ENCYCLOPÆDIA IRANICA

ENCYCLOPÆDIA IRANICA

EDITED BY

EHSAN YARSHATER

Center for Iranian Studies
Columbia University
New York

UNDER THE PATRONAGE OF
THE INTERNATIONAL UNION OF ACADEMIES

Volume XIV

ISFAHAN IX—JOBBĀʾI

Encyclopædia Iranica Foundation
New York, New York
2008

Library of Congress Cataloging-in-Publication Data

Encyclopaedia Iranica/ Edited by Ehsan Yarshater

p. cm.
Includes index
1. Iran—Encyclopedias. I. Yar-Shater, Ehsan
DS253.E531991 91-9733
955´.003—dc20 CIP

 First published in one volume in 2008 by
Encyclopaedia Iranica Foundation, 450 Riverside Drive, New York, N.Y. 10027 U.S.A.

ISBN: 978-1-934283-08-0 (bound volume)
ISBN: 978-1-934283-09-7 (preliminary pages)
ISBN: 978-1-934283-10-3 (binder)

10 9 8 7 6 5 4 3 2 1

This volume is dedicated

to

Dr. Akbar Ghahary

in recognition of two decades of friendship
and generous support of the
Encyclopædia Iranica

ACKNOWLEDGMENTS

The preparation of this volume was made possible in part by a grant from:

The National Endowment for the Humanities, an independent federal agency;

and also by donations from

Dr. Abtin Sassanfar,

The Semnani Foundation, Dr. Akbar Ghahary, Annette and Saman Adamiyatt, Mehdi Metghalchi, Jack Mahfar, Sedigheh Rastegar, Bijan Pakzad, Soudavar Memorial Foundation (Geneva), Dubai Friends of Iranica, The Bahari Foundation (London), Iran Heritage Foundation (London), Mohammad Mohseni, Dr. Fariborz Maseeh (Massiah Foundation), Shirley Elghanian, Friends of Iranica in Montreal, Les Amis de l'Encyclopedie Iranica (Paris), The Iran Society (London), Faranak and Mahyar Amirsaleh, and a number of other donors.

EDITORIAL STAFF

Nicholas Sims-Williams, *Associate Editor for Pre-Islamic Iran*
Christopher J. Brunner, *Associate Editor*
Mohsen Ashtiany, *Associate Editor*

Ahmad Ashraf, *Managing Editor*
Manouchehr Kasheff, *Senior Assistant Editor*
Dagmar Riedel, *Assistant Editor*
Sergei Tourkin, *Assistant Editor*

ADVISORY COMMITTEE

C. Edmund Bosworth (*UK*), Muhammad Dandamayev (*Russia*), Richard N. Frye (*USA*), Gherardo Gnoli (*Italy*), Tsuneo Kuroyanagi (*Japan*), Xavier de Planhol (*France*), Rüdiger Schmitt (*Germany*)

CONSULTING EDITORS

Iraj Afshar, University of Tehran, *Bibliography*
Hamid Algar, University of California, Berkeley, *Islamic Heritage*
Abbas Amanat, Yale University, *Qajar History*
Steven C. Anderson, University of the Pacific, *Fauna*
Daniel Balland, Université de Paris, *Afghanistan*
Stephen Blum, Graduate Center, CUNY, *Music*
C. E. Bosworth, University of Manchester (emeritus), *Early Islamic History*
Gerhard Böwering, Yale University, *Sufism*
Yuri Bregel, Indiana University, *Modern Central Asia*
J. T. P. de Bruijn, University of Leiden, *Classical Persian Literature*
Jean Calmard, Université de Paris, *Popular Religion*
Farhad Daftary, Institute of Ismaili Studies, *Ismailism*
M. Dandamayev, Oriental Institute, St. Petersburg, *Median and Achaemenid History*
Robert H. Dyson, Jr., University of Pennsylvania, *Archeology*
Josef van Ess, Universität Tübingen, *Islamic Theology*
Richard M. Eaton, University of Arizona, *Indo-Persian Studies*
Willem Floor, Bethesda, Md., *Material Culture*
Bert Fragner, Oesterreichischen Akademie der Wissenschaften, Vienna, Austria, *Economic History*
Bahram Grami, Winona, MN, *Flora*
Robert Hillenbrand, University of Edinburgh, *Architecture*
Keith Hitchins, University of Illinois, *Caucasian Studies*
Djalal Khaleghi-Motlagh, Universität Hamburg, *The Shahnama*
Philip G. Kreyenbroek, Universität Göttingen, *Kurdish Studies*
B. A. Litvinsky, Institute of Oriental Studies, Moscow, *Central Asian Archeology*
Maria Macuch, Freie Universität, Berlin, *Sasanian Law and Society*
Wilferd Madelung, Oxford University, *Shiism*
Rudi Matthee, University of Delaware, *Safavid History*
R. D. McChesney, New York University, *Post-Mongol Central Asia*
Eden Naby, Cambridge, Mass., *Assyrians of Modern Iran*
†Amnon Netzer, Hebrew University of Jerusalem, *Jewish Persian Literature*
Pierre Oberling, Hunter College, CUNY (emeritus), *Ethnography*
Mahmoud Omidsalar, California State University, Los Angeles, *Folklore*
Osman Özgüdenli, Marmara Üniversitesi, *Perso-Turkish Literature*
John Perry, University of Chicago, *Zand and Afshar Periods*
Lutz Richter-Bernburg, Universität Tübingen, *History of Medicine*
James Russell, Harvard University, *Irano-Armenian Relations*
Prods Oktor Skjærvø, Harvard University, *Old and Middle Iranian Languages*
Priscilla Soucek, New York University, *Art History*
Brian Spooner, University of Pennsylvania, *Anthropology*
Werner Sundermann, Berlin-Brandenburgische Akademie der Wissenschaften, Berlin, *Manicheism*
Maria Szuppe, Centre National de la Recherche Scientifique, Paris, *Tajikistan*
Gernot Windfuhr, University of Michigan, *Linguistics*
Houra Yavari, Center for Iranian Studies, Columbia University, *Fiction*

ADDENDA AND CORRIGENDA

Volume III

P. 205b AZERBAIJAN, ll. 12-15, *for* region of northwestern Iran, divided between the present-day territories of Iran and the Soviet Union since the treaties of Golestān (1813) and Torkamānčāy (1828) *read*: The historical region of northwestern Iran. The name Azerbaijan was also adopted by the anti-Russian separatist forces of the area for Arrān and Shirvan when in 1918 they declared its independence and called it for the first time Democratic Republic of Azerbaijan. Arrān and Shirvan had been annexed to Russia by the treaties of Golestan (1813) and Torkamānčāy (1828).

P. 476b BAHĀR, MALEK AL-ŠOʿARĀʾ, *add to the bibliography*: Ṣadr-al-Din Elāhi, "Zehi kabutar-e sapid-e āšti. . . ," in *Kayhān* (London), 3 May 2007, p. 11 and 10 May 2007, p. 11.

Volume X

P. 35a FLANDIN, l. -2, *for* 1889 *read* 1876.

Volume XI

P. 104a GOLŠAN ALBUM, l. 23 *for* GOLŠĀN, *read* GOLŠAN.
add to the authors of articles in volume XI, ESLAMI, KAMBIZ, Princeton University, 77, 104.

Volume XIII

P. 609a IRONSIDE, ll. 7-9, *for* MS Persian diary, London University, Liddell Hart Centre for Military Archives. R. Mcleod papers, Public Record Office, Kew, UK *read* MS Persian diary, the National Army Museum, London, UK.

Volume XIV

P. 159b ISLAM IN IRAN xiii, ll. -7–12, *for* Mojahedin of Iran (Mojāhedin-e Ḵalq-e Irān) as well as other Islamic groups, including the Party of Islamic Nations (Ḥezb-e mellal-e eslāmi; for a treatment of this current and other small Islamic groups with militant leftist orientations, see Ḥosaynian . . .), *read* Mojahedin of Iran. Also adhering later to Shariʿati's ideas were a number of small guerrilla groups, including veterans of Ḥezb-e melal-e eslāmi, which was founded in 1962. They were rounded up by the police in early 1964 (see Ḥosaynian . . .).

P. 161a l. 25, *for* and a small group, *read*, with a small number of deputies.

P. 161a ll. -4–5, *for* the leftist Mojahedin, *read* the Mojahedin.

P. 171a l. -13, *delete* and Nancy Pearson.

P. 171a l. -11, *for* Princeton, 1977 *read* tr. N. Pearson, Princeton, 1977.

P. 210a ISMAʿILISM xvi, *add to the author of the entry*, and Zulfikar Hirji.

P. 449a JAMĀLZĀDEH ii, l. 3, *for* Our Iranian Character Traits *read* "Our Iranian Character Traits"
l. -22, for Esḥāque's read Esḥāq's.

P. 474a JĀMI i, l. -11 for Afsahzād read Afṣaḥzād.

P. 474b l. 4 for Afsahzād read Afṣaḥzād.

P. 480 JĀMI iii, after Figure 1. *add* Jāmi, *Haft owrang*, a father advises his son about love. Opaque watercolor, ink, and gold on paper (reduced, orig. size 34.2 x 23.2 cm), probably Mashad. Courtesy of Freer Gallery of Art, Smithsonian Institution, Washington, D.C. MS pers. F1946.12, fol. 52a.

P. 481 After Figure 2. *add* Jāmi, *Haft owrang*, Qays first glimpses Leyli. Opaque watercolor, ink, and gold on paper (reduced, orig. size 34.2 x 23.2 cm), probably Mashad. Courtesy of Freer Gallery of Art, Smithsonian Institution, Washington, D.C. MS pers. F1946.12, fol. 231a.

P. 481b l. -2 *for* (folio 52a, Simpson, p. 26) *read* (Figure 1).

P. 482a ll. 1-2 *for* [Fig. 1] from *Selselat al-ḏahab* (in *Haft owrang*, gen. ed. Alishah et al., p. 265, line 4039 ff.) *read* (*Selselat al-ḏahab* in *Haft owrang*, I, p. 265, line 4046).

P. 482a l. 22 after *Layli o Majnun add* (Figure 2).

P. 482a l. 24 for (Fig. 2, folio 21a; Simpson 1998, p. 65) *read* (*Haft owrang*, II, p. 246, line 444).

P. 482a ll. 29-30 *for* ʿAbd-al-Raḥmān Jāmi, *Haft owrang*, 2 vols., ed. Aʿlāḵān Afṣaḥzād, Tehran, 1999 *read* ʿAbd-al-Raḥmān Jāmi, *Haft owrang*, ed. Aʿlāḵān Afṣaḥzād, 2 vols., Tehran, 1999; for this and older editions, see above Jāmi i., bibliography.

P. 500a JAMʿIYYAT-E MOʾTALEFA-YE ESLĀMI, l. 15, *for* Books. Ḥ Aḵawān *read* Ḥ. Aḵawān.
l. -6, *for* reputed *read* reputable.

P. 500b JAMSHEDJI, l. -11, *for* xfrxnagān *read* āfarinagān

P. 522b JAMŠID i, l. 7, *for* Histoir *read* Histoire.

P. 523b JAMŠID ii, l. 20, *for* gory *read* glory.

CONTRIBUTORS TO VOLUME XIV

ʿĀQELI, BĀQER, Našr-e Goftār, Tehran, 531.

ABISAAB, RULA, McGill University, Montreal, Canada, 305.

ALGAR, HAMID, University of California, Berkeley, 356, 475.

ALI S. ASANI, Harvard University, Cambridge, Mass., 204.

AMANAT, ABBAS, Yale University, New Haven, Conn., 130, 405.

AMIR ARJOMAND, SAID, State University of New York, Stony Brook, 134.

AMIR-MOEZZI, MOHAMMAD ALI, École Pratique des Hautes Études, University of Paris-Sorbonne, France, 136, 146.

ANDERSON, STEVEN C., University of the Pacific (emeritus), Stockton, Calif., 317.

AOKI, TAKESHI, University of Tokyo, Japan, 564.

ASHER, CATHERINE B., University of Minnesota, Minneapolis, 395.

ASHRAF, AHMAD, Columbia University, New York, N.Y., 157.

BABAIE, SUSSAN, University of Michigan, Ann Arbor, 6.

BADANJ, M., Encyclopedia Islamica Foundation, Tehran, 534, 646.

BALABANLILAR, LISA, Rice University, Houston, Tex., 375.

BEELAERT, ANNA LIVIA, Université Libre, Brussels, Belgium, 397.

BERNARDINI, MICHELE, Università degli Studi di Napoli "L'Orientale," Naples, Italy, 250.

†BIRASHK, AHMAD, 468.

BLAU, JOYCE, Institut National des Langues et Civilisations Orientales, Paris, 615.

BOPEARACHCHI, OSMUND, University of Paris-Sorbonne, Paris, 645.

BORJIAN, HABIB, Hofstra University, Hempstead, N.Y., 1, 48, 55, 62, 67, 84, 582, 584, 615.

BORJIAN, MARYAM, Teachers College, Columbia University, New York, 67.

BOSWORTH, C. EDMUND, University of Manchester (emeritus), U.K., 316, 404, 533, 617.

BOURNOUTIAN, GEORGE, Iona College, New Rochelle, N.Y., 602.

BREGEL, YURI, Indiana University (emeritus), Bloomington, 297.

BROOKSHAW, DOMINIC PARVIZ, University of Manchester, U.K., 383.

BROOMAND, MANOUCHEHR, Tehran, 413.

BRUNNER, C. J., Encyclopædia Iranica, New York, 546.

CALLIERI, PIERFRANCESCO, Università di Bologna, Ravenna Campus, Italy, 263.

CASARI, MARIO, Sapienza Università di Roma, Italy, 241, 245, 271, 283, 286, 290.

CERETI, CARLO, Sapienza Università di Roma, Italy, 240, 259, 292.

CHEHABI, HOUCHANG, Boston University, Mass., 366.

CHOKSY, JAMSHEED K., Indiana University, Bloomington, 453, 664.

COOK, DAVID, Rice University, Houston, Tex., 154.

COOPERSON, MICHAEL, University of California, Los Angeles, 386.

DAFTARY, FARHAD, The Institute of Ismaili Studies, London, 173, 176, 178, 298, 403.

DAILAMI, PEZHMAN, Schwerin, Germany, 534.

DAKAKE, MARIA, George Mason University, Fairfax, Va., 312.

DALE, STEPHEN, Ohio State University, Columbus, 374.

DE BRUIJN, J. T. P., Leiden University (emeritus), The Netherlands, 391.

DE JONG, ALBERT, Leiden University, The Netherlands, 618.

DE LA VAISSIERE, ETIENNE, École Pratique des Hautes Études, University of Paris-Sorbonne, Paris, 314.

DE SMET, DANIEL, Katholieke Universiteit Leuven, Leuven, Belgium, 362.

DURAND-GUÉDY, DAVID, CNRS, Ivry-sur-Seine, France, 436.

EBRAHIMNEJAD, HORMOZ, University College London, London, U.K. 420.

EIr, 48, 581, 601.

EKHTIAR, MARYAM, The Metropolitan Museum of Art, New York, 438.

ERNST, CARL W., University of North Carolina, Chapel Hill, 608.

FARHAD, MASSUMEH, Freer Gallery of Art, Smithsonian Institution, Washington D.C., 40.

FLOOD, FINBARR BARRY, New York University, New York, 432.

FLOOR, WILLEM, Bethesda, Md., 43.

FONTANTA, MARIA V., Sapienza Università di Roma, Italy, 277.

FOUACHE, ERIC, University of Paris-Sorbonne, Paris, 648.

GENITO, BRUNO, Università degli Studi di Napoli "L'Orientale," Naples, Italy, 265.

GLEAVE, ROBERT, University of Exeter, U.K., 349, 351.

GRÖTZBACH, ERWIN, Katholische Universität Eichstätt (emeritus), Eichstätt, Germany, 309.

HAJI, HAMID, The Institute of Ismaili Studies, London, 349.

HAMZEH'EE, M. REZA FARIBORZ, Augsburg, Germany, 346, 428.

HANEDA, MASASHI, University of Tokyo, Japan, 568.
HANIFI, M. JAMIL, Michigan State University (retired), East Lansing, 310, 589, 630.
HANIFI, SHAH MAHMOUD, James Madison University, Harrisonburg, Va., 400.
HAUG, ROBERT, University of Michigan, Ann Arbor, 6.
HIJRI, ZULFIKAR, The Institute of Ismaili Studies, London, 208.
HITCHINS, KEITH, University of Illinois, Urbana-Champaign, 339, 371, 419.
HOURCADE, BERNARD, CNRS, Ivry-sur-Seine, France, 399.
IMOTO, EIICHI, Osaka University, School of Foreign Studies, Japan, 558.
JACKSON, PETER, University of Keele, U.K., 305, 415.
JAFARI, SHIVA, The Greater Islamic Encyclopedia, Tehran, 392.
KADHIM, ABBAS, Naval Postgraduate School, Monterey, Calif., 610, 614.
KAMSHAD, HASSAN, Tehran, 444.
KARANJIA, RAMIYAR P., The Athornan Boarding Madressa, Dadar, Mumbai, India, 457, 500.
KARGAR, DARIUSH, Uppsala University, Sweden, 459, 611.
KAZEMI MOUSSAVI, AHMAD, University of Maryland, College Park, 364.
KEENE, MANUEL, Dar al-Athar al-Islamiyyah, Kuwait, 323.
KEYVANI, MAJD-AL-DIN, Teachers Training University, Tehran, 430.
KHALAJI, MAHDI, The Washington Institute for Near East Policy, Washington, D. C., 621.
KIA, CHAD, Columbia University, New York, 479.
KLEMM, VERENA, University of Leipzig, Germany, 143.
KLIER, KLAUS, Freie Universität, Berlin, 427.
KONDO, NOBUAKI, Tokyo University of Foreign Studies, Japan, 547.
KOTWAL, FIROZE, Mumbai, India, 664.
KREYENBROEK, PHILIP, Georg-August-Universität, Göttingen, Germany, 622.
LOSENSKY, PAUL, Indiana University, Bloomington, 469.
MAGGI, MAURO, Instituto Universitario Orientale, Naples, Italy, 592, 664, 666.
MALANDRA, WILLIAM, University of Minnesota (emeritus), Minneapolis-St. Paul, 318, 456.
MARDUKH, ABD-ALLAH, Saint Denis, France, 601.
MARZOLPH, ULRICH, Enzyklopädie des Märchens, Göttingen, Germany, 461.
MATTHEE, RUDI, University of Delaware, Newark, Delaware, 544, 634.
MATTHEWS, DAVID, SOAS, University of London, London, 605.
MELVILLE, CHARLES, University of Cambridge, U.K., 378, 385, 462, 580.
MEMBRADO, MOJAN, CNRS, Ivry-sur-Seine, France, 641.
MENASHIRI, DAVID, Tel Aviv University, Israel, 213.
MENEGHINI, DANIELA, Università Ca' Foscari di Venezia, Italy, 281.
MILSTEIN, RACHEL, The Hebrew University of Jerusalem, Israel, 238.
MIR ʿALINAQI, S. A., Tehran, 532.
MIR-KASIMOV, ORKHAN, École Pratique des Hautes Études, University of Paris-Sorbonne, France, 603.
MITCHELL, COLIN PAUL, Dalhousie University, Halifax, Canada, 313.
MONSUTTI, ALLESANDRO, Graduate Institute of International and Development Studies, Geneva, 373.
MOREEN, VERA B., Bala Cynwyd, Pennsylvania, 643.
MORITA, TOYOKO, Kagoshima University, Japan, 561.
MOZAFFARI, NAHID, New York, 439, 444, 452.
MUSCARELLA, OSCAR WHITE, The Metropolitan Museum of Art, New York, 300, 653.
NANJI, AZIM, The Institute of Ismaili Studies, London, 208, 210.
NASIRI-MOGHADDAM, NADER, Marc Bloch University, Strasburg, France., 593, 629.
†NETZER, AMNON, 75.
NIZAMI, FARHAN, Oxford University, U.K., 410.
NOELLE-KARIMI, CHRISTINE, Die Otto-Friedrichs-Universität Bamberg, Germany, 528.
OBERLING, PIERRE, Hunter College, CUNY (emeritus), New York, 312, 375, 400, 411, 420.
OHTSU, TADAHIKO, Chikushi Jogakuen University, Dazaifu, Japan, 556.
OMIDSALAR, MAHMOUD, California State University, Los Angeles, 71, 522.
ORSATTI, PAOLA, Sapienza Università di Roma, Italy, 273.
ÖZGÜDENLI, OSMAN G., Marmara Üniversitesi, Istanbul, Turkey, 482, 623, 624, 638, 639, 640.
PALSETIA, JESSE S., University of Guelph, Ontario, Canada, 619.
PANAINO, ANTONIO, Università di Bologna, Ravenna Campus, Italy, 294.
PARSI, TRITA, National Iranian American Council, Washington, D.C., 216.
PARVIN, NASSEREDDIN, Geneva, Switzerland, 386.
PERROT, JEAN, CNRS, Ivry-sur-Seine, France, 656.
POONAWALA, ISMAIL K., University of California, Los Angeles, 195, 197.
PORTER, YVES, University of Aix-en-Provence, France, 609.
POTTS, DANIEL T., University of Sydney, Australia, 588, 625.
RAHNEMA, ALI, American University of Paris, France, 483.
RAJABZADEH, HASHEM, Osaka University, School of Foreign Studies, Japan, 556, 569, 574, 577.
RASHOW, KHALIL JINDY, University of Göttingen, Germany, 616.
RICHTER-BERNBURG, LUTZ, Eberhard Karls Universität Tübingen, Germany, 373.
RIZVI, SAJJAD, University of Exeter, U.K., 119, 458.
SADEGHI, ALI, Coquitlam, B.C., Canada, 432.

SCHINDEL, NIKOLAUS, Österreichische Akademie der Wissenschaften, Vienna, 454.
SCHMIDTKE, SABINE, Freie Universität Berlin, Institut für Islamwissenschaft, Berlin, 666.
SCHMITT, RÜDIGER, Universität des Saarlandes, Saarbrucken, Germany, 125, 127.
SCHMUCK, STEPHAN, University of Wales, Aberystwyth, U.K., 627.
SEYED-GOHRAB, A. A., Leiden University, The Netherlands, 438.
SHAKED, SHAUL, The Hebrew University of Jerusalem (emeritus), Israel, 234.
SIMS-WILLIAMS, NICHOLAS, SOAS, University of London, U.K., 314, 372.
SIMS-WILLIAMS, URSULA, The British Library, London, 128.
SIVAN, HAGITH, University of Kansas, Lawrence, 632.
SKJÆRVØ, PRODS OKTOR, Harvard University, Cambridge, Mass., 501.
STAUSBERG, MICHAEL, University of Bergen, Norway, 457, 500.
STILO, DONALD, Max Planck Institute for Evolutionary Anthropology, Leipzig, 77, 93, 112.
SUGIMURA, TOH, Ryukoku University (emeritus), Kyoto, 561, 571.
SZUPPE, MARIA, CNRS, Ivry-sur-Seine, France, 607.
TUCKER, ERNEST, U.S. Naval Academy, Annapolis, Md., 382.
VAN ESS, JOSEF, Eberhard Karls Universität Tübingen, Germany (emeritus), 347, 389.
VANZAN, ANNA, Venice, Italy, 257.
VEJDANI, FARZIN, University of Arizona, Tucsan, 405.
WILLEY, PETER, The Institute of Ismaili Studies, London, 205.
WINDFUHR, GERNOT, University of Michigan, Ann Arbor, 367.
†YAZICI, TAHSIN, 412.
YEROUSHALMI, DAVID, Tel Aviv University, Israel, 223.
ZAKERI, MOHSEN, Orientalisches Seminar, J.W. Goethe-Universität, Frankfurt am Main, Germany, 594.

SHORT REFERENCES AND ABBREVIATIONS OF BOOKS AND PERIODICALS

AAASH
Acta Antiqua Academiae Scientiarum Hungaricae.

Aarne and Thompson
A. A. Aarne, *Verzeichnis der Märchentypen*, tr. and enl. Stith Thompson as *The Types of the Folk-Tale: A Classification and Bibliography*, Helsinki, 1928.

ADTD
Ankara Üniversitesi, Dil ve tarih-coğrafya fa-kültesi dergisi.

Aḡānī **[1,2,3] (Cairo)**
Abu'l-Faraj ʿAlī b. al-Ḥosayn Qorašī Eṣbahānī, *Ketāb al-aḡānī*, I-XX ed. Naṣr Horīnī, Būlāq, 1285/1868-69, XXI ed. R. E. Brünnow, Leiden, 1888; repr., 21 vols., Cairo, 1323/1905-06; 3rd ed., Cairo, 1345-/1926-.

Agathangelos, *History*, tr. Thomson
Agatʿangelay, *Patmutʿiwn Hayocʿ*, tr. R. W. Thomson as *History of the Armenians*, Albany, N.Y., 1976 (except pars. 259-715).

Agathangelos, *Patmutʿiwn Hayocʿ*
Agatʿangelay, *Patmutʿiwn Hayocʿ*, ed. G. Tēr-Mkrtʿean and S. Kanayeancʿ, Tiflis, 1909; repr. Delmar, N.Y., 1979.

Agathangelos, *The Teaching of St. Gregory*
Agatʿangelay, *Patmutʿiwn Hayocʿ*, tr. R. W. Thomson as *The Teaching of St. Gregory, an Early Armenian Catechism*, Cambridge, Mass., 1970 (pars. 259-715).

***Āʾīn-e akbarī*, ed. Blochmann**
Abu'l-Fażl ʿAllāmī, *Āʾīn-e akbarī*, ed. H. Blochmann, Bib. Ind., 2 vols., Calcutta, 1867-77.

***Āʾīn-e akbarī*, ed. Phillott**
Abu'l-Fażl ʿAllāmī, *Āʾīn-e akbarī*, rev. ed. and tr. D. C. Phillott, 3 vols., Calcutta, 1939-49.

***Āʾīn-e akbarī*, tr. Blochmann**
Abu'l-Fażl ʿAllāmī, *Āʾīn-e akbarī* I, tr. H. Blochmann, II-III, tr. H. S. Jarrett, Bib. Ind., Calcutta, 1868-94.

AirWb.
Christian Bartholomae, *Altiranisches Wörterbuch*, Strassburg, 1904; repr. Berlin, 1961.

AIUON
Annali dell'Istituto universitario orientale di Napoli.

AJA
American Journal of Archaeology.

Akbar-nāma
Abu'l-Fażl ʿAllāmī, *Akbar-nāma*, ed. Āqā Moḥammad ʿAlī and Mawlawī ʿAbd-al-Raḥīm, 3 vols., Bib. Ind., Calcutta, 1877-86.

***Akbar-nāma*, tr. Beveridge**
Abu'l-Fażl ʿAllāmī, *Akbar-nāma*, tr. Henry Beveridge, 3 vols., Bib. Ind., Calcutta, 1897-1939.

AKM
Abhandlungen für die Kunde des Morgenlandes.

Aʿlām-al-šīʿa
Āḡā Bozorg Ṭehrānī, *Ṭabaqāt aʿlām al-šīʿa*, Najaf, 1373/1954.

AMI
Archäologische Mitteilungen aus Iran.

***ANRW* II**
Aufstieg und Niedergang der römischen Welt. Geschichte und Kultur Roms im Spiegel der neueren Forschung II: *Principat*, ed. Hildegard Temporini and Wolfgang Haase, Berlin, 1976-.

AOASH
Acta Orientalia Academiae Scientiarum Hungaricae.

AoF
Altorientalische Forschungen.

APAW
Abhandlungen der Preussischen Akademie der Wissenschaften.

ARW
Archiv für Religionswissenschaft.

Āryanpūr, *Az Ṣabā tā Nīmā*
Yaḥyā Āryanpūr, *Az Ṣabā tā Nīmā*, 2 vols., Tehran, 1351 Š./1973.

Ašʿarī, *Maqālāt*
Abu'l-Ḥasan ʿAlī b. Esmāʿīl Ašʿarī, *Maqālāt al-eslāmīyīn*, ed. Helmut Ritter, Istanbul, 1929-33.

Ātaškada
Loṭf-ʿAlī Bīg Āḏar, *Ātaškada*, ed. Ḥasan Sādāt-e Nāṣerī, 3 vols., Tehran, 1337-41 Š./1958-62.

***Avesta*, ed. Geldner**
Avesta: Die heiligen Bücher der Parsen, ed. K. F. Geldner, 3 vols. in 1, Stuttgart, 1886-95.

***Avesta*, tr. Darmesteter**
Le Zend-Avesta: Traduction nouvelle avec commentaire historique et philologique, tr. J. Darmesteter, 3 vols., Paris, 1892-93; repr. Paris, 1960.

ʿAwfī, *Lobāb*
Moḥammad ʿAwfī, *Lobāb al-albāb*, ed. E. G. Browne and M. Qazvīnī, 2 vols., Leiden and London, 1903-06.

ʿAwfī, *Lobāb*, ed. Nafīsī
Moḥammad ʿAwfī, *Lobāb al-albāb*, ed. S. Nafīsī, Tehran, 1335 Š./1956.

ANRW
Aufstieg und Niedergang der römischen Welt, 1972-.

Aʿyān al-šīʿa
Moḥsen al-Amīn Ḥosaynī ʿĀmelī, *Aʿyān al-šīʿa*, 56 parts, Damascus, 1935-1962.

Bābor-nāma
Ẓahīr-al-Dīn Moḥammad Bābor, *Bābor-nāma*, facs. ed. A. S. Beveridge as *The Bábar-náma*, GMS 1, Leiden and London, 1905; repr. London, 1971.

Bābur-nāma, tr. Beveridge
Ẓahīr-al-Dīn Moḥammad Bābor, *Bābor-nāma*, tr. A. S. Beveridge as *Bābur-nāma (Memoirs of Bābur)*, 2 vols., London, 1922; repr. 2 vols. in 1, London, 1969.

Back
Michael Back, *Die sassanidischen Staats-inschriften: Studien zur Orthographie and Phonologie des Mittelpersischen der Inschriften . . .*, Tehran and Leiden, 1978.

Badāʾūnī, _Montaḵab_
ʿAbd-al-Qāder Badāʾūnī, *Montaḵab al-tawārīḵ*, ed. A.-ʿA. Kabīr-al-Dīn Aḥmad and W. N. Lees, 2 vols., Calcutta, 1864-69.

Badāʾūnī, _Montaḵab_, tr. Ranking et al.
ʿAbd-al-Qāder Badāʾūnī, *Montaḵab al-tawārīḵ*, tr. G. S. A. Ranking, W. H. Lowe, and Wolseley Haig, 3 vols., Calcutta, 1884-1925; repr. Patna, 1973.

Baḡdādī, _Farq_, ed. ʿAbd-al-Ḥamīd
Abū Manṣūr ʿAbd-al-Qāher b. Ṭāher b. Moḥammad Baḡdādī, *Ketāb al-farq bayn al-feraq*, ed. M. M. ʿAbd-al-Ḥamīd, Cairo, 1964.

Baḡdādī, _Farq_, ed. Badr
Abū Manṣūr ʿAbd-al-Qāher b. Ṭāher b. Moḥammad Baḡdādī, *al-Farq bayn al-feraq*, ed. Moḥammad Badr, Cairo, 1328/1910.

Bailey, _Dictionary_
Harold W. Bailey, *Dictionary of Khotan Saka*, Cambridge, 1979.

Bailey, _Zoroastrian Problems_
Harold W. Bailey, *Zoroastrian Problems in the Ninth-Century Books*, Oxford, 1943; repr. with a new introd., London, 1971.

Balāḏorī, _Ansāb_
Abu'l-ʿAbbās Aḥmad b. Yaḥyā b. Jāber Balāḏorī, *Ketāb ansāb al-ašrāf* I, ed. M. Ḥamīd-Allāh, Cairo, 1959; II, ed. M. al-Maḥmūdī, Beirut, 1974; III, ed. ʿA.-ʿA. al-Dūrī, Wiesbaden, 1978; IVb, ed. M. Schlössinger, Jersualem, 1935; V, ed. S. D. Goitein, Jerusalem, 1936.

Balāḏorī, _Fotūḥ_
Abu'l-ʿAbbās Aḥmad b. Yaḥyā b. Jāber Balāḏorī, *Ketāb fotūḥ al-boldān*, ed. M. J. de Goeje, Leiden, 1886; repr., Leiden, 1968.

Balāḏorī, _Fotūḥ_, ed. Monajjed
Abu'l-ʿAbbās Aḥmad b. Yaḥyā b. Jāber Balāḏorī, *Ketāb fotūḥ al-boldān*, ed. Ṣalāḥ-al-Dīn Monajjed, 3 vols., Cairo, 1956-61.

Balʿamī, ed. Bahār
Abū ʿAlī Moḥammad Balʿamī, *Tārīḵ-e Balʿamī*, ed. M.-T. Bahār, Tehran, 1341 Š./1962.

Balʿamī, ed. Rowšan
Abū ʿAlī Moḥammad Balʿamī, *Tārīḵ-nāma-ye Ṭabarī gardānīda-ye mansūb be Balʿamī*, ed. Moḥammad Rowšan, 3 vols., Tehran, 1366 Š./1987.

Balʿamī, tr. Zotenberg
Hermann Zotenberg, tr. as *Chronique de . . . Tabari traduite sur la version persane d'Abou-ʿAli Moʿhammad Belʿami*, 4 vols., Paris, 1867-74.

Bāmdād, _Rejāl_
Mahdī Bāmdād, *Šarḥ-e ḥāl-e rejāl-e Īrān dar qorūn-e davāzdahom wa sīzdahom wa čahār-dahom-e hejrī*, 6 vols., Tehran, 1347-57 Š./1966-78.

Barthold, _Turkestan_ [2,3]
W. W. Barthold, *Turkestan Down to the Mongol Invasion*, tr. T. Minorsky and ed. C. E. Bosworth, 2nd ed., London, 1958; 3rd ed., London, 1969.

Bayānī, _Košnevīsān_
Mahdī Bayānī, *Aḥwāl o āṯār-e ḵošnevīsān: Nastaʿlīq-nevīsān*, 3 vols., Tehran, 1345-48 Š./1966-69; IV, ed. H. Maḥbūbī Ardakānī, Tehran, 1358 Š./1979.

Bayhaqī, ed. Fayyāż
Abu'l-Fażl Bayhaqī, *Tārīḵ-e masʿūdī*, ed. ʿA.-A. Fayyāż, Mašhad, 1350 Š./1971.

Bayhaqī, ed. Nafīsī
Abu'l-Fażl Bayhaqī, *Tārīḵ-e masʿūdī*, ed. Saʿīd Nafīsī, 3 vols., Tehran, 1319-32 Š./1940-53.

BGA
Bibliotheca Geographorum Arabicorum, ed. M. J. de Goeje, 8 vols., Leiden, 1870-94.

Bib. Ind.
Bibliotheca Indica, published by the Asiatic Society of Bengal, Calcutta.

Bīrūnī, _Āṯār_
Abū Rayḥān Bīrūnī, *Ketāb al-āṯār al-bāqīa ʿan al-qorūn al-ḵālīa*, ed. E. Sachau as *Chronologie orientalischer Völker von Albêrûnî*, Leipzig, 1878; repr. Leipzig, 1923; repr. Baghdad, 1963.

Bīrūnī, _Āṯār_, tr. Sachau
Abū Rayḥān Bīrūnī, *Ketāb al-āṯār al-bāqīa ʿan al-qorūn al-ḵālīa*, tr. E. Sachau as *The Chronology of the Ancient Nations*, London, 1879; repr. Frankfurt, 1969.

BNF
Beiträge zur Namenforschung.

Borhān-e qāṭeʿ, ed. Moʿīn
Moḥammad-Ḥosayn b. Ḵalaf Tabrīzī, *Borhān-e qāṭeʿ*, ed. M. Moʿīn, 6 vols., Tehran, 1342-52 Š./1963-73.

Bosworth, _Ghaznavids_
C. Edmond Bosworth, *The Ghaznavids: Their Empire in Afghanistan and Eastern Iran 944-1040*, Edinburgh, 1963.

Bosworth, _Later Ghaznavids_
C. Edmond Bosworth, *The Later Ghaznavids, Splendour and Decay: The Dynasty in Afghanistan and Northern India 1040-1186*, Edinburgh, 1977.

Boyce, "Middle Persian Literature"
Mary Boyce, "Middle Persian Literature," in *HO* I/IV, 2/1, Leiden, 1968, pp. 31-66.

Boyce, _Reader_
Mary Boyce, *A Reader in Manichaean Middle Persian and Parthian*, Acta Iranica 9, Tehran and Liège, 1975.

Boyce, _Stronghold_
Mary Boyce, *A Persian Stronghold of Zoroastrianism*, Oxford, 1977.

Boyce, _Zoroastrianism_
Mary Boyce, *A History of Zoroastrianism* I-II, HO

I/VIII/1, 2/2A, Leiden, 1975-82.

Boyce and Grenet, *Zoroastrianism*

Mary Boyce and Frantz Grenet, *A History of Zoroastrianism* III, HO I/VIII/1, 2/2, Leiden, 1991.

Brockelmann, *GAL*

Carl Brockelmann, *Geschichte der arabischen Litteratur*, 2nd ed., 2 vols., Leiden, 1943-49; Supplement (S), 3 vols., Leiden, 1937-42.

Browne, *Lit. Hist. Persia*

Edward G. Browne, *A Literary History of Persia*, 4 vols., London, 1902-24.

Browne, *Persian Revolution*

Edward G. Browne, *The Persian Revolution of 1905-1909*, London, 1910.

Browne, *Press and Poetry*

Edward G. Browne, *The Press and Poetry of Modern Persia Partly Based on the Manuscript Work of Mírzá Muḥammad ʿAlí Khán "Tarbiyat" of Tabríz*, Cambridge, 1914.

BSL

Bulletin de la Société de Linguistique de Paris.

BSO(A)S

Bulletin of the School of Oriental (and African) Studies.

***Bundahišn* (DH)**

The Codex DH, Being a Facsimile Edition of Bondahesh, Zand-e Vohuman Yasht, and Parts of the Denkard, ed. P. K. Anklesaria, Tehran, n.d. (1350 Š./1971).

***Bundahišn* (TD_1)**

The Bondahesh, Being a Facsimile Edition of the Manuscript TD_1, ed. P. K. Anklesaria, Tehran, n.d. (1350 Š./1971).

***Bundahišn* (TD_2)**

The Bûndahishn, Being a Facsimile of the TD Manuscript No. 2 . . . , ed. T. D. Anklesaria, Bombay, 1908.

***Bundahišn*, tr. Anklesaria**

Zand-Ākāsīh: Iranian or Greater Bundahišn, ed. and tr. B. T. Anklesaria, Bombay, 1956.

***CAH*^{2,3}**

Cambridge Ancient History, 2nd ed., 12 vols., Cambridge, 1928-39; 3rd ed., vols. 1 and 2 in 4, Cambridge, 1970-75.

***Čahār maqāla*, ed. Qazvīnī**

Aḥmad b. ʿOmar b. ʿAlī Neẓāmī ʿArūżī Samarqandī, *Čahār maqāla*, ed. M. Qazvīnī, rev. M. Moʿīn, Tehran, 1331 Š./1952.

Camb. Hist. Iran

The Cambridge History of Iran, 7 vols., Cambridge, 1968-91.

Cat. Bankipore

Catalogue of the Arabic and Persian Manuscripts in the Oriental Public Library at Bankipore, 29 vols., Calcutta, 1908-20, Patna, 1918-71.

Cat. Bibliothèque Nationale

Edgar Blochet, *Catalogue des manuscrits persans de la Bibliothèque Nationale*, 4 vols., Paris, 1905-34.

Cat. Bodleian Library

Eduard Sachau, Hermann Ethé, and A. F. L. Beeston, eds., *Catalogue of the Persian, Turkish, Hindustani, and Pushtu Manuscripts in the Bod-leian Library*, 3 vols., Oxford, 1889-1954.

Cat. Chester Beatty Library

The Chester Beatty Library: A Catalogue of the Persian Manuscripts and Miniatures I, ed. A. J. Arberry, M. Minovi, and E. Blochet, Dublin, 1959; II-III, ed. M. Minovi, B. W. Robinson, J. W. S. Wilkinson, and E. Blochet, Dublin, 1960-62.

CDAFI

Cahiers de la Délégation archéologique française en Iran.

Chardin

Jean Chardin, *Voyages du chevalier Chardin en Perse, et autres lieux de l'Orient . . . Nouvelle édition, soigneusement conférée sur les trois éditions originales, augmentée . . . de notes, etc. . . .* , ed. L. Langlès, 10 vols., Paris, 1811.

Christensen, *Contributions*

Arthur Christensen, *Contributions à la dialectologie iranienne*, 2 vols., Copenhagen, 1935.

Christensen, *Iran Sass.*

Arthur Christensen, *L'Iran sous les Sassanides*, 2nd ed., Copenhagen, 1944.

Corpus Inscr. Iran.

Corpus Inscriptionum Iranicarum, London, 1955-.

CSCO

Corpus Scriptorum Christianorum Orientalium.

Curzon, *Persian Question*

George N. Curzon, *Persia and the Persian Question*, 2 vols., London, 1892.

***Dādistān ī dēnīg*, pt. 1**

The Dadistan-i Dinik, Part I, Pursishn I-XL, ed. T. D. Anklesaria, Bombay, 1913.

DAI

Deutsches Archäologisches Institut.

al-Ḏarīʿa

Āqā Bozorg Ṭehrānī, *al-Ḏarīʿa elā taṣānīf al-šīʿa*, 24 vols. in 27, Najaf and Tehran, 1355-98/1936-78.

Dawlatābādī, *Ḥayāt-e Yaḥyā*

Yaḥyā Dawlatābādī, *Tārīḵ-e moʿāṣer yā ḥayāt-e Yaḥyā*, 4 vols., Tehran, n.d.

Dawlatšāh, ed. Browne

Dawlatšāh Samarqandī, *Taḏkerat al-šoʿarāʾ*, ed. E. G. Browne as *The Tadhkiratu 'sh-shuʿará ("Memoirs of the Poets") of Dawlatsháh . . .* , Leiden and London, 1901.

Dehḵodā

ʿAlī-Akbar Dehḵodā, *Loğat-nāma*, Tehran, 1325-58 Š./1946-79.

***Dēnkard*, ed. Dresden**

Dēnkart, a Pahlavi Text: Facsimile Edition of the Manuscript B of the K. R. Cama Oriental Institute Bombay, ed. M. J. Dresden, Wiesbaden, 1966.

***Dēnkard*, ed. Madan**

The Complete Text of the Pahlavi Dinkard, 2 vols., ed. D. M. Madan, Bombay, 1911.

Dēnkard, ed. Sanjana
 The Dinkard, ed. D. P. Sanjana and P. B. Sanjana, 19 vols., Bombay, 1874-1928.

Dīnavarī, ed. Guirgass
 Abū Ḥanīfa Dīnavarī, *al-Aḵbār al-ṭewāl*, ed. V. Guirgass, Leiden, 1888.

Dīnavarī, ed. ʿĀmer and Šayyāl
 Abū Ḥanīfa Dīnavarī, *al-Aḵbār al-ṭewāl*, ed. ʿA.-M. ʿĀmer and J. Šayyāl, Cairo, 1960.

DMBE
 Dāʾerat al-maʿāref-e bozorg-e eslāmī, ed. Kāẓem Mūsawī Bojnūrdī, Tehran, 1367- Š./1988-.

Doerfer, *Elemente*
 Gerhard Doerfer, *Türkische und mongolische Elemente im Neupersischen*, 4 vols., Wiesbaden, 1963-75.

Ebn al-Aṯīr
 ʿEzz-al-Dīn b. al-Aṯīr, *al-Kāmel fiʾl-taʾrīḵ*, ed. C. J. Tornberg, 12 vols., Leiden, 1851-76.

Ebn al-Aṯīr (Beirut)
 ʿEzz-al-Dīn b. al-Aṯīr, *al-Kāmel fiʾl-taʾrīḵ*, ed. C. J. Tornberg, 13 vols., Beirut, 1965-67.

Ebn al-Balḵī
 Ebn al-Balḵī, *Fārs-nāma*, ed. G. Le Strange and R. A. Nicholson as *The Fársnáma of Ibnuʾl-Balkhí*, GMS, Cambridge, 1921.

Ebn Baṭṭūṭa
 Abū ʿAbd-Allāh Moḥammad b. Moḥammad Lawātī Ṭanjī b. Baṭṭūṭa, *Toḥfat al-noẓẓār fī ḡarāʾeb al-amṣār wa ʿajāʾeb al-asfār*, ed. and tr. C. Defrémery and B. R. Sanguinetti as *Voyages dʾIbn Batoutah*, 4 vols., Paris, 1853-58.

Ebn Baṭṭūṭa, tr. Gibb
 Abū ʿAbd-Allāh Moḥammad b. Moḥammad Lawātī Ṭanjī b. Baṭṭūṭa, *Toḥfat al-noẓẓār fī ḡarāʾeb al-amṣār wa ʿajāʾeb al-asfār*, tr. H. A. R. Gibb as *Travels of Ibn Battuta, A.D. 1325-1354*, 4 vols., Cambridge, 1958-94.

Ebn Esfandīār
 Moḥammad b. Ḥasan b. Esfandīār, *Tārīḵ-e Ṭabarestān*, ed. ʿAbbās Eqbāl, 2 vols., Tehran, 1320 Š./1941.

Ebn Esfandīār, tr. Browne
 Moḥammad b. Ḥasan b. Esfandīār, *Tārīḵ-e Ṭabarestān*, tr. E. G. Browne as *An Abridged Translation of the History of Ṭabaristān*, Leiden and London, 1905.

Ebn al-Faqīh
 Abū Bakr Aḥmad b. Moḥammad Hamadānī Ebn al-Faqīh, *Moḵtaṣar Ketāb al-boldān*, ed. M. J. de Goeje, BGA, Leiden, 1886.

Ebn Ḥawqal
 Abuʾl-Qāsem b. Ḥawqal Naṣībī, *Ketāb ṣūrat al-arż*, ed. J. H. Kramers, BGA, 2nd ed., Leiden, 1938.

Ebn Ḥawqal, tr. Kramers and Wiet
 Abuʾl-Qāsem b. Ḥawqal Naṣībī, *Ketāb ṣūrat al-arż*, tr. J. H. Kramers and G. Wiet as *Configuration de la terre*, 2 vols., Paris and Beirut, 1964.

Ebn al-Jawzī, *Montaẓam*
 ʿAbd-al-Raḥmān b. ʿAlī b. al-Jawzī, *al-Montaẓam fī taʾrīḵ al-molūk waʾl-omam*, Hyderabad, 1357-59/1938-40.

Ebn Ḵallekān, ed. ʿAbbās
 Abuʾl-ʿAbbās Aḥmad b. Moḥammad b. Ebrāhīm b. Ḵallekān, *Wafayāt al-aʿyān wa anbāʾ abnāʾ al-zamān*, ed. E. ʿAbbās (Ihsan Abbas), 8 vols., Beirut, 1968-72.

Ebn Ḵallekān, ed. Wüstenfeld
 Abuʾl-ʿAbbās Aḥmad b. Moḥammad b. Ebrāhīm b. Ḵallekān, *Wafayāt al-aʿyān wa anbāʾ abnāʾ al-zamān*, ed. Ferdinand Wüstenfeld, 2 vols., Göttingen, 1835-50.

Ebn Ḵallekān, tr. de Slane
 Abuʾl-ʿAbbās Aḥmad b. Moḥammad b. Ebrāhīm b. Ḵallekān, *Wafayāt al-aʿyān wa anbāʾ abnāʾ al-zamān*, tr. W. M. de Slane as *Ibn Khallikanʾs Biographical Dictionary*, 4 vols., Paris, 1842-71.

Ebn Ḵordāḏbeh
 Abuʾl-Qāsem ʿObayd-Allāh b. ʿAbd-Allāh b. Ḵordāḏbeh, *Ketāb al-masālek waʾl-mamālek*, ed. M. J. de Goeje, BGA, Leiden, 1889; 2nd ed., Leiden, 1967.

Ebn al-Mortażā, *Ṭabaqāt*
 Aḥmad b. Yaḥyā b. al-Mortażā, *Ṭabaqāt al-moʿtazela*, ed. S. Diwald-Wilzer, Beirut and Wiesbaden, 1961.

Ebn al-Nadīm, ed. Flügel
 Abuʾl-Faraj Moḥammad b. al-Nadīm, *Ketāb al-fehrest*, ed. G. Flügel, 2 vols., Leipzig, 1871-72.

Ebn al-Nadīm, ed. Tajaddod
 Abuʾl-Faraj Moḥammad b. al-Nadīm, *Ketāb al-fehrest*, ed. M. R. Tajaddod, Tehran, 1350 Š./1971.

Ebn al-Nadīm, tr. Dodge
 Abuʾl-Faraj Moḥammad b. al-Nadīm, *Ketāb al-fehrest*, tr. B. Dodge as *The Fihrist of al-Nadīm*, 2 vols., New York, 1970.

Ebn Rosta
 Abū ʿAlī Aḥmad b. ʿOmar b. Rosta, *Ketāb al-aʿlāq al-nafīsa*, ed. M. J. de Goeje, BGA, Leiden, 1892; 2nd ed., Leiden, 1967.

Ebn Rosta, tr. Wiet
 Abū ʿAlī Aḥmad b. ʿOmar b. Rosta, *Ketāb al-aʿlāq al-nafīsa*, tr. G. Wiet as *Les atours précieux*, Cairo, 1955.

Ebn Saʿd
 Moḥammad b. Saʿd, *al-Ṭabaqāt al-kobrā*, ed. E. Sachau, 9 vols., Leiden, 1904-40.

Ebn Taḡrīberdī
 Abuʾl-Maḥāsen Jamāl-al-Dīn Yūsof b. Taḡrīberdī, *al-Nojūm al-zāhera fī molūk Meṣr waʾl-Qāhera*, 16 vols., Cairo, 1964-72.

Edrīsī
 Abū ʿAbd-Allāh Moḥammad Edrīsī, *Nozhat al-moštāq fī eḵterāq al-āfāq*, ed. Enrico Cerulli et al. as *Opus Geographicum*, 6 vols., Naples, 1970-76.

Edrīsī, tr. Jaubert
 Abū ʿAbd-Allāh Moḥammad Edrīsī, *Nozhat al-moštāq fī eḵterāq al-āfāq*, tr. P. A. Jaubert as *Géographie dʾEdrisi*, 2 vols., Paris, 1836-40.

***EI*[1,2]**
 The Encyclopædia of Islam, 4 vols. and supplement, London and Leiden, 1908-36; 2nd ed., London and Leiden, 1960-.

EIr.
Encyclopædia Iranica, ed. Ehsan Yarshater, London, Costa Mesa, Calif., and New York, 1982-.

Ełišē, ed. Tēr-Minasean
Vardapet Ełišē, *Vasn Vardanay ew Hayocʿ paterazmin*, ed. Ervand Tēr-Minasean, Erevan, 1957.

Ełišē, tr. Thomson
Vardapet Ełišē, *Vasn Vardanay ew Hayocʿ paterazmin*, tr. R. W. Thomson as *History of Vardan and the Armenian War*, Cambridge, Mass., 1982.

Elliot, *History of India*
The History of India as Told by Its Own Historians: The Muhammadan Period, ed. H. M. Elliot and J. Dowson, eds., 8 vols., Lon-don, 1867-77.

Eskandar Beg
Eskandar Beg Torkamān Monšī, *Tārīḵ-e ʿālamārā-ye ʿabbāsī*, ed. Īraj Afšār, 2 vols., Tehran, 1334-35 Š./1955-56.

Eskandar Beg, tr. Savory
Eskandar Beg Torkamān Monšī, *Tārīḵ-e ʿālamārā-ye ʿabbāsī*, tr. R. M. Savory as *History of Shah ʿAbbas the Great*, 3 vols., PHS 28, Boulder, Colo., and New York, 1979-86.

Eṣṭaḵrī
Abū Esḥāq Eṣṭaḵrī, *Ketāb masālek al-mamālek*, ed. M. J. de Goeje, BGA, Leiden, 1870; 2nd ed., Leiden, 1927; 3rd ed., Leiden, 1967.

Eʿtemād-al-Salṭana, *Maʾāṯer wa'l-āṯār*
Moḥammad-Ḥasan Khan Ṣanīʿ-al-Dawla Eʿtemād-al-Salṭana, *al-Maʾāṯer wa'l-āṯār*, ed. Īraj Afšār as *Čehel sāl tārīḵ-e Īrān dar dawra-ye Pādšāhī-e Nāṣer-al-Dīn Šāh: al-Maʾāṯer wa'l-āṯār*, 3 vols., Tehran, 1363-68 Š./1984-89.

Eʿtemād-al-Salṭana, *Montaẓam-e nāṣerī*, ed. Reżwānī
Moḥammad-Ḥasan Khan Ṣanīʿ-al-Dawla Eʿtemād-al-Salṭana, *Tārīḵ-e montaẓam-e nāṣerī*, ed. M.-E. Reżwānī, 3 vols., Tehran, 1363-68 Š./1984-88.

Eʿtemād-al-Salṭana, *Rūz-nāma-ye ḵāṭerāt*
Moḥammad-Ḥasan Khan Ṣanīʿ-al-Dawla Eʿtemād-al-Salṭana, *Rūz-nāma-ye ḵāṭerāt-e Eʿtemād-al-Salṭana*, ed. Īraj Afšār, 3rd ed., Teh-ran, 2536=1356 Š./1977.

Ethé, *Catalogue*
Hermann Ethé, *Catalogue of Persian Manuscripts in the Library of the India Office*, 2 vols., Oxford, 1903-37.

Eznik, ed. Mariès and Mercier
Eznik Kolbacʿi, *Elc alandocʿ*, ed. and tr. L. Mariès and C. Mercier as *De Deo*, 2 vols., Paris, 1959.

Fasāʾī
Ḥājj Mīrzā Ḥasan Ḥosaynī Fasāʾī, *Fārs-nāma-ye nāṣerī*, 2 vols., Tehran, 1313-14/1896-97; repr. 2 vols. in 1, Tehran, n.d.

Fasāʾī, ed. Rastgār
Ḥājj Mīrzā Ḥasan Ḥosaynī Fasāʾī, *Fārs-nāma-ye nāṣerī*, ed. M. Rastgār Fasāʾī, 2 vols., Tehran, 1367 Š./1988.

Fasāʾī, tr. Busse
Ḥājj Mīrzā Ḥasan Ḥosaynī Fasāʾī, *Fārs-nāma-ye nāṣerī*, tr. H. Busse as *History of Persia under Qajar Rule*, PHS 15, New York, 1972.

Faustus, ed. Patkanean
Pʿawstos Buzandacʿi, *Patmutʿiwn Hayocʿ*, ed. Kʿ. Patkanean, St. Petersburg, 1883; repr. Delmar, N.Y., 1984.

Faustus, tr. Garsoïan
Pʿawstos Buzandacʿi, *Patmutʿiwn Hayoc*, tr. N. G. Garsoïan as *The Epic Histories Attributed to Pʿawstos Buzand (Buzandaran Pat-mutʿiwnkʿ)*, Cambridge, Mass., 1989.

Fehrest. . . Āṣafīya
Fehrest-e kotob-e ʿarabī wa fārsī wa ordū, maḵzūna-ye kotob-ḵāna-ye Āṣafīya-ye Sarkār-e ʿAlī, 3 vols., Hyderabad, 1332-47/1914-28.

Feraq al-šīʿa
Ḥasan B. Mūsā Nawbaḵtī, *Ketāb feraq al-šīʿa*, ed. H. R. Ritter, Leipzig and Istanbul, 1931.

Ferešta
Moḥammad-Qāsem Hendūšāh Astarābādī (Estarābādī) Ferešta, *Golšan-e ebrāhīmī*, ed. J. Briggs, 2 vols., Bombay and Poona, 1831.

Ferešta, tr. Briggs
Moḥammad-Qāsem Hendūšāh Estarābādī Ferešta, *Golšan-e ebrāhīmī*, tr. J. Briggs as *History of the Rise of the Mohammedan Power in India . . .* , 4 vols., London, 1829; repr. Calcutta, 1908-10, 1966.

FIZ
Farhang-e Īrān-zamīn.

Gardīzī, ed. Ḥabībī
Abū Saʿīd ʿAbd-al-Ḥayy Gardīzī, *Zayn al-aḵbār*, ed. ʿA-Ḥ. Ḥabībī, Tehran, 1347 Š./1968.

Gazetteer of Afghanistan
Ludwig W. Adamec, ed., *Historical and Political Gazetteer of Afghanistan*, 6 vols., Graz, 1972-85.

Gazetteer of Iran
Ludwig W. Adamec, *Historical Gazetteer of Iran*, Graz, 1976-.

GMS
E. J. W. Gibb Memorial Series.

Golčīn-e Maʿānī, *Kārvān-e Hend*
Aḥmad Golčīn-e Maʿānī, *Kārvān-e Hend: Dar aḥwāl wa āṯār-e šāʿerān-e ʿaṣr-e ṣafawī ke ba Hend raftand*, 2 vols., Mašhad, 1369 Š./1990.

Golčīn-e Maʿānī, *Taḏkerahā*
Aḥmad Golčīn-e Maʿānī, *Tārīḵ-e taḏkerahā-ye fārsī*, 2 vols., Tehran, 1348-50 Š./1969-71.

Gray, *Foundations*
Louis H. Gray, *The Foundations of the Iranian Religions*, K. R. Cama Oriental Institute Publication 5 (repr. from *Journal of the Cama Oriental Institute* 15, 1929), Bombay, 1930.

Grundriss
Grundriss der iranischen Philologie, ed. Wilhelm Geiger and Ernst Kuhn, 2 vols., Strassburg, 1895-1904.

Ḥabīb al-sīar
Ḡīāṯ-al-Dīn Moḥammad Ḵᵛāndamīr, *Tārīḵ-e ḥabīb al-sīar*, 4 vols., Tehran, 1333 Š./1954.

Ḥabībābādī, *Makārem*
M.-ʿA. Moʿallem Ḥabībābādī, *Makārem al-āṯār dar aḥwal-e rejāl-e do qarn-e 13 wa 14-e hejrī*, 5 vols.,

Isfahan, 1377-96/1958-76.

Haft eqlīm
Amīn Aḥmad Rāzī, *Haft eqlīm*, ed. Jawād Fāżel, 3 vols., Tehran, 1340 Š./1961.

Ḥamza Eṣfahānī
Abu'l-Ḥasan Ḥamza Eṣfahānī, *Ketāb ta'rīḵ senī molūk al-arż wa'l-anbīā'*, ed. and Latin tr. J. M. E. Gottwaldt, 2 vols., St. Petersburg and Leipzig, 1844-48.

Ḥasan Rūmlū, ed. Navā'ī
Ḥasan Rūmlū, *Aḥsan al-tawārīḵ*, ed. ʿAbd-al-Ḥosayn Navā'ī, 2 vols., Tehran, 1349-57 Š./1970-79.

Ḥasan Rūmlū, ed. and tr. Seddon
Ḥasan Rūmlū, *Aḥsan al-tawārīḵ*, ed. and tr. C. N. Seddon, 2 vols., Baroda, 1931-34.

Hedāyat, *Rawżat al-ṣafā*
Reżāqolī Khan Hedāyat, *Tārīḵ-e rawżat al-ṣafā-ye nāṣerī*, 2 vols., Qom, 1339/1960 (= IX-X of Mīrḵʷānd, *Tārīḵ-e rawżat al-ṣafā*; XI = index by M.-J. Maškūr, 1351 Š./1972).

Henning, "Mitteliranisch"
Walter B. Henning, "Mitteliranisch," *HO* I, IV, 1, Leiden and Cologne, 1958, pp. 20-130.

Highlights of Persian Art
Highlights of Persian Art, ed. R. Ettinghausen and E. Yarshater, Boulder, Colo., 1979; repr. Bib. Pers., New York, 1982.

HJAS
Harvard Journal of Asiatic Studies.

HO
Bertold Spuler et al., eds., *Handbuch der Orientalistik.*

***Ḥodūd al-ʿālam*, ed. Sotūda**
Ḥodūd al-ʿālam, ed. M. Sotūda, Tehran, 1340 Š./1961.

***Ḥodūd al-ʿālam*, tr. Minorsky**
Ḥodūd al-ʿālam, tr. V. Minorsky as *Ḥudūd al-ʿĀlam: The Regions of the World*, 2nd ed., GMS, London, 1970.

Honarfar, *Eṣfahān*
Loṭf-Allāh Honarfar, *Ganjīna-ye āṯār-e tārīḵī-e Eṣfahān*, Tehran, 1344 Š./1965.

Horn, *Etymologie*
Paul Horn, *Grundriss der neupersischen Etymologie*, Strassburg, 1893.

Houtsma, *Recueil*
M. Th. Houtsma, *Recueil de textes relatifs à l'histoire des Seljoucides*, 4 vols., Leiden, 1886-1902.

Hübschmann, *Armenische Grammatik*
Heinrich Hübschmann, *Armenische Grammatik*, Leipzig, 1897; repr. Hildesheim and New York, 1972.

Hübschmann, *Persische Studien*
Heinrich Hübschmann, *Persische Studien*, Strassburg, 1895.

İA
İslâm ansiklopedisi, 13 vols., Istanbul, 1961-88.

IF
Indogermanische Forschungen.

IHQ
Indian Historical Quarterly.

IIJ
Indo-Iranian Journal.

IJMES
International Journal of Middle East Studies.

Iran
Iran: Journal of the British Institute of Persian Studies.

Iranian Studies
Iranian Studies: Journal of the Society for Iranian Studies.

Iranisches Personennamenbuch
Manfred Mayrhofer and Rüdiger Schmitt, eds., *Iranisches Personennamenbuch*, Vienna, 1977-.

Ivanov, *Catalogue*
Wladimir Ivanov, *Concise Descriptive Catalogue of the Persian Manuscripts in the Collection of the Asiatic Society of Bengal*, Calcutta, 1924.

JA
Journal asiatique.

Jacoby, *Fragmente*
Felix Jacoby, *Die Fragmente der griechischen Historiker*, 3 vols., Berlin, 1923-58.

Jāmī, *Nafaḥāt*
ʿAbd-al-Raḥmān Jāmī, *Nafaḥāt al-ons min ḥażarāt al qods*, ed. M. Tawḥīdīpūr, Tehran, 1336 Š./1957.

Jāmī, *Nafaḥāt*, ed. ʿĀbedī
ʿAbd-al-Raḥmān Jāmī, *Nafaḥāt al-ons min ḥażarāt al qods*, ed. M. ʿĀbedī, Tehran, 1370 Š./1991.

JAOS
Journal of the American Oriental Society.

JESHO
Journal of the Economic and Social History of the Orient.

JNES
Journal of Near Eastern Studies.

Jovaynī, ed. Qazvīnī
ʿAlā'-al-Dīn ʿAṭā-Malek Jovaynī, *Tārīḵ-e jahāngošāy*, ed. M. Qazvīnī, GMS, 3 vols., Leiden and London, 1906-37.

Jovaynī, tr. Boyle
ʿAlā'-al-Dīn ʿAṭā-Malek Jovaynī, *Tārīḵ-e jahāngošāy*, tr. J. A. Boyle as *The History of the World-Conqueror*, 2 vols., Manchester, 1958.

JPHS
Journal of the Pakistan Historical Society.

JRAS
Journal of the Royal Asiatic Society.

J(R)ASB
Journal of the (Royal) Asiatic Society of Bengal.

JRGS
Journal of the Royal Geographical Society.

Justi, *Namenbuch*
Ferdinand Justi, *Iranisches Namenbuch*, Marburg, 1895; repr. Hildesheim, 1963.

Jūzjānī (Jowzjānī), *Ṭabaqāt*
Menhāj-e Serāj Jūzjānī, *Ṭabaqāt-e nāṣerī*, ed. ʿA.-Ḥ. Ḥabībī, 2nd ed., 2 vols., Kabul, 1342-43 Š./1963-64.

Jūzjānī (Jowzjānī), *Ṭabaqāt*, tr. Raverty
Menhāj-e Serāj Jūzjānī, *Ṭabaqāt-e nāṣerī*, tr. H. G. Raverty, 2 vols., London, 1881-99.

Kaḥḥāla
ʿOmar Reżā Kaḥḥāla, *Moʿjam al-moʾallefīn*, 15 vols., Damascus, 1957-61.

Karatay, *Katalog*
F. E. Karatay, *Topkapı Sarayı Müzesi Kütüp-hanesi farsça yazmalar kataloğu*, Istanbul, 1961.

***Kār-nāmag*, ed. Antia**
Kârnâmak-i Artakhshîr Pâpakân, the Original Pahlavi Text, with Translation in Avesta Characters, Translations into English and Gujarati, and Selections from the Shâhnâmeh, ed. E. K. Antia, Bombay, 1900.

***Kār-nāmag*, ed. Sanjana**
The Kârnâmê î Artakhshîr Pâpakân . . . The Original Pahlavi Text Edited for the First Time . . . Translations into English and Gujarati Languages . . ., ed. D. P. Sanjana, Bombay, 1896.

***Kašf al-ẓonūn*, ed. Flügel**
Ḥājī Ḵalīfa, *Kašf al-ẓonūn*, ed. G. Flügel, 7 vols., Leipzig, 1835-58.

***Kašf al-ẓonūn*, ed. Yaltkaya and Bilge**
Ḥājī Ḵalīfa, *Kašf al-ẓonūn*, ed. Ş. Yaltkaya and K. R. Bilge, 2 vols., Istanbul, 1941-43.

Kašf al-ẓonūn: Ḏayl
Esmāʿīl Pasha Baḡdādī, *Ketāb īżāḥ al-maknūn fi'l-ḏayl ʿalā Kašf al-ẓonūn ʿan asāmī al-kotob wa'l-fonūn*, 2 vols., Istanbul, 1945-47.

Kasrawī, *Āḏarbāyjān*
Aḥmad Kasrawī, *Tārīḵ-e hejda-sāla-ye Āḏarbāyjān*, 2nd ed., Tehran, 1333 Š./1954.

Kasrawī, *Mašrūta*
Aḥmad Kasrawī, *Tārīḵ-e mašrūṭa-ye Īrān*, 3rd ed., 3 vols. in 1, Tehran, 1330 Š./1951.

Kayhān, *Joḡrāfīā*
Masʿūd Kayhān, *Joḡrāfīā-ye mofaṣṣal-e Īrān*, 3 vols., 1310-11 Š./1931-32.

Ḵayyāmpūr, *Soḵanvarān*
ʿAbd-al-Rasūl Ḵayyāmpūr, *Farhang-e soḵanvarān*, Tabrīz, 1340 Š./1961.

Kent, *Old Persian*
Roland G. Kent, *Old Persian: Grammar, Texts, Lexicon*, 2nd ed., New Haven, Conn., 1953.

Lambton, *Continuity*
Ann K. S. Lambton, *Continuity and Change: Aspects of Social and Administrative History in Persia*, Col. Lect. Series, Albany, N.Y., 1988.

Lambton, *Landlord and Peasant*
Ann K. S. Lambton, *Landlord and Peasant in Persia: A Study of Land Tenure and Land Revenue Administration*, London, 1953.

Langlois, *Historiens*
Victor Langlois, tr., *Collections des historiens anciens et modernes de l'Arménie*, 2 vols., Paris, 1868-69.

Laufer, *Sino-Iranica*
Berthold Laufer, *Sino-Iranica: Chinese Contributions to the History of Civilization in Ancient Iran*, Chicago, 1919.

Lazard, *Premiers poètes*
Gilbert Lazard, *Les premiers poètes persans (IXe-Xe siècle): Fragments rassemblés, édités et traduits*, 2 vols., Tehran and Liège, 1964.

Le Strange, *Lands*
Guy Le Strange, *The Lands of the Eastern Caliphate*, 2nd ed., Cambridge, 1930; repr. London, 1966.

***Loḡat-e fors*, ed. Dabīrsīāqī**
Asadī Ṭūsī, *Loḡat-e fors*, ed. M. Dabīrsīāqī from the ed. of P. Horn, Tehran, 1336 Š./1957.

***Loḡat-e fors*, ed. Eqbāl**
Asadī Ṭūsī, *Loḡat-e fors*, ed. ʿA. Eqbāl, Tehran, 1319 Š./1940.

***Loḡat-e fors*, ed. Mojtabāʾī and Ṣādeqī**
Asadī Ṭūsī, *Loḡat-e fors*, ed. F.-A. Mojtabāʾī and ʿA.-A. Ṣādeqī, Tehran, 1365 Š./1986.

Lorimer, *Gazetteer*
J. G. Lorimer, *Gazetteer of the Persian Gulf, ʿOmān, and Central Arabia*, compl. and ed. L. Birdwood, 2 vols., Calcutta, 1908-15; repr., Westmead, U.K., 2 vols. in 6, 1970.

***Maʾāṯer al-omarāʾ* (Calcutta)**
ʿAbd-al-Razzāq Šāhnavāz Khan Awrangābādī, *Maʾāṯer al-omarāʾ*, ed. Mawlawī, Bib. Ind., 3 vols., Calcutta, 1888-91.

***Maʾāṯer al-omarāʾ*, tr. Beveridge**
ʿAbd-al-Razzāq Šāhnavāz Khan Awrangābādī, *Maʾāṯer al-omarāʾ*, tr. Henry Beveridge as *The maāthir-ul-umarā*, rev. Baini Prashad, Bib. Ind., 3 vols., Calcutta 1911-64; repr. Patna, 1979.

***Mādayān*, pt. 1**
Mâdigân-i-hazâr Dâdistân, ed. J. J. Modi (facs. ed. fols. 1-55), Bombay, 1901.

***Mādayān*, pt. 2**
Mâdigân-i-hazâr Dâdistân, ed. T. D. Anklesaria as *The Social Code of the Parsees in Sassanian Times*, pt. 2, Bombay, 1912.

Maḥbūbī, *Moʾassasāt*
Ḥosayn Maḥbūbī Ardakānī, *Tārīḵ-e moʾassasāt-e tamaddonī-e jadīd dar Īrān* I, Tehran, 1354 Š./1975; II, Tehran, 2537=1357 Š./1978; III, ed. Karīm Eṣfahānīān and Jahāngīr Qājārīya, Tehran, 1368 Š./1989.

Majāles al-nafāʾes
ʿAlī-Šīr Navāʾī, *Majāles al-nafāʾes*, tr. Faḵrī Herātī and Ḥakīm Shah Moḥammad Qazvīnī, ed. ʿA.-A. Ḥekmat, Tehran, 1323 Š./1944.

Majmaʿ al-foṣaḥāʾ
Reżāqolī Khan Hedāyat, *Majmaʿ al-foṣaḥāʾ*, ed. Maẓāher Moṣaffā, 6 vols., Tehran, 1336-40 Š./1957-61.

Malekzāda
Mahdī Malekzāda, *Tārīḵ-e enqelāb-e mašrūṭīyat-e Īrān*, 7 vols., Tehran, 1327-35 Š./1948-56; 2nd ed., 3 vols., Tehran, 1363 Š./1984.

Mann, *Kurdisch-persische Forschungen*
Oskar Mann, *Kurdisch-persische Forschungen: Ergebnisse einer von 1901 bis 1903 und 1906 bis 1907 in Persien und die asiatischen Türkei ausgeführten Forschungs-*

reise, pts. 1-2, Berlin, 1909-10; pt. 3, ed. Karl Hadank, 4 vols., Berlin, 1926-32.

Maqdesī, *Bad*ʾ
Moṭahhar b. Ṭāher Maqdesī, *Ketāb al-badʾ wa'l-taʾrīḵ*, ed. and tr. Clément Huart as *Le livre de la création et de l'histoire*, 6 vols., Paris, 1899-1919.

Margoliouth and Amedroz, *Eclipse*
D. S. Margoliouth and H. F. Amedroz, eds. and trs., *The Eclipse of the Abbasid Caliphate: Original Chronicles of the Fourth Islamic Century*, 7 vols., Oxford, 1921-22.

Markwart, *Ērānšahr*
Josef Markwart (Marquart), *Ērānšahr nach der Geographie des Ps. Moses Xorenacʿi*, Abh. Akademie der Wissenschaften zu Göttingen, N.S. 3/2, 1901.

Markwart, *Provincial Capitals*
Josef Markwart, *A Catalogue of the Provincial Capitals of Ērānshahr (Pahlavi Text, Version and Commentary)*, ed. G. Messina, Analecta Orientalia 3, Rome, 1931.

Marshall, *Mughals in India*
D. N. Marshall, *Mughals in India: A Bibliographic Survey* I. *Manuscripts*, Bombay, 1967.

MASI
Memoirs of the Archaeological Survey of India.

Massé, *Croyances*
Henri Massé, *Croyances et coutumes persanes suivies de contes et chansons populaires*, Les littératures populaires de toutes les nations 4 and 6, 2 vols., Paris, 1938.

Massignon, *Essai*
Louis Massignon, *Essai sur les origines du lexique technique de la mystique musulmane*, new ed., Paris, 1954.

Masʿūdī, *Morūj*
Abu'l-Ḥasan ʿAlī Masʿūdī, *Morūj al-ḏahab*, ed. and tr. Charles Barbier de Meynard and Abel Pavet de Courteille as *Les prairies d'or*, 9 vols., Paris, 1861-1917.

Masʿūdī, *Morūj*, ed. Pellat
Abu'l-Ḥasan ʿAlī Masʿūdī, *Morūj al-ḏahab*, rev. ed. Ch. Pellat, 7 vols., Beirut, 1962-79.

Masʿūdī, tr. Pellat
Abu'l-Ḥasan ʿAlī Masʿūdī, *Morūj al-ḏahab*, rev. tr. Ch. Pellat, 3 vols., Paris, 1962-71.

Masʿūdī, *Tanbīh*
Abu'l-Ḥasan ʿAlī Masʿūdī, *Ketāb al-tanbīh wa'l-ešrāf*, ed. M. J. de Goeje, BGA, Leiden, 1894.

***Maṭlaʿ-e saʿdayn*, ed. Šafīʿ**
Kamāl-al-Dīn ʿAbd-al-Razzāq b. Jalāl-al-Dīn Esḥāq Samarqandī, *Maṭlaʿ-e saʿdayn wa majmaʿ-e baḥrayn*, ed. M. Šafīʿ, 2 vols., Lahore, 1360-68/1941-49.

Mayrhofer, *Dictionary*
Manfred Mayrhofer, *A Concise Etymological Sanskrit Dictionary (Kurzgefasstes etymologisches Wörterbuch des Altindischen)*, 3 vols., Heidelberg, 1956-76.

Mayrhofer, *Wörterbuch*
Manfred Mayrhofer, *Etymologisches Wörterbuch des Altindoarischen*, Heidelberg, 1986-.

***MDA* Tabriz**
Majalla-ye Dāneškada-ye adabīyāt (o ʿolūme ensānī)-e Dānešgāh-e Tabrīz.

MDAF
Majalla-ye Dāneškada-ye adabīyāt o ʿolūme ensānī-e Dānešgāh-e Ferdowsī.

MDAFA
Mémoires de la Délégation archéologique française en Afghanistan.

MDAFI
Mémoires de la Délégation archéologique française en Iran.

MDAM
Majalla-ye Dāneškada-ye adabīyāt o ʿolūm-e ensānī-e Dānešgāh-e Mašhad.

MDAT
Majalla-ye Dāneškada-ye adabīyāt o ʿolūm-e ensānī-e Dānešgāh-e Tehrān.

MDOG
Mitteilungen der Deutschen Orient-Gesellschaft.

***Mēnōg ī xrad*, ed. Anklesaria**
Dânâk-u mainyô-i khrad, ed. T. D. Anklesaria, Bombay, 1913.

Meskawayh, *Tajāreb*
Abū ʿAlī Aḥmad b. Meskawayh, *Tajāreb al-omam*. See Margoliouth and Amedroz, *Eclipse*.

***Meyḵāna*, ed. Golčīn-e Maʿānī**
ʿAbd-al-Nabī Qazvīnī, *Taḏkera-ye meyḵāna*, ed. A. Golčīn-e Maʿānī, Tehran, 1340 Š./1961.

MIDEO
Mélanges de l'Institut Dominicain d'Études Orientales du Caire.

Mir. Man.
F. C. Andreas and W. B. Henning, *Mitteliranische Manichaica aus Chinesisch-Turkestan*, SPAW I, 1932, 10; II, 1933, 7; III, 1934, 27.

Mīrḵᵛānd (Bombay)
Mīr Moḥammad b. Sayyed Borhān-al-Dīn Ḵᵛāvandšāh Mīrḵᵛānd, *Tārīḵ-e rawżat al-ṣafā*, Bombay, 1266/1849.

Mīrḵᵛānd (Tehran)
Mīr Moḥammad b. Sayyed Borhān-al-Dīn Ḵᵛāvandšāh Mīrḵᵛānd, *Tārīḵ-e rawżat al-ṣafā*, 8 vols., Qom, 1338-39 Š./1959-60; XI. Index, M.-J. Maškūr, 1351 Š./1972.

MO
Le monde oriental.

Modarres, *Rayḥānat al-adab*
Moḥammad-ʿAlī Modarres, *Rayḥānat al-adab fī tarājem al-maʿrūfīn be'l-konya aw al-laqab*, 8 vols., Tabrīz, n.d.

***Mojmal*, ed. Bahār**
Mojmal al-tawārīḵ wa'l-qeṣaṣ, ed. M.-T. Bahār, Tehran, 1318 Š./1939.

Monzawī, *Nosḵahā*
Aḥmad Monzawī, *Fehrest-e nosḵahā-ye ḵaṭṭī-e fārsī*, 6 vols., Tehran, 1348-53 Š./ 1969-74.

Moqaddasī
Abū ʿAbd-Allāh Moḥammad Moqaddasī (Maqdesī), *Aḥsan al-taqāsīm fī maʿrefat al-aqālīm*, ed. M. J. de Goeje, BGA, Leiden, 1877.

Moreley, *Catalogue*
W. H. Moreley, *A Descriptive Catalogue of the . . . Manu-*

scripts in the Arabic and Persian Languages Preserved in the Library of the Royal Asiatic Society, London, 1854.

Morier, *Journey*
James J. Morier, *A Journey through Persia, Armenia, and Asia Minor, to Constantinople, in the Years 1808-1809 . . .*, 2 vols., London, 1812.

Morier, *Second Journey*
James J. Morier, *A Second Journey through Persia, Armenia, and Asia Minor, to Constantinople, between the Years 1810-1816. With a Journal of the Voyage by the Brazils and Bombay to the Persian Gulf. . .*, London, 1818.

Mošār, *Fehrest*
Fehrest-e ketābhā-ye čāpī-e fārsī, based on the 2-volume catalogue of the same title by Ḵānbābā Mošār and the catalogues of the Anjoman-e Ketāb, 3 vols., Tehran, 1352 Š./1973.

Mošār, *Moʾallefīn*
Ḵānbābā Mošār, *Moʾallefīn-e kotob-e čāpī-e fārsī wa ʿarabī*, 6 vols., Tehran, 1340-44 Š./1961-65.

Moses of Khorene
Movsēs Xorenacʿi, *Patmutʿiwn Hayocʿ*, ed. M. Abelean and S. Yarutʿiwnean, Tiflis, 1913; repr. Delmar, N.Y., 1981.

Moses of Khorene, tr. Thomson
Movsēs Xorenacʿi, *Patmutʿiwn Hayocʿ*, tr. R. W. Thomson as *History of the Armenians*, Cambridge, Mass., 1978.

Mostawfī, *Šarḥ-e zendagānī*
ʿAbd-Allāh Mostawfī, *Šarḥ-e zendagānī-e man yā tārīḵ-e ejtemāʿī o edārī-e dawra-ye qājārīya*, 2nd ed., 3 vols., Tehran, 1343 Š./1964.

MSL
Mémoires de la Société de linguistique de Paris.

MSS
Münchener Studien zur Sprachwissenschaft.

Müller, *Fragmenta*
Karl and Theodor Müller, eds., *Fragmenta Historicorum Graecorum*, 5 vols., Paris, 1841-85.

Nachr.
Nachrichten.

Nafīsī, *Naẓm o naṯr*
Saʿīd Nafīsī, *Tārīḵ-e naẓm o naṯr dar Īrān wa dar zabān-e fārsī*, 2 vols., Tehran, 1344 Š./1965.

Nafīsī, *Rūdakī*
Saʿīd Nafīsī, *Aḥwāl o ašʿār-e Rūdakī*, 3 vols., Tehran, 1309-19 Š./1930-40; 2nd ed., Tehran, 1341 Š./1962.

Naršaḵī
Abū Bakr Jaʿfar Naršaḵī, *Tārīk-e Boḵārā*, ed. M.-T. Modarres Rażawī, Tehran, 1319 Š./1940; 2nd ed. Tehran, 1351 Š./1972.

Naršaḵī, tr. Frye
Abū Bakr Jaʿfar Naršaḵī, *Tārīḵ-e Boḵārā*, tr. R. N. Frye as *The History of Bukhara*, Cambridge, Mass., 1954.

National Census
Āmār-e ʿomumī (Department of Public Statistics), *National and Province Statistics of the First Census of Iran: November 1956*, Tehran, 1961-62; for the following years, see Markaz-e āmār-e Irān (Statistical Center of Iran), *Saršomārī-e ʿomūmī-e nofūs wa maskan/National Census of Population and Housing* (publications of the decennial censuses of Iran, 1966 to 1996, issued for the entire country by provinces [*Ostāns*] and sub-provinces [*Šahrestāns*]).

NC
Numismatic Chronicle.

***NDA* Tabrīz**
Našrīya-ye Dāneškada-ye adabīyāt (o ʿolūm-e ensānī)-e Dānešgāh-e Tabrīz.

Nöldeke, *Geschichte der Perser*
Theodor Nöldeke, *Geschichte der Perser und Araber zur Zeit der Sasaniden, aus der arabischen Chronik des Tabari übersetzt*, Leiden, 1879; repr. Leiden, 1973.

***Nozhat al-qolūb*, ed. and tr. Le Strange**
Ḥamd-Allāh Mostawfī, *Nozhat al-qolūb*, ed. and tr. G. Le Strange, GMS, 2 vols., Leiden and London, 1915-19.

NTS
Norsk tidsskrift for sprogvidenskap.

Nyberg, *Manual*
H. S. Nyberg, *A Manual of Pahlavi*, 2 vols., Wiesbaden, 1964-74.

OGI
Wilhelm Dittenberger, ed., *Orientis Graeci Inscriptiones Selectae*, 2 vols., Leipzig, 1903-05.

OLZ
Orientalistische Literaturzeitung.

Osnovy
Osnovy iranskogo yazykoznaniya, Moscow, 1979-.

***Pahlavi Rivayat*, ed. Dhabhar**
The Pahlavi Rivâyat Accompanying the Dâdestân-î Dînîk, ed. B. N. Dhabhar, Bombay, 1913.

***Pahlavi Texts*, ed. Jamasp-Asana**
The Pahlavi Texts Contained in the Codex MK, ed. J. M. Jamasp-Asana, 2 vols., Bombay, 1897-1913.

Pauly-Wissowa
See under *RE*.

Persian Literature
Ehsan Yarshater, ed., *Persian Literature*, Bib. Pers., Albany, N.Y., 1988.

***Persian Rivayats*, ed. Unvala**
Dârâb Hormazyâr's Rivâyat, ed. M. R. Unvala, 2 vols., Bombay, 1922.

***Persian Rivayats*, tr. Dhabhar**
The Persian Rivayats of Hormazyar Framarz and Others, tr. B. N. Dhabhar, 2 vols., Bombay, 1932.

PHS
Persian Heritage Series.

Pokorny
Julius Pokorny, *Indogermanisches etymologisches Wörterbuch*, 2 vols., Bern and Munich, 1959-69.

PRGS
Proceedings of the Royal Geographical Society.

Qāżī Aḥmad
Qāżī Aḥmad, *Golestān-e honar*, ed. A. Sohaylī Ḵᵛānsārī, Tehran, 1352 Š./1973; 3rd ed., 1366 Š./1987.

Qāżī Aḥmad, tr. Minorsky
Qāżī Aḥmad, *Golestān-e honar*, tr. V. Minorsky and T. Minorsky as *Calligraphers and Painters: A Treatise*

by Qāḍī Aḥmad, Son of Mīr Munshī . . ., Washington, D.C., 1959.

Qodāma, *Ketāb al-ḵarāj*
Qodāma b. Jaʿfar, *Ketāb al-ḵarāj*, ed. M. J. de Goeje, BGA, Leiden, 1889; repr. Leiden, 1967.

RA
Revue d'assyriologie et d'archéologie orientale.

RAA
Revue des arts asiatiques.

Rašīd-al-Dīn, *Jāmeʿ al-tawārīḵ* (Baku)
Ḵᵛāja Rašīd-al-Dīn Fażl-Allāh b. ʿEmād-al-Dawla, *Jāmeʿ al-tawārīḵ* I-II, ed. A. A. Ali-Zade; III, tr. A. K. Arends, Baku, 1957.

Rašīd-al-Dīn, *Jāmeʿ al-tawārīḵ* (Moscow)
Ḵᵛāja Rašīd-al-Dīn Fażl-Allāh b. ʿEmād-al-Dawla, *Jāmeʿ al-tawārīḵ*, ed. A. A. Romaskevicha, A. A. Khetagurova, and A. A. Ali-Zade, Moscow, 1965.

Rašīd-al-Dīn, *Tārīḵ-e ḡāzānī*
Ḵᵛāja Rašīd-al-Dīn Fażl-Allāh b. ʿEmād-al-Dawla, *Tārīḵ-e mobārak-e ḡāzānī*, ed. K. Jahn as *Geschichte Ġāzān-Ḫān's*, GMS, London, 1940; as *Geschichte der Ilḫāne Abāġā bis Gaiḫātū (1265-1295)*, The Hague, 1957.

Razmārā, Farhang
Ḥ.-ʿA. Razmārā, ed., *Farhang-e joḡrāfīā'ī-e Īrān: Ābādīhā*, 10 vols., Tehran, 1328-32 Š./1949-53.

RE
Georg Wissowa, Wilhelm Kroll, and Karl Mittelhaus, eds., *Paulys Real-Encyclopädie der classischen Altertumswissenschaft*, Stuttgart, ser. 1, 24 vols., 1894-1970; ser. 2, 10 vols. and 15 suppl. vols. and index vol., Munich, 1903-80.

REArm.
Revue des études arméniennes.

REI
Revue des études islamiques.

RHR
Revue de l'histoire des religions.

Rieu, *Persian Manuscripts*
Charles Rieu, *Catalogue of the Persian Manuscripts in the British Museum*, 3 vols. and supplement, London, 1876-95.

RlA
Erich Ebeling et al., eds., *Reallexikon der Assyriologie und vorderasiatischen Archäologie*, Berlin and Leipzig, 1928-.

RMM
Revue du monde musulman.

Rypka, *Hist. Iran. Lit.*
Jan Rypka et al., *History of Iranian Literature*, ed. K. Jahn, Dordrecht, 1968.

Ṣadr Hāšemī, *Jarā'ed o majallāt*
Moḥammad Ṣadr Hāšemī, *Tārīḵ-e jarā'ed o majallāt-e Īrān*, 4 vols., Isfahan, 1327-32 Š./1948-53; repr. in 1 vol., Tehran, 1363 Š./1984.

Ṣafā, *Adabīyāt*
Ḏabīh-Allāh Ṣafā, *Tārīḵ-e adabīyāt dar Īrān*, 1332-Š./1953-; I, rev. ed., Tehran, 1335 Š./1956.

***Šāh-nāma*, Borūḵīm ed.**
Abu'l-Qāsem Ferdowsī, *Šāh-nāma*, ed. ʿAbbās Eqbāl et al., 10 vols. in 5, Tehran, 1313-15 Š./1934-36.

***Šāh-nāma*, ed. Khaleghi**
Abu'l-Qāsem Ferdowsī, *Šāh-nāma*, ed. Dj. Khaleghi-Motlagh, Bib. Pers., Persian Text Series, N.S. 1, New York, 1987-.

***Šāh-nāma*, ed. Mohl**
Abu'l-Qāsem Ferdowsī, *Šāh-nāma*, ed. and tr. J. Mohl, 7 vols., Paris, 1838-78.

***Šāh-nāma* (Moscow)**
Abu'l-Qāsem Ferdowsī, *Šāh-nāma*, ed. E. E. Bertel's et al., 9 vols., Moscow, 1960-71.

Šahrastānī
Moḥammad b. ʿAbd-al-Karīm Šahrastānī, *Ketāb al-melal wa'l-neḥal*, ed. W. Cureton, London, 1846.

Šahrastānī, tr. Gimaret and Monnot
Moḥammad b. ʿAbd-al-Karīm Šahrastānī, *Ketāb al-melal wa'l-neḥal*, tr. D. Gimaret and G. Monnot as *Livre des religions et des sectes*, Paris, 1986.

Sāl-nāma-ye āmāri
Sāzmān-e Barnāma wa būdga, Markaz-e āmār-e Īrān (Plan and Budget Organization, Statistical Center of Iran), *Sāl-nāma-ye āmārī-e kešvar* (statistical reports, published annually, Tehran, 1345 Š./1966-).

Samʿānī, ed. Margoliouth
Abū Saʿd ʿAbd-al-Karīm b. Moḥammad Tamīmī Samʿānī, *Ketāb al-ansāb*, facs. ed. D. S. Margoliouth, GMS, Leiden, 1912.

Samʿānī, ed. Yamānī
Abū Saʿd ʿAbd-al-Karīm b. Moḥammad Tamīmī Samʿānī, *Ketāb-al-ansāb*, ed. ʿAbd-al-Raḥmān Yamānī, 7 vols., Hyderabad, 1382-86/1962-76.

Šams-al-Dīn Rāzī, *Moʿjam*
Šams-al-Dīn Moḥammad b. Qays Rāzī, *al-Moʿjam fī maʿāyīr ašʿār al-ʿajam*, ed. M. Qazvīnī and M.-T. Modarres Rażawī, Tehran, 1338 Š./1959.

Sartīpzāda
Bīžan Sartīpzāda, ed., with the collaboration of Kobrā Ḵodāparast, *Fehrest-e rūz-nāmahā-ye mawjūd dar Ketābḵāna-ye mellī-e Īrān*, Tehran, 1336 Š./1957.

Šāyest nē šāyest
Šāyast nē šāyast, a Pahlavi Text on Religious Customs, ed and tr. J. C. Tavadia, Hamburg, 1930.

***Šāyest nē šāyest*, suppl.**
The Supplementary Texts to the Šāyest nē-šāyest, ed. and tr. F. M. Kotwal, Copenhagen, 1969.

Sb.
Sitzungsberichte.

SBE
Sacred Books of the East.

Schlimmer
J. L. Schlimmer, *Terminologie médico-pharmaceutique et anthropologique française-persane*, Tehran, 1874; repr. Tehran, 1970.

Schwarz, *Iran*
Paul Schwarz, *Iran im Mittelalter nach den arabischen*

Geographen, Leipzig, 1969.

Sezgin, *GAS*
Fuat Sezgin, *Geschichte des arabischen Schrifttums*, Leiden, 1957-.

Siroux, *Anciennes voies et monuments*
Maxime Siroux, *Anciennes voies et monuments routiers de la région d'Ispahan*, Cairo, 1971.

Sobkī, *Ṭabaqāt* (Cairo[1])
Abū Naṣr ʿAbd-al-Wahhāb b. ʿAlī Tāj-al-Dīn Sobkī, *Ṭabaqat al-šāfeʿīya al-kobrā*, 6 vols., Cairo, 1906.

Sobkī, *Ṭabaqāt* (Cairo[2])
Abū Naṣr ʿAbd-al-Wahhāb b. ʿAlī Tāj-al-Dīn Sobkī, *Ṭabaqāt al-šafeʿīya al-kobrā*, ed. M. M. Ṭanāḥī and ʿA. M. Ḥelw, 10 vols., Cairo, 1964-76.

Solamī, *Ṭabaqāt*
Moḥammad b. Ḥosayn Solamī, *Ketāb ṭabaqāt al-ṣūfīya*, ed. J. Pedersen, Leiden, 1960.

Solṭānī, *Fehrest*
Mortażā Solṭānī, ed., *Fehrest-e rūz-nāmahā-ye fārsī dar majmūʿa-ye Ketāb-ḵāna-ye markazī wa markaz-e asnād-e Dānešgāh-e Tehrān*, Entešārāt-e Ketāb-ḵāna-ye markazī o markaz-e asnād 6, Tehran, 1354 Š./1975.

SPAW
Sitzungsberichte der Preussischen Akademie der Wissenschaften.

Spuler, *Iran*
Bertold Spuler, *Iran in früh-islamischer Zeit*, Wiesbaden, 1952.

Spuler, *Mongolen* [2,3,4]
Bertold Spuler, *Die Mongolen in Iran*, 2nd ed., Berlin, 1955; 3rd ed., Berlin, 1968; 4th ed., Leiden, 1985.

Stchoukine, *Safavis*
I. V. Stchoukine, *Les peintures des manuscrits de Shâh ʿAbbâs Ier à la fin des ṣafavîs.* Paris, 1964.

Storey
Charles A. Storey, *Persian Literature: A Bio-bibliographical Survey*, Leiden, 1927-53.

Storey-Bregel
Charles A. Storey, *Persidskaya literatura: Bio-bibliograficheskiĭ obzor*, ed. and tr. Yu. E. Bregel, 3 vols., Moscow, 1972.

Storey/de Blois
François de Blois, *Persian Literature: A Bio-bibliographical Survey Begun by the late C. A. Storey*, vols. 2–5, London 1972-94.

Survey of Persian Art
A. U. Pope and P. Ackerman, eds., *A Survey of Persian Art from Prehistoric Times to the Present*, 4 vols., London, 1938-39; 2nd ed., 16 vols., Tehran, 1964, with addenda 1967; 3rd ed. with bibliography and addenda, Tehran, 2535=1355 Š./1977.

Suter, *Mathematiker*
Heinrich Suter, *Die Mathematiker und Astronomen der Araber und ihre Werke*, Leipzig, 1900.

Sykes, *History of Persia*
Percy Sykes, *A History of Persia*, 3rd ed. with suppl. essays, 2 vols., London, 1930.

Ṯaʿālebī, *Ḡorar*
Abū Manṣūr ʿAbd-al-Malek Ṯaʿālebī, *Ḡorar aḵbār molūk al-fors*, ed. and tr. Hermann Zotenberg as *Histoire des rois des Perses*, Paris, 1900.

Ṯaʿālebī, *Yatīma* (Damascus)
Abū Manṣūr ʿAbd-al-Malek Ṯaʿālebī, *Yatīmat al-dahr fī maḥāsen ahl al-ʿaṣr*, Damascus, 1304/1886-87.

Ṯaʿālebī, *Yatīma*, ed. ʿAbd-al-Ḥamīd
Abū Manṣūr ʿAbd-al-Malek Ṯaʿālebī, *Yatīmat al-dahr fī maḥāsen ahl al-ʿaṣr*, ed. M. M. ʿAbd-al-Ḥamīd, Cairo, 1377/1957-68.

Ṭabarī
Moḥammad b. Jarīr Ṭabarī, *Ketāb taʾrīḵ al-rosol wa'l-molūk*, ed. M. J. de Goeje et al., 15 vols., Leiden, 1879-1901; repr. Leiden, 1964.

Ṭabarī (Cairo[1])
Moḥammad b. Jarīr Ṭabarī, *Ketāb taʾrīḵ al-rosol wa'l-molūk*, 13 vols., Cairo, 1326/1908; repr. Beirut, 6 vols., 1970.

Ṭabarī (Cairo[2])
Moḥammad b. Jarīr Ṭabarī, *Ketāb taʾrīḵ al-rosol wa'l-molūk*, ed. M. A. Ebrāhīm, 9 vols., Cairo, 1960-68; repr. Beirut, 6 vols., 1970.

Ṭabarī, tr.
Moḥammad b. Jarīr Ṭabarī, *Ketāb taʾrīḵ al-rosol wa'l-molūk*, tr. by various scholars as *The History of al-Ṭabarī*, ed. E. Yar-Shater, Albany, N.Y., 1985-2007.

***Taḏkerat al-molūk*, tr. Minorsky**
Tadhkirat al-mulūk: A Manual of Ṣafavid Administration (circa *1137/1725*), facs. ed. and tr. V. Minorsky, GMS, London, 1943.

Taʾrīḵ Baḡdād
Ḵaṭīb Baḡdādī, *Taʾrīḵ Baḡdād*, 14 vols., Cairo, 1349/1931.

***Tārīḵ-e bīdārī*, ed. Saʿīdī Sīrjānī**
Nāẓem-al-Eslām Kermānī, *Tārīḵ-e bīdārī-e īrānīān*, ed. ʿA.-A. Saʿīdī Sīrjānī, 2 vols., Tehran, 1346 Š./1967; 2nd ed., Tehran, 1362 Š./1983.

***Tārīḵ-e gozīda*, ed. Browne**
Ḥamd-Allāh Mostawfī, *Tārīḵ-e gozīda*, facs. ed. E. G. Browne, GMS, Leiden and London, 1910.

***Tārīḵ-e gozīda*, ed. Navāʾī**
Ḥamd-Allāh Mostawfī, *Tārīḵ-e gozīda*, ed. ʿA.-Ḥ. Navāʾī, 2 vols., Tehran, 1336-39 Š./1957-60.

Tārīḵ-e Sīstān
Tārīḵ-e Sīstān, ed. M.-T. Bahār, Tehran, 1314 Š./1935.

***Tārīḵ-e Sīstān*, tr. Gold**
Tārīḵ-e Sīstān, tr. M. Gold as *The Tārikh-e Sistān*, PHS, Rome, 1976.

Tārīḵ-e Waṣṣāf
Šehāb-al-Dīn ʿAbd-Allāh Waṣṣāf Ḥażra, *Tajzīat al-amṣār wa tazjīat al-aʿṣār*, ed. M. M. Eṣfahānī, Bombay, 1269/1853.

Tavernier (Paris)
J. B. Tavernier, *Les six voyages de Jean Baptiste Tavernier, ecuyer baron d'Aubonne, en Turquie, en Perse, et aux Indes pendant l'espace de quarante ans . . .*, 2 vols., Paris, 1677-82.

Tavernier (London)
J. B. Tavernier, *The Six Travels of John Baptiste Tavernier . . .*, London, 1684.
TAVO
Tübinger Atlas des Vorderen Orients, Wiesbaden, 1977-.
TDED
Türk dili ve edebiyat dergisi, İstanbul Üniversitesi, Edebiyat fakültesi.
Tedesco, "Dialektologie"
Paul Tedesco, "Dialektologie der westiranischen Turfantexte," *MO* 15, 1921, pp. 184-257.
Thévenot
Jean de Thévenot, *Relation d'un voyage fait au Levant, dans laquelle il est curieusement traité des estats sujets au Grand Seigneur, des moeurs, religions, forces, gouvernemens, politiques, langues et coustumes des habitans de ce grand empire*, 3 vols., Paris, 1665-84.
Thévenot (London)
Jean de Thévenot, *The Travels of Monsieur de Thevenot into the Levant*, 3 vols., London, 1686.
Toḥfa-ye sāmī
Sām Mīrzā Ṣafawī, *Toḥfa-ye sāmī*, ed. Ḥ. Waḥīd Dastgerdī, Tehran, 1314 Š./1935.
TPS
Transactions of the Philological Society.
Ṭūsī, *Fehrest*
Abū Jaʿfar Moḥammad b. Ḥasan Ṭūsī, *Fehrest-kotob al-šīʿa wa asmāʾ al-moʾallefīn*, ed. A. Sprenger, Calcutta, 1853-55.
Ṭūsī, *Rejāl*
Abū Jaʿfar Moḥammad b. Ḥasan Ṭūsī, *Ketāb al-rejāl*, ed. M. Ṣ. Āl Baḥr-al-ʿOlūm, Najaf, 1381/1961.
Vd.
Vidēvdād, Vendidad, a text of the Avesta.
VDI
Vestnik drevniĭ istorii.
Waqāyeʿ-e ettefāqīya
ʿAlī-Akbar Saʿīdī Sīrjānī, ed., *Waqāyeʿ-e ettefāqīya*, Tehran, 1361 Š./1982.
Wolff, *Glossar*
Fritz Wolff, *Glossar zu Ferdosis Schahname*, Berlin, 1935; repr. Hildesheim, 1965.
Wulff, *Crafts*
H. E. Wulff, *The Traditional Crafts of Persia*, Cambridge, Mass., 1966.
WZKM
Wiener Zeitschrift für die Kunde des Morgenlandes.
Y.
Yasna, a group of texts of the Avesta.
Yaʿqūbī, *Boldān*
Aḥmad b. Abī Yaʿqūb Yaʿqūbī, *Ketāb al-boldān*, ed. M. J. de Goeje, BGA, Leiden, 1892; 2nd ed., Leiden, 1967.
Yaʿqūbī, tr. Wiet
Aḥmad b. Abī Yaʿqūb Yaʿqūbī, *Ketāb al-boldān*, tr. G. Wiet as *Les pays*, Cairo, 1937.
Yaʿqūbī, *Taʾrīḵ*
Aḥmad b. Abī Yaʿqūb Yaʿqūbī, *Taʾrīḵ*, ed. M. Th. Houtsma as *Historiae*, Leiden, 1883.
Yāqūt, *Boldān*
Šehāb-al-Dīn Abū ʿAbd-Allāh Yāqūt b. ʿAbd-Allāh Ḥamawī, *Moʿjam al-boldān*, ed. F. Wüstenfeld, 6 vols., Leipzig, 1866-73.
Yāqūt, *Boldān* (Beirut)
Šehāb-al-Dīn Abū ʿAbd-Allāh Yāqūt b. ʿAbd-Allāh Ḥamawī, *Moʿjam al-boldān*, 5 vols., Beirut, 1955-57.
Yāqūt, *Odabāʾ*
Šehāb-al-Dīn Abū ʿAbd-Allāh Yāqūt b. ʿAbd-Allāh Ḥamawī, *Moʿjam al-odabāʾ*, ed. D. S. Margoliouth as *Eršād al-arīb elā maʿrefat al-adīb or Dictionary of the Learned Men of Yāqūt*, GMS, 7 vols., Leiden, 1907-31.
Yt.
Yašt, a text of the Avesta.
ZA
Zeitschrift für Assyriologie.
Zādspram
Vichitakiha-i Zatasparam, pt. 1, ed. B. T. Anklesaria, Bombay, 1964.
ZDMG
Zeitschrift der Deutschen Morgenländischen Gesellschaft.
Zereklī, *Aʿlām*[1,2]
Ḵayr-al-Dīn Zereklī, *al-Aʿlām*, 3 vols., Cairo, 1927-28; 2nd ed., 10 vols., Cairo, 1373-78/1954-59.
Zhukovskiĭ, *Materialy*
V. A. Zhukovskiĭ, *Materialy dlya izucheniya persidskikh narechiĭ*, 3 vols., St. Petersburg, 1888-1922; repr. 1 vol., Tehran, 1976.
ZII
Zeitschrift für Indologie und Iranistik.
ZVS
Zeitschrift für vergleichende Sprachforschung.

TRANSLITERATION OF LANGUAGES

Persian and Arabic

Please note that beginning with volume XI, ī and ū, representing the two long vowels, have been written i and u.

The system employed here aims to achieve simplicity and accuracy. It has been jointly adopted by the Corpus Inscriptionum Iranicarum and Encyclopædia Iranica. Transliteration of Arabic words and words in Persian of Arabic origin follows the system used for Persian, with the exceptions noted below.

	CONSONANT			CONSONANT			VOWEL	
	Persian	Arabic		Persian	Arabic		Persian	Arabic
ء	ʾ		ص	ṣ		آ ، ا ، یٰ	ā	
ب	b		ض	ż		و	u	
پ	p		ط	ṭ		ی	i	
ت	t		ظ	ẓ				
ث	ṯ		ع	ʿ		ـَ	a	
ج	j		غ	ḡ		ـُ	o	
چ	č		ف	f		ـِ	e	
ح	ḥ		ق	q				
خ	k̲		ک	k		ـَة ، ـه	a	a
خو	$\underline{k}^{v}$		گ	g		وَ	ow	aw
د	d		ل	l		یَ	ey	ay
ذ	ẕ	ḏ	م	m				
ر	r		ن	n				
ز	z		و	v	w			
ژ	ž		ه	h				
س	s		ی	y				
ش	š							

Note: When an Arabic word ending in a long vowel iș followed by the definite article *al-*, the macron is omitted and the words are elided: e.g., *fī* and *al-* become *fi'l*; *Abū* and *al-* become *Abu'l*; etc. When the Arabic ending ةٌ is in construct, it is transliterated as *at*. For Darī and early Persian, the *majhūl* vowels و and ی may be transliterated as ō and ē respectively. The Persian *eżāfa* is rendered as *-e* after consonants and *ī* and as *-ye* after other vowels.

Anglicized Forms

Commonly used Arabic and Persian terms and some proper names are cited in the articles in English forms rather than in transliteration. These include:

Titles: amir or emir, aga, atabeg, caliph, jagirdar, khan, pasha, shah, shaikh, sultan.

Religious terms: Ashʿarite, darvish or dervish, Hadith, Hanbalite, imam, Ismaʿili, isnad, jihad, Qur'an, Malikite, molla, Muslim, Muʿtazilite, sayyed, Shafeʿite, Shiʿite or Shiʿi, Sufi, Sunna, Sunnite or Sunni, ulema or olama.

Place Names: Names of countries, major cities, and well-known geographic features, including those of India, Central Asia, and Anatolia, are given in commonly accepted modern forms or anglicized equivalents rather than being transliterated: Ahmadabad, Ankara, Azerbaijan, Baghdad, Bukhara, Herat, Hyderabad, Iran, Iraq, Isfahan, Istanbul, Kabul, Khorasan, Mecca, Medina, Mosul, Samarkand, Samarra, Shiraz, Tashkent, Tehran, Turkestan.

Dynasties: Names of dynasties are regularly anglicized, even when they are not given an English suffix: Mughal, Omayyad, Saljuq, Qajar as well as ʿAbbasid, Buyid, Ghaznavid, Safavid, Samanid, Taherid, Timurid, Ziarid.

ix. The Pahlavi Period and the Post-Revolution Era

THE PAHLAVI PERIOD

The Pahlavi period saw the development of a modern nation-state, rapid urbanization and population growth, establishment of a modern system of national education, and a stronger state-directed economic policy. These all had some repercussions in the province of Isfahan, but most of all in the city itself.

The Reza Shah period, 1925-41. This period, as pertains to Isfahan, consists of two distinct phases: the consolidation of central authority in the 1920s, and social and economic development in the 1930s. In the process of consolidating his power in Isfahan, Reza Shah managed to constrain two powerful social groups: the Shiʿite clergy and the Baḵtiāri tribesmen; in both cases he adopted the same tactics: an initial stage of compromise and then, when the central authority had established its control, the adoption of much harsher measures.

It was hardly surprising that the local clergy, who had played a leading role in the socio-political life of Isfahan in the decades prior to the establishment of the Pahlavi dynasty (Najafi, *passim*; Owrang; Anṣāri, pp. 41-51), were vociferously opposed to the social reforms introduced by Reza Shah in the early part of his reign. The conscription law of 1925 resulted in a general strike in the bazaar of Isfahan, and dozens of mullahs led by Ḥājji Āqā Nur-Allāh Fešāraki, Āqā Najafi, and Sayyed-al-ʿErāqayn set out for Qom to express their protest (December 1927). The dispute was finally settled by the government's concession of a short-term draft relief for the mullahs (Najafi, p. 233; M. Hedāyat, p. 479; Makki, 1980, p. 767; Sayfpur, pp. 640-45). Likewise, the implementation of the uniform dress code from 1928 meant deculturation in a city where not only the clergy but also the members of some guilds wore the turban and the gown, thus giving Isfahan a more palpable aura of religiosity than other Persian urban centers. Another vexatious measure, the 1936 law that prohibited women from wearing the veil, meant that many women avoided appearing in public until they were at liberty to use the veil again after the end of Reza Shah's reign. In the latter years of Reza Shah the reform-minded residents of Isfahan would even dare organize annual carnivals to compensate for the excessive mourning rites of Moḥarram that had been banned nationwide (Sayfpur, pp. 995-97). The chief advocates for the reform policies of the central government were local newspapers such as *Ṣedā-ye Eṣfahān*, *Aḵgar*, *Mokrem*, and *Ḡorreš* (Sayfpur, p. 651). The secularization of the judiciary system and the legal and registry offices (*maḥżars*), which documented transactions, contracts, marriages, and divorces (see DAFTAR-E ASNĀD-E RASMI), deprived the clergy of part of its financial revenue. The traditional *madrasa* students lost their income from established religious endowments when the revenue from these began to be officially earmarked by the state for restoring historical monuments (Sayfpur, pp. 631-52). To undermine further the influential role of the leading madrasas such as Nimāvard and Kāsagarān, in 1927 a new high school of religious sciences (Madrasa-ye ʿolum-e maʿqul o manqul) was established in the Safavid madrasa of Mādar-e Šāh (the Queen Mother; Nurṣādeqi, p. 144). Notwithstanding these policies, Maurice Pernot, in his vivid evocation of the town not long after Reza Shah's accession, recalls the high degree of appreciation among the townspeople towards Reza Shah's policies, particularly in regards to the establishment of security, while the residents of the capital held a more critical view of the new regime (Pernot, 1927a, pp. 109-11; idem, 1927b).

Another major challenge was the Baḵtiāri tribe (q.v.), whose summer pastures were not far from the city to the west and south, and whose chieftains had ruled Isfahan and adjoining provinces since the Constitutional Revolution (Gehrke, 1961). Reza Shah began to end their supremacy by appointing his own officials and officers to run the administration of the city and the province. The tribe reacted in the spring of 1929, when the Baḵtiāri khans launched an assault on Isfahan by bringing 30,000 armed tribesmen to Najafābād, 30 miles west of the city, causing many frightened residents to leave Isfahan. Peace was restored only when two senior khans, Ṣamṣām-al-Salṭana and Sardār Asʿad, were sent from Tehran to mediate. They invited all the khans to the city and granted them an amnesty from the shah. A week later Major General Moḥammad Šāhbaḵti arrived in Isfahan to crush those warlords who had not surrendered. His troops repelled the Baḵtiāris from the city hinterland and took control of their strongholds in Tang-e Bidegān and Qalʿa Safid by mid-July (Sayfpur, pp. 660-67; Anṣāri, p. 76; Gehrke).

Having suppressed the rebellion, the state continued its policy of detribalization, as the tribal system and way of life were considered incompatible with modernization and progress. The enforced sedentarization was pursued through the posting of troops in the migration routes to prevent access. Moreover, the shah launched another series of attacks on the Baḵtiāris, beginning with imprisonment in 1933 of his war minister Sardār Asʿad, resulting in his death. Many other Baḵtiāri khans were detained, exiled, and executed in the remaining years of Reza Shah's reign (Sayfpur, pp. 784-94). Their significance in the affairs of Isfahan was further curtailed when the shah bartered the numerous villages owned by the tribal chiefs with those in Kāšān, Ḵᵛār, Varāmin, and Azerbaijan, far from the Baḵtiāri territory. In addition, the shah himself bought, for a fraction of its real value, the Anglo-Persian Oil Company (q.v.) shares that the Baḵtiāri khans had been awarded as compensation for the conversion of their pastureland to oil fields as well as for their undertaking to maintain the security of the petroleum installations. The abolition of the titles *ilḵāni* and *ilbegi* in 1933, the partition of the Baḵtiāri territory between the provinces of Isfahan and Ḵuzestān in 1936, and the refusal to give the tribe a voice in the parliament from the eighth session of the Majles onwards, were further measures taken by the government to destabilize the tribe. These policies led to the devastation of the tribal confederacy, as indicated by the loss of their livestock, the main source of meat and dairy products of Isfahan during the rule of Reza Shah. However, the sedentarization project was never fully realized, as the migrating Baḵtiāri clans would bribe the gendarmes in return for crossing to their seasonal quarters (Sayfpur, pp. 656, 873). The nomadic way of life returned after the shah's abdication.

The 1930s witnessed major progress in bureaucratic reforms and urban development in Isfahan. As the former municipal order established by the Qajar prince-governor Ẓell-al-Solṭān had virtually vanished by the time of Reza Shah, new provincial and municipal administration, law enforcement, and financial, judicial, and educational systems were created (Anṣāri, pp. 37-39, 389-92; Sayfpur, pp. 958-63). The successive governors appointed by the shah, namely Noṣrat-al-Molk, Solaymān Meykada, Amir Eqtedār, Mošār-al-Dawla Dabir Aʿẓam, Faṭan-al-Molk Jalāli, Reżā Afšār, Ṣur-Esrāfil, Amir-Noṣrat Eskandari, and ʿEzz-al-Mamālek Ardalān, were on the whole men of resolution and accomplishment and were instrumental in encouraging the merchants to invest in textile industries and fund philanthropic institutions such as the branch of the league of the Red Lion and Sun (the Persian equivalent of the Red Cross) which supported an orphanage housing 500 children (ibid, pp. 801, 841-45, 962; Nurṣādeqi, p. 139). As the two existing hospitals (founded by the British Missionary Society and by Amin-al-Tojjār, a leading merchant) proved inadequate given the rising demand, the public hospital Ḵᵛoršid was established (Sayfpur, p. 960). Moreover, the artistic and literary communities of the town, as well as the religious minorities, hitherto isolated and alienated, were welcomed to participate in the social and cultural affairs of the city (ibid, p. 705).

The modern urban planning carried out in this period changed the old layout of the city. The introduction of mechanized transport required wide and straight thoroughfares, the construction of which seems unthinkable, in retrospect, without the uncontested authority of Reza Shah, for these modern arteries invaded the organic texture of the old town by uncompromisingly cutting through the mud structures, markets, and narrow, twisting alleys. The Safavid avenue of Čahārbāḡ (q.v.) was further extended northward and remodeled to become the principal thoroughfare of the town, causing a profound shift of economic activity from the main and local bazaars (cf. Sayfpur, pp. 840, 958). New administrative buildings introduced a metropolitan look to the city: the architecture of the Isfahan branch of the National Bank stands out to this day in sharp contrast to the poorer styles of later periods. Equally impressive in its architecture was the new industrial suburb built with German assistance south of the Zāyandarud. Then, due attention was paid to rehabilitation of historical monuments, notably those of the Meydān-e Naqš-e Jahān (Royal Square) that had suffered from decades of neglect (Sykes; Honarfar, pp. 722, 849).

The crowning achievement of this period was industrialization, and most notably the expansion of the textile industry, which grew so successfully that Isfahan became known as the Manchester of Persia. By 1941 there were at least ten large textile mills employing some 11,000 workers, a sizeable proportion in a city of 210,000 inhabitants. Many wage earners worked in modern factories making paper, matches, cigarettes, and boots, a hosiery, an electric plant, and a grain silo (Floor, p. 59). To this new blue-collar class one may add an equally sizeable white-collar group (about 10,000, according to ʿAbedi, p. 49) of administrators, educators, and healthcare employees, as well as law enforcement agents and armed forces. Thus, within the span of one generation, a whole new working and middle class emerged, financially secure with fixed wages, and new economic needs and social preferences. The large-scale units replacing small workshops and their impersonal bureaucracy brought to an end the erstwhile face-to-face relationship, the patriarchal foundation of the family was undermined, and old norms such as polygamy were rendered socially unacceptable (Anṣāri, pp. 184-87). The streets of Isfahan began to witness rush hours filled with bicycles thrice a day, shortly before and after the simultaneous sound of a dozen factory sirens announcing the change of shift—the fixed rhythm Isfahan followed for most of the twentieth century.

The 1941-53 period. Following the occupation of Persia by the Allied forces in September 1941 and the forced abdication of Reza Shah, Isfahan became an arena of struggle between different local powers. Nomadic and clerical influence resurfaced and the Qajar Prince Akbar Mirzā Masʿud Ṣārem-al-Dawla, heir to Ẓell-al-Solṭān, reappeared as the city's elder statesman. While Isfahan was in the sphere of influence of the British who controlled the southern half of the country, the pro-Soviet Tudeh (Tuda) party entrenched itself in the city, leading the labor movement of 1941-47, which became a political tradition of the city in the subsequent decades.

Outside the city, it did not take long for the Baḵtiāris to reassert their power in their tribal stronghold. Mortażāqoli Khan, the only surviving major chieftain, proclaimed himself patriarch of his Hajji Ilḵāni branch (*bastagān*) and forced the rival Ilḵāni branch to accept his authority. By 1943 he had reclaimed his expropriated estates and persuaded the military and the gendarmerie to withdraw from the Baḵtiāri territories, extending from Dezful in the west to Čahārmaḥāl in the east, and from Rāmhormoz in the south to Faridan (Fereydan) in the north. Eventually, the governorate of Čahārmaḥāl and Baḵtiāri separated from Isfahan province. Another conciliatory measure towards the khans was the restitution of their properties in 1945. Moreover, Mohammad-Reza Shah's marriage in February 1951 to Soraya Esfandiāri, daughter of an Ilḵāni chief residing in Isfahan, was considered a sign of favor to the Baḵtiāris (Abrahamian, p. 196; Sayfpur, pp. 658, 873-76).

The rise of the Tudeh party. Having become a major industrial city, Isfahan proved a fertile ground for the Tudeh party, which emerged in the town immediately after Reza Shah's downfall and quickly recruited members from a wide cross-section of the urban society: factory workers, bazaar wage earners, intellectuals, modern middle class, and the religious minorities (Abrahamian, pp. 330-31).

Very soon the Tudeh party was able to organize mass demonstrations and street parades on May Day, in which tens of thousands took part. Among its many newspapers in Isfahan was *Āhangar*, edited by Mortażā Rāvandi (idem, p. 304). The most notable success of the Tudeh party was in the labor movement, a detailed study of which, based on the British Foreign Office documents, is provided by Ervand Abrahamian (pp. 354 ff.). Assisted by the survivors of the early labor movement, the Tudeh party began to unionize some 10,500 workers of nine large textile factories of the town; it proved successful largely because of the hardship experienced by the workers as a result of the economic impact of high inflation in the early 1940s. The Union of Isfahan Workers (Etteḥādiya-ye kārgarān-e Eṣfahān), formed in August 1942, conducted two strikes that won an unprecedented settlement: not only were the wage demands met but it also gave factory workers an 8-hour workday, monthly medical checkups, food subsidies, two suits per year, and one month's bonus taken from company profits, as well as a ban on child labor. Another major strike was won in July 1943, reconfirming the previous achievements (cf. Sykes, pp. 311-14).

The presence of the Tudeh party and the tribes brought together the rest of the competing forces which were loosely organized under the banner of the royalist National Union party (Ḥezb-e waḥdat-e melli) and Sayyed Żiāʾ's Fatherland party (Ḥezb-e erāda-ye melli). The power distribution was reflected in the electorate's choice of the three Majles members from Isfahan: Taqi Fadākār, the only one of the eight Tudeh members of the 14th parliamentary session who was not from the Soviet-backed north; Sayyed Ḥāšem-al-Din Dawlatābādi, son of a prominent religious leader, supported by the elders of the guilds and bazaar merchants (especially those who had acquired part of the land confiscated from the Baḵtiāri khans during Reza Shah's reign) and the National Union party; and Ḥaydar-ʿAli Emāmi, a wealthy merchant and industrialist, backed by prince Akbar Masʿud and the Fatherland party. Additionally, Faraj-Allāh Meṣbāḥ Sayfpur Fāṭemi, with his family newspaper *Bāḵtar*, won the Najafābād seat with the help of the Baḵtiāris; and the elections of Šahr-e kord and Dezful were won, respectively, by Aḥmadqoli Khan, the son of Mortażāqoli Khan Baḵtiāri, and his cousin Moḥammad-Taqi Khan Asʿad, who had spent a decade in prison (Abrahamian, p. 195; Anṣāri, pp. 324-28).

The power struggle in Isfahan reached its zenith in 1944-46, mostly in reaction to the Tudeh party, which not only kept radicalizing the labor movement but also made a concerted drive into the countryside by organizing the peasants against their landlords. The latter and the mill-owners, who had been retreating in the face of demands, initiated a counter offensive by helping the Fatherland party to create the Union of Peasants and Workers. They also sparked off a major crisis in April 1944 by abruptly locking out workers from factories and mill granaries, thereby depriving them of their source of income; this was followed by a week-long battle in the city, characterized as a "worker's revolt" by the national media. It had major consequences in local and national politics. Qašqāʾis sent contingents to help put down the revolt and formed an alliance with the Baḵtiāri and Ḵamsa tribal chiefs and the government against the Tudeh party (Abrahamian, p. 206). After a short period of suppression, however, the Tudeh party recovered when Aḥmad Qawām (Qawām-al-Salṭana) became prime minister in 1946. In the same year the Union of Isfahan Workers reached its peak, claiming to have 40,000 members (ibid, p. 352). It led a general strike in April and brought out as many as 40,000 supporters into the streets on May Day. By August, according to the report of the British consul, the party controlled much of the local administration and was "ready to seize power in Isfahan as completely as the Democrats had done in Tabriz" (apud Abrahamian, p. 359). Nevertheless, the reoccupation of the northern provinces, the tribal revolts in the south, and Qawām's apparent swing to the right, began a period of intermittent repression for the Tudeh party. In Isfahan, armed tribesmen looted party headquarters and the unionists were drafted into the army (Abrahamian, pp. 305, 366).

Another politically eventful period for Isfahan occurred during the nationalization of the Anglo-Persian Oil Company, reflected in the appearance in the city of 70 to 80 periodicals, mostly politically charged newspapers, from 1950 to 1953 (Ābedi, pp. 234-38; Anṣāri, pp. 341-45). The Tudeh party reemerged as a major political force under the guise of the Coalition of Worker's Syndicates, which organized a series of strikes in Isfahan in conjunction with the strike of refinery workers in Ḵuzestān (Abrahamian, pp. 368-69). The new development in this period was the emergence of the National Front that filled the gap between the traditional royalists in the far right and the Tudeh party in the far left. Formed around the charismatic personality of Moḥammad Moṣaddeq, the Front gained popularity among the modern middle-class, a segment of the intelligentsia and, more particularly, the middle layer *bāzāri*s of Isfahan who not only foresaw economic interests therein but also a political voice they had previously lacked. The popularity of the National Front in Isfahan is reflected in the drastic repercussion the resignation of the prime minister Moṣaddeq in July 1952 had in the city. During 17-21 July the city witnessed the closure of the bazaar, widespread street demonstrations, and a general strike in the factories; according to a report by the chief of police, one thousand men crammed into the Telegraph Office in a show of support for Moṣaddeq (Torkamān, p. 199; Makki, 1987, pp. 254-59). In the course of the next year, as the stalemate in the power struggle dragged on and economic hardship caused by the country's inability to market its oil worsened, many of Moṣaddeq's former supporters lost their enthusiasm. Finally, on 19 August 1953, upon the departure of the shah, the National Front and the Tudeh party organized a large demonstration in Isfahan and the royal statue was brought down in the main square; the turmoil was brought to an end three days later, without any reported resistance.

The period 1953-78. The political arena remained largely calm in these years. Parliamentary elections were generally rigged and hence a mere formality, and the municipal and provincial administration were appointed by the central government, as in the rest of the country. Baḵtiāris retreated for good to their tribal territories and were gradually absorbed into the expanding industries. The major political event of the period was the Land Reform Program, one of the six reform measures of the White Revolution proposed by the shah and backed by a referendum conducted on 26 June 1963. It led to violent protests by a front composed of the ulema, bazaar merchants (*bāzāris*), and landowners at major urban centers. On 5 June urban riots broke out in Shiraz, Tehran, Qom, Mashad, Isfahan, and Kāšān to protest against the reforms; they were suppressed on the same day (Ruḥāni, pp. 492-94, 528, 567, 576).

This was the longest period of prosperity marked by social and economic progress. The national economic boom of 1953-59 resulted in the expansion of Isfahan's textile industry and other privately sponsored factories manufacturing consumer goods for local and national markets. But a profound transformation of production systems and social relationships came with the White Revolution and the two successful economic plans in the period 1963-73, when Isfahan emerged as a major industrial center of the country with a large steel mill, cement and sugar factories, an oil refinery and defense and petrochemical industries. The construction of the Shah Abbas dam on the Zāyandarud and the extension of the national railroad network into the province had a strong impact on its economy (see ISFAHAN xiv.). As these state-sponsored projects brought to Isfahan a large amount of development funds in addition to its usual budget, the city could absorb immigrant workers from all over the country. In the 1970s, Soviet and American employees also had a notable presence in the city, estimated at more than 10,000 families (Anṣāri, p. 102).

In this period Isfahan saw rapid population growth and urbanization, and the expansion of communication, transportation, and education induced radical changes in the social and economic conditions of the city. The urban infrastructure was bolstered by the construction of pipeline water supply and sewage systems in the 1960s, and the province was connected to the national gas network in the ensuing decade. New bridges spanned over the Zāyandarud and its branches and canals were retrofitted to modern needs. The city was outfitted with recreational clubs, theaters, and sport stadiums. Construction activities expanded to what formerly were gardens and farmland encompassing the city, and middle-class neighborhoods flourished on the banks of Zāyandarud; two-story modern houses became a norm, providing a contrast to the inward-oriented older residences (Gulik). Julfa, once a separate town, was now joined legally and physically to the town, as were several surrounding villages like the medieval Jey on the east. Satellite towns such as Šāhinšahr, Malekšahr, and Ḵāna-ye Eṣfahān, with planned geometric layouts, were constructed on the north, and the steelmakers' town of Āryāšahr was connected to the city via a broad freeway. Parallel with industrialization, slums also began to grow around the city, with little urban design or facilities.

The old neighborhoods, on the other hand, had to deal with a clash of the old and the new, where the new had not evolved from the old. The city's master plan attempted in its first five-year program to adapt the old city to the needs of modern citizenry and to keep it alive by placing it inside the future expansion (Shirazi). But these measures could not prevent older quarters such as Jubāra, Dardašt, Šahšahān, Ṭowqči, and Bidābād, with tightly-packed mud-brick houses, to turn into overcrowded shantytowns (cf. Anṣāri, p. 439, Schafaghi, 1979), although the main bazaar survived as a shopping center for cheaper commodities, many of whose items were made on the spot (Anṣāri, p. 307). Moreover, the strictly enforced construction codes, such as those restricting building heights in central Isfahan to four stories, minimized interference with the architectural heritage landscape and skyline. Meanwhile, the extensive restoration of the city's historical monuments continued with the assistance of Maxime Siroux and André Godard (q.v.), and it led to the emergence of a new generation of tile makers, miniature painters, and calligraphers, among other artists (cf. Borjian et al.) As the city grew into a center of tourism, traditional handicrafts flourished once again. They made Isfahan one of the focal points of the Iranian tourist industry from the late 1960s until the Islamic Revolution of 1977-79.

On the whole, Isfahan seemed to have been well equipped with a modern urban infrastructure and the institutions of modern times. But the city was really a developed island surrounded by backward environs, and those who actually benefited from the socio-economic growth were limited to the privileged social groups who did not make up the majority of the residents.

THE POST-REVOLUTION ERA

The 1977-79 Revolution. Isfahan played an important role in the Islamic Revolution. It actively joined the Revolution on 4 August (14 Mordād) 1978, commemorating the fortieth day of mourning for the martyrs of Tabriz. Riots broke out, notably in the older quarters of the city and the rural periphery, where the inhabitants were known for their religious zeal. In the following days, such places as liquor stores, banks, hotels, and cinemas were targeted. As a result of the gravity of the threat, military rule was announced on 8 August, setting a precedence that was followed in other cities. The autumn of the same year saw widespread sabotage and terror. Endemic work stoppages culminated with a strike by thousands of personnel of the steel mill (8 October). The devoutly religious groups that usually organized Moḥarram processions now marshaled political demonstrations. In the winter of 1978-79 Isfahan and other major towns of the province followed the revolutionary course in the country by mobilizing sporadic urban riots, demonstrations, and strikes (ʿĀqeli, I, p. 352, passim).

As the regime began to disintegrate in the course of the upheavals, power passed gradually into the hands of the local ad hoc "revolutionary committees," the first of which was set up by Ayatollah Ḥosayn Ḵādemi, a longtime opponent of the shah who took a moderate position on social issues, and was approved of by the bāzāris and the traditional middle class (cf. Abrahamian, pp. 526 ff.). But he soon found a rival in another leading mullah, Jalāl-al-Din Ṭāheri, who showed his loyalty to the Islamic Revolution and his leadership skills in promoting mass mobilizations both during the Revolution, and later during the war with Iraq, drawing support of young men from the slums and the countryside (cf. Anṣāri, pp. 78, 317). Although he was eventually appointed to lead the Friday congregational prayers (*emām-e jomʿa*; q.v.) in Isfahan, he could never subdue his rivals entirely, and, even after the death of Ayatollah Ḵādemi, polycentrism continued to be the norm in Isfahan. Commensurate with the liberal tendencies of the mainstream townspeople, reflected in successive parliamentary elections, Ṭāheri gradually shifted, over a span of two decades, from his position as a faithful revolutionary with leftist-fundamentalist tendencies to an advocate of liberalism and tolerance. His long tenure came to an end in 2002 with a passionate letter of resignation (published in the newspaper *Nowruz*, 8 July 2002).

As with other cities in Persia, Isfahan experienced a post-revolutionary decade of hardship and regression. As a part of the proscribed "cultural revolution" (enqelāb-e farhangi), universities were closed down for three years, many educators and public employees were dismissed, and professional associations came under attack. Intellectual and recreational life suffered and the number of cinemas, a dozen before the revolution, was halved. Many modern businesses were confiscated; department stores and supermarkets were turned into warehouses, and the traditional small market system emerged once again. The disappearance of foreign tourism resulted in the decline of indigenous arts and crafts.

During the Iran-Iraq War (see IRAQ vii.), Isfahan suffered from recurring bombardments; and a niche at the Friday Mosque dating from the Saljuq era was destroyed in one of the Iraqi bombardments. The war participation rate from Isfahan was exceptionally high, reflected in countless streets and alleys bearing the names of war martyrs. A whole class of family members of martyrs emerged, and they were granted special economic and educational privileges by the state. Isfahan also had its share of war refugees from Ḵuzestān, reported to be in the region of 160,000 in the province in 1982 (Anṣāri, p. 63). The influx of villagers into the town was quantitatively unprecedented, many replacing the middle-class and professional families who either moved to the capital or emigrated abroad (ibid, pp. 60, 75). All in all, an unsophisticated air of provincialism replaced the town's urbane charm.

The most remarkable trait in Isfahan during the last quarter century has been its physical expansion and overpopulation. New satellite towns have been added to the south and north, interconnected with a beltway and a Metro line (under construction) longitudinally traversing the city and its satellites. The widening and extension of older streets and alleys are not sufficient to meet with the ever-growing traffic volume, which is also responsible for considerable air pollution. A striking facet has been the extension of green zones and parks along the Zāyandarud and elsewhere, e.g. the park surrounding the Safavid pavilion-palace Hašt Behešt, the private estate of a Qajar prince before the revolution. Not only horizontal expansion but also vertical growth has been used as a measure to meet the growing demand for housing created by the sudden increase in childbirth immediately after the Revolution. The real estate and construction industry has become extremely profitable, benefiting from cheap construction labor from Afghanistan, and former family dwellings are being systematically replaced by multi-story apartment buildings (cf. *Gozāreš*, 2002, pp. 390-95).

In this regard, the municipal policies are characterized by preservationists as being excessively utilitarian and detrimental to the historical morphology of the city. A major concern is systematic violation of construction codes, such as building of a high-raised shopping center near the Royal Square (renamed Imam Square). Another recent dilemma was the sale of thousands of acres of gardens surrounding textile factories south of the river to real-estate developers; the battle was finally lost by those who tried to save not only an attractive part of the town but what was perceived as monuments of the glorious age of the industrialization of the country (for the arguments, see the local civil engineering quarterly *Dānešnemā*, nos. 83-85, 2000-01). Moreover, for the same social reasons, the implementation of development plans concerning the extension of the street network within the old quarters has proved more difficult than ever before; for instance, the age-old dispute over a Safavid bathhouse near the Royal Square was finally brought to an end in 1995 when the concerned archeologists found it razed to the ground overnight by the municipality. Even the hallowed old cemetery, Taḵt-e pulād, has seen itself intersected by streets. The social confrontation between preservationist intellectuals and pragmatist planners and builders will likely recur in the city for decades to come.

The development of the countryside has been substantial. Soon after the revolution, men of the Construction Corps (Jehād-e sāzandagi) arrived in almost all villages of the province and began to build roads, bridges, schools, and houses, brought electricity and telephone lines to villages and set up a network of producer-and-consumer cooperatives. Thus, rural conditions have changed during the Islamic Republic period beyond recognition. Even the identity of many villages has been subject to change by coining many new Islamic toponyms, arbitrarily imposed on the older "pagan" names to a confusing degree (Mehryār, passim; Borjian, 2005).

Bibliography: Ḥasan ʿĀbedi, *Eṣfahān az leḥāẓ-e ejtemāʿi o eqteṣādi*, Tehran, 1955. Ervand Abrahamian, *Iran Between Two Revolutions*, Princeton, 1982. Hormoz Anṣāri, *Moqaddama-i bar jāmeʿašenāsi-e Eṣfahān*, ed. Aḥmad Jawāheri, Isfahan, 1990. H. Anschütz, "Persische Stadttypen. Eine vergleichende Betrachtung der Städte Esfahan, Tehran, Abadan, Buschir und Chorramshahr in Iran," *Geographische Rundschau* 19, 1967, pp. 105-10. Bāqer ʿĀqeli, *Ruzšemār-e tāriḵ-e Irān*, 2 vols., Tehran, 1990-91. *Asnād-e anjomanhā-ye baladi o ṣenfi-e dawra-ye Reżā Šāh*, ed. Reżā Moḵtāri Eṣfahāni, 2 vols., Tehran, 2001. Wilfred Blunt and W. M. Swaan, *Isfahan: Pearl of Persia*, London, 1966. Habib Borjian, "Eṣfahān dar tāriḵ-e Irān," *Rahāvard* 33, 1993, pp. 74-95. Idem, "Jogrāfiā-ye guyeshā-ye welāyati-e Eṣfahān," *Irānšenāsi* 17/3, 2005, pp. 466-86. Idem, "Isfahan," in *Cities of the Middle East and North Africa: A Historical Encyclopedia*, ed. M. R. T. Dumper and B. E. Stanley, Santa Barbara, CA, 2007, pp. 147-49. Houri Borjian and Habib Borjian (text), and Reza Nour Bakhtiar (photography), *Abbasi Hotel: Museum Within a Museum* (in English and Persian), Tehran, 1997. Judith Brown, "A Geographical Study of the Evolution of the Cities of Tehrān and Iṣfahān," Unpublished dissertation, University of Durham, 1966. Ḥesām-al-Din Dawlatābādi, "Siāsat o talāš," *Majalla-ye ḵāṭerāt-e Waḥid* 9-10, 1972. E. Diez, "Isfahan," *Zeitschrift für bildende Kunst* 25, 1915, pp. 90-104, 113-28. Willem Floor, *Industrialization in Iran: 1900-1941*, University of Durham, Center for Middle Eastern and Islamic Studies, Occasional Paper, no. 23, 1984. Ulrich Gehrke, *Persien in der deutschen Orientpolitik während des Ersten Weltkrieges* I, Stuttgart, 1961. *Gozāreš-e eqtesādi-ejtemāʿi-e ostān-e Eṣfahān*, Sāzmān-e barnāma wa budja, 2002. John Gulik, "Private Life and Public Face: Cultural Continuities in the Domestic Architecture of Isfahan," *Iranian Studies* 7/3-4, 1974, pp. 629-51. Mehdiqoli Hedāyat Moḵber-al-Salṭana, *Ḵāṭerāt o ḵaṭarāt*, Tehran, 1950. Ṣādeq Hedāyat, *Eṣfahān nesf-e jahān*, Tehran, n.d. Loṭf-Allāh Honarfar, *Ganjina-ye āṯār-e tāriḵi-e Eṣfahān*, Isfahan, 1965. Ḥosayn Makki, *Modarres qahramān-e āzādi*, Tehran, 1980. Idem, *Waqāyeʿ-e siom-e Tir-e 1331*, Tehran, 1987. Moḥammad Mehryār, *Farhang-e jāmeʿ-e nāmhā wa ābādihā-ye kohan-e Eṣfahān*, Isfahan, 2003. Moḥammad-ʿAli Musawi-Fereydani, *Do barādar o yek ārezu: Zendaginâma-ye bonyāngoḏārān-e ḵayriya-ye ʿAli o Ḥosayn-e Hamadāniān*, unpublished manuscript. Musā Najafi, *Andiša-ye siāsi o tāriḵ-e nahżat-e Ḥāj Aqā Nur-Allāh-e Eṣfahāni*, 2nd ed. Tehran, 1999. Ḥosayn Nurṣādeqi, *Eṣfahān*, Tehran, 1937. ʿAbd-al-Ḥosayn Owrang (Šayḵ-al-Molk), "Ḵāṭerāt-e gozašta," *Majalla-ye ḵāṭerāt-e Waḥid* 8, 1972. Maurice Pernot, *L'inquiétude de l'Orient: en Asie musulmane*, Paris, 1927a. Idem, "L'inquiétude de l'Orient. ix. A travers la Perse," *Revue des deux mondes* 97, 1927b, pp. 837-70. S.-Ḥ. Ruḥāni, *Barrasi o taḥlil-i az naḥżat-e Emām Ḵomeyni, Qom*, 1977. Naṣr-Allāh Sayfpur Fāṭemi, *Āʾina-ye ʿebrat*, 2nd ed., Tehran, 1999. S. Schafaghi, "Bildung von stadtvierteln in Isfahan," in G. Schweizer, ed., *Interdisziplinäre Iran-Forschung. Beiträge aus Kulturgeographie, Ethnologie, Soziologie und Neuerer Geschichte*, Beihefte zum Tübinger Atlas des Vorderen Orients, Reihe B, no. 40, Wiesbaden, 1979, pp. 169-78. ʿAbd-al-Ḥosayn Sepantā, *Tāriḵča-ye awqāf-e Eṣfahān*, Isfahan, 1967. Bagher Shirazi, "Isfahan, the Old; Isfahan, the New," *Iranian Studies* 7/3-4, 1974, pp. 586-92. Edward Sykes, "Isfahan," *Journal of the Royal Central Asian Society* 33, 1946, pp. 307-17. M. Torkamān, *Qiām-e melli-e siom-e Tir*, Tehran, 1982.

(HABIB BORJIAN)

x. MONUMENTS

In the course of centuries of urbanization, Isfahan has gained a large number of significant monuments. According to the French traveler Jean Chardin, in the late 17th century Isfahan housed some 162 mosques, 48 theological colleges (*madrasa*), 1,802 caravansaries, and 273 bathhouses (see ḤAMMĀM; see Chardin, VII, pp. 343-53, 454-57, 363-67, 463, 321-22, 394; VIII, p. 134; XIX, pp. 198-200). Chardin's numbers reflect the extraordinary expansion of the city begun in 1590-91, when Shah ʿAbbās I the Great (q.v.; r. 1587-1629) embarked on the reconstruction of medieval Isfahan in anticipation of its designation in 1598 as the capital of the Safavid Empire (1501-1722; see vii, above; see also McChesney, pp. 114-15). The magnificent architecture of Isfahan soon gained the city the honorific title of "Isfahan, half the world" (*Eṣfahān, nesf-e jahān*; Eskandar Beg, p. 544), and a number of Isfahan's monuments have been designated by UNESCO as World Heritage Sites. Unfortunately, only some of this rich architectural heritage has withstood the test of time and survived into the present. This entry will be divided into the following sections:

(1) A Historical Survey.
(2) Palaces.
(3) Mosques.
(4) Madrasas.
(5) Bridges.
(6) Bibliography.

(1) A Historical Survey

Isfahan's monuments developed during three major periods in the Islamic era: first, the early medieval period under the ʿAbbāsid Caliphate and Buyid patronage; second, under the Saljuqs; and, finally, under Shah ʿAbbās I and his successors.

THE ʿABBĀSID AND BUYID PERIODS

The architectural history of the city of Isfahan as it developed in the Islamic period from the merger of the towns of Yahudiya and Jay (*šahrestān*), its development into a prosperous trading center under the ʿAbbasids (750-1258), and its role as the princely residence of the Buyid Dynasty (932-1055) can only be archeologically inferred from the continuous occupation of the site of the city's major congregational mosque (Masjed-e Jomʿa) and its nearby *meydān* or urban square (Golombek, pp. 19-20). Buyid patronage had fostered renewed interest in building up Isfahan: a fortification wall with twelve gates enclosed

PLATE I (1)

Hārun-e welāyat, façade. Courtesy of the author.

the central hub of the city surrounding the old (caliphal period) Masjed-e Jomʿa and the nearby marketplace. The addition of a citadel, Ṭabarrak fortress, on the southwestern corner of the Buyid walled city may also be attributed to this period. With the exception of a single, elaborately carved doorway that had belonged to the Jurjir Mosque and was built during the vizierate of Ṣāḥeb Esmāʿil b. ʿAbbād in the second half of the 10th century, the pre- and Buyid constructions in Isfahan are known only through the literary evidence left by medieval travelers and geographers (Ebn Rosta, pp. 160-63; Moqaddasi, pp. 386-90; Māfarokhi, pp. 84-86, tr., p. 63; *Ḥodud al-ʿālam*, ed. Sotuda, p. 140; Honarfar, pp. 40-44). Nevertheless, shadow traces of the old Buyid walls, the inner city arteries and neighborhood subdivisions continued to define the old quarters of Isfahan into modern times. Much of the extant monuments of Isfahan, however, date to two periods in history when the city served as the capital of the ruling dynasties of the Great Saljuqs (1040-1194) and the Safavids (1501-1722).

FROM THE SALJUQS THROUGH THE EARLY SAFAVIDS

After Ṭoḡrel Beg's designation of Isfahan in 1051 as the center of his kingdom, the city acquired several major monuments marking the dynasty's political and cultural ambitions. Among the most renowned aspects of the Great Saljuq patronage in Isfahan were garden residences along the Zāyandarud River, long lost, with their open pavilions, their landscaping and water elements evoking ancient Persian *čahārbāḡ* (q.v.) type. Masjed-e Jomʿa, the Friday or Great Mosque of Isfahan, a royal residence and administrative building, the Neẓāmiya Madrasa and bazaars were clustered around or near a *meydān* that served as the principal urban square of Isfahan under the Saljuqs. The footprint of this public square is still preserved in the Old Square (Meydān-e Kohna, so called since the Safavid addition of a new one), while the Great Mosque remains largely intact in its essential Saljuq outlines and silhouettes and indeed its function, albeit made secondary to the Safavid Royal Mosque for the Friday congregational prayer. Other trace evidence of Saljuq architectural patronage may be found in the site of extinct mosques and sanctuaries still marked with minarets (Honarfar, 1965, pp. 194-204). For example, the imposingly high and elegantly brick-sheathed minaret of Masjed-e ʿAli, an 11th- or 12th-century minaret with an early 16th-century Safavid mosque, most likely locates a hallowed spot, an older mosque perhaps, in the vicinity of the Old Square (Honarfar, 1965, pp. 195-98).

According to the Persian poet-traveler Nāṣer-e K̲osrow (pp. 126-28) and other medieval observers, Isfahan acquired world renown as amongst the most prosperous and populous of its time during the reign of the Saljuq Malekšāh (r. 1072-92), under whose tutelage his grand viziers Neẓām-al-Molk Abu ʿAli Ḥasan of Ṭus and Tāj-al-Molk Abu'l-Ḡanāʾem Pārsi took turns to outdo one another in the grandeur of their architectural patronage. The city walls and gates were refurbished and neighborhood amenities increased as the city's population grew and prospered around the urban hub of the square and the Masjed-e Jomʿa. The Great Mosque of Isfahan was entirely rebuilt to replace the old Arab hypostyle (a pairing

PLATE II (1)

Aerial view of Meydān-e Naqš-e Jahān, with the ʿĀli Qāpu palace on the right, the Shaikh Loṭf-Allāh Mosque on the left, the Shah (Imam) Mosque in the distance, and the Qayṣariya Bazaar at the near front of the Plate. After R. Baḵtiār, p. 34.

of an open courtyard and a covered sanctuary that was roofed with equidistantly-placed pillar supports) with a newly developed Persian mosque plan in which a four-*ayvān* courtyard formed the central focus of the mosque and the sanctuary was marked with a large domed prayer niche (*meḥrāb*) chamber and vaulted bays. Neẓām-al-Molk, the statesman and author of the *Siar al-moluk/ Siāsat-nāma*, the famed manual of princely conduct, initiated the development of some of these key architectural interventions in Isfahan (Grabar, pp. 31-32).

Of this magnificent medieval city, only its Friday Mosque (Masjed-e Jomʿa), a few minarets, and partial ruins have survived. This meager architectural evidence of pre-Safavid Isfahan, so shockingly at odds with the descriptions of the city by Muslim travelers and historians, must be attributed to the devastating impact of successive invasions of Isfahan. Despite vigorous resistance that forced the Mongol hordes to attack the city repeatedly between 1228 and 1240-41, Isfahan fell to the Mongols and its inhabitants were massacred, reputedly because of the betrayal by the Shafeʿite Sunnis, who hoped to gain favor from and ascendancy under the Mongols over their rival Hanafite branch (Rašid-al-Din, *Jāmeʿ al-tawārik̲*, quoted by Šafaqi, p. 280). Again, the 1387 siege of Isfahan under Timur's personal direction ended in the slaughter of some 70,000 denizens of the city (Šāmi, I, pp. 104-5; Ḥāfeẓ-e Abru, II, pp. 666-67). Toward the end of the reign of Jahānšāh, the Qara Qoyunlu (r. 1438-68), 50,000 people of Isfahan were massacred in retaliation for the city's disobedience (Venetian travelers, quoted in Safaqi, p. 283). In all three instances, the slaughter of the people was accompanied with severe damage or destruction of the physical structures of the city along with the devastation of the nearby agricultural lands.

Until the founding of the Safavid dynasty, successive overlords of Isfahan left behind relatively little architectural works, albeit symbolically significant for they stamped political suzerainty. An example of such politically charged markings is the famed carved-stucco prayer niche (*meḥrāb*) commissioned in the name of the Mongol Il-khan Öljeitü/Uljāytu (r. 1304-16) by Moḥammad Sāvi (i.e., K̲ᵛāja Saʿd-al-Din Moḥammad Mostawfi Sāvaji) in 1310 (Honarfar, pp. 115-21; Blair, 1998, pp. 69-70). The prayer niche is placed in a brick vaulted prayer hall behind the western *ayvān* of Friday Mosque and is accompanied with an intricately inlaid and decorated wooden *menbar* (pulpit from which sermons are delivered) that is undated but is clearly the oldest, most significant *menbar* in the whole mosque. The prayer niche is rightly famous for its extraordinarily complex decorative program of alternating and concentric registers of epigraphic and vegetal motifs that are carved with such crispness and ingenuity to impart the illusion of layering of visually exciting bands of decoration in considerable depth. Its fame as the *mehrāb* of Öljeitü, however, is misguided for the recognition of patronage for this magnificent addition to the revered Great Mosque of Isfahan should rightfully belong, as defined by the inscription, to Moḥammad Mostawfi Sāvaji. As one of the grand viziers and principal courtiers (*ṣāḥeb-e divān*) of the Il-khanid G̲āzān Khan

PLATE III (1)

Aerial view of Meydān-e Naqš-e Jahān from Tawḥid-ḵāna and ʿĀli Qāpu Palace looking towards the Shaikh Loṭf-Allāh Mosque. After R. Baḵtiār, p. 11.

and Oljeitü, he followed, with this prayer niche, the well-established Saljuq tradition of architectural patronage by the grandees of the empire.

Notwithstanding the architecturally important Pir Bakrān Tomb (dated 1302-12) in a village of the same name some 30 km outside the city, the other monument of this period in Isfahan, particularly notable because of its great local popularity, is the Menār Jonbān (moving minaret; Honarfar, 1965, pp. 279-82). The structure was built over a tombstone of Il-khanid date and is decorated with tile work that is dateable to this same period. Whatever the shape of the original building, its surviving *ayvān* façade consists of two thin minarets (of the Persian *gol-dasta* style) that flank the corners of the façade and are famous for their ability to vibrate whenever one minaret is shaken. Similar local patronage produced a number of other tombs (Emāmzada Jaʿfar and Bābā Qāsem) and small mosques and *madrasa*s. Of the latter, the Bābā Qāsem Madrasa is better known as the Madrasa-ye Emāmiya, whence has come the famous tiled *mehrāb* now in the Metropolitan Museum of Art (Honarfar, pp. 300-314).

The 15th-century monuments of the Turkmen and Timurid successor states are even more limited in number and remain largely understudied. The most noteworthy is the so-called Darb-e Emām, a shrine over the burial place of two locally venerated descendents of Shiʿite Imams (hence its designation as an emāmzāda; Honarfar, 1965, pp. 341-52). Dating to 1453 and the reign of Jahānšāh, the Qara Qoyunlu, it is the main portal of this monument that is of particular significance, because its intricate mosaic-like tiled patterns are so intense in their blue colors and so fine in their workmanship that they have been compared with the masterpiece of Turkmen-era tile work at the Blue Mosque in Tabriz of this same period (Blair and Bloom, pp. 52-53). The so-called Tālār-e Teymuri, a building located within the royal precinct known as Bāḡ-e Naqš-e Jahān and now occupied by the natural history museum of Isfahan, may have been initiated by Timur, although there is no persuasive evidence of either archeological or textual nature that would support the attribution besides the name by which the building has been known since the 19th century (Honarfar, pp. 327-28; Mehrābādi, pp. 386-89).

The paucity of monumental building in Isfahan continued into the first century of Safavid rule as well. While Tabriz and then Qazvin served as the capital until the end of the 16th century, Isfahan remained vital as one of the major urban centers especially for the promulgation of Twelver Shiʿism, the declared state religion of the Safavids (Jaʿfariān, pp. 305-39). Shah Esmāʿil I (1501-24, q.v.), reportedly visited the city several times in the first decade of the 16th century when he had stayed at the Bāḡ-e Naqš-e Jahān, the then extra-urban royal garden precinct that dated from at least the Timurid period, but he did not commission any constructions (Allāh-Detā Možṭar, facs. ed., p. 184; Quiring-Zoche, pp. 60-67).

Instead, and not unlike earlier examples of significant sub-imperial patronage, the two principal buildings of the 16th century, the Mausoleum of Hārun-e Welāyat

PLATE IV (1)

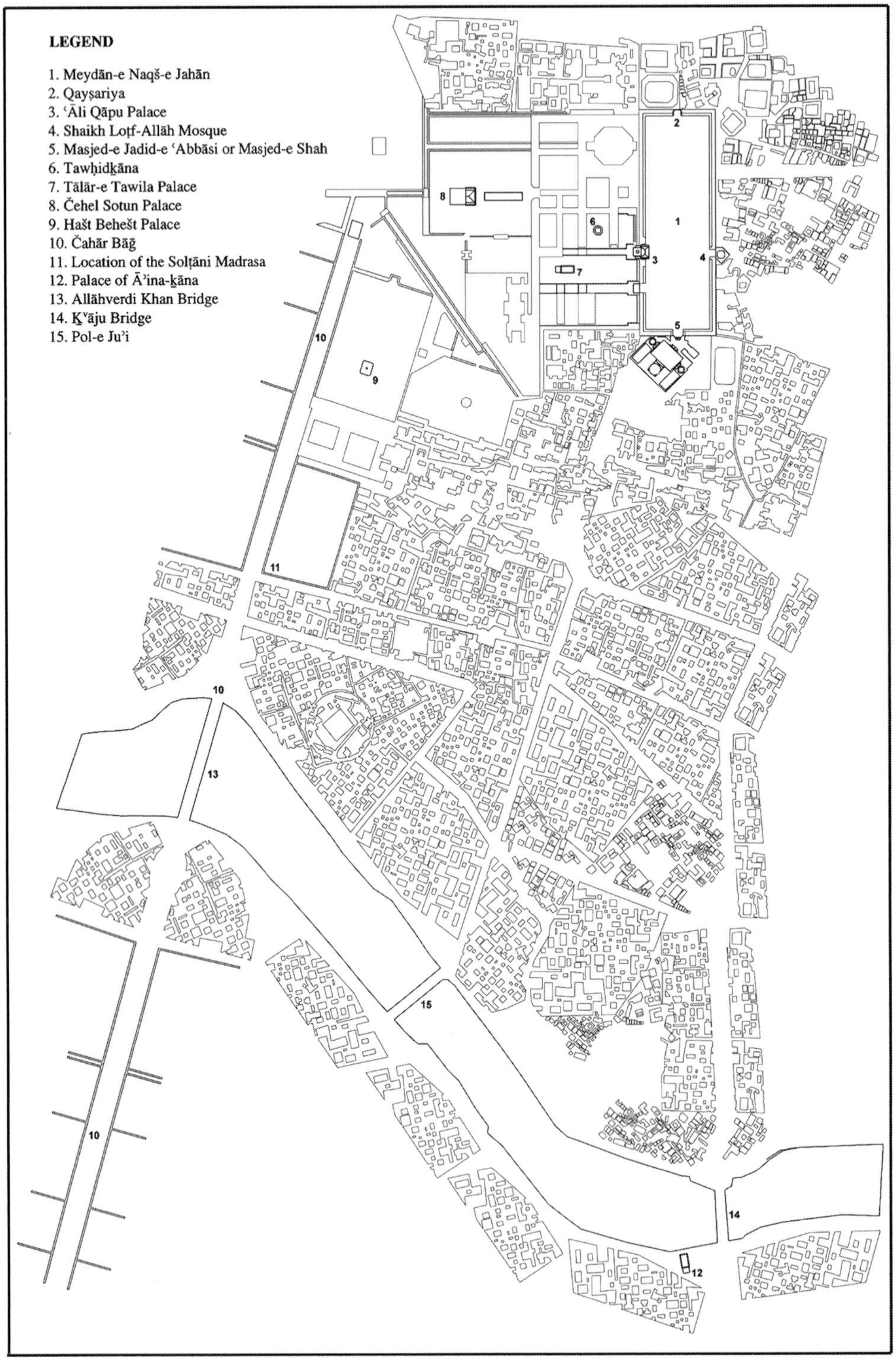

Map of Isfahan, southern area of Meydān-e Naqš-e Jahān, showing the Safavid additions after 1590/91, with some of the lost buildings reconstructed and approximated in their location. © Sussan Babaie and Sam Zeller, after S. Babaie, *Isfahan and its Palaces: Feasting in the City of Paradise*, Edinburgh, forthcoming.

PLATE V (1)

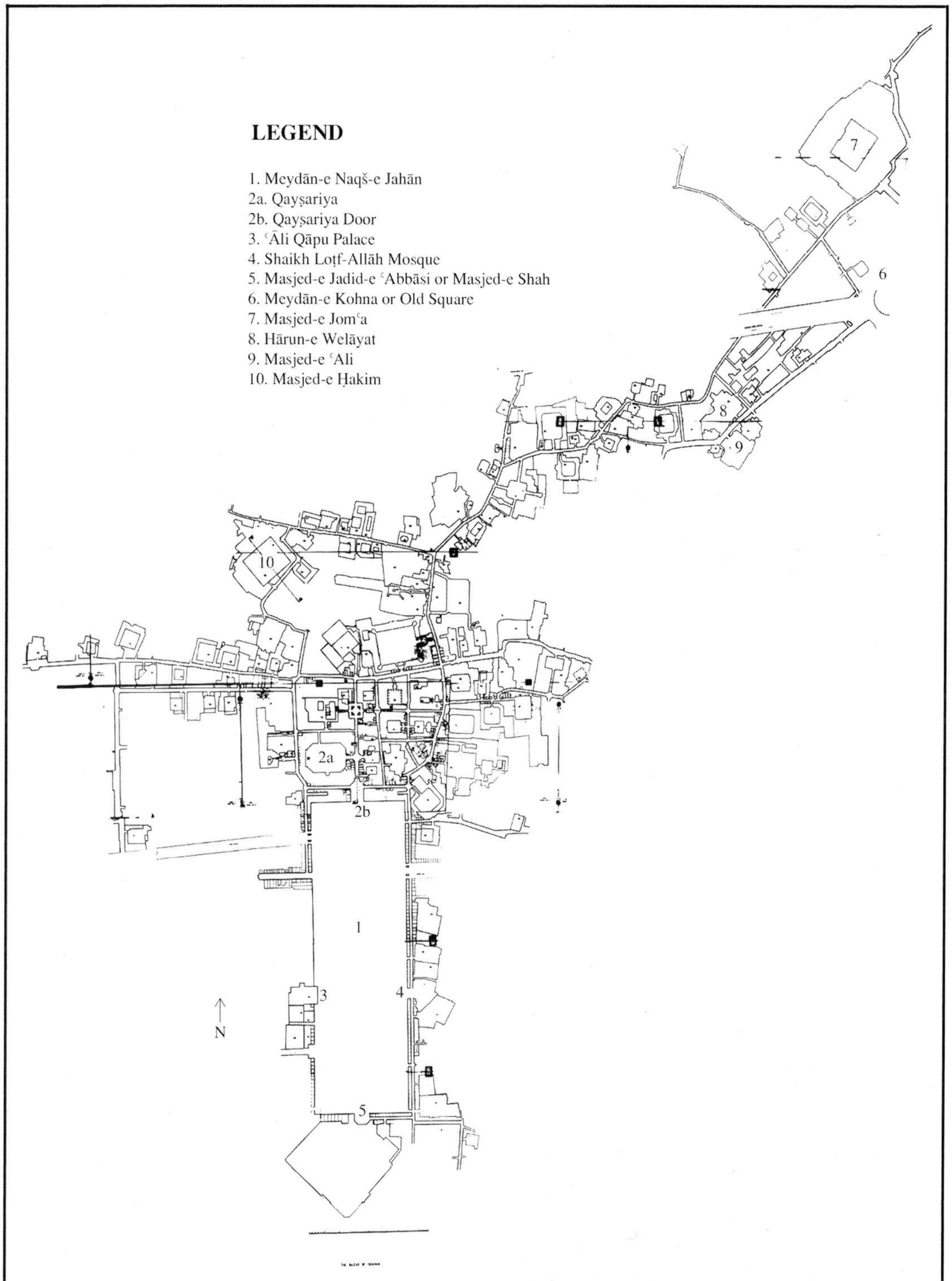

Map of Isfahan, northern area of Meydān-e Naqš-e Jahān, covering the whole bazaar plan with a number of mosques and *madrasas*. Courtesy of John Donat, after *Iranian Studies* 7/1-2, 974, p. 335.

(Plate I [1]) and the Masjed-e ʿAli, issued from the investment of two high-ranking members of the new ruling elite (Hillenbrand, pp. 761-65; Babaie, 2003, pp. 32-36). Durmiš Khan Šāmlu, the governor of Isfahan, sponsored the construction of Hārun-e Welāyat, which an inscription dates its completion to 918/1512. After the death of Durmiš Khan, Mirzā Kamāl-al-Din Šāh-Ḥosayn assumed the regency of Isfahan and built the adjacent Masjed-e ʿAli in 1522 (Honarfar, 1965, pp. 360-79; Mehrābādi, pp. 712-17).

In addition to the shared threads of patronage, these buildings also display in their emphasis on the decoration of the principal façade a compelling aspect of Safavid architectural style. In both cases, but especially in that of the mausoleum, the façade carries the weight of the iconographic import. At the Hārun-e Welāyat, for example, the epigraphic program mentions a tradition, according to which the prophet drew conceptual parallels between the biblical Aaron, presumably commemorated in this shrine, and Imam ʿAli b. Abi Ṭāleb, saying that ʿAli to him was as Aaron had been to Moses (Honarfar, 1965, p. 261; Babaie, 2003, pp. 33-34). It furthermore anchors the multifarious epigraphic content on an equally complex visual composition in which highly accomplished mosaic-tiled floral, vegetal, geometric and bird-of-paradise motifs enunciate an intensely partisan Shiʿite message. This is all well in keeping with the Safavid zeal, especially in this early phase of its dynastic dominion for promoting Twelver Shiʿism as the state religion. In their strategic location on the southern flank of the Saljuq urban center, the mausoleum-mosque duo of Hārun-e Welāyat and Masjed-e ʿAli also demonstrate the Safavid resoluteness in weaving its own imperial beginnings into the fabric of the medieval city.

ISFAHAN: THE CAPITAL OF SHAH ʿABBĀS I

In contrast to the slow pace of construction during the intervening centuries between the Saljuqs and the Safavids, the transition of the capital from Qazvin to Isfahan late in the 16th century propelled the city once again onto the world stage. This most significant phase in the urban history of Isfahan began in 1590-91, when Shah ʿAbbās the Great ordered a series of building campaigns in anticipation of the official transfer of the capital in 1598 (McChesney, pp. 114-15). These works included the refurbishment of the old bazaars and the Meydān-e Kohna. What is more, the shah and his advisors embarked on a radical re-conceptualization of the city as the imperial capital of a reconfigured Safavid household.

Shah ʿAbbās had inherited a considerably weakened foundation of authority after decades of ineffectual rule and civil war amongst the Turkmen Qezelbāš chiefs, whose scrambling for power through alliances forged with Safavid princes and princesses had plagued Persia since the death of Shah Ṭahmāsb (1524-76). Centralization and absolutism, both state-building projects initiated by Shah Esmāʿil and Shah Ṭahmāsb, were revived and reformed by Shah ʿAbbās and found expression in the built environment of the new capital of Isfahan. In this late 16th-early 17th-century period, imperial enterprise shifted emphasis increasingly away from the mystical (Sufi) tendencies of Qezelbāš adherents of Shiʿite Islam and in favor of *šariʿa*-based normative practices of Twelver Shiʿism, spearheaded by the shah and his patronized clerical class, the ulema (Babayan, 2003, pp. 349-402). Concurrently, the reconfiguration of the royal household led to the replacement for the most part of the Qezelbāš companions with a new elite composed mostly of converted Circassian, Armenian, and Georgian military and administrative slaves (*ḡolām*) who owed their positions and their loyalty solely to the shah (Babaie, Babayan, Baghdiantz-McCabe and Farhad, pp. 6-9; Babayan, 2004, pp. 20-48). Seventeenth-century Isfahan was built to facilitate the workings of, and represent the constituent parts of, this new imperial composition of economic, political, religious, and social convergences.

The master plan of Shah ʿAbbās took shape outside the medieval walled city to its southwest. A new public square, Meydān-e Naqš-e Jahān, and a promenade, the Čahārbāḡ (q.v.), formed the armature of the Safavid capital city. Construction of this massive urban project, unprecedented in the concurrence of its extraordinary scale and its integrated planning, took several decades.

The first installment focused on the Meydān-e Naqš-e Jahān, when in 1590-91 the square was formalized as an urban space by virtue of leveling its surface area and containing it within a rectangular perimeter "wall" of a one-story row of shops. A two-story monumental gateway on the western side of the Meydān constituted the ceremonial marking of the threshold between the public urban space and the royal precinct of the Bāḡ-e Naqš-e Jahān, the royal garden retreat of Isfahan in use since at least the Timurid period (15th cent.). This building was expanded within the next decade into the gateway of ʿĀli Qāpu palace (q.v.). The companion to this politico-ceremonial building was the Qayṣariya bazaar (royal marketplace) at the northern side of the Meydān-e Naqš-e Jahān. Together they monumentalized this first phase of construction and facilitated the political and especially economic linkage between the vibrant old commercial hub of Isfahan, the Meydān-e Kohna, and its aspirant rival (Honarfar, 1965, pp. 395-401; idem, 1975).

The next major building campaign began in 1596 with the construction of the Čahārbāḡ promenade on the western flank of the royal precinct of Bāḡ-e Naqš-e Jahān. The avenue, some two kilometers long, connected the palace precinct, the Meydān and Darvāza Dawlat, one of the major city gates to the north, over the Allāhverdi Khan Bridge to a suburban royal retreat, the Hazār Jarib, on the foot of the Ṣoffa Mountain south of the city. Along the way, and developed over the next decade or so, royal gardens and gateway pavilions that were open to public for strolls and picnics lined the avenue on its north side of the river, while mansions and residential quarters for the new elite of Safavid society were developed on the south side of the avenue and the city. The Armenian suburb of New Julfa, begun after 1603-04 to house the forcibly resettled merchant families of Julfa, and the ʿAbbāsābād planned neighborhood (begun in 1611) for the displaced merchants of Tabriz are amongst the most notable of the new urban developments in Isfahan (Honarfar, 1965, pp. 479-93).

Anchored on these earlier building works was the 1602 campaign during which the functionality of the Meydān-e Naqš-e Jahān was enhanced with the addition of a second row of shops and a second-story of rooms above, thus shrinking the area of the Meydān but formalizing and adding more shops and a covered walkway in between the rows (Galdieri, 1970). The palace gateway was raised by another two stories at this point to become not only the seat of the judiciary and the special guards, but also the most accessible of the ceremonial palaces of the royal precinct.

Two other monumental features of the Meydān, the Shaikh Loṭf-Allāh royal chapel-mosque and the Masjed-e Šāh (originally called Masjed-e Jadid-e ʿAbbāsi), reaffirmed the interconnectedness in Safavid imperial discourse of politics and economics on the one hand and Twelver Shiʿism as the state religion on the other. Begun with the other constructions of 1602, the chapel-mosque of Shaikh Loṭf-Allāh stood across from the ʿĀli Qāpu (q.v.) on the eastern side of the Meydān-e Naqš-e Jahān and served to represent the personal piety of the shah and the royal household. Shaikh Loṭf-Allāh was amongst the most noted religious scholars of the time who had been invited from Jabal ʿĀmel in southern Lebanon to Safavid Persia to assist with the (re)composition and teaching of normative *šariʿa*-based Twelver Shiʿism (Honarfar, 1965, pp. 401-15, 425-64; Mehrābādi, pp. 659-710; Abisaab, pp. 81 ff.). To further tie together the bonds of legitimacy, Shah ʿAbbās had married Shaikh Loṭf-Allah's daughter. The positioning of the mosque in the vicinity of the Shaikh's *madrasa*, where he promulgated the teachings of "true" religion, its placement across from the palace gateway where the imperial household resided—to which the Shaikh also belonged through familial ties, and whence justice was dispensed—together these visual-spatial strategies represented the prismatic Safavid claim to legitimacy and authority.

Masjed-e Šāh on the south side of the Meydān-e Naqš-e Jahān formed the climactic conclusion of the major building works under Shah ʿAbbās's patronage. It also completed the monumental articulation of the square as the public space of encounter and exchange—the urban life of the first imperial capital of Twelver Shiʿism. This was the first congregational mosque in a major city to have been built by the Safavid monarchs (Babaie, 2003, pp. 44-46). The first century of Safavid rule had been mired in doctrinal debates over the legitimacy of Friday prayer during the absence of the Hidden Imam (the Mahdi, believed to have been in occultation since 941, and whose return is awaited by the Shiʿites; see Stewart, 1996, pp. 81-103; Abisaab, pp. 20-24). Fiercely opposed theological views had delayed the conclusion of this debate and exposed the Safavids to Sunni, especially Ottoman, accusations of apostasy and illegitimacy. It was the verdict of such authorities of religious law as Shaikh Loṭf-Allāh and Shaikh Bahāʾ-al-Din ʿĀmeli (Shaikh Bahāʾi, himself responsible for having drawn the royal *waqf* or endowment deed for the entire Meydān and closely connected with the urban projects of Isfahan), who had helped resolve this politico-religious dilemma and had paved the way for Shah ʿAbbās to usher in the new order. Thus the construction of the first Safavid Friday mosque at the Meydān-e Naqš-e Jahān represented afresh the legitimacy of the imperial authority of the Safavids.

The Safavid urban scheme of Isfahan is so methodically integrated in its spatial, architectural, functional and iconographic aspects that it discredits the oft-repeated scholarly assumption of its parts having emerged piecemeal because of different building dates. Instead, the urban plan represents the vision of a new order, one that articulates a Twelver Shiʿite conceptualization of kingship and merges the royal glory (*farr*, q.v.) of ancient Persian kings with the aura of legitimacy predicated upon loyalty to the family of the Prophet Moḥammad. The implementation of the visual-spatial aspects of this vision depended on the involvement of more than Shah ʿAbbās, brilliantly imaginative a strategist that he might have been. It was indeed the engagement of the politically empowered *nouveaux riches* of the realm, the new *ḡolām* (slave) elite in particular, that oversaw the realization of the grand plan (Babaie, 2004, pp. 80-113).

These men served as proxy-patrons on behalf of the shahs and funded, supervised and built much of the principal components of the new capital city as well as the infrastructure of the empire at large. For example, Allāhverdi Khan (q.v.), the *sepahsālār* or commander-in-chief of the armies of Shah ʿAbbās, took charge of the construction of his namesake bridge between 1602 and 1607. The bridge spanned the Zāyandarud River and connected the two stretches of the Čahārbāḡ. The fact that such an integral part of the Čahārbāḡ promenade urban project was entrusted to one of the converted Georgian slave grandees bespeaks of the significance of the *ḡolāms* in the reconfigured Safavid household. Other court and government dignitaries, many of whom were indeed of *ḡolām* background, were granted land and ordered to build garden mansions along the Čahārbāḡ. Moḥebb-ʿAli Beg Lala, the tutor of the *ḡolāms* and the "supervisor of the royal buildings in Isfahan" was responsible for a substantial share of the works and funding of the Masjed-e Šāh. He was also in charge of the design and construction of the housing project of the ʿAbbāsābād residential quarter (Honarfar, 1965, p. 429; Mehrābādi, p. 666).

As in earlier centuries of its life, the Isfahan of Shah ʿAbbās witnessed the convergence and coalescence of personal and imperial agendas and interests. This is of course to be expected given the corporate nature of urban development and architecture. Yet, it is the scale and persistence of the coordinated and singular vision of a Shiʿite imperial capital that distinguishes the early 17th-century urban development of Isfahan. The Meydān ensemble, with its cross-axial enunciations of religion, politics, and commerce transformed an old idea for the urban center of activity into an icon of absolutist imperial power. Together with the Čahārbāḡ promenade and the planned residential quarters of the elite, the urban project of Shah ʿAbbās transformed the medieval city of Isfahan into a true capital city, among the most populous and prosperous cities in the 17th century, where the multifarious strands of the early-modern enterprise of absolutism and centralization was made visually and spatially palpable and compelling.

So profoundly effective was this initial framework that subsequent constructions either took cues from its urbanization principles or anchored new and expanded urban functions onto the original layout of Safavid Isfahan. The palace precinct, the vast garden zone of the 16th century, developed into a true abode of felicity (*dawlat-ḵāna*). Shah ʿAbbās II (r. 1642-66), Shah Ṣafi I (r. 1629-42) and Shah Solaymān (r. 1666-94) expanded the functional capacity of the royal precinct with the addition of ceremonial palaces for specific functions. New urban developments on the southwestern side of the city were linked up with new suburban palaces along the Zāyandarud River through the magnificent Ḵᵛāju Bridge and its namesake avenue of Čahārbāḡ-e Ḵᵛāju. Smaller mosques and *madrasas*, many founded by royal women or such powerful officials as the grand vizier Sāru Taqi (d. 1642), dotted both the old and new neighborhoods of Isfahan. An exceptionally large mosque, Masjed-e Ḥakim, was built by the court Physician of Shah ʿAbbās II, while the bazaars were enhanced with the additions of caravansaries and *čahār su* intersections of bazaar arteries and other public amenities. Shah Solṭān-Ḥosayn (r. 1694-1722), the last of the Safavid kings, constructed a complex of *madrasa*-bazaar-caravansary of considerable urban and architectural interest. His proclivities toward extreme religiosity and his abandonment of the reins of authority to the powerful clerical class went hand in hand with his complete retreat into the bosom of the harem, speaking both figuratively and literally. Shah Solṭān-Ḥosayn presided over a capital city in which the influence and power of the clergy was matched only by that of the eunuch *ḡolām* elite of the harem.

The baroque magnificence of the Solṭāni Madrasa of Shah Solṭān-Ḥosayn stands as a testimony to the ways in which the city had shifted gear in the one hundred years since its emergance as the capital of the Safavids. The siege of Isfahan in 1722 by the Afghan invaders, the massacre of its denizens, the pillaging of the city's wealth, and the wholesale destruction of the Safavid symbols of authority, including its buildings, archives of bureaucracy, and structure of polity bracket the end of Isfahan as capital city with tragedy as profound as its beginning was brilliant. The subsequent history of architecture and urbanization in Isfahan pales compared to its Safavid past.

(2) Palaces

None of the royal palaces and pavilions of Isfahan built prior to the 17th century are extant. In contrast, of all the monuments of Isfahan, Safavid palaces represent the most coherent group of buildings to have survived from a single period (Galdieri, 1974). Seventeenth-century palaces in Isfahan, like other principal imperial monuments of the Safavids, served in their architectural and spatial particularities the ceremonial and ritual needs of a reconfigured household. This was a time when the Safavid household increasingly abandoned its peripatetic ways of rule, necessitated in the age of confederacy, for a sedentary demonstration of authority and legitimacy. Whereas in the 16th century, the Safavids entrusted the princes, the family's bloodline, with the powerful *qezelbāš* governors of key provinces of the realm, in the Isfahan phase of imperial rule, the princes were kept at the harem in the capital under the supervision of their concubine-mothers and the tutelage of the eunuch *golām*s (Babayan, 2004 pp. 30-31).

European visitors to Safavid Persia, for example, found themselves increasingly bound by Isfahan, where they were able to gain a royal audience or conduct their business with the court and government bureaucracy without having to follow the itinerant monarchs (Babaie, 1994a, pp. 264-68). Pietro Della Valle (q.v.), who arrived in Persia in 1617, did move from city to city and camp to camp to meet with Shah ʿAbbās I the Great. In contrast, those following him, Jean-Babtiste Tavernier (six journeys to Persia between 1632 and 1668) and Adam Olearius (the secretary of the Holstein envoy in Isfahan in 1637-38), for example, could not have done any of their "official" business outside Isfahan.

Isfahan, more than any other seat of power in the history of Islamic Persia, assumed unique centrality for the performance of kingship during its time as the Safavid capital. A representation of this shift in emphases is the massive urban campaigns carried out during the first half of the 17th century. Its critical imperial role is also clearly reflected in the sheer number of its palaces and the diversity of their architectural articulation of a range of functions. The ʿĀli Qāpu (q.v.), the Tālār-e Ṭawila, the Čehel Sotun (q.v.), and the Hašt Behešt constitute the principal palaces within the Dawlat-ḵāna, the royal precinct of Isfahan. Others, such as Hazār Jarib (reign of Shah ʿAbbās the Great), Āʾina-ḵāna (reign of Shah Ṣafi I), and Faraḥābād (reign of Shah Solṭān-Ḥosayn), served as retreats away from the urban hustle and bustle but still within reach of the city. Instead of moving to Māzandarān summer palaces, for example, which was the habit especially of Shah ʿAbbās the Great, the later Safavids spent the hot summer months at the Hazār Jarib or the Faraḥābād, both garden-palace retreats located south of the city. Centralization had fixed the geography of authority unto the capital city of Isfahan and the convergence of the production and consumption of politics and culture required the architectural accommodation of its operations. The royal precinct and its palaces were at the heart of this imperial enterprise.

Notwithstanding the distinctive Islamic practice of dividing the royal precinct into the private (*andarun*, q.v) and public (*birun*) zones, any discussion of palaces

PLATE I (2)

The ʿĀli Qāpu Palace, view from the Meydān-e Naqš-e Jahān. Courtesy of the author.

in the Islamic world will also have to take note of the different typology that applies to the Western terminology of the architectural experience. The conglomerate that makes up the Dawlat-ḵāna in Isfahan is not a contiguous series of open and closed spaces compounded into a single, albeit massive, building like the Louvre in Paris. Neither is it a barricaded clustering of rooms, halls, and loggias around successive courtyards that is exemplified by the Topkapı in Istanbul. Instead, the Dawlat-ḵāna of Isfahan is composed of a number of large ceremonial palaces and clusters of office buildings, workshops, and residential apartments that are held together through the intermediary of gardens and within boundaries that are marked by "soft" walls.

At the time of the initial constructions, begun in 1590-91, the Safavid royal precinct was the site of the old, extra-urban Bāḡ-e Naqš-e Jahān. As the building campaign progressed, by the official transfer of the capital in 1598, the Dawlat-ḵāna had been flanked by the two urban foci of the Meydān-e Naqš-e Jahān and the Čahārbāḡ Avenue and had become the imperial seat of Safavid dominion (McChesney, pp. 119-20). The boundaries of the Dawlat-ḵāna, unlike in either earlier or contemporary examples, were articulated by the dual function of urban features: the two-story shops and coffeehouses that formed the Meydān periphery and served also as a wall of separation between the royal precinct and the public space; and the verdant gardens along the Cahārbāḡ that lined the western side of the Dawlat-ḵāna.

Access to the precinct was regulated through gates that were strategically positioned to enunciate their multifarious imperial functions: the ʿĀli Qāpu Palace gateway served as the seat of the judiciary as well as for the ceremonial events of the court; the harem gate, just south of the ʿĀli Qāpu, accentuated the inseparable ties in the administration of the centralized empire between the Safavid household and the slave-based political structure. Another gate, known as the Čahār Ḥawż (Four ponds), was located north of the ʿĀli Qāpu and accessed the Daftar-ḵāna or Imperial Chancellery. The Kitchen Gate (Darb-e matbaḵ), located south of the harem gate, brought to the edge of the public sphere the symbol of royal generosity, as it was through this gate that food would be distributed to the poor and dispatched to the guests of the shah. Together, these gates communicated through their architectural mediation of functions the relationship between the Safavid household, the locus of power and authority, and the denizens of Isfahan and, by extension, of the entire Safavid dominion.

ʿĀli Qāpu. The first amongst the urban Safavid palaces in Isfahan was the ʿĀli Qāpu. Its conceptualization coincided with that of the Meydān project (Galdieri, 1979, pp. 1-40; Babaie, 1994a, pp. 99-135; see Plate I [2]). During the initial campaign of 1590-91, the preparation

PLATE II (2)

The ʿĀli Qāpu Palace, the audience hall. Courtesy of the author.

of the Meydān as the new urban center was accompanied by the construction of the Qayṣariya Bazaar and a two-story building that served as the gateway into the royal precinct of the Bāḡ-e Naqš-e Jahān (Galdieri, 1979, pp. 3-15; Babaie, 1994a, pp. 115-24). This initial, modest gateway was to be transformed in the 1602 campaign, during which the first "block" was raised by the addition of two stories. This phase of construction invested the gateway with the monumentality of a palace. It also redefined the functional parameters of this most accessible royal seat of the Dawlat-ḵāna complex.

The first block of two stories, as archeological investigations and extant evidence demonstrate, was an integral part of the Meydān construction. It was designed on a cross-in-square (or nine-fold) plan in which the spaces or rooms formed by the arms of the cross and the intervening spaces in the four corners rotated around a central area. This type of building, known as a *hašt behešt* (eight paradises, for its eight spaces around the central opening; q.v.), was associated with such royal pavilions as the 16th-century so-called Čehel Sotun of Safavid Qazvin and the 15th-century Timurid pavilions in the royal gardens of Samarqand and Herat (known only through descriptions). The initial block of the ʿĀli Qāpu gateway then represented an instance of continuity in architectural traditions of the past.

In contrast, the second block, the additional two stories of 1602, marked a radical departure in the conception of a royal seat, a palace (Plate II [2]). Here the third floor is principally given over to a rectangular audience hall, the narrow side of which faces, through shallow porches (*ayvān*, q.v.), the Meydān and the royal precinct sides. The audience hall rises to the full height of the two stories with its vaulted roof held aloft through an innovative forked-arch system that allowed for fenestration on the upper zone of the side walls (Galdieri, 1979, pp. 16; Ferrante, pp. 142-43; Babaie, 1994a, pp. 101-2). An ingenious double-story mezzanine occupies the sides of the audience hall unit on the fourth floor. This little-known architectural feat is hidden into the floor that was reserved for the women of the harem, who were provided a glimpse of the ceremonial gatherings below through windows that filled the in-between squinch (triangular) surfaces of the forked-arches. The addition of the final fifth floor (comp. by around 1615), of a private cluster of intensely decorated rooms, concluded the first phase of the transition from a gateway into a ceremonial palace during the reign of Shah ʿAbbās the Great (1587-1629).

With its original functions as the seat from which emanated imperial justice, the enhanced functionality of the ʿĀli Qāpu as a ceremonial palace rendered this the uncommon example of the marking of the threshold between the public and the royal arenas of a capital city in the early modern age. Whereas the ceremonial seat of authority and its performance of kingship in the Ottoman Topkapı and the Mughal Red Forts were withdrawn deep inside the fortified royal precincts, the Dawlat-ḵāna of Isfahan placed its most ceremonial palace at the threshold between the royal and the public. The placement of the royal chapel-mosque of Shaikh Loṭf-Allāh (see below) directly across from the ʿĀli Qāpu Palace gateway further illustrated for the denizens of Isfahan and of the imperial dominion of the Safavids the significance of ritual accessibility and humility that was necessitated by the discourse of legitimacy in a Twelver Shiʿite construction of kingship.

Unlike the assumption of aloofness in varying degrees of intensity that befitted a Sunnite, caliphal model of kingship (adopted by the Ottoman sultans and Mughal emperors), the Safavid imperial posture was predicated on the imperative of humility at the threshold of Imam ʿAli. In fact, Shah ʿAbbās the Great, who identified himself as "the dog (or dust or servant) of the threshold of ʿAli" (*kalb-e āstān-e ʿAli, kalb-e āstān-e welāyat*; see, Shah ʿAbbās's poem in Jalāl-al-Din Monajjem, pp. 163, 237; Falsafi, II, the plate facing p. 24) instituted the practice of dismounting before the ʿĀli Qāpu, for this gate was sanctified with the installment of a door from the Shrine of ʿAli in Najaf, and was thus made holy for the shahs ruled on behalf of the Mahdi (Messiah), the Hidden Twelfth Imam.

Tālār-e Ṭawila and Āʾina-ḵāna. Like Shah ʿAbbās, his successor Shah Ṣafi I (r. 1629-42) spent a considerable length of time, especially during the first years of his reign, outside of Isfahan, engaged mostly in the renewed conflicts with the Ottomans on the western frontiers. Shah Ṣafi I's coronation in 1629 took place at the ʿĀli Qāpu, but the waning of the Palace-Gateway's functionality in his reign indicates a shift in Safavid ceremonials (Babaie, 1994a, pp. 234-39). Two palaces are attributable to his reign on the basis of their mention, for the first time, in Persian chronicles of his reign: the Tālār-e Ṭawila (the Hall of the Stables) in the Dawlat-ḵāna and the Āʾina-ḵāna (the Hall of Mirrors) on the southern bank of the Zāyandarud River. Neither one has survived, but descriptions and some engravings help us reconstruct their basic architectural configuration and functions (Babaie, 1994a, pp. 245-53; Honarfar, 1965, p. 752; Mirzā Ḥosayn, p. 23; Floor, pp. 149-63).

According to Adam Olearius, the secretary of the Holstein Embassy, and other European visitors, the Tālār-e Ṭawila was a large elongated building located in a garden a little way to the southwest of the ʿĀli Qāpu. Set at the end of a long pool, the Tālār-e Ṭawila was raised on a platform and was subdivided along its longitudinal axis into three sections, beginning, from the outermost, with a pillared hall with a fountain and concluding at its innermost with an *ayvān* porch for the throne. Wooden pillars held up the roof in all three zones while low wooden banisters separated the sections thus demarcating the degrees of remove and significance (Olearius, 1669, p. 202; Tavernier, 1678, p. 178).

The architectural configuration of this palace is indeed extraordinary, for it is the antithesis of the earlier *hašt behešt* model. Not only is the plan laid out on the longitudinal axis instead of the centralized cross-in-square, it is also here that the traditional ratio between solid and void has been completely reversed in favor of considerable openness. Pillared halls were not a novelty, but the particularity of the pillared halls at the Tālār-e Ṭawila ushers in a new chapter in the Persian palace designs. Unlike the horizontal stretch of pillared halls of Achaemenid palaces or even the contemporary Mughal Divān-e ʿĀmm, the *tālār* in Tālār-e Ṭawila consists of a sequence of pillared spaces that are completely open on three sides, and that are placed one behind the other on the longitudinal axis (Babaie, 1994a, pp. 253-61; Koch, 1994, pp. 143-65). The privileging of the *tālār* in the Tālār-e Ṭawila may in fact be an indication of a consciousness about its architectural novelty.

European descriptions of feasts and audiences at the Tālār-e Ṭawila indicate that this type of palace was especially suited for large gatherings (some describe 500 guests) in a space that could be hierarchically zoned but that also allowed for visibility and access, at least in their potential. The Tālār-e Ṭawila, in fact, became the most frequently utilized building for feasts and audiences during the reign of Shah Ṣafi I and continued to be one of the principal ceremonial palaces in the Dawlat-ḵāna. Equally open and ceremonial was the Āʾina-ḵāna, the other palace built during the reign of Shah Ṣafi I, which is also based on a *tālār* design. The Āʾina-ḵāna was amongst the nearby suburban palaces developed along the southern bank of the Zāyandarud River, and as such the *tālār* there utilized its unobstructed view of the river in the same way that the Tālār-e Ṭawila communicated with the long pool in its garden setting. The Āʾina-ḵāna, better known thanks to 19th-century engravings by Pascal Coste, may also be dated to the 1630s on the evidence

PLATE III (2)

The ʿĀli Qāpu Palace, the tālār level.
Courtesy of the author.

that it was utilized for ceremonial events and was also praised for its beauty in a poem by Moẓaffar Torka (Coste, Pl. XXXV; Babaie, 1994a, pp. 250-51; Honarfar, 1965, pp. 578-80).

ʿĀli Qāpu Tālār. The dominant transparency of the Tālār-e Ṭawila and the Āʾina-ḵāna, as well as their spatial and visual intermingling with the outside (water and garden elements in these cases) mark a new turning point in palace architecture in the Iranian world. Soon after Shah ʿAbbās II ascended the throne in 1642, his grand vizier, Mirzā Moḥammad Sāru Taqi, the most likely mastermind behind the idea of the *tālār* type palace, was entrusted with the construction of a *tālār* in front of the existing five-story tower of ʿĀli Qāpu (Babaie, 2004, pp. 106-7; see Plate III [2]). The addition consisted of a massive two-story unit that provided the gateway with a vaulted passage on the ground floor and the audience hall on the third floor with a *tālār*.

This *tālār* radically altered the functionality of the original palace. As the Safavid court ceremonials had increasingly tended towards enlarged and elaborate feasts and gatherings in the hundreds, the ʿĀli Qāpu's audience hall and its shallow *ayvān* facing the Meydān had seized to be functional. With the *tālār* addition, the ʿĀli Qāpu resumed, as contemporary evidence testifies (e.g., Waḥid, pp. 198, 222), its role as one of the premium ceremonial palaces in the Dawlat-ḵāna. Here, however, the *tālār* at the ʿĀli Qāpu afforded the public an even greater visual access to the performance of kingship.

Čehel Sotun. Following the architectural intervention and the functional updating of the ʿĀli Qāpu, Shah ʿAbbās II (r. 1642-66) sponsored the building of the Čehel Sotun Palace within the grounds of the Dawlat-ḵāna (Honarfar, 1965, pp. 557-74; Mehrābādi, pp. 339-61; Ferrante; see Plate IV [2]). A chronogram by the poet Sāʾeb and other evidence date the building to 1647 while the completion of its mural decorations may have taken until the early 1650s (see Honarfar, 1972b and Babaie, 1994b).

PLATE IV (2)

The Čehel Sotun Palace, Exterior. Courtesy of the author.

PLATE V (2)

Čehel Sotun, view from the alcove before the main hall looking towards an imagined view of the Šāh Mosque. After Flandin and Coste, *Voyage en Perse: Perse modern*, Paris, 1854, Pl. LI.

The Čehel Sotun marks the full architectural realization of the experiments that began with the Tālār-e Ṭawila. It furthermore signals the institutionalization by this mid-century date of the practice of feasting as an imperial ritual that enunciated the particularity of the Safavid kingship that necessitated formal spaces for its performance.

Jean Chardin (q.v.), the French traveler, exemplified the feasting rituals of the Safavids by describing just such an event at the Čehel Sotun, in which the mass of guests were wined, dined, entertained and were engaged in political conversations in the company of the shah (Chardin, V, pp. 468-79). This manner of feasting the multitudes of

PLATE VI (2)

The Hašt Behešt Palace, Exterior. Courtesy of the author.

guests, where the shah himself resided as its host, was the Safavid answer to the symbolic need for accessibility as the deputy of the Imams. As such, it stood in sharp contrast to the aloofness of the Ottoman sultans and Mughal emperors, for example, whose remoteness in the manner of the ʿAbbāsid caliphs prohibited any public display of such earthly and mundane acts as eating, much less sharing food with others of profane status.

The Čehel Sotun is also laid down on its longitudinal axis. Set within a huge garden, its elongated plan is compellingly emphasized by the landscaping of the grounds in which a long pool in front and a smaller one in the back appear as if extensions of the structure itself. A massive *tālār* of twenty wooden pillars (forty with the reflection in the pool and hence the name, Kāḵ-e Čehel Sotun [Forty-Columned Palace]) forms the front of the building (Plate V [2]). This *tālār*, enlivened by a fountain-pool at its center, leads to ever decreasing spaces in size, which are also increasingly more contained by walls and vaults. At the culmination of this processional and hierarchical spacing, which had, for performative purposes, begun at the far end of the long pool, sat the throne *ayvān*. Here, the decorative scheme of painted, gilded and mirrored columns and walls intensified into an explosive, prismatic mirror-work in the vault of the *ayvān* and a pair of mural panels of scenes of courtly pastime on the side walls.

Exceptionally in the Čehel Sotun, a large triple-vaulted audience hall lies behind the *tālār-ayvān* reception area on the west (Babaie, 1994a, pp. 138-39). The hall is a rectangle turned perpendicular onto the main axis of the building. It opened on the sides (north and south) to two verandas (both with a single row of wooden columns and with mural decoration), while at its corners were placed four smaller rooms of intimate decoration and scale, most likely suited for private use. The architectural articulation of the hall and its extensive mural program enunciate its purely ceremonial function. Mural paintings range in size and subject matter: the smaller ones on the lower walls are of scenes of courtly leisure; the four large rectangular panels on the upper walls are of historicized themes in which Safavid monarchs are portrayed as victorious in battle as well as in politics.

The decorative scheme then visualized the centrality of the Safavids as the arbiters in matters of sovereignty within the competitive politics of the Persianate world at the same time that the architectural articulation of the Čehel Sotun facilitated the performance of royal feasts, which had become increasingly the stage for the enunciation of Safavid kingship.

Hašt Behešt. One of the most famous Safavid palaces in Isfahan is the Hašt Behešt, a relatively well-preserved building dated to 1080/1669 (Honarfar, 1965, pp. 622-26; Mehrābādi, pp. 328-39; Naṣrābādi, pp. 487-90; Mirzā Ḥosayn, pp. 25-26; Ferrante, 1968c; see Plate VI [2]). As had been the pattern in the Safavid constructions of palaces in Isfahan, Shah Solaymān (r. 1666-94) also embarked on the construction of a new palace soon after he ascended the throne. His palace, however, was constructed not in the *birun* or public zone of the Dawlat-ḵāna, but in the vast gardens of Bolbol "Nightingale," located to the south of the harem. As such, the Hašt Behešt manifested,

PLATE III (2)

The Hašt Behešt Palace, Interior of the central hall and its vaulted ceiling. Courtesy of the author.

both in its location and its architectural and decorative strategies, the priorities of a more private function than the feasting rituals and ceremonial events held at the Tālār-e Ṭawila or the Čehel Sotun.

As its name indicates, this was a building based on a *hašt behešt* (q.v.) plan. Raised on a platform, the structure reads as a square with its corners cut away to resemble a modified octagon. The corners are accentuated by the massive, two-story rise of pylons that are perforated with stacked pointed-arch niches. Each of the four sides of the building, on the other hand, is given to spacious porches roofed over with the placement of a few tall and thin wooden columns. The large and tall central space is a fully articulated octagon, rising well above the two-story height through an elegantly tapering and mirrored internal lantern (Plate VII [2]). The sensuality of the volumetric alternating of solids and voids within the structure of the Hašt Behešt itself is contrasted with the rich surface articulation through murals, perforated woodwork, prismatic mirrors and extensive tile work of figural subject matter (Luschey-Schmeisser, pp. 7-28). Descriptions of events at this building, of leisurely outings of the harem women and of the private gatherings, clearly synchronize with the architectural and decorative particularities of the Hašt Behešt (Chardin, pp. 39-43).

Suburban palaces. With the Tālār-e Ṭawila, the ʿĀli Qāpu, and the Čehel Sotun, the Dawlat-ḵāna had been equipped by the middle of the 17th century with ceremonial palaces singularly suited to feasting that was accommodated by the *tālār* spaces. These palaces were complemented by the suburban retreats that successive Safavid monarchs built in order to facilitate the need for retreat while still centered at the capital city. The Hezār Jarib (or ʿAbbāsābād) of Shah ʿAbbās the Great, built in the 1590s on the model of gently sloped terraced gardens, mediated the transition from the Čahārbāḡ Avenue and the Ṣoffa Mountain, on the foot of which it was laid out (Honarfar, 1975, pp. 76 ff.; Alemi p. 75; Mirzā Ḥosayn, p. 27).

Palaces along the Zāyandarud River, especially the Āʾina-ḵāna and the so-called Haft Dast ensemble of Shah Ṣafi I and Shah ʿAbbās II lined the southern bank of the river between the two bridges of Allāh-verdi Khan and Ḵᵛāju (see below; Haft Dast was destroyed in the late Qājar period, see Honarfar, 1965, pp. 678, 680). Together with garden retreats and parks on the northern bank, this complex made up the riverfront ensemble of Saʿādatābād, all of which was destroyed during the Qajar period (19th century). Equally large and complex was the Faraḥābād palace-city built by Shah Solṭān-Ḥosayn in the early years of the 18th century (Honarfar, 1965, pp. 722-25; Mehrābādi, pp. 80-81). This, however, was not simply a retreat for the last Safavid king but served as his principal place of residence during a reign that was mired by the delegation of power to the eunuch *ḡolām*s of the harem and the powerful clergy. When Maḥmud the Afghan advanced on Isfahan in 1722, it was from Faraḥābād that he led the siege of the capital city and it was to Faraḥābād that Shah Solṭān-Ḥosayn came to deliver his ancestral crown and the Safavid Empire (Krusinski, II, pp. 36-37, 98-100).

(3) Mosques

Isfahan is known historically for its large number of mosques. According to Abu Noʿaym of Isfahan (I, p. 17), the first large mosque in Isfahan was built by a client (*mawlā*) of ʿOmar b. al-Ḵaṭṭāb during the Caliphate of Imam ʿAli b. Abi Ṭāleb (r. 656-61). The French traveler Jean Chardin had counted one hundred and sixty two mosques during his travels to Isfahan in the middle of the 17th century. The majority in Chardin's account must have been the neighborhood mosques that served, as in every Muslim city, the residential quarters, sections of bazaars, or else were attached to the city's numerous *madrasa*s and shrines. Much of this legacy, however, has been erased through centuries of destructive incursions or urban renewal efforts. Nothing, for example, remains of the oldest amongst these local *masjed* types, while mosques dating to the Safavid and later periods represent, albeit in considerably diminished numbers, the largest extant examples (Haneda, 1996).

Isfahan acquired early in its Islamic history a large mosque that served the male portion of the entire community for congregational Friday noon prayer, hence Masjed-e Jomʿe (Friday Mosque). This has been a principal Islamic practice since the Prophet Moḥammad established the first congregational mosque at his house in Medina (Hillenbrand, 1994, pp. 33-34). Friday mosques

PLATE I (3)

Jāme' Mosque, aerial view. After R. Baḵtiār, p. 16.

of major cities were additional to smaller neighborhood mosques that dotted most large cities in the Islamic world. Ordinarily founded by the king or members of the ruling elite, congregational mosques facilitated the profession of political allegiance through the customary Friday noontime prayer and the sermon (*ḵoṭba*) that was delivered, if not by the king himself, by a representative of the patronized clergy.

Isfahan, however, came to have two congregational mosques: Masjed-e Jāme' (*Jom'a*, Friday Mosque or Great Mosque of Isfahan) founded in the 8th century, and the Masjed-e Jadid-e 'Abbāsi, better known as Masjed-e Šāh (the Royal Mosque; renamed Masjed-e Emām after the Revolution of 1978-79) that Shah 'Abbās I the Great constructed to mark the beginning of a new era of legally-sanctioned practice of Twelver Shi'ite kingship. In addition to these two congregational mosques, four other significant mosques of the city will be considered in this essay, albeit with varying degrees of emphasis: the early 16th-century Masjed-e 'Ali, the royal chapel-mosque Masjed-e Šayḵ Loṭf-Allāh of early 17th-century date, and the mid-17th-century Ḥakim Mosque. It is worth noting, however, that even though this essay focuses on the more important and better-studied mosques, there are many other mosques that present perfectly worthy cases for research. Two mosques built by Sāru Taqi, the grand vizier of Shah Ṣafi I and Shah 'Abbās II and one of the most important patrons of architecture in the 17th-century Persia, deserve further scholarly attention (Babaie, 2004, pp. 97-98). Others, such as the exquisitely decorated, especially in its façade, but totally neglected 19th-century Rokn-al-Molk Mosque represent an opportunity to expand our picture of Isfahan further into the modern period (Babaie, in *EIr.*, p. 500 and Pl. VI; Honarfar, 1965, pp. 805-22; Mehrābādi, pp. 625-40). Among all the mosques of Isfahan, the Masjed-e Jāme' occupies the central position not only in considering the monuments of Isfahan but also in the annals of Persian architecture; it will therefore take a larger share of the following essay.

Masjed-e Jāme'. This mosque was founded in the 8th century by the Taym Arabs of the village Ṭirān (Ṭehrān in Abu No'aym; a village in the Najafābād area) on the outskirts of Yahudiya, one of the then twin towns constituting the city of Isfahan (Plates I [3] and II [3]). The mosque was enlarged with the expansion of the town, which in turn had followed the building of this mosque. It was equipped with a library (*dār-al-kotob*) housing books that were chosen by scholars of the past, covering almost every discipline of knowledge and all registered in a three-volume catalogue. Each time no less than five thousand people congregated for prayer (Abu No'aym, I, pp. 17-19; Māfarruḵi, pp. 84-85). Round plastered columns supported the roof and the minaret on the *qebla* side (Moqaddasi, pp. 388-89). The mosque, which Ebn al-Aṯir describes as among the largest and most beautiful of its kind, burned down in 515/1121 in a fire set to it by the Isma'ilis (Ebn al-Aṯir, Beirut, X, p. 595; Honarfar, 1965, pp. 80-81). The mosque was built anew and became in time the most venerated mosque of the city until the 17th century, when a rival congregational mosque was raised by the Safavid Shah 'Abbās the Great. As the oldest mosque of the city, its aura of ritual sanctity inspired the denizens of Isfahan and its rulers alike to lavish funds and talents on the mosque to enhance its functionality and its prestige and to leave for posterity the imprint of individual and collective patronage (Grabar, pp. 44-60). Nearly every significant architectural and decorative trend of medieval period in Persian history found its monumental representation in this mosque. In fact, so richly diverse, artistically accomplished and technologically inventive are the building and decorative strategies employed in this mosque that it has served as a blueprint for medieval Persian architecture in general. Moreover, in its architectural evolution from an Arab hypostyle type to a four-*ayvān*, courtyard focused mosque plan, this mosque exemplifies the maturation of the Persian style mosque (Honarfar, 1965, pp. 67-168; Mehrābādi, pp. 527-90; Mirzā Ḥosayn Khan, p. 19).

The initial construction of Masjed-e Jāmeʿ was presumably funded by governors who controlled the city on behalf of the ʿAbbāsid caliphs to mark the full establishment of the Islamic community (*omma*) in Isfahan since the city's capture in the early years of Arab conquest (q.v.; According to Abu Noʿaym, I, p. 17, and Māfarruḵi, p. 84, it was first built by the Arabs of the village Ṭehrān). The Masjed-e Jāmeʿ appears to have formed the focal point of ʿAbbāsid constructions in the Yahudiya, the larger of the two settlements (Jay was the other) that developed with its satellite villages into the urban center of early Islamic Isfahan (Golombek, pp. 20-25). The site of the Masjed-e Jāmeʿ has played an important role on the religious landscape of Isfahan since at least the 8th century and quite possibly even earlier as archeological evidence suggests that the location of the prayer niche (*meḥrāb*) and its domed chamber (on the south side of the mosque) are the same as that of a former Zoroastrian fire temple (Galdieri, 1972-84, III, pp. 19-25). Indeed, to appropriate the sanctity of a preexisting site of worship, in this case possibly a Zoroastrian fire temple, would have been in character with the early Islamic discourse of urban conquest; many of the first congregational mosques from Cordova to Delhi occupy the sites of earlier houses of worship.

Archeological investigations of the 1960s and 1970s, carried out by the Italian team of researchers led by Eugenio Galdieri, have revealed the parameters and general configuration of this early mosque (Galdieri, 1972-84, III, pp. 19-25). This was a hypostyle, a classical mosque type developed out of the model of the house-mosque of the Prophet and perfected in such monumental caliphal structures as the Great Mosque of Sāmarrā (comp. 238/852) by al-Motawakkel in the new capital of the ʿAbbasids. The main features of this first hypostyle mosque were its classically proportioned rectangular area subdivided into a covered sanctuary, its roof held atop equidistantly placed pillars, and an open courtyard. This early mosque was purportedly renovated in the 10th-century when the Buyids (932-1055) made Isfahan their major center of political life, yet still little is known about these works. Nevertheless, the mosque remained at the center of urban life of Isfahan throughout the medieval period.

The Masjed-e Jāmeʿ of Isfahan as it stands now is quintessentially a Saljuq mosque. Since 1051, when the city assumed political ascendancy in the vast Saljuq dominion, constructions at the congregational mosque and the Meydān-e Kohna in its vicinity on the southeast had gained momentum. In successive campaigns, the Great Mosque of Isfahan underwent a series of radical architectural alterations that established the basic plan and elevation of the mosque for centuries to come. This mosque covers nearly 17,000 square meters or an area of about four acres, and is centered on a courtyard of approximately 2,500 square meters, making it one of the largest mosques in Iran.

The Saljuq interventions seem to have begun in earnest with the addition, some time between 1072 and 1092 (no firm date is given in the foundation inscriptions), by the great vizier Neẓām-al-Molk (d. 1092) of a domed chamber over the prayer niche of the original hypostyle mosque (Honarfar, 1965, pp. 75-76). Archeological evidence suggests that this structure may have been conceived as a freestanding replacement of the original fire temple idea (Galdieri, III, pp. 19-25). The remains of the South Dome testify to the impressive scale of the brick building; as in the rest of the mosque, this dome is constructed of brick, the traditional building material of the central regions of Persia. Its square chamber is delineated by the placement of massive round pillars clustered into impressive thickness at each corner. As such, the South Dome resembled the *čahār ṭāq* (q.v.) units that have been associated with pre-Islamic Sasanian architecture of Persia in general and with Zoroastrian fire temples in particular.

At the other, northern side of the mosque and well beyond its original compound, the rival and successor of Neẓām-al-Molk, Abu'l-Ḡanāyem Tāj-al-Molk Pārsi (d. 1093), sponsored the construction in 1088 of the North Dome (popularly referred to as Gonbad-e Ḵāki; see Plate IV [3]). This too was a freestanding chamber outside the mosque environs and near the north gate into the mosque. Its function has been debated, but the chamber was most likely intended for some royal function (Grabar, pp. 38-41, 50-52; Honarfar, 1965, pp. 76-78). Such a function may be supported by the architectural, decorative and epigraphic specificities of this small building. While the South Dome of Neẓām-al-Molk would inspire awe with its massive scale and heavy proportions, the North Dome of Tāj-al-Molk achieved its impact through lightness and elegance in the way forms are broken down into geometrically complex patterns. The double-shelled dome allows for a taller external profile and a more tempered rise in the interior. Internally, the dome is held aloft by the ingenious distribution of weight across a system of arches that shrink in size and transform into two and three-dimensional units as they emanate from center to periphery in each area. The patterns of broad arches embracing clusters of smaller arches, of deep-cut corner squinches alternating with shallow niches, of even smaller arches ringing the base of the dome, of intersecting pentagons in the dome are exquisitely integrated into the fabric of the building through the use of brickwork as both structural and decorative material. In this regard, the North Dome of the Great Mosque of Isfahan demonstrates one of the most brilliant examples of what may be said to be a Saljuq specialty in Iranian architecture. Equally inventive and complex is the epigraphic

PLATE II (3)

Jāmeʿ Mosque, Courtyard view toward South. Courtesy of the author.

style and program of the North Dome, in which set brick and carved stucco form Kufic bands of text ornament; Qurʾanic inscriptions on the impost blocks are in a massive cursive script, whereas the foundation inscriptions on the dome itself are in an angular Kufic formed out of brick relief (Galdieri, 1972-84, III, p. 38; Honarfar, 1965, p. 76; Blair, no. 61).

As revolutionary an alteration to the mosque as the addition of these two domes represented, the next Saljuq intervention into the very fabric of the mosque resulted in a total transformation of the original hypostyle into a new mosque type. During the 1120s, pillars and roofs of much of the sanctuary and the courtyard arcade of the mosque were taken down and replaced with vaulted spaces internally and four *pišṭāq-ayvān* compositions facing the courtyard. These deep-set arched openings framed with rectangular bands were placed at the center of each side of the courtyard, both mediating the rhythmic march of the smaller arches along each side and accentuating each courtyard side as an integrated façade (Plate III [3]). In this way, the four-*ayvān* façades of the Great Mosque of Isfahan redistributed ritual and visual attention onto the courtyard. Unlike the rigid separation of the covered sanctuary and open courtyard in a hypostyle mosque, the masterful execution of four-*ayvān* plan of the Great Mosque of Isfahan (not the first in Persia, but the most accomplished) and its use of *ayvān*s to mediate between the inner and outer spaces of the mosque resolved an inherent architectural contradiction between the earlier Arab-Mediterranean solutions and this indigenous Iranian conclusion.

The centrality of the Masjed-e Jāmeʿ in Persian architecture in general, and in the subsequent history of monuments in Isfahan in particular, is illustrated by the fact that successive rulers and patrons left their imprint on this mosque. In the process, however, the mosque complex became an irregularly shaped entity that seems to have grown organically around its constituent parts and into the fabric of the city. During the reign of Öljeitü (Ūljāytū; r. 1304-16) and in the post-Mongol period, the area behind the western *ayvān* of the courtyard was converted into a prayer hall at the *qebla*-side, in which was placed a superb *meḥrāb*. This is dated 710/1310 and claims in its inscriptions credit for Moḥammad Sāvi, an Il-khanid vizier, as the patron and for a Badr as the master calligrapher-designer (Honarfar, 1965, pp. 114-20; Blair and Bloom, pp. 10-11). The *meḥrāb* is rightfully famed for its complex composition and masterful execution in stucco. It is adorned with three-dimensional stucco bands of calligraphy in *ṯolṯ* script that are set against a complex foliate scrollwork and surrounded by borders of twisted vines and a panel featuring lotus-like flowers mentioning the names of the twelve Shiʿite Imams, possibly a reference to Öljeitü's conversion to Shiʿism. The Shiʿite tenor of the commission is also evident in the inclusion of a Hadith that is attributed to the first Imam ʿAli b. Abi Ṭāleb, stating that whoever frequents a mosque will receive one of eight benedictions (Honarfar, 1965, p. 120).

The Mozaffarids (1313–93) added a small *madrasa* to the eastern side of the mosque while the Timurid additions amounted to some significant re-workings of the mosque with a winter prayer hall, a portal, and, what is more, the mosaic-tile sheathing of the courtyard façades that brought to the mainly plain-brick Saljuq building a captivating element of color. The dedication panel of the Timurid prayer hall, dated 851/1447, is an early example of the practice of highlighting with color the names of patrons in foundational inscriptions; here the name of Sultan Moḥammad Bahādor, grandson of Šāhrok̲, is

PLATE III (3)

Jāmeʿ Mosque, Courtyard view toward North-Northeast. Courtesy of the author.

written in ocher against the blue and white background (Honarfar, 1965, pp. 122-23; Mehrābādi, p. 552). This Timurid emphasis on chromatic effects in architecture continued to inspire Safavid and later patrons in their additions to this mosque and in the architecture of Isfahan in general.

The Safavid period also witnessed continued patronage of the Masjed-e Jāmeʿ, whereby successive rulers added their royal imprint both before and after Isfahan became the capital in 1597-98. Among these the most important may be listed here: the four courtyard *ayvāns* received complex *moqarnas* vaulting (or earlier ones were replaced?) with glazed tile facing; the principal south (*qebla*) *ayvān* received a pair of thin minarets that crowned the *pišṭāq* (the *goldasta* type); and the tile work especially on the *meḥrāb* further demonstrates the post-Timurid emphasis on color over the Saljuq preference for bare brickwork. A measure of the continually charged sanctity and social significance of the Great Mosque of Isfahan is the fact that Safavid Shahs used the walls of the mosque to stamp onto the city representations of their dominion; Shah Esmāʿil I and Shah Ṭahmāsb ordered important royal decrees (*farmān*, q.v.) to be affixed strategically onto the mosque. Shah Ṭahmāsb had further ordered repairs to the mosque in 1531-32 to be carried out by one of the patronized clergy acting also as royal representative (Babaie, 2003, p. 39; Honarfar, 1965, pp. 86 ff.). Ṭahmāsb's epigraphic addition to the south *ayvān* contain prayers to the fourteen infallibles (*čahārdah maʿṣum*, q.v.) of Shiʿite belief, thus linking the historic center of religiosity in Isfahan to the new Shiʿite focus of the Safavids. Paradoxically, this change in religious practice contributed, in part, to the attempt to rival the Masjed-e Jāmeʿ with the Royal Mosque during the reign of Shah ʿAbbās the Great early in the 17th century.

Masjed-e ʿAli. This mosque of the early 16th century, dated by inscription to 929/1523, is noteworthy for its pairing with the shrine of Hārun-e Welāyat (1513) and their location on the southern threshold of the Meydān-e Kohna (Hillenbrand, pp. 764-65; Honarfar, 1965, pp. 369-79; Babaie, 2003, pp. 32-33; Mehrābādi, pp. 712-16; see Plate IV [3]). This mosque was built in place of a ruined Saljuq mosque by Mirzā Kamāl-al-Din Shah-Ḥosayn, a professional architect who had also served as a statesman during the reign of Shah Esmāʿil I. In his capacity as the vizier of the *qezelbāš* governor Dormiš Khan Šāmlu, he had built the shrine of Hārun-e Welāyat and had inscribed his own name onto its famous façade (Honarfar, 1965, 361). While the shrine's significance rests on its façade, the mosque represents the aspirations of an architect-patron in its attempt to introduce new architectural elements into the standard four-*ayvān* plan of mosques.

Like the shrine, the epigraphic program of the portal highlights the connection between Shah Esmāʿil and the family of the Prophet Moḥammad, albeit here considerably less intense both visually and iconographically (Honarfar, 1965, p. 372; Babaie, 2003, p. 35; Mehrābādi, pp. 713-14). Recalling Saljuq decorative techniques, Shiʿite sacred names are rendered on the portal in angular Kufic bands of script alongside geometric decoration in alternating glazed and unglazed tiles. A selection of Qurʾanic verses, which interweave numerical symbols of Twelver Shiʿism with the name of Esmāʿil, reference the shah as the recipient of God's grace. An allusion in the inscription to Imam ʿAli as the "opener of gates" reiterates the Safavid devotion to Imam ʿAli as the gate (*bāb*) to

PLATE IV (3)

Masjed-e ʿAli, aerial view. After R. Baḵtiār, p. 74.

PLATE V (3)

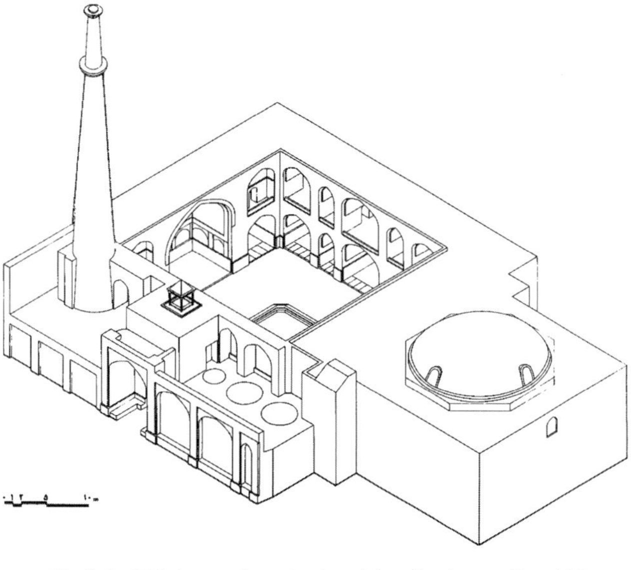

Masjed-e ʿAli, isometric projection. After *Ganj-nāma* II, p. 144.

spiritual knowledge and the dynasty's source of legitimacy (Hillenbrand, p. 765; Babaie, 2003, p. 35).

The mosque's courtyard and four-*ayvān* plan, the familiar Persian form already standardized at the Great Mosque of Isfahan, is relatively modest in size and ordinary in composition (Plate VI [3]). Its domed chamber, however, displays considerable departure from earlier examples (Plate VII [3]). This is the space that contains the *meḥrāb* and constitutes the main prayer hall of the mosque. Two systems, one rooted in the past, and the other prefiguring future developments, coexist in this unusual interior. The multiple arched openings on two stories that

PLATE VI (3)

Masjed-e ʿAli, Courtyard. Courtesy of the author.

PLATE VII (3)

Masjed-e ʿAli, Interior. Courtesy of the author.

surround the sanctuary recall the 15th-century Masjed-e Kabud (Blue Mosque) of Tabriz. The transition from the square chamber walls to the circular base of the dome, on the other hand, is facilitated through four massive pendentives (triangular corner units). Such an expansive architectonic treatment of the domed space anticipates the extraordinarily brilliant square-to-circle solution that will be found at the early 17th-century Shaikh Loṭf-Allāh Mosque in Isfahan.

Shaikh Loṭf-Allāh Mosque. The second, chronologically speaking, of the significant mosques of Isfahan is the mosque that was built across from the ʿĀli Qāpu Palace on the Meydān-e Naqš-e Jahān, which came to be associated with Shaikh Loṭf-Allāh (d. 1032/1623), the father-in-law of Shah ʿAbbās the Great and one of the principal religious doctors of his time (Blair and Bloom, pp. 185-90; Honarfar, 1965, pp. 404-5) (Plate VIII [3]). Shaikh Loṭf-Allāh Mosque is unique among Isfahan's mosques in several respects. Consisting of a single domed chamber, all the standard features of a four-*ayvān* courtyard-centered mosque, including minarets, are foregone here, for this is a mosque designed to serve private royal functions rather than congregational prayer (Honarfar, 1965, pp. 401-15; Mehrābādi, pp. 693-710).

Covering almost 2,500 square meters, the Shaikh Loṭf-Allāh Mosque was conceived as an integral part of Shah ʿAbbās's conversion of Isfahan into his new imperial capital. Construction of the mosque began in 1011/1602-3 and was completed in 1028/1618-19. Epigraphic bands penned by ʿAli-Reżā ʿAbbāsi, the famous calligrapher of this period, grace both the exterior façade and the extensive interior decoration of the mosque (Honarfar, 1965, pp. 402, 407-10) (Plates VIII [3] and IX [3]). The mosque functioned as a private royal-chapel mosque. By placing the royal mosque outside the palace compound on the Meydān and across the ʿĀli Qāpu, Shah ʿAbbās and his urban designers and advisors exploited the symbolic value

PLATE VIII (3)

Shaikh Loṭf-Allāh Mosque, view from Meydān-e Naqš-e Jahān. Courtesy of the author.

PLATE IX (3)

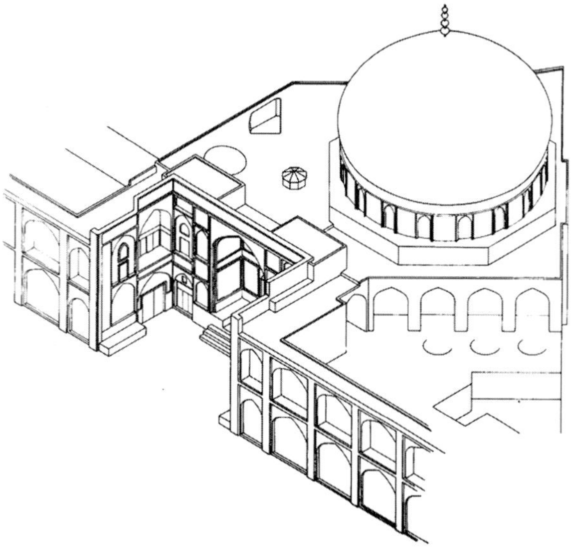

Shaikh Loṭf-Allāh Mosque, isometric projection. After *Ganj-nāma* II, p. 144.

of traversing the public space by the household; to go to the Shaikh Loṭf-Allāh Mosque would become a performative representation of royal piety. The pairing of the ʿĀli Qāpu Palace and the Shaikh Loṭf-Allāh Mosque thus symbolized, both in theory and practice, the worldly and otherworldly sources of Safavid legitimacy. As "the blessed mosque (*al-majed al-mobārak*) of the great sultan," ʿAli-Reżā ʿAbbāsi's epigraphic program on the entrance façade (dated 1012/1603) further enunciated this ideological role of the mosque (Honarfar, 1965, p. 402).

The association of the mosque with Shaikh Loṭf-Allāh, the first chief clergy of the mosque, was to demonstrate the final and firm establishment by Shah ʿAbbās of the legalistic or *šariʿa*-based practice of Twelver Shiʿism as the

PLATE X (3)

Shaikh Loṭf-Allāh Mosque, *mehrāb*.
Courtesy of the author.

religion of the Safavid Empire. It is in this light also that one finds inside the domed chamber epigraphic panels in tiles, wherein the shaikh's name is mentioned at the end of a poem in Arabic, invoking the names of the Fourteen Infallibles and pleading intercession for Shaikh Loṭf-Allāh in the hereafter (done by the otherwise unknown calligrapher Bāqer Bannā; see Honarfar, 1965, pp. 413-15). This oft-overlooked passage is tentatively attributed to Shaikh Bahāʾ-al-Din ʿĀmeli on the basis of a reference in the poem on the other panel.

Like the Masjed-e Šāh (see below), the orientation of the Shaikh Loṭf-Allāh Mosque is skewed in relation to the Meydān, thus allowing the mosque to conform to the direction of prayer. To compensate for the skewed axis, a covered corridor reaches from the entrance façade and wraps around the northern side of the mosque to enter the prayer chamber, so that the façade of the mosque can remain aligned with the Meydān. The façade is covered in tile mosaic work and the portal contains the first monumental variation of the Safavid declaration, standardized by Shah ʿAbbās the Great, of the shah to be the "propagator of the faith of the Infallible Imams" (Honarfar, 1965, p. 402; Babaie, in *EIr.*, p. 499). The façade, much of it restored in the 1930s, was made to be flush with the inner corridor of the Meydān periphery bazaar and was decorated with a mix of marble on the lower half and *haft rangi* tiles of densely interlocking floral and vegetal motifs and bands of inscription on the upper zones. The *haft rangi* technique, also known as *cuerda secca* or burnt-coil, allowed for a more economical and faster production than the laborious and expensive mosaic tile technique favored by earlier Safavid and Timurid periods. Given the massive constructions of the early 17th century and the consequent expansion in the area of building surfaces to be sheathed in tiles, this proved to be the most common technology in Isfahan and practically replaced the mosaic technique.

The Shaikh Loṭf-Allāh Mosque is also distinguished for the elegantly tapered silhouette of its dome, which further stands out for its golden yellow and blue arabesques and inscriptions against a predominantly earth-colored unglazed tile work (Plate VIII [3]). The interior of the domed chamber, on the other hand, is given to an extravagant explosion of tiles predominantly in blue on all surfaces except for the inner dome where a roundel (*šamsa*) in yellow gives the illusion of the sun shining from within. Equally impressive is the ingenious way the dome is held aloft by a ring of windows at the base of the dome, which is itself resting on large corner squinches that rise directly from the floor and are supported by eight-pointed arches. These arches are outlined by a turquoise twisted molding that is framed by a number of inlays of inscriptions and floral patterns. A balcony cut above the entrance into the chamber looks down onto the prayer niche elaborately decorated in tiles and carved marble. In keeping with the royal associations of the mosque, this single chambered structure is a veritable jewel-box, an extravaganza of Safavid architecture and decoration.

Masjed-e Šāh (Masjed-e Jadid-e ʿAbbāsi; renamed Masjed-e Emām after the Revolution of 1978-79). This mosque marked the climax of building campaigns that transformed Isfahan into the new Safavid capital city (Eskandar Beg, II, pp. 831-32; Honarfar, 1965, pp. 427-64; McChesney, "Four Sources," pp. 120-23; Mehrābādi, pp. 659-93; see Plate XI [3]). Built between 1020/1611 and 1039/1630-31, the massive mosque (some 19,000 square meters in area) was positioned at the southern end of the Meydān-e Naqš-e Jahān. In terms of energizing urban spaces, the positioning of the mosque at the southern end was calculated to ensure a steady flow of traffic, for prayer, through the Meydān, thus helping to redirect business and social life away from the Saljuq Meydān-e Kohna to this new urban center. The mosque stood directly across from the monumental royal Qayṣariya bazaar (for this bazaar see Bakhtiar). Since it was intended to serve as the congregational mosque of the new capital city, its placement formed a visual axis between two significant facets of public life, commerce and religion. That these were further placed under and braided with Safavid protection and patronage could not have been missed for this longitudinal axis intersected with the latitudinal link between the icons of imperial authority and justice, the ʿĀli Qāpu Palace on the one hand, and of the personal piety and source of legitimacy of Safavid kingship, embodied in the Shaikh Loṭf-Allāh Mosque on the other (Plate II [1] above).

Masjed-e Šāh was the first congregational mosque to have been built under Safavid royal patronage. The complex theological-legal debates regarding the legitimacy of the congregational Friday prayer during the occultation of the Twelfth Imam had preoccupied Safavid clerical elite throughout the 16th century. The resolution of this

PLATE XI (3)

Shah (Imam) Mosque, aerial view. After R. Baḵtiār, p. 15.

PLATE XII (3)

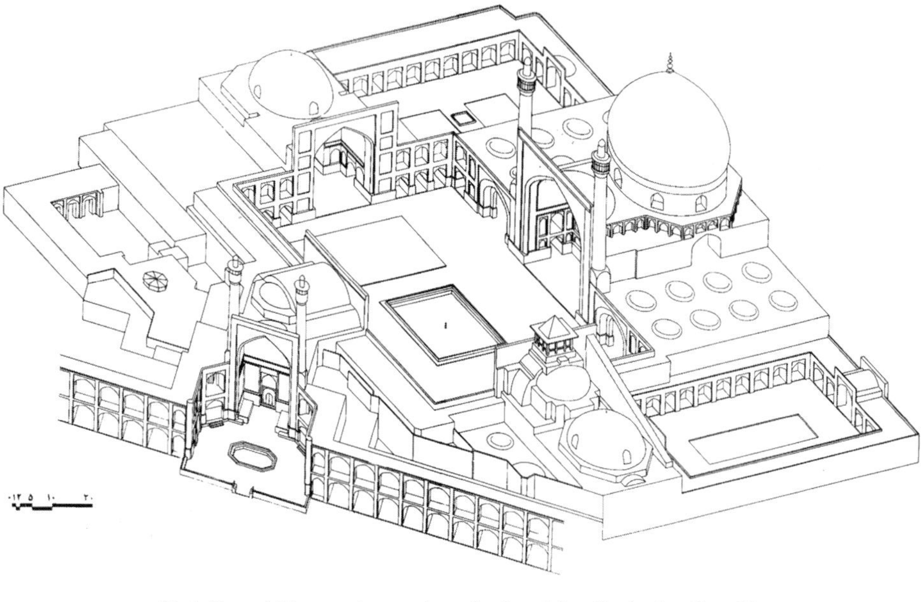

Shah (Imam) Mosque, isometric projection. After *Ganj-nāma* II, p. 23.

debate depended principally on the recognition of the concurrence of kingship and justice under the umbrella of legalistic Twelver Shiʿite doctrine. The vigorous legal arguments and support of such scholars as Shaikh Loṭf-Allāh and Shaikh Bahāʾ-al-Din ʿĀmeli helped to settle the thorny question of legitimacy in favor of the Safavids and hence paved the way for the reinstitution of the Friday congregational prayer. Far from a deliberate affront to the socio-religious centrality of the Masjed-e Jāmeʿ, the venerable old Saljuq congregational mosque of the city, the urban plan of the new imperial capital city incorporated into its chief monuments the Masjed-e Šāh, a new

PLATE XIII (3)

Shah (Imam) Mosque entrance from Meydān-e Naqš-e Jahān. Courtesy of the author.

congregational mosque to mark the Safavid authority to sponsor legitimate performance of this crucial religious obligation of Shiʿite community.

From the architectural viewpoint, the mosque represents a classic Persian four-*ayvān* plan with a domed chamber over the *meḥrāb* sanctuary. In many ways, however, this building represents an exceptionally creative response to a series of pressing needs and preexisting urban constraints. As in the case of the Shaikh Loṭf-Allāh Mosque, the principal façade of the Masjed-e Šāh had to remain flush with the southern side of the Meydān, while at the same time orientating its *meḥrāb*(s) correctly toward Mecca (Plate XIII [3]). Unlike the compacted chapel-mosque, however, this requirement must have posed a difficult challenge for the visual effect of the skewed internal axis, which would be magnified considerably in the royal Masjed-e Šāh. The architects and patrons of the mosque exploited this very potential for theatrical visual impact by creating a crescendo of forms heaped from one side to the other; viewed from a distance in the Meydān, as would have been the case for most denizens busy in the public square, the eye of the beholder is lead from the open-armed portal composition with its massive *pištāq* and soaring *goldasta* minarets to increasingly volumetric and loftier units culminating with the *pišṭāq*-dome-minarets of the *qebla* wall (Plates X-XIII [3]). To the worshipper entering the mosque, the transition from the gorgeously tiled and *moqarnas*-covered *ayvān* on the Meydān side to the courtyard is mediated through a twisted passageway-cum-*ayvān* that serves also as the northern *ayvān* of the courtyard (Plate XIV [3]). This entrance complex corrects the alignment of the mosque by twisting the axis of approach, but it also provides a liminal space passage through which provides the worshipper the opportunity, visually and spatially mediated, to leave the mundane world behind before entering the sanctified space of the mosque.

An overwhelming palette of turquoise-blue tiles covers all the surfaces inside and outside (except what would be the "back" of walls, vaults, etc.). Nearly all the vast surfaces of this mosque are decorated in the *haft rangi* (seven-color) technique, the most economically feasible method of decoration favored in 17th-century Isfahan. Other notable features of the mosque are its two extraordinarily tall pulpits (*menbar*), one open for good weather and another covered for bad weather. The *meḥrāb*, soaring at ten feet, and measuring three feet in width, is made of marble crowned with a gold-encrusted cupboard holding a Qurʾan believed to have been copied by Imam ʿAli al-Reżā as well as the bloodstained robe of Imam Ḥosayn (Chardin, VII, pp. 343-44, 353; Blake, p. 143). Such symbolically charged relics of the Imams further emblazon the legitimacy of the Twelver Shiʿite practice of Safavid kingship embodied in the very conceptualization and construction of this first congregational mosque of the Safavids.

The other extraordinary architectural aspect of this mosque is its integration of a *madrasa* into the fabric of

PLATE XIV (3)

Shah (Imam) Mosque, North of the Courtyard with entrance *merāras*. After *Ganj-nāma* II, p. 29.

the mosque (Honarfar, 1965, pp. 454-57). Two courtyards with adjoining chambers flank the *qebla* sanctuary, the massive domed chamber and its adjacent vaulted prayer halls. While awaiting further research on the mosque in general and the *madrasa* in particular, it may be postulated here that the incorporation of the *madrasa* into this first Safavid imperial congregational mosque was prescribed as another indication of the choice of Isfahan as not only the political capital, but also, and perhaps with more significance, as an imperial capital of Twelver Shiʿism. As the inscribed chronogram, in the poetic decoration on the silver doors, added by Shah Ṣafi I in 1046/1636-37, would indicate, with this mosque the doors of Kaʿba were opened in Isfahan (*šod dar-e Kaʿba dar Ṣefāhān bāz*, which is apparently on the model of the earlier chronogram "*kaʿba-ye ṯāni banā šoda*" on the beginning of the construction in 1020/1611; Mollā Jalāl-al-Din, p. 412; Honarfar, 1965, pp. 433-34), and, as such, Isfahan would stand in rivalry to Constantinople/Istanbul, as Safavid Shiʿite kingship would to Ottoman Sunni caliphate.

The complex enunciations of this braided iconography of kingship, religion and polity, are found throughout the extensive epigraphic program of the Masjed-e Šāh. The principal foundation inscription across the portal was designed by the famous calligrapher ʿAli-Reżā ʿAbbāsi (Honarfar, 1965, pp. 428-29; see Plate XI [3]). It states that Shah ʿAbbās funded the project from the royal treasures (*ḵāleṣa*) for the spiritual benefit of his grandfather Shah Ṭahmāsb, thus linking through this imperial icon of Twelver Shiʿite legitimacy and through the outpouring of the generosity of the Safavid household the two illustrious reigns. An addendum to this inscription, written by Moḥammad-Reżā Emāmi, credits Moḥebb-ʿAli Beg Lala, the trainer of the *ḡolāms* and chief supervisor of imperial buildings, with the supervision over the construction. This same dignitary of the household had joined the Shah by contributing to the endowments of the mosque (*waqf*) a considerable thirty percent of the entire endowment from his personal funds (Honarfar, 1965, pp. 429-30; Babaie, 2004, p. 91). The names of two architects are also associated with this mosque: Ostād ʿAli-Akbar Beg Eṣfahāni as the mosque's engineer (*mohandes*) and architect, whose name appears in the same inscription as that of the royal supervisor, and Ostād Badiʿ-al-Zamān Tuni Yazdi, whose job was to procure the land and construction resources (Mollā Jalāl-al-Din, p. 412; McChesney, pp. 121-22). Several traditions, recorded in contemporary chronicles, spin the story of the difficult task of acquiring the land from an unwilling owner and the miraculous discovery of marbles for the construction into evidence for the protected sanctity of this endeavor by Shah ʿAbbās the Great, whose authority was considered to be based on justice and sanctioned according to legal Twelver Shiʿite precepts. In fact, the entire epigraphic program of the mosque, designed by the most famous calligraphers of the first half of the 17th century, utilize Qurʾanic passages and eulogies

PLATE XVI (3)

Plate XVI. Masjed-e Ḥakim, North of the Courtyard. After *Ganj-nāma* II, p. 43.

PLATE XV (3)

Shah (Imam) Mosque, Entrance.
After *Ganj-nāma* II, p. 29.

to the family of the Prophet Moḥammad and Imam ʿAli b. Abi Ṭāleb to affix onto the surfaces of the mosque the enunciations of the legitimacy of the formation of kingship and hence congregational prayer under the Safavids in this new imperial capital.

Masjed-e Ḥakim. Masjed-e Ḥakim, built in the years 1067-73/1656-63, was commissioned by Ḥakim Moḥammad Dāwud, a converted Jew who served as the royal physician during the reigns of Shah Ṣafi I and Shah ʿAbbās II (Honarfar, 1965, pp. 612-21; Mehrābādi, pp. 604-10; see Plate XVI [3]). Chardin relates that the considerable funds needed for the construction of the mosque had been amassed in India by Ḥakim Dāwud, who had left the Safavid court after his fall from favor during the reign of Shah ʿAbbās II (Chardin, VII, pp. 462-63). His considerably more favorable reception at the court of Shah Jahān, who granted him the title of Taqarrob Khan, the confidant, brought with it wealth. Ḥakim Dāwud never returned to Persia to see his namesake mosque, which carries his name in a poem inscribed on the portal and containing the chronogram "*maqām-e kaʿba-ye digar šod az Dāwud-e Eṣfahān*" indicating the date (1067) of the construction (Honarfar, 1965, p. 613).

PLATE XVII (3)

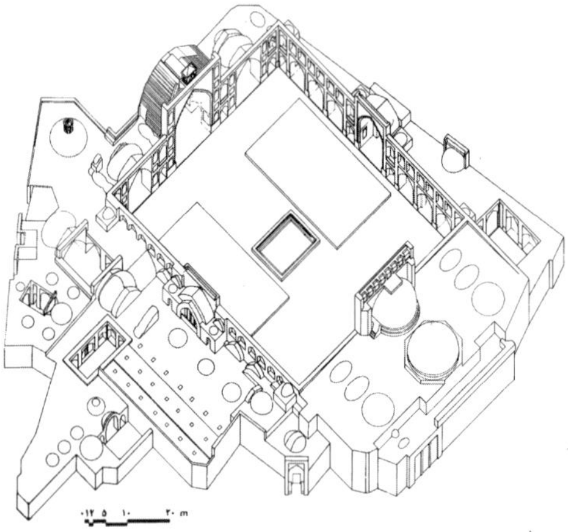

Plate XVI. Masjed-e Ḥakim, isometric projection.
After *Ganj-nāma* II, p. 42.

This mosque is located on the site of the Buyid Jorjir/Rangrezān Mosque, whose construction is credited to the Buyid vizier Ṣāḥeb Esmāʿil b. ʿAbbād (d. 385/995), and of which only a carved doorway has survived (Māfarruḵi, pp. 85-86; Honarfar, 1965, pp. 40 ff., 612). It is nearly four-acres in area, which makes it the largest mosque in Isfahan after the Saljuq and Safavid congregational mosques, thus representing an extraordinary instance of competitively scaled sub-imperial patronage in the capital city. It too is a four-*ayvān*, courtyard-centered mosque of the Persian type. Unlike the two Safavid mosques, here the vast surfaces, especially inside the *ayvān*s and the domed chamber over the *meḥrāb* are decorated with alternating glazed and unglazed tiles. The epigraphic program, designed entirely by Moḥammad-Reżā Emāmi, one of the greatest masters of mid-17th century, records the name of the architect as Moḥammad-ʿAli b. Ostād ʿAli Beg Eṣfahāni (Honarfar, 1965, p. 619; Mehrābādi, p. 606). The architect was the son of the master builder ʿAli Beg of Isfahan, whose name appears in the foundation inscription of the Masjed-e Šāh. By employing the artists and architects associated with royal projects, Ḥakim Dāwud partakes in the same atmosphere of surrogate and competitive patronage that inspired many *ḡolām*s and other elite members of the Safavid household. As the foundation inscription of the mosque indicates, despite his sanctuary at the court of the Sunni Mughal emperor, the physician remained loyal to the protection of Twelver Shiʿism under the auspices of the Safavid Shah ʿAbbās II.

(4) Madrasas

In the pre-modern context, *madrasa*s served as colleges for the teaching of Islamic law with ancillary focus on other Islamic sciences. *Madrasa*, as an architectural type designated specifically for the use of religious learning, did not come into practical use until the 10th century, when the earliest *madrasa*s in Persia were founded and then proliferated under Saljuq patronage. The 11th-century Saljuq Neẓāmiya colleges of Baghdad, Isfahan and other cities, founded by the grand vizier Neẓām-al-Molk were amongst the first to have been state-sponsored. In Isfahan, as elsewhere in Persia, the earliest *madrasa*s were established to spread and solidify Sunni orthodoxy. Isfahan, however, is especially noteworthy for it gave rise also to imperial patronage of the *madrasa*s as institutions of learning for scholarship on and promulgation of Twelver Shiʿism.

The earliest extant *madrasa* in Isfahan is the 725/1325 Emāmi Madrasa, which is also known as the Madrasa-ye Bābā Qāsem after the name of its first teacher, who is buried in a nearby tomb (Honarfar, 1965, pp. 302-10; Mehrābādi, pp. 433-40). As in Persian mosque type, this and most other *madrasa*s in Persia follow the four-*ayvān* courtyard-centered plan. In fact, it has been postulated, although still debated, that the four-*ayvān* plan of Persian mosques may itself derive from the configuration of the needs of a *madrasa* (Grabar, pp. 57-59). At *madrasa* buildings, however, the periphery of the courtyard is articulated with rows of apartments. These served as student cells, as lodging and classroom for both the teachers and their young male students. The self-sufficiency of the *madrasa* as a religious institution is also represented by the fact that, like other religious foundations, it too derived its operating funds from the proceeds of pious endowments (*waqf*).

PLATE I (4)

Madrasa-ye Solṭāni, exterior view.
Courtesy of the author.

Although sufficiently equipped to serve the residents for daily prayers, *madrasa*s were often appended to mosques. Such is the Mozaffarid Madrasa added in 767/1366-67 to the Masjed-e Jāmeʿ of Isfahan (Honarfar, 1965, pp. 136-42; Grabar, 1990, p. 38). While in this case, the single, deep *ayvān*-and-courtyard variation is tucked into one corner of the Great Mosque of Isfahan, at the other prominent example of the Masjed-e Jadid-e ʿAbbāsi, or Masjed-e Šāh (renamed Masjed-e Emām after the revolution of 1978-79) the *madrasa* and the mosque were interwoven into a single integrated structure. There, indeed, the motivating factor for raising such a singularly awesome monument at the apex of the Meydān-e Naqš-e Jahān was the political and religious primacy of enunciating the Twelver Shiʿite creed of the Safavid Empire. Notwithstanding the symbolic and ritual significance of this *madrasa*, the most famous *madrasa* of Isfahan is the unparalleled Solṭāni Madrasa (Royal Madrasa; see PLATE I [4]).

This vast and magnificently decorated *madrasa* is variously known as the Madrasa-ye Mādar-e Šāh (Mother of the Shah) and the Čahārbāḡ Madrasa for its location on the Čahārbāḡ Promenade (Honarfar, 1965, pp. 685-722; Mehrābādi, pp. 444-69). Madrasa-ye Solṭāni was the crowning achievement of the reign of the last Safavid Shah Solṭān-Ḥosayn. With its dependencies, namely a caravanserai and a bazaar, it was also the only monumental project to have been carried out inside the capital city in this period (his other project was the royal palace-city of Faraḥābād located well outside Isfahan to the south). Built largely between 1115/1704 and 1119/1707, the *madrasa* was not finished and formally inaugurated until 1122/1710 (Honarfar, 1965, pp. 688-90, 694-95; Ḵātunābādi, apud Eqbāl, pp. 56-57).

Measuring about 300 by 200 yards in area, the Solṭāni Madrasa appropriated a garden site in the royal precinct that was located just south of the Bāḡ-e Bolbol, at the center of which stood the Hašt Behešt Palace. The rigid symmetry of the cross-axial placement of the four *ayvāns*, and the cell-blocks of one hundred and fifty rooms tucked into the intervening corners dominates and determines the composition of the *madrasa*, despite the fact that its *qebla* orientation is skewed (PLATE II [4]). The southwesterly-facing *meḥrāb* in the principal *ayvān*-domed-chamber is carved into one of the side pillars rather than occupying the central position as in other example. In short, the primacy in this structure is given to the uncompromising regularity of the relationship between the *madrasa* and its urban armature of the Čahārbāḡ.

The large rectangular courtyard is lined with flowing water channel of the Faršādi Canal that also runs through the adjacent Solṭāni Caravansary. Tiled extensively in all its principal façades, the courtyard space of the *madrasa*, with its stately trees and beds of flowers, provides a scholarly retreat worthy of royal patronage. In fact, royal treasury had provided the library with one of the most impressive collections of books on law, philosophy, and religion. The book collections, however, were eventually destroyed after the Afghan invasion, due to the lack of proper maintenance. A special room decorated in gold and located north of the portal was prepared for the personal use of Shah Solṭān-Ḥosayn, to which he could retreat, thus enunciating, as it were, the Shah's personal piety and devotion to religious studies (Mirzā Ḥosayn, p. 81; Honarfar, 1965, pp. 719-20). The emphases on royal patronage and religious piety are further braided through Qurʾanic and Hadith quotations and Persian poetic texts across the entire epigraphic program of the *madrasa*.

The main portal opens onto the Čahārbāḡ Promenade. Not only is the fact of its opening onto the main thoroughfare of the imperial capital an exceptional privilege, the Solṭāni Madrasa's royal precedent under Shah ʿAbbās the Great is also prominently displayed. In the soaring profile of a principal dome and the paired *goldasta* minarets of its *pišṭāq-ayvān*, the Madrasa recalls the composition that culminates the stacked architectural elements at the Masjed-e Šāh in the Meydān-e Naqš-e Jahān. Equally deliberate in drawing parallels with the

PLATE II (4)

Madrasa-ye Solṭāni, south dome.
Courtesy of the author.

Safavid congregational mosque, it appears, is the choice of a pair of silver doors for the tall and prominent principal portal on the Čahārbāḡ (Allen, 1995, pp. 123-37 and pls. XIV-XXII). As in the pair added by Shah Ṣafi I to the portal of the Masjed-e Jadid-e ʿAbbāsi, Shah Solṭān-Ḥosayn ordered ʿAbd-al-Laṭif of Tabriz, the goldsmith of the royal household, to create the door (Honarfar, 1965, pp. 691-94; Mehrābādi, pp. 446-50; Blake, p. 160). No expense seems to have been spared for this later addition (1714). The doors were made of twenty *mans* of silver and cost some eight hundred tomans, indicative of their enormous value; on the day of their installment, the city was illumined with lights (*čerāḡāni*, q.v.). According to Judasz Krusinski, the magnificence of the place "could be imagined by the chief Gate of it only, which is of Massy Silver" (Ḵātunābādi, apud Eqbāl, p. 58; Krusinski, I, p. 127).

Extreme religiosity was never a prerequisite for the founding of *madrasas*, but this institution most eloquently represents the dominant role of the clergy during the reign of Shah Solṭān-Ḥosayn. The Solṭāni Madrasa was built for Mir Moḥammad-Bāqer Ḵātunābādi, the first *mollā-bāši* (chief clergy) of Isfahan who was also closely associated with the shah (Mirzā Rafiʿā, p. 64, tr. pp. 72-73; *Taḏkerat al-moluk*, facs. ed. and tr. Minorsky, fol. 2, tr. p. 41). Although the *madrasa* seems to have been part of a larger urban project—the Solṭāni Caravanserai or Kāravānsarā-ye Mādar-e Šāh (now turned into a hotel called Mehmānsarā-ye Šāh ʿAbbās/ʿAbbāsi; Mehrābādi, pp. 412-13) to the east of the *madrasa* and a single-alley bazaar of a thousand shops to its north—the entire complex was intended to serve the fiscal needs of the *madrasa*. Moreover, the supervision of the *madrasa* constructions was entrusted with Āqā Kamāl, the eunuch-*ḡolām* royal treasurer (Honarfar, p. 686). Together, the evidence points, as it does in most aspects of Shah Solṭān-Ḥosayn's reign, to the complete submersion of royal affairs into the politico-religious sphere of influence of the ulema and of the harem bureaucracy of eunuch *ḡolāms*.

The Solṭāni Madrasa ensemble happened to be the last monumental construction project in Isfahan until the 20th century, and, given the unraveling of Safavid society at the turn of the 18th century, it becomes a befitting testimonial, in the guise of patronage, production, and consumption of architecture, of the compromising conditions presented by the two principal pillars of authority and power in the last decades of Safavid rule.

(5) Bridges

On the southern edge of the city of Isfahan lies the Zāyandarud River, the un-navigable river that has been the major source of water in the region since the earliest settlements in its environs. Until the transfer of the Safavid capital to Isfahan in the late 16th century, the river was well outside the city walls. Bridges, however, have been constructed across the river since as early as Sasanian (224-651) times. The Šahrestān or Jay Bridge, located just outside the city to the east, is the oldest one to span the river in the vicinity of Isfahan, and its construction has been attributed to the period before the Arab conquest in the 7th century, displaying, according to Arthur Upham Pope (pp. 1230-31), features of Roman Bridges. Its name Jay/Šahrestān derives from the name of one of the two original town settlements (Yahudiya was the other) that were subsumed into medieval Isfahan (Abu Noʿaym, I, pp. 15-16; Ebn Ḥawqal, pp. 362-63; Moqaddasi, pp. 388-89; Golombek, pp. 20-22). Presumably the Šahrestān Bridge remained the main point to cross the river for centuries for it had been restored and maintained during the Buyid and Saljuq periods (Moḥammad-Mahdi, pp. 108-9; Honarfar, 1965, pp. 8-9; Mehrābādi, pp. 305-6).

When in 1598 Shah ʿAbbās the Great officially designated Isfahan the new imperial capital of the Safavids, the court historian Eskandar Beg Torkamān gave in his history prominence to the role of the river in the choice of the city, saying that "having gone there often, the special qualities of that paradisial city [*balada-ye jannat nešān*], the suitability of its location, and the waters of the Zāyandarud as well as the Kawthar-like channels [*juyhā-ye Kawṯar meṯāl*] which branch off the aforementioned river and flow in every direction, [all these things] lodged in the resplendent heart [of the shah]" (Eskandar Beg, I, p. 544; tr. McChesney, p. 110). Given the southward direction of the development of the Safavid capital, building bridges became not only a necessity, but it also gave additional opportunities for patronage of architectural and engineering marvels in harmony with the imperial scale of the projects in the Meydān-e Naqš-e Jahān (see PLATE IV [1]). Two major bridges, the Allāhverdi Khan Bridge (1011-15/1602-07) and the Ḵᵛāju Bridge (1060/1650), were added during the reigns of Shah ʿAbbās the Great and Shah ʿAbbās II. A third, known as Pol-e Juʾi or the Rivulet Bridge, a finely wrought stone footbridge with a watercourse running at its center, was also built in 1067/1657-58 by Shah ʿAbbās II. Unlike the other two larger public bridges, Pol-e Juʾi was for the exclusive use of the harem as it connected riverfront palaces across the two banks of the Zāyandarud River (Moḥammad-Mahdi, pp. 108-9; Honarfar, 1965, pp. 575-76; Mehrābādi, p. 303).

Since the Zāyandarud River is not navigable, engineering of the bridges over it need not concern boat traffic. Nevertheless, Safavid bridges demonstrate extraordinary ingenuity in the ways they turn utilitarian dams and slues into architecturally harmonious and visually exciting forms and spaces. The Safavid bridges helped control the flow of water and to manipulate it for the irrigation of agricultural lands and private gardens alike as well as for the regulation and distribution of fresh water for the city's consumption. Most extraordinarily, however, the Safavid bridges of Isfahan were designed to partake in the city's expanded arenas of public entertainment and leisure. Like a promenade, the two Safavid bridges are affixed with wide walkways both open to the elements and covered for poor weather; they have seating niches and royal pavilions for recreation purposes, where royal festivities took place or from where denizens of Isfahan watched regattas and other aquatic entertainment held in the small reservoirs that were created by the bridge dams or along the Zāyandarud River. The Safavid penchant in the monuments of Isfahan for the theatricality of the relationship between architecture and urban space and for the multi-functional acrobatics of buildings and ensembles is brilliantly on display in the two bridges, which serve simultaneously as bridges, dams, promenades, pavilions, and viewing stages.

Allāhverdi Khan Bridge. Already in 1596 when Shah ʿAbbās the Great's campaign for the Čahārbāḡ Promenade (see ČAHĀRBĀḠ) had begun, the project anticipated the building of a bridge to connect the northern and southern stretches of the avenue as well as of the city as it were being developed for the residence of new social groups in Isfahan. (PLATE I [5]). This need was materialized between 1011/1602 and 1015/1607 with the construction of the Allāhverdi Khan Bridge (popularly known as Si-o-seh pol "The bridge of thirty-three spans" and as Pol-e Si-o-seh čašma "The bridge of thirty-three arches;" Moḥammad-Mahdi, p. 108; Honarfar, pp. 487-88; Mehrābādi, pp. 317-27; for new dates, see Melville, p. 71). Eskandar Beg Torkamān called it "A sublime bridge, consisting of forty vaulted arches of a special type that would open so that in time of floods the water would pass through each one of the arches, having been built to span the Zāyandarud," and in the 19th century, Sir Percy Sykes described it

PLATE I (5)

Allāhverdi Khan Bridge, an aerial view. After R. Baḵtiār, p. 44.

as "even in decay must rank among the great bridges of the world" (Eskandar Beg, I, pp. 544-45, tr. in McChesney, p. 111; Sykes, II, pp. 201-2; Pope, pp. 1235-37).

The bridge measures approximately 300 meters in length (388 yards according to Sykes, p. 201). Along its sides are thirty-three arches, giving the bridge its popular name of Si-o-seh Pol. The central lane of the bridge was designed as a path for beasts of burden while the sides were raised for use as pedestrian promenades. Along the walkway the arches form small pavilions, where passersby can rest in shade and take in views of the river and its banks. Until the 19th century, the interior was decorated with paintings (as was that of the Ḵᵛāju Bridge) of subjects often referred to by European travelers to have been erotic (Ouseley, III, pp. 48-49, apud Pope, p. 1235).

This magnificent feat of engineering facilitated linkage through the Čahārbāḡ between the royal precinct (the Dawlat-ḵāna) and the new inner city zones around the Meydān on the one hand, and the suburban palace retreat of Hazār Jarib and the southern suburbs on the other. In addition to connecting the mansions of the elite that lined the southern flank of the Čahārbāḡ, the bridge served to connect to the city the Armenian merchant enclave of New Julfa, an economically vital community incorporated into the household by Shah ʿAbbās the Great and his immediate successors. (Baghdiantz-McCabe, p. 57). The mediatory role of the new elite of the reconfigured Safavid household is similarly exemplified through the surrogate patronage on behalf of Shah ʿAbbās the Great and the royal household, which Allāhverdi Khan (q.v.), the commander-in-chief of the armies, extended in this integral feature of the urban campaign.

Ḵᵛāju Bridge (Pol-e Ḵᵛāju). Located farther to the east, Ḵᵛāju Bridge may have replaced a 15th-century bridge that traversed the river and connected Isfahan to the old road to Shiraz (PLATE II [5]). The bridge is variously known as Pol-e Ḥasanābād for the old neighborhood to its north, as Pol-e Bābā Rokn-al-Din for a nearby shrine, and as Pol-e Šāhi, especially at the time of its construction because of its royal associations. Its construction dates to 1060/1650, during the reign of Shah ʿAbbās II at a time when the monarch had shifted eastwardly the urban development of Isfahan (Waliqoli Šāmlu, p. 517; Pope, pp. 1237-40; Moḥammad-Mahdi, pp. 109-11; Honarfar, pp. 582-85; Mehrābādi, pp. 306-17; Luschey, pp. 143-51).

Some hundred and thirty-two meters long and twelve meters wide, the bridge served several newly expanded urban functions in this area of the city. It connected the Ḵᵛāju Čahārbāḡ and residential quarter to the north of the river to the suburbs on the south including the Zoroastrian neighborhood of Gabrestān (this was the second time Zoroastrian community of Isfahan was forcibly moved; the first was instigated by the Čahārbāḡ of Shah ʿAbbās the Great; Hillenbrand, p. 803).

Like most other Safavid bridges in Isfahan, the Ḵᵛāju Bridge is not only a means for crossing the river but also acts as a space for leisurely strolls and for recreational activities. The bridge is constructed on two tiers. On the lower level, the open niches and closed pylons alternate and accommodate visitors with shaded places to sit and water flow with structures to regulate it; the upper level consists of a "walled" passageway that is lined with an arcade of double niches and is articulated at its center with an embedded octagonal pavilion that looks out onto the riverscape and the pedestrian promenade. The main central aisle on the upper level was slightly lower and was used by horses and carts, while the raised outer vaulted paths on both sides of the bridge were for pedestrian use.

PLATE II (5)

K̲ᵛāju Bridge, an aerial view. After R. Bak̲tiār, p. 50.

PLATE III (5)

K̲ᵛāju Bridge. Courtesy of the author.

The singularly sophisticated engineering of its dams provided the means for the efficient regulation of the water flow and the irrigation of nearby gardens. Utilizing a series of sluice gates, they create retractable dams that could be raised and lowered. The downriver levels were much lower as the water passed over a series of steps under the bridge. When the levels of the river were low enough, either naturally or through usages of the dams incorporated into the bridge, these stepped buttresses reached down to the water from the lower level of the bridge between the weirs and acted as additional social spaces for evening gatherings and picnics. In this regard too, the architectural and engineering of this bridge provides an extraordinary range of visual and aural experiences.

Closing the dams of the two bridges, the Allāhverdi Khan and the K͟ᵛāju, created a lake out of the river in the area of the riverbanks, where Shah Ṣafi I and Shah ʿAbbās II had developed the royal retreat of Saʿādatābād. The K͟ᵛāju Bridge was consequently well positioned to serve not only as a place of recreation for the public but more pointedly for the royal household and their guests and entourage. Persian and European chronicles describe festivities held at the central pavilion of the K͟ᵛāju Bridge and along its length, where the space served as a stage for viewing fireworks, boat races, and the like. For example, Waliqoli Šāmlu, the historian of Shah ʿAbbās II, relates that for the Nowruz celebrations shortly after the completion of the bridge, the shah ordered the bridge of the river to be decorated with lights and flowers, and many of the court and government dignitaries were entrusted with the embellishment of the niches and the pavilion. The king spent about a month there and the event was commemorated in a number of poems, including an ode (*qaṣida*) by Ṣāʾeb of Tabirz (Waliqoli Šāmlu, I, pp. 517-19; Mehrābādi, pp. 311-12; Honarfar, p. 583).

The interior surfaces of the pavilion and the walls of the central alley of the bridge were decorated with tiles, possibly of 18th century date, that are especially noteworthy for their distinctive striped patterns and yellow palette. Nearly all the painted decoration of the pavilion's niches are lost, but Sir William Ousley's observation of "erotic" imagery indicates that at least some of the murals had figural subjects, perhaps of similar leisurely poses that grace the walls of Čehel Sotun Palace, that may have appeared risqué to the Victorian mores of Ousley. The 17th-century traveler Jean Chardin provides us with the text of one of the inscriptions in the mural decoration, which said "The World is truly a Bridge; pass over it. Weigh and measure all that you meet with on your passage. Everywhere Evil encompasses the Good and transcends it" (Blunt, pp. 147-48).

(6) Bibliography

Bibliography: Rula Jurdi Abisaab, *Converting Persia: Religion and Power in the Safavid Empire*, London, 2004. Abu Noʿaym Eṣfahāni, *Ḏekr ak͟bār Eṣfahān*, ed. Sven Dedering, *Geschichte Iṣbahāns*, 2 vols., Leiden, 1931-34. Mahvash Alemi, "The Royal Gardens of the Safavid Period: Types and Models," in Attilio Petruccioli, ed., *Gardens in the Time of the Great Muslim Empires: Theory and Design*, Leiden, New York, and Cologne, 1997, pp. 72-96. James W. Allen, "Silver Door Facings of the Safavid Period," *Iran* 33, 1995, pp. 123-37 and pls. XIV-XXII. Sussan Babaie, "Safavid Palaces in Isfahan: Continuity and Change (1599-1666)," Ph.D. diss., New York University, 1994a. Idem, "Shah Abbas II: The Conquest of Qandahar, the Chihil Sutun, and its Wall Paintings," *Muqarnas* 11, 1994b, pp. 125-42. Idem, "Paradise Contained: Nature and Culture in Persian Gardens," *The Studio Potter*, no. 25, 2 June 1997, pp. 10-13. Idem, "Epigraphy iv. Safavid and Later Inscriptions," in *EIr*. VIII, 1998, pp. 498-504. Idem, "Building on the Past: The Shaping of Safavid Architecture, 1501-76," in Jon Thompson and Sheila Canby, eds., *Hunt for Paradise: Court Arts of Safavid Iran, 1501-1576*, New York and Milan, 2003, pp. 27-47. Idem, "Launching from Isfahan: Slaves and the Construction of the Empire," in Babaie, Babayan, Baghdiantz-McCabe, and Farhad, 2004, pp. 80-113. Idem, *Isfahan and Its Palaces: Feasting in the City of Paradise*, Edinburgh (forthcoming). Sussan Babaie, Kathryn Babayan, Ina Baghdiantz-McCabe, and Massumah Farhad, *Slaves of the Shah: New Elites of Safavid Iran*, London and New York, 2004. Kathryn Babayan, *Mystics, Monarchs and Messiahs: Cultural Landscapes of Early Modern Iran*. Harvard Middle Eastern Monographs 35. Cambridge, Mass., 2003. Idem, "The Safavid Household Reconfigured: Concubines, Eunuchs, and Military Slaves," in Babaie, Babayan, Baghdiantz-McCabe and Farhad, 2004, pp. 20-48.

Ina Baghdiantz-NcCabe, "Armenian Merchants and Slaves: Financing the Safavid Treasury," in Babaie, Babayan, Baghdiantz-McCabe and Farhad, 2004, pp. 49-79. Ali Bakhtiar, "The Royal Bazaar of Isfahan," *Iranian Studies* 7/3-4: *Studies on Isfahan*, 1974, pp. 320-47. Marcel Bazin, "Bāḡ ii: Garden," in *EIr*. III, pp. 393-95. Sheila Blair, *The Monumental Inscriptions from Early Islamic Iran and Transoxania*. Leiden and New York, 1991. Idem, *Islamic Inscriptions*, New York, 1998, pp. 69-70. Sheila Blair and Jonathan Bloom, *The Art and Architecture of Islam 1250-1800*, New Haven, 1995. Stephen P. Blake, *Half the World: The Social Architecture of Safavid Isfahan 1590-1722*, Costa Mesa, Calif, 1999. Wilfred Blunt, *Isfahan: Pearl of Persia*, London, 1966. Jean Chardin, *Voyages du Chavalier Chardin, en Perse, et autres lieux de l'Orient*, ed. L. Langlès, 10 vols., Paris, 1811; parts selected, ed., and tr. Ronald W. Ferrier as *A Journey to Persia: Jean Chardin's Portrait of Seventeenth-Century Empire*, London and New York, 1996. Pascal Coste, *Monuments modernes de la Perse, mesurés, dessinés et décrits par Pascal Coste, publiés par ordre de son excellence le ministre de la maison de l'empereur et des beaux-arts*, Paris, 1867. Ebn al-Aṯir, *al-Kāmel fi'l-tārik͟*. ʿAbbās Eqbāl, "Ketāb-e Waqāyeʿ al-senin wa'l-aʿwām: eṭṭelāʿāt-i dar bāb-e Madrasa-ye Čahār Bāḡ," *Yādgār* 3/3, 1946, pp. 55-58.

Naṣr-Allāh Falsafi, *Zendagāni-e Šāh ʿAbbās-e Awwal*, 4 vols., Tehran, 1955-67. Mario Ferrante, "Quelques précisions graphiques au sujet des ponts séfévides d'Isfahan," in Giuseppe Zander, ed., *Travaux de restauration de monuments historiques en Iran*, IsMEO, Rome, 1968a, pp. 441-64. Idem, "Čihil Sutūn: études, relevés, restaurations," ibid., 1968b, pp. 293-322. Idem, "Notes graphiques sur des monuments islamiques ds la règion d'Ispahan: Le pavillon des Hašt Bihišt, ou les Huit Paradis, a Ispahan, Relevés et problèmes s'y rattachant," ibid., 1968c, pp. 399-420. Willem Floor, "The Talar-i Tavila or Hall of Stables: A Forgotten Safavid Palace," *Muqarnas*, no. 19, 2002, pp. 149-63. A. Gabriel, "Le Madjid-i Djumʿa," *Ars islamica* 4, 1935, pp. 7-44; André

Godard, "Historique du Masdjid-é Djumʿa d'Iṣfahān," *Athār-é Īrān* 1/2, 1936, pp. 213-82; idem, *Athār-é Īrān* 2/1, 1937 (the entire volume is on Isfahan); and the extensive studies published in the *Survey of Persian Art*, vol. 2. Eugenio Galdieri, "Two Building Phases of the Time of Šāh ʿAbbās I in the Maydān-i Šāh of Isfahan, Preliminary Note," *East and West* 20, 1970, pp. 60-69. Idem, "Les Palais d'Isfahan," *Iranian Studies* 7/3-4: *Studies on Isfahan*, 1974, pp. 380-405. Idem, *Esfahān, ʿĀli Qāpū: An Architectural Survey*, IsMEO, Restorations 5, Rome, 1979. Idem, *Esfahan: Masged-i Gumʿa*, 3 vols. Rome, 1972, 1973, and 1984. *Ganj-nāma* II, *Masājed-e Eṣfahān*, Šahid Behešti University, Tehran, 1996. Heinz Gaube and Eugene Wirth, *Der Bazar von Isfahan*, Weisbaden, 1978. Liza Golombek, "Urban Patterns in Pre-Safavid Isfahan," *Iranian Studies* 7/3-4: *Studies on Isfahan*, 1974, pp. 18-44. Lisa Golmbek and Maria Subtelny, eds., *Timurid Art and Culture: Iran and Central Asia in the Fifteenth Century*, Leiden and New York, 1992. Lisa Golombek and Donald Wilber, *The Timurid Architecture of Iran and Turan*. Princeton, New Jersey, 1988. Oleg Grabar, *The Great Mosque of Isfahan*, New York, 1990. Masashi Haneda, "Maydan et Bagh: Reflexion à propos de l'urbanisme du Shah ʿAbbas," in *Documents et Archives Provenant de L'Asie Centrale*, Kyoto, 1990, pp. 87-99. Idem, "The Character of the Urbanization of Isfahan in the Later Safavid Period." in Charles Melville, ed., *Safavid Persia: The History and Politics of an Islamic Society*, Pembroke Persian Papers 4. London, 1996, pp. 369-88. Robert Hillenbrand, "Safavid Architecture," in *Camb. Hist. Iran* VI, 1986, pp. 759-842. Idem, *Islamic Architecture: Form, Function, and Meaning*. Edinburgh, 1994. Loṭf-Allāh Honarfar, *Ganjina-ye āṯār-e tāriḵi-e Eṣfahān: āṯār-e bāstāni wa alwāḥ wa katibahā-ye tāriḵi dar ostān-e Eṣfahān*, Isfahan, 1965. Idem, "Hašt Behešt-e Eṣfahān," *Honar o mardom*, no. 117, 1972a, pp. 2-16. Idem, "Kāḵ-e Čehel Sotun," *Honar o mardom*, no. 121, 1972b, pp. 3-31. Idem, "Bāḡ-e Hazār Jarib wa Kuh-e Ṣoffa (behešt-e Šāh ʿAbbās)," *Honar o mardom*, no. 157, 1975, pp. 73-94.

Mirzā Ḥasan Jāberi Anṣāri, *Tāriḵ-e Eṣfahān*, ed. Jamšid Maẓāheri Sorušiān, Tehran, 1999. Rasul Jaʿfariān, "Pišina-ye tašayyoʿ dar Esfahān," in *Maqālāt-e tāriḵi*, 3 vols. Qom, 1997, pp. 305-39. Moḥammad-Maʿṣum b. Ḵᵛājagi Eṣfahāni, *Ḵolāṣat al-siar*, ed. Iraj Afshar, Tehran, n.d.; tr. Gerhard Rettelbach as *Ḥulasat al-siyar: Der Iran unter Schah Safi (1629-1642)*, Munich, 1978. Hossein Kamaly, "Politics, Economy and Culture in Isfahan, 540-1040," Ph.D. diss., Columbia University, 2004. Ebba Koch, "Diwan-i ʿAmm and Chihil Sutun: The Audience Halls of Shah Jahan," *Muqarnas*, no. 11, 1994, pp. 143-65. Judasz Tadeusz Krusinski, *The History of the Late Revolutions of Persia*, repr. ed., 2 vols. in one, New York, 1973. Thomas W. Lentz and Glenn D. Lowry, *Timur and the Princely Vision: Persian Art and Culture in the Fifteenth Century*, Los Angeles, 1989. H. Luschey, "The Pul-i Khwaju in Isfahan: a Combination of Bridge, Dam and Water Art," *Iran* no. 23, 1985, pp. 143-51. Ingeborg Luschey-Schmeisser, *The Pictorial Tile Cycle of Hašt Bihišt in Iṣfahān and Its Iconographic Tradition*, Rome, 1978. Mofażżal b. Saʿd Māfarruḵi, *Ketāb maḥāsen Eṣfahān*, ed. Sayyed Jalāl-al-Din Ḥosayni Ṭehrāni, Tehran, n.d. Michel M. Mazzaoui, "From Tabriz to Qazvin to Isfahan: Three Phases of Safavid History," *ZDMG*, 1977, pp. 514-22. Robert McChesney, "Four Sources on Shah Abbas's Building of Isfahan," *Muqarnas*, no. 5, 1988, pp. 103-34. Charles Melville, "New Light on the Reign of Shah ʿAbbas: Volume III of the *Afdal al-Tawarikh*," in ed. Andrew J. Newman, *Society and Culture in the Early Modern Middle East. Studies on Iran in the Safavid Period*, Leiden, 2003, pp. 63-96. Moḥammad-Mahdi Eṣfahāni, *Neṣf-e jahān fi taʿrif al-Eṣfahān*, ed., Manučehr Sotuda, Tehran, 1989, pp. 69-73. Mollā Jalāl-al-Din Monajjem, *Tāriḵ-e ʿabbāsi yā Ruz-nāma-ye Mollā Jalāl*, ed. Sayf-Allāh Waḥid-niā, Tehran, 1987. Moqaddasi, *Aḥsan al-taqāsim*. Gülru Necipoglu, *Architecture, Ceremonial and Power: The Topkapi Palace in the Fifteenth and Sixteenth Centuries*, Cambridge, Mass, 1991. Idem, "An Outline of Shifting Paradigms in the Palatial Architecture of the Pre-Modern Islamic World," *Ars Orientalis*, no. 23, 1993a, pp. 3-24. Idem, "Framing the Gaze in Ottoman, Safavid, and Mughal Palaces," ibid., no. 23, 1993b, pp. 303-42. R. Nur Baḵtiār, *Eṣfahān, muza-ye hamiša zenda*, 2nd ed., Tehran, 1974. Adam Olearius, *Vermehrte newe Beschreibung der muscowitischen und persischen Reyse*, Schleswig, 1656, facs repr., Tübingen, 1971; ed. Detlef Haberland, Stuttgart, 1966; tr. A. Behpūr as *Safar-nāma-ye Ādām Oleʾārīūs (bakš-e Īrān)*, Tehran, 1984. Arthur Upham Pope, "Bridges, Forticications, and Caravanserais," in *Survey of Persian Art* II, pp. 1227-51. Rosemarie Quiring-Zoche, *Isfahan im 15. und 16. Jahrhundert: Ein Beitrag zur persischen Stadtgeschichte*, Freiberg, 1980. Mirzā Rafiʿā Moḥammad-Rafiʿ Anṣāri, *Dastur al-moluk*, ed. Moḥammad-Taqi Dānešpažuh, in *MDAT* 16, 1968-69, pp. 62-93, 298-322, 416-40, 540-64; facs. ed. and annotated tr. M. I., Marcinkowski as *Mīrzā Rafīʿā's Dastūr al-mulūk: A Manual of Later Safavid Administration*, Kuala Lumpur, 2002. Hans R. Roemer, "The Safavid Period," in *Camb. Hist. Iran* VI, pp. 189-350. Sirus Šafaqi, *Joḡrāfiā-ye Eṣfahān*, Isfahan, 2003. Roger Savory, "Čahārbāḡ-e Eṣfahān," in *EIr*. IV, pp. 625-26. Waliqoli Šāmlu, *Qeṣas al-ḵāqāni* I, ed. Sayyed Ḥasan Sādāt Nāṣeri, 2nd ed., Tehran, 1996. Devin J. Stewart, "Notes on the Migration of ʿAmeli Scholars of Safavid Iran," *Journal of Near Eastern Studies* 55/1, 1991, 81-103. Idem, "The First Shaykh al-Islam of the Safavid Capital Qazvin," *Journal of the American Oriental Society* 116/3, 1996, 387-405. David Stronach, "Čahārbāḡ," in *EIr*. IV, pp. 624-25. Roy Strong, *Feast: A History of Grand Eating*, London, 2002. *Taḏkerat al-moluk*, facs. ed. and tr. Minorsky. Percy Sykes, *A History of Persia*, 2 vols., London, 1958. Mirzā Ḥosayn Khan b. Moḥammad-Ebrāhim Taḥwildār, *Joḡrāfiā-ye Eṣfahān*, ed. Manučehr Sotuda, Tehran,

1963. Moḥammad Ṭāher Wahid, *ʿAbbās-nāma*, ed. Ebrahim Dehqān, Arak, 1951, pp. 198 and 222. Heidi Walcher, "Face of the Seven Spheres: Urban Morphology and Architecture in Nineteenth-Century Isfahan," *Iranian Studies* 33/3, 2000, pp. 327-47.

(SUSSAN BABAIE with ROBERT HAUG)

xi. SCHOOL OF PAINTING AND CALLIGRAPHY

The "Isfahan" school of painting and calligraphy generally refers to works of art associated with the city of Isfahan from about 1597-98, when the city was chosen as the Safavid capital until the Afghan invasion of 1722. The term was originally coined in the late 1950s as part of an effort to identify and classify Persian painting of the first half of the 17th century, especially the works of Reżā ʿAbbāsi and his followers (Robinson, pp. 153-61). In the second half of the 17th century, many Isfahani artists departed from Reżā ʿAbbāsi's style of painting and began experimenting with Europeanized pictorial concepts, such as modeling and shading. Their distinct work can be described as the second phase of the "Isfahan" school of painting.

PLATE I

Barefoot youth, signed by Reżā ʿAbbāsi (ca. 1565-1635), probably Isfahan, ca. 1600, opaque watercolor, ink, and gold on paper. Courtesy of Arthur M. Sackler Gallery, Smithsonian Institution, Lent by the Art and History Trust, LTS1995.2.78.

One of the most distinguishing features of 17th-century Isfahani style is its format, which, in turn, encouraged the development of new techniques and subject matter. Artists began to focus increasingly on individual drawings and paintings, most of which no longer related to a specific text as in the case of manuscript paintings (PLATE I). Many were assembled in albums (*moraqqaʿ*), together with calligraphic examples (*qeṭʿa*). Although such compositions date back to the late 15th-century, they became a viable alternative to manuscript illustrations only after the 17th century.

Without the stricture of the written text, artists were now able to experiment more freely with different techniques, in particular line drawing. Using both the pen and the brush, they combined sweeping, undulating lines with short, staccato-like strokes, highlighted with washes of color. Their works ranged from spontaneously conceived sketches to meticulously executed compositions and gave a new autonomy to the art of drawing (PLATE II). Like folios of calligraphy, these images were valued as much for their technical virtuosity as for their subject matter.

The repertoire of themes largely comprised idealized and elegantly dressed men and women, as well as elderly male figures in a contemplative mood. The figures are often shown in languid poses with certain props, such as wine bottles, cups, books, or writing materials, which help to identify them as the cupbearer, the scribe, the learned sheikh, and recall well-known poetic conceits. The portrayal of certain well-established types, already familiar from poetry, suggests that association with literary tradition was not completely severed but was now expressed in a different pictorial manner (Babaie, 2001). At the same time, the new format encouraged the development of naturalistic portraiture, and artists began to choose ordinary men and women as their subjects.

Notwithstanding the growing popularity of line drawing, Safavid artists of the 17th century did not abandon the creation of lavish manuscript illustrations and independent figural paintings. The palette is notable for its bright and saturated color scheme, often combining half tones such as purple, orange, and earth colors, lending the compositions a new visual boldness. Many 17th-century works were frequently signed and dated, suggesting the painters' growing sense of independence and self-awareness. An important factor contributing to this development was a shift in the system of patronage. Many Isfahani artists no longer relied on court patronage alone but created works for members of the affluent middle classes, who actively collected the less costly single-page drawings and paintings.

The most celebrated painter associated with the Isfahan school is Reżā ʿAbbāsi, also known as Āqā Reżā (fl. ca. 1565-1635), who worked intermittently at the court of Shah ʿAbbās I throughout his career. Known for his

PLATE II

The pilgrim of Mashad by Reżā ʿAbbāsi (act. 1580s-1635), Mashad, dated 1589, ink on paper. Courtesy of Freer Gallery of Art, Smithsonian Institution, Purchase F1953.12.

PLATE III

Couple Attributed to Moʿin Moṣawwer (act. ca. 1630s-90s), Iran, dated 1642, ink on paper. Courtesy of Freer Gallery of Art, Smithsonian Institution, Purchase F1953.41.

remarkable use of line and harmonious color schemes, his style became synonymous with Isfahan and Safavid artistic efflorescence during the first half of the 17th century (Canby, 1996a). His students and followers emulated his technique and compositions and often added his name to their work to enhance their importance and value.

Among Reżā ʿAbbāsi's most accomplished followers was Afżal Ḥosayni (q.v.), also known as Afżal Tuni, whose compositions have been often erroneously attributed to the master. Moʿin Moṣawwer, active from 1040/1630 until the early 12th/late 17th century, is Reżā ʿAbbāsi's most prolific and well-known student, who created numerous single-page figural compositions and contributed to several illustrated texts (Farhad, 1990). His style remained remarkably consistent throughout his long career, eschewing Western pictorial concepts that became increasingly popular among his contemporaries (PLATE III). Traditionally, artists, such as Moḥammad-Qāsem, Moḥammad-Yusof, and Moḥammad-ʿAli, all of whom worked between 1040-60/1630-50, have also been identified as representative of the "Isfahan" school, although they probably worked in other centers, such as Mashad. Nevertheless, their work was indebted to the style and subject matter that flourished in Isfahan in the early 17th century.

In the 1640s, a number of Isfahani painters turned to Indian art as new sources of inspiration. Mughal and Deccani paintings offered Safavid artists, such as Shaikh ʿAbbāsi (q.v.) and Bahrām Sofrakeš, new themes and pictorial conventions, which they adapted and integrated into their work. While Shaikh ʿAbbāsi continued to explore the potential of line drawing in a more "Indianized" style, Bahrām Sofrakeš's naturalistic floral studies were clearly modeled after mid-17th-century Mughal painting (Soudavar, cat. no. 145).

For other artists, European works of art offered new themes and pictorial concepts. The large Christian Armenian community in New Julfa, a suburb of Isfahan, as well as numerous Italian, Flemish, and Dutch visitors to the Safavid court ensured the availability of Western paintings, drawings, prints, and decorative objects in Isfahan. The presence of several European painters further contributed to the development of a "Europeanized" mode of painting, best represented in the work

PLATE IV

Majnun visited by his father. Signed by Moḥammad Zamān, Ašraf, 1676, opaque watercolor, ink, and gold on paper. Courtesy of Arthur M. Sackler Gallery, Lent by The Art and History Collection, LTS1995.2.120.

PLATE V

Folio of calligraphy, signed by ʿEmād al-Ḥasani (Mir ʿEmād), ca. 1610, ink, opaque watercolor, and gold on paper. Courtesy of Arthur M. Sackler Gallery, Smithsonian Institution, Lent by the Art and History Collection, LTS1995.2.101.

Moḥammad-Zamān and ʿAliqoli Jobbadār (q.v.; see also Canby, 1996b). This pictorial idiom, which flourished during the reigns of Shah Solaymān (1077-105/1666-94) and Shah Solṭān-Ḥosayn (1105-135/1694-722), marks a dramatic departure from the more traditional painting style of Reżā ʿAbbāsi and Moʿin Moṣawwer. Selectively adapting Western pictorial ideals, such as perspective, modeling and shading, Safavid artists developed an innovative, hybrid style that echoed the growing internationalism of the Safavid court towards the end of the 17th century (fig. 4).

Safavid Isfahan is also associated with the art of wall painting as is evident from the extant decoration of the Čehel Sotun and Hašt Behešt (qq.v.) palaces, as well as several Armenian private residences in New Julfa. The compositions depict reception scenes, idealized male and female figures, or iconic literary compositions, known from works on paper, but now adapted to the larger surfaces. Many of the lifesize figures are dressed in European fineries, further attesting to Persia's growing political, diplomatic, and artistic contacts with the West. During the latter part of the 17th century, artists also experimented with oil painting, a technique that was introduced from Europe and became popular in the 18th and 19th centuries. These large-scale compositions, frequently created in pairs, depict idealized Armenian and Georgian couples, who must have played a prominent role in Isfahan's economic and cultural life.

Shah ʿAbbās and his successors were avid patrons of calligraphy, and during the 17th century, scripts such as *ṯolṯ* and *nastaʿliq* (see CALLIGRAPHY) reached new levels of refinement and sophistication. The art of *qeṭʿa* flourished, and Isfahan's many newly erected public monuments were adorned with bold inscription panels. ʿAli-Reżā ʿAbbāsi (q.v.), one of the leading calligraphers of the period, who was appointed head of Shah ʿAbbās I's library in 1598, designed the monumental inscriptions of the Shaikh Loṭf-Allāh Mosque and the Masjed-e Šāh among others (Honarfar, pp. 401-2, 407-10, 428-29, 468). Written in large *ṯolṯ*, these inscriptions are notable for their densely stacked and complex designs that became a powerful visual symbol of later Safavid architecture. Although ʿAli-Reżā ʿAbbāsi also excelled in *nastaʿliq*, it was his rival Mir ʿEmād Ḥasani (q.v.), who is considered the unequaled master of this script (PLATE V). Reserved for poetry since the early 15th century in the Persian-speaking world, Mir ʿEmād brilliantly explored the potential of scale in his calligraphic compositions. His technical skill is most apparent in his monumental *nastaʿliq*, where letters change from fluid, broad strokes to razor sharp lines with utmost control and elegance. Like the painter Reżā ʿAbbāsi, Mir ʿEmād had numerous followers, who emulated his style of writing throughout the 17th century.

Bibliography: Oleg F. Akimushkin, *The St. Petersburgh Muraqqaʿ: Album of Indian and Persian Miniatures from the 16th through the 18th Century and Specimens of Persian Calligraphy by ʿImād al-Ḥasanī*, Milan, 1996. Esin Atil, *Brush of the Master: Drawings from Iran and India*, Washington, D.C., 1978, pp. 50-95. Susan Babaie, "The Sound of the Image/The Image of the Sound," in Oleg Grabar and Cynthia Robinson, eds., *Islamic Art and Literature*, Princeton, 2001, pp. 143-62. Idem, "Abbas II, The Conquest of Qandahar, Chehel Sutun and Its Paintings," *Muqarnas* 11, 1994, pp. 125-42. Mahdi Bayāni, *Aḥwāl wa āṯār-e Ḵošnevisān*, 4 vols., Tehran, 1966-79, II, pp. 456-61, 513-38. Sheila R. Canby, *Persian Painting*, London, 1993, chap. 3. Idem, *The Rebellious Reformer: The Paintings and Drawings of Reza-yi ʿAbbasi of Isfahan*, London, 1996a. Idem, "Farangi Saz: The Impact of Europe on Safavid Painting," *Third Hali Annual*, London, 1996b, pp. 46-60. Idem, *Princes, Poets, Paladins: Islamic and Indian Paintings from the Collection of Prince and Princess Sadruddin Aga Khan*, London, 1998. Richard Ettinghausen, "Stylistic Tendencies at the Time of Shah ʿAbbas I," in *Studies on Isfahan* II, Iranian Studies 7/3-4, 1974, pp. 593-628. Naṣr-Allāh Falsafi, *Zendagāni-e Šāh ʿAbbās dovvom*, 4 vols., Tehran, 1953-67, II, pp. 53-57. Massumeh Farhad, "The Art of Muʿin Musavvir: A Mirror of His Times," in Sheila R. Canby, ed., *Persian Masters: Five Centuries of Painting*, Bombay, 1990, pp. 113-29. Idem, "Military Slaves in the Provinces: Collecting and Shaping the Arts," in *Slaves of Shah: New Elites of Safavid Iran*, London, 2004, chap. 5. Willem Floor, "Dutch Painters in Iran during the First Half of the 17th Century," *Persica* 8, 1979, pp. 145-61. Ernst Grube, "Wall Paintings in the Seventeenth Century Monuments of Isfahan," in *Studies on Isfahan* II, Iranian Studies 7/3-4, 1974, pp. 511-43. Loṭf-Allāh Honarfar, *Ganjina-ye āṯār-e tāriḵi-e Eṣfahān: āṯār-e bāstāni wa alwāḥ wa katibahā-ye tāriḵi dar ostān-e Eṣfahān*, Tehran, 1965. A. A. Ivanov, "The Life of Muhammad Zamān: A Reconsideration," tr. J. M. Rogers, *Iran* 17, 1979, pp. 65-70. Moḥammad-ʿAli Karimzāda Tabrizi, *Aḥwāl wa āṯār-e naqqāšān-e qadim-e Irān wa barḵ-i az mašāhir-e negārgari-e Hend wa ʿOṯmāni*, 3 vols. London, 1985-91. Basil William Robinson, *Persian Painting in the Bodleian Library*, London, 1958, pp. 153-61. E, Sims, "Five Seventeenth-Century Persian Oil Paintings," *Persian and Mughal Art*, London, 1976, pp. 221-48. Idem, "Late Safavid Painting: the Chehel Sutun, the Armenian Houses, the Oil Paintings," in *Akten des VII Internationalen Kongressen für iranische Kunst und Archäologie*, Archäologishe Mitteilungen aus Iran, Ergänsunsband 6, Berlin, 1979, pp. 408-18. Idem, "The European Print Sources of Painting by the Seventeenth-Century Persian Painter Muhammad Zaman ibn Haji Yusuf of Qum," in Henri Zerner, ed., *Le Stampe et la diffusione della imagini e degli stili*, Bologna, 1983, pp. 73-83, pls. 76-83. Abolala Soudavar. *Art of the Persian Courts: Selections from the Art and History Trust Collection*, New York, 1992, chaps. 7 and 9. Ivan Stchoukine, *Les peintures des manuscrits de Shah 'Abbas Ier à la fin de Safavis*, Paris, 1964. Marie Lukens Swietochowski and Susan Babaie, *Persian Drawings in the Metropolitan Museum of Art*, New York, 1989. Anthony Welch, "Painting and Patronage under Shah ʿAbbas I," *Studies on Isfahan* II, Iranian Studies 7/3-4, 1974, pp. 458-98. Idem, *Collection of Islamic Art: Prince Sadruddin Aga Khan*, Geneva, 1978, I, III, IV. Anthony Welch and Stuart Cary Welch, *Arts of the Islamic Book: The Collection of Prince Sadruddin Aga Khan*, Ithaca and London, 1982.

(MASSUMEH FARHAD)

xii. BAZAAR: PLAN AND FUNCTION

The bazaar (see BĀZĀR) of Isfahan is one of the best-preserved examples of the kind of large, enclosed and covered bazaar complex that was typical of most cities in the Muslim world prior to the 20th century. The oldest areas of the present-day bazaar date from the early 17th century, its first stone was laid in 1603. Prior to this date the bazaar of Isfahan was concentrated around the Meydān-e kohna, the old town center (see PLATE II in X [1] above). In 1590 Shah ʿAbbās had decided to move his capital to Isfahan, and although he initially renovated the old bazaar, he later decided to construct a new city center of palaces, mansions for his dignitaries, mosques, and other functional buildings around a new *meydān*, the so-called Meydān-e Naqš-e Jahān. In 1602 work on the new *meydān* began (Blake, p. 23; but 1590-91 according to sources discussed by McChesney, pp. 114-19). First, a one-story façade of arches and porticoes was built, which faced the new square. Through a number of large and small gates people could access the square and the covered bazaar complex behind them. Secondly, an upper-story (*bālā-ḵāna*) was built, with commercial offices and artisan shops that were open to the square. Initially, some 200 shops surrounded the square; each was two stories and about five meters high. The lower-story each contained two shops, and the upper-storey four smaller shops, two facing the square and two at the back, which had a small balcony with a protective brick railing. Most of the original floors were made of marble, while the floors added later were colored tiles and stone (Jonābādi, pp. 759-60). It took, of course, a few decades before the bazaar finally acquired its critical mass. Because the new bazaar at first had to meet the needs of the royal palace complex, the mansions of the Safavid elite as well as of their visitors, the bazaar is often referred to as the royal bazaar. The bazaar at the old square continued mainly to serve the needs of the general population, but it gradually fell into disuse and its entire function was absorbed by

PLATE I

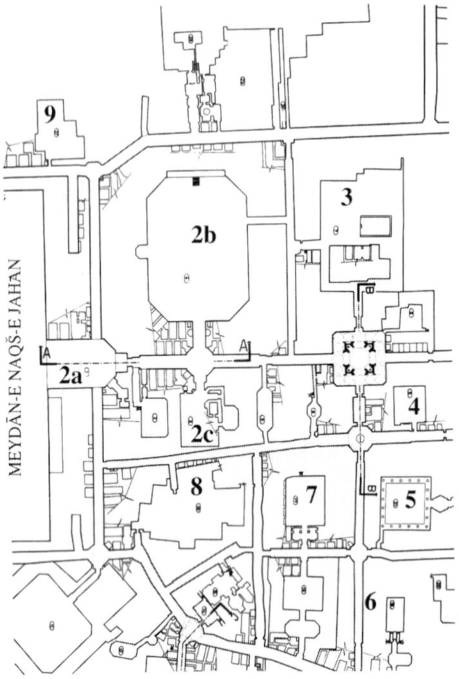

LEGEND

1. Meydān-e Naqš-e Jahān; 2a. Qayṣariya; 2b. Sarāy-e Shah; 2c. Zarrābḵāna; 3. Sarāy-e Čitsāzhā; 4. Sarāy-e Sefidkubhā; 5. Sarāy-e Sangtarāšhā; 6. Bāzār-e Zargarhā; 7. Bārandāz/Timča Malek; 8. Ḥammām-e Shah; 9. Bāzār-e Kaffāšhā.

Bazaar Plan, North of Meydān-e Šāh, Courtesy of John Donat, *Iranian Studies* 7/1-2, 1974, p. 336.

PLATE II

Aerial view of the bazaar. Courtesy of John Donat, *Iranian Studies* 7/1-2, 1974, p. 346.

the new bazaar (for a discussion and maps see Blake, 103, map 9; Soltani-Tirani, p. 4, fig. 1).

The bazaar still forms the commercial heart of Isfahan, because of its location and continued central commercial function. Its importance is further enhanced by the fact that it is surrounded by a number of public shopping thoroughfares which, although formally not part of the original bazaar complex, nevertheless are now an integral and dynamic part it. Like all bazaars it has no residential function at all, for it is only dedicated to a large variety of commercial and socio-religious functions. As to the commercial use of the bazaar there are a great variety of trades, crafts and service providers that work in its many shops and *sarāys*. There are both itinerant and stationary retail activities, private and public services (which include mosques, bathhouses, coffeehouses, public kitchens and simple inns). Wholesale, commissionaires, export and import, finance and credit, crafts and trades as well as the related brokerage activities are to be found there. One may roughly distinguish three major commercial complexes as to the retail trade: (1) the textile sector, from raw material to finished product; (2) food products and spices; and (3) household needs. Furthermore, there is a commercial branch that deals with the needs of the rural areas. There has, of course, been a shift in the relative composition of the trades and crafts that work in the bazaar. Much of the wholesale and import and export trade has moved to other parts of the city, and even to a great extent to Tehran, during the last 50 years. Also, modern Western style shops and supermarkets have drawn away some of the bazaar's business to the various residential quarters of the city. One major positive development is that the bazaar has acquired a new commercial function as a tourist destination, visited for its sights and sounds as well as its goods and services. This has resulted in the proliferation of shops that specifically make, buy and sell products for tourists, while some crafts have even survived largely because their main clientele is tourists (metal work, inlay-work or *ḵātam*, for example; see xiii. below).

Location is, of course, very important. Those shops that sell products with a high unit-value, for example, jewelers, are mostly found at the entrance to the bazaar and at other easily accessible location. Those crafts and traders who are involved in low-unit value production are usually found in less desirable, less accessible locations (e.g., shoemakers, barbers, coffee-houses). Another characteristic is the fact that a variety of different locations account for where a product is sold, traded and stored. For example, an important wholesale company most likely has an office at a prime location in one of the best *sarāys*, but it usually stores its goods in a warehouse in a less well-maintained *sarāy* at a less desirable and less expensive location, i.e., more to the periphery. In addition, the goods that the company trades in are made by artisans who work at another different location in the bazaar (for detailed discussion of the location of shops in the bazaar with maps, see Soltani-Tirani, p. 22-31).

The bazaar complex consists of a large number of bazaar buildings, generally referred to as bazaar or when smaller as *bāzārča*. Next there are the *sarāys* or caravanserais, and their smaller version, the so-called *timčas*.

Often a *sarāy*, which is a uniform, independent construction, usually with an inner court of arcades that is situated within the bazaar complex, includes *timčas* (small arcaded courtyards or halls) with vaulted entrance halls (*dehliz*). All these buildings are interconnected with covered market streets (*rāsta*) and passageways (*dālān*). These streets and lanes are not only market streets, but also communication routes for people and goods to enter and exit the bazaar. Goods, previously brought by caravans of loaded camels, donkeys and mules, now arrive by lorries, and after storage are carried on the back of porters to the various workshops and sales points (Bakhtiar; Gaube and Wirth, pp. 63-66).

In order to create space and light through openings in the dome, so-called domed crossroads or *čahār suq* were built where market streets crossed one another. A similar dome was also built when the bazaar market street gave access to a mosque or *madrasa*. Gaube and Wirth have identified three types of such domes, which are related to Central Asian models. Constructions peculiar to the Isfahan bazaar are domed cellars or windowless, pillared halls that are half subterranean. This type of construction is usually a later addition to a *sarāy*, most of which seem to have been constructed in the 19th century (Gaube and Wirth, pp. 72-74, fig 24). Nowadays these are mostly occupied by workshops using modern machinery. The advent of electricity (see BARQ) has made it possible to work in these dark spaces. Therefore, it is surmised that originally these cellars were used as storage space.

PLATE III

Entrance of the Royal Bazaar. Courtesy of John Donat, *Iranian Studies* 7/1-2, 1974, p. 342.

The bazaar in other Iranian towns mainly consists of a number of smaller bazaars each of which is made up of a large, central *sarāy* with a number of courtyards, *timčas*, halls, bazaar market streets, *dehliz*, and domes that make up a multi-functional, multi-layered construction. The most impressive of these large hybrid buildings date back to the 19th century. However, the number of such hybrids is rather few in Isfahan, probably due to the fixed (endowment) nature of much of the property rights in the city, which did not allow for real estate development as it did elsewhere. However, due to soaring land prices, this seems to be changing somewhat and many buildings that have lost their original function, such as bathhouses, have been torn down and replaced with others serving a different purpose. This shows that the bazaar complex remains a dynamic organism that reacts to the pressures of the world around it (Gaube and Wirth, pp. 66-74; Soltani-Tirani, p. 111 f).

When the bazaar was expanded over time, the original regular, linear structure slowly and subtly adapted itself to the demands of each historical period. The combination of streets, passageways, *sarāys*, *timčas*, mosques, *madrasas* etc., were reproduced many times over within the growing bazaar complex over the course of the centuries. Also, the pattern, whereby each sector of the bazaar was occupied by a single trade or craft, was less strictly adhered to, while there were also movements of trades and craft within the bazaar complex. Moreover, the streets in the newer parts sometimes were not covered, especially in the 20th century, while other vaulted older parts (outside of the central section) have become dilapidated, especially towards the periphery of the bazaar. Over time the bazaar has undergone many changes, including the destruction of parts of the bazaar during the Afghan occupation (1722-29; Floor, 1998, p. 262) as well as during the sacks of Isfahan by various contenders for the throne in the 1750s (Perry, pp. 22, 52, 63). Also, the loss of Isfahan's status as the capital in 1722 as well as the downturn in the economy in the century following the fall of Isfahan negatively impacted the bazaar's condition. Some Safavid parts have disappeared, while later additions have created hybrid mixtures. This makes it difficult to identify the time period when the original vaulted streets were built due to repairs, changes, and extensions, resulting in the presence of several styles belonging to different time periods. For example, regarding the vaulted cover of the bazaar market streets, Gaube and Wirth identified eight different types, of which four clay vault types were only found in Safavid era buildings, while the other four belong to the post-Safavid period, one type of which dated as late as 1900 (Gaube and Wirth, pp. 90-94, fig. 25). These *sarāys* are all of a standard type of construction, and have been used for all kinds of functions including as warehouses, offices, workshops, garages, stables, or even as simple inns to provide sleeping quarters for people from outside Isfahan. The Isfahan bazaar has fewer *timčas* and also of a smaller size than bazaars in other Iranian towns.

Gaube and Wirth have made a similar typology for caravanserais, where they identified five different types:

PLATE IV

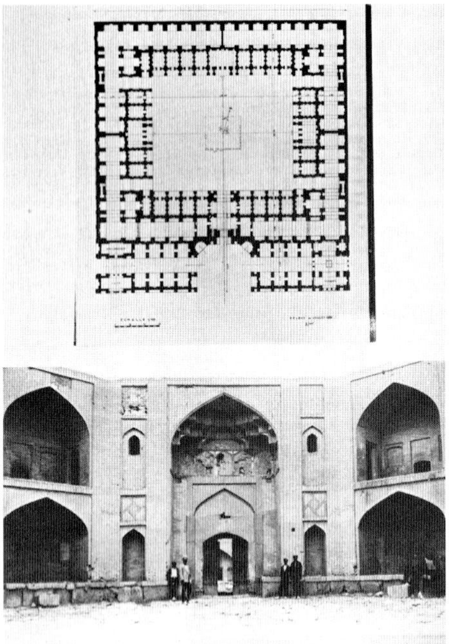

Plan and entrance of Mahyār Caravanserai.
After M. Siroux, p. 370.

(1) The Safavid or arcade group, the main characteristic of which is the arcade in the upper-story. This type of *sarāy* has an *ayvān* (q.v.) that rises above the building elements; it often has a hall (*dehliz*) at the entrance and barrel-vaulted arches as covering of each wall section. Also, they are decorated with geometric patterns with glazed tiles, while later buildings have ceramic mosaics or painted tiles. (2) The one-story Golšan group (named after its first known model, the Sarāy-e Golšan), construction of which was begun during the Zand period. This type of construction is characterized by a one-story alignment, tile decoration in the upper parts of the wall sections, wreathed moulds that surround the courtyard, *dehliz*es and cloistral arches above a long, and rectangular ground plan as roof for the wall sections and recessed corners. (3) The one-story group in the bazaar's periphery. In contrast to the Golšan group, which is the result of historical development, this type of building was functionally determined. They are all to be found at the periphery of the bazaar, and serve as a place for the transshipment of goods. They therefore have very large courtyards for (un)loading, and additional side courtyards where the caravan animals were stabled. This type of construction was built in the 19th and beginning of the 20th century. (4) The *mahtābi* (terrace) type of the 19th century; these are all two-storied, but they do not have a surrounding arcade in the upper-story. The recessed upper-story has a terrace facing the courtyard. Moreover, they all have recessed corners, and covering of the wall sections by cloistral arches over a long-rectangular ground plan. (5) The late Qajar *tārom* (wooden roof) type, which is a product of the early 20th century. The side facing the courtyard has an upper-story that has a wooden roof supported by stone or wooden pillars. This type is divided into two groups—either the upper-story is recessed, or it is aligned with the ground floor (Gaube and Wirth, pp. 94-101; figs. 26-29).

Similarly there are six different types of timčas or domed halls (1). The one-story open- or flat-roofed type; (2) the two-story arcade type; (3) the two-story *mahtābi* type; (4) the two-story *tārom* type; (5) the two-story equilateral octagonal type; and (6) the two-story stretched octagonal type. It is only natural that these types were similar to that of the *sarāy* as a *timča* is but a 'small tim,' which is another word for *sarāy* (Gaube and Wirth, pp. 101-3). These *timča*s are relatively rarer in Isfahan than in the bazaars of other cities in Iran. Gaube and Wirth have suggested that the *qayṣariya* of Isfahan was the forerunner and model for the later *timča*s because from an architectural standpoint it is a more elongated bazaar hall than a bazaar street. The *qayṣariya* was emblematic for the Isfahan bazaar. It functioned both as the gateway (*darb*) to the many streets and passageways of the inner bazaar complex and, at the same time, it was the richest and largest bazaar of Isfahan where merchants sold rich fabrics and cloth. Hence it was also referred to as *bazzāz-ḵāna* or mercers hall. It was a pentagonal semi-circular building around a pond and construction began in 1603 and was completed in 1619. Although it was said to have been modeled after the *qayṣariya* of Tabriz, it may also have borrowed design elements from the *qayṣariya* of the bazaar around the old square of Isfahan that it replaced. It has been suggested that many of the later caravanserais that were built in Iran borrowed their basic design from the gateway of the Isfahan bazaar (Gaube and Wirth, pp. 66-68; Blake, pp.107-10).

Many buildings in the bazaar were decorated, either by mural paintings and/or by tile decorations. There is a large variety of geometrical designs, all variations on cross, diamond, and graded patterns. The mosaic bricks for the post-Safavid period are all smaller and flatter and less color intense. They are quadrangular or bar-shaped. There are also post-Safavid words in mosaic form, albeit barely legible. Another form of decoration was that of tiles, often used on the heads of the wall sections making nine different geometric patterns. The face of the *Qayṣariya* gateway had been decorated with tiles, while in the upper recesses there were mural paintings of Shah ʿAbbās hunting, Shah ʿAbbās defeating the Uzbeks, male and female Europeans having a party, and finally the symbol of Isfahan, the Sagittarius. In the center on top of the gateway there was a clock that was still functional in 1638, but no longer worked in 1670. Within the bazaar complex the vaults of the streets or wall panels were also decorated with epic scenes as well as with arabesques (Floor, 2005a, pp. 122-23, 126; Blake, p. 110; Gaube and Wirth, pp. 105-12, figs. 32-36).

All buildings have a name. Frequently, in the case of bazaars, it indicates a professional group or guild (often of those who traded and worked there), while in the case of *sarāy*s it is usually a person, normally the patron-builder. Others are known by a particular characteristic (e.g., *sarā-ye dālān-darāz* or 'the *sarāy* with a long entrance passageway'), the name of the quarter or of the patron (Masjed-e Sāru Taqi), or some other qualifier. The names have changed over time, of course, just as the function and use of buildings have changed. In the *qayṣariya*, for example, instead of rich fabrics all kinds of tourist products are sold, and the same holds for the *bāzār-e čitsāzhā* (the bazaar of the chintz makers), although there are still some shops that also sell chintzes (Gaube and Wirth, pp. 116-260).

Life in the bazaar is not always about business. Although the bazaar complex is the commercial heart of Isfahan, there are buildings that serve a function other than a commercial one. Today, there are still ten *madrasa*s in the bazaar whose design is very much like that of the *sarāy*s, eight of which date from the Safavid period and two are from the 19th century. In these *madrasa*s religious youths as well as older males receive advanced religious instruction which may lead to a religious career or to serve one's own edification. One also could find some refuge from the hustle and bustle of the bazaar inside a *madrasa*'s courtyard, which is often lined with trees and has a large pond in the middle (Bakhtiyar, pp. 328-31, figs 9-12; Gaube and Wirth, pp. 103-5).

Also, there are a number of mosques, most of which were built in the 17th century and some in the late 19th century. These mosques are characterized by different designs and some, like the Ḥakim Mosque, are as beautiful as the Royal Mosque on the Meydān (see x above). Here the population of the bazaar undertake their daily prayers and participate in religious ceremonies. Some of these mosques had a special relationship with one particular guild that either was its patron and/or had (co-)financed its construction. Such is the case with the Masjed-e k̲ayyāṭhā (tailors and dressmakers mosque), which, apart from its religious function, also served as the administrative office of the said guild. How well integrated these mosques are in the commercial life of the bazaar is evident from the example of the Bāğča-ye ʿAbbāsi Mosque, which has shops flanking its entrance hall. Whereas religion was experienced in an individual and enclosed manner in the mosque and the *madrasa*, this was different in the *takiya*, a type of building where communal *rawża-k̲āni*s were held, and where during Moḥarram and Ṣafar the Shiʿite passion play (*taʿzia-k̲āni*) was performed, often combined with a procession of religiously significant symbols, players, and the general public (Floor, 2005b).

Apart from endowing funds to build mosques, *madrasa*s, and *takiya*s, people also did this for *saqqā-k̲āna*s of water spigots and *maqbara*s or mausolea in the bazaars and elsewhere. Also part of the religious functions were the bathhouses (see HAMMĀM) constructed in the bazaars, where believers regularly came to wash away their impurities so as to be ritually clean and be able to perform their religious duties such as prayer. In addition to the bathhouses where men congregated for relaxation, there were also all kinds of itinerant and shop-based sellers in the bazaar of a large variety of the foods and drinks that made up the supplies for social gatherings. For example, a few shops in Isfahan in the 19th century supplied the entire city with *beriāni* food, all of which was made in one cook shop in the bazaar, (Taḥwildār, p. 119). There also were itinerant sellers of coffee, tea, water, and smokes as well as coffee-houses (*qahvak̲āna*), where the same services were offered. Moreover, these were popular gathering points to exchange news, gossip, and to listen to poetry and story tellers. "Hither repair all those covetous of News, as well as Barterers of Goods; where not only Fame and common Rumour is promulgate, but Poetry too, for some of that Tribe are always present to rehearse their Poems, and disperse their Fables to the Company" (Fryer, III, p. 34; Du Mans/Schefer, p. 244; for coffee-houses in the 19th century, see Floor, 2004). On festive days, shopkeepers would additionally burn oil lamps and decorate their shops so that the entire bazaar area was a sea of light (see ČERĀĞĀNI).

There was also a public government side to the bazaar. North of the *qayṣariya* gateway was a large intersection (*čahār suq*), which led to two major buildings, namely, the *żarrāb-k̲āna* and the *sarāy-e šāhi* (see Plate I), which each had a gateway, albeit less lofty than that of the qayṣariya. The *żarrāb-k̲āna* (the Mint), as its name indicates, was the location where until 1877 silver and copper coins were struck by hand, thus providing the means of exchange for facilitating commercial transactions. On two sides of the qayṣariya gateway balconies protrude (known as *naqqāra-k̲āna*), which were used by the royal music band. This band played at sunrise and sunset as well as after important events had taken place, such as victories. Often condemned men were led through the bazaar, or even executed in a *čahār suq*, in order to convey the government's vigilance to the general population.

Despite the fact that the royal bazaar has long since lost any semblance of its prior courtly association, the bazaar of Isfahan remains a vibrant centerpiece of the city, a place with wide-ranging functions, from the obvious shopping environment to its religious, educational, social, and recreational roles. Because of this, the state of disrepair suffered by many of the bazaar's less central areas, while an unfortunate consequence of the wounds of time and history, have not undermined the bazaar's singular importance, both to the citizens of the city and to outside visitors newly acquainted with its many charms.

Bibliography: Ali Bakhtiyar, "The Royal Bazaar of Isfahan," *Iranian Studies* 7/1-2, 1974, pp. 320-47. Stephen P. Blake, *Half the World. The Social Architecture of Safavid Isfahan, 1590-1722*, Costa Mesa, 1999. Raphael Du Mans, *L'estat de la Perse en 1660*, ed. Ch. Schefer, Paris, 1890. Willem Floor, *The Afghan Occupation of Safavid Persia 1721-1729*, Paris 1998. Idem, "Tea Consumption and Importation in Qajar Iran," *Studia Iranica* 33, 2004, pp. 47-111. Idem, *Wall Paintings in Qajar Iran*, Costa Mesa, 2005a. Idem, *The History of Theater in Iran*, Washington DC, 2005b.

John Fryer, A New Account of East India and Persia. Being nine years' travels, 1672-1681, 3 vols., London, 1909-15 (Hakluyt Society, 2nd Series). Heinz Gaube and Eugen Wirth, *Der Bazar von Isfahan*, Wiesbaden, 1978. Mirzā Beyg b. Ḥasan Jonābādi, *Rawżat al-Ṣafawiya*, ed. Ḡ.-R. Tabāṭabā'i Majd, Tehran, 1999. R. D. McChesney, "Four Sources on Shah ʿAbbas's Building of Isfahan," *Muqarnas* 5, 1988, pp. 103-34. John R. Perry, *Karim Khan Zand, A History of Iran, 1747-1779*, Chicago, 1979. M. Siroux, "Les Carvanserais Routiers Safavids," *Iranian Studies* 7/1-2, 1974, pp. 348-75. Mohammad-Ali Soltani-Tirani, *Handwerker und Handwerk in Esfahan. Räumliche, wirtschaftliche und sociale Organisationsformen*, Marburg/Lahn, 1982. Mirzā Ḥosayn Khan Tahwildār, *Joḡrāfiā-ye Eṣfahān*, ed. M. Sotudeh, Tehran, 1963.

(WILLEM FLOOR)

xiii. CRAFTS

Isfahan has maintained its position as a major center for traditional crafts in Persia. The crafts of Isfahan encompass textiles, carpets, metalwork, woodwork, ceramics, painting, and inlay works of various kind. The work is carried out in different settings including small industrial and bazaar workshops, in the homes of craftsmen and women, and in rural cottage industries.

Isfahan's crafts are clearly rooted in the city's royal past, but to suggest a direct and uninterrupted link to the Safavid era would be too simplistic an assumption. The passing of skills from one generation to the next has been disrupted many times, beginning with the Afghan invasion of 1722, and by later wars, famines, plagues, tribal pillages and the resulting depopulation. During the Qajar period there was a steady outflow of skill and talent from Isfahan to Tehran and Tabriz, where the Qajar court and administration were major consumers and patrons of various crafts (Philipp). Equally detrimental to the crafts of Isfahan was the cheaper mass-produced European merchandise that flooded the Persian markets in ever increasing quantities throughout the 19th century. Mirzā Ḥosayn Khan Taḥwildār reports repeatedly on how the pressure to maintain competitive prices vis-à-vis imports had an adverse effect on the quality of various local products and dented the reputation of Isfahani artisans (p. 97, *passim*). Some crafts disappeared or were significantly reduced due to changes in fashion, market demand, and technology. In particular, changes in fashion hurt those crafts that produced various kinds of embroideries that were only used in traditional clothes and home decorations which were no longer worn or used after 1925 (Floor, 1999a). Changes due to market demand had consequences, for example, for those making helmets, swords, guns, and chain-mail, which given the suppression of the possession of firearms, the development of better modern arms and fighting techniques, and the imposition of general security, had become obsolete (Floor, 2003). This also held for those making copper pots, and of those who tinned them, due to the import and/or local manufacturing of mass-produced metal pots and pans, although by 1920 there were still 200 copper workers (*mesgar*) and 40 tin smiths (*safidgar*; see Janāb, p. 79). Other crafts became obsolete because of the quasi-disappearance of their product such as the water pipe, which was almost entirely displaced by cigarette smoking (Floor, 2002). Other crafts were transformed, such as those that made products for animals, like saddles and horseshoes. These have all disappeared and been replaced by other crafts that serve modern means of conveyance such as carts, cars, and lorries. In short, the result was that in number, output, and quality the craftsmen in Isfahan, like elsewhere in Iran, were on the verge of extinction (for a discussion of these and other crafts in the 19th and early 20th century see Floor, 2003; and 2006).

In the 20th century new social currents and market forces began to interact with traditional techniques and styles to produce new types of objects as well as variations on existing features. In the 1930s, in an attempt to preserve and encourage the local production of handicrafts, the government established a school of arts and crafts (Honarestān) in Isfahan. The growing economy after 1950 had a further positive impact in the area of handicrafts. Between 1952 and 1962 the number of craftsmen doubled, while their output almost quadrupled. To provide structural support to the craftsmen, the government established the Handicrafts Center (Markaz-e ṣanāyeʿ-e dasti) in 1963, to provide loans to craftsmen for the purchase of raw materials and other inputs, organize training courses to acquaint craftsmen with the latest technical developments, to provide them with new designs and other ideas on how to improve their products, and to assist them in marketing their products around the world. In 1974 the Center's export of handicrafts represented ten percent of the total export of handicrafts. The Center's formula of promoting traditional designs and crafts, produced with better quality using traditional as well as modern techniques, worked both abroad and at home (Echo of Iran, *Iran Almanac*, Tehran, 1974, p. 243).

The emphasis on tradition received fresh impetus in the 1960s when Western-educated art students began to return home, eager to revive some of the styles and techniques of the past. Moreover, for emerging middle-class consumers, decorative value was as important as functionality of the crafts. Architectural decoration, which had begun with restoration of public monuments, was sustained by market demand on the part of neo-traditionalism. As the city grew into a center of tourist attraction, handicrafts flourished. Master craftsmen, working with their apprentices in small ateliers along the bazaar, the Royal Square (Meydān-e Naqš-e Jahān), and Čārbāḡ avenue (see Č(AH)ĀRBĀḠ-E EṢFAHĀN; and Soltani-Tirani, pp. 29 ff.), became a tourist attraction themselves.

Architectural decoration. In the past, Isfahan was home to many craftsmen who excelled in the decoration of buildings such as plaster molders, mirror makers (*āʾinasāz*), colored-glass window makers (*orusi*), and tile

PLATE I

Ornamental ceramic at one of the light slits on the dome of Shaikh Loṭf-Allāh Mosque. After R. Baḵtiār, p. 19.

PLATE II

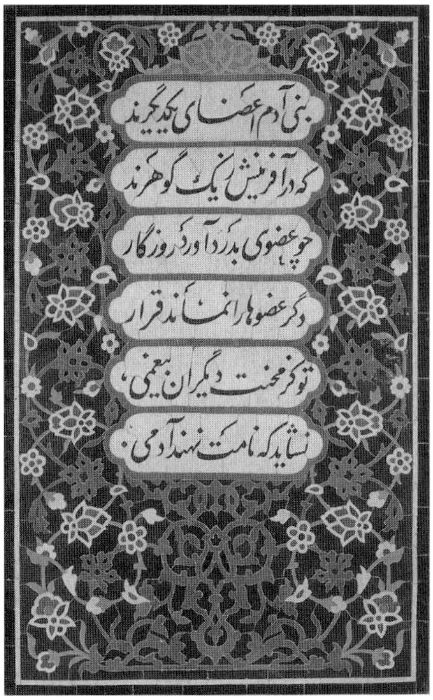

Mosaic panel with Calligraphy, poem of Saʿdi, Shaikh Loṭf-Allah Mosque, by H. Moṣaddeqzāda Kāšikār, 1950. After Gluck, p. 393.

makers (*kāšipaz*), but whose crafts had languished during much of the 19th century. Although the building crafts and their related ancillary crafts in general had seen improvement in their numbers during the second half of the 19th century, the insecurity reigning between 1900 and 1920 stifled their development. For example, in Isfahan in 1920 there were only six tile makers, six mirror makers, and 12 master builders (*meʿmār*; see Janāb, pp. 77-79).

The history of the revival of this craft is closely related to the restoration of the Saljuq and Safavid monuments that had been left to decay for centuries. One of the earliest cases was the refurbishment of the Shaikh Loṭf-Allāh Mosque at the Royal Square in 1926, and the subsequent replication of its dome at the Marmar Palace in Tehran, reviving the abandoned art of mosaic faience (*moʿarraq*) in the process (Gluck et al., pp. 392-93). Many kilns flourished through tile-making in the ensuing decades when a new generation of tile makers, miniature painters, woodcarvers, calligraphers, and other artists emerged thanks to the extensive and longterm program of rehabilitation of the city's historical architecture (Wulff, pp. 118-71).

A milestone in the history of architectural decoration was the renovation and conversion in the 1960s of the Mādar-e Shah caravanserai into a modern hotel named after Shah ʿAbbās the Great—the present-day ʿAbbāsi Hotel (Borjian, 2002). In contrast to the restoration work on mosques, which were carried out by traditional masters, the craftsmen and artists who took part in this project were mostly graduates of the Honarestān. The latter tended to promote innovative techniques and motifs within the framework of traditional decorative arts such as geometric mirror-mosaics, stucco, stained glass, wood, and various combinations thereof that succeeded in welding modernity with tradition, and transformed the modern hotel into a veritable museum of the contemporary and vibrant decorative arts of Isfahan (see Arthur Upham Pope's letter in Borjian et al., p. 10). The hotel decorations were soon imitated in other public buildings, and have had a growing influence on the interior design of private residences as well (Borjian et al.; Gluck et al., pp. 400-402 ff.).

Carpets. Contrary to popular belief, carpets had never been a major export item of Iran, but when almost all other crafts experienced a downturn in their output and numbers in the 19th century, demand for carpets fortuitously increased enormously after 1873 due to a boom with the arrival of a new client—the European and American middle class (Floor, 1999a; Wirth; see CARPETS). The boom spread from the northwestern provinces, and by the 1920s Isfahan had become a major center of carpet weaving (*Camb. Hist. Ir.* I, p. 550; Soltani-Tirani, pp. 75-76 ff.) In this process of renewal, the carpet-weaving tradition in Isfahan adapted itself to new market realities and the requirements of commercial production, leading to Isfahan's own characteristic

PLATE IV

Isfahan Carpet, the central blue lobed medallion on an ivory scrolling vine, forked-leaf and fan palmate design, approximately 11.4 x 9.6 feet. After Sotheby, NY, sale number 4265, p. 156.

PLATE III

The portal of Shah (Imam) Mosque.
After R. Baḵtiār, p. 77.

design that had distinguished itself by 1940. In that year there were 2,000 looms in the city and 500 in its environs (out of some 70,000 looms in the country; Floor, 1984, p. 32). During World War II the carpet industry of Isfahan suffered heavily from the loss of the international market. In the early 1950s the number of looms in the city had fallen to a mere 400, established in about 300 home factories that wove 5,000 m^2 of carpets annually (ʿĀbedi, p. 138). It regained a foothold in the market due to the increasing demands of Tehran market (Edwards, p. 308), and by the 1980s mass production had seen a substantial increase. Among the districts of the province, only Isfahan and Nāʾin produce quality carpets suitable for export (Table 1). Silk carpet weaving workshops are mainly located around Qom, Isfahan, Kāšān and Nāʾin.

Table 1
Carpet industry in the Isfahan Province by looms, production, average price, and percent exported in the early 1980s*

Sub-Province	Number of looms (1,000)	Annual production (1,000 m^2)	Average price (1,000 rials)	Percent exported
Isfahan	18	27	250	80
Najafābād	8	96	25	0
Fereydan	7	42	20	0
Nāʾin	7	21	150	80
Meyma	2	3	23	0
Kāšān	14	150	50	20

*All numbers are estimates with an error margin of 15 percent.
Source: Šurā-ye ʿāli-e barnāmarizi-e ostān-e Eṣfahān, I, ch.11.

The production techniques and organization and commercial practices vary within the province itself (Soltani-Tirani, pp. 75 ff.). Larger factories employing weavers in double figures are few; cottage production has been the norm and is sponsored by subcontractors who supply labor from their own families or other sources, while less than a third of weavers worked for themselves in the early 1980s (ibid, p. 95); weaving of carpets as well as *gelims* (see KELIM) and *jājims* (q.v.), chiefly by women, constituted the bulk of the home industries that existed in 14.1 percent of the houses in the province (*Markaz*, p. 13; Soltani-Tirani, p. 7). As the importance of the cottage industries diminished in the city of Isfahan, where workers preferred the higher wages in other and more modern industries, Isfahani businessmen began to invest in the surrounding rural areas (*Farhang*, p. 18 *passim*) where the carpet industry continues to play a dominant role. It seems that only rug weaving has outlasted the vanishing rural handicrafts. In recent decades, however, the carpet industry of Isfahan has experienced a major setback (Ansāri, pp. 157-60) and machine-made carpets have increasingly replaced hand-woven ones (see CARPETS).

Qalamkār or the craft of woodblock-printing on cotton tablecloths, bedspreads, and curtains has been a specialty of Isfahan for the last two centuries (Gluck et al., pp. 186-88). Indian imports had dominated this branch of the textile industry in the pre-1800 period. Impoverishment and insecurity in the 18th century had created a situation where domestic output had to compensate for the shortfall in imports. As a result there was an initial increase in the output of the textile industry in general, and of *qalamkār* in particular, during the early part of the 19th century, when security returned to Iran. However, this period of growth did not last, for after 1840 domestic *qalamkār* production suffered a structural decline, albeit less so than all other branches of textile crafts, due to the import of fabrics of cheaper and better quality (Floor, 1999a).

In the 1870s the guild of the *qalamkār* makers had four connecting bazaars and between the bazaars there were five caravanserais and *timčas* with 284 shops and offices, but not even half of their number have remained, because trade had declined sharply due to foreign competition and lack of demand at home (Taḥwildār, p. 94). The reason was that the Isfahan output of *qalamkār* was not comparable in quality and price with British and later Russian imports. Production could initially only survive by importing unbleached fabrics from Great Britain and India that were then printed in Iran. This delayed the inevitable decline of the craft for some time, but lack of innovation, continued inferior quality, and the use of chemical dyes meant that by the beginning of the 20th century the craft had all but disappeared (Floor, 1999a). In 1920 there were only 46 *čitsāz* left in Isfahan, where once there had been hundreds (Janāb, p. 78).

Government support seems to have helped another short-lived revival of this labor-intensive craft in the 1920s, just before it declined to the verge of total extinction (Phyllis Ackerman in *Survey of Persian Art*, pp. 2155-56). The craft of *qalamkār* was revived again after World War II thanks to the US Aid program and demand from the international market (Gluck et al., p. 192). In the 1950s in Isfahan and Najafābād there were about thirty *qalamkār* workshops with an annual production of 40,000 pairs of drapery, and 10,000 tablecloth pieces (ʿĀbedi, p. 139). Supported by the Handicrafts Organization, the number of workshops and guild masters multiplied in the bazaar in the next twenty years and new products and techniques were put into practice (Gluck et al., p. 192). The implementation of antipollution laws in the 1970s led to another slowdown of the *qalamkār* industry, but as a result better dyes were developed and production was standardized. Limitation on imports after the 1979 Revolution resuscitated the industry, and *qalamkār* resurfaced as perennial favorites in the bazaar of Isfahan. The main firm involved in the *qalamkār* manufacture is the Čitsāz Company, exporting large quantities of merchandise (see also CRAFTS).

PLATE V

Qalamkār, blocked and painting by Ḥosayn Faḵḵāri, ca. 1955, 130 x 270 cm. After Gluck, p. 189.

PLATE VI

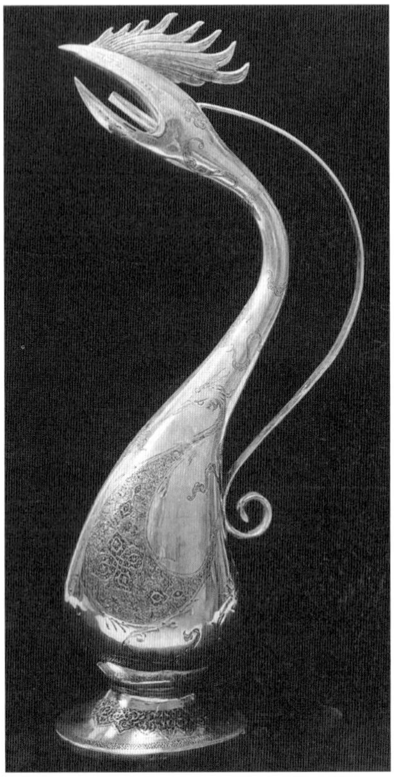

Silver Ewer, engraved, H. 52 cm., 1976.
After Gluck, p. 129.

PLATE VII

Various metalwork on an ʿAlam. After Gluck, p. 143.

Metalwork. Isfahan's prominence in decorative work on metal objects continues today, achieving the highest standards within the country in the past century. The revival of the art in Isfahan was achieved partly thanks to an exodus of artisans from Kerman and Yazd. The metalwork in Isfahan is mainly embossing and engraving (*qalamzani*) on various metals such as iron, copper, brass, and nickel alloys as well as gold and silver (Wulff, p. 35; Westphal-Hellbush and Burns, p. 90).

New market demands in the second half of the 20th century encouraged Isfahani engravers to shift their efforts to silver objects. In the 1950s, chisel work in silver was practiced by more than 800 skilled craftsmen in 110 workshops, while there were 86 silversmith shops with 450 workers making utensils, vases, mirror framing, and the like to be carved or incised by engravers (ʿĀbedi, p. 140-43). Unlike other crafts, that of goldsmiths (*zargar*) did not suffer very much decline, as they were able to compete effectively in both price and product with any foreign import; they also adapted and changed their output in line with market conditions. In 1920 there were still 160 goldsmiths in Isfahan as well as an unknown number of related craftsmen such as gold- and silver-wire drawers (Janāb, p. 78). This number compares favorably with the 500 workers in 169 shops employed by the goldsmith industry in the 1950s, the most notable of which were situated in the Armenian quarter of Julfa (ʿĀbedi, p. 141; Gluck et al., pp. 126-28). A more recent development in the metalwork of Isfahan is the production of large-scale copper sheets for use as interior wall decoration in public and private buildings in the city, and in Tehran. However, the production of copper pots and pans is in decline (Soltani-Tirani, pp. 55-64).

K̲ātamkāri or *k̲ātamsāzi.* This most typical of Persian wood-inlay work has been a specialty of Shiraz and Isfahan since the time of the Zand dynasty in the latter half of the 18th century. During his visit to Persia in 1811, Sir William Ouseley (q.v at *iranica.com*) writes that *k̲ātam* "ensured considerable profit to many artists of Shiraz and Isfahan" (Ouseley, III, p. 65). By 1877, the industry had declined: Taḥwildār reports low quality and poor sales, so much so that European artifact collectors sought old *k̲ātam* pieces, and exports were limited to Anatolia and Istanbul (Taḥwildār, no. 130). However, inlay work was slowly but surely falling out of favor, mainly due to the changing tastes of the elite who wanted fashionable European implements rather than traditional Persian ones. Because the elite were the main market for high-quality inlay work, this had serious consequences for the craftsmen who did not adapt their product. Like Tahwildār, in the beginning of the 20th century Radimsky opined that the quality of work left much to be desired (Radimsky, p. 55). As a result, the craft dwindled, and by

PLATE VIII

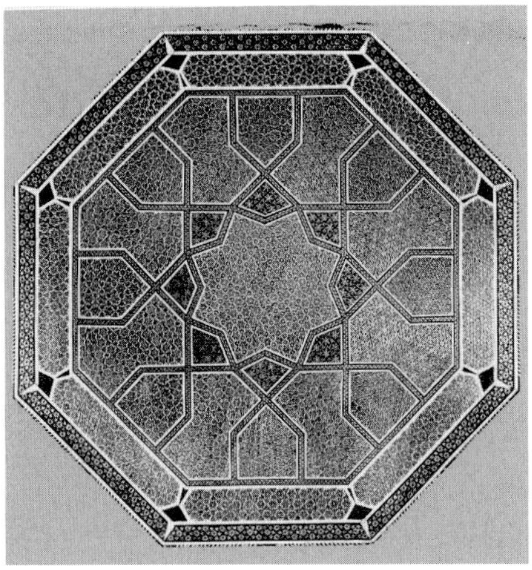

K̲ātamkāri, table top, by Golriz, 1976, D. 50 cm. After Gluck, p. 361.

PLATE IX

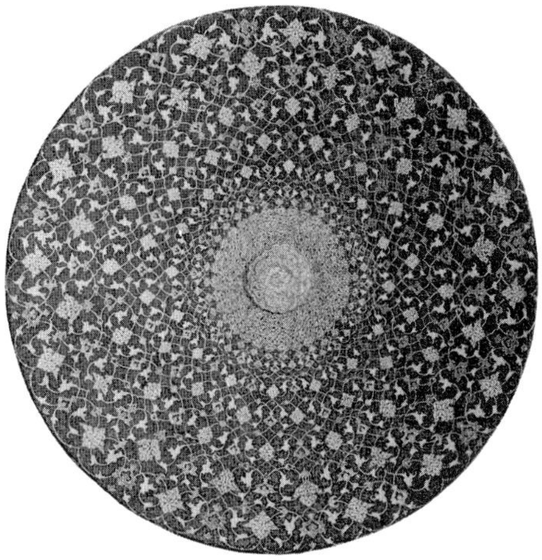

Dome Interior of Shah (Imam) Mosque, enamel plate, adaptation with gold medallion, by Šokr-Allāh Ṣaniʿzādeh. After Gluck, p. 165.

PLATE X

Painting on embossed leather, signed Ḥosayn K̲ata, 1961, W. 80 cm. After Gluck, p. 381.

1920 only six master inlay workers remained in Isfahan (Janāb, p. 78).

The industry began to flourish again when Reza Shah awarded high wages to master *k̲ātamkārs* for the decoration of the walls and furniture of Tehran palaces. But the dominant position of Isfahan was largely due to the migration of the Shirāzi master, Golriz, to the city where he taught at the Honarestān for 36 years, re-establishing the craft in Isfahan (Gluck et al., p. 368). In the 1950s Isfahan had about 100 *k̲ātam* craftsmen working in 40 workshops (ʿĀbedi, p. 144); the numbers had increased to 256 craftsmen and 81 workshops by 1975 (Markaz-e āmār-e Irān, pp. 719-20). According to another estimate there were some 50 masters and 300 skilled workers engaged in the *k̲ātam* industry just prior to the 1979 Revolution (Gluck et al., pp. 362-68). In addition to commercial production, Isfahani artists have decorated several Shiʿite mausoleums with *k̲ātam* decorations and coverings, either through royal benefactions, commissions by wealthy patrons, or at their own cost as an act of faith and devotion (ibid). *K̲ātam* is also widely used in decorating musical instruments, the prominent maker of which at the outset of the Pahlavi era was Yaḥyā, an Armenian from the Julfa district who later moved to the capital. (See also Faryād; Soltani-Tirani, pp. 65-75.)

Enamel and painting. Practiced since the 18th century in Isfahan, the art of enamel (*minākāri*) thrived in Isfahan under the Pahlavis. In the early 1950s there were 15 workshops with 20 enamellers who painted on utensils, vases, frames, bottles, badges, and other objects (ʿĀbedi, pp. 143-44). The trade expanded enormously owing to increasing demand, so that by the 1970s some 500 skilled enamel painters in Isfahan were engaged in decorating a wide variety of objects, from earrings to vases and chandeliers. Many of these artists were apprentices of the master miniaturist Šokr-Allāh Ṣaniʿzāda, who set the standard of the art, and introduced new motifs. Many holy shrines in Persia and Iraq received enamel decoration, some commissioned by the royal family (Gluck et al., pp. 164-66).

In previous centuries, Isfahan had been a major center of the art of painting, where paintings of all kind (miniature, canvas, water colors, lacquer, fresco) were produced for the market, including the tourist trade, and as a consequence the trade employed scores of painters. In particular, the painting of pen-cases (*qalamdān*) was a very popular craft in which many were employed (Floor, 1999a; and 2005). However, this craft was also hit by changes in fashion and a downturn in the economy due to political upheavals between 1900 and 1921, which was inimical to a trade that mainly served the middle-class. As a result, by 1920 only 35 master painters were left in

PLATE XI

Painting on parchment for book cover.
After R. Baḵtiār, p. 69.

PLATE XII

Needlework on leather hammock, 1976.
After Gluck, p. 239.

Isfahan (Janāb, p. 79). Government support for this traditional craft prevented its disappearance until the expanding economy and the resultant growth of the middle-class re-ignited the market for Isfahan's painters.

As a result, Isfahan is home to professional painters from different schools of painting, from traditional miniature to modern designs that are painted on canvas, bone, ivory, wood, and other materials. The number of

PLATE XIII

Golābduzi on wall hanging material, story of Joseph, 19th century. After Gluck, p. 225.

professional artists—some 100 painters in 28 workshops in the early 1950s (ʿĀbedi, pp. 142-43)—rose noticeably with increasing interest from the growing middle-class residents of the city (cf. Gluck et al., pp. 381-82).

Needlecraft. Isfahan is known to have excelled in a wide variety of needlework that was often produced in the context of home industry. In the late 19th-century list of Taḥwildār, however, we find *zaribāf*, *golābatunduz*, *naqdaduz*, *qollābduz* (nos. 39-42), *naqšduz*, and *dah-yakduz* (nos. 56-57) among the professions practiced in Isfahan.

After a period of decline, the art of embroidery was revived in 1920s in Isfahan where traditional designs were applied to homemade or imported materials in old and new techniques (Wulff, p. 219). In the mid-20th century needlework (*sokmaduzi*, *qollābduzi*, *maliladuzi*, *nakduzi*, etc.) was performed in about 500 homes by individual women, typically widows who would sell their artwork to dealers who were mostly Jewish (ʿAbedi, p. 145; for marketing, see Anṣāri, pp. 137-46). Production has been on the rise in recent decades as national demand has risen for luxurious drapery, tablecloths, bedspreads, and the like. At the same time, imports from South and Central Asia seem to be flooding the domestic market. Older pieces are traded as artifacts that have been handed down from generation to generation in Isfahani families as marriage dowry (see also Gluck et al., pp. 217-35).

Bibliography: Ḥasan ʿĀbedi, *Eṣfahān az leḥāẓ-e ejtemāʿi o eqteṣādi*, Tehran, 1955. Hormoz Anṣāri, *Moqaddama-i bar jāmeʿa-šenāsi-e Eṣfahān*, ed. Aḥmad

Jawāheri, Isfahan, 1990. Habib Borjian, "Az kārvānsarā tā mihmānsarā: Sargoḏašt-e bāzsāzi-e kārvānsarā-ye Mādar-e šāh" *Dāneš-nemā* 84-85 (Architects' Society of Isfahan), 2002, pp. 39-44. Idem and Houri Borjian (text), and Reżā-Nur Baḵtiār (photography), *Abbasi Hotel: Museum Within a Museum* (in English and Persian), Tehran, 1997. A. C. Edwards, *The Persian Carpet. A Survey of the Carpet-Weaving Industry of Persia*, London, 1953. *Farhang-e joḡrāfiāyi-e Irān (ābādihā)* X, 1950, repr. 1976. M.-R. Faryād, *Kārgāh-e ḵātamsāzi o pažuheš-i darbāra-ye ḵātamsāzi dar Irān*, Tehran, 1976. Willem Floor, *Industrialization in Iran: 1900-1941*, University of Durham, Center for Middle Eastern and Islamic Studies, Occasional Paper, no. 23, 1984. Idem, *The Persian Textile Industry, Its Products and Their Use 1500-1925*, Paris, 1999a. Idem, "Art (Naqqashi) and artists (Naqqashan) in Qajar Persia," *Muqarnas* 16, 1999b, pp. 129-58. Idem, "The Art of Smoking in Iran and other uses of tobacco," in *Iranian Studies* 35, 2002, pp. 47-86. Idem, *The Traditional Crafts of Qajar Iran*, Costa Mesa, Cal., 2003. Idem, *Wall Paintings in Qajar Iran*, Costa Mesa, Cal., 2005. Idem, "The Importation of Indigo into Qajar Iran," *Studia Iranica* 35/2, 2006a, pp. 237-59. Idem, "The Woodworking Craft and its Products in Iran," *Muqarnas* 23, 2006b, pp.159-89. H. Gaube and E. Wirth, *Der Bazar von Isfahan*, Beihefte zum Tübinger Atlas des Vorderen Orients (TAVO), Reihe B, no. 22, Wiesbaden, 1978. Jay Gluck, Sumi Hiramoto Gluck, and Carl J. Penton, eds., *A Survey of Persian Handicraft. A Pictorial Introduction to the Contemporary Folk Arts and Art Crafts of Modern Iran*, Tehran, 1977; the Persian edition appeared as *Sayr-i dar ṣanāyeʿ-e dasti-e Irān*, Tehran, 1977. H. Grothe, "Der kalamkār—ein Erzeugnis persischen Kunstgewerbes," *Orientalisches Archiv* 2, 1912, pp. 132-36. Mir Sayyed ʿAli Reżā Janāb, *Ketāb al-Iṣfahān*, Isfahan, 1924. Markaz-e āmār-e Irān, *Saršomāri az kārgāhhā-ye kešvar*, Tehran, 1975. Moḥammad-Mehdi Moḥammad-Reżā al-Eṣfahāni, *Neṣf jehān fi taʿrif al-Eṣfahān*, ed. M. Sotuda, Tehran, 1961. William Ouseley, *Travels in Various Countries of the East*, London, 1825. Thomas Philipp, "Isfahan 1881-1891: A Close-up View of Guilds and Production," *Iranian Studies* 17/4, 1984, pp. 391-411. W. Radimsky, *Industrie-und Gewerbeverhältnisse in Persien*, Vienna, 1909. Mohammad-Ali Soltani-Tirani, *Handwerker und Handwerk in Esfahan: Räumliche, wirtschaftliche und soziale Organisationsformen*, Marburg, 1982. Šurā-ye ʿāli-e barnāmarizi-e ostān-e Eṣfahān, *Gozāreš-e ʿamalkard-e goḏašta waważʿ-e mawjud-e bakšhā-ye eqteṣādi, ejtemāʿi, farhangi-e ostān-e Eṣfahān*, 2 vols., 1983-84. Mirzā Ḥosayn Khan Taḥwildār, *Joḡrāfiā-ye Eṣfahān*, ed. M. Sotuda, Tehran, 1963. Sigrid Westphal-Hellbusch and Ilse Bruns, *Metallgefässe aus Buchara*, Berlin, 1974. E. Wirth, *Der Orientteppich und Europa*, Erlangen, 1976. H. E. Wulff, *The Traditional Crafts of Persia: Their Development, Technology, and Influence on Eastern and Western Civilizations*, Cambridge, Mass., 1966. (The author would like to extend his appreciation to Dr. Willem Floor for his useful suggestions and additions to this article.)

(HABIB BORJIAN and EIr.)

xiv. MODERN ECONOMY AND INDUSTRIES

This sub-section is divided into the following parts:

(1) Modern Economy of the Province.

(2) Industries of Isfahan City.

(1) Modern Economy of the Province

On the whole Isfahan is an average province within Persia in terms of general economic indices: in the year 2000 the province contained 6.5 percent of the population of the nation, 6.3 percent of its GDP, 6.5 percent of its total household expense, and 6.5 percent of its budget and public expenditure (Sāzmān-e barnāma, 1997, XXVII/4; cf. Akbari, p. 86). As elsewhere in Persia, the economic infrastructure of the province remains fairly underdeveloped. Modern highways and railways are limited to the transnational arteries crossing the province. The rural economy remains largely peasant-oriented, utilizing traditional irrigation techniques and rudimentary mechanization. The industrial labor is largely untrained, and higher education has become increasingly superficial and does not provide the basic skills needed for a modern economy.

The distribution of economic activities within the province, with an urbanism of 76 percent, is highly uneven. The oasis of Isfahan, watered by the Zāyandarud, is responsible for nearly half of rural activities, while the other half is spread out across the province. The main disparity, however, is the uneven distribution of modern industries, the bulk of which is located in Isfahan proper in a chain of large agglomerations within a fifty-mile radius of the city. This means that Isfahan ranks as the second most important industrialized region in Iran after Tehran. The only other town of the province with some degree of industrial development is Kāšān. The industries of the city of Isfahan will therefore be treated separately (see 2 below; for uneven provincial distribution of natural resources and population see i and iii above).

Labor force. In the province of Isfahan, as illustrated in Table 1, the labor force shows a continuous growth in the last three decades, corresponding to the remarkable increase in population. Between 1971 and 2001 the labor force (i.e., the economically active population ten years of age and older) grew from 540,000 to 1.36 million, while employment rose from 502,000 to 1.17 million, implying that the unemployment rate rose from 7 to 14 percent. The startling unemployment growth after the Revolution is a result of population explosion, compounded by the influx of war refugees from Ḵuzestān (Hourcade, p. 53), and Afghan immigrants (estimated at between 50,000 and 200,000; see DIASPORA x. AFGHAN REFUGEES IN PERSIA) into the labor market (cf. Anṣāri, pp. 62-63). These developments occurred in spite of a substantial decline in the number of women participating in the work force. In the

Table 1

Population of Isfahan Province 10 years of age and over by Economic Activity, 1971-2001 (in 1,000)

		Economically Active			Economically Inactive			
Year	10 Years of Age & Over	Number*	%Employed	%Unemployed	Number	%Student	%Homemaker	%Other**
1971	1,174	540	93.0	7.0	634	n.a.	n.a.	n.a.
1976	1,491	668	96.5	3.5	823	37.1	54.3	8.6
1986	2,233	882	89.5	10.5	1,351	36.0	55.2	8.8
1991	2,611	985	92.2	7.8	1,626	40.0	51.1	8.9
1996	3,074	1,129	92.0	8.0	1,945	45.7	44.0	10.3
2001	3,565	1,362	86.1	13.9	2,203	44.5	45.5	10.0

*The activity rate could be easily calculated by dividing the population 10 years of age and over by the total economically active population: the rate from 1971 to 2001 would be 46, 45, 39, 38, 37, 38 respectively.
**Including income recipients and other categories.
Sources: *National Census*, Isfahan Province and mid-census surveys, 1971, 1976, 1986, 1991, 1996, 2001 as cited in the following: *AOE*, 1975, p. 10; *SAK*, 1980, pp. 68-88; 1990, pp. 71-73; 2003, pp. 94-97; *GEE*, 1995, pp. 20-23; 1998, pp. 31-33; 2002, pp. 77-83; Sāzmān-e barnāma, 1997, XXVII/4, pp. 5, 73; *SAOE*, 2001, pp. 81-113.

post-revolutionary decade the women's share of employment in the province saw a sharp drop from 18.8 to 9.0 percent from 1976-86; it rose, however, in the next ten years to 14.6 percent. This may readily be explained by unfavorable social policies toward women, especially of the first post-revolutionary decade; the ratio of housekeepers (more than 99 percent women) among the inactive population of the province rose 67 percent in 1976-86, compared with a mere 15 percent growth in the next ten-year period. Not as clear is the cause of the decline of women's share in the rural economy that saw a steady drop from 26.6 to 9.1 percent in 1976-91 (Sāzmān-e barnāma, 1997, XXVII/4, pp. 68-72, 99). The economic inactivity of women contributed to the sizeable drop in the general economic activity rate of the province, from 45 percent before the Islamic Revolution to an average of 38 percent in the post 1979 period (ibid), as listed in Table 1.

Similar to many other provinces, the bulk of the growth in employment has been in the service sector, with an increase from 25.6 percent in 1976 to 42.2 percent in 1986 and further to 46.8 percent in 2002. The service sector employed 591,000 persons in 2000, of which a quarter were active in wholesale, retail, and repair, a fifth in construction, a seventh in transportation and communication, and 2 percent in energy (Akbari, pp. 86-87). Despite a slight change in total employment in the agricultural sector, its share in total employment fell from 31.3 percent in 1971 to 12.2 in 2001. Industrial employment declined after the Revolution, before the trend was reversed in the late 1980s. By 2001, however, it constituted 43.0 percent of the total employment, compared with 50.9 in 1976 (see Table 2). There was also a marked shift to the public sector in the structure of employment. Public employees constituted 37.3 percent of the working population in 1991, up from 20.0 percent in 1976 (Sāzmān-e barnāma, 1997, XXVII/4, pp. 45, 48, 88; *SAOE*, 2001, p. 118; cf. ibid, pp. 112-13) and about 4 percent in 1956 (*Edāra-ye āmār-e omumi*, p. 97). While part of this increase comes from extensive nationalization, much of it is due to the creation of new jobs in the state sector.

Table 2

Employed population of Isfahan Province by major industry groups, 1956-2001

Year	Employed Persons (1,000)	Agriculture (%)	Industries (%)	Services (%)
1956	149	54.2	n.a.	n.a.
1971	502	31.3	60.6	8.1
1976	645	23.5	50.9	25.6
1986	789	21.2	35.3	43.5
1991	908	17.2	35.5	43.9
1996	1,039	14.5	42.1	43.4
2001	1,173	12.2	43.0	44.8

*For each year the percentages do not necessarily add up to 100 because of unknown employment.
**In 1956 Yazd was a part of Isfahan province.
Sources: *National Census*, and mid-census surveys of Isfahan Province: 1971, 1976, 1986, 1991, 1996, 2001 as cited in the following: *AOE*, 1975, p. 11; Sāzmān-e barnāma, 1997, XXVII/4, pp. 26, 42, 59; *GEE*, 1998, pp. 33-35; ibid, 2002, pp. 80, 480; cf. ibid, 1995, p. 22.

In 1996 the district of Isfahan alone constituted 41.0 percent of the total working population of the province, followed by Kāšān, Najafābād, and Ḵomeynišahr with 10.3, 8.0, and 5.6 percent, respectively. The district of Isfahan's share in the service, industrial, and agricultural sectors of the province was 50.3, 37.3, and 21.7 percent, respectively (Sāzmān-e barnāma, 1997, XXVII/4, pp. 16-21, 31-38).

Table 3

Large industrial establishments of Isfahan Province by number of units and employees, 1997

Industries	Number of Units**	Number of Employees (in 1,000)	Percent of Employees*
Textile	533	39.9	35.1
Basic metals	72	24.4	21.5
Non-metallic mineral products	656	18.5	16.2
Chemical products	65	7.7	6.8
Food	127	5.6	4.9
Machinery and military	119	4.6	4.0
Fabric metallic products	126	3.7	3.3
Coal	8	2.4	2.1
Rubber and plastic products	75	2.3	2.0
Other	186	4.5	4.0
Total	1,967	113.6	100.0

* Employees as percent of total Industrial Employment of 113.6 thousand.
** Workshops with 10 employees or more.
Source: Markaz-e āmār-e Irān, 1997.

The industrial units and employment in Isfahan province for the workshops with 10 or more employees in 1997 are shown in Table 3. The total of 1,967 such units employing nearly 114,000 workers constitute 14.1 and 13.0 percent of corresponding national figures, respectively, and rank Isfahan the highest after Tehran among all provinces of Persia (Baḵtiāri, p. 22). The textiles, basic metals, and mineral products each employ more than 10 percent of total industrial employment, and chemicals, food, and machinery industries follow suit in rank. Largest of the units are the two gigantic steel mills (see 2 below), which belong to basic metals industry with an average of 339 employees per unit. The same average was 75 for the textile industry which consists of hundreds of small and medium sized workshops distributed throughout the province and a dozen or so large factories in Isfahan. The overall distribution in terms of number of employees was highly uneven: only 27 units employed more than 500 workers, while over 77 percent of the units had less than 30 employees. The state-owned units were as few as 32, but employed nearly a quarter of the industrial labor force (Baḵtiāri, p. 32; cf. Bank-e Markazi, p. 59).

Water management. The province of Isfahan falls into the arid and semi-arid zones and like much of the Iranian plateau suffers from shortage of water, the most important limiting factor in its agriculture (see i. above). The rainfall in the province is half that of the national average and less than one-sixth of the world average (Wezārat-e kešāvarzi, 1997, p. 1). Due to the low rate of precipitation, dry farming is confined to the western highlands for cultivation of wheat and barley.

In areas away from the streams, subterranean waters were utilized through a system of *qanāt*s, but these have been gradually abandoned due to their costly maintenance (cf. Hartl). In the 1940s power pumps were introduced, and the use of deep and semi-deep wells (30 m and more) as well as pumping from rivers rapidly expanded and gained prevalence. The mechanized wells reach to the rather shallow water tables around the traditional water nuclei, many of which have already been sucked dry; nonetheless, the number of deep and semi-deep wells has been on the rise and by the turn of the century had grown to 6,541 and 14,415, respectively (*SAOE*, 2001, p. 231). Diverting water from rivers has been a major source of irrigation in the lower course of the Zāyandarud river (Cordonnier; ʿĀbedi, p. 78; Ṭalāminā'i, p. 117).

Zāyandarud is the only major river in the province. It irrigates the traditional districts (*boluk*s) of Čahārmaḥāl, Fereydan, Lenjānāt, Mārbin, Jay, Barzrud, Karāraj, Barā'ān, and Rudašt, before entering the Gāvḵuni (q.v.) lagoon. From Safavid times, the stretch of the river downstream from Lenjān has been regulated by an elaborate system, the details of which are found in a document known as the Shaikh Bahā'i's *ṭumār*, dated 923/1527. Its underlying principles are based on the requirements for cultivation and the varying need for water of crops sown in each district. The river waters were allotted according to three distinct property rules, each was further divided on principles based on district, irrigation channels (*mādi*s), and villages. This system underwent alteration in 1936, owing to the fact that, on government orders, the cultivation of cotton was substituted in the lands watered by the river for the cultivation of rice (Taḥwildār, pp. 38-41; Lambton). These legal principles are still essentially in effect with certain modification (ʿĀbedi, pp. 68-73).

In order to increase and control the Zāyandarud's flow, two major projects were carried out in the 20th century through heavy investment by the central government. The first one was the construction of the Kuhrang dam and tunnel system to divert the headwaters of the Kārun into the upper reaches of Zāyandarud, thus stabilizing the water supply of Isfahan and its environs. (An early effort in the Safavid period had failed; see Eskandar Beg I, pp. 949-50) The first Kuhrang diverting tunnel (2.7 km long), constructed in 1948-53, increased the river water by a third to an average annual 1,250 million m^3 (*FJI*, p. 163; ʿĀbedi, pp. 74-76). Since then two more tunnels have been dug, and attempts have been made to modernize the agricultural channels. Moreover, a pipeline carries a share of the water surplus as far as Yazd, now benefiting from the water that would otherwise discharge into the Persian Gulf from the Kārun river. The second major project was the construction of a 100 m high, arched concrete dam, named after Shah ʿAbbās the Great, over the Zāyandarud upstream near Čādagān. The dam became operative in 1971. Its reservoir has a capacity of 1.1 km^3 and controls water for irrigation of 95,000 hectares of land, particularly those of the downstream districts which receive little water during the summer, when it is most needed (Šafaqi, pp. 80, 86; U.S. Department of Commerce, p. 74; *GEE*, 2002, p. 493).

Moreover, several earthen dams are constructed to aid irrigation. The Golpāyagān dam, the first modern dam in the nation, was built in 1957, with a reservoir capacity of 0.45 km^3. Other significant embankment dams are the Ḥanā dam in Semirom and Ḵomirān dam on the Morḡāb near Tirān, west of Isfahan, with 0.45 km^3 and 0.06 km^3 reservoirs, respectively (*GEE*, 2002, p. 493).

Farming. Mountains, barren desert, and desert-steppe that cover the biggest expanse of the province are at best usable only for periodic pasturing. The agriculturally usable land is limited to a twentieth of the total land. The most fertile part of the province is the Zāyandarud valley, with the landscape mostly covered by farms and is still dotted by "pigeon towers" once used for collecting pigeon manure to fertilize melon fields (Wulff, p. 270). The agricultural condition of the Isfahan district in the early 1920s is best summed up by Arthur Chester Millspaugh: "The soil is clay and chalk mixed in some section with fine sand. Alfalfa, clover, and maize are cultivated successfully. The climate is favorable for growing mulberry trees and gape. The inhabitants are penurious, credulous and satisfied. Apples, pears, apricots, and peaches are of remarkable size and flavor, and the quinces and melons are the best in Persia. Tobacco and cotton are also important crops. Rice is also produced in some districts" (Millspaugh, p. 256).

Opium was the only cash crop that contributed substantially to the export trade (idem, pp. 191, 258). Much of the commercial activity in the bazaar in the latter half of the 19th century related to the trade of opium which, as the major cash crop, was cultivated in large quantities around Isfahan, with its export paying for the European industrial imports. "Out of a population of approximately eighty thousand, there were at least five thousand who gained all or a large part of their income through the commerce of opium. These included opium-peddlers, brokers, bazaar traders, commission and export merchants, packers, porters, coppersmiths, and the manipulators of the stick and cake opium. If we assume an average of three dependents, which is low, it will be seem that at least a fourth of the entire population of the city was largely dependent on opium trade. The above figures, moreover, do not include the opium-cultivators resident in or near the city" (Millspaugh, p. 190). The fact that the opium sap was used as a means of exchange instead of cash in many businesses demonstrates the significance of opium for the Isfahan economy. When the government centralized the opium trade by taking over its distribution and imposing taxes on revenue from its cultivation in 1923, the fear of loss of jobs prompted a fierce resistance in Isfahan which manifested itself in rioting and turmoil, but the law was ultimately implemented (idem, pp. 191, 259).

Concomitant with the industrial and social development in the 20th century, the agriculture of the province underwent major changes. Industrial crops saw a rapid growth due to Reza Shah's policy of reducing the country's dependence on external supplies of basic products. To provide raw material for the emerging textile factories, the government ordered in 1936 the substitution of cotton in lieu of rice in the mid-course of the Zāyandarud (Lambton). After World War II, sesame and sunflower acreage was extended for oilseed, which have steadily replaced ghee as part of the staple diet. The cultivation of sugar beet was introduced on a wide scale and rapidly became a prime cash crop in Isfahan. These increasingly replaced the cultivation of opium, which was eventually banned by law in the 1960s. During this period, the agriculture of the province was rapidly commercialized in order to satisfy the growing demands of the national market, and primarily those of Tehran, the recipient of a large portion of the fruits and vegetables farmed in Isfahan. The 1970s saw a remarkable expansion of acreage thanks to improvement in water management, as noted above. In that decade, Isfahan saw the introduction of agribusiness (mechanized agriculture), with at least nine large projects in the province (U.S. Department of Commerce, pp. 37-41; cf. Anṣāri, p. 115). The trend came to a halt after the Islamic Revolution, when conditions were no longer favorable to large private investments. On the other hand, the government after the Revolution accorded high priority to the development of agriculture by allocating resources in the form of credit concessions and highly subsidized supplies of fertilizers and machinery. Consequently, in the decade following the Islamic Revolution, there was a marked growth in farm produce (Tables 4 and 5). The notable rise in the yield of certain crops may have resulted from growing mechanization and the use of fertilizers and pesticides. The trend toward specialization of agriculture has continued in the last three decades and the province now exports to the national market and abroad. Nonetheless, the rural economy has largely remained traditional, with little mechanization. A characteristic of the land holding system in the province has been the prevalence of smallholdings of many scattered plots in its 2,470 villages (*SAOE*, 2002, chapter 2). The total average holding has not changed significantly since the Land Reform Law of 1962; it was 3.8 and 3.4 ha in 1964 and 1993, respectively. More than half of the

Table 4
Production of main Agricultural crops, 1971-2001 (1,000 tons)

Year	1971	1974	1986	1996	2001
Vegetables (potatoes, onions, tomatoes)	107	99	852	876	586
Fodder (sainfoin, alfalfa, clover, corn, etc.)	125	134	571	499	401
Orchard fruits	92	88	306	355	353
Wheat	157	189	441	456	209
Corn	n.a.	n.a.	n.a.	252	273
Melons	120	103	300	281	161
Sugar beets	629	682	529	208	146
Barley	29	37	145	243	113
Rice (paddy)	8	10	20	97	29
Other cereals	4.9	9.5	6.6	10.2	n.a.
Beans	2.2	4.6	8.3	15.9	2.9
Cotton	2.2	3.0	9.3	19.0	n.a.
Tobacco	0.60	0.44	2.70	0.75	n.a.
Oilseeds	0.60**	1.32	0.74	4.78	n.a.

Note: Kāšān is excluded in the figures of the 1970s.
**Excluding sunflower seeds.
Sources: *SAOE*, 1975, pp. 40-49; 1996, pp. 241-44; 2001, p. 141; *AOE*, 1986, pp. 213-27; Wezārat-e kešāvarzi. *Āmār-nāma-ye Kešāvarzi*, 1986, p. 75; *GEE*, 1995, pp. 193-94; 2002, p. 464;

Table 5
Major crops by area of cultivation, 1971-2001 (1,000 hectares)

Year	1971*	1974*	1986	1996	2001
Horticulture	10.7	18.2	50.0	47.2**	56.0
Wheat	91.2	121.0	159.5	132.7	74.4
Fodder (sainfoin, alfalfa, clover, corn, etc.)	13.3	20.6	63.1	62.6	42.3
Barley	20.3	28.7	81.7	70.1	37.9
Vegetables (potatoes, onions, tomatoes)	4.7	6.4	30.2	32.5	26.1
Industrial crops	18.7	24.2	21.4	14.1	13.6
Corn	n.a.	n.a.	n.a.	5.5	7.7
Melons	4.7	8.0	11.6	10.6	6.8
Rice (paddy)	1.8	2.4	4.9	19.5	6.5
Beans	1.9	6.1	5.0	10.0	4.5
Other cereals	1.3	3.4	2.5	4.1	n.a.

*Kāšān is excluded in the figures of the 1970s.
**1995 figure.
Sources: *SAOE*, 1975, pp. 40-49; Wezārat-e Kešāvarzi, 1986, p. 75; *AOE*, 1986, pp. 213-28; *GEE*, 1995, pp. 193-94; 2002, p. 462; *SAOE*, 1996, pp. 241-44; 2001, p. 141.

cultivators hold only 6.5 percent of the land, with an average holding of less than half hectare (*GEE*, 2002, p. 483; Wezārat-e jehād-e kešāvarzi, XIX, p. 55).

Of the 10.7 million hectares surface area of the province, some 600,000 ha are arable. In 2002, 535,000 ha of this was under cultivation or fallow, about half of which (263,000 ha) was under cultivation of irrigated annual crops, while orchards occupied 56,000 ha. The total fallow land was 183,000 ha, 85 percent of which was irrigated cropland. Dry farming (rain-fed crops) constitute some 30,000 ha, less than 6 percent of the total farmland, and is limited to western highlands where wheat and barley are cultivated (*GEE*, 2002, pp. 459-65). Cereal grains constitute the most important crops in the province; in the case of irrigated crops, nearly half of the land under cultivation was devoted to wheat, barley, and rice; in the case of dry farming, wheat and barley occupy 87 percent of the cultivated area. The chief orchard fruits are apples, grapes, pomegranates, cherries, apricots, pears, plums, quince, and peaches, and of the nuts almonds, walnuts, and pistachios rank highest in terms of cultivated land. Among natural plants gum tragacanth (*katirā*) has maintained its high importance (Wezārat-e jehād-e kešāvarzi, p. 37; *GEE*, 2002, p. 487).

Animal husbandry. Both the villagers and nomads have traditionally kept livestock. Sheep and goats prevail in most of the province while cattle is raised in the upper Zāyandarud valley. The Baḵtiāri tribesmen still summer in, and exploit the rich pastures of, the western highlands of the province, though they are no longer the main suppliers of meat and dairy to Isfahan, having never fully recovered from the devastation they suffered during Reza Shah's reign, with the loss of about 60 percent of their livestock (see ix above). The villagers feed their domestic animals partly on fodder, but they also rely heavily on natural pastures, which have been diminishing through overgrazing. Drought years have also been responsible for the substantial fluctuation in the number of livestock (Table 6). The expansion of mechanized stock-breeding has been slow and the contemporary proclivity for cattle over sheep has hardly been successful, though selected breeds of cattle have increasingly replaced native ones (*GEE*, 2002, pp. 468, 483). As for poultry, the progress is more striking (Table 7); scores of mechanized chicken breeding units have been established throughout the province in recent decades. The number of beehives and fish farms has also been growing.

Table 6

Number of Main Livestocks 1966-2003 (in 1,000 heads)

Year	Sheep	Goats	Cattle	Donkeys/ Horses	Camels	Fowl
1966	2,450	1,160	510	302	12	1,761
1968	2,638	1,212	518	283	13	1,758
1971	1,105	616	194	98	14	1,095
1984	3,452	1,469	489	n.a.	15	n.a.
1997*	3,500	900	441	68	10	n.a.
2000	2,401	1,031	398	57	6	n.a.
2001	3,080	1,008	433	52	5	n.a.
2003	1,084	500	273	n.a.	3	n.a.

*Estimate.
Sources: *SAK*, 1967, p. 217; *SAK*, 1970, p. 286; *SAOE*, 1975, p. 56; *Iran Yearbook 1977*, p. 503; *GEE*, 1995, p. 199; *SAOE*, 2001, pp. 148-49; Bank Markazi, p. 49; *GEE*, 2002, p. 468; *SAOE*, 2003, Table 4-10.

Table 7

Livestock Produce 1971-2002 (in 1,000 tons)

Products	1971	1995	2002
Red meat	14	52	50
Poultry meat	n.a.	82	70
Milk	128	461	517
Eggs	3	34	35
Honey	n.a.	2.2	2.7
Wool	0.64	2.74	n.a.

Sources: *AOE*, 1975, p. 67; *Iran Yearbook 1977*, p. 503; *GEE*, 1995, p. 200; 2002, p. 469.

Tourism. The existence of numerous historical monuments in Isfahan has made the city a focal point for tourism in the country. The tourist industry was put into motion by the establishment in 1962 of the Organization for Attracting Tourism (Sāzmān-e jalb-e sayyāḥān) that began to train guides and publish maps and brochures for Isfahan. Much was done to encourage tourism by building hotels, by improving roads and air services, and by publicity. A major project was the restoration of a Safavid caravanserai and its conversion into the luxury Shah ʿAbbās Hotel (Borjian, 2002). Isfahan flourished as a hub of tourism in the late 1960s and the 1970s, attracting domestic and international tourists (cf. Ehlers, 1974).

The war with Iraq brought the tourist industry to a virtual halt. Subsequently, the Islamic regime tried hard to revive the tourist industry by investing in the rehabilitation of the riverbed and banks of Zāyandarud and the expansion of the parks along the river as well as improvements in the Royal Square. This has proved effective for domestic tourism, especially during the Persian New Year spring break, when scores of holidaymakers head south from the capital. International tourism, however, has never returned to its pre-revolutionary levels. Foreign sightseers are few, mostly from poorer nations of Asia, despite the fairly inexpensive cost of vacationing in Isfahan. This is not surprising given the limitations imposed by Islamic Law coupled with security and safety concerns for foreign travelers.

The tourist infrastructure of the city and province remains underdeveloped. In 1993 there were 26 hotels and 43 guesthouses (*mosāferḵāna*) in the Isfahan district, with a total of more than 4,500 beds. Among other districts of the province Kāšān had five inns, Fereydan, Golpāyegān, and Šahreżā had three each, Ardestān, Nāʾin, and Ḵᵛānsār had two each, and Naṭanz had one (Sāzmān-e barnāma wa budja, 1997, XV, pp. 42, 69). In 1996, 279,000 tourists visited Isfahan, of which 7.4 percent came from abroad (ibid, p. 62).

Transportation infrastructure. In spite of Isfahan's central location in Persia, its transportation system has experienced a slow growth and still requires major improvements. The Trans-Iranian Railway, opened in the 1930s, bypassed the province. It was only in 1974, in conjunction with the freight needs of the steel industry, that a line was built to traverse the province some 750 km, extending eastward to meet the Tehran-Kerman line at Yazd (cf. *SAK*, 1982, p. 610; *SAOE*, 2001, p. 299). The only airport of the province is in Isfahan.

The most important highway is the Tehran-Isfahan-Shiraz road that traverses the province longitudinally. Constructed in Reza Shah's reign, following the Safavid caravan route for part of the way, its widening was delayed until recently; yet it remains largely substandard, notwithstanding its significance as a transport artery in the country. This deficiency is partly compensated by a recently completed highway connecting Kāšān to Isfahan, competing with the old Kāšān-Yazd road that bypasses Isfahan. Roadways also connect the city eastward to Yazd and westward to Lorestān, and through the latter Isfahan is ultimately linked with Ḵuzestān. The projected shortcut highway to the latter province through the high Zagros range, planned some years ago, is yet to be realized. The network of countryside roads has, in contrast, improved in the past decades thanks partly to the post-revolutionary efforts of the Rural Development Corps (Jehād-e sāzandegi). In 2002 the province had 78 km of freeways, 1,528 km of major roads, and 2,776 km of minor roads, totaling 4,482 km, with the remarkable growth of 10.7 percent in just one year (Bank-e Markazi, 2004, p. 67 cf. Sāsān, pp. 180-84). In spite of this, the underdeveloped nature of the province's transportation infrastructure becomes evident in the number of highway bridges longer than 20 m; they tallied no more than 15 in 2001 (*SAOE*, 2001, p. 303).

Energy infrastructure. For most of the 20th century the production and consumption of energy in Isfahan was quite limited. The electric plant founded by ʿAṭāʾ-al-Molk and Mirzā Fatḥ-Allāh Khan Dehdašti in the early 1930s was supplanted by a larger turbine plant in the 1950s, using diesel fuel to generate electricity for lighting buildings and streets of Isfahan. There were also generator units at individual factories of the city and in a few other towns of the province (*FJI*, p. 23). The fuel needed for these power plants, as well as for heating, transportation, and industrial consumption, was transported by tankers from refineries in Ḵuzestān and Tehran. To these one may add the traditional supply of coal produced from wood, which ultimately led to the destruction of woodlands after centuries of consumption. Villagers also used watermills to generate mechanical energy.

The situation has altered drastically since the 1970s. A hydroelectric power plant, an oil refinery, and several thermal power plants have been put into production and the newly-built heavy industries have become both suppliers and consumers of energy. Networks of oil and natural gas pipelines and electric transmission lines link the city and the province of Isfahan to other energy producing and consuming areas of Iran. Through these networks Isfahan imports crude oil and natural gas from Ḵuzestān and exports petroleum products and electricity to neighboring provinces. More recently the development of nuclear technology has been in progress, but no serious attempt has been made to harness the immense potentials of solar energy and wind power that exist in abundance throughout the province.

Petroleum. The Isfahan refinery was constructed in the second half of the 1970s by a joint venture of Fluor Iran and the German Thyssen Rheinstahl Technik. Initially designed for a daily output of 200,000 barrels (U.S. Department of Commerce, p. 51), the refinery was expanded in phases, apparently to compensate for the destruction of the Ābādān refinery during the war with Iraq. By 2001 the Isfahan refinery was the largest in the country, producing a quarter of the national output. Its production in 2002 reached 550,000 barrels daily (ca. 20 million m^3 annually); it encompasses a wide variety of petroleum products: propane, gasoline, jet fuel, bunker oil, heating oil, diesel oil, lubricants, and asphalt. Only a third of this output is consumed in the province; the surplus is pumped to the Tehran and Tabriz refineries through pipelines. The crude oil comes from Āqājāri in Ḵuzestān via a 435 km pipeline that crosses the Zagros chain at a maximum altitude of 2,700 m. Thus, Isfahan refinery functions as a point of distribution of oil and gasoline for the country and is supplemented by the largest tank farm reserve in Iran (cf. *GEE*, 2002, p. 417; Baḵtiāri, p. 13; Borjian, 1997; Šerkat-e melli-e naft-e Irān).

Natural gas. The consumption of natural gas has been on the rise in recent decades, increasingly replacing petroleum consumption. In 2002 more than 10.2 km^3 was burned in the province, of which 71 percent was consumed by the industrial sector. The heavy industries, including steel, oil-refining, petrochemical, cement, as well as the thermoelectric plants now receive more than 90 percent of their fuel as natural gas. Households make up 26 percent of the consumption, and this has prompted a whole new generation of locally made room heaters for the internal market. A network of pipelines, both steel and polyethylene, distribute natural gas to more than 110 towns and villages in the province (*GEE*, 2002, p. 434).

Electricity. The chief source of electricity production in the province is thermal energy provided by fossil fuel. Two large power plants generate 80 percent of the total output of 19,000 MWhr (2002 figures). Several more thermal power plants are located in the steel mills and other industrial establishments. The hydroelectric generation capacity of the Shah ʿAbbās dam is only 55 MW, i.e. less than 2 percent of the total electricity output of the province. All these sources feed an integrated network that distributes power among the consumers. Electricity consumption has been growing enormously in the recent past; in 2002 some 4,500 MWhr was consumed in the province. Half of this was used by industry while agriculture and household needs consumed less than a quarter each, and the rest went to general public and commercial use. The surplus production is pumped into the nationwide grid through a system of electricity transmitting towers (*GEE*, 2002, p. 420).

Nuclear. Isfahan is known to be the primary location of the national nuclear program. It began in 1975 when Persia signed an agreement with France to build a nuclear research center in Isfahan in conjunction with the University of Isfahan. The program was interrupted by the Revolution and lack of further assistance from the West; but new sources of technical know-how emerged after the disintegration of the Soviet Union. A facility associated with the Center was opened with Chinese assistance in the mid-1980s near Isfahan. As a stepping-stone to achieve nuclear technology, a uranium conversion and enrichment plant has been established in the facility. Additionally, a uranium enrichment facility using gas centrifuges is under construction near Naṭanz (for further discussion, see Bahgat, pp. 307-27).

Bibliography: Ḥasan ʿĀbedi, *Eṣfahān az leḥāẓ-e ejtemāʿi o eqteṣādi*, Tehran, 1955. Neʿmat-Allāh Akbari, *Barrasi-e taḡyirāt-e kammi-e ešteḡāl dar baḵšhā-ye moḵtalef-e eqteṣādi o čašmandāz-e āyanda-ye ān dar ostān-e Eṣfahān* (a report), Sāzmān-e modiriyat o barnāmarizi-e ostān-e Eṣfahān, 2003. Hormoz Anṣāri, *Moqaddama-ʾi bar jāmeʿa-šenāsi-e Eṣfahān*, ed. Aḥmad Jawāheri, Isfahan, 1990. *ĀOE* (*Āmār-nāma-ye ostān-e Eṣfahān*), Markaz-e āmār-e Irān, Isfahan, annually since 1971. Manṣur ʿAṭāʾi, "Gozāreš-e eqteṣādi darbāra-ye zerāʿathā-ye ostān-e dahom," *Taḥqiqāt-e eqteṣādi*, nos. 9-10, 1964. Gowdat Bahgat, "Nuclear Proliferation: The Islamic Republic of Iran," *Iranian Studies* 39/3, 2006, pp. 307-27. Ṣādeq Baḵtiāri, *Barrasi o taḥlil-e sāḵtār-e ṣanʿat dar ostān-e Eṣfahān o jāygāh-e ān dar eqteṣād-e Irān*, Moʾassesa-ye moṭāleʿāt o pažuheshā-ye bāzargāni, Fayż-Allāh Bakāʾi-Jazi, ed., *Gozāreš-e eqteṣādi o ejtemāʿi-e ostān-e Eṣfahān*, Edāra-ye koll-e omur-e eqteṣādi o dārāʾi-e ostān-e Eṣfahān, 1977. Tehran, 2003. Bank-e Markazi, *Gozāreš-e awżāʿ-e eqteṣādi o ejtemāʿi-e ostānhā-ye kešvar dar sāl-e 1381*, Tehran, 2004. ʿAli-Reżā Baṣiri, ed., *Gozāreš-e awżāʿ-e eqteṣādi-e ostān-e Eṣfahān*, Wezārat-e omur-e eqteṣādi o dārāʾi, n.d. Habib Borjian, "Az kārvānsarā tā mihmān-sarā," *Dāneš-nemā*, nos. 84-85, 2002, pp. 39-44. Houri Borjian, ed., *Eṣfahān šahr-e ṣanʿat o honar*, Tehran, 1997. Jean-Claude Codonnier, "Les tendances nouvelles de l'agriculture irriguée dans l'oasis d'Isfahan," *Révue Géographique de l'Est* 4, 1964, pp. 387-92. Edāra-ye āmār-e ʿomumi, *Āmār dar Irān*, 1/1, Jan. 1960. E. Ehlers, "Some geographic and socio-economic aspects of tourism in Iran," *Orient* 15, 1974, pp. 97-105. Eskandar Beg Torkamān Monši, *Tāriḵ-e ʿĀlamārā-ye ʿAbbāsi*, ed. Iraj Afšār, 2 vols., Tehran, 1955-56. Paridokht Fesharaki, "L'oasis d'Isfahan," Doctoral diss., Univ. de Paris-Sorbonne, 1967. *FJI* (*Farhang-e joghrāfiāyi-e Irān, ābādihā*, X, Tehran, 1950, repr. 1976. *GEE* (*Gozāreš-e eqteṣādi-ejtemāʿi-e ostān-e Eṣfahān*), Sāzmān-e barnāma wa budja-ye ostān-e Eṣfahān, annual report from 1995-2002. M. Hartl, *Das Najafabadtal. Geographische Untersuching einer Kanatlandschaft im Zagrosgebrige (Iran)*, Regensburger Geographische Schriften 12, Regensburg, 1979. Bernard Hourcade et al., *Atlas de l'Iran*, Montpellier-Paris, 1998. *Iran Yearbook 1977*, Kayhan Research Associates, 1977. ʿAli Jawāherkalām, *Joḡrāfiā-ye tāriḵi-e Eṣfahān o Jolfā*, Tehran, 1969. Ann K. S. Lambton, "The regulation of the waters of the Zāyande Rūd," *BSOAS* 9/3, 1937-39, pp. 663-73. Moḥammad Maḥmudiān, *Zāyandarud-e Eṣfahān*, Isfahan, 1969. Markaz-e āmār-e Irān, *Natāyej-e āmārgiri az kārgāhhā-ye ṣanʿati-e kešvar*, Tehran, 1997. C. Millspaugh, *The American Task in Persia*, New York, 1925. Xavier de Planhol, "L'oasis d'Isfahan d'après P. Fesharaki," *Revue Géographique de l'Est* 9, 1969, pp. 391-96. Moḥsen Renāni et al., *Gozāreš-e nehāyi-e ṭarḥ-e pažuheši: Barrasi-e sāḵtār-e ešteḡlāl dar bakš-e ḡayr-e rasmi-e ostān-e Eṣfahān* (report), Sāzmān-e modiriyat o barnāmarizi-e ostān-e Eṣfahān, 2004. Sirus Šafaqi, *Joḡrāfiā-ye Eṣfahān*, Isfahan, 1974. *SAK* (*Sāl-nāma-ye āmāri-e kešvar*), Markaz-e āmār-e Irān, various years. *SAOE* (*Sāl-nāma-ye āmāri-e ostān-e Eṣfahān* [substituted *Āmār-nāma-ye ostān-e Eṣfahān*]), Markaz-e āmār-e Irān, annual report, 1975-2003. ʿAbd-al-Ḥosayn Sāsān, *Eqteṣād-e jābajāgari o pažuheši dar rāhhā-ye ostān-e Eṣfahān*, Tehran, 1985. Sāzmān-e barnāma wa budja-ye ostān-e Eṣfahān, *Barnāma-ye ʿomrāni-e ostān-e Eṣfahān*, reports from 1973 to 1991. Idem, *Moṭāleʿāt-e tawseʿa-ye eqteṣādi, ejtemāʿi o farhangi-e ostān-e Eṣfahān*, 2nd ed., 27 vols., 1997. Šerkat-e melli-e naft-e Irān, *Pālāyešgāh-e Eṣfahān*, Tehran, 1992. Brian Spooner, "City and river in Iran: Urbanization and irrigation of the Iranian Plateau," *Iranian Studies* 7, 1974, pp. 681-713. Šurā-ye ʿāli-e barnāmarizi-e ostān-e Eṣfahān, *Gozāreš-e ʿamalkard-e gozašta waważʿ-e mawjud-e bakšhā-ye eqteṣādi, ejtemāʿi o farhangi-e ostān-e Eṣfahān*, 2 vols., Isfahan, 1983-84. Mirzā Ḥosayn Khan Taḥwildār, *Joḡrāfiā-ye Eṣfahān*, ed. M. Sotuda, Tehran, 1963. Aṣḡar Ṭalāmināʾi, *Taḥlil-i az vižagihā-ye manṭaqaʾi dar Irān bar asās-e manṭaqa-ye nemuna-ye Eṣfahān*, Tehran, 1974. U. S. Department of Commerce, *Iran: Country Market Sectoral Survey (A survey of U.S. Business Opportunities)*, Washington, D.C., 1977. Wezārat-e jehād-e kešāvarzi *Moṭāleʿāt-e santez-e ostāni-e tarḥ-e jāmeʿ-e tawseʿa-ye kešāvarzi*, Mohandesin-e mošāver-e Jāmeʿ-e Irān, 19 vols., Tehran, 2001. Wezārat-e Kešāvarzi, *Āmār-nāma-ye Kešāvarzi*, 1986. Idem, *Moṭāleʿāt-e jāmeʿ-e ehyāʾ o tawseʿa-ye kešāvarzi o manābeʿ-e ṭabiʿi-e ḥawżahā-ye ābkiz-e rudḵānahā-ye Zāyandarud o Ardestān*, a report prepared by Mohandesin-e mošāver-e yekom, Tehran, 1997. H. E. Wulff, *The Traditional Crafts of Persia: Their Development, Technology, and Influence on Eastern and Western Civilizations*, Cambridge, Mass., 1966.

(HABIB BORJIAN)

(2) Industries of Isfahan City

The stagnation experienced after the fall of the Safavids was even more marked in the 19th century owing to European competition that had rendered many local industries such as textiles and the manufacture of arms and weapons practically extinct, leaving much of the bazaar industries deserted (Philipp). In the early 1900s, the industries of Isfahan were still steeped in tradition. Small establishments, pre-industrial in nature, were the norm in the manufacturing sector, and were mostly organized into guilds that were concentrated in the bazaar. In 1924 there were 9,555 traditional craftsmen in Isfahan engaged in the following trades and industries: metalwork 1,183, woodwork 220, building and ceramics 317, textile and leather 1,354, food and agro-industry 1,412, transport 370, services and trade 4,784 (Matin-Daftari, p. 30; apud Floor, 1984, p. 12).

Beginning with an overview of the main periods of industrial development in the city of Isfahan, this article will discuss the major modern industries of the city.

AN OVERVIEW OF THE MAIN PERIODS

The Reza Shah period. After the coup of 1921, the government took measures to protect home industries and provide investors with incentives to start new enterprises. The 1923 government decree compelling officials to wear only Persian-made clothes and the 1925 law exempting industrial machinery from import duties for ten years had a positive impact on the local industry: by 1932 a large textile mill, an electric plant for generating electricity, and five cigarette factories had been established by private capital (Floor, 1984, p. 47). The big change, however, came in the mid-1930s, in the form of Reza Shah's protectionist policy, which safeguarded the growth of home industries by setting high tariffs on imports of foreign merchandise and making bank loans and trade credit available to investors (Wilber, p. 134; Sayfpur, pp. 901-4). As a result of these state directed measures, many new factories were built in the country with Isfahan enjoying a substantial share. In the period 1934-38 alone eleven spinning and weaving mills, one hosiery, one boot making, two paper, and one match factory were established with private capital (Floor, 1984, pp. 30, 59). According to a British Foreign Office document "nearly every section of the population of Isfahan and its districts has invested some, if not all of its savings" (FO 371/20050, *Report on Economic Conditions of Esfahan in October 1936*, f. 128, apud Floor, 1984, p. 24). The greater part of the investment in these new ventures was derived from the immense wealth accrued by the affluent merchants through foreign trade, particularly that of opium.

By the end of Reza Shah's reign, Isfahan was an industrial city, highly specialized in textile manufacture and its accessories. The industrial labor encompassed 11,000 textile workers plus those employed in modern factories manufacturing paper, matches, cigarettes, and footwear, the electric plant, and the state-owned grain silo (Floor, 1984, p. 59). Assuming an average of three dependents, as did Arthur Chester Millspaugh in his calculations (see above, 1, under Farming), one finds that a quarter of the city inhabitants (about 210,000) were dependent for their livelihood on the newly established industries. Perhaps most of these wage earners belonged to the same families who were engaged in the opium business just prior to the reign of Reza Shah.

Moḥammad Reza Shah period. From the 1940s through the mid-1960s the consumer good industries grew through private investments, but the textile industry still retained its unique position and vital importance in the economic life of the city. The politically unsettled 1940s were, however, a period of industrial decline for Isfahan. Many new plants were forced to curtail their operations or to shut down completely, largely due to shortages of raw materials and spare parts caused by the war. On the other hand, this situation created an impetus for the redevelopment of small-scale industries, especially textiles and carpet, which continued to be the biggest source of employment in the urban and rural areas. These circumstances changed in the 1950s, when the textile industry of Isfahan began to flourish again (Floor, 1984, p. 18).

Having made a fortune as textile mill owners, the Hamadānián brothers (q.v., Supplement online) emerged as the city's major entrepreneurs. They also diversified their interests by establishing a large cement factory in 1959 to meet the growing demand for the ongoing construction projects. This new venture proved highly lucrative, returning a 60 percent yield of the initial capital to the investors within only two and half years of operation (Musawi-Fereydani, ch. 3). The brothers also opened a sugar refinery, which together with the cement and two textile mills that they owned (Ṣanāyeʿ-e pašm and Šahnāz) employed 8,000 workers in the 1960s, i.e. about a tenth of the entire workforce of the city (idem, *passim*).

The Land Reform Law of 1962 encouraged the traditional landowner-merchants of Isfahan to invest in the industrial sector, mostly in agricultural and food-processing industries, but also in assembly and capital-intensive industries such as non-metal mineral products (cf. Ministry of Industry and Mines, 1959, pp. 159-63; Ministry of Economy, 1968, pp. 15-21).

In the following decades, Isfahan flourished as a major industrial hub of the nation with a marked growth of heavy industries. In the late 1960s and the 1970s, the government invested heavily in steel, cement, defense, and oil-refining and petrochemical industries. These were supplemented by the expansion of transportation, oil and gas pipelines, energy, and irrigation infrastructure of the city and province. The private sector continued to invest in consumer goods and plastic and chemical industries (USDP, pp. 46-47).

The Post-Revolution period. Industrial production in Isfahan, as elsewhere in Iran, went through a period of stagnation in the post-revolutionary years, but the growth resumed after the end of the war with Iraq, with the introduction in 1988 of successive five-year economic plans. Ever since, Isfahan has seen a substantial growth in the steel industry; the hightech industries such as aircraft assembly and nuclear facilities have been expanded; textile manufacturing has been revitalized and synthetic fabrics have achieved a high production; the making of cement and other construction materials as well as processed food and other consumer goods have remained significant; the chemical and pharmaceutical, leather, and machine production are all expanding, while certain older industries such as the garment industry, wood and paper, and glass have experienced a marked decline (cf. Baḵtiāri, p. 197). To increase industrial efficiency, more than ten industrial townships (*šahrak-e ṣanʿati*) have been established outside major towns near Isfahan.

Overall, in the course of the 20th century the center of gravity of the nation shifted from the northwest, where Tabriz had gained importance as the entrepot for European trade and industries, to other parts of Persia, so much so that, by the turn of the century, the cities of Tabriz, Mashad, Isfahan, and, to a lesser degree, Shiraz were in equal footing after the invincible standing of Tehran.

TEXTILE

A dozen or so large textile factories that were financed by private investment in the reign of Reza Shah were the economic mainstay of Isfahan for most of the remaining years of the 20th century. Textile manufacturing was a natural and obvious choice for modern industrial development in Isfahan; it had been the basis of the town's industry for many centuries, though it had sharply declined since the mid-19th century, when Persian textiles suffered under the devastating onslaught of European imports (Philipp; Floor, 1999, pp. 98-127). The "satisfactory fact that Manchester . . . [was] the universal clothier of Isfahan" (Curzon, p. 41) would obviously be perceived as a disgraceful setback by the reform-minded merchants and clerics of Isfahan who were striving to reinstate the indigenous textile industry by founding societies such as Anjoman-e šarqi and Anjoman-e eslāmi. Led by the pioneering entrepreneur Ḥājji Moḥammad-Ḥosayn Kāzeruni, the leading merchants of Isfahan launched the companies Eslāmiya and Masʿudiya in the last years of the 19th century; Eslāmiya manufactured and sold cloth but eventually the enterprise failed (Jamālzāda, p. 98; Najafi, pp. 31-33; Floor, 1984, p. 31; Ašraf, pp. 100-101). Notwithstanding these failures, the endeavor began to be rewarded when the state economy under Reza Shah began to provide extensive support for domestic industries. By the end of his reign, the aspiration of the previous generation of industrialists to bestow Isfahan with the epithet *dār al-ṣanāyeʿ* had been largely realized, as Isfahan became known as the Manchester of Persia. In economic terms, however, these factories were really profitable only for a short while; in the long period of decline after the early boom the survival of the industry was guaranteed only by state intervention. More recently, spinning and weaving of wool and cotton have partly yielded to syntactic fiber, a petrochemical product. Taken as a whole, however, Isfahan's textile industry not only offered employment to many residents but also acted as a catalyst for transforming the socioeconomic fabric of the city from a pre-industrial town to a modern metropolis and set the city on the road towards modernization.

A pioneer attempt in the modern textile industry of Isfahan was Waṭan, the third modern textile factory established in Persia, founded in 1921 by the notable industrialist ʿAṭāʾ-al-Molk Deheš. The setting up of the factory itself proved a challenging task as its machinery had to be transported from Germany by road through a mountainous track via Hamadān, and this took several years. But the ideological drive for domestic manufacture was so high that even with its incomplete modern equipments the factory could boast that it was the first in the country to supply woolen cloth and blankets to the home market. Even when all the necessary machinery had been acquired, the factory was unable to compete commercially with foreign goods, and this in spite of the fact that it was taken over by such a shrewd entrepreneur as Moḥammad-Ḥosayn Kāzeruni. Its survival was critically dependent on government support by both direct financial assistance and governmental directives compelling officials to wear clothes made of domestic cloth (Millspaugh, p. 264). On the anniversary of his coronation in 1930, the king spoke warmly to Kāzeruni, remarking that his factory was the source of the woolen clothes and uniforms that the senior officials were wearing at the ceremony. A few years later the shah paid a visit to the factory in his trip to Isfahan (Wilber, p. 134; Floor, 1984, pp. 16 f.; ʿĀbedi, p. 87; Sayfpur, p. 958).

As a result of the government policy of self-reliance and protectionism, Isfahan witnessed an industrial surge in textiles from 1934-38, when the national industrialization drive was at its peak. The spinning and weaving mills Risbāf, Zāyandarud, Naḵtāb, Ṣanāyeʿ-e pašm, Šahreżā, Barq Deheš (later renamed Nur), Pašmbāf, Etteḥād-e Šahreżā, and Raḥimzāda were launched. They were built in a specially designated industrial suburb on the south bank of the Zāyandarud along the Upper Čāharbāḡ Avenue. The machinery was imported first from England and later from Germany, and was run by German technicians and managers (Sayfpur, pp. 838-40). All these factories were private ventures with a broad investment base; the middle classes could afford the shares, which were issued in small denominations of 1,000 rials. It achieved widespread popularity thanks to the high rates of return and dividends to shareholders (Floor, 1984, pp. 24-25). Nevertheless, by 1936 the danger of overproduction was already imminent, and after 1938 the incentive to start new factories diminished due to the real fear of overproduction as well as governmental attempts to limit profits by introducing new tariffs, which increased the level of duties on most imports (Bharier, p. 174). At any rate, the goal of gaining economical independence in textiles had been achieved by the end of Reza Shah's reign: the import of woolen textiles dropped six fold in just seven years to 124 tons in 1941 (Zāhedi, p. 39; ʿĀbedi, pp. 83-84).

Reza Shah's reign was followed by a period of decline and uncertainty. While some of the factories that were under efficient management were quite successful during World War II, the town's textile industry suffered because government control on imports diminished and cheaper, higher quality commodities flooded the home market. The difficulties over importation of machinery halted the expansion of the industry and left some factories unfinished. These problems were compounded by the lack of spare parts, the withdrawal of the German technicians and managers, and the unprofessional conduct of the *bāzāri* supervisors, factors that adversely affected those factories that were still operating (ʿĀbedi, pp. 107-8; Agah, p. 210; Sayfpur, p. 840). The demands of organized labor, widespread strikes, and vandalism sporadically paralyzed the textile mills. Several factories closed down in spite of state assistance, while those that were still operating experienced financial crises (ʿĀbedi, pp. 59-60, 108). Even in the following decades the survival of the textile factories in the times of hardship was dependent on government subsidies, injection of capital, and state contracts (Floor, 1984, p. 17; ʿĀbedi, p. 87). Some factories eventually came under the direct control of the banks and the state (Sayfpur, p. 840).

The early 1950s was a period of industrial recovery. New factories such as Šahnāz, Nāhid, and Najafābād were built, and the country actually became an exporter of textiles (ʿĀbedi, pp. 109-22, 136-37). A successful factory was Šahnāz; it was owned by the Hamadāniān brothers and grew to become one of the largest in the country by producing 120,000 m^2 of textile daily and employing 5,500 personnel (Musawi-Fereydani, ch. 2). In the mid-1960s nearly half of the national textile production came from Isfahan, where 25 ginning, spinning, and weaving mills employed 18,000 to 20,000 workers, while six of them had over 1,000 workers each. The raw wool came from Kermān, Khorasan, and Ḵuzestān and the cotton from Khorasan and other northern provinces. In addition, merino wool was imported from Australia and raw materials for artificial fibers from Germany, Italy and Switzerland (*Camb. Hist. Ir.* I, p. 107; USDP, pp. 233 ff.; see also Kortum).

The cottage textile industry outlasted the large modern mills. In the 1950s and 1960s there were 25-30,000 traditional handlooms in the Isfahan region, with a daily production of 300,000 m^2, operated in houses and small textile shops. These could survive by producing cheap cloth for rural consumption. They employed throughout the province more than 100,000 workers on low wages and below the poverty line. A successful campaign was launched in the early 1950s to modernize the machinery and organize the workers in the Šerkat-e taʿāwoni-e dastbāfān-e Eṣfahān (ʿĀbedi, pp. 146-53; Bahrāmi, p. 452; *FJI*, p. 28). Many small textile shops equipped with modern machinery continue to operate in Isfahan to this date.

Notwithstanding the relative decline of the textile industry using natural fibers (cotton and wool), in the late 1970s a large synthetic-fiber factory named Polyacryl Iran Corporation was established in Isfahan, in partnership with E. I. Du Pont de Nemours and Co. (USA). In the late 1990s its five production plants manufactured 70,000 metric tons of polyester and acryl staple, yarn, and tops, i.e., nearly 80 percent of the national production of man-made fiber. The dependence on the import of raw materials has been increasingly reduced through the expansion of the petrochemical industry (USDP, pp. 51, 240; Borjian, 1997; cf. *GEE*, 2002, p. 508).

STEEL

After several unsuccessful attempts in establishing the steel industry in Iran, in 1966 an agreement was reached with the Soviet Union to build a steel mill near Isfahan. The site was established at the villages of Čamgardān and Varnāmḵᵛāst, 50 km southwest of the city, which benefited not only from its ready access to a steady supply of water from Zāyandarud, but also from the existing pool of manpower from the densely-populated valley of Zāyandarud, including the city of Isfahan itself. These advantages overruled the alternative of relocating the steel mill to a site closer to the sources of its essential raw materials, i.e., coking coal deposits north of Kermān and iron ore mines of Bāfq, between Kermān and Yazd (Golubev; USDP, pp. 196 ff.). Moreover, the site of Čamgardān met the environmental concerns against possible pollution as the Šāhkuh range acts as a natural barrier for the city (Knübel; cf. Brücher and Kerby).

The National Steel Company was formed to develop and operate the Āryāmehr steel mill (ASM). The construction of the four production units of ASM began in the late 1960s and its smelting plant began production in 1971. Since then the mill has gone through several phases of expansion. The production of the ASM began with a 1,033-m^3 blast furnace having the production capacity of 1,600 tons of pig iron a day, two 80-ton converters, and a continuous casting unit with the capacity to produce 550,000 tons of primary steel products annually. The plant's rolling mills produced steel rods, bands, rails, and various shapes of structural steel (USDP, pp. 175-76). The output of raw steel rose from 400,000 tons to 2 million tons from 1971-98. In addition to producing iron alloys, the plant has two rolling factories with a production capacity of nearly 900,000 tons per annum (Tawḥidi, p. 209; Baḵtiāri, p. 13).

The ASM had a significant impact on the socioeconomic development of the region. It was interlinked with many auxiliary industries, including those feeding it (energy and mining of coal and iron deposits) and those that further developed its products (rolling of steel and semi-fabricated and finished metal products) and byproducts or refuse (chemicals, cement, etc.; USDP, pp. 185-86; Tawḥidi, pp. 26 ff.). The steel complex also encouraged the growth of related industries such as the manufacturing of pipes and mechanical and electrical appliances. Moreover, its transport requirements led to the construction of a railway connecting the mill to the national railway network and of a freeway between the plant and Isfahan. To provide housing for the 10,000 employees of ASM (1975), the nearby town of Āryāšahr (later renamed Pulādšahr) was built on a modernistic radial plan. It was designed to accomodate 50,000 to 80,000 residents, with an ultimate capacity of 300,000 ("Āriāšahr;" Farāsat; cf. Schafaghi, 1975). The neighboring settlements also expanded, most notably the village of Riz, which developed into the present Zarrinšahr with a population above 50,000.

Another large steel complex is Mojtamaʿ-e fulād-e Mobāraka, the biggest industrial project in the country. The complex had initially been designed by a European-American consortium for Bandar ʿAbbās but was eventually built on 35 sq km of terrain near the village of Mobāraka, located 15 km southeast of Zarrinšahr. It had the clear advantage of proximity to the ASM, the source of the raw steel which is then rolled in Mobāraka into steel sheets, plates, rods, and structural profiles of various sizes. These products are used in a large number of different industries, from canning to buildings and machinery (Tawḥidi, pp. 264-71). The production of Mobāraka steel complex began in 1992 and gradually expanded, under a contract with three Italian companies, to an annual output of 4 million tons by the end of the decade (Baḵtiāri, p. 14; Borjian).

The two steel plants in Isfahan together with those in Ḵuzestān and the emerging plants elsewhere have in recent years been producing around 8 million tons of steel annually, which constitutes a meager one-percent share in the world steel production and ranks Iran in the region of 20th worldwide. Yet Iran still needs to import one third of its total domestic consumption that amounts to more than 12 million tons per annum and is increasing rapidly due to the boom in the construction sector (from various Internet sources).

OTHER MAJOR INDUSTRIES

Construction materials. The massive construction projects near Isfahan, like those of the steel mills and dams, necessitated the local production of cement. The first cement factory in Isfahan, owned by the Isfahan Cement Company (Šerkat-e simān-e Eṣfahān), was initiated by the entrepreneur, ʿAli Hamadāniān, who had realized the potential of the market and the availability of minerals. Inaugurated in 1958, it continued to expand in several phases, but was denied further expansion when another, apparently competing, cement factory was built by the government (Musawi-Fereydani, ch. 3). The latter was the Āryāmehr cement plant (now Simān-e Sepāhān), established in conjunction with the ASM, the iron blast furnace of which provided part of the substances consumed in the cement manufacturing process (Sarlak; cf. Pösch). In recent years the annual output of these factories have been 650,000 tons and 2 million tons, respectively. Together, they produce 15 percent of the national cement production (Baḵtiāri, p. 13).

Other major construction materials produced for the national market are tiles, with an average annual production of 6 km^2 (ibid.), and building stones, part of it for export. For local supply, bricks and concrete are made in large amounts to cater for the ever-growing urban construction demands. The fabrication of construction supplies has grown enormously in later years, for rural adobe structures are systematically being replaced with those made from modern materials.

Food processing. Food industries of Isfahan are nationally important and generally belong to the private sector. The vegetable oil from sesame, sunflower, and other seeds was extracted traditionally by large wooden press mechanisms, the last one of which was operating in the bazaar of Isfahan as late as the late 1950s ("Time catches up with Iran bazaar," *New York Times*, 7 Nov. 1961, p. 19). The technology began to modernize after World War II and modern plants were launched in the areas of seed production in the vicinity of Isfahan. The most outstanding plant, Nāz, supplies vegetable oil for the home market. Near Isfahan there are two large sugar refineries processing sugar beetroot. The first was established in 1961 in Ḵᵛorāsgān, east of Isfahan, with a daily beetroot intake of 4,000 tons. The second, initiated by Šerkat-e sahāmi-e qand-e Naqš-e jahān, was built in Dehsorḵ, 40 km south of Isfahan, with Polish assistance. Its output is a third of the one in Ḵᵛorāsgān (Musawi-Fereydani, ch. 4). Their total production of sugar reached 53,000 tons in 1971 (*Iran Yearbook 1977*, p. 504). The horticulture industry revived as dried fruits became a major Persian export. There are many small plants in Isfahan drying grapes for raisins, apricots, figs, mulberry, etc. More recently, canned fruits, jams, lemon and other fruit juice, and tomato paste have been made for the domestic market. Staple industries supplying local consumers are numerous. They include flour-mills and other cereal processing, poultry and livestock meat processing, milk pasteurizing, bottling soft drinks, etc. (Wezārat-e Jehād-e Kešāvarzi, XIX, pp. 49 ff.).

Aviation and defense industries. Isfahan is a major center for the nation's defense industry. These were established, with American and European assistance, in the 1950s-70s. They provided services and repairs and assembled aircrafts, tank overhaul, canons, and other weaponry and munitions. The most well-known complex is Hesa, originally an acronym for *Helicopter-sāzi-e Irān*, now *Ṣanāyeʿ-e havāpeymā-sāzi-e Irān*. Currently, it assembles, with Ukrainian technical assistance, the small passenger aircraft Iran-140 (originally Antonov-140). After the Revolution, the North Koreans and the Chinese assisted in the development of defense industries, which encompass a ballistic missile production facility.

Petrochemicals. Linked to the Isfahan refinery (see 1 above) is a petrochemical plant, which began operation in 1992. Its products (benzene, toluene, orthoxylene, paraxelene, and mixed xylems) are used in downstream line for production of aromatics, detergents, plastics, polyester fiber, paints, among others. The plant has a capacity of 193,000 tons per annum (Company brochure; cf. *GEE*, 2002, pp. 417-24; Baḵtiāri, pp. 13-14).

Bibliography: Ḥasan ʿĀbedi, *Eṣfahān az leḥāẓ-e ejtemāʿi o eqteṣādi*, Tehran, 1955. Manuchehr Agah, "some aspects of economic development of modern Iran," D.Phil. diss., Oxford University, 1958. "Āryāšahr: šahr-e pulādsāzān-e Irān," *Buletan-e māhāna-ye kārḵāna-ye Āryāmehr* 2/4, 1970, pp. 15-20. Aḥmad Ašraf (Ashraf), *Mawāneʿ-e tāriḵi-e rošd-e sarmāyadāri dar Irān*, Tehran, 1980. Taqi Bahrāmi, *Joḡrāfiā-ye kešāvarzi-e Irān*, Tehran, 1954. Ṣādeq Baḵtiāri, *Barrasi o taḥlil-e sāḵtār-e ṣanʿat dar ostāne Eṣfahān o jāygāh-e ān dar eqteṣād-e Irān*, Moʾassesa-ye moṭāleʿāt o pažuheshā-ye bāzargāni, Tehran, 2003. J. Bharier, *Economic Development in Iran: 1900-1970*, Oxford, 1971. Houri Borjian, ed., *Eṣfahān šahr-e sanʿat o honar*, Tehran, 1997. W. Brücher and Wilfried Kerby, "Zur standortfrage von integrierten Hüttenwerken in aussereuropäischen Entwicklungsländern—Die Beispiele Aryamehr/Iran und Paz del Rio/Kolumbien," *Geographische Zeitschrift* 67, 1979, pp. 77-94. George N. Curzon, *Persia and the Persian Question*, London, 1892. Jamšid Farāsat-Šariʿatpanāhi, "Āriāšahr: šahr-e kārkonān-e sanāyeʿ-e mādar," *Pulād-e Irān*, Ḵordād-Tir 1352 Š./1973, pp. 36-43. *FJI: Farhang-e joghrāfiāyi-e Irān (ābādihā)* X, 1950. Willem Floor, *Industrialization in Iran: 1900-1941*, University of Durham, Center for Middle Eastern and Islamic Studies, Occasional Paper, no. 23, 1984. Idem, *The Persian Textile Industry in Historical Perspective: 1500-1925*, Paris, 1999. *GEE* (*Gozāreš-e eqteṣādi-ejtemāʿi-e ostān-e Eṣfahān*), Sāzmān-e barnāma wa budja-ye ostān-e Eṣfahān, per annum for the years 1995-2002. Sergii Golubev, "Mineral raw material resources of the

Aryamehr steel plant," *Pulād-e Irān* 1/1, Esfand 1351 Š./1973, pp. iii-ix. *Iran Yearbook 1977*, Kayhan Research Associates, 1977. Moḥammad-ʿAli Jamālzāda, *Ganj-e Šāyegān*, Berlin, 1917, repr. Tehran 1983. ʿAli Kalbāsi, *Eqteṣād-e šahr-e Eṣfahān*, unpublished diss., Tehran University, 1974. H. Knübel, "Das erste Eidenhüttenwerk im Iran bei Isfahan," *Geographische Rudschau* 23, 1971, pp. 368-70. Gerhard Kortum, "Geographische Grundlagen und Entwicklung der Iranischen Textilindustrie," *Orient* 2, 1972, pp. 68-74. A. Matindaftari, *Kalid-e esteqlāl-e eqteṣādi-e Irān*, Tehran, 1925. A. C. Millspaugh, *The American Task in Persia*, New York, 1925. Ministry of Economy (Ministry of Industry and Mines, from 1972), Bureau of Statistics, *Iranian Industrial Statistics*, (published annually beginning in 1968). Ministry of Industry and Mines, *Industry and Mines Statistical Yearbook*, Tehran, 1957-60. Moḥammad-ʿAli Musawi-Fereydani, *Do barādar o yek ārezu: Zendagināma-ye bonyāngoḏārān-e ḵayriya-ye ʿAli o Ḥosayn-e Hamadāniān*, unpublished manuscript, 2005. Musā Najafi, *Andiša-ye siāsi o tāriḵ-e nahżat-e Ḥāj Aqā Nur-Allāh-e Eṣfahāni*, 2nd ed. Tehran, 1999. Ḥosayn Nurṣādeqi, *Eṣfahān*, Tehran, 1937. Thomas Philipp, "Isfahan 1881-1891: A Close-up View of Guilds and Production," *Iranian Studies* 17/4, 1984, pp. 391-411. H. Pösch, "Ausweitung der Zementindustrie im Iran," *Zement-Kalk-Gips* (Wiesbaden), no. 28, May 1975, pp. 177-88. Maḥmud Qanāʾi, "Ważʿ-e fulādsāzi dar Irān," *Pulād-e Irān*, no. 6, Mordād 1352 Š./1973, pp. 18-21. ʿAlireżā Sarlak, "Sarbāra-ye kura-ye boland o teknōlōži-e mawādd," *Pulād-e Irān*, no. 10-11, Āzar-Dey 1353 Š./1975, pp. 3-7. Naṣr-Allāh Sayfpur Fāṭemi, *Āʾina-ye ʿebrat*, 2nd ed., Tehran, 1999. S. Schafaghi, "Ariashahr. Die neue Eisenhüttenstadt bei Isfahan," *Zeitschrift für Wirtschaftsgeographie* 19, 1975, pp. 190-94. Nāṣer Tawḥidi, *Sayr-e takāmoli-e tawlid-e āhan o fulād dar Irān o jahān*, Tehran, 1985. USDP (U.S. Department of Commerce), *Iran: Country Market Sectoral Survey (A survey of U.S. Business Opportunities)*, Washington, D.C., 1977. Wezārat-e jehād-e kešāvarzi, *Moṭāleʿāt-e santez-e ṭarḥ-e jāmeʿ-e tawseʿa-ye Kešāvarzi*, 19 vols., Tehran, 2001. D. Wilber, *Riza Shah Pahlavi: The Resurrection and Reconstruction of Iran, 1878-1944*, Hicksville, NY, 1975. ʿAli Zāhedi, *Ṣanāyeʿ-e Irān baʿd az jang*, Tehran, 1944.

(HABIB BORJIAN)

XV. EDUCATION AND CULTURAL AFFAIRS

(1) Education.
(2) Cultural Affairs.

(1) Education

Foreign schools. The presence of European educators in Isfahan dates as far back as the reign of Shah Abbas I, when the Carmelites (q.v.) were permitted to open a school for the education of the children of foreign residents in the city (Pietro Della Valle [q.v.] apud Falsafi, III, pp. 68-72). Not until the mid-19th century, however, did Christian missionaries resume their activities in the city. The schools opened in Isfahan by the French Catholics and British Anglicans were often in stiff competition with each other.

French schools. Educational activities by the French began in Qajar Persia through the efforts of a devout Roman Catholic layman, Eugène Boré (1809-78). He successfully established a school in Tabriz in 1839, in competition with the American Protestant missionaries who had already established themselves in northwestern Persia. Having obtained permission to open schools in Persia on the strength of an edict issued in April 1840 by Moḥammad Shah Qajar, Boré opened a school in Isfahan in the same year. To compete with the American missionaries in attracting native students, Boré excluded religious instruction in his school; the four-year curriculum consisted of French, Persian, arithmetic, geography, and philosophy. Of the total of 31 students enrolled in the Isfahan school, five were Muslims and the rest Armenians. Notwithstanding the good reputation Boré had gained and his insistence on a secular curriculum, he encountered severe opposition from the Armenian Church as well as from the ulema, and he was eventually forced to close the school and leave the town. Nevertheless Boré persuaded the French Lazarist Catholics to come to Isfahan (*Yadgār* 3/6-7, 1947, pp. 60-66 Ringer, pp. 113-21; Nāṭeq, pp. 160-63; Hāj Sayyāh, p. 60; CHRISTIANITY viii. CHRISTIAN MISSIONS IN PERSIA).

The Lazarists established themselves in Isfahan in the early 1860s. With the support of the prince-governor Masʿud Mirzā Ẓell-al-Solṭān, they founded in 1875 schools for both boys and girls and an infirmary (Nāṭeq, pp. 182, 191-92). These appear to be the predecessors of the boys school L'Etoile du Matin (Setāra-ye ṣobḥ; opened in 1910 by Father Dimuth) and the girls school Rudāba (from 1904), both closing down completely shortly after the start of World War I (Qafāri, p. 155; apud Qāsemi, pp. 533-34). These schools were reopened later, offering a curriculum in both French and Persian. L'Etoile du Matin was an elementary boarding school for boys with about 100 students, and Rudāba was a twelve-grade school for girls, appended by a unisex kindergarten (ʿĀbedi, p. 224; FRANCE xv. FRENCH SCHOOLS IN PERSIA). They failed to survive the Islamic revolution of 1979.

Aside from the Lazarists' activities, a Francophone Jewish School was founded in Isfahan by Alliance Israélite Universelle (q.v.) in 1901. The number of male students, initially 220, grew to 400 in three years, and during the same period 270 girls were studying in a separate school (FRANCE xv. FRENCH SCHOOLS IN PERSIA). The curriculum for boys included Hebrew, religion, French language and literature, history, physical and natural sciences, mathematics, and Persian, while for girls the emphasis was placed on learning about personal hygiene and home making skills. The Alliance encountered opposition from the local rabbis whose role in education had been undermined by the modern schools. To keep a balance, the teaching of religion was entrusted to rabbis (Ringer, pp. 135, 36). Later on, schools run by the ORT and Otser ha-Torah were opened. In 1961, 150 pupils attended Jewish high schools and 897 attended elementary school; other Jewish children attended non-Jewish schools, while there were about 50 Jews at the University of Isfahan ("Isfahan," *Encyclopaedia Judaica* IX, Jerusalem, 1971, pp. 78-79; ʿĀbedi, p. 220).

British schools. The Church Missionary Society of London (CMS), the most active of all British Anglican missionaries across the Middle East, administered the most successful foreign schools during its presence of more than a century in Isfahan. Competing with their French Catholic and Armenian Orthodox counterparts, the British Anglicans became a close ally of the American Protestant missionaries. An agreement between the CMS and the American Presbyterian mission in 1895 divided the Persian territory into southern and northern halves, preserved for the British and American missionary activities, respectively. Isfahan, though in the center, fell under the influence of the British (Wright, pp. 118-19; Borumand, 2002, pp. 143-45; White, 1996).

The pursuit of the CMS in Isfahan began in the Armenian quarter of New Julfa in 1862 through the efforts of Reverend Robert Bruce and his wife. On behalf of CMS, he took over the Armenian George Joseph school in Julfa, which absorbed, a year later, another Armenian school named Batavian. Despite the ongoing dispute between the CMS, the Armenian Church and the ulama, by 1875 the CMS school had 135 students of a variety of backgrounds, including Catholics, Armenians and as many as thirty Muslim boys. The prince-governor Ẓell-al-Solṭān lent the school official protection against possible provocations from the clergy and even ordered some of his courtiers to enroll their sons there. A decade later, the Society's schools for boys and girls altogether had three hundred students. As the number of the missionaries in Isfahan rose to seventeen by the mid-1890s, more schools were established by the Society in Julfa as well as in Jubāra, the city's Jewish quarter (Ringer, pp. 126-27; Wright, pp. 118-19; GREAT BRITAIN xv. BRITISH SCHOOLS IN PERSIA).

After a period of inactivity during World War I, the Society resumed its activity in 1920, when Bishop William Jameson Thompson reopened the Stewart Memorial College with 27 students in Isfahan with boarding option for nonresident students. It soon gained a good reputation and the enrollment grew steadily. Its faculty rose to some 30 members, 20 of them British. The staff taught some 150 students using a curriculum based on the British secondary school system. The British Oil Company and British Royal Bank offered scholarships to those students who agreed to join the Oil Company at the end of the eighth grade. In order to compete with their European counterparts, including the French schools, the college arranged a contract with London University to accept Persian students upon finishing the twelfth grade as MA prospects (Sayfpur, p. 335). The College placed a strong emphasis on physical education, and annual soccer games with the American College of Tehran were held alternately in each town (Sayfpur, p. 332). The CMS also sponsored the Stileman Memorial College for girls in Isfahan; it became Behešt-āyin high school after the nationalization of foreign schools.

Following the governmental decree in 1939 to close foreign schools and to purchase their properties, the Stewart Memorial College was handed over in July 1940 to the government and placed under the supervision of the Ministry of Education. It eventually became a somewhat mediocre public high school called Adab. The Church Missionary Society itself survived by continuing with its charitable institutions, including a major hospital. Many local and national leaders in various positions were educated in Isfahan College (Sayfpur, pp. 372-77, 589, 622; Thompson, pp. 38-39; Dehqāni-Tafti; cf. Mināsiān; Waterfield, 1973).

Other foreign schools in Isfahan included a finance school (Madrasa-ye māliya) founded in 1912 by the local Belgian finance advisor. It was later renamed Melliya, and eventually Saʿdi public high school (Anṣāri, p. 334; but cf. Sayfpur, pp. 840-41). The joint Perso-German secondary school *Deutsch-Persische Gewerbeschule* (Madrasa-ye ṣanʿati-e Irān o Ālmān) was founded in Isfahan in 1925, offering a combination of science-oriented secondary education, with German as the first foreign language, and technical apprenticeship in several professions. Several years later, the German pastor Ernst J. Christoffel opened a home for the blind in Isfahan. After a period of inactivity during and after World War II, the school resumed its activity in 1955 and eventually joined the Episcopal Church of Persia in 1972 (GERMANY ix. GERMANS IN PERSIA). It was taken over by the Government after the Islamic Revolution.

Educational reforms. Apart from the foreign schools, which involved no more than a tiny fraction of Isfahani children, the educational system of the city remained as a whole under the control of the Shiʿite clergy attached to the traditional curricula. The measures taken during the later Qajar period to introduce modern schools and training facilities, including the establishment of a Ministry of Education in 1910, had little impact on Isfahan. It was not until the rise of Reza Shah that drastic reforms of the educational institutions took place. In 1921 the High Council of Education was created to carry out the necessary reforms, based mainly on the French system. In the same year the first modern secondary school in Isfahan was founded by the Qajar prince Ṣārem-al-Dawla. Ten students graduated from it in 1925. Among its faculty were such eminent scholars as Jalāl-al-Din Homāʾi and Aḥmad Ārām. Several more high schools appeared in the Reza Shah period, including two for girls. In the 1930s the government integrated and centralized the educational system and established a national, tuition-free modern school system. These reforms were most effective in loosening and gradually removing the clerical grip on the educational system and promoting secularism, but they also ended the hitherto existing diversity provided by foreign and minority schools (see BRITISH SCHOOLS above; cf. Chaqueri, ed., p. 391). By 1937 the number of primary schools in the city of Isfahan had reached 19 for boys and 12 for girls (Imāniya, pp. 202-12; Anṣāri, pp. 331-36). The state also founded, with German assistance, a technical-vocational institute in 1936 (cf. GERMANY ix. GERMANS IN PERSIA), where young artisans were trained in the areas of metalwork, carpentry, and painting, among others. Three years later it was split into two institutes: Industrial (Honarestān-e ṣanʿati) and Fine arts (Honarhā-ye zibā); the latter was aimed at protecting and revitalizing native industries and crafts (ʿĀbedi, pp. 227-30) and achieved some success in its mission over the years.

In the following decades the Isfahan saw the expansion of the educational system as a result of the allocation of human resources to education. The enrollment in all levels grew substantially and women's access to education expanded (Table 1). The percentage of relevant age groups enrolled in primary and secondary schools rose from 12.9 in 1966 to 22.3 in 1986 (*Sāl-nāma*, 1972, pp. 114, 124; 1988, pp. 106-8; *SAOE*, 2002, Table 15.2). The drop in enrollment by the turn of the century is apparently due to the drop in the demography of school-attending age group, a consequence of the deceleration of population growth. The adult-literacy program, introduced first in 1936 (Banani, p. 105), grew slowly until the early 1960s, when the establishment of a literary corps in rural areas proved effective in reducing illiteracy.

Table 1
Enrollment in Schools of Isfahan Province by Gender
1953-2003*

Year	Total (in 1,000)	% Male	% Female
1953	58	81	19
1975-76	405	64	36
1986-87	750	55	45
1994-95	1,208	55	45
2000-01	1,116	49	51
2002-03	991	49	51

* Excluding non-Muslim schools.
Sources: ʿĀbedi, pp. 224-26; various issues of the *Āmār-nāma*.

Table 2 shows the literacy rates as percentages of the age group 6 and older; it also bears witness to the gradual tapering of the gender gap. Official statistics claim the literacy rate for the age group 6-39 to have approached 98 percent in 2002 (*Gozāreš*, 2002, p. 263).

Higher education. The Junior College of Medicine and Public Health (Āmuzešgāh-e ʿāli-e behdāri) was opened in 1946 (ʿĀbedi, p. 232) and later expanded its program and was integrated into the University of Isfahan in 1950 as College of Medicine (Dāneškada-ye Pezeški). The University expanded to include schools of pharmacy (1954), literature and the humanities (1958), and sciences (1964). It grew rapidly in the 1970s to a full-grown university with an enrolment of 8,000 in the early 1980s. The university embraces seven faculties with thirty departments as well as an evening school. It is located in a vast campus of 4.5 km^2 in Hazārjarib at the foot of the Kuh-e Ṣofa.

Table 2
Literacy Rate by Gender in Isfahan Province*
1956-2000

Year	Total	Male	Female
1956	14.6	23.9	5.1
1971	40.3	53.6	26.0
1976	52.4	65.3	38.7
1986	71.0	78.5	62.7
1996	84.7	88.3	80.9
2000	90.1	n.a.	n.a.

* Percent of the population 10 years of age and over who could read and write for 1956 and 6 years of age and over for the following years. Yazd included in the province in the 1956 census.
Sources: *Āmār dar Irān/Statistics in Iran* 1, Jan. 1960; Anṣāri, p. 64; *Gozāreš*, 2002, p. 26; cf. *SAOE*, 2002, Table 15.4.

The other major institute of higher education in the city is the Āryāmehr University of Technology (now Dānešgāh-e Ṣanʿati-e Eṣfahān), founded in the 1970s on a secluded piedmont west of the town (Amin). Its 3,000 students in the early 1980s grew threefold by the mid-1990s (*Gozāreš*, 1995, p. 86). Moreover, a teacher's college was opened in 1965, followed by several higher vocational schools both by the state (nursing, accounting, horticulture, food hygiene) and by private investors: Madrasa-ye ʿāli-e Kuroš-e kabir (from 1972) with about one thousand students, granting associate degree in accounting, statistics, surveying, etc. (*Iran*, p. 102; Anṣāri, pp. 357-63; *Āmār-nāma*, 1977, pp. 20-21).

The post-revolutionary decades saw a boom in higher education, mostly due to the high rate of unemployment, similar in this respect to other developing nations experiencing population explosion. Branches of the semi-private Islamic Open University (Dānešgāh-e Āzād-e Eslāmi; see EDUCATION xvii) appeared throughout the province, in Nāʾin, Dehāqān (near Šahreżā), Najafābād, Mobāraka, Falāvarjān, Ḵomeynišahr (formerly Sedeh), Ḵᵛorāsgān, and the Majlesi township near Isfahan. In the academic year 2001-02, the total enrollment in the open universities of the province was 60,000, compared with the 67,500 students who enrolled at the higher institutions under the jurisdiction of the ministry of higher education. The respective figures for the next academic year were 66,500 and 72,600, showing an enormous growth, if the data is to be trusted, with females constituting half of the students (*Gozāreš*, 1995, pp. 86-94; *Gozāreš*, 2002, pp. 279-87; Bank Markazi, pp. 150, 157).

(2) CULTURAL AFFAIRS

Isfahan is distinguished among Persian cities not only for its size, centrality, position in a riverain plain, and numerous historical monuments, but also for the idiosyncratic characteristic of its inhabitant. Their Persian accent is generally perceived as a provincial accent *par excellence*, and their characteristics: wittiness, thriftiness, and industry, attested also in historical sources (Jamālzāda, 1974; Borjian, 1993), are often cited in popular media and jokes. The objectivity of these stereotypes, however, has been questioned by some authors (e.g., Mir-ʿAlāʾi). Indeed, the findings of a national survey, conducted in provincial capitals of 28 provinces in 2001 (Wezārat-e ershād) shows no meaningful pattern that would distinguish values and orientations attested by Isfahanis from those of the inhabitants of other Persian cities of comparable size and status. The private and public life in Isfahan is portrayed by two famous writers from the region, Moḥammad-ʿAli Jamalzāda (q.v.) in *Sar o tah yak karbās yā Esfahān-nāma*, in a traditional setting, and Hušang Golširi (q.v.) in his last novel *Jenn-nāma*.

The first periodical in Isfahan was the official newspaper *Farhang* (q.v.; 1879-90), founded on orders from the Qajar prince-governor Ẓell-al-Solṭān. It was followed by about 39 serial titles initiated during the Qajar period; 27 more during the Reza Shah's reign; and 87 more from 1941-53, of which some 80 percent belonged to the four concluding years alone. No new newspaper was initiated in the ensuing decades. In spite of the impressive quantity, the majority of these newspapers exhibited a lack of professional skills and were a one-man enterprise, which goes some way to explain their short span of publication, their irregular daily appearance, and their inability to maintain even a weekly run. In the mid-1970s there were only four newspapers: *Rāh-e nejāt*, *Mojāhed*, *Eṣfahān*, and *Awliāʾ*, the most enduring and consistent of which were *Eṣfahān*, published from 1942-77 by the noted journalist and scholar Amirqoli Amini, and *Awliāʾ*, run by the Awliāʾ family since 1950. None of these papers, however, could compete with those from the capital, save for their local official advertisements and public statements. Professional journalism never took roots in Isfahan (ʿĀbedi, pp. 234-38; Amini; Anṣāri, pp. 338-47; cf. Moḥammadi, 2003).

More notable were perhaps the literary reviews that have flourished in Isfahan sporadically since the Constitutional Revolution. In the active period of 1933-35 the second series of *Dāneškada-ye Eṣfahān* (q.v.) was published by the poet and calligrapher Mirzā ʿAbbās Khan Dehkordi Šeydā, and the magazine *Bāḵtar* (q.v.) published by the influential Sayfpur Fāṭemi family; the editorship of the latter was entrusted to Amirqoli Amini, who then owned the newspaper *Aḵgar*. These periodicals enjoyed the literary and scholarly advice of Moḥammad-Taqi Bahār (q.v.), who was then living in internal exile in Isfahan (Sayfpur, pp. 771-74). Moḥammad Ṣadr-Hāšemi, an eminent local educator and historian, published *Čehel-sotun* in the early 1950s. Notwithstanding these figures, for most of the 20th century Isfahan suffered a brain drain in favor of the capital city of Tehran, yet remained a hub of traditional Persian literature centered around the literary societies such as Ḥaqāyeq, Adib-e Farahmand, Šeydā, Kamāl Esmāʿil, Ṣāʾeb, Saʿdi, Sarā-ye soḵanvarān (sponsoring the literary review *Nāma-ye soḵanvarān-e Sepāhān*), and many less-recognized circles that often met in the residences of their founders and sponsors. Linked with these circles were scores of poets of various genres, predominantly traditional and, more exclusively, satirists and humorists (cf. Anṣāri, pp. 368-86), with the poet Mokrem as a famous figure.

A modernist circle was formed in the 1960s and published *Jong-e Eṣfahān*, eleven issues of which appeared from 1965-81 (Ḥoquqi, p. 439). Among the members of the circle were such prominent writers, poets, and translators as Hušang Golširi Moḥammad Ḥoquqi, Abu'l-Ḥasan Najafi, Żiāʾ Mowaḥḥed, Aḥmad Mirʿalāʾi, Moḥammad Kalbāsi, Aḥmad Golširi, Moḥammad-Reżā Qānunparvar, Jalil Dustḵʷāh, and Moḥammad-Raḥim Oḵowwat. The circle re-emerged in the late 1980s with the quarterly *Zendarud*.

On the religious side there were Hājia Ḵānom Noṣrat-Bēgom Amin, a leading female *mojtahed* who wrote a fifteen-volume study of the Koran, and equally prolific Sayyed Moṣleḥ-al-Din Mahdawi with mastery in the genre of necrology (*tadkerat al-qobur* "account of the graveyards").

Isfahan is also known as a center of traditional artists. It has its own school of Persian classical music and its contemporary figures have been the vocalists Ḥosayn Ṭāherzāda and Jalāl Tāj and instrumentalists ʿAli-Akbar Šeydā, Jalil Šahnāz and Ḥasan Kasāʾi. Of many painters of the town, Maḥmud Farščiān has gained international recognition owing to his distinguished style. A whole new generation of miniaturists, calligraphers, tile makers, and other visual artists emerged during the restoration of historical monuments and, as the city grew into a center of tourist attraction, handicrafts flourished. Worth mentioning is also the performing arts, most notably the theatrical comic group led by and named after Arḥām-e Ṣadr (Kušān et al., passim).

The Armenian cultural contribution to the city has been demographically disproportional to this small community of a few thousand. The Vank museum and research library were the only ones of their kind in Isfahan until recent past. Several Armenian residents of the town have gained prominence in painting, music, and cinema. The department of Armenian language and literature at the University of Isfahan, founded by the Gulbenkian Foundation in 1974, is the only center of Armenian studies in the country (Mināsiān, pp. 23-28; Lāzāriān, passim; see JULFA).

Bibliography: Ḥasan ʿĀbedi, *Eṣfahān az leḥāẓ-e ejtemāʿi o eqteṣādi*, Tehran, 1955. *Āmār-nāma-ye ostān-e Eṣfahān*, Sāzmān-e barnāma wa budja-ye ostān-e Eṣfahān, Markaz-e āmār-e Irān, annually from 1971. Camron Michael Amin, "Blurring Private and Public Lives by Design: Isfahan University of Technology, 1977-2005," *Comparative Studies of South Asia, Africa, and the Middle East* 26/2, 2006, pp. 279-

302. Amirqoli Amini, "Če angiza-i bāʿeṯ-e ruz-nāma-negāri-e man gardid?" *Majalla-ye ḵāṭerāt-e Waḥid* 9/3, 1972. Hormoz Anṣāri, *Moqaddama-i bar jāmeʿa-šenāsi-e Eṣfahān*, ed. Aḥmad Jawāheri, Isfahan, 1990. Amin Banani, *The Modernization of Iran: 1921-1941*, Stanford, Ca., 1961. Bank Markazi, *Gozāreš-e awżāʿ-e eqteṣādi o ejtemāʿi-e ostānhā-ye kešvar dar sāl-e 1381*, Tehran, 2004. E. Boré, *Correspondance et mémoires d'un voyageur en Orient*, 2 vols., Paris, 1840. Habib Borjian, "Eṣfahān dar tāriḵ-e Irān," *Rahāvard* 33, Spring 1993, pp. 74-95. Ṣafurā Barumand, *Pažuheš-i bar faʿāliyat-e anjoman-e tabliḡi-e kelisā dar dawra-ye Qājāriya*, Tehran, 2002. C. Chaqueri, ed., *The Armenians of Iran*, Cambridge, Mass., 1998. Ḥasan Dehqāni Tafti, "Yād-i az kālej-e Eṣfahān o bonyāngozār-e bozorgvār-e ān Osqof William Jameson Thompson," *Rahāvard* 36, 1994, pp. 253-57. N. Falsafi, *Zendagāni-e Šāh ʿAbbas-e Awwal* III, Tehran, 1960. Abu'l-Ḥasan Ḡaffāri, *Tāriḵ-e rawābeṭ-e Irān o Farānsa, az teror-e Nāṣer-al-Din Šāh tā jang-e jahāni-e awwal*, Tehran, 1989. Moḥammad Ḥoquqi, *Šeʿr o šāʿerān*, Tehran, 1989. *Gozāreš-e eqteṣādi-ejtemāʿi-e ostān-e Eṣfahān*, Sāzmān-e barnāma wa budja-ye ostān-e Eṣfahān, annually in the years 1995-2002. Ḥājj Sayyāḥ, *An Iranian in Nineteenth Century Europe: The Travel Diaries of Haj Sayyah 1859-1877*, tr. Mehrbanoo Nasser Deyhim, Bethesda, Md., 1998. Mojtabā Imāniya, *Tāriḵ-e farhang-e Eṣfahān*, Isfahan, 1978. Moḥammad-ʿAli Jamālzāda, *Goftoguy-e ḵānavādagi dar bāra-ye Eṣfahān*, Tehran, 1974. Nāṣer Kušān et al., *Tāriḵ-e teʾātr dar Eṣfahān*, Isfahan, 2000. Žānet D. Lāzāriān, ed., *Dāneš-nāma-ye Irāniān-e Armani*, Tehran, 2003. L. Mināsiān, *Rāhnemā-ye Jolfā-ye Eṣfahān*, 2nd ed., Isfahan, 1976. Aḥmad Mir-ʿAlāʾi, "Eṣfahān, Eṣfahān-e man," *Hamšahri*, 20 Nov. 1995. Moḥammad Moḥammadi, *Tāriḵča-ye maṭbuʿāt-e Eṣfahān*, Isfahan, 2003. Homā Nāṭeq, *Kārnāma-ye farhangi-e farangi dar Irān*, Paris, 1996. Eqbāl Qāsemi-Puyā, *Madāres-e jadid dar dawra-ye Qājāriya o bāniān o pišravān-e ānhā*, Tehran, 1998. Monica M. Ringer, *Education, Religion, and the Discourse of Cultural Reform in Qajar Iran*, Costa Mesa, Calif., 2001. Aḥmad Šaʿbāni, "Fehrest-e ruz-nāmahā wa majal-lāt-e Eṣfahān," in Iraj Afšār and Karim Eṣfa-hāniān, eds., *Pažuhešhā-ye Irān-šenāsi: Nāmvāra-ye Doktor Maḥmud Afšār* XIV, Tehran, 2002, pp. 180-86. *Statistical Yearbook* (*Sāl-nāma-ye āmāri-e kešvar*), Markaz-e āmār-e Irān, various years. William Jameson Thompson, "Iran: 1939-1944," *Journal of the Central Asiatic Society* 32, 1945, pp. 34-43. Robin E. Waterfield, *Christians in Persia*, London, 1973. Wezārat-e eršād-e eslāmi, *Arzešhā wa negarešhā-ye Irāniān*, Tehran, 2002. Bob White, "Talk about School: Education and the Colonial Project in French and British Africa (1860-1960)," *Comparative Education* 32/1, 1996, pp. 9-25. D. Wright, *The English amongst the Persians*, London, 1977.

(MARYAM BORJIAN AND HABIB BORJIAN)

xvi. ISFAHAN IN THE MIRROR OF FOLKLORE AND LEGEND

Systematic collection of the folklore of Isfahan is mostly due to Amirqoli Amini, whose first publication was a collection of Persian dicta entitled *hazār o yak soḵan*. He followed this book with a more extensive collection of Isfahan's narrative folklore, which led to his best known publication, *Dāstānhā-ye amṯāl*. Amini's approach was to interview mostly illiterate informants, whom he asked about any proverbs or stories associated with proverbs that they might remember; he would then record the data in writing. During eighteen years of research, Amini managed to collect 3,000 proverbs, of which nearly 250 were associated with some explanatory narratives (Amini, 1954, pp. 4-5). In 1935, Amini brought his entire collection to the attention of ʿAli-Aṣḡar Ḥekmat (q.v.), then the minister of education, who concluded an official contract with Amini and charged him with preparing both proverbs and folktales of Isfahan for publication by the Ministry of Education (Amini, 1954, p. 5). Amini arranged his data into three volumes, and turned over the manuscripts to the Ministry of Education in the fall of 1937. Shortly afterwards, however, Ḥekmat was replaced, and Esmāʿil Merʾāt, the new minister, showed no interest in having them published. Amini tried for several years to persuade the ministry to either honor its contract and publish his book, or to return the manuscripts to him so that he could arrange for their publication himself. The officialdom finally relented after seven years, and returned his manuscripts. Eventually, two volumes of his *Dāstānhā-ye amṯāl* were published by the Eṭṭelāʿāt Press (Tehran, 1945), but they soon became difficult to find due to their popularity and also a fire at the press, in which many of them perished. The enlarged second edition containing 277 proverbs and tales (i.e., 34 more than the 1st ed.) was published in 1953. A year later, Amini published another revised edition with 10 additional items, all arranged in alphabetical order. Each proverb was followed by a story that purported to explain its origin and was also provided with the context in which it may be used. Amini also published a collection of thirty Eṣfahāni tales (*Si afsāna*), a number of which he recorded in literary Persian rather than in the dialect he had heard (Amini, 1960, p. ii).

It is true that almost all Iranian studies of folklore name Āqā Jamāl Ḵᵛānsāri (d. 1121/1709 or 1125/1713), a Shiʿite cleric of the 18th century, as the first one to collect the folklore of Isfahan's women (e.g., Enjavi 1972, p. 13; idem, 2002, pp. 234-35; Katirāʾi, pp. 136, n. 3), but in reality Ḵᵛānsāri's short treatise, called *Kolṯum Nana*, is a satirical work in which the author intended to ridicule these beliefs rather than collect them. The book was Ḵᵛānsāri's way of combating superstitious customs and practices, which he, a respected theologian, disliked (Bolukbāši, 1961, no. 19, p. 177). Therefore, one cannot always distinguish between factual folk practices and their caricatures in his account. Authors, such as Mirzā Ḥabib Eṣfahāni (d. toward the end of the 19th century in Istanbul, q.v.) and Moḥammad-ʿAli Jamālzāda (1895-

1997), who are often mentioned in connection with the folklore of Isfahan, are in reality novelists and social critics, who either peppered their writings with folk expressions as a matter of prose style, or used folklore as a vehicle for expressing social and cultural criticism.

Isfahan's folklore has the rich diversity of the folklore of those areas of Iran where different cultures and populations made contact. Natives of Isfahan have themselves become objects of general Persian folklore from very early on. They have been portrayed in folklore as being very clever, business-minded, and thrifty. The association of Isfahan's population with thriftiness must have been a popular notion at least as early as the 10th century, since, according to the 10th-century geographer Moqaddasi, they had been referred to as one of the most tight-fisted people in a text where the Sasanian monarch Qobād described the character of the lands under his rule (Moqaddasi, pp. 257-58, tr, II, pp. 372-73).

Isfahan's reputation as a land of abundance, has been explained by the legend of the refusal of its people to assist Nimrud in his rebellion against God. According to other legends, Nimrud's army was destroyed near Isfahan, whose natives were blessed by Abraham, and thereby the city will always have thirty men to whom God grants every wish they ask for (Abu Noʿaym, I, p. 40; Ebn Rosta, tr. pp. 179, 190; Moqaddasi, p. 397, tr., II, p. 593; Māfarruḵi, pp. 35-36, tr. pp. 80, 82, 144). It is said that ʿAbd-al-ʿAziz ʿEjli in the 10th century found in a village of Isfahan a fully armed man in a tomb, whose body had remained intact. The tomb also contained various artifacts that were turned to dust as soon as they were touched, though the corpse stayed intact (Māfarruḵi, p. 11, tr. p. 22). This is a well known motif that has been related about the Safavid Shah Esmāʿil I (q.v.) and others (Balāḡi, II, p. 24).

Many prominent historical and legendary figures are said to have hailed from Isfahan or to have met their end at or near the city. According to these legends, Anōširvān was born in Ardestān, a village near Isfahan (Ebn Rosta, p. 153, tr. p. 181), as was Moses' pharaoh, Nebuchadnezzar, Bahrām Gōr, and the Prophet's companion Salmān Fārsi (Māfarruḵi, pp. 22-23, tr. pp. 66-67). The legendary king Kay Ḵosrow is said to have been the first king to have held his coronation ceremony there and to also have disappeared in snow near Isfahan at the end of his reign. Likewise, Ardašir Bābakān, the founder of the Sasanian dynasty, was crowned king of Iran there and it was also he who named the city's famous river Zarrinrud (i.e., Zāyandarud) and established the system for the orderly use of its waters in irrigation (Enjavi, 1975, pp. 276, 279, 283, 292; Ebn Rosta, pp., 155, 196, tr., 183, pp. 232-33). Of the heroes of the Šāh-nāma, the chief hero, Rostam, lived in Isfahan as a child and Gōdarz (q.v.) held the region as a fief (Māfarruḵi, tr., p. 79; Enjavi, 1975, p. 100). The tomb of the legendary king Ṭahmuraṯ is said to be atop a mountain called Bandarāb near Isfahan, where there is a room of lapis lazuli in which Adam's ring and Eve's diadem are kept (Hama-dāni, p. 187).

Many festivals and folk ceremonies held in Isfahan have been reported. One, associated with the Nowruz celebration, was held in one of the bazaars near the city at great expense. The varieties of food, dress, and unusual decorations associated with this festival, which continued for seven days, amazed the Arab traveler, Ebn Ḥawqal, in the middle of the 10th century (Ebn Ḥawqal, p. 364, tr., p. 107). Later on, the Buyid monarch ʿAżod-al-Dawla (q.v.), tried to recreate this festival in Shiraz because of his fond childhood memories of it (Māfarruḵi, pp. 93-94, tr., p.17; Faqihi, p. 594). Gardizi in the 11th century reports a popular water festival in Isfahan that commemorated the relief from some ancient draught (Gardizi, pp. 239, 247).

Nowruz festivities in the more recent times involved many folk entertainers such as *ʿamu nowruz, ādam-e čubi*, bear and monkey handlers, and wondering musicians who would entertain people for small fees (Moʿezz-al-Din Mahdawi, p. 66). Religious festivals have also been observed with great relish in Isfahan. Mourning ceremonies associated with the martyrdom of Imam Ḥosyan b. ʿAli (q.v.) were publicly held in a number of predominantly Sunni cities such as Isfahan during the Saljuq period (Faqihi, pp. 452, 457; cf. ʿAbd-al-Jalil Qazvini, p. 371). Under the Qajars, groups of thugs, who had friends in the city jail would go to the governor's house and vigorously self flagellate with of a small sword called *qama*. They used to vow to continue until either they die or the governor would agree to release their imprisoned comrades. It has been reported that this was no idle threat as some of these would continue the flagellation until fainting or death from blood-loss. Sufis would publicly demonstrate their piety during some of these holy periods by placing chains around their necks and limbs while strolling in the streets. Many would use the occasion to extort money from the passers by (Moʿezz-al-Din Mahdawi, pp. 50-51, 66).

There are many landmarks around Isfahan that are believed to have magical power. A field, called Fās, near Harāskān village is said to have been charmed. No wild animals would bother domesticated beasts that might be grazing there. It is said that a rooster that had escaped its coop lived there for four years without being molested by any wild animals (Abu Noʿaym, I, p. 31; Māfarruḵi, p. 16, tr., p. 37; Ebn Rosta, tr., p. 188). A type of water with curative powers oozes out of one of the mountains in the ardahar region near Kāšān. The natives collect the water on the day of Tir of the month of Tir, while, according to Māfarruḵi (pp. 16-17, tr. pp. 37-38), calling upon the mountain saying: "O *Biḏ-doḵt* give me of your water, which I need for the cure of such and such a disease (cf. Moqaddasi, pp. 396-97, tr., II, p. 593; Ebn Rosta, tr., pp. 186-87). There is a different kind of magical water in one of the springs called "The spring of the locusts" (ʿAyn-al-jarād)," near Isfahan, which is used as a charm against locust infestation. When farms are attacked by swarms of locusts, two pious individuals take some of this spring's water and spray it over the infested farms; thereby thousands of birds will appear and destroy the locusts (Fozuni, p. 455). A variety of beads called *mohra-ye taḏark*, "hail beads," found in another village of Isfahan is a potent charm against hale (Abu Noʿaym, I, p. 32; cf. Māfarruḵi, tr., p. 37). Other villages use two rings that are affixed to poles as charms against the devastating power of hailstorms. These rings have the power of turning hail to rain (Ebn Rosta, tr., p. 187). Another village in the vicinity of the city produces a special apotropaic potion that can cure the evil effects of magic as well as madness, provided that it is mixed in the milk of a reddish cow and administered to the victim in one of the three last nights of the lunar month (Māfarruḵi, tr., p. 41). In the past, Eṣfahāni girls who were seeking matrimony would have recourse to several magical practices. The most famous among these is the following: On the last Wednesday evening of the year (Čāhāršanba-suri, q.v.), they would go to a shrine (*emāmzāda*, q.v.) that had a minaret called Monār-e Sar-berenji. Once there, they would climb the staircase in the minaret, place walnuts on each of the stairs and sit on it hard enough to break the shell, while reciting a verse expressing their wishes (Hedāyat, p. 158; Moʿezz-al-Din Mahdawi, p. 92). They might alternatively draw a string across a cross-section and would wait for the passers-by to tear it while passing through (Purkarim, p. 21), or would pour water of an old bathhouse called Ḥammām-e Šayḵ Bahāʾi upon their heads, using a special bowl called *jām-e čel kelid* "the bowl of forty keys" (Hedāyat, p. 159).

Divination by the aid of the tombstone of a saint (Hedāyat, p. 159), tea-leaves (Nafisi), and by interpretation of dreams (*Ketāb-e hafta* 13, pp. 134-35), as well as by other means are common in the folklore of Isfahan. Other magical practices and beliefs, such as those associated with the protection of the newborn infant and its mother from the demoness Āl (q.v.), or protecting a frightened child against becoming a stutterer abound (Moʿezz-al-Din Mahdawi, pp. 8, 10).

Perhaps what natives of Isfahan are most famous for in Persian folklore is their sense of humor and ability to produce clever repartees. Riddles, short folktales, and satires in verse abound in Isfahan's verbal folklore (e.g., see Moʿezz-al-Din Mahdawi, p. 59, who quotes Moḥammad Rāvandi's *Rāḥat al-ṣodur*).

Bibliography: Abu'l-Rašid Naṣir-al-Din ʿAbd-al-Jalil Qazvini Rāzi, *Ketāb al-naqż maʿruf ba Baʿż maṭāleb al-nawāṣeb fi naqż "baʿż fażāʾeḥ al-rawāfeż,"* ed. Jalāl-al-Din Ḥosayni Moḥaddeṯ Ormavi, Tehran, 1979. Abu Noʿaym Aḥmad b. ʿAbd-Allāh Eṣfahāni, *Ketāb ḏekr aḵbār Eṣbahān*, ed. ʿAbd-al-Wahhāb Ḳelji, 2 vol., Delhi, 1985; tr. Nur-Allāh Kasāʾi as *Ḏekr-e aḵbār-e Esfahān*, Tehran, 1998. Amirqoli Amini, *Hazār o yak soḵan*, Berlin, 1920, 2nd ed., Isfahan, 1954. Idem, *Dāstānhā-ye amṯāl-e eṣfahāni*, 2nd ed., Isfahan, 1954. Idem, *Si afsāna az afsānahā-ye maḥalli-e Eṣfahān*, Isfahan, 1960. ʿAbd-al-Ḥojja Balāḡi, *Tāriḵ-e Nāʾin*, 2 vols. in 1, Tehran, 1369/1950. John Chardin, *Voyages du Chevalier Chardin en Perse*, ed. Louis Langlès, 10 vols., Paris 1811; partial tr. Ḥosayn Orayżi as *Safar-nāma-ye Šovālia Šārdan-e farānsavi, qesmat-e šahr-e Eṣfahān*. Isfahan, 1951. "Čistān," *Ketāb-e hafta*, no. 11, 1961, p. 172 (a folk-riddle in verse). Šams-al-Din Moḥammad b. Abi Ṭāleb Anṣāri Demašqi, *Noḵbat al-dahr fi ʿjāʾeb al-barr wa'l-baḥr*, ed. August Ferdinand Mehren, Leipzig, 1923, p. 183; tr. Ḥamid Ṭabibiān, Tehran, 1978. Ebn Ḥawqal, *Ketāb ṣurat al-arż*, ed. Michaël Jan De Goeje, 2nd rev. ed. by J. H. Kramers, Leiden, 1967; tr. and annotated Jaʿfar Šeʿār as *Safar-nāma-ye Ebn Ḥawqal: Iran dar Ṣurat al-arż*, 2nd ed., Tehran, 1987. Ebn Rosta, *Ketāb al-aʿlāq al-nafisa*, ed. Michaël Jan De Goeje, Leiden, 1967; tr. and annototated Ḥosayn Qaračānlu, Tehran, 1986. Abu'l-Qāsem Enjavi Širāzi, *Mardom wa Šāhnāma*, Tehran, 1975. Idem, *Goḏar-i o naẓar-i dar farhang-e mardom*, Tehran, 1992. Idem, "Folklor," in idem, *Jān-e ʿāriat: farhang-e ʿāmma, pažuheshā-ye adabi, mardom-šenāsi-e Sayyed Abu'l-Qāsem Enjavi (Najwā)*, ed. Mahin Ṣadāqat-piša, Tehran, 2002, pp. 226-41 (a collection of Enjawi's articles). Abu Esḥāq Ebrāhim Eṣṭaḵri, *Masālek wa mamālek*, anonymous 5th-6th-cent. Pers. tr. of *Ketāb masālek al-mamālek*, ed. Iraj Afšār, Tehran, 1968. ʿAli-Aṣḡar Faqihi, *Āl-e Buya: naḵostin selsela-ye qodratmand-e Šiʿa wa awżāʿ-e zamān-e išān, bā nemudār-i az zendagi jāmeʿa . . . dar qarnhā-ye čahārom wa panjom*, Tehran, 1986. ʿAbbās Fāruqi, *Dāstānhā-ye maḥalli-e Eṣfahān*, Tehran, 1978. Mir Maḥmud Fozuni Estrābādi/Astarābādi, *Boḥayra*, ed. ʿAbd-al-Karim b. ʿAbbās-ʿAli Qomi, Tehran, 1328/1910. ʿAbd-al-Ḥayy b. Żaḥḥāk Gardizi, *Tāriḵ-e Gardizi*, ed. ʿAbd-al-Ḥayy Ḥabibi, Tehran, 1968. Moḥammad b. Maḥmud Hamadāni, *ʿAjāyeb-nāma: ʿajāyeb al-maḵluqāt wa ḡarāʾeb al-mawjudāt*, ed. Jaʿfar Modarres Ṣādeqi, Tehran, 1996. Ṣādeq Hedāyat, *Neyrangestān*, 2nd ed., Tehran, 1956. *Ḥodud al-ʿĀlam men al-mašreq ela'l-maḡreb*, ed. Manoučehr Sotuda, Tehran, 1961; tr. with commentary Vladimir Minorsky as *Ḥudūd al-ʿĀlam: The Regions of the World*, 2nd ed., London, 1970. Moḥammad-ʿAli Jamālzāda, *Sar o tah yak karbās*, tr. W. L. Heston as *Isfahan Is Half the World: Memories of a Persian Boyhood*, Princeton, 1983. ʿAli Jawāher-Kalām, *Zendarud yā joḡrāfiā-ye tāriḵi-e Eṣfahān wa Jolfā*, 2nd ed. Tehran 1969-70. Āqā Jamāl Ḵᵛānsāri, *Kolṯum Nana*, ed. ʿAli Bolukbāši, in *Ketāb-e hafta*, nos. 17, 1961, pp. 162-68, no. 18, 1961, pp. 169-74, no. 19, 1961, pp. 168-77; ed. Maḥmud Katirāʾi, in idem, ed., *ʿAqāyed al-nesāʾ wa merʾāt al-bolahāʾ: do resāla dar farhang-e tuda*, Tehran, 1970. Maḥmud Katirāʾi, "Ṣādeq Hedāyat wa folklor-e Irān," in idem, *Zabān o farhang-e mardom: naqd*, Tehran, 1978, pp. 131-41. Mofażżal b. Saʿd b. Ḥosayn Māfarruḵi Eṣfahāni, *Ḏekr maḥāsen Eṣfahān*, ed. Sayyed Jalāl-al-Din Ḥosayni Ṭehrāni, Tehran, 1933; tr. Sayyed Ḥosayn b. Moḥammad Āvi as *Tarjama-ye Maḥāsen-e Eṣfahān*, ed. ʿAbbās Eqbāl Āštiāni, Tehran, 1949. Moʿezz-al-Din Mahdawi, *Dāstānhā-i az panjāh sāl awżāʿ-e ejtemāʿi-e nim-qarn-e aḵir*, Tehran, 1969. Moṣleḥ-al-Din Mahdawi, *Taḏkerat al-qobur yā dānešmandān wa bozorgān-e Eṣfāhan*, Isfahan, 1969. Moḥammad-Mahdi b. Moḥammad-Reżā Eṣfahāni (Arbāb), *Neṣf-e jahān fi taʿrif al-Eṣfahān*, ed. Manučehr Sotuda, Tehran, 1961. Moḥammad b. Aḥmad Moqaddasi/Maqdesi, *Aḥsan al-*

taqāsim fi maʿrefat al-aqālim, ed. ed. Michaël Jan De Goeje, Leiden, 1967; tr. ʿAi-Naqi Monzawi, 2 vols., Tehran, 1982. Ḥamd-Allāh Mostawfi, *Nozhat al-qolub*, ed. G. Le Strange, Leiden, 1915; offset printing, Tehran, 1983. Moḥammad Nafisi, "K̲āl wa k̲orāfāt-e mardom-e Eṣfahān," *Ketāb-e hafta*, no. 6, 1961, p. 177. Hušang Purkarim, "Āʾin-e čāhāršanba-suri dar Irān," *Honar o mardom*, New Series, nos. 77-78, 1968, pp. 12-30. Abu'l-Qāsem Ḥosayn Rāġeb Eṣfahāni, *Moḥāżarat al-odabāʾ wa moḥāwarat al-šoʿarāʾ wa'l-bolaġāʾ*, tr. Moḥammad-Ṣāleḥ Qazvini as *Nawāder*, ed. Aḥmad Mojāhed, Tehran, 1992. ʿAbbās Zaryāb K̲oʾi, *Āʾina-ye jām*, Tehran, 1989.

MAHMOUD OMIDSALAR

xvii. ARMENIAN COMMUNITY. See JULFA.

xviii. JEWISH COMMUNITY

The beginning of the Jewish settlement in Isfahan is mixed with legends, but there are fragmentary source materials that enable us to reconstruct the major historical events concerning its Jewish community. According to *The Standard Jewish Encyclopaedia* (s.v. Isfahan), "The Talmud ascribes the foundation of Isfahan to Jews exiled by Nebuchadnezzar." Muslim geographers such as Moqaddasi/Maqdesi (p. 388), Ebn al-Ḥadwqal (pp. 366-67), Ebn al-Faqih (pp. 261-62), and Yāqut Ḥamawi (I, pp. 295 ff., IV, pp. 1044-45) report the tradition that the town of Yahudiya (lit. the town of Jews), the center of Isfahan, was so called, because the exiled Jews of Babylonia chose to settle in that area, which probably would mean during the first phase of the Achaemenian Empire. Ebn al-Faqih records a tradition according to which "When the Jews emigrated from Jerusalem, fleeing from Nebuchadnezzar (Bok̲t-al-Naṣr), they carried with them a sample of the water and of the soil of Jerusalem. They did not settle down anywhere or in any city without examining the water and the soil of each place. This they did all along until they reached the city of Isfahan. There they rested, examined water and soil and found that both resembled Jerusalem. Upon that they settled there, cultivated the soil, raised children and grandchildren, and today the name of this settlement is Yahudiyah" (Ebn al-Faqih, pp. 261-62; cf. Ebn al-Ḥawqal, pp. 366-67, tr., II, p. 358). According to Guy Le Strange, the medieval Yahudiya is the same town that was enlarged under the Safavids (Le Strange, p. 204).

According to Armenian sources, (Moses Khorenatsʿi, tr. Thomson, p. 293) the Sasanian Šāpūr II (r. 309-79) transferred many Jews from Armenia and settled them in Isfahan. According to the Middle Persian text *Šahristānihā ī Ērān*, the Sasanian king, Yazdegerd I (r. 399-421), settled Jews in Jay (Gay) at the request of his Jewish wife Šōšan-dok̲t. Šōšān-dok̲t, who is also credited by the same source with the founding of Šōš (an obvious anachronistic identification) is called the daughter of exilarch (*rēš-gālutak ī Yahudān šāh*) and the mother of Bahrām V Gōr (q.v.; *Šahristānihā ī Ērān*, secs. 47, 53; Darmesteter; Gray). This particular exilarch who is mentioned as the father of Šōšan-dok̲t is not known otherwise. He may have been either Mar Kahana I, Mar Yemar, or Mar Zuṭra I, who successively filled the position of exilarch (*reš galuta*) for brief periods about that time. According to Ḥamza Eṣfahāni, half of the Jewish population of Isfahan were killed and their sons enslaved by the order of the Sasanian king, Pērōz (r. 459-84), when there spread the rumor that Jews had flayed alive two Zoroastrian priests and used their skins in their tanning industry (Ḥamza, ed. Gottwaldt, pp. 55-56; Levy, tr., pp. 144, 147-48; Widengren, p. 143). This incident—if it happened at all, since it is not related by other known primary sources—might have taken place in 472 C.E.

In anticipation for the coming of the Messiah, the Jews of Isfahan celebrated the conquest of the city by the Arabs. According to Abu Noʿaym (I, pp. 21-22) the Jews of Isfahān, while dancing and playing music, went to the gate of the city to receive the Arab conquerors. About a hundred years later, a Jew from Isfahan by the name Abu ʿIsā (q.v.) declared himself a messenger of the expected Messiah (*rasul al-masiḥ al-montaẓar*) and charged by God to rescue the children of Israel from the rule of insubordinate people. He prohibited divorce, eating of meat, and wine drinking and acknowledged the prophethood of Jesus, and Moḥammad. He gathered many thousands armed Jews and rebelled against the rule of the last Omayyad caliph, Marwān II (r. 744-50). Neither the details of his rise are known nor the exact date of his revolution, which is given differently in sources. According to Abu'l-Fatḥ Moḥammad Šahrestāni, he founded a sect called ʿIsawiya after him and was eventually killed along with his followers near Ray (Šahrestāni, p. 168; tr. Haarbrücker, I, pp. 254-55; tr. Ṣadr Torka, pp. 168-69; Pines). The rise of Abu ʿIsā is recorded as an important Messianic movement in Jewish history (Qerqisāni, tr. pp. 382-83). This event together with the report of Abu Noʿaym indicates that Isfahan must have been populated with a large number of Jews who could allow themselves to take hazardous actions. Around the year 1179, another Jewish Messianic movement originated in Isfahan under the leadership of certain Abu Saʿid b. Dāwud. It was reported that Maimonides had sent a special messenger to Isfahan, allegedly to inquire about this movement (Baer, pp. 155 ff.). Benjamin of Tudela (pp. 82, 88), who visited Persia around the 1160s, stated that Isfahan was the seat of the chief rabbi called Sar Šalom, who was appointed by the exilarch of Baghdad over all Jewish communities of Persia. According to this source Isfahan had a Jewish population of 15,000 souls.

At the beginning of the 17th century, Isfahan, located almost in the center of the Safavid kingdom with easy access to the Persian Gulf and at a safe distance from the Ottomon threat, was in the ideal position to become its administrative, political, religious, and commercial center. In 1005/1596-96, Shah ʿAbbās I the Great (r. 995-1038/1587-1629) made it the capital city of Persia and did not spare any efforts to rebuild, beautify, and enlarge it. He turned Isfahan into "the most famous and romantic of the cities of the east" (Curzon, II, p. 22), a cosmopolitan metropolis that became the residential and meeting place of Christian minorities, and European travelers, envoys, emissaries, diplomats, and missionaries, many of whom have left a record of their stay there. Thus we possess more information about the Jews of Isfahan during the Safavid period (1501-1736). According to *Ketāb-e anusi*, a versified history by the Jewish poet of Kāšān, Bābā'i ben Loṭf (q.v.), Jews of Isfahan, like the Jews of many parts of Persia, were severely persecuted under the Safavids (Seligsohn; Bacher; Fischel; Spicehandler; Netzer; Moreen). Nevertheless, they continued to conduct their religious life and cultivate their culture. ʿEmrāni (1454-after 1536, q.v.), one of the two great Judeo-Persian poets, flourished in Isfahan (Netzer, 1973, p. 41; Yeroushalami). In the colophon of an Armenian manuscript written in Isfahan in 1646, the Jews of Isfahan are praised for their knowledge and scholarship: "They know by heart the whole Bible, men and women, boys and girls. For they are very learned and of an inquiring disposition; they ponder over the deep laws of God; they do not pay heavy taxes as is being done in our land of Armenia, nor do all of them devote their time to handicrafts like our own people, for their art is of reading and learning, and to this only do they dedicate their time. Great and small are given to asking questions as did the old Athenians (Ajamian, p. 120). When Nāder Shah Afšār (r. 1148-60/1736-47) decided to have the Bible, and the Qur'an translated into Persian, the rabbi Bābā'i ben Nuri'el (q.v.) of Isfahan was the one chosen to translate the Pentateuch and the Psalms of David from Hebrew with the help of other rabbis.

The number of the Jews of Isfahan decreased to an average estimated of 300 families, or about 1,800 souls (d'Beth Hillel, p. 109; Benjamin, II, pp. 183 ff.), even though, Isfahan in 1889 was considered as the largest of all Jewish communities in Persia (Neumark, p. 85). The turning point for modern education in Isfahan was the opening of the Alliance (q.v.) school in 1901 for the Jews of the city. According to the Alliance, Isfahan was the home of about 6,000 Jews in 1903-04 (Tsadik, 2005, p. 275). In 1948 there were an estimated of 10,000 Jews living in Isfahan, the majority of whom emigrated to Israel. At the beginning of the Islamic regime in Iran, there lived in Isfahan an estimated 3,000 Jews. The Jews of Isfahan bury their dead in a place called Ester (Esther) Ḵātun near Pir Bakrān village, some 30 km southwest of Isfahan (Honarfar, pp. 26, 28-29). The place is known in Hebrew as Seraḥ bat Ašer in the name of the granddaughter of Jacob the Prophet (Genesis 46:17; Targum Yerushalmi on Genesis 49:21, on Numbers 27:46), and as such is revered by Jews all over Persia. Ernst Herzfeld suggested the Jewish origin of the tomb of Pir Bakrān. "In the floor a rock is shown with the impression of a horse's hoof, with which the name of the prophet Elijah is linked . . . The rock, perhaps, originally meant to replace the rock in the temple of Jerusalem. The Sūfī has usurped the Jewish sanctuary" (Herzfeld, quoted by Godard).

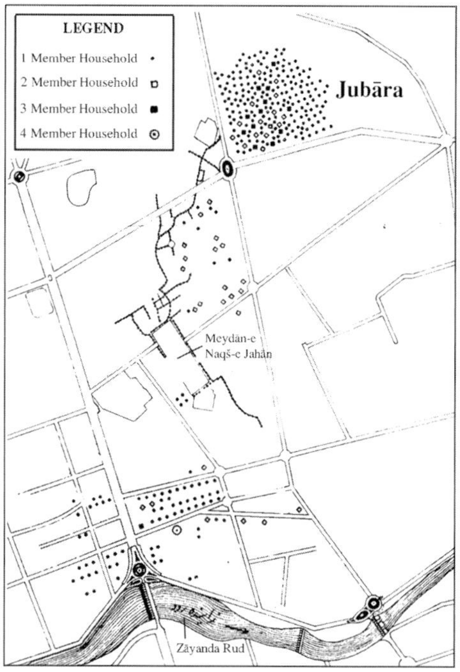

Figure 1. Distribution of Jewish households in the 1970s in the Jewish neighborhood (*maḥalla*) located in Jubāra quarter and other quarters of Isfahan. Adapted from Šafaqi, facing p. 402.

According to the report prepared by the Jewish Central Organization (Anjoman-e kalimiān) in Tehran, there were 1,500 Jews living in Isfahan in 2003, of whom 700 resided in the Jewish neighborhood (*maḥalla*) in Jubāra quarter (see Figures 1 and 2), and the rest were living around the main thoroughfare of Čahārbāḡ. Religious services are carried out in nineteen synagogues, of which eighteen are located in the Jewish quarter and one in the city center; the latter is used for social affairs of the community as well. The Jewish school, now called Madrasa-ye Etteḥād (formerly Alliance) and run by a Muslim principal, is divided into two separate sections, one for boys and one for girls. It provides education from the first to the ninth grade and has the total of about 800 enrollment in each section.

Bibliography: Bishop Sh. Ajamian, "An Armenian Bible, Codex 1934 of the Armenian Library of Jerusalem," *Christian News from Israel* 22, 1972, pp. 119-22. Abu Noʿaym Aḥmad b. ʿAbd-Allāh Eṣfahāni, *Ḏekr aḵbār Eṣbahān*, ed. Sven Deddering as *Geschichte Iṣbahāns nach der Leidener Handschrift*, 2 vols., Leiden, 1934, I, pp. 22-23; tr. Nur-Allāh Kasā'i as *Ḏekr-e aḵbār-e Esfahān*, Tehran, 1998. Wilhelm Bacher, "Un épisode de l'hisoire des Juifs de Perse," *Revue des études juives* 47, 1903, pp. 262-82. Idem, "Les Juifs de Perse aux XVIIe et XVIIIe siècles d'après les chroniques poétiques de Babai b. Loutf et de Babai b. Farhad," *Revue des études juives* 51, 1906, pp. 121-36, 265-79; 52,

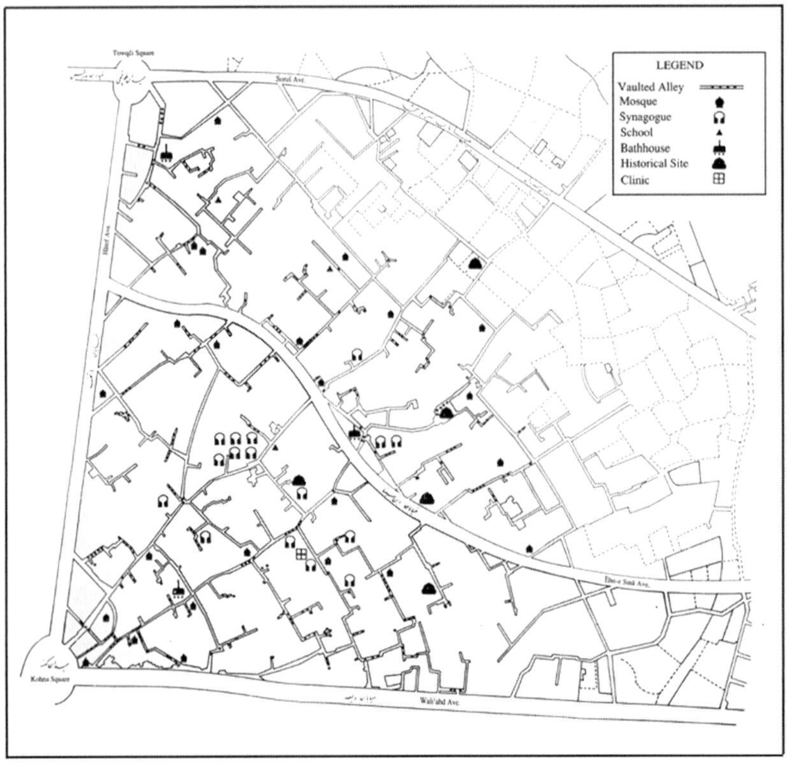

Figure 2. Distribution of various religious and public facilities in the Jewish neighborhood (*maḥalla*), located in Jubāra quarter. Adapted from Šafaqi, facing p. 410.

1906, pp. 77-97, 234-71; 53, 1907, pp. 85-110. F. Baer, "Eine jüdische Messiasprophtie auf das Jahr 1186 und der 3. Kreuzzug," *Montasschrift für Geschichte und Wissenschaft des Judentum* 70, 1926, pp. 155 ff. Israel Joseph Benjamin II, *Cinq années de voyage en Orient 1846-1851, par Israel Joseph Benjamin II*, Paris, 1856, pp. 146-48. Benjamin of Tudela, *The Itinerary of Rabbi Benjamin of Tudela*, ed. and tr. Adolf Asher, 2 vols., New York, 1840-41, pp. 82, 88; repr, New York, 1900. David d'Beth Hilell, *Unknown Jews in Unknown Lands: The Travels of Rabbi David d'Beth Hillel, 1824-1832*, ed. Walter Joseph Fischel, New York, 1973. James Darmesteter, "Textes Pehlevis relatifs au Judaism," *Revue des études juives* 18, 1889, pp. 1-15; 19, pp. 41-56. Idem, "La Rein Shasyân Dôkht," *Actes du VIII Congrès Internationale des Orientalistes*, Leiden, 1892, pp. 193-98. Ebn al-Faqih Hamadāni, *Ketāb al-Boldān*, ed. Michaël Jan de Goeje, Leiden, 1885. Ebn al-Ḥawqal, *Ketāb ṣurat al-arż*, ed. Johannes Hendrik Kramers, Leiden, 1967; tr. Johannes Hendrik Kramers and Gaston Wiet as *Configuration de la terre*, 2 vols., Beirut, 1964-65. Walter Joseph Fischel, Walter Joseph Fischel, "The Bible in Persian Translation," *Harvard Theological Review* 45, 1952, pp. 3-45. Idem, "Isfahan: The Story of A Jewish Community in Persia," *Joshua Starr Memorial Volume: Studies in History and Philology*, New York, 1953, pp. 111-28. Yedda A. Godard, "Le Tombeau de Pīr Bakrān," *Athār-è Īrān: annales du Service Archéologique de l'Īrān* 2/1, 1937, pp. 29-30. Louis H. Gray, "The Jews in Pahlavi Literature," *Jewish Encyclopedia* IX, New York and London, 1905, pp. 462-65. Ḥamza b. Ḥasan Eṣfahāni, *Taʾriḵ seni moluk al-arż wa'l-anbiāʾ*, ed. and tr. J. M. E. Gottwaldt, 2 vols., St. Petersburg and Leipzig, 1844-48; Beirut, 1961, pp. 37, 50. Loṭf-Allāh Honarfar, *Ganjina-ye āṯār-e tāriḵi-e Eṣfahān: āṯār-e bāstāni wa alwāḥ wa katibahā-ye tāriḵi dar ostān-e Eṣfahān*, Tehran, 1965. Josef Markwart (Marquart), *Ērānšahr, nach der Geographie des Ps. Moses Xorenacʿi*, Abhandlungen der Königlichen Gesellschaft der Wissenschaften zu Göttingen, Phil.-Hist. Klasse, N.S. 3/2, 1901, nos. 47, 53. Moses Khorenatsʿi, *Patmutʿiwn Hayotsʿ*, tr. Victor Langlois as *Histoire d'Arménie en trois livres*, Collection des Histoire anciens et modernes de l'Arménie 3, Paris, 1869, part. 3, sec. 35; tr. Robert W. Thomson as History of the Armenians, Cambridge, Mass., 1978. Guy Le Strange, *The Lands of the Eastern Caliphate*, London, 1966. Ḥabib Levy, *Tāriḵ-e Yahud-e Irān*, 3 vols., Tehran, 1955-60; tr. George W. Maschke as *Comprehensive History of The Jews of Iran: The Outset of the Diaspora*, ed. and abridged by Hooshang Ebrami, Costa Mesa, Calif., 1999. Vera Basch Moreen, *Iranian*

Jewry's Hour of Peril and Heroism: A Study of Bābā'i ibn Lutf's Chronicle (1617-1662), New York and Jerusalem, 1987, Index. Šams-al-Din Abu ʿAbd-Allāh Moḥammad Moqaddasi (Maqdesi), *Aḥsan al-taqāsim fi maʿrefat al-aqālim*, ed. Michaël Jan de Goeje, Leiden, 1967, pp. 388, 394, 414, 439. Amnon Netzer, *Montaḵab-e ašʿār-e fārsi az āṯār-e yahudiān-e Irān*, Tehran, 1973. Idem, "Redifot vu-shemadot be-toldot yehudei iran be-meaʾha-17" (Persecutions and forced conversions of Iranian Jewry in the 17th century), *Peʿamim* 6, 1980, pp. 32-56. Idem, "Isfahan and Its People," in *Shofar*, no. 281-91 July 2004-April 1005. E. Neumark, *Masaʿ be-ereẓ ha-qedem* (Journey in the ancient lands), ed. A. Yaʿari, Jerusalem, 1947, p. 85. Jacob Neusner, *A History of the Jews in Babylonia* V: *Later Sasanian Times*, Leiden, 1970, pp. 8-14. S. Pines, "ʿIsāwiyya," in *EI*² IV, p. 96. Yaʿqub b. Esḥāq Qerqisāni, *Ketāb al-anwār wa marāqeb*, ed. Leon Nemoy, 5 vols., New York, 1939-43; partial tr. by Leon Nemoy as "Account of the Jewish Sects and Christianity," *Hebrew Union College Annual* 7, 1930, pp. 382-91. Sirus Šafaqi, *Joḡrāfiā-ye Eṣfahān*, Isfahan, 2003, pp. 400-424. Abu'l-Fatḥ Moḥammad b. ʿAbd-al-Karim Šahrestāni, *Ketāb al-melal wa'l-neḥal*, ed. William Cuerton, London, 1846; tr. Afżal-al-Din Ṣadr Torka Eṣfahāni as *al-Mellal wa'l-neḥal*, ed. Sayyed Moḥammad-Reżā Jalāli Nāʾini, Tehran, 1956; tr. Theodore Haarbrücker as *Religionspartheien und Philosophen-Schulen*, 2 vols., 2nd ed., Hildesheim, 1969. *Šahristānihā ī Ērān*, ed. and tr. with commentary Josef Markwart as *A Catalogue of the Provincial Capitals of Ērānshahr*, ed. Giuseppe Messina, Rome, 1931. Paul Schwarz, *Iran im Mittelalter nach den arabischen Geographer*, Hildesheim and New York, 1969, pp. 582 ff., esp. p. 586. M. Seligsohn, "Quatre poésies judéo-persanes sur les persécutions des juifs d'Ispahan," *Revue des études juives* 44, 1902, pp. 87-103, 244-59. Ezra Spicehandler, "The Persecution of the Jews of Isfahan under Shāh ʿAbbās II (1642-1666)," *Hebrew Union College Annual* 46, 1975, pp. 331-56. *The Standard Jewish Encyclopaedia*, Garden city, New York, 1959. Daniel Tsadik, "Foreign Intervention, Majority, and Minority: The Status of the Jews during the Latter Part of Nineteenth Century Iran (1848-1896)," Ph.D. diss., Yale University, 2002. Idem, "Nineteenth-Century Iranian Jewry: Statistics, Geographical Setting, and Economic Basis," *Iran* 43, 2005, 275-82. Geo Widengren, "The Status of the Jews in the Sassanian Empire," *Iranica Antiqua* 1, 1961, pp. 117-62. David Yeroushalami, *The Judeo-Persian Poet ʿEmrānī and His Book of Treasure*, Leiden and New York, 1995.

(AMNON NETZER)

xix. JEWISH DIALECT

Introduction. The dialect spoken by the Jews of Isfahan (henceforth IsfJ.) belongs to the Central Dialect (CPD) group (also called Median dialects by some scholars) of Northwestern Iranian languages (NWI). The original speech form of the city of Isfahan (see also xxi. PROVINCIAL DIALECTS and xx. GEOGRAPHY OF THE MEDIAN DIALECTS OF ISFAHAN) was probably very similar to IsfJ. and remained in the Jewish community but died out in the Muslim community, not without leaving its influence, however, on the type of Persian spoken in Isfahan. According to Ehsan Yarshater's informants in 1970, there were about 2,500 Jewish residents in Isfahan at the time, a decrease from possibly 13,000 in the heyday of the community, and there were over twenty synagogues, some of which by 1970 were in disuse. The Jewish population is centered in the section of Isfahan known as Jubāra as well as throughout the city. Donald Stilo's notes were also provided by a local rabbi in a synagogue in Jubāra in 1964. While the Jewish community of Isfahan has been greatly reduced, IsfJ. is still spoken among various generations there. In the diaspora, the dialect is still spoken by the older generation in Israel, Los Angeles, and New York City and sporadically in other large urban centers.

History and classification. The Jewish dialects of Isfahan, Kāshān, Hamadān, Borujerd, Yazd, Kermān and others belong to the Central dialect group of Northwestern Iranian. All of Northwestern Iranian languages, in turn, are descended from Median, whereas Persian (including Middle Persian or Pahlavi) belongs to the Southwestern Iranian (SWI) group and are descended from Old Persian. Since Persian and modern "Median" dialects are two completely different linguistic groups within Iranian that diverged over 2,500 years ago, the term "Judeo-Persian," which is sometimes applied to IsfJ. (as well as other dialects spoken by the Jewish communities listed above), is to be considered a misnomer. "Judeo-Persian" is more accurately applied specifically to Persian dialects as spoken (or written) within Jewish communities in different locales and especially at different time periods, beginning with the earliest forms of New Persian in the 8th century C.E. Since IsfJ. and other Central dialects have borrowed extensively from Persian, especially within the lexical domain, they may seem to be very similar to Persian, but a closer look at the diachronics, the native lexicon and grammar as laid out below will suffice to show the radical differences between Persian as opposed to IsfJ. and other Northwestern languages and dialects.

Diachronics. Important differences in the development of proto-Iranian consonants in Median/NWI and Old Persian/SWI show that they were already distinct from each other before the time of the cuneiform inscriptions of the Achaemenian period. The two groups diverged even more in the Middle Iranian and early Modern Iranian periods. Thus, to take one characteristic example, proto-Iranian **dz* (corresponding to Skt. *j-*) yields different reflexes in Old Persian (and its descendants in modern SWI) from those of Median (and its descendants in modern NWI). Words that had a proto-Iranian **dz-*, such as "to know" and "son-in-law," yielded words that begin with *d-* in Southwestern languages (cf. Persian *dān-* and *dāmād*) as opposed to words with *z-* in the Northwestern family (Av. *zan-* "know" and *zāmātar* "son-in-law," cf. Skt. *jān-* and *jāmātar-*, respectively). In examining a sampling of the Central dialects, as well as other Northwestern Iranian languages outside the Central dialects, we find the following forms, all beginning with *z-* and meaning "know (present/past stems)" and "son-in-law," respectively: IsfJ.: *zun-/zunā* and *zumāz*; Hamadāni Jewish: *zun-/zunā* and *dumād* (the latter a borrowing from Persian); Gazi: *zun-/zunāšt* and *zomā*; Anāraki: *zon-/zono* and *zomā*; K̲ᵛānsāri: *zun-/zunā* and *zumā*; Yazdi Zoroastrian: *zon-/zonod* and *zomād*; Āštiāni: *zān-/zānā* and *zāmā*; and beyond the Central dialects, Semnāni: *zun-/zuni* and *zomā* ~ *zumi*; Tāleši (Māsula'i): *zon-/zonoss* and *zemā*; Gilaki: *dān-/ dānəst* (borrowed from Persian) and *zāmā*; Baluchi: *zān-/zānt* and *zamās*; Kurdish (Kurmanji): *zān-/zāni* and *zāvā*. There are many more examples of the differences in sounds that distinguish Persian and other SWI from all NWI languages and dialects, including IsfJ., Gazi, and other Central dialects, some of which are given below.

NWI developments from proto-Iranian in IsfJ. include: **dz > z*, as in IsfJ. *zun/zunā* "know," *zumāz* "son-in-law" (as discussed above), *ezerí* "yesterday"; **tsv- > sp-*: IsfJ. *išpiš* "louse," *esbez* "white"; **dzv- > zb* in IsfJ. *ozun* "tongue," where *-b-* was probably absorbed into the *u* much later (e.g., *zbān > zvān > ozvun > ozun*, or some similar process); **dv- > b-*, as in *bar* "door," *abi* "other"; **y-* remains as *y-* (vs. SWI *j-*) as in IsfJ. *ye* "barley," *yuš-* "boil"; **v-* remains as *v-* (instead of SWI *g-*) in IsfJ. *veyše* "hungry," *v(e)zer-/v(e)zašd* "pass," and as *v-* (vs. SWI *b-*) in IsfJ. *vāzum* "almond," *vārun* "rain," *vij-/vit* "sift," *viye* "widow," *viθ* "twenty," *vāz* "wind"; initial **j-* remains as *j-* (vs. SWI *z-*) in *jan* "wife, play (instrument)," *jande* "alive"; medial **-č- > -j-* (vs. SWI *z-*) as in *tej-* "run," *vij-* "sift," *vājār* "bazaar, market," *jir* "under, down" (< **haca adara-*); $*x^{w} > x$ as in *xunt* "read," *xox* "sister," *xow* "sleep (N)," but note also: $*x^{w} > \phi$ in *owθ-/ofd-* "sleep." The typical NWI change **-xt > -(h)t ~ -(t)t*, is represented in IsfJ. *sowt* "burned," *dot* "daughter, girl," *rit* "poured," *vit* "sifted," *vāt* "said." The usually parallel development of **-ft* > NWI *-(h)t ~ -(t)t*, however, either did not occur in IsfJ. or its absence is possibly due to an effect of Persian or other SWI influence: *dar-kaft* "fall," *i-ofd* "sleep," *i-geft ~ gift* "take" (but cf. Gazi *i-git*).

**fr > r* as in *kāre~gāre* "down" (< Av. *gufra-, ǰafra-*) and possibly **fr- > i-* in the IsfJ. preverb *i-~e-* (see "Preverbs" below). Eṣfahāni Jewish and the dialects of the immediate Isfahan area (specifically Gazi, K̲orzuqi, Sedehi, and Sagzāvi) have an *i- ~ e-* preverb in the same verbs in which other NWI have the corresponding preverb *hā- < *fra-*. Compare IsfJ. *i-gi(r)* "take, get," *i-ni* "sit," *i-owθ* "sleep," *e-tā* "give," *e-n-* "put," *e-band* "hit," *e-parθ* "ask" with the same verbs in: Kafrāni (*hā-gir, hā-ning, ā-xus, hā-t, hā-nā,* —, —), Anāraki (*ha-gir, ha-nik, ha-wsi, ha-t, ha-nā, hab-end,* —), Alviri (a Tāti language) (*hā-gir, hā-neš, hā-xös, ā-d, hā-nā,* —, —), Vafsi (a Tāti language) (*hā-gir, hā-nešin,* —, *hā-d, hā-ni,* —, *hā-pars*) and Māzanderāni (*hā-gir, he-niš,* —, *hā-de,* —, —, *hā-pers*). Other cases of original **fr-* are seen in IsfJ. only as *fr-*, which is typical of SWI (*ferāš/ferāt* "sell," *feresn/-ā* "send"); **θr > r*: *pir* "son" and *ār-ci* "hand mill" (cf. the root minus the diminutive suffix *-ci* with: K̲ᵛānsāri, Jowšaqāni *ār*, Meyma'i *or* "mill" < Av. *ārθra-*, but IsfJ. *āsiow* "mill" < SWI); **xr- >* IsfJ. *ir-*: **xrin-* "buy" > *irin-/irint*, but other examples of this development in initial position were not found. Medial **-xr- >* IsfJ. *-r-*: *θir* "red." See also a longer discussion of the reflexes of **fr-, *θr-, *xr-* under *Diachronics* in xxii, below.

IsfJ. is conservative in preserving medial and final **d*, both medially and finally as *δ~z* and medially occasionally also as *-d-* (equivalents are also given in other Central dialects, where these consonants are either weakened to *-y, -v* or are lost): IsfJ. *vāzum ~ vāδum~vādum* "almond," *cezor~ceδor* "chador," *xód-e~xoz-e ~ xoδ-e* "with" (Farizandi *vāyom, cāyür, xāy*), *bezār ~ beδār* "brother" (K̲ᵛānsāri *berā*), *keze ~ keδe* "house" (Meyma'i *kiye*), *ruze ~ ruδe* "intestine" (Sedehi *ruve*), *v(e)zer/v(e)zašd- ~ v(e)δer/v(e)δašd-* "pass" (Yārandi *viar/viašt-*), *diz ~ diδ* "smoke," *zumāz~δumāδ* "son-in-law" (Zefra'i *dü, zomā*), *esbez ~ eθbeδ* "white" (Sedehi *esbe*), *māz ~ māδ* "mother," *vāz ~ vāδ* "wind" (Naṭanzi *māy, vāy*).

Original **ū*, even in Arabic borrowings, is generally fronted to *i* as in *xin* "blood," *pir* "boy, son," *miš* "mouse," *diz* "smoke," *θir* "red," *āris* "bride," *haθit* "jealous," *til* "length." This change, however, is not universal in IsfJ.: *θuδue* "it burns," *dušnue* "he milks," *gušd* "meat." Original **ā* changes to *u* before nasals: *ume* "come," *zumāz* "son-in-law," (*ve-*) *mun/mund* "stay," *un* "that," *vun* "there."

Phonology. IsfJ. consonants are *p, b, t, d, c, j, k, g, q~γ, f, v, s, z, š, x, h, m, n, r, l, y*, but note that: a) *z, s* alternate freely with interdental *δ, θ* respectively: *δunun~zunun* "I know," *bépez ~ bépeδ!* "cook!," *eδeri~ezeri* "yesterday," *tarsue~tarθue* "he fears," *véroθ ~ véros* "get up!"; b) medial *-d-* sometimes alternates with *-δ* (and occasionally *-z-*): *pírodun~píroδun* "your son," *xód-e~xóδ-e ~ xoz-e* "with," *vāzum~vāδum~vādum* "almond"; c) *č* and *j* (= *ǰ*, which in IsfJ. includes *ž* of other languages) are palatalized to *ć* and *ǰ*: *ćirići* "sparrow, chick," *bijan* "man's name." Noteworthy in the vowel system (*i, e, a, u, o, ā, ey, ew*) is the *ew* diphthong, resulting both from an original glide as well as from the change of *b, f > w*: *mew* "vine," *kewk* "partridge," *lew* "lip," *kewš* "shoe," *kelews* "celery," cf. Persian *mow, kabk, lab, kafš, karafs*, respectively.

Stress in Eṣfahāni Jewish is mostly word-final, but some morphemes, particularly in verbal categories, cause the stress to shift away from final position: the prefix *bé-* (*bé-m-bart* "I carried") and the preverbs of the subjunctive, imperative, preterit, and perfect tenses; the person endings in the present (*ār-ún-e* "I bring," *ber-úv-e* "he carries"); the participial element in the imperfect (*umó-un-e* "I would come," *baθté-š-e* "he would hit," *ve-garté-nd-e* "they would return"). Stress usually contrasts between the present and subjunctive forms with preverbs: *ve-krúne* "I open" vs. *vé-krun* "that I open."

The stress-pitch system of IsfJ. is quite a rare case in that it seems to be the exact opposite of the situation found in most languages of the world: in IsfJ. unstressed syllables have high pitch and the stressed syllables have low pitch. This unusual situation in effect makes the pronunciation of a word sound to the uninitiated ear as if the stress is placed on the unstressed syllable due to the higher pitch. This author thus first heard the words *pírom* "my son" and *beδā́rom* "my brother" as *piróm* and *béδārom* with the stress incorrectly assigned due to the unusual pitch system; compare Rubène Abrahamian's *círi* "sparrow," *ā́lā* "now," *éšnide* "you hear," instead the expected *cirí*, *ālā́*, *ešníde*, possibly incorrectly notated for the same reasons. This unusual pattern is also shared by Isfahani Persian, probably as a leftover from the original dialect of the city. Compare the following parallel patterns of two simple sentences in Tehrani Persian and Isfahani Persian:

Tehrani: (3 levels)

kojā́ míri? xunát nazdík-e?

Isfahani: (2 levels?)

ujā́ míri? xunéd nezík-es?

"Where are you going? Is your house nearby?"

A more careful and detailed analysis of the unusual stress-pitch system patterns of the Persian and NWI dialects in the area from Isfahan to Yazd needs to be conducted.

Noun phrase. Number: IsfJ. nouns and pronouns do not indicate gender or formal case (but see the discussion of *-(r)ā*, below). There is one type of plural ending in *-ā*: *doδδ-ā* "thieves," *gorg-ā* "wolves," *guš-ā* "ears," *kenisā-ā* "synagogues." The two indefinite markers occur either separately or together: *ye* "one" and/or an unstressed *-i*: *xurúθi*, *ye xuruθ*, *ye xurúθi* "a rooster."

Object marking. Definite direct objects are marked with unstressed *-(r)ā*, but less commonly in the tenses of the past system (see *Fronting* below for a discussion of this phenomenon): *bid hāmā-rā bévenid* "come see us," *dandunā-š-ā be-am bé-š-xerāšā* "he pressed (i.e., gritted) his teeth together." The combination of the preposition *še* + the short pronominal suffixes (Set$_2$, see Table 1) also marks (1) direct objects either (a) alone: *še-m bandíe?* "Will you hit me?" or (b) *še* + Set$_2$ along with the full pronoun marked by *-(r)ā*: *mun tó-rā še-d nébandune* "I won't hit you," and (2) indirect objects (*pilā-m-ā še-d nétune* "I won't give you my money"). As will be shown below (see *Person endings*, *Fronting*) the Set$_2$ endings that indicate the past subject are rather mobile and very commonly move off the verb and shift forward in the sentence, hence the designation "Fronting." Thus when a Set$_2$ subject ending is moved from the verb to *še* that already has a Set$_2$ possessive ending, two Set$_2$ endings will then occur together: *še$_1$-š$_2$-om$_3$ baθ$_4$* "I$_3$ hit$_4$ him$_{1\text{-}2}$," *še$_1$-š$_2$-oš$_3$ dā$_4$* "he$_3$ gave$_4$ (it) to$_1$ him$_2$." With indirect objects, the Set$_2$ ending sometimes also moves to an earlier word in the sentence, in which case *še* then stands alone: *še-d* "to you" > *xeδā omr-od še é-tā* "may God give you (long) life." See also *Prepositions* below for more information on indicating indirect objects.

Set$_2$ ending inserted between the suffixes for person (Set$_1$) and tense (*-e*) in the present also optionally indicates pronoun direct objects: *band-ún-ešun-e* "I'll hit them," *keš-end-ed-e* "they'll kill you," but in the subjunctive, optative, and imperative, Set$_2$ as object comes either just before the verb stem (*bé-d-beru* "[that] he takes you," *xeδā bé-š-kešā* "may God kill him," *bé-š-ārid* "bring [pl.] him," *bi-šun-gi* "grab them!") or occasionally at the end: *bétarsen-eš* "frighten him!"). In addition, according to Irān Kalbāsi (1994), two short form pronouns (Set$_2$) can appear together to indicate both subject and object in past tenses: *be-šun$_1$-oš$_2$-ferāt* "they$_1$ sold it$_2$," *pušd-om-oš-e* "I used to wear it," but this construction is not found in any other published sources or field notes for IsfJ., and it may represent a very recent innovation in IsfJ. (most likely under the influence of colloquial Persian among the younger generation, and possibly only from elicited, i.e., translated, examples; it would be informative to track the frequency of this construction in spontaneous speech among speakers of different ages). If only one Set$_2$ ending occurs in a past tense, it obligatorily indicates the subject, never the object. Thus while *peydā-mun kard* in colloquial Persian means "he found us," the equivalent in IsfJ., *peydā-mun kart*, can only mean "we found (him/it)." In sum, to show pronouns as direct objects in the past tense, either the full form of the pronoun or a second Set$_2$ ending is possible: *āmā-rā peydā-š kart* ~ *peydā-š-omun kart* (the latter in Kalbāsi only) "he found us," but the former seems to be preferred, at least in older sources.

As in Gazi (q.v.), IsfJ. also quite commonly indicates full direct objects doubly by both the full noun or pronoun plus the Set$_2$ endings: *doδδe-rā še-š ne-band* "don't hit the thief!," *un-ā be-š-ven* "see him!," *mun tó-rā še-d nébandune* "I won't hit you."

Modifiers follow the noun generally connected by an *eżāfa*, for instance, possessives: *dím-e vece* "the child's face," *váxd-e deróv-e šemā* "the time of your harvest," *bár-e keniθā* "the door of the synagogue," but the *eżāfa* often drops (see also Gazi), especially after a vowel: *keδé xóx-om* "my sister's house," *buvā vece* "the child's father," *beletarā mahalle* "the great (people) of the neighborhood." Possessive pronouns are either full forms or Set$_2$ suffixes: *pír-e mun~pír-om* "my son," but the latter are by far more common: *beδār-om madreθe nešue* "my brother doesn't go to school," *pír-od key be xune yue?* "when will your son come home?," *anšew kami hāl-oš veytar-u* "he feels a little better tonight." Adjective Modifiers with the *eżāfa*: *nasihát-e xab* "good advice," *moallém-e pārisi* "Parisian teacher," *xox-e kuculi dārun* "I have a younger sister," but the *eżāfa* may occasionally drop (*vece-širi* "nursing infant"). The plural suffix may shift from the noun to the adjective: *vece-iθrāel-ā* "the Jewish children."

Demonstratives in IsfJ. are *in* "this," *un* "that," *amin*/*amun* "this/that very (same)": *in mard* "this man," *un kār* "that work," *gumā-bu amin amšew béšim* "we must go this very night."

Pronouns. Table 1 gives three types of pronouns: full pronouns for subject (and various other uses), full direct object forms, and Set_2 suffixes with various functions (described passim throughout this entry), as well as the Set_1 person endings on the verb.

Table 1
Independent Pronouns and Agreement Markers in the Verb

	Independent Pronouns			Set_1 Verb Endings	
	Subject	Object	Short Pronominal Endings	Present	Past (Intransitive)
1st sg.	*mun*	*mún-ā*	*-(o)m*	*-un*	*-(u)n, -wn*
2nd sg.	*to*	*tó-rā*	*-(o)d*	*-e ~ -i*	*-y, -e*
3rd sg.	*un*	*ún-ā*	*-(o)š*	*-u ~ -u(v)-*	*-Ø*
1st pl.	*āmā*	*āmā-rā*	*-(o)mun*	*-im*	*-ym, -im*
2nd pl.	*šemā*	*šemā-rā*	*-(o)dun ~ -(o)δun*	*-id, -it*	*-yd, -yt, -id*
3rd pl.	*unā*	*unā-rā*	*-(o)šun*	*-end, -ent*	*-(e)nd, -(e)nt*
			Set_2 Endings	Set_1 Endings	

Reflexives are *xo-*, *xoc-* + Set_2 endings but the difference between them, if any, is not clear. Both are used in IsfJ. after prepositions (*píš-e xó-š* "to himself," *déwr-e xóc-aš* "around himself"), as possessives (*vece xo-d-u?* "Is he your own child?" *bešā-š fekrhā-ye xóc-aš-ā amali karu* "he can realize his (own) thoughts)," and as emphatics (*xó-mun šíme tu xarman* "we'll go to the harvest ourselves," *mo xóc-am ún-ā tu maδra'e bi-m-di* "I myself saw him in the field," *xóc-aš yúve* "she'll come by herself"). Only two examples of reflexives as direct objects were found in the available corpora: *mun xóc-am-ā be in kār ādat-om e-dā* "I have accustomed myself to this (work)" (Kalbāsi), *amšew gumā-bu xoc-am-rā be ša:r bereθnun* "I must get (lit: deliver) myself to the city tonight" (Borjiān).

Prepositions. Other than *aδ* "from," *še, be* "to," *dā~tā* "until," *tu, der* "in" etc., prepositions usually require an *ezāfa: xód-e* "with," *píš-e* "at, to (person)," *dím-e* "on," etc. Exx: *aδ jir* "from below," *dā šew* "until night," *xód-e cu* "with a stick," *xód-e jan-om* "with my wife," *dím-e áθb-oš* "on his horse." *še, be* and *píš-e* indicate indirect objects: *be āmā buvāid* "tell us," *mun píš-e pír-od bé-m-vāt* "I told your son," *pil-oš-ā še-š de!* "Give him his money!" Prepositions may also take Set_2 endings: *xód-om, xód-ot, xód-oš* "with me, you, him," *gu-m-e xód-ot béngārun* "I want to speak with you." With "to be" of location, especially be_3 (see below), the prepositions indicating "in" are often left unexpressed: *sebāh šew mon keδe der-un* "I'll be home tomorrow night."

Verb phrase. Verb stems. IsfJ. generally has the usual types of past formations seen in other Iranian languages, e.g., *gir-/gifd~gi* "take, catch," *band-/baθθ* "hit," *k-/kafd* "fall," *rij-/rit* "pour," *al~ arz-/ašt* "let," *ven-/di* "see," but most past stems follow two regular patterns: 1) a smaller group in *-t* after an *-r* or *-n* of the root: *jār/-t* "chew," *emar/-t* "break," *xešār/-t* "press," *birin/-t* "cut," *xun/-t* "read," *jan/-t* "hit" (final *-t* is possibly a conservative feature; very few stems take the past formant *-d*, e.g., *mund-an* "stay"); 2) a much larger group in *-ā: zun/-ā* "know," *var-veδ/-ā* "jump," *tanj/-ā* "drink," *kelāš/-ā* "itch." Sometimes a slight change in the root vowel also occurs: *ber-/bart* "take away," *xuθ-/xoθ(θ)* "throw." Roots originally beginning with a vowel often accrue an initial *-r* from a preverb, e.g., **ver-oθ ~ ver-ows > ve-rows* "get up," as seen from the negative forms: *venéroθune* "I don't get up" (= **ver-oθ-un-e > ve-roθ- > ve-né-roθ-*). See also the same process with this root in Caspian languages: Gilaki (Langarudi) *vi-ris (< vir-is) vs. neg: vi-n-ris*, but the original *-r* is not shifted to the root in Māzanderāni *her-est! / néstā!*, "get up! / don't get up!"

Preverbs create finer nuances, lexical extensions, or total meaning changes of a verb root: *bí-gi* "grab! catch!" vs. *vé-gi* "pick up!" vs. *í-gi* "get! buy!"; *gartúne* "I walk around" vs. *vé-gartune* "I return"; *mālúne* "I rub" vs. *var-mālune* "I flee," *cinúve* "he picks (fruit, etc.)" vs. *var-cinúve* "(bird) pecks at (seeds)"; *vé-m-nāšt* "I extinguished" vs. *é-m-nāšt* "I seated." Sometimes the same verb root may occur both with and without a lexical preverb with no real difference in meaning: *dar-kaft ~ bekaft* "he fell." There are two types of preverbs: type 1 (*ve(r)-*, *var-*, *dar-*) appears in all tenses and with negatives; type 2 (*e-~i-*) appears only in the affirmative and only in non-durative forms (subjunctive, preterit and the perfects). Note the use of *e-~i-* in the affirmative imperative (*í-gi* "buy!" *é-parθ* "ask!") and preterit (*í-m-gift, é-m-parθā*), but not in the durative (i.e., present and imperfect) tenses: (present) *gir-un-e, parθ-un-e*, or negatives of any tense (preterit affirmative/negative: *í-m-gift/ná-m-gift, é-m-parθā/ná-m-parθā*). Although both types of preverbs have precedents elsewhere (cf. Māzanderāni, Vafsi where preverbs only appear in non-duratives; and Gilaki, Zefra'i, Gorāni, Tālеši, where the preverb appears in all tenses, no NWI language beyond IsfJ. and three or four immediate neighbors seems to have both types).

The preverbs *i-* and *e-* actually seem to be one preverb whose forms alternate before high and low vowels of the verb root respectively, as the following contrast shows: *í-ni* "sit!" vs. *é-nān* "seat!" Type 2 preverbs only appear in a few roots: (before high vowels) *í-gi(r)* "take," *í-ni* "sit," *í-owθ* "sleep," (before low vowels) *é-de* "give" *é-ne* "put," *é-nān* "seat," *é-band* "hit," *é-parθ* "ask" (see also *Diachronics* above).

Negation. né- ~ ná- comes just before the stem in all present forms and the intransitive preterit (*dar-né-k-un-e* "I don't fall," *né-reθā-un* "I didn't arrive"), but the subject marker (Set_2) in the transitive preterit comes between *né-* and the stem: *ná-š-di* "she didn't see" (the latter, however, may also be fronted out of the verb altogether: *vecé-š-ā né-di* "she didn't see her child"). Negatives occur with type 1 preverbs in all tenses (*dar-né-gin-un-e* "I won't light/kindle," *ve-né-roθā-un* "I didn't get up"). Since the negative particle suppresses both *be-* (subj. *bé-frāš-un/né-frāš-un* "that I sell/not sell") and type 2 preverbs in those tenses, where they occur, verbs with different preverbs (and hence different meanings) merge in the negative: *bé-gir-* "catch/grab" and *í-gir-* "buy/get" both yield the negative forms *né-gir-un-e* "I don't catch/buy." The negative imperative is formed with either *mé-* ~ *má-* (*mé-vāid* "don't say!" *dar-mé-ki* "don't fall!") or *né-* ~ *ná-* (*ná-koš* "don't kill!")

Non-finite forms. Infinitives consist of (preverb) + past stem + *-án: vāt-án* "to say," *dar-kaft-án* "to fall," *und-án* "to come." The *-ā* of a past stem merges with the *-a* of the infinitive: *kešā* > *keš-án* "to pull." Monosyllabic roots ending in a vowel usually retain an original *-z~d~δ* in the stem before the infinitive ending: *še-*, *dā-*, *be-*, also *um(o)-* > *še-δ-an* "to go," *dā-d-an* "to give," *be-δ-an* "to be," *und-an* "to come" (< *um-d-an*). The infinitives in Ḥabib Borjiān's fieldwork are exclusively formed with the ending *–āmun*, but this formation is not found in other sources (but see xxii, below for examples of this formation: *vāt-āmun*, *dar-kaft-āmun*, etc.). This formation sometimes also includes the (unstressed) non-durative marker *be-* in some cases: (*b-ārt-āmun* "to bring," *b-irint-āmun* "to buy," but *paxt-āmun* "to cook," *cint-āmun* "to pick," *reθā-mun* < *reθā-āmun* "to arrive," *ve-roθā-mun* < *ve-roθā-āmun* "to rise, get up," *i-ništ-āmun* "to sit"), and in some cases this formation is based on the present root: *ve-gir-āmun* "to pick up."

The past participle consists of (preverb)/*be-* + past stem + *-é* after consonants (*dar-kaft-é* "fallen"), but the final *-ā* of the stem merges with the *-é* of the participle to form *-á*: *be-* + *reθā* + *é* > *be-reθá* "arrived." The present participle consists of (preverb) + pres. root + *-andé*: *bar-andé* "winning, winner."

Tense markers. General comments. a) The present and imperfect are formed with a suffixed, unstressed *-e*, also called the durative marker (pres.: *band-ún-e*, *band-í-e*, "I hit, you hit," etc.; imperf.: *ārté-d-e* "you used to bring," *še-nd-e* "they used to go"). The suffix *-e* remains on the verb when Set_2 is moved off past transitive verbs to the object, e.g., *xorté-m-e* "I used to eat" vs. *nun-om xort-e* "I used to eat bread," *engliθi-šun-am xunt-e* "they used to study English, too" (for a fuller discussion of the suffixed *-e* and the formation of the durative tenses, see xxi. PROVINCIAL DIALECTS). b) The prefix *bé-* is used to form the IsfJ. subjunctive, optative, imperative, preterit and perfect tenses, but it is suppressed when either type of preverb accompanies the verb root (*bé-gartā* "he walked around," but *vé-gartā* "he returned"; *bí-š-gi* "he caught, grabbed" but *í-š-gi* "he took"), or when the verb is in the negative (see above). It has four alternate forms, *bé-*, *bí-*, *bú-*, and *b-*, of which *bé-* is the most common: *bé-m-ārt* "I brought," *bé-brun* "that I carry," *bé-rew* "sweep!," but *bí-arzu* "that it be worth," *b-ārun* "that I bring." The conditions for *bú-* are not totally clear: *búvā* "say!"; (Yarshater) *bévāun* "that I say," but (Kalbāsi, Borjiān, Stilo) *búvāun*.

Person endings. As with all Central dialects and most Northwestern Iranian languages, IsfJ. makes a crucial distinction between intransitive and transitive conjugations in all past tenses (see Tables 1 and 2). The intransitive forms in all tenses of the past system (preterit, imperfect, and the various perfects) are formed by placing the Set_1 endings consistently after the past stem (preterit: *i-níšd-own*, imperfect: *nišd-own-e*, pres. perf.: *i-nišdówn*, past perf.: *i-nišde-bo*. The tenses of the transitive past system, however, differ from intransitive verbs in three important ways: a) all past transitive tenses are formed with Set_2 endings rather than Set_1; b) the Set_2 endings come *before* the past stem in the preterit and the perfect tenses; c) the Set_2 endings are much more mobile than Set_1. Note the difference in the preterit conjugation of intransitive *tej-*/*tejā* "I ran, you ran, etc." vs. transitive *puš-*/*pušd* "I put on, you put on, etc.":

run:	*be-ttejā-n*	*be-ttejā-y*	*be-ttejā-Ø*
	be-ttejā-ym	*be-ttejā-yd*	*be-ttejā-nt*
put on:	*be-m-pušd*	*be-d-pušd*	*be-š-pušd*
	be-mun-pušd	*be-dun-pušd*	*be-šun-pušd*

The position of the Set_2 endings of the past system is variable according to tense: (1) between the prefixed *bé-* (or the preverb) and the verb stem in the preterit, as we see with *bé-m-pušd* above, or (2) between the verb stem and the suffixed *-e* in the imperfect (*pušdé-m-e* "I would put on"). The position of Set_2 endings seems to depend on the stress placement within the verb and will therefore differ not only according to tense but also according to affirmative versus negative forms due to different stress patterns; that is, they move to that syllable within the verb where the stress falls. The two types of crucial examples that show this phenomenon are those cases where the stress and Set_2 endings follow the stem in the affirmative but precede the stem in the negative: a) (affirmative/negative) imperfect: *pušdé-m-e*/*ná-m-pušd-e*, and b) the forms of the "to want" (all tenses, see *Modals* below): (present) *gú-m-e*/*ná-m-gu-e* "I want/I don't want," (past) past: *gumā́-m-e*/*ná-m-gumā* "I wanted/I didn't want." Note that since *bé-* is always stressed, the stress pattern in other past transitive tenses does not change and the Set_2 endings are consistently placed before the stem: Preterit: *bé-m-pušd*/*ná-m-pušd*, pres. perf.: *bé-m-pušd-e*/*ná-m-pušd-e*, past perf.: *bé-m-pušd-e bu*/*ná-m-pušd-e bo*. Stress is not a determining factor for intransitive verbs as we saw above since the position of Set_1 is always constant.

Important points in the IsfJ. Set_1 endings are: (1) the 1st sg. *-un*, ending in *-n* rather than *-m*, is common within Central dialects (Ardestāni, Meymaʾi *-un*; Gazi, Sedehi, Ḵᵛānsāri, Hamadāni Jewish [q.v.] *-ān*; Delijāni *-on*; Kermāni Jewish *-in*), but other Central dialects have a final *-m* (or no nasal); (2) the 2nd sg. *-e* changes to *-i* when followed by the durative marker *-e*: subjunctive *bé-parθ-e* "that you ask" but present *parθ-i-e* "you ask" (= ask-2sg-durative); (3) the 3rd sg. *-u* is typical of Ḵᵛānsāri, Gazi, Sedehi, Zefraʾi, Vānišāni, Ḵuri, (*-o* in Kermāni Jewish) and of several other, but not of all, Central dialects (note also Gōrāni *-o~-u*).

Fronting. As shown in the previous section, Set_2 endings indicating the subject of transitive verbs are located in a

Table 2
ISFJ. Verb Forms (3rd p. sg; Infinitive)

	Intransitive		Transitive	
	without preverb "to arrive"	with preverb "to fall" (*dar-*)	without preverb "to take (away)"	with preverb "to open" (*ve-*)
Present:	*reθ-úv-e*	*dár-k-uv-e*	*ber-úv-e*	*ve-kr-úv-e*
Neg:	*né-reθ-uv-e*	*dar-né-k-uv-e*	*ná-br-uv-e*	*ve-ná-kr-uv-e*
Subjunctive:	*bé-reθ-u*	*dár-k-u*	*bé-br-u*	*vé-kr-uv-e*
Optative:	*bé-reθ-ā*	*??*	*bé-br-ā*	*??*
Imperative:	*bé-reθ*	*dár-k-i*	*bé-ber*	*vé-ker*
Pres. Prog.:	*dār-u reθ-úv-e*	*dār-u dar-k-uv-e*	*dār-u ber-úv-e*	*dār-u ve-kr-úv-e*
Preterit:	*bé-reθā*	*dar-kafd-Ø*[1]	*bé-š-bart*	*vé-š-kart*
Imperfect:	*reθa*	*dar-ka*	*barté-š-e*	*vé-š-kart-e*
Past Prog.:	*dārt-oš reθa*	*dārt-oš dar-ka*	*dārt-oš barté-š-e*	*dārt-oš vé-š-kart-e*
Pres Perf.:	*be-reθā*	*dar-kafd-e*	*be-š-bart-e*	*ve-š-kart-e*
Past Perf.:	*be-reθā-bo*	*dar-kafd-e-bo*	*be-š-bart-e-bo*	*ve-š-kart-e-bo*
Perf. Subj.:	*be-reθā-bu*	*dar-kafd-e-bu*	*be-š-bart-e-bu*	*ve-š-kart-e-bu*
Past Part.:	*reθā*	*dar-kafd-é*	*bart-é*	*ve-kart-é*
Infinitive:	*reθá-n*	*dar-kafd-án*	*bart-án*	*ve-kart-án*

[1] Abrahamian also lists *dar-kafdā* in two places [pp. 45, 129].

different position in the preterit (*be-m-xo* "I ate") than they are in the imperfect (*xorté-m-e* "I used to eat"). Set$_2$ endings are actually quite mobile and the general (but optional) tendency is for Set$_2$ to move forward in a sentence, hence the term "Fronting." Fronting indicates that the Set$_2$ person endings move off the verb in the various past tenses of transitives to a preceding word, often the direct object (but never to the subject): (preterit) *bí-š-gi* "he caught" > *xurúθ-oš bí-gi* "he caught the rooster"; (imperfect) *xorté-m-e* "I used to eat" > *nāštāi-m-em xort-e* "I used to eat my breakfast," (present perfect) *guθpand-omun né-gifte* "we haven't gotten a sheep." As the above example (*nāštāi-m-em . . .*) also shows, fronting of a Set$_2$ ending to a word that already has a Set$_2$ possessive marker is also possible (see also *še-š-om baθ* above), as opposed to other languages such as Hamadāni Jewish or Vafsi where this is not allowed.

As mentioned above, direct objects more commonly occur without *-(r)ā* in the past tenses than in the present tenses: *mun-od θedā baθ* "you called me." The reason for the lack of *-(r)ā* in the past tenses is that fronting is the most common way of forming sentences with past transitive verbs and it seems that the fronting of Set$_2$ to the object is incompatible with *-(r)ā* marking of the object: *neθf-e xorāk-om bexorte-bo* "I had eaten half of the food." When the person ending of a past tense transitive verb remains with the verb or is fronted to any element other than the direct object, it is then completely permissible for the object to be marked by *-(r)ā*: (remaining on verb) *xár-ā be-šun-bart* "they took the donkey away," *rassi-ā piš-oš ve-m-vāte-bo* "I had told him the truth"; (fronted to element other than direct object) *pil-oš-ā še-š-om dā* (= *pil*$_4$*-oš*$_3$*-ā še*$_5$*-š*$_6$*-om*$_1$ *dā*$_2$) "I$_1$ gave$_2$ his$_3$ money$_4$ to$_5$ him$_6$." Since fronting is always optional, there are very often alternate forms of a sentence with *-(r)ā* (and no fronting) and without *-(r)ā* (but with fronting): *gorgā guθpandā-rā be-šun-xo* ~ *gorgā guθpandā-šun boxo* "The wolves ate the sheep (pl.)," *kudum keδe-rā xoc-aš be-š-sāxt?* ~ *kudum keδe-š xoc-aš be-sāxt?* "which house did he himself build?," *mun un-ā bi-m-di* "I saw him" ~ *mun un-om ne-di* "I didn't see him." It should be noted that there are cases where *-(r)ā* does co-occur with the Set$_2$ in the past tense (e.g., *nāhār-om-ā be-š-ārt* "he brought my lunch"), but the first Set$_2$ (*-om*) in this sentence has a possessive function and the Set$_2$ as subject (agent) marker (*-š*) remains on the verb as in other examples above and thus no fronting occurs in this sentence.

Note also that there is a somewhat common phenomenon for the subject (agent) Set$_2$ marker to be repeated both on the verb and fronted as well (with no meaning change): *ongoθ-om-om bi-m-birint* (= *ongoθ*$_4$*-om*$_3$*-om*$_1$ *bi-m*$_1$*-birint*$_2$) "I$_1$ cut$_2$ my$_3$ finger$_4$," *in perhan-e qašang-ā eδ kuvāy-dun bi-d-irint* "(from) where have you bought this beautiful shirt/dress?" The use of 2nd sg. (*-d*) and 2nd pl. (*-dun*) endings in the latter sentence may either be a slip of the tongue or may show the speaker's ambivalence over how formally he/she should address the hearer.

Set$_2$ may also move farther forward in the sentence over one or more words, a phenomenon that the present author calls "Distance Fronting": *ye bāq-ošun dewr-e un ziāretgā bé-sāte* "they built a garden around that shrine," *θib-ā-šun eδ daraxt bicint* "they picked the apples off the tree," *to-šun eδ keδe ki karte* "they have kicked you out of the house," *píl-om ruδ eδene kam še-š da-bo* "I had given her (too) little money on Friday."

There is a strong tendency in IsfJ. for the Fronted Set$_2$ marker to attach to the direct object, regardless of the position of the object in the clause, hence the occurrences

Table 3
"To Be"

to be$_1$					to be$_2$	to be$_3$	
Pres		Pres	Past	Pres	Pres	Pres	Past
Affirm	Neg	Subj	Affirm	Perf	Affirm	Affirm	
-un	nown	bun	bown	beδown	eθθ-un	der-un	der-bown
-i~-e	ne	be	boy	beδey	eθθ-e	der-e	der-boy
-u	now	bu	bo	beδe	eθθ-u	der-u	der-bo
-im	neym	bim	boym	beδeym	eθθ-im	der-im	der-boym
-id	neyd	bid	boyd	beδeyd	eθθ-id	der-id	der-boyd
-end	nend	bend	bend~	beδend	eθθ-end	der-end	der-bend~
(Yarshater's notes:			boend				der-boend)

Table 4
"To Become"

Pres	Subj	Past	Imperfect	Pres Perfect	Past Perfect
bune	bébun	bébown	bowne	bébdown	bébde-bown
bie	bébe	béboy	boye	bébdey	bébde-boy
buve	bébu	(bé)bo	boi, boe	bébde	bébde-bo
bime	bébim	béboym	béyme~bóyme	bébdeym	bébde-boym
bide	bébid	béboyd	béyde~boyde	bébdeyd	bébde-boyd
bénde	bébend	bébend	bénde/boende	bébdend	bébde-bend

of Distance Fronting mentioned above. This is only a strong tendency, however, and these endings do not obligatorily move to the object. They may also attach to various other words such as adverbs or prepositional phrases: *ar-vaxt-om bedi* "whenever I saw (him), . . ." *mun-ā tu zahmat-oš xoθ* "he threw me into trouble," but the latter type is somewhat rare, and it is much more common for the Set$_2$ endings to remain on the verb when no direct object is present: *xód-oš bé-d-engāšt?* "did you speak with him?" A fuller description of fronting is given under the entry on the Hamadāni Jewish dialect (see HAMADĀN ix) and a further discussion of the tendency of Set$_2$ endings to attach to the direct object is also given under GAZI.

Notes on tenses, aspects, moods. (1) The usual imperative is built with *bé-*/preverbs and the bare root in the singular (the plural imperative and subjunctive are identical): *béxuθ!/béxuθid* "throw!" *vár-māl!/vár-mālid* "flee!" Another common imperative formation uses the 2nd singular ending (identical to the subjunctive; see also GAZI for this formation) and occurs with roots consisting of only one consonant and with all causatives: *bé-š-e!* "go!" *é-d-e!* "give!" *bé-tāy-n-e!* "chase!" *bé-yuš-n-e!* "boil (it)!" There are also irregular imperative formations: a) forms of "to be" (be$_1$: *b-i!* "be!" be$_3$: *dar-b-i!* "be!" and *bé-b-i!* "become!" [for the numbers of verbs, see below]), and b) built either on the imperative of "be" (for the numbers of "to be" verbs, see below): *dār-b-i!* "have!" *δun-b-i!* (usually realized as *δúmbi)* "know!" or on the 3rd pers. subjunctive of "be": *gu-d-bu!* "want!" *béšā-d-bu!* "be able!" (see Modals for the formation of the latter two verbs). Also irregular is "come": *bu ki!* "come out!" (= *b-u*, but present: *y-un-e* "I come"); (2) progressive forms are built with "have" as their auxiliary verb as in colloquial Persian (*ye rubāy aδ dey dārt-oš še, ye xurúθ-oš bidi dāru dun var-cinúve* "A fox was going out of a village (and) he saw a rooster was pecking at seeds"), but they seem to be encountered mostly from elicited sentences and not often in the actual texts, which shows the pattern may be a recent borrowing from Persian. (3) The optative (expressing wishes, used mostly for blessings and curses) occurs only in the 3rd singular and is formed with the optative marker *-ā*, in which case the 3rd sg. *-u* is suppressed (examples from Yarshater): *xeδā bé-š-keš-ā-Ø* "may God kill him," *xeδā ʿomr-ot še t-ā-Ø* "may God give you (long) life." Other persons of the optative are expressed with the subjunctive: (Yarshater) *elāhi bémberun, elāhi bémbere*, but *elāhi bémberā* "God, may I, you, he die!" Note that in purely subjunctive uses, the 3rd sg. *-u* remains: *gumā-š-e be-mber-u* "he was about to (lit: wanted to) die."

To be. IsfJ. has three "to be" verbs (see Table 3): be$_1$, the usual copula, is identical to the Set$_1$ endings on verbs (see Table 1), but it never takes stress: *mun dozd-un* "I am a thief," *xab-un* "I am good," *to mariδ-e* "you are sick," *in aθm-e eθbed-u* "this is a white horse," *kār cetowr-u?* "how is work?," negative: *vaδ now* "it isn't bad." Be_2, *eθθu*, used for existence, emphasis and sometimes location, is probably the Iranian root "to stand" having merged with the alternate copula root *hast-* of other Iranian languages: *cerā guše divār eθθu* "the light is in the corner of the wall." Be_3, *der-u*, is used to express location (*yun der-un* "I am here," *ali kuvā der-u?* "where is Ali?," *pil-omun piš-e mardom der-u* "our money is with (other) people," *ar sāl vis ru der-end* "every year they are (there, here, with us, etc.) for twenty days," *keδe der-bun/ne-der-bun* "I was/wasn't at home," *be-fékr-e θebā né-dar-boend* "they weren't in thoughts of tomorrow." Be_1 may also assume the functions of be_2 and be_3, e.g., existence (*jir-e un ku ye cešme-u ge* . . . "there is a spring at the foot of that mountain that . . . ,") and location (*pošd-e kuy-u* "it is behind the mountain").

Become is built with the forms of "to be_1" (except for the present tense which has its own root, *b-*, also derived from "to be") plus the tense-aspect markers *-e* and *bé-*: pres. *δi-δi xaθθe b-í-e* "you get tired very quickly," *ma:lum b-ú-e* "it will be (become) clear," *bele bé-bo-y* "you got big! (i.e., you grew up!)," *pāre bé-bd-e* "it has become torn," *bihuš bé-bd-e bo-wn* "I had become unconscious" (see also *Passive* below).

Modals. "Want" and "can" are indirect (or dative) verbs, signifying "it is wanting/possible to me," in which the person is expressed with Set_2 endings. Tenses other than the present take the 3rd person of "to be" as an auxiliary (see Imperative above): "can" (pres.: *béšā-m/néšā-m, béšā-d, béšā-š*, etc.; past: *béšā-m-bo/néšā-m-bo, béšā-d-bo*, etc.): *béšāš béxunu* "she can read," *néšām xód-e šemā bešun* "I can't go with you," *kāški béšām-bo ye kāri berā-š békerun* "I wish I could do something for him," *néšām-bo bíun* "I wasn't able to come"; "want" (pres.: *gu-m-e/ná-m-gue, gu-d-e, gu-š-e*, etc.; past: *gumā-m-e/na-m-gumā, gumā-d-e*, etc.): *gu-m-e xód-ot béngārun* "I want to speak with you," *gumā-š-e be-mber-u* "he wanted to die." "Must" is an impersonal, invariable past form of "want" (*gumā-bo*) with no Set_2 endings and is used in both present and past senses (*gumā-bo de timān é-tun* "I must give 10 tomans"). *zun/zunā* "to know" also has the meaning "can": *zunā-m é-t-un* "I was able to give."

Causatives and passives. The causative marker is *-(e)n/(e)nā* added to the present root of the non-causative: *kelāš-/kelāšn-* "itch/scratch," *bíyušā* "it boiled (intrans.)" > *bišyušnā* "he boiled (trans.)," *gumāše mún-ā bétarsenu* "she wanted to scare me," *béθuδu* "let it burn" > *béθunne* "burn (it)! (trans.)," *bémθunnā* "I burned (it)," *m-ofne* "don't put (him) to sleep!" (The latter form seems to be an exception, built on the past stem.) The passive is formed analytically as in Persian with the past participle and "to become" (see Table 4): *bar bas(t)e-buve* "the door closes," *in lebāθ xab dašte nebue* "these clothes will not be sewn well," *qand-eš emarté nebue* "the sugar won't break,"*pādāši bay-aš dā-bebo* "a reward was given to him."

Bibliography: Roubène Abrahamian, *Dialectes des Israélites de Hamadan et d'Isphahan et dialecte de Baba Tahir*, Paris, 1936. Harold W. Bailey "Modern Western Iranian: Infinitives in Gazī and Soī," *TPS*, 1935, pp. 73-74. Ḥabib Borjiān, *Ganjina-ye guyeshā-ye Eṣfahān*, Farhangestān-e zabān o adab-e fārsi series, forthcoming. Irān Kalbāsi, *Fārsi-e eṣfahāni*, Tehran, 1991. Idem, *Guyeš-e Kalimiān-e Eṣfahān*, Tehran, 1994. Pierre Lecoq, "Les dialectes du centre de l'Iran," in Rüdiger Schmitt, ed., *Compendium Linguarum Iranicarum*, Wiesbaden, 1989, pp. 313-26. David Neil MacKenzie, "Jewish Persian from Isfahan," *JRAS*, 1968, pp. 68-75. Manfred Mayrhofer, "Vorgeschichte der iranischen Sprachen; Uriranisch," in Rüdiger Schmitt, ed., *Compendium Linguarum Iranicarum*, Wiesbaden, 1989, pp. 4-24. Rüdiger Schmitt, "Die altiranischen Sprachen im Überblick," ibid., pp. 25-31. Lidia P. Smirnova, *Isfaxanskiĭ govor*, Nauka, Moscow, 1978. A. Sohrābi-Anāraki, *Vāža-nāma-ye Anāraki*, Mashhad, 1994. Donald Stilo, unpublished field notes collected in Isfahan, 1964. Ehsan Yarshater, unpublished field notes collected in Isfahan, 1970, kindly provided to the author. Valentin A. Zhukovskiĭ, *Materialy dlya izucheniya persidskikh narechiĭ*, Petrograd, 1888-1922, II; repr. as *Materials for the Study of Iranian Dialects*, 3 vols. in 1, Tehran, 1976.

(DON STILO)

xx. GEOGRAPHY OF THE MEDIAN DIALECTS OF ISFAHAN

The continuum of Central Plateau Dialects appears along a northwest-souteast axis traversing the modern provinces of Hamadān, Markazi, Isfahan, and Yazd, that is, the area of Ancient Media Major. The lion's share goes to Isfahan, where Median is spoken in many villages scattered throughout the province as well as by Jewish communities in larger towns. Detailed geographical survey is available for only certain parts of Isfahan province; a recent study for the district of Isfahan (Borjian, 2005b) tallies well over a hundred Median-speaking villages, only a fraction whereof had previously been identified. The present article focuses on Isfahan district, but it compiles also all accessible information on the entire province. The following classification of Median dialects is mainly areal, which generally correlates with linguistic classification, except for a few cases that will mentioned.

Geography. The current border of Isfahan province embraces the bulk of Central Dialects (q.v.; South Median or simply Median), save for Ḵomeyn, Maḥallāt, and Delijān just across the northwestern provincial border (yet included in this study) and a few communities, chiefly Zoroastrian, but also Muslim and Jewish, in Yazd province. To achieve a relevant division within the province modern administrative boundaries have been overlooked, for they have been subjected to several major rearrangements in recent decades. Alternatively, resorting to historical divisions together with topographical-communicational attributes will keep the geographical grouping in rather close accord with the linguistic classification.

This linguistic region is clearly bounded by the Central Desert in the east and the massive Central Zagros range in the west. On the foothills of the latter lie, from south, K̲ᵛānsār, Golpāyegān, K̲omeyn, and Maḥallāt, historically secluded valleys away from major highways. Salient within the province is the Karkas range, an offshoot of the Zagros, beginning just east of Maḥallāt and stretching southeast for some 200 miles. On the west of the Karkas, along the Qom-Isfahan highway, lie Delijān and Meyma-Jowšaqān districts, both connected to the districts of Kāšān and Naṭanz across the Karkas by a network of trails and roads leading to many secluded Median villages. Running along the edge of the desert, the Qom-Kāšān-Yazd highway traverses the Median-speaking districts of Ardestān and Nāʾin. These thinly inhabited steppe-deserts are separated from Isfahan by a break-off in the Karkas range which is sometimes called, after its highest peak, Māršnān (Sāzmān-e jog̲rāfiāʾi, p. 167). This short range is dotted on both flanks with villages speaking closely-related dialects, including those of Kuhpāya, a sizeable sub-district of Isfahan. Finally, the riverine plane of Isfahan, irrigated by the Zāyandarud River, constitutes the southern boundary of the Median-speaking province. The grouping of Median dialects in Isfahan proper is best achieved within the well-defined economic units traditionally called *boluk*s (for a list, see Houtum-Schindler, 1896, pp. 125-29). Lori and Turkic surround the Median core in the south and southwest of Isfahan province.

The users of the dialects live in more than 200 villages and in a few towns where Persian is the primary means of communication. These speech communities range in size from a few to hundreds of families, but almost never more than 10,000 speakers; Sedeh, Varzana, and Sagzi are among the largest Median-speaking localities. In larger towns, Median has been limited to less affluent quarters (e.g., Nāʾin and Ardestān) or the fading Jewish communities (e.g., Isfahan; see Yarshater, 1974). The domain of use varies. In the south, where Persianization seems less advanced, the native dialects are used for all in-group communication among the residents, while Persian or the local dialect may be used for inter-village communication, depending on the degree of intelligibility (Krahnke, p. 58). In the north and in larger towns, there is a high degree of use of Persian in all but the most intimate communication (Majidi, passim).

Median in Isfahan province has long been declining in favor of Persian. In certain communities the language shift is well attested by contrasting reports prepared over the past century and a half. Persianization seems to have been more advanced in the Kāšān-Maḥallāt area on the north than in the Isfahan-Nāʾin-Ardestān area (Majidi, passim; Krahnke, p. 59; see also below, under each region). The trend of language loss has been accelerating parallel with the enormous social and economic changes the province has undergone in the last forty years. In many villages where Median is not yet abandoned, the shift seems imminent as the language is becoming increasingly limited to the elders. Consequently, it would be unrealistic to quantify the individuals or even the communities that speak South Median. Nonetheless, some generalizations can be made.

In terms of the number of settlements the center of gravity is east of Isfahan in Rudašt-Kuhpāya area. The most resilient of all appears to be Rudašt, with an uninterrupted continuum of nearly 50 Median-speaking villages. On the southern foothills of Māršnān, in the Kuhpāya-Zefra-Sagzi area, more than three quarters of the total 137 settlements have maintained their native dialects, while in Jarquya, south of Rudašt, only about half of its 23 villages have resisted Persian. Outside of Isfahan district, the Meyma-Jowšaqān area yields the highest ratio, specifically 19 Median-speaking localities out of the total 23. The ratio in the rest of Kāšān district is no more than a quarter of the 73 settlements. (The quantities are calculated from the data published in *ŠGI*.) In the northern and western parts of the province, Median survives in a few isolated communities only. Thus, the Persianization is far more advanced along the northwestern periphery of the province from Kāšān to K̲ᵛānsār.

Isfahan proper. Two distinct Median-speaking areas are noticeable within the Isfahan district: the eastern area, with dozens of Median settlements, in the *boluk*s of Jarquya, Rudašt, and Kuhpāya; and the western area, with only five Median communities in and around the city. This distribution is easily explained if we assume that the entire district was once Median-speaking, and Persian was rooted in the city first and then radiated outward in all directions, overlaying Median. The city has given way to Persian, save for its Jewish residents, who formed a closed community in the quarter of Jubāra until recently. The neighboring villages have also switched to Persian, except (1) Sedeh, or more specifically one of its three parts, namely Varnusfāderān (locally called Benesfōn), in the *boluk* traditionally called Mārbin, west of Isfahan; and (2) in the *boluk* of BorK̲ᵛār north of the city, the three oasis villages of Gaz, K̲orzuq, and Komešča/Komšača. Farther north in Murčak̲ort, only elders could speak the native dialect in 1973 (Majidi, p. 13; cf. *ŠGI* II, p. 36, that reports the village as wholly Persophone).

Jarquya (q.v.; locally Garkuya) is a barren *boluk* stretching from the Šāhkuh range, southeast of Isfahan, to the desert separating it from Abarqu. It is naturally and administratively divided into upper (*ʿolyā*) and lower (*soflā*) halves, each having both Median and Persian-speaking oasis villages. In Upper Jarquya the villages of Dastgerd, Kamālābād, Ḥasanābād, K̲ārā, and Yak̲čāl (Allāhābād) are still largely speaking Median, whereas Mālvājerd and the cluster of six villages to its southwest, including Rāmša(n) and Esfandārān, have lost their vernaculars to Persian. The arrangement in Lower (northwest) Jarquya is somewhat mixed; Median-speaking villages are Ganjābād, Siān, Yangābād (now Nikābād), Peykān, Mazraʿa-ʿArab, and Ḥaydarābād (Šafiʿi Nikābādi, pp. 12-15); the dialect was still alive in Ād̲ark̲avārān (lately renamed Ḥabibābād) as late as 1977 (*ŠGI* II, pp. 50, 55), but is now almost extinct there, as it is in Saʿādatābād and Ḥosaynābād, probably due to the educational careers of their inhabitants. Other causes suggested for language shift are population replacement in Mālvājerd, following the Afghan invasion of Isfahan, and relocation of tribes from Fārs under the Zand dynastic rule; these tribes still have a semi-nomadic life near Narṣābād (locally Givān; cf. Šafiʿi Nikābādi, pp. 150, 202, 446). The Median dialects of Jarquya may clearly be divided into the upper and lower groups of subdialects.

Up to 50 km east and southeast of Isfahan, there stand the thickly populated *boluk*s of Barzrud, Karārej, and Barāʾān, with dozens of Persophone villages, including such old ones as Dašti, Ziār, Gār, and Bersiān, with extant Saljuq monuments. A 1977 survey, however, marks seven settlements as having Median as the idiom of the smaller part of their residents: Bāča/Bāja, Ozvār, Borkān, Espinā, Andelān, Raḥimābād, and Lajanāba (*ŠGI* II, pp. 139-53; cf. Mehryār, 2003, pp. 98, 102, 163, 178, 200). This may throw light on the former language of the area if the Median speakers are not simply recent settlers from Jarquya or Rudašt.

Farther east rests the vast plain of Rudašt with rural settlements arranged roughly linearly around the lower course of the Zāyandarud River toward the Gāvḵuni lagoon. In Lower (west) Rudašt, the Persian-Median border seems to have been shifting since the report of 1977 (*ŠGI* II, pp. 117-21) eastward; in the villages of Mā(de)rkān, Sokān/Sekān, Jombeza, Māči, Qalʿa ʿAbd-Allāh, Kelišād, Siči, and Ḵorram(i) many inhabitants spoke Persian when I visited the area in 2004. The contiguous Median-speaking villages that continue on from there are Ḵorjān/Ḵaračön, Helārta, Sonuči, Pājikābād, Kamandān, Siryān/Seryon, Qalʿa-sārebān, Sidān/Sudon; Šātur (now Emāmzāda ʿAbd-Allāh, whereto the inhabitants of the nearby Sorušān have migrated), Šarifābād, Fayżābād, Kelil, Hāšemābād, Qomšān, Giši, Siān and Qalʿa-bālā, and lastly Ežia/Ži that marks the end of Lower Rudašt. In Upper Rudašt the Median oases appear in clusters: Tāljerd/Dālgerd (now abandoned), Rangi(n)deh; Ṭa(h)mursā(t) and Abu'l-Ḵayr (two contiguous villages), Kafrun, Fārfān, Jondān/Gondun, Kafrud/Kafarved; Baz(a)m, Sohrān, Bahlān, Qurtān/Gurtun, Aškohrān/Šogron, Yasnā (now Qalʿa-Emām), and Varzana, the administrative center and the last settlement of Upper Rudašt (cf. *ŠGI* II, pp. 110, 117-18). The south-north road connecting Ežia to Kuhpāya crosses the oasis villages of Harand and Qehi, the latter having a distinct dialect.

Kuhpāya is a large piedmont *boluk* north of Rudašt. Its administrative center Kupā (local Vir) used to be the second caravan station on the Isfahan-Yazd route and a medium of commerce between Isfahan and more than a hundred hamlets along several valleys to its north and east. An overwhelming majority of these locales speak Median; among them are several Persian-speaking settlements, but without any clear pattern. The central part of Kuhpāya is Jabal (Kuki in the local usage), resting on the southern slopes of Māršnān, with some forty villages, including Ḵʸāja, Pāza, Keriči, Jaza, Mandābād, Daḵrābād, Kerdābād and ʿOlunābād (Allevā in the local dialect; Eilers, 1990, p. 220; *ŠGI* II, pp. 93-94; Wezārat-e jehād-e sāzandagi). In the eastern Kuhpāya, along the road to Nāʾin, lie the village districts of Mašgenān, Tudešk, and Ješuqān/Ješveqān/Gašgun (*ŠGI* II, pp, 68-69, 102), with dialects closely related to those of Nāʾin. The western confines of Jabal consist of Fešārk and its hamlets, with transitional dialects approaching those of Zefra.

In its more general sense Kuhpāya embraces Sagzi and Zefra. Sagzi, now a township, which was the first caravan station on the Isfahan-Yazd road, has a distinct dialect, spoken also in the nearby Mazraʿa-šur (cf. *ŠGI* II, p. 86). Ten kilometers north, approaching Zefra, is Vartun, with a transitional dialect toward Zefra. Zefra is located on the mountainous road to Ardestān. It has more than thirty hamlets, from Āb-gonješk on the south to Bāḡ-gol on the north, apparently with little dialect variation (Borjian, 2005b; cf. Zhukovsiĭ, I, p. viii).

Outskirts of the Kavir. Nāʾin district is situated to the northeast of Isfahan across the Māršnān range, and extends northeastward well into the Dašt-e Kavir. In the town of Nāʾin, now partly deserted, Median was restricted to the older and lower-class residents in the early 1970s (Krahnke, p. 58). The immediate villages of Moḥammadiya, Bāfrān, and Benvid on the road to Ardakān, are reported Median-speaking (Sotuda, pp. ix-xvi). Likewise for Anārak (with the local name Nārestānak), which lies in a basin 50 miles northeast of Nāʾin. Proceeding some 70 miles farther on, one arrives at several oases, among which Ḵur, Farroḵi, and Mehrajān have vernaculars constituting a sub-group of Central Dialects.

Ardestān is chiefly a Median-speaking district. The southern rural sub-district of Barāzvand (north of Zefra) has the Median villages of Ke(y)jān, Nohuj, Mārbin, Neysiān, Nārin, Kesār (Qehsāra), He, Žöugand (current Ẓafarqand?), and Mārču(b)a, among others (Zhukovskiĭ, I, p. viii; *ŠGI* I, pp. 39-40). The town of Ardestān has sub-dialectal variations in various quarters (Lecoq, 2002, p. 3); the surrounding villages, dozens in number, are generally Median (*ŠGI* I, pp. 63-67). The villages in the north of the district bordering the desert are predominantly Persian, including Zavāra (*ŠGI* I; see also Mehryār, pp. 313, 819 and passim).

Karkas region. Northwest of Ardestān on the Isfahan-Kāšān highway rests the district of Naṭanz on the eastern foothills of the Karkas range. The town of Naṭanz was already becoming rapidly Persianized in the early 1930s and had lost many of its Median characteristics by the 1970s (Krahnke, pp. 77, 112). Median is still alive in Bād(rud), a large village abutting the desert to the northeast of Naṭanz, and in its satellite hamlets ʿAbbāsābād, Ḵāledābād, Dehābād, Fami, Matinābād, and Sarāsiā (see BĀDRUDI). Northeast of Naṭanz there are two fairly long and verdant valleys joining at the Median village of Hanjan; the valley of Barzrud traverses the Median villages of Yārand, Komjān/Konjun, Ṭer(r)a, and Abyāna (Joneidi-Jaʿfari), while Barz has become persophone since Zhukovskiĭ's report (I, p. viii). The valley heading south from Hanjan is the seat of Volugerd, Čima, Takia-Sādāt, Bidhand (Vyend), and Fariz(h)and, all Median villages. On a valley (Tarqrud?) south of the Karkas peak (3,900 m) lie the Median villages Ṭāma, Ṭarq, Ṭār, Keša, Mazda/Maz(z)a (Krahnke, pp. 77, 112; Lecoq, 2000, p. 3), and perhaps Bargerun (Zhukovskiĭ, I, p. viii). Further west, on the piedmont of the Karkas, there are the Median villages of So(h), and the nearby Bidešk and Kelahrud (ibid.).

On the west of the Karkas range is the Meyma-Jowšaqān area (Lambton, pp. 1-5), where most villages are Median-speaking. They include Meyma, on the Isfahan-Qom highway, and its satellite villages Vazvān, Ziādābād, Āzān/Azun, Vandāda/Vendāda, as well as Čeqāda/Čegā and Robāṭ to its east, and Muta in the northeast (Majidi, pp. 13, 60; cf. *ŠGI* II, p. 185), while Ḵosr(ow)ābād was no longer reported Median after Zhukovskiĭ (I, p. viii). The sub-district of Jowšaqān (q.v.) has the Median villages Jowšaqān (more specifically Jowšaqān-e qāli), Kāmu, Čugān/Čowqān, Elzag/Alizaq, and Koluḵ, and the cluster on the northeast of Jowšaqān: Varkān, Pandās, Taj(a)ra, Eranjin/Ārenjan, Āzerān (Majidi, pp. 7, 12, 60; *ŠGI* IV, p. 194). Moreover, the villages of Vāžgun/Vājgun (Majidi, p. 12; Krahnke, p. 54; Zhukovskiĭ, I, p. viii) and Gašgun, Qazmābād, Baluḵ, Vāšar, Vadmunā, Tavā (reported to Gernot Windfuhr in 1968 by residents of Kāmu; apud Krahnke, p. 54) are reported as Median-speaking, but they could not be found on the most detailed maps available to me. Jowšaqān borders Kāšān on the northeast and, therefore, may be grouped geographically with Qohrud or Niāsar group, as shown below.

Kāšān district. In the town of Kāšān, Median survived only among its Jewish population, which was on the verge of disappearing in the 1960s (Yarshater, 1974). Immediate neighboring localities are Persianized, most lately Ārān and Bidgol (q.v.), 10 km north of Kāšān (united into the single town temporarily named Golārā in 1977). In the desert east of Kāšān, there is a group of Median oases centered at Abuzaydābād (q.v.), with the hamlets Rijan, Yazdelān, Kāgazi, Faḵra, ʿAliābād, Qāsemābād, Moḥammadābād, Ḥosaynābād-e Šaybāni (*ŠGI* IV, p. 262). Among Kāšān's nearby southern villages only Ḵonb is reported to be Median (*ŠGI* IV, p. 238).

South of Kāšān along the road crossing the Karkas toward Meyma lies Qamṣar, itself Persian-speaking, but most of the villages to its south and east (in Qohrud *dehestān*) were Median: Bonrud, Javinān, Qohrud, Jahaq, Tetmāj/Totmāj, and Zanjānbar/Zangunbar (Majidi, pp. 12, 60); Zanjānbar and Jahaq were reported Persophone in a 1977 survey (*ŠGI* IV, pp. 205-12). In the late Qajar period, the inhabitants of Javinān told Edward Browne that their dialect was spoken in "about a dozen or fifteen villages round about," extending on the one end to Naṭanz and on the other Qamṣar (Browne, 1927, p. 203), implying that Qamṣar was not then Persianized yet. This data may be compared with the nineteen villages the inhabitants of Kāmu (see above) had identified in 1968 as having vernaculars similar to their own (Windfuhr, apud Krahnke, p. 54).

Northwest of Kāšān, in Jowšaqān-e Estark *dehestān*, Estark and Fatḥābād spoke Median (Majidi, p. 60), but both were reported as Persophone only a few years later (*ŠGI* IV, p. 250). Farther up into the valleys, Barz(ābād), Kal(l)a, Armak, Rahak/Rahaq, and the unidentified village of Hesanj used to be Median-speaking (Zhukovskiĭ, I, viii; cf. *ŠGI* IV, p. 220).

West of Kāšān, around a break in the Karkas range, an array of Median villages are identified in the Niāsar *dehestān*: Niāsar, Nešalj, Sādiān, Mar(a)q, Vidjā, Viduj, Azvār, and Barzok/Borzok/Balzoq (Majidi, pp. 46-47). In the early 1970s Median was disappearing in Nešalj and Sādiān (Majidi, pp. 12, 35, 47), both of which, as well as Marq, were reported Persophone a few years later (*ŠGI* IV, pp. 220-21).

Northwestern frontier. Along the crescent-shaped region on the northeast periphery of Isfahan province lie the historically Median-speaking districts of Delijān, Maḥallāt, Ḵomeyn, Golpāyagān, and Ḵᵛānsār.

On the Qom-Isfahan highway, we find the Median-speaking Delijān and the nearby village Nešastābād (Majidi, p. 48). Along a narrow valley of Jāsb running northeast from Delijān lies Bijagān, the Median dialect whereof could only be remembered by seniors in 1973 (Majidi, p. 32); At the head of the valley are located Zor and Vārān (Majidi, pp. 11, 48, 56, 58). In Narāq, east of Delijān, on the way to Kāšān, the dialect was ousted by Persian by 1973; only a few elders could recall that Median had been spoken in two quarters of the village some sixty years earlier (Majidi, p. 24). Median was also being abandoned in Qālhar, an isolated mountain village southeast of Delijān (Majidi, pp. 12, 40).

Maḥallat, Ḵomeyn, and Golpāyagān are now Persophone. The dialect of Maḥallāt, reported by Oskar Mann in 1907, was extinct by 1973, save for several senior residents who could remember a few words (Majidi, p. 11). The towns of Ḵomeyn and Golpāyegān had retained their dialects only within their Jewish communities (Yarshater, 1974). A 1989 report (*ŠGI* IV, pp. 275-343) maintains that no locality in the Golpāyagān district spoke a Median dialect, except Vānešān/Vānišān (*ŠGI* IV, p. 312), halfway along the road to Ḵᵛānsār. Nonetheless, questionnaires filled out in 2000 indicate that the Median vernaculars were still alive in various degrees in the northern villages of Vedāḡ, Konjedjān, Dom-āsemān, and Šeydābād (Wezārat-e jehād-e sāzandagi).

Farther south, approaching Ḵᵛānsār, lie the Median-speaking villages of Ti(d)jān, Qu(d)jān, Bābā-ṣolṭān, Bi(dh)and, Sunaqān, Vādašt, Horestāna, Arasur/Eresil (Zhukovskiĭ, I, p. vi; Mann and Hadank, pp. lxi-lxii; Eilers and Schapka, I, p. 2). Of these only the town of Ḵᵛānsār was reported as having retained the dialect in certain quarters in 1988; Tidjān, Qudjān, Bidhand, Horestāna, and Bābā-ṣolṭān had already lost their native dialects; the last three localities are reported as having been integrated into the town of Ḵᵛānsār (*ŠGI* III, pp. 64-65). Median was also spoken by the fading Jewish community of Ḵᵛānsār (Yarshater, 1974).

SOURCES

Documentation and study of the dialects. There is a fairly long history of notes and reports prepared by scholars and collectors on many localities speaking a South Median dialect. It begins as early as mid-19th century (Polak on Naṭanzi), but more systematically during 1880-1940, and then, after the politically-troubled years that followed World War II, during the 1960s-70s. Since the revolution of 1979 foreigners have been denied of fieldwork, but collections by the local enthusiasts and students have been booming.

The earlier documentations include Friedrich Carl Andreas (1939, q.v.) of Sohi in 1880, whose work was edited by Arthur Christensen and Kay Barr; Albert Houtum-Schindler (1884) of Sohi and Qohrudi; Edward Browne (1893, pp. 188-93; 1927, pp. 203-8) of Qohrudi during his 1887-88 travel to Persia; and Amedeé Querry (1896) of Nāʾini. The major contribution of the 19th century is that of Valentin Alekseevich Zhukovskiĭ (*Materialy* I-II), which is based on his 1880s field notes, embracing the dialects of Vānišān, Qohrud, Keša, Zefra, Gaz, Sedeh, Kafrān (or Kafrud?), and the Jewish community of Kāšān. This extensive and high-quality work has ever since been the backbone of South Median dialect studies. Oskar Mann carried out fieldwork in two trips during 1901-07 to much of the region, collecting data from Maḥallāt, K̲ᵛānsār, Naṭanz, Soh, and, particularly extensively, from Nāʾin (as well as from Sivand and Semnān). His work was edited and published posthumously by Karl Hadank (Mann and Hadank, 1926; for a critical assessment, see Krahnke, pp. 85-88). Vladimir Ivanow's (1926, 1927) reports on Anāraki and the dialects of K̲ur and Mehrajān (as well as Yazd), from trips made by him more than ten years earlier, make him a primary source on the Central Dialects spoken along the edge of the desert. Arthur Christensen's fieldwork (I, pp. 124-294), covering Naṭanzi, Farizandi, and Yārandi, remains unique for the latter two vernaculars. Then there are valuable collections by Ruben Abrahamian (1930) of Isfahani Jewish (but also Judeo-Hamadāni), Harold Bailey (1935a) of Ardestāni, and Ann K. S. Lambton (1938) of Meymaʾi and Jowšaqāni. Wilhelm Eilers' (q.v.) extensive texts from Gaz, K̲ᵛānsār, and Sivand, collected from 1936-40 and then in the 1960s (Eilers and Schapka) renders these dialects the most comprehensively documented of all Central Dialects. His short article on Kupāya (Eilers, 1990) remains the major published source of this dialect to this date.

The next generation includes Kanus-Credé (1971), another contributor to Anāraki, and MacKenzie (1968), who investigated a contemporary text in Isfahani Jewish dialect published by Pažand (1966). Donald Stilo collected field notes in 1963-65 on Isfahani Jewish, Sedehi, Naṭanzi, and Ārāni, (personal communication). Ehsan Yarshater's collected data from various parts of the province remain partly unpublished (Yarshater, 1974, 1985, 1989; see also below, studies by locality). Pierre Locoq's publications (1974, 1975, 2002) are based on his 1969-74 fieldwork on Qohrudi, Abuzaydābādi, Abyānaʾi, Tāri, Bādrudi, Nāʾini, Anāraki, Ardestāni, and Varzanaʾi. Karl John Krahnke carried out fieldwork in 1970-72 in sixteen villages from Naṭanz to Nāʾin to Isfahan, more extensively in Nohuj, Nāʾin, Naṭanz, and Ardestān. His collection, however, has not been published, save for the relevant data used in his comparative study (Krahnke, 1976) of the dialects of Bādrud, Ṭarq, Keyjān, Nohuj, Kupā, Ābčuya, and Sagzi, none of which had been studied before. The fieldwork by foreign scholars was interrupted by the Revolution of 1979; in 2005, however, an expedition from the Department of Iranian Studies of Yerevan State University visited the Kāšān-Karkas region.

Persian publications have been on the rise since the 1970s. A very useful one is Majidi's short survey, sponsored by the second Farhangestān, with sample glosses from the last generation of Median speakers in the Kāšān-Maḥallāt-Meyma area. Several informed locals have published on their home villages, for instance, Moḥammad-Ḥasan Rajāʾi Zefra'i's dozens of short articles on the material culture of Zefra (q.v.), with ample linguistic data, and ʿAli Šafiʿi Nikābādi's monograph on Jarquya, as well as glossaries by Ḥosayn Ṣafari for Delijāni, ʿAbbās Mazraʿati et al. for Abuzaydābādi, etc. The published dialectal poems include, but are not limited to, those of Darviš ʿAbbās in Gazi (see xxii, below), Yusof Bak̲ši (1955, 1997) in K̲ᵛānsāri, Ḡafurzāda (1975) and K̲āsta (2000, 2004) in Sedehi, and Reżā Darviš in Kupāyi (Borjian, 2004). Another source of information on Median dialects can be university theses which have been growing exponentially in the last two decades. Many of these studies suffer from inaccuracies and methodological problems, and most detailed parts of their treatment are limited to the trivial features the dialects share with standard Persian, thus restricting their scholarly merits. One may also occasionally find short notices on individual dialects in literry periodicals such as *Āyanda*.

There still remains a good deal of research and study to be pursued concerning the Central Dialects. The vernaculars of Sedeh and Zefra, for instance, have been virtually ignored after Zhukovskiĭ's introductory survey (1880s). Likewise, the reliable data on the Jewish dialect of Isfahan is confined to the brief study of Abrahamian (1930). The piedmonts and steppes east of Isfahan are only scantily explored; Kuhpāya with dozens of Median villages and several distinct dialects remain largely untouched; and the idioms of Sagzi, Lower Rudašt, and Jarquya are known but poorly.

Identification of the dialects. Some of the studies on individual dialects mention neighboring Median settlements. Persian gazetteers and censuses seldom provide accurate information on the language of various localities, as they often fail to make distinction between Persian and other Iranian languages. Moreover, a serious problem with post-revolutionary atlases is their attempt to Islamicize the 'pagan' toponyms on a broad scale.

Two nationwide projects have been conceived with the goal of generating a linguistic atlas for Persia based on audio-recorded data. The first one began in 1974 under the acronym *Farhangsāz*, standing for Farhangestān (q.v.) and Sāzmān-e jogrāfiāʾi-e arteš (Geographical department of the military), which formed a joint venture to identify dialects nationwide based on a questionnaire consisting of 150 glosses and 20 sentences (Ṯamara). As the Revolution interrupted the project, the amassed data were transferred to Sāzmān-e mirāṯ-e farhangi (Cultural Heritage Organization), which has published at least four volumes, all on Isfahan province (*ŠGI*, covering the districts of Ardestān, Isfahan, K̲ᵛānsār, Kāšān, and Golpāyegān, among other districts where Median is not spoken). Although only a fraction of the collected data is published (19 glosses and two short sentences for two representative dialects in each rural district) in an unmethodical fashion, these volumes are still useful in identifying Median-speaking localities. The second project, sponsored by the Wezārat-e jehād-e sāzandagi, active since 1998, is by and large a duplication of the former project: similar strategy, techniques, and questionnaires are being used, except the number of sentences is now doubled. The greater part of this survey had been completed when the present author visited their Tehran office in 2005; however, the poor quality of workmanship and audio-recordings limit their merits to the mere identification of the language in each surveyed locality, when the audio cassettes are not lost or field notes are legible.

Comparative studies. The main thrust of scholarly interest in the South Median dialects has been comparative, with the intention of clarifying areal or genetic relationships. The following studies include such dialects, often as parts of broader discussions of Iranian dialectology: Zhukovskiĭ, I; Geiger; Mann and Hadank; Tedesko 1921; Ivanow, 1934; Bailey, 1934 and 1936; Morgenstierne; Yarshater, 1974 and 1985; Krahnke; Lecoq, 1989; Windfuhr, 1989, pp. 246-62, 294-95; idem, "Cases" and "Central Dialects" in *EIr*.; Rastorgueva and Moshkalo; and Stilo, "Gazi," "Jewish Dialect," and "Isfahan Dialects" in *EIr*., under "Isfahan."

Historical evidence. The following references, direct or indirect, are available in scattered literary sources on the former dialect of Isfahan. (1) Ḥamza Eṣfahāni in his *Ketāb al-tanbih* (pp. 82-84) describes Persian phonology, apparently that of his hometown Isfahan (cf. K̲ānlari, II, pp. 180-88; Ṣādeqi, 1978, pp. 110, 123-24). He also cites the dialect word *asba* "dog" as the etymon of "Isfahan" (quoted by Yāqut, s.v. "Eṣbahān"); it is now replaced by *ku(y)a* in all Median dialects of Isfahan proper but is retained in many other Central Dialects. (2) Moqaddasi/Maqdesi (p. 398) has a short statement on the dialect of Isfahan. (3) Māfarruk̲i's *Ketāb maḥāsen Eṣfahān* (comp. during 465-85/1072-92) records several words and sentences in the dialect of Isfahan; its Persian translation of 729/1329 by Ḥosayn Āvi adds even more dialect materials to the original Arabic work (Tafażżoli, 1971). (4) The 11th-century *Ḥekāyah Abu'l-Qāsem al-Baḡdādi* preserves two Isfahani sentences and several words (Tafażżoli, 1971). (5) Moḥammad Rāvandi quotes a fragment of a song in an account on the Ismaʿili insurgency in Isfahan in 508/1114 (see Bahār, pp. 840-41). (6) Awḥadi Marāḡaʾi (1274-1338; q.v.) composed three lyrics (*ghazal*, q.v.) in the *fahlavi* of Isfahan (Adib Ṭusi; Awḥadi, *Divān*, pp. 431-32). (7) ʿObayd Zākāni quotes an Isfahani sentence in his 14th-century treatise *Ak̲lāq al-ašrāf* (apud Ṣādeqi, 1996). (8) More materials are available on the Central Dialects other than those of Isfahan proper; see, Shaked on the old texts located among the Cairo Geniza manuscripts; Moḥaqqeq; Ṣādeqi, 2002; Jad̲wa.

In the late 19th century, Sayyed ʿAli Janāb (p. 128) describes the distribution of the *welā(ya)ti* (provincial, i.e., Median) dialects within Isfahan district, which agrees closely with the existing geographical arrangement. Another contemporary report refers to K.linā'i and K.nināni, a tribe who had settled in the quarter of Bidābād of Isfahan, as speaking a distinct variety of Persian (*zabān-e fārsi-e mak̲ṣuṣ*; Taḥwildār, pp. 91-92). From the same time survives the *divān* of Darviš ʿAbbās Jazi (q.v.).

The study of Isfahani Median can be further aided by the study the Persian variant of Isfahan. Various Persian dictionaries include such lexemes, and European travelers to the Safavid capital have quoted many. An important source from the late 17th century, Angelus a Sancto Iosepho, listed phrases and sentences in the contemporary Persian of Isfahan in his extensive vocabulary of Persian (Windfuhr, 1979, p. 159). The current Persian of Isfahan has preserved a considerable number of old words and morphological features, only a few of which are studied, by the late Aḥmad Tafażżoli (1991; see also Ok̲rawi).

Studies and materials on the dialects by locality:

Ābčuya (east of Kuhpāya): Krahnke.

Abuzaydābād: Lecoq, 1975 and 2002; Yarshater, in *EIr*. I, pp. 401-2; Sarafrāzi; Mazraʿati et al.

Abyāna: Lecoq, 1974 and 2002; Yarshater, in *EIr*. I, pp. 404-5; Bolukbāši; Āhani; Amini; Joneidi-Jaʿfari.

Anārak: Ivanow, 1926 and 1927, pp. 57-59; Kanus-Credé; Lecoq, 2002; Windfuhr, in *EIr*. II, pp. 2-3; Sohrābi; Ebrāhimi Anāraki.

Ārān and Bidgol: D̲okā'i, 1972; Yarshater, in *EIr*. IV, pp. 247-49, idem, 1989; ʿAlijānzāda; Maḥbubi.

Ardestān: Bailey, 1935a; Yarshater, 1985; Lecoq, 2002, idem, in *EIr*. II, pp. 387-88; *ŠGI* I.

Bād(rud): Lecoq, 2002; Krahnke; Yarshater, in *EIr*. III, pp. 383-85.

Bāḡ-gol (north of Zefra): Ṭabāʾizāda.

Bidgol: see Ārān and Bidgol, above.

Bijgān (in Jāsb, NE of Delijān): Majidi, pp. 33-34.

Bork̲ᵛār: K̲ān-Aḥmadi; see also Gaz, K̲ᵛorzuq, Komešča.

Delijān: Majidi, pp. 49-55; Yarshater, 1985; Ṣafari; Madani; Peyvandi.

Farizand: Christensen, I.

Gaz: Zhukovskiĭ, II; Bailey, 1935b; Eilers and Schapka, 1979; Moḥammadi et al., 1992; Esmāʿili; Fāżel; Borjian, 2005a.

Golpāyegān: Yarshater (Jewish, unpub.); *ŠGI* IV, pp. 275-343.

Isfahan district: Mehryār, 1977; *ŠGI* II; Sepantā, 1996 and 1997; Borjian, 2005b.

Isfahan Jewish community: Abrahamian; Pažand; MacKenzie; Kalbāsi; Netzer; Sahim; Borjian, forthcoming.

Jarquya: Ḵān-Aḥmadi; Salimi; Šafiʿi pp. 439-568; Ebrāhimi Faḵḵāri; Borjian, forthcoming.

Jowšaqān: Lambton, pp. 43-78; Yarshater, 1985; Zargari.

Ḵᵛānsār: Zhukovskiĭ, I; Mann and Hadank, pp. 3-67; Eilers and Schapka, 1976; Baḵši, 1955 and 1997; Yarshater (Jewery; unpub.); Tasbiḥi; *ŠGI* III, pp. 43-80; Ašraf-al-Kottābi; Tawakkoli; Banihāšemi; Amiri, 2000, 2002a, and 2002b; Ašrafi Ḵᵛānsāri.

Kamandān (in Lower Rudašt): Borjian, forthcoming.

Karfud/Kafrān (two distinct villages in the Upper Rudašt, which are confused in the literature): Zhukovskiĭ, II.

Kāšān district: *ŠGI* IV, pp. 167-270.

Kāšān Jewish community: Zhukovskiĭ, II; Yarshater, 1974; Ṭabari.

Keša (Naṭanz): Zhukovskiĭ, I.

Keyjān: Krahnke.

Komešča: Baḥr-al-ʿOlumi.

Ḵᵛorzuq: Mirʿalāʾi; Borjian, forthcoming.

Kuhpāya: Ḵān-Aḥmadi; Krahnke; Eilers; Almāsi; Borjian, 2004, idem, forthcoming; see also Mašgenān, Ābčuya.

Ḵur and adjoining villages: see CENTRAL DIALECTS.

Maḥallāt: Mann and Hadank, pp. 68-105; Yarshater (Jewery; unpubl.); Majidi, pp. 15-24.

Mašgenān (Kuhpāya): Ṣadri.

Meyma: Lambton, pp. 5-43; Moʿiniān,; Majidi, pp. 61-64; Waṭanḵᵛāh; see also Vazvān.

Nāʾin: Querry; Mann and Hadank, pp. 117-93; Ivanow, 1929; Hadank; Lecoq, 2002; Sotuda; Āqābābāʾi; Purʿābedi.

Narāq: Majidi, pp. 25-32.

Naṭanz: Polak, pp. 264 ff.; Zhukovskiĭ, I; Mann and Hadank, pp. 106-16; Christensen, I.

Nešalj (Kašān): Majidi, pp. 36-39; Yarshater, 1985.

Nohuj: Krahnke.

Qālhar (SE of Delijān): Majidi, pp. 41-46.

Qehi (north of Rudašt): Borjian, forthcoming.

Qohrud: Houtum-Schindler, 1884; Zhukovskiĭ, I; Browne, 1893, pp. 188-93, 1927, pp. 203-8; Mann and Hadank, pp. 265-67; Lecoq, 2002; Yarshater, 1985; Ṣādeqi Qohrudi.

Rudašt: see Kamandān, Kafrud/Kafrān, Qehi, Varzana.

Sagzi: Krahnke; Borjian, forthcoming.

Sedeh: Zhukovskiĭ, II; Farahvaši; Ḡafurzāda (a poem); Ḵāsta, 2000 (poems) and 2004, pp. 71-87 (poems); Ašrafi Varnusfāderāni; Ḵātunābādi (idioms); Esmāʿili, 2001 and 2002; Ṣarrāmi, pp. 128-43; Borjian, forthcoming.

Soh: Andreas, I, pp. 50-110; Houtum-Schindler, 1884; Mann and Hadank; Bailey, 1935b.

Ṭār: Lecoq, 2002; Āhur.

Ṭarq: Krahnke.

Vānešān (near Ḵᵛānsār): Zhukovskiĭ, I; Jalāli; Kefāyati.

Vārān (in Jāsb, NE of Delijān): Majidi, pp. 57-58; Nilipur and Ṭayyeb.

Varzana: Lecoq, 2002.

Vazvān (near Meyma): Ḥosayni-nežād; Samiʿiniā.

Yārand: Christensen, I.

Zefra: Zhukovskiĭ, I; Rajāʾi (and many more articles); Borjian, forthcoming; see also Bāḡ-gol.

Zor (in Jāsb, NE of Delijān): Majidi, p. 59.

Bibliography: Roubene Abrahamian, *Dialectologie iranienne: Dialectes des Israelites de Hamadan et d'Ispahan et dialect des Baba Tahir*, Paris, 1930. Moḥammad-Amin Adib Ṭusi, "Se ḡazal-e eṣfahāni az Awḥadi-e Marāḡi," *NDA Tabriz* 15/4, 1963, pp. 387-400. Moḥammad-Reżā Āhani, "Barrasi-e guyeš-e Abyāna," M.A. thesis, Univ. of Tehran, 1994. Rafʿat-al-Zamān Āhur (or Āhvar), "Taḥlil-e sistem-e feʿli dar guyeš-e qaria-ye Ṭār," M.A. thesis, University of Tehran, 1978. Ḥosayn (ʿAbbās) ʿAlijānzāda, *Zabān-e kavir* I: *taḥqiq dar bāra-ye zabān-e Ārān o Bidgol*, Tehran (?), 1993. ʿAli-Aṣḡar Almāsi Kupāyi, "Tawṣif-e sāḵtemān-e guyeš-e Kuhpāya," M.A. thesis, University of Isfahan, 1995. Farah Amini Abyāna, "Barrasi-e vižagihā-ye dasturi dar guyeš-e Abyāna," M.A. thesis, Allāma Ṭabāṭabāʾi University, 1994. Hušang Amiri Ḵᵛānsāri (Ṣafā), *Farhang-e loḡāt-e Ḵᵛānsār*, Tehran, 2000a. Idem, *Pand o żarb-al-matalhā ba lahja-ye ḵᵛānsāri*, Tehran, 2002b. Idem, ed., *Farhang-e bāstāni-e Ḵᵛānsār: ādāb o rosum o bāzihā wa . . .*, Tehran, 2002. Fredrick C. Andreas, *Iranische Dialectaufzeichnungen aus dem Nachlass von F. C. Andreas*, ed. Kay Barr, Walter B. Henning, and Arthur Christensen, Berlin, 1939. Angelus a Sancto Iosepho (Joseph Labrosse), *Gazophylacium linguae Persarum, triplici linguarum clavi, italicae, latinae, gallicae, nec non specilalibus praeceptic ejusdem linguae referatum (loḡat-e farang va Pārs)*, ed. Jonson Waesberg, Amsterdam, 1684. Reżā Āqābābāʾi Bādafšāni, "Taḥlil-e tāriḵi pirāmun-e vāžahā-ye aṣil-e guyeš-e nāʾini hamrāh bā taḥlil-e āvāʾi o dasturi," M.A. thesis, University of Tehran, 1991. Manučehr Ašraf-al-Kottābi, "Gozida-ye matalhā wa kenāyahā-ye Ḵᵛānsāri," in Fereydun Jonaydi, ed., *Nāma-ye farhang-e Irān* II, Tehran, 1986, pp. 37-48. Mortażā Ašrafi Ḵᵛānsāri, "Vižagihā-ye afʿāl dar guyeš-e Ḵᵛānsāri," in Ḥasan Reżāʾi Bāḡbidi, ed., *Majmuʿa-ye maqālāt-e naḵostin hamandiši-e guyeš-šenāsi dar Irān*, Tehran, 2002, pp. 43-59. Mortażā Ašrafi Varnusfāderāni, "Pažuheš-i dar vāžahā-ye guyeš-e sedehi," M.A. thesis, Dānešgāh-e āzād-e eslāmi/Islamic Azad University, Arāk, 2000. Awḥadi, *Divān-e Awḥadi Marāḡaʾi*, ed. Saʿid Nafisi, Tehran, 1961.

Moḥammad-Taqi Bahār, in *Majalla-ye mehr*, 1927, pp. 840-41. Ḥosayn Baḥr-al-ʿOlumi, "Lahjahā-ye maḥalli-e Irān: Diālekt-e komčaʾi," *Pašutan* 1/8, 1948, pp. 19-20; 1/9 1948, pp. 22-23. Harold W. Bailey,

"Persia. II: Language and Dialects," in *EI*[1] III, pp. 1050-58. Idem, "Western Iranian Dialects," *TPS*, 1933, pp. 46-64, repr. in idem, *Opera Minora* I, pp. 221-39. Idem, "Iranian Studies. IV," *BSO(A)S* 7/4, 1935a, pp. 769-78, repr. in idem, *Opera Minora* I, pp. 163-86. Idem, "Modern Western Iranian: Infinitives in Gazī and Soī," *TPS*, 1935b, pp. 73-74, repr. in idem, *Opera Minora* I, pp. 265-66. Idem, *Opera Minora*, ed. Mahyar Nawabi, 2 vols., Shiraz, 1981. Yusof Bak̲ši, *Tarānahā-ye K̲ᵛānsār*, Tehran, 1955. Idem, *Divān-e Yusof Bak̲ši K̲ᵛānsāri*, Tehran, 1997. Sayyed Mojtabā Banihāšemi K̲ᵛānsāri, *Farhang-e lahja-ye k̲ᵛānsāri*, K̲ᵛānsār, 2000. ʿAli Bolukbāši, "Barrasihā-ye lahja-ye Abyāna," M.A. thesis, University of Tehran, 1970. Ḥabib Borjiān, "Neṣāb-e welāyati-e Reżā Darviš Kupāyi," *Nāme-ye pārsi* 9/3, 2004, pp. 63-80. Idem, "Taṣḥiḥ-e motun-e guyeši: divān-e Darviš ʿAbbās Gazi," *Iranshenasi/ Irān-šenāsi* 17/2, 2005a, pp. 320-37. Idem, "Joḡrāfiā-ye guyešhā-ye welāyati-e Eṣfahān," *Iranshenasi/Irān-šenāsi* 17/3, 2005b, pp. 466-86. Idem, *Ganjina-ye guyešhā-ye ostān-e Eṣfahān* I, Tehran, forthcoming. Edward G. Browne, *A Year Amongst Persians*, London, 1893, 2nd ed., Cambridge, 1927. Arthur Emanuel Christensen, *Contribution à la dialectologie iranienne*, 2 vols., Copenhagen, 1930-35. Nāṣer Dādmān, *Dastur-e zabān o taṭawwor o farhang-e lahja-ye Eṣfahān*, 2nd ed., Isfahan, 1976. Neʿmat-Allāh Ḏokāʾi Bayżāʾi, "Zabān-e rāyeji-e ārāni," in Ḥamid Zarrinkub, ed., *Majmuʿa-ye sok̲anrānihā-ye dovvomin kongera-ye taḥqiqāt-e irāni, Mašhad* II, 1972, pp. 343-45. Moḥammad-ʿAli Ebrāhimi Anāraki, *Ey nār-sina: ašʿār-e maḥalli-e anāraki*, Isfahan, 1999. Ḥamida Ebrāhimi Fak̲kāri, "Tawṣif-e zabān-šenāk̲ti-e guyeš-e manṭeqa-ye Jarquya (garguyi yā welāyati)," M.A. thesis, University of Isfahan, 1997. Wilhelm Eilers, "K̲hpāye, das alte Vir, und seine Mundart," in Carol Altman Bromberg et al., eds., Aspects of Iranian Culture: In Honor of Richard Nelson Frye, Bulletin of the Asia Institute, N.S. 4, 1990, pp. 217-29. Wilhelm Eilers and Ulrich Schapka, *Westiranische Mundarten aus der Sammlung W. Eilers* I: *Die Mundart von Chunsar*, Wiesbaden, 1976; II. *Die Mundart von Gäz*, 2 vols, Wiesbaden, 1979. Moḥammad-Mehdi Esmāʿili, "Guyeš-e gazi," M.A. thesis, University of Shiraz, 1995. Idem, "Guyeš-e sedehi," Ph.D. diss., Dānešgāh-e āzād-e eslāmi/Islamic Azad University, Tehran, 2001. Idem, "Guyeš-e sedehi," in Ḥasan Reżāʾi Bāḡbidi, ed., *Majmuʿa-ye maqālāt-e nak̲ostin hamandiši-e guyeš-šenāsi dar Irān*, Tehran, 2002. pp. 31-41.

Bahrām Farahvaši, "Taḥlil-e sistem-e feʿl dar lahja-ye sedehʾi," *MDAT* 10/3, 1963, pp. 311-23. Sāzmān-e joḡrāfiāʾi-e niruhā-ye mosallaḥ, *Farhang-e joḡrāfiāʾi-e kuhhā-ye kešvar/Gazeteer of Mountains in the Islamic Republic of Iran* II, Tehran, 2000. Ahmad Fāżel, "Barrasi-e vižagihā-ye zabāni o dasturi-e guyeš-e gazi," M.A. thesis University of Isfahan, 1995. Ahmad Ḡafurzāda, "Lahja-ye varnusfādrāni," *Nāma-ye sok̲anvarān-e Sepāhān* 3, 1975, pp. 67-70. Wilhelm Geiger, "Centrale Dialekte," in Wilhelm Geiger and Ernst Kuhn, eds., *Grundriss der iranischen Philologie*, 2 vols., Strassburg, 1895-1904, I, pp. 281-406; repr. Berlin and New York, 1974. Karl Hadank, "Ivanow als Berichterstatter," *Acta Orientalia* 10, 1931, pp. 294-97. Ḥamza Eṣfahāni, *Ketāb al-tanbih ʿalā ḥodut̲ al-taṣḥif*, ed. Moḥammad-Ḥasan Āl Yāsin, Baghdad, 1967. Aḥmad Ḥosayni-nežād, "Lahja wa ādāb o rosum-e mardom-e Vazvān-e Eṣfahān," B.A. thesis, University of Isfahan, 1969. Albert Houtum-Schindler, "Beiträge zum kurdischen Wortschatze," *ZDMG* 38, 1884, pp. 43-116. Idem, *Eastern Persian Irak*, London, 1896. W. Ivanow, "Two Dialects Spoken in the Central Persian Desert," *JRAS*, N.S., 21, 1926, pp. 405-31. Idem, "Notes on the Dialect of K̲ur and Mihrijan," *Acta Orientalia* 8, 1927, pp. 45-61. Idem, "The Gabri Dialect," *Rivista degli Studi orientali* 15, 1934, pp. 1-58. Jadwa, *Vāža-nāma-ye bur-bassa*, ed. Iraj Afšār, Nāma-ye Farhangestān, suppl. 5, Tehran, 1998. Maryam Jalāli Dehkordi, "Barrasi-e guyeš-e Vānešān," M.A. thesis, University of Tehran, 1995. Āqā Mir Sayyed ʿAli Janāb, *Ketāb-e Eṣfahān*, 1924, ed. ʿAbbās Naṣr as *al-Eṣfahān*, Isfahan, 1992. Maḥmud Joneidi-Jaʿfari, "Notes on the Vocabulary of Abyānaʾī," *Iran and the Caucasus* 10/1, 2006, pp. 107-11.

Irān Kalbāsi, *Guyeš-e Kalimiān-e Eṣfahān*, Tehran, 1994. Qodrat-Allāh K̲ān-Aḥmadi, "Vāžahā wa loḡāt-e lahjahā-ye maḥalli-e Bork̲ᵛār, Jarquya, Qohpāya, Eṣfahān," B.A. thesis, University of Isfahan, 1961. Parviz Nātel K̲ānlari, *Tārik̲-e zabān-e fārsi*, 3 vols., Tehran, 1969-; tr. N. H. Ansari as *A History of Persian Language*, New Delhi, 1979-. H. Kanus-Credé, "Notizen zum Dialekt von Anārak," *Iranistische Mitteilungen* 5, 1971, pp. 10-22. K̲āsta (Aṣḡar Ḥāj-Ḥaydari), *ʿAṭr-e gandom, mehr-e mardom*, K̲omeynišahr, 2000. Idem, *Dašt-e šabnam: majmuʿa-ye šeʿr*, Qom, 2004. Afsāna K̲ātunābādi, "Amtāl-e varnusfādrāni," *Nāma-ye Farhangestān* 4/3, 1998 (pub. 2000), pp. 29-31. Ṭāhera Kefāyati, "Barrasi-e guyeš-e Vānešān-e Golpāyegān," M.A. thesis, Dānešgāh-e āzād-e eslami/Islamic Open University, 1999. Karl John Krahnke, "Linguistic Relationships in Central Iran," Ph.D. diss., University of Michigan, 1976. A. K. S. Lambton, *Three Persian Dialects*, London, 1938. Pierre Lecoq, "Le dialect d'Abyāne," *Studia Iranica* 3, 1974, pp. 51-63. Idem, "Le dialect d'Abu Zeyd Ābād," in *Monumentum H. S. Nyberg* II, Acta Iranica 5, Tehran and Liège, 1975, pp. 15-38. Idem, "Les dialects du centre de l'Iran," in Rüdiger Schmitt, ed., *Compendiun Linguarum Iranicarum*, Wiesbaden, 1989, pp. 313-26. Idem, *Recherches sur les dialectes kermaniens (Iran central): grammaire, textes, traductions et glossaires*, Acta Iranica 39, Lovani, Belgium, 2002. David N. MacKenzie, "Jewish Persian from Isfahan," *JRAS*, 1968, nos. 1-2, pp. 69-75. Dāʾud Madani, "Tawṣif-e goruh-e feʿli-e guyeš-e rāji (Delijān)," M.A. thesis, ʿAllāma Ṭabāṭabāʾi University, 1995. Mofażżal b. Saʿd b. Ḥosayn Māfarruk̲i Eṣfahāni, *Ḏekr maḥāsen Eṣfahān*, ed. Sayyed Jalāl-al-Din Ṭehrāni, Tehran, 1933; Pers. tr. by Sayyed Ḥosayn b. Moḥammad Āvi as *Tarjama-ye Maḥāsen-e Eṣfahān*, ed. ʿAbbās Eqbāl, Tehran, 1949. ʿAbbās Maḥbubi Ārāni, "Barrasi-e sāḵt-āvāyi o sāḵt-vāža dar guyeš-e Ārān o Bidgol," M.A. thesis, Dānešgāh-e āzād-e eslāmi/Islamic Azad University, Central Tehran, 2001. Moḥammad-Reżā Majidi, *Guyešhā-ye pirāmun-e Kāšān o Maḥallāt*, Tehran, 1975. Oscar Mann and Karl Hadank, *Kurdisch-persische Forschungen* III/1: *Die Mundarten von Ḵunsar, Mahallat, Naṭanz, Nayin, Samnān, Sivand und Sô-Kohrûd*, Berlin and Leipzig, 1926. ʿAbbās Mazraʿati, ʿAli Mazraʿati, and Moḥammad Mazraʿati, *Farhang-e Bid̲ovoy (Abuzaydābād-e Kāšān)*, Tehran, 1995. Moḥammad Mehryār, "Farhang-nāma-ye vāžahā-ye rustāhā wa deyhhā-ye Eṣfahān," *Nāma-ye soḵanvarān-e Sepāhān*, no. 5, 1977, pp. 133-51. Idem, *Farhang-e jāmeʿ-e nāmhā wa ābādihā-ye kohan-e Eṣfahān*, Isfahan, 2003. Moʿaddab Mirʿalāʾi, "Guyeš-e ḵʸorzuqi (Borḵʸār-e Eṣfahān)," M.A. thesis, Dānešgāh-e āzād-e eslāmi/Islamic Azad University, Tehran, 1995. Moḥammadi, Qowwatmand (or Qutmand), and Ḵāksār, eds., *Ḡazaliyāt-e Darviš ʿAbbās Jazi*, Isfahan, 1992. Mehdi Moḥaqqeq, "Ašʿār-i ba lahjahā-ye maḥalli," *FIZ* 7, 1959, pp. 247-52. Mehdi Moʿiniān, "Taḥqiq dar ādāb o rosum o lahja-ye mardom-e Meyma," B.A. thesis, University of Isfahan, 1969. Moqaddasi (Maqdesi), *Aḥsan al-taqāsim fi maʿrefat al-aqālim*, ed. M. J. de Goeje, Leiden, 1906. Georg Morgenstierne, "Neuiranische Sprache," in Berthold Spuler, ed., *Handbukh der Orientalistik* I/4/1, Leiden, 1958, pp. 155-78.

Amnon Netzer, "Studies in the Spoken Language of the Jews of Iran," in Joseph Dan, ed., *Culture and History: Ino Sciaky Memorial Volume*, Jerusalem, 1987, pp. 19-44 (in Hebrew). Reżā Nilipur and Moḥammad-Taqi Ṭayyeb, "Tawṣif-e sāḵtemāni-e dastgāh-e feʿl-e lahja-ye Vārān," *Majalla-ye zabān-šenāsi* 2/1, 1985, pp. 51-92, 2/2, pp. 81-92. ʿAli Oḵrawi, "Barrasi-e vāžagān o eṣṭelāḥāt-e viža-ye guna-ye fārsi-e Eṣfahāni," M.A. thesis, ʿAllāma Ṭabāṭabāʾi University, Tehran, 2000. ʿAziz Pažand, "Purim," *Našriya-ye Dāneškada-ye adabiyāt-e Eṣfahān*, 1966, nos. 2-3, pp. 163-70. Faribā Peyvandi, "Barrasi-e sāḵtvāži-e guyeš-e Delijān," M.A. thesis, University of Tehran, 1998. Jakob Eduard Polak, *Persien, das Land und seine Bewohner*, 2 vols., Leipzig, 1865-66; tr. Keykāvus Jahāndāri as *Safar-nāma-ye Pulāk: Irān wa irāiān*, Tehran, 1982. Ḥasan Purʿābedi Nāʾini, "Barrasi-e guyeš-e nāʾini," M.A. thesis, University of Tehran, 1993. Masʿud Purriāḥi et al., eds., *Šenāsāʾi-e guyešhā-ye Irān* I-IV, Tehran, 1983-2000. Amedeé Querry, "Le dialecte persan de Nāyīn," *Mémoires de la Société Linguistique de Paris* 9, 1886, pp. 100-124. Moḥammad-Ḥasan Rajāʾi Zefraʾi, "Lahja-ye mardom-e Zefra-ye Kuhpāya-ye Eṣfahān," in Fereydun Jonaydi, ed., *Nāma-ye farhang-e Irān* I, Tehran, 1985, pp. 105-15. V. S. Rastorgueva and V. V. Moshkalo, "Dialekty tsentralnogo Irana," *Osnovy iranskogo yazykoznanya. Novoiranskie yazyki: sever-zapadnaya gruppa* II, Moscow, 1997, pp. 195-329. Moḥammad b. ʿAli Rāvandi, *Rāḥat al-ṣodur wa āyat al-sorur*, ed. Moḥammad Eqbāl, Leiden, 1921; 2nd revised ed. with commentary by Mojtabā Minovi, Tehran, 1985. Ḥasan Reżāʾi Bāḡbidi, ed., *Majmuʿa-ye maqālāt-e noḵostin hamandiši-e guyeš-šenāsi dar Irān*, Tehran, 2002. ʿAli-Ašraf Ṣādeqi, *Takwin-e zabān-e fārsi*, Tehran (?), 1978. Idem, "Fahlaviyāt-e ʿObayd Zākāni," *Majalla-ye zabān-šenāsi* 13/1-2, 1996, pp. 2-8. Idem, *Negāh-i ba guyeš-nāmahā-ye irāni*, Tehran, 2000. Idem, "Guyeš-šenāsi-e Irān bar asās-e motun-e fārsi: guyešhā-ye markazi," *Majalla-ye zabān-šenāsi* 17/1, 2002, pp. 2-8. Nastaran Ṣādeqi Qohrudi, "Guyeš-e qohrudi," M.A. thesis, Dānešgāh-e āzād-e eslāmi/Islamic Azad University, Tehran Central branch, 2003. Jamāl Ṣadri Maškenāni, "Guyeš-e Mašgenān-e Eṣfahān," B.A. thesis, University of Isfahan, 1970. Ḥosayn Ṣafari, *Vāža-nāma-ye rāji yā guyeš-e Delijān*, Tehran, 1994. ʿAli Šafiʿi Nikābādi, *Garkuya: sarzamin-e nāšenāḵta bar karān-e kavir*, 2nd ed., Isfahan, 1997. Haideh Sahim, "Languages and Dialects of the Jews of Iran and Afghanistan," in Houman Sarshar, ed., *Esther's Children: A Portrait of Iranian Jews*, Beverley Hills, 2002, pp. 283-94. ʿAli Salimi, "Folklor yā farhang-e ʿāmma-ye mardom-e Jarquya, ba enżemām-e loḡāt o eṣṭelāhāt-e maḥalli," B.A. thesis, University of Isfahan, 1970. Ḥasan Samiʿi-niā, "Barrasi-e sāḵt-e naḥwi-e guyeš-e Vazvān," M.A. thesis, University of Isfahan, 1995. Sayyed Nāṣer Sarafrāzi, "Tawṣif-e feʿl dar zabān-e bizāvi (Abuzaydābād)," M.A. thesis, Dānešgāh-e āzād-e eslāmi/Islamic Azad University, Tehran Central branch, 1991. Rasul Ṣarrāmi Forušāni, *Sedeh dar god̲ar-e zamān*, Isfahan, 2003. Rüdiger Schmitt, ed., *Compendium Linguarum Iranicarum*, Wiesbaden, 1989. Sāsān Sepantā, "Barrasi-e āzmāyešgāhi-e čand guyeš-e markazi o lahja-ye Eṣfahān," *Nāma-ye Farhangestān* 2/2, 1996, pp. 82-104. Idem, "Barrasi-e gušahāʾ-i az neẓām-e āvāʾi-e čand guyeš-e markazi-e Irān," *Nāma-ye Farhangestān* 3/2, 1997, pp. 69-83. *ŠGI*, see Purirāḥi. Shaul Shaked, "'Do Not Buy Anything from an Aramaean': A Fragment of Aramaic Proverb with a Judaeo-Iranian Version," in Dina Amin, Manouchehr Kasheff, and Shapour Shahbazi, eds., *Iranian Varia: Papers in Honour of Professor Ehsan Yarshater*, Acta Iranica 30, Leiden, 1990, pp. 230-39. Aḵtar Sohrābi Anāraki, *Vāža-nāma-ye anāraki*, Mašhad, 1994. Manučehr Sotuda, ed., *Farhang-e nāʾini*, Tehran, 1986.

Aḥmad Ṭabāʾizāda, "Guyeš-e Bāḡ-gol (Eṣfahān)," M.A. thesis, University of Tehran, 1969. Yaʿqub Ṭabari, "Sipak ḵi-niā," Fereydun Jonaydi, ed., *Nāma-ye farhang-e Irān* I, Tehran, 1985, pp. 142-44. Aḥmad Tafażżoli, "Eṭṭelāʿāt-i dar bāra-ye lahja-ye pišin-e Eṣfahān," in Ḥabib Yaḡmāʾi and Iraj Afšār, eds., *Nāma-ye minovi*, Tehran, 1971, pp. 85-103. Idem, "Some Isfahani Words," in Ronald E. Emmerick and Dieter Weber, eds., *Corolla Iranica: Papers in Honor of Prof. Dr. David Neil MacKenzie on the Occasion of His 65th Birthday*, 1991, pp. 207-10. Mirzā Ḥosayn Khan Taḥwildār, *Joḡrāfiā-ye Eṣfahān*, ed. Manučehr Sotuda, Tehran, 1963. Yad-Allāh Ṯamara, "Moʿarrefi-e do ṭarḥ-e melli-e guyeš-šenāsi," in Ḥasan Reżāʾi Bāḡbidi, ed., *Majmuʿa-ye maqālāt-e noḵostin hamandiši-e guyeš-šenāsi dar Irān*, Tehran, 2002, pp. 135-42. Moḥammad-Ḥosayn Tasbiḥi,

Guyeš-e k̲ᵛānsāri, Rawlpindi, 1975. Moḥammad-Mehdi Tawakkoli, "Barrasi-e sāk̲t-e āvāʾi o ṣarf dar guyeš-e k̲ᵛānsāri," M.A. thesis, University of Tehran, 1995. Paul Tedesco, "Dialektologie der westiranischen Turfantexte, *Le Monde Orientale* 12, 1921, pp. 184-257. Ebrāhim Waṭank̲ᵛāh, *Barrasi-e guyeš-e Meyma*, M.A. thesis, University of Tehran, 1995. Wezārat-e jehād-e sāzandegi, *Ṭarḥ-e jamʿ-āvari-e nemunaʾi-e guyešhā-ye Irān*, unpub. questionnaires and audio cassettes, Tehran. Gernot L. Windfuhr, *Persian Grammar: History and State of Its Study*, The Hague, 1979. Idem, "New Iranian Languages: Overview," in Rüdiger Schmitt, ed., *Compendiun Linguarum Iranicarum*, Wiesbaden, 1989, pp. 246-50. Idem, "New West Iranian," ibid., pp. 251-62. Idem, "Western Iranian Dialects," ibid., pp. 294-95. Šehāb-al-Din Abu ʿAbd-Allāh Yāqut Ḥamawi, *Moʿjam al-Boldān*, ed. Ferdinand Wüstenfeld, 6 vols., Leipzig, 1866-73. Ehsan Yarshater, "The Jewish Communities of Persia and Their Dialects," in Philippe Gignoux and Ahmad Tafazzoli, eds., *Mémorial Jean de Menasce*, Louvain, 1974, pp. 455-66. Idem, "Distinction of Grammatical Gender in the Dialects of Kashan Province and Adjoining Areas," in *Papers in Honour of Professor Mary Boyce*, 2 vols., Acta Iranica 24-25, 1985, II, pp. 727-45. Idem, "The Dialects of Ārān and Bidgol," in Charles-Henri de Fouchécour and Philippe Gignoux, eds., *Études irano-aryennes offertes a Gilbert Lazard*, Paris, 1989, pp. 371-83. Raḥmat-Allāh Zargari, *Tārik̲, farhang o honar-e Jowšaqān-e Qāli*, Tehran (?), 1995. V. A. Zhukovskiĭ, *Materialĭ dlya izuchesniya persidskikh' narechiy*, 3 vols., St. Petersburg, 1888-1922; repr. as *Materials for the Study of Iranian Dialects*, 3 vols. in 1, Tehran, 1976.

(HABIB BORJIAN)

xxi. PROVINCIAL DIALECTS

Within the boundaries of Isfahan Province, in addition to a large number of Iranian languages and dialects, we also find a small minority of non-Iranian languages. The Iranian languages of Isfahan Province are of three basic types: (1) Northwest Iranian (NWI) dialects belonging to the Central Plateau Dialect (CPD) group, also called Central dialects (q.v.) or Median dialects by different authors, and two different types of Southwest Iranian (SWI) languages: (2) slightly divergent dialects of Persian, but intelligible to the standard language, and (3) large pockets of Lori (q.v.), spoken in the vicinity of Faridan (locally: Fereydan) area and Lori-Bak̲tiāri spoken in the arm of Isfahan province reaching directly south past Semirom. Persian dialects are found in the towns and villages south and west of Isfahan and in the larger cities, such as Najafābād [Ād̲ari], Šahreżā [Tāki], etc. In addition, the Central dialect varieties originally spoken by the Muslim populations (but preserved, at least until recently, by the Jewish communities) in cities such as Isfahan, Kāšān, Golpāyegān, and K̲omeyn (the latter, just outside Isfahan province per se) have been replaced by varieties of Persian, in some cases even in recent memory, but in other cases (e.g., Isfahan) this shift came about centuries ago. Without these later shifts to Persian in large, populous areas, the native CPD should be considered the largest group of Iranian dialects original to the area. The present entry will concentrate on the dialects in the immediate Isfahan area but not without relating them to other CPD of Isfahan Province and to the CPD group as a whole.

Aside from the considerable Armenian presence in the township of Jolfā in the suburbs of Isfahan, the non-Iranian languages of Isfahan Province are spoken mostly in the Faridan area (Armenian: *peria*), west of Isfahan. In 1964, while conducting field work in the Faridan area, Donald Stilo encountered Georgian spoken in some eleven villages and also about equal number of Armenian-speaking villages. Both of these groups, along with the Armenians of Isfahan/Jolfā, were introduced into the area during the reign of Shah ʿAbbās I (r. 1587-1629, q.v.). In the upheavals of the 1970s in Persia, there was an Armenian exodus from much of Faridan, leaving their houses empty and some villages totally depleted. Most left for large cities (undoubtedly to Isfahan, but also those contacted by Stilo in Tehran and Southern California). Some of the Georgians of the area (and probably some of the local Armenians as well) also left for the then-Soviet Union. Since the Georgians of the area were Muslim (Georgian informants of Faridan claimed they were converted to Islam during the Afghan invasion of Persia in the early 18th century), many preferred to remain in the area and are still a presence there today. A brief preliminary investigation conducted in the Faridan area by Turkologists in 2005 (see below) showed that Faridani Georgian, local dialects of Armenian, as well as Lori and Turkic-speaking villages still formed a quite vital presence in the Faridan area. Characteristics of the Georgian and the Turkic dialects will be discussed briefly at the end of this entry.

ABBREVIATIONS

The following are the two-letter abbreviations for place names used in Figures 1 and 2, along with the three- or four-letter abbreviations used for each dialect in the text of this entry (only if actual examples appear): aa Ārān (Ārān.), ab Abyāna (Aby.), ac Ābčuba (Ābču.), ak Anārak (Anār.), an Ardakān (Ardk.), ar Ardestān (Ards.), az Abuzeydābād (Abuz.), bd Bādrud (Bādr.), bg Bidgol (Bidg.), bj Bijagān (Bijg.), dj Delijān (Deli.), ff Fārfān (Fārf.), fz Fariz(h)and (Fari.), gp Golpāyegān, gz Gaz (Gazi), Isfahani Jewish (IsfJ.), jq Jarquya (Jrqu.), jv Ješuqān, jw Jowšaqān (Jowš.), kd Kamandān (Kamd.), ke Keša (Keš.), kf Kafrān/Kafrud (Kafr.), kj Keyjān (Keyj.), Kāšāni Jewish (KāšJ.), k̲n K̲omeyn, k̲s K̲ᵛānsār (K̲ᵛān.), ku Kuhpāya/Qohpāya (Kuhp.), k̲z K̲orzuq (K̲orz.), mb Mārbin (Mārb.), mh Maḥallāt (Maḥll.), mm Meyma (Meym.), nj Nohuj (Noh.), nn Nāʾin (Nāʾin), nr Narāq (Nrāq), ns Nešalj (Neš.), nz Naṭanz (NaṭzC. [Christensen], NaṭzS. [Stilo fieldnotes]), ol ʿOlunābād (ʿOlun.), pk Peykān (Peyk.), qh Qohrud (Qohr.), qi Qehi (Qehi), ql Qalhar (Qalh.), sd Sedeh (Sed.), so Soh (Soi), sz Sagzi (Sagzavi, abbreviated Sagz.), tq Tarq (tarq), tr Tār (Tāri), tu Tudešk, vr Vārān (Vār.), vd Vendāda (Vend.), vn Vānišān (Vāniš.), vr Varzana 1 (NW), vz Varzana 2 (SW; Varz.), yg Yangābād/Nikābād (Yang.), yr Yārand (Yār.), zf Zefra (Zefr.), zr Zor (Zori). In addition, Yazdi Zoroastrian (Yaz.), often called "Dari," a CPD of the southeast group, is occasionally mentioned in this entry, but it is not within Isfahan Province and is beyond the boundaries of this figure (see also ISFAHAN i. GEOGRAPHY for a more detailed and comprehensive presentation of the Median-speaking villages of Isfahan Province).

HISTORY AND CLASSIFICATION OF THE CENTRAL PLATEAU DIALECT GROUP

The major division in Western Iranian languages is between Northwestern Iranian and Southwestern Iranian. While the modern SWI languages, for instance, Persian, Lori-Baḵtiāri and others, are derived directly from Old Persian through Middle Persian/Pahlavi, NWI groups are thought to be derived from Median, a language known exclusively through indirect attestation. It is not even known whether Median was actually ever a written language. The only attested NWI language from the Middle period of Western Iranian is Parthian, an independent NWI branch that eventually died out and cannot be considered to be the direct ancestor of any of the known modern NWI languages. Thus the actual histories of the various modern NWI languages are completely unknown in any concrete terms since no data is available on any specific ancestor of these languages. Modern NWI is divided into seven major groups: (1) Caspian (Gilaki, Māzandarāni), (2) Tatic (including Tāti and Tālеši), (3) Kurdish (northern, central, southern), (4) Gurāni (Iran-Iraq border area), (5) Zazaki/Dimli (central Turkey), (6) Baluchi, and (7) the Central Plateau dialects, or simply Central dialects (q.v.), a large group to which most of the dialects of Isfahan Province belong. Parthian is sometimes added as an eighth group, but as an extinct language from the Middle Iranian period, it is not quite parallel with the other groups.

The main concentration of CPD covers a wide area on a northwest-to-southeast axis, extending eastward from Delijān in the northwest through Kāšān and Ārān/Bidgol to Anārak in the east, then south to the dialects of the Zoroastrians and Jews of Yazd and surrounding areas, from there back in a northwesterly direction up to Isfahan and on to Ḵᵛānsār, thence through Golpāyegān and Ḵomeyn to Maḥallāt and again to Delijān. CPD also includes certain more distant outliers (probably the results of later migrations): Sivandi (north of Shiraz), the dialects of the Jews of Kermān, Borujerd, and Hamadān (q.v.), and the somewhat aberrant dialects of the Ḵur area in the southern Dašt-e Kavir (see CENTRAL DIALECTS for more detailed information about the CPD group). The main bulk of CPD is located within Isfahan Province. Pierre Lecoq (1989, p. 313) further divides the CPD group into four subgroups (see Figure 1): (1) northwestern CPD (Maḥallāti, Vanišāni, Ḵᵛānsāri, etc.), (2) northeastern CPD (Naṭanzi, Kāšāni Jewish, Abyāna'i, Abuzeydābādi, Yārandi, Meyma'i, etc.), (3) southeastern CPD (the Jewish and Zoroastrian dialects of Yazd and environs, Kermāni Jewish, Nā'ini, Anāraki, Ardakāni, etc.) and (4) southwestern CPD which includes an area extending from Sedeh (< *seh deh*, "three villages") and Isfahani Jewish (see xix, above) southeast to Peykān, then northeast to Kafrān and Kafrud, northwards through Kuhpāya and ʿOlunābād to Zefra and then back to Gaz (see also Introduction to Isoglosses below for further delineation of the southwest and southeast subgroups of CPD).

Gernot Windfuhr's classification of CPD (see CENTRAL DIALECTS) into western, northern-central, southern, and eastern groups corresponds to Lecoq's classification of northwest, northeast, southwest, and southeast groups, respectively. Both scholars add a fifth group to include the dialects of the Tafreš area, at least Āštiāni, Āmora'i and Kahaki. Lecoq (1989, p. 313) also adds Vafsi and Alviri-Vidari here, although he is ambivalent about their status, because they also resemble the Tāti dialects, also known as Azeri, that is, pre-Turkic "Old Azeri." Windfuhr classifies Āštiāni, Āmora'i and Kahaki among the Central dialects as a fifth subgroup, which he calls northwestern. He does not include Vafsi or Alviri-Vidari but, following Stilo (1981), classifies them with the Tāti family. The present author does not include the dialects of the Tafreš area (Tafreši, Āštiāni, Āmora'i) within CPD but rather reflects Lecoq's ambivalence about their affiliation. While they share a large number of features with both CPD and Tāti, they also exhibit features, especially lexical items, that are highly idiosyncratic and not at all typical of CPD or of Tāti, and their historical development and genetic affiliations are as yet very poorly understood.

The classification and abbreviation of the CPD group as NW, NE, SW, and SE will be used in this entry (see Figure 1). The main thrust of the present entry, as mentioned, will be directed toward the SW subgroup of CPD, located in the immediate area of Isfahan and to the east, northeast, and southeast of the city, but the dialects of other areas of Isfahan Province and a discussion of the relationship of SW to the other CPD subgroups, particularly to the NE group clustered around Kāšān, will also be included.

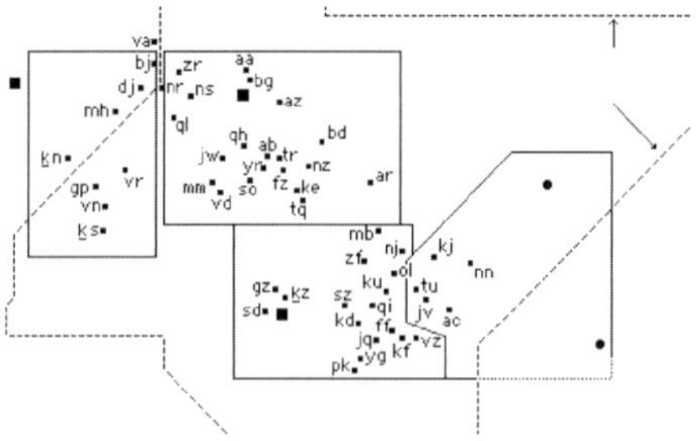

Figure 1. Dialect map of Isfahan area.

Explanation of Figure 1: (1) The name Yangābād is listed on most maps as Nikābād. Razmārā (*Farhang* X) gives both names. (2) Eilers (Eilers and Schapka, 1979) has a few notes on a dialect he calls Jarquya. The *Farhang* only lists this name as a *dehestān* that includes Peykān and Yangābād among others. It is not clear to which village in this *dehestān* Eilers' notes refer. A point on the Figure (jq, SW of Isfahan) was arbitrarily chosen to represent both his data and that of Borjiān (see xx above), who uses the name Jarquya to represent the dialects of both Yangābād and its neighboring village, Ḥosaynābād. (3) The name Sedeh is indicative of three separate villages in this area that became unified into one town. The name was then changed to Homāyunšahr in the 1950s and to K̲omeynišahr after the Islamic Revolution. Moḥammad-Mehdi Esmāʿili (2002) lists a population figure from 1991 of 230,000 for the whole city. The original dialect, while rapidly disappearing, is still spoken in one of the five neighborhoods (*bāvalgun*) of the former village of Varnusfāderān. In the area the dialect is called *velāti* (i.e., *welāyati*); this name also appears in Esmāʿili (2002) and in Ehsan Yarshater's and Ludwig Paul's field notes. (4) Some adjustments to the transcription of place names, as well as of language data throughout this entry, have been made in both Wilhelm Eilers' and Valentin Zhukovskiĭ's transcriptions to compensate for the subphonemic transcription in the former author (see GAZI for further discussion) and the overuse of *o* and *ō* in the latter (e.g., Vonišon, Kafron, etc., where one finds Vānišān, Kafrān in Yarshater's, Krahnke's and others' transcriptions instead).

The Immediate Isfahan area, Isfahan Province, and the Central Plateau dialects. The dialects of the immediate Isfahan area, from Sedeh (present-day K̲omeynišahr) to approximately ʿOlunābād (see the SW subgroup of CPD on Figure 1 as well as the discussion related to composite Figure 5 below) form a rather homogeneous group, but not without the slight range in variation usually found in subdialects extending over a rather large area (for a more detailed discussion of how slight dialect variations generally differ within an extended geographic continuum, see the section entitled "Delineation of the Māzandarāni language zone" under MĀZANDERĀNI.) In order to understand the linguistic position of the dialects of the immediate Isfahan area, one must understand their relationship to the Central Plateau Dialects, the larger group of which they are a subgroup, as well as the further relationship of the whole Central Plateau group, on a larger plane, to NWI in general and how the latter, in turn, are distinguished from Persian and the SWI group.

THE NORTHWEST IRANIAN NATURE OF CENTRAL PLATEAU DIALECTS

Diachrony. The dialects of the immediate Isfahan area (the SW group on Figure 1) exhibit specific features in the historical development of their sound systems that are shared by most CPD and the latter, in turn, have the typical characteristics of NWI that contrast sharply with SWI, typified by Persian. That is, there are various important sound changes that distinguish NWI, and thus also CPD, from Persian and SWI and even Old Persian, the latter already showing typical SWI characteristics as opposed to Median with typical NWI developments. A fuller discussion of one of the key differences between SWI and NWI, the development of original Proto-Iranian **dz* to **d* in SWI and to **z* in NWI, and the prominent examples of these correspondences as seen in the glosses "know" and "son-in-law," are found under ISFAHAN xix. JEWISH DIALECTS. Another important gloss demonstrating this correspondence of NWI *z* to SWI *d* is the IsfJ. word *ezerí* "yesterday" vs. Persian *diruz* (for details, see Table 1).

Table 1
Development of **dz* > *z* in NWI in Words Meaning "Yesterday" in CPD Areas and Beyond

"Yesterday"	Dialects
CPD	
ezerí	Isfahan Jewish
heze	Delijāni, Maḥallāti, Abuzaydābādi, Yārandi, Meymaʾi, Jowšaqāni, Tuyserkān Jewish, Hamadāni Jewish, ʿOlunābādi, Kešaʾi, Zefraʾi, Kuhpāyaʾi Varzanaʾi, Yazdi Zoroastrian
héze	Ardestāni
hizi	Anāraki
(h)eze	K̲ᵛānsāri
eze	Vānišāni, Qohrudi, Sedehi, Gazi, Qehi
hezze	Abyānaʾi, Fārfāni, Peykāni, Kafrudi
haza	Farizandi, Naṭanzi (Christensen)
hazze	Jarquyaʾi
ezza	Sagzābādi
ezze	K̲orzuqi
hezi	Naṭanzi (Stilo)
(h)ezi	Soi
ejer ~ ezer	Ārāni
hezzere	Zori
zirení	Sivandi
Areas Beyond CPD	
zína	N. Tati: Harzani, Keringāni, Kalāsuri C. Tāti: Koluri, K̲oini; Tāleši: Lerik, Vizanaʾi, Jowkandāni,
izər	Asālemi,
zir	Māsāli,
zer	Māsulaʾi;
azinna	C. Tāti: Dikin-Marāgaʾi, Mušqini-Marāgaʾi,
azira	Hazārrudi, Kelāsi, Kabataʾi, Kajali; (S. Tāti) S. Tāti: Tākestāni, Sagzābādi, K̲iāraji, Eštehārdi,
azir(a)	Čāli,
(a)zira	Alviri,
hazíri	Vafsi;
heziri	Tafreš area: Āštiāni,
hezzere	Kahaki,
hezere	Āmoraʾi;
(i)yezze	Semnān area: Aftari,
aza	Sork̲aʾi,
izé	Biābānaki,
azi	Lāsgerdi,
ezi	Semnāni,
izi	Sangesari;
hizi	Gurāni: Tavela, Luhoni, Kandulaʾi, Gāhvāraʾi,
uzera	Bājelāni,
vizēr	Zazaki;
zīk	Baluči

The original NWI form does not appear in Caspian or Northern, Central, or Southern Kurdish, where the initial consonant is *d-* in all cases, borrowed from Persian in the case of the Caspian languages and possibly from another SWI source for Kurdish.

Another typical NWI characteristic, **ts* > *s*, is very rarely represented in CPD, where it has been almost completely replaced by Persian loanwords such as *ā(h)en* "iron," *bahār* "spring," *dah* "ten," all of which are also found in many other NWI languages and represent the SWI development of Proto-Iranian **ts* > *h*. Among CPD only three dialects, for example, have preserved the original NWI form of the word "fish" (Av. *masya-*, Parth. *masyag*), as seen in Abuz. *māsā*, Yazdi, Kermāni Jewish *māsi*, where the NWI development of **ts* > *s* is still retained, while all other CPD, as far as is known, have replaced it with the SWI borrowing *māhi*. Indeed, most NWI have a version of the SWI form and the rare exceptions are, in addition to the CPD forms cited here, Zazaki *māse*, (Tāti) Ḵoʾini *māssā*, (Northern Kurdish) Akre dialect, Farizov: *mesî*, Chyet: *masî* (Central Kurdish), Solaymāniya, (Southern Kurdish) Kermānšahi, (Gurāni) Gahvāraʾi *māsi*, Luhoni *māsāwi*.

The most widespread examples of NWI **ts* > *s* in CPD are the forms *mas* "large" and *kas* "small" (vs. Persian *meh* and *keh*, respectively). *Mas* (and its variants) "large" is found only in the SE and NW subgroups of CPD (and a few other NWI languages); *kas* (in its various forms) "small" is somewhat more widespread. The exact origins of the *keh-kas* pair (small) are somewhat unclear, but it may have been influenced in its formation by the *meh-mas* pair (large). Since their original forms were fairly similar (*mas-/kas-*) and were paired antonyms, they began to mirror each other as rhyming pairs.

LARGE (Av. *masya-*, a comparative form), SMALL (Av. *kasu-*). Within CPD, the NW group generally uses an original comparative form of these roots (but no longer with a comparative meaning), while other CPD areas that have these roots use the plain roots *mas/kas* without *-(s)ar* (see Table 2) These roots show no cognates in Tatic, Caspian, Zazaki, Gurāni, or Northern, Central, and Southern Kurdish and no reflex of *mas* in Baluchi (see Figure 7 for the other forms of "large" in CPD).

Table 2
The Development of **ts* > *s* in the Words "Large" and "Small" in CPD Areas and Beyond

"Large"	"Small"	Dialects
CPD Areas		
A		
mussar	*kessar*	Vānišāni
masar	*küsür*	Maḥallāti
mossar ~ *messar*	*kissara*	Ḵ^{y}ānsāri
messar		Delijāni
maser	*kaser*	Tuyserkāni Jewish
masar	*kasar*	Hamadān Jewish
B		
	kas	Sedehi, Gazi, Ḵorzuqi, Peykāni, Kuhpāyaʾi, Qehi, Kešaʾi, Tāri, Varzanaʾi, Zefraʾi, Kamandāni
	kass	Sagzi, Jarquyaʾi
	kes	Kafrāni, Naṭanzi (Stilo)
	kēs(s)u	Ardestāni
	kasala	Naṭanzi (Christensen)
	kasla	Farizandi
mas(s)e	*kas*	Nāʾini
mas	*kasok*	Kermāni Jewish, Yazdi Zoroastrian
mas(a)	*kas*	Anāraki
	keisu	Ḵuri
Areas Beyond CPD		
masdar	*kastar*	Tafreš area: Āštiāni,
mastar		Kahaki,
masda(r)	*kusda*	Āmoraʾi;
masin	*kasin*	Semnān area: Aftari, Biābānaki, Lāsgerdi, Moʾmenābādi, Semnāni, Sangesari,
māsin	*kāsin*	Sorḵaʾi;
	kasān	Baluči

**ts^W* > *sp*. Retention of the initial *sp-* cluster is found in Old Iranian in the Median word *spaka* "dog" as well as in a form of Scythian (ultimately borrowed from a variety of the latter into Russian as the word *sobaka*). The simplification of this initial cluster to *s-* within Western Iranian is in fact characteristic of SWI (and probably Kurdish), cf. Old Pers. *saka* and its descendant *sag* in New Pers. and Northern, Central, and Southern Kurdish *sa(g)*.

DOG. The forms with retained *-sp-* found in CPD are: Qohr., Abuz. *espa*; Ḵ^{y}āns, Vāniš. *esba*, Yaz. *s(e)va*; and Ārān. *e:sbə*. Similar *sp-* forms of this word are found widely in NWI, (N. Tāti) Kalāsuri, Kajalí, (Cent. Tāti) Koluri, (Tālešī) Asālemi, Māsāli, Māsulaʾi, (Semnān area) Semnāni, Biābānaki, Aftari, (Tafreš area) Āštiāni, Kahaki, Āmoraʾi *esba* ~ *espa*, (S. Tāti) Čāli and others, Vafsi, Alviri, (Semnān area) Lāsgerdi *asba* ~ *espe*, (N. Tālešī) Ṣayyādlari, Jowkandāni *əspa*, (N. Tāti) Harzani *esba*, (Semnān area) Sangesari *əspə*, and with the epenthetic vowel inserted between the first two consonants in (Cent. Tāti) Šāli, Hezārrudi, Ḵoini *seba* (N. Tālešī, various dialects), *sipa* ~ *sepa*. The only two reflexes of this root that are slightly different are found on the one hand in Kabataʾi and Kelāsi *spa* (both Tāromi-type Tāti of the Rudbār area of Gilān) with the unusual initial consonant cluster and on the other hand in Keringāni with the loss of the whole first syllable: *pa* ~ *pā*, but the latter also has the alternate form *espā*. No representatives are found in the Caspian group (where this word has been replaced by the Pers. form), in Northern, Central, or Southern Kurdish (where the change of **ts^w* > *s* may be original), or in Zazaki (probably borrowed from Kurmanji).

In a large central area of the CPD zone (see Figure 2), the original CPD word for "dog" has been replaced by a unique gloss, probably a loanword (< Eastern Iranian?; Krahnke, Isogloss 35): Aby., Fari., Yār., Soi, NaṭzC., Noh. *kuyā*, Anār., Tarq. *kuya*, HamJ., Kuhp., ʿOlun., Keyj., Nāin. *kuye*, Peyk., Fārf., Sagz., Sed., Gazi *kue*, Ards. *küe*, Meym., Jowš., Ābcu., Bādr. *kua*, NaṭzS. *küwa*, Keš., Sagz. *küva*, Tāri *köva*, Zefr., Varz., K̲orz. *kuve*, Kamd., Qehi *ku(v)e*, IsfJ. *kuze~kuδe*). Henceforth, since the lines drawn on the various maps below may also encircle dialects for which no information is available (e.g., Vendādehi, Tudeški, etc.), a white dot will be placed in the middle of each dialect point that yielded actual information on the given feature presented on the map (or at least for one feature on composite figures).

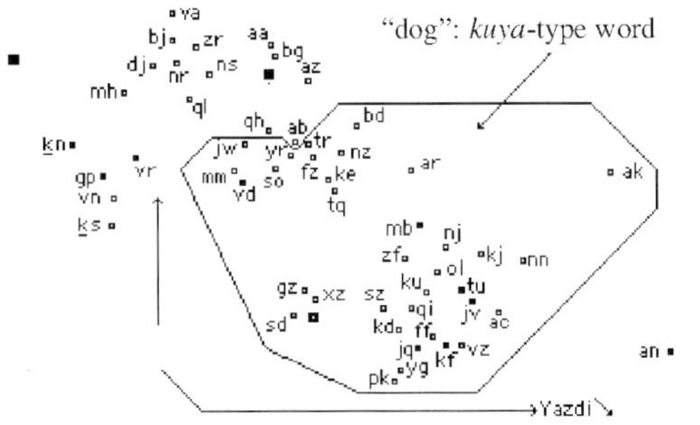

Figure 2. Dialect map of Isfahan area.

Various other sound correspondences that now distinguish NWI from SWI were not yet in effect in Old Persian and often not even in older versions of Middle Persian and/or Parthian, but represent later stages of sound changes that developed in these languages and presumably in the undocumented predecessors of other (non-Parthian) NWI groups, such as pre-CPD, for example. Some of these later changes are in fact areal phenomena that affect predominately NWI or SWI but, depending on their locations, may include some languages from both groups. Below is a selective list with some representative examples of these later changes:

Medial **-rz-* typically remains in NWI, but becomes *-l-* in SWI. There are, however, many words with the SWI *-l-* reflex that were borrowed into various NWI languages at different time periods. Thus the original NWI word for "tall, high" (variations on a root more or less like **barz*) is not retained anywhere in CPD, having been replaced by Persian (or some other SWI source) *boland ~ belend* throughout. A typical NWI example of retained **-rz-* found sporadically in CPD is represented by the present root of the verb "to let, allow" (sometimes also "to put"), although most CPD dialects have a borrowed form with *-l-* e.g., *(h)el-*. Only six CPD dialects were found with the original NWI *-rz-* form. Other NWI groups have the original form quite commonly. It is also found with additional changes of the initial consonant, or the loss of the *-r-* and/or the lengthening of the vowel in Northern Tāti and Gurāni (see Table 3). In the Middle Iranian stage, the Parthian form also retains the medial *-rz-*, but we also find a change in the vowel: *hirz-*. No

Table 3

The Retention of the Medial **-rz-* in the Present Root of the Verb "Let, Allow" in CPD Areas and Beyond

"Let," "Allow"	Dialects
CPD Areas	
harz-	Ārāni, Bidgoli, Abuzaydābādi, Yazdi Zoroastrian
va-hārz- (+ preverb)	Abyānaʾi
al- ~ arz-	Isfahani Jewish
Areas Beyond CPD	
(h)arz-	C. Tāti: Kajali; C. Tāleši: Asālemi
harz-	C. Tāti: Koluri; S. Tāti: Čāli, Vafsi; S. Tāleši: Māsulaʾi;
arz-	C. Tati: K̲oini; S. Tāti: Tākestāni, Eštehārdi;
hārz-	Semnān area: Sangesari
hoz- ~ hož-	N. Tāti: Harzani
faz-	Keringāni,
āz-	Kalāsuri; Gurāni: Luhoni
hāz-	Kandulaʾi

representatives of the NWI form were found in the Caspian group or in Northern, Central or Southern Kurdish.

In CPD, and indeed in most NWI, the original consonant clusters **fr*, **θr*, **xr* generally all merge equally to the same range of consonants: **fr > hr, r, h*, **θr > hr, r, h*, **xr > hr, r, h*. The choice of *hr*, *r*, or *h* depends both on the specific dialect and also on the position of the cluster in the given word. The two clusters **fr*, **xr* have generally remained intact in SWI, whereas **θr* generally becomes *s* in SWI (see GAZI and ISFAHAN, JEWISH DIALECT for a more detailed description of the results of these changes and the alternation of *(h)r~h(r)* in those dialects). Typical examples of these three Proto-Iranian clusters in NWI are represented in the words (**fr*) "sell," "send," and "down" in the immediate Isfahan area (see Figure 5 and accompanying discussion below), (**θr*) "son, boy" "mill," (**xr*) "to buy," "wheel," "red" (see Tables 4-8). Only some of these examples can be demonstrated here.

SELL. In the immediate Isfahan area (and HamJ., which shares a component of its origins with IsfJ.), both "sell" and "send" are generally represented by initial *f(e)r-*, indicating that these words are probably a borrowing from some SWI source, but probably not Persian because of the discrepancy in the vowel of the root, for instance, "sell": Gazi, IsfJ., K̲orz., Qehi, Sagz., Kamd., Zefr. *ferāš-/ferāt*, Sed., Kafr., Jrqu. *f(e)rāš-/f(e)rāt*, ʿOlun. *frāš-/ferāt*, HamJ., Kuhp. *fərāš-/fərāt*, Peyk. *p(e)rāš-/perāt* (see Table 4).

SEND. The verb "send" in many CPD and some other NWI languages has merged with "to deliver" (i.e., the causative of "to arrive"). This is due to the sound change of **fr > (h)r ~ h(r)* leaving the reflex *r-* in initial position in "send" in some dialects yielding a form that was

Table 4
The Verb "Sell" in CPD Areas and Beyond

"Sell"	Dialects
CPD Areas	
ruš- / rut	Vānišani, Kāšāni Jewish, Abuzaydābādi, Ārāni, Sivandi, K̲ʸānsāri
ruš	Delijāni
hruš- / harut	Farizandi
hruš- / horut	Yārandi
ruš- / horut	Meymaʾi
h(o)ruš- / h(o)rut	Naṭanzi (Christensen)
heruš-/ herut	Naṭanzi (Stilo)
(h)araš ~ (h)arāš- / ferāt	Fārfāni
hrāš- / herāt	Tāri
harāš- / harāt	Varzanaʾi
(h)roš- / h(ə)rot	Yazdi Zoroastrian
hroš- / h(i)rāt	Anāraki
hörš- / hörutt	Abyanaʾi
oroš- / orot	Ardestāni
orāš- / orāt	Nāʾini
xruš- / xurut	Qohrudi
xroš- / xrot	Kešaʾi
Areas Beyond CPD	
roš- / rot	Zazaki
hāvāt- / hāvāt	Tāleši: Lerik
heraš- / höröt ~ horat ~ horot	N. Tāti: Harzani,
hirišt	Keringāni,
(h)erāt- / herāt	Kalāsuri;
h(ö)ruš- / höröt	Cent. Tāti: Kajali
xraš- / xrat	Tāleši: Asālemi, Māsāli,
xoroš- / xorot	Māsulaʾi,
x(e)ruš- / x(e)rut	Cent. Tāti: Šāli,
xoruš- / xorut	Karani,
xeriš-	Gandomābi,
x(e)ruš- / xorut	Nowkiāni,
xruš- / xrut	Kelāsi,
(i)ruš- / (i)rut	Kabataʾi,
xaraš- / xarat	K̲oini,
(h)ruš- / yrut	(Ṭālaqāni) Godarkāni,
rut	Owrāzāni;
ruš- / rut	S. Tāti: Čāli, Tākestāni, Razajerdi, Vafsi, Mušqini; Tafreš area: Āštiāni, Tafreši, Āmoraʾi; Semnān area: Lāsgerdi; Caspian: Tonokāboni, Kalārdašti, Velātruʾi, Sāravi, Dodāngaʾi, K̲aṭirābādi
(h)ruš-	S. Tāti: Eštehārdi
rüš- / rüt	Semnān area: Šahmirzādi, Sork̲aʾi,
eyrüš- / eyrüt	Semnāni,
hruš- / hrut	Aftari;
wUraš- / wUrat	(Gurāni) Luhoni, Kandulaʾi;

probably very close to "deliver," for instance, something like pre-CPD **resenā ~ resnā* "deliver" and **restā* "send" (< **frestā(d)*), which then merged in some dialects. The similarity in the semantics of "send" and "deliver" was undoubtedly also a factor contributing to the merger. This merger did not, however, take place throughout CPD as we see in those dialects that retain the initial *h-* (Fari., Tāri, NaṭzC.), including the ones that have lost the initial *h-* but retained an extra syllable with an initial *e-* (Ards.), or that have even strengthened it to *x-* as in Kešaʾi, as well as in (Gilaki) Langerudi, and various Tāti dialects (Table 5).

Table 5
The Verb Send in CPD Areas and Beyond

Send	
CPD Areas	
resn- / resnā	K̲ʸānsāri, Vānišāni, Meymaʾi
rasn- / rasno	Abyānaʾi, Jowšaqāni
rasn- / rasnā	Yārandi, Gazi
erasn- / erasno	Ardestāni
h(a)rasn- / harasnā	Farizandi
harasan- / harasanā	Naṭanzi (Christensen)
harasn- / herasanā	
-farasanā	Tāri
resen- / resenā	Hamadān Jewish
xrasn- / xrasnā	Kešaʾi
Areas Beyond CPD	
rosin- rosni	N. Tāleši: Lerik
xers-	C. Tāti: Gandomābi
xeres-	Nowkiāni
xest	Hazārrudi
xrəst /xrəstā	Kelāsi
(ö)röst	S. Tāti: Čāli
(o)rest	Tākestāni
rëstā	Eštehārdi
röst- / röstānd	Alviri
resd- / resdā	Vafsi, Āmoraʾi
fa-rəsān / rəsāne	Caspian: Rašti
- /xəsāne	Langarudi
rasen- /-	Tonokāboni
resān- / resāni	Kalārdašti
ras- / rest	K̲aṭirābādi
riš- / rišt ~resnā	Zazaki

BOY "SON." **θr > (h)r ~ h(r)*. Most CPD have a word *pür ~ pir* (Av. *puθra-*, OPer. *puça-*, cf. Skt. *putrá*) that in many dialects means both "boy" and "son." In some cases "son" is distinguished from "boy" by the addition of a final vowel (e.g., *püre*; see Table 6). In most cases, however, available sources do not inform us whether this difference between "boy" and "son" is present or absent in a given dialect, since the Persian translation does not specify this distinction. Thus in some dialects only *püre* is given while in others only *pür*. Many may genuinely not have the distinction: boy, son (Avestan: *puθra-*, Old Persian: *puça-*, cf. Skt. *putrá*): Only six CPD dialects (as far as is known) distinguish "boy" from "son": Deli. *pür* vs. *pürə*, Aby. *pür* vs. *püra*, Gazi (Yarshater field notes) *püre* vs. *pür*, Abuz. *pü̃r* vs. *pü̃rja*, Fārf. *poré* vs. *poreci*, Yaz. *porog* vs. *por ~ pórike*, respectively. Maḥll., Vāniš., Meym., Sed., Vār., Neš., Qohr., Keš. *pür*, Zori *püre*,

Table 6
The Words "Boy" and "Son" in CPD and Southern Tāti Areas

"Boy"	"Son"	Dialects
CPD Areas		
pür	*pürə*	Delijāni
pür	*püra*	Abyānaʾi
püre	*pür*	Gazi (Yarshater field notes)
pǖr	*pǖrja*	Abuzaydābādi
poré	*poreci*	Fārfāni
porog	*por ~ porike*	Yazdi Zoroastrian
Southern Tāti Areas		
pura	*pur*	Čāli
fera	*fer*	Tākestāni
fera	*pövr*	Ebrāhimābādi
fera	*fura*	Sagzābādi
pevra	*pevr*	Ḵiāraji
fura	*pur*	Dānesfahāni
pura	*pur*	Esfarvarini
fer	*fer*	Ḵoznini
fura	*fura*	Eštehārdi

Table 7
The Word "Mill" in CPD Areas and Beyond

"Mill"	Dialects
CPD Areas	
ār	Ḵ^{v}ānsāri, Vānišāni, Qohrudi, Jowšaqāni, Kešaʾi, Sedehi, Gazi, Ḵorzuqi, Kamandāni
āra	Abyānaʾi
ahr	Anāraki
ohr	Naṭanzi (Stilo)
or	Ardestāni
ar	Nāʾini, Qehi
ir	Zefraʾi
ēr	Kafrāni
ār	Isfahani Jewish (in *ar-ci* "hand mill," diminutive of original **ār* in this dialect)
Areas Beyond CPD	
ārye	Zazaki
orār	Harzani
ārāqā, orāqā	Keringāni
arga	Ḵoʾini
āxre	Vafsi (Gurčāni)
ārey	Aftari
āri	Sorḵaʾi, Lāsgerdi
āra	Biābānaki
ār	Sangesari
ār(ē)	Semnāni

The Persian word *āsiow* has become rather widespread among many NWI areas.

Bijg., Zori, Fari., Yār. *püra*, KāšJ., Zefr., Anār., Nraq., NaṭzC. *pur*, Kafr., *pure*, Ḵ^{v}āns., Ārān., HamJ., IsfJ. *pir*, Jowš. *pür ~ pur*, NaṭzS. *pohr*, Soi *pǖra*, Yaz., Kermāni Jewish, Ards., Nāin. *por*, Sagz., *pora*, ʿOlun., Kuhp., Peyk. *poré*. This root, while it appears in Parth. *puhr*, is not well represented in NWI outside CPD. It appears only in Southern Tāti (Table 6), where most of the dialects distinguish "boy" and "son" (but not in Vafsi or other forms of Tāti) and the dialects of both the Semnān and Tafreš areas (in both of the latter areas it exclusively means "son"). In the following areas, this root only means "son": (S. Tāti) Alviri *pür*, Vidari *pur*, (Tafreš area) Āštiāni, Tafreši, Kahaki *pur*, Āmoraʾi *pür ~ pur*, (Semnān area) Sangesari, Sorḵaʾi *pür*, Aftari *pur*, Lāsgerdi *pur*, *pür*, Biābānaki *pör*, Semnāni *pir*. Elsewhere it has been replaced either by the Persian word *pesar* or by completely different forms, for instance, Vafsi *leyla* "boy" vs. *lāza* "son."

Table 8
*Development of **xr* > *(h)r ~h(r)*
The Verb "Buy" in CPD Areas and Beyond

"Buy"	Dialects
CPD Areas	
hrin- / hri	Abyānaʾi, Meymaʾi, Jowšaqāni
hrin- / hiri	Tāri
hrin- / hari	Yārandi, Farizandi
hrin- / hrid	Yazdi Zoroastrian
hrin- / hrint	Anāraki
hərin- / hiri(nt)	Kuhpāyaʾi
herin- / herid	Naṭanzi (Stilo)
(h)irin- / (h)rind	ʿOlunābādi
hirind- / hirind	Varzanaʾi
xrin- / xrid	Qohrudi
xrin- / xrind	Kešaʾi
(x)irin- / xirint	Zefraʾi
irin- / irint	Isfahani Jewish, Sedehi, Gazi, Ḵorzuqi
irn- / rit	Ḵ^{v}ānsāri
rin- ~ irn- /eiri	Vānišāni
xarin- / erit	Kāšāni Jewish
rēn- / rid	Abuzaydābādi
rin- / rid	Ārāni
eren- / rid	Ardestāni
Areas Beyond CPD	
xrin- / xri	S. Tāti: Čāli, Sagzābādi,
xrin- / xria	Vafsi (Gurčāni),
rxin- / rxi	Ebrāhimābādi, Dānesfahāni,
rxin ~ rxen- / rxi	Ḵiāraji,
hrin- / hrind	Alviri,
xin- / xi	Rudbāri: Raḥmatābādi;
irin- / iri	Tafreš area: Tafreši,
eirin- / eiri	Kahaki
hin- / he	Caspian: Rašti, Langarudi,
xarin- / x(a)ri	Sāravi;
erin- / erind	Semnān area: Aftari
eyrin- / eyrindi	Semnāni,
ršin- / ršind	Sangesari,
herīn- / herīnā	Zazaki

*Proto-Iranian **xrina-*; cf. Skt. *krīṇā́ti*

Another characteristic sound correspondence between NWI and SWI is the reflex of original Proto-Iranian initial **v- ~ *w-*, which remains as *v-* in NWI but becomes *b-* in SWI. This is a later development in SWI that was not characteristic of Old Persian. The typical cognates that represent this correspondence are "wind" and "willow" (but see also additional examples of NWI *v*- vs. SWI *b*- with the words "snow," "rain," "almond," "sift," "widow," "twenty," "child," "lamb," "nose," "woods," "must," "enough," under the various entries for individual NWI languages, dialects or groups).

WIND (Av. *vāta*-, New Pers. *bād*): CPD: Zefr., Kafr., Gazi, Sed., Nā'in., Anār., Varz. *vā*; Fari., Yār., NatzC., Keš., Tāri *vāy*. Beyond CPD, we find this word with initial *v*- in: (C. Tāti) Koluri, K̠oini, (S. Tāti) Čāli, Alviri, Vafsi, (Tāleši) Jowkandāni, Asālemi, Māsāli, Māsula'i, (Caspian/Māzandarāni) Sāravi, Šahmirzādi, (Semnān area) Semnāni, Aftari, Sork̠a'i, Lāsgerdi, (Lakki) Lakki, (Zazaki/Dimli) Zazaki, (Gurāni) Kandula'i, Tavela *vā*; (Tāleši) Lerik, Anbarān *vo*; (N. Tāti) Keringāni *vu* ~ *voy*; (Semnān area) Sangesari *ve*. Northern and Central Kurdish also underwent the change of **v* ~ *w* > *b*-, and have an initial *b*- in these roots: (N. Kurd.) Kurmanji, (C. Kurd.) Solaymāniya *bā* as does SWI: Pers. *bād*. Within Southern Kurdish, however, Bijāri and Kalhori do have the form *wā*. Certain CPD and other NWI forms are more conservative in that they preserve a final consonant (cf. Pers. *bād*, as also with "son-in-law" above) that is lost in most CPD and other NWI forms: (CPD) Vāniš., Qohr., Jowš., Abuz., Yaz. *vād*, IsfJ. *vāδ* ~ *vāz*, (N. Tāti) Harzani *vör*, Kalāsuri *vur*, (Tafreš area) Āštiāni *vād*, and also the Baluchi form *gwāt* (see the next section).

WILLOW (Av. *vaēti*-): Most CPD and other NWI languages have a form *vi-(dār)* ~ *via-(dār)* ~ *vid* for the word "willow," corresponding to Pers./SWI *bid*, (see Table 9).

**v- > g*: In a development related to the previous one, initial **v*- ~ **w*- remains as *v*- in most NWI languages but has changed to *g*- in SWI. The latter sound change is an areal feature that includes, in addition to Persian, most languages located in eastern Iran, such as K̠uri, Baškardi, Bandari, Fini and Baluchi, where the sound change is the most robust and includes more instances of **v- > g*- than those found in Persian (cf. the Baluchi forms *gist* "twenty," *gēš* "more," *gēt* "willow," or *gwāt* "wind"; K̠uri *gārun* "rain," *gāzi* "game," *gin*- "see (pres.)," *galg* "leaf," *gištar* "more"; Bandari *gin*- "see (pres.)," for all of which Persian has undergone the change of **v- > b*-, presented in the previous section). This is a later development in these languages and was not yet in effect in the Old Iranian period (and thus would not have been a feature separating Old Persian from Avestan or Median). This retention of original **v*- in NWI is typified by the words "to pass" and "wolf," while the New Persian form *gorg* also is derived from this same root via the **v- > g*- sound change (or more fully, **v*- + vowel > *gu*-, which was already in effect in the Middle Iranian period; cf. Middle Persian and Parthian *gurg*). See also additional examples of NWI *v*- vs. SWI (and K̠uri, Baluchi, etc.) *g*- with the words "hungry," "flee," "boar," under the entries for individual NWI languages).

TO PASS (intransitive): derives from Proto-Iranian, Avestan, and Old Persian *vi-tar*- "to cross over, go across"

Table 9
Retention of Initial **v*- ~ **w*- in "Willow" in CPD Areas and Beyond

"Willow"	Dialects
CPD Areas	
vi-	K̠ʸānsāri, Naṭanzi (Christensen), Ardestāni
vē	Zefra'i
via	Anāraki
viye	Varzana'i, Nā'ini
vey	Tāri, Abyāna'i
vid	Jowšaqāni, Yazdi Zoroastrian
vēd	Qohrudi, Abuzaydābādi
Areas Beyond CPD	
via-(dār)	Tāti: Koluri,
vi-dār	Kabata'i,
via-dār	Sagzābādi, Vafsi;
vi	Tāleši: Lerik, Māsāli,
via-dār	Asālemi;
ve-dār	Rudbāri: Jubani
vid	Tafreš area: Āštiāni
vi	Semnān area: Sork̠a'i,
via-(dāra)	Semnāni;
vi	Caspian: Māčiāni
vi-kol	Gurāni: Tavela

(cf. Sanskrit *tṛ*-, pres. *tárati*, lacking the preverb *vi*-), which underwent the following sequence of developments for NWI, with various modern languages stopping at different stages in the process, as indicated: *vi-tar- > vi-dar- > vi-yar- > vi-ar- > ver-* (others, e.g., IsfJ.: *vi-tar- > vi-dar- > vi-δar- > vi-zar-*). On the other hand, Persian and most forms of SWI went through the following stages: *vi-tar- >vi-dar- > vi-δar- > gu-δar- > go-zar* (but note that while contemporary Persian stands at the last stage given here, the written form, with an Arabic *ḏāl*, was codified at the previous stage, *gu-δar*-). We find the forms of the verb stem "to pass" in contemporary CPD (see Table 10), each of which may be compared to one of the stages in the derivation from the Proto-Iranian stem for this word given above. Most Caspian dialects have adopted the Persian word, but Rašti (and possibly other dialects) still has the stem *də-var-/ də-varəst*. While Kurdish dialects have not undergone the **vi > go*- change, they do show instead the typical Kurdish change of **v- > b*- (see wind and Table 7) for the root "pass": (N. Kurdish) Standard Soviet Kurmanji: *buhur/buhurī* ~ *bihur/bihuri* —, Chyet: *buhur/ buhurt*, Akre *bir/biri* —, Zakho *būr/būri* —; (C. Kurdish) Solaymāniya *būr/būrd*, Sorani *bwēr~bör/bward*.

WOLF (cf. Sk. *vṛka*-, Proto-Iran. **vṛka*-, Av. *vəhrka*-): The majority of CPD dialects have borrowed the Persian word *gorg* and have lost their original *varg*- type form of this word. Within CPD, only Jowšaqāni, Farizandi, Yārandi, Abyāna'i, Ardsestāni, Tāri, and Keša'i have retained *varg*; Zefra'i has *verg* and Qohrudi has *var* (but Lecoq, 2002, gives Qohr. *varg*). All in all, the form is

Table 10
Retention of Initial **v-* in "to Pass" (New Pers. *go-δar-*) in CPD Areas and Beyond

"To Pass"	Dialects
CPD Areas	
veder- / vedašt-	K̲ʸānsāri, Vānišāni, Jowšaqāni
vadēr- / vadašt-	Abuzaydābādi
veder- / vedrā-	Nāʾini
uder- / udašt-	Qohrudi
vyer- / veyāšt-	Abyānaʾi
viar- / viašt-	Yārandi, Naṭanzi (Christensen)
veyr- / viyašt-	Anāraki (Form 1)
viyer- / viyešt-	Ardestāni
yver- / yvašt-	Tāri
ivar- / ivašt-	Anāraki (Form 2), Farizandi
iver- / ivašt-	Kešaʾi
iver- / ivešt-	Zefraʾi, Sedehi
ver- / vešt-	Kafrāni
ve-ver- / ve-verā- ~ vašt	Gazi
vezer- / vezerā ~ vezašt-	Isfahani Jewish
Areas Beyond CPD	
da-vard- (both pres. and past)	N. Tāleši: Lerik
da-viar- / da-viara-	S. Tāleši: Māsāli
da-viar- / da-viard-	C. Tāti: Koluri, Kajali; S. Tāleši: Māsulaʾi
viar- /viard-	N. Tāti: Keringāni, C. Tāti: K̲oʾini
verar- / vorord-	Harzani
ā-vir- / ā-višt-	S. Tāti: Alviri,
verr- / verd-	Vafsi;
ho-viyar- / ho-viyarā-	Tafreš area: Āmoraʾi
viar- / viard-	Semnān area: Semnāni, Sork̲aʾi,
vier- / vierd-	Lāsgerdi,
ver- / veri-	Sangesari;
də-var- / də-varest-	Rašti
(rā-)vērēn- / (rā-)vērd	Zazaki
wiar- / wiard- ~ viar- / viard-	Gurāni dialects

well represented in five of the seven modern branches of NWI: (C. Tāti) Koluri, Kelāsi, Kabataʾi, K̲oini, Kajali, (S. Tāti) Tākestāni, Sagzābādi, Dānesfahāni, Vafsi, (N. Tāleši) Anbarāni (C. Tāleši) Asālemi, (S. Tāleši) Tāleš-Dulābi, Māsāli and Māsulaʾi; (Semnān area) Aftari, Semnāni, (Gurāni) Tavela *varg*. Only slightly different is the form *verg* of (S. Tāti) Razajerdi, (Tafreš area) Āštiāni, (Caspian) Tonkāboni, Kelārdašti, Sāravi, Ura'i, K̲aṭirābādi, Shahmirzādi, (Semnān area) Biābānaki, Moʾmenābādi, but (S. Tāti) Čāli has made this word into a feminine noun: *várga*. Other dialects of the Semnān area have: Sangesari *vark*, Sork̲aʾi *vorg*. Within Gurāni we find Luhoni and Bājalāni *warg*, and within Kurdish, Mokri has the form *wurc*. Within the Caspian group, only the Gāleši and Māčiāni dialects of Gilaki, as far as is known, have preserved the original NWI word with *vərg*, whereas all other dialects have replaced it with the Persian variant. With a lengthening and/or other change of the vowel, we find (N. Tāti) Harzani *vorg*, Keringāni *varg* ~ *vārg* ~ *vorg*, Kalāsuri has *vārg* ~ *vorg*, (C. Tāti) the so-called Marāgaʾi dialects of the Alamut area (Mušqini, Garmārudi, Dikini) with *vārg*, (N. Taleši) Archivan *vāg* and Astara with *vāk* ~ *vag*.

Table 11
The Word "Ladder" in CPD Areas and Beyond

"Ladder"	Dialects
CPD Areas	
salt ~ satl	K̲ʸānsāri
salt	Vānišāni
sēdr	Ārāni
sērd	Abuzaydābādi
sárde	Qohrudi
sārd	Abyānaʾi
sert	Zefraʾi
sart	Gazi, Isfahan Jewish, Nāʾini, Tāri, Varzanaʾi
sat	Sedehi
säd	Ardestāni
Areas Beyond CPD	
sɨrd	Northern Tāleši
sərdə	C. Tāleši: Asālemi
serdin	C. Tāti: Koluri,
serti	Gandomābi;
asǿrda	S. Tāti: Čāli,
sǿrda	Sagzābādi,
asélta	Tākestāni,
sérda	Vafsi;
sərdi	Rašti, Gāleši, Langarudi, Tonokāboni
serd	Semnān area: Sork̲aʾi,
sardi	Šahmirzādi, Semnāni, Sangesari;

In Southern Tāti, all forms are grammatically feminine, as seen in their stress pattern. There are no representatives in Zazaki, Gurani or N., C., or S. Kurdish.

**y-* remains as *y-* (vs. SWI *j-*), as is seen in the Isfahani Jewish forms *yuš/-ā* "boil," *yuz/yuss-* "find," *iye* "barley." This last word is also well represented throughout CPD as well as in most NWI groups.

BARLEY (Av. *yava-*): CPD: Deli., Bijg., Qalh., Nrāq., Meym., Qohr., Ards., IsfJ., Olun., Zefr., Nāin. *ye*, Soi, Keš., Anār. *ya*, NatzS. *yah*. In some cases in CPD, an initial *i-* (as in IsfJ.), and occasionally even an extra *hi-*, is added creating an extra syllable: Jowš., Sed., Gazi *ie*, Abuz., Fārf., Jrqu., Peyk. *hie*. Beyond CPD in other NWI we find similar forms in (N. Tāleši) Āstārā, (N. Tāti) Harzani, (C. Tāti) Koluri, Gandomābi, (S. Tāti) Vafsi *yav*, while most other Southern Tāti dialects share the development represented by K̲iāraji *yow*. Gurāni has the forms: Tavela *yav*, Bājalāni *yaw*, Luhoni *yáwa*. No representatives of the original NWI form of this word are found in Caspian or Northern, Central, or Southern Kurdish.

Important Lexical Items. Certain lexical items from CPD, some of which are shared with other NWI while others are unique to CPD, to give only a brief list, include: ladder (Table 11), game, buy (Table 8), cut, lose, lost, break, say (see Tables 13-15).

LADDER is represented by a similar gloss in most NWI, but there are no representatives in Zazaki, Gurāni, or North, Central, or South Kurdish (Table 11).

GAME is clearly attested in Middle Persian (*kādag*) and Sogdian (*kātē*), but it is not found in modern SWI. It, however, still exists in most NWI dialects (see Table 12).

Table 12

The Word "Game" in CPD Areas and Beyond

"Game"	Dialects
CPD Areas	
kāda	Qohrudi
kāya	Keša'i, Anāraki, Tāri
kāye	Abyāna'i, Nā'ini
kaa	Gazi, Sedehi
kā	Isfahani Jewish, Ardestāni
key	Peykāni
kē	Zefra'i
koi	Jowšaqāni
kōw	Ārāni
kuwe	Abuzaydābādi
Areas Beyond CPD	
kay	C. Tāti: Ḵoini
kāwā	S. Tāti: Vafsi
kāi	Caspian: Kalārdašti,
kā	Sāravi,
ku ~ ka ~ ke	Šahmirzādi;
kā	Semnāni area: Sorḵa'i,
cu	Sangesari,
kāy	Zazaki
keyəle	Gurāni: Tavela,
kāy	Kandulā'i

No reflexes of this term are known for N., C., or S. Kurdish.

The two verbs, "buy" and "cut," retain a final *-n* in their present roots in NWI: buy (see above under **xr*; see also Tables 13 and 14).

In addition to the previous section, where we also find special lexical roots in CPD that are typical of other NWI (but not of SWI), the following is a small representative list of lexical items that are typical of CPD as a group but are either not found in other NWI groups or found there only sporadically. Some of these examples represent lexemes that are particular to CPD. One such case is the lexical item "lost" in the compound verbs "to lose, get lost." CPD has a range of variants: *mak ~ max ~ mah ~ māh*. The only dialect beyond CPD to have this word is Vafsi (*mākk-om-ā kard* "I lost (it)"), where it is clearly a borrowing from CPD. Given the close proximity of Vafsi to the CPD group, especially northwestern CPD, Vafsi has an unusually heavy presence of CPD lexical borrowings (see Table 14).

Table 13

Retention of the Final *-n* in the Present Root of Verb "Cut" in CPD Areas and Beyond

"Cut"	Dialects
CPD Areas	
brin-	Keša'i, Gazi, Anāraki, Yazdi Zoroastrian
berīn-	Abuzaydābādi
birin-	Isfahani Jewish
bürn-	Qohrudi, Vānišāni
bürün-	Sedehi
brin- ~ birn-	Ḵᵛānsāri
Areas Beyond CPD	
rbin-	S. Tāti: Čāli, Tākestāni, Ebrāhimābādi, Sagzābādi, Alviri, Ḵiāraji, Dānesfahāni
birin-	S. Tāti: Vafsi,
birrn-	Zazaki;
vrin-	C. Tāti: Kelāsi, Kabata'i; Tafreš area: Āmora'i
birn-	N. Tāti: Harzani
bɨrɨn-	N. Tāleši: Lerik
verin-	Caspian: Kandalusi
rvin-	Semnān area: Šahmirzādi,
buren	Sorḵa'i;
bin-	Rudbāri; Raḥmatābādi; Ṭāleqāni; Goḏarḵāni, Caspian: Rašti, Lāhijāni, Gāleši, Langarudi
verin-	Sāravi
rbin-	Tafreš area: Kahaki; Semnān area: Aftari, Biābānaki, Semnāni, Sangesari, Semnāni; Tajriši, Ṭāleqāni village of Gurān

Table 14

The Verb "lose, lost" in CPD AREAS

"Lose," "Lost"	Dialects
max	Ḵᵛānsāri, Gazi, Isfahan Jewish, Jarquya'i, Tāri, Varzana'i
māx	Hamadāni Jewish
mak	Abyāna'i, Nā'ini, Anāraki
mah	Kafrāni, Sedehi
māh	Vānišāni, Keša'i, Zefra'i
māxe	Yazdi Zoroastrian
mak(vā)	Jowšaqāni
maxi	Ardestāni
maxwā	Meyma'i
mākk	Tāti: Vafsi

An interesting lexical item that is found throughout CPD and seems to be shared only with Gurāni and no other modern groups of NWI is the root "to break" (Table 15).

Table 15
The Verb "Break" in CPD Areas

"Break"	Dialects
h(e)mer-	K̲ᵛānsāri, Meymaʾi, Qohrudi, Zefraʾi
h(e)mar-	Vendādaʾi, Farizandi, Yārandi, Naṭanzi (Stilo), Bidgoli
h(a)mer-	Peykāni, Kafrudi, Hamadāni Jewish, Jarquyaʾi
h(a)mar-	Abyānaʾi, Naṭanzi (Christensen), Kešaʾi, Fārfāni
ahmar-	Zori
hmar-	Tāri
xmar-	Soi, Abuzaydābādi
xmer-	Vānišāni
(h)emar	Kuhpāyaʾi
(h)amer	Kamandāni
emer-	Isfahani Jewish
emar-	Jowšaqāni, Gazi, K̲orzuqi, Nāʾini
amar-	Ardestāni, Sagzi, Qehi
imar-	Sedehi
hmir-	Ārāni
imir-	Maḥallāti
*mar-**	Delijāni, Yazdi Zoroastrian

* This form from the extreme northwest and southeast periphery of CPD is the closest to the Gurāni forms: Luhoni *mărr-*, Tavelaʾi *mar-*, and Kandulaʾi *mirr-* ~ *mar-*.

Another verb that is absent from SWI is *vāj-* ~ *vāž-/vāt* "to say" in NWI. This distinction goes all the way back to the old Iranian stage, where Old Persian is also missing this verb root, but has instead *gaub-*, the source for Modern Persian *gu-/goft*, vs. Av. *vačah-* (Skt. *vac-*) The New Persian word *vāža* "word" is not an original SWI from but a loanword into Persian from Parthian (as is typical of Persian words with the sound *ž*). While Persian does have the SWI form *āvāz*, it is not a verb form.

The root *vāj-/vāt* of the verb "say" is typical for all NWI (except Caspian). Some CPD dialects retain the *-j-* of the present root in all forms of the present system (present, imperative, subjunctive, optative). A significant group in the SW areas of CPD (the Sedeh-Peykān-Ardestān triangle), however, drop the *-j-* of this root throughout the present system (see Table 16). The loss of this *-j-* is in fact one of the minor isoglosses in a rather large complex of isoglosses (also called an "isogloss bundle") that set the immediate Isfahan area apart from the rest of CPD (see also Figure 5 below). Dialects of the transitional areas that have forms both with and without the *-j-* (e.g., Abyānaʾi, Soi, Kešaʾi) are discussed below under *Buffer zone phenomena*.

Introduction to isoglosses. While conducting fieldwork on the dialects of the Isfahan area in 1969, Ehsan Yarshater was told by his informant from ʿOlunābād (90 km east of Isfahan, north of the Isfahan-Nāʾin road) that his dialect was also fairly close to the dialects of Sagzi, Kuhpāya and certain other points along this road and that all these dialects are what the people of the area called "*bure-beše*" dialects. Another informant from the village of Fārfān, east-southeast of Isfahan and south of Kuhpāya, named other villages in his area whose dialects he also called "*bure-beše*" along with his own. In these dialects *bure* means "come!" and *beše* means "go!" and these are typical words that stand in stark contrast to both standard Persian and to the southeastern subgroup of CPD in the area of the Nāʾin-Anārak-Yazd triangle. Except for the dialects within the latter triangle, *bure-beše*-type forms are also found in all other subgroups of CPD (Vāniš. *bure-baš*; Bādr. *bure-baše*; Jowš. *buri-beše;* K̲āns. *búre-baš*). In fact, the words *bure* "come!" and *beše* "go!" are common throughout NWI languages, for instance, Āštiāni, Kahaki, Āmoraʾi *búre*, Vafsi *búri*, Shahmirzādi *búru*, Kalārdašti (Rudbārak district of Māzandarān) *bóro* "come!" (NB: not "go!") and others.

Table 16
The Present Root of the Verb "Say" in CPD Areas

"Say"	Dialects
uāj-	Delijāni
vāj-	Maḥallāti, Ārāni, Abuzaydābādi, Yārandi, Anāraki, Nāʾini
voj-	Meymaʾi, Jowšaqāni
vāž-	K̲ᵛānsāri, Kafrāni,
vāj-, vā-	Farizandi, Kešaʾi, Kāšāni Jewish, Bidgoli, Abyānaʾi, Qohrudi, Soi, Zefraʾi
vā-	Ardakāni, Isfahani Jewish, Sedehi, Gazi, Sagzi, ʿOlunābādi, Fārfāni, Peykāni, Mārbini, Ardestāni, Naṭanzi (Stilo)

The informant from ʿOlunābād then explained that, along the road from Isfahan heading eastward toward Nāʾin, the "*bure-beše*"-type dialects like his own stop at about the villages of Tudešk and Mešgenān (loc. Moškenān), which, according to him, are not of the "*bure-beše*" type but resemble much more the dialect of Nāʾin. The words for "come!" and "go!" in the latter area are, for instance, Naʾin. *yur* (Anār. *iyur*) and *ušo* respectively. An informant of Krahnke's from the village of Ābčuba—also within the latter area, just to the east of the "ʿOlunābād-Tudešk dividing line—told him in the early 1970s that his dialect was of the "*osme-sigā*" type rather than of the "*bure-beše*" type. In these dialects *osme* and *sigā* mean "now" and "thus, this way," respectively. What the speakers of these dialects are doing when they use the terms such as "*bure-beše*" and "*osme-sigā*" to refer to their dialects and others that they can understand vs. the dialects of another group that are not so easy to understand is using a layman's concept of isoglosses to classify their languages.

An isogloss is a certain characteristic feature, whether a lexical item such as *bure*, *beše*, *yur*, *ušo*, *osme*, *sigā*, etc. or a grammatical pattern (e.g., the formation of the present tense, a certain type of noun plural formation), that is in use in the dialects/languages located within a certain geographic area. It is is usually understood as a way of representing the distribution of a certain feature on a map in the form of a line drawn around the area where the given pattern of interest is shared by all the languages or dialects found there. Outside the line, that is, beyond the isogloss, the given pattern is no longer in effect and another isogloss or other isoglosses pick up. The lexical isogloss introduced above in Figure 2 shows the distribution of the *kuya*-type word for "dog" found in a large number of dialects in the CPD area (black dots outside the encircled zone indicate that either the information is known and the response is negative or that no information is available on that dialect). Thus if we plot the occurrence of *bure*, *beše*, *yur*, *ušo*, *osme*, and *sigā* on a map and draw a line around the zones where each of these words occur, the result will be six different isoglosses. Actually, however, these lexical items would turn into more than one isogloss each on a map since, for example, the *osme*-type word is not just opposed to one other word for "now" outside the isogloss, but to three other words: a *zonun*-type word, a *zogun*-type word, and a much more widespread *hat(on)*-type word extending beyond the map to Vafsi and Alviri, resulting in four isoglosses just for the semantic concept of "now" (see Figure 3). Karl Krahnke (pp. 219-22) classifies the *zonun*- and *zogun*-types as one isogloss (*zo*-type, Krahnke Isogloss 36), although it is more convenient to consider them as two separate but similar isoglosses. Likewise, the words meaning "this way, like this, thus" appear in three different forms in the area (see Figure 4), which means that in plotting only "now" and "this way, thus" onto maps, we come up with at least seven different isoglosses.

Krahnke draws thirty-nine isogloss maps, each covering one linguistic feature represented by more than one isogloss and supplies the data along with a discussion of the comparative and historical background on each of them. The present article provides additional new isoglosses, concentrating on Isfahan province and, within that province, on the immediate Isfahan area (see also CENTRAL DIALECTS).

Isogloss bundles. Each isogloss line on a map may seem to differ in a completely random fashion from the next. Some isoglosses, however, may seem more congruent. The northern areas on Figure 3 and Figure 4, for example, centering more or less around Kāšān, show that the two isoglosses "now" and "this way," while they do not conform exactly to each other (but since there are no available data from the northwestern areas of Figure 4, this isogloss may indeed be more consistent with Map Three than the maps currently show), are quite consistent with each other, at least in the large bulk of the area they both cover. The differences on these two figures between the isoglosses for these two words for the southern area, however, show

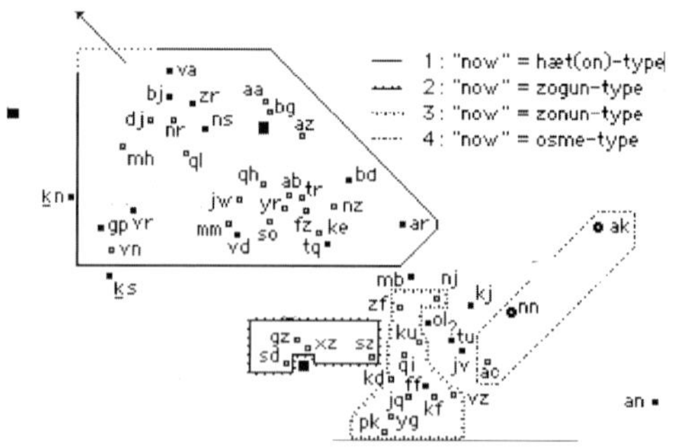

Figure 3. "Now" (four isoglosses).

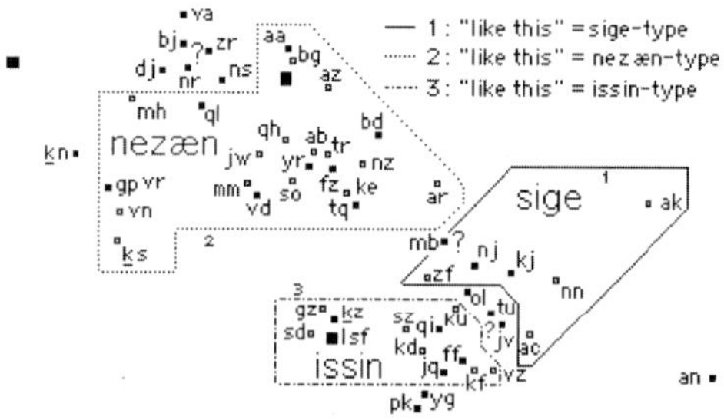

Figure 4. "This way, thus" (three isoglosses).

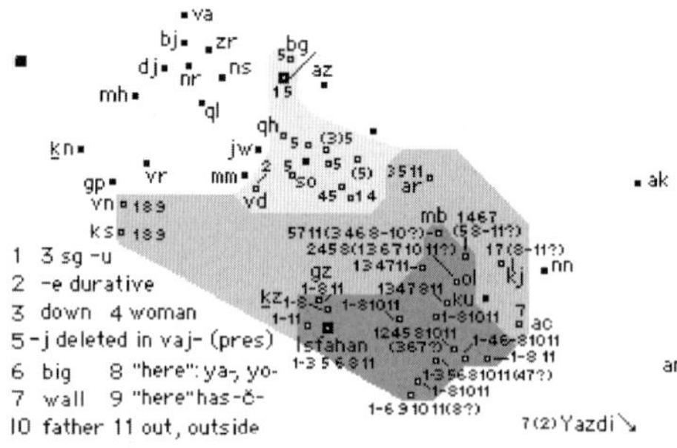

Figure 5. Some isoglosses that define the Isfahan area (SW CPD).

that the dialects from Isfahan towards the east are not as consistent. In other words, the two isoglosses "now" and "this way," at least, do not seem to show any special correlation and thus do not reveal much valuable information about these southern areas on the maps. In order to obtain a truer picture of the relatedness of a group of dialects and the areal bond among them, if there is one, it is necessary to gather and compare a much larger number of isoglosses, preferably by superimposing them on one another, to see if a particular geographic area turns out to be more and more heavily covered by different isoglosses. In this way, as greater numbers of isoglosses pattern over most of the same areas—especially so in the central area, or the "epicenter," and less so in the peripheral areas—they start to form "bundles" and relationships begin to emerge from the picture presented by the convergence of numerous patterns. Figure 5 shows such a bundle of isoglosses centered in the immediate Isfahan area.

In addition to the examples given above (*bure-beše*, *osme-sigā*) that even native speakers use to typify their dialects, Figure 5 shows a total of eleven important isoglosses that set the immediate Isfahan area apart from the rest of CPD. This is a small, representative example of an isogloss bundle. Here the actual isogloss lines have been omitted and only the areas where the majority of them are in effect have been shaded. Numbers referring to the eleven isoglosses are listed for each location where they occur. Given the paucity of adequate materials on CPD and the lack of detailed information on each isogloss in publications (or even unpublished field notes), however, it is not always possible to ascertain whether certain features are present or absent in any given dialect. All features lacking an answer (either affirmative or negative) are put in parentheses with a question mark. The darker the shading on the map, the thicker the bundle which then helps us determine the degree of relatedness of the given dialects or languages. The darkest shading on Figure 5 represents the core area with a bundle of from seven to eleven of these isoglosses. The areas with medium shading have from three to four of the isoglosses in effect and the lightest shading is for areas having only one to two of the isoglosses. Unshaded areas imply that none of the features occur in those dialects. Note that all eleven isoglosses are present in Sedehi, nine are present in Peykāni, Kafrāni, Gazi, and Sagzavi, but as we progress farther to the east (or to the northwest), the number diminishes until we reach Nāʾin and Anārak in the east or Meyma, Jowšeqān, Delijān, Maḥallāt, etc. in the northwest, where none of the isoglosses are in effect.

The eleven isoglosses indicated on Figure 5: (1) The 3rd sing. of the present and subjunctive is formed with a suffixed *-u*, which is also the enclitic of the copula (to be; see Table 17). (2) the durative marker *-e*, the equivalent of Persian *mi-*, is suffixed after person endings to form the durative (i.e., the present and imperfect) tenses (Table 17; see also GAZI and ISFAHAN JEWISH DIALECT for more detailed information on points (1) and (2), ZEFRAʾI and HAMADĀN ix JEWISH DIALECT for point (1)). (3) "Down" is generally a form like Gazi *gāre* (< Av. *gufra-*, *jafra-*, cf. New Pers. *žarf*, and see discussion of **fr > (h)r* above). (4) "Woman, wife" (Krahnke, isogloss 10) has two unusual modifications: in the Isfahan area we find *jinji ~ zinji ~ dzindzi* (the darkest shaded area on Figure (5), while beginning with Tudešk and moving eastwards, the form is *enju* (not included on Figure 5). (5) "Say" (see Table 16); (6) "Large" *bele* (and variants; Krahnke, isogloss 28; see *Diachronics of the gloss "large"* below); (7) "Wall" (Krahnke isogloss 31) has a medial *-z-* in this core area: Gazi, Sed., Sagz., Kamd., Qehi, Zefr. *dezār*, Kuhp. *dəzār*, K̠orz. *dezzār*; (8-9) "Here" generally has an initial *y-*: (8-9) ʿOlun., Jrqu., Kamd., Kuhp., Qehi *yohon*, Sagz. *yon*, Gazi, K̠orz. *yā*, IsfJ. *yun*, but (9) in some cases, there is also a final *-c(e)* (Sed. *yā ~ yāce*). (10) "Father" is a variation on a form found in, for instance, Sed. Jrqu., Kamd., Qehi, Sagz. *puo*, Peyk. *pue* (but does not include forms like *pia*, and variants). (11) "Out" is *kü* in most of the darkest shaded locales, and generally has the following contrasting pairs: Sed., Kafr., K̠orz., Kuhp., Kamd., Qehi, Sagz. *kü* "out," *ku* "mountain" and IsfJ. *ki* "out," *ku* "mountain."

Table 17
Isoglosses

Suffix *u* in the 3rd sing of the Present and Subjunctive		
Gazi	*vā-u-e*	"he says"
	bar kuā-u	"where is the door?"
Qehi	*von-u-e*	"he cuts"
Zefraʾi	*von-u*	"he cuts"
Qehi	*üngür širin-u*	"the grapes are (lit. is) sweet"
Zefraʾi	*engur širin-u*	"the grapes are (lit. is) sweet"
Fārfāni	*gu-š vā-gart-u*	"he wants to return"
	yom bozān nacāk-u	"that goat (sg.) is sick"
The Durative Marker *-e*		
Sedehi	*suz-u-e*	"it burns" (intrans.)
	sote-ye	"it would burn" (trans.)
	vin-ān-e	"I see"
	di-em-e	"I would see"
Kamandāni	*ning-u-e*	"he sits"
	ništ-e	"he would sit
	xos-u-e	"he throws" (trans.)
	xoss-oš-e	"he would throw"

Source: Krahnke, Isoglass 19 and 16.

Buffer zone phenomena. When two opposite or variant isoglosses of the same feature meet, there can sometimes be an overlap in the area (buffer zone) between them. In such a case, the dialects within this overlapping area get both possibilities, and when a language gets two options for the same thing from two different sources, it often takes advantage of both and uses them differently. The dialects in these overlapping areas of CPD have innovated some way of using both isoglosses, thus accommodating both zones simultaneously. A minor buffer zone effect was introduced above with the verb "to say" in those areas that have two forms of the present root both with and without the final *-j-* (Table 16). In the extreme western (Vāniš. *ed-āj-u* and *b-āj!*) and eastern areas (Anār. *e-vāj-a* and *i-vāj!*) we find that the *-j-* is always retained, but deleted throughout the paradigm in the south (Gazi *vā-u-e* and *bé-vā!*, Jrqu. *vo-u-e* and *b-uā!*). In the central areas where the two types overlap, the *-j-* is retained in most forms as in the zones to the east and west, but, in adapting to the areas to the south, they drop the *-j-* only in one form, the imperative, e.g., (present) Qohr., Keš. *a-vāj-un*, Soi *a-vāj-ān*, Fari. *a-vāj-on*, KašJ. *vāj-ān*, Tāri *a-j-ō*, Zefr.

vāž-ān "I say," (subjunctive) Qohr. *bá-vāj-un*, Tāri *be-vāj-ō*, Keš. *bé-vāj-un*, Zefr. *b-ā́ž-ān* "that I say," but (imperative) Keš., Soi, Fari., KašJ., Tāri, Zefr. *bé-vā!* "say!", Qohr., Fari. *bá-vā!* "say!"

Another example consists of the isoglosses showing the distribution of two important variants for "to sit" (both with the preverb *ha-*) in CPD. Some dialects use the verb root (pres./past) *hā-ni(n)(g)/k-/hā-ništ*, while others use the root *hā-cin-/hā-cešt* (see Figure 6; *hā-ni(n)g/k* is a formulaic way of representing the following range of actual verb stems in the area: *hā-ning-*, *hā-nig-*, *hā-nik-*, *hā-nin-*, *hā-ni-*, etc.). In the small overlap area where the two isoglosses meet (the known data on the dialects of this area so far only show that Naṭanzi, Tāri and Keša'i are found within this buffer zone) both patterns are used but are used in different ways. In Naṭanzi, the two roots seem to alternate as optional synonyms in the present (at least in the imperative and possibly in other forms), but have only one choice in the past: *hā-ni(n)* ~ *hā-cin/hā-n(e)šast*. A slightly different situation seems to hold for Keša'i and Tāri, where one root is used for the present and the other is used for the past, but the opposite choice from Naṭanzi is made: (Keša'i) *he-nig-/hā-cašt*, (Tāri) *hā-ng- (imperative: hā-nek!)/hā-cašt*. Keša'i and Tāri also have one more way to use the second root: in the causative form only one root is used for both present and past: (Keša'i) *hā-cān-/hā-cānā*, (Tāri) *hā-cen-/hā-cenā* "to seat, to make sit," but in neither dialect does the causative derive from the alternate stem used in the non-causative present (Tāri *hā-ng-* ~ *hā-nek*). While this buffer zone does not cover a large area, only three locations as far as we know from published material from the area, it does show very neatly how two different isoglosses can overlap and create a buffer zone at the borders where they meet thus causing the common areas to have both patterns and to use them differently.

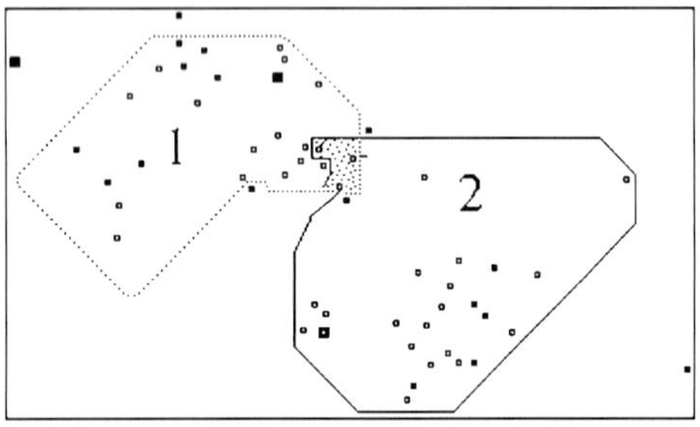

Figure 6. Two major isoglosses for "to sit" (and the overlapping buffer zone between them) (1) *hā-cin/cišt*. (2) *hā-ni(n)(g/k)*.

Diachronics of the durative marker -e. One of the most important grammatical isoglosses that singles out the immediate Isfahan area from the rest of CPD is the placement of the durative marker *-e* of the present and imperfect tenses (Figure 5, isogloss 2). In the Isfahan area a suffixed *-e* is used to form these tenses (see xxii, below), whereas in other areas of CPD, we find a prefixed *e(t)-*, which in the various dialects takes the variants *e-* ~ *a-* ~ *et-* ~ *at-* ~ *ed-* ~ *to-*. It seems that no one has thus far explicitly stated that the suffixed *-e* of the Isfahan area and the prefixed *e(t)-* ~ *a(t)-* of the rest of CPD (and beyond) are, in fact, just variants of the same form. The reasons that have led the present author to this conclusion are as follows:

1) In some dialects, particularly in those of the NW group of CPD, the *-t-* ~ *-d-* of this morpheme appears consistently before both vowels and consonants (Ḵāns. *it-xusān* "I hit," *id-vāzān* "I say," *ít-ārān* "I bring"; Mahll. *at-keron* "I do," *ad-vojon* "I say," *at-iyon* "I come"). This formation before consonants shows that the *-t* is an integral part of the morpheme and not just a transitional consonant to the initial vowel of the verb root. The same *et-* ~ *at-* ~ *ed-* morpheme also appears in the Tafreš area including Vafsi, a clearly Tāti language, whose variants of this morpheme, *at-* ~ *ad-* ~ *ar-* ~ *an-*, etc. (*at-ārom* "I bring," *ar-vinom* "I see," *ar-karom* "I do," *an-nevisom* "I see"), also show that the *-t* is not only retained before roots beginning in consonants but actually adapts to the following consonant and is not simply a transitional consonant to a following vowel (for a detailed discussion see VAFSI as well as Stilo, 2004).

2) It is clear that *e-* ~ *a-* and *et-* ~ *at-* (all prefixed) are originally identical as seen in the consistent use of the *-t* variants in the central areas of CPD before roots that begin with vowels: Jowš. *a-pic-am* "I twist," but *at-ār-am* "I bring"; Qohr. *a-k-ūn* "I fall," but *at-ār-ūn* "I bring"; Tāri *a-ker-ō* "I do," but *at-ār-ō* "I bring"; Aby. *e-kar-ān* "I do," but *et-ōzmar-ān* "I count"; Ards. *e-ker-ō* "I do" but *et-oroš-ō* "I sell." See discussion in Windfuhr (CENTRAL DIALECTS, pp. 249-50); Krahnke [pp. 182-87] also comes to a similar conclusion.

As we move eastward, the durative marker gradually disappears and the form with final *-t* is even less common. Thus in Nā'ini, no tense-aspect marker appears before consonants, for instance, present tenses *biri*, *biri*, *bira* "I, you, he takes/carries away," or *der-k-i*, *der-k-i*, *der-k-a* "I, you, he falls," but the original *-t* still shows up as a remnant before vowels (in the durative tenses): (present) *tāri*, *tārém* (= *t-ār-i*, *t-ār-ém*) "I, we bring" or *tosi* (= *t-os-i*) "I get up" and imperfect *ši-t-ārt* "he would bring" vs. the non-durative tenses, for example, (subjunctive) *yāri* (= *i-ār-i*) "that I bring," and (preterit) *mu-yārt* (= *mu-i-ār-t*) "I brought." Certain dialects have an even rarer remnant of the original *-t*, for example Zefra'i in which the *-t* is generally lost before roots with initial vowels (*v-i-essān* "I stand," *viesson* [= *v-i-essā-un*] "I would stand" (where *i-* < **et-*), but still appears in the imperfect forms of one verb: *t-emon* "I would come," cf. preterit *b-omon* "I came" and *y-ān* "I come."

3) In other cases, while the dialect no longer uses the *t-* in the original *at-*, one can tell that it did have it at some point in its history, but through a process of redivision of the word, the original *t-* of the durative marker was transferred permanently from *at-* to the verb root, just as "an ewt" in an older form of English became today's "a newt." In these dialects the *t-* has become a permanent part of

the verb root and is used even in non-durative tenses that did not originally take *at-* (e.g., Qohr. *tengas-/tangašt* vs. Meym. *enges-/angašt* "look," Soi *angis-* [pres.], and others). Thus while the Qohrudi present tense is *a-tangisun* "I look"—almost identical to Soi *at-angisom*—the Qohrudi subjunctive, *bátengisun* (*bá-tengis-un*) and the preterit *batangaštun* (= *ba-tangašt-un*) show that the initial *t-* is now part of the root (but not in Soi). In another such case, the root of the Nāʾini verb "to hear," which also requires the preverb *ver-* (Krahnke, isogloss 27), originally began with a vowel (i.e., **ver-ašno(v)-/ašnoft*), but both roots now begin with *t-*, which appears even in the non-durative tenses: Nāin. (pres.) *mi ver-tašnovi* "I hear" vs. (imperative) *vér-tašno!* "hear! listen!" and preterit *mi vér-om-tašnoft* "I heard." Thus it is clear that Nāʾini at some point in its history had the *et- ~ at-* marker, at least before vowels, but has since lost the use of this prefix, except for two or three roots in which it still alternates ("bring," "rise"; see Point (2)) and except for (at least) one root shown here in which the *t-* has become lexicalized as part of the root ("hear").

4) The affix *et-* is probably not ancient as a verbal marker in CPD but may have been introduced later, possibly even as a late as the early modern period. There is no way of documenting the emergence of this morpheme in the verbal system, but there is good reason to hypothesize that it developed in a similar process, and possibly even about the same time, by which *mi-/hami* (< Mid. Pers. *hamē*) became part of the verbal paradigm of Modern Persian: *hamē* was at first an unattached and mobile independent word appearing before or after the verb and even at a distance from it. It then became permanently prefixed as *hamē-*, which then changed to *mē-*, then to *mi-*). Like *hamē*, *e(t)-* may derive from some adverbial word—a typical source for the creation of new verbal tense and aspect markers (Heine and Kuteva, pp. 144-47)—which also was most likely an independent, somewhat mobile word that eventually, through a series of stages, became bound to the verb, similar to the development of New Persian *mi/hami*. Although the origin and development of *et-* are unknown, the reasons for positing the original mobility of this affix stem not only from hypothesizing about it based on the example of *hamē* (although it very plausibly was a parallel scenario), but also because, as will be demonstrated in the next three points, *et-* seems to have had its own history of mobility and is still somewhat mobile in the modern languages.

5) It is still mobile in Yazdi Zoroastrian, where it precedes the verb root in the affirmative but follows it in the negative: *evaji* "you say" (= e_1-vaj_2-i_3) vs. *navajie* (na_4-vaj_2-i_3-e_1) "you$_3$ don't$_4$ say$_2$ (durative$_1$)," *etāt* "he comes" (= et_1-$ā_2$-t_3) vs. *nāte* (n_4-$ā_2$-t_3-e_1) "he$_3$ doesn't$_4$ come$_2$ (durative$_1$)." The durative marker in Yazdi Zoroastrian (but not Yazdi Jewish) is thus a prefixed *et-* in the affirmative before a vowel and *e-* before a consonant but a suffix in the negative.

6) Another characteristic of this morpheme that shows its current mobility in CPD is found in the dialects of the immediate Isfahan area, where, as already noted, it always follows the root. Please also note that it does not always *directly* follow the root and can in fact be somewhat distant from it. In other words, both agent and object pronominal affixes may intervene between the verb root and the tense/aspect marker *-e*: (Gazi) present: *yuz-ān-e* "I'll find," *yuz-ān-ež-e* "I'll find him," imperfect: *xorté-m-e* "I used to eat," but *ibize-m xorté-yye* "I was eating melon," and in the modal "want": *gú-d-e* "you want," *har-ci-d gu-e* "whatever you want," (for a detailed description, see xxii, below; and xix, above. JEWISH DIALECT).

7) That the suffixed *-e* in the immediate Isfahan area was at one time more mobile and probably also occurred initially is seen in the verb root "drink" in Isfahani Jewish, where the remainder *t-* from the original durative marker has become a frozen part of the verb root (as in Point 3, above), but fixed to the beginning of the root (e.g., *tanj-/tanjā*) and is now used in both durative and non-durative forms, both present and past (e.g., *tanjuve* "he drinks," *bétanj* "drink!," *be-š-tanj(en)ā* "he drank"). The initial position of the *t-* here shows that the marker **et-* must have been initial in this dialect at some point in its history. Further cognates of this word exist in (C. Tāti) K̲oini (with no initial consonant) *enj-/ent* and (with initial *h-/ x-*) in (S. Tāleši) Māsāli *hinj-/hint*, Māsulai *xənj-/xənt-* and (C. Tāti) Koluri *henj-/hent*, all meaning "to drink," and by extension also in Sangesari *də-(y)inj-/(h)et* "to swallow." This root also occurs as "to pull" in K̲uri *henj-/heid ~ het*, in (Semnān area) Aftari *anj-/a(n)t*, Semnāni *enj-/(h)et*, Sangesari *inj-/(h)et*, and in Zazaki *ānj-/ānt*. This root has other related meanings in other languages as well: Soi *henj-/het* "sprinkle," (S. Tāti) K̲iāraji *hönj-/höt* "to water," and in Gazi *enj-/enjā* "to irrigate," all ultimately derivable from Av. *θang-*, *θanǰaya-* via the semantic shifts: "pull, draw > draw water > irrigate, water, sprinkle > drink," all of which are still attested in NWI as shown here. Note that the Sangesari stem itself conveys the two senses at both ends of this spectrum, which are only distinguished by the use of a preverb: *inj-/(h)et* "to pull," and *də-(y)inj-/(h)et* "to swallow." An alternate analysis of IsfJ. *tanj-/tanjā* sees this form still derived from Avestan *θanj-* "pull," but with the initial *-t-* derived directly from Old Iranian *θ* (cf. the -t- in the Shirazi dialect word *tanj-* "drink," Skjærvø, p.c) rather than through *θanj- > hanj- > anj-* and subsequently accruing an initial *t-* from the tense-aspect marker **et-*.

8) The tense formant *e- ~ a- ~ et- ~ at- ~ ed-* is also the same one that appears in most SWI dialects in a zone that extends from south and southeast of Isfahan to the Persian Gulf. Note the alternate forms of the durative marker before consonants vs. vowels in the Fini dialect (NW of Bandar ʿAbbās) *a-g-am* "I say" but *at-ā-m* "I come," Bandari *a-zan-om* "I hit," *e-gin-i* "you see," but *at-a-m* "I come," and the (Lāri) Bidšahri forms (present) *a-xeləm* "I buy," *a-ger-am* "I take," but *ad-ia-m*, *ad-ie-yš* "I, you come," *ad-ār-əm* "I bring" and (imperfect) *a-xáteda-m* "I would sleep" *m-a-gerɛt* "I would take," but *m-ad-ou* "I would bring." Note also that Kumzari, an Iranian dialect spoken in Oman, due to the metathesis of the final *-t* of this morpheme to initial position, retains *-t*

as *ti-/ta-/t-* (sometimes *it-*) in the present tenses of all verbs (e.g., *ti-kum* "I do").

The Lori-Baḵtiāri durative marker *i-* (and variants) also belongs here but no *t-* appears before vowels (e.g., *i-dē* "you give," *i-kūam* "I pound," *i-yom* "I come"). The use of this morpheme (without *-t*) for the formation of the durative tenses also extends south-southwest from Isfahan, again to the Persian Gulf (cf. Angāli in Bušehr area: *ī-šīn-om* "I sit," *ī-g-om* "I say," *ī-x-om* "I want," but *ī-ā-m* "I come"). Extending to the northwest, it is even plausible that the Kurdish tense-aspect markers (N. Kurdish) *di- ~ da- ~ t-* and (C. Kurdish) *a- ~ da-* are also this same morpheme but this interpretation is far from certain.

This tense formant with the variants *e- ~ a- ~ et- ~ at- ~ ed- ~ to- ~ti- ~ i-* and possibly even *di- ~ da- ~ t-* thus seems to be an isogloss extending northwards from Kumzari and Bandari on both sides of the Persian Gulf in an almost unbroken chain all the way to Hamadāni Jewish and Vafsi, the southernmost Tāti language located just to the east of Hamadān. In addition, it extends to the west along the Persian Gulf to the Bušehr area, and possibly even to Northern and Central Kurdish in the northwest.

A note on the third singular present ending -u. As demonstrated in Figure 5 and accompanying notes above, the person marker *-u* (which is also the enclitic form of the copula) is unique to the immediate Isfahan area within CPD. Outside CPD, it occurs in both Gurāni and Zazaki/Dimli as the masculine 3rd sing. person marker *-o ~ -u* (the feminine is marked separately with *-ā*), for example, (Gurāni) Bājalāni *ma-kar-o*, Kandulai *ma-kar-u* "he does"; Zazaki *ɛst-o* "he is" (but *ɛst-ā* "she is"). Note also the final person ending in the Zazaki sentence *mormɛk āmā ka to-re non byār-o* "a man came to bring you bread" (Stilo field notes, Dersim dialect). This morpheme is probably also the same as the Vafsi feminine copula form *-o(æ)* (e.g., *zene-s-oæ* "she is his wife").

The diachrony of the gloss "large." The seven different isoglosses for the words meaning "large" in CPD, as shown on Figure 7, can all be reduced historically to two sources: (pattern 1, 2) *mas* and *massar*, discussed above under the change **ts > s* (see also Table 2), and (pattern 3-7) the shaded areas on Figure 7: *bale*, *gord*, and three others that are restricted (as far as we have data for) to one locale each, Zefr. *bür(g)*, Kuhp. *vəzārk*, and Ḵuri

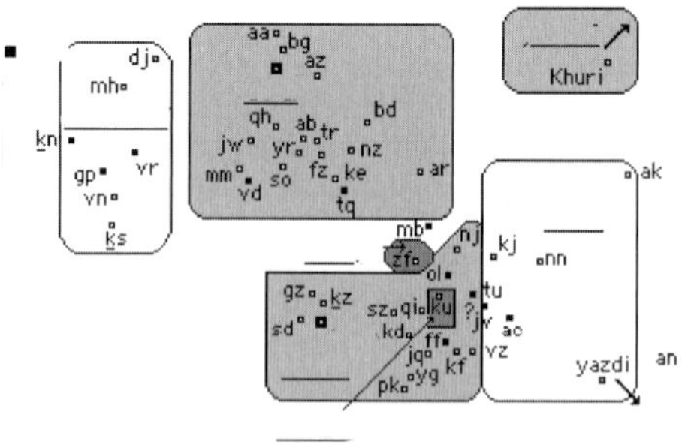

Figure 7. "Large" in Central Plateau Dialects.

gozār, all of which derive from Old Iranian **vadraka-* OPers. *vazraka-* (cf. New Pers. *bozorg*).

Patterns 1 and 2: *mas, massar-type*. The origins of this root and its variants (discussed above) derive from a different root from the forms discussed in the next four points.

Pattern 3: bele-type. Eilers (1979) has already pointed out the derivation of the Gazi form *bele* (isogloss 6 on Figure 5, above) from a probable SWI form,**vardak-* "large," which is a metathesized form of an unattested, but expected, Old SWI word **vadraka-*, paralleling the actually attested Old Persian form *vazraka-*, itself considered to be a borrowing from Median. The attested NWI form *vazraka-* versus the expected SWI word **vadraka-* demonstrate the typical NWI *-z-* vs. SWI *-d-* correspondence that was demonstrated with "know," "son-in-law," and "yesterday" under *Diachrony* above. The forms *bale* and *gord*, because of the presence of an original *-d-*, were probably borrowed into CPD from the hypothetical SWI form, which would have undergone the following stages of development from Old SWI to the borrowing that became the modern form in the Isfahan area: **vadrak(a)- > *vardak- > barda(k) > bala*. The form *bala ~ bale "large"* also involves the two changes of **v- > b-*, as in "wind" and "willow" discussed above, and *-rd- > -l-*, which parallels the change of *-rz- > -l-* (see "allow" (Table 3), above in the *Diachrony* section and also the word "flower," below).

Pattern 4: gord-type of the Kāšān area presents a slightly different outcome of a series of changes derived from the same hypothetical Old SWI word proposed above: **vadrak(a) > *vard(ak) > gurd*, following the sound change of earlier *wa- ~ va- > gu- ~ go-* as was noticed in the forms of "wolf" and "pass" discussed above, and which we also find in **ward ~ *vard > *val >* New Pers. *gol* "rose, flower." In the oldest stage of this word, **ward ~ *vard* "flower," we find the form as it was borrowed into Arabic, Armenian and other languages of the area, whereas the intermediate stage, **val*, is close to Tāleši and Northern Tāti, Semnāni *vel*, as well as to the feminine forms of Vafsi and most Southern Tāti *véla*, and (Gurāni) Tavela *vĭli* "flower" of today.

Pattern 5 and 6: bürg- and vəzārk-types. The Zefraʾi form *bür(g)* would also have a similar history, for instance, **vadrak(a) > vadark > vadarg > bu(d)arg > bürg*. The third stage listed here, *vadarg*, is more or less what we find in the Kuhpāyaʾi form, *vəzārk*, although it may also derive from the form introduced in Pattern 7.

Pattern 7. Gozār-type in Ḵuri may be a modification of an earlier NWI form **vazra(ka)-*: **vazra > vazar > gozār*, also including the change of *vV- > go- ~ gu-*, which is especially typical of Ḵuri and Baluchi.

Faridani Georgian (FG), even though it was brought to the Isfahan area around the very beginning of the 17th century during the reign of Shah ʿAbbās I, was still quite alive and robust in the mid-1960s when Donald Stilo conducted fieldwork on the language and was still reported so in 2005. Villagers of the area in the 1960s reported the existence of some eleven villages with an approximate total of 16,000 Georgians. In fact one of the

Table 18
The Consonantal System of Faridani Georgian

	Labial	Dental	Palatal	Velar	Uvular	Laryngeal
Stops	p^h, p', b	t^h, t', d		k^h, k', g	q^h, q' ~ G	
Affricates		c^h, c', dz	$č^h$, č', j			
Fricatives	f, v	s, z	š, ž		x, g	h
Nasals	m	n				
Liquids		l, r				
Semivowels	[w]	y				

rural districts (*dehestān*) listed in Razmārā's *Farhang* (X, pp. 166-67) (Isfahan Province) is called Gorji (*šahrestān* of Faridan, *bak̲š* of Dārān District, *dehestān* of Gorji) with 25 (22 on page 220) villages and over 24,000 inhabitants. Of these villages, nine were listed as having Georgian either as the primary or a secondary language. Others certainly existed; for instance, Miāndašt, reported in Razmārā (*Farhang* X, p. 189) as Persian-speaking, was in fact the home of one of the Stilo's informants, who reported that it was a Georgian-speaking village (see also GEORGIA viii. GEORGIAN COMMUNITIES IN PERSIA).

While Faridani Georgian has accepted many Persian, Lori and local Turkic loanwords, especially in the areas of material culture and governmental, educational, and adminstrative spheres, it has retained the large mass of the original Georgian lexicon found in normal, everyday speech. Even a brief sketch of the richness of Georgian grammar would be beyond the scope of this article, but a few of the characteristics of phonology, lexicon, and a few verb forms can be listed here. For comparison purposes, the standard Georgian (SG) equivalent of the examples below will be listed in parentheses after each word; the sign (=) indicates that the word is the same in Standard Georgian equivalents as in Faridani Georgian.

The vowels of Faridani Georgian consist of *i*, *e*, *o*, *u* and *a* ~ *æ* (the last two are free alternates, with *æ* often more common in the speech of some individuals, including Stilo's main informant, Moḥammad-ʿAli ʿAṭāʾi of Āk̲ora, now Fereydunšahr).

The features of Faridani Georgian are quite typical for a Georgian dialect and it has not lost any of the defining characteristics of the Georgian language: it has retained a rich consonantal system (see Table 18), all the Georgian cases, and the highly complex verbal system of Georgian, with even further complexity in some areas of verbal aspect than standard Georgian.

The consonantal system of Faridani Georgian (as SG) includes two characteristics that are common among languages of the Caucasus, including Armenian: the contrast of aspirated and glottalized (also called ejective) consonants (aspiration is indicated here by a superscript ^{h} and glottalization with an apostrophe) and a distinction of two sets of affricates: the c-series (c = "ts") and the č-series. Of the consonantal inventory, *q''* and *y* do not occur in standard Georgian but do exist in various dialects; *f* is a phoneme found in loanwords in Faridani Georgian, but not in in standard Georgian. The consonants transcribed here as *v* and *w* are probably alternates of the same sound in Faridani Georgian, with *w* found more commonly, but not exclusively, after vowels. The following pairs show the contrasts of some of the consonants: *p^huri* (=) "cow," *p'uri* (=) "bread," *buri* "blond" (Pers. loanword); *q^hæri* (SG: *xari*) "ox," *k^hæri* (SG: *k^hari*) "wind," *k'æri* (SG: *k'ari*) "door"; *c'ili* (SG: *rc'q'ili*) "louse," *dzili* (=) "to sleep"; *iγo* (SG: *aiγo*) "that you pick up," *iGo* (SG: *iq'o*) "he was"; *Gorebi* (SG: *gogebi*) "girls," *γorebi* (=) "pigs," *gorebi* "mountains" (SG: "hills"); *q^h* of FG is an older sound that has merged with *x* in SG: FG *p^heq^hi* vs. SG *p^hexi* "foot," FG *q^hari* vs. SG *xari* "ox" (see also "calf" below).

Consonant clusters (generally without epenthetic, i.e., transitional, vowels), for which Georgian is renowned, are also quite robust in Faridani Georgian. A small sampling is given: *t^hma* (=) "hair," *k'bili* (=) "tooth," *$č^h$xili* (=) "fingernail," *c^hxori* (SG: *c^hxvari*) "sheep," *dzma* (=) "brother," *k^hmari* (=) "husband," *Gmac^{h}ili* (SG: *q'mac^{h}vili*: "young man in teens") "child," *q^hbo* (SG: *xbo*) "calf," *t^hxa* (=) "goat," *mze* (=) "sun," *c'Gali* (SG: *c'q'ali*) "water," *dγe* (=) "day," *t'Geli* (SG: *brt'q'eli*: "flat") "wide," *č'le* (SG: *mč'le* "lean") "thin," *t^hbili* (=) "warm," *vzivar* (=) "I am sitting," *hč'am [x̌č'am]* (SG: *č'am*) "you eat," There are some longer clusters : (3) *t'k'bili* (=) "sweet," *c'Gran* (SG: *c'q'nari* "quiet") "slowly, quietly," *mq'vanda* ~ *mq'wanda* (SG: *mq'avda*) "I had (animate direct object)," *mt'k'ivis* (SG: *mt'k'iva*) "it hurts me," *gt'k'ivis* (SG: *gt'k'iva*) "it hurts you," *vk'debi* (SG: *vk'vdebi*) "I die," *vsGidop^h* (SG: *vq'idulob*) "I sell," *rc'Gaw* (SG: *rc'q'av*) "you irrigate," *sxnis* (SG: *xsnis*) "he opens," *vk'lav* (=) "I kill," *mc'Gurian* (SG: *mc'q'uria*) "I am thirsty," *c^hxra* (=) "nine," *c'Glis* (SG: *c'q'(a)lis*) "water (genitive)," *vjdebi* (=) "I sit down"; (4) *vt^{h}k^{h}vi* (=) "I said," *vrc'q'aw* (SG: *vrc'q'av*) "I irrigate," *gvt'k'iws* (SG: *gvt'k'iva*) "it hurts us," *vsxni* (SG: *vxsni*) "I open," *hsxni* (SG: *xsni*) "you open," *gvk'lav* (=) "you kill us," *gvc^{h}xela* (=) "we are hot"; (5) *vmč'ldebi* ~ *vč'ldebi* "I become thin."

The verbal system, in addition to having many conjugation types and many irregular patterns within each, is also characterized by a large number of different forms for each verb. Faridani Georgian has eleven different tense-aspect-mood forms (present, future, subjunctive, past, past subjunctive, etc.). In addition, these eleven forms can each be made passive, causative, passivized causative, double causative, passivized double causative, for instance, (future) *gaurec^hxaws* (SG: *gaurec^hxavs*) "he will wash," *gairecxebis* (SG: *gairecxeba*) "he will be washed," *gaarec^hxvinaws* (SG: *gaarecxinebs*) "he will make (someone) wash," *gairec^hxwinebis* (SG: *gairec^hxineba*, rarely used) "he will have it be washed (by someone)."

Faridani Turkic. A brief fieldwork trip to Faridan for gathering recordings of the Turkic dialects by Christiane Bulut of Mainz University during the preparation of this entry has provided data for her preliminary description of some of the characteristics that distinguish these dialects from, or unite them with, Azeri/Azerbaijani Turkish (see AZERBAIJAN viii), "Peripheral Azerbaijani" (Stilo: 1994) of the Hamadān-Sāva area, and Qašqāʾi. While all these Turkic variants of western Persia and the Republic of Azerbaijan are quite close and, for the most part, mutually intelligible, there are some significant features that separate them. Two important features that separate Azerbaijani from Peripheral Azerbaijani and Qašqāʾi is the formation of the 2nd persons singular and plural of the past tenses on the one hand and the non-past forms on the other. In both cases, the older Oghuz Turkic velar nasal, *-ŋ* (the sound of English or German "ng"), still pronounced in some forms of Qašqāʾi (*gediræŋ* "you go" in speech of Stilo's Kaškuli informant; *-ŋ* is also retained in Turkman), has been changed to a dental-alveolar *-n* in Azerbaijani (*gedirsæn*) and Turkish (*gidiyorsun*), but it is generally lost or converted to a diphthong in Central Persia (*gediriy* in Bayādestān Turkic, directly west of Sāva). The latter type is also shared by Faridani Turkic. The second distinguishing characteristic is found in these same forms just quoted: the 2nd persons singular and plural retain the *-s-* in the person ending of the present, the optative/subjunctive and the future in Azerbaijani (*gedæjæk-siniz* ~ [dialectal forms] *gedæjæh-siz*, *gedajax-siz* "you (pl.) will go") and Turkish (*gidecek-siniz*), but eliminate it in Peripheral Azerbaijani, Faridani (*gede-jeg-eyz*), and Qašqāʾi (present, optative/subjunctive). Thus while Faridani Turkic shares most features with Peripheral Azerbaijani dialects spoken farther north, it also shares some features with Qašqāʾi, for instance, the retention of *-n-* in the third person plural pronoun: Qašqāʾi *onlar*, Faridani *onnar* "they" vs. standard and Bayādestān *olar*. Other features separate Faridani from most of the others, for example, the formation of the 1st and 2nd person present perfect forms with the participial form *-ib-* ~ *-ip-*, which is generally characteristic only of the 3rd person, e.g., Faridani *gediblær* "they have gone," but also *gedibæk* "we have gone" vs. Azerbaijani *gedipdilær*, but *getmišik*, respectively. Still other features connect these dialects to most Turkic forms of Persia, for instance, the incorporation of the possessive suffixes into the verb of existence to form an independent "to have" verb-like word: Faridani *var-ïmïz* "we have." Note the following preterit conjugation from the village of Golamir (the source of the other Faridani forms cited above): *getdim*, *getdiy*, *getde*, *getdik*, *getdiyz*, *getdelæ(r)* "I went, you went, etc."

See also DIALECTOLOGY.

Bibliography: Roubène Abrahamian, *Dialectes des Israélites de Hamadan et d'Isphahan et dialecte de Baba Tahir*, Paris, 1936. Forug̲ Āḏari, "Moqāyesa-ye lahja-ye Najafābādi wa Eṣfahāni," in Ḥasan Reżāʾi Bāḡbidi, ed., *Majmuʿa-ye maqālāt-e nak̲ostin hamandiši-e guyeš-šenāsi dar Irān*, Tehran, 2002, pp. 19-30. Jalāl Āl-e Aḥmad, *Owrāzān:ważʿ-e maḥall wa ādāb o rosum wa lahja*, Tehran, 1954. Friedrich Carl Andreas, *Iranische Dialectaufzeichnungen aus dem Nachlass von F. C. Andreas*, ed. Kai Barr, Walter B. Henning, and Arthur Christensen, Berlin, 1939. Koorosh Angali, "The Angāli Dialect," Ph.D. diss., University of California, Berkeley, Calif., 2005. Harold W. Bailey, "Western Iranian Dialects," TPS, 1933, pp. 46-64 repr. in *Opera Minora*, in idem, *Opera minora*, ed. Mahyar Nawabi, 2 vols., Shiraz, 1981, I, pp. 221-39. Idem, "Modern Western Iranian: Infinitives in Gazī and Soī," *TPS*, 1935, pp. 73-74; repr. in idem, *Opera minora*, ed. Mahyar Nawabi, 2 vols., Shiraz, 1981, I, pp. 265-66. Ḥabib Borjiān, unpub. field notes, used for "Eṣfahān dar tārik̲-e Irān," *Rahāvard*, no. 33, spring 1993, pp. 74-95. Idem, "Joghrāfiā-ye guyeshā-ye welāyati-e Eṣfahān," *Iran-šenāsi/Iranshenasi* 17/3, 2005, pp. 466-86. Idem, "Zefra," in *EIr*., forthcoming. Arthur Christensen, *Contributions à la dialectologie iranienne* I: *Dialecte giläki de Recht, dialectes de Färizänd, de Yaran et de Natanz*, Copenhagen, 1930; II, *Dialects de la région de Semnān: Sourkhéi, Lāsguerdi, Sängesäri et Chämerzådi*, Copenhagen, 1930-35. Yaḥyā Ḏokāʾ, *Guyeš-e Keringān*, Tehran, 1953. Desmond Durkin-Meisterernst, *Dictionary of Manichaean Middle Persian and Parthian*, Turnhout, Belgium, 2004.

Edāra-ye jog̲rāfiāʾi-e arteš, *Farhang-e joghrāfiāʾi-e ābādihā-ye kesvar* 72, 1988. Michael L. Chyet, *Kurdish Dictionary: Kurmanji-English/Ferhenga Kurmancî Inglîsî*, New Haven, 2003. Wilhelm Eilers, *Westiranische Mundarten aus der Sammlung W. Eilers* III: *Die Mundart von Sīvänd*, Wiesbaden, 1988. Wilhelm Eilers and Ulrich Schapka, *Westiranische Mundarten aus der Sammlung W. Eilers* II: *Die Mundart von Chunsar*, Wiesbaden, 1976. Idem, *Westiranische Mundarten aus der Sammlung W. Eilers* II: *Die Mundart von Gäz*, 2 vols, Wiesbaden, 1979. Mohammad-Mehdi Esmāʿili, "Guyeš-e sedehi," in Ḥasan Reżāʾi Bāḡbidi, ed., *Majmuʿa-ye maqālāt-e nak̲ostin hamandiši-e guyeš-šenāsi dar Irān*, Tehran, 2002, pp. 31-41. Bahrām Farahvaši, "Taḥlil-e sistem-e feʿl dar lahja-ye sede[h]i," *MDAT* 10/3, 1963, pp. 311-23. Idem, *Vāža-nāma-ye K̲uri*, Tehran, 1976. Ivan Omarovich Farizov, *Russko-kurdsikiĭ Slovar'*, Moscow, 1957. Āḏar Fatḥi, "Sāk̲t-e feʿl dar guyeš-e bandari (Bandar ʿAbbās), lahja-ye maḥalla-ye pošt-e šahr," in Ḥasan Reżāʾi Bāḡbidi, ed., *Majmuʿa-ye maqālāt-e nak̲ostin hamandiši-e guyeš-*

šenāsi dar Irān, Tehran, 2002, pp. 423-40. Farānak Firuzbak̲š, *Barresi-e sāk̲tmān-e dasturi-e guyeš-e Behdinān-e šahr-e Yazd*, n.p., n.d. Jahāngir Hāšemi, "*Guyeš-e Alviri*," Ph.D. diss., Univ. of Tehran, 1974. Bernd Heine and Tania Kuteva, *World Lexicon of Grammaticalization*, Cambridge and New York, 2002. Homādok̲t Homāyun, *Guyeš-e Aftari*, Tehran, 1992. W. Ivanow, "Two Dialects Spoken in the Central Persian Desert [Anāraki and K̲uri]," *JASB* (*JRAS*), N.S. 21, 1926, pp. 405-31. Idem, "Notes on the Dialect of K̲ur and Mihrijan," *Acta Orientalia* 8, 1927, pp. 45-61 [also Anāraki]. Idem, "The Dialect of Gozärkhon in Alamut," *Acta Orientalia* 9, 1931, pp. 352-69. Irān Kalbāsi, *Fārsi-e eṣfahāni*, Tehran, 1991. Idem, *Guyeš-e Kalimiān-e Eṣfahān*, Tehran, 1994. ʿAbd-al-ʿAli Kārang, *Tāti wa Harzani*, Tabriz, 1954. A. A. Kerimova, A. K. Mamedzade, V. S. Rastorgueva, *Gilyansko-Russkiĭ Slovar'*, Moscow, 1980. Ṣādeq Kiā, *Guyeš-e Āštiān* I, Tehran, 1956. Karl John Krahnke, "Linguistic Relationships in Central Iran," Ph.D. diss., University of Michigan, 1976. Anne K. S. Lambton, *Three Persian Dialects*, London, 1938. Gilbert Lazard, "Le dialecte tâleši de Mâsule (Gilān)" *Studia Iranica* 7, 1978, pp. 251-68. Idem, "Textes en tâleši de Mâsule" *Stud. Ir.* 8/1, 1979, pp. 33-66. Idem, "Glossaire Mâsulei," *Stud. Ir.* 8/2, 1979, pp. 269-75. Idem, "Le dialecte des Juifs de Kerman," in *Monumentum Georg Morgenstierne*, 2 vols., Acta Iranica 21-22, Leiden, 1981, II, pp. 333-46. Pierre Lecoq, "Le dialecte d'Abyāne," *Stud. Ir.* 3/1, 1974, pp. 51-63. Idem, "Les dialectes du centre de l'Iran," in Rüdiger Schmitt, ed., *Compendium Linguarum Iranicarum*, Wiesbaden, 1989, pp. 313-26. Idem, *Recherches sur les dialectes kermaniens (Iran central): Grammaire, textes, traductions et glossaires*, Acta Iranica 39, Louvain, 2002. David Neil MacKenzie, *Kurdish Dialect Studies* I, London, 1961. Idem, *The Dialect of Awroman (Hawrāmān-ī Luhōn): Grammatical Sketch, Texts and Vocabulary*, Det Kongelige Danske Videnskabernes Selskab, Historisk-filosofiske Skrifter 4/3, Copenhagen, 1966. Moḥammad-Reżā Majidi, *Guyeshā-ye pirāmun-e Kāšān o Maḥallât*, Farhang-e zabān-e Irān 12, Tehran, 1975. Idem, *Strukturelle Beschreibung des iranischen Dialekts der Stadt Semnan: Phonetik, Morphologie, Syntax, Texte*, Hamburg, 1980. Oscar Mann and K. Hadank, *Die Mundarten von Khunsâr, Mahallât, Natänz, Nâyin, Samnân, Sîvänd und Sô-Kohrûd*, Kurdisch-persische Forschungen, Ergebnisse einer von 1901 bis 1903 und 1906 bis 1907 in Persien und der asiatischen Türkei ausgeführten Forschungsreise von Oskar Mann 3/1 (Nordwestiranisch), Berlin and Leipzig, 1926. Manfred Mayrhofer, "Vorgeschichte der iranischen Sprachen; Uriranisch," in Rüdiger Schmitt, ed. *Compendium Linguarum Iranicarum*, Wiesbaden, 1989, pp. 4-24. Boris V. Miller, *Talyšskiĭ yazyk*, Moscow, 1953. Manučehr Mortażawi, "Nokta-i čand az zabān-e Harzani," *NDA* Tabriz 6, 1954, pp. 304-14. Idem, "Feʿl dar zabān-e Harzani," NDA Tabriz 14, Tabriz, 1962, pp. 543-88; 15, 1963, pp. 61-97. Tatsuo Nawata, "The Masal Dialect of Talishi," *Acta Iranica* 22, 1982, pp. 93-117. Behjat Najibi Fini, *Barresi-e guyeš-e Fini*, Tehran, 2002. Ludwig Paul, *Zazaki, Grammatik und Versuch einer Dialektologie*, Wiesbaden, 1998. A. Querry, "Le dialecte persan de Nâyin," *Mémoires de la Société Linguistique de Paris* 9, 1886, pp. 100-124. Ḥosayn-ʿAli Razmārā, ed., *Farhang-e jog̲rāfiāʾi-e Irān*, 10 vols., Tehran, 1949-53. Ḥasan Rezāʾi Bāg̲bidi, ed., *Majmuʿa maqālāt-e nak̲ostin hamandiši-e guyeš-šenāsi dar Irān*, Tehran, 2002. Reżā Ṣāʾeb, "Guyeš-e Āmora," Ph.D. diss. University of Tehran 1976. Hosayn Ṣafari, *Vāža-nāma-ye rāji yā guyeš-e Delijān*, Tehran, 1994. Hāyeda Sahim, "Guyeshā-ye Yahudiān-e Irān," *Teruʿā* I: *Yahudiân-e irāni dar tārik̲-e moʿāṣer*, Beverly Hills, Calif., 1996, pp. 149-70. Rüdiger Schmitt, "Die altiranischen Sprachen im Überblick," in idem, ed., *Compendium Linguarum Iranicarum*, Wiesbaden, 1989, pp. 25-31. Zülfü Selcan, *Grammatik der Zaza-Sprache, Nord-Dialekt (Dersim-Dialekt)*, Berlin, 1998. Lidia P. Smirnova, *Isfakhanskiĭ govor*, Nauka, Moscow, 1978. Ak̲tar Sohrābi Anāraki, *Vāža-nāma-ye Anāraki*, Mashad, 1994. Manučehr Sotuda, *Farhang-e Semnāni, Sork̲aʾi, Lāsgerdi, Sangesari, Šahmirzādi* I, Tehran, 1963. Idem, "K̲oʾini, yak-i az lahjahā-ye Ād̲ari," *FIZ* 6, 1958, pp. 324-27. Idem, ed., *Farhang-e nāʾini*, Tehran, 1986. Donald Stilo, unpublished field notes collected in Isfahan, 1964. Idem, transcribed, translated and annotated, *Vafsi Folk Tales: Twenty-four Folk Tales in the Gurchani Dialect of Vafsi . . . Collected by Lawrence P. Elwell-Sutton*, Wiesbaden, 2004. Giti Tāki, "Guyeš-e Šahrežā," in Ḥasan Reżāʾi Bāg̲bidi, ed., *Majmuʿa-ye maqālāt-e nak̲ostin hamandiši-e guyeš-šenāsi dar Irān*, Tehran, 2002, pp. 91-110. Gernot L. Windfuhr, *Verbalmorpheme im Sangesari: Ein Beitrag zur neuiranischen Dialektkunde*, Ph.D. diss., University of Hamburg, 1965. Ehsan Yarshater, "Bīdgol and Bīdgoli Dialect," in *EIr.* IV, pp. 247-49. Idem, "The Dialect of Shâhrud (Khalkhâl)," *BSO(A)S* 22, 1959, pp. 52-68. Idem, "The Tâti Dialect of Kajal," *BSO(A)S* 23, 1960, pp. 275-86. Idem, "The Dialects of Alvir and Vidar," in Georges Redard, ed., *Indo-Iranica: Mélanges présentés à Georg Morgenstierne*, Wiesbaden, 1964, pp. 177-187. Idem, *Southern Tati Dialects*, The Hague and Paris, 1969. Idem, "The Tati Dialect of Ṭārom," in Mary Boyce and Ilya Gershevitch, eds., *W. B. Henning Memorial Volume*, London, 1970, pp. 451-67. Idem, "The Jewish Communities of Persia and Their Dialects," in Philippe Gignoux and Ahmad Tafazzoli, eds., *Mémorial Jean de Menasce*, Louvain, 1974, pp. 455-66. Idem, "Distinction of Grammatical Gender in the Dialects of Kāšān Province and Adjoining Areas," in *Papers in Honour of Professor Mary Boyce* II, Acta Iranica 25, 1985, pp. 727-45. Idem, "The Dialects of Ārān and Bidgol," in C.-H. de Fouchécour and Philippe Gignoux, eds., *Études irano-aryennes offertes à Gilbert Lazard*, Paris, 1989, pp. 371-83. Idem, "The Taleshi of Asālem," *Stud. Ir.* 25/1, 1996, pp. 83-113. Valentin A. Zhukovskiĭ, *Materialy dlya izucheniya persidskikh narechiĭ*, St. Petersburg, 1888-1922.

Field notes graciously provided to the author: Ḥabib Borjiān's field notes for: Gazi, Isfahan Jewish, Kamandāni, K̲orzuqi, Kešaʾi, Kuhpāyaʾi, Peykāni, Qehavi, Sagzavi, Sedehi, Tarqi, Varzanaʾi, Yangābādi, and Zefraʾi; Christiane Bulut's field notes for: Faridani Turkic as well as the 2005 survey of other languages spoken in the Faridan area; Ludwig Paul's field notes for: Delijāni, Kahaki, Kuhpāyaʾi, Sagzavi, Sedehi, and Zori; Ehsan Yarshater's field notes for ʿOlunābādi, Āštiāni, Biābānaki, Fārfāni, Isfahan Jewish, Hamadān Jewish, Jowkandāni, K̲oʾini, Keringāni, Mārbini, Mušqini-Marāḡaʾi, Peykāni, Sedehi, Vendādehi, Vizanaʾi. The author's unpublished field notes were used for: Asālemi, Āmoraʾi, Ārāni, Dikin-Marāqaʾi, Kabataʾi, Kelāsi, Koluri, Northern Taleši dialects, Māsāli, Māsulaʾi, Naṭanzi, Vafsi, Yazdi Zoroastrian, and Zazaki.

(DONALD STILO)

xxii. GAZI DIALECT

Gazi, spoken in the city of Gaz in the district of Bork̲ᵛār (dialect: *bolxār*), belongs to the Central Plateau Dialect group (CPD, see CENTRAL DIALECTS) of Northwestern Iranian (NWI) languages. Gazi, the Jewish dialect of Isfahan (see above, xix; henceforth JDI), Sedehi, and probably other uninvestigated dialects of the Gaz-Isfahan area, for instance, Segzi, Jarquyaʾi, and others are grouped together as one subgroup of CPD. The dialect of K̲orzuq, about 3 km from Gaz, is particularly close to Gazi. (see JDI for a fuller description of the subgroups of NWI and CPD and the history and classification of Gazi and its position among these languages). It is not known how many speakers of Gazi there are at present and its current status can only be ascertained by conducting a careful survey of the area. The sources used for this description are abbreviated as follows: WE (Eilers and Schapka, 1979), EY (Yarshater's unpublished field notes), and ZH (Zhukovskiĭ, 1888).

Diachronics. (See the entry on JDI for a brief introduction to the significance of the different sound correspondences that place NWI in contradistinction to Persian and SWI.) The following list details the usual NWI developments from proto-Iranian present in Gazi, but examples typical of Persian and Southwest Iranian (SWI) most likely also borrowed into Gazi will be listed alongside in parentheses: **ts > s: kas* "small," (but > SWI *h*, as in *ā(h)en* "iron," *dah* "ten"); **dz > z: zun/zunāšt* "know," *zomā* "son-in-law," *ezé* "yesterday" (but > SWI *d*, as in *del* "heart," *daryā* "sea"); **tsʷ > sp: üšpüš* "louse," *ösbö* "white"; **dzʷ > zb: ozun ~ uzun* "tongue" (the *-b-* was probably later absorbed by the *u*, e.g., *zbān > ozvān > ozvun > ozun*, or some similar process); **dʷ > b: ber* "door," *ebi, bin* "other"; **y-* remains as *y-* (as opposed to SWI *j-*): *yuš/-ā* "boil," *yuz/yuss* "find," *iye* "barley" and similarly, original **vy > y* in *yā* "place" (cf. MP *gyāg*, NP. *jāy*); **j* remains as NWI *ž* in *žan* "woman," *žen-* "hit, give birth" *žande* "alive." Later developments are: **w-* remains as *v-* in *veše* "hungry," *(i)var ~ (i)vašt* "pass" (but > SWI *g*, in Gazi *gorg* "wolf," *gol* "flower"), and as *v-* in *vorun* "rain," *varf* "snow," *vo* "wind" (but > SWI *b-* in Gazi *biye* "widow," *bid* "willow"); **fr- > (h)r~h(r)-* as in *gāre* "down" (cf. Av. **gufra-, *jafra-*) and possibly the preverb **frā- > i- ~ (h)e-* in *(h)é-nešt* "run," *(h)e-tā-* "give!" *i-git-* "take" (see Preverbs below), but cf. SWI-like reflexes for **fr-* in Gazi *ferāš/ferāt* "sell," *feresn/-ā* "send"; **θr > (h)r ~ h(r)- > -r-* is seen in Gazi *pür* "son," *dār* "sickle," *ār* "mill" (but > SWI *s* in Gazi *se* "three"); **xr > (i)r* in *cār* "wheel," *sür* "red," *irin/irint* "buy." It is possible that **fr, *θr, *xr* are identical developments in Gazi through a merger: **fr, *θr, *xr > NWI *hr > (i)r*, with *-r* after a vowel (e.g., *gāre* "down," *pür* "son," *cār* "wheel," where **fr, *θr, *xr* all have the same reflex), and *ir-* in initial position (*irin-/irint* "buy" and possibly *i-* in the preverb **frā- > ir-* with a subsequent loss of final *-r* in preverbs (?), that is, **ver-, *ir- > ve-, i-*, cf. the Vafsi preverbs *o(r)-, ha(r)-*).

*-xt > -(h)t ~ -(t)t is seen in Gazi *dot* "girl," *ret-* "poured," *urit-* "fled," *vāt-* "said," *vet-* "sifted" (but cf. *pešā ~ paxt* "cooked," possibly a borrowing). The parallel change **-ft > NWI -(h)t ~ -tt*, is seen in *git-* "took," but possibly later influenced by Persian in *darkaft-* "fell," *i-oft-* "slept," *roft-* "swept," *kuft-* "pounded." Most potential examples of **-xt, -ft > -tt* are lost due to re-formations of the past stems with the past formant *-ā* instead of *-t: vāz/-ā* "lose (in games)," *var-sanj/-ā* "weigh," *piš/picā* "twist, wind." **-č- > -ž- ~ -j-* as in *uriž-* "flee," *enj-* "water, irrigate," *rež-* "pour," *vež-* "sift," *ruže* "fast(ing)," *vāžār* "bazaar, market," *žer* "down" (< **haca adara-*), *-ji* "also" (< Av. **cit*), (but > SWI *z*, as in *az* "from" (< **haca*), *suz-* "burn"); **xʷ > x* as in *xox* "sister," *xāss-* "want," *xunt-* "read," and *xow* "sleep" (but see *i-ows*, next); **-x-* is lost before other consonants (*tā* "bitter," *tum* "seed," *bösüre* "father in-law" < *(bā) bā-xsüre*) and initial **x-, *xʷ-, *h-* are also lost (*ibize* "melon," *i-ows/ofd* "to sleep," *al/ašt* "to allow," *ašt* "eight," *em* "together," *ižir* "good," *ürd* "small"), even in words of Arabic origin: *le* "maternal aunt," *emir* "dough" (Ar. *xāl, xamir*). Note loss of medial *-d-* in: *vāum* "almond," *kum* "which," *kaa* "game," *rue* "intestine," in participles from stems in final *-ā* (*pušnāā-* "dressed") and of final consonants in *cu* "wood," *noxo* "chickpea," *dü* "smoke," *du* "buttermilk," *cerā* "lamp," *duru* "lie," *ru* "day," *numā* "prayer."

Vowels. Original **u* is generally fronted to *ü*, even in Arabic loan words: *xün* "blood," *pür* "son," *müš* "mouse," *zü* "early," *pül* "money," *arüs* "bride." As in colloquial Persian, **ā* becomes *u* before nasals: *ume* "came," *xunt* "read," *bun* "roof," *da-mun* "stay," *un* "that." When an original short **a* occurs next to an original back fricative (including Ar. ʿayn), the latter is absorbed into the vowel making it long, as in *cār* "wheel," *arüs* "bride."

Phonology. Gazi consonant inventory (p, b, t, d, c, j, k, g, q, f, v, s, z, š, ž, x, ḡ, h, m, n, r, l, y) is similar to standard Persian. Note that according to WE transcriptions *q* vs. *ḡ* and *j* vs. *ž* seem to be independent phonemes, but many words simply alternate: *ḡaa ~ qaa* "speech" or (WE) *ḡāyde-* (EY) *qāyde* "must" and *jemxow ~ žemxow* "quilt," or *jenúe* ~ *ženúe* "he hits." In both cases the two alternates are probably not independent consonants but upon further investigation will turn out to vary according to position.

Wilhelm Eilers (1979) indicates twenty-six vowels and glides, but the normalized system as in Ehsan Yarshater (*i, e, a, u, o, ā, ü, ö (?), ey, āy, ow* ~ *öy* and possibly *ay*), is probably more realistic; hence transcriptions of Eilers' examples are slightly altered here to conform to the latter system. Even further adjustments have been make to Valentin Zhukovskiĭ's transcriptions. Note the contrasting pairs: *pir* "old," *pür* "son"; *du* "*duq* (buttermilk)," *dü* "smoke, two"; *ru* "day, in," *rü* "spirit"; *dum* "tail," *düm* "face"; *kü* "outside," *ku* "dung, mountain," *küü* "squash." While Eilers, Yarshater, and Zhukovskiĭ usually agree on transcribing *ü* (*kü* "out," *xün* "blood," *üšpüš* "louse," *pür* "son"), there is less agreement on *ö* (WE: *bösürei*-EY and ZH: *bösure* "father-in-law"; WE: *möžö*, ZH: *meže* "eyelash"; WE: *böšoem*, EY: *böšöym* "we went"; WE: *ver-öškoft*, EY: *ver-oškoft*, ZH: *ve-škuft* "split"; but WE, EY, ZH: *cöš* "eye," *böšo* "he went"). The vowel *ö* seems to be most predictable in words with an expected glide (from original *-ow*, *-af*, or *-ab*) as in WE: *möy*, EY: *mö* "vine"; WE *köš*, ZH: *köwš* "shoes"; WE: *šö(y)*, EY and ZH: *šö* "night"; WE: *lö(y)*, ZH: *löv* "lip," cf. Persian *mow*, *kafš*, *šab*, and *lab*, respectively. In addition, *ö* is most common in Eilers' data. Sequences of the same vowel are common (e.g., *küü* "squash," *pāā* "feet," *balee* "the big one"), especially in past participles (*vé-ž-parsaa-bo* "he had asked," *rasaa* "ripe") and even sequences of three vowels occur: *rasaaā* "the ripe ones." Gazi has a strong tendency for vowel harmony (change of a vowel to match a neighboring vowel), especially between verbal affixes and the root: *bé- > bé-be* "carry!," *bü-lül-üd* "move!" *bó-xo* "eat!" *bö-šöym* "we went," *bí-gi* "catch!" *bí-di* "saw."

Stress is mostly word-final, but some prefixes and suffixes shift stress away from final position, for instance, "Set_1" person endings (see Table 1) in the present (*xunā́ne*, *xunéme* "I, we read," *vāíe*, *vāúe* ~ *voúe*, *vāíme* "you, he, we say," *enénde* "they put"); the participial element of the imperfect (*ašnofté-žun-e* "they were hearing," *xunté-m-e* "I would read," *larzā́-yy-e* "he was trembling," *i-ništé-yy-e* "he would sit"); the *bé-* or preverb of the subjunctive (*bǘ-lül-ü* "let it move," *ígiru* "let him get"); the negative (*náfa:māne* "I don't understand," *náunue* "it doesn't cut"). Preverbs seem to attract stress: *mālúe* "he rubs" vs. *vár-mālue* "he flees," *girā́ne* "I grab" vs. *vé-girāne* "I pick up." Note contrasts in *kué* "dog," *kúe* "it falls," *bózā* "the goat (d.o.)," *bozā́* "the goats," *bárāž* "its door," *barā́ž* "for him," *dózzāmun* "our thief," *dozzā́mun* "our thieves," *dozzāmún* "to steal."

Noun forms. Nouns and pronouns do not have gender or formal cases. There is one plural form, *-(v)ā*: *guš-ā́* "ears," *in ādem-ā́* "these people" with an occasional animate plural *-un*, probably borrowed from Persian: *pirún āmā* "our elders," *bozorgún isfoún* "the greats of Isfahan," but only on a sporadic basis, cf. *pürā pādəšā* "the king's sons." The alternate *-vā* sometimes occurs after *-ā*: *berā-vā́* "brothers," but *pāā* "feet." There are two indefinite markers: *ye* "one" (*mo ye kué dārān* "I have a dog") and unstressed-*i* (*be yā́-i nárasā* "he didn't get anywhere"), but for the most part both of these occur together: *mo ye dús-i dārān* "I have a friend."

Object marking. Definite direct objects (as well as indirect objects) are marked with *-(r)ā* in Gazi. Direct objects: *bár-ā dāγ nánāne* "I won't open the door," *buzγālé-rā vé-girue* "he takes the kid." *-(r)ā* is clearly more common in the present system than in the past. When the subject marker in a past transitive verb (see Set_2 endings, Table 1) is moved from the verb to the direct object (see Fronting below), *-(r)ā* must be omitted: *unā-d šehíd ke* "you (*-d*) martyred (*šehíd ke*) them (*unā*)," *kāqez-ām beccösnā* "I stuck/glued the paper up." However, when Set_2 either remains on the verb or is moved to another word other than the object, *-(r)ā* returns (*vazir-āmun-ā vé-mun-numaa* "we have appointed our vazir," *kelíl-o damané-rā hamé-ž zunāšte-biye* "He knew Kalila va Dimna, all of it"), yielding equal alternate structures: *dib dass-āž-ā ru del-āž ke* ~ *dib dassāž-āž ru del-āž ke* "the *div* put his hand in his bosom." Note, however, that moving the Set_2 endings from the verb to the object is by far the most common situation in past transitive verbs and is virtually the primary way of marking the direct object in the past tenses. Set_2 as possessive may cooccur with *-rā*, however, since it appears before *-rā*: *pāā́-ž-ā ru falak nid!* "put his feet in the bastinado!" (*pā-ā́-ž-ā* = foot-plural-his-*rā*). The only suffix that can occur *after* Set_2 as subject marker is *-ji* "also": *dótāžāžji étā* "he_3 also_4 gave away_5 (i.e., married off) his_2 daughter_1" (i.e., dot_1-$\bar{a}\check{z}_2$-$\bar{a}\check{z}_3$-ji_4 $\acute{e}t\bar{a}_5$).

Set_2 on the verb also shows short pronominal direct objects only in the present system (present, subjunctive, imperative). Their position changes according to tense: between the suffixes for person and tense in the present (*yuz-ān-e-ž-e* "I'll find him," *ber-ind-ež-e* "they take him away," *xer-ú-e* "he eats/will eat" vs. *xer-ú-ž-e* "he will eat him"). In the subjunctive/imperative, Set_2 endings occur either just before the verb stem (*bi-ž-yuz!* "find it!" *bé-žun-ber-ān* "that I take them away," *vé-ž-gir-ān* "that I pick it up") or in final position *b-ār-id-āž* "bring him!" *b-ā́r-ān-āž* "that I bring him." The above rules apply only to the affirmative forms as the Set_2 endings always move to the position right after a negative prefix: *keš-ān-ed-e* "I will kill you" > *ná-d-kešāne* "I won't kill you"; *má-ž-koš* "don't kill him!" These Set_2 endings can also move from the verb either to the first part of a compound verb (*vā́ž-āž kerúe* "he calls him," *kü-š kašid!* "pull him out!) or to another preceding word: *ru ša:r-āž mā́rid!* "don't bring him into the city!" Double marking of direct objects with both full pronoun *and* Set_2 endings is also common: *dót-ā bé-ž-berind* "let them take the girl away," *ín-ā b-āru-ž* "let him bring him," *mó-rā bí-m-gi!* "catch me!" In the past tenses Set_2 only indicates the subject, never the direct object; thus *móqr-āmun bí-git* can only mean "we caught a/the chicken, and *not* "he caught our chicken," which is: *móqr-āmun-āy bí-git*. See also *Person endings*, below.

Table 1
Independent Pronouns and Agreement Markers

Pronouns				Verb Endings	
Subject	Object	Short Suffixed		Present	Past (Intrans)
mo	*mún-ā*	*-(ā)m*	*-(e)m*	*-ān*	*-ān*
to	*tó-rā*	*-(ā)d*	*-(e)d*	*-i ~ -e*	*-y*
un, u	*ún-ā*	*-(ā)ž~-āy*	*-(e)ž~-(e)y*	*-u*	*-Ø*
āmā, amā	*āmā́-rā*	*-(ā)mun*	*-(e)mun*	*-im, -em*	*-ym*
šomā	*šomā́-rā*	*-(ā)dun*	*-(e)dun*	*-id*	*-yd*
unā	*unā́-rā*	*-(ā)žun*	*-(e)žun*	*-end*	*-nd, -ynd*
Full Forms		Set$_2$ Endings		Set$_1$ Endings	

Indirect objects have five possibilities: (1) the object marker *-(r)ā* (mostly in the present system): *hakím-ā voúe* "he says to the doctor," *yéki-rā ru kie-ž re ná-tu-e* "he won't let anyone (lit. give one way) into his house"; (2) prepositions (*be* "to," *var (-de)* "to," *bar* "for, to": *de ešrefi-ž be mo etā* "he gave me ten ashrafis," *var xo-ž-de be-ž-vāt* "he said to himself," *bar mardum sargozašt kue-ra voúe* "he tells the people the dog's story"); (3) the pronominal endings (Set$_2$) incorporated into the verb: *bédvān* (< *bé-d-vā-ān*) "let me tell you," *t-ém-ed-e* "we'll give (it) to you," *é-m-te* "give (it) to me!"; (4) fronting the subject Set$_2$ ending to the indirect object in the past system: *rubā-ž bevāt* "he said to the fox," *to mo-d bévāt* "you told me"; (5) with no marking: *egar dót-ā d-ā mo t-í-e* "if you give me your daughter." Set$_2$ as indirect object may also move off the verb to the direct object in the present tenses as well: *ow-āž tinde* "they give him water," *an'um-ām túe* "he'll give me a boon." Double marking of indirect objects is also common: *uštur-ā ow-āž tíe* "you give the camel water." Set$_2$ can sometimes occur two in a row in the past tenses as both indirect object and subject: *nešun-āž*$_1$*-āž*$_2$ *tā* "he$_2$ showed him$_1$."

Modifiers. Modifiers (possessives, adjectives) follow the noun via simple juxtaposition, with no overt connector, for instance, possessives: *nabz šāzde* "the prince's pulse," *berāvā dot* "the girl's brothers," *taxsir to* "your fault," *bar kie hasirbāf* "the door of the mat weaver's house," *taqās xün bābā-ž* "retaliation of (for) the blood of his father." Occasionally an *eżāfa* appears in phrases clearly borrowed from Persian: *xāléγ-e donyā* "creator of the world," *mérd-e kāri* "a working man." Pronoun possessive forms can be either full pronouns or short forms (Set$_2$): *bābā to* ~ *bābā-t* "your father," *xox āmā* ~ *xóx-āmun* "our sister." Adjective modifiers: *pür bale* "old(er) son," *libās nu* "new clothes," *ow garm* "hot water." An *eżāfa* marker also occasionally accompanies an adjective; *sarpúš-e ösbóy* "a white covering." The plural ending of a noun often shifts to the adjective: *söndü naresi-ā* "unripe watermelons," but it may also remain on the noun: *ābādi-ā bale* "the large villages."

Demonstratives. They are *in* "this," *un* "that," *hamin/hamun* "this/that very (same)": *in dot* "this girl," *hamun-vā* "right there," *mo hamun pir-ān* "I am that very same holy man."

Personal pronouns. Table 1 gives the person endings of the verb (Set$_1$) and three types of pronouns: full forms for subject and other functions, full direct objects, and Set$_2$ pronoun suffixes with various functions (described passim throughout this entry).

The reflexive pronoun *xo-* requires Set$_2$ endings and can function as a direct object (*xó-m-ām ru deriā xos* "I threw myself into the ocean," *xó-ž-ā kašúe* "he pulls himself"), with prepositions (*var xo-ž bež-vāt* "he said to himself"), as a possessive (*benā-žun ke ru sar xó-žun xusénd* "they started to hit their heads," *vace xó-d-ā má-š-koš* "don't kill your (own) child!"), and as an emphatic (*mo xo-m bím-di* "I saw it myself").

Prepositions and similar forms. Gazi has a frequent postposition (i.e., a "preposition" that follows the noun), *-de*, meaning both "in" and "from," and some very common circumpositions. For the latter prepositions combine with the suffixed *-de* to form a frame around the object: *ru . . . -de* "in," *düm . . . -de* "on," *az . . . -de* "from," *žer . . . -de* "under," etc. Prepositions are by far the most numerous in Gazi: *az* "from," *be* "to," *tā* "until," *xow* "with" (either instrument, *xow nemarzun* "with a broom," or accompaniment, *xow bābām* "with my father"), *ru* "in, into" (but not "on"), *píš-e* "to, by, near (person)," *var* "in front of; to (as indirect object)," *žer* "under," etc. Examples: (1) prepositions: *ru vāžār*, *ru jeng* "in the bazaar; in the war," *ru xow engārāne* "I talk in (my) sleep," *žer xāk* "under the dirt," *düm xar* "on the donkey"; (2) postposition: *yek yā-ye gármi-de* "in a warm place," *zemin-de í-niue* "he sits on the ground," *inā-t kuāde bā́rte?* "where have you brought these from?"; (3) circumpositions: *düm zimin-de* "on the ground," *az kamár-āž-de* "off his waist," *gal šāx šikār-de* "around the deer's horns," *žir pā-ž-de* "under his foot." Pronouns occurring with prepositions may be either short forms or full forms, thus creating alternate forms (*az-ām* ~ *az mo*, and also: *az-ām-de* ~ *az mo-de*, all meaning "from me").

Verb phrase: Verb stems. Formation of past stems from present stems have the usual types of irregularities as elsewhere in Iranian: *peš-/paxt* "cook," *va-vež-/vet* "pull up, out, off" *zun-/zunāšt* "know," *engār-/engāšt* "speak," *ron-/roft* "sweep." Most past stems are formed from present stems by two regular patterns: (1) addition of *-t* (with *-t* rather than *-d* after *-r* or *-n*, possibly a conservative feature in the area, see also the entry on JDI): *ār/-t* "bring," *kan/-t* (but EY: *kan/kas*) "dig"; (2) addition of *-ā*: *suzn-/suznā* "burn (tr)," *var-māl-/mālā* "flee," *enj-/enjā* "irrigate, water." There are many alternate past stems in *-ā* or *-t* (*ber/berā* ~ *bart* "take away," *ve-ver-/verā* ~ *vašt* "pass," *i-os-/osā* ~ *oft* "sleep"), which often distinguish active in *-t* vs. passive in *-ā*: *emart* "break (trans.)" vs. *emarā* "break (intrans.), get broken," *kant* "dig (up) (trans.)" vs. *kanā* "be dug (up) (intrans.)," but *yuš-/yušā* "boil (intrans.)," *yušn-/yušnā* "boil (trans.)." Present stems in *-r* or past stems in *-rt* or only *-t* optionally lose these consonants when final (but reinstate them before a suffix), for instance, present stems: *í-gi* "take!" *vel ke* "drop!" *kü a* "bring out!" (but note the plural commands: *í-girid!*, *vel kerid!*, *kü arid!*); past stems: *benā-ž ke* ~ *kart* "he started," *kü-ž ā* ~ *kü-ž ārt* "he brought out," *bé-m-xo* ~ *bé-m-xort* "I ate," *ye pür-āž dā* ~ *ye pür-āž dārt* "he had a son," *ve-m-gi* ~ *ve-m-git* "I picked up" (see also *Perfects*, below). Two roots have irregular alternate past stems: "be, become" has *bo* for the preterit (*béboyan* "I became"), *bi-* for the past participle (used in the perfect tenses: *bíbie-bo* "he had become"); "go" has the past stems *št-*, *ši*, *šo*: *be-št-e-bo* ~ *ši-e-bo* (with Participles One and Two) "he had gone," and the short infinitive *šo* (see *Non-finite forms*, below).

Preverbs. Preverbs create finer nuances, lexical extensions, or total meaning changes of a verb root. The preverbs found in Gazi are *dar-*, *de-*, *var-*, *ve-* and possibly *he-*, *e-* ~ *i-*. Note some contrasting examples: *bí-gi* "grab! catch!" *vé-gi* "pick up!," *í-gi* "take! get!"; *bé-cin* "pick!" *vé-cin* "sheer!; gather!" *dé-cin* "stack!"; *gartāne* "I go around," *vé-gartāne* "I return"; *bé-m-xos* "I threw, I hit," *vā́-m-xos* "I threw (down)," *dá-m-xos* "I pinned (him) down (in wrestling)"; *mālāne* "I rub," *vár-mālāne* "I flee." The status of *he-* and *e-~ i-* (*tā jāyeze í-girān* "so that I get a prize," *bṓ-šo í-oft* "he went (and) slept," *é-mun-nāšt* "we seated," *é-ž-tā* "he gave") is not totally clear. In contrast to the Jewish dialect of Isfahan, they occur in the present (*e-n-énde* "they put," *í-ni-ān-e* "I sit"), imperfect (*i-ništ-éy-e* "he would sit"), or even with negatives in Gazi (*i-né-ni-ān* "(that) I not sit," *e-ž-nān-ā́n-e*/ *e-ž-ná-nān-ān-e* "I seat/don't seat him," *e-ná-n-end* "let them not put"), but not always (*e-nān-e~nān-e* "I am putting" *é-t-an* "(that) I give" vs. *t-ān-e* "I give"). *i-* ~ *e-* and *he-* could either be contrastive (*i-nište-bo* "he had sat down" vs. *hé-nešte-bo* "he had run"), or, since some forms vacillate in Eilers' data (e.g., *(h)é-te* "give!" *(h)é-tu* "let him give"), they could just be alternate forms.

Verb roots that had an original initial vowel and a preverb ending in *-r* moved the *-r* from the preverb to the verb root in the modern language. In such forms as *veröškoā* "it split open," *derāyžāne* "I hang," *verossāne* "I get up," or *verašnāne* "I hear," where the position of *-r-* is not apparent in the affirmative forms (but is still part of the preverb in similar preverb-verb combinations in other NWI languages), the past tense or any negative forms in modern Gazi show that the *-r-* has clearly become part of the verb root: *de-ná-rāyžāne* "I don't hang" (cf. *de-má-rāyž!* "don't hang!"), *ve-ná-rossāne* "I do not get up," *vé-m-rašnoft* "I heard," *ve-m-röškoft* "I split (it) open" (see also JDI for a similar process). We can see that the *-r-* is still perceived as part of the preverb even in the modern language, however, in cases when the preverb is occasionally omitted, in which case the initial *-r-* also disappears from the root: *ašnofté-ž-e* "he was hearing."

Negation is formed by *ná-*: *ná-kerāne* "I don't do," *ná-dāru* "he doesn't have," imperfect *e-m-ná-nā-yy-e* "I wouldn't put." *bé-* is suppressed in the negative: *bé-gir-u*/ *ná-gir-u* "that he catch/not catch"; *bé-ž-unt*/*ná-ž-unt* "he cut/didn't cut." The negative command is formed with *na-* (*nam(b)er* "don't die!") or *má-* (*por mángā!* "don't talk so much!" < *angār-*). Preverbs are retained in the negative forms: *mo-ž da-ná-xosse* "he hasn't pinned me down (in wrestling)," *ve-má-ro* "don't get up!" *zun-* "know" has two alternate negative forms: *názunān* ~ *nánān* "I don't know."

Non-finite forms include one present and two past participles and four types of infinitives. Infinitives function as verbal nouns but are, especially types 2 and 3 here, also used with modals (see below). (1) Past stem + *-(ə)mun*: *kār kartəmún* "to work," *gitmún* "to take," *feresnāmún* "to send," e.g.: *mo hāl-e baγdād šo-mún nádārān* "I'm not in the mood for going to Baghdad," *fékri be enāštəmún-āžun ke* "they thought about seating us"; (2) full past stems with no suffix and no loss of final consonants, often called the "short infinitive": *kār kart* "to work," *duru vāt* "to lie," *šo* "to go," e.g.: *cundin sāl dars xunt o kār kart* "several years of studying and working," *az var-mālā́-ž*, *az engā́št-āž xóšnüd bébo* "he was (lit: became) happy with his fleeing, his speaking," *asar vārun ume náu* "there is no sign of rain coming"; (3) another variant of "short infinitive" with similar functions but minus the final *-(r)t*: *kār ke* "to work," *xo* "to eat," usually used with modals (see below); (4) past stem + *-an*, the least common type, probably borrowed from Persian: *unā-d kuštan tā* "you gave them (over) to (being) killed." Note that some verbs have two or three alternate forms as with "to work" and "to go" here.

The formation of Past Participle One (mostly used in the formation of the perfects) is: (preverb/be-) + Past Root + *-é* after consonants (*be-košt-e* "killed," *ve-git-e* "picked up"), but after a vowel, either -Ø, *-ā* or *-a* is added: (*ume* > *b-ume-Ø* "come"; *-ā* of the past root + *-a*/*-ā* of the participle yields either *-aa* or *-āā*, for instance, the past stems *asā*, *e-tā*, *ve-numā* and *ve-pušnā* have the following perfect forms respectively: *béasaayān* "I have looked," *šā farmún-āž e-taa* / *taá-biye* "the shah has commanded/ had commanded," *vazir-āmun-ā vé-mun-numaa* "we have appointed our vazir," *vé-m-pušnāā-bo* "I had dressed (trans)." Past Participle Two is formed exactly like the first but with no initial *be-* or type two preverb (*i-* and (*h*)*e-*) and is used in an optional alternate form of the perfect tenses (see below), or as a noun: *karté-ye xo-ž* "his doing(s) (lit: his own done)," *vāté xodā* "the word of God."

Person endings. The distinction between Set_1 and Set_2 endings in Table One is crucial for the conjugation of verbs in Gazi. Set_1 is reserved for the present system of all verbs (but see *Individual tenses* for the singular command and also *Modals*, below), both intransitive (*xand-end-e* "they laugh") and transitive (*xer-end-e* "they eat"), as well as for the preterit and perfect tenses of intransitive verbs. Set_2 endings (which in Persian may only indicate objects), however, are obligatory in Gazi to indicate the subject in the past system of transitive verbs: trans. *bé-žun-xort* "they ate" vs. intrans. *bé-xandā-ynd* "they laughed." Thus Gazi *qabul-ād kart* only means "you accepted," never "he accepted you." Set_2 endings change position depending on the tense (see Table 4 and the discussion under *Individual tenses* and *Fronting*, below) and even negation: *ašnofté-ž-e* "he was hearing," *né-ž-ašnofté-yy-e* "he wasn't hearing."

Important points in the Gazi Set_1 endings are: (1) 1st sg. *-ān* with *-n* rather than *-m*; (2) the 2nd sg. *-e* changes to *-i* when followed by the tense marker *-e*: subjunctive *bé-xun-e* "that you read," but present *xun-i-e* "you read"; (3) 3rd sg. *-u* is typical of some CPD (see HAMADĀN ix for further discussion); 4) Set_1 plural endings sometimes take an additional suffix *-un* (probably modeled on the Set_2 endings), e.g., *bo-im-un* "we were," *bé-vaz-id-un* "run (pl.)!" *dār-end-un* "they have," *ná-t-end-un-e* "they don't give," *bérasāynd(un)* "they arrived" (see also the imperfect forms below for further discussion). Important points in the Set_2 endings are: (1) the distinction between intransitive (Set_1) and transitive (Set_2) conjugations is lost in the imperfect (see below), a rather unusual case for NWI languages; (2) the difference between the alternate forms *-āž* and *-āy* for the 3rd sg. (see Table 1), if any, is not completely clear. Both are used as possessives: (EY) *pül-āž* "his money" *gušt-āy* "its meat," (WE) *mere-ž*, *mere-y* "her husband"; as subject in past: (ZH) *ún-āy bídi* "he saw him," *in-āž bé-vāt* "he said this"; *vé-y-parsā* ~ *vé-ž-parsā* "he asked"; (WE) *ém-āy yušnā* "he boiled (them) together," *ye žan-āž béxās* "he asked (to marry) a woman"; and as both possessive and fronted agent together: (EY) *āš-āž*$_1$ *-āy*$_2$ *boxorte* "he$_2$ has eaten his$_1$ soup." Note the following alternate forms used by the same speaker (Eilers, pp. 146-48): *be-ž-vāt* ~ *be-y-vāt* "he said," *benā-ž ke*~*benā-y ke* "he began," *gumbā-ž-e* ~ *gumbā-yy-e* "he wanted," *sar-āž* ~ *sar-āy* "his head," *bar kie xo-ž-āž ret* ~ *bar kie xo-ž-āy ret* "he poured (it) in front of his (own) house," *dar dómb-āž*$_1$*-āž*$_2$ *bas* "he$_2$ threw (him) on his$_1$ back," *kúl-āž*$_1$*-āy*$_2$ *git* "he$_2$ took (it) on his$_1$ (upper) back."

Fronting. As shown in the previous section, there are two sets of person endings in Gazi verbs (and most NWI languages). Since Set_2 endings as subject markers are quite different from English, other European, languages and Persian, it is worth reiterating that Set_2 endings show agreement with subject only in the case of transitive verbs and only in the tenses of the past system, as well all tenses of the verb "to want" (see *Modals* below). While the position for the Set_1 endings is fixed and unchangeable in Gazi verbs (just as with all Persian verb forms), Set_2 endings by contrast are quite mobile. As already seen, Set_2 endings indicating the subject are located in different positions in the preterit (e.g., *bé-ž-cint* "he picked," *bé-žun-košt* "they killed") than the imperfect (e.g., *cinté-ž-e* "he was picking," *košté-žun-e* "they would kill"). In addition, there is a general (but optional) tendency for Set_2 to move forward in a sentence, hence the designation "Fronting." This process only occurs in sentences that have words preceding the verb other than the subject. With this process the Set_2 subject markers in the past system of transitives move off the verb to a preceding word (but never to the subject), for instance, (past) *unā-d šehíd ke* "you martyred them," *ibize-m xorté-yy-e* "I was eating melon." Set_2 remains on the verb when it stands alone (*bé-ž-košt* "he killed"), but Fronting to the direct object, when one exists, is the preferred form in the past system, (e.g., preterit: *tofang xo-ž-āmun b-ārt* "we brought (him) his own rifle," *ye pür-bale-žun dā* "they had a big (i.e., grown) son"; imperfect: *araγ-āmun xorté-yy-e* "we were drinking arrack," *numā-m xunté-yy-e* "I was saying (my) prayers"; perfect tenses: *pül-ām-āy ve-ne-git-e* "he hasn't taken my money," *ebādat-āž bé-karte-bo* "he had worshipped"). Set_2 may also remain on the verb (*bar bābā-m xunté-m-e* "I used to read for my father"), especially when there is no direct object. In addition, the verb "want," formed with Set_2 person markers in all tenses, generally moves these markers to a preceding word (pres: *har-ci-d gu-e* "whatever you want," *pül-āžun*$_1$*-āžun*$_2$ *gu-e* "they$_2$ want their$_1$ money"). As the previous example shows, a Set_2 verbal marker may move to a word that already has a Set_2 possessive (*abā-ž-āžun barté-yy-e* "they would take his cloak away").

Set_2 not only moves to the word immediately preceding the verb but also commonly skips to an even earlier word in the sentence: *to-m az qarq nejāt e-tā* "I saved you from drowning," *ye kíe-bale-ž az mo bírinte-bo* "he had bought a big house from me," occasionally even over the subject (*ye emsin cíi-m mo ru tekie bí-di* "I saw such a thing in the *takia*," *ye šāl yazzi nu-ž taže bicāre bí-rinte-bo* "the poor (guy) had just bought a new Yazdi scarf") or out of a relative clause: *in amál-āž ke xow mo bé-karte* "this action that he has done to me." As these examples show, however, the Set_2 endings almost always skip to words earlier in the sentence only so that they can remain attached to the direct object regardless of where it is located, sometimes even quite far from the verb: *cador-āmun šöš kilumetri go sar ye farséngi-u bé-žente-bo* "we had pitched tent six kilometers (away), which is one full parasang." Set_2 endings will usually remain attached to the verb when no overt direct object is expressed even though other words precede the verb (*har ru košté-žun-e* "they would kill (him) every day," *az saadi vé-š-parsā* "he asked Saʿdi"), but this is not a strict rule, cf. *ru ruxune-žun xos* "they threw (it) in the river," *ém-āy yušnā* "he boiled (them) together." Set_2 as agent marker may not be fronted to a subject; thus *refiγ-āž-āž bévāt* can only mean "he told his friend," never "his friend said" (see also *Fronting* under HAMADĀN ix for a more detailed discussion of this phenomenon).

Table 2
Present vs. Subjunctive of Intransitive Verbs and "be, Become"

Without Preverb		With Preverb		"to be"		"to become"	
Present	Subjunctive	Present	Subjunctive	Pres.	Subj.	Present	Sub.
xun-ā́n-e	*bé-xun-ān*	*vé-gart-ān-e*	*vé-gart-ān*	*-ān*	*b-ān*	*b-ā́n-e*	*bé-b-ān*
xun-í-e	*bé-xun-e*	*vé-gart-i-e*	*vé-gart-e*	*-e*	*b-e*	*b-í-e*	*bé-b-e*
xun-ú-e	*bé-xun-u*	*vé-gart-u-e*	*vé-gart-u*	*-u*	*b-u*	*b-u-e*	*bé-b-u*
xun-ém-e	*bé-xun-em*	*vé-gart-em-e*	*vé-gart-em*	*-im*	*b-em*	*b-ém-e*	*bé-b-em*
xun-íd-e	*bé-xun-id*	*vé-gart-id-e*	*vé-gart-id*	*-id*	*b-id*	*b-íd-e*	*bé-b-id*
xun-énd-e	*bé-xun-end*	*vé-gart-end-e*	*vé-gart-end*	*-end*	*b-end*	*b-énd-e*	*bé-b-end*
"I read, etc."		"I return, etc."		"I am, etc."		"I become, etc."	
Imperative:	*bé-xun!*		*vé-gart!*		*b-e!*		*bé-b-e!*
	bé-xun-id!		*vé-gart-id!*		*b-id!*		*bé-b-id!*

Tense Markers. (a) *-e*. The marker of the present and the imperfect tenses (i.e., the durative forms) is a suffixed *-e*: pres. *runú-e* "it grows," *vé-girim-e* "we pick up"; imperf. (intrans.) *vasséym-e* "I used to run," *vārā́-yy-e* "it used to rain"; (trans.) *karté-m-e*, *karté-d-e*, *karté-ž-e*, "I, you, he used to do." With fronting of Set_2, *-e* stays on the verb: *araγ-āmun xorté-yy-e* "we would drink arrack." (b) The prefix *bé-* is used to form the subjunctive, imperative, preterit and perfect forms (i.e., the non-durative forms) but drops when a preverb or a negative is present: *bévān* "let me say" but *vérossān* "let me get up." It has many alternate forms but *bé-* (*bé-ž-vāt* "he said," *bé-m-xunt* "I read") is the most common (see the comment on vowel harmony at the end of *Phonology* above). *Bé-* is sometimes deleted from these tenses, but the reasons for this are not totally clear: *go das dar tilaž mālu* "that he rub his hand on his stomach," *xodā bar kamár-ām xusu* "may God strike my loins (i.e., fertility)," *sar-e yā-ž₁-āy₂ nā* "he₂ put (it) in its₁ place."

Individual tenses. Various comments. (a) Imperatives: "To be" has special subjunctive and imperative forms (see Table 2), which then serve to build the equivalent forms of the modals as well as of "have" (subj. *dār-bān*, *dār-be*, *dār-bu*, etc.; imp. *dār-be!*) and "know" (subj. *zum-bān* (= *zun-bān*), etc.; imp. *zum-be!*). The irregular imperative *búre*/*máwre* "come/don't come!" is typical in NWI. *Véro* "get up!" loses the final *-ss* of the present stem. Alongside *é-m-te*, there is the irregular form *mói*, both meaning "give (it) to me!" The singular imperative of regular verbs, as elsewhere in Iranian, ends simply in the present stem: *bíxus* "hit!" *bírin* "buy!" *bédderaz* "jump!" *bévez* "run!" *vá-darz* "sew!" *dé-cin* "stack!" *í-ni* "sit!" *vé-gi* "pick up!" *máke* "don't do!" *máxus* "don't hit!" Often the second person singular subjunctive also serves as the command form (*báre* "bring!" *béwne* "cut!" *bérone* "sweep!" *béše* "go!" *béase* "look!" *vér-ašne* "hear!" *der-āyže* "hang (it) up!"), including all causative verbs (*bésuzne* "burn (trans.)!" *nátāyne* "don't make run!"); (b) there are no special optative forms for blessings or curses as in the Jewish dialect of Isfahan; the subjunctive forms are used instead: *xodā ömr derāzi-t étu* "may God give you long life," *va:bā bédberu* "may cholera take you!"; (c) Gazi has progressive forms built with "have" as their auxiliary verb as in colloquial Persian (*az dur ye darviš dāru yúe* "a dervish is coming from afar"), but they are rarely encountered in the actual texts: *mo numā-m xunté-yy-e* "I was saying (my) prayers," *cez-u larzíe?* "why are you trembling?"

The transitive preterit has two types, the conditions for which are not totally clear (but in any case Fronting is still the most common pattern): (1) *bé-*/preverb + Set_2 + past root (e.g., "read," "return" in Table 4), and (2) the less common *bé-* + past root + Set_2 (e.g., "brought" in Table 4). On rare occasions when the context is clear, Set_2 markers may be omitted altogether: *be but sujde ke* "he prostrated himself to the idol," *ínā mo xo-m be caš né-die* "I haven't seen this myself with my (own) eyes" (cf. *mo xo-m bí-m-di* "I saw it myself").

The Imperfect of Gazi intransitives shows certain interesting innovations: (1) Set_2 endings are used for intransitive as well as transitive verbs; (2) there seem to be two imperfect markers, one before and one after the person endings (*xandā́-y-m-e*); (3) the 3rd singular uses only the variant *-āy-*, not *-āž*; (4) while Eilers mostly has the usual Set_2 ending for 3rd plural (*xandā-žun-e*), Yarshater (and Eilers, rarely) gives the 3rd pl. as *-ndun* (see Person Endings, point 4 above). Fronting of Set_2 is not allowed for intransitives.

Perfects of most intransitives are formed: Past Participle One + Set_1 + BE (*bérasaa(-u)* "he has arrived"), but a few verbs alternate with Participle Two: "go" (*kuā béšte(-u)* ~ *kuā šiye(-u)?* "where has he gone?) and "become" (*bí-bie(-u)*) vs. "be" (*bie(-u)*). There are two types of transitive perfects (parallel to the two preterit types): (1) *bé-*/preverb + Set_2 + Past Participle + BE: (*bímxosse(-u)* "I have thrown," *bé-ž-rasnaa* "he has delivered") is more

Table 3

Preterit and Imperfect Intransitive Verbs and "Be, Become"

Pretrit No Preverb	Pretrit with Preverb	Past "To be$_1$"	Imperfect No Preverb	Imperfect with Preverb	Imperfect of "to become"
bé-xandā-yān	*vé-gartā-yān*	*bó-yān*	*xandā-y-m-e*	*vé-gartā-y-m-e*	*bó-y-m-e*
bé-xandā-y	*vé-gartā-y*	*bó-i*	*xandā-y-d-e*	*vé-gartā-y-d-e*	*bó-y-d-e*
bé-xandā-Ø	*vé-gartā-Ø*	*bo*	*xandā-y-y-e*	*vé-gartā-y-y-e*	*bó-y-y-e*
bé-xandā-ym	*vé-gartā-ym*	*bó-em*	*xandā́-y-mun-e*	*vé-gartā-y-mun-e*	*bó-y-mun-e*
bé-xandā-yd	*vé-gartā-yd*	*bó-id*	*xandā́-y-dun-e*	*vé-gartā-y-dun-e*	*bó-y-dun-e*
bé-xandā-ynd	*vé-gartā-ynd*	*bó-end*	*xandā́-y-ndun-e*	*vé-gartā-y-ndun-e*	*bó-y-ndun-e*
			~xandā́-žun-e	*~vé-gartā-žun-e*	*~bó-y-žun-e**
⇑Set_1	⇑Set_1		⇑Set_2	⇑Set_2	⇑Set_2
"I laughed"	"I returned"	"I was"	"I would laugh"	"I would return"	"I would become"

* In the 3rd pl., the forms *xandā-y-ndun-e*, *ve-gartā-y-ndun-e*, *bo-y-ndun-e* are as attested in YS and *xandā-žun-e*, *ve-gartā-žun-e*, *bo-y-žun-e* as in WE.

Table 4

Preterit and Imperfect Transitive Verbs

Type One Pretrit	Pretrit Fronted	Pretrit with Preverb	Type Two Pretrit	Imperfect	Imperfect Fronted
bé-m-xunt	*-ā m bé-xunt*	*vé-m-git*	*b-ā́rt-ā m*	*xunté-m-e*	*-ām xunté-yy-e*
bé-d-xunt	*-ād bé-xunt*	*vé-d-git*	*b-ā́rt-ād*	*xunté-d-e*	*-ād xunté-yy-e*
bé-ž-xunt	*-āž bé-xunt*	*vé-ž-git*	*b-ā́rt-āž*	*xunté-ž-e/9*	*-āžxunté-yy-e*
bé-mun-xunt	*-āmun bé-xunt*	*vé-mun-git*	*b-ā́rt-āmun*	*xunté-mun-e*	*-āmun xunté-yy-e*
bé-dun-xunt	*-ādun bé-xunt*	*vé-dun-git*	*b-ā́rt-ādun*	*xunté-dun-e*	*-ādun xunté-yy-e*
bé-žun-xunt	*-āžun bé-xunt*	*vé-žun-git*	*b-ā́rt-āžun*	*xunté-žun-e*	*-āžun xunté-yy-e*
"I read"	"I read"	"I picked up"	"I brought"	"I would read"	"I would read"

common, and (2) the rarer type, Past Participle Two + Set_2 + BE alternates with type one in certain verbs (*bé-ž-vāte-bo ~ vāt-ež bo* "he had said," *b-ārt-ežun-u* "they have brought"). The tense of the auxiliary "be" distinguishes the present, past, and subjunctive perfects (*vémbirinte-(u)* "I have cut," *vémbirinte-bo* "I had cut," *ege mo bé-šte-bān* "if I (may) have gone") and is optional only in the 3rd singular of the present perfect (*dot max bibí-e(-u)* "the girl has gotten lost") and all transitive present perfects (*bímvāte(-u)* "I have said"). Fronting of Set_2 is a further option, most common with direct objects or compound verbs: *mo ta:rif to-m xéli var hākem békarte* "I have praised you to the governor very much," *dessür-ād étaa-bo* "you had commanded." Past verb stems that drop final *-rt* reintroduce these sounds in the perfects before the final *-é: xálγ-ād ke* "you created" vs. *xálγ-ād karté* "you have created." See above under *Verb Stems* and *Non-finite forms* for additional examples of the perfect tenses.

Modals. "Want" and "can" have the following characteristics: (1) they are indirect (or dative) verbs ("it is wanting/possible to me") with the Set_2 endings expressing the person either right in the verb: (want) pres.: *gú-m-e/ná-m-gue*, *gú-d-e*, *gú-ž-e*, etc.; past (two similar variants): *gumā-m-e~gumbā-y-m-e*, *gumā-d-e~gumbā-y-d-e;* (can) pres.: *be-šā-m/ná-šā-m*, *be-šā-d*, *be-šā-ž*; past: *be-šā-m-boyye*, *be-šā-d-boyye*), or with Set_2 fronted to a preceding word (*ű́ccü-mun az to ná-gu-e* "we don't want anything from you," *har bār gu-dun-bu* "whenever you should want," *mo teng araγ-ām ná-šā ürd kerān* "I cannot tolerate arrack"); (2) tenses other than the present are formed with a "be" auxiliary (subj.: *gú-m-bu*, *gú-d-bu*; *bé-šā-m-bu*, *bé-šā-d-bu*, etc.). The main verb is always in the subjunctive following "want" and generally after "can," but the short infinitive may also occur after personal forms of "can." Impersonal forms of "can" always use the short infinitive. Examples: ("want") *xodā gumā́yže emtehún-āž keru* "God wanted to test him"; ("can") personal, with subjunctive: *ű́škü ná-šā-ž xat mó-rā béxunu* "no one can read my handwriting"; personal, with short infinitive: *nášā-žun boyye celgi dót-ā cāk ke* "they couldn't cure the girl's insanity." There are three ways to express personal forms of "must" (i.e., "I, you, he, etc. must") and one way for impersonal forms (i.e., "one must"). Personal: (1) *qāyde* (an invariable form) plus a subjunctive (*qāyde béšān*, *qāyde béše* "I, you must go," *qāyde sālem bu* "he must be healthy); (2) a special form of "want" (*bégu*) minus the Set_2 endings, followed by a subjunctive (*bégu béše* "you must go"). A second form, which is actually a past form, seems to be used also with present sense (*gumā-bo de timān é-t-u* "he must give 10 tumans," etc.); (3) the previous form, *bégu*, or a less common alternate form, *égu* (both with present sense), plus the Set_2 endings (and optional fronting) followed by a short infinitive (*bémgu šo, bédgu šo* "I, you must go," *araγ-ād bégu xo* "you must drink arrack"; *ejāre-ž égu tā* "he must pay (give) the rent"). The impersonal construction uses *bégu* without Set_2 followed by a short infinitive: *sár-āž-ā bégu und* "one must cut the top of it off."

To be. Gazi has possibly four "be" verbs (cited in 3rd sg.): (1) *-u* (neg: *ná-u*), a general copula: *mo mere-d-ān* "I am your husband," *to šöytun-e* "you are the devil," *bár kuā-u?* "where is the door?" *xün sür-u* "blood is red," *mo xasse-yān* "I am tired," *vace go boyān* "when I was a child," *xandedār bo* "it was funny"; (2) While the present form of be_2, *hu*, (cf. Persian *hast-*) is separately listed in Yarshater's data, no examples were found in the various corpora of Gazi. The forms and functions of this verb may have merged with be_3, especially given the Gazi tendency to lose initial *h-*; (3) *ess-u* (i.e., *ess-/essā* "stand") has a copular function: *žer sar to essu* "it is under your charge," *sāt-tā ešrefi ru cante-ž essu* "100 *ašrafi*s (gold coin, q.v.) are in his bag," *ozun vo dandunā ru ayn essu* "the tongue and the teeth are in the mouth"; *essu* sometimes also functions as "become" (see below). (4) *dár-u*, "be in" (neg: *ná-dar-u*) (see also above, ISFAHAN xix and GILĀN ix): *sárāž hamézā ru kitāb dár-bo* "her head was always in a book," *de-vis ru der-end* "they are (around) for ten-twenty days," *mo se raš bumeyān, šoma kie ná-dar-boid* "I came three times (but) you weren't home"). be_1 also alternates with the other "be" verbs: (location) *in deraxt düm xarand bo* "this tree was on the footpath," *ru cante-ž dáru ~ ru cante-ž essu* "it is in her purse."

Become is expressed by two verbs. The more common one consists of "to be_1" plus tense-aspect markers (see Tables 2 and 3): pres. *baletar b-ú-e* "he gets bigger"; imperf. *har vax ibize-m xorté-yy-e, nācāk boym-e* "every time I ate melon, I would get sick." Note the contrast in *nācāk boyān* "I was sick" vs. *nācāk bé-boyān* "I got sick" vs. *nācāk boym-e* "I would get sick." The present perfect is seen in *dot max bibíe(-u)* "the girl has gotten lost." (See also *Passive* below). The second "become" verb is *ve-ess/-ā*, i.e., "be_3" (stand) plus preverb," but seems to occur mostly in the negative form in order to retain a clear distinction between the negative forms of "be" and "become" (which are identical in many NWI languages): *go bozā gar ve-nássend* ". . . so that the goats not get mangy," *mo sir ve-ná-ssāyān* "I have not become full/satiated." There are also occasional affirmative forms: (ZH) *peydā vessā* "it was found," *mah vessaa-bo* "it had gotten lost," (WE) *pir vesse ~ pir bébe* "may you grow (lit: become) old!"

Causatives, Passives. The causative formant *-n/-nā* is added to the present stem of the non-causative: *emus-* "to learn" > *emusn/-ā* "to teach," (WE) *ces-* "to stick (intrans)" > *cesn/-ā* "to stick (trans)." The vowel of the stem may also be lengthened or changed in the causative: *car-* (intrans) > *cārn-* "to graze," *ver-* (intrans) > *vern- ~ vārn-* "to pass," (EY) *cesúe* "it sticks (intrans.) > *cösnāne* "I stick (it) up (on the wall, etc.)." Gazi has no formal passive forms, but four alternatives exist: (1) different past stem formations (see *Verb Stems* above) sometimes distinguish active from passive (with transitive vs. intransitive conjugations): (trans.) *bé-ž-emart, bé-ž-sut (~bé-ž-suzna)* "he broke (it), he burned (it)" vs. (intrans.) *bé-(e)marā-Ø, bé-suz-ā-Ø* "it broke, it burned"; (2) analytic formation with "become" as in Persian: *fárγ-āž öškofte bébie* "his crown (of his head) has (been) split open"; (3) the same verb can have both active/passive or intransitive/transitive senses: *pešúe* "he cooks (trans.)" and "it cooks (intrans.)"; (4) some so-called causative forms are nothing more than a way to convert an intransitive stem to transitive and the resulting pair of verbs serves the same "active/passive" type distinction discussed here: *cesúe* "it sticks" > *cösnāne* "I stick (it)," *xārúe* "it itches" *xārnúe* "he scratches," *girúe* "it lights up, it goes on" > *girnúe* "he lights (it) up, he turns (it) on." As these examples show, "passive" has a much wider range of meanings than simply passive.

Bibliography: Harold W. Bailey "Modern Western Iranian: Infinitives in Gazī and Soī," *TPS*, 1935b, pp. 73-74, repr. in idem, *Opera Minora* I, pp. 265-66. Wilhelm Eilers and Ulrich Schapka, *Westiranische Mundarten aus der Sammlung Wilhelm Eilers* II: *Die Mundart von Gäz*, 2 vols., Wiesbaden, 1979. Pierre Lecoq, "Les dialectes du centre de l'Iran," in Rüdiger Schmitt, ed., pp. 313-26. Manfred Mayrhofer, "Vorgeschichte der iranischen Sprachen; Uriranisch," in Rüdiger Schmitt, ed., pp. 4-24. Rüdiger Schmitt, "Die altiranischen Sprachen im Überblick," in idem, ed., pp. 25-31. Idem, ed., *Compendium Linguarum Iranicarum*, Wiesbaden, 1989. Ehsan Yarshater, Handwritten field notes collected in Gaz, 1969, kindly provided to the author. Valentin A. Zhukovskiĭ, *Materialï dlya izucheshniya persidskikh' narechiy*, 3 vols., St. Petersburg, 1888-1922.

(DONALD STILO)

ISFAHAN SCHOOL OF PHILOSOPHY (l'école d'Isfahan), the term coined by Henry Corbin (1903-78) and Seyyed Hossein Nasr (1933-) to describe a philosophical and mystical movement patronized by the court of Shah ʿAbbās I (r. 1588-1629), centered in the new Safavid capital of Isfahan, and initiated as part of the wider Safavid cultural renaissance associated with his reign. The political power and stability of the Safavid Empire at the turn of the 17th century and material and social conditions afforded by the new capital provided the context, patronage, and opportunities for intellectual flourishing. The Isfahan School of Philosophy (*maktab-e falsafi-e Eṣfahān*) represents the apogee of the "Shiʿite renaissance" of the Safavid period (Landolt, 2003, p. 2). According to Corbin and Nasr, the key elements of the School and its foremost thinkers and proponents shaped the intellectual history of Safavid Persia, often in an adversarial conflict with the rise in power of a juristic hierocracy opposed to metaphysical speculation and mystical experience. The introduction of this phase of post-Avicennian philosophy was designed to further refute the myth that the polemics initiated by Abu Ḥāmed Mo-ḥammad Ḡazāli (d. 1111, q.v.) in his *Tahāfot al-falāsefa* had brought philosophical speculation in Islam to an end. Thus, Corbin and Nasr offered a radically different concept of philosophy in Islam and a method for studying intellectual history that has been influential ever since, whilst also attracting the criticism of a number of detractors. The significance of the notion of the School of Isfahan lies in the methodology that it proposes; as such the question arises whether such a method and notion is coherent, and whether it provides a viable historical-critical and philosophically sensitive understanding of philosophy in the Safavid period.

Origins. The term was first coined by Corbin in an article that he wrote on spiritual visions of Mir Moḥammad-Bāqer Estrābādi, better known as Mir(-e) Dāmād, in the *festschrift* for Louis Massignon (Corbin, 1956). This article had a number of significant aims: first, to insist that our academic understanding of philosophy in Islam was impoverished and that philosophy did not end in Islam with Ḡazāli's famous attack; second, that historians of art and architecture were already familiar with the significance of Isfahan as a cultural center and it was time to recognize its significance as a center of philosophical and theological learning (cf. Corbin, 1962b, p. 85); third, to establish a particular philosophical tradition associated with the Safavid period in the history of philosophy, so that one could learn from the insights of the philosophers of Isfahan; fourth and concomitantly, to introduce important contemporaries of Giordano Bruno, Descartes, and Leibniz to an occidental audience, to make these thinkers of Isfahan as familiar to Western students of philosophy as they were to Persians (Corbin, 1956, pp. 331-33). Corbin identified Mir Dāmād as the founder of the School of Isfahan and its main influence. He saw in him a philosopher who was at once a keen analytic mind and a spiritually enlightened individual aware of the religious foundations of knowledge, a thinker who represented a higher philosophical synthesis beyond the quarrels between Avicennism and Averroism, a philosopher who lived a philosophical life and combined ratiocinative thought with spiritual exercises. The School of Isfahan thus represented a Hegelian synthesis that one ought to engage with to discover the mature thought of spiritual and intellectual Islam (Corbin, 1956, p. 334). Corbin identified the significance of esoteric Shiʿism in the School of Isfahan, a metaphysic of imamology and a form of Sufism that represented a continuity with the primordial spiritual traditions of Persia, and he noted the importance of Neoplatonism to the thought of the School, mainly mediated through the famous adaptation of the *Theology of Aristotle* (Ar. tr. *O̱ṯulujiā*) of Plotinus. He identified the three main figures and thinkers of the School: Mir Dāmād, his colleague Shaikh Bahāʾ-al-Din ʿĀmeli (q.v.), and their student Ṣadr-al-Din Moḥammad Širāzi, better known as Mollā Ṣadrā, and their key works such as *al-Qabasāt* of Mir Dāmād and *al-Asfār al-arbaʿa* of Mollā Ṣadrā. Finally, he completed his description by juxtaposing the esoteric and metaphysical speculation of the thinkers of the School of Isfahan with the "orthodox" Shiʿite theology and jurisprudence of Moḥammad-Bāqer Majlesi (Corbin, 1956, p. 339). The School of Isfahan thus represented the enlightened spiritual and intellectual elite in opposition to the political and theological orthodoxy of the Safavid establishment.

This pioneering article, which included a critical edition of a short Arabic text of the School, was followed about a decade later by "The School of Iṣfahān" by Nasr (Nasr, 1966). This article fleshed out in a more systematic fashion some of the key influences, features, and elements of the School through an exposition of its three main thinkers Mir Dāmād, Shaikh Bahāʾ-al-Din ʿĀmeli, and Abu'l-Qāsem Mir Fendereski. Mollā Ṣadrā was significant enough to merit a separate chapter in the same collection. Nasr considered the School of Isfahan to represent the supreme intellectual achievement of Twelver Shiʿism (Nasr, 1966, pp. 904-5). Thus he situated the philosophical tradition within the spiritual and theological tradition of Islam, whence its inspiration. He characterised the thought of the School as *ḥekmat*, a wisdom and "divine science" that combined gnosis (in particular the sapiential and metaphysical Sufi thought of the school of Ebn al-ʿArabi, q.v.), theosophy, and philosophy (Nasr, 1966, p. 907). To the pantheon of the School, he added the names of Mollā Moḥsen Fayż Kāšāni and ʿAbd-al-Razzāq Lāhiji (qq.v.), both students and sons-in-law of Mollā Ṣadrā. In later works, Nasr would supplement the list with the following generation, in particular the great Shiʿite Neoplatonist Qāżi Saʿid Qomi, following Corbin's lead in his recapitulation of the key thinkers of the School of Isfahan in the fifth section (*livre V*) of his monumental *En Islam iranien*. It was Nasr who critically added the feature of perennial philosophy (*jāvidān-ḵerad, al-ḥekma al-ḵāleda*) to the study of the School of Isfahan, even though Corbin himself was averse to perennialism and traditionalism (Nasr, 2001, p. 50). Like Corbin, Nasr insisted on the prophetic roots of the thought of the School of Isfahan. Furthermore, for them both, the School of Isfahan represented the high point of Persian Shiʿite civilization and thus the totality of the intellectual production was subsumed under this paradigm in the study of intellectual history ever since. The influence of the School of Isfahan was thus seen to extend wherever this civilization imprinted its traces, including significantly India (Nasr, 1986, pp. 696-97; Rizvi, II, pp. 211-24). Nasr also popularized the notion of the five sources of the School of Isfahan: the Peripatetic philosophical tradition, the Illuminationist tradition founded by Shaikh Šehāb-al-Din Sohravardi, the Sufi metaphysics of Ebn al-ʿArabi, the theological traditions of both Sunni and Shiʿite Islam, and esoteric Shiʿism (*ʿerfān-e šiʿi*; Nasr, 1986, p. 658). The thought of the School was thus a higher synthesis of these streams that influenced and nurtured it.

The final significant feature in establishing the School of Isfahan paradigm was the collaborative project initiated by Corbin and Sayyed Jalāl-al-Din Āštiāni (d. 2005) in 1964 to produce editions of the texts written by the major figures of the School "from Mir Dāmād to the present day." Four volumes of texts were published in the 1970s, introducing twenty-eight thinkers and their texts (both in Arabic and Persian) with extensive contextualizations and philosophical introductions written by Āštiāni in Persian and Corbin in French. Making the texts was a critical requisite, given Corbin's desire to make the thought of the School of Isfahan accessible such that "reading Mollā Ṣadrā should become as normal as reading Kant" (Landolt, 2003, p. 3). This collection (*Anthologie des philosophes iraniens . . .*) was, and remains, a major contribution. It extended the scope for studying philosophy in post-Avicennian traditions and provided the material refutation of the idea that philosophy in Islam had died with Averroes as well as proof of the intellectual achievements of Shiʿite Persia. The first thinker included in the anthology was Mir Dāmād, the founder of the School, and the last took the story beyond the Safavid period into the Qajar period, in itself suggesting the intellectual continuity from the Safavid period into the 20th century. The success of the label has meant that the philosophy of the Qajar period is called the School of Tehran and the philosophical-theological movement of the late Timurid and early Safavid period is called the School of Shiraz.

Methodology. The School of Isfahan became a paradigm for the study of Islamic intellectual history. Corbin and Nasr were very clear that they envisaged a particular way of understanding philosophy that was both historically sensitive without becoming "historicist" (Corbin, 1977, p. 25) and philosophically sophisticated so as to demonstrate the value of Irano-Islamic philosophy to the wider world. Embedded within the paradigm were certain key theoretical assumptions, two of which are worth considering in detail. They felt that they were merely representing faithfully the true intentions of the thinkers of the School. Subsequent critics have separated the content of the thought of the School of Isfahan from the methodological paradigm of the "School of Isfahan" as advocated by Corbin and Nasr.

First, Corbin and Nasr had a particular conception of what philosophy is. The pursuit of "wisdom" was neither constrained by the specialization and suspicion of metaphysics of the analytical tradition, nor by the grand designs of the European traditions of philosophy. Philosophy was a lived experience, a way of life that incorporated rational and supra-rational elements and had at its core both a deep spiritual intuition fostered by a meditation on scripture and an esotericism. Corbin used the term "philosophie prophétique" to describe this thought. Corbin states that he discovered this aspect of Islamic philosophy only after a pilgrimage into the spiritual heart of Islam in search of the inner guiding principle of the sapiential tradition of Shiʿite and Iranian Islam (Corbin, 1962a, pp. 49-50). Shiʿite philosophy is privileged not only because it is inspired by the Islamic revelation, but also because it adheres to the principle of eternal presence and the disclosure of being through the person of the Imam from pre-existence through to the age of expectation of the *parousia* (*ẓohur*) of the Twelfth Imam (Corbin, 1971, esp. pp. 62-68). Prophetic knowledge is inherited by the Imams insofar as they are *awliāʾ*, and thus from the niche of prophecy and the light of *walāya*, philosophy spreads forth in the Safavid period (Corbin, 1962a, p. 55). Nasr was less effusively philosophical (and one may say more apologetic): "The roots of Islamic philosophical thought lie in the Quran, the Hadith and the sayings of certain Shiʿite Imams. These roots grew into a tree that was, however, nurtured primarily by the Greco-Alexandrian philosophical tradition" (Nasr, 1999, p. xxvi). Nasr conceived of philosophy as an aspect of a Sufi conceptualization of stages of enlightenment and spheres of human experience, beginning with the law (*šariʿa*), the Sufi path (*ṭariqa*), and metaphysical reality (*ḥaqiqa*). Ḥekmat related to the ultimate level and was the wisdom that was bestowed by God, as the Qurʾān (2:269) says, "He grants wisdom to whom He pleases; and he who is given wisdom is given a great good" (Nasr, 1996, p. 63) Such a conception of philosophy rested on the assumption of a harmony in the School of Isfahan between the claims, dictates and doctrines of revelation, reason and mystical intuition (Nasr, 1999, pp. 6-8), which is the topic of a doctoral dissertation (Moris, *Revelation, Intellectual . . .*) on Mollā Ṣadrā, supervised by Nasr.

Second, Corbin proposed a phenomenological hermeneutics for reading the texts of the School. Prophetic philosophy entailed the deployment of a prophetic hermeneutics of *taʾwil*, of studying the phenomena, the *ẓāher*, while seeking to return to its original essence hidden within, the *bāṭen*. He insisted that this hermeneutics did not forgo the phenomena and in fact was saving the appearances (*sozein ta phainomena*) and engendering what he described as *kašf al-maḥjub*, unveiling the hidden without discarding the veil (Corbin, 1977, pp. 22-33; Nasr, 2001, p. 51). It was in this sense that the method of analysis proposed by Corbin and Nasr was both historical (saving the appearances of the text) and philosophical (disclosing the essence of the text). The text as a symbol is nothing in itself but indicates an essence. At the same time, however, the apparent nature of the text is not a mere transparency that one can forgo (cf. Wasserstrom, pp. 85-90). Everything that exists is thus a symbol of both the word and the world, and this concept was directly related to the Sufi notion representative of the school of Ebn al-ʿArabi that everything was a sign/symbol for the ultimate essence, God. Imagination becomes a key instrument for discovering the essences and underlying forms (Jambet, 1981a, pp. 37-51; hence Corbin's "discovery" of the imaginal as a key ontological bridge between the world of bodies and the world of forms that he considered to be central to the thought of the School of Isfahan, beginning with Mir Dāmād (Corbin, 1986, p. 462). Given the significance of mysticism in their model of philosophy, they recognized that seemingly irrational character of many of the texts that they championed and proposed a concomitant hermeneutic of dealing with apparent contradictions and paradoxes: the *coincidentia oppositorum* (Corbin, 1971-72, IV, pp. 84-105, 134-50; cf. Wasserstrom, pp. 67-82). The coincidence of opposites was a commonly discussed medieval notion that juxtaposed two seemingly contradictory realities. Corbin expressed this in his understanding of two key Safavid thinkers. In his discussion of the eschatology of Mollā Ṣadrā, he argued that the holistic metaphysics of being and presence expounded by this thinker did not allow for the traditional and clear separation of this physical world and the celestial afterlife, the world of the body and the world of the spirit. Historicism insists on the separation; the search for spiritual meaning forgoes the separation (Corbin, 1960, tr., pp. vii-ix). Thus, there were two coincidences of seeming opposites: spiritual body and celestial earth. The study of the imamology of Qāżi Saʿid Qomi raises the second case of the *coincidentia oppositorum*. It is related to the basic paradox of monotheism, the exclusive understanding of divine unicity being considered as unique (Corbin, 1976, pp. 71-72). Esoteric Shiʿism extricates itself by posing the coincidence of the nature of the Imam as at once divine and human, bearing a divine face and a human face. The superior and privileged nature of esoteric Shiʿism is once again central to the understanding of intellectual history. The suggested concept of philosophy and hermeneutics makes this clear. Furthermore, since Corbin and Nasr were not interested in Arab Shiʿite thought or in legal philosophy, esoteric Shiʿism with its symbolic world mediated by the almost imaginal existence of the Hidden Imam, was in itself an illustration of the continuity of the essential spirituality of Persia.

Critiques. Since the paradigm for studying intellectual history proposed by Corbin and Nasr has controversial doctrines relating to hermeneutics, the nature of philosophy, the "essence" of Persia, and the nature of Shiʿism, it is not surprising that there has been a wide range of criticisms. The first and quite common criticism of the School of Isfahan paradigm for studying Islamic philosophy is the description of the philosophical tradition as theosophy. While it was a laudable desire on the part of Corbin and Nasr to insist that philosophy in Islam did not end with Averroes, the shift to theosophy, for some critics, signals an embrace of the irrational and vaguely mystical. If philosophy is supposed to be clear and precise in its articulation of ideas, by contrast theosophy is mystifying and obscure. There are two types of criticisms of this tendency. The first rejects the notion of prophetic philosophy and finds little of value in the works of the Safavid period. Critics such as Dimitri Gutas are quick to point out that philosophy in Islam was neither inherently and essentially mystical nor was it an inquiry rooted in the spiritual tradition of Islam. The real problem is that the Corbin-Nasr approach reduces philosophy to mysticism and theology (Gutas, pp. 17-18). Islamic apologetics cannot explain philosophical traditions in Islam as such, since essentialist arguments about the primordial nature of thought and its divine origins are belied by historical contingencies and contextualizations. Corbin and Nasr, however, were quite careful about the etymology of the term 'theosophy' for labelling the thought of the School of Isfahan; for them, it is a direct rendition of the Arabic term used by these thinkers, *al-ḥekma al-elāhiya* (Corbin, 1986, p. 14) and signals that the conception of philosophy and wisdom in the School of Isfahan is rooted in the Islamic revelation and especially the Shiʿite interpretation of it. Nevertheless, the fact that the term theosophy is associated with the arcane spiritualism movement of the Theosophical Society in the 19th century does not allow for serious engagement. The second type of critique against the paradigm argues that misleading labelling accounts for the neglect of the philosophical importance of the thinkers of the Isfahan period. Hossein Ziai has been at the forefront of this critique insisting that labelling post-Avicennian thought, in particular the School of Isfahan, detracts from the analytical value of the thought (Ziai, 2005, p. 405). The late Fazlur Rahman, the author of so far the best monograph on Mollā Ṣadrā, has similarly argued that to interpret post-Avicennian texts as an ill-defined mysticism or theosophy (he was particularly concerned with the interpretation of Mollā Ṣadrā) would be at the cost of the "purely intellectual and philosophical hard core, which is of immense value and interest to the modern student of philosophy" (Rahman, p. vii).

A second criticism of the Corbin and Nasr approach is that it seems to essentialize the spiritual nature of Persia and to privilege esoteric Shiʿism. This has had an effect on subsequent studies both of Shiʿism and of the intellectual history of Persia. Corbin himself signalled the culmination of the School of Isfahan in the spiritual heterodoxy of the Šayḵi school (Corbin, 1971-72, IV, pp. 205-300). It is thus not surprising that both Mangol Bayat and James Morris have read the oppositional, spiritual dissent of the School of Isfahan as conveying a legacy that filtered through to Bahaʾism and a plethora of spiritual heterodoxies of the present. The spiritual continuity of Persian Islam was thus seen as being radical and oppositional. The Iranian revolution and the political and juridical face of Shiʿism poses a serious challenge, especially when in the form of an individual like Ayatollah Khomeini one encounters a deep affinity to the thought of the School of Isfahan with a radical political agenda that was completely ignored by Corbin and Nasr.

A third criticism relates to the intellectual historiography of the Safavid period. The School of Isfahan paradigm suggests a tension and conflict between the practitioners of law and the spiritual and intellectual elite. It seems to mark a fissure between *eros* and *nomos*. Perhaps the most extreme case of a follower developing this idea is the work of Leonard Lewisohn, who posits an inevitable and essential clash between the law and spiritual and intellectual speculation. Sufism was an integral part of the School of Isfahan and led to its condemnation by anti-Sufi polemicists such as Mollā Moḥammad-Ṭāher Qomi. The clash between these two parties is often noted and cited by specialists of Safavid religious and cultural history. It is worth noting, however, that most of the members of the School of Isfahan were jurists as well, and were appointed to official positions in the hierocracy. The vagaries of shifting patterns of patronage in different reigns as well as the instability of factional politics probably accounts for more than an essential conflict between the "orthodox" jurists and the "heterodox" Sufis and philosophers. Andrew Newman in particular has lamented this problem in the historiography of Safavid Persia that pits "intolerant, orthodox clerics" against the scholars of the reign of Shah ʿAbbās I, who were primarily interested in philosophy and mysticism (Newman, 1986, pp. 165-66). As a corrective, Newman considers the career of Shaikh Bahāʾ-al-Din ʿĀmeli as an engaged political agent and foremost jurist. It is worth noticing, however, that Newman's corrective is more effective against those who have understood Nasr and Corbin as advocating such a split. Nasr in particular has stressed the importance of the thinkers of the School at court, their association with royalty, and their status as major jurists and upholders of the law (*šariʿa*).

Consequently, John Walbridge has argued that the continuity of the Iranian spiritual and philosophical tradition advocated by Nasr and Corbin reflected an ahistorical appreciation of both pre-Islamic Iranian thought and the Illuminationist tradition. Furthermore, he identified the idea of a spiritual core of Persia that is essential and beyond history to be a factor within Pahlavi imperial ideology fostered especially through the Imperial Iranian Academy of Philosophy (Anjoman-e Šāhanšāhi-e Falsafa-ye Irān) that was set up with the patronage of the court and Nasr as its founding director. The stress on the spiritual, in contrast to the political, as the character of Persian intellectuals that the School of Isfahan paradigm suggested was thus exemplified in the career of Nasr himself. One ought to be careful about ascribing political motives of a totalitarian, anti-democratic and fascist nature to Nasr and Corbin; such accusations are quite unfounded (*pace* Wasserstrom, pp. 155, 170-79; Subtelny).

Finally, it may be worth considering what a philosophical school is. Usually the division of the history of philosophy into rival schools and groupings surrounding a thinker, a place, or a textual cycle is shorthand and recognized as a simplification. A school may be a particular institution founded by an individual, or a body of doctrines associated with a particular thinker, or an intellectual movement that comprises an interpretative community of a particular text. We may, for example, talk about the school of Plato as the Academy itself, or his followers who perpetuated his "esoteric" teachings, or the students who taught and studied his dialogues; but once we start talking about Platonism, Middle Platonism, and Neoplatonism, the idea of a unified school certainly begins to break down (cf. Dillon, pp. 1-29). In what sense then can we consider the Isfahan philosophers to constitute a school, especially since Nasr and Leaman used the term to designate thinkers who were not based in Isfahan? There is little doubt that they did not share a central text or a central doctrine or body of doctrines. Is the title merely an indication of Isfahan as the location of the early study of the School, in particular associated with the famous triumvirate of Mir Dāmād, Shaikh Bahāʾi, and Mollā Ṣadrā? It would certainly be foolish to misinterpret Corbin and Nasr's theory as implying that the School of Isfahan was doctrinally united. For them, the School designates a wider movement with common conceptions of philosophy and hermeneutics as they have expounded. It does not entail a rejection of multiple doctrinal schools; in fact, Corbin himself explicitly discussed three different schools within the rubric of the School of Isfahan: the platonic school of Mir Dāmād, the existentialist school of Mollā Ṣadrā, and the apophatic school of Rajab-ʿAli Tabrizi (Corbin, 1977, pp. 63-77; idem, 1986, pp. 462-77). For Corbin, the main uniting factor of these three was not simply the geographical location of Isfahan but the essential and timeless nature of the prophetic philosophy they espoused.

Bibliography: Charles Adams, "The Hermeneutics of Henry Corbin," in Richard C. Martin, ed., *Approaches to Islam in Religious Studies*, Tucson, 1985, pp. 129-50. Nader and Fereshteh Ahmadi, *Iranian Islam: The Concept of the Individual*, Basingstoke, 1998. Zahrā Anāri, *Maktab-e Eṣfahan dar šahr-sāzi*, Tehran, 2001. Said Amir Arjomand, *The Shadow of God and the Hidden Imam*, Chicago 1984. Kathryn Babayan, *Mystics, Messiahs and Monarchs: Cultural Landscapes of Early Modern Iran*, Cambridge, Mass., 2002. Mangol Bayat, *Mysticism and Dissent: Socioreligious Thought in Qajar Iran*, Syracuse, 1982. Mehrzad Boroujerdi, *Iranian Intellectuals and the West: The Tormented Triumph of Nativism*, Syracuse, 1996, pp. 120-30. Browne, *Lit. Hist. Persia* IV, pp. 406-7.

Henry Corbin, "Confessions extatiques de Mir Damad: maître de théologie à Ispahan," in Henri Massé, ed., *Mélanges offerts à Louis Massignon*, 3 vols., Damascus, 1956, I, pp. 331-78. Idem, ed., *Terre céleste et corps de résurrection: de l'Iran mazdéen à l'Iran shîʿite*, Paris, 1960; tr. Nancy Pearson as *Spiritual Body and Celestial Earth: From Mazdean Iran to Shiʿite Iran*, Princeton, 1976. Idem, "De la philosophie prophétique en Islam shîʿite," *Eranos Jahrbuch* 31, 1962a, pp. 49-116. Idem, "La place de Mollâ Sadrâ Shîrâzî dans la philosophie iranienne," *Studia Islamica* 18, 1962b, pp. 81-113. Idem, "Face de Dieu et face de l'homme," *Eranos Jahrbuch* 36, 1967, pp. 165-227. Idem, "Imamologie et philosophie," in Toufic Fahd, ed., *Le Shîʿisme imâmite*, Paris, 1970, pp. 143-74. Idem, "L'idée du Paraclet en philosophie iranienne," in *Problemi attuali di scienzia di cultura. Atti del convegno internazionale sul tema: La Persia nel medievo (Roma 31 Marzo – 5 Aprile 1970)*, Rome, 1971, pp. 37-68. Idem, *En Islam iranien: aspects spirituels et philosophiques*, 4 vols., Paris, 1971-72. Idem, "Le paradoxe du monothéisme," *Eranos Jahrbuch* 45, 1976, pp. 69-133. Idem, *Philosophie iranienne et philosophie comparée*, Académie impériale iranienne de philosophie 25, Tehran, 1977. Idem, *Temple et contemplation*, Paris, 1980; tr. Philip Sherrard as *Temple and Contemplation*, London, 1986. Idem, *La Philosophie iranienne islamique aux XVIIe et XVIIIe siècles*,

Paris, 1981. Idem, *Histoire de la philosophie islamique*, Paris, 1986; tr. Liadain Sherrard as *History of Islamic Philosophy*, London, 1991. Idem, *L'Iran et la philosophie*, Paris, 1990; tr. J. Rowe as *The Voyage and the Messenger: Iran and Philosophy*, Berkeley, Calif., 1998. Idem, *Itinéraire d'un enseignement*, ed. Christian Jambet, Tehran, 1993. Henry Corbin and Sayyed Jalāl-al-Din Āštiāni, eds., *Anthologie des philosophes iraniens depuis le XVIIe siècle jusqu'à nos jours/ Montak̲abāt-i az āṯār-e ḥokamāʾ-e elāhi-e Irān az ʿaṣr-e Mir Dāmād o Mir Fendereski tā zamān-e ḥāżer*, 4 vols., Paris and Tehran, 1971-79.

M. Cruz Hernández, *Historía del pensamiento en el mundo islámico* II, Madrid, 1981, pp. 327-40. Hamid Dabashi, *Theology of Discontent: The Ideological Foundation of the Islamic Revolution in Iran*, New York, 1993. John Dillon, *The Heirs of Plato*, Oxford, 2004. Leili Echghi, *Un temps entre les temps: l'Imam, le Chîʿisme et l'Iran*, Paris, 1992. Mohammad H. Faghfoory, ed., *Beacon of Knowledge: Essays in Honor of Seyyed Hossein Nasr*, Louisville, 2003. Mohamad Reza Fashahi, *Aristote de Bagdad: de la raison grecque à la revelation coranique*, Paris, 1995, pp. 47-54. Dimitri Gutas, "The Study of Arabic Philosophy in the Twentieth Century," *British Journal of Middle Eastern Studies* 29, 2002, pp. 5-25. ʿAbd-al-Rafiʿ Ḥaqiqat, *Tārik̲-e ʿolum wa falsafa-ye irāni*, Tehran, 1993, pp. 285-91, 740-86. Christian Jambet, *La logique des orientaux: Henri Corbin et la science des formes*, Paris, 1981a. Idem, ed., *Henry Corbin*, Cahiers de l'Herne 39, Paris, 1981b. Idem, "Le Soufisme entre Louis Massignon et Henry Corbin," in Sayyid Jalāl al-Dīn Āshtiyānī et al., eds., *Consciousness and Reality: Studies in Memory of Toshihiko Izutsu*, Leiden, 2000, pp. 259-72. Abdolamir Johardelvari, *Iranische Philosophie von Zarathustra bis Sabzewari*, Frankfurt on the Main, 1994, pp. 127-214. Hermann Landolt, "Suhrawardi's 'Tales of Initiation'," *JAOS* 107, 1987, pp. 475-86. Idem, "Henry Corbin, 1903-1978: Between Philosophy and Orientalism," *JAOS* 119, 1999, pp. 484-90. Idem, "Henry Corbin's Understanding of Mulla Sadra," in *Islam-West Philosophical Dialogue: The Papers Presented at the World Congress on Mulla Sadra (May, 1999, Tehran)*, 2 vols., Tehran, 2001, pp. 163-72. Idem, "Introduction," to ʿAbd-Allāh Nurāni, ed., *Moṣannafāt-e Mir Dāmād* I, Tehran, 2003, pp. 1-9. Leonard Lewisohn, "Sufism and the School of Isfahan," in idem, ed., *The Heritage of Sufism*, 3 vols., Oxford and Boston, 1999, III, pp. 63-134. P. Lory, ed., *Henry Corbin: Philosophies et sagesses des religions de livre*, Turnhout, 2005. Muhsin Mahdi, "Orientalism and the Study of Islamic Philosophy," *Journal of Islamic Studies* 1, 1990, pp. 73-98. Maryam Mir-Aḥmadi, *Din o mad̲hab dar ʿaṣr-e Ṣafawi*, Tehran, 1984, pp. 70-73. Zailan Moris, *Revelation, Intellectual Intuition and Reason in the Philosophy of Mulla Sadra*, Richmond, 2001. James W. Morris, *The Wisdom of the Throne*, Princeton, 1981.

Seyyed Hossein Nasr, "Spiritual Movements, Philosophy and Theology in the Safavid Period," in *Camb. Hist. Iran* VI, pp. 656-97. Idem, "The School of Iṣpahān," in Mian Mohammad Sharif, ed., *A History of Muslim Philosophy*, 2 vols., Wiesbaden, 1963-66, I, pp. 904-32. Idem, "*Al-ḥikmat al-ilāhiyyah* and *kalām*," *Studia Islamica* 34, 1971, pp. 139-49. Idem, "Philosophy in Islam," *Studia Islamica* 37, 1972, pp. 57-80. Idem, "Henry Corbin 'L'exil occidental': une vie et une oeuvre en quête de l'Orient des Lumières," in idem, ed., *Mélanges offerts à Henry Corbin*, Tehran, 1977, pp. 3-27. Idem, *Sadr al-Din Shirazi and His Transcendent Theosophy: Background, Life and Works*, Tehran, 1977. Idem, *Traditional Islam in the Modern World*, London, 1987. Idem, "Oral Transmission and the Book in Islamic Education," *Journal of Islamic Studies* 3, 1992, pp. 1-14. Idem, "Introduction," in Seyyed Hossein Nasr and Oliver Leaman, eds., *History of Islamic Philosophy*, 2 vols., London and New York, 1996, I. Idem, "The Meaning and Concept of Philosophy in Islam," ibid., I, pp. 11-26. Idem, "The Place of the School of Isfahan in Islamic Philosophy and Sufism," in Leonard Lewisohn, ed., *The Heritage of Sufism* III: *Late Classical Persianate Sufism (1501-1750)*, Oxford, 1999, pp. 3-15. Idem, "Prolegomenon," in Seyyed Hossein Nasr and Mehdi Amin Razavi, eds., *An Anthology of Philosophy in Persia*, 2 vols., New York and Oxford, 1999, I, pp. xxiii-xxx. Idem, "An Intellectual Autobiography," in L. E. Hahn et al., eds., *The Philosophy of Seyyed Hossein Nasr*, Chicago, 2001, pp. 3-85. Idem, "The Meaning and Role of Philosophy," Seyyed Hossein Nasr and Mehdi Amin Razavi, *The Islamic Intellectual Tradition in Persia*, Richmond, 1996.

Andrew Newman, "Towards a Reconsideration of the 'Isfahān School of Philosophy': Shaykh Bahāʾi and the Role of the Safawid ʿulamā," *Studia Iranica* 15, 1986, pp. 165-99. Idem, "Mirāṯ-e Mollā Ṣadrā dar āṯār-e dānešmandān-e ḡarbi dar zamina-ye moṭālaʿāt-e irāni wa Šiʿi," in *Majmuʿa-ye maqālāt-e hamāyeš-e jahāni-e Ḥakim Mollā Ṣadrā awwal-e k̲ordād māh 1378, Tehran*, Tehran, 2001, pp. 67-80. Fazlur Rahman, *The Philosophy of Mulla Sadra*, Albany, 1975. Yann Richard, *L'Islam Chiʿite: croyances et idéologies*, Paris, 1991; tr. Antonia Neville as *Shiʿite Islam: Ideology and Creed*, Oxford, 1995, pp. 49-76. Saiyid Athar Abbas Rizvi, *A Socio-Intellectual History of the Isnā ʿAshari Shīʿīs in India*, 2 vols., New Delhi, 1986. Ṣafā, *Adabiyāt* V/1, pp. 292-343. Manučehr Ṣaduqi Sahā, *Tārik̲-e ḥokamāʾ wa ʿorafāʾ-e motaʾak̲k̲er bar Ṣadr-al-Motaʿallehin*, Tehran, 1980. Manṣur Ṣefatgol, *Sāk̲tār-e nehād wa andiša-ye dini dar Irān-e ʿaṣr-e Ṣafawi*, Tehran, 2002. Daryush Shayegan, *Henry Corbin: La topologie spirituelle de l'Islam iranien*, Paris, 1990; tr, Bāqer Parhām as *Hānri Korban: ārāq-e tafakkor-e maʿnawi dar Eslām-e irāni*, Tehran, 1992. Maria Subtelny, "History and Religion: The Fallacy of Metaphysical Questions," *Iranian Studies* 36/1, 2003, pp. 91-101. Matthijs Van Den Bos, *Mystic Regimes: Sufism and the State in Iran from the Late Qajar Era to the Islamic Republic*, Leiden, 2002. John Walbridge, *The Wisdom of the Mystic East: Suhrawardi and Platonic Orientalism*, Albany, 2001, pp. 105-10. Steven M. Wasserstrom, *Religion after Religion: Gershom Scholem, Mircea Eliade, and Henry Corbin at Eranos*, Princeton, 1999. Hossein Ziai, "Ṣadr-al-Din Širāzi wa bayān-e falsafi-e ḥekmat-e motaʿālia," *Irān-šenāsi/Iranshenasi* 5, 1993, pp. 353-64. Idem, "Knowledge and Authority in Shiʿi Philosophy," in L. Clarke, tr. and ed., *Shiʿite Heritage: Essays on Classical and Modern Traditions*, Binghamton, 2001, pp. 359-74. Idem, "Recent Trends in Arabic and Persian Philosophy," in P. Adamson and R. Taylor, eds., *The Cambridge Companion to Arabic Philosophy*, Cambridge, 2005, pp. 405-25.

(SAJJAD H. RIZVI)

ISIDORUS OF CHARAX (Gk. Isídōros ho Charakēnós), Greek geographical author, about whose life and person no more is reliably known than that he originated from Characene. Everything else must be derived from the few preserved remains of his writings. Even his lifetime is in dispute. According to the traditional view he flourished in the time of Augustus, shortly before the beginning of the Christian Era (cf. Schoff, p. 17; Herzfeld, pp. 4-8; Tarn, pp. 53-55; Chaumont, pp. 64 f.; Gawlikowski, pp. 78-80; Schuol, pp. 115 f.). The evidence to support this is the following. One of the authors who referred to Isidorus and used his writings was Pliny the Elder in his *Naturalis historia* (see below), even if there are some inconsistencies and inaccuracies. Therefore the date of the completion of this work (77 C.E.) is the fixed terminus ante quem for Isidorus. On the other hand a reliable terminus post quem can be found in the reference to Tiridates' sudden invasion in 26 B.C.E. and his attempt to deprive Phraates IV of the Parthian crown (*Stathmoí* § 1 = Jacoby, p. 780.4); Phraates IV is the latest historical person mentioned there who can be dated with certainty. Tarn (p. 53) recognized another fact in favor of such a date, viz., that Isidorus (*Stathmoí* § 19 = Jacoby, p. 782.1) mentioned the Parthian name of Arachosia as "White India" (*Indikḗ Leukḗ*), which can only mean that at his time Arachosia was part of some Indian kingdom, as actually was the case under the Azes dynasty (30 B.C.E.-19 C.E.).

The main argument is based, however, on an emendation in Pliny, *Naturalis historia* 6.141, where the reading *Isidorum* is proposed instead of manuscriptal *Dionysium*. A "Dionysius of Charax" is totally unknown otherwise and is not given in the lists of Pliny's sources; Isidorus, for his part, is mentioned as a source for books 2-6, and the author referred to in 6.141 is called "the most recent one describing the geography of the world" (*terrarum orbis situs recentissimum auctorem*). From this passage it is clear, if one accepts the emendation, that Isidorus, making inquiries in the Orient before the expedition of Augustus's grandson C. Caesar in the year 1 B.C.E., wrote his book on behalf of this emperor. There is the apparent difficulty, however, that Isidorus is quoted twice in a passage of Ps.-Lucianus, *Makrobioi* 15-17 (= frags. 3-4 in Jacoby, p. 782) mentioning several Oriental kings, among them Artabazus of Characene, who according to Nodelman (p. 107, n. 160; cf. Schuol, p. 388) should be dated to the very end of the 1st century C.E., and who became king only in the year 73 C.E. This difficulty now is cleared up, since a tetradrachm has become known (cf. Alram, p. 158, no. 505) which mentions the name Artabazus and at the same time is dated to the year 264 Seleucid Era = 48/47 B.C.E. (and not with Daffinà, pp. 9 f., to the Arsacid Era). Moreover, it is in no way certain that the passage of Ps.-Lucianus comes from Isidorus in its entirety; because this author is quoted by name only in §§ 15 and 17, and the first of those quotations, referring to "another Artaxerxes," follows directly after an excerpt from Dinon (q.v.) about Artaxerxes Mnemon. It seems more natural to assume that Ps.-Lucianus drew on more than one single source. It is not necessary to think, as often has been done (e.g., by Weissbach; cf. the detailed discussion in Daffinà, pp. 6-13), that two different Characenian authors (whether named Dionysius and Isidorus or being of the same name Isidorus), from whose writings Pliny and Ps.-Lucianus quoted, necessarily lived in different times—i.e., in Augustus's and Pliny's time respectively.

The theoretical foundations on which the writings of Isidorus are based are the discoveries of the late Hellenistic period and in particular the measurement of the world by Eratosthenes. By this it becomes evident that Isidorus had a Greek educational background and perhaps was of Greek descent. In any case he wrote in Greek language, although he also must have had some knowledge of Aramaic, since he used and explained Semitic words and names such as the toponym *Pháliga*, which is translated into Greek *mesoporikón* "half-way" (*Stathmoí* § 1 = Jacoby, p. 779.21).

Under the name of Isidorus of Charax fragments of several writings are preserved: (1) 14 short fragments giving the distances between certain places and particulars on the size of some islands (frags. 6-19 in Jacoby, pp. 782-85; cf. Mullerus, pp. 255 f.; Schoff, pp. 12-15). These belonged to a book, whose title is not given (perhaps *Períplous tês oikouménēs* "Account of a journey around the inhabited world"), a kind of manual of the measurement of the world, from which Pliny drew much information in books 2, 4, and 5 of his *Naturalis historia*. In frag. 19 Pliny (*Naturalis historia* 5.127) refers to Eratosthenes and Isidorus for several Asiatic peoples which have disappeared.

(2) A fragment (no. 1 in Jacoby, pp. 778 f.; cf. Mullerus, pp. 254 f.; Schoff, pp. 10 f.) describing pearl-fishing in the Persian Gulf, which is quoted almost literally by Athenaeus (q.v., *Deipnosophistai* 3.46) from Isidorus's otherwise unknown book *Tò tês Parthías Periēgētikón* "(Geographical) description of Parthia."

(3) Two references in Ps.-Lucianus, *Makrobioi* 15 and 17 (frags. 3-4 in Jacoby, p. 782; cf. Mullerus, p. 256; Schoff, pp. 14 f.; Schuol, pp. 123 f.) concerning two supposedly long-lived Oriental kings—a certain Artaxerxes, most probably Ardaxšīr II of Persis (1st. cent. B.C.E.), and Goaisos, king of Oman. This evidence perhaps belongs to some historical work which dealt with all the kings

ruling Characene and the neighboring kingdoms up to his own time. However, it is not cogent or proven that the entire text between the two mentions of his name goes back to Isidorus, even if it is just in that part that there is discussion of three Characenian kings.

(4) A little, though quite important, work entitled *Stathmoì Parthikoí* (in Latin *Mansiones Parthicae*) "Parthian Stations," which is the only Greek text preserved at all of the genre of the itinerary or route description (frag. 2 in the definitive critical edition by Jacoby, pp. 779-82; cf. also Mullerus, pp. 244-54 and LXXXVI-XCV; Schoff, pp. 2-9 and 22-39). The text, which seems to be complete and which is known from two Paris manuscripts (A and B) of the 13th century (and two inferior copies of the 16th cent.), is a description and measurement of the overland route crossing the Parthian empire in an easterly direction from Zeugma on the Euphrates to Alexandria in Arachosia, the so-called "Parthian Royal Road," which had some significance both for strategic reasons and as a trade route. The text gives the frontiers of each province crossed and the names of the principal supply stations and, quite exactly, also the distances between the stations (*stathmoí*) mentioned. (*Stathmós* is a technical term used already in Herodotus's description [5.52-54] of the Achaemenid Royal Road from Sardis to Susa.) Presumably the text follows older models such as the (lost) list of stations along the route from Ephesus to Bactria and India in the last book of Ctesias's *Persika* (frag. 33), but Chaumont (p. 66) suspected that Isidorus also made use of Aramaic documents. It is not only possible, but, in view of the striking textual difference between § 1 and the remainder of the text, very likely, that the *Stathmoì Parthikoí* is only an excerpt from a more exhaustive geographical account of the Parthian empire, i.e., of the *Periēgētikón* (above, no. 2), and that this book, apparently a description of all the regions from the Red to the Caspian Sea and from the Euphrates almost to the Indus River, is Isidorus's major work. The scant information of the second part, given without elaboration—i.e., in a certain province the number of villages is such and such—is a clear sign that the text in front of us is the poor work of an excerptor. In such a scenario, which cannot simply be dismissed, questions arise (and remain unanswered) as to who excerpted the *Stathmoí*, who chose this title, and the like.

In the manuscripts the text of the *Stathmoí* proper is preceded by a concise listing (not printed in Jacoby, p. 779) of all the 19 regions through which the road leads, and of the distances, which are given in *schoînoi* (a variable, originally Egyptian, measure indicating, not the length, but the distance covered in a certain time, thus ca. 5.5 km on average, as experience shows): Mesopotamia and Babylonia 171 *schoînoi*, Apollōniâtis 33, Chalōnîtis 21, Media 22, Kambadēnḗ 31, Upper Media 38, Media Rhagiana 58, Choarēnḗ 19, Komisēnḗ 58, Hyrcania 60, Astauēnḗ 60, Parthyēnḗ 25, Apauarktikēnḗ 27, Margiana 30, Aria 30, Anaúōn 55, Zarangianḗ 21, Sakastēnḗ 63, Arachosia 36—in all, 858 *schoînoi*. Thus the course of this great route starting in Antiochia on the Orontes and reaching the Parthian frontier at Zeugma (Seleucia on the Euphrates) can be pursued in broad outline. It runs from there along the Euphrates via Nikēphórion, Doûra and the "Royal Canal" to Seleucia on the Tigris, then in an easterly direction to Ecbatana, Rhágai, Nísaia (the ancient Parthian capital Nisā), and Margiana, before turning southwards to Aria, Sistan, and finally Arachosia, "as far as the rule of the Parthians extended" (so in § 19). Because this was the state of affairs only under Mithridates II, and not at Isidorus's own time, the conclusion (suggested also by other data concerning the division into provinces) cannot be avoided, that Isidorus here was drawing on a much older document, probably an official survey of the Parthian Empire (cf. Tarn, pp. 54 f.). For identifying the names of the districts, towns, and villages, some difficulties arise from the fact that the distances are given in *schoînoi* and not in a fixed unit of length; and because the numbers are written with alphabetic numerals, errors of the scribes and copyists relating to this also must be taken into account.

The western part of the route along the Euphrates up to Seleucia on the Tigris (frag. 2, § 1 in Jacoby, pp. 779.6-780.11; text and German tr. also in Schuol, pp. 116-18) is described in much greater detail than the following sections (about Iran proper) and covers more than a third of the entire text. Only here is found also a rather complete list of the stations, including the distances between them and now and then also additional remarks concerning, e.g., historical facts. Of some interest is the expression *stathmòs basilikós* "royal (posting or supply) station," which is found twice, only in this western section, applied to the fortified place Álagma and to Thilláda Mirráda. A certain place with a temple of Artemis, i.e., Anāhitā, the name of which either has fallen out or has been translated into Basíleia (literally "royal palace or treasury"), is expressly said to have been founded by Darius; it seems to be identical (cf. Chaumont, pp. 82-84) with Ptolemy's (5.18.6) Aphphadána, which for its part is nothing other than the Iranian term *apadāna-* "palace" (Parth. *appaδan*; see APADĀNA). This first part of the text has been commented upon in recent times, in particular from the historical-geographical point of view, by Chaumont (with maps on pp. 72, 81, and 94) and Gawlikowski (with map on p. 76).

The description of the eastern part of the route is much more succinct and actually is no more than a brief account, which does not give the individual stations, but only the separate provinces, the overall distance of the route within the individual provinces, and summary information on the number of towns, villages, and stations. Therefore, strictly speaking, the route itself, with the exception of only a few stations, is not given at all; and its course, though in part going back to the Assyrians and used also in Achaemenid times, for several sections cannot be reconstructed exactly and is at issue. To make matters worse, several of the provinces mentioned by Isidorus are not attested elsewhere (e.g., Kambadēnḗ and Apauarktikēnḗ, but also the subdivision of Upper and Lower Media). From § 13 on, only provinces (those east of Parthyēnḗ) and cities or villages are listed; there are no more stations and no distances between the inhabited places. This may be explained by assuming that for those last parts of the text the excerpt either is based on a different source or was made by a different person, for whom those matters were of minor interest. More recent treatments of this, as it were, Iranian stage of the route from the viewpoint of historical geography are by Khlopin (to be used with the utmost caution) and Walser (with map near p. 147), for the easternmost provinces (§§ 15-19) also by Daffinà (pp. 87-106).

Some details of interest may be specified. It is remarkable that in Media (probably we have to read: Lower Media, *Mēdía hē kátō*) there was not one single *pólis* (§ 4 = Jacoby, p. 780.20). – In § 5 (Jacoby, p. 780.22) mention is made of a town *Bagístana* (emendation of *Báptana*) "situated at a mountain, where there are a relief and a pillar of Semiramis." This information reminds us of Diodorus 2.13.1-2, who (after Ctesias) says nearly the same, but actually means (as does Isidorus) the relief and inscription of Darius at the mountain of Bisotun (q.v.). – It is regrettable that all attempts at localizing the city of *Asaák* (or whatever the true form of the name may be) have failed so far (§ 11 = Jacoby, p. 781.12); there Arsaces I had been crowned the first Parthian king and "an eternal fire is attended". – In § 12 (Jacoby, p. 781.14 f.) the Parthian royal city, where the "royal tombs" are found, is mentioned by the name *Parthaúnisa* (which looks like some "Parthian Nisā") and with the additional remark, that the Greeks call it *Nísaia*. – Otherwise unknown is the royal capital of the Sakas mentioned in § 18 (Jacoby, p. 781.28), *Sigál*, in whose neighborhood is the city Alexandrópolis (thus Tarn, pp. 470 f., who in contrast to former editors correctly eliminated the dittographic toponym Alexandria in this passage and not vice versa).

On the whole, the data and in particular the forms of the names given in the *Stathmoí* are not always reliable. One more example may be sufficient for illustrating this: In § 17 (Jacoby, p. 781.26) the province is named *Drangianḗ*, whereas the summary index preceding the text has *Zarangianḗ*, which obviously is the original form, because manuscript A has the unmotivated abbreviation *z´* before *Drangianḗ* (which apparently resulted from misreading ZAPA- as ZΔPA-). Similar problems arise with Ptolemy's *Geography* and other Greco-Roman geographic writings (including maps such as the Tabula Peutingeriana), so that the total useable evidence they contain tends to be in small proportion to the amount of detail, and the comparison of the various texts mostly is not as helpful as one may expect.

Bibliography: M. Alram, *Iranisches Personennamenbuch. IV: Nomina propria Iranica in nummis. Materialgrundlagen zu den iranischen Personennamen auf antiken Münzen*, Wien, 1986. M.-L. Chaumont, "Études d'histoire parthe. V: La route royale des Parthes de Zeugma à Séleucie du Tigre d'après l'itinéraire d'Isidore de Charax," *Syria* 61, 1984, pp. 63-107. P. Daffinà, *L'immigrazione dei Sakā nella Drangiana*, Roma, 1967. M. Gawlikowski, "La route de l'Euphrate d'Isidore à Julien," in P.-L. Gatier et al., eds., *Géographie historique au Proche-Orient (Syrie, Phénicie, Arabie, grecques, romaines, byzantines)*, Paris, 1988, pp. 77-98. E. Herzfeld, "Sakastān," *AMI* 4, 1932, pp. 1-116. Jacoby, *Fragmente*, vol. IIIC, Leiden, 1958, pp. 777-85 ("FgrHist 781"). I. Khlopin, "Die Reiseroute Isidors von Charax und die oberen Satrapien Parthiens," *Iranica Antiqua* 12, 1977, pp. 117-65. C. Mullerus, *Geographi Graeci Minores*, vol. I, Paris, 1855 (repr., Hildesheim, 1965), pp. LXXX-XCV, pp. 244-56. S. A. Nodelman, "A Preliminary History of Characene," *Berytus* 13, 1959-60, pp. 83-121. W. H. Schoff, *Parthian Stations by Isidore of Charax. An account of the overland trade route between the Levant and India in the first century B.C.: The Greek text, with a translation and commentary*, Philadelphia, 1914 (repr., Chicago, 1976). M. Schuol, *Die Charakene: Ein mesopotamisches Königreich in hellenistisch-parthischer Zeit*, Stuttgart, 2000. W. W. Tarn, *The Greeks in Bactria and India*, Cambridge, 1938; 2nd ed., 1951 (repr., New Delhi, 1980). G. Walser, "Die Route des Isidorus von Charax durch Iran," *AMI* 18, 1985 (1986), pp. 145-56. [F. H.] Weissbach, "Isidoros. 20," in Pauly-Wissowa, *RE* IX/2, 1916, cols. 2064-68.

(RÜDIGER SCHMITT)

IŠKATA, in the Avesta the name of a mountain (*Yt.* 19.3; *Y.* 10.11) and in *Yt.* 10.14 that of the land (situated in the Hindu Kush region) which is dominated by this mountain. It is mentioned in the list of the mountains of the Iranian countries at the beginning of *Zamyād Yašt* (*Yt.* 19.1-8); in stanza 3 the words *iškatā-ca upāiri.saēna* obviously must be interpreted as a dvandva compound in nom. dual "and (Mt.) Iškata (and) (Mt.) Upāirisaēna" (cf. Humbach and Ichaporia, p. 70), and *iškatā* is neither nom. plur. nor an epithet to *upāiri.saēna* (*pace* Hintze, p. 418). The same dual dvandva is found in *Hōm Yašt* (*Y.* 10.11) in a passage enumerating all the mountainous regions which the birds bringing the haoma cross in flight: *auui iškata upāiri.saēna* "over (Mt.) Iškata (and) (Mt.) Upāirisaēna." Both times Iškata is connected with the name of the Hindu Kush range, Upāiri.saēna (cf. MPers. *kōf ī Aparsēn* in *Bundahišn* 12.9),which only by folk etymology is understood as meaning "(the mountain) above the eagles' (flight)"; despite the close parallel of Ved. *upariśyena-* it actually goes back to an original like **upārisaina-* "covered with juniper" (cf. Humbach, 1995; Humbach and Ichaporia, 1998, p. 71).

In addition, Iškata is attested in a passage of *Mihr Yašt* describing the lands surveyed by the god Mithra, where "the entire Aryans' abode" (*Yt.* 10.13 *vīspəm . . . airiiō.šaiianəm*) is named first, after which the names of several particular countries follow, beginning with *ā iškatəm pourutəm-ca* "Iškata and Pouruta" (*Yt.* 10.14; no common noun *iškata-* "rock," as Bartholomae, *AirWb.*, col. 376 has it). In this list, Iškata seems to be the name of a land (as does the coordinated Pouruta, which *pace* Gershevitch, 1959, p. 81, is no ethnical adjective). As to the comprehension of that passage, Gnoli (1966, p. 72;

1967, pp. 83 f.; 1980, p. 86, n. 148) was the first to interpret the preceding *ā* as resuming the verbal prefix *ā-* of *ādiδāiti* "he surveys" (in stanzas 13 and 15) and thus to understand the lands Iškata, etc., as not being included in the "Aryans' abode." Neither Iškata nor Pouruta is the plural of an ethnonym at any rate, as Christensen (1943, p. 68) had proposed. Besides, Pouruta is usually identified with the names of the Aparýtai (Herodotus 3.91.4) and/or the Paroûtai (or Párautoi) located in Areia next to the Hindu Kush by Ptolemy (6.17.3).

There has been some dispute as to the correct form of the name Iškata, because in all of the three passages the various manuscripts have variant readings, with *š́* (thus one reads, e.g., in *Yt.* 19.3 *iš́atā-ca* in Geldner's edition after F1) or with the ligature *šk* quite similar in appearance (the two signs being confused even in good old manuscripts and actually being interpretable in either way) or with *šk* written as separate signs (see, e.g., Hintze, pp. 76 f.). As Humbach and Ichaporia (1998, p. 71) recognized, the Pahlavi rendering by *škuft* "hardness" (though being erroneous) makes clear by its initial *šk-* that *iškata-* and not *iš́ata-* is the correct reading. In consequence the reading *iš́(ii)ata-* and the etymology based on it (IndoIr. **īč-i̯a-ta-* "[widely] visible"), which Hintze (1994, p. 77) had suggested, must be given up. For the time being, there is no alternative to Karl Hoffmann's admittedly somewhat strange proposal "house/home of refreshments" (see ibid.; Humbach and Ichaporia, 1998, p. 70).

Iškata must be located to the south of the western Hindu Kush, on the slope where the Helmand has its source; so it may probably be identified with Kūh-e Bābā (see Marquart, 1905, p. 74; Gershevitch, 1959, p. 175; Gnoli, 1980, p. 85; see AVESTAN GEOGRAPHY). Gershevitch even went further and supposed that it is the country located between Haraiva and Gandhara, viz., ancient Sattagydia (OPers. *Θataguš*). The alternative identification as proposed by Eggermont (1982; 1991, pp. 22-37) with the mountain range of the *Askatá(n)kas*, along which the Massagetae live in the land of the Sakas (thus Ptolemy 6.13.1, 3), is in every respect unfounded. Christensen (1943, p. 69) suspected that the name Iškata is also preserved in *Kyréschata* (only in Ptolemy 6.12.5), the name of the most north-easterly town of Cyrus's empire on the Iaxartes River (otherwise called CYROPOLIS, q.v.), which he consequently understood as "Kura of the Iškatā." A more convincing etymology of the name *Kyréschata*, however, was proposed by Benveniste (followed by Gershevitch, 1959, p. 175, n. †; most recently by Bernard, 1999, pp. 276 f., n. 2), **Kuru(š)-kaθa-* (or possibly **Kurauš kaθa-*) "Cyrus's town," which is supported by the Transoxanian toponym *Kurkaθ* known from Arab geographers (cf. Barthold, *Turkestan*[2,3], p. 166) and the Persian *Hodūd al-ʿālam* (tr. Minorsky, p. 115).

Bibliography: E. Benveniste, "La ville de Cyreschata," *JA* 234, 1943-45 (1947), pp. 163-66. P. Bernard, "Compte rendu," *Topoi* 9/1, 1999, pp. 275-90. A. Christensen, *Le premier chapitre du Vendidad et l'histoire primitive des tribus iraniennes*, Copenhagen, 1943. P. H. L. Eggermont, "Kyreschatè en Ptolemaeus Geographicus," *Persica* 10, 1982, p. 277. Idem, "Cyrus the Great, Alexander the Great and the Identification of the Avestan Iskata [sic] Mountain," *Pakistan Archaeology* 26, 1991, pp. 1-47. I. Gershevitch, *The Avestan Hymn to Mithra, with an Introduction, Translation and Commentary*, Cambridge, 1959. Gh. Gnoli, "Airyō.šayana," *RSO* 41, 1966, pp. 67-75. Idem, *Ricerche storiche sul Sīstān antico*, Rome, 1967. Idem, *Zoroaster's Time and Homeland: A Study on the Origins of Mazdeism and Related Problems*, Naples, 1980. A. Hintze, *Der Zamyād-Yašt: Edition, Übersetzung, Kommentar*, Wiesbaden, 1994. H. Humbach, "Der alte Name des Hindukusch," *AOASH* 48, 1995, pp. 67-69. Idem, and P. R. Ichaporia, *Zamyād Yasht: Yasht 19 of the Younger Avesta. Text, Translation, Commentary*, Wiesbaden, 1998. J. Marquart, *Untersuchungen zur Geschichte von Eran. II*, Leipzig, 1905.

(RÜDIGER SCHMITT)

ISLAM AKHUN (Eslām-āḵūn), treasure-seeker and swindler active in Khotan and neighboring areas between 1894 and 1901, best known, however, as an adept forger of manuscripts and block prints in various pseudo-scripts. He was eventually unmasked by Sir Aurel Stein (1862-1943) in 1901.

Following the discovery in 1889 of the "Bower manuscript," a fifth-century medical treatise in Sanskrit, the Government of India and Russia became intense rivals in acquiring manuscripts and other antiquities. Until then manuscripts from Central Asia were virtually unknown; and, when George Macartney (1867-1945), acting for the Government of India in Kashgar, and Nikolai Petrovsky (1837-1908), the Russian Consul, were offered material discovered at remote desert sites, they had little reason to suspect that some of them were not genuine.

Already before 1894, Islam Akhun had been in the habit of collecting coins, seals, and similar antiques from Khotan villagers. When he learned from Afghan traders the price that was being given for manuscripts, he decided to make them himself in preference to the hazardous business of scouring the desert for ancient sites. Between 1895 and 1898 he supplied Macartney, Petrovsky, and several European travelers with a steady stream of books and manuscripts. His collaborators were Muhammad Tari, Mulla Muhammad Siddiq, and Ibrahim Mullah, who apparently specialized in the Russian market (Stein, 1907, pp. 509, 511).

The first manuscript they produced was sold by Islam Akhun in 1895 to Munshi Ahmad Din, who was temporarily in charge of the Assistant-Resident's office at Kashgar. It was written by hand, and an attempt had been made to imitate the Brāhmī (q.v.) characters found in a genuine, probably Khotanese, manuscript from Dandan Uiliq (q.v.). Since, however, at this time, none of the Europeans could read the scripts, the forgers soon realized that it was unnecessary to bother with imitating genuine manuscripts. Thus each individual freely invented his own characters, as is shown by the diversity of different

PLATE I

Or.13873/70. Forgery, ca. 1897; this manuscript was examined in 1897 by Sir Aurel Stein, who had begun his career as an Iranian scholar; he decided the script was Pahlavi, though he could not fully understand it (Hoernle, 1899, p. 63).
Courtesy of the British Library Board.

scripts which were based loosely on Brāhmī, Aramaic (PLATE I), Uighur, Cyrillic, Arabic, and Chinese (see Sims-Williams for examples of these).

Islam Akhun's ingenuity is evident not only from the forgeries themselves, but also from the elaborate details he supplied regarding the provenance and circumstances of each find (Hoernle, 1899, pp. xii-xxiii). His descriptions were passed on with the manuscripts and block prints for decipherment to the Sanskritist Rudolf Hoernle (1841-1918, q.v.) in Calcutta. Hoernle, who by then had started to decipher the genuine Khotanese manuscripts amongst them, neverthless believed, on balance, that the ones in "unknown characters," were also genuine. Hoernle's article of 1897 discusses the manuscript forgeries (pp. 250-56; plates 17-26), and section 2 of his 1899 report is devoted to block prints (pp. 45-110; plates 5-18).

By 1897, however, Islam Akhun's goods were beginning to be regarded with suspicion. Magnus Bäcklund (1866-1903), the Swedish missionary in Yarkand, had severe doubts as to their authenticity (Hoernle, 1899, pp. 57-58; Deasy, pp. 149-50), and Hoernle had himself written to Captain S. H. Godfrey (1861-1941), Assistant to the Resident in Kashmir, on 21 July 1898 "not to purchase any more Khotan books" (BL/IOR/MSS EUR F 302/13). It seems likely that full-scale production ceased shortly after this.

In the early summer of 1898 Islam Akhun acted as an unwilling guide for the explorer Captain H. H. P. Deasy (1866-1947) on an expedition to look for ancient sites near Guma (Deasy, pp. 150-55). By the third day Islam Akhun had absconded, leaving the travelers to make their own way back. On his return he forged a note in Deasy's handwriting to get money from Badruddin, the Aqsaqal (official who looked after the interests of the Indian traders, reporting to the Consul-General in Kashgar) in Khotan; he was famous for providing Stein and others with numerous manuscripts (Sims-Williams, p. 112). For this, Islam Akhun was sentenced to wear the cangue, a large square board, weighing about 30 lbs., round his neck for a month (see photograph in Deasy, p. 155).

After this Islam Akhun moved to the area south of Khotan and Keriya (Stein 1903, pp. 472-73), where he blackmailed hillmen while masquerading as a British agent searching for illegal slaves. His credentials were two large sheets of a Swedish newspaper, the *Svenska Morgonbladet*, one of which contained the photo of a Swedish missionary in China whom he claimed to be. During the winter of 1901 he practiced as a "hakim" in Chira near Keriya. His bizarre medical kit included several leaves of a French novel, which Stein suggested (1903, p. 473) he might have read aloud as imaginary charms, or even administered in pieces for internal consumption!

In 1900 Stein made a special point of trying to locate, without success, some of the sites Islam Akhun had mentioned in his reports (Stein, 1907, pp. 100-103). Before leaving Khotan in 1901 he spent several days interviewing him, and eventually extracted a full confession (Stein, 1903, pp. 469-81; 1907, pp. 507-14). When Islam Akhun asked Stein to let him accompany him to Europe, Stein refused, and nothing more is known of him after that.

Bibliography: British Library IOR/MSS EUR F 302/13: Register of Hoernle's Central Asian correspondence between 1895 and 1914. H. H. P. Deasy, *In Tibet and Chinese Turkestan: being the Record of Three Years' Exploration*, London, 1901. A. F. R. Hoernle, "Three Further Collections of Ancient Manuscripts from Central Asia," *Journal of the Asiatic Society of Bengal* (*JASB*) 66, pt. 1, 1897, pp. 213-60; repr., Calcutta, 1897. Idem, "A Report on the British Collection of Antiquities from Central Asia: Part I," *JASB* 68, pt. 1, 1899, extra no., Calcutta, 1899. S. Rosen, "Suwen Hedin korekushon ni okeru izō Saka monjo/The Forged Saka Documents in the Sven Hedin Collection," in *Ryūsa shutsudo no moji shiryō/Written Materials Excavated from the Sands*, ed. Itaru Tomiya, Kyoto, 2001, pp. 161-75. U. Sims-Williams, "Forgeries from Chinese Turkestan in the British Library's Hoernle and Stein collections," *Bulletin of the Asia Institute* 14, 2000, pp. 111-29. M. A. Stein, *Sand-Buried Ruins of Khotan: Personal Narrative of a Journey of Archæological and Geographical Exploration in Chinese Turkestan*, London, 1903. Idem, *Ancient Khotan: Detailed Report of Archaeological Explorations in Chinese Turkestan*, 2 vols., Oxford, 1907.

(URSULA SIMS-WILLIAMS)

ISLAM IN IRAN. Although a large number of articles in this *Encyclopaedia* are devoted to specific aspects of Sunnite Islam in general and Shiʿite Islam in particular, the following series of articles provide an overview of some historical, contemporary, and especially political aspects of the topic that are of special interest and relevance in the world today. The series consists of the following three broad sections:

1. The Advent and Spread of Islam in Iran.
   - i. *The advent of Islam in Iran*. See IRAN ix/2.1.
   - ii. *Conversion to Islam*. See CONVERSION iii.
   - iii. *Late medieval period*. See IRAN ix/2.2.
   - iv. *Shiʿite states since the Safavids*. See IRAN ix/2.3.
2. Messianism and Millenarianism in Islam.
   - v. *Messianic Islam in Iran: A general survey*.
   - vi. *The concept of Mahdi in Sunni Islam*.
   - vii. *The concept Mahdi in Twelver Shiʿism*.
   - viii. *The occultation of Mahdi*. See ḠAYBA.
   - ix. *The deputies of Mahdi*.
3. Islamic Political Movements.
   - x. *The roots of political Shiʿism in Iran*.
   - xi. *Jihad in Islam*.
   - xii. *Martyrdom in Islam*. Forthcoming online.
   - xiii. *Islamic political movements in 20th-century Iran*.
   - xiv. *Islam and democracy*. Forthcoming online.
   - xv. *Islam and socialism*. Forthcoming online.
   - xvi. *Islam and fundamentalism*. Forthcoming online.
   - xvii. *Islamic Revolution of 1977–79*. Forthcoming online.
   - xviii. *Islamic Republic of Iran*. Forthcoming online.

1. The Advent and Spread of Islam in Iran

The series of entries in this section provide a general survey of historical geography of the advent and spread of Islam in the lands of Iran and related territories from the early period to the present time, including the Iranian plateau, Central Asia and Afghanistan, and Mesopotamia.

i. THE ADVENT OF ISLAM IN IRAN. See IRAN ix/2.1.

ii. CONVERSION TO ISLAM. See CONVERSION iii.

iii. LATE MEDIEVAL PERIOD. See IRAN ix/2.2.

iv. SHIʿITE STATES SINCE THE SAFAVIDS. See IRAN ix/2.3.

2. Messianism and Millenarianism in Islam

With the rise of political Islamic movements in the latter half of the 20th century, and the increasing politicization of theological conceptions of messianism and millenarianism in Islam, the concept and significance of the Mahdi in Islam in general and in Shiʿism in particular needs to be examined and understood in order to contextualize the central themes of militant Islamic movements, both Sunni and Shiʿite. These issues are discussed in the following sub-entries: "A General Survey of the Concept," "Mahdi in Sunni Islam," "Mahdi in Shiʿism," "Mahdi's Occultation," and "Mahdi's Deputies."

v. MESSIANIC ISLAM IN IRAN: A GENERAL SURVEY

Messianism is one of the most powerful, diverse and enduring expressions of Islam in Iran throughout its long history. Messianic speculations are evident especially in Shiʿite literature ranging from Hadith, theology, and philosophy to occult sciences, and folklore. Messianic yearnings also motivated a number of epoch-making popular movements with political ambitions and lasting influence on Iranian cultural identity. Shiʿism is the prevalent locus for such activities—though not the only one—extending over thirteen centuries of advocacy for the advent of the Mahdi, and at times striving to fulfill such expectations. Though only conceptualized as a mode of religious expression in the 20th century, through what is often referred to as *Mahdawiyat* (Mahdism), the Shiʿite authors were well aware of it, as attested by the existence of numerous "books of Occultation" (*ketāb al-ḡayba*; see vii, below). Thriving in the Iranian environment, messianic speculations go even beyond the religious space, as this cultural environment has shown a paradigmatic propensity for the messianic mode since antiquity (see below). Expressions such as "yearning for the manifestation" (*enteẓār-e ẓohur*), waiting for the "signs of final salvation" (*ʿalāmat-e faraj*) and support for the "Lord of the Time" (*Ṣāḥeb al-Zamān*), often intertwined with millennial and apocalyptic motifs, denote the presence of such aspirations not only in the classic works of Shiʿite Hadith and as one of principals beliefs of Shiʿism, but also surpass normative religion to include mystical, literary, and, in the 20th century, revolutionary religion (see vii, below; see also Amir Arjomand, 1996; Amir-Moezzi; Modarresi; Sachedina, 1981).

Pre-Islamic influences. Such expressions are rooted in Iran's per-Islamic past and its memories as conveyed through myth and legend. In early centuries, Islam in Iran incorporated the rich apocalyptic tradition of its Zoroastrian past especially on the advent of the savior *Saošiant*, the millennial cycles (*hazārag*), the renewal of the world (see FRAŠŌ.KƎRƎTI), the ensuing events of the Day of the Judgment and to the eternal residence in paradise (*ferdows*), all purely Zoroastrian notions (see IRAN ix/1). They found their way into the Shiʿite Hadith and more often into the *aḵbār* (reports) of the Shiʿite Imams. Apocalyptic motifs also seem to have reached Iranian Muslims through the medium of Jewish and Christian prophecies, especially as upheld by the Karaite Jewish community of Iran. The Zoroastrian-Jewish cross-cultural exchanges dating back to the Babylonian era influenced formative Shiʿism. Traces of Jewish Messiah (*Māšiaḥ*) are evident as early as in the Kaysāniya movement of the 8th century in Mesopotamia and southwestern Iran. The Judeo-

Christian influence also helped augmenting the millenarian aspiration for the Christ's Second Coming. The Shiʿite image of Jesus as the Mahdi, and later as the lieutenant to the Mahdi, looms large in early Hadith possibly through the medium of Byzantine and Eastern churches (see IRAN ix/1).

Non-Shiʿite Iranian messianism of the 8th and 9th centuries, most notably in the anti-Islamic Ḵorramiya and Abu-Moslemiya and the anti-Ummayad Zaydi revolts in the 8th century were, on the other hand, influenced by Mazdakite and other pre-Islamic dissident beliefs and ideologies of Sasanian Iran. The communistic egalitarianism of the Mazdak movement remained an inherent undercurrent of Iranian messianism and time and again reemerged in later movements. More characteristically, Iranian messianic space allowed the synthesis of two or more trends, notably in Khorasan in the eve of the ʿAbbasid revolution (750 CE), and later in early Ismaʿili-Qarmaṭi movement of the 9th and 10th centuries (see IRAN ix/1.1; Yarshater; Sadighi; Madelung in *EI*[2]: "Ismailiyya" and cited sources).

Mahdi in Shiʿite denominations. Unlike normative Sunni Islam, where belief in Mahdi is often associated with folk religion, in Shiʿism belief in the Mahdi and expectations for his return is incorporated into the fundamentals of belief (*oṣul al-din*) and a significant part of the principle of Imamate. In Shiʿism, whether Zaydi, Ismaʿili, or Twelver Shiʿism (Eṯnā-ʿašari or Imami), and the extremists (see ḠOLĀT), expectations for the Mahdi are a central part of the religious awareness. The doctrine of Occultation (*ḡayba*, q.v.), and its corollary, the Manifestation (*ẓohur*) of the Hidden Imam in Ismaʿili and in Twelver Shiʿism are doctrinally linked to the eschatological belief in the Return (*maʿād*) and the Resurrection (*qiāma*). As a precursor to the End of the Time, the Mahdi is an inseparable part of the Shiʿite apocalyptic narrative able to transform political and social conditions and initiate cyclical renewal. He is the divine agency that brings the old revelatory cycle to its ultimate totality and potentially stands to start a new religious dispensation (even though the latter aspect is often passed over in silence in the Shiʿite literature). In historical reality such potentiality is often translated into revolutionary aspirations to transform society's political, social, moral, and religious order and offers one of the few perceivable means of protest against political repression, social injustice, and clerical tyranny. Such yearnings thus aspired for a utopian alternative to the prevailing religio-political order. Chronologically, this was a challenge first to the Sunni institution of the Caliphate, Sunni sultans, their conservative *divān* establishment, and the Ashʿarite theology and later to the state-clergy pact of the Safavid and Qajar eras (see vii, below; see also Amir Arjomand, 1996; Amir-Moezzi).

MAIN PHASES OF MESSIANIC MOVEMENTS IN IRAN

Five periods of messianic activities may be identified in Islamic Iran.

The first phase. This phase is marked by proto-Shiʿite trends of the 7th century, the Iranian revivalist movements, and anti-Ummayad *mawāli* movement culminating in the ʿAbbasid revolution of 750 CE. Most notable among these are the movement of Moḵtār Ṯaqafi (k. 687), the leader of a pro-Alid movement, and the Kaysāniya, the Abu-Moslemiya and a range of persecuted Zaydi claimants, all displaying some form of proto-Mahdi status (see ḠOLĀT; ABŪ MOSLEM; ʿABBASID CALIPHATE).

The second phase. This phase embraces a range of movements with a concrete Mahdistic idea often reflecting frustrated hopes that came in the wake of the ʿAbbasid caliphate's monopoly of power and exclusion of the followers of the Shiʿite Imams and their subsequent persecution in the latter part of the 8th and the early 9th centuries. While the Twelver Shiʿites benefited from the patronage of the pro-Shiʿite Iranian Buyids (q.v.) and their hegemony over the ʿAbbasid caliphate of Baghdad, they eventually resorted to the doctrine of Occultation of the 12th Imam, and the unspecified day of his return in the distant future, especially after the Greater Occultation in 941. Such a quietist position allowed the development of Twelver Shiʿites' theology, and major figures of the period such as Shaikh Jaʿfar Ṭusi and Shaikh Moḥammad Mofid allocated extensive space to the theory of the Occultation (see vii, below). Their work manifests an evident attempt to combat popular messianic aspirations for the return of the Imam. The early Ismaʿili-Qarmaṭi Shiʿism, on the other hand, adopted a clear messianic course with revolutionary potentials advocating the imminent advent of the Imam of the age. Though the Qarmaṭi missionary activity was played out in the Iranian periphery, the Ismaʿili *daʿwa* (q.v.) ultimately came to fruition in the Fatimid caliphate of North Africa and Egypt (q.v.) in the 10th century. The Iranian upsurge of unfulfilled Ismaʿili messianism had to wait another century before the Nezari-Mostaʿli split (see ISMAʿILISM ii) precipitated the emergence of Alamut (q.v.) in 1090 as the nerve center of a network of Ismaʿili mountain fortresses in Iran and Syria with the revolutionary objective of combating the Sunni Saljuq state and the emerging Ashʿarite orthodoxy under its aegis. The inner dynamics of the Nezāri messianism of Alamut eventually culminated in the declaration of *qiāma* (resurrection) under Ḥasan II in 559/1162 (for him see Daftari, pp. 385-91, 410-11). Though the Ismaʿilis of Alamut soon reverted back to the Islamic fold, and even for a while to Sunnism, the messianic spirit of the movement persisted in the Iranian environment. The hermeneutical binary of the inward (*bāṭen*), silent (*ṣāmet*) Imam, and his speaker (*nāṭeq*) in the outward (*ẓāher*) sphere offered the ideal theological format. The fall of Alamut and the collapse of the Ismaʿili fortress "state" in 1258 during the second wave of the Mongol invasion brought this phase to an end (Daftary, pp. 281-98; see also IRAN ix/2.1 and 2.2).

The third phase. The catastrophic Mongol invasion and destruction of major Iranian cities of Khorasan and central Iran during the first half of the 13th century, and the collapse of the ʿAbbasid caliphate of Baghdad in 1260, generated dispersed messianic currents often within the broad framework of popular Sufism and was instrumental in shaping radical Sufi orders both in the Iranian center and on the western periphery (see IRAN ix/2.2. Mongol Period). This phase of messianic activities has not yet been fully explored. It is possible that the post-Alamut dispersed Isma^cilism influenced the Mahdi aspirations of the Ilkhanid and the Timurid periods through the doctrine of the Perfect Man (*ensān-e kāmel*). More explicitly, it may have contributed to the thriving apocalyptic synthesis of the late 14th- and early 15th-century Iran and Anatolia ranging from Horufism (q.v.) to the Noqṭawi, the Nurbaḵši, and the Mošaʿšaʿi movements—often with ultra-Islamic aspirations. Other trends such as the Qalandari movement and the more politically active Juriya dervish order and the associated Twelver Shiʿite Sarbadāri state in Khorasan also manifested strong messianic aspirations. This most intense episode of apocalyptic activity in the history of Iran, especially after the fragmentation of the Timurid Empire, may be attributed to a new revolutionary synthesis that aimed to embrace Iran's geopolitical and cultural identity at the beginning of the early modern times. The Safavid dynasty, the final product of this grand synthesis, came about as a result of a slow transformation of a Sufi quietist Sunni order in the 13th century to a militant Shiʿite messianic movement in the latter half of the 15th century. The Safavid revolution successfully fused the extremist (*ḡolow*) tendency of the Qezelbāš military confederacy—itself charged with anthropomorphic aspirations of the Ahl-e Ḥaqq (q.v.) pastoral religion of northwestern Iran—with the Shariʿa-oriented Twelver Shiʿism of Iran proper and the adjacent Arab lands. The latter current, which was on the rise since the late Il-khanid era, though devoid of any messianic contingency, condoned the claims of Esmāʿil I (q.v.; r. 1501-24), the founder of the Safavid dynasty, to a Mahdi status and even his implied claims to divine manifestation. The Qezelbāš, on the other hand, were devoted to Esmāʿil as their Perfect Guide (*moršd-e kāmel*) who in their eyes equaled or even rose above the status of the Mahdi (see IRAN ix/2.3; see also ḠOLĀT).

The fourth phase. This phase of Iranian messianic activities stretches from the middle of the 16th century to late 19th century. With the ascendancy of Twelver Shiʿite juristic and later ritualistic orthodoxy in the 16th and 17th centuries and the Safavid patronage for the jurist class, came first the suppression of the revived Noqṭawi movement at the turn of the Islamic millennium (1593-94) and soon after the elimination of the Qezelbāš and by the late 17th century the purging of nearly all other Sufi tendencies that often harbored latent anti-clerical sentiments along with messianic aspirations. Likewise, the millennial speculations of philosophers of the School of Isfahan were safely aborted. Later, with the collapse of the Safavid state in 1722, and the ensuing crisis of legitimacy that continued on and off until the end of the 18th century, latent messianic aspirations were rekindled. Some pretenders to the Safavid throne, shrouding themselves in Sufi garb, entertained vague messianic claims. The revived Neʿmat-Allāhi order in the latter part of the 18th century was also infused with messianic aspirations. Mir ʿAbd-al-Hamid Maʿṣum-ʿAlišah and Mohammad-ʿAli Nur-ʿAlišah Eṣfāhani made claims to the deputyship of the Mahdi (*niābat*) and even to the status of being a latent Mahdi (see IRAN ix/2.3; Amanat, 1989, pp. 71-83 and cited sources).

The prevalence of the Oṣuli school and the emergence of the *mojtahed* (see EJTEHĀD) establishment in the early Qajar period, and the tacit alliance forged with the Qajar state, created an atmosphere of growing intolerance for alternative thought, which included Aḵbāriya (q.v.) school, Sufism, and the Šayḵi school of theology (see AḤSĀʾĪ), whose doctrines of the Perfect Shiʿa (*šiʿa-ye kāmel*) became the prominent loci for speculative messianism in early 19th century. The Babi movement (see BABISM), no doubt the most conscious and the most explicit messianic current since the rise of the Safavids, was the outcome of nearly half a century of millennial speculations and renewed engagement with Shiʿite hermeneutics within and outside the Šayḵi school. The claim of Sayyed ʿAli-Mohammad Širāzi first to be the Bāb "Gate" (see BĀB) to the Imam of the Age and in 1264/1848 his open claim to be the promised millennial Mahdi, opened the way for an apocalyptic break with Islam and the beginning of a new Bayāni dispensation (see BAYĀN). The movement's broad appeal to the socially deprived and discontented within the clerical class and beyond to include women, petty merchants, and the guilds, made Babism the most explicitly messianic current in modern Iranian history. Harassed and persecuted by both the Shiʿite ulama and the Qajar state, the Babis (see BABISM) shift to radical millenarianism eventually resulted in armed confrontation with the state, culminating in the destruction of its leadership, exile and banishment, and more than half a century of underground dissent (see Amanat, 1989). In the later Bahai phase (see BAHAI FAITH), the claim of Bahāʾ-Allāh (q.v.) to be the "locus of all divine manifestations" can be seen as further unfolding of the Babi messianic break with Islam. In due course, the formative Bahai thought adopted in the latter half of the 19th century a universalistic message of moral humanism and religious reconciliation, while the rival Azali Babis advocated political dissent and active engagement with the progressive Shiʿite clerical elements, thereby exerting some influence in the early shaping of the Constitutional Revolution (q.v.). The Babi movement and its aftermath may be considered as a unique experience not only in the Shiʿite context but also in the history of Muslim reform movements for attempting to forge an endogenous form of religious modernity beyond the accepted precepts of normative Islam (see Amanat, 1998, pp. 241-48).

The fifth phase. The final period of Iranian messianic activity may be traced back to militant Islamic activism of the 1970s culminating in the Islamic revolution of 1979 and its aftermath. The invasion of Iran by the Iraqi forces in particular helped sharpen the revolution's latent messianic and apocalyptic aspirations. Even though the leader of the revolution, Ayatollah Khomeini, never entertained an explicit messianic claim, he was viewed by his followers as the deputy of the Imam (*nāʾeb-e emām*) and was recognized as such in the literature and propaganda of the Islamic Republic. This is distinct from the collective deputyship of the Imam of the Age (*niābat-e ʿāmm*) claimed by the Shiʿite mojtaheds at least since the 16th century. More commonly, he came to be known with the popular title of "Imam," the first ever in the history of Twelver Shiʿism, which also implied a latent messianic status, albeit an ambiguous one. Moreover, familiar messianic motifs of Qurʾānic origin also emerged during the revolution with great evocative power including the labeling of the Pahlavi establishment as the apocalyptic Evil (*Ṭāḡut*) and that of the United States as the Great Satan (*Šayṭān-e bozorg*). The revolution itself, and the assumed struggle against the forces of "global arrogance" (*estekbār-e jahāni*), was seen as an apocalyptic challenge. Some factions within the revolutionary forces such as the Ḥojjatiya Society (q.v.), which since the 1960s harbored messianic beliefs infused with anti-Bahai sentiments, viewed the revolution as a prelude to the advent of the Imam of the Age. Persistence of messianic motifs in the post-revolutionary years may be attributed to the potency of messianic paradigm in the Iranian religious culture that were once more triggered by frustrated expectations regarding the outcome of the Islamic Revolution and the apparent failure of the government to tackle the current economic and social problems. At the same time, the recent resort to messianic motifs may also be seen as part of a calculated policy to compensate for the diminishing fervor of the ideological Islam of the revolutionary days by actively encouraging among other things the thriving cult of Jamkarān (q.v.) shrine near the city of Qom, which is dedicated to the Hidden Imam (see Moṭahhari, 1975, IV, pp. 62-840, for his discussion on resurrection [*maʿād*] and his debates with Mahdi Bāzargān during late 1960s).

State of scholarship. Critical episodes of Iranian messianism, including early Islamic era, development of Ismaʿili and Twelver Shiʿite messianism, the Safavid movements, and the Babi movement have been subject of numerous Western studies from as early as the middle of the 19th century. Late medieval trends such as Ḥorufi, Noqṭawi, Nurbaḵši, and Sarbadāri movements have also received scholarly attention in recent years, as have aspects of speculative messianism and the doctrine of Occultation in the Twelver Shiʿite tradition. Muslim authors of the past, such as Ebn Ḵaldun (q.v.), also devoted some attention to the phenomenon of the Mahdi in Shiʿism. Yet theoretical study of Iranian messianism as a cultural paradigm and its social, political, and cultural implications remains to be further explored (see Amanat, 2002).

Bibliography: For a selection of primary sources on Mahdism, see John Alden Williams, ed., pp. 189-251; J. Macdonald, a series of seven articles.

For surveys on Messianism in Islam and Iran, see Abbas Amanat, 1998; Jan-Olaf Blichfeldt; James Darmesteter; Wilferd Madelung; Abdulaziz A. Sachedina.

On Shiʿi Mahdism and the Occultation, see Said Amir Arjomand, 1996; Mohammad Ali Amir-Moezzi; Hossein Modarresi, pp. 53-105; Abdulaziz A. Sachedina, pp. 78-183.

For Shiʿite messianism in the early modern period, see Said Amir Arjomand, 1984, pp. 66-104; Heinz Halm, tr., pp. 71-91; Abbas Amanat, 1998.

For a summary of the Babi-Bahaʾi doctrine, see Bahāʾ-Allāh; Browne, 1889; Cole; Peter Smith.

For Khomeini and the ideology of the Islamic Revolution, see Said Amir Arjomand, 1988, pp. 91-102, 147-88; Shaul Bakhash; Henry Munson.

Sources. Abbas Amanat, *Resurrection and Renewal: The Making of the Babi Movement in Iran, 1844-1850*, Ithaca, 1989. Idem, "The Nuqṭawī Movement of Maḥmūd Pisīkhānī and His Persian Cycle of Mystical-Materialism," in Farhad Daftary, ed., *Mediaeval Ismaʿili History and Thought*, Cambridge, 1996, pp. 281-97. Idem, "The Emergence of Apocalyptic in Modern Islam," in Stephen J. Stein, ed., The *Encyclopedia of Apocalypticism* III: *Apocalypticism in the Modern Period and the Contemporary Age*, New York, 1998, pp. 230-64. Idem, "Apocalyptic Anxieties and Millennial Hopes in the Salvation Religions of the Middle East," in A. Amanat and M. Bernhardsson, eds., *Imagining the End: Visions of Apocalypse from the Ancient Middle East to Modern America*, London and New York, 2002, pp. 1-22. Said Amir Arjomand, *The Shadow of God and the Hidden Imam: Religion, Political Order and Societal Change in Shiʿi Iran from the Beginning to 1890*. Chicago, 1984. Idem, *The Turban for the Crown: Islamic Revolution in Iran*, New York, 1988. Idem, "The Crisis of Imamate and the Institution of Occultation in Twelver Shiʿism: A Sociohistorical Perspective," *IJMES* 28, 1996, pp. 491-515. Mohammad Ali Amir-Moezzi, *Le guide divin dans le Shîʿisme original: aux sources de l'ésotérisme en Islam*, Lagrasse, 1992; tr. David Stright as *Divine Guide in Early Shi'ism: The Sources of Esotericism in Islam*, Albany, 1994. Kathryn Babayan, *Mystics, Monarchs and Messiahs: Cultural Landscape of Early Modern Iran*, Cambridge, Mass., 2002. ʿA. Bāqi, *Dar šenāḵt-e ḥezb-e qāʾedin-e zamān*, Tehran, 1984. Bašir-al-Din Maḥmud Aḥmad, *Daʿwat al-amir*; tr. as *Invitation to Ahmadiyyat: Being a Statement of Beliefs, a Rationale of Claims, and an Invitation on Behalf of Ahmadiyya Movement for the Propagation and Rejuvenation of Islam*, London, 1980. Mahdi Bāzargān, *Rāh-e ṭayy šoda*, Tehran, 1959. Idem, *Zarra-ye bi-entehā*, Tehran, 1966. Jan-Olaf Blichfeldt, *Early Mahdism: Politics and Religion in the Formative Period of Islam*, Leiden, 1985. Edward G. Browne, "The Babis of Persia II: Their Literature and Doctrines," *JRAS* 21, 1889, pp. 881-933; repr. in idem, *Selections from the Writings of E. G. Browne on the Bābī and the Bahāʾī Religions*, ed. Moojan Momen, Oxford, 1987, pp. 187-239. Idem, ed., *Kitáb-i Nuqṭatu'l-Káf: Being the Earliest History of the Babis Compiled by Hájjí Mírzá Jáni of Káshán Between the Years A.D. 1850 and 1852*, Leyden, 1910 (Pers. original of an early history of the movement and apologia with introduction and index of the Bab's Persian *Bayān*). S. Bashir, *Messianic Hopes and Mystical Visions: the Nurbaskhshiya between Medieval and Modern Islam*, New York, 2003. Juan Ricardo I. Cole,

Modernity and the Millennium: The Genesis of the Bahaʿi Faith in the Nineteenth Century Middle East, New York, 1998. Idem, "Millenarianism in Modern Iranian History," in A. Amanat and M. Bernhardsson ed. *Imagining the End*, London and New York, 2002, pp. 282-311. Henri Corbin, *Terre céleste et corps de resurrection de l'Iran mazdéen à l'Iran shîʿite*, Paris, 1960; tr. Nancy Pearson as *Spiritual Body and Celestial Earth from Mazdean Iran to Shiʿite Iran*, Princeton, 1977 (a broad selection of philosophical writings on eschatology and apocalypse with two introductory chapters demonstrating continuity in the Iranian millennial tradition). Farhad Daftary, *The Ismaʿilis: Their History and Doctrines*, Cambridge, 1990. James Darmesteter, *Le Mahdi depuis les origines de l islam jusqu'r nos fours*, Paris, 1885. Heinz Halm, *Die Schia*, Darmstadt, 1988; tr. as *Shiism*, Edinburgh, 1991. Marshall G. S. Hodgson, *The Venture of Islam*, 3 vols. Chicago, 1974. Idem, *The Order of Assassins*, The Hague, 1955. Ayatollah Ruḥ-Allāh Musawi Ḵomeyni, *Welāyat-e faqih*, Tehran, 1978; tr. and annotated by Hamid Algar as *Islam and Revolution: Writings and Declarations of Imam Khomeini*, Berkeley, Cal., 1981. J. Macdonald, "The Creation of Man and Angels in the Escatological Literature," *Islamic Studies* 2, 1964, pp. 285-308 (tr. of excerpts from an unpublished collection of traditions). Idem, "The Angel of Death in Late Islamic Tradition," *Islamic Studies* 3, 1964, pp. 485-519. Idem, "The Twilight of the Dead," *Islamic Studies* 4, 1965, pp. 5.5-102. Idem, "The Preliminaries to the Resurrection and Judgment," *Islamic Studies* 4, 1965, pp. 137-79. Idem, "The Day of Resurrection," *Islamic Studies* 5, 1966, pp. 129-97. Idem, "Paradise," *Islamic Studies* 5, 1966, pp. 331-83. Wilferd Madelung, "al-Mahdi," in *EI*² V, pp. 1230-38. Hossein Modarresi, *Crisis and Consolidation in the Formative Period of Shiʿite Islam: Abū Jaʿfar ibn Qiba al-Rāzī and His Contribution to Imamite Shiʿite Thought*, Princeton, 1993, pp. 53-10. Mortażā Moṭahhari, *Qiām wa enqelāb-e mahdi az didgāh-e falsafa-ye tāriḵ*, Tehran, 1975. Idem, *Majmuʿa-ye āṯār*, 4 vols., Tehran, 1995. Henry Munson, *Islam and Revolution in the Middle East*, New Haven, 1988. Abdulaziz A. Sachedina, *Islamic Messianism: The Idea of the Mahdi in Twelver Shi'ism*, Albany, 1981. Golam Hossein Sadighi, *Les mouvements religieux iraniens au IIe et au IIIe siècle de l'hégire*, Paris, 1938; incomp. Pers. version by the author as *Jonbešhā-ye dini-e Irāni dar qarnhā-ye dovvom wa sevvom-e hejri*, pub. posthumously, Tehran, 1993. Ṣadr-al-Din Širāzi (Mollā Ṣadrā), *Ḥekmat al-ʿaršiya*, tr. with commentary, James W. Morris as *The Wisdom of the Throne: An Introduction to the Philosophy of Mulla Sadra*, Princeton, 1981. Peter Smith, *The Babi and Bahaʾi Religions from Messianic Shiism to a World Religion*, Cambridge, 1987. John Alden Williams, ed., *Themes of Islamic Civilization*, Berkeley, Cal. 1971. Ehsan Yarshater, "Mazdakism," in *Camb. Hist. Ir.* III/2, 1983, pp. 991-1024.

(ABBAS AMANAT)

vi. THE CONCEPT OF MAHDI IN SUNNI ISLAM

The Savior is a descendant of the Prophet whose expected return to rule the world will restore justice, peace, and true religion. The Twelver Shiʿites believe him to be the Twelfth Imam who is in occultation (see ḠAYBA) until his reappearance at the end of time (see 2 below).

Although derived from the root, *h-d-y*, which appears many times and in a variety of forms in the Qurʾān, the actual term *mahdi*, meaning "the rightly-guided one," does not occur in the Qurʾān. Most probably, it entered Islam as an apocalyptic term from the southern Arabian tribes who settled in Syria under Moʿāwiya (governor during the caliphate of ʿOṯmān b. ʿAffān, r. 644-56). They expected "the Mahdi who will lead the rising people of the Yemen back to their country" (Marwazi, p. 244) in order to restore the glory of their lost Himyarite kingdom. It was believed that he would eventually conquer Constantinople. This Mahdi would be followed by the "Qaḥṭāni" (also called the "Yamāni"), who would lead the Yemenite tribes in fierce warfare against the Qorayš, destroying the latter (ibid., pp. 236-39, 242, 246). The Qaḥṭāni is said to be the brother of the Mahdi in some traditions, while other traditions separate him from a second Mahdi who would be the conqueror of Constantinople (ibid., pp. 243-45, 247, 249).

The more generally recognized appearance of the term dates from the Second Civil War (*fetna*; 680-92). It was first used in a messianic sense during the rebellion of Moḵtār in Kufa in 683 on behalf of a son of ʿAli b. Abi Ṭāleb (q.v.), Moḥammad b. al-Ḥanafiya (d. 700). Its messianic connotation probably emerged from two distinct groups of his supporters who became known as the Kaysāniya: southern Arabian tribes settled in Iraq, and Persian and Mesopotamian clients (*mawāli*) who were new converts to Islam.

The Kaysāniya spread two other ideas that became closely associated with the belief in the Mahdi. The first was the idea of *rajʿa* (q.v.), or return of the dead, especially of the Imams. The second was the idea of *ḡayba* (occultation). When Moḥammad b. al-Ḥanafiya died in 700, the Kaysāniya maintained that he was in occultation in the Rażwā mountains west of Medina, and would one day return as the Mahdi and the Qāʾem (q.v.). The Kaysāni poet Koṯayyer (d. 723) hailed him as "the Mahdi, whom Kaʿb, the brother/fellow of the Aḥbār, had told us about," and affirmed that "he has vanished in the Rażwā, not to be seen for a while, and with him is honey and water" (Masʿudi, III, p. 277).

It is probably in connection with the expectation of the return of this Mahdi from occultation that the term *Qāʾem* (the Standing One, the Riser) gained currency in the Shiʿite apocalyptic tradition. What is certain is that the apocalyptic figure in the early Shiʿite traditions is the Qāʾem (Modarresi, p. 6). He is represented as the expected redresser of the cause of God (*al-qāʾem be amr Allāh*), and the riser by the sword (*al-qāʾem be'l-sayf*). He is the Lord of the Sword (*ṣāḥeb al-sayf*, see Ṣaffār, p. 151) and the avenger of the wrong done to the House of Moḥammad by the usurpers of their rights. This picture can be supplemented by the early Imami Shiʿite traditions which present the Qāʾem as the redresser of the house of Moḥammad (*qāʾem āl Moḥammad*; see Majlesi, LI, pp. 49-54, and Arjomand 1998, p. 252, for further references). The Qāʾem would establish the Empire of Truth (*dawlat al-ḥaqq*; see Majlesi, LI, pp. 62-63).

It should be noted that the apocalyptic politics of the Second Civil War prompted its pious opponents to promote an anti-apocalyptic conception of the Mahdi. The most important proponent of the anti-apocalyptic idea of the Mahdi was ʿAbd-Allāh, son of the famous disciple Zobayr, who declared himself caliph in Mecca. The dispersal in the desert in 683 of an army sent by the Umayyad caliph Yazid (r. 680-83) against the anti-caliph ʿAbd-Allāh b. al-Zobayr, upon hearing the news of Yazid's death, generated what may be the first *ex eventu* prophecy about an unnamed restorer of faith who was later taken to be the Mahdi. Two notable historical features of the event—the pledge of allegiance by the people of Mecca between the Rokn Yamāni and the Maqām Ebrāhim, and the swallowing up (*ḵasf*) of an army in the desert (between Mecca and Medina)—were absorbed into the apocalyptic literature as parts of the image of the Mahdi (Madelung, 1981). Musā (son of the disciple Ṭalḥa), too, was proposed by his circle as the Mahdi after he fled from Kufa during Moḵtār's rebellion to Basra (Ebn Saʿd V, pp. 120-21). Two generations later, the Umayyad ʿOmar II b. ʿAbd-al-ʿAziz (r. 717-20) was said to be the Mahdi. In a conversation between him and ʿAbd-Allāh b. ʿOmar, even Moḥammad b. al-Ḥanafiya himself is made to say that any man who is with integrity (*ṣāleḥan*) can be called "the rightly-guided one" (Marwazi, pp. 229-30). Furthermore, the pious opposition to the revolutionary Mahdism of the followers of Moḥammad b. al-Ḥanafiya found a resource in the belief in the Second Coming of Jesus. A tradition attributed to Ḥasan al-Baṣri (d. 728), who was a leading figure in this opposition, categorically states: "There will be no Mahdi other than Jesus son of Maryam" (Marwazi, pp. 230-31). This tradition has survived the avalanche of later traditions that affirm the return of both Jesus and the Mahdi. The appropriation of the notion of Mahdi in a non-apocalyptic form by Sunni Islam was largely the result of this pious opposition to the Shiʿite notion of the Qāʾem, which remained emphatically apocalyptic.

The image of the Prophet was also projected unto the Mahdi. An enormously influential tradition attributed to ʿAbd-Allāh b. Masʿud has Moḥammad foretell the coming of a Mahdi coined in his own image: "His name will be my name, and his father's name my father's name" (Marwazi, p. 227). Furthermore, widespread traditions assert that the number of the Mahdi's companions in battle is exactly the same (usually put at 313) as those of Moḥammad in the apocalyptic Battle of Badr (ibid., p. 213; Majlesi LI, pp. 44, 55, 58). One Sunni tradition goes even further and affirms that "on his shoulder is the mark of the Prophet" (Marwazi, p. 226), while some Shiʿite traditions have the Archangel Gabriel to the right of the Mahdi on the battlefield, and the Archangel Michael to his left, just as with Moḥammad at Badr (Majlesi LII, p. 311).

It is well known that the ʿAlid and the ʿAbbasid branches of the House of Moḥammad (see AHL-E BAYT) vied for the leadership of the revolutionary movement that overthrew the Umayyad caliphate. However, the intense apocalyptic character of the ʿAbbasid revolution (744-63) remains largely unrecognized. There is firm evidence for the assumption of the title of Mahdi by the first ʿAbbasid caliph, Abu'l-ʿAbbās (r. 749-54), and for his claim to be the Qāʾem, even though this evidence has been generally overlooked (Duri, pp. 128, 136; see Arjomand 1998, p. 278, n. 34 for other references). The culmination of the revolutionary apocalypticism of the period for the ʿAlids was the uprising, in 762, of Moḥammad b. ʿAbd-Allāh al-Nafs al-Zakiya (the "Pure Soul"), the namesake of the Prophet foretold in the above-mentioned Mahdist tradition whom the ʿAbbasids themselves had accepted as the Qāʾem and the Mahdi of the House of Moḥammad before coming to power. ʿAbd-Allāh, the father of the Mahdi and the head of the Hasanid descendants of ʿAli, claimed to be in possession of the sword and the armor of the Prophet, which would evidently be put at the disposal of his son as the Lord of the Sword. The long delayed rebellion of the Mahdi of the House of Moḥammad in Arabia in 762 was followed by that of his brother Ebrāhim, who assumed the title of the *Hādi*, in Iraq. The wide following of the Hasanid Mahdi included an "extremist" (*ḡāli*, see ḠOLĀT) group, the Moḡiriya, who considered him the Qāʾem-Mahdi and with whom he had been in hiding in the mountain of Tamiya before his uprising. After his death and the suppression of his uprising, the Moḡiriya claimed that he was alive and immortal, and was residing in the same mountain (Ašʿari, p. 76). A large number of traditions about the return of the Qāʾem that had been generated by the followers of al-Nafs al-Zakiya were absorbed into the corpus of Imami Shiʿite traditions, the most notable being the above-mentioned ʿAbd-Allāh b. Masʿud tradition which made him the namesake of the Prophet: "The name of the [divinely-] guided Qāʾem (*al-qāʾem al-mahdi*) is my name, and his father's name, the name of my father. He will fill the world with justice as it is filled with oppression" (Ašʿari, p. 76; Ṭusi, p. 112).

Although Jaʿfar al-Ṣādeq (d. 765), the sixth Imam of the Imami Shiʿites and head of the Ḥosaynid branch of the ʿAlids, denied his Hasanid cousin's claim, and reportedly asserted that he himself had inherited the sword and armor of the Prophet from his grandfather and was holding them in his house (Ṣaffār, pp. 150-53, 184), he was apparently not able to prevent his own sons from joining the uprising of the al-Nafs al-Zakiya. Jaʿfar's son and later the seventh Imam, Musā al-Kāẓem (d. 799), is reported among the participants, and in fact learned to harness its persisting political Messianism to longer term designs of his own, albeit more subtly. Musā al-Kāẓem competed in clandestine political activism with the surviving Zaydi followers of his cousin, the al-Nafs al-Zakiya. There is ample evidence in the early Shiʿite books on sects to prove that he followed the example of the latter in claiming to be the

Qāʾem-Mahdi, although the Imami compendia of traditions have systematically expunged the traces of this claim. His two periods of imprisonment gave rise to the idea, circulated by his followers, that the Qāʾem would undergo two occultations, a short one followed by a longer one extending to his rising. (Modarresi, pp. 10, 87) Several groups of Musā's followers who became known as the Wāqefiya (cessationists) refused to accept that he had died, and/or maintained instead that he was the Qāʾem and the Mahdi and had gone into occultation (Modarresi, pp. 60, 87; Arjomand 1996a; 1996b, p. 557).

The Wāqefiya's identification of the Qāʾem with the Mahdi was resisted for quite some time, prompting an inquisitive believer to ask the ninth Imam, Moḥammad al-Jawād (d. 835), if the Qāʾem was in fact the Mahdi or someone else (Ebn Bābawayh, p. 377; Modarressi, p. 91). Modarressi considers the introduction of the idea of the Mahdi to have taken place very slowly after the death of the eleventh Imam and the severe crisis of succession that resulted from it, and he gives (p. 89, n. 194) some illustrations of later insertions of the term Mahdi into the Qāʾem traditions. In any event, during the indefinite occultation of the twelfth Imam (see ĠAYBA; Arjomand, 1997) many of the Mahdi traditions were eventually absorbed into the collection of Imami traditions by being assimilated to, or compounded with, the Qāʾem traditions. According to the Imami doctrine that took shape in the 10th and 11th centuries, the Twelfth Imam is the Mahdi, who is in occultation and will reappear at the end of time (Arjomand, 1996b).

The development of the doctrine of the Imamate (q.v.) as a central component of Imami rational theology (*kalām*) in the same period allowed for the development of religious juristic authority that upheld a Shiʿite nomocracy against future claimants to Mahdi-hood. Nevertheless, Mahdism is more endemic in the Shiʿite tradition, especially in the Persianate world. Notable among the later claimants to Mahdi-hood in the period following the massive spread of Sufism were Sayyed Fażl-Allāh Astarābādi (q.v., d. 1394), the founder of the Ḥorufi (see ḤORUFISM) movement (Bashir, 2000, pp. 292-93), Sayyed Moḥammad b. Fallāḥ (d. 1462), the founder of the extremist Mošaʿšaʿ sect, and Sayyed Moḥammad Nurbaḵš (d. 1464), the initiator of the Nurbaḵšiya Sufi movement in Persia and Central Asia (Bashir, 2003, chap. 2; see also Arjomand, 1984, chap. 2). The Safavid Empire, founded in 1501, had its origins in a similar Mahdist movement (Arjomand, 2005), and the Qajar era was marked by the claim of Mirzā ʿAli-Moḥammad of Shiraz (see BĀB, d. 1850) to be the Qāʾem-Mahdi, and the millennial uprisings it generated.

Numerous claimants to Mahdi-hood have risen in Sunnism, too, especially, as Ebn Ḵaldun (d. 1406) noted (Ebn Ḵaldun, pp. 342-48), in the milieu of Sufism. The Sunni Mahdis include Ebn Tumart (d. 1130), the founder of the Almohad movement, and the Sudanese Mahdi, Moḥammad Aḥmad (d. 1885); John Voll has constructed a distinct ideal type of "frontier Mahdism" for the modern period (Voll, pp. 145-66).

Bibliography: S. A. Arjomand, *The Shadow of God and the Hidden Imam: Religion, Political Organization and Societal Change in Shiite Iran from the Beginning to 1890*, Chicago and London, 1984. Idem, "Crisis of the Imamate and the Institution of Occultation in Twelver Shiʿism: A Sociohistorical Perspective," *IJMES* 28/4, 1996a, pp. 491-515. Idem, "The Consolation of Theology: The Shiʿite Doctrine of Occultation and the Transition from Chiliasm to Law," *Journal of Religion*, 76/4, 1996b, pp. 548-71. Idem, "Imam *Absconditus* and the Beginnings of a Theology of Occultation: Imami Shiʿism Around 900 CE/280-290 AH," *JAOS* 117/1, 1997, pp. 1-13. Idem, "Islamic Apocalypticism in the Classical Period," in B. McGinn, ed., *The Encyclopedia of Apocalypticism*, New York, 1998, II, pp. 238-83. Idem, "The Rise of Shāh Esmāʿil as a Mahdist Revolution," *Studies on Persianate Societies* 3, 2005 (forthcoming). Saʿd b. ʿAbd-Allāh Ašʿari Qomi, *Ketāb al-maqālāt wa 'l-feraq*, ed. M.-J. Maškur, ed., Tehran, 1963. Sh. Bashir, "Enshrining Divinity: The Death and Memorialization of Fażlallāh Astarābādī in Ḥūrūfī Thought," *The Muslim World* 90/3-4, 2000, pp. 289-308. Idem, *Messianic Hope and Mystical Visions: The Nurbakhshiyya Between Medieval and Modern Islam*, Columbia, S.C., 2003. ʿA.-ʿA. Duri, "al-Fekra al-mahdiya bayn al-daʿwa al-ʿabbāsiya wa 'l-ʿaṣr al-ʿabbāsi al-awwal," in Wadād al-Kadi, ed., *Studia Islamica and Arabica: Festschrift for Iḥsān ʿAbbās*, Beirut, 1981. ʿAbd-al-Raḥmān Ebn Ḵaldun, *Tāriḵ-e Ebn Ḵaldun (Ketāb al-ʿEbar)*, Beirut, vol. 1, pp. 342-48. Abu Jaʿfar Moḥammad b. ʿAli Ebn Bābawayh Qomi, *Kamāl al-din wa tamām al-neʿma fi eṯbāt al-ġayba wa kašf al-ḥayra*, ed. ʿA.-A. Ğefāri, Tehran, 1975. Ebn Saʿd. W. Madelung, "ʿAbd Allāh b. al-Zubayr and the Mahdi," *JNES* 40/4, 1981, pp. 291-305. Idem, "Mahdi," in *EI²* V, pp. 1230-38. Moḥammad-Bāqer Majlesi, *Beḥār al-anwār*, 110 vols., Beirut, 1983. Noʿaym b. Ḥammād al-Marwazi, *Ketāb al-fetan*, ed. S. Zakkār, Mecca, 1991. Masʿudi, *Moruj*, ed. Pellat. H. Modarressi, *Crisis and Consolidation in the Formative Period of Shiʿite Islam*, Princeton, N.J., 1993. Moḥammad b. Ḥasan Ṣaffār al-Qomi, *Baṣāʾer al-darajāt*, Qom, 1983-84. Moḥammad b. Ḥasan al-Ṭusi, *Ketāb al-ġayba*, ed. A. B. Tehrāni, Najaf, 1965. John Voll, "The Sudanese Mahdi: Frontier Fundamentalism," *International Journal of Middle East Studies* 10/2, 1979, pp. 145-66.

(SAID AMIR ARJOMAND)

vii. THE CONCEPT OF MAHDI IN TWELVER SHIʿISM

Mahdism in Twelver Shiʿism inherited many of its elements from previous religious trends. Without necessarily going back to Zoroastrianism, Manichaeism, Judaism, and Christianity, to which generally eschatology, messianism, and the apocalyptic in Islam owe many of their doctrines and elements (Darmesteter, introduction; Margoliouth, pp. 125-28), one can think of numerous Shiʿite and non-Shiʿite sects that existed prior to the definitive transition from earlier Imamism to Twelver Shiʿism in the first half of the 10th century (Kohlberg 1976, passim). In the study that follows, a descriptive introduction to the doctrines will be accompanied by an overview of the contribution of these borrowed elements in order to better appreciate the historical development and evolution of the articles of faith.

Hesitation and progressive development of Mahdism. According to the traditional date most often retained, Imam Ḥasan ʿAskari (q.v.), the eleventh Imam, died in 874. His death, like that of previous Imams, gave rise to a period of turbulence among the faithful, but this time the crisis seemed even more serious and the Imamis did not themselves hesitate to call the decades that were to follow "the period of perplexity" or "confusion" (*ḥayra*; Modarressi, introduction). The mysterious fate of the presumed son of the eleventh Imam led to several schisms with notable doctrinal variances. Some groups claimed that his son died at a very young age, others that he had lived until a certain age and then died, and still others simply denied his very existence, believing that Ḥasan ʿAskari never had a son. Only a small minority supported the idea that the son of the eleventh imam was alive, that he was in "occultation," and that he was to reappear as *mahdi* (Ar. "the Guided One") at "the end of time" (*āḵer al-zamān*). This idea was gradually adopted by all Imamis, who thus became known as "Twelvers" (Nowbaḵti, pp. 90 ff.; Ašʿari Qomi, pp. 102 ff.: Kohlberg, 1976, passim; Sachedina 1981, pp. 42-55; Hussain, pp. 56-67). Sources from this period, reflect, in their particular manner, the hesitation and crisis believers experienced. A close study of these sources indeed seems to show that profound uncertainties and serious lacunae existed regarding a substantial number of important doctrinal elements that became articles of faith. First, the definitive number of Imams and even the notion of "occultation" (*ḡayba*, q.v.): Abu Jaʿfar Barqi (d. 887 or 893), in his *Ketāb al-maḥāsen*, contributes no information regarding these two points. In the first chapter, dedicated to different interpretations of numbers, he takes into account the numbers 3 to 10, but says nothing about the number 12 (Barqi, I, pp. 3-13). A few decades later, Ebn Bābuya (Ebn Bābawayh, q.v.; 923-91), known as Shaikh Ṣaduq, in his *Ketāb al-ḵeṣāl*, reported many traditions regarding the number 12, some among them about twelve Imams (Ebn Bābuya, 1950, II, pp. 264-329). Barqi's contemporary, Ṣaffār Qomi (d. 902-3) in his *Baṣāʾer al-darajāt* (pp. 280, 319-20, 372) mentions only five traditions from a total of almost 2,000 regarding the notion that the Imams were to be twelve in number, and he reports nothing about the occultation. The oldest text of certain authenticity that we have, in which a complete list of the twelve Imams is found, seems to be the *Tafsir* by ʿAli b. Ebrāhim Qomi (d. ca. 919; Qomi, II, p. 44), a work written some years after what would finally be termed the "Minor Occultation" (see below).

It is only from Kolayni's (d. 940-41) hadith collection onwards that traditions regarding the definitive number of Imams, and the occultation of the twelfth Imam became more frequent. Even so, a study of chains of transmission (*esnād*) of these traditions, not only in Kolayni, but also in the two voluminous monographs by his famous successors, namely *Ketāb al-ḡayba* by Ebn Abi Zaynab Noʿmāni (d. ca. 956 or 971), and *Kamāl al-din* by Ebn Bābuya (see bibliography), reveal that elements of older books on the *ḡayba* belonging to other Shiʿite trends had been appropriated in the service of the cause, and were adapted to Twelver Shiʿite doctrines (Hussain, pp. 2-6; Amir-Moezzi, 1996, esp. pp. 115 ff.). As examples, one can cite the following names of transmitters: Ebrāhim b. Ṣāleḥ Anmāṭi, disciple of the fifth Imam, Moḥammad Bāqer, authored a book on the occultation and considered the latter as the hidden Mahdi (Najāši, pp. 12, 19; Ṭusi, 1972, p. 14). Among the Wāqefis of the seventh Imam Musā Kāẓem (i.e., those who ended the lineage of the Imams at the latter and considered him as the Mahdi), were ʿAli b. Ḥasan Ṭāṭari Ṭāʿi and Ḥasan b. Moḥammad b. Somāʿa, both authors of works on the *ḡayba* (Najāši, pp. 193 and 39 respectively; Ṭusi 1972, pp. 216-17 on the first mentioned author). Another "Sevener" transmitter (Wāqefi or Ismaʿili?), Moḥammad b. Moṯannā Ḥażrami (fl. 9th cent.), author of a *Ketāb* that is part of the "400 original texts" (*al-oṣul al-arbaʿomeʾa*) of the Imamis, reports a tradition by Jaʿfar Ṣādeq according to which the number of Imams is limited to seven, with the final one to be the Mahdi (*al-oṣul al-arbaʿomeʾa*, fol. 53b; regarding this collection see Kohlberg, 1987). Ḥasan b. ʿAli Baṭāʾeni Kufi, like his father, served as Wāqefi of the eighth Imam ʿAli al-Reżā (q.v.). He was the author of a work bearing the title *Ketāb al-Ḡayba* (Ṭehrāni, XVI, p. 76, no. 382). Abu Saʿid ʿOṣfuri (d. 864), a contemporary of the tenth and eleventh Imams is the author of another *Ketāb* from the "400 original texts" in which he speaks of eleven Imams (though avoiding naming them), with the last to be the Mahdi (*al-oṣul al-arbaʿomeʾa*, fol. 10a ff.; also *Ketāb Abu Saʿid al-ʿOṣfuri*, p. 34). The book, already mentioned by the Imami Ṣaffār Qomi, even contains two traditions that seem to indicate that the Imams will be seven in number (Ṣaffār, pp. 146, 150).

One also encounters signs of hesitation and grasping for ideas concerning the nature and modalities of the occultation. Different theories appear to have co-existed in the decades following the death of the eleventh Imam. One discerns a trace of this in reports regarding a character as influential as Abu Sahl Nowbaḵti (d. 923), who would have played a determining role in the establishment of a definitive form of the theology of occultation (Eqbāl, *s.v.*; Arjomand 1996a and 1996b). Indeed, the sources attribute two different conceptions of the occultation to him. According to the first, cited by Ebn Bābuya, based on *Ketāb al-tanbih wa'l-emāma*, a work by Abu Sahl now apparently lost, the Hidden Imam "exists in the world by his spiritual substance thanks to a subsisting essence" (*mawjud al-ʿayn fi'l-ʿālam wa ṯābet al-ḏāt*: Ebn Bābuya 1985, I, pp. 90 ff.). According to a second theory reported by Ebn Nadim (d. 990; see also AL-FEHREST), Abu Sahl is said to have maintained that the twelfth Imam died, but secretly left behind a son as a successor to him; the lineage of Imams would thus be perpetuated in occultation from father to son until the final Imam manifests himself publicly as the Mahdi (Ebn al-Nadim, p. 225). Eventually, none of the theories were sustained, but here one recognizes tentative efforts (undoubtedly among the oldest) to rationalize the concept of occultation. During the same period, Abu Jaʿfar Ebn Qebba (d. before 931) wrote some texts with the same objective, such as his *Masʾala fi'l-emāma* and *al-Naqż ʿalā Abi 'l-Ḥasan ʿAli b. Aḥmad b. Baššār fi'l-ḡayba* (both edited in Modarressi, 1993). The rationalizing theorization of the concept of occultation continued in full force with Shaikh Mofid (d. 1022) and his disciples, Šarif Mortażā (d. 1044), Moḥammad b. ʿAli Karājaki (d. 1057), and Shaikh Abu Jaʿfar Ṭusi, known as Šayḵ al-Ṭāʾefa (d. 1067), thinkers who explicitly had recourse to dialectical demonstration drawing notably from some older Muʿtazilite principles (Sachedina 1981, pp. 108 ff.; see bibliography).

Other uncertainties and contradictions concern the notion of the "double occultations" and belief in the "delegation" (*niāba, sefāra, wekāla*) and the "four delegates or deputies" (*nowwāb / sofarāʾ arbaʿa*) of the Hidden Imam. We shall consider them further on.

All this tends to show that during this period the Imami community underwent what one might consider a serious identity crisis. This "time of confusion" is one of groping in the dark, of research, development, and the more or less painful establishment of doctrines related to the authority and legitimacy of the twelfth Imam. These doctrines were faced with, and overcame, much resistance before eventually standing as articles of faith. The transition from Imami Shiʿism to Twelver Shiʿism was certainly not achieved seamlessly (Kohlberg, 1976). In the introduction of his *Ketāb al-Ḡayba*, Ebn Abi Zaynab Noʿmāni laments the fact that a large majority of his co-religionists still did not know the identity of the Hidden Imam, or even go so far as to contest his existence (Noʿmāni, pp. 18-32). Ebn Bābuya makes a similar observation when he says that he was inundated by questions from the Shiʿites of Khorasan regarding the identity of the Hidden Imam and this, in fact, was what prompted him to write his *Kamāl al-din* (Ebn Bābuya 1985, I, pp. 2 ff.). In this confused atmosphere in which schisms were growing in number (Sachedina, 1981, pp. 42 ff.) and adversarial movements, particularly the Ismaʿilis, justifiably benefited from the situation, propaganda intensified and as a consequence the Twelver Shiʿite trend saw a large number of its faithful, including some notable personalities, abandon its ranks (Halm, 1981, passim). The main preoccupation of Twelver Shiʿite thinkers at this time was to demonstrate the actual existence of the son of Imam Ḥasan al-ʿAskari, and to establish his legitimate authority as the Hidden Imam. This objective was attained thanks to the sustained efforts of a certain number of thinkers and transmitters of traditions, some of whom have already been cited: Nowbaḵti, Abu Jaʿfar Ebn Qebba, Kolayni, Noʿmāni, and especially Ebn Bābuya and his masterly *Kamāl al-din*, the principal architect of the canonization of elements relating to the Hidden Imam, his occultation, and status as eschatological Savior (Amir-Moezzi, 1996, pp. 122 ff.). Still, one can list some authors and their works that were decisive in the definitive establishment of doctrines regarding the Mahdi of the Twelvers: the father of Ṣaduq, ʿAli b. Ḥosayn Ebn Bābuya (d. 940) and his book, *al-Emāma wa'l-tabṣera men al-ḥayra*; Ebn Quluya (Ebn Qulawayh, q.v., d. 979) and his *Kāmel al-ziārāt*; Ḵazzāz Rāzi (2nd half of 10th cent.) and his *Kefāyat al-aṯar*; and Ebn ʿAyyāš Jawhari (d. 1011) and his *Moqtażab al-aṯar* (see bibliography). Consequently, when Shaikh Ṭusi (d. 1067) wrote his *Ketāb al-Ḡayba*, a substantial monograph on the subject, articles of faith regarding the Mahdi of the Twelver Imamis appeared already well established: that the son of the eleventh Imam is indeed the twelfth and final Imam; that he had two occultations: during the first and much shorter one, he communicated with believers through the intermediary of four delegates. During the second, which is to last until the end of time, he remains providentially living in his physical body in order to return to save the world as Mahdi. We shall now examine these points in greater detail.

Birth and occultation of the Mahdi. What precisely do traditional accounts of the Mahdi relate? Versions that would eventually be considered "orthodox" began to emerge in the first half of the 10th century and only attained their definitive form in the following century. For what follows, we base our information mainly on the works of authors such as Noʿmāni, Ebn Bābuya (1985), and Shaikh Ṭusi (1965), to cite only the most important monographs on the subject.

The eschatological Savior of Imamism is presented as Abu'l-Qāsem Moḥammad b. Ḥasan al-ʿAskari, twelfth and last among the Imams. He therefore bears the same name and *konya* as the Prophet, thus fulfilling the hadith that probably goes back to ʿĀṣem b. Bahdala (d. 744-45) from Kufa. It undoubtedly owes its origin to Moḵtār's rebellion in favor of Moḥammad b. al-Ḥanafiya, son of ʿAli, who, once when he was described as Mahdi, declared that his privilege consisted in bearing the same name and *konya* as the Prophet (Ebn Saʿd, V, p. 68; Madelung, "al-Mahdī," p. 1223a). However, it was inadvisable to call the Mahdi by his name, according to a ban attributed to many among the imams (*al-nahy ʿan al-esm/al-manʿ ʿan al-tasmiya*), the aim of which was to protect the Savior (commissioned to put an end to injustice) from the threat posed by the ʿAbbasid court (Kolayni, n.d., II, pp. 126 ff.; Noʿmāni, chap. 16; Ebn Bābuya, 1985, I, pp. 333 ff., 370; II, p. 648; Amir-Moezzi, 1992, pp. 257-59). This also reflected uncertainties that weighed upon the identity of the Mahdi. The latter is thus called by any one of his surnames: *mahdi* (the Guided One), *montaẓar* (the Awaited One), *ṣāḥeb al-zamān* (Lord of the Time), *al-ḡāʾeb* (the Occulted/Hidden One), *ḥojjat Allāh* (Proof of God), *ṣāḥeb al-amr* (Lord of the Cause), *baqiyat Allāh* (Remainder of God) and, most often, *qāʾem* (a complex term meaning among other things: the standing, one who stands up, one who rises, the resurrector). The latter title, which among the Imamis gradually replaced that of Mahdi, was employed in Shiʿite circles to designate the

Imam who "stood up" to fight against unjust and illegitimate power. In this sense, it contrasted with *qāʿed*, literally "the seated one," a term designating previous imams who did not participate in rebellious movements against Umayyad and ʿAbbasid rule (Nowbaḵti, pp. 90 ff.; Ašʿari Qomi, pp. 102 ff.; Sachedina, 1981, *s.v.*; Madelung, "Ḳāʾim Āl Muḥammad").

According to some accounts, his mother, to whom various names are given (Narjis, Rayḥāna, Sawsan, Maryam), was a black slave of Nubian origin (the first three names, being those of flowers and plants, and often given to female slaves, seems to confirm this version); according to other accounts, undoubtedly legendary and hagiographic, she was the grand-daughter of the Byzantine emperor, himself a disciple of the Apostle Simon. According to this version, the Byzantine princess was captured by Muslim troops and sold as a slave in Baghdad to a man belonging to the entourage of the tenth Imam, ʿAli al-Naqi (see ʿALI AL-HĀDI) who then came to Sāmarrāʾ and offered the girl to Ḥakima, the latter's sister. Even before her captivity, the princess had a dream vision of Mary, mother of Jesus, as well as of Fāṭema (q.v.), daughter of the Prophet Moḥammad, both of whom had asked her to convert to Islam and let herself be captured by the Muslim armies as she was destined for a glorious life. In Sāmarrāʾ, the tenth Imam, having by clairvoyance recognized in her the future mother of the Mahdi, gave her in marriage to his son Ḥasan, the future eleventh Imam. Signs of the mother's pregnancy as well as the birth of the child were miraculously concealed, since the ʿAbbasids sought to eliminate an expected child whom persistent rumors described as a Savior. The date most often cited for his birth is 15 Šaʿbān 256/18th July 870 (one of the most important Imami festivals). The father showed the newborn to some forty intimate disciples, and then the child was hidden. According to many accounts, the eleventh imam is said to have adopted a two-fold tactic to guarantee the child's security. First, apart from his intimate circle, the Imam kept the birth of the child secret, going so far as to designate his mother, Ḥodayṯ, as his sole heir. Now, it is known that according to Imami law, under some conditions the inheritance belongs to the mother of the deceased when the latter does not leave behind a child. Secondly, Imam Ḥasan al-ʿAskari had recourse to a ruse to cloud the issue and distract attention. Some time before his death in 874, he allowed a rumor to spread that his servant Ṣaqil was pregnant with his child. Informants of the caliph al-Moʿtamed (r. 870-92) closely observed the activities of the Imam, who was kept under surveillance in the military camp at Sāmarrāʾ. When, following a serious illness, the Imam's death seemed inevitable, the caliph dispatched his trusted men to the site. After the eleventh Imam died, his servant was arrested for observation. During the year that followed, she showed no signs of pregnancy and was released and promptly forgotten. The caliph and his entourage were then convinced that the deceased eleventh Imam left behind no descendants. According to Imami authors, divine providence had been accomplished. The twelfth Imam, the awaited Savior, was thus saved and grew up in hiding (for these accounts and a critical analysis of them, see Amir-Moezzi, 1992, pt. IV-1 and IV-2). This "gilded legend" meets the obvious hagiographic requirements, but at the same time it reflects the uncertainties that continued to be felt in Imami circles regarding the very existence of a child of Imam Ḥasan al-ʿAskari. This led, as we have seen, to a number of schisms. It is certainly no accident that the sources present "the concealed birth" as one of the distinctive signs of the Savior (Noʿmāni, chap. 10, no. 7, p. 244; Ebn Bābuya, 1985, I, chap. 32, no. 2, p. 325).

Not unlike previous imams, the Mahdi had a birth and childhood bathed in the miraculous. Supernatural signs, divine lights, and celestial messengers accompanied him from his very birth. From his early childhood on, he demonstrated initiatory knowledge and manifested supernormal powers. Our sources regularly relate that even while in hiding, the young twelfth Imam was visited by initiated adepts of his father, and the latter never missed an occasion to reveal to his followers that his son was indeed the *qāʾem*. Upon the death of his father in 260/874, the twelfth Imam entered his first occultation while still a child, later termed the Minor Occultation (*al-ḡaybat al-ṣoḡrā*), which lasted 70 lunar years, i.e., until 329/940. During this period, the Hidden Imam is said to have communicated with his believers through four intermediary delegates or representatives: (1) Abu ʿAmr ʿOṯmān b. Saʿid ʿAmri/ʿOmari; (2) Abu Jaʿfar Moḥammad ʿAmri/ʿOmari, son of the above; (3) Abu'l-Qāsem Ḥosayn b. Ruḥ, from the influential family of the Banu Nowbaḵt; and (4) Abu'l-Ḥasan ʿAli b. Moḥammad Semmari (regarding these representatives and the sources see Ali, pp. 197 ff.; Hussain, chap. IV-VII; on the vocalization of the fourth name, usually erroneously pronounced Samarri, see Halm, 1988, chap. 4, *s.v.*).

The most important activities of these "representatives" would have included ensuring that canonical precepts were respected by the believers, the collection and distribution of taxes, delivering questions of a religious nature to the Hidden Imam, making his responses known in public and, finally, performing miracles to convince those believers who were prey to perplexity and confusion. Ebn Bābuya dedicates several pages of his *Kamāl al-din* to enumerating and describing the supernatural powers of the representatives, perceived by the faithful to be the result of direct initiation by the Hidden Imam (Ebn Bābuya, 1985, II, pp. 486-520; Amir-Moezzi, 1992, pp. 272-75).

According to official tradition, in 329/940, the fourth and last delegate received a final letter signed by the Hidden Imam in which he declared that henceforth and "until the end of time," no one will see him or be his representative, and that whosoever declares otherwise is no less than an imposter. This important document, apparently reported for the first time by Ebn Bābuya in his *Kamāl al-din* (II, chap. 45, no. 44, p. 516), heralds the second, or Major Occultation (*al-ḡaybat al-kobrā*), which according to Twelver Shiʿite doctrine still continues and will last until the eschatological return of the Mahdi (regarding this letter, reports concerning it in ancient sources, and translations of it into Western languages, see Amir-Moezzi 1996, pp. 122-23 and n. 51). Thus, for more than a thousand years the Imamis have lived in a period of Major Occultation of the Hidden Imam. Imami tradition cites four principal reasons to prove the necessity of the occultation: safeguarding the life of the Hidden Imam; independence with regard to temporal powers which, according to some traditions, will all be unjust until the return of the Mahdi; testing believers in order to measure the degree of their faith; and finally, a secret reason not to be revealed until the end of time (Kolayni, n.d., II, pp. 127-45; Noʿmāni, chap. 10; Ebn Bābuya, 1985, chap. 44; idem, 1966, chap. 179; Ebn ʿAyyāš, pp. 34-36; Ṭusi 1965, pp. 73 ff. pp. 109-11, 214-15). It must be emphasized that the concept of two occultations, the first shorter than the second, originated in the beliefs of the Wāqefis of the seventh Imam Musā al-Kāẓem. For them, these two occultations constituted a distinctive sign of the Mahdi, obviously here alluding to the two periods of imprisonment of the seventh Imam, the first of a shorter period under the caliphate of the ʿAbbasid caliph al-Mahdi (r. 775-85), and the second, lasting until the death of the Imam, ordered by Hārun al-Rašid (r. 786-809; Madelung, "al-Mahdī," p. 1226b). This Wāqefi origin also seems at issue in a hadith, preserved by the Twelver Shiʿite corpus, that mentions the imprisonment of the Savior (Noʿmāni, p. 288; Ebn Bābuya, 1985, II, p. 548; Ṭusi, 1965, p. 181). As a corollary to the preceding concept, belief in the delegation of four official representatives of the Hidden Imam during the first occultation seems to have started to take form long after the proclamation of major occultation, most likely in the second half of the 10th century. As we have seen, Barqi and Ṣaffār do not even deal with the theme of occultation. With two authors from the end of the 9th century, namely Nowbak̲ti in his *Feraq al-šiʿa*, and Ašʿari Qomi in his *Maqālāt*, there is still no mention of any representative. The same is true of Noʿmāni, who wrote in the first half of the next century. During the same period, Kolayni in his *Kāfi*, and Kašši in his *Rejāl*, provide names of several "representatives" (for example the two ʿAmri/ʿOmari, Ebrāhim b. Mahziyār, Marzbāni Ḥāret̲i, Ḥājez b. Yazid, etc.), but never speak of an official list of four individuals (Kolayni, n.d., II, pp. 449 ff.; Kašši, s.v.). In her well-documented study, V. Klemm convincingly demonstrates that Ḥosayn b. Ruḥ Nowbak̲ti (d. 938), the "third" *nāʾeb*, would have been the first to claim to be the only representative of the Hidden Imam, and as a consequence, the supreme leader of the community in the absence of the latter. According to Klemm, the dogma of delegation to the Hidden Imam by a sole representative seems to have been invented and spread by the powerful Nowbak̲ti family in Baghdad. The two previous claimants, the two ʿAmri/ʿOmaris, were no doubt elevated to the status of sole representative posthumously to prove to believers the continuity of this institution since the presumed beginning of the occultation (Klemm, passim). This conception of the *niāba* was far from being accepted without hesitation or resistance, and one has to wait almost half a century until the *Kamāl al-din* by Ebn Bābuya has it take its more or less definitive canonical form for the first time. "More or less," indeed, since even Ebn Bābuya, who provides the list of "four representatives," speaks of other trusted men of the Hidden Imam in different cities (Ebn Bābuya, 1985, II, pp. 432, 442).

Let us end this section by recalling an interesting phenomenon at the time of the occultation that increases devotion to the Hidden Imam and strengthens faith in his invisible presence: accounts of meetings with the Mahdi. Hagiographic literature dedicated to the twelfth Imam has always accorded a special place to accounts of meetings with the Mahdi. It covers a period of almost one thousand years, ranging from some decades after the occultation with, for example, Kolayni, until the contemporary period with monographs by Mirzā Ḥosayn Ṭabarsi/Ṭabresi Nuri (d. 1902), which are veritable encyclopedias of this genre, and *Beḥār al-anwār* by ʿAllāma Moḥammad-Bāqer Majlesi (d. 1699-1700: see bibliography). Regarding encounters during the Major Occultation, henceforth a question arises to which some Imami thinkers have responded: how to consider accounts of meetings during the Major Occultation authentic when in his final letter to his last representative the Imam declares any encounter to be impossible until the end of time? It is important to note that Ebn Bābuya, who reports this letter in his *Kamāl al-din*, does not hesitate to relate in the same work some accounts of meetings with the Hidden Imam after his Major Occultation. From the very beginning, ocular vision of the imam, to which the letter refers, seems to have been understood not in a general sense, but as a condition of the Hidden Imam's representative. Thus, what is declared impossible during the major occultation (thus until the end of time) is not an encounter with the Hidden Imam as such, but laying claim to the *niāba* of the latter by citing a meeting with the Hidden Imam as grounds. A believer may be granted the privilege of meeting the Imam, but if following this he declares himself to be the "representative" of the Imam due to the encounter, he is considered (according to terms of the letter) no less than a liar and impostor (Šarif Mortażā, n.d., pp. 233 ff.; Ebn Ṭāwus, 1931, pp. 34, 48, 73-75; Majlesi, LII, p. 151; Ṭabarsi/Ṭabresi Nuri, 1991, chap. 8, pp. 559 ff.).

These encounters may occur anywhere, but certain sites seem to be more propitious: Mecca; beside the Imams' mausoleums; the Cave (*sardāb*) in Sāmarrāʾ where the Hidden Imam is said to have begun his occultation; the mosque of Sahla in Najaf, and the sanctuary of Jamkarān, not far from Qom (Amir-Moezzi, 1997, first part). Typologically, one can distinguish three categories of narratives of encounters, based on the principal dimension promoted: a humanitarian dimension in which the great generosity of the Hidden Imam towards his believers and his concern for their well-being are emphasized; an initiatory dimension in which the Imam teaches his believers prayers, transmits spiritual knowledge, and bears secrets etc.; and finally, an eschatological dimension, presented mainly by late mystical sources, in which the encounter prompts a believer's individual spiritual resurrection (Amir-

Moezzi, 1996, passim, esp. pp. 127-35; see also Corbin, 1963-64, pp. 67 ff., and idem, 1972, book VII, esp. pp. 346-67).

The end of time and rising of the Mahdi. These subjects have been discussed at length in the article dedicated to Twelver Shiʿite eschatology (Amir-Moezzi, 1998). Here we mostly summarize this work, contributing additional information where necessary. The "end of time" or, in other words, the date of the final advent of the Hidden Imam, is unknown and believers are urged to await deliverance (*faraj*) patiently and piously. The future coming of the Savior is the most frequently cited subject in predictions made by the Prophet, Fāṭema, and the Imams: entire lengthy chapters are dedicated to the topic in the sources. This coming is heralded by a number of signs (*ʿalāmāt*). The universal signs are the widespread invasion of the earth by Evil, the overcoming of knowledge by ignorance, and the loss of a sense of the sacred and all that links man to God and his neighbors. These, in some measure, require the manifestation (*ẓohur*) and the rising (*ḵoruj, qiām*) of the Qāʾem, or else humanity will be overwhelmed by darkness. Furthermore, there are certain specific signs among which five recur more regularly and are hence justifiably called the "five signs": (1) the coming of Sofyāni, the enemy of the Qāʾem, who will command an army in battle against the latter (Madelung, 1986, passim, and 2000); (2) the advent of Yamāni, who appears in the Yemen to preach support for the Qāʾem; (3) the Cry/Scream (*ṣayḥa, nedāʾ*) of supernatural origin, coming from the sky and calling man to defend the Imam's cause; (4) the swallowing (*ḵasf*) of an army composed of the Imam's enemies in a desert often located between Mecca and Medina, according to a hadith most likely propagated by ʿAbd-Allāh b. Zobayr during his war propaganda against the Umayyad caliph Yazid (r. 680-83), during the latter's campaign against Mecca and Medina, popularized by the traditionist of Basra, Qatāda (d. 773-74; see Madelung, 1981, pp. 293-95); and (5) the assassination by the Meccans of the messenger to the Qāʾem, often called Nafs or al-Nafs al-Zakiya (echoing the messianic rebellion and death in 762 of the Hasanid Moḥammad b. ʿAbd-Allāh, surnamed al-Nafs al-Zakiya).

The Mahdi thus becomes manifest, all the while having miraculously maintained his youth. He fights and definitively uproots Evil and pervasive ignorance, re-establishing the world to its original pure state (Amir-Moezzi, 2000, passim). For this to occur, he must first avenge the assassination of Imam Ḥosayn in order that the majority of Muslims be purged of the most villainous crime that it ever committed. Moreover, according to the eschatological doctrine of *rajʿa* (q.v.), a certain number of past saints, victims of their community's injustice, and their persecutors come back to life in order that the good may take revenge on the evil ones. The Savior will thus not only re-establish Islam, but all religions, to their purity and original integrity, making "submission to God" (Ar. *eslām*) the universal religion. He will also bring wisdom to mankind by revealing the esoteric secrets of sacred Scriptures (Amir-Moezzi, 1992, pt. IV-3).

In this final battle against the forces of Evil, the Qāʾem is obviously not alone. First, he will be accompanied by certain important characters from the sacred history of humanity; thus, according to different hadiths one finds various prophets of the past such as Jesus and the Prophet Moḥammad, and various Imams, most often ʿAli and/or Ḥosayn. In this war, the Mahdi commands an army in which, apart from the masses of oppressed who enlist depending on the progress of his victories, three kinds of "warriors" are present: (1) angels, especially the 313 angels that accompanied the 313 fighters from Badr, the site of a battle of the Prophet against the Meccans; (2) a terrifying celestial entity named Fear (*roʿb*; see ESCHATOLOGY iii. IMAMI SHIʿISM) who marches at the head of the Mahdi's army and terrifies his enemies; and (3) most importantly, 313 Companions of the Qāʾem forming his militia (*jayš*), a term whose letters also add up to the value of 313. These are specially initiated disciples bearing secret knowledge and possessing miraculous powers. The Savior will no doubt triumph, and the entire world will be brought to submission. Forces of injustice and ignorance will once and for all be exterminated, the earth embellished with justice and wisdom, and humanity revived by knowledge. The Mahdi thus prepares the world for the ultimate trial of the final resurrection of the Last Judgment. According to some traditions, he will reign upon the earth for some time (7, 9, 19 . . . years), after which occurs the death of all humanity just prior to the Judgment. Other traditions report that after the death of the Qāʾem, the government of the world will remain in the hands of the initiated for a certain period before the Day of Resurrection.

Influence and consequences. Unlike in Sunnism, where belief in the Mahdi, although present, never became an essential article of faith, in Shiʿism in general, and Twelver Imamism in particular, it is made a constitutive dogma of its religious doctrine, its dualist vision of the world and more specifically, its conception of *maʿād*, "place of return" or the hereafter (see SHIʿITE DOCTRINE). During the course of time, Imami panegyric as well as hagiographic literature dedicated to the Hidden Imam tried hard to demonstrate that the figure of the Mahdi, present in Sunni hadith, referred to the twelfth Imam (Madelung, "al-Mahdī"). Imami arguments gained momentum during the 13th century when some great Sunni scholars contributed their support to the Imami dogma of identifying the Mahdi with the twelfth Imam: the two Syrian Shafiʿite scholars Moḥammad b. Yusof Ganji in his *Bayān fi aḵbār ṣāḥeb al-zamān*, composed in 1250-51, and Kamāl-al-Din Moḥammad ʿAdawi Naṣibini in his *Maṭāleb al-soʾul*, completed in 1252, and the renowned Sebṭ Ebn al-Jawzi (d. 1256) in his *Taḏkerat al-ḵawāṣṣ* (see bibliography). Given the dates of these authors and their works, coinciding with the arrival of the Mongols, the end of Sunni caliphal power and the increasing political influence of the Imamis, one wonders if this doctrinal reversal was not dictated by a certain opportunism. One might note in this respect that Moḥammad b. Yusof Ganji was assassinated in Damascus in 1260 for having collaborated with the Mongol conquerors. In any case, it is from this period onward that one notices, from time to time, some learned Sunnis rallying to Imami Mahdism. The phenomenon is also noticeable among Sunni mystics. Already in the 11th century, Abu Bakr Bayhaqi had denounced the consent of some Sufis concerning the identification of the Mahdi with the last Imam of the Twelvers (Madelung, "al-Mahdī"). Setting aside the influence of Imamism upon the eschatological hagiology of Ebn al-ʿArabi (q.v.; Elmore, pp. 111-40), one can cite the disciple of the latter, Saʿd-al-Din Ḥammuya in his *Farāʾed al-semṭayn*, the Egyptian ʿAbd-al-Wahhāb Šaʿrāni in *al-Yawāqit wa'l-jawāher* (1551) or, more recently, the Naqšbandi master from Balkh, Solaymān Qonduzi (d. 1877) in his *Yanābiʿ al-mawadda* (see bibliography). Finally, let us note that some doctrinal issues regarding the person of the twelfth Imam, his occultation, his final advent, his companions, and accounts of encounters with him have been interpreted in terms of spiritual and esoteric hermeneutics (*taʾwil*) in the Imami mystical schools and texts, particularly among the Šayḵis and Neʿmat-Allāhis (Amir-Moezzi 2001, 2003).

Bibliography: Āḡā Bozorg, *al-Ḏariʿa*. J. Aguade, *Messianismus zur Zeit der frühen Abbasiden: Das* Kitāb al-Fitan *des Nuʿaim b. Ḥammād*, Tübingen, 1979. Javad Ali, "Die beiden ersten Safire des Zwölften Imams," *Der Islam* 25, 1939, pp. 197-227. M. A. Amir-Moezzi, *Le Guide divin dans le shi'isme originel*, Paris, 1992; tr. David Streightas, *The Divine Guide in Early Shi'ism*, New York, 1994. Idem, "Contribution à la typologie des rencontres avec l'imam caché (Aspects de l'imamologie duodécimaine II)," *JA* 284, 1996, pp. 109-35. Idem, "Jamkarân et Mâhân: deux pèlerinages insolites en Iran," in idem, ed., *Lieux d'islam: cultes et cultures de l'Afrique à Java*, Paris, 1997, pp. 154-67. Idem, "Eschatology in Imami Shiʾism," in *EIr*. VIII, 1998, pp. 575-81. Idem, "Fin du Temps et Retour à l'Origine (Aspects de l'imamologie duodécimaine VI)," in M. Garcia Arenal, ed., *Mahdisme et millénarisme en Islam*, Revue des mondes musulmans et de la Méditerranée, 91-94, 2000, pp. 53-72. Idem, "Une absence remplie de présences: herméneutiques de l'Occultation chez les Shaykhiyya (Aspects de l'imamologie duodécimaine VII)," *BSOAS* 64, 2001, pp. 1-18; tr. in R. Brunner and W. Ende, eds., *The Twelver Shia in Modern Times: Religious Culture and Political History*, Leiden, 2001, pp. 38-57. Idem, "Visions d'Imam en mystique duodécimaine moderne et contemporaine (Aspects de l'imamologie duodécimaine VIII)," in E. Chaumont et al., eds., *Autour du regard: Mélanges Gimaret*, Louvain, 2003, pp. 97-124. S. A. Arjomand, "The Crisis of the Imamate and the Institution of the Occultation in Twelver Shi'ism: A Sociohistorical Perspective," *IJMES* 28, 1966a, pp. 491-515. Idem, "The Consolation of Theology: Absence of the Imam and Transition from Chiliasm to Law in Shi'ism," *The Journal of Religion* 76, 1996b, pp. 548-71. Saʿd b. ʿAbd-Allāh Ašʿari Qomi, *Ketāb al-maqālāt wa 'l-feraq*, ed. M. J. Maškur, Tehran, 1963.

Abu Jaʿfar Barqi, *Ketāb al-maḥāsen*, ed. J. Moḥaddeṯ Ormavi, Tehran, 1950. H. Corbin, "Au pays de l'imam caché," *Eranos Jahrbuch* 32, 1963-64, pp. 31-87. Idem, *En Islam iranien. Aspects spirituels et philosophiques*, Paris, 1971-72. J. Darmesteter, *Le Mahdi depuis les origines de l'Islam jusqu'à nos jours*, Paris, 1885. Ebn ʿAyyāš Jawhari, *Moqtażab al-aṯar fi'l-naṣṣ ʿalā ʿadad al-aʾemmat al-eṯnā ʿašar*, Tehran, 1927. ʿAli b. Ḥosayn Ebn Bābuya [Bābawayh], *al-Emāma wa'l-tabṣera men al-ḥayra*, Qom, 1984. Moḥammad b. ʿAli b. Ḥosayn (Shaikh Ṣaduq), *al-Ḵeṣāl*, ed. M.-B. Kamareʾi, Tehran, 1950. Idem, *ʿElal al-šarāʾeʿ*, Najaf, 1966. Idem, *Kamāl al-din wa tamām al-neʿma*, ed. ʿA.-A. Ḡaffāri, repr. Qom, 1985. Ebn al-Nadim, *Fehrest*, ed. R. Tajaddod, Tehran, 1971. Ebn Quluya [Qulawayh], *Kāmel al-ziārāt*, lithograph, Iran, n.d. Ebn Saʿd, *al-Ṭabaqāt al-kobrā*, ed. E. Sachau, Leiden, 1904-17. Ebn Ṭāwus, *Kašf al-maḥajja*, n.p. (Iran), 1931. Idem, *al-Malāḥem wa'l-fetan*, Najaf, 1963. G. Elmore, *Islamic Sainthood in the Fullness of Time: Ibn al-ʿArabī's Book of the Fabulous Gryphon*, Leiden, 1999. ʿA. Eqbāl, *Ḵāndān-e Nowbaḵti*, Tehran, 2nd ed., 1966. Moḥammad b. Yusof Ganji, *Bayān fi aḵbār ṣāḥeb al-zamān*, ed. M.-H. Amini, Najaf, 1970. Ṣāfi Golpāyegāni, *Montaḵab al-aṯar fi'l-emām al-ṯāni ʿašar*, Tehran, 1953. ʿAbd-al-Karim Ḥāʾeri Yazdi, *Elzām al-nāṣeb fi eṯbāt ḥojjat al-ḡāʾeb*, Tehran, 1932. H. Halm, "Die *Sīrat Ibn Ḥaushab*: Die ismailitische *daʿwa* im Jemen und die Fatimiden," *Die Welt des Orients* 12, 1981, pp. 107-35. Idem, *Die Schia*, Darmstadt, 1988. Saʿd-al-Din Ḥammuya, *Farāʾed al-semṭayn*, Tehran, 2001. J. M. Hussain, *The Occultation of the Twelfth Imam: A Historical Background*, London, 1981. Moḥammad b. ʿAli Karājaki, *al-Borhān ʿalā ṣul ʿomr ṣāḥeb al-zamān*, in the margins of idem, *Kanz al-fawāʾed*, Tabriz, n.d. Kašši, *Eḵtiār maʿrefat al-rejāl*, Mašhad, 1970. Ḵazzāz Rāzi, *Kefāyat al-aṯar fi'l-naṣṣ ʿalu'l-aʾemmat al-eṯnā ʿašar*, Tehran, 1888. *Ketāb Abu Saʿid al-ʿOṣfuri*, Tehran, 1951. V. Klemm, "Die vier *sufarāʾ* des Zwölften Imam. Zur formativen Periode der "Zwölferšīʿa," *Die Welt des Orients* 15, 1984, pp. 126-43; Engl. tr. in E. Kohlberg, ed., *Shīʿism*, Aldershot, England, 2003, pt. VI. E. Kohlberg, "From Imāmiyya to Ithnā-ʿashariyya," *BSOAS* 39, 1976, pp. 521-34; repr. in his *Belief and Law in Imāmī Shīʿism*, Aldershot, England, 1991, pt. XIV. Idem "Al-Uṣul al-arbaʿumiʾa," *Jerusalem Studies in Arabic and Islam* 10, 1987, pp. 128-66; reprint in his *Belief and Law*, pt. VII. Idem, "Early Attestations of the Term *ithnā ʿashariyya*," *Jerusalem Studies in Arabic and Islam* 24, 2000, pp. 343-55. Moḥammad b. Yaʿqub Kolayni, *al-Rawża men al-Kāfi*, ed. H. Rasuli Maḥallāti, Tehran, 1969. Idem, *Oṣul men al-Kāfi*, 4 vols., ed. J. Moṣṭafawi, Tehran, n.d.

W. Madelung, "ʿAbdallāh b. Zubayr and the Mahdī," *JNES* 40, 1981, pp. 291-305. Idem, "The Sufyānī between Tradition and History," *Stud. Isl.* 43, 1986, pp. 5-48. Idem, "Apocalyptic Prophecies in Ḥimṣ in the Umayyad Age," *Journal of Semitic Studies* 31, 1987, pp. 141-85. Idem, "Ḳāʾim Āl Muḥammad," EI^2 IV, 1978, pp. 456-57. Idem, "Al-Mahdī," EI^2 V, 1978, pp.

1230-38. Idem, "Abū'l-ʿAmayṭar the Sufyānī," *Jerusalem Studies in Arabic and Islam* 24, 2000, pp. 327-42. Moḥammad-Bāqer Majlesi, *Beḥār al-anwār*, Tehran and Qom, 1956-72. H. Modarressi Tabataba'i, *Crisis and Consolidation in the Formative Period of Shi'ite Islam*, Princeton, 1993. E. Moeller, *Beiträge zur Mahdilehre des Islams*, Heidelberg, 1901. Moḥammad b. Moḥammad b. Noʿmān Mofid, *al-Foṣul al-ʿašara fi'l-ḡayba*, Najaf, 1951. Najāši, *Rejāl*, Tehran, n.d. Kamāl-al-Din Naṣibini, *Maṭāleb al-so'ul*, Tehran, 1870-71. Ḥasan b. Musā Nowbaḵti, *Feraq al-šiʿa*, ed. H. Ritter, Istanbul, 1931. Noʿaym b. Ḥammād, *Ketāb al-fetan*, ed. S. Zakkār, Beirut, 1993. Ebn Abi Zaynab Noʿmāni, *Ketāb al-ḡayba*, ed. ʿA.-A. Ḡaffāri, Tehran, 1977. Mirzā Ḥosayn Ṭabarsi/Ṭabresi Nuri, *Jannat al-ma'wā*, at the end of vol. 53 of al-Majlesi's *Beḥār al-anwār*. *Al-Oṣul al-arbaʿome'a*, University of Tehran, MS no. 962. ʿAli b. Ebrāhim Qomi, *Tafsir*, ed. Musawi Jazā'eri, Najaf, 1966-68. Qonduzi, *Yanābi' al-mawadda*, Qom, 2000. Ṣaffār Qomi, *Baṣā'er al-darajāt*, ed. M. Kučebāḡi, Tabriz, 1960. A. A. Sachedina, "A Treatise on the Occultation of the Twelfth Imamite Imam," *Stud. Isl.* 68, 1978, pp. 109-24. Idem, *Islamic Messianism: the Idea of the Mahdi in Twelver Shiʿism*, Albany, 1981. ʿAbd-al-Wahhāb Šaʿrāni, *al-Yawāqit wa 'l-jawāher*, Cairo, 1932. Šarif Mortażā [Abu'l-Qāsem ʿAli b. Ḥosayn], *Mas'ala wajiza fi'l-ḡayba*, in *Nafā'es al-maḵṭuṭāt*, ed. Āl Yāsin, IV, Baghdad, 1955. Idem, *Tanzih al-anbiā'*, Qom, n.d. Sebṭ Ebn al-Jawzi, *Taḏkerat al-ḵawāṣṣ*, Najaf, 1964. Abu Jaʿfar Moḥammad (Šayḵ al-Ṭā'efa) Ṭusi, *Ketāb al-ḡayba*, Najaf, 1965. Idem, *Fehrest kotob al-šiʿa*, ed. Sprenger and ʿAbd-al-Ḥaqq, Mašhad, 1972, repr.

(MOHAMMAD ALI AMIR-MOEZZI)

viii. THE OCCULTATION OF MAHDI. See ḠAYBA.

ix. THE DEPUTIES OF MAHDI

According to Twelver Shiʿite tradition, the deputies of Mahdi (Ar. *al-nowwāb al-arbaʿa*) consist of the four intermediaries between the Hidden Imam and the faithful during his "Minor Occultation" (*al-Ḡaybat al-ṣoḡrā*), 874-941 (see ḠAYBA). In Imami sources, the *nowwāb* (lit. deputies, sing. *nā'eb*) were called *sofarā* (official mediators, sing. *safir*; first attested in Noʿmāni [d. 956 or 971], pp. 113-15). After a period of intermediation, which lasted about 70 years, the Imam is believed to have severed links with his community in order to retreat into the 'Major Occultation' (*al-Ḡaybat al-kobrā*) that is said to last until his final reappearance as *Mahdi* or the Guided One.

According to recent research (Arjomand; Klemm), Shiʿite traditional accounts about the activities of four successive *nowwāb* during the 'Minor Occultation' appear to be partially unsound. The concept of mediation reflects rather the crisis, or 'confusion" (*ḥayra*), of the Imami Shiʿites after the death of the eleventh Imam, Ḥasan al-ʿAskari, who died in prison in Sāmarrā', Iraq, in 873-74. The answer as to whether he left a son remains in dispute. Ḥasan ʿAskari's death resulted in a series of differing opinions regarding the issue of succession to the Imamate. Just as after the deaths of the previous Imams, followers of Imami Shiʿism once again splintered into various subgroups that held differing views regarding the identity of the new bearer of the Prophet's heritage as the legitimate leader of the Muslim community. One group, the later Twelver Shiʿites, adhered to the lineal continuation of the chain of Imams in the person of a young son of the deceased Imam al-ʿAskari who, as he could not be found nor seen anywhere, was assumed to have been sent into occultation after his father's death through divine providence. Shiʿite Traditions (Nowbaḵti, pp. 84-91; Mofid, p. 345; for a Sunni heresiographical source see Ašʿari, *Maqālāt*, p. 30) give the name of the child as 'Moḥammad,' and his age at the time of his Occultation as around five years. However, the de facto absence of the Imam who, according to Shiʿite thought, had the elementary function of serving as 'God's Proof' (*Ḥojjat Allāh*) on Earth, plunged Imami Shiʿism into a deep theological and political crisis: How long would the occultation last? Could it last longer than a natural human lifetime? Could the Imam have died in occultation? How could his ever-increasing period of absence be plausibly explained? Was it certain that the Twelfth Imam would also be the last? Could the Imamate have ceased to continue? Moreover, who could be the authorized leader of the community in a period during which God had removed the proof of His guidance from Earth?

Several books and theological treatises of varying lengths on the issue of occultation appeared a few decades after the disappearance of the eleventh Imam, Ḥasan ʿAskari (Arjomand, pp. 504 f.; Klemm, pp. 137 ff.). However, the principle of the hierarchic leadership of four successive deputies, who could provide convincing arguments in favor of the continued existence of a Twelfth Imam, is nowhere mentioned in the sources of that time. Most of the works dealing exclusively with the *ḡayba* are not extant (for those which did survive, see Nowbaḵti and Qomi). The pre-eminent Persian traditionist, Moḥammad b. Yaʿqub Kolayni (q.v.; var. Kolini, d. 941, in the last year of the Minor Occultation), for instance, whose monumental *al-Kāfi fi ʿelm al-din* constitutes a collection of much older material of Shiʿite Traditions, presents Traditions which refer only vaguely to written decrees (*tawqiʿāt*) sent from the Twelfth Imam to some pious men who had been active in the Imami community (Kolayni, I, pp. 517-25).

Among them, Abu ʿAmr ʿOṯmān b. Saʿid ʿAmri (or ʿOmari, d. 880) and Abu Jaʿfar Moḥammad b. ʿOṯmān ʿAmri (or ʿOmari, d. 917) functioned as the first two official deputies of the Hidden Imam (see below). In Kolayni's *Kāfi*, they are recommended by the eleventh Imam to the Shiʿites as exceedingly loyal, honest and trustworthy. Furthermore, Abu ʿAmr ʿOṯmān claims to have seen al-ʿAskari's son with his own eyes. However, there appears to be no direct indication of his appointment as an intermediary (ibid., pp. 329-30, no. 1, p. 331 no. 4).

The notion of intermediation (*sefāra*) was either not known or not shared by eminent Imamite scholars or hadith compilers in the first decades of the absence of the Twelfth Imam. Instead, the *Ketāb al-tanbih* by Abu Sahl Nowbaḵti (written between 903 and 913 and partially preserved in Ebn Bābawayh's *Ekmāl al-din* (pp. 88, 91), describes the worsening crisis at the time when, twenty years after the eleventh Imam's death, nearly all his close companions had died. These men had claimed to be in contact with the Hidden Imam and had conveyed his orders to the Shiʿites. But now, after their death, there were no more signs from the Imam, and the Shiʿites had no more proof of his existence that they could have shown to skeptics and opponents. All they could do was to refer to the traditional analogies and predictions of the earlier Imams in order to justify the ever-increasing duration of the Occultation. There is no mention at all of a continuously functioning *sefāra*, as described by Shiʿite authors who wrote decades after that time.

We first meet the notion of four successive deputies of the Twelfth Imam who represented him among the Shiʿites, in the *ḡayba* books of Ebn Bābawayh (q.v.; d. 991-92) and Abu Jaʿfar Moḥammad b. Ḥasan Ṭusi, known as Shaikh al-Ṭāʾefa (d. 1067). In their works, the information on the *sefāra* is a weighty argument in favor of the actual existence of the Hidden Imam. According to them, the first of the deputies was Abu ʿAmr ʿOṯmān, also known as Sammān, "the butter dealer," who secretly carried the money collected from Iraq's suppressed Shiʿite communities, hidden in a butter bag, to the caliphal residential town Sāmarrāʾ, where the Shiʿites lived under the strict control of ʿAbbasid rulers. Abu ʿAmr ʿOṯmān was considered a tried and trusted long-serving companion of the eleventh Imam Ḥasan al-ʿAskari. The latter had conferred on him the leadership for the time after his death, which occurred in 873. As the head of the Shiʿites in Sāmarrāʾ, he is said to have organized the funeral rites for the deceased Imam. Furthermore, he has been able to understand the mysteries surrounding the disappearance of the Twelfth Imam and even to come into contact with him in some way. It was incumbent on him to convey commandments from the Hidden Imam, and he was also the authority to be approached by the Shiʿites with their requests, questions, and concerns if they wanted to receive an answer from the Mahdi. After the death of the first deputy, in about 880, his exalted position was occupied by his son Abu Jaʿfar Moḥammad b. Oṯmān ʿAmri (d. 917), who handed it down to Abu'l-Qāsem Ḥosayn b. Ruḥ Nowbaḵti (d. 938). The latter's successor, Abu'l-Ḥosayn ʿAli b. Moḥammad Somerri (for this spelling see Amir-Moezzi, p. 110; another, less frequent, variant is Semarri, see Halm, p. 37 n. 16), died in 941. Just before his death, he is said to have received a command from the Twelfth Imam not to designate any further successor, for the 'complete' *ḡayba* (*al-Ḡaybat al-tāmma*) had begun. Thereupon the connection between the Imam and the Shiʿites was severed (Ebn Bābawayh, 1970, pp. 466 ff.; Ṭusi, pp. 214 ff., 242).

Apart from this, Shiʿite sources offer very little biographical information about the first two deputies, the father and son ʿAmri. Concerning them, we are told by Ṭusi that they were scions of the Bānu Asad, and that their *nesba*, ʿAmri or ʿOmari, referred to the grandfather of the first deputy ʿOṯmān b. Saʿid (Ṭusi, pp. 214-18). Further information on the two first *nowwāb* follows rather standardized patterns. The same is true with respect to the information provided on the fourth deputy Somerri, which is as vague as that on the ʿAmris.

The sources are far more transparent and varied on Abu'l-Qāsem Ḥosayn b. Ruḥ Nowbaḵti, a member of the Shiʿite family Nowbaḵt, who had become famous as writers, poets, statesmen, and theologians. The Banu Nowbaḵt played a significant and influential role at the ʿAbbasid court (Eqbāl's *Ḵānadān-e Nowbaḵti* is still the most comprehensive study on them). One of their ancestors had been the court astrologer of the second ʿAbbasid caliph al-Manṣur (r. 754-75). In the 10th century, especially during the caliphates of al-Moqtader (r. 908, 908-29, and 929-32) and al-Rāżi (r. 934-40), members of the clan served as state secretaries and viziers in the offices of the central administration in Baghdad. A relative of Ebn Ruḥ was the Shiʿite author Abu Sahl Esmāʿil b. ʿAli Nowbaḵti (851-923). As a high-ranking civil servant and poet, he is considered to have been the most prominent member of the family at that time. In the years following the beginning of the Major Occultation of the Twelfth Imam, Abu Sahl was the leader of the Twelver Shiʿites in Baghdad, where many of their notables had moved to after the abandonment of Sāmarrāʾ by the ʿAbbasids at the end of the 9th century. The titles of Abu Sahl's theological and theoretical writings bear witness to disputes with the Muʿtazilites and to his dissociation from certain Shiʿite views on the Imamate that were at one time supported by some of the followers of the seventh Imam Musā al-Kāẓem (d. about 800) and the extremists (*ḡolāt*, q.v.). Furthermore, he tried to find a theological solution to the issue of the Occultation, using rational arguments rather than Traditions (Arjomand, pp. 503 ff.).

According to Ebn Bābawayh and Ṭusi, Ebn Ruḥ Nowbaḵti was established as *safir*, i.e., official intermediary between the Hidden Imam and his community, in 917. Soon thereafter, he produced the first decree issued by the Twelfth Imam in occultation. The subject was the confirmation of the *safir* as new head of the hierarchy of the Shiʿites (Ṭusi, pp. 227 f.). Thus, communication with the Hidden Imam was reopened after decades of worsening crisis, evident before Ebn Ruḥ's designation, as described by Abu Sahl Nowbaḵti in *Ketāb al-tanbih*.

Ebn Ruḥ's term of office as deputy of the Twelfth Imam began during the caliphate of al-Moqtader, spanned that of al-Qāher, and ended during the reign of al-Rāżi. The attitude of their viziers toward the Twelver Shiʿites alternated between favor and disfavor. Temporarily, Ebn Ruḥ was forced underground for unknown reasons. He was only able to reappear when, in 923, al-Moqtader's vizier ʿAli b. Moḥammad b. Forāt, coming from a Shiʿite family himself, was generous towards him and supported him financially. This enabled Ebn Ruḥ to gain respect and continue his work undisturbed. He was also in favor with the next caliph, Rāżi. One of Ebn Ruḥ's relatives, Ḥosayn b. ʿAli Nowbakṯi, was even promoted to vizier for a short time (936-37). Other members of the clan held good positions at court (for details see Klemm, pp. 142 ff.). Shiʿite sources reveal Ebn Ruḥ's activities as *safir*, which are somewhat better known than those of his two predecessors, the ʿAmris. It becomes clear that he was in contact with the theologians in the central Persian town of Qom, the stronghold of the traditionalist wing of Shiʿite scholarship. Letters from Qom, with petitions or questions to the Twelfth Imam, found their way to him in Baghdad, and he would reply on behalf of the Imam and sometimes even pronounced judgment in cases pertaining to Islamic law (Ṭusi, pp. 228 ff.). He also published several formal proclamations and decrees, usually on request, concerning law and worship (ibid. pp. 230-36). Although legal decisions were not pronounced exclusively by Ebn Ruḥ, he nevertheless sent a work on Islamic law to Qom for the guidance of the Shiʿite scholars there (ibid., p. 240). Ebn Ruḥ died on 19 June 938, and was buried in the Nowbakṯiya quarter in Baghdad (ibid., p. 238).

An analysis of the accounts of Ebn Ruḥ Nowbakṯi and their transmitters (see Klemm, pp. 147 ff.) leads one to assume that Ebn Ruḥ seems to have laid claim to recognition as the only deputy of the Twelfth Imam in his time. On the other hand, available information about the ʿAmris suggests that they were forced posthumously into the institution of 'deputyship' or *sefāra*, which, in order to be credible, had to begin as early as the death of the eleventh Imam. On a personal level, the two families were indeed close to each other, since Ebn ʿAmri's daughter Omm Kolṯum was married to a Nowbakṯi, who was the secretary of Ebn Ruḥ. It is worth noting that a grandson of Omm Kolṯum, Ebn Barniya, can be identified as the chief source of information about the *sefāra* in the *ḡayba* books of Ebn Bābawayh and Ṭusi, where that institution and its four succeeding representatives are presented for the first time as a proof for the continuous guidance of the Hidden Imam after he was removed by God away from the believers into occultation.

It is therefore doubtful whether the institution of *sefāra* was founded and propagated by the Nowbakṯis themselves. At the time of Abu Sahl and Ebn Ruḥ, the Nowbakṯi family exercised a dominant influence over the Shiʿite community and the ulema. Furthermore, it was only during the period of the "crisis management" of the Nowbakṯis that the *sefāra* had any effective control over the Shiʿites. In Somerri's time, this control collapsed again, since it was apparently not generally recognized. Ṭusi describes the prevailing consensus, according to which all those who laid claim to the *sefāra* after Somerri were "secret unbelievers and confused" (Ṭusi, p. 255). This had led some modern scholars to speak of the "failure" of the *sefāra* as a central hierarchic authority in Twelver Shiʿism (Arjomand, pp. 508 f.).

Thus the death of Somerri in 941 marked the onset of the second, total *ḡayba*. Once again, perplexity and the sense of trial were deepened in the community and their leadership. Shiʿite theologians and scholars, among them Mofid Šarif Mortażā, had to struggle until the 11th century, when they finally arrived at an explanation of the Occultation of the Twelfth Imam in rational theology.

Bibliography: Primary sources: Ašʿari, *Maqālāt*. Moḥammad b. ʿAli b. Ḥosayn Ebn Bābawayh al-Šayḵ al-Ṣaduq Qomi, *Ketāb ekmāl al-din wa tamām al-neʿma fi eṯbāt al-ḡayba wa kašf al-ḥayra*, ed. Moḥammad Mahdi Musawi Ḥerṣān, Najaf, 1971. Idem, *Eʿteqādāt al-emāmiya*, tr. A. A. A. Fyzee, as *A Shīʿite Creed*, Tehran, 1982; Ebn al-Nadim, ed. Tajaddod. Abu ʿAmr Moḥammad b. ʿOmar b. ʿAbd-al-ʿAziz Kašši, *Eḵtiār maʿrefat al-rejāl*, ed. Ḥasan Moṣṭafawi, Mashad, 1969-70. Abu Jaʿfar Moḥammad b. Yaʿqub b. Esḥāq Kolayni, *Al-Kāfi fi ʿelm al-din*, ed. ʿAli-Akbar Ḡaffāri, 8 vols., Tehran, 1968 (especially vol. 1). Moḥammad b. Moḥammad b. Noʿmān [Šayḵ] Mofid, *Ketāb al-eršād*, ed. Moḥammad-Kaẓem Kotobi, Najaf, 1962; tr. I. A. K. Howard as *The Book of Guidance*, Dubai, n.d. Moḥammad b. Ebrāhim Noʿmāni, *Ketāb al-ḡayba*, Beirut, 1983. Ḥasan b. Musā Nowbakṯi, *Feraq al-šiʿa*, ed. H. Ritter, Istanbul, 1931. Saʿd b. ʿAbd-Allāh Qomi, *Al-Maqālāt wa 'l-feraq*, ed. Moḥammad-Jawād Maškur, Tehran, 1973. Abu ʿAbd-Allāh Moḥammad b. Aḥmad b. Abi Bakr Qorṭobi, "Ṣilat *Taʾriḵ al-Ṭabari*," in *Ḏoyul Taʾriḵ al-Ṭabari*, ed. Moḥammad Abu'l-Fażl Ebrāhim, Cairo, 1977. Abu'l-Fatḥ Moḥammad b. ʿAbd-al-Karim Šahrestāni, *Al-Melal wa 'l-neḥal*, ed. W. Cureton, London, 1846; repr. Leipzig, 1923. Moḥammad b. Yaḥyā Ṣuli, *Aḵbār al-Rāżi be'llāh wa'l-Mottaqi le'llāh aw Taʾriḵ al-dawla al-ʿabbāsiya* [. . .], ed. Heyworth Dunne, Cairo, 1935. Abu Jaʿfar Moḥammad b. Ḥasan Ṭuṣi, *Ketāb al-ḡayba*, ed. Āḡā Bozorg Moḥammad-Moḥsen Ṭehrāni and Moḥammad-Sādeq Musawi, Najaf, 1965.

Secondary Sources: Saiyad Nizamuddin Ahmad, "Twelver Šiʿi Hadiṯ: From Tradition to Contemporary Evolution," *Oriente moderno* 21/1, 2002 [special issue "Hadith in Modern Islam"], pp. 125-45. Wahid Akhtar, *The Early Imamiyyah Shiite Thinkers*, New Delhi, 1988. Jawad Ali, "Die beiden ersten Safîre des Zwölften Imâms," *Der Islam* 25, 1939, pp. 197-227. M. A. Amir-Moezzi, *The Divine Guide in Early Shiʿism. The Sources of Esotericism in Islam*, tr. David Streight, Albany, N.Y., 1994. Said Amir Arjomand, "The Crisis of the Imāmate and the Institution of Occultation in Twelver Shi'ism: A Sociohistorical Perspective," *IJMES* 28, 1996, pp. 491-515. J. Eliash, "The Ithnaʿashari-Shiʿi Juristic Theory of Political and Legal Authority," *Stud. Isl.* 29, 1969, pp. 17-30. ʿAbbās Eqbāl, *Ḵānadān-e Nowbakṯi*, 2nd ed., Tehran, 1966. T. Fahd, ed., *Le shîʿisme imâmite. Colloque de Strasbourg*, Paris, 1970 (esp. the first chapters). Heinz Halm, *Shiism*, Edinburgh, 1991; first published in Ger. as *Die Schia*, Darmstadt, 1987. J. M. Husain, "The Role of the Imamite *Wikala* with Special Reference to the First *Safir*," *Hamdard Islamicus* 5/4, 1982, pp. 25-52. Idem, *The Occultation of the Twelfth Imam: A Historical Background*, London, 1982. A. Kazemi-Moussavi, *Religious Authority in*

Shiʿite Islam. From the Office of Mufti to the Institution of Marjaʿ, Kuala Lumpur, 1996 (esp. chap. 1). Verena Klemm, "The Four *sufarāʾ* of the Twelfth Imām: On the Formative Period of the Twelfer Shiʿa," in Etan Kohlberg, ed., *Shiʿism*, The Formation of the Classical Islamic World 33, Aldershot, UK, 2003, pp. 135-52; first published in German as "Die vier *sufarāʾ* des Zwölften Imām. Zur formativen Periode der Zwölfersschiʿa," *Die Welt des Orients* 15, 1984, pp. 126-43. Etan Kohlberg, "From Imāmiyya to Ithnā ʿAshariyya," *BSOAS* 39, 1976, pp. 521-34. Idem, "Ṣafīr i," *EI²* VIII, 1995, 811-12. Wilferd Madelung, "Kas̲h̲s̲h̲ī," *EI²* IV, 1978, pp. 711-12. Idem, "Authority in Twelver Shiism in the Absence of the Imam," in *La notion d'autorité au Moyen Age: Islam, Byzance, Orient. Colloques internationaux de la Napoule 1978*, Paris 1982, pp. 163-73. Idem, "Mahdī," *EI²* V, 1986, pp. 1230-33. Louis Massignon, "Les origins shîʿites de la famille vizirale des Banû'l-Furât," in idem, *Opera minora*, Beirut, 1963, pp. 484-87. A. Sachednia, "A Treatise on the Occultation of the Twelfth Imamite Imam," *Stud. Isl.* 48, 1978, pp. 108-24. Idem, *Islamic Messianism: The Idea of the Mahdi in Twelver Shiʿism*, Albany, N.Y., 1981.

(VERENA KLEMM)

3. Islamic Political Movements

A series of articles on Political Islam in Iran can be viewed in two categories: One, consisting of "Roots of Political Shiʿism," "Jihad in Islam," and "Martyrdom in Islam," examine the historical and theological antecedents of modern Islamic political ideas.

The above entries will thus facilitate a deeper understanding of contemporary Islamic political movements, which are then discussed in detail in the following six entries: "Islamic Movements in 20th Century Iran," "Islam and Democracy," "Islam amd Socialism," "Islam and Fundamentalism," "Islamic Revolution of 1977-79," and "Islamic Republic of Iran."

x. THE ROOTS OF POLITICAL SHIʿISM

By "political Shiʿism" we mean here the politicization of theological and legal doctrines of Twelver Shiʿism among some thinkers, often *motakallem* and/or *faqih*, in certain specific historical contexts, in order to make of these doctrines an ideology of legitimization of religious authority and power. Excluded from our study are contemporary revolutionary movements because separate articles are dedicated to them (see xiv-xvii, below), and the philosophers—especially Hellenistic thinkers—whose political thought, often without any original Imami specificity, also requires a separate article in itself (Vakili, pp. 14-16; Jambet, 2000, passim and 2004, pp. 241-78). The present study is comprised of three parts: The initial quietism, the ancient roots of political Shiʿism, and aspects of theologian-jurist power.

THE INITIAL QUIETISM

The study of different categories of sources that have come down to us seem to show that the imams of Twelver Shiʿism would have largely opted for a quietist attitude, isolated from political power. This attitude seems to have prevailed, more particularly, after the tragedy of Karbalāʾ and the massacre of Imam Ḥosayn and his dependents in 61/680 (Amir-Moezzi, 1992, part III-1, with the special case of the eighth Imam, al-Reżāʾ, an exception that confirms the rule). The technical term for this attitude is *qoʿud*, literally remain "seated"; whence the surname *al-qāʿed* (the Seated), of imams, as opposed to *al-qāʾem* (the Standing), the twelfth and final imam, the only imam permitted to "rise" as "insurgent" (*qiām, ḵoruj*) against injustice, as the Mahdi (see section 2, above). The impression that emerges from the earliest corpus of Imami sources is that after Karbalāʾ the period of understanding between spiritual and temporal power had forever changed. The imams, based on traditions that are attributed to them, seem to have concluded that henceforth "the religion of truth" (*din al-ḥaqq*), i.e., Shiʿism and temporal power had become two poles forever irreconcilable: "Forever" since "the ideal city," governed by a just ruler, can only be realized at the end of time, with the Mahdi, the eschatological savior as the only truly just sovereign (*al-solṭān al-ʿādel*). He is the only being authorized to legitimately fight the unjust, the only one able to avenge the oppressed and establish a world of knowledge and justice. Thus, according to the tradition attributed to many among the imams: "Any banner raised before the end of time and the uprising of the *qāʾem* belongs to a rebel against God" (*ṭāḡut*; see Kolayni, 1969, II, pp. 121-22; Noʿmāni, chap. 5, pp. 161-68 and chap. 14, p. 393, no. 53). From now until then the world will be governed irrevocably by the unjust and any attempt at rebellion, even apparently legitimate, is inevitably doomed to failure and suffering: "Dust always falls upon him who raises it" (i.e., the rebel is bound to be the victim of his own revolt), says a tradition going back to Imam Jaʿfar al-Ṣādeq, "any revolt from one among us (the Shiʿites) will be no more than additional suffering for us (the Imams) and our believers" (*al-Ṣaḥifat al-Sajjādiya*, "esnād," p. 22, no. 62; Kašši, pp. 262-63, 290-93; Noʿmāni, pp. 244, 48, 283, 286, 291). In order to maintain the purity of his faith, the Imami believer is urged to tolerate patiently the injustice of the world until the advent of the Mahdi. Not only is he forbidden from rebelling against established power (as we have just seen) but he is also forbidden from seeking to establish power, since in general, any power before the Return of the Hidden Imam is illegitimate. Kolayni went as far as to dedicate an entire sub-chapter of "The Book of Faith and Infidelity" from his *Oṣul men al-Kāfi*, to traditions forbidding Shiʿite believers any kind of leadership (*reʾāsa*), religious and/or political (Kolayni, *K. al-imān wa'l-kofr*, chap. on *ṭalab al-reʾāsa*, in idem, n.d., III, pp. 405-7). Similarly, apart from exceptional cases in which his or his co-religionist's life is endangered, the believer is forbidden from collaborating with power (Kolayni, 1980, V, pp. 105-12; Ebn Bābuya (see BĀBAWAYH) 1970,

III, pp. 106 and 108; Ṭusi, 1980, VI, pp. 330-36; Madelung, 1980, passim; Karimi Zanjāni-Aṣl, pp. 199 ff.). How was it then that a religious movement, presented in its sacred texts as essentially initiatory, esoteric, mystical and quietist (Amir-Moezzi, 1992, passim), was within its own ranks able to give rise to a politico-religious ideology justifying the taking of power by jurist-theologians, and assuming power, as recently illustrated by the principal political theory of Ayatollah Khomeini and the Iranian Islamic Revolution, namely the doctrine of the power of the jurist (*welāyat-e faqih*)? This paradox of Shiʿism is the result of a long doctrinal process based upon certain major historical turning points.

THE ROOTS OF POLITICAL SHIʿISM

The first turning point, and perhaps the most important, occurred in the 10th century. This golden age of "the Renaissance of Islamic Humanism," the period of "the Iranian intermezzo," to quote Vladimir Minorsky's description (see Minorsky, p. viii), between the end of the Arab domination and the arrival of the Ghaznavids (q.v.) and later the Seljuk Turks in the following century, was also the Shiʿite century of Islam. With Buyids (q.v.) at the center of the empire, Hamdanids in Syria and northern Iraq, Fatimids (q.v.) in North Africa, Zaydis in the Yemen and finally Carmatians (q.v.) in Southern Iran, Bahrain and parts of Arabia, the most important regions in the land of Islam were governed by different Shiʿite branches and families.

This period was also the rationalizing turning point of Islam. Learned and intellectual Muslims had now assimilated the subtleties of Hellenic culture and thought, and texts had begun to be translated in great numbers since the previous century. Among the many contributions of this translated literature, scholars were particularly fascinated by Aristotelian dialectic, logical reasoning, dialectical reasoning and its various intellectual tools. It was especially the jurists and theologians of different Schools that discovered in dialectical reasoning a particularly efficient weapon to convince and overcome their adversaries in their frequent polemical sessions. The term *ʿaql*, meaning henceforth "reason" (and not "intelligence"/"intellect" as had been the case hitherto) became a key term for this entire century (Kraemer, introduction).

Finally, for Twelver Shiʿites, this century represents the end of the period of historical imams. According to tradition, the twelfth and final imam disappeared definitively in 329/940-41, only four or five years before the arrival of the Buyids in Baghdad. The Imamis from then on found themselves deprived of a physical leader. For a doctrine entirely dominated by the figure of the imam and different aspects of his authority, this state of affairs proved to be highly awkward. This disturbing situation was also felt by the Buyid princes, and especially by those religious scholars who desired to justify their power, since, as we have seen, numerous texts attributed to the imams explicitly forbade believers to engage in positive political activities. Moreover, the Shiʿite scholars were also embarrassed since in this century of triumphant reason and well-established Sunni orthodoxy, they found themselves legatees of a body of sacred texts, the corpus of Hadith, strongly distinguished by esoteric, mystical and even magical traits, that is to say, "non-rational" elements and doctrines perceived as deviant and heretic.

It was in this lively context within Imamism that a "rationalist" movement led by brilliant jurist-theologians trained by Shaikh al-Mofid (413/1022) and his disciples was firmly established. This movement, called the "School of Baghdad," was to progressively distance itself from the original esoteric tradition represented especially by the traditionalists (*moḥaddeṯ*) of "the School of Qom and Rayy" (Amir-Moezzi, 1992, parts I-1 and I-2; idem, 1993, pp. 69 ff.). These jurist-theologians presented themselves as the only legitimate authorities permitted to fill the void left by the Occultation. In order to enable Twelver Shiʿism to survive as an organized religion, compromises, doctrinal redefinitions, as well as dogmatic and legal redevelopments seemed indispensable. Adapting Shiʿism to the prevailing rationalism, trimming doctrines deemed too deviant so as not to offend the recently formed orthodoxy, providing justifications for the exercise of power shared with the Buyids and through them with the ʿAbbasids—these seem to have been the primary objectives of the Doctors of rationalist law in the School of Baghdad.

At first, the School distanced itself from esoteric doctrines considerably in the name of reason (*ʿaql*). It is indeed in the name of reason that Shaikh al-Mofid dedicated a critical commentary to the "Profession of Faith" (*Resālat al-eʿteqādāt*) by his master Ebn Bābuya (381/991; Mofid, 1951a, passim; Idem, 1951b, pp. 11 ff.; McDermott, chaps. II, XII and XIV). His disciple, al-Šarif al-Mortażā (436/1044), also educated in rationalist Moʿtazelite theology, went as far as to request his co-religionists to censor for themselves entire passages from Kolayni's *Kāfi*, one of the most prestigious collections of Hadith, containing, according to the new rationalist norms, several absurd traditions with regard to reason (Mortażā, 1863, introduction and pp. 98 ff.). Irrational, these could only be inauthentic, such is al-Mortażā's line of argument briefly stated (Mortażā, 1954, pp. 81-83). Thus begins to develop in Shiʿite milieu what had already existed a century before in Sunnism: the science of criticism of Hadith (*ʿelm al-ḥadiṯ*), a discipline whose purpose is to develop the criteria for authenticity in traditions (Hadith). Thus, in the name of reason, the rationalist scholars were to remain silent about a number of esoteric traditions, initiatory and mystical, mainly regarding imamology, and bearing in them all the Shiʿite particularity, in order that divergences with Sunnism could be attenuated and the rationalist movement could associate with circles of power without encountering obstacles too formidable to surmount. Very often, these kinds of traditions were to be taxed with heresy and attributed to those "extremist" (*ḡālin* pl. *ḡolāt*, q.v.) who fabricated Hadith (Amir-Moezzi, 1997, pp. 18 ff.).

Another case of rupture with the past was the practice of *ejtehād*. According to the original Shiʿite point of view, as it appears in the earliest corpus of remaining texts, the Qurʾān and Hadith (traditions going back to the Fourteen Impeccable Ones, the *Čahārdah Maʿṣum* [q.v.]) are the only authoritative sources in religious matters. Any other system or criteria is rejected. Any new legal case, not foreseen by the Qurʾān or Hadith, remains "in suspension" (*waqfa, tawaqqof al-ejrāʾ, soquṭ*) until the imam provides his solution (one of the imams during the period of historic imams or the Hidden Imam after his advent). In conformity with explicit guidance by the imams, any other personal effort by jurist-theologians is rejected and declared forbidden, and this encompasses analogical reasoning (*qiās*), individual reasoned opinion (*raʾy*), or the effort of personal interpretation (*ejtehād*) (Kolayni, n.d., I, pp. 73 ff.; Noʿmāni, p. 77 ff.; Ebn Bābuye, 1984, pp. 6-7; also Brunschvig, pp. 202-3; Amir-Moezzi, 1992, pp. 37-38; idem 1997, pp. 7-16). However, ever since the first half of the 10th century, a certain kind of rationalizing *ejtehād* was exercised in the field of law by such thinkers as Ebn Abi ʿAqil and Ebn Jonayd Eskāfi (Baḥr al-ʿOlum, II, pp. 211-20, III, pp. 301-8; Modarressi, pp. 35-39). After Mofid's ambivalent stance in this regard (Mofid, 1962, 50 f.; idem, 1971b, pp. 115-16) al-Šarif al-Mortażā explicitly presents *ejtehād* as the field for the application of reason in cases left in suspense by the Qurʾān and Tradition (Mortażā, 1967-68, p. 646, 672, 760, 786 ff.; McDermott, iii, chap. 17; Arjomand, pp. 52 f.). Another great figure of the rationalizing Buyid School of Baghdad, Shaikh al-Ṭusi (460/1067), specialist in the science of Hadith and theoretician of the prerogatives of the Doctor of Law, is the author, among other works, of two renowned compilations of traditions with tellingly significant titles: *Tahḏib al-aḥkām* (Rectification of the principles) and *al-Estebṣār fi māʾḵtolefa fih men al-aḵbār* (Clarification of the problem relating to traditions subject to divergence; see bibliography). These compilations seem to have had two main objectives: to provide a systematic revision of ancient compilations and to present law (*feqh*) as by far the most important religious discipline (Amir-Moezzi, *EI²*). With his intelligent attenuation of the sometimes extremely radical positions of his master al-Mortażā, Shaikh al-Ṭusi is able to offer to law and therefore to jurists (*faqih*, pl. *foqahāʾ*), a status and field of action almost independent of the figure of the imam. Indeed he systematically presents the entire body of jurist-theologians as delegates of the imams during Occultation (Ṭusi, 1896, pp. 25 ff., pp. 51-57, 61-63; Idem, 1970, p. 278). The monumental work by Ṭusi sealed the definitive dominance by the jurist-theological rationalist tradition later known as *Oṣuliyya* or the School of the *mojtaheds*, practitioners of *ejtehād*. This dominance that continues to this day, led to the marginalization, and at times the violent repression of the original tradition whose tenants are the Traditionalist *Akbāriyya*, the esotericists and the mystics, including some among the philosophers (regarding the history of the latter, from the medieval period to modern times, see Amir Moezzi and Jambet, 2004, chaps. 3 and 4 of part III, pp. 221-78).

Another sign of the distance of the rationalist tendency in relation to foundational texts: political activity. The Occultation and its consequence—the absence of an "infallible" authority providing leadership for the believers—drove the Doctors of Law to exercise their own authority, in order to ensure that the community had a collective and organized religious life (Eliash, passim; Madelung, 1982, pp. 164-65). Thinkers and jurists attempted to provide solutions in order to resolve the flagrant contradiction that existed between the Hadith forbidding believers from collaborating with those in power and their participation in the Buyid government and thus in the Abbasid State. It is again from the tenth century onwards that the rationalist Doctors open a distinct chapter in their works, a chapter entitled "collaboration with power" (*al-ʿamal maʿa'l-solṭān*) or "the exercise of power" (*ʿamal al-solṭān*). It is interesting to note that the science of Hadith criticism, development of the Shiʿite theory of *ejtehād*, and justification of political power of the jurist-theologian by means of this literary genre, had always been in close connection and underwent strictly parallel developments in the historical evolution of the rationalist movement. The reason for this is relatively simple: the criticism of Hadith, political activity and the practice of *ejtehād* had been explicitly rejected in the early corpus attributed to the imams. To be able to put them into practice, in order to consolidate the foundation of the jurists' authority, the jurists had no other choice but to distance themselves from this corpus. The recourse to rationalism enabled them to develop a critical science of Hadith to be able to declare disturbing traditions as inauthentic or to subject them to biased interpretations precisely by having recourse to *ejtehād* (Amir-Moezzi, 1997, pp. 21 ff.). It is true that ever since the period of the imams, some believers or groups did not follow quietist directives of the imams and devoted themselves to political activities. One can mention those who launched or participated in revolutionary insurrections of a messianic nature. For example, some notable families (Āl-e Nawbaḵt, Āl-e Jonayd, Āl-e Forāt, Āl-e Yaqṭin) were very active in the administration of the state (Monzavi, pp. 748-50) and some religious scholars in the region of Rayy attempted to set up a small independent state at the end of the 9th century (Yāqut, III, pp. 121 ff.). Yet, these cases seem to have been exceptional and the great majority of believers, including the learned and religious scholars, refrained from any actual political activity. Here too, one must await al-Mofid's work to witness the first attempts at theoretical justification for large-scale collaboration of religious Shiʿites with Buyid power. The "founder" of the rationalist movement qualifies and imparts nuances to the famous tradition according to which any power, prior to the Return of the Hidden Imam, is unjust: unjust power is either illegitimate (such is the case with the Abbasids and in general with non-Shiʿites), or legitimate (the case of the Buyids, since it is a matter of staunch Shiʿites, ready to render power to the Hidden Imam in the event he were to return). According to Shaikh al-Mofid, it is permitted for the Shiʿite jurist-theologian to collaborate with legitimate albeit unjust power if this collaboration leads to the promotion of the rights of the Shiʿite community and prevention of its repression (Mofid, 1971b, pp. 40-42; idem, 1989, pp. 811-12). Henceforth, the notions of justice and injustice are to occupy a central position in political Shiʿite thought.

The two most famous disciples of Shaikh Mofid, the brothers Šarif, al-Rażi (406/1016) and al-Mortażā (already mentioned), occupied, one after the other and succeeding their father, a number of important posts as senior civil servants in the administration of the Abbasid State, controlled by the Buyids (Ebn al-Jawzi, VII, pp. 255 ff.; Ebn al-Aṯir, IX, pp. 236 ff.). Inspired by Moʿtazelite ideas regarding evil, al-Mortażā developed fresh thinking concerning the notions of justice and injustice of political power, most notably in his treatise *al-ʿamal maʿa l-solṭān*. There he goes as far as to declare collaboration with the authorities to be obligatory if it enables the re-establishment of neglected rights of the Shiʿites. Basing his argument on a Hadith attributed to imam Jaʿfar according to which "(the sin of) collaboration with power may be expiated by meeting the needs of brothers (Shiʿites)," he declares that he who assumes the responsibility to defend the rights of Shiʿites under the authority of an unjust or illegitimate sovereign, indeed does so tacitly upon the order of the true just sovereign—the Hidden Imam; which is why believers owe him absolute obedience (Madelung, 1980). The ambiguity of al-Mortażā ʿAlam al-Hodā's character, assiduously frequenting the court and the caliphs, becomes apparent in another text, *al-Resāla fi'l-ḡayba*, in which he explains or rather accounts for the duration of the Occultation in terms of the tyranny of the caliphs and persecution of the Shiʿites (Sachedina, 1978). A little while later, Shaikh al-Ṭusi will complete this development by implicitly setting aside the classical doctrine of universal reign of injustice until the advent of the Mahdi. Indeed, according to him any ruler can be considered just if he commands good, forbids evil, and distributes religious taxes equitably and according to Shiʿite law. This is the doctrine of Divine Grace (*loṭf*), according to which God, in his justice, cannot let his worshippers live indefinitely under unjust governments (Ṭusi, 1970, pp. 356 ff.; Idem, 1983, pp. 208-21). Thus, the great theoretician at the end of the Buyid period introduced a new theory that rendered legitimate the establishment of a "just power" during the Occultation.

The fall of the Buyids. The fall of the Buyids, the re-establishment of a rigorous form of Sunnism, and the violent repression of the Shiʿites in the capital were the main reasons for the progressive transfer of the intellectual center of Shiʿism from Baghdad towards another Iraqi city, Ḥella. During the entire 12th and 13th centuries, the learned men of the Ḥella School, almost all belonging to the rationalist movement, were to consolidate even further the speculative bases of the *Oṣuli* tendency (Calder, 1989, pp. 64-68). The Mongol invasion during the middle of the 13th century, the fall of the Sunni caliphate and of the Ismaʿili strongholds, constitute a second major historical turning point from which once again Imami rationalist jurist-theologians were to benefit greatly. After Ebn Edris Ḥelli (598/1202), the first to present, next to the Qurʾān and the Tradition, reason (*ʿaql*) and consensus of jurists (*ejmāʿ*) as the methodological bases for law (Ebn Edris, p. 3; Löschner, index *s.n.*; Modarressi Tabātabāʾi, pp. 3 ff.), Moḥaqqeq Ḥelli (676/1277), author of a monumental work on law, *Šarāʾeʿ al-Eslām*, and the first to have given the Four Books (*al-kotob al-arbaʿa*) their status as authoritative books in Hadith, marked another decisive step in the establishment of an increasingly invasive canonical law in Shiʿite science (Moḥaqqeq Ḥelli, 1859, pp. 378-410; idem, 1900, pp. 7-8). Similarly, the social role of the jurist and perception of his authority as an intellectual and spiritual necessity occupied an increasingly greater place. At the same time, the theory of *ejtehād* is clarified and developed further in the monumental work by ʿAllāma Ḥelli (q.v.; 726/1325), a disciple of Moḥaqqeq. According to him, *ejtehād* constitutes the logical step following imamate/*walāya* of imams to the extent that the fallibility of jurists follows the infallibility of imams. If the imams did not practice *ejtehād*, it was because as inspired and infallible they simply had no need to. "The effort of personal interpretation in matters of faith," the shortest path towards certainty in legal cases unforeseen by Revelation and Tradition, constitutes the jurist-theologian's duty. The fallibility of the latter is as a consequence one of the essential components of *ejtehād* and the jurist who commits an error at the moment of his "personal effort" does not commit a sin (ʿAllāma Ḥelli, 1970, pp. 241 ff.; Halm, pp. 85 ff.; Kazemi Moussavi, 1985, pp. 37 ff.; Calmard, "Mardjaʿ," p. 533b). ʿAllāma Ḥelli thus provides the *mojtahed* with great freedom of action. The infallible authority, reserved for the Hidden Imam, is projected into an indefinite and distant future. From this point onward, it is to the fallible "representatives" (*nāʾeb*, pl. *nowwāb*) of the imam that "legal responsibility" (*wilāya*/*walāya*) falls to resolve practical questions of the present (ʿAllāma Ḥelli, 1970, p. 244 ff.). Simultaneously, ʿAllāma Ḥelli develops a corollary concept of *ejtehād*, namely *taqlid*, imitation or emulation. One who does not meet the conditions to exercise *ejtehād* for himself—i.e., mainly the mass of believers—leaves it to the professional religious scholars. He thus becomes an "imitator" of a jurist-theologian *mojtahed*. The Shiʿites are thus divided into two categories: the *mojtahed*s, those who possess legal knowledge (therefore holders of authority), and their imitators who are supposed to scrupulously apply their directives to remain on the right path (Arjomand, pp. 139 ff.; Halm, pp. 88-89; Schmidtke, 1991, index s.v.). It is also interesting to note that a number of rationalist scholars of the Ḥella School were also collaborators of the Mongol Khans and Ilkhanid rulers.

The Safavid period. Another historical turning point was the reign of the Safavids (907-1135/1501-1722) and the declaration of Twelver Shiʿism as the religion of state. Drawing legitimacy from its religious affiliation, seeking to convert all of Iran to Shiʿism in order to create a credible politico-religious axis in opposition to the Sunni caliphate of the Ottomans, Safavid power felt the need to assure itself of a firm religious ideological weapon. Thus, an entire religious system, if not an official "church" controlled by the state, was instituted. At the same time, the religious system gave rise to a group of professional religious jurists who progressively claimed its independence from power (Aubin, passim; Richard, pp. 39 ff.). This represents the beginning of what came to be known as the Shiʿite "clergy," a clergy that with time was to become more organized, increasingly hierarchic and powerful (Calmard, "Mudjtahid"; Idem, 1982). It was especially from the Safavid period onwards that the *mojtaheds* were to effectively obtain great prerogatives that Tradition had reserved exclusively for the imams: leading collective prayers, collecting specific religious taxes, monitoring justice, etc. (We return to this below). An innovation with considerable implications was the attribution by Shah Ṭahmāsb I of the title "the Representative of the Hidden Imam" to the jurist Moḥaqqeq al-Karaki (940/1534). This promotion occurred at the same time as a reformulation by Zayn-al-Din al-ʿĀmeli known as "the Second Martyr" (965/1557) according to which representatives of the hidden imam during the Minor Occultation (See MAHDI IN TWLEVER SHIʿISM) are allowed to be called "particular representatives" (*nowwāb ḵāṣṣ*) whereas the *mojtaheds* are to be considered as "general representatives" (*nowwāb ʿāmm*) of the imam during the Major Occultation (Arjomand, pp. 229 ff.). This reformulation of traditional elements authorized the jurist-theologians to preside "in the name of the imam" over religious tribunals and to collect certain religious taxes, as had done, according to tradition, the four representatives during the Minor Occultation (Calder, 1981, pp. 479-80; 1982, pp. 4 ff.). The application of these legal redefinitions, accompanied with the management of profits from endowments (*waqf*) assured the religious clergy substantial social influence and great financial independence.

The Qajar period. Under the rule of the Qajars (1209-1346/1794-1925) other decisive steps were to be taken. Although relations between the shahs and the *mojtaheds* had been problematic and at times even adversarial, it is undeniable that one party sought the confirmation of its legitimacy from the other. Although for some time, the title, "special representative of the Hidden Imam" was held by the sovereign, with the agreement of the most influential clerics, the prerogatives of the latter were in return emboldened with the initiative of the powerful leader of the *mojtaheds*, Jaʿfar Kāšef al-Ḡeṭāʾ (1227/1812) of Najaf who authorized Fatḥ-ʿAli Shah to lead the holy war against the army of the Tsar in the name of the Hidden Imam (Lambton, passim; Kohlberg, 1976, pp. 82 f.; Hairi, pp. 280 ff.).

During the same period, the jurist Mollā Aḥmad Narāqi (1245/1830), for the first time it seems in his *ʿAwāʾed al-ayyām*, employed the expression *wilāyat* (or *walāyat*) *al-faqih* to designate the delegation with decision making power given to the jurists, in the name of the Hidden Imam and due to privileges related to the exercise of *ejtehād*. However, the expression in Narāqi refers only to certain specific areas of law (the power to manage particular inheritances or responsibility for orphans, etc.) and does not at all include the right to govern (Kazemi Moussavi, pp. 40 ff.; Kadivar, pp. 17 ff.). At the same time, it is evident that leaving the management of believers' affairs in the hands of the jurists makes the *welāyat al-faqih* vulnerable to politicization. At any rate, henceforth it features in all major legal works of the Oṣuli. Still during the early 19th century, two new complementary concepts, implying the authority of the jurist-theologian, are developed: *aʿlamiyat* (theory of the most learned *mojtahed*) and *marjaʿiyat* (institution of the "source of imitation" par excellence). According to these theories, which are direct extensions of those developed by scholars at the School of Ḥella, the mass of believers must follow or "imitate" the directives and precepts of the most learned Doctor of Law. Although in theory based on theologico-legal competence, in reality the actual influence and hierarchy of the clerics is established based on the notion of leadership, a notion practically defined by popular acclamation and confidence of the believers as illustrated by the payment of religious taxes (Calmard, "Mardjaʿ"). A controversial notion, since, as we have seen, vigorously rejected by the imams, this leadership is exercised mainly by control over socio-professional and ethnic communities. Thus, from Moḥammad-Ḥasan Najafi, (1266/1849-50) to Ayatollah Borujerdi (1380/1961), the Twelver community experienced ten generations of "a unique and universal source of imitation" (Calmard, "Mardjaʿ;" Cole, pp. 40 ff.). At the same time, the formation of a network of theological seminaries (*ḥawza ʿelmiya*) in the holy cities of Iraq and Iran provided the religious authority a considerable social and intellectual foundation. Upon the death of Ayatollah Borujerdi, the collapse of the *marjaʿiyat* institution led to the establishment of several sources of imitation that were often discreetly competing with each other. The contained anger of certain religious milieu opposed to the policy of secularization and modernization of Reżā Shah, founder of the Pahlavi dynasty (1925-79), discovered its most virulent expression in the emphatic 'idealogization' of religious leadership carried out under the influence of Ruḥ-Allāh Ḵomeyni (d. 1989), later to become Ayatollah. The Khomeinist doctrine and at its core "political and charismatic power of the jurist-theologian" (the expression employed with new meaning—and nothing specifically Shiʿite about it—is indeed *welāyat al-faqih*) was thus to follow directly in the historical evolution of the Oṣuli movement. As such, it may be considered as the accomplishment of a long millenary process from rationalization to idealogization (Calder, 1982b, passim; Amir-Moezzi, 1993, pp. 79-81).

The dominance of the theological-legal rational tendency was to ensure the permanence of Shiʿism as an organized religion after the profound crisis provoked by the Occultation. The life and work of great authors of this movement contributed to an intellectual dynamism and a lively debate of ideas that to this day characterizes Shiʿite thought. But at the same time, the rationalist religious system, developed ever since the Buyid period and applied generally from the Safavid period onwards, put into place an entire process of substitution, at least within the Oṣuli movement and its supporters: professional religious jurists replaced the imams, esoteric teachings of the imams were substituted by scholastic theology and law, and the initial quietism gave way to political activism (Amir-Moezzi, 2004, pp. 181-206).

ASPECTS OF JURIST-THEOLOGIAN POWER

The figure of the imam is at the center of all Shiʿite doctrines. For everything that has to do with individual religiosity and inner aspects of faith during the Occultation, the believer must maintain his mystical relation with "the living imam" of the time, i.e., the Hidden Imam, or more generally with the Fourteen Infallible Ones to whom he feels linked by an intense devotion. But absence of the physical person of the imam renders collective practices highly problematic for in order to be properly followed according to ancient Shiʿite law, they need either the direction of the imam or of an individual specifically designated by the latter. According to tradition transmitted by the earliest corpus of Hadith, these prerogatives exclusively reserved for the imam remain "suspended" during the entire duration of his absence since no one else has the right to claim them. It is especially the case with what is termed "the four legal domains" (literally the Four Precepts, *al-aḥkām al-arbaʿa*), most likely of Zaydi origin (Madelung, 1965, p. 154), namely: religious justice (*ḥo-kuma šarʿiya*) and legal punishments (*ḥadd*, pl. *ḥodud*); collection of certain religious taxes; collective prayers (on Fridays and of the two festivities i.e., sacrifice and at the end of the month of Ramadan); and finally, holy war (*jehād*) (Ṭusi, 1955-56 and 1980, s.v.; Ebn Edris, pp. 63, 70, 151-56, 161, 191, 197; Amir-Moezzi, 2004, pp. 207-20).

Absence of the imam, the needs of an organized religious community, especially in legal and economical affairs, as well as the increasing influence of jurist-theologians in the social and political life from the 10th century onward, quite rapidly provoked a revision of ancient law. As we have seen, the seizure of power by the rationalist Doctors of Law, thanks to scholars from the Schools of Baghdad and Ḥella as well as of Safavid Iran, took place by a process of appropriating prerogatives of the imam. This gradual appropriation and thus politicization of Shiʿism are clearly illustrated by problems presented by the "four legal domains."

The first legal domain. According to early Shiʿite law, Shiʿite judges-theologians must be personally nominated by the imam. For legal punishments foreseen by the Qurʾān (amputation of a thief's hand, death sentence of an assassin, application of Talion Law, etc.) the imam is considered as the sole individual authorized to properly apply the Qurʾānic precepts to individual cases (Ebn Edris, p. 203). As a consequence, in the absence of the imam and therefore of an individual specifically designated by him, religious jurisdiction and application of the *ḥodud* became prone to polemical debate. Whereas the Traditionalists were to attempt more or less successfully to keep away from judicial matters, the Rationalists, prominent on the socio-political scene since the Buyid period, confronted the problem. Their embarrassment and the ambiguity of their attitude are evident ever since the work of al-Šarif al-Mortażā. Whereas in his *Masʾala fi'l-ʿamal maʿa'l-solṭān*, he states that the Shiʿite judge, working tacitly under instructions from the Hidden Imam, is authorized to apply legal punishments (Madelung, 1980, pp. 22-23), on the other hand, in his *Resāla fi'l-Ḡayba* he writes that before the Return of the Hidden Imam, legal punishment cannot be applied and blame for this abnormal situation falls upon those who compelled the imam to enter Occultation (Sachedina, 1978, passim). After him, Shaikh Ṭusi saw no obstacle for a religious judge to assume his function if the latter met four conditions: sound mind; knowledge of the Qurʾān and Shiʿite Hadith; proficiency in Arabic; piety and moral rectitude (Ṭusi, 1970, I, pp. 303 ff.). In order to justify the assumption of this role by a jurist-theologian, Ṭusi, and after him almost all his successors, often based their argument on the famous Hadith of Imam Jaʿfar al-Ṣādeq reported by ʿOmar b. Ḥanẓala according to which Shiʿite judges are the representatives and the spokesmen of the imam. These scholars, however, failed to specify that the Hadith in question dealt with the period during the presence of the imam and did not foresee the Occultation (Kadivar, pp. 17-18). These theories of the founder of the School of Baghdad were rejected by certain religious scholars from the School of Ḥella, particularly Ebn Edris and Moḥaqqeq (Ebn Edris, p. 197; Moḥaqqeq, 1982-84, I, p. 138) for whom Qurʾānic sentences are impracticable in the absence of the imam and judges during Occultation can only serve as non-religious, civil servants (*ʿorfi, madani*). On the other hand, ʿAllāma Ḥelli supported Ṭusi's theories by declaring that, since capable of *ejtehad* Doctors of Law are authorized to apply legal punishments (ʿAllāma Ḥelli, n.d., pp. 83-84; Idem, 1989, I, p. 353). Of course, during the Safavid period great figures of the Shiʿite clergy were to follow Ṭusi and ʿAllāma's path. From the 17th century, the clergy presided over religious tribunals and applied legal punishments. From the following century onwards, their power to excommunicate (*takfir*) adversaries was to be added; which explains why these prerogatives are found to be at the basis of numerous offences and repressive actions, at times bloody: from putting to death of adepts of the traditionalist Akbāriyya movement ordered by Waḥid Behbahāni, the leader of the Oṣuliyya in the 18th century, and the fierce repression of Sufis by the sons of the latter (Algar and Arjomand, s.v.), to the execution of intellectuals and "servants of the West" after the Islamic revolution of 1978-79, to say nothing of the massacres of Babis and Baha'is in the 19th and 20th centuries.

The second legal domain. Another critical question: religious taxes, "the Fifth" (*ḵoms*), income taxes and property tax (*ḵarāj*) more precisely. Still according to early Shiʿite law, collection and distribution of these taxes are rights exclusively reserved for the imam and to individuals specifically designated by him. From the Occultation onward, leaders of the religious hierarchy stopped paying the *ḵoms*. (Sachedina, 1980; Madelung, 1981, pp. 193-94; Calder, 1981, pp. 470-71; Idem, 1982a, pp. 39-43). According to a commentary on the Qurʾānic verse 8:41, *k̲oms* consists of two equal parts. The first, called, "the share of the imam," belongs to God, the prophets and the Imams. The other half, "the share belonging to descendants of the imams," is transferred to orphans, the poor and to travelers among the *sayyed*. After Shaikh al-Mofid and his disciples, such as Shaykh al-Ṭusi or Abu'l-Ṣalāḥ al-Ḥalabi, jurist-theologians suggest to believers that they burn or bury the first part if not save it until the Return of the Hidden Imam (Mofid, 1989, p. 277; Ṭusi, 1977, p. 255; Ḥalabi, index, s.v.). As for the second part, they ought to distribute it themselves or pay it to jurist-theologians trusting the latter to re-distribute it properly. Moḥaqqeq Ḥelli in the 13th century, was to have been the first to justify collection by clerics, two parts of the *k̲oms*, as well as the alms-giving (*zakāt*), by the prolongation of the period of the Occultation and the impossibility to hoard this tax until the Return of the Hidden Imam (Moḥaqqeq, 1900, p. 298 f.). From then onward, the rationalist-jurists almost unanimously agreed that it is the *mojtahed*'s duty to levy these taxes on income to be used in the best interests of the community. Property tax posed an even thornier problem to the extent that according to Islamic law in general, it is used mainly to support the State and its functionaries. Well, what to do if this rule is unjust? During the entire medieval period and until the advent of the Safavids, countless and technically detailed discussions were held by the jurists to address this problem but without ever arriving at a definitive solution (Madelung, 1981, passim). This came much later with Moḥaqqeq Karaki, (940/1534) referred to, as noted earlier, as the "representative of the Hidden Imam" by the Safavid ruler Ṭahmāsb I, for he was the first to offer a systematic justification for regarding the *mojtaheds* as the beneficiaries of this tax. One must specify that these donations, sometimes quite considerable sums, that rulers offered to clerics originated mainly from the *k̲arāj*. Karaki thus found himself responsible for an immense fortune, which is why he felt obliged to justify himself by writing an entire treatise dedicated to the collection of *k̲arāj* (Karaki, 1895). Although these theories became the official doctrine of the Shiʿite clergy (Madelung, 1981, passim), it also had its significant opponents such as Ebrāhim b. Solaymān Qaṭifi of Bahrayn (945/1538) and Moqaddas Ardabili (993/1585) (see Bibliography) (Madelung, 1981; Newman, passim).

The third legal domain. Collective prayers, especially those of Fridays accompanied by a sermon (*k̲oṭba*) in which problems of communal life are exposed, have an undeniable political dimension. According to early Shiʿite law, these prayers can only be led by the imam or someone specifically designated by him. Once the latter is absent, the Shiʿites seem to have accepted that these prayers cannot be carried out and must remain "suspended" until the Return of the Hidden Imam. This state of affairs prevailed during the entire medieval period since one of the most frequent accusations from Sunni authors against Shiʿite "heresies" relate precisely to this non-execution of collective prayers (Ṭehrāni, 1990, pp. 69-71). Here too, things begin to change with the establishment of Imami clergy during the Safavid period. From the very beginning of this period, more than a hundred books and treaties were written for or against the legality of collective prayers, the Friday prayer specifically, during the Occultation (Ṭehrāni, 1934-78, XV, pp. 62-82). Again, the role played in this regard by Moḥaqqeq Karaki proved to be decisive. Not only did he declare the Friday prayer and its direction by a cleric to be legal but also obligatory. For this position, he had recourse to the exegesis of some works of rationalist masters of the past, in this case, the two Ḥelli, Moḥaqqeq and ʿAllāma, as well as Moḥammad Ebn Makki known as "the First Martyr" (786/1384), thinkers however, who had never explicitly declared that collective prayer was practicable in the absence of the imam (Karaki, 1988, passim). The obligatory nature of the Friday prayer was henceforth to become a dogma defended by the Safavid State. Throughout Iran, Karaki appointed mullahs to posts as "Friday imam" and "leader of prayer". Those who opposed this doctrine were arrested, reduced to silence or still yet, violently forced to direct the collective prayer (Newman, passim; Karimi Zanjāni Aṣl, p. 237 ff.; see EMĀM-E JOMʿA).

The fourth legal domain. With regard to holy war, one witnessed the same kind of evolution. Based on fundamental texts of Shiʿite law, holy war can only be declared and led by the imam in person or by someone specifically designated by him. The classical authors had established a clear distinction between offensive jihad (*jehād*) declared "in suspense" during the Occultation, and defensive jihad considered legal, if not obligatory in case of external attack. Linking offensive holy war to the Return of the Mahdi once again provided Sunni heresiographers with an opportunity to condemn the Shiʿite by comparing them to the Jews. The numerous argumentative works on the subject, written after the advent of the Safavids, show, here again, that from this period onward the Doctors of Oṣuli Law sought to appropriate this other prerogative of the imam. And this is actually what does occur in the 19th century: for the first time, a Shiʿite jurist-theologian summoned the State to offensive holy war; in the event, as already noted, the *mojtahed* and "representative of the Lord of the Time (i.e., the Hidden Imam)" Shaykh Jaʿfar Kāšef-al-Ḡeṭāʾ authorized the Qajar ruler Fatḥ-ʿAli Shah to lead a holy war against the Tsar. Some years later, another *mojtahed*, Sayyed Moḥammad Eṣfahāni drove the same Shah to undertake a second holy war. The result turned out to be disastrous for Iran which had to definitively surrender the entire Transcaucasian territories to the Russians (Lambton, passim; Kohlberg, 1976; Arjomand, p. 221 ff.).

Bibliography: Hamid Algar, *Religion and State in Iran, 1785-1906. The Role of the Ulama in the Qajar Period*, Berkeley and Los Angeles, 1969. ʿAllāma Ḥelli, *al-woṣul Mabādeʾ elā ʿelm al-oṣul*, ed. A. Ḥ. Moḥammad ʿAli, Najaf, 1390/1970. Idem, *Eršād al ad̲hān elā aḥkām al-imān*, ed. F. Ḥassun, Qom, 1410/1989. Idem, *Tab-ṣerat al-motaʿallemin*, ed. A. Ḥosayni and H. Yusofi, Qom, n.d. (circa 1995). M. A. Amir-Moezzi, *Le Guide divin dans le shi'isme originel*, Lagrasse, 1992

(English transl. *The Divine Guide in Early Shi'ism*, New York, 1994). Idem, "Réflexions sur une évolution du shiisme duodécimain: tradition et idéologisation," in E. Patlagean and A. LeBoulluec, eds., *Les retours aux Ecritures: fondamentalismes présents et passés*, Bibliothèque de l'Ecole des Hautes Etudes, 99, Louvain and Paris, 1993, pp. 63-82. Idem, "Remarques sur les critères d'authenticité du hadîth et l'autorité du juriste dans le shi'isme imâmite," *Studia Islamica* 85, 1997, pp. 5-39. Idem, "Ṭūsī," *EI*² X, pp. 745-46. Idem, and C. Jambet, *Qu'est-ce que le shi'isme?*, Paris, 2004. S. A. Arjomand, *The Shadow of God and the Hidden Imam*, Chicago and London, 1984. Jean Aubin, "La politique religieuse des Safavides," *Le shi'isme imamite*, Paris, 1970, pp. 235-44. Baḥr al-ʿOlum, *al-Fawāʾed al-rejāliya*, n.p. Iran, 1404/1987. Robert Brunschvig, "Les *uṣul al-fiqh* imamite à leur stade ancien (Xe-Xie siècles)," in *Le shîʿisme imâmite*, ed. T. Fahd, Paris, 1970, pp. 201-13. Norman Calder, "*Zakāt* in Imāmi Shiʿite Jurisprudence from the Tenth to the Sixteenth Century A.D.," *BSOAS* 44, 1981, pp. 468-80. Idem, "*Khums* in Imāmi Shiʿi Jurisprudence from the Tenth to the Sixteenth Century A.D.," *BSOAS* 45, 1982(a), pp. 39-47. Idem, "Accommodation and Revolution in Imami Shi'i Jurisprudence: Khumayni and Classical Tradition," *Middle East Studies* 18, 1982(b), pp. 3-20. Idem, "Doubt and prerogative: the emergence of an Imami Shi'i theory of *ijtihād*," *Studia Islamica* 70, 1989, pp. 57-78. J. Calmard, "Le chiisme imamite à l'époque seldjoukide d'après le *kitâb al-Naqḍ*,"*Le Monde Iranien et l'Islam* 1,1971, pp. 43-67. Idem "Mardjaʿ-i taḳlīd," *EI*² V, pp. 533-34. Idem, "Mudjtahid," *EI*² VI, pp. 300-301. Idem, "Les Olamâ, le pouvoir et la société en Iran: le discours ambigu de la hiérocratie," in J. P. Digard, ed., *Le cuisinier et le philosophe: Hommage à Maxime Rodinson*, Paris, 1982, pp. 253-61. Juan Cole, "Imami Jurisprudence and the Role of the Ulama: Morteza Ansari on Emulating the Supreme Exemplar," in N. Keddie, ed., *Religion and Politics in Iran*, New Haven and London, 1983, pp. 33-46. Ebn al-Aṯir, *al-Kāmel*, Beirut, 1385-86/1965-66. Ebn Bābuya, *Ketāb man lā yaḥżoroho'l-faqih*, ed. al-Musawi al-Ḵarsān, 5th ed., n.p., 1390/1970. Idem, *Amāli*, ed. M. Kamareʾi, Tehran, 1404/1984. Ebn Edris Ḥelli, *al-Sarāʾer*, Tehran, lithograph ed., 1270/1853-54. Ebn al-Jawzi, *al-Montaẓam*, Haydarabad, 1357/1938. J. Eliash, "The Ithnāʿashari Shiʿi Juristic Theory of Political and Legal Authority," *Studia Islamica* 29, 1969, pp. 132-54. A. H. Hairi, "The Legitimacy of Early Qajar Rule as Viewed by the Shi'i Religious Leaders," *Middle Eastern Studies* 24, 1988, pp. 271-86. Ḥalabi, *al-Kāfi fi'l-feqh*, ed. R. Ostādi, Isfahan, 1983. H. Halm, *Die Schia*, Darmstadt, 1988. C. Jambet, "Idéal du politique et politique idéale selon Naṣir al-Din Ṭusi," in Ž. Vesel and N. Poorjavady, eds., *Naṣir al-Din Ṭusi, philosophe et savant du XIIIe siècle*, Tehran and Paris, 2000, pp. 31-58. Idem and M. A. Amir-Moezzi, *Qu'est-ce que le shi'isme?*, Paris, 2004. Moḥsen Kadivar, *Naẓariya-hā-ye dawlat dar feqh-e šiʿe*, Tehran, 1997. Karaki, *Qāṭeʿat al-lejāj fi taḥqiq ḥall al-ḵarāj*, in *Kalemāt al-moḥaqqeqin*, lithograph ed., Tehran, 1313/1895. Idem, *Resāla fi ṣalāt al-jomoʿa*, in *Rasāʾel al-moḥaqqeq al-Karaki*, ed. M. Ḥassun, Qom, 1409/1988. M. Karimi Zanjāni Aṣl, *Emāmiye va siyāsat dar naḵostin sadehhā-ye ḡaybat*, Tehran, 2002. Kašši, *Eḵtiyār maʿrefat al-rejāl*, ed. J. Moṣṭafawi, Mashad, 1970. S. A. Kazemi Moussavi, "The Establishment of the Position of *marjaʿiyat-i taqlid* in the Twelver-Shi'i Community," *Iranian Studies* 18/1, 1985, pp. 35-51. Etan Kohlberg, "The Development of Imāmi Shiʿi Doctrine of *Jihād*," *ZDMG* 126, 1976, pp. 64-86 (= *Belief and Law in Imāmi Shiʿism*, Aldershot, 1991, art. no. 15). Moḥammad b. Yaʿqub Kolayni, *al-Rawża men al-al-Kāfi*, ed. H. al-Rasuli Maḥallāti, Tehran, 1389/1969. Idem *al-Oṣul men al-Kāfi*, ed. J. Moṣṭafawi, 4 vols., Tehran, n.d. Idem, *al-Foruʿ men al-Kāfi*, ed. ʿA. A. Ḡaffāri, repr. Beirut, 1401/1980. J. L. Kraemer, *Humanism in the Renaissance of Islam: the Cultural Revival during the Buyid Age*, Leyden, 1992. A. K. S. Lambton, "A Ninteenth Century View of Jihâd," *Studia Islamica* 32, 1970, pp. 181-92. H. Löschner, *Die dogmatischen Grundlagen des schiʿitischen Rechts*, Erlangeṇ, 1971. P. J. Luizard, *La formation de l'Irak contemporain. Le rôle politique des ulémas chiites à la fin de la domination ottomane et au moment de la construction de l'Etat irakien*, Paris, 1991. M. McDermott, *The Theology of al-Shaikh al-Mufid (d. 413/1022)*, Beirut, 1978. Wilferd Madelung, *Der Imam al-Qāsim ibn Ibrāhim und die Glaubenslehre der Zaiditen*, Berlin, 1965. Idem, "A Treatise of the Sharif al-Mortażā on the Legality of Working for the Government (*Masʾala fi'l-ʿamal maʿa l-solṭān*)," *BSOAS* 43, 1980, pp. 18-31 (repr. in *Religious Schools and Sects in Medieval Islam*, London, 1985, art. 9). Idem, "Shi'ite Discussions on the Legality of the Kharāj," R. Peters, ed., *Proceedings of the Ninth Congress of the Union européenne des arabisants et islamisants (Amsterdam 1978)*, Leiden, 1981, pp. 193-202 (= *Religious Schools and Sects*, art. 11). Idem, "Authority in Twelver Shiism in the Absence of the Imam," *La notion d'autorité au Moyen Age: Islam, Byzance, Occident (Colloque internationale de Napoule 1978)*, Paris, 1982, pp. 163-73 (= *Religious Schools and Sects*, art. 10). Vladimir Minorsky, *Iranica*, Tehran, 1964, p. viii. Ḥosayn Modarressi Tabātabāʾi, *An Introduction to Shiʾi Law*, London, 1984. Mofid, *Ketāb šarḥ ʿaqāʾed al-Ṣaduq*, ed. Wajdi, 2nd ed., Tabriz, 1972(a). Idem, *Awāʾel al-maqālāt*, ed. Wāʿeẓ, 2nd ed., Tabriz, 1972(b). Idem, *al-Foṣul al-moktāra men al-ʿoyun wa l-maḥāsen*, Najaf, 1382/1962. Idem, *al-Moqneʿa*, Qom, 1410/1989. Moḥaqqeq Ḥelli, *Nokat al-nehāya* in *al-Jawāmeʿ al-feqhiyya*, lithograph ed., Tehran, 1276/1859. Idem, *al-Moʿtabar*, litho., Tehran, 1318/1900. Idem, *Šarāʾeʿ al-Eslām*, transl. Abu'l-Qāsem b. Ḥasan Yazdi, ed. M. T. Dānešpažuh, Tehran, 1982-84. ʿA.-N. Monzawi, "Irān-dusti dar sadehhā-ye sevvom wa čahārom-e hejri," in Y. Mahdawi and I. Afšār, eds., *Haftād maqāla (armaḡān-e farhangi ba Doktor Ḡolām Ḥosayn Ṣadiqi)*, Tehran, 1990, pp. 743-52. Moqaddas

Ardabili, *al-Ḵarājiya* in *Kalemāt al-moḥaqqeqin*, lithograph ed., Tehran, 1313/1895. Mortażā ʿAlam-al-Hodā, *al-Šāfi fi'l-emāma*, lithograph ed., Tehran, 1301/1863. Idem, *al-Amāli*, Cairo, 1954. Idem, *al-Ḏariʿa elā oṣul al-šariʿa*, ed. Gorji, Tehran, 1967. Andrew Joseph Newman, "The Myth of the Clerical Migration to Safawid Iran: Arab Shiite Opposition to ʿAli al-Karaki and Safawid Shiism," *Die Welt des Islams* 33, 1993, pp. 66-112. Ebn Abi Zaynab Noʿmāni, *Ketāb al-ḡayba*, ed. ʿA. A. Ḡaffāri, Tehran, 1397/1977. Qaṭifi, *al-Serāj al-wahhāj le-dafʿ ʿajāj qāṭeʿat al-lejāj* in *Kalemāt al-Moḥaqqeqin*, lithograph ed., Tehran, 1313/1895. Yann Richard, *Le shi'isme en Iran: Imam et revolution*, Paris, 1980. A. A. Sachedina, "A Treatise on the Occultation of the Twelfth Imamite Imam," *Studia Islamica*, 68, 1978, pp. 109-24. Idem, "Al-Khums: The Fifth in the Imami-Shi'i Legal System," *Journal of the Near Eastern Studies*, 39, 1980, pp. 76-96. *Al-Ṣaḥifat al-Sajjādiya*, attributed to the Imam Zayn-al-ʿĀbedin, ed. and Pers. tr. with commentaries ʿA. N. Fayż-al-Eslām, Tehran, 1375/1955. Sabine Schmidtke, "Modern Modification in the Shiʾi Doctrine of the Expectation of the Mahdi (*inti̤ẓār al-mahdi*): the case of Khumaini," *Orient* 28, 1987, pp. 389-406. Idem, *The Theology of al-ʿAllāma al-Ḥilli*, Berlin, 1991. Āḡā Bozorg Ṭehrāni, *al-Ḏariʿa*, Tehran and Najaf, 1353-98/1934-78. Idem, *al-Rawża al-nażira fi ʿolamāʾ al-meʾat al-ḥādiya ʿašara*, Beirut, 1411/1990. Ṭusi, *ʿOddat al-oṣul*, Tehran, 1314/1896. Idem, *al-Estebṣār fi mā ḵtalafa men al-akbār*, ed. Musawi Ḵarsān, Najaf, 1375-76/1955-56. Idem, *al-Nehāya fi mojarrad al-feqh wa l-fatāwā*, Beirut, 1390/1970. Idem, *K. al-Ḡayba*, ed Āḡā Bozorg Ṭehrāni, Tehran, 1398/1977. Idem, *Tahḏib al-aḥkām*, ed. Musawi Ḵarsān, repr. Beirut, 1401/1980. Idem, *Tamhid al-oṣul*, ed. ʿA. Meškāt-al-Dini, Tehran, 1983. V. Vakili, *Debating Religion and Politics in Iran: The Political Thought of Abdolkarim Soroush*, New York, 1996. Yāqut Ḥamawi, *Moʿjam al-boldān*, Beirut, 1955-57. L. Walbridge ed., *The Most Learned of the Shiʾa: The Institution of the Marjaʿ Taqlid*, Oxford, 2001.

(MOHAMMAD ALI AMIR-MOEZZI)

xi. JIHAD IN ISLAM

The term jihad (Ar. *Jehād* "struggle, striving") occurs (either in its root or derivatives) about forty times in the Qurʾān with the secondary, but dominant, meaning of "regulated warfare with divine sanction." Doctrine concerning jihad in the Qurʾān does not use this word but instead favors the alternate word *qetāl* "fighting." Traditional Islamic exegesis of the Qurʾān divides the doctrine of jihad into four distinct phases, all except the first one dating from the Medinan period of the Prophet Moḥammad's ministry (ca. 622-32). These phases are: (1) nonconfrontation (Qurʾān 15:94-95); (2) defensive fighting (Qurʾān 22:39-40); (3) initiating attack allowed but within strictures (Qurʾān 2:217); (4) unrestricted warfare against all pagans (and perhaps against all unbelievers) at all times (Qurʾān 9:5: schema according to Firestone, chap. 3).

In general, the final phase of the Qurʾānic doctrine of jihad was held to be 9:29: "Fight those who do not believe in Allāh and the Last Day, do not forbid what Allāh and His Apostle have forbidden, and do not profess the true religion, (even if they are) of the People of the Book, till they pay the poll-tax (*jezya*) out of hand and with submission." This limitation of jihad to the period prior to accepting the protection (*ḏemma*) of the Muslims is good for *ahl al-ketāb* "the People of the Book" (i.e., Jews, Christians, Sabeans, later Zoroastrians and Hindus). However, protection is not accorded to pagans, who have only the choice between conversion to Islam and fighting.

In order for jihad to be legitimate, it has to be sanctioned by an authoritative personality (in Sunni Islam, either the caliph or an imam: in Shiʿite Islam, the Imam or one of his representatives and, later, the ulama), directed against a legitimate target, fought according to the rules laid down by the Qurʾān and tradition, and concluded in a manner according with verse 9:29 cited above. These facts mean that, although there are a great many wars associated with Muslims throughout their history, only a limited number of them constitute jihad. However, because of the spiritual prestige of jihad, it is not unusual for there to be disputes concerning the question of whether or not a given battle or conflict constitutes a legitimate jihad.

There exists a general consensus among Muslims that the Prophet Moḥammad's jihad against the polytheists of Mecca, and other Arab polytheists during his lifetime, was legitimate. Questions begin to arise once the prophetic authority was removed. In the immediate wake of his death, most of the Arab tribes revolted against the authority of Abu Bakr (632-34), and some refused to pay their *zakāt* tax. Abu Bakr's uncompromising attitude towards those who refused this Islamic obligation has made it normative to see the *redda* "apostasy" wars (632-33) as a legitimate jihad as well.

Shortly after the *redda* wars, the Arabs began to attack and conquer most of the regions bordering on Arabia: Iraq, Syria, Egypt, etc. These conquests (from 634 to ca. 740) transformed the Middle East, caused a linguistic shift from Aramaic and Greek to Arabic, a religious transformation from Christianity, Zoroastrianism, and Judaism to Islam (over a period of centuries), and formed the territorial basis for the region bound together by the high Islamic culture. Presumably these conquests were jihad; if so, then they would be the best available example of offensive jihad (other prominent Muslim military advances such as the Ottoman conquests are not usually portrayed in the contemporary sources as jehad). Since the boundaries reached by the early Muslim conquerors were in many cases natural ones (mountain ranges, seas, or deserts) with few exceptions there was no pressing need for offensive jihad during the period in which Muslim law was codified (8th through 11th cents.). In general, beyond this initial period jihad was declared in order to repel an invader, to preempt an invasion, or to conquer an area that had been missed by the first Muslim conquerors.

As the doctrine of jihad coalesced in the middle Islamic period, jurists usually divided the world into either two or three sections: *dār al-Eslām*, the area in which Islam was predominant, and *dār al-ḥarb*, the area where war (jihad) was permitted. Sometimes a third area, *dār al-ṣolḥ*, the area with which there was a peace agreement or truce, was included in this list (Khadduri, pp. 49-73). The laws of jihad make elaborate provisions for those non-Muslims from the *dār al-ḥarb* or the *dār al-ṣolḥ* to travel in Muslim lands with safe-conduct (*amān*), usually for the purposes of commerce or pilgrimage. In essence, laws concerning jihad govern all aspects of the relations between Muslims and non-Muslims, whether there is hostility or peace between the two groups.

Jihad is portrayed in both the Sunni and Shiʿite sources as a spiritual exercise leading to redemption. The Sunni authority Moḥammad b. Esmāʿil Bok̲āri (d. 870) in his *Ketāb al-ṣaḥiḥ* (IV, p. 263, no. 2782) gives jihad a rank immediately after prayer and filial piety (*birr al-walidayn*). The spiritual value of jihad is legitimate only when one fights for raising the Word of Allāh to the highest (Bok̲āri, IV, p. 272, no. 2810). Likewise, the Shiʿite author Moḥammad Kolayni (d. ca. 941) states: "Jihad is the most meritorious [action] after the [sacred religious] obligations" (V, p. 4, no. 5; Ṭusi, VI, p. 105). Jihad is usually said to be incumbent upon those who fulfill six criteria. that is, they must be Muslim, male, adult, sane, free, and able-bodied. Although it is imperative that the community as a whole conduct jihad in order to enjoy these spiritual blessings (*farż kefāya* "communal obligation") at all times, during an invasion this obligation becomes incumbent upon each and every Muslim (*farż ʿayn* "individual obligation"). Whether this includes women is debatable; most classical scholars follow Bok̲āri, who cites a tradition that states that a woman's jihad is a righteous performance of the *ḥajj* pilgrimage (Bok̲āri, IV, p. 264, no. 2784).

Beyond these spiritual aspects, jihad as warfare is governed by a number of regulations in both Sunni and Shiʿite law. Declaration of war must be accompanied by a call to convert to Islam, with the other two options being to surrender and pay the *jezya* tax or to fight. Killing of civilians, including women and children, elderly non-combatants and monks, is strictly prohibited. Excessive forms of warfare, such as indiscriminant killing, desecration of bodies, or wanton destruction are also forbidden. Spoils taken in warfare are divided in accordance with Qurʾān 8:41: "And know that whatever booty you take, the fifth thereof is for Allāh, the Apostle, the near of kin, the orphan, and the wayfarer." According to Sunni law this fifth goes to the caliph, while according to Shiʿite law it goes to the rightful Imam (today distributed by the ulama). The religious authorities are responsible for distributing this fifth to others in need. Other laws concerning jihad involve the question of captives. Sunni law affirmed that it was the responsibility of the caliph or the commander in the field to decide what to do with them: they could be held for ransom, sold as slaves, killed, or set free according to his discretion. Laws concerning the ending of jihad are less clear; it seems that this was also up to the discretion of the commander or was decided upon the basis of benefit for the Muslim community.

The most tangled questions concerning jihad focus upon the locus of authority to declare a jihad, and the issue of fighting other Muslims. In general, Sunnis held that the caliph or rightful Imam had the right to declare jihad, but that when an invader invades Muslim lands there is no need for a formal proclamation of jihad as it is *farż ʿayn*. Since the destruction of the Sunni caliphate by the Mongols in 1258, the caliph has had little role in the declaration of jihad (despite occasional attempts by the Ottomans to prove otherwise), and effectively the right to declare jihad has fallen to the ulama. In Shiʿite Islam the right to declare jihad was always vested in the Imam; since the occultation, that right has also devolved upon the *marjaʿ al-taqlid* or the ulama (Kohlberg, pp. 69, 81-82).

The question of against which Muslims jihad is possible is problematic. In a widely cited (both Sunni and Shiʿite) tradition, ʿAli b. Abi Ṭāleb (q.v.) said: "I was ordered to fight those who leave [Islam] (*al-māreqin*), those who broke their oaths (*al-nāketin*), and the unjust ones (*al-qāsetin*)" (Sarak̲si, V, p. 4). The first group is usually said to be the Kharijites (exemplified by the Battle of Nahrawān in 658), the second, those such as Zobayr, Ṭalḥa, and ʿĀʾeša whom ʿAli fought in the Battle of the Camel in 656, and the final group was the Umayyads (the Battle of Ṣeffin in 657). When the implications of this tradition are considered, there are a wide range of possibilities of waging jihad against heretical Muslims or against corrupt and unjust Muslim rulers. In Shiʿite literature the heretical group is usually referred to as *ahl al-baği* "the people of iniquity." This term comes from the well-known tradition associated with the Prophetic Companion ʿAmmār b. Yāser, who was told by Moḥammad that "*al-feʾat al-bağiya* would kill you" (Kohlberg, p. 73). The term *al-feʾat al-bağiya* "the iniquitous band," has some importance in Shiʿite jihad discussions, and tends to be used in place of other terms. It indicates non-Shiʿite Muslims against whom Shiʿites fight. They are unbelievers, but are not actual apostates, and their relatives and property outside the battlefield are not to be harmed because these relatives might be true Muslims (i.e., Shiʿites). However, possessions of the *feʾat al-bağiya* or *boğāt* on the battlefield can be looted in the same way as with non-Muslims (Kohlberg, p. 76).

Jihad is also foundational within Muslim society because of the confrontation against evil that is implicit in it. One widely cited tradition that indicates this type of confrontation is: "The best type of jihad is a word of truth [or justice] in the presence of the sultan" (Abu Dāwud Sejestāni, IV, p. 122, no. 4344). The great Sufi synthesizer Abu Ḥāmed Ğazāli (q.v.; d. 1111) in his *magnum opus*, *Eḥyāʾ ʿolum al-din*, included a section on the importance of the principle of *al-amr beʾl-maʿruf waʾl-nahy ʿan al-monkar* "enjoining the right and forbidding the wrong" for jihad (Ğazāli, II, 314-55; see AMR BE MAʿRUF). According to his analysis, jihad was part of the process of creating a just and ethical society. Without this positive, militant action the believer would be unable to enforce Muslim norms. Thus, by the end of the classical period, jihad was divided into several categories: jihad of the hand or of the sword (militant jihad), jihad of the tongue (speaking truth to power), which sometimes includes jihad of wealth, and jihad of the heart, the Sufi "greater jihad."

Gradually, with the appearance of ascetic groups in early Islam that would later develop into Sufism, a doctrine of non-violent jihad emerged. This doctrine became known as the "greater jihad" (*al-jehād al-akbar*) after the formative tradition: "A number of fighters came to the Messenger of Allāh, and he said: "You have done well in coming from the lesser jihad to the greater jihad." They said: "What is the greater jihad?" He said: "For the servant [of God] to fight his passions" (Bayhaqi, p. 165). By the period of Ḡazāli, the idea of the "greater jihad" had developed into a process by which the believer fought and dominated his soul (in Sufi traditions, usually said to be the locus of evil passions). This idea was developed considerably in the Persian Sufi tradition of Jalāl-al-Din Moḥammad Rumi (d. 1274), who, in his *Maṯnawi-e maʿnawi*, retold the story of the famous fighter Fożayl b. ʿEyāż who gave up his fighting career (*jehād-e aṣḡar* "the smaller jihad") career and spent his time fighting the greater jihad: I threw myself into the Greater Warfare [*jehād-e akbar*] (which consists) in practicing austerities [*riāżat kardan*] and becoming lean.

(One day) there reached my ear the sound of the drums of the holy warriors; for the hard-fighting army was on the march.
My fleshly voice [*nafs*] cried out to me from within:
at morningtide I heard (its voice) with my sensuous ear,
(Saying): 'Arise! 'Tis time to fight.
Go devote thyself to fighting the holy war!'
I answered, 'O wicked perfidious soul, what hast thou to do with the desire to fight? . . .'
Thereupon my soul, mutely eloquent, cried out in guile from within me,
'Here thou art killing me daily, thou art putting my (vital) spirit (on the rack), like the spirits of the infidels.
No one is aware of my plight—how thou art killing me (by keeping me) without sleep and food (Rumi, ed. Barzigar Ḵāleqi, pp. 858-59, ed. and tr. Nicholson, III, pp. 240-41, VI, pp. 227-28).

Many other Sufi writers continued on this vein (Renard, pp. 225-42). A great many of the problematic issues concerning Shiʿite jihad came to the fore in Persia during the Russo-Iranian wars of 1722-23, 1796, 1804-13, and 1826-28 and the *fatwā*s (q.v.) that were issued during that time (see Lambton). Until that time most Shiʿite discussions of jihad had been theoretical; since Shiʿites were rarely in control of a state, and when the Safavids gained control of Persia they arrogated to themselves much of the Imam's authority without discussing the problems with the ulama. Etan Kohlberg cites one of these *fatwa*s to indicate the position of the ulama, who stated: "It is possible to say that *Jihad* during the Imam's concealment is more praiseworthy than during his presence" (Kohlberg, p. 83). This type of authority is further amplified by the *fatwa*s issued during the first part of the 20th century (Rajabi, pp. 247-348).

Modern interpretations of jihad have usually been either apologetic or radical and aggressive. The apologetic trend began in India during the 19th century, when Muslims were first exposed to the polemics of Christian missionaries under the protection of the British raj. A number of the missionaries polemicizing against Islam characterized the entire religion as violent and aggressive. In order to counteract this polemic, Muslim apologists sought to highlight the defensive nature of jihad and its spiritual aspects (the greater jihad). The more radical and aggressive interpretations of jihad have been common among radical Muslims, especially since the 1960s. Most of these interpretations have centered around the idea that because of the unwillingness of Muslim governments to impose the *šariʿa*, they are apostate and jihad against them is necessary. Radical Sunni interpretations of this type usually do not emphasize the role of spiritual jihad. However, the radical Shiʿite interpretation of Ayatollah Ruḥ-Allah Khomeini combines the militant and the spiritual aspects of jihad (*al-jehād al-akbar*; see also Khomeini, 1981, pp. 130, 385-88).

Bibliography: Abu Dāwud Solaymān b. Ašʿaṯ Sejestāni, *Sonan*, 4 vols., Beirut, 1988. Aḥmad b. Ḥosayn Bayhaqi, *Ketāb al-zohd al-kabir*, ed. Amir Aḥmad Ḥaydar, Beirut, 1987. Moḥammad b. Esmāʿil Boḵāri, *Ṣaḥiḥ al-Boḵāri*, ed. ʿAbd-Allāh b. Baz, 5 vols., Beirut, 1991. David Cook, *Understanding Jihad*, Berkeley, 2005. Reuven Firestone, *Jihād: The Origin of Holy War in Islam*, Oxford, 1999. Abu Ḥamid Moḥammad Ḡazāli, *Eḥyāʾ ʿolum al-din*, 5 vols., Beirut, n.d. Majid Khadduri, *War and Peace in the Law of Islam*, Baltimore, 1955. Ayatollah Ruḥ-Allāh Ḵomeyni, *Jehād al-nafs aw al-jehād al-akbar*, n.p., n.d. Idem, *Islam and Revolution: Writings and Declarations of Imam Khomeini*, tr. Hamid Algar, Berkeley, 1981. Etan Kohlberg, "The Development of the Imami Shiʿi Doctrine of *jihad*," *ZDMG* 126, 1976, pp. 64-86. Moḥammad b. Yaʿqub Kolayni, *Foruʿ al-kāfi*, ed. ʿAli-Akbar Ḡaffāri, 6 vols., Beirut, 1996. A. K. S. Lambton, "A Nineteenth Century View of Jihād," *Studia Islamica* 32, 1970, pp. 181-92. Moḥammad-Ḥasan Rajabi, *Rasāʾel wa fatāwā-ye jehādi*, Tehran, 1999. John Renard, "*al-Jihad al-akbar*: Notes on a Theme in Islamic Spirituality," *Muslim World* 78, 1988, pp. 225-42. Jalāl-al-Din Moḥammad Rumi, *Maṯnawi-e maʿnawi*, ed. Moḥammad-Reżā Barzigar Ḵāleqi, Qazvin, 2002; ed. and tr. Reynold A. Nicholson as *The Mathnawí of Jalálu'ddín Rúmí*, 6 vols., London, 1977. Šams-al-Din Abu Bakr Moḥammad Saraḵsi, *Ketāb al-mabsuṭ*, 15 vols., Beirut, 2000. Abu Jaʿfar Moḥammad b. Ḥasan Ṭusi, *Tahḏib al-aḥkām fi šarḥ al-moqnia le'l-Šayḵ Mofid*, ed. Moḥammad-Jaʿfar Šams-al-Din, 11 vols., Beirut, 1992.

(DAVID COOK)

xii. MARTYRDOM IN ISLAM.
Forthcoming online.

xiii. ISLAMIC POLITICAL MOVEMENTS IN 20TH CENTURY IRAN: A GENERAL SURVEY

New Islamic political movements first emerged in the Near East, the Indian Subcontinent, and Indonesia in the middle of the 19th century in response to European imperial expansion and encounter with European intellectual currents, social values, political thought, and technological advances. They represented, at least in part, the weakness of Islamic societies in resisting Western encroachment and its accompanying modes of modernity. A variety of religious responses and political ideologies emerged in this context with pro-democracy, fundamentalist, and socialist tendencies each having an elective affinity with the interests of different social classes and strata. These movements paved the way for subsequent Islamic movements that emerged in early 20th century Iran and in other Islamic societies, and have continued to the present time (for earlier "Muslim" reactions to and engagements with Western political influences, ideologies, and "modernity," see Hairi, 1988; see also Hourani, pp. 57-160; for a comparative treatment of these broad categories of Islamic ideologies, see Enayat, pp. 93-159).

Following a brief discussion of the historical background to the emergence of the above movements in a number of Muslim societies, this entry will focus only on Iran's Islamic political movements. Examining the main phases in the development of various Islamic political movements in 20th-century Iran—before and after the 1977-79 Revolution—this entry will treat the main ideological orientations of pro-democracy Islamic groups and those leaning toward Islamic socialism and fundamentalism. The final section of the entry focuses on the three ideological platforms in practice since the 1979 Revolution.

A HISTORICAL BACKGROUND

Under the influence of Western liberal ideas, the underlying political-religious discourses of the early Islamic movements asserted the compatibility of Islam with democracy—for example, in cases of Refa'a Rafi' Tahtawi (1801-73) in the early-19th century and the al-Nahda (al-Nahża) movement in the latter half of that century in Egypt. Some of these discourses advocated the rights of the citizenry to free and equal participation in national political processes. Another contemporary example of a modernizing movement was the "Islamic Reformist" platform of Sir Syed Ahmad Khan Bahadur (1817-98) in Aligarh, India. These movements, in turn, influenced Iranian lay and religious intellectuals in the course of the 1905-11 Constitutional Revolution (q.v.). The translation in 1909 of Adolrahman Kawakebi's work, *Tabāyeʿ al-estebdād* (The Nature of Tyranny), by Mirzā Moḥammad-Ḥosayn Nāʾini, a prominent clerical figure in Najaf religious center, was another source of influence on the Iranian constitutionalists (see below; for intellectual influences from Egypt and India, see CONSTITUTIONAL REVOLUTION i; INDIA ix).

Other forms of religiously inspired responses to European imperial expansion and various aspects of modernity included a broad spectrum of ideological movements characterized by "traditionalist," "revivalist," and "fundamentalist" attributes. Some of these movements emerged with messianic undertones, such as the Babi movement in Iran (q.v.) and the Qadiri Sufi resistance to Dutch rule in Indonesia in mid-19th century, and the Mahdist movement in Sudan in late 19th century (see ISLAM IN IRAN 2. MILLENARIANISM AND MESSIANISM IN ISLAM). An example of the traditionalist movement with a fundamentalist leaning was the Deobandi/Devbandi movement, which emerged in British-controlled India in the second half of the 19th century in opposition to British domination as well as the Islamic reformist tendencies, and the pro-British stance of the Aligarh movement (see Metcalf, 1982). The news of these movements also had some influence on the new generation of emerging Iranian intellectuals in the late 19th and early 20th centuries (see INDIA ix).

The most influential and distinctly Islamic fundamentalist movement to emerge in reaction to European imperial ambitions, secular political ideologies, and Western modernity was Hasan al-Banna's Muslim Brotherhood (Ek̲wān al-moslemin), which began in Egypt in 1928, and quickly spread to Syria, Jordan, and Palestine. In Iran it contributed to the formation of the Devotees of Islam (see FEDĀʾIĀN-E ESLĀM) in the mid-1940s. A younger generation of Muslim Brotherhood further radicalized in the 1960s-70s and moved from right-wing fundamentalism of Banna to the left-wing fundamentalism of Sayyed Muhammad Qutb (1903-66). Qutb had set forth his leftist ideas in a popular work, *ʿAdālat al-ejtemāʿiya fi'l-Eslām* (Social justice in Islam), which was translated into Persian as *ʿAdālat-e ejtemāʿi dar Eslām*, and reprinted several times from 1962 to 2001 (8th printing). Qutb's other works were also translated into Persian and frequently reprinted during this period.

Islamic movements with socialist leanings emerged later in the Near East and Iran. Mustafa al-Siba'i (Moṣṭafā al-Sebāʾi), Dean of the Law School of Damascus University in late 1950s, and the author of a highly acclaimed socialist textbook in the Arab world, *Ešterākiyat al-Eslām* (The Socialism of Islam), is widely viewed to be the pioneering figure of both Arab and Islamic socialism (see Enayat, 1982, p. 144-50), whose ideas influenced a number of radical Islamic movements. The traditionalist, revivalist, fundamentalist, and socialist religious movements challenged Western ideas of modernity, including the notion of the compatibility of Islam with Western democracies.

In practice, the various Islamic movements partly adhered to ideal-typical forms of democracy and socialism or even traditionalism and fundamentalism. Some sought to combine Islamic fundamentalism and Islamic socialism, as in the case of al-Siba'i, the leader of the Syrian organization of the fundamentalist Muslim Brotherhood.

Compared with Sayyed Qutb, Siba'i leaned more toward socialism than Islam, as can be seen by the name he selected for his fundamentalist organization, the "Islamic Socialist Front" (see Enayat, 1982, p. 144-50). Others have sought to fuse Islam with fascist ideologies, as in the case of the Egyptian Nationalist Islamic Party, founded in 1940 (formerly Young Egypt; see Gershoni and Jankowski, 1995).

In the broader discourse of Islamic modernism, one must include the recent contributions of those who have advocated democracy for Islamic societies, including Harun Nasusion, Mohammed Arkoun, Abdolkarim Soroush (ʿAbd-al-Karim Soruš) and Mohammad Mojtahed Shabestari (Moḥamamd Mojtahed Šabestari). Drawing from modern hermeneutics in theology (see HERMENEUTICS), these "neo-Mu'tazelite" thinkers emphasize the primacy of "reason" in addressing modern social and political problems instead of relying on the "authentic sources" of scripture and tradition (see further below; for the advocates of neo-Mu'tazelism in Islamic societies, see, e.g., Martin and Woodward).

DEVELOPMENT DURING THE PERIOD OF 1905-79

This period may itself be divided into several phases with respect to the development of Islamic political ideas and movements.

The 1905-1911 Constitutional Revolution. The platform of liberal nationalism, which was introduced in the second half of the 19th century, flourished in the course of the Constitutional Revolution. The idea of popular sovereignty, in particular, became the rallying call for the advocates of constitutionalism, progress, and equality. A rudimentary form of liberal nationalism, advocating the compatibility of Islam with democracy, also found a few adherents among high-ranking Shiʿite clerics who supported the Constitutional Revolution. These included Sayyed Moḥammad Ṭabāṭabāʾi and Mirzā Moḥammad-Ḥosayn Nāʾini as well as influential preachers, including Sayyed Jamāl al-Din Eṣfahāni (see CONSTITUTIONAL REVOLUTION i-ii; see also Yaḡmāʾi), though some members of this group later abandoned the liberal tenets of the constitutionalist movement, such as some degree of tolerance toward secularism and equality of all faiths before the law.

An Islamic fundamentalist orientation, led by Shaikh Fażl-Allāh Nuri, also emerged in this period. This was in response to liberal nationalism and in direct opposition to the clerical and lay supporters of constitutionalism. In his *lawāyeḥ* (pamphlets), published in 1907 in the form of leaflets, treatises, and manifestos, Nuri argued that a constitutional regime and the key ideas of "modernity" are contrary to the tenets of Islam. His condemnation of constitutionalism—attacking liberty, equality, and representative government as "un-Islamic innovations" (*bedʿa*)—provided Moḥammad-ʿAli Shah with a religious justification for the bombardment of the Majles premises and the suspension of the constitutional regime in June 1908. Nuri's orientation shared certain key characteristics with other fundamentalist movements of the 20th century (see below). It differed from other contemporaneous movements in the Islamic world, such as those espoused by Sayyed Jamāl-al-Din Asadābādi (see AFḠĀNI) in the 19th century and his disciple, the Egyptian Muhammad Abduh, in being "reactive" rather than "revivalist" (for the revivalist ideas of Jamāl-al-Din and Abduh, see Hourani, 1983, pp. 71-160; for comprehensive original, primary sources on Nuri's ideas see Nuri, ed., Torkamān, 2 vols., 1983–84, which includes a revealing debate on the fundamental principles of "pro-democracy Islam" and "Islamic Fundamentalism" between Ṭabāṭabāʾi and Nuri, see Nuri, II, 1984, pp. 172-75; for English tr. of one of Nuri's major manifestos, see Hairi, 1977b, pp. 327-39; Martin, 1989, pp. 181-96; see further ISLAM IN IRAN xvi. ISLAM AND FUNDAMENTALISM, forthcoming, online).

To refute Nuri's criticisms of the constitutional regime as incompatible with the fundamental principles of Islam, Nāʾini published *Tanbih al-omma wa tanzih al-mella* (The Admonition of the Religious Community and the Refinement of the Nation) in 1909. With a preface written by two leading *mojtahed*s of Najaf's important Shiʿite religious center, Ākund Mollā Moḥammad-Kāẓem Ḵorāsāni (q.v.), and Shaikh ʿAbd-Allāh Māzandarāni, this book became an influential treatise in the constitutionalist period. However, like other works of the time in support of pro-democracy ideas in Islamic societies of the Middle East and the Indian Subcontinent, Nāʾini's treatise was criticized by some on the grounds that he misunderstood the Western concepts of freedom, equality, democracy, and separation of powers, and therefore glided over the problem of reconciling them with Muslim scripture (see, e.g., Hairi, 1977b, pp. 218-22; cf. Enayat, p. 134).

The 1941-53 period. Islamic protest movements in Iran, which had waned in the 1910s-30s, re-emerged during the 1940s. A significant development in this period was the appearance of religious intellectuals with ideological leanings toward democracy or socialist platforms at the University of Tehran, and in high schools in response to the challenge of the pro-Soviet Tudeh Party's propaganda campaign among the intelligentsia, and the increasing popularity of the Party's Youth Organization (Sāzmān-e javānān) among students (see COMMUNISM ii). The adherents of both democracy and socialism in Muslim societies attempted to offer ideological alternatives to Marx's then-popular historical materialism, which claimed to offer a "scientific" interpretation of social problems and historical development (Rahnema, 1998, pp. 6-7, 12-19, 40-41, 50-51, 100-101; Jaʿfariān, pp. 15-46).

The ideas of the compatibility of Islam with democracy in the Constitutional Revolution also gained a new generation of adherents among the religious intelligentsia, mostly rallied around Mehdi Bazargan (Bāzargān), Yad-Allāh Ṣaḥābi, and Ayatollah Sayyed Maḥmud Ṭāleqāni. The continuity of these Islamic ideas from the Constitutional era may be seen in the reprint of Nāʾini's *Tanbih al-omma* in 1955, with an introduction by Ṭāleqāni (see Bazargan, 1998, pp. 73-84; for Ṭāleqāni's "Last Sermon," see Kurzman, 1998, pp. 46-48; for a detailed survey of the movement in this period, see Chehabi, pp. 103-39).

The Devotees of Islam (see FEDĀʾIĀN-E ESLĀM) was a fundamentalist Islamic movement that was founded during the 1940s and early 1950s, led by a young, charismatic religious student, Nawwāb Ṣafawi. The movement held a hostile attitude toward the then secular Iranian state and the highest-ranking Shiʿite leader and source of emulation, the Grand Ayatollah Sayyed Ḥosayn Ṭabāṭabāʾi Borujerdi (q.v.), on the grounds of the latter's accommodating stance toward the regime. The Devotees of Islam influenced the course of political events in this critical period by carrying out two political assassinations: that of ʿAbd-al-Ḥosayn Hažir (q.v.), a former prime minister and powerful minister of the royal court, on 4 November 1949, which led to the suspension of the elections of the 16th Majles, and calls for new elections in Tehran. The assassination of Hažir, and the active participation by the Fedāʾiān in protecting the ballot boxes from tampering by professional thugs, were instrumental in the successful election of Moḥammad Moṣaddeq and a number of other National Front candidates to the 16th Majles from Tehran (ʿErāqi, pp. 41-45). Furthermore, with the assassination of Prime Minister Ḥāj-ʿAli Razmārā on 17 March 1951, the Fedāʾiān paved the way for the approval of Moṣaddeq's proposal for the nationalization of the oil industries by the Majles, and his appointment to the premiership on 2 May 1951 (for a detailed account of their role in the politics of the early 1950s, see Rahnema, 2005, pp. 53-97).

An Islamic movement with socialist leanings, seeking the egalitarian transformation of society within an Islamic framework, also emerged in 1943 with the publication of a manifesto by Moḥammad Nakšab, "Divine-worshipping socialists" (*Sosiālisthā-ye Kodāparast*). Although this movement remained in the shadow of liberal nationalism in this period, it significantly influenced the next generation of religious intellectuals in the radicalized era of the 1960s-70s, with the number of its adherents surpassing the adherents of Bazargan's Iran Liberation movement in universities at this period. Nakšab's ideas were a form of "humanist Islamic socialism" based on the teachings of the Qurʾān, emphasizing social justice and equality of all pious Muslims based on the teachings and examples from the life of the Prophet, Imam ʿAli b. Abi Ṭāleb (q.v.), and Imam Ḥosayn (see further, ISLAM IN IRAN XV. ISLAM AND SOCIALISM, forthcoming, online; Nekuruh, 1998; for an account of this movement, see Rahnema, 1998, pp. 24-34).

The 1960s-70s period. Following a relatively dormant phase after the 1953 coup d'état (q.v.), the period of 1960s-70s saw the revitalization and expansion of all brands of political Islam, inspired by the rise of Ayatollah Khomeini as the charismatic political source of emulation (with access to religious networks and financial resources). Incited by his increasingly militant rhetoric, scores of veterans and sympathizers of the Devotees of Islam and other like-minded religious activists organized in a number of mourning religious groups (*hayʾathā-ye ʿazādāri-e ḥosayni*) during the 1950s-early 1960s, founded the Coalition of Mourning Islamic Groups in 1963 (Hayʾathā-ye moʾtalefa-ye eslāmi, changed later to Jamʿiyat-e moʾtalefa-ye eslāmi [q.v.] and to Ḥezb-e moʾtalefa-ye Eslāmi in 2004). They played a key role in the 1963 urban riots in reaction to Khomeini's arrest, as well as in the assassination of Prime Minister Ḥasan-ʿAli Manṣur in 1964. They also participated in the revolutionary movement of 1977-79, forming a powerful right-wing fundamentalist camp following the revolution (for two insiders' accounts of the development of the Coalition of Islamic Groups by their founders and leaders, see Mehdi Erāqi; Bādāmčiān; see further ISLAM IN IRAN XVI. ISLAM AND FUNDAMENTALISM, forthcoming online).

Also reemerging in this period was Bazargan's pro-democracy nationalist movement that began in the 1940s adhering to the idea of the compatibility of Islam with democracy. It became a political party in 1961 as the Liberation Movement of Iran (Nahżat-e āzādi-e Irān). In its 1961 platform, the Liberation Movement advocated national sovereignty, freedom of political activity and expression, social justice under Islam, respect for Iran's constitution, the Universal Declaration of Human Rights, and the Charter of the United Nations. Although this movement had lost the support it enjoyed in the 1940s-50s in the University of Tehran, it played an important role in the political religious movements of this period, and also later in the 1977-79 Revolution. The popularity of Mehdi Bazargan and Yad-Allāh Ṣahābi stemmed from their presumed mastery of modern sciences. They were seen as examples of a pious Muslim, modern scientist, and pro-democracy nationalist all rolled into one. Bazargan and Saḥābi endeavored to theorize the idea of the compatibility of Islam with democracy through discovering the basis of human rights and democracy in "pristine Islam," that is, through obtaining the needed theological and jurisprudential support from scripture and the deeds of the fourteen infallible Shiʿite leaders (see further, ISLAM IN IRAN XV. ISLAM AND DEMOCRACY, forthcoming, online; for a comprehensive treatment, see Chehabi, pp. 140-312).

Of all Islamic political orientations, "militant Islamic socialism" became most popular in the 1960s-70s, the period that also witnessed a surge in the popularity of secular socialist ideologies among the youth throughout the world. Beginning in the mid-1960s, Ali Shari'ati (ʿAli Šariʿati), influenced in part by Nakšab's ideas, became a source of inspiration to many religious-minded students and, more specifically, the members of the guerrilla organization, People's Mojahedin of Iran (Mojāhedin-e kalq-e Irān) as well as other Islamic leftist groups, including the Party of Islamic Nations (Ḥezb-e melal-e eslāmi; for a treatment of this current and other small Islamic groups with militant leftist orientations, see Ḥosaynian, pp. 499-543, 806-74; see also Jaʿfariān, pp. 92-94, 145-70). The increasing popularity of Shari'ati among religious students derived from his passionate and mesmerizing style of sermons and writings, which featured a radical reading of the Shiʿite idea of human commitment to revolt against tyranny through martyrdom and jihad, combined with the revolutionary ethos of the French left in the era of rising radical movements throughout the world (see below).

The Islamic leftist currents emphasized the ideas of an Islamic classless society as well as solidarity with third-worldist national liberation movements and the Palestinian cause. Shariʿati made many bold innovations in the interpretation of Shiʿite doctrines, particularly as it applied to the relationship between religion and politics, and he supported the use of violence in transforming society into an Islamic utopia. He envisaged a classless society of Muslims (*jāmeʿa-ye biṭabaqa-ye tawḥidi*) under the leadership of committed religious intellectuals with no room for the clergy (*Eslām bedun-e ruḥāniyat*). Shariʿati's ideology was a blueprint for a social revolution and a radical transformation of the social order, and his followers were primarily made up of young students (see further ISLAM IN IRAN XV. ISLAM AND SOCIALISM, forthcoming, online; for a detailed discussion of Shariʿati and his ideas, see Rahnema, 1998, pp. 35-370; for his relation with various Islamic orientations, see also Ḥosaynián, pp. 762-98; for his ideological orientations, see below).

With the emergence of Ayatollah Khomeini as a militant populist in the 1960s-70s, combining personal charisma and the will to power with the spiritual charisma embedded in the office of the Shiʿite source of emulation, all variants of Islamic political currents gradually found a place under the canopy of his leadership. They were later joined by a large number of leftist and liberal political forces in the final years of the 1970s, contributing in various ways to the success of the 1977-79 Revolution (see ISLAM IN IRAN xvii. ISLAMIC REVOLUTION OF 1977-79, forthcoming, online; for Khomeini's charismatic authority, see Ashraf, 1994, pp. 101-55; for a discussion of various urban forces in revolution, see Ashraf and Banuazizi, 1985, pp. 3-40; idem, 2001, p. 237. Bazargan, 1982, pp. 16-76; for the role of clerical forces in the revolution, see Ruḥāni, 1985; Ḥosayniān, pp. 551-902; Jaʿfariān, pp. 47-91, 171-92).

DEVELOPMENT DURING THE PERIOD OF 1979-2000

With the founding of the Islamic state in 1979, many of the leaders and cadres of the revolutionary struggle representing the competing "Islamic" political orientations emerged as the elites of the new regime and began engaging in intense factional politics that continue to this day.

Revolutionary honeymoon. The immediate aftermath of the February 1979 Revolution was a brief period of revolutionary honeymoon. In this period, the liberal factions of both religious and secular currents in the revolutionary coalition, including Mehdi Bazargan's Liberation Movement and secular veterans of Moḥammad Moṣaddeq's National Front, occupied most upper and middle-echelon positions within the official bureaucracy. Yet from the beginning the "unofficial" bureaucracy was taking shape behind the scenes made up of both right-wing fundamentalists and socialist Islamic forces, which controlled local revolutionary committees (Komitahā-ye enqelāb-e eslāmi), and the newly founded Islamic Revolutionary Guards Corp (Sepāh-e pāsdārān-e enqelāb-e Eslāmi; hereafter, the Revolutionary Guards or Guards) and its affiliated organization, Mobilization Resistance Force (Niru-ye moqāwemat-e Basij or Basij-e Mostażʿafin, hereafter Paramilitary forces). The militants also controlled various foundations, which were established to manage confiscated property and nationalized enterprises with enormous assets. The militant groups monitored and obstructed the daily activities of the government (see Bazargan, 1982, pp. 79-209; idem, 1983, passim).

Constitution of the Islamic Republic. As early as August 1979, Ayatollah Khomeini banned twenty-one newspapers of liberal-nationalist and secular-leftist groups who were critical of certain provisions of the new Constitution. The main controversial issue at this time was the nature of the Constitution of the new republic: either an outright republican regime with sovereignty of the people or a hybrid of republican super structure and Islamic substructure with the supreme authority of the guardian jurist (*welāyat-e faqih*). A sharp division evolved between the followers of Khomeini's platform (Ḵaṭṭ-e Emām), who supported his concept of the sovereignty of the guardian jurist or supreme spiritual leader, and those who opposed it, including Bazargan's Liberation Movement and his cabinet, National Front supporters, People's Mojahedin of Iran, and most secular leftist forces, including the Fedāʾiān-e ḵalq, who had a large group of followers among the students and youth (see COMMUNISM iii). Yet, the Assembly of Experts, whose members were popularly elected and predominantly supporters of Khomeini, approved the Constitution of the Islamic Republic in August, establishing rule by the Jurisconsult, consolidating the power of the highest political authority and the highest religious authority under Ayatollah Khomeini. According to the Constitution, the supreme leader is commander in chief of the armed forces and security forces, appoints the clerical members of the Guardianship Councils, a body of six cleric and six lay members, to approve the laws enacted by the Majles with veto power, and also appoints the head of the judiciary. He is the official arbiter between competing camps and separation of powers and, more specifically, between the Revolutionary Guards and other branches of the government. In other words, the Islamic Republic was founded as a hybrid of a Western type republican regime with an elected president, elected parliament, and elected Assembly of Experts, combined with an Islamic fundamentalist apparatus with no accountability to the Majles (see CONSTITUTION ii; for the debate on the Constitution, see Montaẓeri, pp. 522-57; Schirazi; Bakhash, pp. 71-91; for the structure of power in the Islamic Republic, see Buchta).

The radicalization process. In the years immediately following the revolution, several circumstances contributed to an atmosphere of terror, a resort to brutal repression, violent confrontations with the armed opponents of the regime, and, more generally, a move toward radicalization of politics in the Islamic Republic. These included the takeover of the American Embassy by Islamic leftist students in November 1979 and the ensuing hostage crisis, which led to the collapse of the liberal provisional government of Prime Minister Bazargan, and helped mobilize the radical forces of the secular and Islamic left in a new "anti-imperialist" front against the United States and the West in general (see Bazargan, 1982 pp. 77-154; idem, 1983, passim; Chehabi, pp. 253-304). Also of help to the radicalization process was Iraq's invasion of the Iranian territory in September 1980 and the onset of the Iran-Iraq War (q.v.), which required a massive mobilization of nearly every segment of Iranian society for support of the war effort.

In January 1980, the first presidential elections were held and Abul Hasan Bani Sadr (Abu'l-Ḥasan Bani Ṣadr), who had leaning toward the Islamic left and liberal nationalism, emerged as the victor. His victory, in spite of intense objections by the Islamic republican party (IRP: Ḥezb-e jomhuri-e eslāmi, whose nominee was Ḥasan Ḥabibi), would have not been possible if Bani Sadr had not enjoyed the outright support of Ayatollah Khomeini. As a result from the beginning of his presidency Bani Sadr faced increasing obstructions by the IRP (see Montaẓeri, pp. 258-59). The subsequent elections of the First Islamic Consultative Assembly (Majles-e šurā-ye eslāmi), held in March, resulted in the landslide victory of the IRP and Mojahedin of Islamic Revolution (Mojāhedin-e enqelāb-e eslāmi) and a small group from Liberation Front, Bani Sadr's supporters, and others (see Ḥajjāriān, pp. 140-41).

Following the hostage crisis and the outbreak of the Iran-Iraq War of 1980-88, the Islamic regime faced a period of intense crisis marked by internal conflict and instability, which culminated in the impeachment of President Bani Sadr. This event led to a series of assassinations, masterminded and implemented by the People's Mojahedin of Iran. They assassinated the powerful head of the judicial system, Ayatollah Moḥammad Ḥosayni Behešti, Prime Minister Moḥammad-Jawād Bāhonar, and President Moḥammad-ʿAli Rajāʾi as well as scores of powerful provincial clerics, cabinet members, and Majles deputies, most of whom were members of the Islamic Republican Party (for a diary of this critical period, see Hashemi Rafsanjani [ʿAli-Akbar Hāšemi Rafsanjāni], 1998).

The rise of Islamic left: 1981-89. This period saw a shift toward the left when Majles approved the appointment of Mir Hosayn Musavi (Mir Ḥosayn Musawi) as prime minister. In this period, the leftist Islamic forces rose to prominence with the support of Ayatollah Khomeini (hereafter referred to as "leftists"). During the last years of Khomeini's life, the infighting between these leftist forces and the right-wing fundamentalist groups within the regime intensified over a number of basic socio-economic and cultural issues as well as over which faction monopolized the powerful state agencies and the media. An increasing factional conflict led to the dissolution of the Islamic Republican Party (1979-87), the bastion of the right-wing camp, as well as the leftist Mojahedin of the Islamic Revolution (Mojāhedin-e enqelāb-e eslāmi). Meanwhile, the left-wing clerics left the Militant clerics association (Jāmeʿa-ye ruḥāniyat-e mobārez) and formed a new organization, the Combatant clerics society (Majmaʿ-e ruḥāniun-e mobārez). These developments led to a sweeping victory of the left in the elections for the Third Majles in 1988. Now in command of all branches of the government, the leftist cabinet of Musavi championed the interests of the peasants and workers. However, the Guardianship Council rejected a number of radical laws enacted by the Majles, including a progressive labor law, a law for imposing a ceiling on agricultural lands as well as urban commercial lands and real estates, and nationalization of foreign trade. To pave the way for the approval of these laws, Khomeini declared the absolute authority of the spiritual leader (*welāyat-e moṭlaqa-ye faqih*) and created the "Expediency Council" (Majmaʿ-e tašḵiṣ-e maṣlaḥat-e neẓām) in 1988 to review controversial bills, in the event the Majles (at the time dominated by the left-wing camp) and the Guardian council (dominated by right-wing camp) failed to reach a consensus on theological and legal matters. The members of the Expediency council, in addition to the conservative members of the Guardian council, included the heads of the legislative and judicial branches, as well as the then Prime Minister Musavi, who frequently supported the aforementioned radical laws. Khomeini's son Aḥmad, as well as his chief of personal bureau, Majid Anṣāri, who supported the radical laws, also became members of the Expediency council. President Ali Khamenei (ʿAli Ḵāmenaʾi) was the only relatively moderate addition to the new review board. The absolute authority of the *faqih* (Shiʿite guardian jurist; now specifically Khomeini as the supreme leader), it was now argued, would augment the powers of the legislative bodies, including both the Majles and the Guardian Council (see Ashraf, 1994).

At least four factors contributed to the leftward gravitation of the regime in the 1980s: the legacy of both the secular and religious left in Iranian society during the 1960s-70s; the exigencies of the Iran-Iraq War and Iran's worsening international relations in the aftermath of the American hostage crisis, as well as the antagonism of regional regimes to Khomeini's revolutionary stance, the revolutionary aura and prestige of Khomeini around the world and the expectations of militant Islamic movements in different parts of the world (irrespective of sectarian divisions in Islam) for emulating the example of the Islamic Republic; and, above all, the preservation and cultivation of Khomeini's charismatic authority, intended to transcend all competing Islamic political currents in Iran.

The post-War/post-Khomeini era. The early post-war/post-Khomeini era, from 1989 to the mid-1990s, witnessed the demise of the Islamic left and the formation of Islamic pragmatism, a process inaugurated by the presidency of Hashemi Rafsanjani (1989-97) and the incorporation of the offices of president and prime minister. Under these circumstances, a new centrist and pragmatist faction, seeking to strike a balance between the right and the left, was formed. The right-wing fundamentalists and their base of support in the bazaar-mosque alliance tactically supported this more moderate, pragmatist camp.

Iran's many setbacks in the long and costly war with Iraq and the eventual acceptance of a UN-sanctioned settlement by Ayatollah Khomeini, who had previously declined all offers of a cease-fire after having publicly declared the overthrow of the Iraqi regime as one of Iran's war objectives (referring to the humiliation of the cease-fire as "swallowing a chalice of poison"), led to the disillusionment of the people and discontent among the Revolutionary Guards (see IRAN-IRAQ WAR; for blaming the Guards for the setbacks, see Reżāʾi, pp. 9-11). Furthermore, the heavy death toll suffered, the destruction of cities and the country's ravaged infrastructure, and the shattered economy all contributed to the growing sense of frustration among people from all walks of life.

The main issue in the immediate post-war period was the path to be followed in reconstructing the country. The pragmatists, enjoying the support of the new middle classes, promoted an economic policy of greater privatization and international trade, combined with a social policy of relative tolerance. The pragmatists advocated a mixed economy based on the coexistence of public and private sectors. However, they also wanted rapid economic development with foreign investments and assistance. This policy proved unsavory not only to the "left," which pushed for a state-dominated economy, but also to the conservative forces opposed to Iran's opening up to foreign powers, keeping in mind also reliance of some prominent members of the conservative camp on the traditional bazaar middle class who were wary of outside competition. The pragmatists' social bases of support consisted of the new middle classes, the industrial entrepreneurs, modern commercial bourgeoisie, government employees, and the intelligentsia (Ashraf, 1994, pp. 101-55). However, following the victory of the right-wing fundamentalist factions such as the Militant Clerics Association and the Coalition of Islamic Groups in the elections of the Fourth Majles (1991-95), they obstructed moderate policies of the pragmatist president Hashemi Rafsanjani.

The new pro-democracy ideas and the 1997 reform movement. The period of the 1990s ushered in two new Islamic discourses in Iran: the "new pro-democracy" and the "new fundamentalist," both either substantively or instrumentally informed by the new philosophical and social science discourses.

The most eloquent expression of the new Islamic pro-democracy reformist discourse may be found in the publications of the "Kiān circle" (Ḥalqa-ya *Kiān*), formed around the weekly intellectual journal *Kiān*, founded by Abdolkarim Soroush, Mojtahed Shabestari, Moḥsen Kadivar, ʿAli-Reżā ʿAlawitabār, Saʿid Ḥajjārian, and ʿAbbās ʿAbdi (see below; for details of their ideas, see ISLAM IN IRAN xiv. ISLAM AND DEMOCRACY, forthcoming, online; see also Soroush, 2000a; 2000b; Mojtahed shabestari, 2002; ʿAlawi-tabār, 2000; idem, 2007; Ḥajjāriān; Bāqi). The new "reformist" political discourse broadened the social base of support for pro-democracy Islamic forces. While the old, pristine "pro-democracy" discourse of Bazargan had lost its appeal for the intelligentsia, the new reformist ideology enjoyed overwhelming support among the younger generation of religious and even secular intelligentsia and, more specifically, among a large group of religious "leftist" forces who now shifted their ideological orientation from Shariʿati's emotional discourse of authenticity to the rational political philosophy of Soroush and Mojtahed Shabestari as well as the modern social sciences. This ideological shift, which began in the late 1980s, was also influenced by the increasing disillusionment of many younger religious intellectuals with the authoritarian and repressive character of the post-revolutionary Islamic-leftist-dominated government, and coincided with the collapse of the Soviet Union and the emergence of pro-democracy movements in countries such as China.

The coalition of the new pro-democracy currents, the reformed Islamic-socialist currents (including Mojahedin of Islamic Revolution and the Bureau of Consolidating Unity [Daftar-e taḥkim-e waḥdat]), and Hashemi Rafsanjani's pragmatist clique, known as the Executives of Construction (Kārgozārān-e sāsandagi), succeeded in securing the confidence of the people, which led to the sweeping victory of Muhammad Khatami (Moḥammad K̲ātami) in the presidential elections of 1997 over Nāṭeq Nuri, the nominee of the right-wing fundamentalist camp. The 1997 presidential elections ushered in a new era in post-revolutionary Iranian politics. Mohammad Khatami's campaign platform emphasized the rule of law, establishment of a civil society, a moderation in foreign policy and improved international relations, and the protection of civil liberties guaranteed under the Islamic constitution (see Bāqi, pp. 32-90; Ḥajjāriān; ʿAlawi-tabār).

Khatami's election victory in 1997 was followed by the triumphant performance of reformist candidates in both the municipal elections of 1999 and the Majles elections of 2000. This unmistakably pro-reform popular mandate at the polls, however, did not translate into the legislative authority and effectiveness of the reformists. This failure can be attributed in part to internal divisions over the extent and priority of pro-democracy reforms among the main constituents of the reformist coalition. But the chief reason for this failure was that the new fundamentalists retained control of the security forces as well as the judiciary and, along with their allies from extremist currents, staged an offensive against the more popular reformers in the three elections. The offensive by the Paramilitary forces consisted of various tactics of intimidation, vigilantism, and acts of terror directed against their political rivals. They also launched a systematic crackdown against the pro-reformist press, intellectuals, students, and the pro-reform political activists, as well as the growing number of outspoken critics of the regime. These circumstances manifested the emergence and rapid expansion of a "garrison-state" (*dawlat-e pādgāni*) with the new fundamentalist orientation. The garrison-state is primarily concerned with maintaining control over the key political positions and the enormous economic resources they have appropriated, without any accountability as required in a democracy (see Ḥajjāriān, pp. 237-45, 596-603, 689-703; Bāqi, pp. 121-205; ʿAlawi-tabār, 2000, pp. 187-98; Yazdi, pp. 179-84; and Banuazizi, 1995, pp. 563-78).

The new fundamentalist current. After the mid-1990s a substantial discursive shift also occurred in the formulation and presentation of "fundamentalist" ideas, with the soon-to-be principal fundamentalist faction adopting a new language in order to reach the younger generation of devout Muslims. Notably, this transformed fundamentalist discourse also included an appeal to the Western philosophical tradition of anti-Humanism. This marked a major rupture with the former discourse of fundamentalism reminiscent of the Fedāʾiān-e Eslām, Hayʾathā-ye moʾtalefa (originally formed to commemorate the martyrdom of Imam Ḥosayn), Militant Clerics Association, and Preachers Association of Tehran (Jāmeʿa-ye woʿāẓ-e Tehran). Immersed in traditional religious jurisprudence (*feqh-e sonnati*) and the popular religion of the masses, the right-wing fundamentalist discourse of these earlier organizations not only had no appeal to the university students, it was even unable to evoke support among the young veterans of the Iran-Iraq War who, with a populist agenda, found an organizational base in the Revolutionary Guards and its Paramilitary forces. Instead, these veterans were attracted to the new fundamentalist discourse as articulated, among others, by the Imam Khomeini Education and Research Institute at Qom (Moʾassesa-ye āmuzeši wa taḥqiqāti-e Emām Ḵomayni), directed by Ayatollah Mohammad Taqi Mesbah Yazdi (Meṣbāh Yazdi). This new fundamentalist discourse was heavily influenced by the discourses of anti-Humanism and anti-modernism in Western philosophy (see below). Equipped with these instruments of ideological debate, the leading new fundamentalist thinkers could claim to provide philosophically more sophisticated and fundamental critiques of the reformist and pro-democracy Islamic ideologies, as well as of the Islamic currents with socialist leanings (for ideological orientation of new fundamentalists, see below).

As the new Islamic reformist and pro-democracy forces were engaged in a bitter factional struggle with the older right-wing fundamentalist groups (symbolized by Khatami and Nāṭeq Nuri) in the latter half of the 1990s, the new fundamentalists appeared on the scene from within the Paramilitary forces as an Islamic third current ("*jarayān-e sevvom*," see Reżāʾi, pp. 9-11; for ideological orientation of new fundamentalism, see below; see further, ISLAM IN IRAN xvi. ISLAM AND FUNDAMENTALISM, forthcoming, online).

IDEOLOGICAL DIVISIONS IN ISLAMIC MOVEMENTS

The opposition and rivalry between Islamic pro-democracy reformist ideas, Islamic socialism, and Islamic fundamentalism—in addition to the vested material, as well as the more immediate political and cultural, interests of their adherents—also stems from their disparate ideological orientations vis-à-vis four key related issues: Islam and modernity; Islam and militancy; Islam and economic policy; and above all, the degree of an individual's freedom in relation to God and the compatibility of Islam with democracy, human rights, gender equality, and the rights of minority groups.

Islam and modernity. Notwithstanding the diversity of Islamic political movements in contemporary Iran, their conception of "modernity" was, and remains, relatively stable: it refers to certain ideas, institutions, norms, and practices associated with the West since the late 18th century. While the various Islamic movements differ in their analyses of the particular European historical processes and perspectives comprising "modernity," they nonetheless are shaped considerably by their respective response to Western influences. The pro-democracy Islamic movements emphasize Islam's doctrinal recognition of the ideas of freedom and political participation, hence Islam's receptiveness to "modern" concepts of constitutionalism and individual rights (for different pro-democracy perspectives, see below). The "socialist" Islamic movements, on the other hand, equate modernity with social and economic development combined with social justice and egalitarian distribution of wealth (similar to Liberation Theology, often characterized as a form of "Christian socialism" and enjoying widespread support in Latin America). For their part, the fundamentalist Islamic movements (similar to their Christian, Hindu, and Jewish counterparts) vilify Western "humanism" and, more specifically, the underlying "subjectivism" inherent in modernity. The fundamentalist movements also uphold a moderate or deep belief in messianic millenarianism. In modern Iranian history the deep conviction in the imminent coming of the Mahdi emerged for the first time in its extremist form in the ideological pronouncements of the new-fundamentalists (see below). Meanwhile, fundamentalists criticize modernity as a product of Christianity and/or Western imperialism. Fundamentalist and socialist Islamic movements—like their Western counterparts—often criticize the stagnant conservative religious establishment for not utilizing modern technologies and modes of mass mobilization to fight back against anti-Islamic elements of the political establishment and modernity. Their more radical elements even advocate an "Islam without clerics" (e.g., Ali Shariʿati and the People's Mojahedin of Iran; see below).

In Iran, as elsewhere in the Islamic world, an ongoing debate is raging over which modern institutions, practices, and ideologies may be deemed to be consistent with the Islamic faith. Pro-democracy and socialist Islamic movements, despite their embrace of modernity, agree that some elements of Western modernity are inconsistent with Islamic doctrines and ought to be rejected; for pro-democracy Islam these would include totalitarian state ambitions and even secular liberalism, and for Islamic socialism the tenets of imperialism, capitalism and consumerism are seen as counter to many egalitarian and puritan Islamic values. Fundamentalist Islamic movements, despite their outright hostility toward the Western model of modernity, nevertheless agree that some elements of modernity are essential under new circumstances, such as modern science and technology and organizational skills. The essential cause of the animosity between fundamentalists, on the one side, and religious modernists—with both pro-democracy and socialist leanings—on the other, stems from controversy over Humanism, as a main element of modernity (see below, "*The compatibility of Islam with democracy*").

Islam and militancy. Militant Islamic movements, whether with fundamentalist or socialist leanings, have significantly diverged from the moderate worldview of the mainstream religious establishment of the ulama and the popular Shiʿism of the masses. To mobilize their followers for radical political action, both fundamentalists and Islamic socialists have interjected the spirit of revolt into their interpretive framework of the principle of *amr be maʿruf* (q.v.)—"enjoining what is proper or good" (a principle religious duty in Islam)—radicalizing the otherwise quietist discourses of millenarianism, jihad, and martyrdom.

Amr be'l maʿruf. Since the advent of Islam in the 7th century, the topic of the legitimacy of resorting to physical force in resistance to oppression has been a key debate in interpreting the principle of *amr be'l maʿruf.* From the very early days, two polarized perspectives emerged: those who viewed *amr be'l maʿruf* merely as a moral standard for admonishing corrupt and unjust rulers and members of the Muslim community; and those who proclaimed it a mandatory religious justification for armed revolt against unjust rulers and their loyal subjects. The Majority of Sunnite and Shiʿite scholars generally have upheld the former quietist reading of *amr be'l maʿruf*, while certain movements since the early years of the advent Islam—ranging from Kharijites to more recent "militant" Islamic currents—have espoused the activist "combative" reading of this principle (see further AMR BE'L MAʿRUF).

Millenarianism and Messianism. The "quietist millenarianism" of the majority of the ulama and of the masses simply anticipates the return of the Mahdi before an unspecified millennium to commence it. This "expectant" (*enteẓār*) perspective had nurtured an attitude of quietism among most Twelver Shiʿites for centuries and, more specifically, since the Safavids. This orientation led to non-involvement in protest movements and accommodation with the established political order during the "Greater Occultation" of the Mahdi (see ḠAYBA). The active millenarianism of the militants, on the other hand, anticipates the return of the Mahdi only after the millennium, having been inaugurated by the faithful themselves. Yet, the earlier "political" fundamentalists such as Fedāʾiān-e Eslām and Jamʿiyat-e moʾtalefa, as well as the Islamic socialists, adopted a more moderate version of militant millenarianism, primarily against the quietist stand of the Ḥojjatiya Association (q.v.; see also ḤALABI), and other admirers of the Mahdi (*welāyatis*) who ardently advocated an accommodationist stand vis-à-vis the temporal authority. Therefore, the doctrine of millenarianism and the return of the Mahdi remained at the periphery of Islamic political movements and the Islamic regime in the period of the 1980s-90s (for a detailed survey, see ISLAM IN IRAN 2. MILLENARIANISM AND MESSIANISM IN ISLAM).

Militant conception of jihad. The activist idea of *amr be'l-maʿruf* and militant conception messianic millenarianism requires a new reading of the principles of jihad and martyrdom. There are two basic views of jihad in Islam: defensive and offensive (for other views, see ISLAM IN IRAN xi. JIHAD). A fight to defend Islamic society (*dār al-Eslām*) against the aggression of enemies of the faith is incumbent upon the faithful in Islam. The ulama and the masses adhere to the defensive idea of jihad. The legitimacy of offensive jihad and, more specifically, a revolutionary call for jihad during the greater occultation of the Mahdi, is questionable in Twelver Shiʿism. It has been strongly prohibited by numerous Hadith attributed to the Imams (see ISLAM IN IRAN X. THE ROOTS OF POLITICAL SHIʿISM; xi. JIHAD IN ISLAM). While the ulama cast doubt on the legitimacy of offensive and revolutionary jihad during the absence of the Mahdi, militants have appropriated the idea of jihad to mean not only a duty to defend the Islamic community (*omma*), but also an offensive revolutionary strategy.

Ayatollah Mortaza Motahhari (Mortażā Moṭahhari), who, along with Shariʿati, is considered as the ideologue of the Islamic Revolution, declares that, "There is a complete agreement amongst scholars that the essence of jihad is defensive, not offensive." However, he extends the notion of "defensive" jihad to rebellion against the tyrannical regimes, to the export of Islamic revolution, and even against cultural aggression. "Islam says that we must fight those tyrants so as to deliver the oppressed from the claws of tyranny." This militant conception of jihad is also extended to the export of revolution: "Rushing to the defense of the oppressed, especially if they are Muslims, such as the Palestinians, is certainly permissible; in fact it is obligatory." Finally, the idea of jihad is also extended to the defense of Islamic society against cultural aggression, "So, when we say that the basis of jihad is defensive, we do not mean defensive in the limited sense of having to defend oneself when one is attacked with the sword, gun or artillery shell. No, we mean that if one's being, one's material or spiritual values are aggressed or in fact, if something that mankind values and respects and which is necessary for mankind's prosperity and happiness, is aggressed, then we are to defend it" (all quotations from Motahhari, 1991, online, see bibliography). The new fundamentalists go even further and propagate the idea that jihad is necessary and essential in expediting the coming of the Mahdi (see Saviyon). Another conception of jihad, which is also popular among many Shiʿites and most Sufis, is spiritual jihad, the idea of individual struggle to elevate the mundane existence of the faithful up to the realm of the sacred, leading to refinement and concern with the higher things in life (see ISLAM IN IRAN X. THE ROOTS OF POLITICAL SHIʿISM; xi. JIHAD IN ISLAM).

Militant conception of martyrdom. The activist reading of *amr be'l-maʿruf*, millenarianism and jihad, in turn, has evolved into an innovative interpretation of the meaning and significance of the martyrdom of Imam Ḥosayn. The popular Shiʿism of the masses is marked by such symbolic religious rituals as "passion play," commemorating the martyrdom of Imam Ḥosayn (*taʿzia*), and collective mourning, which includes such practices as self-mutilation and flagellation by mourners (see DASTA). Whereas the militants' interpretation of the martyrdom evolved in the 1970s to become a rallying call for making individual sacrifices to propagate the establishment of a utopian Islamic society or against the tyranny of the existing order. The turning point was the dissemination of Shari'ati's idea of martyrdom in his lectures in Ḥosayniya-ye eršād in early 1970s, later published as *Šahādat*, and publication of a provocative and controversial book, *Šahid-e jāvid, Ḥosayn b. ʿAli*, (The immortal martyr, Hosayn b. Ali) by Neʿmat-Allāh Ṣāleḥi Najafābādi, with two prefaces by Ayatollahs Ḥosayn-ʿAli Montaẓeri and ʿAli-Akbar Meškini, both ardent supporters of Ayatollah Khomeini.

The interpretation of the martyrdom of Imam Ḥosayn by Shari'ati and Neʿmat-Allāh Ṣāleḥi Najafābādi initiated a new debate on the subject in the 1970s. Ṣāleḥi believed that the Imam possessed a clear religio-political agenda when he mobilized a war against the usurpers of the Islamic government. Thus, he did not intend to attain martyrdom for its own sake, as understood by the masses and disseminated by the ulama, but rather, Ṣāleḥi argued, the Imam acted as the exemplar for his faithful followers for generations to come to make permanent revolutionary sacrifices until the establishment of the "divinely guided" Islamic government. This bold innovation on a pre-existing deep-rooted quietist belief was met with the overwhelming indignation of the religious hierarchy on the pulpit, turning the masses against the author (see Ṣāleḥi Najafābādi; for a discussion on Ṣāleḥi's idea, see Modarresi, chap. 2; Enayat, pp. 190-94). Like the traditionalist conception of martyrdom, Shari'ati propagated the idea that Ḥosayn b. ʿAli, The Lord of Martyrs (*Sayyed-al-Šohadāʾ*), believed in "martyrdom for the sake of martyrdom," and that he was aware that he would be martyred when he staged a war with a small force of 72 against the large and well-equipped army of the tyrannical government. He deviated from the traditionalist reading of martyrdom, however, when he glorified martyrdom by propagating the idea that the Imam staged a war to set an exemplar for his faithful Shiʿites to be martyred as a dramatic act of protest and revolt against the tyranny of the established order, "if you are not able to be a victor, be a martyr" (see Shari'ati, 1973; Rahnema, 1998, pp. 312-27).

The new apocalyptic mood. The recent rise to power of new fundamentalists brought different readings to the activist conceptions of *amr be'l-maʿruf*, millenarianism, jihad, and martyrdom. The radicalization of Shiʿite millenarianism, leading to the rise in the cult of the Mahdi, may be seen as a bold innovation by the new-fundamentalists. It originates in a sort of extremist Shiʿism (see ḠOLĀT), a well-known and recurrent movement in the history of Shiʿism. The new apocalyptic mood helped the burgeoning of Jamkarān edifice near Qom, believed to be the abode of the Hidden Imam. Believing that the well of the mosque in Jamkarān is the host of the Mahdi, the faithful Shiʿites drop prayers and personal requests therein. The new fundamentalists brought, for the first time, the idea of imminent anticipation of the return of the Hidden Imam to a central place in the politics of the Islamic Republic. They have expressed, on various occasions, their deep belief in the universality of the return of the Mahdi, his imminent return to form a divinely ordained state throughout the world. To expedite the appearance of the Hidden Imam, they call for revolutionary mobilization and confrontation with the enemies of Islam through jihad and *šahādat*. The cult of the Mahdi is replacing the historical place of the drama of the Martyrdom of Imam Ḥosayn. The drama of martyrdom for the return of the Mahdi is even more inciting and more "real" in the mind of believers than the commemoration of the Martyrdom of Imam Ḥosayn. It shifts the orientation from the past to the imminent future. The new cult of the Mahdi, however, encountered growing criticism from the sources of emulation to religious intellectuals of both pro-democracy and socialist camps. They often accuse it of spreading superstition in society (for a survey of the emerging cult of the Mahdi in primary sources, see Saviyon and Mansharof).

Islam and economic policy. The controversy over the priority of public or private sectors became the main point of contradiction and dividing lines in factional politics during the period of 1982-89. In control of the state apparatus during wartime, the radical left championed land distribution among the peasantry, nationalization of foreign trade, imposing limitations on the ownership of urban real estate, and progressive labor laws. Both Shari'ati and Motahhari provided the Islamic left with a socialist platform. While Shari'ati contributed to such rhetorical slogans as "divinely ordained classless society" or "wretched of the earth," Moṭahhari's contribution was mainly a moderate and systematic treatment of an Islamic economic system as mediating between socialism and capitalism, public and private sectors of economy (see Motahhari, 1989; for Shari'ati, see above). On the other side were pro-democracy groups, right-wing fundamentalists, and pragmatists with modern capitalist agendas who fought for private ownership and freedom of economic activities. The right-wing fundamentalists even opposed the establishment of a minimum wage or any control by the state over economic enterprises, arguing that capital and labor are in constant interaction in the Islamic free market, and that labor accepts the proposed wage on its own free will. Thus, no intervention by the state in the economic life of the community should be permitted (see Ashraf, 1994). However, the new fundamentalists, with their populist agenda, have adopted more support for the public sector at the cost of private enterprises.

Compatibility of Islam with democracy. A more fundamental and controversial aspect of modernity for Islamic movements is Humanism and, more specifically, the degree of freedom of human agency and compatibility of Islam with democracy. Modern Humanism can be simply defined as "a system of thought that rejects all supernaturalism and relies primarily upon reason and science as well as a concern with the needs, well-being, and interests of people." Secular Liberalism and Marxism may be considered as the two major political manifestations of Humanism, both having influenced particular Islamic movements. In Abrahamic religions, there evolved two polarized perspectives in response to the spread of modern secular Humanism: an uncompromising outright rejection of Humanism by fundamentalists versus a more moderate, compromising view that propagates the compatibility of religious faith with a modified conception of humanism as mediated by God. The receptive attitude toward modified definitions of humanism is evident in the pronouncements of the compatibility of Islam with democracy and socialism (see below).

Fundamentals of Fundamentalism. As with the adherents of fundamentalist movements in Abrahamic faiths in general—Judaism, Christianity, and other branches of Islam—a primary target of Iranian Shiʿite new fundamentalists is "humanism," conceiving Man to be "the center of the universe." The cardinal objective of fundamentalism is, therefore, to reinstate the idea and practice that "God, not man, is the center of the universe." They also maintain that the path to social justice lies in a return to the original, fundamental message of the scripture (for Islamic fundamentalists, the *šariʿa* law), and the formation of a religious state combined with the rejection of "innovations" (*bedʿa*) and perceived anti-religious ideas and practices stemming from the secularization of the world. The targeted innovations include the modern secular state with its tolerance towards institutions of a pluralistic civil society, and the separation of "church" and state. In addition, most fundamentalist movements bitterly scorn any tolerance, much less the collaboration of their religious establishments with, the secular state. In the same vein, they oppose all religious intellectuals with pro-democracy or socialist orientation, accusing them of succumbing to the evils of "Humanism" and the ostensibly false belief of the compatibility of Western forms of democracy or socialism with Islam (for a comparative survey of fundamentalism in Judaism, Christianity and Islam, see Almond, Sivan and Appleby; see further ISLAM IN IRAN xvi. ISLAM AND FUNDAMENTALISM, forthcoming, online).

This stance also signifies the fundamentalists' conviction of being the guardians of 'absolute truth'—founded upon immutable and historically unchanging religious principles in pursuit of the right path enjoined by God (*al-ṣerāt al-mostaqim*)—as well as possessing the sole blueprint for establishing the perfect society in all its aspects of life (political, social, economic, religious, and cultural). The concept of "absolute truth" is evident, for example, in the title of the manifesto by the Fedāʾiān-e Eslām, "The Guide to truths" (*Rāhnemā-ye ḥaqāyeq*). Such a rigid notion of an invariable "absolute truth" rests upon a dualistic Manichean vision of the world and its division into two opposing forces of good and evil, faith and blasphemy, Allāh and *ṭāqūt*, true Islam (*Eslām-e rāstin*) and false Islam, and friends and foes of Islam. This worldview justifies extreme and violent political action without constraints in defense of Truth, serving as a rationalization for the envisaged totalitarianism of the Fedāʾiān-e Eslām and Jamʿiyat-e moʾtalefa, or even the extremist totalitarian worldview of the new fundamentalists. Another feature of fundamentalism in this regard has been the frequent recourse to violent enforcement of "prescribed" religious codes of conduct when and where possible by resorting to a principle of religious duty in Islam, *al-amr be'l-maʿruf*. It should be noted that the belief in the existence and knowledge of "absolute truth" also exists among the adherents of secular as well as religious left such as certain trends within Liberation Theology in Latin America and Islamic left, including People's Mojahedin of Iran, who justify recourse to violence in bringing about their own order of truth in the form of "social justice" (see above section on militancy).

The new fundamentalist discourse and Western philosophy. The underlying epistemological difference between secular humanism and fundamentalism in Iran has been intensified by the new fundamentalists' adoption of anti-humanist ideas, drawn from Western philosophy. These ideas could be treated in two related currents: perennial Traditionalism and Heideggerian anti-Humanism. The perennial Traditionalist perspective—which can be characterized as essentially metaphysical, esoteric, and primordial—began to emerge in Europe and America at the beginning of the 20th century through the work of René Guénon (1886-1951), and Ananda Coomaraswamy (1877-1947). It was developed further by Guénon's disciple Frithjof Schuon (1907-98), and their followers, including Sayyed Hossein Nasr, who edited *The Essential Writings of Frithjof Schuon* (New York, 1986). Most of the adherents of perennial Traditionalism converted to Islam, including Guénon, who adopted the name, Abd al-Wahid Yahya, and Schuon, who adopted the name, Isa Nur al-Din. A number of the works by these Traditionalist figures have been translated into Persian in the last two decades and have further bolstered the ideological position of new fundamentalism in Iran.

Martin Heidegger's anti-humanism and anti-modernism has also influenced Persian religious thought through Henri Corbin (q.v.), an influential scholar in Islamic philosophy, and his disciple, Sayyed Hossein Nasr and, more specifically, through Aḥmad Fardid (Corbin was the first to translate Heidegger into French; for the influence of Heidegger on Corbin, see Nemo, "From Heidegger to Suhravardi: An Interview with Henri Corbin," and Green, pp. 219-26; Corbin, 1983; Nasr, 1990; idem, 1998).

Heidegger's ideas of the decadence of the West through the concept of the "Darkening of the world"—a recurring theme in his philosophy—introduced and articulated by Fardid through the coinage of its Persian equivalent, "*ḡarb-zadagi*." This term means, metaphorically, the dusk of illumination (the Sun) in the West (translated as Occidentosis or Westoxication, meaning Darkening of the Western world, which has also contaminated the East). Drawing from this concept, Fardid and his disciple, Reżā Dāvari Ardakāni founded a new version of Heideggerian fundamentalism in post-revolution Iran (see Fardid, 2000). Heidegger spoke of a "darkening of the world," to mean the loss of humanity or enfeeblement of the spirit and forgetfulness of Being in the modern world. Following Heidegger, Fardid emphasized that the decadence of the West had already begun with Greek philosophy which marked a human being's (*wojud*) loss of "oneness" with spiritual consciousness (*del-āgāhi*). Western man, immersed in technology, is more concerned with his being than with his spiritual calling in the world. The Liberal conception of civil society and democracy are illusions in a world in which being and spiritual consciousness are no longer in unison but at odds (for an influential vulgarization of Fardid's Heideggerian concept of *ğarb-zadagi*, see Āl-e Aḥmad, 1977, and its English tr. as *Occidentosis*, 1983). Fardid claimed that the Islamic Revolution served as the vehicle for a return to the authentic spiritual ethos of the Orient. Fardid asserted, "Heidegger is the only philosopher whose thought corresponds to the fundamental ethos of the Islamic Republic, founded by Imam Khomeini." Fardid gained followers among a circle of people in seminaries and the intelligence forces, as well as in the editorial staff of the major daily *Kayhān* newspaper, and in journals such as *Ṣura*, *Ḥawza-ye andiša*, and *Honar-e eslāmi* (for Fardid's ideas, see the posthumous publication of his lectures by one of his loyal students in 2000, particularly pp. 12, 347-65; Dāvari, 1984; idem, 2000).

These ideas, drawn from anti-modernist currents in Western philosophy and religious thought, were transmitted to Iranian audience through translation of a number of works of Western adherents of anti-Humanist ideas and by such scholars as Sayyed Hossein Nasr. Following the perennial Traditionalism of Guénon and Schuon, as well as the Heideggerian-Corbinian anti-Humanist ideas, Nasr advocated an apolitical Traditionalist Islam vis-à-vis both modernism and fundamentalism. Yet his ideas of anti-modernism have substantively buttressed the ideological position of new fundamentalism with a hard-line political agenda in the last two decades. These ideas are also transmitted to Iranian advocates of new-fundamentalism by such instructors as Gary Muhammad Legenhausen, among others, who have further equipped the proponents of new fundamentalism, such as Mesbah Yazdi, in developing discursive ammunition against humanism and the "pro-democracy" ideas of such religious intellectuals as Soroush and Mojtahed Shabestari (Legenhausen, an American student of philosophy with perennial traditionalist and new fundamentalist leanings, who converted from Catholicism to Shiʿism, has taught and propagated Western traditionalist and anti-modernist ideas at the Imam Khomeini Education and Research Institute at Qom since 1996; see Legenhausen, 1999; see further ISLAM IN IRAN xvi. ISLAM AND FUNDAMENTALISM, forthcoming, online).).

Consequently, the main division within the respective political factions since the 1990s has come to be defined by the conflicting ideological poles of "new fundamentalism," with its totalitarian proclivity, on the one hand, and the "new Islamic pro-democracy thought," on the other hand.

The pro-democracy and socialist Islamic ideas. The proponents of pro-democracy and socialist oriented Islamic platforms often resort to the idea that man, as God's caliph (emissary) on earth, has been entrusted by God with a relative freedom of action (for a concise treatment of the basic ideas of religious intellectuals, see Narāqi, pp. 177-200). They often refer to Article 56 in the opening section of Chapter V of the constitution of the Islamic Republic on "the right of national sovereignty" and the powers deriving therefrom: "Absolute sovereignty over the world and man belongs to God, and it is He Who has made man master of his own social destiny. No one can deprive man of this divine right, nor subordinate it to the vested interests of a particular individual or group. The people are to exercise this divine right in the manner specified in the following articles" (Blaustein and Glanz, p. 39).

Referring to this Article, the proponents of varying brands of Islamic humanism occupy a middle ground between secular humanism and religious fundamentalism. This stance, in contrast to the absolute and diametrically opposed worldviews of religious fundamentalists and secular humanists, asserts the centrality of both God and man at the center of the universe. In this way, religious intellectuals with pro-democracy and socialist orientations rationalize the idea of human agency mediated by God's will and God's endowment of humanity with the capacity for freedom and creativity (for an application of Jurgen Habermas's theory of inter-subjectivity to these debates, and the use of the notion of "mediated subjectivity," see Vahdat, 2000; see also Narāqi, pp. 171-88).

The proponents of mediated humanism can be divided into two distinct orientations: First, those like Bazargan and Shariʿati, who meditate the distance between man and God by referring to the original sources, thereby demonstrating the compatibility of Islam with democracy or socialism through the adoption of universalistic Western political principles and their Islamic textual corroborations. Second, those like Mojtahed Shabestari and Soroush who, transcending the above old way, reconstructed a new theological approach concerning the question of the compatibility of Islam with the ideas of freedom and democracy (see below).

Compatibility of Islam with democracy through authentic sources. As a French educated engineer in the 1930s who was familiar with the modern sciences and political philosophy, Bazargan developed a pristine approach in a number of influential books, expounding the compatibility of Islam with Western science and technology, freedom and democracy. In *Ensān o Ḵodā* (Man and God), Bazargan sought to bridge the deep chasm between the place of God and Man in the center of the universe (*pol-e bozorg miān-e do binahāyat-e dur*). Bazargan maintained that the common element in both religion and democracy is the principle of "Man's nobility," from which the ideas of human freedom and human rights, responsibilities, and political participation are derived. In his view, Islam along with the monotheistic religions bestows great respect on human rights and considers mankind as free, responsible and autonomous agency. He makes a sharp distinction between the essence and precepts of religion, which belongs to God, and the administration of the polity, which belongs to the people. The former falls under religious rules and the latter under man's rules. He concludes that "freedom to oppose and criticize and object" is vital and necessary for both government and religion. "When freedom is banished then tyranny will take its place" (Bazargan, 1976a; idem, 1998, pp. 78-82).

Religious intellectuals with socialist tendencies such as Shari'ati, have shown a similar inclination towards mediated humanism and authenticity. Shari'ati, given his emphasis on "authentic man" and his own version of attacking "West-toxification," as evident in works such as *Fāṭema, Fāṭema ast* (Tehran, 1971), that were heavily influenced by Louis Massignon, has shown a strong leaning toward authenticity (see also Afary, 2003, pp. 7-35). Inspired by Jean Paul Sartre's existentialist conceptions of "being" and "becoming," Shari'ati developed a theory that found equivalents of Sartre's concepts with the Qur'anic terms "*bašar*" and "*ensān*," arguing that God has created man as *bašar*, or merely "a being," but with the ability and potential of "becoming" human "*ensān*." Thus, he claimed, "from among all humans, everyone is as much *bashar* as the rest, but there are some who have attained *insaniyat*, and there are others who are in the process of becoming an *ensān*. . . . *bashar* is a "being" while *ensan* is a "becoming" (Shari'ati, "Humanity and Islam," 1998, p. 188). Divine revelation, Shari'ati argued, has left certain matters up to human creative and inventive intervention, not because the revelation is incomplete or imperfect but because humans have been granted the capacity for rational and moral action. He argued that we are justified in using these powers to create a "social-democratic" system because these powers are what make us truly human (*ensān*). Shari'ati maintained that man is created by God with the ability to make choices and to create social and political systems in keeping with their authentic values, including the rejection of "traditional" clergy.

Islamic socialists may even go so far as advocating Deism, a belief in God based on reason rather than revelation, subscribing to the view that God has created the universe but does not interfere with how it proceeds, thereby underscoring the primacy and creativity of human agency and recognizing the role of socio-economic factors as a driving force of history (see, e.g., Mojāhedin-e ḵalq, *Tabyin-e jahān* [Explaining the world]).

A theological breakthrough. Both Soroush and Mojtahed Shabestari have constructed a novel theory of the compatibility of Islam with democracy, which seems to be based on a new theological approach. The old pro-democracy approaches—from the Constitutional Revolution to Bazargan's Liberation Movement—referred mostly to the ideas of freedom, human rights, and democracy as contained in the original sources of scripture and tradition. This new paradigm, however, advances a "pro-democracy" Islamic theory by focusing on extra-religious sources. The new theory's main objective is to seek answers to the following questions: "How is a system of democracy, freedom, and human rights possible in Islam?"; and "By what theological method and in what sources may one find an answer to the preceding question?"

Soroush begins his argument in support of the compatibility of Islam with democracy with the premise that human beings aspire to freedom in the modern age and that the best way to attain freedom is democracy. Yet, since the values of freedom and democracy and its criteria are extra-religious values, democracy cannot be reconciled with Islam without unearthing available sources for rationalization of the basis of democracy in religion. The task of the political philosophers in the world of Islam, Soroush believes, is to reconcile religion and freedom by giving a new interpretation of religion to make it possible to link religion with democracy (Soroush, 2000a, chap. 1).

Inspired by Iqbal Lahury (1877-1948) and new Mu'tazilite theology, Soroush calls for an essential reconstruction of the archaic orientation of Islamic philosophy (*ḥekmat-e elāhi*), theology (*ʿelm-e kalām*), and traditional jurisprudence (*feqh-e sonnati*). His mode of reconstruction recognizes the autonomy of the sphere of human values from that of religion (Soroush, 2000a, pp. 30-32). Resorting to philosophical and theological traditions in medieval Islam, Soroush shows that there are ideas which "could be independent of Islam without being incompatible with the faith." To this end, Soroush constructs a new interpretation of religious ideas and principles by making a distinction between the absolute, immutable principles of religion and its mutable aspects. The main task for Soroush is, therefore, to unfold the basic purposes of the *šariʿa* by way of interpreting the concepts, theories, and principles of religious texts. Once we unfold the basic purposes of Divine law, Soroush contends, we would be able to undertake a new reading of the mutable aspects of the text. To meet the requirements of modern times, he suggests the theory of interpretation of Islamic theology, known as the "contraction-and-expansion of *šariʿa*" (*teʾori-e qabż o basṭ-e šariʿat*; see Soroush, 2000a, pp. 30-38).

In expounding his theory, Soroush makes a distinction between maximalist and minimalist perspectives of religion. Maximalists believe that all aspects of Islamic social life must be derived from religion. Soroush contends that most of the current problems in Islam can be traced to such a perspective. It leads, he maintains, inexorably down a path towards a totalitarian regime. Replacing this position with a minimalist view would solve the problem. He argues that some values cannot be derived from religion, such as respect for human rights and even freedom. Therefore, freedom has to be treated from the favorable sources of theology. Islamic philosophers, Soroush says, should change their conception of man and focus on the idea of justice (*ʿadl*), connoting man's freedom of action in his relation with God's justice—one of the five principles of Shiʿism and one of the key concepts in Mu'tazilite theology. Mu'tazilite theologians, Soroush argues, "have already explored this area extensively and provided us with the tools to solve many of our problems" (citations from Soroush, 2000b; see also Soroush, 2000a; and ʿAlawitabār, 2000, pp. 124-36).

Mojtahed Shabestari, a pro-democracy theoretician of clerical background, maintains that "democracy" and "human rights" are historically-evolving concepts and as such were not, either in their current form or substance, conceived at the time of the revelation of the Qurʾān and the formation of Islamic "traditions." The foundational religious sources cannot, therefore, be expected to contain guidelines on attaining democracy and human rights in our time (for the very recent formulation and definition of "human rights," as enshrined in the charter of the United Nations, see Ishay; Donnelli). The answer to the compatibility of Islam with democracy and human rights, Mojtahed Shabestari contends, should therefore be sought not in the foundational "religious sources," but in "extra-religious sources." He further suggests that in order to bring about democracy and human rights one must consult and follow models outside the foundational religious sources, even if these models tend to be secular and grounded in Western modernity and humanism. Not unlike Soroush, Mojtahed Shabestari espouses the view that, due to the limited capacity of religious dogmas to address the many complex issues and needs of the modern world, religion should be complemented with the extra-religious rational values and practices that have emerged in response to the new circumstances, challenges and requirements of modern societies. The complex political, social, economic, and cultural characteristics of modern times are historically specific and evolving variables and thus distinguishable from the "eternal values of religion," which by definition are assumed to be unchangeable (Mojtahed Shabestari, 2000, pp. 143-44). Refuting Mojtahed Shabestari's theory, new fundamentalist ideologues such as Mesbah Yazdi argue that, as an integrated system, the *šariʿa* does not allow any distinction between the eternal values of religion and the evolving values of democracy and human rights (Mesbah Yazdi, 1999a).

With the application of modern hermeneutics (q.v.) to Islamic theology and jurisprudence, Mojtahed Shabestari has thus made a significant methodological breakthrough in the controversy between pro-democracy religious intellectuals and those advocating Islamic fundamentalism. He constructs his concept of "variability of religious knowledge," by refuting the validity ascribed to the totalitarian concept of political jurisprudence (*feqh-e siāsi*) and "official reading of religion" (*qerāʾat-e rasmi az din*), as advocates of new fundamentalism such as Mesbah Yazdi, who claim exclusive knowledge of the absolute truth (see Mesbah Yazdi, 1999a). Drawing on modern hermeneutics, Mojtahed Shabestari debunks any claim that God's absolute truth could ever be accessible to man. In his view, the ideas of freedom and democracy are compatible with Islam not, as Bazargan believed, because one finds parallel terms in the Qurʾān or the traditions, but because one can rationally assume that these modern ideas are compatible with the spirit of Islam and its concept of justice (see Mojtahed Shabestari, 1996).

In a telling debate on Islamic democracy between Mojtahed Shabestari and two new fundamentalist disciples of Mesbah Yazdi (Moḥammad Fatāʾi Oskuʾi and ʿAli Ḏuʿelm), presented in four articles published in 1998, Mojtahed Shabestari summarizes their argumentations in a seminal article, entitled "Democracy of Muslims, Not Islamic Democracy" ("Demokrāsi-e mosalmānān, na demokrāsi-e eslāmi"). He suggests that his detractors, in their criticism of his article on "Democracy and Religiosity" (Demokrāsi wa din-dāri), claim that on the basis of the following considerations they endorse "Islamic democracy, but not absolute democracy." Firstly, Mesbah Yazdi's followers believe that "in an Islamic democracy, the state functions as the guardian of Islam, and cannot, therefore, afford to view other religions and worldviews indiscriminately." Secondly, "Muslims must follow the divine laws, and the laws of Islam have not sanctioned such concepts as the equality of Muslims and non Muslims or gender equality. . . . Muslims, therefore, are not allowed to seek a democracy which is not bound by principles and rules of *šariʿa*." Thirdly, "democracy, particularly in its absolute form, far from being merely a framework for a political system, derives its inner substance from humanistic concepts such as freedom, equality and the citizen's right and ability to make rational choices." And last, but not least, that "absolute democracy is based on the sovereignty of the people, which affirms the priority of man's will over divine will, and the primacy of Man's laws over divine laws" (see Mojtahed Shabestari, 2000, pp. 143-44; for the above four articles, see ibid, pp. 107-51). These arguments are intimately informed by anti-modernist ideas of perennial Traditionalist school and anti-Humanist ideas of Heidegger and Corbin (see above).

Mojtahed Shabestari suggests, however, that the preceding considerations laid out by Mesbah Yazdi and his followers are based on a fundamental misunderstanding of the concept of democracy. Whether people should follow divine laws and values in establishing a political order is in the domain of the philosophy of law and ethics and is, therefore, irrelevant to the nature of government itself. He further suggests that, "democracy is not divisible into Islamic and non-Islamic forms." The nature of government in any society is either "democracy or dictatorial." Summing up his arguments, Mojtahed Shabestari concludes that "although there are various models of democracy, any attempt to constrain the form of government by religious laws and beliefs would lead not to the establishment of a specific form of democracy, but to the emergence of a specific model of dictatorship" (see Mojtahed Shabestari, 2000, p. 144).

ISLAMIC POLITICAL IDEOLOGIES IN PRACTICE

Considerable differences and animosities have emerged among the various proponents of Islamic pro-democracy ideas, Islamic socialism, Islamic fundamentalism, and a newcomer, Islamic pragmatism in the post-Revolution era, when their position was transformed from opposition forces, mobilizing against the previous regime, to one of competing factions for scarce political, economic, and social resources within the Islamic Republic. They often deny the shared elements of their ideas and practices, and their competition for the same Islamic political space has frequently involved denunciations and violence. Does this antagonism stem merely from their material interests and thirst for political power or is it born out of their conflicting ideas and utopian beliefs, or combinations thereof?

To answer this question one must note that ideology as an organized collection of ideas—forming the basis of a political philosophy or program—often shows an elective affinity with the material and non-material interests of certain social classes and groups who adopt them. This selection of ideas in turn influences the mode of thinking and behavior of the people. Political ideology either offers a rationalization for the survival of an established order or suggests blueprints for a desired change in social, political, or economic systems. A shift in conflicting ideological issues in society may also influence the competing political currents in modifying their ideological orientations. For example, the question of religiosity versus non-religiosity or allegiance to Islam versus anti-Islamic or even non-Islamic orientations became the main controversial issue during the early post-revolutionary period, whereas focusing on the priority of public versus private sectors of the economy became the main conflicting ideological issue during the period of Iran-Iraq War under the leftist government of Musavi (1981-89). Finally, democracy versus totalitarianism became the main controversial issue in factional politics during the period of the 1990s-2000s.

The proponents of various Islamic ideologies often formed coalitions and counter-coalitions depending on the political imperatives of the time. They have engaged in continuous intra—and inter-factional competitions and rivalries that have reflected their material and political interests no less than their ideological positions. A telling example is the coalition of the Islamic reform movement formed in the latter half of the 1990s by pro-democracy, pro-socialist, and pragmatist currents to compete in the 1995 and 1997 elections with the right-wing fundamentalist faction, who dominated the Fourth Majles and much of the security forces. Each current in the new coalition had its own political or politico-ideological agendas of either maintaining their hold on power or returning to power or changing the structure of power. The pragmatist "Executives of Construction," organized around President Hashemi Rafsanjani, and the resourceful mayor of Tehran, Ḥosayn Karbāsči, as their campaign manager, were primarily concerned with maintaining their hold on political power by dominating Khatami's government. The socialist currents, particularly the Mojāhedin-e enqelāb-e eslāmi and Majmaʿ-e ruḥāniyun-e mobārez, who lost their hold on political power following Khomeini's death and the fall of Musavi's Cabinet in 1989, were fighting a life and death struggle to return to power. Neither the pragmatists nor the Islamic left could be considered to have genuine pro-democracy intentions in their ideological formation. Yet a large number of reformed socialists and, more specifically, the students organized around Daftar-e taḥkim-e waḥdat, who were influenced by the new pro-democracy ideas of Ḥajjārian, ʿAbbās ʿAbdi, Soroush and Mojtahed Shabestari, became the sincere supporters of democracy in the reformist coalition. Religious intellectuals, student activists, and the Islamic Participation front (Jebha-ye mošārakat), were the only segment of the coalition who were genuinely concerned with effecting basic changes in the structure of power in the Islamic Republic. Yet instead of entering a coalition with Bazargan's Liberation movement, with whom they shared a genuine ideological affinity, they made it with the pragmatist and socialist leaning forces, in a well-thought out and rational political choice (for a round table discussion on factional politics in post-revolution period, see Yazdi, 2000, pp. 251-92; ʿAlawitabār, 2007; Yusofi Eškevari).

Since its formation in the early years of the revolution, the Revolutionary Guard Corps and its affiliated agencies, including the Paramilitary forces, intelligence services, security forces, and large commercial and industrial enterprises has vastly expanded its powers in relation to all other parts of the state. In the first phase of this expansion, which took place during the Iran-Iraq War in the 1980s, the Revolutionary Guards served as a military force that was entirely subordinate to the top leadership of the Islamic Republic, that is, Ayatollah Khomeini, as the commander-in-chief. In the last years of the war and, more specifically after the death of Khomeini, the Guards' performance was criticized often by some leading figures of the clerical establishment (*bozorgān-e enqelāb*, in the words of Moḥsen Reżāʾi, the Guards' commander during most of the war period; see Reżāʾi, pp. 9-11) for the War's prolongation and setbacks. This prompted some commanders of the Guards to seek a relatively independent power base from the clerical leadership of the regime. By the late 1990s, the Guards had succeeded in achieving considerable power and were fast becoming a semi-independent force, "a state within the state." As such, they exerted increasing influence over most government agencies and in many instances managed to appoint senior officers to key positions in the civilian bureaucracy. They also promoted a new hard-line fundamentalist ideological orientation, one that had emerged from within the Guards and its Paramilitary forces in the 1990s. In the ensuing years, and particularly since the defeat of the reformist movement in the 2005 presidential elections, the Guards and its affiliates and allies seem to have gained a near complete monopoly of power and control over the entire state.

Bibliography: Mehdi Abedi and G. Legenhausen, trs. and eds., *Jihad and Shehadat: Struggle and Martyrdom in Islam* (articles by, Ṭāleqāni, Moṭahhari, and Shariʿati), Houston, 1986. Janet Afary, "Shiʿi Narratives of Karbala and Christian Rites of Penance: Michel Foucault and the Culture of the Iranian Revolution, 1978-1979," *Radical History Review* 86, Spring 2003, pp. 7-35. Ḥ. Aḥmadi and M.-Ḥ. Fattāḥiān, eds., *Jarayān-e rowšanfekri wa rowšanfekrān dar Irān*" (Intellectual Current and Intellectuals in Iran), Tehran, 2000. ʿAli-Reżā ʿAlawitabār, *Rowšanfekri, din-dāri, mardom-sālāri* (Intellectualism, Religiosity, and Democracy), Tehran, 2000. Idem "ʿAqaba-ye fekri-e eṣlāḥ-ṭalabān, in *Irān emruz* (Iranian political online magazine), 7 March 2007. Jalāl Āl-e Aḥmad, *Ḡarb-zadagi*, Tehran, 1977. Idem, *Occidentosis, a Plague from the West (Ḡarb-zadagi)*, tr. R. Campbel, Berkeley, 1984. Gabriel A. Almond, Emmanuel Sivan, and R. Scott Appleby, "Fundamentalism: Genus and Species," in Martin E. Marty and R. Scott Appleby, eds., *Accounting for Fundamentalisms*, Chicago, 1994, pp. 403-24. A. Ashraf, "Charisma, Theocracy and New Men of Power in Iran," in M. Weiner and A. Banuazizi, eds., *The Politics of Social Transformation in Afghanistan, Iran, and Pakistan*, Syracuse, 1994, pp. 101-55. A. Ashraf and A. Banuazizi, "The State, Classes and Modes of Mobilization in the Iranian Revolution," *State, Culture and Society* 1/3, 1985, pp. 3-40. Idem, "Iran's Tortuous Path Toward 'Islamic Liberalism' in *Politics, Culture and Society* 15/2, 2001, pp. 237-55. "Āsibšenāsi-e 'Rošanfekri-e dini'" (Pathology of Religious Intellectualism), ed. M.-R. Jalāʾipour, special issue of *Eʿtemād-e melli* (daily newspaper), Tehran, 11 September 2007.

Asad-Allāh Bādāmčiān, *Heyʾathā-ye moʾtalefa-ye eslāmi* (Coalition of Islamic [Mourning] Groups), Tehran, 1992. Shaul Bakhash, *The Reign of the Ayatollahs, Iran and the Islamic Revolution*, New York, 1984. Ali Banuazizi, "Faltering Legitimacy: The Ruling Clerics and Civil Society in Contemporary Iran," *International Journal of Politics, Culture and Society* 8, 1995, pp. 563-78. ʿEmād-al-Din Bāqi, *Jonbeš-e eṣlāḥāt-e demokrātik dar Irān: enqelāb yā eṣlāḥ* (Pro-Democracy Reform Movement in Iran: Revolution or Reform), Tehran, 2004. Mehdi Bazargan (Bāzargān), *Ensān o Ḵodā*, (Man and God), Tehran, 1976a. Idem, *Enqelāb-e Irān dar dow ḥarakat* (Iran's Revolution in Two Moves), Tehran, 1982. Idem, *Moškelāt wa masāʾel-e awwalin sāl-e enqelāb* (The Difficulties and Problems of the First Year of the Revolution), 2nd ed., Tehran, 1983. Idem, "Religion and Liberty," in Kurzman, ed., 1998, pp. 73-84. Richard Bernstein, Heidegger on Humanism, in *Praxis International* 5/2, 1985, pp. 95-114. Albert P. Blaustein and Gisbert H. Glanz, eds., *Constitutions of the Countries of the World: Islamic Republic of Iran (1980-1992)*, Dobbs Ferry, New York, 1992, p. 39. Wilfried Buchta, *Who Rules Iran: Structure of Power in the Islamic Republic*, Washington, DC, 2000. H. E. Chehabi, *Iranian Politics and Religious Modernism: The Liberation Movement of Iran under the Shah and Khomeini*, Ithaca, NY, 1990.

Henry Corbin and Nancy Pearson, *Spiritual Body and Celestial Earth, From Mazdean Iran to Shi'ite Iran*, Princeton, 1977. Daftar-e tabliḡāt-e eslāmi-e Ḥawza-ye ʿelmiya-ye Qom, wāḥed-e siāsi, *Nahżat e āzādi dar andiša wa ʿamal* (Liberation Movement in Theory and Practice), Qom, 1989. Reżā Dāvari Ardakāni, *Šemmaʾi az tāriḵ-e ḡarb-zadagi-e mā* (A Historical Sketch of Our West-toxification), 2nd ed., Tehran, 1983. Idem, "Rowšan-fekri wa rowšan-fekrān" (Intellectualism and Intellectuals), in Ḥ. Aḥmadi ed., 2000, pp. 9-34. Jack Donnelly, *Universal Human Rights in Theory and Practice*, Ithaca, 2002. Hamid Enayat, *Modern Islamic Political Thought*, Austin, TX, 1982. Mehdi ʿErāqi, *Nāgoftahā: Ḵāṭerāt-e šahid Ḥājj Mehdi ʿErāqi* (The Untold: Memoirs of Martyr Hājj Mehdi ʿEraqi), Tehran, 1978. Aḥmad Fardid, *Didār-e farrahi wa fotuḥ-e āḵer al-zamān* (Visionary Gift of Grace and Conquests of the Last Day), ed. M. Madadpur, Tehran, 2002. I. Gershoni and J. Jankowski, *Redefining the Egyptian Nation, 1930-1945*, Cambridge, UK, 1995. Nile Green, "Between Heidegger and the Hidden Imam: Reflections on Henry Corbin's approaches to mystical Islam," *Method and Theory in the Study of Religion* 17/3, 2005, pp. 219-26.

A.-H. Hairi, "Shaikh Fazlollah Nuri's Refutation of the Idea of Constitutionalism," *Middle Eastern Studies* 23/3, 1977a, pp. 227-39. Idem, *Shiʿism and Constitutionalism in Iran. A Study of the Role Played by the Persian Residents in Iraq in Iranian Politics*, Leiden, 1977b. Idem, *Noḵostin ruyāruʾihā-ye andišagarān-e Irān bā do rawiya-ye tamaddon-e buržuāzi-e Ḡrb* (Early Encounter of Iranian Intellectuals With Two Orientations of Western Bourgeois Civilization), Tehran, 1988. Saʿid Ḥajjāriān, *Jomhuriyat, afsun-zedāʾi az qodrat* (Republicanism, Demystification of Power), Tehran, 2000. ʿA.-A. Hashemi Rafsnjani, *ʿObur az boḥrān: Kārnāma wa ḵāṭerāt-e Hāšemi Rafsanjāni* (Passing the Crisis: Diaries of Hashemi Rafsnjani), Tehran, 1999. Ruḥ-Allāh Ḥosaynīān, *Čahārdah sāl reqābat-e ideʾoložik dar Irān, 1343-56* (Fourteen Years of Ideological Competition in Iran, 1964-77), Tehran, 2004. Albert Hourani, *Arab Thought in the Liberal Age: 1797-1939*, London, 1962, rep., 1983. Micheline Ishay, *The History of Human Rights: From Ancient Times to the Globalization Era*, Berkeley, 2004. ʿJamileh Kadivar, *Taḥawwol e goftmān-e siāsi-e Šiʿa dar Irān* (The Change of Shiʿite Discourse in Iran), Tehran, 1998. Moḥsen Kadivar, *Naẓariyahā-ye dawlat dar feqh-e Shiʿa* (The Theories of State in the Shiʿite Feqh,), Tehran, 1998. Idem, Ḥokumat-e welāʾi [*welāyat-e faqih*], (Government of the Guardian Jurist), Tehran, 1999. Idem, *Dağdağahā-ye ḥokumat-e dini* (Tribulations Concerning Religious Government, a Collection of Political Papers and Lectures), Tehran, 2000. Ruhollah Khomeini, *Ḥokumat-e eslāmi* and *welāyat-e faqih*, (Islamic Government Under the Guardian Jurist), Najaf, 1972. Idem, *Islam and Revolution: Writings and Declarations of Imam Khomeini*, tr. and annot. Hamid Algar, Berkeley, 1981. Idem, *Ṣaḥifa-ye nur: majmuʿa-ye rahnemudhā-ye Emām Ḵomeyni* (Imam Khomeini's Collected Guidelines) 16 vols., Tehran, 1983-90. Charles Kurzman, ed., *Liberal Islam: A Sourcebook*, New York, 1998.

Gary Muhammad Legenhausen, *Islam and Religious Pluralism*, London, 1999. Idem, *Contemporary Topics of Islamic Thought*, London, 2000. R. Martin and M. Woodward, *Defenders of Reason in Islam, Muʻtazilism from Medieval School to Modern Symbol*, Oxford, 1997. V. A. Martin, Islam and Modernism: *The Iranian Revolution of 1906*, London, 1989. M. Marty and R. Appleby, eds., "The Fundamentalist Project," 5 vols., Chicago, 1991-1995, I, *Fundamentalisms*

Observed, Chicago, 1991. M.-T. Mesbah Yazdi, *Naẓariya-ye siāsi-e Eslām* (Islamic Political Theory), Tehran, 1999a. Idem, *Tahājom-e farhangi* (Cultural Aggression), ed. ʿA. Ebrāhimi, Qom, 1999b. Barbara D. Metcalf, *Islamic Revival in British India: Deoband 1860-1900*, Princeton, 1982. Hossein Modarressi, *Crisis and consolidation in the formative period of Shiʿite Islam*, Princeton, 1993. Mojāhedin-e ḵalq-e Irān, *Ideʾoloži I: takāmol* (Ideology I, Evolution), n.p., n.d. Idem, *Ideʾoiloži II: šenāḵt* (Ideology II, Knowledge), n.p., n.d. M. Mojtahed Šabestari, *Hermenotik, ketāb wa sonnat* (Hermeneutics, Book and Tradition), Tehran, 1996. Idem, *Naqd-i bar qerāʾat-e rasmi az din: boḥrānhā, čālešhā, rāh-e ḥalhā* (A Critique of Official Reading of Religion: Crises, Challenges, and Solutions), Tehran, 2002. Ayatollah Ḥosayn-ʿAli Montaẓeri, *Matn-e kāmel-e ḵāṭerāt-e Āyat-Allāh Ḥosayn-ʿAli Montaẓeri*, Sweden, 2000. Mortaza Motahhari, *Jihād dar Eslām wa mašruʿiyat-e ān dar Qurʾān*, Tehran, 1985, Eng. tr. Mohammad Salman Tawhidi as *The Holy War of Islam and Its Legitimacy in the Qurʾān*, online: www.al-islam.org/short/jihad. Idem, *Naẓari be neẓām-e eqteṣādi-e Eslām* (A Look at the Islamic Economic System), Tehran, 1989. Idem, *Eslām wa moqtażiyāt-e zamān* (Islam and Requirements of Times), Tehran, 1991.

Moḥammad-Ḥosayn Nāʾini, *Tanbih al-omma wa tanzih al-mella dar lozum-e mašruṭa* (The Admonition of the Religious Community and the Refinement of the Nation on Necessity of Constitutionalism), Baghdad, 1909; 2nd ed., Tehran, 1910; ed., Sayyed Maḥmud Ṭāleqāni, Tehran, 1955. Aḥmad Narāqi, "Dar bāra-ye rowšanfekr-e dini" (About Religious Intellectual), in Ḥ. Aḥmadi and M.-Ḥ. Fattāḥiān, pp. 177-88. Sayyed Hossein Nasr, *Man and Nature: the Spiritual Crisis of Modern Man*, Chicago, 1998. Idem, *Religion and the Order of Nature*, Oxford, 1996. Maḥmud Nekuruḥ, *Nahżat-e ḵodaparastān-e sosiālist* (Divine Worshiping Socialists), Tehran, 1998. Philippe Nemo, "From Heidegger to Suhravardi: An Interview with Henri Corbin," online: www.amiscorbin.com/textes/anglais/interview nemo.htm. Shaikh Fażl-Allāh Nuri, *Majmuʿaʾi az rasāʾel-e ʿelmiya, mokātabāt, wa ruz-nama-ye Šayḵ-e šahīd Fażl-Allāh Nuri*, ed. M. Torkamān, 2 vols., Tehran, 1983-84.

Sayyed Muhammad Qutb, *ʿAdālat al-ejtemāʿiya fiʾl-Eslām* (Social Justice in Islam), tr. Pers., Hādi Ḵosrowšāhi and M.-ʿA. Gerāmi Qomi, as *ʿAdālat-e ejtemāʿi dar Eslām*, Tehran, 1962; 8th repr., 2001. Ali Rahnema, *An Islamic Utopian: A Political Biography of Ali Shariʿati*, London, 2000. Idem, *Niruhā-ye maḏhabi bar bestar-e ḥarakat-e nahżat-e melli* (Religious Forces in the Context of Nationalist Movement), Tehran, 2005. Moḥsen Reżāʾi, "Jaryān-e sevvom" (The third current), an interview published in *Šarq al-awsaṭ* in early 2001, its tr. published in *Kayhān* (London), 1 August 2001, pp. 9-11. Sayyed Ḥamid Ruḥāni, *Nahżat-e Emām Ḵomeyni* (Imam Khomeini's Movement), 2 vols., Tehran, 1985. Neʿmat-Allāh Ṣāleḥi Najafābādi, *Šahid-e jāvid, Ḥosayn b. ʿAli* (The Immortal Martyr, Hosayn b. Ali), Tehran, 1970. A. Saviyon and Y. Mansharof, "The Ideological and Political Philosophy of Mahmoud Ahmadinejad and Ayatollah Mesbah-e Yazzdi, *Inquiry and Analysis Series* 357, The Middle East Media Research Institute, May 31, 2007 (available online). Ali Shariʿati, *Šahādat* (Martyrdom), Tehran, 1973. Idem, "Humanity and Islam," in Kurzman, ed., 1998, pp. 187-95. Asghar Schirazi, *The Constitution of Iran: Politics and the State in the Islamic Republic*, London, 1998. Mostafa al-Sibaʾi, *Ešterākiyat al-Eslām* (The Socialism of Islam), Damascus, 1959. Abdolkarim Soroush, *Reason, Freedom, and Democracy in Islam*, trs. and eds., M. Sadri and A. Sadri, Oxford and New York, 2000a. Idem, "Reason and Freedom in Islamic Thought," 2000b (in www.dsoroush.com). M. Tāleqāni, "Taleqani's Last Sermon," in Kurzman, ed., 1998, pp. 46-48. Farzin Vahdat, "Post-Revolutionary Islamic Discourse on Modernity in Iran: Expansion and Contraction of Human Subjectivity," in *IJMES* 35, 2003, pp. 599-631. Idem, "Post-Revolutionary Discourses of Mohammad Mojtahed Shabestari and Mohsen Kadivar: Reconciling the Terms of Mediated Subjectivity," *Critique: Journal for Critical Studies of the Middle East* 16, Spring 2000, pp. 31-54; 17, Fall 2000, pp. 135-57. Eqbāl Yaḡmāʾi ed., *Šahid-e rāh-e āzādi, Sayyed Jamāl al-Din Eṣfahāni*, Tehran, 1978. Ebrāhim Yazdi, *Se jomhuri*, Tehran, 2000. Ḥasan Yusofi Eškevari, *Yād-e ayyām: ruykardhā-ye siāsi dar jonbeš-e eṣlāḥāt* (Memory of Those Days: Political Events in the Reform Movement), Tehran, 2000.

(AHMAD ASHRAF)

xiv. ISLAM AND DEMOCRACY.
Forthcoming online.

xv. ISLAM AND SOCIALISM.
Forthcoming online.

xvi. ISLAM AND FUNDAMENTALISM.
Forthcoming online.

xvii. ISLAMIC REVOLUTION OF 1977–79.
Forthcoming online.

xviii. ISLAMIC REPUBLIC OF IRAN.
Forthcoming online.

ISMAʿILISM, a major Shiʿite Muslim community. The Ismaʿilis have had a long and eventful history dating back to the middle of the 2nd/8th century when the Emāmi Shiʿis split into several groups on the death of Imam Jaʿfar al-Ṣādeq. The earliest Ismaʿilis from amongst the Emāmi Shiʿis traced the imamate in the progeny of Esmāʿil b. Jaʿfar al-Ṣādeq, the eponym of the Esmāʿiliya. Subsequently, the Ismaʿilis themselves became subdivided into a number of major branches and minor groupings. Currently, the Ismaʿilis are comprised of the Nezāri and Ṭayyebi Mostaʿlian branches, and they are scattered as religious minorities in over twenty-five countries of Asia, the Middle East, Africa, Europe and North America. Numbering several millions, the Ismaʿilis represent a diversity of ethnic groups and literary traditions, and speak a variety of languages and dialects, including especially Arabic, Persian as well as a number of Indic and European languages.

Until the middle of the 20th century, the Ismaʿilis were studied and judged almost exclusively on the basis of evidence collected or fabricated by their enemies. Consequently, a variety of myths and legends circulated widely, both in Muslim societies and in the West, regarding their teachings and practices. The breakthrough in Ismaʿilis studies occurred with the recovery and study of genuine Ismaʿili texts on a large scale—Arabic and Persian manuscript sources which had been preserved in numerous private collections in the Yemen, Syria, Persia, Central Asia, and South Asia. As a result of the findings of modern scholarship in Ismaʿili studies, we now have a much better understanding of Ismaʿili history and thought. The Ismaʿilis elaborated a diversity of intellectual and literary traditions in different languages and made important contributions to Islamic civilization, especially during the Fatimid period of their history when they possessed an important state, the Fatimid caliphate, and the classical Ismaʿili texts on a range of exoteric and esoteric subjects were produced. At the same time, a distinctively Ismaʿili school of jurisprudence was founded under the early Fatimid caliph-imams. Later, the Nezāri Ismaʿilis, under the initial leadership of Ḥasan Ṣabbāḥ (q.v.), founded their own state in Persia and Syria, also elaborating their teachings in response to changing circumstances.

A number of specialized articles on the Ismaʿilis and their heritage have already appeared in the *Encyclopaedia Iranica*. The articles of this main multi-authored section on Ismaʿilism cover central aspects of Ismaʿili history and thought in addition to surveys of Ismaʿili historiography and literature as well as the Ismaʿilis communities of modern times.

This entry will be divided into the following sections:

i. *Ismaʿili Studies*.
ii. *Ismaʿili historiography*.
iii. *Ismaʿili history*.
iv. *Qarāmeta*. See CARMATIANS.
v. *Ismaʿili daʿwa and dynasty of Fatimid*. See FATIMIDS.
vi. *Ismaʿili ideas of time*. See DAWR.
vii. *Ismaʿili ideas of cosmology and cosmogony*. See COSMOLOGY AND COSMOGONY vii.
viii. *Free will in Ismaʿilism*. See FREE WILL ii.
ix. *Ismaʿili Missionaries*. See DĀʿI.
x. *Ismaʿili Myths and Legends*. See FEDĀʾIS.
xi. *Ismʿili jurisprudence*.
xii. *Ismaʿili Hadith*. See HADITH iii.
xiii. *Ismaʿilism in Arabic and Persian literature*.
xiv. *Ismaʿilism in Ginān literature*.
xv. *Nezāri Ismaʿili monuments*.
xvi. *Modern Ismaʿili communities*.
xvii. *The Imamate in Ismaʿilism*.

i. ISMAʿILI STUDIES

In its modern and scientific form, dating to the 1930s, Ismaʿili studies represents one of the newest fields of Islamic studies. Before this time, the Ismaʿilis were almost exclusively studied and evaluated on the basis of evidence collected, or often fabricated, by their enemies. As a result, they were persistently misrepresented with a variety of myths and legends circulating about their teachings and practices. The perceptions of outsiders of the Ismaʿilis in the pre-modern period, in both Muslim and Christian milieus, contrast with modern developments in Ismaʿili studies to make the history of this field particularly fascinating.

As the most revolutionary wing of Shiʿism with a religio-political agenda that aimed to uproot the ʿAbbasids and restore the caliphate to a line of ʿAlid imams, the Ismaʿilis from early on aroused the hostility of the Sunnite establishment. With the foundation of the Fatimid state in 297/909, the potential challenge of the Ismaʿilis to Sunnite "orthodoxy" became actualized, and thereupon the ʿAbbasids and the Sunnite ulama launched what amounted to an official anti-Ismaʿili propaganda campaign. The overall purpose of this prolonged campaign was to discredit the entire Ismaʿili movement from its roots, so that they could be readily condemned by other Muslims as *molḥeds*, heretics or deviators from the true religious path. In particular, several generations of Sunnite polemicists, starting with Abu ʿAbd-Allāh Moḥammad b. ʿAli b. Rezām Ṭāʾi Kufi, known as Ebn Rezām, who lived in Baghdad during the first half of the 4th/10th century, began to fabricate evidence that would provide justification for the condemnation of the Ismaʿilis on specific doctrinal grounds. Ebn Rezām's book on the refutation of the Ismaʿilis has not survived, but it was used extensively by another polemicist and early ʿAlid genealogist Šarif Abu'l-Ḥosayn Moḥammad b. ʿAli, better known as Aḵu Moḥsen, who wrote his own anti-Ismaʿili work to refute the doctrines of the Ismaʿilis and the ʿAlid genealogy of their imams. Aḵu Moḥsen's treatise, too, written around 372/982, has not survived directly. However, the Ebn Rezām-Aḵu Moḥsen accounts have been preserved fragmentarily in the writings of Nowayri (pp. 187-317), Ebn al-Dawādāri (pp. 6-21, 44-156), and Maqrizi (pp. 22-29, 151-202). These polemical writings were used as a major source of information by Sunnite heresiographers, such as Abu Manṣur ʿAbd-al-Qāher b. Ṭāher Baḡdādi (pp. 265-99), who produced another important category of source material against the Ismaʿilis. The earliest Twelver Shiʿite heresiographers Nowbaḵti and Qomi, who were better informed than their Sunnite counterparts about the internal divisions of Shiʿism, were less hostile toward the Ismaʿilis while upholding the legitimacy of the rival Ḥosaynid line of ʿAlid Imams recognized by the Twelver Shiʿites.

Polemicists also fabricated travesties in which they attributed a variety of shocking beliefs and practices to the Ismaʿilis. These travesties circulated widely in the guise of genuine Ismaʿili works and were used as source materials by later polemicists and heresiographers. Aḵu Moḥsen claims to have read one of these forgeries, the anonymous *Ketāb al-siāsa*, quoted also by Baḡdādi (pp. 277-79), which expounded the procedures allegedly followed by Ismaʿili *dāʿi*s (missionaries; q.v.) to attract converts and instruct them through seven stages of initiation (*balāḡ*), leading ultimately to libertinism and atheism (see Stern, pp. 56-83). The same book, or another travesty entitled *Ketāb al-balāḡ*, was seen by Ebn al-Nadim (pp. 238, 240). In fact, the Ismaʿili tradition itself only knows these travesties from the polemics of its enemies. Nonetheless, the anti-Ismaʿili polemical and heresiographical traditions, in turn, influenced the historians, theologians and jurists who wished to comment on the Ismaʿilis. By their misrepresentation of the Ismaʿilis, the anti-Ismaʿili authors in fact produced a "black legend" in the course of the 4th/10th century. Thus, Ismaʿilism was portrayed as the arch-heresy of Islam, carefully designed by some non-ʿAlid impostors, or possibly even a Jewish magician disguised as a Muslim, with the aim of destroying Islam from within (see, for instance, Ivanow, 1946). By the 5th/11th century, this "black legend," with its elaborate details and stages of initiation, had been accepted as an accurate and reliable description of Ismaʿili motives, beliefs and practices, leading to further accusations against the Ismāʿiliya, or Bāṭeniya, another designation coined in reference to the Ismaʿilis by their enemies.

The revolt of the Persian Ismaʿilis led by Ḥasan-e Ṣabbāḥ (q.v.) against the Saljuq Turks provoked another round of Sunnite reaction against the Ismaʿilis in general and the Nezāri Ismaʿilis in particular. The new literary campaign was initiated by the all-powerful Saljuq vizier Neẓām-al-Molk, who devoted a long chapter in his *Siāsat-nāma* (pp. 282-311; trans., pp. 208-31) to the condemnation of the Ismaʿilis. At the same time, Ḡazāli was commissioned by the ʿAbbasid caliph al-Mostaẓher to write a major polemical tract against the Bāṭenis and their doctrine of *taʿlim* (authoritative instruction from the Imam; see Ḡazāli, *Fażāʾeḥ al-Bāṭeniya*). It was under such circumstances that the Nezāri Ismaʿilis of Syria were referred to by the term of abuse *ḥašišiya* (Abu Šāma, I, pp. 240, 258; Ebn Moyassar, p. 102). The Persian Nezāris, too, were designated as *ḥašiši* in some contemporary Zaydi sources written in northern Persia (Madelung, pp. 146, 239). However, it should be pointed out that all Muslim sources which refer to the Nezāris as *ḥašiši*s use this term in its pejorative sense of "low-class rabble," without accusing the Nezāris of actually using the narcotic hashish.

It was in the time of Rāšed-al-Din Senān, who led the Syrian Nezāris for three decades until his death in 589/1193, that occidental chroniclers of the Crusades and a number of European travelers began to write about the Nezāri Ismaʿilis, better known in medieval Europe as "the Assassins." The very term "Assassin" was evidently based on local variants of the Arabic word *ḥašiši* (plural, *ḥašišiya*) picked up in the Levant by the Crusaders and their European observers. The Crusader circles, who remained completely ignorant of Islam and the Ismaʿilis, now began to produce reports about the alleged secret practices of the Nezāri Ismaʿilis, with whom they had come into contact in Syria. Eventually, medieval Europeans themselves began to fabricate and put into circulation both in the Latin Orient and in Europe a number of tales, rooted in their "imaginative ignorance," about the secret practices of the Assassins and their leader, the so-called "Old Man of the Mountain"—another term coined by the Crusader circles and originally applied to Senān (see, e.g., Arnold of Lübeck, pp. 178-79, 240; Daftary, 1994, p. 116). These imaginative tales revolved around the recruitment and training of the Nezāri *fedāʾi*s (q.v.). The so-called Assassin legends consisted of a number of interconnected tales which developed in stages and finally culminated in a synthesis popularized by Marco Polo (I, pp. 139-46). Different Assassin legends were "imagined" independently and at times concurrently by different authors, such as Arnold of Lübeck (d. 1212) and James of Vitry (d. 1240); and by the 8th/14th century, these legends had acquired wide currency and were accepted as reliable descriptions of secret Nezāri practices (Daftary, 1994, pp. 88-127). Henceforth, the Nezāris were portrayed in medieval European sources as a sinister order of hashish-crazed "assassins" bent on senseless murder and mischief.

The orientalists of the 19th century, led by A. I. Silvestre de Sacy (1758-1838), correctly identified the Ismaʿilis as a Shiʿite Muslim community, but they were still obliged to study them exclusively on the basis of the hostile Sunnite sources and the fanciful tales of the Crusader circles. Consequently, the orientalists, too, lent their seal of approval to the medieval myths about the Ismaʿilis, including the anti-Ismaʿili "black legend" of the Sunnite polemicists and the Assassin legends of the Crusaders. It was under such circumstances that von Hammer-Purgstall (q.v.; 1774-1856) wrote the first Western book on the Persian Nezāris of the Alamut period. This book, permeated with misconceptions and misrepresentations, received much acclaim in Europe and continued to be treated as the standard history of the Nezāris until the 1930s. With rare exceptions, notably the studies of Charles F. Defrémery (1822-83) on the Nezāris of Syria and Persia and those of Michael J. de Goeje (1836-1909) on the Carmatians (q.v.), the Ismaʿilis continued to be misrepresented to varying degrees by later orientalists. Even a distinguished scholar like Edward Browne (q.v.) could not resist reiterating the orientalistic tales of his predecessors about the Ismaʿilis (I, 391-415; II, 190-211, 453-60). Meanwhile, Westerners retained the habit of referring to the Nezāri Ismaʿilis of the Alamut period as the Assassins, a misnomer rooted in a medieval pejorative appellation.

The breakthrough in Ismaʿili studies occurred with the recovery and study of genuine Ismaʿili texts on a relatively large scale—manuscript sources which had been preserved secretly in scattered private collections. A few Ismaʿili manuscripts of Syrian provenance had already surfaced in Paris during the nineteenth century, and some fragments of these Arabic texts were published by S. Guyard among others. At the same time, Paul Casanova (1861-1926), who produced important studies on the Fatimids, was the first European orientalist to recognize the Ismaʿili connection of the *Rasāʾel Eḵwān al-Ṣafāʾ*. More Ismaʿili manuscripts preserved in the Yemen and Central Asia were recovered in the opening decades of the twentieth century (see Griffini, pp. 80-88; Ivanow, 1917, pp. 359-86). However, by 1922, when the first Western bibliography of Ismaʿili works was compiled by Louis Massignon, who erroneously used the terms Carmatian and Ismaʿili interchangeably, scholars clearly still possessed only a very limited knowledge of Ismaʿili literature.

Modern scholarship in Ismaʿili studies was initiated in the 1930s in India, where significant collections of Ismaʿili manuscripts are preserved within the Ṭayyebi Ismaʿili Bohra community. The breakthrough resulted mainly from the pioneering efforts of Wladimir Ivanow (1886-1970; q.v.) and a few Ismaʿili Bohra scholars, notably Asaf A. A. Fyzee (1899-1981), Ḥosayn F. Hamdāni (1901-62) and Zāhed ʿAli (1888-1958), all of whom possessed family collections of important manuscripts. It was indeed Fyzee who through his studies of Qāżi Noʿmān's legal treatises made modern scholars aware of the existence of an independent Ismaʿili school of jurisprudence (see Daftary, 1984, pp. 49-63). Ivanow found access not only to the Arabic manuscripts preserved by Ṭayyebi Ismaʿili Bohras but also to the Persian Ismaʿili literature of the Nezāris of Persia, Afghanistan and Central Asia. As a result, he compiled the first detailed catalogue of Ismaʿili works, attesting to the hitherto unknown richness and diversity of Ismaʿili literature and intellectual traditions. This catalogue (Ivanow, 1933) provided a scientific framework for modern Ismaʿili studies. Ismaʿili scholarship received another major impetus through the establishment in 1946, in Bombay, of the Ismaili Society, or Anjoman-e Esmāʿili (q.v.).

By 1963, when Ivanow published a revised edition of his catalogue, many more Ismaʿili sources had been discovered and progress in Ismaʿili studies had been astonishing. Numerous Ismaʿili texts had now begun to be critically edited and studied, laying a solid foundation for further progress in the field. In this connection, other than the Persian Nezāri texts edited and translated by Ivanow and published by the Ismaili Society, mention should be made of the editions and translations of the texts of the Fatimid and later times by Henry Corbin (q.v.), published in his *Bibliothèque Iranienne* series, and the Arabic Ismaʿili texts edited by the Egyptian scholar Moḥammad Kāmel Ḥosayn (1901-61) in his *Selselat Maḵṭuṭāt al-Fāṭemiyin* series. At the same time, ʿĀref Tāmer (1921-98) published numerous Ismaʿili texts of Syrian provenance, though often in flawed editions. Meanwhile, a group of Egyptian scholars, notably Ḥasan Ebrāhim Ḥasan (1892-1968), Jamāl-al-Din al-Šayyāl (1911-67) and ʿAbd-al-Monʿem Mājed (1920-99) made important contributions to Fatimid studies, while in the West, Bernard Lewis, Samuel M. Stern (1920-69), Wilferd Madelung and Abbas Hamdani produced important studies on the early history of the Ismaʿilis and their relations with the Carmatians; and Marshall Hodgson (1922-68) produced the first scholarly study of the Nezāris of the Alamut period.

The rapid progress in the recovery and study of Ismaʿili literature in the course of the 20th century is reflected well in I. K. Poonawala's *Biobibliography* (1977), which identifies some 1300 titles written by more than 200 authors. Progress in Ismaʿili studies promises to continue at an even greater pace as many Ismaʿilis themselves are now becoming interested in the study of their own history and literary heritage, and as The Institute of Ismaili Studies (q.v.), with its unique collection of manuscripts (see Gacek; Cortese), continues to serve as a central forum for furthering progress in this field of Islamic studies.

Bibliography: Abu Šāma, *Ketāb al-rawżatayn fi aḵbār al-dawlatayn*, 2 vols., Cairo, 1287-88/1870-71. Abū Manṣūr ʿAbd-al-Qāher b. Ṭāher Baḡdādī, *al-Farq bayn al-feraq*, ed. Moḥammad Badr, Cairo, 1328/1910. Arnold of Lübeck, *Chronica Slavorum*, in G. H. Pertz et al., eds., *Monumenta Germaniae Historica: Scriptores*, Hanover, 1826-1913, XXI, pp. 100-250. E. G. Browne, *Lit. Hist. Persia*. D. Cortese, *Ismaili and other Arabic Manuscripts: A Descriptive Catalogue of Manuscripts in the Library of The Institute of Ismaili Studies*, London, 2000. F. Daftary, "The Bibliography of Asaf A. A. Fyzee," *Indo-Iranica* 37, 1984, pp. 49-63. Idem, *The Assassin Legends*, London, 1994. Idem, "Introduction: Ismaʿilis and Ismaʿili Studies," in F. Daftary, ed., *Mediaeval Ismaʿili History and Thought*, Cambridge, 1996, pp. 1-12. Idem, "Moṭālaʿāt-e Esmāʿili," *Iran Nameh* 18, 2000, pp. 257-71. Ebn al-Dawādāri, *Kanz al-dorar* VI, ed. I. Monajjed, Cairo, 1961. Charles F. Defrémery, "Nouvelles recherches sur les Ismaéliens ou Bathiniens de Syrie," *JA* 5, S 3, 1854, pp. 373-421; 5, 1855, pp. 5-76. Idem, "Essai sur l'histoire des Ismaéliens ou Batiniens de la Perse," *JA* 8, S 5, 1856, pp. 353-87; 15, 1860, pp. 130-210. Ebn al-Nadim, ed. Tajaddod, 2nd ed. Ebn Moyassar, *Aḵbār Meṣr*, ed. A. Foʾād Sayyed, Cairo, 1981. A. Gacek, *Catalogue of Arabic Manuscripts in the Library of The Institute of Ismaili Studies* I, London, 1984. Abu Ḥāmed Moḥammad Ḡazāli, *Fażāʾeḥ al-Bāṭeniya*, ed. ʿA. Badawi, Cairo, 1964. M. J. de Goeje, *Mémoire sur les Carmathes du Bahraïn et les Fatimides*, 2nd ed., Leiden, 1886. E. Griffini, "Die jüngste ambrosianische Sammlung arabischer Handschriften," *ZDMG* 69, 1915, pp. 63-88. J. von Hammer-Purgstall, *Die Geschichte der Assassinen*, Stuttgart and Tübingen, 1818; tr. J. Hellert and P. A. de la Nourais, *Histoire de l'ordre des Assassins*, Paris, 1833; tr. O. C. Wood, *The History of the Assassins*, London, 1835; reprinted, New York, 1968. M. G. S. Hodgson, *The Order of Assassins*, The Hague, 1955. V. A. Ivanov [Ivanow], "Ismailitskiya rukopisi

Aziatskago Muzeya. Sobranie I. Zarubin, 1916g.," (Ismaʿili Manuscripts, Asiatic Museum: Collection of I. Zarubin) *Bulletin de l'Académie des Sciences de Russie* 11, S 6, 1917, pp. 359-86. Idem, *A Guide to Ismaili Literature*, London, 1933. Idem, *The Alleged Founder of Ismailism*, Bombay, 1946. Idem, *Ismaili Literature: A Bibliographical Survey*, Tehran, 1963. W. Madelung, ed., *Arabic Texts Concerning the History of the Zaydī Imāms of Ṭabaristān, Daylamān and Gīlān*, Beirut, 1987. Marco Polo, *The Book of Sir Marco Polo, the Venetian*, ed. and tr. H. Yule, 3rd rev. ed. by H. Cordier, 2 vols., London, 1929. Taqi-al-Din Aḥmad b. ʿAli Maqrizi, *Etteʿāẓ al-ḥonafāʾ* I, ed. J. al-Šayyāl, Cairo, 1967. L. Massignon, "Esquisse d'une bibliographie Qarmaṭe," in T. W. Arnold and R. A. Nicholson, ed., *A Volume of Oriental Studies Presented to Edward G. Browne*, Cambridge, 1922, pp. 329-38; reprinted in L. Massignon, *Opera Minora*, ed. Y. Moubarac, Paris, 1969, I, pp. 627-39. Neẓām-al-Molk, *Siar al-moluk (Siāsat-nāma)*, ed. H. Darke, 2nd ed., Tehran, 1347 Š./1968; tr. H. Darke, *The Book of Government or Rules for Kings*, 2nd ed., London, 1978. Aḥmad b. ʿAbd-al-Wahhāb Nowayri, *Nehāyat al-arab* XXV, ed. M. J. ʿAbd-al-Āl al-Ḥini et al., Cairo, 1984. I. K. Poonawala, *Biobibliography of Ismāʿīlī Literature*, Malibu, Calif., 1977. A. I. Silvestre de Sacy, "Mémoire sur la dynastie des Assassins, et sur l'étymologie de leur Nom," in *Mémoires de l'Institut Royal de France* 4, 1818, pp. 1-84; tr. A. Azodi, "Memoir on the Dynasty of the Assassins, and on the Etymology of their Name" in F. Daftary, *The Assassin Legends*, London, 1994, pp. 129-88. S. M. Stern, *Studies in Early Ismāʿīlism*, Jerusalem and Leiden, 1983. Paul E. Walker, *Exploring an Islamic Empire: Fatimid History and Its Sources*, London, 2002.

(FARHAD DAFTARY)

ii. ISMAʿILI HISTORIOGRAPHY

Ismaʿili historiography has been closely related to the very nature of the Ismaʿili mission, or *daʿwa*, and the changing fortunes of the Ismaʿilis during the various phases of their history. The Ismaʿilis were usually persecuted by their numerous enemies, necessitating the observance of *taqiya* by them. The Ismaʿili *dāʿis*, who were at the same time the scholars and authors of their community, often operated in hostile territories and were obliged to observe utter secrecy in their activities. These dāʿi-authors were, moreover, normally trained as theologians and as such, they were not interested in compiling annalistic or other types of historical accounts. The general lack of Ismaʿili interest in historiography is well attested by the fact that only a few works of historical nature have been found in the rich corpus of Ismaʿili literature recovered in modern times, which comprises mainly of theological works, with a substantial number of treatises related to the so-called esoteric, or *ḥaqāʾeq*, subjects, as well as numerous titles utilizing the methodology of esoteric interpretation (*taʾwil*), the hallmark of Ismaʿili thought (see Majduʿ; Ivanow, pp. 17-173; Poonawala, pp. 31-297). It should be added, however, that the religious works of the Ismaʿilis, written in Arabic, Persian and Indic languages, do occasionally shed light on aspects of Ismaʿili history, while at the same time they serve themselves as sources for understanding the nature and development of the intellectual and literary traditions of the Ismaʿilis.

Among the few historical works produced by Ismaʿili authors mention may be made of Qāżi Noʿmān's *Eftetāḥ al-daʿwa* (Beirut, 1970; Tunis, 1975), completed in 346/957, which is the oldest known Ismaʿili history covering the background to the establishment of the Fatimid state in North Africa. In later medieval times, only one general history of Ismaʿilism, covering from the earliest period until the mid-6th/12th century, was written by an Ismaʿili author, namely, the seven-volume *ʿOyun al-aḵbār* (Beirut, 1973-84) of Edris ʿEmād-al-Din (d. 872/1468), the 19th *dāʿi-e moṭlaq* of the Mostaʿli-Ṭayyebi Ismaʿilis in Yemen. This dāʿi produced two more historical works, the *Nozhat al-afkār* and the *Rawżat al-aḵbār* (Sanaa, 1995), which continue the history of the Ṭayyebi daʿwa until 870/1465. There are also certain brief, but highly significant, accounts of particular events in Ismaʿili history, notably the *Estetār al-emām* (ed. W. Ivanow, 1936a), written by the dāʿi Nisāburi, relating the settlement of the early Ismaʿili imam ʿAbd-Allāh al-Akbar in Salamiya, and the subsequent prolonged journey of ʿAbd-Allāh al-Mahdi from Syria to North Africa where he was installed to the Fatimid caliphate in 297/909.

In spite of the general absence of an Ismaʿili historiographical tradition, there were two periods during which the Ismaʿilis concerned themselves with historical writings and produced or encouraged works which in a sense served as official chronicles. During the Fatimid and Alamut periods of their history, the Ismaʿilis possessed states of their own and ruling dynasties whose achievements needed to be recorded by reliable chroniclers. In Fatimid times (297-567/909-1171), especially after the transference of the seat of the Fatimid state to Cairo in 362/973, numerous histories of the Fatimid caliphate and dynasty were written by contemporary historians, both Ismaʿili and non-Ismaʿili, such as Ebn Zulāq (d. 386/996), Mosabbeḥi (d. 420/1029) and Qażāʿi (d. 454/1062). With the exception of a few fragments, however, none of these chronicles survived the demise of the Fatimid dynasty. The Sunnite Ayyubids who succeeded the Ismaʿili Shiʿite Fatimids, systematically destroyed the renowned Fatimid libraries, including the collections of the Dār al-ʿElm in Cairo, also persecuting the Ismaʿilis of Egypt (see Daftary, 1990, pp. 144-52; Walker, pp. 152-69).

In addition to historical writings, the Ismaʿilis of the Fatimid period who enjoyed the protection of their own state, also produced certain biographical works of the *monāẓara* and *sira* genres with great historical value. Among the extant examples of such works, special mention may be made of the *Ketāb al-monāẓarāt* (ed. and tr. W. Madelung and P. E. Walker, London, 2000) of the dāʿi Ebn Hayṯam, containing unique details on the first year of Fatimid rule in Efriqiya; the *Sira* of Jaʿfar b. ʿAli (ed. W. Ivanow, 1936b), chamberlain (*ḥājeb*) to the first Fatimid caliph-imam al-Mahdi; and the *Sira* (Cairo, 1954) of Ostad̲ Jawd̲ar (d. 363/973), who served the first four Fatimid caliph-imams. There is also the important autobiography of al-Moʾayyad fi'l-Din Širāzi (d. 470/1078), who held the office of the chief dāʿi in Cairo for almost twenty years (Walker, pp. 131-51).

The Nezāri Ismaʿilis, too, maintained a historiographical tradition during the Alamut period of their history (483-654/1090-1256), when they had a territorial state in Persia centered at the mountainous fortress of Alamut (q.v.), with a subsidiary branch in Syria. During this turbulent period, they compiled chronicles in Persian recording the events of their state according to the reigns of the successive lords of Alamut (Daftary, 1990, pp. 324-33; idem, 1992, pp. 91-97). This historiographical tradition commenced with the *Sargod̲ašt-e Sayyednā*, a work describing the life and the events of the reign of Ḥasan-e Ṣabbāḥ (q.v., d. 518/1124) as the first lord of Alamut. The first part of this work, which has not survived directly, may have been autobiographical. The reign of Kiā Bozorg-Omid (518-532/1124-1138), Ḥasan's successor as the leader of the Nezāri state and daʿwa, was covered in another chronicle entitled *Ketāb-e Bozorg-Omid*. The events of the Persian Nezāri state during the subsequent times until the reign of the eighth and final lord of Alamut, Rokn-al-Din K̲oršāh and the Mongol destruction of that state in 654/1256, were narrated by other Nezāri chroniclers such as Dehk̲odā ʿAbd-al-Malek b. ʿAli Fašandi and Raʾis Ḥasan Ṣalāḥ-al-Din Monši Birjandi. All these chronicles held at the libraries of Alamut and other Nezari castles in Daylamān and Qohestān perished in the Mongol invasions or soon afterwards, during the period of Ilkhanid rule over Persia. However, these chronicles as well as other Nezāri writings and documents were seen and used extensively by three Persian historians of the Ilkhanid period, namely, Joveyni (d. 681/1283), Rašid-al-Din Fażl-Allāh (d. 718/1318) and Abu'l-Qāsem Kāšāni (d. ca. 736/1335), in their own histories of the Ismaʿilis. Indeed, these histories remain our most important primary sources on the Nezāri Ismaʿili state in Persia; and they provided the main sources of reference for later Persian historians, like Ḥamd-Allāh Mostawfi (d. after 740/1339) and Ḥāfeẓ-e Abru (d. 833/1430), writing on the subject. Unlike their Persian coreligionists, the Syrian Nezāris and the Nezāri K̲ojas of the Indian subcontinent did not elaborate historiographical traditions.

In the turbulent conditions of the post-Alamut period, when the Persian Nezāris often had to resort to practicing taqiya, and the Nezāri imams remained in hiding for several generations, their literary activities almost ceased to exist and the Nezāris of different regions, who now developed independently of each other, remained largely ignorant of their historical heritage. The situation ameliorated somewhat during the Anjedān (q.v.) revival in Nezāri daʿwa and literary activities, which coincided almost exactly with the Safavid period in Persian history. However, the Nezāri works of this period, such as those produced by Abu Esḥāq Qohestāni (d. after 904/1498) and K̲ayrk̲ᵛāh-e Harāti (d. after 960/1553), although doctrinal in nature, do contain some historical information. In Badak̲šān and other regions of Central Asia, the Nezāris of later medieval times elaborated a distinctive literary and doctrinal tradition, based especially on the teachings of Nāṣer-e K̲osrow as well as certain Sufi traditions. However, the Central Asian Nezāris, too, did not develop any interest in historiography. Indeed, in the entire extant literature of the Nezāris of Persia and Central Asia, written in the Persian language and preserved mainly in private libraries of Badak̲šān now divided between Tajikistan and Afghanistan, there are no historical works worth mentioning, with the major exception of the *Hedāyat al-moʾmenin* of Fedāʾi K̲orāsāni (q.v; d. 1342/1923).

On the other hand, the Mostaʿli-Ṭayyebi Ismaʿilis, especially those belonging to the majority Dāʾudi branch, have produced a number of works in Arabic on the history of their daʿwa and the dynasties of their dāʿis in Yaman and India. In order to make them more accessible to the Dāʾudi Bohra community, some of these histories produced in modern times have been written in Gujarati and transcribed in Arabic (Daftary, 1990, pp. 256-61). Amongst more reliable histories of this kind, mention may be made of the *Montazaʿ al-ak̲bār* (Beirut, 1999) of Qoṭb-al-Din Solaymānji Borhānpuri (d. 1241/1826), and the *Mawsem-e bahār* (Bombay, 1301-1311/1884-93) of Moḥammad-ʿAli Rāmpuri (d. 1315/1897). In more recent times, a number of learned Dāʾudi Bohras such as Zāhed-ʿAli (1888-1958) and members of the scholarly Hamdāni family have produced historical works in Arabic, Urdu and English on the basis of their ancestral collections of Ismaʿili manuscripts. Since the 1960s, a growing number of Ismaʿilis, belonging mainly to the Nezāri community, have written doctoral dissertations on aspects of Ismaʿili history.

Bibliography: Qoṭb-al-Din Solaymānji Borhānpuri, *Montazaʿ al-ak̲bār*, partial ed. S. F. Traboulsi, Beirut, 1999. F. Daftary, *The Ismāʿīlīs: Their History and Doctrines*, Cambridge, 1990 (with full references); Persian tr. F. Badraʾi, *Tārik̲ va ʿaqāʾed-e Esmāʿiliya*, Tehran, 1996. Idem, "Persian Historiography of the Early Nizārī Ismāʿīlīs," *Iran* 30, 1992, pp. 91-97. Idem, "Intellectual Life among the Ismailis: An Overview," in F. Daftary, ed., *Intellectual Traditions in Islam*, London, 2000, pp. 87-111. Ebn Hayt̲am, *Ketāb al-monāẓarāt*, ed. and tr. W. Madelung and P. E. Walker as *The Advent of the Fatimids: A Contemporary Shiʿi Witness*, London, 2000. Edris ʿEmād-al-Din b. Ḥasan, *ʿOyun al-ak̲bār wa fonun al-āt̲ār* IV-VI, ed. M. Ḡāleb, Beirut, 1973-84; VII, ed. and summary English by A. F. Sayyid in collaboration with P. E. Walker and M. A. Pomerantz as *The Fatimids and their Successors in Yaman*, London, 2002. Idem, *Rawżat al-ak̲bār*, ed. M. al-ʿAkwa, Sanaa, 1995. Moḥammad b. Zayn-al-ʿĀbedin Fedāʾi K̲orāsāni, *Ketāb-e hedāyat al-moʾmenin al-ṭālebin*, ed. A. A. Semenov, Moscow, 1959. Ḥāfeẓ-e Abru, *Majmaʿ al-tawārik̲ al-solṭāniya, qesmat-e k̲olafāʾ-e ʿAlawiya-e Maʾreb wa Meṣr wa Nezāriān wa rafiqān*, ed. M. Modarresi-e

Zanjāni, 1985. A. Hamdani, "Fatimid History and Historians," in M. J. L. Young et al., ed. *Religion, Learning and Science in the ʿAbbasid Period*, Cambridge, 1990, pp. 234-47. W. Ivanow, *Ismaili Literature: A Bibliographical Survey*, Tehran, 1963. Abu ʿAli Manṣur al-ʿAzizi al-Jawḏari, *Sirat al-ostaḏ Jawḏar*, ed. M. Kāmel Ḥosayn and M. ʿAbd-al-Hādi Šaʿira, Cairo, 1954; French tr. M. Canard as *Vie de l'Ustadh Jaudhar*, Algiers, 1958. Jovayni, ed. Qazvini, III, pp. 106-278. Idem, tr. Boyle, II, pp. 618-725. Abu'l-Qāsem ʿAbd-Allāh Kāšāni, *Zobdat al-tawārīḵ, baḵš-e Fāṭemiān wa Nezāriān*, ed. M. T. Dānešpažuh, 2nd ed., Tehran, 1987. B. Lewis, "Sources for the History of the Syrian Assassins," *Speculum* 27, 1952, pp. 475-89. Esmāʿil b. ʿAbd-al-Rasul Majduʿ, *Fehrest al-kotob wa'l-rasāʾel*, ed. ʿAli-Naqi Monzavi, Tehran, 1966. Al-Moʾayyad fi'l-Din Širāzi, *Sirat al-Moʾayyad fi'l-Din dāʿi al-doʿāt*, ed. M. Kāmel Ḥosayn, Cairo, 1949. Aḥmad b. Ebrāhim Nisāburi, *Estetār al-emām*, ed. W. Ivanow, in *Bulletin of the Faculty of Arts, University of Egypt*, IV/2, 1936a, pp. 93-107; English tr. in W. Ivanow, *Ismaili Tradition Concerning the Rise of the Fatimids*, London, etc., 1942, pp. 157-83. Qāżi Noʿmān b. Moḥammad, *Eftetāḥ al-daʿwa*, ed. W. al-Qāżi, Beirut, 1970; also ed. F. Dašrāwi, Tunis, 1975. I. K. Poonawala, *Biobibliography of Ismāʿīlī Literature*, Malibu, Calif., 1977. Moḥammad ʿAli b. Mollā Jiwābhāʾi Rāmpuri, *Mawsem-e bahār fi aḵbār al-ṭāherin al-aḵyār*, 3 vols., Bombay, 1301-11/1884-93. Rašid-al-Din Fażl-Allāh, *Jāmeʿ al-tawārik, qesmat-e Esmāʿiliān*, ed. M. T. Dānešpažuh and M. Modarresi-e Zanjāni, Tehran, 1959. P. E. Walker, *Exploring an Islamic Empire: Fatimid History and Its Sources*, London, 2002. A. F. Sayyid, "Lumières nouvelles sur quelques sources de l'histoire Fatimide en Egypte," *Annales Islamologiques* 13, 1977, pp. 1-41. Moḥammad b. Moḥammad Yamāni, *Sirat al-Ḥājeb Jaʿfar b. ʿAli*, ed. W. Ivanow, in *Bulletin of the Faculty of Arts, University of Egypt*, IV/2, 1936b, pp. 107-33; English tr. in W. Ivanow, *Ismaili Tradition*, pp. 184-223. Zāhed-ʿAli, *Tāriḵ-e Fāṭemiyin-e Meṣr*, 2nd ed., Karachi, 1963.

(FARHAD DAFTARY)

iii. ISMAʿILI HISTORY

ORIGINS AND EARLY HISTORY

On the death of Imam Jaʿfar al-Ṣādeq in 148/765 his followers from among the Imami Shiʿites split into six groups of which two may be identified as proto-Ismaʿilis or earliest Ismaʿilis. Imam al-Ṣādeq had originally designated his second son Esmāʿil (the eponym of the Esmāʿiliya) as his successor to the imamate, but as related in the majority of the sources, Esmāʿil had predeceased his father. The two proto-Ismaʿili groups, which were based in Kufa and supported the claims of Esmāʿil b. Jaʿfar (q.v.) and his son Moḥammad, had already appeared in the lifetime of Imam al-Ṣādeq but they separated from other Imamis only in 148/765. One of these groups denied the death of Esmāʿil and awaited his return as the Mahdi. The members of this group, designated as *al-Esmāʿiliya al-ḵāleṣa*, or the 'pure Esmāʿiliya' by the earliest Imami heresiographers, Nawbaḵti and Qomi, who are our main sources for the initial phase of Ismaʿilism, held that Imam al-Ṣādeq had announced Esmāʿil's death as a ruse to protect him against ʿAbbasid persecution as he had been politically active against them. The second group, designated as the Mobārakiya, affirming Esmāʿil's death, now recognized his eldest son Moḥammad b. Esmāʿil as their imam (*Feraq al-šiʿa*, pp. 57-58; Qomi, pp. 80-81, 83; Ašʿari, *Maqālāt*, pp. 26-27; Daftary, 1991, pp. 220 ff.). It seems likely that the Mobārakiya, derived from Esmāʿil's epithet al-Mobārak, the Blessed One (Sejestāni, *Etbāt*, p. 190; Edris, *Zahr*, p. 199; Ḥ. F. al-Hamdāni, 1958, text p. 10; Ivanow, 1946, pp. 103-12), were originally supporters of Esmāʿil before acknowledging Moḥammad as their Imam. At any rate, Mobārakiya was thus one of the original names of the nascent Esmāʿiliya, a term coined by later heresiographers.

Nawbaḵti (pp. 58-59) and Qomi (p. 81), who are generally hostile towards the Ismaʿilis, identify al-Esmāʿiliya al-Ḵāleṣa with the early Ḵaṭṭābiya, the followers of Abu'l-Ḵaṭṭāb (q.v.), the most famous *ḡāli* (a term used pejoratively by heresiographers for those who attribute divine qualities to Imams; see ḠOLĀT) in the entourage of Jaʿfar al-Ṣādeq, who was eventually repudiated by the Imam. They further hold that on the death of Abu'l-Ḵaṭṭāb in 138/755 a group of his *ḡolāt* followers joined the supporters of Moḥammad b. Esmāʿil (*Feraq al-šiʿa*, pp. 60-61; Qomi, p. 83). Some later sources, too, refer to close relations between the earliest Ismaʿilis and the Ḵaṭṭābis (Lewis, 1940, pp. 33-35). On the other hand, Abu'l-Ḵaṭṭāb is condemned as a heretic by the Ismaʿilis of the Fatimid times (see, for example, Qāżi Noʿmān, *Daʿāʾem*, I, pp. 49-50; tr. Fyzee, I, pp. 65-66; idem, *Ketāb al-majāles*, pp. 84-85). Be that as it may, relations between al-Esmāʿiliya al-ḵāleṣa and the Mobārakiya, on the one hand, and between these groups and the Ḵaṭṭābis, on the other, remain rather obscure due to lack of reliable sources. It is certain, however, that all these groups were politically active against the ʿAbbasids and they originated within the radical milieus of Imami Shiʿism in Kufa.

Little is known about the life and career of Moḥammad b. Esmāʿil, the seventh imam of the Ismaʿilis. The relevant biographical information contained in early Ismaʿili sources has been preserved by the *dāʿi* (q.v.; Ismāʿili missionary) Edris (*ʿOyun*, IV, pp. 351-56; idem, *Zahr*, pp. 204-8). Soon after al-Ṣādeq's death, and after the recognition of the imamate of his uncle Musā al-Kāẓem by the majority of the Imamis, Moḥammad b. Esmāʿil left Medina, seat of the ʿAlids, and went into hiding. His decision marked the initiation of the *dawr al-satr*, or period of concealment, in early Ismaʿilism that lasted until the foundation of the Fatimid state when the Ismaʿili Imams emerged from their concealment. Henceforth, Moḥammad acquired the epithet of al-Maktum, the Hidden One, in addition to al-Maymun, the Fortunate One. Nonetheless, Moḥammad maintained his contacts with the Kufan-based

Mobārakiya from different localities in southern Iraq and Persia. He seems to have spent the latter part of his life in Ḵuzestān, where he had some following. He died not long after 179/795 during the caliphate of the ʿAbbasid Hārun al-Rašid. On the death of Moḥammad b. Esmāʿil, the Mobārakiya split into two groups (*Feraq al-šiʿa*, p. 61; Qomi, p. 83). A majority refused to accept his death; they recognized him as their seventh and last imam, and awaited his return as the Mahdi or *qāʾem*. A second, small and obscure group, acknowledging Moḥammad's death, traced the imamate in his progeny. Almost nothing is known with certainty regarding the subsequent history of these earliest Ismaʿili groups until shortly after the middle of the 3rd/9th century, when a unified Ismaʿili movement appeared on the historical stage.

It is certain that for almost a century after Moḥammad b. Esmāʿil, a group of leaders who were well placed within Ismaʿilism worked secretly for the creation of a unified, revolutionary Shiʿite movement against the ʿAbbasids. These leaders did not openly claim the Ismaʿili imamate for three generations. They had, in fact, hidden their true identity in order to escape ʿAbbasid persecution. ʿAbd-Allāh al-Akbar, the first of these hidden leaders, had organized his campaign around the central doctrine of the majority of the earliest Ismaʿilis, namely, the Mahdism of Moḥammad b. Esmāʿil. Organizing a revolutionary movement in the name of a concealed imam who could not be chased by ʿAbbasid agents represented an attractive strategy. At any rate, the existence of such a group of early Ismaʿili leaders is confirmed by both the official version of the Ismaʿilis of the Fatimid period regarding the pre-Fatimid phase of their history (Edris, *ʿOyun*, IV, pp. 357-67, 390-404) as well as the hostile account of the Sunni polemicists Ebn Rezām and Aḵu Moḥsen preserved in later sources (Ebn al-Dawādāri, VI, pp. 44-156; Maqrizi, *Etteʿāẓ*, I, pp. 151-201; idem, *al-Ḵeṭaṭ*, I, pp. 391-97; Nowayri, XXV, pp. 187-317). Indeed, with minor variations, the names of these leaders, viz., ʿAbd-Allāh, Aḥmad, Ḥosayn, or Moḥammad and ʿAbd-Allāh al-Mahdi, who were members of the same family and succeeded one another on a hereditary basis, are almost identical in the accounts of the later Fatimid Ismaʿilis (Ḥ. F. al-Hamdāni, 1958, text pp. 10-12; Nisāburi, p. 95; see also Hamdani and de Blois, pp. 173-207) and in the lists traceable to Aḵu Moḥsen and his source Ebn Rezām (Ebn al-Nadim, ed. Tajaddod, p. 238; tr. Dodge, I, pp. 462-64; Ebn al-Dawādāri, VI, pp. 17-20; Maqrizi, *Etteʿāẓ*, I, pp. 22-26; Nowayri, XXV, p. 189; Ḥammādi Yamāni, *Kašf*, pp. 16 ff.). However, in the Ismaʿili sources these leaders are presented as ʿAlids descending from Imam al-Ṣādeq while in anti-Ismaʿili accounts their ancestry is traced to a certain Maymun al-Qaddāḥ. Modern scholarship has shown that the Qaddāḥid ancestry of the early Ismaʿili leaders was constructed by hostile polemicists, soon after the establishment of the Fatimid caliphate, in order to refute the ʿAlid genealogy of the Fatimid caliph-imams. Maymun al-Qaddāḥ and his son ʿAbd-Allāh (see ʿABDALLĀH b. MAYMŪN) were, in fact, associated with Imams al-Bāqer and al-Ṣādeq and had nothing to do with the leaders or imams of early Ismaʿilism (see Ivanow, 1946, pp. 61-103; Daftary, 1990, pp. 105-16).

ʿAbd-Allāh al-Akbar, the first of the early Ismaʿili leaders after Moḥammad b. Esmāʿil, settled in ʿAskar Mokram, in Ḵuzestān, where he lived as a wealthy merchant. From there he began to organize a reinvigorated Ismaʿili *daʿwa* sending *dāʿis* to different districts around Ḵuzestān. At an unknown date, still in the first half of the 3rd/9th century, ʿAbd-Allāh found refuge in Syria, where he eventually re-established contact with some of his *dāʿis*, and settled in Salamiya, continuing to pose as a Hāšemid merchant. Henceforth, Salamiya, situated some 35 km southeast of Ḥamā, served as the secret headquarters of the Ismaʿili *daʿwa*. The efforts of ʿAbd-Allāh, and his successors, began to bear fruit in the 260s/870s, when numerous *dāʿis* appeared in Iraq and adjacent regions. It was around 261/874 that Ḥamdān Qarmaṭ (q.v.) was converted to Ismaʿilism by the *dāʿi* Ḥosayn Ahvāzi (Ebn al-Nadim, ed. Tajaddod, p. 238; Masʿudi, *Tanbih*, p. 395). Ḥamdān, in turn, organized the *daʿwa* in the Sawād of Kufa, his native locality, and in other districts of southern Iraq. Ḥamdān's chief assistant was his brother-in-law ʿAbdān (q.v.). A learned theologian, ʿAbdān enjoyed a certain degree of independence and was responsible for training and appointing numerous *dāʿis*, including Abu Saʿid Jannābi (q.v.), who later founded the Qarmaṭi state of Baḥrayn.

Centered on the expectation of the imminent return of Moḥammad b. Esmāʿil as the Mahdi who would establish justice in the world, the revolutionary and messianic Ismaʿili movement appealed to underprivileged groups of different social backgrounds. It achieved particular success among the Imami Shiʿites who were disillusioned with the quietist policies of their imams and were left without a manifest imam after the death of the eleventh Imam, Abu Moḥammad Ḥasan al-ʿAskari (q.v.; d. 260/874). It was under such circumstances that Ḥamdān won many supporters in southern Iraq and embarked on his anti-ʿAbbasid activities (Ebn al-Dawādāri, VI, pp. 44 ff.; Maqrizi, *Etteʿāẓ*, I, pp. 151 ff.; Nowayri, XXV, pp. 189 ff.; Ṭabari, III, pp. 2124, 2126-27; Ṭabari, tr. XXXVII, pp. 169, 171-73). The Ismaʿilis of southern Iraq became generally known as the Qarāmeṭa or Carmatians (q.v.), named after their first chief local leader. This term was soon applied to other Ismaʿili communities not organized by Ḥamdān and ʿAbdān. At the time, there was a single Ismaʿili movement directed from Salamiya in the name of Moḥammad b. Esmāʿil as the Mahdi (Stern, 1961, pp. 99-108; Madelung, 1961, pp. 43-65). In fact, in order to prepare the ground for the emergence of the Mahdi, in 277/890 Ḥamdān established a *dār al-hejra*, or abode of migration, near Kufa, where his followers gathered weapons and other provisions. This abode was to serve as the nucleus of a new society for the Ismaʿilis. Similar *dār al-hejra*s were later established for the Ismaʿili communities of Yemen, Bahrain and North Africa. The Ismaʿilis (Qarmaṭis) now referred to their movement simply as *al-daʿwa* (the mission) or *al-daʿwa al-hadia* (the rightly guiding mission), in addition to using expressions such as *daʿwat al-ḥaqq* (summons to the truth) or *ahl al-ḥaqq* (people of the truth).

In the meantime, the Ismaʿili *daʿwa* had appeared in many other regions in the 260s/870s. ʿAbdān's brother Maʾmun was active as a *dāʿi* in Fars, where the Ismaʿili converts became known as the Maʾmuniya (Daylami, p. 21). The *daʿwa* in Yaman was initiated by Ebn Ḥawšab (q.v.), later known as Manṣur al-Yaman. He arrived there in 268/881, accompanied by his collaborator ʿAli b. al-Fażl. By 293/905-6, when ʿAli occupied Ṣanʿāʾ, these *dāʿis* were in control of almost all of Yaman (Qāżi Noʿmān, *Eftetāḥ*, pp. 32-54; Janadi, *Ketāb al-soluk*, in Kay, 1892, text pp. 139-52, tr. pp. 191-212). Yaman also served as a base for the extension of the *daʿwa* to other regions. In 270/883, Ebn Ḥawšab sent his relative Haytam as a *dāʿi* to Sind, initiating the *daʿwa* on the Indian subcontinent (Qāżi Noʿmān, *Eftetāḥ*, pp. 45, 47; S. M. Stern, 1949, pp. 298 ff.; Hamdani, 1956). On Ebn Ḥawšab's instructions, the *dāʿi* Abu ʿAbd-Allāh al-Šiʿi was active among the Kotāma Berbers of Lesser Kabylia in the Maghreb by 280/893. Ebn Ḥawšab sent other *dāʿis* to Yamāma, Egypt and Baḥrayn. After his initial activities in Fars, Abu Saʿid Jannābi was sent to Baḥrayn by Ḥamdān and ʿAbdān in 273/886, or a few years later. He rapidly won converts there from among the bedouins and the Persian emigrants (Ebn al-Dawādāri, VI, pp. 55-62, 91 ff.; Maqrizi, *Etteʿāẓ*, I, pp. 159 ff.; Nowayri, XXV, pp. 233 ff.; Ṭabari, III, pp. 2188 ff., 2196-97, 2205, 2232; Ṭabari, tr. XXXVIII, pp. 77 ff., 86-89, 98, 128-29; Masʿudi, *Moruj*, VIII, pp. 191 ff.; de Goeje, pp. 33-47, 69 ff.)

In the early 260s/870s, the *daʿwa* was taken to the region of the Jebāl in Persia by Ḵalaf al-Ḥallāj, who established himself in Ray. There, the Ismaʿilis became known as the Ḵalafiya. Under Ḵalaf's successors as chief *dāʿis* of the Jebāl, the *daʿwa* spread to Qom, Kāšān, Isfahan, Hamadān and other towns of that region. Ḡiāṯ, the third *dāʿi* of Ray, extended the *daʿwa* to Khorasan and Transoxania on his own initiative. But the *daʿwa* was officially established in Khorasan during the last decade of the 3rd century (the first decade of the 9th century) by Abu ʿAbd-Allāh Ḵādem who set up his secret headquarters at Nišābur. A later chief *dāʿi* of Khorasan, Ḥosayn b. ʿAli Marwazi was an eminent amir in the service of the Sāmānids and he succeeded in extending the *daʿwa* to Herat, Ḡur and other localities under his control, (Neẓām-al-Molk, pp. 282-95, 297-305; tr. Darke, pp. 208-18, 220-26; Ebn al-Nadim, ed. Tajaddod, p. 239; Baḡdādi, *Farq*, ed. Badr, p. 267; Stern, 1960, pp. 56-90; repr. in idem, 1983, pp. 189-233).

By the early 280s/890s, a unified Ismaʿili movement had replaced the earlier Ismaʿili groups. But in 286/899, soon after ʿAbd-Allāh al-Mahdi, the future Fatimid caliph, had succeeded to leadership in Salamiya, Ismaʿilism was wrought by a major schism. Ḥamdān now noticed significant changes in the doctrinal instructions he received from Salamiya, and dispatched ʿAbdān there to investigate the matter. Ḥamdān found out that instead of advocating Moḥammad b. Esmāʿil as Mahdi, the new leader now claimed the imamate for himself and his predecessors, the central leaders of the Ismaʿili *daʿwa* in the *dawr al-satr*. Ḥamdān and ʿAbdān refused to accept this doctrinal change, allowing for continuity in the imamate. They renounced their allegiance to the central leadership of Ismaʿilism and suspended all *daʿwa* activities in Iraq. Soon after, Ḥamdān disappeared while ʿAbdān was murdered at the instigation of a subordinate *dāʿi*, Zekrawayh b. Mehrawayh, who initially remained loyal to Salamiya (Ebn al-Dawādāri, VI, pp. 65-68; Maqrizi, *Etteʿāẓ*, I, pp. 167-68; Nowayri, XXV, pp. 227-32; Ebn Ḥawqal, p. 295; tr. Kramers and Wiet, II, p. 289; Madelung, 1961, pp. 59-65, 69 ff.; Daftary, 1993, pp. 123-39).

ʿAbd-Allāh al-Mahdi's reform is explained in a letter he later sent to the Ismaʿili community in Yaman (see Ḥ. F. al-Hamdani, 1958; also Hamdani and de Blois, 1983), in which an attempt is made to reconcile his reform with the actual course of events in pre-Fatimid Ismaʿili history. He explains that as a form of *taqiya*, the central leaders of the *daʿwa* had assumed different pseudonyms, such as al-Mobārak and al-Maymun, also assuming the rank of *ḥojja*, proof or full representative, of the absent Imam Moḥammad b. Esmāʿil. ʿAbd-Allāh, whose own pseudonym had been al-Saʿid, the Happy One, further explained that the earlier propagation of Moḥammad b. Esmāʿil as Mahdi was itself another dissimulating tactic and that this was in reality another collective pseudonym for every true imam in the progeny of Jaʿfar al-Ṣādeq. The statements of ʿAbd-Allāh are corroborated by the few surviving early Ismaʿili sources (see, for instance, Jaʿfar b. Manṣur al-Yaman, *Ketāb al-kašf*, pp. 97-99, 102 ff., 109-10, 135, 160; also Madelung, 1961, pp. 254-58).

The doctrinal reform of ʿAbd-Allāh al-Mahdi split the Ismaʿili movement into two rival factions. One faction remained loyal to the central leadership and acknowledged continuity in the imamate, recognizing ʿAbd-Allāh and his ʿAlid ancestors as their imams, which was in due course incorporated into the Fatimid Ismaʿili doctrine of the imamate. These Ismaʿilis now allowed for three hidden imams (*al-aʾemma al-masturin*) between Moḥammad b. Esmāʿil and ʿAbd-Allāh al-Mahdi. This loyalist faction came to include the bulk of the Ismaʿilis of Yaman and those communities in Egypt, North Africa and Sind, founded by *dāʿis* dispatched by Ebn Ḥawšab. On the other hand, a dissident faction, originally led by Ḥamdān, rejected ʿAbd-Allāh's reform and maintained their original belief in the Mahdiship of Moḥammad b. Esmāʿil. Henceforth, the term Qarmaṭi came to be applied more specifically to the dissidents, who did not acknowledge ʿAbd-Allāh al-Mahdi, as well as his predecessors and successors in the Fatimid dynasty, as their imams. The dissident Qarmaṭi faction, which lacked central leadership, soon acquired its most important stronghold in the Qarmaṭi state of Baḥrayn, founded in the same eventful year 286/899 by Abu Saʿid Jannābi who sided with Ḥamdān and ʿAbdān (Ebn Ḥawqal, p. 295). There were also Qarmaṭi communities in Iraq, Yaman, Persia and Central Asia. The subsequent history of Qarmaṭism is not treated here (see F. Daftary, "Carmatians," in *EIr*, IV, pp. 825-32; Madelung, "Ḳarmaṭī," in *EI²*, IV, pp. 660-65; idem, 1959; idem, 1996).

Meanwhile, the *dāʿi* Zekrawayh b. Mehrawayh had gone into hiding following the events of the year 286/899, possibly fearing reprisals by ʿAbdān's supporters in Iraq. From 288/901 he sent several of his sons as *dāʿis* to the Syrian desert where large numbers of bedouins were converted. Zekrawayh now aimed to establish a Fatimid state in Syria for ʿAbd-Allāh al-Mahdi without his authorization. Soon Zekrawayh's sons summoned their bedouin followers to proceed to Salamiya and declare their allegiance to the imam who was still guarding his identity. In the event, ʿAbd-Allāh, whose position had now been dangerously compromised, secretly left Salamiya in 289/902 to escape capture by the ʿAbbasid agents sent after him. He first went to Ramla, in Palestine, and then in 291/904, following the defeat of Zekrawayh's movement in Syria by an ʿAbbasid army, he embarked on a historic journey which ended several years later in North Africa where he founded the Fatimid caliphate (see Yamāni, *Sirat al-Ḥājeb*, pp. 107-33; tr. in Ivanow, 1942, pp. 184-223; French tr. Canard, 1952, pp. 279-324). After their defeat in Syria in 291/904, Zekrawayh and his sons turned against ʿAbd-Allāh al-Mahdi and joined the Qarmaṭi camp. Zekrawayh was finally defeated and killed in 294/907 by the ʿAbbasids while his Qarmaṭi movement lingered on for a while longer (Ṭabari, III, pp. 2218-46, 2255-75; tr. XXXVIII, 113-44, 157-79; ʿArib, pp. 9-18, 36, 137; Masʿudi, *Tanbih*, pp. 370-76, 391; Ebn al-Dawādāri, VI, pp. 69-90; Maqrizi, *Etteʿāẓ*, I, pp. 168-79; Nowayri, XXV, pp. 246-76; Halm, 1979, pp. 30-53; idem, *Empire of the Mahdi*, pp. 66-88, 183-90).

The early Ismaʿilis elaborated the basic framework of a system of religious thought, which was further developed or modified in the Fatimid period. Central to this system was a fundamental distinction between the exoteric (*ẓāher*) and the esoteric (*bāṭen*) aspects of the sacred scriptures and religious commandments and prohibitions. Accordingly, they held that the Qurʾān and other revealed scriptures, and their laws (*šariʿa*s), had their apparent or literal meaning, the *ẓāher*, which had to be distinguished from their inner meaning hidden in the *bāṭen*. They further held that the *ẓāher*, or the religious laws, enunciated by prophets underwent periodical changes while the *bāṭen*, containing the spiritual truths (*ḥaqāʾeq*), remained immutable and eternal. These truths, representing the message common to Judaism, Christianity and Islam, were explained through *taʾwil* or esoteric exegesis, which often relied on the mystical significance of letters and numbers. In every age, the esoteric truths would be accessible only to the elite (*Ḵawāṣṣ*) of humankind as distinct from the ordinary people (*ʿawāmm*) who were only capable of perceiving the apparent meaning of the revelations. Consequently, in the era of Islam, the eternal truths of religion could be explained only to those who had been initiated into the Ismaʿili *daʿwa* and as such recognized the teaching authority of the Prophet Moḥammad and, after him, that of his *waṣi*, ʿAli b. Abi Ṭāleb, and the rightful imams who succeeded him; these authorities were the sole sources of *taʾwil* in the era of Islam. Initiation into Ismaʿilism, known as *balāḡ*, was gradual and took place after the novice had taken an oath of allegiance, *ʿahd* or *mitāq*. The initiates were also obliged to keep secret the *bāṭen* imparted to them by a hierarchy (*ḥodud*) of teachers (see Jaʿfar b. Manṣur al-Yaman, *Ketāb al-ʿālem*; Halm, "Ismaʿili Oath of Allegiance," pp. 91-115). By believing in the *bāṭen* aspect of religion, the Ismaʿilis came to be regarded by the rest of the Muslim community as the most representative of the Shiʿites propounding esotericism in Islam and, hence, their common designation as the Bāṭeniya (q.v.). This designation was also used in a derogatory sense accusing the Ismaʿilis of generally ignoring the *ẓāher*, or the *šariʿa*.

The esoteric truths or *ḥaqāʾeq* formed a gnostic system of thought for the early Ismaʿilis, representing a distinct worldview. The two main components of this system, developed by the 280s/890s, were a cyclical history of revelations or prophetic eras and a gnostic cosmological doctrine. They applied their cyclical interpretation of time and the religious history of humankind to Judaeo-Christian revelations as well as a number of pre-Islamic religions such as Zoroastrianism with much appeal to non-Muslims. This conception of religious history, reflecting a variety of influences such as Hellenic, Judaeo-Christian, Gnostic as well as eschatological ideas of the earlier Shiʿites, was developed in terms of the eras of different prophets recognized in the Koran. This cyclical conception was also combined with the Ismaʿili doctrine of the imamate inherited from the earlier Imamis.

According to their cyclical view, the Ismaʿilis held that the religious history of humankind proceeded through seven prophetic eras (*dawrs*, q.v.) of various duration, each one inaugurated by a speaker or enunciator (*nāṭeq*) of a divinely revealed message which in its exoteric (*ẓāher*) aspect contained a religious law (*šariʿa*). Each *nāṭeq* was, in turn, succeeded by a spiritual legatee (*waṣi*), also called the silent one (*ṣāmet*) and later the foundation (*asās*), who revealed to the elite the esoteric truths (*ḥaqāʾeq*) contained in the *bāṭen* dimension of that era's message. Each *waṣi* was succeeded by seven imams, who guarded the true meaning of the sacred scriptures and laws in their *ẓāher* and *bāṭen* aspects. The seventh imam, also called *motemm*, of every era would rise in rank to become the *nāṭeq* of the following era, abrogating the *šariʿa* of the previous era and enunciating a new one. This pattern would change only in the seventh, final era of history. As the seventh imam of the sixth era, the era of the Prophet Moḥammad and Islam, Moḥammad b. Esmāʿil was initially expected to return as the Mahdi (or *qāʾem*) as well as the *nāṭeq* of the seventh eschatological era when, instead of promulgating a new law, he would fully reveal the esoteric truths of all the preceding revelations. This original cyclical view of religious history was modified after ʿAbd-Allāh al-Mahdi's doctrinal reform. Recognizing continuity in the imamate, the seventh era now lost its earlier messianic appeal for the Fatimid Ismaʿilis, for whom the final eschatological era, whatever its nature, was postponed indefinitely into the future. On the other hand, the Qarmaṭis of Baḥrayn and elsewhere continued to consider Moḥammad b. Esmāʿil as their

Mahdi who, on his reappearance as the seventh *nāṭeq*, was expected to initiate the final age of pure spirituality (see F. Daftary, "Dawr," in *EIr*, VII, pp. 151-53; also Ebn Ḥawšab Manṣur al-Yaman, *Ketāb al-rošd*, pp. 185-213; tr. Ivanow, 1955, pp. 29-59; Jaʿfar b. Manṣur al-Yaman, *Ketāb al-kašf*, pp. 14 ff., 103-4, 109-10, 113-14, 132-33, 138, 143, 150, 169-70; Qāżi Noʿmān, *Asās al-taʾwil*; Sejestāni, *Eṯbāt*, pp. 181-93; Corbin, 1983, pp. 1-58; Madelung, 1961, pp. 51 ff., 82-90; Halm, 1978, pp. 18-37; Walker, 1978, 355-66).

The cosmological doctrine of the early Ismaʿilis may be reconstructed from the fragmentary evidence preserved in later Ismaʿili texts (see especially Stern, 1983, pp. 3-29; Halm, 1978, pp. 18-127, 206-27; idem, "The Cosmology of the Pre-Fatimid Ismāʿīliyya," in Daftary, ed., 1996, pp. 75-83). This doctrine, representing a gnostic cosmological myth, was espoused by the entire Ismaʿili (Qarmaṭi) movement until it was superseded by a new cosmology of Neoplatonic provenance. According to this doctrine, through His intention (*erāda*) and will (*mašiʾa*), God first created a light (*nur*) and addressed it with the Qurʾānic creative imperative *kon* (be!). Through the duplication of its two letters, *kāf* and *nun*, the name acquired its feminine form Kuni. On God's command, Kuni created from its light Qadar, its male assistant. Kuni and Qadar were thus the first two principles (*aṣlān*) of creation. It was out of the original heptad of consonantal letters of Kuni-Qadar, also called the higher letters (*al-ḥoruf al-ʿolwiya*), that all other letters and names emerged; and with the names there simultaneously appeared the very things they symbolized. This doctrine explained how God's creative activity, through the intermediary of Kuni and Qadar, brought forth the beings of the spiritual world, also accounting for the creation of the lower physical world which culminated in the genesis of Man.

THE FATIMID PERIOD TO 487/1094

In this period, often referred to as the "golden age" of Ismaʿilism, the Ismaʿilis possessed an important state of their own and Ismaʿili thought and literature as well as *daʿwa* activities attained their summit. After his stay in Ramla, ʿAbd-Allāh al-Mahdi arrived in Egypt in 291/904 where he spent a year. Subsequently, he was prevented from going to the Maghreb, where the *dāʿi* Abu ʿAbd-Allāh al-Šiʿi had been successfully active among the Kotāma Berbers from 280/893 (see Qāżi Noʿman, *Eftetāḥ*, pp. 71-222; Dachraoui, pp. 57-122; Halm, *Empire of the Mahdi*, pp. 9-128; M. Talbi, *L'Émirat Aghlabide 184-296/800-909*, Paris, 1966, pp. 579-672), because the Aḡlabid rulers of the region and their ʿAbbasid overlords had discovered the Imam's plans and awaited to arrest him. ʿAbd-Allāh now headed for the remote town of Sejelmāsa, in southern Morocco, where he lived quietly for four years (292-96/905-9), maintaining his contacts with Abu ʿAbd-Allāh who had already commenced his conquest of Efriqia (the eastern part of the Maghreb) with the help of his Kotāma soldier-tribesmen. By 296/908, this Kotāma army had achieved much success signaling the fall of the Aḡlabids. On 1 Rajab 296/25 March 909, Abu ʿAbd-Allāh entered Raqqāda, the royal city outside of the Aḡlabid capital of Qayrawān, from where he governed Efriqia, as al-Mahdi's deputy, for almost a whole year. In Ramażān 296/June 909, he set off at the head of his army for Sejalmāsa to hand over the reins of power to the Ismaʿili imam himself. ʿAbd-Allāh al-Mahdi was acclaimed as caliph in a special ceremony in Sejelmāsa on 7 Du'l-Ḥejja 296/27 August 909. With these events the *dawr al-satr* in early Ismaʿilism had also ended. ʿAbd-Allāh al-Mahdi entered Raqqāda on 20 Rabiʿ II 297/4 January 910 and was immediately acclaimed as caliph (for a detailed eyewitness account of the establishment of Fatimid rule, see Ebn al-Haytam, *Ketāb al-Monāẓarāt*). The Ismaʿili Shiʿite caliphate of the Fatimids had now officially commenced in Efriqia. The new dynasty was named Fatimid (Fāṭemiya) after the Prophet's daughter, Fāṭema, to whom al-Mahdi and his successors traced their ʿAlid ancestry.

The Fatimids did not abandon the Ismaʿili *daʿwa* on assuming power, as they entertained universal aspirations aiming to extend their rule over the entire Muslim community. However, the early Fatimid caliph-imams, ruling from Efriqia, encountered numerous difficulties while consolidating their power. In particular, they confronted the hostility of the Kharijite Berbers and the Sunni inhabitants of Qayrawān and other cities of Efriqia led by their Māleki jurists. Under the circumstances, the Ismaʿili *daʿwa* remained rather inactive in North Africa for some time (Madelung, 1999, pp. 97-104). Fatimid rule was established firmly in the Maghreb only under al-Moʿezz le-Din Allāh (341-365/953-975), who succeeded in transforming the Fatimid caliphate from a regional state into a great empire. He was also the first Fatimid caliph-imam to concern himself significantly with the propagation of the Ismaʿili *daʿwa* outside the Fatimid dominions, especially after the transference of the seat of the Fatimid state in 362/973 to Egypt, where he founded Cairo as his new capital city. The *daʿwa* policy of al-Moʿezz was based on a number of religio-political considerations. In particular, he was apprehensive of the success of the Qarmaṭi propaganda which not only undermined the efforts of the Fatimid Ismaʿili *dāʿis* operating in the same lands, notably Iraq, Persia and Transoxania, but also aroused the general anti-Ismaʿili sentiments of the Sunni Muslims who did not distinguish between the Ismaʿilis and the Qarmaṭis who had acquired a reputation for irreligiosity and lawlessness. Al-Moʿezz's policies soon bore fruit as the Ismaʿili *daʿwa* and Fatimid cause were reinvigorated outside the Fatimid state. Most notably, Abu Yaʿqub Sejestāni (q.v.), the *dāʿi* of Sistān, Makrān and Khorasan, who had earlier belonged to the dissident Qarmaṭi faction, transferred his allegiance to the Fatimids; and, consequently, many of his followers in Persia and Central Asia acknowledged the Fatimid caliph-imam. Ismaʿilism also acquired a stronghold in Moltan, Sind, where an Ismaʿili principality was established.

The caliph-imam al-Moʿezz also permitted into the teachings of the Fatimid *daʿwa* the Neoplatonic cosmology elaborated by the *dāʿis* of the Iranian lands.

Henceforth, this Neoplatonized cosmology was advocated by the Fatimid *dāʿis* in preference to the earlier mythological doctrine. In the course of the 9th/10th century, Moḥammad Nasafi, Abu Ḥātem Rāzi and Sejestāni had set about harmonizing their Ismaʿili Shiʿite theology with Neoplatonic philosophy. This led to the development of a unique intellectual tradition of philosophical theology in Ismaʿilism. These *dāʿis* wrote for the educated classes of society and aimed to attract them intellectually. This is why they expressed their theology, always revolving around the central Shiʿite doctrine of the imamate, in terms of the then most intellectually fashionable terminologies and themes. The Iranian *dāʿis* elaborated complex metaphysical systems of thought with a distinct Neoplatonized emanational cosmology. In this cosmology, fully elaborated in Sejestāni's *Ketāb al-yanābiʿ* and other works, God is described as absolutely transcendent, beyond being and non-being, and thus unknowable (Sejestāni, *Kašf al-maḥjub*, pp. 4-15). Here, the Neoplatonic dyad of universal intellect (*ʿaql*) and universal soul (*nafs*) in the spiritual world replace Kuni and Qadar of the earlier cosmology; and the emanational chain of creation is traced finally to Man, while recognizing that God created everything in the spiritual and physical worlds all at once (Sejestāni, *Etbāt*, pp. 2-3, 28; Nāṣer-e Ḵosraw, *Jāmeʿ al-ḥekmatayn*, pp. 210-32). These *dāʿis* also expounded a doctrine of salvation as part of their cosmology. In their soteriology, the ultimate goal of salvation is the human soul's progression towards his Creator in quest of a spiritual reward in an eternal afterlife. This depended on guidance provided by the authorized sources of wisdom in every era of history (see Daftary, 1990, pp. 234-45; Walker, 1993, pp. 67-142; idem, 1996, pp. 26-103). Neoplatonic philosophy also influenced the cosmology elaborated by the Ismaʿili-connected Eḵwān al-Ṣafāʾ (q.v.). It was also in al-Moʿezz's time that Ismaʿili law was codified and its precepts began to be observed by the judiciary throughout the Fatimid state.

The Ismaʿilis had high esteem for learning and created distinctive traditions and institutions of learning under the Fatimids. The Fatimid *daʿwa* was particularly concerned with educating the converts in Ismaʿili esoteric doctrine, known as the *ḥekma* or "wisdom". As a result, a variety of lectures or "teaching sessions," generally designated as *majāles* (singular, *majles*), were organized. The private lectures on Ismaʿili esoteric doctrine, known as the *majāles al-ḥekma* or "sessions of wisdom," were reserved exclusively for the Ismaʿili initiates who had already taken the oath of allegiance and secrecy. The lectures, delivered by the *dāʿi al-doʿāt* at the Fatimid palace, were approved beforehand by the imam. Only the imam was the source of the *ḥekma*; and the chief *dāʿi*, commonly called *bāb* (the Gate) in Ismaʿili sources, was merely the imam's mouthpiece through whom the Ismaʿilis received their knowledge of Ismaʿili esoteric doctrines (see Kermāni, *Rāḥat al-ʿaql*, pp. 135, 138, 143, 205-8, 212-14). Many of these *majāles* were in due course collected and committed to writing. This Fatimid tradition of learning culminated in the *Majāles al-Moʾayyadiya* of the *dāʿi* al-Moʾayyad fi'l-Din Širāzi (see Maqrizi, *al-Ḵeṭaṭ*, I, pp. 390-91; Qalqašandi, X, pp. 434-39; Halm, "The Ismaʿili Oath of Allegiance," pp. 98-112; idem, 1997, pp. 23-29, 41-55; Walker, 1997, pp. 182-86). Another main institution of learning founded by the Fatimids was the Dār al-ʿElm, the House of Knowledge, sometimes also called Dār al-Ḥekma. Established in 395/1005 by the caliph-imam al-Ḥākem (386-411/996-1021), a variety of religious and non-religious subjects were taught here and it was also equipped with a major library. Many Fatimid *dāʿis* received at least part of their training at the Dār al-ʿElm (Maqrizi, *al-Ḵeṭaṭ*, I, pp. 458-60; Halm, 1997, pp. 71-77; Walker, 1997, pp. 189-93).

Information on the structure and functioning of the Ismaʿili *daʿwa* organization was among the most guarded secrets of Ismaʿilism. The religio-political messages of the *daʿwa* were disseminated by networks of *dāʿis* within the Fatimid dominions as well as in other regions referred to as the *jazāʾer* (singular, *jazira*, "island"). Each *jazira* was placed under the charge of a high-ranking *dāʿi* referred to as *ḥojja*; and every *ḥojja* had a number of *dāʿis* of different ranks working under him. Organized in a strictly hierarchical manner, the Fatimid *daʿwa* was under the overall supervision of the imam and the *dāʿi al-doʿāt*, or *bāb*, who acted as its administrative head. The *daʿwa* organization developed over time and reached its full elaboration under the caliph-imam al-Mostanṣer (see Daftary, "Dāʿī," in *EIr*, VI, pp. 590-92; idem, 1990, pp. 224-32; Stern, 1972, pp. 437-50; Hamdani, 1976, pp. 85-114). It was in non-Fatimid regions, in the *jazāʾer*, especially Yaman, Persia and Central Asia, that the Fatimid *daʿwa* achieved lasting success (Daftary, 1999, pp. 29-43; idem, "Medieval Ismaʿilis," pp. 48-61). The *daʿwa* was intensified in Iraq and Persia under al-Ḥākem. Foremost among the *dāʿis* of this period was Ḥamid al-Din Kermāni (q.v.). A learned philosopher, he harmonized Ismaʿili theology with a variety of philosophical traditions in developing his own metaphysical system. In fact, Kermāni's thought represents a unique tradition within the Iranian school of philosophical Ismaʿilism. He expounded a particular cosmology, replacing the Neoplatonic dyad of intellect and soul in the spiritual world by a system of ten separate intellects in partial adaptation of Fārābi's Aristotelian cosmic system (Kermāni, *Rāḥat al-ʿaql*, pp. 134 ff.) Kermāni's cosmology was not adopted by the Fatimid *daʿwa*; it later provided the basis for the fourth and final stage in the evolution of Ismaʿili cosmology at the hands of Ṭayyebi Mostaʿli *dāʿis* of Yaman (see W. Madelung, "Cosmogony and Cosmology. vi. In Ismaʿilism," in *EIr*, VI, pp. 323-24; de Smet, 1995, pp. 16-377; Walker, 1999, pp. 80-117). Al-Ḥākem's reign also coincided with the initial phase of what was to become known as the Druze religion, founded by a number of *dāʿis* who had come to Cairo from Persia and Central Asia, notably Aḵram, Ḥamza, and Darzi. These *dāʿis* proclaimed the end of the era of Islam and declared the divinity of al-Ḥākem. Kermāni was officially invited to Cairo around 405/1014 to refute the new extremist doctrines from a theological perspective (M. G. S. Hodgson, "Duruz," in *EI*², II, pp. 631-34; Bryer).

The Ismaʿili *daʿwa* activities outside the Fatimid dominions reached their peak in the long reign of al-Mostanṣer (427-487/1036-1094), even after the Sunni Saljuqs had replaced the Shiʿite Buyids as overlords of the ʿAbbasids in 447/1055. The Fatimid *dāʿis* won many converts in Iraq and different parts of Persia and Central Asia. One of the most prominent *dāʿis* of this period was al-Moʾayyad fe'l-Din Širāzi who after his initial career in Fars settled in Cairo and played an active role in the affairs of the Fatimid *dawla* and Ismaʿili *daʿwa*. In 450/1058, al-Mostanṣer appointed him as *dāʿi al-doʿāt*, a post he held for twenty years, with the exception of a brief period, until his death in 470/1078 (see al-Moʾayyad fe'l-Din, *Sirat*; Klemm, pp. 2-63, 136-92). Al-Moʾayyad established closer relations between Cairo and several *jaziras*, especially Yaman where Ismaʿilism had persisted in a dormant form throughout the 4th/10th century. By the time of al-Mostanṣer, the leadership of the *daʿwa* in Yaman had fallen into the hands of the *dāʿi* ʿAli b. Moḥammad al-Ṣolayḥi, an important chieftain of the Banu Hamdān in the mountainous region of Ḥarāz. ʿAli al-Ṣolayḥi rose in Ḥarāz in 439/1047, marking the effective foundation of the Ṣolayḥid dynasty ruling over different parts of Yaman as vassals of the Fatimids until 532/1138. On ʿAli's death in 459/1067, Lamak b. Mālek Ḥammādi was appointed as chief *dāʿi* of Yaman while ʿAli's son Aḥmad al-Mokarram succeeded his father merely as head of the Ṣolayḥid state. The *dāʿi* Lamak had earlier spent five years in Cairo, studying with the chief *dāʿi* al-Moʾayyad. From the latter part of Aḥmad al-Mokarram's reign, during which time the Ṣolayḥids lost much of Yaman to Zaydis there, effective authority in the Ṣolayḥid state was transferred to al-Mokarram's consort, al-Maleka al-Sayyeda Ḥorra. She also played an increasingly important role in the affairs of the Yamani *daʿwa* culminating in her appointment as the *ḥojja* of Yaman by al-Mostanṣer. This represented the first application of a high rank in the *daʿwa* hierarchy to a woman (ʿOmāra b. ʿAli al-Ḥakami, *Taʾrik̲ al-Yaman*, in Kay, 1892, text pp. 1-102, tr. pp. 1-137; Ḥ. F. al-Hamdāni, 1955, pp. 62-231). The Ṣolayḥids also played an active part in the renewed efforts of the Fatimids to spread the *daʿwa* on the Indian subcontinent (see al-Mostanṣer, *al-Sejellāt*, pp. 167-69, 203-6). The Ismaʿili community founded in Gojarāt by *dāʿis* sent from Yaman in the second half of the 5th/11th century evolved into the modern day Ṭayyebi Bohra community.

Meanwhile, the Ismaʿili *daʿwa* had continued to spread in many parts of the Iranian world, now incorporated into the Saljuq sultanate. By the early 460s/1070s, the Persian Ismaʿilis in the Saljuq dominions were under the leadership of ʿAbd al-Malek b. ʿAṭṭāš who had his secret headquarters in Isfahan. He was also responsible for launching the career of Ḥasan-e Ṣabbāḥ (q.v.) who in due course led the Ismaʿili *daʿwa* in Persia. In Badak̲šān and other eastern parts of the Iranian world too the *daʿwa* had continued to spread after the downfall of the Sāmānids in 395/1005 (Ebn al-Atir, IX, pp. 211, 358, X, pp. 122 ff., 165-66; Barthold, pp. 251, 304-5, 316-18). One of the most eminent *dāʿis* of al-Mostanṣer's time, Nāṣer-e K̲osrow played an important part in propagating Ismaʿilism in Central Asia as the *ḥojja* of Khorasan; he also spread the *daʿwa* to Ṭabarestān and other Caspian provinces. It was mainly during his period of exile in Yomgān that Nāṣer extended the *daʿwa* throughout Badak̲šān while maintaining his contacts with the *dāʿi* al-Moʾayyad and the *daʿwa* headquarters in Cairo. In fact, the Ismaʿilis of Badak̲šān, now divided between Tajikistan and Afghanistan, and their offshoot groups in the Hindu Kush region, now situated in Hunza and other northern areas of Pakistan, regard Šāh Nāṣer-e K̲osraw as the founder of their communities (Ivanow, 1948; Berthels, *Nasir-i Khosrov*; Corbin, "Nāṣir-i Khusrau," pp. 520-42; Daftary, 1990, pp. 215-18; Hunsberger, pp. 220-54). By the time the Qarmaṭi state of Baḥrayn was finally uprooted in 470/1077-78 by some local tribal chieftains, other Qarmaṭi groups in Persia, Iraq, and elsewhere too had either disintegrated or switched their allegiance to the Ismaʿili *daʿwa* of the Fatimids. There was now, once gain, only one unified Ismaʿili *daʿwa* under the supreme leadership of the Fatimid caliph-imam.

During the long reign of al-Mostanṣer the Fatimid caliphate had already embarked on its decline resulting from factional fighting in the Fatimid armies and other political and economic difficulties. The unruliness of the Turkish troops led to a complete breakdown of law and order, and drove al-Mostanṣer to appeal to Badr al-Jamāli, an Armenian general in the service of the Fatimids, for help. Badr arrived in Cairo in 466/1074 and soon assumed the leadership of civil, judicial and religious administration in addition to being "commander of the armies" (*amir al-joyuš*), his main source of power. He managed to restore peace and relative prosperity to Egypt in the course of his long vizierate of some twenty years, as the de facto ruler of the Fatimid state. Badr died in 487/1094, having arranged for his son Afżal to succeed him in the vizierate. Henceforth, real power in the Fatimid state remained in the hands of the Fatimid viziers who also commanded the troops, whence their title of "Vizier of the Sword" (*wazir al-sayf*). They were also in charge of the *daʿw* organization and activities.

Al-Mostanṣer, the eighth Fatimid caliph and eighteenth Ismaʿili imam, died in Du'l-Ḥejja 487/December 1094, a few months after Badr al-Jamāli. Thereupon, the unified Ismaʿili *daʿwa* split into two rival factions, as al-Mostanṣer's son and original heir-designate, Nezār, was deprived of his succession rights by Afżal who quickly installed Nezār's younger half-brother to the Fatimid throne with the title of al-Mostaʿli be'llāh (487-95/1094-1101). The two factions were later designated as the Nezāriya and Mostaʿliya. Afżal immediately obtained for al-Mostaʿli the allegiance of the notables of the Fatimid court and the leaders of the Ismaʿili *daʿwa* in Cairo who now also recognized al-Mostaʿli's imamate. Nezār refused to pay homage to al-Mostaʿli and fled to Alexandria where he rose in revolt, but he was defeated and killed in 488/1095. The imamate of al-Mostaʿli was recognized by the Ismaʿili communities of Egypt, Yaman, and western India. These Ismaʿilis, who depended on the Fatimid regime, later traced the imamate in the progeny of al-Mostaʿli. The bulk of the Ismaʿilis of Syria, too, joined the Mostaʿli camp. On the other hand, the Ismaʿilis of Persia who were then already under the leadership of Ḥasan-e Ṣabbāḥ supported the succession rights of Nezār. The Central Asian Ismaʿilis seem to have remained uninvolved in the Nezāri-Mostaʿli schism for quite some time (al-Mostanṣer, *al-Sejellāt*, pp. 109-18; Ebn al-Qalānesi, p. 128; Ebn Moyassar, pp. 59 ff., Ebn al-Dawādāri, VI, pp. 443 ff.; Maqrizi, *Etteʿāẓ*, III, pp. 11 ff.; idem, *al-Ḵeṭaṭ*, I, pp. 422-23; Ebn Tağriberdi, V, pp. 142-45).

MOSTAʿLI ISMAʿILISM

The Fatimid state survived for another 77 years after the Nezāri-Mostaʿli schism of 487/1094. These decades witnessed the rapid decline of the Fatimid caliphate which was beset by continuing crises. Al-Mostaʿli and his successors on the Fatimid throne, who were mostly minors and remained powerless in the hands of their viziers, continued to be recognized as imams by the Mostaʿli Ismaʿilis who themselves soon split into Ḥāfeẓi and Ṭayyebi branches. After al-Mostaʿli's premature death in 495/1101, the all-powerful vizier Afżal placed his five-year-old son on the throne with the caliphal title of al-Āmer be-Aḥkām Allāh. Afżal was murdered in 515/1121; and when al-Āmer himself was assassinated in 524/1130, the Mostaʿli Ismaʿilis were confronted with a major crisis of succession. A son, named Ṭayyeb, had been born to al-Āmer a few months before his death; and he had been designated as the heir. But on al-Āmer's death, power was assumed by his cousin, ʿAbd-al-Majid, the eldest member of the Fatimid family, and nothing more was heard of Ṭayyeb. After a brief confusing period in Fatimid history, when Twelver Shiʿism instead of Ismaʿilism was adopted as the official religion of the Fatimid state by Afżal's son Kotayfāt who had succeeded to the vizierate, ʿAbd al-Majid re-emerged on the scene in 526/1132, proclaiming himself as caliph and imam with the title of al-Ḥāfeż le-Din Allāh; and Ismaʿilism was reinstated as the state's religion (Ebn al-Qalānesi, pp. 203, 229, 242 ff., 262, 270, 272-73, 295-96, 308; Ebn Ẓāfer, pp. 94-101; Ebn Moyassar, pp. 113-41; Ebn al-Dawādāri, VI, pp. 506-56; Maqrizi, *Etteʿāẓ*, III, pp. 135-92; Ebn Tağriberdi, V, pp. 237-87).

The irregular proclamation of al-Ḥāfeẓ as imam, whose father had not been imam previously, caused a major schism in Mostaʿli Ismaʿilism. As in the case of the Nezāri-Mostaʿli split, the Mostaʿli *daʿwa* headquarters in Cairo endorsed the imamate of al-Ḥāfeẓ, who claimed al-Āmer had personally designated him (see Qalqašandi, IX, pp. 291-97). Therefore, it was also acknowledged by the Mostaʿli Ismaʿilis of Egypt and Syria as well as a portion of the Mostaʿlis of Yaman. These Ismaʿilis, who recognized al-Ḥāfeẓ and the later Fatimid caliphs as their imams, became known as the Ḥāfeẓiya. On the other hand, the Ṣolayḥid queen of Yaman, al-Sayyeda, who had already drifted away from Cairo, upheld Ṭayyeb's cause and recognized him as al-Āmer's successor to the imamate. As a result, the Mostaʿli community of the Ṣolayḥid state, too, recognized Ṭayyeb's imamate. These Mostaʿli Ismaʿilis of Yaman, with some minority groups in Egypt and Syria, initially known as the Āmeriya, became later designated as the Ṭayyebiya. Ḥāfeẓiya Ismaʿilism disappeared completely soon after the collapse of the Fatimid dynasty and caliphate. The Ayyubid Ṣalāḥ al-Din, the last Fatimid vizier, ended Fatimid rule in 567/1171 and thereafter persecuted the Ismaʿilis of Egypt. Henceforth, Mostaʿli Ismaʿilism survived only in its Ṭayyebi form (Casanova, pp. 415-45; Stern, 1951, pp. 193-255; Daftary, 1990, pp. 256-84).

Ṭayyebi Ismaʿilism found its permanent stronghold in Yaman, where it received the initial support of the Ṣolayḥid queen al-Sayyeda who had been looking after the affairs of the Mostaʿli *daʿwa* there with the help of the *dāʿi* Lamak b. Mālek Ḥammādi and then his son Yaḥyā (d. 520/1126). It was soon after 526/1132 that the Ṣolayḥid queen broke her relations with Cairo and declared Yaḥyā's successor Doʾayb b. Musā as the *dāʿi moṭlaq*, or *dāʿi* with absolute authority, to lead the affairs of the Ṭayyebi Mostaʿli *daʿwa* on behalf of Ṭayyeb, who was thought to be in hiding. This marked the foundation of the Ṭayyebi *daʿwa* independently of the Ṣolayḥid state. On Doʾayb's death in 546/1151, Ebrāhim Ḥāmedi succeeded to the headship of the Ṭayyebi *daʿwa* as the second *dāʿi moṭlaq*. The Ṭayyebi *daʿwa* spread successfully in the Ḥarāz region even though it did not receive the support of any Yamani rulers after the death of the Ṣolayḥid queen in 532/1138. After Ebrāhim Ḥāmedi (d. 557/1162), the position of *dāʿi moṭlaq* remained hereditary among his descendants until 605/1209 when it passed to ʿAli b. Moḥammad al-Walid of the Banu al-Walid al-Anf family of the Qorayš, and it then remained in this family, with minor interruptions, until 946/1539. The Ṭayyebi Ismaʿilis are of the opinion that in the current period of *satr*, initiated by Ṭayyeb's own concealment, their imamate has been handed down among his descendants down to the present time. All these imams have remained in concealment, and in their absence the *dāʿi moṭlaq*s lead the affairs of the Ṭayyebi *daʿwa* and community (Hamdani, 1970, pp. 279 ff.; Daftary, 1990, pp. 285-91; idem, "Sayyida Ḥurra: The Ismāʿīlī Ṣulayḥid Queen of Yemen," in G. R. G. Hambly, ed., *Women in the Medieval Islamic World*, New York, 1998, pp. 117-30).

In the doctrinal field, the Ṭayyebis maintained the Fatimid traditions, and preserved a good portion of the Ismaʿili texts of the Fatimid period. Similarly to the Fatimids, they emphasized the equal importance of the *ẓāher* and *bāṭen* aspects of religion, also retaining the earlier interest of the Ismaʿilis in cyclical history and cosmology which served as the basis of their gnostic, esoteric *ḥaqāʾeq* system of religious thought with its distinctive eschatological themes. This system was founded largely by Ebrāhim Hāmedi who drew extensively on Kermāni's *Rāḥat al-ʿaql* and synthesized its cosmological doctrine of the ten separate intellects with gnostic mythical elements (see Hāmedi, *Kanz al-walad*). This represented the final modification of Neoplatonic cosmology in Ismaʿili thought (Corbin, 1983, pp. 37-58, 65 ff., 76 ff., 103 ff.,

173-81; Daftary, 1990, pp. 291-97). The Ṭayyebi *daʿwa* organization has drawn on Fatimid antecedents with certain modifications. As in the case of imams, every *dāʿi moṭlaq* has appointed his successor by the rule of the *naṣṣ*. The *dāʿi moṭlaq* was normally assisted in the affairs of the Ṭayyebi *daʿwa* by several subordinate *dāʿis* designated as *maʾdun* and *mokāser*.

Meanwhile, the Ṭayyebi *dāʿi moṭlaqs* in Yaman maintained close relations with the Ṭayyebi community in western India. There, the Ismaʿili converts, mostly of Hindu descent, were known as Bohras, a name believed to have been derived from the Gojarāti term *vohorvu* meaning "to trade," since the *daʿwa* originally spread among the trading community of Gojarāt. The Ismaʿili Bohras of Gojarāt were persecuted under the Sunni sultans of the region from 793/1391, forcing them to observe *taqiya* in the guise of Sunnism. With the establishment of Mongol rule in 980/1572, however, Bohras began to enjoy a certain degree of religious freedom and conversions to Sunni Islam ended.

On the death of the twenty-sixth *dāʿi moṭlaq*, Dāʾud b. ʿAjabšāh, in 997/1589, his succession was disputed, leading to the Dāʾudi-Solaymāni schism in the Ṭayyebi *daʿwa* and community. The great majority of Ṭayyebis, then located in India, acknowledged Dāʾud Borhān al-Din (d. 1021/1612) as their new *dāʿi* and became known as Dāʾudis. A small number of Yamani Ṭayyebis, too, supported the Dāʾudi cause. On the other hand, a minority of all Ṭayyebis, who accounted for the bulk of the community in Yaman, recognized Solaymān b. Ḥasan (d. 1005/1597) as their new, twenty-seventh *dāʿi*; they became known as Solaymānis. Henceforth, the Dāʾudi and Solaymāni Ṭayyebis followed separate lines of *dāʿis*. The Dāʾudi *dāʿis* continued to reside in India, while the headquarters of the Solaymāni *daʿwa* were established in Yaman (Moḥammad ʿAli, *Mawsem-e bahār*, III, pp. 169-259; Misra, pp. 27-31; Daftary, 1990, pp. 299-306). Subsequently, the Dāʾudi Bohras were further subdivided in India due to periodical challenges to the authority of their *dāʿi moṭlaq*.

In 1200/1785, the headquarters of the Dāʾudi *daʿwa* was transferred to Surat, where the forty-third *dāʿi*, ʿAbd ʿAli Sayf al-Din (1213-32/1798-1817), founded a seminary known as Sayfi Dars, also Jāmeʿa Sayfia, for the education of Dāʾudi scholars and the functionaries of the community. This seminary, with a major library, has continued to serve as an institution of traditional Islamic learning for the Dāʾudi Bohras. Since 1232/1817, the office of the *dāʿi moṭlaq* of the Dāʾudi Ṭayyebis has remained among the descendants of Šayḵ Jiwanji Awrangābādi, while the community has experienced intermittent strife and crisis rooted in opposition to the *dāʿi*'s authority. The present *dāʿi moṭlaq* of the Dāʾudi *daʿwa*, Sayyednā Borhān al-Din, succeeded to his position as the fifty-second in the series in 1385/1965. The total Dāʾudi population of the world is currently (2002) estimated at around 900,000, located mainly in South Asia. Since the 1920s, Bombay, with its largest single concentration of Dāʾudi Bohras, has served as the permanent administrative seat of the Dāʾudi *dāʿi moṭlaq*. The Ṭayyebi Bohras, together with the Nezāri Khojas, were also among the earliest Asian communities to settle, during the nineteenth century and subsequently, in East Africa (Amiji, 1969, pp. 141-81; idem, 1975, pp. 27-61).

In Yaman, the leadership of the Solaymāni Ṭayyebis has remained hereditary, since 1088/1677, with few exceptions, in the same Makrami family. Unlike the Dāʾudis, the Solaymānis have not experienced succession disputes and schisms. The Solaymāni *dāʿis* established their headquarters in Najrān, in northeastern Yaman, and ruled over that region with the military support of the local Banu Yām. In the twentieth century, the political prominence of the Solaymāni *dāʿis*, checked earlier by the Ottomans, was further curtailed by the Saʿudi family; Najran was, in fact, annexed to Saudi Arabia in 1353/1934. The present *dāʿi moṭlaq* of the Solaymānis, the forty-ninth in the series, Sayyednā Šarafi Ḥosayn Makrami who succeeded to office in 1396/1976, lives in Saudi Arabia. At present, the Solaymāni Ṭayyebi Ismaʿilis of Yaman number around 70,000 persons. The Solaymāni Bohras represent a very small community of a few thousands in India (Daftary, 1990, pp. 318-23).

NEZĀRI ISMAʿILISM OF THE ALAMUT PERIOD

By 487/1094, Ḥasan-e Ṣabbāḥ (q.v.), who preached the Ismaʿili *daʿwa* on behalf of the Fatimids within the Saljuq dominions in Persia, had emerged as the leader of the Persian Ismaʿilis. He had already been following an independent policy, and his seizure of the mountain fortress of Alamut (q.v.) in 483/1090 signalled the commencement of an open revolt against the Saljuq Turks as well as the foundation of what was to become the Nezāri Ismaʿili state. As an Ismaʿili Shiʿite, Ḥasan-e Ṣabbāḥ could not have tolerated the anti-Shiʿite policies of the Saljuqs, who as the new champions of Sunni Islam aimed to uproot the Fatimids. Ḥasan's revolt was also an expression of Persian "national" sentiments, as the alien rule of the Saljuq Turks was intensely detested by the Persians of different social classes. This may explain why he substituted Persian for Arabic as the religious language of the Ismaʿilis of Persia (see Daftary, "Ḥasan-i Ṣabbāḥ and the Origins of the Nizārī Ismaʿili Movement," in Daftary, ed., 1996, pp. 181-204). It was under such circumstances that in al-Mostanṣer's succession dispute Ḥasan supported Nezār's cause and severed his relations with the Fatimid regime and the *daʿwa* headquarters in Cairo which had supported al-Mostaʿli. By this decision, Ḥasan had founded the independent Nezāri Ismaʿili *daʿwa* on behalf of the Nezāri imam. As a result of this decision, the Nezāri *daʿwa* survived the downfall of the Fatimid dynasty, a pattern similar to the subsequent fate of the Ṭayyebi *daʿwa* in Yaman (Jovayni, III, pp. 186-216; tr. Boyle, II, pp. 666-83; Rašid al-Din, pp. 97-137; Kāšāni, pp. 133-72; Hodgson, 1955, pp. 41-98; Daftary, 1990, pp. 324-71).

The revolt of the Persian Ismaʿilis soon acquired a distinctive pattern and method of struggle, adapted to the decentralized power structure of the Saljuq sultanate and their much superior military power. Ḥasan devised a strategy to overwhelm the Saljuqs locality by locality and from a multitude of impregnable mountain strongholds. Ḥasan Ṣabbāḥ did not divulge the name of Nezār's successor to the imamate. In fact, numismatic evidence shows that Nezār's own name appeared on coins minted at Alamut for about seventy years after his death in 488/1095, while his progeny were blessed anonymously (Miles, pp. 155-62). The early Nezāri Ismaʿilis were thus left without an accessible imam in another *dawr al-satr*; and, as in the pre-Fatimid period of concealment, the absent imam was represented in the community by a *ḥojja*, his chief representative. Ḥasan and his next two successors at Alamut as heads of the Nezāri *daʿwa* and state, were recognized as such *ḥojja*s (*Haft bāb-e Bābā Sayyednā*, pp. 21-22; Abu Esḥāq Qohestāni, text p. 23). It seems that already in Ḥasan Ṣabbāḥ's time many Nezāris believed that a son or grandson of Nezār had been secretly brought from Egypt to Persia, and he became the progenitor of the line of the Nezāri imams who later emerged at Alamut (Jovayni, III, pp. 180-81, 231-37; tr. Boyle, II, pp. 663, 691-95; Rašid al-Din, pp. 79, 166-68; Kāšāni, pp. 115, 202-4).

From early on in the Alamut period, the outsiders had the impression that the Persian Ismaʿilis had initiated a "new preaching" (*al-daʿwa al-jadida*) in contrast to the "old preaching" (*al-daʿwa al-qadima*) of the Fatimid times. The "new preaching" did not, however, represent any new doctrines; it was merely a reformulation of the old Shiʿite doctrine of *taʿlim*, or authoritative teaching by the imam. It was mainly Ḥasan Ṣabbāḥ himself who restated this doctrine in a theological treatise entitled *al-Foṣul al-arbaʿa*, or *The Four Chapters*. This treatise, originally written in Persian, has been preserved only in parts (see Šahrastāni, pp. 150-52; tr. Gimaret and Monnot, I, pp. 560-65; Jovayni, III, pp. 195-99; tr. Boyle, II, pp. 671-73; Rašid-al-Din, pp. 105-7; Kāšāni, pp. 142-43; Hodgson, 1955, pp. 51-61, 325-28). The doctrine of *taʿlim*, emphasizing the autonomous teaching authority of each imam in his own time, became the central doctrine of the Nezāris who, henceforth, were designated also as the Taʿlimiya. The intellectual challenge posed to the Sunni establishment by the doctrine of *taʿlim*, which also refuted the legitimacy of the ʿAbbasid caliph as the spiritual spokesman of all Muslims, called forth the reaction of the Sunnis. Many Sunni scholars, led by Ḡazāli, attacked the Ismaʿili doctrine of *taʿlim* (see Ḡazāli, *Fażāʾeḥ al-Bāṭeniya*, ed. ʿA. Badawi, Cairo, 1964; Mitha, pp. 28-102).

By 489/1096, when the fortress of Lamasar was seized, Ḥasan had acquired or built numerous mountain strongholds in Rudbār, the center of Nezāri power. At the same time, the Ismaʿilis had come to possess a network of fortresses and several towns in Qohestān, in southeastern Khorasan, which remained the second most important territory of the Nezāri state. Later, the Nezāris acquired Gerdkuh (q.v.) and other fortresses in the regions of Qumes, Arrajān and Zagros. By the opening years of the 6th/12th century, Ḥasan had begun to extend his activities into Syria by sending Persian *dāʿi*s from Alamut. By the final years of Ḥasan's life, the anti-Saljuq revolt of the Persian Nezāris had lost its effectiveness, much in the same way that the Saljuqs under Barkiāroq and Moḥammad Tapar had failed in their prolonged military campaigns to uproot the Persian Ismaʿilis from their strongholds. The Ismaʿili-Saljuq relations had now entered a new phase of "stalemate" (Daftary, 1990, pp. 340-44, 361-65; Hillenbrand, pp. 205-20).

After Ḥasan Ṣabbāḥ's death in 518/1124, Kiā Bozorg-Omid (q.v.) followed as the head of the Nezāri *daʿwa* and state. A capable administrator like his predecessor, Bozorg-Omid (518-32/1124-38) maintained the policies of Ḥasan and further strengthened and extended the Nezāri state. The Ismaʿili-Saljuq stalemate essentially continued during the long reign of Bozorg-Omid's son Moḥammad (532-57/1138-62) as the third lord of Alamut (Jovayni, III, pp. 216-22; tr. Boyle, II, pp. 683-86; Rašid al-Din, pp. 137-61; Kāšāni, pp. 172-99; Daftary, 1990, pp. 371-86). By then, the Nezāri state had acquired its distinctive administrative structure. Each Nezāri territory was placed under the overall leadership of a chief *dāʿi* appointed from Alamut; the leader of the Qohestāni Nezāris was known as *moḥtašam*. These *dāʿi*s, as well as the commanders of major strongholds, enjoyed a large degree of independence and local initiative, contributing to the dynamism and resilience of the Nezāri movement. Being preoccupied with their struggle and survival in an extremely hostile environment, the Nezāris produced military commanders rather than learned theologians of the types operating under the Fatimids. Consequently, the literary activities of the Nezāris were rather limited during the Alamut period. Nevertheless, the early Nezāris did maintain a sophisticated outlook and a literary tradition, elaborating their teachings in response to changed circumstances. Ḥasan Ṣabbāḥ himself is credited with establishing an impressive library at Alamut. Other major fortresses in Persia and Syria, too, were later equipped with significant collections of manuscripts, documents and scientific instruments. Firmly united with a remarkable sense of mission, the Nezāris acknowledged the supreme leadership of Alamut and obeyed without any dissent the religious policies initiated at that fortress initially by the Nezāri imam's *ḥojja*s and, subsequently, by the imams themselves. Meanwhile, the Nezāris had been eagerly expecting the appearance of their imam, who had remained inaccessible since Nezār's murder in 488/1095.

The fourth lord of Alamut, Ḥasan II (q.v.), to whom the Nezāris referred with the expression *ʿalā ḏekrehe'l-salām* (on his mention be peace), succeeded to leadership in 557/1162 and, soon after, declared the *qiāma* or resurrection initiating a new phase in the religious history of the early Nezāris. On 17 Ramażān 559/8 August 1164, in the presence of the representatives of different Nezāri communities who had gathered at Alamut, he delivered a sermon in which he proclaimed the *qiāma*, the long awaited Last Day. About two months later, a similar ceremony was held at the fortress of Moʾmenābād, near Birjand, and the earlier *ḵoṭba* and message were read out by Raʾis Możaffar, the *moḥtašam* in Qohestān. There, Ḥasan II's position was more clearly equated with that of al-Mostanṣer as God's caliph (*kalifa*) on earth, implicitly claiming the status of imam for the lord of Alamut (Jovayni, III, pp. 222-39; tr. Boyle, II, pp. 686-97; Rašid-al-Din, pp. 162-70; Kāšāni, pp. 199-208; Abu Esḥāq Qohestāni, text pp. 19, 24, 38-39, 40-44, 46-47, 53, 58, tr. pp. 19, 23, 38, 40-44, 46-47, 53-54, 58; Hodgson, 1955, pp. 146-59; Lewis, 1967, pp. 70-75, Daftary, 1990, pp. 385-91).

Ḥasan II relied heavily on Ismaʿili *taʾwil* and earlier traditions, interpreting *qiāma* symbolically and spiritually for the Nezāris. Accordingly, *qiāma* meant nothing more than the manifestation of unveiled truth (*ḥaqiqa*) in the person of the Nezāri imam; it was a spiritual resurrection only for the Nezāris who acknowledged the rightful imam of the time and were now capable of understanding the truth, the esoteric essence of Islam. It was in this sense that Paradise was actualized for the Nezāris in this world. The Nezāris, like Sufis, were now to rise to a spiritual level of existence, from *ẓāher* to *bāṭen*, from *šariʿa* to *ḥaqiqa*, or from the literal interpretation of the law to an understanding of its spiritual essence and the eternal truths. On the other hand, the "outsiders," the non-Nezāris who were incapable of recognizing the truth, were rendered spiritually non-existent. The imam proclaiming the *qiāma* would be the *qāʾem al-qiāma*, or the lord of resurrection, a rank which in Ismaʿili religious hierarchy was always higher than that of an ordinary imam.

Ḥasan II's son and successor Nur-al-Din Moḥammad devoted his long reign (561-607/1166-1210) to a systematic doctrinal elaboration of the *qiāma*. The exaltation of the autonomous teaching authority of the present Nezāri imam now became the central feature of the Nezāri thought; and *qiāma* came to imply a complete personal transformation of the Nezāris who were expected to perceive the imam in his true spiritual reality. Nur-al-Din Moḥammad also made every Nezāri imam potentially a *qāʾem*, capable of inaugurating the era of *qiāma*. In the spiritual world of resurrection there would no longer be any need for ranks of the *daʿwa* intervening between the imam-*qāʾem* and his followers. There would now remain only three categories of persons, reflecting different levels of existence in terms of relationships to the Nezāri imam. There are the "people of opposition" (*ahl-e tażādd*), the non-Nezāris who exist only in the realm of appearances (*ẓāher*) and are spiritually non-existent. Secondly, there are the ordinary followers of the Nezāri imam, the "people of gradation" (*ahl-e tarattob*), who have penetrated the *šariʿa* to its inner meaning. However, they have access only to partial truth, as they still do not fully understand the *bāṭen*. Finally, there are the "people of union" (*ahl-e vaḥdat*), the Nezāri super-elite, or the *akaṣṣ-e kāṣṣ*, who perceived the imam in his true spiritual reality as the epiphany (*maẓhar*) of the word (*kalema*) of God (Ṭusi, *Rawża*, text pp. 104-5, 112, tr. pp. 119, 128-29; idem, *Sayr*, text pp. 17-18, tr. pp. 47-48); only they arrive at the realm of the *ḥaqiqa*, in a sense the *bāṭen* behind the *bāṭen*, where they find full truth and as such, they enjoy full salvation in the paradisal state actualized for them in this world. It seems that the privileged state of the *ahl-e vaḥdat* was attainable by only a few. Nur-al-Din Moḥammad also explicitly affirmed the Nezārid Fatimid descent of his father and, therefore, himself, explaining that Ḥasan II was in fact imam and the son of a descendant of Nezār b. al-Mostanṣer who had earlier found refuge in Alamut. Henceforth, the Nezāris recognized the lords of Alamut, beginning with Ḥasan II, as their imams (*Haft bāb-e Bābā Sayyednā*, pp. 4-42; tr. Hodgson, in his *Order of Assassins*, pp. 279-324; Ṭusi, *Rawża*, text pp. 42, 44-45, 47-56, 98-99, 101-2, tr. pp. 46-47, 49-50, 52-63, 111-12, 115-16; Jovayni, III, 240-42; tr. Boyle, II, pp. 697-99; Rašid-al-Din, pp. 170-73; Kāšāni, pp. 208-14; Hodgson, 1955, pp. 160-84, 210-17).

Meanwhile, the Syrian Nezāris had entered into an important phase of their history under Rāšed-al-Din Senān, their most famous leader who had been appointed as chief *dāʿi* in Syria by Ḥasan II soon after his own accession in 557/1162. Senān reorganized and strengthened the Syrian Nezāri *daʿwa*, also consolidating their network of fortresses in the Jabal Bahrāʾ, in central Syria. Aiming to safeguard his community, he entered into intricate and shifting alliances with the major neighboring powers and rulers, notably the Crusaders, the Zangids and Ṣalāh-al-Din. Senān taught his own version of the doctrine of *qiāma*, which did not acquire deep roots in the Syrian Nezāri community. The only one of the Syrian *dāʿis* to act somewhat independently of Alamut, Senān led the Syrian Nezāris for almost three decades to the peak of their power and fame until his death in 589/1193 (Abu Ferās Šehāb al-Din Maynaqi, *Faṣl*, in Guyard, pp. 387-489; B. Lewis, "Kamāl al-Dīn's Biography of Rāšid al-Dīn Sinān," *Arabica* 13, 1966, pp. 225-67; idem, 1967, pp. 110-18; Hodgson, 1955, pp. 185-209; Mirza, pp. 22-39; Daftary, 1994, pp. 67-74, 94 ff.).

Nur-al-Din Moḥammad's son and successor, Jalāl-al-Din Ḥasan (607-18/1210-21), proclaimed his own daring religious policy, aimed at redressing the isolation of the Nezāris from the larger world of Sunni Islam. Consequently, he publicly repudiated the doctrine of *qiāma* and ordered his followers to observe the *šariʿa* in its Sunni form, inviting Sunni jurists to instruct his people. Indeed, Jalāl-al-Din Ḥasan did his utmost to convince the outside world of his new policy. In 608/1211, the ʿAbbasid caliph al-Nāṣer acknowledged the Nezāri imam's rapprochement with Sunni Islam and issued a decree to that effect. Henceforth, the rights of Jalāl-al-Din Ḥasan to Nezāri territories were officially recognized by the ʿAbbasid caliph, as well as by the Kᵛārazm-Šāhs, who were then establishing their own empire in Persia as successors to the Saljuqs, and by other Sunni rulers. The Nezāris accepted their imam's new instructions without any opposition. They evidently viewed Jalāl-al-Din Ḥasan's declarations as a reimposition of *taqiya*, which had been lifted in *qiāma* times; the observance of *taqiya* could, thus, imply any type of accommodation to the outside world as deemed necessary by the infallible imam. Be that as it may, the Nezāri imam had now successfully achieved peace and security for his community and state (Jovayni, III, pp. 243-49; tr. Boyle, II, pp.

699-704; Rašid-al-Din, pp. 174-78; Kāšāni, pp. 214-17; Hodgson, 1955, pp. 217-25; Daftary, 1990, pp. 404-7).

Under ʿAlāʾ-al-Din Moḥammad (618-53/1221-55), Jalāl-al-Din Ḥasan's son and successor as the penultimate lord of Alamut, the Sunni *šariʿa* was gradually relaxed within the community and the Nezāri traditions associated with *qiāma* were revived, although the Nezāris continued to appear to outsiders in Sunni guise. The Nezāri leadership now also made a sustained effort to explain the different doctrinal declarations and religious policies of the lords of Alamut. All these teachings were interpreted comprehensively within a coherent theological framework, aiming to provide satisfactory explanations for the seemingly contradictory policies adopted at Alamut. Intellectual life indeed flourished in the long reign of ʿAlāʾ-al-Din Moḥammad, receiving a special impetus from the influx of outside scholars, who fled the first waves of the Mongol invasions and took refuge in the Nezāri fortress communities. Foremost among such scholars, who availed themselves of the Nezāri libraries and patronage of learning, was Naṣir-al-Din Ṭusi, who made major contributions to the Nezāri Ismaʿili thought of the late Alamut period during his three decades amongst them in Qohestān and Rudbār.

It is mainly through Ṭusi's extant Ismaʿili writings, notably his *Rowżat al-taslim*, that we have an exposition of Nezāri thought of the Alamut period as it developed during *qiāma* and its aftermath. *Qiāma*, Ṭusi explained, was not necessarily a final eschatological event, but a transitory condition of life when the veil of *taqiya* would be lifted to make the unveiled truth accessible. In the current cycle of history, however, the full *qiāma*, or Great Resurrection (*qiāmat-e qiāmāt*) would still occur at the end of the era initiated by the Prophet Moḥammad. Be that as it may, the identification between *šariʿa* and *taqiya*, implied by the teachings of Ḥasan II, was now made explicit by Ṭusi who also identified *qiāma* with *ḥaqiqa*. Thus, the imposition of the Sunni *šariʿa* by Jalāl-al-Din Ḥasan was presented as a return to *taqiya*, and to a new period of *satr* or concealment, when the truth (*ḥaqiqa*) would be once again concealed in the *bāṭen* of religion. The condition of *qiāma* could, in principle, be granted by the current Nezāri imam at any time, because every imam was potentially also an imam-*qāʾem*. Thus, Ṭusi now expounded a new doctrine of *satr*. In his integrated theological presentation, human life could alternate between periods of *qiāma*, when reality is manifest, and *satr*, when it would be concealed, requiring the observance of *taqiya*. In this sense, the term *satr* was redefined to imply the concealment of the religious truths and the true spiritual reality of the imam, and not the physical inaccessibility of his person, as had been the cases in the pre-Fatimid and early Alamut periods (Ṭusi, *Rawża*, text pp. 61-63, 101-2, 110, 117-19, 132-33, 143, 145, 147, tr. pp. 67-69, 115-16, 126, 136-38, 154-55, 173, and elsewhere; Hodgson, 1955, pp. 225-38; Daftary, 1990, pp. 407-12). The teachings of the late Alamut period brought the Nezāris even closer to the esoteric traditions more commonly associated with Sufism.

Nezāri fortunes in Persia were rapidly reversed when the collapse of the Ḵᵛārazmian Empire brought them into direct confrontation with the invading Mongols. When the Great Khan Möngke decided to complete the Mongol conquests of western Asia, he assigned a priority to the destruction of the Nezāri Ismaʿili state, a task completed with some difficulty in 654/1256 by Hülegü who led the main Mongol expedition into Persia. Shortly before, in 653/1255, ʿAlāʾ-al-Din Moḥammad had been succeeded by his eldest son Rokn-al-Din Ḵoršāh, who would rule for exactly one year as the last lord of Alamut (Jovayni, III, pp. 259-78; tr. Boyle, II, 712-25; Rašid-al-Din, pp. 185-95; Kāšāni, pp. 224-33; Daftary, 1990, pp. 416 ff., 421-30). The youthful imam engaged in a complex, and ultimately futile, series of negotiations with Hülegü. On 29 Šawwāl 654/19 November 1256, Ḵoršāh descended from the fortress of Maymundez in Rudbār in the company of Naṣir-al-Din Ṭusi and Nezāri dignitaries, and surrendered to the Mongols. With the fall of Alamut a month later, the fate of the Nezāri state was sealed. Alamut and many other fortresses were demolished. In the spring of 655/1257, Ḵoršāh himself was killed by his Mongol guards in Mongolia, where he had gone to see the Great Khan. By then, the Mongols had massacred large numbers of Nezāris in their protective custody. Shortly afterwards, the Nezāri castles in Syria submitted to the Mamluks; Kahf was the last Nezāri outpost there to fall in 671/1273. However, the Syrian Nezāris were permitted to remain in their traditional abodes as loyal subjects of the Mamluks and their successors. Having lost their political prominence, the Nezāris henceforth lived secretly in numerous scattered communities.

POST-ALAMUT NEZĀRI ISMAʿILISM

In the wake of the Mongol debacle, the Persian Nezāri Ismaʿilis survived the downfall of their state and strongholds. Many migrated to Central Asia and Sind, where Ismaʿili communities already existed. Other isolated groups in Persia soon disintegrated or were assimilated into the religiously dominant communities of their locality. The centralized *daʿwa* organization and direct leadership of the Nezāri imams had also disappeared. Under these circumstances, Nezāri communities developed independently while resorting to the strict observance of *taqiya* and adopting different external guises. Many Nezāri groups in the Iranian world disguised themselves as Sunni Muslims. Meanwhile, a group of Nezāri dignitaries had managed to hide Rokn-al-Din Ḵoršāh's minor son, Šams-al-Din Moḥammad, who had then succeeded to the Nezāri imamate. Subsequently, Šams-al-Din was taken to Azerbaijan, where he and his next few successors to the imamate lived secretly.

Šams-al-Din, who in certain legendary accounts has been confused with Mawlānā Jalāl-al-Din Rumi's spiritual guide Šams-e Tabriz, died around 710/1310. An obscure dispute over his succession split the line of the Nezāri imams and their following into the Qāsem-šāhi and Moḥammad-šāhi (or Moʾmen-šāhi) branches (Ivanow, 1938, pp. 57-79; Daftary, 1990, pp. 446 ff., 451-52). The

Moḥammad-šāhi imams, who initially had more followers in northern Persia and Central Asia, transferred their seat to India in the 10th/16th century and by the end of the 12th/18th century this line had become discontinued. The sole surviving Moḥammad-šāhi Nezāris, currently numbering about 15,000, are to be found in Syria where they are locally known as the Jaʿfariya (Daftary, 1990, pp. 532-34). The Qāsem-šāhi branch has persisted to the present time. The last four Qāsem-šāhi imams have enjoyed prominence under their hereditary title of Āqā Khan (also Āghā Khan and Aga Khan). It was also in the early post-Alamut times that Persian Nezāris, as part of their *taqiya* practices, disguised themselves under the cover of Sufism, without establishing formal affiliations with any of the Sufi *ṭariqa*s. The practice soon gained wide currency among the Nezāris of Central Asia and Sind as well. The earliest manifestation of this phenomenon is found in the writings of the poet Ḥakim Saʿd al-Din Nezāri Qohestāni (d. 720/1320). He is the earliest known post-Alamut Nezāri author to use poetic expressions and Sufi idioms for concealing Ismaʿili ideas, a model adopted later by many Nezāri authors of Persia, Afghanistan and Central Asia.

In early post-Alamut times, a most obscure phase in Ismaʿili history, the Nezāris had some success in regrouping in Daylam, where they remained active throughout the Ilkhānid and Timurid periods. A certain Ḵodāvand Moḥammad (d. 807/1404), a Moḥammad-šāhi imam, even occupied Alamut for a while, before he was dislodged by Sayyed ʿAli, the powerful Zaydi ruler of Daylamān. The Nezāris did not survive in the Caspian region after the 10th/16th century (Ẓahir al-Din Marʿaši, *Tāriḵ-e Gilān va Daylamestān*, ed. M. Sotuda, Tehran, 1347 Š./1968, pp. 52-68, 69-70, 76 ff., 81 ff., 89, 121, 123-30). Soltan Moḥammad b. Jahāngir (d. 998/1589) and his son Soltan Jahāngir (d. 1006/1597), belonging to Banu Eskandar rulers of Kojur, adhered to Nezāri Ismaʿilism and spread it in their dominions; they represent the last known references in the sources to Ismaʿilism in northern Persia (Šayḵ ʿAli Gilāni, *Tāriḵ-e Māzandarān*, ed. M. Sotuda, 1352 Š./1973, pp. 88-89, 100). Only a few isolated Nezāri groups survived a while longer in Daylam during the Safawid period when Alamut was used as a prison. In Badaḵšān and other parts of Central Asia, the Ismaʿilis evidently acknowledged the Nezāri imamate only during the late Alamut period as a result of the activities of *dāʿi*s dispatched from Qohestān. These *dāʿi*s founded local dynasties of *pir*s and *mir*s who ruled over Šoḡnān and other districts of Badaḵšān. Later, the Nezāris of Badaḵšān were severely persecuted by the region's Timurid and Özbeg rulers.

By the middle of the 9th/15th century, Ismaʿili-Sufi relations had become well established in the Iranian world. Indeed, a type of coalescence had emerged between Persian Sufism and Nezāri Ismaʿilism, two independent esoteric traditions in Islam which shared close affinities and common doctrinal grounds. This explains why the Persian-speaking Nezāris have regarded several of the greatest mystic poets of Persia, such as Sanāʾi, ʿAṭṭār and Jalāl-al-Din Rumi, as their co-religionists (see, for instance, Fedāʾi Ḵorāsāni, pp. 113-16). The Nezāri Ismaʿilis of Persia, Afghanistan and Central Asia have continued to use verses of the mystical poets of the Iranian world in their religious ceremonies. The dissimulating Persian Ismaʿilis also adopted visible aspects of the Sufi way of life. Thus, the imams appeared to outsiders as Sufi masters or *pir*s, while their followers adopted the typically Sufi guise of disciples or *morid*s (see F. Daftary, "Ismāʿīlī-Sufi Relations in Early Post-Alamūt and Safavid Persia," in L. Lewisohn and D. Morgan, ed., *The Heritage of Sufism*, Oxford, 1999, III, pp. 275-89).

By the middle of the 9th/15th century, the Nezāri imams of the Qāsem-šāhi line emerged in the village of Anjedān (q.v.), in central Persia, in the guise of Sufi *pir*s, initiating the so-called Anjedān revival in Nezāri Ismaʿilism that lasted some two centuries. With Mostanṣer be'llāh II (d. 885/1480), who adopted the Sufi name of Šāh Qalandar, the Qāsem-šāhi imams became definitely established in the locality where their tombs are still preserved. Taking advantage of the changing religio-political climate of Persia, including the spread of ʿAlid loyalism and Shiʿite tendencies through Sunni Sufi orders, the imams successfully began to reorganize and reinvigorate their *daʿwa* to win new converts and reassert their authority over various Nezāri communities. These communities, notably those in Afghanistan, Central Asia and India, had been led for long periods by independent hereditary dynasties of *pir*s. The imams now gradually replaced these powerful autonomous figures with their own loyal *dāʿi*s who would also regularly deliver the religious dues to them.

The Anjedān period also witnessed a revival in the literary activities of the Nezāris, especially in Persia where authors such as Abu Esḥāq Qohestāni and Ḵayrḵᵛāh Harāti produced the earliest doctrinal works of the post-Alamut period. In the context of Nezāri-Sufi relations during the early Anjedān period, valuable details are preserved in the *Pandiāt-e javānmardi*, containing the religious admonitions of Imam Mostanṣer be'llāh II. In this book, the Nezāris are referred to with Sufi expressions such as *ahl-e ḥaqiqat*, or the "people of the truth," while the imam is designated as *pir* or *moršed*. The imam's admonitions start with the *šariʿat-ṭariqat-ḥaqiqat* categorization of the Sufis, describing *ḥaqiqat* as the *bāṭen* of *šariʿat* which would be attained by the believers (*moʾmen*s) through following the spiritual path or *ṭariqat*. The *Pandiāt* (text pp. 2-3, 11, 13, 14, 34-36, 54-58, 65-68 and elsewhere) further explains, in line with the earlier Nezāri teachings of *qiāma* times, that *ḥaqiqat* consists of recognizing the spiritual reality of the imam of the time. The Nezāris now essentially retained the teachings of the Alamut period, especially as elaborated after the declaration of *qiāma*. The current imam retained his central importance in Nezāri doctrine, and the recognition of his true spiritual reality remained the prime concern of his followers (Abu Esḥāq Qohestāni, text pp. 19-20, 37-38, 53-54, 58, 67-68, tr., pp. 19-20, 37-38, 53-54, 58, 67-68; Ḵayrḵᵛāh, *Kalām-e pir*, text pp. 46, 72-73, 86, 95-96, 100, 114-16; idem, *Taṣnifāt*, pp. 18 ff.).

The advent of the Safavids and the proclamation of Twelver Shiʿism as the state religion in 907/1501, promised a more favorable atmosphere for the activities of the Nezāris and other Shiʿite communities in Persia. The Nezāris did, in fact, initially reduce the intensity of their *taqiya* practices. However, this new optimism was short-lived as the Safavids and their *šariʿat*-minded *ʿolamāʾ* soon persecuted all popular forms of Sufism and those Shiʿite movements which fell outside the confines of Twelver Shiʿism. The Nezāris, too, received their share of persecutions. Šāh Ṭāher Ḥosayni (d. ca. 956/1549), a learned religious scholar and the most famous imam of the Moḥammad-šāhi line, was persecuted in Shah Esmāʿil's reign (907-30/1501-24). However, Šāh Ṭāher, whose religious following and popularity had proved unacceptable to the Safavid ruler and his Etnāʿašari scholars, fled to India in 926/1520 and permanently settled in the Deccan where he rendered valuable services to the Neẓām-šāhs of Aḥmadnagar. It is interesting to note that from early on in India, Šāh Ṭāher advocated Twelver Shiʿism, which he had obviously adopted as a form of disguise. He achieved his greatest success in the Deccan when Borhān Neẓām-šāh proclaimed Twelver Shiʿism as the official religion of the state in 944/1537. Šāh Ṭāher's successors as Moḥammad-šāhi imams continued to observe *taqiya* in India mainly in the form of Twelver Shiʿism (see Freešta, *Tāriḵ-e Ferešta*, ed. J. Briggs, Bombay, 1832, II, pp. 213-31; ʿAli b. ʿAziz Ṭabāṭabā, *Borhān-e maʾāter*, Hyderabad, 1936, pp. 251-70, 274 ff., 281 ff., 291, 308, 324-26, 338-39, 448-50, 452-53, 584; Daftary, 1990, pp. 487-91).

Meanwhile, Shah Ṭahmāsp persecuted the Qāsem-šāhi Nezāris of Anjedān and had their thirty-sixth imam, Morād Mirzā, executed in 981/1574. By the time of Shah ʿAbbās I (995-1038/1587-1629), the Persian Nezāris had successfully adopted Twelver Shiʿism as a second form of disguise. Šāh Ṭāher may have been the first Nezāri imam to have conceived of this new form of dissimulation, which was now adopted by the Qāsem-šāhi Nezāri imams and their followers (see Daftary, 1990, pp. 471-74). By the end of the 11th/17th century, the Qāsem-šāhi *daʿwa* had gained the allegiance of the bulk of the Nezāris at the expense of the Moḥammad-šāhis. The *daʿwa* had been particularly successful in Afghanistan, Central Asia and several regions of the Indian subcontinent. In South Asia, the Hindu converts became known as Khoja, derived from the Persian word *ḵᵛāja* (Nanji, 1978, pp. 50-83). The Nezāri Khojas developed an indigenous religious tradition, known as Satpanth or the "true path" (to salvation), as well as a devotional literature known as the *ginān*s (q.v.). With the fortieth Qāsem-šāhi imam, Šāh Nezār (d. 1134/1722), the seat of this branch of the Nezāri *daʿwa*, then representing the only branch in Persia, was transferred from Anjedān to the nearby village of Kahak, near Qom and Maḥallāt, ending the Anjedān period in post-Alamut Nezāri Ismaʿilism.

By the middle of the 12th/18th century, in the unsettled conditions of Persia after the demise of the Safavids and the Afghan invasion, the Nezāri imams moved to Šahr-e Bābak in Kermān, a location closer to the pilgrimage route of the Khojas who regularly traveled from India to see their imam and deliver their religious dues. Soon, the imams acquired political prominence in the affairs of Kermān. The forty-fourth imam, Abu'l-Ḥasan, also known as Sayyed Abu'l-Ḥasan Kahaki, was appointed around 1170/1756 to the governorship of the Kermān province by Karim Khan Zand; earlier he had been the *beglerbegi* or governor of the city of Kermān (Vaziri, pp. 543-65). It was in his time that the Neʿmat-Allāhi Sufi order was revived in Persia. Imam Abu'l-Ḥasan had close relations with Nur-ʿAli-šāh and Moštāq-ʿAli-šāh among other Neʿmat-Allāhi Sufis in Kermān (Daftary, 1990, pp. 498-503). After Abu'l-Ḥasan's death in 1206/1792, his son Šāh-Ḵalil-Allāh succeeded to the Nezāri imamate and eventually settled in Yazd. In 1232/1817, he was murdered in a mob attack on his house. Šāh-Ḵalil-Allāh was succeeded by his eldest son Ḥasan-ʿAli-šāh who was appointed to the governorship of Qom by Fath-ʿAli-Šāh and also given properties in Maḥallāt. In addition, the Qājār monarch gave one of his daughters in marriage to the young imam and bestowed upon him the honorific title of Āqā Khan (q.v.), meaning lord and master—this title has remained hereditary among Ḥasan-ʿAli-šāh's successors.

Ḥasan-ʿAli-šāh was appointed to the governorship of Kermān in 1251/1835 by Moḥammad Shah Qājār. Subsequently, after some prolonged confrontations between the imam and the Qājār establishment, Āqā Khan I, also known as Āqā Khan Maḥallāti, left Persia in 1257/1841. After spending some years in Afghanistan, Sind, Gojarāt and Calcutta, he settled permanently in Bombay in 1265/1848, marking the advent of the modern period of Nezāri Ismaʿilism. As the spiritual head of a Muslim community, Āqā Khan I received the protection of the British in India. The Nezāri imam now engaged in a widespread campaign for defining and delineating the distinct religious identity of his Khoja following. The Nezāri Khojas, too, had dissimulated for long periods as Sunnis and Twelver Shiʿites while their religious traditions had been influenced by Hindu elements. With the help of the courts in India, Āqā Khan I's followers were legally defined as Šiʿa Imami Ismaʿilis (see Ḥasan-ʿAli-šāh, Āqā Khan, *ʿEbrat-afzā*, Bombay, 1278/1862, pp. 8-49; Vaziri, pp. 60-64, 608-13; Algar, pp. 61-81; Daftary, 1990, pp. 504-13).

Āqā Khan I died in 1298/1881 and was succeeded by his son Āqā ʿAli Šāh, who led the Nezāris for only four years (1298-1302/1881-85). The latter's sole surviving son and successor, Solṭān Moḥammad Šāh, Āqā Khan III, led the Nezāris for seventy-two years, and also became well known as a Muslim reformer and statesman. Āqā Khan III, too, made systematic efforts to set his followers' identity apart from other religious communities. The Nezāri identity was spelled out in numerous constitutions that the imam promulgated for his followers in different regions, especially in India, Pakistan and East Africa. Furthermore, the Nezāri imam became increasingly concerned with reform policies that would benefit not only his followers but other Muslims as well. He worked vigorously for consolidating and reorganizing the Nezāris into a modern Muslim community with high standards of both male and female education, health and social well-being, as well as developing a new network of councils for administering the affairs of his community. The participation of women in communal affairs also received a high priority in the imam's reforms.

Āqā Khan III died in 1376/1957 and was succeeded by his grandson, Mawlānā Ḥāżer Imam Šāh Karim Ḥosayni, as he is addressed by his followers. The present imam of the Nezāris, the forty-ninth in the series, has continued and substantially expanded the modernization policies of his predecessor, also developing numerous new programs and institutions of his own which are of wider interest to the Muslims and the Third World countries (Daftary, 1990, pp. 518-32, 537-48). He has created a complex institutional network generally referred to as the Aga Khan Development Network (AKDN), which implements projects in a variety of social, economic and cultural areas. Prince Karim Aga Khan IV, as he is known internationally, has his secretariat near Paris. Numbering several millions, the Nezāri Ismaʿilis are scattered as Muslim minorities in more than twenty-five countries of Asia, Middle East, Africa, Europe and North America.

Bibliography: Primary Sources. Abu Esḥāq Qohestāni, *Haft bāb*, ed. and tr. W. Ivanow, Bombay, 1959. ʿArib b. Saʿd Qorṭobi, *Ṣelat taʾrik̲ al-Ṭabari*, ed. M. J. de Goeje, Leiden, 1897. Ašʿari, *Maqālāt*. Baḡdādi, *Farq*, ed. Badr. Qoṭb al-Din Solaymānji Borhānpuri, *Montazaʿ al-ak̲bār*, ed. S. F. Traboulsi, Beirut, 1999. Ebn al-Atir. Ebn al-Dawādāri, *Kanz al-dorar wa jāmeʿ al-ḡorar*, VI, ed. I. al-Munajjed, Cairo, 1961. Moḥammad b. Ḥasan Daylami, *Bayān madhab al-Bāṭeniya*, ed. R. Strothmann, Istanbul, 1939. Ebn ʿEdāri, *al-Bayān al-moḡreb*, ed. G. S. Colin and É. Levi-Provençal, new ed., Leiden, 1948-51. Ebn Ḥammād, *Ak̲bār moluk Bani ʿObayd*, ed. and tr. M. Vonderheyden, Algiers and Paris 1927. Ebn Ḥawšab Manṣur al-Yaman, *Ketāb al-rošd wa'l-hedāya*, ed. M. Kāmel Ḥosayn, in W. Ivanow, ed., *Collectanea* I, Leiden, 1948, pp. 185-213; tr. W. Ivanow as "The Book of Righteousness and True Guidance," in Ivanow, 1955, pp. 29-59. Ebn al-Haytam, *Ketāb al-monāẓarāt*, ed. and tr. W. Madelung and P. E. Walker as *The Advent of the Fatimids*, London, 2000. Ebn Moyassar, *Ak̲bār Meṣr*, ed. A. F. Sayyed, Cairo, 1981. Ebn al-Nadim, ed. Tajaddod. Idem, tr. Dodge. Ebn Taḡriberdi. Ebn al-Qalānesi, *Ḏayl taʾrik̲ Demašq*, ed. H. F. Amedroz, Leiden, 1908. Ebn Ẓāfer al-Azdi, *Ak̲bār al-dowwal al-monqaṭeʿa*, ed. A. Ferré, Cairo, 1972. Edris ʿEmād al-Din b. Ḥasan, *ʿOyun al-ak̲bār wa fonun al-āṯār*, IV-VI, ed. M. Ḡāleb, Beirut, 1973-84. Idem, *Rawżat al-ak̲bār*, ed. M. al-ʿAkwah, Ṣanʿāʾ, 1995. Idem, *Zahr al-maʿāni*, ed. M. Ḡāleb, Beirut, 1991. Moḥammad b. Zayn al-ʿĀbedin Fedāʾi K̲orāsāni, *Ketāb hedāyat al-moʾmenin al-ṭālebin*, ed. A. A. Semenov, Moscow, 1959. Ḥāfeẓ Abru, *Majmaʿ al-tawārik̲ al-solṭāniya, qesmat-e k̲olafāʾ-e ʿAlawiya-e Maḡreb va Meṣr va Nezāriān va rafiqān*, ed. M. Modarresi Zanjāni, 1364 Š./1985. *Haft bāb-e Bābā Sayyednā*, ed. W. Ivanow, in his *Two Early Ismaili Treatises*, Bombay, 1933, pp. 4-44. Ḥ. F. al-Hamdāni, ed., *On the Genealogy of Fatimid Caliphs*, Cairo, 1958. Ebrāhim b. Ḥosayn Ḥāmedi, *Ketāb kanz al-walad*, ed. M. Ḡāleb, Wiesbaden, 1971. Moḥammad b. Mālek Ḥammādi Yamāni, *Kašf asrār al-bāṭeniya wa ak̲bār al-Qarāmeṭa*, ed. M. Zāhed Kawtari, Cairo, 1357/1939. Jaʿfar b. Manṣur al-Yaman, *Ketāb al-ʿālem wa'l-ḡolām*, ed. and tr. J. W. Morris as *The Master and the Disciple*, London, 2001. Idem, *Ketāb al-kašf*, ed. R. Strothmann, London, etc., 1952. Idem, *Sarāʾer wa asrār al-noṭaqāʾ*, ed. M. Ḡāleb, Beirut, 1984. Abu ʿAli Manṣur al-ʿAzizi al-Jawdari, *Sirat al-ostād Jawdar*, ed. M. Kāmel Ḥosayn and M. ʿAbd al-Hādi Šaʿira, Cairo, 1954; French tr. M. Canard as *Vie de l'ustadh Jaudhar*, Algiers, 1958. Jovayni, ed. Qazvini. Idem, tr. Boyle. Abu'l-Qāsem ʿAbd-Allāh Kāšāni, *Zobdat al-tavārik̲, bak̲š-e Fāṭemiān wa Nezāriān*, ed. M. T. Dānešpažuh, 2nd ed., Tehran, 1366 Š./1987. H. C. Kay, ed., *Yaman, its Early Mediaeval History*, London, 1892. K̲ayrk̲ᵛāh-e Harāti, *Faṣl dar bayān-e šenāk̲t-e emām*, ed. W. Ivanow, 3rd ed., Tehran, 1960; tr. W. Ivanow as *On the Recognition of the Imam*, 2nd ed., Bombay, 1947. Idem, *Kalām-e pir*, ed. and tr. W. Ivanow, Bombay, 1935. Idem, *Taṣnifāt*, ed. W. Ivanow, Tehran, 1961. Ḥamid- al-Din Kermāni, *Ketāb al-riāż*, ed. ʿĀ. Tāmer, Beirut, 1960. Idem, *Majmuʿat rasāʾel*, ed. M. Ḡāleb, Beirut, 1983. Idem, *Rāḥat al-ʿaql*, ed. M. Kāmel Ḥosayn and M. Moṣṭafā Ḥelmi, Leiden and Cairo, 1953. Esmāʿil b. ʿAbd al-Rasul Majduʿ, *Fehrest al-kotob wa'l-rasāʾel*, ed. ʿAli N. Monzavi, Tehran, 1966. ʿAbd-al-Ḥākim Maliji, *al-Majāles al-Mostanṣeriya*, ed. M. Kāmel Ḥosayn, Cairo, 1947. Taqi al-Din Aḥmad b. ʿAli Maqrizi, *Etteʿāẓ al-ḥonafāʾ*, ed. J. al-Šayyāl and M. Ḥ. M. Aḥmad, 3 vols. Cairo, 1967-73. Idem, *Ketāb al-mawāʿeẓ wa'l-eʿtebār be-dekr al-k̲eṭaṭ wa'l-āṯār*, Bulāq, 1270/1853-54. Masʿudi, *Moruj*. Idem, *Tanbih*. Al-Moʾayyad fe'l-Din Širāzi, *al-Majāles al-Moʾayyadiya*, I, III, ed. M. Ḡāleb, Beirut, 1974-84; I and II, ed. Ḥamid-al-Din, Bombay, 1395-1407/1975-86. Idem, *Sirat al-Moʾayyad fe'l-Din dāʿi al-doʿāt*, ed. M. Kāmel Ḥosayn, Cairo, 1949. Moḥammad ʿAli b. Mollā Jiwābhāʾi, *Mawsem-e bahār fi ak̲bār al-ṭāherin al-ak̲yār*, 3 vols., Bombay, 1301-11/1884-93. Moḥammad b. ʿObayd Allāh Mosabbeḥi, *Ak̲bār Meṣr*, ed. A. F. Sayyed et al., Cairo, 1978-84. Abu Tamim Maʿadd al-Mostanṣer be'llāh, *al-Sejellāt al-Mostanṣeriya*, ed. ʿA. Mājed, Cairo, 1954. Nāṣer-e K̲osrow, *Gošāyeš wa rahāyeš*, ed. and tr. F. M. Hunzai as *Knowledge and Liberation*, London, 1998. Idem, *Jāmeʿ al-ḥekmatayn*, ed. H. Corbin and M. Moʿin, Tehran and Paris, 1953; tr. I. de Gastines as *Le Livre réunissant les deux sagesses*, Paris, 1990. Idem, *Šeš faṣl*, ed. and tr. W. Ivanow, Leiden, 1949. Idem, *Vajh-e din*, ed. Ḡ. R. Aʿvāni, Tehran, 1977. Idem, *Zād al-mosāferin*, ed. Badl-al-Raḥmān, Berlin, 1341/1923. S. H. Nasr and M. Aminrazavi, ed., *An Anthology of Philosophy in Persia*, II, Oxford, 2001. Neẓām-al-Molk, *Siar al-moluk (Siāsat-nāma)*, ed. H. Darke, 2nd ed.,

Tehran 1347 Š./1968; tr. H. Darke as *The Book of Government or Rules for Kings*, 2nd ed., London, 1978. Aḥmad b. Ebrāhim Nisāburi, *Estetār al-emām*, ed. W. Ivanow in *Bulletin of the Faculty of Arts, University of Egypt* IV, part 2, 1936, pp. 93-107; English tr. in Ivanow, 1942, pp. 157-83. Aḥmad b. ʿAbd al-Wahhāb Nowayri, *Nehāyat al-arab*, XXV, ed. M. J. ʿAbd al-Āl al-Ḥini, Cairo, 1984. *Pandiāt-e javānmardi*, ed. and tr. W. Ivanow, Leiden, 1953. Šehāb al-Din Aḥmad Qalqašandi, *Sobḥ al-aʿšā*, Cairo, 1331-38/1913-20. Qāżi Noʿmān b. Moḥammad, *Asās al-taʾwil*, ed. ʿĀ. Tāmer, Beirut, 1960. Idem, *Daʿāʾem al-Eslām*, ed. A. A. A. Fyzee, Cairo, 1951-61; Eng. tr. A. A. A. Fyzee, revised by I. K. Poonawala, as *The Pillars of Islam* I, Oxford, 2002. Idem, *Eftetāḥ al-daʿwa*, ed. W. al-Qāżi, Beirut 1970. Idem, *Ketāb al-majāles wa'l-mosāyarāt*, ed. al-Ḥabib al-Faqi et al., Beirut, 1978. Idem, *Taʾwil al-daʿāʾem*, ed. M. Ḥ. al-Aʿẓami, 3 vols., Cairo, 1967-72. Saʿd b. ʿAbd-Allāh Qomi, *Ketāb al-maqālāt wa'l-feraq*, ed. M. J. Maškur, Tehran, 1963. Rašid al-Din Fażl-Allāh, *Jāmeʿ al-tavāriḵ, qesmat-e Esmāʿiliān*, ed. M. T. Dānešpažuh and M. Modarresi Zanjāni, Tehran, 1338 Š./1959. Abu Ḥātem Rāzi, *Aʿlām al-nobowwa*, ed. Ṣ. al-Sāwi and Ḡ. R. Aʿvani, Tehran, 1977. Idem, *Ketāb al-eṣlāḥ*, ed. Ḥ. Minučehr and M. Moḥaghegh. Tehran, 1998. Šahrastāni. Idem, tr. Gimaret and Monnot. Šehāb al-Din Šāh-Ḥosayni, *Ḵetābāt-e ʿālia*, ed. H. Ojāqi, Bombay, 1963. Abu Yaʿqub Esḥāq b. Aḥmad Sejestāni, *Etbāt al-nobowwāt*, ed. ʿĀ. Tāmer, Beirut, 1966. Idem, *Kašf al-maḥjub*, ed. H. Corbin, Tehran and Paris, 1949; French tr. H. Corbin as *Le Dévoilement des choses cachées*, Lagrasse, 1988; Eng. tr. H. Landolt as *Unveiling of the Hidden*, in S. H. Nasr and M. Aminrazavi, ed., *An Anthology of Philosophy in Persia*, II, Oxford, 2001, pp. 71-137. Idem, *Ketāb al-efteḵār*, ed. I. K. Poonawala, Beirut, 2000. Idem, *Ketāb al-yanābiʿ*, ed. and French tr. H. Corbin, in his *Trilogie Ismaélienne*, Tehran and Paris, 1961, text pp. 1-97, tr. pp. 1-127; Eng. tr. P. E. Walker as *The Book of Wellsprings*, in his *The Wellsprings of Wisdom*, Salt Lake City, 1994, pp. 37-111. R. Strothmann, ed., *Gnosis Texte der Ismailiten*, Göttingen, 1943. Ṭabari. Idem, tr. Naṣir al-Din Moḥammad Ṭusi, *Rawżat al-taslim*, ed. and tr. W. Ivanow, Leiden, 1950; French tr. C. Jambet as *La Convocation d'Alamût*, Lagrasse, 1996. Idem, *Sayr va soluk*, ed. and tr. S. J. Badakhchani as *Contemplation and Action*, London, 1998. Aḥmad ʿAli Ḵān Vaziri, *Tāriḵ-e Kermān*, ed. M. E. Bāstāni-Pārizi, 2nd ed., Tehran 1352 Š. /1973. ʿAli b. Moḥammad al-Walid, *Tāj al-ʿaqāʾed*, ed. ʿĀ. Tāmer, Beirut, 1967. Moḥammad b. Moḥammad Yamāni, *Sirat al-Ḥājeb Jaʿfar b. ʿAli*, ed. W. Ivanow, in *Bulletin of the Faculty of Arts, University of Egypt*, IV, part 2, 1936, pp. 107-33; English tr. in Ivanow, 1942, pp. 184-223. S. Zakkār, ed., *Akḇār al-Qarāmeṭa*, 2nd ed., Damascus, 1982.

Studies. H. Algar, "The Revolt of Āghā Khān Maḥallātī and the Transference of the Ismāʿīlī Imamate to India," *Stud. Isl.* 29, 1969, pp. 55-81. H. M. Amiji, "The Asian Communities," in J. Kritzeck and W. H. Lewis, ed., *Islam in Africa*, New York, 1969, pp. 141-81. Idem, "The Bohras of East Africa," *Journal of Religion in Africa* 7, 1975, pp. 27-61. A. S. Asani, *Ecstasy and Enlightenment: The Ismaili Devotional Literature of South Asia*, London, 2002. Barthold, *Turkestan* 3. A. E. Berthels, *Nasir-i Khosrov i ismailizm*, Moscow, 1959; Persian tr. Y. Ārianpur as *Nāṣer-e Ḵosrow va Esmāʿiliān*, Tehran, 1346 Š./1967. T. Bianquis, "La prise du pouvoir par les Fatimides en Egypte (357-363/968-974)," *Annales Islamologiques* 11, 1972, pp. 49-108. M. Boivin, *Les Ismaéliens*, Paris, 1998. M. Brett, *The Rise of the Fatimids*, Leiden, 2001. D. R. W. Bryer, "The Origins of the Druze Religion," *Der Islam* 52, 1975, pp. 47-84, 239-62; 53, 1976, pp. 5-27. M. Canard, "L'Autobiographie d'un chambellan du Mahdi ʿObeidallāh le Faṭimide," *Hespéris* 39, 1952, pp. 279-324; repr. in idem, *Miscellanea Orientalia*, London, 1973, article V. Idem, "Fāṭimids," in *EI*[2], II, pp. 850-62. P. Casanova, "Les Derniers Fāṭimides," *Mémoires de la Mission Archéologique Française du Caire* 6, 1897, pp. 415-45. H. Corbin, "Nāṣir-i Khusrau and Iranian Ismāʿīlism," in *Camb. Hist. Iran* IV, pp. 520-42. Idem, "L'Initiation Ismaélienne ou l'ésotérisme et le Verbe," *Eranos Jahrbuch* 39, 1970, pp. 41-142; repr. in idem, *L'Homme et son ange*, Paris, 1983, pp. 81-205. Idem, *Cyclical Time and Ismaili Gnosis*, tr. R. Manheim and J. W. Morris, London, 1983. D. Cortese, *Ismaili and other Arabic Manuscripts: A Descriptive Catalogue of Manuscripts in the Library of The Institute of Ismaili Studies*, London, 2000. F. Dachraoui, *Le Califat Fatimide au Maghreb, 296-365 H./909-975 Jc.*, Tunis, 1981. F. Daftary, *The Ismāʿīlīs: Their History and Doctrines*, Cambridge, 1990 (with full references); Persian tr. F. Badraʾi, *Tāriḵ wa ʿaqāʾed-e Esmāʿiliya*, Tehran, 1375 Š./1996. Idem, "The Earliest Ismāʿīlīs," *Arabica* 38, 1991, pp. 214-45. Idem, "Persian Historiography of the Early Nizārī Ismāʿīlīs," *Iran* 30, 1992, pp. 91-97. Idem, "A Major Schism in the Early Ismāʿīlī Movement," *Stud. Isl.* 77, 1993, pp. 123-39. Idem, *The Assassin Legends: Myths of the Ismaʿilis*, London, 1994; Persian tr. F. Badraʾi, *Afsānahā-ye ḥašāšin*, Tehran, 1376 Š./1997. Idem, ed., *Mediaeval Ismaʿili History and Thought*, Cambridge, 1996. Idem, "The Ismaili *Daʿwa* outside the Fatimid *Dawla*," in M. Barrucand, ed., *L'Égypte Fatimide, son art et son histoire*, Paris, 1999, pp. 29-43. Idem, "Intellectual Life among the Ismailis: An Overview," in F. Daftary, ed., *Intellectual Traditions in Islam*, London, 2000, pp. 87-111. Idem, "The Medieval Ismāʿīlīs of the Iranian Lands," in C. Hillenbrand, ed., *Studies in Honour of Clifford Edmund Bosworth*, II, Leiden, 2000, pp. 43-81. Idem, "Esmāʿiliya," in *DMBE* VIII, pp. 681-702. A. Foʾād Sayyed, *al-Dawla al-Fāṭemiya fi Meṣr*, 2nd ed., Cairo, 2000. W. Frischauer, *The Aga Khans*, London, 1970. S. Guyard, "Un Grand maître des Assassins au temps de Saladin," *JA* 7 série, 9, 1877, pp. 324-489. H. Halm, *Kosmologie und Heilslehre der frühen Ismāʿīlīya*, Wiesbaden, 1978. Idem, "Die Söhne Zikrawaihs und das erste fatimidische Kalifat (290/903)," *Die Welt des Orients* 10, 1979, pp. 30-53. Idem, "Les Fatimides à Salamya," *REI* 54, 1986, pp. 133-49. Idem, *Shiism*, tr. J. Watson, Edinburgh, 1991, pp. 162-205. Idem, *The Empire of the Mahdi: The Rise of the Fatimids*, tr. M. Bonner, Leiden, 1996. Idem, "The Ismaʿili Oath of Allegiance (*ʿahd*) and the 'Sessions of Wisdom' (*majālis al-ḥikma*) in Fatimid Times," in Daftary, ed., 1996, pp. 91-115. Idem, *The Fatimids and their Traditions of Learning*, London, 1997. A. Hamdani, *The Beginnings of the Ismāʿīlī Daʿwa in Northern India*, Cairo, 1956. Idem, "The Dāʿī Ḥātêm Ibn Ibrāhīm al-Ḥāmidī (d. 596H./1199A.D.) and his *Tuḥfat al-Qulūb*," *Oriens* 23-24, 1970-71, pp. 258-300. Idem, "Evolution of the Organisational Structure of the Fāṭimī Daʿwah," *Arabian Studies* 3, 1976, pp. 85-114. A. Hamdani and F. de Blois, "A Re-Examination of al-Mahdī's Letter to the Yemenites on the Genealogy of the Fatimid Caliphs," *JRAS*, 1983, pp. 173-207. Ḥ. F. al-Hamdāni, *al-Ṣolayḥeyyun wa'l-ḥaraka al-Fāṭemiya fe'l-Yaman*, Cairo, 1955. C. Hillenbrand, "The Power Struggle between the Saljuqs and the Ismaʿilis of Alamut, 487-518/1094-1124: The Saljuq Perspective," in Daftary, ed., 1996, pp. 205-20. M. G. S. Hodgson, *The Order of Assassins*, The Hague, 1955; Persian tr. F. Badraʾi, *Ferqa-ye Esmāʿiliya*, 2nd ed., Tehran, 1369 Š./1990. Idem, "The Ismāʿīlī State," in *Camb. Hist. Iran*, V, pp. 422-82. J. N. Hollister, *The Shiʿa of India*, London, 1953. A. C. Hunsberger, *Nasir Khusraw, The Ruby of Badakhshan*, London, 2000. ḤasanʿAli Ismāʿilji, *Akbār al-doʿāt al-akramin*, Rajkot, 1937. W. Ivanow, "A Forgotten Branch of the Ismailis," *JRAS*, 1938, pp. 57-79. Idem, *Ismaili Tradition concerning the Rise of the Fatimids*, London, etc., 1942. Idem, *The Alleged Founder of Ismailism*, Bombay, 1946. Idem, *Nasir-i Khusraw and Ismailism*, Bombay, 1948. Idem, *Studies in Early Persian Ismailism*, 2nd ed., Bombay, 1955. Idem, *Ismaili Literature: A Bibliographical Survey*, Tehran, 1963. N. Eboo Jamal, *Surviving the Mongols: Nizārī Quhistānī and the Continuity of Ismaili Tradition in Persia*, London, 2002. C. Jambet, *La Grande résurrection d'Alamût*, Lagrasse, 1990. V. Klemm, *Die Mission des fāṭimidischen Agenten al-Muʾayyad fī d-dīn in Šīrāz*, Frankfurt, etc., 1989. Y. Lev, *State and Society in Fatimid Egypt*, Leiden, 1991. B. Lewis, *The Origins of Ismāʿīlism*, Cambridge, 1940. B. Lewis, *The Assassins*, London, 1967; Persian tr. F. Badraʾi, *Fedāʾiān-e Esmāʿili*, Tehran, 1348 Š./1969. S. T. Lokhandwalla, "The Bohras, a Muslim Community of Gujarat," *Stud. Isl.* 3, 1955, pp. 117-35. W. Madelung, "Fatimiden und Baḥrainqarmaṭen," *Der Islam* 34, 1959, pp. 34-88; English version, "The Fatimids and the Qarmaṭīs of Baḥrayn," in Daftary, ed., 1996, pp. 21-73. Idem, "Das Imamat in der frühen ismailitischen Lehre," *Der Islam* 37, 1961, pp. 43-135. Idem, "Aspects of Ismāʿīlī Theology: The Prophetic Chain and the God Beyond Being," in Nasr, ed., 1977, pp. 51-65; repr. in idem, *Religious Schools and Sects in Medieval Islam*, London, 1985, article XVII. Idem, *Religious Trends in Early Islamic Iran*, Albany, NY, 1988, pp. 93-105. Idem, "The Religious Policy of the Fatimids toward their Sunnī Subjects in the Maghrib," in M. Barrucand, ed., *L'Égypte Fatimide, son art et son histoire*, Paris, 1999, pp. 97-104. Idem, "Ismāʿīliyya," in EI^2, IV, 1973, pp. 198-206. G. C. Miles, "Coins of the Assassins of Alamūt," *Orientalia Lovaniensia Periodica* 3, 1972, pp. 155-62. N. A. Mirza, *Syrian Ismailism*, Richmond, Surrey, 1997. S. C. Misra, *Muslim Communities in Gujarat*, Bombay, 1964. F. Mitha, *Al-Ghazālī and the Ismailis*, London, 2001. A. Nanji, "Modernization and Change in the Nizari Ismaili Community in East Africa—A Perspective," *Journal of Religion in Africa* 6, 1974, pp. 123-39. Idem, *The Nizārī Ismāʿīlī Tradition in the Indo-Pakistan Subcontinent*, Delmar, NY, 1978. Idem, "Ismāʿīlism," in S. H. Nasr, ed., *Islamic Spirituality: Foundations*, London, 1987, pp. 179-98. Idem, "Ismāʿīlī Philosophy," in S. H. Nasr and O. Leaman, ed., *History of Islamic Philosophy*, London, 1996, I, pp. 144-54. S. H. Nasr, ed., *Ismāʿīlī Contributions to Islamic Culture*, Tehran, 1977. I. K. Poonawala, *Biobibliography of Ismāʿīlī Literature*, Malibu, Calif, 1977. N. Pourjavady and P. L. Wilson, "Ismāʿīlīs and Niʿmatullāhīs," *Stud. Isl.* 41, 1975, pp. 113-35. D. de Smet, *La Quiètude de l'intellect: Néoplatonisme et gnose Ismaélienne dans l'oeuvre de Ḥamīd ad-Dīn al-Kirmānī (X^e/XIes.)*, Louvain, 1995. S. M. Stern, "Ismāʿīlī Propaganda and Fatimid Rule in Sind," *Islamic Culture* 23, 1949, pp. 298-307. Idem, "The Succession to the Fatimid Imam al-Āmir, the Claims of the Later Fatimids to the Imamate, and the Rise of Ṭayyibī Ismailism," *Oriens* 4, 1951, pp. 193-255; repr. in idem, *History and Culture in the Medieval Muslim World*, London, 1984, article XI. Idem, "Heterodox Ismāʿīlism at the Time of al-Muʿizz," *BSOAS* 17, 1955, pp. 10-33. Idem, "The Early Ismāʿīlī Missionaries in North-West Persia and in Khurāsān and Transoxania," *BSOAS* 23, 1960, pp. 56-90. Idem, "Ismāʿīlīs and Qarmaṭians," in *L' Élaboration de l'Islam*, Paris, 1961, pp. 99-108. Idem, "Cairo as the Centre of the Ismāʿīlī Movement," in *Colloque international sur l'histoire du Caire*, 1972, pp. 437-50. Idem, *Studies in Early Ismāʿīlism*, Jerusalem and Leiden, 1983. L. V. Stroeva, *Gosudarstvo ismailitov v Irane v XI-XIIIvv.*, Moscow, 1978; Persian tr. P. Monzavi, *Tārik-e Esmāʿiliān dar Īrān*, Tehran, 1371 Š./1992. P. E. Walker, "Eternal Cosmos and the Womb of History: Time in Early Ismaili Thought," *IJMES* 9, 1978, pp. 355-66. Idem, *Early Philosophical Shiism: The Ismaili Neoplatonism of Abū Yaʿqūb al-Sijistānī*, Cambridge, 1993. Idem, *Abū Yaʿqūb al-Sijistānī: Intellectual Missionary*, London, 1996. Idem, "Fatimid Institutions of Learning," *Journal of the American Research Center in Egypt* 34, 1997, pp. 179-200. Idem, "The Ismāʿīlī Daʿwa and the Fāṭimid Caliphate," in M. W. Daly, ed., *The Cambridge History of Egypt*: Volume 1, *Islamic Egypt, 640-1517*, ed. C. F. Petry, Cambridge, 1998, pp. 120-50. Idem, *Ḥamīd al-Dīn al-Kirmānī: Ismaili Thought in the Age of al-Ḥākim*, London, 1999. Idem, *Exploring an Islamic Empire: Fatimid History and Its*

Sources, London, 2002. Zāhed ʿAli, *Hamāri Esmāʿili maḏhab*, Hyderabad, 1373/1954.

(FARHAD DAFTARY)

iv. QARĀMEṬA. See CARMATIANS.

v. ISMAʿILI DAʿWA AND DYNASTY OF FAṬEMIDS. See FATIMIDS.

vi. ISMAʿILI IDEAS OF TIME. See DAWR.

vii. ISMAʿILI IDEAS OF COSMOLOGY AND COSMOGONY. See COSMOLOGY AND COSMOGONY vii.

viii. FREE WILL IN ISMAʿILISM. See FREE WILL ii.

ix. ISMAʿILI MISSIONARIES. See DĀʿI.

x. ISMAʿILI MYTHS AND LEGENDS. See FEDĀʾIS.

xi. ISMAʿILI JURISPRUDENCE

A distinct Ismaʿili system of jurisprudence was founded after the establishment of the Fatimid dynasty in North Africa. The pre-Fatimid Ismaʿilis, as a secret revolutionary organization, were preoccupied in various parts of the ʿAbbasid empire with missionary activities, promising the advent of the expected messianic figure called Mahdi and Qāʾem who would restore justice and equity. Toward this goal, they developed a highly sophisticated gnostic system of thought, wherein the *bāṭeni* (esoteric) sciences were more emphasized than the *ẓāheri* (exoteric) sciences (see BĀṬENIYA). Law not only belonged to the latter category. but also had very little practical use as long as the Ismaʿilis had not obtained political power. Hence, it was not a priority at that stage. This, however, does not mean that they completely neglected law. The early Ismaʿilis shared a common heritage with other Shiʿites, especially the Imamis up to the death of the Imam Jaʿfar al-Ṣādeq in 148/765. Thus, they shared with the Zaydis as well as the Imamis certain rituals and practices that had evolved until then. Recent scholarship has demonstrated that Imam Moḥammad al-Bāqer (q.v.) played a major role in the shaping of Shiʿite jurisprudence (Lalani, pp. 114-26), which became crystallized during the time of his son Imam Jaʿfar al-Ṣādeq and was known as *maḏhab Ahl al-Bayt* (rite of jurisprudence from the family of the Prophet; see AHL-E BAYT). It should be also noted that both the Ismaʿilis and the Imamis consider Imam Moḥammad al-Bāqer and his son Imam Jaʿfar al-Ṣādeq as the founders of their respective systems of law, because most of the traditions in Qāżi Noʿmān's *Daʿāʾem al-Eslām* and Abu Jaʿfar Moḥammad Kolayni's *Ketāb al-kāfi* are traced back to these Imams. This school of jurisprudence was not in favor of *raʾy* (personal opinion) or *qiās* (analogical deduction), both of which prevailed in the contemporary circles of the Sunni jurisconsults (*faqih*). The Ismaʿilis share certain ritualistic features with other Shiʿites, such as the wiping of the feet in ablution, saying *basmala* (i.e., the formula *beʾsm Allāh al-raḥmān al-raḥim*) aloud in recitation of the Qurʾan and during obligatory prayers, and addition of the formula *ḥayya ʿalā ḵayr al-ʿamal* (come to the best of work) in the call to prayer (*aḏān*; Lalani, pp. 120-24).

Soon after his triumphant entry into Qayrawān in 296/909, Abu ʿAbd Allāh Šiʿi, the founder of the Fatimid dynasty, appointed Moḥammad b. ʿOmar Marvazi, a local Shiʿite figure, as judge (*qāżi*). Marvazi imposed strict adherence to the above Shiʿite rituals and legal practices. Moreover, he ordered the omission of *al-ṣalāt ḵayr men al-nawm* (prayer is better than sleep) from the morning call to prayer and prohibited the *tarāwiḥ* prayers led by an imam during the month of Ramażān. In the Friday sermon (*ḵoṭba*) he added the blessings (*ṣalāt*) on Imam ʿAli, Fāṭema, Imam Ḥasan, and Imam Ḥosayn immediately after the blessings on the Prophet. He also issued an order forbidding jurists to give legal opinions except according to the Shiʿite *maḏhab* (school); declared *ṭalāq al-batta* (irrevocable divorce) invalid, and upheld the right of a daughter to inherit the whole of her father's estate, to the exclusion of *ʿaṣāba* (agnates), in the absence of a son (Ebn al-Hayṯam, pp. 64-67; Māleki, II, pp. 41, 55-56, 60-62; Ebn ʿEẕāri, I, pp. 151, 159, 173).

Unfortunately, we have no information about legal compositions of Marvazi or his immediate successors in the office of *qażāʾ Efriqiya*. One can only surmise that some of those judges might have written law manuals hoping that their works would be recognized officially. Even if they did, their works were overshadowed by that those of Qāżi Noʿmān and soon fell into disuse and were lost.

Qāżi Noʿmān, an Ismaʿili Shiʿite from Qayrawān, entered the service of the Fatimid dynasty at an early age and served the first four caliphs consecutively for over half a century, from 312/924 until his death in 363/974, in various capacities. He was commissioned by the fourth caliph al-Moʿezz le-Din-Allāh (r. 341-65/953-75) to compose the *Daʿāʾem al-Eslām*, his magnum opus, which was officially promulgated as the Fatimid code. He is, therefore, rightly regarded by the Ismaʿilis as the one who propounded their law. Qāżi Noʿmān had also composed several legal works based on the *maḏhab* of the Ahl al-Bayt. In his first and voluminous *Ketāb al-iżāḥ*, which has reached us in abridged versions, his efforts were directed to the collection and classification of a vast number of legal traditions transmitted from the family of the Prophet. He compiled this work from all the available sources. This early and massive work consisting of 3,000 folios could be seen as an attempt by Qāżi Noʿmān to lay the foundation on which Ismaʿili law could then be built. Consequently, he made several abridgments of the *Ketāb al-iżāḥ*, namely *Ketāb al-aḵbār* (or *al-eḵbār*), *Moḵtaṣar al-iżāḥ*, *al-Orjuza al-montaḵaba*, *Ketāb al-eqteṣār*, and *Ketāb al-eḵteṣār* (or *Moḵtaṣar al-āṯār*, or *Eḵteṣār al-āṯār*). In addition to those legal texts he also wrote refutations of the Sunni schools of jurisprudence and their founders, such as Mālek b. Anas, Abu Ḥanifa, and Šāfeʿi (for the chronology of these works and the development of Noʿmān's thought, see Poonawala, 1996, pp. 119-24). In his *Eḵtelāf oṣul al-maḏāheb* (p. 22), Qāżi Noʿmān cites the decree of al-Moʿezz le-Din-Allāh, wherein he is instructed by the latter about the roots of jurisprudence. It states that, in issuing his legal decisions, Qāżi Noʿmān should first follow the Qurʾān, next, the tradition (*sonna*) of the Prophet, and for what is not found in either of them he should turn to the *mad̲hab* of the Imams from the family of the Prophet. If something still remains doubtful and difficult to resolve, he should refer the matter to the Imam. In his *Ketāb al-eqteṣār* (p. 167) and *Ketāb al-ek̲teṣār*, Qāżi Noʿmān proposes the same principles for issuing legal decisions and rejects *raʾy* and *qiās*.

The *Daʿāʾem*, according to ʿEmād-al-Din Edris (d. 872/1468), a Mostaʿli-Ṭayyebi *dāʿi* and a historian, was closely supervised by the Caliph-Imam al-Moʿezz himself (Edris, p. 44). The work follows the general pattern of law manuals and is divided into two volumes. The first deals with the acts of devotion and religious observances (*ʿebādāt*) while the second with laws pertaining to human intercourse (*moʿāmalāt*). Qāżi Noʿmān states on the authority of Imam Jaʿfar al-Ṣādeq that Islam was founded on seven pillars, that is, *walāya* (devotion to the imam), *ṭahāra* (ritual purity), *ṣalāt* (prayers), *zakāt* (welfare tax), *ṣawm* (fasting in the month of Ramażān), *ḥajj* (pilgrimage to Mecca), and *jehād* (holy war). *Walāya*, the corner-stone of Ismaʿili faith, embodies the doctrine of the imamate that lies at the basis of Shiʿism, and Qāżi Noʿmān transformed it into a dynamic principle after the establishment of the Fatimid caliphate. It is considered the highest and the noblest of the seven pillars, without which no human acts of devotion and worship are acceptable to God. It should be noted that, unlike with the Ismaʿilis, *walāya* did not become part of the Imami legal works. The *Daʿāʾem* was therefore the first juristic text to give *walāya* a legal status in Islamic law. For the Ismaʿilis and the newly founded Fatimid dynasty, it was not merely a religious belief but was the very basis of their claim to the political leadership of the Muslim community. In the chapter on *jehād*, Qāżi Noʿmān included the *ʿahd* (a command document) ascribed to Imam ʿAli b. Abi Ṭāleb (Daʿāʾem, tr., I, pp. 436-56), which deals with the ruler's conduct with his subjects. This document, according to Wadād al-Qāżi (p. 104), represents the Ismaʿili theory of the state. *Ṭahāra*, which implies physical and spiritual purification and is a necessary requirement for the valid performance of prayers, was raised by Qāżi Noʿmān to the status of an independent pillar (*deʿāma*, pl. *daʿāʾem*).

The *Daʿāʾem*, as a law manual, addresses matters of substantive law, hence, Qāżi Noʿmān restricted the authorities to Imam Jaʿfar al-Ṣādeq and his predecessors. In this work he does not deal with the day-to-day running of the state, where the ultimate authority was the ruling imam. The sources of law, according to Qāżi Noʿmān, are the Qurʾān, the tradition (*sonna*) of the Prophet, and the teachings or rulings of the Imams. The major differences with Imami (Twelver Shiʿites) law are that Qāżi Noʿmān admitted the prohibition of temporary marriage (*motʿa*), and the introduction of a fixed calendar rather than sighting the new moon for the beginning and end of Ramażān (*Daʿāʾem*, tr., I, p. 339, II, p. 214). The *Daʿāʾem* is considered by the Mostaʿli-Ṭayyebi Ismaʿilis as the greatest authority on their law and has remained until today a source of supreme authority in legal matters.

Ebn Kelles (d. 380/991), vizier of the caliph al-ʿAziz, is credited to have composed a legal work based on the pronouncements of al-Moʿezz and al-ʿAziz (r. 365-86/975-96), but the work did not survive. After Qāżi Noʿmān, there was no significant development in Ismaʿili law either during the remainder of the Fatimid rule in Egypt or in Yemen, where the Mostaʿli-Ṭayyebi community survived for the next four centuries after the fall of the Fatimids in Egypt (567/1171) and the Ṣulayhids in Yemen (532/1138). It was in India that the works of Qāżi Noʿmān were glossed. Aminji b. Jalāl (d. 1010/1602), an eminent jurist, deserves special mention in this respect. His *Ketāb al-soʾāl wa'l-jawāb* (Majduʿ, pp. 37-38) is an interesting collection of legal questions and their answers. Another noteworthy work is the anonymous *Ketāb al-soʾāl wa'l-jawāb le-mašāʾek̲ al-Hend maʿ al-ḥawāši men kotob al-Qāżi al-Noʿmān* (Majduʿ, p. 37), which consists of questions put to the contemporary *dāʿis* and other *daʿwa* dignitaries and the answers given by them. In addition, it contains extensive excerpts from the works of Qāżi Noʿmān that have not survived, especially *Ketāb al-iżāḥ* and *Mok̲taṣar al-iżāḥ*. Another anonymous work worth mentioning is *Taqwim* (or *Taqāwim*) *al-aḥkām* (Majduʿ, pp. 36-37), wherein various topics in law concerning what is permitted and what is forbidden are arranged in a novel way. All the latter three works reiterate that *raʾy* and *qiās* are not permitted. Hence, they give answers to the questions posed in the form of a ruling, however, without going into the details of methodology as to how the authorities arrived at those answers.

One can thus conclude that Ismaʿili jurisprudence began with Qāżi Noʿmān and ended with him. Before him, there was no distinct Ismaʿili jurisprudence, and after him there was no significant development except glosses, repetition, and restatement.

Bibliography: Anonymous, *Ketāb al-soʾāl wa 'l-jawāb le-mašāʾek̲ al-Hend maʿ al-ḥawāši men kotob al-Qāżi al-Noʿmān*, 2 vols., ms. in the collection of Mollā Qorbān Ḥosayn Godhrawala. Anonymous, *Taqwim al-aḥkām*, Ms. in the collection of Mollā Qorbān Ḥosayn Godhrawala. Aminji b. Jalāl, *Ketāb al-soʾāl wa'l-jawāb aw Masāʾel Aminji b. Jalāl*, ms. in the collection of Mollā Qorbān Ḥosayn Godhrawala. Ebn al-Hayṯam, *Ketāb al-monāẓarāt*, ed. and tr. Wilferd Madelung and Paul Ernest Walker as *The Advent of the Fatimids: A Contemporary Shiʿi Witness*, London, 2000, pp. 66-67. Ebn ʿEẕāri Marrākoši, *al-Bayān al-mog̲reb fi ak̲bār moluk al-Andalus wa'l-Mag̲reb*, ed. G. S. Colin and E. Lévi-Provençal as *Histoire de l'Afrique du nord et de l'Espagne musulmane . . . et fragments de la Chronique de ʿArib*, new ed., 2 vols., Leiden, 1948-51, I, pp. 151, 159, 173. ʿEmād al-Din Edris b. ʿAbd-Allāh, *ʿOyun al-akbār wa-fonun al-āṯār* VI, ed. Moṣṭafā G̲āleb, Beirut, 1404/1984, pp. 35-50. Asaf A. A. Fyzee, *Compendium of Fatimid Law*, Simla, 1969. Arzina R.

Lalani, *Early Shiʿi Thought: The Teachings of Imam Muḥammad al-Bāqir*, London, 2000, pp. 114-26. Wilferd Madelung, "The Sources of Ismāʿili Law," *JNES* 35, 1976, pp. 29-40. Idem, "ʿAbd Allāh b. ʿAbbās and Shiʿite Law," in U. Vermeulen and J. van Reeth, eds., *Law, Christianity and Modernism in Islamic Society: Proceedings of the Eighteenth Congress of the Union Européenne des Arabisants et Islamisants*, held at the Katholoieke Universiteit Leuven, Sept. 3-9, 1996, Leuven, 1998, pp. 13-25. Esmāʿil b. ʿAbd-al-Rasul Majduʿ, *Fahrasat al-kotub wa'l-rasāʾel*, ed. ʿAli-Naqi Monzawi, Tehran, 1966, pp. 18-38. ʿAbd Allāh b. Moḥammad Māleki, *Riāż al-nofus fi ṭabaqāt ʿolamāʾ al-Qayrawān wa Efriqiya*, ed. Bašir Bakkuš, 3 vols., Beirut, 1983, II, pp. 41, 55-56, 60-62. Abu Ḥanifa Qāżi Noʿmān b. Moḥammad Tamimi, *Daʿāʾem al-Eslām fi ḏekr al-ḥalāl wa'l-ḥarām wa'l-qażāya wa'l-aḥkām*, ed. ʿĀṣaf A. A. Fayżi (Fyzee), 2 vols., Cairo, 1951-61; tr. A. A. A. Fyzee, as *The Pillars of Islam*, completely revised and annotated by Ismail K. Poonawala, 2 vols., New Delhi, 2002-4. Idem, *Ketāb al-eqteṣār*, ed. Moḥammad Waḥid Mirzā, Damascus, 1376/1957, p. 167. Idem, Idem, *Ketāb eḵtelāf oṣūl al-maḏāheb*, ed. S. T. Lokhandwalla, Simla, 1972. pp. 19-24. Ismail K. Poonawala, *Biobibliography of Ismāʿili Literature*, Malibu, Calif., 1977, pp. 48-68, 78-79, 185. Idem, "Al-Qāżi al-Nuʿmān and Ismaʿili Jurisprudence," in Farhad Daftary, ed., *Medieval Ismaʿili History and Thought*, Cambridge, 1996, pp. 117-43. Rudolf Strothmann, "Recht der Ismailiten," *Der Islam* 42, 1954, pp. 131-46. Wadād al-Qāżi, "An Early Fāṭimid Political Document," *Studia Islamica* 48, 1978, pp. 71-108.

(ISMAIL K. POONAWALA)

xii. ISMAʿILI HADITH. See HADITH iii.

xiii. ISMAʿILI LITERATURE IN PERSIAN AND ARABIC

Ismaʿili literature ("literature" is used here in its wider sense to include all the written products of scholarly disciplines delineated by learning, religion, and science) refers to the literary production of more than a millennium, from the middle of the 3rd/9th century (i.e., before the advent of the Fatimids in 909 in North Africa) to recent times. It deals with the writings of Ismaʿili missionaries (*doʿāt*, pl. of *dāʿi*) and religious dignitaries, either sponsored by the *daʿwa* (religio-political organization), or the Fatimid regime, or composed independently. Geographically, it covers wide regions stretching from North Africa to India, wherever Ismaʿili missions operated actively and were able to maintain a foothold through local converts and their support. The Fatimids (297-567/909-1171) were great patrons of learning and their newly founded capital, Cairo (al-Qāhera, i.e., the victorious), soon became a rival of older centers like Baghdad as a seat of learning and intellectual activity. Ismaʿili literature produced during the pre-Fatimid and Fatimid periods, often referred to as the classical period, with the exception of Nāṣer(-e) Ḵosrow's works, is almost exclusively in Arabic.

After the fall of the Fatimids in Egypt, the Ismaʿilis of Yemen, known as the Mostaʿli-Ṭayyebi daʿwa, continued this tradition of producing Ismaʿili works in Arabic. It should be noted that from the very beginning of the Ismaʿili religio-political movement, Yemen had become an Ismaʿili stronghold. Although the first Ismaʿili state founded there by Ebn Ḥawšab (q.v.), generally known as Manṣur al-Yaman, disintegrated through inner dissentions at the beginning of the 10th century, and hence before the advent of the Fatimids in North Africa, the religious component of the mission survived and achieved new success under ʿAli b. Moḥammad Ṣolayḥi, who founded the Sulayhid dynasty in 439/1047. The Sulayhids, adherents of Ismaʿili faith and nominal vassals of the Fatimids of Egypt, ruled Yemen until 1138, first from their capital Ṣanʿāʾ, in the north, and then from Ḏi Jebla, in the south. With the waning of their power, the Ismaʿili Mostaʿli-Ṭayyebi community not only survived, but their stronghold in Ḥaraz became the headquarters of the daʿwa for the next four centuries. It was this Yemeni community that preserved a great portion of the classical Ismaʿili heritage and writing by copying and studying those works; as well as augmenting and enriching this literature through their own original contributions in various disciplines of learning. In 1567, following the death of the first Indian dāʿi, Yusof b. Solaymān, in Ṭayba in Yemen, the headquarters of the Mostaʿli-Ṭayyebi daʿwa was moved to Gujarat, on the west coast of India. In the wake of this move most of the Ismaʿili literature, preserved from the classical period and produced later in Yemen, was also transferred to India. The Bohras, Indian converts to Mostaʿali-Ṭayyebi daʿwa, continued the Arabic tradition by diligently copying and studying those earlier works, and at times commenting on them. Al-Jāmeʿa al-Sayfiya, a well-known seminary for the Dāʾudi Bohras, established by the dāʿi ʿAbd-e ʿAli Sayf-al-Din in 1814 for the religious education of the community, has continued the Arabic tradition to the present day. Beside preserving a major portion of Ismaʿili literature produced in North Africa, Egypt, Yemen and elsewhere, the learned Bohra shaiks have put their own stamp on whatever they have added. The Arabic tradition also prevailed in the Nezāri Ismaʿili communities of Syria. They had succeeded in acquiring fortresses in the mountains of central Syria where they ruled from about 1100 to 1273, the year when their power was terminated by the Mamluk ruler of Egypt and Syria, Malek Ẓāher Baybars. Though the Syrian Nezāri community survived the adversity, they only succeed in preserving a very minute portion of the Fatimid heritage.

The Persian tradition in Ismaʿili literature, started by Nāṣer(-e) Ḵosrow, on the other hand, was continued exclusively by the reformed Ismaʿilism of Alamut, that is, the Persian Nezāris. The Nezāri branch originated from internal dissension among the Ismaʿilis over the issue of succession to the caliph-Imam Monstanṣer in 1094.

Ḥasan(-e) Ṣabbāḥ (q.v.), an Ismaʿili dāʿi who had succeeded in gaining control of the strong mountain fortress of Alamut in Rudbār, in 1090, later broke off his relations with the Fatimids of Egypt in support of the claims of Nezār b. al-Mostanṣer. Ḥasan Ṣabbāḥ expounded in Persian his new doctrine of *taʿlim*, that in religious faith one has to accept absolute authority of the teacher, that is, the Imam. Persian continued to be the language of the Nezāri state founded by Ḥasan Ṣabbāḥ until its destruction by the advancing Mongols in 1256. The Persian Nezāris used Persian in their religious writings. They not only abandoned Arabic but also did not show much interest in the preservation of the earlier heritage that was in Arabic. The Persian tradition continued among the Nezāri communities that survived the Mongol onslaught in various parts of Persian speaking regions. Considerations of space do not allow a detailed description of Ismaʿili literature, hence only the most prominent aspects will be highlighted and only their most outstanding representatives will be enumerated here.

In Arabic. In their classification of various "sciences" or fields of learning, Muslim writers generally make a distinction between the "religious sciences" (*al-ʿolum al-šarʿiya* also called *al-ʿolum al-naqliya*, "traditional sciences") and the "foreign sciences" (*ʿolum al-ʿajam min al-Yunāniyin wa-ḡayrehem men al-omam*, also called *al-ʿolum al-ʿaqliya*). The former includes Qurʾānic exegesis (*tafsir*), tradition (Hadith), theology (*ʿelm-e kalām*), jurisprudence (*feqh*), and other sciences, such as Arabic grammar, philology, rhetoric, and historiography that developed from them. The latter, that is, the so-called "foreign sciences," include mathematics, natural sciences, medicine, astronomy, philosophy, etc. The Ismaʿilis, on the other hand, draw a fundamental distinction between the *ẓāher* and the *bāṭen*, the two aspects of religion. The ẓāher consists of exterior expressions of religion as laid down in the law (*šariʿa*) and explains the literal meaning of the Qurʾān. The ẓāher changes with each prophet in accordance with time and circumstances, whereas the bāṭen, comprised of the inner, true meaning of the Qurʾān and the šariʿa, remains unchanged. The prophet receives the revelation (*tanzil*), transmits it to the people and lays down the šariʿa, while it is the Imam who expounds the inner, esoteric meaning of the Qurʾān and the šariʿa through *taʾwil* (hermeneutics). The principle of hermeneutics developed by a number of outstanding dāʿis, such as Jaʿfar b. Ebn al-Ḥawšab, Qāżi Noʿmān b. Moḥammad, and Abu Yaʿqub Sejestāni, became the major method of Ismaʿili doctrine, so much so that it has come to be regarded as typical and characteristic of Ismaʿili thought. It was for this reason that the Ismaʿilis were often called *bāṭeniya*. Taʾwil begins as a method of verbal interpretation and consists in going from the surface level (ẓāher, exterior) of a given linguistic term or expression to the depth (bāṭen, interior) of its meaning. Ismaʿili taʾwil is not, therefore, a simple matter of verbal interpretation, rather it has an important ontological significance. For in Ismaʿili doctrine, whatever exists in the physical world conceals in its ontological depths an inner reality. Thus, the Is-maʿilis classify sciences into two major categories: *ẓāheri* sciences, and *bāṭeni* sciences. The former comprises of Arabic language and grammar, poetry, history, jurisprudence, and related disciplines; while the latter comprises of taʾwil and *ḥaqāʾeq* (lit. truth, reality). The highest level of knowledge is, therefore, called ḥaqāʾeq or *ʿelm al-ḥaqāʾeq* (the knowledge of the truth) which represents the ultimate cosmological and eschatological system of the Ismaʿili doctrine. Despite this twofold division of sciences and religion, they emphasize that both are complimentary to each other, and one cannot exist without the other. Ismaʿili literature is therefore overwhelmingly religious in character. In other words, it is heavily tinged with their particular ideology.

The earliest extant writings, such as the *Ketāb al-kašf* (The book of revelation), *Ketāb al-rošd wa'l-hedāya* (The book of proper conduct and guidance), and *Ketāb al-ʿālem wa'l-ḡolām* (The book of the master and the disciple), ascribed either to Ebn al-Ḥawšab or his son Jaʿfar, give us insights into the theory of the imamate, the practices of the mission, the technique used for the esoteric interpretation, and a partial picture of the entire framework of their doctrines. Another important work from the early period that occupies a unique position in the history of Islamic thought and exercised a great influence on the Muslim elite is *Rasāʾel ekwān al-ṣafāʾ wa-kollān al-wafāʾ* (the epistles of the brethren of purity). *Ekwān al-ṣafāʾ* (q.v.) was a pseudonym assumed by the authors of this well-known encyclopedia who described themselves as a group of fellow-seekers after truth. They deliberately concealed their Ismaʿili identity so that their treatises could gain wider currency and appeal to a broader cross-section of the society. The philosophical system of the *Rasāʾel* is a synthesis of reason (*ʿaql*) and revelation (*waḥy*), wherein the cosmos is viewed as a unified whole. The philosophical structure and the cosmology are derived from Neoplatonic and Neo-Pythagorean sources. The *Rasāʾel* offered a new political order headed by an ʿAlid Imam. Their utopia, referred to as *al-madina al-fāżela al-ruḥāniya* (the spiritual, virtuous city) or *dawlat ahl al-kayr* (the governance of virtuous people), was to be governed by a lawgiving philosopher-prophet or his spiritual successor. The organization and arrangement of the *Rasāʾel* and their classification of the sciences, although somewhat different from the twofold division into the ẓāheri and the bāṭeni, reflect their ultimate objective.

Conspicuously absent from Ismaʿili literature are the two important branches of Islamic sciences, Hadith and tafsir, classified as branches of the ẓāheri sciences. The reason for their absence could be explained by the fact that, after the establishment of the Fatimid dynasty, the imamate as conceived by Ismaʿili doctrine, unlike what happened in the case of the Imāmis (i.e., the Twelver Shiʿites), became a living institution. It implied that as long as the Imam (i.e., the Fatimid caliph-imam), who represented the living *sonna* of the Prophet was accessible, there was no need for the compilation of Hadith and tafsir. The traditions needed for clarification of the šariʿa and handed down by the Imams, were collected by Qāżi Noʿmān in his *Daʿāʾem al-eslām*, hence there was no further need for them. As for the external philological meaning of the Qurʾān, any tafsir could be used. Its inner true meaning, however, could be obtained only through the taʾwil derived from the rightful Imam. For this reason, the Imam, the repository of true knowledge and the authoritative interpreter of the Qurʾān, is often called "the speaking Qurʾān" (*Qorʾān-e nāṭeq*), while the Qurʾān, since it needs an interpreter, is called "the silent Qurʾān" (*Qorʾān-e ṣāmet*). There are numerous works on taʾwil that deal with specific verses or chapters of the Qurʾān. Qāżi Noʿmān's *Asās al-taʾwil* (the foundation of taʾwil), *Taʾwil al-daʿāʾem* (Taʾwil of the pillars), and *Taʾwil al-šariʿa* (Taʾwil of the canon law of Islam) and Jaʿfar b. Manṣur al-Yaman's *Sarāʾer al-noṭaqāʾ* or *Asrār al-noṭaqāʾ* (Secrets of the *noṭaqāʾ*, i.e., the major prophets), *Ketāb al-farāʾeż wa ḥodud al-din* (the book of religious duties and the hierarchy of the daʿwa), *Ketāb al-reżāʿ fi'l-bāṭen* (the book of the inner meaning of foster relationship), *Ketāb taʾwil al-zakāt* (the book of the esoteric interpretation of the alms tax), and *Taʾwil surat al-nesāʾ* (the esoteric interpretation of the Qurʾānic chapter on women) are noteworthy works of taʾwil from the early period. Sejestāni's *Ketāb al-efteḵār* (The book of glory) is the best example of the whole range of taʾwil applied to the basic beliefs of Islam and its šariʿa; as well as being a compendium of Ismaʿili doctrine. *Mezāj al-tasnim* (medley of a fountain in Paradise) by Żiāʾ-al-Din Esmāʿil b. Hebat-Allāh, a partial tafsir from *Surat al-tawba*, verse 94, to *Surat al-ʿankabut*, verse 44, was compiled during the second half of the 18th century in Yemen.

Ismaʿili literature of pre-Fatimid and Fatimid periods reflects the general concern of Muslims and of Islamic theology, which was being developed and debated among scholars of various schools of thought, such as the Muʿtazilite, Ashʿarite, and the Imāmi theologians (*motakallemun*). The major Ismaʿili contribution to Islamic thought is their formulation of a new synthesis of reason and revelation based on Neoplatonic cosmology and Shiʿite doctrine. Thus, they offered a new world order under the Imam who resembles Plato's philosopher-king. The classic formulation of this synthesis, as indicated above, is found in the *Rasāel Eḵwān-al-Ṣafā* (Epistles of the Brethren of Purity).

The philosophical trend was the most dominant in the Iranian school of the Ismaʿili daʿwa and it has contributed the lion's share to this discipline. The elaboration of theoretical and doctrinal discourse among major dāʿis varied to a certain extent in keeping with their social and intellectual environment as well as their textual sources. The spirit of intellectual inquiry fostered by the daʿwa allowed some degree of freedom. In his *Ketāb al-eṣlāḥ* (The book of correction; lost), Abu Ḥātem Aḥmad Rāzi (q.v.) wrote a correction of Abu'l-Ḥasan Moḥammad b. Aḥmad Nasafi's views expounded in his *Ketāb al-maḥṣul* (The book of the harvest). Rāzi disagreed with the latter concerning several issues, such as the precedence of *qażāʾ* (fate, predestination) over *qadar* (freedom of will), the imperfect nature of emanation (*fayż*) of the Soul (*nafs*) from the Intellect (*ʿaql*), and the dissociation of šariʿa from the first *nāṭeq*, that is, Ādam. In his *Ketāb al-noṣra* (The book of support; lost), Abu Yaʿqub Esḥāq Sejestāni (q.v.) disagreed with Rāzi's corrections and upheld Nasafi's opinions. In his *Ketāb al-riāż* (The book of the meadow), Ḥamid-al-Din Aḥmad Kermāni tried to harmonize the acrimonious debate that had raged within the daʿwa. He criticized the previous views and offered his own solutions. In his *magnum opus*, *Rāḥat al-ʿaql*, Kermāni modified the earlier Neoplatonic cosmology he had inherited by introducing the Ten Intelligences and their astronomical counterparts that had been current in philosophic circles since Abu Naṣr Fārābi (q.v.). In accordance with this system Kermāni revised the structure of the spheres, the hierarchies of the physical world and of the daʿwa, known as *ḥodud-al-din*. The refined cosmology of Kermāni was adopted with some modifications by the Mostaʿli-Ṭayyebis of Yemen. Again, considerations of space prevent one from elaborating on this except for citing some important works on *ḥaqāʾeq* during the Yemeni period: *Kanz al-walad* (The treasure of the offspring) by Ebrāhim Ḥāmedi, *al-Anwār al-laṭifa* (Delicate lights) by Moḥammad b. Ṭāher Ḥāreṯi, *Ketāb al-ḏaḵira* (The book of the treasure) by ʿAli b. Moḥammad b. Walid, and *Zahr al-maʿāni* (The blossoming of [spiritual] concepts) by ʿEmād-al-Din Edris. Numerous small treatises entitled *al-mabdaʾ wa'l-maʿād* or *al-ebtedāʾ wa'l-entahāʾ* (the beginning and the end) compiled during the Yemeni period attempt to summarize the ḥaqāʾeq system very much like the account of the soul's initial downfall and its subsequent ascent through "knowledge."

The Ismaʿilis view history as a progressive cycle, which advances through seven major cycles, each inaugurated by a *nāṭeq* (speaking prophet; pl. *noṭaqāʾ*) or *ulu'l-ʿazm* (endowed with resolution) who brings revelation and promulgates law in its external form. Ādam, (Adam), Nuḥ (Noah), Ebrāhim (Abraham), Musā (Moses), ʿIsā (Jesus), and Moḥammad were the six noṭaqāʾ. Each succeeding nāṭeq abrogates the law of his predecessor and brings a new law. Nāṭeq is followed by *asās* (foundation), or *ṣāmet* (one who remains silent) who promulgates the bāṭen through taʾwil. Šiṯ (Seth), Sām (Shem), Esmāʿil (Ishmael) or Esḥāq (Isaac), Hārun (Aaron), Yušaʿ (Joshua) the son of Nun, Šamʿun al-Ṣafāʾ (Simon Peter), and ʿAli were the six *osos* of the aforementioned six *noṭaqāʾ*. The *asās*, in turn, is followed by series of seven imams; the last rises in rank and becomes the nāṭeq of the following era. Thus, each major cycle contains seven minor cycles. The length of each cycle varies. Moḥammad b. Esmāʿil b. Jaʿfar al-Ṣādeq, considered by some groups of Ismaʿilis as the seventh nāṭeq would abrogate the *ẓāheri šariʿa* of Moḥammad and promulgate the bāṭen. This doctrine, however, has undergone many modifications in the course of Ismaʿili history. During the Fatimid period, ẓāher and bāṭen together were considered two complimentary aspects of religion and both were emphasized. However, dormant antinomian tendencies have resurfaced from time to time throughout Ismaʿili history.

Given this view of history one finds very few historical works in Ismaʿili literature. Qāżi Noʿmān was an early exception to this rule; and although he composed several historical works, only the following have survived: *Eftetāḥ al-daʿwa wa-ebtedāʾ al-dawla* (Commencement of the daʿwa and the establishment of the [Fatimid] state; Dachraoui has analyzed and summarized it in his edition in French) deals with the beginning of the Ismaʿili mission in Yemen and North Africa, leading to the establishment of the Fatimid dynasty. Noʿmān's account is based on contemporary sources that have not survived. It is, therefore, a primary source for that period and has been exploited extensively by modern historians. *Šarḥ al-ak̲bār* (The elucidation of the traditions), in three volumes, is a detailed account of the outstanding traits of ʿAli b. abi Ṭāleb and early Imams up to Imam Jaʿfar al-Ṣādeq, based on the traditions of the Prophet. It is followed by a brief account of the advent of the Fatimid Mahdi and the traditions concerning this event. *Ketāb al-manāqeb wa'l-maṯāleb* (the book of virtues and defects) treats the history of the two powerful clans, Banu Hāšem and Banu Omayya, from pre-Islamic times up to the reign of the Fatimid Caliph-Imam al-Moʿezz. As the title indicates, Noʿmān exposes immoral traits and vices of the Banu Omayya by juxtaposing them with the piety and learning of the Imams from the House of Banu Hāšem. *Ketāb al-majāles wa'l-mosāyarāt* is a collection of Noʿmān's intimate conversations with al-Moʿezz during their strolls together as well as through the correspondence between them.

Ismaʿili literature of the Fatimid period contained at least half a dozen autobiographies and biographies. Unfortunately, two important ones, *Sirat Ebn Ḥawšab*, and *al-Sira al-Kotāmiya*, used by Qāżi Noʿmān for his *Eftetāḥ al-daʿwa*, have not survived. *Sirat al-Ḥājeb Jaʿfar* (tr. into English and French), written by a scribe during the reign of ʿAziz, describes the journey of the Fatimid Mahdi from his hiding place in Salamiya, Syria, to Sejelmāsa and his subsequent arrival at Raqqāda. *Sirat al-Ostād̲ Jawd̲ar* (tr. into French) was written by a scribe who served Ostād Jawd̲ar, the chamberlain of Moʿezz. *Sirat al-Moʾayyad* is an autobiography of the famous dāʿi Abu Naṣr Moʾayyad fi'l-Din of Shiraz during the reign of the Caliph-Imam Mostanṣer, who played a leading role as an intermediary between the Turkish military leader Abu'l-Ḥāreṯ Arsalān Basāsiri and the Fatimid government in the campaign against the Saljuqs after the fall of the Buyids in Baghdad.

ʿEmād-al-Din Edris was another noted historian of the daʿwa during the Yemeni period. His *ʿOyun al-ak̲bār* (The fountainheads of history), in seven volumes, narrates the history of the Prophet and the Ismaʿili Imams until the occultation of the twenty-first Mostaʿli-Ṭayyebi Imam, son of the Fatimid caliph-Imam Āmer, following the latter's assassination in around 524/1130. Some of the sources used by Edris have not survived. The first three volumes still remain unedited. Although volumes four, five, and six have been edited, they cannot be regarded as definitive editions. The seventh volume, which also contains the history of the Sulayhid dynasty in Yemen, is available in a critical edition with an English summary. *Nozhat al-afkār wa-rawżat al-ak̲bār* (The promenade of reflection and the meadow of history), in two volumes, is a political history of Yemen after the collapse of the Sulayhid dynasty up to the year 853/1449. It is considered a most important primary source for the three-hundred-year history of the Mostaʿli-Ṭayyebi community in Yemen. In his third work, entitled *Rawżat al-ak̲bār wa nozhat al-asmār* (The meadow of history and the promenade of stories), Edris continued the history of Yemen where he had left off in the *Nozhat al-afkār* up to the year 870/1465. During the Indian period, the following works should be noted for the beginning and the early history of the Mostaʿli-Ṭayyebi daʿwa in Gujarat. *Majmuʿ al-rasāʾel al-sett* by K̲awj b. Malek and *Ketāb pali midu* by Shaikh Ādam Ṣafi-al-Din. *Montazaʿ al-ak̲bār*, in two volumes, by Qoṭb-al-Din Borhānpuri is a comprehensive history of the daʿwa. The first volume deals with the history of twenty-one Mostaʿli-Ṭayyebi Imams, and the second volume with the history of the dāʿis beginning with the first *dāʿi moṭlaq*, D̲oʾayb b. Musā Wādeʿi, to the year 1824. It is an important source for the later Yemeni and early Indian periods.

Another genre peculiar to the Ismaʿilis is that of sermons (*majāles*; pl. of *majles*), prepared by the chief dāʿi to be delivered to the faithful at special sessions. Usually these lectures were written and submitted to the caliph-Imam for approval. Qāżi Noʿmān's *Taʾwil al-daʿāʾem* is composed in this form and was delivered as sermons. The most famous is *al-Majāles al-moʾayyadiya*, in eight volumes, each volume with a hundred *majles*, composed by Moʾayyad fi-Din of Shiraz. Ḥātem Ḥāmedi abridged those eight volumes in his *Jāmeʿ al-ḥaqāʾeq* and divided it, according to the subject matter, into eighteen chapters. The *al-Majāles al-monstanṣeriya* of Abu'l-Qāsem Maliji were written during the reign of Mostanṣer, and the *Majāles Abi'l-Barakāt* were composed by Abu al-Barakāt Ḥalabi during the reign of Āmer. In addition to these works the following should be noted. The *Majāles Sayyedenā Ḥātem Ḥāmedi*, *Majāles al-nosḥ wa'l-bayān* of ʿAli b. Moḥammad b. Walid, and an anonymous work entitled *Majāles ʿĀšuriya*, containing sermons to be delivered during the first ten days of Moḥarram.

Among the anthologies of Ismaʿili literature three deserve special mention. The *Majmuʿ al-tarbia*, compiled by Moḥammad b. Ṭāher Ḥāreṯi, in two volumes, and *Ketāb al-azhār wa majmaʿ al-anwār* by Ḥasan b. Nuḥ Bharuchi in seven volumes. Both these anthologies have preserved extensive excerpts as well as complete treatises of some of the earlier works which are no longer extant. *Ṣanduq al-laʾāliʾ* is another anthology that was compiled by an anonymous author (Poonawala, 1977, pp. 144-48, 179-82).

Ismaʿili literature is rich in religious and devotional poetry. *Diwāns* of Moʾayyad of Shiraz and Solṭān K̲aṭṭāb are just two outstanding examples among several of this genre of poetry. *Semṭ al-ḥaqāʾeq* by ʿAli b. Ḥanẓala is a versified version of Ismaʿili doctrines. *Al-Orjuza al-mok̲tāra* by Qāżi Noʿmān, in 2,375 verses, deals with the imamate. His *Montak̲aba* is yet another attempt at versifying the Pillars of Islam and law. Among the several treatises on the question of the imamate the following should be noted: *Taṯbit al-emāma* by the caliph-Imam Manṣur, *Eṯbāt al-emāma* by Aḥmad Nisāburi, *Resāla fi'l-emāma* by Abu'l-Fawāres, and *Ketāb al-maṣābih* by Ḥamid-al-Din Kermāni.

Qāżi Noʿmān, the founder of Ismaʿili law, wrote numerous books on jurisprudence, with the *Daʿāʾem* as the most famous. Among the chancery documents, *al-Sejellāt al-mostanṣeriya*, and *al-Hedāya al-āmeriya*, are worth noting from the Fatimid period. *Qarāṭis al-Yaman* contains letters exchanged between the daʿwa dignitaries in Yemen and India (Poonawala, 1977, pp. 326-28). *Ketab al-zina* (The book of ornament) of Abu Ḥātem Rāzi is a dictionary of Islamic theological terms, which also contains a section on Islamic heresiography. It is a comprehensive work on Islamic nomenclature and Rāzi's philological method of discussing the etymologies of those terms sheds light on the history of Arabic linguistics. His other work, *Aʿlām al-nobuwa* (The distinguishing marks of prophecy), records Ismaʿili views in defense of religion and the principle of prophethood while refuting the arguments of his opponent, Abu Bakr Moḥammad b. Zakariyāʾ Rāzi. In his *al-Aqwāl al-ḏahabiya fi'l-ṭebb al-nafsāni*, Ḥamid-al-Din Kermāni supported Abu Ḥātem's criticism of Abu Bakr Rāzi's views on the therapy of the mind expounded in the latter's *al-Ṭebb al-ruḥāni*. Lastly, Esmāʿil b. ʿAbd-al-Rasul Majduʿ's *Fehrest*, compiled during the second half of the 18th century, provides a detailed catalog of extant Ismaʿili literature.

In Persian. Nāṣer(-e) K̲osrow's works were preserved by the Nezāris of Persia and Central Asia, and most of his extant works are edited and some translated into French, English, and Russian. He was the first Ismaʿili dāʿi to have used Persian exclusively for his intellectual and poetic discourse. His poetry is didactic. His *Safar-nāma* depicts a vivid picture of the 11th century Islamic world from Transoxania to Egypt and includes visits to Mecca and Jerusalem. He first traveled across the Caspian coast of Persia into eastern Anatolia and southward to Syria and Palestine. He spent three years in Cairo and returned taking the southern route down to Aswān and crossing the Red Sea to the Ḥejāz, the Arabian peninsula to Basra, and passing through the Carmathian (Qarmaṭi) state in Lahsā; finally arriving at Balk̲ through southern Persia. His role in the establishment of Persian as a language of philosophical discourse is yet to be assessed.

The Persian Nezāris used Persian exclusively in their religious writings and did not develop any interest in the copying and preservation of the classical Arabic heritage of the Fatimid period. Ḥasan Ṣabbāḥ expounded his new teaching (*al-daʿwa al-jadida*), often called the doctrine of taʿlim, by formulating four propositions. The first demonstrates the need for a teacher in order to know God by refuting rationalism in its contention that human reason by itself is capable of obtaining the absolute truth. Once the need for a teacher is established, the second proposition poses the question: Is any teacher acceptable or must the teacher be a trustworthy person? When the Sunni position that any teacher will do is refuted, the need for a trustworthy teacher (*moʿallem-e ṣādeq*) is established. The third proposition, directed against non-Ismaʿili Shiʿites, poses the question as to whether it is necessary to know that teacher and acquire knowledge through him. The fourth and the final proposition attempts to answer the issue raised in the third proposition by proving that a particular Imam, that is, an Ismaʿili Imam of Ḥasan Ṣabbāḥ, could be the authentic teacher. He expounded his doctrine in a Persian treatise, *Čahār faṣl*, which has been preserved only in fragments This doctrine had a great impact on the Sunni population, hence Abu Ḥamed Ḡazāli in his *Mostaẓheri* tried to wrestle with the intellectual issues posed by this doctrine (see ḠAZĀLI and THE BĀṬENIS).

A major shift in the Nezāri doctrine came during the time of Ḥasan II, the fourth ruler of Alamut, who proclaimed the doctrine of the *qiāma* (resurrection). From then on the lords of Alamut also claimed the imamate for themselves. With the new doctrine the imam became the focal point, and qiāma meant seeing God in the spiritual reality of the imam. The elaboration of this teaching with its cosmological implication and the development of the doctrine of the Perfect Man in contemporary Sufism paved the way for the future relationship of the post-Alamut Nezāris with Sufism. The Syrian Nezāris do not seem to have been affected by the qiāma doctrine, and they continued the earlier Fatimid tradition.

Naṣir-al-Din Ṭusi, a major intellectual figure of the 13th century, a scientist, a philosopher, and a theologian, should be mentioned here for his long association with the Nezāris. It appears that during that period he himself had embraced the Ismaʿili Nezāri faith. In his spiritual autobiography entitled *Sayr wa soluk*, he describes how his search for knowledge led him to embrace Ismaʿili esoteric philosophy. In it he also elaborates Ḥasan(e) Ṣabbāḥ's doctrine of taʿlim. Another work, *Rawżat al-taslim*, also known as *Taṣawworāt*, an ethico-eschatological guide for ascending from the physical to the spiritual world, is an important testimony to Ṭusi's Ismaʿili-oriented philosophy.

Despite the Mongol massacres, the Persian Nezāri communities did survive in certain areas, especially in Rudbār and Qohestān and they lived clandestinely under the cover of Sufism. The Nezāris of Badak̲šān and other remote regions succeeded in preserving the bulk of the extant Nezāri literature of the Alamut period. The widely scattered communities of post-Alamut period, differentiated in terms of their vernacular language and socio-ethnic background, more or less developed their own particular religious literature, independently of one another. Nezāri history, for the first two centuries after the fall of Alamut, remains quite obscure. The poet Nezāri Qohestāni was the first post-Alamut author who chose the verse and Sufi forms of expression to conceal his Ismaʿili identity and views; and later authors followed in his footsteps. The period known as Anjedān (q.v.; from the name of this village in central Persia), lasting about two centuries from the second half of the 15th century marks a revival in Nezāri thought and its missionary activities. It was during this period that the Nezāri Imams of the Qāsemšāhi line developed close associations with the Neʿmat-Allāhi Sufi order and attempted to extend their control over the remaining Nezāri communities. Most noteworthy poets and authors of this period are Abu Esḥāq of Qohestān and Ḵayrḵᵛāh of Herat. They were followed by Kāki of Ḵorāsān and his son ʿAliqoli Raqqāmi.

Bibliography: Primary sources (this bibliography is not exhaustive and it should be noted that very few Arabic texts are available in scholarly editions; dates in paranthesis are in CE). ʿAbdān (fl. 9th cent.), *Ketāb šajarat al-yaqīn*, ed. ʿĀref Tāmer, Beirut, 1982. Abu Esḥāq Ebrāhim Qohestāni (after 1498), *Haft Bab or Seven Chapters*, ed. and tr. Wladimir Ivanow, Bombay, 1959. Abu'l-Fawāres Aḥmad b. Yaʿqub (d. 1020), *Resāla fi'l-emāma*, ed. and tr. Sami Nasib Makarem as *The Political Doctrine of the Ismaʿīlīs (The Imamate)*, Delmar, New York, 1977. Šehāb-al-Dīn Abu Ferās b. Naṣr (fl. 16th cent.), *Ketāb al-iżāḥ*, ed. ʿĀref Tāmer, Beirut, 1965. Idem, *al-Šāfeya*, ed. and tr. Sami N. Makarem as *Ash-Shâfiya, The Healer: An Ismâʿîlî Poem Attributed to Shihâb Ad-dîn Abû Firâs*, Beirut, 1966. Abu Tammām (fl. 10th cent.), *Bāb al-šayṭān men ketāb al-šajara*, eds. and tr. Wilferd Madelung and Paul E. Walker as *An Ismaili Heresiography: The 'Bāb al-shayṭān' from Abū Tammām's Kitāb al-shajara*, Leiden, 1998. ʿAli b. Ḥanẓala (d. 229), *Ketāb semṭ al-ḥaqāʾeq*, ed. ʿAbbās ʿAzzāwi, Damascus, 1953. ʿAli b. Moḥammad Walid (d. 1215), *Resāla fī maʿnā al-esm al-aʿẓam*, in Rudolf Strothmann, ed., *Gnosis Texts der Ismailiten/Arbaʿa kotob Esmāʿiliya: Arabischen Handschrift Ambrosiana*, Abhandlungen der Akademie der Wissenschaften in Göttingen, Philologisch-Historische Klasse 3/28, Gottingen, 1943, pp. 171-77. Idem, *Resālat al-īżāḥ wa'l-tabyīn*, in Rudolf Strothmann, ed., op. cit., pp. 137-58. Idem, *Resālat toḥfat al-mortād wa ḡoṣṣat al-ażdād*, in Rudolf Strothmann, ed., op. cit., pp. 159-70. Idem, *al-Resāla al-mawsūma be-jelāʾ al-ʿoqūl wa zobdat al-maḥṣul*, ed. ʿĀdel ʿAwwā, in idem, ed., *Montaḵbāt Esmāʿīlīya*, Damascus, 1958, pp. 87-153. Idem, *Tāj al-ʿaqāʾed wa maʿdan al-fawāʾed*, ed. ʿĀref Tāmer, Beirut, 1967; abridged Eng. tr. by Wladimir Ivanow as *A Creed of the Fatimids*, Bombay, 1936. Idem, *Ketāb al-ḏaḵira fil-ḥaqīqa*, ed. Moḥammad-Ḥasan Aʿẓami, Beirut, 1971. Idem, *Dāmeḡ al-bāṭel wa ḥatf al-monāżel*, ed. Moṣṭafā Ḡāleb, 2 vols., Beirut, 1982. al-Āmer be-Aḥkām Allāh (died 1130), *al-Hedāya al-āmeriya fī eṯbāt daʿwat al-Nizāriya*, ed. Āṣaf A. A. Fayżi (Fyzee), London, 1938; repr. in Jamāl-al-Din Shayyāl, ed., *Majmuʿat al-waṯāʾeq al-Faṭemiya*, Cairo, 1958, pp. 203-30. Idem, *Resāla īqāʿ ṣawāʿeq al-erḡām*, ed. Āṣaf A. A. Fayżi, in *al-Hedāya al-āmeriya*, pp. 27-39; repr. in Jamāl-al-Din Shayyāl, ed., op. cit, pp. 231-47. Ḥasan b. Nuḥ Bharuchi (d. 1533), *Ketāb al-azhār wa majmaʿ al-anwār* I, ed. ʿĀdel ʿAwwā, in idem, ed., *Montaḵbāt Esmāʿīlīya*, Damascus, 1958. Qoṭb-al-Din Solaymānji Borhānpuri (d. 1826), *Montazaʿ al-aḵbār fī aḵbār al-doʿāt al-aḵyār*, ed. Samer F. Traboulsi (partially edited up to the Dāʾudi-Solaymāni schism), Beirut, 1999. Ebn Hāni Andalosi (d. 973), *Diwān*, ed. with commentary Zāhed ʿAli as *Tabyin al-maʿāni fi šarḥ Diwān Ebn Hāni al-Andalusi al-Maḡrebi*, Cairo, 1352/1933. Ebn Ḥawšab (d. 914), *Ketāb al-rošd wa'l-hedāya*, in Wladimir Ivanow, ed., *Collectanea* I, Leiden, 1948, pp. 185-213. Ebn Hayṯam (fl. 10th cent.), *Ketāb al-monāẓarāt*, eds. and tr. Wilferd Madelung and Paul Ernest Walker as *The Advent of the Fatimids: A Contemporary Shiʿi Witness*, London, 2000. Emād-al-Din Edris b. ʿAbd-Allāh (d. 1468), *Nozhat al-afkār wa-rawżat al-aḵbār fi ḏekr man qāma be'l-Yaman* (in ms.). Idem, *Rawżat al-aḵbār wa nozhat al-asmār fi ḥawādeṯ al-Yaman* (in md.; for these two mss., see Poonawala, 1977, pp. 172-73). Idem, *ʿOyun al-aḵbār wa fonun al-āṯār* IV-VI, ed. Moṣtfā Ḡāleb, Beirut, 1973-84; VII (part of), ed. Moḥammad Yaʿlāwi as *Taʾrīḵ al-ḵolafāʾ al-Fāṭemīyīn be'l-Maḡreb*, Beirut, 1985; VII, ed. Ayman Fuʾād Sayyid as *The Fatimids and Their Successors in Yaman: The History of An Islamic Community*, London, 2002 (Eng. summary by Paul E. Walker and Maurice A. Pomerantz). Idem, *Zahr al-maʿāni*, ed. Moṣṭafā Ḡāleb, Beirut, 1991. Moḥammad Fedāʾi Ḵorāsāni (d. 1923), "*Maṯnawi-e negārestān*," ed. Alexsandr A. Semenov, *Iran* 3, 1929, pp. 51-70. Idem, *Ketāb al-hedāyat al-moʾmenīn al-ṭālebin maʿruf ba tāriḵ-e Esmāʿiliya*, ed. Alexsandr A. Semenov, Moscow, 1959. Ebrāhim b. Ḥosayn Ḥāmedi (d. 1162), *Kanz al-walad*, ed. Moṣṭafā Ḡāleb, Beirut and Wiesbaden, 1971. Ḥātem b. Ebrāhim Ḥāmedi (d. 1192), *Resālat zahr badr al-ḥaqāʾeq*, ed. ʿĀdel ʿAwwā, in idem, ed., *Montaḵabāt Esmāʿilīya*, Damascus, 1958, pp. 155-80. Idem, *Jāmeʿ al-ḥaqāʾeq* (an abridged reduction of Moʾayyad's *Majāles*), partial ed. Moḥammad ʿAbd-al-Qāder ʿAbd-al-Nāṣer, Cairo, 1975. Abu'l-Qāsem Jaʿfar b. Manṣur Yaman (d. 957), *Ketāb al-kašf*, ed. Rudolf Strothmann, London, 1952; ed. Moṣṭafā Ḡāleb, Beirut, 1984. Idem, *Ketāb farāʾeż wa ḥodud-al-din*, ed. and tr. Husayn F. Hamadani as *On the Geneology of Fatimid (Statement on Mahdi's Communication to the Yemen on the Real and Esoteric Names of His Hidden Predecessors)*, Cairo, 1958. Idem, *Sarāʾer wa-asrār al-noṭaqāʾ*, ed. Moṣtafā Ḡāleb, Beirut, 1984. Idem, *Ketāb al-ʿālem wa'l-ḡolām*, ed. and tr., James Winston Morris as *The Master and the Disciple: An Early Islamic Spiritual Dialogue*, London, 2001. Abu ʿAli Manṣur Jawḏari (d. 996), *Sirat al-Ostāḏ Jawḏar*, ed. Moḥammad Kāmel Ḥosayn and Moḥammad ʿAbd-al-Hādi Šaʿira, Cairo, 1954; tr. Marius Canard as *Vie de l'Ustadh Jaudhar (contenant lettres et rescrits des premiers califes Fâtimides)*, Algeria, 1958. MKMK Moḥammad-Reżā Ḵayrḵᵛāh Herāti (d. after 1553), *Kalām-e pir*, ed. and tr. Wladimir A. Ivanow as *Kalām-e Pir: A Treatise on Ismaili Doctrine*, Bombay, 1935. Idem, *Faṣl dar bayān-e šenāḵt-e emām*, ed. Wladimir A. Ivanow, Tehran, 1959; tr. W. A. Ivanow as *On the Recognition of the Imam*, Bombay, 1947. Idem, *Taṣnifāt-e Ḵayrḵᵛāh Herāti*, ed. Wladimir Ivanow, Tehran, 1961. Aḥmad Ḥamid-al-Din Kermāni (d. after 1020), *Rāḥat al-ʿaql*, ed. Moḥammad Kāmel Ḥosayn and Moḥammad-Moṣṭafā Ḥelmi, Cairo, 1952. Idem,

Ketāb al-riāż fi'l-ḥokm bayn al-ṣādayn ṣāḥebay al-eṣlāḥ wa'l-noṣra, ed. ʿĀref Tāmer, Beirut, 1960. Idem, *Ketāb al-maṣābīḥ fi eṯbāt al-emāma*, ed. Moṣṭafā Ḡāleb, Beirut, 1969. Idem, *al-Aqwāl al-ḏahabīya fi'l-ṭebb al-nafsāni*, ed. Ṣalāḥ Ṣāwi, Tehran, 1977; ed. Moṣṭafā Ḡāleb, Beirut, 1977. Idem, *Majmūʿat rasāʾel al-Kermānī*, ed. M. Ḡāleb, Beirut, 1983 (a collection of eleven treatises). Emāmqoli Ḵāki Ḵorāsāni (d. 1646), *Diwān*, ed. Wladimir A. Ivanow as *An Abbriviated Version of the Diwan of Khaki Khorasani*, Bombay, 1933. Esmāʿil b. ʿAbd al-Rasul Majduʿ (d. 1769 or 1771), *Fahrasat al-kotob wa 'l-rasāʾel (Fehrest)*, ed. ʿAli-Naqi Monzawi, Tehran, 1966. Abu'l-Qāsem ʿAbd-al-Ḥakim Maliji (fl. 11th cent.), *al-Majāles al-monstanṣeriya*, ed. Moḥammad Zinhom and Moḥammad ʿAzab, Cairo, 1992. Abu Naṣr Hebat-Allāh Moʾayyad fi'l-Din Širāzi (d. 1078), *Dīwān*, ed. Moḥammad Kāmel Ḥosayn, Cairo, 1949. Idem, *Sīrat al-Moʾayyad fi'l-Din dāʿi-al-doʿāt*, ed. Moḥammad Kāmel Ḥosayn, Cairo, 1949; for partial Eng. tr., see "The Autobiography of al-Muʾayyad," in Dwight F. Reynolds et al., eds., *Interpreting the Self: Autobiography in the Arabic Literary Tradition*, Berkeley, 2001, pp. 132-44. Idem, *al-Majāles al-Moʾayyadiya* I-II, ed. Ḥātem Ḥamid-al-Din, Bombay and Oxford, 1975-86; I and III, ed. Moṣṭafā Ḡāleb, Beirut, 1974-84. Abu Tamim al-Mostanṣer Be'llāh (d. 1094), *al-Majāles al-mostanṣerīya* (ascribed to al-Mostanṣer, the Fatimid caliph), ed. Moḥammad Kāmel Ḥosayn, Cairo, n.d. Idem, *Pandiyāt-e jawānmardī or Advices of Manliness*, ed. and tr. Wladimir Ivanow, Leiden, 1953. Idem, *al-Sejellāt al-mostanṣerīya*, ed. ʿAbd-al-Monʿem Mājed, Cairo, 1954. Nāṣer-e Ḵosrow (d. after 1070), *Safar-nāma*, ed. Maḥmud Ḡanizāda, Berlin, 1922; ed. Nāder Wazinpur, Tehran, 1971; tr. Charles Schefer as *Sefer Nameh, relation du voyage de Nassiri Khosrau*, Paris, 1881; tr. Wheeler M. Thackston as *Nāṣer-e Khosraw's Book of Travels (Safarnāma)*, Albany, New York, 1986. Idem, *Zād al-mosāferin*, ed. Moḥammad Badl-al-Raḥmān, Berlin, 1923. Idem, *Wajh-e din*, ed. Maḥmud Ḡanizāda and Moḥammad Qazvini, Berlin, 1924; ed. Ḡolām-Reżā Aʿwāni, Tehran, 1977. Idem, *Šeš faṣl yā rowšanāʾi-nāma-ye naṯr*, ed. and tr. Wladimir Ivanow, Cairo and Leiden, 1948. Idem, *Jāmeʿ al-ḥekmatayn/Le livre réunuissant les deux sagesses, ou harmonie de la philosophie Grecque et de la théosophie Ismaélienne*, ed. Henry Corbin and Moḥammad Moʿin, Bibliothèque Iranienne 3, Tehran and Paris, 1953; Ar. tr. by Ebrāhim Dasuqi Šatā, Cairo, 1974; tr. Isabelle de Gastines as *Les Livre réunissant les deux sagesses*, Paris, 1990. Idem, *Ḵʾān al-eḵwān*, ed. ʿAli Qawim, Tehran, 1959. Idem, *Ketāb-e gošāyeš wa rahāyeš*, ed. Saʿid Nafisi, rev. ed., Tehran, 1961; ed. and Eng. tr. Faquir Hunzai as *Knowledge and Liberation: A Treatise on Philosophical Theology*, London, 1998; tr. Pio Filippani-Ronconi as *Il libro dello scioglimento e della liberazione*, Instituto Universitario Orientale di Napoli, Naples, 1959; Idem, *Divān*, eds. Mojtabā Minovi and Mahdi Moḥaqqeq, Tehran, 1974; partial Eng. tr. Peter Lamborn Wilson and Ḡolām-Reżā Aʿwāni (Aavani) as *Forty Poems from the Dīvān*, Tehran, 1977; partial Eng. tr. Annemarie Schimmel as *Make a Shield from Wisdom: Selected Verses from Nāṣir-i Khusraw's Dīvān*, London, 2001. Aḥmad Nisāburi (d. after 996), *Estetār al-emām wa tararroq al-doʿāt fi'l-jazāʾer le-ṭalabehi*, ed. Wladimir Ivanow, *Bulletin of the Faculty of Arts of the University of Egypt* 4/2, Cairo, 1936, pp. 93-107. Idem, *Eṯbāt al-emāma*, ed. Moṣṭafā Ḡāleb, Beirut, 1984. Abu Ḥanifa Qāżi Noʿmān b. Moḥammad Tamimi (d. 974), *Daʿāʾem al-Eslām fi ḏekr al-ḥalāl wa'l-ḥarām wa'l-qażāya wa'l-aḥkām*, ed. ʿĀṣaf A. A. Fayżi (Fyzee), 2 vols., Cairo, 1951-61; tr. A. A. A. Fyzee, as *The Pillars of Islam*, completely revised and annotated by Ismail K. Poonawala, 2 vols., New Delhi, 2002-4. Idem, *Ketāb al-eqteṣār*, ed. Moḥammad Waḥid Mirzā, Damascus, 1957. Idem, *Asās al-taʾwīl*, ed. ʿĀref Tāmir, Beirut, 1960. Idem, *al-Orjuza al-moḵtāra*, ed. Ismail K. Poonawala, Beirut, 1970; ed. Yusof Beqāʿi, Beirut, 1999. Idem, *Ketāb eḵtelāf oṣūl al-maḏāheb*, ed. S. T. Lokhandwalla, Simla, 1972. Idem, *Taʾwil al-daʿāʾem*, ed. Moḥammad-Ḥasan Aʿẓami, 3 vols., Cairo, 1968-72; ed. ʿAref Tamir, 3 vols., Beirut, 1995. Idem, *Eftetāḥ al-daʿwa wa-ebtedāʾ al-dawla*, ed. Farḥat Dašrāwi (Dashraoui), Tunis, 1975. Idem, *al-Majāles wa'l-mosāyarāt*, ed. Ḥabib Faqi et al., Tunis, 1978. Idem, *Šarḥ al-aḵbār fī fażāʾel al-aʾemma al-aṭhār*, ed. Moḥammad Ḥosayni Jalāli, 3 vols., Qom, 1409-12/ 1988-92. Idem, *Ketāb al-manāqeb wa maṯāleb*, ed. Majid ʿAṭiya, Beirut, 2002. Saʿd-al-Din Nezāri Qohestāni (d. 1320), *Dastū-nāma*, ed. and tr. Evgeniĭ E. Berthels in *Vostochniy Sbornik*, Leningard, 1926, pp. 37-104. *Rasāʾel Eḵwān-al-Ṣafā wa Ḵollān-al-Wafā*, ed. ʿAref Tamir, 5 vols., Beirut and Paris, 1995. Abu Ḥātem Aḥmad Rāzi (d. 934), *Ketāb al-zina fi'l-kalemāt al-eslāmiya al-ʿarabiya*, ed. Ḥosayn Hamdāni, 2 vols., Cairo, 1957-58, repr. by ʿAbd-Allāh Sallūm Sāmarrāʾi with an addition of a section on Islamic sects, in ʿA. Sallum, *al-Ḡolow wa'l-feraq al-ḡāliya fi'l-hazāra al-Esmāʿiliya*, Baghdad, 1972. Idem, *Aʿlām al-nobuwa*, ed. Ṣalāḥ Ṣāwi and Ḡolām-Reżā Aʿwāni, Tehran, 1977. Idem, *Ketāb al-eṣlāḥ*, ed. Ḥasan Minučehr and Mahdi Moḥaqqeq, Tehran, 1998. Jamāl-al-Din Šayyāl, ed., *Majmūʿat al-waṯāʾeq al-Fāṭemīya*, Cairo, 1958 (23 documents issued by the Fatimid state chancery). Abu Yaʿqub Sejestāni (d. after 971), *Kašf al-maḥjūb*, ed. Henry Corbin, Tehran and Paris, 1949; tr. Henry Corbin as *Le dévoilement des choses cachées: Kasf al-Maḥjub*, Recherches de Philosophie Ismaélienne, Lagrasse, 1988. Idem, *Ketāb al-yanābīʿ*, ed. and tr. Henry Corbin, in idem, *Trilogie Ismaélienne*, Bibliothèque Iranienne 9, Tehran and Paris, 1961; tr. Paul E. Walker as *The Wellsprings of Wisdom*, Salt Lake City, 1994. Idem, *Eṯbāt al-nobūʾāt*, ed. ʿĀref Tāmer, Beirut, 1966. Idem, *Ketāb al-efteḵār*, ed. Moṣṭafā Ḡāleb, Beirut 1980; ed. Ismaʿil K. Poonawala, Beirut, 2000. Solṭān al-Ḵaṭṭāb, *Dīwān*, ed. Ismail K. Poonawala, 2nd ed., Beirut, 1999. Naṣir-al-Din Ṭusi (d. 1274), *Rawżat al-taslim*, ed. and tr. Wladimir Ivanow as *Rawżatu't-Taslim Commonly Called Taṣawworāt*, Leiden, 1950; ed. and tr. Sayyed

Jalāl Ḥosayni Badakšāni as *Rawżat al-taslim yā taṣawworāt/Paradise of Submission: A Medieval Treatise on Ismaili Thought*, London and New York, 2005. Idem, *Sayr wa soluk*, in *Majmuʿa-ye rasāʾel-e Kᵛāja Naṣir-al-Din Moḥammad Ṭusi*, ed. Moḥammad-Taqi Modarres Rażawi, Tehran, 1956, pp. 36-55; ed. and tr. S. J. Badakhchani as *Contemplation and Action: The Spiritual Autobiography of a Muslim Scholar*, London, 1998. Amir Tamim b. al-Moʿezz, *Diwān*, ed. Moḥammad-Ḥasan Aʿẓami et al., Cairo, 1957. Sohrāb Wali Badakšāni, *Si o šeš ṣaḥifa*, ed. Hušang Ojāqi, Tehran, 1961. Moḥammad b. Moḥammad Yamāni (fl. 10th cent.), *Sīrat al-Ḥājeb Jaʿfar b. ʿAli wa korūj al-Mahdi men Salamiya*, ed. Wladimir Ivanow, in *Bulletin of the Faculty of Arts of the University of Egypt* 4/2, Cairo, 1936, pp. 107-33; tr. W. Ivanow, in idem, *Ismaili Tradition Concerning the Rise of the Fatimids*, London and New York, 1942, pp. 184-223; tr. Marius Canard as "L'autobiographie d'un chambellan du Mahdî ʿObeidallâh le Fâṭimide," *Hespéris* 39, 1952, pp. 279-324, repr. in Marius Canard., *Miscellanea Orientalia*, London, 1973, art. V.

Ziāʾ-al-Din Esmāʿil b. Hebat-Allāh, *Mezāj al-tasnim/Ismailitischer Koran-Kommentar*, ed. Rudolf Strothmann, Gottingen, 1944.

Secondary Sources: 1. Henry Corbin, "Nāṣir-i Khusrau and Iranian Ismāʿīlism," in *The Cambridge History of Iran* IV: *The Period from the Arab Invasion to the Saljuqs*, ed. Richard N. Frye, Cambridge, 1975, pp. 520-42. Della Cortese, *Ismaili and Other Arabic Manuscripts*, London and New York, 2000. Farhad Daftary, *The Ismāʿīlīs: Their History and Doctrines*, Cambridge, 1990. Idem, *The Assassin Legends: Myths of the Ismaʿilis*, London, 1994. Idem, *Ismaili Literature: A Bibliography of Sources and Studies*, London and New York, 2004. Husain F. Hamdani, "The History of the Ismāʿīlī *Daʿwat* and Its Literature during Biobibliographical sources: The Last Phase of the Fāṭimid Empire," *JRAS*, 1932, pp. 126-36. Marshal G. S. Hodgson, *The Order of Assassins*, The Hague, 1955. Alice C. Hunsburger, *Nasir Khusraw, The Ruby of Badakhshan: A Portrait of the Persian Poet, Traveller and Philosopher*, London, 2000. Wladimir Ivanow, ed., *Collectanea* I, Leiden, 1948. Idem, *Studies in Early Persian Ismailism*, Bombay, 1955. Nadia Eboo Jamal, *Surviving the Mongols: Nizārī Quhistānī and the Continuity of Ismaili Tradition in Persia*, London, 2002. Verena Klemm, *Memoirs of a Mission: The Ismaili Scholar, Statesman and Poet al-Muʾayyad fi'l-Dīn al-Shīrāzī*, London, 2003. Farouk Mitha, *Al-Ghazālī and the Ismailis: A Debate on Reason and Authority in Medieval Islam*, London, 2001. Ismail K. Poonawala, *Biobibliography of Ismāʿīlī Literature*, Malibu, Calif., 1977 (for details concerning authors and their works). Idem, "Ismāʿīlī *taʾwīl* of the Qurʾān," in Andrew Rippon, ed., *Approaches to the History of the Interpretation of the Qurʾān*, Oxford, 1988, pp. 199-222. Idem, "Al-Qāḍī al-Nuʿmān and Ismaʿili Jurisprudence," in Farhad Daftary, ed., *Mediaeval Ismaʿili History and Thought*, Cambridge, 1996, pp. 117-43. Idem, "The Beginning of the Ismaili *Daʿwa* and the Establishment of the Fatimid Dynasty as Commemorated by al-Qāḍī al-Nuʿmān," in Farhad Daftary and Josef W. Meri, eds., *Culture and Memory in Medieval Islam: Essays in Honour of Wilferd Madelung*, London, 2003, pp. 338-63. Jan Rypka, "History of Persian Literature up to the Beginning of the 20th Century," in idem et al., *History of Iranian Literature*, ed. Karl Jahn, Dordrecht, 1956, pp. 185-89, 255-56. Paul E. Walker, *Early Philosophical Shiism: The Ismaili Neoplatonism of Abū Yaʿqūb al-Sijistānī*, Cambridge, 1993. Idem, *Abu Yaʿqub al-Sijistani: Intellectual Missionary*, London, 1996. Idem, *Ḥamīd al-Dīn al-Kirmānī: Ismaili Thought in the Age of al-Ḥākim*, London, 1999.

(ISMAIL K. POONAWALA)

xiv. ISMAʿILISM IN *GINĀN* LITERATURE

A conspicuous feature in the intellectual history of Nezāri Ismaʿili Shiʿism has been the fundamental impulse to translate the concept of the Imam, which is the central aspect of their faith, within the frameworks of the various philosophical and theological systems it encountered as the movement spread geographically. As a result, Ismaʿili religious texts are frequently characterized by their use of motifs from multiple streams of thought. Thus, works written during the political heyday of Fatimid Ismaʿili rule in Egypt and North Africa in the 9th and 10th centuries draw upon Islamic, Gnostic, Neoplatonic, and Manichean elements to elaborate the concept of the Imam. Similarly, Ismaʿili treatises written in Persia and Central Asia from the 15th century onward explain the significance of the Imam utilizing the Sufi discourse that had become so widespread in these areas.

Not surprisingly, Nezāri Ismaʿili texts from the Indian Subcontinent exhibit a similar adaptive response to the region's complex religious, literary, and cultural environment. A significant element in this response was the creation of a unique genre of devotional songs called *ginān*s. The Indic term *ginān* is commonly believed to be derived from Sanskrit *jñāna* "knowledge derived from meditation." Composed in the several northwestern Indic languages (such as Gujarati, Sindhi, Punjabi, Hindi) and sung in various Indian *rāga*s, or melodies, *ginān*s form an important element in the liturgy and devotional life of the subcontinent's Nezāri Ismaʿili communities to our day. The authorship of these devotional hymns is traditionally attributed to Ismaʿili *dāʿi*s (q.v.), or *pir*s, of Persian ancestry who were sent to the subcontinent by Ismaʿili Imams living in Persia, in order to propagate the Ismaʿili form of Islam and to provide spiritual guidance to Ismaʿili communities living there (Daftary, pp. 414-15, 442-43).

There is very little accurate information about the reputed authors of the *ginān*s and their activities, as most of what we know about them derives from hagiographic accounts. As a result, we are not certain about significant biographical details such as birth and death dates of many *pir*s, particularly the earlier ones. In any case, the vast majority of *ginān*s are attributed to the four great *pir*s who lived between the 12th and 15th centuries: Pir Satgur Nur, Pir Šams, Pir Ṣadr-al-Din, and Pir Ḥasan Kabir-al-Din. A fifth figure, Emāmšāh, who lived in the late 15th and early 16th century, was allegedly the founder of a "schismatic" movement that broke away from the main group to form a separate sect. Each *pir* was regarded as a tangible symbol of the Imams' authority in the subcontinent, the "door" to the Imam, without whose guidance and instruction access to religious truths would be impossible. Hagiographic accounts assert that, to overcome cultural and linguistic barriers between themselves and the local populations, the Ismaʿili *pir*s composed songs to explain fundamental Ismaʿili doctrines to Indian disciples in their native languages and idioms. It is these songs that eventually came to constitute the corpus of what is now called the *ginān* literature.

In more recent times, community traditions have come to regard these compositions as providing the faithful with an understanding of the "true meaning" of the Qurʾān and serving to penetrate its inner or spiritual (*bāṭen*, q.v.) significance. The *pirs* were not ordinary missionaries and evangelists; in the community's understanding they were spiritually enlightened individuals whose religious authority had been endorsed by the Imams living in the "west" (i.e., Persia). In order that their Indian disciples should fully comprehend the theological significance of the Imam, the *pirs* taught that the Imam, specifically ʿAli b. Abi Ṭāleb (q.v.), was the long-awaited tenth incarnation (*avatāra*) of the deity Vishnu. In this manner they created an ostensible correspondence, or bridge, between the Ismaʿili concept of the Imam with the concept of *avatāra* as understood in the Vaishnavite form of Hinduism. The translation of the Ismaʿili concept of Imam into a Vaisnavite framework is best represented in the classic *ginān*, *Dasa Avatāra* "Ten Incarnations," of which there are several versions attributed to different *pir*s (see Khakee).

In the *ginān*s the *pir*s exhort their disciples to follow *Satpanth* "the true path," the name used in the texts to refer to the Ismaʿili tradition. The essence of Satpanth lay in its emphasis on the esoteric and spiritual over the exoteric and material, and the interiorized form of religious practice over mere ritual practice. Satpanth teachings asserted that attachment to the material and transitory world along with negative, egotistical qualities such as anger, greed, and jealousy result in individual souls being trapped in endless cycles of rebirth in the material world. The spiritual enlightenment that is necessary to break these cycles of rebirth is, however, possible only through the allegiance to the Imam (often called *Sat Guru* "True Guru" or *moršed* "[Spiritual] Guide") and his representatives the *pirs*. It is the *Sat Guru* who provides the guidance necessary for an ethical and moral life and who also bestows on the disciple the sacred word (*shabd/nam/bol*) on which to meditate. If successful in the spiritual quest, the disciple would be blessed with the vision (*didār/darshan* [< Sk.. *darśana*]) of the Divine Light, the most sublime experience of the spiritual life.

A key aspect of Satpanth Ismaʿili tradition is the spiritual relationship between the Imam and the individual disciple (*rikhīsar* [Ind.], *moʾmen*, *morid*), often portrayed as a bond of love. Indeed, the tradition views love and devotion to the Imam as important preconditions for spiritual enlightenment and salvation. Borrowing images and metaphors from the realm of human love, the *pirs* frequently invoke in *ginān*s the symbol of the *virahinī* (Ind.), or woman separated from her beloved, and the *viraha*, or the longing she feels for him. Based on this symbolism, many *ginān*s represent the disciples of the Imam as *virahinī*s longing for their beloved Imam. While the representation of the soul as a female longing for vision (*didār/darshan*) of the Imam is certainly unusual by the standards of the Arabic and Persian literary traditions, it is perfectly in keeping with local Indian literary conventions. Traditions of Indian devotional poetry contemporaneous with the *ginān*s, such as the *sant*, *bhakti*, or Sikh traditions, all employ the symbol of the *virahinī*. Even Sufi poetry written in the Indian vernacular languages adopts this Indic topos. In this way, the *ginān*s explicate core Ismaʿili ideas about the Imam within religious and devotional frameworks that strongly resonated with the broader Indian religious ethos.

Bibliography: Ali Sultaan Ali Asani, "The Ismāʿīlī Ginān Literature: Its Structure and Love Symbolism," MA thesis, Harvard University, 1977. Idem, *Ecstasy and Enlightenment. The Ismaili Devotional Literature of South Asia*, London, 2002. Farhad Daftary, *The Ismāʿīlīs: Their History and Doctrines*, Cambridge, New York, and Melbourne, 1990, esp. pp. 414-15, 442-43, 478, 479, 484-85. Wladimir Ivanow, ed., *Collectanea* I, Leiden, 1948, pp. 1-145. Tazim R. Kassam, *Songs of Wisdom and Circles of Dance: Hymns from the Satpanth Ismāʿīlī Muslim Saint, Pīr Shams*, Albany, N.Y., 1995. Gulshan Khakee, "The Dasa Avatāra of the Satpanthi Ismailis and the Imam Shahis of Indo-Pakistan," Ph.D. diss., Harvard University, 1972. Azim Nanji, *The Nizārī Ismāʿīlī Tradition in the Indo-Pakistan Subcontinent*, Delmar, N.Y., 1978. Christopher Shackle and Zawahir Moir, *Ismaili Hymns from South Asia: An Introduction to the Ginans*, London, 1992; rev. new ed., Richmond, 2000.

(ALI SULTAAN ALI ASANI)

xv. NEZĀRI ISMAʿILI MONUMENTS

The principal monuments of the Nizāri Ismaʿili state, which also defined and defended its boundaries, were the exceptionally well-constructed and provisioned castles that dominated the surrounding valleys and countryside. These castles varied in size from the massive fortified complex built on the sides and the top of a spur of the Alborz Mountains at Gerdkuh (q.v.) near Dāmḡān to a cluster of smaller independent fortified sites in Khorasan or the Anṣariya Djebel in Syria. Sometimes three or four large castles were built at a strategic site, such as Ferdows, to protect the southwest flank of the Ismaʿili state.

Although many of these castles in Persia were taken and demolished by the Mongols, the ruins still give an impression of their immense power. As far as we know there are no other Ismaʿili monuments still extant with the exception of isolated remains of pottery kilns, for instance at Andij in Alamut. It should be remembered that Ismaʿili castles, especially the larger ones, were used not only for defensive military purposes, but often constituted complete towns in themselves, acting as the seat of the local governor and his officials, and centers of learning and study, with extensive libraries built within the castle walls and containing valuable manuscripts and scientific instruments. They were also bases from which *dāʿis* (q.v.; the Ismaʿili missionaries) could be sent to other parts of the state.

From 483/1090, when Ḥasan-e Ṣabbāḥ gained control of the castle of Alamut, until 654/1256, when Rokn-al-Din Ḵoršāh surrendered to the Mongols, the Ismaʿili state consisted of four principal semi-autonomous areas—Rudbār in which Alamut and Lamasar were the principal fortresses, Qumes, the area around Dāmḡān and Semnān, which contained the formidable castles of Gerdkuh and Soru, and Qohestān, in the south of Khorasan, in which most of the recent discoveries of castles have been made. There were also additional sites in Ḵuzestān, Arrajān in particular, where the Ismaʿilis established their hegemony for a few years. The fourth important Ismaʿili area was in Syria where the Ismaʿilis were able to retain their independence until 671/1273, when the last of their castles surrendered to Baybars. The most important Syrian fortress was Maṣyāf, though the castle of Kahf was probably the main residence of the Ismaʿili leader, Rāšed al-Din Senān. This impressive stronghold remained a military post until Ottoman times and was destroyed only at the beginning of the nineteenth century. Another important Ismaʿili center was the cluster of castles around Qadmus including Ḵawābi, Roṣāfa, Qolayʿa, Maniqa and ʿOlleyqa.

In their attempts to persuade their fellow-citizens to join them in their fight against the Seljuqs, the Ismaʿilis often gained control of large fortresses that eventually had to be relinquished after a few years occupation. The outstanding example was their infiltration and occupation of the great castle of Šāhdiz overlooking the Seljuq capital of Isfahan, a considerable blow to the prestige of the Seljuqs. Almost at the same time, around 598/1100, the Ismaʿilis seized Ḵān Lanjān, only seventeen miles south of Isfahan and over 1,000 feet above the valley. Although the capture of Šāhdiz ended tragically, we must admire the verve and ingenuity of the Ismaʿilis.

From the very earliest days of its inception, the boundaries of the new Ismaʿili state had been firmly fixed and the main line of fortresses did not change during the next 166 years. From Alamut the line stretched east to Firuz Kuh and then along the road to Mašhad, past the great complex of strongholds between Semnān and Dāmḡān (q.v.). In Khorasan the line ran southward to Qohestān and the border with Sistān, and westward to Ferdows and Ṭabas. The Ismaʿilis well understood the need for quick communications between each of the centers and these were provided by means of smaller forts, watchtowers and beacons. The vital line of communication between Alamut and the Ismaʿili community in Syria was always kept open and there was regular interchange between these two centers.

The Ismaʿili fortresses are notable examples of military architecture. Their strategic position, and the skilled use of natural resources, ensured that despite the difficulties of the terrain the residents were well supplied with food and water and able to withstand a prolonged siege of many months, even years. Several major considerations were observed in the construction of Ismaʿili castles: The area chosen for fortification was in a strong and naturally defensive position, and in a terrain sufficiently remote and inaccessible to discourage attacks by their far more numerous Seljuq foe and other enemies. The complex of fortresses within the chosen area were able to support each other in the event of attack and possessed an efficient system of communication, whether by beacon or other means. The chosen area usually contained enough natural material, especially wood and stone, to allow for any construction or reconstruction to be carried out expeditiously and with the minimum labor force. The terrain was self-sufficient in water and food supplies—that is to say there was fertile ground and water near by.

The strategy was thus a defensive one and, in the mountains of Qohestān, Alamut, and in Syria, it worked admirably. It differed from that of the Crusaders, who built strong bases from which they pursued an offensive strategy. The Ismaʿilis were able to overcome, often in an astonishing way, the difficulty of building large fortresses on the rugged crest of a high mountain and solidly anchoring the fortress into the hard and unyielding rock. As precipitous an approach as possible was important as this avoided the need for extensive outer walls, and a steep angle of slope made it very difficult for an enemy to set up his ballistae or rely on conventional siege tactics such as sapping and mining. Of course, the Ismaʿilis took every precaution to block off any approach that lay in dead ground and so made their castles virtually impregnable.

Several of the castles were already in existence at the time of the Ismaʿili uprising in the early 480s/1090s and after declaring his allegiance to Ḥasan-e Ṣabbāḥ the new governor would set about rebuilding and enlarging his castle. This was an urgent matter as it was not long before Seljuq troops set out to defeat the "heretics." The imminent task was to build underground storage rooms containing sufficient food for the garrison for several years. These were so well built that ʿAlāʾ-al-Din ʿAṭā Malek Jovayni, the historian of the Mongol era, complains bitterly how difficult it was to demolish the castle of Alamut after it had surrendered to the Mongols. He is clearly astonished at the amount of stores, both liquid and solid, the castle contained, all still in very good condition.

The military genius behind the construction of Ismaʿili castles seems to have been Bozorg-Omid, Ḥasan-e

Ṣabbāḥ's successor (518-32/1124-38). He rebuilt the castle of Lamasar, the largest Ismaʿili castle, with its complex and highly efficient water storage system. Wherever the slope of a fortified hill was large enough, a well-constructed water catchment area was constructed. When the present author located the site of Soru, not far from Dāmḡān, it was noted that in addition to the water catchment area, which needed to be defended by strong thick walls, water had also been channeled to the main castle from a smaller castle a mile away. The Ismaʿilis were skilled water engineers and agriculturists. Every Ismaʿili castle had a large number of deep limestone-lined water storage cisterns, which were roofed over. Steps led down to the water. Many of the valleys below the castles are now barren and infertile, but some still contain flourishing little farms. Soru is a prime example. In 1972, the present author and his team estimated that the castle of Lamasar was able to rely on almost 400,000 liters of water stored in the castle's water cisterns and that supplementary water supplies could easily be obtained from the nearby Naina Rud. This amount would be sufficient to keep 500 men and 50 mules or horses in water for three months.

The Ismaʿili castles in Syria, apart from Kahf and Maṣyāf, were not built on the same massive scale as those in Persia. It was some time before the Ismaʿilis were able to acquire their own castles (524-34/1130-40) and often there was insufficient space available to enlarge them greatly, although the walls, entrances and outworks were often rebuilt or strengthened considerably. Thus the Syrian castles tended to be more compact, although they were well provisioned and able to withstand a prolonged siege. The castle of Ḵawābi, for instance, was never taken by Crusaders and the site was reoccupied at the beginning of the 20th century by Syrians who continue to live in the castle ruins. An epigraph shows the date of 708/1308.

Kahf and Maṣyāf are the two most interesting castles in the area. Kahf was the headquarters of Rāšed-al-Din Senān and the last Ismaʿili stronghold to submit to Baybars. It is set on a rocky hill, almost completely covered by undergrowth, overlooking a deep valley and is over 600 meters long. The most important building still standing is the *ḥammām* or bathhouse, a large and exceptionally well proportioned and elaborate complex, hewn from solid rock on the south side of the castle. Water was brought from a spring 2 kilometers away. Three gates lead into the castle, again hewn from the rock, on which are carved important inscriptions and Qurʾanic verses.

Maṣyāf is the best preserved of the Ismaʿili castles in Syria. It had its origins in Seleucid, Roman and Byzantine eras, and was acquired by the Ismaʿilis in 535/1140 and together with Kahf became the center of Ismaʿili power. It was, however, more exposed than Kahf, besieged unsuccessfully by Saladin in 571/1176, and eventually surrendered to Baybars. The castle was surveyed by Michael Braune in 1983-84 in conjunction with the German Archaeological Institute in Syria and he has compiled a list of thirteen epigraphs in Maṣyāf, most of them dating from 646-47/1248-49, although there is an earlier one of 621/1224. The latest was 1191/1777. Such epigraphs are not found in Persian Ismaʿili castles, but are fairly common in Syria. The defensive arrangements of Maṣyāf are very impressive, and include extensive use of the bent entrance and the concentric principle of fortification.

When the Mongols under Hulagu Khan invaded the Alamut Valley in November 654/1256, they wisely made for the weakest Ismaʿili castle from the military point of view, Maymun Dez. The castle was not set on a great ridge like Alamut and the Mongols were able to use their mangonels with devastating effect. The Ismaʿili Imam, Rokn-al-Din Ḵoršāh, like most other rulers, stood in awe of the Mongols, and soon agreed to surrender all his castles to them. Some of his garrison commanders were reluctant to follow and Lamasar did not surrender for a year. Gerdkuh held out for 17 years. It would have been interesting to see what the outcome would have been if the Ismaʿilis had been able to offer a more spirited resistance. Many of the castles could have withstood a prolonged siege without much difficulty.

The present author has identified the location of a large number of Ismaʿili castles in the last decades of the 20th century, thus making it possible to appreciate more fully the power and influence of the Ismaʿili state, especially the part played by Qohestān. The fortresses at Qāʾen, Fourk, and Šāhdiz are particularly impressive. The ruins of Moʾmenābād cover a large area and this must have been a particularly impressive fortress and city. It was not far from the borders of Qohestān and because of its importance needed to be strongly protected. The Mongols set about its destruction with ferocity. The main curtain wall stretched for about 2 miles over sandy dunes. The track leading to it was closed in 1997 and declared impassable.

Bibiliography: Max Van Berchem, "Épigraphie des Assassins du Syrie," *JA*, série, 9, 1897, pp. 453-501; repr. in idem, *Opera Minora*, Geneva, 1978, vol. I, pp. 453-501. Michael Braune, *Untersuchungen zur mittelalterlichen Befestigung in Nordwest-Syrien: Die Assassinenburg Masyāf*, Damascus, 1985. Bernard Hourcade, *Alamut*, *EIr.*, I, pp. 797-801. Wladimir Ivanow, *Alamut and Lamasar: Two Mediaeval Ismaili Strongholds in Iran*, Tehran, 1960. ʿAlāʾ-al-Din ʿAṭā Malek Jovayni, *Tāriḵ-e jahāngošā*, tr. John Andrew Boyle as *The History of the World-Conqueror*, 2 vols., Manchester, 1958. M. Kervran, "Une Forteresse d'Azerbaidjan: Samirān," *REI* 41, 1973, pp. 71-93. Caro O. Minasian, *Shah Diz of Ismaʿili Fame, Its Siege and Destruction*, London, 1971. J. Phillips, "Assassin Castles in Syria," *The Connoisseur*, No. 770, 1976, pp. 287-89. Samuel M. Stern, with E. Beazley, and A. Dobson, "The Fortress of Khān Lanjān," *Iran* 9, 1971, pp. 49-57. Manučehr Sotuda, *Qelāʿ-e Esmāʿiliya*, Tehran, 1966. Peter Willey, *The Castles of the Assassins*, London, 1963. Idem, "The Valley of the Assassins," *Royal Central Asian Journal* 48, 1961, pp. 147-51. Idem, "Further Expeditions to the Valleys of the Assassins," *Royal Central Asian Journal* 54, 1967, pp. 156-62. Idem, "The Assassins in Quhistan," *Royal Central Asian Journal* 55, 1968, pp. 180-83. Idem, "The 1972

Assassin Expedition," *Royal Central Asian Journal* 61, 1974, pp. 60-70. Idem, *University Lectures in Islamic Studies*, Vol. II, Altajir World of Islam Trust, 1998, pp. 167-81. Idem, *The Eagle's Nest: Ismaili Castles in Iran and Syria*, London, 2004.

(PETER WILLEY)

xvi. MODERN ISMAʿILI COMMUNITIES

The Ismaʿilis consist of two main branches—the Nezāri Ismaʿilis and the Mustaʿlian Ṭayyebi Ismaʿilis. Both have their roots in the Fatimid period of Ismaʿili history and differ primarily over their respective belief in the Imamat, spiritual leadership of the community. The Nezāri branch believes in a living physically present Imam, Ḥāżer Imam. Their present and forty-ninth Imam is Prince Karim Aga Khan. The Mustaʿlian Ismaʿilis believe that their twenty-first Imam, al-Ṭayyeb went into physical concealment (*satr*) and that while the Imamat continues in his line, authority in his physical absence is fulfilled by a vice-gerent, *dāʿi moṭlaq*, who acts on his behalf. In their encounter with modernity therefore, the two communities reflect a different pattern of historical and institutional development.

THE MUSTAʿLIAN ṬAYYEBI ISMAʿILIS

From the 10th/16th century onward the Mustaʿlian Ṭayyebi community became divided into Dāʾudi and Solaymani factions over allegiance to a particular line of *dāʿis*. The present *dāʿi* of the major group, the Dāʾudi Ṭayyebis, also known popularly as Bohras, is Sayyednā Borhan-al-Din, the fifty-second in a line of authorities. They are found mostly in South Asia, to a lesser extent in Yemen and in small immigrant communities living in Britain, North America and Sri Lanka.

The other group, called the Ṭayyebi Solaymānis, followed a different line and their present fiftieth *dāʿi* is al-Ḥosayn b. Esmāʿil al-Makrami, headquartered in the Yemen. Following the annexation of Najrān from the Yemen to Saudi Arabia a community of Solaymānis is also to be found there and an even smaller number lives in India.

Two major *dāʿis* have played an important role in the modern Dāʾudi Ṭayyebi community. Sayyednā Ṭāher Sayf-al-Din became leader in 1915 and was succeeded in 1965 by the present leader Sayyednā Moḥammad Borhān-al-Din (b. 1915). They have continued to emphasize the strong tradition of learning in the community, as reflected in the further development of the two major libraries in Mumbai and Surat; and the enlargement of the seminary, Jāmeʿa Sayfiya in Surat, an academy of studies and training for religious scholars of the community. There are well established madrasas for the religious education of all followers as well as schools for secular education. The tradition of preserving the heritage of learning through manuscript study has been well preserved and scholarly and literary works, primarily in Arabic, continue to be developed within the community.

The Dāʾudi community is organized under the leadership of the *dāʿi*, with its headquarters in Mumbai, and with the assistance of the brothers and sons of the *dāʿi*. The 'Wazarat al-Safiyya', the central administrative office, appoints local representatives called *ʿāmel*, throughout the world. Each *ʿāmel* heads the local community, organizing religious and social life, including maintenance of places for religious worship and ritual, as well as communal buildings. The legal framework of practice is based on the *Daʿāʾem al-Eslām* of the Fatimid jurist al-Qāżi al-Noʿmān (d. 363/974). Bohra congregational religious practices include sessions called *majāles*, where sermons are given, religious poems are recited and other practices distinctive to the tradition are performed. The majority of the Dāʾudi Bohras are in business and industry and have a well-deserved reputation for entrepreneurship and public service. They also run many charitable organizations for the welfare of their communities world-wide.

The Solaymāni community, of predominantly Arab origin in the Yemen, is found in both urban and rural areas, with strong tribal roots. The community of Najrān in Saudi Arabia, has often found it difficult to practice its faith openly and freely. The community in India has produced noted public officials and scholars, the most prominent was Asaf A. A. Fyzee (1899-1981), a lawyer, diplomat, and scholar.

THE NEZĀRI ISMAʿILIS

The modern Nezāri Ismaʿili community which is more numerous has a global presence. Historically, the community reflects the geographical and ethnographic diversity based on the various cultural regions of the world, where its members originated and lived. These heritages are Central Asian, Persian, Arab and South Asian. They are found in some thirty different countries ranging from Iran, Afghanistan, various countries in Africa, Bangladesh, India, Pakistan, Syria and Tajikistn. During the 19th and 20th centuries many Ismaʿilis from South Asia migrated to Africa and settled there. In more recent times there has been migration from all the parts of the Ismaʿili world to North America and Europe. The shared values that unite the Nezāris are centered on allegiance to a living Imam, at present the forty-ninth hereditary Imam, Prince Karim Aga Khan. The role and guidance of the Imam provides the enabling framework for the development of the community and for the continuity of its Muslim heritage.

The modern phase of the Nezāris Ismaʿili history, as in general with other Muslims, can be dated to the 9th century and to the significant historical changes arising from the growth and enlargement of European presence and power in the Muslim world. Following a period of change and turmoil in Iran during the 1840s, the forty-sixth Imam, Āḡā Ḥasan-ʿAli Šāh (Aga Khan I, q.v.), went to India, where he was the first Imam to bear the title of Aga Khan, granted by the Persian ruler Fatḥ-ʿAli Shah Qajār. His leadership enabled the community in India to lay the foundations for institutional and social developments and also fostered more regular contacts with Ismaʿili communities in other parts of the world. He was succeeded on his death in 1881 by his son Āḡā ʿAli Šāh (Aga Khan II, q.v.) who continued to build on the institutions created by his father, with a particular emphasis on providing modern education for the community. He also played an important role in representing Muslims in the emerging political institutions under British rule in India and encouraging philanthropic efforts to enlarge opportunities for them in social and educational fields. Following his early death in 1885, he was succeeded by his eight-year-old son, Imam Solṭān Moḥammad Šāh, Aga Khan III. He was Imam for 72 years, the longest in Ismaʿili history and his life spanned dramatic political, social and economic transformations among Muslims, as in much of the world at large.

Aga Khan III's long term involvement in international affairs, including the Presidency of the League of Nations, his advocacy of Muslim interests in troubled times and his commitment to advancing education, particularly for Muslim women, reflect his many and varied contributions. It was however at the level of his leadership as Imam that he was able to transform the modern history of the Ismaʿilis, enabling them to adapt successfully to the challenges and changes of the twentieth century.

Particularly in the Subcontinent and Africa, where enabling conditions existed for the development of the community, the Ismaʿilis established administrative structures, educational institutions, health services and built on economic opportunities in trade and industry. The educational institutions included instruction from early childhood through secondary schooling, with scholarships made available for advanced studies. Schools for girls were established separately, where necessary and female education was given a high priority.

In 1905, the Nezāri Ismaʿili community in East Africa adopted a constitution which laid the basis for an organized framework of institutions and governance at local, national and regional levels. Similar constitutions became part of other Ismaʿili communities and appropriately revised over time, provided guidance for the conduct of personal law and its relationship with other communities in the context of the laws of the land. In 1986, the present Imam, Prince Karim Aga Khan, extended the practice to the world-wide community. The revised Constitution which serves the social governance needs of the Ismaʿilis facilitates a united approach to internal organization and external relations, while taking account of regional diversity and local differences. As in the past, Nezāri Ismaʿilis continue a strong tradition of voluntary service, contributions and donations of time, expertise and personal resources to the Imam and the institutions.

The present Imam assumed his role in 1957 at a time when much of the developing world, including the Muslim world, was going through an important period of transition, often marked by political change and upheaval. These continued throughout the 12th century, making it particularly vital that the Ismaʿilis were guided appropriately through periods of crises and tumultuous changes, as in the case of East Africa and then later Tajikistan, Iran, Syria and Afghanistan. Dislocation often meant that humanitarian concerns for refugee rehabilitation and resettlement took priority, and a significant number of Ismaʿilis also immigrated to Britain, Canada, Europe and the United States. More recently, many refugees have returned to Afghanistan to contribute to nation-building there.

While the internal institutional organizations of the Nezāri community continued to be strengthened and variously reorganized to respond to changing conditions, the Imam also created new institutions to better serve the complex development needs of the community as well as the societies in which the Ismaʿilis lived. This gave rise to the establishment and growth of the Aga Khan Development Network (AKDN), an international and inter-denominational group of agencies with the goal of pioneering values and strategies for sustainable human development conducive to the fulfilment of cultural, economic, social and spiritual needs and aspirations of individuals and communities. A number of institutions within AKDN pursue a variety of non-denominational programmes in economic development, education, social development, culture and the environment and poverty eradication, across the world, in rural and urban settings, with a particular emphasis on populations that are disadvantaged.

The Nezāri Ismaʿilis and their Imam view the entire spectrum of their engagement in the world as an expression of an encompassing ethic of Islam and a long standing faith and historical tradition going back to the teachings of the Prophet and the early Imams as reflected in various periods of history, such as that of the Fatimids. Some of these institutions, which work closely with international agencies, national governments, local communities and charitable organizations, have become acknowledged world-wide for successfully addressing critical developmental needs through programmes in Architecture and the Environment, Education and in particular childhood and girls' education, Economic Development and Health Services. This has enabled the Ismaʿili community and the Imamat to become catalysts for innovative approaches to problems of society, without losing the grounding in their Muslim traditions of ethical commitment and interpretations of faith and practice.

The creation of an Institute of Ismaili Studies (q.v.) in London in 1977 has enabled the development of a significant program of research, publications and education to promote scholarship and learning on Islam, Shiʿism and Ismaʿilism. The Institute is increasingly becoming an important international academic forum and reference point for Ismaʿili studies in Arabic, Persian, English and several other languages as well as an important resource for Ismaʿilis for the preservation and study of their heritage.

Each Ismaʿili Jamat, or congregation, is generally served by an Ismaʿili Center called the *Jamatkhana*, an institutional category of religious spaces common to many Muslim communities. It is a space reserved for tradition and practices specific to the Ismaʿili *ṭariqa* of Islam. In several cities around the world, such as London, Vancouver, Lisbon, Dubai and Dushanbe, Ismaʿili centers built in the recent past became well-known for their architectural design and for the promotion of cultural, educational and social programmes serving Ismaʿilis and the larger society.

In their modern historical development, the various Ismaʿili communities, Mustaʿlian and Nezāri, represent a case among cases, of how Muslim religious communities might through appropriate interpretation of their heritage create new opportunities to affirm and further some of the positive gains of modernity.

Bibliography: Materials on the contemporary period in Ismaʿili history is increasingly available on institutional, academic websites, such as the website (www.iis.ac.uk) of the Institute of Ismaili Studies, and the official website (www.mumineen.org) of the Dāʾudi Bohra community.

Aga Khan III, Sultan Muhammad Shah. *Selected Speeches and Writings*. Edited by K. K. Aziz, London, 1998. 2 vols. Jonah Blank, *Mullahs on the Mainframe: Islam and Modernity among the Daudi Bohras*. Chicago and London, 2001. Farhad Daftary, *The Ismāʿīlīs: Their History and Doctrines*. Cambridge, 1990. Rafiq Keshavjee, *Mysticism and the Plurality of Meaning: The Case of the Ismailis of Rural Iran*. London, 1998. Azim Nanji, "Modernization and Change in the Nizari Ismaʿili Community in East Africa—A Perspective" *Journal of Religion in Africa*, 6 (1974) pp. 123-39. Idem, "The Nizari Ismaili Muslim Community in North America: Background and Development" in Earle H. Waugh et al., ed. *The Muslim Community in North America*. Edmonton, 1983, pp. 149-64. Tahera Qutbuddin, "The Daudi Bohra Tayyibis: Ideology, Literature, Learning and Social Practice" in F. Daftary, ed., *A Modern History of the Ismailis* (London, forthcoming).

(Azim Nanji)

xvii. The Imamate in Ismaʿilism

In common with all major Shiʿite groups, the Ismaʿilis (q.v.) believe that the Imamate is a divinely sanctioned and guided institution, through whose agency Muslims are enabled to contextualize the practice of their faith and to understand fully the exoteric and esoteric dimensions of the Qurʾān. The Imamate exists to complement prophethood and to ensure that the divine purpose is fulfilled on earth at all times and in all places.

The principle of the Imamate

The historical underpinning for this vision of Islam is based on the cardinal principle of Shiʿite belief that, after the death of the Prophet Moḥammad, his cousin and son-in-law, ʿAli (q.v.), became Imam following a specific designation (*naṣṣ*) made by the Prophet, based on divine command, before his death (see Ḡadir Ḵomm). Shiʿite historical understanding thus locates itself within a framework of interpretation supported by Qurʾanic verses and Prophetic Hadith. The institution of the Imamate is to continue thereafter on a heredity basis through ʿAli and his wife, Fāṭema (q.v.), the Prophet's daughter, succession being based on designation by the Imam of the time. Adherence to the doctrine of the Imamate as a pillar of faith meant not only acceptance of, but also devotion to, the legitimate successors of the Prophet. The Imamate is therefore linked to the concept of *welāya*, devotion to the Imams. The two major branches of the Ismaʿilis, the Nezāris and the Mostaʿlis, affirm a shared belief in the Imamate, but give allegiance to different lines of Imams. The Nezāri Ismaʿilis believe in the physical presence of a living Imam, who for them today is Prince Karim Aga Khan IV, the 49th Imam in direct descent from the Prophet through ʿAli and Fāṭema. The Mostaʿlis believe that their 21st Hidden Imam went into physical concealment around 524/1130; while the Imamate continues in his line, in his physical absence authority is fulfilled by a vicegerent who acts on his behalf. At present this role is held by the 52nd *dāʿi* (q.v.), Sayyednā Borhān-al-Din (b. 1333/1915) who leads the Dāʾudi Ṭayyebi Bohras, while a smaller Solaymāni Bohra community found in Yemen is headed by their 51st *dāʿi*, ʿAbdallāh b. Moḥammad (Daftary, pp. 353-57).

One of the most systematic and succinct expositions of Ismaʿili ideas of the Imamate is to be found in a work of Qāżi Noʿmān (d. 363/974) called *Daʿāʾem al-eslām*. Noʿmān, a leading jurist of the Fatimid period of Ismaʿili history, played a key role in the formation and elaboration of several legal as well as theological works that were regarded as definitive in his time. *Welāya*, as the basis for belief in the Imamate as defined by Qāżi Noʿmān, is the foremost among the pillars of Islam. However, prior to discussing the question of *welāya*, he differentiates between *eslām* (submission) and *imān* (faith), basing himself on a Qurʾānic verse: "The desert Arabs say 'we believe.' Say (to them) 'You have no faith (*imān*).' But rather they should say 'we have submitted (*aslama*)'" (Qurʾān 49:14). From this he deduces that one can thus be a Muslim (*moslem*, i.e., a member of the religion of Islam) without necessarily being a *moʾmen*. The latter implies belief in and devotion to the rightful Imam; this, in fact, constitutes true faith. The Shiʿite and Ismaʿili claim to *welāya* is deduced by Noʿmān on the basis of historical events revealing ʿAli's close proximity to the Prophet, as well as his being the most worthy among the Companions to succeed the Prophet. Then follows a discussion of the indications of preference for ʿAli made by the Prophet throughout his life and confirmed in the declaration at Ḡadir Ḵomm after the so-called Farewell Pilgrimage (*ḵoṭbat al-wadāʿ*): "He whose *mawlā* (trustee, helper, lord) I am, ʿAli is his *mawlā*." According to this view, having been attached to the establishment of the Imamate, ʿAli was granted the authority to interpret the Qurʾān and to initiate change in society in accordance with these principles adapted to the context of the time. The importance of *welāya* in Noʿmān's scheme lies in the fact that the Imam deserves the love and allegiance of the community, quite apart from whether, at a given time, the Imamate is a political office or not (Qāżi Moʿmān, *Daʿāʾem* I, pp. 14-98; tr., I, pp. 18-122).

Noʿmān then goes on to give the Ismaʿili concept far wider scope by relating it to Qurʾānic analogies and

Islamic tradition. He argues that the tradition of designating and establishing the succession has been adhered to throughout the history of the earlier prophets and quotes the specific Qurʾānic instance where Jesus announced the coming of Moḥammad; he also cites other cases of prophets who had designated their legatee (*waṣi*). The Imamate therefore complements the cycle of prophethood (*nobuwwa*), sustaining the continuity of divine guidance until the Day of Judgment. In the Ismaʿili view, the function of prophethood to convey God's message had ended, but the need for affirmation, interpretation, stewardship and spiritual leadership was not yet over: the Imamate fulfils this role.

While the juridical view, as stated in the *Daʿāʾem*, establishes the foundational Qurʾānic and historical basis for the Imamate, Ismaʿili thought also developed a philosophical approach for this concept. Ḥamid-al-Din Aḥmad Kermāni (d. ca. 411/1021), the Ismaʿili philosopher and *dāʿi*, who lived during the reign of the Fatimid al-Ḥākem (r. 386-411/996-1021), discusses the fusion of the philosophical basis of Imamate with its juridical aspects. For him, the essence of governing involves the organization of human beings, with all the variety of individual opinions and prejudices they represent, into a divinely ordered pattern. If such a pattern were to become understood and then followed, society as a whole would reflect greater order and consequently greater happiness. According to Kermāni, therefore, the *Imam* interprets the elements of the divine revelation so that each has its proper place within the integrity of the whole, assuming thereby that human beings and society will find proper equilibrium in both material and spiritual matters. Justice (*ʿadl*) then comes to be conceived as this state of equilibrium, at the individual and social levels. In the general definitions given by al-Noʿmān, as well as the philosophical exposition of Kermāni, a significant aspect of the Imamate links it to the achievement of justice in society, which in turn reflects the proper intellectual, spiritual, and social maturity of individuals in society. The concepts of *din* "religion" and *donyā* "the world," are both elements in the proper ordering of society and the Imam's guidance sustains a balance between the two dimensions of life (Walker, pp. 16-24, 62-79).

A further philosophical discourse is represented in Persian Ismaʿili writings such as those of Nāṣer-e Ḵosrow (d. after 462/1070) and Naṣir-al-Din Ṭusi (d. 672/1274), where, in connection with their discussion of the concept of higher truths (*ḥaqāʾeq*, sing. *ḥaqiqa*), or according to their work, it was through teaching (*taʿlim*) from the Imam that knowledge (*ʿelm*), in the fullest sense of the word, could be attained. Such knowledge encompassed the dimension of *ẓāher*, exemplifying the outward expression of Islam and its practice (as in the *Daʿāʾem* of Qāżi Noʿmān) and the *bāṭen*, as embodied in the inner meaning of the *ḥaqāʾeq* of revelation. The Imamate, through the symbolic interpretation (*taʾwil*) of the Qurʾān, enabled an understanding of the metaphysical, philosophical and symbolic dimensions of the faith, which is a composite of shariʿa and *ḥaqiqa* (Hunsberger, pp. 72-90).

Nāṣer-e Ḵosrow's philosophical writings and his literary work, the *Divān* (collection of poems), as well as the devotional literature preserved in several vernacular languages in the Ismaʿili tradition, provide passages that illustrate how the Imamate is the gateway through whose intercession, an individual passes through the stages of knowledge that bring about attainment of spiritual goals and knowledge. In his work *Sayr wa soluk*, Ṭusi relates the concept of taʿlim to the instructional role of the Imamate. He states that after having reached a certain stage through action and individual intellectual effort, an individual becomes aware of the necessity of an authoritative teacher. He states: "Since the circumstances of this world are (always) changing, if at a certain time or under certain circumstances, the speaker of truth (*moḥeqq*) shows himself to Mankind in a different form expresses himself differently, manifests the truth differently, or institutes the divine law differently (from that of his predecessor), it will not mean that there is any difference in his truthfulness, because (in his essence) he is free from transformation and alteration. Transformation and alteration are the necessary attributes of this world" (Ṭusi, *Sayr*, text, pp. 4-18; tr., pp. 27-48).

History in Ismaʿili thought, therefore, reflects varied patterns through which institutional order can be realized, according to the guidance of the Imam of the time. The dominant patterns of this process are characterized in the two eras that unfold over time and space: (1) periods of quiescence and interiorization, when circumstances may limit a broader engagement with the world, and (2) a more enabling time when it is possible to engage intellectually and institutionally in the world. In historical and human terms, society during these eras reflects a model of history in which justice remains a constant goal and the function of the Imamate is to give that goal personal meaning and institutional expression and coherence, within the context of faith and reason, applied in diverse and changing circumstances.

The metaphors that underpin this view of history can be considered as elements that give a permanent imprint to Ismaʿili understanding of the sacredness of spiritual authority and knowledge, and to the view that, even when the processes of history might appear to temporarily inhibit the fulfilment of justice, the idioms inherent in these symbols retain their universality. The metaphors connect the social world, in this sense, with the cosmic world and represent a quest for, and the hope of, attaining "higher stages of perfection," inner and outer, through the Imamate.

THE IMAMATE IN HISTORY

The early Imams. Following the death in 40/661 of ʿAli, whom all Shiʿites regard as the first Imam, the Ismaʿilis acknowledge his son Ḥosayn as having inherited the full authority of Imamate. Although ʿAli's eldest son Ḥasan is also acknowledged as a successor (in most Shiʿite accounts), the Nezāri Ismaʿilis regard his role as having been custodial, until such time as Ḥosayn assumed the Imamate. Following Ḥosayn's tragic death at Karbalā in 61/680, he was succeeded by his son ʿAli Zayn-al-ʿĀbedin and then Moḥammad al-Bāqer and Jaʿfar al-Ṣādeq who died in 148/765). Though none of them exercised a political role, this early period is considered significant, as it is around the Imamate that the identity of the Shiʿites as a group within the Muslim community comes to be consolidated.

The Fatimid Caliph-Imams. After the death of Imam Jaʿfar-al-Ṣādeq, the Shiʿites became eventually divided into two main groups. One accepted Musā al-Kāẓem, one of Imam Jaʿfar's sons, and these eventually came to be known as Imamis or Twelver Shiʿites (*q.v.), and others acknowledged another son Esmāʿil (q.v.) and his descendants. It is in this time that the Imamate appeared during the rise of the Fatimids, beginning with the public proclamation in 297/909 of the Imamate of ʿAbd-Allāh b. Ḥosayn al-Mahdi (r. 297-322/909-34), the first Fatimid caliph. The group of Imams prior to this, between Esmāʿil and al-Mahdi, are regarded as part of the period of public quiescence and concealment (*satr*), as they sought to escape persecution.

The Imams of the Fatimid era are well known, and this period of Imamate reflects the flowering of intellectual, cultural, and economic life that became the hallmark of the vast Fatimid empire. The Ismaʿili Imams now ruled as Fatimid caliphs, and their authority was acknowledged in many parts of the Muslim world of the time. Ismaʿili communities flourished in the Middle East, Central Asia, Persia, South Asia, and North Africa (Daftary, pp. 152-222).

The Imamate in Persia. Following the death of the Fāṭimid Caliph-Imam al-Mostanṣer Be'llāh in 487/1094 (r. 427-97/1036-94), the Ismaʿilis became divided into two major groups, one acknowledging continuity of the Imamate in his son Nezār (d. 488/1095), while others recognized a younger son, al-Mostaʿli (r. 487-95/1094-1101). The latter group continued to follow al-Mostaʿli's son al-Āmer (r. 495-524/1101-30). On al-Āmer's death in 524/1130, the majority of followers accepted his infant son al-Ṭayyeb, but believed that he went into concealment and that subsequent Imams succeeding him remain hidden, awaiting manifestation of the end of time.

The successors of Nezār inaugurated the Nezāri Ismaʿili Imamate and a state in Persia and Syria, with its main base in the fortress of Alamut (q.v.). This period of the Imamate lasted until the Mongol invasion and destruction of the Ismaʿili state in 654/1256. The Imamate continued thereafter in various parts of Iran, with the Imams maintaining a discrete profile and providing continuity and guidance through their representatives to the scattered communities in Persia, Syria, and Central and South Asia (Daftary, pp. 386-429; see also FATIMIDS, relations with Persia).

The modern period. The modern period, from the middle of the 19th century, is marked by the transition of the Imamate from Persia to India and then to Europe. It is largely dominated by the lives and activities of three Imams: Ḥasan ʿAli Šāh, Aga Khan I (q.v., d. 1881), Solṭān Moḥammad Šāh, Aga Khan III (d. 1957), and the present Imam, Prince Karim Aga Khan IV (b. 1936).

In its modern and contemporary context, the Imamate has been able to provide Ismaʿili communities with guidance and structures to contextualize and implement their faith in a changing world. Among the Nezāri Ismaʿilis, who have emerged in the last hundred years as a well-organized and coherent Muslim community, the Imamate has created new institutions for the governance, social development and religious continuity of the various worldwide communities, spread in some thirty countries. In addition, by creating a global network of institutions, under the umbrella of the Aga Khan Development Network (AKDN), the Imam of the time, Prince Karim Aga Khan, building on the groundwork laid by his grandfather, the previous Imam, has sought to realize the social conscience of Islam, through programs that promote social, cultural, and educational development, encompassing some of the poorest areas of Africa and Asia, to serve significant populations, regardless of their origin, gender, or religion. In this way, the Imamate continues to provide guidance and support to Ismaʿili communities and the populations among whom they live (Daftary, pp. 504-48).

Bibliography: Mian Bhai Mulla Abdul Husain, *Gulzare Daudi for the Bohras of India: A Short Note on the Bohras of India, their 21 Imams and 51 Dais*, Ahmedabad, 1920; repr., Surat, 1977. Aga Khan III [Solṭān Moḥammad Šāh], *The Memoirs of Aga Khan: World Enough and Time*, London, 1954. Mohammad-Ali Amir-Moezzi, *The Divine Guide in Early Shiʿism: The Sources of Esotericism in Islam*, tr. D. Streight, Albany, N.Y., 1994. Henry Corbin, *Cyclical Time and Ismaili Gnosis*, London, 1983. Farhad Daftary, *The Ismāʿilis: Their History and Doctrines*, Cambridge, 1990. Aziz Esmail, *A Scent of Sandalwood: Indo-Ismaili Religious Lyrics (Ginans)*, Richmond, Surrey, UK, 2002. Sumaiya Hamdani, *Between Revolution and State. Al-Nuʿman and the Construction of Fatimid Legitimacy*, forthcoming. Alice C. Hunsberger, *Nasir Khusraw, The Ruby of Badakhshan. A Portrait of the Persian Poet, Traveller and Philosopher*, London, 2000. Ḥamid-al-Din Aḥmad Kermāni, *Rāḥat al-ʿaql*, ed. M. K. Ḥosayn and M. M. Ḥelmi, Leiden, 1953. Wilferd Madelung, *The Succession to Muḥammad: A Study of the Early Caliphate*, Cambridge, 1997. Azim Nanji, *The Nizāri Ismāʿili Tradition in the Indo-Pakistan Subcontinent*, Delmar, N.Y., 1978. Qāżi Moʿmān b. Moḥammad, *Daʿāʾem al-eslām*, ed. A. A. Fyzee, Cairo, 1951-61; tr. A. A. A. Fyzee, *The Pillars of Islam*, rev. I. K. Poonawala, New Delhi, 2000-04. Naṣir-al-Din Ṭusi, *Rawżat al-taslim, yā taṣawwurāt*, ed. W. Ivanov, Tehran, 1984; ed. and tr. S. J. Badakhchani as *Paradise of Submission*, London, 2005. Idem, *Sayr wa soluk*, in idem, *Majmuʿa-ye rasāʾel*, ed. M.-T. Modarres-Rażawi, Tehran, 1956, pp. 36-55; tr. S. J. Badakhchani as *Contemplation and Action. The Spiritual Autobiography of a Muslim Scholar*, London, 1998. Paul E. Walker, *Hamid al-Din al-Kirmani: Ismaili Thought in the Age of al-Hakim*, London, 1999.

(AZIM NANJI)

ISRAEL, Relations with Iran. This entry is divided into the following four sections.

i. *Diplomatic and political relations.*
ii. *The Jewish Persian community.*
iii. *Iranian Studies in Israel.*
iv. *Persian art collections in Israel.*

i. Diplomatic and Political Relations with Iran

The relationship between Israel and Iran has since the very inception of the Jewish state in 1948 been a complex function of Iran's geo-strategic imperatives as a non-Arab, non-Sunni state in an overwhelmingly Arab and Sunni environment, and its need to find an appropriate relationship with its Arab/Sunni neighbors in order to materialize Iranian regional leadership aspirations.

Though military and intelligence cooperation with Israel has at times been seen as necessary to advance Iran's geo-strategic goals primarily the balancing of threats emanating from Iran's Arab neighbors ties to the Jewish state has impeded the attainment of Iran's second goal; that of achieving long-term security by befriending the Arab/ Sunni states in its immediate neighborhood and gaining legitimacy for Iran's quest for supremacy.

This entry is divided into two separate sections: the Pahlavi period and the Post-Revolution period.

(1) The Pahlavi Period (1948-78).
(2) Post Revolution Period (1979-2007).

(1) The Pahlavi Period (1948-78)

Under the Pahlavi regime, and particularly since the 1960s, Israel and Persia enjoyed close ties, resulting in informal strategic alliance. While seeking close ties with the West and striving for modernization, Mohammad Reza Shah Pahlavi (r. 1941-79) viewed Israel as a natural ally. Israel's strength and progress fascinated him, and its conflict with the Arab world and opposition to Communist influence in the region further promoted the strengthening of ties. The shah also believed that through relations with Israel, Persia would benefit in the United States, gaining the support of American Jewry, the congress, media, business community, and the administration. Persia then felt threatened by its Arab neighbors, some of which, like Nasserist Egypt and Baʿathist Iraq, were common adversaries of both countries. Although domestic concerns regulated relations in the initial years of Israel's independence, later regional and domestic developments encouraged the expansion of ties.

Israel, then seeking legitimacy in the Middle East, viewed Persia an ideal ally. While the intent to befriend Persia existed prior to independence, it intensified in the late 1950s when Prime Minister David Ben-Gurion coined the "periphery concept." It prescribed that in the absence of relations with its neighbors, Israel should seek the friendship of "the neighbors of the neighbors." This was translated into a close, though informal, alliance with Persia (Gilad, 2002, p. 252; Gilboa, p. 257; Welāyati, 2001, pp. 97-103; Fallāḥ-nežād, pp. 121-27). Gradually, as the shah gained further power and expanded his ties with Washington, in conjunction with the enticing Iranian oil income and lucrative development plans, Israel had even better reasons to cultivate ties with Persia. Although several regional developments (declining Arab nationalism, Persia's improved ties with Egypt, and the Algier Accord with Iraq) joined to diminish Israeli significance for Persia's interests in the 1970s political, economic and strategic ties continued to expand. This period of close ties came to an abrupt end with the fall of the Pahlavi regime and the establishment of the Islamic Republic in February 1979. Fierce hostility still continues to define their "relations" twenty-eight years later. Moreover, Persia's Islamic stance has placed the Arab-Israeli conflict on a different footing, projecting it rather as a religious crusade than merely a political-national conflict. Persia's involvement in Lebanon and support for Islamist movements (Hamas, Hizballah and Islamic Jihad) has made it more directly involved it in the Arab-Israeli conflict. Its nuclear and missile programs were viewed as a major threat to Israeli security, as was its alleged engagement in terrorism. Thus, while Persia views Israel as the enemy of Persia, Islam, and mankind, Israel regards Persia as the primary threat to its existence and to the safety of the free world; and whereas Persia volunteered to hoist the anti-Israel flag, Israel undertook to lead the anti-Persian camp.

Early contact, 1948-63. In the Jewish collective memory, Persia is cherished as a friendly nation. This goes back to the days of Cyrus the Great (q.v.), who granted the Jewish people significant liberties. The close ties between the two countries under the last shah reinforced such perceptions. This image of Persia existed despite the fact that over history Persian Jews frequently suffered periods of persecution and harassment to a greater extent than they did under Ottoman rule.

Since the emergence of the Zionist movement in the late 19th century, Persia's attitude has been ambivalent, if not hostile, to the idea of Jewish statehood. While Persia's national interests and the last shah's pro-Western tendencies have led to a somewhat tolerant approach, as a Muslim state influenced heavily by the ulama, hostile attitudes remained prevalent. Israel's initial contacts with Persia focused on issues relating to the Persian residents in Israel and the Jewish inhabitants of Persia. In 1942, Zionist agencies sent emissaries to provide Persian Jewry with education and indoctrination. Yet, paradoxically, the immediate stimuli for this interest was both the misfortune of European Jewry, many of whom arrived in Persia after fleeing the European Holocaust, and the growing threat to the Jews of Iraq who wished to immigrate to Israel via Persia.

Prior to Israel's independence, Persian policy toward a Jewish state was unfavorable. Persian ulama (some of them residing in shrine cities of Iraq), took the lead in expressing vehement criticism (Welāyati, 1997, pp. 163-69). In 1947, serving on the UN Special Committee for Palestine, Persia was one of the three states that voted against Palestine's partition, favoring a federal solution. When the General Assembly endorsed the partition plan (29 November 1947), Persia again voted against it. It later sided again with the Arab states (11 May 1949) voting against Israel's admission to the United Nations. During the 1948 war, Persia showed tacit solidarity with the Arab states, but proved reluctant to involve itself in combat. Ayatollah Abu'l-Qāsem Kāšāni worked to recruit volunteers to fight on Israeli fronts, but the Persian government resisted Arab demands for support in the war efforts, preferring indirect involvement (Welāyati, 2001, pp. 68-74; Fallāḥ-nežād, pp. 24-26).

Gradually, political realities forced a measure of contact between Israel and Persia. During the 1948 war, some Persian residents of Palestine fled the country and their properties, like those of the Arabs who had left, were put under government custody. These Persian refugees asked Tehran to interfere on their behalf to redeem their properties. In March 1949 Persia sent an unofficial envoy, ʿAbbās Ṣayqal, without official invitation or formal portfolio, to manage these claims. Israel attempted reciprocation, asking to send one of its diplomats in Ankara to Tehran as non-resident minister, but Persia refused (Gilad, 2002, pp. 251-52; Bialer, 1985, p. 300). The persecution of Iraqi Jews and their immigration restrictions added to the urgency of forming Persian contacts, as Persia had become a transit point for Iraqi Jews (Sobhani, pp. 27-40).

In 1949 Israel's foreign ministry asked the head of its UN mission, Abba Ebban, to initiate talks with the Persian ambassador, Naṣr-Allāh Enteẓām (q.v.), and stress the good will Israel has shown toward Persian nationals in Israel. Enteẓām, in turn, promised to work to improve relations. Responding to yet another Israeli initiative, after the Israeli-Arab cease-fire talks in Rhodes, the Persian ambassador to Washington, said his country will consider recognition of Israel, though doubted that it could be achieved soon (Hacham, pp. 83-89). The Persian efforts to get support from the United States, combined with American interest in securing Persian recognition of Israel, provided fertile ground for Israeli lobbying. During the shah's visit to the United States in late 1949, Israel's recognition was discussed. Turkey's recognition of Israel in September 1949, made Persia's recognition more appealing as they could not be accused of breaking the Israeli blockade first. Israel also stressed the financial benefit to Persia, as Israel would supply Persia with the raw materials it needed to import. A peculiar scheme was also underway to pay a considerable sum of money to interested parties to help expedite the recognition (Hacham, pp. 90-100; Bialer, 1985, pp. 301-8; Welāyati, 2001, pp. 57).

On 6 March, 1950 while the Majlis was in New Year recess, the government recognized Israel de facto, without formal announcement. On 7 March Enteẓām informed Abba Eban of the recognition (Hagana Archives, 14/13A; Hacham, p. 95). On 26 March, Reżā Ṣafiniā, a Persian diplomat with ministerial rank, presented his credentials as a "special envoy." The recognition led to fierce opposition at home (mainly clerics and nationalists) and abroad in Arab countries. On 7 July 1951, shortly after taking power, Moḥammad Moṣaddeq's government closed its Jerusalem consulate, due to "financial difficulties," but did not revoke the de facto recognition (Israel Government Archives, 2410/11/A; Hacham, pp. 101-6). Economic cooperation continued, and Persia offered agricultural products in exchange for the importation of industrial goods, medical equipment, and for additional technical assistance. On 11 June 1953, an agreement was signed between the respective National Banks for opening a line of credit (Hacham, p. 109; Gilad, 1953, p. 294). To encourage business ties an Iranian-Israeli trading company IRIS was also founded in 1953 (Bialer, 1988, p. 193).

Following the fall of Moṣaddeq government through the coup d'état of 1953 (q.v.), the prevailing Cold War and regional tensions bolstered an improvement in Persian-Israeli relations. The Egyptian revolution (July 1952) presented Israel and Persia with a common enemy: Gamal/Jamāl ʿAbd-al-Nāṣer and Egypt's arms deal with the Soviet Union (September 1955) illuminated the challenges of regional subversive activity and Soviet penetration in the Middle East. The shah, then, based his "positive nationalism" on maximizing Persian security and promoting economic development through alignment with the United States. The Baghdad Pact (q.v.) of 1955 also provided him with the sense of security that he needed to pursue his regional goals. Israel fit these goals perfectly: it could help Persia's economic programs, balance Egyptian-Soviet alliance, and be instrumental in strengthening his ties with the United States. Persia also needed oil-markets following the 1954 agreement with the Consortium (an international body of companies that replaced Anglo-Persian Oil Company, q.v.), and Israel was viewed as a potential partner. It was not surprising then that Israel's diplomat, Zvi Duriel, arrived in Persia (early 1956) under the cover of an IRIS representative, settling in an indistinguishable office with no flag or official sign (Gilad, 2002, p. 252).

The next impetus for extending relations was the impressive Israeli military show in the Sinai campaign (October 1956), which also opened the port of Eilat to the Red Sea shipping, thus further assisting trade. The shah considered Israel a valuable tool for preoccupying ʿAbd-al-Nāṣer in the Arab-Israeli front, thereby preventing the spread of his creed to the Persian Gulf region. The strategic value of Israel for Persia in meeting the challenges of internal subversion and regional aggression further encouraged the cultivation of closer economic ties as well as security and intelligence cooperation since the late 1950s. The opening of the Tiran Straits turned Eilat into a natural route for importing oil to Israel and later to Europe. In 1957, Israel started buying Persian oil through alien ships unmarked with the Israeli flag. Over the years, Israeli export expanded and El-Al Airline eventually opened a direct line to Tehran. The assignment in Persia of two Israeli officials further enhanced their mutual cooperation. Meir Ezri, a Persian native, was sent by the Israeli foreign ministry to Tehran in 1958 and remained there as minister and ambassador until 1973 (Ezri, pp. 58-169; Welāyati, 2001, p. 41; Fallāḥ-nežād, pp. 140-42).

Jackob Nimrodi, an intelligence officer, was originally assigned to Persia on a Mossad mission, and later returned to Persia as military attaché and private businessman (Nimrodi, pp. 142-343; Fallāḥ-nežād, pp. 142-47). These men were instrumental in translating the general understandings between the two parties into a network of intimate cooperation. In September 1957, General Teymur Baḵtiār, deputy prime minister and head of the newly established SAVAK (Sāzmān-e eṭṭelāʿāt wa amniyat-e kešvar) met in Paris with the Israeli ambassador (Yaacov Zur) offering cooperation in the exchange of intelligence, a suggestion Israel warmly welcomed (Hacham, p. 81; Sobhani, pp. 57-60; Nimrodi, I, pp. 170-93).

The regional occurrences of 1958 (the formation of the United Arab Republic of Egypt and Syria in February, the collapse of Iraq's pro-Western monarchy in July, and the subsequent collapse of the Baghdad Pact) augmented Persian concerns about Communist penetration and Arab radicalism and reinforced Persian decisions to enhance Israeli-Persian relations. On 24 July 1960, the shah reiterated publicly his country's recognition of Israel. ʿAbd-al-Nāṣer responded with harsh criticism, breaking all diplomatic ties with Persia (to be restored only in 1970). Ben-Gurion described relations between Persia and Israel then as friendly, informal, "but not hidden," and based on "mutual benefit" (Gilad, 2002, pp. 252-53). Ben-Gurion was the first Israeli prime minister to visit Tehran (December 1961), setting the precedent for visits of prominent officials on both sides. Although these hesitant initial steps gained significant momentum since the White Revolution (a series of economic and social reforms announced by the shah in January 1963), they remained informal. Even so, their relations gradually developed into what one Persian official described it to me as "relations of love without a marriage contract."

The White Revolution growing alliance. The culmination of the events of the early 1960s engendered deeper bonds between Israel and Persia. The shah, who began his career as a mere figurehead and was harshly scrutinized by local powers and super-powers, emerged as an absolute monarch determined to proceed in his development plans. His ideology, basing itself on westernization, secularization, nationalism, and edging closer to the West permitted increasingly greater Persian-Israeli cooperation. Viewing himself as a benevolent leader following in the footsteps of Cyrus the Great probably reinforced his tolerant approach to religious minorities and his friendship with Israel, whose officials persistently made flattering comparisons between the two men in their joint-meetings. It is also apparent that his close ties with Israel stemmed from an overestimation of the power of world Jewry. After 1967, with ʿAbd-al-Nāṣer considerably weakened and incapable of conducting subversive activities, the shah was able to expand ties with Israel with less anxiety and with the support of Unites States. The new realities were seen as a golden opportunity for Israel, to promote its economic interests and strategic schemes.

The strengthening of ties since the early 1960s corresponded with Ben-Gurion's "periphery concept," or an alliance between Israel and each of Persia, Turkey, and Ethiopia. Persia was perceived as an especially important country due to its strategic location, size, and economic potential; it is a Muslim (but not Arab) state and had no ostensible reason for conflict with Israel. Although the precise scope of the economic and military cooperation remained unclear, they were most profound in the 1960s and 1970s. Israel trained Persian students and officers, sent experts in various fields (agricultural development and modernization, medical services, exploration of water resources, road pavement, and reconstruction, most significantly of the Qazvin region after an earthquake). In the last two years of the shah's rule, the present writer resided in Persia conducting research and noticed a wide range of Israeli business, and numerous representatives of leading Israeli firms active in Persia. The Israeli presence was in fact so large that it necessitated the opening of an Israeli school in Tehran. Intimate cooperation between the security agencies developed and economic ties rocketed forward (Gilboa, pp. 257-58; Nimrodi, I, pp. 289-332; Ezri, pp. 181-255; Welāyati, 2001, pp. 203-28). From the interviews conducted by the present author with former officials (e.g., ambassadors, military attachés in Persia), it seems resonable to conclude that much remains to be told about the extent and depth of the relations.

In the years 1958-67, while Israel helped develop Persia's armed forces, Persia accelerated its sale of crude oil to Israel. Although certain projects aimed at transferring oil through pipelines (from Eilat to Beer Sheva) were examined previously, after the closure of the Suez Canal in 1967, Persia and Israel embarked on a joint venture to construct the Eilat-Ashkelon Pipeline. This pipeline initially transferred annually more than ten million tons of oil, which was more than Israel's annual consumption (Ezri, pp. 341-51; Sagev, pp. 94-102, 121). Israeli imports from Persia, as shown in the official Israeli statistics, grew from $1.3m in 1967 to $2.7m in 1969, $4.5m in 1975, reaching $5.8m in 1977 (Israel Central Bureau of Statistics, XXI, p. 219, XXIX, p. 222). Israeli exports to Persia grew from $22.3m in 1970 to $92.4m in 1975, reaching $103.2m by 1977, higher than its rate of export to Japan and Turkey (99.5m and $33.6m, respectively; Israel Central Bureau of Statistics, XXI, p. 219, p. 223). Between 1973 and 1974 alone, Israeli exports to Persia almost doubled (State of Israel, p. 101; see also data in Welāyati, 2001, pp. 159-201; Fallāḥ-nežād, pp. 207-45). It should be noted, however, that the figures cited above do not include the entire scope of trade and can only illustrate the general trend in trade business.

In the early 1970s, several regional developments threatened to obstruct their flourishing relations. The death of ʿAbd-al-Nāṣer (September 1970) followed by the rise of Moḥammad Anwar-al-Sādāt significantly altered the shah's negative attitude toward Egypt. Unlike ʿAbd-al-Nāṣer, the shah trusted Anwar-al-Sādāt and supported his Middle East policy. Subsequently, the October War (1973) diminished the prestige of the Israeli army. Moreover, in March 1975, Persia and Iraq signed the Algiers

Accord (see BOUNDARIES iv), putting (a temporary) end to the Persian-Iraqi conflict and closing a chapter in Persian-Israeli common support for (Iraqi) Kurds. The incentives for close relations with Israel were less compelling in this new conciliatory atmosphere, although extensive cooperation continued in various fields.

Throughout this period of friendship, anti-Israeli attitudes continued to prevail, particularly among the clergy and the anti-shah and anti-western elements. Most prominent among these spokesmen was the Ayatollah Ruḥ-Allah Ḵomeyni, who, in a speech on 3 June 1963, gave vent to such views: Israel wishes "to seize your economy, to destroy your trade and agriculture, to appropriate your wealth"; it "does not wish" the Qurʾān, the ulama, or any learned man "to exist in this country." Addressing *ḥajj* pilgrims in 1971, Ayatollah Ḵomeyni typically portrayed Israel as "the universally recognized enemy of Islam and the Muslims," that has "penetrated all the economic, military, and political affairs" of Persia, turning the country into "a military base for Israel" and "by extension, for America" (Ḵomeyni, 1981, pp. 177-80, 197; Fallāḥ-nežād, pp. 191-94). As long as the shah was behind the wheel, domestic distaste for close relations with Israel was largely ignored, but the instatement of the Ayatollah Ḵomeyni signaled the termination of an alliance that had continued over two decades.

Bibliography: ʻA. R. Ahmadi, *Sāvāk wa dastgāh-e eṭṭelāʿāti-e Esrāʾil*, Tehran, 2002. Uri Bialer, "The Iranian Connection in Israel's Foreign Policy: 1948-1951," *Middle East Journal*, 39/2, Spring 1985, pp. 292-315. Idem, *Oil and the Arab-Israeli Conflict, 1948-63*, London, 1988. Meir Ezri, *Mir vaḵem mi-kol ʿamo/ Anyone of His People Among You: Mission in Iran*, Or Yehuda, 2001 (in Hebrew). ʿAli Fallāḥ-nežād, *Monasabāt-e Irān wa Esrāʾil dar dawra-e Pahlavi-e Dovvom*, Tehran, 1982. B. Gilad, "Paras," *Ha-Miazrah ha-Hadash* 4/4, 1953. Idem, "Iranian-Israeli relations (1949-1979): Diplomacy under cover," in M. Yager, Y. Govrin and A. Oded, eds., *Ministry of Foreign Affairs: The First Fifty Years*, Jerusalem, 2002, I, pp. 251-54 (in Hebrew). M. Gilboa, "Iranian-Israeli relations: The first 50 years," in Yager, Govrin and Oded, eds., *Ministry of Foreign Affairs: The First Fifty Years*, Jerusalem, 2002, I, pp. 257-60. Government Archives, Hagana Archives. U. Hacham, "Iranian-Israeli Relations in the Years 1947-1957," M.A. Thesis, Tel Aviv, 1989 (in Hebrew). ʿAli-Akbar Hāšemi Rafsanjāni, *Esrāʾil va Qods-e ʿaziz*, Qom, n.d. Israel Central Bureau of Statistics Ayatollah Ruḥ-Allāh Ḵomeyni, *Islam and Revolution: Writings and Declarations of Imam Khomeini*, tr. Hamid Algar, Berkeley, 1981. Idem, *Dar Jostoju-ye rāh az kalām-e Emām: az bayānāt wa eʿelāmiyahā-ye Emām Ḵomeyni* XIX: *Felestin wa Sahionism*, Tehran, 1984. David Menashri, "Reflections on the Immigration of Iranian Jews to Israel," *The History of Contemporary Iranian Jews*, Los Angeles, 1997, pp. 3-17. Idem, *Post-Revolutionary Politics in Iran: Religion, Society and Power*, London, 2001. Moʾassasa-ye Moṭālaʿāt wa Pažuheshā-ye Siāsi, *Sāzmānhā-ye Yahudi wa Saḥyunisti dar Irān*, Tehran, 2002. Jackob Nimrodi, *My Life's Journey*, Or Yehuda, 2003 (in Hebrew). ʿAbd-Allāh Nuri, *Šowkarān-e eṣlāḥ: defāʿiyāt-e ʿAbd-Allāh Nuri dar dādgāh-e viža-ye ruḥāniyat*, Tehran, 1999. Robert B. Reppa, *Israel and Iran: Bilateral Relations and Effect on the Indian Ocean Basin*, New York, 1974. S. Sagev, *The Iranian Triangle: The Untold Story of Israel's Role in the Iran-Contra Affair*, tr. Haim Watzman, New York, 1988. Eshaq Emran Shaoul, "Cultural Values and Foreign Policy Decision-Making in Iran: The Case of Iran's Recognition of Israel," Ph.D. diss., George Washington University, 1971. Sohrab Sobhani, *The Pragmatic Entente: Israeli-Iranian Relations, 1948-1988*, New York, 1989; tr. A. M. Šāpuriān as *Tawāfoq-e maṣlaḥatāmiz: rawābeṭ-e Irān wa Esrāʾil (1948-1988)*, Los Angeles, 1988. Eliezer Tsafrir, *Big Satan, Small Satan: Revolution and Escape in Iran*, Or Yehuda, 2002 (in Hebrew). State of Israel, Ministry of Industry and Trade, *Israel Industry 1973-1974*, Jerusalem, 1975. ʿAli-Akbar Welāyati, *Irān wa masʾala-ye Felestin*, Tehran, 1997. Idem, *Irān wa taḥawwolāt-e Felestin: 1939-1979*, Tehran, 2001.

(DAVID MENASHRI)

(2) Post Revolution Period (1979-2007)

The impact of Iran's change to an Islamic state on Israeli-Iranian relations must be seen within the context of Iran's geo-strategic imperatives as a non-Arab, non-Sunni state in an overwhelmingly Arab and Sunni environment beyond the camouflage of Islamic rhetoric and exaggerated threat depictions in order to assess the changes that the Revolution of 1977-79 brought about and the continuities that it failed to end.

The legacy of the Pahlavi era. In the Pahlavi era, Iran and Israel formed strategic ties based on their common threat perceptions; both states felt threatened by Arab nationalism and Soviet influence in the Middle East. Nevertheless, in spite of extensive Israeli-Iranian intelligence and military cooperation, Iranian government refrained from recognizing Israel de jure, precisely due to the need to win regional approval and support for Iran's leadership ambitions. Distancing Iran from Israel was the primary political vehicle used by the shah to reconcile Iran with the region's Arab states. As Iran's power rose and the need for Israel decreased, the shah increasingly sought to distance Iran from Israel in order to translate Iran's increased capabilities into an acceptance of its preeminence.

The shah's efforts to distance Iran from Israel went so far that Israel feared that the Iranian monarch would severe all ties with the Jewish State (Segev, p. 89). These fears turned out to be unfounded, however. Though the Israeli-Iranian entente had weakened due to Iran's rise in the early 1970s, and though the threat from the Arab world and the Soviet Union had been reduced, neither threat had been neutralized.

These geo-political realities survived the birth of the Islamic Republic, which put Iran's clerical leaders in the awkward position of finding themselves on the same side, geo-politically, as Israel. Iran continued to fear Soviet intentions, and the threat from the Arab block, particularly Iraq, was greater in 1980 than it ever had been in the previous decade. In addition, Iran had since 1976 experienced a relative decline, fueled by the rise of Iraqi power. Israel assessed regional threats similarly. Publicly, the Islamic Republic took an uncompromising position on Israel, calling for its destruction and vehemently criticizing any Muslim country that negotiated with Tel Aviv. In a symbolic move, only six days after Ayatollah Khomeini's return to Iran, the compound of the Israeli mission to Iran was handed over to Yassir Arafat, and the street on which it was located was renamed Palestine Street (Entessar, p. 5).

Much like the shah, Iran's religious leaders sought a central role for Iran in the affairs of the region, but while the language through which the shah articulated Iran's ambitions was one of Iranian nationalism, the clerics expressed the same aspirations through a religious lexicon. While the shah sought approval and legitimacy for his hegemony through financial aid to, and military protection of, the surrounding Arab states, the revolutionary regime sought the same through the instrument of political Islam. The shah believed that his aspirations could be achieved within the framework of the existing order. The revolutionaries, on the other hand, needed to redefine the guiding principle of state to state interaction in order to reverse Iran's decline and restore its bid for regional leadership. The export of the revolution was key to the restructuring of the region for the enablement of Iranian leadership. The shah's quest to legitimize Iran's hegemony through American backing, strong ties and military aid to the regions moderate Arab government, and financial aid to the more radical Arab states, combined with public distancing from Israel, ultimately failed to persuade the Arabs to grant Iran the role it aspired. Historic Arab-Iranian suspicions, as well as resentment for the shah's entente with Israel, served to deny Iran that role. Furthermore, pan-Arab thought dominated the Arab states; an ideology that by definition excluded Tehran due to Iran's non-Arab nature.

The Islamic Revolution. Through political Islam, however, the revolutionaries hoped to bridge the Iranian-Arab divide and establish a normative framework that included, rather than excluded Iran from the peoples of the region; but Islamic unity and an Islamic order hardly suited the existing regimes in the region, particularly the Arab kingdoms. The Arabs had been wary of the shah's ambitions, but they were terrified by Khomeini's revolutionary designs (Menashri, p. 207). Rather than restructuring the political order of the region, Iran found itself increasingly isolated. Iran's pro-Arab stance and venomous rhetoric on Israel won it few, if any, Arab friends (Hunter, p. 104). As a result, in spite of its anti-Israeli ideology and rhetoric, geo-strategic forces compelled Iran to avoid any direct confrontation with Tel Aviv.

According to a former Iranian official who worked closely with Khomeini, the Ayatollah's view was that the Palestinian issue was primarily a Palestinian issue. At the second level, it should involve the Arab states neighboring Israel, and only at the third level should it involve Iran. Consequently, Iran should never be a front-line state against Israel (Interview, former Iranian official, Tehran, August, 2004). In the words of former deputy foreign minister, Maḥmud Wāʾeẓi, Iran never operationalized its rhetoric into actual policy, since it aimed "to avoid getting entangled in the Palestinian conflict" (Interview, Tehran, 16 August 2004; the same view was also related by Eqbāl Ahmad, a Pakistani political scientist, who visited Khomeini in Qom during the early weeks after the victory of revolution [interviewed by Ahmad Ashraf, Fall 1985, Bennington, Vermont]).

This distinction between Iran's public posture and operational policy was exemplified by Khomeini's blocking of attempts by more radical elements in the government to dispatch 10,000 Iranian soldiers to southern Lebanon to fight the Israelis (Chehabi, pp. 211-13). Khomeini prevented this potentially disastrous operation by declaring that the road to Qods (i.e., Jerusalem) went through Karbalā, thus, reaffirming Iran's ideological goals while ensuring that these goals would not be acted upon. The "liberation" of Jerusalem would remain an ideal to be used in Iran's rhetoric to win legitimacy in the Arab world, but not to be operationalized for its own purposes. This intricate and perilous balancing act was intended to ensure the pursuit of Iran's role ambitions without jeopardizing its short-term security needs. Primarily, Iran needed Israel's assistance in procuring American weaponry and spare parts for Iran's American-built air force. Iran's behind the scenes dealings with Tel Aviv accentuated the continuation of Iran and Israel's geo-strategic commonalities, in spite of Iran's Islamic rhetoric and anti-Israeli ideology.

The extent of these dealings came to light through the Iran-Contra Affair (q.v.), in which Israel lobbied the United States to arm Iran in its war efforts against Saddam Hussein in order to achieve a "broader strategic relationship with Iran" (Segev, p. 249). Unconfirmed reports claim that Israeli military advisors even visited the Iranian frontline to evaluate Iran's capabilities and needs. All in all, according to Aḥmad Ḥaydari, a Iranian arms dealer, roughly 80 percent of the weaponry bought by Tehran immediately after the onset of the war originated from Israel (Entessar, p. 7). Israel's motivations for supporting a state that officially called for its destruction also lied in the continuity of these geo-strategic realities.

Israel had great difficulties coming to terms with the Revolution and the strategic setback of losing the shah's support. After twenty-five years of Israeli investments into the relations with Iran, the ties to Tehran had become a crucial element of Israel's regional strategy. In the words of David Kimche, the former head of the Israeli Foreign Ministry: "We had very deep relations with Iran, cutting deep into the fabric of the two peoples. It was difficult for people to accept the fact that all of this intimacy was thrown out of the window. So there were a lot of attempts during the first year after the Revolution, to see if we could revive the relations with [Iran]" (Interview, Tel Aviv, 22 October, 2004). Israel believed that the Revolution and Iran's Islamic orientation was a historical parenthesis; the real, geo-strategically oriented Iran would resume and the shah's cooperation with Israel would soon reemerge.

From Israel's perspective, it was Iraq and not Iran that constituted the greatest threat to its security. Tel Aviv was very concerned about Baghdad's rise and looked toward Iran as a potential partner to contain Saddam's ambitions (Alpher, p. 155). Iran continued to be viewed as a non-threat due to its lack of offensive capabilities. "Throughout the 1980s, no one in Israel said anything about an Iranian threat—the word wasn't even uttered," according to David Menashri of Tel Aviv University (Interview, Tel Aviv, 26 October 2004).

Iran-Iraq War. The outbreak of the Iraq-Iran War (q.v.) was seen as a setback in Tel Aviv due to the risk of an Iraqi victory, which would leave the Jewish state in a far more vulnerable position (Entessar, p. 7). A Iranian victory, on the other hand, was not seen as negative since Iran's ability to participate in a war against Israel remained minimal (Segev, p. 22). According to David Kimche, "We weren't happy with the idea of exporting the Revolution, but between the two, Iraq was a greater threat and we didn't want to see Iraq win" (Interview, 22 October 2004).

Three days after Iraqi troops invaded Iran, Israeli Foreign Minister Moshe Dayan urged Washington to forget the past and help Iran keep up its defenses (Sick, p. 114). Two days later, Deputy Defense Minister Zippori announced that Israel would provide military aid to Iran if it changed its hostile approach to the Jewish state (Associated Press, 28 September 1980).

The Iran-Iraq War reinforced the common Israeli-Iranian threat picture and increased hopes in Israel that Iran would realize the utility of an alliance with Tel Aviv. In the words of Joseph Alpher, a former senior Mossad official, "certainly there was a strong sense that the Iranians are fighting the Arabs again, aren't we their natural allies? Why don't they understand that? Why don't they overcome their religious ideological compunctions and understand that?" (Interview, Tel Aviv, 27 October 2004). According to Israel former ambassador to the United States, Itamar Rabinovich, "in strict geo-political terms, if you don't consider regimes, our friend should be Iran, and we should never forget that" (Interview, Tel Aviv, 17 October 2004).

To Iraq's surprise, however, Iran was no push-over, and Iraqi expectations of a swift victory soon proved false. Though Israel initially supported Iran, it came to appreciate the way the war absorbed Arab resources and prevented the Arabs from focusing on the Palestinian issue. Tel Aviv reasoned that providing military assistance to Iran contributed to Israel's security by further splitting the Arabs (Sobhani, p. 150).

According to David Kimche, "our big hope was that the two sides would weaken each other to such an extent that neither of them would be a threat to us" (Interview, 22 October 2004). Balancing between continued warfare (Israel's preferred outcome at the time) and an Iraqi victory was an imprecise science. An Iraqi victory would make Baghdad the undisputed hegemonic power in the Persian Gulf, with the world's third largest oil reserves and an army more than four times the size of Israel's. It was not until 1987, when Iraqi prospects for victory had grown substantially that Tel Aviv concluded that a continuation of the war would be too risky and viewed a stalemate as the best possible outcome. Although Iraq did not win the war, by the time of its conclusion, Baghdad emerged as the most potent military power in the region, save Israel. As a result, Iraq remained Israel's primary threat, and Iran its preferred partner in balancing Iraq. This underlined the endurance of the geo-strategic forces bringing Israel and Iran together. According to an Israeli official, "the basic geo-political interests, which originally dictated an Israeli-Iranian link were far from being a mere whim of the Shah's. These common interests will remain valid" (*Manchester Guardian Weekly*, 7 December 1986).

Nevertheless, though Iran utilized its contacts with Israel in order to boost its military, it avoided the formation of strategic ties with Tel Aviv, due to its second strategic goal, that of improving relations with Iran's immediate neighborhood in order to satisfy its hegemonic inclinations. Thus, Khomeini preferred a cold peace with Israel, in which it opposed the Jewish state at the rhetorical level without translating that rhetoric into operational policy. Albeit not a whim, the geo-political forces that provided a basis for the Iranian-Israeli cold peace only endured for three more years after the end of the war. By 1991, the geo-strategic map of the Middle East was significantly transformed by two critical events, namely, the collapse of the Soviet Union and the demolition of the Iraqi army in the 1991 Persian Gulf War. Indeed, the real turning point in Israeli-Iranian relations was not in 1979, but in 1991, since the end of the Cold War also ended the Iranian-Israeli cold peace. The distribution of relative power shifted towards Iran and Israel and formed a nascent bipolar structure in the region. The defeat of Iraq and the collapse of the Soviet Union evaporated Iran and Israel's common threats and improved their security environments, but it also left both of them unchecked. Without Iraq balancing Iran, Tehran would become a threat, so argued Israeli hawks. This initiated a Iranian and Israeli redefinition of their respective roles and positions in the emerging Middle Eastern order under the hegemony of the United States. Since the United States was seeking to establish an order based, not on a realist assessment of the power distribution in the region, but on its own ideological disposition and bilateral relations with individual states, powerful countries like Iran and Iraq with justified role aspirations could be the biggest losers in the new Middle East order, due to their tense relations with Washington.

For Iran, the second Persian Gulf War provided an opportunity to improve its relations with Washington in order to break out of its isolation and return to a state in which Iran's power in the region would be recognized and its role objectives met. Tehran adopted a policy of "positive neutrality" during the war, but was in essence allied with the United States by, amongst other things, permitting Washington to use Iranian airspace to attack Iraq (Interview, Wāʿeẓi). Iran expected to be rewarded by the Unites States for its tacit support and be granted what it believed to be its rightful role in the formation of the new Middle East order. Israel, on the other hand, had its continued alliance with the United States to thank for its avoidance of complete isolation. Now, it feared that the United States reorientation towards the Arabs and a possible U.S.-Iran rapprochement would leave it isolated. With the Soviet Union gone, Israel usefulness for the United States had diminished significantly.

By the time the Labor Party swept the June 1992 elections, the need for bold action was evident. Labor's landslide victory, the Arabs' military weakness, and the PLO's near-collapse led the Labor Party to conclude that Israel's long-term security would be better served by befriending the Arab states of Israel's vicinity, instead of the non-Arab states in its periphery. This strategy reflected the new geo-strategic realities. The redistribution of power had caused Iran to become a rival rather than a potential allie, which in turn necessitated improved relations with Israel's Arab neighbors. By befriending the underdeveloped Arab states, Israel could become the economic engine of the Middle East, the producer for the 250 million consumers in the Arab countries. Israel could become the dominant economic power in the Middle East in addition to its military domination, which would help regain its strategic importance in Washington. This was at the heart of Peres' vision of the "New Middle East," which had little room for Iranian prominence.

Israel's vision of the new Middle East order came at the expense of Iran since Yitzhak Rabin believed that the Israeli population would be unlikely to accept peace with the Arabs unless a greater and more ominous threat, namely Iran and Islamic fundamentalism, was looming in the horizon. Moreover, the Arab states would be more inclined to make peace with Israel if they felt more threatened by Iran's fundamentalist ideology than by Israel's occupation of Palestinian land and its nuclear arsenal. According to Ephraim Inbar of the Begin-Sadat Center for Strategic Studies, "there was a feeling in Israel that, because of the end of the Cold War, relations with the U.S. were cooling and we needed some new glue for the alliance. And the new glue was radical Islam. And Iran was radical Islam. So Rabin played [the Iranian threat] more than it was deserved in order to sell the peace process" (Interview, Jerusalem, 19 October 2004). In the words of an Israeli diplomat, the Israeli gambit was to establish a new Middle East order in which Iran would "have no choice but to accept" its own isolation and Israel's leadership (Interview, Israeli UN diplomat, New York, 31 March, 2004).

Israel adopted a very aggressive posture on Iran, echoing Iran's venomous rhetoric against the Jewish state. The view of Iran as an unredeemable terrorist state became an integral part of Israeli political rhetoric to the extent that that any act of terrorism anywhere in the world was automatically blamed on Iran (White and Logan, eds., p. 218). Prime Minister Yitzhak Rabin missed no opportunity to stress the "Iranian danger," Iran's "dark murderous regime," and the "turbid Islamic wave" that it produced. Shimon Peres followed the same line and even made open threats directed at Iran, stressing that Israel could take action against Iran (Menashri, p. 295). Peres also urged Erope to "stop flirting" with Iran, declaring that Iran "is more dangerous than Hitler," and that "Iran is the center of terrorism, fundamentalism, and subversion" (Reuter, 7 March 1996). This stands in stark contrast to Rabin's view of Iran at the height of Iran's export of Islamic fundamentalism in 1987, when he said "Iran is Israel's best friend and we do not intend to change our position in relation to Tehran" (Agence France-presse, 28 October 1987).

Exclusion and confrontation. The first indication that Washington was not inclined to include Iran in future regional decision making was President George H. W. Bush's justification of the decision not to dethrone Saddam. Bush argued that Saddam was needed to balance Iran (Interview, Wilkerson). The other watershed event was the United Stated did not invite Iran to the multilateral talks at the Madrid conference in October 1991. These two events had a profound impact on Iranian decision makers, who concluded that Washington would not include Iran in the formation of the new Middle East order unless the exclusion of Iran makes the execution of its policies too costly.

As Iran began to realize the implications of Israel's New Middle East, it reassessed its long-standing position of avoiding direct confrontation with Israel. Iran, which in the early 1990s reduced its financial support to Hezbollah and lacked strong ties and presence in the Palestinian territories, started to reach out and develop relations with rejectionist Palestinian groups after the Madrid conference. Suddenly, Iran's geo-strategic imperatives and ideological disposition no longer collided. Tehran began translating its anti-Israeli ideology into operational policy in order to undermine the American-Israeli push for the new Israel-centric Middle East by attacking its weakest link, the peace process. According to an Israeli diplomat, Iran's active participation against Israel began after its exclusion from the formation of the new Middle East order (Interview, Israeli UN diplomat, New York, 31 March 2004). In the view of Itamar Rabinovich, Iran's anti-Israeli acts began in 1994 with the bombings of the Israeli embassy in Buenos Aires and a Jewish community center in Argentina (Interview, Itamar Rabinovich, Tel Aviv, 17 October 2004), although no evidence has yet been presented to tie Iran to these bombings. Peres said that the Iranians "are doing whatever they can to bring an end to peace and bring an end to the government that goes for peace" (Reuters, 8 April 1996.); and according to Keith Weissman of the American Israel Public Affairs Committee (AIPAC), "it's not an unreasonable assertion that the Iranians understood that by electing Netanyahu, you would slow-down the peace process. And that's exactly what happened" (Interview, 25 March 2004).

In May 1996, Benjamin Netanyahu defeated Peres on an anti-Oslo platform. As the Likud government put an effective freeze on the peace process, it also initiated a re-examination of its relations with Iran. A political source in the Israeli prime minister's office told Israel Radio Station (IDF Radio) in late 1996 that the era of dual containment (i.e., the Oslo process) was over and that Israel had changed its approach toward Tehran (IDF Radio, 10 November 1996.). The Israeli accounts were confirmed by the Islamic Republic's News Agency (IRNA), which reported that the Likud was seeking to settle its political issues with Tehran through the assistance of Iranian Jews (IRNA, 24 July 1996). Through these conciliatory measures, Netanyahu sought to avoid any unnecessary provocation against Iran that could lead to similar attacks with unpredictable political consequences. He didn't want to use rhetoric that would just antagonize the Iranians for no reason. A decision was made at the highest political levels to lower Israel's profile on issues concerning Iran.

Netanyahu and the Likud Party were ideologically opposed to the Oslo process and did not conceal their mistrust of the Palestinians. Therefore, they subscribed to the view that since peace with the Arabs remained highly unlikely, Israeli security was best achieved by forging alliances with the Middle East's non-Arab states, that is, a return to the pre-1991 strategy of Israel. In their view, not only was Peres' vision of the New Middle East inherently flawed, his strategy of demonizing Iran was also contrary to Israel's national interest in the sense that it significantly reduced the possibility of reviving the Iranian-Israeli entente, which the Likud viewed as next to inevitable in case of a failure to reach an accord with the Palestinians. Accordingly, the Likud strategists needed to keep the Iran option alive. According to Dore Gold, "The Likud tended to be more open to the idea [that] maybe there are residual elements in the revolutionary regime that see things geo-politically the same way as it was during the shah's time" (Interview, Jerusalem, 28 October 2004).

Moreover, Israel wanted to avoid a scenario in which Iran and the United States would resume diplomatic ties while Iranian-Israeli relations were still hostile, since improved relations between them under such circumstances could come at the expense of Israel (IDF Radio, 10 November 1996). Finally, from a domestic political perspective, Netanyahu's aim was to turn the Israeli public against the Oslo process and end the land for peace formula. In the words of an AIPAC representative, "Blaming the Iranians for Palestinian terrorism would be counterproductive to his message that terror was coming from the Palestinians" (Interview, AIPAC representative, 25 March 2004). In short, whereas the Iranian threat depiction served Rabin's efforts to convince the Israeli public to support reconciliation with the Arabs, the very same Iranian threat depiction undermined Netanyahu's efforts to convince Israelis to oppose that very same reconciliation. From the Iranian perspective, Likud was preferred over Labor for this very reason: an Israel that doesn't pursue the peace process won't need to confront Iran. As argued by a Iranian political strategist, "in Iran, the perception was that Likud is not serious about peace, so they do not need a scapegoat [Iran]. Labor, however, needed a scapegoat" (Interview, 26 February 2004).

In the end, the Likud's attempt to reduce tensions with Iran failed. By 1997, Iran announced the production of Šahāb-3 ballistic missiles, which would put Israel within Iran's reach. Furthermore, Israeli intelligence reports indicated that Iran was swiftly moving towards a nuclear weapons capability. To many Israelis, the alarmists' exaggerated view of the "Iranian threat" from the early 1990s started to be reflected in reality by the late-1990s. At the same time, Iran increasingly felt sufficiently confident about the doomed destiny of the peace process to readopt the policy of not translating Iran's anti-Israeli rhetoric into actual policy. The more Iran became politically integrated into the region through improved relations with the outside world, the less of a strategic threat it perceived the peace process to be.

The effect of the decrease in the tension on Tehran's perception of the peace process was crystallized one year later when Iran's new president, Moḥammad Ḵātami, reinstated the policy of accepting any deal agreeable to the Palestinians, including a two-state solution (Interview, Ambassador Nežād-Ḥosaynīān, Tehran, 12 August, 2004). In addition, the eruption of the second Intifada in 2000 and the deterioration of the situation in the Palestinian territories were met by a lowering of Iran's profile on the Palestinian issue. Eventually, however, Ḵātami's efforts were hampered by his inability to improve relations with the United States, which in turn prevented Iran from gaining recognition for its rising power and moderated foreign policy. This failure cost the Ḵātami government dearly and paved the way for the rise of the Iranian isolationists who opposed Ḵātami's policy of détente.

After September 11, officials in the Ḵātami government convinced the conservative clerical establishment to provide Washington with considerable assistance in the war against the Taliban (Ṭālebān) and in the reconstruction of Afghanistan's political system. A high-level channel was set up in which Washington and Tehran coordinated their policies in Afghanistan in order to establish a stable and representative government in Kabul. Iran permitted the United States to use Iranian airfields and helped repair America's relations with the Northern Alliance. The Iranians also used intelligence provided by the United States to find and kill Al-Qaeda (al-Qāʾda) leaders that were slipping into Iran from Afghanistan. Tehran's assistance was instrumental, a fact recognized by the White House officials testifying in the Senate Foreign Relations Committee (Pollack, pp. 346-49). Iran also played a critical role in the reconstruction efforts after the Iraq war and instructed its proxy groups in Iraq to cooperate with the US forces. According to Kenneth Pollack, Iran's "willingness to stay the course when initial American mistakes created tremendous problems with lawlessness, economic chaos, and the threat of a political collapse was critical in keeping the [Iraqi] situation from spiraling out of control" (Pollack, p. 355).

The Ḵātami government hoped that its constructive cooperation in Afghanistan and Iraq would pave the way for a new chapter in U.S.-Iran relations. Instead, President George W. Bush labeled Iran on 29 January 2002 as part of the "Axis of Evil," and the Iranian diplomats who spearheaded the efforts to open up to the United States were reprimanded by conservative factions in Tehran. This strengthened the hands of those in the Iranian leadership who maintained that the United States was not interested in anything less than weakening Iran and replacing its regime. No Iranian policy change could accommodate the Bush administration. Proponents of this school of thought pointed out that Ḵātami's efforts at détente with the United States and the Arab governments had failed to win Iran recognition for its security interests in the region. As a result, they argued, Iran should return to investing in the discontented Arab streets and Muslim masses, just as it did in the early 1980s.

Radicalzation of Iranian government. Muslim masses were increasingly anti-American and opposed to their own pro-American regimes. Accordingly, strategists on the Iranian side contended that investing politically in the possibility of friendly relationship with the United States and in the Arab governments could not be a successful long-term strategy for Iran. Instead, mindful of Washington's unwilling to accept Iran's rise in power and its claims for a role commensurate with its geopolitical weight, Iran should seek to build a new order in the region based on Islamic principles and the support of the discontented "Muslim Streets," through which Iran's role aspirations could be materialized.

This camp captured the Iranian presidency with the election of Maḥmud Aḥmadi-nežād in June 2005. Only months into his term, amid intensified American and Israeli threats against Iran over its nuclear program, Aḥmadi-nežād heated up Iran's anti-Israel rhetoric by making inflammatory statements. Aḥmadi-nežād's rhetorical excesses are a throwback to the Ayatollah Khomeini era. Yet, for Iran to escalate tensions with Israel and intensify its rhetorical excesses at a time when it is facing increased pressure from Washington and Tel Aviv shows continuity rather than discontinuity in the behavior of Iranian government. Much like what Ayatollah Khomeini did in the early 1980s, Tehran is using the guise of its ideology to fight its real-political battles in order to conceal its true interests and the geo-strategic nature of its conflict with Israel.

Currently, this rivalry, set in motion by the dramatic redistribution of power in the region following the Persian Gulf War and the ensuing efforts to establish a new regional order, is still in effect and has hampered the attainment of the United States foreign policy objectives in the Middle East. While Iran has actively sought to undermine any peace settlement between Israel and the Palestinians that would intensify Iran's isolation, Israel has actively undermined efforts to improve U.S.-Iran relations due to its fear that Washington would betray Israeli interests in order to patch up its relations with Tehran. Both Iran and Israel have proven to be effective spoilers, yet inadequate builders of a new order. Mindful of the decline in Arab power, those nostalgic about the strong Israeli-Iranian relationship during the Pahlavi era will have a daunting task rebuilding those ties since the bedrock of that entente is lacking in the current geopolitical environment, to wit the existence of common threats to Iran and Israel and a well-entrenched regional order.

Lebanon connection. The struggle between Iran and Israel has primarily been manifested in confrontations through proxies, of which the Lebanese Hezbollah has been the most potent and dangerous one. Though it is often believed that Iran helped form Hezbollah to target Israel, Iranian calculations regarding Hezbollah had far more to do with spreading the Iranian revolution than countering the Jewish state. In fact, Israel inadvertently handed Iran its only success in exporting its revolution in the Arab world by invading Lebanon. The invasion of 6 June 1982 was ostensibly in response to an attempt by Palestinian militants to assassinate Shlomo Argov, Israel's ambassador to the United Kingdom, but Ariel Sharon, then Israel's defense minister, had been planning a Lebanon invasion to wipe out the PLO presence there for many months, at least as early as late 1981 (Smith, p. 377).

Southern Lebanon had traditionally been the home of Lebanon's disenfranchised Shiʿite Muslim community. The Shiʿites initially welcomed the Israelis because of their own competition with Palestinian refugees for local resources and their resentment of the PLO's often heavy-handed rule of the south, but they were dismayed when the Israelis overstayed their welcome by creating a "security zone" in the south. They soon turned against Israel as it blocked the Shiʿites' access to northern markets and began dumping Israeli goods into their local economy, causing indigenous economic interests to suffer (Smith, p. 284). In addition, Israel's invasion had been immensely destructive and only adding to the misery of Lebanese who had already been suffering from seven years of civil war. Close to 20,000 Lebanese were killed in the invasion and another 450,000 were displaced. In September 1982, under direction of Defense Minister Sharon, a Lebanese Christian militia unit entered the Palestinian refugee camps of Sabra and Shatila in Beirut, and, with tacit Israeli approval, raped, killed, and maimed as many as several thousand civilian refugees. Approximately one quarter of those refugees were Shiʿites who had fled the violence in the south (Deeb, 2006). The plight of the Shiʿites under Israeli occupation made them receptive to Tehran's message. Faced with a mighty Israeli opponent, the Shiʿites desperately needed an external ally, and Tehran was more than willing to play the part, not so much to act out its anti-Israeli sentiments but rather to find a stronghold in an Arab country. Tehran badly needed progress in exporting its revolution. It had failed in Iraq and Bahrain, in spite of the majority Shiʿite populations of those countries. Now, thanks to the Israeli invasion of Lebanon, Iran was given the opportunity to plant the seeds of Islamic revolution in the Levant.

Out of the Israeli invasion emerged a new and invigorated Shiʿite movement, inspired by Iran's Islamic Revolution. Initially just a small number of armed groups of young men organized under the banner of Islam and dedicated to fighting the Israeli occupation, over time they banded together into what has proved to be one of Israel's most formidable foes, the Lebanese Hezbollah. The Israeli-Iranian proxy war through Hezbollah culminated during the summer war of 2006, which signified a new and heightened phase in this conflict.

The Summer War of 2006. America's position and credibility in the region has significantly suffered due to the ever-increasing chaos in Iraq that followed the fall of Saddam in 2003. Iran, on the other hand, inadvertently benefited from America's policies. The fall of Saddam, Iran's deadly enemy who engaged it in an eight-year war (see IRAQ VII.), and the emergence of a pro-Iranian Shiʿite leadership in Iraq, the removal of the Taliban regime in Afghanistan, America's unpopularity in the region, the Arab governments' perceived inability to act independently of Washington or oppose its policies, America's perceived inability to push back Iran militarily, and Tehran's unhindered march towards a nuclear capability all served to strengthen Iran's position in the region and increase Israel's strategic vulnerability.

These developments significantly increased Israeli fears that American inaction against Iran may leave Israel alone in facing a strong, nuclear Iran riding on a wave of anti-American and anti-Israeli sentiments in the region at a time when Israel still appeared incapable of easing regional tensions by improving relationships with its immediate Arab neighbors, including the Palestinians.

The summer war between Israel and Lebanon took place against this backdrop. The fighting may have been sparked by Hezbollah's cross-border raid, but Israel's decision to expand a border clash into a full scale war was likely motivated by an intent to preempt Iran. Israel, with a potential future showdown with Iran in mind, seemed to have sought an opportunity to neutralize Hezbollah and Hamas in order to weaken Iran's deterrence and retaliation capabilities. (The summer war was preceded by heavy Israeli bombardment of Gaza.) Through these groups, Iran could bring the war to Israeli territory, a scenario that further accentuated Israel's vulnerability to asymmetric warfare. By launching preemptive attacks on Hamas and the Hezbollah, Israel could significantly deprive Iran of its capabilities to retaliate against Israel in the event of an American assault on Iran. In fact, Israel had been planning for war against Hezbollah for more than two years. In 2005, a senior Israeli army officer began giving off-the-record Power-Point presentations to American diplomats, journalists, and think tanks, setting out in great detail the plan for the expected operation. "Of all of Israel's wars since 1948, this was the one for which Israel was most prepared" (Gerald Steinberg, quoted by Matthew Kalman).

According to a former deputy defense minister of Israel, Major General Ephraim Sneh, "War with Iran is inevitable. Lebanon is just a prelude to the greater war with Iran" (author's conversation with Ephraim Sneh, 28 July 2006). Once Iran obtained a nuclear capability, however, this option would no longer be available to Israel. Moreover, in the absence of an American assault on Iran, such a strategic pushback against Iran would be beneficial to both Israel and the United States. In fact, Tehran was expecting some form of Israeli offensive against its Shiʿite allies in Lebanon, though the Iranian intelligence services had predicted a much smaller Israeli campaign that would occur in the fall of 2006 (interview with senior Iranian official, 12 October 2006).

As it became increasingly likely that Israel would fail to debilitate Hezbollah quickly through its massive air campaign, Washington and London provided for it the political support and cover to continue the war, in spite of the international protests and calls for an immediate ceasefire. Secretary of state, Condoleezza Rice, referring to the fighting, remarked on 21 July 2006 two days before her official trip to Israel to meet with Prime Minister Olmert: "What we are seeing here, in a sense, is the growing, the birth pangs of a new Middle East, and whatever we do we have to be certain that we are pushing forward to the new Middle East, not going back to the old one" (see www.state.gov/secretary/rm/2006).

After some initial successes, the Israelis were stunned at Hezbollah's powerful response, including its firing of thousands of Katyusha rockets into northern Israel. Rather than facing an amateur militia, the Israelis soon realized that they were fighting a well-trained and well-equipped guerilla army. Hezbollah even used a Chinese-made C-807 missile against an Israeli warship off Lebanon's coast, catching the Israelis off guard and disabling the ship. Israeli intelligence had failed to discover in full before the war what Hezbollah had amassed in its arsenals. The Lebanese fought a high-tech war and paid as much attention to the media battle as they did to the fighting on the ground. Hezbollah fighters cracked the codes of Israeli radio communications, intercepting reports on the casualties they had inflicted. Whenever an Israeli soldier was killed, Hezbollah confirmed it by listening to the Israeli radio and then sent the reports immediately to its satellite TV station, Al-Manar, which broadcast the news live. Thus Arab audiences knew the names of Israeli casualties and where they had been killed well before the Israeli army had a chance to inform the soldiers' families. The psychological impact of this on the Israelis, who had grown accustomed to superiority over the armies of their Arab neighbors, was devastating. By the end of the thirty-four day war, Hezbollah had won a stunning victory by simply having withstood and survived Israel's onslaught. Rather than strengthening and reinforcing the image of Israel's invincible deterrence, the war that was to weaken Iran only made Israel itself more vulnerable.

With Washington unwilling to recognize Iran as a regional powerhouse with legitimate security interests, with Israel insisting on maintaining military disparity with its neighbors while clinging on to its arsenal of 200 nuclear warheads, and with Iran openly professing the military exodus of the United States from the region, open war may be avoided, but peace will remain elusive. A sustainable peace in the Middle East can only be achieved if it be coupled with a sustainable security order. Such an order must, by definition, be all-inclusive and reflect the reining geopolitical balance. The order that the United States pursued in the 1990s under the policy of Dual Containment, was based on the exclusion of two of the strongest powers in the region, namely Iran and Iraq. The order it seeks today is equally disconnected from regional realities.

From Israel's perspective, the rise of a nuclear Iran and the defeat that Israel suffered in 2006 indicate that time may no longer be on its side. Moderate elements in Israel recognize that the security of Israel is no longer served by this balance of power paradigm, because Israel cannot indefinitely balance its more populous neighbors, particularly as they, as in the case of Iran, begin to master nuclear technology. Shlomo Ben-Ami, Israel's former foreign minister, argued that "the question today is not when Iran will have nuclear power, but how to integrate it into a policy of regional stability before it obtains such power. Iran is not driven by an obsession to destroy Israel, but by its determination to preserve its regime and establish itself as a strategic regional power, vis-à-vis both Israel and the Sunni Arab states. The Sunnis are Iran's natural foe, not Israel. The answer to the Iranian threat is a policy of detente, which would change the Iranian elite's pattern of conduct. . . . A detente policy with Iran would have far-reaching implications for the chances for peace between Israel and its Arab neighbors."

Save any major shift in the balance of power in the Middle East, the geopolitical rivalry between Iran and Israel is likely to endure regardless of the ideological predispositions of the Iranian leadership, though a change in the nature of the regime in Tehran may cause the manifestation of this rivalry to vary significantly.

Bibliography: Books: Joseph Alpher, *The Iran-Iraq War: Impact and Implications*, New York, 1989. Houchang Chehabi, *Distant Relations: Iran and Lebanan in the Last 500 Years*, New York, 2006. Shireen Hunter, *Iran and the World: Continuity in A Revolutionary Decade*, Bloomington, 1990. David Menashri, *Post-Revolutionary Politics in Iran: Religion, Society, and Power*, London, 2001. Kenneth Pollack, *The Iranian Puzzle: The Conflict between Iran and America*, New York, 2004. Samuel Segev, *The Iranian Triangle: The Untold Story of Israel's Role in the Iran-Contra Affair*, tr. Haim Watzman, New York, 1988. Gary Sick, *October Surprise: America's Hostages in Iran and the Election of Ronald Reagan*, New York, 1991. Charles D. Smith, *Palestine and the Arab-Israeli Conflict*, New York, 1996. Sohrab Sobhani, *The Pragmatic Entente: Israeli-Iranian Relations, 1948-1988*, New York, 1989. Paul J. White and William S. Logan, eds., *Remaking the Middle East*, Oxford, 1997.

Signed Articles: Shlomo Ben-Ami, "The Basis for Iran's Belligerence," *Haaretz*, 7 September, 2006. Ian Black, "Israel's Longstanding Links with Iran," *Manchester Guardian Weekly*, December 7, 1986. Lara Deeb, "Hizballah: A Primer," *Middle East Report Online*, July 31, 2006. Nader Entessar, "Israel and Iran's National Security," *Journal of South Asian and Middle Eastern Studies* 27/4, Summer 2004. Matthew Kalman, "Israel Set War Plan More Than a Year Ago: Strategy Was Put in Motion As Hezbollah Began Increasing Its Military Strength," *San Francisco Chronicle*, 21 July 2006. R. K. Ramazani, "Iran and the Arab-Israeli Conflict," *The Middle East Journal*, 1978.

Unsigned Articles: Agence France-presse, 28 October 1987. Associated Press, 28 September 1980. IDF Radio, 10 November 1996. Reuter, 7 March 1996 and 8 April 1996. *Washington Post*, 10 January 1978.

Interviews: Yossi Alpher, former Mossad official and senior advisor to Ehud Barak, Tel Aviv, 27 October 2004. ʿAli-Naqi ʿĀliḵāni, former minister of finance under the shah, Washington, D.C., 7 April 2004. American Israel Public Affairs Committee (AIPAC) representative, Washington, D.C., 25 March 2004. Ephraim Inbar, Jerusalem, 19 October 2004. Former Iranian official, Tehran, August, 2004. Iranian political strategist, New York, 26 February 2004. Israeli UN diplomat, New York, 31 March 2004. David Kimche, Tel Aviv, 22 October 2004. David Menashri, Tel Aviv University, Tel Aviv, 26 October 26, 2004. Nežād-Ḥosaynīān, Iran's former ambassador to the UN 1997-2002, Tehran, 12 August 2004. Itamar Rabinovich, former advisor to Rabin and Israeli ambassador to the US, Tel Aviv, 11 October 2004. Maḥmud Wāʿeẓi, former Deputy Foreign Minister, Tehran, 16 August 2004. Lawrence Wilkerson, Secretary of State Colin Powell's chief of staff, Washington, D.C., 6 October, 2006.

(TRITA PARSI)

ii. THE JEWISH PERSIAN COMMUNITY

Definition and background. Jews of Persian origin and their descendants who live in the State of Israel and constitute an integral and active part of its general population. As a convenient but rather too broad and loosely defined ethno-cultural and demographic notion, the designation "Jewish Persian Community in Israel" refers to diverse and considerably different groups of Persian and Neo-Aramaic speaking Jews of Persia who immigrated to Palestine-Israel from a large number of highly scattered urban, provincial, and rural communities and settlements across Persia. The latter emigrants and immigrants settled in Ottoman and British-controlled Palestine (roughly ever since the 1820s until the termination of the British Mandate in Palestine in 1948) and in much larger numbers ever since the establishment of the State of Israel and its declaration of independence on 14 May 1948. Because of numerous objective obstacles, chief among them lack of documentation, absence of comprehensive research on the subject and difficulties in devising sound criteria required for defining and estimating the size of this community, at this stage of research one cannot provide any definitive figures as to the number of Persian Jews and their descendants who presently live in the State of Israel.

However, on the basis of the available information and estimates regarding the numbers of those who immigrated from Persia before and after Israel's establishment, and taking into account the number of those who were born to families in which either one or both of the parents were born in Persia, it appears that the number of Jews of Persian extraction in Israel today may cautiously be put at some 200 to 250 thousand souls. The latter estimate is indeed provided by some scholars and community activists of Persian descent who are closely involved in the lives of Persian Jews in Israel (Menashri, p. 6). The estimated figure of some 250 thousand Jews of Persian extraction living currently in Israel would roughly represent 3.7 percent of Israel's total population of 6.7 million, and about 4.8 percent of the country's Jewish population of 5.1 million counted in 2003 (Central Bureau of Statistics, *Statistical Abstract*, no. 55, 2004, tables 2-10). In terms of their sheer numbers, Jews of Persian origin and their descendants living presently in Israel constitute by far the largest concentration of Persian Jews living either in or outside Persia's borders. Moreover, in terms of their relative size within Israel's multi-ethnic and increasingly multi-cultural population, and when compared with the other main groups of Jewish immigrants from the Muslim countries of the Middle East and North Africa in Israel, Jews of Persian origin constitute the fourth-largest immigrant group after the Jews of Morocco, Iraq, and Yemen (Peres, p. 47). Nevertheless, despite the importance of the Jewish Persian community both in the recent and contemporary history of Persian Jewry as well as in the context of Israel's own genesis and transformation in the course of the last decades, the annals, experiences and the present condition of Persian Jews living in Israel have remained largely neglected and uninvestigated. The generally poor state of available sources and documentation on the one hand and the dearth of systematic research and broader academic and public interest on the subject on the other hand stand in sharp contrast to the state and level of research and publication (particularly in the Hebrew language) devoted over the past years to Israel's other Middle Eastern and North African immigrant communities. With the exception of some very few in-depth studies, articles and surveys of general nature that deal with partial and mostly isolated subjects related to the general history of Jewish Persian immigration to Israel (see particularly Netzer, Mizrahi, Levy, Ha-Cohen, Klein, Menashri, and Yeroushalmi), some of the most basic areas and aspects of general history, society, economy, community, family, education, culture, and ethnicity among the Jews of Persian origin in Israel still await systematic data collection and examination. Owing to the latter gaps in information and perspective, the present article and the diverse data and observations contained in it run the risk of being incomplete and as such tentative.

Early migrations and community until 1917. The biblical land of Israel and its sacred sites, ccupying an exalted position in the religious beliefs and messianic yearnings of Persian Jews, have always attracted Jews of Persian origin throughout their documented history. The religious and spiritual bonds of Persian Jews to the land they deemed as the cradle of their ancestral religion and ethnic identity were historically preserved and nurtured by means of a variety of sources, practices, and channels. Chief among the latter were: (1) The diverse sources of Jewish religion, liturgy, annual cycle and commemorative holidays (particularly the ninth of the Hebrew month of Āv, on which day, according to Jewish tradition, both the First and the Second Temples in Jerusalem were destroyed in 586 BCE and 70 CE, respectively); (2) the literary and religious writings of the Persian-speaking Jews themselves, in which both the biblical and post-biblical land of Israel as well as the events, memories and legends associated with them in Jewish writings are extensively treated (Moreen, pp. 123-36; Yeroushalmi, 1995, pp. 34-38, 134-36); (3) visits to Persia's scattered Jewish communities and settlements by rabbis and emissaries from the main centers and institutions of religious learning in Palestine. The latter visits, which fulfilled a variety of religious and inter-communal needs (documented mainly in the course of the 16th-20th cents.) contributed considerably to the maintenance of ongoing contact between the Jewish centers in Palestine and the Jewish communities in various parts of Persia (Yaʿari, 1977, pp. 4, 12, 21, 265-66, 381-85). The earliest written record attesting to the migration of some Jewish sectarians (Karaites) from the northeastern Persian town of Dāmḡān (q.v.) to Jerusalem dates from the end of the 9th century (Yaʿari, 1943, pp. 56-59; Netzer, 1981, p. 281). We also know of several Persian Jews who made pilgrimage to Jerusalem and to other holy sites and localities in Palestine in the course of the 16th century (Netzer, 2002, p. 365). In addition to Jerusalem, the capital of ancient Israel and the site of its ruined temple, Jews from various communities in Persia made journeys and pilgrimages also to tombs and holy sites in the Ottoman-controlled cities of Safed and Tiberias (in Upper Galilee) and Hebron (Ar. al-Ḵalil), formerly called Qeriat Arbaʿ (Judges, 1:10-15), the first capital of King David (2 Samuel 2:4), located 30 km to the south of Jerusalem. These four Palestinian cities and towns, known among the Jews of Palestine and diaspora by the Hebrew title of "Arbaʿ Arasot" or (The Four Lands), and their respective sacred sites, tombs, synagogues and local institutions of religious learning and charity enjoyed a considerable aura and veneration among the Jews across Persia. A few of those who made these expensive and highly hazardous pilgrimages in pre-modern times, are known to have settled in the various Jewish communities of Ottoman-controlled Palestine (conquered by the Ottomans in 1517). We know specifically of Persian Jews who settled in Safed and Jerusalem in the course of the 16th-18th centuries (Netzer, 1981, pp. 282-86), although dearth of information and documentation prevents us from forming any clear view of all those who settled in Palestine during those years. On the basis of the scanty available evidence and in the light of what we know about the plights, poverty, and harsh living conditions that prevailed in the Jewish settlements of Palestine in the course of the 17th-18th centuries (Dubnow, IV, pp. 1710-14), it is reasonable to assume that the number of Persian Jews who migrated to Palestine during those years was negligible. All the available sources of information, which grow considerably and progressively in the course of the 19th century and onward, clearly indicate that a significant process of Jewish migration from Persia to Ottoman Palestine began during the last two decades of the 19th century. The latter trend, so it appears, grew gradually and steadily during the years 1892-1917, and increased further following the actual termination of the Ottoman rule in Palestine (October 1917) and during the three decades of de facto British control of the land (1917-48).

According to various accounts, and particularly on the basis of oral testimonies and memoirs written by the descendants of Persian emigrants who had settled in Palestine prior to the 1880s (Ha-Cohen, pp. 47-51; Mizrahi, 1959, pp. 200-201; Levy, 1976, p. 18), several families from Persia's larger Jewish communities (among them those of Yazd, Shiraz, and Isfahan) migrated and settled in a number of Jewish settlements in Palestine during the first decades of the 19th century. Among the latter emigrants were some who settled in Tiberias and Hebron and even in other small settlements such as Še̲kem (Ar. Nablus), located in Samaria (Ha-Cohen, p. 47), but the largest known group of Persian emigrants who settled in Palestine during the 1840s-1860s lived in the town of Safed. They consisted of some fifty to sixty families (Levy, 1976, p. 18), many of whom, much like the vast majority of the Persian emigrants who settled in Palestine in the course of the 19th century and the first two decades of the 20th century, were extremely poor. In Safed of the 1840s-1860s, however, they enjoyed the local patronage and support of a wealthy Jewish Persian merchant by the name of Yiṣḥāq Šālom Cohen, commonly known by his nickname as Abū Geršon. An enterprising merchant, landowner and banker, Abū Geršon (b. ca. 1810 d. 13 April 1896) is said to have been born in Yazd (or, according to a family tradition, in Shiraz), and while a youngster, emigrated with his family to Palestine. He settled in Safed and soon amassed a large fortune, and by virtue of his influence and connections both with Ottoman officials and Persian dignitaries, was appointed, in about 1858, as Persian consul in Safed (Levy, 1976, pp. 17-18; Netzer, 1982, pp. 332-34; Tidhar, XII, p. 4102). Many among the Persian emigrants in Safed were employed and supported by Abū Geršon and his many descendants. His third son, by the name of Raphael, also served as Persian consul in Safed at the beginning of the 20th century (Levy, 1976, p. 19). A communal leader and a devout Jew, Abu Geršon is said to have urged and encouraged Jews of Persia to emigrate to Palestine (Mizrahi, 1959, p. 201). The Persian emigrants who arrived in rather small numbers during the 1820s-70s, as well as those who began arriving in larger numbers during the 1880s-1910s, were, according to all evidence, driven by diverse personal, communal, and religious motivations and impulses. Religious, messianic and Jewish national yearnings undoubtedly played an important role in the decision of these emigrants throughout the 19th century and the first decades of the 20th century (Kashani, pp. 39-40), yet all the available and so far little studied primary sources at our disposal indicate that wide-ranging plights, insecurities, and deeply rooted discriminations that affected the lives of the vast majority of Persia's Jewish communities and settlements throughout the 19th century and the first years of the 20th century also contributed to the flight and migration of Persian Jews from their centuries-old native communities in Persia (Fischel, pp. 119-24). A variety of primary and secondary sources (chief among them the 19th-century Jewish press of Europe, the writings of the Persian Jews themselves, and the accounts of Christian missionaries who conducted evangelical activity among the Jewish communities of Persia during the 1820s-1910s) evidence that Persian Jews abandoned their communities in substantial numbers and migrated or fled to countries and territories adjacent to or far beyond Persia's borders. Afghanistan, Turkistan, Bukhara, and the Ottoman-controlled cities of Baghdad and Basra as well as the British colonies of India were among the main destinations to which tens of hundreds of Persian Jews migrated in the course of the 19th century and beginning of the 20th century (Wolff, p. 83; the Hebrew weekly *Hamaggid*, Lyck, Prussia, 12 January 1876, pp. 12-13; Yehoshua-Raz, pp. 110-11; Yeroushalmi, 2003, pp. 97-98). The emigration of the Persian Jews to Ottoman-controlled Palestine appears to have been part of the larger migratory trends and impulses among the Jewish communities of Persia during the 19th century and first two decades of the 20th century. Diverse local distresses and legal and socio-economic inequalities and discriminations on the one hand, and hopes for improving one's personal and family living conditions and prospects abroad on the other, were intermingled with religious yearning and together formed the major driving forces that led growing numbers of Persian Jews to abandon their native settlements and towns and set out on the long journey to Ottoman Palestine.

These emigrants used three routes to travel from Persia to Palestine in the course of the 19th century (roughly through the 1940s). First, the western overland route that led to Iraq, mainly Baghdad, and from there, through the Syrian Desert, to Damascus, where it turned southward to Palestine. Second, the northern route, which connected northwestern Persia (via the Caspian port of Anzali, q.v., and through the Black Sea) to the Ottoman territories in the west and from there to Greater Syria and Palestine. Third was the southern route, which was inaugurated with the opening of the Suez Canal in November 1869 (Klein, pp. 98-99), connecting the ports of the Persian Gulf (esp. Bušehr) with Egypt and the Mediterranean sea-ports of Palestine. It provided a safer and relatively more convenient and affordable means of traveling, thereby contributing significantly to the expansion of Jewish migration from Persia to Palestine in the course of the 1880s-1940s. This was particularly so with respect to the Jewish communities and settlements in Persia's southern provinces, particularly those of the province of Fārs, mainly Shiraz and its adjacent towns and settlements. Indeed, the growing migration of Jews from Shiraz and other localities in southern Persia (among them Jahrom and Bušehr) during the 1880s-90s marks an important turning point in the history of Jewish migration and emigration to Palestine. These emigrants of Shiraz, estimated at some 500 to 1,000 souls by 1892 (Mizrahi, 1959, p. 202), constituted the largest group of Persian emigrants that arrived and settled in Palestine prior to the beginning of World War I in 1914. Moreover, despite Ottoman restrictions imposed on Jewish traffic and emigration to Palestine, particularly the law of 1887, which required each emigrant family to provide proof that it was capable of supporting itself economically, and an earlier law (enacted in 1882), which allowed for organized groups of up to 200-250 Jewish emigrants to settle in all districts of Palestine with the exception of the district of Jerusalem (Netzer, 1981, pp. 289-90; Lipman, pp. 200-202), the vast majority of these emigrants succeeded in settling in Jerusalem. The Persian emigrant community in Jerusalem constituted the largest concentration of Persian Jews throughout Palestine, and until 1917 (other much smaller numbers were found in Safed, Tiberias, Jaffa and in some of the newly founded Jewish colonies in the Mediterranean coastal plain), it played a major role in attracting additional families and semi-organized groups of newcomers from Persia's various urban and provincial communities. Despite a temporary slow-down in emigration during 1909-17 (caused, *inter alia*, by prospects of change inside Persia following the Constitutional Revolution, q.v., in 1906, educational and communal improvements resulting from the activities of the Alliance Israélite Universelle in Persia's larger Jewish communities, and harsh security and economic conditions in Palestine during World War I), tens of additional families, mainly from Mashad, Tehran, Kāšān, Yazd, Isfahan, Shiraz, Jahrom, and Lār had arrived and settled predominantly in Jerusalem (Mizrahi, 1959, pp. 200-216). By the end of the Ottoman rule in Palestine in 1917, the number of Persian Jews living in Jerusalem was estimated at 1509 souls (Ben-Arieh, p. 407). The emigration of Persian Jews to Palestine during the 19th century until 1917, and to a large extent until Israel's independence in 1948, was carried out in a sporadic manner and lacked any central organization or coordination. Single families and at times semi-organized groups consisting of a handful of extended families from the same town or settlement in Persia were ordinarily stirred and led by a local charismatic rabbi or some other well-respected figure in the community to emigrate. They would then liquidate their possessions and embark on the journey to Palestine bearing the entire expenses of the journey, which would last three to four months, by land, or some five-six months, by ship, the latter through the Persian Gulf to India and from there to Egypt and Palestine. Lack of central organization and absence of external financial and welfare support weighed heavily on the vast majority of these emigrants. The considerable expenses and fees of travel and the physical hardships and threats in the course of the journey (e.g., widespread illness, malnutrition, assaults by robbers, etc.) ordinarily exhausted the limited resources of these emigrants even before they arrived and began their existential struggles in Palestine (Ha-Cohen, pp. 48-49; Mizrahi, 1959, pp. 214-15). A notable exception to the latter mostly poor or impoverished arriving emigrants were the wealthy Jewish merchants of Mashad, descendants of Jews who had been forcibly converted to Shiʿite Islam in 1839 (Levy, 1985, p. 135). Returning openly to Judaism, the latter emigrants settled in a prosperous and newly built neighborhood of Jerusalem during the years 1901-03 and onward. The latter Jews of Mashadi origin, together with some very few well-to-do merchants and businessmen from other Persian towns (among them Bušehr and Yazd), formed the rather small group of affluent Persian Jews in Palestine until 1917. According to all evidence, the overwhelming majority of the Persian emigrants and their children in Jerusalem, who according to another source numbered 1760 souls in 1916 (Levy, 1985, p. 137), were steeped in poverty. They grappled with a wide range of physical, communal, and socio-cultural hardships and distresses. Not least among the latter difficulties were the language barriers, as these emigrants during the 1880s-1920s did not speak any of the three main languages of Arabic, Ladino (or Judaeo-Spanish), and Yiddish, which served as the main languages of communication, business, and social intercourse among the diverse ethno-religious and national denominations in Ottoman Jerusalem and in other parts of Palestine.

All but a few of these emigrants lived in the newly built neighborhoods of Jerusalem, and to the west of the walls of the Old City as of the 1860s. The first of such neighborhoods built and occupied by the Persian emigrants, called Ševet Ṣedeq (located nearby the city's present-day down-town market of Mahaneh Yehudā), was an overcrowded shanty town consisting of shabby rooms made of sheets of tin and empty wood-boxes erected on an uninhabited plot of land. Eventually the emigrants, aided by some well-to-do Persian donors, managed to buy a plot of land (to the west of Ševet Ṣedeq) and, in 1900, laid the foundations for a new neighborhood for the Persian emigrants, named Neveh Šalom (Ha-Cohen, pp. 89-90). In both neighborhoods, however, the emigrants faced many hardships, including diseases, poor sanitary conditions, lack of insulation in hot summers and without protection against cold in winter. Most of them had not received any modern professional training, and the vast majority of them in the 1880s-1920s (and a large number of those who arrived in the 1930s-1940s) eked out a living by means of various physical and menial labors. Many among these first-generation emigrants worked as construction-workers, builders, masons, water-drawers and peddlers (Ben-Arieh, p. 407; Ha-Cohen, p. 37). Others were occupied as retailers and shop-keepers, vegetable-sellers, butchers, bakers, as well as buyers and sellers of used clothes, etc. (Levy, 1985, p. 137). Some of the children of these emigrants acquired vocational education in the school of the Alliance Israélite in the city during the 1890s-1910s and onward. These young emigrants and their older family members, who were mostly from Shiraz and trained as shoemakers, carpenters, blacksmiths, masons, and particularly as builders, were among the main builders and craftsmen who built some of the new neighborhoods, public buildings, and hospitals in the western part of the city. These buildings, together with the aforementioned Persian neighborhoods, which were converted subsequently into permanent stone houses, as well as a number of synagogues and communal buildings constructed during this period in those neighborhoods, are today among the more attractive architectural and historical sites of western Jerusalem (Shalev-Khalifa, pp. 252-56, 263-69). The wealthy Jews of Mashad built a number of luxurious homes for their own families as well as a large rental building and other communal endowments for the use of the needy members of their community. The latter residential and communal buildings, built during the years 1900-1905, were located in the quarter of the very affluent Persian-speaking Jews of Bukhara. Known until today as the Bukharan Quarter, the latter neighborhood was the most modern and luxurious Jewish quarter built outside the walls of the Old City of Jerusalem during the last decade of the 19th century (Kroyanker, pp. 125-28).

The communal lives and internal organization of the Persian emigrants during the 1880-1917 (and to a large extent until the establishment of the State of Israel) centered mainly around synagogues and their affiliated bodies. Between the years 1894 and 1913 these emigrants built six synagogues in the midst of their Jerusalem neighborhoods (Netzer, 1891, p. 293). These synagogues, which were headed by Persian-speaking rabbis, were assisted by volunteering functionaries and were supported mainly by well-to-do Persian donors from Jerusalem and from the Jewish communities inside Persia. Most of these synagogues were hard pressed, but, despite their limited material resources and the fact that they received little support from the local Jewish institutions and authorities, they did their best to attend to the diverse needs of the Persian emigrants in the areas of religion, education and social services. As early as 1900, a welfare and educational society by the name of "the Society for the Lovers of Zion" was founded by the Persian-speaking Jews of Jerusalem (Ha-Cohen, pp. 48-49). By 1906, they had established two traditional religious schools for the Persian-speaking children in the city, in which some 80 children were enrolled by 1907. Another society, named "the Association for Peace and Fellowship," was founded by some young descendants of the Jewish emigrants from Bušehr, with a view to provide educational and welfare assistance to the growing community (Netzer, 1981, p. 292). These and some other similar communal and organizational activities of the emigrants, however, did not succeed in turning the community of the Persian-speaking Jews in and outside Jerusalem into an independent and officially recognized ethnic community vis-à-vis the Ottoman and local Jewish authorities and institutions. For many years to come (roughly until 1948), the community of Persian Jews in Jerusalem remained subordinated to the jurisdiction of the Committee of the Sephardic Community in Jerusalem, which was the recognized representative organization of Jews of Middle-Eastern and North-African extraction in Jerusalem. Moreover, despite the different communal bodies and functions that were established by the Persian emigrants in Jerusalem and in the few other towns and colonies of Palestine during the years 1882-1917, by and large the community did not possess the material, organizational, and human resources and connections to cope with the diverse needs and distresses of its predominantly poor population.

From 1917 to 1948. The Balfour Declaration, which was a British declaration of sympathy with Zionist aspirations, marked a new chapter in the history of Jewish migration from Persia to Palestine. In the form of a letter signed and dated 2 November 1917, the British Foreign Secretary Arthur James Balfour (1848-1930) officially announced to Lord Lionel Walter Rothschild (1868-1937) that "His Majesty's [i.e., the British] Government view with favour the establishment of a national home for the Jewish people, and will use their best endeavours to facilitate the achievement of this object" (Stein, p. V). Similar to many other Jewish communities across the world, the latter declaration soon aroused national and religious aspirations among the Jews of Persia and led to the establishment of Zionist associations, first in Tehran (in 1918) and thereafter in Persia's other larger Jewish communities. Among their other Jewish nationalist-oriented activities in the various communities, which included the instruction of modern Hebrew, the Zionist bodies and activists were engaged in encouraging emigration from Persia to Palestine as well as in raising funds and donations for various Jewish colonization, settlement, and development projects in Palestine. The Zionist associations in Persia were also engaged in collecting funds in order to provide assistance to those Persian Jews who had already settled in Palestine as well as to those who were planning to emigrate (Mizrahi, 1971, p. 584; Netzer, 1994, pp. 662-63). Shortly after the Balfour Declaration, the Persian community in Jerusalem elected the "General Committee of the Community of Persian Jews in Jerusalem," (*Voʿad kelali la-ʿadat Yehudei Paras be-Yerušalayim*) to serve as a representative body of Persian Jewry in Palestine and to act as a liaison with outside Jewish and governmental institutions and authorities (Mizrahi, 1959, pp. 221-22). Among the Committee's other main objectives were administering the assets and properties of the community, procuring funds and loans for housing, tending to the educational and general welfare of the Persian emigrant community, and raising the public standing and profile of Persian Jews in Jerusalem and other parts of Palestine (Levy, 1985, pp. 138-39). The Committee was active among the old and new emigrants who continued to arrive in larger numbers; it was also assisted in its endeavours by a small number of other communal welfare and cultural bodies that were set up and run mainly by the younger generation of Persian emigrants in Jerusalem during the 1920s-30s.

The Balfour Declaration, the termination of Ottoman rule in Palestine (Jerusalem was conquered by British troops on 9 December 1917), and the institution of the British Mandate for Palestine, ratified by the League of Nations in April 1920, led to a considerable expansion in the activities, investments, and enterprises of the Jewish national institutions in Palestine. These changes and developments were conducive to a significant growth in the volume of emigration from Persia during the three decades of de-facto British control in Palestine. According to official figures published in 1949 by the State of Israel's Central Bureau of Statistics, some 3,632 Jews from Persia emigrated to Mandatory Palestine during the years 1917-48 (*Statistical Abstract*, no. 2, 1950-51, p. 27; Sicron, II, p. 27). On the basis of other sources, however, it appears that the numbers were considerably higher (Mizrahi, 1971, pp. 549-50). Owing to emigration and natural growth, the number of Jews of Persian origin in Palestine is said to have reached 7,275 in 1926 and some 16,000 souls in 1935 (Netzer, 1994, pp. 663-64). Although we do not possess reliable figures and documentation on the number of Persian emigrants and their descendants living in Palestine on the eve of Israel's independence, based on various estimates and conjectures, their numbers are put at some twenty to thirty thousand souls in May 1948 (Netzer, 1994, p. 664; Yeroushalmi, 2001, p. 9). Out of an estimated population of some 20,000 to 30,000 Persian emigrants in 1948, about 18,000 lived in Jerusalem, and the rest, which according to all accounts constituted a very small minority (Levy, 1985, p. 134), lived in the old and some of the newly established Jewish colonies and towns along the Mediterranean coastal plain, including Jaffa, Tel-Aviv, Petah-Tiqva, Rehovot, Haifa, etc. (*Hed Hamizrah*, 29 April 1949, p. 11). Their synagogues and communal associations provided assistance and services in the areas of housing, welfare, education, and religion, but they lacked the means to provide solutions for the old and newly arriving emigrants. Some of the emigrants who arrived and settled in Jerusalem during the 1930s and onward received financial and other forms of social and welfare assistance from the local Jewish organizations and authorities (Levy, 1985, p. 134), but the vast majority of the old and new emigrants during the years 1917-48 were poor, and many had to support large families. A good number of Persian families and individuals (e.g., mainly merchants and businessmen from Mashad, Hamadān, Tehran, Yazd, Isfahan, and Bušehr) who emigrated to Palestine and particularly to Jerusalem in the third and fourth decades of the 20th century, enjoyed substantial financial means, while some others had received modern education at the Alliance (q.v.) and state institutions in Persia (mainly in Hamadān and Tehran), but the great majority, particularly women, had no modern education or professional and technical training and belonged to the lower socio-economic, educational, and professional strata of the Jewish population in Palestine. Given the predominantly modern and European-dominated nature of the Jewish national institutions and structures that were laid in Palestine during the formative years of the British Mandate, the traditional and premodern qualifications of the vast majority of Persian emigrants had significant implications with respect to their general condition and standing. Much like the Persian emigrants during the 1880s-1920s, the bulk of the emigrants who arrived during the 1930s-1948 made a living as unskilled or semi-skilled laborers. Many were occupied as construction workers, road-pavers, and porters as well as carpenters, blacksmiths and shoemakers. Another large group among them worked as peddlers, vegetable vendors, and traders of fabric and used clothes. Among them were found numerous retailers, shop-keepers, and small merchants as well as a few trained artisans (e.g., weavers, printers, and metal casters) and dozens of elementary school teachers, clerks, and policemen (Tahon, p. 205; Levy, 1985, p. 137).

The Jews of Mashad and their descendants and an unknown number of merchants and businessmen from Persia's larger cities (among them Hamadān, Tehran, Yazd and Bušehr) stood in sharp contrast to the vast majority of Persian Jews living in Jerusalem and in other localities during the British Mandate. The Jews of Mashad, numbering some 1,000 souls in 1946 and an estimated 1,200 in 1948 (*Hed Ha-Mizrah*, 3 March 1946, p. 14, 29 April 1949, p. 11), constituted the most organized and prosperous concentration of Persian emigrants in Palestine before and after the establishment of the State of Israel. Headed by well-to-do communal leaders and businessmen engaged in international trade (mainly in rugs, precious stones, and finances), they formed (and still continue to form) a closely knit community. Owing to their collective experiences and tribulations as Jews who preserved their religious identity in secret, by and large they avoided marital or close inter-communal ties with the rest of the Persian emigrants. Much like the vast majority of the Persian emigrants and their descendants prior to the establishment of the State of Israel, however, the bulk of the Jews of Mashad, some 900 out of an estimated 1,000 in 1946, lived in Jerusalem, and the remainder in the greater Tel-Aviv area (*Hed Ha-Mizrah*, 15 March 1946, p. 14).

Immigration since 1948 and its characteristics. The gradual development and strengthening of the Jewish national institutions and settlements under the British Mandate resulted in a significant growth in the size of the Persian emigrant community in Palestine. The establishment of the State of Israel, the international recognition accorded to it by the United Nations on November 29, 1947, and particularly the declaration of its independence on 14 May 1948 caused a profound change in the common attitudes and sentiments of Persian Jews toward the newly established state. Although we do not have accurate figures on the size of Jewish population of Persia in 1948, nor do we possess reliable documentation and research concerning those among them who intended to immigrate to Israel, it has been suggested that out of Persia's estimated Jewish population of some 90,000-100,000 souls at the time of Israel's independence, some 60,000 were intending to immigrate to Israel (Ha-Cohen, p. 202). The estimated 20,000 to 30,000 Jews of Iranian origin who lived in Palestine on the eve of Israel's independence (see above) were joined by an estimated body of some 80–85,000 new immigrants during the years 1948-2004. According to official figures provided by Israel's Central Bureau of Statistics and by the Jewish Agency (i.e., the executive body of the World Zionist Organization responsible for immigration), the number of Persian immigrants who arrived in Israel between May 1948 through the end of December 1989 (i.e., the first decade of the Islamic Revolution in Iran) amounted to 74,148 souls (see Central Bureau of Statistics, *Statistical Abstract*, no. 46, 1990, p. 180). This figure should be increased by 8,000-10,000, which is a conservative estimate of the number of immigrants who arrived in Israel during 1990-2004 (Yeroushalmi, 2001, p. 15). Out of the above estimated total of some 85,000 Persian immigrants who are reported to have arrived directly from Persia (and some proportionately few from other countries), an unknown number left Israel. They left mainly during the 1950s due to the harsh living conditions that prevailed in Israel during the first years of Israel's establishment. Most of the latter group, and an unknown number of immigrants in the 1960s-70s, returned to Persia. The average rate of negative immigration among all immigrant groups in Israel during the years 1948-53, which were particularly difficult years, has been estimated at some 7 percent (Sicron, I, p. 30). Taken as a general and rather inaccurate measure, the latter rate would suggest that among the estimated 85,000 Persian immigrants who arrived in Israel during 1948-2004, at least 6,000 left the country. Out of this estimated total of some 80,000 Persian immigrants who arrived and evidently settled in Israel between 1948 and 2004, 38,876 people, or about 49 percent, came during the first twelve years of Israel's existence (1948-60), among whom 30,756 souls (ca. 79 percent) had come during the first five years (Central Bureau of Statistics, *Statistical Abstract*, no. 21, 1970, p. 49; Netzer, 1982, pp. 351-52). Both numerically as well as in terms of the length of their residence in Israel and the extent and depth of their acculturation and absorption in the diverse spheres of life in Israel, these immigrants and their descendants constitute a major and dominant part of the Persian immigrant community in Israel. Together with the descendants of immigrants who settled in Palestine before 1948, they form the two major and highly integrated Israelis of Persian origin in the present-day State of Israel. The majority of the prominent and influential public figures of Persian origin in Israel today, among them the former president of the State of Israel, Mr. Moshe Katsav, the defense minister, Lieutenant-General Shaul Mofaz, the chief of the general military staff, Lieutenant-General Dan Halutz, and some others (see below) belong to the veteran families of immigrants who settled in the pre-state and independent Israel during the 1920s-1960s.

Since the early 1960s until the establishment of the Islamic Republic in Iran in February 1979, there was an average annual immigration of some 1,000 to 1,500 souls from Persia. The average did not increase in the wake of the Islamic Revolution, which was followed by a major wave of Jewish immigration from Persia to various destinations, chief among them the United States and Europe. The number of immigrants who reportedly arrived from Persia to Israel in the course of the first decade of the Islamic Republic (1979-89) amounted to 8,487 souls, or roughly about 850 people per year, which declined progressively in the course of the 1990s-2004 (e.g., 323 in 1999, 420 in 2000, and 133 in 2003; see Central Bureau of Statistics, *Statistical Abstract*, no. 46, 1995, p. 180; no. 47, 1996, p. 150; no. 48, 1997, p. 158; ibid., no. 51, 2000, sec. 5.3; no. 52, 2002, sec. 5.3; no. 55, 2004, sec. 5.3). A salient characteristic of the Persian immigrants to Israel, including both those who arrived prior to 1948 as well as those who settled in the country ever since Israel's establishment, is the comparatively young age of the immigrants at the time of their immigration. Similar to other immigrant groups from Asia and Africa, and in contrast to immigrants from Europe, North America and other Western communities, about 85 percent of all the Persian immigrants during the massive immigration influx of 1948-53 were less than forty-five years old (Sicron, I, Table 8, p. 48). Among the latter immigrants, about 39 percent were children below the age of fourteen. Moreover, only 3.6 percent of these newcomers were sixty years old and over (Sicron, I, Table 10, p. 49). The large proportion of children, youth, and young adults among these immigrants explains the high degree of adaptability among them to the predominantly new and modern-oriented systems and institutions of education, culture, society and economy in the State of Israel. It appears that a relatively high percentage of children and youngsters among the immigrants characterizes also those who arrived from Persia in the course of the 1960s and 1970s, although, on the basis of a general impression, the average size of a Persian immigrant family in the 1980s-2000 is smaller in comparison to those who arrived in the 1940s-1960s and earlier (Tahon, p. 204).

The establishment of the State of Israel fundamentally altered and transformed the structure and nature of immigration from Persia. Whereas until 1948 sporadic families and semi-organized groups of immigrants had to rely mostly on themselves and on the limited communal resources of Persian-speaking Jews and philanthropists in and outside Palestine, following the establishment of the State of Israel the physical relocation and the processes of absorption of the vast majority of the Persian immigrants were (and still are) facilitated, and to a large degree directed and implemented, by the state and its affiliated arms and institutions. As such the state took over, replaced, and expanded the roles and services that had hitherto been provided by a few and mostly strapped communal and external Jewish bodies and volunteers. In contrast with the older semi-organized groups of families or extended families (ordinarily from the same settlement or district in Persia) that arrived and settled together in the same community or neighborhood of Persian-speaking Jews until 1948, following the establishment of the State of Israel, immigrant families and individuals originating from diverse locations in Persia and characterized by vastly different linguistic, socio-cultural and occupational histories and backgrounds arrived in Israel as separate individual units and not as part of an organized communal, religious, or ideological framework. For the vast majority of the Persian immigrants ever since 1948, the bonds and resources of the nuclear family have been serving as the most important framework and vehicle with which they deal with the diverse demands and challenges of relocation, acculturation, and absorption into their new environment. Chief among the national goals and policies of the State of Israel, particularly during the first three decades of its existence, were the creation of a melting pot which would assimilate the diverse groups of immigrants and mold them into a new and homogenous state, society, and national culture. One of the main instruments for achieving this goal was to settle the immigrant families from the various countries and cultural backgrounds in ethnically mixed settlements, towns, and housing projects across the country. The considerable geographical diffusion of the immigrants ever since 1948, and the fact that in most parts of Israel today Persian immigrants and their descendants are found in relatively diluted numbers in the midst of Hebrew-speaking multi-ethnic neighborhoods and settlements, account for the fact that, strictly speaking, one cannot speak of a cohesive and distinct community of Persian Jews in Israel. Rather than a community whose members ordinarily reside in the same locality and maintain various degrees of common ties and interests, the Persian immigrants, similar to most other groups of veteran and increasingly assimilated immigrants in Israel today, consist mostly of diffused families of Persian origin and their descendants whose social bonds, economic activities, and cultural and religious affiliations take place predominantly within the frameworks and institutions created over the years within the state of Israel.

Hand-in-hand with the latter family-based (and not communal) pattern of immigration and relocation that has characterized the immigration and absorption processes of the great majority of Persian immigrants ever since 1948, the immigration from Persia brought to Israel also a significant number of organized groups of pioneers, youths and children, particularly during the years 1948-1960s. Since early 1940s there were direct contacts between Persia's larger Jewish communities, particularly that of Tehran, and the representatives and emissaries of the various Zionist institutions, political movements, and establishments in Mandatory Palestine. Among the latter bodies and ideological currents (mostly of secular socialist orientation), which appealed particularly to the Jewish Persian youth during the 1940s-1950s, was the Jewish socialist Kibbutz movement (Saʿidi, pp. 48-74). Known as the "Halutz" or "Pioneer" movement, the youth socialist branch of the Kibbutz movement was officially established in Persia in 1946, with the aim of educating and preparing groups of Jewish youth in Persia to immigrate to Israel and take part in the Zionist enterprise by settling in the land's collective and socialist communities, known as kibbutz. Soon after Israel's declaration of independence, the Halutz movement had some 4,000 young male and female members in Tehran and a similar number of affiliated activists and sympathizers in Persia's other Jewish communities (Saʿidi, p. 48; Ben-David, pp. 91-97). The first organized group of these young socialist pioneers of Persia, consisting of some forty members, arrived in Israel in 1949 and joined a newly founded kibbutz (by the name of Maʿagan Mik̲āel), located some 20 km to the south of Haifa. Other similar groups, estimated at some two dozens or more, arrived subsequently during the first years of the 1950s and settled mostly in kibbutz settlements and some few in agricultural cooperatives in the north, center, and south of Israel. The majority of the latter organized groups of pioneers, whose numbers are estimated at about one thousand or more, joined existing or newly founded collective settlements and none were involved in setting up settlements of their own. Moreover, a large number of the latter Persian settlers soon abandoned their collective settlements and chose to live in other parts, mostly towns and cities, across Israel. In addition to those rather few Persian Jews who still live in various kibbutz settlements, the members of the Halutz movement who immigrated to Israel on their own, as well as those who gave up the collective lifestyle were, and some still are, active in diverse professions, including business, public and government services, academia, education, welfare, etc. Some are active in nonprofit communal organizations which deal exclusively with the needs and interests of Persian immigrants in Israel.

To the groups of young socialist-oriented pioneers and immigrants we should add a relatively large number of teenagers and children who immigrated to Israel within the framework of the Youth Immigration (Hebrew: *ʿAliyat Ha-Noʿar*) Department of the Jewish Agency. Beginning in 1949 and continuing during the 1950s-1960s, hundreds of Jewish children and youth (both boys and girls) immigrated to Israel. Arriving in Israel in small organized groups without their parents, they received vocational, agricultural or general high-school education within the boarding schools of the Youth Immigration Department. These youths and numerous children of the Persian immigrant families who were sent by their parents to these boarding schools (or to the kibbutz) due to economic or other considerations, were highly adaptable and talented (Yeroushalmi, 2001, pp. 12-13), and, upon the completion of their primary and secondary education, were soon fully integrated into the general fabric of the society. Many of Persian-born children and youths of the 1950s-1960s who went to these schools still are productive in diverse areas and levels of public and economic activities such as (industry, technology, military, business, education, civil services, etc. There were also a significant number of high-school graduates (estimated at a few hundreds) who arrived from Persia as non-immigrants during the 1950s-70s, with the purpose of pursuing their studies at institutions of higher education in Israel. Many among them settled in Israel following the completion of their studies (mostly at the undergraduate level) and joined the academic work-force in various locations across Israel.

Finally, we know of several families and individuals of Persian origin who immigrated to Israel not directly from Persia, but from various countries and Jewish communities in Western Europe, North America and elsewhere, mostly since the 1970s. In comparison to the immigrants of the 1940s-60s, these immigrants, and particularly those among them who arrived in Israel after some years of residence, education, and professional careers in the West, are better educated and arrived in Israel with larger economic and material means.

The organized groups of pioneers, despite their importance and contribution in the history of Persian immigration and settlement in Israel ever since its establishment, constitute a rather small and non-typical segment among the larger population of Persian immigrants in Israel. Out of the estimated total of some 80,000 immigrants who reportedly arrived and settled in Israel ever since its establishment (see above), the overwhelming majority (over 95 percent) consisted of families and individuals who lacked any communal, ideological, or religious organization or framework at the time of their immigration. This reality, combined with numerous other economic, socio-cultural, and psychological characteristics and limitations among these immigrants, resulted in a high degree of dependency on the part of these immigrants upon the various institutions, projects, and decisions of the state of Israel. This was particularly true with respect to the vast majority of the immigrant families who arrived from Persia and several other Middle Eastern and North African countries during the years 1948-67. The comparatively larger economic means and higher educational and professional qualifications of the Persian immigrants who arrived since the 1970s (hand-in-hand with political, economic, and structural changes inside Israel that have led to increasing economic liberalization and cultural pluralism and decreasing bureaucratic centralization over the last three decades) reduced to some extent the need and dependency of the immigrants on the settlement priorities and decisions of the central government in the important areas of housing, employment, professional training, access to higher education, and so forth. Moreover, because of a variety of historical conditions inside Persia, mainly the absence of state-wide persecution or popular harassment of Jews, freedom of movement and immigration from and into Persia during the years 1948-79 (and actual possibilities for immigration from Persia since the establishment of the Islamic Republic), the Persian immigrants who moved to Israel ordinarily did so out of their own free will. These immigrants, as well as those who settled in Mandatory Palestine, did not perceive themselves as victims, refugees or displaced individuals whose immigration was imposed on them by events or forces beyond their personal control. The latter factors, combined with the existence of close bilateral relations and ongoing traffic between Persia and Israel until 1979, seem to have been of major psychological importance favorably affecting the broader processes of immigration and absorption among the vast majority of the Persian immigrants. These conditions and factors may also explain the generally high degree of positive motivation and optimism demonstrated by these immigrants and their descendants in dealing with the entailing various difficulties, challenges, and opportunities. A fundamental sense of free choice and a perceived ability to control and improve one's lot through the process of immigration appear as common characteristics among the vast majority of Persian immigrants and their descendants in Israel. Coupled with a number of other cultural and sociological dispositions (among them pragmatism, diligence, compliance, social conformism, as well as loyalty and dedication to the needs and concerns of one's family members), these factors seem to have further facilitated the general processes of immigration and absorption among these immigrants over the last decades. The same socio-cultural factors also appear to have nurtured a profound sense of belonging and identification among the vast majority of these immigrants with the common goals, causes, and challenges of the Jewish state.

Jews of Persian origin in Israel today. Despite the historical conditions and socio-cultural traits of the Persian Jews that facilitated and enhanced the overall processes of immigration and absorption among these immigrants ever since Israel's establishment, numerous communal, socio-economic, and educational characteristics among their vast majority placed them in a difficult and disadvantageous position in comparison with some other groups of immigrants from the Muslim countries, and particularly in relation with Jews of European and Western countries who were the principal originators and founders of the State of Israel. First, while the Jewish immigrants from the Arab lands (among them those of Iraq and Yemen) left their countries of residence almost in their entirety and together with their traditional leaderships, the Persian Jews, much like the Jews of Morocco, left Persia without their leadership, which consisted mostly of the elite of the wealthy and well-educated classes, who continued to live and prosper in Persia (Menashri, p. 8). This reality persisted both before and after the establishment of the Islamic Republic in Iran, in the wake of which the vast majority of the traditional and modern-educated economic and communal leadership of Persian Jewry migrated to North America and Europe and preferred not to settle in Israel. Second, the immigration from Persia during 1948-60, which accounts for some forty thousand souls, or roughly half of all the Persian Jews who have settled in Israel over the years 1948-2004, consisted mostly of Jews from Persia's scattered provincial towns and rural districts, stretching from Persia's north and northwest (Western Azerbaijan and Persian Kurdistan) to the smaller towns of central Persia (e.g., Nehāvand, Borujerd, Golpāyagān, and K̲ᵛānsār) and the provinces and districts of Iran's south (mainly Fārs) and the southwest (Ben-Zvi, pp. 42-43). The immigration during these early years of Israel's independence brought to the country also large numbers of economically hard-pressed immigrants from Persia's larger towns and cities (mainly Urmia, Kermānšāh, Sanandaj, Hamadān, Tehran, Kāšān, Isfahan, Shiraz, and Yazd). Thus, the vast majority of these immigrants arrived in Israel without significant (and at times no) modern education, professional training, or capital. Although the average educational qualifications and economic resources of the immigrants who arrived in Israel in the 1970s-2004 grew considerably in comparison to those who came during the 1940s-1960s (primarily as a result of the social, educational, and economic improvements in the lives of the Jews inside Persia during those years), nevertheless, for the vast majority of the Persian Jews who moved to Israel ever since its establishment, the immigration required considerable change or adjustment in occupation as well as in general cultural and societal orientations. This was particularly the case with the immigrants in the 1950s-1960s. Owing to a lack of modern education, vocational training, or significant economic resources in a fundamentally modern-oriented and rapidly developing country, the latter newcomers from Persia had to relinquish their old trades and occupations, among them peddling, shop-keeping, and petty trade as well as traditional Jewish-persian occupations such as weaving, dyeing, handling of gold and silver, traditional medicine, etc. (Sicron, I, pp. 75-76). The great majority of these immigrants, including a large number of young adults, youths, and women, had to make a living by taking up physical and semi-skilled jobs in an array of projects and work-places offered by the newly-founded state. Many of them took part in the construction of Israel's physical infrastructures and facilities, among them roads, public buildings, housing-complexes, factories, as well as afforestation, farming, and settlement projects across the country. Others were employed as laborers in a growing number of public- and private-owned companies, factories, and industrial complexes. Directed by the government, a sizeable number of these families, mainly Neo-Aramaic and Kurdish speaking Jews of Persian Kurdistan, joined agricultural settlements in Galilee, in the north, and in the Negev, in the south (Netzer, 1994, p. 664). This was a major transformation for the Persian Jews, who for centuries had not been engaged in farming and agriculture. Together with some few Persian families who had become farmers in the 1880s-1910s (Klein, pp. 146-47), some second and third generation of the latter Persian agriculturalists are still engaged in modern and advanced agriculture in the agricultural cooperatives (Hebrew: *mošav*) which their parents had joined or founded in the 1950s (Kanka-Shekalim, pp. 101-4). In the latter capacities, mainly as physical laborers, semi-skilled workers and farmers, these immigrants of the 1948-1960s and their children were part and parcel of the work-force which participated in numerous construction and development projects in the areas of economy and industry, agriculture, settlement, security, etc. during the early and crucial years of Israel's independence.

The vast majority of the Persian immigrant families during the first decade of Israel's independence became diffused and housed in a large number of transit camps, settlements, and development towns throughout the country, but, already in the 1950s and increasingly during the 1960s and 1970s, many of these families and their children moved and relocated in towns and outskirts of the larger cities, mainly in the center of the country and along the Mediterranean coastal plain. Together with the large and old concentration of Persian Jews in Jerusalem, they attracted, in the course of the 1960s-1990s, additional family members from Persia and from other parts of Israel. First and second generation Persian Jews are found today in all parts of Israel and in all existing forms and frameworks of settlement and residence, but they are found in comparatively larger numbers in towns and urban areas. In the coastal towns and cities of Hadera and Netanya (to the south of Haifa), in the larger Hasharon area in the center of Israel, and more notably in metropolitan Tel-Aviv and its nearby towns of Ramat-Gan, Holon, Rishon-Letzion, Bat-Yam, and some others, relatively large numbers of veteran and more recent immigrants live and work.

Although Jews of Persian origin and their descendants in present-day Israel are found in diverse areas and levels of professional and economic activity across the country, a proportionately high percentage of those who live in Israel's larger towns and cities (chief among them Tel-Aviv and its satellite towns and Jerusalem) are engaged in the private sector and make a living in a wide range of small and medium-size businesses. Quite a large number of the Persian-born immigrants and their children are store-owners and shop-keepers (selling clothes and shoes, food products, gifts, souvenirs, jewelry, antiques, and rugs) in the main commercial centers and streets of Israel's larger towns and cities. Others are engaged in medium-size businesses and commercial enterprises such as manufacturing of clothes, imports and distribution of foreign commodities and products (such as textile and electronic appliances), ownership and management of wedding halls, real-estate, construction companies, etc. The gradual and significant progress of the second and third generation of Persian immigrants in the areas of primary and secondary education, professional training, and college and university education over the last five decades have resulted in considerable improvement in the educational and professional qualifications among the children and descendants of Persian Jews in Israel. The improvements have provided their children with increasingly better and more variegated opportunities in the areas of employment and economic activity, income, housing and general living conditions, in comparison with the generation of their parents and grandparents (Tahon, pp. 207-8; Menashri, pp. 9-10; Yeroushalmi, 2001, pp. 42-45). However, despite these significant improvements, major gaps still remain between the average educational and professional level of Israelis of Western origin and those of Persian and other Middle-Eastern and North-African immigrants and their descendants (Hever, pp. 17-18; Shavit, pp. 115-26). While there are a relatively large number of university and college graduates of Iranian extraction in Israel (among them physicians, engineers, and graduates in the various fields of natural sciences, technology, social sciences, and humanities who have completed their studies both in and outside Israel over the last three decades or so), the percentage of Persian Jews among the academic and research staffs of the Israeli universities and research institutes is very low and far below their relative share in the general population. So is the situation in numerous other areas of professional activity and positions of influence, among them ownership and directorship of large commercial, financial and technological companies, media and telecommunications, journalism, and diverse areas of cultural and intellectual activity grounded in Israel's fundamentally European and Western-oriented hegemonic culture. A relatively low level of representation characterizes the Persian immigrants and their descendants also in the spheres of public life, national politics, and local government. The number of Persian immigrants and their descendants in the Israeli parliament, as well as in the institutions of local government, also appears to have been below their demographic share over the last five decades (Netzer, 1994, p. 664).

The gradual but consistent progress and integration of Persian Jews and their descendants in the diverse areas of professional, economic, and cultural activities are likely to result in a larger degree of presence and prominence on their part in the various spheres of life in Israel. Indeed, Persian-born immigrants and their children have risen to some very high positions of prominence and public recognition, particularly over the last two decades. Among the more outstanding and nationally known figures of Persian origin in present-day Israel mention should be made particularly of the following: Mr. Moshe Katsav, the former President of the State of Israel (elected in 2000). Born in Yazd in 1945, Mr. Katsav immigrated to Israel with his parents in 1951. Among his numerous elected and appointed positions on behalf of the Likud party, he served as a member of the Israeli Parliament for seven consecutive terms (1977-2000), as minister of labor and welfare (1984-1988), transportation (1988-1992), and tourism, and deputy prime minister (1996-1999). The current defense minister, Lt. General Shaul Mofaz, was born in Isfahan in 1948 and immigrated to Israel with his parents in 1957. Enlisted in the Israeli army in 1966, his long military career peaked with his appointment as deputy chief and chief of the joint military staff (in 1997 and 1998, respectively). As a member of the governing Likud party, General Mofaz joined the Israeli cabinet as minister of defense in November 2002. No less impressive in his military rank and professional career has been Lt. General Dan Halutz, the current chief of the joint military staff. Born in Tel-Aviv in 1948 to a family of mixed Persian-Iraqi background (his father immigrated from Shiraz to the British-controlled Palestine in 1936), Dan Halutz was enlisted in the Israeli army in 1966. Trained as a combat-pilot in the Israeli air force, he pursued his military career in numerous operational and command capacities. He was appointed as commander in chief of the air force (April 2000) and was subsequently promoted to the position of deputy chief of staff (in July 2004) and chief of staff (in June 2005). A rather similar successful military career characterizes also Major General Eitan Ben Eliyahu, a former commander in chief of the Israeli air force (July 1996-April 2000). Born in Jerusalem in 1944 to a family of immigrants from Persia and Macedonia (his father immigrated from Hamadān to Palestine in 1921), he began his military service in 1962. He was trained also as a combat pilot and, following numerous combat and command positions, was promoted to the rank of Major General (April 1995) and served as commander in chief of the air force (July 1996-April 2000). Among the descendants of Iranian-born immigrants in Israel who have occupied prominent official positions over the last two decades reference should also be made to Rabbi Eliyahu Bakshi Doro, scholar of Jewish law and the former chief Sephardic rabbi of Israel (1993-2003). He was born in Safed in 1941 to parents who had immigrated to Mandatory Palestine from Shiraz; he served as chief Sephardic rabbi of the city of Bat-Yam in 1972 and was appointed to the prestigious position of chief Sephardic Rabbi of Israel in 1993. Among the important but nationally less known individuals who made significant contributions in the areas of scholarship and public and communal leadership mention should be made particularly of the late Ezra Sion Melammed (b. Shiraz, 1903; d. Jerusalem, 1994), the distinguished scholar of biblical and rabbinic studies; rabbi, scholar, poet, and Zionist leader, Rabbi Menahem Ha-Levy (b. Hamadān 1884; d. Jerusalem, 1940); and a leader of the Persian community in Jerusalem during the first half of the 20th century, Mr. Raphael Haim Ha-Cohen (b. Shiraz 1883; d. Jerusalem 1954). Among the younger generation of Persian extraction in Israel who have established themselves on a national level we should point particularly to the highly popular singer and performer known by her first name as Rita (b. Tehran 1962), who immigrated to Israel in 1970, and the gifted writer and novelist Dorit Rabinyan (b. Israel in 1972 to Persian parents). The author of the two acclaimed Hebrew novels, entitled *The Almonds Alley in Omrijan* (pub. in 1994) and *Our Weddings* (1999), Rabinyan's novels incorporate Persian and Jewish-Persian cultural and literary elements.

Bibliography: Yehoshua Ben-Arieh, *ʿIr bi-Rʾi Tequfāh: Yerušālayim ba-Meʾāh ha-Tesaʿ ʿEsreh*, Jerusalem, 1977. N. Ben-David, "Ha-Peʿilut ha-Ṣiyyonit ve-ha-Ḥaluṣit be-Irān bi-Šenot ha-Arbaʻim," in Amnon Netzer, ed., *Yehudei Iran*, Tel-Aviv, 1988, pp. 91-97. Itzhak Ben-Zvi, *Nidḥei Yisrāel*, Tel-Aviv, 1953. Central Bureau of Statistics, *Statistical Abstract of Israel* / Šenāton Stātisti le-Yisrāel, Jerusalem (compiled annually). Simon M. Dubnow, *Divrei Yemei ʿAm ʿOlām*, 5 vols., Tel-Aviv, 1956. W. J. Fischel, "The Jews of Persia, 1795-1940," *Jewish Social Studies* 12, 1950, pp. 119-60. Dvorah Hacohen (sic), *ʿOlim bi-Sʿārāh, ha-ʿaliyāh ha-gedolāh u-qelitātah be-Yisrāel, 1948-1953*, Jerusalem, 1994; tr. Gila Brand as *Immigrants in Turmoil: Mass Immigration to Israel and Its Repercussions in the 1950s and after*, Syracuse, New York, 2003. Raphael Hayyim Ha-Cohen, *Avānim ba-Ḥomāh*, Jerusalem, 1970. Hannan Hever et al., eds., *Mizraḥim be-Yisrāel: ʻiyun biqorti meḥudāš*, Jerusalem, 2002. E. Kanka-Shekalim, "Mivṣaʻ Koreš," in Amnon Netzer, ed.,

Yehudei Irān, Tel-Aviv, 1988, pp. 98-104. Reuben Kashani, *Yehudei Pārās, Bukarā ve-Afgānistān*, Jerusalem, 2001. D. Klein, ʿAliyot Yehudei Pārās le-Eres Yisrāel bein ha-šanim 1884 ve-ʿad Hașharat Balfur be-1917" (The immigration of Persian Jews to Israel between the years 1884 and the Balfour Declaration), unpub. thesis, University of Haifa, 1997. D. Kroyanker, *Yerušalayim*, Jerusalem, 1996. A. Levy, "Abu-Geršon Ha-Consul mi-Șefat," *ʿEtmol*, no. 4, March 1976, pp. 18-19. Idem, "Yehudei Pārās bi-Yerušālayim," *Kivunim*, no. 27, 1985, pp. 133-44. V. D. Lipman, "Britain and the Holy Land: 1830-1914," in Moshe David and Yehoshua Ben-Arieh, eds., *With Eyes Toward Zion* III: *Western Societies and the Holy Land*, New York, 1991, pp. 195-207. David Menashri, "Reflections on the Immigration of Iranian Jews to Israel," in H. Sarshar, ed., *Teruā: The History of Contemporary Iranian Jews / Yahudiān-e Irān dar tārik-e moʿāșer*, Beverly Hills, Calif., 1997, pp. 3-16. H. Mizrahi, *Yehudei Pārās*, Tel-Aviv, 1959. Idem, "Iranian Jews in Israel," in R. Patai, ed., *Encyclopedia of Zionism and Israel*, New York, 1971, I, pp. 549-50. Vera Basch Moreen, tr., *In Queen Esther's Garden: An Anthology of Judeo-Persian Literature*, New Haven, 2000. Amnon Netzer, "ʿAliyat yehudei Pārās ve-Hityašvutām be-Ereș Yisrāel mi-Šilhei ha-Meʾāh ha-Yod-Tet ʿad Hakrazat Balfur," *Miqqedem Umiyyam* 1, 1981, pp. 281-94. Idem, *Tārik-e Yahud dar ʿașr-e jadid*, Jerusalem, 1982. Idem, "Iranian Jews in Israel," in G. Wigoder, ed., *New Encyclopedia of Zionism and Israel*, London and Toronto, 1994, I, pp. 663-64. Idem, "ʿAliyat Yehudei Irān le-Ereș Yisrāel ba-Šānim 1922-1948," in Z. Harvey et al., eds., *Zion and Zionism among Sephardi and Oriental Jews*, Jerusalem, 2002, pp. 365-79. Yohanan Peres, *Yahasei ʿedot be-Yisrāel*, Tel-Aviv, 1976. A. Saʿidi, *Tenuʿat he-Hāluș be-Irān, Tequmātāh u-Nefilātāh 1942-1963*, Rishon Letzion, 1996. Nirit Shalev-Khalifa, *Nahlā'ot be-Lev ʿIr*, Jerusalem, 2003. Y. Shavit, "Segregation, Tracking, and the Educational Attainment of Minorities: Arabs and Mizrahi Jews in Israel," *American Sociological Review* 55, 1990, pp. 115-26. Moshe Sicron, *Ha-ʿaliyāh le-Yisrael, 1948 ʿad 1953*, 2 vols., Jerusalem, 1957. Leonard Stein, *The Balfour Declaration*, Jerusalem and London, 1961. H. Tahon, "Olei Pārās be-Yerusālayim," in M. Lissak et al., eds., *ʿOlim be-Yisrāel*, Jerusalem, 1969, pp. 203-8. David Tidhar, *Encyclopedia le-Halusey ha-Yisuv u-Vonāv*, 19 vols., Tel-Aviv, 1947-71, XII, 1962, p. 4102. J. Wolff, *The Eighteenth Report of the London Society for Promoting Christianity amongst the Jews*, London, 1826. A. Yaʿari, *Igerot Ereș Yisrael*, Tel-Aviv, 1943. Idem, *Šeluhei Ereș Yisrāel*, Jerusalem, 1977. Marzia Yazdāni, ed., *Asnād-e mohājerat-e Yahudiān-e Irān be-Felastin (1300-1330 Š. H.)*, Tehran, 1995. B. D. Yehoshua-Raz, *Mi-nidhei Yisrāel be-Afgānestān le-ānusei Mashad be-Irān*, Jerusalem, 1992. David Yeroushalmi, *The Judeo-Persian Poet ʿEmrānī and His Book of Treasure*, Leiden, 1995. Idem, "Yoșʾei Irān be-Yisrāel," in A. Mizrahi and A. Ben-David, eds., *ʿEdot-ʿedut le-Yisrāel*, Netanya, 2001, pp. 27-49. Idem, "Yehudei ha-İmperiah ha-ʿOtmānit ve-ha-Qehilot ha-Yehudiot be-Iran ba-Meʾāh ha-Tesaʿ ʿEsreh," *Sefunot* 8, 2003, pp. 239-76.

(DAVID YEROUSHALMI)

iii. IRANIAN STUDIES IN ISRAEL

A department of Iranian Studies was only formally established in Israel in 1970, but scholars working in Israel have been interested in aspects of Iranian history and culture since long before that date. The Hebrew University of Jerusalem, the first university in Israel, was established in 1926, with two institutes of research and teaching relevant to our topic, one for Jewish Studies and another for Oriental Studies (the latter was later renamed Asian and African Studies). Scholars of ancient Judaism, in disciplines such as Bible studies, Talmudic literature, Gnosticism and early Christianity, the Dead Sea Scrolls, and similar fields, investigated the possible connections between Jewish religious history and the Iranian world. For the medieval period, the poetry composed and transmitted in Persian-speaking lands in Hebrew as well as in Judeo-Persian (q.v.) attracted interest. Historians of the modern world felt the need to understand the role of Iran in the Middle East, and the existence of a sizeable population in Israel whose personal and cultural roots were in Iran was a further incentive for developing the study of Persian language, literature, and history.

The teaching of Iranian languages, with special emphasis on Old and Middle Iranian, was begun at the Hebrew University in 1965 with the appointment of Shaul Shaked, who had obtained a Ph.D. in Iranian philology from the University of London. In 1970 a Department of Iranian and Armenian Studies, afterwards enlarged to include Indian Studies, was established. Shaked and Amnon Netzer (the latter holds a Ph.D. from Columbia University) taught Old and Middle Iranian as well as Persian language, literature, and history. Some time later, Michael Zand (originally from Moscow) and Soroud Soroudi (with a Ph.D. from UCLA) were appointed to teach Persian language and literature. Armenian was taught by M. E. Stone, and Sanskrit and other Indian languages and literatures by David Shulman.

The later books of the Bible deal with historical and conceptual developments in Jewish society in the Achaemenid period. These include the latter half of the Book of Isaiah, composed after the exile to Babylonia and relects awareness of the newly established Persian kingdom. The books of Ezra and Nehemiah, Esther and Daniel also belong to the priod after the creation of the Achaemenid kingdom. Among scholars who have worked on this period in Jewish history and literature are M. Z. Segal (Hebrew University), Israel Grintz (Tel Aviv University), S. Shaked (Hebrew University), and Ran Zadok (Tel Aviv). The archeology of the Achaemenid priod in the Land of Israel was studied by Ephraim Stern (Hebrew University) in his book *Ha-tarbut ha-homrit shel Yisrael ba-tequfa ha-parsit (538-332)* (Jerusalem, 1968; tr. as

Material Culture of the Land of the Bible in the Persian Period 538-332. B.C., Warminster, UK, 1982). Issues relating to the art and archeology of the Parthian period were discussed by Michael Avi-Yonah (Hebrew University) in his monograph *Oriental Art in Roman Palestine* (Rome, 1961).

The discovery of the Dead Sea Scrolls in the late 1940s caused a whole new branch of studies to be created. The existence of a strong dualism and a developed doctrine of spirits and other elements reminiscent of Zoroastrianism suggested the possibility of Persian influence on certain Jewish groups of the period. Among Israeli scholars discussing these issues mention may be made of David Flusser, S. Shaked (both of Hebrew University), and J. Licht (Tel Aviv University). The Dead Sea Scrolls could not be separated from the Apocrypha and Pseudepigrapha of the Old Testament, on which Flusser wrote extensively. The notion of the Sefirot or the emanations of the Divine Presence, a central idea in the Kabbalah, is derived, it was suggested by G. G. Stroumsa (Hebrew University), from the Iranian theme of the Aməša Spəntas (q.v.). The same scholar also studied several aspects of Manicheism, a topic discussed in depth by J. C. Polotsky (1905-91; Hebrew University), who edited some of the Coptic Manichean texts and wrote the masterly exposition on Manicheism in the *Realenzyklopädie für Altertumskunde* (Pauly-Wissowa; see Bibliography).

Much important work was done by Ran Zadok (Tel Aviv University) on the onomastics of the Achaemenid Empire and on the ethnic composition of the people mentioned in the ancient documents.

The field of Aramaic, with special awareness of the Iranian impact on Aramaic, enjoyed considerable expansion by E. Y. Kutscher (Hebrew University). He studied, in particular, the passive or ergative construction in Aramaic in comparison with Old Persian. J. C. Greenfield made important contributions to the study of Aramaic formulae and lexical items. Shaked has mostly written on lexical connections between Aramaic and Iranian. B. Porten and A. Yardeni have checked the readings of the Aramaic documents of the Achaemenid period; Greenfield and Porten edited the Aramaic version of the Bisotun (q.v.) inscription.

The period of the Babylonian Talmud (ca. 2nd-5th centuries C.E.), a period of enormous formative creativity in Judaism, corresponds to the late Parthian and the Sasanian eras in Iranian history. A knowledge of Iranian languages, culture, and history is obviously a help for understanding Talmudic literature, but awareness of this has taken long to set in. One of the earliest publications on this subject in Israel was by Samuel Krauss, who collected references to Persia and Rome in the Babylonian Talmud. It is necessary to mention J. N. Epstein (Hebrew University), one of the founders of the critical school of Talmudic philology; he also dealt with the Aramaic magic bowls and with Persian loanwords in Aramaic. Another scholar who worked in this philological domain was E. S. Rosenthal (Hebrew University), chiefly on Iranian words in the Talmud. David Rosenthal (Hebrew University), son of the latter scholar, also contributed to this field, as did some of their students (e.g., Mordechai Sabato). The religious ideas encountered in the Talmud were discussed by E. E. Urbach, with particular attention to an Iranian connection, where appropriate, in his monumental *The Sages* (1969, in Hebrew; English tr., 1975). Other scholars who contributed to this field include Moshe Beer (Bar-Ilan University), Isaiah Gafni, and Eliyahu Ahdut (the latter in an unpublished Ph.D. dissertation on Jewish marital conditions in Babylonia). The topography of Sasanian Babylonia was studied from Talmudic sources by A. Oppenheimer (Tel Aviv University).

Themes in Zoroastrian religion were the object of studies by Shaked and Dan Shapira (Bar-Ilan University). The latter dealt with the Zand writings in Pahlavi in an unpublished Ph.D. thesis, and is preparing an edition of the *Bundahišn* (q.v.).

Questions relating to the interaction between Greeks and Persians in Asia Minor in the Achaemenid period formed the theme of a monograph by David Asheri (Hebrew University), who is also responsible for an edition and commentary of Herodotus in Italian.

Classical Persian language and literature were taught at the Hebrew University initially by scholars of Arabic and Turkish such as S. D. Goitein (1900-85) and Uriel Heyd (1913-68). With the appointment in 1970 of Amnon Netzer, and later with that of Michael Zand and Sorour Soroudi, the study of Classical and modern Persian was formally established. Soroudi studied, in particular, aspects of folk culture among Iranians, both Jews and Muslims. At Tel-Aviv University the teaching of Classical and modern Persian was assured by David Menashri, a historian of modern Iran, and David Yeroushalmi, who has contributed to the study of Judeo-Persian literature by editing and translating the work of the great Judeo-Persian poet ʿEmrāni (q.v.), *Ganj-nāma*. Julia Rubanovich (Hebrew University) worked, in an unpublished thesis, on the popular epic works in Persian, in particular the *Eskandar-nāma* and the *Hamza-nāma*.

Much of the scholarly effort concentrated on Judeo-Persian. The collection of the Judeo-Persian manuscripts at the Ben-Zvi Institute in Jerusalem was described by Netzer, who introduction to the volume constitutes the most comprehensive survey of Judeo-Persian literature. The same scholar also published a philosophical text in Judeo-Persian, *Ḥayāt al-ruḥ*, a work of the sixteenth century, as well as an anthology of Judeo-Persian poetry done in Standard Persian (1352), and numerous articles on the history and literature of the Jews of Iran written in Persian, English, and Hebrew. Early Judeo-Persian texts have become a field of research following the discovery by Shaked of a substantial number of writings dating back to the 10th-11th centuries among the treasures of the Cairo Geniza and in the Firkowicz Collection in St. Petersburg. Not all of these writings have yet been published. Ludwig Paul (Hamburg University) has worked on the grammar of these texts. Thamar E. Gindin (Hebrew University) prepared an edition of the extensive *tafṣir* (translation with commentary) of Ezekiel from St. Petersburg and studied its language in a Ph.D. thesis, 2005). She earlier worked on the language of the Jewish dialect of Yazd. Dan Shapira edited the Story of Daniel (*Qeṣṣa-ye dāniyāl*), a legendary history based on the Biblical Book of Daniel, the *Tafsir* of Hosea, and other Judeo-Persian compositions.

Other scholars who worked on Judeo-Persian literature include W. J. Fischel (1902-73, q.v.; University of California at Berkeley), who started his scholarly career at the Hebrew University, and wrote extensively on Judeo-Persian literature and in particular on Bible translations. Abraham Yaari published a bibliography of Judeo-Bukharan books printed in Jerusalem. The Ben-Zvi Institute published an early translation of the Pentateuch from a British Library manuscript edited by H. H. Paper, and the Israel Academy of Sciences and Humanities published a version of the Book of Job from a private collection, edited by the same scholar. A manuscript of a Judeo-Persian prayer book, preserving a tradition which is otherwise lost, was edited by Shlomo Tal.

A series of conferences on the Judeo-Persian heritage and on aspects of contacts between Iran and Judaism are held in Jerusalem and elsewhere under the auspices of the Ben-Zvi Institute. The papers presented in these colloquia are published under the title *Irano-Judaica*; 5 volumes have been published since 1982. A series of volumes in Persian, under the title *Pādyāvand*, also dedicated to the themes of Jewish-Iranian contacts, have been issued since 1996 by A. Netzer.

A descriptive book on the Jews of Afghanistan was published by B. Z. Yehoshua-Raz (1992), and a history of the Jews of the Eastern Caucasus, known as Tats or Mountain Jews, was written by M. Altshuler (1990). A dictionary of Tat, compiled by Yaakov Yitshaki at the turn of the nineteenth and twentieth century, is being prepared for publication by M. Zand. Work on Jewish education in Iran was carried out by A. Cohen.

The Israel Museum has put up over the years a series of exhibitions displaying the art and costumes of Jews living in Persian-speaking countries. Each exhibition is accompanied by a thoroughly researched catalogue.

Several non-scholarly books in Hebrew on the history and culture of the Persian Jews, as well as some local histories (e.g., of the Jews of Yazd), have been published. Among authors of such books mention should be made of Hanina Mizrahi and Yosef Sharga. During the late nineteenth and early twentieth century, Jerusalem was an important center for printing Judeo-Persian texts, especially in the dialect of the Jews of Bukhara. The most prominent writer and printer in that period was Shim'on Ḥakham, who, among other books, brought out the works of the poet Šāhin and his own version of the Pentateuch in the Bukharan dialect.

Interest in Classical Persian literature has led several scholars and poets to translate monuments of Persian poetry into Hebrew. The most ambitious project of this kind is the complete translation of the *Šāh-nāma* of Ferdowsi, done by E. Cagan (1912-2000). Two volumes of this work, edited by Shaked, with the help of J. Rubanovich, have been published. Other works, mostly excerpts and anthologies, have been published over the years. The most prominent translators have been Ben-Zion Benshalom (Katz), from the *Šāh-nāma*; Shim'on Levi (1988), and Raphael Loewe (1982), from ʿOmar Ḵayyām; Parviz Behruzi, two anthologies (1974, 1978) of Classical Persian poetry.

The field of Shiʿite doctrine and literature was explored by Etan Kohlberg (Hebrew University) in a series of books and articles. Early Shiʿite history was dealt with by M. Sharon, who has also worked on the Baha'i religion, and who is the first incumbent of a Chair for Baha'i Studies at the Hebrew University, the first of its kind. Meir Bar-Asher (Hebrew University) has worked on the Yazidis. Sabine Schmidtke (Freie Universität Berlin), who did part of her studies at the Hebrew University, has worked on aspects of Shiʿite doctrine.

The modern history of Iran is a major field of study by scholars in Israel. Special mention should be made of David Menashri (Tel Aviv University), who has studied the Iranian educational system. Bar-Ilan University, Haifa University and Ben-Gurion University have scholars dedicated to research of modern Iranian history. A Center for Modern Iranian history has been established in Tel Aviv University, to encourage research and teaching in this field.

As for Iranian art, it was studied and taught by L. A. Mayer (Hebrew University). A museum carrying his name, where an impressive collection of Iranian art is displayed, was established in Jerusalem with the expertise of Richard Ettinghausen. Myriam Rosen-Ayalon, Rachel Milstein and Raya Shani produced several works on aspects of Iranian art, archaeology and architecture as well as on Judeo-Iranian themes in art.

Collections of Persian and Judeo-Persian manuscripts exists in several centers. The Jewish National and University Library possesses about 250 manuscripts in Judeo-Persian in addition to their collection in New Persian. About 250 manuscripts in Judeo-Persian are held by the Ben-Zvi Institute. The Israel Museum and the L. A. Mayer Memorial Museum also have collections of Persian and Judeo-Persian illuminated manuscripts.

Jewish-Iranian music has been collected at the Israel National Sound Archives in the Jewish National and University Library. This was done over the years by E. Gerson-Kiwi, and includes, among other things, a recording of the Persian *dastgāh*s performed by Netzer on violin in 1956-57 (a similar recording by the same performer is in the Department of Musicology at the University of Illinois in Urbana); there are also recordings of Morteżā Neydāvud (d. 1990).

The Center for the Study of Jewish Language Traditions at the Hebrew University holds recordings of Jewish-Iranian recitations of various texts.

The Archive of Jewish Folk-Stories in Haifa comprises a large collection of stories told by informants from various Jewish communities, including many from the Persian-speaking areas.

Bibliography (selected, in addition to sources given in the body of the article): M. Altshuler, *The Jews of the*

Eastern Caucasus. The history of the "Mountain Jews" from the beginning of the nineteenth century, Jerusalem, 1990 (in Hebrew). D. Asheri, *Fra ellenismo e iranismo. Studi sulla società e cultura di Xanthos nella età achemenide*, Bologna, 1983. Idem, introd. and comm., *Le storie / Erodoto* I. *Libro I: La Lidia e la Persia*, Milan, 1989; III. *Libro III: la Persia*, 2nd ed., 1997. M. M. Bar-Asher, *Scripture and Exegesis in Early Imami-Shiism*, Leiden, 1999. Idem and A. Kofsky, *The Nuṣayrī-'Alawī Religion: an Enquiry into its Theology and Liturgy*, Leiden, 2002. A. Cohen, "Significant Changes in Jewish Education in Iranian," *Pādyāvand* 1, 1996, pp. 19-31 (in English and Persian). J. N. Epstein, "Gloses babylo-araméennes," *Revue des Etudes Juives* 73 1921, pp. 27-58; 74, 1922, pp. 40-72; repr. in Hebrew tr. in idem, *Meḥqarim besifrut hattalmud uv-safot šemiyyot*, Jerusalem, 1984. W. J. Fischel, *Jews in the Economic and Political Life of Medieval Islam*, London, 1937; New York, 1969. Idem, *The Jews of Persia*, New York, 1950. Idem, "The Bible in Persian Translation," *Harvard Theological Review* 45, 1952, pp. 3-45. D. Flusser, *Judaism and the Origins of Christianity*, Jerusalem, 1988.

I. M. Gafni, "Expressions and Types of 'Local Patriotism' among the Jews of Sasanian Babylonia," *Irano-Judaica* 2, 1990, pp. 63-71. Idem, *The Jews of Babylonia in the Talmudic period*, Jerusalem, 1990 (in Hebrew). E. Gerson-Kiwi, *The Persian Doctrine of Dastgah-Composition*, Tel Aviv, 1963. J. C. Greenfield, *'Al kanfei yonah. Collected studies of J.C. Greenfield*, Leiden, 2001. Idem and B. Porten, *The Bisitun Inscription of Darius the Great. Aramaic version*, Corpus Inscriptionum Iranicarum, Part I, vol. V, London, 1982. E. Kohlberg, *Belief and Law in Imami Shī'ism*, Aldershot, UK, 1991. Idem, *A Medieval Muslim Scholar at Work: Ibn Tawus and his Library*, Leiden, 1992. S. Krauss, *Persia and Rome in the Talmud and Midrashim*, Jerusalem, 1948 (in Hebrew). Y. E. Kutscher, *Hebrew and Aramaic Studies*, Jerusalem, 1977.

D. Menashri, *Education and the Making of Modern Iran*, Ithaca, 1992. R. Milstein et al., *Stories of the Prophets: Illustrated Manuscripts of Qisas al-anbiya*, Costa Mesa, 1999. A. Netzer, *Montaḵab-e aš'ār-e fārsi az āṯār-e yahudiyān-e irān*, Tehran, 1973. Idem, "Dāniyāl-nāme: an Exposition of Judeo-Persian," in *Islam and its Cultural Divergence*, ed. G. L. Tikku, Urbana, 1971, pp. 145-64. Idem, "Dāniyāl-nāma and its Linguistic Features," *Israel Oriental Studies* 2, 1972, pp. 305-14. Idem, "A Judeo-Persian Footnote: Šāhīn and 'Emrānī," *Israel Oriental Studies* 4, 1974, pp. 258-64. Idem, "An Isfahānī Jewish Folk-Song," in *Irano-Judaica*, Jerusalem, 1982, pp. 180-203. Idem, *Jewish Persian Manuscripts at the Ben-Zvi Institute*, Jerusalem, 1985 (in Hebrew). Idem, "Rashid al-Din and his Jewish Background," in *Irano-Judaica* 3, 1994, pp. 118-26. Idem, *Duties of Judah by Yehudah ben El'azar*, Jerusalem, 1995 (in Hebrew). Idem, "An Early Judaeo-Persian Fragment from Zefreh," *Jerusalem Studies in Arabic and Islam* 27, 2002, pp. 419-38. Idem, "The Jewish Poet Aminā of Kashan and his Sacred Poems," in *Irano-Judaica* 5, Jerusalem, 2003, pp. 68-81.

A. Oppenheimer, *Babylonia Judaica in the Talmudic Period*, Beihefte zum Tübinger Atlas des Vorderen Orients, Wiesbaden, 1983. H. H. Paper, *A Judeo-Persian Pentateuch*, Jerusalem, 1972. Idem, "A Judeo-Persian Book of Job," *The Israel Academy of Sciences and Humanities. Proceedings* 5, 1976. Idem, "Proverbs in Judeo-Persian," in *Irano-Judaica*, Jerusalem, 1982, pp. 122-47. J. C. Polotsky, "Manichäismus," in Pauly Wissowa, *Realenzyklopädie der classischen Altertumswissenschaft*, Supplement 6, Stuttgart, 1935, cols. 240-71; repr. in idem, *Collected Papers*, Jerusalem, 1971. B. Porten, "Persian Names in Aramaic Documents from Ancient Egypt," in *Irano-Judaica* 5, 2003, pp. 165-86. Idem and Ada Yardeni. *Textbook of Aramaic Documents from Ancient Egypt*, The Hebrew University, Dept. of the History of the Jewish People, 4 vols., Jerusalem, 1986-99. M. Rosen-Ayalon, "A Judeo-Persian Amulet," in *Irano-Judaica* 2, Jerusalem, 1990, pp. 199-216. D. Rosenthal, two articles in *Tarbiz* 61, 1992; also an article in *Meḥqarim belašon* 5-6, 1992 (in Hebrew). E. S. Rosenthal, "Talmudica Iranica," in *Irano-Judaica*, Jerusalem, 1982, pp. 38-134.

S. Schmidtke, *The Theology of al-'Allāma al Ḥillī*, Islamkundliche Untersuchungen 152, Berlin, 1991. Eadem, *Correspondence Corbin-Ivanow*, Travaux et mémoires de l'Institut d'études iraniennes 4, Paris, 1999. S. Shaked: see bibliography in *Jerusalem Studies in Arabic and Islam* 26, 2002. R. Shani, "A Judeo-Persian Talismanic Textile," *Irano-Judaica* 4, 1999, pp. 251-73. D. Shapira, "Manichaios, jywndg gryw and Some Other Manichaean Terms and Titles," *Irano-Judaica* 4, 1999, pp. 122-50. Idem, "Qissa-ye Daniyal in Judaeo-Persian," *Sefunot* 22, 1999, pp. 337-66 (in Hebrew). Idem, "Was There Geographical Science in Sasanian Iran?" *Acta Orientalia Hung.* 54, 2001, pp. 319-38. Idem, "On Biblical quotations in Pahlavi," *Henoch* 23, 2001, pp. 175-83. Idem, "Zoroastrian Sources on Black People," *Arabica* 49, 2002, pp. 117-22. Idem, "Bel and the Dragon in Judeo-Persian," *Irano-Judaica* 5, 2003, pp. 52-67. Idem, "Judeo-Persian Translations of Old Persian Lexica," in *Persian Origins—Early Judaeo-Persian and the Emergence of New Persian*, Iranica 6, ed. L. Paul, Wiesbaden, 2003, pp. 221-42. M. Sharon, *Black Banners from the East. The Establishment of the 'Abbāsid State—Incubation of a Revolt*, Jerusalem, 1983. Idem, *Revolt: the Social and Military Aspects of the 'Abbāsid Revolution*, Jerusalem, 1990. Idem, ed., *Studies in Modern Religions and Religious Movements and the Babi-Baha'i Faiths*, Leiden, 2004. S. S. Soroudi, "Shīrā-ye ḥātānī. A Judeo-Persian Wedding Song," in *Irano-Judaica*, 1982, pp. 204-64. Idem, "Folk Poetry and Society in Nineteenth-Century Iran," *Proceedings of the First European Conference of Iranian Studies*, Rome, 1990, II, pp. 541-52. Idem, "Judeo-Persian Religious Oath Formulas as Compared with non-Jewish Iranian Traditions," *Irano-*

Judaica 2, 1990, pp. 167-83. Idem, "The Concept of Jewish Impurity and its Reflection in Persian and Judeo-Persian Traditions," *Irano-Judaica* 3, 1994, pp. 142-70. Idem, "*Sofreh* of Elijah the Prophet: a pre-Islamic Iranian Ritual?" *Jerusalem Studies in Arabic and Islam* 27, 2002, pp. 463-74. G. G. Stroumsa, "A Zoroastrian origin to the Sefirot?" *Irano-Judaica* 3, 1994, pp. 17-33.

S. Tal, *The Persian Jewish Prayer-Book*, Jerusalem, 1980 (in Hebrew). A. Yaari, *Sifrei yehudei bukharah* (The books of the Bukharan Jews), in *Kiryat Sefer* 18, 1941/2 and 19, 1942/3. B. D. Yehoshua-Raz, *From the lost tribes in Afghanistan to the Mashad Jewish converts of Iran*, Jerusalem, 1992 (in Hebrew). D. Yeroushalmi, *The Judeo-Persian Poet Emrani and his "Book of Treasures,"* Leiden, 1995. R. Zadok, "On the Connections between Iran and Babylonia in the Sixth Century B.C.," *Iran* 14, 1976, pp. 61-78. Idem, "A Tentative Structural Analysis of Elamite Hypocoristica," *Beiträge zur Namenforschung*, N.F. 18, 1983, pp. 93-120. Idem, *The Elamite Onomasticon*, Naples, 1984. Idem, "Elamite Onomastics," *Studi Epigrafici e Linguistici* 8, 1991, pp. 225-37.

(SHAUL SHAKED)

iv. PERSIAN ART COLLECTIONS

Persian art in most of the Israeli collections represent the entire history of Iran, with a strong emphasis on the Islamic period, and including Judaic-Persian ethnography. The following article is arranged in a chronological order.

The Bible Lands Museum, Jerusalem. This museum houses an important collection of ancient Near Eastern artifacts, starting with a decorated clay chalice from Tepe Silak III, dated to 4200-3400 B.C.E.; painted jars and vases from the 3rd millennium B.C.E. in Central Western Iran; a shaft-hole axe with modeled figures; and a spouted ritual goblet from Susa from about 2000-1800 B.C.E. Iron Age II-III is represented by a few clay rhytons, including one with human face and hands; anthropomorphic and zoomorphic vessels; tiny animals made of baked clay and frit; a metal figurative comb; an Elamite figure of a goddess; a finial of a standard portraying two lions from Luristan; and various kinds of daily objects.

The Achaemenid collection includes a unique alabaster vessel bearing a royal inscription of Darius I (r. 522-486 B.C.E.) in four languages. Other important objects from this period are: a small silver statue of a Persian nobleman holding a flower; a fragment of stone relief from Persepolis; a gilded silver incense altar; a rare sword guard; some wonderful pieces of jeweler; coins from the province of Judea and an ostracon of baked clay with an Aramaic inscription. Parthian objects include a number of New Year festival silver bowls and alabastrons, and a bronze mirror, while some magnificent silver bowls, two incantation bowls made from clay with Aramaic inscriptions, seals, a gold medallion decorated with the image of an eagle, and a gold coin with portrait of Shapur II represent the Sasanian period.

PLATE I

Female-headed bird, unglazed painted baked brick, Urartu, 800-700 B. C. E., Height, 33.5 cm, width, 34 cm, thickness: 8.2 cm. Courtesy of The Bible Land Museum, inv. no. BLMJ 4230.

Israel Museum in Jerusalem. This museum has the most comprehensive array of Persian Art and Judaic-Persian ethnography among the Israeli collections. The early periods are represented by a 13th-cenury clay model of a sacred enclosure; Middle Elamite objects, including pieces of architectural decoration; and further Iranian material in the Ternbach Collection. A few Achaemenid carved fragments from Persepolis and Pasargadae, some of them with inscriptions, are followed by Parthian metal or terra cota statues, and a large collection of seals; many silver coins; an important group of some 250 glyptic finds; several silver plates; and one helmet from the Sasanian period.

A single post Sasanian silver plate portraying a royal feast leads to the Islamic collection, which starts with 9th and 10th centuries. Vessels made of cut glass; a Buyid burial stretcher and burial shirts; and a large collection of glass vessels from the 8th to the 11th century, representing a variety of functions, forms and techniques. The Saljuq period is represented by beautiful metalic zoomorphic incense burners; lighting vessels; and magnificent pieces of jewelry. Perfect silver and gold coins of all the periods are included in the Balog collection. Equally inclusive is the large ceramic collection, the highlights of which are a group of *mināʾi* vessels); a complete Safavid *meḥrāb* of mosaic-tiles; and lovely Qajar tiles with figurative decoration. The late period is also represented by a glass collection from Shiraz; a silk rug depicting a hunting party; and some carpets from early 20th century. An unusual object, of an unknown date, is a carved wooden

Mashaddoor from an unknown religious monument, apparently Shiʿite.

In addition to the decorative arts, the *Israel Museum* possess also Islamic illuminated and illustrated manuscripts and a large collection of detached miniatures. An illustrated Judeo-Persian manuscript, *Musā-nāma* of Sahin, makes part of the very important Judaica collection. Other illustrated Judeo-Persian manuscripts are found at the L. A. Mayer Museum and at the collection of the Ben-Zvi Institute, in Jerusalem.

Eretz Israel Museum, Tel Aviv. Although in a much smaller scale, this interdisciplinary museum, too, hosts archeological, ethnographical, and decorative art objects. The earliest items, hollowed bicolored glass rods for door decoration, originate from the temple near the ziggurat of Čoḡā Zanbil (q.v.). Glazed ceramic tiles from the same site are on loan at the Bible Lands Museum. Other objects, notably glass vessels, beads, seals, and apothropaic amulets, represent the Eastern Mediterranean regional production during the Achaemenid period, 6th-4th century B.C.E. An unusual ceramic drinking horn portraying the king of Egypt as Amun-Re belongs to this group. From Iran came a few Achaemenid darichs and one sigloi; many Sasanian drachmas; seals and bulai; and a huge hoard of bronze coins.

The Islamic collection comprises of several high quality ceramic vessels from the 11th-13th century; one 14th-century molded and glazed tile depicting hanging lamps within niches; a few long-necked glass bottles from the 10th-13th century Gorgān; Saljuq metal vessels from Khorasan, including a beautifully decorated ink-well; Safavid and Qajar metal works; and a group of glass bottles dating to the 18th-19th century.

Late 19th-century metal objects in the ethnographic department include vessels for daily use and mirror-boxes which were used by the Jewish community as marriage presents; metal amulets and printed maps for the Saturday table with Hebrew Inscriptions; and Jewish marriage contracts (*ketuba*), among which those made in Isfahan are decorated with lions and suns.

The Authority of Antiquities of Israel. This institution possess a few examples of Luristan metalwork from 1200-1000 B.C.E., including a number of Sasanian engraved seals and ceramic incantation bowls, one Islamic apothropeic metal bowl, and a few glazed ceramic vessels from the late 12th to the 14th century C.E.

The Museum of Regional and Mediterranean Archaeology, Gan-Hashlosha. This archeological museum exhibits seventeen large and small clay vessels, decorated with monochrome painting, from the end of the 2nd millennium and the first half of the 1st millennium B.C.E.; and a fragment of stone relief from the Achaemenid palace at Persepolis, portraying a head of a man. The Islamic period is represented by an important collection of soft stone vessels, probably from the Persian Gulf area, and a nice collection of richly decorated glazed ceramic vessels in various techniques.

L. A. Mayer Museum for Islamic Art, Jerusalem. The exquisite collection of this museum, purchased mostly by Richard Ettinghausen (q.v.), represents the best of all the Islamic periods in Iran. It starts with early Islamic metal and glass objects of the transitional period, such as a gilded silver pomegranate cut on a wheel. Next come glass vessels and bottles carved and engraved with animal and bird motifs, and a large group of excellent glass from Nishapur, blown into a mold and decorated in the beveled style. The ceramic collection, representative of all the techniques, includes: an important Samanid group from Nishapur, decorated with inscriptions, birds and animals; colorful vessels and tiles from Ray and Kāšān; small sculptured figurines, mainly zoomorphic; fine Safavid wares; and a few iconographic Qajar tiles.

The highlight of metal work is the 10th-11th century Harari hoard of magnificent gold vessels decorated with gold and niello, found in Nehāvand and published by Arthur Upham Pope and Phyllis Ackerman (pp. 1349-52). Other groups of metalwork include: Saljuq and Il-khanid brass vessels and candlesticks inlayed with silver and red copper; a rare collection of early gold and silver jewelry, mainly from the 10th-13th century; an inlayed *kaškul* from the Safavid period; various swards, daggers and a fancy Qajar armor set of steel, incrusted with gold and silver threads; and gold and silver coins representing all the periods. An important group, in a different material, consists of ivory and bone chess pieces of various shapes, from the 9th-11th-century Nishapur.

PLATE II

Silver sprinkler from the "Harari Hoard" L. A. Mayer Museum for Islamic Art, Jerusalem, inv. no. M.32.68. The hoard is from Nehāvand, 10-12th century.

The Persian collection is completed with one 17th-century "Polonaise" carpet from Isfahan; beautifully illuminated Qurʾān pages from the 11th to 14th century; a few illustrated manuscripts; and many detached miniatures, including folios from *Manāfeʿ al-ḥayawān*, small *Šāh-nāma* manuscripts, and the dispersed 14th-century "Demotte" *Šāh-nāma* (q.v.).

The Jewish National Library of Jerusalem. This library houses the art of the book, which holds thirteen illustrated manuscripts from Iran: eight from the 15th to the 17th centuries, and five from the Qajar period.

Bibliography: Bible Lands Museum, Jerusalem, *Guide to the Collection*, Jerusalem, 2002. Naʿma Brosh, *Biblical Stories in Islamic Painting*, Jerusalem, 1991. Idem. "Glass in the Islamic Period," in Museon Yisrael, *Ancient Glass in the Israel Museum: The Eliahu Dobkin Collection and Other Gifts*, Jerusalem, 2003, pp. 319-80. Rachel Hasson, *Early Islamic Jewellery*, Jerusalem, 1987. Idem, *Later Islamic Jewellery*, Jerusalem 1987. Idem, *Masterworks from the Collections of the L. A. Museum for Islamic Art*, Jerusalem, 2000. P. Kletter, I. Ziffer, and O. Segal, "A Ryton with a Human Face from the Persian Period at Tel Ya'oz," *Qadmoniot* 34, 2001, pp. 49-52 (in Hebrew). Rivka Merhav, ed., *A Glimpse into the Past: the Joseph Ternbach Collection: Israel Museum Catalogue no. 218*, Jerusalem, 1981. Rachel Milstein, *Islamic Painting in the Israel Museum*, Jerusalem, 1984. Vera Basch Moreen, *Miniature Paintings in Judeo-Persian Manuscripts*, Cincinnati, 1985. Joseph Naveh and Shaul Shaked, *Amulets and Magic Bowls: Aramaic Incantations of Late Antiquity*, Jerusalem, 1998. Arthur Upham Pope and Phyllis Ackerman, *A Survey of Persian Art from Prehistoric Times to the Present*, 4 vols., London, 1938-39; 3rd ed. in 16 vols., Tehran, 1977. Shalom Sabar, *Ketubba: The Art of the Jewish Marriage Contract*, New York, 2000. Hana Taragan, "The 'Speaking' Inkwell from Khorasan: Object as 'Words' in Iranian Medieval Metalwork," *Muqarnas* 25, 2005, pp. 27-42. Joan Goodnick Westenholz and Matthew W. Stolper, "A Stone Jar with Inscriptions of Darius I in Four Languages," in *Arta* 2002.005, Achemenet November 2002.

(RACHEL MILSTEIN)

ISRĀʾILIYĀT. See QEṢAṢ AL-ANBIĀʾ.

ITALY, Relations with Iran. This entry is divided into the following sections:

i. *Introduction.*
ii. *Diplomatic and commercial relations.*
iii. *Cultural relations.*
iv. *Travel accounts.*
v. *Iranian Studies, pre-Islamic.*
vi. *Excavations in Iran.*
vii. *Iranian Studies, Islamic period.*
viii. *Persian manuscripts.*
ix. *Persian art collections.*
x. *Lirica Persica.*
xi. *Translations of Persian works into Italian.*
xii. *Translations of Italian works into Persian.*
xiii. *Iranians in Italy.*
xiv. *Current centers of Iranian Studies in Italy.*
xv. *IsMEO.*

i. INTRODUCTION

Direct commercial and political relations between the Italian peninsula and the Iranian plateau date at least from the Parthian period when, after the fall of the Seleucids, the border between the Arsacids and the Roman Empire was set on the Euphrates, while Mesopotamia and Anatolia provided the setting for trade and commerce, contact and war. In the surviving sources a long silence follows the fall of the Sasanian Empire, though we may surmise the existence of commercial relations of the Papacy, and later the maritime republics (Amalfi, Genoa, Pisa, and Venice), with Iran. However, it is only in the thirteenth century, during the Il-khanid period, that we again have positive proof of the presence of Italian travelers in Iran. Through the late Middle Ages and the early modern era we know of a few travelers, mainly men of religion and merchants, who journeyed to Iran and Central Asia. Still later we have reliable information about trade between Safavid Iran and Venice and other Italian states. Both the Papacy and Venice tried to establish diplomatic relations with the Safavid court, which they viewed as a possible ally against the Ottomans. Later, in the nineteenth century, it was the turn of the Savoia, rulers of the kingdom of Piedmont-Sardinia, who sought to establish diplomatic relations with the Qajars. These efforts continued after the unification of the kingdom of Italy and led to a visit by Nāṣer-al-Din in 1873, during his first European tour. Earlier, in 1862, Marcello Cerruti had traveled to Iran to obtain the permission to export the renowned silk worms of Gilan (see below, ii. DIPLOMATIC AND COMMERCIAL RELATIONS and iv. TRAVELOGUES).

Not being a colonial power, Italy played a very minor role in the events of the Qajar period limited to the presence of a few Italians, such as General Enrico Andreini, who were active in training the army of the shahs. Italy's economic involvement in Iran grew strong during the Pahlavi period, when Italian concerns obtained significant contracts in Iran and made considerable investments in the country. One example for all: the Italian petroleum company ENI (Ente Nazionale Idrocarburi), has had a presence in Iran since 1957, when, together with the National Iranian Petroleum Company (NIOC), it created the Société Irano-Italienne des Pétrols (SIRIP). Commerce between the two nations continued to flourish after the birth of the Islamic Republic of Iran—although with fluctuations due to the international political context—to a degree that in 1999 the Camera di Commercio Italo-Iraniana (Italo-Iranian Chamber of Commerce) was created in Rome; and two years later the Iranian Bānk-e

Markazi and the Arab Italian Bank signed an agreement aimed at increasing trade between the two countries. As a consequence commerce increased by nine percent during 2001-03, due mainly to the increased demand for products "Made in Italy." At present Italy is one of the main commercial partners of Iran; it is the third-ranking source of Iran's imports (six percent of the total) and second among importers from Iran, receiving 17.1 percent of total Iranian exports (Alessandro Marrone, "L'Italia in Iran tra affari (molti) e politica (poca)," at http://www.magna-carta.it/node/1372, 5 February 2007).

Italy has also been particularly active in the study of the cultural heritage of Iran, especially through the activities of the Istituto Italiano per il Medio ed Estremo Oriente (IsMEO, now Istituto Italiano per l'Africa e l'Oriente, IsIAO). It opened its first archeological mission in Iran in 1957, thanks to the efforts of Giuseppe Tucci, and contributed significantly to the restoration and conservation of the monumental complex of Persepolis; it also conducted archeological excavations in Sistān and at the Masjed-e Jomʿa of Isfahan (the latter is ongoing; see below, xv. ISMEO INSTITUTE). Finally it should be mentioned that the oldest existing manuscript of Ferdowsi's *Šāh-nāma*, unfortunately incomplete and dating to 1217 C.E., is today preserved in the Italian National Library of Florence (see below, viii. PERSIAN MANUSCRIPTS IN ITALY).

(CARLO G. CERETI)

ii. DIPLOMATIC AND COMMERCIAL RELATIONS

A privileged relationship between Iran and Italy dates back to the age of the ancient Roman and Persian Empires. Despite their ever-changing internal affairs, the two political centers of Europe and Asia, throughout the entire ancient time, experienced long lasting contacts that produced political and military rivalries as well as economic and cultural relations of mutual interest (see BYZANTINE-IRANIAN RELATIONS). In the Middle Ages, the powers in Italy with an international horizon belonged first to the Papacy and later to the maritime republics of Pisa, Amalfi, and particularly Genoa and Venice. Documentation of direct contact is lacking for a long time, although the exchange of material goods is always testified (see GENOA, VENICE). Evidence of renewed diplomatic and commercial contacts between the two regions date back to the period when Persia was under the Il-khanid (q.v.) dynasty, as a part of the great Trans-Asiatic Empire of the Mongols (see Spuler, pp. 86, 229, 235, 435, 436). The reasons inducing Italian states towards Persia were of three natures: religious, economic, and political, not to mention "those travelers who passed through (Persia) on their way to or from India or beyond" or "visited the country merely out of curiosity" (Lockhart, pp. 373-75). The first was missionary activity, urged on by the Papacy further east beyond the Holy Land, especially after the foundation of the Dominican (1216) and Franciscan (1223) Orders. The economic reason was the trade of exotic products, particularly silk, which had never completely stopped. The political incentive, which came into play at a later stage, was the continuous attempt to establish an alliance with Persian rulers against the common Ottoman enemy.

The will of Pietro Vioni, possibly a business agent, redacted in Tauris (Tabriz) in 1264, is the first document attesting Italian presence in Persia (Cecchetti). There are more substantial traces concerning the existence of a Genoese colony in Persia at the end of the 13th century. From this environment came the Genoese Buscarello di Ghisofili, a member of the royal guards (*qurči*), who was sent by the Il-khan Arḡun (r. 1284-91, q.v.) as ambassador to the pope and the king of France, bringing proposals for an alliance against the Mamluks of Egypt (Mostaert and Cleaves, eds., pp. 18, 29; Spuler, pp. 229-30). At that time Genoa and Venice had their own consulate in Tabriz. Because during the Mongol domination travel throughout Asia was relatively easy, many Italians passed through Persia with commercial aims. Some left accounts of their travels, such as the Venetian Marco Polo, author of the celebrated *Il Milione*. At the same time, through missionary activity, diplomatic relations between the Papacy and the Il-khanid sovereigns were developed. From 1289 one Dominican and two Franciscan convents were set up in Tabriz. Pope Nicholas IV (r. 1288-92) kept close contact with the Il-khan Arḡun, an allegedly pro-Christian king. Nicholas sent many missionaries to Asia, who often crossed Persia. Among the others were Guglielmo and Matteo from Chieti, and the Franciscan missionary Giovanni Montecorvino (1247-1333), who later became the first archbishop of China's Catholic Church (1307) in Peking (Ḵānbāleḡ). In 1318 Pope John XXII (r. 1316-1334) issued a bull establishing Soltani (Solṭāniya) a metropolitan see with jurisdiction over the whole of Persia, and he nominated as its first archbishop the Dominican Francus of Perugia. His successors were all Dominicans. In the next decade, bishopries were set up in Tabriz and Marāḡa, all supervised by Dominicans (Spuler, pp. 233-34). In 1330 an important missionary expedition ordered by Pope John moved towards many oriental potentates, including Persia (Richard, pp. 180-83).

The fall of the Il-khanid dynasty towards the end of the 14th century reduced contacts between the two regions, and the age of Timur seriously damaged the traditional communication system, but Timur sent Johannes de Galonifontibus, the Archbishop of Solṭaniya to Venice, Genoa, Paris, and London with the news of his victory over the Ottomans in 1402 (Lockhart, p. 375). Travelers and merchants also appear in this difficult era, such as Nicolò de' Conti (1395-1469), who visited the east in the 1420s and wrote some observations on Persia (Cusmai Belardinelli). A new and substantial leap was made in the Italian-Persian relationship in 1459 with the rise to power of the Āq Qoyunlu Uzun Ḥasan (r. 1457-78). The Papacy and the Republic of Venice tried independently or together to build a political and military alliance with him against the Ottomans. Many diplomatic missions were exchanged between 1463 and 1477 (see Berchet;

Woods, pp. 18-19, 127-28, 271, n. 117). In December 1463, the Venetian senate opted to enter an alliance with Uzun Ḥasan and Lazzaro Quirini was sent to Persia, who remained there for seven years, returning in February 1471. In the same year, the Persian ambassador Ḥāji Moḥammad was sent to Rome for the inception of the pontificate of Sixtus IV (1471-84) and then to Venice, and Caterino Zeno was dispatched by the senate on a similar mission to Persia. Zeno, having married a niece of Uzun Ḥasan's wife (Lockhart, Morozzo della Rocca, and Tiepolo, eds., p. 12; Caraci, p. 52), in a way counted as a member of his family and was very well liked at his court. Uzun Ḥasan later sent him as an envoy to European allies. Two Venetian envoys in Persia, Giosafat Barbaro and Ambrogio Contarini, left highly regarded accounts of the country, rich in detail and of high literary quality (see Gabriel, pp. 49-51). In Rome, Pope Sixtus IV, following the strategy introduced by his predecessor Calistus III (1455-58), was among the major supporters of establishing connections with Persia. He confirmed Rome's confidence in Ludovico Severi of Bologna, a Franciscan who served as the Papal ambassador (nuncio) in Armenia, Persia, and elsewhere (1455-79), and sent to Persia some other nuncios charged with particular missions. Marino Saxo was appointed as ambassador to Uzun Ḥasan and then dispatched to the Duke of Milan, Galeazzo Maria Sforza (1444-76), in order to exhort him to participate in the forging of the alliance (Piemontese, 1998, pp. 93-94). In the exchange of embassies between Uzun Ḥasan and the Papacy, the Duke of Urbino Federico da Montefeltro also played an important role (Piemontese, 2004). The alliance between the Italian States and Persia was actually established, many times confirmed, and enforced with military supplies. Uzun Ḥasan was promised control of all Anatolia on the condition that he would not construct any fortresses on the coastline and would allow free passage for Venetian ships (Woods, p. 271; Inalcik, p. 28). Nevertheless, Uzun Ḥasan's hesitations and rare success at war, in particular his total defeat at the battle of Baškent in August 1473, limited the results, and by the end of his reign, disillusionment had set in and he was out of the international arena. With his death in 1478, all hope of an alliance vanished. In that same year, Venice signed a peace treaty with the Ottomon Turks.

New hopes arose with the rise of Shah Esmāʿil I (q.v.) and the establishment of the Safavid dynasty. Their vehement Shiʿism was initially interpreted by the Italian side as a kind of Catholic religion in their own style, able to overthrow the Muslim religion as embodied by the power of the Sunni Ottoman Turks. Relations between Venice and Shah Esmāʿil can be followed in the fragmentary collection of documents of the *Diarii* by Marin Sanudo (1531-32). After the negative valuation of a possible alliance by the envoy Constantino Lascaris, the first initiative was taken by Esmāʿīl himself, who in 1508 sent a legation to Venice, proposing an agreement like that drawn up with Uzun Ḥasan. Venice was engaged in the struggle against the Cambrai League and was unable to take advantage of the opportunity. Friendship and an intention for an alliance was repeatedly reaffirmed, but nothing actually happened, neither with Esmāʿīl (r. 1501-24), nor with his successor Shah Ṭahmāsb (r. 1524-76). An important embassy was dispatched to the latter in 1539, led by the Venetian-Cypriote Michele Membré. This embassy is not recorded in Persian sources, but two magniloquent letters on the subject by the Shah survive in the State Archive of Venice (Scarcia, 1968; *Le relazioni tra l'Italia e l'Iran*, pp. 72-74) and, moreover, a detailed and objective account was left by Membré himself. Meanwhile, the Venetians and Ottomans started peace negotiations, which eventually led to the 1540 peace treaty. These contacts adversely influenced Membré's mission and caused its failure. The indecisiveness of Ṭahmāsb's character is depicted by numerous Venetian accounts, the last by Vincento degli Alessandri, the envoy extraordinary sent to Persia in 1570 in order to propose a joint military action, but he was not even received at court (see Berchet). In the second half of the 16th century the Papal States sent an envoy, Gian Battista Vecchietti, to examine the possibility of an Asian front against the Ottomans. This mission failed as well, but Vecchietti was able to collect a large number of precious literary texts. However, a friendly letter of Shah Moḥammad was brought to Pope Sixtus V by Vecchetti himself in 1586 (Piemontese, 2007a).

Increasingly, the idea of a political and military understanding waned, although strong commercial ties between Persia and many Italian states remained, especially during the reign of Shah ʿAbbās I the Great (r. 1587-1629, q.v.). An important embassy reached Venice in 1603, and the meeting between the Persian envoy and the Doge Marino Grimani is depicted in the Doge's Palace (PLATE I; Berchet, pp. 44-47). In 1609 two other ambassadors of Shah ʿAbbās, ʿAliqoli Beg and Robert Sherley, were received by Pope Paulus V: the event is magnificently

PLATE I

Shah ʿAbbās's envoy to Venice in 1603 meets with the Doge Marino Grimani, depicted in the Doge's Palace. After Berchet, pp. 44-47.

PLATE II

Shah ʿAbbās's ambassador, ʿAliqoli Beg, being received by Pope Paulus V in 1609, depicted in the Palace of Quirinale in Rome. After Piemontese, 2005.

PLATE III

Shah ʿAbbās's ambassador, Robert Sherley, being received by Pope Paulus V in 1609 (depicted in the Palace of Quirinale in Rome). After Piemontese, 2006.

depicted in the Palace of Quirinale in Rome (See PLATES II and III; Piemontese, 2005 and 2006).

It is said that during this period Venetians imported from Persia the secret of the glass coloring substance called "Venetian blue." In turn, Persians imported from Venice, among other things, the blown glass mirrors. While the Armenian Kᵛāja Ṣafar served as Shah ʿAbbās's ambassador in Venice, the missionary Giovanni Taddeo exerted influence at the king's court. He was able to collect a number of Shah ʿAbbās's personal letters, which are preserved in Naples. Shah ʿAbbās also maintained cordial relationships with the Dukes of Tuscany Ferdinand 1 (1587-1609) and Cosmo II (1609-21) (Pontecovro).

The second half of the 17th century witnessed the decline of both Venice's intense diplomatic and commercial activity and the Safavid expansion. Persia entered a long period of decay, while Italy as a whole entered a time of troubled crisis that would result in its national unity. Sporadic missions continued during the 18th century, especially from Venice and the Papacy (see Chick; Vanzan). A semblance of contact between the two countries was resumed after the rise of a new strong Italian state whose political horizon touched Asian shores again, and at the same time the establishment of a new stable dynasty on the Persian throne. The kingdom of Piedmont-Sardinia, ruled by the Savoias, made some attempts to establish diplomatic contacts with Persia (ca. 1830-50), especially through the action of Romualdo Tecco, a diplomat and Orientalist settled in Istanbul (D'Erme). The first concrete result came after a Persian initiative encouraged by Nāṣer-al-Dīn Shah (r. 1848-96). In 1857, a Persian delegate led by Farrok̲ Khan Amin-al-Dawla Ḡaffāri (q.v.) signed a friendship and business treaty in Paris with the kingdom of Piedmont-Sardinia. A year later, Farrok̲ Khan went to Turin where he met Prime Minister Cavour and King Vittorio Emanuele II. Then he went traveling through Italy, thus occasioning one of the first direct descriptions of Italy in Persian (Sarābi, pp. 387-401). A periodic exchange of letters began between Vittorio Emanuele II and Nāṣer-al-Dīn Shah, who also kept friendly correspondence with Pope Pius IX and his successors (see Piemontese, 1969; idem, 2007b). In 1862, a large scale Italian mission, organized in three sections of diplomatic, military and scientific, and led by Marcello Cerruti, set out for a serious exploration of the possibilities offered by Persia. A new agreement signed in September followed faithfully that of 1857, but additionally conceded to Italy the right to export the valuable

Gilān silkworms, a privilege that Persia had previously refused to France and Russia (Piemontese, 1968; idem, 1972). Yet the agreement was not actualized for many different reasons, and, besides, the Italian state had to first settle its internal situation resulting from the unification, which came in 1861, before undertaking intended international initiatives again. Nāṣer-al-Dīn Shah visited Italy in 1873 on the occasion of his first European journey (Piemontese, 1970). In 1886 the first permanent Italian chargé d'affaires, A. de Rege di Donato, was sent to Tehran. The Persian chargé d'affaires, Narimān Khan, arrived in Rome in 1896. From 1899 to 1908, Malkom Khan was in Italy as envoy extraordinary and minister plenipotentiary. During this period, up to the first decades of the 20th century, Italian representatives stayed in Persia as neutral observers of the struggle of interests played by the two great powers, Russia and Great Britain.

Mention must also be made of the Italian army officers working as instructors of the Persian army. Besides Neapolitans Luigi Pesce, Antonio Giannuzzi, Michele Materazzo, and Benedetto Barbara, all of whom had left Italy after the fall of the Venetian Republic, arriving in Persia in 1852, a relevant role was played by Captain (later General) Enrico Andreini, from Lucca, who arrived in Persia in 1857. For many years, starting in 1872, Andreini was the chief instructor of the Persian army, and until 1886 he also served as the actual intermediary between the Italian and Persian governments, taking the singular initiative to write periodical reports on Persia to Italian ministers of foreign affairs (1871-86) (see Piemontese, 1969). Military relations entered a new phase between 1926-36, when the Italian royal army contributed to the creation of the first nucleus of modern Persian navy with providing supplies and by having young Persian cadets trained at the Naval Academy in Livorno. This practice lasted, with a break during the period 1941-55, until the late 1970s. From the rise to power of Reżā Shah Pahlavi (r. 1925), the two governments showed, in different ways, friendly intentions towards each other, the Persians in order to find European support away from the interferences of Great Britain, and the Italians aiming to gain a considerable role in the Persian Gulf (Pasqualini, 1992b).

The Second World War vicissitudes interrupted all projects, and in the aftermath, Italy was dedicated to its own reconstruction and eventually integrated into NATO for its foreign policy. Since the end of the 1950s, however, Italy has been able to make some autonomous choices, which have had a significant influence on relations between Persia and the West. In 1957, the ENI (Ente Nazionale Indocarburi), the Italian state oil agency, and the NIOC (National Iranian Oil Company) signed an agreement in which, for the first time, the so-called Fifty-Fifty rule was established, recognizing equal rights for the producing country and the concessionary firm (see *Le relazioni tra l'Italia e l'Iran*, pp. 175-76). Italian participation increased in many other Persian projects, such as the construction of the Dez hydroelectric power plant (completed in 1963). Also, after the revolution of 1978-79 and during the war with Iraq, the relations between the two countries continued, with Italian firms and skilled workers engaged in different sectors on Persian soil. In the last decade of the 20th century, relations between Italy and Persia seem to have taken a relatively friendly and independent course. After the crisis in European Union-Iran relations (1997), and its solution (1998), Italy was the first European country to send its Foreign Minister and its Prime Minister to Tehran. Moreover, with Mohammad Khatami's visit in 1999, Italy was the first Western country to host a President of the Islamic Republic.

Bibliography: Guglielmo Berchet, *La repubblica di Venezia e la Persia*, Torino 1865. Annibale Bugnini, *La Chiesa in Iran*, Rome 1981. G. Caraci, "Viaggiatori italiani in Persia nel Medioevo," in *Le relazioni tra l'Italia e l'Iran*, compendium issue of *Il Veltro*, 1970, pp. 39-60. Bartolomeo Cecchetti, "Testamento di Pietro Vioni veneziano fatto a Tauris (Persia) MCCLXIV, X Dicembre," *Archivio Veneto* 26, 1883, pp. 161-62. Hubert Chick, *A Chronicle of the Carmelites in Persia and the Papal Mission of the XVIIth and XVIIIth Centuries*, 2 vols., London, 1939. Ambrogio Contarini and Josafa Barbaro, *Travels to Tana and Persia by Josafa Barbaro and Ambrogio Contarini: A Narrative of Italian Travels in Persia in the 15th and 16th Centuries*, tr. William Thomas and S. (Eugene) Armand Roy, ed. with an introd. by Lord Stanley of Alderley, Hakluyt Society 49, London, 1873, repr. New York, 1964; ed. Laurence Lockhart, Raimondo Morozzo della Rocca, and Maria Francesca Tiepolo as *I Viaggi in Persia degli ambasciatori veneti Barbaro e Contarini*, Rome, 1973. Nicolò de Conti, in Mario Langhena, ed., *Viaggi in Persia, India e Giava di Nicolò de' Conti, Giralmo Adorno et Girolamo da Santo Stefano*, Milan, 1929. Renata Cusmai Belardinelli, "Discorso sopra il viaggio di Nicolò Di Conti Veneziano", *Accademie e Biblioteche d'Italia* 13, 1985, pp. 155-70. Giovanni D'Erme, "Romualdo Tecco (1802-1867) diplomatico sardo orientalista," *Annali della Facoltà di Lingue e Letterature Straniere di Ca' Foscari* 9/3, Serie Orientale 1, 1970, pp. 107-22. Valeria Fiorani Piacentini, "Le relazioni tra Italia e Persia (1852-1862)," *Rassegna Storica del Risorgimento* 57/4, 1969, pp. 587-640. P. Francesco da Vicenza, *P. Felice Maria Severini da Sellano ambasciatore del Papa al Re di Persia*, Venice, 1930. Alfons Gabriel, *Die Erforschung Persiens: Die Entwicklung der abendländischen Kenntnis der Geographie Persiens*, Vienna 1952. Maria Gabriella Pasqualini, *L'Italia e le prime esperienze costituzionali in Persia (1905-1919)*, Naples, 1992a. Idem, "La Marina italiana e la Persia (1925-1938)," *Bolletino dell'Archivio dell'Ufficio Storico della Marina* 6, 1992b, pp. 53-105. Charles Grey, tr., *A Narrative of Italian Travels in Persia, in the Fifteenth and Sixteenth Centuries*, London, 1873. Halil Inalcik, *The Ottoman Empire: The Classical Age, 1300-1600*, tr. Norman Itzkowitz and Colin Imber, New York, 1973. Moḥammad-Ḥasan Kāvusi, *Asnād-e rawābeṭ-e dawlat-e Ṣafawi bā ḥokumathā-ye Itāliā*, Tehran, 2000.

Le relazioni tra l'Italia e l'Iran, compendium issue of *Il Veltro, Rivista dealla civiltà italiana* 14/1-2, 1970. Laurence Lockhart, "European Contacts with Persia, 1350-1736," in *The Cambridge History of Iran* VI: *The Timurid and Safavid Period*, ed. Peter Jackson, Cambridge, 1986, pp. 373-411. Michele Membré, *Relazione di Persia (1542)*, ed. Giorgio R. Cardona, with an introduction by Gianroberto Scarcia, Naples, 1969; tr. A. H. Morton as *Mission to the Lord Sophy of Persia (1539-1542)*, London, 1993. Vladimir Minorsky, "Uzun Ḥasan," in *EI*[1] IV, pp. 1065-69. Antoine Mostaert and Francis W. Cleaves, eds., *Les lettres des 1289 et 1305 des ilkhan Arγun et Öljeitü à Philippe le Bel*, Cambridge, Mass., 1962. Angelo M. Piemontese, "Le relazioni fra Italia e Persia nel XIX secolo: I trattati del 1857 e del 1862," *Oriente Moderno* 48, 1968, pp. 537-66. Idem, "Le relazioni fra Italia e Persia nel XIX secolo: La corrispondenza reale," *Oriente Moderno* 49, 1969, pp. 1-20. Idem, "An Italian Source for the History of Qāǧār Persia: The Reports of General Enrico Andreini (1871-1886)," *East and West*, New Series 19/1-2, 1969, pp. 147-75; tr. K̲osrow Fāniān as "Yak mak̲zan-e tārik̲i dar bāra-ye tārik̲-e Qājāriya: gozārešhā-ye Ženerāl Enrico Āndreʾini," *Barrasihā-ye tārik̲i* 9/1, 1974, pp. 37-70. Idem, "Per una biografia di Malkom Xan: Materiali e documenti," *Annali dell'Istituto Universitario Orientale di Napoli*, Nuova Serie 19, 1969, pp. 361-85. Idem, "Descrizioni d'Italia in viaggiatori persiani del XIX secolo," *Annali della Facoltà di Lingue e Letterature Straniere di Ca' Foscari, Venezia* 9/3, Serie Orientale 1, 1970, pp. 63-106. Idem, "The Photograph Album of the Italian Diplomatic Mission to Persia (Summer 1862)," *East and West*, New Series 22/3-4, 1972, pp. 249-311. Idem, "Gli ufficiali italiani al servizio della Persia nel XIX secolo," in Giogio Borsa and Paolo Beonio Brocchieri, eds., *Garibaldi, Mazzini e il Risorgimento nel risveglio dell'Asia e dell'Africa*, Milan, 1984, pp. 65-130. Idem, "The Nuncios of Pope Sixtus IV (1471-84) in Iran," in Kambiz Eslami, ed., *Iran and Iranian Studies: Essays in Honor of Iraj Afshar*, Princeton, 1998, pp. 90-108. Idem, "L'ambasciatore di Persia presso Federico da Montefeltro, il cardinale Bessarione e Ludovico Bononiense O.F.M.," *Miscellanea Bibliothecae Apostolicae Vaticanae* XI, Città del Vaticano, 2004, pp. 539-65. Idem, "I due Ambasciatori di Persia ricevuti da Papa Paolo V al Quirinale," *Miscellanea Bibliothecae Apostolicae Vaticanae* XII, Città del Vaticano, 2005, pp. 357-425. Idem, "Les célébrités du Janicule et les diplomates Safavides immigrés à Rome," in Michele Bernardini, Masashi Haneda, and Maria Szuppe, eds., *Liber amicorum: Études sur l'Iran médiéval et moderne offertes à Jean Calmard*, Eurasian Studies 5/1-2, 2006, pp. 271-95. Idem, "La diplomazia di Gregorio XIII e la lettera del Re di Persia a Sisto V," *Miscellanea Bibliothecae Apostolicae Vaticanae* XIV, Città del Vaticano, 2007a, pp. 539-65. Idem, "*Amicitiae nexus*. Lettere tra i Papi e i Re di Persia (1874-1922)," *Dall'Archivio Segreto Vaticano: Miscellanea di testi, saggi e inventari* II, Città del Vaticano, 2007b, pp. 385-462. Virgilio Pontecorvo, "Relazioni tra lo Scià ʿAbbās e i Granduchi di Toscana Ferdinando I e Cosimo II," *Atti della Accademia Nazionale dei Lincei*, Serie 8/4, 1949, pp. 157-82. Jean Richard, *La papauté et les missions d'orient au Moyen Age (XIII*e*-XV*e *siècles)*, Rome, 1977. Marin Sanuto, *Diarii*, ed. Biancamaria Scarcia Amoretti as *Šāh Ismāʿīl I nei "Diarii" di Marin Sanudo*, Roma, 1979. Ḥosayn b. ʿAbd-Allāh Sarābi, *Safar-nāma-ye Farrok̲ K̲ān Amin-al-Dawla: Mak̲zan al-waqāyeʿ*, ed. Karin Eṣfahāniān and Qotrat-Allāh Rowšani, Tehran, 1382. Gianroberto Scarcia, "Un documento persiano del 946/1539 nell'Archivio di Stato di Venezia," *Annali dell'Istituto Universitario Orientale di Napoli*, N. S. 18, 1968, pp. 338-42. Manučehr Sotuda and Iraj Afšār, eds., *Asnād-e Pādriān-e Karmeli, bāzmānda az ʿaṣr-e Šāh ʿAbbās Ṣafawi*, Tehran, 2004. Berthold Spuler, *Die Mongolen in Iran: Plitik, Verwaltung und Kultur der Ilchanzeit 1220-1350*, 3rd ed., Berlin, 1968. U. Tucci, "Una relazione di Giovan Battista Vecchietti sulla Persia e sul Regno di Hormuz (1587)," *Oriente Moderno* 34/4, 1955, pp. 149-60. Anna Vanzan, "Commerci fra Venezia e la Persia nel Settecento," *Islàm Storia e Civiltà* 18, 1987, pp. 31-38. ʿAli-Akbar Welāyatī, *Tārīk̲-e rawābeṭ-e k̲āreji-e Irān dar ʿahd-e Šāh Esmāʿīl Ṣafawī*, Tehran, 1996. Anthony Welch, "Safavi Iran as Seen Through Venetian Eyes," in Andrew J. Newman, ed., *Society and Culture in the Early Modern Middle East: Studies on Iran in the Safavid Period*, Leiden and Boston, 2003, pp. 97-124. John E. Woods, *Aqquyunlu: Clan, Confederation, Empire*, Minniapolis and Chicago, 1976. Lewon B. Zekiyan, "Xoǧa Safar ambasciatore di Shāh ʿAbbās a Venezia," *Oriente Moderno* 58/7-8, 1978, pp. 357-67. Caterino Zeno, *Storia curiosa delle sue avventure in Persia*, Venice, 1783.

(MARIO CASARI)

iii. CULTURAL RELATIONS

Artistic influences. Italy and Persia have hardly ever had a direct and continuous cultural exchange. During the Middle Ages, when Italy and Persia were not clearly definable cultural entities, the translated works of significant Persian literature had a great influence on Italian and European culture. This, however, was part of the greater process by which Islamic heritage flowed into Christian and European culture mainly in Arabic and through Latin translation. Only approximate traces can be identified of a more direct relationship between Persian and Italian works until the introduction of Amir K̲osrow Dehlavi's *Hašt behešt*, as the famous *Peregrinaggio* (1557) by Cristoforo Armeno, which had an enormous cultural influence throughout Europe. Its heritage in Italy is most noticeable in the work of Carlo Gozzi (the tragicomic theatrical fable *Il Re Cervo*, 1762; see Cerulli, 1975, pp. 335-58). A possible link between the Pahlavi account of the celestial journey of Ardā Wīrāz (q.v.) and the oriental material on which Dante Alighieri's *Divina Commedia* was based has been the source of much discussion (see Blochet). This possibility, however, has been rejected by scholars who prefer to view the episode regarding Ardā Wīrāz as belonging to a type of tale which spread throughout the Indian world and filtered into primitive Christian and Islamic spheres. The *Ketāb al-Meʿrāj*, an Arab folk tale about the Prophet's ascension to Heaven, which was translated into Castilian and then into Latin in the 12th century as the famous *Libro della Scala*, is more easily identifiable as the direct reference text for Dante's work, even if to a lesser degree than was initially suggested (Cerulli, 1949). These conclusions are now almost unanimously accepted by scholars, who also disregard the question of a possible relationship between the *Sayr al-ʿebād ela'l-maʿād*, a mystic *maṯnawi* by the Persian poet Sanāʾi, and the Italian masterpiece (Bausani, 1979).

Analogously, it was certainly through the mediation of the Arabic language that a typical theme of the Persian cultural and literary tradition established itself as a semiotic map for ethical and intellectual literature in the West, and in particular in Humanist and Renaissance Italy. This was the symbol of the garden. The garden-paradise, an ancient symbol of Persian monarchic power, a framework and structural model for major works in Persian literature, arrived in medieval Italy via Arab architecture and literature. There, combined with the strong Greco-Roman tradition, it gave rise to an original symbolic literary model, which can be found in important works such as Giovanni Boccaccio's *Decamerone* (1349-51), Francesco Colonna's *Hypnerotomachia Poliphili* (1499), and numerous other works (including the *Peregrinaggio*), as well as at the heart of Leon Battista Alberti's (d. 1472) architectonical reflections (Tornesello, 2002). This consideration can be extended to much of the literary material in circulation between the ancient and medieval eras between the East and the West. Through many different kinds of linguistic and cultural mediation, various themes and motifs, probably of Persian origin, though not always perfectly identifiable, reached the Italian literary milieu. Italian texts made use of Eurasian expansive narrative cycles such as the *Arabian Nights*, the *Book of Sinbad*, the *Book of Kalila and Demna* (absorbed in the works of the prominent humanist and writer Anton Francesco Doni [d. 1574]), the *Vis o Rāmin* (a love story of Parthian origin) of Faḵr-al-Din Gorgāni (q.v.), which was perhaps reflected in the story of Tristan and Isotta, and which is also present in Italian literature (Minorsky; Piemontese, 1999).

As the effects of medieval literary circulation faded and the modern era dawned, direct influences appeared less frequently. Even the excellent divulgation of Ḥāfeẓ by Pietro Della Valle does not appear to have left any evident traces in Italian literature, although it is certainly at the origins of European masterpieces such as Johann Goethe's *West-Östlicher Divan* (see GEOTHE). Della Valle himself composed a brief epigram inspired by a visit to his mausoleum in Shiraz (Bertotti, 1990). Perhaps the only writer to have an explicit effect on the Italian literary scene was Omar Khayyam (ʿOmar Ḵayyām), whose work reached Italy from England and mostly through the filter of French and German languages. The very personal interpretation of Khayyam by Edward Fitzgerald (q.v.) found an ideal fertile terrain in Italian decadentism, where Khayyam's poetry earned critical attention and underwent several indirect translations. The themes and the character of Khayyam's poetry were picked up again in poetic texts by esteemed writers such as Arturo Graf (d. 1913), Giovanni Pascoli (d. 1912), Vincenzo Cardarelli (d. 1959), as well as in specially written musical compositions (see Piemontese, 2002-2003). Besides the beginning of a work of translation of Persian literary works (see ITALY xi), other signs of the absorption of Persian literary influence can be found in the works produced within the rising academic circle of Iranian studies, for example in the novel *Miro e Naida: romanzo orientale*, by Italo Pizzi (Turin, 1901), and in the poetry of the authors who had had personal contact with Persia, such as Gina Labriola and Alessandro Coletti (1970-80).

Perhaps it was through a rather indirect historical approach that Persia and Persian culture made a mark on Italian artistic expression. From classical sources (Greek, Latin, and Biblical), the Italian Renaissance brought back the names of the ancient sovereigns, Cyrus, Darius I, Darius III (qq.v.; the adversary of Alexander; q.v.), Artabanus, Tiridates, Šāpur, and Ḵosrows (Chosroe), especially Ḵosrow II Parvēz (adversary of Heraclius, emperor of Byzantium; q.v.); the names of the ancient cities, Ekbatana (q.v.), Susa, Ctesiphon (q.v.); the names of emblematic figures such as the *Sibilla Persica*, who was the first among the sibyls scattered around the ancient world, according to Latin tradition. The figurative representation of these characters through bass-reliefs and frescoes in Italian art between the 15th and 18th centuries (the Persian Sybil was produced twice for Pope Julius II by Bernardino Pinturicchio in Santa Maria del Popolo and by Michelangelo in the Sistine Chapel) was accompanied by a flood of ancient Persian themes in the literature of the day, spanning all genres (chivalric legends, heroic, festive or jousting poems, baroque novels, comedies, tragedies, dramas for music, oratorios) with thousands of works. The systematic diffusion of this literary and figurative usage appears as an implicit proto-nationalistic awareness of Persia as the paramount counterpart to the ancient glory of Imperial Rome. The particular influence of this thematic category on the formation of drama for music can be seen in more than 270 works of the genre produced in Italy, or by Italians, in the 17th and 18th centuries, and particularly in the theaters of Venice. In-depth research on this important matter has yet to be completed, however (Piemontese, 1982, pp. 803-60; idem, 1993; idem, 2003, pp. 29-30).

Alongside this ancient evocation, there also was the representation of current affairs. On 2 March 1473, Rome witnessed the performance of a play based on the victory of Uzun Ḥasan, the ideal ally of Pope Sixtus IV, against the common Ottoman enemy (Piemontese, 1991). In the same period, a milestone of relations between Italy and Persia, envoys and presents of the Persian king are portrayed in outstanding works of art (paintings, miniatures) dedicated to the Duke of Urbino Federico da Montefeltro, one of the main weavers of the anti-Ottoman alliance (Piemontese, 2004). Following this, the term Sofi (the distorted name of the Safavid king, whose application was later extended), the king of Persia, became a common figure in both scholarly and folk Italian literature, and was immortalized in the 19th century in a sonnet by the Romanesque poet Giuseppe Gioachino Belli (d. 1863), *Er re de nov'idea* (The king of the New Idea, 1834), written upon the news of Fatḥ-ʿAli Shah Qājār's death. As the political situation grew more distant, this exotic taste gradually wore out and the 20th century, which began with the institutionalization of Iranian Studies in Italy, has not yet witnessed the foundation of a relationship of direct literary or artistic influence.

In the other direction, sporadic examples of the influence of Italian literature on Persian works can be identified only from the 20th century onwards, with the first translations of Italian works (see ITALY xii. TRANSLATIONS), and within a relatively limited range. While the introduction of Giovanni Boccaccio and Nicolo Machiavelli to Persia had some effect on the development of sociological and political thinking in that country, the main example of a piece of Persian literature inspired by the *Divina Commedia*, the *Jāvid-nāma* by Indo-Persian philosopher and poet Moḥammad Eqbāl (which came two decades earlier than the translation of Dante's work into Persian) derived from the long standing worldwide fame of the Italian poem, known through translations into many other languages (Bausani, 1952). As occurred in the rest of the world, the introduction of Carlo Collodi's *Le avventure di Pinocchio* certainly appears to have played a significant role, especially in a phase of re-foundation of literature for children in Persia, following the earlier progressive pedagogical ideas. This role was brought to the readers' attention in the preface of the book by the first translator, Ṣādeq Čubak (tr. as *Ādamak-e čubi*, Tehran, 1955; see also Casari). Only a careful study, which has yet to be carried out, will determine the influence of 20th-century Italian literary works (imported since the end of the Second World War) on recent Persian literature, whereas it is unanimously acknowledged that an important contribution was made on its development by the acquisition of English and French literary models for story-telling and novels.

A field in which it is perhaps possible to identify a more direct relationship between the two countries is that of dramaturgy in its wider sense. There are similarities between the Italian and Persian traditions of the so-called *Commedia dell' Arte* and folk theater (including puppet shows), which could provide important parallels between distant characters such as *Pahlavān(-e) kačal* and the Florentine mask of Stenterello. Nevertheless the various attempts, which have been made to mark out direct routes, have not yet borne any fruit. The trend is to be satisfied with imagining a common origin (perhaps Greek?) and parallel developments. It does, however, appear certain that modern Italian theatre (from Machiavelli's *Mandragola* to Carlo Goldoni, from Pirandello to Dario Fo) did fascinate Persian intellectuals of the post-Second World War. They imported texts, plays, and radio play-readings, using them as a model and a support for the rising Persian theater and for modern literature in general (Piemontese, 2003 pp. 69-71). In an important performance of Pirandello's *Sei personaggi in cerca d'autore* in Tehran in 1964, the role of the protagonist was played by the already established poet Forūḡ Farroḵzād (q.v.; see Ṣāberi). During the 1970s, the number of performances of Italian musical operas multiplied, but this approach, which was interrupted by the advent of the Islamic Republic, does not seem to have interacted either with the deep rooted tradition of Persian music, nor with the dramaturgical forms which were developing.

Italian neo-realist and auteurial cinema in the 1950s and 1960s, famous all over the world, had a definite influence on the Persian movie industry. From the beginning of the 1960s onwards, the importation of the masterpieces of Roberto Rossellini, Vittorio de Sica, Federico Fellini, and Michelangelo Antonioni, dubbed into Persian, were accompanied by the publication of screenplays, interviews, and critical literature, establishing itself as a structural and ideological model for the so-called nouvelle vogue of directors such as Dāriuš Mehrjuʾi and Masʿud Kimiāʾi, and later as an inspiration for the post-revolutionary cinema of the likes of Amir Nāderi, Moḥsen Maḵmalbāf, ʿAbbās Kiārostami, Jaʿfar Panāhi, whose international recognition has often been associated with reference to the great Italian masters, requested by the Iranian directors themselves (Piemontese, 2003, p. 76; Tornesello, 2003). In 1975 the citadel of Bam in southeastern Persia was the set for the Italian-French movie production, *Il deserto dei Tartari*, directed by Valerio Zurlini and based on the celebrated novel of Dino Buzzati.

Institutional relations. While this complex web of reciprocal influences often spread through the abstract and indirect routes of art, concrete, internationally recognized cultural relations only began to take shape around the middle of the 19th century, when the Persian government hired Italian instructors to serve at state institutions and a number of Persians studied at Italian universities. Initially, this took place in a sporadic and casual manner, but subsequently became increasingly organized and structured. Besides those serving as instructors of the Persian army (see ITALY ii. DIPLOMATIC AND COMMERCIAL RELATIONS), there were several Italian teachers at Dār al-fonun (q.v.), a modern school founded in Tehran in 1851 by Mirzā Taqi Khan Amir(-e) Kabir. Included among them were Captain Zatti, engineering lecturer (who died suddenly in 1852) and Focchetti, instructor of Physics and Chemistry at the Dār al-fonun from its foundation until 1862. Focchetti also accompanied Farroḵ Khan Ḡaffāri on his mission to Italy in 1858. Also some of the Italian military instructors, such as Michele and Francesco Materazzo, Luigi Pesce, Enrico Andreini, occasionally taught at the Dār al-fonun. An institutional agreement signed in 1927 established the despatch of Persian cadets to the Naval Academy in Livorno, where they were mainly taught (up to diploma level) scientific subjects with the aim of serving in the new Persian Royal Navy. This agreement remained in effect, with a few interruptions, until the end of the 1970s. However, the first official confirmation of cultural relations between Italy and Persia was the Cultural Agreement signed in Rome on 29 November 1958 by the two ministers of foreign affairs, A. Fanfani and ʿAli-Aṣḡar Ḥekmat. This agreement encouraged the exchange of cultural material between the two countries (books, publications, radio programs, scientific or educational films, works of art for exhibitions, etc.) as well as exchange trips combined with various forms of financial aid and grants for the students, researchers, and cultural personalities of the two countries (see *Accordi culturali*, pp. 326-32).

The agreement was also designed to spread the historical, linguistic, and cultural knowledge of each country with the institution and the development of teaching and readership positions in the relative subjects. This agreement laid the basis for the foundation of respective cultural institutes in each country. The Italian Cultural Institute was founded in 1962 through the collaboration between the Italian Foreign Ministry and IsMEO (Istituto Italiano per il Medio ed Estremo Oriente), transforming the Italian Cultural Center, which had been founded in 1960 by Giuseppe Tucci. The IsMEO has worked for many years with the Institute, setting up both excavation and restoration projects. The Institute had organised various cultural initiatives, in particular to stimulate the study of Italian culture and language, even in Persian university systems. These initiatives led to various types of scientific collaboration, in particular in the field of architecture, exhibitions, concerts, plays, cinema festivals, and numerous publications regarding Italian and Iranian cultures. In 1986, however, the Cultural Institute was closed to the public, following a dispute between the Persian authorities and the Italian state-run television. The institute was shut down definitively in 1994, leaving the embassy's cultural attaché as the only figure of its kind (Ministerial Decree 2518 of 17 January 1994; see also Piemontese 2003, p. 10).

Also during the 1960s, on the basis of the above-mentioned Cultural Agreement, the Iranian Cultural Institute was founded in Rome, first located in the building of the embassy. In 1991 the Institute moved to an autonomous residence in Monte Mario, where it is still situated. An Iranian school, called "Šahid Bāhonar," with official Persian curriculum, was established in Rome in 1995, and is mainly attended by children of Persian diplomatic staff.

The agreement of 1958, which was renewed and enlarged by a subsequent agreement in 1970, is designed to promote technical and scientific cooperation in Persia and is to this day the cornerstone of cultural cooperation between the two countries. This cooperation was confirmed in 1996 and again in 2000 with an executive program presenting a detailed extension into numerous fields and sectors, including universities and related study grants, music, theatre, cinema, exhibitions, archives, libraries, publications, measures for the conservation of cultural heritage, as well as scientific and technological cooperation. The theoretical basis of this new long-term project is the concept of historical and cultural affinity and links between the two countries, established between 1999 and 2001 by a series of parliamentary dialogues on ancient Mediterranean civilizations (Egypt, Greece, Italy, Persia) held in each of the countries. In the context of the above mentioned executive programme of 2000, and in order to support a cultural policy of exchange and integration, Persian authorities recently (2004) decided to include Italian as an elective subject in the curriculum of certain schools at the same levels that English and French are offered, while Italian authorities introduced Persian as one of the optional languages valid for the open competition finalized to diplomatic career.

Persian students. Despite the lower degree of familiarity concerning recent history and politics, compared to other European countries such as France, Great Britain, or Germany, Persians have always felt and demonstrated an instinctive sense of closeness to the Italian cultural and artistic spheres, perceived in many ways as having a high degree of affinity to their own. It is mainly for this reason that, from the middle of the 19th century, a small but constant number of Persian students chose Italy as the country for their university education, particularly in the field of fine arts. After the Second World War, this flow of Persian students to Italy increased notably, mainly towards the arts faculties (fine arts, architecture, music) and some specific fields of science (engineering, medicine, agronomy). Since the signing of the Cultural Agreement in 1958, these students in Italy have been eligible for study grants, though the distribution of the grants was never constant and was suspended many times.

The number of Persian students in Italy at any one time appears to have never risen above 10,000 and at the present time (2004) is lower than 5,000. Of the Persian students who have finished their studies in Italy, many have chosen to remain in the country, joining one of many Italian institutions, including newspapers, publishing firms, art galleries, and theaters, as well as becoming engaged in movie production. Among those who returned to Persia, there are some, almost all with an artistic or literary education, whose translations of Italian works contributed to widening the horizon of Italian literature in Persia (see ITALY xii. TRANSLATIONS; Piemontese, 2003, pp. 126-44).

Italian schools. The formation of Italian educational nucleuses can be attributed to the Salesian missionaries, who have been present and active in Persia since 1936. Most of these schools have remained affiliated to the church, and their size is proportionate to the small parish communities of each locality. The history of the Salesian school of Tehran is, however, more complex. It was founded as soon as the missionaries arrived in the capital, initially as part of the parish of the Consolata. The school, which had been closed during the Second World War, was reopened in 1944 and then moved to a series of different locations, until it found a permanent home in a building that had been erected to house it in 1958 on the Andiša hill in Tehran. The school came to be known as the Don Bosco College. The number of pupils attending the nursery, elementary, middle and high schools grew to around 1,700 by the middle of the 1970s. From an administrative point of view, the school had a private statute and was attended not only by the children of Italian workers and diplomats living in Persia, but also by many young Persians as well as those of other nationalities. At a certain point, a managing committee, established by the Italian companies present in the country, took on the administration of the school. Around the 1970s, the increase in the school's prestige, and in the number of students attending, made it necessary to open a new building, specially commissioned by this committee, at Farmāniya in a space allocated by the Italian embassy in Tehran. At the same time, in 1976, the school was officially recognized by the Italian Ministry of Foreign Affairs. In 1980 the Persian authorities banned all Catholic schools and consequently the Italian school, still a Salesian institution, closed down only to re-open immediately as the official school of the Italian Ministry of Foreign Affairs. Nevertheless, the ban on attending foreign schools for children with Persian fathers, enacted by the Persian authorities of the Islamic Republic, meant that the school was attended almost exclusively by Italians. It included a nursery school, elementary school, middle school, and a science high school. In December 1995, the school was renamed "Pietro Della Valle" as a tribute to the famous Roman traveler. Many schools teaching in Italian on a smaller scale and with a precarious statute have opened in areas where Italian companies operate, but they have almost always been used by the children of the employees of these companies.

Bibliography: Some of the official documents concerning schools and institutional relations are kept in various archives, including the Italian Ministry of Foreign Affairs, Rome.

Accordi culturali e di cooperazione scientifica e tecnica fra l'Italia e altri Stati, Rome, Ministry of Foreign Affairs, 1972. Alessandro Bausani, "Dante and Iqbâl," *East and West*, N.S. 2, 1952, pp. 77-81; repr. in *Crescent and Green: A Miscellany of Writings on Pakistan*, London, 1955, pp. 62-70. Idem, "Sanāʾī precursore di Dante? Osservazioni sul *Seir al-ʿIbād*," in *Colloquio italo-iraniano sul poeta mistico Sanāʾī (Roma, 29-30 marzo 1978)*, Accademia nazionale dei Lincei, Rome, 1979, pp. 5-22. Giuseppe Gioachino Belli, *I soneti*, ed. Maria Teresa Lanza, 4 vols., Milan, 1965, III, p. 1468. Filippo Bertotti, "Un viaggiatore romano e un poeta persiano: Pietro Della Valle estimatore e divulgatore di Ḥāfiz," *Islàm: Storia e Civiltà* 9/2, 1990, pp. 121-27. Edgar Blochet, *Les sources orientales de la Divine Comédie*, Paris, 1901. Annibale Bugnini, *La Chiesa in Iran*, Rome, 1981. Mario Casari, "Pinocchio persiano," *Oriente Moderno*, N.S. 22, 83/1, 2003, pp. 57-91. Enrico Cerulli, ed., *Il "Libro della Scala" e la questione delle fonti arabo-spagnuole della Divina Commedia*, Studi et testi 150, Città del Vaticano, 1949; repr., 1970 (Tr. of *Ketāb al-meʿrāj* in Latin and French). Idem, "Una raccolta persiana di novelle tradotte a Venezia nel 1557," *Atti della Accademia nazionale dei Lincei: Memorie della Classe di Scienze morali, storiche e filologiche*, 8th series 18/4, 1975, pp. 247-365. *Le relazioni tra l'Italia e l'Iran*, compendium issue of *Il Veltro. Rivista della civiltà italiana* 14/1-2, 1970. Vladimir Minorsky, "Vis u Ramin: A Parthian Romance," *BSO(A)S* 11, 1946, pp. 741-63; 12, 1947, pp. 20-35; 16, 1954, pp. 91-92. Angelo Michele Piemontese, "ʿOmar Khayyām in Italia," *Oriente Moderno* 54, 1974, pp. 275-97. Idem, *Bibliografia italiana dell'Iran (1462-1982)*, 2 vols., Naples, 1982. Idem, *The Italian Embassy in Tehran*, Tehran 1990. Idem, "La représentation de Uzun Hasan sur scène à Rome (2 mars 1473)," *Turcica. Revue d'études turques* 21-23, 1991, pp. 191-203. Idem, "Persia e Persiani nel dramma per musica veneziano," *Opera e Libretto* 2, Firenze, 1993, pp. 1-34. Idem, *Gli otto paradisi di Amir Khusrau da Delhi: una lezione persiana del Libro di Sindbad fonte del Peregrinaggio di Cristoforo Armeno*, Rome, 1995. Idem, "Narrativa medioevale persiana e percorsi librari internazionali," in Antonio Pioletti and Francesca Rizzo Nervo, eds., *Medioevo romanzo e orientale: Il viaggio dei testi. Colloquio internazionale, Venezia, 10-13 ottobre 1996*, Soveria Mannelli (Catanzaro), 1999, pp. 1-17. Idem, "Poèmes lyriques italiens consacrés à Omar Khayyam," in *Mélanges in memoriam Javād Ḥadidi*, Loqmān: Annales des Presses Universitaires d'Iran 19/1, 2002-2003, pp. 127-39. Idem, "L'antica Persia veduta in Roma," in Laura Biancini et al., eds., *Roma memoria e oblio*, Rome 2001, pp. 71-81. Idem, *La letteratura italiana in Persia*, Atti della accademia nazionale dei Lincei, classe di scienze morali, storiche e filologiche, Memorie, 9th series 17/1, Roma, 2003. Idem, "L'Ambasciatore di Persia presso Federico da Montefeltro, il cardinale Bessarione e Ludovico Bononiense O.F.M.," in *Miscellanea Bibliothecae Vaticanae* 11, 2004, pp. 539-65. Italo Pizzi, "L'origine persiana del romanzo di Tristano e Isotta," *Rivista d'Italia* 14, 1911, pp. 5-21. Ettore Rossi, "Poesie inedite in persiano di Pietro Della Valle," *Rivista degli Studi Orientali* 28, 1953, pp. 108-17. Pari Ṣāberi, "Pirāndello wa Forug: do gostāḵ-e nowpardāz ba donbāl-e wāqeʿiyat," *Gardun*, no. 44-45, Bahman-Esfand 1373/February-March 1995, pp. 42-47. Natalia L. Tornesello, "Una mappa semiotica iranica nella letteratura del Rinascimento: il giardino," in Michele Bernardini, et al., eds., *Europa e Islam tra i secoli XIV e XVI*, 2 vols., Naples 2002, I, pp. 203-34. Idem, *Il cinema persiano*, Roma, 2003. Idem, ed., *La letteratura persiana contemporanea tra novazione e tradizione*, Naples, 2003.

(MARIO CASARI)

iv. Travel Accounts

(1) A General Survey

Italian travel accounts represent a major source for the history of Iran, especially that of the Middle Ages and the Renaissance. Collections of Italian travel accounts, together with biographical and bibliographical details, have been published from the Renaissance up to the present day.

The first attempt to assemble this kind of material was made by the Venetian humanist, historian, and geographer Giovan Battista Ramusio (1485-1557), who in 1520 began to bring together the main Italian travel accounts in his *Navigationi et viaggi* (3 vols., Venice, 1550, 1556, 1559). Ramusio's work was published in expanded editions between 1566 and 1606, and during the 20th century the entire corpus was re-edited (M. Milanesi, ed., *Navigazioni e viaggi*, 6 vols., Turin, 1978-88; English ed., *Navigationi et viaggi, Venice 1563-1606*, ed. by G. B. Parks and R. A. Skelton, Amsterdam, 1970-71). Rightly considered one of the main collections of medieval and Renaissance travel literature on the East (Del Piero, 1902; Parks, 1955), Ramusio's work represented a model for other collections of European travel literature, such as those of Richard Hakluyt and Samuel Purchas in England, Théodore de Bry and his sons in France, and Levinus Hulsius and Jan Huygen van Lischoten in Holland. A new, systematic attempt to list such material was made during the 19th century by the geographer and cartographer Pietro Amat di S. Filippo (1822-95), author of several works dedicated to Italian travelers from the Middle Ages to the 19th century (Amat di S. Filippo, 1882, 1895). Angelo Michele Piemontese's *Bibliografia Italiana dell'Iran* includes a chapter on travelers that is the most accurate bibliographical list of such sources, containing all the printed material from the 15th to the 20th century (Piemontese, 1985, I, "Viaggi e viaggiatori," pp. 131-77). Other, more specialized collections exist, such as the Venetian reports from Persia during the Safavid period, which are collected together in the works of Alberi (1840-55) and Berchet (1865). An extensive list of missions to the East during the Middle Ages was made by G. Golubovich, who produced a rich compendium of Franciscan sources (Golubovich, 1906-28). Certain encyclopedias are also useful, especially for research on the biographies of the travelers. Of such encyclopedias, the *Dizionario Biografico degli Italiani* is the most complete for Italian authors (57 vols., Rome, 1960-).

Italian travel accounts can be broadly divided into five periods, and the volume of production is different for each. The first period, that of Mongol and Timurid rule in Iran and Central Asia, which takes in works such as merchants' reports and descriptions by religious missionaries, can be considered, together with the second period, as a kind of Golden Age of Italian travel literature on Persia. The second period coincides with the Renaissance and begins with the special relations between Italy and the Āq Qoyunlu ruler Uzun Ḥasan. It gives way to the third with the successors of Shah ʿAbbās I, in whose reigns the Italian presence in Iran began to change. There was a substantial revival of religious missions, in which the Carmelites played a particular role, although there were also independent travelers at this time. A fourth period, in which there is evidence of a new Italian diplomatic presence at the Qajar court, coincides with the unity of Italy and with a new attitude, which included the beginning of a scientific interest (in the modern sense) in the subject of Iran. This attitude continues in the last phase of the history of Italian travelers and runs from about the beginning of the 20th century until the present day.

The Mongol and Timurid period. The first Italian travelers to Iran and Central Asia during the Middle Ages were religious missionaries sent by the popes to spread the Christian faith in Mongol lands. We have some traces of the journey made during this period by the Lombard Ascelino, who was sent to the East by Pope Innocent IV. Together with André de Longjumeau and other friars, Ascelino met Baiju, the commander of Mongol forces in western Asia, in 1247 near Tiflis, after a journey to Aleppo, Mosul, and Tabriz. The report of this mission, probably the *Historia Tartarorum* of Simon of Saint-Quentin, is now lost, but references to it are found in chapters of Vincent of Beauvais' *Speculum historiae* (Pelliot, 1924, p. 277; Petech, 1962; Richard, 1977, pp. 373-74). In 1246-47 the same pope sent Giovanni da Pian del Carpine [John of Plano Carpini] to the court of Ögödey, and he reached Karakorum when Güyük was in power (Golubovich, 1906, I, pp. 190-213; P. Daffinà et al., eds., *Storia dei Mongoli*, Spoleto, 1989).

Italian merchants were established in Tabriz from the early Il-khanid period (Petech, 1962, pp. 550-51; Paviot, 1997, pp. 74-75). Marco Polo's presence in Persia is attested after the years 1271-72, even if the description of the country is dated 1298, when he described Persia as he remembered it while on his journey to the court of Qubilay in China (Franchi, 1941; Gabriel, 1963). Polo followed the journey of his father Niccolò and his uncle Matteo (1261-69), who were in Persia and Bukhara; and he left again with them for Cathay. His journey started from Ayas (Lajazzo) in 1271, and he returned to Venice in 1295. Although the difficult question of the various versions of the *Milione* cannot be addressed here, it is important to note it provided a model for later travelers; because it included historical, geographical, and anthropological aspects of the journey (see POLO). During the pontificate of John XXI, Friar Gherardo of Prato was sent to the court of Abaqa (1278), who was considered to be inclined favorably towards the Christians. We have traces of this embassy from letters written by the pope (Golubovich 1913, II, pp. 426-28). Franciscan missions in Persia also played an important role in the embassy to Rome in 1288 of the Nestorian monk Rabban Sauma (Borbone, 2000), who carried several letters for the pope from the Franciscans of Tabriz (Golubovich, 1913, II, pp. 437-40). Unfortunately the important role played by Genoese travelers, such as Buscarello de Gizolfi (q.v., ambassador during the reigns of Arḡun, Gayḵatu, and Ghazan), Benedetto Vivaldi, who traveled in Persia and

Afghanistan in 1315, and Tommasino Gentile, who tried to reach China but was forced by illness to abandon his journey in Hormuz in 1344 (Lopez, 1952, pp. 92-93), is attested only in passing in sources such as letters, diplomatic notes, and notarial deeds (Petech, 1962, pp. 562-65; Paviot, 1991; Borbone, 2000, p. 256).

Probably the most important description of Baghdad in this period was that written by the Dominican Ricoldo da Montecroce (d. 1320; q.v.), who began his long journey in 1288, traveling through Palestine, Syria, northern Mesopotamia, Sivas, Erzurum, and on to Persia, visiting Tabriz. From there he traveled to Baghdad, where he remained for six months during the reign of Arḡun (Ricoldo da Montecroce, *Itinerario ai paesi orientali di Fra Ricoldo da Monte Croce domenicano. Scritto del XIII secolo dato ora in luce da Fra Vincenzo Fineschi sacerdote dello stesso ordine*, Florence, 1793; U. Monneret de Villard, "La vita le opere e i viaggi di frate Ricoldo da Montecroce O.P.," *Orientalia Christiana Periodica* 10, 1944, pp. 227-74; idem, *Il libro della peregrinazione nelle parti dell'Oriente di Frate Ricoldo da Montecroce*, Rome, 1948). The embassy of the friar Giovanni da Montecorvino (1247-1330), sent to Arḡun by Pope Nicholas IV to evangelize among the Mongols (1279-89), is not attested in any travel account; but Giovanni himself later wrote two letters describing his second journey to China (1289): he went from Ayas (Lajazzo) to Sis and Tabriz, where he met Arḡun in 1290-91, and then to Hormuz. From there he sailed for China, where he became the first Catholic archbishop of Peking (Amat di S. Filippo, 1882, pp. 79-80; Golubovich, III, 1919, pp. 86-96; R. Almagià, "Giovanni da Montecorvino," *Rivista Geografica Italiana* 33/1-2, 1926, pp. 61-65; A. van der Wyngaert, *Jean de Mont Corvin O.F.M. premier évêque de Khanbaliq [Peking], 1247-1328*, Lille, 1924). There are few references to the journey of the Franciscans Guglielmo of Chieri and Matteo of Chieti, who visited Tabriz around 1291 (Golubovich, 1906, I, pp. 354-55, 472-77).

Another Franciscan, Odorico da Pordenone (q.v.), who visited Armenia, Tabriz, Solṭāniye, Kāšān, Yazd, Mesopotamia, and Hormuz (1314-30), is one of the more interesting sources on Persia during the Il-khanid period. This journey must be connected with the foundation of the archbishopric of Solṭāniye in 1318 by Pope John XXII and subsequently that of the archbishoprics of Marāḡe (1328) and Tabriz (1329). Archbishops such as Bartolomeo of Poggio (better known as Bartolomeo of Bologna), archbishop of Marāḡe (1328-33), played an important role in the spread of knowledge about the Persian language in Western countries through translations of the Gospels into Persian and the production of the *Codex cumanicus* ("Viaggio del B. Odorico da Udine, dell'Ordine de' Frati Minori, Delle usanze, costumi, & nature, di diverse nationi, & genti del Mondo, et del martirio di quattro frati dell'Ordine predetto, quali partirono tra gl'Infedeli," in Ramusio, *Navigazioni et viaggi*, Venice, 1583, II, foll. 245b-253a; Golubovich, 1919, III, pp. 205-7, 374-93; Piemontese, 2001, pp. 322-23). The friar Tomaso da Tolentino traveled in Persia between 1305 and 1307 with letters written by Giovanni da Montecorvino (Golubovich, 1919, III, pp. 219-21). From Francesco Petrarca's *Epistles* we know also of the travels of Giovanni Colonna (ca. 1298-1332), who traveled in Persia presumably between 1324 and 1332 (Ciampi, 1874, pp. 870-79; Surdich, 1982). The itineraries traced by the Florentine Francesco Balducci Pegolotti (q.v.) in his *Pratica della Mercatura* form one of the most important sources on Persian and Central Asian commercial routes during the last part of the Il-khanid period (around 1335 and 1340). Pegolotti never visited the countries he describes, relying instead on the accounts of merchants who had been in the East (Pegolotti, *La pratica della mercatura*, ed. by A. Evans, Cambridge, Mass., 1936). Some years later, in 1339-53, Giovanni de' Marignolli (see MARIGNOLLI) passed through Hormuz and Mesopotamia before returning to Avignon in 1353. During the last years of the Il-khanid Empire, there was a revival of Christian missions by Dominicans and Franciscans together with a strengthening of the bishopric in Persia. The bishop of Tabriz, Guglielmo Zigio, reached Persia during the last part of Abu Saʿid's reign and there assisted in the appointment of Giovanni da Cori as bishop of Solṭāniye. About the same time, Tommaso Mancasole became the first bishop of Samarkand (Golubovich, 1919, III, pp. 350-59; on this period see also pp. 424-541).

After the fall of the Il-khanid Empire and the troubles of 1340, there followed a period of obscurity in relations between Italy and Persia, until the Italian presence there revived during the reign of Timur—in particular at the end of the fourteenth century, after the first encounters between the Central Asian sovereign and the Italians. Italians, however, did not entirely stop visiting Persia in the interim period. The Venetian ambassadors Giovanni Querini and Giuffredo Morosini traveled to various courts in Persia between 1345 and 1346 (Donazzolo, 1929, p. 19).

The first meeting between Italians and Timur occurred in 1395 near Azaq and is referred to in the *Cronaca di Treviso* of Andrea de Redusiis ("Chronicum tarvisinum ab anno MCCCLXVIII usque annum MCCCCXVII," in *Rerum Italicarum Scriptores* XIX, Milan, 1731, cols. 802-04; Bernardini, 2002, pp. 395-98). The Sienese merchant Beltramo Mignanelli (q.v.; Fischel, 1956. Piemontese, 1996) wrote a *Vita Tamerlani*, in which he included his impressions of the military events of the years 1401-02. Although Timur was the object of special interest in Italian courts (Knobler 1995), the meeting between him and the Italians did not lead to any further developments in Italian relations with the Timurids after Timur's death in 1405. Nevertheless Italians continued to cross Persia, following the southern routes (on land or by sea). in particular as Niccolò de' Conti (see CONTI) did when on his way to India through Birecik (Turkey), Mosul, Bandar ʿAbbās, and Hormuz at the beginning of the 15th century ("Viaggio di Nicolo di Conti Venetiano scritto per Messer Poggio Fiorentino," in Ramusio, *Navigationi et Viaggi*, Venice, 1550, I, foll. 365a-371b; V. Bellemo, *I viaggi di Nicolò de' Conti riscontrati ed illustrati con proemio storico, documenti originali e carte geografiche*, Milan, 1883; idem, *La cosmografia e le scoperte geografiche del secolo XV e i viaggi di Nicolò de' Conti*, Padua, 1908; G. Caraci, "Il Quattrocento e Nicolò de' Conti," in *Nuove questioni di storia medievale*, Milan, 1969, pp. 448-51; idem, "Viaggiatori italiani in Persia nel Medioevo," *Il Veltro* 14, 1970, pp. 39-60).

From Uzun Ḥasan to Shah 'Abbās I. The appearance of Uzun Ḥasan on the scene in the 15th century was heralded by Western, and in particular Italian, powers as a great opportunity for their anti-Ottoman policy (Woods 1999, pp. 87-123). The travel account of the Venetian diplomat Josapha Barbaro (1473-78; q.v.; L. Lockhart, R. Morozzo della Rocca, and M. F. Tiepolo, *I viaggi degli ambasciatori veneti Barbaro e Contarini*, Rome, 1973) was one of the first pieces of evidence in the West of the power of the Āq Qoyunlu in this period. To this work we should add the account of Ambrogio Contarini (1474-75; q.v.), which was first published in Venice in 1487 and subsequently included, together with Barbaro's account, in Ramusio's *Navigationi et Viaggi* (see also N. Di Lenna, *Ambrogio Contarini politico e viaggiatore del secolo XV*, Padua, 1921). Later Venetian material should also be mentioned, such as the report by Lazaro Quirini (1471; Berchet, 1865, pp. 1-6; Donazzolo, 1929, p. 47) and that of Giovanni Dario, who gave information on the state of Persia at the end of the 15th century in his dispatches sent to the Venetian Senate (Berchet, 1965, pp. 150-53; F. Babinger, *Johannes Darius [1414-1494]: Sachwalter Venedigs im Morgenland, und sein griechischer Umkreis*, Munich, 1961). Another writer who was at the court of Uzun Ḥasan, Giovanni Maria Angiolello (ca. 1451-1524; q.v.), who was in the entourage of Meḥmed II as *defterdār*, probably went to the Āq Qoyunlu court (Babinger, 1961) during the reign of Bayezid II. Even though the work of Angiolello is considered more important for the history of the Ottoman Empire, his *Vita e fatti del signor Usuncassano* (in "Breve narrazione della vita et fatti del Signor Ussuncassano fatta per Giovan' Maria Angiolello" in Ramusio, *Navigazioni et Viaggi*, Venice, 1559, II, foll. 66a-78a; *Navigazioni e viaggi*, ed. by M. Milanesi, III, 1980, pp. 359-420) offers important data on events relating to the Āq Qoyunlu, such the battle of Baškent (1473). Barbaro, Angiolello, and Domenico Romano were later included in the *Historia turchesca* of Donato da Lezze (*Historia turchesca [1300-1514]*, ed. by I. Ursu, Bucharest, 1909). To these accounts must be added that of the Venetian ambassador in Persia, Caterino Zeno, who was in the court of Uzun Ḥasan between 1471 and 1473 (Berchet, 1865, pp. 6-8, 130-35; *De i Comentari del Viaggio in Persia di M. Caterino Zeno il K. & delle guerre fatte nell'Imperio Persiano, dal tempo di Ussuncassano in quà*, Venice, 1558; V. Formaleoni, *Caterin Zeno. Storia curiosa delle sue avventure in Persia tratta da un antico originale manoscritto ed ora per la prima volta pubblicata*, Venice, 1873). During the last years of the 15th century, the Genoese merchant Geronimo da S. Stefano wrote a letter from Tripoli in Syria in which he recounts his travels from Hormuz through Persia with Armenian and *Azami* (Persian) merchants. He passed through Shiraz, Kāšān, Solṭāniye, and Tabriz before reaching Aleppo ("Viaggio di Hieronimo da Santo Stephano Genouese dirizzato à Messer Giouan Iacobo Mainer, di lingua portoghese tradotto nell'Italiana," in Ramusio, *Navigationi et Viaggi*, Venice, 1563, I, foll. 345-46; P. Peregallo, "Viaggio di Geronimo da Santo Stefano e di Geronimo Adorno in India nel 1494-99," *Bollettino della Società Geografica Italiana* 38, 1901, pp. 24-40; M. Longhena, "Il testo originale del viaggio di Geronimo Adorno e Geronimo da S. Stefano," in *Studi Italiani di Filologia Indo-Iranica diretti da Francesco Pullè* 5, 1905, appendici, pp. 1-56; *Viaggi in Persia India e Giava di Nicolò de' Conti. Girolamo Adorno e Girolamo da Santo Stefano*, ed. by M. Longhena, Milan, 1929).

A significant source for the beginnings of the Safavid period was written by a Venetian, known formerly as the "Anonimo Mercante" (for example, by Ramusio who published his travel account, "Viaggio di un mercante che fu nella Persia," *Navigationi et viaggi*, II, Venice, 1583, foll. 78a-91a; "The Travels of a Merchant in Persia," in *A Narrative of Italian Travels in Persia*, transl. by C. Grey, London, 1873, pp. 141-207); he has been identified by Jean Aubin (1988, p. 129; 1995, p. 258) as Domenico Romano (q.v.). This merchant was in Persia from 1507 to 1510. He describes several places, mainly in Azerbaijan, and gives important information on Uzun Ḥasan, Šayḵ Ḥaydar, and Šāh Esmāʿil I. Although Domenico Romano can be considered the more important traveler of the period of Shah Esmāʿil I, one must also mention the *Itinerario* of Ludovico Varthema (or Bathema, as Ramusio calls him; see VARTHEMA). His account of a journey to India and Southeast Asia between 1502 and 1508 (the years when he passed through Hormuz) includes descriptions of Ḵorāsān (Herat) and Transoxania (Samarkand) which do not seem to reflect actual visits there ("Itinerario," in Ramusio, *Navigationi et Viaggi*, Venice, 1550, I, foll. 159a-188b; Varthema, *Itinerario dallo Egypto alla India*, ed. by E. Musacchio, Bologna, 1991). Some years later, the Florentine astronomer and geographer Andrea Corsali traveled through Persia on his long journey to India. His descriptions of Hormuz and the Shiʿites reflect a rationalistic approach (A. Corsali, "Lettera d'Andrea Corsali Fiorentino allo illustrissimo Signor Duca Giuliano de Medici scritta in Cochin terra dell'India, nell'anno MDXV alli VI di Gennaio. Della Navigazione del Mar Rosso & sino persico fino a Cochin città nella India, scritta alli XVII di Settembre MDXVII," in Ramusio, *Navigationi et Viaggi*, Venice, 1550, I, pp. 192a-203b). Other Italian reports are mentioned in the *Diarii* of Marin Sanudo the Younger (d. 1536; q.v.), in which there is much information for the reign Shah Ismāʾil (*Šāh Ismāʾil I nei "Diarii" di Marin Sanudo*, ed. by B. Scarcia Amoretti, Rome, 1979; see also: Marin Sanuto il Giovane, *I Diarii*, ed. by R. Fulin, F. Stefani, N. Borozzi, et al., 58 vols., Venice, 1578-1903; F. Babinger, "Marino Sanuto's Tagebucher als Quellen zur Geschichte der Safawiyya," in T. W. Arnold, R. A. Nicholson, eds.,

A Volume of Oriental Studies Presented to Edward G. Browne, Cambridge, 1922, pp. 28-50).

Several Italian travelers were in Iran during the reign of Ṭahmāsp I (1524-76). Alberi and Berchet have not included the *Relazione* of Michele Membré (q.v.), written in 1542 (*Relazione di Persia [1542]. Ms. inedito dell'Archivio di Stato di Venezia*, ed. by F. Castro, G. R. Cardona, and A. M. Piemontese, Naples, 1969; English transl. by A. H. Morton, *Mission to the Lord Sophy of Persia [1539-1542]*, London, 1993). This *Relazione* is an important report on the first period of the reign of Ṭahmāsp I. The edition of 1969 also contains other important evidence, such as the *Viaggio di Colocut* of the Venetian Giovanni Veneziano (pp. 105-114), which was first published in 1543 (L. Runcinotto, "Viaggio di Colocut descritto per messer Aloigi di Messer Giovanni Venetiano, nel quale si narra le mirabil forze, provincie, terre, & città del gran Signore Sophi et come passò infiniti Spagnoli in soccorso di esso signore contra Turchi: & etiam narra le meravigliose isole che producono Oro & pietre preciose: cosa invero molto curiosa da intendere," in *Viaggi fatti, da Vinetia, alla Tana, in Persia, in India, et in Costantinopoli: con la descrittione particolare di città, luoghi, siti, costumi, et della Porta del Gran Turco: et di tutte le intrate, spese et modo di governo suo, et della ultima impresa contra portoghesi*, Venice, 1543, foll. 108a-120a). Other information useful for the reign of Ṭahmāsp I are found in the *Vita di Ismael e Thomas Sofì* of Theodore Spandugino (Spandugino, "La vita di Sach Ismael et Tamas re di Persia chiamati Soffi, nella quale si vede la cagione della controversia ch'è tra il Turco e il Soffi," in F. Sansovino, *Dell'Historia Universale dell'origine et Imperio de Turchi. Parte Prima*, Venice, 1560, foll. 125-34; also in Membré, 1969, pp. 143-75) and in the report of Vincenzo degli Alessandri (q.v.), who was sent to Persia in 1570 by the Venetian Senate on the unsuccessful diplomatic mission which gave rise to his polemic remarks about the Safavids (V. Alessandri, "Relazione presentata al Consiglio dei Dieci il 24 settembre 1572 e letta l'11 ottobre da Vincenzo Alessandri veneto legado a Tahmasp re di Persia," in E. Alberi, *Relazioni degli Ambasciatori veneti*, ser. III, II, Florence, 1844, pp. 103-27; "Narrative of the most noble Vincentio Alessandri, ambassador to the King of Persia from the most illustrious Republic of Venice," in *Narrative of Italian Travels in the fifteenth and sixteenth centuries*, ed. by C. Gray, London, 1873; Berchet, 1865, pp. 29-38; Berengo, 1960). The adventurous travels of the merchant Cesare Federici (or de' Federici), originally from Val Camonica near Brescia, who was in Persia between 1563 and 1581 and who journeyed through Birecik, Aleppo, Baghdad, and then Hormuz on his way to India, merits special mention for his rational objectivity. Particularly interesting is his description of the coronation of the King of Hormuz (*Viaggio di M. Cesare dei Federici nell'Indie Orientali et oltra l'India*, Venice, 1587; C. de' Federici, "Viaggio di M. Cesare de i Federici nell'India Orientale et oltra l'India per via di Soria," in Ramusio, *Navigazioni e viaggi*, Venice, 1605, III, foll. 386b-398b; "The voyage and travel of M. Caesar Fredericke into the East India and beyond the Indies," in R. Hakluyt, *The second volume of the Principal Navigations, Voyages, traffiques and discoveries of the English Nation made by Sea or over Land, in the South and South-east part of the World*, London, 1599, pp. 213-44). Later, Gasparo Balbi, a Venetian merchant and jeweler, traveled in Persia (1579-88) on his way to India. His description of Hormuz, which he passed through in 1580, offers a considerable amount of information about navigation and pearl production in the area, together with various somewhat fantastic details (*Viaggio dell'Indie Orientali, di Gasparo Balbi, Gioielliero Venetiano. Nel qual si contiene quanto egli in detto viaggio hà veduto per lo spatio di 9 anni consumati in esso dal 1579 al 1588*, Venice, 1590; O. Pinto, "Il veneziano Gasparo Balbi ed il suo viaggio in Mesopotamia," *Rendiconti dell'Accademia dei Lincei, classe Scienze morali etc.*, ser. VI, vol. 8, 1932, pp. 665-734; idem, "Viaggi di Cesare Federici e Gaspare Balbi in Oriente nel secolo XVI," *Bolletino della Reale Società Geografica Italiana* 83, 1946, pp. 1-5; idem, ed., *Viaggi di C. Federici e G. Balbi alle Indie Orientali*, Rome, 1962). For the reigns of Shah Ismāʿil II (1576-77) and Moḥammad Ḵudābanda (1578-87), mention can be made of the important report of Giovanni Minadoi (q.v.), who refers to the war between Murad III and Moḥammad Ḵudābanda in his *Historia*. This text also offers extensive information on the Safavid Empire (G. T. Minadoi, *Historia della guerra fra Turchi, et Persiani, descritta in quattro libri da Gio. Tomaso Minadoi; cominciando dall'anno MDLXXVII nel quale furo li primi mouimenti di lei, seguendo per tutto l'anno MDLXXXV*, Rome, 1587; idem, *The History of the wares betweene the Tyrkes and the Persians*, trans. by A. Hartwell, London, 1595).

A revival of political and diplomatic relations between the Italian courts and Persia occurred during the reign of ʿAbbās I (1587-1629), when three travelers in particular played a noteworthy role in the spread of knowledge of Persia. Two brothers from Cosenza, Giovan Battista (1552-1619) and Girolamo Vecchietti (1557-1640; qq.v.), left a collection of material that demonstrates their deep knowledge of Persia and the Persian language, together with their special diplomatic ability. Cardinal Ferdinando de Medici, the future Grand duke of Tuscany, following a commission of Pope Gregory XIII, sent Giovan Battista to the Safavid kingdom with the aim of forming an alliance against the Turks. He reached Tabriz in 1586. In 1590, he again traveled through Persia on his way to India, where he was joined by his brother Girolamo. They returned separately to Italy, Girolamo in 1608 and Giovan Battista, who had been a prisoner of the Turks in Tunis, in 1618. Their detailed report on Persia and the kingdom of Hormuz represents a very important source for the last period of Moḥammad Ḵudābanda and the beginnings of the reign of ʿAbbās I (H. F. Brown, "A report on the condition of Persia in the year 1586", *The English Historical Review* 7, 1892, pp. 314-21; U. Tucci, "Una relazione di Giovan Battista. Vecchietti sulla Persia e sul Regno di Hormuz, 1587," *Oriente Moderno* 35/4, 1955, pp. 149-60.

R. Almagià, "Giovanni Battista e Girolamo Vecchietti viaggiatori in Oriente," *Rendiconti dell'Accadermia Nazionale dei Lincei*, ser. VIII, 11, 1956, pp. 313-50; P. Donazzolo, "Gerolamo Vecchietti e la sua 'Peregrinazione d'Oriente'," *Rivista di Geografia* 12, 1932, pp. 391-97). The period of Shah ʿAbbās I is also described in the accounts of travels in Persia by the Roman noble Pietro Della Valle (q.v.), who left Italy for a 12-year journey in the East in 1614. His descriptions of Baghdad (1616), Isfahan (1617), where he met Shah 'Abbās I, Persepolis, and Shiraz are certainly unique for their objectivity and acuteness. The important information given by this traveler has been published only in part. While his *Viaggi*, travels, have been variously edited, his *Diari* needs further extensive research (see Piemontese, 1982, vol. I, nos. 831-85; see also P. Della Valle, *In viaggio per l'Oriente: Le mummie, Babilonia, Persepoli*, ed. by A. Invernizzi, E. Lesopo, and F. Pennacchietti, Alessandria, 2001). For this period one must also mention the *Relatione* of Gian Francesco Sagredo, Venetian consul in Syria from 1608 to 1611, who gives an account of the Safavid Empire (Donazzolo, 1929, pp. 78-79).

The late Safavid period. During the reign of Shah ʿAbbās I, Pope Clement VIII sent the first Carmelite mission to Persia (1604); this order would be followed later by the Augustinians, Capuchins, Dominicans, and Jesuits (see CARMELITES and P. Ambrosius a S. Teresia, *Bio-bibliographia ordinis carmelitarum discalceatorum*, Rome, 1941; H. Chick, *A Chronicle of the Carmelites in Persia and the Papal Missions of the XVIIth and XVIIIth Centuries*, 2 vols., London, 1939; see also Richard, 1993). A discalced Carmelite, Phillipe de la Sainte Trinité, was dispatched to a mission in Persia. He left Italy in 1629 and traveled through Persia to India, where he arrived in 1631. His long travel account was translated into Italian from the original Latin and contains several chapters on the Persian Empire, the role played by the Portuguese, and the customs and manners of the Persians (*Viaggi orientali del Reverendissimo P. Filippo della SS. Trinità Generale de' Carmelitani Scalzi Da lui composti nella lingua latina e nuouamente tradotti nell'Italiana da un Padre del medesimo Ordine*, Rome, 1666). The Carmelites played an important role in the spread of knowledge of Persia in this period. Other travel accounts include those of Father Giuseppe di S. Maria (1620-89) from Caprarola (*Prima spedizione alle Indie Orientali del P.F. Giuseppe di Santa Maria Carmelitano Scalzo, delegato apostolico ne' regni de' Malavari Ordinata da Nostro Signore Alessandro VII*, Rome, 1666; *Seconda spedizione all'Indie Orientali di Monsignor Sebastiani Fr. Giuseppe di S. Maria dell'Ordine de' Carmelitani Scalzi Ordinata da Alessandro VII di gloriosa memoria*, Rome, 1672) and the report written by Vincenzo Maria di S. Caterina (d. 1680; *Il viaggio alle Indie Orientali del P.F. Vincenzo Maria di S. Caterina da Siena Procuratore Generale de' Carmelitani Scalzi*, Rome, 1672; see also V. Prinzivalli, *Viaggiatori e missionari nell'Asia a tutto il secolo XVII. Appunti di storia della geografia pubblicati nel IV centenario della scoperta d'America*, Rome, 1892).

The 17th century closes with some travel accounts of special importance because of their interest in archeology. The first is that written by Angelo Legrenzi, a physician from Venice, who joined a caravan in Syria and traveled through Tabriz, Solṭāniye, Qazvin, Isfahan, and Persepolis. In 1678 he left Persia via Hormuz for India. He returned to Venice in 1694 (Legrenzi, *Il pellegrinaggio nell'Asia cioè viaggi del Dottor Angelo Legrenzi Fisico, e Chirurgo, Cittadino Veneto. Con i ragguagli dello Stato dell'Imperio Ottomano, dei Rè di Persia, de Mogori, e Gentili loro leggi, vite e costumi*, II, Venice, 1705). A similar journey was undertaken by the Calabrian Giovanni Francesco Gemelli Careri (1648-1724). This magistrate of the kingdom of Naples returned in 1700 after a long journey, in which he also visited India and China. Gemelli Careri reached Isfahan in 1694 and, as a member of the Polish delegation, witnessed the coronation of Sultan Ḥosayn. He visited Persepolis and traveled along the southern coast of Iran before his departure for India in 1695. His travel account achieved particular success during the 18th century (G. F. Gemelli Carreri, *Giro del mondo del Dottor D. Gio. Francesco Gemelli Carreri. Parte seconda contenente le cose più ragguardevoli vedute nella Persia*, 2nd ed., Naples, 1708 [1st ed., 1699-1700]; P. Doria, "Gemelli Carreri, Giovanni Francesco," in *Dizinario Biografico degli Italiani* LIII, Roma, 1999, pp. 42-45). Another non-religious traveler was the Venetian noble Ambrogio Bembo (1652-1705), who was in Persia in 1674 and remained there for four months. Modeled on Polo's *Milione*, Bembo's travel account gives important information on Persia, paying particular attention to the monuments of Persepolis, Naqš-e Rostam, Kermānšāh, and Kordestān. In Isfahan Bembo met Chardin and the illustrator G.-J. Grelot (J. Morelli, *Dissertazione attorno ad alcuni viaggiatori eruditi veneziani poco noti*, Venice, 1803; A. Welch, "Safavi Iran through Venetian eyes," in *Society and Culture in the Early Modern Middle East. Studies on Iran in the Safavid Period*, ed. by A. J. Newman, Leiden, 2003, pp. 97-121; Tucci, 1966). In 1693 the Lombard Carmelite Francesco Maria di S. Siro (Antonio Gorla di Portalbera) visited Tabriz, Solṭāniye, and Qom, where he witnessed the celebration of Āšura, and Isfahan where he assisted in the expulsion of the Carmelites from Julfa (P. Donazzolo, "Viaggi in Oriente ed in Occidente [sec. XVII e XVIII] del fratello Francesco Maria di S. Siro, [Carmelitano Scalzo], al secolo Antonio Gorla di Portabbera [Pavia]", *Rivista Geografica Italiana* 19, 1912, pp. 337-54, 423, 436, 530-37, 584-605). At the end of the 17th century, the Carmelite Fulgenzio di S. Giuseppe (1696-1703) visited Persepolis and wrote about the coronation of Sultan Ḥosayn (Alberto Dallolio, "Un viaggiatore in Oriente alla fine del secolo XVII," *L'Archiginnasio* 2, 1907, pp. 73-106). During the first half of the 18th century, Florio Beneveni was sent by Tsar Peter I to Bukhara; from there he sent several letters published in 1986 in a Russian translation (*Poslannik Petra I na Vostoke. Posol'stvo Florio Beneveni v Persiyu i Bukharu v 1718-1725*, ed. by V. G. Volovnikova, Moscow, 1986;

see C. Poujol, "L'ambassade à Boxârâ de Florio Beneveni. ou comment contourner en vain la Mer Caspienne: Chronique," in J. Calmard, ed., *Études Safavides*, Paris and Tehran, 1993, pp. 247-49).

In the 18th century another Carmelite, Leandro di S. Cecilia (Giovanni Augusto Cottalorda), left a series of travel writings. He was in Persia between 1736 and 1738 and traveled in Kermanšāh, where he visited Ṭāq-e Bostān. He also visited Bisotun, Hamadān, and Baghdad (*Persia ovvero Secondo Viaggio di F. Leandro di Santa Cecilia Carmelitano Scalzo in Oriente scritto dal medesimo, e dedicato a Sua Altezza Serenissima il Principe Arciduca d'Austria*, Rome, 1757 [which reproduced his drawing of Ṭāq-e Bostān]; *Mesopotamia ovvero Terzo Viaggio di F. Leandro di Santa Cecilia Carmelitano Scalzo in Oriente scritto da lui medesimo, e dedicato a Sua Altezza Serenissima il Principe Leopoldo Arciduca d'Austria*, Rome, 1757; B. Genito, "Un Carmelitano Scalzo del XVIII secolo: tra ideologia medievale e coscienza moderna del reale in alcune interpretazioni e disegni di resti archeologici," *La conoscenza dell'Asia e dell'Africa in Italia nei secoli XVIII e XIX*, ed. by U. Marazzi and A. Gallotta, I/1, Naples, 1984, pp. 489-501; P. Orsatti, "Il Carmelitano Leandro di S. Cecilia, viaggiatore in Oriente (1731-1751)," in *La conoscenza dell'Asia e dell'Africa in Italia nei secoli XVIII e XIX*, ed. by U. Marazzi and A. Gallotta, II/2, Naples, 1985, pp. 509-31").

The Qajar period. At the beginning of the 18th century Italian men of letters began to show a certain interest in Persia. Antonio Ranieri Biscia (1780-1839), a native of Forlì, traveled in Iran and translated several Persian works, although he apparently left no account of his long journey in Persia from 1804-14 (M. Nallino, "Un orientalista dei primordi del sec. XIX: Antonio Ranieri Biscia (1780-1839)," in *A Francesco Gabrieli. Studi Orientalistici offerti nel suo sessantesimo compleanno*, Rome, 1964, pp. 175-88). An important travel account was written by the professional traveler Gaetano Osculati (1808-84), who was with Felice De Vecchi in Iran in 1841. During his travels he visited Tabriz, Solṭāniye, Tehran, Shiraz, Bušehr, and Hormuz (De Vecchi, *Giornale di carovana o Viaggio dell'Armenia, Persia ed Arabia fatto negli anni 1841-42 da Felice De Vecchi e G. Osculati*, Milan, 1847. Bandini, Pietro, *Un viaggio nella Persia e nelle Indie Orientali intrapreso dal chiarissimo signore Gaetano Osculati negli anni 1841 e 1842*, Udine, 1845).

The new political conditions under the reign of Nāṣer al-Din Shah (1848-96) brought about a change in the Italian approach towards Iran, and renewed attention was given to the diplomacy which had been interrupted at the beginning of the 18th century. The first attempt to conclude a treaty was made in 1848 by Romualdo Tecco, a Sardinian minister in Constantinople, who had a good knowledge of Persian and was clearly interested in Persian matters (G. D'Erme, "Romualdo Tecco (1802-1867). Diplomatico sardo «Orientalista»," *Annali di Ca'Foscari* 9/3, 1970, pp. 107-22). Diplomatic relations flourished particularly in the second half of the century, especially after the Persian embassy to Europe in 1856 of Farroḵ Khan Amin al-Molk. This ambassador met the plenipotentiary minister of the kingdom of Sardinia, S. Villamarina, in Paris and in 1857 signed an important treaty; this was followed in 1862 by an embassy to the court of Nāṣer al-Din Shah headed by Marcello Cerruti. The details of this diplomatic mission were recorded by the naturalist Filippo De Filippi (1814-67), who took part in it together with other scientists (Michele Lessona, Giacomo Doria, Camillo Ferrati). An important album of photographs also records this embassy (F. De Filippi, "Note di un viaggio in Persia nel 1862," *Il Politecnico* 20, 1864, pp. 28-63, 168-222; 22, 1864, pp. 5-37, 233-54; 23, 1864, 233-45; 25, 1865, pp. 5-32, 154-94; 26, 1865, pp. 5-32, 261-76; idem, *Note di un viaggio in Persia*, Milan, 1865; A. M. Piemontese, "Le relazioni tra Italia e Persia nel XIX secolo. I trattati del 1857 e del 1862," *Oriente Moderno* 48, 1968, pp. 537-66; idem, "Le relazioni fra Italia e Persia nel XIX secolo. La corrispondenza reale," *Oriente Moderno* 49, 1969, pp. 1-20; idem, "Profilo delle relazioni italo-persiane del XIX secolo," *Il Veltro* 14/1-2, 1970, pp. 1-20; idem, "The Photograph Album of the Diplomatic Mission to Persia (Summer 1862)," *East and West* 22, 3-4, 1972, pp. 249-311; G. Branca, "I viaggiatori italiani del nostro secolo. C) Viaggi in diverse parti dell'Asia: Brocchi nella Siria e nell'Egitto, Osculati e De Vecchi in Persia, Dandolo in Palestina e nel Sudan, De Bianchi nel Curdistan, Botta nelle rovine di Ninive, la Missione italiana in Persia nel 1862, Gavazzi a Bucara, Guzmani nell'Arabia, gli Italiani in Palestina. Conclusione," *Bollettino della Reale Società Geografica Italiana* 3, 1869, pp. 345-409). In 1863 the Lombard patriot Modesto Gavazzi (1828-68), together with P. Litta and F. Meazza, undertook an adventurous journey to Bukhara in search of silkworms. Gavazzi was taken prisoner by the local khan and left a vivid account of his year in detention there (Gavazzi, *I prigionieri italiani a Bocara. Lettera di Modesto Gavazzi al comm. Cristoforo Negri*, Turin, 1864; idem, *Alcune notizie raccolte in un viaggio a Bucara*, Milan, 1865). During the same period, A. de Bianchi traveled in Armenia and Kurdistan and wrote a travel account, *Viaggi in Armenia, Kurdistàn e Lazistàn* (Milan, 1863), while Giuseppe Anaclerio recorded his journey in his work, *La Persia descritta. Relazione di un viaggio* (Naples, 1868).

In 1857 Captain Enrico Andreini from Lucca went to Persia, where he worked as an instructor in the Qajar army in which he served until 1886. Andreini wrote a series of reports to the Italian Foreign Ministery that were rightly considered an invaluable source on Qajar history. There are 437 reports, about 100 having been lost, which give details not only on the army but also on the economy, commerce, and administrative structure of the Iranian state in this period (A. M. Piemontese, "An Italian Source for the History of Qajar Persia: the Reports of General Enrico Andreini (1871-1886)," *East and West* 19/1-2, 1969, pp. 147-75; idem, "L'esercito persiano nel 1874-75 organizzazione e riforma secondo E. Andreini," *Rivista degli Studi Orientali* 49/1-2, 1975, pp. 71-117).

Another Italian instructor of the Qajar Army was Antenore Perini (1855-1934), who was sent by the Austrians on a diplomatic and military mission to Persia from 1882 to 1884. He left a rich collection of his travels with some photos (*Un trentino alla corte dello Scià di Persia. Le memorie di Antenore Perini 1882-1884*, ed. by Mir Gialal Hashemi, Trento, 1997).

The 20th century. The end of the Qajar period and the constitutional period produced a certain interest in Italy and occasioned further travels by Italians to Persia. Such interest is shown by the reports of the various ambassadors, especially between 1907 and 1914, including those of Camillo Romano Avezzana (ambassador from 1907 to 1910), Giulio Cesare Montagna (1910-14) and Carlo Arrivabene Valenti (1914-18). These reports offer important data on the changes in Iran during this period (Maria Gabriella Pasqualini, *L'Italia e le prime esperienze costituzionali in Persia (1905-1919)*, Naples, 1992; see also A. Rizzini, "Un paese in agonia: la Persia," *La Lettura* 12, 1912, pp. 150-58).

During the period of Reżā Shah, Italian interest was frequently scientific. Ardito Desio, for example, explored the region and prepared an important report on the mountains of the Zarda Kuh in the Zagros and on Mount Damāvand (Desio, "Una spedizione italiana ai monti della Persia," *Nuova Antologia* 49, August 1934, pp. 338-51; idem, "Appunti geografici e geologici sulla catena dello Sardeh Kuh in Persia," *Memorie Geologiche e Geografiche di Giotto Danielli* 4, 1933-34, pp. 139-67; G. Polvara, P. Righini, "La spedizione alpinistica italiana in Persia," *L'Illustrazione Italiana* 60, 1933, II, pp. 562-63, 700-701; G. Polvara, A. Desio, A. Prosperi, L. Bonzi, "La spedizione italiana ai Monti della Persia 1933," *Bollettino del Club Alpino Italiano* 43/76, 1936, pp. 39-78). Father Giuseppe Messina investigated the ancient religious background of Iran during his travels (Messina, "Viaggio in Iran. I. Impressioni e riflessioni. II. Iran antico. Iran moderno," *La Civiltà Cattolica* 88, 1937, I, pp. 227-42, 319-31). The participation of a large group of Italians in the construction of the Trans-Iranian Railway (1939) resulted in various Italian reports, such as that written by P. M. Bardi ("La ferrovia transiriana [sic, for transiraniana]," *L'Ingegnere* 1935, pp. 905-17). This new approach to Iran required a certain regional knowledge of the country, exhibited, for example, by Giuseppe Capra, who wrote an account about Mashad and the Persian Gulf (Capra, "Mashhed la città santa sciita [Persia]," *Le Vie d'Italia e del Mondo* 2, 1934, pp. 223-37; idem, "Una via maestra tra occidente e oriente. Il Golfo persico," *Le Vie d'Italia e del Mondo* I, 1933, pp. 1057-84; idem, "Il Golfo persico e gli interessi italiani," *Rassegna Italiana* 17, 1934, pp. 561-75 and 649-70; see also V. Pozzi, "Vagabondo nel Tagikistan," *L'Illustrazione italiana* 60, 1933, I, pp. 808-09). Such writings were paralleled by a new political and cultural stance taken during the period of fascism. This involved also a revival of the classical and medieval glories of the East. Capra, for example, retraced the old Italian merchant journeys in Persia ("La 'strada dei Genovesi' nell'Asia Minore," *Le Vie del Mondo* 1, 1933, pp. 939-70; see also A. Cipolla, *Sulle orme di Alessandro Magno [dal Granico al Caspio]*, Verona, 1933). This kind of revivalism appeared again after World War II and obviously involved the rediscovery of Marco Polo (A. Gaudio, "Sulle tracce di Marco Polo. II. Dall'Anatolia Orientale all'Iran. III. Iran Meridionale e Belucistan. VI. La via del ritorno," *L'Universo* 35, 1955, pp. 250-56, 369-82, 892-904). During this period the more traditional travelers also continued to travel to Iran. Gastone Tanzi traveled in Afghanistan during the reign of Amān Allāh and left a very vivid account of his journey (G. Tanzi, *Viaggi in Afghanistan*, Milan, 1929; for Afghanistan in this period, see also C. M. Pecorella, *Fardà. Tavolozza di Afghanistan sotto l'Emiro Amanullah*, Palermo, 1930). Other travelers were influenced by the strong ideological background of the time (A. Cipolla, *Asia Centrale Sovietica contro India. Viaggio in Turchestan ed Afghanistan*, Milan, 1935; see also idem, *Sino al limite segreto del mondo. Per terra e per aria dall'Oriente all'India, Viaggi terrestri ed aerei nel Vicino Oriente. Iran, Afghanistan, India*, Florence, 1937; idem, *Sugli altipiani dell'Iran*, Milan, 1926).

Some journals, like *Le Vie d'Italia e del Mondo*, became an important means of publishing travel accounts and descriptions of Iran in Italy, even after World War II (see e.g., O. Maier, "Attraverso la Persia settentrionale," *Le Vie del Mondo* 13, 1951, pp. 801-18; idem, "Teheran capitale dell'Iran," *Le Vie del Mondo* 13, 1951, pp. 1279-92; idem, "Attraverso la Persia meridionale," *Le Vie del Mondo* 14, 1952, pp. 987-1002). After World War II authors were struck by the social and economic conditions in Persia. Vincenzo Bianchini, for example, left an impressive account of the rural society of Iran during the reign of Moḥammad Reżā Shah which has been compared with the work of Jamālzādeh for its realism (V. Bianchini, *L'Acqua del Diavolo*, Bari, 1962; N. L. Tornesello, *Šurābād e il "realismo" di Seyyed Moḥammad 'Ali Jamālzāde. Funzione letteraria e veridicità storica*, Rome, 2000). This interest was paralleled by the anthropological approach to Persia of travelers such as G. C. Castelli Gattinara (*L'Islam dei nomadi afghani. Note di viaggio*, Rome, 1967 and *I nomadi Kuci dell'Afghanistan*, Rome, 1970). The revolution of 1979 and the emergence in Iran of the new Islamic Republic resulted in a particular interest in the country on the part of journalists. Filippo Bertotti, using the nickname Filippo Rumi, has written several articles in the newspaper *Il Manifesto*. His "Sciismo e politica nell'Iran contemporaneo" (in *L'Iran e i suoi schermi*, Venice, 1990, pp. 29-39) contains a memoir that represents a synthesis of his experiences in that country. More recently, the role of several Italians involved in Afghanistan as volunteers was evidenced by books in which they described their experiences. A representative example is the *Storie da Kabul*, (Turin, 2003) by Alberto Cairo, who worked as a physical therapist in the orthopedic centers of the Red Cross in Afghanistan.

Bibliography: E. Alberi, *Relazioni degli ambasciatori veneti al Senato durante il sec. XVI*, Serie III, Relazioni di Costantinopoli, 3 vols, Florence, 1840, 1844, 1855.

P. Amat di S. Filippo, *Studi biografici e bibliografici sulla storia della geografia in Italia pubblicati in occasione del III° Congresso Geografico Internazionale*, vol. I, *Biografia dei viaggiatori colla bibliografia delle loro opere*, Rome, 1882; *Appendice*, Rome 1884. Idem, *Gli illustri viaggiatori italiani con una antologia dei loro scritti*, Rome, 1885. J. Aubin, "L'avènement des Safavides reconsidéré (Études Safavides III)," *Moyen Orient et Océan Indien* 5, 1988, pp. 247-59. Idem, "Chroniques persanes et relations italiennes: notes sur les sources narratives du regne de Šâh Esmâʿil Ier," *Studia Iranica* 24/2, 1995, pp. 247-59. F. Babinger, "Angiolello, Giovanni Maria," *Dizionario Biografico degli Italiani*, Rome, 1961, III, pp. 275-78. R.-H. Bautier, "Les relations économiques des occidentaux avec les Pays d'Orient au Moyen ŕge. Point de vue et documents," in M. Mollat, ed., *Sociétés et compagnies de commerce en Orient et dans l'Océan Indien*, Paris, 1970, pp. 263-351. G. Berchet, *La repubblica di Venezia e la Persia*, Turin, 1865. M. Bernardini, "Tamerlano, i Genovesi e il favoloso Axalla," in *Europa e Islam tra i secoli XIV e XVI, Europe and Islam between the 14th and 16th centuries*, ed. by M. Bernardini et al., Naples, 2002, I, pp. 391-426. P. G. Borbone, *Storia di Mar Yahballaha e di Rabban Sauma. Un orientale in Occidente ai tempi di Marco Polo*, Turin, 2000. N. Broc, *La géographie de la Renaissance. 1420-1620*, Paris, 1986. I. Ciampi, "Viaggiatori italiani men noti," *Nuova Antologia di lettere, arti e scienze* 26, 1874, pp. 863-66, 870-79; 27, 1874, pp. 74-83. A. Del Piero, *Della vita e degli studi di Giovanni Ramusio*, Venice, 1902. P. Donazzolo, *I viaggiatori veneti minori. Studio bio-bibliografico*, Rome [1929]. J. W. J. Fischel, "A new Latin source on Tamerlane's conquest of Damascus, 1400-1401: B. de Mignanelli's 'Vita Tamerlani' 1416. Translated into English with an Introduction and a Commentary," *Oriens*, 9, 1956, pp. 201-32. S. Franchi, *L'itinerario di Marco Polo in Persia*, Turin, 1941. A. Gabriel, *Marco Polo in Persien*, Vienna, 1963. G. Golubovich, "Fr. Giovanni Colonna di San Vito viaggiatore in Oriente (c. 1260-1343-44)," *Archivum franciscanum historicum* 11, 1918, pp. 32-46. Idem, *Biblioteca bio-bibliografica della Terra Santa e dell'Ordine Francescano*, Quaracchi, 1906-28. A. Knobler, "The Rise of Tīmūr and Western Diplomatic Response (1390-1405)," *JRAS*, 1995, pp. 341-49. R. S. Lopez, "Nuove luci sugli italiani in Estremo Oriente prima di Colombo," *Studi colombiani nel V centenario della nascita* III, Genoa, 1952, pp. 337-98. G. Masturzi, *Dal Mar Rosso al Caspio*, Bologna, 1928. G. A. Menavino, *I costumi et la vita de Turchi di Gio: Antonio Menavino Genovese da Vultri*, Florence, 1551. *Mostra dei navigatori veneti del Quattrocento e del Cinquecento. Catalogo a cura della Biblioteca Nazionale Marciana e dell'Archivio di Stato di Venezia*, Venice, 1957. L. Olschki, *Storia letteraria delle scoperte geografiche*, Florence, 1937. G. B. Parks, *The Contents and sources of Ramusio's Navigationi*, New York, 1955. J. Paviot, "Buscarello de Ghisolfi, marchand génois intermédiaire entre la Perse Mongole et la Chrétienté latine (fin du XIIIe début du XIVe s.), in *La storia dei Genovesi*, Genoa, 1991, pp. 107-17. Idem, "Les marchands italiens dans l'Iran Mongol," in D. Aigle, ed., *L'Iran face à la domination mongole*, Tehran, 1997, pp. 71-86. P. Pelliot, "Les mongoles et la papauté II, I, Ascelin," *Revue de l'Orient chrétien* 24, 1924, pp. 335-62. L. Petech, "Les marchands italiens dans l'empire Mongol," *JA* 250, 1960, pp. 549-74. Idem, "Ascelino," in *Dizionario Biografico degli Italiani* IV, Rome, 1962, pp. 373-74. A. M. Piemontese, *Bibliografia italiana dell'Iran*, 2 vols., Naples, 1982. Idem, "Beltramo Mignanelli senese biografo di Tamerlano," in M. Bernardini, ed., *La civiltà Timuride come fenomeno internazionale* (Oriente Moderno 15 [77]/2), Rome, 1996, I, pp. 213-26. Idem, "Le glosse sul Vangelo persiano del 1338 e il Codex Cumanicus," *Miscellanea Bibliothecae Apostolicae Vaticanae* 8, 2001, pp. 313-49. O. Pinto, "Viaggiatori veneti in Oriente dal secolo XIII al XVI," in A. Pertusi, ed., *Venezia e l'Oriente fra tardo Medioevo e Rinascimento*, Venice, 1966, pp. 389-401. M. Polo, *Milione*, ed. by V. Bertolucci Pizzorusso and G. R. Cardona, Milan, 1975. J. Reinhard, *Angiolello historien des Ottomans et des Persans*, Buenos Aires and Besançon, 1913. F. Richard, "L'Apport des missionaires europeens à la connaissance de l'Iran en Europe et de l'Europe en Iran," in J. Calmard, ed., *Études Safavides*, Paris and Tehran, 1993, pp. 247-49. J. Richard, *La papauté et les missions d'Orient au Moyen ŕge (XIIIe-XIVe siècles)*, Rome, 1977, pp. 157-63. C. Serena, *Hommes et choses en Perse*, Paris, 1883. F. Surdich, "Colonna, Giovanni," in *Dizionario Biografico degli Italiani* XXVII, Rome, 1982, pp. 337-38. G. Tanzi, *Viaggi in Afghanistan*, Milan, 1929. [Gir. Vecchietti,] "Della sua peregrinazione d'Oriente," Ms. Athens, Gennadios Library, no. 73, foll. 48-160. U. Tucci, "Bembo Ambrogio," *Dizionario Biografico degli Italiani* VIII, Rome, 1966, pp. 101-2. Idem, "Mercanti veneziani in Asia lungo l'itinerario poliano," in *Venezia e l'Oriente*, ed. by L. Lanciotti, Venice, 1987, pp. 307-21. J. E. Woods, *The Aqquyunlu. Clan, Confederation, Empire, revised and expanded*, Salt Lake City, 1999. S. Yerasimos, *Les voyageurs dans l'Empire ottoman (XIVe-XVIe siècle)*, Ankara, 1991. P. Zurla, *Di Marco Polo e degli altri viaggiatori più illustri. Dissertazioni del P. Ab. D. Placido Zurla con appendice sulle antiche mappe idrografiche lavorate in Venezia*, Venice, 1818-19.

(MICHELE BERNARDINI)

(2) Qajar Period

There is ample evidence of an Italian presence in Persia throughout the Qajar period, when many Italians went to work there as physicians, military advisors, or merchants. They left little written testimony of their Persian experience until the second half of the 19th century, when the number of Italians who went to Persia increased, and with them the bulk of recorded data. The most salient aspect of the accounts written by Italians who lived in Persia between 1850 and the turn of the century is that almost all of them had official assignments. In fact, most of the Italian material published are the reports of military officials who were in Persia to train the Persian army, of natural scientists researching the zoological world, or of financial advisors to the Persian government.

The first Italian travelers who left significant accounts of their visits to Qajar Persia were the members of the 1862 mission, which included diplomats, scientists and military officers. The greatest contributions in terms of scientific articles and general information about Persia were brought by Filippo de Filippi (q.v.) and the physician Michele Lessona (1823-1894). Lessona was particularly interested in zoology and his essays are basically devoted to natural life in Persia, such as its landscapes and "magnificent nature [that is] so great and excellent that I cannot describe it properly" (letter written in 1865, in Camerano, pp. 25-26). He also became very interested in the Bahai religion, so much so that he wrote a book on it (*I Babi*).

In the second half of the 19th century, Qajar governors employed Italian officers both as teachers at the Dār al-Fonun (q.v.) in Tehran and as advisors within the ranks of the military. The first Italian officer who left a written account of Persia was Count Luigi Serristori (1793-1857), in whose brief account one finds information on Persian geographical and economic conditions, on the trade and commerce, as well as many comments on Persian people with whom the author sympathized, because they were "repressed by the monarch's endless tyranny" (p. 211), but whom he also accused of barbarous customs and of falsehood and vanity, although they were also "intelligent, quick learning, cordial, and merry tempered" (p. 214).

More substantial and responsible are the accounts by two other officers, Alessandro de Bianchi and Enrico Andreini. De Bianchi was a captain of the Italian army, who served in the Ottoman armed forces in the 1850s and came into contact with the Persians who lived on the borders between the Ottoman and the Qajar domains. Most of de Bianchi's observations concerned the Kurds, whose way of life he described in detail, especially their bellicose recreations.

De Bianchi presented himself as an expert on Muslim manners and languages (p. 38) and enriched his narrative with historical notes, legends, anecdotes and linguistic annotations. Muslim women were another interesting topic for de Bianchi, who reflected on their ways and manners among the Turks, Armenians, Kurds and Persians. He scorned the overall confusion made by books on the Middle Eastern people, and he was particularly critical of the Christian missionaries (such as the Italian Father Maurizio Garzoni, author of the first vocabulary of the Kurdish language, who would antagonize everyone who professed a non-Christian religion; de Bianchi, p. 225). He also labeled the Christians who resided in the Levant as "ignorant, full of prejudices, fanatically attached to their religion and therefore hostile to other religions' believers" (p. 226).

The Captain Enrico Andreini, who lived in Persia from 1857 until his death in 1895, was an instructor of the Persian army and also taught at the Dār al-Fonun. He was appointed general in 1872, soon after his proposal to the Italian governor to become the Italian correspondent for Persian affairs. His 437 reports are a very complete account of the most important Persian events in those crucial years. Andreini's main concern was the reform of the Persian armed forces, and in 1864 he translated into Persian a French manual on infantry maneuvers (*Ḥarakāt-e afwāj*; see Piemontese, 1969, p. 156, and n. 14), one of the first works of this genre to be published in Persia. In May 1875 he also wrote in French a project of reform of the Persian army, which he addressed to Nāṣer-al-Din Shah, whom he highly esteemed. Andreini also had a great interest for the Central Asia question and devoted many dispatches to the analysis of the various components involved in the Great Game (q.v.), in which he showed his political and diplomatic acumen (see Piemontese, 1972).

Very little is known abut Giuseppe Anaclerio, who spent three years (1862-65) in Persia working in the army. His account, *La Persia descritta*, although much influenced by his prejudices and preconceptions about Persian civilization, nonetheless gives interesting descriptions of life in Persia. Particularly remarkable is his description of Tehran prisons, which he had the chance to visit.

Some 19th-century travelers to Persia went to investigate the Persian methods of silk-worm cultivation for the Italian government, such as Giulio Adamoli (1840-1926), an engineer and mathematician, who was extremely knowledgeable about Middle Eastern countries and who lived in Ḵoqand for about one year (1870). He only wrote some articles in which he described the Ḵoqand Khanate in great detail: its mosques and sanctuaries, the bazaar, the Khan's residence and private dwellings, the administrative system, the local customs and celebrations, including the ceremony for the circumcision of a dignitary's son and some *ruhawzi* performances. He was very critical of the conditions of women and ascribed all the faults of Ḵoqand's society to the "most fanatic and stubborn ignorance" ("Un'escursione," p. 442) and to the superstition that abided among every social group.

More ponderous is the account written by Eteocle Lorini (1805-1919), a professor of Financial Sciences at the University of Pavia who spent the years 1897-98 in Persia. His extensive monograph, *La Persia*, covers a variety of topics, ranging from religion to political institutions, from the world of work and business to that of art and literature, from the public realm to the private. It is an interesting, readable guidebook, in which Lorini showed his familiarity with, and knowledge of, both past and present Persia. His chapters on Persian administrative hierarchy is a model of clarity and accuracy, as are his economic and financial observations, which reveal both his wit and capacity for perceiving and analyzing the complex Persian situation. Another outstanding aspect of Lorini's study is a collection of authoritative assertions aimed at correcting and eliminating many prejudices about Persia and her people. He contradicted the common Western bad opinion about Muslim education (p. 103).

He also had a series of provocative assertions on Persian women, whom he described as the sovereigns of Persia, happy with their position in the harem, and protected by Muslim law (pp. 107-9). He is also the author of reports on Persian commerce (Lorini, 1887, 1888, 1983).

More extensive was the Persian experience of Carlo Chiari, who had previously studied Persian and other Asian and African languages at the Institute of Oriental Languages in Paris. At the turn of the century he went to Persia and entered the Persian financial services under the directorship of the Belgian Josef Naus. In 1910 he was appointed director of customs of Persian Kurdistan, where he lived for about thirty years. His autobiography, *Notti persiane*, describes at length the Kurdish way of life and the manners of Christian populations dwelling on the fringes of the Qajar realm; but it is also rich in episodes regarding the eventful period of civil war in western Persia in the first decades of the 19th century.

The writings of Italian travelers in Qajar Persia reveal some common characteristics: the majority of the writers showed a sympathetic attitude towards the country they visited and its people. Though they were critical of certain events and situations, they were usually not affected by the prejudices and preconceptions of the time; moreover, they were eager to make a good impression in the foreign country. This attitude and the way it is expressed in these accounts is important as these writings fostered other Italian interests towards Persia and Persian studies. They offered information about Persian matters which were virtually unknown in Europe, such as the richness of Persian zoological and botanical life, the organization of the Persian army, and the life of the people who lived on the periphery of the Persian world.

Moreover, the material provided about Persian politics benefited from the authorship of politically impartial observers; Italy had no immediate or direct interest in the rivalry among European powers, for it was too small and too weak a state to entertain such ambitions.

Bibliography: Giulio Adamoli, "Un'escursione nel Kokan [sic], Aprile-Maggio 1870," *Nuova Antologia di lettere, arti e scienze* 22, 1873, pp. 411-48. Idem, "Una spedizione militare in Asia Centrale, Agosto-Settembre 1890," ibid., pp. 917-53. Giuseppe Anaclerio, *La Persia descritta: relazione di un viaggio*, Naples, 1868. Enrico Andreini, "Relazione sull'industria ed il commercio della Persia del Generale Andreini," *Bollettino consolare* 2, 1884, pp. 493-536. Alessandro de Bianchi, *Viaggio in Armenia, Kurdistàn, Lazistàn*, Milan, 1863. Lorenzo Camerano, "Michele Lessona, notizie biografiche e bibliografiche," *Bolettino dei Musei di Zoologia e di Anatomia Comparata della R. Università di Torino* 9, no. 188, 1894. Carlo Chiari, *Notti persiane: Mezzo secolo di vita sugli altipiani dell'Iran*, Rome, 1946. Maurizio Garzoni, *Grammatica e vocabolaria della kurda . . .*, Rome, 1787. Michele Lessona, *I Babi*, Conferenza tenuta alla Societa Filotecnica di Torino addi 5 e 12 dicembre 1880, Torino, 1881. Eteocle Lorini, "Commercio in Persia," *L'Esplorazione commerciale* 2, 1887, p. 374. Idem, "La produzione della seta in Persia," ibid., 3, 1888, pp. 151-52. Idem, *La Persia economica contemporanea e la sua questione monetaria: Monografia fatta per incarico del Ministero del tesoro (1897-1898)*, Rome, 1900; repr., Pahlavi commemorative reprint series, Tehran, 1976. Idem, "Da Roma a Teheran: Note di un viaggio in Persia," *Nuova Antologia di letter, arti e scienze*, no. 84, 1899, pp. 327-47. Idem, "La Persia all'esposizione mondiale," *Minerva* 5, 1983, pp. 461-62. Idem, "Economia e finanza e commercio della Persia" ibid., pp. 468-69. Angelo M. Piemontese "An Italian Source for the History of Qāǰār Persia: The Reports of General Enrico Andreini (1871-1886)," *East and West* 19, 1969, pp. 45-79; tr. Ḵosrow Fānīān as "Yak maʾḵaḏ-e tāriḵi dar bāra-ye Qājāriya: gozārešhā-ye Ženeral Enriko Āndreʾini," *Barrasihā-ye tāriḵi* 9, 1974, pp. 37-70. Idem, "La questione centroasiatica in E. Andreini (1872-'86)," *Il Veltro* 16, 1972, pp. 475-530. Idem, "L'esercito persiano nel 1874-75: organizzazione e riforma secondo E. Andreini," *Rivista degli Studi Orientali* 49, 1975, pp. 71-117. Luigi Serristori, "Notizie geografiche e statistiche della Persia: Memoria del colonnello conte L. Serristori," *Annali Universali di Statistica* 65, 1840, pp. 207-15.

(ANNA VANZAN)

v. IRANIAN STUDIES, PRE-ISLAMIC PERIOD

The only comprehensive bibliographical repertory of studies on Iranian subjects, both pre-Islamic and Islamic, published in Italy is the *Bibliografia Italiana dell'Iran* by Angelo Michele Piemontese (1982). Though providing a very informative guide to the subject, it cannot be regarded as complete due to the vast time span (1462-1982) that it covers. Some information on Iranian studies in the 19th century can be found in a little-known article by Italo Pizzi (1897a), which outlines the course of Iranian studies in his time. The half-century 1861-1911 was not particularly fruitful for Iranian studies, so much so that in 1913 L. Bonelli could summarize the results in a series of brief notes. In 1935 Giuseppe Gabrieli published a bibliographical study of Oriental studies, which included Iranian studies. Subsequently Francesco Gabrieli (1950) briefly discussed Iranian studies in his "Cinquant'anni di studi orientali in Italia," while Alessandro Bausani devoted an article to the studies that had appeared between 1940 and 1950 (Bausani, 1950) and provided the chapter on Iran in a volume detailing the Italian contribution to Oriental studies (Bausani 1962). Two informative surveys of a more general scope were the article by Jacques Duchesne-Guillemin (1962) on ancient Iranian studies and the book by Adriano Valerio Rossi (1975) discussing the bibliography of Middle Persian linguistics between 1966 and 1973. Iranian studies, both pre-Islamic and Islamic, were the subject of works by Giorgio Raimondo Cardona (1970) and Angelo Michele Piemontese (1982, 1988); these are rich in citations of earlier bibliographies. For more recent contributions of Italian scholars, one may consult, among others, the important bibliographies by Ursula Weber and Josef Wiesehöfer (1996), focused on the Achaemenid period and by Gunner B. Mikkelsen (1996) on Manicheism. Classical studies and other related fields are not considered here. On Zoroaster's character as represented by authors who flourished during the Renaissance and early modern period, one may profitably consult the first volume of the work by Michael Stausberg (1998).

Although Italian contacts with Iran date from ancient times, scientific interest in pre-Islamic Iran cannot be traced earlier than the second half of the eighteenth century. Early works which touched on the Avestan ("Zend") language were published by Lorenzo Hervás (1735-1809; e.g., Hervás, 1767). Also, the discoveries of Anquetil Duperron (q.v.) found an echo in the journal *Novelle letterarie pubblicate in Firenze* as early as 1762. But these were isolated cases. The first Italian scholar to study Iranian languages in depth was the philologist Giacomo Lignana (1827-91), who took part in the embassy, which the newly unitified Kingdom of Italy sent in 1862 to the Qajar court. Lignana was both a scholar and politician (he served as counselor to one of the main builders of the modern Italian state, Camillo Benso Count of Cavour), and had studied Indian languages under Christian Lassen and Iranian languages under Friederich von Spiegel. Professor of historical linguistics ("Lingue e letterature comparate"), first in Naples (1861-71), and then in Rome (from 1871), he was to open the way not only to the teaching of Persian language and literature but also to the philological and linguistic study of other Iranian languages. Despite his friendship with Graziadio Isaia Ascoli, a man considered the founder of Italian linguistic studies, Lignana opposed his idea of separating the teaching of linguistics from literary studies, and succeeded in maintaining his Roman chair as the only one where both subjects could be taught. His unpublished papers on Iranian subjects are now preserved in the Fondo Pullé of the Italian National Library in Florence (Dovetto, 1989 and 1991). Ascoli himself wrote a number of contributions on Old Persian, as well as on other aspects of Iranian languages, although Iranian was far from being his main interest. Almost a generation later Leone Caetani (1869-1935), well known as a scholar of Islam and author of the monumental work *Annali dell' Islam*, took an interest in pre-Islamic Iran, although it was limited to the fate of Christianity in that region (Caetani, 1906).

The first Italian scholar to entirely devote himself to Iranian studies was Italo Pizzi (1849-1920). From 1885 onwards he taught Iranian subjects at the University of Turin, first as Chair of Persian language and literature, then teaching Iranian philology as well. He was more a man of letters than a scholar in the modern sense of the word, not being influenced in the least by the great achievements attained by European philology and historical linguistics in that century. He did, however, write a grammar of the two known Old Iranian languages (1897), and translated passages from the Avesta (1914) and occasional excerpts from Pahlavi literature. A less known scholar, also active between the 19th and 20th century was Francesco (Franz) Cannizzaro (1867-1914; q.v.) who met an untimely death at the age of forty-six. He published a translation of the third chapter of the *Vidēvdād* (1913), but his main contribution to Iranian studies, the complete translation of this same book, was put together from his handwritten notes by his father, Tommaso, and I. Pizzi, and appeared in 1916.

Two linguists born at the end of the 19th century were bound to play a very active role in establishing Iranian languages as an independent field of study in Italy: Vittore Pisani (1899-1991) and more importantly, Antonino Pagliaro (1898-1973). Pisani's interest in Iranian studies was only secondary, a small component of his broader interests which focused mainly on Indo-European linguistics and Indian languages. Conversely, one of Pagliaro's main fields of interest was Iranian studies, to which he contributed widely. He had studied ancient and Middle Iranian languages under the renowned German scholar Christian Bartholomae (q.v.) in Münster. After returning to Rome, he taught Filologia Iranica (Iranian philology) for many years while officially in charge of the chair called Glottologia (general linguistics) at the Faculty of Humanities of the University of Rome "La Sapienza." In the field of Iranian studies, Pagliaro's main interest was the Book of Pahlavi, though he also contributed a number of important articles on Old Iranian languages, on the Zoroastrian religion, and on the so-called irano-graeca, that is, Iranian loanwords in the works of Greek authors (see Belardi, 1992, pp. 75-78). Particularly interesting are his articles in the field of Middle Iranian (such as the contributions to the study of the Middle Persian juridical vocabulary) and his in-depth study of the history of the game of chess. Very early in his life, Pagliaro began the study of the Book of Pahlavi, a field in which he was to become one of the main experts of his age. At the age of 26, he prepared an edition of the *Ayādgār ī Zarērān* (1925), Two years later he published a translation of the same text as well as of the *Kārnāmag ī Ardaxšīr ī Pābagān* in a series meant for a wider literary public. Later in his life he edited the *Wizārišn ī čatrang* (1951), a text which in 1936 had been the subject of a dissertation by his pupil and subsequently teaching assistant, Mario Lucidi. The same text has recently been the subject of a detailed study by Antonio Panaino (1999). Though mainly interested in the non-religious Pahlavi texts, Pagliaro also wrote an important synthesis of pre-Islamic Iranian literature for a volume improperly named *La letteratura persiana* ("Persian literature"), which he wrote together with Alessandro Bausani, who was responsible for the Islamic section (cf. Belardi, 1992).

Among Pagliaro's students, it was Walter Belardi who took up the task of continuing Iranian studies in Rome. A specialist in historical and general linguistics, like his teacher, Belardi always considered Iranian, and more particularly Middle Iranian, as one of his favorite fields of research. Among his main contributions to the study of the Pahlavi texts we may instance his significant edition of the first two chapters of the *Ardā Wīrāz nāmag*

(1979). Two years earlier he had published the important, but not sufficiently well-known volume which goes under the title of *Studi mithraici e mazdei*, in which he discussed problems related to the figure of Mithra, theology and astronomy in the Zoroastrian calendar, the *corpus* of the Avestan *Yašt*s, and the manuscript tradition of the *Bundahišn*. Not least among his merits was his ability to transmit his passion for Iranian studies to a number of his former students. Walter Belardi shares with Giancarlo Bolognesi, a pupil of Vittore Pisani, an enthusiasm for the Armenian language. Both have published important articles on Iranian loanwords in Armenian, but Bolognesi's book on the dialectology of Iranian loans in Armenian (1960) is especially significant for this field. Among the earlier studies on pre-Islamic Iran, the contribution by the Arabist Carlo Alfonso Nallino (1872-1938) is particularly stimulating. He profoundly studied the translation movement in the caliphate period and the character of Ebn al-Moqaffaʿ (q.v.), and while engaged in this he wrote a seminal work on the role played by Middle Persian in transmitting a number of Greek texts to the Arabs (1922).

Father Giuseppe Messina (1893-1951) belonged to the same generation as Pagliaro. He studied under Josef Markwart (Marquart) and edited posthumously a few of his mentor's works (*inter alia* Markwart, 1930, 1931). Active at the Pontificio Istituto Biblico in Rome, he bestowed his private library—containing many of Markwart's books—on the Institute, where they are still preserved. In the field of pre-Islamic Iran he dedicated many efforts to the understanding of Zoroastrian eschatology, publishing an important essay on the *Saošiānt-* (1932) and editing the *Ayādgār ī Jāmāspīg*, thus naming the text which he had obtained by collating a number of Middle Persian, New Persian and Pāzand texts belonging to the *Jāmāspi* tradition previously studied by Jivanji Jamshedji Modi, among others. He also studied with useful results the tradition relative to the Zoroastrian Magi and their connection with the Christian tradition (1930, 1933). In his later years Father Messina devoted himself to the study of a New Persian *Diatesseron* and was able to prove that this Harmony of the Gospels was translated from a Syriac original.

Though principally an Assyriologist, Giuseppe Furlani (1885-1963) also wrote extensively on the Elamite and Parthian civilizations, as well as on the Mandean religion and the modern Yazidis, the latter a subject also touched upon by the Islamist Michelangelo Guidi (1886-1946; cf. Piemontese, 1982, pp. 792-804 and passim). Another scholar of Islamic studies, Mario Grignaschi, has discovered and accurately described Arabic translations of important Sasanian-based texts such as the *Kār-nāmag of Anōširavān* and the *Testament of Ardašir* (1966). Moreover, he has studied the administrative reform of Ḵosrow I and the influence of Sasanian statecraft on Islamic practice (1970, 1976).

More at home in the field of art history, the orientalist Ugo Monneret de Villard (1881-1954) shared Messina's interest in the Magi and keenly studied the various Oriental legends which contributed to the art of the establishing of the traditional image of the gospel Magi (1952). He also devoted his time to Manichean art, particularly to that religion in eastern areas. Though capable of making innovative contributions to the topics he tackled, his main field of interest remained art, and he wrote an interesting introduction to history of Iranian art of both the pre-Islamic and Islamic periods (1954). Another art historian deeply interested in history was Mario Bussagli (1917-88), who worked at the school of Oriental studies of the University of Rome, specializing in Indian and Central Asian art and culture (1963, 1970). Though Italian scholars have not actively participated in the systematic investigation of Iranian numismatics, Alberto M. Simonetta and Bono Simonetta have produced a number of interesting studies mainly focused on the Parthian period.

The contribution of the school of religious studies of the University of Rome was also particularly important, both in volume and quality. Among the various scholars who wrote on Iranian and related subjects, several are particularly noteworthy. The first to take an active interest in Iranian religions was Uberto Pestalozza (1872-1966), who wrote mainly on Manicheism (1964), soon followed by Raffaele Pettazzoni (1883-1963), who was to analyze both Zoroastrianism and the Mithraic cult, publishing an informed and innovative volume on Zoroaster's religion (1920). He was followed by Ugo Bianchi (1922-95), who studied Gnosticism and dualism with particular attention to the Iranian world (1958a, 1978). Mithraism, both in the Roman and in the Eastern world, was likewise central to his interests (1979). He also contributed greatly to our understanding of the question of Zurwanism. In fact, he devoted many articles and a thought-provoking volume to the question of Time in Iranian religion (1958b).

Alessandro Bausani (1921-88) is no doubt the most important Italian scholar of Islamic Iran. From 1957 he taught at the Istituto Universitario Orientale of Naples from where he moved to the University "La Sapienza" of Rome in 1971. It is fair to state that every Italian Iranist has been his student, either directly or indirectly. Less well known is his contribution to the understanding of pre-Islamic Iran. His most important contribution to Iranian studies is the volume *Persia Religiosa* (1959) recently translated into English (2000), a seminal work in which he sets out to prove the trends of continuity in the discontinuity that characterize the Iranian religious world of both pre-Islamic and Islamic periods without surrendering to the then current nationalistic interpretation of religious history. He further underlined the contribution of Mesopotamian and Near Eastern thought to Iranian religion, a contribution which he understood as complementary to the Indo-European heritage. In the field of pre-Islamic Iran he also published an interesting booklet containing a complete translation of the *Dādestān ī Mēnōg ī xrad* (q.v.) and *Čēdag andarz ī pōryōtkēšān* (see ANDARZ) and excerpts from the *Bundahišn* and *Dēnkard* (qq.v.).

One of Italy's more prominent orientalists, Giuseppe Tucci (1894-84) began his scholarly career with pre-

Islamic Iran. His earliest publications concerned the second *fargard* of the *Vidēvdād* (1913-14) and the funerary customs of the ancient Persians (1914). Later he pursued interests in other fields of Oriental studies, but as President of IsMEO (now IsIAO), the Institute he led from 1947 to 1978, he returned to the Iranian world and launched major archeological and restoration programs in Iran. The IsMEO first sent an archeological mission to Ghazni in 1957, and then carried out substantial investigations and conservation works in Sistān (1959), at Persepolis and Isfahan (1964). (See below, vii and viii.)

Prof. Gherardo Gnoli (1937-), President of IsIAO, who at present holds a chair of Iranian Studies at the University of Rome "La Sapienza," is the undisputed founder of contemporary pre-Islamic studies in Italy; he sponsored this field first as professor and rector of the Istituto Universitario Orientale of Naples and subsequently in his present responsibilities.

Bibliography: Alessandro Bausani, "Les études d'iranistique et turcologie en italie depuis 1941," *Archiv Orientální* 19, 1951, pp. 85-93. Idem, *Testi religiosi zoroastriani*, Rome, 1957. Idem, *La Persia religiosa. Da Zaratustra a Bahá'u'lláh*, Milan, 1959; tr., *Religion in Iran. From Zoroaster to Baha'u'llah*, New York, 2000. Idem, "Iran," in *Contributo italiano alla conoscenza dell'Oriente. Repertorio bibliografico dal 1935 al 1958*, Florence, 1962, pp. 195-202. Alessandro Bausani and Antonino Pagliaro, *La letteratura persiana*, Milan, 1960. Walter Belardi, *Studi mithraici e mazdei*, Rome, 1977. Idem, *The Pahlavi Book of the Righteous Viraz* I, *Chapters I-II*, Rome, 1979. Idem, *Antonino Pagliaro nel pensiero critico del novecento*, Rome, 1992. Ugo Bianchi, *Il dualismo religioso. Saggio storico ed etnologico*, Rome, 1958a. Idem, *Zamān-i Ōhrmazd. Lo zoroastrismo nelle sue origini e nella sua essenza*, Turin, 1958b. Idem, *Selected Essays on Gnosticism, Dualism and Mysteriosophy*, Leiden, 1978. Idem, ed., *Mysteria Mithrae: atti del Seminario internazionale su 'La specificità storico-religiosa dei Misteri di Mithra, con particolare riferimento alle fonti documentarie di Roma e Ostia,'* Rome, 1979. Luigi Bonelli, "Gli studi orientali in Italia durante il cinquantenario 1861-1911. V. Persiano," *Rivista degli Studi Orientali* 5, 1913-27, pp. 215-18, 362, 372-73, 382-84, 386. Giancarlo Bolognesi, *Le fonti dialettali degli imprestiti iranici in armeno*, Milan, 1960. Mario Bussagli, *La peinture de l'Asie centrale*, Genoa, 1963. Idem, *Culture e civiltà dell'Asia Centrale*, Turin, 1970. Leone Caetani, "I popoli cristiani sottomessi ai Sassanidi," *Bessarione* 11, 1906, pp. 232-54. Francesco Cannizzaro, *Il capitolo georgico dell'Avesta. Vendidad III*, Messina, 1913. Idem, *Il Vendidad reso italiano sul testo zendico di C.F. Geldner . . .*, Messina, 1916; 2nd ed., Milan, 1990. Giorgio R. Cardona, "Studi di iranistica in Italia dal 1880 ad oggi," *Il Veltro. Rivista di civiltà italiana* 14/1-2, 1970, pp. 99-107; repr. in *Acta Iranica* I, Leiden, 1974, pp. 348-59. Francesca M. Dovetto, "Gli inediti di Giacomo Lignana," *Atti dell'Accademia Pontaniana*, N.S. 38, 1989, pp. 51-62. Idem, "Giacomo Lignana: studioso e uomo politico," in *Giacomo Lignana, Atti del Convegno Tronzano V. se 17 febbraio 1991*, Tronzano Vercellese, s.d. [1992] pp. 7-19. Jacques Duchesne-Guillemin, "L'étude de l'iranien ancien au vingtième siècle," *Kratylos* 7 1962, pp. 1-44.

Giuseppe Gabrieli, *Bibliografia degli studi orientalistici in Italia dal 1912 al 1934*, Rome, 1935. Idem, "Cinquant'anni di studi orientali in Italia," in C. Antoni and R. Mattioli, eds., *Cinquant'anni di vita intellettuale italiana*, Naples, 1951, II, pp. 89-111; repr. in F. Gabrieli, *Dal mondo dell'Islàm*, Milan and Naples, 1954, pp. 228-55. Gherardo Gnoli, *Ricerche storiche sul Sīstān antico*, Rome, 1967. Idem, *The Idea of Iran: An Essay on its Origin*, Rome, 1989. Idem, *Zoroaster in History*, New York, 2000. Mario Grignaschi, "Quelques spécimens de la littérature sassanide conservés dans le bibliothéques d'Istambul," *JA* 214, 1966, pp. 1-142. Idem, "La riforma tributaria di Ḫosro I e il feudalesimo sassanide," in *La Persia nel Medioevo*, Rome, 1970, pp. 87-147. Idem, "La 'Siyāsatu-l-ʿāmmiya' et l'influence iranienne sur la pensée politique islamique," in *Monumentum H.S. Nyberg* III, Acta Iranica 6, Leiden, 1976, pp. 33-287. Lorenzo Hervás, *Vocabolario poliglotta con prolegomeni su più classi di lingue*, Cesena, 1787. Josef Markwart (Marquart), *Das erste Kapitel der Gāthā uštavati (Jasna 43). Nach dem Tode der Verfassers herausgegeben von Ios. Messina S.I.*, Rome, 1930. Idem, *A Catalogue of the Provincial Capitals of Ērānshahr (Pahlavi Text, Version and Commentary)*, ed. G. Messina, Rome, 1931. Giuseppe Messina, *Der Ursprung der Magier und die zarathuštrische Religion*, Rome, 1930. Idem, "Il Saušyant nella tradizione iranica e la sua attesa," *Orientalia* 1, 1932, pp. 149-76. Idem, *I Magi a Betlemme ed una predizione di Zoroastro*, Rome, 1933. Idem, *Libro apocalittico persiano Ayātkār ī Žāmāspīk*, Rome, 1939. Idem, *Diatesseron persiano*, Rome, 1951. Gunner B. Mikkelsen, *Bibliographia Manichaica. A Comprehensive Bibliography of Manichaeism through 1996*, Turnhout, 1997. Ugo Monneret de Villard, *Le leggende orientali sui Magi evangelici*, Città del Vaticano, 1952. Idem, *L'arte iranica*, Verona, 1954.

Carlo A. Nallino, "Tracce di opere greche giunte agli Arabi per trafila pehlevica," in *A Volume of Oriental Studies presented to Professor Edward G. Browne*, Cambridge, 1922, pp. 345-63. Antonino Pagliaro, "Il testo pahlavico Ayātkār-ī Zarērān," *Rendiconti della R. Accademia dei lincei, Classe di scienze morali, storiche e filologiche*, Serie sesta, 1, 1925, pp. 550-604. Idem, *Epica e romanzo nel Medioevo persiano*, Florence, 1927. Idem, "Il testo pahlavico del giuoco degli scacchi," in *Miscellanea G. Galbiati* III, Milan, 1951, pp. 97-100. Raffaele Pettazzoni, *La religione di Zarathustra nella storia religiosa*, Bologna, 1920. Angelo M. Piemontese, *Bibliografia italiana dell'Iran (1462-1982)*, Naples, 1982. Idem, "Italian Scholarship in Iran (An Outline, 1557-1987)," *Iranian Studies* 20/3-4, 1988, pp. 99-130. Italo Pizzi, *Grammatica elementare dell'antico iranico (zendo e persiano antico) con antologia e vocabolario*, Turin, 1897a. Idem, "Gli studi iranici in Italia," *Studi italiani di filologia indo-iranica* 1, 1897b, pp. 58-72. Idem, *Zarathustra. L'Avesta tradotto, premessa una introduzione storica*, Milan, 1914. Adriano Valerio Rossi, *Linguistica mediopersiana 1966-1973*, Naples, 1975. Michael Stausberg, *Faszination Zarathushtra. Zoroaster und die Europäische Religionsgeschichte der Frühen Neuzeit*, Berlin and New York, 1998. Giuseppe Tucci, "Osservazioni sul Fargard II del Vendīdād," *Giornale della Società Asiatica Italiana* 26, 1913-14, pp. 243-51. Idem, "Nota sul rito di seppellimento degli antichi persiani," *Rivista di Antropologia* 19, 1914, pp. 315-19. Ursula Weber and Josef Wiesehöfer, *Das Reich der Achaimeniden eine Bibliographie*, AMI, Erganzungsband 15, Berlin, 1996.

(CARLO G. CERETI)

vi. ITALIAN EXCAVATIONS IN IRAN

(1) General Survey

From the early 20th century on, Italians participated in the scholarly investigation of ancient Iranian history and culture, most notably Ugo Monneret de Villard, but Italy's direct involvement in field archeology in Iran dates from relatively recent times. The first agreement between the Iranian Archeological Services and the Institute for the Middle and Far East (Istituto Italiano per il Medio ed Estremo Oriente, IsMEO, q.v.) was reached only in 1959. Under its learned and dynamic director, Giuseppe Tucci (q.v.), IsMEO had already started archeological research in Pakistan (1956) and Afghanistan (1957).

Tucci played a leading role in Italian archeological investigations in Asia. He was primarily a scholar of the history and culture of Tibet and the religions of the Indian subcontinent and Eastern Asia, but he was also interested in Iranian cultures of the proto-historic, pre-Islamic, and Islamic periods (Scerrato, 1995, pp. 99-105). While not an archeologist, he keenly recognized that the discipline offered new sources of information for solving important cultural problems, especially in relation to the history of Buddhism. Through the combination of IsMEO's organizational flexibility and his own ability to promote large-scale enterprises, Tucci succeeded in organizing a Center for Archeological Excavation and Research in Asia (Centro Scavi e Ricerche Archeologiche in Asia). From that point, diverse projects began to be initiated abroad. These were noted for thorough, up-to-date research methodologies in all aspects—stratigraphic methods of excavation, careful attention to the conservation of buildings and artifacts, and study of all of the archeological evidence, both material culture and paleozoological and paleobotanical remains; together, these approaches provided a holistic perspective that for its time was truly revolutionary. The publication of the results obtained were always timely, rich in descriptive details, and lavishly illustrated with plates of superb quality. They opened a new phase in the proper dissemination of archeological research.

In its early phases the Center received some support from the cultural organizations of the city of Turin, but from 1962 IsMEO became the sole support of its archeological work. In 1962 also, IsMEO made a commitment to architectural restoration, setting up a new Center for Conservation and Restoration (Centro per la Conservazione ed il Restauro) under the directorship of G. Zander.

Since 1960 the Center for Archeological Excavation has organized large-scale excavations in the region of Sistān (discussed separately; see SISTĀN ii.); the Center for Conservation carried out especially significant research at Persepolis and Isfahan.

Conservation and restoration work at Persepolis began in 1964. In 1965 it came under the guidance of the conservation expert Giuseppe Tilia, who worked with his wife, A. B. Pettersson-Tilia, on all aspects of preliminary site research, as well as on restoration (Tilia, 1972, 1978). Collaborating in the effort to lay down a comprehensive methodological framework were the two Center directors, G. Zander and D. Faccenna (of the Center for Archeological Excavation), and, from 1973, A. Shapur Shahbazi, who had founded The Institute of Achaemenid Research at Persepolis. This work of IsMEO's Italian expedition has come to be recognized as a fundamental contribution to clarification and verification, following the American and Iranian excavations. The following achievements of the Tilias are especially noteworthy: (1) complete investigation of the Terrace Wall (Tilia, 1978, p. 1 ff.); (2) discovery that the two orthostats bearing audience scenes, which were found in the Treasury (one is now in the National Museum of Iran, Tehran), originally decorated the central facades of the Apadāna staircases (Tilia, 1972, pp. 173 ff.); (3) understanding of the construction techniques of the foundation level of the complex (Tilia, 1968; 1972, pp. 125 ff.); (4) ascertaining of the main plan of the staircase of Palace H (Tilia, 1972, pp. 241 ff.); (5) reconstruction of the parapet along the southwest corner of the terrace's retaining wall, characterized by a coping with horn-like elements which were uncovered just in front of the wall; (6) identification of the techniques of construction and decoration for various buildings in which the color scheme played an important role both for the plaster elements and for the carved stone surfaces (Tilia, 1978, pp. 29 ff.; Tilia, 1995); (7) restoration from fragments of three columns in the Gate of All Lands, east Apadāna portico, and north portico of the Hundred Column Hall; (8) discovery of the original entrance to Persepolis (from the south). Additionally, some work was done on the Achaemenid bridge at Dorudzan and at Pasargadae (q.v.): (9) cleaning and restoration of the Tomb of Cyrus the Great; (10) reassembling of a number of columns in Cyrus's palaces there. Also important was G. Tilia's training of a number of Iranian artisans in restoration and conservation techniques, which made it possible to continue his plans even after he left the site in 1978.

As with Persepolis, the conservation activity at Isfahan, led by E. Galdieri and begun in 1970 in the Friday Mosque (Masjed-e Jomʿa), was based on a stratigraphic analysis of the architectural structures and on soundings conducted underneath the main floor. These contributed to reveal some architectural elements from the pre-Islamic period, to determine the original hypostyle structure as a 9th-century Abbasid mosque in the "Arab" style, and to document architectural activity from the Buyid (10th-11th centuries) and Saljuqid (11th-12th centuries) periods (Galdieri, 1972-84). The need for a more thorough understanding of the most ancient phases led to the start of a series of investigative stratigraphic excavations, conducted during 1972-78 by U. Scerrato, that threw light on basic characteristics of the building (Scerrato, 1973-78; 2001). They also clarified the Sasanian-period phase of Yahudiya, one of the predecessor towns of the city of Isfahan. (The other was Jay: see GABAE.) "Yahudiya" sometimes was synonymous with Isfahan; see Moqaddasi, p. 388, where he also describes the Friday Mosque. (See also ISFAHAN.) According to the sources, the Friday Mosque of Isfahan was constructed on the site of a Nestorian church, which might correspond to the monumental building discovered below the north section of the mosque along the south side of a broad, open space. (The space was also lined with other monumental buildings prior to the mosque and did not function as the courtyard for the Friday Mosque.) Above this pre-Islamic building, remains were found of an 8th-century mosque, which appears to be the first one, founded in 772. The mosque's *qeble* wall (i.e., that oriented towards Mecca) has a particular importance in that its luxuriant foliage decorations in carved and painted stucco constitute a primary source of evidence for pre-Samarra Iranian art. The excavations also produced evidence for the Saljuq period indicating that, under the domed room of Neẓām al-Molk, an earlier project had been begun and later was abandoned.

Another IsMEO project was the survey of the proto-historic site of Shahdad (Šahdād: Salvatori, 1978; Salvatori and Vidale, 1982), the cemetery of which had already been excavated by ʿAli Ḥākemi (Hakemi, 1997) of the Iranian Center for Archeological Research. The survey was conducted in 1977, thanks to the availability of Ḥākemi, who was then directing an archeological expedition at Lut. Time limitation prevented use of the most advanced techniques and strategies in the survey. Nevertheless, more than half of the site was systematically explored, and 37 areas containing large concentrations of material culture were identified. The results were important for chronology, because they confirmed that the site definitely was occupied by the beginning of the 4th millennium B.C.E., without excluding the possibility of an even earlier settlement similar to that of Tepe Yaḥyā, dating to the end of the 5th millennium B.C.E. In terms of topography, it was found that the nucleus of the settlement moved from east to west during the 4th millennium, and again in the 3rd millennium B.C.E., when it appears to have also moved from south to north. From the results of the archeological excavation it was possible to define areas used for artisanal production, with the important further recognition of areas for the production of ceramics, metals, and semiprecious stones.

Italian archeology in Iran is not limited to IsMEO, for from the mid-1970s other Italian institutions also established field research projects in various regions of Iran. In 1976 the University of Turin participated in a joint program with the University Museum of Pennsylvania and the Iranian Center for Archeological Research, known as the Hesar Restudy Project (Dyson and Howard, 1989); it was undertaken out of a need to study this fundamental site, uncovered in the region of Dāmḡān during the 1930s, more thoroughly (Dyson & Howard, 1989). After various visits to the site by scholars in the 1950s, G. M. Bulgarelli had conducted a limited surface survey in 1972 (Bulgarelli, 1974), followed by a re-examination of the pottery by J. Deshayes. Unlike the earlier studies, the Hesar Restudy Project was a structured program of architectural and stratigraphic investigations, intended to analyze the site in terms of its environment and economics, to highlight the changes in the settlement pattern, to identify different production areas through the analyses of slag, to collect carbon samples for the creation of an absolute chronology, and to study in a more complete manner the architectural remains and the ceramic artifacts. As part of the activities of the University of Turin, R. Biscione conducted a stratigraphic study of the westernmost mound of the "Twins"; M. Tosi with G. M. Bulgarelli and I. Reindell completed an architectural and stratigraphic study of the South Hill; M. G. Bulgarelli studied the lithics and lapis lazuli; and M. Tosi was responsible for the collection of the paleobotanical and zoological research materials.

The University of Turin Expedition also undertook a study of the upper valley of the Atrek in northern Khorasan, directed by R. Venco Ricciardi. From 1976 to 1978 a complete survey was performed of the valley bottom, to an elevation of 1500 m above sea level; there followed two stratigraphic soundings at Tepe Yam and Tepe Ḵorramābād, made possible through financial aid from the Iranian Center for Archeological Research (Venco Ricciardi, 1980; Biscione, 1981). A total of 180 mounds were identified, indicating an almost uninterrupted occupation from the Chalcolithic Period to recent times. The lack of identifiable materials from the Neolithic Period may be due to the limited topography covered during the survey, and the same reason may be given in the case of the materials from the Late Bronze Age, which were discovered only in the soundings of Tepe Yam. From the first archeological evidences, it was apparent that this area had a strong connection with southern Turkmenistan and the Central Asian world, rather than with other regions of the Iranian Plateau. A detailed analysis was made of the ceramic materials at the main sites in comparison with those of the region and of areas beyond; thus the settlement patterns of the various proto-historic and historic periods were outlined with sufficient clarity. This was also done for the Parthian and Sasanian periods, which previous surveys had not been able to fully clarify.

From 1976 to 1978 Italian researchers from the Institute of Mycenaean and Aegean-Anatolian Studies (a branch of the National Research Council [Consiglio Nazionale delle Ricerche]) conducted surface surveys, directed by P. E. Pecorella and M. Salvini, in the Urmia and Ušnaviye plains, as well as in the area between Lake Urmia and the Zagros Mountains in Iranian Azerbaijan (Pecorella, 1984). The field research was comprehensive in approach, leading to the documentation of every trace of human occupation from the prehistoric to the present, but with a specific concern for the Urartian culture. The complexity of the initial data, which is very rich for the pre- and proto-historic periods and extremely poor for Parthian and Sasanian times, made a continuous "story" impossible, and as a result the majority of studies have concentrated on the period between the 4th and the 1st millennia B.C.E. and on the Islamic period. Thus the material culture of the pre- and proto-historic phases has been clearly defined (Neolithic, Chalcolithic, IV millennium, III millennium, II millennium B.C.E., Iron Age I, Iron Age II, Iron Age III); those for the phases later than Iron Age III and prior to Islam were classified under a generic definition of "Late Period" pottery. The paucity of material obtained from the archeological survey prompted further investigations. Two soundings were carried out, supervised by M. R. Belgiorno, R. Biscione, and P. E. Pecorella, at the Uratian fortress of Qālʿa-ye Esmāʾil Āqā in 1977, and at the site of Tepe Gijlar in the Urmia plain in 1978. The paleo-botanical remains and the obsidian artifacts found at these two sites were investigated in detail (see, respectively, Costantini and Biasini, in Pecorella and Salvini, 1984, pp. 397-402; Capannesi and Palmieri, in ibid., pp. 385-95).

An important highlight of Italian archeological work in Iran lies in the area of paleobotanical research, which formed part of the studies in Sistān and later at Tepe Yaḥyā, Tepe Ḥesār, Qālʿa-ye Esmāʿil Āqā, and Tepe Gijlar. For L. Costantini, Director of the Laboratory of Bioarcheology of the Museum of Oriental Art and of IsMEO/IsIAO (Istituto Italiano per l'Africa e l'Oriente), this work was an opportunity to collect a considerable amount of information on the arboreal population and general paleoenvironment of various regions of Iran, as well as on proto-historical agriculture (Costantini, 1975; Costantini and Dyson, 1990).

Bibliography: R. Biscione, "Ricognizioni e ricerche nell'Iran orientale dall'età preistorica ad oggi. Le ricerche archeologiche italiane nell'Iran orientale ed il problema dell'urbanizzazione turanica," *Memorie dell'Accademia delle Scienze di Torino*, serie V, vol. 5, 1981, II, Classe di scienze morali, storiche e filologiche, pp. 81-89. G. M. Bulgarelli, "Tepe Hisar: Preliminary Report on a Surface Survey, August 1972," *East and West* 24, 1974, pp. 15-27. L. Costantini, "Methodological Proposals for Palaeobiological Investigations in Iran," in *Proceedings of the IIIrd Annual Symposium on Archaeological Research in Iran*, Tehran, 1975, pp. 311-31. L. Costantini and R. H. Dyson, Jr., "The ancient agriculture of the Damghan Valley," in N. F. Miller, ed., *Economy and Settlement in the Near East: Analyses of Ancient Sites and Materials* (MASCA Research Papers in Science and Archeology, Suppl. V.7), Philadelphia, 1990, pp. 46-68. R. H. Dyson, Jr. and S.M. Howard, eds., *Tappeh Hesar. Reports of the Restudy Project, 1976*, Florence, 1989. E. Galdieri, *Iṣfahān: Masgǐd-i Gǐumʿa. I-III* (IsMEO Restorations, I. 1-3), Rome, 1972-84. A. Hakemi, *Shahdad: Archaeological Excavations of a Bronze Age Centre in Iran* (IsMEO Reports and Memoirs, XXVII), Rome, 1997. P. E. Pecorella and M. Salvini, eds., *Tra lo Zagros e l'Urmia. Ricerche Storiche ed Archeologiche nell'Azerbaigian Iraniano* (Incunabola graeca 78), Rome, 1984. S. Salvatori, "Problemi di protostoria iranica: Note ulteriori su di una ricognizione di superficie a Shahdad (Kerman, Iran), *Rivista di Archeologia* 2, 1978, pp. 5-15. S. Salvatori and M. Vidale, "A Brief Surface Survey of the Protohistoric Site of Shahdad (Kerman, Iran): Preliminary Report," *Rivista di Archeologia* 6, 1982, pp. 5-10. U. Scerrato, "IsMEO Activities: Reports of Archaeological Researches in Masgǐd-i Gǐum'a at Iṣfahān," *East and West*, 23, 1973, pp. 416-18; 24, 1974, pp. 475-77; 25, 1975, pp. 538-40; 27, 1977, pp. 465-67; 28, 1978, p. 329. Idem, "Ricerche archeologiche nella moschea nel Venerdì di Isfahan della Missione Archeologica Italiana in Iran dell'IsMEO (1972-1978)," in *Antica Persia. I tesori del Museo Nazionale di Tehran e la ricerca italiana in Iran*, Rome, 2001, pp. XXXVII-XLIII, with bibliography. Idem, "Giuseppe Tucci, l'archeologia islamica ed altri parerga," in *Giuseppe Tucci. Nel centenario della nascita, Roma 7-8 giugno 1994* (Conferenze IsMEO, 8), ed. by B. Melasecchi, Rome, 1995, pp. 85-111. A. B. Tilia, "New Contribution to the Knowledge of the Building History of the Apadāna. Discovery of a wall in the inside of the façade of the Eastern Apadāna Stairway," *East and West* 18, 1968, pp. 96-108. Eadem, "Reconstruction of the Parapet of the Terrace Wall at Persepolis, South and West of Palace H," *East and West* 19, 1969, pp. 9-43. Eadem, *Studies and Restorations at Persepolis and Other Sites of Fārs* (IsMEO Reports and Memoirs 16), Rome, 1972. Eadem, *Studies and Restorations at Persepolis and Other Sites of Fārs. II* (IsMEO Reports and Memoirs 18), Rome, 1978. G. Tilia, "Appunti sull'uso del colore nella Sala del Consiglio di Persepolis," in M. Bernardini, ed., *L'arco di fango che rubò la luce alle stelle. Studi in onore di Eugenio Galdieri per il suo settantesimo compleanno*, Lugano, 1995, pp. 321-22. Idem, "Ponte-Diga sul fiume Kor – Fārs, Iran," in B. Magnusson et al., eds., *Ultra Terminum Vagari. Scritti in onore di Carl Nylander*, Roma, 1997, pp. 331-38. R. Venco Ricciardi, "Archaeological Survey in the Upper Atrek Valley (Khorassan, Iran), Preliminary Report," *Mesopotamia* 15, 1980, pp. 51-72.

(PIERFRANCESCO CALLIERI)

(2) Excavations in Sistān

The Italian archeological activity of IsMEO (Istituto Italiano per il Medio ed Estremo Oriente), Rome (now

Istituto Italiano per l'Africa e l'Oriente, IsIAO), in Iran began in 1959 when Prof. U. Tucci opened a long and rich series of activities that ended only in 1978. Three geographical areas constituted IsMEO's main interest in Iran: Sistān, Fārs, and Isfahan. In Sistān, G. Gullini and U. Scerrato started surveying the whole territory, one of the most important regions for Iranian history. The starting point was the work of Tate in 1906, who had identified many archeological sites in the area that were later also investigated by Sir Aurel Stein and E. Herzfeld (q.v.). The Italian activities from 1959 to 1978 were mainly at the following sites: Šahr-e Suḵta (Bronze Age), Dahan-e Ḡolāmān (q.v., Achaemenid period), Kuh-e Ḵᵛāja (Parthian), Qalʿa-ye Sām (Parthian), Qaḷʿa-ye Tappe (Sasanian and Islamic), Tappe Šahrestān (Parthian), and Bibi Dust (Islamic). In order to understand the regional history of Sistān, the Italian fieldwork and studies were at first devoted to the historical and geographical context of ancient Drangiana (q.v.). The name of the territory, first attested in Old Persian in the great Bisotun (q.v.) inscription of Darius I as "Zranka," is reflected in the Elamite, Akkadian, and Egyptian versions of the Achaemenid royal inscriptions, as well as in Greek and Latin sources. The Drangians were listed among the peoples ruled by the legendary King Ninus, before the Achaemenids, but there is no evidence for the situation of the country during the Median period; it may well have belonged to the Median Empire, or it may instead have been part of an eastern Iranian proto-state centered on Mary (Marv) and Herat (q.v.). In the Achaemenid royal inscriptions, Drangiana is listed as a separate province, but its position varies. The land was historically characterized as rich in tin, a crucial element for the manufacture of bronze weapons.

First in the chronological sequence of Italian activities was the work on a basaltic island in the Hāmun-e Helmand (see HĀMUN, DARYĀČE-YE), the location of a majestic palace/sanctuary, Kuh-e Ḵᵛāja, first dateable to the Achaemenid period. Successive trenches on the site revealed, on the basis of the pottery found there, a dating to the Hellenistic-Parthian period. Particularly significant was the removal and restoration in 1975-76 of a small fresco from the Kuh-e Ḵᵛāja palace. In 1963 an excavation was carried out at the fortified center of Qalʿa-ye Sām, whose encircling wall has approximately the same shape as that at Parthian Nisa. Besides the characteristic painted pottery (termed *dipinta storica sistana*) which is useful for dating the deepest layers of Kuh-e Ḵᵛāja, other pottery evidently related to Hellenistic ware and a number of ostraca with Greek epigraphy were brought to light. These inscriptions reveal that the citadel dates to the 3rd-2nd century B.C.E. Particularly interesting were the activities at Qalʿa-ye Tappe, where a long chronological sequence from the 3rd century B.C.E. to the 11th-12th century C.E. was recognized.

The Islamic period was the subject of the field survey at the site of Bibi Dust. The site takes its name from the grave of a saintly woman located under a large, miraculous tree. The pottery collected there, which is dateable from the ʿAbbāsid period to the 15th-16th century, indicates that the Timurid invasion, contrary to what had been believed up to then, was not the main reason for the abandonment of Sistān.

Amongst the most important sites investigated and extensively excavated by the Italians in Sistān are Šahr-e Suḵta and Dahan-e Ḡolāmān.

The excavation of the protohistoric center of Šahr-e Suḵta, identified earlier by Stein, began in 1967. A well-established set of cultural relations with various, and distant, geographical and cultural areas is documented from its foundation at the end of the 4th millennium B.C.E.; thus the city is one of the key sites for the study and analysis of the formative cultural processes of Central Asian civilization between the end of the 4th and the 3rd millennium B.C.E. and for the study of the recent prehistory of Central Asia. From Period I, the material culture is known either from settlements or from an extensive cemetery, which shows close connections with the late Chalcolithic centers of southern Turkmenistan, the Kandahar (Qandahār) region in Afghanistan, the Quetta valley in southern Baluchistan, the Bampur valley in southeastern Iran, and the Proto-Elamite cities of Ḵuzestān and Fārs. During Period II, the city kept in contact with the pre-Harappan centers of the Indus valley, the cities of southern Turkmenistan, and the Bampur valley. It seems highly likely that relations with Mundigak in Afghanistan were close, and it was probably from here that lapis lazuli came during this period, reaching Šahr-e Suḵta from the distant mines of Badaḵšan. For that reason, scholars began to speak of a "Helmand Civilization."

Period III (phases 4, 3, and 2) is marked by great change in the archeological sequence. The city changes its architectural form completely with the construction of large buildings enclosed by massive encircling walls. The pottery production becomes standardized and loses the characteristic painted ornamentation of the previous period; in the burials one can note a widening socio-economic gap between the various sectors of the population. At the end of Phase 4, the materials imported from Mesopotamia and western Iran disappear, and this suggests an interruption in the relationships with those regions, while the communication and trade routes with Mundigak, Bampur, and the Indus valley cities remain open. In Period IV, up to now known only through the excavation of the so-called "Burnt Palace" and of the pottery kilns of Tappe Rud-e Biābān 2 in the southern delta of the Helmand, Šahr-e Suḵta maintained contacts with only the Bampur valley (as shown by numerous close relationships with typical Bampur V-VI pottery) and the Kandahar area. A group of lapis lazuli processing sites was discovered in 1972 in the western quarters of the city. On the surface, a consistent concentration of flint, lapis lazuli, turquoise, and other types of stone fragments was observed. These workshops still remain unique in the whole Near and Middle East with regard to the level of conservation thirty years after their discovery. The excavations at Šahr-e Suḵta yielded other important evidence about the role played by the process of working semi-precious stones. In some graves, instruments and half-finished products were buried along with the corpse; the chalcedony and lapis lazuli cutters thus exercised their profession for the "other world" as well as for this one.

About 2500 B.C.E., the area of the old settlement and many other city quarters were occupied again by a large building, of which, unfortunately, only the massive foundation walls remain. In traditional societies, both European and Oriental, craft specialization was an economic activity of a familiar type, organized within precise urban spaces around courtyards, and it involved adults and children, both male and female. Probably, with the birth of the State at the end of the 4th millennium B.C.E., the most specialized manufacture was placed under the control of the elite, and workshops started to develop around the palace and temple areas. The study of the wooden remains collected during the excavation of the eastern, residential area should provide evidence of the industrial activities within family units. Up to now, we have known of no other proto-urban settlement anywhere in the Middle East that has preserved hundreds of wooden finds in residential deposits.

Around 2700 B.C.E., the major part of the city was destroyed by a fire, which marked the end of Phase 7. Rooms with burnt plaster, filled with ash and burnt remains of roof beams have been excavated in the eastern residential quarter and in the central quarter. The reasons for the disaster are unknown, but there is no evidence that the fire was due to an enemy attack. The old cities were easy prey to fires, and Šahr-e Sukta was probably not an exception. During phase 6, the city was soon reconstructed, although some destroyed houses were left abandoned for more than a century, until the time of the great expansion of the site during phases 5 and 4.

In 1962, the discovery of Dahan-e Ḡolāmān, ca. 40 km northeast of Šahr-e Sukta, revealed macroscopic remains of a city that was considered to be the old Zranka of the Achaemenid inscriptions, Zarin of the classical sources (see DAHAN-E ḠOLĀMĀN), the capital of the satrapy of Drangiana. The presence of roads, private houses, and public buildings testifies to the urban character of the remains, something unusual for the Achaemenid period in Iran. A religious building (no. 3) relates the town to a possible fire cult in the area, later related to Zoroastrianism. The location of Dahan-e Ḡolāmān in a peripheral area, far from the center of the empire, allows one to consider it from a very different perspective from the one usually applied to Achaemenid culture. A new conception of the first half of the 1st millennium B.C.E. in Iran emerges, of which the main aspects can be summed up as follows: (1) an urban core with groups of buildings around it; (2) frequent use (though not very well attested) of water supply channels; (3) precise distinction between public and private spaces.

The presence of a zone close to the urban center where numerous remains of pottery production (Namaki) have been identified, and of a square precinct, suggest in the first case a craftsmen's quarter, and in the second, a military garrison. The city would have had a complex system of functions, amongst which one would be ceremonial-religious (no. 3), one ceremonial-civil (no. 2), one economic (Namaki), and finally, one military-administrative. The basic idea underlying the foundation of Dahan-e Ḡolāmān was clearly related to the history of an Oriental satrapy progressively and slowly absorbed into the political and administrative system. The palatial architecture of Dahan-e Ḡolāmān represents a sort of meeting point of different building traditions and experiences from widely separated geographical areas, that is, those of the palaces of Bactria and Chorasmia, of northwestern Iran, of Fārs, and of Susiana. All of these seem to be reflected in a perfect synthesis at Dahan-e Ḡolāmān. The particular nature of building no. 3, with the presence of different fire installations, leads one to think of a building in some manner related to a fire-oriented cult.

In the last few years, new excavations at Šahr-e Sukta and some trenches at Dahan-e Ḡolāmān have been carried out by the Iranian Cultural Heritage Organization. The first results seem to confirm the extraordinary importance of the sites, adding significant new aspects to our knowledge of the material culture.

Bibliography: P. Amiet and M. Tosi, "Phase 10 at Shahr-i Sokhta: Excavations in Square XDV and the Late 4th Millennium B.C. Assemblage of Sistan," *East and West* 28, 1978, pp. 9-31. P. Amiet, "Les sceaux de Shahr-i Sokhta," in *South Asian Archaeology 1975*, ed. J. E. van Lohuizen-de Leeuw, Leiden, 1979, pp. 3-6. Piero Basaglia, *La Città Bruciata nel Deserto Salato. Archeologi e naturalisti italiani alla riscoperta di una civiltà protourbana nel Sistan iraniano: dieci anni di ricerche archeologiche, presentazione di G. Tucci*, Venice, 1977. I. Behnam, "Šahr-e Sukta," *Honar wa mardom* 126, 1974, pp. 2-6. P. Bernard, "Les traditions orientales dans l'architecture gréco-bactrienne," *JA* 264, 1976, pp. 246-75. R. Biscione, "Dynamics of an Early South Asian Urbanization: the First Period at Shahr-i Sokhta and its Connections with Southern Turkmenia," in *South Asian Archaeology*, ed. N. Hammond, London, 1973, pp. 105-18. Idem, "The Burnt Building of Period IV at Shahr-i Sokhta IV. An Attempt of Functional Analysis from the Distribution of Pottery Types," in *Iranica*, ed. G. Gnoli and A. V. Rossi, Naples, 1979, pp. 291-306. Idem, "Baluchistan Presence in the Ceramic Assemblage of Period I at Shahr-i Sokhta," in *South Asian Archaeology 1981*, ed. B. Allchin, Cambridge, 1984, pp. 118-23. Idem, "The Elusive Phase II at Shahr-i Sokhta," in *South Asian Archaeology 1987*, ed. M. Taddei and P. Callieri, Rome, 1990, pp. 391-409. Idem, G. M. Bulgarelli, L. Costantini, M. Piperno, and M. Tosi, "Archaeological Discoveries and Methodological Problems in the Excavations of Shahr-i Sokhta, Sistan," in *South Asian Archaeology 1973*, ed. J. E. van Lohuizen-De Leeuw and J. J. M. Ubaghs, Leiden, 1974, pp. 12-52. R. Biscione, G. M. Bulgarelli, M. Piperno, and M. Tosi, "Shahr-i Sokhta," *Iran* 11, 1973, pp. 203-5. S. Bökönyi, and L. Bartosiewicz, "A Review of Animal Remains from Shahr-i Sokhta (Eastern Iran)," in *Archaeozoology of the Near East IV B. Proceedings of the 4th International Symposium on the Archaeo-*

zoology of Southern Asia & Adiacent Areas. ARC-P.32, ed. M. Mashkour et al., Groningen, 2000, pp. 116-52. S. Bökönyi, "Preliminary Results of a Thorough Evaluation of the Mammal Bone Material from Shahr-i Sokhta. IsMEO Activities," *East and West* 35, 1985, pp. 426-29. L. Bondioli, and A. Lazzari, "Some Aspects of Data Treatment of the Shahr-i Sokhta and Related Records, in *South Asian Archaeology 1987*, ed. M. Taddei, Rome, 1990, pp. 377-90. G. L. Bonora, C. Domanin, S. Salvatori, and A. Soldini, "The Oldest Graves of the Shahr-i Sokhta Graveyard," in *South Asian Archaeology 1997*, ed. M. Taddei and G. De Marco, Rome, 2000, pp. 495-520. C. E. Bosworth, *Sistan under the Arabs, from the Islamic Conquest to the Rise of the Saffarids (30-250/651-864)*, Rome, 1968. C. Bovington, A. Mahdavi, R. Masoumi, "Tehran University Nuclear Center Radiocarbon Dates II: Shahr-i Sokhta Series," *Radiocarbon* 15/3, 1973, pp. 593-94. G. M. Bulgarelli, "La lavorazione delle perle in pietre dure nel III millennio a.C.: testimonianze da Shahr-i Sokhta (Sistan, Iran)," in G. Lombardo, *Perle orientali. Tradizione antica e artigianato moderno nella lavorazione delle pietre semipreziose in Medio Oriente*, Rome, 1998, pp. 57-70. S. Buson, and M. Vidale, "The Pear-Shaped Beakers of Shahr-i Sokhta: Analysis of the Relationships Between Technological and Morphological Evolution through Experimental Simulation," *East and West* 33, pp. 31-51.

L. Caloi, "The Bone Remains of Small Carnivores from Shahr-i Sohkta," in Meadow and Zeder, eds., 1978, pp. 129-32. Idem, and B. Compagnoni, "Preliminary Remarks on the Bovine Remains at the Archaeological Site of Shahr-i Sokhta (Iranian Sistan) (3200-1800 B.C.)," in *South Asian Archaeology 1979*, ed. H. Härtel, Berlin, 1981, pp. 182-90. G. Cattini, "Administrative Indicators in the Shahr-i Sokhta Eastern Residential Area of Period II (2800-2600 BC)," in *South Asian Archaeology 1997*, ed. M. Taddei and G. De Marco, Rome, 2000, pp. 485-94. J. Chaline, and D. Heimer, "Les rongeurs de la cité antique de Shahr-i Sokhta (Iran) et leur signification paleoethnologique," *Studi di Paletnologia, Paleoantropologia, Paleontologia e Geologia del Quaternario* 2, 1974, pp. 261-78. R. Ciarla, "A Preliminary Analysis of the Manufacture of Alabaster Vessels at Shahr-i Sokhta and Mundigak in the 3rd Millennium BC," in *South Asian Archaeology 1979*, ed. H. Härtel, Berlin, 1981, pp. 45-63. Idem, "New Material in the Study of the Manufacture of Stone Vases at Shahr-i Sokhta. IsMEO Activities," *East and West* 35, 1985, pp. 418-25. B. Compagnoni, "The Bone Remains of *Equus hemionus* from Shahr-i Sokhta," in Meadow and Zeder, eds., 1978, pp. 105-18. Idem, "The Bone Remains of *Gazella subgutturosa* from Shahr-i Sokhta," in Meadow and Zeder, eds., 1978, pp. 119-28. Idem, and M. Tosi, "The Camel: Its Distribution and State of Domestication in the Middle East during the Third Millennium B.C. in the Light of Finds from Shahr-i Sokhta," in Meadow and Zeder, eds., 1978, pp. 91-103. B. Compagnoni, "On the Probable Presence of the Urial (Ovis vignei Blyth) at the Protohistoric Site of Shahr-i Sokhta (Sistan, Iran)," *East and West* 30, pp. 9-15. L. Costantini, M. Tosi, and A. Vigna Taglianti, "Typology and Socioeconomical Implications of Entomological Finds from Some Ancient Near Eastern Sites," *Paléorient* 3, 1977, pp. 247-58. M. Cucarzi, and M. Piperno, "The Possibility to Distinguish Some Classes of Tombs in the Shahri-i Soktha Graveyard," *Rivista di archeologia* 3, 1979, pp. 12-13. P. Daffinà, *L'immigrazione dei Saka nella Drangiana*, Rome, 1967. R. De Nicola, L. Bondioli, A. Lazzari, S. Laurenza, "Uno strumento ipermediale per la visita di un antico sito urbano dell'Asia Medio-orientale," in *1st International Congress on "Science and Technology for the Safeguard of Cultural Heritage in the Mediterranean Basin", Catania, 27 November-2 December 1995*, Palermo, 1998, pp. 1779-85. S. Durante, "The Utilization of Xancus pyrum (L.) at Shahr-i Sokhta: a Further Evidence of Cultural Relations between India and Iran in the the-3rd Millennium BC," in *South Asian Archaeology 1975*, ed. J. E. van Lohuizen-de Leeuw, Leiden, 1979, pp. 27-42.

D. Faccenna, "A New Fragment of Wall-Painting from Ghaga Shar (Kuh-i Khwaga - Sistan, Iran)," *East and West* 31, pp. 83-97. P. Ferioli, E. Fiandra, and S. Tusa, "Stamp Seals and Functional Analysis of their Sealings at Shahr-i Sokhta II-III (2700-2200 BC.)," in *South Asian Archaeology 1975*, ed. J. E. van Lohuizen-de Leeuw, Leiden, 1979, pp. 7-26. E. Fiandra, and C. Pepe, "Typology and Distribution of the Administration Indicators in Eastern Residential Area of Shahr-i Sokhta During Period II (2800-2600 BC). The Sealings," in *South Asian Archaeology 1997*, ed. M. Taddei and G. De Marco, Rome, 2000, pp. 467-83. B. Fishman, and B. Lawn, "University of Pennsylvania Radiocarbon Dates XX: Shahr-i Sokhta Series," *Radiocarbon* 20/2, 1978, pp. 223-24. B. Fishman, H. Forbes, and B. Lawn, "University of Pennsylvania Radiocarbon Dates XIX: Shahr-i Sokhta Series," *Radiocarbon* 19/2, 1977, pp. 204-7. L. Foglini, "L'area di lavorazione del lapislazzuli nei quadrati EWK-EWP," in G. Lombardo, *Perle orientali. Tradizione antica e artigianato moderno nella lavorazione delle pietre semipreziose in Medio Oriente*, Rome, 1998, pp. 71-75. M. Forte, P. Mozzi, and M. Zocchi, "Immagini satellitari e modelli virtuali: interpretazioni geoarcheologiche della regione del Sistan meridionale," *Archeologia e calcolatori* 9, 1998, pp. 271-90. B. Genito, "Una città achemenide tra centro e periferia dell'impero," *Oriens Antiquus* 25/3-4, 1987, pp. 287-317. Idem, "Altari a gradini nell'Iran antico," in G. Gnoli, and L. Lanciotti, eds., *Orientalia Iosephi Tucci Memoriae Dicata*, Rome, 1987, pp. 475-84. Idem, "The Most Frequent Pottery Types at Dahan-e Ḡolāmān and their Spatial Variability," in M. Taddei, and P. Callieri, eds., *Proceedings of the Ninth International Conference of the Association of South Asian Archaeologists in Western Europe, held in the Fondazione Giorgio Cini, Island of San Giorgio Maggiore, 6th-10th July Venice, 1977* II, Rome, 1990, pp. 587-

604. Idem, "The Iranian Empires and Central Asia: an Archaeological Perspective," in *Accademia Nazionale dei Lincei Atti dei Convegni Lincei 127, La Persia e l'Asia Centrale da Alessandro al X secolo, in collaborazione con l'Istituto Italiano per il Medio ed Estremo Oriente, Rome, 9-12 November 1994*, Rome 1996, pp. 401-21. Idem, "The Achaemenids and their Artistic and Architectural Heritage: an Archaeological Perspective," in *Proceedings of the First International Congress on the Archaeology of the Ancient Near East, May 18-23, 1998*, ed. P. Matthiae et al., Rome, 2000, pp. 533-54. Idem, "Dahan-i Ghulaman: una "vicina" periferia dell'Impero Achemenide, " in *Antica Persia, I tesori del Museo Nazionale di Teheran e la ricerca italiana in Iran*, Rome, 2001, pp. XXI-XXXVI. Idem, "Dahan-i Ghulaman," in *Enciclopedia Archeologica Treccani, Asia*, dir. Gherardo Gnoli, sect. Iran e Asia Centrale, coord. Pierfrancesco Calmieri, *1. La protostoria: l'altopiano iranico: l'età del ferro e l'apogeo dei Medi*, Rome, 2004.

G. Gnoli, "Additional Note to the Paper by U. Scerrato," in *La Persia e il mondo greco-romano*, Rome, 1966, pp. 471-76. Idem, *Ricerche Storiche sul Sistān antico*, Rome, 1967. G. Gullini, *Architettura Iranica dagli Achemenidi ai Sasanidi*, Turin, 1964. A. Hauptmann, "Zur frühbronzezeitlichen Metallurgie von Shahr-i Sokhta (Iran)," *Der Anschnitt*, 32/2-3, 1980, pp. 55-61. Idem, and G. Weisgerber, "The Early Bronze Age Copper Metallurgy of Shahr-i Sokhta (Iran)," *Paléorient* 6, 1980, pp. 120-23. A. Hauptmann, T. Reheren, and S. Schmitt-Strecker, "Early Bronze Age Copper Metallurgy at Shahr-i Sokhta (Iran), Reconsidered," in *Man and Mining. Mensch und Bergbau. Studies in Honour of Gerd Weisberger*, ed. I. Stöllner et al., special volume of *Der Anschnitt* 26, Bochum, 2003, pp. 1-16. "IsMEO Activities," *East and West*, 25, 1975, pp. 550-52. P. L. Kohl, "A Note on Chlorite Artefacts from Shahr-i Sokhta, *East and West* 27, 1977, pp. 111-27. C. C. Lamberg-Karlovsky, and M. Tosi, "Shahr-i Sokhta and Tepe Yahya: Tracks on the Earliest History of the Iranian Plateau," *East and West* 23, 1973, pp. 15-53. N. Laneri, "Analisi radiografica e macrostrutturale delle ciotole tronco-coniche dell'inizio del III millennio a.C., Shahr-i Sokhta (Iran)," *Orient Express* 1, 1996, pp. 17-19. Idem, and M. Vidale, "An Anatomy of the Truncated-Conical Bowl of Shahr-i Sokhta," *East and West* 48, 1998, pp. 225-64. A. Lazzari, "Bibliography of Shahr-i Sokhta (Sistan) 1968-1997," *Journal of Humanities. University of Sistan and Balouchestan* 5/1, 1999, pp. 168-89. E. C. Lombardi Pardini, and E. Pardini, "Sexual Dimorphism in an Ancient Sistan Population (Shahr-i Sokhta)," in *South Asian Archaeology 1989*, ed. C. Jarrige, Madison, Wisc., 1992, pp. 223-25.

R. Macchiarelli, and P. Passarello, "Analisi paleodemografica comparativa della popolazione di Shahr-i Sokhta (Sistan, Iran, III millennio a.C.)," *Rivista di Antropologia* 66, 1988, pp. 5-36. L. Mariani, *The Operation Carried out by the Italian Restoration Mission in Sistan 1975-1976 (2534-2535) Campaigns. Conservation of the Mud-Brick Structures in the Sacred Building QN3 at Dahan-i Ghulaman, and the Detachment of the Fresco in the Palace at Kuh-i Khwağa*, Rome and Tehran, 1977. Idem, "Conservation Work on Building 3 at Dahan-e Ghulaman," in *South Asian Archaeology 1977*, ed. M. Taddei, Naples, 1979, pp. 737-54. Idem, "Conservation Work on Building 3 at Dahan-e Ghulaman, Sistan," in *South Asian Archaeology 1977*, ed. M. Taddei, Naples, 1979, pp. 737-54. Idem, "Problems and Methods in Resource Mapping for the Paleoeconomic Study of the Hilmand Valley in Proto-Historic Times, in *South Asian Archaeology 1979*, ed. H. Härtel, Berlin, 1981, pp. 13-27. Idem, "Craftsmen's Quarters in the Proto-Urban Settlements of the Middle East: the Surface Analysis," in *South Asian Archaeology 1981*, ed. B. Allchin, Cambridge, 1984, pp. 118-23. Idem, and M. Tosi, "L'universo familiare a Shahr-i Sokhta," in *Orientalia Iosephi Tucci Memoriae Dicata*, ed. G. Gnoli and L. Lanciotti, II, Rome, 1987, pp. 853-79. L. Mariani, "The Monumental Area of Shahr-i Sokta: Notes from a Surface Reconnaissance. *South Asian Archaeology 1985*, ed. K. Frifelt, and P. Sørensen, London, 1989, pp. 114-36. Idem, "An Overview of the Architecture Techniques at Shahr-i Sokhta," in *South Asian Archaeology 1987*, ed. M. Taddei, Rome, 1990, pp. 411-26. Idem, "The Eastern Residential Area at Shahr-i Sokhta," in *South Asian Archaeology 1989*, ed. C. Jarrige, Madison, Wis., pp. 181-93. R. H. Meadow and M. A. Zeder, eds., *Approaches to Faunal Analysis in the Middle East*, Peabody Museum Bulletin 2, Cambridge, Mass., 1978. O. Nalesini, "Social Implication of the Morphological Variability of the Decorative Motifs of Shahr-i Sokhta II Buff Ware: an Outline," in *South Asian Archaeology 1981*, ed. B. Allchin, Cambridge, 1984, pp. 108-17. S. Nishimura, and M. Tosi, "Fission-Track Ages of the Remains Excavated at Shahr-i Sokhta and Kangavar, Iran," in *The Memorial Volume of the VIIth International Congress of Iranian Art & Archaeology*, ed. M. Y. Kiāni, Tehran, 1976, pp. 221-85.

E. Pardini, and A. A. Sarvari-Negahban, "Craniologia degli inumati di Shahr-i Sokhta (Sistan, Iran)," *Archivio per l'antropologia e l'etnologia* 106, 1976, pp. 273-321. Idem, "Gli inumati di Shahr-i Sokhta (Sistan, Iran). Studio osteologico preliminare," *Archivio per l'antropologia e l'etnologia* 107, 1977, pp. 159-235. Idem, "Gli inumati di Shahr-i Sokhta (Sistan, Iran)," *Archivio per l'antropologia e l'etnologia* 109-10, 1979-80, pp. 521-608. Idem and E. C. Lombardi Pardini, "La struttura biologica della popolazione di Shahr-i Sokhta (III millennio a.C., Sistan, Iran)," in *Orientalia Iosephi Tucci Memoriae Dicata*, ed. G. Gnoli and L. Lanciotti, II, Rome, 1988, pp. 1061-78. E. Pardini, and E. C. Lombardi Pardini, "The Somatic Aspect of the Shahr-i Sokhta Inhabitants from Inhumed Skeletal Remains," in *South Asian Archaeology 1987*, ed. M. Taddei and P. Callieri, Rome, 1990, pp. 453-57. M. Piperno, "Micro-Drilling at Shahr-i Sokhta: the Making and Use of Lithic Drill-Heads," in *South Asian Archaeology*, ed. N. Hammond, London, 1973, pp. 119-29. Idem, "Grave 77 at Shahr-i Sokhta: Evidence of Technological Specialization in the 3rd millennium B.C.," *East and West* 26, 1976, pp. 9-12. Idem, "Socio-Economic Implications from the Graveyard of Shahr-i Sokhta," in *South Asian Archaeology 1977*, ed. M. Taddei, Naples, 1979, pp. 123-40. Idem, "Aspects of Ethnical Multiplicity Across the Shahr-i Sokhta Graveyard," *Oriens Antiquus* 25, 1986, pp. 257-70. Idem, and S. Salvatori, "Evidence of Western Cultural Connections from a Phase 3 Group of Graves at Shahr-i Sokhta," in *Mesopotamien und seine Nachbarn (XXV Rencontre Assyriologique Internationale) Berlin 3.-7. Juli 1978*, ed. H.-J. Nissen and J. Renger, Berlin, 1982, pp. 79-85. M. Piperno, and S. Salvatori, "Recent Results and New Perspectives from the Research at the Graveyard of Shahr-i Sokhta, Sistan, Iran," *AIUON* 43/2, 1983, pp. 173-91. M. Piperno, and M. Tosi, "The Graveyard of Sahr-e Suxteh (A Presentation of the 1972 and 1973 Campaigns)," in *Proceedings of the 3rd Annual Symposium on Archaeological Research in Iran*, ed. F. Bagherzadeh, Tehran, 1975, pp. 121-40. M. Piperno, and M. Tosi, "The Graveyard of Shahr-i Sokhta, Iran," *Archaeology* 28, 1975, pp. 186-97. S. Pracchia, "Preliminary Analysis of the Shahr-i Sokhta II Buff Ware Painted Figuration: Some Observations for a Systematic Classification," in *South Asian Archaeology 1981*, ed. B. Allchin, Cambridge, 1984, pp. 98-107. Idem, "Shahr-e Sokhta," *Enciclopedia dell'arte antica, classica orientale. Secondo supplemento 1971-1994*, IV, Rome, 1997, pp. 59-61. G. Pugliese Carratelli, "Greek Inscriptions of the Middle East," *East and West* 16, pp. 34-35.

S. M. Sajjadi, "Negāhi beh farhanghā-ye nāšenāḵta-ye nima-šarqi-ye falāt-e Iran: Šahr-e Suḵta, Irān," *Farāvahar* 1/276, 1983, pp. 86-109. Idem, "Negāhi beh farhanghā-ye nāšenāḵta-ye nima-šarqi-ye falāt-e Iran: Šahr-e Suḵta, Irān," *Farāvahar* 2/277, 1983, pp. 208-37. Idem, "Negāhi beh farhanghā-ye nāšenāḵta-ye nima-šarqi-ye falāt-e Iran: Šahr-e Suḵta, Irān," *Farāvahar* 3/278, 1983, pp. 273-83. Idem, "Šahr wa Šahrnešini dar nima-šarqi-ye falāt-e Irān, Šahr-e Suḵta," in *Naẓar-e ejmāli beh šahrnešini wa šahrsāzi dar Irān*, ed. M. Y. Kiāni, Tehran, 1986, pp. 51-77. S. Salvatori, and M. Vidale, *Shahr-i Sokhta 1975-1978: Central Quarters Excavations. Preliminary Report*, Rome, 1997. Idem, "Sequential Analysis and Architectural Remains in the Central Quarters of Shahr-i Sokhta," in *South Asian Archaeology 1977*, ed. M. Taddei, Naples, 1979, pp. 141-48. G. Santini, "A Preliminary Note on Animal Figurines from Shahr-i Sokhta," in *South Asian Archaeology 1987*, ed. M. Taddei and P. Callieri, Rome, 1990, pp. 427-51. U. Scerrato, "A Probable Achaemenid Zone in Persian Sistān, *East and West* 13, pp. 186-97. Idem, "A Lost City of Seistan," *Illustrated London News*, Archaeological sec. 2255, 29 October 1966, pp. 20-21. Idem, "Excavations at Dahan-i Ghulaman (Seistān-Iran), First Preliminary Report (1962-1963)," *East and West*, N.S., 16/1-2, 1966, pp. 9-30. Idem, "L'edificio sacro di Dahan-e Ghulaman (Sistan)," in *La Persia e il mondo greco-romano*, Rome, 1966, pp. 457-70. Idem, "La missione archeologica italiana nel Sistan persiano," *Il Veltro* 14/1-2, February-April 1970, pp. 123-40. Idem, "Missions archéologiques italiennes au Sistan," in *The Memorial Volume of the Vth International Congress of Iranian Art & Archaeology, Tehran, Isfahan, Shiraz, 11th-18th April 1968*, Tehran, 1972, pp. 200-203. Idem, "A proposito dello Airyana Vaejah. Notizie sulla possibilità di allevamento del bovino nella Drangiana come attività autonoma," in *Gururajamanjarika. Studi in onore di Giuseppe Tucci*, I, Naples, 1974, pp. 101-12. Idem, "Evidence of Religious Life at Dahan-i Ghulamān, Sistān, in *South Asian Archaeology 1977*, Naples, 1979, pp. 709-35.

M. Tosi, "Excavations at Shahr-i Sokta, a Chalcolithic Settlement in the Iranian Sistan, Preliminary Report on the First Campaign," *East and West* 18, 1968, pp. 9-66. Idem, "Excavations at Shahr-i Sokhta. Preliminary Report on the Second Campaign," *East and West* 19, 1969, pp. 109-22. Idem, "Shahr-e Sukhteh," *Bastan chenasi va honar-e Iran* 4, 1969, pp. 29-42. Idem, "Shahr-i Sokhta: Un insediamento protostorico nel Sistan iraniano," in *Atti del convegno internazionale "La Persia nel Medioevo*," Accademia dei Lincei, Quaderno 160, Rome, 1971, pp. 405-17. Idem, "Seistan v bronzovom veke. Raskopki v Shahri-Sokhte" (Sistān in the Bronze Age. Excavations at Šahr-e Suḵta), *Sovetskaya Arkheologiya* 3, 1971, pp. 15-30. Idem, "Shahr-i Sokhta: un contributo degli archeologi italiani allo studio delle più antiche civiltà urbane ad oriente della Mesopotamia, " *La Parola del Passato* 142-44, 1972, pp. 186-208. Idem, "La lavorazione degli elementi di collana a Shahr-i Sokhta," *Rivista di geo-archeologia* 1, 1973, pp. 15-20. Idem, "The Cultural Sequence of Shahr-i Sokhta," *Bullettin of the Asian Institute of the Pahlavi University* 3, 1973, pp. 64-80. Idem, "The Lapis Lazuli Trade across the Iranian Plateau in the 3rd mill. B.C.," in *Gururājamañjarikā, Studi in Onore di Giuseppe Tucci*, Naples, 1974, pp. 3-22. Idem, "A Topographical and Stratigraphical Periplus of Sahr-e Suxteh," in *Proceedings of the IVth Annual Symposium on Archaeological Research in Iran*, ed. F. Bagherzadeh, Tehran, 1976, pp. 130-58. Idem, "Shahr-i Sokhta," *Iran* 14, 1976, pp. 167-68. Idem, "Ricerche archeologiche sulla protostoria del Sistan," in *Un decennio di ricerche archeologiche*, Quaderni de "La Ricerca Scientifica" 100, Rome, 1978, pp. 519-48. Idem, "The Development of Urban Societies in Turan and the Mesopotamian Trade with the East: the Evidence from Shahr-i Sokhta," in *Mesopotamien und seine Nachbarn (XXV Rencontre Assyriologique Internationale) Berlin 3.-7. Juli 1978*, ed. H.-J. Nissen and J. Renger, Berlin, 1982, pp. 57-77. Idem, ed., *Prehistoric Sistan* 1, Rome, 1983. Idem, "Shahr-i Sokhta: 5000 Jahre städtische Kultur in der Seistan-Wüste," *Bild der Wissenschaft* 10, 1983, pp. 47-62. Idem, "The Joint ICAR/IsMEO Delivering Program: a Constrained Return to Shahr-i

Sokhta. IsMEO Activities," *East and West* 34, 1984, pp. 466-82 (in coop. with S. Pracchia and R. Macchiarelli). Idem, "Gli Italiani a Shahr-i Sokhta," in *Antica Persia. I tesori del Museo Nazionale di Tehran e la ricerca italiana in Iran*. Rome, 2001, pp. XXI-XXV. M. Vidale, "The Pear-Shaped Beaker of Shahr-i Sokhta: Evolution of a Ceramic Morphotype During the 3rd Millennium BC," in *South Asian Archaeology 1981*, ed. B. Allchin, Cambridge, 1984, pp. 81-97. Idem, and M. Tosi, "The Development of Wheel Throwing at Shahr-i Sokhta. Slow and Fast Revolutions Towards Statehood," *East and West* 46, 1996, pp. 251-69.

(BRUNO GENITO)

vii. IRANIAN STUDIES, ISLAMIC PERIOD

The earliest known references to Persia by Italian writers are gleaned from numerous notes in the oldest medieval travel accounts, dating from the 13th century onwards. Marco Polo's *Il Milione* (comp. 1298), which is a great inventory of literary traditions (see Gabriel, pp. 35-39), contains interesting observations on Persia, particularly on the cities Tabriz, Solṭāniya, Sāva, Kāšān, Yazd, and Kerman). So does the *Itinerarium* of the Dominican monk Ricoldo da Monte Croce (1243-1320). The first scientific study of the Persian language began in the context of Franciscan and Dominican missionaries in Iran, Armenia, and the Crimea, from which originated the so-called *Codex Cumanicus* (Cod. Mar. Lat. DXLIX, Biblioteca Marciana, Venice). This is a Persian-Latin-Cuman Turkish dictionary, which was probably redacted around 1330 (it may have belonged to the personal library of Francesco Petrarca, 1304-74). The first attempt to render a formal transcription system of Persian in Latin characters, and with diacritic signs, has been found on the margins of a manuscript of a Persian translation of the Four Gospels dated 738/1338 (Vatican Apostolic Library, MS Borg. Pers. 19). The glosses, especially those inserted in St. John's Gospel, reveal a deep knowledge of Persian lexicon and syntax, and show an advanced method of transliteration. The author of the glosses may possibly be identified as Giovanni of Florence (d. 1347), a Dominican priest who served as the bishop of Tiflis and was active for many years in the monastery of Kirnë in Azerbaijan (Piemontese, 2000, p. 125).

Outside of these restricted circles, knowledge of Persian long remained superficial. In cultivated European milieus, the existence of another literary language of the Islamic Orient distinct from Arabic was not really clear. A new process of conscious political observation and of the cultural discovery of Persia emerged with the accession of Uzun Ḥasan (r. 1457-78). The interest, particularly of the Republic of Venice and the Papacy, in the possibility of establishing a common alliance with Persia against the Ottomans, led to an active exchange of embassies (see above, ii). A secondary result of this activity on the Italian side was the publication of numerous accounts of Persia, mainly geopolitical in character. The travel diaries of the Venetian envoys Giosafat Barbaro (1413-94, q.v.) and Ambrogio Contarini (1429-99, q.v.), although mainly concerned with the figure of Uzun Ḥasan and his reign, also recount the general situation of the country and contain detailed descriptions of the towns they visited (Lockhart et al, 1973). The documents and considerations collected in the *Diarii* of Marin Sanudo il Giovane deal with the rise to power of Shah Esmāʿil (see Scarcia Amoretti, 1979), and Michele Membré's *Relazione di Persia* (1542) is a most objective source on Safavid power under Shah Ṭahmāsp I. The period between the rise of Uzun Ḥasan and the death of Shah Esmāʿil is also treated in an interesting, firsthand chronicle ascribed to Giovanni Maria Angiolello (d. 1525, q.v.), a Venetian merchant enslaved by the Ottomans and then sent twice on missions to Persia. The accession of Shah Esmāʿil, the "Sofi," was widely noticed in Italy, where he was even popularly seen (as a recently discovered note by Leonardo da Vinci indicates) as a "new prophet" (Ponte, 1977). (For bibliography of the travelers and their works, see above, iii.)

From the middle of the 16th century, the acquisition of an increasing number of Persian manuscripts laid the basis for direct research on Persian language and literature as distinct from Arabic and Turkish, and thereby for penetration into the heart of Persian culture. A first step was taken in 1548 when Stefan V, patriarch of the Christian province of Greater Armenia, whose capital was at the time Tabriz, presented Pope Paul III with a rare Persian Gospel, now conserved in Florence. Of greater impact was the introduction inside an erudite Venetian circle, via a certain Christoforo Armeno, of the reworked translation of some Persian text that was based, it appears, primarily on the poem *Hašt behešt* (comp. 700/1301) by Amir Ḵosrow Dehlavi (q.v.). The translation was published as *Peregrinaggio di tre giovani figliuoli del re di Serendippo* (Pilgrimage of the three princes of Serendip; Venezia 1557). This, the first Persian literary text to be published in a European language, was an enormous success and was translated elsewhere in Europe (Cerulli, 1975), contributing to the birth of the genre of the detective novel and occasioning the coinage (by Horace Walpole in 1754) of the new word "serendipity."

Also in the 16th century, some Oriental works were published, for the first time in Europe, in several Italian towns. In 1584 Giovan Battista Raimondi (ca. 1536-1614), professor of mathematics and philosophy, founded in Rome the Medici Oriental Press (Stamperia orientale Medicea), which printed several Arabic and Persian texts; these included the first printing of Avicenna's (q.v.) medical Canon (*al-Qānun fe'l-ṭebb*) in 1593. Raimondi, the "greatest Italian Orientalist of the age defined the Persian language as the most beautiful in the world, divinely endowed with the spirit of expression of concepts in poetry" (Piemontese, 1988, p. 101). Yet the majority of Raimondi's editions and translations of Persian texts and lexicons, as well as his studies, including a noteworthy Persian grammar, remained in draft form. His print sample of a *ḡazal* by Šāhi Sabzavāri (d. 857/1453) survives in Florence, even though not published, and represents the first Persian text ever printed. Between 1591 and 1607, Giovan Battista Vecchietti and his brother, Gerolamo, traveled to Egypt, Persia, and India and collected Arabic and Persian manuscripts, they collaborated with Raimondi. Giovan Battista had a good knowledge of Persian, and he laid the foundations for the study of Judeo-Persian literature (q.v.). Gerolamo brought to Italy from Cairo a codex (Florence, Biblioteca Nazionale Centrale, Fondo Magliabechi, MS C1. III.24) which is the oldest extant manuscript of the (first half of the) *Šāh-nāma* of Ferdowsi, dated 614/1217 (Piemontese, 1980). The pioneering works of these three scientists and philosophers-turned-orientalists had a great impact on "the European scientific and Orientalist circles" (Piemontese, p. 101).

In the 17th century, with the decline in Venetian power, Italian Oriental studies tended to return to the dominion of ecclesiastical institutions, such as the Sacra Congregatio de Propaganda Fide, whose main attention continued to be devoted to practical linguistic matters, and which in 1654 printed the first Persian grammar by an Italian scholar. The work was written by the Carmelite Ignazio di Gesù, a missionary and author of a Latin-Persian lexicon and of another interesting transliteration system for Arabic script (on him, see also MANDAEANS i. HISTORY at *iranica.com*). Another Christian missionary, Maurizio Garzoni, published the first European grammar of the Kurdish language in 1787. The other field of ecclesiastical engagement was the Islamic-Christian controversy, in which the Roman traveler and scholar Pietro Della Valle (1586-1652, q.v.) also took part. Yet Della Valle's activity went further. Besides writing valuable accounts of his stay at the court of Shah ʿAbbas I in Isfahan, he collected and studied several Persian manuscripts. He was among the first Europeans to write Persian in Arabic script, and probably the first to spread Hafez's fame through European literary circles (Bertotti, 1990). Thereafter, to the end of the 18th century, Iranian studies in Italy on the whole waned, although some important manuscript collections were acquired, such as those of the scientist, L. F. Marsili (1658-1730), of Bologna and of the antiquarian, J. Nani (1725-1797), in Venice.

A renewed interest in Iran followed the rise to political ascendancy of the Kingdom of Piedmont-Sardinia (from the 1830s on), and the expansion of its political aim to encompass unification of the Italian states. To the Sardinian diplomat and orientalist, Romualdo Tecco, we owe the formation of the collection of Persian manuscripts in the Royal Library in Turin. The Italian diplomatic mission to Persia in 1862 had important implications for scholarship. For the occasion G. Berchet was commissioned to produce his book *La repubblica di Venezia e la Persia* (Torino, 1865), which documented the relations between the Republic of Venice and Persia, from Uzun Ḥasan's time onward. Moreover, one of the embassy's members, Giacomo Lignana (1827-91), on his return laid the foundation for teaching Persian at the Naples Oriental Institute [Istituto Universitario Orientale] (1863-65), a task later continued by G. de Vincentiis (1845-1907), and Luigi Bonelli (1865-1947). The chair for teaching Iranian languages at Rome University was established in 1871. In Turin, Italo Pizzi (1849-1920), a scholar of classical Persian literature, completed his verse translation of Ferdowsi's *Šāh-nāma*. Among his students were V. Rugarli (1860-1900) and C. A. Nallino, who both contributed in different fields of Iranian studies. Until the middle of the 20th century, however, Iranian studies in Italy were not conducted by specialists, but by scholars of other fields associated in varying degrees with the Iranian world and culture: islamists, arabists, turcologists, historians of religion, linguists, and others. During this period contributions to the study of Islamic Iran were made by Leone Caetani (1896-1935), U. Monneret de Villard (1881-1954), Ettore Rossi (1894-1955), E. Cerulli (1898-1988), and F. Gabrieli (1904-96). Caetani collected the Persian manuscripts now in the Lincei Academy in Rome. Cerulli brought to Italy a collection of 1,055 manuscripts and some lithographed books concerned with the passion plays (*taʿzia*); housed in the Vatican Library (Rossi and Bombaci), these have constituted the basis for specialized contributions on the subject by Italian scholars. In addition to the above collections, thirty Italian libraries in fifteen different towns at present count over 400 other Persian manuscripts (Piemontese, 1989, pp. XV-XX).

After World War II, the transformation of Italy from a prevalently agricultural into an industrial country had consequences also on university structure. In the area of Iranian studies, study groups and single researchers have developed increasingly specialized fields and methodologies, at a pace with the contemporary world's scientific tendencies. In 1957, for the first time a chair of Persian language and literature was set up at the Naples Oriental Institute (now L'Università degli Studi di Napoli "L'Orientale"), first held by A. Bausani (1921-88). Since the middle of the 20th century, all aspects of Persia in the Islamic period—language, literature, history, religious history, law, etc.—have been subjects of study in Italy, and many classical and less renowned literary texts have been translated from Persian into Italian. At present four Italian universities (Naples, Rome, Venice, Bologna) house chairs devoted to different fields of studies on Islamic Iran, and since 1984 a specialized Ph.D. program in Iranian studies has treated subjects related to both the pre-Islamic and the Islamic periods. A scholarly association, Societas Iranologica Europaea (see www.societasiranologicaeu.org), was founded in 1983 in Rome, at the Istituto Italiano per il Medio ed Estremo Oriente [IsMEO] (now Istituto italiano per l'Africa e l'Oriente [IsIAO]; for these, see below, vii.a and b), to promote Iranian studies with the participation of scholars worldwide. Its first congress was held in Turin in 1987.

See also below, xvi. CURRENT CENTERS OF IRANIAN STUDIES IN ITALY.

Bibliography: See also bibliographies above, ii. DIPLOMATIC AND COMMERCIAL RELATIONS WITH PERSIA; iii. TRAVELOGUES.

R. Almagià, "Giovan Battista e Gerolamo Viaggiatori in Oriente," *Atti della Accademia Nazionale dei Lincei.*

Rendiconti. Classe di scienze morali, Serie 8, 11, 1956, pp. 313-50. F. Bertotti, "Un viaggiatore romano e un poeta persiano: Pietro Della Valle estimatore e divulgatore di Ḥāfiẓ," *Islàm Storia e civiltà* 9/2, 1990, pp. 121-27. Enrico Cerulli, "Una raccolta persiana di nonelle tradotte a Venezia nel 1557," *Atti della Accademia Nationale dei Lincei*, Memorie classe di science morali, storiche e filologiche, Ser. VIII, 18, 1975, pp. 247-363. Alessandro Coletti, "Maurizio Garzoni padre della linguistica curda," in U. Marazzi ed., *La Conoscenza dell 'Asia et dell 'Africa in Italia nei secoli XVIII e XIX*, I/1, Naples, 1984, pp. 535-41. Maurizio Garzoni, *Grammatica e vocabolario della lingua kurda*, Roma, 1787. A. de Gubernatis, *Matériaux pour servir à l'histoire des etudes orientales en Italie*, Paris, 1876. N. di Lenna, "Ricerche intorno allo storico Giovanni Maria Angiolello (degli Anzolelli), patrizio Vicentino, 1451-1525," *Archivio veneto-tridentino* 5, 1924, pp. 1-56. Alfons Gabriel, *Die Erforschung Persiens*, Vienna, 1952. F. Gaeta and L. Lockhart, eds., *I Viaggi di Pietro Della Valle. Lettere dalla Persia* I, Rome, 1972. G. Gnoli, "Italian Contributions to the Study of Persian Drama," *East and West*, N.S, 15/1-2, 1964-65, pp. 79-88. Ignatius di Gesù, *Grammatica linguae Persicae*, Rome, 1661. L. Lockhart et al, eds., *I viaggi in Persia degli ambasciatori veneti Barbaro e Contarini*, Rome, 1973.

U. Monneret de Villard, "La vita, le opere e i viaggi di frate Ricoldo da Montecroce, O.P.," *Orientalia Christiana Periodica*, 9, 1944, pp. 227-74. P. Orsatti, "Grammatica e lessicografia persiana nell'opera di P. Ignazio di Gesù," *Rivista degli Studi Orientali* 55, 1981, pp. 55-85. A. M. Piemontese, "La 'Grammatica Persiana' di G. B. Raimondi," *Rivista degli Studi Orientali* 53, 1979, pp. 141-52. Idem, "Nuova luce su Firdawsī: uno 'Šāhnāma' datato 614 H. 1217 a Firenze," *Annali dell'Istituto Universitario Orientale di Napoli*, Nuova Serie 30, 1980, pp. 1-91. Idem, *Bibliografia italiana dell'Iran (1462-1982)*, 2 vols., Napoli, 1982. Idem, "Italian Scholarship on Iran (An Outline, 1557-1987)," *Iranian Studies* 20, 1987, pp. 99-130. Idem, *Catalogo dei manoscritti persiani conservati nelle biblioteche d'Italia*, Roma, 1989. Idem, ed., *Amir Khusrau da Dehli. Le otto novelle del paradiso*, Soveria Mannelli, 1996. Idem, "Un testo latino-persiano connesso al Codex Cumanicus," *AAASH* 53/1-2, 2000, pp. 121-32. G. Ponte, "Attorno a Leonardo da Vinci: L'attesa popolare del Sofì di Persia in Venezia e Firenze all'inizio del Cinquecento," *La Rassegna della Letturatura Italiana*, 81, 1977, pp. 5-19. E. Rossi, *Elenco dei manoscritti persiani della Bibliotheca Vaticana: Vaticani, Barberiniani, Borgiani, Rossiani*, Città del Vaticano, 1948. E. Rossi and A. Bombaci, *Elenco di drammi religiosi persiani (fondo mss. Vaticani Cerulli)*, Città del Vaticano, 1961. B. Scarcia Amoretti, *Šah Ismail nei "Diarii" di Marin Sanudo*, Rome, 1979. U. Tucci, "Una relazione di Giovan Battista. Vecchietti sulla Persia e sul Regno di Hormuz, 1587," *Oriente Moderno* 35/4, 1955, pp. 149-60.

(MARIO CASARI)

viii. PERSIAN MANUSCRIPTS

Italy houses 439 Persian manuscripts in two public archives and thirty public libraries located in fifteen different cities. All of them have been catalogued by Angelo Michele Piemontese (1989). Three more manuscripts are preserved at the Harvard University Center for Italian Renaissance Studies at Villa "I Tatti" in Florence, which, besides the three bound codices, possesses some loose folios from Persian manuscripts as well. Paintings in Persian manuscripts from the Harvard University Center (the Berenson collection) have been studied by Richard Ettinghausen (q.v.) in 1962, and their description is given by Piemontese (1984a). Additionally, within Vatican City, 189 Persian manuscripts are preserved at the Biblioteca Apostolica Vaticana (hereinafter the Vatican Library): 158 are part of the Vatican collection, 23 of the Borgia collection, 6 of Barberini collection, and 2 of Rossi collection. These manuscripts were catalogued by Ettore Rossi (1948). The Vatican Library also owns an important collection of Persian religious dramas (*taʿzia*). This collection was acquired by Enrico Cerulli (q.v.) during one of his sojourns in Iran in 1950-54 as the Italian ambassador. It was catalogued by Ettore Rossi and Alessio Bombaci (1961) and includes 1055 manuscripts, of which 15 are in Turkish, and a few others are written in both Turkish and Persian. Finally, 13 Persian manuscripts are part of a collection, mostly Arabic, purchased by the Vatican in 1927 and known as the Sbath collection, so called after the Syrian priest, Paul Sbath (1887-1945), whose original name was Bulos Sbāṭ al-Soryāni al-Ḥalabi, and who himself was a collector of manuscripts. Persian manuscripts of the Sbath collection were described by Piemontese (1978).

Apart from the Vatican Library, other Italian libraries that own the larger number of Persian manuscripts are: the Medicean-Laurentian Library in Florence (83 MSS); the Library of the University of Bologna and the Library of the National Academy of the Lincei in Rome (60 MSS each); the Marciana National Library in Venice (46 MSS); and the Ambrosiana Library in Milan (37 MSS). In fact, Persian manuscripts preserved in Italy are parts of larger collections of Oriental codices which, starting in the Renaissance period, were acquired for different reasons by various Italian courts, or through the initiative of noble families, religious institutions, and important members of the Catholic church, as well as individual scholars and travelers. The geographical dispersion of the manuscripts, which had been usually kept in Oriental funds without any linguistic distinction (except for the funds of the Vatican Library), has been a major obstacle for identifying and cataloguing them (for an updated report on the localization of Islamic manuscripts with references to the published and unpublished catalogues see Heine for the Vatican; and Orsatti, Pirone, and Gallotta for Italy).

Italy was the first European country to collect Oriental manuscripts. The history of acquiring Persian manuscripts for Italian collections is discussed in the studies of Giorgio Levi Della Vida (1939), Ettore Rossi (1948, pp. 11-16),

Angelo Michele Piemontese (1979a, 1982, 1989), Stephan Roman (pp. 140-65), and Paola Orsatti (1996b, pp. 168-73). The first Persian manuscript in an Italian library appears to have been a copy of the Gospel of Matthew in Persian dated 712/1312 (MS Vat. Pers. 4), acquired by the Vatican Library before 1570 (Levi Della Vida, pp. 167-69; Rossi, 1948, pp. 29-30; for the Persian copies of the Gospels preserved in Italy and in the Vatican see Rossi, 1948, index; Piemontese, 1989, esp. pp. 228-29; Gulbenkian).

It was also in Rome, during the late 16th and early 17th century, that an important initiative led to an interest in collecting Oriental manuscripts in general, including the Persian ones. Under Pope Gregory XIII (1572-85), the printing house 'Stamperia Orientale Medicea' was founded by Cardinal Ferdinando I de' Medici (1549-1609, Grand Duke of Tuscany from 1587) in order to print texts that could be used in promoting Catholicism among Muslims, and for refuting the rites of Eastern Christians. In 1586 Ferdinando I de' Medici acquired a collection of more than 100 Oriental manuscripts, including some Persian, from the Jacobite Patriarch Ignazio Neʿmat-Allāh Aṣfar of Mardin. Other Persian manuscripts were purchased for the 'Stamperia Orientale Medicea' by the brothers Giovan Battista Vecchietti (1552-1619), and Gerolamo Vecchietti (1557-ca. 1640), during their several missions to the East commissioned by the papacy. Furthermore, Giovan Battista reached Persia and India during one of his Oriental journeys (1598-1608) and became particularly excited by the Persian translations of Biblical texts and by the Judaeo-Persian texts which he collected (Almagià, pp. 321-23, 339). The manuscripts, either specially acquired by the Vecchietti brothers for the 'Stamperia Orientale Medicea' or collected on their own, are at present scattered among different libraries: the Medicean-Laurentian Library and the National Library in Florence, the Vatican Library, the National Libraries in Naples and Venice, and the Bibliothèque nationale de France in Paris (Richard, 1980).

Gerolamo Vecchietti purchased in Cairo the most remarkable Persian manuscript preserved in Italy—a copy of the *Šāh-nāma* dated 30 Moḥarram 614/9 May 1217 (Florence, National Library, MS Cl.III.24; Piemontese, 1989, no. 145), which contains the first part of the epic only. The manuscript, identified and described by Piemontese (1980), is the earliest known dated manuscript of Ferdowsi's poem, and it was used as the basis for the critical edition of the *Šāh-nāma* by Djalal Khaleghi-Motlagh (8 vols., New York, 1988-2007; see also idem, 1985-86, I, pp. 380-81; II, pp. 31 ff.). The manuscript has been reproduced in Tehran both in facsimile (Ferdowsi, 1369 Š./1990) and as a typeset edition (Ferdowsi, 1996-98, 2 vols., publication still continues at the time of writing this article).

Among the manuscripts brought to Italy by Giovan Battista Vecchietti, mention should be made of a copy of the Judaeo-Persian Pentateuch, preserved at the Vatican Library as MS Vat. Pers. 61 (Rossi, 1948, p. 87). Ignazio Guidi (q.v.) made a preliminary study of it, and Herbert Paper published the text in Latin transliteration (1965-68). The National Library in Naples possesses a copy of the Persian version of the Book of Psalms (MS III.G.34; Piemontese, 1989, no. 233), which was made in Lār in 1601 under the supervision of Giovan Battista Vecchietti (an identical 'twin' manuscript is preserved in Bibliothèque nationale de France in Paris as MS Supplément persan 1; see Richard, 1980, pp. 295-96). In 1602 Vecchietti brought from Hormuz a copy of Asadi-Ṭusi's (ca. 1000-1072/73, q.v.) Persian lexicon entitled *Loḡat-e fors*, which is dated to 733/1332-33 and is preserved in the Vatican Library as MS Vat. Pers. 22 (Rossi, 1948, pp. 49-51). This manuscript was used as the main copy in Paul Horn's edition of the text published in Berlin in 1897 (Horn).

The collection of manuscripts that once belonged to the Patriarch Ignazio Neʿmat-Allāh Aṣfar includes a 16th-century copy (dated 8 Šawwāl 954/21 November 1547) of a 13th-century Persian *Diatessaron*, that is a compilation in which the four Gospels are 'harmonized' in a single work. At present, it is preserved as MS Or. 81 in the Medicean-Laurentian Library in Florence (Piemontese, 1989, no. 140; studied and edited by Messina in 1943 and 1951).

The superintendent of the 'Stamperia Orientale Medicea', Giovan Battista Raimondi (d. 1614), left behind numerous texts on Persian linguistics in manuscript form, which are at present dispersed as separate manuscripts between libraries in Florence and Venice (Piemontese, 1979b). Based on Raimondi's studies and translations of Persian lexicons and grammars, Flamino Clementino Amerino—one of Raimondi's collaborators, who worked in the convent of the Chierici Regolari Minori in Rome and is otherwise unknown—compiled a grammatical text in 1614 that is considered the earliest unpublished Persian grammar written in Europe. It is preserved as MS Vat. Pers. 24 in the Vatican Library (Kromov; Piemontese, 1989, p. 93; Orsatti, 1996a, pp. 559-61).

In the 17th-century Italy, the interest towards Persian studies and towards collecting Persian manuscripts became mainly the prerogative of the religious and missionary circles. The Borgia collection, which the Vatican Library acquired in 1902 from Propaganda Fide (founded in 1622), perfectly represents this type of interest, mostly religious and linguistic, that the missionary community had in Oriental cultures (Orsatti, 1996b). Among the 23 Persian manuscripts of the Borgia collection, particularly important are some lexicographical works (MSS Borg. Pers. 2, Borg. Pers. 11, Borg. Pers. 12, Borg. Pers. 14, Borg. Pers. 15, and Borg. Pers. 17), and two copies of Persian versions of the Gospels (MSS Borg. Pers. 18 and Borg. Pers. 19; for the latter see Piemontese, 2000 and 2001).

An important group of Persian manuscripts in the Vatican library comprises 29 codices brought from the East by Pietro Della Valle (1586-1652, q.v.). These manuscripts have been preserved in the Vatican since 1718 and were identified as part of the Vatican collection by Rossi (1948, pp. 12-13). This group of manuscripts includes copies of the works of Persian classical poets, such as Neẓāmi Ganjavi, Saʿdi, Ḥāfeẓ (Della Valle was the first who introduced Ḥāfeẓ in Europe; see Bertotti), Jāmi, and Hātefi; works of religious disputes, including a treatise written in Persian by Della Valle himself during his stay in Isfahan in 1621 (for works on Islamic-Christian disputes in Persian see Piemontese, 1989, esp. pp. 201-2; Orsatti, 1992); works that document Persian linguistic studies at the Carmelite (see CARMELITES IN PERSIA) mission in Isfahan where Della Valle himself studied Persian; and a copy of Persian lexicographical work *Majmaʿ al-fors* of Soruri, transcribed for Della Valle under the supervision of the author (MS Vat. Pers. 69; Rossi, 1948, pp. 91-92). Finally, Pietro Della Valle brought to Italy two apparently unique manuscripts—two historical poems composed by Qadri Širāzi (first half of the 17th century) that describe historical events of Della Valle's time, like the fights between the Portuguese and Safavid forces in 1622 for gaining control over islands in the Persian Gulf. These texts are the *Jang-nāma-ye Kešm* (MS Vat. Pers. 30; Rossi, 1948, pp. 56-57; published by Bonelli), and the *Fatḥ-nāma* (Modena, Biblioteca Estense, MS γ.F.6.22; Piemontese, 1989, no. 216; Pudoli, 1985; Pistoso; published by Pudioli in 1987-88). Another poem by Qadri Širāzi entitled *Jarun-nāma* speaks about the Safavids taking the island of Hormuz (Jarun) back from the Portuguese; it is preserved in the British Library in London as MS Add. 7801 (Rieu, II, p. 681).

Most of the Persian manuscripts preserved in the Bologna University Library come from the collection of Oriental manuscripts (mainly Arabic and Turkish) acquired by the scientist, Luigi Ferdinando Marsili (or Marsigli, 1658-1730), during his participation in the wars against the Ottomans in Europe (surrender of Buda in 1686 and the siege of Belgrade in 1688). Besides scientific works, which must have been the primary interest of the collector, this group of manuscripts also includes literary texts (mainly copies of the *Pand-nāma* attributed to Farid-al-Din ʿAṭṭār), an interesting poetic anthology (MS 3283; Piemontese, 1989, no. 3), several lexicographical texts, and a beautiful album of calligraphy (*moraqqaʿ*) datable to the late 15th or early 16th century (MS 3574PP; Piemontese, 1989, no. 37).

Persian manuscripts in the Marciana National Library in Venice are of different provenance. Some of them come from the Dominican convent of St. John and St. Paul in Venice, others are from the collection of philologist and Orientalist Emilio Teza (1831-1912), but the greater part (36 MSS) originate from the collection of the Oriental codices of the Venetian aristocrat, Jacopo Nani (1725-97), who acquired them during his journeys to the East and through the expeditions of the Venetian fleet. Among the Persian manuscripts preserved in Venice, the following bear larger importance: several scientific works (mainly medical); works of classical Persian literature (the *Pand-nāma*, the *Golestān* of Saʿdi, *divān* of Ḥāfeẓ, and poems of Jāmi); an early copy (allegedly dated to early 14th century) of Balʿami's (q.v.) translation of the history of Ṭabari (MS Or. CXXVIII; Piemontese, 1989, no. 380; more details in Piemontese, 1977); lexicographical works; religious treatises of missionaries and Christian apologetics. The Marciana Library also possesses the famous *Codex Cumanicus* (MS Lat. DXLIX; for bibliography and history of the studies on the manuscript see Piemontese, 1989, no. 393; Stojanow), whose first part contains a Latin-Persian-Comanian dictionary compiled in Solḡat in the Crimea within the years 1324-25. The copy in the Marciana Library is dated to 1330 and was probably transcribed in the convent of St. John in Sarāy (Ligeti; Richard, 1981, pp. 227, 244-45).

A small but valuable collection of 15 Persian manuscripts is preserved at the Royal Library of Turin. They mainly come from the collection of Oriental manuscripts, which was owned by Carlo Alberto di Savoia (1798-1849, king of Sardinia from 1831). One of them—a beautiful illuminated manuscript of the *Manṭeq al-ṭeyr* of ʿAṭṭār, dated to Ṣafar 857/February-March 1453 (MS Or. 40; Piemontese, 1984b; Idem, 1989, no. 338)—has been reproduced in facsimile in Tehran in 1994 (ʿAṭṭār).

In Rome, the Library of the National Academy of the Lincei and Corsiniana has only four Persian manuscripts which derive from an early collection of the Corsini Library. A beautiful manuscript containing three poems of Hātefi, which once belonged to Federico Cesi (1585-1630), the founder of the Academy of Lincei, had been owned by the Barberini Library which in 1902 became the core part of the Vatican Library (MS Barb. Orient. 104; Rossi, 1948, pp. 159-60). Nearly all (56 out of 60) Persian manuscripts preserved in the Library of the Academy of the Lincei come from the collection of Prince Leone Caetani (1869-1935), a distinguished Orientalist who in 1921 established the Caetani Foundation for Islamic Studies housed at the Library of Academy of Lincei, to which he donated his private collection of manuscripts. Particularly important among this group of Persian manuscripts are those containing works of Persian historiography and classical literature, such as a copy of the collected works (*kolliāt*) of Amir Ḵosrow Dehlavi dated 908/1503 (MS Caetani 38-39; Piemontese, 1989, no. 296; codicological study in Orsatti, 1993, pp. 322-23); two beautiful illustrated copies of the *Ḵamsa* of Neẓāmi, namely MS Caetani 36 (15th century; Piemontese, 1989, no. 286) and MS Caetani 58 (2nd half of the 16th century; Piemontese, 1989, no. 287); a copy of the *Negārestān-e Moʿini* (MS Caetani 62; Piemontese, 1989, no. 315; see also Tornesello) composed by Moʿin-al-Din Joveyni (q.v.) in 735/1335 in imitation of Saʿdi's *Golestān*.

The Italian collections of Persian manuscripts, scattered in various cities and distributed between many libraries, are a mirror of the different types of interest that brought forth in the establishment of Persian studies in Italy. Besides, they form a valuable part of the multifaceted Italian cultural history.

Bibliography: R. Almagià, "Giovan Battista e Gerolamo Vecchietti viaggiatori in Oriente," *Atti della Accademia Nazionale dei Lincei, Rendiconti della classe di Scienze morali, storiche e filologiche*, Series 8, no. 11/11-12, pp. 313-50. Farid-al-Din ʿAṭṭār Nišāpuri,

Manṭeq al-ṭayr be ḵaṭṭ-e Naṣir b. Ḥasan al-Makki, fascim. ed. of the manuscript preserved at the Royal Library in Turin (Italy), ed. N. Purjavādi, Tehran, 1994. F. Bertotti, "Un viaggiatore romano e un poeta persiano: Pietro Della Valle estimatore e divulgatore di Hafiz," *Islam. Storia e civiltà* 9/2, 1990, pp. 85-98. L. Bonelli, "Il poemetto persiano Jangnāma-yi Kišm," *Atti della R. Accademia Nazionale dei Lincei, Rendiconti della classe di Scienze morali, storiche e filologiche*, Series 4, no. 6, 1890, pp. 291-303. R. Ettinghausen, *Miniature persiane nella collezione Bernard Berenson*, Milan, 1962. Abu'l-Qāsem Ferdowsi, *Šāh-nāma-ye Felorāns, čāp-e ʿaksi az ru-ye nosḵa-ye ketābḵāna-ye melli-e Felorāns mowarraḵ-e 614 hejri-e qamari*, Tehran, 1990. Idem, *Šāh-nāma az dastnevis-e muza-ye Felorāns*, 2 vols., ed. ʿA. Joveyni, Tehran, 1996-98. I. Guidi, "Di una versione persiana del Pentateuco," *Atti della Accademia Nazionale dei Lincei, Rendiconti della classe di Scienze morali, storiche e filologiche*, Series 1, no. 1, 1885, pp. 347-55. R. Gulbenkian, "The Translation of the Four Gospels into Persian," *Neue Zeitschrift für Missionswissenschaft* 36, 1980, pp. 186-218, 267-88; 37, 1981, pp. 35-37. A. Heinen, "Vatican City State," in *Worldwide Survey of Islamic Manuscripts*, 4 vols., ed. G. Roper, vol. I, London, 1991, pp. 145-59. P. Horn, "Asadī's neupersisches Wörterbuch 'Lughat-i Furs' nach der eingingen Vaticanischen Handschrift," *Abhandlungen der königlischen Gesellschaft der Wissenschaften zu Göttingen, Phil.-Hist. Klasse*, N.S. 1, no. 8, 1897, pp. 133-37. Djalal Khaleghi-Motlagh, "Moʿarrefi wa arzyābi-e barḵ-i az dastnevishā-ye Šāh-nāma," *Irān-nāma/Iran Nameh* 3/3, 1985, pp. 378-406; 4/1, 1985, pp. 16-47; 4/2, 1986, pp. 225-55. A. Kromov, "Darbāra-ye awwalin ketāb-e ṣarf o naḥw-e zabān-e fārsi dar Orupā," *Soḵan* 20/1, 1970, pp. 83-84. G. Levi Della Vida, *Richerche sulla formazione del più antico fondo dei manoscritti orientali della Biblioteca Vaticana*, Vatican City, 1939. L. Ligeti, "Prolegomena to the Codex Cumanicus," *Acta Orientalia Academiae Scientarium Hungaricae* 35, 1981, pp. 1-54. G. Messina, S. J., *Notizia su un Diatessaron persiano tradotto dal siriaco*, Rome, 1943. Idem, *Diatessaron Persiano. I. Introduzione II. Testo e traduzione*, Rome, 1951.

P. Orsatti, "Uno scritto ritrovato di Pietro Della Valle e la polemica religiosa nella storia degli studi sul persiano," *Rivista degli Studi Orienali* 64, 1992, pp. 267-74. Idem, "Le manuscrit islamique: caractéristiques, matérielles et typologie," in *Ancient and Medieval Book Materials and Techniques, Proceedings of the Conference at Erice, 18-25 September 1992*, ed. M. Maniaci and P. F. Munafò, 2 vols., Vatican City, 1993, vol. II, pp. 269-331; Pers. tr. "Nosḵehā-ye ḵaṭṭi-e eslāmi: vižegihā-ye māddi wa gunešenāḵti," *Nāma-ye Bahārestān* 6/1-2, nos. 11-12, 2005-06, pp. 35-74. Idem, "Prodromi degli studi europei sul persiano nel Rinascimento," in *Italia ed Europa nella linguistica del Rinascimento: confronti e relazioni/Italy and Europe in Renaissance Linguistics: Comparisons and Relations, Proceedings of the International Conference, Ferrara, 20-24 March 1991*, ed. M. Tavoni, 2 vols., Modena, 1996a, vol. II, pp. 551-67. Idem, *Il fondo Borgia della Biblioteca Vaticana e gli studi orientali a Roma tra Sette e Ottocento*, Vatican City, 1996b. P. Orsatti, B. Pirone, and A. Gallotta, "Italy," in *World Survey of Islamic Manuscripts*, 4 vols., ed. J. Roper, vol. II, London, 1993, pp. 67-116. H. H. Paper, "The Vatican Judeo-Persian Pentatech," *Acta Orientalia* 28/3-4, 1965, pp. 263-340; 29/1-2, 1965, pp. 75-181; 29/3-4, 1966, pp. 253-310; 31, 1968, pp. 56-113. A. M. Piemontese, "Il codice marciano della Tārix-e Ṭabari," *Annali. Istituto Universitario Orientale* 37, 1977, p. 463-74. Idem, "I manoscritti persiani del fondo Sbath nella Biblioteca Vaticana e un nuovo "Barzūnāma," *Atti della Accademia Nazionale dei Lincei, Rendiconti della classe di Scienze morali, storiche e filologiche*, Series 8, no. 33/7-12, 1978, pp. 447-64. Idem, "I fondi dei manoscritti arabi, persiani e turchi in Italia," in *Gli Arabi in Italia: cultura, contatti e tradizioni*, ed. F. Gabrieli and U. Scerrato, Milan, 1979a, pp. 661-88. Idem, "La 'Grammatica persiana' di G. B. Raimondi," *Rivista degli Studi Orientali* 53, 1979b, pp. 141-50. Idem, "Nuova luce su Firdawsi: uno 'Šāhnāma' datato 614 H./1217 a Firenze," *Annali. Istituto Universitario Orientale* 40, 1980, pp. 1-91. Idem, "Les fonds de manuscrits persans conserves dans les Bibliothèques d'Italie," *JA* 270/3-4, 1982, pp. 273-93. Idem, "I manoscritti persiani della collezione Berenson," in *Studi in onore di Francesco Gabrieli nel suo ottantesimo compleanno*, 2 vols., ed. R. Traini, Rome, 1984a, vol. II, pp. 631-39. Idem, "Un codice miniato del 'Manṭiq al-Ṭayr' di ʿAṭṭār (857 H./1453) a Torino," *Atti della Accademia Nazionale dei Lincei, Rendiconti della classe di Scienze morali, storiche e filologiche*, Series 8, no. 39/3-4, 1984b, pp. 55-78. Idem, *Catalogo dei manoscritti persiani conservati nelle biblioteche d'Italia*, Rome, 1989. Idem, "Un testo latino-persiano connesso al Codex Comanicus," *Acta Orientalia Academiae Scientarium Hungaricae* 53/1-2, 2000, pp. 121-32. Idem, "Le glosse sul Vangelo persiano del 1338 e il Codex Cumanicus," in *Miscellanea Bibliothecae Apostolicae Vaticanae* 8, Vatican City, 2001, pp. 313-49.

M. Pistoso, "Qadri di Širāz e l'Epica' safavide," *Oriente Moderno* 58, 1978, pp. 321-25. M. C. Pudioli, "Un inedito *maṣnavi* persiano nella Biblioteca Estense di Modena," in *Contributi alla storia dell'orientalismo*, ed. G. R. Franci, Bologna, 1985, pp. 39-44. Idem, "Qadri di Siraz e la 'Guerra di Kešm'," *Studi orientali e linguistici* 4, 1987-1988, pp. 66-95. F. Richard, "Les manuscrits persans rapportés par les frères Vecchietti et conservés aujourd'hui à la Bibliothèque Nationale," *Stud. Ir.* 9, 1980, p. 291-300. Idem, "Un lectionnaire persan des Évangiles copié en Crimée en 776 H./1374," *Stud. Ir.* 10/2, 1981, pp. 225-45. S. Roman, *The Development of Islamic Library Collections in Western Europe and North America*, London, 1990. E. Rossi, *Elenco dei manoscritti persiani della Bilbioteca Vaticana. Vaticani, Barberiniani, Borgiani, Rossiani*, Vatican City, 1948. E. Rossi and A. Bombaci,

Elenco dei drammi religiosi persiani (fondo mss. Vaticani Cerulli), Vatican City, 1961. V. Stojanow, "Der *Codex Cumanicus* in der Forschungsgeschichte," in *Il Codice Cumanico e il suo mondo: atti del colloquio internazionale, Venezia, 6-7 dicembre 2002*, ed. F. Schmieder and P. Schreiner, Rome, 2005, pp. 3-44. C. A. Storey, *Persian Literature. A Bio-bibliographical Survey*, vol. III/1, *A. Lexicography. B. Grammar. C. Prosody and Poetics*, Leiden, 1984. N. L. Tornsello, "Un Negarestan di Moʿini Joveyni conservato al'Accademia Nazionale dei Lincei a Roma," *Oriente Moderno*, N. S. 15/2, 1996 (monographic volume: *La civiltà timuride come fenomeno internazionale*, 2 vols., ed. M. Bernardini), pp. 351-77.

(PAOLA ORSATTI)

PLATE I

A brass bowl, engraved and inlaid in silver and gold, Iran (Fārs), 14th century. Courtesy of the Museo Nazionale del Bargello, Florence, Inv. Bronzi 7161.

PLATE II

A detail of PLATE I

ix. PERSIAN ART COLLECTIONS

Since the Middle Ages, Italians have been some of the greatest collectors of Islamic art in Europe. The Islamic market that Italy drew on was very large and some of the most opulent works were imported from Persia. Among the five most stunning are the early 14th century Central Asian textiles (lampas weave, silk, gold thread) used to make the burial cloths of Cangrande I della Scala (d. 22 July 1329), held by the Museo di Castelvecchio in Verona since 1922 (similar ones used for the dalmatic robe of Pope Benedict XI are preserved in the Church of San Domenico in Perugia; Magagnato; Wardwell). Dating from the late 8th or early 9th century is a large piece of red silk with *senmurv* designs used in the Carolingian period to make a whole chasuble housed in the Abbey of San Salvatore near Siena. This textile was venerated as a relic of Pope St. Mark (first half of the 4th century; but to be dated, in all probability, to Pope John VIII (872-82; Dolcini). Until World War II, the façade of the Church of San Frediano (first half of the 12th century) in Lucca was surmounted by an engraved, cast bronze incense burner from the 9th century in the shape of a bird, fitted with a whistle that when the *libeccio* (south-west wind) blew emitted a very shrill sound (Treasury of San Frediano, Lucca; Scerrato, 1979, p. 491).

A bowl in relief-cut glass of an opaque turquoise color, perhaps previously in the possession of the Byzantines, appears to have been offered as a gift to the Signoria of Venice by Uzun Ḥasan (1453-78), leader of the Āq-Qoyunlū (q.v.), and has the word *Khorāsān* carved in relief underneath its base. It is a magnificent 10th century specimen, created in imitation of a carved turquoise bowl now in the Treasury of St. Mark in Venice (Inv. no. 140; Erdmann, pp. 103-4). The Treasury of St. Markalso holds a carved rock crystal dish (Inv. no. 102; Iran or Iraq, 9th-10th century), which is probably the one described in the inventory of 1325, as "*Platinam unam de cristallo intaiatam*" (Alcouffe, pp. 222-23; cf. also Erdmann, pp. 115-17).

One of the earliest, and most famous families to collect Islamic art was undoubtedly the Medici, in Florence who, from the 15th century onwards, collected Islamic metalwork. The collection was lost in 1494-95 when the Medici were driven out of Florence; nevertheless, when they re-entered the city in the following century, a limited number of the pieces were retrieved. A cast brass jug engraved and inlaid with gold and silver, produced in the late 15th-early 16th century, was acquired by Ferdinand I de' Medici, Grand Duke of Tuscany (1587-1609) in 1589, and has been kept in the Sala della Tribuna at the Uffizi Palace (Florence Museo Nazionale del Bargello, Inv. Bronzi 289); Curatola and Spallanzani, 1981b, pp. 13-16). The most recent inventory, in which its lid and its handle with a zoomorphic head (both later lost) are still recorded, is that of 1733. The jug is part of a remarkable group of Timurid pieces characterized by the same sub-spherical shape and elaborately decorated with arabesques (Komaroff, pp. 153-62, 169-83, 219-21). The same museum houses a hammered brass bowl, engraved and inlaid in silver and gold, depicting a series of horsemen and dated to the 14th century (PLATES I AND II; Inv. Bronzi, 7161; Curatola, ed., 1993, pp. 265-66, cat. 152); an inscription on the base possibly refers to a Safavid collector of objects from Fārs (Melikian-Chirvani, pp. 77-78).

The Medici of Florence also collected precious objects such as vessels in crystal and in semiprecious stones; these include an outstanding sardonyx jug with a handle in the shape of a panther (Persia, 8th century), listed in an inventory compiled in the 15th century uponthe death of Lorenzo the Magnificent (1492) and copied in 1512: *Uno bochale di sardonio chol manicho di detta pietra, col piè et bechuccio d'ariento dorato, pesa lib. xi once 3, vale f. 2000* 'A jug in sardonyx with a handle in the said stone, with foot and spout in gilded silver, weight 11 pounds, 3 ounces, value fl. 2000' (Spallanzani and Gaeta Bertelà, p. 34), at present in the Museo degli Argenti in Florence (Inv. Gemme 777; Damiani and Scalini, eds, p. 79, cat. 51) and a jade bowl (probably from Central Asia, 15th century) also from the collection of Lorenzo the Magnificent (Grote, p. 127). The latter was perhaps transferred from the Treasure of S. Lorenzo or from the Uffizi to the Museo di Fisica e Storia Naturale in the 18th century and, at the end of the 19th century, to the Museo di Mineralogia e Litologia of the University of Florence (Inv. no. 1947, 1336/565; Curatola, ed., 1993, pp. 360-61, cat. 217). A small engraved serpentine bowl with a handle in the shape of a dragon was, in all probability, one of the gifts presented by Johan Georg I, the Elector of Saxony, to the Grand Duke Ferdinand II of Tuscany in 1654; it is perhaps the same bowl listed in a Medici inventory of 1666-70 (Florence, Museo degli Argenti, Inv. Gemme 745; Curatola, ed., 1993, pp. 359-60, cat. 216).

A beautiful ewer in hammered and embossed brass, engraved and inlaid in copper and silver (Khorasan, late 12th to early 13th century), comes from the ancient collection of the Este (from 1288 Lords, and from 1452 Dukes of Modena, until 1796); it is presently in the Galleria Estense in Modena (Inv. no. 6921; Curatola, ed., 1993, pp. 234-37, cat. 125). The ewer, one of a fairly large extant group, has alternately fluted and concave faces, a pierced lid surmounted by a projecting feline, and many other ornaments (including harpies and falconers) projecting out from the body; some inscriptions in animated *nasḵi* on the body and in animated kufic on the foot. The inscriptions wish upon the owner glory, good fortune, and the like. The Galleria Estense holds another important example of Persian metalwork (Inv. no. 8082): an engraved cast brass bowl inlaid in gold and silver, inscribed "work of ʿAbd-al-Qāder al-Ḵāleq Širāzi" and dated Moḥarram 705/August 1305. On the body, epigraphical cartouches (*nasḵ*) alternate with medallions showing fighting, hunting, and court scenes (Curatola, ed., 1993, pp. 266-67, cat. 153).

Cardinal Cesare Borgia (1731-1804), Prefect of Propaganda Fide, collected enough antiquities and curios from all over the world to fill a museum in Velletri (Rome); the objects in the Islamic collection included an outstanding engraved cast bronze bowl inlaid in silver, with an animated *nasḵi* inscription around the rim; we read on the body the name of its owner, Ḵalif b. al-Julāki (Khorasan, late 12th to early 13th century; now in the Museo di Capodimonte in Naples, Inv. A.M. 112114; Scerrato, 1968, pp. 2-3). A later (13th to 14th century) bowl of similar shape, with a kufic inscription running around the rim, from the Carrand collection, is in the Museo Nazionale del Bargello in Florence (Inv. C 363; Damiani and Scalini, eds, p. 126, cat. 100). Some objects from collections of Islamic antiquities belonging to important Italian families are now housed in various museums abroad. Noteworthy is the so-called "Vaso Vescovali" from the Vescovali collection (see M. Lanci, *Trattato*), bought on the antiques market in 1950 by the British Museum. It is an important cast bronze bowl with lid (probably not originally part of the object), inlaid in silver, with complex astrological ornamentation (Khorasan, late 12th to early 13th century; London, The British Museum, Inv. OA 1950-7-2511; Curatola, ed., 1993, pp. 237-39, cat. 127).

There is also a collection of Islamic metalwork in the Museo Civico Medievale in Bologna, which includes a superb engraved, cast bronze bowl inlaid with silver (Inv. no. 2128), inscribed on the inside in animated kufic and on the outside in *nasḵi*, executed for a member of the retinue of Badr-al-Din Loʾloʾ, *atābeg* of Mosul (1222-59), probably from northwestern Persia and dated to the first half of the 13th century (Scerrato, 1979, p. 508).

Hunting scenes are depicted both on the outside, in medallions and on the inside, on the base. Some of the above-mentioned museums also house Persian objects in other materials, mainly ceramics, in their collections of Islamic art. Excellent examples of painted luster tiles (12th-14th century) are to be found, for instance, in the Museo Nazionale del Bargello in Florence (Curatola and Spallanzani, 1981a, pp. 6-17), and the Museo di Capodimonte in Naples (Scerrato, 1968, pp. 42-46, cat. 50-59), and also in the Scuola Grande di S. Rocco in Venice, the Museo Internazionale delle Ceramiche in Faenza and the Museo Nazionale d'Arte Orientale in Rome. In addition to cross, star, and quadrangular-shaped tiles with figures, there are many with verses from the *Šāh-nāma* by Ferdowsi. In Naples, there is a good collection of Safavid and Qajar tiles, not only in the Museo di Capodimonte, but also in the Museo Artistico Industriale, a 19th century establishment with a triple function (museum, school, and workshop where replicas of Islamic prototypes were made; Fontana, 1988, p. 12). Apropos of ceramics, it should be noted that the aforementioned museums in Faenza and Rome also hold large and important collections of Samanid, Seljuq, Il-khanid, Timurid, and Safavid vessels (Torre, ed., pp. 41-115; Curatola, ed., 1993, pp. 93-94, 222-34, 255-56, 263-64, 354, 424-26). Among the finest works in the Museo Nazionale d'Arte Orientale in Rome (established in 1957), is a large Samanid bowl of so-called buff animated ware on which three horsemen hunting with a cheetah are depicted (Inv. no. 2629), some Seljuq turquoise glazed house-models (Inv. nos. 1417), a beautiful turquoise-glazed, molded ewer with a series of interlaced dancers (Inv. no. 4863; Ventrone), some luster and *minā'i* pieces, and a magnificent *lājvardina* bottle (Inv. no. 1977). A good collection of Samanid, Seljuq, and Il-khanid ceramics, as yet unpublished, is housed in the Department of Asiatic Studies of the University of Naples "L'Orientale." The collection of the Museo Nazionale d'Arte Orientale in Rome also includes some of the oldest pieces produced in Persia, not only ceramics, but also other handicrafts: e.g., a turquoise-glazed ceramic storage jar with applied relief (Inv. no. 12749; Curatola, ed., 1993, p. 66, cat. 1), dated to the early Islamic period (late 7th-early 8th century), and a small bowl in greenish glass with applied or molded disks (Inv. no. 2705; Genito, p. 6) belonging to the same period. There are still some doubts, however, concerning the Persian or Byzantine origin of a group of glasses with wheel-cut disks in the Treasury of St. Mark in Venice (Grabar, pp. 70-71, 75-76, cat. 65, 78, 80-81). An engraved cast bronze jug (Khorasan or Transoxiana, 9th-10th century), with a stylized pomegranate serving as a thumb-rest (Rome, Museo Nazionale d'Arte Orientale, Inv. no. 877/695; Curatola, ed., 1993, pp. 97-98, cat. 25), belongs to a slightly later period, as does a cast bronze jug with an attached spout ending in the shape of a zoomorphic head, from the Church of San Lorenzo fuori le Mura (Rome), now in the Museo Sacro, Vatican City (Scerrato, 1979, p. 455). This museum also houses an important silk from eastern Persia (8th-9th century), displaying pairs of lions set face to face in oval medallions (Inv. no. 1251; Scerrato, 1979, p. 454).

Italian collections hold other textiles, some little known, including a beautiful silk from the Tomb of St. Cyriacus in Ancona, now in the local Museo Diocesano. The design, consisting of roundels containing pairs of lions set back to back, is most probably from Central Asia, mid-13th century (Curatola, ed., 1993, pp. 244-45, cat. 132). In the Museo Nazionale del Bargello in Florence there are two fragments of silks contemporary with the above, most probably from western Persia, dated to around 1340-80, both with a blue background, one with animal and vegetal designs (Inv. no. 2312 Carrand), the other with floral motifs (Inv. no. 609 Franchetti; for both see Suriano and Carboni, pp. 38-44, cat. 9-10). An earlier Central Asian silk (8th century), belonging to the so-called "Zandaniji" textiles, has oval medallions containing a pair of lions set face to face, alternating with trees of life and quadrupeds; it is also in the Museo Nazionale del Bargello in Florence (Inv. no. 633 Franchetti; Suriano and Carboni, pp. 18-21, cat. 2). Some Safavid textiles are to be found in the same museum, as well as in the Museo Correr in Venice, the Museo Civico in Turin, the Museo Nazionale d'Arte Orientale in Rome, and the Museo Poldi Pezzoli in Milan (PLATE III; Curatola, ed., 1993, pp. 428-33, cat. 274-76, 278; Suriano and Carboni, pp. 117-27, cat. 39-42). At the end of the 16th century, and particularly from the 17th century on, following the establishment of close diplomatic relations between Safavid Persia and major Italian cities, including Venice and Florence, many gifts were exchanged between Persia and Italy. In this manner, a

PLATE III

Detail of an Isfahan carpet, 1521, or, more probably, 1541. Courtesy of the Museo Poldi Pezzoli, Milan, Temporary Loan.

number of Persian carpets found their way to both these cities.

From 1603 on, some carpets were presented by Shah Abbās I (1587-1629) to the Serenissima of Venice, and are housed in the Basilica of St. Mark (Erdmann, pp. 123-24); while five Safavid examples known as "Polonaise" carpets, produced mainly in Isfahan but also in Kāšān, are in the Treasury of St. Mark in Venice (Inv. nos 23-27; Erdmann, pp. 123-27, cat. 133-37). A pair of "Polonaise" carpets, formerly owned by the Italian Doria family, are in two major foreign museums: the Carpet Museum in Tehran (King), and the Metropolitan Museum of Art in New York (Inv. no. 50.190.5; Dimand and Mailey, pp. 60-61, 103, cat. 18). Three carpets, woven with silk and gold and silver threads, entered the Florentine Grand Ducal collections in the 18th century at the time of the Grand Dukes of Lorraine, and are now in the Museo degli Argenti in Florence (Boralevi, 1980). Florence also boasts important collections of Persian carpets assembled by antique dealers during the 19th and 20th century. The most notable was Stefano Bardini, who bequeathed to the city of Florence a museum that bears his name (Museo Bardini), whose holdings include twenty Persian carpets, some of exquisite craftsmanship (Boralevi, 1981). A carpet in the Museo Nazionale del Bargello in Florence (Inv. no. 2203 Carrand; Curatola and Spallanzani, 1983, pp. 20-21, 26) and others in the Museo Poldi Pezzoli in Milan (Balboni Brizza, pp. 40-59) are magnificent examples of 16th century workmanship. Those in Milan include a particularly outstanding carpet with hunting scenes from Isfahan, dating to 1521, or, more probably, 1541 (PLATE III, Temporary Loan); abandoned by papal troops in the Quirinal Palace in 1870, it became part of the furnishings of the royal palace of Victor Emmanuel III in Monza, who donated it to the Pinacoteca di Brera in Milan in 1919, which, in turn, lent it to the Museo Poldi Pezzoli in

1923); and another with medallions and dragons, probably made for Shah Ṭahmāsp, (Kāšān, 1524-76: Inv. No. 424). A contemporary carpet fragment from Herat with animal and floral motifs is in the Museo Civico in Turin (Curatola, 1983, p. 80).

The two Italian museums that hold the largest number of Islamic armor are the Museo Stibbert in Florence and the Armeria of the Royal Palace in Turin. Some of the Safavid pieces in these collections are of exquisite quality. The Museo Stibbert houses entire suits of armor and a fine knife with an ivory handle, and blade decorated with gold, dating to the 16th to 17th century (Inv. no. 6459), while the Armeria has two swords with blades inlaid in gold and silver, dating to the 16th century (Inv. nos G. 98 and G. 99; Curatola, ed., 1993, pp. 435-36, cat. 283). Armor and weapons from the 18th and 19th century are held by other Italian collections, such as those in the Museo Nazionale d'Arte Orientale and the Fondazione Caetani *apud* the Accademia Nazionale dei Lincei (Di Flumeri Vatielli, pp. 329-37), both in Rome, and in the Museo di Palazzo Fortuny in Venice (Curatola, ed., 1993, pp. 433-35, cat. 280, 282).

There are many illustrated manuscripts preserved in Italian collections, such as those from the Il-khanid and Timurid periods in the Berenson Collection at Villa "I Tatti" in Settignano (Florence), which houses a leaf of the Great Mongol *Šāh-nāma* showing Esfandiār approaching Goštāsp (qq.v.), a leaf from a manuscript of a *Ẓafar-nāma* (Shiraz, June-July 1436) illustrating Timur receiving guests at the marriage of his son, Jahāngir, and an anthology from Herāt (1 Šawwāl 830 A.H./26 July 1427), copied for the Timurid prince Bāysonqor (Curatola, ed., 1993, pp. 271-72, 364-65, cat. 157, 220). An important Timurid illustrated manuscript of the *Šāh-nāma*, from Shiraz, dated to the second half of the 15th century (Ms. C1.III.48; Curatola, ed., 1993, pp. 368-69, cat. 223), is in the Biblioteca Nazionale Centrale in Florence. A Safavid *Šāh-nāma* of good quality, dating to 20 Rabiʿ I 977 A.H./ 2 September 1569, is in the Biblioteca Nazionale in Naples (Ms. III.G.68; Fontana, 1980).

Safavid illustrated manuscripts are also preserved in other collections, and in the Library of the Accademia Nazionale dei Lincei and the Casanatense Library, both in Rome, and the Biblioteca Comunale in Palermo (see Piemontese). Special mention must be made of the collection of archaeological finds of the Italian Archaeological Mission in Ghazni, at present lent by the Istituto Italiano per l'Africa e l'Oriente (IsIAO) to the Museo Nazionale d'Arte Orientale in Rome. There are many marble slabs, architectural elements in terracotta and alabaster, and objects in ceramic and metalwork from the Ghaznavid Palace of Masʿud III (1099-1115; PLATE IV), and some pottery vessels from the so-called "House of Luster-Painted Wares" (Bombaci; Scerrato, 1959). There are also a few marble tombstones from Ghazni and its environs, belonging to a long period between the 12th and 16th century, in the same museum (Giunta, pp. 9, 109-11, 169-70, 217-18, 232-37, cat. 16, 30, 47, 53-54).

PLATE IV

A painted terracotta from the excavation of the Palace of Masʿud III at Ghazni (Afghanistan), 505/1112. Museo Nazionale di Arte Orientale Rome, on loan by the IsIAO, Rome. Courtesy of the IsIAO.

Bibliography: D. Alcouffe, "La glittica islamica," in *Il Tesoro di San Marco*, (Exhibition Catalog, Paris, 1984), Italian edit. by R. Cambiaghi, Milan, 1986, pp. 215-35. G. A. Bailey, "The Bernard Berenson Collection of Islamic Painting at Villa i Tatti: Turkman, Uzbek, and Safavid Miniatures," *Oriental Art* 48/1, 2002, pp. 2-16. M. T. Balboni Brizza, *Tappeti*, Museo Poldi Pezzoli, Milan, 1993. A. Bombaci, "Introduction to the Excavations at Ghazni," *East and West* 10, 1959, pp. 3-22. A. Boralevi, "Three Rugs in the Museo degli Argenti in Florence," *Halı* 3, 1980, p. 48. Idem, "I tappeti orientali del Museo Bardini a Firenze," *Halı* (Italian Suppl. 1), Sept. 1981, pp. 2-15. G. Curatola, *Oriental Carpets*, London, 1983. Idem, ed., *Eredità dell'Islam, Arte islamica in Italia*, (Exhibition Catalog, Venice, 1993-94), Milan, 1993. G. Curatola and M. Spallanzani, *Mattonelle islamiche / Islamic Tiles*, Museo Nazionale del Bargello, Florence, 1981a. Idem, *Metalli islamici dalle Collezioni Granducali / Islamic Metalwork from the Grand Ducal Collection*, Museo Nazionale del Bargello, Florence, 1981b. Idem, *Tappeti / Carpets*, Museo Nazionale del Bargello, Florence, 1983. G. Damiani and M. Scalini, eds., *Islam, specchio d'Oriente, Rarità e preziosi nelle collezioni statali fiorentine*, (Exhibition Catalog, Florence, 2002), Florence, 2002. G. Di Flumeri Vatielli, "Metalli tardo-islamici nella Fondazione Caetani (Roma)," *Rivista degli Studi Orientali* 70, 1996, pp. 303-52. M. Dimand and J. Mailey, *Oriental Rugs in the Metropolitan Museum of Art*, New York, 1973. L. Dolcini, "San Marco papa o Giovanni VIII. Nuove ipotesi per due sciamiti post-sasanidi e una confezione carolingia," in L. Dolcini, ed., *La casula di San Marco papa. Sciamiti orientali alla corte carolingia*, Florence, 1992, pp. 1-51. K. Erdmann, "III. Opere islamiche," in H. R. Hahnloser, ed., *Il Tesoro di San Marco* II, *Il Tesoro e il Museo*, Florence, 1971, pp. 99-127. M. V. Fontana, *La collezione ceramica islamica e l'imitazione ottocentesca del Museo Artistico Industriale di Napoli* (Museo Artistico Industriale), Naples, 1988. Eadem, "Un manoscritto safavide dello *Šāh-nāma* conservato alla Biblioteca Nazionale di Napoli," *Annali dell'Istituto Orientale di Napoli* 40, 1980, pp. 39-48. B. Genito, *Vetri iranici*, Museo Nazionale d'Arte Orientale, Rome, 1977. R. Giunta, *Les inscriptions funéraires de Ġaznī (IVe-IXe/X^e-XVe siècles)*, Naples, 2003. A. Grabar, "II. Opere bizantine," in R. H. Hahnloser, ed., *Il Tesoro di San Marco* II, *Il Tesoro e il Museo*, Florence, 1971, pp. 13-97. A. Grote, "I Medici collezionisti nel Quattrocento," in N. Dacos, A. Grote, A. Giuliano, D. Heikamp, U. Pannuti, *Il tesoro di Lorenzo il Magnifico. Repertorio delle gemme e dei vasi*, Florence, 1980, pp. 125-30. E. J. Grube, "Piattino in cristallo di rocca," in Curatola, ed., 1993, entry no. 53 at pp. 143-44. D. King, "The Doria 'Polonaise' Carpet," in *Persian and Mughal Art*, (Catalog of exhibition at Colnaghi's, 7 April-20 May 1976) London, 1976, pp. 301-10. L. Komaroff, *The Golden Disk of Heaven, Metalwork of Timurid Iran*, Costa Mesa, Calif., 1992. M. Lanci, *Trattato delle simboliche rappresentanze arabiche*, Paris, 1846. L. Magagnato, ed., *Le stoffe di Cangrande*, Florence, 1983. A. S. Melikian-Chirvani, *Le bronze iranien*, Paris, 1973. A. M. Piemontese, *Catalogo dei manoscritti persiani conservati nelle biblioteche d'Italia*, Rome, 1989. U. Scerrato, "The First Two Excavation Campaigns at Ghazni, 1957-1958," *East and West* 10, 1959, pp. 23-55. Idem, *Arte islamica a Napoli, opere delle raccolte pubbliche napoletane*, (Exhibition Catalog, Naples, 1967), Naples, 1968. Idem, "Arte islamica in Italia," in F. Gabrieli and U. Scerrato, *Gli Arabi in Italia*, Milan, 1979, pp. 275-571. Idem, M. Spallanzani and G. Gaeta Bertelà, eds., *Libro d'inventario dei beni di Lorenzo il Magnifico*, Florence, 1992. C. M. Suriano and S. Carboni, *La seta islamica, temi ed influenze culturali / Islamic Silk, Design and Content, 9th International Conference on Oriental Carpets* (Museo Nazionale del Bargello), Florence, 1999. P. Torre, ed., *Le Mille e una Notte, ceramiche persiane, turche e ispano moresche* (Exhibition Catalog, Faenza, 1990), Faenza, 1990. G. Ventrone, "Una brocca selgiuchide con scena di danza," in *Arte Orientale in Italia* I, Museo Nazionale d'Arte Orientale, Rome, 1971, pp. 31-46. A. E. Wardwell, "*Panni tartarici*: Eastern Islamic Silks woven with Gold and Silver (13th and 14th Centuries)," *Islamic Art* 3, 1989, pp. 95-173.

(M. V. FONTANA)

x. LIRICA PERSICA

The name of a project set up in 1989 by the School of Persian Literary Studies at Venice University. The aim of the project was to create a database for Persian lyric verse by following a computer-assisted and linguistic-statistical approach in a semiotic-structuralist perspective. The work preparing the ground for the project included a methodological essay on the modes of versification and interpretation of Persian poetry (Zipoli, 1988), and the first computer-generated concordances of the *divān* of Ḥāfeẓ (Meneghini Correale, 1989).

The project is being developed along three major lines. Firstly, the continuous increase in the database mainly made up of texts and lexical material of 1,000-line samples taken from the *ḡazal* collections of Persian poets (the only exception is the sample taken from Farroḵi Sistāni's *nasib*s "lyrical introduction to the *qaṣida*s"). The decision to work on quantitatively uniform samples ensures that statistical comparisons can be made of the lexical material. In addition to the samples (for the list, see below), the database is made up of all the *ḡazal*s of Ḥāfeẓ (Meneghini Correale, 1989), and Aṯir-al-Din Aḵsikati (q.v.), in addition to 104 *ḡazal*s by Sanāʾi Ḡaznavi according to the seven oldest manuscripts (Zanolla, 2003).

The second main line of activity involves the construction of a software package dedicated to analyzing the texts. The main tools offer the possibility to search for contexts, morphological elements, and lexical solidarities; to identify rhyme structures and figures of speech; to calculate lexicon exhaustion; and to compare processed data (vocabularies, frequencies, etc.) besides other functions.

The third line of activity consists of analysis and research into the texts in the database at various levels (statistical-lexical, rhetorical, semantic, philological, etc.), using the dedicated software. These kinds of assays are not part of a systematic program, but are meant to demonstrate how the experience of the Lirica Persica project may be put to good use in different contexts.

The work carried out in the Lirica Persica project has led to the publication of a number of books and CD Roms (Lirica Persica Series) and articles in various journals (see Bibliography). The first volume in the Series is the project handbook, to be referred to for information not only on the structure, problems, and aims of the Series, but also the underlying principles, whose methodological criteria have subsequently been partly revised (Meneghini, Zanolla, and Zipoli, 1997). The Series includes eleven volumes containing the computer-processed texts by individual *ḡazal* authors (Farid-al-Din ʿAṭṭār, Bābā Feḡāni, Bidel, Faḵr-al-Din ʿErāqi, Ḥāfeẓ, Kamāl Ḵojandi, Naẓiri Nišāburi, Saʿdi, Salmān Sāvaji, Sanāʾi, and Ṭāleb Āmoli), one volume with a sample of Farroḵi's *nasib*s, two volumes in which the data are analyzed (Zipoli, 1992; Meneghini Correale, 1993), and a presentation of comparative data of the first ten *ḡazal* samples (Meneghini and Zipoli, 1998). The database was later extended by adding the computer-processed texts of another nine samples of *ḡazal*s (Ahli Širāzi, Amir Ḵosrow Dehlavi, Anwari Abivardi, ʿAbd-al-Raḥmān Jāmi, Ḵᵛāju Kermāni, Ḵāqāni Šarvāni, Rumi, Ṣāʾeb Tabrizi, Waḥši Bāfqi) bringing the number of *ḡazal* samples up to twenty for a corpus of 20,000 lines (2,437 *ḡazal*s, 370,053 tokens,

16,312 types, and 9,866 lemmas). The material processed from this database (texts in both Persian characters and transliteration, complete with lexical, prosodic, and statistical material; a collection of more than 500 files, with internal and external links) was stored on a CD Rom (Meneghini, 2000) and given with a hypertext system of navigation and search (to retrieve contexts, morphological elements, and lexical solidarities). This database has two different levels, Authors and Corpus. The Authors level enables the user to browse and search the 20 separate samples of 1,000 lines; the Corpus level enables the user to browse and search the 20,000 lines as a whole, thus as a sample of the Persian *ǧazal* lexical system.

Another research area of the Lirica Persica project deals with developing a system for the computer-assisted collation and analysis of manuscripts. The outcome of this work is the publication of the second CD Rom in the Series (Zanolla, 2003), containing the electronic edition of a corpus of 104 *ǧazal*s by Sanāʾi, organized in a hypertext (links added to the poems lead to the transcription of each witness, to the digitized images of the folios, to the single-witness and all-witness spelling databases, and to the word-by-word collation of the texts).

The Lirica Persica project has a website www.liricapersica.it, presenting its activities and publications.

Bibliography: Lirica Persica (LP) series. Daniela Meneghini Correale, Giampaolo Urbani, and Riccardo Zipoli, *Handbook of Lirica Persica*, LP 1, Eurasiatica 12, Venezia, 1989. Daniela Meneghini Correale, *Hafez: Concordance and Lexical Repertories of 1000 Lines*, LP 2, Eurasiatica 13, Venezia, 1989. Roscinach Habibi and Riccardo Zipoli, *Faghani: Concordance and . . .*, LP 3, Eurasiatica 17, Venezia, 1990. Daniella Meneghini Correale, *Taleb: Concordance and . . .*, LP 4, Eurasiatica 18, Venezia, 1990. Narges Samadi and Riccardo Zipoli, *Naziri: Concordance and . . .*, LP 5, Eurasiatica 20, Venezia, 1990. Daniela Meneghini Correale, *Farroxi: Concordance and . . .*, LP 6, Eurasiatica 25, Venezia, 1991. Riccardo Zipoli, *Statistics and Lirica Persica*, LP 7, Eurasiatica 26, Venezia, 1992. Setrag Manoukian and Riccardo Zipoli, *Saʿdi: Concordance and . . .*, LP 8, Eurasiatica 32, Venezia, 1992. Daniela Meneghini Correale and Valentina Zanolla, *ʿAttar: Concordance and . . .*, LP 9, Eurasiatica 34, Venezia, 1993. Daniela Meneghini Correale, *The Handling of Āb/Water in Farruḫī, Ḥāfiẓ and Ṭālib*, LP 10, Eurasiatica 36, Venezia, 1993. Riccardo Zipoli, *Bidel: Concordance and . . .*, LP 11, Eurasiatica 41, Venezia, 1994. Daniela Meneghini Correale, *Salman: Concordance and . . .*, LP 12, Eurasiatica 44, Venezia, 1995. Valentina Zanolla, *Sanaʾi: Concordance and . . .*, LP 13, Eurasiatica 47, Venezia, 1997. Riccardo Zipoli, *Kamal: Concordance and . . .*, LP 14, Eurasiatica 50, Venezia, 1997. Daniela Meneghini Correale and Riccardo Zipoli, *The Collected Lirica Persica (ʿAttar, Bidel, Faghani, Hafez, Kamal, Naziri, Saʿdi, Salman, Sanaʾi, and Taleb)*, 2 vols., LP 15, Eurasiatica 53, Venezia, 1998. Daniela Meneghini Correale and Valentina Zanolla, *ʿEraqi: Concordance and . . .*, LP 16, Eurasiatica 60, Venezia, 1999. Daniela Meneghini Correale, *Lirica Persica Hypertext: Browse and Search 20,000 Lines of Persian Ghazals*, LP 17, HyperFolia 1, Venezia, 2000 (CD-Rom). Valentina Zanolla, *The Ghazals of Sanaʾi in the Most Ancient Manuscripts*, LP 18, HyperFolia 2, Venezia, 2003 (CD-Rom).

Related studies. Daniela Meneghini Correale, *The Ghazals of Hafez: Concordance and Vocabulary*, Rome, 1989. Idem, "Quelques observations sur la structure lexicale des ghazals de Hafiz," in Michael Glünz and J. Christoph Bürgel, eds., *Heavenly and Earthly Drunkenness: Seven Studies on the Poet Hafiz of Shiraz*, Schweizer Asiatische Studien 12, Bern, 1991, pp. 105-36. Idem, "Some Support Programs Used in the Lirica Persica Project," in *Proceedings of the 4th International Conference and Exibition on Multilingual Computing*, London 1994, pp. 5.2.3.1-5.2.3.10. Idem, "Repérage automatique des *tajnis* dans la poésie lyrique néo-persane," *Studia Iranica Mesopotamica et Anatolica* 1 (1994), 1995, pp. 189-230. Idem, "La ripetizione lessicale nei ghazal di Salmân i Sâwajî," *Annali di Ca' Foscari* 36, Serie orientale 28, 1997, pp. 215-52. Idem, "Potential of the Vocabulary and Actuality of the Text: Computer Assisted Procedures for the Study of the Anagram in Classical Persian Verse," *Annali di Ca' Foscari* 39, Serie orientale 31, 2000, pp. 201-14. Idem, "Lexical Solidarity and Textual Cohesion in the Classical Persian Ghazal: Research Methodology and Preliminary Data," *Annali di Ca' Foscari* 36, Serie orientale 34, 2003, pp. 169-202. Daniela Meneghini Correale, Valentina Zanolla and Riccardo Zipoli, *Outline* of a Persian-English Dictionary*, Eurasiatica 51, Venezia 1997. Valentina Zanolla, "*Chashm* in Sanâʾî, ʿAṭṭâr e Rûmî," in *Quaderni 3 dell'Istituto Culturale della Repubblica Islamica dell'Iran in Italia*, Roma, 1995, pp. 39-136. Riccardo Zipoli, *Encoding and Decoding Neopersian Poetry*, Rome, 1988. Idem, "Tecniche informatiche e lirica neopersiana: dalle concordanze di Hafez a Lirica Persica," *Annali di Ca' Foscari* 29, Serie orientale 21, 1990, pp. 169-91. Idem, "Lirica Persica's Typical Vocabularies," in *Proceedings of the Second European Conference of Iranian Studies*, Rome, 1995, pp. 759-79. Idem, "Processing Word Pairs in Samples from the Lirica Persica Series," *Studia Iranica Mesopotamica et Anatolica* 1 (1994), 1995, pp. 247-97. Idem, "Textual Solidarity in the Ghazals of Hafez," in Iraj Afšār and Hans R. Roemer, eds., *Soḵanvāra: panjāh o panj goftār-e pažuheši ba yād-e Doktor Parviz Nātel Ḵānlari*, Tehran, 1997. Idem, "Syntagma Cohesion in the Neopersian Ghazal as Microtext," *Edebiyât* 9, 1998, pp. 101-27. Idem, "The Syntagmatic Cohesion between 'Wind' and 'Hair' in Hâfiz's Ghazals," *Annali di Ca' Foscari* 40, Serie orientale 32, 2001, pp. 93-110. Idem, "Comparing Typical Vocabularies of Persian Ghazal Authors," forthcoming.

(DANIELA MENEGHINI)

xi. Translations of Persian Works into Italian

With a few rare exceptions, Persian literature has never been widely circulated or made commercially available in Italy—a fact that is more visible in this country than in other European countries with more uninterrupted political, economic, and cultural ties with Persia. The approach adopted toward Persian texts in Italy has been almost exclusively academic, with the consequence that many important works of Persian literature have never been translated into Italian, as they are accessible to scholars in other European languages. On the other hand, the highly erudite level of certain individuals of the Italian Orientalist tradition, which dates back to Renaissance times, has guaranteed the production of some translations of significant historical value and of very high literary and academic quality.

The first Persian work translated into Italian was actually also the first to be translated into any European language. It was the poem *Hašt behešt* by Amir Ḵosrow Dehlavi (q.v.) written in 1300, which was translated by Cristoforo Armeno (16th century) as the *Peregrinaggio di tre giovani figliuoli del Re di Serendippo*, and published in Venice in 1557. In accordance with the custom of the time, it is not a literal translation but rather a re-casting, probably the result of the collective work of a group of Venetian scholars through comparison with two other kindred Persian texts: Neẓāmi's *Haft peykar* and Hātefi's *Haft manẓar* (qq.v.). Since these three Persian texts are different variants of the 'Romance of Bahrām,' the first Persian text in Italian (and in any other European language) thus represents the genre of the 'mirror for princes' (Cerulli; Amir Ḵosrow, 1996).

In Papal Rome—the other center of Oriental Studies in Italy—the efforts of Giovan Battista Raimondi (d. 1614) would have offered further rare and early Persian texts, and from less frequented areas such as those of the sciences and religious literature, but his project for translations and publications through the 'Stamperia Orientale Medicea' printing house encountered a series of obstacles of both personal and logistic nature. The contribution of the erudite Roman scholar Pietro Della Valle (1586-1652, q.v.) to the field of translations from Persian to Italian was also to remain only potential. From what can be determined from his papers at present, his love for Ḥāfeẓ, whose fame he was the first to bring to Europe, produced translations of only a few poems, read at a gathering after his return from Persia, of which no written trace has remained (Bertotti, 1990).

Such outstanding scholars as Cristoforo Armeno, Raimondi, and Della Valle had planted the seeds of the culture of translation that would only bear fruit on a regular basis when the seats of Iranian studies were officially established in the Italian university system. With the establishment of a continuous tradition of academic activity dedicated to Persia, the production of translations of Persian texts into Italian gradually became more necessary and frequent (an overview in Piemontese, 1982, pp. 575-654).

The first significant translations of pre-Islamic Persian literary texts are the works of Francesco Adolfo Cannizzaro (1867-1914, q.v.) and Italo Pizzi (1849-1920), written in the period between the last two decades of the 19th and the early 20th century. They both concentrated almost exclusively on translating passages from the Avesta (q.v.), which culminated in a broad anthology by Pizzi (1916). Moreover, the Avesta has been particularly fortunate among the pre-Islamic Persian texts, for reasons independent of its Persian origins, being republished partially or entirely in 1943-44 and later in translations from European languages with an accent on its universal spiritual teachings. Since Pizzi was primarily a specialist in Islamic Persian literature, the real initiator of a period of systematic translations from pre-Islamic literature was Antonino Pagliaro (1898-1973). Pagliaro translated excerpts from the Avesta and passages of Old Persian inscriptions from the Achaemenid era, mainly for his compendium of literary history (Pagliaro and Bausani). He also devoted much of his time to the translation of passages and entire works of Pahlavi literature, in particular the *Ayādgār ī Zarērān*, the *Kār-nāmag ī Artaxšēr ī Pāpakān* (qq.v.; Pagliaro, 1927), and the *Vičārišn ī čatrang* (1951). Besides Pagliaro's works, few other Italian translations of such comprehensiveness were produced in this field until recent times, and these were made by non-specialists in the field. Some examples are the translation of the *Ayādgār ī Jāmāspīg* (q.v.) by Giuseppe Messina (1939), a series of passages from Zoroastrian Pahlavi religious texts (*Pand-nāmag ī Zarduxšt*, *Bundahišn*, *Dādestān ī mēnog ī xrad*, *Dēnkard* [qq.v.]) translated by Alessandro Bausani (1957), and a later, isolated version of the *Gathas* (q.v.) translated by Marcello Meli (1996). The lack of a greater output of Italian translations in this field is due to three factors: the abovementioned tendency towards an almost exclusively academic approach to the texts, which is particularly true for pre-Islamic studies; the availability of translations of most of the works in question into other European languages; and, finally, the spread of the use of English for scientific publications, even among Italian scholars. Nevertheless, in recent times there have been some additions to the list, such as a new translation of the *Vičārišn ī čatrang* by Antonio Panaino (1999), an anthology of Pahlavi texts for the compendium of literary history by Carlo Cereti (2001), and a completely new translation of the Avesta carried out by Arnaldo Alberti from the original texts (2004).

The period of Italian translations of Persian literary works from the Islamic era began, and not by accident, in the post-Risorgimento (Italian unification) age (1880s) with epic poetry. In fact, apart from the appearance of occasional literary passages (lyrical, didactic, a travel diary, a treatise on falconry), the first truly representative translation is the monumental version of the *Šāh-nāma* by Italo Pizzi (1886-88). Rendered in eight-line stanzas of non-rhyming hendeca syllables, which has often been subject of criticism, Pizzi's *Libro dei Re* ('Book of Kings') is one of the greatest efforts of translating a Persian text in the history of Iranian studies worldwide (PLATE I). Pizzi

PLATE I

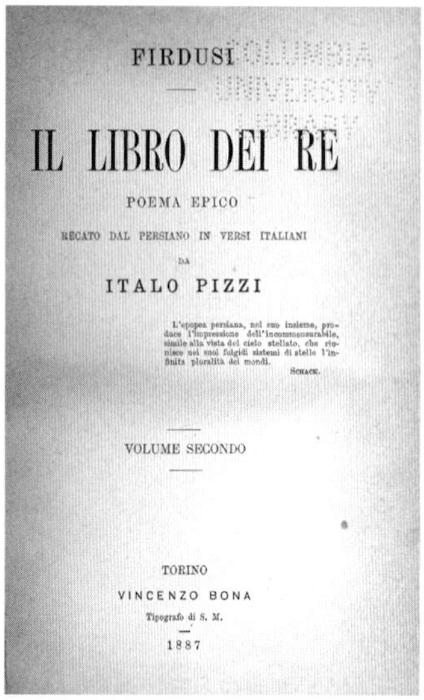
FIRDUSI

IL LIBRO DEI RE

POEMA EPICO

RECATO DAL PERSIANO IN VERSI ITALIANI

DA

ITALO PIZZI

L'epopea persiana, nel suo insieme, produce l'impressione dell'incommensurabile, simile alla vista del cielo stellato, che riunisce nei suoi fulgidi sistemi di stelle l'infinita pluralità dei mondi.

SCHACK.

VOLUME SECONDO

TORINO

VINCENZO BONA

Tipografo di S. M.

1887

Frontispiece and title page of Italo Pizzi's translation of the *Šāh-nāma* II (see Ferdowsi, 1886-88).
Courtesy of Butler Library, Columbia University, New York City.

has also translated numerous other works which were published either separately or as parts of his handbooks on the history of Persian prose and poetry (lyric poems by many poets, excerpts from narrative poems by Neẓāmi and ʿAṭṭār, historical texts, didactic pieces, a version of the *Golestān* of Saʿdi made in 1917; see Pizzi, 1887 and 1894). Nevertheless, his translation of Ferdowsi's *Šāh-nāma* remains his most important contribution, arousing interest and admiration in Italy even among non-Orientalists (Carducci, 1886). Two other, incomplete, Italian translations of the *Šāh-nāma* (1989 and 2003) do nothing more than paraphrase, and often summarize, Pizzi's work. Vittorio Rugarli (1860-1900), Pizzi's disciple and brother-in-law, also worked on the epic narratives, producing valuable, well-written translations of the *Šāh-nāma*, the *Barzu-nāma*, the *Kuk-nāma*, and long sections from the *Garšāsp-nāma* of Asadi Ṭusi (qq.v.).

A large hiatus separates this initial phase of Italian academic translations from the second cycle initiated by the following generation, in particular Francesco Gabrieli (1904-96, q.v.) and Alessandro Bausani (1921-88 q.v. at *www.iranica.com*), who focused on narrative, epic, and romantic literature with a short series of partial translations of the *Marzbān-nāma*, Gorgāni's *Vis o Rāmin*, and Neẓāmi's *Haft Peykar* (q.v.). Bausani's complete translation of the *Haft Peykar* in 1967 (incorporating passages translated by Gabrieli) marked an important point from which two different paths opened up. One was a specific interest in the works of Neẓāmi, whose *Leyli o Majnun* and *Eqbāl-nāma* were also translated into Italian and published commercially in 1985 and 1997, respectively. The other was a line of study that concentrated on the structural form of the book, which led to the Italian translation of the answers (*jawāb*) to *Haft Peykar* in *maṯnawi* form by Hātefi and Amir Ḵosrow, which came out in 1995 and 1996. Thus, considering also the section of Pizzi's *Libro dei Re* related to Bahrām, Italy can boast of four complete versions of the 'Romance of Bahrām.' The attention paid to this narrative model is clearly related to the first Venetian translation of the *Peregrinaggio* in 1557. With Angelo Michele Piemontese's translation of a second poem by Amir Ḵosrow, *Āʾena-ye Eskandari* (*Lo Specchio Alessandrino*, 1999), Italy consolidated a pioneering role in the filed, as the works of this important Indo-Persian poet had not yet been translated into any other European language. Along with this line of work, and besides the translations of excerpts published as individual studies or in volumes on literary history, such as those of Alessandro Bausani (Pagliaro and Bausani, 1960), Gianroberto Scarcia (1969), and Angelo Michele Piemontese (1970), only a few other complete translations of works of this genre appeared in Italian, notably the translation of Ebn Ḥosām's (see EBN ḤOSĀM ḴʷĀFI) version of the *Ḵāvar-nāma*, published in 1979.

To date, Persian historiography has received insufficient attention in Italy. Translations of brief fragments can be found in individual studies or in the usual general handbooks, beginning with the work on universal literature by Angelo De Gubernatis and in some anthologies (Piemontese and Scarcia, 1973). Lengthier versions in commercial editions, translated from intermediary languages, include: *Tāriḵ-e Jahāngošā* by Joveyni (q.v.; 1962, translated from English), some excerpts of *Tāriḵ-e Ṭabari* by Balʿami (q.v.; 1985 and 1993, from French), and a long excerpt from *Rowżat al-ṣafā᾽* by Mirḵᵛānd (1996, from French). In 2000, the *Homāyun-nāma* by Golbadan Bēgom (q.v.) was translated from the Persian original by Anna Vanzan.

In the field of didactic literature, mention should be made of complete translations of some masterpieces of Persian prose: Saʿdi's *Golestān* (four complete versions: 1917, 1965, 1979, and 1991), *Čahār Maqāla* by Neẓāmi ʿArużi Samarqandi (1977), *Qābus-nāma* (1981), *Safar-nāma* of Nāṣer-e Ḵosrow (1991), and *Siāsat-nāma* of Neẓām-al-Molk (1999). At the same time, academic circles showed a growing interest in the satiric works of ʿObeyd-e Zākāni, which appear to be quite well suited to the Italian sense of humor: examples are translations by Bausani (1964), Piemontese (1973), and D'Erme (1979, reprinted in 2005).

Due largely to a deep-rooted tendency in Italian culture to favor a generally aesthetic approach to literary history, the greatest number of translations from Persian have been those of lyric poetry. The first examples of the translated poetry appeared in the beginning of the 19th century in the context of academic research: odes of Jāmi, Saʿdi, Ḥāfeẓ, and Ḵāqāni were translated by scholars such as, among others, Romualdo Tecco (1802-67), and Angelo De Gubernatis (1840-1913). However, in this area too, truly representative translations began with Italo Pizzi and Vittorio Rugarli. Besides translations of various classical Persian authors, often published as celebratory books for the weddings of noble Italian families, Pizzi and Rugarli were the first to introduce the works of ʿOmar Khayyam (Ḵayyām) to Italy. Following the European success of Edward FitzGerald's (q.v.) translations, in Italy Khayyam represented the rare exception of a Persian author whose poetry appealed not only to academics but also to a vast and heterogeneous public, especially within the 'decadent' movement. There are over thirty publications containing selections of Khayyam's quatrains translated into Italian, ranging from small excerpts in booklets edited by Rugarli to various complete editions that were published throughout the 20th century. The latter include translations based on the original texts and accompanied by scholarly introductions (especially Gabrieli, 1944 and Bausani, 1956, both of which have been re-edited and printed many times), as well as those made from intermediate languages, particularly FitzGerald's English version. Khayyam is certainly the most widely known Persian poet in Italy and is recognized as a classic of world literature (Piemontese, 1974).

Once again, it was A. Bausani who began a new round of translations of lyric poetry, increasing the number of poets represented, even if by a single poem. To the anthology of classical poets (Rudaki, Farroḵi, ʿOnṣori, Manučehri, Sanāʾi, ʿAṭṭār, Masʿud-e Saʿd-e Salmān, Azraqi, Moʿezzi, Anwari, Ḵāqāni, Saʿdi, Rumi, ʿErāqi, Ḥāfeẓ, ʿObeyd-e Zākāni, Jāmi, Ṣāʾeb, and Qāʾāni, who constitute more or less the classical framework of all subsequent literary histories and anthologies) presented in his history of Persian literature (Pagliaro and Bausani, 1960), which also provides a review of the main motifs of Persian lyrics, Bausani added some of his own personal favorites, such as a translation of the Persian work of Avicenna and an ample selection of Rumi's mystical poems. Important translations of lyric poetry were also produced by Gianroberto Scarcia, who similarly included excerpts in literary histories (Scarcia, 1969; Piemontese, 1970), individual studies, and collections; his personal favorites included poets from the later Indian style such as Ṣāʾeb and Bidel (Zipoli and Scarcia). So far, monographs have been quite rare; Ḥāfeẓ was treated in 1966 (a small volume edited by Eva Giardina), in 1998 (edited by Carlo Saccone), and two complete editions appeared in the early 2000s—one by Giovanni D'Erme (2004, so far first volume only), and the other by Stefano Pellò and Gianroberto Scarcia (2005). Other monographs concern Bābā Ṭāher (1988), Bidel (1995), and Mahsati Ganjavi (1999).

Anthologies for the commercial market have been published more frequently since the 1970s: the most comprehensive editions date to 1973 (edited by A. M. Piemontese and G. Scarcia, including Turkish poetry), 1986 (*Divano Occidentale* by G. Scarcia), 1995 (*Antologia della pleiade ghaznavide* by Rita Bargigli), 2003 (*Ti amo di due amori*, together with Arabic, Turkish, and Hebrew poems, Persian section edited by Mario Casari), and 2004 (*Poesia dell'Islam* by G. Scarcia).

The collection of Rumi's poems edited by Bausani also marks another area of translation of Persian works into Italian: that of philosophical-religious literature, especially of mystical nature. The approach to this subject, sometimes carried out in an academic context, as in the case of the translation of religious texts by Nāṣer-e Ḵosrow (1959 and 1990), the *Omm al-Ketāb* (1966), and the *Ḥosn o del* by Fattāḥi (1974), has more often been driven by the choice of texts that might attract interest among a broader, more general audience seeking a less familiar spirituality. This trend also includes the many Sufi anthologies containing Persian material (1951, 1964, 1991, and 1999), the publications dedicated to ʿAṭṭār (*Taḏkerat al-awliāʾ*, 1964; *Manṭeq al-ṭeyr*, 1986; *Elāhi-nāma*, 1990; and the dubiously attributed *Gol o bolbol*, 2003), Sanāʾi (1992 and 1993), Sohravardi (1990 and 2000), and the numerous anthologies inspired by Rumi's *maṯnawi* or *divān*, most of which were translated from French or English versions. The first complete translation of Rumi's *maṯnawi* was made by Gabriele Mandel Khan and published in 2006. Other publications, which were the result of a political-religious approach, include those concerning Bahai (q.v.) literature and, more recently, the works of thinkers and ideologues of the Islamic Republic such as M. Moṭahhari and R. Khomeini.

There have also been some cautious attempts to make contemporary Persian literature better known to a wider public than strictly academic. While theatrical works (a handful of comedies from the Akhundov (1812-78, see ĀḴUNDZĀDA) school and a few passages from *taʿzia*s and poetry (the Indo-Persian poet Moḥammad Eqbāl, introduced by A. Bausani, and poems by modern Persian poets such as Sohrāb Sepehri and Forūḡ Farroḵzād, q.v.)

have appeared only sporadically, certain prose writers have fared better, particularly Ṣādeq Hedāyat (q.v.), whose works came in the 1960s and 1970s via French, and in 2007 a new revised edition of his works was published on the basis of the original Persian texts. Besides a few novellas by authors like Čubak, Jamālzāda, and Behrangi, translated and published within some academic articles, the best attempt to introduce modern Persian literature to the Italian public was through an anthology of 20th-century Persian literature edited by Filippo Bertotti (1989), followed by an anthology of works by Ḡolām-Ḥosayn Sāʾedi (1990). Recently, some attention has been paid to contemporary Persian female writers, particularly Šahrnuš Pārsipur, who were presented by stressing a sociological approach to the status of women in Persia (1998, 2000, 2002, and 2004).

Following a similar pattern, which reveals the persistent methodological barriers to the diffusion of knowledge of Persian literature in Italy, an anthropological and ethnological, rather than literary, approach has favored the publication of many volumes of Persian fables, presented in popular 'exotic' editions that most often derive from anthologies in other European languages.

Bibliography: Amir Ḵosrow Dehlavi, *Hašt behešt*, tr. A. M. Piemontese as *Le otto novelle del paradiso*, Soveria Mannelli, 1996. Idem, *Āʾina-ye Eskandari*, tr. A. M. Piemontese as *Lo specchio alessandrino*, Soveria Mannelli, 1999. C. Armeno, *Peregrinaggio di tre giovani figliuoli del re di Serendippo, per opra di M. Christoforo Armeno dalla Persiana nell'Italiana lingua trapportato*, Venice, 1557. Farid-al-Din ʿAṭṭār, *Manṭeq al-ṭeyr*, tr. G. Saccone as *Il verbo degli uccelli*, Milan, 1986. R. Bargigli, ed., *I poeti della pleiade ghaznavide*, Milan, 1995. A. Bausani, *Testi religiosi zoroastriani*, Milan, 1957. F. Bertotti, ed., *I minareti e il cielo. Racconti persiani del Novecento*, Palermo, 1989. Idem, "Un viaggiatore Romano e un poet persiano: Pietro Della Valle estimatore e divulgatore di Ḥāfiẓ," *Islàm. Storia e Civiltà* 9, 1990, pp. 121-27. Bidel—see Zipoli and Scarcia. G. Carducci, "Arte e poesia," *Nuova antologia di lettere, arti e scienze* 88, 1886, pp. 5-21. C. G. Cereti, *La letteratura pahlavi. Introduzione ai testi con riferimenti alla storia degli studi e alla tradizione manoscritta*, Milan, 2001. E. Cerulli, "Una raccolta persiana di novelle tradotte a Venezia nel 1557," *Atti della Accademia Nazionale dei Lincei. Memorie della Classe di Scienze morali, storiche e filologiche*, Serie 8, vol. 18/4, 1975, pp. 247-365. *Dāstān-e Kok-e kuhzād*, tr. V. Rugarli as *Kuk il Montanaro*, Bologna, 1891. G. M. D'Erme, "Opere satiriche di 'Ubayd Zākānī," in *Iranica*, ed. G. Gnoli and A. V. Rossi, Naples, 1979, pp. 3-160. Ferdowsi, *Šāh-nāma*, tr. I. Pizzi as *Il Libro dei Re*, 8 vols., Turin, 1886-88. Golbadan Begom, *Homāyunnāma*, tr. A. Vanzan as *La storia di Humāyūn raccontata da Golbadan Begum, principessa dell'harem Moghul*, Milan, 2000. Ḥāfeẓ, *Divān*, tr. G. D'Erme as *Canzoniere*, vol. 1, Naples, 2004; tr. S. Pellò and G. Scarcia as *Canzoniere*, Milan, 2005. Hātefi, *Haft manẓar*, tr. M. Bernardini, as *I sette scenari*, Naples, 1995. Key-Kāʾus b. Eskandar, *Qābus-nāma*, tr. R. Zipoli as *Il libro dei consigli*, Milan, 1981. ʿOmar Ḵayyām, *Robāʿiyāt*, tr. F. Gabrieli as *Le Rubàiyyàt*, Florence, 1944; tr. A. Bausani as *Quartine*, Turin, 1956. G. Messina, *Libro apocalittico persiano «Ayātkār-I Zāmāspik» I. Testo pehlevico, pārsi e pāzend restituto, tradotto e commentato*, Rome, 1939. Neẓāmi, *Haft Peykar*, tr. A. Bausani as *Le sette principesse*, Bari, 1967. Idem, *Leyli o Majnun*, tr. G. Calasso as *Leylā e Majnun*, Milan, 1985. Idem, *Eqbāl-nāma*, tr. C. Saccone as *Il libro della fortuna di Alessandro*, Milan, 1997. A. Pagliaro, *Epica e Romanzo nel Medioevo Persiano*, Florence, 1927. A. Pagliaro and A. Bausani, *Storia della letteratura persiana*, Milan, 1960. A. Panaino, *La novella degli scacchi e della tavola reale. Un'antica fonte orientale sui due giochi da tavola più diffusi nel mondo eurasiatico tra Tardoantico e Medioevo e sulla loro simbolica militare e astrologica*, testo pahlavi, traduzione e commento al *Wizārišn ī čatrang ud nihišn ī nēw-ardaxšīr "La spiegazione degli scacchi e la disposizione della tavola reale*," Milan, 1999. A. M. Piemontese, *Storia della letteratura persiana*, 2 vols., Milan, 1970. Idem, "ʿOmar Khayyām in Italia," *Oriente Moderno* 54, 1974, pp. 275-97. Idem, *Bibliografia italiana dell'Iran (1462-1982)*, 2 vols., Naples, 1982. A. M. Piemontese and G. Scarcia, *Poesia d'amore turca e persiana*, Novara, 1973. I. Pizzi, *Manuale di letteratura persiana*, Milan, 1887. Idem, *Storia della poesia persiana*, 2 vols., Turin, 1894. *Rūmī, Poesie mistiche*, ed. A. Bausani, Milan, 1980. Jalāl-al-Din Rumi, *Maṯnawi-e maʿnawi*, tr. G. Mandel Khan as *Mathnavi. Il poema del misticismo universale*, Milan, 2006. Saʿdi, *Golestān*, tr. P. Filippani-Ronconi as *Il Roseto*, Turin, 1965; tr. R. Bargigli as *Il Roseto*, Rome, 1979. G. Scarcia, "Letteratura persiana," in *Storia delle letterature d'Oriente*, vol. II, ed. O. Botto, Milan, 1969, pp. 243-451. Idem, *Divano Occidentale*, Bologna, 1986. A. Vanzan, *Parole svelate. Racconti di donne persiane*, Padua, 1998. R. Zipoli, ed., "Da Onsori a Hatefi. Antologia poetica," *Quaderni dell'Istituto Culturale della Repubblica Islamica d'Iran in Italia* 1, 1989, *Majmuʿa-ye Bahāria*, pp. 7-43. R. Zipoli and G. Scarcia, eds., *Il canzoniere dell'alba. 50 ghazal di Bidel*, Milan, 1997.

(MARIO CASARI)

xii. TRANSLATIONS OF ITALIAN WORKS INTO PERSIAN

Two texts by Italian authors appear to be the first known translations of European literary works into Persian carried out in the modern age. They are the *Idea del giardino del mondo*, a treatise on natural medicine by Tommaso Tomai (d. 1593), and the *De christiana expeditione apud Sinas* (in Latin), a report about China by the Jesuit missionary (see JESUITS IN SAFAVID PERSIA), Matteo Ricci (1552-1610). The translator of both texts was Moḥammad Zamān (b. 1618), known as *Farangiḵʷān* ('reader of the Frankish language')—an Iranian who converted to Catholicism in Isfahan in 1641 and subsequently emigrated to India. The excellent Persian translations of the Italian (*Ḥadiqa-ye ʿālam*, ca. 1642-50) and Latin (*Tāriḵ-e Čin*, ca. 1650-65) texts exist in two unique manuscripts (Paris, Bibliothèque nationale de France, MS Persan 158; and Calcutta, Asiatic Society of Bengal, MS Curson I.124). It seems highly probable that a missionary (in the second case, probably, the Jesuit father Enrico Uwens who was stationed in India and died in Delhi in 1667) may have aided Moḥammad Zamān in his translation. Nonetheless, whether or not he was helped by others, if these works were personally translated by Moḥammad Zamān, he should be recognized not only as the first Persian translator from Italian, but also as the first and, to date, the only known translator from Latin (Blochet, II, pp. 108-9; Richard, pp. 287-88; Piemontese, pp. 28-35).

Though both significant and praiseworthy, Moḥammad Zamān's works were neither distributed in Persia nor were they followed by any similar endeavor and should therefore be considered unique and apparently occasional. It was not until the first half of the 19th century when Persian culture turned its attention to the languages and literatures of Europe once again, although it tended to concentrate primarily on French and, to a lesser extent, on English. These two languages were also to become the main intermediary channels for the subsequent approach towards Italian literature which, however, remained sporadic and discontinuous.

Indeed, it was with the translation from French of Giovanni Boccaccio's (1313-75) *Decameron* by Aḥmad Khan Daryābeygi (governor of Bušehr and then of other ports in the Persian Gulf), that Italian literature stepped back into Persia at the beginning of the 20th century (Boccaccio, 1905). In this case, however, the work was recast rather than simply translated. It was stripped of its textual and contextual complexity, and the stories were presented in a simplified narrative sequence. This illustrated lithographic volume stemmed from a growing interest in literature of libertine character under the Qajars, which was not well received by the Shiʿite religious authorities. As Boccaccio's work was at the center of such a substantial divergence from the norm, it did not circulate regularly in Persia, and, despite the occasional appearance of a few individual novellas, two new translations from French made by Ḥabib Šonuqi (1966) and by Moḥammad Qāżi (1986) were censored and have never been printed.

In much the same vein, Gabriele D'Annunzio (1863-1938) was presented as a hero and poet capable of both military and erotic achievements, rather than solely as a literary artist. His name and fragments of his writings appeared mostly during the decade of fervent publishing between the abdication of Reżā Shah Pahlavi (r. 1925-41) and the fall of the Moṣaddeq government (1943-53). D'Annunzio was mentioned in various journals (particularly in the widely distributed *Eṭṭelāʿāt-e haftegi*), in which other important Italian poets and writers, such as Dante, Petrarch, Machiavelli, Michelangelo, and Galileo, began to appear more frequently.

Among these newly introduced writers, Nicolò Machiavelli (1469-1527) represented an important step forward in presenting the Italian culture, and his ideas left a distinct mark. The translation of his *Il principe* from English by Maḥmud Maḥmud (1882-1965; a publisher of historical and political writings who also held various political posts) was printed in 1945. The translator presented Machiavelli's masterpiece, emphasizing the cynical element in the Italian writer's reflections in an updated, anti-British light. The book was well received and was reprinted several times until 1968, along with Persian translations of Machiavelli's two other works: *Belfagor* (1963) and *Mandragola* (1966). Machiavelli's theories in the history of political thought were also discussed (Piemontese, pp. 101-8). Iranian scholar and linguist Dāryuš Āšuri compared one German and two English translations to produce an admirable new Persian translation of *Il Principe*, accompanied by a thorough critical analysis (1987, rev. ed. 1996). This led to the translation of another important work of Machiavelli, the *Discorsi sopra la prima deca di Tito Livio* (1998).

The works of Tomai, Boccaccio, and Machiavelli represent three landmarks, albeit isolated and motivated by different factors, in the approach of Persian intelligentsia toward Italian literature. It was, however, not until after World War II that Italian literature really took hold in Persia as a result of the strengthening of political and economic relations with Europe and the United States, the increase in travel to and from Persia, and the foundation of libraries and cultural institutions that made international literature available more easily. Nonetheless, Italian literature continued to be mediated mostly by French and English translations. Various cultural reviews began to publish Persian translations, often fragmentary, of 20th-century Italian authors and of critical reflections on their works. These were chosen according to the criteria that suited the elements and predispositions of Persian taste: the surreal compassion of Luigi Pirandello's novels (in *Soḵan*, 1948, 1955; *Eṭṭelāʿāt-e māhāna*, 1948, 1950; *Mehregān*, 1952, 1955; *Ferdowsi*, 1955-56), the crude realism of Alberto Moravia (*Mehregān*, 1953, 1955; *Kāviān*, 1954; *Ferdowsi*, 1956; *Soḵan*, 1957; *Tehrān-e moṣawwar*, 1957-59), the bitter lyrical naturalism of Grazia Deledda (*Eṭṭelāʿāt-e māhāna*, 1952; *Soḵan*, 1954), and the magic and alienation of Dino Buzzati (*Soḵan*, 1955).

A name that often appears in association with some of these translations is that of Šojāʿ-al-Din Šafāʾ (b. 1918), who was one of the first to translate directly from Italian, although he amply complemented this with a constant comparison of French, English, and German versions. The most substantial undertaking in Šafā's vast output was his translation of the masterpiece of Italian literature, Dante Alighieri's (1265-1321) *Divina Commedia* (1956). Despite the abundant criticism directed against him, especially regarding the lack of any attempt to use poetic expression in the Persian language, Šafā's translation should be regarded as highly successful because it corresponds meticulously to the original and is often annotated, either directly in the text or within explanatory notes. This translation enjoyed great popular success and was reprinted four times up to 1978. With the advent of the Islamic Republic, Dante's work was removed from circulation (Bertotti and Orsatti, pp. 257-69). This situation has recently been reversed with a reprint of Šafā's translation (1999) and, more importantly, with the publication of a new full translation of the work (based on French and English translations) by Farida Mahdavi-Dāmḡāni (2000, repr. 2001). Although this translation has brought important new contributions, there is still room for improvement. The same translator also published *La Vita Nuova* (1997), Dante's only other work to be translated into Persian in full.

The translation of the *Divina Commedia* can also be regarded as a milestone in the Persian awareness of Italian poetry. Previously, Italian poetry had lacked broad and thoughtful attention and had been treated in a fragmentary manner, mainly through short extracts and comments translated from English and French, which were published in reviews and anthologies. Until then, except for Dante, publishers have only briefly touched on the great Italian authors of the Middle Ages and the Renaissance, such as Petrarch, Ariosto, Tasso, and Metastasio, preferring instead collections of a wide range of 19th- and 20th-century authors, whose appeal is more immediate as Persians discover more of European culture. Moreover, if one leaves aside some significant exceptions (the translation of Giacomo Leopardi's *Canto notturno di un pastore errante dell'Asia* in the review *Bahār* of 1922, the curiosity about Salvatore Quasimodo in some of the reviews published after he was awarded the Nobel Prize in 1959, some interest in the poetry of Cesare Pavese in reviews and collections from the 1970s onwards, and a volume dedicated to the poetry of Giuseppe Ungaretti in 1991), the main examples of Italian poetry in Persian can be found in two anthologies edited by the Cultural Institute of the Italian Embassy in Tehran. One of them was edited by Nāder Nāderpur in collaboration with Gina Labriola Caruso (*Haft čehra*, 1974), and concentrated on the 20th-century works, while the other, by A. Mohājer Irvāni (*Bargozidegān-e šeʿr-e Itāliā*, 1991), focused on the 19th-century authors.

Beginning in the 1960s, the popular success of some Italian authors, although limited almost exclusively to those of the 20th century, took a firmer hold. Writers such as Grazia Deledda, Alba De Céspedes, Carlo Cassola, Giovanni Guareschi, Curzio Malaparte, and Elio Vittorini appeared sporadically on the cultural scene in reviews and in the occasional volume, while others were introduced more systematically and, consequently, greater attention was paid to their literary development. The translation and publication of Pirandello's short stories in reviews and magazines went on without interruption, accompanied by the appearance of volumes containing tales, novels, and plays: *Bist dāstān* (1956), *Enrico IV* and *Il fu Mattia Pascal* (1967 and 1969), *Non si sa come* (1970), *Uno, nessuno e centomila* and *Il turno* (1993), and *L'esclusa* (1995), although the latter work was censored before it was distributed. Similarly, the fame of Moravia continued to spread, and his stories appeared frequently in literary reviews. His works also appeared in volumes with substantial print runs, although they were almost exclusively translated from English: there are four different translations of *La ciociara* (in installments in *Tehrān-e moṣawwar* in 1960, then in separate volumes in 1964, 1985, and 1990); translations were also published of *Gli indifferenti* (1967), *Racconti romani* (1985), and *Il conformista* (1995). Buzzati's works continued to appear too: some of his short stories in reviews and collections (1972, 1995, 2000, and 2003), and some of his novels, in particular the well-known *Il deserto dei Tartari*, which has seen three translations (1970, 1986, and 2000; see Vanzan, 2000; Ebrāhim, 2002).

To these three authors, who were already quite well known, other significant names may be added, each having a specific appeal for the Persian audience. Ignazio Silone, whose collection of essays *Testimonianze sul comunismo* had already been published in 1950, gained renown with the publication of his novel *Pane e vino*, translated from French by Moḥammad Qāżi (1966), which reached its twelfth printing in 1995. Critical reflections and radio readings accompanied the publication of numerous other writings by Silone, at times carried out by some of the most outstanding translators of Italian: *Fontamara* (1968, by Manučehr Ātaši, from English), *Una manciata di more* (1971, by Bahman Farzāna), *L'avventura di un povero cristiano* (1973, by Moḥammad Qāżi, from French), *La volpe e le camelie* (1977, by Bahman Farzāna), *Il seme sotto la neve* (1982), *Uscita di sicurezza* (1983), and *La scuola dei dittatori* (1984, the latter three by Mehdi Saḥābi).

The many aspects of Cesare Pavese's works, including his poetry, received great attention, especially his short stories and several novels (two translations of *La luna e i falò* in 1967 and 1991, *Paesi tuoi* in 1974, and *Il compagno* in 1975). Some of Natalia Ginzburg's best-known novels have been translated (*Caro Michele*, 1978 and *Lessico famigliare*, 1985), along with her many articles on culture and customs (*Le piccole virtù*, in installments in various reviews, and collected together in 1997).

Great attention was paid to Italo Calvino, already internationally celebrated, through the publication of articles and essays regarding him, and translations of his better-known works: *Il visconte dimezzato* (1967), *Il barone rampante*, *Se una notte d'inverno un viaggiatore*, *Sei lezioni americane* (1984, 1990, and 1996, in each case from French by Leyli Golestān), *Le città invisibili* (1988), *Marcovaldo* (1991), *Palomar* (1998), and even an anthology from his collection of tales entitled *Fiabe italiane* (1999).

The most striking publishing phenomenon regarding an Italian writer, however, is that of Oriana Fallaci, whose journalistic writing became the best known of all Italian voices in terms of both the number of copies sold and editions printed. After *Niente e così sia* (1971) and *Se il sole muore* (1973), the great success of *Lettera a un bambino mai nato* (four different translations between 1976 and 1977) and *Intervista con la storia*, which contained the interview with Moḥammad-Reżā Shah Pahlavi (four translations between 1977 and 1978), earned her the honor of being the most important foreign writer in Persia during the 1970s.

During the period in which these writers gained reputation in Persia, the names of a few prolific translators from Italian became familiar (Piemontese, pp. 126-44): Bahman Moḥaṣṣeṣ (b. 1931; translated works of Pirandello, Pavese, and also *La pelle* by Curzio Malaparte, which in 1964 created a certain scandal), Bahman Farzāna (b. 1938, translated works of Deledda, D'Annunzio, Ginzburg, De Céspedes, Pirandello, Buzzati, Silone, and also Vasco Pratolini's *Cronaca Familiare* in 1975), Reżā Qeyṣariya (b. 1941, translated works of Moravia, Buzzati, Pirandello, Pavese, Calvino, and Leonardo Sciascia, as well as *Il giorno della civetta* in 1979), Mehdi Saḥābi (b. 1944, translated works of Silone, Calvino, Pavese, Sciascia, together with Gavino Ledda's *Padre padrone* in 1987), and Moḥsen Ṭāher Nowkanda (b. 1947, translated works of Quasimodo, Pavese, Fenoglio, and Baricco).

A particularly influential factor in the awareness of Italian culture in general was the international success of Italian cinema and, in particular, the neorealist genre of the 1950s and 1960s. Numerous articles and essays on the subject were not, however, accompanied by an equivalent degree of effort in translating the screenplays (with the exception of a few by Federico Fellini, Luchino Visconti, and Michelangelo Antonioni). Italian playwriting has received slightly more attention. Translated plays were sometimes printed, but mostly performed either in theaters or as radio readings: above all, works of Pirandello (in particular translations by the director and translator Pari Ṣāberi), although other playwrights attracted attention too, like Goldoni (*La locandiera*, 1957) and, from the 1990s, the Nobel Prize winner Dario Fo (*Morte accidentale di un anarchico* in 1992).

An exceptional case is the introduction of the wooden puppet Pinocchio into the Persian cultural scene, with a mixture of cinematographic, theatrical, and literary influences at its roots. Carlo Collodi's *Le avventure di Pinocchio* is, moreover, a worldwide 'steady-seller' and one of the books that can boast the highest number of translations around the world. The first translation into Persian was made by the writer Ṣādeq Čubak (1916-88). It was published in 1955 and has continuously stayed in print. Besides this incomparable version, four other unabridged translations have appeared to date (1977-95), along with innumerable reduced versions, all pointing to the literary success with a degree of influence on the development of Persian literature for children in the second half of the 20th century (Casari, pp. 57-91). In this specific area of literature, which is very important in Persian publishing, another noteworthy Italian writer is Gianni Rodari, two of whose works have enjoyed good print runs: *La torta in cielo*, translated by Piruz Maleki (1985), and *Tante storie per giocare*, translated by Čengiz Dāvarpanāh (1992).

In the last years of the 20th century, besides the attention paid to contemporary authors particularly in vogue in Italy and Europe such as Umberto Eco, Susanna Tamaro, and Alessandro Baricco, the appreciation of the 20th-century Italian prose has been increased by two systematic anthologies: *Gozida-ye dāstānhā-ye kutāh az nevisandegān-e moʿāṣer-e Itāliā*, compiled by Firuza Mohājer and Kāmrān Širdel (1989), and *Adabiyāt wa nevisandegān-e moʿāṣer-e Itāliā* (1997)—a wide-ranging collection assembled by the translator Moḥsen Ebrāhim, who also translated some of the works of Buzzati, Ginzburg, and Calvino. The latter anthology also contains a long introductory essay which is the first history of Italian literature to be written in Persian originally.

Bibliography: M. Afšār, *Ketābšenāsi-e romān wa majmuʿehā-ye dāstāni-e motarjam*, 2 vols., Tehran, 1998. Dante Alighieri, *Komedi-e elāhi. Duzak̠. Barzak̠. Behešt*, tr. Š. Šafāʾ, 3 vols., Tehran, 1956; tr. F. Mahdavi-Dāmḡāni, 3 vols., Tehran, 2000. F. Bertotti and P. Orsatti, "Dante in Iran," in *L'opera di Dante nel mondo. Edizioni e traduzioni del Novecento. Atti del Convegno internazionale di studi, Roma, 27-29 aprile 1989*, ed. E. Esposito, Ravenna, 1992, pp. 257-69. E. Blochet, *Catalogue des manuscrits persans de la Bibliothèque nationale*, 4 vols., Paris, 1905-34. G. Boccaccio, *Ketāb-e Dekāmeron*, tr. A. K̠. Daryābeygi, Bushehr, 1905. D. Buzzati, *Biābān-e Tātārhā*, tr. S. Ḥabibi, Tehran, 1970. Idem, *Ṣaḥrā-ye Tātārhā*, tr. M. Ebrāhim, Tehran, 2000. I. Calvino, *Viskont-e šakkesoda*, tr. B. Moḥaṣṣeṣ, Tehran, 1967. Idem, *Agar šab-i az šabhā-ye zemestān mosāfer-i*, tr. L. Golestān, Tehran, 1990. M. Casari, "Pinocchio persiano," *Oriente Moderno*, N.S. 22 (83), 2003, pp. 57-91. C. Collodi, *Pinokio. Ādamak-e čubi*, tr. Ṣ. Čubak, Tehran, 1955. M. Ebrāhim, *Adabiyāt wa nevisandegān-e moʿāṣer-e Itāliā*, 2 vols., Tehran, 1997. Idem, "Riflessioni su alcuni aspetti della ricezione di Buzzati in Iran," *Studi buzzatiani* 7, 2002, pp. 83-94. O. Fallaci, *Nāma be kudak-i ke hargez motawalled našod*, tr. V. Mošfeq, Tehran, 1985. N. Ginzburg, *Alefbā-ye k̠anevāda*, tr. F. Mohājer, Tehran, 1985. N. Machiavelli, *Šahryār*, tr. M. Maḥmud, Tehran, 1945; tr. D. Āšuri, Tehran, 1987, rev. ed. Tehran, 1996. F. Mohājer and K. Širdel, *Gozida-ye dāstānhā-ye kutāh az nevisandegān-e moʿāṣer-e Itāliā*, Tehran, 1989. A. Mohājer Irvāni, *Bargozidegān-e šeʿr-e Itāliā*, Tehran, 1991. A. Moravia, *Dāstānhā-ye romi*, tr. R. Qeyṣariya, Tehran, 1985. K̠. Mošār, *Fehrest-e ketābhā-ye čāpi-e fārsi az āḡāz tā āk̠ar-e sāl-e 1345*, 3 vols., Tehran, 1971-73. N. Nāderpur and G. Lābriolā Kāruso, *Haft čehra az šāʿerān-e moʿāṣer-e Itāliā*, Tehran, 1974. A. M. Piemontese, "La letteratura italiana in Persia," *Atti della Accademia Nazionale dei Lincei, Classe di Scienze morali, storiche e filologiche, Memorie*, Series 9, vol. 17/1, 2003, pp. 1-251. L. Pirandello, *Henri-e čahārom*, tr. B. Moḥaṣṣeṣ, Tehran, 1967. Idem, *Yek-i, hičkas, ṣadhezār*, tr. B. Farzāna, Tehran, 1971. F. Richard, "Une traduction persane d'un ouvrage italien au XVIIe siècle," *Stud. Ir.* 7, 1978, pp. 287-88. Š. Šafāʾ, *Montak̠ab-i az zibātarin šāhkārhā-ye šeʿr-e jahān*, Tehran, 1952. I. Silone, *Nān wa šarāb*, tr. M. Qāżi, Tehran, 1966. A. Vanzan, "*Sahra-ye Tatarha*: traduzione in lingua persiana de *Il deserto dei Tartari* di Dino Buzzati, a cura di Mohsen Ebrahim, Teheran, 1379/2000; *Shast dastan*, traduzione in lingua persiana de *I sessanta racconti* di Dino Buzzati, a cura di M. Ebrahim, Teheran, 1379/2000," *Studi buzzatiani* 5, 2000, pp. 187-91.

(MARIO CASARI)

xiii. IRANIANS IN ITALY

It is difficult to speak about a true Persian community in Italy. The presence of Persians in Italy has always been fragmentary and discontinuous, which never led to any extended, cohesive social groups of permanent residents. Even during the periods when the migratory flow from Persia towards other countries was at its peak (India until the 18th century, France from the middle of the 18th century, Sweden and the USA, for different reasons, after World War II and especially following the Revolution of 1978-79), few Persians arrived in Italy. Unlike other countries, Italy has not been an especially favored destination for a long stay abroad or for exile, due to its fewer cultural and diplomatic links and the less developed legislation on immigration, work availability, and refugee asylum.

Recent research is now casting light upon the presence in Rome, in ancient times, of important personalities from the Persian court as well as members of the nobility, in particular during the Parthian and the early Sasanian eras. They included sometimes hostages or refugees staying for long periods of time as guests of the Roman imperial court and later on also newly converted Christian pilgrims (Nedergaard; Ricci 1996; Piemontese, 2001; idem, 2003). The scant information available concerning Persian merchants and ambassadors who came to Italy (especially Rome and Venice) between the Middle Ages and the modern era does not reveal either a steady presence or lengthy stays. It seems that the first group of Persians to settle in Italy followed the arrival of the first Persian *chargé d'affaires*, Narimān Khan Qawām-al-Salṭana (1896) and then with the entourage of the minister plenipotentiary, Malkom Khan, in Rome (1899-1908), but about whom very little is known. The creation of a diplomatic seat gave a degree of continuity to a small-scale, but significant, Persian presence in Italy, which was represented by diplomatic staff and their families. The period of their residence in Italy, however, depended on the length of their assignment to their diplomatic posts, and, besides, they tended to isolate themselves from the Italian society in general, mainly residing within the areas around the embassy and the consulates. This has remained relatively constant even throughout crucial political and institutional changes. At present (2004), the Persian diplomatic corps, divided between Rome and Milan, consists of about forty individuals, including officers and clerical staff and their respective families. Since the mid-1980s, the Persian embassy to the Vatican has become a point of reference for the Shiʿites in Italy, and, as the European Islamic Cultural Centre, has published numerous religious works.

Historically, students have always constituted the main body of Persians residing in Italy. Fragmentary information indicates that since the 17th century, although still very sporadically, there has been the custom of spending spells in Italy to pursue artistic studies. Uncertain information indicates an educational voyage of a certain Moḥammad-Zamān to Rome in the first half of 1600. It is not clear whether he is the same Moḥammad-Zamān Farangiḵᵛān, who translated into Persian the *Idea del giardino del mondo* of Thomaso Tomai (see ITALY xii. TRANSLATIONS), or the famous painter living in India at the Mughal court (see Manucci 1901, II, pp. 16-18; Tucci 1949, pp. 79-80). Another known name is that of the intellectual and painter Mirzā Abu'l-Ḥasan Khan Saniʿ-al-Molk Ḡaffāri (q.v.), who spent five years (1846-50) in Italy studying at the *Accademia delle Belle Arti* in Rome and copying the works of Italian masters. In 1860, he became the editor of the first Persian newspaper, the *Ruz-nāma-ye waqāyeʿ-e ettefāqiya*, published in Tehran (Davarpanah; Ḏokāʾ, pp. 18-19). Alongside these students of the arts (who remained very few until the 1950s), since 1927 another kind of Persian student could be found at the Naval Academy in Livorno, where Persian cadets received military and naval training (together with technical training in a variety of specializations up to university level), with the objective of creating the Persian Royal Navy. The influx of students to the Academy was, however, interrupted by the advent of the Revolution of 1970. In any case, both of these projects were temporary, and, with a few rare and not statistically significant exceptions, most students returned home after completing their studies.

A greater flux of Persian students to Italy can be identified from the 1950s onwards. This new flux was soon helped by the creation of study grants established in accordance with the Cultural Agreement signed between the two countries in 1958. Exact figures are not available, but between 1950 and 1970 some tens of thousands of Persian students came to settle for varying periods of time in Rome, Florence, Turin, Venice, Perugia, and other major Italian cities, to study architecture, fine arts, music, engineering, medicine, and agronomy.

In Italy, as in the rest of Europe, among these students, who were mainly children of the wealthy classes from Tehran, opposition groups began to form against the politics of the shah. These groups were linked to the international network of the Confederation of Iranian Students, National Union. The activities of these student associations, such as the Federation of the Unions of Iranian Students in Italy, was never comparable to that of their equivalent groups in France, Great Britain or Germany, and in terms of publications, it never went much further than a few pamphlets.

During the same period, in particular during the late 1970s, Italy witnessed a boom in the importation of Persian carpets, with an increase in the number of Persian tradesmen coming to Italy. The trade in carpets and the vast network of shops and related activities (cleaning, repairs, etc.) has also represented the main working opportunity for the new generations of Persians in Italy during the twenty-five years following the Islamic Revolution.

With the advent of the Revolution of 1978-79, the majority of the last generation of students who had arrived during the monarchy regime decided to stay on in Italy, and many eventually started new lives there, mostly obtaining Italian citizenship (currently, approximately 5,000 Persians who were born in Persia have Italian citizenship). At times, these new residents have responded to the need to express their identity through cultural activities connected to their language and world (small publishing companies such as *Entešārāt-e Bābak*, which has been active for several years, the Persian bookshop, *Nimā*, active in Rome since 1994, several cultural associations, the longest standing of which is the *Associazione culturale Italia-Iran* in Florence, magazines with a few issues, concerts, recording of traditional Persian music, etc.). Others have integrated into Italian environments and working situations, using the training they have acquired in cultural and technical fields such as medicine and engineering. On the whole, it is particularly noticeable that since the second half of the 20th century, a rather significant number of artists and intellectuals (writers, musicians, painters, sculptors, illustrators, photographers, actors) who completed their education in Italy settled there, assuming a productive role in their respective fields of expertise. This recent Persian contribution to Italian culture has yet to be duly recognized.

Since the beginning of the 1980s, as an aftermath of the outbreak of the Iran-Iraq war, a new migratory influx from Persia started to move towards Italy, although on a smaller scale compared to the same phenomenon towards other Western countries, especially the United States (see DIASPORA viii). According to information provided by the Ministry of the Interior (the only available data), the number of Persians in Italy rose from 10,131 in 1981 to 13,536 by 1986, who were fairly evenly spread throughout the country. Part of a sociological investigation carried out between the end of the 1980s and the beginning of the 1990s on the Persian immigrants in Italy highlighted some of the characteristics of this migration. The immigrants came almost exclusively from the middle class of Tehran and displayed the features of first generation immigrants: young people (80% under 30 years of age), mainly male (71.1%), and mostly unmarried (58.3%). A common feature seems to be the temporary nature of their immigration. As already mentioned, Italy's legislation and employment situation do not make it an ideal country either for exile or for a long-term integration project. The pretext for coming to Italy has always been to study, though this is often neglected in favor of some form of temporary employment. Employment is still perceived as temporary even when it lasts over ten years, since the final and constant objective is to return to Persia as soon as the conditions permit.

The link with Persia is never broken and is often reinforced by economic ties with the family. A feature that characterizes Persian immigrants in the 1980s and 1990s is a sense of national identity common both to those who come from a religious background and culture and those who have arrived with secular or lay backgrounds and positions. The former, even when politically opposed to the authorities of their country, consider the return to the homeland as absolutely fundamental, whilst the latter seem to be more open to integration in the context of Italian society, even if in a state of continuous uncertainty. In any case, partly due to this constant "utopia of returning home" and also due to the higher than average level of culture and social conscience, Persians in Italy do not consider themselves "immigrants" and tend not to lay down the foundations for the creation of a real Persian social network. Work—always present even if often temporary, especially for those who have arrived most recently (and particularly in the carpet sector, as already mentioned)—, personal relations within a limited range, and the distant but rooted link with their homeland have been main features of the Persian identity in Italy in the last two decades of the 20th century and the beginning of the 21st.

Persians of the Bahai religion are an exception. Though overall a minority, they put their religious faith with its ecumenist characteristics before their national identity. They consider themselves citizens of the world and brothers of the Italians (or people of other nationalities) sharing the same religion. Consequently, they pursue social integration in the country where they are guests, supported by an efficient network of assistance from their own community, which in Italy is focused mainly in Rome and the surrounding area.

This context of the Persian presence in Italy, small-scale and fragmentary, is reflected in the low rate of political dynamism that can be seen. Despite the presence of almost all the opposition factions to the Islamic Republic, from Marxists to liberals, from monarchists to the Mojāhedin-e Ḵalq (probably the most active, with periodic demonstrations and radio broadcasts), as well as the supporters of the Tehran government, political debate has never turned into any particularly noteworthy activity, either in periodicals or in noteworthy occasional publications.

This framework, together with the most recently published figures from the Italian National Institute of Statistics, which indicate 8,371 Persian citizens (5,041 males and 3,330 females) legally present in Italy in 1999, confirm the notion that Persians in Italy, while representing a significant presence, especially due to their integration at certain professional and cultural levels, have not yet constituted a true "community."

Bibliography: Data has been used from the Italian Ministries of Foreign Affairs and the Interior, from the Italian National Institute of Statistics, and from private archives. Stefano Allievi, "Sciiti d'Europa: Una minoranza senza visibilità," in Arnaldo Nesti, ed., *Laboratorio Iran: Cultura, religione, modernità in Iran*, Milan,

2003, pp. 113-26. Changiz Davarpanah, "Il primo giornale a stampa iraniano e l'Italia (1853-56)," *Rivista degli Studi Orientali* 70, 1996, pp. 199-225. Yaḥyā Ḏokāʾ, "Mirzā Abu'l-Ḥasan Ḵān Ṣaniʿ-al-Molk Ḡaffāri, moʾsses-e naḵostin honarestān-e naqqāši dar Irān," *Honar o mardom*, no. 10, 1963, pp. 14-27. Niccolao Manucci, *Storia do Mogor*, tr. William Irvine as *Storia do Mogor or Mogul India 1653-1708*, 4 vols., London, 1907-1908; repr. Calcutta, 1965. E. Nedergaard, "The Four Sons of Phraates IV in Rome," *Acta Hyperboraea* 1, 1987, pp. 102-15. Angelo Michele Piemontese, "L'antica Persia veduta in Roma," in Laura Biancini et al., *Roma memoria e oblio*, Rome, 2001, pp. 71-81. Idem, *La memoria romana dei santi martiri persiani Mario, Marta, Audiface e Abaco*, Rome, 2003. Cecilia Ricci, "*Principes et Reges externi* (e loro schiavi e liberti) a Roma e in Italia: Testimonianze epigrafiche di età imperiale," in *Atti della Accademia Nazionale dei Lincei. Rendiconti. Classe di scienze morali*, S 9/7, 1996, pp. 561-92. Chantal Saint-Blancat, "L'immigrazione iraniana in Italia: vera o falsa parentesi?," in Giovanni Cocchi, ed., *Stranieri in Italia: caratteri e tendenze dell'immigrazione dai paesi extracomunitari*, Bologna, 1989, pp. 109-25. Idem, "La presenza iraniana in Italia," *Inchiesta*, no. 90, 1990, pp. 59-67. Giuseppe Tucci, *Italia e Oriente*, Milan, 1949.

See also bibliographies above: i. CULTURAL RELATIONS WITH PERSIA; ii. DIPLOMATIC AND COMMERCIAL RELATIONS WITH PERSIA.

(MARIO CASARI)

xiv. CURRENT CENTERS OF IRANIAN STUDIES IN ITALY

Studies on subjects related to the Iranian cultural world can boast an ancient tradition in Italy, but not as an independent field of study at academic level. The earliest scholar to hold a chair whose main focus was Persian language and literature, to which he later added the teaching of Iranian philology, was Italo Pizzi in Turin, whose main claim to fame was a verse translation of the *Šāh-nāma* in eight volumes (Pizzi, 1886-88). But things have considerably changed in recent times. The last forty-five years have witnessed the growth of the scholarly tradition investigating Persian language and literature, as well as the birth of a school focusing on the study of Iranian philology, history, and religion.

The beginning of contemporary Iranian studies may be set in 1957. In that year Alessandro Bausani won the chair of Persian Language and Literature at the Istituto Universitario Orientale of Naples (IUO, now Università degli Studi di Napoli "L'Orientale"), and Giuseppe Tucci, President of the Istituto Italiano per il Medio ed Estremo Oriente (IsMEO, now Istituto per l'Africa e l'Oriente; see xvii, below), inaugurated the first archeological expedition at Ghazni, which was to be followed by expeditions in Sistān (1959), and at Isfahan and Persepolis (1964). In 1967 Gianroberto Scarcia was appointed chair of Persian Language and Literature at the Faculty of Foreign Languages and Literatures at the University of Venice "Ca' Foscari," and in 1968 Gherardo Gnoli was called to cover the newly established chair of Iranian Philology at the IUO, Bausani left Naples in 1971 for the "Scuola Orientale" of the Faculty of Humanities at the University of Rome "La Sapienza," where he taught Islamic studies, with particular attention to Iran, until his retirement in 1987. In 1975 Angelo M. Piemontese, previously in Naples, was appointed chair of Persian Language and Literature in Rome. Thus by 1975 all three historical seats of Oriental research in Italy saw the presence of at least one chair focusing on one or other aspect of Iranian culture and civilization. Today this field of study is fortunately present also in universities with a weaker tradition in Middle Eastern and Asian studies. Giovanni M. D'Erme, who was elected in 1980 as chair of Persian language and literature at the Istituto Universitario Orientale, had inaugurated Persian studies at the Faculty of Humanities of the University of Bologna as early as 1973. Iranian studies were pursued from the start in the newly founded Faculty of Cultural Heritage, located in the Ravenna branch of the University of Bologna. In 1996 Antonio Panaino moved from Bologna to Ravenna, where he obtained the full chair of Iranian Philology in 2000. Since 1986 Iranian studies have also been pursued at the University of Pisa, in the Faculty of Humanities, where Elio Provasi, previously at the Orientale in Naples, teaches Iranian philology and linguistics. This scholar, a specialist of different fields of Middle and New Iranian linguistics, is now actively preparing a comprehensive dictionary of the Sogdian language. In 2002, the University of the Tuscia in Viterbo, through the effort of its Rector, Marco Mancini, himself a student of Walter Belardi, opened a new position and appointed Elina Filippone chair of Iranian Studies. A collaborator and former student of Adriano Rossi, she is mainly interested in modern Iranian linguistics. Iranian studies are also pursued, though marginally, at the Catholic University in Milan, where Giancarlo Bolognesi and Valeria Fiorani-Piacentini teach. The former is a linguist, the latter principally a modern historian.

Many scholars belonging to the older generation had studied in Rome, but in more recent times this University was joined by Naples and Venice in preparing a significant number of prospective scholars in the field of Iranian studies. The most significant recent development was the establishment in 1984 of a doctoral course in Iranian Studies at the Istituto Universitario Orientale, with a curriculum covering both pre-Islamic and Islamic studies. A number of students have completed the program, and in fact all scholars who have been able to pursue an academic career in Iranian studies in recent years are graduates of it. A second doctoral course, which covers pre-Islamic Iran as part of Ancient Near Eastern studies, is active in Rome.

Iranian studies in Italy are divided academically into two broad divisions. The first goes under the name of Persian Language and Literature, a field inaugurated by Italo Pizzi, mastered by Alessandro Bausani, and continued by Angelo Michele Piemontese, Giovanni Maria D'Erme, Riccardo Zipoli (Chair, 1987), Maurizio Pistoso (Chair, 1987), Rahim Raza, Daniela Meneghini, Michele Bernardini, Paola Orsatti, and Carlo Sacconi. It specializes in literary and linguistic studies of the Persian language, but also covers literary and linguistic studies concerning other modern Iranian languages. The second is more concerned with philological, historical, religious, and linguistic studies and has its roots in historical linguistics, history of religions, and ancient history; it now encompasses Islamic Iran as well. Although many scholars have turned their attention to problems in these subjects since the birth of Iranian studies, the collective field of studies only gained independent status in the second half of the 20th century, thanks to the impressive works of such giant Iranists as Walter Bruno Henning (q.v.), Sir Harold Bailey (q.v.), and Georg Morgenstierne (q.v. at *iranica .com*). In Italy it was introduced by Gherardo Gnoli and later continued by Adriano Rossi (Chair, 1980) and more recently by Antonio Panaino (Chair, 2000), Carlo G. Cereti (Chair, 2001), Elina Filippone (Chair, 2002), Elio Provasi, Mauro Maggi, and Andrea Piras.

The number of international congresses hosted in Italy covering both the pre-Islamic and the Islamic periods is evidence of the the strong interest in Iran. Particularly noteworthy are four conferences organized jointly by the Istituto Italiano per l'Africa e l'Oriente (IsIAO, ex IsMEO) and the Accademia Nazionale dei Lincei: Persia and the Graeco-Roman World, 1966; Persia in the Middle Ages, 1971; Persia and Central Asia from Alexander the Great to the 10th Century, 1994; and Persia and Byzantium, 2002. In 1983 (18-20 June) the First European Colloquium of Iranology met in Rome. On that occasion, the participating scholars came together in the evening of the 19th to found the Societas Iranologica Europaea (SIE), which still has its legal seat at the Istituto Italiano per l'Africa e l'Oriente in Rome. A few years later IsMEO and the Piedmontese Centro per gli Studi Medio ed Estremo Orientali (CeSMEO) jointly hosted the first Europaean Conference of Iranian Studies in Turin (7-11 September 1987); the fifth met in Ravenna (6-11 October 2003). During April 9-11, 2003, the IsIAO, the Faculty of Humanities of the University of Rome "La Sapienza," and the Consiglio Nazionale delle Ricerche jointly organized an international conference under the title "Middle Iranian Lexicography. The Vocabulary of the Middle Iranian Languages." The IsMEO has further organized in Venice, in collaboration with that city's Fondazione Giorgio Cini, three conferences on various aspects of Iranian culture. The first (Incontro di religioni in Asia tra il III ed il X secolo d.C., 1981) was devoted to selected problems in the study of religions in Asia between the 3rd and the 10th century C.E. The second (Turfan and Tun-Huang. The Texts, 1990) and the third (Cina e Iran. Da Alessandro Magno alla dinastia Tang, 1994), were organized together with the IUO and UNESCO, and in both the discussion focused on the vast region of Central Asia linking Iran to China. Luigi Cirillo has organized four conferences on Manichean studies, though only the last two had relevance for Iranian studies. The first two were held at the University of Calabria in 1984 and 1988, both on the *Codex Manichaicus Coloniensis* (see COLOGNE MANI CODEX). The third, held at the same place in 1993, was entitled Manicheismo e Oriente Cristiano Antico. The latest was held at the IUO in 2001, under the title The Fifth International Conference of Manichaean Studies. In the 1970s, the Caetani Foundation, closely linked to the Accademia Nazionale dei Lincei, organized a number of symposia on classical Persian poetry: in 1974 on Rumi, in 1975 on Neẓāmi, in 1976 on Ḥāfez, in 1977 on ʿAṭṭār, and in 1978 on Sanāʾi. Italy has also hosted a few exhibitions of Iranian art. The first was held in Rome in 1956, followed by a second and more eleborate one in Milan in 1963 (called 7000 Anni d'Arte Iranica-). The third exhibition was hosted many years later at the Museo Nazionale d'Arte Orientale in Rome (Antica Persia, 2000).

At present Iranian studies in Italy represent a fairly thriving field of research, encompassing all its different branches. The main centers of research are the Istituto Italiano per l'Africa e l'Oriente, the Department of Oriental Studies of the University of Rome "La Sapienza," the Department of Asian Studies of the University of Naples "L'Orientale" (formerly Istituto Universitario Orientale), the Department of Eurasian Studies at the University of Venice. The University of Bologna presents a peculiar situation, with Iranian studies divided between three different faculties: the Faculty of Cultural Heritage in Ravenna, and those of Humanities and Foreign Languages and Literatures in its historical seat of Bologna.

In Rome, Persian language and literature as well as Iranian studies are taught, the first subject by Angelo Michele Piemontese, Paola Orsatti, and Simone Cristoforetti, the second by Gherardo Gnoli and Carlo G. Cereti. The main focuses of teaching are Persian literature, codicology, and history of Iranian studies in Italy (taught by A. Piemontese, Paola Orsatti, and Mario Casari), history of Zoroastrianism, both ancient and modern, history of Manicheism and Iranian philology and linguistics (G. Gnoli and C.G. Cereti), and also studies on the Iranian calendars and other anthropological subjects (S. Cristoforetti). Umberto Scerrato, Bianca Maria Alfieri, and Francesco Noci teach Islamic archeology and art history with particular attention to the Iranian world. Biancamaria Scarcia Amoretti, Professor of Islamic Studies, in her youth devoted time and energy to the history of Islamic Iran. The Roman school of linguistics traditionally shows a particular interest in Iranian languages, and still today Walter Belardi, Palmira Cipriano, Paolo Di Giovine, and Claudia Ciancaglini are active in the study of Iranian lexicography and historical linguistics. An international research project aimed at the compilation of a Middle Persian Dictionary has recently been started in collaboration with the Hebrew University, Jerusalem. This project, coordinated at an international level by Shaul Shaked, enjoys the participation of the Faculty of Humanities in Rome, IsIAO, and the University of Naples "L'Orientale."

The University "L'Orientale," in Naples, has chairs for Persian language and literature (Persian linguistics and literature, taught by G. M. D'Erme; Persian literature in India, taught by R. Raza; Persian and Turkish literature and history, taught by M. Bernardini; Modern Persian literature, taught by L. Tornesello) and for Iranian Studies, which are the fields of A.V. Rossi (Iranian philology and linguistics) and M. Maggi (Khotanese, Buddhist studies, and comparative Indo-Iranian grammar). Mario Vitalone studies the contemporary Zoroastrian communities in Iran and India, while Felicetta Ferraro concerns herself with modern Iranian history seen from an anthropologist's point of view. Maria Vittoria Fontana teaches Islamic art and archeology with specialization in the Iranian world, and Bruno Genito holds the chair of Iranian archeology and actively participates in a number of archeological excavations in Iranian lands. Another art historian, Giovanna Ventrone Vassallo, who had worked in Isfahan, was until very recently at the Orientale of Naples. Among the scholars of Islamic studies, both Alberto Ventura and Claudio Lo Iacono are interested in Iran. A major research project run by the Orientale and the IsIAO is the Baluchi Etymological Dictionary (see BALUCHISTAN at *iranica.com*).

Ca' Foscari in Venice is a third important center for the teaching of Iranian subjects, although there is no chair specified as such. Persian language and literature, and New Persian linguistics and prosody, are taught by R. Zipoli and D. Meneghini. However, the chair of Islamic studies in Venice is held by one of Bausani's former disciples, G. Scarcia, who is principally an Iranist, although, like his teacher, quite adept in a wide range of subjects. G. Vercellin, an expert in modern Iranian history, formerly held the chair for Afghan language and literature but now teaches History and Institutions of Asia. A very important research project run in this university is *Lirica Persica*, aimed at creating a vast electronic database of Persian poetry (see xii, above).

Two specialists of pre-Islamic Iran are teaching at the relatively new Faculty of Cultural Heritage of Ravenna: Antonio Panaino (Avestan, history of Zoroastrianism, and intercultural relations in antiquity and late antiquity), and Andrea Piras (Avestan and Zoroastrian religion). They collaborate with a group of Byzantinists and ancient historians. New Persian is taught in Bologna, at the Faculty of Humanities by Maurizio Pistoso and at the Faculty of Foreign Languages by Carlo Saccone. Pierfrancesco Callieri and Maurizio Tosi, both archeologists and experts in the Iranian area, also teach at the Faculty of Cultural Heritage in Ravenna. The Melammu research project, studying the continuity of Mesopotamian cultural heritage in different historical contexts, is run by the Department of History and Methods for the Preservation of the Cultural Heritage in collaboration with the Department of Oriental Studies of Rome, the Department of Asian Studies of Naples, and the Department of Ancient History of Padua.

Bibliography: 7000 Anni d'Arte Iranica. Mostra realizzata in collaborazione con l'Istituto Italiano per il Medio e l'Estremo Oriente, Milano-Palazzo Reale, Maggio – Giugno 1963, Milan, 1963. *Antica Persia. I tesori del Museo Nazionale di Tehran e la ricerca italiana in Iran, Museo Nazionale d'Arte Orientale 29 maggio-22 luglio 2001*, Rome, 2001. *Atti del convegno sul tema: La Persia e il Mondo Greco-Romano, Roma 11-14 aprile 1965*, Accademia dei Lincei, Rome, 1966. *Atti del convegno Internazionale sul tema: La Persia nel Medioevo, Roma, 31 marzo-5 aprile 1970*, Accademia dei Lincei, Rome, 1971. Alfredo Cadonna, ed., *Turfan and Tun Huang: The Texts. Encounter of Civilizations on the Silk Route*, Florence, 1992. Alfredo Cadonna and Lionello Lanciotti, eds., *Cina e Iran. Da Alessandro Magno alla dinastia Tang*, Florence, 1996. *Colloquio italo-iraniano sul poeta mistico Fariduddin 'Aṭṭār, Roma, 24-25 marzo 1977*, Rome, 1978. *Colloquio italo-iraniano sul poeta mistico Sanā'i, Roma, 29-30 marzo 1978*, Rome, 1979. *Colloquio sul poeta persiano Nizāmī e la leggenda iranica di Alessandro Magno, Roma, 25-26 marzo 1975)*, Rome, 1977. *Convegno internazionale sulla poesia di Hāfez, Roma, 30-31 marzo 1976*, Rome, 1978. *Convegno internazionale sul tema: La Persia e l'Asia Centrale da Alessandro al X Secolo, Roma, 9-12 novembre 1994*, Accademia dei Lincei, Rome, 1996. L. Cirillo, ed., *Codex Manichaicus Coloniensis. Atti del Simposio Internationale. Rende-Amantea 3-7 settembre 1984*, Constance, 1986. Idem, ed., *Codex Manichaicus Coloniensis. Atti del secondo Simposio Internationale (Cosenza 27-28 maggio 1988)*, Constance, 1990. L. Cirillo and A. van Tongerloo, eds. *Atti del Terzo Congresso Internazionale di Studi "Manicheismo e Oriente Cristiano Antico," Arcavacata di Rende-Amantea 31 agosto-5 settembre 1993*, Louvain and Naples, 1997. Ferdowsi, *Il libro dei re. Poema epico recato dal persiano in versi italiani da Italo Pizzi*, 8 vols, Turin, 1886-88. Gherardo Gnoli, ed., *The First European Colloquium of Iranology, Rome, June 18th-20th, 1983*, Orientalia Romana 6, Rome, 1985. Gherardo Gnoli and Antonio Panaino, eds., *Proceedings of the First Euroapean Conference of Iranian studies held in Turin, September 7th-11th, 1987 by the Societas Iranologica Europaea*, 2 vols, Roma, 1990. Lionello Lanciotti, ed., *Incontro di religioni in Asia tra il III e il X secolo d.C.*, Florence, 1984. *Nel centenario del poeta mistico persiano Ǧalāl-ad-Dīn Rūmī, Conferenze, Roma, 18-19 Gennaio 1974*, Rome, 1975.

(CARLO G. CERETI)

xv. IsMEO

IsMEO is an acronym for the Istituto Italiano per il Medio ed Estremo Oriente ('Italian Institute for Middle and Far East'). The IsMEO was founded in 1933 by Royal Decree no. 142 as a moral institution (*Ente Morale*) under the inspiration and encouragement of Giuseppe Tucci, then a young scholar but already well-known as an Indologist and Tibetologist. Its first President was Professor Giovanni Gentile, a famous Hegelian philosopher who, as the Minister of Culture in the Fascist government, exerted enormous influence in the field of cultural politics. With Gentile's strong support, Tucci was appointed the executive Vice-president of IsMEO. The creation of the IsMEO was clearly seen by the leadership of the Italian state at that time as the answer to the political need for developing cultural relations with the entire Asiatic world. That its aim was in fact the promotion of Italian presence in these countries with a deep interest for the politico-economic affairs, is documented by a number of IsMEO's monographs as well as its official periodicals, such as *Bollettino dell'Istituto italiano per il Medio ed Estremo Oriente* ('Bulletin of the Italian Institute for Middle and Far East' 1935 only), and *Asiatica* (1936-43). Although these perspectives doubtless represented an objective interest associated with the politics of the Fascist government, in the actual realization of the cultural projects of the IsMEO, they never formed its primary goals. In reality, the scholarly activity of the staff leading the Institute was kept, as far as possible, independent, and came increasingly to be devoted to purely scientific programs, all directed by Tucci with the official support and protection of Gentile. This explains the impressive results obtained by the IsMEO in the field of Tibetology, mainly owing to a number of long and repeated expeditions by him to Tibet, which had started in 1929, before the birth of the IsMEO, but continued with the direct support of the Institute in a more systematic way until 1948.

Between1943 and 1947, the IsMEO remained inactive. Then it resumed its scholarly goals, thanks to the reestablishment of democratic life in Italy, and also on the other hand, to its own traditional scientific orientation which was enormously greater than its earlier political role, the institute was finally able to mainly focus its interests on research activities. Under the chairmanship of Professor Tucci, a new phase in the life of the Institute was opened in November 1947. The year 1950 saw the beginning of the well-known monographic serial "Series Orientale Roma" ('Rome Oriental Series') and of the quarterly *East and West*, which took new shape from 1958 with publication exclusively in English; the periodical *Cina* started in 1956, while *Il Giappone* was started by the IsMEO, with the collaboration of the Japanese Cultural Institute of Rome, in 1963. In 1951 the courses of Oriental languages were organized on a new basis. Between 1950 and 1955 a number of new expeditions to Nepal were organized while, beginning in 1956, the archaeological campaigns in Pakistan took place, followed by other archaeological missions and campaigns in Afghanistan (from 1957) and in Iran (from 1959). From 1954 the IsMEO organized various Oriental art exhibitions, opening the treasuries of many ancient Eastern cultures to the Italian and Western world (Chinese art, 1954; Iranian art, 1956; Gandhara art, 1958; Afghanistan, 1961). The increasing archaeological activities of the Institute were soon supplemented from 1960 with a program of restoration and conservation of the cultural heritage of many countries, in particular at Kabul and Ghazni (Afghanistan), Persepolis and Isfahan (Iran). The results of these works were made public from 1960 through the publication of two new series of the IsMEO "Reports and Memoires," (in two Series: Major and Minor) and "Restorations" (also in two Series: Major and Minor). After Professor Tucci's retirement in 1978, Professor Sabatino Moscati was elected president of the IsMEO; he was succeeded in 1979 by Professor Gherardo Gnoli who maintained his function till 1995, when the IsMEO was finally merged by a law passed by the Italian Parliament (Act no. 5054 of 25 November 1995) with the IIA (acronym for the Istituto Italo-Africano, 'Italian-African Institute') into a new Institute called IsIAO (Istituto Italiano per l'Africa e l'Oriente, 'Italian Institute for Africa and the East'). Professor Gherardo Gnoli was elected as the chairman of this new institution. The IsIAO actually has its main office in Rome (via Ulisse Aldrovandi 16, 00197), in the building which was the place of the IIA, while the offices of Palazzo Brancaccio (via Merulana 248) have been moved to the new address (with the exception of the Centre for Excavations and the Office of the Editorial Staff). Two further branches of the Institute exist at the moment: one in Milan (dating back to February 1937) and the second in Ravenna (activated in 1999). Further information on the IsIAO are available on the website of the Institute (www.isiao.it). In addition to the periodicals *East and West*, *Cina*, *Il Giappone*, the IsIAO publishes other journals: *Yemen: studi archeologici, storici e filologici sull'Arabia meridionale*; *Ming Qing Yanju* and *Newsletter of Baluchistan* (both in collaboration with the Istituto Universitario Orientale di Napoli); and *Africa: rivista mensile di interessi africani.*

The investigations of the IsMEO (and now of the IsIAO) in Iran have been considerable and fruitful. Already in 1959 Tucci focused the main archaeological researches in Iran on two sites: the city of Isfahan and the Sistān basin. In Isfahan the archaeological mission headed by Professor Umberto Scerrato shed new light on the oldest phases of the most important mosque of the city, the Masjed-e Jomʿe, finding stratigraphical levels of the 8th century as well as those belonging to the Sasanian period. In Sīstan, excavations in the Kuh-e K̲ᵛāja (an architectural complex attributed to Parthian-Sasanian periods and situated on the island in the middle of Hāmun lake) and in Qalʿa Tape started in 1960, and were continued in 1962 with the inclusion of the Achaemenid site of Dahāna-ye Ḡolāmān, probably the location of the capital of the ancient Persian satrapy of Zranka. In this place, excavations directed by Professor Scerrato and continued till 1966, found some of the main monumental religious and civil structures of the area. The stronghold of Qalʿa-ye Sām, with stratigraphical levels of the post-Achaemenid and Sasanian periods, was excavated in 1963, while some additional archaeological research was devoted to the Islamic site of Bibi Dust. Under the direction of Professor Maurizio Tosi the study of the protohistorical phases of Sistān began in 1967 and continued until 1972, with the main focus being the excavation of Šahr-e Suk̲ta "The burned Town," the largest inhabited area of the Bronze Age in Southwestern Asia (151 ha). This mission did not limit itself to illuminating the status of the material culture in the third millennium B.C. but introduced an original multidisciplinary approach in the field with an impressive development of scientific knowledge spanning from the field of Palaeo-botany to that of physical anthropology, etc. A very significant analysis of the necropolis of Šahr-e Sukta, which covers a surface of ca. 29 ha. and contains some 20,000 to 30,000 graves, has been carried out by Marcello Piperno and Sandro Salvadori. From 1964, the IsMEO (with the direct involvement of its "Centro Restauri") undertook, with the support of the Ministero per gli Affari Esteri ('Ministry of Foreign Affairs' = MAF), a long series of restoration and conservation activities in Iran. In Isfahan itself, the architect Eugenio Galdieri directed the restoration of the Safavid pavillons of ʿĀli Qāpu and Čehel Sotun and of that of Hašt Behešt; further restorations there were conducted in the Masjed-e Jomʿe, in the Meydān-e Šāh, in the Sardar-e Qeyṣariya, and in the Kāravānsarā-ye Šāh. In the Isfahan area, the Pir-e Bakrān of Lenjān and Masjed-e Jomʿe of Bersiyān were subjects of investigation and exploration. In Fārs, thanks to the brilliant works of Giuseppe Tilia (and the cooperation of Domenico Faccenna, Giuseppe Zander, and others), a great work of restoration and conservation was achieved in the monumental area of Persepolis, and significant improvements resulting from scientific investigations and systematic restorations were brought about in the following monuments: the *Tačara* or Palace of Darius, the *Hadiš* or Palace of Xerxes, the Hundred-Column Hall, the "Unfinished Gate," the Gate of All Lands, the "Harem of Xerxes," the Apadāna, and the tombs of Artaxerxes II and Artaxerxes III. Other repairs were made in Pasargadae, at the tomb of Cyrus, in the palaces P and S, while in Marvdašt other Achaemenid pavillons were studied and preserved. Of particular importance was the transferring of an Achaemenid bridge at Dorudzan, which was moved and reconstructed down the valley in order to avoid its submersion by a hydroelectric dam. Unfortunately, all these activities were interrupted in 1979, and despite many diplomatic and scholarly attempts to maintain the cultural and scientific collaboration in this field (see the chronology of the relations between the IsMEO [and after by the IsIAO] and the Sāzemān-e mirās-e farhangi-ye kešwar [= SMFK] between 1979-1999 in the booklet *Il contributo dell'Istituto . . .*, pp. 10-14), their resumption has not materialized. In the meantime a great archaeological recognition of the ancient Margiane (in Turkmenistan, in the area around Mary, the old Merw) has been directed by M. Tosi with the fresh publication of a detailed archaeological map (*The Archaeological Map of the Murghab Delta. Preliminary Reports 1990-5*, ed. by A. Grubaev, G. Koshelenko and M. Tosi, Rome, 1998). The outlook for the future is bright. Already new forms of collaboration have been established with the Iranian cultural institutions resulting in the organization in Rome (May 29-July 22, 2001) of a great exhibition of the treasuries of the National Museum of Tehran (following one held in Vienna), and of the Italian collection of Iranian art and archaeology. Furthermore, the publication of the results obtained by the IsMEO's archaeological mission in Iran prior to 1979 has been started anew in collaboration with Iranian scholars and authorities. In addition to all these activities the IsMEO and its successor, the IsIAO, have conducted many philological, historical and religious researches in the field of Iranian studies, which have been mainly published in the Rome Oriental Series and in *East and West*. Likewise, the Institute strongly supported the birth of the *Societas Iranologica Europaea* (SIE), which was officially founded in Rome (at the Institute) on the June 19, 1983 on the occasion of the First European Colloquium of Iranology. The IsIAO organized the first Conference of Iranian Studies (Turin, 7-11 September 1987) and has supported in many forms many other activities of the SIE. Actually, the legal seat of the SIE is at the address of the IsIAO. The Institute in addition cooperates with many scientific, cultural and academic institutions for the promotion of Iranian studies.

Bibliography: On the history of the IsMEO, and the tenure of Giuseppe Tucci and Giovanni Gentile see V. Ferretti, Politica e cultura: origini e attività dell'IsMEO durante il regime fascista, *Storia Contemporanea*, 17, 1986, pp. 779-819; *Giuseppe Tucci: nel centenario della nascita, Roma, 7-8 giugno 1994*, edited by B. Melasecchi, Roma (IsMEO), 1995. Gh. Gnoli, *Nel cinquantenario dell'IsMEO: discorso tenuto a Palazzo Brancaccio il 16 febbraio 1983*, Roma (IsMEO), 1983. *Giuseppe Tucci*, Ancona (Istituto Marchigiano-Accademia di Scienze Lettere e Arti), 1985. Gh. Gnoli, "Giovanni Gentile fondatore e presidente dell'IsMEO," in *Giovanni Gentile: la filosofia, la politica, l'organizzazione della cultura*, Venezia (Marsilio), 1995 (Engl. tr. Giovanni Gentile, Founder and President of IsMEO, *East and West*, 44, 1994, pp. 223-29). R. Gnoli, *Ricordo di Giuseppe Tucci*, with contributions by L. Petech, F. Scialpi, G. Galluppi Valauri, Roma (IsMEO), 1985 (Engl. tr. in *Purana*, 26, 1994). *Centenario della nascita di Giuseppe Tucci: discorsi pronunciati da Sabatino Moscati e Gherardo Gnoli il 6 giugno 1994 in Campidoglio*, Roma (IsMEO), 1995. *Statuto dell'Istituto Italiano per il Medio ed Estremo Oriente*. Approvato con Decreto del Presidente della Repubblica 9 ottobre 1987, Gazzetta Ufficiale n. 37 del 15 febbraio 1988.

On the scientific activities of the IsMEO (and of the IsIAO) see *Il Contributo dell'Istituto allo studio della Civiltà Iranica*. Una breve presentazione. (IsIAO), Roma 1999. *IsIAO. Istituto Italiano per l'Africa e l'Oriente*. (Italian version of a booklet of presentation of the Institute), Rome (IsIAO), 1996, (containing a catalogue of the scientific Iranological activities of the Institute till 1999). See also many individual contributions concerning IsMEO archeological activities in Iran published in the catalogue of the exibition *Antica Persia. I tesori del Museo Nazionale di Tehran e la ricerca italiana in Iran*, Museo Nazionale d'Arte Orientale, Roma, 2001.

(ANTONIO PANAINO)

IVANOV, PAVEL PETROVICH, (b. Siberia, February 1893; d. Leningrad, 3 February 1942). In the early 1900s his family moved to Central Asia, where his father worked at railroad construction. Ivanov finished a teacher's seminary in Tashkent in 1914 and then taught in a "Russian-Kirghiz" (i.e., mixed Russian-Kazakh) school. After a brief service in the Russian army in 1916-18, he studied in the Iranian Department of the Turkestan Oriental Institute in Tashkent, from which he graduated in 1924. In 1929 he moved to Leningrad, where he first taught Oriental languages, but in 1934 he began to work as a researcher at the Institute of Oriental Studies (Institut Vostokovedeniya) of the Soviet Academy of Sciences. He died on 3 February 1942, during the German siege of Leningrad in World War II.

Ivanov's first scholarly works concerned mostly archeology, as well as some problems of the historical geography of Central Asia. He published two articles on the historical topography of Sayram (medieval Esfijāb; see ASFĪJĀB), which he visited three times in 1924-26 (see his "Saĭram" and "Kvoprosu ob istoricheskoĭ topografii"). In the late 1920s he participated in archeological explorations in the Lake Issyk-Kul basin (his detailed report on this work was only published posthumously; see "Materialy") and in the upper Talas valley (see his "Kvoprosu o drevnostyakh"). His work "Kistorii razvitiya gornogo promysla v Sredneĭ Azii" (1932), although based on written sources, was also connected with his archeological interests. After his move to Leningrad, however, his research concentrated exclusively on the history of Central Asia in the 16th-19th centuries, and during just eight years (1935-42) he made major contributions to the study of this period. He took part, as a principal editor and translator, in the publication of two major collection of excerpts, in Russian translation, from Persian and Turkic historical works dealing with the history of the Qaraqalpaqs (*Materialy po istorii karakalpakov*, 1935) and the Turkmens (*Materialy po istorii turkmen i Turkmenii* II, 1938). Both these collections served for many years as the basis for subsequent historical works dealing with the Qaraqalpaqs and the Turkmens.

His first major historical work was "Ocherk istorii karakalpakov" (Outline of the history of the Qaraqalpaqs), which laid the foundation for all later research on the history of this people; he also devoted two more articles to their history ("Novye dannye" and "Karakalpaki"). In an article published in 1939 Ivanov analyzed the relationships between another Central Asian nomadic people, the Kazakhs, and the Khanate of Ḵoqand (Qoqand, q.v. at *iranica.com*) in the 19th century ("Kazakhi i Kokandskoe khanstvo"). But Ivanov's main interest was the social and economic history of Central Asia. Although he approached this subject (as did all the Soviet historians) from the Marxist standpoint, most of his works dealt, not so much with sociological generalizations, but mainly with the study of specific events and topics based on primary sources—Central Asian chronicles and documents. His work "Vosstanie kitaĭ-kipchakov," containing an analysis of the situation of the Uzbek tribes in the Khanate of Bukhara under the Manḡïts, included a description, with a Russian translation of excerpts, of some previously unstudied Central Asian narrative sources of the 19th century. An article on the "crown lands" in the Khanate of Khiva ("Udel'nye zemli") was based on the Khivan chronicle, excerpts from which were translated by him for *Materialy po istorii karakalpakov* and *Materialy po istorii turkmen i Turkmenii*.

In 1936 Ivanov discovered a large collection of documents in the Leningrad Public Library captured by Russian troops in the palace of the khan of Khiva upon the conquest of the Khanate of Khiva in 1873; the documents had been brought to St. Petersburg and then forgotten. After his discovery, Ivanov was busy for five years with the sorting and description of the documents. The result of this work was the book *Arkhiv khivinskikh khanov XIX v*. published in 1940; it contains a systematic and detailed description of 137 documents, mostly tax registers (*daftars*), written in Čaḡatay. The documents proved to be an invaluable source for the study of the social and economic history of the Khanate of Khiva in the 19th century, and Ivanov's description was extensively used by other scholars. Later many more Khivan documents were discovered in Leningrad and Tashkent, but these discoveries did not diminish the importance of Ivanov's work.

While still working on the Khivan archives, Ivanov began new research related to another documentary source—a collection of copies of documents (preserved in Leningrad) related to the land properties of the Juybāri shaikhs of Bukhara (16th-17th centuries). The Persian text of the documents was prepared for publication by a Leningrad Iranologist, F. Rostopchin, and published in 1938 (*Iz arkhiva*); the name of Rostopchin was suppressed from this publication because he was a victim of Stalin's purges of the 1930s. Ivanov wrote an introduction to the Russian translation of the documents (also prepared by Rostopchin), and it became an important monographic study in its own right. In it he traces the history of the Juybāri family and the ways they accumulated and managed their land possessions (see *Khoziaĭstvo dzhuĭbarskikh sheĭkhov*). This work, written in 1938-40, remained unpublished because of the war and Ivanov's death; it was only published posthumously, in 1954, together with Rostopchin's translations of the documents (without the name of the translator).

During the same years Ivanov wrote a more general work on the history of Central Asia in the 16th-19th centuries, which was also not published immediately because of the war. It appeared posthumously in 1958 under the title *Ocherki po istorii Sredneĭ Azii (XVI – seredina*

XIX v.) in an abridged form; out of ten original chapters, the last three, dealing with the second half of the 19th century (Russian conquest and rule), were omitted. The book was written as a popular work, without references to the sources (a brief survey of the most important Persian and Turkic sources is attached as an appendix), although Ivanov did utilize primary sources. The history of Central Asia is interpreted in this book in accordance with the Marxist approach. In many cases (especially in the sections concerning the nomads), Ivanov's conclusions mostly reflected some general constructs current in Soviet historical literature of that time. Despite this weakness, *Ocherki* has one great advantage, for which it stands out in the Soviet literature on Central Asia: it treats Central Asia as one historical and cultural entity, as distinct from all later general works, both Soviet and post-Soviet, in which Central Asian history is parceled out among the various Soviet Republics.

Bibliography: Published works of P. P. Ivanov. *Archiv khivinskikh khanov XIX v.: Issledovanie i opisanie dokumentov s istoricheskim vvedeniem. Novye istochniki dlya istorii narodov Sredneĭ Azii* (Archive of the 19th-century Khivan khans: analysis and description of the documents with a historical introduction. New sources for the history of the peoples of Central Asia), Leningrad, 1940. "Iz oblasti sredneaziatskoĭ khozyaĭstvennoĭ terminologii" (From the field of Central Asian economic terminology), *Izvestiya Akademii nauk SSSR, Otdelenie obshchestvennykh nauk*, 1935, No. 8, pp. 745-58. "Kvoprosu o drevnostyakh v verkhov'yakh Talasa" (On the question of the antiquities in the upper reaches of the Talas), *S. F. Ol'denburgu k 50-letiyu nauchno-obshchestvennoĭ deyatel'nosti*, Leningrad, 1934, pp. 241-51. "Kvoprosu ob istoricheskoĭ topografii starogo Saĭrama" (On the question of the historical topography of old Sayram), *V. V. Bartol'du turkestanskie druz'ia, ucheniki i pochitateli*, Tashkent, 1927, pp. 151-64. "Kazakhi i Kokandskoe khanstvo: K istorii ikh vzaimootnosheniĭ v nachale XIX v." (The Kazakhs and the khanate of Ḵoqand: toward the history of their mutual relations at the beginning of the 19th century), *Zapiski Instituta vostokovedeniya Akademii nauk SSSR* 7, 1939, pp. 92-128. *Khozyaĭstvo dzhuĭbarskikh sheĭkhov: Kistorii feodal'nogo zemlevladeniya v Sredneĭ Azii v XVI-XVII vv.* (The economy of the Juybari shaikhs: on the history of feudal landholding in Central Asia in the 16th-17th centuries), Moscow and Leningrad, 1954. "Materialy po arkheologii kotloviny Issyk-Kulya" (Materials on the archeology of the Issyk-Kul basin), *Trudy Instituta istorii Akademii nauk Kirgizskoĭ SSR* 3, Frunze, 1957, pp. 65-107. "Novye dannye o karakalpakakh" (New data on the Qaraqalpaqs), *Sovetskoe vostokovedenie*, vol. III, Moscow and Leningrad, 1945, pp. 59-79. "Ocherk istorii karakalpakov" (Outline of the history of the Qaraqalpaqs), *Materialy po istorii karakalpakov* [see below], pp. 9-89. *Ocherki po istorii Sredneĭ Azii (XVI-seredina XIX v.)* (Outline of the history of Central Asia, 16th to mid-19th centuries), Moscow, 1958. "Saĭram: Istoriko-arkheologicheskiĭ ocherk" (Sayram: historical-archeological essay), *Sbornik Turkestanskogo Vostochnogo instituta v chest' prof. A. È. Shmidta*, Tashkent, 1923, pp. 46-56. "'Udel'nye zemli' Seĭid-Mukhammed-khana khivinskogo (1856-1865)" (The crown lands of Sayyed Mohammad Khan of Khiva [1856-1865]), *Zapiski Instituta vostokovedeniya Akademii nauk SSSR* 6, 1937, pp. 27-59. *Vosstanie kitaĭ-kipchakov v Bukharskom khanstve 1821-25 gg.: Istochniki i opyt ikh issledovaniya* (The revolt of the Kitai Kipchaqs in the khanate of Bukhara 1821-25: sources and an approach to their study), Moscow and Leningrad, 1937 (Trudy Instituta vostokovedeniya AN SSSR 28). *Iz arkhiva sheĭkhov Dzhuĭbari: Materialy po zemel'nym i torgovym otnosheniyam Sredneĭ Azii XVI veka* (From the archives of the Juybari shaikhs: materials on the landholding and commercial relations of Central Asia in the 16th century), Moscow and Leningrad, 1938. *Materialy po istorii karakalpakov: Sbornik* (Materials for the history of the Qaraqalpaqs: a collection), Moscow and Leningrad, 1935. *Materialy po istorii turkmen i Turkmenii* II. *XVI-XIX vv. Iranskie, bukharskie i khivinskie istochniki* (Materials for the history of the Turkmen and Turkmenia 2: 16th-19th centuries. Iranian, Bukharan, and Khivan sources), Moscow and Leningrad, 1938 (Trudy Instituta vostokovedeniya AN SSSR 29).

Literature on P. P. Ivanov. A. Borovkov, "Vmesto vvedeniya (Neskol'ko predvaritel'nykh zamechaniĭ ob 'Ocherkakh po istorii Sredneĭ Azii' P. P. Ivanova)" (In place of an introduction [some preliminary observations about P. P. Ivanov's 'An outline of the history of Central Asia']) in P. P. Ivanov, *Ocherki po istorii Sredneĭ Azii*, pp. 3-12. V. A. Romodin, "Vklad leningradskikh vostokovedov v izuchenie istorii Sredneĭ Azii" (The contribution of the Leningrad orientalists to the study of the history of Central Asia), *Uchenye zapiski Instituta vostokovedeniya AN SSSR*, vol. XXV, Moscow, 1960, pp. 38-41. A. Yu. Yakubovskiĭ, "Pavel Petrovich Ivanov kak istorik Sredneĭ Azii" (P. P. Ivanov as a historian of Central Asia), *Sovetskoe vostokovedenie*, vol. V, Moscow and Leningrad, 1948, pp. 313-20 (with a portrait).

(YURI BREGEL)

IVANOW, VLADIMIR ALEKSEEVICH (b. St. Petersburg, Russia, 3 November 1886, d. Tehran, 19 June 1970; variously spelt Ivanov and Wladimir), Russian orientalist and leading pioneer in modern Ismaʿili studies. His father was a military doctor, and he spent his youth in his native city and Moscow, graduating in 1907 with distinction as a gold medalist from a gymnasium in St. Petersburg. From 1907 to 1911 he studied at the Faculty of Oriental Languages of the University of St. Petersburg. After studying Arabic with the noted Russian scholar Victor Rosen

(1849-1908), Ivanow read Islamic and Central Asian history with Vasiliĭ Vladimirovich Barthold (1869-1930, q.v.), while specializing in Persian dialects under the eminent Russian authority Valentin A. Zhukovsky (1858-1918; Barthold, p. 320). In 1910, Ivanow visited Persia for a few months on a scholarship to improve his knowledge of Persian. After graduating from the University of St. Petersburg with a first class diploma in 1911, he joined the Persian subsidiary of the State Bank of Russia and served in Persia from 1912 to 1914, a career decision primarily motivated by his scholarly interests. Sent initially to Birjand and later to Kermānšāh, Ivanow embarked on his field research into Persian dialects as well as the folk poetry of Khorasan and elsewhere in Persia. The results of these linguistic and related ethnological and folkloric studies, which he pursued intermittently until the 1920s, were later published in some twenty articles (Daftary, 1971, pp. 62-63). They retain their importance as works of reference in the field of Iranian languages.

In 1914 Ivanow resigned from the bank in Persia and returned to Russia where a year later he joined the Asiatic Museum of the (Imperial) Russian Academy of Sciences in St. Petersburg. The Asiatic Museum, then under the directorship of the eminent philologist Karl Salemann (1849-1916), had built up an important library. In the next year, 1915, Ivanow was sent to Bukhara to collect manuscripts and acquired over a thousand Arabic and Persian manuscripts for the museum. He was described as a "fanatical lover of manuscripts" by Ignatiĭ IUlianovich Krachkovskii (p. 68), who was at the time working on the Arabic collection of the museum. In 1916 Sergei Fedorovich Oldenburg (1863-1934), Salemann's successor at the museum, appointed Ivanow as an assistant keeper of oriental manuscripts. His lifelong interest in Islamic manuscripts provided him with the basis for his pioneering work in Ismaʿili studies.

It was at the Asiatic Museum that Ivanow had his first contacts with Ismaʿili literature, his main research interest in later years. He catalogued a small collection of Persian Ismaʿili manuscripts acquired for the museum by Ivan Ivanovich Zarubin (1887-1964), the renowned Russian scholar of Tajik dialects and ethnology (Ivanow, 1917, pp. 359-86). These, like other Persian Ismaʿili manuscripts dating from the Alamut and post-Alamut periods in the history of Nezāri Ismaʿilis, had been preserved in Šoḡnān, Rušān and other districts of Badaḵšān (q.v.) in Russian Central Asia, a region now divided between Tajikistan and Afghanistan.

In the spring of 1918 Ivanow was once again sent to Central Asia to enlarge the Asiatic Museum's so-called Bukharan collection of Islamic manuscripts, but the mission was cut short because of the unsettled conditions of Russia in the wake of the October Revolution. For the same reason, Ivanow had to abandon his plans to visit the Samarkand region to conduct field research in certain local dialects related to Sogdian. Unable to return to St. Petersburg, he decided to go to Persia. He arrived at Mashad in June 1918, and served there during 1919-1920 as a Persian interpreter to Major-General W. E. R. Dickson, commander of the Anglo-Indian forces in Eastern Persia in World War I. During these years, he also met many Persian Ismaʿilis and acquired valuable details about their community and literature.

In November 1920 Ivanow went to India in the company of an Anglo-Indian force which was about to be disbanded. Thus began his long residency of some four decades in the Indian Subcontinent. Soon after, Ivanow settled in Calcutta, where Sir Ashutosh Mukerji, president of the Asiatic Society of Bengal (see BENGAL ii.), commissioned him to catalogue the extensive collection of Persian manuscripts in the Society's library. He completed this task meticulously in two annotated volumes and two supplements, which were published during 1924-28 in the *Bibliotheca Indica* series (Daftary, 1971, p. 64). The same decade saw the appearance of his first major Ismaʿili publication ("Ismailitica," in *Memoirs of the Asiatic Society of Bengal* 8, 1922, pp. 1-76), which contained first editions of certain Nezāri Ismaʿili texts. In 1928 Ivanow went to Persia to collect manuscripts for the Asiatic Society, as he had done frequently in India. On this occasion, he made the first of several visits to Alamut (q.v.) and other Ismaʿili strongholds in northern Persia. Having done considerable work also on a catalogue of the Asiatic Society's Arabic manuscripts, later completed by H. Husain and published in 1939, Ivanow ended his association with the Asiatic Society in 1930 and moved to Bombay. This initiated a new phase in his scholarly career, a phase devoted exclusively to his path-breaking Ismaʿili studies.

In the meantime, Ivanow had established relations with some members of the Nezāri Ḵoja community of Bombay who, in turn, introduced him to Solṭān Moḥammad Šāh, Āqā Khan III (1877-1957, q.v.), the forty-eighth imam of the Nezāri Ismaʿilis. In January 1931, the Āqā Khan employed Ivanow on a permanent basis to research into the literature, history, and teaching of the Ismaʿilis. Henceforth, Ivanow rapidly found access to the private collections of Ismaʿili manuscripts held secretly by the Nezāri Ismaʿilis of India, Afghanistan, Central Asia, Persia and elsewhere. At the same time, he established scholarly contacts with Asaf Ali Asghar Fyzee (1899-1981), the leading authority on Ismaʿili law, and a few other scholars of the Ismaʿili Bohrā community of Bombay, who placed at his disposal their valuable family collections of Arabic Ismaʿili manuscripts dating to the Fatimid and Mostaʿli Yamani phases of Ismaʿili history. It was in Bombay of the early 1930s that these scholars, led by Ivanow, brought about a breakthrough in Ismaʿili studies. Through the network of his Ismaʿili connections, Ivanow managed to identify a large number of Ismaʿili texts, which he described in an annotated catalogue (*A Guide to Ismaili Literature*, London, 1933). This catalogue was the first pointer to the hitherto unknown richness and diversity of the literary heritage of the Ismaʿilis and remained an indispensable research tool for several decades, providing the material for the advancement of Ismaʿili scholarship. By 1963, when Ivanow published a second edition of his Ismaʿili catalogue (*Ismaili Literature: A Bibliographical Survey*, Tehran, 1963), he had identified a few hundred more manuscript sources while the field of Ismaʿili studies as a whole had undergone a revolution thanks to the concerted efforts of Ivanow and a few other scholars, notably A. A. A. Fyzee, Ḥosayn F. al-Hamdāni (1901-1962), Zāhed ʿAli (1888-1958) and Henry Corbin (q.v.).

Ivanow was also instrumental in founding the Islamic Research Association in Bombay in 1933. Several of Ivanow's early Ismaʿili works, including his major study on early Ismaʿilism (*Ismaili Tradition Concerning the Rise of the Fatimids*, London and New York, 1942), appeared in the Association's series of publications. In these seminal Ismaʿili studies, Ivanow used archeological and epigraphic evidence, as well as literary sources. In 1937 he discovered the tombs of several Nezāri imams in the villages of Anjedān (q.v.) and Kahak, in Central Persia, enabling him to fill important gaps in the post-Alamut history of the Nezāris (see V. Ivanow, "Tombs of some Persian Ismaili Imams," *Journal of the Bombay Branch of the Royal Asiatic Society*, N.S. 14, 1938, pp. 49-62). In 1957-58, building on his earlier work carried out in 1928 and 1937, he undertook extensive archeological studies of the fortress of Alamut, the seat of the Nezāri Ismaʿili state (483-654/1090-1256), and Lamasar, producing what still remains the most comprehensive monograph on the subject (*Alamut and Lamasar*, Tehran, 1960).

Ivanow's systematic efforts in recovering Ismaʿili manuscripts and facilitating research and publication in the field led to the creation in 1946 of the Ismaʿili Society of Bombay (see ANJOMAN-E ESMĀʿĪLĪ), under the patronage of Āqā Khan III, and with Ivanow as the Society's honorary secretary and the editor of its series of publications. The bulk of Ivanow's numerous Ismaili monographs and editions and translations of Ismaʿili texts appeared in the same series. It was also mainly through Ivanow's efforts that the Ismaili Society came to possess an important library of manuscripts in Bombay; these manuscripts were subsequently transfered, in the late 1970s, to the Institute of Ismaili Studies Library in London, which currently holds the largest single collection of Ismaʿili manuscripts in the West. In 1959, Ivanow settled permanently in Tehran where he spent his final years.

Ivanow was the moving spirit behind the modern progress in Ismaʿili studies; and as his associate of four decades has observed, his work will endure and constitute the basis for further studies in almost every major field of Ismaʿilism (Fyzee, p. 93). It was, however, the Nezāri branch of Ismaʿilism to which he devoted most of his attention. He identified, recovered, edited, translated and indefatigably studied a good portion of the extant literature of the Nezāri Ismaʿilis, a literature produced mainly in the Persian language (see Daftary, 1971, pp. 58-62), and he stands as the unrivaled founder of modern Nezāri Ismaʿili studies (Hodgson, pp. 30-32; Berthel's, pp. 51-52). Largely thanks to his pioneering research and numerous contributions, the Nezāri Ismaʿilis of the Alamut period are no longer judged on the basis of medieval crusader legends and Marco Polo's fantasies as a band of drugged assassins led by a fanatical "Old Man of the Mountain."

Bibliography: V. V. Barthold, *La Découverte de l'Asie*, tr. Basil Nikitine, Paris, 1947. Andrei Evgen'evich Bertel's, *Nasir-i Khosrov i Ismailizm*, Moscow, 1959. Farhad Daftary, "Bibliography of the Publications of the late W. Ivanow," *Islamic Culture* 45, 1971, pp. 56-67; 56, 1982, pp. 239-40. Idem, "W. Ivanow: A Biographical Notice," *Middle Eastern Studies* 8, 1972, pp. 241-44. Idem, "Vladimir Ivānof," *Āyanda* 9, 1983, pp. 665-74. Idem, *The Ismāʿīlīs: Their History and Doctrines*, Cambridge, 1990. A. A. A. Fyzee, "Wladimir Ivanow (1886-1970)," *Journal of the Asiatic Society of Bombay* 45-46, 1970-71, p. 92-97. Marshall G. S. Hodgson, *The Order of Assassins*, The Hague, 1955. V. A. Ivanow, "Ismailitskiya rukopisi Aziatskago Muzeya. Sobranie I. Zarubina, 1916 g.," *Bulletin de l'Académie [Impériale] des Sciences de Russie*, série 6, 11, 1917, pp. 359-86; abr. Eng. tr. E. Denison Ross, in *JRAS*, 1919, pp. 429-35. Idem (Ivanow), *Fifty Years in the East: An Autobiographical Sketch* (unpublished manuscript). I. IU. Krachkovskii, *Among Arabic Manuscripts, Memories of Libraries and Men*, tr. Tatiana Minorsky, Leiden, 1953. Sabine Schmidtke, ed., *Correspondance Corbin-Ivanow: lettres échangée entre Henry Corbin et Vladimir Ivanow de 1947 à 1966*, Paris, 1999.

(FARHAD DAFTARY)

IVORY AND ITS USE IN PRE-ISLAMIC IRAN. Prior to the 1st millennium B.C.E. ivories are not commonly documented from excavations in Iran. Whether this reflects an actual unavailability of ivory and hence ivory carving, or is a result of the incompleteness of archeological recovery, is unknown. In Mesopotamia ivory carvings have been excavated at a number of sites dating to the 3rd and 2nd millennia B.C.E., and in Anatolia especially from the 2nd millennium B.C.E. In Iran, ivory beads are reported from excavations from early 2nd millennium B.C.E. at Tepe Hissar (Ḥeṣār) IIIC in northeast Iran, but remain to be analyzed. During the Middle Elamite period in the 2nd millennium B.C.E., a small number of ivory artifacts occur in Elam in southwestern Iran. At Susa there are four small sculptures, a headless clothed female, a kilted male figure, and two female heads. From nearby Chogha Zanbil (see ČOĠA ZANBEL) from the 13th century B.C.E. derive mosaic fragments, forming an inlaid panel of a winged female and caprids flanking trees. Elephant bones (but no tusks, as has erroneously been reported several times), were recovered from Haft Tepe, 15th-14th centuries B.C.E.

As in Mesopotamia, ivory artifacts are more commonly excavated in Iran in the first millennium B.C.E. The largest and best-known collection from Iran is the corpus recovered from the citadel site of Ḥasanlu in northwestern Iran; its ancient name and ethnic and linguistic background remain unknown. The site was destroyed ca. 800 B.C.E., an event that sealed all the contemporary artifacts, thus dating them. Among the thousands of excavated disparate artifacts manufactured from many materials were hundreds of carved and sculpted ivory fragments, and a smaller number of sculpted wood fragments, the latter preserved because they had burned to charcoal. All had been housed and utilized in several large, manifestly elite structures, but most derive from the second storey of the largest and richest, named Burned Building II, which may have been a temple. Not one piece was recovered intact; all had been broken or shattered by the collapse of the structure's walls, ceilings and roof.

Four cultural styles of carving were recognized. (1) Outstanding in quantity and in cultural significance was a distinct "local style" corpus depicting scenes carved in relief on plaques and other forms, depicting battle scenes involving cavalry, chariots, and foot soldiers, a besieged city; and genre events, the hunt, royal ceremonies, processions, animals. Also recovered were statuettes of male and female deities, some standing on animals, and animals in the round. (2) Another stylistic group consisted of carved plaques depicting animals (no humans) elaborately and concisely executed. Based on stylistic and parallels with Iranian metalwork known outside of Ḥasanlu, these ivories are associated with another, separate Iranian workshop. They (or their craftsmen) were imported into Ḥasanlu from another Iranian polity.

Also recognized were two well-known non-Iranian ivory groups. (3) One is an Assyrian assemblage of plaques that included representations of an Assyrian king at sacrifice and other classic Assyrian-style motifs. (4) The second foreign group consists of units of the classic north Syrian style corpus that include here *pyxides* (lidded boxes), statuettes, animal figurines, and handles. These foreign-made, expensive ivory artifacts were luxury items that probably came to Ḥasanlu, not as a result of commercial trade, but as royal gift exchanges (which often reflected state treaties and marriages)—certainly the presence of royal Assyrian plaques indicate close cultural and political relations with that powerful western polity.

The source of the raw ivory at Ḥasanlu remains unknown, but probably it also arrived from the west via Assyria, via either trade or gifts. Based on carving details, one recognizes that several workshops, or perhaps just several individuals, functioned at Ḥasanlu, and also that the same craftsmen carved the ivories and the few wood sculptures preserved. These workshops/individuals were aware of and adapted both Assyrian and north Syrian iconography, very clear in the warfare representations.

Not one ivory artifact was recovered in its original functional locus, and only comparanda can help determine their precise function. These suggest that most of the plaques, and possibly some of the animal statuettes, probably decorated furniture, beds and chairs, or boxes. The statuettes of deities, sometimes standing on an animal, which feature identifies them as deities, were apparently freestanding; they surely had been situated in sacred areas.

In the 1970s Iranian archeologists excavated a number of fragmentary ivories at Ziwiye, a mound in northwestern Iran, some 130 km southeast of Ḥasanlu; only a few examples have been recorded. Plaques with depictions of birds, animals, rosettes, and human figures were reported. There is also a large number of very fragmentary ivory objects scattered in many museums and private collections in a number of United States and European museums and collections that over many years have been claimed (by dealers and curators, followed by scholars) to have derived from a plunder at Ziwiye in 1947. Most examples consist of carved plaques depicting Assyrian- or Assyrianizing-style scenes representing hunting, ceremonial, and heraldic animals, also animal and human statuettes. However, not one of this large corpus had been excavated, and it is therefore impossible to establish with archeological certainty which may have been plundered and acquired at Ziwiye, or even at other sites in Iran, or even that all derived from Iran (given the absolute lack of reliability of dealers' and curators' claims). At least two plaques from this corpus reflect a style that indicates they may have been carved in Iran; one depicts a royal figure accompanied by a parasol-bearer receiving individuals (Godard, 1950, figs. 91, 92; Muscarella, 1980, pp. 205, 208, 174). The chronology of the use of the excavated Ziwiye ivories is 7th century B.C.E., based on a sealing of the Urartian king Rusa II recovered there; some may have been carved slightly earlier.

Judging from cemetery sites and one mounded site, Luristan produced both ivory and bone carving in the 2nd and 1st millennium B.C.E. At Sorḵ Dom there are a number of artifacts published (Schmidt et al., 1989, pp. 363-69). As bone carved in the form of sculpted flat- or round-headed pins, also buttons, small animal sculpture, a few incised decorated plaques, and small decorative objects. However (*pace* Schmidt et al., 1989, pp. 368 ff.) the carved and sculpture objects published in Muscarella 1981 are ivory, not bone (nos. 25, 26, 27: hippo ivory; nos. 28-30: elephant ivory). Bone carving for small objects existed at Nuš-e Jān during the Median period.

From the Achaemenid period there is evidence of ivory carving both from excavations and site destructions. At Susa a number of ivory fragments, along with other material, including two Greek sherds, were recovered in a pit dated to the Seleucid period (but its chronology is unclear). Among the fragments (consciously broken and discarded by an enemy?) are examples of Achaemenid workmanship: a female head, possibly a female statuette, and eight double-sided combs, some with classic Achaemenid canonical representations on their frames. Other ivory fragments recovered in the pit derived from western workmanship—Syria, Egypt and Greece; and the cultural background of other fragments remains unidentified. Little can be said from the fragmented nature of the find regarding functions except for the combs, also that for some furniture decoration seems to have been involved. The inscription DSf of Darius I, celebrating the building of his palace (OPers. *hadiš*) at Susa, boasts that its costly prestige goods were brought from afar (l. 23), including ivory (OPers. *piru* from Akk. *pilu*; Kent, *Old Persian*, p. 197): "the ivory which was fashioned here was brought from Ethiopia [q.v., OPers. Kūša "Kush"] and from India and from Arachosia" (ll. 43-45).

A masterfully carved ivory akinakes scabbard depicting in relief a classic Achaemenid court-style rampant feline holding a stag was excavated on the Oxus river in Tajikistan; whether locally made or received from the Achaemenid heartland cannot be determined.

Persepolis itself (sacked in antiquity) yielded not many artifacts, including a few fragmented ivories that make up part of a human and an animal head, hands, and a bird head. Achaemenid-period material in the Louvre, acquired from the collector Clot Bey, who purchased them in Egypt in the early 19th century, include wood and ivory combs (a few surely Achaemenid), and a number of Achaemenid-period sword chapes. If indeed they had been locally recovered in Egypt (aside from having been purchased there), they could have been either locally made or imported.

Ivories thereafter in Iran seem to be non-existent from excavations. From the Parthian period there is the well-known group of ivory rhytons from the early Parthian site of Nisa in Turkmenistan. Representations of furniture, couches, stools, and chairs are known from coins and reliefs; that some parts were made of ivory is known from examples recovered at Nisa. Similar furniture representations continued into the later Sasanian period; bronze furniture remains exist but are rare.

For the ivory plaques of later date found in Afghanistan, see AFGHANISTAN viii., BEGRĀM, KABUL MUSEUM.

Bibliography: Susa: P. Amiet, "Les Ivories achéménides de Suse," *Syria* 49, 1972, pp. 167-91 and 319-37. Idem, *Elam*, Auvers-sur-Oise, 1966, figs. 217, 325, 327. P. O. Harper et al., eds., *The Royal City of Susa*, New York, 1992, nos. 84, 86. Chogha Zanbil: P. Amiet, *Elam*, fig. 271. Haft Tepe: E. O. Neghaban, *Excavations at Haft Tepe*, Philadelphia, 1991, p. 18. Tepe Hissar: E. F. Schmidt, *Excavations at Tepe Hissar, Damghan*, Philadelphia, 1937, pp. 223, 232, 312. Ḥasanlu: Oscar White Muscarella, *The Catalogue of Ivories from Hasanlu, Iran*, Philadelphia, 1980. Ziwiye/ "Ziwiye": "Exposition des dernieres decouvertes archaeologiques 1975-1976," Tehran, 1976, p. 28, no. 184. "Exposition . . . 1976-1977," Tehran, 1977, p. 37, nos. 338, 339, 340, 341. A. Godard, *Le Trésor de Ziwiyé*, Haarlem, 1950, pp. 78 ff., figs. 66, 68-70, 72-89, 91, 92. R. Ghirshman, *Tombe princiére de Ziwiyé*, Paris, 1979, p. 11, pls. VII-XIV, XVII-XIX, XXII. In the Tehran Museum: Stefana Mazzoni, *Studi sugli avon di Ziwiye*, Rome, 1977. Oscar White Muscarella, "'Ziwiye' and Ziwiye: The Forgery of a Provenience," *Journal of Field Archaeology* 4, 1977, pp. 197-219. C. K. Wilkinson, *Ivories from Ziwiye*, Bern 1975.

Luristan: Oscar White Muscarella, "Surkh Dum at the Metropolitan Museum of Art: A Mini-Report," *Journal of Field Archaeology* 8, 1981, pp. 327-59. Erich F. Schmidt et al., *The Holmes Expeditions to Luristan*, Chicago, 1989.

Persepolis: Erich F. Schmidt *Persepolis* II, Chicago, 1957, p. 71, pl. 40, la-g. Rolf Stucky, "Achamenidische Wilzer und Elfenbeine aus Agypten und Vorderasien im Louvre," *Antike Kunst* 28, 1985, pp. 7-32. Parthian and Sasanian periods: Vesta Sarkhosh Curtis, "Parthian and Sasanian Furniture," in *The Furniture of Western Asia Ancient and Traditional*, ed. G. Herrmann, Mainz, 1996, pp. 233-44.

(OSCAR WHITE MUSCARELLA)

J

JABA (Jebe; Jovayni uses the Turkish form Yeme), 13th-century Mongol general of the Besüt (Bisut) tribe under Čengiz Khan (q.v.). His original name was Jirḡoʾadai ("sixth"; Jirqutāy), but when, having deserted the Tayičiʾut tribe, he joined Čengiz Khan, the latter renamed him Jebe, a Mongolian term meaning "weapon" (*Secret History*, I, p. 69, par. 147; Rašid-al-Din gives a different etymology: *Jāmeʿ al-tawārik̲* [Moscow], p. 488; ed. Rowšan and Musawi, I, p. 188). He rose from commanding a unit of ten to be commander of *a tümen* (10,000; Rašid al-Din, *Jāmeʿ al-tawārik̲* [Moscow], pp. 551-53; ed. Rowšan and Musawi, I, pp. 207-8), and he distinguished himself in the war against the Chin Empire in northern China, taking Tung-ching (the modern Liao-yang), its eastern capital, by a ruse that involved a false retreat (*Secret History*, I, pp. 175-76, par. 247; Rašid-al-Din, *Jāmeʿ al-tawārik̲* [Moscow], p. 563 ed. Rowšan and Musawi, I, pp. 210, 443). His most celebrated operations fell during the great seven-year campaign to Western Asia (1218-24), when he was first sent against Čengiz Khan's enemy, the Naiman (Nāymān) chief Küčlüg (Kušluk), who had usurped the throne of the Qara-Khitay Empire. Jebe fomented a rising by the oppressed Muslim population with a proclamation of religious freedom (Rašid-al-Din, ed. Rowšan and Musawi, I, pp. 465-66; cf. Jovayni, ed. Qazvini, I, pp. 49-51). After Jebe's success in hunting down and killing Küčlüg on the frontier of Badak̲šān, Čengiz Khan warned him against excessive self-confidence (Rašid-al-Din, *Jāmeʿ al-tawārik̲* [Moscow], p. 554; ed. Rowšan and Musawi, I, p. 208). From Samarkand in 1220, Čengiz Khan dispatched Jebe and another general, Sübeʾetei (Subatāy), with an army of 30,000 men in pursuit of the K̲ᵛārazmšāh Moḥammad b. Tekeš (Jovayni, ed. Qazvini, I, pp. 92, 113-16; tr. Boyle, I, pp. 118, 143-49), who had fled to the Caspian coast; they were ordered to complete the task within three years, but did so in two-and-a-half (Rašid al-Din. *Jāmeʿ al-tawārik̲* [Moscow], p. 557, ed. Rošwan and Musawi, I, pp, 209, 505). As the two generals moved rapidly through northern Persia, Jebe received the submission of Balk̲, Nišāpur, Ray, and Hamadān, but sacked towns such as Zāva, Āmol, and Ardabil, which offered resistance. The Mongol army then ravaged Azerbaijan, defeated the Georgian king and the Alans, and crossed the Caucasus to crush the Qepčāq (Cumans) and their Russian allies on the Kalka River before withdrawing eastwards to rejoin Čengiz Khan on his homeward march to Mongolia (Rašid-al-Din, ed. Rowšan and Musawi, I, pp. 501, 504-10, 521-25, giving slightly different details from Jovayni; Jovayni, ed. Qazvini, I, pp. 112-17). Garbled reports of these operations, reaching the Fifth Crusade in Egypt, brought the Mongols to the attention of Christian Europe for the first time. The Chinese dynastic history of the Mongol era, the *Yuan Shih* (chap. 120), suggests that Jebe died towards the close of the expedition (tr. Pelliot and Hambis, p. 270). An isolated reference in the *Secret History* (I, p. 202, par. 272) to his participation in a campaign in northern China in 1231 is therefore probably anachronistic.

Bibliography: Histoire des campagnes de Gengis Khan: Cheng-wou ts'in-tcheng lou, tr. Paul Pelliot and Louis Hambis, Leiden, 1951, pp. 154-56. Rašid al-Din Fażl-Allāh, *Jāmeʿ al-tawārik̲*, ed. Moḥammad Rowšan and M. Musawi, 4 vols, Tehran, 1994. Paul Ratchnevsky, *Činggis-Khan: Sein Leben und Werken*, Wiesbaden, 1983; tr. Thomas Nivison Haining as *Genghis Khan: His Life and Legacy*, Oxford, 1991, index. *Secret History of the Mongols: A Mongolian Epic Chronicle of the Thirteenth Century*, tr. Igor de Rachewiltz, 2 vols, Leiden, 2004. B. Spuler, *Mongolen*[4], pp. 23-25.

(PETER JACKSON)

JABAL ʿĀMEL, SHIʿITE ULAMA OF, in the Safavid Period. Two decades after the establishment of the Safavid state in Persia in 1501, the Safavid monarchs sought prominent clerics who would strengthen their rule by promoting a standard urban system of Shiʿite worship and lend them political legitimacy against their Sunnite Ottoman foes. Neither the Qezelbāš who adhered to heterodox militant Shiʿism, nor the erudite Persian notables who had a general Sunnite training were capable of providing the Safavid state with a collective social consciousness congenial to empire building and stability. The shahs, who were widely perceived as divinely guided charismatic leaders, gradually transformed their rule from a communal Shiʿism to a state-operated Shiʿism. Meanwhile, several Arab theologians from Jabal ʿĀmel in southern Lebanon (see also SHIʿITES IN LEBANON), along with their families, were emigrating from Ottoman Syria to Iraq, Mecca, India, and Persia. A number of historical factors motivated this emigration, namely, a surplus of jurists who could not find a professional outlet to their expertise, first due to a decrease in opportunities within the Ottoman learning system, and second, due to their limited ability to implement and formally spread their Shiʿite legal rulings in ʿĀmeli villages and towns, and third, due to the Ottoman suppression and threat against publicly active Shiʿite *mojtahed*s. In addition, a few ʿĀmeli scholars who were professing and implementing *ejtehād* (q.v. "legal inference") came under close Ottoman scrutiny and at least one eminent scholar, Zayn-al-Din ʿĀmeli (see Kohlberg), among Shiʿites widely known as al-Šahid al-T̲āni "the Second martyr" (1506-58), was put to death by the Ottomans. The Safavids, in contrast, found the ʿĀmelis' use of *ejtehād* helpful in developing new theological positions that supported dynastic authority and projected an image of Islamic "authenticity" to their Ottoman rivals to the west.

The nature, scope and reasons for the emigration of ʿĀmeli theologians and their families to Safavid Persia has been the center of academic debate in the last decade. Said Amir Arjomand was the first scholar in the West to highlight the significance and implications of the integration of ʿĀmeli scholars into the Safavid religious structure (see Arjomand, pp. 105-211). Albert Hourani, inspired by Ḥosayn Modarresi Ṭabāṭabāʾi, followed his lead by emphasizing the large-scale emigration of ʿĀmeli scholars to Persia in the 16th and 17th centuries. To this, Andrew Newman, who looked at the early Safavid rule, responded by a denial of the ʿĀmeli emigration altogether, arguing that the Syrian Arab scholars of Jabal ʿĀmel found Qezelbāš Shiʿite beliefs too 'heterodox' to accept and rejected association with the Safavid monarchs (Newman). Rula Jurdi Abisaab challenged Newman's position after examining the historical circumstances of the ʿĀmeli ulama in Ottoman Syria and followed their careers throughout the Safavid period. She suggested that the presence of more than 158 first- and second-generation émigré ʿĀmeli scholars and their families in Safavid Persia, and their advent from a small region like Jabal ʿĀmel, confirmed the emigration theory. She also pointed to the fluid and multifaceted nature of socio-political exchange between the Qezelbāš *amirs* and the ʿĀmeli clerics (Abisaab, 1994, 2004). The latter supported the proclamation of the first Safavid ruler Shah Esmāʿil I (q.v., r. 1501-24) that Twelver Shiʿism, mainly of an urban legal nature, would become the foundation of his new kingdom (even if conversion to Shiʿism happened much later). Devin Stewart, too, suggested that the ʿĀmeli scholars were not reluctant to associate with the Safavid court, but he noted that the emigration from Jabal ʿĀmel to Persia was limited in scope (Stewart).

Beyond the scholastic-social ties that bound the founders of the *madrasas* (religious schools) of Jabal ʿĀmel and their disciples together, there was a marked network of kinship relations, both consanguinal and marital, that reinforced the solidarity and elitism of this community. Access to knowledge of Islamic law (*šariʿa*) tended to concentrate in tightly knit family groups and became the esteemed possession of their immediate descendants. By the early 16th century, Jabal ʿĀmel became the foremost center for Shiʿite learning and an accrediting institution, producing and influencing hundreds of theologians who lived or settled in Syria, Mecca, Iraq, Persia, and India. Among the most prominent of these ulama were ʿAli b. ʿAbd-al-ʿĀli Karaki (d. 1534), Ḥosayn b. ʿAbd-al-Ṣamad (d. 1576), Ḥosayn Mojtahed (d. 1592), Bahāʾ-al-Din ʿĀmeli (q.v., d. 1621 or 1622), known as Shaikh Bahāʾi, Mir Moḥammad-Bāqer b. Šams-al-Din Moḥammad Ḥosayni Astarābādi, known as Mir(-e) Dāmād (d. between 1631 and 1632, see DĀMĀD), Aḥmad b. Zayn-al-ʿĀbedin (d. between 1644 and 1650; see Aḥmad ʿAlawi), Loṭf-Allāh Maysi (d. 1622-23), ʿAli b. Moḥammad b. Ḥasan b. Zayn-al-Din ʿĀmeli (d. 1691), and Moḥammad b. Ḥasan Ḥorr ʿĀmeli (d. 1693; see representative works in bibliography). Except for ʿAli b. Moḥammad b. Ḥasan b. Zayn-al-Din, all of the above theologians enjoyed close ties with the Safavid court, occupied the highest religious offices in Persia, and created the principal tools for the consolidation of Safavid rule. They never, however, acted independently or determined the Safavids' policies as such. They accommodated the sovereign's agendas while simultaneously manipulating the judicial domain and reworking vital social alliances among Persian elites to achieve some social autonomy and political power. During the reign of Shah Ṭahmāsp I (r. 1524-76) and Shah Esmāʿil II (q.v., r. 1576-77), influential Qezelbāš *amirs* welcomed the ascendancy of ʿĀmeli clerics to the religious posts in order to undermine their rivals, namely, the Persian *ṣadrs* and bureaucrats.

Unlike Sayyed Ebrāhim Qaṭifi (fl. 16th cent.) and Iraqi Shiʿite scholars at the time, the ʿĀmelis were prepared to transform Shiʿism from a religion of the community to that of the state, proposing significant modifications in political theory and becoming highly equipped to circumvent Ottoman and Uzbek propaganda and ideological expansion. They espoused, with differing degree, a close affinity with secular sovereignty. This is best illustrated in their distinct approaches toward the issue of the performance of Friday prayers (*ṣalāt al-jomʿa*) at the time of the Major Occultation of the Twelfth Imam (see Karaki, *Resālat ṣalāt al-jomʿa*; Ḥosayn b. ʿAbd-al-Ṣamad, *al-ʿEqd al-ṭahmāsbi*; Ḥasan b. ʿAli Karaki, *al-Bolḡa*; Mir Dāmād, *Resāla fi ṣalāt al-jomʿa*). The enactment of Friday prayers, which required the presence of a jurist further aimed at restoring the Shiʿite community to political normalcy concomitant with state formation. Whether as rationalists (*oṣulis*) who favored the use of rational inference in deriving legal rulings or as traditionists (*akbāris*, see AḴBĀRIYA) who relied solely on Hadith for religious guidance, leading ʿĀmeli scholars strengthened the foundation of Safavid rule. In terms of their involvement in converting Persia from Sunnism to Shiʿism, the ʿĀmelis promoted anti-Sunnite rituals for practical political reasons, namely, to popularize Shiʿite creed, create collective religious emblems, and advocate emotional immersion in experiences distinguished as Shiʿite. Several competing and complementary versions of both Sunnism and Shiʿism existed at the time. On their part, the ʿĀmeli clerics distinguished their version of legalistic Islam from popular heterodox and Sufi leanings and made the relevance of the sacred law to everyday life more pronounced for the layperson.

Far from remaining self-absorbed legal experts, the ʿĀmeli jurists communicated their ideas through a network of students and followers who translated their juridical rulings into Persian, and state officials who turned them into decrees. The ulama's doctrinal, legal, and philosophical works reflected alterations in the monarchs' sources of legitimacy, a measure of control over the Qezelbāš, and centralization efforts at the hands of some sovereigns, particularly Shah ʿAbbās I (r. 1587-1629). Legal and doctrinal works also reflected issues of economic stability and political conflict with the Ottomans, depopulation and forced migration aimed at thwarting Ottoman invasions in frontier areas heavily inhabited by Christians. The clerics' writings also reflected internal class conflicts, expressed in distinct ideological terms. At the time of Shah Taḥmāsp I (r. 1524-76), but mainly under Shah ʿAbbās I, the translation from Arabic into Persian and abridgment of major Shiʿite texts of doctrine and positive law carried the legal-political debates from the exclusive circles of theologians to a vast community of low-ranking scholars, political figures, merchants and artisans (on translations from Arabic into Persian, see ĀZARNUŠ; Abisaab, 2004, pp. 27-29).

Encouraged by his teacher, the "Second Martyr," Ḥosayn b. ʿAbd-al-Ṣamad left Jabal ʿĀmel for Iraq and finally settled in Persia. With an eagerness to bring Persian society under the fold of Shiʿite legalism, Ḥosayn started actively to spread and propagate Shiʿite Hadith. Karaki had argued that observing Friday prayer was optional for Shiʿite Muslims and must only be held during the presence of a jurist who functions as the deputy of the Twelfth Imam. The social and political importance which Karaki gave to such a jurist created much resistance among Persian bureaucrats against the observance of Friday prayers, which was halted after his death. Ḥosayn, however, convinced Shah Ṭahmāsp that holding Friday prayers was a powerful weapon against the anti-Shiʿite campaign of the Ottomans and their Uzbek allies, because it embellished the Islamic character of his kingdom. Ḥosayn also tried to disentangle *ejtehād* from court politics, warning against accepting the opinions of Karaki and his grandson, Mir Sayyed Ḥosayn, both of whom took on the title "seals of *mojtahed*s." Ḥosayn held steadfastly to the idea of a pluralism of authority, reflected in the rationalist renewal of legal rulings and a rejection of the opinions of dead *mojtahed*s. Indirectly, Ḥosayn's support for the renewal of Shiʿite law validated the position of the Persian notables who opposed Karaki's assumption of supreme *ejtehād*. More importantly, however, Ḥosayn resisted attempts by the Safavid sovereign to control questions of clerical leadership or to designate a "seal" of *mojtahed*s. Ultimately, he hoped to promote the autonomy of the jurists and high-ranking ulama in deciding such matters and defending them from court politics.

Safavid scholars have debated the motives for the favorable approach of Shah Esmāʿil II toward Sunnism, assigning various psychological, political, and economic motives for it. They have accepted, for the most part, the court historians' claims, based on accusations by the Qezelbāš and ulama, according to which Shah Esmāʿil II attempted to eliminate Twelver Shiʿism as the official "state religion." A close examination of these accusations, however, shows that Shah Esmāʿil II, for political expediency, aimed to suppress extreme anti-Sunnite rituals, particularly cursing, as a way to normalize Sunnism as one of many Islamic expressions in Persia. He did not truly attempt to uproot Twelver Shiʿism, but rather to perpetuate conciliatory approaches toward Sunnism. After all, in the post-Il-khanid and the early Safavid periods, a fluid exchange between Sunnism and Shiʿism (in their various forms) ensued. Ḥosayn Mojtahed, Karaki's grandson and the main ʿĀmeli scholar who, in alliance with the Qezelbāš, led the opposition against Shah Esmāʿil II, supported ritual cursing of the first three caliphs, Abu Bakr, ʿOmar, and ʿOṯmān, who are considered as rightly guided (*rāšedun*) by the Sunnites, as an essential tool for "being truly Shiʿite" and for solidifying a distinctive identity and memory for Twelver Shiʿites as separate from that of Sunnites.

Under Shah ʿAbbās I, the social and ethnic composition of the military and the administrative staff underwent fundamental changes, mainly due to a systematic replacement of Qezelbāš leaders with Circassian and Georgian slave soldiery (*ḡolām*s, q.v.). Safavid society was arguably shaped by forced migration and the depopulation policies in the face of Ottoman military expansion in the west and Uzbek opposition in the east. More extensively than his predecessors, Shah ʿAbbās used depopulation and a scorched earth policy to prevent Ottoman occupation of frontier regions and cities. One would also add forced conversion of frontier populations, particularly Christians, to Islam.

As new Christian regions and groups came under Safavid control, thorny legal issues about Muslim-Christian relations surfaced. During one of ʿAbbās's court assemblies, the Ottoman envoy criticized the shah for prohibiting the consumption of meat from animals slaughtered by Christians and Jews, pointing to a long-established Sunnite tradition proclaiming the consumption of such meat licit. Shah ʿAbbās then ushered in Shaikh Bahāʾ-al-Din ʿĀmeli (Shaikh Bahāʾi) to elucidate, from a Shiʿite legal viewpoint, the sovereign's support for such prohibition. In eighteen legal questions that Shah ʿAbbās put forth to Bahāʾ-al-Din, he seemed particularly concerned with providing a clear legal framework for the social and economic exchanges among Muslims and Christians. On another occasion, Bahāʾ-al-Din ruled that it was impermissible to destroy a church that functioned as a mosque in the "land of infidels" or even to interrupt its activities and source of funding. The church, Bahāʾ-al-Din argued, cannot become any person's property. It is possible that such views reflected Shah ʿAbbās' hope to promote social integration in depopulated areas, particularly those with a Christian majority. Jean Chardin (q.v.), a French traveler, noted that a strict observation of purity rituals among Muslims was a clear hindrance to traveling abroad to engage in trade with Europeans, because theoretically the *šariʿa* prohibited the consumption of meat or the wearing of clothes made by non-Muslims and, in extreme cases, coming in direct touch with them (Chardin, p. 281). Bahāʾ-al-Din's rulings, however, showed that in reality, when the need arose, there were ways to work around such laws. For instance, he expounded the unique conditions under which it is possible to consider grape syrup, honey, or vinegar to be religiously pure, if offered to a Muslim by a Georgian Christian.

High-ranking theologians like Bahāʾi and Mir(-e) Dāmād expressed a keen interest in scientific and philosophical thought. They also appropriated traditions of 'high' Sufism even while popular Sufi practices and heterodoxy were suppressed. Shah ʿAbbās welcomed this elitist eclecticism as long as it promoted outward conformity to the political order. On his part, Mir Dāmād supported his philosophical arguments by statements in the Qurʾān and Hadith. In the fourth *qabas* (lit. firebrand) of his book *Qabasāt*, for instance, he referred to the Qurʾān and the statements of Shiʿite scholars and Imams, noting that philosophy is not an independent or superior method for knowing God, but rather a supplemental and exegetical one.

Mir Dāmād advocated a hierarchy of consciousness and gradations of knowledge and emphasized the necessity for humans to be ruled by those who are more knowledgeable and able. What society labels 'evil' in reference to injustice or adultery, he wrote, was constructed and as such has no absolute reality. Evil then describes the person who is lacking in justice, uprightness, or goodness, or it simply describes the standpoint of civic political law (*al-siāsa al-madaniya*) whose order is disrupted due to such imperfection. Mir Dāmād suggested that it was necessary for humans to fear divine retribution against "abominable acts," that is, acts held to be abominable by legal experts and the disciplining state (Mir Dāmād, *Qabasāt*, pp. 437, 440-41).

Shaikh Loṭf-Allāh Maysi, another scholar of ʿĀmeli background, gained wide acclaim under the patronage of ʿAbbās I. His treatise on spiritual seclusion became an occasion for him not only to establish his credibility as a court *mojtahed* but also to confirm the shah's authority in Isfahan's refashioned public space known as the Meydan-e Naqš-e Jahān. The debate over the congregational qualities of the Loṭf-Allāh Mosque, or their lack thereof, brought to the fore the social struggle between the old Isfahani business elite of Meydān-e Hārun-e Welāyāt and the shah's rivaling and authoritative new business center, the Meydān.

As the impetus for conversion to Shiʿism weakened by the 17th-century, Sunnite-Shiʿite polemical confrontations between Safavid and Ottoman scholars lost much steam. Shah Ṣafi I (r. 1629-42) and Shah ʿAbbās II (r. 1642-66) cut off the economic grants of leading legal rationalists, *mojtahed*s, and replaced the latter with another branch of the Persian clerical elite, which promoted *akbāri* approaches (see above).

When scholars of a Sufi or a philosophical bent joined the clerical ranks and were welcomed by the Safavid court, conventional jurists bemoaned the monarch's retreat from the sacred Shiʿite law of his ancestors. Behind their attacks on the Safavids' moral laxity and supposed hypocrisy, lurked the *mojtahed*s' anger at being displaced by such scholarly hybrids who proved politically useful to the Safavid sovereigns of the late 17th century.

Overall, the clerics of ʿĀmeli background honored their alliance with the temporal rulers, fitting a *šariʿa*-guided sociopolitical order to Safavid sovereignty despite their inclination to achieve a measure of autonomy from the state. Gradually, clerical Shiʿism, advocated by the émigré ʿĀmelis, found eager followers not only among a learned Persian elite, but also among the populace, giving way to a distinct and multifaceted form of Twelver Shiʿism.

Bibliography: For the written works of the ulama of Jabal ʿĀmel, see Abisaab, 2004, Appendices I and III and their footnotes, pp. 147-52, 156-73, 216-19.

ʿAbdi Beg Širāzi, *Takmelat al-akbār: tārik-e ṣafawiya az āḡāz tā 978 hejri-e qamari*, Tehran, 1990. Rula Jurdi Abisaab, "The ʿUlama of Jabal ʿAmil in Safavid Iran, 1501-1736: Marginality, Migration and Social Change," *Iranian Studies* 27/1-4, 27, 1994, pp. 103-22. Idem, *Converting Persia: Religion and Power in the Safavid Empire*, London, 2004. Mirzā Afandi Eṣfahāni, *Riāż al-ʿolamāʾ wa ḥiāż al-fożalāʾ*, Qom, 1981. Idem, *Taʿliqat amal al-Āmel*, Qom, 1991. Maḥmud b. Hedāyat-Allāh Afuštāʾi Naṭanzi, *Noqāwat al-āṯār fi ḏekr al-akyār*, ed. Eḥsān Ešrāqi, Tehran, 1971. Āḡā Bozorg Ṭehrāni, *al-Ḏariʿa elā taṣānif al-šiʿa*, 25 vols., Beirut, 1983. Aḥmad b. Zayn-al-ʿĀbedin ʿAlawi ʿĀmeli, *Laṭāʾef-e ḡaybiya*, ed. Jamāl-al-Din Mirdāmādi, Tehran, 1976. Qāżi Aḥmad Qomi, *Kolāṣat al-tawārik*, ed. Eḥsān Ešrāqi, 2 vols., Tehran, 1980-84; ed. and tr. Hans Müller, *Die Chronik Ḫulāṣat al-Tawāriḫ des Qāżī Aḥmad Qumī, Der Abschnitt über Schāh ʿAbbās I*, Wiesbaden, 1964. ʿAli b. ʿAbd-al-ʿAli Karaki ʿĀmeli, "Resāla fi ṣalāt al-jomʿa," in idem, *Rasāʾel al-Moḥaqqeq al-Karaki*, ed. M. Hassun, 2 vols., Qom, 1988. ʿAli b. Zayn-al-Din ʿĀmeli, *al-Dorr al-manṯur men al-maʾṯur wa ḡayr al-maʾṯur*, 2 vols., Qom, 1977. Ḥasan Amin, ed., *Dāʾerat al-maʿāref al-eslāmiya al-šiʿiya*, 5 vols., Beirut, 1981. Idem, *Mostadrakāt Aʿyān al-šiʿa*, 4 vols., Beirut, 1987. Said A. Arjomand, *The Shadow of God and the Hidden Imam*, Chicago, 1984. Āzartāš Āzarnuš, *Tārik-e tarjama az ʿarabi ba fārsi az āḡāz tā ʿaṣr-e ṣafawi*, Tehran, 1996. Shaikh Bahāʾ-al-Din ʿĀmeli, *Ḥormat ḏabāʾeh ahl al-ketāb*, ed. Zohayr Aʿraj, Beirut, 1990. Idem, *Jāmeʿ-e ʿabbāsi*, n.p., n.d. (1980s). Sir John Chardin, *Sir John Chardin's Travels in Persia*, tr. Edmond Lloyd, ed. R. Percy Sykes, 2 vols., London, 1927. Raphaël Du Mans, *Estat de la Perse en 1660*, ed. Charles Schefer, Paris, 1890. Willem Floor, *Safavid Government Institutions*, Costa Mesa, Calif., 2001. Ḥasan b. ʿAli Karaki ʿĀmeli, *al-Bolḡa fi bayān eʿtebār eḏn al-Emām fi šarʿiyat ṣalāt al-jomʿa*, MS kept at Ketāb-kāna-ye ʿomumi-e Marʿaši, Qom, collection 4697, see Aḥmad Ḥosayni, ed., *Fehrest-e noskahā-ye kaṭṭi-e Ketāb-kāna-ye ʿomumi-e Marʿaši*, Qom, 1975. Ḥosayn b. ʿAbd-al-Ṣamad Ḥāreṯi Jobbāʿi ʿĀmeli, *al-ʿEqd al-ṭahmāsbi aw al-ḥosayni*, ed. Sayyed Jawād Modarresi Yazdi, Yazd, n.d. Ḥosayn b. Šehāb-al-Din Karaki ʿĀmeli, *Hedāyat al-abrār elā ṭariq al-aʾemma al-aṯhār*, ed. Raʾuf Jamāl-al-Din, Baghdad, 1977. Moḥammad Ḥorr ʿĀmeli, *Amal al-āmel fi ʿolamāʾ Jabal ʿĀmel*, 2 vols, Najaf, 1965. Albert Hourani, "From Jabal ʿĀmil to Persia." *BSO(A)S* 49, 1986, pp. 133-40. Rasul Jaʿfariān, *Safawiya dar ʿarṣa-ye din, farhang wa siāsat*, 3 vols., Qom, 2000. Etan Kohlberg, "al-Shahīd al-Thāni," in *EI*[2] IX, pp. 209-10.

Moḥammad-Maʿṣum Maʿṣum-ʿAlišāh Širāzi, *Ṭarāʾeq al-ḥaqāʾeq*, ed. Moḥammad-Jaʿfar Maḥjub, 3 vols., Tehran, 1960. Rudi Matthee, "The Career of Mohammad Beg, Grand Vizier of Shah ʿAbbas II (r. 1642-66)," in *Iranian Studies* 24/1-4, 1991, pp. 17-36. Idem, *The Politics of Trade in Safavid Iran: Silk for Silver, 1600-1730*, London, 1999. Loṭf-Allāh Maysi ʿĀmeli, *al-Eʿtekāfiya*, MS kept at Ketāb-kāna-ye āstāna-ye Qom, collection 2244; see Moḥammad-Taqi Dānešpažuh, ed., *Fehrest-e nosak̲-e k̲aṭṭi-ye ketāb-k̲āna-ye āstāna-ye moqaddasa-ye Qom*, Qom, 1976. Michele Membré, *Relazione di Persia (1542)*; tr. A. H. Morton as *Mission to the Lord Sophy of Persia (1539-1542)*, London, 1993. Moḥsen Amin Ḥosayni ʿĀmeli, *K̲eṭaṭ Jabal ʿĀmel*, Beirut, 1983. Idem. *Aʿyān al-šiʿa*, ed. Ḥasan al-Amin, 10 vols., Beirut, 1986. Mir Dāmād [Mir Moḥammad-Bāqer b. Šams-al-Din Moḥammad Ḥosayni Astarābādi], *Qabasāt*, ed. Mehdi Moḥaqqeq, Tehran, 1954. Idem, "Resāla fi ṣalāt al-jomʿa," MS kept at Ketāb-k̲āna-ye ʿomumi-e Marʿaši, Qom, collection 7036; see Aḥmad Ḥosayni, ed., *Fehrest-e nosk̲ahā-ye k̲aṭṭi-e Ketāb-k̲āna-ye ʿomumi-e Marʿaši*, Qom, 1975.

Andrew Newman, "The Myth of the Clerical Migration to Safavid Iran," *Die Welt des Islams* 33, 1993, pp. 66-112. Ḥasan Beg Rumlu, *Aḥsan al-tawārik̲*, tr. C. N. Seddon as *Aḥsanu't-Tawārikh: A Chronicle of the Early Safawis*, 2 vols., Baroda, 1934. Sayyed Ḥasan Ṣadr, *Takmelat amal al-āmel*, ed. Aḥmad Ḥosayni, Qom, 1985. Waliqoli b. Dāwudqoli Šāmlu, *Qeṣaṣ al-k̲āqāni*, ed. Sayyed Ḥasan Sādāt-e Nāṣeri, 2 vols., Tehran, 1992-95. Devin Stewart, "Notes on the Migration of ʿAmili Scholars to Safavid Iran," *JNES* 55, 1996, pp. 81-103. Mirzā Moḥammad-Ṭāher Waḥid Qazvini, *ʿAbbās-nāma*, ed. Ebrāhim Dehgān, Tehran, 1951. Yaḥyā b. ʿAbd-al-Laṭif Qazvini, *Lobb al-tawārik̲*, n.p., 1943.

(RULA ABISAAB)

JABAL-E SERĀJ, a small town in the province of Parvān in Afghanistan, located at the mouth of the Sālang Valley in Kabul Kohestān to the north of the city of Charikar (Čārikār). On official maps, the name of the city was also given in the Arabic manner as Jabal al-Serāj. Its geographical location allowed the town to control southern access to the Sālang and Bājgāh passes across the Hindu Kush mountains, thus giving it strategic and commercial importance at the time when the routes were safe and controlled.

Various objects, among them a stone Buddhist relief found in 1913 during construction works, indicate that the place was already settled in pre-Islamic time (Ball and Gardin, I, p. 131). Many more objects date from later periods, when the locality was known under the name of Parvān, or Barvān, Farvān, or Fervān. Ebn Ḥawqal (according to Le Strange, p. 350) mentioned it as a large town with a mosque, and mistakenly reported it to be situated on the banks of the Panjshir River. According to the *Ḥodud al-ʿĀlam* (tr. Minorsky, p. 112) it was "a pleasant town and a resort of merchants," being "the gate of Hindustan." The *Ṭabaqāt-e Nāṣeri* by Menhāj-al-Din Juzjāni mentions Parvān several times, but Henry George Raverty in the notes of his translation expresses doubts that this corresponds to Parvān on the Panjshir River to the north of Kabul (Juzjāni, I, pp. 288, 1042). Ẓahir-al-Din Bābor (r. 1526-1530, q.v.) described it as one of the fruit-bearing villages on the skirts of the mountains, whose inhabitants produced "cheering wines" and practiced a special method of catching fish in the Sālang River (Bābor, pp. 214-15, 226). He also mentions a "full of difficulties" road that leads through Parvān to the pass of Bājgāh, one of the seven roads across the Hindu Kush (Bābor, pp. 204-5). During the 19th century, when Kohestān was rather unsafe for most of the time, Parvān was rarely mentioned by Western travelers. Charles Masson (III, p. 166) only referred to it as "a city of great magnitude" in ancient times, where coins were discovered in large numbers.

The city gained new importance under the Emir of Afghanistan, Habibullah (Ḥabib-Allāh, r. 1901-19, q.v.), who shifted the governor's seat to it. Moreover, he built a palace and a large fortified cantonment nearby (Adamec, VI, p. 274), giving them the name Jabal al-Serāj, which gradually replaced the old name of Parvān. This change of name has produced some confusion about the location of the former Parvān. The new gazetteer even confuses it with Charikar, located 12 km further south (Adamec, VI, p. 639).

Habibullah also initiated the modern development of Jabal al-Serāj by constructing the first (1911-18) water-power station in the country, fed by the Sālang River, which supplied electricity mainly to the royal palace and to a few small factories in Kabul. In 1938 a small cotton-weaving mill was opened there which used the locally produced electric power and benefited from the traditional cotton crafts of Kohestān. The industrial function of the city grew further when a cement factory was put into operation in 1957. Finally, Jabal al-Serāj became an important transit place in the transportation system of Afghanistan, being the southern base of the new Sālang highway completed in 1964 (Grötzbach, p. 212).

Bibliography: L. W. Adamec, ed., *Historical and Political Gazetteer of Afghanistan*, 6 vols., Graz, 1972-85; vol. 6 *Kabul and Southeastern Afghanistan*, Graz, 1985. Ẓahir-al-Din Bābor, *Bābur Nāma* (Memoirs of Bābur), tr. A. S. Beveridge, London, 1922; repr. Lahore, 1979. W. Ball and J.-C. Gardin, *Archaeological Gazetteer of Afghanistan, Catalogue de Sites Archéologiques d'Afghanistan*, 2 vols., Paris, 1982. E. Grötzbach, *Afghanistan: eine geographische Landeskunde*, Darmstadt, 1990. *Ḥudūd al-ʿĀlam: 'The Regions of the World,' A Persian Geography 372 A.H.-982 A.D.*, tr. V. Minorsky, pref. by V. V. Barthold, ed. C. E. Bosworth, 2nd ed., London, 1970. M. Jewett Bell, ed., *An American Engineer in Afghanistan: from the letters and notes of A. C. Jewett*, Minneapolis, Minn., 1948. Menhāj-al-Din Abu-ʿOmar ʿOṯmān b. Serāj-al-Din Juzjāni, *Ṭabak̲āt-i-Nāṣirī: a General History of the Muhammadan Dynasties of Asia, Including Hindustan, from A.H. 194 (810 A.D.) to A.H. 658 (1260 A.D.), and the Irruption of the Infidel Mughals into Islam*, tr. H. G. Raverty, 2 vols., London, 1881; repr. New Delhi, 1970 and Osnabrück, 1991 (3 vols.). G. Le Strange, *The Lands of the Eastern Caliphate*, London, 1905; repr. London, 1966. Ch. Masson, *Narrative of various Journeys in Balochistan, Afghanistan and the Panjab*, 3 vols., London, 1842; repr. Graz, 1975.

(ERWIN GRÖTZBACH)

JABBĀR KḎĒL (or Jabar Ḵēl or Khan Ḵēl), the leading lineage of the Solaymān Ḵēl Paxtun tribe of the Ḡalzi/Ḡilzi (q.v.) tribal confederation of eastern and southeastern Afghanistan. *Ḵēl* in Pashtu generally means a small (minimal lineage, 3-4 generations) or large (maximal lineage, 5 or more generations) segment of a tribe that may occasionally refer to a whole tribe and its constituent lineages, as in the Solaymān Ḵēl (cf. *zay* "lit. descendant" in Aḥmadzay, tribe, and Bārakzay, lineage).

During the past three centuries the Jabbār Ḵēl maximal lineage has provided political and military leadership for the eastern Paxtuns, especially eastern and southeastern Ḡalzi tribes. This leadership role was triggered by increased contacts between the tribal Paxtuns of Afghanistan and the expanding Persian and Mughal empires during the first quarter of the 17th century, corresponding roughly to the reigns of Shah ʿAbbās I (1588-1629) in Persia and Emperor Jahāngir (1605-27) in India.

The Jabbār Ḵēl lineage has played military and political roles in opposition to and, occasionally, in collaboration with the state structures centered within and outside Afghanistan. On occasion, they have participated in joint resistance and organized military operations with Western Ḡalzi, Hōtak, and Tōḵi Paxtuns against Persians, Mughals, and, during the first and second Anglo-Afghan wars (qq.v.), British encroachments into Paxtun tribal territories.

The tribal Paxtuns of Afghanistan have been engaged with centralized polities at least as far back as the rule of Sultan Maḥmud Ghaznavi (998-1030) and his Ghaznavid successors (1030-87; see ʿOtbi, pp. 467-71). During these early periods and, continuing throughout the 16th century, Paxtun tribes generally remained marginal to state structures, but, by virtue of proximity to trade routs and/or other state-controlled strategic locations, some tribal segments, especially in the aftermath of European colonialism and global capitalism during the past three centuries, experienced regular close political and economic contacts with these structures. These relations induced segmentation (and occasionally fusion) and political and economic rankings in the otherwise egalitarian and cohesive organization of tribal societies. An important outcome of this process of transformation has been tribal access to state power structure and resources, triggering the emergence of dominant tribal segments and individuals.

Among western Ḡalzis of Afghanistan, Khan Ḵēl lineages emerged among the Hōtak and Tōḵi tribes during the late 17th and early 18th centuries leading to the conquest of Isfahan in 1722 by Shah Maḥmud and his cousin Shah Ašraf (q.v.) of the Shah ʿAlam Ḵēl (Khan Ḵēl) lineage of the Hōtak tribe. The prominence of Hōtak and Toḵi Ḡalzis in western Afghanistan began to decline with the rise of Nāder Shah Afšār (q.v.) and his invasion of Afghanistan and subsequent emergence of the Dorrāni (q.v.) consortium of lineages (mainly Sadozay and Bārakzay) among the Popalzay tribal Paxtuns of southwestern Afghanistan. These Dorrāni lineages have had a long-standing collaborative relationship with the Persian and Mughal empires as far back as the early 16th century. As the Dorrāni state structure in Afghanistan was gradually being consolidated during the 19th and 20th centuries, the Ḡalzi opposition to this structure, led by their Khan Ḵēl segments, assumed increased intensity and frequency.

The emergence of the Jabbār Ḵēl as a dominant lineage among the eastern Ḡalzi was an outcome of tribal contacts with the Persian, Mughal, British imperial structures, and the Dorrāni state in Afghanistan. After the decline of the Hōtak Ḡalzis in western Afghanistan during the 1730s and the ascendance of the Dorrānis a decade later, the leadership of Ḡalzi Paxtuns passed on to the eastern Ḡalzis, among whom the Jabbār Ḵēl evolved as the leading lineage. During the reign of Aḥmad Shah Dorrāni (1747-73), Moḥammad-ʿAli Khan Jabbār Ḵēl was appointed the head of the Ḡalzi tribes. Timur, Aḥmad Shah's son (r. 1773-93), appointed Ṣafā Khan Jabbār Ḵēl and later his son, Aḥmad Khan, to the leadership of the Ḡalzis. Aḥmad Khan died near Herat in a battle against the Persian forces. His son, ʿAbd-al-ʿAziz Khan, became chief of the Ḡalzis during the 1790s and early 1800s.

The Ḡalzis, led by the Hōtaks and Jabbār Ḵēls, posed regular opposition to the Dorrāni rule in Afghanistan. In 1801, a western Ḡalzi force, led by ʿAbd-al-Raḥim Khan Hōtak, captured Kandahar and then, joined by eastern Ḡalzi contingents led by the Jabbār Ḵēl, defeated the governor of Ḡazni (October 1801). Then the combined army advanced through Lōgar to within ten miles of Kabul but was defeated by the Dorrāni's Qezelbāš force. (Malleson, p. 317; Elphinstone, II, p. 329; Ḡobār, p. 392)

Jabbār Khan, the eponym of the Jabbār Ḵēl, lived during the first quarter of the 17th century and died at an unknown date in a military operation against the Safavid. He is buried in the village of Ḵāk-e Jabbār, about 30 miles southeast of Kabul. The village is the center of the *ʿalāqadāri*, the smallest unit of a provincial government in Afghanistan, of the same name in Kabul Province. The locality is mentioned in non-Paxtun Kabuli and Fārsiwān lore for its harsh winters, robbery, and molestation of strangers by local Paxtuns (*Gazetteer of Afghanistan* VI, p. 315).

Most available written Paxtun tribal genealogies were originally produced by outsiders in Persian. British authors, while making modifications of their own and adding augmentations from local sources, have reproduced these genealogies in available English versions. In these genealogies, Jabbār Khan is usually linked through five ascending generations to the putative Ḡalzi ancestor: Jabbār Khan, nested in the Aḥmadzi tribe, nested in the Solaymān Ḵēl tribe, descendants of Izab, descendant of Ebrāhim, son (or descendant) of Ḡalzi, eponym of Ḡalzi tribal confederation. Three minimal lineages are nested in the Jabbār Ḵēl section: Aḥmad Ḵēl (descendants of Aḥmad Khan, Jabbār Khan's eldest son), Maryam Ḵēl (descendants of Maryam, Jabbār Khan's daughter; unusual for the patrilineal Ḡalzi, and hence their claim to Jabbār Ḵēl identity is considered dubious), and Ḵogiāni Ḵēl. Aḥmad Ḵēl, the senior lineage of the Jabbār Ḵēl, has in turn branched into three sections, each headed by one of the three great grandsons of Aḥmad Khan: Ṣafā Khan, Langar Khan, and Moḥammad Khan whose descendants have been prominent in the modern political history of Afghanistan. A descendant of these individuals who lived through the first half of the 20th century would be usually linked in eight ascending verifiable generations to Jabbār Khan. For example, Moḥammad Jān Khan (d. 1956, a high ranking government official in Kabul), son of Mehrdel Khan, son of Moḥammad Hanif Khan, son of Moḥammad-ʿAli Khan, son of Moḥammad Khan, son of Sarmast Khan, son of Esḥāq Khan, son of Ahmad Khan, son of Jabbār Khan.

The Jabbār Ḵēl are mostly engaged in growing wheat and other cash crops. They live in an area stretching from Ḵāk-e Jabbār eastward along the Sorḵrōd River, roughly paralleling the northern foothills of Spin Ghar mountain, to the western vicinity of Jalālābād, and from there northward throughout the southern part of Laḡmān Province. Leading families live in the villages of ʿAziz Khan Kats, Ka Kats, Moḥammad-ʿAli Khan Kats (all in southern Laḡhmān), and the districts of Ḥesārak and Sorḵrōd, all along major historical trade routs in this part of Afghanistan.

The Jabbār Ḵēl led the armed opposition during the First Anglo-Afghan War (1839-42, q.v.) to the installation of Shah Šojāʿ by the British as the ruler of Kabul. During winter 1842 the Jabbār Ḵēl were prominent in (save for a few women and a medical doctor) the total destruction of the retreating British force consisting of about 700 Europeans, over 3,800 Indian infantry and cavalry, and over 12000 camp followers between Ḵāk-e Jabbār and Gandomak, a distance of about 45 miles. During his second reign (1843-63), Amir Dōst Moḥammad and his sons fought several battles against the Ḡalzis, led, in the east, by the Jabbār Ḵēl. To cope with the Ḡalzi opposition, the Dorrāni rulers made marital alliances with the Jabbār Ḵēl (e.g., Amir Dōst Moḥammad married a sister of ʿAbd-al-ʿAziz Khan, grandson of Ṣafā Khan) and encouraged intermarriages between the latter and the Qezelbāš community in Kabul, a major base of Dorrāni support in Afghanistan (e.g., ʿAbd-al-ʿAziz Khan Jabbār Ḵēl married a daughter of Esmāʿil Khan Bayāt, a leading member of the Qezelbāš community in Kabul). During the reign of Amir Šēr ʿAli (1868-79), several leading Jabbār Ḵēl were appointed to high positions at his court in Kabul. They included ʿEṣmat-Allāh Khan, son of ʿAbd-al-ʿAziz Khan, as a member of the state council and Arsala Khan, son of Langar Khan, as vizier and governor of Zormat. Three grandsons of Arsala Khan, Amin-Allāh Khan, ʿAbd-al-Jabbār Khan, and Fāteḥ Moḥammad Khan were high-ranking officials in the Afghan government during the middle years of the 20th century. Virtually all their descendents have now migrated to the United States. Wazir Tāj Moḥammad, a khan of Jabbār Ḵēl, commanded Afghan troops at the battle of Maywand in 1879 (Adamec, pp. 253-54).

ʿEṣmat-Allāh Khan, the chief of the Jabbār Ḵēl during early 1880s, rose several times against the government of Kabul and attacked government communication lines. He and his eldest son, Moḥammad-Hāšem Khan, were executed by Amir ʿAbd-al-Raḥmān (r. 1880-1901), while other sons were exiled to India. The Ḡalzi rebellion of 1886-87 against Amir ʿAbd al-Raḥmān was also led by the Jabbār Ḵēl. Prominent in the leadership of the rebellion were four Jabbār Khel brothers: Mehrdel Khan, Purdel Khan, Sherdel Khan, and General Najm al-Din Khan commanded Sardār Moḥammad Es-ḥāq Khan's army against his cousin, Amir ʿAbd al-Raḥmān in 1888. After the rebellion was crushed, thousands of Jabbār Ḵēl families were forced to move to Afghan Turkestan, seeding the ethnic tensions that to date beset Afghanistan.

During the destabilization of Afghanistan in the 1980s and 1990s, large numbers, including many leading families of the Jabbār Ḵēl, migrated to Pakistan, some of whom joined the groups fighting the then government of Kabul.

See also AFGHANISTAN iv, vi, x; GHILZI.

Bibliography: Ludwig W. Adamec, *Historical and Political Who's Who of Afghanistan*, Graz, 1975. James Sutherland Broadfoot, *Reports on Parts of the Ghilzi Country, and on Some of the Tribes in the Neighborhood of Ghazni . . .* , ed. William Broadfoot, *JRGS*, Supplementary Papers 1, 1886, pp. 341-400. Louis Dupree, "The Retreat of the British Army from Kabul to Jalalabad in 1842: History and Folklore," *Journal of the Folklore Institute*, 1967, 4/1, pp. 50-74. Idem, "The First Anglo-Afghan War and the British Retreat of 1842: The Function of History and Folklore," in *East and West*, 26/3-4, 1976, pp. 503-29. Mountstuart Elphinstone, *An Account of the Kingdom of Caubul*, 2 vols., Karachi and New York, 1972. Fayẓ Moḥammad Kāteb, *Serāj al-tawārīḵ*, 3 vols., Kabul, 1333/1915. Šēr Moḥammad Khan Gandāpur, *Tawārīḵ-e ḵoršid-e jahān*, Lahore, 1894. *Gazetteer of Afghanistan* VI, pp. 271-73. Mir Ḡolām Moḥammad Ḡobār, *Afḡānestān dar masir-e tāriḵ*, Kabul, 1967. Ḥafiẓ-Allāh Xād Jabbār Ḵēl, *De Ḡaljāʾi ḥesārak zini farhangi arkhuna*, Kabul, 1987. W. Jenkyns, *Report on the District of Jalalabad, Chiefly in Regard to Revenue*, Calcutta, 1879. *Kabul Newsletters*, no. 135, 1886, National Archives of India. Mirzā Yaʿqub ʿAli Ḵᵛāfi, *Pādšāhān-e motaʾḵḵer-e Afḡānetsān*, 2 vols., Kabul, 1957. J. R. Leech, "An Account of the Early Ghiljaees," *Journal of the Asiatic Society of Bengal* 14, 1845, pp. 306-28. C. M. MacGregor, *Central Asia (Part II): A Contribution Towards the Better Knowledge of the Topography, Ethnology, Resources, and History of Afghanistan*, Calcutta, 1871, rep. 1995. George Bruce Malleson, *History of Afghanistan from the Earliest Period to the Outbreak of the War of 1878*, London, 1879. Moḥammad-Ḥayāt Khan, *Ḥayāt-e afḡān*, tr. H. Priestly as *Afghanistan and its Inhabitants*, Lahore, 1874. Jamiat Rai, *Rough Notes on the Nasar, Kharot, and Other Afghan Pawindas*, Quetta, 1922. Henry George Raverty, *Notes on Afghanistan and Part of Baluchistan: Geographical, Ethnographical, and Historical*, London, 1988, esp. appendix, pp. 2-75. J. A. Robinson, *The Powindahs*, Peshawar, 1934; repr. as *Notes on Nomad Tribes of Eastern Afghanistan*, Quetta, 1978. Percy Sykes, *A History of Afghanistan*, 2 vols., London, 1940. R. Warburton, *Report on the District of Lughman, Chiefly in Regard to Revenue*, Simla, 1880.

(M. JAMIL HANIFI)

JABBĀRA, a group of Shiʿite Arabs in Fārs province who, together with the Šaybāni. form the Arab tribe of the Ḵamsa tribal confederation (q.v.). In all likelihood, these Arabs came to southern Persia by way of the Fertile Crescent, for there is a tribe by the name of Jabbāra in western Iraq (Oppenheim, p. 119), as well as a clan of the Šaybāni of Fārs by the name of Takriti. Both the Jabbāra and the Šaybāni could be descendants of a tribe of Syrian Arabs which the Buyid ruler ʿAżod-al-Dawla (r. 949-83; q.v) transplanted to Fārs (Le Strange, *Lands*, p. 321).

The following list of the Jabbāra clans given by Ḥasan Fasāʾi (1821-98) in his *Fārs-nāma-ye Nāṣeri* (q.v.) shows that the group has absorbed many Lor and Turkic elements: Āl-e Saʿdi, Abu'l-Ḥosayni, Abu'l-Ḡani, Abu'l-Moḥammadi, Arboz, Borbor Čārboniča, Boz Sorḵi Čārboniča, Pir-e Eslāmi, Bahluli, Tāti, Torbor, Jāberi, Jaheki, Jelowdāri Čarboniča, Ḥannāʾi, Darāzi, Sādāt-e Ḥosayni, Šāhiseven, Šaʿbāni (who might be related to the Āl Bu Šaʿbān of northern Syria), Širi, Ṣafari, ʿAzizi, ʿIsāʾi, Qarāʾi, Qaraḡani, Qanbari, Lon (*Lor* in lith. ed., 2 vols., Tehran, 1895), Čārboniča, Lavārdān, Faridi (Mazidi in lith. ed., 1895), and Naqd ʿAli (Fasāʾi, ed. Rastgār, pp. 1579-80). Referring to the Ḵamsa Arabs in general, Ḥasan Fasāʾi points out that, as a result of their ethnic diversity, their language "has undergone so many changes both in form and in pronunciation that it is no longer Arabic, nor is it ordinary Persian, Turkish or Lori" (ibid., p. 1578).

The Ḵamsa Arabs suffered great hardship during the reign of Reżā Shah Pahlavi (r. 1925-41). When Oliver Garrod visited Fārs province in 1945, he observed that "many sections are in a miserable plight, having been reduced to a state of beggary and petty robbery," and he concluded that "they suffered, perhaps more than any other tribe in Fārs, from the oppression and enforced settlement of the past ten years, the misery of many sections having been accentuated by the somewhat arid and barren nature of their lands compared with those of the Qashqai" (p. 44). Because of a lack of cohesion and effective leadership, the Jabbāra have remained among the poorest nomads of Fārs province. According to a list of the tribes of Fārs sent to me by the Persian court minister in 1958, the Jabbāra numbered some 2,490 families. During the winter, they occupy a large swath of land southeast of Shiraz, from Sarvestān to Forg. During the summer, their grazing lands stretch all the way from Deh Bid, on the Shiraz-Isfahan road, to Bešna, 78 kilometers northeast of Neyriz.

Bibliography: Oliver Garrod, "The Nomadic Tribes of Persia To-Day," *Journal of the Royal Central Asian Society* 33, 1946, pp. 32-46. Max Freiherr von Oppenheim, Erich Bräunlich, and Werner Caskel, *Die Beduinen: Band I*, Leipzig, 1939; repr., Hildesheim, 1982.

(P. OBERLING)

JĀBER JOʿFI, ABU ʿABD-ALLĀH (or Abu Moḥammad b. Yazid b. Ḥāreṯ), a Kufan traditionist and companion of the fifth and sixth Shiʿite Imams, Moḥammad al-Bāqer and Jaʿfar al-Ṣādeq. Jāber belonged to the to the first generation of Muslims after Moḥammed, likely dying in 128/745-46 (other reports date his death in 127/744-45 or 132/749-50; Moḥsen al-Amin, p. 158). He is well-known in both Sunni and Shiʿite circles, but, while his transmissions are considered reliable by some, others have suspected their accuracy or have rejected them altogether. A number of prominent Sunni traditionists, including Sofyān Ṯawri, considered Jāber honest (*ṣaduq*), a highly scrupulous traditionist, and related traditions on his authority (Ḏahabi, 1987, VIII, pp. 59-60; Ebn Ḥajar, II, p. 47; Ṭusi, p. 196), but others (e.g., Yaḥyā b. Maʿin, Abu Ḥanifa, Ebn Ḥanbal) denounced him as a liar and an extremist Shiʿite who believed in the doctrine of *rajʿa* (return of the Mahdi; see Ebn Ḥajar, II, pp. 48-50; Ḏahabi, 1987, I, pp. 379-84; Ebn Qotayba, p. 480; Moḥsen al-Amin, pp. 158-59).

Among Shiʿites, his reputation is equally mixed. He was clearly a close companion of Imam Moḥammad al-Bāqer (q.v.), from whom he narrates most of his traditions. Other Shiʿites, however, reportedly questioned Imam Jaʿfar al-Ṣādeq (q.v.) about him. Imam al-Ṣādeq generally endorsed him as a sound transmitter from the Imams (Mofid, p. 216; Ṭusi, p. 192; Moḥsen al-Amin, p. 158), but a report from Jāber's contemporary, Zorāra b. Aʿyān, casts doubt on Jāber's claims of proximity to the Imams (Ṭusi, p. 191). According to Ḥasan Nawbaḵti, ʿAbd-Allāh b. Ḥāreṯ, the leader of the followers of the Talebid rebel ʿAbd-Allāh b. Moʿāwia (q.v.), propagated such extremist ideas as metempsychosis (*tanāsoḵ*) and cyclical history (*dawr*) and attributed them to Jāber (Nawbaḵti, p. 47, tr. p. 59), while other reports suggest that the Imam did not wish the Hadith Jāber transmitted to reach the spiritually unqualified, lest they be misunderstood (Ṭusi, pp. 192, 193). Sunni heresiographies connect him with the executed extremist Shiʿite Moḡira b. Saʿid, who had acknowledged Imam al-Bāqer's imamate (Ašʿari, p. 8; Ebn Ḥazm, pp. 118-19), but at least one Shiʿite Hadith explicitly separates Jāber from Moḡira (Mofid, p. 204; Ṭusi, p. 192).

Works attributed to Jāber include a book of Qurʾān commentary (*Ketāb al-tafsir*), likely a redaction of Imam al-Bāqer's *tafsir* known from other sources; books on the events of the First Civil War (*Ketāb al-Jamal*, *Ketāb Ṣeffin*, *Ketāb al-Nahrawān*); books on the deaths of Imam ʿAli (*Ketāb al-maqtal Amir-al-Moʾmenin*) and Imam Ḥosayn (*Ketāb al-Ḥosayn*); and other collections of praise traditions and rare Hadith or "*nawāder*" (Najāši, pp. 93-94; see Modarressi, I, pp. 94-103, for a list of extant material from these works that survive in other sources). Prominent themes among his traditions include Qurʾānic commentary, the virtues of the believers, and the esoteric nature of the Imams' knowledge. He is a primary transmitter of the well known Hadith that the Imams' traditions are difficult, and that only prophets, archangels, and true believers can comprehend them (Ṭusi, p. 193; Kolayni, I, p. 466). He also reportedly heard tens of thousands of traditions from the Imams that he related to no one (Ṭūsi, p. 194; Ebn Ḥajar, II, p. 48; Tostari, II, pp. 535, 542), apparently implying that they were too esoteric in nature to be shared with others; he also reportedly complained to Imam al-Bāqer that the burden of these secrets would make him appear mad (Mofid, pp. 66-67; Ṭusi, p. 194). In other accounts, Jāber is reported to have displayed public madness, with most traditions suggesting that he feigned insanity to avoid arrest by the Umayyads (Ṭusi, pp. 192, 194-95; Tostari, II, pp. 538-39, 541). A number of material and epistemological miracles are also attributed to him, undoubtedly from extremist sources (Ṭusi, pp. 195-98; Tostari, pp. 535-41).

Bibliography: Moḥsen al-Amin Ḥosayni ʿAmeli, *Aʿyān al-šiʿa*, ed. Ḥasan al-Amin, Beirut, 1962, XV, pp. 156-70. Moḥammad b. ʿAli Ǧarawi Ḥāʾeri Ardabili, *Jāmeʿ al-rowāt wa ezāḥat al-eštebāhāt ʿan al-ṭoroq wa'l-esnād*, 2 vols., Beirut, 1403/1983. Abu'l-Ḥasan ʿAli b. Esmāʿil Ašʿari,. *Ketāb maqālāt al-eslāmiyin wa ek̲telāf al-moṣellin*, ed. Helmut Ritter, Cairo, 2000. Moḥammad b. Aḥmad Ḏahabi, *Mizān al-eʿtedāl*, ed. ʿAli-Moḥammad Bajāwi, 4 vols., Cairo. 1964. Idem, *Taʾrik̲ al-Eslām wa wafāyāt al-mašāhir wa'l-aʿlām*, ed. ʿOmar ʿAbd-al-Salām Tadmor, 10 vols., Beirut, 1987. Ebn Ḥajar ʿAsqalāni, *Tahḏib al-tahḏib*, 12 vols., Beirut, 1968. Ebn Ḥazm, *al-Faṣl fi'l-melal wa'l-ahwāʾ wa'l-nehal*, ed. Aḥmad Šams-al-Din, 3 vols., Beirut, 1996. Ebn Qotayba, *Ketāb al-maʿāref*, ed. Ṯarwat ʿOkāša, Cairo, 1960. Ignaz Goldziher, *Muslim Studies*, tr. C. R. Barber and S. M. Stern, 2 vols., London, 1967, I, pp. 110, 134. Abu Jaʿfar Moḥammad b. Yaʿqūb b. Esḥāq Rāzi Kolayni, *al-Kāfi*, ed. Moḥammad-Jaʿfar Šams-al-Din, 7 vols., Beirut, 1990. Wilferd Madelung, "Jābir b. Yazīd al-Juʿfī," in *EI*^{2}, supplement, pp. 232-33. Hossein Modarressi, *Tradition and Survival: A Bibliographical Survey of Early Shiʿite Literature* I, Oxford, 2003. Shaikh Moḥammad b. Moḥammad b. Noʿmān Mofid, *al-Ek̲teṣāṣ*, ed. ʿAli-Akbar Ğaffāri, Qom, 1980. Aḥmad b. ʿAli Najāši, *Fehrest asmāʾ moṣannefi'l-šiʿa*, Qom, 1977. Ḥasan b. Musā Nawbak̲ti, *Ketāb feraq al-šiʿa*, ed. ʿAbd-al-Monʿem Ḥefni, Cairo, 1992; tr. Moḥammad-Jawād Maškur as *Tarjama-ye Feraq al-šiʿa-ye Nawbak̲ti*, Tehran, 1974. Abu Jaʿfar Moḥammad b. Ḥasan b. ʿAli Ṭusi, *Ek̲tiār maʿrefat al-rejāl* (= *Rejāl al-Kašši*), ed. Ḥasan Moṣṭafawi, Mashad, 1969. Moḥammad-Taqi Tostari. *Qāmus al-rejāl*, 10 vols., Qom, 1990.

(MARIA DAKAKE)

JĀBERI, MIRZĀ SALMĀN, vizier and prominent statesman during the reigns of Shah Esmāʿil II (1576-77) and Shah Moḥammad K̲odābanda (1577-88). Mirzā Salmān began training as an administrator under the tutelage of his father who was the vizier to the governor of Shiraz, Ebrāhim Khan, in the latter years of Shah Ṭahmāsp's reign. After his father died, Mirzā Salmān moved to the central court in Qazvin, and thanks to political sponsorship from Mirzā ʿAṭāʾ-Allāh, the powerful vizier of Azerbaijan, he soon entered Shah Ṭahmāsp's service as both an intimate (*moqarrab*), and supervisor of the departments in the service of the royal household (*nāẓer-e boyutāt-e sarkār-e k̲āṣṣa-ye šarifa*). After Esmāʿil II ascended the throne, Mirzā Salmān was made the *vazir-e aʿlā* on June 13, 1577 after Mirzā Šokr-Allāh was dismissed from the post. Mirzā Salmān proved himself to be a wily operator in the turbulent politics and machinations of the day, initially aligning himself with Esmāʿil II's sister, Pari K̲ān K̲ānom (q.v. at *iranica.com*), but later abandoning her and joining the retinue of Moḥammad K̲odābanda and his wife, Mahd-e ʿOliyā, in Shiraz after Esmāʿil II died mysteriously less than a year later. The new shah confirmed Salmān in his post as *vazir-e aʿlā*, but the Persian administrator involved himself in a number of military campaigns, the most spectacular of which resulted in the defeat of a joint Ottoman-Tatar force and capture of the Tatar prince, ʿĀdel Gerāy Khan. Mirzā Salmān succeeded in handling the shifting political relationships skillfully upon learning that the de facto ruler, Mahd-e ʿOliyā, was targeted by disgruntled Qezelbāš amirs for elimination; he promptly joined the opposition (led by Pira Moḥammad Khan Ostājlu and Moḥammad Khan Torkmān) and secured a new sponsor from the royal family by marrying his daughter to the heir apparent, Ḥamza Mirzā.

There is little doubt that Mirzā Salmān Jāberi transgressed boundaries in terms of the traditional division between Turks and Tajiks; in fact, he was described by al-Qommi (p. 685) as "lord of [both] the sword and pen" (*ṣāḥeb al-sayf wa'l-qalam*). This was best manifested in 1581 when he emerged as the principal architect of a major diplomatic arrangement whereby the Georgian Kārtel and Kāketi dynasties, led by Simon Khan and Alexander Khan respectively, were subordinated to the Safavid household. This new suzerain status, whereby each Georgian ruler sent a son and a daughter to the Safavid court (the daughters were married to Ḥamza Mirzā and the sons were held as hostages) was negotiated by Mirzā Salmān, and it was he who personally presided over the ceremony in Georgia when robes of honor were exchanged and monies were remitted (Falsafi I, p. 70; Eṣfahāni, p. 636). The most serious threat to Salmān's position came in 1582 when Moršedqoli Khan and his charge, prince ʿAbbās Mirzā, revolted in Herat. Despite the waning appeal of Shah Ḵodābanda, Salmān exhorted the Qezelbāš amirs in the court to join their liege and march against these royal rebels to the east. A number of lengthy sieges ensued at Herat and Torbat, but Šāmlu and Ostājlu amirs circumvented Mirzā Salmān and secretly concluded a cease-fire with Moršedqoli Khan. Mirzā Salmān's brinkmanship in Khorasan (sources such as *Ḵolāṣat al-tawāriḵ* and *Noqāwat al-āṯār* emphasize his control over the Qezelbāš amirs) contributed to the coalescing of a conspiracy around the *qorči bāši* (commander of royal cavalry) Qoli Beg Afšār, the *mohrdār* (seal holder), Šāhroḵ Khan Ḏu'l-Qadar, and Moḥammad Khan Torkmān. Assassins were dispatched after Mirzā Salmān on May 12, 1583 when he left Herat to organize a celebratory feast at the shrine of his ancestor, ʿAbd-Allāh Anṣāri, in Gāzorgāh (q.v.), but supporters alerted him to this threat. He quickly returned to Herat and sought asylum in the *madrasa* of Solṭān-Ḥosayn Bayqarā where Ḵodābanda and Ḥamza Mirzā had set up their royal apartments. Surrounded by Qezelbāš amirs who argued that only strife and civil war would result from Salmān's continued presence, the shah acceded to the conspirators' demands. Qezelbāš amirs killed the Persian vizier in the Bāḡ-e Zāḡān, after which his head was sent to ʿAliqoli Khan Šāmlu and his body was hung publicly in Herat. Later, a military judge (*qāżi-e moʿaskar*), Mir Abu'l-Wāli Inju, decreed that his body be interred properly at the Gonbad-e Mir Wāli in Mashad (al-Qommi, pp. 746-47). Mirzā Salmān was not noted for any scholarly or literary endeavors, but the text of one of his letters, to the Ottoman noble Sinān Pasha, was preserved by al-Qommi in *Ḵolāṣat al-tawāriḵ* (pp. 717-21).

Bibliography: Qāżi Aḥmad b. Šaraf-al-Din al-Ḥosayn al-Qommi, *Ḵolāṣat al-tawāriḵ*, 2 vols., ed. E. Ešrāqi, Tehran, 1980. Maḥmud b. Hedāyat-Allāh Afušta'i Naṭanzi, *Noqāwat al-āṯār*, ed. E. Ešrāqi, Tehran, 1971. Eskandar Beg Monši, *Tāriḵ-e ʿālamārā-ye ʿAbbāsi*, 2 vols., ed. and tr. R. Savory, Boulder, 1978. Moḥammad Yusof Vāleh Eṣfahāni, *Ḵold-e barin*, ed. M. H. Moḥaddeṯ, Tehran, 1993. Manučehr Pārsādust, *Šāh Esmāʿil-e dovvom: šojāʿ-e tabāh šoda*, Tehran, 2002. Naṣr-Allāh Falsafi, *Zendagāni-e Šāh ʿAbbās-e awwal* I, Tehran, 1966. R. Savory, "The Significance of the Political Murder of Salman Mirza," *Islamic Studies* 3, 1964, pp. 181-91.

(COLIN PAUL MITCHELL)

JABḠUYA, Arabo-Persian form of the Central Asian title *yabḡu*. This article will be divided into two sections.

i. Origin and early history.

ii. In Islamic sources.

i. ORIGIN AND EARLY HISTORY

Although *yabḡu* is best known as a Turkish title of nobility, it was in use many centuries before the Turks appear in the historical record. The earliest form of the word attested is the Chinese *xihou* (ancient *i̯əp-g'u*; Karlgren, pp. 675 q [and variants] + 113a, Early Middle Chinese *xip-γəw*), which is found as a title of various "barbarian" (Wusun, Yuezhi, etc.) rulers in texts referring to events from the 2nd century B.C.E. onwards. The title seems first to have been brought to the Iranian world by the Kushans. The *Han shu*, (chap. 96A, p. 3891), tells that the Yuezhi were ruled by five *xihou*, to which the *Hou Han shu* (chap. 88, p. 2921), adds an account of how Qiujiuque, the "Guishuang *xihou*," that is Kujula Kadphises the "Kushan *yabḡu*," obtained supremacy over the other four *xihou* and thus established the Kushan Empire (Chavannes, 1907, pp. 189-92; Hulsewé and Loewe, pp. 121-23). As is to be expected, the title is also attested on the coins of Kujula, where it written *yavuga-* or *yaüa-* in Prakrit and *zaoou* (genitive of **zaoos* or **zaoēs*) in Greek. The identity of these forms with the Chinese *xihou* was first recognized by Alfred von Gutschmid (p. 114). Another Prakrit variant, *jaüva-*, may be attested in an inscription from Taxila (see Konow, p. 27), but the context is not entirely clear. The Bactrian form *iabgo* is also attested in the Kushan period (Livshits and Kruglikova, p. 103); much later, probably at the end of the 5th century, it reappears as a Hephthalite title (Sims-Williams, 1999, p. 255). The personal name Yapḡu in the Kharoṣṭhī documents from Niya (e.g., Burrow, passim on pp. 92-95; cf. Lüders, p. 789) and the Tocharian B title **yapko* (attested via the adjective *yapkoñe*; see Pinault, p. 12) are likely to derive from the Bactrian form. However, the supposed form *iapgu* in a Bactrian coin legend of the Turkish period (Ghirshman, p. 50) is a misreading, probably for *tagino*, that is, Turk. *tegin* "prince" (Davary, p. 98).

Among the Turks, the title *yabḡu* gained a new lease of life. In the Turkish inscriptions of Mongolia, it refers to a noble ranking immediately after the *qaḡan*, but in the West the title seems to have been used more generally of tribal chiefs, and was so characteristic that the Chinese came to refer to the Western Turks by expressions such as "the tribes of the *yabḡu*" (Chavannes, 1903, p. 95 n. 3). In Tang times, Turkish *yabḡu* was retranscribed into Chinese as *yehu* (archaic *i̯äp-γuo*, see Karlgren, nos. 633d + 784k, Late Middle Chinese *jiap-xɦuǝ̆*), showing that the equivalence with *xihou* was by then forgotten. In the Sogdian version of the Karabalgasun inscription, the Turkish title is transcribed as *ypγw*. In the 7th century, the spelling *cpγw* [*ǰabγu*] is attested on Sogdian coins of Chach (Shagalov and Kuznetsov, 2006, pp. 84-86). In a ninth-century colophon to a Manichean hymn-book, *jβγw* [*žaβγu*] is attested as the title of the ruler of Parvān (Āqsu) and the variant *yβγw* as part of a Turkish personal name. (Müller, p. 11, ll. 77, 93; cf. also Bailey, 1985, p. 130, where Tibetan, Armenian, and Pahlavi forms are cited).

The ultimate origin of the word *yabḡu* has been much disputed. A useful survey of the older literature is provided by Richard Frye, pp. 356-58, who refers to suggested Altaic etymologies but himself favors an Iranian source. Two different Iranian etymologies were proposed by Harold W. Bailey (**yam-uka-* "leader," Bailey, 1958,

p. 136, and **yāvuka-* "troop-leader," idem, 1985, pp. 32, 130), but the phonetic equivalence would not be close and both forms are quite hypothetical. A "Tocharian" origin has been suggested by several scholars (e.g., Pulleyblank, 1966, p. 28, who tentatively compares Toch. A *ype*, B *yapoy* "land, country"; Bosworth and Clauson, pp. 9-10), an idea which depends on the doubtful assumption that peoples such as the Wusun and Yuezhi were ethnically related to the speakers of what we now call Tocharian.

Although the title *xihou* is only borne by non-Chinese rulers and is invariably regarded by Sinologists as a transcription of a foreign form, Helmut Humbach (pp. 24-28) has argued that the word is in fact Chinese in origin, the syllable *hou* being a Chinese title often translated "marquis." Elaborating on this view, Nicholas Sims-Williams (2002, p. 229) has proposed to interpret *xihou* as "allied prince." Such an interpretation is particularly suited to some of the earliest attestations of *xihou*. According to the *Shiji* (chap. 19, p. 1021, and chap. 20, p. 1027), the title was bestowed twice by the Chinese emperor, in 147 B.C.E. on a Xiongnu prince and in 129 B.C.E. on a prince of the western barbarians (Hu), both of whom had allied themselves with the Han. However, the *Han shu* provides evidence for the even earlier use of this title: amongst the Wusun in the 170s B.C.E., a period before they were in direct contact with the Chinese (chap. 61, p. 2692; Hulsewé and Loewe, p. 215), and amongst the Yuezhi of Bactria, who had left Gansu or Turfan in the 170s B.C.E. and would therefore be unlikely to use a Chinese title of more recent origin (*Han shu*, chap. 96A, p. 3891; Hulsewé and Loewe, pp. 121-23). Moreover, *xi* "joined, harmonious, etc." would not have been an obvious word to employ in the political sense "united" or "allied." The earliest Chinese interpretation of *xihou* (already in the first century C.E., see the *Han shu*, chap. 17, pp. 640, 642) was "marquis of Xi," Xi being understood as the name of a village in the Huang region (Henan). Although this association must be due to folk etymology or secondary association (cf. Hirth, p. 49), its mere existence is a clear indication that the syllable *xi* was not felt to be meaningful. Later commentators of the Tang period define *xihou* as a Wusun title for a high-ranking general. It seems most likely that this view is essentially correct and that *xihou* is a Chinese transcription of a title used by the Wusun and Yuezhi, peoples from the Gansu or Turfan regions, of whose languages hardly anything is known.

Bibliography: Chinese dynastic histories are quoted according to the pagination of the Zhonghua shuju edition, Beijing, 1972-. Reconstructed Chinese forms are quoted according to Bernhard Karlgren (1957) and Edwin G. Pulleyblank, 1991. Harold W. Bailey, "Languages of the Saka," in *Handbuch der Orientalistik* I.IV.1, Leiden, 1958, pp. 131-54. Idem, *Khotanese Texts* VII, Cambridge, 1985. Clifford E. Bosworth and G. Clauson, "Al-Xwārazmī on the Peoples of Central Asia," *JRAS*, 1965, pp. 2-12. Thomas Burrow, *A Translation of the Kharoṣṭhi Documents from Chinese Turkestan*, London, 1940. Édouard Chavannes, *Documents sur les Tou-kiue (Turcs) occidentaux*, St. Petersburg, 1903. Idem, "Les pays d'occident d'après le *Heou Han chou*," *T'oung Pao*, Series 2/8, 1907, pp. 149-234. Gholam Djelani Davary, *Baktrisch: Ein Wörterbuch auf Grund der Inschriften, Handschriften, Münzen und Siegelsteine*, Heidelberg, 1982. Richard Nelson Frye, "Some Early Iranian Titles," *Oriens* 15, 1962, pp. 352-59. Roman Ghirshman, *Les Chionites-Hephtalites*, Mémoires de la Délégation archéologique française en Afghanistan 13, Cairo, 1948. Alfred von Gutschmid, *Geschichte Irans und seiner Nachbarvölker von Alexander dem Grossen bis zum Untergang der Arsaciden*, Tübingen, 1888. F. Hirth, "Nachworte zur Inschrift von Tonjukuk," in W. Radloff, ed., *Die alttürkischen Inschriften der Mongolei*, 2nd Series, St Petersburg, 1899. Anthony F. P. Hulsewé and Michael A. N. Loewe, tr., *China in Central Asia: The Early Stage 125 B.C.-A.D. 23*, Leiden, 1979 (annotated tr. of chaps. 61 and 96 of "The history of the former Han Dynasty"). Helmut Humbach, *Baktrische Sprachdenkmäler* I, Wiesbaden, 1966. Bernhard Karlgren, "Grammata Serica Recensa," *Bulletin of the Museum of Far Eastern Antiquities* 29, Stockholm, 1957. Sten Konow, ed., *Kharoshṭhī Inscriptions*, Corpus Inscriptionum Indicarum, II, part 1, Calcutta, 1929. V. A. Livshits and I. T. Kruglikova, "Fragmenty baktriĭskoĭ monumental'noĭ nadpisi iz Dil'berdzhina (Fragments of a Bactrian monumental inscription from Dilberjin)," in I. T. Kruglikova, ed., *Drevnyaya Baktriya* (Ancient Bactria) II, Moscow, 1979, pp. 98-112. Heinrich Lüders, *Philologica Indica*, Göttingen, 1940. Friedrich W. K. Müller, "Ein Doppelblatt aus einem manichäischen Hymnenbuch (Maḥrnâmag)," *APAW*, 1912, pp. 1-40. Georges-Jean Pinault, "Economic and Administrative Documents in Tocharian B from the Berezovsky and Petrovsky Collections," *Manuscripta Orientalia* 4/4, 1998, pp. 3-20. Edwin G. Pulleyblank, "Chinese and Indo-Europeans," *JRAS*, 1966, pp. 9-39. Idem, *Lexicon of Reconstructed Pronunciation in Early Middle Chinese, Late Middle Chinese, and Early Mandarin*, Vancouver, 1991. V. D. Shagalov and A. V. Kuznetsov, *Katalog monet Chach III-VIII vv.* (Catalogue of coins of Chach, III-VIII C.E.), Tashkent, 2006. Nicholas Sims-Williams, "From the Kushan-shahs to the Arabs: New Bactrian Documents Dated in the Era of the Tochi Inscriptions," in Michael Alram and Deborah E. Klimburg-Salter, eds., *Coins, Art and Chronology: Essays on the pre-Islamic History of the Indo-Iranian Borderlands*, Vienna, 1999, pp. 245-58. Idem, "Ancient Afghanistan and Its Invaders: Linguistic Evidence from the Bactrian Documents and Inscriptions," in idem, ed., *Indo-Iranian Languages and Peoples*, Proceedings of the British Academy 116, Oxford, 2002, pp. 225-42.

(NICHOLAS SIMS-WILLIAMS and ÉTIENNE DE LA VAISSIERE)

ii. In Islamic Sources

The title, found in early Turkic languages from the 8th century (stone stellae in the Orkhon River in Mongolia) onward as *yabğu*, appears as *jabğuya* or *jab(b)uya* in early Islamic sources dealing with the Eastern Iranian fringes and the steppe lands beyond. Since these sources connect the title in the first place with the Oghuz (see ĞOZZ) and Qarluq tribes of the Turks, the initial sound change *y* > *j* of the form in Arabic presumably accords with the statement by Maḥmud Kāšḡari that the Oghuz and Qıpčaq change every initial *yāʾ* into *alef* or *jim* (Kāšḡari, I, p. 31; tr. Dankhoff and Kelly, I, p. 84).

In the old Turkic Empire, the Yabḡu was a close relative of the Qaḡan and, on the evidence of the Orkhon inscriptions, he held a high administrative rank (Clauson, p. 873). The title had also been borne by Turkic princes in the upper Oxus region in post-Hephthalite (see HEPHTHALITES) times, appearing on their coins (Ghirshman and Ghirshman, pp. 50-51), and it is at Qondoz in Ṭok̲ārestān that the Chinese Buddhist pilgrim Hüen-Čuang located Šad, the eldest son of the Yabḡu of the Western Turks. At this time (7th century C.E.), the Yabḡus ruled over a principality to the south of the upper Oxus, and it is as opponents of the Arabs in Ṭok̲ārestān that the Jabbuyas or Jabḡuyas appear in such Arabic sources as Yaʿqubi and Ṭabari (Gibb, pp. 8-11). The operations of Qotayba b. Moslem in the upper Oxus region in 90-91/708-10 against the Hephthalite chief Ṭark̲ān Nizak involved the Jabbuya's eventual deportation to Syria as a hostage by Qotayba after Nizak's death (Ṭabari, III, pp. 1206-7, 1220-21, 1225; tr. Hinds, pp. 155, 166, 168, 172; cf. Gibb, pp. 37-38; Bosworth, 1986, pp. 541-42).

Subsequently, it is in connection with the relations of the Arab governors in Transoxania with the Turks of the adjacent regions that the Yabḡu of the Oghuz tribe is mentioned there. Thus in the early Abbasid period, the caliph al-Mahdi (r. 775-85) received the submission of various princes of the Transoxanian fringes and the lands beyond, including the Yabḡu of the Qarluq and the K̲āqān of the Toghuz-Oghuz; and in 195/810-11, the caliph al-Maʾmun (r. 813-33), faced with a coming struggle for the caliphate with this brother al-Amin (r. 809-13), had to conciliate various rulers of the East who had fallen away in their nominal allegiance, including Jabḡuya, K̲āqān, the ruler of Tibet, and the king of Kabul (Yaʿqubi, *Taʾrik̲*, II, p. 478; Ṭabari, III, pp. 815-16, tr. Fishbein, pp. 71-72; cf. Barthold, p. 202). In the early 10th century, geographical works mention Jabḡukat̲, "the town of the Yabḡu," located on the middle Syr Daryā in the neighborhood of Šāš (Eṣṭak̲ri, p. 330; Ebn Ḥawqal, p. 461; Ebn Ḥawqal, tr. Wiet, p. 445; *Ḥudūd al-ʿĀlam*, p. 117; cf. Barthold, p. 173).

The title *Yabḡu* for the chiefs of the Oghuz and Qarluq is listed by K̲ᵛārazmi, who wrote ca. 366/977 and probably used a Samanid source for this (Bosworth and Clauson, p. 6). The Yabḡu, as the head of the Oghuz, who lived as nomads in the steppes between the lower Syr Daryā and the Aral Sea and the Ural River, is well-known from historical and geographical sources of the 10th and early 11th centuries. The caliphal envoy Aḥmad b. Fażlān (q.v.) traversed these lands in 309-10/921-23, and he describes the chief of the Oghuz as the Yabḡu (Togan, p. 33, tr. p. 28, Excursus 33a, pp. 140-41; Bosworth, *The Ghaznavids*, pp. 217-18).

The Oghuz in the proximity of Transoxania did not become Muslims until towards the end of the 10th century, and in the early 11th century we find the Yabḡu of the Oghuz ruling from Yengi-kent ('new town') on the lower Syr Daryā. It is also at this time that we learn of the hostility between the two branches of the Oghuz under the Yabḡu and the Saljuq family respectively. In the 1030s, Šāh-Malek b. ʿAli of Yengi-kent and Jand (q.v.) became the ally of the Ghaznavid (see GHAZNAVIDS) ruler Masʿud (r. 1031-40) in his struggle with the Saljuqs who were harrying Khorasan. He conquered Khwarazm for Masʿud in 432/1041, but by that time the latter was already dead; and very soon Šāh-Malek was dislodged by the victorious Saljuqs, who forced him to flee and then killed him (Pritsak, pp. 406-10; Bosworth, *The Ghaznavids*, p. 239).

The Saljuqs had already appropriated the title of Yabḡu for a member of their own family, Musā, but after the middle of the 11th century, with the constituting of the Saljuq state as a Perso-Islamic empire, this old Turkish title disappeared from use.

Bibliography: See Short References for Ebn Ḥawqal; Eṣṭak̲ri; and Yaʿqubi, *Taʿrik̲*. W. W. Barthold, *Turkestan Down to the Mongol Invasion*, with additions, tr. T. Minorsky, ed. C. E. Bosworth, 3rd ed., London, 1968. C. E. Bosworth, *The Ghaznavids: Their Empire in Afghanistan and Eastern Iran 944-1040*, Edinburgh, 1963. Idem, "K̲utayba b. Muslim," in *EI*² V, 1986, pp. 541-42. C. E. Bosworth and G. Clauson, "Al-Xwārazmī on the Peoples of Central Asia," *JRAS*, 1965, pp. 2-12. G. Clauson, *An Etymological Dictionary of Pre-Thirteenth Century Turkish*, Oxford, 1972. R. N. Frye, *The History of Bukhara*, Cambridge, Mass., 1954. H. A. R. Gibb, *The Arab Conquests in Central Asia*, London, 1923. R. Ghirshman and T. Ghirshman, *Les Chionites-Hepthalites*, Cairo, 1948. *Ḥudūd al-ʿĀlam: 'The Regions of the World,' A Persian Geography 372 A.H.-982 A.D.*, tr. V. Minorsky, pref. by V. V. Barthold, ed. C. E. Bosworth, 2nd ed., London, 1970. Maḥmud Kāšḡari, *Divān loḡāt al-tork*, ed. R. B. Kilisli, Istanbul, 1333/1917; tr. R. Dankoff and J. Kelly as *Compendium of the Turkic Dialects (Dīwān Luγāt at-Turk)*, Cambridge, Mass., 1984. O. Pritsak, "Der Untergang des Reiches des Oğuzischen Yabğu," in *60. doğum yılı münasebetiyle Fuad Köprülü armağani. Mélanges Fuad Köprülü*, Istanbul, 1953, pp. 397-410. Ṭabari, *Ketāb taʾrik̲ al-rosol waʾl-moluk*, ed. M. J. de Goeje et al., 15 vols., repr., Leiden, 1964; tr. M. Hinds as *The Zenith of the Marwānid House*, in *The History of Tabari: an annotated translation*, vol. 23, Albany, N.Y., 1990; tr. M. Fishbein as *The War between Brothers*, in *The History of Tabari: an annotated trans-*

lation, vol. 31, Albany, N.Y., 1992. A. Z. V. Togan, *Ibn Faḍlāns Reisebericht*, Leipzig, 1939.

(C. EDMUND BOSWORTH)

FIGURE 1. Golden Jackal, *Canis aureus*. H. Żiāʾi, *Rāhnemā-ye ṣaḥrāʾi-e pestāndārān-e Irān*, table 11.

JACKAL, Golden or Asiatic (*Canis aureus*, MPers. *tōrag*, NPers. *tura*, *šaḡāl* [cf. Skt. *śṛgāla-* and related IAr. forms; Mayrhofer, 1976, p. 368]; FIGURE 1), a medium-size member of the dog family (Canidae) occurring throughout Afghanistan and Iran. It also extends east through India to Myanmar and Thailand and west through southern Europe to Italy and throughout North Africa, south throughout the Arabian peninsula and East Africa to Tanzania. Weighing 7-15 kg, it has a head and body length of 60 to 106 cm, and the tail measures 20-30 cm. The coat color is variable, but usually golden-brown or brown-tipped yellow; the back is black and gray; the tail is black-tipped. *Canis aureus* is the northernmost of four jackal species. The other three are confined to Africa. Our jackal doubtless has persisted in its present range owing to its adaptation to arid habitats. The most active recent student of jackal biology is Patricia D. Moehlman (1994), whose work has been carried out in Africa. Information specific to Iran and Afghanistan is to be found in Harrington (1977), Hassinger (1968, 1973), Lay (1967), Misonne (1959), and Żiāʾi (1996). The type locality for the original description of *Canis aureus* was restricted to "Benná Mts., Laristan [Lārestān] (now in Fārs Province), S. Persia" (Wozencraft, 1993, p. 280).

The jackals usually occur in monogamous mated pairs, sometimes accompanied by yearling young, who assist in hunting and the raising of young. The family group will carry food in the stomach from a large carcass for regurgitation to pups or a nursing mother. Cooperative hunting during the period when pups are provisioned facilitates the killing of hares and occasionally larger prey, such as young gazelles. In Iran, Afghanistan, and elsewhere in the Middle East, scavenging supplies a small percentage of the diet, especially in habitats away from humans; and carrion consists mainly of road kill and, around villages, garbage. Jackals are omnivorous, opportunistic feeders, eating fruits and vegetables as well as hunting small animals such as reptiles, amphibians, birds and eggs, rodents, and various invertebrates.

The time of mating varies from region to region, but usually occurs sometime from October to February in the area of Iran. Usually, 5-6 pups are born after a 63-day gestation and are nursed for 8-10 weeks. They are born in a den within the pair's defended territory of 2-3 km^2. Both males and females mark territorial boundaries with urine. Jackals are known to live up to 13 years in the wild when conditions are consistently good. Females are sexually mature at 11 months, males at up to two years, but they may delay mating, particularly those that remain as "helpers" with their family. They are active both day and night, although, where they are in contact with humans, they tend to become nocturnal. Jackals have an extensive vocal repertoire to locate one another, communicate with pups, and in other social interactions. Howling together apparently strengthens the pair's bond.

There are both negative and positive aspects in their interactions with humans. They raid crops and occasionally kill sheep (lambs) and chickens. They may be involved in the spread of rabies. On the other hand, they control rodent and hare populations and often serve an important role in removal of animal carrion and garbage around villages. They play an important role in folklore and fables throughout the Middle East.

Bibliography: (Websites were accessed 26 October 2004.) G. B. Corbet, and J. E. Hill. *A World List of Mammalian Species*, 3rd ed., New York, 1991. R. F. Ewer, *The Carnivores*, Ithaca, N.Y., 1973. Michael W. Fox, ed., *The Wild Canids. Their Systematics, Behavioral Ecology, Evolution*, London and New York, 1975. Bernard Grzimek, *Encyclopedia of Mammals*, New York, 1990, IV, pp. 107-14. Fred A. Harrington, *A Guide to the Mammals of Iran*, Tehran, 1977 (Department of the Environment, 89 pp.). D. L. Harrison, "Carnivora Artiodactyla Hyracoidea," in *The Mammals of Arabia*, London, 1968, II, pp. 193-381. Jerry D. Hassinger, "Introduction to the Mammal Survey of the 1965 Street Expedition to Afghanistan," *Fieldiana: Zoology* 55/1, 1968, pp. 1-81, figs. 1-25, table 1. Idem, "A Survey of the Mammals of Afghanistan Resulting from the 1965 Street Expedition (excluding bats)," *Fieldiana: Zoology* 60, 1973, pp. i-xi and 1-195. R. T. Hatt, "The Mammals of Iraq," in *Miscellaneous Publications, University of Michigan* 106, 1959, pp. 1-113. International Union for the Conservation of Nature, "Golden or Asiatic Jackal (*Canis aureus*)," available on the internet at http://www.canids.org/SPPACCTS/caureas.htm. Alicia Ivory, "*Canis aureus*" in *Animal Diversity Web*, available on the internet at http://animaldiversity.ummz.umich.edu/site/accounts/information/Canis_aureus.html. Douglas M. Lay, "A Study of the Mammals of Iran Resulting from the Street Expedition of 1962-63," *Fieldiana: Zoology* 54, 1967, pp. 1-282. X. Misonne,

"Analyse zoogéographique des mammiferes de l'Iran," *Mem. Inst. Roy. Sci. Nat. Belgique*, 2nd ser., 167/59, 1959, 3 pls., 24 figs., 8 pp., distribution maps, 1 folding map. M. Mayrhofer, *Kurzgefasstes etymologisches Wörterbuch des Altindischen* III, Heidelberg, 1976. Patricia D. Moehlman, "Jackals," in David Macdonald, ed., *The Encyclopedia of Mammals*, New York, 1994, pp. 64-67. Ronald M. Nowak, *Walker's Mammals of the World*, 5th ed., Baltimore and London, 1991, pp. 1065-68. D. J. Osborn, and I. Helmy, "The Contemporary Land Mammals of Egypt (including Sinai)," *Fieldiana: Zoology*, N.S. 5, 1980, pp. 1-579. Robert K. Wayne, Raoul E. Benveniste, Dianne N. Janczewski, and Stephen J. O'Brien, "Molecular and Biochemical Evolution of the Carnivora," in John L. Gittleman, ed., *Carnivore Behavior, Ecology, and Evolution*, Ithaca, N.Y., 1989, I, chap. 17, pp. 465-94. Lars Werdelin, "Carnivoran Ecomorphology: a Phylogenetic Perspective," in John L. Gittleman, ed., *Carnivore Behavior, Ecology, and Evolution*, Ithaca and London, 1996, II, chap. 17, pp. 582-624. W. Christopher Wozencraft, "Order Carnivora," in D. E. Wilson and D. M. Reeder, ed., *Mammal Species of the World*, Washington, D.C., 1993, p. 280. H. Żiāʾi, *Rāhnemā-ye ṣaḥrāʾi-e pestāndārān-e Irān*, Tehran, 1996.

(STEVEN C. ANDERSON)

JACKSON, ABRAHAM VALENTINE WILLIAMS (b. New York City, 9 February 1862; d. New York City, 8 August 1937), pioneer of Iranian studies in America and prominent Iranist for half a century, twice president of the American Oriental Society, honorary president of the American Institute for Persian Art and Archaeology, and honorary member of the Royal Asiatic Society and of the Société Asiatique; he was honored by the king of Persia with the decoration (*nešān*) of the lion and the sun (see DECORATIONS) and was recipient of an honorary degree from Dār al-Fonun, Tehran. He married twice, Dora Ritter in 1889 (d. 1909), and Kate Brigham in 1911; he had no children.

Biography. Jackson was born into an old New York family and was given the name of his maternal grandfather, Abraham Valentine Williams, former president of the Board of Aldermen of New York City. Jackson attended both public and private schools in the city and, in 1879, he entered Columbia College as a freshman, marking the beginning of a long and productive academic career, during which, to the time of his death, he never left Columbia University, save for numerous trips abroad. He studied Classics as an undergraduate, but he also developed a lively interest in comparative philology and studied Anglo-Saxon, Persian, and Sanskrit, the latter under Edward Delaven Perry (d. 1938). Together with other upperclassmen, he also organized a lecture series on "Comparative Philology," a subject to which he was to return later in life in his 1908 pamphlet entitled "Philology." He began the study of Sanskrit in his senior year in college and, inspired by Perry, continued his graduate study after receiving the bachelor's degree with honors at the top of his class in 1883. Following a path trod by many, the study of Sanskrit led him to Avestan (q.v.), taught for the first time in America by E. Washburn Hopkins. His graduate career was short, as he went from A.M. (1884) to L.H.D. (doctor of humane letters; 1885) to doctor of philosophy (1886) in two years. In 1904 he received the honorary LL.D. (doctor of laws) from Columbia University.

Figure 1. Detail, portrait of A. V. Williams Jackson by his friend (Bakhmeteff, p. 180), the artist William J. Whittemore (1860-1955). Courtesy of Columbia University, Center for Iranian Studies; full portrait in Jackson, 1931, and Perry, 1938.

A year after receiving the doctor of philosophy, Jackson was employed for a year at Columbia as an Assistant in Anglo-Saxon and Instructor in Indo-Iranian language. A personal and unsolicited letter from the Harvard Sanskritist, Charles Rockwell Lanman, to the president of Columbia, recommending that the young Jackson be sent to Germany to deepen his knowledge, resulted in the granting of leave from the university to spend a year and a half at Halle, Germany, where he studied Avestan and Sanskrit with Karl Friedrich Geldner (q.v.), Sanskrit and Prakrit with Richard Pischel, and Anglo-Saxon with Eduard Sievers, and in the summers of 1891 and 1892 again with Geldner in Berlin. It was Geldner whom he particularly always regarded both as a guru and a friend. At a time when there was disagreement among Sanskritists over the value of native traditions in the interpretation of Sanskrit texts, Geldner and Pischel carried the banner of "Indien für die Inder." Their influence is evident in the importance that Jackson attached to understanding and valuing native Iranian traditions, as seen especially in his *Zoroaster*, his several extended journeys to Persia and India, and his two travel books, *Persia Past and Present* and *From Constantinople to the Home of Omar Khayyam*.

Jackson's appointment in 1891 as Adjunct Professor of English is testimony both to his breadth of learning and to an attitude toward disciplinary boundaries different from that prevailing in America a century later. A heavy teaching load, as much as twenty hours per week, forced him to pursue his researches late into the night, as he had done as a student (cf. Jackson, 1931, pp. 151-52, and Haas, p. 242). The year 1895 marked his appointment as professor and head of the new Department of Indo-Iranian Languages and Literatures, and the Oriental studies component of his teaching began to outweigh English literature (Jackson, 1931, p. 155).

Although he was born and raised, went to college and graduate school, and taught all his life in New York, Jackson was no stay-at-home. Beyond his early years studying in Germany and frequent trips to Europe to attend international conferences, the spirit of scientific curiosity and adventure led him to Persia and India on seven separate journeys between 1901 and 1926. The first of these was to India, where he established lifelong contacts with members of the Parsi community there. The most arduous and adventurous of his travels came in 1903 in an extensive tour of Persia and Central Asia, an account of which was given in his *Persia, Past and Present* (1906). That trip was followed by two more trips in 1907 and 1910. The latter two were woven together to form the narrative of his *From Constantinople to the Home of Omar Khayyam* (1911). He returned to India in 1911. He returned to Persia in 1918-19 as a member if the American Relief Mission to Persia at the time of World War I, eventually traveling around the world. In 1926 he made his final journey to Persia and India. In his last three trips he enjoyed the company of his wife.

Jackson was afflicted by a severe illness in the summer of 1931 which made him unable to engage in extensive travel and generally forced him to limit his activities. In 1935 he retired to become Professor Emeritus in Residence, in recognition of his ongoing scholarship and involvement with Columbia. He died on 8 August 1937 before he could complete a second book on Manicheism. Reminiscences of those who knew him paint a picture of a great gentleman, always impeccably dressed, a humane yet demanding teacher, whose fair judgment was revered throughout the university. He avoided writing book reviews out of a gentleman's respect for colleagues and desire not to provoke acrimonious controversy. A former student and later editor of the *Columbia University Quarterly* recalled a lecture that Jackson gave to a student group, The King's Crown. Doubtful that this old philologist would have anything interesting to say to a cross-section of undergraduates, they were won over "when we discovered that the most disreputable and untrustworthy looking of the caravan shown in the lantern slides was none other than our professor himself" (Bakhmeteff, p. 181).

Works. Between 1888 and 1893 Jackson published two short monographs and two books dealing with the Avestan language and literature, all with the publisher Kohlhammer who possessed the elegant Avestan fonts used in the Niel Westergaard and later the Geldner editions of the Avesta. These works, especially the *Reader* (1893), used the original script to a far greater extent than in subsequent scholarly works to the present. The first (1888) is a study of *Yasna* 31, which presents the text in Avestan script with a translation on opposite pages. The philological notes have transliterated verses at the head of the commentaries of the individual verses. The provisional system of transliteration employed here was to be significantly revised in his short monograph on the Avestan alphabet (1890), the latter then providing the model for his *Avestan Grammar* (1892) and *Reader* (1893). More on Avestan was planned. The *Avestan Grammar* was published as Part I, and in his preface (p. x) he stated that a second volume, Part II, which would contain "a sketch of the syntax, with a chapter also on Metre, is already half in print and is shortly to appear." Unfortunately this was never published. Further, Montgomery Schuyler, in the preface to his publication of an index to the Avestan fragments mentions "the Avestan dictionary which Professors Geldner and Jackson are to make" (p. ix). With the appearance, first of Christian Bartholomae's comprehensive grammar of Avestan and Old Iranian in the *Grundriss* (1895), then of his *Wörterbuch* (1904; see BARTHOLOMAE), the dictionary project was, apparently, abandoned. Extensive marginalia in Jackson's copy of Ferdinand Justi's *Handbuch* (in the possession of the present author) point to such a lexicographical undertaking. It may well be that the imminent publication of Bartholomae's grammar caused the cancellation of Jackson's *Avestan Grammar*, Part II. Although Bartholomae's transliteration system became the standard in the field and remained so until the recent revisions of Karl Hoffmann (1989, q.v.), Jackson's remarks on the Avestan alphabet are significant for the history of Avestan studies. Particularly interesting is the table showing sixteen different scholarly systems of transliteration going back to Anquetil du Perron (q.v.). Jackson himself had gone over to Bartholomae's system in his *Zoroaster* (1898).

As a student of Sanskrit under Edward Perry, Jackson was certainly familiar with the latter's *Sanskrit Primer*, as have been many generations of American Sanskritists; yet it was the example of William Dwight Whitney's *Sanskrit Grammar* and Charles Rockwell Lanman's *Sanskrit Reader* that provided the models for Jackson's *Grammar* and *Reader* It is clear from the plan of the *Grammar* that Jackson had as his objective a comprehensive reference work, like Whitney's, that would be accessible to students taking their first steps in Avestan. To this pedagogical end, he relegated matters of philological detail that need not burden the beginner to small print. As its subtitle declares, the *Grammar* presupposes that the user has a basic knowledge of Sanskrit and employs Sanskrit as the constant frame of reference for much of Avestan grammar. While this approach risks giving the impression that Avestan is a peculiar form of Sanskrit, the pedagogical advantage is superior over Hans Reichelt's *Elementarbuch*. The thirty-three page Introduction provides sufficient cultural and linguistic background to show that Avestan is a thoroughly Iranian vehicle of cultural expression.

In a way, Jackson's works on Avestan have been the victims of history. First, Bartholomae's grammatical chapters in the *Grundriss* and then his *Wörterbuch*, as they became standards in the field, marginalized Jackson's works. Later, after the publication of Hans Reichelt's *Awestisches Elementarbuch* (1910) and later of his *Avesta Reader*, Jackson's contributions seemed all the more outmoded. Nevertheless, Jackson's *Grammar* has maintained its usefulness not only for those unable to read German, but also for the vast majority of students who come to Avestan through the prior study of Sanskrit.

The most important book of Jackson perhaps was *Zoroaster, the Prophet of Ancient Iran* (1898). As suggested above, Jackson was not among those who belittled indigenous traditions, nor did he embrace positivistic historiography. Not so naive as to believe in the fabulous accounts contained in traditional sources and in Classical and Arabic histories, he had, nevertheless, an abiding faith in basic historicity of these sources. As he put it: "This mass of Zoroastrian patristic literature [recently translated by West in the series SBE] tends largely to substantiate much that was formerly regarded as somewhat legendary or uncertain. This has resulted in placing the actual tradition on a much firmer basis and in making Zoroaster seem a more real and living personage. . . . In taking a position so much in accord with tradition with regard to Zarathushtra I might adopt the plea which the old Armenian annalist, Moses of Khorene, employs in another connection: 'there may be much that is untrue in these stories, there may be much that is true; but to me, at least, they seem to contain truth'" (pp. vii-viii). These remarks may strike the reader as naive. If the attempt had been to establish an historically verifiable biography, the book would have been short, indeed. What Jackson wished to accomplish was to create a narrative of the life of the prophet based on the sources and "to lay these down for reference and judgment" (p. 4). Whether one will want to follow him to the extent that he endorsed the historical veracity of the traditions, will depend on one's critical judgment. A lasting achievement of the book is that it lays out a synthesis of the sources that allows us to perceive the prophet as his tradition perceived him.

Zoroaster is divided into two major sections. The first section is the biography of the prophet in eleven chapters and a conclusion (pp. 1-143) designed for the general reader. The second contains in seven appendices (pp. 147-294) both detailed studies and collections of data that are of interest mostly to the specialist and which, in one way or another, support or document the positions taken in the biographical section. Here one finds extensive discussions of Zarathushtra's dates and of his native land and his place of ministry. Even if one does not agree with Jackson's conclusions, the mass of evidence brought to bear in each case can still serve as a point of departure for anyone researching these issues. Concerning Zarathushtra's dates, the traditional figure of 258 years before Alexander is defended, with obvious consequences for the chronology of events in the life of the prophet. Concerning his homeland, a bipartite solution is offered. The preponderance of evidence from the Pahlavi sources points to the northwest, specifically Atropatene (i.e., Azerbaijan, q.v.), yet the Avesta together with the later sources seem to exclude the northwest in favor of eastern Iran. Jackson's explanation of this is that modern Azerbaijan was indeed Zarathushtra's natal home (*Zoroaster*, pp. 16-17, 205 ff.). A prophet exiled by his own people, he eventually gained a favorable reception in the east and it was from there that the new religious movement returned to the West. Other appendices which give all passages containing references to Zarathushtra's name by Greek and Latin authors, as well as allusions to him is various literatures, remain excellent sources for research (*Zoroaster*, pp. 182-225).

During the first decade of the 20th century, most of Jackson's energies were devoted to traveling and writing two major books reflecting his experiences in Asia and Persia. He also managed to edit a nine-volume *History of India*, the ninth volume of which is his collection of "Historic Accounts of India by Foreign Travelers." *Persia, Past and Present* (1906) and *From Constantinople to the Home of Omar Khayyam* (1911) were written as companion volumes. The former follows an itinerary that began in Moscow, descended through the Caucuses into the western Iranian plateau as far as Shiraz, then doubled back through Yazd, Tehran, and the western Caspian. There was also an eastward excursion as far as Samarkand, but its description was left out. The latter is actually a synthesis of the two trips of 1907 and 1910, insofar as their itineraries partially overlapped as far east as Mashad and Ṭus. Although a third volume was planned to cover the itineraries through Central Asia, it never appeared.

As its subtitle, *A Book of Travel and Research*, suggests, *Persia Past and Present* was a bold attempt to combine a traveler's journal with a scholar's observations and reflections concerning events of the distant past. Not far removed from his *Zoroaster*, in which many pages had been devoted to establishing the place of Zarathushtra's birth in Azerbaijan, of his missionary activity in the east, and the triumphant return of his faith to western Persia under the Achaemenids, Jackson plotted his itinerary to follow the steps of the prophet and the course of the Good Religion. Even if one does not agree with his geographic reconstructions, one reading *Persia* a century after its writing cannot help but to be caught up in the author's enthusiasm as the land of Zarathushtra and of Cyrus and Darius (qq.v.) unfolded before him. There is a quaint 19th-century romanticism in much of Jackson's writing. For example, while approaching the Caucuses by train, he is caught in a reverie of Prometheus Bound. "Far in the distance I could picture the desolate vulture peak, where the demigod lay chained in fetters . . . I could hear faint echoes of the dialogue with Io and mutterings of the titan's curse against the wrath of Zeus . . . For a moment, Greek mythology, classic reminiscences, and thoughts of college days made me forget that the land of my quest was Iran, not Hellas" (p. 3). In contrast, the book is also full of down to earth descriptions of the hardships and perils he encountered, when, after leaving the railroad behind in Erivan, he traveled by carriage and horse along caravan routes through the ice and blizzards of March. Of the road from Aḥmadābād to Tak̲t-e Solaymān (q.v.), he wrote: "The snow lay two feet deep on the side of the hills and sometimes three or four in the gullies. Twice that day the horse which I rode went down under me in the treacherous depths. The glare from its white surface . . . was dazzling and set up a painful inflammation in my eyes . . . As darkness began to fall, the mountain gorges became dangerous because of robbers, and at each turn of the road it interested me to watch the two guards lower their guns to the saddle-bow" (p. 122).

Among the many fascinating descriptions of ancient sites, a report of a visit with the Zoroastrians of Yazd, and details of all sorts of aspects of the life of the contemporary Persia, the two chapters devoted to Behistun/Bisotun (q.v.) illustrate well the way Jackson was able to sustain a narrative weaving together adventure, ancient history and recondite paleography (*Persia*, pp. 175 ff., 353-400). Half a century had passed since Henry C. Rawlinson had personally examined under great duress the inscription of Darius. His work had been pioneering and solid, but many questions and problems with the decipherment remained, and no one since had undertaken a reexamination. For Jackson it was a four-day journey by horse from Hamadān (q.v.). As an introduction to that journey, he devoted a chapter, giving an excellent review of the site from Classical references through the stages of decipherment of Georg F. Grotefend (q.v.) and Henry Rawlinson (*Persia*, pp. 176-79). A wonderful description of the approach to the mountain still covered in April snow sets the scene for the arduous ascent to the high ledge that gives access to the inscription and sculptures. One can understand the thrill of the philologist to witness at last the actual cuneiform that rendered him insensitive to the peril to his life, as when he was drawn up by ropes or held by his Persian companions as he leaned out over the abyss to snap a photograph. Yet, for Jackson this was all incidental "to the far more interesting and important matter of what I was able to note, verify, or restore" (*Persia*, p. 196). Twelve pages of learned paleographic commentary is then devoted to sometimes verifying Rawlinson's reading, sometimes offering different readings of his own. Only "the westering sun . . . warned me that I must descend for the last time from the rocky height" (*Persia*, p. 208).

"Zoroaster, the founder of Persia's ancient religion, ran as a minor chord through the pages of the earlier volume; in the present volume Alexander the Great, upon whose track I have followed so extensively, adds another connecting link between the interests of East and West, while Omar's home, as goal to visit, gave to the journey the semblance, at least, of a pilgrimage" (*From Constantinople*, p. viii). So wrote Jackson in the Preface to his second book of travels in Persia. While this volume continues the plan of the first, in weaving present observations with Persia's past, it is much more about the present. Whereas *Persia* tended to give a picture of an archaic country rooted in ancient traditions, *From Constantinople* presents a view of a nation beginning to move forward into the 20th century along with its rich cultural heritage. There is a greater awareness of the strategic position of Persia in global politics, particularly in respect to imperial Russian and British imperialistic objectives. Chapters on "Baku, the City of Oil Wells" and "Teheran and the Newer Persia" stand in contrast to "On the Track of Alexander the Great" and "The Tomb of Omar Khayyam." The lasting value of the book is the eyewitness account and photo documentation of Persia at a particular time in its modern history. As a literary composition it is not as successful as *Persia*. Because it is a conflation of two trips, the narrative is sometimes confusing and a bit artificial. The digressions into Zoroastrianism and Persia's past, which are more integral to the flow of the narrative in *Persia*, often seem forced or uncontrolled. A case in point is a long digression on a patently Hindu temple in Baku (established by traders) that was thought locally to be Zoroastrian. In excruciating detail over fifteen pages Jackson established the curiosity's Hindu credentials. One wonders whether the project had become too tedious to sustain the third volume which he envisioned.

Jackson's love of classical Persian poetry, first aroused in his college days, begins to show in the pages of the two travel books, where places visited evoked quotations from the great poets. Already, in 1908, he delivered seven lectures at John Hopkins University and then in 1919 three lectures at the University of Chicago, all on early Persian poetry. The publication in 1920 of a small volume entitled *Early Persian Poetry form the Beginnings down to the Time of Firdausi* presented the substance of those ten lectures. Indeed, the style in which most of the chapters are written suggest public oratory. The book stands somewhere between a brief literary history and an anthology, with a greater emphasis on the poets and their background, than on their poems. Only two samples of pre-Islamic poetry are given: a Gathas (q.v.) of Zarathushtra (*Y*. 44) and a brief passage from the *Mehr yašt* (*Yt*. 10.13-14), both in Avestan, not Persian. The short discourse on Pahlavi literature betrays the general lack of understanding of the principles of Middle Persian verse, which was prevalent at the time. In his own translations of selected fragments of the early poets and of three longer passages from Ferdowsi (q.v.), Jackson demonstrated a real talent for transforming the Persian into elegant English verse. An example of his translation of the following quatrain by Abu Šakur (q.v.) Balk̲i will illustrate the point:

Ey gašta man az ḡam-e farāwān-e to past,
Šod qāmat-e man ze dard-e hejrān-e to šast.
Ey šosta man az farib o dastān-e to dast,
K̲od hič kas-i ba-sirat o sān-e to hast?

Through grievous pangs for thee I am bowed low;
Neath separation's burden bent I go.
But ah! with hands wash'd of thy guile and wile!
None e'er had moods and whims like thine, I know.

Zoroastrian Studies (1928) is a collection of various writing. The bulk (215 pages) is taken up with the publication of the original English text which was translated into German for the chapter "Die iranische Religion" in the *Grundriss* (1903). Although Jackson claimed in the Preface (p. vii) that the original had "undergone so many alterations or has been expanded by so many additions [usually indicated by enclosure in square brackets], that this part may be regarded in large measure as a new contribution," a comparison of the two texts shows that, except for the additions so indicated, little was done to revise the text itself. The bracketed material is mostly confined to further bibliography, with comments on developments in scholarship relevant to the topics at hand. The one major addition is an addendum of seven pages dealing with Manicheism, the subject of his last major publication. In any case, the monograph length essay presents a comprehensive history of Iranian religion, almost exclusively defined as Zoroastrianism, from the Indo-Iranian period to contemporary Zoroastrianism in Persia and India, with emphasis on the latter, though it will be remembered that he had visited Zoroastrians in Yazd in the course of his travels. Jackson's approach to the religion is similar to what he had followed in his *Zoroaster*. That is, there is a marked reliance on traditional sources of the Sasanian and Islamic periods to illuminate the often fragmentary testimony of the Avesta; and there is also a concerted effort to portray continuity in Zoroastrian theology throughout the faith's history. The remainder of the book (pp. 219-86) contains a long essay on "The Zoroastrian Doctrine of the Freedom of the Will" and miscellaneous notes on a variety of subjects.

Studies in Manicheism was Jackson's final major work. It was completed at the end of 1930 but was not published until 1932. The dates are significant, as he could only refer to unpublished materials of Friedrich C. Andreas. Just at this time, these texts, thoroughly edited by Walter B. Henning (q.v.), were about to be published as *Mitteliranisches Manichaica aus Chinesisch-Turkestan*. In addition, Henning's groundbreaking *Das Verbum* appeared in 1933. The work itself is a collection of various studies, some previously published, which Jackson made over the period of a decade. There is a general survey of Manicheism, followed by six philologically detailed studies of several Turfan and Book Pahlavi texts covering some 200 pages. Study VIII is a translation of Theodore Bar Khoni on Mani by Abraham Yohannan ("On Mānī's Teachings Concerning the Beginning of the World") with notes by Jackson. The remaining five studies are essays on a variety of subjects. One suspects that Jackson's deteriorating health may have been decisive in leading him to construct his last two books as studies, that is, as collections of already published material and previously unpublished short pieces on loosely related subjects. In the preface to *Studies in Manichaeism*, he alludes to a comprehensive work on Manicheism to which he regarded the present work as prolegomena. Sadly he passed away before bringing this to completion.

Bibliography: Works. (For complete writings, in all areas, see Haas.) (1) Books and Monographs. *The Avestan Alphabet and its Transcription*, Stuttgart, 1890. *An Avesta Grammar in Comparison with Sanskrit*, Part I: *Phonology, Inflection, Word-Formation*, Stuttgart, 1892, repr. New York, 1975. *Avesta Reader: First Series*, Stuttgart, 1893. *Zoroaster, the Prophet of Ancient Iran*, New York, 1898, repr. New York, 1965, tr. with notes Palanji B. Desai as *A New Zaratosht Nameh: An Account of the Life of Zoroaster, the Prophet*, Bombay, 1900. "Die iranische Religion," in *Grundriss* II, pp. 612-708, revised, expanded version in English in his *Zoroastrian Studies*, pp. 3-212. *Persia Past and Present: A Book of Travel and Research*, New York, 1906, repr. New York, 1975. *From Constantinople to the Home of Omar Khayyam: Travels in Transcaucasia and Northern Persia for Historic and Literary Research*, New York, 1911, repr. New York, 1975. *Early Persian Poetry, from the Beginnings down to the Time of Firdausi*, New York, 1920, repr., New York, 1975. *Zoroastrian Studies: The Iranian Religion and Various Monographs*, New York, 1928, repr. New York, 1965. *Researches in Manichaeism, with Special Reference to the Turfan Fragments*, New York, 1932.

(2) Articles. "Herodotus VII.61: The Arms of the Ancient Persians Illustrated from Iranian Sources," in *Classical Studies in Honour of Henry Drisler*, New York, and London, 1894, pp. 95-125. "Avesta," in *International Cyclopaedia*, New York, 1894, rev. repr. as the Introduction to his *Grammar*, pp. xi-xxxiii. "The Ancient Persian Doctrine of Future Life," *Biblical World* 8, 1896, pp. 149-63. "The Religion of the Achaemenian Kings: The Religion According to the Inscriptions," *JAOS* 21, 1900, pp. 160-84. *Philology*, New York, 1908 (a lecture published in a pamphlet series by Columbia University Press). "Avesta," in James Hastings, ed., *Encyclopædia of Religion and Ethics* II, New York, 1909, pp. 266-72. "The Ancient Persian Conception of Salvation According to the Avesta, or Bible of Zoroaster," *American Journal of Theology*, April-May 1913, pp. 195-205. "The Location of Farnbāg Fire, the Most Ancient of the Zoroastrian Fires," *JAOS* 41, 1921, pp. 81-106. "The Persian Dominions in Northern India," in *The Cambridge History of India* I, Cambridge, 1922, pp. 319-42. "The 'Second Evocation': The Manichaean System of Cosmogony," *JRAS*, Centenary supplement, 1924, pp. 137-55. "The Doctrine of Metamorphosis in Manichaeism," *JAOS* 45, 1925, pp. 246-68. "Voices that Called Eastward Ho!" *Columbia University Quarterly* 23, 1931, pp. 151-58 (a memoir). "Traces of Biblical Influence in the Turfan Pahlavi Fragment M 173," *JAOS* 56, 1936, pp. 198-207.

Jackson published fifty-one articles and notes in the *JAOS* between 1885 and 1938; for references see *JAOS* 21, 1902, and *Index to the Journal of the American Oriental Society* XX-LX, New Haven, 1955.

(3) Editions and translations. Tr. with comments, *A Hymn of Zoroaster, Yasna 31*, Stuttgart, 1888. Tr. with comments, "The Āfringān Rapitwin on the Avesta," *JAOS* 13, 1889, pp. clxxxvii-cxciii. Ed., *History of India*, 9 vols., London, 1906-07 (repr., New York, 1975;

New Delhi, 1987, etc.), of which he compiled vol. 9 as *Historic Accounts of India by Foreign Travellers, Classical, Oriental, and Occidental*, 1907. Ed. and prepared with Abraham Yohannan, *A Catalogue of the Collection of Persian Manuscripts, Including Also Some Turkish and Arabic, Presented to the Metropolitan Museum of Art, New York, by Alexander Smith Cochran*, New York, 1914. Ed. and tr. (with Gushtaspshah K. Narimanand, and Charles J. Ogden), King Harsha's *Priyadarśikā* as *Priyadarśikā, A Hindu Drama Ascribed to King Harsha*, New York, 1923. Tr. (from *Dēnkart*) "The So-called Injunction of Mani," *JRAS*, 1925, pp. 213-19.

He was also the founder and editor of the *Columbia University Indo-Iranian Series*, 13 vols., New York, 1901-32 (listed in Haas, p. 257).

Obituaries and biographical sketches. B[oris] A. B[akhmeteff], obituary in *Columbia University Quarterly*, 29, 1937, pp. 180-82. Edward D. Perry, "Abraham Valentine Williams Jackson," *JAOS* 58, 1938, pp. 221-24. George C. O. Haas, "Bibliography of A. V. Williams Jackson," *JAOS* 58, 1938, pp. 241-57. Charles J. Ogden "Biographical Sketch of Prof. Jackson," in *Prof. Jackson Memorial Volume*, Bombay, 1954, pp. iii-viii. *Who's Who*, London, 1916 [and years following].

References. Friedrick C. Andreas and Walter B. Henning "Mitteliranische Manichaica aus Chinesisch-Turkestan I" *SPAW*, Phil.-hist. Kl., Berlin, 1932, pp. 175-222; II, ibid., 1933, pp. 294-363; III, ibid., 1934, pp. 848-912; repr. in Henning, *Selected Papers* I, pp. 1-48, 191-260, 275-339. Christian Bartholomae "Vorgeschichte der iranischen Sprachen" in *Grundriss* I, pp. 1-151. Idem, "Awestische und Altpersisch" in *Grundriss* I, pp. 152-246. Idem, *Altiranisches Wörterbuch*, Strassburg, 1904. Wilhem Geiger and Ernst Kuhn *Grundriss der iranischen Philologie*, 2 vols., Strassburg, 1895-1904. Walter Bruno Henning, "Das Verbum des Mittelpersischen der Turfanfragmenta," *ZII* 9, 1933, pp. 158-253; repr. in idem, *Selected Papers* I, pp. 65-160. Idem, *Selected Papers*, 2 vols., Acta Iranica 14-15, Leiden, Tehran, and Liège, 1977. Karl Hoffmann and Johanna Narten *Der Sasanidische Archetypus: Untersuchungen zu Schreibung und Lautgestalt des Avestischen*, Wiesbaden, 1989. Hans Reichelt, *Awestisches Elementarbuch*, Heidelberg, 1909. Idem, *Avesta Reader*, Strassburg, 1911. Montgomery Schuyler, *Index Verborum of the Fragments of the Avesta*, New York, 1901.

(WILLIAM W. MALANDRA)

JADE (nephrite; Pers. *yašm, yašb, yašf, yaṣb*). For at least two and a half millennia, Jade has been carved in the lands where Iranian languages have prevailed in various eras. The known material is often of extraordinary refinement, and testifies to an extensive influence on other jade-carving cultures, including the Chinese. Most of the major lapidary regions were in the eastern Iranian world, particularly in ancient and medieval Central Asia (q.v.), encompassing Sogdiana, Khotan (Ḵotan), and Bactria, as far as Farḡāna (qq.v.). This entry will be divided into three sections:

i. *Introduction.*
ii. *Pre-Islamic Iranian Jades.*
iii. *Jade Carving, 4th century B.C.E to 15th century C.E.*

i. INTRODUCTION

Regional overview. Jade carving in pre-Islamic Central and Western Asia was largely an east Iranian and Turkic phenomenon, and the same holds true for the Islamic tradition. Under Muslim rule jade carving was probably widespread in the eastern parts of Persia, and it is likely that Samarqand, Balkh, Herat, and Nishapur (Nišāpur) were particularly important centers. This is not surprising, given the sophisticated and age-old lapidary traditions in the region, and the relative proximity to Khotan, the great classic source of rough jade.

The jades of India may be seen as a major but highly individualistic and prolific branch of the Iranian school. In the sixteenth and seventeenth centuries, the Indian school was much influenced by the European hardstone carving tradition, while continuing to develop within the overwhelming nurture of the Indian artistic tradition and genius. The jade artifacts that originated in India between the 16th and 18th centuries were highly sophisticated, exhibiting refined craftsmanship. They were much appreciated in China, and many pieces have survived in former imperial collections; that of the emperor Qianlong (r.1735-96) is known to have been extensive and distinguished, and particularly noted for his commissioned inscriptions carved on many of the pieces (cf. Skelton, 1972, pp. 106-8; Teng, 1983, 2004).

Mineralogy and technology. The jade of objects that originated in Iran is nephrite. The mineral belongs to the tremolite-actinolite series of the amphibole family; it is slightly less hard than the quartzes (at 6 1/2 on Moh's scale), but is extraordinarily tough due to the interlocking felt-like structure of its crystals (Webster, pp. 223-24). Like other hardstones, it is worked by drilling, grinding, sanding and polishing with grits and powders, typically harder than itself and delivered on, or as a component of, mostly rotary tools, such as discs, points, tubes, and rods. These tools may be composed of a variety of materials, depending on their intended use: from lac and wood—attested by Jawhari of Nishapur in his treatise, *Jawāher-nāma-ye Neẓāmi*, dated 592/1195-96 (Jawhari, p. 218)—through copper and soft iron. The grits and powders involved range from quartz through garnet, corundum, and diamond. Exceptionally detailed and valuable information on the cutting and polishing of gemstones is to be found in Abu'l-Qāsem Kāšāni's treatise, *ʿArāyes al-jawāher wa nafāyes al-aṭāyeb*, dated 700/1301. Kāšāni mentions, in connection with the cutting of rubies, wheels of lac, lead, wood, and copper (p. 42), and describes a long process of cutting, polishing, and tests, involving such abrasives as emery, shell, marcasite, and clay.

The myth that jade presents exceptional technical difficulties not encountered when dealing with other hardstones is remarkably persistent. Yet the technology is exactly the same as that used for other hardstones. Indeed, in some ways jade is easier to cut than, for example, the quartzes. Compared to them, not only is jade slightly less hard, but its toughness reduces the likelihood of breakage in the process of cutting, as well as later. Problems may arise at the polishing phase of finishing jade pieces, especially if a highly glossy surface is required, but these are neither significant nor insurmountable. Moreover, for most of the West Asian material, such a surface was never sought.

Terminology. In Persian and Arabic literary sources, the words *yašm*, *yašf*, *yašb*, and *yaṣb* are used for jade, though *yašb* and *yaṣb* are generally understood to refer more precisely to jasper, a variety of cryptocrystalline quartz closely related to the chalcedonies such as carnelian and agate. Assadullah Souren Melikian-Chirvani (1997/2000, esp. pp. 123-26; cf. Pelliot, p. 424) has collected extensive material, tracing apparent cognates of these words to Old Babylonian and Old Assyrian texts. The overwhelming likelihood is that essentially all of the ancient Near Eastern use of *yashpu/ashpu*, even if cognate with *yašf/yašb*, must actually refer to the cryptocrystalline quartzes chalcedony (including agate) and jasper. This is borne out by any extensive survey of the thousands upon thousands of extant hardstone objects from the period in question.

Jade has always been noted for its beneficial properties, a lore which in East Asia stretches back into prehistory. In medieval Arabic, Persian, and Turco-Mongol sources, these purported properties are mainly apotropaic and medicinal, ranging from assuring victory in combat and protection from lightning to the prevention and cure of ailments of the internal organs. The modern English word *jade* is derived from the French *pierre de l'éjade*, resp. *l'éjade* and *le jade*, which in turn is derived from the Spanish *piedra de ijada* resp. *hijada*, a stone which cures internal ailments of the area of the small ribs resp. flanks. This was once seen as a cure for all sorts of colic, and became conflated with *piedra de los riñones* (kidney stone). In the sixteenth century, after the discovery of the use of jade in Central America, the stone "seems rapidly to have acquired a reputation as a treatment for kidney diseases" (Middleton and Freestone, p. 413). The eighteenth-century use of *nephrite* for jade reflects the same medicinal presumption, as it is derived from *nephroi*, the Greek word for kidneys (cf. Lat. *lapis nephriticus*: kidney stone).

But the ultimate derivation of the Spanish name for jade, and the issue of its supposed powers, bristle with controversy arising from a series of ancient associations of words in the Turkic, Mongol, Iranian, and Sanskrit languages. Some of the Spaniards who discovered the Native Americans using jade may have been aware of these connections, the Asian names and beliefs, and the medicinal and apotropaic powers already associated with them in Asia. Muslim dynasties had ruled over parts of the Spanish peninsula from the beginning of the 8th century to the end of the 15th century; and European Christian rulers sent their ambassadors, such as Clavijo (d. 1412; q.v.), to the Timurids and the Mongols. Words such as *yāt*, *yāi*, *yadā/jada/yadeh*, *jādu*, and *jādi* occur in the context of Turkish and Mongol ceremonies in which a shaman uses stones to induce rain, storms, and the like; the association of *yadā/jada/jādu* with magical powers is illustrated by *yada-taš* (Turk. magic rain stone, possibly, at least at times, of jade—see below). In all likelihood any envoy to Central Asia would have heard stories about these wondrous practices, as well as jade's putative medicinal properties for the internal organs, and the similarity between *yada* and *ijada* would not have been lost on a Spaniard. In today's Mongolian folklore (personal communication from an elder jade connoisseur and dealer of Ulan Bator, 2006), jade (*haš*) is considered most beneficial for the kidneys (*bur*), and this is probably an extremely ancient belief (for the characterization of *haš* as Qalmuq and *qas* as Mongolian, see Pelliot, p. 424; cf. Turk. *qāš* and Pers. *yašm/yašb*).

An etymological connection between Old Turkic *yat* and *yada/jada* and similar-sounding words in modern Western European languages has been ruled out (Clauson, p. 883; cf. Pelliot, p. 424). Moreover, it has been asserted that "the *yada* or *jada* stone is a bezoar and has nothing to do with 'jade', either with the word or the thing" (Pelliot, p. 424). But this claim does not accord with the literature on the Bezoar-stone (Pers. *bāzahr*), which is a well-documented agent for neutralizing poison, including occasionally poisonous stings (Ruska and Plessner, pp. 1155-56). Nor is it supported by the medieval literature about the weather-influencing properties of the *yada-taš*, mentioned above. It should be remembered in this context that in Chinese culture as late as Tang times (Schafer, p. 225), it was the emperor, in his role as chief shaman, "who compelled the attendance of the rain-dragons with his wand of green nephrite;" and the awareness in 12th-century eastern Iran of stories revealing the importance in China of the shamans' role in bringing beneficial rain is well attested by Marvazi (p. 25) and others. The use of *qāš* for jade in Turkish is attested since the 11th century, first by Biruni (p. 198), and later by Kashghari (Kāšḡari, p. 511). Jade was probably extracted at Kashghar (Kāšḡar) by this time, but the passage in *Kashghari's Dictionary* (of the 1070s) is apparently based on the corresponding one in Biruni's book, *Ketāb al-jamāher fi maʿrefat al-jawāher*. Biruni uses the terms *Qāš* and *Qārā Qāš* for the two rivers of Khotan from which jade was extracted, whereas Kashghari calls them the *Urung Qāš Okuz* and the *Qārā Qāš Okuz*.

Mines and varieties. The acknowledged classic source of nephrite for both the Chinese and Western Asian worlds for millennia was Khotan, near the foot of the Kunlun mountains, on the southwest side of the Tarim Basin. The mineral appears in a wide range of greens (typically more or less dull and blending with other colors), as well as colors ranging from a pure, translucent white (the rarest and the most sought after both in western and eastern Asia) through various shades of off-white, to yellowish, tan, iron-red (normally occurring in the pebble's rind, where the iron content is strongly oxidized), to brown and black (the last almost invariably a very dark green when viewed through strong transmitted light). Even relatively small pieces of nephrite are very often variegated both in color and degree of translucency. Biruni states: "Jade (*yašm*) is extracted from two river valleys in Khotan where the reeds (or canes) form thickets. One of the river valleys is called Qāš, and there *the superior white material* is extracted, and it is not taken from its ultimate source [i.e., it is found as rollers in the streambed and not at its origin, from which it is washed down]. *The big pieces of it are reserved for the king personally*, and the small ones are for the populace" (p. 198; italics added). The author of the *Ḥodud al-ʿālam* (372/982) had earlier reported that "the jade stone (*sang i yashm*) comes from the rivers of Khotan" (*Ḥodud al-ʿālam*, tr. p. 86)

It seems now established that in early times the Chinese had other sources of nephrite in China itself (Middleton and Freestone, pp. 414 and 417, apud Guang and Zhichun). Another major source, Kashghar, seems to have been feeding jade into the supply stream, probably starting as early as the 11th century, and in any case not later than the 13th. In a Persian panegyric from the late 11th or early 12th century by Lāmeʿi of Gorgān, a warrior wears "Kashghar jade" on his arms (Melikian-Chirvani, 1997/2000, p. 132). But as indicated above, Kashghari does not expand on Biruni's information. Jawhari of Nishapur, writing about a hundred years after Kashghari, also repeats Biruni, and adds that Khotan is the only known source of jade (*yašb*, p. 219). Aḥmad b. Yusof al-Tifāši (1184-1253), however, indicates only Kashghar as the source of jade, from where it was exported "to all countries" (p. 195). Although for a number of reasons Tifāši is not the best-informed of authorities, his account, in a manner similar to and combined with literary evidence like the aforementioned panegyric, indicates that Kashghar was a source of jade, whose deposits must have been exploited in a significant manner before his time in order for him to have heard of it. At the beginning of the 14th century, Kāšāni (p. 139) observes that jade (*yašb*) "comes in varieties, and its mines are in Ḵitāy and Ṭuḡmāj." Ḵitāy/ Khitay, Anglicized to Cathay, is an old name for northern China, and was derived from the name of the Ḵitāʾ confederation, while Ṭuḡmāj, also spelled Ṭugmāj, is a region in Turkistan. Kāšāni's usage of "Ḵatāy" may not, however, have referred to northern China but to the former territory of the Qārā Ḵatāy, a branch of the Ḵatāʾ who moved to the south and west in the 12th century and were the overlords of much of Turkistan in the period leading up to the conquests of Chingiz Khan. Nevertheless, the possibility that northern China may have been an important source of nephrite is suggested by the fact that on a recent visit to Mongolia the author became aware that jade is retrieved there and was able to acquire significant amounts of rough nephrite, including sizable pieces of fine white material. Its source does not seem to be officially documented, but according to word of mouth this material is sold on the Chinese market. It appears plausible that this source was already exploited long ago, but escaped scholarly attention.

ii. Pre-Islamic Iranian Jades

An extremely small range of pre-Islamic Iranian jades have thus far been published, despite the very ancient employment of jade in eastern Iran. The overwhelming majority consists of a conjugation of sword pommel, quillon, and scabbard slide types. They are associated with the development of the long iron sword (Trousdale 1975, p. [iv]) and are thought to have originated with a northern nomadic group, most likely the Yuezhi (Yüeh Chih; see KUSHAN DYNASTIES at *iranica.com*), who were well-established in China by the 5th century B.C.E. (Trousdale, 1975, pp. 110-13; and on early developments in China, Trousdale, 1975, pp. 11-70). Between the 2nd century B.C.E. and the 5th century C.E., this sword type and its associated accoutrements spread to West Asia and Europe in association with the dominance of the Kushans and their immediate predecessors and successors (Trousdale, 1969; 1975; 1988). These jade scabbard slides, quillons, and pommels are important, because they demonstrate the widespread employment of jade and its substitutes, and yet in the literature on non-Chinese jades they tend to be ignored as a phenomenon apart. The wearers of these swords and accoutrements would have been aware of jade's appropriateness for such mounts due to its great toughness. But, apart from its aesthetic appeal, jade's purported apotropaic properties (especially its ability to assure its wearer of victory in combat) would also explain part of its popularity among those who could afford it. Ralph Pinder-Wilson (in Pinder-Wilson and Watson, p. 19; 1976, p. 122—for his role in jade scholarship, see Skelton 1991, p. 369, n. 15) was the first to point out jade's reputation for such qualities, based on Biruni's statement (p. 198) that these properties were an important reason for the wearing of jade fittings by the "Turks." Extant scabbard slides of softer and more brittle stones (e.g., lapis lazuli, rock crystal), as well as wood, suggest that the toughness of jade was not an essential requirement for this function. A number of other types of jade fittings on the warrior and his horse would often accompany the weapon's mounts.

Two vessels found in Iran in the 20th century had seemed potentially very important for the history of ancient Iranian jades, though at this point neither object can be accepted as such. The first is a circular, flattish dish with a wide, flat rim, found near Shiraz at Qaṣr-e Abu Naṣr and preserved in the National Museum of Iran, Tehran (2.2 × 21.1 cm, inv. no. 2512). It may or may not be of jade; it has been described as jasper by both Upton (1934, p. 21 and fig. 27, showing the bottom) and Wilkinson (1965, p. 344 and figs. 19 and 20, illustrating both top and bottom; for color photo of top, see Curtis, 2005, p. 130 no. 147); the latter work characterizes it as of "dark speckled stone." The main basis for these authors' "Achaemenian" attribution is its alleged closeness to the stone vessels excavated in the Treasury at

Persepolis and elsewhere (for the Persepolis pieces, see Schmidt, 1957, pls. 59-61; cf. Wilkinson, 1965, p. 344). Although several of the Persepolis pieces exhibit a general similarity to the Qaṣr-e Abu Naṣr plate, none has in fact the same profile, and until careful measurements and a mineralogical examination are made available, the piece remains in limbo. While Melikian-Chirvani (1997/2000, p. 135) seems to be of two minds regarding the date when the vessel was made, research by the present contributor suggests that the Achaemenid attribution is unlikely to be correct and that the piece is probably of the 10th century. This will be taken up again below in connection with the discussion of the charger in the Cleveland Museum of Art (PLATE V).

The second vessel which has been put forward as an ancient Iranian jade is a small elliptical dish excavated at Susa (see SASANIAN SUSA at *iranica.com*), and exhibited for many years at the Louvre Museum (inv. no. Sb 3792; l. 82, w. 42, ht. 15 mm). Specialists have placed it in the Sasanian era between the 4th and 7th centuries—the later end of this range is most likely—and identified its material as jadeite. The dish belongs to a group of hardstone vessels of the same shape and identical or related decoration (for its early comparison to a similar rock crystal piece, see Christie's London, 5 July 1995, lot 118). While Melikian-Chirvani (1997/2000, pp. 135-36, figs. 1-2), suggests nephrite as its material, this contributor's personal examination (Paris, 30 June 2006) has revealed that the vessel was carved from bloodstone, a variety of fine, dark green cryptocrystalline quartz with red spots or larger blotches (sometimes termed heliotrope), which was a popular material for hardstone carvings in the ancient world. On the Louvre Museum piece, the spots are tiny, and so the confusion with jade is an understandable mistake. Despite the occasional superficial resemblance to jade, however, bloodstone is entirely different in composition, crystal structure, fracture, and aspect from both jadeite and nephrite. Moreover, before the 18th century, nephrite was the jade of the entire Old World, jadeite playing no part (excluding certain Neolithic instances of tools and weapons).

Thus the first of the two most famous objects claimed to be ancient Iranian jades is possibly not jade and was probably made in the medieval eastern Islamic world, and the second is not jade at all. But there are other ancient Iranian jades which are properly so characterized, in addition to the iron sword ensemble discussed above. The earliest hitherto published piece known to the author has been described as an edged-weapon pommel (Litvinskiy and Pichikiyan, p. 163 pl. XII; *Oxus*, no. 14). It was found in the Takht-i Sangin temple deposit on the right bank of the Oxus river (see ĀMU DARYĀ), near the site where the famous Oxus Treasure was found. Here, the head of a wolf or wolf-dragon is rendered in a highly abstract, Steppe art manner, and has inlay which apparently consists of lapis lazuli and glass (shell?). The piece is possibly from the 2nd century B.C.E.

Not much later, but very different in handling, is a dragon's head (Keene, 2004, pp. 196-97, fig. 1), putatively from Afghanistan. The subject embodies local and Steppe traditions, but, in contrast with the Takht-i Sangin piece, the artistic style is dominated by the anatomical verisimilitude brought to the area by the Greeks of the 4th to 2nd centuries B.C.E. (see GREECE. viii. GREEK ART IN CENTRAL ASIA, AFGHANISTAN, AND NORTHWEST INDIA). The Greek style (see esp. PLATE I) persisted for centuries, spreading, in one form or another over much of Asia, revolutionizing the arts from Syria to China, a phenomenon that will be further discussed below.

Another published ancient Iranian jade is a plaque incusely carved on both sides (Rtveladze). Although the object is not finely made (figs.1-3), its origin in modern-day Uzbekistan reinforces the likelihood of the concentration of the industry in the region from ancient times. One side shows a ruler's bust of the Bactrian Greek type, and the other the Bull-King Gopatshah. It has been placed "in North-Eastern Bactria at the juncture of the Yueh-chi and Early Kushan periods" (Rtveladze, p. 294), and dated between the 1st century B.C.E. and the 1st century C.E. (p. 299). This attribution is argued in great detail (using particularly numismatic evidence), and other early nephrite pieces found in Central Asia are cited in an excursus which forms part of Rtveladze's paper. He considers an uncharacterized item from Uzbekistan (Aibek Museum of the History of the Peoples of Uzbekistan, inv. no. 259/666) to date to the 1st millennium B.C.E. and regards it as "probably the earliest known article fashioned from nephrite to have been found in Central Asia" (p. 304). A seal from Fargāna has been attributed to the Achaemenid period (p. 305). A small bowl from Kirghizia is said to date from between the 2nd century B.C.E. and the 1st century C.E. (p. 305). A dagger quillon-block and jade scabbard slide, excavated together in the Samarqand region, belong to the sword type which was discussed above, and are dated between the 2nd and 1st centuries B.C.E. (p. 305).

iii. JADE CARVING, 4TH CENTURY B.C.E. TO 15TH CENTURY C.E.

The eleven ancient and medieval jades illustrated in the plates are representatives of a very large and expanding corpus of ancient and medieval Iranian jades. They are primarily discussed as works of art, but the ways in which they document the technological sophistication of the hardstone industries in Iran, and Iran's cultural interrelationships with neighbors and far-off contacts, are also examined.

Since the Al-Sabah Collection in Kuwait is the only center known to have systematically sought and secured West Asian jades, most of the illustrations and the ensuing discussion focus on pieces in this collection. In the legends, the order of measurements is height (ht.), width (w.), thickness (th.); weights are also given. Unless otherwise stated, the pieces in the Al-Sabah Collection have not been published before. Brief publication histories are provided for pieces not in the Al-Sabah Collection.

The figurine of a couchant hound bitch of a breed for hunting fierce prey such as lions (PLATE I) is the earliest

PLATE I

Figurine of a couchant hound bitch. Jade, highly translucent, zoned light russet to yellowish off-white: 9.0 × 17.7 × 6.7 cm, wt. 1200.0 gm. Probably Samarqand (from Samarqand according to a previous owner), 4th-3rd century B.C.E. Al-Sabah Collection, Kuwait, LNS 654 HS.

piece among the presently known ancient Iranian jades. This is a large piece of astounding quality, carved by a supreme artist thoroughly schooled in Greek art, but probably of the Samarqand region, or, possibly, of what is now northern Afghanistan or southern Tajikistan. The artistic quality embodied in the piece (including the mastery of anatomy and the rendering of detail) is unsurpassed in the finest of Hellenistic Greek marbles, indeed of Greek art generally; yet the artist was almost certainly a native Central Asian, as is shown by the treatment of the end of the tail and the extreme exaggeration of the vertebrae of the spine. Although such stylization of the spine was inspired by realistic Greek examples, the only parallels for what we see here are Chinese examples of later date and comparatively inferior quality. The only other possibility, that this was carved by a Greek artist, would entail the supposition that he was a longtime resident in Central Asia and schooled in Central and East Asian art, a much less plausible conjecture than the above. Aside from its beauty, this most impressive carving is of prime importance for the history of Asian art generally, ranking alongside the horses of the terracotta army uncovered in the tomb of the first Chinese emperor, Qin Shihuangdi (d. 210 B.C.E.). Like these horses, the jade piece demonstrates some of the earliest phases of the enormous and lasting but little-recognized influence of Greek art on that of China. It is evident that this influence in certain cases (notably that of the terracotta army) can only have been direct.

On the whole, Chinese art does not fundamentally evince a great interest in the literal appearance of things in this world. It is overwhelmingly expressionistic and visionary, brilliantly suggesting moods or materializing other worlds. There are Chinese objects, particularly renditions of animals, which embody wonderful observation and highly sophisticated training from long before the era of Classical Greece, yet nothing in earlier Chinese art presages the art of Shihuangdi's tomb. In general approach as well as with respect to a number of tell-tale motifs or preoccupations, this Qin art has earlier Greek models. Therefore, it is a reasonable conclusion that just as the artistic achievements of the Greeks—especially in the realm of realism—had spawned hybrid Greek-Steppe art schools in South Russia and Central Asia, this process, at least for a brief period, found a home as far north and east as the present-day Chinese province of Shanxi. Although the fall of the Qin dynasty in 207 B.C.E. seems to have marked the end of a strongly Greek art in China proper, the art of China was imprinted by the phenomenon in a myriad of ways and for millennia afterward. Seen within the context of the comparative study of Greek and Chinese art, the terracotta army, and especially the horses, document an intensive training in Greek traditions. These horses embody anatomical interest and knowledge that could not have originated outside the Greek school of art.

One specific element, which is highly characteristic of these horses, as well as of Tang ceramic horses and, to a lesser extent, of Han horse figures in various media, is a pronounced, stylized, bifurcated forelock which sweeps out from between the ears and around their bases on either side. This is also a feature of earlier Greek art, notably the "Satrap Sarcophagus" of the 5th century B.C.E. and the "Alexander Sarcophagus" of the last quarter of the 4th, both in the Archaeological Museum, Istanbul, and both from the Royal Necropolis of Sidon (inv. nos. 367 T and 370 T, respectively: for the Satrap Sarcophagus, cf. Hamdy and Reinach, pl. XX, Kleeman, pls. 2 and esp. 10; for the Alexander Sarcophagus, Hamdy and Reinach, pls. XXVII; Winter, pls. X-XI, XVII; Boardman, 1993, pp. 172-73 pls. 162A, XIII; Boardman, 1995, figs. 228.1-2; Jidejian, pls. on pp. 277, 279-80). The bifurcated forelock is also well represented on coinage from the 4th and 3rd century B.C.E. (e.g., Kraay, no. 874; Head, pl. 31, no. 21; and Parrot, pp. 210-11 pl. 231). In the Oxus region, representation of this type of forelock continued, and was probably the direct source of inspiration of its use for Tang horses. It seems that depiction of the bifurcated forelock died out during the Han period and thereafter was not present in Chinese art until the Tang. On the other hand, a very well-modeled stucco horse with the forelock in this fashion was excavated at Khalchayan (Pugachenkova, 1966, pl. XX; Pugachenkova and Rempel', p. 48 color pl.), and it appears again later at Varakhsha (Shishkin, fig. 104).

In line with their intense study of anatomy and its representation, as well as with the lessons learned from Pharaonic art, Greek artists rendered not only the hair, skin, and muscles of the creatures forming their subjects, but also their skeletal structure. Hundreds of extant sculptures show strongly rendered ribs, and there are examples of vertebrae taking a prominent, serially knobbed form. In the white jade bitch this has been taken to an intensified, stylized level, but it certainly started from Greek originals (e.g., the lion pair from the Nereid Monument at Xanthos, British Museum, inv. nos. BM Sc. 929-30; cf. Childs, pls. 156-58; Boardman, 1995, fig. 218.2). Large numbers of Chinese jade figurines of dogs and other animals, real and imagined, are modeled on this white jade bitch (considered as a type), though none is as early or as anatomically informed. A large percentage of these are most easily compared with the Sogdian original because of their highly stylized spines. But various pieces, especially the hound figurines, share other characteristics as well: the couchant position, often with crossed front feet; the general breed type; large paws with prominent claws, often sharply detailed; the treatment of the ears; the prominently modeled ribs; the curlicue tail, and so on. Uniquely comparable, though very decidedly inferior to the piece under discussion, is a carving that appeared recently in the art market (Tajan, 21 Nov. 2005, lot 143). That hound figurine should also be from Sogdiana, and probably was carved about a century or two later than our white jade one. The Tajan piece shows conclusively that our piece was not without descendants, which in turn form a bridge to the later Chinese tradition.

Of all the areas which had been influenced by Greek art, Sogdiana preserved the Classical and Hellenistic achievements for the longest duration, in terms of both finesse and the anatomical information incorporated in artworks. This situation even persisted during the early Islamic period. Further examples of classical-period Sogdian models for Chinese jade types could be cited, and Sogdiana served as a reservoir of classical knowledge of the rendering of anatomy when Samarqand was a Tang protectorate. Greek influence is recognizable in the sharp turn toward realism in Tang art generally, which in turn furnished important models for the Chinese art of later periods.

The sizable and powerfully expressive mare (PLATE II) is probably the only known example of a fully in the round rendition of the Steppe art subject of a contorted horse; she rolls on the ground and is twisted in multiple dimensions. What the piece reveals of artistic currents in early Central Asia makes it of extremely high interest for the history of art. As indicated, the subject was popular in Steppe art, and the artist was deeply steeped in this tradition. Large numbers of low-relief and two-dimensional Steppe art pieces are known in which a sinuous bodied animal, most commonly a horse, is seen in side view, with the fore- and hindquarters twisted with respect to each other by a full 180°. This kind of stylization reflects an ingrained tendency in Steppe art; for example, there is the early tradition of a quadruped whose serpentine body forms a circle, with the head ending up behind the rump. And the present piece also has descendants in Chinese jades; noteworthy is a horse performing a similar type of trick, but carved centuries later and devoid of the expressive power, the anatomical interest, and the art-historical importance of our mare (Sotheby's Hong Kong 23 Oct., 2005, lot 17, attributed to the Ming period). Its knobby spine also represents the heritage in Chinese art from pieces such as the jade bitch (PLATE I).

A contorted horse in Steppe art is typically executed in low relief or two dimensions, and the existence and character of this subject's three-dimensional version indicates the impact of Classical tradition. A number of general and individual features further testify to the strength of this impact: these include the spatial conceptualization and general full-roundness, and details such as the eyes, the teeth, the tongue, and the bottoms of the hooves. On the other hand, this plastically conceived horse exhibits a pervasive stylization; but despite the fact that the artist took liberties with the animal (especially the rubbery insect-like legs and the hippopotamus-like head), the mare's position is still a possible one. The figurine betrays an intimate knowledge of the behavior of the horse, which, among large ungulates, is especially fond of rolling on the ground, and even of contortion. The subject was sure to have wide appeal at the time, and the fact that the fore- and hindquarters are only torqued by 90° with respect to each other—a feat which poses no problem even for human beings—probably enhanced this appeal. Still, it is the artistic value that impresses most about this piece, and its inventiveness and expressionism are especially remarkable. The compositional and representational elements are cleverly found within the boulder, which is fully exploited to create the levels and internal details, while the orchestration of all elements convey the subject's frenzy.

PLATE II

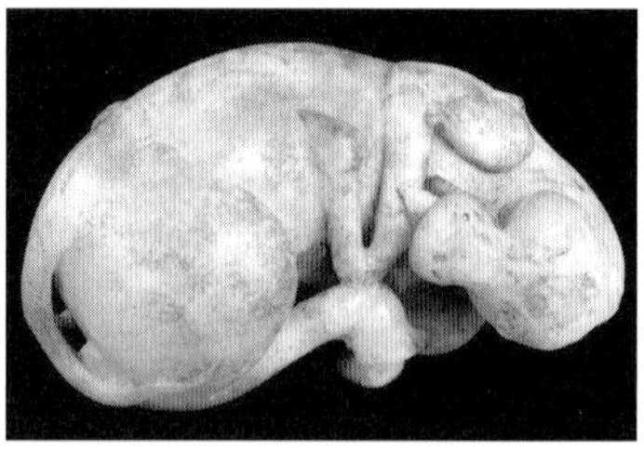

Figurine of a rolling mare. Hard and tough jade simulant (unidentified), slightly off-white with minor areas more grayish and translucent, some small areas of iron stain, but all the brown, tan and black consists of surface accretions: 8.0 × 14.8 × 9.2 cm, wt. 1230.0 gm. Central Asia, perhaps Ferghana or Khotan (from Khotan according to a previous owner), probably 2nd-1st century B.C.E. Al-Sabah Collection, Kuwait, LNS 816 HS.

The figurine is slightly off-white, with superficial dark accretions. The stone is not jade, though it is of a very similar appearance, and the material has not yet been identified. It is almost as hard as nephrite, and there are various indications that its toughness is comparable with jade as well. The material exhibits tiny sparkling points, and microscope observation reveals in the stone large, elongated blocky structures, presumably some sort of crystals. Since these two features do not accord with jade as it is known up to now, only examination by a mineralogist will resolve the issue.

The figurine of a warrior, mounted on a lion (PLATE III), is not among the finest Central Asian jades that were

PLATE III

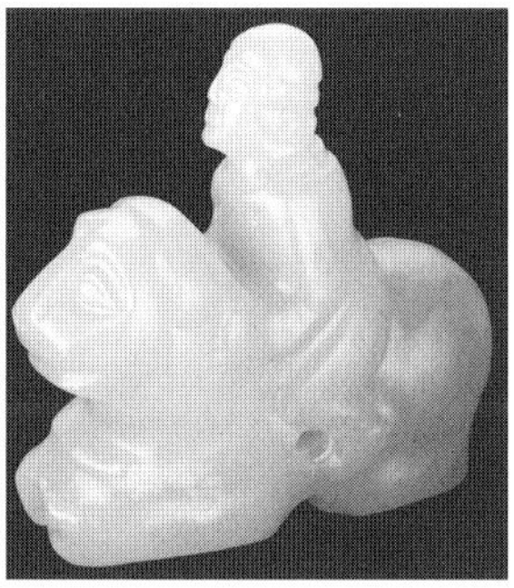

Figurine of a helmeted man riding a lion. Jade, translucent, light grayish green with a darker area at the back: 4.9 × 5.0 × 2.3 cm, wt. 71.8 gm. Oxus region (from Balkh according to an associate of a previous owner), ca. 7th-8th century C.E. Al-Sabah Collection, Kuwait, LNS 3988 J.

produced shortly before the Islamic conquest. Yet the piece is of great interest on several counts. The subject of a helmeted man riding a lion is highly unusual, and supports its attribution to the Oxus region. The iconography of Nana astride a lion was a standard image in the area's art, and appears, for example, in a mural at Panjikant (q.v. at *iranica.com*), dated to the 8th century C.E. (Azarpay, p. 68, fig. 32). Literature attests that lions raised their young in the thickets along the Oxus river system, and that they were often captured young and tamed (Rossabi, 1983, pp. 55-56). In 628 C.E., a tame lion was sent from Samarqand to the Chinese court (Juliano in Juliano, p. 325) The Samanid ruler Aḥmad b. Esmāʿil (r. 907-14) is reported to have had a lion guarding his door as he slept (Naršaḵi, pp. 94-95). In 1413, the Chinese court is documented as having received lions as part of the "tribute payments" of Samarqand and Herat (Rossabi, 1976, p. 30). That the practice of depicting humans with tame lions at the leash goes back to ancient times in Central Asia is documented by the fragment of a rhyton from Nisa. This is in repoussé-worked silver, and dated to the 2nd century C.E. (Pugachenkova, 1986, p. 106, upper illus.).

The artistic style and indications of costume are most convincing for the figurine's placement. Domical caps and helmets (see HELMET) were common in the region in the period in question. The rider's helmet has an apparently quilted neck defense, and this headgear is close in form to the known examples from the period, both extant and recorded in depictions. A number of preserved helmets, attributed to the Sasanian period, are of this general form, while depictions in Central Asian paintings of the first several centuries C.E. provide close analogues. Tall conical and rounded helmets, many with suspended mail to protect the neck—and often the shoulders and face as well—abound in the murals of Panjikant (Azarpay, figs. 43-45 and pl. 4). Caps similar in form to that in the jade carving also appear frequently; some include a cloth element that is suspended down the back of the neck, in the manner of the jade figurine (Azarpay, fig. 43, note the far left figure, lower register, right panel, and pl. 8).

Three other jade lion figurines in a similar style are in the Al-Sabah Collection, and these are also putatively from Central Asia. Taken together, these four pieces suggest the existence of a particular school of jade carving in the Oxus region, immediately before the period of the Islamic conquest. They deal with subjects and stories current in the area at the time, and are unlikely to be the products of a princely atelier. The presence of the transverse hole in our figurine suggests that the piece was threaded on a cord or leather strip, perhaps as part of a fob, securing a purse or other necessary item suspended on a sash or belt.

PLATE IV

Bowl with everted lip and ring foot. Jade, white with greenish undertones, of variegated translucency: ht. 6.5, diam. 16.0 cm, wt. 196.6 gm. Probably Samarqand (from Central Asia according to a previous owner), probably 9th century Al-Sabah Collection, Kuwait, LNS 721 HS.

The form of this fine, thin bowl of translucent white jade with greenish undertones (PLATE IV) is a close analogue with one of the most popular shapes of Islamic ceramics between the 8th and 10th centuries. These Islamic vessels include the prestigious Mesopotamian types of ceramics covered with opaque white glazes, among which are the following: undecorated; with cobalt blue overglaze-painted decoration; and monochrome and polychrome overglaze luster-painted wares. Unfortunately, a great deal of uncertainty surrounds the dating and placement of most types of plain jade vessels, particularly of simple bowls. Far too little attention has been paid to careful study of matters related to forms, and far too much weight has been given to Chinese manufacture in general, and the Qing period (1644-1911/1912) in particular. But poems of the great Qing emperor and jade connoisseur Qianlong testify that exceptionally fine jade bowls were made to the west of China, and that many of these were in his collection.

The prevailing conventional wisdom is that because early Chinese porcelains enjoyed an unrivalled status, they inspired both the use of the white glaze and the form of the wares in the Islamic world. While this is surely true for the white glaze, much work remains to be done on comparative dating and careful study of form, in conjunction with the best evidence for the dating of shape evolution, both Chinese and Islamic. It is intriguing that pottery of essentially this form was made in the Oxus region in the centuries on either side of the B.C.E./C.E. divide (Pugachenkova, 1966, figs. 11, 17, 19, 33, 40 and 53; 1978, fig. 56, left). This evidence could significantly neutralize the mystique built around the bowl's shape in the literature on Islamic ceramics.

The most likely place of manufacture of this elegant, masterfully cut bowl is Samarqand, particularly in light of its status as an ancient lapidary center, including its fame at the Chinese court in the period as a source of worthy hardstone objects (cf. Schafer, pp. 226-28; Teng 1983, p. 77 and n. 22-23 on p. 106; Pinder-Wilson, 1992, p. 36).

PLATE V

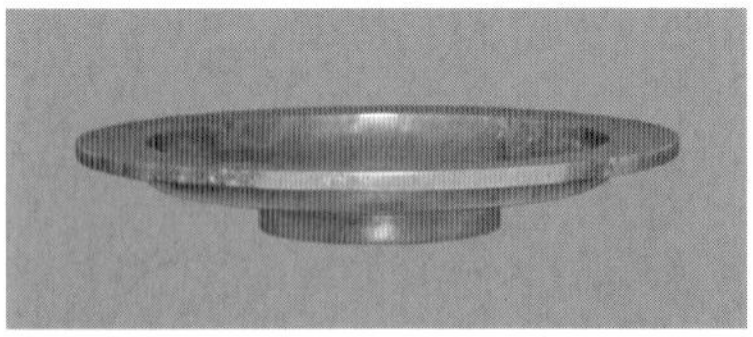

Large platter with flattish rim and ring foot. Jade, middle green with blackish veins and patches: ht. 6.5, diam. 41.0 cm, wt. 4200.0 gm. Probably Samarqand (no putative origin available), 10th century Cleveland Museum of Art, Cleveland, Ohio, USA, inv. no. 1976.73, reproduced by permission. *Publ.*: Lee, fig. 163; Markel, fig. 1.

The magnificent large platter of dark green jade (PLATE V) in the Cleveland Museum of Art has generally been taken to be of Mughal Indian manufacture (see INDIA v-vi). Until recently it was generally accepted in the Islamic art-historical literature that jade was not carved in West and South Asia before the 15th century; and since this piece did not fit in well with the known Iranian or Turkish corpus, India seemed the obvious candidate. S. E. Lee (p. 42, fig. 163) identified the vessel as Mughal Indian, and dated it to the 17th century. S. Markel (pp. 52, 54, fig. 1) essentially followed Lee, though he placed it approximately in the last quarter of the 16th century. Markel (pp. 52 and 54, fig. 4) argued for his attribution by citing dark green vessels depicted in Mughal miniatures, and analogies with Chinese porcelain of generally related form. But it is not certain that the depicted dark vessels are jade, and, even more importantly, their shapes do no relate them usefully to this piece. Markel's suggestion of possible inspiration from Chinese porcelains, generally of the earlier 15th century and decorated with cobalt-blue painting, has also been considered. The present author has taken detailed measurements of such a Chinese piece in the Al-Sabah Collection (inv. no. LNS 769 C; cf. Watson, no. W.1). These measurements show that the shape cannot be used to support the attribution of the Cleveland jade. Moreover, such porcelains would have been in the collections of every prince and sovereign in the central and eastern Islamic world. The drift of Markel's argument for the Cleveland charger could, for example, have led him to attribute it to Ottoman Turkey, which is also known to have had a long-lasting jade-cutting industry, as well as a thriving production of ceramics of generally similar form to the cited Chinese porcelains. Still, this proposition of possible Ottoman origin cannot be entertained for a variety of reasons, which are beyond the scope of this survey.

The jade platter does, however, have such precise, interrelated and very carefully executed proportions that any really close parallel in ceramics would make a strong argument; in such a case, the suggestion that the jade and ceramics would have been made in the same milieu must be taken seriously. Uniquely, Samanid ceramic types of the 10th century do show close shape analogies with this grand dish. A simple visual comparison already shows that the shape is identical, and no other vessels, in ceramics or otherwise, can provide so close an analogy. The author's personal examination of the Cleveland jade has furthermore made possible the conclusion that certain members of this class of Samanid ceramics hew uncannily close to the charger's proportions and ratios. They have not only the exact shape, but also the exact same proportional relationship between the whole and the parts, specifically the overall diameter, the foot diameter, and the rim width.

The high level of planning and control in execution embodied in the jade piece allows the demonstration of its remarkably close relationship with the Samanid ceramics in question. The vessel features a wide, near-flat rim, a well that plunges sharply downward and then inward in a quarter-arc, and afterwards continuously increases the diameter of the arc to a near-flat center. It has an assertive, sharp, relatively high foot-ring. The author's drawings and calculations on the basis of his measurements show that this piece embodies an extraordinary set of extremely close and quite intriguing proportional consonances. On the top surface, the width of the rim is 1/10 of the overall diameter; and two incised, linear grooves around the rim are each 0.4 cm from the rim edge which it parallels, which is 1/10 of the width of the rim itself. On the bottom surface, the lip width, like that of the top, is 1/10 of the overall diameter; the diameter of the belly from the point at which it drops sharply from the underside of the rim is 4/5 (8/10) of the overall diameter; the outside diameter of the footring is 2/5 resp. 4/10 of the overall diameter; and the thickness of the footring at its edge is 1/2 of its height. The closest shape parallels possible are to be found in some pieces of the Samanid pottery excavated at Nishapur. The correspondences between the jade charger and one plate in particular among the Nishapur ceramics (Wilkinson, 1973, no. 5:36) are identical. Working from the platter's published photos (Wilkinson, 1973, p. 175 top and bottom views; profile drawing p. 167), the author calculated that it embodies the same mathematical ratios. Specifically, the plate's belly is 4/5 resp. 8/10 of the diameter of the piece, leaving the width of the rim 1/10 of that overall diameter; and the outside diameter of the footring is .40 or 2/5 of the overall diameter. It is also noteworthy that the excavations at Varakhsha again unearthed a model distinctly similar in form to the Samanid dishes (Shishkin, fig. 63, top).

The size and perfection of the Cleveland jade, in conjunction with the above comparisons, strongly suggest that in the 10th century the Samanids supported a developed and sophisticated jade-carving industry, even though specialists of both Islamic and Chinese art may find this difficult to accept. But this attribution is further supported by the prolific and sophisticated hardstone industry that is attested in eastern Iran, specifically Nishapur, for the early Islamic period (Keene, 1981). The very first pre-Timurid Islamic jade to be published came from the excavations at Nishapur (Keene in Jenkins and Keene, no. 12). Furthermore, the region, as mentioned above, was almost certainly the main west Asian jade-working area in both ancient and Islamic times, with Samarqand and Balkh as probably its greatest centers. The already discussed jades, notably the white jade bitch (PLATE I) show that this industry was of long standing and of the highest order of sophistication, technically and artistically. Large jade objects of the first centuries after the Islamic conquest are mentioned in the contemporary literary sources; with regard to the early Islamic lapidary establishments in general, pieces such as the huge rock crystal vase with a Kufic inscription in the Treasury of St. Mark's Cathedral (Alcouffe in *Trésor*, no. 37), attest to their high sophistication and technical capabilities.

Three other very large jade platters (two of them approximately one-and-one-half times the size of the Cleveland example) in the National Palace Museum, Beijing, are clearly representatives of the same school which produced the Cleveland piece (Teng, 2004, pp. 41-43, pls. 44-46). To judge from the illustrations, the closest piece is that in fig. 44; and measurements from the photo and calculations based thereon indicate, again, that the rim width is 1/10, and the well diameter 8/10, of the overall diameter. Teng draws the parallel between these pieces and the Cleveland platter (p. 41), and she refers to Qianlong's own stated opinion that the likes of these had been passed down for generations in Central Asia, concluding: "From what we know of the three pieces . . . it is probably safe to assume that the plate in the Cleveland Museum was also used by the ancestors of the Mughal emperors in the Central Asian plains" (p. 41).

The Qaṣr-e Abu Naṣr dish (discussed above under "Pre-Islamic Iranian Jades") seems to be more at home with the present piece than in the Achaemenian context which has been proposed for it, and calculations made from its illustrations reveal a similar concern for mathematical ratios. The fact that, among other indications, the diameter of the base is 3/4 that of the dish overall reveals a similar concern with ratios internal to the piece.

The fine seal ring (PLATE VI), made from a single piece of white jade (i.e., hololithic) is inscribed with the name Moḥammad b. ʿAbd-al-ʿAziz. Such rings have been Near Eastern luxury accoutrements since Pharaonic times. "Hololithic" rings were made not only of hardstones such as carnelian, agate and rock crystal, but also of soft stones and other materials such as shell, horn, faience, and glass, for those who could not afford one cut from semiprecious stones harder than steel. Due to its toughness, jade is the most perfect of the available choices for hololithic finger rings, and the indications are that they were made in the thousands, especially in the eastern parts of the Islamic world. The majority of the known examples were inscribed in reverse, on the top of their bezel, to serve as seal rings, and normally the style of the inscription's calligraphy is extremely helpful in determining place and date of manufacture. Another very useful tool for dating is comparison of hololithic rings' form with those executed in metal, mostly gold, silver, and various copper alloys (bronze, brass). Surviving rings of metal exist in much greater numbers, and are very frequently shaped or decorated in styles which can be attributed with some accuracy.

PLATE VI

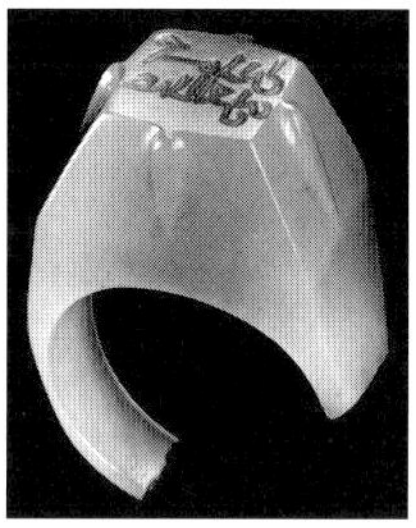

Hololithic finger seal-ring, fragmentary. Jade, translucent white, with four "claws," double-line of mirror-reversed *nasḵ* inscription reading "Moḥammad b. ʿAbd-al-ʿAziz": 3.0 × 2.2 × 1.1 cm, wt. 6.5 gm. Probably northern Afghanistan (from Herat according to a previous owner), ca. 11th century Al-Sabah Collection, Kuwait, LNS 2698 J.

This jade ring exhibits two features that are frequently encountered in finger rings from eastern Iran. The first is a marked fondness for very high bezels, which is often much more radically expressed than here. The second feature is the use of wedge-shaped "claws" on the upper bezel, the original purpose of which was to keep a set stone in place. In hololithic rings such as this one, the non-functional "claws" are, of course, a visual pun, but such non-functional claws were popular as part of the form and decoration not only of hololithic rings but of cast metal rings without stones as well.

The pear-shaped belt-fitting (PLATE VII) is made of translucent jade with a pale, grayish green hue. Belt-fittings were among the objects most commonly made of jade: the stone's toughness guaranteed the fitting's serviceability in the rugged life of the cavalier, while jade's putative status as the "victory stone" further insured its popularity (Keene, 2004, p. 208 n. 5).

PLATE VII

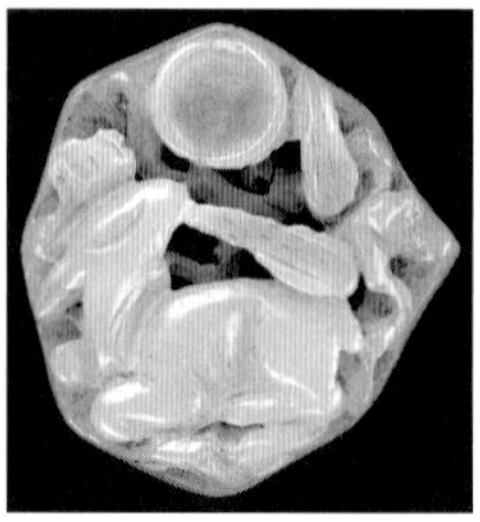

Belt fitting. Jade, translucent, pale grayish green, diagonal connecting holes in the back for attachment: 3.0 × 2.9 × 0.8 cm, wt. 7.8 gm. Probably Balkh region (from Balkh according to a previous owner), 13th-14th century, Al-Sabah Collection, Kuwait, LNS 377 HS.

On the basis of stylistic criteria, the belt-fitting can be dated to the 13th or 14th century, when the Mongol dynasty of the Il-khanids (q.v.) dominated the region. The Il-khanid style was heavily influenced by that of the Liao of northern China, and that influence is reflected here. The fitting's imagery draws on the iconography of the backward-looking hare that the Mongols inherited from Chinese symbolism (for the pre-Tang Chinese tradition of associating the hare with the moon, see Rawson, p. 335). The story of the hare whose image is put on the moon because he was willing to sacrifice himself as food when King Shakra had appeared in the disguise of a beggar (Beal, pp. 59-60) belongs to the Buddhist narrative tradition. A Chinese jade, dated to the 12th or 13th century (Rawson, no. 25:11) shows closely related imagery: a hare, amidst lingzhi fungi, is looking at the moon. The two jades constitute yet another piece of evidence for a trans-Asian artistic sharing, which is particularly well documented in Eastern Iranian jades. During the Mongol period, however, this phenomenon is less surprising than in earlier times, when it is also evidenced.

The thick-walled hemispherical vessel (PLATE VIII), which is missing its lid and precious-metal interior lining, is made of waxy middle-green jade, and retains some of its gold inlay. The piece is of great art-historical importance, because it is the earliest precious-metal-inlaid hardstone object known. In the Islamic tradition of inlaid hardstones, as well as in the Islamic tradition of precious-metal inlay in objects of copper alloy, the inlay is mechanically locked in place by forcing the precious metal into grooves, undercuts, and sometimes drilled holes in the areas excavated in the substrate. Most of the linear inlay in Iranian jades—on this vessel as well as the subsequently discussed examples of inlaid jade—exhibits a concave V-shaped cross-section, imparted by the presumably V-shaped tool used to force the inlay down into the recesses prepared by wheel-cutting.

This vessel was presented as an Ottoman object in two auction sales (Christie's London 24 April 1990, lot 366; Christie's London 25 April 1997, lot 316), even though it exhibits no close parallels with any artifact known to be Ottoman. Its decoration, in fact, places it squarely in the decorative tradition that derived from the highly creative schools of art of the Ghaznavids. The author's very comprehensive collection of comparative material, which strongly supports the Ghaznavid attribution, can in this context only be summarized (see the introductory paragraphs preceding the Bibliography below).

PLATE VIII

Hemispherical vessel with solid, slightly splayed foot. Jade, waxy middle green with blackish areas and vuggy voids, inlaid with gold, though only seven tiny preserved segments have been observed: ht. 5.1, diam. 7.7 cm, wt. 232.5 gm. Eastern Iranian world, perhaps Ghazni (no putative origin available), 12th century, Al-Sabah Collection, Kuwait, LNS 249 HS. *Publ.*: Christie's London, 24 April 1990, lot 366; Christie's London 25 April 1997, lot 316; Melikian-Chirvani, 2000, pp. 146-48, figs. 10-11; Keene, 2001, figs. 11-12. *Exhibited: Treasury of the World*, suppl. material to sec. 2, no. S2.1.

The gold inlay was intentionally removed in ancient times, as is revealed by microscopic examination: the recesses cut to hold the inlay are filled with the dark accretions of the ages, but seven tiny remaining bits of gold have been observed under these accretions (Keene, 2001, p. 5 and figs. 11-12, the latter a photomicrograph of one remaining bit of inlay). The vessel's inlay was definitely not set with precious stones, as has been asserted repeatedly (both auction catalogues cited above; Melikian-Chirvani, 1997/2000, p. 147). The setting of stones into the inlay of hardstones is a 15th century Timurid development, and in any case it would have been physically impossible for this piece, as study of the cut recesses shows.

This piece's decoration is unique with regard to its position in developments that ultimately led to the highly influential Timurid classical type of arabesque, while at the same time being of a singularly particular nature. It constitutes an important early monument in this line of development, and it cannot, for a variety of reasons, be made to fit in with the decoration of the Timurid School or its descendants in Iran, Turkey, and India. It belongs, rather, to an early, inventive, and formative stage, full of features that were to prove fundamental for much of what was to come in later centuries. The creation of overlapping compartments of arch-like aspect, filled with arabesque designs, and featuring "hipped," or "lump-jawed" half-palmettes, appears in scores of examples of the carved-marble dado panels from the Palace of Masʿud III (r. 1099-1115), which was built at Ghazni (q.v.), in the second decade of the 12th century (e.g., Bombaci, 1966, pls. V.6, VI.8, IX.12-13, X.14-15, XII.18-19, XIII.20-21, XXXIX.137-39, XL.140-41, XLI.142).

The design of one panel not among those unearthed in the official archeological excavations of the palace but very much of the same suite (in the Kabul museum—see Bombaci, pl. XLI.142), is composed in a way which is especially close to our jade piece. Like the rest of the panels from the palace, from which it must also have come, it has the running repetition of trefoil arches that interweave with ogival networks of split-leaf resp. split-palmette arabesques. In this panel, however, the upper, undulating segment of the vines has a prominence and visual aspect that is particularly reminiscent of the same feature on the jade. The similarity between this panel and the vessel is further strengthened by the resolutely round form of the ends of split-leaf lobes. On this and the other panels from Masʿud's palace, the skeletal structure of the design consists of a running trefoil arch system, current in Iran at the time, and overlaid on another widely evidenced running design of counterchanging heart-shaped compartments.

This earliest known example of inlaid jade was unquestionably made in eastern Iran in the 12th century. It is worth noting that it was in this same historical and regional context that the inlaying of copper-alloy objects was enjoying an efflorescence. According to contemporary literary evidence (Melikian-Chirvani, 1997/2000, p. 129) jade was even used in the decoration of a Ghaznavid palace, this time built for Amir Yusof, brother of Maḥmud (r. 998-1030); and in light of the discussed parallels in the relief-carved marbles of Masʿud III's palace, there is a distinct possibility that our vessel was made there as well.

PLATE IX

Squat jug with handle and ring foot. Jade, variegated darkish green, inlaid with gold: ht. 9.2, max. w. 10.9, diam. belly 10.2 cm, wt. 489.2 gm. Probably Samarqand (no putative origin available), late 13th-3rd quarter 14th century, Freer Gallery of Art, Smithsonian Institution, Washington, D.C., Purchase, inv. no. F1955.7, reproduced by permission. *Publ.*: Atil, 1973, no. 25; Skelton, 1978, fig. 3.

The small jug (PLATE IX) is made from darkish green jade and inlaid with gold. The author places its origin in Central Asia in the period leading up to the rise of the Timurid dynasty (1370-1507). This jade is preserved in the Freer Gallery, and the museum's official attribution, as well as the piece's previous publication, place its manufacture in early Ottoman Turkey. It would seem that the Ottoman attribution has persisted, unchallenged, due to insufficiencies in both the study of arabesque development and of observation and understanding of technical matters.

Robert Skelton in particular has argued the case for the vessel's Ottoman context. He states (1978, p. 796) that its excavated areas are solidly and completely filled, so that the gold inlay is flush with the surface of the jade. This description indeed fits one of two main types of Ottoman hardstone gold inlay, although this had some precedence in Timurid and earlier inlay in steel (e.g., Melikian-Chirvani, 1976, fig. 3; and several 12th century knife blades in the Al-Sabah Collection). This flush style of inlay was also used for hardstones in India, especially in certain fine pieces of the reign of Shah Jahan (r. 1628-57). But the author's personal examination (Washington, D.C., 2 July 2002) has revealed that this type of gold inlay is not present in the Freer jug.

The jug's inlay is far from flush with the surface; it is composed of gold so thin that it may best be characterized as foil. The inlay's general technical nature (as well as aspects of its design) places it in the same east Iranian tradition as the previous vessel (PLATE VIII) and presages the classic Timurid inlay of the 15th century, the character of which has been summarized above. Close observation of such inlay reveals the undercuts at the sides of the excavated areas and, occasionally, (e.g., the probably Ghaznavid vessel just mentioned) drilled holes. Both undercuts and holes are measures to lock the inlay in place. In these earlier pieces, the central area of each excavated mass has a kind of gabled profile, the center being higher than the edges. In none of the work in this tradition, including the later Timurid and Safavid material, does the inlay actually lie flush and smooth with the surface.

Architectural decoration again provides helpful comparisons for the context from which the Freer jug must issue. The Sogdian school of architecture of the 14th century exhibits in its tilework numerous examples of the kind of arabesque that covers the jug's body, in which overlapping systems of scrolls and compartments form a maze and carry half-palmettes, often straddled by elaborated crescent-like brackets. Among the closest comparisons is the field of the third stage of the cenotaph of Qoṯām b. ʿAbbās (Golombek and Wilber, I, p. 235; for illustrations, see Pugachenkova, 1959, pl. [20]; Voronina, pl. 74; Chuvin, pl. 544). Qoṯām, whose tomb formed the nucleus around which the Shāh-e Zenda complex at Samarqand developed, died in 677 C.E. The cenotaph bears an inscription identifying the interred and giving the year of his death, but none dating its manufacture. Golombek and Wilber refer to this as the "original" cenotaph, just as they refer to the present *ziārat-ḵāna* as the "original mausoleum." The latter is dated 735/1334-35 in a tile band at the top of the wall, and Golombek and Wilber seem to imply that the two are of the same date. The cenotaph's decorative and technical features make this a distinct possibility.

The neck of the jug is encircled by a three-filament half-palmette plait. This motif does appear in Ottoman art, and this may have influenced the previous attributions to Ottoman Turkey. At first glance, the motif on the neck of a similarly shaped silver jug preserved in the Victoria and Albert Museum, London (Atil, 1987, no. 51) might be taken as the same as that on the Freer jug, but closer examination reveals that they are in fact fundamentally different in structure. The scroll on the silver jug is actually a one-filament scroll, with complex curling side-branches that bear half-palmettes, giving the illusion of more than one main filament. Although the three-filament half-palmette scroll does indeed occur to the west of Iran, including Anatolia, as early as the 13th century, it originated and developed earlier in eastern Iran. Of course, multi-element plaits *per se*, often with a great number of filaments, were widespread in the ancient world long before and during the Classical period. In eastern Iran, the plain three-filament plait was certainly in vogue in the 11th century, and probably in the 10th (cf. the interlace around the middle of a pair of unpublished copper-alloy vases, Al-Sabah Collection, LNS 966 M). The fashion continued into the late 12th to early 13th century, and can be observed on east Iranian silver-inlaid bronzes of this period. The most important early occurrence of plaits composed of vines bearing half-palmettes is in the borders of practically all the already mentioned marble dado panels from the palace of Masʿud III in Ghazni (Bombaci); but in these panels, the half-palmette scrolls are based on a two- and not a three-filament plait.

Thus, all the elements for the three-filament half-palmette scroll were present in eastern Iran, and those which are very close in structure and appearance to the scroll on the Freer jug are found in the already mentioned school of 14th-century Sogdian architectural decoration. They are to be seen in the narrow horizontal borders of colonnettes at the corners of the entrance blocks of two mausolea in the above mentioned Shāh-e Zenda burial complex. The earliest of these is popularly known as Qotluq Āqā (thus ascribing it to one of the wives of Timur, though this is not supported by any reliable record; Hill and Grabar, fig. 89). This mausoleum is dated 13 Ṣafar 762/23 December 1360 (the date is given as 12 December 1361 in Golombek and Wilber, I, p. 237). The second mausoleum, that of Shad-e Molk Āqā, was built in 1371 or shortly thereafter (Cohn-Wiener, pls. XXVI, XXIX-XXX; Knobloch, pl. 70; Golombek and Wilber, I, p. 237, II, pl. 22; Chuvin and Degeorge, p. 53; Degeorge and Porter, 2002, pp. 112 and 114). The same close similarity to the scroll on the Freer jug is also to be seen in a horizontal band encircling a 14th century wooden column in the Baghbanly Mosque at Khiva (Pugachenkova, 1981, pl. 160; the date is wrongly published as 15th century). A cup in the Topkapi Museum (Rogers and Köseoglu, cat. 62) shows that this type of scroll was applied to Timurid inlaid jades; the original Timurid borders around the foot-ring and the lip take the form of this motif, while the side-walls have subsequently been inlaid and set with stones in the typical Ottoman salient technique and style, with many examples from the 16th century onward. The practice of "adorning" earlier objects in the Ottoman Imperial collections in this fashion is attested in multitudes of objects, including Chinese porcelains (e.g., Rogers and Köseoglu, cat. 63-64, 67; Atil, 1987, cat. 68-69, pp. 135-36).

The shape of the Freer jug can be seen as an ancestor of all the Timurid, Safavid, and Ottoman examples, but the whole series must in fact rely on silver and pottery jugs that were made between the 9th and early 11th centuries. An early group of these are earthenware jugs, mostly unglazed, which were excavated at Nishapur and dated to the 9th century (Wilkinson, 1973, cat. nos. 7.15-16, esp. 12.12, 12.15). Silver vessels with a similar shape—in this case a spheroidal body with a neck which begins cylindrically and then flares at the lip, but without a handle—appear in the Tang period (Thorp, fig. 76). A hoard found near Hamadān included an Islamic silver vessel essentially of the shape of the jade examples. This piece is dated to the beginning of the 11th century and thought to be of west Iranian manufacture (Allan, fig. 1, left; for the comparison with a 10th century glazed jug from Samarqand, see Raby, p. 186, fig. 18). It is not clear that this silver jug and the Samanid pottery are derived from Chinese models such as the Tang silver vase. It is noteworthy that certain of the pottery pieces cited for their similarity in shape to the Freer jug, as well as an analogous relief-cut rock crystal cup excavated at Samarqand and made in the 9th or 10th century (see Chuvin, pl. 495, but disregard the mistaken description as "verre soufflé, décor taillé"), have a molding at the base of the neck. Such a molding is a standard feature of the Timurid jade pieces of this form, although it is absent from the Freer jug. Finally, one should note here that a further question is raised by a bronze vessel (British Museum, inv. no. ANE 136355; cf. Curtis, 1977) whose form is identical to the Tang silver vessel. This bronze dates to the 9th or 8th century B.C.E. and is attributed to western Iran. It has a semicircular bail handle, and engraved figures in Assyrian-style dress just under the rim. Due to the shape analogy, including the molding at the base of the neck, it poses the question whether the shape enjoyed a continued existence over the one-and-a-half millennia involved.

The gold-inlaid slab pendant of darkish, middle-green jade (PLATE X) incorporates, as part of the original inlay, the date 868/1463-64, and so, in contrast to the already discussed jade vessels with gold inlay (PLATES VIII-IX), there is no room for argument about the date of manufacture. Thus, the piece provides a fixed point of reference for other jades, inlaid and otherwise, which share features embodied in it. Yet, the pendant's significance is far from having been widely understood and exploited by scholars.

While the pendant type descends from certain 11th-12th century Islamic jade examples, lobed escutcheon-shaped slab pendants of the present type are characteristic for Iran and India between the 14th and 16th centuries. These are not normally inlaid but variously decorated by incuse carving, featuring vegetal motifs that are at times supplemented by inscriptions. Their decoration often also includes the outline of other pendants or necklace elements of the general type, and this curious feature is also present on this inlaid pendant.

PLATE X

Pendant. Jade, translucent, darkish middle green, inlaid with gold, *nask* inscription of Qur'ān 68:51-52: 6.4 × 7.9 × 0.3 cm, wt. 35.0 gm. East Iranian world (no putative origin available), dated 868/1463-64. Al-Sabah Collection, Kuwait, LNS 205 HS. *Publ.*: Christie's London, 19 October 1993, lot 355. *Exhibited: Treasury of the World*, suppl. material to sec. 2, no. S2.2.

The piece's inlay—like that of the other inlaid pieces here (PLATES VIII-IX)—descends from its edge toward the center of the inlaid area, and the linear elements finish in a V-shaped cross-section. But the centers of the flowers are raised in a manner reminiscent of jades and other luxury objects of the Timurid school, in which the inlay is scooped downward and lifted up and over to form a setting for small gemstones (Pope, VI, pl. 1428D; Lentz and Lowry, 1989, no. 121; *Anatolian Civilizations*, no. E.87; Atil, 1987, pp. 141-42; no. 77).

Another hardstone, which is dated by association, displays a second and more well-known style of Timurid gold inlay. Melikian-Chirvani (1976, fig. 1; cf. Lentz and Lowry, 1989, p. 353, footnote of no. 121) has identified this as jade. Yet it is in fact a translucent, colorless chalcedony (which has also been called agate, despite the absence of contrasting colors forming patterns; Laking, no. 1414). This example forms the hilt of a dagger that is dated in an inscription on the blade. There is little reason to doubt that blade and hilt are original to each other, though a gem-set collar was added around the hilt's lower end in the late 19th or early 20th century. In addition to the already discussed incuse V-section inlay, this hilt features nearly flush-set inlaid split-palmettes with relief introduced in the form of tiny volutes cut as interior details, a style that is much associated with Timurid hardstone inlay.

The superb belt-fitting entirely composed of a contorted, writhing five-toed dragon (PLATE XI) is unique in the published corpus of Iranian jades. Executed in multilevel open-work from pure translucent white jade, it belongs to the early, highly sinicizing phase of Timurid art, which provides many parallels, especially in drawings and paintings. This belt-fitting would conventionally be taken as of the Ming period, but careful study of its features and manner of execution shows that it does not belong with the known Chinese pieces of any period. Of course, in a general sense, the dragon is of Chinese type in essentially all its disposition, composition, and general details, and quite close typological parallels for this fitting occur in Chinese jades *per se*, including examples roughly contemporary with the Timurid period. For example, certain of the white jade belt plaques from the tomb of Wang Xingzu, Marquis of Dongsheng, who died in 1371 (Nanjing City Museum; cf. Thorp, pp. 156-57) are very similar in their general composition and subject matter. They exhibit all the elements of the Iranian belt-fitting, with the addition of a pearl in the sole which is presented to the viewer. Incidentally, they also comprise a kind of high point in one aspect of the development of the Chinese dragon, since these have six toes, rather than five, which was the typical number in later Chinese art.

This classic version of the five-toed Chinese dragon was fully developed at least as early as the Yuan dynasty (1206-1368), and was standard by the time the discussed pieces were made. Five-toed dragons are featured, for example, on two outstanding objects that belong to the Yuan period: a silk embroidery of the Heavenly King of the West (National Museum of Chinese History, Beijing; cf. *China*, no. 84); and the justly celebrated jade wine vessel in the Round Fort, Beijing (Watt, p. 22 fig. 2; for color reproduction of different views, Yang, p. 130 fig. 5; Cang, fig. 50). It is noteworthy that the dragon on this enormous (182 × 135 × 70 cm) and truly wonderful jade has turned the sole of one of its front feet toward the viewer, just as in our belt-fitting, and like the Ming fittings, it is holding up a pearl. In another Yuan jade, a five-toed dragon is cavorting amid lotus blossoms (Imperial Collection of the National Palace Museum, Taipei; cf. Toyka-Fuong, no. 162).

One point of comparison between the belt-fitting in PLATE XI and east Asian as well as Sogdian dragons is the manner in which the tusks come out over the lip. This is seen in a number of pieces of the period. Examples include a Yuan marble architectural finial (Inner Mongolia Museum, Hohhot; cf. Komaroff, no. 204, fig. 21) and a large Yuan jade dragon-head finial (Arthur M. Sackler Gallery, Washington; cf. Komaroff, no. 206, fig. 23). A particularly interesting instance of this usage is in a Sogdian mural painting at Panjikant (see SOGDIANA. v. SOGDIAN ART at *iranica.com*), dated to the 6th century (Azarpay, pp. 43-44, pl. 27, fig. 13). Here, both canines extend over the lip of an Oxus-type dragon (wolf-dragon) on which the four-armed goddess rides.

PLATE XI

Belt fitting. Jade, highly translucent, pure white with no hint of undertones of other colors, diagonal connecting holes in the back for attachment: 5.7 × 6.5 × 1.3 cm, wt. 63.0 gm. Probably Balkh region (from Dawlatābād-e Balkh, according to a previous owner, purchased in Peshawar), 2nd half of 14th-early 15th century. Private Collection, Kuwait.

As indicated at the outset, the closest analogues to this belt-fitting are to be found in the distinctive and powerful renditions of Timurid art, even though the general dragon type is modeled on Chinese examples. We have also indicated that the overall handling, and especially that of the dragon, is not close to the Ming belt-fitting cited. Therefore, it would be extremely interesting to see a high level of detail, if such be present, of the fittings that are depicted in an early Timurid drawing of a bearded man (*Islamic Art* 1, fig. 86). His belt is extensively mounted with lobed plaques which must be of white jade, and at least one of these is surely depicted as consisting of a writhing dragon, immediately calling to mind the present piece.

In jades, probably the closest comparison piece for the head of this dragon is found on a near-black Timurid quillon-block (Metropolitan Museum of Art, inv. no. 02.18.765; cf. Lentz and Lowry, no. 51, p. 143). The rendering of the dragon heads which form the terminals of the quillon-block is very similar, especially noticeable in the strongly modeled form of the jaws and the curls which encircle the jaws' back end. A number of instances which are close in the treatment of the jaws can also be seen in the dragon heads that top a series of copper-alloy Timurid candlesticks (e.g., Grube, 1989a, figs. 1-2, 7-8, 12-14, 18; Lentz and Lowry, no. 122, p. 223).

For comparison with the drawing of the dragon as a whole, one can point to the one carved in relief on the lid of a Timurid sandalwood box (Grube, 1989b, figs. 24 and 31; for color photo of the lid, see Lentz and Lowry, no. 49, p. 207, bottom). The box was made for Ulugh Beg (1394-1449), who was the governor of Samarqand between 1408 and 1447, when he became Timurid sultan, for a brief and troubled reign before being killed in 1449. The dragons' most notable similarities include the following: the manner of containment within the shape; the dragons' general lines and posture; the saw-tooth spine fin; and the foot with the sole displayed toward the viewer. On the box, the creature presents three pearls on the soles of both the left front and right rear feet. Another feature of the dragon on the box which is more closely Chinese than in the fitting is the head, with its long, elephant-like snout, curled downward, whereas in the jade the dragon head is of the well-exampled Iranian type. Another closely related dragon is depicted in a Shirazi miniature painting (Topkapi Saray Library, MS Pers. hazine 1511, fol. 203 verso; cf. Gray, p. 63; dated to approximately the last decades of the 14th century), which shows Bahrām Gur (see BAHRĀM V) in combat with the dragon.

The belt-fitting seems to be earlier than the casket of Ulugh Beg and the cited candlesticks. It could very well have been one of the plaques mounted on the jade belts of young princes, the sight of which scandalized the Chinese ambassador Ch'en Ch'eng during his mission to the court of Ulugh Beg's father, the Timurid sultan Šāhrok̲ (Shah Rukh), in Herat about 1414. Ch'en Ch'eng, a high-level bureaucrat in the highly regulated Chinese society, was not prepared to see "young boys wearing richly embroidered robes cinched in with solid jade belts." By contrast, this ambassador "wore a simple dark blue silken gown embroidered only on the chest and back with an egret insignia designating his official rank" (Hecker, p. 94).

In Ming society, belts with jade plaques belonged to the emblems of rank which distinguished court officials; official regulations were issued, as for example in 1393, to control their use. A cap with seven ridges, a leather belt with jade plaques, and a sash of four-colored silk embroidery were restricted to officials of the First Rank, who dressed in red robes. Belts with rhinoceros horn plaques were worn by Second Rank court officials, while belts with gold, silver, or horn ornaments were allowed for officials of lower ranks (Thorp, p. 155). The passage from Ch'en Ch'eng is particularly interesting, because it suggests that belts covered with jade fittings were much in evidence in Herat at the court of Šāhrok̲. This impression is strengthened by a number of drawings and paintings—in addition to the one discussed above—in which men wear belts with plaques which are probably jade, the shapes of which are analogous to the one under discussion.

This fitting is one of the two purest white jade pieces that the author has seen. The other example is the hilt of a 17th-century Indian dagger and has the form of a masterfully carved horse's head (Al-Sabah Collection, inv. no. LNS 70 HS; cf. Keene and Kaoukji, no. 8.17). Both jades are of a very high level of translucency, and—a most unusual circumstance—have not the slightest hint of any color undertones. Objects of such ultimate material can be taken as made for those at the highest rank of society, whenever and wherever they occur.

After the Timurid period, the use of jade declined in the Iranian world, and from the 16th to the end of the 19th century India was the main Asian area of jade carving west of China. Of course, it can be assumed that jade cutters from the Iranian world found patronage in India, as they did in Ottoman Turkey. And although much of courtly and learned culture in India at the time was Persian, this truly must, for a variety of reasons, be treated as a separate subject. The Iranian tradition in jade cutting is among the most distinguished in world history, but it is yet to be fully credited for its accomplishments and influence.

In the past two decades, however, there have been some attempts to redress the situation. In April and November 1998, the present contributor delivered a lecture on "Pre-Timurid Islamic Jades" before the Islamic Art Circle at the School of Oriental and African Studies, London, and in the lecture series of the Dār-al-Aṯār al-Eslāmiya, Kuwait, respectively. The lecture covered in excess of one hundred ancient Western Asian, Islamic, and Chinese specimens to demonstrate the history of Iranian jade carving, with comparison material in other media, and included a review of the literary evidence. The jade examples comprised buckles and other belt and strap fittings, horse trappings, sword and quiver fittings, hololithic finger rings, seal-stones, stamp seals, beads, necklace pendants, earring pendants, figurines, chess pieces and vessels, including the provision of material for the identification of the earliest development of gold-inlay technique in Iranian jades (the vessel in PLATE VIII). A brief summary of the lecture was published in 2001, and is listed below.

This contributor also curated *Treasury of the World*, an exhibition of Mughal era jeweled arts from the Al-Sabah Collection, which opened at the British Museum, London, in 2001, and then traveled to seven museums in North America and Europe. This exhibition broke new ground not only for the understanding of Indian jewelry, but also of Iranian jades. It was accompanied by a catalog (also listed below), but the supplemental early background and comparison material exhibited was not included in this catalog, nor were most of the texts incorporated in the exhibition.

Bibliography: Auction catalogs. Christie's, *Important Islamic, Indian, Himalayan and South-East Asian Art*, London, 24 April 1990. Christie's, *Islamic Art and Indian Miniatures*, London, 19 October 1993. Christie's, *Fine Antiquities*, London, 5 July 1995. Christie's, *Islamic Art and Indian Miniatures*, London, 25 April 1997. Sotheby's, *Scholarly Works of Art from The Mary and George Bloch Collection*, Hong Kong, 23 October 2005. Tajan, *Arts de l'Asie*, Paris, 21 November 2005.

Exhibition catalogs: *The Anatolian Civilizations: III-Seljuk, Ottoman*, European Art Exhibitions of the Council of Europe 18, Istanbul, 1983. Esin Atil, *Exhibition catalogue of Turkish Art of the Ottoman Period*, Washington, D.C., 1973. Idem, *The Age of Sultan Süleyman the Magnificent*, Washington, D.C., and New York, 1987. *China, 5,000 Years: Innovation and Transformation in the Arts*, New York, 1998. John Curtis et al, *Forgotten Empire: The World of Ancient Persia*, London, 2005. Annette L. Juliano et al, *Monks and Merchants: Silk Road Treasures from Northwest China, Gansu and Ningxia, 4th-7th Century*, New York, 2001. Manuel Keene and Salam Kaoukji, *Treasury of the World: Jewelled Arts of India in the Age of the Mughals*, London, 2001. Linda Komaroff et al, *The Legacy of Genghis Khan: Courtly Art and Culture in Western Asia, 1256-1353*, New York, 2002. Thomas W. Lentz and Glenn D. Lowry, *Timur and the Princely Vision: Persian Art and Culture in the Fifteenth Century*, Los Angeles, 1989. *Oxus: Tesori dell'Asia Centrale*, Rome, 1993. R. H. Pinder-Wilson, "Rock Crystal and Jade," in *The Arts of Islam*, (Catalogue of the Hayward Gallery Exhibition 8 April-4 July 1976), The Arts Council of Great Britain, London, 1976, pp. 119-24. Jessica Rawson, *Chinese Jade from the Neolithic to the Qing*, London, 1995. Teng Shu-p'ing, *Catalogue of a Special Exhibition of Hindustan Jade in the National Palace Museum*, Taipei, 1983. *Le trésor de Saint-Marc de Venise*, Paris, 1984. Robert L. Thorp, *Son of Heaven: Imperial Arts of China*, Seattle, 1988; VHS tape. Ursula Toyka-Fuong, *Schätze der Himmelssöhne: Die Kaiserliche Sammlung aus dem Nationalen Palastmuseum, Taipeh, Die Grossen Sammlungen*, Bonn, 2003. James C. Y. Watt, *Chinese Jades from Han to Ch'ing*, New York, 1980.

Sources and Studies: J. W. Allan, "The Survival of Precious and Base Metal Objects from the Medieval Islamic World," in M. Vickers, ed., *Pots & Pans: A Colloquium on Precious Metals and Ceramics in the Muslim, Chinese and Graeco-Roman Worlds, Oxford 1985*, Oxford Studies in Islamic Art 3, Oxford, 1986, pp. 57-70. Guitty Azarpay et al, *Sogdian Painting: The Pictorial Epic in Oriental Art*, Los Angeles, 1981. Samuel Beal, *Si-yu-ki; Buddhist Records of the Western World of Hiuen Tsiang, AD 629*, London, 1884, repr., New Delhi, 2004. Abu Rayḥān Biruni, *Ketāb al-jamāher fi maʿrefat al-jawāher*, ed. F. Krenkow, Hyderabad, 1936, repr., Beirut, 1984. John Boardman, ed., *The Oxford History of Classical Art*, Oxford, 1993. Idem, *Greek Sculpture: The Late Classical Period and Sculpture in Colonies and Overseas*, London, 1995. Alessio Bombaci, *The Kūfic Inscription in Persian Verses in the Court of the Royal Palace of Masʿūd III at Ghazni*, Rome, 1966. Cang Shi, ed., *Dragons of China*, Beijing, 2000 (in Chinese). William A. P. Childs et al., *Le monument des Néréides: Le décor sculpté*, Fouilles de Xanthos 8, 2 vols., Paris, 1989. Pierre Chuvin et al., *Les arts de l'Asie centrale*, Paris, 1999. Idem and Gérard Degeorge, *Samarkand, Bukhara, Khiva*, Paris, 2001. Gerard Clauson, *An Etymological Dictionary of Pre-Thirteenth-Century Turkish*, Oxford, 1972. Ernst Cohn-Wiener, *Turan: Islamische Baukunst in Mittelasien*, Berlin, 1930. J. E. Curtis, "A Bronze Bucket from Western Iran," *Collectors and Collections: British Museum Yearbook* 2, pp. 253-56. Gérard Degeorge and Yves Porter, *The Art of the Islamic Tile*, Paris, 2002. Lisa Golombek and Donald Wilber, *The Timurid Architecture of Iran and Turan*, 2 vols., Princeton, 1988; all monuments cited herein are part of the 14th-century Transoxiana school, and the extensive bibliography is particularly useful for further research.

Basil Gray, *Persian Painting*, Geneva, 1961. Ernst J. Grube, "Notes on the Decorative Arts of the Timurid Period, II: A Group of Timurid Candlesticks," *Islamic Art* 3, 1989a, pp. 175-78. Idem, "Notes on the Decorative Arts of the Timurid Period, II: A Wooden Casket Made for Ulūgh Beg," *Islamic Art* 3, 1989b, pp. 178-80. Guang Wen and Zhichun Jing, "Chinese Neolithic Jade: A Preliminary Geoarchaeological Study," *Geoarchaeology* 7, 1992, pp. 251-76. O. Hamdy and T. Reinach, *Une nécropole royale à Sidon*, Paris, 1892. Barclay V. Head, *A Guide to the Principal Coins of the Greeks, from circ. 700 B.C. to A.D. 270*, London, 1965. Felicia J. Hecker, "A fifteenth-century Chinese diplomat in Herat," *JRAS*, 3rd series, 3, 1993, pp. 85-98. Derek Hill and Oleg Grabar, *Islamic Architecture and its Decoration, A.D. 800 - 1500*, 2nd ed., London, 1967. *Ḥodud al-ʿĀlam* (Anon.), tr. V. Minorsky as *Ḥudūd al-ʿĀlam, 'The Regions of the World' A Persian Geography 372 A.H.-982 A.D.*, 2nd. ed., London, 1970. *Islamic Art* 1, 1981. Marilyn Jenkins and Manuel Keene, *Islamic Jewelry in the Metropolitan Museum of Art*, New York, 1982. Nina Jidejian, *Sidon Through the Ages*, Beirut, 2006. Maḥmud b. Ḥosayn Kāšḡari, *Diwān loḡāt al-tork*, Ankara, 1990; facsimile ed., Fatih National Library, Istanbul, MS Ar. 4189; partially tr. and arranged alphabetically into Persian by Sayyed Moḥammad Dabir-siyāqi, Tehran, 1996. Manuel Keene, "The Lapidary Arts in Islam: An Underappreciated Tradition," *Expedition* 24, 1981, pp. 24-39. Idem, "Medieval Islamic Jades: Pre-Tîmūrid Islamic Jades," *Hadeeth ad-Dar* 12, 2001, pp. 2-6; cited illustrations are referenced to the number in the text, and not to the figure number associated with the misplaced captions. Idem, "Old World jades outside China, from ancient times to the fifteenth Century: Section One," *Muqarnas* 21, 2004, pp. 193-214. Roger Keverne, ed., *Jade*, London 1991. Ilse Kleeman, *Der Satrapen-Sarcophag aus Sidon*, Berlin, 1958. Edgar Knobloch, *The Art of Central Asia*, with photos by Milos Hrbas, tr. Roberta Finlayson-Samsour, London, 1965. Colin M. Kraay, *Archaic and Classical Greek Coins*, Berkeley, 1976. Guy Francis Laking, *Oriental Arms and Armour*, London, 1964. Sherman E. Lee, "The Year in Review for 1976," *The Bulletin of the Cleveland Museum of Art*, February 1977, pp. 42, 61, 79. B. A. Litvinskiy and I. R. Pichikiyan, "The Temple of the Oxus," *JRAS* 2nd series, 1981, pp. 133-85. Stephen Markel, "Inception and Maturation in Mughal Jades," *Marg* 44, no. 2, December 1992, pp. 49-64; also sep. pub. as *The World of Jade*, ed. Stephen Markel, Bombay 1992. Sharaf al-Zamān Ṭāhir Marvazī (Šaraf-al-Zamān Ṭāher Marvazi), *On China, the Turks and India*, ed. and tr. Vladimir Minorsky, London, 1942. A. S. Melikian-Chirvani, "Four Pieces of Islamic Metalwork: Some Notes on a Previously Unknown School," *Art and Archaeology Research Papers* 10, 1976, pp. 24-30. Idem, "Precious and Semi-Precious Stones in Iranian Culture, Chapter I. Early Iranian Jade," in *Bulletin of the Asia Institute*, NS 11, 1997 (published 2000), pp. 123-73. Andrew Middleton and Ian Freestone, "The Mineralogy and Occurrence of Jade," in Rawson 1995, pp. 413-23. Narshakhi (Abu Bakr Moḥammad b. Jaʿfar Naršaḵi), *The History of Bukhara*, tr. R. Frye, Cambridge, Mass., 1954. Jawhari Nišāburi, *Jawāher-nāma-ye Neẓāmi*, ed. Iraj Afšār and Moḥammad Rasul Daryāgašt, Tehran, 2004. André Parrot, Maurice H. Chéhab, and Sabatino Moscati, *Les Phéniciens: L'expansion phénicienne. Carthage*, Paris, 1975. Paul Pelliot, *Notes on Marco Polo*, Paris, 1959. R. H. Pinder-Wilson, "A Persian Jade Cup," *British Museum Quarterly* 26, 1962, pp. 49-50. Idem and William Watson, "An Inscribed Jade Cup from Samarqand," *British Museum Quarterly* 23, 1960, pp. 19-50. A. U. Pope and P. Ackerman, eds., *A Survey of Persian Art from Prehistoric Times to the Present*, 6 vols., London and New York, 1938-39. G. A. Pugachenkova, *Zodchestvo Uzbekistana* (*Architecture of Uzbekistan*), Tashkent, 1959. Eadem, *Khalchayan*, Tashkent, 1966. Eadem, *Les trésors de Dalverzine-Tépé*, Leningrad, 1978. Eadem, *A Museum in the Open: The Architectural Treasures of Uzbekistan*, Tashkent, 1981 (in Uzbek, Russian, and English). Eadem, *Shedevri Srednei Azii* (*Masterpieces of Central Asia*), Tashkent, 1986. G. A. Pugachenkova and L. I. Rempel', *Ocherki iskusstva Srednei Azii* (*Surveys of Central Asian Art*), Moscow, 1982. Abu'l-Qāsem ʿAbd-Allāh Kāšāni, *ʿArāyes al-jawāher wa nafāyes al-aṭāyeb*, ed. Iraj Afšār, Tehran, 1966. Julian Raby, "Looking for Silver in Clay: A New Perspective on Sāmānid Ceramics," in Vickers, *Pots & Pans*, pp. 179-203. J. M. Rogers and Cengiz Köseoglu, *The Topkapi Saray Museum: The Treasury*, Boston, 1987. Morris Rossabi, "Two Ming Envoys to Inner Asia," *T'oung Pao*, 62, 1976, pp. 1-34. Idem, "A translation of Ch'en Ch'eng's *Hsi-yü fan-kuo chih*," *Ming Studies* 17, 1983, pp. 49-59. E. V. Rtveladze, "Gopatshah of Bactria: A Nephrite Plate with Depictions of a Bactrian Ruler and a Bull-Man," *Ancient Civilizations from Scythia to Siberia* 4, 1997, pp. 294-305. J. Ruska and M. Plessner, "Bāzahr," EI^2, I, pp. 1155-56. Edward H. Schafer, *The Golden Peaches of Samarkand: A Study of T'ang Exotics*, Berkeley, 1963. Erich F. Schmidt, *Persepolis II: Contents of the Treasury and Other Discoveries*, Chicago, 1957. V. A. Shishkin, *Varakhsha*, Moscow, 1963. Robert Skelton, "The Relations between the Chinese and Indian Jade Carving Traditions," in *The Westward Influence of the Chinese Arts from the 14th to the 18th Century*, ed. William Watson, London, 1972, pp. 98-110. Idem, "Characteristics of Later Turkish Jade Carving," in *Proceedings of the Fifth International Conference of Turkish Art*, ed. G. Fehér, Budapest, 1978, pp. 795-807. Idem, "Islamic and Mughal Jades," in Keverne, pp. 272-95. Teng Shu-p'ing, "On the Eastward Transmission of Islamic-style Jades during the Ch'ien-lung and Chia-ch'ing Reigns," in *National Palace Museum Bulletin* 37, no. 2, 2004, pp. 25-138. Aḥmad b. Yusof al-Tifāši, *Azhār al-afkār fi jawāher al-aḥjār*, ed. Moḥammad Yusof Ḥasan and Maḥmud Basyuni Ḵaffāji, Cairo, 1977; tr. Samar Najm Abul

Huda as *Arab Roots of Gemology: Ahmad ibn Yusuf Al Tifaschi's Best Thoughts on the Best of Stones*, Lanham, Md., 1998 (defective tr.). William Trousdale, "A Possible Roman Jade from China," *Oriental Art*, NS 15, no. 1, 1969, pp. 58-64. Idem, *The Long Sword and Scabbard Slide in Asia*, Washington, D.C., 1975. Idem, "A Kushan Scabbard Slide from Afghanistan," *Bulletin of the Asia Institute*, NS 2, 1988, pp. 25-30. Joseph M. Upton et al, "The Persian Expedition, 1933-1934," *Bulletin of the Metropolitan Museum of Art* 29, no. 12, pt. 2, December 1934, pp. 3-22. Michael Vickers, ed., *Pots & Pans: A Colloquium on Precious Metals and Ceramics in the Muslim, Chinese and Graeco-Roman Worlds, Oxford 1985*, Oxford Studies in Islamic Art 3, Oxford, 1986. V. Voronina, *Arkhitekturniye Pamyatniki Srednei Azii: Bokhara, Samarkand/Architectural Monuments of Middle Asia: Bokhara, Samarkand*, with photos by A. Aleksandrov, Leningrad, 1969. Oliver Watson, *Ceramics from Islamic Lands*, London, 2004. Robert Webster, *Gems: Their Sources, Descriptions and Identification*, 3rd ed., London, 1975. Charles K. Wilkinson, "The Achaemenian Remains at Qaṣr-i-Abu Naṣr," *JNES* 24, 1965, pp. 341-45 and pls. 66-77. Idem, *Nishapur: Pottery of the Early Islamic Period*, New York, 1973. Idem, *Nishapur: Some Early Islamic Buildings and their Decoration*, New York, 1986. Franz Winter, *Der Alexander-Sarkophag aus Sidon*, Strasburg, 1912. Boda Yang, "The Glorious Age of Chinese Jades," in Keverne, pp. 126-187.

In addition to the above, the reader is referred to the contributor's forthcoming catalogue raisonné of the hundreds of other jades in the Al-Sabah Collection, the overwhelming majority of which are Iranian and cover a span of more than 2,000 years.

(MANUEL KEENE)

JADIDISM, a movement of reform among Muslim intellectuals in Central Asia, mainly among the Uzbeks and the Tajiks, from the first years of the 20th century to the 1920s. It took its name from *oṣul-e jadid* (new method), which was applied to the modern schools that the reformers advocated in place of the "old" (*qadim*) schools: the traditional *maktab*s and *madrasas*. "*Jadid*" or "*jadidči*" became a synonym for reformer, while "*qadim*" or "*qadimči*" meant a conservative opposed to change. These terms also suggested a generational divide: the *jadid*s were, on the whole, younger men and looked to the future, whereas leading *qadim*s were older and embraced tradition (Khalid, p. 93).

The origins of Central Asian Jadidism are diverse. It belongs within the broad framework of reformist and revolutionary movements among the Muslims of Russia and the neighboring Islamic countries in the late 19th and early 20th century. The efforts among the Volga Tatars beginning in the 1880s and by Esmāʿil Bey Gasprali/Gasprinski (d. 11 Sept. 1914), the founder of a new-method school in Bakhchisaray (Bāḡča Sarāy), the capital of the Tatars in the Crimea in 1884, and the publisher of the influential reformist newspaper *Terjümān* beginning in 1883, were crucial sources of ideas for the Jadids (*Ismoil Gasprinskiy va Turkiston*, pp. 40-100). So were publications from Istanbul, Cairo, Beirut, and cities in India and Persia. Numerous books in Persian were imported from India, especially the classics of Persian poetry (e.g., Saʿdi, Rumi, Ḥāfeẓ, Jāmi) and the works of ʿAbd-al-Qāder Bidel (q.v.; Dmitriev, pp. 243-47), and Persian-language newspapers came from Calcutta, Kabul, and Cairo. The Jadids were also inspired by political movements in the Islamic world: the anti-colonial struggles in India, the constitutional movement in Persia (1905-1911, q.v.), and, above all, the Young Turk movement in the Ottoman Empire. They could not but feel a strong sense of solidarity with their fellow Muslims. Yet, however much they may have owed to others, their programs, organizations, and enthusiasms were primarily responses to the social and economic changes and the cultural initiatives introduced by Russia in Central Asia from the middle of the 19th century on. The Jadids had to confront colonialism as circumstances required in the governorate-general of Turkestan, which was under direct Russian administration, and in the Emirate of Bukhara, which maintained its own governmental institutions under a Russian protectorate. In both areas the connection with Russia suggested new models of development and raised cultural and moral challenges that called into question traditional institutions and values.

The Jadids by no means constituted a unified movement. They were conservatives, radicals, and moderates, but, above all, they were individuals, and each one professed his own ideas about culture and identity, social change, religion, and the state. Although the notion of youth is usually associated with the Jadids, two generations are, in fact, discernible within their ranks. The first generation consisted of those who undertook their education mainly in Muslim institutions, who used Persian as their language of written expression, and who were subject to only modest Russian influences before 1917. A second generation began to assert itself in the years around World War I. Its members had received educations less tied to the traditional *madrasa* and more exposed to Russian influences, and were harsher than their somewhat older colleagues in their criticism of customs and institutions. Yet, the Jadids as a whole shared certain beliefs and aspirations that endowed their drive for reform with both coherence and idealism. They displayed a critical attitude towards the society around them, an abiding commitment to learning, and an eagerness for change that were all framed by a vision of the future that was essentially optimistic. They were, in short, modernizers and enlighteners.

The Jadids were determined, first and foremost, to bring Central Asia into the modern age. They were, in essence, Muslim modernists as their perception of the contemporary world and their attention to its problems originated in the culture and society of Muslim Central Asia. Thus, they belonged to a common Muslim modernist community that extended from the Ottoman Empire and Egypt to Persia and India, and they could converse with one another in their common Turkic and Iranian languages, but, unlike the Young Turks, they did not reject Islam. Rather, they sought to bring Islamic teachings into harmony with the norms of modern society.

At first, the Jadids perceived their cause as educational, and they assumed moral and cultural leadership as a matter of right, because they were certain that the path they had chosen would lead to an enlightened and prosperous future. They were equally certain about who their opponents were, and they waged a resolute campaign against the conservatives within the ulama. The contest between them took on the attributes of a Kulturkampf, as both sides recognized how high the stakes were, nothing less than the power to decide what Muslim culture would be. The mullahs had no intention of relinquishing the cultural dominance they had exercised for centuries, while the Jadids were filled with anxiety, lest ignorance and hidebound tradition condemn Central Asian Muslims to eternal backwardness and subordination to others.

The Jadids also merit the epithet, "enlighteners," because they had complete faith in knowledge as the most effective means of solving society's problems, and because they were inveterate dispensers of knowledge. Dismayed by the deficiencies of the *maktab*s and many *madrasa*s, they committed themselves, first of all, to the new-method schools. But they conceived of their didactic mission in broad terms: they wrote school textbooks, founded newspapers and filled their columns with exhortations to learn and to reform, wrote poetry and plays and experimented with new forms of fiction to popularize their ideas and to create a new mental climate, and founded publishing houses to print their works and bookstores to disseminate them.

The Jadids had no formal, written program at first. Yet, their actions made clear their determination to overcome ignorance and backwardness by establishing new schools and creating a new literature, by combating the entrenched ulama and widening the horizons of students in the *madrasa*s, and by exposing the corruption and tyranny of the emir and his officials (ʿAyni, 1987, pp. 69-70). Thus, even under the emir's oppressive regime in Bukhara and the vigilance of Russian colonial administrators in Turkestan, the Jadids prepared themselves for political struggle.

A measure of the unity and diversity of Jadidism may be gleaned from the biographies of its leading proponents. Mahmudḵoja Behbudiy (Maḥmud Ḵᵛāja Behbudi, 1874-1919) was by all accounts the most prominent figure among the Jadids. He came from a family of means; his father was a mufti, and he himself, well educated in both religious and secular subjects, became a mufti. He had traveled extensively, including the *ḥajj* pilgrimage in 1899 and had spent time in Russia in 1903-4; he was an enthusiastic founder of new-method schools and an ardent promoter of the indigenous press. ʿAbd-al-Raʾuf Feṭrat (1886-1937 or 1938, q.v.) also enjoyed great esteem among his contemporaries. He was a true enlightener who was engaged simultaneously in many projects, including social criticism, literary creativity, journalism, and politics. He studied in a *madrasa*, but the four years he spent at the University of Istanbul (1909-13) and his direct acquaintance with the Young Turk movement proved decisive. He became one of the more radical Jadid leaders and was an early critic of the Emirate of Bukhara's regime in such works as *Monāẓara-ye modarres-e boḵārāʾi* (1911). After 1917, he participated in the reconstruction of Central Asia under Soviet auspices, but he could not reconcile his own aspirations with the demands of the new regime. Ṣadr-al-Din ʿAyni (1878-1954, q.v.) came from a modest family of village craftsmen, but attended several *madrasas* and became engrossed in the study of classical Persian poetry. He attended small gatherings of intellectuals in Bukhara and was attracted to the Jadid cause early on, committing himself fully to educational reform. Later he accommodated himself to the Soviet regime and became the leading literary figure of the new Soviet Tajikistan. Monawwar Qori (Qāri; 1878-1931) was from a cultured family. He had an elite *madrasa* education and was a faithful activist in all the Jadid enterprises, particularly as a pioneering founder of new-method schools and a founder and editor of newspapers. Abdulla Avloniy (ʿAbd-Allāh Awlāni, 1878-1934), born into a prosperous family, was educated in the *maktab* and *madrasa*. He founded new-method schools, edited two short-lived newspapers, was an author of great versatility (poetry, plays, and school textbooks), and after 1917 played an important role in education. Tolagan Khojamiyorov, known as Tavallo (Tawallā; 1882-1939), came from a family of ulama and literary people and received a traditional Islamic education. He was an advocate of Muslim cultural renewal and the modernization of Muslim education and was best known as a poet. In his small book of poems, *Ravnaq al-Islom* (*Rawnaq al-Eslām*, 1916), he urged his readers to strive for a cultural and economic renaissance in Turkestan. After 1917, though reserved toward the new Soviet order, he was eager to create a flourishing intellectual life. Hoji Mu'in Shukrulla (Ḥāji Moʿin Šokr-Allāh, 1883-1942), raised in modest circumstances, contributed regularly to the Jadid press and was a well-known author and producer of plays on Jadid themes.

The members of what may be called the second Jadid generation were more radical in their social activism and more experimental in their literary creativity than their elders. Hamza Hakimzoda Niyoziy (Ḥamza Ḥakimzāda Niāzi, 1889-1929), from a prosperous family, was educated in a *maktab* and *madrasa* in Kokand, but he also probably attended a Russian-native school, where he learned Russian. He opened numerous new-method schools and wrote textbooks for them. He wrote poetry and the first Uzbek novel in addition to plays on reformist and revolutionary themes, thereby becoming the leading playwright of the new Uzbekistan. Abdulla Qodiriy (ʿAbd-Allāh Qāderi, 1894-1938) studied in traditional schools and in a Russian-native school to learn Russian and was much influenced by the reformist press. He was a prolific writer and the founder of the modern Uzbek novel in the 1920s. Fayzulla (Fayż-Allāh) Khojaev/Khodzhaev (1896-1938) came from a well-to-do, religious family and combined a traditional *maktab* education with studies and association with liberal Russians in Moscow before 1917. He was a radical activist who emphasized political struggle, and, allying himself with the Bolsheviks, eventually became the political leader of Soviet Uzbekistan in the 1920s and 1930s. Abdulhamid Sulaymon (ʿAbd-al-Ḥamid Solaymān) Čolpan (1897-1938) was born into a wealthy and prominent family. He received a traditional Islamic education and also attended a Russian-native school and learned Russian, which, as he gratefully acknowledged, opened European literature and culture to him. His debt to Jadid thought is evident throughout his poetry and prose.

Of all the instruments the Jadids used to achieve their goals, new-method schools most absorbed their energies at the beginning. They wanted to replace the rote learning of the *maktab* with the phonetic method of teaching the Arabic alphabet, thereby teaching pupils actually how to read. They were also intent upon expanding the curriculum in order to provide pupils with the knowledge they would need to take their place in the modern world and thus to survive the competition from outside Central Asia. Arithmetic, the natural sciences, history, and geography became regular subjects of study, and Arabic and Persian and, here and there, Russian, were taught systematically (Dudoignon, pp. 161-68; Dolimov, pp. 88-115).

The Jadids by no means eliminated religion from their schools. Indeed, they devoted much attention to instruction in the tenets of Islam and the recitation of the Qurʾān, but the approach had changed. New textbooks written in the vernacular (Uzbek Turkish or Tajik) were used, and, instead of having pupils memorize sacred texts, teachers strove to instill in them a genuine understanding of the doctrines and practices of their faith. In the *madrasa*s the Jadids emphasized the need to focus on the sources of Islam as the proper subject of study rather than on commentaries and interpretations, as was the prevailing practice. Yet, they also, in a sense, separated Islam from the rest of the curriculum. Under the old system, religion had pervaded every subject, but in the new-method schools it became a distinct discipline alongside history, geography, and other subjects (Khalid, pp. 172-74).

As the number of new-method schools grew, from the first one founded in Tashkent by Monawwar Qāri in 1901 to the probably several hundred in Bukhara, Samarkand, Tashkent, Kokand, and other places at the outbreak of World War I, the Jadids spared no effort to support them. In Bukhara in 1908, they formed Širkati Buḵoroi šarif (Šerkat-e Boḵārā-ye šarif "The association of noble Bukhara"), a joint-stock company whose main purpose was to publish textbooks. Among them were ʿAyni's *Tahzib-us-sibyon* (*Tahḏib al-ṣebyān* "The Education of Children;" 1910), which emphasized the importance of study and the role of the family in learning, and *Zaruriyoti din* (*Żaruriyāt-e din* "The requirements of religion;" 1914), which presented the fundamental teachings of Islam in straightforward language (Gafarov, pp. 102-5).

Jadid newspapers and periodicals made their appearance after the Russian Revolution of 1905, when restrictions on the press were loosened. Their founders were much influenced by reformist Tatar and Azeri publications, notably *Terjümān*, *Waqt* (Orenburg), and *Eršād* and *Ḥayāt* (Baku), which circulated widely in Central Asia; but the Jadids of Tashkent, Bukhara, and other cities were eager to create outlets of their own for their ideas. The most striking characteristic of all their publications was their didactic contents and tone. They covered a great variety of subjects, but they concentrated on education and the ways of achieving social and economic progress (Jalolov and Ozganboev, pp. 60-82). Editors favored the informative and critical essay, which sometimes took up to a quarter of each issue and was almost always committed to a moral or social cause. In these newspapers, poets (Awlāni and Tawallā) and prose writers (ʿAyni, Behbudi, Čolpan, and Feṭrat) early on tested their ideas and honed their literary skills.

The first Jadid publications, in Turkic published in Tashkent, were short-lived. Among them was Qāri's *Ḵoršid* (1906) and Awlāni's *Šohrat* (1907), both of which were closed by government order after only ten issues each, because of their outspokenness. In 1912, after a four year absence of the Jadid press, reformers in Bukhara obtained the emir's permission, apparently through the intervention of the Russian agent, to publish a Tajik-language newspaper, *Buḵoroi šarif* (*Boḵārā-ye šarif*). It was a true organ of enlightenment, informing its readers about a wide range of topics, almost always in a didactic vein. It was also a staunch advocate of material progress, which it made dependent on the growth of literacy. Authors regularly dwelt on ways of developing industry and improving agriculture and irrigation and, especially, trade, which they thought essential if Bukhara's economy was to flourish and poverty be eliminated. Feṭrat was a frequent contributor. Along with admonitions to raise the general level of learning in the *madrasa*s, he urged that more attention be paid to agriculture, specifically that farmers receive specialized instruction in their "trade" and that schools specializing in agricultural studies be established. Behbudi frequently wrote in praise of new-method schools, but underlying his expressions of hope for the future were nagging doubts about the ability of his fellow Muslims to take responsibility for their own destiny. He lamented the absence among them of "invigorating thought" and "Muslim science," and he feared that they were losing their creativeness (Gafarov, pp. 128-29). The editors of *Buḵoroi šarif*, to promote their ideas among Uzbek-speakers, published *Turon* (*Turān*), at first as a supplement and then as a separate newspaper. Both papers, which appeared three times a week, were constantly beset by financial problems, because of the small number of subscribers. The emir closed both on 2 January 1913, because of their unrelenting criticism of conditions in the emirate.

Among other important Jadid periodicals was Behbudi's *Oina* (*Āyna*; 1913-15), which was published in Uzbek and Tajik. A clear voice of reform, it was noteworthy for Behbudi's commitment to sow enlightened ideas in every possible form; no branch of knowledge escaped his attention. *Sadoi Turkiston* (*Ṣadā-ye Torkestān*; 1914-17), highly influential among intellectuals, brought together as editors Qāri, Awlāni, Niāzi, and Čolpan and published on a wide range of subjects, including religious questions and events in Muslim countries (Jalolov and Ozganboev, pp. 82-113). *Sadoi Ferġona* (*Ṣadā-ye Farġāna*; 1914-1915) disseminated moderate Jadid views on political, commercial, and literary questions in Kokand and the Farġāna Valley. The influence of Jadid newspapers was undoubtedly limited, because of the small number of subscribers and the hostility of the authorities. But they are indispensable for tracing the evolution of the Jadids' ideas on politics, society, and culture before 1917, and for explaining their creativity and their stands on important public issues in the 1920s and 1930s.

In their zeal to enlighten and to reform, the Jadids turned also to literature. They were eager to create a new prose and poetry to serve as yet another means of persuading a broader public to accept their vision of a modern society. Traditional literature struck them as unsuited to their times, because it placed entertainment and artistic formulas ahead of enlightenment and social and economic progress. They used new themes and new genres to criticize prevailing social, political, and moral evils, and their early works, especially, were full of earnestness and fervor. These changes were evident in poetry. While many poets remained faithful to the traditional metric system (see ʿARŪŻ), Feṭrat and Čolpan began to write in other styles, drawing on the spoken language and the prosody of Turkic folk poetry. Feṭrat's collection of poems, *Ṣayḥa* "Outcry" (1912), and Awlāni's collections, *Adabiyot yok̲ud milliy šeʿrlar* (*Adabiyāt yā k̲od melli šeʿrlar*, 4 parts, 1909-16), displayed new forms and had as themes, besides the importance of learning and science, the urgent need for justice and liberty.

The most profound literary effects of Jadidism were felt in fiction. Two writers in particular, Qodiriy (Qāderi) and Čolpan, exemplified the Jadid approach to literature before 1917, but while they placed their talents in the service of social activism, they were also conscious of themselves as literary artists. Qāderi's short story, *Juvonboz* (*javānbāz* "pederast:" 1915), purely Jadid in content, reveals the corruption and lack of freedom in Turkestan society. In two other stories of the same year, *Ulogda* "At the goat game" and *Jinlar bazmi* "The Jinni's party," he is clearly more concerned with literature as art than with the defects of the surrounding society. His attention to character, his descriptions of place, and his humorous approach to diverse situations, all amply on display here, assured his popularity as a novelist in the next two decades (Mirbaliev, pp. 46-56).

Čolpan began his literary career with the publication of his first two short stories, *Qurboni jaholat* (*Qorbān-e jahālat* "The victim of ignorance"), and *Dok̲tyr Muhammadyor* (*Doktor Moḥammadyār*) in 1914. Both betray his Jadidist sympathies and accord literature a social function. In the first story the young hero is made aware of the ignorance and depravity around him through his reading of the enlightened press, and he must wrestle with the ideas espoused by reformers and conservatives. In the second story, Čolpan portrays the quintessential Jadid of the time, D. Moḥammadyār, who is not satisfied merely to lament the backwardness and torpor that pervades his Turkestan, but assumes responsibility for reform. He establishes new schools and benevolent societies and publishes a daily newspaper and a weekly journal. Thus, he spreads knowledge and enlightens minds in order to arouse people to take the tasks of reform into their own hands. He is the archetype of the Jadid, because he combines the two main constituents of Jadidism. On the one hand, he thinks about life in modern terms, but, on the other, he remains true to the conservative family from which he comes, preserving the wholesome ethical values it taught him (Karimov, pp. 34-40). Čolpan himself is the Jadid par excellence, because he sees hope for the future in the commitment of the socially conscious, enlightened individual to change society. Yet, he is unlike many Jadids, too, because of his idea of the autonomy of art. He thought that form and language and style were as important as content, and he insisted that a writer must be creative and have imagination, if his literary work was to fulfill its purpose (Čolpan, pp. 35-37).

The theater offered the Jadids a unique opportunity to bring their ideas before a larger public. Building upon a popular theater tradition, the *mask̲arabozlik* (*mask̲ara-bāzlik* "buffoonery"), they wrote and produced some thirty plays in the modern, "European" style between 1911 and 1916. Almost all of them were social dramas with a clear message excoriating ignorance, religious fanaticism, and government oppression and corruption. Focused mainly on the shortcomings of the prevailing political and social order and brimming with solutions, all in accordance with the Jadid credo, these plays were deficient in character development, as both heroes and villains were there primarily as the bearers of ideas (Rizaev, pp. 101-34). Often at the end of the play, to make certain that the audience had grasped the message, one of the characters would summarize the author's ideas, sometimes at length. Yet despite, or perhaps because of, their didactic qualities, these Jadid dramas were immensely popular, and numerous companies of amateur actors, often composed of *madrasa* students, were organized, beginning in 1914, to perform them in Samarkand, Tashkent, Kokand, and smaller towns. The Jadids used the proceeds from performances to support their favorite causes, notably the new-method schools.

Behbudi laid the foundations of the Jadid and the modern Turkestan theater with his play, *Padarkuš* (*Pedarkoš* "The patricide"), a true literary manifesto of the Jadids, written in 1911 and performed in Samarkand in 1914. A great success, it became a staple of the Jadid repertoire. The plot revolves around a rich man and his son, who, denied an education, leads a dissolute life and, in the end, kills his father. He thus fulfils the prophecy of Intelligent, a Jadid-like figure serving as the author's spokesman, who points out that Muslims must become learned people in both secular and religious subjects, if they are to survive. Related to *Padarkuš* in its emphasis on enlightenment is Ḥāji Moʿin Šokr-Allāh's *Eski maktab – yangi maktab* (old school - new school; 1916). Critical of the existing state of education, it lauds a wealthy patron of new-method schools who understands why Central Asia must get in step with the modern world and its secular learning and industry, if it is ever to overcome poverty and suffering.

Harsher in their judgments of Turkestan society were Awlāni and Qāderi. Awlāni's *Advokatlik osonmi?* "Is it easy to be a lawyer?" (1916) portrays poor and downtrodden petitioners who tell their stories to a lawyer in the desperate hope that he can rescue them from unscrupulous moneylenders and officials. In *Baḵtsiz kuyov* "The unfortunate bridegroom" (1915), Qāderi condemns a corrupt financial system that drives a young bridegroom to suicide when he cannot repay a loan. Ḥamza, perhaps the most radical of all the Jadid playwrights, questioned the moral foundations of Turkestan society. In *Zaharli hayot* "A poisioned life," (1915) he tells of two young people in love from different social classes, whose families forbid their marriage. When the parents of the girl promise her to an elderly rich man, she and her lover see no other way out than suicide. In their tragedy, Ḥamza says, they represent the enlightened who stand for social and gender equality; only people like them can save society from ignorance and sinister traditions (Rahmonov, 1959, pp. 100-117, 292-98).

As time passed, a new sense of community took form among the Jadids. They spoke often about *mellat* (nation). Sometimes they applied the term to the Muslims of Central Asia and sometimes, more narrowly, to the Muslims of Turkestan. Thus, at first, ethnic identities were encompassed by the broader Muslim community. For example, the history taught in the new-method schools was of Islam, not of Turks and Turkestan, and the language was called *Musulmān tili* (Muslim language). Many Jadids also used the term *waṭan*, which traditionally had referred to one's birthplace, that is, a city or region, but increasingly after 1900 it designated a larger territory united by a common culture. In Čolpan's *Doḵtyr Muhammadyor* and in the works of Awlāni and Ḥamza *waṭan* meant "Turkestan." An ethnic differentiation was also present in the thought of many Jadids, as they identified the Muslims of Turkestan as Turks, thereby excluding the Tajiks. Although these new categories did not become explicit until after 1917, language was already becoming a distinctive mark of ethnicity. Turkic Jadids insisted that Turkic (Uzbek) alone was appropriate for their new-method schools because their pupils did not understand Persian, the traditional language of instruction.

The Jadids' sense of social community remained all-inclusive. They admitted the lower classes into the *mellat* and accepted their own responsibility to improve the lot of the poor through education and other reforms, but they left no doubt that only the intellectuals, that is, they themselves, were capable of leading society on the road to progress.

The Jadids regarded women as members of the community, too, and they strove to improve their status in two areas in particular: education and marriage. They were united in urging equal opportunities for women to study, and Ḥamza in his novel, *Yangi saodat: melli roman* "The new happiness: A national novel" (1915), emphasized the importance of a bride's good education. Although many hesitated to change existing marriage customs, Ḥāji Moʿin Šokr-Allāh in his play, *Maẓluma ḵāten* "The oppressed woman" (1916), condemned polygyny, and Ḥamza in *Yangi saodat* praised marriage based on the free choice of the bride and groom. Yet, on the whole, the Jadids took a conservative approach to women's issues.

The most consistent advocates of women's rights were women writers who shared Jadid principles, such as the Uzbek poetess Anbar Otin (Atun) (1870-1916). She was anxious to end the practice of arranged marriages between young girls and older men, and she urged the sending of more girls to the *maktab*s and *madrasa*s. Like the Jadids, she expressed warm feelings for the *waṭan* (for her, the Farḡāna Valley) and welcomed the influence of Russian culture and education, but she condemned the effects of colonialism (Qodirova, pp. 21-25, 32-36, 38-50).

Islam, too, defined community for the Jadids, but it is difficult to discern the precise boundaries between their thought and religion. Many had a comprehensive knowledge of Islam, gained from study in the *madrasa*, and they maintained contacts with the ulama. They were also convinced that religion was the moral and ethical foundation of society, and, thus, they retained it in the new-method schools. Yet, however important a place Islamic religion and culture had in their thought and writings, they showed little interest in purely theological debate, preferring instead to focus their attention on cultural reform. The majority were anti-clerical because, in the interest of intellectual and social progress, they wished to limit the influence of organized religion in public affairs, especially education.

In their discussions of community and identity the Jadids had to take into account the presence of Russia in Central Asia. Their attitude was ambivalent. On the one hand, they were not separatists; they wanted to take part in the political and economic renewal of the Russian Empire after 1905 and accepted Russia and its connection to Europe as a means of modernizing their own society (Khalid, pp. 217-18). Yet, they were determined to maintain their own identity, as their strivings for autonomy and their insistence on the cultivation of their own languages, not Russian, suggest. Some Jadids put matters bluntly. Feṭrat in the original Persian text of his *Monāẓara*, published in Istanbul in 1911, expressed strong anti-colonial, anti-Russian feelings, which were omitted from the Uzbek version published by Ḥāji Šokr-Allāh in Tashkent in 1914.

The Russian Revolution of February and, more strongly, the Bolshevik Revolution of October 1917 forced the Jadids to make crucial decisions about their immediate and long-term goals and the means of achieving them. The most urgent tasks before them were political mobilization and alliances.

The Jadids were by no means novices in either organization or politics, even though before 1917 they had had to avoid open, coordinated confrontation with the emir and the Russian administration. They had formed an association in Bukhara in 1910, Tarbiyai atfol (Tarbiat-e aṭfāl) "The education of children," primarily to promote their educational reforms. It had twenty-eight members, fourteen of whom were mullahs, and it remained secret until its dissolution in April 1917, because the authorities treated the work of enlightenment as revolutionary. The association helped students in various ways, and since there was no new-method *madrasa* in Bukhara, it undertook to send students to Orenburg, Kazan, Urfa, Istanbul, and Cairo (Gafarov, pp. 88-99). Its members also harbored long-term political goals, notably the transformation of the emirate into a modern state by transforming its fiscal system and combating corruption. These two directions, the cultural and the political, over time caused serious divergences within the association. A number of activists, led by Feṭrat, became impatient with its concentration on cultural matters and demanded economic and social reforms to improve the lives of the common people.

The years between 1917 and 1920 were marked by upheaval in Central Asia. They were decisive for the Jadids, as revolution changed the very character of their project; the era of classical Jadidism was at an end. In the previous decade they had acted as a small intellectual elite. Now they were forced to adjust their program and methods to the demands of mass political and social struggle, and they had not only to confront the emir and the conservative ulama, but also to maneuver among competing Russian political forces in Tashkent and other cities. As their involvement in the affairs of the new Russia deepened, political activism became the defining feature of Jadidism, and new men came to the fore. One of them was Fayzulla Khojaev, who renounced Jadidism in favor of revolutionary change (Alimova, 1997, pp. 37-47).

The Jadids welcomed the February Revolution as the beginning of a new era in the history of Central Asia. They pressed forward with educational reforms and founded newspapers, but in March they formed a new party, that of the Young Bukharans, as they came to be known, whose main goals were political. No longer satisfied to pursue change by private, cultural means, they recognized the advantages of using state power. They were thus eager to drive the emir from Bukhara and to replace him by a democratic order that would allow Muslims to be fully represented in administrative and legislative bodies. They wrung liberal decrees from an embattled emir, but when they challenged him with public demonstrations in Bukhara, he arrested large numbers and withdrew his reforms (ʿAyni, 1987, pp. 139-99). When in the spring and summer the Russian Provisional Government in Petrograd failed to support them, they turned elsewhere for allies.

Many Jadids associated themselves with the Bolsheviks after October 1917. Bolshevik promises of social and economic emancipation and, especially, their "Declaration of the Rights of the Peoples of Russia" of 2 November made an enormous impression on the Young Bukharans. Typical of their endorsement of the Bolshevik Revolution was Čolpan's poem, *Qizil bayroq* (*Qezel bayrāq* "The red flag;" 1918), which hailed it as the harbinger of "freedom" and "prosperity," and ʿAyni's *Marshi khurriyat* (*Mārš-e ḥorriyat* "The freedom march;" 1918), based on La Marseillaise (the French national anthem composed during the French Revolution), which proclaimed the advent of "liberty" and "justice."

The link between the Young Bukharans and the Bolsheviks was tenuous from the start. The basis for their cooperation lay in the realization that they needed one another to achieve their respective goals. They agreed on getting rid of the emir and his regime, but whereas the Young Bukharans wanted autonomy and self-determination (A'zamkhojaev), as promised in the "Declaration of Rights," the Bolsheviks were intent on bringing Central Asia under their own control. The result was growing despair among some Young Bukharans, notably Behbudi and Awlāni, particularly after forces controlled by the Russian-dominated Tashkent Soviet, the center of power in Turkestan, crushed the Kokand Autonomy, the short-lived Muslim experiment in self-government from December 1917 to February 1918. Behbudi, who had hoped for the establishment of an autonomous Turkestan within a Russian federated republic, was thoroughly disillusioned, and Awlāni condemned the suppression of that autonomy in a series of poems published in the newspaper *Ishtirokiyun* (*Ešterākiyun* "The Communists") in 1919. Other, more radical Young Bukharans, led by Fayzulla (Fayż-Allāh) Khojaev, who emerged as their political leader, and Feṭrat, continued to see in the Bolsheviks their main hope for the future. Thus, when the Bolsheviks founded the Communist Party of Turkestan in June 1918, many Young Bukharans, including Awlāni and Tawallā, became members.

Decisive for the Young Bukharan movement was the overthrow of the emir of Bukhara by the Red Army, which entered the city on 2 September 1920. Young Bukharans returned the following day and formed a revolutionary committee. It became the foundation of the Bukharan People's Soviet Republic with Khojaev as chairman of the Council of Ministers (Khodzhaev, pp. 163-94).

For many Young Bukharans the experience of managing the affairs of the new republic between 1920 and 1924 proved bitterly disappointing. They had entered office with high hopes of advancing enlightenment and creating new political and social institutions. True to their Jadid origins and guided by Feṭrat as minister of education, they immediately formulated ambitious plans to increase literacy and to establish colleges to train the teachers for their projected network of modern schools, but here and in other areas they accomplished little, in part because they lacked funds and skilled people. Nor did they have the support of the new Soviet leaders. Their supposed mentors were pursuing their own agenda for centralization and judged the Young Bukharans' strivings for self-determination as inimical to their purposes. Matters came to a head in 1923 when they dismissed most of the officials of the Bukharan Republic, including Feṭrat, in order to make way for a new political order in Central Asia.

Alongside these political struggles other changes of great consequence for the future of Central Asia were taking place within the Young Bukharan circle itself. Uzbek-Tajik bilingualism, one of the pillars of early Jadidism, was dissolving. It could not survive the growing national feeling and the burgeoning separate ethnic identities, all of which received added impetus from the Soviet state's division of Central Asia into ethnically based republics and its support for indigenous languages and literatures.

ʿAyni and Feṭrat had been leading representatives of the linguistic and literary ties that united Tajiks and Uzbeks, but after 1917 they became ardent promoters of separate cultures. Feṭrat, who had earlier used Persian almost exclusively, turned to Uzbek. He now spoke of Turkestan as the homeland of Turkic Muslims, and in 1918 he organized a circle, the Chaghatoy Gurungi, to promote Turkic self-consciousness and Turkic culture. For his part, ʿAyni, who grouped Tajik intellectuals around the weekly Communist newspaper, *Šuʿlai inqilob* (*Šoʿlaye enqelāb* "The flame of revolution"), published in Samarkand from 1919 to 1921, promoted a distinct Tajik literature and an awareness of the Tajiks' deep Iranian roots in Central Asia. He strove to make his prose more Tajik by using the vernacular and folk sayings and by avoiding the use of Uzbek words (Naby, pp. 150-52, 193). Yet, despite the enthusiasm of Uzbek and Tajik intellectuals for the new *mellat*s (nations), relations between them remained cordial. At the same time they both bore witness to the passing of Persian as the lingua franca of Central Asian intellectual life and the introduction of Russian as its eventual replacement.

Many Young Bukharans, including ʿAyni, Qāderi, and Čolpan, turned away from political engagement to literature in the 1920s. In so doing, they laid the foundations of modern Uzbek and Tajik fiction. In the four novels ʿAyni wrote in the 1920s and 1930s, notably *Doḵunda* (1930) and *Gulomon* (*Ḡolāmān* "The Slaves;" 1934 in Uzbek; 1935, in Tajik), he was chiefly responsible for laying down the norms of the modern Tajik literary language; Qāderi experimented with new prose forms in his novels, *Utkan kunlar* "Past days" (1922) and *Mehrobdan čayon* "A scorpion from the mehrāb" (1929), and became the inspiration of later Uzbek novelists (Kleinmichel, pp. 201-59); and, like his colleagues, Čolpan in short fiction such as *Taraqqi* "Progress" (1924), remained faithful to the Jadid tradition in his advocacy of education, the renewal of society, and the emancipation of women. The course of their literary careers, however, was far from smooth (Sharafiddinov). When Qāderi and Čolpan and other Young Bukharans challenged the prevailing Soviet literary theory that came to be known as socialist realism, they suffered the harsh criticism of proletarian critics for their "nationalist" and "bourgeois" ideas.

Literary controversy was merely a symptom of deeper rifts. The incompatibility between the Young Bukharans' aspirations and Stalin's Soviet regime widened on all fronts in the 1930s and assumed violent forms. Feṭrat, Qāderi, Čolpan, Tawallā, and even Khojaev were among those who perished in the Stalinist purges; ʿAyni, almost alone, survived. By 1939 the great Jadid generation had been largely wiped out. Soviet authorities tried for several decades afterward to expunge the memory of them, too, but a few writers, such as Qāderi, returned to print in the 1950s. Interest in the Jadids revived in the 1980s with 'perestroika' and then flourished after 1991.

Bibliography: A. Works on Jadidism: Adeeb Khalid, *The Politics of Muslim Cultural Reform: Jadidism in Central Asia*, Berkeley, 1998, is an indispensable starting point for a study of Jadidism. Useful general surveys are Hèlène Carrere d'Encausse, *Réforme et revolution chez les musulmans de l'Empire Russe*, 2nd ed., Paris 1981 (tr. Quintin Hoare as *Islam and the Russian Empire: Reform and Revolution in Central Asia*, Berkeley, 1998), which covers political, economic, and cultural development from the second half of the 19th century to the end of the Bukharan People's Soviet Republic in 1924; and Namoz Khotamov, *Sverzhenie emirskogo rezhima v Bukhare* (The overthrow of the emirate of Bukhara), Dushanbe, 1997, which traces events in Bukhara from the beginning of the 20th century through the formation of the Bukharan Republic in 1920. On Jadidism specifically: Numandzhon Gafarov, *Istoriya kul'turno-prosvetitel'skoĭ deiatel'nosti dzhadidov v bukharskom emirate* (History of the cultural and enlightenment activity of the Jadids of the Emirate of Bukhara), Khojand, 2000, is based on the extensive use of Jadid writings; Dilorom Agzamovna Alimova, ed., *Jadidčilik: eslahot, yangilaniš, mostaqillik va taraqqiyot učun kuraš*, Tashkent, 1999; and Rustam Sharipov, *Turkiston jadidčilik harakati tariḵidan*, Tashkent, 2002, investigate important aspects of Jadid thought and activities. Succinct appraisals of Jadidism are to be found in Hisao Komatsu, "The Evolution of Group Identity among Bukharan Intellectuals in 1911-1928: An Overview," *Memoirs of the Research Department of the Toyo Bunko*, no. 47, Tokyo, 1989, pp. 115-44; and Begali Qosimov, "Sources littérarires et principaux traits distinctifs du djadidisme turkestanais (début du XXe siècle)," *Cahiers du monde russe* 37/1-2, 1996, pp. 107-32. Stéphane A. Dudoignon, "La Question scolaire à Boukhara et au Turkestan russe, du 'premier renouveau' à la sovietisation (fin du XVIIIe siècle-1937)," *Cahiers du monde russe* 37/1-2, 1996, pp. 133-210 and Ulughbek Dolimov, *Turkistonda jadid maktablari*, Tashkent, 2006, focus on the Jadids' commitment to education. The Jadid press and the influences on it are covered in M. Babakhanov, *Iz istorii periodicheskoĭ pechati Turkestana* (From the history of the periodical press of Turkestan), Dushanbe, 1987; Alexandre Bennigsen and Chantal Lemercier-Quelquejay, *La Presse et le mouvement national chez les Musulmans de Russie avant 1920*, Paris, 1964; and G. L. Dmitriev, "Rasprostranenie indiĭskikh izdaniĭ v Sredneĭ Azii v kontse XIX-nachale XX vekov (The dissemination of Indian publications in Central Asia at the end of the 19th century and the beginning of the 20th)," *Kniga. Issledovaniya i materialy* 6, Moscow, 1962, pp. 239-54. Especially valuable is A. Jalolov and H. Ozganboev, *Ozbek maʿrifatparvarlik adabiyotining taraqqiyotida vaqtli matbuotning orni*, Tashkent, 1993, which analyzes in detail *Taraqqi* and other Jadidist newspapers.

The influence of Ismail Gasprinski on the Jadid press and on prominent Jadids is covered in articles in *Ismoil Gasprinsky va Turkiston/Ismail Gasprinsky i Turkestan*, Tashkent, 2005. On Jadid prose and poetry Edward Allworth, *Uzbek Literary Politics*, The Hague, 1964, is wide-ranging and judicious; Eden Naby, "Transitional Central Asian Literature: Tajik and Uzbek Prose Fiction from 1909 to 1932," unpub. Ph.D diss., Columbia University, 1975, is full of insights and valuable comparisons; and Sigrid Kleinmichel, *Aufbruch aus orientalischen Dichtungstraditionen: Studien zur usbekischen Dramatik und Prosa zwischen 1910 und 1934*, Budapest, 1993, is indispensable. Akademiia Nauk Uzbekskoi SSR, *Istoriya uzbekskoĭ sovetskoĭ literatury* (History of Uzbek Soviet literature) I, Tashkent, 1987, pp. 17-175, surveys literature from a specific ideological and aesthetic perspective. A. Jalolov, *XIX asr oḵiri XX asr bošlaridagi ozbek adabiyoti*, Tashkent, 1991, on the period up to 1917, is an invaluable guide. Drama is covered in Shuhrat Rizaev, *Jadid dramasi*, Tashkent, 1997, which describes the evolution of Jadid dramas and presents the texts of representative plays; and in B. Imomov, Q. Joraev, and H. Hakimova, *Ozbek dramaturgiyasi tariḵi*, Tashkent, 1995, pp. 14-77. One may also consult *Uzbekskiĭ sovetskiĭ teatr* (The Uzbek Soviet theater), ed. A. M. Rybnik, Tashkent, 1966, and Mamadhzan Rakhmanov, *Uzbekskiĭ teatr s drevneishikh vremen do 1917 goda* (The Uzbek theater from the earliest times to 1917), [?] Tashkent, 1968.

B. Works about and by individual Jadids (alphabetically): Sirojiddin Ahmad (Serāj-al-Din Aḥmad), "Munawwar Qori," *Šarq yulduzi*, 1992, no. 5, pp. 105-19. Ahmad Aliev, *Mahmudḵoja Bihbudiy* (*Maḥmud Ḵᵛāja Behbudi*), Tashkent, 1994. Dilorom Agzamovna Alimova, "Fayzulla Kojaev va Jadidčilik," in idem, ed., *Fayzulla Kojaev hayoti va faoliyati haqida yangi mulohazarlar*, pub. with Fayzulla Khojaev, *Buḵoro inqilobining tariḵiga materiallar*, Tashkent, 1997, pp. 37-47. Dilorom Agzamovna Alimova and D. Rashidova, *Makhmudkhodzha Bekhbudiy i ego istoricheskie vozzreniya* (Mahmudkoja Behbudi and his historical views), Tashkent, 1998. Idem, *Mahmudḵuja Behbudiy va uning tariḵi tafakkuri*, Tashkent, 1999. Edward Allworth, *The Preoccupations of Abdalrauf Fitrat, Bukharan Nonconformist*, Berlin, 2000 (an exhaustive bibliography of Feṭrat's works). Idem, *Evading Reality: The Devices of Abdalrauf Fitrat: Modern Central Asian Reformist*, Leiden, 2002. Abdulla Avloniy (ʿAbd-Allāh Awlāni), *Tanlangan asarlar*, 2 vols., Tashkent, 1998, vol. one contains a study of Avloniy's life and works by B. Qosimov, pp. 5-78. Ṣadr-al-Din ʿAyni, "Jallodoni Buḵoro" (Jallādān-e Boḵārā), *Kulliyot* (*Kolliyāt*) I, Stalinabad (Dushanbe), 1958, pp. 101-82. Idem, *Taʾriḵi inqilobi Buḵoro* (*Tāriḵ-e enqelāb-e Boḵārā*), Dushanbe, 1987. Idem, *Yaddoshtho*, 4 vols., Stalinabad (Dushanbe), 1949-54; ed. ʿAli-Akbar Saʿidi Sirjāni as *Yāddāšthā*, 4 vols. in one, Tehran, 1983. S. S. A'zamkhojaev, "Turkiston mukhtoriiati-jadidlar milliy-demokratik davatchilik ghoialarining amaldagi ifodasi," in Dilorom Agzamovna Alimova, ed., *Jadidčilik: Islahot, yangilaniš, mustaqillik va taraqqiyot učun kuraš*, Tashkend, 1999, pp. 152-73. I. Braginskiĭ, *Sadriddin Aini: Zhizn'i tvorchestvo* (Sadriddin Aini, "Life and Works"), 2nd ed., Moscow, 1978. Abdulhamid Suleyman (ʿAbd-al-Ḥamid Solaymān) Čolpan, *Adabiyot nadir*, Tashkent, 1994. ʿAbd-al-Raʾuf Feṭrat, *Monāẓara-ye modarres-e boḵārāʾi bā yak nafar farangi dar Hendustān dar bāra-ye makāteb-e jadida*, Istanbul, 1911. Keith Hitchins, "ʿAynī, Ṣadr-al-Din," in *EIr*. III, pp. 144-49. Faizulla Khodzhaev (Khojaev), "K istoriĭ revoliutsiĭ v Bukhare i natsonal'nogo razmezhevaniya Srednei Azii (On the history of the revolution in Bukhara and the national boundary delimitation of Central Asia)," in Idem, *Izbrannye trudy* (Selected works) I, Tashkent, 1970, pp. 68-194. Naim Karimov, *Abdulhamid Sulaymon uğli Čulpon*, Tashkent, 1991. Hamza Hakimzoda Niyoziy (Ḥamza Ḥakimzāda Niāzi), *Tola asarlar toplami*, 5 vols., Tashkent, 1988-89. Sobir Mirbaliev, *Abdulla Qodiriy (Hayoti va ijodi)*, Tashkent, 2004. Ibrohim Mirzaev, *Abdulla Qodiriyning ijodiy evoliutsiyasi*, Tashkent, 1977. Anbar Otin, *Sheʿrlar: risola (Šeʿrlar: resāla)*, Tashkent, 1970. Abdulla Qodiriy (ʿAbd-Allāh Qāderi), *Tola asarlar toplami* I, Tashkent, 1995. Habibulla Qodiriy (Ḥabib-Allāh Qāderi), *Otam haqida*, Tashkent, 1983. Mahbuba Qodirova, *Shoira Anbar Otin*, Tashkent, 1991. Begali Qosimov, *Maslakdošlar. Behbudiy, Ajziy, Fitrat*, Tashkent, 1994. M. Rahmonov, *Hamza Hakimzoda Niyoziy va ozbek sovet teatri*, Tashkent, 1959. O. Sharafiddinov, "20-30 yillardagi hukmron 'mafkura' va jaded adabiyoti," in Dilorom Agzamovna Alimova, ed., *Jadidčilik: Islahot, yangilaniš, mustaqillik va taraqqiyot učun kuraš*, Tashkent, 1999, pp. 188-200. Iusuf Sultanov, *Khamza. Ocherk zhizni i tvorchestva* (Hamza. A sketch of his life and works), Tashkent, 1984. Tolagan Khojamiyorov Tavallo (Tawallā), *Ravnaq ul-Islom* (*Rawnaq al-Eslām*), Tashkent, 1993 (A short introduction to Tawallā's life by B. Qosimov, pp. 3-12).

(K. HITCHINS)

JĀF, designation of a once large Kurdish nomadic confederation living in south Iraqi Kurdistan and in the Sanandaj area of Iranian Kurdistan. The former used to be called Morādi, because they had helped the Ottoman Sultan Morād IV to capture Baghdad in about 1638 (Nikitine, p. 171, tr. p. 369). The latter is known as Javānrudi after the main area of their concentration.

Jāf tribal confederation must have been formed some time in the early 17th century, since Šaraf-al-Din Bedlisi (q.v.), the author of the first written history of Kurdistan (comp. 1595), makes no mention of such a tribe, although it is referred to in the Perso-Ottoman peace treaty of 14 Moḥarram 1049/17 May 1639 (Hurewitz, tr. and ed., I, p. 27). The Jāf are culturally related to the the inhabitants of central Kurdsistan, like the Mokri, Bābān, and Sōrān. They are Sunnite Muslims of Shafeʿite persuasion, with a good number of them belonging to the Qāderi and Naqšbandi Sufi orders. According to the oral traditions of the Tāyšaʾi branch, the members of this branch were originally Christians and came from Armenia (Sanandaji, p. 460). According to Moḥammad Marduḵ (I, pp. 78, 102), Timur brought the Qobādi and Bāwajāni (Bābājāni) branches of Jāf from the Ottoman territories in Mesopotamia to their present location in Persia.

During the Constitutional Revolution of 1907-09 (q.v.), the Jāf of Iraq and some southern Kurdish tribes supported Prince Abu'l Fatḥ Mirzā Sālār-al-Dawla, who had married a daughter of the chief of Iraqi Jāfs chief, Maḥmud Pāšā, and was planning to move in force against the constitutional government in Tehran. They were, however, routed at about ninety miles southeast of Tehran at the end of September 1911 by an army of the Constitutionalists led by Epʿrem Khan (q.v.; Kasravi, pp. 186-94; Marduḵ, II, pp. 278 ff.; Malekzāda, VII, pp. 53 ff.).

In the past, the seasonal migrations of this large tribe across the Perso-Ottomman border, had made them a significant factor in the political relations between the two countries. The movement of the tribe, whose large size and nomadic habits often disturbed the peace and disrupted the economic activities in the areas along their migrating route, was always a cause of grave concern for local governments. Eventually Farhād Mirzā Moʿtamed-al-Dawla, the governor of Kurdistan in the years 1284-91/1867-74, prevented the sections stationed in the Ottoman territories from entering Persia (Sanandaji, p. 326).

The Jāf of Javānrud staged a few rebellions during the reigns of Reżā Shah Pahlavi (1925-41) and his son and successor Moḥammad-Reżā Shah (1941-79), which were mainly due to the relentless centralization policy of the government. None of these uprisings, however, lasted long or spread widely enough to cause any serious concern for the government. Their last rebellion was a brief one in 1956.

The Jāf are to be found settled everywhere in the region between Sanandaj and Kermānšāh, an area bordering Iraq on the west and once a part of the Ardalān district. The main body of the tribe moved to the Ottoman territory toward the end of the 17th century, after a battle with the governor (*wāli*) of Ardalān, in which their chief and his son were taken prisoner and killed. They settled in the Solaymāniya district, whose governor gave them protection and let them graze their flocks in a region south of this city down to a region of Ḵāneqin in present-day Iraq. The sections that remained behind in Persia gradually joined the Gurān (q.v.) and became a part of their tribal confederation.

The language of the Jāf belongs to the group of Kurdish dialects known as Sōrāni, but it has adopted many elements of Gurāni and south Kurdish, especially in regions like "Māhidašt" and Qaṣr-e Širin, where they live next to the south Kurdish speakers in many towns and villages.

Bibliography: Iraj Afšār Sistāni, *Ilhā, čadornešinān wa ṭawāyef-e ʿašāyeri-e Irān*, 2 vols., Tehran, 1987, I, pp. 248-50. Amir Šaraf-al-Din Bedlisi, *Šaraf-nāma: tāriḵ-e mofaṣṣal-e kordestān*, ed., Moḥammad ʿAbbāsi, 2nd ed., Tehran, 1988. Jacob C. Hurewitz, "The Treaty of Peace and Frontiers: The Ottoman and Empire of Persia 17 May 1639," in idem, tr. and ed., *The Middle East and North Africa in World Politics: A Documentary Record*, 2 vols., New Haven, 1975-79, I, pp. 25-28. Aḥmad Kasrawi, *Tāriḵ-e hejdah-sāla-ye Āḏarbāyjān*, Tehran, 1954. Mahdi Malekzāda, *Tāriḵ-e enqelāb-e mašruṭiyat-e Irān*, 7 vols., Tehran, n.d. Moḥammad Marduḵ Kordestāni, *Tāriḵ-e Kord wa Kordestān wa tawābeʿ yā tāriḵ-e Marduḵ*, 2 vols., Sanandaj, n.d., pp. 78, 278 ff. Basile Nikitine, *Les Kurdes: étude sociologique et historique*, Paris, 1956; tr. Moḥammad Qāżi as *Kord wa Kordestān*, Tehran, 1988. Faḵr-al-Kottāb Mirzā Šokr-Allāh Sanandaji, *Toḥfa-ye nāṣeri dar tāriḵ wa joḡrāfiā-ye Kordestān*, ed., Ḥešmat-Allāh Ṭabibi, Tehran 1988, pp. 326, 460.

(M. REZA FARIBORZ HAMZEH'EE)

JAʿFAR B. MOḤAMMAD B. **ḤARB**, ABU'L-FAZL AL-HAMDĀNI (d. 236/850 at the age of 59), also called al-Ašajj ('scar-face' or 'skull-broken'), Muʿtazilite theologian who lived in Baghdad. His family was of Yemeni descent, as is shown by the *nesba* (cf. Masʿudi, *Moruj*, ed. Pellat, V, p. 21), and the reading *Hamadāni*, which would turn him into a Persian (Nader, p. 373; Sezgin, *GAS* I, p. 619), has to be abandoned. The ancestral relations of Jaʿfar b. Ḥarb are difficult to reconstruct. His name is normally shortened to Jaʿfar b. Ḥarb, but Ḥarb was, in fact, the name of his grandfather or great-grandfather (cf. Tawḥidi, IV, p. 215, no. 783), who seems to have been a person of some renown and was possibly identical with an Abbasid general who died in 147/764 (Masʿudi, *Moruj*, ed. Pellat, V, p. 21; cf. van Ess, 1991-97, III, p. 12). His father, a certain Moḥammad b. Ḥarb, may have been the chief of police in Basra for some time, and this would, at least, best explain why, in his youth, Jaʿfar b. Ḥarb studied with Abu'l-Hoḏayl ʿAffāf (ca. 135-227/752-841; q.v.), who lived there, and not with Bešr b. al-Moʿtamer (for him see van Ess, 1991-97, III, pp. 107-30), the head of the Muʿtazilite movement in Baghdad. At a later date, the Abbasid governor Qoṯam b. Jaʿfar invited Jaʿfar b. Ḥarb to Basra again for a disputation with his former teacher, when Abu'l-Hoḏayl was already at a rather advanced age (van Ess, 1994, pp. 14 f.). For some time Jaʿfar b. Ḥarb had a position in the army, and the scar on his forehead may have been the trace of a wound, which he had got in battle. However, the Muʿtazilite tradition avoids the nickname Ašajj and rather presents him as somebody who, because of his piety, was invited to the court of the Abbasid caliph al-Wāṯeq (r. 227-32/842-47) and had discussions there with the Ibadite (*Ebāżi*; see Lewicki, pp. 648-60) scholar Yaḥyā b. Kāmel, the contents of which seem to have been subsequently published as *al-Masāʾel al-jalila* ('The Important Questions'; see Ebn al-Nadim, ed. Tajaddod, pp. 213, 233). Both theologians are said to have been friends, which would be all the more plausible, if we can assume that Jaʿfar's father was identical with Moḥammad b. Ḥarb, who is mentioned as an Ibadite theologian by Ašʿari (pp. 108, 120, line 7). But this suggestion, again, necessarily remains highly hypothetical (van Ess, 1991-97, IV, pp. 173 ff.). Before al-Wāṯeq came to power, however, Jaʿfar b. Ḥarb had already passed through a religious crisis which had made him renounce his military job (and perhaps his pecuniary security too). He had passed under the influence of Abu Musā Mordār (q.v.; see van Ess, 1991-97, III, pp. 134-35 and 138 f.), a Muʿtazilite with a Persian nickname (*mordār* means 'carrion'), who had strong ascetic leanings and died in 226/841. Mordār called on him to do penance for his former life, and by diving into the river Tigris Jaʿfar b. Ḥarb washed off his sins; afterwards he put on new clothes offered to him by Mordār (ʿAbd-al-Jabbār, p. 278). These may have been Sufi garments, because the group of Baghdadi intellectuals, whom he joined, was named *Ṣufiyat al-moʿtazela* at that time (van Ess, 1991-97, III, pp. 130 ff.). The main sin, however, from which he wanted to be absolved was probably that of having worked for the government, and in the army at that.

The crisis affected Jaʿfar b. Ḥarb's theological outlook. Trained by Abu'l-Hoḏayl, he had started as an atomist; unlike his contemporary Jāḥeẓ (q.v.), he did not feel tempted by the "naturalist" approach of Abu Esḥāq Naẓẓām (q.v.). Yet he had attacked Abu'l-Hoḏayl because of the latter's idea that even in paradise all human actions will come to an end, and, therefore, the blessed have to remain in eternal immobility. This may have been the subject of his *Ketāb towbiḵ Abi'l-Hoḏayl* (van Ess, 1991-97, III, pp. 260 f.). In Baghdad, Jaʿfar b. Ḥarb had to take notice of Bešr b. al-Moʿtamer's theory of benevolence, which purported that, since the Muʿtazilites could not uphold God's "creating" belief or unbelief, they had to explain the difference between Muslims and pagans by an act of God's benevolence (*lotf*) being accorded to those who have the true faith (van Ess, 1991-97, III, pp. 121 f.). This, however, seemed to contradict the Muʿtazilite idea that God always acts in the most salutary (*aṣlaḥ*) way for everybody, that is, even for unbelievers. The geographical expansion of the Muʿtazilites had resulted in a certain incongruity of the "system," which expressed itself in the rise of two different schools of Basra and Baghdad, and Jaʿfar b. Ḥarb may therefore have felt reduced to merely adding footnotes to insolvable problems. In any case, the sources confirm that, after his "conversion," he did not deal with doctrinal niceties any more, but rather decided to write about broad subjects for a large audience. Mordār had taken the same step before him.

The titles of a few books which belong to this late period are quoted, via Ebn Yazdād, the early historian of the Muʿtazilite school, by Qāżi ʿAbd-al-Jabbār (p. 282): *Naṣiḥat al-ʿāmma, al-Iżāḥ, al-Mostaršed, al-taʿlim*, and *al-Diāna*. Furthermore, he lists a *Ketāb al-oṣul* which, however, may have pertained to a different literary genre, for it seems highly probable that, as W. Madelung has suggested (pp. 220-36), the *Ketāb oṣul al-neḥal*, edited under the name of a relatively well-known later Muʿtazilite al-Nāšiʾ al-Akbar, was in reality written by Jaʿfar b. Ḥarb. This book would then be, to date, the oldest specimen, at least partially preserved, of Islamic heresiography, and the fact that it is the only work where the *Ṣufiyat al-moʿtazela* are mentioned under this expression and are extensively treated as a separate group would be of special significance. In another treatise entitled *Ketāb motašābeh al-Qorʾān*, Jaʿfar b. Ḥarb seems to have commented upon the predestinarian verses of the Qurʾān; the text was still known to the Muʿtazilite Ebn al-Ḵallāl (Sezgin, *GAS* I, 624) when, more than one century later, he wrote his *Radd ʿalā al-jabriya*.

As the head of the Baghdad school, Jaʿfar b. Ḥarb was followed by Eskāfi (q.v.) who, however, survived him by a few years only. He remained a provocative figure for Shiʿite and Sunnite theologians alike. Ḥasan b. Musā Nowbaḵti (q.v. at *www.iranica.com*) and Mofid criticized him because of his concept of leadership (*emāmat*), for, in spite of having high respect for Imam ʿAli (whom he seems to have regarded as the founder of Islamic theological thinking), he did not believe in the prerogatives of the imams. He was also attacked by ʿAbd-al-ʿAziz b. Moḥammad b. Esḥāq Ṭabari, known as Dommal, a pupil of Ašʿari (Ebn ʿAsāker, XLIII, pp. 7, 16 f.), and by ʿAbd-al-Qāher Baḡdādi (q.v.) in his *Ketāb al-ḥarb ʿalā Ebn Ḥarb*, but we do not know for what reasons (for more details on books and refutations, see van Ess, 1991-97, VI, pp. 288-90; for doxographical material, see VI, pp. 290-300).

Bibliography: Qāżi ʿAbd-al-Jabbār, *Fażl al-eʿtezāl*, ed. Foʾād Sayyed, Tunis, 1974. ʿAli b. Esmāʿil Ašʿari, *Maqālāt al-eslāmiyin*, ed. H. Ritter, 3 vols., Istanbul, 1927-33, index, s. n. Ebn ʿAsāker, *Taʾrik Demašq*, ed. ʿOmar b. Ḡarāma ʿAmrawi, 70 vols., Damascus 1402/1981. J. van Ess, *Theologie und Gesellschaft im 2. und 3. Jahrhundert Hidschra: eine Geschichte des religiösen Denkens im frühen Islam*, 6 vols., Berlin and New York, 1991-97; IV, pp. 68-77 for Jaʿfar b. Ḥarb. Idem, "Abu l'Hudhayl in Contact: The Genesis of an Anecdote," in *Islamic Theology and Philosophy: Studies in Honor of George F. Hourani*, ed. M. E. Marmura, Albany, 1984, pp. 13-30. D. Gimaret, *La doctrine d'al-Ash'ari*, Paris, 1990, pp. 105, 306 f., 317. T. Lewicki, "al-Ibāḍiyya," in *EI*[2] III, 1971, pp. 648-60. W. Madelung, "Frühe mu'tazilitische Häresiographie: das *Kitāb al-Uṣūl* des Ǧaʿfar b. Ḥarb," *Der Islam* 57, 1980, pp. 220-36. A. N. Nader, "D̲jaʿfar b. Ḥarb," in *EI*[2] II, 1965, p. 373. C. Schöck, *Koranexegese, Grammatik und Logik*, Leiden, 2006, pp. 210 f. Šahrastāni, *Livre des Religions et des Sectes*, tr. D. Gimaret and G. Monnot, 2 vols., Paris, 1986-93; I, pp. 218 f., 243 f. Abu Ḥayyān Tawḥidi, *Al-baṣaʾer wa'l-ḏaḵāʾer*, ed. W. Qāżi, 9 vols. in 5, Beirut, 1408/1988. C. Tunç, "Ca'fer b. Harb," *Türkiye diyanet vakfı İslâm ansiklopedisi* VI, 1992, pp. 549-51.

(JOSEF VAN ESS)

JAʿFAR B. **MANṢUR**-AL-**YAMAN**, a high-ranking Ismaʿili author who flourished during the reigns of the first four Fatimid caliphs. His father, Ebn Ḥawšab (d. 302/914, q.v.), originated from a learned Shiʿite family of Kufa, and pioneered the Ismaʿili *daʿwa* (see FATIMIDS) in the Yemen, where his conquests earned him the honorific title of Manṣur-al-Yaman (Conqueror of Yemen). Jaʿfar's detailed account of his father's life (*Sirat abihi*) has been largely preserved through quotations. After Ebn Ḥawšab's death, Jaʿfar was his only son to remain faithful to the mission (*daʿwa*). Antagonism between him and his disgruntled brother, Abu'l-Ḥasan, eventually forced him to emigrate to the Maḡreb, where he arrived during the reign of the second Fatimid caliph al-Qāʾem (r. 322-34/933-46; see Ḥammādi, pp. 39-41.). Jaʿfar witnessed the serious anti-Fatimid rebellion led by the Kharijite Abu Yazid (d. 336/947), which rattled the Fatimid state during the last two years of al-Qāʾem's reign and the beginning of the reign of his successor al-Manṣur (r. 334-41/946-53). Jaʿfar's fervent support for the Fatimids is expressed in his poems, composed during the years 333-36/945-48 and celebrating Fatimid victories (Stern, pp. 146-52). After defeating Abu Yazid, al-Manṣur founded, near Qayrawān, his new residential town Manṣuriya, where Jaʿfar had a fine house. His financial situation led him to mortgage his house, and he was in danger of losing it when the caliph al-Moʿezz (r. 341-65/953-75) saved him from his predicament by paying off his debt in recognition of his and his father's services (ʿAzizi Jawḏari, pp. 126-27; tr. pp. 193-94). Jaʿfar died at an unknown date in the early period of al-Moʿezz's reign.

Jaʿfar's works were often copied and incorporated in later anthologies of Ismaʿili literature (Poonawala, pp. 71-75, 144, 150, 317, 323). They are largely devoted to allegorical interpretation (*taʾwil*) in which he relates words and expressions from the Qurʾān, Islamic rituals, and letters of the Arabic alphabet, to the grades of the hierarchy of the Fatimid *daʿwa* (*ḥodud al-din*); the numbers seven and twelve feature prominently in his scheme. Among Jaʿfar's early works are *Ketāb al-ʿālem wa'l-ḡolām*, a dialogue of spiritual initiation, and *Ketāb al-kašf* containing six short pre-Fatimid *taʾwil* treatises dealing mainly with the subject of the imamate. Jaʿfar viewed the imamate as a continuation of prophecy. His works on stories of the prophets were written particularly with this view. These include *al-Šawāhed wa'l-bayān* supporting ʿAli's succession to the imamate, *Sarāʾer al-noṭaqāʾ* and its sequel *Asrār al-noṭaqāʾ*, as well as the interpretation of the *sura* Yusof contained in his *Ketāb al-farāʾeż wa ḥodud al-din*. One epistle of Jaʿfar, *Šarḥ dalālāt ḥoruf al-moʿjam* (or *Resālat taʾwil ḥoruf al-moʿjam*), is devoted to the interpretation of the letters of the Arabic alphabet.

Bibliography: Works. *Ketāb al-farāʾeż wa ḥodud al-din*, The Institute of Ismaili Studies Library (IISL), London, MS no. 928; *al-Reżāʾ fi'l-bāṭen*, London, IISL, MS no. 1143; *Šarḥ dalālāt ḥoruf al-moʿjam*, London, IISL, MS no. 141; *al-Šawāhed wa'l-bayān*, London, IISL, MS no. 142; *Taʾwil surat al-nesāʾ*, London, IISL, MS no. 1103; *Ketāb al-ʿālem wa'l-ḡolām*, ed. and tr. James W. Morris as *The Master and the Disciple: An Early Islamic Spiritual Dialogue*, London, 2001; *Ketāb al-kašf*, ed. Rudolf Strothmann, London, 1952; *Sarāʾer al-noṭaqāʾ* and *Asrār al-noṭaqāʾ*, ed. Moṣṭafā Ḡāleb as *Sarāʾer wa asrār al-noṭaqāʾ*, Beirut, 1984.

Studies: Abu ʿAli Manṣur ʿAzizi Jawḏari, *Sirat al-ostād Jawḏar: wa behi tawqiʿāt al-aʾemma al-fāṭemiyin*, ed. Moḥammad Kāmel Ḥosayn and Moḥammad ʿAbd-al-Hādi Šaʿira, Cairo, 1954; tr. Marius Canard, as *Vie de l'Ustadh Jaudhar (contenant sermons, lettres et rescrits des premiers califes fatimides*, Algiers, 1958. Farhad Daftary, *Ismāʿīlīs: Their History and Doctrines*, Cambridge, 1990. Heinz Halm, "D͟jaʿfar b. Manṣūr al-Yaman," in *EI²*, suppl, pp. 236-37. Ḥosayn b. Fayż-Allāh Hamdāni, *al-Ṣolayḥiyun wa'l-ḥaraka al-fāṭemiya fi'l-Yaman*, Cairo, 1955. Moḥammad b. Mālek Ḥammādi, *Kašf asrār al-bāṭeniya wa akḇār al-Qarāmeṭa*, ed. Moḥammad Zāhed b. Ḥasan Kawṯari, Cairo, 1939. Ismail K. Poonawala, *Biobibliography of Ismāʿīlī Literature*, Malibu, 1977. Edris ʿEmād-al-Din Qoraši, *ʿOyun al-akḇār wa fonun al-āṯār fi fażāʾel al-aʾemma al-aṭhār*, vols. 4-6, ed. Moṣṭafā Ḡāleb, Beirut, 1973-84; vol. 5 and part of vol. 6 ed. Moḥammad Yaʿlāwi, Beirut, 1985. Fuat Zezgin, *Geschichte des arabischen Schrifttums*, 8 vols., Leiden, 1967-82, I, pp. 578-79. Samuel Stern, *Studies in Early Ismāʿīlism*, Max Schloessinger Memorial Series, Monograph 1, Jerusalem, 1983.

(HAMID HAJI)

JAʿFAR B. **YAḤYĀ BARMAKI**. See BARMAKIDS.

JAʿFAR KHAN AZ FARANG ĀMADEH. See MOQADDAM, ḤASAN. Forthcoming, online.

JAʿFAR KHAN BAKṮIĀRI. See BAKṮIĀRI.

JAʿFAR AL-**ṢĀDEQ**, ABU ʿABD-ALLĀH, the sixth imam of the Imami Shiʿites. He was the eldest son of Imam Moḥammad al-Bāqer (q.v.) and, on the side of his mother, Omm Farwa, a descendent of Abu Bakr by four generations (Ṭabari, III/IV, p. 2509; Yaʿqubi, II, p. 458; Ebn Qotayba, p. 215). He spent most of his life in Medina, where he built up a circle of followers primarily as a theologian, Ḥadith transmitter, and jurist (*faqih*).

i. *Life*.
ii. *Teachings*.
iii. *And Sufism*.
iv. *And Esoteric sciences*.
v. *And herbal medicine*.
vi. *And Shiʿite jurisprudence*. See SHIʿISM. Forthcoming, online.

i. Life

The most extensive biographical sources for Jaʿfar al-Ṣādeq are to be found amongst the various Shiʿite branches, though the exact date of his birth, or his accession to the imamate are uncertain. Most sources mention 83/702 for his birth (though 80/699 and 86/705 are also recorded; e.g., Yaʿqubi, II, p. 458; Masʿudi, IV, p. 132; ʿĀmeli, IV/2, p. 29). Similarly, the date when he became imam (that is, the death of his father, the fifth imam, Moḥammad al-Bāqer) is recorded as 117/735 in most sources (though 114/732 and 126/743 are also found in some sources; e.g., Ebn Qotayba, p., 215; ʿĀmeli, IV/2, p. 3). His death date is almost universally agreed to have been 148/765.

Imam Jaʿfar al-Ṣādeq's life spanned the latter half of the Umayyad dynasty ruling from Damascus, which was marked by various rebellions (mainly by Shiʿite movements), the rise of the ʿAbbasids (a movement that drew on Shiʿite themes), and the establishment of the ʿAbbasid caliphate in Baghdad. Throughout this period, he appears to have maintained the politically quietist stance of his father, Imam Moḥammad al-Bāqer. Whether the revolt of Imam al-Bāqer's half-brother Zayd b. ʿAli in 122/740 was during Jaʿfar al-Ṣādeq's imamate or that of his father depends on which of the various dates for the latter's death is taken. It is clear, however, that Jaʿfar al-Ṣādeq did not wish to be associated with the revolt and, according to a number of reports Shaikh Mofid (*Eršād* II, pp. 174-75) condemned the uprising, since he believed that the rebellion would be counter-productive and ultimately harmful to the true community of believers (i.e., the Shiʿites). Similarly, he refused to be involved in the ʿAbbasid uprising and offered no support even after the ʿAbbasids gained power in 132/750. His motives for this refusal were grounded in his belief that he alone was the imam, having been designated as such by the preceding imam, his father. This belief was founded on the doctrine of *naṣṣ* (clear designation) of the incumbent imam of his successor. *Naṣṣ* was in turn based on the notion that the incumbent imam was protected from error by God (*ʿeṣma* "inerrency"; see ČAHĀRDAH MAʿṢUM). Therefore, the incumbent imam's designation was, in effect, a revealing of God's will for the future leadership of the Shiʿites. Some, particularly the followers of Zayd (the Zaydiya), did not recognize this doctrine and branched off to form their own distinct Shiʿite tradition, with quite different notions of the functions of an imam.

Apart from those traditions that record the explicit designation of Jaʿfar al-Ṣādeq as imam by his father, there is also a bundle of historical accounts of Jaʿfar al-Ṣādeq acting as Moḥammad al-Bāqer's traveling companion. Such stories reinforce the closeness of the father-son relationship and further secure Jaʿfar al-Ṣādeq's imamate in the face of Zaydi attack. In particular, thre is the story of Imam al-Bāqer being summoned to Damascus by Hešām b. ʿAbd-al-Malek (r. 724-43) after besting Nāfeʿ in debate over the powers of Imam ʿAli b. Abi Ṭāleb (q.v.). Jaʿfar al-Ṣādeq accompanied his father on this journey (for an account of the debate and its aftermath, see Qomi, II, pp. 246-86). Such explicit confrontations with the ruling power were, however, rare for both of them. Just as he had refused to be involved in the uprisings of Zayd or the ʿAbbasids against Umayyad rule, Jaʿfar al-Ṣādeq offered no support to the uprising of his own cousin Moḥammad b. ʿAbd-Allāh b. Ḥasan, called al-Nafs al-Zakiya (the Pure Soul) and referred to as al-Mahdi (Ebn al-Ṭeqṭaqā, pp. 132-33), in 145/762 against the ʿAbbasids after they had gained power in Baghdad.

Jaʿfar al-Ṣādeq was, it seems, happy to pursue a scholarly imamate, studying and teaching in Medina. He acquired a number of followers and supporters, most (though not all) of Shiʿite persuasion. He is respected by the Sunnis as a transmitter of Hadith and a jurist (*faqih*), while the Shiʿites, who consider him an imam and as such infallible (see ČAHĀRDAH MAʿṢUM), record his sayings and actions in works of Hadith and jurisprudence (*feqh*, q.v.). The Ismaʿili jurist Qāżi Abu Ḥanifa Noʿmān b. Moḥammad Qayrawāni (d. 363/974), has preserved a number of Jaʿfar al-Ṣādeq's legal opinions, presenting them as authoritative expositions of the Islamic religious law (*šariʿa*; see, e.g., *Daʿāʾem* I, p. 4). In imami Shiʿite writings, his legal dicta constitute the most important source of imami law. Indeed, imami legal doctrine is called *al-Maḏhab al-Jaʿfari* by both Imamis and Sunnis in recognition of his legal authority. A number of works are attributed to him, though none of these can be securely described as authored by Jaʿfar al-Ṣādeq. Included in this list is a Qurʾān commentary (*tafsir*), a work on divination (*Ketāb al-jafr*), various versions of his will, and a number of collections of legal dicta (Sezgin, I, pp. 528-32, IV, pp. 128-31, VII, pp. 323-24; ʿĀmeli, IV/2, pp. 52 ff.; Āḡā Bozorg Ṭehrāni, III, p. 121, XXI, pp. 110-11). In addition to these, there are many reports attributed to him in the early Shiʿite Hadith collections; he features as a central source of imami doctrine, for example, in Moḥammad b. Yaʿqub Kolayni's *al-Kāfi*.

Jaʿfar al-Ṣādeq's circle of followers included two of the most important imami theologians, namely, Abu Moḥammad Hešām b. Ḥakam (d. 179/796) and Abu Jaʿfar Moḥammad b. Noʿmān (d. after 183/799). Hešām proposed a number of doctrines that later became orthodox imami theology, including the rational necessity of the divinely guided imam in every age to teach and lead God's community. Moḥammad b. Noʿmān (nicknamed Šayṭān al-Ṭāq) held anthropomorphist doctrines, which on occasions clashed with later imami theology (influenced as it was by Moʿtazelite thought; for their works see Ebn al-Nadim, pp. 223-24, tr. pp. 437-38). The "extremist" (*ḡāli*; see ḠOLĀT) Abu'l-Ḵaṭṭāb Moḥammad Asadi (executed ca. 138/755) is also said to have been associated with Jaʿfar al-Ṣādeq. According to the heresiographers, Abu'l-Ḵaṭṭāb claimed to have been appointed as the representative of Jaʿfar al-Ṣādeq, receiving secret doctrines from him. His extreme views on the divinity of Jaʿfar al-Ṣādeq and his own status as the prophetic emissary of God (i.e., Jaʿfar al-Ṣādeq) seem to have led Jaʿfar al-Ṣādeq to repudiate him, though Abu'l-Ḵaṭṭāb supposedly maintained that the repudiation was part of Jaʿfar al-Ṣādeq's technique at preserving his true nature. The followers of his doctrine were called K̲aṭṭābiya (Ašʿari, pp. 10-13; Šahrastāni, pp. 136-38, tr. Afżal-al-Din Torka, pp. 140-41, tr. Haarbrücker, I, pp. 206-8; Nawbak̲ti, pp. 68 ff.). In any case, imami tradition rejects any association between Jaʿfar al-Ṣādeq and Abu'l-K̲aṭṭāb's eccentric views.

Jaʿfar al-Ṣādeq is also recorded as having taught with, or studied under Abu Ḥanifa and Mālek b. Anas, two of the eponyms of the Sunni legal schools (the Ḥanafiya and the Mālekiya respectively). More is recorded concerning the relationship between Abu Ḥanifa and Jaʿfar al-Ṣādeq. Shiʿite sources portray Jaʿfar al-Ṣādeq as consistently humbling Abu Ḥanifa, pointing out defects in his reasoning and his incompetence in legal argument (see, e.g., Ebn Bābawayh, *ʿElal al-Šariʿa* I, p. 86). They clearly arose out of a Shiʿi-Sunni (and more specifically Shiʿi-Ḥanafi) polemic, though they may reflect the character of the relationship between the two jurists.

According to most sources, Jaʿfar al-Ṣādeq died in 148/765 (e.g., Masʿudi, IV, pp. 132-33), supposedly poisoned by the ʿAbbasid caliph al-Manṣur, though to what political end is unclear. He left behind him uncertainty about the future of the imamate. He had designated Abu Moḥammad Esmāʿil (q.v.), his eldest son by his first wife, Fāṭema, as the next imam, but Esmāʿil had predeceased him. Some claimed that Esmāʿil had not died, but was in hiding; others claimed that Esmāʿil's son, Moḥammad, should be the next imam. Both of these groups went on to form the Ismaʿiliya (q.v.) Shiʿite (Daftary, pp. 93-99). Others claimed that after Esmāʿil, Jaʿfar al-Ṣādeq had designated his second eldest son ʿAbd-Allāh al-Afṭaḥ as the next imam. The majority, though, supported the imamate of Musā al-Kāẓem, son of Ḥamida (or Ḥomayda, a Berber slave) and Jaʿfar al-Ṣādeq, as the imam. It was this line which went to form the Twelver (imami) Shiʿite, which has predominated in Persia since the 16th century (Daftary, pp. 93-99; ʿĀmeli, IV/2, p. 80).

Bibliography: ʿAbd-al-ʿAziz Sayyed-al-Ahl, *Jaʿfar b. Moḥammad*, Beirut, 1954. Āḡā Bozorg Ṭehrāni, *al-Ḏariʿa elā taṣānif al-šiʿa*, 24 vols. in 27, Najaf and Tehran, 1936-78. Moḥsen al-Amin Ḥosayni ʿĀmeli, *Aʿyān al-šiʿa*, ed. Ḥasan al-Amin, Beirut, 1962, IV/2, pp. 29-79. Abu'l-Ḥasan ʿAlī b. Esmāʿīl Ašʿarī, *Ketāb maqālāt al-eslāmīyīn wa ek̲telāf al-moṣellīn*, ed. Helmut Ritter, Cairo, 2000. Farhad Daftary, *The Ismāʿīlīs: Their History and Doctrines*, Cambridge etc., 1990. Ebn al-Nadim, *Ketāb al-fehrest*, ed. Reżā Tajaddod, Tehran, 1971; tr. Bayard Dodge as *The Fihrist of al-Nadīm: A Tenth-Century Survey of Muslim Culture*, 2 vols., New York, 1979. Ebn Qotayba, *Ketāb al-maʿāref*, ed. Ṯarwat ʿOkāša, Cairo, 1960. Ebn al-Ṭeqṭaqā, *al-Fak̲ri fi'al-ādāb al-solṭāniya wa'l-dowal al-eslāmiya*, Egypt, n.d. S. H. M. Jafri, *The Origins and Early Development of Shiʿa Islam*, London and New York, 1979, pp. 259-79. Ahmad Kazemi Mousavi, *Religious Authority in Shiʿite Islam: From the Office of Mufti to the Institution of Marjaʿ*, Kuala Lampur, 1996. Moḥammad b. Yaʿqub al-Kolayni, *al-Kāfi fi ʿlm al-din*, Tehran, 1994. Abu'l-Ḥasan ʿAli Masʿudi, *Moruj al-ḏahab wa maʿāden al-jawhar*, ed. Charles Pellat, 7 vols., Beirut, 1962-79; tr. Barbier de Meynard and Pavet de Courteille as *Les prairies d'or*, rev. and corrected by Charles Pellat, 3 vols., Paris, 1965. Ḥasan b. Musā Nawbak̲ti, *Ketāb feraq al-šiʿa*, tr. Moḥammad-Jawād Maškur as *Tarjama-ye Feraq al-šiʿa-ye Nawbak̲ti*, Tehran, 1974. Abu Ḥanifa Qāżi Noʿmān b. Moḥammad Tamimi, *Daʿāʾem al-Eslām fi ḏekr al-ḥalāl wa'l-ḥarām wa'l-qażāya wa'l-aḥkām*, ed. ʿĀṣaf A. A. Fayżi (Fyzee), 2 vols., Cairo, 1951-61; tr. A. A. A. Fyzee, as *The Pillars of Islam*, completely revised and annotated by Ismail K. Poonawala, 2 vols., New Delhi, 2002-04. ʿAli b. Ebrāhim Qomi, Tafsir al-Qomi, Najaf, 1387/1967. Abu'l-Fatḥ Moḥammad b. ʿAbd-al-Karim Šahrastāni, *Ketāb al-melal wa'l-neḥal*, ed. William Cureton, Leipzig, 1928; tr. Theodore Haarbrücker as *Religionsparthien und Philosophen-Schulen*, 2 vols. in 1, Hildesheim, 1969; tr. Afżal-al-Din Ṣadr Torka Eṣfahāni, ed. Sayyed Moḥammad-Reżā Jalāli Nāʾini, Tehran, 1956. Fuat Sezgin, *Geschichte des arabischen Schrifttums*, 8 vols., Leiden, 1967-82. Moḥammad b. Jarir Ṭabari, *Ketāb taʾrik̲ rosol wa'l-moluk*, ed, M. J. de Goeje et al., 15 vols., Leiden, 1964, III/IV, pp. 2059-60; tr. by various scholars as *The History of al-Ṭabari*, 40 vols., Albany, 1985-2007, XXXIX, pp. 248-49. Aḥmad b. Abi Yaʿqub Yaʿqubi, *Taʾrik̲*, ed. M. Th. Houtsma, 2 vols., Leiden, 1969, pp. 458-60.

(ROBERT GLEAVE)

ii. TEACHINGS

Any attempt to summarize Imam Jaʿfar al-Ṣādeq's teaching is hampered by the fact that his views are reported in support of a number of contradictory theological and legal positions. These conflicting reports emerged as scholars from different schools of thought used his legacy for their own ends. Particular views are attributed to Jaʿfar al-Ṣādeq by one group, often prompting counter-attributions by their rivals. It is clear that nearly all the early intellectual factions of Islam (with the exception perhaps of the Kharijites) wished to incorporate Jaʿfar al-Ṣādeq into their history in order to bolster their schools' positions. The use of Jaʿfar al-Ṣādeq by conflicting and rival theological and legal traditions, obviously a testimony to his perceived importance, complicates any attempt to describe his teachings with certainty and makes the identification of his actual views difficult.

The potential sources for Jaʿfar al-Ṣādeq's teaching fall under a number of categories. First, there is an extensive list of attributed works (both extant and summarized or quoted by later writers), including works of Qurʾānic exegesis, so-called "occult sciences" (dream interpretation, divination by other means and hemerology), theology (normally transmitted through "extremist" or *ḡāli* sources; see GOLĀT), and reflections on Islamic law (*feqh*). Second, there are a large number of oral reports attributed to him. Many of these are to be found in imami

Hadith collections amongst traditions from the other imams constituting legal and theological statements. There are also some accounts of his views found in non-imami Hadith collections (including Prophetic reports in Sunni collections, transmitted through Jaʿfar al-Ṣādeq as well as his own legal views). Third, there are works by (or attributed to) his followers who claim to be representing Jaʿfar al-Ṣādeq's views, or to have written the work on Jaʿfar al-Ṣādeq's orders. In others, Jaʿfar al-Ṣādeq is portrayed as dictating a work to a follower. Finally, there are descriptions of his views found in hagiographic and heresiographical sources. It is not always easy to assess the reliability and authenticity of any of these sources, and even if they can be identified as reliable (or even as reliable summaries of his views), there is always the doctrinal problem of *taqiya* (precautionary dissimulation), where an individual is permitted, for the purposes of personal protection, to express outwardly one opinion, while inwardly holding another. According to most Shiʿite groups, Jaʿfar al-Ṣādeq is said to have advocated *taqiya*, and therefore even an accurate report of his words may not exactly reflect his real views. Consequently, an account of Jaʿfar al-Ṣādeq's teaching is, to a large extent, an account of what others considered his teaching to be within the framework of their own intellectual traditions.

Within what can be described as the Sufi/mystical tradition, Jaʿfar al-Ṣādeq's influence can be seen most obviously in Qurʾānic exegesis. His extent writings include a number of exegetical works, all broadly "mystical" in character. There exists a lengthy Qurʾānic commentary entitled *Tafsir al-Qorʾān*, together with shorter works entitled *Manāfeʿ ṣowar al-Qorʾān* and *Ḵawāṣṣ al-Qorʾān al-aʿẓam* (Āḡā Bozorg Ṭehrāni, VII, p. 273; Sezgin, IV, pp. 529-30). Gerhard Bowering considers the attribution of these works to Jaʿfar al-Ṣādeq as "suspect" (Shaikh Mofid, *Eršād* II, pp. 174-75) In particular the more extensive *Tafsir al-Qorʾān* is accompanied by what, in his view, is a "cryptic" chain of transmission (*esnād*). The style of these commentaries demonstrate a mastery of the lexicon of Muslim mysticism, in particular Sufi *tafsir*, which might indicate a composition date sometime after Jaʿfar al-Ṣādeq's death. There is also an independent tradition of Qurʾānic exegesis attributed to Jaʿfar al-Ṣādeq, found first in the two Sufi *tafsirs* of ʿAbd-al-Raḥmān Solami and extensively cited by later Sufis. Whether these came from a literary or oral source is not clear, although Jaʿfar al-Ṣādeq is identified as one of the master exegetes of the early period of Islam in both of Solami's *tafsirs*. In the *Ḥaqāʾeq al-tafsir* and his *Ziādāt Ḥaqāʾeq al-tafsir*, ʿAbd-al-Raḥmān Solami cites Jaʿfar al-Ṣādeq as one of his major (if not the major) source of knowledge concerning the meaning of Qurʾānic verses.

Jaʿfar al-Ṣādeq's *Meṣbāḥ al-šariʿa wa meftāḥ al-ḥaqiqa* is a work on personal conduct, with chapters on a variety of topics. Issues which are of strictly legal interest (such as pilgrimage, alms, ritual purity) are interspersed with general ethical topics (thankfulness, truthfulness, sincerity) and advice on how to lead a spiritual life and thereby purify the soul (fearing God, guarding oneself against evil, remembrance of God). Moḥammad-Bāqer Majlesi considered the work to have been written not by Jaʿfar al-Ṣādeq but by the famous Sufi Šaqiq b. Ebrāhim Balḵi (d. 194/810, see Majlesi, I, p. 32; Āḡā Bozorg Ṭehrāni, XXI, pp. 110-11). Majlesi's basis for this claim is one of the *esnāds* of the book, which goes back to Šaqiq al-Balḵi, who supposedly related it from "one of the people of knowledge," and not explicitly Jaʿfar al-Ṣādeq. Majlesi states that the *Meṣbāḥ al-šariʿa* is full of Sufi terminology and owes much to the ideas of Sufi shaikhs. There is a distinctively Shiʿite chapter on "Recognizing the Imams," in which the names of all the imams are listed (both those before Jaʿfar al-Ṣādeq and those after him) during a reported exchange between the Prophet and Salmān Fārsi (d. 33/654). If this passage is seen as a later interpolation, then the work may well have had its origins in a Sufi environment, though not necessarily that of Šaqiq Balḵi, since he also predates the occultation. For the faithful, of course, the inclusion of such an exchange is evidence of the Prophet's foreknowledge of the names and fates of his successors. Despite Majlesi's doubts as to its authenticity, the work continues to be extremely popular as a manual of personal devotion and has been the subject of a number of commentaries by famous Shiʿite and Sufi scholars. It has also been translated into various languages, the most popular probably being the Persian *Meṣbāḥ ul-Šariʿa*, a *maṯnawi* by Neẓām ʿAli-šāh Aḥmad Kermāni (d. 1242/1826-27). The work itself does appear to be in the style of legally-inclined Sufis (the so-called sober Sufis), who advocated adherence to the law, whilst at the same time encouraged spiritual reflection on the performance of religious obligations such as purity law, alms, and the like. In a similar vein, the ethical work entitled *al-Ḥekam al-jaʿfariya* consists of a series of sayings by Jaʿfar al-Ṣādeq, divided into chapters ("Good manners," "Rebellion," "Avarice," etc.). This, however, is not so much a work by Jaʿfar al-Ṣādeq, but a collection of his sayings, transmitted through Mofażżal b. ʿOmar Joʿfi (on whom, see below).

An attributed text, also of clear Sunni sectarian leanings, is the *Monāẓara Jaʿfar b. Moḥammad al-Ṣādeq maʿa'l-rāfeżi*. The text is prefaced by an *esnād* (recording it as having been written down in 435/1043) by ʿAbd-al-Raḥmān Anṣāri Boḵāri, a Hanafite scholar of minor importance. The text itself is the record of fourteen question posed by a Shiʿite (the *rāfeżi*), with their replies by Jaʿfar al-Ṣādeq. Jaʿfar al-Ṣādeq dissociates himself from standard Shiʿite doctrines, announces his belief in the superiority of Abu Bakr and rejects the Shiʿite interpretation of numerous Qurʾānic verses. He chastises the Shiʿite *rāfeżi* for failing to understand both the words of the Prophet and the proclamations of the previous imams. The text is obviously an element of the Sunni polemic against the Shiʿite, in which Jaʿfar al-Ṣādeq is reclaimed as a good Sunni scholar, who was not part of the Shiʿa and was not responsible for Shiʿite doctrines of imamate and the illegitimacy of the first three rightly guided caliphs. The general Sunni appraisal of Jaʿfar al-Ṣādeq is positive.

He is remembered as a transmitter of Hadith and a jurist (*faqih*) of some importance.

Within the tradition of scientific Muslim writings, Jaʿfar al-Ṣādeq also holds a central role. There are also a large number of works on the "occult" sciences attributed to him. A work on auspicious and inauspicious days of the year has been edited by Ebied and Young and described as of Persian origin (Ebied and Young, but their characterization of the work has been corrected by Witkam). The editors consider it most likely to be *Ektiārāt ayyām al-šahr*. There is also a work on the interpretation of dreams, popularly known as *Taqsim al-roʾyā* and attributed to Jaʿfar al-Ṣādeq. It is almost certainly identical with the work attributed to Jaʿfar al-Ṣādeq, entitled *Ketāb al-taqsim fi taʿbir al-ḥolm*. In this work, Jaʿfar al-Ṣādeq interprets eighty different categories of dream sightings from the religious (dreams of God, angels, the prophets, and imams) to the profane (dreams of meat, fat, and cheese). There are also a large number of attributed books on divination (given the various titles *Faʾl-nāma, Ketāb al-jafr, al-Kāfiya fi'l-jafr*, see British Museum, MS 426 and Browne, p. 246). Whether these can be considered works attributed to Jaʿfar al-Ṣādeq, or works attributed to Imam ʿAli b. Abi Ṭāleb and transmitted through Jaʿfar al-Ṣādeq is not always clear. From a Shiʿite position, this is unproblematic since there is, religiously, no recognized division between the knowledge of one imam and another. The authenticity of these works, as indicated already, is questionable, but their attribution to Jaʿfar al-Ṣādeq demonstrates that he became associated in later Muslim tradition with esoteric knowledge and the means whereby it might be obtained.

Jaʿfar al-Ṣādeq's work on medicine (*Ṭebb al-Emām al-Ṣādeq*) can also be included in this category (see v. below) , as can his work of various invocations (*Ketāb al-saʿādāt*) that are meant to be used as cures. He allegedly had a close relationship with Jāber b. Ḥayyān (d. 2nd/8th cent.); Jaʿfar al-Ṣādeq is described in a number of sources as Jāber's master (shaikh). Jāber b. Ḥayyān reports that all his knowledge comes from Jaʿfar al-Ṣādeq (though he does mention other masters as well). Jāber is famous as an alchemist, scientist, and natural philosopher. His writings, if authentic, also reveal him to have devised a blend of Neoplatonism and Shiʿism, not dissimilar to that found amongst the Ismaʿilis (particularly the Qarāmeṭa) and certain extremist Shiʿite sects (*ḡolāt*, q.v.). He proposes a division of world history into cycles, the most recent witnessing the seven imams of the Muslims. Jaʿfar al-Ṣādeq, in line with some Ismaʿili views, is counted as the sixth imam in this latest cycle (the seventh being Jaʿfar al-Ṣādeq's eldest son, Esmāʿi; see Rusca).

Through the writings of Jāber and others, Jaʿfar al-Ṣādeq is linked with so-called "extremist" Shiʿism, and figures largely in key texts of the *ḡolāt*. Jaʿfar al-Ṣādeq is said to have had a number of extremist Shiʿites among his followers and, thus, a number of works attributed to these followers supposedly record the teaching of Jaʿfar al-Ṣādeq (either by the normal citation of reports, or through dictation to the follower by Jaʿfar al-Ṣādeq himself). Most famous among these is the *Ketāb al-haft wa'l-aẓella*, attributed to Mofażżal b. ʿOmar Joʿfi. Mofażżal is sometimes described as a follower of the extremist Abu'l-Kaṭṭāb Moḥammad Asadi, though he is also recorded as having direct contact with Jaʿfar al-Ṣādeq. According to heresiographical works, Mofażżal and his followers, called Mofażżaliya, considered Jaʿfar al-Ṣādeq a god and themselves as his prophets (Ašʿari, p. 13). According to imami tradition, however, he was appointed by Jaʿfar al-Ṣādeq to rein in the excesses of the Kaṭṭābiya (the followers of Abu'l-Kaṭṭāb; Šahrastāni, pp. 136-38, tr. Afżal-al-Din Torka, pp. 140-41, tr. Haarbrücker, I, pp. 206-8; Nawbakti, pp. 68 ff.). Mofażżal is also recorded as having aided Imam Musā al-Kāẓem after Jaʿfar's death. Whichever is the case, the principal work attributed to Mofażżal display a clear extremist character. In the *Ketāb al-haft wa'l-aẓella* (p. 32), Mofażżal records his conversations with Jaʿfar al-Ṣādeq, referring to him as "our lord" (*mawlānā*). The conversations are divided into sixty-seven chapters, and cover a range of topics. The emphasis throughout is on the secret knowledge of religion that Jaʿfar al-Ṣādeq is passing on to Mofażżal. Mofażżal is, then, charged with establishing the true sect of the Muslims (called *moʾmenin* "believers") who hold fast to Jaʿfar al-Ṣādeq's doctrines. These include a belief in the transmigration of souls (*tanāsok*), a commitment to dis-associating from the rest of the unbelievers, and the constant need for secrecy with regard to doctrine. Also found in the *Ketāb al-haft* are Jaʿfar al-Ṣādeq's supposed views on the cycles of seven Adams and Imams, which demonstrate a certain gnostic and (and possibly Ismaʿili) influence upon the text (pp. 160-77). The *Ketāb al-ehlilaja* is also presented as Jaʿfar al-Ṣādeq's views transmitted through Mofażżal b. ʿOmar (Moḥsen al-Amin, IV/2, p. 53). The work is supposedly a reply to a request of Mofażżal for a refutation of those who deny God. In it, Jaʿfar al-Ṣādeq recounts his own debate with an Indian doctor who denied God. The debate occurred whilst the doctor was making medicine from the myrobalan plant (known in Arabic as *ehlilaja*, and hence the title of the work).

The *Ketāb al-tawḥid* (also known as *Ketāb al-fekr*, and *Kanz al-ḥaqāʾeq wa'l-maʿāref*), often thought to be identical with the above (see Sezgin, I, p. 530), is presented as Mofażżal's questions with Jaʿfar al-Ṣādeq's answers. The work is also more orthodox in doctrine, with Jaʿfar al-Ṣādeq giving proofs as to the unity of God. Both these book can be seen as works intended to rehabilitate Mofażżal b. ʿOmar as a reliable transmitter of Jaʿfar al-Ṣādeq's writings, countering the portrayal of him as an extremist (*ḡāli*) in works such as *Ketāb al-haft wa'l-aẓella*.

As indicated above, the use of Jaʿfar al-Ṣādeq's name as an authority within the Sufi, scientific, Sunni legal, Ismaʿili and extremist writings demonstrate his importance as a figure within the development of early Muslim thought in that most groups wished to recruit his legacy for their own cause. Yet, the most extensive source for his teachings is to be found within the imami Shiʿite tradition. For Imami Shiʿites Jaʿfar al-Ṣādeq is the sixth imam who established the imamiya as serious intellectual force in the late Umayyad and early ʿAbbasid periods. His most important contribution was in the legal sciences, as reports of his sayings and actions form the major source for imami legal scholars. It is for this reason that the imami legal school is often called *al-Maḏhab al-Jaʿfari*. He also continued to develop imami theological doctrine, a task begun by his father, Imam Moḥammad al-Bāqer, who died, by the earliest reckoning, in 114/732.

For the imami theologians, Jaʿfar al-Ṣādeq's theological doctrine perfectly accords with later relevant discourses. His scattered statements in imami Hadith collections do not, however, reveal a systematic theological tradition. Sunni commentators (see, for example, Abu Zahrā) aim to portray the imamiya as infected by Moʿtazelite doctrine and, therefore, straying from the theologically orthodox position (which later became associated with Abu'l-Ḥasan Ašʿari) advocated by Jaʿfar al-Ṣādeq (van Ess, I, pp. 274-82). This cleavage, however, is part of a Sunni polemic, and there is inconclusive evidence for both the continuity of imami theological doctrine from the time of the imams onwards, and for a cleavage between the thoughts of Jaʿfar al-Ṣādeq and later imami theologians. On the standard questions of *kalām* (theology), Jaʿfar al-Ṣādeq's statements are open to interpretation. For example, concerning the question of predestination and free will, Jaʿfar al-Ṣādeq is attributed with the statement: "Whoever claims that God has ordered evil (*al-faḥšāʾ*), has lied about God. Whoever claims that both good and evil are attributed to him, has lied about God" (Kolayni, 1994, I, pp.156-57). This would appear to absolve God of the responsibility for evil in the world, in line with general Muʿtazilite (and later imami) theological doctrine. Jaʿfar al-Ṣādeq is also credited with the statement that God does not "order created beings to do something without providing for them a means of not doing it, though they do not do it, or not do it without God's permission (Kolayni, 1994, I, p. 160)." This would seem to indicate a more orthodox Sunni (later Ašʿari) position, that God's power is supreme and it is only through His power that human beings perform actions. That Jaʿfar al-Ṣādeq's statements can be interpreted as supporting either position is confirmed by the reported exchange between him and an unknown interlocutor. The interlocutor asks if God forces (*ajbara*) his servants to do evil or whether he had delegated (*fawważa*) power to them. Jaʿfar al-Ṣādeq answers negatively to both questions. When asked "What then?" he relies, "The blessings of your Lord are between these two" (Kolayni, 1994, I, p. 159). Such doctrinal ambiguity can be found in Jaʿfar al-Ṣādeq's statements concerning most of the standard questions of early *kalām* including the nature of creation, God's knowledge, the definition of faith and unbelief, and the created/uncreated nature of speech (and particularly the Qurʾān). The one doctrine in which a reasonably coherent doctrine merges from Jaʿfar al-Ṣādeq's statements is on the imamate. The imam for Jaʿfar al-Ṣādeq (as portrayed in the imami Hadith collections) is clearly not only a supreme legal authority, but also a means whereby the individual believer can gain knowledge of God. The supremacy of the imam's knowledge is such that the individual believer need not embark on detailed theological argumentation himself, but instead should refer all disputes over theological doctrine to the imam. The manner in which these doctrines are expressed by Jaʿfar al-Ṣādeq in the collections are sufficiently vague for them to be cited both by later orthodox imamis and by more extremist Shiʿites. For example, a report of Jaʿfar al-Ṣādeq, transmitted through Mofażżal b. ʿOmar and found in the standard imami Hadith collections, claims for the imams all human knowledge: "We have knowledge of the Torah, the Gospel, and the Psalms, and the explanation of all that is on the Tablets." When asked if this was all of knowledge (*al-ʿelm*), he replied, "This is not knowledge. Knowledge is that which happens day after day, and hour after hour" (Kolayni, 1994, I, pp. 224-25). From such a statement it is not clear whether the imam has both knowledge of the past scriptures and of worldly events, or only the former. The extremists (and indeed some more daring imami theologians) interpret the statement as meaning that the imam has both types of knowledge, and hence as further supporting evidence for the divinational knowledge of Jaʿfar al-Ṣādeq found in the pseudographical literature mentioned above. More conservative imamis interpret Jaʿfar al-Ṣādeq as stating that whilst they have knowledge of past scriptures, they do not have knowledge of future events.

In legal matters, the corpus of Jaʿfar al-Ṣādeq's statements form the major source of imami jurisprudence. He is presented as one who denounces the legal reasoning of his contemporaries. Personal opinion (*raʾy*), personal juristic reasoning (*ejtehād*), and analogical reasoning (*qiās*) are roundly condemned as human attempts to impose conformity, regularity, and predictability onto the Shariʿa of God. Jaʿfar al-Ṣādeq, in these statements, argues that God's law is occasional and unpredictable, and that the servants' duty is not to embark on reasoning in order to discover the law, but to submit to the inscrutable will of God as revealed by the imam. This position is most obviously seen in the various exchanges between Jaʿfar al-Ṣādeq and Abu Ḥanifa (q.v.), after whom the Ḥanafi school of Islamic law is named. Abu Ḥanifa supposedly studied with Jaʿfar al-Ṣādeq, but the reports recorded in imami Hadith collections do not portray him in a positive light. He is recorded as having employed analogical reasoning in his legal judgements, and Jaʿfar al-Ṣādeq is well known as one who rejected this approach. In one exchange Jaʿfar asked Abu Ḥanifa whether it is true that he uses *qiās*. Abu Ḥanifa confirms this, to which Jaʿfar al-Ṣādeq replies, "Do not use *qiās* for the first to use *qiās* was the Devil himself" (Kolayni, 1994, I, p. 58). In another exchange, Abu Ḥanifa asked Jaʿfar al-Ṣādeq about temporary marriage (*motʿa*), and received the reply that this is what is referred to in the Qurʾānic verse "For what you have enjoyed from them, give them their due as a duty" (4:24). Abu Ḥanifa replies "By God, I have never read this verse" (or alternatively "it is as if I had never read this verse"; see Ḥorr Āmeli, *Wasāʾel*, XXVIII, p. 8).

Reports such as this, where Abu Ḥanifa is bested by Jaʿfar al-Ṣādeq and exposed as of inferior intellect, are extremely common, and clearly function as part of an anti-Sunni (and more specifically, anti-Ḥanafi) polemic. References in imami literature to the relationships between Jaʿfar al-Ṣādeq and Mālek b. Anas are less narrative, and Mālek is normally portrayed simply as one who relates Hadith from Jaʿfar al-Ṣādeq (e.g., Ebn Bābawayh, p. 128). Non-imami Shiʿite sources, especially the *Daʿāʾem al-Eslām* of the Ismaʿil Qāżi Noʿmān, also contain reports of the legal opinions of Jaʿfar al-Ṣādeq, along with those of his father Moḥammad al-Bāqer. In general, the reports here agree with those of the imami sources, and, according to Wilferd Madelung, provide a common legal source for the two Shiʿite groupings, and (more tantalizingly) a core of legal teaching which might be more assuredly traced back to Jaʿfar al-Ṣādeq himself.

Despite Jaʿfar al-Ṣādeq's emphasis on the imam's supreme legal authority in the imami sources, there are also hints at a more devolved system of legal authority. Most famous amongst Jaʿfar al-Ṣādeq's saying in this regard is known as the *Maqbula* of ʿOmar b. Ḥanẓala. Ebn Ḥanẓala was a disciple of Jaʿfar al-Ṣādeq and is cited in the *esnāds* as relating a number of sayings from his master, and through intermediaries from Imam al-Bāqer. In the *Maqbula*, Ebn Ḥanẓala asks how legal disputes within the community should be solved, and whether one should take such cases to the ruler (sultan) and his judges. Jaʿfar al-Ṣādeq replies in the negative, indicating that he considered at least the Umayyad and ʿAbbasid caliphates illegitimate. He describes the state apparatus as *ṭāḡut* (an idol or demon) in the *Maqbula* and says that those who take their disputes to the rulers and their judges get only *soḥt* (unlawful decision; Ebn Bābawayh, *Man lā yaḥḍoroho al-faqih* III, p. 3). This is a common motif in subsequent imami juridical literature, as most jurists considered any state not led by the imam himself to be illegitimate, citing the *Maqbula* (amongst other reports from the imams) as evidence of this. In place of the state system, Jaʿfar al-Ṣādeq appears to recommend an informal, and unofficial system of justice for the Shiʿite community. The disputants, he claims, should turn to "those who relate our [i.e., the imams'] Hadiths." The reason for this is that the imams have "made such a one a judge (*ḥākem*) over you." Subsequent questions within the report prompt Jaʿfar al-Ṣādeq to list the means whereby a believer might choose between apparently equally qualified Hadith transmitters (see, for example, Ṭusi, VI, p. 218). The report itself has been variously interpreted by subsequent imami scholars. Some considered it to confer general legal (and for some, political) authority upon the scholars after the occultation (*ḡayba*) of the twelfth imam. Others considered Jaʿfar al-Ṣādeq to be referring solely to Hadith transmitters and not to the *ʿolamāʾ* in general. Whichever interpretation one favors, however, it is clear that the ultimate legal authority of the imam, in this case Jaʿfar al-Ṣādeq, is to be tempered through his appointment of judges of the people in his place. While the imam has optimum community legal authority, he also may, when the need arises, appoint certain persons to act as judges in his stead. Whether this delegation applies only to the time of the imams' presence, and whether it refers to all scholars or just one subset of the *ʿolamāʾ* was the subject of much subsequent debate amongst the imamiya. Jaʿfar al-Ṣādeq's words may have enabled the imamiya to develop an internal means of dispute resolution (and therefore avoid involvement in the judicial system of the ruling state). They did not, however, describe this alternative system in detail. That task was left to subsequent imami thinkers.

The variety of uses to which Jaʿfar al-Ṣādeq's name has been put, and the ideas and teachings which have been attributed to him, are significant not only because they establish him as an important figure in the history of early Islamic thought, but also because they demonstrate the malleability of his legacy. The works attributed to him may be of dubious authenticity, but they do establish his name at least as indicating a mastery of learning generally, and the Islamic sciences in particular. It is the manner in which his contribution has been recast and, at times, re-invented that enables him to be employed by writers in the different Islamic sciences as integral to their development.

Bibliography: (A) Published works attributed to Imam Jaʿfar al-Ṣādeq or allegedly written on his command: *Faʾl-nāma*, ed. Robert Ambelain as *Le fal nameh, ou, Livre des sorts*, Paris, 1984. *al-Ḥekam al-jaʿfariya*, ed. ʿĀref Tāmer, Beirut, 1957. Mofażżal b. ʿOmr Joʿfi (attr. to), *Ketāb al-haft wa'l-aẓella: talmiḏ al-Emām Jaʿfar b. Moḥammad al-Ṣādeq*, ed. ʿĀref Tāmer, Beirut, 1981. *Meṣbāḥ al-šariʿa wa meftāḥ al-ḥaqiqa*, Beirut, 1980; tr. Muna Bilgrami as *The Lantern of the Path*, Shaftesbury, 1989; tr. Ḥasan Moṣṭafawi as *Meṣbāḥ al-šariʿa . . . : ṣad bāb dar ḥekmat wa maʿāref wa siar wa soluk wa aḵlāq wa ādāb wa sonan*, Tehran, 2003. *Monāẓarāt Jaʿfar ibn Moḥammad al-Ṣādeq maʿa'l-rāfeżi fi'l-tafżil bayna Abi Bakr wa ʿAli*, ed. ʿAli Āl Šebl, Riyadh, 1996 or 1997. *Ketāb al-taqsim fi taʿbir al-holm*, ed. ʿAli Zayʿur, Beirut, 2004. *Ṭebb al-Emām al-Ṣādeq*, ed. Moḥsen ʿAqil, Beirut, 1998. *Ketāb al-Tawḥid* (also known as *Tawḥid al-Mofażżal*), Beirut, 2002; tr. Muhammad Ibrahim and Abdullah Shahin as *Tawheed al-mufadhdha: As Dictated by Imam Ja'far As-Sadiq*, Qom, 2004. *Ketāb al-Ehlilaja*, found in Moḥammad-Bāqer Majlesi, *Behār al-anwār*, Beirut, 1983, III, pp. 152-97.

(B) A selection of the unpublished works attributed to Imam Jaʿfar al-Ṣādeq referred to above. *Ketāb al-saʿādāt*, Princeton, Garrett MS no. 229Y, folios 188b-89a. *Faʾl-nāma*, Cambridge MS no. 2.47. *Ketāb al-jafr*, British Museum, MS no. 426.

Studies. Moḥammad Abu Zahrā, *al-Emām al-Ṣādeq: ḥayātoh wa-ʿaṣroh, ārāʾoh wa-feqhoh*, Cairo, 1964. Āḡā Bozorg Ṭehrāni, *al-Ḏariʿa elā taṣānif al-šiʿa*, 24 vols. in 27, Najaf and Tehran, 1936-78. Moḥsen al-Amin Ḥosayni ʿĀmeli, *Aʿyān al-šiʿa*, ed. Ḥasan al-Amin, Beirut, 1962, IV/2, pp. 29-79. Abu'l-Ḥasan ʿAli b. Esmāʿil Ašʿari, *Ketāb maqālāt al-eslāmiyin wa ekteläf al-moṣellin*, ed. Helmut Ritter, Cairo, 2000. Gerhard Bowering, "Isnad, Ambiguity and the Qurʾān Commentary of Jaʿfar al-Ṣādiq," in Lynda Clarke, ed., *Shiʿite Heritage: Essays on Classical and Modern Traditions*, Binghampton, 2001. E. G. Browne, *A Catalogue of the Persian Manuscripts in the Library of the University of Cambridge*, Cambridge, 1896. Ronald Paul Buckley, "Jaʿfar al-Ṣādiq as a Source of Šhiʿi Traditions," *Islamic Quarterly* 43/1, 1999, pp. 37-58. Idem. "The Imam Jaʿfar al-Ṣādiq, Abu'l-Khaṭṭāb and the Abbasids," *Der Islam*, 79/1, 2002, pp. 118-140. Leonardo Capezzone, "Un aspetto della critica imamita alle tradizioni eterodosse: il *Kitāb al-haft wa'l-azilla* e le molteplici redazioni di un *Kitāb al-azilla*," *Annali di Ca' Foscari (Ann. Ca' Foscari)* 38/3, 1999, pp. 171-93. L. Clarke, "Early Doctrine of the Shiʿah, According to the Shiʿi Sources," Ph.D. diss., McGill University, 1995. Rifaat Y. Ebied and M. J. L. Young, "A Treatise on Hemerology Ascribed to Ǧaʿfar al-Ṣādiq," *Arabica* 23, 1976, pp. 296-307. Ebn Bābawayh, *ʿElalal-Šariʿa*, Najaf, 1966. Idem, *al-Amāli*, Qom, 1984. Taufic Fahd, "Ǧaʿfar aṣ-Ṣādiq et la tradition scientifique arabe," in idem, ed., *Le Shîʿisme imâmite: colloque de Strasbourg (6-9 1968)*, Paris, 1970, pp. 131-42. Marshall G. S. Hodgson, "Djaʿfar al-Ṣādiq," in EI^2 II, pp. 374-75. Moḥammad b. Yaʿqub al-Kolayni, *al-Kāfi*, Tehran, 1994. Paul Kraus, *Jābir Ibn Ḥayyaān: contribution à l'historie des idées scientifiques dans l'islam, Jābir et la science grecque*, Paris, 1986. Judith Loebenstein, "Miracles in Šiʿi Thought: A Case Study of the Miracles Attributed to Imām Jaʿfar al-Ṣādiq," *Arabica* 50/2, 2003, pp. 199-244. Wilferd Madelung, "The Sources of Ismaili Law," *JNES* 35/1, 1976, pp. 29-40. Moḥammad-Bāqer Majlesi, *Beḥār al-anwār*, 111 vols., Beirut, 1983. Ensieh Nasrollahi Zadeh, "The Qurʾan Commentary Attributed to Imam Jaʿfar Sadiq (a.s.): A Study of its Dating and Interpretive Method," Ph.D. diss., University of Birmingham, UK, 2003. Ḥasan b. Musā Nawbaḵti, *Ketāb feraq al-šiʿa*, tr. Moḥammad-Jawād Maškur as *Tarjama-ye Feraq al-šiʿa-ye Nawbaḵti*, Tehran, 1974. Paul Nwyia, "Le Tafsir mystique attribué à Ǧaʿfar Ṣādiq: edition critique," *Mélanges de l'Université St.-Joseph*, no. 43, 1967, pp. 179-230 Abu Ḥanifa Qāżi Noʿmān b. Moḥammad Tamimi, *Daʿāʾem al-Eslām fi ḏekr al-ḥalāl wa'l-ḥarām wa'l-qażāya wa'l-aḥkām*, ed. ʿĀṣaf A. A. Fayżi (Fyzee), 2 vols., Cairo, 1951-61; tr. A. A. A. Fyzee, as *The Pillars of Islam*, completely revised and annotated by Ismail K. Poonawala, 2 vols., New Delhi, 2002-4. Julius Ruska, "Ǧābir ibn Ḥajjān und seine Beziehungen zum Imām Ǧaʿfar aṣ-Ṣādiq," *Der Islam*, no. 16, 1927, pp. 264-66. Abu'l-Fatḥ Moḥammad b. ʿAbd-al-Karim Šahrastāni, *Ketāb al-melal wa'l-neḥal*, ed. William Cureton, Leipzig, 1928; tr. Afżal-al-Din Ṣadr Torka Eṣfahāni, ed. Sayyed Moḥammad-Reżā Jalāli Nāʾini, Tehran, 1956; tr. Theodore Haarbrücker as *Religionsparthien und Philosophen-Schulen*, 2 vols. in 1, Hildesheim, 1969. Fuat Sezgin, *Geschichte des arabischen Schrifttums*, 8 vols., Leiden, 1967-84. Abu ʿAbd-al-Raḥmān Solami, *Majmuʿa-ye āṯār-e Abu ʿAbd-al-Raḥmān Solami*, comp. Naṣr-Allāh Purjawādi, Tehran, 1996. Shaikh Moḥammad b. Ḥasan Ṭusi, *Tahḏib al-aḥkām*, 10 vols., Tehran, 1970. Josef van Ess, *Theologie und Gesellschaft im 2. und 3. Jahrhundert hidschra: eine Geschichte des religiösen Denkens im frühen Islam*, 6 vols, Berlin, 1991. Januarius J. Witkam, "An Arabic Treatise on Hemerology Ascribed to Jaʿfar al-Ṣādiq," *Arabica*, no. 26, 1979, pp. 100-102.

(ROBERT GLEAVE)

iii. AND SUFISM

With a single exception, that of the Naqšbandiya, all the Sufi orders claim initiatic descent from the Prophet exclusively through ʿAli b. Abi Ṭāleb, the first imam of the Ahl al-Bayt (q.v.), and many speak also of a *selselat al-ḏahab* (golden chain), linking them with all of the first eight of the Twelve Imams. Jaʿfar al-Ṣādeq, the sixth imam, occupies, however, a position of particular significance in Sufi tradition. A number of Sufis are said to have associated with him; he is lauded for his knowledge of the Path in several foundational works of Sufi literature; and numerous utterances and writings on the topic of spiritual progress have been attributed to him. What has been asserted concerning him in these respects is in some cases clearly apocryphal and has been the subject of dispute, especially on the part of Shiʿite authors ill-disposed to Sufism, even in its Shiʿite manifestations. Thus, Moqaddas Ardabili (d. 993/1585), probable author of *Ḥadiqat al-šiʿa*, dismisses the alleged links between Imam Jaʿfar al-Ṣādeq and Sufism as an attempt on the part of some early Sufis to gain the authority of the imam for the teachings they began to elaborate during his lifetime. By way of refutation, Ardabili cited a tradition of the imam condemning Abu Hāšem Kufi, generally regarded as the first person to be designated as Sufi (quoted in Maʿṣum-ʿAlišāh, I, p. 190). Given the duration of Jaʿfar al-Ṣādeq's imamate and the influence and appeal he exerted beyond the circle of his specifically Shiʿite following, it is, however, likely that he played some role in the gestation of Sufism, even if the nature and extent of that role were distorted in later tradition.

In the *Ḥelyat al-awliāʾ*, one of the earliest hagiographical compendia, the author Abu Noʿaym Eṣfahāni (d. 430/1038) mentions Jaʿfar al-Ṣādeq immediately after his father, Imam Moḥammad al-Bāqer, and he lauds him for his devout concentration on worship, his chaste abstention from the pursuit of power, and insistence on feeding the poor, even to the detriment of his own family (III, pp. 192-193). Jaʿfar al-Ṣādeq is the last in the succession of imams of the Ahl al-Bayt acknowledged by Abu Bakr Kalābāḏi (d. 380/990), as foremost, after the companions of the Prophet, in manifesting the truths of Sufism "in word and deed" (Kalābāḏi, p. 27). ʿAli Hojviri (d. ca. 463/1071), author of the first Persian compendium on Sufism, likewise includes the first six imams among the forerunners of the Sufis, and he describes Jaʿfar al-Ṣādeq as "the sword of the Sunna, the beauty of the Path, the interpreter of gnosis, and the adornment of pure devotion" (*sayf-e sonnat wa jamāl-e ṭariqat wa moʿabber-e maʿrefat wa mozayyen-e ṣafwat*; Hojviri, p. 94). The most eloquent testimony to the prominence of Jaʿfar al-Ṣādeq in the Sufi imagination is provided, however, by Shaikh Farid-al-Din ʿAṭṭār (d. 618/1221). He invokes him in the very first section of *Taḏkerat al-awliāʾ* as a figure who will bring blessing on his enterprise and mention of whom will suffice as an indication of the centrality to the Sufi path of the Prophet, his Companions, and all the Ahl al-Bayt. Jaʿfar al-Ṣādeq was, moreover, the one "who spoke more than the other imams concerning the Path (*ṭariqat*)," who "excelled in writing on innermost mysteries and truths and who was matchless in expounding the subtleties and secrets of revelation (*laṭāyef-e asrār-e tanzil wa tafsir*)." Given his own emphatic loyalty to Sunnism, ʿAṭṭār felt it necessary at the same time to emphasize that love of the Ahl al-Bayt was not the preserve of Shiʿites, and he even claimed that Sunnis are the true devotees of the Prophet's household (pp. 12-13). This assertion foreshadowed attempts by later Sufis of Sunni bent to detach Jaʿfar al-Ṣādeq from Shiʿism entirely and appropriate him in exclusivity for their own tradition.

Both Abu Noʿaym and ʿAṭṭār narrate several encounters between Jaʿfar al-Ṣādeq and Sufis (or, to be more precise, proto-Sufis) with whom he was contemporary. Thus according to Abu Noʿaym, Sofyān Ṯawri (d 161/776), celebrated both as a jurist and as an ascetic, met with him at least twice. On the first occasion, the imam bestowed threefold pious counsel on Sofyān at his request; he responded gratefully by seizing his hand in a gesture implying submission and loyalty (Abu Noʿaym, III, p. 193). Later, however, Sofyān permitted himself to reproach the imam for the silken raiment he found him to be wearing, only for him to reveal beneath it a modest white woolen cloak and to explain that the finery is for men to behold and the woolen cloak for God; he therefore displays the former and conceals the latter (Abu Noʿaym, III, p. 193). A similar account is given by ʿAṭṭār (p. 15), except that the hidden garb is of coarse linen, not of wool, and the visitor beholding the duality of dress is left unnamed. (Given the reprehensibility of silken clothing for men, it is remarkable that Shiʿite tradition similarly reports that Jaʿfar al-Ṣādeq could be seen wearing a silk cloak at the Prophet's Mosque in Medina; Majlesi, XLVII, p. 17). ʿAṭṭār also speaks of an occasion when Sofyān suggested to Jaʿfar al-Ṣādeq that he should emerge from his self-imposed isolation in order to benefit men with his utterances. The imam replied that the nature of the times necessitated such isolation, and he proceeded to recite two lines of verse to the effect that the hearts of men had become full of scorpions (ʿAṭṭār, p. 15).

Another proto-Sufi, Dāʾud Ṭāʾi (d. 160/775), is said to have heard Jaʿfar al-Ṣādeq express fear that his ancestor, the Prophet, would reproach him in the hereafter for not sufficiently following (*motābaʿat*) his model, for—said the imam—it was not lineage that mattered, but deeds (ʿAṭṭār, p. 14). Belittling as it does one of the central values of Shiʿism, that is, descent from the Prophet, this utterance seems of dubious authenticity. Two further stalwarts of early Sufism, Mālek-e Dinār (d. 131/748) and Ebrāhim b. Adham (d. 261/875) are said by a Shiʿite author, Abu Jaʿfar Moḥammad Ṭusi (d. 460/1067), to have been the servants (*ğelmān*) of Jaʿfar al-Ṣādeq (Ṭusi, *al-Amāli*, cited in Ebn Šahrāšub, IV, p. 248); the case of the former is undocumented, and that of the second involves a chronological impossibility. Probably apocryphal, also for reasons of dating, is the story of an encounter between Jaʿfar al-Ṣādeq and Šaqiq Balḵi (d. 194/810). To the imam's request for a definition of *fotowwat* (spiritual chivalry), Šaqiq replied that if sustenance came his way, he would give thanks, and if it did not, he would be patient. The imam retorted that even the dogs of Medina comported themselves thus; true *fotowwat* was not only to be patient when lacking sustenance, but also to dispense it freely when having it at one's disposal (Afšār and Omidsālār, eds., fol. 36b).

The most widespread but also least plausible tradition is that linking Imam Jaʿfar al-Ṣādeq to Bāyazid Besṭāmi (q.v.), for the Sufi in question was born not earlier than 234/848, that is eighty-six years after the death of the imam. ʿAṭṭār recounts nonetheless that Jaʿfar al-Ṣādeq was the culminating figure among the one hundred and thirteen elders from whose company Bāyazid benefited. One day the imam instructed him to fetch a book from a nearby shelf, to which Bāyazid responded, "what shelf?" indicating that he had been absorbed in the presence of the imam to the exclusion of all else. Jaʿfar al-Ṣādeq thereupon pronounced his training complete and sent him home to Besṭām (ʿAṭṭār, pp. 161-62). Ḥaydar Āmoli (d. after 787/1385), a proponent of the absolute identity of true Sufism and true Shiʿism, elaborated on the theme by having Bāyazid function as the gatekeeper, water carrier, and confidant of the imam during a sojourn in Baghdad (Āmoli, p. 224); according to a certain Abu ʿAbd-Allāh Moḥaddeṯ, Bāyazid was in his service for precisely thirteen years (cited in Ebn Šahrāšub, IV, p. 248). Nur-al-Din Jaʿfar Badaḵši (fl. 8th/14th cent.), a Kobrawi author, repeats the anecdote of the shelf and attributes to Besṭāmi the confession: "if I had not met al-Ṣādeq, I would have died an unbeliever;" and he claims that he was persuaded to join the circle of the imam by a consideration of two of the key textual proofs of Shiʿism: Qurʾān, 42:23 ("I ask for this no reward save love of my kinsfolk"), and the *ḥadiṯ al-ṯaqalayn*, which links the imams to the Qurʾān as guarantors for the correct practice of Islam (cited by Nur-Allāh Šuštari, I, p. 21).

From the 8th/14th century onwards, the main initiatic line of the Naqšbandiya places Jaʿfar al-Ṣādeq intermediate between his maternal grandfather, Qāsem b. Abi Moḥammad b. Abi Bakr (d. 101/719-20 or 102/720-21), and Bāyazid. The assertion that Qāsem had been the spiritual preceptor of Jaʿfar al-Ṣādeq was not new, having already been made by Abu Moḥammad Ṭāleb Makki (d. 386/996) in his *Qut al-qolub*. The imam may well have studied with Qāsem, who attained renown in Sunni tradition as one of "the seven jurists" (*foqahā-ye sabʿa*) of Medina, and he definitely transmitted Hadith from him.

Qāsem is not numbered, however, among the proto-Sufis, and the attribution to him of a preceptorial function seems therefore fanciful. As for the supposed initiatic relation between Jaʿfar al-Ṣādeq and Besṭāmi, Naqšbandis were aware from the outset of the chronological problem and therefore affirmed that the imam's training of Bāyazid took place inwardly by means of his spiritual being (*ruḥāniyat*), not outwardly through the meeting of their bodily forms (Pārsā, pp, 12-13; Kāšefi, I, pp. 11-12). The same was asserted by Sufis of the ʿEšqiya, a Central Asian order, and its Indian derivative, the Šaṭṭāriya, who similarly included Jaʿfar al-Ṣādeq and Bāyazid Besṭāmi in the ancestry to which they laid claim (Maʿṣum-ʿAlišāh, II, p. 151; Rizvi, II, p. 151; Trimingham, pp. 97-98).

Others sought to solve the problem posed by the occurrence of Jaʿfar al-Ṣādeq's demise before the birth of Bāyazid by positing the existence of two Bāyazid Besṭāmis, elder and younger. Describing his visit to Besṭām, Yāqut Ḥamawi (d. 626/1229) mentions two personages with remarkably similar names: the celebrated Sufi, Abu Yazid (i.e., Bāyazid) Ṭayfur b. ʿIsā b. Sorušān Zāhed Besṭāmi, whose tomb he records having seen, and the far less well-known Abu Yazid (i.e., Bāyazid) Ṭayfur b. ʿIsā b. Ādam b. ʿIsā b. ʿAli Zāhed Besṭāmi al-Aṣḡar (the younger; Yāqut, I, p. 421). Nur-Allāh Šuštari (d. 1019/1610) therefore hypothesizes that tradition may have confused the elder Bāyazid with the younger, thereby disqualifying the Sufi from being a contemporary of the imam; if the chronology be corrected, it remains possible that Bāyazid indeed kept the company of Jaʿfar al-Ṣādeq (Nur-Allāh Šuštari, II, p. 24). He also suggests, somewhat contradictorily, that Bāyazid's link to the imam consisted simply of a turn to Shiʿism at a certain point in his life; this, he claims, is the sense of Šarif ʿAli b. Moḥammad Jorjāni's statement in his *Šarḥ al-Mawāqef* (a commentary on ʿAżod-al-Din Iji's *Ketāb al-mawāqef fi ʿlm al-kalām*) that the Sufi benefited spiritually (*estefāża*) from the spiritual being of the imam. Jorjāni's statement reflects his Naqšbandi and, therefore, Sunni affiliation, but, in accordance with his own standard procedure, Šuštari imposes a Shiʿi identity on Jorjāni (d. 816/1413) himself so that his formulation of the matter can be interpreted as an exercise in *ṭaqiya* (prudential dissimulation). With a single deft maneuver, Nur-Allāh Šuštari thus claims both Jorjāni and Bāyazid Besṭāmi for Shiʿism (Nur-Allāh Šuštari, II, p. 22).

The supposed link between Jaʿfar al-Ṣādeq and Bāyazid has also received architectural expression. It is said that when Bāyazid returned to Besṭām, he was accompanied by one of the imam's sons, Moḥammad by name; he predeceased Bāyazid, who was wont to spend much time in meditation at his tomb. Centuries later, a descendant of Bāyazid successfully petitioned the Oljāytu (Öljeitü) the Il-khanid for funds to construct a dome over the tomb, making it the nucleus of a shrine that was repeatedly restored and expanded in Safavid and Qajar times (Nur-Allāh Šuštari, II, pp. 23-24; see BESṬĀM). As for the tomb of Bāyazid himself, it has remained to this day a modest affair, standing in the courtyard of the shrine of Moḥammad b. Jaʿfar al-Ṣādeq and surmounted by nothing more than an iron grille, as if acknowledging the subordination of the Sufi to the Ahl al-Bayt.

With respect to Jaʿfar al-Ṣādeq and Naqšbandi tradition, it may finally be noted that a late source, the *Ḵazinat al-aṣfiāʾ* of Ḡolām Sarvar Lāhuri, ascribes to Bahāʾ-al-Din Naqšband, the eponym of the order, genealogical as well as spiritual descent from the imam (I, p. 545); and that once the Sunni identity of the Naqšbandiya received new emphasis by way of reaction to the Safavid promotion of Shiʿism in Persia, at least one Naqšbandi, Sayyed Moḥammad Bādāmyāri, sought to deny all connection of Jaʿfar al-Ṣādeq to Shiʿism and claimed him, however incongruously, for Sunni Islam (Qazvini, fol. 19b). A similar assertion had earlier been made by the Kobrawi, Nur-al-Din Esfarāʾeni (d. 717/1317); Jaʿfar al-Ṣādeq would be repelled, he claimed, by the doctrines put forth in his name by the Shiʿites (Landolt, introd. to his ed. of Esfarāʾeni, pp. 18-19). Like Bāyazid at the hands of Šuštari, the imam thus became an object of sectarian appropriation and debate.

The Bektāšiya (q.v.), an order professing a Shiʿism of a certain type and therefore utterly different from the emphatically Sunni Naqšbandiya, also invoked the authority of Jaʿfar al-Ṣādeq for various aspects of its doctrines and practices. It thus attributed to him the origin of its fourfold scheme of the ascending stages of religion (*šariʿat*, *ṭariqat*, *maʿrefat*, *ḥaqiqat*), as well as the initiatic belt known as the *tiğbent* girded on by the neophyte (Birge, pp. 106, 234). The initiatic ceremony included the recognition of the *maḏhab* of Jaʿfar al-Ṣādeq as true and correct, although this rarely resulted in any substantial knowledge or practice of Shiʿi jurisprudence on the part of the Bektāšis, notoriously lax as they were in the fulfillment of canonical duties (Sertoğlu, p. 263). Of particular interest is the patently false attribution to Jaʿfar al-Ṣādeq of one of the few prose texts to which Bektāšis have traditionally referred, the *Buyruk* (Command). Circulating in different recensions, the book includes doctrinal elements reminiscent of early Safavid Shiʿism as well as several evocations of Ḵaṭāʾi, the pen-name of Shah Esmāʿil I Ṣafawi (q.v.), features which suggest an early 16th century origin for the text (Mélikoff, pp. 135-36). The purpose behind its original composition may indeed have been to recruit Bektāšis for the Safavid cause, but the book contains much that is distinctively Bektāši: rites of initiation (*ikrar âyini*) for males and females (Jaʿfar al-Ṣādeq [attrib. to], 1989, pp. 85-88); prayers and proclamations known as *gülbank* (Pers. *golbāng*) to be recited on various occasions (ibid., pp. 281-85); and the fantastic legend of the Prophet's dealings with the *kırklar*, a forty-man conclave of the saintly who, initially reluctant to admit him to their midst, ultimately consented to drink wine with him out of a luminous bowl brought from paradise by Salmān Fārsi (ibid., pp. 9-17). Much of this material is attributed to Jaʿfar al-Ṣādeq, a circumstance difficult to explain. Given his status as eponym of the Jaʿfari *maḏhab*, perhaps it was thought appropriate to invoke his authority additionally for the rites and doctrines of the Bektāšiya. Alternatively, elements of extremist (*ḡolāt*, q.v.) teaching that had claimed to enjoy Jaʿfar al-Ṣādeq's approval, despite his best efforts to disown them throughout his life, may have found their way to Anatolia, by routes unknown, some time during or before the gestation there of the Bektāši order.

More worthy of serious consideration is the contribution that Jaʿfar al-Ṣādeq reputedly made to the Sufi exegesis of the Qurʾān. Traditions ascribed to him are a major component of the *Ḥaqāʾeq al-tafsir*, a compilation of sayings on various Qurʾānic verses assembled by Abu ʿAbd-al-Raḥmān Moḥammad Solami (d. 412/1021); they have been culled from its text and edited by Paul Nwyia (1968, pp. 188-230) and ʿAli Zayʿur (pp. 73-177). Solami inaugurates his commentary with Jaʿfar al-Ṣādeq's dictum that the Qurʾān has four aspects: *ʿebāra*, the explicit verbal meaning; *ešāra*, implicit or allusive meaning; *laṭāʾef*, subtleties; and *ḥaqāʾeq*, ultimate truths, each aspect being intended for a separate class of humanity: the *ʿawāmm* (masses), the *ḵawāṣṣ* (elite), the *awliāʾ* (friends of God), and the *anbiāʾ* (prophets) respectively. This fourfold scheme is not, however, implemented anywhere in the body of Solami's *tafsir*, where no more than two levels are ever proposed. He then proceeds to cite a series of traditions from Jaʿfar al-Ṣādeq analyzing the *basmalah*, the invocation that precedes every chapter of the Qurʾān but one, in terms of its component letters; each is treated as the initial of one or more significant words (Nwyia, 1968, pp. 188-89; Zayʿur, pp. 73-74). Insofar as Jaʿfar al-Ṣādeq is regarded as the founder of *jafr*, the arcane science of the letters, the attribution to him of these traditions does not entirely lack plausibility. The other material ascribed in Solami's commentary to Jaʿfar al-Ṣādeq consists of brief glosses on miscellaneous verses, mostly interiorizing in nature; nothing reminiscent of Shiʿism is to be discerned in them. *Ziyādāt Ḥaqāʾeq al-tafsir*, Solami's addenda to his *tafsir*, preserved in an apparently unique manuscript dating from the 13th or 14th century held by the Gazihusrevbegova Library in Sarajevo (Dobrača, I, p. 139), also contains no fewer than two hundred and forty two citations from Jaʿfar al-Ṣādeq (index, s.v. Jaʿfar al-Ṣādeq, in Solami, 1995). In his introduction to this later work, Solami cites two further traditions from Jaʿfar al-Ṣādeq bearing on the multiplicity of meanings to be found in the Qurʾān: one to the effect that it has seven principal topics (*sabʿat anwāʿ*), and the other proclaiming it to have nine aspects (*tesʿat awjoh*; Solami, 1995, p. 2).

Solami may not have been the first Sufi to cite mystically tinged traditions from Jaʿfar al-Ṣādeq relating to commentary (*tafsir*) on the Qurʾān. He had been preceded by Fożayl b. ʿEyāż (d. 187/803) and Ḏu'l-Nun Meṣri (d. 246/861); the latter claimed to have heard the traditions in question from Fażl b. Ḡonaym Ḵozāʿi, and he in turn narrated them from Mālek b. Anas, the imam of the Māleki *maḏhab*, who had heard them from Jaʿfar al-Ṣādeq himself. Louis Massignon, the first Western scholar to draw attention to Solami's commentary, dismisses this chain of transmission as improbable, and suggests instead, without providing much evidence, that the initial compilation was the work of either Jāber b. Ḥayyān or Ebn Abi'l-ʿAwjāʾ (Massignon, pp. 205-6). The only authority mentioned by Solami himself for his citations from Jaʿfar al-Ṣādeq is a chain of authorities (*esnād*) reaching back to the imam by way of Manṣur b. ʿAbd-Allāh, Abu'l-Qāsem Eskandarāni, Abu Jaʿfar Malaṭi, Imam ʿAli al-Reżā, and Imam Musā al-Kāẓem. The identity of the first link in this chain is uncertain; very little is known of the second; and the third laid no claim to direct contact with Imam ʿAli al-Reżā (Böwering, 1991, pp. 52-53; idem, 1996, pp. 44-52). The case is somewhat different with the *esnād* cited by Solami in the *Ziādāt* for material from Jaʿfar al-Ṣādeq, for the persons comprising it can be identified with certainty as transmitters of Shiʿite Hadith; they are: Aḥmad b. Naṣr Ḏāreʿ (d. after 365/975), Solami's immediate source; ʿAbd-Allāh b. Aḥmad b. ʿĀmer (d. 324/936) and his father, Aḥmad b. ʿĀmer. Again, however, there is no direct linkage to Imam ʿAli al-Reżā and through him to Jaʿfar al-Ṣādeq, for all that Aḥmad b. ʿĀmer claimed was to be in possession of a written text attributed to the imam (Böwering, 1996, pp. 52-56). Gerhard Böwering seems ultimately to have concluded that the material attributed by Solami to Jaʿfar al-Ṣādeq is inauthentic, for in his final pronouncement on the subject, without providing further argumentation, he speaks of a "pseudo-Jaʿfar aṣ-Ṣādiq" (Böwering, 2001, p. 135).

Whatever conclusions may be reached concerning the chains of transmission, it is highly improbable that all the exegetical utterances attributed to Jaʿfar al-Ṣādeq actually stemmed from him. In commenting on the "Light Verse" (23:35), he is, for example, supposed to have spoken of four terrestrial lights (i.e., Abu Bakr, ʿOmar b. Ḵaṭṭāb, ʿOṯmān, and ʿAli) rising up to merge with their celestial counterparts, the archangels Jebril, Mikāʾil, Esrāfil, and ʿAzrāʾil (Nwyia, 1968, p. 212; Zayʿur, p. 126). Likewise comprising an endorsement of the first four caliphs, is the pronouncement elsewhere ascribed to Jaʿfar al-Ṣādeq that on the leaves of each of the four trees of Paradise—the Lote Tree of the Limit (*sedrat al-montahā*), Ṭubā, the Eternal Abode (*al-maʾwā*), and the Tree of Immortality (*šajarat al-ḵold*)—is written the name of one of the four, complete with a laudatory invocation (Afšār and Omid-sālār, eds., fol. 76a-b). These statements might be interpreted as an exercise in *taqiya*, were it not that the concept of the Rightly Guided (*rāšedun*) caliphs, as a harmonious and normative quartet, in chronologically descending order of merit, had not fully crystallized even among Sunnis in the time of Jaʿfar al-Ṣādeq.

The definitive evaluation of the material in Solami's two collections is rendered particularly difficult by the existence of other exegetical works ascribed to Jaʿfar al-Ṣādeq but compiled by Shiʿite scholars, and all except one unpublished (Böwering, 1991, p. 54; Ateş, 1974, p. 50; Sezgin, I, p. 529). That exception is a text related by Moḥammad b. Ebrāhim Noʿmāni (d. 360/971), the last link in a chain of authorities going back to Jaʿfar al-Ṣādeq and entirely different from that invoked by Solami. It constitutes the entire chapter of Moḥammad-Bāqer Majlesi's *Beḥār al-anwār* entitled "Traditions concerning the various types of verse found in the Qurʾān" ("Bāb mā wareda fi aṣnāf āyāt al-Qorʾān"; Majlesi, CXIII, pp. 3-97).

Although slightly similar in content to the tradition enumerating the "nine aspects" cited by Solami at the beginning of his *Ziādāt*, it is not an assemblage of discrete traditions but a separate treatise (*resāla mofrada*) that deals systematically with categories of Qurʾānic verses such as the abrogating and the abrogated; the general and the specific; the Meccan and the Medinan; and verses relating to commanding and prohibiting. In other words, it is in the nature of a general introduction to the contents of the Qurʾān rather than a commentary on its specific verses, and it has much in common with the prefatory parts of an earlier *tafsir*, that of ʿAli b. Ebrāhim Qomi, on which Noʿmāni may have drawn; alternatively, Qomi and Noʿmāni may have derived their material independently from the same source (Bar-Asher, pp. 64-67). What is certain is that the text associated with the name of Noʿmāni has little in common with the material attributed to Jaʿfar al-Ṣādeq by Solami, and it cannot therefore be taken as even circumstantial evidence for its authenticity. Even a cursory comparison of the two would invalidate Massignon's assertion that there are "remarkable doctrinal coincidences" between the works in question (Massignon, p. 204), as well as Nwyia's still bolder claim that "we are in the presence of one and the same work, having the same inspiration, the same style, and the same spiritual content" (Nwyia, 1970, pp. 159-60).

However the question of authenticity may be adjudicated by modern scholarship, the material presented by Solami as emanating from Jaʿfar al-Ṣādeq was unquestioningly reproduced in a number of other Sufi Qurʾān commentaries, notably the *Kašf al-asrār* of Abu'l-Fażl Rašid-al-Din Meybodi (d. late 6th/12th century) and the *ʿArāʾes al-bayān* of Ruzbehān Baqli (d. 606/1209), with attribution to the imam. The first of these two, however, sometimes places the citations from Jaʿfar al-Ṣādeq in a Qurʾānic context different from that chosen by Solami (Keeler, p. 22; for a complete listing of the thirty-nine traditions narrated from the imam by Meybodi, see Šariʿat, p. 923). Contrastingly but perhaps not surprisingly, Ebn Taymiya (d. 728/1328), who, despite his reputation was not totally averse to Sufism, rejected the authenticity of all the material that Solami attributed to Jaʿfar al-Ṣādeq (Ebn Taymiya, I, p. 29).

Another text marked by the emphasis of Sufism and ascribed to Jaʿfar al-Ṣādeq is *Meṣbāḥ al-šariʿa wa meftāḥ al-ḥaqiqa*, consisting of one hundred brief homilies on various virtues and devotional practices arranged in no particular order; the first is humble submission to God and the hundredth, the avoidance of backbiting. A detailed examination of its contents might reveal correspondence between certain parts of this work and verified Hadith of the imam, but the likelihood of the book as a whole having emanated from him is slim (Šibi, I, p. 210).

The most fully verifiable and certainly the longest lasting connection of Jaʿfar al-Ṣādeq with Sufism is to be sought in a number of lineages descended from him both genealogically and, to some degree, spiritually. They all originate with ʿAli ʿOrayżi, the youngest offspring of Jaʿfar al-Ṣādeq, who was still an infant when his father died but came to gain a reputation for Hadith scholarship (Majlesi, XLVIII, p. 258). At some point, either he or one of his descendants came to settle in Basra, where the family remained until 317/929 when ʿOrayżi's great-great-grandson, Aḥmad b. ʿIsā b. Moḥammad b. ʿAli "al-Mohājer," left for the Ḥejāz in order to escape an impending Qarmaṭi raid. His intention was also to perform the Ḥajj, but he was compelled to tarry a year in Medina on account of the Qarmaṭi sacking of Mecca that took place not long after his arrival. In 318/930, he moved on to Yemen, and then, in 340/951, to the region of Tarim in the Hażramawt in south Arabia. This was the final stage in his migratory journey, and although previously a stronghold of the Ebāżi sect (an offshoot of the Kharijites), Tarim now became the center from which various branches of the family went forth to disseminate religious knowledge. This they did in accordance with the Shafiʿite *madhab*, a curious circumstance which may have originated as a form of *taqiya* before becoming a permanent and actual choice of legal rite. The principal clan, descended from Aḥmad b. ʿIsā, was that of the Bā ʿAlawi, named after one of his grandsons, ʿAlawi (this name, often shortened to ʿAlwi, is not to be confused with the *nesba* belonging to Imam ʿAli; it is evidently the name of "a well-known bird;" Löfgren, "Bā ʿAlawı," p. 828).

It is with ʿAlawi's great-grandson, Moḥammad b. ʿAli b. Moḥammad b. ʿAli b. ʿAlawi (d. 653/1255), known as al-Ostad al-Aʿẓam (the great master), that this line of descent from Jaʿfar al-Ṣādeq acquires a Sufi dimension; from his time onward, it is possible to speak of an ʿAlawi *ṭariqa*, characterized by hereditary transmission of the leadership. Descended genealogically from the ʿAlawiya but counting more importantly as an offshoot of the Kobrawiya is the ʿAydarusiya, the order established by Abu Bakr b. ʿAbd-Allāh ʿAydarus (d. 914/1508), who has been described as the "patron saint" of Aden (Löfgren, "ʿAydarūs," p. 781). Several shaikhs of the ʿAydarusiya bore the complete name of their distant ancestor, Jaʿfar al-Ṣādeq, indicating thereby a claim to spiritual as well as genealogical descent from the sixth imam of the Shiʿites (Zabidi, fols. 80b-81a). Although the Hażramawt preserved its centrality for both the ʿAlawis and the ʿAydarusis, many members of both lineages either visited or settled in various parts of Southeast Asia, primarily Java, Sumatra, and the Malay peninsula. Although they participated there in the propagation of Islam, their spiritual influence on the indigenous population, particularly in the case of the ʿAlawiya, was limited by the consistent exclusion of non-*sayyed*s from membership (Attas, p. 32). Some of them, nonetheless, enjoyed great prestige in a number of Muslim principalities in Pontianak, Sulawesi, and the Sulu Archipelago, often intermarrying with the ruling families (Atjeh, 1977, pp. 35-37). With respect to these far-flung Sufi descendants of Jaʿfar al-Ṣādeq, it may finally be noted that, impressed by the triumph of the 1978-79 Islamic Revolution in Iran, some have abandoned their affiliation to the Shafiʿite school and indeed, to Sunnism as a whole, and embraced Twelver

Shiʿism, with which their ancestor is, after all, definingly associated (Alatas, pp. 337-39).

Entirely mythical is, by contrast, the purported connection between Jaʿfar al-Ṣādeq and another distant part of the Muslim world, namely eastern Turkestan. Traditions circulating there depict him as a warrior who was martyred while propagating Islam in Khotan and China (*Tezkire-i Imam Jaʿfar-i Sadiq*), and a shrine attributed to him to the south of the ancient city of Khotan remains an object of pious visitation down to the present time (Baumer, p. 69). Since there is no trace of Shiʿism in the history of the area, it seems reasonable to speculate that the legend was first cultivated, and the shrine first built, by Sufis who cannot be presently identified.

Bibliography: Abu Noʿaym Aḥmad Eṣfahāni, *Ḥelyat al-awliāʾ*, 10 vols. in 5, Beirut, 1387/1967, III, pp. 192-206. Abu Ṭāleb Moḥammad Makki, *Qut al-qolub: fi moʿāmalāt al-maḥbub wa waṣf ṭariq al-morid elā maqām al-tawḥid*, ed. ʿAbd-al-Moʾmen Ḥefni, Cairo, 1991. Iraj Afšār and Maḥmud Omidsālār, eds., *Hazār ḥekāyat-e Ṣufiān*, a facs. ed., Tehran, 1993 (comp. in the 9th/15th cent.). Syed Farid Alatas, "The *Ṭariqat al-ʿAlawiyyah* and the Emergence of the Shiʿi School in Indonesia and Malaysia," *Oriente Moderno* 18/2, 1999, pp. 322-39. Ḥaydar Āmoli, *Jāmiʿ al-asrār wa manbaʿ al-anwār/La philosophie shiʿite*, ed. Henry Corbin and Oṯmān Esmāʿil Yaḥyā, Bibliothèque iranienne 16, Tehran and Paris, 1969. Süleyman Ateş, *Sülemî ve tasavvufî tefsîrî*, Istanbul, 1969. Idem, *Işari tefsir Okulu*, Ankara, 1974, pp. 50-55. Aboebakar Atjeh, *Pengantar Ilmu Tarekat (Uraian Tentang Mystik)*, Bandung, 1964, pp. 346-64. Idem, *Aliran Syiʿah di Nusantara*, Jakarta, 1977. Farid-al-Din ʿAṭṭār, *Taḏkrat al-awliāʾ*, ed. Moḥammad Esteʿlāmi, 3rd. ed., Tehran, 1981. Syed Muhammad Naguib Attas, *Some Aspects of Sufism as Understood and Practised among the Malays*, ed. Shirle Gordan, Singapore, 1963. Meir M. Bar-Asher, *Scripture and Exegesis in Early Imāmī Shiism*, Leiden, 1999. Christoph Baumer, *Die südliche Seidenstrasse: Inseln im Sandmeer: Versunkene Kulturen der Wüste Taklamakan*, Mainz, 2002. John Kingsley Birge, *The Bektashi Order of Dervishes*, London, 1937; repr. 1982. Edgar Blochet, "La Conquête des États Nestoriens de l'Asie Centrale par les Schiites," *Revue de l'Orient Chrétien* 25, 1925-26, pp. 36-41. Gerhard Böwering, "The Qurʾān Commentary of al-Sulamı," in Wael Hallaq and Donald P. Little, eds., *Islamic Studies Presented to Charles J. Adams*, Leiden, 1991, pp. 41-56. Idem, "The Major Sources of Sulamı's Minor Commentary," *Oriens* 35, 1996, pp. 35-56. Idem, "The Light Verse: Qurʾānic Text and Sufi Interpretation," *Oriens* 36, 2001, pp. 113-44. Kasim Dobrača, *Katalog Arabskih, Turskih i Persijskih Rukopisa/Catalogue of the Arabic, Turkish, Persian, and Bosnian Manuscripts* I, Sarajevo, 1963. Ebn al-Jawzi, *Taḏkerat al-ḵawāṣṣ*, Najaf, 1964, pp. 342-43. Idem, *Ṣefat al-ṣafwa*, eds. Ebrāhim Ramażān and Saʿid al-Laḥḥām, 4 vols., Beirut, 1989, II, pp. 114-15. Ebn Šahrāšub, *Manāqeb Āl Abi Ṭāleb*, 4 vols., Qom, n.d. Ebn Taymia, *Majmuʿat al-rasāʾel wa'l-masāʾel*, ed. Moḥammad Rašid Reżā, 5 vols., Beirut, 1983. Nur-al-Din ʿAbd-al-Raḥmān Esfarāʾeni, *Kāšef al-asrār*, ed. Hermann Landolt, Tehran, 1979; ed. and tr. H. Landolt as *Le révélateur des mystères*, Lagrasse, 1986. Alan Godlas, "The *ʿArāʾis al-Bayān*: The Mystical Qurʾānic Exegesis of Rūzbihān al-Baqlī," Ph.D. diss., University of California, Berkeley, 1991. Fernand Grenard, *Mission Scientifique dans la Haute Asie, 1890-1895, Troisieme Partie*, 2 vols., Paris, 1898, pp. 27-31. Ḡolām Sarvar Lāhuri, *Ḵazinat al-aṣfiāʾ*, 2 vols., Bombay, 1873. Abdurrahman Habil, "Traditional Esoteric Commentaries on the Quran," in Seyyed Hossein Nasr, ed., *Islamic Spirituality* I: *Foundations*, New York, 1987, pp. 24-47. ʿAlwi Ṭāher Ḥaddād, *ʿOqud al-almās*, Singapore, 1991. ʿAli b. ʿOṯmān Hojviri, *Kašf al-maḥjub*, ed. Valentin Zhukovskii, repr., Tehran, 1979. Imam Jaʿfar al-Ṣādeq (attr.), *Meṣbāḥ al-šariʿa wa meftāḥ al-ḥaqiqa*, Beirut, 1980; tr. Muna Bilgrami as *The Lantern of the Path*, Shaftesbury, 1989; tr. Ḥasan Moṣṭafawi as *Meṣbāḥ al-šariʿa . . . : ṣad bāb dar ḥekmat wa maʿāref wa siar wa soluk wa aḵlāq wa ādāb wa sonan*, Tehran, 2003. Idem (attr. to) *Tam ve Hakiki Imam Cafer-i Sadık Buyruğu*, Istanbul, 1989. Abu Bakr Moḥammad Kalābāḏi, *al-Taʿarrof le maḏhab ahl al-taṣawwof*, eds. ʿAbd-al-Ḥalim Maḥmud and Ṭaha ʿAbd-al-Bāqi Sorur, Cairo, 1960. Faḵr-al-Din Kāšefi, *Rašaḥāt ʿayn al-ḥayāt*, ed. ʿAli-Aṣḡar Moʿiniān, 2 vols., Tehran, 1977. Annabel Keeler, *Sufi Hermeneutics: The Qurʾān Commentary of Rashīd al-Din Maybudī*, Oxford, 2006. O. Löfgren, "ʿAydarūs," in EI^2 I, pp. 780-82. Idem, "Bā ʿAlawī," in EI^2 I, pp. 828-30. Moḥammad-Bāqer Majlesi, *Beḥār al-anwār*, Tehran, 1965, XLVII. Cesar Adib Majul, *Muslims in the Philippines*, Quezon City, 1973. Louis Massignon, *Essai sur les origines du lexique technique de la mystique musulmane*, Paris, 1968. Moḥammad Maʿṣum-ʿAlišāh, *Ṭarāʾeq al-ḥaqāʾeq*, ed. Moḥammad-Jaʿfar Maḥjub, 3 vols., Tehran, n.d. Irène Mélikoff, *Hadji Bektach: un mythe et ses avatars, Genèse et évolution du soufisme populaire en Turquie*, Leiden, 1998. Aḥmad Moqaddas Ardabili, *Ḥadiqat al-šiʿa*, ed. Ṣādeq Ḥasanzāda, Qom, 1998. Nur-Allāh Šuštari, *Majāles al-moʾmenin*, 4th. ed., 2 vols., Tehran, 1998. Paul Nwyia, "Le *tafsır* mystique attribué à Ǧaʿfar Ṣādiq," *Mélanges de l'Université Saint-Joseph* 43/4, 1968, pp. 181-230. Idem, *Exégèse coranique et langage mystique: Nouvel essai sur le lexique technique des mystiques Musulmans*, Beirut, 1970. Moḥammad Pārsā, *Qodsiya: kalemāt-e Bahāʾ-al-Din Naqšband*, ed. Aḥmad Ṭāheri ʿErāqi, Tehran, 1975. Moḥammad b. Ḥosayn Qazvini, *Selsela-nāma-ye ḵᵛājagān*, ms. Bibliothèque Nationale, supplèment persan, 1418. S. A. A. Rizvi, *A History of Sufism in India*, 2 vols., Delhi, 1983. Ruzbehān Baqli Širāzi, *ʿArāʾes al-bayān fi ḥaqāʾeq al-Qorʾān*, Lucknow, 1898. Moḥammad-Jawād Šariʿat, *Fehrest-e tafsir-e Kašf al-asrār wa ʿoddat al-abrār*, Tehran, 1984. Robert Bertram Serjeant, *The Saiyids of Hadramawt*, London, 1957. Murat Sertoğlu, *Bektaşilik*, Istanbul, 1969. Kāmel Moṣṭafā Šibi, *al-Ṣela bayn al-taṣawwof wa'l-tašayyoʿ*, 2 vols.,

Beirut, 1982. Abu ʿAbd-al-Raḥmān Moḥammad Solami, *Ziādāt Ḥaqāʾeq al-tafsir*, ed. Gerhard Böwering as *The Minor Qurʾān Commentary of Abū ʿAbd ar-Raḥmān b. al-Ḥosayn as-Sulamī*, Beirut, 1995. Idem, *Ḥaqāʾeq al-tafsir*, ed. Sayyed ʿOmrān, Beirut, 2001. Mark Aurel Stein, *Ancient Khotan: Detailed Report of Archaeological Explorations in Chinese Turkistan*, 2 vols., London, 1907, I, pp. 417-18. John B. Taylor, "Jaʿfar al-Sādiq, Spiritual Forebear of the Sufis," *Islamic Culture* 40/2, April 1966, pp. 97-113. *Tezkire-i Imam Jaʿfar-i Sadiq*, uncatalogued Turki manuscript, Bancroft Library, University of California, Berkeley. J. Spencer Trimingham, *The Sufi Orders in Islam*, Oxford, 1971. L. W. C. van den Berg, *Le Hadhramout et les Colonies Arabes dans l'Archipel Indien*, Batavia, 1886, pp. 192-212. Ferdinand Wüstenfeld, "Die Çufiten in Süd-Arabien im XI. (XVII.) Jahrhundert," *Abhandlungen der historisch-philologischen Classe der königlichen Gesellschaft der Wissenschaften zu Göttingen* 30/4, 1883, pp. 1-148. Šehāb-al-Din Abu ʿAbd-Allāh Yāqut Ḥamawi, *Moʿjam al-boldān*, 6 vols., Beirut, n.d. Abu Jaʿfar Moḥammad Ṭusi, *al-Amāli*, Qom, 1995. Mortażā Zabidi, *ʿEqd al-jawhar*, ms. Dār-al-Kotob al-Meṣriya: Taṣawwof Taymur 332. Thierry Zarcone, "Le Culte des Saints au Xinjiang de 1949 à nos Jours," *Journal of the History of Sufism* 3, 2002, pp. 138-39. ʿAli Zayʿur, *Kāmel al-tafsir al-Ṣufi al-ʿerfāni le'l-Qorʾān be ḥasb Ḥaqāʾeq al-tafsir wa Ziādāt Ḥaqāʾeq al-tafsir le'l-Solami*, Paris 2002.

(HAMID ALGAR)

iv. AND ESOTERIC SCIENCES

Imam Jaʿfar al-Ṣādeq, a major figure in Shiʿite esotericism, is purported to be the founder of occult science in Islam. According to Imami-Shiʿite tradition, his knowledge concerned "the exoteric (*al-ẓāher*), the esoteric (*al-bāṭen*), and the esoteric of the esoteric (*bāṭen al-bāṭen*)" (Āmoli, p. 33; Corbin, pp. 188-89). "Our science, Jaʿfar is reported to have said, is immemorial and written in venerable books; it is engraved in the hearts and fixed in the ears. We have in our possession the red *Jafr*, the white *Jafr*, the Book of Fāṭema (*Maṣḥaf Fāṭema*) and *al-Jāmeʿa* (the "Encompassing")" (Shaikh Mofid, p. 274). These books, containing knowledge of all things past, present, and future, were transmitted from one prophet and imam to another, the *Jafr* even going back to Adam, and reached Jaʿfar al-Ṣādeq through Imam ʿAli b. Abi Ṭāleb and the other Shiʿite imams. Written on colored tablets made of pearl (white), ruby (red), emerald (green) or gold (yellow), they evoke both by their content and their material substrate the two esoteric sciences in which Imam Jaʿfar al-Ṣādeq is said to have excelled: divination and alchemy (Kolayni, I, pp. 344-46; Straface, pp. 347-49; Amir-Moezzi, pp. 186-88, 196-97, tr. pp. 73-74, 78).

Several pseudo-epigraphical works in Arabic, covering different sciences of divination, were transmitted under the name of Jaʿfar al-Ṣādeq (Sezgin, I, pp. 530-31; Ullmann, pp. 195-96). The *Ketāb al-jafr* deals with a Shiʿite science par excellence, being considered a privilege of the imams. It contains apocalyptic predictions on the advent of the Mahdi, the final triumph of Shiʿism, and the annihilation of Sunni rule, using divinatory techniques such as gematria (*ḥesāb al-jommal*) and the occult power of the letters of the alphabet. According to Ebn K̲aldun, Jaʿfar al-Ṣādeq possessed its original copy written on the skin of a young bull. It allowed him to reveal the hidden meaning of the Qurʾān (Ebn K̲aldun, pp. 264-65, tr. Monteil, pp. 524-25, tr. Rosenthal, II, pp. 209-10; Kolayni, p. 348; Fahd, "D̲jafr," p. 377; idem, 1966, pp. 219-24). Closely related to the science of *jafr* are books on the "salutary properties" of the Qurʾān (*Manāfeʿ ṣowar al-Qorʾān*, *K̲awāṣṣ al-Qorʾān al-aʿẓam*; Sezgin, I, p. 530), a method of divination based on the "mysterious letters" at the beginning of certain chapters (*sura*), the *basmala* or the names and attributes of God (Fahd, 1966, pp. 241-43). Jaʿfar al-Ṣādeq was also well versed in the *ʿelm al-faʾl*, the "science of omens," teaching how to interpret natural phenomena as good or bad presages (Fahd, 1966, pp. 450-83). To this discipline belongs hemerology (*ektiārāt*), a divinatory technique based on astrological calculations in order to determine the auspicious and inauspicious nature of specific years, months, days, or hours (Fahd, 1966, pp. 483-88; see Jaʿfar al-Ṣādeq, *Faʾl-nāma*; idem, *Ek̲tiārāt al-ayyām wa'l-šohur*). Moreover, Jaʿfar al-Ṣādeq is reported to have introduced in Islam the science of palmomancy (*ektelāj al-aʿżāʾ*), enabling one to take presages about the future of a given person from the spontaneous pulsations and contractions of all parts of his body (Fahd, 1966, pp. 397-402; see Jaʿfar al-Ṣādeq, *Ketāb ek̲telāj al-aʿżāʾ*, containing his predictions and those of Daniel, Alexander, and Persian and Greek sages).

Imam Jaʿfar al-Ṣādeq is known in Islamic esoteric tradition as the father of Arabic alchemy. According to Ebn al-Nadim (p. 420, tr. II, pp. 853-54), the Shiʿites claim that he was the master of Jāber b. Ḥayyān. The alchemical corpus transmitted under Jāber's name is indeed presented as written under the direct inspiration of Jaʿfar al-Ṣādeq, who initiated his disciple into the secrets of alchemy. The historical relations between Jaʿfar al-Ṣādeq and Jāber b. Ḥayyān remain very controversial, as they are linked to still unresolved questions about dating, composition, and authorship of the texts attributed to Jāber. Scholars such as Julius Ruska, Paul Kraus, and Pierre Lory consider Jaʿfar al-Ṣādeq's involvement in the transmission of alchemical knowledge as a literary fiction, whereas Fuat Sezgin, Toufic Fahd, and Nomanul Haq are rather inclined to accept the existence of alchemical activity in Medina in Jaʿfar al-Ṣādeq's time, although they remain cautious regarding the authenticity of the attribution of the Jaberian corpus to Jāber b. Ḥayyān and of the alchemical works to Jaʿfar al-Ṣādeq (Ruska, 1924, pp. 40-52; idem, 1927, pp. 264-66; Kraus, I, pp. LV-LVII; Lory, pp. 14-21, 57-59, 101-7; Sezgin, I, p. 529, IV, pp. 128-31; Fahd, 1970, pp. 139-41; Nomanul Haq, pp. 3-47). Among several apocryphal works attributed to Jaʿfar al-Ṣādeq figures a *Resāla fi ʿelm al-ṣenāʿa wa'l-ḥajar al-mokarrem*, also known under the title *Resālat al-waṣāyā lesayyedenā al-Emām Jaʿfar al-Ṣādeq* (for manuscripts, see Sezgin, I, p. 531, IV, p. 131; Ullmann, pp. 195-96, 221). Ruska, who translated this text (in Ruska, 1924), showed that it is nearly identical with the *Ketāb taʿwiḏ al-Ḥākem fi ʿelm al-ṣanʿat al-ʿāliya*, containing two receipts for the elaboration of the elixir, allegedly transcribed from the bracelet of the Fatimid caliph al-Ḥākem, who inherited it from his ancestors and thus ultimately from Jaʿfar al-Ṣādeq (Ruska, 1924, pp. 67-113, combines both texts in his German translation and gives a facsimile edition of the *Taʿwiḏ* from a Gotha manuscript).

Jaʿfar al-Ṣādeq is supposed to have revealed his esoteric knowledge to a small circle of privileged disciples, such as Abuʾl-Ḵaṭṭāb Moḥammad Asadi and Mofażżal b. ʿOmar Joʿfi (eponyms of al-Ḵaṭṭābiya and al-Mofażżaliya), both considered by later Imami-Shiʿite tradition as extremists (see ḠOLĀT). Jaʿfar al-Ṣādeq's "secret revelations" to Mofażżal are transmitted in the *Ketāb al-haft waʾl-aẓella* (partial Ger. tr. in Halm, 1982, pp. 246-74) and in the *Ketāb al-ṣerāṭ* (ed. Capezzone, pp. 318-415). These texts played an important role in the elaboration of the esoteric doctrine of the Noṣayris (Halm, 1978, pp. 253-65; 1981, pp. 72-84; Capezzone, pp. 265-73), who consider Jaʿfar al-Ṣādeq as one of their main authorities (Bar-Asher and Kofsky, pp. 8, 22-23, 26-27, 32, 37, 80, 84, 129, 134).

Bibliography: Mohammad Ali Amir-Moezzi, *Le guide divin dans le Shiʿism e originel*, Lagrasse, 1992; tr. David Steight as *The Divine Guide in Early Shiʿism: The Sources of Esotericism in Islam*, New York, 1994. Ḥaydar Āmoli, *Jāmiʿ al-asrār wa manbaʿ al-anwār/La philosophie shiʿite*, ed. Henry Corbin and Oṯmān Esmāʿil Yaḥyā, Bibliothèque Iranienne 16, Tehran and Paris, 1969. Meir M. Bar-Asher and Aryeh Kofsky, *The Nuṣayrî-ʿAlawî Religion: An Enquiry into Its Theology and Liturgy*, Jerusalem Studies in Religion and Culture 1, Leiden, Boston, and Cologne, 2002. Leonardo Capezzone, "Una nuova fonte per lo studio dell'eterodossia islamica: il *Kitāb al-ṣirāṭ* attribuito a Mufaḍḍal b. ʿUmar al-Ǧuʿfī," *Rivista degli Studi Orientali* 67, 1993, pp. 265-73. Henry Corbin, *En Islam iranien: aspects spirituels et philosophiques* I: *Le shîʿisme duodécimain*, Paris, 1971. Rifaat Y. Ebied and M. J. L. Young, "A Treatise on Hemerology Ascribed to Ǧaʿfar al-Ṣādiq," *Arabica*, 23, 1976, pp. 296-307. Ebn Ḵaldun, *al-Moqaddema*, tr. Franz Rozenthal as *The Muqaddimah: An Introduction to History*, 3 vols., Princeton, 1967; tr. Vincent Monteil as *Discours sur l'histoire universelle: al-Muqaddima*, Paris, 1997. Ebn al-Nadim, *Ketāb al-fehrest*, ed. Reżā Tajaddod, Beirut, 1988; tr. Bayard Dodge as *The Fihrist of al-Nadīm*, 2 vols., New York, 1970. Toufic Fahd, "Djafr," in *EI*² II, pp. 375-77. Idem, *La divination arabe: Etudes religieuses, sociologiques et folkloriques sur le milieu natif de l'islam*, Leiden, 1966. Idem, "Ǧaʿfar aṣ-Ṣādiq et la tradition scientifique arabe," in *Le Shîʿisme imāmite: Colloque de Strasbourg (6-9 mai 1968)*, Paris, 1970, pp. 131-42. Heinz Halm, *Die islamische Gnosis: Die extreme Schia und die ʿAlawiten*, Bibliothek des Morgenlandes, Zürich and Munich, 1982. Idem, "Das Buch der Schatten: Die Mufaḍḍal Tradition der Gulat und die Ursprunge des Nuṣairiertums," *Der Islam* 55, 1978, pp. 219-66; 58, 1981, pp. 15-86. Imam Jaʿfar al-Ṣādeq (attr. to), *Eḵtiārāt al-ayyām waʾl-šohur*, ed. and tr. Rafaat Y. Ebied and M. J. L. Young as "A Treatise on Hemerology Ascribed to Ǧaʿfar al-Ṣādiq," *Arabica* 23, 1976, pp. 296-307. Idem, *Eḵtelāj al-aʿżāʾ*, tr. Julius Lippert and Friedrich Kern as *Arabische Zuckungsliteratur*, in Hermann Diels, ed., *Beiträge zur Zuckungsliteratur des Okzidents und Orients*, Berlin, 1907-8, II, pp. 57-91. Idem, *Faʾl-nāma*, ed. Robert Amberlain as *Le fal nameh, ou, Livre des sorts*, Paris, 1984.

Mofażżal b. ʿOmar Joʿfi (attr. to), *Ketāb al-haft waʾl-aẓella: talmiḏ al-Emām Jaʿfar b. Moḥammad al-Ṣādeq*, ed. ʿĀref Tāmer, Beirut, 1960, new ed., Beirut, 1981; ed. Moṣṭafā Ḡāleb as *Ketāb al-haft al-šarif men Mawlānā Jaʿfar al-Ṣādeq*, Beirut, 1964. Idem, *Ketāb al-ṣerāṭ*, ed. Leonardo Capezzone as "Il *Kitab al-sirat* attribuito a Mufaddal b. ʿUmar al-Guʿfi: Edizione del ms. unico (Paris, Bibliothèque Nationale) e studio introduttivo," *Rivista degli Studi Orientali* 69/3-4, 1995, pp. 318-416; ed. Monṣef b. ʿAbd-al-Jalil, Beirut, 2005. Abu Jaʿfar Moḥammad b. Yaʿqub Kolayni, *al-Oṣul men al-Kāfi*, ed. and tr. with commentary Sayyed Jawād Moṣṭafawi, 4 vols. in 2, Tehran, n.d. Paul Kraus, *Jābir Ibn Ḥayyān: contribution à l'histoire des idées scientifiques dans l'islam* I: *Le corpus des écrits jābiriens*, Mémoires de l'Institut d'Égypte 44, Cairo, 1942. Julius Lippert and Friedrich Kern, "Arabische Zuckungsliteratur," in Hermann Diels, *Beiträge zur Zuckungsliteratur des Okzidents und Orients* II: *Weitere griechische un aussergriechische Literatur und Volksüberlieferung*, Berlin, 1909, pp. 53-91. Pierre Lory, *Alchimie et mystique en terre d'Islam*, Lagrasse, 1989. Shaikh Moḥammad Mofid, *Ketāb al-eršād*, Najaf, 1962; tr. I. K. A. Howard as *The Book of Guidance into the Lives of the Twelve Imams*, Elmhurst, New York, 1981. Syed Noma-nul Haq, *Names, Natures and Things: The Alchemist Jābir ibn Ḥayyān and his Kitāb al-Aḥjār (Book of Stones)*, Boston Studies in the Philosophy of Science 158, Dordrecht, Boston, and London, 1994. Julius F. Ruska, *Arabische Alchemisten* II: *Ǧaʿfar Alṣādiq, der sechste Imām*, Heidelberger Akten der Von-Portheim-Stiftung, Arbeiten aus dem Institut für Geschichte der Naturwissenschaft 10, Heidelberg, 1924. Idem, "Ǧābir ibn Ḥajjān und seine Beziehungen zum Imām Ǧaʿfar aṣ-Ṣādiq," *Der Islam* 16, 1927, pp. 264-66. Fuat Sezgin, *Geschichte des arabischen Schrifttums*, 8 vols., Leiden, 1967-82. Antonella Straface, "Simbolismo ermetico e letteratura religiosa shiʿita," in Paolo Lucentini, Ilaria Parri, and Vittoria Perrone Compagni, eds., *Hermetism from Late Antiquity to Humanism/La tradizione ermetica dal mondo tardo-antico all'umanesimo*, Instrumenta Patristica et Mediaevalia 40, Turnhout, 2003, pp. 339-53. Manfred Ullmann, *Die Natur-und Geheimwissenschaften im Islam*, Handbuch der Orientalistik, Abt. I, Der Nahe und der Mittlere Osten Ergänzungsband VI/2, Leiden, 1972.

(DANIEL DE SMET)

v. And Herbal Medicine

Imam Jaʿfar al-Ṣādeq's work on medicine (*Ṭebb al-Emām al-Ṣādeq*) belongs to a genre of traditional herbal medicine attributed to the Shiʿite imams and known as the Medicine of the imams (*ṭebb al-aʾemma*), whose salient figure is Imam Jaʿfar al-Ṣādeq. Imam Ṣādeq's narrated dictums (Hadith) are central to Shiʿite medical literature as it enhanced, in the course of time, the spiritual image of the imam in popular religion. Imam Jaʿfar, indeed, was not the only imam who contributed to Shiʿite traditional medical wisdom, but the variety of his ethical instructions on the priorities of foods and drinks has significantly extended the chapter of "eating and drinking" (*bāb al-aṭʿema wa'l-ašreba*) in Shiʿite jurisprudence (see FEQH; Āqā Bozorg Ṭehrāni, XV, pp. 139-40). Before juridical rearrangements of Imami traditions by Shiʿite authors of the 4th/10th century (particularly by Abu Jaʿfar Kolayni, d. 329/940 and Ebn Bābuya, d. 381/991, q.v.), Imam Jaʿfar's medical instructions were compiled by some of his companions under the rubric of *ṭebb al-aʾemma* (Āqā Bozorg Ṭehrāni, XV, pp. 139-42; Ebn Besṭām, tr., p. xv). A similar rubric *ketāb al-ṭebb* (the book of medicine) appears in the earliest collection of Hadith of the Prophet Moḥammad by Moḥammad Bok̲āri (d. 256/870; Bok̲āri, IV, pp. 8-23), whose contents, too, were rearranged and renamed with different designations in Sunnite jurisprudence.

Another main reshuffling of Shiʿite medical traditions occurred in the late Safavid period by two renowned authors, Moḥammad Ḥorr ʿĀmeli (d. 1104/1693, q.v.), and Moḥammad-Bāqer Majlesi (d.1111/1699), who refashioned the imam's traditions not only with more popular flavor, but also with religious sanctions. The juridical instructions of the imam appear with medical sanctions in the language of Majlesi. Based on the above-mentioned sources, Imam Jaʿfar al-Ṣādeq's medical statements were re-collected in the modern period (see Āqā Bozorg Ṭehrāni, XV, p. 141). The most recently published collection, compiled by Moḥsen ʿAqil, endeavors to support the imam's instructions with today's scientific medical evidence.

Following a summary of Imam Jaʿfar al-Ṣādeq's traditional herbal medicine according to Moḥsen ʿAqil's arrangement, this article will deal with intellectual reactions to the traditional herbal medicine and comments by various observers and scholars.

IMAM AL-ṢĀDEQ'S POPULAR MEDICINE

Imam Jaʿfar al-Ṣādeq's medical traditions are concerned with three spheres: a variety of beneficial and harmful food items and drinks; some commonly known diseases and their remedies; corroboration of some traditional methods of treating illness.

Useful and harmful foods and drinks. Beneficial fruits reportedly mentioned by Imam al-Ṣādeq include apple (10 Hadiths), dates (7 Hadiths), quince (6 Hadiths), pomegranate (5 Hadiths), citrus fruits (4 Hadiths), pear, walnut, and raisins (3 Hadiths each), grape, melon, and olive (2 Hadiths each; ʿAqil, pp. 7-79, quoting Majlesi, LXIII, pp. 133-74, 181-82, 188, 196, 198; Ḥorr ʿĀmeli, XXV, pp. 124, 151,156, 164, 167-68, 170-71, 174, 177; Nuri, XVI, pp. 397-98, 400-2, 405-6).

Vegetables, legumes, and grains with health benefits reportedly recommended by Imam al-Ṣādeq include barley, lentil, and rice (16 Hadiths), rice (13 Hadiths), wild chicory (5 Hadiths), eggplant (5 Hadiths), black cumin and chard (4 Hadiths each), onion (3 Hadiths), radish, harmal peganum, marshmallow, turnip, beans, and pumpkin (2 Hadiths each), carrot, lettuce, leek, garlic, and frankincense (1 Hadith each; ʿAqil, pp. 80-161, 187-89, quoting Majlesi, LIX, pp. 220 234, LXIII, pp. 208, 215, 221, 227-28, 237, 239, 248-49, 280-81, 444, LXXIII, p. 86; Ḥorr ʿĀmeli, XXV, pp. 14-18, 21, 129-31, 189, 195-96, 199-200, 205-6, 212; Nuri, XVI, pp. 337, 339, 416-17, 423, 428-30).

Imam Jaʿfar al-Ṣādeq is also credited with naming a number of juices and beverages as being beneficial to one's good health. They include water (12 Hadiths), milk, and vinegar (7 Hadiths each), honey (3 Hadiths), and rose water Hadiths; ʿAqil, pp. 162-63, 213-59, 291 460-67, quoting Nuri XVI, pp. 363-64, 369; Ḥorr ʿĀmeli XXV, pp. 88-92, 112, , 115, 302-3; Majlesi, LIX, pp. 145-47, 221-29, 236, LXIII, pp. 95, 101, 302-3; Kolayni, VI, pp. 336-39).

Beneficial kinds of meat and other animal products, reportedly remarked by Imam al-Ṣādeq, include general references (13 Hadiths), fish (7 Hadiths), egg (4 Hadiths; see ʿAqil, pp. 268, 278, 446-47, quoting Majlesi, LXII, pp. 190, 207-8, 212, 215, LXIII, pp. 46-47; Ḥorr ʿĀmeli, XXV, pp. 39-41, 44-45, 77). Harmful drinks and foods which cannot be used even for medical treatment include alcoholic beverages, specifically wine (13 Hadith), blood, pork, and dead meat (1 Hadith each; see ʿAqil, pp. 410, 594, quoting Majlesi, LIX, p. 89).

Commonly known diseases and their remedies. In cases of certain pain in the waist, honey and cumin are advised (3 Hadiths;ʿAqil, p. 325, quoting Majlesi, LIX, p. 170). In cases of certain stomach pains, honey, cumin, rice, and sumac are advised (4 Hadiths; ʿAqil, p. 327, quoting Majlesi, LIX, p. 177). For treating certain hemorrhoids, it is advised to eat rice, leek, especially white leek (3 Hadiths; ʿAqil, pp. 337-38, quoting Majlesi, LIX, pp. 195-96). In case of head cold, among other things, violet oil is advised (3 Hadiths; ʿAqil, p. 341, quoting Majlesi, LIX, pp. 183-84). For treating tapeworm, freckles, throat pain, cough, chest pain, nightmares or anxiety during sleep, herbal medicine are mostly advised (1 Hadith each; see ʿAqil, pp. 354-61, quoting Majlesi, LIX, pp. 165, 182). For treating fever, in general, twenty-one Hadiths are quoted in which footbath and eating fruits such as apple and, on occasion, onion and honey are advised (ʿAqil, pp. 372-76, quoting Majlesi, LIX, pp. 93-99, 101-4). For the remedy of eye disease, washing, cleaning, nail-cutting, and eating specific foods are advised (9 Hadiths; ʿAqil, pp. 291-92, quoting Majlesi, LIX, pp. 145-47).

Methods of treating some illnesses. Imam Jaʿfar al-Ṣādeq has corroborated some traditional methods of treating illness and health problems. He has sometimes supported his instructions with God's blessing and *šariʿa* law; treatment of the eyes with kohl (9 Hadiths; ʿAqil, p. 390, quoting Majlesi, LXIII, pp. 94-96); vento treatment (*ḥejāma*) or art of cupping (39 Hadiths; ʿAqil, pp. 394-402, quoting Majlesi, LIX, pp. 108-31; see BLOODLETTING); cauterization (*kayy*) or burning the skin (1 Hadith; ʿAqil, p. 410, quoting Majlesi, LIX, p. 74); cutting down on food (11 Hadiths; ʿAqil, pp. 481-82, quoting Ḥorr ʿĀmeli, XXIV, pp. 239-40, 242-43, 247; Nuri, XVI, p. 213; Majlesi, LXIII, p. 232; 336); taking a bath (8 Hadiths; ʿAqil, pp. 281-82, as cited by Majlesi, LXXIII, pp. 70-71, 76-79).

PERSPECTIVES ON THE IMAM'S TRADITIONAL MEDICINE

On the authenticity of the above-mentioned Hadiths, Āqā Bozorg Ṭehrāni quotes Majlesi's view that the imams' traditions on food and drinks do not need strong documentation (*al-asānid al-qawiya*) on the part of transmitters, because their ignorance does not spoil what they have heard and quoted from the imam (Ṭehrāni, XV, p. 140). This argument is in line with the opinion articulated by the pioneering scholar of early Shiʿism, Shaikh al-Ṭāʾefa Abu Jaʿfar Moḥammad Ṭusi (d. 460/1067), who adopted weak traditions from ignorant or exaggerative narrators relying on their general knowledge of the religion (Ṭusi, p. 349). An example of a weak transmitter in Imam Jaʿfar al-Ṣādeq's medical traditions is Mofażżal b. ʿOmar Joʿfi (q.v.), who, as a companion of the imam, figures repeatedly in the imam's traditions, but whom the famous biographer of the early period Aḥmad b. ʿAli Najāši (d. 450/1058-9) described as "weak" (Ebn Besṭām, tr., p. xxii, quoting Najāši).

Unlike the Shiʿite position that regards the imams' statements as *aḥkām* (rulings) or parts of divinely inspired ordinances, Ebn Ḵaldun (d. 809/1406, q.v.) characterized the Prophet Moḥammad's medical statements as something customarily practiced among the Arabs. According to him, "the medicine mentioned in religious tradition is of the (Bedouin) type. It is in no way part of the divine revelation. (Such medical matters) were merely (part of) Arab custom and happened to be mentioned in connection with the circumstances of the Prophet, like other things that were customary in his generation. They were not mentioned in order to imply that that particular way of practicing (medicine) is stipulated by religious law. Moḥammad was sent to teach us the religious law. He was not sent to teach us medicine or any other ordinary matter. In connection with the story of fecundation of palms, he said: "'You know more about your worldly affairs (than I)'" (Ebn Ḵaldun, III, p. 150).

Ebn Ḵaldun's quotation of the above tradition of the Prophet refers to three Hadiths documented by Abu'l-Ḥosayn Moslem b. Ḥajjāj (d. 261/875) saying, "I am a human, follow me when I order you something concerning your religion, when I order you something out of my opinion, [be aware] I am a human. You know more about your worldly affairs [than I])" (Moslem, XV, pp. 116-17). Neither is Imam Jaʿfar al-Ṣādeq's overall language so juridical in his medical statements as they are in religious matters. Today's Shiʿites, however, make use of the imam's medical traditions mostly for invocation, good omen, and recently to prove the miraculous insight of the imam that can be ascertained by contemporary scientific evidence (ʿAqil, p. 6).

Michael Dols has characterized the origin and contents of the imams' medical traditions as a blend of three distinct elements, "The folk medicine of the Arabian Bedouin, the borrowing of Galenic concepts (see JĀLINUS; HUMERISM) that had become common parlance (such as humours, temperaments, and qualities), and the overacting principle of divine or supernatural causation" (Dols, p. 421, as cited in Ebn Besṭām, editor's Introd., p. xvi).

Commenting on the *ṭebb al-aʾemma*, Fazlur Rahman observes that the Shiʿites "underplay the natural cures and emphasize the value of suffering." Such tendencies, he argues, were "undoubtedly connected with the passion motif and the stress on martyrdom, of which Sunni Islam has little trace" (Rahman, 1987, pp. 37-38, as cited in Ebn Besṭām, editor's Introd., p. xv). In Imam Jaʿfar al-Ṣādeq's collection of medical traditions, however, we do not find any obvious trace of such value in suffering or martyrdom.

Given the high priorities of fruits and vegetables prescribed by Imam Jaʿfar al-Ṣādeq, one may conclude that the imam was essentially concerned with herbal-based remedies then current in Mesopotamia, where he traveled in the latter part of his life. He occasionally combined his food and drug instructions with invocation to God, or recitation of passages from the Qurʾān; but, in his medical stipulations he did not ascertain his remarks by attributing them, even by implication, to divine inspiration, neither did he ascribe them to a tradition of the Prophet Moḥammad. It is noteworthy that some of the his instructions, such as drinking three sips of hot water of the reservoir of a public bath wherein one enters (ʿAqil, p. 468, quoting Majlesi, LXIII, p. 451), are common among Muslims where public baths are still in use.

Bibliography: Moḥammad b. Ḥasan Ḥorr ʿĀmeli, *Wasāʾl al-Šiʿa*, 30 vols., Beirut, 2003. Moḥsen ʿAqil, *Ṭebb al-Emām al-Ṣādeq*, Beirut, 1998. Moḥammad b. Esmāʿil Boḵāri, *Ṣaḥiḥ al-Boḵāri*, pub. with notes of ʿAbd-al-Hādi Sendi as *Matn al-Buḵāri maškul be-ḥāšiat al-Sendi*, 4 vols. in 2, Cairo, 1981. Michael Dols, "Islam and Medicine," *History of Science* 26, 1988, p. 421. Ebn Besṭām, *Ṭebb al-Aʾemma*, tr. Batool Ispahany as *Islamic Medical Wisdom: The Tibb al-A'immah*, ed. Andrew J. Newman, London, 1991. Ebn Hendu, *Meftāḥ al-ṭebb wa menhāj al-ṭollāb*, Beirut, 2002. Ebn Ḵaldun, *The Muqaddimah: An Introduction to History*, tr. Franz Rosenthal, 2nd ed., 3 vols., Princeton, 1967. Abu Jaʿfar Moḥammad Kolayni, *Foruʿ al-Kāfi*, 8 vols., Beirut, 1993. Moḥammad-Bāqer Majlesi, *Beḥār al-anwār*, 110 vols., Beirut, 1983. Moslem b. Ḥajjāj Qošayri, *Ṣaḥiḥ moslem be šarḥ al-Emām al-Nowawi*, 18 vols., Beirut, 1994. Abu'l-ʿAbbās Aḥmad b. ʿAli Najāši, *Rejāl al-Najāši*, ed. Moḥammad-Jawād Nāʾini, 2vols., Beirut, 1988. Mirzā Ḥosayn Nuri, *Mostadrak al-wasāʾel wa mostanbaṭ al-masāʾel*, 18 vols. Beirut, 1987. Fazlur

Rahman, *Health and Medicine in the Islamic Tradition: Change and Identity*, New York, 1987. Āqā Bozorg Ṭehrāni, *al-Ḏariʿa elā taṣānif al-Šiʿa*, 25 vols. Beirut, 1983. Šayḵ-al-Ṭāʾefa Abu Jaʿfar Moḥammad b. Ḥasan Ṭusi, *ʿOddat al-oṣul*, 2 vols. Najaf, 1983.

(AHMAD KAZEMI MOUSSAVI)

vi. AND SHIʿTE JURISPRUDENCE.
See SHIʿISM. Forthcoming online.

JAʿFARI, ŠAʿBĀN (known in Persia as Šaʿbān Bimoḵ [simple-minded]; b. Tehran 1921, d. Santa Monica, Calif., 19 August 2006), a *luṭi* (*q.v.) of the *jāhel* variety, athlete, and rightwing political agent from the early 1940s to the early 1950s, who later headed Persia's traditional sports establishment (*zur-ḵāna*).

Early years. Šaʿbān Jaʿfari was the last of fourteen children. When the Sangelaj quarter of Tehran where the family lived was razed by order of Reżā Shah to be replaced by a municipal park, they moved to nearby the Dabbāḡ Ḵāna quarter, where his father had a grocery store. As a young child he worked in his father's shop, but ended his formal education after only four grades, having been expelled from several schools for unruly behavior. It was at school that one of his teachers called him *bimoḵ* (simple-minded), a sobriquet, which would stick to him for the rest of his life. He then worked briefly in a foundry, a smithy, and the arsenal. His father died when he was twelve, and soon thereafter he started frequenting the Darḵungāh *zur-ḵāna* of Sangelaj (see Jaʿfari). He quickly gained a reputation as a brawler, and at the age of fifteen went to prison for the first time. In 1940 he started his two-year military service, but ran away from the barracks so often that it took him four years to complete it (Saršār, pp. 21-55). When Ḥabib-Allāh Bolur, a successful wrestler who would in later years become a coach, official, and actor, founded the Āhan Club in 1942 (ʿAbbāsi, p. 383), Jaʿfari joined it (Saršār, p. 51). In 1943 he became national champion in *kabbāda* and *čark*, two *zur-ḵāna* (q.v.) exercises (*Sāl-nāma-ye Pārs*, 1944, p. 93). By now Jaʿfari was a typical *luṭi* (q.v.) of the *jāhel* variety, and would often start or get involved in fights. One evening, when the Ferdowsi Theatre had a private show by leftist artists to which the owners refused him admission, he became violent and was arrested and exiled to Lāhijān, where he married a local girl and ran a *zur-ḵāna*.

Rightwing political agent. After the war Jaʿfari briefly became a sympathizer of the Fedāʾiān-e Eslām (q.v.) and would often attack the pro-Soviet Tudeh Party (see COMMUNISM ii) activists on the streets of Tehran on behalf of the political establishment (Saršār, pp. 59-65). Jaʿfari lived in the same neighborhood as the politician and historian Sayyed Ḥosayn Makki, gravitated towards him, and supported his electoral campaign for the Majles. Through Makki he met Ayatollah Sayyed Abu'l-Qāsem Kāšāni, whose supporter he became. In addition to Makki and Kāšāni, he was also in touch with Moẓaffar Baqāʾi (Saršār, pp. 77-78, 110, Rahnemā, p. 164). Jaʿfari continued brawling with Tudeh sympathizers. When on 5 December 1951 pro-Kāšāni and pro-Moṣaddeq demonstrators, who included a sizable contingent of *jāhels*, clashed with Tudeh sympathizers in Tehran and attacked the editorial offices of a number of anti-Moṣaddeq newspapers, both conservative and pro-Tudeh, Jaʿfari was among them (Mowaḥḥed, I, pp. 391-93; Rahnemā, pp. 345, 563-67). There are plausible indications that he had been put on the payroll of the police (Rahnemā, pp. 565, 573, 576, and 578), but Jaʿfari himself claimed that he accepted no money from the government. He was arrested and went to prison for about five months (Saršār, pp. 91-95, 104. Cf. Rahnemā, pp. 573-74). Some months later, when the Shah dismissed Moṣaddeq as prime minister on 30 Tir 1331 Š./21 July 1952, and appointed Aḥmad Qawām in his stead, Jaʿfari was one of the ringleaders of the demonstrations that led to Qawām's resignation and Moṣaddeq's reappointment. According to his own account, he took a few men to the Sinā hospital and stole a few corpses, which they paraded on the streets of Tehran shouting that they were the remains of people Qawām had ordered to be killed (Saršār, pp. 110-11). To show their appreciation, a delegation of National Front leaders visited Jaʿfari's sports club on 19 September 1952 (*Bāktar-e emruz*, 20 September 1952, reproduced in Saršār, p. 119). Throughout all these eventful months, Jaʿfari took his cue in political matters from Ayatollah Kāšāni, and when Kāšāni parted company with Moṣaddeq, Jaʿfari followed his lead.

In late February 1952, the Shah, exasperated by the power struggle with Moṣaddeq, decided to leave the country. Although he did not say that he would abdicate, Kāšāni and Ayatollah Sayyed Moḥammad Behbahāni spread rumors to that effect, and invited their followers to congregate at the gates of the palace to prevent the Shah's departure. In the morning of 9 Esfand 1330 Š./28 February 1952, Kāšāni warned a group of supporters who had assembled in his house that if the Shah left the country, the *ulama*'s turbans would go too. Jaʿfari thereupon went to the bazaar to rouse the bazaaris, but most of these supported Moṣaddeq, and so his efforts proved fruitless. Jaʿfari then led a crowd to Moṣaddeq's house under the pretext of forcing him to prevent the Shah's departure. When they were refused entry, he personally led the attack on the prime minister's house by ramming a jeep into the gate; in the scuffle his nephew was killed (Saršār, pp. 82, 123-28; Rahnemā, pp. 822-35; *New York Times*, 23 August 1953). But Moṣaddeq prevailed in that crisis, and Jaʿfari was arrested, tried, and given a one-year prison sentence. He was still in prison when the conflict between Moṣaddeq and the Shah came to a head in the summer of 1953.

It is widely believed that Jaʿfari was one of the ringleaders of the demonstrations that accompanied the coup d'état of 28 Mordād 1332 Š./19 August 1953 (q.v.). The fact is that he was still in prison when the events began to unfold, and the demonstrations were led by *jāhels* close to Ayatollah Behbahāni (Rahnemā, pp. 956-60). In the afternoon of that day he was freed by order of General

Fażl-Allāh Zāhedi (Saršār, pp. 161-62) and joined the pro-Shah street demonstrations. When the Shah returned from his brief exile on 22 August, Jaʿfari organized crowds to welcome him.

After the restoration of the Shah, Jaʿfari continued his strong-armed activism on behalf of the ruler, for which purpose he founded an organization named Jamʿiyat-e javānmardān-e jānbāz (Society of Chivalrous and Selfless Men; Mowaḥḥed, III, pp. 107-8, 130). On 13 March 1954 he roughed up Moṣaddeq's erstwhile foreign minister, Ḥosayn Fāṭemi, in front of the police building, injuring him to the point that he had to be taken to a hospital to be treated for knife wounds. In the elections to the 18th Majles he physically intimidated opponents of General Fażl-Allāh Zāhedi's regime, which was blatantly rigging the elections (*Life*, 22 March 1954, pp. 38-40).

Šaʿbān Jaʿfari and traditional athletics. After the coup, the Shah helped Jaʿfari establish a modern sports facility dedicated to traditional athletics on the northern edge of the municipal park (Park-e sahr), in the neighborhood in which he grew up, and personally came to inaugurate it in November 1957. The Bāšgāh-e Šaʿbān-e Jaʿfari had far more elaborate and well appointed facilities than traditional *zur-ḵānas*, and included not only showers and training rooms for other disciplines such as wrestling, boxing, and karate, but also a small museum in which Jaʿfari exhibited objects related to traditional athletics (Partow Beyżāʾi Kāšāni, pp. 245-46, Jaʿfari, personal interview). On 5 June 1963 the club was set on fire during the riots caused by the arrest of Ayatollah Khomeini in Qom, but Jaʿfari managed to rebuild it expeditiously. On most evenings Jaʿfari personally led the exercises in the pit (*gowd*), and the club was regularly visited by foreign dignitaries and celebrities (Saršār, pp. 254-68). Jaʿfari broke with tradition by allowing women to attend these sessions (ibid, p. 225), for which he was criticized by many veteran athletes (Rochard, p. 71). Until the early 1970s Jaʿfari enjoyed personal access to the Shah, and on his birthday (4 Ābān/26 October) would organize mass displays of traditional *zur-ḵāna* exercises involving up to 1,800 athletes as part of the celebrations in Tehran's main stadiums (Saršār, pp. 215, 249-51).

In the 1970s Jaʿfari lost his access to the court (Saršār, p. 310). The men and women who now led Iran were embarrassed to be associated with a ruffian like him and gave him the cold shoulder (Forugī, p. 47). In the course of the 1978 confrontation between the Shah's regime and its opponents, Jaʿfari made half-hearted attempts to recruit *luṭis* to counter the anti-regime demonstrators, but did not have any success (Mirzāʾi and Ḥosayni, p. 151). He himself claimed that his proposals to organize a countermobilization against the revolutionaries did not meet the approval of the government (Saršār, pp. 337-38).

In the course of the anti-government riots the Jaʿfari Club was again attacked and the museum looted. Jaʿfari himself fled Iran in January 1979, and after a few peripatetic years spent in Japan, Israel, Germany, Britain, France, Belgium, and Turkey, he settled in Santa Monica, California, where he was looked after in his old age by former acolytes, his wife and only son having remained in Iran (Jaʿfari; Saršār, pp. 337-73). He refused to grant interviews about his role in Iranian politics to anyone until 1999, when he consented to tell the story of his life to Homā Saršār. He died on 19 August 2006, the anniversary of the coup against Moṣaddeq.

Concluding remarks. For Mohammad Reza Shah's opponents, be they leftists, Moṣaddeqists, or Islamists, Šaʿbān Jaʿfari is one of the most hateful figures of 20th-century Iran, a man who served reactionary causes. While there is general agreement that he had originally been a *čāqukeš* (thug), from the mid-1950s onwards his demeanor became more respectable as he came to concentrate on traditional athletics. As *sarparast-e varzeš-e bāstāni* (head of ancient sport) he played a major part in keeping alive Iran's athletic tradition at a time when the country's physical education establishment was mostly committed to propagating Western disciplines and looked down on Jaʿfari and the *zur-ḵāna* tradition (Jaʿfari; Saršār, pp. 304-5). His tireless efforts to recruit young Iranian men for what was by now called "ancient" (*bāstāni*) sports played a major part in ensuring the generational renewal of that tradition at a time when most young people were attracted to Western sports. The Jaʿfari club was Iran's first modern *zur-kānā* and paved the way for others, such as that of the Bānk-e Melli and the ones built after the revolution. Since the revolution, the premises of his club have housed the National Federation of Ancient Sports.

Bibliography: ʿA. ʿAbbāsi, *Tāriḵ-e košti-ye Irān*, I, Tehran, 1995. Ḵ. Forugī, "Naqdi bar ketāb-e 'Šaʿbān-e Jaʿfari'," *Negin* 24, 2006, pp. 41-51. Š. Jaʿfari, personal interview, 15 May 1997, Santa Monica, California. S. Mirzāʾi and S. M. Ḥosayni, *Az sargoḏašt-e luṭihā*, Tehran, 2004. M.-ʿA. Mowaḥḥed, *Ḵāb-e āšofta-ye naft: Doktor Moṣaddeq wa nahżat-e melli-ye Irān*, I, Tehran, 1999 and III, Tehran, 2004. H. Partow Bayżāʾi Kāšāni, *Tārik-e varzeš-e bāstāni-e Irān: Zur-ḵāna*, Tehran, 1957, 2nd ed., 2003. A. Rahnemā, *Niruhā-ye maḏhabi bar bastar-e ḥarakat-e nahżat-e melli*, Tehran, 2005. Ph. Rochard, "Le 'sport antique' des zurkhâne de Téhéran. Formes et significations d'une pratique contemporaine," PhD dissertation, Université Aix-Marseille, 2000. H. Saršār, *Šaʿbān-e Jaʿfari*, Los Angeles, 2002.

(H. E. CHEHABI)

JAʿFARQOLI KHAN BAḴTIĀRI, Sardār Asʿad. See BAḴTIĀRI TRIBE.

JAFR, a term of uncertain etymology (for which, see below) used to designate the major divinatory art in Islamic mysticism and gnosis, the *ʿelm al-jafr* (the science of *jafr*) also simply *al-ʿelm*, of discovering the predestined fate of nations, dynasties, religions, and individuals by a variety of methods and is represented by a vast literature that is well documented already during the Umayyad period, and more so during the ʿAbbasid period (Fahd, pp. 375-77; idem, pp. 595-96; idem, 1966, pp. 219-45; Colin; Knysh; see also BĀṬEN).

Given the underlying thrust of this science, an important component of *jafr*-literature is the *malāḥem*, apocalyptic predictions (or *ḥedṯān*), prophetic and apocalyptic speculations in prose or verse concerning past, present, and future events up to the coming of the Mahdi (Macdonald; Editors, p. 216; Hartmann). For *Jafr* proper, the major tool is the science of letters, *ʿelm al-ḥoruf*, based on the numerical values of the twenty-eight letters of the Arabic alphabet in the order of the Abjad (q.v.). It is applied to words, phrases, and letters of the Qurʾān, the prophetic traditions (Hadith), and other sources considered divinely inspired (Fahd, pp. 595-96; Colin; Knysh). Specific subsets include the ninety-nine Beautiful Names of God (Gardet), the seven letters not found in the *Surat al-fāteḥa*, and the fourteen mysterious letters of the Qurʾān that open twenty-nine of the *suras* (Welch, pp. 412-14).

Table 1
NUMERICAL VALUES OF THE
ARABIC LETTERS
ABJAD

أ	ب/پ	ج/چ	د	ه	و	ز/ژ	ح	ط	
alef	*be/pe*	*jm/če*	*dāl*	*he*	*vāv*	*ze/že*	*ḥā*	*ṭā*	
ʾ	*b/p*	*j/č*	*d*	*h*	*v*	*z/ž*	*ḥ*	*ṭ*	
1	2	3	4	5	6	7	8	9	
ى	ک/گ	ل	م	ن	س	ع	ف	ص	
y	*k/g*	*l*	*m*	*n*	*s*	ʿ	*f*	*ṣ*	
yā	*kāf/gāf*	*lām*	*mim*	*nun*	*sin*	*ʿayn*	*fe*	*ṣād*	
10	20	30	40	50	60	70	80	90	
ق	ر	ش	ت	ث	خ	ذ	ض	ظ	غ
q	*r*	*š*	*t*	*ṯ*	*ḵ*	*ḏ*	*ż*	*ẓ*	*ḡ*
qāf	*re*	*šin*	*te*	*ṯe*	*ḵe*	*ḏāl*	*żād*	*ẓā*	*ḡayn*
100	200	300	400	500	600	700	800	900	1000

As such, *jafr* intersects with letter magic, *simiā* (Macdonald and Fahd, pp. 612-13), the interpretation of the primordial lettered *lawḥ-e mahfuẓ* "safely preserved tablet" (Wensinck and Bosworth p. 698), containing all knowledge of the preordained course of the world; the art of lettered magic squares (Sesiano, pp. 28-31), and with astrology. A skeptic account of the art is given by Ebn Ḵaldun (q.v.; d. 1406) in the chapter: "Forecasting the future of dynasties and nations, including a discussion of predictions (*malāḥim*) and an exposition of the subject called 'divination'" (*jafr*; Ebn Ḵaldun, tr., II, pp. 200-31).

The divine gift of *Jafr* is foremost correlated with the Shiʿite notion of the prophetic afflatus transmitted from Adam through Moḥammad to the descendants of Fāṭema, that is, the Alids. The secret *Ketāb-e jafr* is supposed to have been in the possession of the sixth Shiʿite Imam, Jaʿfar al-Ṣādeq (d. 765, q.v.). It is said to have been handed down from Imam ʿAli b. Abi Ṭāleb, assumed to have been the first to have practiced *jafr*. Other sources mentioned, particularly regarding apocalyptic, are attributed to the prophet *Dāniāl*. By fanciful interpretation and etymology, the noun *jafr* in the title of Jaʿfar al-Ṣādeq's book, which among other meanings may refer to a weaned lamb or kid (Lane, II, s.v. "*jfr*"), is related to the leather bag believed to have contained secret scrolls or to the leather on which the secret texts were written (Ebn Ḵaldun, tr., II, p. 210; Kolayni, I, pp. 348-49).

Jafr, while representing a long indigenous Islamic intellectual and cognitive endeavor focused on the prophetic texts, continues and develops the gnostic-mystical theory, or technique, of Hellenistic Neo-Pythagorean and Neo-Platonic cosmological letter and number speculations (for these, including Jewish traditions, see Dornseiff, pp. 142-45, still the most detailed treatment of these subjects). The numerological principles and operations for revealing the message hidden in the Qurʾān ultimately derive from the mathematics of the Pythagoreans, as does the spiritual and dialectic style which is inseparable from its sacred form which, nevertheless, only aided the intrinsically Islamic approach (Nasr, pp. 75-76). From among the various pre-Islamic Near Eastern schools and traditions, an important input into the emergence and development of *jafr* quite likely came from the extensive divinatory and apocalyptic literature of pre-Islamic Iran (see DIVINATION; APOCALYPTIC i. In Zoroastrianism, ii. in Muslim Iran). The latter ultimately reflects the dialectic teachings of the Gathas (q.v.) of Zarathustra, which are the archetype of emanational cosmology and apocalyptic vision and ethics. Such input would suggest the possibility that the Arabic term *jafr* was influenced, at least, by an Iranian term, most directly Parthian *žafr* "deep," assuming adjustment of *ž* to Arabic *j* (Av. *jafra-* [also *gufra-*] "deep, mysterious," Mid. Pers. *žufr*, New Pers. *žarf*).

Within Islamic tradition, *jafr* is an exegetical method that complemented *taṭbiq*, the discovery of correspondences (foremost between ontological levels), and *taʾwil*, the allegorical exegesis of the Qurʾān and prophetic sayings, often based on associated meanings derived from the root letters of words. This approach to revealing insights into the ontological continuum between the levels of the macro-cosmos and micro-cosmos seeks patterns of allusion (*ešāra*) accessible to the spiritual elite, which transcend the explicit literal expression (*ʿebāra*) intended for the masses (*ʿawāmm*), but are still below the subtleties (*laṭāʾef*), accessible to *awliāʾ* (q.v.), the friends of God, and the level of the *ḥaqāʾeq* "profound realities," accessible only to prophets, according to the commentary attributed to Jaʿfar al-Ṣādeq, which is included in Moḥammad Solami's *Ḥaqāʾeq al-tafsir* (Nwyia, 1968, pp. 181-230; idem, 1970, pp. 210-11).

There has been a continuous line of mystic and gnostic movements and prominent individuals engaged in certain or most aspects of numerological speculations and *jafr*. Omitting theologians such as Abu Ḥāmed Moḥammad Ḡazāli (d. 505/1111, q.v.) and Qurʾānic commentators who wrote on the *al-asmāʾ al-ḥosnā* and/or the *ḥoruf*, these include: (1) the late 5th-century Mazdakites and the later Ḵorramdinis (see Madelung); (2) the Ismaʿilis (q.v.); the

Table 2
THE ALPHA-NUMERIC HIERARCHY OF THE UNIVERSE

A	1	alef	al-bāriʾ	Creator	
B	2	bāʾ	al-ʿaql	Intellect	
J	3	jim	al-nafs	Soul	
D	4	dāl	al-ṭabiʿa	Nature	
H	5	hāʾ	al-bāriʾ (be'l-eżāfa)	Creator re what is below it	
W	6	wāw	al-ʿaql (be'l-eżāfa)	Intellect re what is below it	
Z	7	zāʾ	al-nafs (be'l-eżāfa)	Soul re what is below it	
Ḥ	8	ḥāʾ	al-ṭabiʿa (be'l-eżāfa)	Nature re what is below it	
Ṭ	9	ṭāʾ	al-hayulāʾ	material world, no relation to below	
Y	10	yāʾ	al-ebdāʿ	plan of the Creator	5 × 2
K	20	kāf	al-takwin	structure to created realm	5 × 4
L	30	lām	al-amr	divine commandments	5 × 6
M	40	mim	al-ḵalq	created universe	5 × 8
N	50	nun	two-fold aspect of *wojud* "being"		M + Y
S	60	sin	double relation to *ḵalq* and *takwin*		M + K
ʿ	70	*ʿayn al-tartib*	chain of being of universe		M + L
Ṣ	90	ṣād	triple relation *amr*, *ḵalq*, *takwin*		M + L + K
Q	100	qāf	assembly of things in divine plan		2M = Ṣ + Y
R	200	rāʾ	return of all things to One		2Q

Source: Nasr, p. 210.

10th-century Eḵwān al-Ṣafāʾ (q.v.); (3) individuals, including Avicenna (Ebn Sinā d. 428/1037; q.v.), Šehāb-al-Din Sohravardi (d. 587/1191); Abu'l-ʿAbbās Aḥmad Buni (d. 622/1225; see Dietrich), Ebn al-ʿArabi (d. 638/1240; q.v.); and ʿAbd-al-Raḥmān Besṭāmi (d. 858/1454; q.v.); (4) later movements, including the Ḥorufis (see HORUFISM), a Muslim sect founded by Fażl-Allāh Astarābādi (d. 796/1394, q.v.), who distinctly added the four Persian letters ("*p*," "*č*," "*ž*," "*g*") to the twenty-eight Arabic letters; the Bektāšiya (q.v.); Maḥmud Pasiḵāni (d. 831/1427), the founder of the Noqṭawiya "Pointers" Order (Babayan, pp. 57-117; Algar), who believed that all creation and knowledge is ultimately contained in the first emanative differentiating power point, the one under the Arabic letter "*b*" of the initial *besmellāh* (q.v.) "in the name of God," of the first Sura of the Qurʾān, the *Surat al-fāteḥa*; Shaikhism, founded by Shaikh Aḥmad Aḥsāʾi (d. 1826; q.v.); Babism, founded by Mirzā Moḥammad-ʿAli, known as the Bāb (executed 1850, q.v.; see also BABISM); and Bahaism.

Similar to cabbalistic *gematria* in Jewish tradition, the quasi-alchemical divinatory techniques to find hidden dates and connections involve two distinct aspects of letters, numerical and non-numerical. A simple additive examples is the foretelling by Ebn al-ʿArabi of the Almohads' victory over the Christians at Alarcos (al-Arak) on the Iberian Peninsula, when pointed by a mysterious friend to the phrase *fatḥan mobinan* "clear victory" (Qurʾān 48:1; the numerical value of the phrase, according to Abjad [q.v.] table, is 592, corresponding to 1195-96 C.E.; Ebn al-ʿArabi, 1971, p. 29). Another example is the association of two names with the same date, for instance, the birth year of Timur, 736/1336, which is also the year that the last Il-khan, Abu Saʿid (q.v.) died, for which was found the chronogram *lawḏ* (LVḎ) "refuge" (3+6+700; Roemer, p. 181; Browne, III, p. 58). Or, two fundamental terms are found to have the same numerical value, such as the sacred number 19 in Babism and Bahaism, which is encoded in the equation of *wāḥed* (VĀḤD; 6+1+8+4) "the One," with *wojud* (VJVD; 6+3+6+4) "existence." More complex operations include addition and subtraction (e.g., *dud az Ḵorāsān bar āmad* "smoke came up from Khorasan" for the death year of the poet Jāmi, obtained by subtracting the numerical value of "*dud*" [14] from that of "Ḵorāsān" [912]; Brown, III, p. 512); anagrammatic transposition; replacement of letters by others from various types of alphabetic arrangements; the combination with letters from significant words, such as the ninety-nine most beautiful names of God with those of the names of the desired object; the *notaricon*, that is, acronymic exegesis by which each letter is replaced by a different significant word (for a variety of chronograms, see Naṣrābādi, pp. 468 ff.).

On a metaphysical cosmic scale, letters are assigned an ontological status of active creative constituents (for the Greco-Roman tradition of this concept, cf. "*Stoichaion*-Element," in Dornseiff, pp. 14-16). The emanated cosmos is perceived as a hierarchical, multi-level dynamic matrix, each level of which is coded by a distinct letter of the Arabic alphabet. Thereby the sacred texts become accessible for exegesis by establishing the correspondence of the macro-cosmic and micro-cosmic hierarchies with the alpha-numerical hierarchies (e.g., see Cole, pp. 1-23, on the cognitive frameworks of this world view). An example is the above alpha-numerical table of Ebn Sinā (Nasr, p. 210), here modified by spacing to highlight the main ontological sets (Table 2).

This cosmic-hierarchical Table encodes two significant numbers. The total number of levels is 19. Level 19 (R), as the all-inclusive highest level, embraces the other levels,

(A-Q) = 18. These two numbers evidently imply reference to the much discussed set of 18 or 19 letters of the *besmellāh* (B-SM ALLH ALRḤMN ALRḤYM), and, considering the Muslim lunar calendar, are also reminiscent of the eighteen-year "Saros" cycle of lunar eclipses and the nineteen-year "Metonic" lunar cycle. At the same time, the number 19 is associated with the basic nine-house magic (Saturn) square, known in Islamic tradition by its corner letters as *boduḥ* (BDWḤ; Macdonald, p. 153) and in China as the "Nine Steps of Jü" (Nasr, p. 211), steps that in fact trace stars of *Ursa Major* (cf. Schafer, p. 240).

Table 3
BASIC MAGIC SQUARE

D 4 د	Ṭ 9 ط	B 2 ب
J 3 ج	H 5 ه	Z 7 ز
Ḥ 8 ح	A 1 ا	W 6 و

Source: Nasr, p. 211.

This square encodes multiple hidden correlations to the alphabet, to arithmetic series and geometric figures, and to other patterns. Among others, the number of the gnomon of 4-9-2-7-6 = 28 (top and right sides of the magic square) equals the number of the Arabic alphabet. The remaining sub-square, crosswise 1-8-3-5, sequentially 1-3-5-8 = 17, is another sacred number related to the four natures of metals, and of other fundamental cosmic sets (Nasr, 1976, p. 195).

Not all of the alpha-numerical cosmic hierarchies adhere to the strict sequence or number of the Arabic alphabet. Louis Massignon (tr., pp. 68-72) includes a synoptic "Table of the 'Philosophical' Alphabet (JAFR)" that collates the various symbolic values assigned to each of the Arabic letters by select Islamic thinkers with those assigned to the corresponding letters in the Hebraic, Christian, and Greek traditions. In essence then, specific sacred words and names of the prophetic texts were seen as a divine logogram "*moʿammā*" or chronogram (q.v.) "*mādda tāriḵ*," that needs to be deciphered (Windfuhr, forthcoming). In doing so, the mystic adepts, illustrious or not, used the same techniques by which names and dates are encoded into pleasing phrases and verse in the Islamic art of riddling, just as they produced their own logograms and chronograms in their poetry and writings.

Bibliography: Hamid Algar, "Noḵṭawiyya," in *EI*[2] VIII, pp. 114-17. R. Austin, *The Sufis of Andalusia*, London, 1971. Alessandro Bausani, "Ḥurūfiyya," in *EI*[2] III, pp. 600-01. Kathryn Babayan, *Mystics, Monarchs and Messiah: Cultural Landscape of Early Modern Iran*, Harvard Middle Eastern Monographs 35, Cambridge, Mass., 2002. Edward G. Browne, *A Literary History of Persia*, 4 vols., Cambridge, 1929-30, III, pp. 282-83, 385-87. J. R. I. Cole, "The World as Text: Cosmologies of Shaykh Aḥmad al-Aḥsāʾi," *Studia Islamica* 80, 1994, pp. 1-23. G. S. Colin, "Ḥisāb al-Djummal," in *EI*[2] III, p. 468. ʿAli-Akbar Dolfi, *Taṣwir-e ʿadad dar āʾina-ye ʿerfān*, Tehrān, 1983. A. Dietrich, "Būnī," in *EI*[2], suppl., pp. 156-57. Franz Dornseiff, *Das Alphabet in Mystik und Magie*, Leipzig and Berlin, 1922 (also includes the section "Islam. 1. Alphabetspekulation," and "2. Ketzeriche Buchstabenanbeter"). Ebn al-ʿArabi, *The Sufis of Andalusia: Ruḥ al-qods and al-Durra al-fāḵera*, tr. R. W. J. Austin, London, 1971. Idem, *al-Fotuḥāt al-makiyya*, selected texts ed. and tr., Michel Chodkiewicz, Cyrille Chodkiewicz and Denis Gril as *Les Illuminations de la Mecque/The Meccan Illuminations*, Paris, 1998. Ebn al-Ḵaldun, *al-Moqaddema*, tr. Franz Rosenthal as *The Muqaddimah: An Introduction to History*, 3 vols., Princeton, 1967. Editors, *EI*[2] "Malāḥīm," in *EI*[2] VI, p. 216. Gerald T. Elmore, *Islamic Sainthood in the Fullness of Time: Ibn al-ʿArabī's Book of the Fabulous Gryphon*. Leiden and Boston, 1999. Toufic Fahd, "Djafr," in *EI*[2], II, pp. 375-77. Idem, "Ḥurūf," in *EI*[2] III, pp. 595-96. Idem, *La divination arabe: études religieuses, sociologiques et folkloriques sur le milieu natif d'Islam*, Leiden, 1966. Louis Gardet, "al-Asmāʾ al-Ḥusnā," in *EI*[2] I, pp. 714-17. Denis Gril, "La science des lettres," in Ebn ʿArabi, *Les Illuminations de la Mecque*, Paris, 1998, pp. 335-487. Abu'l-Ḥasan Ḥāfeẓiān, *Šarḥ wa tafsir-e lawḥ-e maḥfuẓ*, Tehran, 1996. R. Hartmann, "Eine arabische Apokalypse aus der Kreuzzugszeit: Ein Beitrag zur *Gafr*-Literatur," *Schriften der Königsberger Gelehrten Gesellschaft, Geisteswissenschaftliche Klasse*, Berlin 1924, pp. 89-116 (extract of Ebn al-ʿArabi, *Moḥāżarat al-abrār*). A. Knysh, "Ramz 3: Mystical and Other Esoterical Discourse," in *EI*[2] VIII, pp. 428-30. Abu Jaʿfar Moḥammad b. Yaʿqub Kolayni, *al-Oṣul men al-Kāfi*, ed. and tr. with commentary Sayyed Jawād Moṣṭafawi, 4 vols. in 2, Tehran, n.d., pp. 344-50. Edward William Lane, *Arabic-English Lexicon*, 8 vols., Beirut, 1997. Pierre Lory, *La science des lettres en Islam*, Paris, 2004. D. B. Macdonald, "Malāḥim," in *EI*[1] III, pp. 188-89. Idem, "Bodūḥ," in *EI*[2], Suppl., pp. 153-54. D. B. Macdonald, and Toufic Fahd, "Sīmiyā" in *EI*[2] IX, pp. 612-13. Wilferd Madelung, "Khurramiyya," in *EI*[2] V, pp. 63-65. Louis Massignon, *Essai sur les origines du lexique technique de la mystique musulmane*, tr. Benjamin Clark as *Essay on the Origins of the Technical Language of Islamic Mysticism: Conceptions of Nature and Methods Used for Its Study by the Ikhwān al-Ṣafā, al-Bīrūnī, and Ibn Sīnā*, Notre Dame, Indiana, 1997. Seyyed Hossein Nasr, *An Introduction to Islamic Cosmological Doctrines: Conceptions of Nature and Methods Used for Its Study by the Ikhwān al-Ṣafā, al-Bīrūnī, and Ibn Sīnā*, Boulder, Colorado, 1978. Mirzā Moḥammad Ṭāher Naṣrābādi, *Taḏkera-ye Naṣrābādi*, ed. Ḥasan Waḥid Dastgerdi, 2nd ed., n.p., n.d. Paul Nwyia, "Le tafsīr mystique attribué à Gaʿfar Sādiq, edition critique," *Mélanges de l'Université Saint-Joseph* 43/4, 1968, pp. 181-230. Idem, *Exégèse coranique et langage mystique: Nouvel essai sur le lexique technique des mystiques Musulmans*, Beirut, 1970. Hermann Römer, *Die Bābī-Behāʾi: Die jüngste mohammedanische Sekte*, Potsdam, 1912. Jacque Sesiano, "Wafḳ," in *EI*² XI, pp. 28-31. Edward H. Schafer, *Pacing the Void: T'ang Approaches to the Stars*, Berkeley, Los Angeles, and London, 1977. Jaʿfar Sharīf, *Qanoon-e-Islam, or the Customs of the Mossulmans of India: Comprising a Full and Exact Account of Their Various Rites and Ceremonies from the Moment of Birth Till the Hour of Death*, composed under the direction of, and translated by G. A. Herklots, London, 1832. Annemarie Schimmel, "Letter Symbolism in Sufi Literature," in idem, *Mystical Dimensions of Islam*. Chapel Hill, 1975, pp. 411-25. A. T. Welch, "al-Ḳurʾān," in *EI*², pp. 400-419, esp. pp. 412-14. A. J. Wnsinck and C. E. Bosworth, "Lawḥ," in *EI*² V, p. 698. Gernot Windfuhr, "Riddles and Chronograms," in J. T. P. de Bruijn, ed., *History of Persian Literature* I: *A General Introduction to Persian Literature*, forthcoming.

(GERNOT WINDFUHR)

JAGARḴWIN (or Cegerxwin), pseudonym of Şêxmûs Hesen (b. 1903, d. Stockholm, 22 October 1984), considered by many the leading Kurdish poet of the 20th century writing in Kurmanji. He was born into a poor family in the village of Hesar in present-day Turkey, and was orphaned at an early age. He was unable to attend a regular school because of poverty and his family's frequent moves, but he received lessons in reading from the Qurʾān from mullahs in the villages where his family settled. He earned his living as an agricultural laborer and shepherd, and from these early experiences he began to absorb impressions of Kurdish life and to memorize the poems and songs he heard from dervishes that later were to inspire his social poetry (*Hayat hikâyem*, pp. 59-60, 82). Beginning in 1920, he studied in traditional schools (*madrasa*) in Syria, Iraq, and Iran. He got married in 1927, and from 1928 until 1936 he served as a mullah in several villages. He also composed his first *divān*, now lost, during the same period (Özalp, ed., p. 25). His first published divān, *Agir û pirûsk*, appeared in 1945 (Khaznadar, p. 539).

From the 1930s on he devoted himself to social activism and poetry. The plight of peasants struggling to make ends meet convinced him that the prevailing social and political order was unjust. He witnessed the brutal suppression of the Shaikh Saʿid Pirān rebellion in Turkey in 1925, which profoundly affected him as both an activist and a poet (*Hayat hikâyem*, pp. 157-67). Deeply moved by these experiences, he adopted as his pseudonym, Jagarḵwin (Cegerxwin "bleeding heart"). Eager to bring about change, he helped to found various associations, including "Ciwankurd" (Young Kurd) in 1938 to promote the study of the Kurdish language and history, and in 1946 "Civata Azadî (Society of Freedom) and "Yekîtiya Kurd" (Kurdish Unity), which had pronounced political goals. He joined the Communist Party of Syria in 1949 and thus associated himself with the international Communist movement, becoming a strong supporter of the Soviet Union's campaign against Western colonialism. Such activities led to several arrests, the first in 1949. He eventually broke with the Communists in 1957 over principle, as he had made the emancipation of his people his chief goal and joined the Kurdish Democratic Party of Syria as an alternative (*Hayat hikâyem*, pp. 307-14, 343-44).

Jagarḵwin's commitment to Kurdish emancipation never wavered, but it increasingly took on cultural and literary forms. He moved from Syria to Iraq in 1958 following the overthrow of the royal regime and became a lecturer in Kurmanji language and literature at the University of Baghdad (from 1959 to 1963). In 1961 he published a grammar of the Kurdish language, *Destûra zimanê kurdi*, for his students. It was followed in 1962 by two volumes of his Kurdish dictionary, *Ferhenga kurdi Ceger-xwîn*, a work that reveals his sensitivity to the expressiveness and nuances of his native language. In the same year the Iraqi government forced him to return to Syria.

He spent some years in Syria, went again briefly to Iraq, and then to Lebanon before settling in Stockholm in 1979, where he died. He continued to write poetry, publishing four divans before his death, and worked on his autobiography, *Jînenîgariya min*, and his history of Kurdistan, *Tarîxa Kurdistan*, both published posthumously. The latter covered the history of the Kurds from their origins down to the 13th century in striking detail, although he modestly described it as a work of intuition.

As a poet Jagarḵwin was both a classicist and a modernist, a mystic and, at the same time, an atheist, and a patriot and socialist; but, above all, he was a seeker of truth, a mission that led him to explore all corners of the Kurdish homeland and all layers of Kurdish society. He came out of the tradition of Kurdish classical poetry and was thus thoroughly familiar with the works of Eli Heriri (10th-11th cent.), Emed Mele Batê (1417-91), Meleyê ceziri (1570-1640), Ehmede Ḵāni (ca. 1650-1706), and Nāli (Mela Ḵidir;1791-1855), among others. To some extent, he followed in their footsteps. His classicism undoubtedly owed much to his studies in the traditional schools (*madrasa*). Another potent source of inspiration was folk poetry, which he avidly collected during his travels back and forth across Kurdistan.

The language of his poetry is varied but, above all, simple and straightforward. He uses a natural, colloquial language because he is addressing, in the first instance, the general reading public, but it is also literary, as many poems display a charming elegance of expression (e.g., see *Şefaq*, p. 159). He uses modern Kurdish and excels at putting new and old words together, thus creating almost a parallel language (e.g., see *Hêvî*, p. 11). His modes of expression are socially engaged; he takes sides, always favoring the poor and downtrodden over the rich and powerful, but his language is also nurturing and comforting, as he freely offers hope and encouragement to his fellow Kurds.

The dominant theme of his poetry is his Kurdish homeland. He writes of its beauties and its bountiful nature, but these sentiments are often clouded by the knowledge that the Kurd is not master in his own land. He is unforgiving in his criticism of the Turkish authorities, because of their repression of Kurdish aspirations, and he wonders what kind of Muslims they can be who refuse fellow Muslims even the right to study their own language (*Sewra azadî*, p. 181). Yet, political liberation for him also meant the achievement of social justice within the Kurdish community itself, that is, the liberation of the Kurdish peasant from the exploitation of shaikhs and aghas (*Sewra azadî*, pp. 116-20). He also perceived an international dimension to the Kurds' struggle, as he condemned British and American imperialism and praised the Soviet Union as the protector of oppressed peoples.

Even though he wrote many beautiful love poems and touching poems about everyday life, it was his militancy on behalf of freedom for Kurdistan that assured his recognition as a national poet. The poems themselves constitute a national epic of the Kurdish people in the 20th century.

Bibliography: Works. Poetry: *Agir û pirûsk (Dîwana 1an)*, 1st ed., Damascus, 1945, 3rd ed., Istanbul, 2003. *Sewra Azadî (Dîwana 2an)*, Damascus, 1954, 3rd ed., Istanbul, 2003. *Kîem Ez (Dîwana 3an)*, Beirut, 1973, 3rd ed., Istanbul, 2003. *Salar û Mîdya*, Beirut, 1973, 3rd ed., Istanbul, 2003. *Ronak (Dîwana 4an)*, Stockholm, 1980, 3rd ed., Istanbul, 2003. *Zend-Avista (Dîwana 5an)*, Stockholm, 1981, 3rd ed., Istanbul, 2003. *Şefaq (Dîwana 6an)*, Stockholm, 1982, 3rd ed., Istanbul, 2003. *Hêvî (Dîwana 7an)*, Stockholm, 1983, 3rd ed., Istanbul, 2003. *Aşitî (Dîwana 8an)*, Stockholm, 1985, 3rd ed., Istanbul, 2003. *Şerefnameya menzûm*, Beirut, 1977, 2nd ed., Istanbul, 2003.

Other Works: *Cîm û Gulperî: ji keç u xortan re diyari*, Çîroka Yekem, Damascus, 1948. *Reşoyê darê*, Çîroka Duyem, Damascus, 1956, [Zurich] 1973. *Destûra zimanê kurdi*, Baghdad, 1961. *Ferhenga kurdi Ciger-xwîn*, 2 vols., Baghdad, 1962. *Tarîxa Kurdistan*, 3 vols., 3rd ed., Stockholm, 1985-99. *Folklora kurdi: Kurmanci*, Stockholm, 1988. *Jînenîgariya min*, Stockholm, 1995; tr. into Turk. by Gazi Fincan as *Hayat Hikâyem/Jînenîgariya min*, Istanbul, 2003.

Studies: Ordîxanê Celîl, *Cegerxwîn'in Yaşami ve şiir anlayaşi*, Istanbul, 2004. Marouf Khazandar, *Mêjui edebi kurdi* VI, Erbil, 2006, pp. 537-45. Davut Özalp, ed., *Jînenîgarî, têkoşîn û berhemdariya Cegerxwîn*, Istanbul, 2003. Bavê Zozanê, *Dengê Cegerxwîn*, n.p., 1990.

(KEITH HITCHINS)

JAǦATU, an archaeological site in Ḡazni (q.v.) province, Afghanistan, situated about 20 km north of Ḡazni (lat. 33°47'N, long. 68°22'E) on the route between Ḡazni and Wardak. The site includes a group of small mounds situated on either side of the caravan road that skirts the Bād-e Āsiā mountain, remains of fortifications on the slopes of the mountain, and two rock-inscriptions in Bactrian cursive script. The most detailed report on the site so far is that of Umberto Scerrato (for further references see Ball, I, p. 43, site no. 71, and p. 131, site no. 461). Nearby sites include the high mound of Dobaḵ-sar, also referred to as Tabaḵ-sar or Taḵt-e Solṭān, the remains of a fortified town (Scerrato, pp. 13-15), where fragments of jars with cursive Bactrian inscriptions are said to have been found (Ball, I, p. 94, site no. 303), and the Ghaznavid dam known as Band-e Solṭān (Scerrato, p. 12; Ball, I, p. 52, site no. 103).

In 1958 Umberto Scerrato dug some trial trenches in the mounds at the foot of the Bād-e Āsiā. The excavations revealed vaulted mud brick structures on stone foundations (Scerrato, pp. 18-20). Amongst the small finds were coins of the Nēzak type (Scerrato, p. 21, and figs. 44-45; see hunnic coinage) and potsherds with stamped decoration (Scerrato, pp. 20, 22, and figs. 47-49; Verardi, Paparatti, and Inaba, p. 91).

The most important antiquities of Jaḡatu are the two inscriptions, which were first noticed by Alessio Bombaci and Umberto Scerrato in 1957 (see Scerrato). One is inscribed on a rock high on the northeast side of the Bād-e Āsiā. As recognized by Olaf Hansen (apud Scerrato, p. 16 n. 7; see also Humbach, 1967, pp. 25-26), it consists of the Buddhist *triratna* formula "Homage to the Buddha, homage to the law, homage to the community." Although the inscription is written in Bactrian script, it is doubtful whether its language should be regarded as Bactrian, since the text is entirely made up of Indian words: *namōo* = Sanskrit *namo* "homage" (occurring three times), *bodo* = *buddha*, *dauarmo* (or perhaps *ddharmo*) = *dharma* "law," and *saggo* = *saṅgha* "community."

The second inscription, consisting of five short lines scratched on a boulder beside the caravan road, has not yet been plausibly read or interpreted; attempts such as those of Helmut Humbach (1966-67, I, p. 104; idem, 1967, p. 26) and Davary (p. 69) have been rendered obsolete by progress in the understanding of the Bactrian script and its historical development. A possible reading of the first three lines is *baio taiamšo p(?)oro* "Bay son of Tayamsh." The name Bay is also known from a 7th-century Bactrian document (Sims-Williams, pp. 12-13), while Tayamsh may be understood as a compound name whose second element is the divine name Yamsh, the Bactrian counterpart of Persian Jamšid (q.v.). The last two lines are less well preserved and no meaningful reading can be proposed at present. It should, however, be noted that Humbach's reading of the last word as Turkish *uluḡ* "great," on the basis of which he assigned this inscription to the "Turkish period of Eastern Iranian history" (Humbach, 1967, p. 26), is impossible.

Usable photographs of both inscriptions can be found in Humbach (1966-67, II, pl. 23; idem, 1967, fig. 1-2; MacDowall and Taddei, p. 242, figs. 5.3 and 5.4 (the latter printed upside-down).

Bibliography: Warwick Ball, *Archaeological gazetteer of Afghanistan: catalogue des sites archéologiques d'Afghanistan*, 2 vols., Paris 1982. Gholam Djelani Davary, *Baktrisch: Ein Wörterbuch auf Grund der Inschriften, Handschriften, Münzen und Siegelsteine*, Heidelberg, 1982. Helmut Humbach, *Baktrische Sprachdenkmäler*, 2 vols., Wiesbaden 1966-67. Idem, "Two Inscriptions in Graeco-Bactrian Cursive Script from Afghanistan," *East and West* 17, 1967, pp. 25-26. David W. MacDowall and Maurizio Taddei, "The pre-Muslim Period," in Frank Raymond Allchin and Norman Hammond, eds., *The Archaeology of Afghanistan from Earliest Times to the Timurid Period*, London, 1978, pp. 233-99. Umberto Scerrato, "A Note on Some pre-Muslim Antiquities of Ğaġatū," *East and West* 17, 1967, pp. 11-24. Nicholas Sims-Williams, "Bactrian Legal Documents from 7th- and 8th-Century Guzgan," *Bulletin of the Asia Institute* 15, 2001 [2005], pp. 9-29. Giovanni Verardi, Ellio Paparatti, and Minoru Inaba, *Buddhist Caves of Jāghūrī and Qarabāgh-e Ghaznī, Afghanistan*, Rome, 2004.

(NICHOLAS SIMS-WILLIAMS)

JAGHATAY. See CHAGHATAY.

JAĞMINI (or Čağmini), **MAḤMUD** b. Moḥammad b. ʿOmar, an astronomer from Jağmin, a village in K̲ᵛārazm (d. 745/1344). He is mentioned as the author of a brief Arabic survey of mathematical astronomy under the title *al-Molak̲k̲aṣ fi'l-hayʾa* (purportedly written in K̲ᵛārazm in 618/1220) and of an Arabic extract of Avicenna's al-*Qānun fi'l-ṭebb*, named *al-Qānunja* (i.e., Pers. *Qānunča* "the little *Qānun*").

Nothing specific is known about his life, but it would seem plausible (but no more) to speculate that the author of *al-Qānunja* was a linear descendent of his earlier namesake, considering conservative family traditions in passing on forefathers' names to subsequent generations. In any case, the early date of the astronomical treatise is attested by two manuscripts, the later of the two being dated to 644/1246-47, whereas the medical author's death-note is owed to a reader's gloss. It does bear mention, however, that a more intensive study of either text, as reflected in the existent commentaries, did not begin much before the turn of the 9th/15th century, only to last well into the 13th/19th century. Their wide dissemination attests to their practical usefulness rather than to any outstanding scientific merit.

The astronomical treatise, *al-Molak̲k̲aṣ fi'l-hayʾa*, elicited interest in Ulugh Beg's circle of specialists. It became the subject of an Arabic commentary (comp. 814/1411) by the mathematician and astronomer Ṣalāḥ-al-Din Musā b. Moḥammad b. Maḥmud, known as Qāżizāda Rumi (d. after 1440). Another member of Ulugh Beg's entourage, Ḥosayn b. Ḥosayn (?) K̲ᵛārazmi (d. ca. 839/1436-37), dedicated a Persian commentary to him. Another Persian commentary was compiled in India as late as the early 12th/18th century.

Qānunja's conciseness was a major cause of the great popularity it enjoyed, demonstrated by its numerous Arabic copies and the string of translations from the Timurid period onward in Iran and India. It was commented upon in a book called *Mofarreḥ al-qolub* by the medical author Moḥammad-Akbar Arzāni (d. Delhi, 1722), who alternated between Safavid Iran and Mughal India. His commentary went through several Indian editions during the 19th century (e.g., Lucknow, 1886). Another commentary, anonymous, was prepared in India as late as 1822-23, and an English version of one of the Persian translations was published in Calcutta in 1782.

Bibliography: Carl Brockelmann, *Geschichte der arabischen Literatur*, 2nd ed., 2 vols., Leiden, 1943-49; Supplement, 3 vols., Leiden, 1937-42, I, pp. 598, 624; II, pp. 212-13; Supp. I, pp. 826, 865. F. Jamil Ragep, "Ḳāḍī-Zāde Rūmī," in *EI*^{2}, Supplement, p. 502. Maḥmud Jağmini, *al-Molak̲k̲aṣ fi'l-hayʾa*, Tehran, 1880; tr. G. Rudloff and Adolf Hochheim as "Die Astronomie des Maḥmûd ibn Muḥammed ibn ʿOmar al-Ğagmînî," *ZDMG* 4, 1893, pp. 213-75. Idem, *Qānunja*, tr. Moḥammad-Taqi Mir as *Qānunča dar ṭebb*, Shiraz, 1971. Lutz Richter-Bernburg, *Persian Medical Manuscripts at the University of California, Los Angeles*, Humana Civilitas 4, Malibu, Cal., 1978, pp. 28-29, 155-56, nos. 19, 134, resp. (*al-Qānunja*, Ar. ms of 1261/1845), p. 152 ff., no. 132 (Moḥammad Arzāni's Persian commentary). Rudolf Sellheim, *Materialien zur arabischen Literaturgeschichte* Teil 1, Verzeichnis der Orientalischen Handschriften in Deutschland 17, Arabische Handschriften Reihe A, Wiesbaden, 1976, pp. 158-68. Charles A. Storey, *Persian Literature: A Bio-biographical Survey*, 2 vols., London, 1927-39, II, pp. 50-51, no. 88 (*al-Molak̲k̲aṣ*), 219-20, no. 377 (*al-Qānunča*; cf. pp. 8, 67, 73, nos. 16, 103, 106 resp.). Heinrich Suter (rev. Juan Vernet), "al-D̲j̲aghmīnī," in *EI*^{2} II, p. 378.

(LUTZ RICHTER-BERNBURG)

JĀĞORI, a term of uncertain etymological origin, is both a tribal section of the Hazāras and a district (*woluswāli*) of Ğazni province in Afghanistan. In Hazārajāt (q.v.), former tribal names tend nowadays to refer to territories. This evolution mirrors the general breakdown of social organization based on descent groups after the conquest of the region by the Amir ʿAbd-al-Raḥmān at the end of the 19th century (see AFGHANISTAN x).

Situated somewhere between 2000 and 3600 m, the district of Jāğori covers 1,855 square km in the upper Arğandāb (q.v.) valley and is bounded in the west by Mālestān and Dāʿi-čopān, in the north by Nāwor, in the east by Qarabāğ and Moqor, and in the south by Gelān and Arğandāb. Non-governmental organizations and the United Nations' agencies active in the region estimate the total population between 99,126 (AVICEN, p. 20) and 150,000 (GRSP, p. 5; Johnson, p. 46). In spite of the climate, the altitude, and the rare precipitation (less than

300 mm per year), population density is very high. The demographic pressure is intense, which accounts for a constant migratory flux. This trend increased dramatically after the Communist coup of 1978. The government troops and the Red Army did not control the district, which was nevertheless the theater of bitter internal conflicts. The economy is essentially based on the remittances of the men who work in Kabul, Quetta (Pakistan), or Persia, and on irrigated agriculture. Autumn wheat dominates, but spring wheat, barley, potatoes, beans, onions, carrots, turnips, and fodder plants are also cultivated. Other crops are almonds, mulberries, apricots and apples. In local discourses and representations, but also by the social practices, the district of Jāḡori can be divided into more than twenty regions (*manṭeqas*), which have never, however, been officially acknowledged. The list may vary, but includes Almetu, Anguri, Bābā, Busaʿid, Čilbāḡtu-ye Oqi, Čilbāḡtu-ye Paši, Dahmarda, Dāwud, Ḥaydar, Heča, Hutqol, Kamarak, Lumān, Maska, Pātu, Sang-e Māša, Sapāya (or Ḵodādād), Sayyed Aḥmad, Šašpar, Šerzāda, Šolḡla, Siā Zamin (or Pošt-i Čob), Taberḡān, Uliātu, and Zerak. Available sources (Leech, p. 336; Maitland, pp. 369-75; Ḡarjestāni; Poladi, pp. 37-38) have drawn slightly different pictures of the tribal sections of Jāḡori. It would be misleading to impose an arbitrary order on this diversity, which expresses the changing political coalitions in genealogical terms. The following list is only indicative (Monsutti, 2002, pp. 125-26): Ātā (Oqi, including the Mir section, Bābā, Maska, Dahmarda, Koša, Heča); Bāḡočari (Lumān, Busaʿid, Nedām, Ḵodādād); Ezdari (Mirdād, Ḵᵛaja ʿAli, Ḵāṭer); Gari (Anguri, Dawlatšāh, Qara, Dāwud, Zirak, Ḥaydar). Two other groups present in the region have a distinct origin; they are Paši, which are sometimes said to be of remote Pashtun descent, and Qalandar, who were refugees arriving from Daʾi-čopān and Arḡandāb at the end of the 19th century.

Bibliography: Ludwig W. Adamec, ed., *Historical and Political Gazetteer of Afghanistan* VI: *Kabul and Southeastern Afghanistan*, Graz, 1985, pp. 279-80. Afghanistan Vaccination and Immunisation Centre (AVICEN), Hazarajat, *The Development of the EPI Programme in the Central Provinces*, Peshawar, 1990. Maḥmud ʿIsā Ḡarjestāni, *Tāriḵ-e Hazāra wa Hazārestān*, Quetta, 1989. Ghazni Rural Support Programme (GRSP), *Report of Hazarajat Mini Survey on Jaghori District 1995*, Ghazni, 1996. C. Johnson, *Hazarajat Baseline Study: Interim Report*, Islamabad, 2000. R. Leech, "A Supplementary Account of the Hazarahs," *JASB* 14, no. 161, 1845, pp. 333-40. P. J. Maitland, "The Hazáras of the Country Known as the Hazáraját, and Elsewhere," *Afghan Boundary Commission Report* IV, Shimla, 1891, pp. 277-450. A. Monsutti, "Soziale und politische Organisation im südlichen Hazarajat," in Paul Bucherer and Cornelia Vogelsanger, eds., *Gestickte Gebete: Gebetstüchlein*-dastmal-e mohr *der afghanischen Hazara und ihr kultureller Kontext*, Schriftenreihe der Stiftung Bibliotheca Afghanica 13, Liestal, 2000a, pp. 263-77. Idem, "Nouveaux espaces, nouvelles solidarities: la migration des Hazaras d'Afghanistan," in Pierre Centlivres and Isabelle Girod, eds., *Les défis migratoires: actes du colloque CLUSE*, Neuchâtel, 1998, Zurich, 2000b, pp. 333-42. Idem, *Guerres et migrations: réseaux sociaux et strategies économiques des Hazaras d'Afghanistan*, Neuchâtel, 2002. S. A. Mousavi, *The Hazaras of Afghanistan: An Historical, Cultural, Economic and Political Study*, Richmond, 1998. Hassan Poladi, *The Hazâras*, Stockton, Calif., 1989.

(A. MONSUTTI)

JAHĀNĀRĀ BEGUM, (1614-81) the eldest surviving daughter of the Mughal Emperor Šāh Jahān and his favorite wife, Momtāz Mahal, for whom Šāh Jahān commissioned the Tāj Mahal. Born in 1614, Jahānārā became the head of the imperial harem when her mother died in 1631, and she played a pivotal role in Mughal domestic politics throughout her life. Šāh Jahān favoured Jahānārā over his other daughters, just as he preferred Dārā Shekoh, one of Jahānārā's younger brothers, over his other surviving sons. Šāh Jahān granted her the titles: Sāḥebat al-Zamāni (Lady of the Age), and Pādšāh Begum (Lady Emperor), and she repaid her father with her loyalty during the war of succession in 1657-58, when another of her brothers, Awrangzēb, seized the throne, executed Dārā Shekoh and another brother, and imprisoned Šāh Jahān in the Red Fort at Agra. Jahānārā cared for her father until his death in 1666 when Awrangzēb, despite her loyalty to her father and Dārā Shekoh, granted Jahānārā a sizeable stipend and allowed her to live in comfort for the remainder of her life, initially in Agra but also, evidently, in her father's newly constructed city of Šāh Jahānābād in Delhi.

Apart from her acknowledged role within the Mughal household, Jahānārā is know for sharing the dynasty's commitment to Sufism and for her patronage of buildings in and around Šāh Jahānābād. Although an adherent of the Qāderi Selsela, she revered members of the well-known Češti Order, and in 1640 wrote a biography of the Indian founder of the Order, Moʿin-al-Din Češti titled *Moʾnes al-arwāh*.

As is true of other Mughal princesses she is known to have written some Persian verses and a few of her verse letters to Awrangzēb have survived, but she is best known for commissioning five building and garden projects in and around Šāh Jahānābād, rivalling perhaps the patronage of the famous Herati Timurid princess, Gowhar Šād (q.v.). Jahānārā's projects included a typical royal Muslim architectural complex: a mosque, a public bath and a caravanserai. However, she is most famous for her construction of the bazaar known as Chandni Chauk, which was bisected by the "Paradise Canal." This bazaar quickly became Delhi's principal commercial center, and it still functions as a major commercial artery in Old Delhi. In addition, Jahānārā continued the well-established Timurid-Mughal patronage of Persian gardens (see GARDEN III; ČAHĀRBĀḠ), by commissioning a *čahārbāḡ* adjacent to the bazaar, which was reserved, however, for imperial women and children.

Bibliography: Andrea Butenschon, *The Life of a Mogul Princess Jahanara Begum*, Delhi, 2004. Kathryn Lasky, *Princess of Princesses of India 1627*, New York, 2002. D. N. Marshall, *Mughals in India, A Bibliographical Survey* I, *Manuscripts*, Bombay, 1967. Jadunath Sarkar, "Jahanara: the Indian Antigone," in *Studies in Aurangzib's Reign*, repr., London, 1989, pp. 99-107.

(STEPHEN DALE)

JAHĀNBEGLU (or Jānbeglu), one of several Kurdish tribes transplanted from northwestern Persia to Māzandarān by Āḡā Moḥammad Khan Qajar (r. 1789-97, q.v.) at the end of the 18th century to protect the province from Turkmen raids (Fortescue, p. 316). Together with the Kurdish Modānlu tribe and the Turkic Usānlu and Gerāyli tribes, they formed a loose tribal confederation called "Kord o Tork," which the British officer L. S. Fortescue estimated at 2,000 households after World War I (p. 316). According to Fortescue, both the Jahānbeglu and the Modānlu were offshoots of the Mokri tribe of Sāvojbolāḡ (Mahābād). The Jahānbeglu settled in a handful of villages between Ašraf and Lārim, north of Sāri, where they became engaged chiefly in cotton and rice cultivation (Fortescue, p. 316). But G. Melgunof, who traveled in Māzandarān between 1858 and 1860, also mentions a group of Jahānbeglu dwelling in a village southwest of the provincial capital (p. 195). Although in 1922 the Jahānbeglu and Modānlu still retained their original Kurdish dialect, they had become "more or less assimilated to the Māzandarānis" (Fortescue, p. 313). Today they have lost their tribal identity to such an extent that they are not even mentioned by Iraj Afšār-Sistāni on his list of the tribes of Māzandarān (pp. 1078-80).

Bibliography: Iraj Afšār-Sistāni, *Ilhā: Čādornešinān o tawāyef-e ʿašāyeri-e Irān*, 2 vols., Tehran, 1987. L. S. Fortescue, *Military Report on Tehran and Adjacent Provinces of North-West Persia*, Calcutta, 1922. G. Melgunof [Grigoriĭ Mel'gunov], *Das südliche Ufer des Kaspischen Meeres, oder: Die Nordprovinzen Persiens*, tr. from Russian by J. Th. Zenker, Leipzig, 1868; repr., Islamic Geography 244, Frankfurt am Main, 1995; orig., St. Petersburg, 1863; tr. Masʿud Golzāri from the German as *Safar-nāma be sawāḥel-e janub-e Daryā-ye Ḵazar (1858 o 1860)*, Tehran, 1984.

(P. OBERLING)

JAHĀNGAŠT, SHAIKH JALĀL-AL-DIN BOḴĀRI. See BOḴĀRI, SHAIKH JALĀL-AL-DIN.

JAHĀNGIR, SĀLEM MOḤAMMAD NUR-AL-DIN, the fourth Mughal emperor, and the first of his dynasty to have been born in India (b. 17 Rabiʿ I 977/30 August 1569; d. 28 Ṣafar 1037/7 November 1627). His court remained strongly influenced by the Persianate political, cultural, and aesthetic traditions of the refugee Timurid elite who had fled the Uzbek invasion of Transoxiana to found the Mughal Empire. Jahāngir's glittering peripatetic court maintained a tolerant and eclectic character, welcoming merchants, artists, poets, and political refugees from across the Subcontinent, Central Asia, Persia, and Europe. His palace ateliers produced the finest examples of Mughal miniature painting, while he himself authored an intimate personal memoir in the tradition of his great grandfather, Ẓahir-al-Din Moḥammad Bābor (q.v.; d. 1530). Although Jahāngir's reign began and ended in princely rebellion, he ruled the Subcontinent for twenty-two years in relative peace and stability.

Born in the rocky hills of Sikri, near the Mughal capital of Agra, Jahāngir was the first son of the Mughal Emperor Akbar (q.v.; d. 1605). The child was named Sālem after the Sufi Shaikh Sālem Čišti, who had foretold his birth and whose hermitage had housed Akbar's Rajput wife during her pregnancy, in order that the long awaited birth might take place under the auspices of the revered holy man. Prince Sālem was raised in the new capital city of Fathpur Sikri which had been built in part to commemorate his birth. In a break with Timurid dynastic tradition, Sālem and his brothers were not sent out as children to govern imperial appanages but were educated and remained at the imperial court well into adulthood.

In later years, an uneasy relationship developed between father and son. Prince Sālem rebelled in 1600, proclaiming his virtual independence in Allahabad, where he assembled his own army, distributed *jagirs* (*jāgirs*; land grants) to members of his personal retinue and had the *khutba* (*ḵoṭba*; bidding prayers) read in his name. Two years later, Sālem, who resented and feared his father's closest friend and advisor, Abu'l-Fażl, arranged to have him assassinated as Abu'l-Fażl made his way from the Deccan to Akbar's court. Akbar was horrified by the murder, but his pool of possible successors had become dramatically narrowed by the early deaths of Sālem's two younger brothers, related to excessive drinking. Still, Sālem remained in drugged dissipation in Allahabad until the death in 1603 of his grandmother, the venerable dowager Ḥamida Bānō Begum, induced him to return to his father's court. The errant prince was publicly welcomed but immediately afterwards imprisoned by his father for ten days in an effort to break his addiction to wine and opium. The abrupt treatment proved temporarily effective and Sālem, publicly acknowledged as his father's successor, settled down quietly at his father's side. Before his death, Akbar had Sālem formally invested with the robes of imperial office. He ascended the Mughal throne at the age of 36, on Jomādā II 1014/October 23, 1605, taking the regnal name of Nur-al-Din Moḥammad Jahāngir (Conqueror of the World).

Less than a year later, Jahāngir's eldest son, Ḵosrow, rebelled. Fleeing westward, his undisciplined army of the disaffected passed through the Punjab, where Ḵosrow begged for financial assistance from the Sikh patriarch, Guru Arjun Singh (d. 1606). The guru finally offered the desperate prince a charitable gift of 5,000 rupees. Jahāngir would later interpret this act as support for the princely rebellion and order the guru's execution, in what would prove to be a disastrous and divisive moment in the history of Mughal-Sikh relations.

Jahāngir was able to rapidly quell his son's rebellion. Three hundred of the captured soldiers of his son's army were impaled alive, forming an avenue through which K̲osrow was led on an elephant to review the anguish of his followers. Only one year later K̲osrow was again involved in a plot to overthrow his father's rule, but in this instance a member of the cabal informed Jahāngir of the conspiracy and it was easily crushed, and the ringleaders executed. K̲osrow was imprisoned and partially blinded, eventually dying under somewhat mysterious circumstances in 1622 in Burhanpur while in the custody of his younger brother, K̲orram, the future Emperor Shah Jahān.

Jahāngir inherited a relatively stable empire. His father had managed to centralize imperial control across most of the Subcontinent, successfully recruiting a diverse aristocracy of Persian nobles, Uzbek and Turāni Begs, indigenous Indian Muslims, Afghans, and Hindu Rajput chieftains. The relative tolerance displayed and encouraged by the Emperor Akbar resulted in the creation of a stable and unified nobility, which was respectfully maintained by Jahāngir even as he added his own followers to the imperial service.

In his sixth regnal year, Jahāngir married a thirty-four year old Persian widow, Mehr-al-Nesā. Her father, Mirzā G̲iāt̲-al-Din, an immigrant from Safavid Persia, had risen to the rank of 1,000 at the court of Emperor Akbar and, as Eʿtemād-al-Dawla, became Jahāngir's most important advisor. Mehr-al-Nesā was the last of Jahāngir's several wives; they had no children together. Given the title Nur-Jahān (light of the world), she displayed exceptional political and administrative acumen, quickly earning the admiration and trust of her husband. Jahāngir went so far as to grant her the right of sovereignty, allowing coins to be minted in her name and drums beaten at her advance. Although the emperor is seen by some commentators to have abdicated imperial authority to his wife, Jahāngir remained deeply involved in the political affairs of his realm until the last five years of his reign. Nur-Jahān served as co-regent to a king who did not so much neglect as delegate authority to a trusted and able partner.

The imperial court of Jahāngir and Nur-Jahān was, even by the standards of his nomadic ancestors, remarkably mobile. On the move during more than half of his reign, Jahāngir's court operated out of duplicate imperial camps that leapfrogged across the countryside. Lacking the drive and ambition of his father, Jahāngir managed to combine imperial duties with life in a garden setting as the court wove slowly through magnificent countryside, pausing for pleasure trips to famous sights, visits to local mystics, personal distribution of alms, dispensation of imperial justice, and the daily hunt. Jahāngir was a passionate sportsman and Nur-Jahān regularly accompanied him on these expeditions, during one of which she killed four lions with six shots. Her proud husband showered a thousand *ašrafi* coins over her head and gave her a pair of pearls and a diamond worth a lac of rupees (*Jahāngir-nāma*, p. 214, tr. Thackston, p. 219). Yet even in the golden middle years of his reign, when no princely rebellion marred the emperor's peace, Jahāngir remained deeply dependent on drugs and alcohol, even retaining a court official whose sole charge seems to have been the care and keeping of the imperial intoxicants. The emperor held regular wine parties at court at which, he claimed, his courtiers became "intoxicated with the wine of loyalty" (*Jahāngir-nāma*, p. 212, tr. Thackston, p. 218).

Jahāngir was fascinated by the classic Perso-Islamic model of sovereignty and its demands for imperial justice and royal charity. His first legislation, the Twelve Decrees, eliminated non-Islamic taxes, such as the Mongol customs impost, the *tamḡā* and port duties, the *mirbaḥri*, as well as locally improvised taxes imposed by village headmen and governors. He also banned non-Islamic punishments, such as the disfigurement of a convicted criminal by the removal of his ear or nose. In a deliberately symbolic act, following the celebrated exemplar of royal justice, the pre-Islamic Persian monarch Anuširvān, Jahāngir's first act as sovereign was to order a golden "Chain of Justice" (*zanjir-e ʿadl*) strung with bells and hung between the banks of the river and the peak of the citadel at Agra. This would enable petitioners to gain direct access to the royal court, bypassing those public servants who "were slack or negligent in rendering justice to the downtrodden" and appealing directly to the imperial court in times of need (*Jahāngir-nāma*, p. 5; tr. Thackston, p. 24).

Jahāngir's regular public acts of piety and religious patronage, in both Muslim and Hindu communities, may have been particularly valuable to the emperor who, although ostensibly a Sunni Muslim, denied the ulema substantial influence at his court. On the other hand, he regularly referred to the *yāsā* and *tamḡā* of his ancestor, Čengiz Khan (q.v.), and seems to have had no more qualms or concerns over the awkward reconciliation of Islamic and Mongol legal systems than had his Timurid predecessors, whose religious beliefs his most closely resembled: pragmatic, informal and statist. Jahāngir remained loyal to the Čištiya Order of Sufis, maintaining a close relationship with Shaikh Sālem Čišti's sons, his childhood playmates at Sikri. He also nurtured the historical Timurid alliance with the Naqšbandis, exchanging rich gifts and lines of poetry with the Transoxiana-based Sufi Order, and described his relationship with the hereditary leader of the Order in Transoxiana as "one of his devotees and his sincere servant" (Moṭrebi; tr. Folz, p. 40). His imprisonment in 1619 of the Naqšbandi Shaikh Aḥmad Serhendi, known as *Mojadded-e alf-e t̲āni* (Renewer of the Second Millennium), was not a rejection of his family's alliance with the Naqšbandi Order but a reflection of the emperor's personal religious skepticism, mistrust of insincere piety, and fear of public disturbance. No evidence exists of a late conversion to Serhendi's spiritual path by Jahāngir.

Jahāngir was deeply influenced by his Timurid imperial legacy, which expressed itself in a nostalgic yearning for Transoxiana, referred to by the emperor as "my ancestral dominions" and "my hereditary territories" (*Jahāngir-nāma*, p. 14; tr. Thackson, p. 33). His court artists produced a series of dynastic portraits showing Jahāngir in the company of his illustrious Turco-Mongol ancestors; his genealogical charts linked him back to Alanqoa, the mythical mother goddess of the Mongols. In the middle of his reign Jahāngir made a pilgrimage to Kabul, Bābor's long-time capital, which he described in his memoirs as "like a home to us" (*Jahāngir-nāma*, p. 53; tr. Thackston, p. 68).

The highly cultivated Jahāngir encouraged poets and literary figures at his court, where Persian predominated as the language of high culture. He was well read in the medieval classics of Persian literature and quoted widely from the works of Sa'di, Hafez and Rumi. Although his own poetic compositions were rather mediocre, much more significant a legacy is that of his extraordinarily intimate imperial memoir, modeled on the diary of his Timurid great-grandfather Bābor, but written in the court Persian of Mughal India. The *Jahāngir-nāma* constitutes the most significant record of his reign.

Jahāngir emulated and replicated the Persianized cultural and aesthetic understandings of the late Timurid milieu, resulting in munificent and enthusiastic imperial patronage of the arts. The emperor was intimately involved in the artistic output of his palace ateliers and it was during his reign that Mughal miniature painting reached its apogee. Priding himself on his knowledge of individual painters and their styles, he personally directed the production of illustrations for his memoir. Jahāngir's beneficence and relative benevolence made the Mughal court a refuge for those in search of wealthy benefactors, including the Isfahan trained Āqā Reżā Heravi (q.v.) and his son Abu'l Ḥasan, who painted the frontispiece of the *Jahāngir-nāma* and was given the title of Nāder-al-Zamān (The Rarity of His Time) by his patron, the Emperor Jahāngir. Other noted examples include the painter Bišn Dās, who accompanied a diplomatic mission to Persia with the commission to paint a portrait of Shah ʿAbbās for Jahāngir; the miniaturist Manṣur, known as Nāder-al-ʿAṣr (The Rarity of the Age), famous for his detailed studies of birds and animals, and Jahāngir's calligraphers from Persia, Solṭān ʿAli Mašhadi and Mir ʿAli Heravi. Thousands of Persian and Central Asian artists and intellectuals found patrons at court and among the Mughal nobility, adding to an artistic and literary efflorescence in Mughal India that has been described as a Timurid renaissance.

Jahāngir's reign ended much as it had begun, with princely rebellion. In 1622, the Safavid Shah ʿAbbās took Kandahar (Qandahār), a territory much disputed between the royal families of India and Persia since his grandfather, the Emperor Homāyun, had conquered it for Shah Ṭah-māsp in 1545. Jahāngir, who throughout his reign had maintained very cordial relations with the Shah, ordered Ḵorram, entitled Shah Jahān, to command a Mughal army against the Safavids. Instead, the prince dallied in India, seizing territories assigned to his brother Šahriār and Nur-Jahān. An outraged Jahāngir cancelled the military campaign against the Safavids and spitefully renamed his former favorite *bi-dawlat*, "wretched." The thirty-year old Shah Jahān was quickly cowed by his father's response and sent apologies to the court, but Jahāngir did not accept his son's emissary. The rebellion grew in military scope with Jahāngir's implacability, and Shah Jahān was forced to flee, eventually seeking help from the Safavid Shah who, still occupying Kandahar, advised filial obedience. After three years, a defeated Shah Jahān surrendered and was grudgingly welcomed back to his father's court though forced to leave his sons behind as hostages when he returned to military duties in the Deccan.

Mahābat Khan, the general who had successfully pursued Shah Jahān, was accused by Āṣaf Khan, the ambitious brother of Nur-Jahān, of not reporting the entire spoils of the campaign. Recalled from Bengal to account for his alleged misdeeds, he arrived at the imperial encampment on the Jhelum River on Jomādā II 1035/ March 1626, accompanied by 5,000 Rajput soldiers. The court had begun a leisurely shift towards its next destination, leaving the imperial household isolated on the eastern bank alone with the indignant Mahābat Khan, who impulsively captured the emperor. Nur-Jahān's attempt to rescue her husband failed disastrously in the river crossing and Āṣaf Khan, who had most to fear from a Mahābat Khan ascendancy, deserted, leaving Nur-Jahān to join her husband in captivity. Over time, however, the acquiescence of the royal couple lulled Mahābat Khan into lowering his guard. On returning from Kabul in late 1626, the imperial household managed to become separated from Mahābat Khan's forces. Realizing that control had been irretrievably lost, he fled with 2,000 Rajput troops, eventually joining forces with the still rebellious Shah Jahān.

Although no longer captive, Jahāngir, after years of excessive drug and alcohol abuse, was an invalid. Turning north to his beloved Kashmir, the emperor became too ill even for opium, his life-long companion, managing only to take a few sips of wine. In Bairamkala, on the road to Lahore, they paused for a hunt. When a foot soldier, chasing a deer wounded by the emperor, fell from a cliff to his death, the emperor was very deeply affected. "It seemed he had seen the angel of death" (*Eqbāl-nāma*, p. 292). Jahāngir, the peripatetic king, continued his journey but at Čengiz Hatli, near Bhimbar, soon after sunrise on Sunday, 28 Safar 1037/7 November 1627, he died. He was fifty- eight years old and had reigned as emperor for twenty-two years. Shah Jahān was enthroned in Agra on 22 Jomādā I, 1037/23 January 1628.

Bibliography: Primary sources. Abu'l-Fażl ʿAllāmi, *Akbar-nāma (The Akbar Nama of Abu-l-Fazl)*, 3 vols, tr. Henry Beveridge, 1902-39; repr., Delhi, 1979. Elliot and Dawson, *The History of India as Told by Its Own Historians*, 8 vols., London, 1837; repr., New York, 1966. Nur-al-Din Moḥammad Jahāngir Gurkāni, *Jahāngir-nāma (Tuzok-e Jahāngiri)*, ed. Moḥammad Hāšem, Tehran, 1980; tr. into Eng. by Alexander Rogers, and ed. Henry Beveridge as *The Tūzuk-i-Jahāngīrī or Memoirs of Jahangir*, Delhi, 1968; ed. and tr., Wheeler M. Thackston as *The Jahangirnama, Memoirs of Jahangir, Emperor of India*, New York, 1999. Khwaja Kamgar

Husaini, *Maasir Jahangiri*, New York, 1978. Sir Thomas Roe, *Embassy to the Court of the Great Mogul, 1615-1619*, ed. W. Foster, Hakluyt Society Series, London, 1899. Moṭrebi al-Aṣamm Samarqandi, *Ḵātema-e moṭrebi*, ed. ʿAbd-al-Ḡani Mirzoyef, Karachi, 1977; tr. Richard C. Foltz as *Conversations with Emperor Jahangir*, Costa Mesa, Calif., 1998. Moḥammad Šarif Moʿtamad Khan Baḵši, *Eqbāl-nāma-ye Jahāngiri*, Calcutta, 1820. Francis Pelsaert, *A Dutch Chronicle of Mughal India*, tr. and ed., Brij Narain and Sri Ram Sharma, Lahore, 1978. Also tr. as *Jahangir's India: The Remonstrantie of Francisco Palsaert*, tr. by W. H. Morelan and P. Geyl, Cambridge, 1925. Fernao Guerreiro, *Jahangir and the Jesuits*, London, 1930.

Secondary sources. Stephen Dale, *The Garden of the Eight Paradises: Babur and the Culture of Empire in Central Asia, Afghanistan and India (1483-1530)*, Leiden, 2004. Idem, "*The Legacy of the Timurids*," *JRAS* 8/1, 1998, pp. 43-58. Beni Prasad, *The History of Jahangir*, London and Bombay, 1922. John F. Richards, "The Formulation of Imperial Authority Under Akbar and Jahangir" in Idem, *Power, Administration and Finance in Mughal India*, Variorum Collected Studies Series, Brookfield, Vt., 1993. Sanjeev P. Srivastave, *Jahangir, A Connoisseur of Mughal Art*, New Delhi, 2001.

(LISA BALABANLILAR)

JAHĀNGIR KHAN ŠIRĀZI. See ṢUR-E ESRĀFIL.

JAHĀNGOŠĀ-YE JOVAYNI, TĀRIḴ-E, the title of the history of the Mongols composed during the years 650-58/1252-60 (Qazvini's introd., pp. *fd-fh*) by the Il-khanid Persian vizier, ʿAlāʾ-al-Din Abu'l-Moẓaffar ʿAṭā-Malek Jovayni (623-81/1226-83, q.v.). It is the first major historical work to be written in Persian in the Mongol period, and an invaluable source on the formation of the Mongol Empire and its early administration in Persia by someone who observed or participated in some of these momentous developments. According to Vladimir Minorsky (1952, p. 221), Jovayni represents the tradition of writing elaborated in the Saljuq chanceries and his mental field is the Islamic world: "He ventures into the Outer Darkness with some reluctance." Nevertheless, he provides a very immediate account of the contemporary Mongol Empire. His achievement was to record the events of the Mongol invasions from an Iranian and Islamic perspective and to come to terms with the great changes taking place in Persian government and society, within a coherent view that both celebrated past traditions and sought positive aspects of Mongol rule for the future.

Context. Jovayni, descended from a long line of officials who had served with distinction under previous regimes, entered goverment services (I, pp. 5-6) when hardly twenty years old, against the advice of his own father, Bahāʾ-al-Din Moḥammad (d. 651/1253). In 1249, he traveled with Arḡun to the Mongol court, and made a second journey between 1251 and 1253, during which time he spent over a year at Möngke (Manku) Qāʾān's capital. This gave him personal experience of the perils and possibilities associated with Mongol service, since Arḡun had been obliged, like his predecessor Körgüz, to defend himself from hostile factions at court, a preview of Jovayni's own fate under the Il-khanids (q.v.). Apart from his firsthand observations, it is possible that Jovayni had indirect access at Qara Qorum to the *Secret History of the Mongols*, whether completed at this time or earlier, and evidently a source for some of his information, although the similarities may simply represent a common source (Boyle, 1962, pp. 136-37; Bira, pp. 86-87). In November 1255, Jovayni entered the service of Hulāgu (Hülegü) Khan (q.v.) and accompanied him on his westward expedition. Following the capture of Baghdad in 1258, Jovayni was appointed governor of the city and former ʿAbbasid lands in Mesopotamia and Khuzestan, a post he retained almost without interruption until his death in 681/1283 (Qazvini, pp. *ya-sin*, tr. Browne, pp. xix-xlvii; Jovayni, tr. Boyle's, intro., pp. xxx-xxxvii).

Jovayni started the *Tariḵ-e Jahāngošā-ye Jovayni* at the age of twenty-seven, while he was at Qara Qorum in 650/1252-53, at the invitation of his "faithful friends . . . whose definite command he could not refuse," his motive being to immortalise the glorious actions of the "lord of the age" (*pādšāh-e waqt*, i.e., Möngke Qāʾān; Jovayni, I, pp. 2-3, 7, tr., pp. 5, 10); that is, the work was evidently an imperial commission (cf. Bira, p. 85). In a famous passage (Jovayni, pp. I, 3-7, tr., pp. 5-10) lamenting the current state of patronage and learning, and his own neglect of his education by entering government service, he accepts the task in hand, using many rhetorical devices to excuse his own inadequacies, while drawing attention to his firsthand acquaintance with the subject. He also sets out the premise of the book, to make intelligible the change in fortune of the Muslims, punished for their sins, but showing also the benefits to Islam that could be discerned in the situation. The work thus has an explicitly didactic element in its purpose to achieve both spiritual and temporal advantage (I, 7, tr., p. 11). This message is reinforced throughout the text, not only in the repeated advocacy of harmony over discord (e.g., I, pp. 30, 143, III, pp. 66-68, tr., pp. 41, 181, 593-94), but in pointed observations about the consequences of treachery and oppression and the lessons to be learned from his narration of events (I, pp. 32, 45, 202, II, pp. 207, 263, tr., pp. 43, 60, 247, 474, 527). As noted by Claude-Claire Kappler (p. 191), by inviting "men of discernment" to understand the situation, he encourages his learned audience to read between the lines of his text, in which he juxtaposes tales of disaster with signs of hope and encouragement to maintain Iran's traditional values.

Jovayni complained of having only a few hours at night "when the caravan halts" (*yak sāʿat-i dar forṣat-e nozul*) to compose his history (I, p. 118, tr., p. 152), which must nevertheless have been completed after his appointment to the governorship of Baghdad. John Andrew Boyle, in the introduction to his translation (1958, pp. xxxviii-xxxix), notes several indications of the unrevised and unfinished nature of the work, and uncertainty as to its intended final form. Some support for this is provided by Ebn Bibi, who alludes to an unfulfilled historiographical project by Jovayni (Ebn Bibi, p. 12-13; cf. Melville, 2006, p. 140). Nevertheless, the *Tariḵ-e Jahāngošā-ye Jovayni* remains a polished and complete literary creation, evidence of the considerable erudition and sophistication of the author.

Structure and contents. The work is normally divided into three sections or volumes, covering (I) the rise and career of Čengiz Khan and his successors down to the deaths of Güyük and Čaḡatāy, (II) the history of the Ḵᵛārazmšāhs, especially Qoṭb-al-Din Moḥammad and his son Jalāl-al-Din, besides the pre-Mongol Turkish dynasties in Central Asia and the Mongol governors before the arrival Hulāgu Khan, (III) the rest of Mongol history to Hulāgu Khan's westward expedition besides a history of Ḥasan-e Ṣabbāḥ (q.v.) and the Ismaʿilis (Qazvini's introd., pp. *fā-fj*). Jovayni himself seems to have originally intended the early history of the Mongols and the history of the Ḵᵛārazmšāhs to become the first book, and the reign of Möngke Qāʾān, the expedition of Hulāgu to the west, and an account of the other rulers of the time the second book (III, p. 2; tr., p. 548). Either way, the overall structure of the work is clear; it would be the history of the two Mongol invasions of Iran, framing an account of the powers previously established there and their destruction. Nevertheless, the composition of the work in its details is rather loosely conceived. David Morgan (1982, p. 118) considers it to be "more of a collection of material on the Mongol invasions, and other matters, than a coherent history of them."

The narrative develops essentially in chronological order, but not in annalistic format and only loosely by reign; it is characterized by various diversions and asides. It is to some degree held together by internal cross-referencing (e.g., I, 199, II, 45, III, 61; tr., pp. 243, 312, 590), though as noted by Boyle (1958, p. xxxviii), this serves also to highlight the unfinished nature of the work. Jovayni himself, however, does have a sense of the proper place for things, as in his account of the Uighurs, which is included in the first volume (p. 34, tr., p. 48) as appropriate, although in chronological terms it should be placed after the accession of Möngke; he deals with other matters too as they arise, rather than in a rigid sequential way (e.g., the popular uprising in Bukhara in 636/1238-39; Jovayni, I, pp. 85 ff., tr., pp. 109 ff.; Barthold, pp. 269-71). This gives the work a rather immediate and engaging quality, achieved also by other means (see below), though especially in the second volume Jovayni uses the technique of frequent "flashbacks," which punctuate the flow of the narrative in a fairly logical manner, but without any bridging passages to guide the reader and clarify his chain of thought. His method leads also to repetitions and sometimes conflicting statements (II, p. 74, tr. p. 341, and II, pp. 230 ff., tr., pp. 494 ff. concerning his arch-enemy, Šaraf-al-Din Ḵᵛārazmi, cf. II, pp. 270 ff., tr., pp. 534 ff.; see also Barthold, p. 37).

Overall, the *Tariḵ-e jahāngošā* is informed by a unifying vision of the justice and sagacity of the ruling emperor, Möngke Qāʾān, and the legitimacy of the new Ilkhanid regime established in Iran by Hulāgu Khan, expressed somewhat ironically with respect to concepts associated with pre-Islamic Iranian kingship (in frequent references to Ḵosrow Anōširvān and other Iranian heroes), although also making great efforts to portray the Mongol Qāʾāns as favorable towards Islam (e.g., III, pp. 32, 60-61, 79-80, tr. pp. 569, 589, 600 and Boyle's intro., pp. xxxiv-xxxv).

The contents of the work have been summarized by the editor, Mirzā Moḥammad Qazvini (introd., pp. *fā-fj*, tr. Browne, pp. lxi-lxiii; Browne, 1904). After a brief word on the conditions of the Mongols before Čengiz Khan, Jovayni includes an important chapter on his *yāsā*, which, like much of Jovayni's material, gives a valuable insight into the conditions of Mongol military life and society (I, pp. 16-25, tr., pp. 23 ff.). This section has given rise to much scholarly debate (see Ayalon; Morgan, 1986; de Rachewiltz; Aigle, 2004). There follows a very brief account of the rise of Čengiz (I, pp. 25-29), his early dealings with Ong Khan, Khan of Kerāyets, and the poisoning of relations between them, which is blamed on the envious calumnies of the latter's close associates (a familiar enough theme in Persian history). Jovayni paints a rosy and idealized picture of the harmony among the sons and descendants of Čengiz Khan, thus setting a pattern for the moral framework of the whole book.

Much of the first volume is taken up with the conquests of Čengiz Khan, preceded by the actions of Kučlok the Naiman (Nāymān), who is wrongly identified as the son of Ong Khan, and the Ḵᵛārazmšāh against the Qara Ḵetāy in removing what Jovayni saw as the mighty wall (*sadd-e bozorg*) defending Islam from the turbulent hordes of the steppe (I, pp. 52, II, pp. 80, 89, tr., pp. 70, 347, 357). Jovayni's account includes many celebrated passages on the fall of the major cities of Transoxiana and Khorasan, such as the description of Čengiz Khan mounting the pulpit (*menbar*) in the *moṣallā-ye ʿid* (prayer grounds used on the occasion of the *ʿid al-feṭr*) at Bukhara, calling himself the scourge of God (*ʿaḏāb-e Ḵodā*) and explaining his conquests as God's will and a punishment for the sins of the people (p. 81, tr., p. 105), rightly viewed as one of the ways whereby Jovayni sought to make sense of the calamity that had struck the Muslim world. He narrates the complex parallel but distinct campaigns in different theaters without great loss of clarity, and his brief accounts of events in the Golden Horde (q.v.) and the Čaḡatāy Khanate (see CHAGHATAYID DYNASTY) that conclude the first volume bring the history of the different regions of the empire to the same point on the eve of the accession of Möngke Qāʾān. In both cases, it is also true that it would be helpful if he made it clearer what he was doing. Jovayni's juxtaposition of unconnected passages does, however, create a powerful and occasionally cathartic literary effect (see below). The first volume nevertheless ends abruptly and the author's chain of thought is not picked up later.

The second volume starts with a chronological history of the Ḵᵛārazmšāhs in a more annalistic framework, especially following the career of the heroic Jalāl-al-Din Ḵᵛārazmšāh, frequently compared with champions in the *Šāh-nāma*. There follows the history of the Mongol viceroys (pp. 218 ff; tr., pp. 482 ff.), evidently based on first hand knowledge and doubtless drawing also on the experiences of his father, Bahāʾ-al-Din (e.g., p. 247, tr., p. 511).

The last volume is considered by Bira (2002, p. 93) the most important part of the work, largely because Jovayni here relies almost entirely on his own observations. After the contested election of Möngke, the work continues with Hulāgu Khan's westward expedition and his attack on the Ismaʿilis (pp. 89 ff.; tr., 607 ff.). This is followed, logically enough, by an account of their doctrines. The fall of the Ismaʿilis is taken as evidence of the hidden significance of Čengiz Khan and his successors (*ḥaqiqat-e serr-e elāhi dar ḵoruj-e Čengiz Ḵān*; pp. 138-39, tr. p. 638), yet the whole work ends with an implied threat also to his imperial patrons: "This is a warning for all who reflect . . . may God do likewise to all tyrants" (p. 278, tr., p. 725).

As frequently noted, despite being completed in 658/1260, the *Tariḵ-e jahāngošā-ye Jovayni* does not cover the fall of Baghdad that had occurred two years earlier. Jovayni contents himself with ending on the more propitious note of the destruction of the Ismaʿilis (Morgan, 1997, p. xxi), but many manuscripts contain as a supplement the account of the fall of Baghdad written by Naṣir-al-Din Ṭusi (Jovayni, III, pp. 280-92; Wickens; Boyle, 1961).

Sources. Jovayni mentions very few written sources, though there are occasional hints (I, 27, II, 44, tr., pp. 37, 312-13; cf. also Qazvini's footnote at III, pp. 355-57, tr., p. 651 n. 55). Apart from his possible familiarity with material in the *Secret History of the Mongols* (see above), he refers to one of Möngke's *yarliḡs* as being kept in the archives (III, P. 75, tr. p. 598), implying he had access to them. At the outset of the second volume, he mentions some sources on the Ḵᵛārazmšāhs (II, p. 1, tr., p. 277), but these cannot account for all his material. A detailed comparison with the chronicle of Ebn al-Aṯir (ca. 630/1233) and others has yet to be made. Jovayni knew Šehāb-al-Din Moḥammad Nasawi, whose history of the life of Jalāl-al-Din Ḵᵛārazmšāh (in Arabic) was written in 639/1241-42, but it seems he did not use it, though he quotes Nasawi's *Fatḥ-nāma* after the fall of Aḵlāt (II, pp. 153, 177-80, tr. pp. 420, 445-49), which is not included in Nasawi's own book. This, as also the earlier writings of Rašid-al-Din Watwāṭ, quite extensively quoted (II, pp. 6 ff., tr., pp. 280 ff.), reveals his interest in the linguistic and stylistic models familiar to any scribe, rather than in factual information. References to the historians of the Ghaznavids, Abu'l-Fażl Bayhaqi (II, p. 44, tr., p. 313) and Abu Naṣr Moḥammad ʿOtbi (II, p. 122, tr., p. 393), who wrote well before the period covered by Jovayni, also suggest their literary relevance to his own work (see below). For the history of the Ismaʿilis, he used materials found in the library at Alamut, including the celebrated "biography" of Ḥasan-e Ṣabbāḥ (III, pp. 186-87, 269-70, tr., pp. 666, 719; Daftary, pp. 94-95).

Jovayni must have relied heavily on oral sources, occasionally alluded to (e.g., I, pp. 28, 45, 86, 185, tr., pp. 39, 60, 110, 228), and particularly on information from his father (I, p. 134, tr., p. 170) and other relatives (II, p. 79, tr., p. 347), who in turn could draw on the experiences of their own forebears, which are frequently referred to. Mainly, however, he drew on his personal experience, which surfaces occasionally in the narrative, for instance, encounters at the court of the Chaghatayid khan Yesü on his return from the camp (*ordu*) in 1251-52 (I, pp. 231-32, tr. pp. 275-76), and on many other occasions (II, pp. 217, 225, 248-50, III, p. 101, tr., pp. 481, 489, 512-13, 615). It is his own involvement in many of the affairs he describes that lends his work its authority and value.

Place in Persian historiography. Fażl-Allāh Ruzbehān Ḵonji (p. 91, tr. Minorsky/Woods, p. 10) puts Jovayni's history in the category of those who focus on a particular dynasty (*ferqa*), but without concentrating only on their leader or chief (*sarvar*); Jovayni, "pride of the learned and choice of the eloquent," covers all the affairs of the Chengizid rulers, together with the kings (*moluk*) of other groups (*ṭawāʾef*). Ḵonji notes that Šehāb-al-Din ʿAbd-Allāh Waṣṣāf followed this lead, while a second group including Abu Naṣr ʿOtbi and Šaraf-al-Din ʿAli Yazdi discuss the fortunes only of one great king or ruler (p. 92). On the one hand, Jovayni was certainly the model and inspiration for the work of Ebn Bibi (see above) and Waṣṣāf, who wrote a continuation of the *Jahāngošā-ye Jovayni*; it was also the source of emulation for Yazdi's *Ẓafar-nāma*, supposed to be entitled *Tāriḵ-e jahāngir* (Woods, p. 101), and the *Jahāngošā-ye nāderi* of Mirzā Mahdi Khan Estrābādi/Astarābādi. On the other hand, Jovayni was also extensively drawn upon both by Bar Hebraeus (q.v.; Ayalon, 1971, p. 127; Borbone, cited by Aigle, in press) and by Rašid-al-Din Fażl-Allāh, who supplemented his work with additional sources (Boyle, 1962; Daftary); the later author is generally fuller in his information, the earlier, Jovayni, in his "opinions" or judgments. There is still no detailed study dedicated purely to the relationships between these works. Ebn al-Ṭeqṭaqā (q.v.) also made lesser, and contentious, use of Jovayni (Boyle, 1952). As for the precursors of Jovayni, his subject matter led him to depart from previously established models of historiography, which were structured around the history of Muslim rulers (cf. Bira, p. 88); his antecedents are more in the literary realms of rhetorical prose, which acquired its definitive features in his work (Poliakova, p. 244, citing Bahār).

Style. Ḵonji's classification of Jovayni is accurate not only so far as his focus is concerned, but also for his style; it is no accident that the authors with whom he is bracketed share his flair for ornate literary language and the ornate style of writing (*naṯr-e monšiāna*). This is exemplified in the *Fatḥ-nāma* penned on the fall of Alamut by the author, who here calls himself a *mostawfi* (III, pp. 114-15, tr., pp. 622-23). The text is full of wordplays, allusions and tropes appealing to highly educated readers, although as noted by Julie Meisami (1999, p. 294), such language is also a perfect vehicle for irony. In fact, he intersperses passages of panegyric and flattering personal epithets into a narrative that is otherwise artful but restrained. Jovayni's language is vivid, and his metaphors are always colourful and fresh. Among its notable features are the descriptions of spring, which break up the narrative and also carry the promise of a fresh departure, as at the start of the account of Čengiz Khan's return to Mongolia, and also before Ögedei's *quriltāy* (assembly of Mongol princes) of 1235 and the accession of Güyük (I, pp. 109-10, 155, 204, tr., pp. 138, 197, 249). Some of these juxtapositions create a sense of relief from the dark import of the events chronicled; the optimistic tone set before the accession of Ögedei, mentioned even before Čengiz Khan's death (I, pp. 141, tr., p. 178), follows the grim narrative of the devastation of Nišāpur, and the very long section of anecdotes about Ögedei (I, pp. 158-91, tr., pp. 201-36; copied by Rašid-al-Din, pp. 684-705) are entertaining as well as edifying, doing much to dispel the brutal impressions of the account of Čengiz Khan and the subsequent bloody conquest of north China.

Another feature is Jovayni's frequent quotation of the *Šāh-nāma*, in such a way as to provide a commentary on the events he describes, rather than purely for ornament in the manner of Moḥammad Rāvandi (see Meisami, 1994), who quotes entire *qaṣidas*. As noted by Asadullah Melikian-Chirvani (esp. pp. 70-71; Jovayni, II, pp. 136, 139, tr., pp. 406, 409), his deliberate use of Ferdowsi drives home the identification of Čengiz Khan and the Mongols with Afrāsiāb (q.v.) and the Turks, Iran's traditional enemies in the *Šāh-nāma*, and underlines the durability of Iranian civilization. He also cites many other verses, in Arabic and Persian, sometimes from memory (e.g., II, p. 79, tr., p. 346), but also perhaps drawing on Abu Manṣur Ṯaʿālebi's *Tatemmat al-Yatima* for many quotations (see the footnotes to Boyle's intro. to his translation, relying largely on Qazvini's notes).

Appraisal. The *Tariḵ-e jahāngošā-ye Jovayni* is a sophisticated literary work and an essential, often first-hand, account of the expansion of the Mongol Empire. The unflattering assessment by David Ayalon (1971, p. 133) is wide of the mark, and although there is no doubt that Jovayni benefited from his association with the new ruling class, as in the development of his investment at Ḵabušān (III, 105, tr., p. 617), he was also unsparing in his comments on the evils of the times (e.g., I, p. 198, II, pp. 260, 269, tr. pp. 243, 523, 533) and in his aim to seek potential benefits to Islam from the situation. His pro-Toluid bias (I, pp. 211, 215, III, p. 7, tr., pp. 256, 260, 552; Ayalon, 1971, pp. 151-66; Jackson) merely reflects the political realities of the time and puts him in the same position as many generations of official court chroniclers (see Melville's review of Boyle's tr.). While we may agree with E. A. Poliakova (pp. 245-47) that Jovayni's language of "canonized verbal formulae" tends to cloak concrete or naturalistic details in generalised and artificial descriptions, this has not yet reached the point at which the language itself determines the factual contents of the work. Although his manner is suggestive rather than explicit, his valuable and highly personal view of the Mongol conquests of Iran leaves little doubt about their impact on Iranian society.

Large numbers of surviving manuscripts testify to the favorable reception and wide dissemination of the work (over 50 listed by Storey, tr., pp. 760–62); at least two of these were illustrated (e.g., Paris, Supplément persan 206, with other dispersed folios in the British Museum and the Art Museum of Worcester, U.S.A), including the celebrated copy of 689/1290 in Paris, both used by Moḥammad Qazvini for his edition (see Fitzherbert, esp. pp. 69-75; Richard, pp. 41, 79).

See also HISTORIOGRAPHY iv. MONGOL PERIOD.

Bibliography: Editions and translations. ʿAlāʾ-al-Din ʿAṭā-Malek Jovayni, *Tariḵ-e jahāngošāy*, ed. Moḥammad b. ʿAbd-al-Wahhāb Qazvini, E. J. W. Gibb Memorial Series 16/1-3, with a substantial introduction (I, pp. *j-fkv*), tr. by Edward G. Browne (I, pp. xv-xciii), 3 vols., London, 1912-37; tr. John Andrew Boyle as *The History of the World-Conqueror by Ata-Malik Juvaini*, 2 vols., Manchester, 1958; repr. in one vol. as *Genghis Khan. The History of the World-Conqueror*, with an introd. and bibliography by David O. Morgan, Manchester and Seattle, 1997; reviewed by Charles Melville, in *Iranian Studies*, 32/3, Summer 1999 [2000], pp. 435-37. Aḥmad Monzawi, *Fehrest-e nosḵahā-ye ḵaṭṭi-e fārsi*, 6 vols., Tehran, 1969-74, VI, pp. 4306-309. Charles A. Storey, *Persian Literature: A Bibliographical Survey*, 2 vols., London, 1970, I, pp. 260-64; II, p. 1272; ed. and tr. Yuri E. Bregel as *Persidskaya literature: Biobibliograficheskiĭ obzor*, 3 vols., Moscow, 1972, pp. 760-62.

Studies. Denise Aigle, "Le 'grand *yasa*' de Gengis-Khan, l'Empire, la culture mongole et la shariʿa," *JESHO* 47/1, 2004, pp. 31-79. Idem, "Le Prêtre Jean et le processus d'intégration des Mongols dans la conscience de la chrétienté occidentale," in M. Tardieu, ed., *Le Prêtre Jean: Modèles et transformations d'une légende médiévale*, Bures-sur-Yvette, in press. David Ayalon, "The Great *Yasa* of Chingiz Khan: a Re-examination," *Studia Islamica* 33, 1971, pp. 97-140; 34, 1971, pp. 151-80. Moḥammad-Taqi Malek-al-Šoʿarāʾ Bahār, *Sabk-šenāsi yā tāriḵ-e taṭawwor-e naṯr-e fārsi*, 3 vols., Tehran, 1958, III, pp. 51 ff. Vasiliĭ (W.) Vladimirovich Barthold, *Turkestan down to the Mongol Invasion*, 3rd revised ed., E. J. W. Gibb Memorial Series 5, London, 1968. Shagdaryn Bira, *Mongolian Historical Writing from 1200 to 1700*, tr. John R. Kreuger, 2nd ed., Studies on East Asia 24, Bellingham, Wash., 2002. Pier Giorgio Borbone, "Barhebraeus e Juvayni: un cronista siro e la sua fonte Persiana," *Egitto e Vicino Oriente* 27, 2004, pp. 121-44. John Andrew Boyle, "Ibn al-Tiqtaqā and the Ta'rīkh-i Jahān-Gushāy of Juwaynī," *BSO(A)S* 14/i, 1952, pp. 175-77. Idem, "The Death of the Last ʿAbbasid Caliph: A Contemporary Muslim Account," *Journal of Semitic Studies* 6, 1961, pp. 145-61. Idem, "Juvaynī and Rashīd al-Dīn as Sources on the History of the Mongols," in Bernard

Lewis and Peter Malcolm Holt, eds. *Historians of the Middle East*, London, 1962, pp. 133-37. Edward G. Browne, "Note on the Contents of the *Ta'ríkh-i-Jahán-Gushá*, or History of the World-Conqueror, Chingíz Khan," *JRAS*, January 1904, pp. 27-43. Farhad Daftary, "Persian Historiography of the Early Nizari Ismaʿilis," *Iran* 30, 1992, pp. 91-97. Ebn Bibi, *Awāmer al-ʿalāʾiya fi'l-omur al-ʿalāʾiya*, ed. ʿAdnān S. Erzi, Ankara, 1957. Teresa Fitzherbert, "Portrait of a Lost Leader: Jalal al-Din Khwarazmshah and Juvaini," in Julian Raby and Teresa Fitzherbert, eds., *The Court of the Ilkhans 1290-1340*, Oxford, 1996, pp. 63-77. Peter Jackson, "The Dissolution of the Mongol Empire," *Central Asiatic Journal* 22, 1978, pp. 186-244. Claude-Claire Kappler, "Regards sur les Mongols au XIII-ème siècle: Joveyni, Rubrouk," *Dabireh* 6, 1989, pp. 183-94. Fażl-Allāh b. Ruzbehān Ḵonji, *Tāriḵ-e ʿālamārā-ye amini*, abridged tr. by Vladimir Minorsky as *Persia in A.D. 1478-1490*, London, 1957; ed. John E. Woods (with Vladimir Minorsky's tr. rev. and enlarged), London, 1992. Mirzā Mahdi Khan Estrābādi/Astarābādi, *Jahāngošā-ye nāderi*, ed. ʿAbd-Allāh Anwār, Tehran, 1962. Julie Scott Meisami, *Persian Historiography to the End of the Twelfth Century*, Edinburgh, 1999. Idem, "Rāvandi's *Rāhat al-sudūr*: History or Hybrid?," *Edebiyat*, N.S. 5, 1994, pp. 181-215. Asadullah Souren Melikian-Chirvani, "Le Livre des Rois, miroir du destin II: Takht-e Soleymān et la symbolique du *Shāh-Nāme*," *Studia Iranica* 20/I, 1991, pp. 33-148. Charles Melville, "The Early Persian Historiography of Anatolia," in Judith Pfeiffer, ed., *History and historiography of post-Mongol Central Asia and the Middle East: Studies in Honor of John E. Woods*, Wiesbaden, 2006, pp. 135-66. Vladimir Minorsky, "Caucasia III: The Alan Capital *Magas and the Mongol Campaigns," *BSO(A)S*, 14/2, 1952, pp. 221-38. David O. Morgan, "Persian Historians and the Mongols," in idem, ed., *Medieval Historical Writing in the Christian and Islamic Worlds*, London, 1982, pp. 109-21. Idem, "The 'Great Yasa of Chinggis Khan' and Mongol Law in the Ilkhanate," *BSO(A)S* 49, 1986, pp. 163-76. Šehāb-al-Din Moḥammad Nasawi, *Sira Jalāl-al-Din*, ed. and tr. Octave V. Houdas as *Histoire de Sultan Jelal ed-Din Mankobirti*, 2 vols., Paris, 1891-95. Abu Naṣr ʿOtbi, *al-Taʾriḵ al-yamini*, ed. with commentaries A. Manini, 2 vols., Cairo, 1869. E. A. Poliakova, "The Development of A Literary Canon in Medieval Persian Chronicles: The Triumph of Etiquette," *Iranian Studies* 17/2-3, 1984, pp. 237-56. Moḥammad Qazvini, "Yādāšthā-ye Moḥammad Qazvini bar *Jahāngošā-ye Jovayni*," ed. Moḥammad Rowšan, *FIZ* 15, 1968, pp. 161-221. Igor de Rachewiltz, "Some Reflections on Chinggis Qan's *jasagh*," *East Asia History* 6, 1993, pp. 91-104. Rašid-al-Din Fażl-Allāh Hamadāni, *Jāmeʿ al-tawāriḵ*, ed. Moḥammad Rowšan and Moṣṭafā Musawi, 4 vols., Tehran, 1994. Moḥammad b. ʿAli b. Solaymān Rāvandi, *Raḥat al-ṣodur wa āyat al-sorur dar tāriḵ-e Āl-e Saljuq*, ed. Muhammad Iqbāl, Leiden, 1921; 2nd rev. ed. with commentary by Mojtabā Minovi, Tehran, 1985. Francis Richard, *Splendeurs persanes: manuscrits du XIIe au XVIIe siècle*, Paris, 1997. Ḏabiḥ-Allāh Ṣafā, *Tāriḵ-e adabiyāt dar Irān* III/2, Tehran, 1974, pp. 1209-12. Żiāʾ-al-Din Sajjādi, "*Šāh-nāma dar Tāriḵ-e jahāngošā-ye Jovayni*," in *Šāhnāma-šenāsi*, Tehran, 1978, pp. 241-60 (collection of papers presented at a symposium on the *Šāh-nāma*). Šaraf-al-Din ʿAli Yazdi, *Żafar-nāma*, ed. Moḥammad ʿAbbāsi, 2 vols., Tehran, 1957. Abu Manṣur ʿAbd-al-Malek Ṯaʿālebi, *Tatemmat al-Yatima*, ed. ʿAbbās. Eqbāl, Tehran, 1934. G. M. Wickens, "Nasir ad-Din Tusi on the Fall of Baghdad: A Further Study," *Journal of Semitic Studies* 7, 1962, pp. 23-35. John E. Woods, "The Rise of Timurid Historiography," *Journal of Near Eastern Studies* 42/2, 1987, pp. 81-108.

(CHARLES MELVILLE)

JAHĀNGOŠĀ-YE NĀDERI, TĀRIḴ-E (or *Tāriḵ-e nāderi*), one of the most important chronicles of the reign of Nāder Shah Afšār (r. 1736-47) by his court secretary, Mirzā Moḥammad-Mahdi Khan Estrābādi/Astarābādi (q.v.). It closely follows the conventions of Safavid historiography in its depiction of Nāder's life and ends during the chaotic period that ensued upon Nāder's assassination in 1160/1747 (Lockhart, pp. 262-63). The work appeared in its finished form in the 1750s, some three decades after the Afghan invasion of Iran and a decade after Nāder's death. It was based on Nāder's official court chronicle as recorded by Astarābādī, who had served as his main official historiographer. This work, originally titled *Tāriḵ-e nāderi*, later became known as the *Tāriḵ-e jahāngošā-ye nāderi*, a title reminiscent of ʿAlāʾ-al-Din ʿAṭā Malek Jovayni's history of the Mongol era, *Tāriḵ-e jahāngošā* (q.v.), with which it does not have many obvious stylistic or structural parallels. Moreover, Astarābādī himself did not use this phrase to describe his own text.

Jahāngošā-ye nāderi is divided into two major parts. Its first section provides a general overview of the chaotic situation in Iran after the Afghan invasion in 1722, followed by a detailed account of Nāder's life and career. The second part of the work is described in its introduction as a "*ruz-nāmča-ye ẓafar*" (diary of victory), perhaps alluding to the *Ẓafar-nāma*s of Šaraf-al-Din ʿAli Yazdi and Neẓām-al-Din Šāmi, both written about Timur. Astarābādi's stylistic debt to these authors as well as to Safavid chroniclers is fairly clear, as reflected particularly in his florid language and stylized battle accounts. The *Tāriḵ-e nāderi*/*Jahāngošā-ye nāderi* displayed great structural similarity to the well-known Safavid chronicle, Eskandar Beg Monši's *Tāriḵ-e ʿālamārā-ye ʿabbāsi*. Astarābādī mimicked Eskandar Beg's annalistic division of his history in terms of Turko-Mongol years almost exactly, and, like Eskandar Beg, he offered detailed florid descriptions of spring immediately followed by accounts of courtly *nowruz* festivities.

In Astarābādi's work, these accounts of spring became almost as important as the actual narrative of events themselves. The chronicle's role as a decorative celebration of the ruler's charisma and royal glory (*farr*) now began to overshadow its function as a record of his actual accomplishments. Descriptions of spring in this work do not merely evoke the natural process of change, but rather foreshadow and parallel the accounts of historical events that they precede.

The succession struggles that erupted in Persia after Nāder's assassination created uncertainty for the author as to how to memorialize him. Some versions of Astarābādi's work ended with a short passage explaining that the author's goal was to record the events of Nāder's life, not to discuss the chaos that had arisen after his death. A few copies of the text end with a brief tribute, dated 1171/1758, to Moḥammad-Ḥasan Khan Qājār (Ṣafā, V, pp. 1807-8; Tucker, 2006, p. 107). The lack of continuity in dynastic rule in the 18th century made the task of celebrating rulers through panegyric tributes more complicated for court chroniclers of the time.

The *Tāriḵ-e nāderi* served as a stylistic model for numerous Persian court histories through the early Qajar period. The continuing popularity of this work in Asia and the Middle East is evidenced by the numerous lithographic editions of it that began to appear in the mid-19th century. Its appearance, too, at a time when Europeans were becoming increasingly aware of Persia's importance in world affairs, made it one of the first early modern Persian histories to be translated into a European language. A French translation of this work was made for the king of Denmark and published in 1770 by Sir William Jones, a British Orientalist who later achieved fame as a translator and scholar of Sanskrit and other Indian languages. Versions of the Jones translation then quickly appeared in German and English a few years later.

Bibliography: Mīrzā Mahdī Khan Estrābādi/Astarābādī, *Tāriḵ-e Jahāngošā-ye nāderi*, ed. Sayyed ʿAbd-Allāh Anwār, Tehran, 1962; ed. Adib Barumand as *Tāriḵ-e Jahāngošā-ye nāderi: noska-ye ḵaṭṭi-e moṣawwar motaʿalleq ba 1171 H.Q*, Tehran, 1991; tr. William Jones as *Histoire de Nader Chah, connu sous le nom de Thahmas Kuli Khan, empereur de Perse*, 2 vols., London, 1770; abr. tr. by William Jones as *The History of the Life of Nadir Shah, King of Persia*, London, 1773; tr. Thomas Heinrich Gaderbusch as *Geschichte des Nadir Schah, Keysers von Persen*, Greifswald, 1773 (based on the Fr. tr.). Laurence Lockhart, *Nadir Shah: A Critical Study Based Mainly upon Contemporary Sources*, London, 1938, pp. 292-96. Aḥmad Monzawi, *Fehrest-e nosḵahā-ye ḵaṭṭi-e fārsi*, 6 vols., Tehran, 1969-74, VI, pp. 4309-14. Ḏabiḥ-Allāh Ṣafā, *Tāriḵ-e adabiyāt dar Irān*, 5 vols. in 8. Tehran, 1954-92. Charles A. Storey, *Persian Literature: A Bio-bibliographical Survey*, 2 vols., London, 1927-39, I, pp. 322-24. Ernest Tucker, "Religion and Politics in the Era of Nādir Shāh: The Views of Six Contemporary Sources," Ph.D. diss., University of Chicago, 1992, pp. 130-85. Idem, *Nadir Shah's Quest for Legitimacy in Post-Safavid Iran*, Gainsville, Florida, 2006.

(ERNEST TUCKER)

JAHĀN-MALEK ḴĀTUN (b. after 724/1324, d. after 784/1382), Injuid (see INJU DYNASTY) princess, poet, and contemporary of Ḥāfeẓ (715-92/1315-90, q.v.). Jahān-Malek Ḵātun was the only child of the Injuid ruler Jalāl-al-Din Masʿudšāh (k. 1342) to survive to adulthood. On her mother's side, Jahān-Malek was descended from the Chobanids (q.v.) of Azerbaijan and the Il-khanid (see IL-KHANIDS) vizier Rašid-al-Din Fażl-Allāh (Moʿin-al-Din Naṭanzi, pp. 170-72). She married Amin-al-Din Jahromi, a boon companion (*nadim*) of her uncle, Shaikh Abu Esḥāq (r. 1343-53, k. 758/1357, q.v.), some time between 1343 and 1347 (Jahān-Malek Ḵātun, editors' Introd., pp. iii-x; Ādamiyat, II, pp. 151-53; Ṣafā, III/2, p. 1047). Her pen name (*taḵalloṣ*), which she often mentions more than once in a given poem, was Jahān. The style and quality of her poetry suggest that she was acquainted with famous male contemporaries Ḥāfeẓ and ʿObayd Zākāni (d. 1371), as do also the anecdotes related by Dawlatšāh Samarqandi (pp. 289-90) and Faḵri Heravi (pp. 122-23).

After Masʿudšāh was killed in 1342, Shaikh Abu Esḥāq acted as Jahān-Malek Ḵātun's guardian, and he may well have encouraged her to compose poetry. Shiraz was conquered by the Mozaffarid Amir Mobārez-al-Din Moḥammad b. Moẓaffar (r. 1314-58) in 1353, and even after the Mozaffarid conquest Jahān-Malek appears to have stayed in Shiraz. Jahān-Malek mocks Mobārez-al-Din in at least one poem (*ḡazal* no. 1321; presumably composed after his death) but, in contrast, she praises Shah Šojāʿ, Mobārez-al-Din's eldest son and successor, who ruled in Shiraz twice, in 1358-63 and in 1366-84, and who was much more inclined to poetry and the arts than his father. It seems likely that Jahān-Malek Ḵātun lived at least until 1382, since in her poetry she also praises the Jalayerid (see JALAYERIDS) ruler, Solṭān-Aḥmad b. Shaikh Oways (r. 1382-1410), who ruled in Isfahan from that year. In another *ḡazal* (no. 404), Jahān-Malek appears to praise Mirānšāh b. Timur (r. 1367-1408), who was appointed governor of Khorasan in 1380 and later governor of Azerbaijan in 1393. If this *ḡazal* was indeed written for Mirānšāh, this could suggest an even later date of her death.

In the 13th- and early 14th-century Salghurid Shiraz, several women played decisive roles in the running of the city, most notably Ābeš Ḵātun (d. 1286, q.v.) and her daughter Kordujin/Kordučin (d. 1338; see Jonayd, pp. 281-82, esp. Qazvini's n. 8, tr., pp. 324-26, Qazvini's comm., p. 324, n. 193; Ḡani, pp. 64-65). Sources contemporary with Jahān-Malek mention that a number of Injuid women were active in the cultural life of 14th-century Shiraz (Ebn Baṭṭuṭa, pp. 218-22). Tāši Ḵātun, Shaikh Abu Esḥāq's mother, founded the Ḵātuniya *madrasa*, developed the Šāh-e Čerāḡ shrine complex, donated a number of valuable Qurʾāns to that same shrine, and regularly attended public theological assemblies (*majāles*; see Jonayd, pp. 289-92, esp. Qazvini's comm., p. 290, n. 2, tr., pp. 335-37, Qazvini's comm, p. 335, n. 23). Some of Jahān-Malek's female relatives even played important political roles in the Mozaffarid period. One such woman was Jahān-Malek's cousin Ḵānsolṭān, who was married to Shah Maḥmud (r. 1364-66, d. 1375), Shah Šojāʿ's younger brother, and who secretly supported her brother-in-law against her husband (Moʿin-al-Din Naṭanzi, pp. 175, 182, 190; Limbert, pp. 41, 76, 148). Given that Injuid women were both culturally and politically active, it is probable that they were also active participants in the literary scene of the city.

Jahān-Malek's *divān* is the largest known *divān* to have reached us from any poetess of pre-modern Iran (1st ed., Tehran, 1995). She is primarily a *ḡazal* poet. Her *divān* contains 4 odes (*qaṣida*), one strophe-poem (*tarjiʿband*) a lengthy elegy (*marṯia*), 12 fragments (*moqaṭṭaʿ*), 357 quatrains (*robāʿi*), and 1,413 love lyrics (*ḡazal*, q.v.).

Four manuscripts of Jahān-Malek Ḵātun's *divān* are known to exist. The most complete is in the Bibliothèque nationale de France in Paris (MS Supplément persan 763; see Blochet, III, p. 222, no. 1580). This manuscript, which is dedicated to the Jalayerid ruler Solṭān-Aḥmad Bahādor b. Shaikh Oways, reportedly contains more than 14,000 verses (*bayt*; an estimation questioned by Ṣafā; p. 1051) and appears to date from Jahān-Malek's lifetime. Edgar Blochet believed that this was the original copy of Jahān-Malek's *divān* (Blochet, III, p. 222). Henri Massé argued that this manuscript must have been copied during the lifetime of the author, and that, given the fine nature of the gold illumination (*taḏhib*), it may in fact be the same copy that was originally presented to Solṭān-Aḥmad Bahādor, a known bibliophile (Massé, pp. 4-5).

Another manuscript of Jahān-Malek's poetry in the Bibliothèque nationale de France (MS Supplément persan 1102, see Blochet, III, pp. 222-23, no. 1581) contains a selection of her poetry (*ḡazal*s, *moqaṭṭaʿ*s, *robāʿi*s, and *qaṣida*s, a total of about 1,300 verses) bound together with a similar number of verses by another (possibly female) poet with the pen name Binešān. According to Edgar Blochet, MS Supplément persan 763, illuminated after the fashion of the schools of western Iran, dates from the late 14th century, and MS Supplément persan 1102 has been copied in Herat around 1460 (Blochet, III, pp. 222-23).

The second most complete manuscript of Jahān-Malek's poetry, containing about 5,000 verses, is preserved at the Topkapi Palace Library in Istanbul (MS H. 867). Fehmi Karatay dates this manuscript to 1437 (Karatay, p. 215), that is, within four to five decades after Jahān-Malek's death.

The fourth extant manuscript of Jahān-Malek's poetry contains about 500 *bayt*s and is dated to around 1618. This manuscript opens with a preface in praise of Shah Šojāʿ; it was acquired by Edward G. Browne (q.v.) and is now preserved at the University Library in Cambridge as MS V.32(6) (Browne, pp. 237-38).

None of the libraries inside Iran seem to contain a manuscript copy of Jahān-Malek's *divān*, which explains why her poetry has received relatively little academic attention. The small number of extant manuscripts would also suggest that her *divān* was not widely disseminated, either during her lifetime or after her death, although a small number of her poems do appear in fairly early *taḏkera*s (e.g., Dawlatšāh, pp. 289-90; Faḵri Heravi, pp. 122-23). Like the works of many other poets of 14th-century Iran, Jahān-Malek's poetry has been overshadowed by that of Ḥāfeẓ, perhaps even more so in her case because she was a woman.

Jahān-Malek's poetry reflects the influence of Saʿdi (d. 691/1292), to whom she refers directly at least once (*ḡazal* 230). Many more of her *ḡazal*s, however, bear a striking similarity to those of Ḥāfeẓ. There is a noticeable degree of overlap in terms of rhyme, meter, and metaphor; and it is not clear who is drawing on whom. Given that Ḥāfeẓ and Jahān-Malek Ḵātun were active at the same court, it is not unreasonable to assume that they may have influenced each other's poetry. It should be noted, however, that Jahān-Malek's *ḡazal*s (in contrast to a good number of Ḥāfeẓ's poems) have little (if any) Sufi or mystical content, whether covert or overt. Jahān-Malek is also less critical of the hypocrisy of the clergy and the Sufis than either Ḥāfeẓ or ʿObayd Zākāni (d. 771/1370), her other contemporary poet.

In language and style, her poetry is similar to the works of her contemporaries, but, compared to them, she makes fewer references to the tavern (*ḵarābāt*) and the life of the *rend*s "libertine." According to Ḏabiḥ-Allāh Ṣafā (p. 1048), her poerty clearly reflects the love passion of a woman, and the poet Kamāl Ḵojandi (q.v.) seems to have satirized Jahān-Malek, claiming that it is obvious to anyone who reads her poetry that it is written by a woman (Kamāl Ḵojandi, pp. 394-95). Dowlatšāh's attribution of these vulgar one-line poems (*mofradāt*) to ʿObayd Zākāni appears to be erroneous (Dawlatšāh, pp. 289-90), and are not included in the edited version of his *divān*.

Jahān-Malek Ḵātun's *divān* is prefaced by an eloquent prose introduction that seems to have been penned by the poet herself. In this introduction, Jahān-Malek says that she composed poems now and then in her free moments, and that, at first, she was reluctant to compile her verses, thinking that it did not befit noblewomen (*ḵavātin*). However, when she learned that some Arab and Persian noblewomen of the past had composed poetry, she decided to write down her verses so that her name would live on. She laments that so few women of Iran have written poetry, although she does mention the Qutlugh-khanid princess Pādšāh Ḵātun (k. 1295), who ruled in Kerman from 691/1292 to 695/1295, and Qotloḡšāh Ḵātun (the wife of the Il-khanid ruler Öljeitü/Uljāytu; see Blochet, III, p. 222; Ṣafā, pp. 658, 1047). In her introduction, Jahān-Malek also refers to an earlier female poet by the name of ʿĀʾeša Moqria and quotes two of her quatrains.

Bibliography: Moḥammad Ḥosayn Roknzāda Ādamiyat, *Dānešmandān o soḵansarāyān-e Fārs*, 5 vols., Tehran, 1958-61. ʿAli Āl-e Dāwud, "Abu Esḥāq-e Inju," in *Dāʾerat al-maʿāref-e bozorg-e eslāmi* (*DMBE*) V, Tehran, 1993, pp. 161-65. Idem, "Āl-e Moẓaffar," in *DMBE* VII, Tehran, 1995, pp. 140-53. Idem, "Inju," in *DMBE* X, Tehran, 2001, pp. 719-20. Edgar Blochet, *Catalogue des manuscrits persans de la Bibliothèque nationale*, 4 vols., Paris, 1905-34. Clifford Edmund Bosworth, *The New Islamic Dynasties: A Chronological and Genealogical Manual*, Edinburgh, 1996. John A. Boyle, "Indju," in *EI*[2] III, 1965, p. 1208. Dominic

Parviz Brookshaw, "Odes of A Poet-Princess: the *Ghazals* of Jahān-Malik Khātūn," *Iran* 43, 2005, pp. 173-95. Edward Granville Browne, *A Descriptive Catalogue of the Oriental MSS. Belonging to the Late E. G. Browne*, ed. Reynold A. Nicholson, Cambridge, 1932. Parvin Dawlatābādi, *Manẓur-e ḵaradmand: barrasi-e aḥwāl wa gozida-ye ašʿār-e Jahān-Malek Ḵātun*, Tehran (?), 1989 (?). Dawlatšāh Samarqandi, *Taḏkerat al-šoʿarāʾ*, ed. Edward G. Browne as, The *Tadhkiratu'sh-shuʿará ("Memoirs of the Poets") of Dawlatsháh . . .*, Leiden and London, 1901. Ebn Baṭṭuṭa, *Reḥlat Ebn Baṭṭuṭa: toḥfat al-noẓẓār fi ḡarāʾeb al-amṣār wa ʿajāʾeb al-asfār*, ed. Ṭalāl Ḥarb, Beirut, 1987. Ebn Zarkub, *Širāz-nāma*, ed. Bahman Karimi, Tehran, 1932. Solṭān-Moḥammad Faḵri Heravi, *Taḏkera-ye Rawżat al-salāṭin wa jawāher al-ʿajāʾeb*, ed. Sayyed Ḥosām-al-Din Rāšedi, Karachi, 1968. Purān Farroḵzād, *Nimahā-ye nātamām: negāreš-i now dar šeʿr-e zanān az Rābeʿa tā Foruḡ*, Tehran, 2001. Qāsem Ḡani, *Tāriḵ-e ʿaṣr-e Ḥāfeẓ: baḵt dar āṯār o afkār o aḥwāl-e Ḥāfeẓ*, Tehran, 2001. Aḥmad Golčin-e Maʿāni, *Tāriḵ-e taḏkerahā-ye fārsi*, 2 vols., Tehran, 1984. ʿAbd-al-Karim Golšani, "Pādšāh Ḵātun," *Däneš-nāma-ye jahān-e eslām* V, Tehran, 2000, pp. 363-64. ʿAli-Asḡar Ḥalabi, *ʿObayd Zākāni*, Tehran, 1998. Marle Hammond, "Literature: 9th to 15th Century," in *Encyclopedia of Women and Islamic Cultures*, ed. J. Suad et al., 4 vols., Leiden, 2003-07. Peter Jackson, "Muẓaffarids," in *EI2* VII, 1993, pp. 820-22. Jahān-Malek Ḵātun, *Divān-e kāmel-e Jahān-Malek Ḵātun, qarn-e haštom-e hejri*, ed. Purāndoḵt Kāšāni Rād and A. Aḥmad-nežād, Tehran, 1995. Moʿin-al-Din Abu'l-Qāsem Jonayd Širāzi, *Šadd al-ezār fi ḥaṭṭ al-awzār ʿan zowwār al-mazār*, ed. with commentary, Moḥammad Qazvini and ʿAbbās Eqbāl, Tehran, 1949; tr. ʿIsā b. Joneyd Širāzi as *Taḏkera-ye hezār mazār*, ed. ʿAbd-al-Wahhāb Nurāni Weṣāl, Shiraz, 1985. Fehmi Karatay, *Topkapı Sarayı Müzesi Kütüphanesi Farsça yazmalar kataloğu: no. 1-940*, Istanbul, 1961. Kamāl Ḵojandi, *Divān*, ed. ʿAziz Dawlatābādi, Tabriz, 1958. John Limbert, *Shiraz in the Age of Hafez: The Glory of a Medieval Persian City*, Seattle, 2004. Henri Massé, "Le divan de la princesse Djehane," in Parimarz Nafisi, ed., *Yād-nāma-ye Saʿid Nafisi/Mélange d'iranologie en memoir de feu Said Naficy*, ed. Parimarz Nafisi, Tehran, 1972, pp. 1-42. Fatima Mernissi, Sultanes oubliées, tr. May Jo Lakeland as *The Forgotten Queens of Islam*, Cambridge, 1993. Vladimir Minorsky, "Ḳutlugh-Khānids," in EI^2 V, 1986, pp. 553-54. Moʿin-al-Din Yazdi, *Mawāheb-e elāhi dar tāriḵ-e Āl-e Moẓaffar*, ed. Saʿid Nafisi, Tehran, 1947. Nāṣer-al-Din Monši Kermāni, *Semṭ al-ʿolā le'l-ḥażrat al-ʿolyā*, ed. ʿAbbās Eqbāl, Tehran, 1983. Parimarz Nafisi, "Divān o šarḥ-e ḥāl-e šāʿera-ye qarn-e haftom, [zic] Jahān-Malek Ḵātun-e Injuʾi," in Ḥamid Zarrinkub, ed., *Majmuʿa-ye soḵanrānihā-ye dovvomin kongera-ye taḥqiqāt-e Irāni*, Mašhad, 1972, pp. 137-46. Saʿid Nafisi, *Tāriḵ-e naẓm o naṯr dar Irān*, 2 vols., Tehran, 1965, I, p. 216. Idem, "Ḥāfeẓ wa Jahān-Malek Ḵātun," *Rāhnemā-ye ketāb* 11/7, 1968, pp. 369-72. Moʿin-al-Din Naṭanzi, *Montaḵab al-tawāriḵ-e moʿini*, ed. Jean Aubin, Tehran, 1957. Ḏabiḥ-Allāh Ṣafā, *Tāriḵ-e adabiyāt dar Irān*, 5 vols. in 8, Tehran, 1959-92, III, pp. 1045-56. Bertold Spüler, "Ābeš Ḵātun," in *EIr*. I, 1982, p. 210. Idem, "Atābakān-e Fārs," in *EIr*. II, 1987, pp. 894-96. Maria Szuppe, "The 'Jewels of Wonder': Learned Ladies and Princess Politicians in the Provinces of Early Safavid Iran," in Gavin R. Hambly, ed., *Women in the Medieval Islamic World: Power, Patronage, and Piety*, London, 1998, pp. 325-47.

(Dominic Parviz Brookshaw)

JAHĀNŠAH QARĀ QOYUNLU. See QARĀ QOYUNLU DYNASTY. Forthcoming, online.

JAHĀN TIMŪR (TEMÜR), son of Alafrank (q.v.) son of Gaikhatu Khan (q.v.). A phantom Il-khan, previously known as ʿEzz-al-Din, Jahān Timūr was recognized briefly in Iraq and Mesopotamia in 1339-40 during the period of the collapse of the Il-khanate following the death of Abu Saʿid (q.v.) in 736/1335.

The evidence for Jahān Timūr's career is extremely scarce, reflecting his own insignificance and the brevity of his place in the spotlight. Neither the pro-Jalayerid *Tāriḵ-e Šayḵ Ovays* of Ahari, nor Faryumadi's continuation of the chronicle of Šabānkāra'i mention Jahān Timūr, and some of the information we possess is conflicting. According to Mostawfi (tr. pp. 108-9, text, pp. 448-49), his elevation followed the failure of Šayḵ Ḥasan-e Bozorg's initiative to recognize the Khorasanian candidate, Ṭaḡāy Timūr, as Il-khan and the collapse of the second Khorasanian invasion of western Iran in the summer of 739/1339. This also marked a new rift with the Chobanid, Šayḵ Ḥasan-e Kuchek, whose subtle diplomacy had broken up an alliance that was anyway beginning to unravel (see CHOBANIDS, p. 500). Returning towards Iraq from Sāva, Ḥasan-e Bozorg stopped at a settlement called Aqtaq near Talbar (or Talambar, near Šahr-e Naw of Hamadan) and turned to prince Jahān Timūr as an alternative Chinggisid figurehead to the Chobanid Sati Beg (shortly to be married to, and replaced by, Solaymān Khan, a grandson of prince Süge). Mostawfi was himself at Sāva at this time, in the service of Ḥasan-e Bozorg's newly appointed vizier, Ḵᵛāja Šams al-Din Zakariā (tr. p. 111, text, p. 451). This must have been early in 740/autumn 1339, for Šayḵ Ḥasan is then reported to have gone to Baghdad for the winter. Most of this information is followed by Ḥāfeẓ-e Abru (p. 208).

Confirmation is provided by the issue of coins in the name of Jahān Timūr Khan throughout the area controlled by Šayḵ Ḥasan and his allies (notably Ḥāji Ṭaḡāy of Diyarbakır [Diarbekr] and Eretna in E. Anatolia), in the year 740 A.H.: in Baghdad, Basra, Erzincan, Hella, Arbīl, Jazirat b. ʿOmar, Khilat (Ahlat), Mosul, perhaps Samsun (read by Album as an issue for Ṭaḡāy Timūr), Sinjar, and Wastan (Album I, pp. 84-87, Album II, pp. 65-70, Aykut, pp. 109-10). On the other hand, Ebn Fatḥ-Allāh (p. 75) states that Ḥasan-e Bozorg elevated the previously unknown Jahān Timür to the Khanate in 743/1342-43 at Noʿmāniya (S. Iraq): possibly, therefore, a second 'coronation' in Iraqi territory, though the date must be disregarded, despite the fact that Ebn Fatḥ-Allāh is citing a contemporary source.

Jahān Timür's dismissal was as abrupt as his rise. Mustering his forces in the spring of 740/1340, Ḥasan-e Bozorg marched together with his protégé on Azerbaijan. They fought a pitched battle at Aqtash near Küitü (for which see Melville, p. 55 n. 165) on Wednesday 29 Ḏu'l-Ḥejja 740/21 June 1340 and the Jalayerids were defeated and fled (Mostawfi, tr. p.122, text p. 459). At some stage after this, returning to Baghdad, Ḥasan-e Bozorg recognized that Jahān Timür was of no use and deposed him before returning to the attack with a new campaign to Azerbaijan in the spring of 741/1341 (*ibid.*, tr. p. 125, text p. 462). In the interval, according to the same source, Chobanid forces attacked Baghdad but were repulsed. The same events, though in a different order, are reported by Ḥāfeẓ-e Abru (pp. 209-10, 212). Whatever the exact date of Jahān Timür's dismissal, it is significant that no coins in his name were minted in Iraq in the year 741/1340, though there are a few from Jazirat b. ʿOmar early in the year, before local allegiance was instead given to the Chobanid Solaymān Khan (Album, II, pp. 57, 67-68). As noted by Album (I, p. 85), the coinage of Jahān Timür, with a lighter standard (double dirham of 10 *qirāts*), departed from the standard established by Ḡāzān Khan's coinage reform and retained elsewhere, so that now a single currency no longer prevailed in the Il-khanid empire.

The removal of the wholly insignificant Jahān Timür is generally considered to mark the start of Ḥasan-e Bozorg's independent rule, although on occasions, as circumstances dictated, he did briefly offer allegiance to other figurehead Il-khans outside his own control (cf. J. M. Smith, *Sarbadārs*, pp. 99, 110-11; Roemer, p. 5).

Bibliography: S. Album, "Studies in Ilkhanid history and numismatics I. A late Ilkhanid hoard (743/1342)," *Studia Iranica* 13, 1984, pp. 49-116. Idem, "Studies in Ilkhanid history and numismatics II. A late Ilkhanid hoard (743/1342)," *Studia Iranica* 14, 1985, pp. 43-76. T. Aykut, "The Yapı Kredi coin collection, in *Ak Akçe. Mongol and Ilkhanid coins*, Yapı Kredi coin collections I, Istanbul, 1992, pp. 41-120. Š. Bayāni, *Tāriḵ-e Āl-e Jalāyer*, Tehran, 1966, repr. 2002, pp. 26-27. ʿAbd-Allāh b. Fatḥ-Allāh, *al-Taʿriḵ al-Ḡiāṯi*, ed. T. N. al-Hamadāni, Baghdad, 1975. Ḥāfeẓ-e Abru, *Ḏayl-e Jāmeʿ al-tawāriḵ*, 2nd ed., ed. Ḵ. Bayāni, Tehran, 1971. Charles Melville, *The fall of Amir Chupan and the decline of the Ilkhanate, 1327-37: A decade of discord in Mongol Iran*, Indiana, 1999. Ḥamd-Allāh Mostawfi, *Ḏayl-e Żafar-nāma*, facs. ed. Z.V. Pirieva, Baku, 1978; Russ. tr. by M. D. Kazimova & Z. V. Pirieva, Baku, 1986 (entitled *Ḏayl-e Tāriḵ-e gozida*) . Hans Roemer, "The Jalayrids, Muzaffarids and Sarbadārs," in *Cam. hist. Iran*, VI. *The Timurid and Safavid periods*, Cambridge, 1986, pp. 1-41. J. M., Smith, "Ḏjalāyir, Ḏjalāyirid," in *EI*², II, pp. 401-2. Idem, *The History of the Sarbadār Dynasty 1336-1381 A. D. and its Sources*, The Hague and Paris, 1970.

(CHARLES MELVILLE)

JAHĀN-E ZANĀN (Women's World), a magazine published first in Mašhad (four issues, 25 Jomādā I-17 Šaʿbān 1339/15 Dalw 1299-6 Ordibehešt 1300 Š./4 Feb.-26 April 1921) and, after a lapse of about five months, in Tehran (one issue only, Moḥarram 1340/Sept. 1921). It started as a biweekly journal but became monthly after the second issue. In Mašhad, the journal dealt with topics such as the necessity of education for women, cooking recipes, child rearing, notices about famous women, and the like. Nevertheless, in its only issue published in Tehran, it printed an article titled "Az ḥālā" (From now on) that advocated education for women and called for their active involvement in society. This article created a great deal of angry protests in Tehran by conservative clergy and led to the banning of the magazine and the banishment of its founder, Farroḵdin Pārsā, and his family (Ṣadr Hāšemi, II, pp. 183-84). The paper was managed in Mašhad by Faḵr-e Āfāq Batul Pārsā, a teacher by profession and Farroḵdin's wife, who later, in Tehran, functioned as its chief editor. Farroḵdin Pārsā was a civil servant but also worked for a number of newspapers, journals, and magazines as editor, columnist, and correspondent.

Jahān-e zanān was printed in Mašhad, in 28-32 two-column pages of 13.5×22 cm, first at Ṭus Printing House and then at Ḵorāsān Printers, and in Tehran at Bāqerzāda Brothers Press. Annual subscription was 30 *qerāns*. Complete sets are accessible at the Central Library (Ketāb-ḵāna-ye markazi) of Tehran University and at the Ebn Meskuya Library in Isfahan. A single issue is kept in Āstān-e Qods Library, Mašhad.

Bibliography: Kāva Bayāt and Masʿud Kuhestāni-nežād, ed., *Asnād-e maṭbuʿāt (1286-1320 H. Š)*, 2 vols., Tehran, 1993, I, pp. 416-17. Moḥammad Moḥiṭ Ṭabāṭabāʾi, *Tāriḵ-e taḥlili-e maṭbuʿāt-e Irān*, Tehran, 1987, pp. 175-76. ʿAbd-al-Ḥosayn Nāhid, *Zanān-e Irān dar jonbeš-e mašruṭa*, Tabriz, 1981, pp. 121-22. Ali No-Rouze [Ḥasan Moqaddam], "Registre analytique annoté de la presse Persane [depui la guerre)," *RMM* 60, 1925, pp. 35-62, no. 191. Faḵr-al-Zamān Nuri Eṣfahāni, Rāhnemā-ye maṭbuʿāt: Fehrest-e našriyāt-e mawjud dar Ketāb-ḵāna-ye ʿomumi-e Ebn Meskuya Eṣfahān, Isfahan, 2001, p. 114. Moḥammad Ṣadr Hāšemi, *Tāriḵ-e jarāʾed wa majallāt-e Irān*, 4 vols., Isfahan, 1984, II, no. 456, pp. 181-85. Mortażā Solṭāni, *Fehrest majallahā-ye fārsi az ebtedā tā sāl-e 1320 šamsi*, Tehran, 1976, nos. 73-74, pp. 41-42.

(NASSEREDDIN PARVIN)

JĀḤEẒ, ABU ʿOṮMĀN ʿAMR B. BAḤR (b. *ca.* 160/776; d. 255/868-9), the leading Arabic prose writer of the 9th century. His father, who may have been of East African descent, was a client of the Arab tribe of Kināna.

Jāḥeẓ grew up in Baṣra, where he studied with a number of leading scholars, including the Muʿtazilite theologian Abu Esḥāq Ebrāhim b. Sayyār al-Naẓẓām (d. between 220/825 and 230/825, q.v.) and the philologists Abu ʿObeyda Maʿmar (d. 209/824-25, q.v.) and al-Aṣmaʿi (d. 213/828). His essays on the imamate brought him to the attention of the Abbasid caliph al-Maʾmun (r. 198-218/813-33), who invited him to Baghdad. Jāḥeẓ joined the caliph in condemning literalist scholars of the Hadith (the statements and opinions attributed to the Prophet Muhammad, see HADITH) as anthropomorphists and wrote several polemical tracts against them (al-Qadi). Under the caliphs al-Moʿtaṣem (r. 218-27/833-42) and al-Wāṯeq (r. 227-32/842-47), he enjoyed the patronage of the vizier Ebn al-Zayyāt (d. 233/847), the Muʿtazilite judge Ebn Abi Doʾād (d. 240/854), and the latter's son Abu'l-Walid Moḥammad (d. 239/854). In 237/851, the caliph al-Motawakkel (r. 232-47/847-61) reversed his predecessors' anti-Sunnite stance; but Jāḥeẓ, now under the protection of the courtier al-Fatḥ b. Ḵāqān, continued to attack the literalist Hadith-scholars. After his protector was assassinated in 247/861, Jāḥeẓ returned to Baṣra, where he apparently remained until his death. The Arabic sources flesh out his biography with a number of anecdotes. Reportedly, he was strikingly ugly: the name Jāḥeẓ means 'pop-eyed.' He is said to have sold fish for a time in Baṣra during his youth, and to have paid rent to booksellers in order to be allowed to spend the night reading in their shops. Several sources report that he died of a stroke, but tradition claims that he was killed by a collapsing bookshelf.

Jāḥeẓ has been credited with up to 245 works, although the true total may be closer to 190. Approximately 90 of his works have survived, either completely or in fragments (Montgomery, p. 234). Many take up theological issues, notably the createdness of the Qurʾān, or political controversies, particularly the nature of the imamate. The largest surviving works are *al-Ḥayawān* ('Living creatures'), ostensibly on zoology, but full of miscellaneous religious, scientific, and literary observations; and *al-Bayān wa al-tabyin* ('Clarity and clarification'), on language and eloquence, especially as manifested in Arabic. Of his other works, the most famous include *al-Boḵalāʾ* ('The Misers'), *Manāqeb al-Tork* ('The virtues of the Turks'), *Resālat al-qiān* ('Epistle on singing slave women'), and *Faḵr al-sudān ʿalā al-biżān* ('The boasting of blacks over whites'). As a stylist, he is famous for his incessant quotation of sources, his evident delight in arguing both sides of a question, his penchant for *reductio ad absurdum*, and his love of digression. His works constitute a rich source of information on contemporary opinions and practices, including those of the Persians. This information is, however, scattered throughout several works, all of them in one way or another polemical, and none of them devoted to Persians as such. One must therefore beware of insisting upon a particular interpretation of his attitudes toward Persians or any other ethnic group. Only in connection with certain religious and political topics does he appear to be speaking in his own voice and to be entirely serious. Otherwise, he makes a point of concealing his opinions behind a farrago of citations, many of them humorous.

Jāḥeẓ was familiar with what he calls the 'books of the non-Arabs' (*kotob al- ʿajam* or *al-aʿājem*), that is, the Middle Persian writings that had been available in Arabic translations since the first half of the 8th century. He condemns the books of the Manicheans (*zanādeqa*), which, despite being most impressively decorated, speak of nothing but "light and darkness, coupling demons, rutting devils," and other "nonsense" (*Ḥayawān*, I, p. 75). Yet he has great respect for those works he calls *ādāb*, a term which—to judge by his comments elsewhere—refers to well-expressed observations about man and the world, insightful arguments about intellectual matters, and practical advice for improving one's lot in life. For all its beauty, Arabic poetry, he claims, contains no wisdom that cannot be found in the works of the Persians (*Ḥayawān*, I, p. 75). His citations from the Persian tradition include a definition of eloquence attributed to Ebn al-Moqaffaʿ (d. *ca.* 757, q.v.), the famous translator of Middle Persian (*Bayān*, I, pp. 115-17); and the comments of Sahl b. Hārun (d. 215/830), the well-known Shuʿubite (Šoʿubi), to the effect that audiences are often more impressed by a shabby and ill-favored orator than by an elegant and comely one (*Bayān*, I, pp. 89-90). In other cases, Jāḥeẓ alludes (usually without specifying the source of his information) to practices characteristic of the Persians, such as their kings' love of hunting (*Ḥayawān*, II, p. 140) or their favorite foods (*Boḵalāʾ*, p. 179).

Despite his generally laudatory comments about Persian literature, Jāḥeẓ takes a dim view of those whose reading extends to nothing else. In an epistle entitled *Ḏamm aḵlāq al-kottāb* ('A condemnation of the character of secretaries'), he sketches a portrait of a typical Abbasid bureaucrat—one whose learning is thoroughly Persian in character. Such learning, says Jāḥeẓ, consists of the aphorisms of Bozorgmehr (see BOZORGMEHR-E BOḴTAGĀN), the testament of Ardašir (r. ?-242 C.E., see ARDAŠIR I), the *adab* of Ebn al-Moqaffaʿ, the epistles of ʿAbd-al-Ḥamid b. Yaḥyā b. Saʿd (d. 132/750, q.v.; the secretary to the last Umayyad caliph Marwān II b. Moḥammad [r. 127-32/744-50]), the *Book of Mazdak* (or *Mardak*), and *Kalila wa Demna* (q.v.). The secretaries who have mastered these texts feel qualified to speak with authority on all subjects, including scriptural exegesis, Islamic law, philosophy, and Arabic style. Full of confidence in their own judgment, they impugn the language of the Qurʾān and express doubt about the authenticity of the Hadith. The common people, dazzled by the secretaries' air of learning, revere them (*Rasāʾel*, II, pp. 187-209). This polemic against the secretaries seems contrived: elsewhere, Jāḥeẓ claims—with greater plausibility—that the common people revere *ḥadiṯ*-scholars, not secretaries (e.g., *Rasāʾel*, III, pp. 298 and 300).

In his epistle on the virtues of the Turks—by which is meant their usefulness as soldiers in the caliph's army—Jāḥeẓ describes three groups of Persians, or Persianized Arabs and Arameans, associated with the Abbasid dynasty. These are the *banawi*s (the descendants of the *abnā*ʾ *al-dowla*, the first Abbasid revolutionaries), the *mawlā*s ('clients,' pl. *mawāli*), and the Khorasanis (people from Khorasan). The *banawi*s boast of their ancestors who brought the Abbasids to power. They also speak of their own ability to fight in trenches, on bridgeheads, at gates, in alleyways, and in prisons—a claim that suggests that they served as an urban police force (*Rasāʾel*, I, pp. 25-28; Crone). The *mawlā*s, for their part, pride themselves on their long-standing and intimate connection to the ruling family but also of their ability to understand the common people (*Rasāʾel*, I, pp. 23-25). They are thus probably to be identified with the Iranian or Persianized Aramean class that supplied the Abbasid dynasty with its scribes and viziers. The Khorasanis, finally, appear to be the partisans of the "second call to allegiance," that is, the warriors recruited by al-Maʾmun to overthrow the caliph al-Amin (which they did in 198/813). Like the *banawi*s, the Khorasanis claim descent from the original partisans of the Abbasids. In the speeches Jāḥeẓ attributes to them, they vaunt their skill in battle and their spectacular record of victory over the enemies of the caliphate. They describe themselves as having long hair, curling mustaches, and broad shoulders; and as riding into battle with drums, banners, curved swords, clubs, battleaxes, and daggers. They were "created to topple dynasties" and the sound of their shouting is enough to cause a miscarriage (*Rasāʾel*, I, pp. 14-23).

Jāḥeẓ's work *al-Boḵalāʾ* ('Misers') contains a good deal of detail—real or invented—about the famous penny-pinchers of Khorasan. Khorasanis eat alone instead of sharing meals (*Boḵalāʾ*, pp. 24-26); they pretend not to recognize old friends in order to avoid treating them (*Boḵalāʾ*, p. 22, with the miser's final remark given in Persian; see further Mahdavi-Dāmġāni, p. 250); and they walk for three months on their heels and three months on their toes in order to save shoe leather (*Boḵalāʾ*, p. 28). In one anecdote, a man from Marv (Merv)—a town famous for its misers—refuses to help pay for lighting oil, so his friends blindfold him in order to deny him the benefit of the lamp (*Boḵalāʾ*, p. 18). In another yarn, a Khorasani refuses to lend his frying pan to a neighbor but then regrets his refusal when he learns that the neighbor planned to fry meat and would therefore have returned the pan with a layer of grease on it (*Boḵalāʾ*, p. 23). These anecdotes, along with the epistle in defense of penny-pinching ascribed to the Shuʿubite Sahl b. Hārun (d. 215/830; *Boḵalāʾ*, pp. 9-16), have led some modern critics to conclude that the *Misers* ridicules Persians by contrasting their supposed stinginess with the proverbial generosity of the Arabs (Pellat, 1953, p. 229). Yet it is not the Persians but rather the Khorasanis—some of whom were or were considered to be Arabs—who are collectively described as misers. Of the other figures in the book, some are Persians, some—including the caliph Hešām b. ʿAbd-al-Malek (r. 105-25/724-43)—are Arabs, and many are simply unidentified (*Boḵalāʾ*, introd., p. 33). The work does contain a complaint, attributed to a miser, that Arabic poetry has declined because of the ascendancy of the *ʿajam* (non-Arabs; *Boḵalāʾ*, p. 177), but the likeliest conclusion is that the speaker means the Turkish soldiery of Samarra.

Jāḥeẓ has much to say about the Shuʿubites, that is, those of his contemporaries who argued that Persians were superior—or at least not inferior—to Arabs. Some may have advocated the view that Persians of noble lineage should enjoy the same privileges as the Arab elite (Mottahedeh), or at least maintain some of the privileges they enjoyed before the Arab conquest (Enderwitz, pp. 16-25). The Shuʿubites reportedly mocked elements of traditional Arab culture, saying for example that the Arab orator's staff was a crude prop and that the ancient Arabs lacked even the most basic weapons and military tactics. Jāḥeẓ devotes a long section of his *Bayān* to rebutting these attacks, citing poems and other testimony to show that the Arabs could indeed use saddles, fight at night, and the like; and that the staff is a noble and useful implement (*Bayān*, III, pp. 5-124). Although it contains a good deal of information on Shuʿubite arguments, the discussion says relatively little about Persian culture itself. The exceptions are the claims (attributed anonymously to the Shuʿubites) that the most gifted orators are the Persians in general and the people of Fārs in particular; that the most fluent and masterful speakers come from Merv; that the most eloquent speakers of Dari and Pahlavi (qq.v.) languages come from Ahvāz; that "the intonation of the herbeds and the language of the mobeds" may still be learned from "the interpreter of the *zamzamah*" (*ṣāḥib tafsir al-zamzama*, apparently a transmitter of the Zand); and that eloquence may be attained from reading a work called the *Book of Kārwand* (*Bayān*, III, pp. 13-14).

To these claims Jāḥeẓ responds by saying that, while the Persians have their orators, all their productions are the result of long study and preparation, while Arab eloquence is spontaneous. He adds that the best-known works of Persian literature may well have been invented by those who, like Ebn al-Moqaffaʿ, claim merely to have translated them (*Bayān*, III, pp. 27-29). What he most deplores, in any case, is the tendency of the Shuʿubites to criticize not only Arabs but also Islam. In *al-Ḥayawān*, he declares that a major cause of resentment is *ʿaṣabiya*, 'group feeling.' The Shuʿubites begin by hating the Arabic language, then they come to hate Arabia and finally renounce Islam because it was brought by the Arabs (*Ḥayawān*, VII, p. 220). "You will never see any people more miserable than these Shuʿubites, nor any more hostile to their own religion," as a result of jealousy and resentment (*Bayān*, III, pp. 29-30). In the essay *Fi al-nābeta* ('On the upstarts'), however, he strikes a more conciliatory note. After attacking the arguments of those clients (*mawāli*) who use specious logic to claim that they are superior to Arabs and Persians both, he describes ethnic chauvinism as corrosive and pernicious. He also hopes that a certain (now lost) work of his will put the clients in their place while nevertheless giving them their due (*Rasaʾel*, II, pp. 20-22).

Among the works attributed to Jāḥeẓ is one devoted to the rights of kings according to the Persians. This work, entitled *Ketāb al-tāj* ('Book of the crown'), consists of a list of precepts, each of which is illustrated by one or more historical reports about the Sasanian kings, the caliphs, or both. The list of principles and the Sasanian examples come from unspecified "books of the non-Arabs" (*kotob al-aʿājem*) and "the lives of their kings" (*siar moluke-hā*; *Ketāb al-tāj*, pp. 138 and 163). The principles have mostly to do with the various forms of deference one should display toward the king (riding behind him, not taking medicine on the same day he does, never telling him the same story twice, and the like), although some have to do with the king's duties toward his subjects (for example, forgiving their drunkenness and pilfering). The work contains a number of Sasanian historical legends, such as the tale of Bahrām Gur (see BAHRĀM V.) and his manhandling of two lions (*Ketāb al-tāj*, pp. 164-67). It describes Sasanian administrative practices, including the ranking of courtiers (*Ketāb al-tāj*, pp. 23 ff.), the giving of gifts on the days of the festivals of Mehregān and Nowruz (qq.v.; *Ketāb al-tāj*, pp. 146 ff.), and the king's annual reception of petitioners (*Ketāb al-tāj*, pp. 159-63). It also contains some examples of Persian language, including two sentences (*Šab bešod* and *Ḵorram ḵoftār*) purportedly spoken by Sasanian kings as a signal that they wanted to go to bed (*Ketāb al-tāj*, p. 118).

The *Ketāb al-tāj* appears to have been composed during the reign of al-Motawakkel (r. 232-47/847-61), whose immediate predecessor, al-Wāṯeq (r. 227-32/842-47), is the last caliph to be named (p. 153). Even so, the work is almost certainly not by Jāḥeẓ. He doubtless agreed with its premise, namely that "the felicity of the common people consists in obedience to the sovereign while the felicity of the sovereign consists in obedience to God" (attributed to Ardašir Bābakān [see ARDAŠIR I]; *Ketāb al-tāj*, p. 2). As is clear from his known works, however, he supported an Abbasid imamate that made exclusive claims to religious authority. Accordingly, he had no particular reverence for the ancient Iranian kings, and none at all for the Umayyad caliphs. On stylistic grounds, too, the work is unlikely to be his (Moḥammadi, pp. 209-28). In his surviving works, no matter what their subject, he relies on arguments that are clever, sometimes to the point of perversity; and all his known works ramble and digress. The *Ketāb al-tāj*, by contrast, is focused and systematic; and it never swerves from its tone of earnest servility.

Even when the *Ketāb al-tāj* is dropped from the list, the works of Jāḥeẓ remain among the richest available sources of information on the cultural history of the Iranian peoples in the 9th century. His systematic interest in comparing different peoples has been attributed to his desire to see them united in one community under a single imam. He is said to have welcomed the unique contributions of each ethnic group to the totality of knowledge available to the Muslim community. Nevertheless, he supposedly had little patience for the Shuʿubite attempt to revive Sasanian traditions (which, it is argued, they did not necessarily make as a reaction to Islam but rather as part of an effort to maintain aristocratic privilege; Enderwitz, pp. 5-13, 16-25, 178). Whether or not this characterization of his opinions is accurate, it should be remembered that his remarks on Persian culture and traditions do not in the first instance constitute documentary evidence of lived reality. Rather, they reflect attitudes adopted by Arabs and Persians alike in the course of 9th-century arguments over the meaning of God's decision to divide the human race into distinct ethnic groups.

Bibliography: Patricia Crone, "ʿAbbasid Abnāʾ and Sasanid Cavalrymen," *JRAS*, Series 3/8, No. 1, 1998, pp. 1-19. Susanne Enderwitz, *Gesellschaftlicher Rang und ethnische Legitimation. Der arabische Schriftsteller Abu ʿUthmān al-Ǧāḥiẓ (gest. 868) über die Afrikaner, Perser und Araber in der islamischen Gesellschaft*, Freiburg, 1979. al-Jāḥiẓ, *al-Bayān wa al-tabyin*, ed. ʿAbd-al-Salām Moḥammad Hārun, 4 vols., Cairo, 1949; excerpts tr. J. Montgomery in *Writing and Representation in Medieval Islam: Muslim Horizons*, ed. J. Bray, London, 2006, pp. 443-56. Idem, *al-Boḵalāʾ*, ed. Ṭāhā al-Ḥājeri, 5th ed., Cairo, 1990; tr. R. B. Serjeant as *The Book of Misers*, Reading, 1997; tr. J. Colville as *Avarice and the Avaricious*, London, 1999. Idem, *Ketāb al-ḥayawān*, ed. ʿAbd-al-Salām Moḥammad Hārun, 7 vols., Cairo, 1947. Idem (attr.), *Ketāb al-tāj = Djâhiz, Le livre de la couronne*, ed. Aḥmad Zaki Bāshā, Cairo, 1914; repr. Baghdad, n.d.; tr. Ch. Pellat as *Le livre de la couronne*, Paris, 1954. Idem, *Rasāʾel al-Jāḥeẓ*, ed. ʿAbd al-Salām Moḥammad Hārun, 4 vols., Cairo, 1964; repr. Beirut, 1991; excerpts tr. W. Hutchins in *Nine Essays of al-Jahiz*, New York, 1989. Aḥmad Mahdawi-Dāmḡāni, "Fāresiyāt," *EIr* IX/3, 1999, pp. 249-51. James Montgomery, "al-Jahiz," in *Dictionary of Literary Biography*, Volume 311: *Arabic Literary Culture, 500-925*, ed. M. Cooperson and Sh. M. Toorawa, Detroit, 2005, pp. 231-42. Roy P. Mottahedeh, "The Šoʿubiyah Controversy and the Social History of Early Islamic Iran," *IJMES* 7, 1976, pp. 161-82. Moḥammad Moḥammadi, *al-Tarjama wa al-naql ʿan al-fāresiya fi al-qorun al-eslāmiya al-ulā*, Beirut, 1964. Charles Pellat, *Le Milieu basrien et la formation de Ǧāḥiẓ*, Paris, 1953. Idem, *The Life and Works of Jāḥeẓ*, tr. D. M. Hawke, London and Berkeley, 1969. Wadad al-Qadi, "The Earliest Nābita and the paradigmatic nawābit," *Stud. Isl.* 78, 1993, pp. 27-61.

(MICHAEL COOPERSON)

JAHM B. ṢAFWĀN, ABU MOḤEZ, Islamic theologian of the Umayyad period (d. Marv 128/746). Documentation about him is scarce and not entirely reliable. He was a client (of the Banu Rāseb), but probably not of Persian descent, for his name seems to indicate that he, as well as his father, grew up in an Arabic speaking environment. Ebn Ḥanbal connected him with Ḥarrān in Upper Mesopotamia. He may have been trained there as an administrator for later on, in Khorasan, he was responsible among other things for collecting the bridge-toll at Termeḏ where traders used to cross the Oxus.

During the period of anarchy that preceded the Abbasid revolution, he came into conflict with the last Umayyad governor, Naṣr b. Sayyār. At a certain moment, probably around 126/744, he sided with al-Ḥāreṯ b. Sorayj who had been leading a rebellion since 116/734 and who, though an Arab himself, propagated ideas that had appeared at the turn of the century concerning a just treatment of the *mawāli* and the neophytes. We hear that he had to read Ebn Sorayj's political "program" (*sira*) to the latter's adherents in his army and elsewhere (Ṭabari II, p. 1918; tr. XXVII, p. 29); Jahm seems to have been his scribe (*kāteb*), and he may have composed this text. At that time, i.e. in the year 128 A.H., he was so influential (and the Umayyad government so weak), that when it came to negotiations, he could propose a *šurā*, i.e. a referendum by the population, which would have placed Ebn Sorayj and the Umayyads on an equal footing (Ṭabari II, p. 1919; tr. XXVII, p. 31). The plan failed, not simply because Naṣr b. Sayyār refused to accept it, but more significantly because Ebn Sorayj became involved in an intertribal dispute with Joday^c al-Kermāni who ultimately killed him in battle. Deprived of his protector, Jahm fell into the hands of Salm b. Aḥwaz al-Māzini al-Tamimi, the chief of Naṣr b. Sayyār's police force and a hard-liner on the government's side. In spite of his personal attachment to Salm's son, he was executed at once (Ṭabari II, p. 1924; tr. XXVII, p. 35).

Ebn Sorayj's plea for equality between the Arabs and the neophytes, Iranian as well as Turkish, was perceived as Murji^ʾism (cf. Naṣr b. Sayyār's poem from the year 117, in Ṭabari II, p. 1576; tr. XXV, p. 114). This implied that the very act of belief undertaken by a convert entitled him to all the benefits enjoyed by a Muslim. Jahm is said to have developed the most minimal definition for this purpose: Belief is already achieved by knowing God in one's heart, without *eqrār*, i.e. without expressing it in correct Arabic speech. He may have done so out of political necessity; Ebn Sorayj had to collaborate with Soghdian or Turkish allies who were not able to pray in the language of the Qurʾān. In Ebn Sorayj's army he may have played the same role as did the *motakallemun* mentioned in connection with Abu Moslem's conquest of Marv (*Akḇār al-dawla al-ʿAbbāsiyya*, p. 310); people like him were obviously expected to explain how Ebn Sorayj's beliefs accorded with the Qurʾān and the Sunnah (Ṭabari II, p. 1567, tr. XXV, p. 105; p. 1571, tr. p. 109). His contemporaries, on the other hand, might have identified him as a popular story-teller and preacher (*qāṣṣ*); significantly, his opponent on the side of Naṣr b. Sayyār was Moqātel b. Solaymān, the famous Qurʾānic exegete (Ṭabari II, p. 1921; cf. *Taʾrik Baḡdād* XIII, p. 162). The authors of later doxographical works (e.g., Ašʿari, *Maqālāt*, p. 279 f.) present him as a systematic thinker who upheld a rigid determinism: God being the absolute Other directs everything, even the forces of nature and human will. This is why man's belief in God cannot be the result of a personal decision but is created and given by God himself. Since God is beyond all Being (*šayʾ*) He cannot be defined or recognized, and He has no attributes. If He reveals Himself to man in the Qurʾān He does so only in time, and if He knows all things and events He does so only insofar as He comes to know them when He creates them. This amounted to saying that God has no foreknowledge; but He is eternal: He is "the First and the Last" (Q. 57:3). The Creation is therefore only an interlude, and Paradise as well as Hell will not last forever.

Positioning this "system" in the development of Islamic theology presents considerable problems. We know of no earlier synthesis of this kind, and we are far from sure that anything that was later on subsumed under the term "Jahmiyya" derived from it. Jahm's concept of God could have been neo-Platonic; this would fit in well with Ḥarrān and the ideas of the Ṣābians who were living there. But it is also possible to explain him through Indian parallels. In a widespread though probably apocryphal report he is said to have had discussions with Buddhist monks (Sumaniyya); but everything that has been reported about him is refracted through later interpretations. The only original text we have from his hand, a quotation in Jāḥiẓ's *Manāqeb al-Tork* (*Rasāʾel*, ed. Hārun I, p. 82), deals with the relationship between Turks, Persians, and Byzantines; it attests to his interest in the history of the area where he lived. At Termeḏ, his doctrine survived for centuries (cf. Moqaddasi, *Aḥsan al-taqāsim* p. 323, and Esfarāʾeni, *al-Tabṣir fi'l-din*, ed. Kawṯari p. 97).

Bibliography: Primary sources. Anon., *Akḇār al-dawla al-ʿAbbāsiya wa-fihi Akḇār al-ʿAbbās wa-wuldih*, ed. ʿAbd al-ʿAziz al-Duri and ʿAbd- al-Jabbār al-Moṭṭalebi, Beirut, 1971. Abu Helāl al-ʿAskari, *Awāʾel*, ed. Moḥammad al-Meṣri and Walid Qaṣṣāb, Vol. II, Damascus 1976 (quoting Abu'l-Qāsem al-Kaʿbi al-Balḵi, pp. 126, 7 ff.) Abu'l-Ḥasan ʿAli b. Esmāʿil al-Ašʿari, *Maqālāt al-Islāmiyyin (Die Dogmatischen Lehren der Anhänger des Islam)* ed. H. Ritter, 3rd. printing, Wiesbaden, 1980. al-Jāḥiẓ, *Rasāʾel al-Jāḥeẓ*, ed. ʿAbd-al-Salām Moḥammad Hārun, 4 vols., Cairo, 1965-1979. Moḥammad b. Jarīr Ṭabarī, *Ketāb taʾrīḵ al-rosol wa'l-moluk*, ed. M. J. de Goeje et al., 15 vols., Leiden, 1879-1901; repr. Leiden, 1964; tr. by various scholars as *The History of al-Ṭabarī*, ed. Ehsan Yar-Shater, Albany, N.Y., 1985-. Abu Tammām, *K. al-Šajara*, in: W. Madelung and P. E. Walker, *An Ismaili Heresiography*, Leiden, 1998.

Secondary literature. Saleh Said Agha, "A Viewpoint of the Murji'a in the Umayyad Period: Evolution through Application," *Journal of Islamic Studies* 8/i, 1997, pp. 1-42. Idem, *The Revolution which Toppled the Umayyads*, Leiden, 2003. Ḵāled al-ʿAsali, *Jahm b. Ṣafwān wa-makānatuhu fi'l-fekr al-eslāmi*, Baghdad, 1965. J. van Ess, *Theologie und Gesellschaft im 2. und 3. Jh. Hidschra*, II, pp. 493-508; V, pp. 212-23, Berlin, 1992-97. R. M. Frank, "The Neoplatonism of Gahm Ibn Ṣafwān," *Le Muséon* 78, 1965, pp. 395-424. M. J. Kister, art. "al-Ḥariṯẖ b. Suraydj" in *EI*[2] III, pp. 223-24. W. Madelung, *Religious Trends in Early Islamic Iran*, Albany, 1988. F. W. Zimmermann: "The Origins of the So-Called 'Theology of Aristotle,'" in J. Kraye et al. eds., *Pseudo-Aristotle in the Middle Ages*, London, 1986, pp. 110-240.

(JOSEF VAN ESS)

JAHN, KARL EMIL OSKAR (b. Brno, 26 March 1906; d. Utrecht, 7 November 1985), Czech Orientalist who specialized in Central-Asian history, Persian historiography, and Turcology; he lived and worked in Czechoslovakia, Austria, Germany, and the Netherlands. His father's family originated from German Silesia and emigrated to the Austria-Hungarian Empire, first to Vienna and then to Brünn (or Brno, presently in the Czech Republic), where his father, Oskar Jahn, held the post of Oberfinanzrat—a high-ranking revenue officer. Karl Jahn started his academic education in chemistry at the University of Brno, but after one year he went to Prague where he took up art history, history, and archaeology. He then moved on to Oriental studies, taking Semitic and Arabic studies with Alfred Grohmann and Max Grünert, and Persian and Turkish with Jan Rypka (q.v. at *iranica.com*) and Max Grünert. He also developed a lively interest in Slavic languages and literatures, in particular Czech and Russian. In 1929 he continued his education at the University of Leipzig, where he studied Arabic with August Fischer, Assyriology with Heinrich Zimmern, and Hittitology with Johannes Friedrich, while Hans Summe introduced him to Arabic dialectology. In 1931, after his promotion in Prague on the thesis *Studien zur arabischen Epistologie* ('Studies on Arabic Epistology,' published in 1937), Jahn briefly studied in Berlin with the Iranologist Hans-Heinrich Schaeder and with Willy Bang, a specialist on Central Asian languages and history. His interest in the history of Central Asia was intensified through his meeting with Zeki Velidi Toğan (1890-1970)—a Turkish scholar who, as a political exile, studied at the University of Vienna and became a lifelong friend of Jahn.

Having first intended to write a history of the reign of Maḥmud Ḡāzān Khan (r. 1295-1304, q.v.), the zenith of the Il-khanid rule in Iran, Jahn soon realized that the most essential source, the *Jāmeʿ al-tawārik̲* (q.v.) written by the Il-khanid vizier Rašid-al-Din Fażl-Allāh (1247-1318, q.v.), had not yet been properly edited. From that moment onwards, philological research became the focus of his scholarship. His most important contribution to Persian, as well as to Central-Asian studies, was the edition and translation of parts of the monumental *Jāmeʿ al-tawārik̲*—a chronicle of the Mongol history and a world-history of an exceptionally wide scope. In 1934 Jahn visited Istanbul for the first time and worked in the manuscript collections of its libraries. His Habilitation, presented at the German University of Prague in 1938, was based on a critical edition of the section of the *Jāmeʿ al-tawārik̲* that deals with the reign of the Il-khan Maḥmud Ḡāzān. This work, accompanied by a summary of the contents in German, was printed in London in 1940 as a volume of the Gibb Memorial Series (Jahn, 1940), but it only came into the hands of the author after the end of World War II.

Having taught Turkish in Prague for a few years (1936-42), Jahn was appointed as an Assistant Librarian at the University Library of Halle in 1942. However, in 1943 he was drafted into the German army and sent to occupied Netherlands as an interpreter attached to the unit of Azerbaijanis who were set to work on German fortifications along the Dutch coast. During the final months of the war he went on a brief leave to Prague for an academic promotion, but on his return to the Netherlands in April 1945 he was unable to join his unit again. After the Germans capitulated, he came into contact with Orientalists at the University of Utrecht, and in 1948, thanks to the help of his Dutch colleagues, notably the Indologist Jan Gonda and the Leiden professor of Arabic, Johan Hendrik Kramers, Jahn was employed there as a teacher and, later, as an extraordinary professor of Turkish and Slavic languages. After the death of Kramers in 1951, Jahn was appointed extraordinary professor of Turkish at the University of Leiden in 1953, and was also charged with teaching Persian, while still continuing his assignments at the University of Utrecht.

For more than two decades Karl Jahn taught three different disciplines at the two Dutch universities. His classes covered an impressively wide range of subjects, including history of Central Asia from the earliest times until the reign of Timur and his successors, Persian historiography, reading Ottoman diplomatic documents, Islamic art and architecture, and nearly every Turkic language. During the 1960s he supervised the preparation of *History of Iranian Literature*, written by his former teacher, Jan Rypka, and other Iranologists in Czechoslovakia, of which two Czech editions (1956 and 1963) and one German (1959) had already been published. This English edition was based on the second, much enlarged Czech edition, and was printed by the Dutch publisher D. Reidel in Dordrecht in 1968. It very soon gained the status of the standard textbook for the remainder of the 20th century. One of its merits was that it made internationally accessible important contributions of Eastern European and modern Iranian scholars to the study of Persian literature.

In 1969 Jahn made his first journey to Persia to take part, as a guest of honor, in the symposium on the works of Rašid-al-Din Fażl-Allāh held at Tehran and Tabriz. The proceedings of this conference were jointly edited by Karl Jahn and John Andrew Boyle (*Rashīd Al-Dīn commemoration volume*). He visited the country again in 1971, when the 2500th anniversary of the Persian monarchy was celebrated. He traveled regularly to Turkey for the purpose of studying Persian and Turkish manuscripts there. As a Turcologist, he did much to promote the study of Central Asian culture—as one of the founders of the Permanent International Altaic Conference (1957); and, from 1955 until the end of his life, as the sole editor of the *Central Asiatic Journal*. In 1965 and 1967, he lectured as a guest professor at Istanbul University and was awarded the honorary membership of the Türk Tarih Kurumu (Turkish Historical Society). In 1979 he received the Indiana University Prize for Altaic Studies.

From 1969 onwards, Jahn would spend more and more of his time in Vienna, the city where he felt most at home. In 1973, after his retirement from the two Dutch professorships, he went to live in Vienna permanently. Already a few years earlier (1970), he had become a Corresponding Member of the Österreichische Akademie der Wissenschaften (Austrian Academy of Sciences)—the institution that published a series of his editions and translations of parts from Rašid-al-Din's world history (Jahn 1971, 1973, 1977, and 1980). At the same time, he held a guest professorship at the University of Vienna (1969-83). At the invitation of the Soviet Academy of Sciences, he traveled to Uzbekistan and visited Samarqand and Bukhara around 1980. In 1983 Karl Jahn returned to the Netherlands where he died two years later in Utrecht.

The variety of Jahn's teaching is also reflected in the range of subjects that he studied and about which he published. Special mention should be made of his contributions to Turcology, which include a volume on the eighteenth-century documents in the Austrian National Archive concerning the release of the slaves (*Türkische Freilassungserklärungen*, 1963). However, by far the major place among his scholarly works is occupied by the many books and articles he wrote about the great Persian historiographer of the Mongol period, Rašid-al-Din Fażl-Allāh, often nicknamed *ṭabib* ('doctor') after the profession he had had before entering the service of the Il-khans Ḡāzān and Uljāytu (qq.v.), and his universal history *Jāmeʿ al-tawāriḵ*.

At the beginning of his academic career Karl Jahn joined the efforts of several generations of scholars to make this major historical source accessible to modern historical research, and he continued to devote most of his working life to Rašid-al-Din. At first, he set himself the task of publishing the section of *Jāmeʿ al-tawāriḵ* which directly concerns the period of Rašid-al-Din's own career, and the period of Maḥmud Ḡāzān (r. 1295-1304), who ordered his vizier to write a history of the Mongol Empire up to and including his own reign. This work, which eventually became the first volume of the *Jāmeʿ al-tawārik*, is also known under the separate title *Tāriḵ-e mobārak-e Ḡāzāni*. The section published in the Gibb Memorial Series in 1940 contains the famous description of the measures envisaged under the rule of Ḡāzān to reform his realm into a well-organized Islamic state. Shortly afterwards, Jahn published another section of the same volume treating the Il-khans who immediately preceded Ḡāzān (Jahn, 1941 and 1957). During World War II, most of the copies of this edition, which had been printed in Vienna in 1941, were lost so that the book had to be reprinted after the war in 1957. In these early publications Jahn exhibited his great skill as a philologist, presenting the versions of the manuscripts he used comprehensively, and in a very accessible manner.

Having contributed significantly to the sources available to the historians of the Mongol period, Jahn turned his attention to the second volume of Rašid-al-Din's work, which is primarily of interest as a cultural document of an exceptional nature. It is the first truly universal history in the Islamic tradition, which also included the nations outside the boundaries of the Muslim world. In the publications of the Austrian Academy of Sciences appeared a series of books prepared by Jahn which contain the parts of this world history dealing with the history of China (1971), the Children of Israel (1972), the Francs (1977), and India (1980). The volume on India encompasses an interesting account on the life of Buddha, based on information Rašid-al-Din received in Tabriz from a Buddhist scholar. In addition to a full German translation with detailed commentary, each volume contains facsimiles of the most important manuscripts of Rašid-al-Din's work. These publications were accompanied by a number of monographic studies that appeared mostly as articles in the *Anzeiger* of the *Östereichische Akademie der Wissenschaften*. In these essays Jahn examined the sources used by Rašid-al-Din and emphasized the significance of this monumental work of Persian historiography.

Bibliography: Selected works: *History of Ghāzān Khān. Geschichte Ġāzān-Ḫān's aus dem Ta'rīh-i-Mubārak-i- Ġāzānī des Rašīd al-Dīn Faḍlallāh b. ʿImād al-Daula Abūl-Hair*, London, 1940 (E. J. W. Gibb Memorial New Series, XIV). *Ta'rīh-i-Mubārak-i-Ġāzānī des Rašīd al-Dīn Faḍl Allāh Abīl-Hair. Geschichte der Ilhāne Abāġā bis Gaihātū (1265-1295)*, Prague, 1941; repr. The Hague, 1957. *Türkische Freilassungserklärungen des 18. Jahrhunderts (1702-1776)*, Naples, 1963. "The still missing works of Rashīd al-Dīn," *Central Asiatic Journal* 9, 1964, pp. 113-22. *Rashīd al-Din's History of India: collected essays with facsimiles and indices*, The Hague, 1965 (reprints of articles published between 1956 and 1963). "Rashīd al-Dīn as World Historian," in *Yádnáme-ye Jan Rypka*, ed. J. Bečka, Prague, 1967, pp. 79-87. *Die Geschichte der Oġuzen des Rašīd ad-Dīn*, Vienna, 1969. *Rashīd Al-Dīn commemoration volume (1318-1968): to the memory of our friend and colleague A. Zeki Velidi Toğan (1890-1970)*, eds. J. A. Boyle and K. Jahn, Wiesbaden, 1970 (*Central Asiatic Journal* 14, 1970). "Paper currency in Iran. A contribution to the cultural and economic history of Iran in the Mongol Period," *Journal of Asian History* 4, 1970, pp. 101-35 (an extended version of an article in German, published in 1938). *Die Chinageschichte des Rašīd ad-Dīn*, Vienna, 1971. *Die Geschichte der Kinder Israels des Rašīd ad-Dīn*, Vienna, 1973. *Die Frankengeschichte des Rašīd ad-Dīn*, Vienna, 1977. *Die Indiengeschichte des Rašīd ad-Dīn*, Vienna, 1980.

Obituaries of Karl Jahn: Ilse Laude-Cirtautas, *Central Asiatic Journal* 30, 1986, pp. 1-6. Walther Heissig, *Der Islam* 64, 1987, pp. 4-5. Andreas Tietze, *Almanach der Österreichischen Akademie der Wissenschaften*, 136, Jahrgang (1986), Vienna, 1987, pp. 421-25.

(J. T. P. DE BRUIJN)

JAHROM, city and sub-province (*šahrestān*) in central Fārs Province, covering an area of 4,517 sq. km. The entire area includes four cities (Jahrom, Bāb Anār, Ḵāvarān, and Qoṭbābād), three districts (*baḵš*; Ḵafr, Kordiān, Simakān) and twelve rural districts (*dehestāns*; see Ṭufān, p. 45; Wezārat-e kešvar, p. 32). It is bounded by Shiraz sub-province to the north and northwest, the Fasā sub-province to the east, the Lārestān sub-province to the south, and the sub-provinces of Firuzābād and Qir o Kārzin to the west (Baḵtiāri, p. 137). In 1996 the population of Jahrom sub-province was 197,128 (Markaz-e āmār, p. 16).

The economy of Jahrom sub-province is based mainly on agriculture (using traditional and semi-mechanized methods), horticulture, and carpet weaving. The principal crops are dates and citrus fruit, which are produced in high volume and exported. Other crops include cotton, cereals, and tobacco (Sāzmān-e joḡrāfiāʾi, p. 36; Ṭufān, pp. 88, 110). The sub-province is also home to coal and white stone mines (Ṭufān, p. 89).

The city of Jahrom, the administrative center of the sub-province, is situated between 28° and 38' N and 33° and 53' E, on the road from Firuzābād and Lār to Fasā, and Dārāb (Jaʿfari, p. 353; Pāpoli Yazdi, p. 169). In 1996 the population of the city of Jahrom was 94,185 (Markaz-e āmār, p. 39)

Jahrom is mentioned in the *Kār-nāmag ī Ardašīr ī Bābakān* (6.18, ed. Ântia, pp. 62-63) as Zarham. It is probable that the word Zarham referred to green spaces, which, given the geographical position of Jahrom and its thriving agriculture, would be a fitting description. According to Aḥmad Kasravi (pp. 275-76, 280), the name "Jahrom" is derived from the same root as *gahrān*, a word used in the northern dialects of Iran, composed of the word *gah* (warmth) and the word *rān* (the suffix of place), and meaning a warm place or an area with a warm climate. It could also be surmised that the name of the area was initially Jarham (< Mid. Pers. Zarham), which transformed into Jahram by metathesis (Ebn Ḵordādbeh, p. 46; Yāqut, II, p. 167) and finally into Jahrom.

History. Ḥamd-Allāh Mostawfi has attributed the founding of Jahrom to Bahman b. Esfandiār (1915-19, p. 125, tr., p. 124), while Ferdowsi traces the history of Jahrom back to the Achaemenid period, mentioning the city in the story of Dārā – the last Kayanid king, who historically mirrors the Achaemenid king Darius III – and his battle against Alexander of Macedonia (*Šāh-nāma* VI, p. 392). Based on the information in the *Kār-nāmag* (ed. Ântia, p. 62), Jahrom must have been a thriving city ruled by a certain Mihrak Anōšagzātān towards the end of the Arsacid (q.v.) period in the early 3rd century CE. The temple of Āḏur Faranbāg (q.v.), one of the three major fire temples in the Sasanian period, in Kāriān in the nearby Lār, and the existence of Sasanian remains in the area point to the prosperity of the city during this period (Moṣṭafawi, pp. 86, 94, 314; Afsar and Musawi, p. 314). Jahrom is mentioned in the early Arabic geographies as a town in the district (*kura*) of Dārābgerd (q.v.; Ebn Ḵordādbeh, p. 46; Eṣṭaḵri, p. 107, tr. p. 127; Ebn Ḥawqal, p. 268; Ebn al-Faqih, p. 410)

Towards the end of Omar's caliphate and the beginning of the rule of Oṯmān (ca. 23/644), Jahrom was captured by an Arab army under Oṯmān b. Abi'l-ʿĀṣi (Balāḏori, p. 388; Ebn al-Aṯir, III, p. 40). Coins excavated in the Dārābgerd region indicate that, during the first century of Islamic rule, Jahrom was ruled by semi-independent local rulers who were appointed by Ummayyad local governors (*wāli*; Daryaee, 2002, pp. 75-77). Upon a high mountain top at about five leagues from Jahrom stood the fortress of Ḵorša, so called after the name of Ḵorša, the man who had been assigned as the local governor by the brother of Ḥajjāj b. Yusof, the then governor of the province. Relying on the impregnable position of the fortress, Ḵorša rebelled against Ḥajjāj, which was why no other governor was allowed to take possession of this fortress (Ebn al-Balḵi, p. 157; Mostawfi, 1915-19, p. 133, tr., p. 132; Ḥāfeẓ-e Abru, II, p. 150).

Jahrom is described by Arab geographers as a cultivated and economically robust town with a variety of industrial products including colorful and highly designed fabrics, flat-woven carpets (*gelim*; see CARPETS v), prayer rugs, and *zilu*s (flat cotton weavings, known as *zilu-ye jahromi*), which were exported to other areas; it was also known for its cotton and grain products (Eṣṭaḵri, p. 153; *Ḥodud al-ʿālam*, p. 135, tr. p. 129; Moqaddasi, p. 442; Ebn al-Balḵi, p. 131; Ḥāfeẓ-e Abru, II, p. 118). During this period Jahrom was considered one of the major industrial centers of Fārs Province (Daryaee, 2003, p. 46; Le Strange, p. 294). Jahrom is now best known for producing dates of excellent quality, but there is no mention of its date palm groves until the 18th century, when its dates are praised for quality by Majd-al-Din Ḥosayni Majdi (p. 795; Ṭufān, p. 106).

According to Abu Esḥāq Eṣṭaḵri (p. 139), in the 11th century the majority of Jahrom's population was Muʿtazilite. It was perhaps for this reason that Moqaddasi, who traveled to Fārs and wrote a detailed account of his observations, did not visit Jahrom and has not written much about the city in his travelogue (Schwartz, p. 103), mentioning only its exports to other areas. Fārs fell under the Buyids (q.v.) in 322/934, when ʿEmād-al-Dawla ʿAli (q.v.) captured Shiraz and made it the center of Buyid power in south, but with the rise of the Saljuqids the Buyid power began to decline. In 448/1056, Abu'l-ʿAbbās Fażluya b. Ḥasnuya, the chief of the Šabānkāra Kurds, rebelled against Abu Manṣur Fulād Sotun, the last Buyid amir of Fārs, defeating and imprisoning him in the fortress Pahan Dez, where he died (Šābānkāraʾi, pp. 94-95; Ebn Balḵi, p. 166; Mostawfi, 1970, p. 425; Ḡaffāri, p. 127; Ḥāfeẓ-e Abru, II, p. 118; Le Strange, p. 245). Fażluya was confirmed as ruler of Fārs by Alp Arslān (q.v.), but he rebelled in 464/1072 and took refuge in the Fortress Ḵorša. Alp Arslān dispatched an army under his vizier Neẓām-al-Molk, who captured the fortress after a brief siege (Ebn al-Balḵi, p. 166; Ḡaffāri, pp. 127-28). During the reign of Malekšāh, Jahrom was considered one of the crown prince's holdings (*mawājeb*; Ebn al-Balḵi, p. 131; Lambton, pp. 238-39).

Sources provide no significant information about the town and its dependencies in the following centuries until the rise of the Safavids, except that it was a medium-sized city with a hot climate and many dependencies (*tawābeʿ*), and got its water from running streams and subterranean channels (*kāriz*; Mostawfi, 1915-19, p. 125, tr., p. 124; Ḥāfeẓ-e Abru, II, p. 118). With the arrival of Europeans in the Persian Gulf and the establishment of trade with Europe following the rise of the Safavids, Jahrom, due to its location on a route from the Persian Gulf to Shiraz and further to Isfahan, once more became a notable town (Pohanka, pp. 302, 306; Ferrier, p. 476). Two caravanserais on this route were the Banāruba caravanserai, between Lār and Jahrom, and the Mut Ḵun caravanserai, between Jahrom and Shiraz (Kiāni, p. 207, 261). European travelers considered the road to Jahrom as one of the most difficult to traverse (Tavernier, p. 315; Gabriel, p. 367).

During the Safavid era, and particularly in the reign of Shah ʿAbbās I (r. 1587-1629), Jahrom was a part of the crown lands (*ḵāleṣa*; Roeherborn, tr., p. 178; Bāstāni Pārizi, p. 78) and did not escape unscathed during the violent turmoil following the fall of the Safavid dynasty and the Afghan occupation of Iran (Floor, tr., 1986, pp. 137-38; idem, tr., 1987, p. 49).

In 1275/1858-59 Mirzā ʿAli-Moḥammad Khan Qewām-al-Molk Širāzi was appointed the governor of Jahrom, the rural district (*boluk*) of Bidšahr, and Juyom of Abi Aḥmad. He brought the unruly tribes of Ḵamsa under his control, pacified the region, and took strong measures in the improvement of the living conditions (Fasāʾi, II, p. 967; Širvāni, p. 236). Authors in the Qajar period have described Jahrom as a township with two to three thousand households and numerous date palm groves. Moḥammad-Ḥasan Khan Eʿtemād-al-Salṭana (IV, p. 2309) estimated the number of town's households at 5,500. In the 19th century, the town was divided into ten neighborhoods. In 1255/1839, Moḥammad-Ḥasan Khan Jahromi, the local governor, built a wall fortified with towers around six of them, separating them from the other four out, which were left without a wall. The poet Mirzā Ḥabib Qāʾāni commemorated the event in one of his odes (*qaṣida*; Fasāʾi, II, pp. 1278-79). The construction of a bazaar, styled after Bāzār-e Wakil in Shiraz, is indicative of the region's robust economy during the Qajar period (Sahāmpur, pp. 37-38).

Jahrom is mentioned as the hometown of Bārbad (q.v.), the minstrel-poet of the court of the Sasanian king Khosrow II Parvēz (Šams-al-Din Rāzi, p. 200). This is contradicted by earlier sources, such as Eṣṭaḵri (p. 262), Ṯaʿālebi (p. 694), and Mostawfi (1915-19, p. 157, tr., p. 154), who say that Bārbad was from Marv, while Ferdinand Jusi (p. 63) mentions Nišāpur as his city of residence.

Bibliography: Karāmat-Allāh Afsar and Aḥmad Musawi, *Pāsdāri az āṯār-e bāstāni dar ʿaṣr-e Pahlavi*, Tehran, 1976. Saʿid Baḵtiāri, ed., *Aṭlas-e gitā-šenāsi: ostānhā-ye Irān*, Tehran, 2004. Aḥmad b. Yaḥyā Balāḏori, *Ketāb fotuḥ al-boldān*, ed. Michaël Jan de Goeje, Leiden, 1866; repr., Leiden, 1968. Moḥammad-Erāhom Bāstāni Pārizi, *Siāsat wa eqteṣād-e ʿaṣr-e ṣafawi*, Tehran, 1978. Touraj Daryaee, *The Fall of the Sāsānian Empire and the End of Late Antiquity: Continuity and Change in the Province of Persis*; tr. Manṣura Ettehādiya and Farahnāz Amirḵāni as *Soquṭ-e Sāsāniān: fātehin-e ḵāreji, moqāwamat-e dāḵeli, wa taṣwir-e pāyān-e jahān*, Tehran, 2002. Idem, *The History and Culture of Sasanians*; tr. Mehrdād Qodrati Dizaji as *Tāriḵ va farhang-e Sāsāni*, Tehran, 2003. Ebn al-Aṯir, *al-Kāmel fiʾl-taʾriḵ*, ed. C. J. Tornberg, 13 vols., Beirut, 1966. Ebn al-Balḵi, *Fārs-nāma*, ed. Guy Le Strange and Reynold A. Nicholson, Cambridge, 1921. Ebn al-Faqih Hamadāni, *al-Boldān*, ed. Yusof Hādi, Beirut, 1996. Ebn Ḥawqal, *Ketāb ṣurat al-arż*, ed. Johannes Hendrik Kramers, Leiden, 1938; repr., 1967; tr. Johannes Hendrik Kramers and Gaston Wiet as *Configuration de la terre*, 2 vols., Beirut, 1964-65. Ebn Ḵordādbeh, *Ketāb al-mamālek wa masālek*, ed. Michaël Jan de Goeje, Leiden, 1873, repr., 1967. Abu Esḥāq Ebrāhim Eṣṭaḵri, *Ketāb masālek al-mamālek*, ed., Michaël Jan De Goeje, Leiden, 1967; tr. Moḥammad b. Asʿad Tostari as *Masālek wa mamālek*, ed. Iraj Afšār, Tehran, 1974. Moḥammad-Ḥasan Khan Eʿtemād al-Salṭana, *Merʾāt al-boldān*, ed. ʿAbd-al-Ḥosayn Navāʾi and Mir-Hāšem Moḥaddeṯ, Tehran, 1989. Mirzā Ḥasan Fasāʾi, *Fārs-nāma-ye nāṣeri*, ed. Manṣur Rastgār Fasāʾi, 2 vols., Tehran, 1988, II, 1277-78. Abu'l-Qāsem Ferdowsi, *Šāh-nāma*, ed. Evagniĭ E. Bertel's et al., 9 vols., Moscow, 1960-71. Ronald Ferrier, "Trade From the Mid-14th Century to the End of the Safavid Period," in *Cambridge History of Iran* VI, ed. Peter Jackson, Cambridge, 1986, pp. 412-90. Willem Floor, "The Revolt of Shaikh Ahmad Madani in Laristan and the Garmsirat (1730-1733)," *Studia Iranica* 8, 1983, pp. 63-93; tr. Abu'l-Qāsem Serri, "Šureš-e Šayḵ Aḥmad Madani," in idem, *Jostārhāʾ-i az tāriḵ-e Irān* 9, Tehran, 1986. Idem, *The Afghan Occupation of Persia, 1722-1730*, Paris, 1998; tr. Abu'l-Qāsem Serri, *Bar oftādan-e Ṣafaviān, bar āmadan-e Maḥmud-e Afḡan: rewāyat-e šāhedān-e holandi*, Tehran, 1987 (according to the author it was translated from a manuscript before the original version was published later in 1998). Alfonse Gabriel, *Die Erforschung Persien: Die Entwicklung der abendländischen Kenntnis der Geographie Persiens*, Vienna, 1954; tr. Fatḥ-ʿAli Ḵᵛājanuri as *Taḥqiqāt-e joḡrafiāʾi rājeʿ ba Irān*, Tehran, 1969. Qāżi Aḥmad Ḡaffāri, *Tāriḵ-e jahānārā*, Tehran, 1964. Ḥāfeẓ-e Abru, *Joḡrāfiā*, ed. Ṣādeq Sajjādi, 3 vols., Tehran, 1999. *Ḥodud al-ʿālam*, ed. Manoučehr Sotuda, Tehran, 1962; tr. with commentary Vladmir Minorsky, London, 1937. ʿAbbās Jaʿfari, *Gitā-šenasi-e Irān: daʾerat al-maʿāref-e joḡrāfiāʾi-e Irān*, Tehran, 1963. Ferdinand Justi, *Iranisches namenbuch*, Marburg, 1895; repr. Hildesheim, 1963. *Kār-nāmag i Ardašir i Bābakān*, ed. and tr. Edalji Kersâspji Ântia, as *Kârnâmak Artakhshîr Pâpakân: The Original Pahlavi Text, with Translation in Avesta Characters, Translations into English and Gujarati, and Selections from the Shâhnâmeh*, Bombay, 1900; ed. and tr. Bahrām Farahvaši as *Kār-nāma-ye Ardašir-e Bābakān*, Tehran, 1975. Aḥmad Kasravi, *Kārvand-e Kasravi*, ed. Yaḥyā Ḏokāʾ, Tehran, 1973. Moḥammad-Yusof Kiāni and Wolfram Kleiss, *Kārvānsarāhā-ye Irān/ Iranian Caravansarais*, Tehran, 1994. A. K. S. Lambton, "The Internal Structure of the Saljuq Empire," in *Cambridge History of Iran* V, ed. John A. Boyle, Cambridge, 1968. Guy Le Strange, *The Lands of the Eastern Caliphate*, London, 1966; tr. Maḥmud

ʿErfān as *Sarzaminhā-ye ḵelāfat-e šarqi*, Tehran, 1958. Majd-al-Din Moḥammad Ḥosayni Majdi, *Zinat al-majāles*, Tehran, 1983. Markaz-e āmār-e Irān, *Saršomāri-e nofus o maskan, 1375* (Census of Population and Housing, 1996) *Natāyej-e tafṣili-e šahrestān-e Jahrom* (Census Report of Jahrom Sub-Province), Tehran, 1997. Abu ʿAbd-Allāh Moḥammad Moqaddasi, *Aḥsan al-taqāsim fi maʿrefat al-aqālim*, ed. Michaël Jan De Goeje, Leiden, 1906, repr., 1967. Moḥammad-Taqi Moṣṭafawi, *Eqlim-e pārs: āṯār-e tāriḵi wa amāken-e bāstāni-e Fārs*, Tehran, 1964. Ḥamd-Allāh Mostawfi, *Nozhat al-qolub*, ed. and tr. Guy Le Strange as *The Geographical Part of the Nuzhat-al-qulūb*, 2 vols., Leiden and London, 1915-19. Idem, *Tāriḵ-e gozida*, ed. ʿAbd-al-Ḥosayn Navāʾi, Tehran, 1970. Moḥammad-Ḥosayn Pāpoli Yazdi, *Farhang-e ābādihā wa makānhā-ye maḏhabi-e kešvar*, Mašhad, 1988. Reinhard Pohanka, "Karavanenweg und Karavanserails in Laristan: Die Strassenabschnitte Lar – Djahrom, Lar – Khung und Lar – Bastak," *AMI* 17, Berlin, 1984, pp. 258-308. Šams-al-Din Moḥammad b. Qays Rāzi, *al-Moʿjam fi maʿāyir ašʿār al-ʿajam*, ed. Moḥammad Qazvini and Moḥammad-Taqi Modarres Rażawi, Tehran, 1948. Klaus Michel Roehrborn, *Provinzen und Zentralgewalt Persiens im 16. und 17. Jahrhunder*, Berlin, 1966; tr. Kaykāvus Jahāndāri as *Neẓām-e eyālāt dar dawra-ye Ṣafawiya*, Tehran, 1970. Moḥammad b. ʿAli Šabānkāraʾi, *Majmaʿ al-ansāb*, ed. Mir-Hāšem Moḥaddeṯ, Tehran, 1984. Hušang Sahāmpur, *Tāriḵča-ye ilāt wa ʿašāyer-e ʿarab-e ḵamsa-ye Fārs*, Shiraz, 1998. Sāzmān-e joḡrāfiāʾi-e niruhā-ye mosallaḥ, *Farhang-e joḡrāfiāʾi: ābādihā-ye kešvar-e Jomhuri-e eslāmi-e Irān* CXII, Tehran, 1990. Paul Schwartz, *Iran im Mittelalter nach den arabischen Geographen*, Leipzig, 1896-35; repr., 9 vols. in 4, Frankfurt on the Main, 1993; tr. Kaykāvus Jahāndāri as *Joḡrāfia-ye tāriḵi-e Fārs*, Tehran, 1993. Mast-ʿAlišāh Zayn-al-ʿĀbedin Širvāni, *Bostān al-siāḥa*, ed. ʿAbd-Allāh Mostawfi, Tehran, 1897-98. Abu Manṣur ʿAbd-al-Malek Ṯaʿālebi, *Ḡorar aḵbār moluk al-fors*, ed. and tr. Hermann Zotenberg as *Histoir des rois des Perses*, Paris, 1900. Jean-Baptiste Tavernier, *Voyages en Perse et description de ce royaume par Jean-Baptiste Tavernier, marchand français*, Paris, 1930. Jalāl Ṭufān, *Šahrestān-e Jahrom*, šāmel-e eṭṭelāʿāt-e joḡrāfiāʾi, tāriḵi, eqteṣādi, ejtemāʿi wa folklori-e Jahrom wa tawābeʿ-e ān, Shiraz, 2001. Wezārat-e kešvar, *Našriya-ye ʿanāṣer wa wāḥedhā-ye taqsimāt-e kešvari*, Tehran, 2005. Šehāb-al-Din Abu ʿAbd-Allāh Yāqut Ḥamawi, *Moʿjam al-boldān*, 5 vols., Beirut, 1955-57.

(Shiva Jaʿfari)

JAIPUR, city in northwestern India, founded in 1727 by the Kachhwaha prince (raja) and Mughal officer Sawai Jai Singh Kachhwaha (1688-1743), as his state began to slowly distance themselves from the Mughals with whom they had been close allies. Without Mughal permission Sawai Jai Singh was able to take control of considerable lands adjacent to his capital, thus bolstering his basis of power. The name of the city reflects its patron's status (in Hindi and Urdu Jaipur means City of Victory and City of Jai [Singh Kachhwaha), and it is another sign of his state's increasing distance from the Mughals. In spite of this, Sawai Jai Singh continued to perform loyal service as a high-ranking military officer who was frequently consulted for his sound opinions by both the Mughals and other Rajput princes.

The new Kachhwaha capital, Jaipur, replaced the older one of Amber which was ten kilometers to the south. Jaipur is located in eastern Rajasthan, and today it is the capital of the modern Rajasthan state. Probably inspired by the broad avenues of Isfahan and Shahjahanabad (Šāhjahānābād, Delhi), Jaipur was a completely planned and walled city based on a grid plan possibly inspired by Indic Shastric texts (Erdman, pp. 220-21). The city's main streets were broad enough for six elephants abreast to traverse them, thus making it ideal for processions. Jai Singh and his successors would often process in a chariot or on the back of an elephant to visit temples or to celebrate festivals (Bhatnagar, pp. 339-40), giving his subjects the auspicious opportunity to behold him, a particularly Indic concept known as *darshan* that had been adopted earlier by the Mughals. The visual impact of these royal processions was guaranteed for Sawai Jai Singh mandated uniformity in the city's architecture. Although today Jaipur's buildings are painted pink and it is often described as the Pink City, until the late 19th century the city had a uniform cream color (Roy, p. 80). Against this bland background the raja and his bejeweled entourage were the focus of attention.

Jaipur's uniformity was further enhanced by the introduction of a new temple type. Earlier temples in the area, including those at Amber, featured high towering superstructures. Beginning in about 1730 with the construction of Jaipur's most important temple, the Govinda Deva (PLATE I), a new temple type evolved that was modeled on a flat-roofed Mughal Public Audience Hall (Asher, p. 74). This flat-roofed pillared audience hall had originally been inspired by the pillared halls of Persepolis (Koch, p. 148). Over time, Sawai Jai Singh considered the god Govinda Deva to be the true ruler of Jaipur and regarded himself, the king, only as the god's prime minister (Bahura, p. 67). The new Govinda Deva temple reflected the god's new role as Jaipur's ruler. This temple then was the model for all Jaipur's temples, both Hindu and Jain, because of its simplicity. The adoption of a standard style for temple architecture further enhanced the city's uniformity ultimately enhancing the king during processions.

Sawai Jai Singh was a righteous (dharmic) ruler who supported Indic institutions, but at the same time he continued to serve the Mughal emperor loyally. He wanted to create a city which would be inhabited by a variety of peoples practicing multiple professions to ensure its economic well-being. Sawai Jai Singh issued invitations to Hindus, Muslims, Jains, and Sikhs to relocate to Jaipur to practice their professions, crafts, and skills. Among them were Muslim musicians, paper makers, cloth printers, and

PLATE I

Govinda Deva Temple, c. 1730.
Courtesy of Sawai Pratap Singh, Jaipur.

PLATE II

Hawa Mahal, 1799.
Courtesy of Sawai Pratap Singh, Jaipur.

soldiers, Hindu and Jain scholars and businessmen, and Sikhs who specialized in enameled gold jewelry. As these people and their families came to Jaipur, land was provided for housing, and they were instructed on the required appearance to ensure a sense of homogeneity (Roy, pp. 51-52).

The palace, first erected by Sawai Jai Singh and later expanded by subsequent rajas, was located in the center of the city. Like Mughal and other Islamic palaces, the king's residence, known today as the City Palace, consisted of multiple courtyards with buildings on all four sides. Today the courtyards are paved with cement, but originally they must have been planted with gardens, as are those at Amber and at the Mughal palaces both of which served as sources of inspiration for the Jaipur palace. The complex is large and roughly can be divided into three sections. One is the large terraced Mughal-inspired garden containing the Govinda Deva temple, the second is the administrative and residential section, and the third is an area accommodating the observatory (commonly known as Jantar Mantar, from *yantra mantra*, 'chanting instrument') built by Sawai Jai Singh. The most famous of the residential buildings is known as the Hawa Mahal (*Havā Maḥall*, 'palace of air') built in 1799 by Maharaja Sawai Pratap Singh. It was built as a viewing platform for the court's harem, so that the ladies could watch Jaipur's many processions, and over time it has become a symbol of the city (PLATE II).

Sawai Jai Singh had a passionate interest in astronomy and, inspired by Ulugh Beg's (1394-1449) astronomical observations and tables (*zij*), he wrote the *Zij-e Moḥammad-Šāhi* (Sharma, p. 241) and built an observatory in Jaipur with enormous instruments for observing and calculating celestial phenomena (PLATE III). Scholars are often perplexed as to his motivation in building observatories (he constructed several of them in Delhi, Jaipur, Ujjain, and Varanasi or Benares), but it must have been intimately linked to his interest and performance of Hindu ritual rites and sacrifices where precise timing of conjunctions of certain planets in the commencement of such ritual is paramount. Among other Vedic rites, Sawai Jai Singh twice performed the Ashvameda (horse sacrifice), a Vedic ritual that could only be performed by a great king and had not been practiced since the 9th century.

PLATE III

Jantar Mantar Observatory, 1728-34.
Courtesy of Sawai Pratap Singh, Jaipur.

Sawai Jai Singh, the founder of Jaipur, was aware of both the Persianate and Indic cultural trends and established the city in both traditions. His successors continued many of these traditions until the discontinuation of the Kachhwaha royal house in 1949. Since the middle of the 19th century the city has spread far outside its original walls, and nowadays it features notable religious, educational, health care, and cultural institutions. In the early 2000s the population of Jaipur was about 2.7 millions of people.

Bibliography: Catherine B. Asher, "Amber and Jaipur: Temples in a Changing State," in *Stones in the Sand: The Architecture of Rajasthan*, ed. G. Tillotson, Mumbai, 2001, pp. 68-77. G. N. Bahura, *The Literary Heritage of the Rulers of Amber and Jaipur*, Jaipur, 1976.

Joan L. Erdman, "Jaipur: City Planning in 18th Century India," in *Shastric Traditions in Indian Arts*, ed. A. L. Dallapiccola, Stuttgart, 1989, vol. I, pp. 219-33. Monika Horstmann, *In Favour of Govinddevji: Historical Documents Relating to a Deity of Vrindaban and Eastern Rajasthan*, New Delhi, 1999. Ebba Koch, "Diwan-i 'Amm and Chihil Sutun: The Audience Halls of Shah Jahan," *Muqarnas* 11, 1995, pp. 153-65. Asim Kumar Roy, *History of the Jaipur City*, New Delhi, 1978. Virendra Nath Sharma, *Sawai Jai Singh and His Astronomy*, Delhi, 1995. G. H. R. Tillotson, *The Rajput Palaces: The Development of an Architectural Style, 1450-1750*, New Haven and London, 1987.

(CATHERINE B. ASHER)

JĀJARMI, MOḤAMMAD B. BADR, Persian poet and anthologist. His father Malek-al-Šoʿarāʾ Badr-al-Din ʿOmar Jājarmi (d. 686/1287; q.v.), a poet from Jājarm, a small town in the district of Jovayn in Khorasan, had moved to Isfahan. There, Badr-al-Din entered the services of Ḵᵛāja Bahāʾ-al-Din Moḥammed b. Šams-al-Din Jovayni (q.v.), the governor of Isfahan and ʿErāq-e ʿAjam in the Il-khanid kingdom.

Moḥammed was a poet himself, but his fame rests only on his *Moʾnes al-aḥrār fi daqāʾeq al-ašʿār* ("The Free Men's Companion to the Niceties of Poems"), a voluminous anthology which is his only surviving work and the only source about his life. In the *Moʾnes* he includes eight of his own poems, none of which can be dated from before the death of the Il-khanid Abu Saʿid (q.v.) in 736/1335 (Morton, in Swietochowski and Carboni, p. 49).

At the beginning of the 20th century, the art dealer Hagop Kevorkian (see below) acquired an incomplete illustrated autographed copy of this anthology, dated Ramadan 741/February-March 1341. Morton (in Swietochowski and Carboni, p. 51) convincingly argued that the manuscript was written and illustrated in Isfahan.

The *Moʾnes al-aḥrār* is divided into thirty chapters (*bāb*), according to criteria of form or content, and begins, like thematically arranged *divān*s, with chapters containing poems devoted to praises of God and the Prophet and those of ethical content. The majority of the chapters contain almost exclusively *qaṣida*s, while separate chapters are devoted to strophic poems (*mosammaṭāt* and *tarjiʿāt*, respectively), "fragments" (*moqaṭṭaʿāt*), *ḡazal*s, *robāʿi*s, and isolated single verses (*fardiyāt*).

Most of the chapters containing *qaṣida*s are concerned with devices that would appear rather frivolous in the view of modern critics and hardly include first-rate poems (e.g., the chapter on *maṣnuʿāt* "artificial poems," containing, amongst others, poems which have a different figure of style in each verse, or which can be scanned in more than one meter). Fortunately, the subject of some chapters is general to the point of being all-inclusive, such as those on *tašbihāt*, "poems containing similes" (I, pp. 214-369), *ašʿār-e moqaffā*, "rhyming poems" (II, pp. 453-663), and *ašʿār-e moraddaf*, poems with *radif* (II, pp. 664-778). These chapters contain also by far the most *qaṣida*s, and very beautiful ones among them (e.g., several by Anwari and two prison poems [*ḥabsiyāt*] by Masʿud-e Saʿd). The order of the poems within these chapters is mainly associative. Poems follow one another because of a common rhyme, meter, or theme, and thus this anthology is an ideal source for a study of the phenomenon of *naẓira*. Jājarmi includes few poets from the earliest period (e.g., Daqiqi and Rudaki are represented by only a single *qaṣida* each). Likewise, the poets attached to the court of the early Ghaznavids (e.g., ʿOnṣori, Farroḵi and Manučehri) are represented by only one or two *qaṣida*s each. Poets from the Saljuq period fare a little better, but unevenly (Anwari and Ẓahir-al-Din Fāryābi [qq.v.] get much more attention than Ḵāqāni Šarvāni, for example). The *Moʾnes al-aḥrār*, however, is particularly rich in *qaṣida*s of some 13th-century poets, such as Kamāl-al-Din Esmāʿil Eṣfahāni, Šams-al-Din Moḥammad Ṭabasi, Najib-al-Din Jorbādaqāni, Rafiʿ-al-Din Lonbāni (the younger), and Farid-al-Din Aḥwal. Understandably, Jājarmi pays much attention to poets attached to the Il-khans and their entourage like his own father, Badr-al- Din, and Saʿid Heravi.

The chapter on the *ḡazal* (II, pp. 952-1133), containing nearly three hundred poems by more than a hundred poets (most of them known only because of the *Moʾnes*), gives us a picture not entirely in keeping with modern critical consensus. There are, curiously enough, only three *ḡazal*s by Farid-al-Din ʿAṭṭār (q.v.), and five by Jalāl-al-Din Moḥammad Balḵi Rumi; the latter's contemporary, Saʿdi, however, is better served with sixteen *ḡazal*s. Jājarmi includes many poets who were his (near)-contemporaries when they had some connections with the Il-khans, such as Awḥadi Marāḡaʾi (q.v.), and, most of all, Ḵᵛāju Kermāni, who are represented with sixteen and nineteen *ḡazal*s, respectively. On the other hand, Amir Ḵosrow Dehlavi (q.v.), who had lived in far-away India and died there less than two decades before the composition of *Moʾnes al-aḥrār*, appears to have been unknown to Jājarmi. Ḥāfez (q.v.), still in his teens, had yet to enter the stage.

The chapter on the *robāʿi* (II, pp. 1134-1216) is divided into thirty-five sections (*faṣl*s), with quatrains that are either thematically related, share the same figure of style, or are considered to be by the same author, like those by Mahsati (the collection has been used by Fr. Meier, pp. 117-18), or ʿOmar Ḵayyām (thirteen *robāʿi*s, published as an appendix by Fr. Rosen to his edition of *Robāʿiyāt*).

One short chapter (II, pp. 841-60) is devoted entirely to selections from the *Šāh-nāma*; it contains no narrative passages, but primarily ethical and panegyrical ones. Others deal with light verse and facetiae (*hazliyāt, moṭāyabāt*), divination based on the twitching of a part of the body (*eḵtelāj*; poems by the author's father), and riddles. Chapter 29, known well to art-historians, contains two fully illustrated didactic works.

The first, *ašʿār-e moṣawwar*, under the name of Ostād Moḥammad Rāvandi, is to be considered, as has been demonstrated by Morton, as a riddle of which the illustrations give the clue. The second, *eḵtiārāt-e qamar*, by Badr-al-Din Jājarmi, a poem on ascertaining the (in)auspiciousness of the different lunar months, consists of a suite of quatrains with a short introduction in *ramal* (II, pp. 1217-21; Morton, in Swietochowski and Carboni, pp. 54-57).

Even if the *Moʾnes al-aḥrār* offers a rather idiosyncratic choice of poems (the extensive quoting of his own father is an example), it gives an idea of what was known and loved in Isfahan at the time. Moreover, it is an important source because, unlike most works belonging to the *tadkera*-genre, it gives the full text of all the poems (although no particulars on the authors) instead of excerpts. Of many of the poets mentioned here no manuscript of a *divān* older than this autograph is extant.

There seems to be no information about precisely where and when Kevorkian acquired the autographed copy of the *Moʾnes al-aḥrār*. Six of the eight illustrated folios (that is, not the frontispiece, but all those making up chapter 29) were detached, and purchased by public collections in the United States (details in Carboni, in Swietochowski and Carboni, p. 9). The rest of the manuscript was sold in 1979, at Sotheby's in London, and is now in the Dār-al-aṯār al-Eslāmiya in Kuwait (LNS 9 MS). In all probability the manuscript was not well known in the centuries after its completion and may have been part of a private collection during a long period. Apparently, no *tadkera* earlier than the mid-19th-century *Majmaʿ al-foṣaḥā* by Reżāqoli Khan Hedāyat mentioned it explicitly (author's Introd., p. xi). When Kevorkian acquired the autograph copy, it was bound together both with a full index of all the poems it should have contained, and thirty-five pages of poems missing in the autograph copy (even so the text was not complete). He offered the non-autograph part of the manuscript to the Persian scholar Moḥammad Qazvini (q.v.), who bequeathed it to the University Library in Tehran. Moḥammad-Taqi Dānešpažuh dated it from the 17th century, which would make it older than all the other manuscripts (pp. 504-6, MS no. 144b; full text of Qazvini's note on the provenance and the value of these pages, Jājarmi, I, pp. *yā-kāf*).

The published text edited by Mir Ṣāleḥ Ṭabibi is based not only on various manuscripts (none of which is older than the 18th century, except for the autographed copy and the pages mentioned above), but also on other material: an untitled anthology dated 1021/1612 which itself heavily depends on the *Moʾnes* (II, pp. iii-iv), and both the published and unpublished *divāns* of the poets. The complete index which had been bound together with the autograph provided the information about the poems originally included. Curiously enough, whenever the editor was unable to find the complete text of the original poem, he added another poem by the same poet (on this procedure, Jājarmi, II, pp.vi-vii; examples a.o. II, pp. 795, 960, 961).

At least one more anthology, titled *Daqāʾeq al-ašʿār* by a certain ʿAbd al-Wahhāb Dawlatābādi, which is not dated, is dependent on the *Moʾnes* (Bodleian library, Elliot 37, Cat. Sachau/Ethé 1333: presumably 18th century; for the relation between the two texts, see Dānešpažuh, p. 505; Monzawi, *Noskahā* IV, pp. 2813, 3249; Storey/de Blois, V/2, p. 437, n. 3). Another anthology titled *Mo'nes al-aḥrār*, composed in 702/1302 by a certain Laṭif al-Din Kalāmi (or Kalāti), has been considered as the original version of Jājarmi's text; this was disproved later on (Nafisi, *Naẓm o naṯr*, I, pp. 176, 204; Jājarmi, II, pp. v-vi).

Bibliography: Arthur J. Arberry, "Handlist of Islamic Manuscripts Acquired by the India Office Library 1936-38," *JRAS*, 1939, no. 4600, pp. 380-81. Taqi Bineš, "*Moʾnes al-aḥrār fi daqāʾeq al-ašʿār*," *Rāhnemā-ye ketāb* 2/5, 1960, pp. 713-16; 16/4-6, 1973, pp. 265-74 (reviews of Ṭabibi's edition). Hugo Buchthal, Otto Kurz, and Richard Ettinghausen, "Supplementary Notes to K. Holter's Check List of Islamic Illustrated Manuscripts before AD 1350," in *Ars Islamica* 7, 1940, no. 48, p. 155. Stefano Carboni, "The Muʾnis al-Ahrar Manuscript in the al-Sabah Collection, Illustrated Poetry for a Princely Patron," in *The Newsletter of Dar al-Athar al- Islamiyyah* 6, Fall 1997, pp. 14-16. *Catalogue of Important Oriental Manuscripts and Miniatures the Property of the Hagop Kevorkian Fund (. . .) which Will be Sold by Auction by Sotheby . . . London (. . .) 23rd April, 1979*, no. 144, pp. 84-87. Moḥammad-Taqi Dānešpažuh, *Fehrest-e noskahā-ye kaṭṭi-e Ketābkāna-ye dāneškada-ye adabiyāt*, MDAT 8/1, Tehran, 1960. J. T. P. de Bruijn, "Djādjarmī," in *EI*², Suppl. (with bibl., read K. Holter for K. Hilter), pp. 235-36. *Exhibition of the Kevorkian Collection (. . .) Exhibited at the Galleries of Charles of London*, New York, March-April 1914, nos. 68 and 264. Reżāqoli Khan Hedāyat, *Majmaʿ al-foṣaḥāʾ*, ed. Mażāher Moṣaffā, Tehran, 1957-61. Kurt Holter, "Die islamischen Miniaturhandschriften vor 1350," in *Zentralblatt für Bibliothekswesen*, Leipzig, 1937, no. 48, p. 19. Moḥammad b. Badr-al-Din Jājarmi, *Moʾnes al-aḥrār fi daqāʾeq al-ašʿār*, ed. Mir Ṣāleḥ Ṭabibi, 2 vols., Tehran 1959-71.

Georges Marteau and Henri Vever, *Miniatures persanes: tirées des collections de MM. Henry d'Allemagne, Claude Anet . . . exposées au Musée des Arts Décoratifs*, Paris 1913, pl. xlix, fig. 55. Fritz Meier, *Die Schöne Mahsatī: Ein Beitrag zur Geschichte des persischen Vierzeilers* I, Wiesbaden, 1963. Aḥmad Monzawi, *Noskahā* IV, pp. 3249-50. Sa'id Nafisi, *Naẓm o naṯr*, Moḥammad Qazvini, "*Moʾnes al-aḥrār*," in idem, *Bist maqāla-ye Qazvini*, 2 vols., ed. ʿAbbās Eqbāl, Tehran, 1928-34, II, pp. 138-55; 2nd ed., Tehran, 1954, II, pp. 184-206. repr. in the edition of the *Moʾnes al-aḥrār* I, Introd., pp. *bā-yā*. Idem, "An Account of the *Muʾnisuʾl-ahrar*: A Rare Persian MS. Belonging to Mr. H. Kevorkian," *BSO(A)S* 5, 1928-30, pp. 97-108 (not a translation of his Persian article). Friedrick Rosen, *Robāʿiyāt-e Ḥakīm ʿOmar Kayyām*, Berlin, 1925. Eduard Sachau and Hermann Ethé, *Catalogue of the Persian . . . Manuscripts in the Bodleian Library* I, Oxford, 1889. Storey/de Blois, V. Marie Lukens Swietochowski and Stefani Carboni (with essays by A. H. Morton and Tomoko Masuya), *Illustrated Poetry and Epic Images: Persian Painting of the 1330s and 1340s*, New York, 1994 (contains photographs and a discussion of all the miniatures in the autograph, as well as the text and translation of the poems they illustrate).

(ANNA LIVIA BEELAERT)

JĀJRUD, a major river of the southern slopes of central Alborz (q.v.) in the Central Plateau (140 km. long, basin of 1890 km^2), running from the mountains of Šamirānāt at Rudbār-e Qaṣrān to the plain of Varāmin and eventually joins the salt lake of Qom (Daryāča-ye Qom), at about 89 km to the northwest of the city.

The name of Jājrud is mentioned as Jāyejrud (lit. the river of Jāyej, a village in the Lavāsān district; Razmārā, I, p. 50) in the 14th century by Ḥamd-Allāh Mostawfi as "a river rising from Mount Damāvand and flowing through the province (*welāyat*) of Rey . . ." (Mostawfi, I, p. 312, II, p. 312). In the next century, it is already referred to as Jājrud by Ẓahir-al-Din Marʿaši (p. 154). Under the Qajars, the name Jājrud was better known as the royal hunting ground near Qaṣr-e Firuza east of Tehran, where Fatḥ-ʿAli Shah and Nāṣer-al-Din Shah had each built a royal residence (Eʿtemād-al-Salṭana, 1989a, p. 86; idem, 1989b, s.v. Jājrud). Numerous travelers going to Tehran by the roads of Harāz or Firuzkuh have mentioned this river, which they used to cross at Pol-e Jājrud, two leagues (*farsaḵ*) before reaching the capital city.

With an average annual discharge of 317 million cubic meters at Latiān, Jājrud is the second major river of Southern Alborz, after the river of Karaj. The annual discharge is very irregular, for instance, fluctuating from 127 million m^3 in 1969 to 731 million in 1969; the seasonal variations are even wider, with 61 percent of the discharge in spring, due to the heavy rainfalls and the melting of the snow. According to Moḥammad-Ḥasan Khan Eʿtemād-al-Salṭana (1989b, s.v. Jājrud), the meaning of Jājrud "is "the angry river," which can probably be explained by its rapid flow and the casualties caused by the spring floods when the flow reaches 130 m^3 per second, while the average is only 9.3 m^3 per second. The amount of sediments transported by the rapid flow of this strong river is very high, making the lands irrigated by it quite fertile but, at the same time, causing serious erosions in the highlands of the upper valley (Ehlers, p. 120; Kayhān, I, p. 87).

The Latiān Dam, built in 1967 (altitude 1610m., 110m. high, ca. 35 km NE of Tehran) with the original capacity of 95 millions m^3, cannot store the largest part of the water of Jājrud that flows down and reaches the central desert (*kavir*) during major spring floods. This medium size dam provides the city of Tehran with 80 million m^3 of piped water through an 11-km. long tunnel, which since 1990 has also been the conduit of the water coming from the dam of Lār. A small power station below the dam provides electricity. Four small villages, including Latiān, were destroyed by the dam's lake (4 km long), where now numerous migratory birds rest near the villages of Laškarak and Galanduak and the new city of Lāvasān.

The watercourse of Jājrud can be divided into three parts. The Upper Jājrud valley (45 km long, 692 km^2) above the Latiān Dam, where two main streams join at Fašam (altitude 1920m); they come from mountains of more than 4000m. high above the ski resort of Šemšak (Kolumbastak, Dizin Pass) and the village of Garmābdar and the pass of Qātumbārgāh. It joins the river of Āhār (annual discharge of 20 million m^3) at Ušān (altitude 1850m.) and near the Latiān Dam connects with the Lāvorak River (Ḵizrudbār River in Jaʿfari, 1997) coming from Lavāsān (annual discharge of 35 million m^3). The narrow mountainous valley of Jājrud has numerous old villages, where people used to have large flocks of sheep and cultivate rich orchards of apples (see Hourcade, 1975; Lambton, pp. 213, 250). The rural district (*dehestān*) of Rudbār-e Qaṣrān (*šahrestān* "provincial district" of Šamirānāt) is well known in history as the mountainous region of Rey (see Karimān, II, pp. 566-67, 601) and has now become a very popular and crowded summer resort (*yeylāq*) of Tehran, with numerous villas and restaurants and a picnic place along the river bank (Hourcade, 1975, 1976, 1978). The former villages of Fašam, Ušān, and Meygun are now cities, and, near the lake formed by the Latiān Dem, the new township (*šahrak*) of Lavāsān has become a suburb of Tehran.

In the middle valley between Latiān and Pārčin, the river flows across the bare lands of Hazār-darra and the mountains of Qara-āğāč (see ANTI-ALBORZ). In the upper part are located the ruins of the Safavid bridge and the caravanserai of Pol-e Jājrud which were the last stages before Tehran on the road from Māzāndarān. At Māmālu, the river joins the small stream of Damāvand, coming from this city and the mountains of Emāmzāda Hāšem. There are only some hamlets along this middle section of Jājrud, because the access has been restricted since the 19th century, when Nāṣer-al-Din Shah Qājār (r. 1264-1313) took over these mountains as a royal hunting area (*šekargāh-e salṭanati*) and made it off-limits (*qoroq*) to the general public (Lambton p. 258). The only inhabitants allowed to live there with their flocks were some semi-nomadic families of the tribe of Hedāvand, a Lor tribe living in small hamlets (Yurd-e Šāh, Ḥammāmak). Soon after the revolution of 1978-79, access was restricted again because of the development of the military-industrial compound of Pārčin (1180m) at the exit of the valley in the plain, where a large new city has been built at about 30 km southeast of Tehran. The highway linking western Tehran (Damāvand road) to Khorasan road in the plain along Jājrud valley is not open to the public for reasons of military security.

The lower Jājrud valley is the large alluvial fan of the plain of Varāmin. From Pārčin downward, the river branches off into numerous streams that feed countless brooks (*juy*) irrigating the plain of Varāmin, one of the largest irrigated lands of the Central Plateau. The major stream crosses the city of Qarčak and joins in the Kavir-e Namak the lower course of the Karaj River and sometimes the Rud-e Šur stream during major spring floods. There are also many subterranean channels (*qanāt*) using underground water, but since the construction of the Latiān Dam in 1967, which diverts the water to the city of Tehran, the level of underground water has fallen, drying up many *qanāt*s and wells. The agriculture of the plain of Varāmin was thus deeply upset and irrigated lands were abandoned. Now only deep wells equipped with water pumps are able to use the underground water provided by Jājrud.

A large canal has been under construction for years to collect the polluted waters of the capital city and bring them back to Jājrud River and the plain of Varāmin after de-pollution in a large sewage system. This comprehensive program for the management of the water of Jājrud was proposed when the Latiān Dam was built, but it never materialized. Consequently, a great part of the water of Jājrud that is diverted to Tehran is lost in the desert and in the surrounding areas of the city of Rey, which are flooded at spring time because of the height of the water table, especially after the diversion of the water of the Lār River to the Latiān Dam and Tehran in 1990. Another part of the flood of Jājrud is collected by the canal near Rey and lost in the new large lake of Band-e ʿAli K̲ān between Rey and the Kavir near Qom.

Bibliography: Ludwig W. Adamec, ed., *Historical and Political Gazetteer of Iran* I: *Tehran and Northwestern Iran*, Graz, 1976, p. 267. Eckart Ehlers, *Iran: Grundzüge einer Geographischen Landeskunde*, Darmstadt, 1980. Moḥammad-Ḥasan Khan Eʿtemād-al-Salṭana, *al-Maʾāṯer wa'l-āṯār*, ed. Ī. Afšār as *Čehel sāl tārīḵ-e Īrān dar dawra-ye pādšāhī-e Nāṣer-al-Dīn Šāh*, 3 vols., comments by Ḥosayn Maḥbūbī Ardakānī, Tehran, 1989a, I, pp. 86, 106. Idem, *Merʾāt al-boldān-e nāṣeri*, ed. ʿAbd-al-Ḥosayn Navāʾi and Mir-Hāšem Moḥaddeṯ, 4 vols. in 3, Tehran, 1989b. Bernard Hourcade, "La haute vallée du Djādj-e Roud, Elbourz central, étude de géographie humaine," Paris, Unpublished doctorate thesis, Université de Paris, Sorbonne, 1975, p. 268. Idem, "Le processus de déprise rurale dans l'Elbourz de Téhéran (Iran)," *Revue de géographie Alpine* 64/3, 1976, pp. 365-88. Idem, "Migrations de travail et migrations de loisir dans l'Elbourz de Téhéran," *Revue de géographie de Lyon* 3, 1978, pp. 229-40. ʿAbbās Jaʿfari, *Šenās-nāma joḡrāfiāʾi-e ṭabiʿi-e Irān*, 4th ed., Tehran, 1995. Idem, *Gitā-šenāsi* II: *Rudhā wa rudnāmahā-ye Irān*, Tehran, 1997, pp. 163-64. Ḥosayn Karimān, *Rey-e bāstān*, 2 vols. Tehran, 1966-70. Masʿud Kayhān, *Joḡrāfiā-ye mofaṣṣal-e Irān*, 3 vols., Tehran, 1932-33, I, pp. 86-87; II, pp. 356-57. A. K. S. Lambton, *Landlord and Peasant in Persia*, Oxford, 1953. Ẓahir-al-Din Marʿaši, *Tāriḵ-e Ṭabarestān o Ruyān o Māzandarān*, ed. Moḥammad-Ḥosayn Tasbiḥi, Tehran, 1966. Ḥamd-Allāh Mostawfi Qazvini, *Nozhat al-qolub*, ed. and tr. Guy Le Strange as *The Geographical Part of the Nuzhat al-Qulūb*, 2 vols., Leiden and London, 1915-19, I (text), p. 220; II (tr.), p. 213. Moḥsen Ranjbar, "Jājrud," in *Dāneš-nāma-ye jahān-e Eslām* IX, Tehran, 2005, pp. 199-203. Ḥosayn-ʿAli Razmārā, *Farhang-e joḡrāfiāʾi-e Irān*, 10 vols., Tehran, 1949-53.

(BERNARD HOURCADE)

JĀKI, a group of Lor tribes in the Kuhgiluya region of eastern Khuzesan. They comprise the tribal confederations (q.v.) of the Čahārboniča (or Čarboniča) and the Lirāvi. The Čahārboniča, in turn, comprises the Boir Aḥmadi (q.v.), Čorām (see ČERĀM), Došmanziāri (q.v.), and Novi tribes. The Lirāvi, on the other hand, comprise the Bahmaʾi (q.v.), Šir ʿAli, Ṭayyebi , and Yusofi tribes.

Bibliography. Fasāʾi, ed. Rastgār, p. 1466-1501. Masʿud Kayhān, *Joḡrāfiā-ye mofaṣṣal-e Irān II: Siāsi*, Tehran, 1932, pp. 88-89. Maḥmud Bāvar, *Kuh-e Giluya o ilāt-e ān*, Gač-e Sārān, 1945, pp. 86 ff. Jawād Ṣafi Nežād, *ʿAšāyer-e markazi-e Irān*, Tehran, 1990, pp. 133-66.

(P. OBERLING)

JALĀLĀBĀD, a city, a valley, and an administrative unit of fluctuating scope within the Afghan state structure. The city is located in eastern Afghanistan at 34°25'28" N latitude and 70°26'53" E longitude at 1,885 feet above sea level in the north-central portion of an elongated oval valley that stretches approximately 80 miles east to west and an average of about 30 miles north to south in the province of Nangrahār in eastern Afghanistan (Adamec, pp. 284-300). Jalālābād district is one of twenty districts of Nangrahār province, of which Jalālābād city is the capital. Today Nangrahār Province is bounded by the K̲aybar Agency of Pakistan's Federally Administered Tribal Areas (FATA) in the east, the Korram Agency of FATA in the southeast, and its remaining boundaries are shared with the Afghan provinces of Paktiā in the south, Logar in the southwest, Kabul in the west, and Laḡmān and Konār in the north. The main water body of the Jalālābād region is the Kābol River that enters from Laḡmān and is joined by its primary tributary the Sork̲rud/Sork̲āb River approximately four miles west of Jalālābād city. After flowing through the northern outskirts of Jalālābād city the Kābol River continues its prevailing easterly course through the Hindu Kush (q.v.) mountain range, streaming north of the Khyber (K̲aybar) Pass before debouching near Warsak in the Peshawar valley (Adamec, pp. 338-39).

The city of Jalālābād is strategically situated near the western entrance of the Khyber Pass and as such the locality has been an important dimension in and significantly effected by a large set of economic, cultural, and political relations between Central and South Asia. Jalālābād assumes particular significance in the context of the historic relations between the cultural groups oriented towards and the political economies revolving around Kabul and Peshawar, the former approximately 73 miles to the west and the latter approximately 69 miles to the east of Jalālābād as the crow flies; the most direct road between Kabul and Peshawar passing through Jalālābād was estimated at 170 miles during the Second Anglo-Afghan War (1878-80, q.v.). At present there are four main roads between Jalālābād and Kabul, and from north to south; they are (all but the first merge and diverge in Jagdalak): the road completed in 1960 that runs through the Ḡāru Gorge (Tangi-e Ḡāru) and tunnel; the road through the Latahband Pass; the road via the K̲ord Kābol Pass and Botk̲āk; and the road via Tezin, K̲āk-e Jabār, and Begrāmi. The primary channel of communication between Jalālābād and Peshawar is the Khyber main road via Dakka, Tork̲am,

Landi Kotal, ʿAli Masjed, and Jamrud, while secondary routes include those through the Tartāra and Ābsuna passes. While connected to and meditating relations between Kabul and Peshawar, in general terms, Jalālābād appears economically more oriented towards Peshawar, but more politically connected to Kabul.

From approximately the third century B.C.E., the Jalālābād area was exposed to Hellenist and Buddhist influences (L. Dupree, 1980, pp. 282-95). This ancient encounter between two surging global forces involved significant local cultural influences, and this interaction led to the emergence of the Gandharan civilization (see GANDAHARA) that prospered in the midst of continuing cultural and political influences emanating from the wider Indian, Iranian, and Chinese worlds (e.g., under the Kushans during the first centuries C.E.; see http://depts.washington.edu/ebmp/index.php; http://www.bl.uk/onlinegallery/themes/asianafricanman/budscrolls.html). Archeological and textual data reveal the cultural synthesis characterizing Gandhara, which had flourished between approximately the first and seventh centuries C.E. The Chinese Buddhist travelers Fa-hsien in the fifth century and Hsuang-tsang in the seventh century record a number of sites of Buddhist pilgrimage, worship, and cultural production in the Jalālābād region (N. Dupree, 1971, pp. 215-17). Hadda, located approximately seven miles south of Jalālābād city, was particularly renowned for shrines said to contain part of the skull bone, a tooth, some hair, and the staff of the Buddha (N. Dupree, loc. cit.). A significant volume of the artistic and archeological remains from this period was extracted and exported from stuppas, topes, and mounds of various sorts by Europeans in the 19th century. The French Archeological Delegation to Afghanistan excavated Hadda in the 1920s and a Japanese team worked at a proximate site in Lalma in the 1960s (N. Dupree, 1971, p. 219; L. Dupree, 1980, p. 306; Ball, I, pp. 116-18). Much of Hadda's archeological heritage was lost as a result of Soviet aerial bombardment in the 1980s.

On his first excursion from Kabul into India in 1505, Ẓahir-al-Din Bābor, the founder of the Mughal Empire described Nangarhār and noted the differences between the Nangarhār and Kabul region in terms of climate, plants, trees, animals, birds, and people and their customs (Bābor, fols. 132a-33a, tr. Beveridge, pp. 207-10, tr. Thackston, III, pp. 271-375). The Mughal Emperor Jalāl-al-Din Akbar (r. 963-1014/1556-605; q.v.) simultaneously transformed and integrated the localities of Jalālābād and Attak, the latter being where the royal Grand Trunk road to Delhi and Bengal crossed the Indus (MacGregor, p. 295). Further Mughal investment in the region came in 1019/1610 when Akbar's son and successor, Nur-al-Din Jahāngir (r. 1014-37/1605-27; q.v.) built gardens at Nimla at approximately twenty five miles southwest of Jalālābād city (N. Dupree, 1971, pp. 227-28). During the reign Jahāngir's son, Shah Jahān (r. 1037-68/1628-57), ʿAli-Mardān Khan, the governor of Kabul built a bridge over the Sorḵrud River, with an inscription on the bridge commemorating its building. The bridge is described as being of brick-work and masonry, having one arch, spanning sixty feet, and standing thirty feet above the river (Lal, p. 207; Moorcroft et al, II, p. 370). Shah Jahān and ʿAli-Mardān Khan are responsible for the construction of two bridges in Jalālābād valley, one bridge to the east of Peshawar (Habib, Notes to Sheets 1-A and 1-B, p. 3), and the Kabul covered bazaar, which was destroyed by General Pollock and the British "army of retribution" in 1842 (Burnes, I, p. 145; Norris, p. 415).

Jalālābād region figured prominently in the first Anglo-Afghan War (1839-42; q.v.; N. Dupree, 1975, passim; Norris, pp. 361-419). The final remnants of the decimated British army of the Indus, in full and fatal retreat, made their last stand about thirty miles from Jalālābād city at the village Gandamak on the morning of 2 Ḏu'l-ḥejja 1257/13 January 1842 (N. Dupree, 1967, p. 74; L. Dupree, 1976, pp. 523-24). The sole survivor of the entire force of roughly 15,530 that had set out from the Kabul cantonment to Peshawar a week earlier (approximately 690 British soldiers, 2,840 Indian soldiers, and 12,000 camp followers), Dr. William Brydon, arrived in Jalālābād city that evening. A British force commanded by General Sale had fallen under siege in the city the previous day and remained in that condition until being relieved by General Pollock's army in April 1842 (Sale, passim; Sale in Stocquelor, pp. 215-21). In October 1842, General Pollock left Kabul for Peshawar, en route destroying General Sale's fortifications in Jalālābād (Norris, p. 416).

During the second Anglo-Afghan War (1878-80), the British established Fort Sale on the western outskirts of Jalālābād city. The treaty signed between Moḥammad Yaʿqub Khan (r. 1296/1879) and the British at the village Gandamak (4 Jomādā II 1296/26 May 1879; M. J. Hanifi, passim; for the text of treaty, see Hurewitz, II, pp. 417-19) during the second British invasion imposed humiliating terms which provoked a rebellion that culminated in Yaʿqub Khan's abdication and subsidized refuge in India. Upon his accession to a now heavily British-subsidized (S. M. Hanifi, pp. 255-98, passim) emirate of Kabul in 1880, ʿAbd-al-Raḥmān (r. 1280-1319/1880-1901) acquiesced to the Gandamak treaty terms with the sole exception that the British representative in Kabul be an Indian Muslim, not a European.

ʿAbd-al-Raḥmān built a garden complex in Jalālābād but devoted proportionally less attention to that city and region than the rulers preceding and succeeding him in Kabul. ʿAbd-al-Raḥmān instead used material and political resources to suppress revolts in Afghan Turkestan, the Hazārajāt (q.v.), Kāferstān (which was renamed Nurestān) and in the south and east of Afghanistan. The second British occupation of Jalālābād resulted in the first publicized photographs of the city (Khan, pp. 107, 111) and its inhabitants, and the publication of a handbook in the gazetteer tradition that lists or briefly describes the resources, revenue, administration, demography, and history of the city and region (Jenkyns). In this report Jalālābād's demography is notable for the numeric preponderance of Hindus among the approximately 2,000 permanent residents of the city. The region itself produced an array of fruits and nuts (pomegranates, melons, and walnuts), many prized strains of rice, wheat (the Gandamak variety being particularly celebrated), and some so-called cash crops including cotton, opium, silk, and tobacco, the quality of which did not particularly impress British Indian officials. Good crops of sugar cane were grown along the Sork̲rud River (Jenkyns, p. 9; Vigne, pp. 231-34); the Jalālābād region continues to be recognized for a variety of brown sugar (*gora* in Pashto), which in lumped form is well-known and highly valued in Kabul and Peshawar.

In the late 19th century Jalālābād was populated by a number of ethnic and tribal groups, among whom Paštuns (Ḡalzi particularly, but also K̲ugiānis, Mohmands, Ṣāfis, Šenwāris, and others) appear to be most numerous among a large constellation of sedentary and nomadic communities including populations of Arabs, Dehqāns, Hindus, Moḡols, Tājiks, Kashmiris, Parāčas, Qezelbāš, and sayyids (Jenkyns, pp. i-xvi). Colonial authorities viewed the nomadic Kučis as the distinguishing element of the region's demography. The British occupation report also indicates nearly all Ḡalzi villages remitted their revenue directly to Kabul, not to or through the local provincial government in Jalālābād.

The near tropical climate of the area attracts an influx of winter residents, including Kučis and other nomadic and semi-nomadic people, which swells the population of Jalālābād (Burnes, I, pp. 122-23). Jalālābād has long-served along with Peshawar as a winter retreat for the Kabul elite (Bosworth, p. 237; Jenkyns, p. 3). Amir Ḥabib-Allāh (r. 1901-19, q.v.) built a palace, Serāj-al-ʿEmārāt (Bell, pp. 163-64), in the center of the city, but it was ransacked during the revolts leading up to the abdication of Ḥabib-Allāh's son and successor, Amir Amān-Allāh (r. 1919-29, q.v.; N. Dupree, 1971, pp. 212-13). Ḥabib-Allāh, Amān-Allāh, and Amān-Allāh's wife T̲orayyā are buried on the grounds of a golf course that Ḥabib-Allāh constructed in Jalālābād (Gregorian, p. 201) in a mausoleum facing the remains of Serāj-al-ʿEmārāt.

The Jalālābād medical school was founded in 1963 (Seraj). Until the 1980s the Jalālābād region's many shrines were sites of pilgrimage for Muslims, Hindus and Sikhs. The shrine of Miān ʿAli at ʿAli Buqān was notable for the popular belief that it cured insanity; and the week-long Waisak festival held each April at Solṭānpur that celebrated Guru Nanāk's generation of the local springs attracted Hindus and Sikhs from all over Afghanistan and south Asia, who came to visit the temple there (N. Dupree, 1971, pp. 227-28). The United States' ongoing Operation Enduring Freedom, which includes most particularly the bombardment of the Tora Bora mountains in the southern portion of Nangrahār province, has introduced significant levels of depleted uranium into eastern Afghanistan (Project Censored) in addition to causing significant damage to the region's ancient and sophisticated irrigation system through subterranean channels (*kārēz/qanāt*). Jalālābād city, with an estimated population of 96,000 in 2002, is presently the seat of a Provincial Reconstruction Team under the International Security and Assistance Force umbrella in Afghanistan.

Bibliography: Louis W Adamec, ed., *Historical and Political Gazetteer of Afghanistan* VI: *Kabul and Southeastern Afghanistan*, Graz, 1985. Ẓahir-al-Din Moḥammad Bābor, *Bābor-nāma*, facs. ed., Annette S. Beveridge, London, 1971; tr. Annette S. Beveridge as *The Bābur-nāma in English (Memoirs of Bābur)*, London, 1922, repr. New Delhi, 1970; ed. and tr. with annotation Wheeler M. Thackston, Jr. as *Bâburnâma: Chaghatay Turkish Text with Abdul-Rahim Khankhanan's Persian Translation, Turkish Transcription*, 3 vols., Cambridge, Mass., 1993. Warwick Ball, *Archaeological Gazeteer of Afghanistan: Catalogue des sites archéologiques d'Afhanistan*, 2 vols., Paris, 1982. Fredrik Barth, *Political Leadership among Swat Pathans*, London, 1965. Marjorie Jewett Bell, *An American Engineer in Afghanistan: From the Letters and Notes of A. C. Jewett*, Minneapolis, 1948, repr., Kabul, 2004 [1948]. Clifford E. Bosworth, "D̲jalālābād," in *EI*² Supplement, pp. 237-38. Alexander Burnes. *Travels into Bokhara: Being the Account of A Journey from India to Cabool, Tartary, and Persia; Also A Narrative of A Voyage on the Indus from the Sea to Lahore*, 3 vols, London, 1834, repr. New Delhi, 1992. Louis Dupree, "The Retreat of the British Army from Kabul to Jalalabad in 1842: The Role of History in Folklore," *Journal of the Folklore Institute* 4/1, 1967, pp. 50-74. Idem, "The First Anglo-Afghan War and the British Retreat of 1842: The Functions of History and Folklore," *East and West* 26/3-4, 1976, pp. 503-29. Idem, *Afghanistan*. Princeton, 1980. Nancy Hatch Dupree, *An Historical Guide to Afghanistan*, Kabul, 1971; rev. and enlarged ed., Kabul, 1977. Idem, "Will the Sikhs Take Jalalabad?," *Afghanistan Journal* 1975, pp. 53-59. David B. Edwards, *Heroes of the Age: Moral Fault Lines along the Afghan Frontier*, Berkeley, Calif., 1996. Mountuart Elphinstone, *An Account of the Kingdom of Caubul and Its Dependencies in Persia, Tartary and India*, London, 1815; 3rd. ed. with corrections, Karachi, 1972. Fayż Moḥammad Kāteb, *Serāj al-tawārik̲*, 3 vols. Kabul, 1913-15. *Gandharan Scrolls (Early Buddhist Manuscripts)* at the British Library and the University of Washington (joint project) Vartan Gregorian, *The Emergence of Modern Afghanistan: The Politics of Reform and Modernization, 1880-1946*, Stanford, Calif., 1969. Irfan Habib, *An Atlas of the Mughal Empire: Political and Economic Maps with Detailed Notes, Bibliography, and Index*, 2nd. ed., Delhi and New York, 1986. Shah Mahmoud Hanifi, "Inter-Regional Trade and Colonial State Formation in Nineteenth-Century Afghanistan," Ph.D. Diss. The University of Michigan, 2001. Jacob C. Hurewitz, tr. and ed., *The Middle East and North Africa in World Affaris: A Documentary*, 2 vols., New Haven, 1975-79. W. Jenkyns, *Report on the District of Jalalabad Chiefly in Regard to Revenue*, Calcutta, 1879. Omar Khan. *From Kashmir to Kabul: The Photographs of John Burke and William Baker, 1860-1900*. Munich, 2002. M. Lal, *Travel in the Punjab, Afganistan and Turkistan to Balk, Bokhara and Herat and a Visit to Great Britain and Germany*, Calcutta, 1977. Charles M. MacGregor, *Cen-*

tral Asia, Part II: A Contribution Towards the Better Knowledge of the Topography, Ethnology, Resources, and History of Afghanistan, Calcutta, 1871, repr., Petersfield, 1995. W. Moorcroft, G. Trebeck, and H. H. Wilson, *Travels into The Himalayan Provinces of the Hindustan and the Panjab from 1819 to 1825*. Karachi, 1979. James Alfred Norris, *The First Afghan War, 1838-1942*, Cambridge, 1967. Robert Henry Sale, "Account of the Jellalabad Siege," in Joachim H. Stoqueler, ed., *Memorials of Afghanistan: Being State Papers, Official Documents, Dispatches, Authentic Narratives, etc. Illustrative of the British Expedition to, and Occupation of, Afghanistan and Scinde, between the Years 1838 and 1842*, Calcutta, 1843, Peshawar, 1983. Robert Henry Sale, Charles Joseph Hullmandel, and W. L. Walton, *The Defence of Jellalabad*, London, 1846. Godfrey Thomas Vigne, *A Personal Narrative of a Visit to Ghuzni, Kabul, and Afghanistan, and of A Residence at the Court of Dost Mohamed: with Notices of Ranjit Sing, Khiva, and the Russian Expedition*, London, 1840, repr., New Delhi, 1986. André Wink, *al-Hind: The Making of the Indo Islamic World* I: *Early Medieval Indian and the Expansion of Islam, 7-11th Centuries*, Leiden, 1990.

Online sources. M. Jamil Hanifi. "The Treaty of Gandomak," *EIr*, *Supplement*, accessed via http://www.iranica.com/articles/sup/Gandomak.html.

I. Seraj. "The Past History of Health Care in Afghanistan," http://www.afghanmed.org/dr__seraj_presentation.htm

http://depts.washington.edu/ebmp/index.php http://www.bl.uk/onlinegallery/themes/asianafricanman/budscrolls.html

Project Censored (multiple authors on the uranium contamination issue)

http://www.projectcensored.org/publications/2005/4.html

(SHAH MAHMOUD HANIFI)

JALĀL-AL-DIN DAVĀNI. See DAVĀNI.

JALĀL-AL-DIN ḤASAN III (b. 562/1166-67; d. 15 Ramażān 618/1 November 1221), Nezāri Ismaʿili imam and the sixth lord of Alamut (q.v.). He succeeded to the leadership of the Nezāri *daʿwa* ('propaganda' or 'mission,' see DĀʿI) and state on the death of his father, Nur-al-Din Moḥammad II b. Ḥasan II (r. 561-607/1166-1210), on 10 Rabiʿ I 607/1 September 1210, and, as was then customary for the lords of Alamut, he carried the honorific title of Jalāl-al-Din. Weary of the isolation of the Nezāris, he devoted his brief reign of some eleven years to establishing better relations with Sunni Muslims and their rulers.

Following the failure of the earlier Nezāri revolts against the Saljuqs and the subsequent stalemate between them, the Nezāri community had become further isolated from the rest of the Muslim world by the spiritual *qiāma* ('resurrection') declared by Jalāl-al-Din Ḥasan III's grandfather, Ḥasan II ʿAlā Ḏekrehe'l-Salām (r. 557-61/1162-66, q.v.), a declaration that had effectively rendered the outside world irrelevant. Jalāl-al-Din, who had grown dissatisfied with the doctrine and practices of *qiāma*, had evidently communicated his own new ideas to a number of Sunni leaders even before his accession (Jovayni, III, p. 242; Jovayni, tr. Boyle, II, pp. 698-99; Daftary, pp. 385-91). At any rate, upon his accession, Jalāl-al-Din publicly repudiated the doctrine of *qiāma*, proclaimed his adherence to Sunni Islam and ordered his followers to observe the *šariʿa* ('religious law') in its Sunni form.

He sent messengers to the Abbasid caliph al-Nāṣer (r. 575-622/1180-1225), to the Ḵᵛārazmšāh Moḥammad b. Tekeš (r. 596-617/1200-20), and to other Sunni rulers informing them of his reform. Indeed, Jalāl-al-Din did his utmost to convince the Sunni world of his new religious policy and to end the isolation of his community. He invited Shafʿite *faqih*s ('experts of Islamic law') from Iraq and Khorasan to instruct his followers, and he also permitted Sunni scholars from Qazvin to remove any books deemed "heretical" from the library at Alamut. Finally, in Rabiʿ I 608/August 1211, the caliph al-Nāṣer acknowledged Jalāl-al-Din Ḥasan III's new dispensation and issued a decree to that effect.

Jalāl-al-Din now became known as the "New Muslim" (*now-mosalmān*; Jovayni, III, p. 243), and his rights to the Nezāri territories were officially recognized for the first time by the Abbasid caliph, who showed him all manner of favors. Jalāl-al-Din's mother went on pilgrimage to Mecca in 609/1213 under Abbasid patronage; and the caliph also intervened to persuade the nobility of Gilān (q.v.) to allow four of their daughters to marry Jalāl-al-Din. Amongst these wives was a sister of Kaykāʾus b. Šāhanšāh, the ruler of Kutom (present-day Kohdom in western Gilān), who bore Jalāl-al-Din's sole son and successor ʿAlāʾ-al-Din Moḥammad III (r. 618-53/1221-55, q.v.; Jovayni, III, pp. 242-45; Daftary, pp. 404-6).

The Nezāri Ismaʿilis of Persia and Syria accepted Jalāl-al-Din's reform without any dissent, continuing to regard him as the infallible imam who guided his community and contextualized the interpretation of the *šariʿa* as he saw fit. As it was more comprehensively explained at the time of his successor, especially by Naṣir-al-Din Ṭusi (1201-74; see Ṭusi, 1950, text, pp. 61, 110; and Ṭusi, 1996, pp. 214, 290-91), the Nezāris had evidently viewed their imam's declarations as a reimposition of *taqiya* ('dispensing with or concealing someone's true religious beliefs') which had been lifted in the *qiāma* times; and the observance of *taqiya* could be taken to imply any sort of accommodation to the outside world as deemed necessary by the Nezāri imam.

Jalāl-al-Din's rapprochement with Sunni Muslims had obvious advantages in terms of peace and security for the Nezāri state and community, which hitherto had been under constant attacks by their Sunni neighbours. In particular, the Ghurid (see GHURIDS) attacks on the Nezāris of Qohestān ceased, and, in Syria, where the Nezāris confronted renewed Frankish campaigns, they received timely assistance from the Ayyubids (q.v.; Daftary, pp.

419-20). The improved relations were also beneficial to the Sunnis, as the Nezāri imam played an active role in the caliphal alliances of al-Nāṣer. In 610/1213, Jalāl-al-Din personally led his army to Azerbaijan to join forces with Moẓaffar-al-Din Özbeg (r. 607-22/1210-25), the last Ildegozid ruler of Azerbaijan and Arrān (see ATĀBAKĀN-E ĀḎARBĀYJĀN) and one of the Abbasid caliph's major allies. Jalāl-al-Din helped Moẓaffar-al-Din Özbeg in his campaign against a rebellious lieutenant, Nāṣer-al-Din Mengli. After victory, as a reward for his efforts, Jalāl-al-Din was given the towns of Abhar and Zanjān with their environs.

After an absence of one and a half years, Jalāl-al-Din returned to Alamut and maintained his close relations with the caliph al-Nāṣer and Moẓaffar-al-Din Özbeg (Jovayni, III, pp. 245-47; Jovayni, tr. Boyle, II, pp. 701-2). Towards the end of his reign, many Sunnis and Sunni scholars, who were fleeing from the Mongol invasion of Khorasan, found refuge in the Nezāri fortress communities of Qohestān where they were treated lavishly by the Nezāri leaders (*moḥtašams*; Juzjāni, II, pp. 182-83; Juzjāni, tr. Raverty, II, pp. 1197-98). Jalāl-al-Din was evidently also the first Muslim ruler to engage successfully in negotiations with the Mongols after they crossed the Oxus (see ĀMU DARYĀ) River (Jovayni, III, p. 248; Jovayni, tr. Boyle, II, p. 703).

Jalāl-al-Din Ḥasan III died of dysentery in the middle of Ramażān 618/November 1221, but his vizier accused the imam's sister and wives of having poisoned him; and they were all put to death (Jovayni, III, p. 249; Jovayni, tr, Boyle, II, pp. 703-4).

Bibliography: Ḥāfeẓ-e Abru, *Majmaʿ al-tawāriḵ al-solṭāniya: qesmat-e ḵolafāʾ-e ʿAlawiya-ye Maḡreb wa Meṣr wa Nezāriān wa Rafiqān az tāriḵ-e Ḥāfeẓ-e Abru bā maṭāleb-e eżāfi-e hamin bakš az Jāmeʿ al-tawāriḵ-e Rašid-al-Din Fażl-Allāh Hamadāni wa Zobdat al-tawāriḵ-e Abu'l-Qāsem Kāšāni*, ed. M. Modarresi-Zanjāni, Tehran, 1985, pp. 264-66. F. Daftary, *The Ismāʿīlīs: Their History and Doctrines*, Cambridge, 1990; tr. F. Badraʾi as *Tāriḵ wa ʿaqāʾed-e Esmāʿiliya*, Tehran, 1996. M. G. S. Hodgson, *The Order of Assassins*, The Hague, 1955, pp. 217-25. Idem, "Ismāʿīlī State", in *Camb. Hist. Iran* V, 1968, pp. 422-82. ʿAlāʾ-al-Din ʿAṭā-Malek Jovayni, *Tāriḵ-e jahāngošā*, ed. M. Qazvini, 3 vols., Leiden and London, 1906-37; tr. J. A. Boyle as *The History of the World Conqueror*, 2 vols., Manchester, 1958. Menhāj-al-Din b. Serāj-al-Din Juzjāni, *Ṭabaqāt-e Nāṣeri*, ed. ʿA.-Ḥ. Ḥabibi, 2nd ed., 2 vols., Kabul, 1963-63; tr. H. G. Raverty, 2 vols., London, 1881-99. Abu'l-Qāsem ʿAbd-Allāh Kāšāni, *Zobdat al-tawāriḵ, bakš-e Fāṭemiān wa Nezāriān*, ed. M.-T. Dānešpažuh, 2nd ed., Tehran, 1987, pp. 214-17. B. Lewis, *The Assassins*, London, 1967, pp. 78-81. Ḥamd-Allāh Mostowfi, *Tāriḵ-e gozida*, ed. ʿA.-Ḥ. Navāʾi, Tehran, 1960, pp. 524-25. Rašid-al-Din Fażl-Allāh, *Jāmeʿ al-tawāriḵ, qesmat-e Esmāʿiliān*, ed. M.-T. Dānešpažuh and M. Modarresi-Zanjāni, Tehran, 1959, pp. 174-78. Naṣir-al-Din Moḥammad Ṭusi, *Ketāb-e rowżat al-taslim yā taṣawworāt*, ed. and tr. W. Ivanow, Bombay, 1950; tr. Ch. Jambet as *La Convocation d'Alamût*, Lagrasse, 1996.

(FARHAD DAFTARY)

JALĀL-AL-DIN ḴᵛĀRAZMŠĀH(I) MENGÜBIRNI, the last Ḵᵛārazmšāh of the line of Anuštigin Ḡarčaʾi (q.v.), reigned in 1220-31 as the eldest son and successor of ʿAlāʾ-al-Din Moḥammad (q.v.). His Turkish personal name remains enigmatic, as no more satisfactory interpretation of the Arabic consonant *ductus* MNK-BRNY has been seriously suggested than *mengü birti* ('the Heavens [i.e., God] gave'), propounded by d'Ohsson in the early 19th century (d'Ohsson, I, p. 195, n. 1; Boyle, 1965, p. 392). Recently, however, Peter Jackson has tentatively put forward as a possibility the reading of *Mingīrinī* ('having a thousand men'), which can be an equivalent to Persian *hazārmard* with the same meaning (Bosworth, p. 179).

Jalāl-al-Din was in fact never able to reign in his ancestral kingdom for more than a brief time. When his father died on an island off the Caspian coast in December 1220, Jalāl-al-Din and various members of his family made their way via the Mangyshlak peninsula on the eastern side of the Caspian to the Ḵᵛārazmian capital Gorgānj, just before it was invested by the Mongol commanders Čaḡatay and Ögedey in 1221 and destroyed after a lengthy siege (Nasavi, pp. 120-22, 170-73; Ebn al-Aṯir, Beirut ed., XII, pp. 394-95; Jovayni, tr. Boyle, I, pp. 123-28; Barthold, *Turkestan²*, pp. 433-37; Kafesoğlu, pp. 274-75, 283-84). Suspecting treachery against himself in Gorgānj by discontented Turkish commanders, who were unable to accept ʿAlāʾ-al-Din's last-minute change of the succession from the previously appointed heir Qoṭb-al-Din Uzlaḡšāh to his elder brother Jalāl-al-Din, the latter left the capital and headed southwards. He eluded Mongol watchmen in northern Khorasan, defeated a force of Mongol cavalry near Nasā, and reached the appanage which his father had previously allotted to him, i.e., the lands conquered by ʿAlāʾ-al-Din from the Ghurids (q.v.), corresponding roughly to modern Afghanistan. At Ghazna (see ḠAZNI) he gathered together a large force of Ḵᵛārazmians, Turks, and Ghurids, marched out to inflict a serious defeat on the pursuing Mongols of Chinghiz Khan (see ČENGIZ KHAN) at Parvān, but was forced by Chinghiz Khan to retreat to northwestern India. A battle took place on the banks of the Indus, and Jalāl-al-Din escaped the Mongols only by riding his horse across the river either in August-September 1221 or two months later (Nasavi, pp. 126-34, 152-62; Jovayni, tr. Boyle, I, pp. 133-35; Juzjāni, *Ṭabaqāt*, tr. Raverty, II, pp. 1012-23; Barthold, *Turkestan²*, pp. 437-46; Spüler, *Mongolen*, pp. 31-32; Boyle, 1968, pp. 317-21). He was never to see Khwarazm again.

He managed to get some 4,000 of his troops safely across the Indus and spent the next three years in India, being involved in negotiations and warfare with local rulers including the ruler of Sind, Nāṣer-al-Din Qubača, but then he made his way to western Persia where his brother Ḡiāṯ-al-Din Piršāh had established himself as a ruler. He passed through Kerman in 1224, confirming the position of the Qutlugh-khanid Baraq Ḥājeb (r. 1222-35) as his governor there; in Fārs he married a daughter of the Salghurid Atabeg Saʿd I b. Zangi (r. 1198-1226; see ATĀBAKĀN-E FĀRS). Jalāl-al-Din made Ḡiāṯ-al-Din Piršāh his vassal and clashed with the army of the resurgent Abbasid caliph al-Nāṣer (r. 1180-1225). In Azerbaijan he expelled the Ildegizid Atabeg Uzbek b. Jahān-Pahlavān (r. 1210-25; see ATĀBAKĀN-E ĀḎARBĀYJĀN) from his capital Tabriz in 1225 before going on in 1226 to invade the Christian kingdom of Georgia, defeating its king, sacking the Georgian capital Tbilisi (Teflis), and massacring its inhabitants (Nasavi, pp. 163-69, 174-79, 192-200, 211-12; Jovayni-Boyle, II, pp. 411-35; Ebn al-Aṯir, Beirut ed., XII, pp. 425-28, 432-36, 450-52; Spüler, *Mongolen*, pp. 32-33; Boyle, 1968, pp. 322-28).

After a lightning march back to Kerman to subdue the rebellious Baraq Ḥājeb, Jalāl-al-Din turned to invade eastern Anatolia and unsuccessfully besieged the town of Ak̲lāṭ (q.v.) on lake Van, at that time under Ayyubid (see AYYUBIDS) control. In 1227 he reduced the Ismaʿilites of Alamut in northern Persia to tributary status (Nasavi, pp. 228-31, 246; Ebn al-Aṯir, Beirut ed., XII, p. 470; Daftary, pp. 414, 416-18). The Mongols re-appeared in central Persia in this same year, and Jalāl-al-Din engaged them in battle outside Isfahan. The result was technically a Mongol victory, but their losses were so severe that they withdrew from Persia back to Transoxania (Nasavi, pp. 232-38; Ebn al-Aṯir, Beirut ed., XII, pp. 470, 476-77; Jovayni, tr. Boyle, II, pp. 436-38; Boyle, 1968, pp. 329-32). Jalāl-al-Din was forced to return to Ak̲lāṭ in the hope of carving out for himself a principality in Anatolia. He captured the town at last in 1230, but then he had to face the combined forces of the Ayyubid ruler of Diyarbakır al-Malek al-Ašraf I Musā (r. 1229-37) and the Saljuq sultan of Rum ʿAlāʾ-al-Din Kay-Qobād I b. Kay-K̲osrow (r. 1220-37). He was defeated by them at Arzinjān in July-August 30. Peace was agreed in face of the common threat from the Mongols, and he withdrew to Azerbaijan. However, a new Mongol army under Čormaḡun appeared in northern Persia, and Jalāl-al-Din, pursued by the Mongols, had to flee westwards to Ak̲lāṭ, Āmid, and then Mayyāfāreqin, but he was unable to recruit an army to face the Mongols and was mysteriously killed in a nearby Kurdish village in August 1231, perhaps for reasons of gain or for revenge (Nasavi, pp. 299-335, 374-83; Ebn al-Aṯir, Beirut ed., XII, pp. 454-55, 459-63, 481, 487-91, 495-504; Spüler, *Mongolen*, pp. 33-34; Boyle, 1968, pp. 328-35). His troops stayed in Anatolia and Syria, where for a considerable time they formed a distinct ethnic element. Jalāl-al-Din would have been the only ruler in the eastern Iranian world with the statesmanship and military expertise to possibly withstand the Mongols, if he had been able to assemble a coalition of the local rulers of Persia, Iraq, and Anatolia, but divisions and jealousies made such an aim impossible, and the line of K̲ᵛārazmšāhs ended with his death.

Bibliography: C. E. Bosworth, *The New Islamic Dynasties, a Chronological and Genealogical Manual*, Edinburgh, 1996, pp. 178-80, no. 89. J. A. Boyle, "D̲jalāl al-Dīn K̲h̲ʷārazm-S̲h̲āh," *EI*² II, 1965, pp. 392-93. Idem, "Dynastic and Political History of the Il-K̲h̲āns," in *Camb. Hist. Iran*, V, 1968, pp. 303-421. F. Daftary, *The Ismāʿīlīs: their History and Doctrines*, Cambridge, 1990. İbrahim Kafesoğlu, *Harezmşahlar devleti tarihi (485-617/1092-1229)*, Ankara, 1965. Moḥammad b. Aḥmad Nasavi, *Sirat al-solṭān Jalāl-al-Din Mengobirti*, ed. Ḥ. A. Ḥamdi, Cairo, 1953. C. d'Ohsson, *Histoire des mongols, depuis Tchinguiz-Khan jusqu'à Timour Bey ou Tamerlan*, 4 vols., The Hague and Amsterdam, 1834-35. B. Spüler, *Die Mongolen in Iran: Politik, Verwalting und Kultur der Ilchanzeit 1220-1350*, Leipzig, 1939.

(C. EDMUND BOSWORTH)

JALĀL-AL-DIN MIRZĀ, Qajar historian and freethinker (b. 1242/1827; d. 1279/1872). Born at the court in Tehran, he was the fifty-fifth son of Fatḥ-ʿAli Shah (r. 1797-1834, q.v.) from Homāʾi K̲ānum, a Kurdish woman from Māzandarān with some education and influence in Jalāl-al-Din Mirzā's upbringing and pro-Western orientation (Amanat, 1999, pp. 6-7). Jalāl-al-Din Mirzā's early education in Qajar princely circles was further complemented through studying classical Persian literature and the French language. As an adult he seems to have attended the Tehran Polytechnic (Dār-al-fonun, founded in 1851, q.v.) and for a while was associated with the European instructors of the Polytechnic and exposed to European intellectual trends (Divān-Beygi, I, pp. 370, 372).

Jalāl-al-Din Mirzā
After *Nāma-ye k̲osrovān*, ed. Vienna, 1880, p. 2.

Beside European influences, the intellectual sources of Jalāl-al-Din Mirzā's acknowledged freethinking are not entirely known, though allusions in the sources to his "broad association" (*woṣʿat-e mašrabi*) and making "remarks contrary to the spirit of pure *šariʿa*" (Divān-Beygi, I, p. 370) may suggest not only traces of possible indebtedness to the European Enlightenment, for instance through the perusal of works by Voltaire, but also exposure to the indigenous Persian antinomian tradition found in Sufi circles and the heterodox (*bāṭeni*) milieux of the time. This tradition culminated in the emergence of the Babi movement (see BABISM) in the middle of the 19th century, with its advocacy of a break with Islam and the founding of a new circle of revelation (Amanat, 1999, pp. 8-9; Idem, 1989, pp. 48-105).

Jalāl-al-Din Mirzā's unorthodox proclivities found further exposure through association with Mirzā Malkom

Khan (1833-1908) and his secret society, the Farāmuš-ḵāna ('house of oblivion,' see FREEMASONRY), which made strident efforts to recruit members from the Qajar family, the ulema, and students from the Dār-al-fonun. Established in 1289/1861-62, the Farāmuš-ḵāna was a semi-clandestine political organization which aimed at bringing about reforms based on the ideas of Mirzā Malkom Khan and his father, Yaʿqub Khan (Amanat, 1997, pp. 358-64, 383-94). Its founding coincided with a series of administrative reforms such as the dissolution of the office of the Chief Minister (*ṣadr aʿaẓam*, *ṣadārat*) in 1274/1858 and the formation of a consultative council (*majles-e mašwarat* or *mašwarat-ḵāna*). Eventually, however, the more conservative elements convinced the shah that the Farāmuš-ḵāna was a den of heresy and support for European ways, bent on overthrowing the government itself (Amanat, 1997, pp. 351-54, 358-83). Jalāl-al-Din Mirzā's connections with the Farāmuš-ḵāna might in part be attributed to his dissatisfaction with the line of succession that had side-stepped the Fatḥ-ʿAli Shah branch of the Qajar dynasty. In the aftermath of the dissolution of this semi-secret organization, clandestinely produced and distributed pamphlets (*šab-nāmas*) began to appear, criticizing the shah and the conservative elements within the court. These broadsheets were perhaps the first examples of explicit criticism of the government during Nāṣer-al-Din Shah's (r. 1848-96) reign (excluding the earlier Babi example), and ultimately led to the repression of former members of the Farāmuš-ḵāna. Jalāl-al-Din Mirzā, fearing for his life, took refuge at the shrine of Šāh ʿAbd-al-ʿAẓim near Tehran while other prominent members, including Mirzā Malkom Khan, sought refuge abroad. Jalāl-al-Din Mirzā, as a member of the royal family, was eventually pardoned (Divān-Beygi, I, p. 370).

Nāma-ye ḵosrovān. While remaining critical of the Qajar government, towards the end of his short life Jalāl-al-Din Mirzā turned to writing a history textbook noted for its attention to the Iranian pre-Islamic past and written in "pure Persian" prose shorn of Arabic loanwords. The initial instigation for embarking on such a venture is not entirely clear although in a letter to Mirzā Fatḥ-ʿAli Āḵundzāda (1812-78, q.v.), Jalāl-al-Din Mirzā suggests that he was driven to write a history of his Iranian ancestors in pure Persian in order to restore their greatness which had long "disappeared as a result of the Arab invasion" (Āḵundzāda, p. 373). Initially, the text was meant to comprise of four volumes, but only three were ever completed and published in Tehran. The first volume (1285/1868) covered the ancient history of Iran until the end of the Sasanian dynasty. The second volume (1287/1870) dealt with Islamic Iran from the Taherid dynasty to the demise of the Ḵᵛārazmšāhs. The third volume (1288/1871) covered the period from the Mongol invasion to the Zand dynasty. The fourth volume, which was meant to bring the events to his time, never materialized, perhaps out of concern for the outcome if it ventured to criticize the Qajar establishment in its narrative.

Figure 1. Hušang (Hōšang), mythical father of the Iranians and founder of the Pišdādiān dynasty. After *Nāma-ye ḵosrovān*, ed. Vienna, 1880, p. 26.

The two main foreign culprits in Iranian history, according to the *Nāma-ye ḵosrovān*, were the Arabs and the Mongols. Surprisingly, the Greeks are not included in the list. Such a view of history, particularly in its depiction of Islam and the Arab invasion as a great calamity, stands well apart from traditional Qajar historiography, as manifested in works by Reżāqoli Khan Hedāyat (1800-71, q.v.) or Moḥammad-Taqi Sepehr (1792-1879). Stylistically, *Nāma-ye ḵosrovān* was written in simple Persian, free of foreign words (particularly Arabic). It was intended "for the general public (*mardomān*), especially children" (*Nāma-ye ḵosrovān*, I, p. 6), and might have been written with French textbooks in mind. Another exceptional aspect of the text was the inclusion of portraits of the kings mentioned in the book, often modeled on Sasanian coins, although for the Islamic period he complains of not being able to find pictorial representations of Iranian kings since such realistic portraiture was discouraged in the Islamic era and considered "idol-worshiping" (*Nāma-ye ḵosrovān*, II, pp. 7-9). Despite Jalāl-al-Din Mirzā's claim to having read recent Western scholarship on Iran, he apparently was not familiar with the Persian translation of the Bisotun inscription (see BISOTUN iii), originally translated by the British archeologist Henry Rawlinson (1810-95). He was also apparently unaware of the history of the Achaemenids, through sources like Herodotus (q.v.), since he follows the *Dabestān-e maḏāheb* (q.v., and see below) with a brief recital of the five mythical dynasties as recounted there (Ābādiān, Jiān, etc.) before arriving at the more familiar traditional accounts of the Pišdādiān dynasty and the Kianids whose dynasty was supposedly terminated by Alexander (q.v.) and his invasion of Iran.

Figure 2. Jamšid, mythical king of Iran, believed to be the father of human civilization. After *Nāma-ye ḵosrovān*, ed. Vienna, 1880, p. 60.

While the writing of such an Iran-centered history was unique during the Qajar era, it was not completely without precedence. The 14th-century historian and geographer Ḥamd-Allāh Mostawfi Qazvini (1280-1350, q.v.) in his *Tāriḵ-e gozida* demonstrates his acute awareness of pre-Islamic dynasties of Iran, often drawing on *Tāriḵ-e Ṭabari* and the *Šāh-nāma*. The *Šāh-nāma* had a major impact on Jalāl-al-Din Mirzā's work, not only as a source, but insofar as both narratives mixed legends with history. A more recent influence came from the school of Āḏar Kayvān (see ĀẔAR KAYVĀN, b. circ. 1529-33; d. circ. 1609-18) a neo-Zoroastrian movement originating in Iran and thriving in the Mughal court of Akbar (r. 1556-1605, q.v.), which tended to emphasize the superiority of Persian-Zoroastrian legacy over Arab-Islamic elements. Jalāl-al-Din Mirzā draws upon the pseudo-historical text *Dabestān-e maḏāheb* associated with this school, as a crucial source for the early period of Iran's ancient history, although much of the details provided are mythical and legendary. In the absence of proper historical sources for ancient Iran, Jalāl-al-Din Mirzā often turned to texts inspired by Āḏar Kayvān's school. Although these texts have been dismissed by many scholars as historically unreliable, they are still important for the light they shed on the intellectual formation of the authors of the time, including Jalāl-al-Din Mirzā, and their attempt to retrieve the Iranian national identity and heritage. In terms of European sources, Jalāl-al-Din Mirzā makes some mention of European travelers to Persepolis (*taḵt-e jamšid*) alluding perhaps to Sir Gore Ouseley (1770-1844, q.v. at *iranica.com*) and Sir William Ouseley (1769-1842, q.v. at *iranica.com*) or to the British painter and traveler Robert Ker Porter (1777-1842). His use of European sources for the Sasanian period is also evident from his references to European calendar dating.

Figure 3. Ardašir Bābakān, the founder of Sasanian dynasty. After *Nāma-ye ḵosrovān*, ed. Vienna, 1880, p. 210.

The sources for the second and third volumes of the *Nāma-ye ḵosrovān* appear to have been drawn mainly from two popular universal histories: Ḡiāṯ-al-Din Ḵ^v^āndamir's (ca. 1475—ca. 1535, q.v.) *Ḥabib al-siar* (q.v., printed in Tehran in 1263/1846-47) and Moḥammad b. Ḵ^v^āndšāh Mirḵ^v^ānd's (1433-98) *Rowżat al-ṣafāʾ* (qq.v.), supplemented by Reżāqoli Khan Hedāyat's addendum (printed in Tehran in 1270-74/1853-58). He generally follows these sources closely in outline and chronology, though with a more plain and simple diction than that of his medieval or contemporary counterparts. For the third volume he also appears to draw on Mirzā Moḥammad-Mahdi Khan Astarābādi's (d. between 1759-68) *Tāriḵ-e Jahāngošā-ye Nāderi*.

Jalāl-al-Din Mirzā's narrative is unique among Persian historical sources for the manner in which it connects the pre-Islamic period to the Islamic era. While there were other Persian texts establishing continuity with pre-Islamic past, this was often done through stories from the Hebrew Bible, the Qur'ān, Hadith narratives, and even accounts of the Jāheliya period and Hellenistic philosophers. *Nāmā-ye ḵosrovān*, on the other hand, was probably the first to observe continuity in the political and cultural narrative of the Perso-Islamic past. Islam thus received little exposure in the narrative of the *Nāma-ye ḵosrovān*. Moreover, the Arab conquest and the subsequent destruction of the Sasanian Empire is given central importance. Turco-Mongol tribal dynasties were also blamed alongside the Arabs for bringing havoc in their wake (*Nāma-ye ḵosrovān*, I, p. 10 and II, p. 12). Such an emphasis on the destructive character of the Arab and Mongol invasions was rooted in the nineteenth century European Orientalist scholarship. More broadly, it stemmed from European Romanticist historiography that tended to see the shaping of national identity through the prism of national conflict against foreign and tyrannical powers. The ancient and glorious past, therefore, was held up as an emblematic model for a better future while the present was interpreted as being oppressive in light of injustices emanating from abroad.

While Jalāl-al-Din Mirzā might not have been directly influenced by European romanticism, he certainly conjured up an idealized image of the past, the shaping of which took precedence over historical accuracy. This becomes palpable in his uncritical praise for the pre-Islamic shahs of Persia, an implicit counterpart to his criticism of Nāṣer-al-Din Shah and the Qajar establishment, and perhaps intended to serve also as kind of counsel to the king (*naṣiḥat-nāma*). This is not to say, however, that Jalāl-al-Din Mirzā sympathizes with historical anti-state movements in pre-Islamic Iran. Mazdak and Mani are assessed negatively and so are other heterodox movements of later centuries. Indeed, at no point does he appear to question the royal institution itself and its claims to inherent legitimacy (*Nāma-ye ḵosrovān*, I, pp. 251, 318-40).

While foreigners, mainly the Arabs and Turks, are blamed for the Iranian decline, there are some exceptions. Surprisingly, he is sympathetic towards the Ghaznavid ruler Maḥmud (r. 998-1030; *Nāma-ye ḵosrovān*, III, p. 49), Chinghiz Khan (d. 1227, see ČENGIZ KHAN), and Timur (1336-1405, q.v.), although he remains critical of the Il-khanids (q.v.). Among more recent monarchs, Jalāl-al-Din Mirzā praises Shah Abbas I (r. 1588-1629, q.v.; *Nāma-ye ḵosrovān*, III, p. 99), Nāder Shah (r. 1736-47, q.v.; *Nāma-ye ḵosrovān*, III, pp. 117-38), and Karim Khan Zand (r. 1751-79; *Nāma-ye ḵosrovān*, III, pp. 139-48). His praise for Karim Khan, the great rival of the early

Figure 4. Ḵosro I Anušaravān, the last great Sasanian king. After *Nāma-ye ḵosrovān*, ed. Vienna, 1880, p. 325.

Qajars, as a "victorious and brave king" who showed considerable kindness to his subjects, testifies to Jalāl-al-Din Mirzā's ability to distance himself from entrenched pro-Qajar loyalties.

Jalāl-al-Din Mirzā's commitment to employing exclusively words of Persian origin should be understood within the broader context of his desire to revive Persia's pre-Islamic heritage. The origins of such a nostalgic return to pure Persian harks back, as suggested above, to at least the 16th-century Āḏar-e Kayvān movement that was possibly known to Jalāl-al-Din Mirzā through reading Mollā Firuz's *Dasātir* (q.v.). Among his near contemporaries, several men of letters could have also had some influence on him. Yaḡmā Jandaqi (1781-1859) noted for his epistolary style, was known for employing pure Persian in his letters. But, unlike him, Jalāl-al-Din Mirzā's pure Persian was aimed to be simple and accessible. In this respect, he should be seen as a forerunner of the 20th-century writers of simple Persian prose, but, contrary to later figures such as Aḥmad Kasravi (1890-1946), Jalāl-al-Din Mirzā made no attempt to coin Persian neologisms. He did however employ new expressions with skill, including *dāstān* for history, *dāstānsarā* for historian, and *peyḡambar* instead of *rasul* for prophet or messenger. Jalāl-al-Din Mirzā's style was praised by Mirzā Eskandar Kāẓem Beg (*Nāma-ye ḵosrovān*, II, preface) and Fatḥ-ʿAli Āḵundzāda (Āḵundzāda, p. 221), both of whom wrote to the Qajar prince expressing their admiration. Āḵundzāda in particular commended Jalāl-al-Din Mirzā for having liberated Persian from the ungainly shackles of adopted Arabic words and expressions in Persian. Jalāl-al-Din Mirzā, however, was open in his criticism of Āḵundzāda's naive usage of Arabicized French words. His aversion to Arabic made him hope that, in the future, Persian children would learn French rather than Arabic in schools (Āḵundzāda, pp. 376-77). While Jalāl-al-Din Mirzā's purified Persian appears to have had few immediate imitators, yet it in due course he foreshadowed similar attempts during the Pahlavi era (see FARHANGESTĀN).

Death and legacy. Jalāl-al-Din Mirzā had already lost his sight at the time of publication of the second volume of his history (*Nāma-ye ḵosrovān*, III, p. 386). He had also contracted syphilis (possibly contributing to his blindness) which eventually led to his death at the age of forty-six in 1872 (Bāmdād, I, p. 255). Towards the end of his life, the Qajar prince expressed a desire to perform the pilgrimage to Mecca (Āḵundzāda, p. 252). One interpretation for this apparent conversion may have been his hope for recovery and the urge to absolve himself from accusations of heresy. It is also possible that his request to leave the country for *ḥajj* might, in reality, have been a mere pretext for gaining royal permission to leave Persia and possibly visit Europe. Such hope may have been spurred by the appointment of Mirzā Ḥosayn Khan Mošir-al-Dawla to the premiership in 1869. Indeed, the liberalizing cultural climate of the early 1870s allowed the publication of the third volume of the *Nāma-ye Ḵosrovān*, possibly with the premier's patronage.

After his death, Jalāl-al-Din Mirzā's work was largely forgotten by the general public. *Nāma-ye ḵosrovān* was published twice abroad, in Bombay in 1319/1899 and then in Lucknow in 1931, where it may have been assigned as a history textbook. Khan Ṣāḥeb Moḥammad Širāzi, Malek-al-Kottāb, the publisher of the Bombay edition, also produced the fourth volume of the *Nāma-ye ḵosrovān* in the style of Jalāl-al-Din Mirzā and brought the events up to date, albeit in an inferior quality. The conclusion of volume four of the Bombay edition states that the text was assigned for Persian examination (presumably the Indian Civil Service) from 1901 to 1904.

In spite of the apparent neglect, the influence of *Nāma-ye ḵosrovān* can be traced in historical writing of the Constitutional Revolution (1905-11, q.v.) and after. Although no longer published in Iran, it served as a prototype for modern Persian textbooks and the emphasis on dynastic history continued into the nationalist histories of the early Pahlavi period. Like the *Nāma-ye ḵosrovān*, historiography of the Pahlavi period tended to glorify the pre-Islamic era at the expense of the Islamic era—particularly the recent past, which received less attention. Likewise, the Arab conquest and the Turkish and Mongol invasions were blamed for Iran's decay and destruction. In such reading, the West was held up as a model of renewal. In the linguistic project of the Pahlavi era there also existed a tendency, similar to that of the *Nāma-ye ḵosrovān*, of expunging Arabic and Turkish elements from Persian.

Jalāl-al-Din Mirzā's focus of blame on the twin forces of emasculated traditional kingship and conservative religious establishment is emblematic of liberal intellectuals of his age. Like his contemporaries, he, too, was enamored of the modern Western secular culture and saw it as the panacea for Persia's ills, but like many he failed to see the West's hegemonic presence as a political threat. Like Āḵundzāda, he tended to emphasize culture and language as the key to the country's renewal. Yet his work marked a new age in Persian historiography. It differs markedly not only from court chronicles of his time, but also from the Shiʿite *rejāl* literature or martyrology and from the Sufi hagiographies of the period. As such, his works should be seen as one of the earliest examples of modern Iranian national narrative standing between the legendary memory of the past, as in the *Šāh-nāma*, and the first glimpses of European studies of ancient Iran popularized for Iranian audiences. Although in popular appeal it came nowhere near such contemporary chronicles as Sepehr's *Nāseḵ al-tawāriḵ* and Hedāyat's *Rowżat al-ṣafāʾ-e Nāṣeri*, the *Nāma-ye ḵosrovān* nonetheless seems to have been the source of inspiration for the popular painters of the so called "coffeehouse school" (see ṢAQQĀ-ḴĀNA School of Painting) of the late Qajar and early Pahlavi periods.

Bibliography: Fatḥ-ʿAli Āḵundzāda, *Alefbā-ye jadid wa maktubāt*, ed. Ḥamid Moḥammadzāda and Ḥamid Arasli, Baku, 1963. Fereydun Ādamiyat, *Andišehā-ye Mirzā Fatḥ-ʿAli Āḵundzāda*, Tehran, 1960. Hamid Algar, *Mirza Malkum Khan: A Biographical Study of Iranian Modernism*, Berkeley, Calif., 1973. ʿAbbās Amānat, "Hamrāh-e Mirzā Ṣāleḥ az Eṣfahān be Tehrān," *Āyanda* 9/1, 1983, pp. 36-49. Idem, *Resurrection and Renewal: The Making of the Babi Movement in Iran, 1844-1850*, Ithaca, N.Y., 1989. Idem, *Pivot of the Universe: Nasir al-Din Shah and the Iranian Monarchy, 1831-1896*, Berkeley, Calif., 1997. Idem, "Eʿteżād-al-Salṭana," *EIr* VIII, 1998, pp. 669-72. Idem, "Pur-e ḵāqān wa andiša-ye bāzyābi-e tāriḵ-e melli-e Irān: Jalāl-al-Din Mirzā wa *Nāma-ye Ḵosrovān*," *Irān-nāma/Iran Nameh* 17/1, Winter 1999, pp. 5-54. Moḥammad-Mahdi Khan Astarābādi, *Tāriḵ-e Jahāngošā-ye Nāderi*, Tehran, 1989. Solṭān Aḥmad ʿAżod-al-Dawla, *Tāriḵ-e ʿAżodi*, ed. ʿAbd-al-Ḥosayn Navāʾi, Tehran, 1977. Mehdi Bāmdād, *Šarḥ-e ḥāl-e rejāl-e Irān dar qorun-e davāzdahom wa sizdahom wa čahārdahom-e hejri*, 6 vols., Tehran, 1968-78. *Čehel sāl-e tāriḵ-e Irān*, ed. Iraj Afšār, 3 vols., Tehran, 1984-89. Henry Corbin, "Āẕar (Aḏar) Kayvān," *EIr* III, 1987, pp. 183-87. *The Dasatir or Sacred Writings of the Ancient Persian Prophets*, ed. Mollā Firuz b. Kāvus, Bombay, 1818. Aḥmad-ʿAli Divān-Beygi, *Ḥadiqat al-šoʿarāʾ: dar šarḥ-e ḥāl wa āṯār-e šāʿerān wa ṣufiān wa honarmandān-e dowra-ye Qājāriya az sāl-e 1200 tā 1300 hejri-e qamari*, ed. ʿAbd-al-Ḥosayn Navāʾi, 3 vols., Tehran, 1985-87. Moḥammad-Ḥasan Khan Eʿtemād-al-Salṭana, *Merʾāt al-boldān*, ed. ʿAbd-al-Ḥosayn Navāʾi and Jalāl Moḥaddeṯ, 4 vols., Tehran, 1988-89. Reżāqoli Khan Hedāyat, *Tāriḵ-e rawżat al-ṣafā-ye Nāṣeri*, 10 vols., Tehran, 1959-60. Idem, *Majmaʿ al-foṣaḥāʾ*, ed. Maẓāher Moṣaffā, 6 vols., Tehran, 1960. Jalāl-al-Din Mirzā, *Nāma-ye ḵosrovān: dāstān-e pādšāhān-e Pārs be zabān-e pārsi ke sudmand-e mardomān be viže kudakān ast*, 3 vols., Tehran, 1868-72; ed. Vienna, 1880 ed. Moḥammad Malek-al-Kottāb, Bombay, n.d. [1889-90?], repr. Lucknow, 1931. Abu'l-Ḥasan Yaḡmā Jandaqi, *Kolliāt-e Yaḡmā'-e Jandaqi*, Tehran, 1960. Ḡiāṯ-al-Din Ḵᵛāndamir, *Tāriḵ-e ḥabib al-siar fi aḵbār-e afrād-e bašar*, ed. Jalāl-al-Din Homā'i, 4 vols., Tehran, 1954. Moḥammad-Jaʿfar Ḵurmuji, *Tāriḵ-e Qājār: ḥaqā'eq al-aḵbār-e Nāṣeri*, ed. Ḥosayn Ḵadivjam, Tehran, 1965. Moḥammad-Taqi Sepehr Lesān-al-Molk, *Tāriḵ-e Qājāriya [Nāseḵ al-tawāriḵ]*, ed. Moḥammad-Bāqer Behbudi, Tehran, 1996. Ḥosayn Maḥbubi Ardakāni, *Tāriḵ-e mo'assasāt-e tamaddon-e jadid dar Irān*, 3 vols., Tehran, 1975-89. Fatḥ-Allāh Mojtabā'i, "Dabestān-e Maḏāheb," *EIr* VI/5, 1993, pp. 532-34. Idem, "Dasātir," *EIr* VII, 1994, p. 85. Ḥamd-Allāh Mostawfi-Qazvini, *Tāriḵ-e gozida*, ed. ʿAbd-al-Ḥosayn Homā'i, 3rd ed., Tehran, 1985. William Ouseley, *Travels in Various Countries of the East, More Particularly Persia, etc.*, 3 vols., London, 1819. George Rawlinson, *The Seventh Great Oriental Monarchy*, London, 1876. Rašid Šahmardān, *Farzān-egān-e Zartošti*, 2nd ed., Tehran, 1984. Ṭāher Ša'ri Eṣfahāni, *Ganj-e šāyegān*, Tehran, 1855-56, lithogr. Moḥammad-Maʿṣum Širāzi, *Ṭarā'eq al-ḥaqā'eq*, ed. Moḥammad-Jaʿfar Maḥjub, 3 vols., Tehran, 1966. Denis Wright, *The English Amongst the Persians*, London, 1964. ʿAbd-al-Raḥim Kalāntar Żarrābi (Sohayl Kāšāni) *Tāriḵ-e Kāšān (Mer'āt al-Qāsān)*, ed. Iraj Afšār, Tehran, 1956, repr., 1962.

(ABBAS AMANAT and FARZIN VEJDANI)

JALĀL-AL-DIN MOḤAMMAD BALḴI, MAWLAWI. See RUMI. Forthcoming, online.

JALĀL-AL-DIN ABU'L-QĀSEM **TABRIZI** (b. Tabriz, early 13th century; d. Bengal, 642/1244-45), a prominent Sufi of the Sohravardiya Order. He started his education in Tabriz under Badr-al-Din Abu Saʿid Tabrizi. After his teacher's death, he moved to Baghdad where he studied with Šehāb-al-Din Abu Ḥafṣ ʿOmar Sohravardi (539-632/1145-1234). Jalāl-al-Din stayed with Sohravardi for several years and, as it is reported in the *Aḵbār al-akyār*, accompanied him on the annual pilgrimages to Mecca and Medina (Sobieroj). Through Sohravardi, Jalāl-al-Din became close to another disciple of his, Bahā'-al-Din Zakariyā (d. 661/1262). When Sohravardi ordered Bahā'-al-Din Zakariyā to migrate to Multan (Molṭān, in modern Pakistan), he permitted Jalāl-al-Din to travel with Bahā'-al-Din. Jalāl-al-Din and Bahā'-al-Din are to be considered the founders of the Sohravardiya Order in India (Sobieroj, quoting Rizvi, I, p. 190). On the way to India, at Nišapur, they met the famous Persian poet Farid-al-Din ʿAṭṭār (d. 618/1221, q.v.). Thereafter, some disagreement must have ensued between the two traveling companions and, while Bahā'-al-Din went on to Multan, Jalāl-al-Din set off for Delhi. En route, at Kahtwal (near Multan), he met the famous Cheshti (see ČEŠTIYA) Sufi, Farid-al-Din Masʿud Ganj-e Šakar (d. 664/1265; see GANJ-E ŠAKAR, FARID-AL-DIN MASʿUD; Čerāḡ-e Dehli, pp. 219-20).

Jalāl-al-Din was received with much ceremony at the outskirts of Delhi by the reigning sultan, Šams-al-Din Eltotmeš (r. 1211-36; see ELTOTMEŠ, ŠAMS-AL-DIN), who brought him to the palace. Jalāl-al-Din was lodged nearby, so that the sultan could call on him more easily. Jalāl-al-Din visited the famous Cheshti Sufi Qoṭb-al-Din Baḵtiār Kāki (d. 1236) on the occasion of a *samāʿ*. The respect he enjoyed, particularly from Eltotmeš, made him an object of envy. The Shaikh-al-Islam of Delhi, Najm-al-Din Ṣoḡrā, contrived to discredit Jalāl-al-Din by bribing a local dancer and a moneylender to lay charges of adultery against him (*Siar al-ʿārefin*). In 1228, the sultan convened an investigation to test the charges. Najm-al-Din Soḡrā proposed Bahā'-al-Din Zakariyā to preside at the proceedings—no doubt counting on his disagreement with the accused to sway his judgment. Many distinguished ulema and Sufis attended. In the event, the dancer's nerve failed her, and she withdrew her allegations and confessed the plot with Najm-al-Din Soḡrā. Though exonerated in this way, Jalāl-al-Din Tabrizi was profoundly disillusioned with Delhi and withdrew from the city and its intrigues.

He moved to Badā'un (modern Budaun or Badaun in Uttar Pradesh, India), where he is credited with founding a mosque and with converting many Hindus and Buddhists to Islam (Rizvi, II, p. 398; Trimingham, p. 232). There he passed the mantle to ʿAlā'-al-Din Oṣuli, who later became famous as the teacher of the Cheshti Sufi Neẓām-al-Din Moḥammad Awliyā' Badā'uni (d. 726/1325). The names of two of his deputies (*ḵalifa*) from Badā'un are recorded, Shaikh Borhān-al-Din and Shaikh ʿAli Mowlānā.

From Badā'un, Jalāl-al-Din moved on to Bengal, settling (according to later writers) in Pandua (in modern West Bengal state of India), where he founded a mosque, a garden, and a *ḵāneqāh* (hospice reserved for Sufi mystics) much frequented by the poor, wayfarers, and Hindu yogis. He is said to have had many students and disciples but, despite his personal prestige, the *ḵāneqāh* did not evolve into a major Sohravardi center. Nevertheless, his memory was greatly cherished, and many successive rulers renovated in his honor the buildings in Pandua that were associated with him—the Friday mosque (*masjed-e jāmeʿ*), the *ḵāneqāh*, and the *čella-ḵāna* (premises to spend time at during the 40-day period of fasting, see ČELLA ii). An inscription on the *čella-ḵāna* in Deotala (in modern West Bengal state of India) indicates that a mosque was built in Deotala under his initiative and that the place was renamed to Tabrizābād, after Jalāl-al-Din Tabrizi's name.

It is recorded (Sejzi, pp. 99-100) that Jalāl-al-Din Tabrizi exchanged letters with Bahā'-al-Din Zakariyā on the evils of wealth, any rancor between them presumably long since forgotten. He is credited with having had an enduring impact in Bengal and inspiring many people to take the journey to God through Islam. According to Ḡolām Sarvar Lāhuri's *Ḵazinat al-aṣfiā'*, he died in 642/

1244-45, but this is not certain. Ebn Baṭṭuta (d. 770/1368-69, q.v.) must have confused Jalāl-al-Din Tabrizi with Shah Jalāl of Sylhet (Sobieroj, quoting Rizvi, I, p. 341) whom he met in western Assam around 740/1340 (Ebn Baṭṭuṭa, IV, pp. 216-22; cf. Storey, I/2, p. 971, n. 7).

Bibliography: Karim Abdul, *Social History of the Muslims of Bengal, down to A.D. 1538*, 2nd ed., Chittagong, 1985. S. Moḥammad Mobārak ʿAlawi-Kermāni (Amir-e Ḵord), *Siar al-owliyaʾ*, Delhi, 1884-85. *Anwār-e aṣafiya*, 4th ed., Lahore, 1985. Naṣir-al-Din Maḥmud Čerāḡ-e Dehli, *Ḵeyr al-majāles: malfuẓāt-e ḥażrat-e šeyḵ Naṣir-al-Din Maḥmud Čerāḡ-e Dehli*, ed. K. A. Nizami and H. Qalandar, Aligarh, 1959. ʿAbd-al-Raḥmān Češti, *Merʿāt al-asrār*, Lahore, 1990; ed. and tr. V. B. Siyal as *Miratulasrar: qadim o ghair matbu'ah tazkirah-yi Sufiyah ka avvalin Urdu tarjumah*, 2 vols., Lahore, 1982. ʿAbd-al-Ḥaqq b. Seyf-al-Din Moḥaddeṯ Dehlawi, *Aḵbār al-aḵyār fi asrār al-abrār*, Delhi, 1863, repr. 1891; ed. ʿAlim Ašrafḵān, Tehran, 2004. Abu ʿAbd-Allāh Moḥammad b. Moḥammad Lawāti Ṭanji Ebn Baṭṭuṭa, *Toḥfat al-noẓẓār fi ḡarāʾeb al-amṣār wa ʿajāʾeb al-asfār*, tr. H. A. R. Gibb as *The Travels of Ibn Battuta, A.D. 1325-1534*, 5 vols., vol. IV by C. F. Beckingham, vol. V by A. D. H. Bivar, London, 1958-2000. Muhammad Enamul Haq, *A History of Sufi-ism in Bengal*, Dacca, 1975. Moḥammad Ḡowṯi-Šaṭṭāri, *Aḏkār-e abrār*, tr. F. A. Jiyuri as *Urdu tarjumah Gulzar-i abrār: Jahangiri 'ahd ke ek ghair matbu'ah tazkire ka nayab tarjumah*, 2nd ed., Lahore, 1975. ʿAbd-al-Ḥayy b. Faḵr-al-Din al-Ḥasani, *Nozhat al-ḵawāṭer wa bahjat al-masāmeʿ wa al-nawāẓer, yatażammān tarājem ʿolamāʾ al-Hend wa aʿyāne-hā . . .*, 8 vols., 2nd ed., Hyderabad, Deccan, 1951-70. Ḥāmed b. Fażl-Allāh Jamāli, *Siar al-ʿārefin*, Delhi, 1893-94; ed. M. A. Qadri, Lahore, 1976; repr. Chicago, 1993. Ḡolām Moʿin-al-Din ʿAbd-Allāh Ḵalifa, *Maʿārij al-walāyat*, 2 vols., MS from Khaliq Ahmad Nizami's collection, Aligarh, India. Ḡolām Sarvar Lāhuri, *Ḵazinat al-aṣfiāʾ*, 2 vols., Kanpur, 1914. K. A. Nizami, *Some Aspects of Religion and Politics in India during the Thirteenth Century*, Bombay and New York, 1961. I'jazulhaq Quddusi, *Tazkirah-yi Sufiyā'e Bangāl*, Lahore, 1965. S. A. A. Rizvi, *A History of Sufism in India*, 2 vols., New Delhi, 1978-83. Amir Ḥasan Sejzi, *Fawāʾed al-foʾād*, Lucknow, 1884-85. F. Sobieroj, "Tabrīzī, Djalāl al-Dīn, Abu'l-Ḳāsim," EI^2 at www.encislam.br.nl/subscriber/entry?entry=islamSIM-8916, accessed 29 November 2007. C. A. Storey, *Persian Literature: a Bio-bibliographical Survey*, repr. ed., London, 1970. J. S. Trimingham, *The Sufi Orders in Islam*, Oxford, 1971; repr. with a new introduction by J. O. Voll, New York, 1998.

(FARHAN NIZAMI)

JALĀL-AL-DIN TURĀNŠĀH. See MOZAFFARIDS.

JALĀLI,

a Kurdish tribe of eastern Anatolia and northwestern Persia. Basile Nikitine (p. 162) believed that the Jalāli were Kurdicized Armenians. An Armenian connection was also suggested by Moritz Wagner (II, p. 232). The Jalāli of Anatolia have settled down in the vicinity of Diyadin, west of Dogu Beyazit (Blau, 1862, p. 609). According to Nikitine, their clans (*tiras*) are (his spelling): Kotanli, Soranli, Saganli, Hassananli, Ketchananli, Doutkanli, Kapdekanli and Djinankanli (p. 162). The Jalāli of Persia have settled down around Māku in Azerbaijan. According to Ḥosayn-ʿAli Razmārā (*Farhang* IV), they occupy fifteen villages in the rural district (*dehestān*) of Sārisubāsār (northeast of Māku), four villages in the district of Qalʿa Daresi (south of Māku), four villages in the district of Aras-kenār (along the Aras river), two villages in the district of Čāybāsār (east of Māku), and two villages in the district of Āvājiq (west of Māku). According to Komisiun-e melli (I, p. 118), their clans are: Ḵalikānlu, Ḥasuḵalaf, ʿAli Maḥvolu, Miṣrkānlu, Eṭāblu, Qezelbāš, Sākān, Balḵkānlu, Jenikānlu, and Qandkānlu (I, p. 118).

The Jalāli on both sides of the Ottoman-Persian border regularly raided caravans along the main road from Erzurum to Tabriz which, as today, passed through Dogu Beyazit and Māku (Blau, 1858, pp. 586-87). When the Russian offensive into eastern Anatolia was launched in 1915, the Jalāli of Diyadin took refuge on Mount Ararat (q.v.), where they sustained a prolonged siege until they were finally rescued by Ottoman forces in 1918 (Arfa, p. 40). After the war, a substantial number of the Jalāli of Diyadin moved to Persia (Eagleton, p. 17). On 30 June 1930, the Jalāli on both sides of the border revolted. They were soon joined by several other Kurdish tribes and occupied Morādiya and Čālderān. This led to a prolonged and widespread Kurdish uprising, which required the combined efforts of Turkish and Persian troops to subdue. Once more, many Jalāli sought refuge on the slopes of Mount Ararat, but this time they were not able to resist for long, owing to the effective use of aircraft by the Turkish Army (Arfa, pp. 39-42). As a result of this rebellion, Reza Shah Pahlavi (r. 1925-41) issued a *farmān* ordering the entire Jalāli tribe of Māku to move to an area between Tehran, Hamadān and Varāmin in central Persia. After Reza Shah's abdication in September 1941, the Jalāli returned to their ancestral grazing grounds (Komisiun-e melli, I, p. 185). During World War II, the Jalāli of Māku established cordial relations with Soviet authorities (Douglas, p. 70), and, in 1946, they contributed (together with the Milān tribe) a force of 400 mounted warriors to the insurgent Kurdish leader Qāżi Moḥammad (Eagleton, p. 91). Since then, most of the Jalāli on both sides of the border have become sedentary.

The population of the Jalāli tribe of Māku was estimated at 5,000 families by Otto Blau (1858, p. 586), and 25,000 individuals by William Eagleton (p. 17). The Jalāli are Sunnis of the Shafiʿite denomination (Maškur, p. 185).

There is also a small group of Jalāli Kurds in the Jānaki Garmsir, north of Ahvāz (Qāʾem-maqāmi, pp. 66-69). But it is not known whether or not they are related to the Jalāli of Māku.

Bibliography: Iraj Afšār Sistāni, *Ilhā, čadornešinān wa ṭawāyef-e ʿašāyeri-e Irān*, 2 vols., Tehran, 1987, pp. 148 ff. Hassan Arfa, *The Kurds: An Historical and Political Study*, London, 1966. Otto Blau, "Die Stämme des nordöstlichen Kurdistan," *ZDMG* 12, 1858, pp. 584-98. Idem, "Nachrichten über kurdische Stämme," *ZDMG* 16, 1862, pp. 607-27. William Orville Douglas, *Strange Lands and Friendly People*, New York, 1951. William Eagleton, *The Kurdish Republic of 1946*, London, 1963. Komisiun-e melli-e Yunesko (UNESCO) dar Iran, *Irānšahr*, 2 vols., Tehran, 1963-65. Moḥammad-Jawād Maškur, *Naẓar-i ba tāriḵ-e Āḏarbāyjān*, Tehran, 1971, pp. 185-88. Basile Nikitine, *Les Kurdes: étude sociologique et historique*, Paris, 1956; tr. Moḥammad Qāżi as *Kord wa Kordestān: barrasi az naẓar-e jāmeʿa-šenāsi wa tāriḵ*, Tehran, 1999. Jahāngir Qāʾem-maqāmi, "ʿAšāyer-e Ḵuzestān: Jalāli," *Yādgār* 3/10, 1947, pp. 26-37. Friedrich Spiegel, *Eranische Altertumskunde*, 3 vols., Leipzig, 1871-78; repr. Amsterdam, 1971, I, pp. 755-57. Moritz Wagner, *Reise nach Persien and dem Lande der Kurden*, 2 vols., Leipzig, 1852.

(PIERRE OBERLING)

JALĀL-AL-MOLK, See IRAJ MIRZĀ.

JALĀLZĀDA, MOṢṬAFĀ ÇELEBI, also known as "Koja Nişancı" (Ḵᵛāja Nešānči), Ottoman historian and administrator (b. Tosya, ca. 895-900/1490-94; d. Istanbul, 975/1567), It is surmised that he was born in the Tosya district of the city of Kastamonu. The eldest son of the judge Qāżi Jalāl-al-Din, he began his education in Tosya, before continuing at the *madrasa* in the court of the Fetih Mosque in Istanbul (Aşık Çelebi, f. 134a). Upon completion, he was appointed as the Secretary of the Council of State, before being assigned to the post of private secretariat of Piri Pāšā. Following the retirement of the latter in 929/1523, he became the private secretary of Piri Pāšā's successor as Governor General of the Rumeli provinces, Ebrāhim Pāšā.

After the rebellion of Aḥmad Pāšā in 1524, he went to Egypt with Ebrāhim Pāšā. There he contributed to the preparation of the statutes designed to regulate the affairs of Egypt. Upon his return in 931/1525, he replaced the minister of foreign affairs, Ḥaydar Čalabi (*Ṭabaqāt al-mamālek*, p. 129b). After serving for ten years in this post, Jalālzāda joined Süleyman the Magnificent's Baghdad campaign in 951/1534, and later in the same year he was appointed as the *nešānči* (officer whose duty it was to inscribe the Sultan's imperial monogram over all imperial letters). He is famous for excelling in this post, which he held for twenty-three years before his retirement in 964/1551, after which he devoted most of his time to his scholarship. For a short period, Jalālzāda served in the *motafarreqa* office (the department of the police dealing with petty offenses, licenses, etc.), and he also took part in Süleyman the Magnificent's Zigetvar campaign in 974/1566. After the latter's death, he served as the *nešānči* of his son, Selim II, for thirteen months. He died in Istanbul in Rabiʿ I 975/ October 1567. The area around the mosque where "Koja Nişancı" is buried is called "Nişancı" after him.

Works in Turkish, Persian and Arabic: (1) *Ṭabaqāt al-mamālek wa darajāt al-masālek*. This work is a chronicle of Sultan Süleyman the Magnificent's reign and gives information about the organization of the Ottoman state and its institutions. It is comprised of 35 sections and 375 sub-sections. The sections recounting the campaigns in Mohāj, Rodos and Karabāg, which are particularly prominent, exist also as separate manuscripts. The *Ṭabaqāt al-mamālek* has been translated into German by Petra Kappert (1974), and has been published as a facsimile edition (ed. Kappert, 1981; for details of manuscripts, see ibid, pp. 42-50). (2) *Salim-nāma*, a chronicle covering events from Selim I's governorship in Trabzon until his death. It has been published by Ahmed Uğur and Mustafa Çuhadar as *Selim-Nâme* (Ankara, 1990). (3) *Manṣur-Šāh-nāma*. Even though Bursalı Tahir claims that Jalālzāda refers to this work in another work of his own, no copy of this work have yet been found. (4) *Dalāʾel-e nobowwat-e moḥammadi wa šamāʾel-e fotowwat-e aḥmadi*, a translation of the Persian biography of the Prophet Moḥammad, *Maʿāref al-nobowwa fi madārej al-fotowwa* by Moʿin-al-Din Ḥāj Moḥammad Farahi, popularly known as Mollā Meskin. The translation was dedicated to Sultan Süleyman and presented to him as a gift at Edirne in 956/1547. (5) *Estānbol wa maʿbad-e Āyā-Sofya*. This work, which has been translated by an unknown Persian author, is about the Ayasofya Mosque. There is a single copy of this work at the Istanbul Municipal Library, but its attribution to Jalālzāda is uncertain.

Although a complete set of his letters have not survived, the letter Jalālzāda wrote on behalf of Süleyman the Magnificent to Shah Tahmāsp demonstrates his talent in this genre. He did not write any poetry apart from the occasional verses he included in his prose works. An anthology of poetry that he had compiled can be found at Süleymaniye Library (*Ašir Efendi*, no. 1004), and he is also attributed with two minor religious works, called *Hadiat al-moʾmenin* and *Jawāhir al-aḵbār*.

Bibliography: Aşık Çelebi, *Mašāʾer al-šoʿarāʾ*, ed. G. Meredith-Owens. London, 1971. Sehi Bey, *Heşt Bihişt: the Tezkire*, ed. Günay Kut, Cambridge, Mass., 1978, ff. 33a-34b (pp. 135-38). M. Tayyib Gökbilgin, "Celâlzâde," *İA* III, pp. 61-64. Latifi, *Tezkire*, Istanbul, 1898, pp. 335-37. Moṣṭafā Jalālzāda, *Ṭabakât ül-memâlik ve derecat ül-mesâlik*, ed. Petra Kappert, Wiesbaden, 1981, ff. 10a-b, 20b, 57b, 69a, 109b, 111b, 163b, 172b, 250a-b, 251a, 260a, 334a-b, 367b, 428a, 454a-b, 479b-481b, 482a, 485b, 528a. Idem, *Selim-Nâme*, eds. Ahmed Uğur and Mustafa Çuhadar, Ankara, 1990, foreword and pp. v-xxi. Petra Kappert, "Mustafa b. Celals "Tabakat al-mamalik" als Quelle für die Osmanische Geschichte des 16. Jahrhunderts," in A. Gallotta, ed., *Studi Preottomani et Ottomani, atti del Convegno di Napoli (24-26 settembre 1974)*, Naples, 1976. Celia J. Kerslake, "A Critical Edition and Translation of the Introductory

Section and First Thirteen Chapters of *Selimnâme*," unpublished PhD Dissertation, Oxford University. Agâh Sırrı Levend, *Gazavatnameler*, Ankara 1956, p. 27. Joseph Matuz, *Das Kanzleiwesen Sultan Süleymans des prächtigen*. Wiesbaden, 1974, pp. 30-32. V. L. Menage, "D̲jalālzāde Muṣṭafā Çalabi," *EI*² II, p. 400. *Türkiye Diyanet Vakfı İslâm Ansiklopedisi*, Istanbul, 1993, VII, pp. 262-64 (Celâlzâde Sâlih Çelebi). Hakkı Uzunçarşılı, "Onaltıncı asır ortalarında yaşamış olan iki büyük şahsiyet: Tosyalı Celalzâde Mustafa ve Salih Çelebiler," *Türk Tarih Kurumu Belleteni* 22, 1958, pp. 391-422.

(TAHSİN YAZICI)

JALĀYER. See KHORASAN, TRIBES.

JALĀYER, ESMĀʿIL KHAN, a prominent painter of the Qajar era who lived during the reign of Nāṣer-al-Din Shah (r. 1848-96). He was particularly noted for his work in two popular though different genres of Qajar paintings of the period, *irāni-sāzi* (concentrating on Iranian subjects, drawing on facial features, make-up, costume, and relatively unaffected by European influences) and *ṭabiʿat-sāzi* (concentrating on fauna and flora in a European naturalistic mode, aiming at verisimilitude).

Life. He was the son of Ḥāji Moḥammad Khan Jalāyer Kalāti from an ancient and eminent family of Khorasan (Hedāyat, *Majmaʿ al-foṣaḥāʾ* IV, p. 429; Ḏokāʾ, p. 662) but there is no precise information about the dates of his birth and death or place of burial (for further information about his son and other descendants and his own lineage see Fatḥi, *Rāhnemā-ye ketāb*, pp. 655-56; Ḏokāʾ, p. 662). Moreover, only a few of his paintings bear a date: one is a portrait of Nāṣer-al-Din Shah in watercolor, dated Rabiʿ II, 1279 A.H./1862 C.E., others include a depiction of a scene from the battle of Herat (1856; see HERAT. vi) drawn by Esmāʿil Jalāyer to complete work originally begun by an earlier famous painter, Moḥammad-Ḥasan Afšār, on a pen-box (for further details, see below). The date inscribed on the box is 8 Šaʿbān 1296/17 May 1878 (Robinson, *Muqarnas*, pp. 131-46). Further information about his work and apprenticeship can be gleaned from accounts given by two of his contemporaries, Ḵalil Khan Ṯaqafi (Aʿlam-al-Dawla) and Dust-Moḥammad Khan (Moʿayyer-al-Mamālek). He was a student at the Dār-al-fonun (q.v.; Ṯaqafi, p. 163) during ʿAliqoli Mirzā Eʿteżād-al-Salṭana's (q.v., 1822-80) long directorship of the college (1857-80). He was taught painting there by Monsieur Constant (Maḥbubi Ardakāni, I, pp. 283, 329, 331) and Mirzā ʿAli-Akbar Khan Kāšāni (Mozayyan-al-Dawla). He graduated as one of the top-ranking students (*Irān* newspaper, No. 55), his work attracting the attention and patronage of the Shah as well as some of his courtiers including ʿAli-Aṣḡar Khan Atābak-e Aʿẓam (q.v.), and Dust-Moḥammad Khan (Moʿayyer-al-Mamālek). As well as at the Dār-al-fonun itself, Jalāyer taught and worked at two other ateliers, one in the Atābak Park (*Pārk-e Atābak*), and the other in the public quarters (*biruni*, q.v.) of the Ferdows Garden (*bāḡ-e ferdows*), residence of Moʿayyer-al-Mamālek (Fatḥi, *Rāhnemā-ye ketāb*, p. 655). He must have continued with his artistic activities at least until 1307/1889 when reportedly the fifteen-year old Moʿayyer-al-Mamālek was taking lessons from him at his workshop in the Ferdows Garden (Moʿayyer-al-Mamālek, *Yaḡmā* 12, p. 74).

Esmāʿil Jalāyer was a most fastidious man with a pleasing countenance and a fondness for witty anecdotes and repartees. He led a frugal life and was a habitual smoker of opium. Because of his family background (his father belonged to the Ḏahabiya [q.v.] Order of Sufis; Ḏokāʾ, p. 662) as well as his own deep personal faith, many of his paintings represent religious themes and subjects, including the Prophet and his family and companions and those of the founders and luminaries of Sufi sects and dervishes.

Works. He was skilled in different techniques and branches of painting. His watercolors, pen-and-ink, and oil drawings, his work in portraiture and landscape, and his paintings on lacquered boxes and pen-cases, can all be regarded as masterpieces in their own right. However, his critical eye and perennial quest for perfection meant that once he detected the slightest flaw in one his canvasses, he would tear it up, and this explains why so few of his works have survived (Fatḥi *Rāhnemā-ye ketāb*, pp. 654-55). His work may be divided into different groups on the basis of their subject matter and style:

Portraits of royalty and notables. The list includes Nāṣer-al-Din Shah, Mirzā Ḥosayn Khan Sepahsālār, ʿAli-Aṣḡar Khan (Atābak-e Aʿẓam), and other courtiers and men of eminence. Oil, watercolor and pen-and-ink using the technique of *noqṭa-pardāzi*, a method that uses almost imperceptible dots to induce a chiaroscuro [*sāya rowšan*] effect while creating a meticulously detailed and realistic likeness of the subject. The portraits depict the sitters in different moods and bring out their personal traits; be it pensive, cheerful, or magnanimous, with a dignified and commanding aura. Those of Nāṣer-al-Din Shah himself include an undated but signed pen-and-ink drawing of the monarch on horseback in the Museum of Decorative Arts in Tehran, as well as a watercolor of the Shah seated on a chair in full regal attire with a bejeweled belt and sword and bearing the Sun decoration on his chest, with the inscription, "Esmāʿil Jalāyer; the month of Rabiʿ II of the year 1279."

Portraits of notables include a 90 x 70 cm. oil portrait of Mirzā Ḥosayn Khan Sepahsālar with the signature "Work of the painter to the Exalted Government of Iran, Esmāʿil, son of the late Ḥājj Zamān Khan Jalāyer." The subject is depicted astride a finely drawn horse with a garden and some rustic huts in the background.

There is also an oil painting of Mirzā ʿAli-Aṣḡar Khan Atābak (Amin-al-Solṭān), sitting on a chair, and wearing a jewel-studded medallion depicting the picture of Nāṣer-al-Din Shah. The room with its furniture and decorations are drawn in some detail. Colorful fruit trees fill the outer space and there is also an inscription in the *nastʿaliq* style (see CALLIGRAPHY) in black ink with white margins containing a line from Ḥāfeẓ, "If the grace of the Holy Ghost grants his aid anew/Others can achieve what the Messiah was accustomed to do" (*Fayż-e ruḥ ol-qodos ar bāz madad farmāyad/digarān ham bekonand ānča Masiḥā mikard*). In the background that displays a garden, there is a lion with a sword under an image of the sun, with the single word *zamāmdāri* (rule, sovereignty) inscribed on its sheath. In the foreground there is another piece of writing stating that "this single verse of Hafez has been inscribed by copying the handwriting of His Most Exalted Excellency Amin-al-Solṭān, may one be sacrificed for him!" This portrait too depicts the same person.

Paintings with religious and mystical subjects and themes. As already pointed out, these include images of the prophets and religious and mystical luminaries, and are mostly in watercolor or pen-an-ink, but occasionally also in oil. In some cases the result is a fusion of Persian traditional painting and European naturalistic style. Sometimes, as in the oil painting on canvas of Nur-ʿAli Šāh as a young dervish, presently in the Decorative Arts Museum of Tehran, despite the very Persian way the face is made up, and the Sufi garb donned by the subject, it is the European naturalistic aspect of the style that catches the eye (Figure 1). The young mystic has his long hair scattered over his shoulders, and sits in the middle of a garden, holding an ornate walking stick with one hand and the chain of a *kaškul* (a dervish's begging bowl) in the other. This and other portraits of Nur-ʿAli Šāh by the painter have been copied on many a carpet from Kerman and in all sizes (Ḏokāʾ, p. 664).

Figure 1. The portrait of Nur-ʿAli Šāh.
Courtesy of the Decorative Arts Museum, Tehran.

Two other portraits of Nur-ʿAli Šāh deserve mention. One, in the Golestān Palace (q.v.) collection, has an autograph, "drawn by the humble Esmāʿil," and another, in the private collection of Amir Bahman Ṣamṣām, also shows the young Sufi with all the trappings of a dervish (see *Camb. Hist. Iran* VII, pl. 37). It is also signed.

An album (*moraqqaʿ*) comprising of pictures of leading Sufi luminaries and masters belonging to the library of Golestān Palace, signed "Esmāʿil Jalāyer ebn al-Ḥāji Zamān Ḵan," and dated 1286 A.H. with idealized depictions of Bāyazid Besṭāmi, Bābā Ṭāher, Awḥadi (qq.v.), Šams of Tabriz, Nur-ʿAli Šāh, Moštāq of Kerman, and Maʿṣum-ʿAli Šāh; as well as two paintings of flowers and grapes (Ātābāy, p. 386).

A painting inspired by the story of Yusof and Zolayḵā (Joseph and the Potiphar's wife), in the Victoria and Albert Museum, London, and exhibited in the famous Burlington House exhibition of 1931, though misdated there (Robinson, *Camb. Hist. Iran* VII, p. 887, n. 57) with a group of Zolayḵā's female companions in Persian costumes sipping tea by a samovar. Yusof and Zolayḵā stand amongst them with the former accepting a cup offered to him by Zolayḵā. Other details include a young woman smoking a water pipe (*ḡalyān*, q.v.), and another playing a stringed instrument (*tār*). On the upper part of the painting there is a brief inscription and signature in nastaʿliq with the name Esmāʿil and an often repeated tag on Persian artifacts to the effect that the work should be considered a memento to commemorate its maker ("*Esmāʿil; ḡarаż naqšist k'az mā bāz mānad.*")

There is a painting with the approximate dimensions of 220 x120 cm. in the Decorative Arts Museum of Tehran depicting Abraham's sacrifice of his son, surrounded by angels, one of whom holds the sacrificial ram (Figure 2). It is painted in the *siāh qalam* manner, a method using mostly black watercolor with tiny touches of white here and there. Traditionally, in the city of Isfahan, they used soot and other products to make little grains that were then ground and mixed with water. Sometimes oil paint was also used. The technique produced a good quality texture unaffected by humidity and could evoke an atmosphere imbued with spirituality.

A horizontally rectangular painting exists in the collection of Mr. Adib Borumand, depicting Imam ʿAli, his sons Imam Ḥasan and Ḥosayn, as well as one of the most celebrated Companions of the Prophet, Salmān-e Fārsi. The painting also contains images of cherubs in the European style.

Paintings with a variety of subjects. A painting approximately 50 x 80 cm., commissioned by the merchant Ḥāji Mirzā ʿAbd-al-Wahhāb and now in the Decorative Arts Museum of Tehran, copies using a brush, the calligraphy of the famous calligrapher Āqā Mirzā Ḡolām-Reżā of a verse from the poet Saʿdi (for the text see Ḏokāʾ, p. 663), with scenes from a traditional coffee-house, a festive gathering of women musicians, and other scenes including the athletes of a *zurḵāna* (the traditional Persian gymnasium). It too bears the signature "the work of Esmāʿil Jalāyer" in a fine nastaʿliq hand and is dated 1284 A.H.

Figure 2. Abraham sacrificing his son.
Courtesy of the Decorative Arts Museum, Tehran.

A pen-box that was completed by the painter has already been referred to above. It had begun as the work of the celebrated painter Moḥammad Beg Afšar of Urmia (sometimes referred to as "the mute master painter," *Naqāšbāši-e lāl*) who showed the unfinished work to the French traveler Xavier Hommaire de Hell (q.v.) in Tabriz on November 15, 1847 (see Khalili, Robinson et al, *Lacquer of the Islamic Lands*, p. 149, for a long extract from Hommaire de Hell who provides a detailed description of the encounter and the illustrations on the pen-box). The box was exhibited in Cairo in 1935 (Wiet, *Exposition d'art persan*, p. 87) and appeared twice at Sotheby's auctions in London (9 October 1978, lot no. 187; and 12 October 2000, lot no. 89). There is a long inscription by Jalāyer in nastaʿliq script on the base clarifying which parts were the original work of "*Naqāšbāši-e lāl*" and which were Jalāyer's own. More comprehensive lists and descriptions of his paintings are to be found in the works by Mohammad-ʿAli Karimzāda-Tabrizi, ʿAbbās Sarmadi and Yaḥyā Ḏokāʾ, cited in the bibliography.

Bibliography: Badri Ātābāy, *Fehrest-e moraqqaʿāt-e Ketābḵāna-ye Salṭanati*, Tehran, 1974. Yaḥyā Ḏokāʾ, in "Esmāʿil Jalāyer," *The Great Islamic Encyclopaedia*, VIII, Tehran, 1998, pp. 662-65. Naṣr-Allāh Fatḥi, *Negin*, 59, 1970; repr. as "Naqāšihā-ye Esmāʿil-e Jalāyer," *Rāhnemā-ye ketāb* 15, 1972, pp. 653-57. Reżāqoli Khan Hedāyat, *Majmaʿ al-foṣaḥā*, ed. Maẓāher Moṣaffā, 6 vols. Tehran 1957-61. Xavier Hommaire de Hell, *Voyage en Turquie et en Perse . . .* , compiled Jules Laurens, Paris, 1854-60, vol. 3, p. 18. *Irān* newspaper, no. 55, 17 Ramażān 1288/30 November 1871. Nasser D. Khalili, B. W. Robinson et al., *Lacquer of the Islamic Lands*, II, The Nasser Khalili Collection of Islamic Art XXII, London, 1997. Ḥosayn Maḥbubi Ardakāni, *Tāriḵ-e moʾassasāt-e tamaddoni-e jadid dar Irān* I, Tehran, 1975, pp. 283, 329, 331. Dust-ʿAli Khan Moʿayyer-al-Mamālek, "Rejāl-e ʿaṣr-e nāṣeri," *Yaḡmā* 10, 1957, pp. 168-75. Idem, "Haštād o panj sāl zendegi dar čand ṣafḥa," (part one) *Yaḡmā* 12/2, April-May 1959, pp. 78-83. Basil William Robinson, "Qajar Lacquer," *Muqarnas* VI, 1989, pp. 131-46; repr. in Idem, *Studies in Persian Art*, I, London, 1993. Moḥammad-ʿAli Karimzāda-Tabrizi, *Aḥwāl wa āṯār-e naqqāšān-e qadim-e Irān*, 3 vols., London, 1983, I, pp. 77-81. ʿAbbās Sarmadi, *Dāneš-nāma-ye honarmandān-e Irān o Islām*, Tehran, 2000, pp. 83-84. *Sotheby's Catalogue*, "Arts of the Islamic World," 12 October 2000, No. 89. Ḵalil Khan Ṯaqafi Aʿlam-al-dawla, *Maqālāt-e gunāgun*, Tehran, 1943, pp. 163-66. Gaston Wiet, *Exposition de d'art persan*, Société des Amis de l'Art, Cairo, 1935.

(MANOUCHEHR BROOMAND)

JALAYERIDS (sometimes called the Ilakāni by Persian historians), a dynasty of Mongol origin which ruled over Iraq, and for several decades also over northwestern Persia, from the collapse of the Il-khanate in the late 1330s until the early 9th/15th century. Its history can be divided into four phases: (1) the early years, in which the dynasty was in practice autonomous but theoretically acknowledged the authority of a series of feeble Il-khans; (2) the apogee of the Jalayerids, coinciding with the reign of Šayḵ Ovays (1356-74); (3) an era of incipient decline following his death, marked by internecine conflict; and (4) a final phase, beginning in 1385, in which the Jalayerid territories were subjected to external attack by the Central Asian conqueror Timur (Temür/Tamerlane) and by the rising power of the Qarā Qoyunlu ('Black Sheep') Türkmen, at whose hands the dynasty met its end. The principal sources are the history produced (c. 1359) for Šayḵ Ovays by his court chronicler, Ahari, and the continuation (down to 1391) which Zayn-al-Din appended to the *Ḏayl-e Ẓafar-nāma* of his father Ḥamd-Allāh Mostawfi Qazvini and which in turn was utilized by Ḥāfeẓ-e Abru for his *Ḏayl-e Jāmeʿ al-tawāriḵ* (see Melville, 1998, pp. 1-4). Additional material can be gleaned from the late 9th/15th-century Iraqi author al-Ḡiāṯ, although his chronology is sometimes at variance with that of the Persian accounts. The numismatic evidence for the history of the period has more recently been collected by Stephen Album, while accounts of the Jalayerid monuments and artists are found in the dated but still useful study by ʿAbbās ʿAzzāwi.

Origins and early history. The amir (or *noyan*) Ilge (Ilkā), known as Köke (Kukā, 'Blue') Ilge, from whom the Jalayerids were descended, belonged to the Jalair

(Jalāyer) tribe, which had occupied pasturelands along the River Onon in Mongolia prior to Genghiz (Čengiz) Khan's time and produced several important military commanders during the Mongol era (Rašid-al-Din, *Jāmeʿ al-tawārik̲* (Moscow), pp. 130-49, tr. Thackston, I, pp. 37-41; *Tārik̲-e Waṣṣāf*, p. 423). Accompanying Hülegü (Hulāgu, q.v.) on his great expedition to Western Asia in the 1250s, Ilkā was among the generals who reduced the Assassin strongholds in Qohestān in 1256 (Jovayni, ed. Qazvini, III, p. 102, tr. Boyle, II, pp. 615-16; Rašid-al-Din, *Jāmeʿ al-tawārik̲* (Baku), p. 29, tr. Thackston, II, p. 482); subsequently he participated in the campaign against Baghdad and after the city's fall in 1258 he was ordered to supervise its reconstruction (Rašid-al-Din, *Jāmeʿ al-tawārik̲*, Baku, pp. 52, 55, 62, tr. Thackston, II, pp. 493, 496, 499). He was in joint command of the forces operating against Mayyāfāreqin, and was sent into Syria late in 1260 to avenge the defeat at ʿAyn Jālut, but withdrew into Anatolia on the approach of the Mamluk Sultan Baybars (ibid., pp. 76, 77, 79, tr. Thackston, II, pp. 506, 507). Ilkā was in charge of the *ordos* ("royal encampment") when Abaqa (q.v.) ascended the throne in 1265 and is described as a veteran amir (ibid., p. 100, tr. Thackston, III, p. 517). He must have died soon afterwards.

A number of his sons were in the service of Abaqa's successors. One of them, Aqbuqa (Āqbuqā), whom the Il-khan Gayk̲ātu (q.v.) promoted to the rank of *mir-e mirān* or chief amir (*Tārik̲-e Waṣṣāf*, pp. 264-5), was executed by the supporters of Bāydu (q.v.) in 1295 (Rašid-al-Din, *Jāmeʿ al-tawārik̲* (Baku), p. 291, tr. Thackston, III, p. 615; *Tārik̲-e Waṣṣāf*, p. 282; Ahari, p. 146). He had married a daughter of the Il-khan Arḡun (q.v.) named Öljetei (Uljatāi) who bore him a son, Ḥosayn (Rašid-al-Din, *Jāmeʿ al-tawārik̲* (Baku), p. 197, tr. Thackston, III, p. 562). Ḥosayn was in attendance on his maternal uncle Öljeitü (Uljāitu, q.v.), prior to his accession as Il-khan, and during his reign stood high in his favor (Ahari, pp. 148-49), receiving the governorship of Arrān in 1313 (*Tārik̲-e Waṣṣāf*, p. 610). He subsequently served Öljeitü's son and successor, Abu Saʿid (q.v.), as governor of Khorasan until his death in 1322 (Ahari, p. 151). His son Ḥasan was the real founder of the Jalayerid dynasty. Having been promoted to the dignitary of *amir-e olus* (or *olus-beg* 'chief amir') under Abu Saʿid, he was accused in 1331 of conspiring against the Il-khan with his former wife, a granddaughter of Čoban (Čobān, q.v.) named Baḡdād k̲ātun, whom Abu Saʿid had misappropriated. Dismissed from office, he was imprisoned in the fortress of Kemāk̲, but was released the following year and sent to Anatolia as governor (Ḥāfeẓ-e Abru, pp. 186-87; Ahari, p. 156). After Abu Saʿid's death in 1335, he married that monarch's widow, Delšād K̲ātun, and the new Il-khan, Arpa (q.v), restored him to the position of senior *amir-e olus* (Ahari, p. 159).

In the chaos that followed the death of Abu Saʿid, the great amirs and provincial governors vied with one another for power. Ḥasan took part in this conflict, at first in opposition to the late Il-khan's maternal uncle, ʿAli Pādšāh, and subsequently against Čoban's progeny, the Chobanids (q.v.). Known as Ḥasan-e Uljatāi, or more often as Ḥasan-e Bozorg to distinguish him from his Chobanid rival Ḥasan-e Kučak, he first entered the struggle after Arpa's downfall in 1336 when, at the instigation of the Oirad (Uyrāt) amir Ḥājji Taḡai (Ṭaḡāy), governor of Diār Bakr, he enthroned Moḥammad in opposition to the puppet Il-khan Musā set up by ʿAli Pādšāh. After Moḥammad's death in battle with the Chobanids (1338), Ḥasan-e Bozorg recognized Taḡai Timur (Ṭaḡā Temür), a descendant of one of Čengiz Khan's brothers and a more powerful prince, who sough to conquer western Iran from his base in Khorasan. A few months later Ḥasan switched his support to Jahān Timur (1339-40), a grandson of the Il-khan Geykhatu (Gayk̲ātu). Thereafter his allegiance is unclear, though he struck coins in the name of his last known Il-khanid protégé, Solaymān, in 745-46/1344-46 (Album 1984, pp. 83, 100). In order to strengthen his position against Ḥasan-e Kučak, he may have acknowledged the sovereignty of the Mamluk Sultan al-Nāṣer Moḥammad just prior to that ruler's death in 1341, striking coins and making the *k̲oṭba* in his name at Baghdad (al-Šojāʿi, pp. 68, 98-101, 115, tr. pp. 95, 128-31, 147-48). Whatever the case, at no time during his own autonomous rule in Baghdad did Ḥasan-e Bozorg claim sovereign status; rather, he contented himself with the title *olus-beg* right until his death in Rajab 757/July 1356. For a brief interval in 1337-38 his authority had been recognized in every part of the Il-khanid Empire except Khorasan (Album 1984, pp. 70-71), but during his later years he held power only in Iraq, having been forced to evacuate Azerbaijan in the winter of 1338-39 by Ḥasan-e Kučak and his brother Malek Ašraf (see CHOBANIDS).

The dynasty's apogee. Ḥasan's son by Delšād k̲ātun, Šayk̲ Ovays (1356-74), was the first of the dynasty to take the title of Sultan. Any internal challenge to the new ruler's position was removed with the early death (in 1359) of his brother Ḥosayn. Soon after his accession, however, Jānibeg, khan of the Mongols of the Golden Horde (q.v.) in the Pontic steppe, which had long coveted Azerbaijan and other territories south of the Caucasus, defeated and killed the Chobanid Malek Ašraf, occupying Tabriz and forcing Ovays to recognize his overlordship. The khan died shortly after returning to the north, and his son Berdibeg, whom he had left in command in Azerbaijan, hurried off to secure the succession, though he reigned only briefly. One of Ašraf's former officers named Ak̲ičoq (Ak̲ičuq) now usurped control in Tabriz (1357). For a time Tabriz was contested between Ak̲ičuq, the Mozaffarid (q.v.) Mobārez-al-Din Moḥammad of central and southern Persia, and Ovays himself, but it was the Jalayerid who achieved the definitive conquest of Azerbaijan in 1359. Ak̲ičuq, who had at first been treated generously, was soon executed for conspiracy (Zayn-al-Din, pp. 66-70). A bid by Malek Ašraf's son Temürtaš (Timurtāš) to recover his father's territories with the aid of the new khan of the Golden Horde, K̲eżr, was frustrated in 1360 when the latter handed him over to Ovays (ibid., p. 71; Ḥāfeẓ-e Abru, pp. 238-39). Several campaigns were required before Ovays enforced the submission of the Šarvānšāh Kāvus (1366-67), but thereafter the whole of Šarvān as far north as Darband remained obedient to him until his death, and he was able to install Kāvus' compliant brother as ruler in 1372-73 (Zayn-al-Din, pp. 81-2, 90; Ḥāfeẓ-e Abru, p. 242).

Šayḵ Ovays intervened in the disputes among the Mozaffarid princes, who had deposed their father Mobārez-al-Din Moḥammad. At the request of Šāh Maḥmud, who ruled in Isfahan, he dispatched an army in 1368-69 to expel Šāh Šojā from Shiraz (Zayn-al-Din, p. 85; Ḥāfeẓ-e Abru, p. 243), but the brothers' reconciliation prevented him in the longer term from establishing his own influence in central Persia. Greater success attended the campaign Ovays headed in person against Amir Vali, who had supplanted the heirs of the Il-khan Ṭaḡā Timur in Gorgān, Astarābād and western Khorasan and from whom he took Ray in 1370-71 (Zayn-al-Din, pp. 87-88; Ḥāfeẓ-e Abru, p. 244). If we can believe al Ḡiāṯ (p. 88), the *ḵoṭba* was made in Ovays's name at Mecca. But his reign was not devoid of problems. In 1363 his governor in Baghdad, Ḵᵛāja Marjān, profited from the absence of Ovays in Šarvān and rebelled in collusion with the Šarvānšāh. Šayḵ Ovays suppressed the rising only with some difficulty in the following year (Zayn-al-Din, pp. 74-78; Ḥāfeẓ-e Abru, pp. 240-41); Marjān, spared at the intercession of the religious class in Baghdad, was later reinstated as governor in 1367-68 (Zayn-al-Din, pp. 78, 83; Ḥāfeẓ-e Abru, p. 243). In the far west Šayḵ Ovays's reign witnessed the first clashes with the rising power of the Qarā Qoyunlu Turkmens of the Diār Bakr region, from whose leader, Bayram ḵᵛāja, he wrested Mosul (al-Mawṣel) in 1365 or 1366 (ibid., p. 79; Ḥāfeẓ-e Abru, pp. 241-42; Cahen, pp. 80-81).

Decline. When Šayḵ Ovays died in Tabriz on 2 Jomādā I 776/9 October 1374 at the age of thirty, the amirs killed his eldest son and heir, Ḥasan, and enthroned another son, Ḥosayn I (1374-82). The new reign began auspiciously with a successful campaign in 1375 to secure the submission of the Qarā Qoyunlu amir Qarā Moḥammad (Zayn-al-Din, p. 94). But under Ḥosayn, whose government was dominated by the chief amir, ʿĀdel Āqā, decline swiftly set in. Amir Vali recovered Ray (ibid., p. 104), which he retained in the ensuing peace settlement of 1377-78 (ibid., pp. 97-98; Ḥāfeẓ-e Abru, p. 252), and in 1376-77 the Qarā Qoyunlu retook Mosul (al-Ḡiāṯ, p. 99). In the latter year Šāh Šojā invaded Jalayerid territory. Owing to the antipathy between ʿĀdel Āqā and the other amirs, no concerted resistance was offered and in September-October 1376 the Mozaffarid ruler occupied Tabriz itself for four months before retiring on the news of Ḥosayn's advance (Zayn-al-Din, pp. 95-96; Ḥāfeẓ-e Abru, pp. 247-50).

Ḥosayn was also confronted by disaffection on the part of his brothers, one of whom, Šayḵ ʿAli was at the center of an uprising in 1378-79 and temporarily gained control of Baghdad in 1380 (Zayn-al-Din, pp. 99-102); the Khorasani chronicler Faryumadi (p. 313) says that he was older than Ḥosayn and that his father had intended him to rule the city. Early in 1382 another brother, Solṭān Aḥmad, suddenly withdrew to his appanage of Ardabil and mustered an army in Muḡān and Arrān, with which he marched on Tabriz. Most of Ḥosayn's troops were absent at Solṭāniya with ʿĀdel Āqā, and Solṭān Aḥmad encountered no resistance. He was proclaimed sultan, and Ḥosayn was put to death (Zayn-al-Din, pp. 106-7). This alarmed a number of amirs, who fled to Baghdad to join Šayḵ ʿAli (al-Ḡiāṯ, p. 102).

Although the latter was overthrown thanks to the aid of the Qarā Qoyunlu, Solṭān Aḥmad was unable at first to establish himself in Tabriz in the face of strong opposition from Ḥosayn's former lieutenant, ʿĀdel Āqā, who now championed another brother named Solṭān Bāyazid. In an attempt to mediate, it was proposed that Solṭān Aḥmad hold Azerbaijan, Muḡān and Arrān; ʿErāq-e ʿAjam should fall to Bāyazid, while the revenues of ʿErāq-e ʿArab should be divided between them. The plan fell through, however, and Solṭān Aḥmad occupied Baghdad (Zayn-al-Din, pp. 107-10). In 1383 he was able to enter the town of Solṭāniya and invest the citadel. Later that year Šāh Šojā, who had advanced to Hamadān and had been joined by ʿĀdel Āqā and Solṭān Bāyazid, brought about a peace whereby Bāyazid secured ʿErāq-e ʿAjam and ʿĀdel Āqā accompanied the Mozaffarid ruler to Shiraz; but in the spring of 1384 Solṭān Bāyazid, deprived of his protector, finally surrendered Solṭāniya to Solṭān Aḥmad (ibid., pp. 111-13).

The attacks by Timur and by the Qarā Qoyunlu. By this juncture western Iran lay under the shadow of the Central Asian conqueror Timur, who had welded together the forces of the Chaghatayid (q.v.) khanate in Transoxania and aspired to recreate Čengiz Khan's empire; and like the other dynasties which had supplanted the Il-khans, the Jalayerids met his attack in a state of utter disunity and debilitation. In 1384-85 Solṭān Aḥmad's lieutenants at Solṭāniya abandoned the town on the approach of Timur's forces, an act for which their furious master publicly humiliated them in Tabriz. Timur conferred the governorship of Solṭāniya on ʿĀdel Āqā, who had left Shiraz and had submitted to him at Ray (Zayn-al-Din, pp. 113-14; al-Ḡiāṯ, pp. 104-5). When Solṭān Aḥmad sent an army to recover Solṭāniya, ʿĀdel Āqā vigorously defended the citadel on Timur's behalf (Zayn-al-Din, pp. 114-15).

The installation in Azerbaijan of a client of Timur brought down on the province a savage attack by Toqtamiš, khan of the Golden Horde, who in 1384 sacked Tabriz and Marāḡa and devastated the regions of Marand and Nakhchivan (Naḵjavān) before withdrawing with allegedly 200,000 captives (ibid., pp. 115-18). This was shortly followed by Timur's own first major assault on the Jalayerids. In the spring of 1386 his forces entered Tabriz and installed ʿĀdel Āqā there; Solṭān Aḥmad's army was put to flight. On Timur's own approach, Solṭān Aḥmad, who had briefly entered Tabriz, fled back to Baghdad. Tabriz had to pay the conqueror a heavy ransom (*māl-e amān*), which ʿĀdel Āqā had dutifully collected, though this did not prevent his execution by Timur on suspicion of embezzlement (Zayn-al-Din, pp. 120-22). The dynasty now suffered the almost permanent loss of Azerbaijan, since when Timur withdrew to Khorasan in 1387, he left his son Mirānšāh as viceroy of the province.

In 1393 Timur renewed the struggle with the Jalayerids, occupying Baghdad without a fight when Solṭān Aḥmad fled to Mamluk Syria. The city was plundered and a heavy ransom was extorted; on his departure, the conqueror took with him not only Solṭān Aḥmad's son, ʿAlāʾ-al-Dawla (Salmāni, *Šams al-ḥosn*, tr. p. 96), but Baghdad's artists and scholars, to embellish his capital at Samarqand. On Solṭān Aḥmad's return the following year, however, the Timurid garrison withdrew; nor was Mirānšāh successful in his attempt to take the city in 1398. In 1399 the thirteen- (or fifteen-)year siege of Alenjaq by Mirānšāh's troops was raised by the Georgian King Giorgi VII (Sanjian, p. 118), and its commander, Solṭān Aḥmad's son Ṭāher, made his way to Baghdad, though this brought no amelioration in the Jalayerids' position, since he then rebelled against his father and was drowned in the Tigris (ibid., p. 155). In 1400, during Timur's operations in Syria and before the conqueror moved on Baghdad, Solṭān Aḥmad again abandoned his capital, this time to find shelter with the Ottoman Sultan Bāyezīd Yïldïrïm. Timur, already angry that the Jalayerid ruler had escaped him, was further infuriated by the spirited resistance of the city during a forty-day siege. Taken by storm on 27 Ḏuʾl-qaʿda 803/9 July 1401, Baghdad was ruthlessly sacked and its fortifications and most of the public buildings were destroyed. The entire population was massacred, with the exception of sayyids, ulama and dervishes, and pyramids were formed of their skulls as a grisly memento.

Unlike the other successor dynasties, the Jalayerids survived Timur's onslaught, but only to fall victim to the Qarā Qoyunlu. For a time Solṭān Aḥmad collaborated against Timur with the Qarā Qoyunlu leader, Qarā Yusof, who, like the Jalayerids themselves, had suffered a series of attacks by the conqueror. They were both for a time guests of the Ottoman Sultan, and returned to Baghdad together after the Timurid sack in 1401. But their rivalry continued to resurface. Having spelled Solṭān Aḥmad from Baghdad, Qarā Yusof was himself ousted by Mirānšāh's son Abu Bakr, and fled to Syria, where he found Solṭān Aḥmad. The two men were imprisoned together and made an agreement whereby the Jalayerids would retain Iraq while Azerbaijan was to form the Qarā Qoyunlu sphere of influence. After they returned from captivity in 1404, however, they again clashed because Solṭān Aḥmad could not be satisfied merely with Iraq. In an attempt to wrest Tabriz from Qarā Yusof in 1410, he was captured and executed; his son ʿAlaʾ-al-Dawla, who had rejoined him after being released by the Timurid ruler of Samarqand, shared his fate (al-Ḡiāṯ, p. 136). The Qarā Qoyunlu's seizure of Baghdad in 1412 from Solṭān Aḥmad's nephew and successor, Šāh Valad b. Šayḵ ʿAli, marked the effective end of the dynasty.

The Jalayerids were not completely eliminated, however, since minor scions of the family maintained themselves in Ḵuzestān and southern Iraq, where their history is documented by al-Ḡiāṯ (pp. 137-44). On the fall of Baghdad, Šāh Valad's son Solṭān Maḥmud fled to Šuštar, where he ruled for two years and was succeeded by his brother Solṭān Ovays. The latter made two attempts to recover Baghdad from the Qarā Qoyunlu in 1421, in the second of which he was killed in battle with their ruler Jahānšāh. Yet another of Šāh Valad's sons, Solṭān Moḥammad, was dislodged from Šuštar in 1423 by Ebrāhim Solṭān, the Timurid ruler of Fārs, and fled first to Wāseṭ and later to al-Ḥella. From here he made the dynasty's final bid to regain Baghdad, but after an abortive siege of the city, he died in July 1424. The licentious behavior of the last Jalayerid ruler, Ḥosayn II b. ʿAlāʾ-al-Dawla, alienated his amirs, who invited in the Qarā Qoyunlu prince Aspān; al-Ḥella was taken in October 1431, and Ḥosayn was hunted down and killed on 3 Rabiʿ I/9 November.

Cultural aspects. Although certain scholars have imputed Shiʿite sympathies to the Jalayerids, the strongest grounds for this view lie in the dynasty's preference for names such as ʿAli, Ḥasan and Ḥosayn and in the expressed desire of Ḥasan-e Bozorg to be buried in Najaf. It is true that Ḥasan-e Bozorg was also on excellent terms with Shaikh Ṣafi-al-Din, the ancestor of the later Safavid dynasty, at Ardabil, and that friendly relations with Ṣafi-al-Din's successors persisted under Šayḵ Ovays. Yet at this early stage it is doubtful whether the Ardabil order itself can be described as Shiʿite in any real sense. The evidence of Jalayerid coins, on the other hand, suggest a more Sunni stance: the overwhelming majority carry the names of the Orthodox Caliphs, and only rarely does a coin, like that struck by Ḥasan-e Bozorg at Āmol in 741/1340, bear the names of the Twelve Imams.

The Jalayerids gained a reputation as patrons of literary activity and the arts, and under their rule both Baghdad and Tabriz were centers of flourishing schools of miniature painting. Baghdad in the time of Šayḵ Ovays was the home of the miniaturist Šams-al-Din, and later of ʿAbd al-Ḥayy, whom Timur carried off to his capital, Samarqand. Šayḵ Ovays was a skilled calligrapher and painter who also wrote verse and patronized the poet Salmān-e Sāvaji, the dynasty's principal panegyrist. Solṭan Aḥmad was a musician and painter, but his efforts to lure into his service the poet Ḥāfeẓ from Shiraz were unsuccessful. Regrettably, as a result of Timur's activity little trace remains of the buildings raised by the Jalayerids and listed by al-Ḡiāṯ (pp. 91-96), who alleges that Šayḵ Ovays's reign was especially notable in this regard. The Jāmeʿ-e Marjān, the madrasa erected in Baghdad by the Jalayerid governor Marjān (d. 1373-74), whom the literary sources describe as an active builder (Zayn-al-Din, p. 83; al-Ḡiāṯ, pp. 91-93), survives; not so the Dawlat-ḵāna or palace which Šayḵ Ovays constructed outside Tabriz and which greatly impressed the Castilian envoy Clavijo in 1404 (Clavijo, p. 107; tr. Le Strange, p. 153).

The efforts of Šayḵ Ovays to promote economic recovery following the upheavals of the late Il-khanid and Chobanid periods, did not always materialize. He wrote twice to the Venetians at Trebizond with the aim of inducing them to return to Tabriz and assume the role they had enjoyed in the days of the Il-khan Abu Saʿid, but they were wary; attacks upon caravans demonstrated that the roads were still unsafe for merchants (Heyd, II, pp. 130-31). The plague struck Azerbaijan in 1360 and took an especially heavy toll of the population of Tabriz in 1369-70 (Zayn-al-Din, pp. 72, 86); in Baghdad thousands of people perished during severe floods in 1374-75 (ibid., p. 92). Yet posterity looked benignly upon Šayḵ Ovays's reign. The historian al-Ḡiāṯ heard that both he and Ḥasan-e Bozorg had been commendably just rulers (pp. 87, 88), while Zayn-al-Din (pp. 82, 94, 105) pays tribute to the happiness and prosperity that characterized the eras of Šayḵ Ovays and Ḥosayn I. Even if this were largely conventional hyperbole, this earlier period stands in sharp contrast to the upheavals of Solṭān Aḥmad's reign, when Tabriz changed hands repeatedly, when Toqtamiš's attack desolated much of Azerbaijan, and when Timur's campaign harried both Azerbaijan and Iraq and severely damaged the economy of both provinces. According to al-Ḡiāṯ (p. 128), Baghdad had still not recovered in his own day (late 15th century) from its sack at the hands of Timur's army.

Table 1

THE JALAYERID DYANSTY

(rulers in capitals; m. = married)

Ilge (Ilkā)

Aqbuqa (Āqbuqā)

Ḥosayn

1. ḤASAN-E BOZORG

Ḥosayn

2. ŠAYḴ OVAYS

Ḥasan

3. ḤOSAYN I

Šayḵ ʿAli

4. SOLṬĀN AḤMAD

Solṭān Bāyazid

5. ŠĀH VALAD m. Tandu ḵātun

Ṭāher, ʿAlāʾ-al-Dawla

6. SOLṬĀN MAḤMUD

7. SOLṬĀN OVAYS

8. SOLṬĀN MOḤAMMAD

9. ḤOSAYN II

Biliography: ʿAbbās ʿAzzāwi, *Tāriḵ al-ʿErāq bayn al-eḥtelālayn* II, Baghdad, 1936. Abu Bakr Qoṭbi Ahari, *Tāriḵ-e Šayḵ Ovays*, ed. (and tr.) J. B. Van Loon, The Hague, 1954. Stephen Album, "Studies in Ilkhanid history and numismatics, I. A late Ilkhanid hoard (743/1342)," *Stud. Ir.* 13, 1984, pp. 49-116. Idem, "Studies in Ilkhanid history and numismatics, II. A late Ilkhanid hoard (741/1340) as evidence for the history of Diyār Bakr," *Stud. Ir.* 14, 1985, pp. 43-76. C. E. Bosworth, "Uways," *EI*[2], pp. 957-58. J. A. Boyle, in *Camb. Hist. Iran* V, pp. 414-16. Cl. Cahen, "Contribution à l'histoire du Diyār Bakr au quatorzième siècle," *JA* 243, 1955, pp. 65-100. Ruy González de Clavijo, *Embajada a Tamorlán*, ed. F. Lopez Estrada, Madrid, 1943; tr. G. Le Strange, *Embassy to Tamerlane*, London, 1930. Eqbāl, *Tāriḵ-e Moḡol*, Tehran, 1962, pp. 455-65. Faryumadi, *Ḏayl-e Majmaʿ al-ansāb*, ed. in Šabānkāraʾi, *Majmaʿ al-ansāb*, ed. Mir Hāšem Moḥaddeṯ, Tehran, 1984. al-Ḡiāṯ ʿAbd-Allāh b. Fatḥ-Allāh, *al-Tarʾriḵ at-Ḡiāṯi*, partial ed. Ṭāreq Nāfeʿ al-Ḥamadāni, Baghdad, 1975, pp. 81-144. Ḥāfeẓ-e Abru, *Ḏayl-e Jāmeʿ al-tawāriḵ-e rašidi*, ed. ḵānbābā Bayāni, 2nd ed., Tehran, 1971. Ḥamd-Allāh Mostawfi Qazvini, *Ḏayl-e Ẓafar-nāma*, tr. (Russian and Azeri) M. D. Kazymov and V. Z. Piriiev as *Ḏayl-e Tāriḵ-e gozida*, Baku, 1986. Wilhelm Heyd, *Geschichte des Levantehandels im Mittelalter*, Stuttgart, 1879. A.K. Markov, *Katalog dzhelairidskikh monet*, St. Petersburg, 1897. Charles Melville, "Ḥamd Allāh Mustawfī's *Ẓafarnāmah* and the historiography of the late Ilkhanid period," in Kambiz Eslami, ed., *Iran and Iranian studies: essays in honor of Iraj Afshar*, Princeton, 1998, pp. 1-12. Idem, *The fall of Amir Chupan and the decline of the Ilkhanate, 1327-37: a decade of discord in Mongol Iran*, Bloomington, Indiana, 1999. H. L. Rabino da Borgomale, "Coins of the Jalāʾir, Ḳara Ḳoyūnlū, Mushaʿshaʿ and Aḳ Koyūnlū dynasties," *Numismatic Chronicle*, 6th series, 10, 1950, pp. 94-139. Rašid-al-Din, *Jāmeʿ al-tawāriḵ* (Moscow), and Rašid-al-Din, *Jāmeʿ al-tawarīḵ* (Baku); tr. Wheeler M. Thackston, *Jāmi'u't-tawārikh. Compendium of chronicles*, 3 vols., Cambridge, Mass., 1998-99. H. R. Roemer, in *Camb. Hist. Iran* VI, pp. 5-10, 64-69, 160-62. Tāj-al-Din Salmāni, *Šams al-ḥosn*, ed. and tr. Hans Robert Roemer, Wiesbaden, 1956. Avedis K. Sanjian Jr., *Colephous of Armenian Manuscripts, 1301-1480*, Cambridge, Mass., 1969. J. M. Smith, "Ḏjalāyir, Ḏjalāyirid," *EI*[2], pp. 401-2. Šams-al-Din al-Šojāʿi, *Taʾriḵ al-Malek al-Nāṣer Moḥammad b. Qalāwun al-Ṣāleḥi*, ed. and tr. Barbara Schäfer as *Die Chronik aš-Šuǧāʿīs*, 2 vols., Wiesbaden, 1977-85. B. Spüler, *Mongolen*[4], pp. 109-15. Zayn-al-Din b. Ḥamd-Allāh Mostawfi Qazvini, *Ḏayl-e Ẓafar-nāma*, ed. Iraj Afšār as *Ḏayl-e Tāriḵ-e gozida*, Tehran, 1993.

(PETER JACKSON)

JALĀYER-NĀMA. See QĀʾEM-MAQĀM.

JALIL, RAHIM, Soviet Tajik writer (b. 3 June 1909 in Ḵojand; d. 10 October 1989 in Ḵojand), Born into a family of shoemakers, he remained true to his class origins throughout his career. He became a teacher in 1927 after a one-year training course, but was soon drawn to journalism. From 1931 to 1951 he worked on various newspapers, including *Tojikistoni surkh*, the main party and state organ, and *Sharqi surkh*, the leading literary journal. He joined the Communist Party in 1943, and from 1952 he was a secretary of the Union of Writers of Tajikistan. In 1979 he was accorded the title of People's Writer of Tajikistan.

Jalil's literary career began with the publication of poetry in 1931. He soon recognized prose as his true calling, and in 1936 he published his first collection of short stories, *Orzu*, and in 1941 his first large-scale work, part one of the novel *Gulru*. After World War II he revised the novel, adding a second part and publishing both as *Odamoni jovid* in 1949. Two other major prose works followed: the novel, *Shurob* (pt. 1, 1959; pts. 2 and 3, 1967), perhaps his most important creation, and *Ma'voi dil* (pt. 1, 1970; pt. 2, 1982), essentially his memoirs of the places and people of his native Ḵojand. Between 1932 and 1975 he also wrote stories for children and a number of plays.

Jalil was a master of the short story. He excelled at satirical portraits, which revealed his ear for the spoken language and his appreciation for the oral literature of ordinary people, as in the collection *Hissa az qissa* (1941) and his novels (Ghafforov, pp. 22-37). The stories he wrote during World War II describing the heroism of Tajiks in defending the common Soviet homeland and published as *Hikoiahoi zamoni jang* (1944) were, like much of the literature of the time, patriotic and propagandistic. Then, between 1949 and 1978 he published nine more collections of stories depicting the most varied aspects of Tajik society of his time (Sayfulloev and Fayzulloeva, pp. 175-93).

As a novelist Jalil aligned himself with the proponents of socialist realism, using his skills to promote the official Soviet interpretation of the past and vision of the new society in process of formation. *Odamoni jovid* is set in the time of the Bolshevik Revolution and the early years of the new Soviet regime, and its themes are standard fare in the works of Jalil's contemporaries: the role of the Russian Bolsheviks in tutoring the first Tajik revolutionaries; the contribution of Russian and Ukrainian workers to awakening Tajik workers to class consciousness and the struggle for liberation; and the heroic efforts of a new generation of Tajiks, led by Communists to build a new life. The main characters, Pulod, who represents the revolutionary Tajik proletariat, and Gulru, his wife, who is the new Soviet woman actively engaged in production, are Jalil's ideal family of the new Tajikistan (Otakhonova, pp. 92-95). *Shurob* belongs to the same genre of the historical-revolutionary novel and treats the Russian Revolution and Civil War and the creation of a new society in the same socialist-realist fashion. In describing the struggles of the miners in northern Tajikistan, Jalil is at his best in depicting the complex Communist revolutionary in the person of Khol and in showing how simple workers in critical situations are raised to the level of committed revolutionaries (Sayfulloev and Fayzulloeva, pp. 270-73).

Rahim Jalil was a writer of his own time and place, and he himself acknowledged Maxim Gorky, "the great founder of socialist realism," as one of his mentors. His best work will undoubtedly endure as the embodiment of a distinct era in the evolution of Tajik culture.

Bibliography: Rahim Jalil, *Asarho*, 4 vols., Dushanbe, 1967-71. L. N. Demidchik, *Nasri solhoi 30 (Ta'rikhi adabiyoti sovetii tojik*, 2), Dushanbe, 1978, pp. 204-8, 259-75. R. Ghafforov, *Zabon va uslubi Rahim Jalil*, Dushanbe, 1966. Khursheda Otakhonova, *Rahim Jalil va ejodiyoti u (Hikoiaho va "Odamoni jovid")*. Dushanbe, 1962. Atakhon Sayfulloev and Mavluda Fayzulloeva, *Akhtari toboni adabiyot*, Ḵujand, 1999. M. Shukurov, *Nasri solhoi 1945-1974 (Ta'rikhi adabiyoti sovetii tojik*, 4), Dushanbe, 1980, pp. 264-80, passim.

(K. Hitchins)

JALILAVAND, a small Shiʿite Kurdish tribe of the Kermānšāh and Qazvin regions. Hyacinth Louis Rabino (1877-1950) informs us that in 1905 some 200 or 300 sedentary families of them dwelt in the district of Dinavar, northeast of Kermānšāh (p. 22). He also noted that, in the course of time, many had moved to the Qazvin region, fleeing from oppression in Kermānšāh. According to the UNESCO survey from the 1960s, the remaining Jalilavand of Dinavar form a section of the Sanjābi tribal confederation (p. 137). As regards to the Jalilavand in the Qazvin region, Rabino in 1909 estimated their number at 800 families (Adamec, p. 268). By 1932, according to Masʿud Kayhān, their number had shrunk to only 300 families (p. 112). In the late 1960s Parviz Varjāvand observed that they comprised a mere 150 to 200 families, and were settled in the villages of Āqčakand, Bašgol, Qarabāḡ, and Yangija Pāʾin in the rural district (*dehestān*) of Qāqazān (p. 459).

Bibliography: Ludwig Adamec, ed., *Tehran and Northwestern Iran*, Historical Gazetteer of Iran 1, Graz, 1976. Masʿud Kayhān, *Joḡrāfiā-ye mofaṣṣal-e Irān: II – Siāsi*, Tehran, 1932. Komisiun-e melli-ye Yunesku (UNESCO) Iran, *Iran-Shahr: A Survey of Iran's Land, People, Culture, Government and People* I, Tehran, 1963 (in Persian). Hyacinth Louis Rabino, "Kermanchah," *RMM* 38, 1920, pp. 1-40. Parviz Varjāvand, *Sarzamin-e Qazvin*, Tehran, 1970.

(Pierre Oberling)

JĀLINUS (Galen), the Arabic form of Greek Galenos, the name of the illustrious authority on medicine of ancient Greece, a physician, pharmacologist, anatomist, philosopher, physiologist, surgeon, and author of a good number of medical works. His fame grew in the following centuries and he became the most influential figure in the development of medical sciences in the Islamic world. He was born in August or September 129 C.E., in Pergamon, a thriving city in northwestern Asia Minor. Until the age of fourteen, Galen studied literature, grammar, arithmetic, geometry, and rudiments of philosophy with his father, a rich and cultivated man. At the age of fifteen, he was sent to study the four main philosophical schools of the time with four masters, a Platonist, an Aristotelian, a Stoic, and an Epicurean (Sarton, p. 16). While pursuing his philosophical study, Galen began learning medicine at the age of sixteen, following his father's dream in which Asclepius, god of healing, had told him that he should guide the boy to the study of medicine (for

Galen's biography see Wissowa, Kroll, and Mittlehaus, VII/1, cols. 578-91, tr., V, pp. 651-63; Nutton, 2004, pp. 216 ff.; Sarton, p. 16; Nuland, pp. 31 ff.).

In 151 C.E., after his preliminary medical studies in Pergamon, Galen went to Smyrna, where he stayed one year attending, among others, the anatomy lectures of Satyrus and visiting his clinics; from him Galen learned also surgery and internal medicine (Sarton, p. 40). Satyrus' lectures induced Galen to pursue his anatomical studies further, so he went to Corinth to attend the course of another anatomy master, Numisianus, but, according to some Greek traditions, Numisianus had just died (Boudon-Millot, 2007, p. xxxv; Nutton, 1987, pp. 235-39; Garcia-Ballester, chap. I, p. 16). Towards the end of 152 C.E., Galen reached Alexandria, which was famous for its tradition of human and animal dissection. Galen, later in his career, advised his students to go to Alexandria to observe the human skeleton (Kühn, II, pp. 220-22, cited in Vegetti, 1995, p. 77), as only in Alexandria were human bones still used for demonstration by the teachers of anatomy, while elsewhere any systematic dissection of human cadavers had ceased since the second part of the 3rd century B.C.E. (Temkin, pp. 3-4; Guerrini, p. 13).

Galen returned to Pergamon in 158; by then he had, for about twelve years, studied mainly anatomy and written several books on the subject. In summer 161, Galen went to Rome, the capital of the empire, a city of a million inhabitants and several thousands of physicians of different persuasions. His public dissection of animals attracted a large audience and consequently aroused the hostility of many established physicians who saw in him a rival as well as an opponent to their methods and ideas. These incessant hostilities first brought an end to his public anatomical demonstrations and finally prompted his departure from Rome in summer 166 to Sicily and from there to Pergamon (Nutton, 2004, p. 224; idem, 1972; Wissowa, Kroll, and Mittlehaus, col. 580, tr., V, pp. 653-61). Galen stayed in Pergamon for about two years before being summoned in 168 by Emperor Marcus Aurelius (r. 161-80) to accompany him and his army in a campaign against the invasion of Germanic tribes. From this period onward, Galen served as one of the court physicians in Rome and took up residence there to the end of his life. There is no clear mention of the date of his death but, in his recent study on Galen, Vivian Nutton sets his death about 216 (Nutton, 2004, p. 226). Neither is there any definite indication of the place where he was buried. According to an Islamic tradition, he was buried in Farmā in Egypt (Eṣṭaḵri, p. 53; Ebn Ḥawqal, p. 105, tr. p. 158), while other traditions hold that he was buried in Sicily or in Jerusalem. It is more likely, however, that he was buried in Rome, where in all probability he had died (Boudon-Millot, pp. lxxv-lxxvii).

Galen and Hippocratic medicine. Throughout the Hellenistic period various medical approaches developed including Hippocratic medicine (On Hippocrates (q.v.) and Hippocratic medicine, see Jouanna, 1992 and 1995). During the first four years of his medical studies, Galen attended the courses of almost all of the then-active medical schools (or rather approaches), the Dogmatic, Empiric, Methodic, and the Pneumatic in Pergamon. It seems, however, that from the time he was studying at Pergamon, he was more influenced by the Dogmatics, who, while following principles of the Hippocratic teachings, believed that the mere observation of the exterior of the body was not sufficient and a knowledge of anatomy was critical to medical practice (Guerrini, p. 7). Although Galen criticized the Empirics, believing that knowledge of inner structures and functions was essential to successful medical practice (Guerrini, pp. 13-14), he combined the two approaches of dogmatism and scientific experimentation, a method that was followed by Islamic physicians (Ebn Reżwān, p. 21).

Works. Galen began writing from when he was a teenager (Sarton, p. 14) and continued until nearly the end of his life. His surviving works include more than 120 titles, published in 22 hefty octavo volumes by Carolus Gottlob Kühn in the original Greek with accompanying Latin translation. Ḥonayn b. Esḥāq (d. ca. 873) provides details of about 129 works of Galen that he and his collaborators translated from Greek into Syriac and/or Arabic (Savage-Smith and Pormann, p. 25). Donald Campbell (II, pp. 13-220) records 272 titles of Galen, including those that have been lost. None of these figures, however, represent the entirety of Galen's work, neither does the list provided by Galen himself, since, as noted by Ḥonayn b. Esḥāq, some of them Galen had lost already (Ḥonayn b. Esḥāq, apud Véronique Boudon, 2002, pp. 10-11; Galen, 2007b, pp. 134-73). Galen's works became known to the Medieval Islamic world mainly through the translations of Ḥonayn b. Esḥāq and his followers, such as his own son Esḥāq b. Ḥonayn (d. 910) and Ṯābet b. Qorra (d. 901; see Sezgin, pp. 247-56, 260-63, 268-69). In the interest of clarity and readability, Ḥonayn intended his translations to be idiomatic rather than literal, at times achieving greater lucidity than Galen himself, but at the cost of occasional errors (Savage-Smith and Pormann, pp. 30 ff.; Montgomery, p. 119). The content of Galen's lost works can also be found in the works of later physicians, such as Moḥammad b. Zakariyāʾ Rāzi, who in his *Šokuk ʿalā Jālinus* quotes Galen literally, or Ebn Sinā (Avicenna, q.v.), who in his *al-Qānun fi'l-ṭebb* (the *Canon*) paraphrases him without specifying from which book of Galen (Strohmaier, 1981, pp. 191-92). We might also find works that are wrongly attributed to Galen, for instance, the *Ṭāleʿ-nāma-ye Jālinus*, which obviously belongs to the genre of commentary in which Galen's ideas are presented through the prism of Islamic or folk astrology. In Iran, the number of those who knew Arabic varied depending on region, period, and education, but, generally speaking, it was small and Arabic medical texts, including those of Galen, were more accessible in commentaries written in Persian (Elgood, 1970, p. 18).

The translations of Galen's works were made from both Galen's original texts and from the summaries and commentaries used at the school of Alexandria in late antiquity. According to Šams-al-Din Moḥammad Šahrazuri (fl. 13th cent.), "from nearly 400 small and large tracts of Galen, [a summary made in] sixteen volumes were [the most] read by medical students" (p. 332). Šahrazuri's reference here is evidently to the so-called sixteen (*setta ʿašara*) books of Jālinus, which ʿOnṣor-al-Maʿāli Kaykāvus b. Eskandar and Neẓāmi ʿArużi recommended to medical students (Ebn al-Nadim, pp. 348-50; Ebn Qefṭi, p. 123; Kaykāvus b. Eskandar, pp. 179-81; Neẓāmi ʿArużi, text, p. 110, comm., p. 384). These sixteen books are sometimes mistaken for another set of textbooks based on Galen's works, called *Jawāmeʿ al-Eskandar-āniyin* or *Summaria Alexandrinorum* (for this book, see Sezgin, pp. 140-50). According to Savage-Smith (2002, pp. 126-27, 131, 138), these sixteen books were written by Galen himself for "the beginners," while, according to Ebn al-Qefṭi, the so-called *Jawāmeʿ al-Eskandarān-iyin* were the abridged versions of the works of Galen, made by four leading physicians (*ʿomdat al-aṭebbāʾ*) of Alexandria who also compiled commentaries (Ebn al-Qefṭi, pp. 71-72, tr. p. 97; Savage-Smith and Pormann, 2007, p. 13; Sezgin, p. 143). Manfred Ullmann maintains that the prolixity and partial contradictions in the original Galen's works led the Islamic physicians to have recourse rather to their summarized or coherent translation (Ullmann, p. 10). It seems, however, that, as far as the *Jawāmeʿ-e Eskandarāniyin* is concerned, its significance for the Islamic physicians was more fundamentally related to the importance of both Alexandrian medicine and Aristotelian philosophy in Islam.

Galen's influence on Persian medicine. Galen's long-lasting influence on Persian medicine is linked to the wider impact of Greek sciences in both pre-Islamic and Islamic periods in Iran. In pre-Islamic Iran, this was partly due to the introduction, or formation, of Hellenistic culture in the aftermath of the conquest of Iran by Alexander of Macedonia (q.v.) in 333 B.C.E., and partly to the translation of Greek sciences into the Middle Persian under the Sasanians. The mention of the four humors (*āb*)—blood (*xōn*), phlegm (*drēm*), red bile (*wiš ī suxr*), and black bile (*wiš ī syā*)—by the 9th-century author, Zātspram, echoes Greek humoral physiology and may be indicative of Greek influence on Sasanian medicine (Zātspram; Savage-Smith and Pormann, p. 17). According to some scholars, the statement in the 9th-century Middle Persian text of *Dēnkard* (q.v.), which refers to Greek sciences as parts of the Zoroastrian canon, is an indication of the pre-Islamic origin of Greek influence in Iran (Gutas, p. 1998). The city of Gondēšāpur (q.v.) in Khuzestan was a major center of the learning and practice of Galenic medicine, where a hospital had been founded under the Sasanians, probably by Ḵosrow I Anōšarvān. The city was founded by Šāpur I (r. 242-72), and soon became an institution (Ebn Qefṭi, pp. 132-33), where Persian, Indian, and Greek traditions of medical practice and theory were maintained well into the early phases of the ʿAbbasid caliphate. The medical literature in Iran in the Islamic period, however, was a largely different development. A possible continuation of an Iranian tradition in medical writings without passing through Arabic texts in this period remains to be ascertained (Richter-Bernburg, 1999, p. 142).

The question of why the Muslims assimilated Greek sciences and in particular Greek medicine continues to be an outstanding topic of historical research. It is often held that Greek sciences were transmitted to Islam through the Sasanian channel insofar as the ʿAbbasid Caliphate inherited the Sasanian state apparatus and its scientific legacy (Ebn Reżwān, tr., pp. 5-8), deemed to be largely based on Greek science. This transmission, according to Dimitri Gutas, was structurally framed in what he called the "imperial ideology" that the ʿAbbasid Caliphate borrowed from the Sasanians for the establishment of their own empire (Gutas, pp. 40-45). It should be noted, however, that the Sasanians were highly eclectic in acquiring foreign sciences, and that the Indian sciences, for instance, were no less introduced than the Greek sciences (Ebrahimnejad, 2004, pp. 19 ff.; Montgomery, pp. 79-80). Although the transmission of Greek medicine into Iran followed an earlier tradition of translation of Greek texts into Middle Persian under the Sasanians (Ullman, pp. 17-18), its systematic development after Islam represented a new phenomenon. Its predominance in Islam seems to stem primarily from the fact that the integration of Greek sciences was part of the ideological and intellectual process in the course of the development of Islamic sciences (Ebrahimnejad, 2005).

The origin of the integration of Greek medicine in Iran after Islam should also be sought in the regions that had undergone hellenization since their conquest by Alexander of Macedonia before being conquered by Islam. It seems that the conquest of Egypt in the first decades of the Islamic expansion constituted the first major step in the integration of Galenic medicine into Islamic sciences, as Alexandria was by that time not only the cultural center of Hellenism (Garcia-Ballester, I, p. 17), but also the place where Galenism had become the predominant medical system. The fact that the region where Islamic medicine was first developed had already inherited a selective portion of Hellenistic sciences—Aristotle and Plato in philosophy and Hippocratic medicine at the expense of theoretical developments of other schools (Nutton, 2004, p. 140)—might explain why from a range of philosophical and medical schools of the Hellenistic period, Aristotelian, and then Neoplatonic, philosophy and Galenic medicine became predominant in the Islamic world. Already, by the middle of the 4th century C.E., Galen's medicine had become completely dominant in the east of the Hellenistic world (Temkin, p. 61).

For Galen, philosophy and syllogistic reasoning were fundamental in medicine. His maxim that a good physician is a philosopher (Daremberg, in Galen, 1854, I, pp. 1-7) is reminiscent of the internal debates between "philosophical medicine" and medicine *tout court* during the pre-Hellenistic Hippocratic medicine (Jouanna, 1995, pp. 49-51). But more fundamentally, by accentuating the importance of philosophy, Galen represented the epistemological shift that occurred during the Hellenistic period, principally during the 3rd century B.C.E., under Aristotle's influence, a shift from the Hippocratic tradition that was centered on the "problem of illness and clinic" and therefore prone to "approximation and empiricism" to a medicine that dealt also with the state of health and was thus eager to penetrate the opacity of the body by anatomy and dissection (Vegetti, pp. 68-71, 78). Aristotelian anatomy had, for theoretical background, teleological approach that established relation between structure of the organs and their normal function, explaining each organ in terms of its purpose. Galen borrowed this approach and advocated it in his *De usu partium* or *Manāfeʿ al-aʿżāʾ* and his other works (Sarton, p. 70; Temkin, pp. 41-42; Galen, 1854). It was this approach that was transmitted through translations of Galen's works to Islamic physicians. Several physicians, including Ebn Sinā, wrote treatises entitled *Manāfeʿ al-aʿżāʾ*, emulating Galen's book (see the short treatise of Ebn Sinā, Arabic manuscript, Majles Library, Tehran, ms. no. 14, pp. 27-36; Sezgin, pp. 106-8).

Anatomy was the foundation of Galen's physiopathology and it was this Aristotelian heritage, developed later on by Herophilus (ca. 320 to ca. 260 B.C.E.) and his contemporary Erasistratus (fl. ca. 260 B.C.E.) that revolutionalized Hippocratic medicine, which was transmitted through Galen to Islamic medicine. The teleological approach of Aristotle was not only rooted in his philosophy but also resulted from the technical necessity of filling the gap that was created when zoological anatomy, practised by Aristotle, was to be used to explain organs and their functions in the human body. But the incapacity of the followers of Herophilus and Erasistratus to solve the other problem that resulted from Aristotle's influence, namely the lack of theoretical connection, or continuity, between anatomophysiology and clinical therapeutic, led to the abandonment of anatomy based on observation and dissection and a return to (the commentary of) Hippocratic texts (Vegetti, pp. 83-84).

It should be noted that the terms *mošāhada* (observation) and *qiās* (analogical/syllogistic reasoning) in medicine were based on Greek concepts but, due to both the philological problem coming from translation and the epistemological and experimental gap between Islamic anatomists and Galen, to some extent they differed from Greek concepts. Galen insisted on dissection and anatomical experience, but they were exclusively carried out on animals (mainly apes, pigs, sheep, and goats) and not on human cadavers, as Roman authorities forbade human dissection and vivisection (Grant, p. 85). As a result, Galen's description of human anatomy was based on analogical reasoning. It is, however, safe to suggest that unlike Galen, for whom observation meant both physically and theoretically observable practice, for Islamic anatomists *qiās* (syllogistic reasoning) was predominantly at work, even in an original development such as Ebn al-Nafis' discovery of pulmonary transit of blood (Ṣafā, III, p. 275; Savage-Smith, 1995; for a detailed discussion, see Savage-Smith and Pormann, pp. 46-48).

Galen always recommended physicians to see nature by carrying out individual dissection rather than accepting the ideas and writings of their predecessors or contemporaries. Almost all of Galen's principles and rationale for the necessity of anatomy and dissection were accepted and underlined by Persian physicians. Abu'l-Majd Ṭabib Bayżāwi (writing before 1646), in the introduction to his book on anatomy (*tašriḥ*), sets two reasons why anatomy is important: first, because by knowing the human body one realizes the power of God; and second, if a physician knows about description of the human body, he would avoid mistakes when providing cure and medication. Bayżāwi in fact repeats here exactly the two reasons put forward by Galen for the necessity of anatomy, but he does not give any indication as to how a physician should proceed to acquire anatomical knowledge or surgical skill and, unlike Galen, does not refer to any dissections that he might have undertaken (Bayżāwi, fols. 1-2).

ʿAbd-al-Razzāq, in his *Ḵolāṣat al-tašriḥ*, underlines the priority of anatomy in medicine by stating that without this knowledge a physician cannot accurately carry out his practice, but, just like Bayżāwi, his source is not his own anatomical experience but the writings of Ebn Sinā, ʿAli b. ʿAbbās Majusi (d. ca. 994, q.v.), Ebn al-Nafis Qoraši (d. 1288), etc. (ʿAbd-al-Razzāq, fol. 3). Likewise, Aḵawayni (10th cent.) states that the number of muscles were observed by Galen and that he did not [need to] proceed himself to observe them (p. 60). Almost all anatomical texts by Persian physicians are compilation from other books and do not reflect any practice of anatomy and surgery (e.g., ʿAqili, p. 31).

While theoretical exercise in Hellenistic medicine was grounded on anatomical observation, which after a period of abandonment from the second part of the 3rd century B.C.E. was taken up by Galen in the 2nd century C.E., in Islamic medicine, anatomy-based theoretical innovation practically did not occur. This may explain why ʿAbd-al-Razzāq, just as Ebn Elyās (q.v.), accepted the incorrect theories of Galen and Ebn Sinā rather than the correct one of Ebn al-Nafis on blood circulation (ʿAbd-al-Razzāq, fol. 51; Elgood, 1966, p. 336; idem, 1970, p. 136). Lack of anatomical observation led outstanding physicians such as Bahāʾ-al-Dawla Nurbaḵši (d. 1508-9) and ʿEmād-al-Din Maḥmud Širāzi (physician of Shah ʿAbbās I), to continue repeating, following Ebn Sinā, the millenary theory according to which the arteries carried blood and the soul (*ruḥ*; Ebn Sinā, tr., IV, p. 5; ʿEmād-al-Din, fol. 1; Bahāʾ-al-Dawla, fol. 35). The hiatus between medicine and/or anatomy on the one hand, and philosophy on the other, finds expression in Rāzi's *Šokuk ʿalā Jālinus*, where Rāzi, who is known for his clinical/experimental approach, addressed and criticized Galen's thought from philosophical dimension and not from a medical viewpoint (Moḥaqqeq, p. 53).

The fact that Galen was the most respected medical reference in Iran did not prevent the development of a gap between Galen's ideas, on the one hand, and the application or perception of these ideas, on the other. This might explain the fact that, although Galen was more referred to in Iran than Hippocrates was, Hippocratic bedside medicine was favored at the expense of practical anatomy and surgery, which were fundamental for Galenic physiology. Bahāʾ-al-Dawla Nurbaḵši (d. 1508-09; see

Richter-Bernburg, 1978, p. 64), for instance, did not practice surgery but advised calling in a surgeon for a surgical case (Elgood, 1970, p. xiv). This was in conformity with Hippocratic Oath that advised physicians not to undertake incisions and to confer such practices to specialists.

It seems that Islamic anatomists, despite the Aristotelian influence, never grasped the epistemological link between animal dissection and medical knowledge. Often lack of dissection in Islam is attributed to religious prohibition, but this prohibition has always been a matter of interpretation rather than based on a formal and legal ban. Galen did not proceed to human dissection either, no matter what was the rationale behind such avoidance. The fundamental difference between Galen and his Islamic followers resided, however, in the fact that the former widely practiced animal dissection and the latter did not. The reason seems to be that not only Muslim anatomists in general based their anatomical knowledge on text rather than on experience, but more importantly, unlike Galen who, given his pagan culture, or his attachment to Aristotle's anatomy, established a biological affinity between animal and human structure and extrapolated the function of human body from his research on animal cadavers, the Islamic anatomists never believed in any affinity between animals on the one hand and the human body, on the other, which they considered as the noblest creature of God.

In the matter of humoral theory too, Galen's influence was represented with speculative repetition or, in a few cases, reinterpretation or misinterpretation. The theory of humors that goes beyond Hippocrates took its final shape in Galen's works (Sarton, pp. 52-54). Just as in anatomy, Galenic humoral theory was influenced by Aristotelian philosophy (Nutton, 2004, p. 145). Galen conceived of things as composed of the four elements of fire, air, earth, and water that are formed by the union of matter and the four qualities of hot, cold, dry, and moist. These elements are not found as such in the body but represented by the four humors respectively, blood, phlegm, black bile, and yellow bile (*ḵun*, *balḡam*, *sawdāʾ*, and *ṣafrāʾ*). These humors are produced by the process of digestion of food and drink, and only air enters the body through respiration. What is found in the vein is in fact a mixture of the four humors and not only blood (Temkin, p. 17). The balance between the quantities or qualities of the humors maintains health and their imbalance causes disease (see HUMORALISM).

According to Galen, there are nine types of temperaments: One ideal, in which all qualities are balanced; four, in which one of the qualities, hot, cold, dry, or moist predominates; and four others, in which the predominant qualities appear in couples of hot and moist, hot and dry, cold and moist, or cold and dry. Following Galen, Persian physicians believed in nine types of nature (*mezāj*). The absolutely balanced nature (*mezāj-e moʿtadel-e ḥaqiqi*), in which all humors are equal in quantity and quality, does not exist in ordinary people. In reality, however, natures are twofold, *basiṭa* (simple) and *morakabba* (compound). Simple natures are four: hot, cold, moist, and dry. The compound natures are also four: hot and dry, cold and dry, hot and moist, cold and moist (Bahāʾ-al-Dawla, fol. 2a; Solṭān-ʿAli Ṭabib, fol. 13; Kaykāvus b. Eskandar, pp. 175-76; Temkin, p. 19). For both Galen and Persian physicians, the balanced temperament was a point of reference to diagnose illness but, while for the former balanced temperament could be found in ordinary people, for the latter it was the characteristic of the Imams (Bahāʾ-al-Dawla, fol. 2a).

Humoral theory also permeated folk medicine and Galen's influence is clearly discernable in manuals of popular medicine. In the anonymous *Ḵawāṣṣ al-ašyāʾ*, (written in or before the 17th cent.), a short treatise on the medicinal, as well as magical, properties of objects, animals, and various parts of animal and human bodies, references are also made to Galen's idea about humoral qualities of the substances discussed (St. Petersburg MS, fols. 4, 12, 13, 36). A mixture of natural properties and magical powers of drugs is mentioned in Pliny's work (1st cent. C.E.), and also in Galen's writings despite the assumption that Galen's idea was all rational (Keyser, p. 179). This indicates that the origin of this influence predates Galen.

Quite similar to the Roman Empire, where the compilation, summaries and commentaries on Galen's works dominated medical literature (on the analogous social and intellectual context between Byzantine and the medieval Islamic world, see Strohmaier, 1995, pp. 124-25; Ullmann, p. 22), in Iran compilation rather than creation characterized medical literature. Commentary became the dominant form of medical literature, especially after Ebn Sinā, on whose *Canon* several commentaries were written (Elgood, 1951, pp. 336-37, 375; Elgood, 1970, p. 77; Ṣafā, III, pp. 274-77). Some commentaries were written in order to make the original text more readable, while others were instigated by spirit of criticism.

Occurrences of new ideas within the framework of humoral theories were rather exceptions to the predominant exercise of compilation and respect for tradition. The common presumption dividing Islamic medicine into two periods of Golden Age and stagnation needs to be reassessed insofar as "relative independence from transmitted learning or textual authorities" (Richter-Bernburg, 1994, pp. 387-88) did not end with Rāzi and Ebn al-Nafis. For instance, one finds this independence in Bahāʾ-al-Dawla Nurbaḵši, who gave the first description of whooping cough (Elgood, 1970, pp. xii, xiv) and in Mirzā Qāżi b. Kāšef-al-Din Moḥammad Yazdi (d. ca. 1664-65), who, refuting ʿEmād-al-Din Maḥmud's idea that the chinaroot was hot, contended that the china-root was cold, and, besides, that it was not the quality of hot or cold in the drugs that operated, but another property that had nothing to do with hot and cold. He also refuted the dominant Galenic theory according to which every disease should be cured by its opposite. As proof, he mentions the curing effect of *teryāq-e fāruq* that is hot but is good for typhus (*ḥaṣba-ye siāh*) that is also hot (Mirzā Qāżi Yazdi, fol. 2). Thus, by objecting to the idea of ʿEmād-al-Din Maḥmud about chinaroot, Mirzā Qāżi seems to be suggesting a new concept, if not a new reading, of humoral pathology that obviously differed from that of the Galenic hot-cold paradigm, for he maintained that each drug had its own quality made of a specific composition of different properties (*morakkab al-qowā*).

The two trends, one guided by the spirit of criticism and research and the other characterized by respect of tradition and authority, continued side by side. Despite criticism, however, the humoral paradigm was never called into question until Ṣāleḥ b. Naṣr-Allāh Ḥalabi (d. 1670-71), called Ebn Sallum, the physician at the court of the Ottoman ruler, Sultan Moḥammad IV (r. 1648-87), introduced the Paracelsian notion of iatrochemistry (chemical medicine) into Islamic medical literature and developed pathology not based on Galen's humoral theory but on three basic substances, salt, mercury, and sulphur (Ullmann, p. 50; Savage-Smith, 1987). Several Persian translations of Paracelsian medicine were made in the 19th century, including the *Kimiā-ye bāsāliqā* made from the Arabic text of Ebn Sallum (1810), and the *Kimiā-ye šefā* translated by Moḥammad-ʿAli Širvāni from a Turkish text (1252/1836; see Richter-Bernburg, pp. 167-71).

The preference of Islamic medicine for Aristotelian universals to the detriment of Galenic experimental medicine played an enduring role in the way that medicine developed in Iran in the Islamic period until the sweeping waves of modernization in the 19th century, and the pressure of the increasing number of soldiers injured by gunshot, emphasized the importance of surgery and anatomy in medicine. An army physician of traditional education in mid-19th-century Iran, advocating the improvement of surgical skills, criticized Hippocrates for downgrading the importance of surgery in medicine (*Dar ḵoṣuṣ-e ta'sis*, apud Ebrahimnejad, 2004, pp. 227-28). Significantly, he did not blame Galen, who not only based his medical knowledge on *tašriḥ* (dissection/anatomy), but also practiced surgery in military campaigns (Ebn al-Qefṭi, tr., p. 172) and took care of the gladiators in Pergamon by cleaning and stitching their wounds (Sarton, p. 20; Nutton, 2004, p. 223).

See also GREECE x. GREEK MEDICINE IN PERSIA.

Bibliography: ʿAbd-al-l-Razzāq *Ḵolāṣat al-tašriḥ*, Pers. MS, Khanikoff 154, St Petersburg National Library. Abu Bakr Rabiʿ b. Aḥmad Akawayni Boḵāri, *Hedāyat al-motaʿallemin fi'l-ṭebb*, ed. Jalāl Matini, Mašhad, 1965. Anonymous [on the refutation of *bad'at*] Persian manuscript, National Library, St Petersburg, P.N.S. 285. Moḥammad-Ḥosayn b. Hādi ʿAqili Širāzi, *Ḵolāṣat al-ḥekma*, lithog. ed., Bombay, 1845. Bahāʾ-al-Dawla Nurbaḵši, *Ḵolāṣat al-tajāreb*, WMS Per. 602, Wellcome Trust Library, London. Abu'l-Majd Ṭabib Bayżāwi, *Moḵtaṣar-i dar ʿelm-e tašriḥ*, MS, Add. 26307, Oriental and India Office, London. Donald Campbell, *Arabian Medicine and Its Influence on the Middle Ages*, 2 vols., London , 1926; repr., London, 2000. *Dar ḵoṣuṣ-e taʾsis-e mariż-ḵāna-ye dawlati*, undated ms., Tehran, Majles Library, MS 505. Bertrand Thierry De Crussol des Eppess, "Buḫārī et l'abord des troubles psychiques," in Nasrollah Pourjavadi and Živa Vesel, eds., *Sciences techniques et instruments dans le monde Iranian (Xe-XIXe siècle)/Tāriḵ-e ʿelm o ṣanʿat wa abzār-e ʿelmi dar Irān (az qarn-e čahārom tā sizdahom h.q.)*, Actes du colloque tenu à l'Université de Téhéran (7-9 juin 1998), Tehran, 2004, pp. 239-51. Véronique Boudon, "Galen's On My Own Books: New Material from Meshed, Rida, Tibb, 5223," in Vivian Nutton, ed, *The Unknown Galen*, London, 2002, pp. 9-18.

Ebn Elyās, *Tašriḥ-e manṣuri*, Pers. MS IO Isl. 1379, British Library, London; pub. Delhi, 1864. Ebn Ḥawqal, *Ketāb ṣurat al-arż*, ed. Johannes Hendrik Kramers, 3rd ed., Leiden, 1967; tr. Johannes Hendrik Kramers and Gaston Wiet as *Configuration de la terre*, 2 vols., Paris and Beirut, 1964. Ebn al-Nadim, *Ketāb al-fehrest*, ed. Reżā Tajaddod, Tehran, 1971, pp. 347-50; tr. Bayard Dodge as *The Fihrist of al-Nadīm: A Tenth-Century Survey of Muslim Culture*, 2 vols., New York and London, 1970, II, pp. 680-86. Ebn al-Qefṭi, *Taʾriḵ al-ḥokamāʾ*, ed. Julius Lippert, Leipzig, 1903, pp. 122-32; Pers. tr. of 1688 as *Tarjama-ye Tāriḵ al-ḥokamā-ye Qefṭi*, ed. Bahman Daryāʾi, Tehran, 1992. Ebn Reżwān, *Resāla fi dafʿ al-mażārr al-abdān be-arż Meṣr*, ed. ʿĀdel Solaymān Jamāl (Ar. text) and tr. Michael Dols as *Medieval Islamic Medicine: Ibn Ridwan's Treatise "On the Prevention of Bodily Ills in Egypt,"* Berkeley, Los Angeles, and London, 1984. Ebn Sallum, see Paracelsus. Ebn Sinā, *Ketāb al-qānun fi'l-ṭebb*, tr. ʿAbd-al-Raḥmān Šarafkandi (Hažār) as *Qānun dar ṭebb*, ed. Moḥammad-Reżā Ḡaffāri and Abu'l-Qāsem Pākdāman, 5 vols., Tehran, 1986-91. Hormoz Ebrahimnejad, *Medicine, Public Health and the Qājār State: Patterns of Medical Modernisation in Nineteenth-Century Iran*, Boston and Leiden, 2004. Idem, "The Development of Galenico-Islamic Medicine: Assimilation of Greek Sciences into Islam," *Disquisition on the Past and Present*, 13 October 2005, Institute of History and Philosophy, Academia Sinica, Taiwan, pp. 127-40. Cyril Elgood, *A Medical History of Persia and the Eastern Caliphate*, Amsterdam, 1951. Idem, *Safavid Surgery*, Oxford, London, and New York, 1966. Idem, *Safavid Medical Practice or The Practice of Medicine, Surgery and Gynaecology in Persia between 1500 A.D. and 1750 A.D.*, London, 1970. ʿEmād-al-Din Maḥmud Širāzi, *Resāla-ye čub-e čini*, WMS 293A, Wellcome Trust Library, London. Abu Esḥāq Ebrāhim Eṣṭaḵri, *Ketāb masālek al-mamālek*, ed., Michaël Jan De Goeje, Leiden, 1967; tr. Moḥammad b. Asʿad Tostari as *Masālek wa mamālek*, ed. Iraj Afšār, Tehran, 1974.

Galen, *Que l'excellent médecin est aussi philosophe*, ed. and tr. Véronique Boudon-Millot, Paris, 2007a, pp. 283-92. Idem, *Sur ses propres livres*, ed. and tr. Véronique Boudon-Millot, Paris, 2007b. (attr. to), *Ṭāleʿ-nāma-ye Jālinus*, WMS., Per. 417 (A), Wellcome Trust Library, London. Idem, *Oeuvres anatomiques, physiologiques et médicales de Galien*, tr. Charles Daremberg with summaries and notes, 2 vols., Paris, 1854 (a selection of Galen's works). Idem (attr. to), *De usu partium*, tr. with commentary Margaret Talmadge May as *On the Usefulness of the Parts of the Body*, 2 vols., Ithaca, 1968. Luis Garcia-Ballester, "Galen's Medical Works in the Context of His Biography," in idem, *Galen and Galenism: Theory and Medical Practice from Antiquity to the European Renaissance*, ed. Jon Arrizabalaga et al, Variorum collected studies, Aldershot, 2002, chap. I, pp. 1-53. Isam Ghanem, *Islamic Medical Jurisprudence*, London, 1982; 2nd enlarged ed. as *Islamic Medical Jurisprudence: Comparative Forensic Medicine*, London, 1987. Bayron Good and Mary-Jo Del Vecchio Good, "The Comparative Study of Greco-Islamic Medicine: The Integration of Medical Knowledge to Local Symbolic Contexts," in Charles Leslie and Allan Young, eds., *Paths to Asian Medical Knowledge*, Berkeley, Los Angeles, and Oxford, 1992, pp. 257-71. Edward Grant, *Science and Religion, 400 B.C. to A.D. 1550: From Aristotle to Copernicus*, Westport (Conn.) and London, 2004. Anita Guerrini, *Experimenting with Humans and Animals From Galen to Animal Rights*, Baltimore and London, 2003. Dimitri Gutas, *Greek Thought, Arabic Culture: The Graeco-Arabic Translation Movement in Baghdad and Early ʿAbbāsid Society (2nd-4th/8th-10th Centuries)*, London and New York, 1998. Ḥonayn b. Esḥāq, *Resāla elā ʿAli b. Yaḥyā fi ḏekr mātorjema men kotob Jālinus be-ʿelmeh wa baʿż māyatarjam*, ed. and tr. Gotthef Bergsträsser as *Ḥunayn Ibn Isḥāq: Über die Syrischen und Arabischen Galen-Übersetzungen*, Leipzig, 1925.

Jacques Jouanna, *Hippocrate*, Paris, 1992. Idem, "La naissance de l'art médicale occidental," in Mirko D. Grmek, ed., *Storia del pensiero medico occidentale* I: *Antichità e mdioevo*, Rome, 1993; tr. Maria Laura Bardinet Broso as *Histoire de la pensée médicale en Occident* I: *Antiquité et Moyen Age*, ed. Mirko D. Grmek et al., Paris, 1995, pp. 25-66. *Ḵawāṣṣ al-ašyāʾ*, Pers. MS, St Petersburg, National Library, P.N.S. 283, undated, fols. 4, 12; another copy in the British Library, Add. 23558 (not to be mistaken for a treatise of this name by Qoṭb-al-Din Ebrāhim Meṣri, dated 22 Šaʿbān 1004/ April 1596, kept at Majles Library, Tehran). ʿOnṣoral-Maʿāli Kaykāvus b. Eskandar, *Qābus-nāma*, ed. Ḡolām-Ḥosayn Yusofi, Tehran, 1973, comm. pp. 398-406; tr. Reuben Levy as *A Mirror for Princes*, New York, 1951. Krzysztof Pomian, *Ibn Khaldun au prisme de l'Occident*, Paris, 2006. Paul T. Keyser, "Science and Magic in Galen's Recipes (Sympathy and Efficacy)," in Armelle Debru, ed, *Galen on Pharmacology: Philosophy, History and Medicine*, Proceedings of the 5th International Galen Colloquium, Lille, 16-18 March 1995, Leiden, New York, and Cologne, 1997, pp. 175-98. Carlos Gottlab Kühn, ed. and tr., *Medicorum Graecorum opera quae exstant: Claudii Galeni opera omnia*, 26 vols., Leipzig, pp. 1821-33.

George Makdisi, *Ibn ʿAqil: Religion and Culture in Classical Islam*, Edinburgh, 1977. Max Meyerhof and Joseph Schacht, *The Medico-Philosophical Controversy between Ibn Butlan of Baghdad and Ibn Ridwan of Cairo*, Cairo, 1937. Mahdi Moḥaqqeq, "Šokuk-e Rāzi bar Jālinus wa masʾala-ye qedam-e ʿālam," *MDAT* 15, 1967-68, pp. 155-206. Scott M. Montgomery, *Science in Translation: Movements of Knowledge through Cultures and Time*, Chicago and London, 2000. Aḥmad Monzawi, *Fehrest-e noskahā-ye ḵaṭṭi-e fārsi*, 6 vols. in 7, Tehran, 1969-74, I, pp. 415, 507, 527-28, 529, 535-36. Abbas Naficy, *La medicine en Perse des origins à nos jours: ses fondements théoriques d'après l'Encyclopédie médicale de Gorgani*, Paris, 1933. Aḥmad b. ʿOmar b. ʿAli Neẓāmi ʿAruzi Samarqandi, *Čahār maqāla* ed. Moḥammad Qazvini, rev. ed. with additional notes by Moḥammad Moʿin, Tehran, 1954. Vivian Nutton, "Galen and Medical Auto-biography," *Proceedings of the Cambridge Philological Society* 18, 1972, pp. 50-62. Idem, "Numisianus and Galen," *Suddhof Archive Zeitschrift für wissenschaftsgeschichte* 71, 1987, pp. 235-39. Idem, ed., *The Unknown Galen*, London, 2002. Idem, *Ancient Medicine*, London and New York, 2004. Mirzā Qāżi b. Kāšef-al-Din Moḥammad Kāšef Yazdi, *Resāla dar qahwa wa čāy wa pāzahr wa čub-e čini*, manuscript, WMS Per. 293(B), Wellcome Trust Library, London.

Paracelsus, *Ḡāyat al-etqān fi tadbir badan al-ensān*, tr. Ebn Sallum, n.p., 1826. Lutz Richter-Bernburg, *Persian Medical Manuscripts at the University of California, Los Angeles: A Descriptive Catalogue*, Humana Civilitas 4, Malibu, Cal., 1978. Idem, "Abû Bakr Muḥammad al-Rāzi's (Rhazes) Works," *Medicina nei Secoli* 6/2, 1994, pp. 377-92. Idem, "Medicina Ancilla Philosophiae: Ibn Ṭufayl's Ḥayy ibn Yaqẓān," in Lawrence Conrad, ed., *The World of Ibn Ṭufayl: Interdiciplinary Perspective on Ḥayy ibn Yaqẓān*, Leiden, New York, and Cologne, 1996, pp. 90-113. Idem, "Iran's Contribution to Medicine and Veterinary Science in Islam AH 100-900/ AD 700-1500" in John A. C. Greppin, Emilie Savage-Smith, and John L. Gueriguian, eds, *The Diffusion of Greco-Roman Medicine into the Middle East and the Caucasus*, Delmar, New York, 1999, pp. 139-68. Charles Rieu, *Catalogue of the Persian Manuscripts in the British Musium*, 3 vols., London, 1966, II, pp. 467-68, 851-52, 844. Ḏabiḥ-Allāh Ṣafā, *Tāriḵ-e adabiyāt dar Irān*, 5 vols. in 8, Tehran, 1959-92. Šams-al-Din Moḥammad b. Maḥmud Šahrazuri, *Nozhat al-arwāḥ wa rawżat al-afrāḥ fi taʾriḵ al-ḥokamāʾ wa'l-falāsefa* (comp. in the 13th cent.), ed. Sayyed Ḵoršid Aḥmad, 2 vols., Hyderabad, 1976; tr. Żiāʾ-al-Din Dorri as *Kanz al-arwāḥ*, Tehran, 1937; tr. Maqṣud-ʿAli Tabrizi (in 1602) as *Nozhat al-arwāḥ . . .*, ed. Moḥammad-Taqi Dānešpažuh and Moḥammad Sarvar Mawlāʾi, Tehran, 1986. George Sarton, *Galen of Pergamon*, Lawrence, Kansas, 1954. Emilie Savage-Smith, "Drug Therapy of Eye Diseases in Seventeenth-Century Islamic Medicine: The Influence of the 'New Chemistry' of the Paracelsians," *Farmacy in History* 29/1, 1987, pp. 3-28. Idem, "Attitudes toward Dissection in Medieval Islam," *The Journal of the History of Medicine and Allied Sciences* 50, 1995, pp. 67-110. Idem, "Galen's Lost Ophthalmology and The Summaria Alexandrinorum," in Vivian Nutton, ed., *The Unknown*

Galen, Bulletin of the Institute of Classical Studies, suppl 77, London, 2002, pp. 121-38. Emilie Savage-Smith and Peter Pormann, *Medieval Islamic Medicine*, Edinburgh, 2007. Fuat Sezgin, *Geschichte des arabischen Schriftttums* III: *Medizin, Pharmazie, Zoologie, Tierheilkunde*, Leiden, 1970, pp. 68-150. Solṭān-ʿAli Ṭabib Ḵorāsāni, *Dastur al-ʿelāj*, WMS. Per 159, Wellcome Trust Library, London (see also Mon-zawi, I, p. 535); publ. Lucknow, 1885. *Sowgand-nāma-ye Boqrāṭ* (Pers. tr. of Hippocrates Oath), Pers. manuscript, Majles Library, Tehran, No. 242, fols. 124-26. Gotthard Strohmaier, "Galen in Arabic: Prospects and Projects," in Vivian Nutton, ed, *Galen: Problems and Prospects: A Collection of Papers Submitted at the 1979 Cambridge Conference*, London, 1981, pp. 187-212. Idem, "Réception et tradition: la médecine dans le monde byzantin et arabe," in Mirko D. Grmek, ed., *Histoire de la pensée médicale en Occident: antiquité et Moyen Age*, Paris, 1995, pp. 123-49.

Oweisi Temkin, *Galenism: Rise and Decline of a Medical Pholosophy*, Ithaca and London, 1973. Manfred Ullmann, *Islamic Medicine*, Edinburgh, 1997. Mario Vegetti, "Entre le savoir et la pratique: la mèdecine hellénistique," in Mirko D. Grmek, ed, *Histoire de la pensée médicale en Occident* I: *antiquité et Moyen Age*, Paris, 1995, pp. 67-94. George Wissowa, Wilhelm Kroll, and Karl Mittlehaus, eds., *Paulys Real-Encyclopädie der classicschen Altertumswissenschaft* VII/1, Stuttgart, 1910, cols. 578-91; Eng. tr. with updates as *Brill's New Pauly: Encyclopaedia of New Pauly*, ed. Hubert Cancik, Helmuth Schneider, and Christine F. Salazar, Leiden and Boston, 2004, V, pp. 653-61. Aḥmad b. Abi Yaʿqub Yaʿqubi, *Taʾriḵ*, ed. M. Th. Houtsma as *Historiae*, 2 vols., Leiden, 1989, I, pp. 130-33. Zātspram, *Wizīdagīhā ī Zātspram*, ed. and tr. Philippe Gignoux and Ahmad Tafazzoli as *Anthologie de Zādspram: Edition critique du texte pehlevi*, Studia Iranica, Cahier 13, Paris, 1993.

For one of the commentaries written on the *Manāfeʿ al-aʿżāʾ*, see Persian MSS, Malek Library, Tehran, microfilm.

(HORMOZ EBRAHIMNEJAD)

JALLĀD. Forthcoming, online.

JALULĀ, the site of a major battle between the Sasanian and Muslim forces. This locale is a medium-sized town in the Diāla Province of Iraq, situated on the middle course of the Diāla River. In Sassanid times Jalulā was the center of a subdistrict of Šāḏ Qobāḏ Province, later known as al-ʿĀl (or al-ʿĀli) Province (Ostān al-ʿĀl/ʿĀli; Ebn Faqih, p. 199). It marked the eastern fringes of the Babylonian *sawād*, with the foothills of the Zagros mountains rising further east. The important Khorasan Road, which linked Ctesiphon to the north-east of the empire, ran through the town and continued to Ḵāneqin, Qaṣr-e Širin, and Hamadān. Jalulā is mostly referred to in Islamic sources as the scene of a battle that took place between the invading forces of the Arabs and a Sasanian army.

Setting the contradictory reports in the sources aside, one can take a battle between Persian and Muslim forces at an unspecified date between the fall of Ctesiphon and the battle of Nehāvand for granted. After their defeat at Qādesiya and after the fall of Ctesiphon, (q.v.) or Madāʾen of Islamic sources, the remnants of the Persian army retreated along the Khorasan Road. The Sasanian king, Yazdegerd III, stopped for a while in Ḥolwān, leaving his rear-guard in Jalulā. The Muslims, on the other hand could not feel safe in Ctesiphon as long as the Persians controlled the eastern *sawād* (i.e., Iraq in early Ar. sources).

Almost every Arab historiographer provides information about "the great battle" of Jalulā, Ḵalifa b. Ḵayyāṭ (p. 108), even calling it the victory of victories (*fatḥ al-fotuḥ*), but, as in other cases of the *fotuḥ* history, the reports are highly redundant and contradictory. Therefore, it is hard to extract a convincing description of the events. A likely scenario, relying mainly on Ṭabari's account on the authority of Sayf b. ʿOmar, would be: After the conquest of Madāʾen (Ṣafar 16/March 637), the caliph ʿOmar b. Ḵaṭṭāb ordered Saʿd b. Abi Waqqāṣ to follow the fleeing Persians, and also appointed Saʿd's nephew, Hāšem b. ʿOtba the leader of the pursuing forces. A troop of some 12,000 Muslim fighters marched northeast to Jalulā, where a strong Persian army (about 100,000 fighters, clearly an exaggeration, see below) had gathered. They had dug a trench around their position and enforced it with iron-covered stakes. Mehrān Rāzi is often mentioned as the commander of the Persian army. The Muslims laid siege to the stronghold and forced the Persians finally to come out and deliver battle. The Persians were utterly routed, 100,000 of them were killed and only a few escaped the onslaught, which is referred to as *Jalulāʾ al-waqiʿa*. The victors found a tremendous amount of booty in the Persian camp, including a number of women who were taken captive (Ṭabari, I/IV, pp. 2456-60; tr., pp. 36-39; cf. Balāḏori, pp. 264-65; Dinavari, 1960, pp. 127-29). An Arab vanguard was despatched to follow the Persians and reached Ḥolwān, which was taken and garrisoned. The caliph objected to any further advance, saying in a letter to Saʿd: "because I prefer peace for the believers to great booty" (*anfāl*; Ṭabari, I/IV, pp. 2463-64, tr., p. 43; Ebn al-Aṯir, II, p. 363; 2nd ed., III, p. 521). Therefore, the army returned to Madāʾen.

One finds a great deal of discrepancies in the accounts of the battle in the primary sources, not to mention some information (e.g., 100,000 Persians killed) that is at best questionable. For instance, most sources refer to Hāšem b. ʿOtba as the Arab commander at Jalulā, while, according to Hešām b. Moḥammad Kalbi (apud Balāḏori, p. 265), it was ʿAmr b. ʿOtba b. Nawfal, the grandson of Saʿd b. Abi Waqqāṣ, who led the Arab army; Abu Ḥanifa Dinavari (1960, p. 127) mentions ʿAmr b. Mālek b. Najaba, and Abu Yusof give the command to Saʿd b. Abi Waqqāṣ himself. More outright discrepancies turn up in connection with the names of the commanders of certain contingents, which tend to discredit the entire account. The date of the battle is also given differently in various reports. The earliest date is 635 (Ṭabari, I/IV, p. 2359, on Ebn Esḥāq's authority and the latest is 640, Yaʿqubi, II, p. 173). Many authors speak of the end of Ḏu'l-qaʿda 16 (Dec. 637), which most modern scholars consider a plausible date of the battle. The Sayf tradition, which features prominent in Ṭabari's account, is centered on the valor of Qaʿqāʿ b. ʿAmr (for him, see Zettersteén). In the Jalulā saga this so-called Arab hero is again portrayed as the warrior who almost single-handedly decided the battle by his courage (Ṭabari, I/IV, 2459-61, tr., pp. 38-40). The only author who provides a different story is Ebn Aʿṯam Kufi, but he is mostly deemed unreliable.

Hidden under the surface of the seemingly authentic reports lays an abyss of highly questionable information, so that one can discard nearly every detail of the story of Jalulā. Neither is the date certain, nor are the circumstances, the commanders, the number of the fighting troops, or the outcome of the battle (see Noth's study). Furthermore, two standard features of the *fotuḥ* reports are missing in the Jalulā stories, namely, the usual obituary of martyred Muslims and the mentioning of any treaty with the local population after the battle.

Noth took the reports about Jalulā as evidence for his observation that Arab authors sometimes constructed a story only to give an explication for an otherwise inexplicable name of a locality, in this case Jalulā, which was traced back to allusions to the Ar. root √*j-l-l*, which conveys, among others, the meaning "to cover the ground." In order to "cover the ground" with slain bodies, they invented the colossal number of 100,000 Persians killed.

Contrary to the traditional interpretation of Jalulā as a decisive blow to the power of the Persian king, the fighting seems to have been just one more setback in a long run of defeats. For the Muslims the battle of Jalulā was only the final stage of the conquest of the Babylonian *sawād*, but it was not the first stage of the conquest of Iran.

Bibliography: Abu'l-ʿAbbās Aḥmad Balāḏori, *Fotuḥ al-boldān*, ed. Michaël Jan de Goeje, Leiden, 1886; new ed., Leiden, 1968. Abu Yusof, Abu Ḥanifa Dinavari, *al-Aḵbār al-ṭewāl*, ed. V. Guirgass, Leiden, 1888; ed. ʿAbd-al-Monʿem ʿĀmer and Jamāl-al-Din Šayyāl, Cairo, 1960. Fred McGraw Donner, *The Early Islamic Conquests*, Princeton, 1981. Ebn Aʿṯam Kufi, *Ketāb al-fotuḥ*, ed. ʿAli Širi, 8vols. in 4, Beirut, 1991; incomp. Pers. tr. by Moḥammad b. Aḥmad Mostawfi Heravi as *Tarjama-ye Ketāb al-fotuḥ*, Bombay, 1882. Ebn al-Aṯir, *Ketab al-kāmel fi'-taʾriḵ*, ed. Carl Johann, Tornberg as *Ibn-el-Athiri cronicon*, 15 vols., Leiden, 1851–76; new ed., 13 vols., Beirut, 1956-67. Ebn al-Faqih, *Ketāb al-boldān*, ed. Michaël Jan de Goeje, Leiden, 1967. Ebn Meskawayh (Meskuya) Rāzi, *Tajāreb al-omam* I, ed. Abu'l-Qāsem Emāmi, Tehran, 1987, pp. 224-26. Ḵalifa b. Ḵayyāṭ ʿOṣrufi, *Taʾriḵ Ḵalifa ebn Ḵayyāṭ*, ed. Akram Żiāʾ ʿOmari, Najaf, 1967. Michael G. Morony, *Iraq after the Muslim Conquest*, Princeton, 1984. Albrecht Noth, *Quellenkritische Studien zu Themen, Formen und Tendenzen frühislamischer Geschichtsüberlieferung*, Bonn, 1973. Moḥammad b. Jarir Ṭabari, *Ketāb akbār al-rosol wa-'l-moluk*, ed. Michaël Jan de Goeje et al., 15 vols., Leiden, 1879-1901; tr. by various scholars as *The History of al-Ṭabarī* XIII: *The Conquest of Iraq, Southwestern Persia, and Egypt*, tr. Gautier H. A. Juynboll, Albany, 1989. Yaʿqubi, *Taʾrik*, ed. Martijn Theodor Houtsma, *as Historiae*, 2 vols., Leiden, 1883; 2nd ed., Leiden, 1969. K. V. Zettersteén, "al-Ḳaʿḳāʿ b. ʿAmr," in *EI*² IV, p. 464.

(KLAUS KLIER)

JAM, name given to a religious ceremony performed among two important religious communities living traditionally in the same historical region on the Zagros Mountain chain, which for a long time has been located in the core of several Mesopotamian and Iranian civilizations. Today, the same region is within the national borders of Iran, Iraq and Turkey. This term, according to Nur-ʿAli Elāhi (p. 27), is the Arabic word *jamʿ* (gathering, assembly), which is pronounced by the non-Arabs of the region without its last letter "*ʿayn*," thus sounding exactly like Persian *jam*, the name of a king in Iranian mythology.

Jam is the most important religious ceremony among the Yāresān or Ahl-e Ḥaqq (q.v.) of Iran and Iraq as well the Alevis of Turkey, but it does not exit among the Yazidi or Ezdi Kurds (Kreyenbroek, p. 103), although they share many of their religious tenets with the other two communities. Jam is performed by both Yāresāns and Alevis as a ceremony for periodical meetings, but it also includes many other rituals. The ritual is structurally performed, with some notable variations, in a similar manner by all branches of these two communities. The place where Jam is performed is called *Jam-ḵāna*. In both communities Jam is accompanied by music and religious dances; sacrificial food and other offerings are also made and distributed among the participants (author's own fieldwork material). Their instrument of choice is *tanbur*, a plucked instrument of the lute family. Both groups seem to be using the same instrument, but the one played by the Yāresān is of more traditional form, while the one played by the Alevis (also called *sāz* or *divān*) seems to have undergone several modifications (for various forms of *tanbur*, see Mallāḥ, pp. 192-218, 386-87; Setāyešgar, I, pp. 284-86).

The ideal number of participants to perform a Jam by the Yāresān is three, five, or seven male adults. The women and children are allowed to attend a Jam, but they stand outside of the circle. This is usually for the sake of educating their children in religious matters. The children are not allowed to sit and are expected to stand throughout the ceremony. Women are not allowed to enter the Jam, even the one who is being ceremonially initiated; for her the ceremony is performed by a proxy (author's own fieldwork material).

Nur-ʿAli Elāhi (q.v.), the leader of a branch of the Yāresān, states that both men and women can attend the

Jam ceremony, but women are not allowed to sit with men; they may, however, gather behind a partition that would separate them from the men (Elāhi, p. 81). Considering relatively high position of the women among this community, the prohibition of women folk to participate directly in the Jam ritual seems to be a recent decision. Probable previous participation of the women could have been the reason for the outsiders to accuse them of holding orgies. For instance, Henry Rawlinson, writing in 1839, stated that orgiastic nights had existed among the Yāresān "until within the last half century" (Rawlinson, p. 110; cf. De Bode, II, p. 180 and Sāʿedi, p. 127). In any case, the participation of the women is still current among the Alevis of Turkey, who even take part in their religious dances.

The sociological function of Jam may be both uniting and dividing the Yāresān as a whole. The performance of the ritual as well as its many latent and apparent symbols can bring about a strong sense of solidarity among the participants, who, in theory, should forget all kinds of resentful and rivalrous feelings that they might have entertained. At the same time, the members of each one of eleven branches (*ḵānadān*; Elāhi, pp. 53, 66-72) attend only their own ceremony, which is performed slightly different from those of others and which may lay grounds for alienation.

Another important motive emphasized in the Jam ceremony is the principal of absolute equality among the participants, which is also repeated in their songs (*kalām*), and which should be observed to the extent that a king and a beggar be treated equally (Elāhi, p. 84). Every participant covers his head, either wearing a hat or using a piece of cloth or a handkerchief. He also must gird his waist, either by a belt or with a length of cloth. This is usually done over their clothes, whether over their shirts and jackets, or under their coats or *ʿabā* (a kind of loose outer garment for men, q.v.). Since no kinds of ranking is recognized, no one is allowed to have a special place to sit, except those who are in charge of directing the ceremony (author's own fieldwork material).

When a participant enters, he prostrate himself, kisses the threshold and says: "The Beginning and the End is the *Yār*" (*Yār* "the Friend" is one of the names of God among the followers of the Yāresān). This is in accordance to their religious philosophy, which does not believe in death, rather comparing it with the diving of a duck into water. He then goes first to the *sayyed* or the religious guide in charge of the ceremony to perform the hand kissing rite. He then goes from the right to the left, kissing the hands of those already seated. To take the correct prescribed position, he gets down on his knees and sits back, resting his weight on his lower legs and feet. Otherwise, especially for those who do not have enough physical strength to go through the motion, it is enough to bend down before each participants in order to perform the hand kissing rite. In practice, however, the former way is not commonly performed. The participants in a Jam always sit on the floor and chairs are never used. Normally in the regions west of Kermānšāh city, the participants remain seated by kneeling, whereas those inhabiting the regions west of this city are seated cross legged (author's own fieldwork material).

They then hold each others right hands, palms touching each others. While still holding each others' right hands, they simultaneously bring them to the level of their lips in such a way that each one is able to kiss the back side of the other's right hand. In the version described by Nur-ʿAli Elāhi, while right hands are holding, each participant should place his left hand on the back of the other person's right hand and kiss the back side of the other's left hand (Elāhi, p. 78). The first version, however, is more commonly followed.

Each newcomer goes round the room from right to left, and after kissing the hands of all those already seated one by one, he takes the first vacant place to sit. As already mentioned, only those in charge of directing the ceremony have their prescribed places in the Jam to sit. These are, the *sayyed*, the leader of the assembly, who sits opposite the entrance; his representative (called *ḵalifa*), who sits on the left side of the sayyed; and the person in charge of reciting the kalām, who sits on his right side. These three, as well as a person in charge of serving the Jam (*ḵādem*) are the necessary authorities for a Jam to be performed (author's own fieldwork material). Therefore, the prescriptive rule of holding a Jam with the minimum number of three can only mean three participants added to these four, making the total number at least seven. Some believe that, although a Jam can be performed with the minimum number of three participants, at least seven participants are required if the ceremony is accompanied by an initiation rite (Hamzeh'ee, p. 156).

The ḵādem should remain standing in the doorway opposite of the sayyed throughout the ceremony. He is required to have already washed his feet and to serve the Jam bare-footed. In the absence of a sayyed, the ḵalifa recites prayer when offerings are made, but he is not allowed to recite prayer for sacrifices, which can only be done by a sayyed. Once everyone is seated in a circle, the ḵādem declares the beginning of the ceremony by saying "The Beginning and the End is the *Yār*." From the beginning to the end of a Jam, all participants are required to remain seated in the manner already described. No movements or changing positions are allowed once the ḵādem declares the official beginning of the Jam, except in the case of urgent or unexpected situations (author's own fieldwork material).

A Jam is often accompanied by other rituals such as offerings and sacrifices as well as initiation rites. In case that a sacrifice is made, first a bowl and a ewer are brought to the Jam by the ḵādem, who takes them around for the participants to wash their hands. Then they touch their faces with the palms of their hands (*masḥ*) and recite the above mentioned formula. The ḵādem also washes his own hands after all participants. Then a white table cloth (*sofra*) is brought in and spread before the sayyed. The pot containing cooked sacrificial meat is placed on the *sofra*, and the sayyed separates the meat from the bones without the bones being broken. Then equal portions of the meat are put on a type of bread (called *tiri*) and rolled up. In case that offerings of rice are made, some cooked rice may be added to each portion of meat. These sacrificial shares are called *baš* or *nawāla*. The shares are distributed by the ḵalifa among the participants, including men, women, and children outside of the Jam. The first *baš* is a holy one and is called *māl-e Dāwud* (belonging to Dāwud). This is regarded as that of the Divinity and would be put in the middle of the Jam. While doing so, all the participants say *Hu* "He" (i.e., God). In case the Jam is performed at night, the second share called "*māl-e čerāḡ*" may be offered to the light and it would be kept in front of a burning candle or an oil lamp. Except for tasting or eating the holy share received, nothing should be eaten throughout the ceremony. Similarly, no private word should be exchanged or the prescribed sitting position altered. This is not applicable for those who are in charge of the performance. The ḵādem is not allowed to leave the room, and the works outside are done by his assistants. He may, however, leave the room when no assistants are available, but he has to leave his headgear in the Jam each time he goes out (author's own fieldwork material).

Throughout the ceremony, the *kalām* is recited or music is played on the *tanbur*. Just like the Alevis, the Yāresān may merely listen to the music meditatively or move their bodies with its rhythms. The whole atmosphere of the Jam and religious songs as well as the sound of *tanbur*, often leads several of the participants to experience deep moments of ecstasy. A Jam might be performed without music as well, when no one is present to play music or recite the religious songs. After the sacrificial shares are distributed, the ḵādem brings in a bowl of drinking water, offering water to each participant one by one, from the right to the left. Each person takes a sip of water from the same bowl and returns it to the ḵādem, who turns the bowl a little bit around before offerring it to the next person, so that the lips of the next participant do not touch the same point where those of the previous one has done. The ceremony is called *āw-e čarḵ-e Jam*, meaning the circulating water of the Jam (Hamzeh'ee, pp. 175, 177, 203).

After the *sofra* is collected and taken away, the *sofra* prayer is recited by the sayyed. Then at the end of the ceremony, the ḵādem and his helper call the Permission Prayer (*Doʿā-ye roḵṣat*), after which they go to kiss the hands of all the participants from the right to the left, starting from the sayyed. Finally the sayyed, who is called *sarjam*, declares the completion of the ceremony.

The Jam ceremony is an extremely important ritual for both the Alevis and the Yāresān. The latter regard Jam as a Mecca of their own and believe that there is a divine manifestation wherever it is held. Thus, all participants are believed to be in the presence of the Holy Essence (*ḏāt* or *ḏarra*) of God, and any person attending the Jam is required to observe the purity of both body and mind (for detailed description of the ceremony, see Hamzeh'ee, chap. 6.1). The great importance that the Yāresān attach to the Jam is illustrated in a myth in which a son of Solṭān Ṣaḥāk, one of the main theophanies of the Yāresān religion, is said to have been wrestling with a believer. He called out for his father to give him strength, but the believer called on the magnanimity of the Jam and won. The youth went and complained to his father. Solṭān Ṣaḥāk said: "Quite right, for my right arm is always with the Jam" (Saeed Khan, p. 37). It is believed that, in a Jam, all problems of the participants would receive solutions, as promised by the Divinity. This can be one of the reasons for the followers to use a particular language with many symbolic expressions while describing the Jam.

Bibliography: C. A. Baron De Bode, *Travels in Luristan and Arabistan*, 2 vols., London, 1845; tr. Moḥammad-Ḥosayni Āriā as *Safar-nāma-ye Lorestān wa Ḵuzestān*, Tehran, 1992. Nur-ʿAli Elāhi, *Borhān al-ḥaqq*, Tehran, 1994. M. Reza (Fariborz) Hamzeh'ee, *The Yaresan: A Sociological, Historical and Religio-Historical Study of a Kurdish Community*, Berlin, 1990. Philip G. Kreyenbroek, "Religion and Religions in Kurdistan," in Philip Kereyenbroek and Christine Allison, eds., *Kurdish Culture and Identity*, London, 1996. *Majmuʿa-ye rasāʾel wa ašʿār-e Ahl-e Ḥaqq*, ed. and tr. Wladimir Ivanow with commentary as *The Truth Worshippers of Kurdistan*, Leiden, 1953, pp. 75-88, 172. Ḥosayn-ʿAli Mallāḥ, *Farhang-e sāzhā*, Tehran, 1977. Ziba Mir-Hosseini, "Faith, Ritual and Culture among the Ahl-e Haqq," in Philip Kereyenbroek and Christine Allison, eds., *Kurdish Culture and Identity*, London, 1996, pp. 111-34. Henry C. Rawlinson, "Notes on a March from Zohab, at the Foot of Zagros along the Mountains of Khuzistan (Susiana) and from Thence through the Province of Luristan to Kirmanshah, in the Year 1836," *Journal of the Royal Geographical Society* 9, 1839, pp. 26-116. Ḡolām-Ḥosayn Sāʿedi, *Ilḵči: yak deh-e ṣufinešin dar Āḏar-bāyjān*, Tehran, 1978. Saeed Khan, "The Sect of Ahl-i Haqq (Ali Ilahis)," *The Moslem World* 17/1, January 1927, pp. 31-42. Mahdi Setāyešgar, *Vāža-nāma-ye musiqi-e Irān-zamin*, 2 vols.,Tehran, 1995-96.

(M. REZA FARIBORZ HAMZEH'EE)

JAM, MAḤMUD, titled Modir-al-Molk (b. Tabriz, 1885; d. Tehran, 1969), prime minister under Reżā Shah. He maintained that his family had originally come from Kermān, while he also claimed to be descended from Shaikh Maḥmud Šabestari, the 13th-century mystic and poet from Azerbaijan. Jam received his elementary education in the Rošdiya and Kamāliya schools in Tabriz and studied French on his own. He began work as a schoolteacher of French and was hired as a translator to work with Henry Renar, the French teacher of the crown prince Moḥammad-ʿAli Mirzā in Tabriz, and subsequently with his personal physician Dr. Coppin (Taqizāda, pp. 139, 141). Later he moved to Tehran, where he entered the civil service as a translator at the Customs Office in 1909 and before long moved up to more senior positions. He, however, left the Custom Office shortly before World War I in order to become the translator to the Attaché at the French Embassy, and during the war he acted as the translator in the negotiations that took place between the French Embassy and the Persian government. In 1919, he went to the Ministry of Finance as the head of the state-owned grain storage and distribution. It was at this time that, on the suggestion of Mirzā Ḥasan Khan Woṯuq-al-Dawla, then the prime minister, and the agreement of Aḥmad Shah Qājār, he received the title of Modir-al-Molk. He served as the head of the treasury department (*ḵazāna-dāri*) in the cabinets of Mošir-al-Dawla Ḥasan Pirniā and Manṣur Sepahdār Rašti.

In 1921, during the short-lived government of Sayyed Żiāʾ-al-Din Ṭabāṭabāʾi, Jam served as foreign minister, which led many to believe that he was a close political ally of the prime minister. Among the political elite of the time, many of whom were arrested by Sayyed Żiāʾ-al-Din, feelings against Jam ran high. Despite this, he was appointed deputy minister of finance in the cabinet of Mošir-al-Dawla (in January 1922), and minister of finance in the cabinet of Reza (Reżā) Khan Sardār-e Sepah, the future Reza Shah, when he became prime minister (November 1923). Jam remained loyal to Reza Shah throughout the latter's reign and served for four years (1929-33) as the governor of Khorasan, minister of interior (1933), and as prime minister between December 1935 and October 1939. His period in office as prime minister coincided with perhaps the darkest hour in Reza Shah's reign after a number of distinguished politicians and notables such as ʿAbd-al-Ḥosayn Teymurtāš, Noṣrat-al-Dawla Firuz Mirzā, Sayyed Ḥasan Modarres, and ʿAli-Akbar Dāvar had been eliminated in various ways, while others, like Moḥammad-ʿAli Forugi (qq.v.), were forced to leave the political stage. It was during this period that he traveled to Egypt with a number of other politicians to make arrangements for the marriage between Princess Fawzia, King Fāruq's sister, and Moḥammad-Reżā, the crown prince. Two more significant events of his tenure as prime minister were the universal removal of veils (enforced January 1936, see ČĀDOR) and the signing in Tehran of the Saʿdābād Pact between Persia, Turkey, Iraq, and Afghanistan (8 July 1937). His removal from office in 1939 was interpreted by some as a move by Reza Shah to draw closer to Nazi Germany by appointing a more pro-German prime minister. Jam acted as minister of court from 1939 to September 1941. Under Mohammad Reza Shah, Jam served as ambassador to Egypt, minister of court, minister of war, ambassador to Italy, and finally as a senator in 1956. Except for a few casual articles in the daily *Eṭṭelāʿāt* and the annual journal *Sāl-nāma-e donyā*, Jam never published any writings.

Bibliography: Bāqer ʿĀqeli, *Naḵost-wazirān-e Irān az Mošir-al-Dawla tā Baḵtiār*, Tehran, 1991, pp. 444-61. Idem, *Šarḥ-e ḥāl(l)-e rejāl-e siāsi wa neẓāmi-e moʿāṣer-e Irān*, 3 vols., Tehran, 2001, I, pp. 547-51. Mahdi Bāmdād, *Šarḥ-e ḥāl(l)-e rejāl-e Irān*, 6 vols., Tehran, 1968-78, V, pp. 283-85. Hušang Etteḥād, *Pažuhešgarān-e moʿāṣer-e Irān* III, Tehran, 1999, pp. 166-68. Cyrus Ghani, *Iran and the Rise of Reza Shah: From Qajar Colapse to Pahlavi Power*, London and New York, 1998, pp. 201, 250, 291-92. Qāsem Ḡani, *Yādašthā-ye Doktor Qāsem Ḡani*, ed. Cyrus Ghani, 12 vols., London, 1980-82, II, pp. 16-19. Mahdi Mojtahedi, *Rejāl-e Āḏarbāyjān dar ʿaṣr-e Mašruṭiyat*, ed. Ḡolām-Reżā Ṭabāṭabāʾi Majd, Tehran, n.d., pp. 114-15. Aḥmad Nikuhemmat, "Rašid Yāsami," *Armaḡān* 25/6, 1949, p. 325. Ebrāhim Ṣafāʾi, *Naḵost-wazirān* I, Tehran, n.d., pp. 43-44, 59-65. Sayyed Ḥasan Taqizāda, *Zendagi-e ṭufāni: ḵāṭerāt-e Sayyed Ḥasan Taqizāda*, ed. Iraj Afšār, 2nd ed., Tehran, 1993.

(ALI SADEGHI)

JĀM, a mountainous, hard to access, region at about 200 km to the east of Herat on the way from this city to Kabul, and a historically important village in the province of Ghur (Ḡur, q.v.) in western Afghanistan (lat. 34°23′ N, long. 64°30′ E). It is located near the historical monument, the minaret of Jam. This entry is divided into the following two sub-entries:

i. *Jām region and village.*
ii. *Jām Minaret.*

i. JĀM REGION AND VILLAGE

Lying 45 km northeast of Šahrak, the village of Jām is located on the barren foothills of the remote narrow valley of Jām, close to the celebrated Ghurid monument, the minaret of Jām (see below). The village of Jām abounds in cornfields, willow trees, and orchards, particularly of apricots and apples (Adamec, III, p. 183; Pažvāk, p. 16, no. 1; Stark, pp. 65-66; Massé, p. 406).

The history of Jām is virtually interwoven with that of its minaret, which stands at the confluence of the Harirud River and one of its tributaries, Tagao Gonbaz (or Jam-rud; see ii. below). Emphasizing its cultural significance, in 2002 UNESCO declared the minaret of Jām and the surrounding archeological remains as Afghanistan's first World Heritage Site, but, due to the status of the minaret, it was also put on UNESCO's List of World Heritage in Danger or List of Endangered Sites (Thomas, Pastori, and Cucco, 2004, p. 89; "Endangered Minaret . . ."; Manhart, pp. 406-8; for more details see http://whc.unesco.org/en/list/211/).

Because of the brevity of historical evidence, some confusion has arisen regarding the position of Jām and its minaret in relation to the now non-existent city of Firuzkuh (see FIRUZKUH i. The Ghurid Capital) and its Friday Mosque (*masjed-e jāmeʿ*). Menhāj-al-Din Juzjāni (1193-1260?), the main source on the Ghurids (q.v.), states that, when the Ghurid Malek-al-Jebāl Qoṭb-al-Din Moḥammad b. Ḥosayn decided to have a well-fortified castle (*qalʿa-ye ḥaṣin*) built, he sent his people around to find a suitable place. He eventually chose the spot where the city and the castle of Firuzkuh were constructed (Juzjāni, I, pp. 335-36). Juzjāni further reports that Firuzkuh's Friday Mosque was washed away in a flash flood (Juzjāni, I, p. 375). Apparently, for both natural and human reasons, the city itself disappeared completely. The minaret is evidently the only significant piece of architecture left from the Ghurid dynasty, which ruled for some sixty years a vast area extending from Khorasan in the west to the Bay of Bengal in the east.

Due to its inaccessibility, local conflicts, as well as devastating Mongol incursions in the 13th century, the village of Jām seems to have been lost to the outside world for centuries until it "was 're-discovered' during a survey of the Afghan Boundary Commission in 1886" (Thomas, Pastori, and Cucco, p. 89, with reference to Holdich). In the mid-1950s, the governor of Herat reported to the Afghan Historical Society of his sighting of a minaret on the banks of the Harirud River, thus drawing some attention to Jām again. In 1957, an expedition led by the president of the Afghan Historical Society, Aḥmad-ʿAli Kohzād, and by the Belgian archeologist, André Maricq, visited the minaret of Jām. Since one of the two inscriptions on the minaret glorifies Ḡiāṯ-al-Din Moḥammad, Maricq came to identify Jām with Firuzkuh (Maricq and Wiet, pp. 21-55), the summer capital of the Ghurids, assuming accordingly that the minaret belonged to the Friday Mosque of Firuzkuh (Leshnik, pp. 37, 40-41; Jilāni Dāvari, p. 44). Maricq thus called the whole area Firuzkuh (Jilāni Dāvari, p. 52; Massé, p. 406). However, the view that the flood had destroyed Firuzkuh's mosque but left its minaret intact has been seriously challenged. It appears highly improbable that the Jām minaret could survive so strong a flood that had devastated the rest of the mosque. Besides, because of its mountainous condition and the lack of land space, the area of Jām could not have possibly afforded such enormous monumental buildings as Firuzkuh's Friday Mosque. Nor could it have possessed the capacity of becoming the capital of the Ghurid dynasty, as some have assumed (Jilāni Dāvari, pp. 55-56).

Bibliography: Louis W. Adamec, ed., *Historical and Political Gazetteer of Afghanistan* III: *Herat and Northwestern Afghanistan*, Graz, 1975. Moḥammad-ʿAli Bar, *Afḡānestān men al-fatḥ al-Eslām elā al-ḡazw al-rusi*, Jeddah, 1985. Clifford E. Bosworth, "Ghūrids," in *EI*[2] II, 1965, pp. 1099-104. Idem, "The Early Islamic History of Ghūr," *Central Asiatic Journal* 6, 1961, pp. 116-33; repr. in *The Medieval History of Iran, Afghanistan, and Central Asia*, Variorum Reprints Collected Studies 56, London, 1977. A. Bruno, "Notes on the Discovery of Hebrew Inscriptions in the Vicinity of the Minaret of Jām," *East and West*, N.S. 14/3-4, 1963, pp. 206-8. G. D. Davary, "Jam and Feroz-koh: A New Study," *Afghanistan* 30/4, 1968, pp. 69-91. Louis Dupree, *Afghanistan*, Princeton, N.J., 1973; new ed., Karachi and Oxford, 1997. ʿAbd-al-Ḥayy Ḥabibi, "The City of Firuzkuh: Where Was It?" *Afghanistan* 331, 1980, pp. 34-44. W. Herberg, "Topograpische Feldarbeiten in Ghor: Bericht über Forschungsarbeiten zum Problem Jam-Ferozkoh," *Afghanistan Journal* 3/2, 1976, pp. 57-69. W. Herberg and D. Davary, "Das Land Ghor in Afghanistan: Auf der Suche nach einem verschollen Imperium," *Die Waage* 175, 1978, pp. 216-20. Derek Hill, "Journey to Jam," Apollo, N.S. 84, pp. 390-96. Thomas Hungerford Holdich, *Geographical Results of the Afghan Boundary Commission: India Office Political Department Memoranda*, London, 1886. Ḡolām Jilāni Dāvari, "Taḥqiq-e jadid dar bāra-ye Jām wa Firuzkuh," *Aryāna* 33/1, 1975, pp. 43-58. Charles M. Kieffer, "Le minaret de Ghiyath al-Din à Firuzkuh," Afhanistan 15/4, pp. 16-60. Menhāj-al-Din b. Serāj-al-Din Juzjçni, *Ṭabaqāt-e nāṣeri*, ed. ʿAbd-al-Ḥayy Ḥabibi, 2 vols., 2nd ed., Kabul, 1963. L. S. Leshnik, "Ghor, Firuzkuh and the Minar-i Jam," *Central Asiatic Journal* 12, 1968, pp. 36-49. Christian Manhart, "UNESCO's Mandate and Recent Activities for the Rehabilitation of Afghanistan's Cultural Heritage," *IRRC* 86, no. 854, June 2004, pp. 401-14; available at www.icrc.org/Web/eng/siteeng0.nsf/htmlall/634JK5/$File/irrc_854_Manhart.pdf (accessed on 17 August 2007). André Maricq and Gaston Wiet, *Le minaret de Djam: la découverte de la capitale des sultans Ghorides (XIIe-XIIIe siècles)*, Paris, 1959. Henri Massé, "Djām," in *EI*[2] II, 1965, p. 406. ʿAtīq-Allāh Pažvāk, *Ḡuriān*, Kabul, 1966. R. Pinder-Wilson, "Ghaznavid and Ghurid Minarets," *Iran* 39, 2002, pp. 155-86. Freya Stark, *The Minaret of Djam: An Excursion in Afghanistan*, London, 1970. D. Thomas, "Looting, Heritage Management and Archaeological Strategies at Jam," *Culture Without Context* 14, 2004, pp. 16-20. David Thomas, Giannino Pastori, and Ivan Cucco, "Excavations at Jam, Afghanistan," *East and West* 54/1-4, 2004, pp. 87-119. Giorgio Vercellin, "The Identification of Firuzkuh: A Conclusive Proof," *East and West* 26/3-4, 1976, pp. 337-40.

Online sources: "Endangered Minaret Puts Afghanistan on World Heritage List," available at www.portal.unesco.org/culture/en/ev.php-URL_ID=25620&URL_DO=DO_TOPIC&URL_SECTION=201.html (accessed on 17 August 2007). "Minaret of Jam (12th century)" at www.orientalarchitecture.com/afghanistan/minaretjamindex.htm (accessed on 17 August 2007). David Thomas, Giannino Pastori, and Ivan Cucco, "The Minaret of Jam Archaeological Project (MJAP)," *Antiquity* 79/303, March 2005, Article no. 79010, available at http://www.antiquity.ac.uk/projgall/thomas/index.html (accessed on 17 August 2007).

(MAJD-AL-DIN KEYVANI)

ii. JĀM MINARET

A pre-eminent 12th-century monument of the Šansabāni sultans of Ḡur in central Afghanistan. The minaret stands 65 meters high near the confluence of the Harirud and Jāmrud rivers in a remote mountain valley once protected by a series of defensive towers (Ball, 2002; PLATE I). The first major publication on the monument appeared in 1959 (Maricq and Wiet), but its existence was reported as early as the 1880s (Ball, 1982, I, p. 133). It was discussed in Afghan publications in the 1940s (Herberg and Davary, p. 57), and an image of it appeared on the cover of the *Majalla-ye Kābul* in 1932-33 and 1933-34, anticipating its subsequent adoption as an Afghan national symbol. In 2002, the minaret of Jām was added to

PLATE I

Jām Minaret, view from the east showing distinctive arched panel on the eastern face. Courtesy of MJAP, 2005.

UNESCO's World Heritage List. It is widely recognized as the cynosure of Ghurid architectural patronage (see ĀL-E ŠANSAB, GHURIDS, ĠUR; cf. Hillenbrand), remnants of which are scattered across Afghanistan (q.v.), Pakistan, and north India.

Historical context. The minaret bears the name of the Šansabāni sultan Ġiāṯ-al-Din Moḥammad b. Sām (r. 1163-1203), during whose reign Ghurid control extended from Nishapur in the west to Benares in the East. Although it is not mentioned in the medieval sources, it is widely believed to mark the site of Firuzkuh (q.v.), the Ghurid summer capital (Maricq and Wiet, pp. 55-64). Despite objections to this identification (Leshnik), attempts have been made to correlate the topography of the site to medieval descriptions of Firuzkuh (Vercellin, 1976; Pinder-Wilson, 2001, pp. 166-71). Recent illegal excavations on the hills surrounding the site have reportedly uncovered evidence for a great density of occupation in small multistoried structures, recalling medieval accounts of Firuzkuh as heavily populated (Stewart, pp. 168-78). Moreover, the existence of a small 12th-century Jewish community at the site, attested by a series of Judaeo-Persian tombstones (Bruno, 1963; Gnoli, 1962, 1964; Rapp), and the reported retrieval of shards of luster and *minai* ceramics (q.v.) probably imported from Kāšān (Sourdel-Thomine, 2004, p. 41), indicate a degree of cosmopolitanism and a local market for luxury goods.

The minaret stands isolated today, but the probable remains of an associated mosque have been identified on a riverine terrace to the northeast (Sourdel-Thomine, 2004, pp. 31-32; Thomas et al., pp. 92-93). As with other apparently free-standing 11th- and 12th-century brick (q.v.) minarets in Ġazna (q.v.) and Iranian Sistān, the mosque may have been built with more ephemeral materials (O'Kane, pp. 89-97); it is reported that the Friday Mosque of Firuzkuh was destroyed by flooding just before 1200, at the zenith of Ghurid power (Juzjāni, I, p. 375, tr. I, p. 404).

The minaret bears a foundation text. Scholarship has long been split between a reading of 1174-75 and 1193-94, but recent research has confirmed that the former is correct (Sourdel-Thomine, 2004, pp. 135-39), casting doubt on the oft-cited idea that the monument was erected to commemorate Ghurid victories in India. If the minaret had a commemorative function, it may memorialize the capture of Ġazna, the former capital of the Ghaznavid sultans (see GHAZNAVIDS), from the Ġozz (q.v.) Turks in 1174. This was a pivotal event for the development of the Ghurid sultanate, after which Moʿezz-al-Din Moḥammad b. Sām, the brother of the Jām minaret's patron, was installed as co-sultan in Ġazna (r. 1203-06). The choice of monument may have reflected the nature of the victory that it commemorated, for it seems likely that the minarets of Masʿud III (r. 1099-1115) and Bahrāmšāh (r. 1117-57) at Ġazna provided the inspiration for the monument at Jām (Pinder-Wilson, 1985, p. 100; idem, 2001, pp. 155-66). The early date of construction points to the precocious development of a distinctive Ghurid architectural style otherwise witnessed in a mausoleum at Češt (q.v.), which is dated 1167 (Blair, p. 82), and the spectacular *madrasa* of 1176 at Šāh-e Mašhad in Ġarjestān (Glatzer).

Construction. The minaret is constructed from baked brick, with occasional wooden courses and the use of stucco and terracotta for decoration. It stands on an octagonal socle, which supports three superimposed cylindrical shafts of decreasing girth crowned by a small pavilion. The interior is occupied by two staircases that do not communicate but once originated in a single entrance oriented towards the northeast, the probable location of the mosque with which the minaret was originally associated. The reason for this idiosyncratic arrangement is unclear. The exterior transitions between different sections of the shaft were originally masked by projecting balconies borne on wooden armatures adorned with stucco revetment in the form of *moqarnas* vaulting. The complex brick and terracotta geometric ornament of the lowest shaft is not integral to its structure, but applied with a thin course of mortar, a separation between structural medium and applied ornament that is characteristic of Ghurid architectural decoration as whole (Sourdel-Thomine, 1960).

Inscriptions. The surface of the minaret bears a series of inscriptions (see EPIGRAPHY) contained in five encircling bands that range in height from 1.5 to 3 meters. The inscriptions terminate on the eastern face, which one would have beheld when facing toward the west, the direction of the conventional *qebla* (Sourdel-Thomine, 2004, pp. 93-95; Flood, p. 276). The two uppermost bands of the minaret contain religious texts, culminating in the profession of faith. Below is an extract from the Quʾrān 61:13-14. The three lower bands are occupied by increasingly elaborate and bombastic renditions of the name and titles of sultan Ḡiāt al-Din. The inscriptions are executed in angular *kufi* script rather than the cursive scripts that were gaining popularity during the 12th century (see CALLIGRAPHY). Here the sole use of cursive is reserved for the signature of the architect (*meʿmār*), who bore the *nesba* Nišāpuri (Sourdel-Thomine, 2004, pp. 133-34). Nevertheless, a concern with legibility reveals itself in the positioning of the inscriptions, and in the use of turquoise blue glaze for the letters of the central historical text, the earliest recorded use of this feature in Ghurid architecture (PLATE II). The epigraphic ensemble culminates in a spectacular but poorly preserved rendition of the sultan's titles surrounding the octagonal socle. The inscription demonstrates a stunning calligraphic virtuosity, with the verticals (*hastae*) of three-meter high letters forming three alternating knot patterns at their centers, and terminating in dense scrolls, each filled with a single palmette.

The most extraordinary inscription appears, however, on the surface of the lowest shaft, where the entire text of the Qurʾān's nineteenth sura (Maryam) is inscribed in a series of narrow ribbon-like bands that overlap and intersect to form panels filled with geometric ornament (PLATE II). The form and content of this inscription are unusual, and have fueled speculation that the epigraphic program reflects the particular historical circumstances of the minaret's construction (Grabar).

Interpretation. Taken in conjunction with the interpretation of the minaret as a monument to the Indian victories of the Šansabānis, denunciations of idolatry in the Surat Maryam (19:49, 19:81) have been read as references to the Indian subjects of the Ghurids (Pinder-Wilson, 2001, pp. 170-71). The recent re-dating of the minaret precludes such an interpretation, however, since its construction predates Šansabāni expansion into north India. Instead, analysis of the content of the verses and their spatial deployment suggests that they may have been chosen for their ability to promote the doctrinal position of the Karrāmiya. This pietistic Sunnite sect flourished in Ḡur, which Karrāmi preaching is said to have been instrumental in converting to Islam (Bosworth, 1961, 1969).

PLATE II

Minaret of Jām, detail of epigraphic bands on lower section. Courtesy of MJAP, 2003.

The Karrāmiya enjoyed widespread popularity in the eastern Islamic world in the 11th and 12th centuries, competing for patronage, material resources, and spiritual adherents with representatives of other Sunnite legal schools (*maḏhabs*), chief among them the Hanafites and Shafiʿites. The sect was closely associated with the Šansabāni sultans in the decades before the sultans ended the relationship in 1199 (Juzjāni, I, p. 362; tr. I, p. 384). Among the very few material remains of this relationship is a superb four-volume Qurʾān with commentary (*tafsir*) included at the end of each sura. The manuscript, now in the Archeological Museum of Iran (q.v. under MUSEUMS OF IRAN), was commissioned by Sultan Ḡiāṯ-al-Din and completed 584/1189, and is the only manuscript that can be confidently ascribed to Ghurid patronage (Afround Flood). Like the Jām minaret, the manuscript bears the signature of a scribe with the *nesba* Nišāpuri. The included *tafsir* is by Abu Bakr ʿAtiq b. Moḥammad Surābādi (d. ca. 1101), one of the leading Karrāmis of Nishapur (Gilliot), and this choice suggests that the manuscript comprised a Šansabāni bequest to a Karrāmi foundation (Flood, pp. 268-70, 279).

The opponents of the Karrāmiya depict them as anthropomorphists, and even accuse them of harboring quasi-Christian beliefs concerning an embodied Godhead (El-Galli, p. 73; Bosworth, "Karrāmiyya," p. 667). The Qurʾānic phrase "kon fa-yakun" (*Be! And it is*) occupied a central position in Karrāmi polemics concerning the relationship between divine nature and the created universe (Flood, pp. 275-76, 279). The phrase occurs eight times in the Qurʾān, including verse 34 of the Surat Maryam. This verse is emphasized on the eastern side of the Jām minaret, where the densest and the most lavishly appointed ornament appears, and which one would have beheld when facing the *qebla*. Here a unique rhomboidal knot is formed by the intersection of different epigraphic strands containing verses 19:34-35, directly above a singular arched panel that seems to represent a *meḥrāb* (PLATES I-II; cf. Sourdel-Thomine, 2004, pp. 93-95). These verses deny the divinity of Jesus while asserting the ability of God to call whatever He wills into being with his command "kon" (*Be!*). The focal verses thus highlight the contentious issue of anthropomorphism, emphasizing the relationship between God's eternal essence and His temporal creative powers, but in a manner that rebuts the critics of the Karrāmiya by underlining that these powers did not extend to the production of divine progeny.

The construction of the Jām minaret and the careful orchestration of its sophisticated epigraphic program suggest active collaboration between artisan, theologian, and perhaps patron. The use of Qurʾānic citation to promote a specific polemical position underlines the way in which the sacred text could acquire particular valences related to contemporary exegesis and its deployment in specific historical contexts. This use of Qurʾānic scripture as both text and contextual commentary was later exported to India and is manifest in the choice of Qurʾānic verses that adorn the Qoṭb Mosque, the Ghurid Friday mosque of Delhi (Welch et al., pp. 17-26; Flood, pp. 288-89). Adjoining this mosque the Qoṭb Menār (1199 onwards), a massive multi-tiered stone minaret, is perhaps the most enduring, and certainly the most visible, legacy of the Jām minaret, which evidently inspired it (Maricq and Wiet, pp. 65-67; Pinder-Wilson, 1985, p. 100).

Bibliography: Q. Afround, "Qorʾān-e mawqufa-ye torbat-e Šayḵ Aḥmad Jāmi," *Mirāṯ-e farhangi* 15, 1996, pp. 4-14. W. Ball, *Archaeological Gazetteer of Afghanistan*, 2 vols., Paris, 1982, I, pp. 133-34; a full bibliography of publications on Jām until 1982. Idem, "The Towers of Ghur: A Ghurid 'Maginot Line'," in *Cairo to Kabul: Afghan and Islamic Studies Presented to Ralph Pinder-Wilson*, ed. W. Ball and L. Harrow, London, 2002, pp. 21-45. Sh. S. Blair, "The Madrasa at Zuzan: Islamic Architecture in Eastern Iran on the Eve of the Mongol Conquest," *Muqarnas* 5, 1985, pp. 75-91. J. Bloom, *Minaret: Symbol of Islam*, Oxford, 1989, pp. 170-74. C. E. Bosworth, "The Early Islamic History of Ghūr," *Central Asiatic Journal* 6, 1961, pp. 116-33; repr. in *The Medieval History of Iran, Afghanistan, and Central Asia*, Variorum Reprints Collected Studies 56, London, 1977. Idem, "The Rise of the Karāmiyyah in Khurasan," *Muslim World* 50, 1969, pp. 5-14; repr. in *The Medieval History of Iran, Afghanistan, and Central Asia*, Variorum Reprints Collected Studies 56, London, 1977. Idem, "Karrāmiyya," EI^2 IV, pp. 667-69. A. Bruno, "Le minaret de Jam," *Monumentum* 26, 1983, pp. 189-200. Idem, "The Minaret of Jam: A UNESCO Project to Restore an Historic Afghan Monument," *UNESCO Courier* 20, 1979, pp. 32-34. Idem, "Notes on the Discovery of Hebrew Inscriptions in the Vicinity of the Minaret of Jām," *East and West* 14, 1963, pp. 206-08. G. D. Davary, "Jam and Feroz-koh: A New Study," *Afghanistan* 30, no. 4, 1968, pp. 69-91. G. Donini, "L'orografia del Ghūr secondo Jūzjānī (sec. XIII)," *Annali di Ca'Foscari* 11, no. 3, 1972, pp. 191-95. A. H. El-Galli, "The History and Doctrines of the Karrāmiyya Sect with Special Reference to ar-Rāzī's Criticism," M.Litt. thesis, University of Edinburgh, 1970. F. B. Flood, "Ghurid Monuments and Muslim Identities: Epigraphy and Exegesis in Twelfth Century Afghanistan," *Indian Economic and Social History Review* 42 no. 3, 2005, pp. 263-94. C. Gilliot, "L'éxègese du Coran en Asie Centrale et au Khorasan," *Studia Islamica* 89, 1999, pp. 129-64, esp. p. 147; abbreviated tr. as "Works on *ḥadith* and its Codification, on Exegesis and on Theology," by A. Paket-Chy in *The Achievements*, ed. C. E. Bosworth and M. S. Asimov, History of Civilizations in Central Asia 4.2, Paris, 2000, pp. 91-131, esp. p. 107. B. Glatzer, "The Madrasah of Shah-i-Mashhad in Badgis," *Afghanistan* 25, no. 4, 1973, pp. 46-68. G. Gnoli, "Jewish Inscriptions in Afghanistan," *East and West* 13, 1962, pp. 311-12. Idem, *Le inscrizioni Giudeo-Persiane del Ḡūr (Afghanistan)*, Rome, 1964. O. Grabar, Review of *Le minaret de Djam* by A. Maricq and G. Wiet, *Ars Orientalis* 4, 1961, p. 419. A. H. Habibi, "The City of Firuzkuh: Where Was It?" *Afghanistan* 33, no. 1, 1980, pp. 34-44. W. Herberg, "Topograpische Feldarbeiten in Ghor: Bericht über Forschungsarbeiten zum Problem Jam-Ferozkoh," *Afghanistan Journal* 3, no. 2, 1976, pp. 57-69. W. Herberg and D. Davary, "Das Land Ghor in Afghanistan: Auf der Suche nach einem verschollen Imperium," *Die Waage* 17, no. 5, 1978, pp. 216-20. G. Herrman, "A Golden Tower in the Hindu Kush: The Minaret of Djām," *The Connoisseur*, no. 159, 1965, pp. 230-31. D. Hill, "Journey to Jam," *Apollo*, N.S., 84, 1966, pp. 390-96. R. Hillenbrand, "The Architecture of the Ghaznavids and Ghurids," in *Studies in Honour of Clifford Edmund Bosworth* II: *The Sultan's Turret: Studies in Persian and Turkish Culture*, ed. C. Hillenbrand, Leiden, 2000, pp. 124-206. Menhāj-al-Din Juzjāni, *Ṭabaqāt-e Nāseri*, ed. ʿAbd al-Ḥayy Ḥosayni Ḥabibi, 2nd ed., 2 vols.,

Kabul, 1963-64, I, pp. 318-414; tr. H. G. Raverty, as *Ṭabaḳāt-i Nāṣiri: A General History of the Muhammadan Dynastics of Asia, Including Hindustan*, 2 vols., London, 1881, I, pp. 300-507. C. M. Kieffer, "Le minaret de Ghiyāth al-Din à Firouzkoh," *Afghanistan*, 15 no. 4, 1960, pp. 16-46. L. S. Leshnik, "Ghor, Firuzkoh and the Minar-i-Jam," *Central Asiatic Journal* 12, 1968-69, pp. 36-49. A. Maricq, "The Mystery of the Great Minaret: The Remarkable and Isolated 12th-Century Tower of Jam Discovered in Unexplored Afghanistan," *Illustrated London News* 10, 1959, pp. 56-58. A. Maricq and G. Wiet, *Le minaret de Djam: La découverte de la capitale des sultans Ghourides XIIe-XIIIe siècles*, Mémoires de la Délégation archéologique française en Afghanistan 16, Paris, 1959. J. Moline, "The Minaret of Ğām (Afghanistan)," *Kunst des Orients* 9, 1973, pp. 131-48. B. O'Kane, "Salǧūq Minarets: Some New Data," *Annales Islamologiques* 20, 1984, pp. 89-97. R. Pinder-Wilson, "The Minaret of Masʿūd III at Ghazni," in *Studies in Islamic Art*, London, 1985, pp. 89-102. Idem, "Ghaznavid and Ghurid Minarets," *Iran* 39, 2001, pp. 155-86. E. L. Rapp, *Die Jüdisch-Persisch-Hebräischen Inschriften aus Afghanistan*, Munich, 1965. J. Sourdel-Thomine, "L'Art Ġūride d'Afghanistan à propos d'un livre récent," *Arabica* 7, 1960, pp. 273-80. Eadem, *Le Minaret Ghouride de Jām: Un chef d'oeuvre du XIIe siècle*, Mémoires de l'académie des inscriptions et belles-lettres 29, Paris, 2004. R. Stewart, *The Places in Between*, London, 2004. D. C. Thomas et al., "Excavations at Jam, Afghanistan," *East and West* 54, nos. 1-4, 2004, pp. 87-119. W. Trousdale, "The Minaret at Jam: A Ghorid Monument in Afghanistan," *Archaeology* 18, no. 2, 1965, pp. 102-8. G. Vercellin, "Appunti su Firuzkuh e Šahr-e Dāvar," *Annali di Ca' Foscari* 14, no. 3, 1975, pp. 367-76. Idem, "The Identification of Firuzkuh: A Conclusive Proof," *East and West* 26, nos. 3-4, 1976, pp. 337-40. Idem, "Sulle voce 'Firūzkūh' in E.I.," *Rivista degi Studi Orientali* 50, 1976, pp. 319-28. A. Welch et al., "Epigraphs, Scripture, and Architecture in the Early Delhi Sultanate," *Muqarnas* 19, 2002, pp. 12-43.

(F. B. FLOOD)

JĀM (Cup in Persian Art and Literature). Forthcoming online.

JAMĀL-AL-DIN MOḤAMMAD b. ʿAbd-al-Razzāq **EṢFAHĀNI**, poet and painter of the second half of the 12th century. His exact name is given by his contemporary Moḥammad Rāvandi, who also called him Jamāl-al-Din Naqqāš (Rāvandi, pp. 33, 57, see the correction of Waḥid, p. *jim*). However, according to Ebn al-Fowaṭi (IV, p. 129), his name was ʿAbd-Allāh and his patronymic (*konya*) was Abu Moḥammad.

Almost all we know about Jamāl-al-Din is based on his *Divān*, but some elements of information can be found in the writings of Rāvandi and Kamāl-al-Din Esmāʿil (and to a lesser extent Zakariyāʾ Qazvini, ʿAwfi, Dawlatšāh and Āḏar Bigdeli). He was born in Isfahan and spent most of his life there. He attended a local *madrasa* (Kamāl-al-Din Esmāʿil, p. 191, verse 3119). It was without doubt a Hanafite *madrasa* since he himself was a follower of that *maḏhab* (*Divān*, p. 285). He affirms that he was once more familiar with religious law (*šarʿ*) than with poetry (*šeʿr*; *Divān*, p. 264). Despite his education, he worked as a painter (*naqšband*) and a goldsmith (*zargar*) in the Isfahan bazaar (*Divān*, p. 335), probably as did his father (Kamāl-al-Din Esmāʿil, verse 3119). Jamāl-al-Din's skill was great and in 1184-85 he was commissioned by the Saljuq Sultan Ṭoḡrel b. Arslān to illustrate a poetical anthology (Rāvandi, p. 57). In his poetry he makes frequent references to this activity and even boasts about it ("I am not a beggar, I am a poet without cupidity and I have a craft," *Divān*, p. 247). Nonetheless, although this manual activity must have provided him with a certain degree of financial independence, the extent of his wealth is still a matter for conjecture (Dāmādi, p. 32). In the second part of the 12th century, Isfahan was no longer the seat of royal court. We do not know whether Jamāl-al-Din was reluctant to leave his native town on account of his activity in the bazaar, or whether he failed to find a permanent position of court poet outside Isfahan; perhaps his stammering (*Divān*, pp. 21, 300) prevented him from occupying such a position. He did, however, make at least one trip to Ganja, the capital of the Atābegs of Azerbaijan, who ruled Isfahan at that time. He dedicated several *qaṣidas* to the Bavandid Espahbad Ḥosām-al-Dawla Ardašir (r. 1172-1206), who granted him the title (*laqab*) of Sayyed-al-Šoaʿrāʾ (*Divān*, p. 34), but he might not have actually traveled to Māzandarān (Nafisi, 1921, p. 113). Likewise, he speaks on several occasions about his desire to live a more ascetic life, but there is no evidence that he actually took the plunge (Nafisi, 1921, p. 117). On the contrary, it seems that at the end of his life he was close to the last Saljuq sultan, Ṭoḡrel b. Arslān (d. 1194).

Jamāl-al-Din's earliest datable qasida is from spring 1160 and his last from 1187-88. Thus his poetical activity spans a period of at least twenty-eight years. He alludes to his old age in numerous verses and was alive at the age of fifty-five (*Divān*, p. 292). We know that he passed away before 1202-03, because at that date Rāvandi (p. 33) speaks of him as if he was dead. The date of death given as 1192-93 by Charles Rieu (II, 581, apud Taqi-al-Din Kāšāni, *Ḵolāṣat al-afkār*) is plausible but not confirmed by other sources. Dowlatšāh's assertion (p. 156) that Jamāl al-Din began to write "at the time of Ḵᵛārazmšāh Jalāl-al-Dīn" (i.e., 1220-31) is obviously not correct. Jamāl al-Din's tomb is supposed to be in the graveyard of Ṭoqči Gate (Jāberi Anṣāri, p. 169). Of the four children he may have had (Glünz, p. 9), we know only of Kamāl-al-Din Maḥmud, who died before him, and Kamāl-al-Din Esmāʿil, whose fame as a poet overshadowed his.

Jamāl-al-Din is said to have composed more than twenty thousand verses (Hedayāt, 1937, p. 292), but

Waḥid Dastgerdi recovered only half of them. The affirmation that he also wrote a *Divān* in Arabic (Nafisi, 1921, p. 112; Waḥid, p. *yah*) is very unlikely, since ʿEmād-al-Din Moḥammad Eṣfahāni does not mention in the section on Isfahan of his *Ḵaridat al-qaṣr*, an anthology of 6th-century poets who wrote in Arabic. Jamāl-al-Din's *Divān* contains 175 lyrics (*ḡazal*, q.v.) and 122 quatrains (*robāʿi*), but the bulk of his poetry is made of eulogies in the form of *qaṣida* and strophe poems (*tarkib-band*, 143 in total). These were dedicated to four kinds of *mamduḥ*s: (1) The Prophet Moḥammad (see Dāmādi); (2) contemporary poets, such as Ḵāqāni and Mojir-al-Din Beylaqāni, with whom Jamāl-al-Din had turbulent relations (see de Khanikof, p. 177; Ṣafā, 1960, pp. 721-22); (3) rulers of Isfahan (Saljuq sultans, Atābeg of Azerbaijan Pahlavān b. Eldigüz) and their local representatives (Turkish amirs and Persian servants, such as Šehāb-al-Din Ḵāleṣ) and their allies (the Bavandid Espahbad Ardašir, who was allied to Atābeg Pahlavān); (4) notables of Isfahan, especially the Ṣāʿed family, leaders of the local Hanafites (thirty *qaṣidas* and *tarkib-bands* are explicitly dedicated to Rokn-al-Din Masʿud b. Qewām-al-Din Ṣāʿed). For a brief period, Jamāl-al-Din also praised Ṣadr-al-Din Ḵojandi, leader of the Shafeʿite camp, but he later admitted his mistakes when he came back at the court of the Ṣāʿeds (*Divān*, p. 288).

In his *Divān*, Jamāl-al-Din acknowledges his debt to Anwari (q.v.), Sayyed Hasan Ḡaznavi, and Rašid-al-Din Waṭwāṭ; he was also clearly influenced by Sanāʾi. Although all these poets were from Khorasan, he affirms the preeminence of "ʿErāq," that is, ʿErāq-e ʿAjami (Western Iran). His own *qaṣidas* stand out for their simplicity of expression (especially when compared to those of his contemporary Ḵāqāni) and the visual strength of the poet's descriptions (e.g., his description of the famine of Isfahan, in *Divān*, pp. 192-96). On the whole, his poetry reflects the troubled times in which he lived (see his *qasidas* "šekāyat az ruzgār," *Divān*, pp. 25, 56, 250, 347, 354). Modern scholars are agreed on the high quality of his *ḡazal*s, considered as a precursor of Saʿdi's (Ṣafā, p. 733; Waḥid, p. *yad*; Rypka, 1968, p. 214; Maẓāheri and Qānuni, pp. 233-34). There are, however, differing opinions on his eulogistic production. Saʿid Nafisi (1921, p. 120) considers him as "the greatest Iranian poet of the 6th/12th century" and "the most eloquent poet of Iran after ʿOnṣori."Waḥid Dastgerdi (p. *yā*) affirms that only Jamāl-al-Din could compete with Sanāʾi; on the other hand, Foruzānfar and Rypka judge him more harshly.

The first edition of Jamāl-al-Din's *Divān*, based on a single manuscript, was compiled by Adib Nišāburi and printed between 1926 and 1929. In 1941, Waḥid Dastgerdi delivered a more complete edition (quoted as *Divān* in this article), but it is sometimes faulty and it omits substantial parts of Jamāl-al-Din's poetry, such as fifty-seven quatrains (*robāʿi*) contained in Šarvāni's *Nozhat al-majāles* and a little *maṯnawi* (Maẓāheri and Qānuni, pp. 240-48). A critical edition is still awaited

Bibliography: The pioneer studies on Jamāl-al-Din were done by Saʿid Nafisi (1921) and Adib Nišāburi's introd. to his edition of the *Divān*, both of which have been superseded by the studies of Waḥid Dastgerdi and Moḥammad Dāmādi and Maẓāheri and Qānuni.

Loṭf-ʿAli Big Āḏar Bigdeli, *Ātaškada*, ed. Ḥasan Sādāt Nāṣeri, 3 vols., Tehran, 1958-62, III, pp. 929-39, esp. p. 930, n. Moḥammad ʿAwfi, *Lobāb-al-albāb*, ed. Edward G. Browne and Moḥammad Qazvini, 2 vols., London and Leiden, 1903-06, II, pp. 402-4. Moḥammad Dāmādi, "Moʿarrefi-e ejmāli-e sargoḏašt-e Jamāl-al-Din ʿAbd-al-Razzāq," *Gowhar* 3, 1975, pp. 198-201, 320-25, 864-69, 982-87; 4, 1976, pp. 91-97; repr in idem, *Šarḥ bar tarkib-band-e Jamāl-al-Din Moḥammad b. ʿAbd al-Razzāq dar setāyeš-e payāmbar*, Tehran, 1990, pp. 25-60. Dawlatšāh Samarqandi, *Taḏkerat al-šoʿarāʾ*, ed. Edward G. Browne as *Tadhkiratu 'sh-shuʿarāʾ (Memoirs of the Poets) of Dawlatshāh*, London and Leiden, 1901, pp. 156-64. D. Durand-Guédy, "Iṣfahān de la conquête salǧūqide à la conquête mongole," Ph.D. diss., Aix-en-Provence, 2004, pp. 380-81. Ebn al-Fowaṭi, *Majmaʿ al-ādāb fi moʿjam al-alqāb*, ed. Moḥammad Kāẓem, 6 vols., Tehran, 1994-95, IV, p. 129. ʿEmād-al-Din Moḥammad Eṣfahāni, *Ḵaridat al-qaṣr wa jaridat alʿaṣr*, ed. ʿAdnān Moḥammad Āl-e Ṭoʿma, 3 vols., Tehran, 1999. Badiʿ-al-Zamān Foruzānfar, *Soḵan o soḵvarān*, Tehran, 1944, pp. 547-78. Michael Glünz, *Die Panegyrische qaṣīda bei Kamāl ud-dīn Ismāʿīl aus Isfahan: Eine Studie zur persischen Lobdichtung um den Beginn des 7./13. Jahrhunderts*, Beirut, 1993, pp. 8-9. Reżāqoli Khan Hedāyat, *Riāż al-ʿārefin*, 2nd ed., Tehran, 1937, pp. 292-95. Idem, *Majmaʿ al-foṣaḥā*, ed. Maẓāher Moṣaffā, 6 vols., Tehran, 1957-61, I, pp. 470-96. Jalāl-al-Din Homāʾi, *Tāriḵ-e Eṣfahān: mojallad-e abnia wa ʿemārāt*, ed. Mahdoḵt Bānu Homāʾi, Tehran, 2005, pp. 355-56.

Mirzā Ḥasan Jāberi Anṣāri, *Tāriḵ-e Eṣfahān*, ed. Jamšid Maẓāheri Sorušyār, Tehran, 1999, p. 169. Jamāl-al-Din Ḵalil Šarvāni, *Nozhat al-majāles*, ed. Moḥammad Amin Riāḥi, 1st ed., Tehran, 1989 (contains 57 *robāʿis* of Jamāl-al-Din that are not in his *Divān*). Jamāl-al-Din Moḥammad b. ʿAbd-al-Razzāq Eṣfahāni, *Divān*, ed. ʿAbd-al-Jawād Adib Nišāburi, Tehran, n.d.; ed. Ḥasan Waḥid Dastgerdi, Tehran, 1941, repr. 1982 and 2001 (the latter with a different pagination). Kamāl-al-Din Esmāʿil Eṣfahāni, *Divān*, ed. Ḥosayn Baḥr-al-ʿOlumi, Tehran, 1969. Nicolas de Khanikof, "Mémoires sur Khâcâni, poëte persan du XIIe siècle," *JA* 6/4, 1864, pp. 167-200. Jamšid Maẓāheri and Ḥamid-Reżā Qānuni, "Negareš-i-e now ba zabān wa šeʿr-e Jamāl-al-Din ʿAbd-al-Razzāq Eṣfahāni," *Majalla-ye ʿelmi-pažuheši-e Dāneškada-ye adabiyāt wa ʿolum-e ensāni-e Dānešgāh-e Eṣfahān*, no. 41, 2006, pp. 229-50. Saʿid Nafisi, "Jamāl-al-Din ʿAbd-al-Razzāq," *Armaḡān* 6, 1921, pp. 109-18, 153-63. Idem, *Tāriḵ-e naẓm o naṯr dar Irān wa dar zabān-e fārsi tā pāyān-e qarn-e dahom-e hejri*, 2 vols., Tehran, 1965, I, pp. 101-2. Abu Yaḥyā Zakariyāʾ Qazvini, *Āṯār al-belād*, ed. Ferdinand Wüstenfeld, as *Zakarija ben Muhammed ben Mahmud el-Cazwini's Kosmographie*, 2 vols., Göttingen, 1848, p. 197. Moḥammad b. ʿAli Rāvandi, *Rāḥat al-sodūr wa āyat al-sorur dat tāriḵ-e Āl-e Saljuq*, ed. Muḥammad Iqbál, London, 1921, index. Charles Rieu, *Catalogue of the Persian Manuscripts in the British Museum*, 3 vols. and Supplement, London, 1881-95. J. Rypka et al., *History of Iranian Literature*, ed. Karl Jahn, Dordrecht, 1968, pp. 213-14. *Idem*, "Poets and Prose Writers of the Late Saljuq and Mongol Periods," in *Camb. Hist. Iran* V, 1968, pp. 584-85. Ḏabiḥ-Allāh Ṣafā, *Tāriḵ-e adabiyāt dar Irān* II, Tehran, 1960, pp. 731-40. Idem, tr., *Anthologie de la poésie persane, XIe-XXe siècle*, Paris, 1964, pp. 170-75. Maḥmud Šafiʿi, "Naẓar-i ba ejmāl az laḥāẓ-e sabk wa dastur-e zabān dar divān-e Ostād Jamāl-al-Din Eṣfahāni," *Armaḡān* 44, 1975, pp. 644-54; 45, 1976, pp. 38-48, 88-96, 171-79, 214-20, 316-22, 387-92. Moḥammad-Ḥasan Semsār, "Jamāl-e Naqqāš Eṣfahāni," *Honar o Mardom*, no. 71, 1968, pp. 7-13. Ḥasan Waḥid Dastgerdi, "Ostād Jamāl-al-Din Moḥamad b. ʿAbd-al-Razzāq Eṣfahāni," *Armaḡān* 22, 1940, pp. 65-76, 169-82, repr. as the Introd. to his edition of the *Divān*.

(D. DURAND-GUÉDY)

JAMĀL-AL-DIN ʿASADĀBĀDI. See AFGHANI.

JAMĀL-AL-DIN WĀʿEZ-E EṢFAHĀNI. See forthcoming, online.

JAMĀLI ṢUFI, PIR YAḤYĀ, calligrapher of the mid-14th century who worked in Shiraz in the 1340s. He was reputedly a pupil of Aḥmad Rumi and of Mobārakšāh b. Qoṭb (Zarrin Qalam), renowned students of the master calligrapher Yāqut Mostaʿsemi (d. 1297 or 1299 C.E.), who is credited with canonizing the proportions of the six chief Arabic scripts (*aqlām-e setta*; Bayāni, 1984, IV, p. 1233).

Before settling in Shiraz, where he served at the court of the Injuids (1303-53; see INJU DYNASTY) and later of the Muzaffarids (1314-93), Pir Yaḥyā worked under various patrons, including Amir Čobān Solduz (Süldüs), the Il-khanid warlord (Fażāʾeli, p. 320; Bayāni, 1984, IV, p. 1233; James, 1988, p. 163). He transcribed several calligraphy specimens and manuscripts of the Qurʾān that range in date from 731/1330 to 746/1345 (Blair, p. 44). The earliest Qurʾān manuscript by Pir Yaḥyā is dated 739/1338-39 and kept at the Türk ve Islam Eserleri Muzesi (Bayāni, 1966-79, IV, p. 223; James, 1988, p. 164)

One of his most notable works is a Qurʾān commissioned in 1344-68 by Tāši Ḵatun, the mother of the Injuid ruler, Abu Esḥāq (q.v.), at the time of the construction of the Šāh-e Čerāq Mosque in Shiraz (James, 1988, p. 163). His finest work is a large, multi-volume Qurʾān manuscript in gold *moḥaqqaq* script, dated 745-46/1344-45, part of which is currently in the Pārs Museum in Shiraz (ms. 456; Bayāni, 1966-79, p. 224; Fażāʾeli, p. 320; James, 1988, pp. 162-63). This manuscript demonstrates the continuation of traditions developed at the Il-khanid capitals of Baghdad and Tabriz in Shiraz in the mid-14th century.

Pir Yaḥyā also designed monumental inscriptions for buildings in Najaf and Shiraz. One inscription is an eleven-line carved text on the entrance of a wall of the small stone palace built by the Achaemenid Darius the Great at Persepolis. It commemorates a visit to the site by the Injuid ruler of the area, Abu Esḥāq, in June 1347 and his reverence to the great ancient kings of Persia (Moṣṭafawi, pp. 346-47; Blair, p. 45). He was also responsible for a *ṯulṯ* inscription in brick and glazed tile running around the upper part of the Ḵodā-ḵāna or Bayt al-Moṣḥaf (Qurʾān repository) at the center of the old Mosque (Masjed-e ʿAtiq) in Shiraz (Moṣṭafawi, pp. 65-66; Wilber, p. 28; James, 1988, p. 164).

Pir Yaḥyā was a contemporary of Iran's master poet and lyricist, Ḵᵛaja Šams-al-Din Moḥammad Ḥāfeẓ (b. circa 1325). Although Shiraz endured stormy periods of political upheaval in the middle and late 14th century, art and culture continued to thrive, and eminent scholars, men of letters, poets and calligraphers remained active (Rypka, p. 271).

Other calligraphic works by Pir Yaḥyā can be found in the collections of the Chester Beatty Library, Dublin, Türk ve Islam Eserleri Muzesi, and the Topkapı Saray Library in Istanbul.

Bibliography: Mehdi Bayāni, *Aḥwāl wa āṯār-e ḵošne-visān*, 4 vols., Tehran, 1966-79; new ed., 4 vols in two, Tehran, 1984. Sheila Blair, "Yaqut and His Followers," *Manuscripta Orientalia* 9/3, September 2003. Ḥabib-Allāh Fażāʾeli, *Aṭlas-e ḵaṭṭ*, Tehran, 1984, pp. 319-21. David Lewis James *Qurʾans and Bindings from the Chester Beatty Library*, London, 1980. Idem, *Qurʾans of the Mamluks*, NY, 1988, pp. 162-64. Martin Lings, *Splendours of Qurʾan Calligraphy and Illumination*, Liechtenstein, Thesaurus Islamicus Foundation, 2005. Moḥammad-Taqi Moṣṭafawi, *Eqlim-e Pārs: Āṯār-e tāriḵi wa amāken-e bāstāni-e Fārs*, Tehran, 1964. Jan Rypka et al., *History of Iranian Literature*, ed. Karl Jahn, Dordrecht, 1968. Donald N. Wilber, *The Masjid-i Atiq of Shiraz*, Asia Institute of Pahlavi University Monograph 2, Shiraz, 1972.

(MARYAM EKHTIAR)

JAMĀLI, ḤĀMED B. FAŻL-ALLĀH (b. Delhi, ca. 1457; d. Gujarat, 942/1535), a Persian-speaking Indian poet. The information about his life is scarce. Jamāli was born around 1457 in Delhi. He traveled widely in Islamic lands, visiting scholars, mystics, and religious figures, with several of whom he formed friendships (Seyed-Gohrab in Jamāli, 2002, pp. xi-xix; Hameed-ud Din in Jamāli, 1984, pp. 13-14; Storey, I/2, No. 1280, pp. 968-72; Nafisi, I, pp. 312, 404-5). ʿAbd-al-Raḥmān Jāmi (d. 1492, q.v.) was one of his friends. ʿAli-Aṣḡar Ḥekmat states that Jamāli was Jāmi's student, and that he returned to India after Jāmi died in Herat in 1492 (Ḥekmat, p. 55).

Jamāli's spiritual teacher, Shaikh Samāʾ-al-Din Kanbuh (d. 1495), was affiliated to the Sohravardiya Sufi order (Trimingham, pp. 33-37). He was also Jamāli's uncle and father-in-law. Jamāli venerated his teacher immensely and paid homage to him in one of his poems (Jamāli-Dehlavi, 2002, pp. 10-12; Purjawādi, pp. 30-33).

Initially, Jamāli had no significant relationship with the Lodi sultans, who ruled over northern India from the middle of the 15th century until the first quarter of the 16th century. Later, however, his spiritual guide, Shaikh Samāʾ-al-Din, advised him to function as poet-laureate to the Lodi sultan Sekandar II b. Neẓām Khan (r. 1489-1517). They had a dervish-king or philosopher-king relationship, in which the king respected the dervish/philosopher for his high spiritual status and consulted him on earthly and godly matters.

Jamāli died in 1535 in Gujarat and was buried in Delhi. His burial-place, called *Dargāh-e Jamāli* ('The Court/Shrine of Jamāli'), has been visited by many pilgrims. We have little information about Jamāli's personal life. He had three sons: Ḥasan, Šeyḵ-Gadāʾi (d. 1568-69), and ʿAbd-al-Ḥayy Ḥayāti. The latter was a famous poet and historian who wrote the history of Eslām Shah b. Šir Shah Suri (r. 1545-54). Šeyḵ-Gadāʾi was a poet and the chief chancellor at the court of Ebrāhim II b. Sekandar II Lodi (r. 1517-26) and later attended the court of Akbar (r. 1556-1605, q.v.; see Siddiqui).

Jamāli's writings. Jamāli wrote a number of works in verse and prose. Some works ascribed to Jamāli were, in fact, written by Pir Jamāl Ardestāni (d. 1474), the founder of the famous Sufi order Pir-Jamāliya. The confusion is based on the fact that in various works Jamāli is referred to under different names, such as Darviš Jamāli, Mowlānā Jamāli, Mollā Jamāli, Šayḵ Jamāli-e Kanbuh, and Jalāl Khan. Jamāli is, above all, famous for his two books. The first, entitled *Siar al-ʿārefin* (The Virtues of the Mystics), is a memoir of Indian mystics of the Češtiya (q.v.) Sufi order (Purjawādi in Jamāli, 2005, pp. 127-62). The second book is the collection of his poems (*divān*, q.v.), which comprises nine thousand odd lines and includes three *maṯnawi* poems. One of the latter, *Mehr o Māh* (The Sun and the Moon), is a poetical imitation of Moḥammad Aṣṣār Tabrizi's (d. 1382-83) famous romantic poem *Mehr o Moštari* (The Sun and Jupiter). Jamāli's second *maṯnawi* poem is titled *Bayān-e ḥaqāʾeq-e aḥwāl-e sayyed-e morsalin* (The Explanation of the True States of the Lord of Messengers) and consists of two parts which describe the spiritual journey of the Prophet Muhammad. The third *maṯnawi* poem is *Merʾāt al-maʿāni* (The Mirror of Meanings); it is composed in the same way as *Golšan-e rāz* (The Rose-garden of Mystery) of Maḥmud Šabestari (686-720/1287-1320). This poem can be divided into three parts: a) chapters one to three are devoted to the doxology, the praise of the Prophet, and the praise of the Master of the Path; b) chapters four to nineteen depict the beloved's anatomy from head to foot; and c) chapters twenty to thirty-eight expound several terms connected to mystical states (*aḥwāl*), stations (*maqāmāt*), wine (*šarāb*), and love-play through the contemplation of a beautiful beardless youth (*šāhed-bāzi*; see Seyed-Gohrab in Jamāli, 2002, pp. xix-xlvi).

Bibliography: Jamāli's selected works: Ḥāmed b. Fażl-Allāh Jamāli-Dehlavi, *Maṯnawi-e Mehr o Māh: 905 h[ejri]*, ed. Ḥosām-al-Din Rāšedi, Rawalpindi, 1974. Idem, *Siar al-ʿārefin*, ed. M. A. Qaderi, Lahore, 1976. Idem, *Masnawī Mirʾātul Maʿānī = Mirʾātül-Maʿānī mesnevisi / Shaikh Jamālī Dihlavī; facsimiles of all existing manuscripts with an introduction and annotation by Hameed-ud Din*, ed. Gönül Alpay Tekin, Cambridge, Mass., 1984. Idem, *The Mirror of Meanings = Merʾāt al-maʿāni: a parallel English-Persian text* tr. A. A. Seyed-Gohrab, critical Persian text N. Pourjavadi, Costa Mesa, Calif., 2002. Idem, *Merʾāt al-maʿāni, be enżemām-e gozida-ye Siar al-ʿārefin*, ed. N. Purjawādi, Tehran, 2005.

Studies: Nazir Ahmad, "The *Lahjat-i Sikandar Shahi*, A Unique Book on Indian Music of the Time of Sikandar Lodi (1489-1517)," *The Islamic Culture* 28/1, January 1954, pp. 410-17. ʿAli-Aṣḡar Ḥekmat, *Naqš-e pārsi bar aḥjār-e Hend: fehrest-i az katibehā wa ḵoṭuṭ-e fārsi bar lowḥ-sanghā-ye Hendustān*, Calcutta, 1957; 2nd ed., Tehran, 1958. Saʿid Nafisi, *Tāriḵ-e naẓm o naṯr dar Irān wa dar zabān-e fārsi tā pāyān-e qarn-e dahom-e hejri*, 2 vols., Tehran, 1965. Naṣr-Allāh Purjawādi, "Merʾāt al-maʿāni," *Maʿāref* 11/1-2, November 1994, pp. 3-64. S. A. A. Rizvi, *A History of Sufism in India*, 2 vols., New Delhi, 1978-83. I. H. Siddiqui, "Gadāʾī Kambō, Shaykh," *EI²*, at *www.encislam.br.nl/subscriber/entry?entry=islam SIM-8554*, accessed 28 November 2007. C. A. Storey, *Persian Literature: a Bio-bibliographical Survey*, repr. ed., London, 1970. J. S. Trimingham, *The Sufi Orders in Islam*, Oxford, 1971; repr. with a new introduction by J. O. Voll, New York, 1998. I. Yaḡmāʾi, *Dāstānhā-ye ʿāšeqāna-ye adabiyāt-e fārsi*, Tehran, 1995.

(A. A. SEYED-GOHRAB)

JAMALZADEH, MOHAMMAD-ALI (Moḥammad-ʿAli Jamālzāda; b. Isfahan, 1892; d. Geneva, 1997), a prominent Iranian intellectual and a pioneer of modern Persian prose fiction, and of the genre of the short story. Jamalzadeh's long and productive life spanned over a century in a vital period in modern Iranian history, from the Constitutional Revolution of 1906, to the Islamic Revolution of 1979 and beyond. The publication in 1921 of his collection of short stories *Yeki bud yeki nabud* (Once Upon a Time), notable for its direct, colloquial language, remarkable use of Persian idiom, and immense sociological, political, and critical insight, signaled a major turning point in the development of modern fiction in Iran. Yet, Jamalzadeh's contributions to Persian culture go beyond the genre of the short story. In the span of his long life (1892-1997), Jamalzadeh published novels, short stories, political and social essays, scholarly research articles, literary reviews and criticism, and autobiographical and biographical essays. His world view, reflected in almost all of his writings, is informed by his unique experience as a "product of two worlds" (Moayyad, 1985, p. 1; Cuypers, 1998, p. 68), the world of the Persian language, culture, history and customs, including the memories of his experiences in Iran during a period of upheaval, revo-

Jamalzadeh in 1973. Courtesy of Iraj Afšār.

lution and turmoil, and the world he inhabited in the West as a product of a Western education, acquaintance with European languages and research methods, and as an advocate of the European Enlightenment and modernity. His lifelong dedication, discernible from his stories, essays, interviews and letters, was to bridge these two worlds and to combine the best of both in the advancement of modern education as the main weapon in the struggle against ignorance, poverty, oppression, and injustice for the people of Iran (Yarshater, 1985, p. x). This entry is divided into the following sections:

i. *Life*.
ii. *Works*.
iii. *Bibliography*.

i. Life

Early Life and Education. Mohammad-Ali, the eldest of five children, was born in 1892 in Isfahan. His father was the famed cleric and preacher, Sayyed Jamāl-al-Din Wāʿeẓ (Hamadāni) Eṣfahāni (1863-1908), whose family had come to Isfahan from Lebanon via Hamadān and Tehran. His mother was Maryam Ḵānom, daughter of Mirzā Ḥasan-Bāqer Khan, an Eṣfahāni notable. Along with Malek-al-Motekallemin, Sayyed Jamāl-al-Din was among the most prominent of the radical clerics of the constitutional movement. He was a passionate and effective orator with a large following and was instrumental in the contextual definition and popularization of constitutionalist ideas such as freedom, justice and the rule of law for the ordinary people and the poor (Taqizadeh, in Jamalzadeh, 1999, pp. 14-15). Together with Malek-al-Motekallemin, he wrote the secret pamphlet "*Roʾyā-ye ṣādeqa*" (the Truthful Dream) which was an indictment of the corrupt despotism of Prince Ẓell-al-Solṭān, the governor of Isfahan, and the ignorant, self-serving short-sightedness of Āqā Najafi and other followers of conservative religion. He was among the *ulama* who founded Anjoman-e Taraqqi (Society for Progress) and the clerical secret society (Šerkat-e Eslāmi) advocating the ideas of modernization and reform associated with Sayyed Jamāl-al-Din Afghani (q.v.), Malkom Khan, and Ṭāleboff (Moayyad, 1985, p. 3; Mangol Bayat, 1982, p. 186). Sayyed Jamāl-al-Din was also a close associate of Sayyed Hasan Taqizadeh (Sayyed Ḥasan Taqizāda) in the years leading up to and through the first constitutional period.

While in Isfahan, Sayyed Jamāl-al-Din spoke out against oppression, injustice, and regressive religion based on blind faith. He was thus accused of blasphemy (*kofr*) and of Babi (q.v.) sympathies by the conservative *ulama*, and was compelled to travel to Tehran and Tabriz for much of his preaching (Ādamiyat, 1976, p. 266). Jamalzadeh attended a series of traditional schools (*maktab*) in Isfahan, including a religious school for training clerics. He was then transferred to a school established by an enlightened cleric, where he and the two sons of Malek-al-Motekallemin were taught arithmetic and some English in addition to the traditional curriculum. In his memoirs, Jamalzadeh recounts that this school was closed by a mob of religious zealots, and the principal Hāji Jawād was publicly beaten by order of Āqā Najafi. He also relates witnessing the mob burning of two merchants accused of Babi beliefs (Jamalzadeh, 1999, p. 22, 51-52).

In 1902, Sayyed Jamāl-al-Din moved to Tehran along with his family, and began preaching and giving speeches in favor of constitutionalism in the Shah mosque. The young Jamalzadeh first attended the modern Ṯerwat school, where he was taught geography and mathematics by Solaymān Mirzā (Eskandari), Arabic by Shaikh Moḥammad Borujerdi, and French by Mirzā ʿAbbāsqoli Khan Qarib (Jamalzadeh, 1999, pp. 53-54). He later attended the Adab School, another modern school with a similar curriculum established by Mirzā Yaḥyā Dawlatābādi and known for its outstanding curriculum and teaching staff (Jamalzadeh, 1999, pp. 54-55; Maḥbubi Ardakāni, 1975, pp. 389-90; Yaḥyā Dawlatābādi, I, pp. 254-57). Along with a few other students of Tehran's modern schools, Jamalzadeh was selected to attend chemistry, botany and zoology classes taught by French teachers at the Dār al-Fonun (q.v.; Jamalzadeh 1999, p. 55). Jamalzadeh later noted that though they taught Arabic and French in these modern schools, they did not have a course or a teacher for the Persian language. He later taught himself Persian through his years of diligent reading and research when he was abroad (Cuypers, 1998, pp. 64-65).

Being the eldest living son in the family, Jamalzadeh also received much of his education by accompanying his father to his meetings, sermons and speeches. He thus met many of the intellectuals and leaders of the constitutional movement and as much as his young age would permit, became familiar with the current discussions about freedom, justice and the rule of law. His father's simple and direct style of speech undoubtedly influenced the young Jamalzadeh as did his probable exposure to the constitutional newspapers such as *Ṣur-e Esrāfil*, and its satirical *Čarand parand* column by Dehḵodā (q.v.; Cuypers, 1998, p. 80). The extent of Sayyed Jamāl-al-Din's influence on the young Jamalzadeh must be underscored; his mosque speeches contained not only discussions of equality, freedom, meritocracy, and social justice but even a definition of the novel, roman, as a vehicle to convey knowledge and wisdom in story form that is more accessible to the whole population (Yaḡmāʾi, 1978, pp. 98-101)

With the ascent to the throne of Moḥammad-ʿAli Shah Qajar (1872-1925) and the bombardment of the Majles on June 23, 1908, prominent and vocal constitutionalists were sought and many were executed, notably, Mirzā Jahāngir Khan the editor of *Ṣur-e Esrāfil*, and Malek-al-Motekallemin. Others, including Taqizadeh and Dehḵodā took sanctuary in various embassies and were later exiled. Sayyed Jamāl-al-Din escaped to Hamadān with the aim of fleeing to the holy cities in Iraq, but he was caught, imprisoned in Borujerd, and shortly thereafter, strangled by order of Amir Afḵam, the local governor (Afšār in Jamalzadeh, 1999, p. 272; Bāstāni Pārizi, 1978, pp. 8-9).

In April 1908, a few months before the anti-constitutionalist coup, and the execution of Sayyed Jamāl-al-Din by the forces of despotism, Jamalzadeh was sent to Beirut to study at the 'Antoura School, run by Lazarite missionaries. There, he learned French, and began to write some poetry and articles in the school newspaper. His school companions in Beirut were Ebrāhim Purdāwud and Mehdi Malekzādeh, the son of Malek-al-Motekallemin (Jamalzadeh, 1999, p. 30, p. 272).

In 1910, following a brief stay in Cairo, Jamalzadeh went first to Paris, and then settled in Lausanne to study law. After experiencing financial difficulties and a clandestine love affair, he moved to Dijon, in 1911, where he graduated from the Faculty of Law in 1914. He married Josephine, a Swiss woman and a fellow student in Dijon, in the same year (Jamalzadeh, 1999, pp. 34-35).

Berlin Committee. As the First World War broke out in 1914, Taqizadeh, prominent constitutionalist and one of the leaders of the Democrat Party who was in exile, invited a number of Iranian exiles in Switzerland, France, Britain, and the Ottoman Empire to establish the Committee of Iranian Nationalists (Komita-ye Melliyun-e Irāni) in Berlin. Prominent members of this group, which first met in January 1915, included Mirzā Maḥmud Khan Qazvini, Ebrāhim Purdāwud, Ḥosayn Kāẓemzāda Irānšahr (q.v.), Esmāʿil Nobari, Ḥājj Esmāʿil Amirḵizi, Reżā Afšār, Maḥmud Khan Ašrafzāda, and Naṣr-Allāh Jahāngir (nephew of Mirzā Jahāngir Khan). Jamalzadeh was among the youngest members of the group. With financial, political, and military aid from the government of Germany, the group's goal was to fight against the colonial interests and aims of Britain and Russia in Iran (Jamalzadeh, 1999, p. 69, Taqizadeh, 1989, pp. 181-88). Similar groups were formed by Indian nationalists and others, since German policy in this period was to encourage unrest in the British, French, and Russian spheres of control (Taqizadeh, 1989, p. 186). Jamalzadeh was first dispatched to Baghdad via Istanbul, where he was joined by several other members of the committee as well as various anti-British activists and German officers. In Baghdad, Jamalzadeh, Purdāwud, and Amirḵizi established a newspaper called *Rastāḵiz* (which lasted from August 1915 to March 1916). They proceeded to Kermānšāh and Lorestān with the specific mission to recruit militias from the Kurdish and Luri tribes, and to instigate an uprising against British and Russian control and interests in the region. Once they established a militia called the Nāderi army in Kermānšāh, Jamalzadeh traveled to Tehran in disguise to meet with the leaders of the Democrat Party, Solaymān Mirzā Eskandari and Sayyed Moḥammad Reżā Mosāwāt, to enlist a leader for that militia (Jamalzadeh, 1999, p. 36). The efforts of Jamalzadeh and the other members of the Nationalist Committee in the tribal regions lasted for sixteen months but did not ultimately meet with success. With the advance of the Russian armies in Iran and the British armies in Baghdad, the activists fled to Berlin. En route in Baghdad, Jamalzadeh met the constitutionalist poet ʿĀref Qazvini, the renowned social democratic leader Ḥaydar Khan ʿAmu Oqlu (q.v.) and the scholar and educator Sayyed ʿAbdul Raḥim Ḵal-ḵāli. In his difficult passage from Baghdad to Istanbul, Jamalzadeh noted the condition of turmoil, and witnessed terrible scenes of the death and starvation of large numbers of Armenians (Jamalzadeh, 1972; pp. 211-17, Jamalzadeh 1963, in Mehrin, pp. 55-69).

Among the interesting episodes in Jamalzadeh's life during this period was his participation in the Socialist Congress of 1917 in Stockholm along with Taqizadeh, Yaḥyā Dawlatābādi and Waḥid-al-Molk Šaybāni as representatives of the Committee of Iranian Nationalists (Taqizadeh, 1989, p. 188; Jamalzadeh, 1999, p. 43). This conference had been organized by various socialist parties and groups to negotiate a peaceful solution to end World War I, but as the governments of France, Britain, and the United States did not permit their delegations to participate, it became a forum for discussion rather than a platform for action. Jamalzadeh and his colleagues used this forum to draw attention to the disastrous effects of British and Russian colonialism and interference in Iran (Jamalzadeh, 1999, pp. 43-44; Kamshad 1966, p. 93).

The Kāveh period. During his absence from Berlin, Taqizadeh and Qazvini had established the Persian journal *Kāveh*, which was published from January 24, 1916 to March 30, 1922. In the first thirty five issues which were published during and shortly after the First World War, *Kāveh* was primarily a political magazine with openly pro-German sympathies. It advocated Iranian independence from the colonial manipulations of Britain and Russia, contained reports and critiques of the political situation in Iran, and reported the activities of the Nationalist Committee. There were also a few articles on history and literature. In its second period of publication (January 22, 1920-December 11, 1921) Taqizadeh declared that *Kāveh* would now be mainly devoted to scientific, literary and historical discussions. The new guiding philosophy of the journal was the adoption of European civilization in Iran, resistance to fanaticism, defense of national unity and integrity, the promotion of the Persian language and literature and when possible, the quest for liberty both within and outside of Iran (Aryanpur, pp. 231-32; Jamalzadeh 1962, pp. 3-18). The emphasis on the necessity to adopt and promote modern education was evident from the editorials and the articles that appeared in the journal.

In what proved to be an extremely productive period in his life, Jamalzadeh began researching and writing articles for *Kāveh* from his return to Berlin in 1916 until the last issue of the journal in 1921. The erudite group of exiles who had gathered in Berlin included Mirzā Moḥammad Khan Qazvini, Sayyed Hasan Taqizadeh, Mirzā Fażl-ʿAli Tabrizi, Mirzā Moḥammad-ʿAli Khan Tarbiat, Kāẓemzādeh Irānšahr (q.v.), Ḥājj Sayyed Abu'l-Ḥasan ʿAlawi (father of Bozorg-e Alavi), ʿAbbās Khan Aʿẓam-al-Salṭaneh, Maḥmud Qanizādeh, and Ebrāhim Purdāwud. They organized a literary and scientific association for the presentation of lectures and met for weekly and monthly discussions (Jamalzadeh, 1999 pp. 171-232) Jamalzadeh frequently names Taqizadeh and Qazvini as the two most influential people in the development of his mind and talent. Taqizadeh provided him with wisdom, energy, moral courage, tenacity, and access to his wealth of knowledge and curious mind. He attributes Qazvini with teaching him the European methods of research based on reason, attention to detail, and critical thinking. He also mentions the influence of E. G. Browne on Qazvini's approach to scholarship. Both expressed admiration and praise for his scholarship and for his great talent as a writer of fiction (Jamalzadeh, 1999, pp. 212, 214-15). During this period, he also had the opportunity to meet and/or become familiar with the work of a number of important German orientalist scholars such as Josef Markwart (1864-1930), Wilhelm Geiger (1856-1943), Eugen Mittwoch (1876-1942), and Oskar Mann (1867-1917; Jamalzadeh, 1999, p. 275).

Devoting his full energies to writing and research, between January 1916 and December 1921, Jamalzadeh wrote *Ganj-e šāyegān* (Priceless Treasure): The Economic History of Iran (Berlin, 1918), a series of fifteen articles on the history of relations between Russia and Iran (1918-21), and articles on various topics in Persian language, poetry and history. His methodic use of European as well as Iranian sources and his direct language was commended by many, including Qazvini and Taqizadeh. The Economic History of Iran, hailed as the first work of scholarship in Persian using European methods of research, received praise from the Journal of the Royal Asiatic Society; it was translated into German, but its publication was halted due to wartime difficulties (Jamalzadeh, 1999, pp. 275, 278; Kamshad, 1966, p. 93)

The publication in *Kāveh* in 1921 of "*Fārsi šekar ast*" (Persian is Sweet), the first modern short story in Persian, catapulted Jamalzadeh to fame. In the preamble to its publication in *Kāveh*, he states that he had written it "for his amusement, to present a sampling of ordinary Persian as it is spoken today" (Jamalzadeh, *Kāveh* 1, 11 January, 1921, p. 8). The story was immediately identified as a novelty in Persian literature in several respects: it was narrated in a simple, direct, satirical, and colloquial prose style; language was utilized to present a biting social and cultural critique, and it was the first instance of European realism in Persian fiction. "*Fārsi šekar ast*" and five other stories that Jamalzadeh had written between 1915 and 1921 were combined into a collection entitled *Yeki bud yeki nabud* and published in Berlin and Tehran in 1921. His more serious intentions were spelled out in the introduction to the book where he pointed to the need for writers to rejuvenate the Persian language, to refrain from using stylized, specialized, circuitous language, to write for a larger audience, and to bring social relevance into Persian prose (Jamalzadeh, 1954. pp. 5-21).

The reaction to the book in Tehran was tumultuous. Some regarded it as an insult to language and religion, while others hailed it as a great innovation in Persian literature (see ii. below). The combination of fame and controversy, and accusations of blasphemy (*kofr*) by the *ulama* must have had a bitter but familiar ring to Jamalzadeh; his father had been the object of conservative clerical wrath throughout his childhood. The uproar led Jamalzadeh to decide not to publish another work of fiction in Iran for the next twenty years (Kamshad, p. 95).

By the end of 1921, the Berlin group ran out of money and resources, and the last issue of *Kāveh* was published in December of that year. Jamalzadeh found full time employment in the Iranian embassy in Berlin first as a translator and then as the director of student affairs from 1922 until 1931. During this period, he did not give up writing scholarly articles. From May 1924 until April 1925, he collaborated with the Iranian students' journal *Farangestān*, along with Mortażā Yazdi, Ḡolām-Ḥosayn Foruhar, Ḥasan Nafisi, Mošfeq Kāẓemi, Aḥmad Farhād and Taqi Arāni. After the closing of this journal, he began to publish articles in journals such as *Šafaq-e sorḵ*, *Kušeš* and *Eṭṭelāʿāt* in Iran. He also became the director of the journal *ʿElm o honar* in Berlin, but it only lasted for seven issues. This seems to have been an unstable and difficult period of his life. He lost his wife Josephine due to an illness; he was unhappy with the persistence of clerical fanaticism in Iranian society at large, and dissatisfied with the reappearance of autocracy, Aryan nationalism, and the imposition of strict censorship for writers under Reza Shah Pahlavi (Kamshad, p. 94; Moayyad, 1985, p. 7. Katouzian, 2003, pp. 20-22.)

The Geneva period. In 1931, Jamalzadeh married his second wife, the German Margaret Eggert, and moved to Geneva to work for the International Labor Organization of the United Nations (ILO). He remained at that post until his retirement in 1956. His job consisted of documenting and monitoring work conditions, compiling labor statistics, and devising labor regulations and laws in industry and agriculture, mainly in the Middle East and South Asia. He traveled to India, Iraq, Iran and Turkey with ILO delegations on several occasions, and wrote reports on the dire condition of industrial workers in Isfahan and oil workers in Ābādān (Mehrin, pp. 77-81).

His literary and scholarly output, which aside from a few essays on classical literature, had diminished during the 1930s, flourished again after the abdication of Reza Shah in 1941. From 1942, Jamalzadeh wrote and published many novels, such as *Dār al-majānin* (Lunatic Asylum, Tehran, 1942), *Qoltašan divān* (Neighborhood Bully, Tehran, 1946), *Ṣaḥrāy-e maḥšar* (The Plain of Resurrection, Tehran, 1947), and *Rāheāb-nāmeh*, (The Drainage Chronicles, Tehran, 1948). He also published a drama/novella entitled *Maʿsume-ye Širāzi* (Massoumeh of Shiraz, Tehran, 1954), and several collections of short stories, such as *Sargozašt-e ʿAmu Ḥosayn-ʿAli* (The Story of Uncle Hossein-Ali, Tehran, 1942), *Talḵ o širin* (Bitter and Sweet, Tehran, 1956), *Šāhkār* (Masterpeice, Tehran, 1957), *Kohneh o now* (Old and New, Tehran, 1959), *Ḡayr az Ḵodā hičkas nabud* (There Was No One but God, Tehran, 1960). Other collections of stories followed such as *Āsemān o rismān* (Tehran, 1964), *Qeṣṣehā-ye kutāh barā-ye bačehā-ye rišdār* (Short Tales for Bearded Children, Tehran, 1974) and *Qeṣṣe-ye mā be sar resid* (The End of the Story, Tehran, 1978). Jamalzadeh also compiled a dictionary of colloquial terms, *Farhang-e loḡāt-e ʿāmiāneh* (Tehran, 1962), and compiled a volume on the characteristics of Iranians entitled *Ḵolqiyāt-e mā Irāniān* (Tehran, 1966; for a survey of his work, see ii. below).

With the reemergence of many journals and the establishment of new ones after 1942, Jamalzadeh also contributed articles and stories to *Soḵan*, *Yaḡmā*, *Waḥid*, *Armaḡān*, *Honar o mardom*, and *Rahnemā-ye ketāb*. In 1945, he resumed writing for a new version of *Kāveh* which was established in Munich by Mohammad Asemi (Afšār in Jamalzadeh, 1999, pp. 276-77).

He is one of the few Iranian writers who spoke and wrote candidly about his life, and who frequently used his life observations and experience in his work. For example, ʿAmu Ḥosayn-ʿAli in *Šāhkār* is based on Shaikh Abu'l-Qāsem Širāzi, a merchant he met and admired in Cairo. He also wrote and spoke about many of the important personalities that he encountered in his life, including his father Sayyed Jamāl-al-Din, his mentors, friends, and colleagues Sayyed Hasan Taqizadeh, Moḥammad Qazvini, Ebrāhim Purdāwud, ʿĀref Qazvini, Yaḥyā Dawlatābādi, Sayyed Ziāʾ-al-Din Ṭabāṭabāʾi, and Sadeq Hedayat.

Fluent in French, German and Arabic, Jamalzadeh was an able translator. His translations of Bernardin de Saint Pierre, Moliere, Ibsen, Schiller and Van Loon were published in various Persian periodicals throughout his working years. He also showed a commitment to writing articles on European intellectuals and writers such as Maxim Gorky, Friedrich Nietzsche and James Joyce, and Anatole France in order to introduce them to the Persian reading public (Kamshad, p. 104). Jamalzadeh continued to write well into the end of the 1970s, although most critics agree that with advancing age, his later writings became repetitive and lacked cohesion (for criticism of his work, see ii. below).

Although Jamalzadeh lived in Geneva until his death in 1997, visiting Iran for only short periods of time, he kept in touch with intellectual and literary developments in Iran by reading books and periodicals and earnestly corresponding with authors. Consequently, he produced a massive volume of correspondence, which has been published in various books during his life and since his death (for example, Bahārlu, 1994, Afšār, 1996; Dehbāši, 1998).

Jamalzadeh's devotion to the advancement of education in Iran did not cease with his death on November 8, 1997. From 1977 onwards, he began donating his book collections and his papers to the Tehran University library and archives, and gave a percentage of the royalties from his books to be spent on scholarships, educational institutions and various charities in Isfahan (Afšār, in Jamalzadeh, 1999, pp. 7-8). He died on November 8, 1997, and is buried in Geneva, Switzerland.

Conclusion. Developments in prose and fiction writing in the late 19th and early 20th centuries, notably the work of Abdu'l-Raḥim Tāleboff, Zayn-al-ʿĀbedin Marāgaʾi's Siāḥat-nāma-ye Ebrāhim Beg (The Travels of Ibrahim Beg), Mirzā Ḥabib Eṣfahāni's Persian translation of James Morier's, *The Adventures of Haji Baba of Isfahan* (q.v.), Dehḵodā's critical and humorous articles in Ṣur-e Esrāfil, all reflected a modern outlook and a didactic use of fiction and travel literature as an instrument of social change. These books and essays prefaced Jamalzadeh's innovation in the use of language, humor, and social criticism in fiction. As he remarked in his customary unassuming manner, the ground had been prepared for his innovation (Kamshad, p. 106). Nevertheless, his contribution was a watershed in the development of modern Persian fiction.

Jamalzadeh's stories, memoirs and prose reflect his life experiences. He grew up in the "shadow of the mosque" (Cuypers, 1998, p. 68) as the son of an expert orator and preacher, observing the speech and wit of the people of Isfahan in his childhood; he experienced the Iranian constitutional revolution and absorbed the prevailing anti-despotic discourse criticizing backwardness and fanaticism, demanding justice, law and modern education; he studied the French Enlightenment (Bernardin Saint Pierre, Voltaire), the French language and literature (Anatole France, Marcel Proust, Abel Hermant, Henri Lavedan) in ʿAntoura and later in Lausanne and Dijon; he persisted in teaching himself Persian by reading and rereading the great classical texts. His political and human observations in Iran and the Ottoman Empire during World War I, and his higher education in research and writing under the tutelage of Taqizadeh and Qazvini in Berlin—all fed his creative talent as a writer and his lifelong dedication to the Persian language and education.

Besides being a consummate and talented storyteller, Jamalzadeh seems to have retained his didactic purpose in the writing of literature throughout his life. Many of his stories and novels were prefaced with introductions that put the work in a sociological, cultural (and consequently always bordering on a political) context. The main themes in his stories involve exposing the multi-faceted malaise of despotism, corruption, and fanaticism, and extolling the benefits of a modern education. He remained committed to contributing to the Enlightenment project that the secular intellectuals and the progressive clergy—notably his admired friend Taqizadeh and his father —had advocated during the constitutional revolution. The main features of this project were the promotion of parliamentary democracy based on meritocracy, the development of the resources and economic potential of the country, and the constant vigilance of an educated, critical population against the habits of corruption, dogmatism, and abuse that had developed over the centuries among all segments of the population. Though Jamalzadeh was an admirer of Western modernity, industry, progress, and education, he never advocated blind imitation of the West. His professional focus on the intricacies of the Persian language and the meticulous critique of its culture was aimed at its progress and advancement.

Jamalzadeh insisted on the removal of dictatorship and corruption, and the pursuit of economic development as the only conditions which could substantially improve the condition of Iran over time (letter to Qāsem Ḡani, in Dehbāši, 1998, pp. 660-61; letter to Pišdād, in ibid, p. 709) As such, he welcomed the Iranian revolution of 1979 because it removed the monarchy which he perceived as the embodiment of despotism in Iranian history (Afšār, 1996, p. 133). Even as late as 1980, he continued to believe that a form of socialism or social democracy, not copied from the east or west, but well thought out and adapted to the traditions and conditions of Iran, would be the ideal form of government for the country. (letter to Pišdād in Dehbāši, 1998, pp. 697-701). In his eagerness to celebrate the removal of the monarchy, and perhaps with a degree of naiveté that came with his old age, he could not or did not imagine the development of another form of dictatorship within the framework of a republic with a nativist ideology.

Jamalzadeh's depiction of the lives, mentalities, and language of the common people and the poor in a realistic, yet satirical manner opened the way for the development of modern Iranian prose fiction and influenced the work of writers such as Sadeq Hedayat, Moḥammad Masʿud, Ṣādeq Čubak, and Jalāl Āl-e Aḥmad.

Bibliobraphy: See iii. below.

(NAHID MOZAFFARI)

ii. WORKS

Jamalzadeh holds a place of singular distinction in the history of modern Persian literature and letters. An innovator of the modern literary language, he was the first to introduce the techniques of European short-story writing in Persian literature. He was only twelve when he left his country—he produced the entire bulk of his work abroad—yet the impression left upon him by his childhood training and environment proved indelible, and in his compositions one senses the life, spirit, and atmosphere of Iran. The oratorical talent and modernist outlook of his father Sayyed Jamāl-al-Din Wāʿeẓ Eṣfahāni, the Catholic school education in Lebanon that introduced him to western fiction, the process of his politicization that began with the Iranian Constitutional Revolution, the murder of his father by the forces of despotism, his political and intellectual associations with Taqizadeh and Moḥammad Qazvini—all led to a life-long and conscious attempt to bring about progressive change in the polity and culture of his homeland through language and discourse. Along with many intellectuals of his generation he feared that with the adoption of western science and education, the imitation of western words would follow, leading to the decline of the Persian language, the loss of its unique character and beauty, and the subsequent loss of Iranian identity (Jamalzadeh, 1941, p. 5). Thus, the modernization of language while preserving its unique character and idioms was one of Jamalzadeh's main goals (Sprachman in Jamalzadeh, 1985, p. 17, Qazvini in Jamalzadeh, 1985, pp. 27-29).

This feat was all the more remarkable considering he left Iran at a young age, before he could gain a good command of the Persian language. With much self-discipline and dedicated study of the classical texts, he gradually gained an impressive command of the language while he lived abroad (Jamalzadeh, 1999, pp. 53-56).

Jamalzadeh's writing has been categorized into works of fiction, and other works which include essays on history, socio-political and cultural studies, literary criticism, translations and biographies/memoirs.

WORKS OF FICTION

Yeki bud yeki nabud. Jamalzadeh's career as a storyteller began with the publication of "*Fārsi šekar ast*" (Persian is Sweet), the first modern Persian short story. This, together with five other stories which were written between 1915 and 1920, appeared later in the celebrated collection, *Yeki bud yeki nabud* in 1921. This book laid the foundation of modern prose, set the direction for the first generation of fiction writers in Iran and established Jamalzadeh's reputation as a literary figure. The first story of *Yeki bud yeki nabud*, "*Fārsi šekar ast*" (Persian is Sweet), is about the encounter in a prison between an ordinary provincial Iranian and two stylized types of his countrymen—one a religious-minded, pompous cleric or *āḵund*, the other a Western-educated modernist just back from Europe—who confuse the simple man by the jargon they fling at him as Persian. The high-flown Arabic-Persian phrases of the cleric, then the strange foreign terms used by the francophone youth, flabbergast and bewilder the poor simple man who has been put in jail for no reason and is seeking an explanation from these eminent characters. It is a clever and extremely funny story with exquisite parodies of the Eurocentric and the religious establishment's modes of speaking Persian. Its linguistic subtleties render translation very difficult, nonetheless this feat has been accomplished in whole or in parts into Russian, French, and English (Zakhoder 1936; Corbin and Lotfi, 1959; Moayyad and Sprachman, 1985).

"*Dusti-e ḵāle ḵerse*" (With Friends Like That) is the tragic story of a kind-hearted, cheerful, and gallant cafe waiter who, despite the advice of traveling companions, saves the life of a Russian Cossack laying wounded in the snow on the road to Kermānšāh (the incident takes place during the First World War). The wounded soldier learns that his rescuer is carrying a small sum of money with him, and when he is conveyed to safety he incites a group of drunken Russian troops to arrest the waiter and have him shot by a firing squad. Except for some inessential details, the movement and pathos of this story achieve the standard of some of the best short stories of European literature.

In another story, "*Dard-e del-e Mollā Qorbān-ʿAli*" (Mulla Qurban-Ali's Complaint), an infatuated *mullah* tells us about his reckless love for the daughter of a neighboring merchant. The girl dies and the unfortunate Qorbān-ʿAli, of whose love the girl's family knows nothing, is invited to spend the night beside the coffin praying for her soul. During the night he cannot quench the temptation to see the beautiful face of his beloved once more. He is caught kissing the lips of the dead girl and ends up in jail.

"*Bila dig bila čoḡondar*" (What's Sauce for the Goose) is a piquant satire on the despotic order, way of life, ruling circles, and class distinctions of the late Qajar times. Fate takes a European bath-attendant to Persia, where he becomes adviser to a minister, and his memoirs about life in Persia remind one of some of the most amusing passages of James Morier's *Hajji Baba of Isfahan* (q.v). It was mainly the remarks made in this story that disturbed religious and state dignitaries in 1921 when the book was first published (Jamalzadeh, 1999, pp. 99-101).

The remaining stories of *Yeki bud, yeki nabud* are "*Rajol-e siāsi*" (The Political Figure) and "*Veylān-al-Dawla*" (Vagrant of the Realm). *Rajol-e siāsi* is a satirical account of how political figures can emerge through opportunism and deceit in times of social upheaval. "*Veylan al-Dawleh*" is a tragic lampoon of a vagabond symbolizing annoying but harmless people who are do-nothings, and who live off of the charity, and face, on occasion, the callousness of others (Balay and Cuypers 1983, pp. 201-6).

In his exuberant letter of praise, Moḥammad Qazvini the leading scholar and critic of the time wrote that in his stories, Jamalzadeh had succeeded in portraying the best representation of the current Persian language of the time—spoken by literati as well as by the common people (Jamalzadeh, 1985, pp. 25-29). While other intellectuals and educated people praised the book, according to a letter written to Jamalzadeh by ʿAbd-al-Raḥim Kalkāli, some of the *ulama*, some members of parliament, and groups of people congregated in Jāmeʿ mosque in Tehran in condemnation of the book and its allegedly insulting images of the clergy, leaders, and state officials, particularly in the stories "*Fārsi šekar ast*," "*Bila dig, bila čoḡondar*," and "*Dard-e del-e Mollā Qorbān-ʿAli*" (Katouzian, 2003, pp. 190-91). The protestors demanded that the book and its author be accused of *kofr* (apostasy), and that its publishers be punished and exiled. Most of the resentment came from the conservative *ulama*, their students and followers who were already embroiled in an effort to pass a law in the Majles to impose censorship on whatever was deemed as insulting to Islam in the press. Meanwhile, a counter demonstration in defense of the book was held in the Sepahsālār Mosque. (Moayyad, 1985, pp. 10-11). While initially, socio-political reasons attracted attention to the book, its literary merits ultimately established Jamalzadeh's reputation as a major writer of fiction.

These literary merits can be summarized as follows. First, the stories of *Yeki bud yeki nabud* demonstrate a focus on fiction and literary style over other considerations, a departure from the predominantly didactic and political nature of the fiction produced in the constitutional and post-constitutional era (Katouzian, 2003, pp. 191-96). As the critic Reza Barāheni has stated, with Jamalzadeh, the literature of the constitutional period entered the realm of the short story, and Dehkodā's caricatures in the *Čarand parand* columns of *Ṣur-e Esrāfil* evolved into the fictional characters in *Yeki bud yeki nabud*. (Barāheni, 1983, p. 550; Balay and Cuypers, 1983, p. 110, ʿĀbedini in Dehbāši, 1998, p. 151). Second, the stories were the first introduction of the modern genre of the short story to Persian fiction. This genre differed from traditional tales in that each story was situated in a particular time and place, each character had distinctive features including his or her voice or language, and events occurred according to a structured plot (Barāheni 1983, p. 551). Preceded by attempts to develop the genre of the novel in works such as Marāḡaʾi's *Ebrāhim Beg*, various works by Ṭālebof and Ḵosrovi's *Šams o Ṭoḡrā*, the short story proved to be popular with readers and writers alike, as it was similar in length to traditional folkloric tales, but did not require the complexity of plot and character development necessary for a novel. To this day, the short story has been more successful for Iranian writers than the novel (Raḥimi in Dehbāši 1998, pp. 375-76; Katouzian, 2003, pp. 194-95). Third, Jamalzadeh's stories comprise the first instance of the Western style of critical realism with its focus on mirroring society and its immediate problems, and interest in the representation of average people in Persian fiction. As such, they made a lasting impact in the body of literature and influenced several subsequent generations of writers like Sadeq Hedayat, Ṣādeq Čubak and Hušng Golširi (qq.v.; Balay and Cuypers, 1983, pp. 107-8; Katouzian, 2003, p. 191). Fourth, the particular and conscious employment of language in the stories is a departure from the traditional styles of prose writing in Persian. The language of the narrative is direct, unadorned, and colloquial, and the choice of words varies according to the class and educational level of the characters (Katouzian, 2003, pp. 192-93; Mirṣādeqi in Dehbāši, 1998, pp. 295-303). Scholars correctly trace the origin of this type of language use to the newspapers of the constitutional period, particularly to satirical essays and poetry of Dehkodā in the *Čarand parand* column in *Ṣur-e Esrāfil* and the poetry of Sayyed Ašraf-al-Din in *Nasim-e šemāl* (Balay, 1998, p. 29; Katouzian, 2003, p. 192).

Like other modernist intellectuals, Jamalzadeh had both political and cultural intentions in the conscious use of a language that would be comprehensible to people of different classes and educational levels. These intentions, which are expressed in a manifesto-like introduction to

Yeki bud yeki nabud by the author, state that it is incumbent on writers and intellectuals to emerge from the limited inner circles of their patrons and colleagues and to create a new literature that would expose the ills of society, and address, include, and give a voice to the people (Jamalzadeh, 1921; 1954 edition, pp. 3-21; Balay 1998, pp. 77-8). He highlights European successes in technological, scientific, and social development, and the instrumental role of literature in the transmission of a common language, education, and knowledge (Balay 1998, p. 78). In essence, his argument pointed to the responsibility of Iranian writers and intellectuals to create a common national language in order to conduct the national discourse necessary in the construction of a modern society and state in the beginning of the 20th century (Navabpour 1996, p. 71).

To highlight the importance of words and language, Jamalzadeh, ended the book *Yeki bud yeki nabud*, with a glossary of colloquial Persian words and phrases. He continued to collect and document colloquial terms through much of his life, and his collection was later published as a book in 470 pages entitled *Farhang-e loġāt-e ʿamiāna* (Dictionary of Colloquial Words; Afšār in Jamalzadeh, 1999, p. 278).

Dār al-majānin (Lunatic Asylum). Despite the critical acclaim of intellectuals and modernists, the uproar in religious and government circles after the publication of *Yeki bud yeki nabud*, and the re-imposition of censorship by the state led Jamalzadeh to refrain from publishing fiction for the next twenty years (Kamshad 1966, pp. 94-95). He resumed his literary activities in earnest in 1942, proving to be one of the most prolific authors of modern Iran. The first of his new books was the novel *Dār al-majānin* (Tehran, 1942), the engaging story of a madhouse in which some interesting characters, each with his own philosophy, habits and idiosyncrasies, are in custody. While throwing light on the abnormalities of his characters, the author also tries to criticize the conditions of a society in which sensitive men prefer taking refuge in an asylum rather than being at large. But this critical note is only incidental: it is droll humor that forms the driving force of the novel. Among the crowd of bedlamites the reader can recognize one unmistakably: a certain Hedāyat-ʿAli Khan, known as Monsieur, who calls himself *Buf-e kur*. He is a writer, and some of the passages and hallucinations of Hedayat's *Buf-e kur* (q.v.; The Blind Owl) are given as samples of his writings. The allusions are clear enough, and the author's love and respect for the late Sadeq Hedayat are touching. The book also contains a good selection of quotations from classical Persian poetry about wisdom and insanity.

Qoltašan divān. Jamalzadeh's second novel, *Qoltašan divān* (Tehran, 1946), concerns the age-old struggle between good and evil. The book opens with a neat description of a little street and its residents in Tehran that resemble many other streets and people in the country. The following chapters scrutinize the life of two inhabitants of the little street: first the hero, Ḥāji Shaikh, a wholesale dealer in tea and sugar; a virtuous, patriotic man with a good reputation among the people, he has been a deputy in the first Majles. Then there is the villain, *Qoltašan divān*, a cunning and ruthless opportunist who would stop at nothing to attain his personal aims. The villain fails in his first attempt to use the good name of Ḥāji Shaikh for his own ends, by marrying off his own compromised daughter to the son of old Hajji. Embittered by Ḥaji's refusal, he waits for an opportune moment to take his revenge. During the First World War, when Hajji's trade and financial strength are badly disrupted, the villain reappears asking for a huge consignment of sugar to be bought and kept for him. In the following months the acute shortage of provisions brings the people to the doorstep of Ḥaji, who they know has a whole store loaded with sugar. But he cannot sell the stuff and the real owner refuses to show up. Cursed and despised by everybody, defamed as a vicious hoarder, Hajji dies in grief and misery, without being able to defend his innocence. The villain, on the other hand, having made his fortune in this bargain, builds an orphanage and throws a lavish party for ministers and notables in his newly constructed, sumptuous house. At the height of his career *Qoltašan divān* dies peacefully in his sleep of a stroke. The newspapers devote their front pages to the glorification of his benevolence and service to culture; his name is whispered on every lip as that of a great man, and all the dignitaries mourn his death as a grave national loss.

The principal characters of the book, like many other characters created by this author, belong to the middle class; and their ideas, ambitions, and personal dilemmas, as well as the tragedy of an honest man entangled in an unbalanced society, are skillfully portrayed. This has led some critics to consider *Qoltašan divān* to be Jamalzadeh's most mature novel in its poignant utilization of humor to highlight injustice (Kamshad 1966, p.97).

Ṣaḥrā-ye maḥšar (Plain of Resurrection, Tehran, 1947) is a fantasy about the day of resurrection, possibly inspired by the pamphlet *Roʾyā-ye ṣādeqa* (A Truthful Dream) composed in part by Jamalzadeh's father some fifty years before. His father's "Plain of Resurrection" had a serious intention: to prophesy the hard times that were awaiting certain despotic rulers and political opponents of the time when they finally reached the presence of their Maker. The son's flight of fancy, however, is primarily in the realm of humor and satire: he is amusing himself by visualizing the position of people of various walks of life when they stand before the divine scales in which their deeds are to be weighed. Implicit, however, is a traditional Islamic dogma, which runs through the medieval Persian works that offer counsel to rulers and princes: the dogma that we are answerable for all our misdeeds in this life. So to understand the salient points of this satire, the reader should have a fair knowledge of Shiʿa doctrine. But even then he is likely to be confounded by some of the things happening in the heavenly kingdom. We learn, for example, that influential connections, string pulling and even bribery play a considerable part in the placement and promotion of angels and other ministering spirits. The prophets, on the other hand, are dispatched to heaven straight away without any demur or interrogation. Some smart sinners, by reciting an appeasing Qurʾānic verse or an apostolic tradition, are let off lightly; and a great number of people escape the blazing fires of Hell by reciting an appropriate line of poetry or even by cracking a joke that amuses God. But, in general, moderation and compromise seem to be the order of the day: moral issues and human values, not the religious dogmas, are the criterion of divine justice.

But when it comes to *āḵunds*, mullahs, and religious pretenders, the handling of affairs take a different turn: the gates of mercy are shut, for the sins of this group weigh much heavier than their good deeds. Among the crowd who line up for questioning, the reader may recognize some familiar faces. One delightful moment is the appearance of Omar Khayyam. Despite his apparent mischief, the celebrated poet-philosopher is granted celestial bliss.

In the final section the narrator meets Satan in a lonely corner, and after some exchange of views on a number of scriptural topics, Satan, who is on good terms with God, obtains permission to take him back to earth endowed with eternal life. But before long the narrator grows tired of this troublesome gift and asks to be given liberty instead; liberty in its fullest sense, including that of dying when he chooses.

Rāheāb-nāma (The Drainage Controversy). For social criticism, a study of the characteristics of different social classes, for humor and excellence of style and language, Jamalzadeh's *Rāheāb-nāma* (The Drainage Controversy," 1948) stands high above his other novels. The framework of the book is rather similar to that of *Qoltašan divān*, the scene is a cul-de-sac in Tehran; the characters are members of the six households living there. But the problem this time is the repairing of a blocked water channel, without which they cannot have a drop of water-so precious in the days before the capital was equipped with a piped water system.

The hero is a European-educated Iranian student spending his summer vacation at home. Having learned about the hitch in the drainage he calls a meeting of the neighbors, who unanimously authorize him to make arrangements for the necessary repairs. He thanks them for their confidence in him and promptly sets to work. After endless troubles with the architect, the mason, and other workmen, with all expenses having been paid from his own pocket, the job is completed and he sends the neighbors the bill. But they, unfamiliar with the principle of "business is business," find it hard to lend themselves to such extravagance. They start dilly-dallying, each one making various excuses and all refusing to pay their share. With his meager allowance floating down the drain, the kind-hearted, civilized student is unable to return to Europe to resume his studies. He leaves his ancestral home and finds shelter in a cozy little room in the courtyard of a holy shrine, away from any neighbors, disillusioned at all the lectures he had received on good neighborly relations, and cursing his compatriots for their moral degradation.

Contrary to the general pattern of Jamalzadeh's novels, *Rāhāb-nāma* is concise, coherent and very much to the point. Three sketches at the beginning of the book-the unbearable heat of a Persian summer day, the active life of the bazaar and the peaceful atmosphere of the holy shrine-are portrayed with mastery. There are many other pages of skilful writing; and the author's knowledge of and deep insight into the inner lives, habits and thinking of middle-class families deserve praise. The unrestrained criticism of the national character with which the book ends, however, is not entirely free from exaggeration (Kamshad 1966, p. 100)

Sar o tah yek karbās. In the two-volume work *Sar o tah yek karbās* (Cut From the Same Cloth, Tehran, 1956) or *Esfahān-nāma*, the first chapter is an account of the author's childhood. The rest of the book is devoted to episodes in the life of a friend, which, though immensely rich and interesting, deny us the pleasure of learning more about the later years of the author's life.

Jawād Āqā is the son of a merchant, and after the death of his father he becomes interested in mysticism and ascetic teachings. After divorcing his wife and abandoning his home, he joins a Sufi guide (*moršed*) whose daily life is full of spiritual sublimities. What follows is an account of the adventurous life these two, the guide and follower, go through. Their tireless wayfaring, their experiences with people of different creeds and social standing, all imbued with the recollections, beliefs, and instructions of the dervish, form the chapters of the book. But the book is not a close-knit, consistent piece: several stories, some historical details, and many mystical speculations are woven into the overall texture of the narrative.

The first chapter, about the childhood of the author, is written with a sincerity and innocent candor rare, if not absent, in the works of any writer living inside Iran. In two other chapters, one on the history of Isfahan and the other a description of the old Persian polestars or wrestling houses, their amiable ceremonies and traditional customs, a great deal of valuable information is offered. Of the various stories and anecdotes included in both volumes, some (in particular, *Jahannam-e taʿaṣṣob* (The Hell of Fanaticism), about the hypocrisy of an *āḵund*, and *bāj-e sibil* (extortion), illustrating the thuggish character of army officers, are in fact independent pieces superimposed on the narrative. Taken as a whole, *Sar o tah yek karbās* is the most erudite work by Jamalzadeh. Meditations on philosophy, metaphysics, religious instructions, mysticism, and their expression in Persian ethics and literature are to be found throughout.

STORY COLLECTIONS

In addition to his novels, Jamalzadeh published several collections of short stories. *Sargozašt-e ʿAmu-Ḥosayn-ʿAli yā šāhkār* (The Story of Uncle Hussein Ali or The Masterpiece, Tehran, 1942), *Talḵ o širin* (Bitter and Sweet, Tehran, 1956), *Kohna o now* (Old and New, Tehran, 1959), and *Ḡayr az Ḵodā hičkas nabud* (There was no one but God, Tehran, 1961). The first was republished in 1957 in a two-volume enlarged edition called *Šāhkār* (Masterpiece). Some of the pieces in the second volume of this collection had been written much earlier and published in the periodicals of the time. Among them "*Kabāb-e ḡāz*" (Roast Goose), "*Ḡayr az Ḵodā hičkas nabud*", "*Palang*" (Leopard), "*Noparast*" (Modernist), and "*Došman-e ḵuni*" (Mortal Enemy) are famous either for their abundant humor or for the freshness, vigor, and pathos that characterized Jamalzadeh's earlier writings. But save for the title-piece "*ʿAmu-Ḥosayn-ʿAli*," written with ingenuity and brilliance, the contents of the first volume exemplify some of the author's later trends: prolixity, effusion, and reverie laden with poetic and proverbial quotations.

These tendencies are also detectable in the second collection, "*Talḵ o širin*," especially in the first three stories, "*Yak ruz dar Rostamābād-e Šemirān*" (A Day in Rustamabad of Shemiran), "*Ḥaqq o nāḥaqq*" (Just and Unjust) and "*Darviš-e mumiāʾi* (Mummified Dervish), where the main emphasis is on poetry and philosophical speculation. Other pieces in this book, together with six stories and one play collected in "*Kohna o now*," deal with social problems such as the difficulties of life for honest families living in a corrupt society, and the credulity of young intellectuals when they first come in contact with the rough and tumble, resulting in their bitterness and disillusionment later. Other collections include *Ḡayr az Ḵodā hičkas nabud* (There was no one but God, Tehran, 1961), "*Asmān o rismān*" (From Here and There, Tehran, 1964); "*Qeṣṣahā-ye kutāh barā-ye bačahā-ye rišdār* (Short Tales for Bearded Children, Tehran, 1974) and "*Qeṣṣa-ye mā be sar rasid*" (The End of the Story, Tehran, 1978). Within the latter collections, the story "*Šurābād*" met with critical acclaim and was translated into German, French, and Italian. Along with "*Namak-e gandideh*" (Rotten Salt) these stories reflected the prevailing despotism and social problems of Iran in the 1960s and 1970s (Jamalzādeh, 1999, p. 282; Cornesello, pp. 20-48).

In general, there appears a sharp distinction between the early works of fiction written by Jamalzadeh and his later compositions. Conciseness, novelty of form, originality of ideas, a biting sense of humor, and, above all, observance of the conventional divisions in storytelling (development, climax, and denouement) mark the earlier writings. His later works, however, show a tendency toward prolixity, sage remarks and mystical and philosophical speculations; there is frequent use of classical poetry and at times a lack of shape and order. Common to all his compositions is the language he uses: the charm of his prose discourses cast in a familiar yet individual style. Everyday expressions adorn almost every line, to the extent that his care for juxtaposing idioms seems to override other considerations. Years of hard work have equipped him with masses of slang and colloquial proverbs, and he has the gift to use them with skill; but his indiscreet dwelling on these terms appears over-righteous at times. A single idea is normally expressed in a variety of ways, in as many roundabout phrases as the author happens to remember; as if the flow of the story mattered less than the recording of expressions. The frequently synonymous phrases render a kind of superficiality to his description and a certain amount of immobility to the progress of the narrative. Moreover, Jamalzadeh believed in imbuing his stories with incidental acts of personal perception, which again hold up the plot. From the technical point of view, then, the majority of his novels lack a firm and continuous narrative: they are episodic, and in this regard he displayed more talent for short- than long-story writing. In his later works he grew increasingly intent on abandoning fiction for erudition.

OTHER WORKS

Historical, Social, and Political Studies. Jamalzadeh began writing historical, social and political essays in the period when he was writing for the journal *Kāveh* (1916-22) in Berlin. His first contribution to this paper, an article entitled "*Vaqti ke yek mellat asir mišavad*" (When a Nation is Reduced to Slavery), condemned the policies of Britain and Russia in Iran before and during World War I. A translation of this article appeared in some German newspapers of the time. It was also during this period that he published his first book, *Ganj-e šāyegān yā awżāʿ-e eqteṣādi-e Irān* (The Worthy Treasure, or the Economic Situation of Iran, Berlin, 1916-17), which deals with the physical geography of Iran, a history of commerce, customs, transportation, mines, arts and crafts, reforms, finances, weights and measures, post and telegraph system, life in the capital, and a great deal of other useful information about the country. This work was praised by the Journal of the Royal Asiatic Society (January 1921), and was translated into German.

Jamalzadeh's second work of research entitled, "*Tāriḵ-e rawābeṭ-e Rus o Irān*" (The History of Russo-Persian Relations), appeared serialized in *Kāveh*, but was in fact never completed because of the journal's closure. "*Bolševism dar Irān-e qadim*" (Bolshevism in Ancient Iran), was a study of the beliefs and preaching of Mazdak, which has been translated into Russian and published in Moscow. To introduce European men of letters and their way of thought to the Iranian public, he wrote articles in various papers; his subjects included Maxim Gorky in *Yaḡmā* 6/7 1953, pp. 265-72, "Ničeh and Jeyms Joys" (Nietzsche and James Joyce) in *Soḵan* 5/1 1953, pp. 25-31 and 5/2, pp. 99-108), and "Kont do Gobino" (Comte de Gobineau; in *Yaḡmā*, 1960, pp. 478-84; and 14, 1961, pp. 17-20, 63-68).

While Jamalzadeh had written mostly fiction in the period of intense politicization and turmoil in Iranian society between 1941 and the coup of 1953, he resumed his critical writing about society and politics in the early 1960s when the issue of land reform and other reforms had been raised. His "*Āzādi o ḥayṯiyat-e ensāni*" (Freedom and Human Dignity), an anthology of prose and poetry on these subjects from Western and Persian literature was published in 1960, followed by "*Ḵāk o ādam*" (Earth and Man, Tehran, 1962), and "*Zamin, o arbāb o dehqān*" (Land, Landowner, Peasant, Tehran, 1963). *Ḵolqiyāt-e mā Irāniān* (Our Iranian Character Traits) a compendium of writings on the positive and negative traits of Iranians by foreigners and Iranians in history was first published in a serial form in the magazine *Masāʾel-e Irān* (Problems of Iran) in 1965, and then in book form in 1967. The aim of this book and of the others mentioned above was to shed light on the social problems of Iran, and to provide a self-critique, which would pave the way for finding solutions. Our Iranian Character Traits was subsequently criticized by the government and eventually banned in Iran (Jamalzadeh, 1999, p. 283; Matini, in Dehbāši 1998, pp. 445-57). Before his death, Jamalzadeh also published *Taṣwir-e zan dar farhang-e Irāni* (The Image of Women in Iranian Culture) in 1979, which predominantly consists of the image of women in Persian poetry.

Literary Criticism. Throughout his literary career Jamalzadeh was either closely associated with or an ardent contributor to the Persian press inside and outside the country. A list of the articles and shorter pieces he wrote for various journals has been compiled by Iraj Afšār (1999, pp. 271-87). Another longer bibliography by Nāhid Ḥabibi Āzād includes books, articles, translations and works about Jamalzadeh (Iraj Afšār and ʿAli Dehbāši, eds., pp. 651-97). These bibliographies list the numerous articles and book reviews that Jamalzadeh wrote on classical and modern Iranian literature including the examples below.

Golestān-e nikbakti yā pand-nāma-ye Saʿdi (The Garden of Prosperity, or The Counsel of Saʿdi, Tehran, 1938), published on the seven hundredth anniversary of publication of the *Golestān*, is a compilation of the prose-counsels laid down in that immortal book. In the book entitled *Bāng-e nay* (Lamentation of The Reed; Tehran, 1959), Jamalzadeh tried to collect some of the scattered stories of Rumi's great *Divān*, the *Maṯnawi*, and by putting them together he produced one smooth amalgam of all the verses related to each story. *Qeṣṣa-ye qeṣṣahā* (The Tale of Tales, Tehran, 1948) is a compendium of the biographical work *Qeṣaṣ al-ʿolamāʾ* (Stories of the Learned), written by Moḥammad b. Solaymān of Tonokābon in 1873. It throws light on the life and works of some Shiʿa scholars who lived between the 10th and 19th centuries. Jamalzadeh's ideas about the modern trends in Persian poetry are expressed fully and candidly in his Introduction to Moḥammad Esḥāque's *Sokanvarān-e Irān dar ʿaṣr-e-ḥāżer* (Poets and Poetry of Modern Persia, I, Delhi, 1933), and later, in a detailed review of the work of one of the younger poets in *Rāhnemā-ye ketāb*, the journal of the Book Society of Persia.

Hazār piša (The Pigeon Hole, Tehran, 1948) is a kind of work-box containing a thousand interesting and amusing notes made from the author's reading of various books and articles. This, the first of two volumes, includes part of the first thousand jottings; the second volume, containing 309 different items, appeared in 1960 under the title *Kaškul-e Jamāli* (Beggar's Cup of Jamāl). The final collection was published as *Sanduqča-ye asrār* (Chest of Secrets, Tehran, 1964). Jamalzadeh continued to write and publish reviews of classical poetry and modern prose in Persian journals until late in life.

Jamalzadeh's translations of other works. With his excellent knowledge of French, German and Arabic, Jamalzadeh translated a large number of books and articles into Persian. The best known among these are the following: Hendrik Willem van Loon, *The Story of Mankind* (*Dāstān-e bašar*, Tehran, 1955); Friedrich Schiller, *Wilhelm Tell* (*Vilhelm Tell*, Tehran, 1955, 2nd ed., 1969) and *Don Carlos* (*Don Kārlos*, Tehran, 1956); Bernardin de Saint-Pierre, *Le Cafe de Surat* (*Qahvekāne-ye surāt yā jang-e haftādo do mellat*, Berlin, 1961); Moliere, *L'avare* (*Kasis*, Tehran, 1957); and Henrik Ibsen, *En folkefiende* (*Došman-e mellat*, Tehran, 1961).

Translations of Jamalzadeh's works. Because of his colloquial style and the wealth of idiomatic phrases in Jamalzadeh's works, the translation of his books into foreign languages is a formidable task. This is probably why, despite the literary value and great significance of his writings for modern Persian letters, attempts at introducing him to foreign readers have been relatively few. The untidiness of his novels and the cultural specificity of many of the situations in his stories are two other problems facing the translator. Hence, apart from an unpublished German translation of *Ganj-e šāyagān*, only some of the short stories published in the collection *Yeki bud yeki nabud*, and a few other stories, have appeared in foreign languages. An English translation of *Dard-e del-e Mollā Qorbān-ʿAli* was first printed in the magazine *Āhang* (Delhi, April 1944). *Yeki bud yeki nabud* was translated into English by Heshmat Moʾayyad and Paul Sprachman and published in its entirety as *Once Upon a Time* in 1985. *Sar o tah yek karbās* or *Eṣfahān-nāma* (Cut from the Same Cloth) was translated by W. L. Heston and published as *Isfahan is Half the World: Memories of a Persian Boyhood*, Princeton, 1983.

In his book *Kulturskitser fra Iran*, Arthur Christensen included a Danish translation of "*Rajol-e siāsi*" (Christensen 1931, pp. 179-84). This story has also been translated into German, as *Mein debut in der Politik*, and published in Austria in *Die Reise zum wonnigen Fisch: die besten Humoresken der zeigen; ossischen Weltliteratur* (Trip to the Jolly Fish; The Best Humorous Short Stories from Contemporary World Literature, Vienna, 1960). In addition, an Austrian professor, Karl Stolz, has translated "*Veylān-al-Dawla*" into German. This piece was also broadcast from Vienna Radio in October 1951 under the title "*Der Tod des Vagabunden*."

In the first issue of the journal *Fikr o naẓar*, published by the Association of Letters of Aligarh in India, there appeared Munibur Rahman's translation in Urdu of the short story "*Dusti-e kāle kerse*." Rudolf Gelpke's German rendering of this and another of Jamalzadeh's stories were included in a collection called *Persische Meistererzähler der Gegenwart* (Zurich, 1961). The volume entitled Im Garten des Hadschis: persische Erzählungen (The Haji's Garden: Persian Stories) contains a collection of Jamalzadeh's stories translated by Touraj Rahnama (Frankfurt, 1993). A recent dissertation which includes a German translation of *Ganj-e šāyegān ya awżāʾ-e eqteṣādi-e Irān* has been published by Leila Nabieva, *Der unermessliche Schatz, oder die wirtschaftliche Lage Irans: Galazades Studie zur iranischen Volkswirtschaft am Vorabend des Ersten Weltkrieges* (Berlin, 2006).

The Russian translation of *Yeki bud yeki nabud* (Byli i nebylitsy) by Boris Nikolaevich Zakhoder appeared in Moscow in 1936. The book contains some useful explanatory notes and a detailed preface by A. Bolotnikoff about the writer, the stories in the collection, and some general observations on the literary revival of the period in Iran. Discussing the influence that Jamalzadeh's first collection of stories had on Iran's contemporary literature, Bolotnikoff, quoting K. Chaikine, attributes the beginning of the style of realism in Persian literature to Jamalzadeh in *Yeki bud yeki nabud*. More recently, Jahangir Dorri has translated *Bila dig bila čoḡondar*, in a volume entitled *Chudesa v reshete* (Wonders in a Sieve), which was published in Moscow in 1989. Further Russian scholarship on Jamalzadeh includes a bio-bibliographical index by Jahangir Dorri and N. M. Safarova (Dzhamal-'zade: bibliograiceski ukazatel', Moscow, 1972) and a book about the life and works of Jamalzadeh (Mokhammad Ali Dzhaml'zade, Moscow, 1983) by Jahangir Dorri.

Finally, a collection containing eight of Jamalzadeh's better-known stories appeared in French in 1959. The book, entitled *Djamalzadeh: choix de nouvelles*, was translated by Stella Corbin and Hassan Lotfi and published by UNESCO (Paris, 1959). It contains a preface by Andre Chamson, member of the French Academy, and an informative introduction about Jamalzadeh's work and life written by Professor Henri Massé, the celebrated French Orientalist and expert on Persian folklore.

BIOGRAPHIES/MEMOIRS

Jamalzadeh wrote and spoke extensively about friends, colleagues, intellectuals, and writers who were his contemporaries such as Ebrāhim Purdāwud, Sayyed Ḥasan Taqizādeh, Yaḥyā Dawlatābādi, Moḥammad Qazvini and writers, poets, and scholars from a younger generation like Ṣādeq Hedāyat, Parvin Eʿteṣāmi, Moḥammad Moʿin and Mojtabā Minovi.

He also wrote and spoke at length about his memories of his father and his own long life. These memoirs and interviews—along with many of his thousands of letters—have been published in various journals and books (see bibliography).

MAJOR THEMES IN JAMALZADEH'S WORK

Almost all of Jamalzadeh writing reflects his didactic purpose in the writing of literature as evidenced by the essays he wrote as a preface or introduction to his stories. His main themes explore the negative consequences of the combination of despotism, poverty, and fanaticism—prevalent in twentieth century Iran—on the lives of normal people, predominantly from the middle and lower classes. A corollary of this unfortunate combination in many of Jamalzadeh's works is the prevalence of corruption and insecurity among all social groups (Kamshad 1966, p. 110). He had a particular distaste for despotism and the culture of subservience that it perpetuated (Katouzian, 2003, pp. 15-17).

In his social criticism he was principally concerned with exposing the ills of despotism, and with probing with sympathetic insight into its shortcomings, of middle-class elements. He blamed the young middle-class students for their *naivete*. He showed them victimized by old charlatans of power and influence, thwarted by fear and seduced by vain fancies. In this he was speaking as a middle-class Iranian who had lived abroad for many years. He was concerned about the outmoded practices and beliefs in education, and the rights of women, and questioned the reactionary aspects of religious practice.

Wholesale imitation of Western ways was always a source of concern to Jamalzadeh. Apart from frequent references in his works, he expressed these apprehensions in the Preface to *Sar o tah yek karbās*, where he indicated that not only the cultural products, but names, manners, even foods and drinks were indiscriminately influenced, or often replaced, by their European counterparts.

The dilemma of Western-educated Iranians who returned to their country often appeared in Jamalzadeh's novels and stories. Numerous characters of this type were depicted in different situations and with different potentialities, but none of them were able to tolerate the prevailing conditions, accommodate to the requirements of their milieu, or even to feel at home once they returned to their own country. Not only in their social environment but often in their own family circle they seemed like outsiders. All of them, even if endowed with exceptional learning and capabilities, failed in whatever they took up and generally ended up as morbid and useless members of society. For example, there was the strange creature in "*Fārsi Šekar Ast*," the Francophone youth, whose absurd imitation of Western ways and language became a great subject for ridicule. Then there was the hero of *Rāhāb-nāma*, who wanted to be civil and helpful to his neighbors but was easily swindled by them. Or Raḥmat-Allāh, in "*Ātaš-e zir-e ḵākestar*" (The Fire under Ashes), trained as a skilled carpenter in Germany, he opened a factory in Tehran after his return home. As he was a master-craftsman, his trade flourished rapidly. But rival firms could not tolerate the success of their young colleague and their plotting lost Raḥmat-Allāh both the factory and his profession.

The hero of "*Darviš-e mumiāʾi*" was another outcast. Though a learned and conscientious student, he locked himself up in his room in Geneva and without proper food or sleep brooded on abstract ideas such as the existence of God, the secret of creation, and free-will and predestination. In contrast to this bookworm living like a hermit, we have the son of a wealthy merchant in "*Dār al-majānin*" who was sent to Paris to study commerce; but after three years' stay in that city, he could not yet identify the building of his school.

A slightly happier situation can be found by looking at another of Jamalzadeh's heroes, one who finally did achieve a position of honor, though in an unorthodox manner, after going back to his country. Aḥmad Āqā, the hero of "*Ḵāna-beduš*" (The Wanderer), returned to Iran from Europe with a Ph.D. degree in education. But the job he was given by the government was that of sticking labels on bars of opium. Even in this menial employment he found occasion to complain of the prevailing bribery and corruption. His complaints were ridiculed by his friends and his own father. He felt an absolute stranger at home and finally, giving up the attempt to settle down with his own people, found a teaching job among the wandering tribes. He completely identified himself with the nomads, living and moving with them and winning their love and gratitude for teaching their children. When he died his tomb became venerated as a place of pilgrimage for the people of the tribe.

Jamalzadeh's preoccupation with cultural alienation and the clash of cultural identities as symbolized by the tragedy of the returned student points to a major sociological problem in Iran's state of social flux from the end of the 19th century until the revolution of 1979 (and perhaps beyond). The unhappy Westernized, idealistic, and ambitious young student returning home faces a situation where poverty, illiteracy, and adherence to outdated traditions coexist with the predominance of selfish, dominant classes with no sense of civic responsibility, and corruption prevails at all levels. Jamalzadeh was most admirably suited to handle this theme, for he was the archetype of that Iranian student who could never again adapt himself to prevailing conditions in his own country. In this regard, Jamalzadeh spoke for his time and for a number of young Iranian intellectuals in the first half of the twentieth century.

Another theme that looms large in Jamalzadeh's works is criticism of Muslim clerics and the religious institutions. Jamalzadeh was brought up with a religious as well as a modern education; the *ʿabā* (q.v.; cloak), *ʿammāma* (turban) and *menbar* (pulpit) occupy a more prominent place in his vision of Iran than they did in the minds of most other secular writers between the Constitutional Revolution and the 1979 Revolution. But unlike Hedāyat, who hated the religious institution as something alien, and as part of the evil resulting from the Arab conquest which suppressed true Iranian ideals, Jamalzadeh believed that ignorance, outdated interpretations, greed, and corruption among the clergy made them fall short of the ideals and requirements of a just and forward looking religion. It is for this reason that Jamalzadeh exposed the clergy to ruthless satire. Perhaps Jamalzadeh could not forget that some of the supporters of popular and progressive causes during the Constitutional Revolution—among them his own father—were clerics, whom he considered to be an essential element in the life and culture of his people. Jamalzadeh was by birth a member of the clerical-professional element of the middle class. Thus he could portray middle-class people with an accuracy and vividness born only of the most intimate acquaintance; and he could beat the *āḵund* with the *āḵund*'s own stick, defeating him with the clerics' own techniques and terminology, as in the argument with the mullah in the story "*Jahannam-e taʿaṣṣob*." With the skill of a Moliere, he made his characters fulfill the worst charges against them.

Finally, reference should be made to Jamalzadeh's preoccupation with language. When he left Iran for good, before the First World War, the state of the language was chaotic. Some practiced the elaborate and convoluted traditional style of writing, and others, supporting the idea of a literary revival, were pushing for a simpler and more concise mode of expression. With literacy gaining ground, the written word was ceasing to be the preserve of a traditionally educated few; the growing number of newspapers and importance of the press was an important factor. Contacts with the modern and technically more advanced states of the West were on the increase. People educated abroad, like the young man in "*Fārsi šekar ast*," went too far in the pretentious use of foreign terms and suffered from either having forgotten, or never having learned, the resources of their own language. The reactionary clergy indulged in pretentious and almost incomprehensible use of an Arabic jargon associated with *feqh* (q.v.) and *oṣul*.

Against this background Jamalzadeh began writing his *Yeki bud yeki na-bud*, and the Persian literati of Berlin, with whom he was associated in the 1920s, began consciously, through their journal *Kāveh* and other publications, to reform the language and to establish a suitable modern medium of communication. However, Jamalzadeh continued to harp on linguistic circumstances that no longer prevailed. He continued to write and discuss language as if the old battle of styles were still being fought with its former intensity, whereas, in fact, due to him and Hedayat more than others, from the 1940s and 1950s, writers committed neither the linguistic solecisms nor the anachronisms that Jamalzadeh was criticizing in "*Farsi šekar ast*" (and later in certain passages of "*Rāhāb-nāma*," *Ḵāstegāri*," "*Roʾyā*," "*Ṣahrā-ye maḥšar*," etc.). The contemporary writer gradually became equipped with a settled brand of modern Persian, with which he or she could be intelligible and inoffensive to the majority of readers.

In its overall effect, Jamalzadeh's writing is powerful enough to conceal his defects of style; yet these defects are serious. In introducing his characters, for instance, he often uses the method of a dramatist: depicting them at the outset of the story rather than letting them develop gradually (see, for example, *Dār al-majānin*, *Qoltašan-Divan*, *Rāhāb-nāma*, *and Namak-e gandida*). He also presents them as types rather than as individuals through whose actions their type may be perceived. Another aspect of Jamalzadeh's technique is his almost Dickensian flow of words, with adjectives piled up, numerous repetitions, and popular phrases never omitted where they can possibly be squeezed in. Also, particularly in his later works, he seized every opportunity for quoting maxims, poems, proverbs, and popular sayings, as well as Qurʾānic verses and quotations from the Traditions. He allowed his copious literary memory to run freely when he took pen in hand.

CRITIQUES OF JAMALZADEH'S WORKS

The body of criticism on Jamalzadeh's work focuses on three major points. First, that after his major literary contribution with *Yeki bud yeki nabud*, he essentially regurgitated the same themes with the same forms and styles and language but in different configurations. In other words, his early spurt of genius and innovation was not developed any further, yet he kept writing. Second, that Jamalzadeh's work became increasingly cut off from the social and political realities of Iran and the experiences of its people. He lived abroad and rarely visited Iran but kept on writing about Iran and Iranians. Third, it is alleged that by not challenging the despotic authorities in Iran and their allies in the west, he was essentially collaborating with them. He claimed to be an advocate of the people, but he acted as an accomplice of the oppressors. The first of these points is the only one that directly addresses literary concerns. The second and third are essentially political in nature.

Among post-war writers, Jalāl Āl-e Aḥmad has been most vociferous in his criticism of Jamalzadeh: he openly accused Jamalzadeh of producing worthless and insignificant work for decades, of being out of touch with Iran and its realities, and of collaborating with the pro-Pahlavi writers (Āl-e Aḥmad, 1988, pp. 65-76; Hillmann, 1988, p. 311; Dehbāši 1988, pp. 65-77). The political tone of Āl-Aḥmad's critique outweighed his specific literary arguments. Alternately, Navabpour states that although Jamalzadeh writes often about the poor and conditions of injustice, like his contemporary European thinkers, he talks to the poor from above, in effect, with the goal of dominating them with his own ideological vision (Navabpour, 1996, pp. 72-74).

Writer and critic Reżā Barāheni's analysis of Jamalzadeh's work is more grounded in literary criticism. Considering him to be stranded in the tradition of 19th century European literature, he acknowledges Jamalzadeh's talent as a writer not in exploring depths, but in examining outward manners and exposing moral and material corruption through satire (Barāheni, 1983, pp. 551-53). He accuses him of predominantly regurgitating his outdated memories in his later works (Baraheni, 1983, p. 560). Other critics of Jamalzadeh's fiction such as Ahmad Karimi-Hakkak have contended that after his initial innovation with *Yeki bud yeki nabud*, he lost his creativity and produced writing that was tedious and obsolete (Karimi-Hakkak, 1985, pp. 423-24). Heshmat Moayyad stated that his language was too archaic and verbose, and that his stories and novels, particularly the later ones lacked even plot development and technical refinement (Moayyad, 1992, p. 14). Ḥasan ʿĀbedini argued that Jamalzadeh's didactic approach to storytelling and his deliberate use of language as a method of social reportage evokes the religious and political discourses of the constitutional period (ʿĀbedini in Dehbāši, 1998, pp. 151-53). Paul Sprachman noted that "[Jamalzadeh's] fiction at times serves as an advanced species of dictionary" (Jamalzadeh, 1985, p. 19).

The charge that Jamalzadeh never came back to live in Iran, that his work demonstrated that he was out of touch with the real problems of Iranians (Dastḡayb, 1977, pp. 5-6), or that he served Mohammad Reza Shah's regime or the West by his refusal to take a firm political stand, stemmed from the fact that his work did not fit into the mold of any of the prevailing ideologies in Iran. Though his fiction was often socio-political, and though he remained deeply involved and interested in Iranian culture, Jamalzadeh was not a proponent of the romantic Iranian nationalism (Aryanism) in the 1920s and 1930s; he was not leftist or a "committed" writer in the 1950s, 1960s, and 1970s. His writing was thus considered to be irrelevant by many of the revolutionary writers and intellectuals. Furthermore, he was never a monarchist, and did not join the establishment before the revolution. He was generally timid about taking a firm political stand perhaps because he hated dictatorship but feared it at the same time (Katouzian, 2003, pp. 17-20). This tendency to be politically non-committal can possibly be explained by his deep disappointment, during his early revolutionary days, in the outcome of national and international events from the Constitutional Revolution to the aftermath of the First World War.

Nevertheless, all critics point to Jamalzadeh as the indisputable innovator who introduced modern, realist writing to Persian prose literature, and who demonstrated great ability and creativity in using the Persian language and the genre of fiction as a means of communication with all Iranians.

Bibliography: See iii. below.

(HASSAN KAMSHAD and NAHID MOZAFFARI)

iii. BIBLIOGRAPHY

Most of Jamalzadeh's work is presented in the body of the texts (i and ii above). Some of his work and major works on his life and writings are included in this bibliography. For a comprehensive list of his works in Persian, particularly the numerous articles he wrote in the press, please see the bibliography by Nāhid Ḥabibi Āzād in Dehbāši, 1998, pp. 607-51).

Iraj Afšār, *Nāmehā-ye dustān*, Tehran, 1996. Isā Arbābi, *Čahār sarv-e afsāneh*, Tehran, 1999. Yaḥyā Āryanpur, *Az Ṣabā tā Nimā* II, Tehran, 1995. Moḥammad Bahārlu, ed., *Gozida-ye āṯār-e Moḥammad-ʿAli Jamālzādeh*, Tehran, 1994. Christoph Balay and M. Cuypers, *Aux Sources de la nouvelle persane*, Paris, 1983. Idem, *La Genese du Roman Persan Moderne*, Tehran, 1998. Reżā Barāheni, *Qeṣṣa-nevisi*, Tehran, 1983. M.-E. Bāstāni Pārizi, "Naqš-e k̲unin" in Eqbāl Yaqmāʾi, *Šahid-e rāh-e āzādi, Sayyed Jamāl Wāʿeẓ Eṣfahāni*, Tehran, 1978, pp. seven-twenty five. Mangol Bayat, *Mysticism and Dissent: Socioreligious Thought in Qajar Iran*, Syracuse, 1982. Idem, *Iran's First Revolution*, Oxford, 1991. Stella Corbin and Hassan Lotfi, *Choix de Nouvelles*, UNESCO, Paris, 1959. Michel Cuypers, "The Birth of a Writer" and "Outline of Jamalzadeh's Life," tr. A. Karimi Hakkak, in ʿA. Dehbāši, *Yād-e Sayyed Moḥammad-ʿAli Jamālzādeh*, Tehran, 1998, pp. 63-86. ʿAbd-al-ʿAli Dastḡayb, *Naqd-e āṯār-e Moḥammad-ʿAli Jamālzādeh*, Tehran, 1977. Yaḥyā Dawlatābādi, *Ḥayāt-e Yaḥyā* I, Tehran, 1950. ʿAli Dehbāši, ed., *Nāmahā-ye Jalāl Āl-e Aḥmad*, Tehran, 1988. Idem, *Bargozide-ye āṯār-e Sayyed Moḥammad-ʿAli Jamālzādeh*, Tehran, 1999. Idem, *Yād-e Sayyed Moḥammad-ʿAli Jamālzādeh*, Tehran, 1998. Dzhekhangir Khabibullaevich Dorri, *Persidskaya Satiricheskaya proza. Traditsiya i novatorstvo* (Persian satirical prose: Tradition and innovation), Moscow, 1977, pp. 88-113. Idem, *Mokhammad Ali Dzhamalzade*, Moskva, 1983. Idem, *Chudesa v reshete*, Moskva, 1989. Idem and Naderova Safarova, *Dzhamal'zade: Bibliograficeskij ukazatel*, Moskva, 1972. Idem, *Persidskie yumoristicheskie i satiricheskie rasskazy* (Persian humorous and satirical stories), Moscow, 1988, pp. 1-94. Mohammad Reza Ghanoonparvar, *Prophets of Doom: Literature as a Socio-Political Phenomenon in Modern Iran*, Lanham, Md., 1984. Nāhid Ḥabibi Āzād, "Ketābšenāsi-e ketābhā wa maqālāt-e Sayyed Moḥammad-ʿAli Jamālzādeh wa maqālāti keh dar bāre-ye vey montašer šodeh ast" (A Bibliography of Books and Articles by Mohammad Ali Jamalzadeh, and Articles Published About Him) in Dehbāši, 1998, pp. 607-51. Walter B. Henning and E. Yarshater, *A Locust's Leg: Studies in Honor of S. H. Taqizadeh*, London, 1962. Michael C. Hillmann, "Persian Prose Fiction: An Iranian Mirror and Conscience," in Ehsan Yarshater, ed. *Persian Literature*, New York, 1988, pp. 291-317. Idem, "Review of *Once Upon a Time*," in *Journal of Near Eastern Studies* 47/4, 1988, pp. 311-13.

Mohammad-Ali Jamalzadeh, *Yeki bud, yeki nabud*, Tehran, 1954. Idem, *Yeki bud, yeki nabud*, tr. Russian, B. N. Zakhoder, Moscow, 1936. Idem, "Preface" (*Yeki bud, yeki nabud*) tr. Haideh Daraghi, *The Literary Review* 18/1 pp. 24-35. Idem, "Taqizadeh, tel qui je l'ai connu" in Walter B. Henning and Ehsan Yarshater, *A Locust's Leg: Studies in Honor of S. H. Taqizadeh*, London, 1962, pp. 1-18. Idem, "Qatl o ḡārat-e Arāmaneh dar Torkiya," in ed. Mehrdad Mehrin, *Sargozašt o kār-e Jamālzādeh*, 1963, pp. 55-69. Idem, "Qatl-e ʿĀmm-e Armaniān" in E. Rāʾin, *Qatl-e ʿāmm-e Armaniān*. Tehran, 1972, pp. 211-17. Idem, *Sar o tah yek karbās*, tr. H. L. Heston as *Isfahan is Half the World: Memoirs of a Persian Boyhood*, Princeton, 1983. Idem, *Once Upon a Time*, tr., H. Moayyad and P. Sprachman, New York, 1985. Idem, *Ḵāṭerāt-e Sayyed Moḥammad-ʿAli Jamālzādeh*, eds., Iraj Afšār and ʿAli Dehbāši, Tehran, 1999.

Hasan Kamshad, *Modern Persian Prose Literature*, Cambridge, 1966. Ahmad Karimi-Hakkak, "Book Review: *Isfahan is Half the World: Memories of a Persian Boyhood* by Sayyed Mohammad Jamalzadeh," *Iranian Studies* 18, 1985, pp. 423-27. Homa Katouzian, "Sadeq Hedayat i. Life and Work," in *EIr.*, XII, 2004, pp. 121-27. Idem. *Dar Bāre-ye Jamālzādeh wa Jamālzādeh šenāsi*, Tehran, 2003. Ḥosayn Maḥbubi Ardakāni, *Tāriḵ-e moʾassesāt-e tamaddoni-e jadid dar Irān* I, Tehran, 1975. Henri Massé, "Introduction," in ed. S. Corbin et H. Lotfi, *Choix de nouvelles, tradition Du Persan*, Paris, 1959, pp. 7-25. Mehrdād Mehrin, *Sargozašt o kār-e Jamālzādeh*, Tehran, 1963. Jamāl Mirṣādeqi, "The Fiction of Moḥammad-ʿAli Jamālzādeh" in Dehbāši, 1998, pp. 295-303. Heshmat Moayyad, ed., *Stories from Iran*, Bethesda, Md., 1992. Idem and P. Sprachman, tr., *Once Upon a Time*, New York, 1985. Reza Navabpour, "The 'Writer' and the 'People': Jamalzadeh's *Yeki bud yeki nabud*: a Recast," *British Journal of Middle Eastern Studies* 23/1, 1996, pp. 69-75. Basile Nikitine, "Seyyed Mohammad Ali Djamalzadeh, pionnier de la prose moderne persane' in *Revue des Etudes Islamiques* 27, Paris, 1959, pp. 23-33. Masʿud Rażawi, *Laḥẓaʾi wa soḵani bā Moḥammad-ʿAli Jamālzādeh*, Tehran, 1994. Jalāl Matini, "Dar Bāre-ye Ḵolqiyāt-e mā Irāniān" (Comments on Our Iranian Character Traits) in Dehbāši, 1998, pp. 445-58). K. Pārsinežād, *Naqd o taḥlil wa gozida-ye dāstānhā-ye Sayyed Moḥammad-ʿAli Jamālzādeh*, Tehran, 2002. Reżā Raḥimi, "Negāhi be yeki bud, yeki nabud" (A Glance at Once Upon a Time) in Dehbāši, 1998, pp. 375-82. Sayyed Ḥasan Taqizadeh, *Zendegi-e ṭufāni, Ḵāṭerāt-e Sayyed Ḥassan Taqizāda*, ed. I. Afšār, Tehran, 1989. Natalia Tornesello, *Surabad e il realismo di Seyyed Mohammad Ali Jamaālzādeh*, Finzione Letteraria e Veridicita Storica. Quaderni di Oriente Moderno, 2000. Eqbāl Yaḡmāʾi, *Šahid-e rāh-e āzādi, Sāyyed Jamāl Wāʿeẓ Eṣfahāni*, ed. I. Afšār, Tehran, 1973. Ehsan Yarshater, "The Development of Iranian Literatures: Historical Perspective" in idem, ed. *Persian Literature*, New York, 1988, pp. 3-37.

Websites. *www.farhangsara.com/jamalzadeh.htm*
www.caroun.com/Literature/Iran/Writers/Jamalzadeh.html

(NAHID MOZAFFARI)

JĀMĀSP, Sasanian king for a short period (ca. 496-97 CE). This entry is divided into two sections.

i. *Reign*.
ii. *Coinage*.

i. REIGN

Jāmāsp or Zāmāsp (Middle Persian yʾmʾsp, zʾmʾsp; Greek Zamásphēs; Arabic Jāmāsb, Zāmāsb, Zāmāsf; New Persian Jāmāsp, Zāmāsp) ascended to the Sasanian throne in 496 (or possibly early 497) when his brother, the king of kings Kawād I, was deposed. Jāmāsp, like Kawād, was a son of the Sasanian ruler Pērōz (r. 459-84). Jāmāsp's name associated this short-reigned Sasanian king with the legendary seer Jāmāspa (q.v.), who supposedly served the Kayanian Vīštāspa (Kay Vīštāsp). On his coinage, the name is inscribed as Jām (Mid. Pers. gʾm) perhaps also linking him with the mythical Pishdadian monarch Jam or Jamsēd (Av. Yima Xšaēta).

The period just prior to Jāmāsp's reign witnessed waxing influence of Mazdakism, raids by Arab tribes in the province of Asuristan (see ĀSŌRISTĀN) to the southwest and along the border with Arabia, rebellion by Armenians in Armin to the northwest, deteriorating relations with the Byzantines in the west, and an uprising by members of the Iranian nobility and clergy angered by socioeconomic and religious changes. The rebellion by feudal nobles and magi resulted in Kawād's ouster, trial, and imprisonment, and produced Jāmāsp's elevation as *šāhān šāh* "king of kings." Kawād escaped from captivity in Khuzestan, fled eastward, and found safe haven with the Hephthalites (q.v.), among whom he had been raised. After having gathered forces under his command, Kawād fought back for the throne with the assistance of those Hephthalite troops. Famine caused much hardship across the Sasanian empire, adding to the social, political, and religious tumult of that period (see overview in SASANIAN DYNASTY at *iranica.com*). Jāmāsp, probably realizing he lacked support to retain the monarchy, chose not to confront Kawād in battle. Thereby, rule of Iran was relinquished back to Kawād I in late 498 or early 499.

Limited details of Jāmāsp's reign can be gleaned from historical records. Jāmāsp's reign marked the standardization of regnal year notation on the reverses of Sasanian coinage. However no gold coinage or *dēnārs* are attributable to the king's brief reign, perhaps due to the scarcity of bullion in that economically challenged time. Christian documents, such as *The Chronicle of Joshua the Stylite* (sections 23-24) composed in Syriac in 507, briefly mentioned Jāmāsp's royal rise and fall within the context of Kawād I's reigns. So did later Muslim writers like Ṭabarī (d. 923) (*Taʾrik̲ al-rosol wa'l-moluk* I, pp. 886-87), who mistakenly recorded the reign as six years (I, p. 887). Kawād's life and times obscure Jāmāsp's in Ferdowsi's *Šāh-nāma* as well. The Byzantine historian Agathias (ca. 536-82) recorded that Jāmāsp was selected for the throne because of his calm and fair disposition but that he chose to abdicate, after four years in power, upon Kawād's return to Iran rather than confront his brother and so was pardoned to a life of obscurity (*History*, sections 268b-270b). Dinawari (d. ca. 894-903) (*Ketāb al-ak̲bār al-ṭewāl*, p. 66) noted a similar set of events. However, Elias the Nestorian Metropolitan of Nisibis (d. ca. 1049) claimed that Jāmāsp was executed by Kawād, perhaps confusing Kawād's punishment of the rebellious nobles and magi with the fate allotted to his submissive brother.

Bibliography: C. E. Bosworth, tr., *The History of al-Ṭabarī* V, Albany, 1999, pp. 133-36 and notes. Averil Cameron, "Agathias on the Sasanians," *Dumbarton Oaks Papers* 23, 1969-70, pp. 67-183. *The Chronicle of Joshua the Stylite*, ed. and tr. W. Wright, London, 1882; repr., Piscataway, N.J., 2003. Abū Hanīfa Aḥmad b. Dāwud al-Dinawari, *Ketāb al-ak̲bār al-ṭewāl*, ed. A. M. ʿAmir and J. D. al-Shayyal, Cairo, 1960. Richard N. Frye, *The History of Ancient Iran*, Munich, 1984, p. 150. *RE* IXA2, Stuttgart, 1968, cols. 2308-9.

(JAMSHEED K. CHOKSY)

ii. COINAGE

Typology. The obverses of Jāmāsp's coins are notable for the addition of a small bust, to the right of the king's own, which wears a mural crown with a *korymbos* (a cloth element enclosing the hair). The figure faces left and holds a diadem. Göbl has argued that it represents the god Ahura Mazdā and not, as was earlier believed, a

PLATE I

(a) (b)

Drachm coins of Jāmāsp. a. AR-Drachm, type Ia/1a, mint AW, RY 1. Münzkabinett, Staatliche Museen zu Berlin; Schindel, 2004, no. 4. b. AR-Drachm, type Ib/1b, mint GW, RY 3. Numismatic Central Card File, Institute for Numismatics and Monetary History, University of Vienna; Schindel, 2004, no. A11.

crown prince (Göbl, 1952; Göbl, 1971, p. 51). Even if his arguments are not fully convincing, the fact that the depiction under Jāmāsp has very close parallels in the coinage of Bahrām II (276-293), in which the bust certainly represents the goddess Anāhitā handing over the diadem to the king on the obverse—thus repeating the investiture (q.v.) scene on the reverse—is a very strong argument for interpreting the bust on Jāmāsp's coins as Ahura Mazdā (Schindel, 2004, pp. 450-51). This depiction certainly can be seen in the context of the internal struggles after the deposition of Kawād I, most likely to emphasize the legitimacy of Jāmāsp's reign. During regnal year one and the earlier part of regnal year two, the diadem which the bust holds is depicted with two short ribbons showing to the left and to the right (PLATE I.a, Figure 1-1.Ia), whereas in the latter half of regnal year two and in regnal year three, the ribbons are much broader and ribbed, and show to the right (PLATE I.b, Figure 1-1.Ib). The king's crown basically follows the model of that of Wahrām V, which most likely has a propagandistic meaning. The main difference is that Jāmāsp adds a second crescent on a pearl between the two mural elements. The obverse legend consists only of Jāmāsp's name in the abbreviated form gʾm *Gām*; the absence of any royal title has parallels in the first reign of Kawād I (488-96). As in that period, on breast and shoulders various combinations of dots, crescents, and the like occur, which were used empire-wide.

On the reverse, the attendant figures face the altar and raise their respective right hand in a gesture of adoration towards the altar. Typologically, Jāmāsp does not alter the reverse depiction of Kawād I's first reign (see Figure 1-4.1a-b). Two minor reverse variants occur: On type 1a,

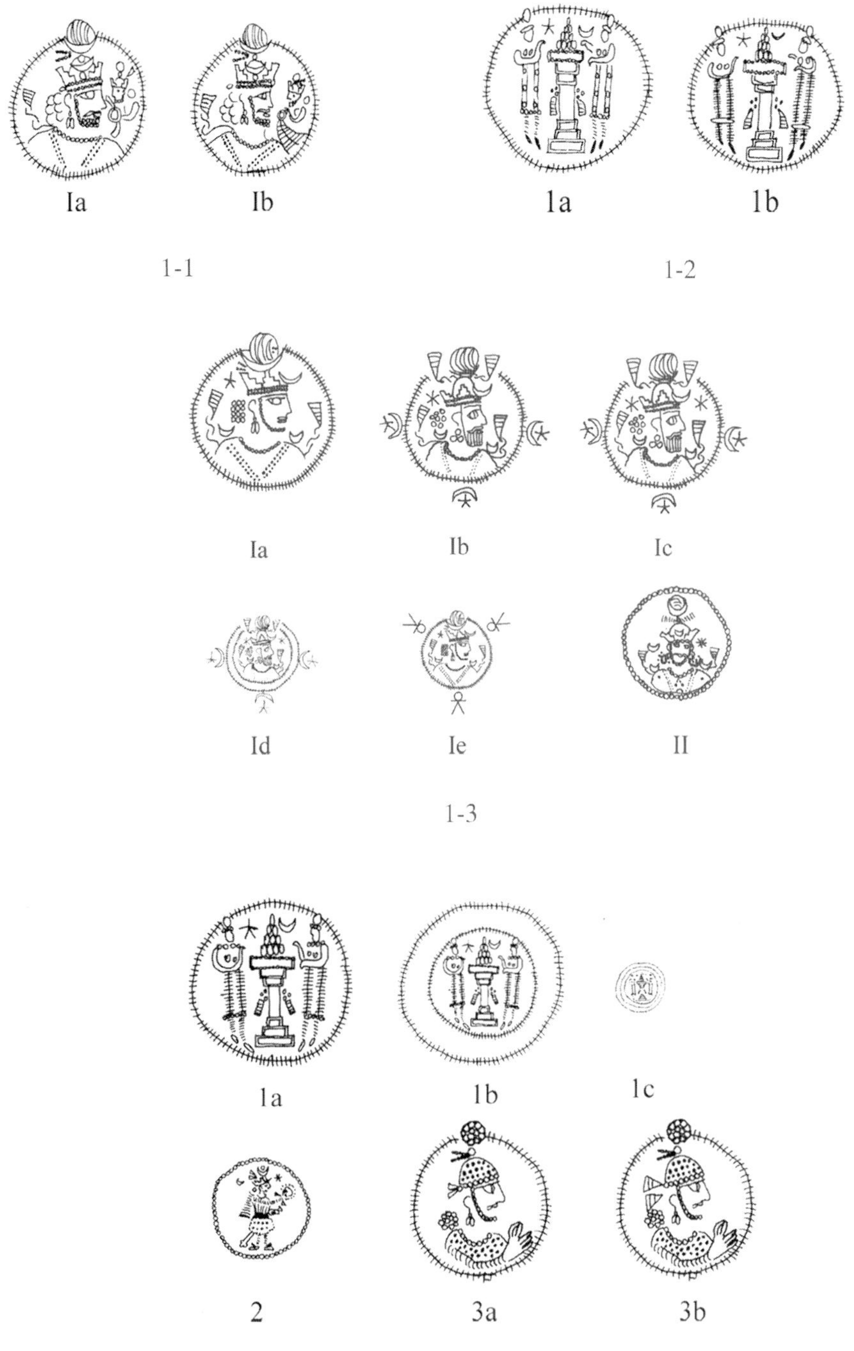

Figure 1. Coin types of Jāmāsp and Kāwād. Group 1-1: obverse types of Jāmāsp. Group 1-2: reverse types of Jāmāsp. Group 1-3: obverse types of Kāwād. Group 1-4: reverse types of Kāwād. (Source: Schindel, 2004.)

the bodies of the assistant figures are shown with two parallel lines adorned with three dots (PLATE I.a, Figure 1-2.1a), whereas on type 1b their bodies are built up with a number of fine, parallel strokes (PLATE I.b, Figure 1-2b.1b). Apart from some precursors in AS (Āsuristān) and WH (Veh-Antiok-Šāpur in Ḵuzestān), in most other mints type 1b commences in regnal year three. Combinations of obverse type Ib with reverse type 1a are certainly hybrid. An important feature is the canonical introduction of regnal years at 9h (year 1-3). Dates had been placed on the same location already during regnal years two to seven of Pērōz (457-84), but their use was discontinued thereafter. From Jāmāsp until the end of Sasanian-style coinage, the date indication—together with the mint indication at 3h—was to remain canonical.

Denominations. No gold coins are attested so far for Jāmāsp. Apart from the silver drachms, sixths of a drachm, or obols, are known from the mints DA (Dārābgerd) and LD (Ray). All the DA specimens are dated to regnal year one, and perhaps are connected with the king's coronation, which thus may have taken place in Dārābgerd. One bronze coin has turned up so far (Schindel 2004, no. 29). Both silver and copper fractions feature the same typology as the drachms.

Mints. So far, 18 different mints are attested for Jāmāsp, which are were active also under other rulers. In contrast to Balāš and the first reign of Kawād I, under whom GW (Gorgān) was the most prolific mint in the empire, the center of monetary production under Jāmāsp is located in the center of the Sasanian realm. The most common mint is WH (Veh-Antiok-Šāpur), followed by AY (Erān-xwarrah-Šāpur) and AS (Āsuristān).

Bibliography: R. Göbl, *Sasanian Numismatics*, Braunschweig 1971. Idem, "Die Investitur des Djamasp," *Schweizer Münzblätter* 3, 1952, pp. 57-58. N. Schindel, *Sylloge Nummorum Sasanidarum Paris–Berlin–Wien. Band III. Shapur II.–Kawad I. / 2. Regierung*, Vienna, 2004.

(NIKOLAUS SCHINDEL)

JĀMĀSPA (GAv. Dəjāmāspa; Elam. Zamašba, Zamišba; Arm. Zmsp; Gk. Zamaspes; Akk. Za-ma-as-pa-a'), name of an official at the court of Vīštāspa and an early convert of Zarathushtra, who, in the tradition became widely known for his wisdom.

Etymology. There is no certain etymology of the name. It is a compound whose final member is *aspa-* "horse." In metrical contexts (*Y.* 46.17; 51.18; *Yt.* 5.68), the name must be read as tetrasyllabic *jāma-aspa-* (cf. Ved. *ṛjrá-aśva-* proper noun; Mayrhofer, 1956, I, p. 121). A favored etymology of *jāma-* has been to compare it with OInd. *kṣāmáh-* "burnt, singed," but Prakrit *jhāma-* points to IE *$d^{h}g^{wh}$-*eH*-, which one would expect to give Av. **γžā/žγā* (Mayrhofer, 1979, p. 55; 1992, p. 430). Ilya Gershevitch (pp. 177 ff.) proposed "leading horses" to Parth. *žām-* "to lead," while Martin Schwartz (1975, p. 10; idem, 1980, p. 203) seemed to favor "he who bridles horses," in view of Arm. *cim* "bridle."

In the Avesta. Jāmāspa is mentioned twice in the Gathas (q.v.) in close connection with his brother Frašaoštra and with Kavi Vīštāspa. There is no reason to doubt that the two brothers, belonging to the Hvō.gva (YAv. Hvōva) family, were officials at the court of Vīštāspa and were among Zarathustra's early converts to whom he preached (Jackson, pp. 20-22, 76-77). Specifically, in *Yasna* 46.17 Zarathustra addresses Jāmāsp directly, commanding him "Go where I shall proclaim to you (pl.) praises in verse, not non-verse, O Jāmāspa the Hvōgvid!" (*yaθrā wə̄ afšmānī sə̄nghānī nōiṯ anafšmąm də̄jāmāspā hwō.gwā . . . wahmə̄ng*). The fame that Jāmāspa enjoys in the later tradition as the wise vizier of Goštāsp is, perhaps, foreshadowed in *Yasna* 51.18, where Zarathustra says of him: "He chooses through Aša, this insight (and) this power" (*tąm cistīm . . . ašā wərəntē taṯ xšaθrəm*). In *Yašt* 5.68, Jāmāspa is among the many hero supplicants of Arədvī Sūrā Anāhita (see ANĀHĪD), where "he sacrificed to her, as he perceived the army of *daēva*-worshiping liars approaching from afar in battle array" (*tąm yazata jāmāspō yaṯ spāδəm pairi.awaēnaṯ dūrāṯ āyantəm rasmaoyō drwatąm daēwayasnanąm*). It is puzzling why he is placed at this point in the *Yašt*, in that one might expect, on the basis of the later royal epic tradition, that he would have been placed in the Vīštāspa, Zairi.vairi, Arəjaṯ.aspa (in Mid. Pers. and the *Šāh-nāma*: Vīštāsp/Goštāsp, Zarēr, Arjāsp; qq.v.) sequence of *Yašt* 5.108-18. Jāmāsp appears in the longer *frawarānā* (confession) of *Yasna* 12.7 in a dvandva compound with his brother (*frašaoštrā-jāmāspā*) immediately after Vīštāspa; and the dual formation is repeated in the *Vīštāsp Yašt* 11 (*frašaoštraēibya jāmāspaēibya*). In the *fravaši* (q.v.) lists of *Yašt* 13, Jāmāsp's *fravaši* is worshiped immediately after Frašaoštra's (103), but at some distance from those of Vīštāspa (99-100) and Zairi.vairi (101), for the reason that they belonged to different families. In the late text, *Āfrīn ī Zardošt* 2 his name appears in two benedictions given by Zarathustra to Vīštāspa: "May you be just like Jāmāspa . . . powerful like Jāmāspa (*aēvaθa bavēhi yaθa jāmāspō . . . amava yaθa jāmāspō*); and in the closely related *Vīštāsp Yašt* 3 there is a benediction that Vīštāspa have ten sons: three priests, three warriors and three agriculturalists, plus "one son of yours (like) Jāmāspa" (*zayånte tanukəhrpa dasa puθra θrāyō yaθa aθaurunō θrāyō yaθa raθaēštārahe θrāyō yaθa vāstryehe fšuyantō aēva te puθrō <yaθa> jāmāspō*). In contrast to his association with royal power, Jāmāsp was also thought to have exercised a priestly function, as seen in the passage from the N. 89: "He who strews the *barəsman* according to these (rules) as righteous Jāmāspa used to strew (it), is a *ratufriš*" (*yō anu aēšąm barəsma frastarənte yaθa ašawa jāmāspō frastarənaēta ratufriš*).

In Pahlavi literature. As an actor in the epic drama of the establishment of Zoroastrianism, Jāmāsp is remembered in *Dēnkard* (q.v.) together with Zarēr, Spandyād (Av. Spəntōδāta; *Šāh-nāma* Esfandiār, q.v.) and Frašōštar, as one of the first princes (*wāspuhragān*) to propagate the religion (*Dēnkard*, ed. Madan, p. 436.14-15) and as the one who received the teaching of Zarthustra (*zarduxšt-*

āmōg; ibid, p. 437.14-20), which was written on oxhides in Avestan and Zand, according to the familiar story (see Bailey, pp. 149 ff.). In the *Ayādgār ī Zarērān* (q.v.), he is featured prominently, as he is later in the *Šāh-nāma*, as the wise vizier (*bidaxš*, q.v.) of Kay Wištāsp, capable of foreseeing the outcome of the great battle with Arjāsp and ever ready to give counsel. His fame for wisdom lent his name to a late Pahlavi compendium of lore, the *Ayādgār ī Zarērān*. The name was known in antiquity, appearing already as Zamašba on Persepolis tablets (Hallock, p. 722), later in Sasanid royal nomenclature (though not at Paikuli), and has remained a common name among Zoroastrians.

Bibliography: Harold W. Bailey, *Zoroastrian Problems in the Ninth Century Books*, London, 1943, p. 149 ff. Ervand Bahmanji N. Dhabhar, "Jamasp Bitaxsh or Jamasp Hakim," in *Poure Davoud Memorial Volume* II: *Papers on Zoroastrian and Iranian Subjects in Honour of Ebrahim Poure Davoud*, Bombay, 1951, pp. 57-61. Ilya Gershevitch, "Amber at Persepolis," in *Studia classica et orientalia Antonino Pagliaro Oblata*, 3 vols., Roma, 1969, II, pp. 167-251. Philippe Gignoux, *Glossaire des Inscriptions Pehlevies et Parthes*, Corpus Inscriptionum Iranicarum, London, 1972, pp. 38, 68. Richard Hallock, *Persepolis Fortification Tablets*, Chicago, 1969. Walther Hinz, *Altiranisches Sprachgut der Nebenüberlieferungen*, Wiesbaden, 1975, p. 143. Helmut Humbach and Prods O. Skjærvø, *The Sassanian Inscription of Paikuli*, pt. 3.1, 2, Wiesbaden, 1983, p. 123. A. V. Williams Jackson, *Zoroaster: The Prophet of Ancient Iran*, New York, 1965. Ferdinand Justi, *Iranisches Namenbuch*, Marburg, 1895, p. 109; repr., Hildesheim, 1963 [esp. for references to Pers. and Ar. sources]. Manfred Mayrhofer, *Kurzgefasstes etymologisches Wörterbuch des Altindischen/A Concise Etymological Sanskrit Dictionary*, 3 vols., Heidelberg, 1956. Idem, *Onomastica Persepolitana: Das altiranische Namengut der Persepolis-Täfelchen*, Vienna, 1973, p. 253. Idem, *Iranisches Personennamenbuch* I: *Die altiranischen Namen*, Vienna, 1979; rev. Martin Schwartz, in *Orientalia* 49, 1980, p. 125. Idem, *Etymologisches Wörterbuch des Altindoarischen* I, Heidelberg, 1992. Henrik Samuel Nyberg, *Irans forntida religioner*, tr. Hans Heinrich Schaeder as *Die Religionen des Iran*, Osnabrük, 1966, pp. 254-55, 296-97. Ebrāhim Pur-e Dāwud, "Jāmāsb," in idem, ed. and tr., *Yašthā*, 2 vols., Bombay, 1928, I, pp. 227-30. Martin Schwartz "Proto-Indo-European √ĝem-," in *Monumentum H. S. Nyberg*, 4 vols., Acta Iranica 4-7, Tehran and Liège, 1975, II, pp. 195-207. Fritz Wolff, *Glossar zu Firdosis Schahname: Festgabe des deutschen Reiches zur Jahrtausendfeier für den persischen Dichterfürsten*, Berlin, 1935; repr., Hildesheim, 1965, s.v. Jāmāsp.

(W. W. MALANDRA)

JĀMĀSPASA, DASTUR JAMASPJI MINOCHERJI (b. Bombay, 1830; d. Bombay, 26 September 1898), Parsi priest and Iranologist.

Dastur Jamaspji Minocherji JāmāspAsa was the offspring of a priestly family from the Bhagaria group/lineage (*panth*) from Navsari in Gujarat, India. Throughout the 19th century, the JāmāspAsa family rivaled with the fellow Bhagaria Sanjana family for priestly pre-eminence in Bombay. His paternal grandfather, Khurshedji Jamshedji (1749-1829), had arrived in Bombay in 1801 and became the leading Zoroastrian priest of his time there. Unlike the Sanjana family, whose authority was grounded in the Wadia Atash Bahram Temple (consecrated 17 November 1830), the JāmāspAsa family were referred to as *Anjuman Dasturs*, that is, high priests for the entire Parsi community, as they were not yet bound to any particular fire temple.

Dastur Jamaspji began his studies in Zoroastrian language and literature under the supervision of his grandfather and father. Sponsored by Sir Jamsetji Jijibhoy (1783-1859), he studied Avesta (q.v.), Pahlavi, Persian, and Sanskrit (the latter under the guidance of a Pundit). In 1861, he succeeded his father as *Anjuman Dastur*. As a high priest, Jamaspji became controversial, when, in 1882, he took an active part in nine initiations (*navjote*) of children of Parsi fathers and non-Parsi mothers from Mazagon, which became a contentious issue in the community (Patel, III, p. 41). His rival, Dastur Peshotanji Behramji Sanjana (1828-98), published a pamphlet to show that the ceremonies "were not properly performed" (Desai, p. 12), which was followed by Dastur Jamaspji's rejoinder. Despite this incident, he was nominated high priest of Parsis of Aden in 1883, of Surat in 1898, and of Lahore and Punjab in 1893 (Patel, III, p. 573).

From the age of 30, Dastur Jamaspji gave religious instructions in schools. He also regularly held religious discourses in and outside Bombay (Patel, II, pp. 131, 169, 184, 196, passim). As a high priest he guided and supervised the consecration of several fire temples, not only in Bombay but all over India (Patel, II, pp. 305, 309; III, pp. 432, 554). In this respect, his crowning achievement was the consecration of the Anjuman Atash Bahram Temple in Bombay in 1897, for which in 1898 he was appointed the first Dastur (Patel, III, pp. 651-55), a position inherited by his offspring ever since. For the consecration of this fire temple not only were there financial difficulties to overcome, but public opinion was not entirely in favor of the venture, and Dastur Sanjana objected that the new temple was located much too close to the other Shehenshai Atash Bahram Temple in the city. The two families of priests had many clashes, some of which had to be resolved by civil courts.

Dastur Jamaspji also acted as the Officer of the Parsi Law Association (1861), worked for the Directorate of Public Instruction of Bombay region (1864), and was a delegate of the First Parsi Chief Matrimonial Court (1866-

74; see Patel, II, p. 164). As *Anjuman Dastur*, he prayed for royalty and high-ranking dignitaries. In 1875, for instance, he honored the Prince of Wales (later His Imperial Majesty King Edward VII, r. 1901-10) with an address in Avestan, specially composed for the occasion of the latter's visit to India (Patel, II, p. 545). Dastur Jamaspji was a member of the working committee of the World's Parliament of Religions (1893), but because of his age and health he was not able to travel to Chicago to attend its first formal gathering.

Dastur Jamaspji possessed a vast collection of important Zoroastrian manuscripts. His publication of the *Pahlavi texts* (1897-1913) made these manuscripts available to a larger audience. Among his contributions to Pahlavi philology, mention should be made of his decipherment and translation into Gujarati of the Pahlavi inscriptions at the Kanheri caves in 1866 and a Pahlavi Dictionary in Gujarati entitled *Pehelvi, Gujarāti ane Ingreji shabdakosh* (Pahlavi, Gujarati and English Dictionary, 3 vols., 1877-78). The work is incomplete and goes up to the word *omānāg*. In 1881 he published an annotated Gujarati translation of the Persian Saddar entitled *Saddare behre tāvil, yāne so bāb athwā so darwājāni kitāb* (Saddar-e Behr-e Tavil, that is, the book of a hundred chapters or doors). His other publications include: *Radiyā ī farmān ī dīn* (On the disqualification of the injunctions of religion, 1867); *Jeh Shekan, yāne badfelinā felavāne todnār, jarthostione vākef thavā sāu* (Jeh shekan, that is, annihilating the spread of evil, for the information of Zoroastrians, 1870); *Khurdeh Avesta (Khurdād, Behrām tathā āvā yasht sāthe)* (Khordeh Avesta [with Khordad, Behram and Avan Yashts], 1873); and two collection of sermons, one comprising three Gujarati sermons and entitled *Yazdānparasti ane jarthoshti dharma pālvāni agat* (Worship of God and the necessity of practicing the Zoroastrian religion, 1874), and the other containing seven sermons and entitled *Vāejo, Dastur Jāmāspji Minicherji Jamaspāsānāe gayā farvardegān nā divaso par kidheli* (Sermons delivered by Dastur Jamaspji Minicherji Jamaspasa on the previous Farvardegan days, 1874; see Patel, II, pp. 336, 462, 504, 510, 589; III, p. 7).

Dastur Jamaspji was in close touch with Western scholars, like Martin Haug (1827-76, q.v.) and Lawrence Mills (1837-1918). He was a member of such scholarly associations as the German Oriental Society (as of 1884), the American Oriental Society at Baltimore (as of 1887; see Patel, III, p. 231), and the Italian Oriental Society (as of 1887). Moreover, he attended and read a paper ("A study of certain important Avestan words") at the International Congress of Orientalists held in London in 1883. In 1884 he was awarded an Honorary Doctorate by the University of Tübingen in Germany for his contribution to Pahlavi philology and for the generosity in sharing his rich collection of ancient manuscripts (Patel, III, p. 103). He was also awarded the honorary degree of D.C.L. (Doctor of Civil Law) by Oxford University in 1889. Since he had presented a manuscript of the Pahlavi translation of the *Yasna* dated 1323 C.E. to the Bodleian Library in Oxford, his portrait was installed in the Reading room of the Indian Institute at the Bodleian Library.

Dastur Jamaspji Minocherji JamaspAsa passed away in Bombay on 26 September 1898, at the age of 68, on account of illness resulting from kidney stones, as well as general debility (Dasturna, p. 277).

Bibliography: Selected works (more works are mentioned in the text). *Farhang i oîm yak/An Old Zand-Pahlavi Glossary*, Bombay, 1867; repr. Osnabrück, 1973. *Pahlavi, Gujarâti and English Dictionary*, 3 vols., London, 1877-82. *A Short Treatise on the Navjot Ceremony: Compiled into English from the Original Zoroastrian Scrotures . . .*, Bombay, 1887. *Pahlavi Texts*, ed. J. M. Jamasp-Asana and B. T. Anklesaria, 2 vols., Bombay, 1897-1913; repr. Tehran, 1969, 2 vols. in 1. *Arda Viraf Nameh: the Original Pahlavi Text*, Bombay, 1902.

Studies. Anonymous, *A Brief History of Anjuman Atash Bahram—Mumbai (1897-1996)*, n.p., n.d. Mehervanji BehramKamdin Dasturna, *Athornan Namu* (The Book of Priests), Bombay, 1923. S. P. Desai, *History of the Bombay Parsi Punchayet (1860-1960)*, Bombay, 1977. Bomanjee Byramjee Patel, *Parsee Prakash, Being a Record of Important Events in the Growth of the Parsee Community in Western India, Chronologically Arranged from the Date of their Immigration to India*, 3 vols., Bombay, 1888-1920.

The portrait of Jamaspji Minocherji JamaspAsa is taken after: Anonymous, *A Brief History of Anjuman Atash Bahram—Mumbai (1897-1996)*, n.p., n.d., p. 26.

(RAMIYAR P. KARANJIA and MICHAEL STAUSBERG)

JĀMĀSPI. See AYĀDGĀR I JĀMĀSPIG.

JĀMĀSP-NĀMA. See AYĀDGĀR I JĀMĀSPIG.

JĀMEʿ-E ʿABBĀSI, a Persian manual on *foruʿ al-feqh* (positive rules derived from the sources of legal knowledge) in Shiʿism written by the Safavid *šayk-al-Eslām* of Isfahan, Shaikh Bahāʾ-al-Din ʿĀmeli (d. 1621, q.v.), in response to a commission from Shah ʿAbbās I (q.v.; hence the title of the text). A key aspect of Safavid religious policy was the communication of the Shiʿite tradition in Persian to a population that was in the process of being converted. Before the Safavid period, Shiʿite sources in the religious sciences were almost exclusively written in Arabic and were available to scholars; *feqh* manuals in Arabic dominated, in particular *al-Nehāya fi mojarrad al-feqh wa'l-fatāwā* of Abu Jaʿfar Moḥammad Ṭusi (d. 1067) and *al-Qawāʿed* of Šams-al-Din Abu ʿAbd-Allāh Moḥammad ʿĀmeli known as al-Šahid al-Awwal (d. 1384). *Jāmeʿ-e ʿabbāsi* was the first Shiʿite manual written in Persian and established the shift to the use of the vernacular that has become more popular in the last two centuries (Modarressi, pp. 51, 85).

The *Jāmeʿ* was designed as a comprehensive and practicable text for the average believer, written in clear and simple Persian so that all the "slaves of the Commander of the faithful [i.e., ʿAli]," both elites and the common people, could understand the legal obligations and rules of their faith (*Jāmeʿ*, 1868, pp. 2-3). It played a key role in the development of a Persian Shiʿite law, ethics, and spirituality as it sought to cover issues beginning with ritual purity required in the performance of normative practices such as prayer, to discussions of blood money and vengeance in criminal law. ʿĀmeli had originally planned to write a text divided into twenty chapters (*bāb*), namely ritual purity, prayer (both compulsory and supererogatory), alms and religious dues, fasting, pilgrimage to Mecca, endowments, pilgrimage to shrines, vows and oaths, sale transactions, marriage, divorce, hunting, ritual slaughter, eating and drinking, justice system, wills and inheritance, funerary issues and rites, prescribed punishments in criminal law, and blood money and vengeance. By the time of his death in 1621, however, he had only completed the first five chapters on *ṭahārat* (ritual purity), *namāz* (compulsary prayer), *ḵoms* and *zakāt*, (religious dues and alms), *ruza*, (fasting), and *ḥajj* (pilgrimage to Mecca). At the same time, he wrote a series of Arabic treatises on the same topics called *Resāla eṯnā-ʿasriya fi feqh al-ṣalāt*. The text was thus completed, fulfilling the royal command, by his student Neẓām-al-Din b. Ḥosayn Sāvaji (*Jāmeʿ*, 1909, p. 93; Ṣefatgol, p. 182). The contents of the original chapters reflect the clear use of language and the articulation of an easy to understand set of terms as well as examples of ritual utterances and supplications required in the formulation of the ritual. Alongside these features, ʿĀmeli often included sayings of the Imams justifying and explaining the rules that were lacking on the whole from such *feqh* manuals. The result was a practical work of reference for believers, akin to the modern *resāla ʿamaliya*, and this is indeed how it was used into the Qajar period. Moḥammad-ʿAli Shah Qājār (r. 1907-09) commissioned a printing of it for this reason, as did the religious establishment in Avadh in India. One *mojtahed* in Lucknow, Sayyed Moḥmmad-Bāqer, even issued an epitome of the text as a manual in 1898 "practice according to whose rules was permissible and the source of reward in this life and the afterlife" (Reżawi, frontispiece).

Bibliography: Āqā Bozorg Ṭehrāni, *al-Ḏariʿa elā taṣānif al-šiʿa*, Tehran, 1968-, III, pp. 62-63. Bahāʾ-al-Din ʿĀmeli, *Jāmeʿ-e ʿabbāsi*, ed. Moḥammad-Hāsem, lithograph, Tehran, 1285/1868 (only 5 *bāb*s with tr. of *Ṣalāt* of Moḥammad-Bāqer Majlesi on the margin; ed. Jamāl-al-Din Eṣfahāni, Tehran, 1909. Hossein Modarresi, *An Introduction to Shīʿī Law: A Biobibliographical Study*, London, 1984. Moḥammad-Bāqer b. Abu'l-Ḥasan Reżawi, *Ḵolāṣa-ye Jāmeʿ-e ʿabbāsi*, Lucknow, 1898. Manṣur Ṣefatgol, *Sāḵtār-e nehād wa andiša-ye dini dar Irān-e ʿaṣr-e Ṣafawi*, Tehran, 2002.

(SAJJAD RIZVI)

JĀMEʿ AL-ḤEKĀYĀT (lit. Compiler of stories), one of the oldest and most common titles of mostly anonymous Persian story collections, dating from the 13th to the 19th century. Although various manuscripts of such collections have different titles, such as *Jāmeʿ al-masāʾel* and *Jāmeʿ al-ḥekāyāt* (Berlin, 1031; Pertsch, IV, p. 988), *Jāmeʿ at-takāyāt* (Blochet, Paris, Supp. Pers. 2039), *Majmʿ al-ḥekāyāt* (Dushanbe, Orientalistics 11.338; Dānešpažuh), *Majmuʿa-ye ḥekāyāt* (Dushanbe, Orientalistics 649), the title of most manuscripts is just *Jāmeʿ al-ḥekāyāt*.

Most of the comprising texts of *Jāmeʿ al-ḥekāyāt* are parables, a genre with a long tradition in the Persian literature, the record of which goes back to the Arsacids (*Draxt ī asūrik*) and Sasanid (*Baḵtiār-nāma*, *Sindbād-nāmag*) literature. For instance, one may mention "Ḥekāyat-e dur oftādan-e Bahrām Gōr az laškar . . ." (Ṣafā, 1984b, V/3, p. 1531) and the story about Bahrām and his vizier Rāst Rowšan, related by Ḵᵛāja Neẓām-al-Molk (pp. 31-41) as relatively recent narrations and transcript of two episodes from the adventures of Bahrām V Gōr (q.v.; Ṣafā, 1984b, V/3, pp. 1531-32). Some of the parables of *Jāmeʿ al-ḥekāyāt* in the manuscript D327 in Saint Petersburg (Akimushkin et al., I, p. 139) are so similar to the stories found in the *Marzbān-nāma* of Saʿd-al-Din Varāvini that it led Breshovskii to believe that this copy was another version of *Marzbān-nāma* (Akimushkin et al., I, p. 11).

The striking similarity of the title of *Jāmeʿ al-ḥekāyāt* with *Jawāmeʿ al-ḥekāyāt*, the shortened form of the *Jawāmeʿ al-ḥekāyāt wa lawāmeʿ al-rewāyāt* of Sadid-al-Din Moḥammad ʿAwfi (late 12th-early 13th cent. C.E.; q.v.), has caused *Jāmeʿ al-ḥekāyāt* to be overshadowed by the latter and to remain relatively unknown.

The most prominent characteristic of *Jāmeʿ al-ḥekāyāt* that singles it out among all Iranian books of this genre, is the extensive divergence of different manuscripts, to the point that one hardly finds two manuscripts of this title that consist of similar parables or have the same number of parables. This obvious variety of the content is due to the fact that various collections bearing the same title were compiled by authors at different times since the 13th century; the most recent collection was compiled in the 19th century.

ʿAwfi compiled his *Jawāmeʿ al-ḥekāyāt wa lawāmeʿ al-rewāyāt*, using a variety of sources including Abu ʿAli Moḥassen Tanuḵi's *al-Faraj baʿd al-šedda*, which he had translated into Persian (ʿAwfi, Moʿin's Intro., p. 34; Nafisi, I, pp. 97-98; Ṣafā, 1984b, V/3, p. 1028). The next author to translate Tanuḵi's book into Persian was Ḥosayn Asʿad Dahestāni, who carried out the translation during the years 1253-74 (ʿAwfi, Moʿin's Intro., p. 35) and called his book *Jāmeʿ al-ḥekāyāt fi tarjamat al-faraj baʿd al-sedda wa'l-żiqa* (Ṣafā, 1984b, III/2. p. 1236; Dahestāni, editor's intro., p. xiv). Of all the collections that were compiled after Dahestāni, forty-one manuscripts are known to exist in the libraries of Tashkent (11 MSS), Dushanbe (9 MSS), Saint Petersburg (4 MSS), Bibliothèque nationale de France in Paris and Ketāb-ḵāna-ye melli-e Malek (3 MSS each), India Office and Berlin

(2 MSS each), Āstān-e Qods in Mashad, Elāhiyāt in Mashad, Mar῾aši in Qom, Qāżi private collection in Tehran, Ganj-bakš in Pakistan, Ann Arbor in Michigan, and Bengal Asiatic Society in Calcutta (1 MS each).

The oldest manuscript of *Jāme῾ al-ḥekāyāt* is the manuscript A103 (902F; Akimushkin et al., I, p. 137) of the Russian Academy of Sciences in Saint Petersburg. It was evidently compiled some time during the reign of ῾Alā᾽-al-Din Moḥammad Shah, the Ḵalji ruler of Delhi (r. 1295-1316), to whom the book is dedicated. The youngest collection is apparently the manuscript kept at the Bibliothèque nationale de France, Supp. Pers. 2039 (Blochet, IV, pp. 374-78), which bears the date 1862 and also contains several stories in verse (for a sample of verses, see Ṣafā, 1984b, V/3, p. 1542).

Alongside the noticeable divergence that differentiates various manuscripts of *Jāme῾ al-ḥekāyāt*, one also finds some clear points of similarity and even connection. The most evident sign of the texts being related to each other is the common use of some parables (e.g., "Dorudgar wa julā wa doḵtar-e pādšāh-e ῾Ommān," "Shah Bahrām Gōr wa ῾āšeq šodan be Bānu Ḥosn doḵtar-e šāh-e pariān," "Māni-e naqqāš wa šāhzāda-ye Boḵārā," "Farroḵšāh wa Farroḵruz wa Farroḵnāz," "Šāhzāda Moslem wa Maleka Hezār-gisu," etc.; for the brief summaries of some stories, see Ṣafā, 1984b, V/3, pp. 1520 ff.). Some manuscripts also contain the stories of *Baḵtiār-nāma* attached to the end of the collection. In the view of Evagniĭ Eduardovich Berthels (q.v.), the purpose behind some of the late collections was to popularize the main tenets of the Shi῾ite doctrine in a way that would be accessible to common folks (Berthels, pp. 83-84, apud Cejpek, p. 681).

The number of parables varies in different manuscripts of *Jāme῾ al-ḥekāyāt*. The smallest volume in the India Office (India Office 798) contains only four parables and the largest one (India Office 797) fifty three (Ethé, I, pp. 524-26).

Unfortunately, most of *Jāme῾ al-ḥekāyāt* collections remain anonymous, as the first and last pages, which might have contained the compiler's name, are missing in many manuscripts, while some other manuscripts seem to have been compiled without recording any indication of the compiler's name. A number of compilers, however, have mentioned their own names, for instance Shaikh Moḥammad-῾Aẓim Baldāsi (Bibliothèque nationale, Paris, Supp. Pers. 907; Blochet, IV, pp. 84-85; Ṣafā, 1984b. V/3, pp. 1535-36) and Mašhadi ῾Abd-al-Raḥim Beg Me῾mār Širāzi in Manuscript 42 (Petermann 718) in Berlin (Pertsch, IV, pp. 94-95).

The *Jāme῾ al-ḥekāyāt* of Ketāb-ḵāna-ye melli-e Malek in Tehran (1044), apparently following suit the format of *Jawāme῾ al-ḥekāyāt wa lawāme῾ al-rewāyāt* of Moḥammad ῾Awfi, is divided into one hundred chapters, each one made of ten parables. This manuscript can be considered unique for the fact that it does not have any resemblance to the manuscripts of Saint Petersburg, Pakistan, or Mashad (Ḥojjati and Monzawi, p. 389). It consists of 998 parables written in *nasta῾liq* calligraphy (see CALIGRAPHY) on 414 sheets, which makes it an incomplete manuscript of *Jāme῾ al-ḥekāyāt* with the largest number of parables.

There exists three translations of *Jāme῾ al-ḥekāyāt* into Kāšḡari Turkish; the oldest one was done by Mollā Sanjar b. Ebrāhim Kāšḡari in 1849-50 and the most recent one by Ḥāji Yusof Safarbay in 1906-07 (Mughinuv, pp. 99-100).

The first edition of a *Jāme῾ al-ḥekāyāt* manuscript, in which the first and the last pages are missing, was published by Abu'l-Fażl Qāżi in 1976 as *Āvarda-and ke* (ed. Qāżi). Roxane Haag-Higuchi chose the manuscript of Āstān-e Qods as the subject of her thesis (Afšār, p. 748); her study and German translation of the text was published in 1984 (Haag-Higuchi, pp. 117-200). A selection of nine parables of the copy of Āstān-e Qods was edited and published as *Qeṣṣa-ye hezār-gisu* by Sayyed ῾Ali Rażawi Behābād in 2001.

Bibliography: Iraj Afšār, "Didār-i digar az seminār-e Ferāyburg," *Āyanda* 7/9-10, 1981, pp. 746-49. O. F. Akimushkin et al., *Persidskie i tadzhikskie rukopisi Instituta Narodov Azii AN SSSR* (Persian and Tajik manuscripts of the Institute of the peoples of Asia, USSR Academy of Sciences), 2 parts, Moscow, 1964. Sadid-al-Din Moḥammad ῾Awfi, *Jawāme῾ al-ḥekāyāt wa lawāme῾ al-rewāyāt*, 1st part, ed. Moḥammad Mo῾in, 2nd ed., Tehran, 1961. Evagniĭ Èduardovich Bertheles (Bertel's), Persidskaya 'lubochnaya' Literatura (The popular literature in Persian)," in *S. F. Ol'denburgu k pyatidesyatiletiyu nauchno-obshchestvennoĭ deyatel'nosti, 1882-1932* (To the fiftieth anniversary of scholarly and social activities of S. F. Ol'denburg, 1882-1932), St. Petersburg, 1934, pp. 83-94. Edgar Blochet, *Catalogue des Manuscrits Persans de la Bibliothèque nationale*, 4 vols., Paris 1905-34. J. Cejpek, "Iranian Folk-Literature," in Jan Rypka et al., *History of Iranian Literature*, ed. Karl Jahn, Dordrecht, 1968, pp. 680-81. Moḥammad-Taqi Dānešpajuh, "Nosḵahā-y ḵaṭṭi dar ketābḵānahā-ye Etteḥād-e Jamāhir-e Šawrawi," *Našriya-ye nosḵahā-ye ḵaṭṭi* 8-10, 1979, pp. 27-29, 1-47, 71-221, respectively. Hermann Ethé, *Catalogue of Persian Manuscripts in the Library of the India Office*, 2 vols., Oxford, 1903, I, pp. 524-27. Aḥmad Golčin-e Ma῾āni, *Fehrest-e kotob-e ḵaṭṭi-e ketāb-ḵāna-ye Āstān-e Qods-e Rażawi*, Mashad, VII 1970-, pp. 68-75. Roxane Haag-Higuchi, *Untersuchungen zu einer Sammlung Persischer Erzählungen, čihil wa-šiš ḥikāyat yā Ğāmi῾ al-ḥekāyāt*, Berlin, 1984. Moḥammad-Bāqer Ḥojjati and Aḥmad Monzawi, *Fehrest-e ketābhā-ye ḵaṭṭi-e ketāb-ḵāna-ye melli-e Malek, wābasta be Āstān-e Qods-e Rażawi*, Tehran, 1975. Aḥmad Monzawi, *Fehrest-e nosḵahā-ye ḵaṭṭi-e fārsi*, 6 vols. in 7, Tehran, 1969-74, V, pp. 3664-67. Idem, *Fehrestvāra-ye ketābhā-ye fārsi*, 3 vols, Tehran, 1995-97, pp. 304-5. A. M. Mughinuv, *Opisanie uĭgurskikh rukopiseĭ Instituta Narodov Azii* (Description of Uighur manuscripts of the Institute of the peoples of Asia), Moscow, 1962. Sa῾id Nafisi, *Tāriḵ-e naẓm o naṯr dar Irān wa dar zabān-e fārsi*, 2 vols., Tehran, 1965. Ḵᵛāja Abu ῾Ali Ḥasan Ḵᵛāja Neẓām-al-Molk Ṭusi, *Siar-al-moluk (Siāsat-nāma)*, ed. Hubert

Darke, Tehran, 1976. Wilhelm Pertsch, *Die Handschriften-Verzeichnisse der Königlichen Bibliothek zu Berlin* IV, Berlin, 1888, pp. 988-89. Abu'l-Fażl Qāżi, ed., *Āvarda-and ke: majmuʿ-ye dāstānhā-ye kohan-e irāni*, Tehran, 1976; 2nd ed., Tehran, 2000. Sayyed ʿAli Rażawi Behābādi, *Qeṣṣaye hezār-gisu*, Yazd, 2001. Ḏabiḥ-Allāh Ṣafā, *Ganjina-ye soḵan, pārsinevisān-e bozorg wa montaḵab-e āṯār-e ānān* I, 4th ed., Tehran, 1984a. Idem, *Tāriḵ-e adabiyāt dar Irān*, 5 vols. in 8, Tehran, 1984b, III/2, pp. 1234-36; V/3, pp. 1502-50. Saʿd-al-Din Varā-vini, *Marzbān-nāma*, ed. Moḥammad Qazvini, Leiden, 1909. Abu ʿAli Moḥassen Tanuḵi's *al-Faraj baʿd al-šedda*, tr. Ḥosayn b. Asʿad Dahestāni, tr., *Faraj baʿd az šeddat*, ed. Esmāʿil Ḥākemi, 2 vols., Tehran, 1976. D. G. Voronofsk, *Sobranie vostochnykh rukopiseĭ Akademii nauk Uzbekskoĭ SSR* (Collection of Oriental manuscripts of the Academy of science of the Uzbek SSr), Tashkent, VI, 1963, p. 366; VIII, 1967, p. 199; X, 1975, pp. 95-98; XI, 1987, pp. 232-36.

(DARIUSH KARGAR)

JĀMEʿ AL-ḤEKMATAYN. See NĀṢER-E ḴOSROW

JĀMEʿE MOFIDI. See forthcoming, online.

JĀMEʿ AL-ʿOLUM. See ENCYCLOPAEDIAS.

JĀMEʿ AL-TAMṮIL, a collection of Persian proverbs and their stories compiled in 1045/1644 by Moḥammad-ʿAli Ḥablarudi (variant readings Ḥilarudi, Jabalrudi). The only known biographical information about the author is that he apparently originated from Māzandarān, lived in Golkonda, and evidently was attached to the court of ʿAbd-Allāh Qoṭbšāh (r. 1626-83). The denomination Ḥablarudi is said to refer to the Ḥablarud, a river rising in the Firuzkuh mountain range in Māzandarān (Jaʿfari, pp. 199-201). As a mature man Ḥablarudi appears to have been attracted by contemporary Muslim Indian civilization, in which Persian was the language of court and literature. The author himself mentions that he compiled two books during the reign of ʿAbd-Allāh Qoṭbšāh while residing in the Deccan kingdom of Golkonda, situated in the vicinity of the South Indian city of Hyderabad. Ḥablarudi's first collection, *Majmaʿ al-amṯal*, was compiled in 1049/1639 (ed. Ṣādeq Kiā, Tehran, 1965). Being the first scholar ever to do so in Persian, he assembled as many proverbs as they became available to him and eventually compiled them in an alphabetically arranged collection, titled *Majmaʿ al-amṯāl*, listing some 2,100 proverbs.

Ḥablarudi himself must already have been aware of the fact that the task of mere documentation was only a first step, since many of the proverbs were hard to understand without explanation, and with the passing of time were likely to become altogether unintelligible. Accordingly, his next step was to elaborate and expand on his first work, adding many new proverbs and incidents or stories connected with their use. The ensuing work, titled *Jāmeʿ al-tamṯil* (or, less commonly, *Majmaʿ al-tamāṯil*) was compiled in 1644. Though *Jāmeʿ al-tamṯil* is, according to Ṣādeq Kiā's enthusiastic assessment, probably the most often printed book in the Persian language, no reliable modern prints or critical editions are available. Manuscripts of both of Ḥablarudi's works are numerous, the oldest one dating from the 17th century (Monzawi, V, pp. 3549 ff.), yet *Jāmeʿ al-tamṯil* still today is primarily available in the cheap and uncritical editions produced for bazaar bookstalls, sidewalk peddlers, and itinerant merchants (Shcheglova, no. 1491; Marzolph, 1994, no. XVII). The earliest printed edition, lithographed, and containing a total of thirty-three illustrations, dates from the year 1269/1852 (Marzolph, forthcoming).

In contrast to the additive technique of *Majmaʿ al-amṯāl*, the *Jāmeʿ al-tamṯil* does not simply add stories to the proverbs wherever feasible. Instead, it offers a choice of proverbs arranged alphabetically in twenty-eight chapters (*bāb*), while specific topics are dealt with more extensively in separate paragraphs (*faṣl*). These elaborations (on *boḵl* "stinginess," *tawakkol* "trust in God," *ṯawāb* "heavenly reward," etc.) stress the essential moral quality of Ḥablarudi's work, which is further underlined by the interpretations added to many stories, expressly reading "My dear friend, I have quoted this proverb in order to make you understand that . . . ." Within this framework, and somewhat reminiscent of the European catalogues of virtues and vices, Ḥablarudi quotes a large number of popular stories and folktales from such sources as *Barlaam and Josaphat* (q.v.; Pers. *Belawhar o Budāsaf*) and *Kalila wa Demna*. Other sources he expressly acknowledges include *Majmaʿ al-amṯāl* by Abu'l-Fażl Aḥmad Maydāni, *Rabiʿ al-abrār wa foṣuṣ al-aḵbār* by Abu'l-Qāsem Maḥmud Zamaḵšari, and the unidentified works *Baḥr al-saʿāda* and *Meftāḥ al-daʿawāt*. The link between a story and a specific proverb or proverbial expression is not always a close one. Often, and increasingly so towards the latter half of the book, the author quotes stories in connection with a certain range of proverbs or a specific moral theme. In this way, *Jāmeʿ al-tamṯil* not only constitutes a unique indigenous compilation inaugurating the field of Persian paremiology but also an important document for the international dissemination of popular tales.

Bibliography: Iraj Afšār, "*Jāmeʿ al-tamṯil*," *Āyanda* 5/1, 1979, pp. 132-33. Hermann Ethé, "Neupersische Literatur," in Wilhelm Geiger and Ernst Kuhn, eds., *Grundriss der iranischen Philologie*, 2 vols., Strassburg, 1896-1905, II, pp. 212-368, esp. p. 351. ʿAbbās Jaʿfari, *Gitā-šenāsi-e Irān* II: *Rudhā wa rud-nāmahā-ye Irān*, Tehran, 1997. Ulrich Marzolph, *Dāstānhā-ye širin: Fünzig persische Volksbüchlein aus der zweiten Hälfte des zwanzigsten Jahrhunderts*, Wiesbaden, 1994. Idem, "Illustrated Exemplary Tales: A Nineteenth Century Edition of the Classical Persian Proverb Collection *Jāmeʿ al-tamṯil*," *Proverbium* 16, 1999, pp. 167-91. Aḥmad Monzawi, *Fehrest-e noskahā-ye ḵaṭṭi-e fārsi*, 6 vols. in 7, Tehran, 1969. Ḵānbābā Mošār, *Fehrest-e ketābhā-ye čāpi-e fārsi az āḡāz tā āḵer-e sāl 1345 Š.*, 3 vols., Tehran,

1973, I, cols. 988-89. Ḏabiḥ-Allāh Ṣafā, *Tāriḵ-e adabiyāt dar Irān wa dar qalamrove-e zabān-e fārsi* V: az āḡāz-e sada-ye dahom tā miāna-ye sada-ye davāzdahom, Tehran, 1992, pp. 1497-498. Olimpiada P. Shcheglova, *Katalog litografirovannykh knig na persidskom jazyke v sobranii Leningradskogo otdeleniya Instituta vostokovedeniya AN SSSR*, 2 vols., Moscow 1975, II.

(ULRICH MARZOLPH)

JĀMEʿ AL-TAWĀRIḴ (The Compendium of chronicles), the historical work composed in the period 1300-10 by Ḵᵛāja Rašid-al-Din Fażl-Allāh Ṭabib Hamadāni, vizier to the Mongol Il-khans Ḡāzān (r. 1295-1304) and Öljeitü (Uljāytu; r. 1304-16), in response to commissions by both rulers. As its title suggests, the work is a compilation of materials not only on Islamic and Persian history, but also on the Mongols and other peoples with whom they came into contact: Turks, Franks, Jews, Chinese, and Indians, which has caused it to be called the "first world history" (Boyle, 1962, 1971b; Jahn, 1967; Morgan, 1982). This is indeed justified, given its coverage and reflecting its composition at one of the courts of what could equally be called the first world Empire.

Rašid-al-Din (ca. 1247-1318) entered Mongol service as a physician, but he came to prominence and power in 1298 with his appointment as co-vizier with Saʿd-al-Din Sāvaji. He remained joint vizier until his dismissal at the start of Abu Saʿid's reign, only to be coaxed out of retirement by Amir Čobān (q.v.) and ultimately to his death from the intrigues of his rivals (Melville, 1997, pp. 93-94). The details of his life have been fully studied elsewhere (e.g., ed. Quatremère, pp. i-xliv; Morgan, 1994; Amitai-Preiss; Rajabzāda, pp. 30-65), as has his Jewish background (Fischel, pp. 118-25; Netzer; ed. Rowšan and Musawi, Intro., pp. 73-81); one possible consequence of the latter may be that he was comfortable approaching Islamic history from a different perspective than was usual; this is certainly reflected in his work. It is perhaps also seen in his inclusion of a history of the Jews in the second volume (see below). He was a prolific author and wrote on many practical and theoretical subjects aside from the *Jāmeʿ al-tawāriḵ* (see, e.g., Jahn, 1964; van Ess; Allsen, 1996, pp. 14-15; Rajabzāda, pp. 302-25). Although several aspects of his life and background may have affected his historical writing, the most important factors are his intimate access to the two Mongol rulers, Ḡāzān and Öljeitü (Uljāytu), and his high position at the center of government. He also supported the work of other historians; in 1303, for example, he presented the historian Šaraf-al-Din ʿAbd-Allāh Waṣṣāf-e Ḥażrat and his work to Ḡāzān at ʿĀna on the Euphrates (Waṣṣāf, pp. 305-7), and inspired several later authors (see below).

While there is little reason to doubt Rašid-al-Din's overall authorship of the *Jāmeʿ al-tawāriḵ*, the work has generally been considered a collective effort, partly carried out by research assistants (Bira, pp. 96-97). The best evidence of this is the notorious claim by Abu'l-Qāsem Qāšāni that Rašid-al-Din had "stolen" his work (see Qāšāni, 1969, esp. pp. 54-55, 240-41; Zaryāb, pp. 134-35; Morgan, 1997, esp. pp. 182-83; Rajabzāda, pp. 351-53). The context of the final complaint is a story praising Öljeitü's generosity, none of which, however, benefited Qāšāni. The work in question is here called the *Ḏayl-e Jāmeʿ al-tawāriḵ*, and could therefore refer either to the second part of the chronicle, commissioned by Öljeitü, concerning Islamic history and the people of the world, or to the history of Öljeitü himself, which has not been recovered. In the first instance, it is worth recalling that Qāšāni did write a general history (entitled *Zobdat-al-tawāriḵ*) that covers much the same ground as Rašid-al-Din (Blochet, 1910, pp. 132-57). Secondly, Qāšāni's history of Öljeitü, as it stands, in the same format as the histories of the previous Il-khans, could resemble the drafts for those earlier reigns. It seems unlikely that Rašid-al-Din's version was ever completed; the copy reportedly sighted by Togan in Mashad turns out to be the text continued by Ḥāfeẓ-e Abru (q.v.; see Ṣayyād, pp. 279-80). As noted by A. H. Morton (in Ẓahir-al-Din Nišāpuri, Introd., pp. 25-27), there are other grounds for believing that Qāšāni's claims are not entirely baseless. Certainly, assistants were used, together with named collaborators and informants, for the sections outside Rašid-al-Din's area of knowledge, such as the Kashmiri monk Kamālashri for the life and teachings of Buddha (Jahn, 1956), and Chinese, Uighur, Qepčaq, and other scholars resident at court (on Rašid-al-Din's sources, see, e.g., idem, ed. Rowšan and Musawi, Intro., pp. 57-63). It was probably written, like the contemporary Chinese histories of the Chin and Liao, by a committee of historians, as part of an empire-wide project to record the early history of the dynasty (Allsen, 2001, pp. 95-101).

For the first part of the chronicle (see below), apart from the ruler himself, Rašid-al-Din acknowledges the crucial role played by the Yüan envoy in Iran, Bolad Ch'eng-hsiang, an unrivalled authority on the early history of the Mongols, in giving him access to the Mongols' own record of their history (ed. Rowšan and Musawi, pp. 35, 1338; Boyle, 1971a, p. 3; see also Allsen, 1996, p. 13, and idem, 2001, pp. 84-85, concerning Bolad's own use of assistants). Zeki Velidi Togan (1962, pp. 63-68) proposed that this "Mongol" part of the world history is little more than a Persian translation of a Mongolian original, an idea that has attracted both criticism and support (Morgan, 1997, pp. 183-84; Bira, p. 98). Rašid-al-Din's use of Mongol sources has been analyzed by John Andrew Boyle (1962, 1971a), Thomas Allsen (2001, pp. 88-91), and Shagdaryn Bira, and is revealed also by his use of the animal calendar (Melville, 1994). It is clear at least that much scattered material, both archival and orally transmitted by Bolad and including information found in the so-called *Altan debter* "Golden register" (see ed. Rowšan and Musawi, pp. 186, 227, 235) was combined with sources such as ʿAlāʾ-al-Din ʿAṭā-Malek Jovayni, (see, e.g., Minorsky, pp. 222-28, for his account of the Mongol conquests in Russia and the Caucasus) and Ebn al-Aṯir (q.v., to whom Rašid-al-Din himself refers; ed. Rowšan and Musawi, p. 306), to produce a narrative with a very distinctive idiom, terminology, and structure, quite unlike anything produced by previous Muslim historians.

Contents. *Jāmeʿ al-tawāriḵ* is divided into two volumes of unequal length, which prompted Edward G. Browne (1929-30, III, pp. 72-74) to propose a different scheme of contents. Rašid-al-Din's own structure, however, addresses two fundamental questions that correspond to the circumstances of the empire at the time of writing: who were these nomadic people who conquered the world, and what was that world? (Toynbee, X, pp. 75, 79). The set had also a third volume that was devoted to geography, but is not known to be extant.

Volume one. This volume, divided into five parts, has been published in a composite edition by Bahman Karimi and in a new complete edition by Rowšan and Musawi; a complete English translation by Wheeler M. Thackston (pp. vii-x) includes references to other partial editions and translations (for the Russ. publications, see Arends, pp. 42-43, 50-51; see also Rajabzāda, pp. 331-33, 358-60).

The first part is a history of the Mongolian and Turkic peoples and tribes (ed. Berezin, 1861; Russ. tr. idem, 1858; ed. Romaskevitz et al., 1965; Russ. tr. and commentary, Khetagurov and Semenov, 1952), followed first by the history of the Mongols before the rise of Čengiz Khan (q.v.; tr. Brezin, 1868; ed. idem, 1888) and then his times and life (ed. and Russ. tr. Berezin, 1888; Russ. tr. and commentary, Smirnova and Pankratov, 1952) in the next two parts. The final two parts are devoted to Čengiz Khan's successors from Ögedei to Temür Khagan (ed. Blochet, 1911; ed. Karimi, 1934; partial ed., ʿAlizāda, 1980, "Ögedei" only; Russ. tr. Verkhovskii, 1960; Eng. tr. Boyle, 1971) and the history of the Il-khans of Persia from Hülegü to the death of Ḡāzān (ed.ʿAlizāda, 1957; Russ. tr. Arends, 1946, 2nd ed. 1957; partial ed., with Fr. tr., Quatremère, 1836, "Hülegü" only; Jahn, 1940, "Ḡāzān;" Jahn, 1957, "Abaqa to Gayḵātu;" partial tr. Martinez, 1986-88, 1992-94).

Volume two. This volume, which has not yet been edited in its entirety (for mss., see Bibliography), was originally divided into two parts. The first part, on the history of of Öljeitü, is missing, and the second part is divided into a couple of sections, each one made of a number of subsections:

The second part starts with a preface on Adam, the Patriarchs, and the biblical prophets (uned.), followed by a history of pre-Islamic rulers in four subsections (uned.; mss. in John Rylands University Library, Manchester, no. 406; Punjab University Library, Lahore, ms. 94/25; Arabic version in Edinburgh University Library, Arabic ms. 20). The next section treats the Islamic history from the time of the Prophet Moḥammad and the caliphate (uned.; mss. at Tehran University, Faculty of Letters, ms. 76-b; Institute of Oriental Studies, St. Petersburg, E. 5; partly in Edinburgh, Arabic ms. 20; part in Khalili MSS 727, facs. ed. Sheila Blair, 1995) to the year 1258. This section also treats Persian independent dynasties, including the Ghaznavids and their predecessors (ed. Ateş, 1957, repr. Dabirsiāqi, 1959), the Saljuqs (ed. A. Ateş, 1960; Eng. tr. Luther, 2001), Ḵᵛārazmšāhs (uned.; mss. at Bibliothèque nationale, Suppl. persan 1364; British Library, Or. 1684; St. Petersburg, Institute of Oriental Studies, C. 374, fragment; partly in Edinburgh, Arabic ms. 20), the Salghurids (uned.; mss. at Bibliothèque nationale, Suppl. persan 1364; British Library, Or. 1684), and a Supplement on the Fatimids and Ismaʿilis, (ed. Dabirsiāqi, 1958; ed. Dānešpažuh and Modarresi Zanjāni).

The second section of this part is on the (other) people of the world encountered by the Mongols, including Oghuz Turks (Ger. tr. Jahn, 1969, with facs. illustrations; tr. Zeki Validi Togan, 1972; tr. Shukyurova; ed. Rowšan, 2005a), the Chinese (facs. ed. of Topkapı Saray, Istanbul, H. 1653 and Royal Asiatic Soc. ms. A.27 = Khalili MSS727, with Ger. tr. Jahn, 1971; ed. Wang Yidan, 2000; Rowšan, 2006), Jews (facs. ed. of Topkapı Saray, Istanbul, H. 1654, and Royal Asiatic Soc. A.27 = Khalili, MSS727, with Ger. tr., Jahn, 1973), Franks, their emperors, and popes (ed. and Fr. tr. Jahn, 1951; Pers. text, repr. Dabirsiāqi, 1960; facs. ed. of Topkapı Saray, Istanbul, H. 1654, H. 1653, and Sultan Ahmed III, no. 2935, with Ger. tr., Jahn, 1977; ed. M. Rowšan, 2005b), and Indians (facs. ed. of Royal Asiatic Soc. ms. A.27 = Khalili MSS727, British Library, Add. 7628, and Topkapı Saray, Istanbul, H. 1654, in Jahn, 1965; 2nd ed., with Ger. tr., Jahn, 1980; ed. Rowšan, 2005c).

Rašid-al-Din does not specify when his work began, though he seems to have been collecting material for some time before he was invited to compose his history. Ḥamd-Allāh Mostawfi appears to link the commission with Ḡāzān's calendar reform, initiating the Ḵāni era in 701/1302 and his desire to leave a good name in the world (*Ẓafar-nāma*, p. 1414; cf. Šams-al-Din Kāšāni, fol. 4r). Ḡāzān's stated aim was to preserve the Mongols' identity and knowledge of their past, but also to make it more widely known. Much material concerning the Mongols was until then secret and kept in archives that consisted of books and scrolls with no particular order and in danger of being forgotten (Rašid-al-Din, ed. Rowšan and Musawi, pp. 34-36; cf. Toynbee, X, pp. 75-78).

One reason for preserving this memory was certainly highly practical, and explains the strong emphasis not only on the tribal origins and genealogies of the leading Mongol families but also especially on the genealogy of the ruling dynasty. As the political unity of the empire dissolved and succession crises became more frequent, it was important to reaffirm not only the identity of the ruling clan (in its descent from the mythical Alan Qoa) but also its dynastic legitimacy. Detailed genealogical information runs like a strong thread through the core of the *Jāmeʿ al-tawāriḵ*, not only in the remarkably full accounts of the Turkish and Mongol tribes with which the work begins, but also appearing again at the outset of every reign: the principles of the organization of the work and its aims being explained again at the start of the section on the life of Čengiz Khan (ed. Rowšan and Musawi, p. 306). To these genealogical charts, incidentally, Rašid-al-Din also intended to add portraits of the rulers and their families, an element that has scarcely survived in the remaining manuscripts of his work (see below). In addition, a whole volume of genealogical information seems to have been conceived as an appendix to the work, in the *Šoʿāb-e panjgāna*, which still remains unedited (Topkapı Saray, Istanbul, ms. Ahmet III, 2937; see Togan, 1962, pp. 68-71; Quinn; Allsen, 2001, p. 92).

The *Jāmeʿ-al-tawāriḵ*, then, is an official history, but it is characterized by a matter-of-fact tone and a refreshing absence of sycophantic flattery, even in the sections on Ḡāzān Khan himself, though the description of his reign is the main goal and purpose of the work (ed. Rowšan and Musawi, pp. 30-31, 307). At one moment, Rašid-al-Din is moved to consider Ḡāzān to be a Muslim saint (*wali*; idem, p. 1317), but he is praised chiefly for bringing Islam to the Mongols and thereby revealing and accomplishing God's purpose in the career of Čengiz Khan and the destruction that he wrought. The narrative of historical events and anecdotes is lively and gains immediacy from many passages of direct speech and conversation (e.g. concerning the episode of Barāq, in the reign of Abaqa; ed. Rowšan and Musawi, pp. 1065-96). This, no doubt, reflects the important role of his oral sources of information, which in this case probably included the Amir Nowruz, who is specifically mentioned as an informant (ed. Rowšan and Musawi, p. 627). The organization of material does lead to some duplication (the story of Barāq is a case in point), and also some confusion in the histories of the rulers contemporary with the various Mongol khans; but, unlike the writings of Jovayni, his immediate predecessor, Rašid-al-Din's work has a strong structural coherence to which the author regularly draws attention, while, at the same time, never failing to provide short, helpful passages linking the various sections of the chronicle.

Rašid-al-Din is remarkably frank about the shortcomings of early Mongol rule in Persia, but he is seldom overtly judgmental, offering little by way of personal opinion and even less of the moralizing tone that was a conspicuous aspect of the work of earlier historians such as Jovayni. One rare exception is his verdict on the reign of Aḥmad Takudār, whom he characterizes simply as a ruler unable to deliver justice, using personal experience from the time when he was in the service of the Jovaynis in Baghdad to illustrate the point (tr. Thackston, pp. 559-60; omitted from the edition of Rowšan and Musawi). The *Jāmeʿ al-tawāriḵ* does, nevertheless, have something of the style of a mirror for princes in the final third section of each reign, in which the author relates the character and customs, good deeds and words of the ruler, starting with the *biligs* (adages or maxims) of Čengiz Khan and Ögedei (Ukatāy; ed. Rowšan and Musawi, pp. 581-91, 676-705, the latter lifted directly from Jovayni, pp. 161-91). This section is particularly prominent in its account of Ḡāzān, describing in detail the ruler's various reforms. This undoubtedly provides an idealized vision of the state that owes much to Rašid-al-Din's own initiative; nevertheless, he could not have written in the way he did without a very real respect for Ḡāzān's ability and character, and absolute confidence in his support.

Ḡāzān Khan's history, as the first part of the *Jāmeʿ al-tawāriḵ* is called, was not completed before Ḡāzān's death in 1304. His brother and successor Öljeitü ordered it to be finished in two further volumes: one including an account of his reign, to be compiled as it progressed, a general history of the (Muslim) world, and an account of the peoples with whom the Mongols came into contact; the other was to be a geography describing the different climes of the world and the routes linking them. Although Rašid-al-Din speaks of the latter as being completed (see also his reference to it in ed. Jahn, 1951, p. 11, tr. p. 24), no copy has yet been found. It is possible that elements of this were incorporated into the work of Ḥāfeẓ-e Abru (Rašid-al-Din, tr. Thackston, p. 11 n. 3), and more immediately into the geography of Ḥamd-Allāh Mostawfi (q.v.), though neither author refers specifically to this debt (see also ed. Rowšan and Musawi, Intro., p. 53; Allsen, 2001, pp. 103-4, 112-13).

Although most scholarly attention has focused on volume one, which is a fundamental source for the history of the rise and establishment of the Mongol Empire, from a historiographical point of view, the second volume is far more significant as the first attempt to write a universal history: an achievement not aspired to again in subsequent centuries (cf. Jahn, 1965, pp. ix-x). It attests to the remarkable global imperial vision of the Mongol rulers. Rašid-al-Din was aware of the unique quality of his work, referring to its unprecedented nature and as an assembly of all branches of history (ed. Rowšan and Musawi, pp. 8, 9, 14, 307; Barthold, pp. 44-49; Allsen, 2001, p. 83).

The general history of the world (in practice, the Muslim world) follows the pattern established by Qāżi Bayżāwi in his *Neẓām-al-tawāriḵ*, with sections on the prophets, the four dynasties of the pre-Islamic rulers of Persia, the prophet Moḥammad, and the Caliphs, and then the dynasties that flourished under the ʿAbbasids; it thus provides a similarly Perso-centric view of Islamic history (see Melville, 2000). Much of this remains unpublished and, until this is rectified, it is premature to offer remarks on Rašid-al-Din's use of his sources and the message that his history of the caliphate conveys. It is clear that the sections on the Ghaznavids and the Saljuqs made use of the work of Abu Naṣr ʿOtbi and Ẓahir-al-Din Nišāpuri respectively (for the latter, see Luther, 1971; Morton). The section on the Ismaʿilis is borrowed in large amount from Jovayni, but with the addition of new material; Rašid-al-Din's treatment of the sect is also much more objective than was the norm among Sunni historians (see Levy; Daftary, p. 95). Certainly, the language was also modified, especially that of ʿOtbi's translator, Jorfāḏaqāni, probably the version used by Rašid-al-Din (Šahidi, esp. pp. 186-91). Behind this part of the *Jāmeʿ al-tawāriḵ* lies the interesting historiographical question of the relationship between Rašid-al-Din and the *Zobdat al-tawāriḵ* of Qāšāni (cf. above), still to be thoroughly investigated (for the Ismaʿilis, see Qāšāni, 1987, which also provides the parallel passages in Ḥāfeẓ-e Abru).

The following sections, in contrast, contain much information that had previously not been available to Muslim scholarship. As in the first volume, Rašid-al-Din starts with a history of the Turks, thus vicariously linking the comparatively insignificant Mongols to the far more ancient and illustrious legends of the Oghuz (Turan); there is once more a concern with genealogies (tr. Jahn, 1969, pp. 44-47). This material derives entirely from oral sources. The recent history of China had also already been included in the first volume, but Rašid-al-Din now prepared a separate account of the Chinese, containing general information on the country and its customs, followed by the history and stories of the emperors of China, in annalistic form. Rašid-al-Din's own engagement with Chinese civilization continued, particularly in his *Tansuq-nāma*, chiefly concerning medicine (Jahn, 1970). Rašid-al-Din's Chinese informants, from the Buddhist tradition, are named but still not identified (see also, Franke, pp. 21-24; Menges).

As with China, Persia's long contacts with the West had not generated a real Muslim history of Europe. The impulse of empire building led to an expansion of knowledge here, too; political circumstances and Mongol religious tolerance were particularly favorable to the exchange of goods and cultural wares (Jahn, 1971, pp. 12-13; Allsen, 2001). In contrast with the case of China, however, volume one of the *Jāmeʿ-al-tawāriḵ* contains almost nothing of contemporary interest, such as the Mongol missions to the West, and there is only a single enigmatic reference to the Crusades; the section on the West in volume two stands in no sort of organic relationship with the work as a whole (Boyle, 1970, p. 63). The section on the Franks derives from conversations with unnamed clerics in Tabriz, including perhaps Isolo the Pisan (Nizami, p. 37). Its introductory descriptions of Europe's geography and politics concentrate on the Mediterranean countries, and emphasize the power of the king of France, third only to the Pope and the Holy Roman Emperor; there are also various interesting items of information (Jahn, 1971, pp. 19-20; Jackson, pp. 329-30). One example is the suggestion that the killing of the Christian community in Lucera was in response to the Muslim capture of Acre and the destruction of churches in Il-Khanid Iran (ed. Rowšan, 2005b, pp. 46, 122). The second part, on the history of the Popes and emperors, is based on the popular history by Martin of Troppau (d. 1278), and supplemented by a few extra legends and sagas (Jahn, 1951, pp. 8-10; idem, 1971, p. 21). It originally resembled a Western work not only in its contents, but also in its page layout and illustration (cf. Jahn, 1951, pp. 12-13).

As with the previous sections, Rašid-al-Din's history of India is in two parts, the first containing information about the geography, habits, and religious beliefs of the people, based largely on Abu Rayḥān Biruni's celebrated study. There follow chapters on the Sultans of Delhi, the rulers of Kashmir, and the four *yuga*s "ages" and the kings who reigned in them; this account contains the remarkable claim that Čengiz Khan was descended from one of the legendary dynasties of India (see Jahn, 1965, pp. lxxviii-lxxxvi; Nizami, p. 41; ed. Rowšan, 2005c, p. 100). The second part of book is on Buddha and his teachings, with a supplement on transmigration (*tanāsoḵ*); as noted, the main source of information was the Buḏdhist Lama from Kashmir, Kamālashri. Mongol interest in the subject is natural given the fact that this was the religion of Arḡun (q.v.) and his son Ḡāzān for a time, and the work might reflect the syncretist conceptions held by the Mongols in Iran (Jahn, 1956, pp. 83, 127); but there is also an attempt to fit Buddhism into the wider context of medieval religious thought and to approximate Buddhist to Muslim theological concepts (e.g., concerning angels, prophethood).

Rašid-al-Din made elaborate provisions for the preservation and transmission of his work. In an addendum to the endowment deed (*waqfiya*) for the quarter he established in Tabriz, the Rabʿ-e Rašidi, dated 1 Rabiʿ I, 709/9 August 1309, he stipulates that two copies of the *Jāmeʿ al-tawāriḵ* were to be made every year in the *ketāb-ḵāna*, one in Arabic and one in Persian, and distributed throughout the cities of the Arab world and Iran. His collected works were also to become part of the curriculum of the *madrasa*s he had founded. This addendum is dated Ḏu'l-ḥejja 713/April 1314 (see Rašid-al-Din, *Waqf-nāma*, pp. 237, 239, 241, 252; Afšār, pp. 12-13; Blair, 1995, pp. 14, 114-15; Blair, 1996; Hoffmann, p. 200, with further bibliography).

In view of these precautions, it is ironic that so few early manuscripts have survived. This is particularly unfortunate given the fact that they were intended to be illustrated, and the surviving examples are of crucial importance for the development of Persian manuscript painting: a departure as original as the nature of the text itself. The earliest surviving copy is part of an Arabic version, to be dated 714/1314, now preserved in Edinburgh University Library and the Khalili Collection, and must thus have been one of the first to be produced according to the stipulations of the author's endowment instructions. It comprises about half of part 2 of the second volume. Many of the illustrations show a strong influence of Chinese painting (see Blair, 1995, with full bibliography; Hillenbrand, pp. 145-50). The subjects chosen to illustrate the text are partly for pedagogical purposes and partly reflect current interests at the Il-khanid court (Blair, 1996, esp. pp. 51-53), a notion developed further by Abolala Soudavar, to suggest that illustrations in a contemporary copy of the *Šāh-nāma* were used to depict events recorded in the *Jāmeʿ al-tawāriḵ* rather than in Ferdowsi's work itself (Soudavar; cf. Grabar and Blair).

Later historians recognized that Rašid-al-Din stood apart from other Muslim universal historians, in style if not in intention (Ḵonji Eṣfahāni, p. 87, tr., p. 8), although his intention was also quite different from that of his predecessors; like Bayhaqi's work, Rašid-al-Din's work found no later emulators, though many admirers. Both Faḵr-al-Din Banākati and Ḥamd-Allāh Mostawfi acknowledged their very full use of the *Jāmeʿ al-tawāriḵ*, which was also put into verse by Kāšāni in the reign of Öljeitü (Banākati, p. 107, 338, 340; Blochet, 1910, pp. 94-106; Mortażawi, pp. 590-625; Paris ms. Supplément persan 1443), and summarized in the later 14th century (ms. St. Petersburg University Library, OP. 950B). The most important means of the transmission of the *Jāmeʿ al-tawāriḵ* was its absorption into the work of Ḥāfeẓ-e Abru, also a native of Hamadān (born in Ḵᵛāf, Khorasan, and raised in Hamadān; see Aḏkāʾi), giving rise to an extremely complicated textual tradition that, despite the painstaking work of Felix Tauer, has still not been entirely clarified. Ḥāfeẓ-e Abru's compilation reflects the fact that Ḡāzān and Öljeitü's universalist vision was shared by his patron, Šāhroḵ b. Timur, but it is nevertheless significant that Rašid-al-Din's work on the peoples of the world was merely reproduced, not updated. It is probably via the work of Ḥāfeẓ-e Abru that Rašid-al-Din's history was exploited by later Timurid universal historians, such as Mirḵᵛānd and Ḵᵛāndamir (qq.v.).

Edward G. Browne's assessment of the *Jāmeʿ al-tawāriḵ* (e.g., 1929-30, III, p. 75) is as valid now as a century ago and is echoed by all subsequent writers (for a thorough survey of early authorities, see Mortażawi, 1980, pp. 405-544). *Jāmeʿ al-tawāriḵ* presents a vast amount of data on East Asia and gave the Muslim world a quantum leap in their knowledge of the region and the wider world about them (Allsen, 2001, p. 85) at the unique moment in history when Persia was, with China, at the cultural heart of a great world empire. The passing of the moment once more restricted the intellectual horizons and vision of Persian historians. It thus remains all the more regrettable that there is still no complete critical edition of the whole text, a fundamental requirement for a full evaluation of the relationships between the *Jāmeʿ al-tawāriḵ* and the work of previous and subsequent historiographers.

Bibliography: Manuscripts. For the numerous cataloged manuscripts of the *Jāmeʿ-al-tawāriḵ*, see Storey I/1, pp. 71-78, supplemented by Bregel, I, pp. 301-20; Monzawi, VI, pp. 4133-35. Four of these manuscripts were produced in the author's lifetime (cf. Thackston, tr., pp. xii-xiii). Several excerpts from the illustrated Istanbul mss. H. 1653 and 1654, together with others, have been reproduced in the publications by Karl Jahn (Jahn, 1951, 1971, 1973, 1977, 1980); the fragment of the Arabic text in the Khalili Collection (MSS727) has been reproduced and studied by Sheila Blair.

Manuscripts of the second volume, which has not yet been edited in its entirety, are accessible for almost the whole text in Topkapı Saray, Istanbul, Hazine 1654 and 1653; Süleymaniye, Istanbul, Damad Ibrahim Paša 919; British Library, Add. 7628, and I. O. Islamic 3524 (Ethé, no. 2828); Bibliothèque nationale, Paris, Suppl. persan, 2004; and Reza Library, Rampur (see Bregel, p. 310).

Editions (arranged alphabetically by editor's name). ʿA. A. ʿAlizāda, II/2 (Ögedei), Moscow, 1980; III, ed., with Russ. tr. by A. K. Arends, Baku, 1957. Ahmed Ateş, as *Cāmiʿ al-tavārīh (Metin) II. Cild, 4: Cüz, Sultan Mahmud ve devrinin tarihi*, and *Cild, 5. Cüz, Selcuklular Tarihi*, Ankara, 1957-60; repr. 1999. I. N. Berezin, as "Sbornik letopiseĭ: Istoriya Mongolov, sochinenie Rashid ad-Dina . . . (Collection of Chronicles: History of the Mongols, work by Rašid-al-Din . . .)" *Trudy Vostochnogo Otdeleniia Imperatorskogo Russkogo Arkheologicheskogo Obshchestva* 5, 7, 13, 15, St. Petersburg, 1858, 1861, 1868, 1888. Egar Blochet, as *Djami el-Tévarikh/Histoire gènèrale du monde: Tarikh-i moubarek-i ghazani/Histoire des Mongols*, Leiden, 1911. Moḥammad Dabirsiāqi, *Faṣl-i az Jāmeʿ-al-tawāriḵ: tāriḵ-e ferqa-ye rafiqān wa Esmāʿiliān-e Alamut*, Tehran, 1958; repr. Tehran, 1987. Idem, ed., *Faṣl-i az Jāmeʿ-al-tawāriḵ (Tāriḵ-e Ğaznaviān wa Sāmāniān wa Āl-e Buya)*, Tehran, 1959. Idem, *Tāriḵ-e Afranj, yā faṣl-i az Jāmeʿ-al-tawāriḵ*, Tehran, 1960. Moḥammad-Taqi Dānešpažuh and Moḥammad Modarres Zanjāni, *Jāmeʿ-al-tawāriḵ, qesmat-e Esmāʿiliān wa Fāṭemiān wa Nezāriān wa dāʿiān wa rafiqān*, Tehran, 1960.

Karl Jahn, as *Geschichte Ġāzān-Ḫān's: taʾriḫ-i-mubārak-i-ġāzānī des Rašid al-Din Faḍlallāh*, London, 1940. Idem, as *Taʾriḫ-i mubārak-i ġāzāni des Rašid al-Din Faḍlallāh: Geschichte der Ilḫāne Abāġā bis Gaiḫātū (1265-1295)*, Prague, 1941; 2nd ed., Gravenhage, 1957. Idem, ed. and tr. with commentary as *Histoire universelle de Rašīd al-Dīn Fadl Allāh Abul-Khair* I: *Histoire des Francs*, Leiden, 1951. Idem, in *Rashīd al-Dīn's History of India: Collected Essays with Facsimiles and Indices*, The Hague, 1965. Idem, ed. and tr., *Die Chinageschichte des Rašīd ad-Dīn*, Vienna, 1971. Idem, ed. and tr., *Die Geschichte der Kinder Israels des Rašīd ad-Dīn*, Vienna, 1973. Idem, ed. and tr. as *Die Frankengeschichte des Rašīd ad-Dīn*, Vienna, 1977. Idem, ed. and tr. as *Die Indiengeschichte des Rašīd ad-Dīn*, Vienna, 1980. Bahman Karimi, *Tāriḵ-e pādšāhān-e Moğol az Uketāy Qāʾān tā Teymur Qāʾān*, Tehran, 1934. Idem, *Ferqa-ye Esmāʿiliān-e Alamut*, 2 vols., Tehran, 1959. Etienne M. Quatremère, ed. and tr. as *Raschid-Eldin: Histoire des Mongols de la Perse*, Paris, 1836, repr. Amsterdam, 1968 (probably the source of the anonymous *Extraits de l'histoire des Mongols de Raschid-eldin, Texte persan*, Paris, 1847). A. A. Romaskevitz, L.A. Khetagurov, and ʿA. A. ʿAlizāda, eds., Moscow, 1965; 2nd ed., Moscow, 1968. Moḥammad Rowšan, ed., *Tāriḵ-e Oğoz*, Tehran, 2005a. Idem, ed., *Tāriḵ-e Afranj, Pāpān wa Qayāṣera*, Tehran, 2005b. Idem, ed., *Tāriḵ-e Hendustān wa Kašmir*, Tehran, 2005c. Idem, ed., *Tāriḵ-e aqwām-e pādšāhān-e Ḵatāy*, Tehran, 2006. Moḥammad Rowšan and M. Musawi, eds., 4 vols., Tehran, 1994. Wang Yidan, ed., *Tārik-e Čīn*, Tehran, 2000.

Translations. John A. Boyle, as *The Successors of Genghis Khan*, 2 vols., New York, 1971. Karl Jahn, ed. and tr., 1951, 1965, 1971, 1973, 1977, 1980 (see above). Idem, as *Die Geschichte der Oguzen des Rašīd ad-Dīn*, Vienna, 1969. Kenneth A. Luther, as *The History of the Seljuq Turks from the Jamiʿ al-tawarikh: An Ilkhanid Adaptation of the Saljuq-nama of Zahir-al-Din Nishapuri*, ed. C. Edmund Bosworth, Richmond, 2001. A. P. Martinez, as "The Third Portion of the History of Gāzān Xan in Rašīdu'd-Dīn's Taʾrīx-e mobārak-e Gāzānī," *Archivum Eurasiae Medii Aevi* 6, 1986-88, pp. 129-242. Idem, "The Third Portion of the History of Gāzān Xan in Rašīdu'd-Dīn's Taʾrīx-e mobārak-e Gāzānī," *AEMA* 8, 1992-94, pp. 99-206. Etienne M. Quatremère, 1836 (see above). R. M. Shukyurova, as

Oguz-name, Baku, 1987. Wheeler M. Thackston, as *Rashiduddin Fazlullah's Jami^cu't-tawarikh, A Compendium of Chronicles: A History of the Mongols*, 3 vols., Cambridge, Mass., 1998-99. A. Zeki Velidi Togan, as *Oguz destan. Reşideddin Oguznâmesi, Tercüme ve Tahlili*, Istanbul, 1972.

Studies. Parviz Adḵāʾi, *Tāriḵnegārān-e Irān* I, Tehran, 1994. Iraj Afshar, "Autograph Copy of Rashīd-al-Dīn's Vaqfnāmeh," *CAJ* 14/1-3, 1970, pp. 5-13. Thomas T. Allsen, "Biography of a Cultural Broker: Bolad Ch'eng-Hsiang in China and Iran," in Julian Raby and Teresa Fitzherbert, eds., *The Court of the Ilkhans 1290-1340*, Oxford, 1996, pp. 7-22. Idem, *Culture and Conquest in Mongol Eurasia*, Cambridge, 2001. Reuven Amitai-Preiss, "New Material from the Mamluk Sources for the Biography of Rashid al-Din," in Julian Raby and Teresa Fitzherbert, eds., *The Court of the Ilkhans 1290-1340*, Oxford, 1996, pp. 23-37. A. K. Arends, "The Study of Rashīd ad-Dīn's Jāmi^cu't-Tawārīkh in the Soviet Union," *CAJ* 14/1-3, 1970, pp. 40-61. Faḵr-al-Din Dāwud Banākati, *Tāriḵ-e Banākati: Rawżat ule'l-albāb fi ma^crefat al-tawāriḵ wa'l-ansāb*, ed. Ja^cfar Še^cār, Tehran, 1969. Vasiliĭ V. Barthold, *Turkestan down to the Mongol Invasion*, ed. Clifford Edmund Bosworth, 4th ed., London, 1977. Širin Bayāni, "Barrasi-e awżāʿ-e ejtemāʾi-e Irān az ḵelāl Jāme^c al-tawāriḵ," in Sayyed Hossein Nasr et al., eds., *Majmu^ca-ye ḵaṭābahā-ye taḥqiqi dar bāra-ye Rašid-al-Din Fażl-Allāh Hamadāni*, Proceedings of the Colloquium on Rashid-al-Din Fadlallah, Tehran-Tabriz, 11-16 Abān 1348 (2-7 November 1969), Tehran, 1971, pp. 59-79. Shagdaryn Bira, *Mongolian Historical Writing from 1200 to 1700*, tr. John R. Kreuger, 2nd ed., rev. and updated by the author, Bellingham, 2002. Abu Rayḥān Biruni, *Ketāb taḥqiq mā le'l-Hend men maqula maqbula fi'l-^caql aw marḏula*, Hyderabad, 1958; tr. Eduard Sachau as *Albiruni's India*, 2 vols., London, 1888-1910. Sheila S. Blair, *A Compendium of Chronicles: Rashid al-Din's Illustrated History of the World*, London, 1995. Idem, "Patterns of Patronage and Production in Ilkhanid Iran: The Case of Rashid al-Din," in Julian Raby and Teresa Fitzherbert, eds., *The Court of the Ilkhans 1290-1340*, Oxford, 1996, pp. 39-62. Edgar Blochet, *Introduction à l'histoire des Mongols de Fadl Allah Rashid ed-Din*, Leiden, 1910. John A. Boyle, "Juvayni and Rashīd al-Dīn as Sources on the History of the Mongols," in Bernard Lewis and Peter M. Holt, eds., *Historians of the Middle East*, London, 1962, pp. 133-37. Idem, "Rashīd al-Dīn and the Franks," *CAJ* 14/1-3, 1970, pp. 62-67. Idem, "The Significance of the *Jāmi^c al-tawārīkh* as a Source on Mongol History," in Sayyed Hossein Nasr et al., eds., *Collected Works of Rashid-al-Din Fadlallah*, Proceedings of the Colloquium on Rashid-al-Din Fadlallah, Tehran-Tabriz, 11-16 Aban 1348 (2-7 November 1969), I, Tehran, 1971a, pp. 1-8. Idem, "Rashīd al-Dīn: the First World Historian," *Iran* 9, 1971b, pp. 19-26. Edward G. Browne, "Suggestions for a Complete Edition of the Jāmi'u't-tawārīkh of Rashīdu'd-Dīn Faḍlu'llāh," *JRAS*, January 1908, pp. 17-37. Idem, *Literary History of Persia*, 4 vols., Cambridge, 1929-30. Farhad Daftary, "Persian Historiography of the Early Nizārī Ismā^cīlīs," *Iran* 30, 1992, pp. 91-97. ^cAbbās Eqbāl, "Nosḵahā-ye moṣawwar-e *Jāme^c al-tawāriḵ*," *Yādgār* 2/3, 1945, pp. 33-42. Walter J. Fischel, *Jews in the Economic and Political Life of Mediaeval Islam*, London, 1937. H. Franke, "Some Sinological Remarks on Rashîd al-Dîn's History of China," *Oriens* 4, 1951, pp. 21-26.

Oleg Grabar and Sheila Blair, *Epic Images and Contemporary History: The Illustrations of the Great Mongol Shahnama*, Chicago and London, 1980. Ḥāfeẓ-e Abru, *Ḏayl-e Jāme^c al-tawāriḵ-e rašidi*, ed Ḵānbābā Bayāni, Tehran, 1971. Robert Hillenbrand, "The Arts of the Book in Ilkhanid Iran," in Linda Komaroff and Stefano Carboni, eds., *The Legacy of Genghis Khan: Courtly Art and Culture in Western Asia, 1256-1353*, New York, 2002, pp. 134-67. Birgitt Hoffmann, "The Gates of Piety and Charity: Rašīd al-Dīn Fadl Allāh as Founder of Pious Endowments," in Denise Aigle, ed., *L'Iran face à la domination mongole*, Tehran, 1997, pp. 189-202. Peter Jackson, *The Mongols and the West, 1221-1410*, Harlow, 2005. Karl Jahn, "Kamālashrī-Rashīd al-Dīn's 'Life and Teaching of Buddha: A Source for the Buddhism of the Mongol Period," *CAJ* 11/2, 1956, pp. 81-128; repr. in idem, *Rashīd al-Dīn's History of India*, The Hague, 1965, pp. xxxi-lxxvii. Idem, "The Still Missing Works of Rashīd al-Dīn," *CAJ* 9, 1964, pp. 113-22. Idem, "Rashīd al-Dīn as World Historian," in *Yádnáme-ye Jan Rypka: Collection of Articles on Persian and Tajik Literature*, Prague, 1967, pp. 79-87. Idem, "Some Ideas of Rashīd al-Dīn on Chinese Culture," *CAJ* 14/1-3, 1970, pp. 134-47 (printed as "Rashīd al-Dīn and Chinese Culture"). Idem, "Rashīd al-Dīn's Knowledge of Europe," in S. Hossein Nasr et al., ed., *Collected Works of Rashid-al-Din Fadlallah* I, Tehran, 1971, pp. 9-25. ^cAlāʾ-al-Din ^cAṭā-Malek Jovayni, *Tāriḵ-e jahāngošā*, ed. Moḥammad Qazvini, 3 vols., London, 1912-37. Šams-al-Din Kāšāni, *Chengiznāma*, ms. Bibliothèque nationale de France, Suppl. pers. 1443. Fażl-Allāh Ḵonji Eṣfahāni, *Tāriḵ-e ^cālamārā-ye amini*, ed. John E. Woods, London, 1992 (with Vladimir Minorsky's tr. rev. and enlarged). Reuben Levy, "An Account of the Ismā^cīlī Doctrines in the *Jāmi^c al-tawārīkh* of Rashīd al-Dīn Faḍlallāh," *JRAS*, 1930, pp. 509-36. Kenneth A. Luther, "The Saljuqnamah and the Jami^c al-tawarikh," in S. Hossein Nasr et al., eds., *Collected Works of Rashid-al-Din Fadlallah* I., Tehran, 1971, pp. 26-35.

Charles Melville, "The Chinese Uighur Animal Calendar in Persian Historiography of the Mongol period," *Iran* 32, 1994, pp. 83-98. Idem, "Abū Sa^cīd and the Revolt of the Amirs in 1319," in Denise Aigle, ed., *L'Iran face à la domination mongole*, Tehran, 1997, pp. 189-120. Idem, "From Adam to Abaqa: Qāḍi Baydāwī's Rearrangement of History," *Studia Iranica* 30, 2000, pp. 67-86. Karl H. Menges, "Rašīdu'd-Dīn on China," *JAOS* 95, 1975, pp. 95-98. Vladimir Minorsky, "Caucasia III: The Alan Capital Magas and the Mongol Campaigns," *BSO(A)S* 14, 1952, pp. 221-38. Aḥmad Monzawi, *Fehrest-e nosḵahā-ye ḵaṭṭi-e fārsi*, 6 vols., Tehran, 1969-74. D. O. Morgan, "Persian Historians of the Mongols," in idem, ed., *Medieval Historical Writing in the Christian and Islamic Worlds*, London, 1982, pp. 109-24. Idem, "Rashīd al-Dīn Ṭabīb," in *EI*² VIII, 1994, pp. 443-44. Idem, "Rašīd al-Dīn and Gazan Khan," in Denise Aigle, ed., *L'Iran face à la domination mongole*, Tehran, 1997, pp. 179-88. Manučehr Mortażawi, "*Jāmeʿ al-tawāriḵ* wa moʾallef-e wāqeʿi-e ān," *Naŝriya-ye Dāneškada-ye adabiyāt-e Tabriz* 13, 1961, pp. 31-92, 311-50, 516-26. Idem, *Masāʾel-e ʿaṣr-e Ilḵānān*, Tehran, 1980. Ḥamd-Allāh Mostawfi, *Ẓafar-nāma, ba enżemām-i Šāh-nāma-e . . . Ferdawsi* (as ed. by Mostawfi), facs. ed. Naṣr-Allāh Purjawādi and Noṣrat-Allāh Rastegār, 2 vols., Vienna and Tehran, 1999. Sayyed Hossein Nasr, et al., eds., *Collected Works of Rashid-al-Din Fadlallah*, Proceedings of the Colloquium on Rashid-al-Din Fadlallah, Tehran-Tabriz, 11-16 Aban 1348 (2-7 November 1969), I, Tehran, 1971. Amnon Netzer, "Rashīd al-Dīn and His Jewish Background," in Shaul Shaked and Amnon Netzer, eds., *Irano-Judaica: Studies Ralating to Jewish Contacts with Persian Culture throughout the Ages* 3, Jerusalem, 1994, pp. 118-26. K. A. Nizami, "Rashid al-Din Fazl Allah and India," in S. H. Nasr, et al., eds., *Collected Works of Rashid-al-Din Fadlallah* I, Tehran, 1971, pp. 36-53. Abu Naṣr ʿOtbi, *al-Taʾriḵ al-yamini*, ed. with commentaries A. Manini, 2 vols., Cairo, 1286/1869; tr. Abu'l-Šaraf Nāṣeḥ b. Ẓafar Jorfādaqāni as *Terjama-ye Tāriḵ-e yamini*, ed. Jaʿfar Šeʿār, Tehran, 1966.

Abu'l-Qāsem Qāšāni, *Tāriḵ-e Uljāytu*, ed. Mahin Hambly, Tehran, 1969. Idem, *Zobdat al-tawāriḵ, baḵš-e Fāṭemiān wa Nezāriān*, ed. Moḥammad-Taqi Dānešpažuh, Tehran, 1987. S. A. Quinn, "The *Muʿizz al-ansab* and the *Shuʿab-i Panjganah* as Sources for the Chaghatayid Period of History: A Comparative Analysis," *CAJ* 33, 1989, pp. 229-53. H. Rajabzāda, *Ḵᵛāja Rašid-al-Din Fażl-Allāh*, Tehran, 1998. Rašid-al-Din Fażl-Allāh, *Waqf-nāma-ye Rabʿ-e Rašidi*, ed. Mojtabā Minovi and Iraj Afšār, Tehran, 1976. Sayyed Jaʿfar Šahidi, "Sabk-e āṯār-e fārsi-e Ḵᵛāja Rašid-al-Din," in Sayyed Hossein Nasr et al., eds., *Majmuʿa-ye ḵaṭābahā-ye taḥqiqi dar bāra-ye Rašid-al-Din Fażl-Allāh Hamadāni*, Proceedings of the Colloquium on Rashid-al-Din Fadlallah, Tehran-Tabriz, 11-16 Abān 1348 (2-7 November 1969), Tehran, 1971, pp. 183-202. Foʾād ʿAbd-al-Moʿṭi Ṣayyād, *Moʾarreḵ al-Moḡul al-kabir Rašid al-Din Fażl-Allāh al-Hamaḏāni*, Cairo, 1967. Abolala Soudavar, "The Saga of Abu-Saʿid Bahādor Khān: The Abu-Saʿidnāmé," in Julian Raby and Teresa Fitzherbert, eds., *The Court of the Ilkhans 1290-1340*, Oxford, 1966, pp. 95-218. Charles A. Storey, *Persian Literature: A Bio-Bibliographical Survey*, 2 vols., London, 1972; tr. Yuri E. Bregel as *Persidskaya literatura . . .*, 3 vols., Moscow, 1972. Felix Tauer, "Ḥāfiẓ-i Abrū," in *EI*² III, pp. 57-58. A. Zeki Velidi Togan, "The Composition of the History of the Mongols by Rashīd al-Dīn," *CAJ* 7, 1962, pp. 60-72. Arnold J. Toynbee, *A Study of History*, 12 vols., London, 1934-61. Osman Turan, "Rashid üd-dîn et l'Histoire des Turcs," in S. Hossein Nasr et al., eds., *Collected Works of Rashid-al-Din Fadlallah* I, Tehran, 1971, pp. 68-80. Josef Van Ess, "Der Wesir und siene Gelehrten: Zu Inhalt und Entstehungsgeschichte der theologischen Schriften des Rasiduddin Fazlullāh (gest. 718/1318)," *AKM* 45/4, Wiesbaden, 1981. Šehāb-al-Din ʿAbd-Allāh Waṣṣāf Ḥażra, *Tajziat al-amṣār wa tazjiat al-aʿṣār*/ *Tāriḵ-e Waṣṣāf*, Bombay, 1269/1853; repr., Tehran, 1959; partial tr. with text by Josef von Hammer-Purgstall as *Geschichte Wassafs*, Vienna, 1856. Ẓahir-al-Din Nišāpuri, *The Saljūqnāma*, ed. A. H. Morton, London, 2005. ʿAbbās Zaryāb Ḵoʾi, "Seh nokta dar barā-ye Rašid al-Din Fażl-Allāh," in Sayyed Hossein Nasr et al., eds., *Majmuʿa-ye ḵaṭābahā-ye taḥqiqi dar bāra-ye Rašid-al-Din Fażl-Allāh Hamadāni*, Proceedings of the Colloquium on Rashid-al-Din Fadlallah, Tehran-Tabriz, 11-16 Abān 1348 (2-7 November 1969), Tehran, 1971, pp. 123-35.

(CHARLES MELVILLE)

JĀMEʿA. See ZIĀRAT-E JĀMEʿA.

JĀMEʿA-YE LISĀNSIAHĀ-YE DĀNEŠ-SARĀ-YE ʿĀLI, the Association of graduates of the Teacher Training College, founded on 28 Mehr 1311/21 Oct. 1932 by its first two graduating classes, at the suggestion of ʿIsā Ṣadiq, the dean of the Teachers Training College (see EDUCATION xix) at that time. It was originally known as Jāmeʿa-ye Lisānsiahā-ye Dār-al-Moʿallemin-e ʿāli, but, after the name Dār-al-Moʿallemin was changed to Dāneš-sarā, the association changed its name too. It chose a five-point star for its emblem, symbolizing the five fields of study offered at the college.

Moḥsen Ḥaddād and Mahdi Bayāni, two of the first alumni of the college, were elected the first and second president of the association, each one serving for two years. In the third election (1936), the general assembly elected Aḥmad Birašk, one of the second group of graduates, as its president. He was twice reelected in 1938 and 1940.

In the 1942 elections, Moḥsen Haštrūdi (q.v.), an alumnus of the college and professor of mathematics at Tehran University, was elected president. Haštrūdi was succeeded by Aḥmad Mehrān in 1944, who was also among the second group of mathematics graduates. The association pursued a cordial, cooperating relationship with the Ministry of Education, and on numerous occasions the association was consulted by the ministry on questions concerning education (e.g., drawing up regulations, devising procedural provisions, etc.). In the 1946 elections, Moḥammad Deraḵšeš was elected president of the association, In 1948, Deraḵšeš founded the weekly *Mehragān* as the organ of the association; it was banned twice by the government during its seven years of existence.

Derak̲šeš, who was more of a politician than a teacher, however, pursued a different policy, and a rift developed between the association and the Ministry of Education. The minister of education urged a few of the old graduates, such as Moḥsen Ḥaddād and Moḥammad-Mahdi Rādserešt, the first president and vice-president of the association, who were unhappy with Derak̲šeš's leadership, to undermine him by establishing a second such association. This was an unfortunate development, which would seriously damage the feeling of solidarity in the association and lead to factional discord among teachers. In an effort to remedy the situation, Birašk called on the two associations to unite and hold a new general election. Derak̲šeš welcomed the idea, but the second association did not agree to it and continued its separate existence as Jāmeʿa-ye Maʿrefat, after the name of its second president, Reżā Maʿrefat, while the first society came to be known as Jameʿa-ye Derak̲šeš. In order to centralize various activities of the members, Derak̲šeš established on 29 Bahman 1330/18 February 1952 a club called Bāšgāh-e Mehragān, which was rather a political club, and in practice he transformed the Association of Graduates into the Mehragān Club. Discord in the boards of directors of the two associations spread to other cities as well, and the teachers who were graduates of the Teacher Training College were divided into two rival factions, which hurt teachers' interests and also had a negative effect on education in general.

During the premiership of Jaʿfar Šarif Emāmi (Šahrivar 1339-Ordibehešt 1340/September 1960-May 1961), teachers went on strike at the request of the Mehragān Club, in protest against the low scale of their pay, which was among the lowest received by government employees. This led to confrontation with security forces and the death of a teacher by the name of K̲ān-ʿAli, who was shot by police during a demonstration in front of the parliament. Šarif Emāmi resigned (Ordibehešt 1340/May 1961) and the cabinet of the new premier, ʿAli Amini, included Derak̲šeš as the minister of education. In Tir 1341/July 1962, the Cabinet of Amini fell and Derak̲šeš left the political scene, but the Mehragān Club survived. In Mordād 1341/August 1962, the minister of education, and on his request the shah, proposed to Birašk, then the deputy minister of education, to organize a new association to replace the two existing ones, but Birašk refused on the grounds that it would be detrimental to teachers' interests and would only result in further discord among them.

In Bahman 1341/January 1963, in the course of the events that led to the so-called White Revolution (*Enqelāb-e safid*), the shah's power increased and in practice any sort of assembly not officially condoned was prohibited and condemned. Without being dissolved by the government or declaring their own dissolution, the two associations of graduates of the Teacher Training College gradually diminished and eventually disappeared.

Bibliography: Sāl-nāma-ye Dāneš-sarā-ye ʿāli (Yearbooks of Daneshsara-ye Ali), various years, and author recollections, who was directly involved in and had first-hand knowledge of the history of the Association throughout the years of its existence.

(AHMAD BIRASHK)

JĀMI, ʿABD-AL-RAḤMĀN NUR-AL-DIN b. Neẓām-al-Din Aḥmad-e Dašti, Persian poet, scholar, and Sufi of the 15th century (b. K̲arjerd-e Jām, November 7, 1414/d. Herat, November 9, 1492).

i. *Life and works.*
ii. *Jāmi and Sufism.*
iii. *Jāmi and Persian art.*

i. LIFE AND WORKS

LIFE

Though born in the hamlet of K̲arjerd, Jāmi would take his penname from the nearby village of Jām (lying about midway between Mashad and Herat), where he spent his childhood. Before coming to Khorasan sometime in the 14th century, the family resided in the Dašt district of Isfahan, with which Jāmi's father, Aḥmad Dašti, was still identified. In Jām, Aḥmad was a prominent member of the community, and his house was frequented by the learned and the pious. One of Jāmi's biographers, Neẓāmi Bāk̲arzi (p. 50), relates that the renowned Naqšbandi Shaikh K̲ᵛāja Moḥammad Pārsā stopped there on his way to Mecca, showing special favor to the five-year-old ʿAbd-al-Raḥmān. Though this story was probably invented to explain Jāmi's later spiritual affiliation, it does indicate that his father had the learning and wherewithal to provide Jāmi with his earliest education in Persian and Arabic letters. When Jāmi entered his teens, he and his father moved to Herat where he pursued further education in theology, Arabic grammar, and literature. Here the young Jāmi soon established himself as a brilliant, though somewhat arrogant young scholar, a reputation he consolidated in Samarqand (Samarkand), the principal center of learning in Khorasan in the first half of the 15th century (Māyel-Heravi, pp. 33-35). Jāmi continued his studies in Samarqand and Herat throughout his twenties, displaying a prodigious memory and powerful intellect in all fields of learning from Hadith study to astronomy and mathematics.

It was during this period of his life, according to Ṣafi Kāšefi (I, p. 238-39), that Jāmi fled Herat after an unsuccessful love affair and again sought refuge in scholarship in Samarqand. But no sooner had he arrived there than he saw the Naqšbandi Shaikh Saʿd-al-Din Kāšḡari in a dream; the shaikh instructed him to leave his studies, go back to Herat, and take up the Sufi path. Though we may question this explanation, Jāmi does seem to have gone through a spiritual crisis sometime in his thirties, and he did, in fact, return to Herat, give up his scholarly career, and embark upon the Sufi path under Saʿd-al-Din's direction. The close relations between the Naqšbandi order and the Timurid dynasty would decisively shape the rest of Jāmi's life. It was apparently at about this time and through the influence of Saʿd-al-Din that Jāmi was first introduced to the royal court; one of his earliest surviving works, *Ḥelya-ye ḥolal*, dates from 1452 and is dedicated to the Timurid ruler, Abu'l-Qāsem Bābor (q.v.). Jāmi maintained his affiliation with the court in Herat when the Timurid Abu Saʿid b. Moḥammad came to power in 1457, and he dedicated the first recension of his *divān* to this ruler in 1463. Abu Saʿid's religious advisor and spiritual counselor was, in turn, the Naqšbandi Shaikh Ḵᵛāja ʿObayd-Allāh Aḥrār (q.v.), and he and Jāmi would maintain a close and mutually beneficial relationship for most of the next three decades. Ḵᵛāja Aḥrār filled the spiritual void in Jāmi's life left by the death of Saʿd-al-Din in 1456, and Jāmi apparently lent Ḵᵛāja Aḥrār and his order a cultural and scholarly legitimacy while serving as its semi-official representative in Herat. Under the impact of meeting Ḵᵛāja Aḥrār, Jāmi began his first major poetic work, the first book of *Selselat al-ḏahab* ('The Chain of Gold'), and wrote the first of his Arabic commentaries (*Naqd al-noṣuṣ fi šarḥ naqš al-foṣuṣ*, 1459) on the works of the great Andalusian theosopher Ebn al-ʿArabi (q.v.), whose ideas played a central role in Naqšbandi teachings. Ḵᵛaja Aḥrār was active primarily in Transoxiana, and he and Jāmi did not have the face-to-face relationship typical of the Sufi master-disciple relationship, but Jāmi did travel north from Herat on several occasions to meet with Ḵᵛāja Aḥrār in Samarqand, Merv, and Tashkent.

When Sultan Ḥosayn Bāyqarā (q.v.) seized power in Herat in 1470, Jāmi was a respected teacher and spiritual leader in the city and had already established close ties with Sultan Ḥoseyn's powerful advisor and vizier, ʿAlišir Navāʾi. When Jāmi was setting out to go on pilgrimage to Mecca in 1472, he entrusted ʿAlišir with his personal affairs in his absence, and Sultan Ḥoseyn equipped Jāmi's entourage and provided him with letters of introduction to the local rulers he would encounter on his way (Bāḵarzi, pp. 160-64). Traveling west through Nishapur, Semnān, and Qazvin, Jāmi received a warm welcome from Shah Manučehr, the governor of Hamadān, to whom he dedicated his famous mystical treatise *Lawāyeḥ* ('Flashes,' see Māyel-Heravi, p. 44). From Hamadān, Jāmi proceeded to Baghdad, where he resided for some six months in 1472-73. When Jāmi went to visit the shrine city of Karbala, a disgruntled servant capitalized on verses from *Selselat al-ḏahab* that attack religious 'dissenters' (*rawāfeż*), to stir up the Shiʿite population of Baghdad against him. Jāmi was brought before a public assembly in the presence of local authorities to defend himself (Ṣafi Kāšefi, I, pp. 256-57). Although he was able to exculpate himself from the charges against him, his bitter feelings against the city and its populace are evident from a ghazal he wrote about this time (*Divān*, ed. Afsaḥzād, I, p. 778-79). Nevertheless, Jāmi stopped at the tomb-shrine of ʿAli b. Abi Ṭāleb in Najaf, and the poem memorializing his visit shows a devotion to the family of the Prophet that transcends sectarian differences (see *Divān*, ed. Afsaḥzād, I, pp. 54-56). After performing the rites of the *ḥajj* in May 1473, Jāmi began his return trip to Khorasan, stopping in Damascus and Aleppo. While in Aleppo, he received an invitation from the Ottoman Sultan Moḥammad II (Mehmet the Conqueror) to join his court in Istanbul. Not swayed by the money and gifts that accompanied this invitation, Jāmi moved quickly to avoid these golden shackles and headed to Tabriz and the court of Uzon Ḥasan. Although he was warmly welcomed by the Āq Qoyunlu ruler, Jāmi declined his invitation to remain in the city and finally arrived back in Herat in January 1474. In addition to its religious purposes, Jāmi's pilgrimage served to enhance his reputation and establish a network of political and scholarly connections that extended across the Persianate world.

Shortly after his return to Herat, an event took place that helped consolidate his standing with Sultan Ḥosayn and ʿAlišir. According to Bāḵarzi (pp. 196-98), the sons of Abu Saʿid in Transoxiana regarded Herat as part of their patrimony and planned a campaign against Sultan Ḥosayn. Despite the rumor that his mentor Ḵᵛāja Aḥrār had given his blessing to this campaign, Jāmi stood in defense of Sultan Ḥosayn. His position with the court was further strengthened when ʿAlišir joined the Naqšbandi order, with Jāmi as his spiritual director. For the last fifteen years of Jāmi's life, he, Sultan Ḥosayn, and ʿAlišir constituted a religious, military, and administrative 'triumvirate' governing Khorasan. Despite his status, wealth, and influence, Jāmi lived simply and unostentatiously in the district of Ḵiyābān-e Herāt, just outside of the city. Sometime after his return from the pilgrimage, he married the granddaughter of his first spiritual guide, Saʿd-al-Din Kāšḡari. Of the four children born of this marriage, only one survived infancy. Jāmi composed a strophic elegy on the death of his second child, Ṣafi-al-Din Moḥammad in 1475 (*Divān*, ed. Afsaḥzād, I, pp. 164-69). His third and surviving son, Żiyāʾ-al-Din Yusof, was born in 1477, and Jāmi would eventually write the *Bahārestān* (q.v.; 1487) and a treatise on Arabic grammar, *al-Fawāʾed al-żiyāʾiya* (1492), as manuals for his education. Although Jāmi often complains of the ills of old age (Afsaḥzād, p. 136), he made a final trip to Samarqand to visit Ḵᵛāja Aḥrār (Ṣafi Kāšefi, I, pp. 249-51) and, as will be seen below, entered his most productive period as a writer and scholar in the 1480s. Two years after mourning the death of his spiritual guide, Ḵᵛāja Aḥrār, in 1490 (*Divān*, ed. Ahsaḥzād, II, p. 454-59), Jāmi died after a brief illness on November 9, 1492. He was over eighty years old, and at the time he was the most renowned writer in the Persian-speaking world, receiving appreciation and payment for his works from as far away as India and Istanbul.

LITERARY WORKS

Jāmi's active career as a writer extended over almost fifty years, and he wrote a prolific amount of poetry and prose in both Persian and Arabic. He turned his hand at one time or another to every genre of Persian poetry and penned numerous treatises on a wide range of topics in the humanities and religious sciences. Wāleh of Daghestan (I, p. 487) and other later biographers have claimed that the number of Jāmi's works matches the numerical value of his name according to the *abjad* system, for a total of 54, but such a happy coincidence is no doubt too good to be true, and Sām Mirzā's list of 47 titles (pp. 144-46) is probably closer to the truth. Accurately ascertaining the extent of Jāmi's corpus, however, is made difficult by the sheer number of surviving manuscripts and the multiple titles by which some of his works are known. Aʿlāḵān Afsaḥzād provides the most reliable inventory to date (*Divān*, ed. Afsaḥzād, II, pp. 8-12; Afsaḥzād, pp. 154-241), and his findings provide the basis for the following account.

Poetic Works. In its final recension, prepared at the request of ʿAlišir Navāʾi in 1491, Jāmi's divān is divided into three separately titled sections: *Fāteḥat al-šabāb* ('Opening of Youth'), *Wāsiṭat al-ʿeqd* ('Middle of the Necklace'), and *Ḵātemat al-ḥayāt* ('The End of Life'). The titles and arrangement, however, are somewhat misleading. Containing more than 9,000 verses, the first section is longer than the other two sections combined. A prose introduction preserved in some manuscripts shows that Jāmi first compiled his (untitled) divān in 1463 and dedicated it to Sultan Abu Saʿid. Afsaḥzād argues (*Divān*, ed. Afsaḥzād, I, pp. 7-17) that Jāmi revised this divān in 1468 and again in 1475, when he added the poems that he had written on his pilgrimage; a final version of this divān was then completed in 1479, for which he wrote a new introduction dedicating the work to Sultan Ḥosayn Bāyqarā. Despite its title, then, *Fāteḥat al-šabāb* contains the lyric poetry that Jāmi wrote from the beginning of his writing career to his mid-60s, a period of some three decades. The bulk of the volume consists of some 1,000 *ḡazal*s, but it also includes poems in all the prevalent shorter forms: *qaṣida*, *tarjiʿ*- and *tarkib-band*, *qeṭʿa*, and *robāʿi*, as well as thirteen short *maṯnawi*s. In addition to poems on the sort of mystical and religious themes most associated with Jāmi, this divān also contains a number of panegyrics to various rulers, such as Abu Saʿid, Jahānšāh Qarā Qoyunlu, Sultan Yaʿqub, and Mehmet the Conqueror, thanking them for gifts or congratulating them on the completion of building projects. According to the datable occasional poems it contains, Jāmi's second divān, *Wāsiṭat al-ʿeqd*, was apparently compiled around 1489. Again consisting mostly of ghazals, it is half as long as its predecessor and less diverse formally and thematically; perhaps its best-known poem is the autobiographical qaṣida entitled *Rašḥ-e bāl be-šarḥ-e ḥāl* (*Divān*, ed. Afsaḥzād, II, pp. 35-39). Half as long again is the third divān, compiled a year or two later; in addition to ghazals, qeṭʿas and a few qaṣidas, it contains Jāmi's famous stanzaic elegy on the death of Ḵᵛāja Aḥrār.

Jāmi's seven long maṯnawis are known collectively as *Haft owrang (awrang)* ('The Seven Thrones' or 'The Constellation of the Great Bear'). The first of these maṯnawis, *Selselat al-ḏahab* ('The Chain of Gold'), is the most lengthy of the set and took the longest to compose. Although all three of its three books or *daftar*s are modeled after Sanāʾi's *Ḥadiqat al-ḥaqiqat* (q.v.), they might almost be considered independent works. The first *daftar* was written between 1468 and 1472, and it was verses from this work that caused Jāmi so much trouble in Baghdad. Like its model, the work treats a variety of ethical and didactic themes, illustrated by short anecdotes, and is notable for its critique of contemporary society. The second *daftar* of *Selselat al-ḏahab*, composed over a decade later in 1485, is of similar structure, but more unified in theme, dealing throughout with the varieties of carnal and spiritual love. The third *daftar* was written a year later and dedicated to the Ottoman Sultan Bāyazid II and serves as a short conclusion to the whole work.

The remaining six works of the *Haft owrang* were completed in an intensive creative outburst of little more than five years. *Salāmān o Absāl* was dedicated to another distant patron, Sultan Yaʿqub Āq Qoyunlu; the year of its composition is usually given as 1480, but Māyel-Heravi has argued for a date as late as 1484 (pp. 173-76). Based on an allegorical tale first alluded to in Avicenna's *al-Ešārāt wa'l-tanbihāt* and narrated in full in Naṣir-al-Din Ṭusi's commentary, *Salāmān o Absāl* tells the story of the misguided carnal love of the Greek prince Salāmān for his nurse Absāl, and the purification of his desires in a conflagration that consumes his lover (Dehghan, pp. 118-22). The work gained some renown outside Persia thanks to the English version by Edward FitzGerald (q.v.), the famous translator of ʿOmar Ḵayyām (London, 1856; see Arberry, 1956).

The year 1481 saw the composition of two maṯnawis similar in both title and structure. Written in response to Neẓāmi Ganjavi's *Maḵzan al-asrār* (and Amir Ḵosrow's *Maṭlaʿ al-anwār*), *Toḥfat al-aḥrār* ('Gift of the Free') contains twenty discourses (*maqāla*) on various religious and moral themes paired with illustrative anecdotes and, as its title suggests, was dedicated to Jāmi's spiritual guide, Ḵᵛāja Aḥrār. *Sobḥat al-abrār* ('Rosary of the Pious') is similarly divided into forty "knots" (*ʿaqd*), each of which is devoted to a principle of the Sufi way. The central work of the *Haft owrang*, it is written in a meter that has no precedent in the maṯnawi tradition.

In 1483, Jāmi again undertook a single continuous narrative in *Yusof o Zoleyḵā*, the most celebrated of his maṯnawis. It follows the meter of Neẓāmi's *Ḵosrow o Širin* (q.v. at *iranica.com*), but its story is based on the twelfth chapter of the Qurʾān, the story of Joseph (Yusof), narrating the passionate, unrequited love of Zoleyḵā (Potiphar's wife) for the prophet Joseph, but extending the story to the eventual union and death of the protagonists. As Browne (III, p. 531) notes, this work was translated several times into European languages in the 19th century. Like Neẓāmi and Amir Ḵosrow before him, Jāmi took up the famous Bedouin tale of *Leyli o Majnun* (q.v. at *iranica.com*) for the sixth volume in the *Haft owrang*, completing the work in 1484. Finally, a year later, after completing the last installments of *Selselat al-ḏahab*, Jāmi turned to the Alexander legend for the final volume of his heptad, *Ḵerad-nāma-ye Eskandari* ('The Alexandrian Book of Wisdom'). While this work adopts the heroic *motaqāreb* meter utilized by Neẓāmi in his *Eskandar-nāma*, Jāmi devotes relatively few verses to the story of Alexander's adventures and instead turns his attention to stories and teachings of the various philosophers and wise men whom Alexander encounters on his journeys.

Prose works. The nearly 39,000 lines of verse that make up Jāmi's poetic oeuvre already make him one of the most prolific poets in the classical tradition. But when one considers the thirty-plus prose works that survive from his pen, his literary productivity is truly staggering. Mention has already been made of the *Bahārestān* (q.v.), a work in mixed prose and verse in imitation of Saʿdi's *Golestān* that Jāmi ostensibly wrote for his son's education in 1487 (most recently ed. Afsaḥzād, Tehran, 2000).

Given his long affiliation with and high standing in the Naqšbandi order, it is not surprising that many of Jāmi's prose works are devoted to the practice and teaching of Sufism. One of the earliest and most famous of such works is the *Lawāyeḥ* (The Flashes), composed in 1465-66 and dedicated to the Qarā Qoyunlu ruler Jahānšāh. Modeled on Aḥmad Ḡazāli's *Sawāneḥ*, it consists of a series of mystical meditations in mixed prose and poetry. It has been edited several times in recent years (ed. Moḥammad Ḥosayn Tasbiḥi, Tehran, 1964; Yann Richard, Paris, 1982; and most recently Afsaḥzād in *Bahārestān*, pp. 445-81), and has been translated into both English (E. H. Winfield, London, 1928; William Chittick, in Sachiko Murata, *Chinese Gleams of Sufi Light*, Albany, 2000) and French (Yann Richard, Paris, 1982). Perhaps even more widely known is the large collection of Sufi hagiographies that Jāmi composed after returning from his pilgrimage to Mecca, *Nafaḥāt al-ons men ḥażarāt al-qods* (Breaths of intimacy from presences of sanctity). It was translated into Ottoman Turkish (Istanbul, 1872) shortly after its completion by Lameʿi Çelebi (d. 1532) and into Arabic a few decades later by Moḥammad b. Zakariyā b. Solṭān ʿAbšami (d. 1640) (Cairo, 1989). The Persian text appeared in numerous lithograph editions in India, and there are two modern print editions (ed. Mehdi Towḥidipur, Tehran, 1958; and ed. Maḥmud ʿĀbedi, Tehran, 1991). The unpublished *Jāmeʿ-e soḵanān-e Ḵᵛāja Pārsā* (date unknown, in Persian and Arabic) collects the sayings and sermons of the famous Naqšbandi shaikh, accompanied by Jāmi's own commentary. The practice of *ḏekr*, the communal recitation of pious formulas often ending in ecstatic transport, was a controversial doctrinal issue in Naqšbandi circles, and Jāmi treated the topic in his *Resāla-ye šarāyeṭ-e ḏekr* (date unknown; ed. Juyā Jahānbaḵš in *Bahārestān*, pp. 483-91); the work is also known as *Resāla-ye ṭariq-e Ḵᵛājagān* and was published under the title *Resāla-ye sar-rešta* in Kabul in 1963. Finally, the *Resāla fi'l-wojud* (in Arabic, date unknown) deals with the concept of the "unity of being," central to the teachings of Ebn al-ʿArabi and taken up by the Naqšbandi order.

Many of Jāmi's mystical writings take the form of commentaries on earlier works. Two commentaries on Ebn al-ʿArabi's magnum opus, *Foṣuṣ al-ḥekam*, mark the beginning and end of Jāmi's career. *Naqd al-noṣuṣ fi šarḥ-e Naqš al-foṣuṣ*, a commentary on Ebn al-ʿArabi's own abridgement of *Foṣuṣ al-ḥekam*, was written in 1458-59, around the time when Jāmi first came under the influence of Ḵᵛāja Aḥrār (ed. William Chittick, Tehran, 1977). In 1490-91 near the end of his life, Jāmi undertook an Arabic commentary on the full text of the *Foṣuṣ* entitled *Šarḥ Foṣuṣ al-ḥekam*, his last major mystical work (ed. ʿĀṣem Ebrāhim al-Kayyāli al-Ḥoseyni al-Šāḏeli al-Darqawi, Beirut, 2004). The Egyptian poet Ebn al-Fāreż was one of the earliest Arabic poets to give literary expression to the theosophy of Ebn al-ʿArabi, and Jāmi wrote commentaries on two of his most famous poems: *Šarḥ-e qaṣida-ye tāʾiya-ye Ebn Fāreż* (in *Bahārestān*, pp. 409-38), and *Lawāmeʿ fi šarḥ-e qaṣida-ye mimiya-ye ḵamriya-ye Fāreżiya* (ed. Ḥekmat Āl-āqā, Tehran, 1962; in *Bahārestān*, pp. 339-406). Both works apparently date from the 1470s. In Persian, Ebn al-ʿArabi's earliest poetic proponent was Faḵr-al-Din ʿErāqi (q.v.), and Jāmi wrote a commentary on his famous treatise *Lamaʿāt* in 1481, entitled *Ašaʿʿāt al-lamaʿāt* (ed. Ḥāmed Rabbāni in *Ganj-e ʿerfān*, Tehran, 1973). The first two verses of the *Maṯnawi-ye maʿnawi* of Mowlānā Rumi are the subject of a brief treatise entitled *Resāla-ye nāʾiya*, also known as *Ney-nāma* (in *Bahārestān*, pp. 325-36). *Šarḥ-e beyt-e Amir Ḵosrow*, as its title indicates, is a short treatise on a verse from one of Amir Ḵosrow's qaṣidas and interprets the Islamic profession of faith from the perspective of Ebn al-ʿArabi's teachings. Finally, Jāmi subjected his own poetry to an extensive mystical commentary in *Šarḥ-e robāʿiyāt*, a commentary on 46 of his own quatrains, which draws on numerous works of the school of Ebn al-ʿArabi and his Naqšbandi followers (ed. Najib Māyel-Heravi, Kabul, 1964).

Aside from his works on Sufism, Jāmi also wrote a number of works on more traditional topics of Islamic theology. *Šawāhed al-nobuwwa*, 'Witnesses of Prophethood,' was written at the request of ʿAlišir Navāʾi as a sequel to *Nafaḥāt al-ons*, extending the spiritual history of Islam back to the Prophet and his companions (for a summary of its contents, see Browne, III, p. 513). Commonly known as *al-Dorra al-fāḵera* ('The Splendid Pearl'), the epistle *Taḥqiq al-maḏāheb* was written in Arabic at the request of Mehmet the Conqueror around 1481. In it, Jāmi compares the perspectives of Sufis, theologians (*motakallemin*), and philosophers with regard to a number of key doctrinal issues. An edition of the text has been published by Nicholas Heer and ʿAli Musavi-Behbehāni (Tehran, 1979) and translated into both Italian (Martino Mario Moreno, Naples, 1981) and English (Nicholas Heer, Albany, 1979). Also dating from 1481 is *Čehel ḥadiṯ*, or *Arbaʿeyn ḥadiṯ*, a versified Persian translation of forty of the sayings of the Prophet (ed. Kāẓem Modir-Šānači, Mashad, 1984; in *Bahārestān*, pp. 311-23). Jāmi also wrote a guide to the pilgrimage during his journey to Mecca in 1473, entitled *Resāla-ye manāsek-e ḥajj*. A longer work on the same topic, reported by Lāri (p. 39), is lost. Finally, mention should be made of two very brief theological works *Šarḥ-e ḥadiṯ-e Abi Zarrin al-ʿAqili* and *Resāla-ye soʾāl o jawāb-e Hendustān*, as well as two uncompleted works: a *tafsir* on the Qurʾān and a commentary on *Meftāḥ al-ḡeyb* by Ṣadr-al-Din Qonyavi, an early student of Ebn al-ʿArabi.

In addition to his mystical and theological writings, Jāmi's oeuvre contains a variety of treatises on literary topics. He composed no less than four treatises on *moʿammā* ('riddles' or 'logogriphs'), which were the height of literary fashion in the 15th century (Losensky, pp. 154-60). The first and longest of these, *Ḥelya-ye ḥolal* (The Ornament of Ornaments) is Jāmi's earliest datable prose work. Also known as *Resāla-ye kabir dar moʿammā*, it sets out to clarify some of the obscure points in an earlier treatise on the topic by Šaraf-al-Din ʿAli Yazdi and was dedicated to the Timurid ruler Abu'l-Qāsem Bābor in 1452 (ed. Najib Māyel-Heravi, Mashad, 1982). The *Resāla-ye motawasseṭ dar moʿammā* explicates the logogriphs contained in a twelve-verse ghazal, which yield the name and titles of Sultan Ḥoseyn Bāyqarā. A summary of the *Ḥelya-ye ḥolal*, known as the *Resāla-ye ṣaḡir dar moʿammā*, was composed in 1480. Finally, *Resāla-ye aṣḡar-e manẓum dar moʿammā* summarizes the basic rules for deriving the solutions of riddles in 68 rhymed couplets. Apart from this specialized topic, Jāmi wrote treatises on the two most basic elements of classical Persian poetic form—the concise *Resāla-ye qāfiya* on rhyme and the more comprehensive *Resāla-ye ʿaruż* on prosody (in *Bahārestān*, pp. 223-85 and 289-303).

Jāmi's interests extended to other areas of scholarship as well. His *Resāla-ye musiqi* treats both the modal and rhythmic systems of traditional Persian music (*Bahārestān*, pp. 181-220; facsimile edition and Russian translation by A. N. Boldyref, Tashkent, 1960). As an aid to the education of his son Żiāʾ-al-Din, Jāmi composed a textbook on Arabic grammar entitled *Fawāʾed Żiyāʾiya fi šarḥ al-Kāfiya* in the last year of his life. As the title indicates, this is a commentary on Ebn Ḥājeb's *al-Kāfiya fi'l-naḥw*, and it continued to be used as a textbook through the 19th century; it soon accumulated its own set of commentaries and was perhaps the most frequently published of all of Jāmi's works with lithograph editions appearing in Istanbul, India, and Persia. Although less popular as a textbook, *Ṣarf-e Fārsi-ye manẓum va manṯur* seems to have been written as a companion piece to the *Fawāʾed* and deals with Arabic morphology in Persian prose and verse. Finally, Jāmi also prepared a collection of his letters and extensive correspondence (*Monšaʾāt*), which helps map his vast network of colleagues, friends, and patrons (*Nāma-hā va monšaʾāt-e Jāmi*, ed. A. Urunbaev and Asrār Rahmanof, Tehran, 1999).

JĀMI'S POETICS AND HIS LITERARY REPUTATION

Perhaps the most striking feature to emerge from even a cursory survey of Jāmi's vast oeuvre is its constant reference to the literary past. This is obviously true of his commentaries, but nearly all of his poetic writings too are modeled in one way or another on earlier works. The *Bahārestān* looks back to Saʿdi's *Golestān*, his maṯnawis revisit stories, themes, and structures first developed by Sanāʾi, Neẓāmi, and Amir Ḵosrow, and even his autobiographical qaṣida *Rašḥ-e bāl be-šarḥ-e ḥāl* takes its cue from a similar poem written by Kasāʾi some five centuries before. Jāmi's comprehensive knowledge of the earlier poetry and the traditional canons of criticism is also evident throughout the seventh chapter of *Bahārestān*, devoted to the lives of poets. Classical Persian poetry is, of course, defined by its conventions, and there are few works in the tradition that do not draw on earlier precedents to some extent. What distinguishes Jāmi's poetics, however, is the effort to codify and consolidate the entire literary tradition up to his time, a largely conservative project that might be best characterized as neo-classical. In his ghazals, for example, Jāmi responded repeatedly to poems by Saʿdi, Amir Ḵosrow, Kamāl of Khojand, and Ḥāfeẓ in the same rhyme and meter (Afsaḥzād, pp. 377-428). However, it is not the writing of response poems itself, but the way of writing them that distinguishes Jāmi's poetics. In general, his responses stick close to the theme of their model, regularize its structure, and elaborate on its images and topoi (Losensky, pp. 166-90).

Jāmi's vast neo-classical project was met with nearly universal acclaim during his lifetime. His works spread quickly throughout Persian speaking regions and were warmly received in Ottoman Turkey, where they were translated into Turkish and widely imitated. His life was celebrated in a series of biographies by his close friend ʿAlišir Navāʾi and his students ʿAbd-al-Ḡafur Lāri, ʿAbd-al-Wāseʿ Neẓāmi Bāḵarzi, and Faḵr-al-Din ʿAli Ṣafi Kāšefi. His profound impact on the literary scene of the Uzbek courts in Transoxiana is evidenced by the constant references to him throughout Wāṣefi's *Badāyeʿ al-waqāyeʿ*. The large numbers of high quality manuscripts of his works preserved in the libraries of Central Asia, Turkey, and India testify to his continuing popularity in these areas over the next several centuries (Māyel-Heravi, pp. 299-300). In Persia proper, however, profound changes in politics, religion, and literary taste cast a shadow over Jāmi's reputation. The rise of the Safavids and the propagation of state-sponsored Shiʿism in effect again subjected Jāmi to a trial of his religious affiliations, similar to the one that had taken place in Baghdad. Poets of the 'realist school' (*maktab-e woquʿ*) in the 16th century consciously turned away from the Sufistic symbology of Jāmi's lyric poetry, while their successors in the 'fresh style' (*šiva-ye tāza*) looked past Jāmi to the classical tradition itself to find sanction for their innovations in poetic diction and imagery. It is indicative of the indifference of the seventeenth century poets to Jāmi that among the hundreds of references to several dozen poets found in Ṣāʾeb's divan, Jāmi is mentioned only once.

However, toward the end of the 18th century, Persian poetry in Persia again entered a neo-classical period with the *bāzgašt* or 'return movement' (see BĀZGAŠT-E ADABI) and Jāmi's reputation rose accordingly. In the rejection of the stylistic norms of their immediate predecessors, Qajar critics dubbed Jāmi 'the seal of the poets' (*ḵātam al-šoʿarā*), the last great representative of a classical tradition that died along with him at the end of the 15th century. It is in this spirit that the modern literary historian Ḏabiḥ-Allāh Ṣafā writes that Jāmi "must be accounted the last truly great master of Persian poetry" (IV, p. 360). But only a couple of decades later an equally prominent literary critic, Moḥammad Reżā Šafiʿi Kadkani, would write: "Those who have termed Jāmi the last in the line of poets of the Persian language have been greatly mistaken;" whoever was responsible for this notion "was ignorant or ill-informed as far as direct contact with the course of [the] history of Persian poetry was concerned" (pp. 135-36). When Jāmi's reputation is judged in such terms it is impossible to reconcile the disagreement; for those ages and critics that place a high value on poetic experimentation and innovation, Jāmi makes a clear target for the attack on conservative complacency. On the other hand, to use Jāmi's accomplishments to condemn all the poetry written after him is no less a distortion of his work and his place in literary history. Any balanced evaluation of Jāmi's legacy must recognize his goals and aims as a neo-classicist. He was a prodigious and prolific talent with a vast knowledge of earlier tradition who devoted his energies throughout his long life, not to blazing new directions in the tradition, but to consolidating what had already been achieved. His success in doing so provided a solid basis for later innovations of the poets of the 'fresh style' and even for the modern study of classical Persian literature. Jāmi placed a high premium on the formal qualities of poetry, fluency and elegance of diction, and immediate comprehensibility. At the same time, he rarely goes beyond a stock treatment of the standard images and metaphors of the tradition, and his works sometimes seem a comprehensive digest of literary convention. In retrospect, it appears that his reputation as a master poet during his lifetime owed much to his scholarship and political position. In his works, however, one does find perhaps the fullest summation of the long history of the integration of the Sufi theosophy of Ebn al-ʿArabi with the Persian literary tradition, and it is here that his vast erudition is seen to its best advantage.

Bibliography: Poetic works. Over 130 manuscripts of Jāmi's divān are listed in Monzawi, *Nosḵahā* (III, pp. 2264-70), a list that does not include most of the copies kept in libraries across the former Soviet Union. Given the number of manuscripts and their wide dispersal, it is not surprising that a fully comprehensive critical edition has yet to be published. There are three modern editions of Jāmi's divān. The editions of Ḥ. Pežmān (Tehran, 1955) and Hāšem Reżā (Tehran, 1962) are based on manuscripts of a relatively late date and make little effort to list variant readings; Reżā's edition also completely rearranges the original tripartite organization of the divān. The most reliable edition is that of Aʿlāḵān Afsaḥzād, based on nine of the oldest surviving manuscripts. Originally published in Moscow, 1978 (*Fātehat al-šabāb*) and 1980 (*Wāseṭat al-ʿeqd* and *Ḵātemat al-ḥayāt*), it was thoroughly revised and reissued in 2 volumes in Tehran (1999). The textual history of the maṯnawis contained in *Haft owrang* is perhaps even more complicated. In addition to 70 manuscripts of the entire collection (Monzawi, *Nosḵahā*, IV, pp. 3312-16), numerous independent copies exist of each maṯnawi. Monzawi (*Nosḵahā*, IV, pp. 3331-40) inventories over two hundred manuscripts of *Yusof o Zoleyḵā* alone. The older edition of Mortażā Modarres-Gilāni (Tehran, 1982) can now be set aside in favor of an edition prepared by a group of Tajik scholars under the direction of Aʿlāḵān Afsaḥzād (2 vols., Tehran, 1999). This edition, too, is a revised reprint of editions previously published in Moscow. Recent critical editions also exist for a number of individual maṯnawis, such as *Yusof o Zoleyḵā* (ed. Nāṣer Nikubaḵt, Tehran, 1998) and *Salāmān o Absāl* (ed. Zahrā Mohājeri, Tehran, 1997). Editions of Jāmi's prose works are given in the text, but special note should be made of the recent publication of *Bahārestān va rasāʾel-e Jāmi*, ed. Aʿlāḵān Afsaḥzād, et al., Tehran, 2000, which includes the work of a number of Tajik and Soviet scholars.

Secondary sources. Aʿlāḵān Afsaḥzād, *Naqd va barrasi-ye āṯār va šarḥ-e aḥwāl-e Jāmi*, Tehran, 1999. A. J. Arberry, *FitzGerald's Salaman and Absal: A Study*, Cambridge, 1956. ʿAbd-al-Wāseʿ Neẓāmi Bāḵarzi, *Maqāmāt-e Jāmi*, ed. Najib Māyel-Heravi, Tehran, 1992. E. G. Browne, *Lit. Hist. Persia*, III, pp. 507-48. J. T. P. de Bruijn, "Chain of gold: Jāmī's defence of poetry," *Journal of Turkish Studies* 26/1, 2002, pp. 81-92. J. C. Bürgel, "Ǧāmī's epic poem on Alexander the Great: an introduction," *Oriente Moderno* 15/76, 1996, pp. 415-38. Iraj Dehghan, "Jāmī's Salāmān and Absāl," *JNES* 30/2, 1971, pp. 118-26. Dawlatšāh Samarqandi, *Taḏkerat al-šoʿarāʾ*, ed. Moḥammad Ramażāni, Tehran, 1958, pp. 245-48. Ch.-H. de Fouchécour, "Djâmi, conseiller des princes, ou Le Livre de la Sagesse Alexandrine," *Kâr-Nâmeh* 5, 1999, pp. 11-32. ʿAli-ʿAṣḡar Ḥekmat, *Jāmi: motażammen-e taḥqiqāt dar tāriḵ-e aḥwāl wa āṯār-e manẓum va manṯur-e ḵātam al-šoʿarā*, Tehran, 1941. Cl. Huart, "Djamī," in EI^2 vol. II, pp. 421-22 (rev. H. Massé). "Jāmi" in *Dānešnāma-ye adab-e Fārsi*, ed. Ḥasan Anuša, Tehran, 1999, III, pp. 272-74. ʿAbd-al-Ḡafur Lāri, *Takmela-ye ḥawāši-e Nafaḥāt al-ons: šarḥ-e ḥāl-e Mawlānā Jāmi*, ed. ʿAli-Aṣḡar Bašir-Heravi, Kabul, 1964. Paul Losensky, *Welcoming Fighānī: Imitation and Poetic Individuality in the Safavid-Mughal Ghazal*, Costa Mesa, Calif., 1998. Najib Māyel-Heravi, *Sheyḵ ʿAbd-al-Raḥmān Jāmi*, Tehran, 1998. ʿAlišir Navāʾi, *Ḵamsat al-motaḥayyirin*, trans. (from Chaghatay into Persian) Moḥammad Naḵjavān, ed. Mehdi Farhāni-Monfared, *Nāma-ye Farhangestān*, supplement 12, 2002. F. Richard, "Un cas de 'succès littéraire:' la diffusion des œuvres poétiques de Djâmî de Hérât à travers tout le Proche-Orient," in Idem, *Le livre persan*, Paris, 2003, pp. 61-77. J. Rypka, *Hist. Iran. Lit.*, pp. 286-88. Ṣafā, *Tāriḵ-e adabiyāt*, IV, pp. 347-68. Faḵr-al-Din ʿAli b. Ḥoseyn Ṣafi Kāšefi, *Rašaḥāt-e ʿeyn al-ḥayāt*, ed. ʿAli-Aṣḡar Moʿiniyān, 2 vols., Tehran, 1977. Sām Mirzā, *Tohfa-ye Sāmi*, ed. Rokn-al-Din Homāyun-farroḵ, Tehran, 2005, pp. 143-52. Moḥammad-Reżā Šafiʿi-Kadkani, "Persian Literature (Belles-Lettres) from the Time of Jāmi to the Present Day," in *Handbuch der Orientalistik*, IV/2, fasc. 2, *History of Persian Literature from the beginning of the Islamic Period to the Present Day*, ed.

George Morrison, pp. 135-206, Leiden, 1981. ʿAliqoli Wāleh of Daghestan, *Tad̲kera-ye Riyāż al-šoʿarā*, ed. Sayyed Moḥsen Nāji Naṣrābādi, 5 vols., Tehran, 2005. Zeyn-al-Din Maḥmud Wāṣefi, *Badāyeʿ al-waqāyeʿ*, ed. Alexander Boldyrev, 2 vols., 2nd ed., Tehran, 1970.

(PAUL LOSENSKY)

ii. AND SUFISM

Among the several facets of Jāmi's persona and career—Sufi, scholar, poet, associate of rulers—it may be permissible to award primacy to the first mentioned. This would certainly correspond to Jāmi's own view and to that of one of his closest disciples, ʿAbd-al-Ḡafur Lāri: both the practice of scholarship and the composition of poetry served for Jāmi, Lāri reports, as veils for his inward state, as guarantors for the concealment of spiritual absorption that is mandated by the Naqšbandiya (Lāri, p. 3, 9; Bāḵarzi, p. 125). As for Jāmi's dealings with rulers in Herat and elsewhere, they generally consisted of interventions on behalf of petitioners seeking the redress of grievances or the remission of taxes (Urunbayev and Epifanova, pp. 156-59), consonant with the practice of his friend and fellow Naqšbandi, Ḵʷāja ʿObayd-Allāh Aḥrār (d. 1490; see further below). It must also be said, however, that Jāmi was by no means averse to receiving of costly gifts from the powerful.

Jāmi's affiliation to the Naqšbandiya, an order swiftly rising to prominence at the time in both Transoxiana and Khorasan, was central to his understanding and practice of Sufism. His association with the order began when he was still a child: when Ḵʷāja Moḥammad Pārsā (d. 1419), one of the principal associates of its eponym, Ḵʷāja Moḥammad Bahāʾ-al-Din Naqšband (q.v.; d. 1389), was passing through Herat in 1419 en route to the Hajj; Jāmi's father had hoisted him onto his shoulders to receive Pārsā's blessing. Recalling the event in later years, Jāmi affirmed that this encounter had already linked him indissolubly to the Naqšbandiya (Kāšefi, I, p. 242; Jāmi, *Nafaḥāt*, pp. 397-98). The linkage became manifest when Jāmi joined the following of Saʿd-al-Din Kāšḡari (d. 1456), who was joined to Bahāʾ-al-Din Naqšband by two generations in the initiatic chain. Jāmi had with difficulty extricated himself from an amorous attachment in Herat in order to follow a course of study in Samarqand, and one night, when tormented by the pangs of separation, he dreamt of Kāšḡari who instructed him to take God as his beloved and as the one indispensable (*nāgozir*) companion. Hastening back to Herat, he submitted himself to Kāšḡari with immediate and permanent transformative effect. This was an outcome Kāšḡari himself had long desired. It was his wont to hold forth in the Masjed-e Jāmeʿ of Herat before and after each of the five daily prayers, and whenever Jāmi passed by, before his departure for Samarqand, he would remark to his followers: "This is a young man of remarkable talent; I am enchanted by him, and know not how to ensnare him." After Jāmi's return, he proclaimed with satisfaction: "Now a royal falcon has fallen into my trap; God has granted me a favor with the company of this young man" (Kāšefi, I, pp. 239-40). The tie thus forged between the two men was soon palpably fortified by Jāmi's marriage to a granddaughter of Kāšḡari.

Jāmi initially submitted himself, however, to austerities of separation from the world so extreme that on his re-emergence he had temporarily forgotten the niceties and forms of social intercourse. This retreat was intended to serve as a purgative measure, and did not represent a permanent choice; fully in accord with the Naqšbandi principle of *ḵalvat dar anjoman* ("solitude within society"), Jāmi soon resumed involvement in a broad range of social, intellectual and even political activities, in Herat and beyond. Indeed, while confessing to his own predilection for solitude, he frequently expressed his disdain for those who, under the pretext of piety, sought isolation from their fellows (Bāḵarzi, p. 226). Neither did Jāmi's Sufi initiation bring to an end his endeavors in formal scholarship, the sphere in which he had displayed precocious brilliance in both Herat and Samarqand (nor, it seems, did it free him from the arrogance that frequently accompanies unusual scholarly attainment). This did not necessarily imply a contradiction, for as Kāšefi reports, there were many who believed that "engagement with the path of the Ḵʷājagān [the Naqšbandi masters and their immediate predecessors in Transoxiana] reinforces the powers of intellectual and rational perception" (Kāšefi, I, p. 237; one of his early teachers in Herat, Šahāb-al-Din Moḥammad Jājarmi, nonetheless expressed dissatisfaction with his recourse to Kāšḡari; Kāšefi, I, p. 240). Also in full conformity with Naqšbandi precepts was Jāmi's disdain for miraculous visions and feats (*karāmāt*); the only such feat worth aspiring to was, he said, to experience a state of intense awareness of God (*jad̲ba*) in the company of one blessed by Him (Kāšefi, I, p. 240). In one respect, however, Jāmi seems to have dissented from Naqšbandi norms, for he did not advocate exclusive recourse to the silent *d̲ekr* that had been normative for the order ever since the time of its eponym. He even discerned in vocal *d̲ekr* qualities lacking in its silent counterpart, embracing as it does in cyclical fashion the faculties of the imagination (*motaḵayyela*), speech, hearing, and then again the imagination; and he rejected suspicions that its practice partook of hypocrisy (Kāšefi, I, p. 266). Another sign of individual preference at variance with Naqšbandi norms was his occasional indulgence in *samāʿ*, ecstatic circular motion to the accompaniment of music and song, in particular when stimulated by the composition of his romantic mat̲nawi, *Yusof o Zoleyḵā* (Lāri, p. 7).

Equally important for Jāmi's practice of Sufism, especially after the death of Kāšḡari in 1456, were his links with the already mentioned Naqšbandi shaykh, Ḵʷāja ʿObayd-Allāh Aḥrār, resident in Samarqand, where he wielded considerable influence in the affairs of the Timurid dynasty. Aḥrār was Jāmi's senior by some twelve years, but the two men appear to have regarded each other as equals, judging by the compliments exchanged between them. Jāmi praised Aḥrār for his skill in the fluent exposition of Naqšbandi principles, dedicated to him one of his didactic maṯnawis, the *Tohfat al-aḥrār*, and lauded him when he died. For his part, Aḥrār would encourage aspirants on the Sufi path to study with Jāmi (Kāšefi, I, p. 251). They first met in 1460 when Aḥrār came to Herat in order to appeal to Sultan Abu Saʿid for the abolition of a tax, the *tamḡā*, not authorized by the *šariʿa* (Bāḵarzi, p. 116). More significant and prolonged interaction took place some five years later in Samarqand, Jāmi having gone there expressly to visit Aḥrār. They spent whole days together for close to six months, engaged in learned and uplifting discourse. Two years later, they met again in Marv, where Aḥrār had been invited by Sultan Abu Saʿid; and Aḥrār suggested that Jāmi should join him there (Bāḵarzi, pp. 142-43). Their fourth encounter took place in 1479. Aḥrār was once again absent from Samarqand, busy with mediating between the warring sons of Abu Saʿid, but ultimately the two men met in Šāš (Tashkent) and were able to commune anew without significant disruption. Much of their time was spent in meaningful and mutual silence, but it was on this occasion that Aḥrār was able to help Jāmi understand certain problematic passages in Ebn al-ʿArabi's *Fotuḥāt* (Kāšefi, I, pp. 249-50). Jāmi and Aḥrār also corresponded with each other, some of their letters being little more than concise and formulaic expressions of esteem but others recommending their bearers for some form of assistance (Jāmi, *Pis'ma-avtografy*, letters 121, 197, 208, 263, 267, 279; Gross and Urunbaev, p. 131, 168-69, 335, 345; Kāšefi, I, pp. 248-49). Jāmi also paid public tribute to Aḥrār with the encomia he included in the prefatory matter of several of his maṯnawis (*Yusof o Zoleyḵā*, in *Haft owrang (awrang)*, pp. 588-89; *Leyli o Majnun*, in *Haft owrang*, pp. 753-55; and *Ḵerad-nāma-ye Eskandari*, in *Haft owrang*, pp. 918-19).

Jāmi expounded the fundamental principles of the Naqšbandiya in a brief treatise entitled *Sar-rešta-ye ṭariq-e Ḵ*ʷ*ājagān* ("The Quintessence of the Path of the Masters"). He sets forth as the goal of their path "permanent presence with God" (*davām-e ḥożur maʿa'l-Ḥaqq*); once such presence has become fully assimilated, the result is witnessing (*mošāheda*), i.e., a witnessing of the divine manifestation in all things. The paths to this goal are threefold: ceaseless and silent *ḏekr*, accomplished in such fashion that one seated next to the person engaged in it would be unaware of his state; *tawajjoh*, interpreted in this context to mean orientation to the heart as the locus of a divine presence resulting from *ḏekr*; and *rābeṭa*, a constant state of inward attachment to the spiritual guide. The attribution to Jāmi of another, somewhat longer treatise on the Naqšbandiya (*Resāla-ye Naqšbandiya*, ms. Esad Ef. 3702 [Süleymaniye]), is uncertain, for no mention of it occurs in lists of his writings drawn up by contemporaries, and it seems to rest on little more than the citation of a line of his verse at the very end of the work. Jāmi gathered some of the sayings of Ḵʷāja Moḥammad Pārsā and supplemented them with commentary in a brief treatise, *Soḵanān-e Ḵ*ʷ*āja Pārsā*, and he also prepared a précis of the main source for the life of Bahāʾ-al-Din Naqšband, the *Anis al-ṭālebin wa ʿoddat al-sālekin* (q.v.) of Ṣalāḥ-al-Din b. Mobārak Boḵāri; what appears to be an autograph copy of his version is to be found in the Khudabakhsh Library in Patna (Moḥammad Ḏāker Ḥosayn, introduction, Jāmi, *Ḵolāṣa-ye Anis al-ṭālebin*, p. xiii). Finally, the title of Jāmi's longest maṯnawi, *Selselat al-ḏahab* ("The Golden Chain") may be an allusion to a secondary line of Naqšbandi initiatic descent so designated, that consisting of the first eight Imams of the Prophet's Household. This diffuse work does, in any event, sometimes address itself to matters of distinctively Naqšbandi concern, such as the true nature of the silent *ḏekr* (*Selselat al-ḏahab* in *Haft owrang*, pp. 20-29). It also includes Kāšḡari's account of how his master, Neẓām-al-Din Ḵāmuš, had swiftly freed himself from the love of a handsome young man (*Selselat al-ḏahab* in *Haft owrang*, pp. 164-66). More informative, however, than all the foregoing for Jāmi's understanding and personal practice of the Naqšbandi path are the dicta and anecdotes recorded by his biographers, especially ʿAbd-al-Ḡafur Lāri in his *Takmela*.

Although authorized by Kāšḡari to inculcate the distinctive *ḏekr* of the Naqšbandis in aspirants to the path and fulfill all the other tasks of formal spiritual guidance, Jāmi was notoriously averse to the tasks of preceptorship. After the death of Kāšḡari, he customarily assigned those who sought training in the path to Moḥammad Ruji, another of his *ḵalifa*s, and similarly referred Ṣonʿ-Allāh Kuzakonāni, who customarily led the prayer at the mosque where his circle would gather, to still another successor, ʿAlāʾ-al-Din Maktabdār (Algar, 2003, p. 13, 24-25). News of this reached Aḥrār in Samarqand, and he accordingly asked Faḵr-al-Din Kāšefi, newly arrived from Herat, whether it was true that Jāmi did not accept *morid*s, by contrast with Ruji. Kāšefi responded that this was the case, whereupon, with a mixture of regret and approval, Aḥrār cited this dictum of ʿAbd-al-Ḵāleq Ḡojdovāni (q.v.), an initiatic ancestor of the Naqšbandiya: *dar-e šayḵi-rā beband, dar-e yāri begošāy/ dar-e ḵalvat-rā beband, dar-e ṣoḥbat-rā gošāy* ("close the door of shaikhhood, open the door of friendship/ close the door of retreat, open the door of companionship"; Kāšefi, I, pp. 251-52). Nonetheless, again according to Faḵr-al-Din Kāšefi, "if a sincere person should suddenly appear, he [i.e., Jāmi] would secretly enlighten him about this path," a case in point being his own father, Ḥosayn Wāʿeẓ Kāšefi. The elder Kāšefi had come to Herat in the hope of joining the following of Kāšḡari, but the shaikh had expired not long before his arrival. He therefore beseeched Jāmi to accept him as his disciple. Jāmi demurred, but "by way of allusion pointed him to a certain spiritual practice" (*šoḡli*; Kāšefi, I, pp. 253-54); the wording seems to convey a high degree of reluctance. Perhaps anxious to enhance his spiritual legacy, Jāmi changed course toward the end of his life and began to look actively for authentic seekers (*arbāb-e ṭalab*), but he was disappointed, for, he said, "seekers are many, but what they seek is only the gratification of their own souls" (Kāšefi, I, p. 252).

Despite all the foregoing, several persons are said to have been formally trained by Jāmi in the *ṭariqa*: Rażi-al-Din ʿAbd-al-Ḡafur Lāri (d. 1506), renowned for a number of writings, especially the supplement (*takmela*) he wrote to Jāmi's *Nafaḥāt al-ons*, an engaging and detailed portrayal of his master as a near-perfect embodiment of the Naqšbandi ideal; Mawlānā Šahidi Qomi, who took refuge in Gujarat once the Safavids conquered Khorasan; and K̲ʷāja Żiāʾ-al-Din Yusof, Jāmi's third son (d. 1513) (Algar, 2003, pp. 24-25). Others include ʿAlāʾ-al-Din Sāvaji (d. 1559); Masʿud Širvāni (d. 1531); Ḥāfez-al-Din Bayhaqi, whose son, Moḥammad Hāšem, having received the *ṭariqa* from him, passed it on to some five other persons, at least one of whom trained another generation of disciples (Kešmi, *Nasamāt*, pp. 108-109, 110-14, 122-23). As for ʿAlišir Navāʾi (d. 1501), minister to Mirzā Ḥosayn Bayqarā and celebrated for his poetry in both Persian and Chaghatay Turkish, he openly proclaimed his loyalty to Jāmi in this unambiguous verse: *Nevâyî kim mürid ve bendesidir/ irâdet yolıda efkendesidir* ("Navāʾi, his [i.e., Jāmi's] disciple and slave/ is prostrate before him in the path of discipleship," quoted in Lâmiî, *Nefehat Tercemesi*, p. 458).

In addition to these individuals, two relatively late sources, *al-Entebāh fi salāsel awliyāʾiʾllāh* by Šāh Wali-Allāh Dehlavi (q.v.; d. 1762), and the *Tebyān wasāʾel al-ḥaqāʾeq* of Kamāl-al-Din Ḥaririzāda (d. 1882) mention the Jāmiya as a distinct branch of the Naqšbandiya, leading from ʿAlāʾ-al-Din Maktabdār through his son, Ḡiyāṯ-al-Din Aḥmad, to Jāmi's nephew, Mawlānā Moḥammad Amin (*al-Entebāh*, p. 32, *Tebyān*, III, f. 201b). This account presupposes that Maktabdār had an initiatic relationship with Jāmi as well as with Kāšḡari, something not borne out by the sources. The Jāmiya is said to have spread to the Hejaz, becoming entwined there with other lines of Sufi transmission and therefore losing its independent significance. What is certain is that Jāmi's posthumous influence on Sufism was exerted more by the broad literary corpus he carefully and deliberately assembled than by any Naqšbandi lineage descended from him.

Jāmi joined to his Naqšbandi affiliations an enthusiastic, even combative devotion to the teachings and textual legacy of Ebn al-ʿArabi (q.v.). Not only had he been preceded in this devotion by other Naqšbandis, notably Moḥammad Pārsā; he also saw a clear affinity between the two foci of his loyalty: "Uttering the *ḏekr* softly is the method of some shaikhs, including the great master Moḥyi-al-Din Ebn al-ʿArabi . . . The method of most shaikhs is uttering the *ḏekr* loudly, whereas the method of imagining (*tak̲ayyol*), i.e., the silent *ḏekr*, is the foundation of the path of the [Naqšbandi] masters" (Lāri, *Takmela*, p. 28). Jāmi saw in him the supreme exponent of gnostic wisdom for the Arabs, just as Jalāl-al-Din Rumi had been for the Persians; defended in public debate Ebn al-ʿArabi's view that the Pharaoh had died a believer; and rejected as misconceived the criticisms made of some of his teachings by the Kobrawi, ʿAlāʾ-al-Dawla Semnāni (q.v.; d. 1336) (Bāk̲arzi, pp. 90, 96, 103).

He nonetheless confessed to an initial inability to grasp certain of Ebn al-ʿArabi's writings, and it was not until he had studied the works of Ebn al-ʿArabi's foremost pupil, Ṣadr-al-Din Qonavi/Qunyavi (d. 1234), that matters were clarified for him. According to Lāri, he had vowed that "if this gate be opened for me, I will expound the meanings intended by this group [the Sufis of Ebn al-ʿArabi's school] in such a way that people will easily understand them," and all that he wrote thereafter on that subject was in fulfillment of that vow (Lāri, p. 17). There is indeed an unmistakable pedagogical intent in much of Jāmi's writing on Sufi matters. He wrote first a commentary on *Naqd al-noṣuṣ fi Šarḥ naqd al-noṣuṣ*, Ebn al-ʿArabi's own digest of the *Foṣuṣ al-ḥekam*, drawing on both Qonavi and other previous commentators such as Moʾayyed-al-Din Jandi (d. 1291), Saʿd-al-Din Farḡāni (q.v.; d. ca. 1299-1300), ʿAbd-al-Razzāq Kāšāni (d. 1335) and Dāʾud Qayṣari (d. 1350), from whose works he includes pages of verbatim quotation. Far bulkier than the original work, the *Naqd al-noṣuṣ* serves effectively as a general introduction to the mysticism of Ebn al-ʿArabi, with particular attention to the concept of the "Perfect Man" (*al-ensān al-kāmel*; Chittick, pp. 142-51). Later Jāmi wrote a commentary on the *Foṣuṣ al-ḥekam* itself, a relatively modest enterprise in that he restricts himself to elucidating the immediate meaning of each sentence in the original text and shuns theoretical digressions.

The role of Jāmi in propagating the mysticism of Ebn al-ʿArabi in the Persian-speaking world was by no means limited to these two commentaries. More accessible and aesthetically attractive was his *Lawāyeḥ* ("Illuminations"), a series of thirty-six meditations of varying length on metaphysical topics such as the relation of the divine attributes to the Essence (*Lawāyeḥ*, ed. Richard, no. 15, p. 78), the plurality of the modes of the Essence and their "inclusion" within Its unity (no. 19, p. 96), and the connection between degrees of existence and degrees of knowledge (no. 33, p. 154). Here, too, he cites previous authorities, above all Qonavi, as well as Ebn al-ʿArabi himself (pp. 123, 147, 154, 163). Jāmi is moved on several occasions in this work to criticize both the Ašʿari theologians and the philosophers (*ḥokamāʾ*), finding their views inferior to the insights of the Sufis (*Lawāyeḥ*, ed. Richard, pp. 122-24, 152). He took up the same comparative theme, systematically and in detail but more prosaically, in *al-Dorrat al-fāk̲era fi taḥqiq maḏhab al-Ṣufiyya wa'l-Motakallemin wa'l-Ḥokamāʾ al-Motaqaddemin*, a work commissioned by Sultan Mehmed Fatih but only completed after his death in 1481. Eleven principal topics are examined in turn, with the theologians represented by Šarif Jorjāni (d. 1413) and Saʿd-al-Din Taftazāni (d. 1390), the philosophers by Naṣir-al-Din Ṭusi (d. 1274), and the Sufis by Qonavi, Mollā Fanāri (d. 1431), and Dāʾud Qayṣari, as well as Ebn al-ʿArabi himself. Not all the copious citations from these authorities are explicitly identified by Jāmi (Heer, Introduction to *al-Dorrat al-fāk̲era*, pp. 6-9).

The *Lawāyeḥ* is written in a mixture of rhymed prose and verse, mostly quatrains appended to the end of each section and serving to summarize it. The relationship between poetry and prose is the exact opposite in the case of his *Šarḥ-e robāʿiyāt*: here, the quatrains come first, forty-eight in number, and they are each followed by an average of one page of commentary. The quatrains express concisely some gnostic or metaphysical theme, which is then developed in greater detail in the commentary. Similarly compounded of prose and verse are two commentaries Jāmi wrote on the works of others: *Lawāmeʿ* ("Gleams"), on the celebrated wine poem of Ebn al-Fāreż (d. 1235); and *Ašeʿat al-lamaʿāt* ("Rays from the Flashes"), on the *Lamaʿāt* of Fak̲r-al-Din ʿErāqi (q.v.; d. 1289). Both of these address themselves primarily to the theme of love (*ʿešq*) as articulated by Ebn al-ʿArabi and his school.

The same topic is frequently encountered in the vast body of ghazals that make up about three quarters of Jāmi's three successive divāns, later assembled into a single whole. Many of the poems in question are suffused with homoerotic undertones that were by then conventional in Persian Sufi poetry. By way of explanation, Jāmi had recourse to the equally conventional adage that love of the metaphorical—the divine beauty as manifested in a human—serves as a bridge to love of the Real, but it seems that Jāmi tarried indefinitely on the bridge in question, for he confessed that even in old age he was appreciative of the beauty of young men (Bāk̲arzi, p. 138). Certain of the ghazals do, however, lend themselves reasonably to allegorical explanation, given the inclusion in them of technical terms of gnosis and metaphysics such as *momken* and *wājeb* (contingent and necessary [being]) or *mabdaʾ* and *maʿād* (the beginning and return [of all things]) (*Divān-e Kāmel, ğazal*s 292 (392), p. 283, and 879 (979), p. 509).

Jāmi's most substantial and widely read contribution to the Sufi canon was perhaps his *Nafaḥāt al-ons men ḥażarāt al-qods*, a hagiographical compendium that marked the apex of this genre in Persian. Here as in several of the instances already enumerated, he built carefully and respectfully on the work of his predecessors. The foundation had been laid by ʿAbd-al-Raḥmān Solami (d. 1021) with his *Ṭabaqāt al-Ṣufiya* in Arabic. This book was then rendered by K̲ʷāja ʿAbd-Allāh Anṣāri (q.v.; d. 1089), using the same title, into the Persian dialect of Herat; he rearranged much of the contents and added material of his own. Jāmi recounts this history in his introduction to the *Nafaḥāt*; the language used by Anṣāri, he claimed, had become incomprehensibly archaic and liable to misinterpretation, apart from which Sufis of the four centuries that had elapsed since Anṣāri had completed his work also deserved to be memorialized. Hence the *Nafaḥāt*, a compendium based on the *Ṭabaqāt al-Ṣufiya* but incorporating material from other "reputable books;" the final impetus for its composition was supposedly provided by an earnest request from Navāʾi (Jāmi, *Nafaḥāt*, p. 2). Before proceeding thus to update the *Ṭabaqāt al-Ṣufiya* in terms of both content and language, Jāmi takes care to define key concepts relating to the history of Sufism: the meanings of sainthood (*walāya*) and the saint (*wali*); the difference between the Sufi (the fully accomplished wayfarer), the *motaṣawwef* (the one still striving on the path); the *malāmati* ("the seeker of blame"); various levels of *tawḥid*; and the charismatic feats (*karāmāt*) of the saints (Jāmi, *Nafaḥāt*, pp. 3-25).

Among the new biographies he includes are those of numerous Naqšbandis and their immediate ancestors, beginning with Yusof Hamadāni (d. 1140) and ending with Aḥrār, who was still alive at the time of writing; the inclusion of a living figure in a work of this type was unusual, and it may be taken as another mark of Jāmi's esteem for Aḥrār (Jāmi, *Nafaḥāt*, pp. 380-416). He allots even more space to the other order important at the time in the eastern Persian world, the Kobrawiya, together with its Sohrawardi antecedents (pp. 420-55). Remarkable, too, is that he includes towards the end of his work notices of eleven poets, ranging chronologically from Sanāʾi (d. ca. 1131) to Hafez (Ḥāfeẓ, pp. 593-612). It is by no means certain, as Jāmi would have it, that Sanāʾi was a disciple of Yusof Hamadāni, or that ʿAṭṭār (d. 1221) followed Majd-al-Din Bağdādi (d. 1220) (Jāmi, *Nafaḥāt*, p. 593, 596), still less that some of the poets he refers to can with confidence be identified as Sufi. Jāmi's efforts to make a Sufi of K̲āqani (d. 1199) are particularly unconvincing (Jāmi, *Nafaḥāt*, p. 605); but to his credit he confesses to uncertainty whether Hafez "ever stretched out the hand of discipleship to an elder" (Jāmi, *Nafaḥāt*, p. 612). In all, what have been termed "eight clusters" of entirely new entries can be discerned in the *Nafaḥāt* (Mojaddedi, p. 169).

Copious mention in the *Nafaḥāt* of one's near ancestors was evidently a matter of prestige for some of Jāmi's contemporaries in Herat, for they complained to him that he had not written enough concerning them. He was, however, deliberate in his exclusions as well as inclusions, and he claimed to rely only on the most trustworthy authorities. He was particularly adamant in excluding from the *Nafaḥāt* Moḥammad Nurbak̲š (d. 1464), eponym of the Nurbak̲šiya, an offshoot of the Kobrawiya, and a claimant to Mahdihood, despite the appeal of the son, Qāsem Nurbak̲š, that he make mention of him; were he to do so, Jāmi responded, Qāsem would find the result highly displeasing (*Maqāmāt*, pp. 195-96). The absence from the *Nafaḥāt* of Šāh Neʿmat-Allāh Wali (d. 1431), an undeniably eminent figure, cannot be ascribed to any doctrinal deviance comparable to that of Moḥammad Nurbak̲š, for he was indubitably a Sunni. The fact that Neʿmat-Allāh's descendants had moved in the direction of Shiʿism must, however, have sufficed for Jāmi—bitterly hostile to all manifestations of that creed—to expunge him from the roster of the Sufis. A similar explanation might be advanced for the omission of Ṣafi-al-Din Ardabili (d. 1334), were it not that his immediate successor, Ṣadr-al-Din (d. 1393), is respectfully mentioned in the context of Jāmi's notice of Qāsem-e Tabrizi (d. 1433), better known as Qāsem al-Anwār (Jāmi, *Nafaḥāt*, p. 590).

Some three years after the death of Jāmi, ʿAlišir Navāʾi translated the *Nafaḥāt* into Chaghatay Turkish as *Nesâyimüʾl-Mahabbe min Şemâyimiʾl-Fütüvve* (ed. Kemal Eraslan). On the one hand, he abbreviated some of the entries found in the original, and on the other, he expanded it by including material on Jāmi himself as well as his companions, some Indian Sufis, and, most importantly, numerous Turkic shaykhs of Central Asia. In 1520, Lâmiî Çelebi completed a translation of the *Nafaḥāt* into Ottoman Turkish. His version was originally entitled *Futûhu'l-Mücahidîn li Tervîhi Kulûbi'l-Müşâhidîn* because its completion happily coincided with the Ottoman conquest of Belgrade but it became popularly known simply as *Nefehat Tercemesi* (first printed Istanbul, 1872); and includes entries on early Ottoman Sufis, including those who brought the Naqšbandiya to Anatolia and Istanbul. A still unpublished Arabic translation of the *Nafaḥāt* was made by Tāj-al-Din Zakariā ʿOṯmāni (d. 1592), an Indian Naqšbandi shaikh resident in Mecca.

In sum, whether by design or not, with his affiliations and enthusiasms, his original works and his commentaries, Jāmi represented a summation of the learned and spiritual traditions of the Persian-speaking world, especially Khorasan, on the eve of the transformations wrought by the Safavid conquest.

Bibliography: Works by Jāmi. *Ašeʿat al-lamaʿāt*, in *Ganjina-ye ʿerfān*, ed. Ḥamid Rabbāni, Tehran, 1974. *Divān-e kāmel*, ed. Hāšem Rażi, Tehran, 1962. *al-Dorrat al-fāḵera fi taḥqiq maḏhab al-Ṣufiyya wa'l-Motakallemin wa'l-Ḥokamāʾ al-Motaqaddemin*, ed. Nicholas Heer, Tehran, 1979. *Haft Owrang*, ed. Modarres Gilāni, Tehran, 1984. *Ḵolāṣa-ye Anis a-ṭālebin*, ed. Moḥammad Ḏāker Ḥosayn, Patna, 1996. *Lawāmeʿ*, in *Majmuʿa-ye Monlā Jāmi*, Istanbul, 1309 A.H.; repr. in *Seh resāla dar taṣawwof* with introduction by Iraj Afšār, Tehran, 1981, pp. 104-89. *Nafaḥāt al-ons*, ed. Maḥmud ʿĀbedi, Tehran, 1991. *Lawāyeḥ*, in *Majmuʿa-ye Monlā Jāmi*, Istanbul, 1309 A.H.; repr. in *Seh resāla dar taṣawwof* with introduction by Iraj Afšār, Tehran, 1981, pp. 3-103; ed. and tr. Yann Richard as *Les Jaillissements de Lumière*, Paris, 1982; ed. Moḥammad Ḥosayn Tasbiḥi, Tehran, n.d. *Naqd al-noṣuṣ fi Šarḥ Naqš al-foṣuṣ*, ed. William C. Chittick, Tehran, 1977. *Pis'ma-avtografy Abdarrakhmana Dzhami iz "Al'boma Navoi,"* ed. A. Urunbaev, Tashkent, 1982 (Persian text in facsimile and Russian translation). *Resāla-ye Naqšbandiyya*, ms. Esad Ef. (Süleymaniye), 372. *Sar-rešta-ye Ṭariq-e Ḵ^vājagān*, ed. ʿAbd-al-Ḥayy Ḥabibi, Kabul, 1965. *Šarḥ-e Robāʿiyāt*, ed. Māyel Heravi, Kabul, n.d.; ibid, in *Majmuʿa-ye Monlā Jāmi*, Istanbul, 1309 A.H.; repr. in *Seh resāla dar taṣawwof* with introduction by Iraj Afšār, Tehran, 1981, pp. 42-103. *Soḵanān-e Ḵ^vāja Pārsā*, in "Quelques Traités Naqshbandis," ed. Marijan Molé, *FIZ* 6 1958, pp. 294-303. *Tafsir Surat al-Fāteḥa*, ed. Sajjad Rizvi, forthcoming.

Other sources. Susan Āl-e Rasul, *ʿErfān-e Jāmi dar majmuʿa-ye āṯāraš*, Tehran, 2006. Hamid Algar, "Reflections of Ibn ʿArabi in Early Naqshbandi Tradition," *Journal of the Muhyiddin Ibn ʿArabi Society* 10, 1991, pp. 45-66. Idem, "Naqshbandis and Safavids: A Contribution to the Religious History of Iran and Her Neighbors," in Michel Mazzaoui, ed., *Safavid Iran and Her Neighbors*, Salt Lake City, 2003, pp. 28-31. ʿAbd-al-Wāseʿ Neẓāmi Bāḵarzi, *Maqāmāt-e Jāmi*, ed. Najib Māyel Heravi, Tehran, 1992. Ye. E. Bertel's, *Navoi i Džami*, Moscow, 1965. William C. Chittick, "The Perfect Man as the Prototype of the Self in the Sufism of Jâmî," *Studia Islamica* 49, 1979, pp. 135-57. Šāh Wali-Allāh Dehlawi, *al-Entebāh fi salāsel awliyāʾiʾllāh*, Lyallpur, n.d. Jo-Ann Gross and Asom Urunbaev, eds., *The Letters of Khwāja ʿUbayd Allāh Aḥrār and his Associates*, Leiden, 2002. Kamāl-al-Din Ḥaririzāda, *Tebyān wasāʾel al-ḥaqāʾeq*, ms. Ibrahim Efendi (Süleymaniye) 432. Najib Māyel Heravi, *Jāmi*, Tehran, 1998. Faḵr-al-Din Wāʿeẓ Kāšefi, *Rašaḥat-e ʿayn al-ḥayāt*, ed. ʿAli-Aṣḡar Moʿiniān, Tehran, 1978, 2 vols., I, pp. 235-86. Moḥammad Hāšem Kešmi, "*Nasamāt al-qods men ḥadāʾeq al-ons*," ed. Monir-e Jahān Malek, Ph.D. diss., University of Tehran, 1996. Lâmiî Çelebi, *Nefehat Tercemesi*, Istanbul, 1872. ʿAbd-al-Ḡafur Lāri, *Takmela-ye Ḥavāši-ye Nafaḥāt al-ons*, ed. Bašir Heravi, Kabul, 1964. Esmāʿil Moballeḡ, *Jāmi va Ebn ʿArabi*, Kabul, 1964. Jawid Mojaddedi, *The Biographical Tradition in Sufism: the Ṭabaqāt Genre from al-Sulami to Jāmi*, Richmond, U.K., 2001, pp. 151-76. ʿAlišir Navāʾi, *Ḵamsat al-motaḥayyerin*, ms. Institut Vostokovedeniya po imeni Biruni Tashkent, 2242. Moḥammad b. Ḥosayn Qazvini, *Selsela-nāma-ye Ḵ^vājagān*, ms. Bibliothèque Nationale, supplément persan, 1418. Necdet Tosun, *Bahâeddîn Nakşbend: Hayatı, Görüşleri, Tarikatı*, Istanbul, 2002, pp. 135-45. A. Urunbayev and L. Epifanova, "The Letters of Abdarrahman Jami as a Source of the Characteristics of the Poet's Personality," *Yádnáme-ye Jan Rypka*, Prague and the Hague, 1967, pp. 155-59.

(HAMID ALGAR)

iii. AND PERSIAN ART

Jāmi's writings are among the most frequently illustrated in the history of Persian manuscript painting. By the fifteenth century, the intense devotion of Timurid warlords and princes to Sufi elders had created the most favorable conditions for the spread of Sufism and an increase in the influence of Sufi orders. Whether in prose or verse, books and treatises on Sufism, its ideology, and exposition of its goals, continued to be written both in Arabic and Persian (Yarshater, pp. 19-20; Ṣafā, pp. 66-78). The popularity of Sufism led to the ascendance of literary works with Sufi contents among texts that were commissioned for illustration (Sims, p. 57). During the reign of the Timurid Ḥosayn Bāyqarā (q.v.; 1470-1506), Herat, where Jāmi resided for most of his life, became the center of literature and book production in the Iranian world (Sām Mirzā Ṣafavi, pp. 14-15; Blair and Bloom, p. 63). The later years of Jāmi's life thus coincided with the high point in the history of Persian miniature painting. The last decade of Jāmi's life also corresponds with the emergence, as master miniaturists, of a number of individuals known by name, including Kamāl-al-Din Behzād (q.v.; d. 1535-36), whose name was to become proverbial for skill in painting. Wide scale patronage of

Figure 1.

poetry and painting by members of the court at Herat, most notably, Ḥosayn Bāyqarā, and his confidant and childhood companion, Mir ʿAliŠir Navāʾi (1441-1501), and Jāmi's own eminent position, as a poet and a master of the Naqšbandi order of Sufis, must have contributed to the desirability of his works as subjects for book illustrations while he was still alive (Subtelny, 1988, p. 488; and 1979, pp. 81-97, 98-110). This desirability did not diminish during the Safavid period and in fact increased during the latter part of the 16th century (Simpson, 1998, p. 12; Galerkina, p. 231).

The fact that Jāmi's works were illustrated during his lifetime distinguishes him from most other major literary figures of the so-called classical period. Completed by Jāmi in 1483 (Arberry, p. 442) a manuscript copy of the mystical romance *Yusof o Zoleyḵā*, dated 1488—four years before Jāmi's death—contains two spaces reserved for paintings, in one of which a sketch can be seen representing Yusof and Zoleyḵā in the latter's palace (Simpson, 1997, p. 371; Simpson, 1998, p. 11). One often noted miniature painting from this same year was likewise inspired by Jāmi's *Yusof o Zoleyḵā*. This illustration, depicting the attempted seduction of Yusof by Zoleyḵā, is not in a manuscript of Jāmi's own works but is rather one of four paintings, undisputedly by Behzād, in a *Bustān* (q.v.) of Saʿdi that was made for the library of Ḥosayn Bāyqarā, with a text colophon of 893/1488. Although the scene illustrated corresponds with Saʿdi's text regarding Zoleyḵā's seduction scheme, the elaborate architectural setting illustrated by Behzād is that described in Jāmi's romance, where Zoleyḵā's palace, its conception, building, decoration, and completion are detailed (Afṣaḥzād, p. 123, line 2183 ff.; Golombek, p. 28). Following Jāmi's description, the painting shows Yusof who, having been led from room to room, at last flees from Zoleyḵā's reach to make his escape through all the rooms that according to Jāmi's text, she had carefully bolted as she led him through the building.

Inspired by the often illustrated *Ḵamsa* of Neẓāmi and with strong Sufi content, the seven maṯnawis comprising the *Haft owrang* (awrang), whether as individual poems, selections of poems or compilations of all seven, have been the most popular of Jāmi's works for illustrations, as evidenced by at least two hundred manuscripts held in collections around the world (Simpson, 1998, p. 12; Simpson, 1997, p. 369). However, among his works commissioned for illustration his divan of poems (Richards, pp. 69-74), his work *Bahārestān* (q.v.), modeled on Saʿdi's *Golestān* (q.v.), his *Nafaḥāt al-ons* on the lives and works of Sufi saints, and his *Lawāyeḥ*, a treatise on Sufism (Galerkina, p. 232) can be mentioned. Popularity of Jāmi is particularly prominent in Bukhara during the sixteenth and seventeenth centuries. Under the Uzbek rulers, numerous manuscripts of his works, such as selections from his Divān, copied by Solṭān ʿAli Mašhadi (d. 1519) with later miniatures attributed to Maḥmud and Ḵʷājakak Naqqāš, were copied and illustrated (now at the New York Public Library; Schmitz, p. 59). From Bukhara is also a manuscript of *Bahārestān* (at the Calouste Gulbenkian Foundation Museum in Lisbon), which has illustrations that have been dated to circa 1525-30 (Hillenbrand, pp. 70-71). An illustration belonging to a copy of the *Nafaḥāt al-ons* (presently at Chester Beatty Library in Dublin) was also executed in Bukhara circa1650s for ʿAbd-al-ʿAziz Bahādor Khan (r. 1645-91; see ABU'L-ḠAZI BAHĀDOR KHAN) and is attributed to Farhād (Soudavar, p. 221). A copy of *Bahārestān*, dated 1595 and made in the imperial atelier at Lahore and now at the Bodleian Library, Oxford, has been cited as one of the finest books produced under the Mughals in India (Blair and Bloom, p. 292).

Perhaps the most noteworthy and elaborately illustrated among works of Jāmi is the *Haft owrang* manuscript at the Freer Galley of Art in Washington DC (accession number 46.12), with its twenty-eight remarkable miniatures executed between 1556 and 1565 (Simpson, 1998, p. 13). This luxury manuscript was commissioned by the Safavid Ebrāhim Mirzā (q.v.; 1540-77), who at the age of sixteen was appointed the governor of Mashad by his uncle Shah Ṭahmāsp in 1554-55 (Qāżi Aḥmad, pp. 93-94). The calligrapher Moḥebb-ʿAli, who was the head of the *ketāb-ḵāna* of Ebrāhim Mirzā must have been responsible for delegating different segments of the project to various artists, not all of whom resided in Mashad. Other calligraphers known to have participated in this nine-year long project are Rostam-ʿAli, Malek-al-Daylami, and Ayši b. Ešrāti. The illuminator ʿAbd-Allāh al-Širāzi's signature also appears on the manuscript. Only two painters have been identified provisionally on stylistic grounds as having illustrated certain of the miniatures, Shaikh Moḥammad and ʿAli-Aṣḡar (Simpson, pp. 308-14).

Stylistically the illustrations in this manuscript, with large-scale compositions running over into the margins; bright, polished colors; sophisticated landscape or architectural settings; and idealized figures belong to the so-

Figure 2.

called classical tradition of Persian manuscript painting that by the second half of the fourteenth century had moved beyond merely advancing the narrative it accompanied, evolving through the fifteenth century into a complex art form in its own right. Especially noteworthy in the Freer Jāmi paintings is the phenomenon whose origins can be traced back to the last decade of Jāmi's life in the late fifteenth century and to the workshop of Ḥosayn Bāyqarā in Herat, where the familiarity of the artists with Sufi literature has been acknowledged (Galerkina, pp. 237-41; Lentz and Lowry, p. 285), and where certain depictions in Sufi manuscripts transcended subordination to the signified text. It might be relevant that this was also a period when composition, in verse form, of *moʿammā* (riddle) had become extremely popular (Subtelny, 1986, p. 77). Some of the twenty-eight miniatures in the Freer Jāmi seem barely to relate to the subject of their scenes, which in every case involves the precise moment narrated in the verses that are incorporated within each painting, and are in every case of selected anecdotes that Jāmi has used, allegorically, to elaborate or explain his often abstract and didactic theme (Simpson, 1998, p. 21). Literary works with Sufi content, such as Jāmi's *Haft owrang*, are rich in metaphorical images and mystical symbols that are open to a wide range of interpretation. In the case of the illustration (folio 52a, Simpson, p. 26) of the anecdote about the father who advises his son about love [Fig. 1] from *Selselat al-ḏahab* (in *Haft owrang*, ed. Alishah, p. 265, line 4039 ff.), it is not exactly clear which two figures among the twenty-three depicted are those of the father and son. Several figures depicting youths engaged in conversation with other men, though not at all described specifically in Jāmi's text could be understood as various examples of the types of suitors that are courting the favor of the son and about whom the father's advice is sought; but certain figures, having no apparent link to the meaning of the story could also be understood as Sufi symbols connoting secondary, or more oblique references that are signified by Jāmi's parable of the father and son. The figure of the kneeling man on the right, playing the flute, is an example in this case (Schimmel, pp. 273-75). As the spokesman of his time for the theosophy of Ebn ʿArabi (q.v.) and his school, Jāmi uses the pervasive influence of mystical currents, ideas, symbols, and images in his narrative and lyric poems, so that various interpretations for the recurrent depictions found in paintings that illustrate his texts may be possible (Chittick, p. 140). In the case of the illustration from the romance of *Leyli o Majnun*, where Qayṣ, visiting Leyli's tribal encampment catches a glimpse of her for the first time (Fig. 2; folio 231a; Simpson, 1998, p. 65), a Sufi allusion should be read into both the figure of the man playing the flute at the top-center of the painting, and the man with his spindle at the right-center, neither of whom are directly mentioned in Jāmi's text (Brend, pp. 174-76).

Bibliography: ʿAbd-al-Raḥmān Jāmi, *Haft owrang*, 2 vols., ed., Aʿlāḵān Afsaḥzād, Tehran, 1999. A. J. Arberry, *Classical Persian Literature*, London, 1958. Sheila S. Blair and Jonathan M. Bloom, *The Art and Architecture of Islam 1250-1800*, New Haven, 1995. Barbara Brend, *Perspectives on Persian Painting: Illustrations to Amir Khusrau's Khamsah*, New York, 2000. W. C. Chittick, "The Perfect Man As the Prototype of the Self in the Sufism of Jami," *Studia Islamica* 49, 1979, pp. 135-57. Olympiada Galerkina, "Some Characteristics of Persian Miniature Painting in the Later Part of the 16th Century," *Oriental Art* 21/3, 1975, pp. 231-41. Lisa Golombek, "Toward a Classification of Islamic Painting," in *Islamic Art in the Metropolitan Museum of Art*, ed., Richard Ettinghausen, New York, 1982, pp. 23-34. Robert Hillenbrand, *Imperial Images in Persian Painting*, Edinburgh, 1977. Thomas W. Lentz and Glenn D. Lowry, *Princely Vision: Persian Art and Culture in the Fifteenth Century*, Los Angeles, 1989. Qāżi Aḥmad, *Golestān-e honar: Taḏkera-ye ḵošnevisān wa naqqāšan*, ed., Aḥmad Sohayli Kʷānsāri, Tehran, 1987. Francis Richard, *Le livre persan*, Paris, 2003. Ḏabiḥ-Allāh Ṣafā, *Tāriḵ-e adabiyāt dar Irān* IV, Tehran, 1990. Sām Mirzā Ṣafavi, *Taḏkera-ye toḥfa-ye Sāmi*, ed. R. Homāyun-farroḵ, Tehran, 1960. Annemarie Schimmel, *A Two-Colored Brocade: The Imagery of Persian Poetry*, Chapel Hill, 1992. Barbara Schmitz, "Miniature Painting in Harat, 1570-1640," Ph.D. Diss., New York University, 1981. Eadem, *Islamic Manuscripts in the New York Public Library*, New York, 1992. Marianna Shreve Simpson, *Sultan Ibrahim Mirza's Haft Awrang: A Princely Manuscript from Sixteenth-Century Iran*, New Heaven, 1997. Eadem, *Persian Poetry, Painting and Patronage: Illustrations in a Sixteenth-Century Masterpiece*, New Heaven, 1998. Eleanor Sims with Boris I. Marshak and Ernst Grube, *Peerless Images: Persian Painting and its Sources*, New Haven, 2002. Abolala Soudavar, *Art of the Persian Courts: Selections from the Art and History Trust collection*, New York, 1992. Maria E. Subtelny, "The Poetic Circle at the Court of the Timurid, Sultan Husain Baiqara, and Its Political Significance," Ph.D. Diss., Harvard University, 1979. Eadem, "A Taste for the Intricate: The Persian Poetry of the Late Timurid Period," *ZDMG* 136/1, 1986, pp. 56-79.

Eadem, "Socioeconomic Bases of Cultural Patronage under the Later Timurids," *IJMES* 20, 1988, pp. 479-505. Ehsan Yarshater, *Šeʿr-e fārsi dar ʿahd-e Šāhroḵ ya aġaz-e inḥeṭāṭ dar šeʿr-e fārsi*, Tehran, 1956.

(CHAD KIA)

JĀMI RUMI (or Jāmi Meṣri), **AḤMAD**, Ottoman official, poet, and translator (fl. 10th/16th century). Next to nothing is known about him beyond his career as a ranking official of the Ottoman state, even the dates and places of his birth and death are not recorded. He was a professional soldier in the service of the royal court. In the reign of Sultan Süleymān (Solaymān) the Magnificent (r. 1520-66), he worked as a treasurer (*ḵazīna-ye ʿāmera kātebi*) in Egypt, where he lost four sons during a plague epidemic. He was sent to Mecca in order to renovate the Kaʿba, where he stayed for three years (ca. 1551-55). Upon returning to Istanbul he was promoted and once again sent to Egypt. During this time he translated Wāʿeẓ Kāšefi's *Rawżat al-šohadāʾ* from Persian into Ottoman Turkish under the title of *Saʿādat-nāma* for Süleymān the Magnificent. He became famous for this translation and became governor of a *sanjaq* (provincial district) in Egypt, the position in which he also served under Sultan Murād III (r. 1574-94).

His poetical works were apparently never collected in a *divān*, but some of his poems can be found in *taḏkera*s and anthologies. In *Saʿādat-nāma* he used simple language but adorned it with poems of Turkish and Persian poets. There are many manuscripts of *Saʿādat-nāma*; the oldest known manuscript dates from 986/1578 and is kept at Topkapı Palace Library in Istanbul (Revan, no. 1092; see Uzun, p. 103).

Bibliography: Meḥmed-Ṭāhir Bursalı, *ʿOtmānlı müʾellifleri* I, Istanbul, 1914, pp. 273-74. "Câmî-i Rûmî," in *Türk Dili ve Edebiyatı Ansiklopedisi* II, Istanbul, 1977, p. 14. M. Cunbur, "Câmî-i Rûmî," in *Türk Dünyası Edebiyatçıları Ansiklopedisi* II, Ankara, 2002, pp. 383. *Dāneš-nāma-ye adab-e fārsi* VI: *Adab-e fārsi dar Ānāṭuli wa Bālkān*, ed. Ḥasan Anušah, Tehran, 2004, pp. 270-71. Sadeddin Nüzhet Ergun, *Türk şairleri* II, Istanbul, 1936, pp. 900-02. Fehmi Edhem Karatay, *Topkapı Sarayı Müzesi kütüphanesi Türkçe yazmalar kataloğu* I, Istanbul, 1960, p. 367; II, Istanbul,

1961, pp. 7-78. ʿAbd-al-Laṭif Čelebi Laṭifi, *Taḏkerat al-šoʿarāʾ*, ed. Mustafa İsen as *Latifi tezkiresi*, Ankara, 1990, pp. 141-42. Ḥasan Čelebi Qenālizāda (Kınalızāde), *Teḏkeret al-šoʿarā*, ed. İbrahim Kutluk, I, Ankara, 1989, p. 245. Moḥammad Ṯorayyā (Meḥmed Süreyyā) Bey, *Sejell-e ʿOtmāni: Taḏkera-ye mašāhir-e ʿOṯmāniya*, 4 vols., Istanbul, 1890-97, II, p. 66; repr., 1971. Charles A. Storey, *Persian Literature: A bio-bibliographical Survey*, 2 vols., London, 1927-39; tr. Yu. E. Bregel as *Persidskaya literatura . . . , Bio-bibliograficheskiy Obzor*, 3 vols., Moscow, 1972; Pers. tr. Yaḥyā Ārinpur, Sirus Izadi, and Karim Kešāvarz as *Adabiyāt-e fārsi, bar-mabnā-ye taʾlif-e Estori, tarjama-ye Y. Bregel*, ed. Aḥmad Monzawi, 2 vols., Tehran, 1983, II, p. 909. Āqā Bozorg Ṭehrāni, *al-Ḏariʿa elā taṣānif-al-šiʿa*, 24 vols. in 27, Najaf and Tehan, 1936-78, XII, p. 181. Mustafa Uzun, "Câmî-i Rûmî," in *Türkiye Diyanet vakfı İslâm Ansiklopedisi* VII, 1993, pp. 102-3. Taḥsin Yāziji (Tahsin Yazıcı), *Pārsinevisān-e Āsiā-ye Ṣaḡir*, Tehran, 1992, p. 28.

(OSMAN G. ÖZGÜDENLİ)

JAMʿIYAT-E MOʾTALEFA-YE ESLĀMI

(Society of Islamic Coalition), was a religious-political organization founded in 1963 to propagate Ayatollah Khomeini's vision of an Islamic-Iranian state and society and to mobilize the population to implement that vision. This society was initially entitled the Islamic Coalition of Mourning Groups (Hayʾathā-ye moʾtalefa-ye eslāmi; hereafter, Hayʾathā-ye moʾtalefa). These small religious mourning groups (hayʾathā-ye ʿazādāri), were originally formed to commemorate the martyrdom of Imam Ḥosayn and other religious rituals in the late 1950s and early 1960s. Deeply inspired by Ayatollah Ruhollah Khomeini, when he rose to prominence as the "sole political" source of emulation (marjaʿ-e taqlid) in the early 1960s, this coalition of religious groups played an important role in the uprising of 1963 and the assassination of prime minister Ḥasan-ʿAli Manṣur in 1965. They participated in the Islamic Revolution of 1977-79 and emerged as the most organized and coherent political force in the powerful right-wing fundamentalist faction in the Islamic Republic. They changed the name of the organization first to the Society of Islamic Coalition (Jamʿiyat-e Moʾtalefa-ye eslāmi) in 1987, and formed the Party of Islamic Coalition (Ḥezb-e moʾtalefa-ye eslāmi) in 2004. This article is divided into the following two sections:

i. *Hayʾathā-ye moʾtalefa-ye eslāmi: 1963-79.*
ii. *Jamʿiyat-e moʾtalefa-ye eslāmi: 1979-2000.*

i. HAYʾATHĀ-YE MOʾTALEFA-YE ESLĀMI

The Islamic Coalition of Mourning Groups was born almost two years after the death of Ayatollah Ḥosayn Ṭabāṭabāʾi Borujerdi (q.v.) in 1961. The absence of Borujerdi, the uncontested source of emulation (marjaʿ-e taqlid) of Iranian Shiʿities, created a decision-making and leadership vacuum in Iran's religious establishment (ruḥāniyat). Hoping to take advantage of the disarray among the clergy, traditionally a very important force to contend with, the Shah was intent on pushing ahead with his modernization policies. A sequence of events, starting with the government's Bill on the formation of Local Councils (Anjomanhā-ye eyālati wa welāyati) on 6 October 1962 led to an escalating open confrontation between Ayatollah Khomeini – who took the helm of the politics of the Qom Religious Center – and the Shah. The birth of the Islamic Coalition of Mourning Groups can be considered as one of the by-products of this confrontation, which in turn impacted the course of this face-off.

According to this Bill candidates were no longer required to be Muslims, elected representatives were not obliged to take their oath on the Qurʾan and women were given the right to vote for the local councils. Khomeini immediately rallied the high ranking clergy or the *ulema* of Qom (Grand Ayatollahs Sayyed Kāẓem Šariʿatmadāri, Moḥammad Golpāyegāni, and Sayyed Šehāb-al-Din Najafi Marʿaši) to oppose the Bill and demanded its repeal. To take the clergy's oppositional stand among the people and sensitize them, Khomeini insisted that the letters of objection written by the religious dignitaries be made public and widely distributed (Ruhāni, pp. 149-50). The widespread publicizing of the leading clergy's religious opposition to the Shah's policies was of great importance to Khomeini, who wished to sensitize, mobilize and rally the people to the cause championed by the *ulema*. To this end, Khomeini sent an emissary to the mosques, religious circles, associations and mourning groups in Tehran, heeding them to go to Qom and establish regular contact with the leading clerics (Moqaddam, p. 132). The impetus to build a bridge between dispersed Islamic religious groups in Tehran and the clergy in Qom in a systematic and organizational form came directly from Ayatollah Khomeini (Qāsempur, p. 32).

THE FORMATION PROCESS

As of around October 1962, key members of the mourning group of the Šayḵ-ʿAli Mosque in Tehran, such as Ṣādeq Amāni and Moḥammad Ṣādeq Eslāmi came into contact with Ayatollah Khomeini. Their first mission was to print, reproduce and distribute Khomeini's declarations and letters. The second mourning group establishing regular contact with Khomeini in Qom was that of the Amindawla (Amin-al-Dawla) Mosque, known as Heyʾat-e bāzār-e darvāzeʾihā. This group, led by Mehdi ʿErāqi and Ḥabib-Allāh Asgarawlādi claimed some fifty members. Members of this group also became involved with the reproduction and distribution of Khomeini's declarations and letters. The third group was the Eṣfahānis. This group was closely affiliated with Tehran's bazaar and had sought Ayatollah Morteżā Moṭahhari's guidance in order to organize itself and actively support the political clergy (āḵund-e siāsi) after the issue of the Bill on the Local Councils. Moṭahhari had subsequently introduced Moḥammad Ḥosayni Beheští (later Ayatollah

Behešti) to the group (Moqaddam, pp. 130-32, 140-42, 150; Bādāmčiān and Banāʾi, pp. 34, 127-28).

From the autumn of 1962, Ayatollah Khomeini directly and systematically challenged the ambitions and policies of the Shah. During two highly charged years, culminating in Khomeini's exile to Turkey on 4 November 1964, tension between the Shah and the Ayatollah constantly escalated and Iran became a theatre of confrontation between the two men and their followers. On 9 January 1963 the Shah announced the Six Principles of his "White Revolution" (*Enqelāb-e safid*). He also announced that to stave off the false accusations and denunciations of the "black reactionary agents" and "destructive red forces" against his reforms, he would put the Six Principles to a national referendum. In anticipation of a major political showdown on the issue of the "White Revolution" and the referendum, which he opposed, Khomeini mobilized, coordinated and directed the previously wasted and unfocused energies of Islamic zealots into an effective organization.

The attack on the Fayżiya Seminary School by government forces on 22 March 1963 highlighted the urgency of Ayatollah Khomeini's directive to the scattered Islamic groups in Tehran to coordinate their resources. In the early spring of 1963, members of the Eṣfahāni group and the mourning group of the Amin-al-Dawla Mosque, both operating in Tehran, were convened to Ayatollah Khomeini's residence in Qom (Moqaddam, pp. 127, 147). Both religious groups had been independently in contact with Ayatollah Khomeini. Uninformed about the agenda of the meeting, Ayatollah Khomeini introduced them to one another, merged them into an operational coalition and charged them with carrying out his directives (Moqaddam, p. 35). The exact official date of the formation of the Islamic Coalition of Mourning Groups is not known, but is said to be around April 1963 (Moqaddam, pp. 131-32, 149; ʿErāqi, p. 168).

Social profile of the coalition members. The rank and file of the Coalition were non-clerical Muslim zealots who held regular religious meetings once or twice a week. Professionally, a good majority of the members were engaged in commerce and petty trade primarily in Tehran's bazaar. It could be surmised that other than the few who had some seminary school training, the majority had a high school education at best. The Coalition had neither female nor intellectual members (*ʿErāqi*, pp. 166-72). A salient feature of the members was their sincere attachment to the politico-religious leadership of the clergy. They firmly believed that the sphere of obedience to and emulation from the clergy could not be strictly limited to the religious and spiritual realm and naturally included the social and political domains.

Contact with Khomeini. To establish a secure and effective channel of communication with the clergy, receive their directives and implement them, two groups, the Eṣfahānis as well as members of the Amindawla Mosque were in contact with Ayatollah Moṭahhari and held regular weekly meetings with Behešti, both of whom were students of Ayatollah Khomeini. Members of the Šayḵ-ʿAli Mosque, under the leadership of Ṣādeq Amāni, seem to have been directly in contact with Khomeini. Ṣādeq Amāni had studied a regular seminary school educational program for twelve years while working in the bazaar and taught a class on morals (Moqaddam, pp. 23, 25, 135, 139). Explaining the attraction of Khomeini's message to certain members of the Coalition, Shaikh Fażl-Allāh Mahallāti, a veteran of the Devotees of Islam, maintains that once Nawwāb Ṣafawi's old friends realized that someone had come forth whose words and vision were similar to that of Nawwāb Ṣafawi, they immediately united under his banner (Mahallāti, p. 43).

Networks of religious procession. Aside from providing a space for worship, mosques organized religious gatherings and functions, engaged in charity and social works and possessed their own preachers as well as their respective mourning groups. The mourning groups, to which the majority of the Coalition members belonged, played an important religious, cultural and social role. During Tāsuʿā and Ašurā, the religious mourning groups take to the streets and display the passion, might and sense of self-sacrifice that religious ardor and conviction can summon among zealots. On these two days and especially Ašurā, Shiʿites commemorate, mourn, glorify and exalt the martyrdom of Imam Ḥosayn (q.v.) and his companions (see DASTA).

THE CHARTER AND ORGANIZATIONAL STRUCTURE

The Coalition formulated its own charter and organizational structure. In its preamble, it posited that the spiritual and material welfare of society, as well as its physical and moral well-being were contingent upon following Islamic injunctions and their application. The preamble concluded that once the people realized that they were striving in God's cause, they would welcome sacrifices (Moqaddam, p. 156). Acknowledging the fact that all across the country devout and enlightened Muslims gathered in regular weekly religious meetings, the charter called upon them to enter into a rigorous organizational structure and pave the way for the attainment of their objectives. The charter stipulated four objectives around which Muslims were invited to join forces and cooperate within the structure of the coalition: attainment of a better understanding of Islamic teachings in the private and social realm, an improved exposition and presentation of Islamic teachings, greater application of these teachings in the practical realm and finally charting a clear and practical way for creating a model Islamic society (Bādāmčiān, pp. 50-51). The Charter was written by Eslāmi from the Šayḵ ʿAli group and Ḥabib-Allāh (Mehdi) Šafiq from the Amindawleh group. The charter was subsequently edited by two clerics, Behešti and Moḥammad Bāhonar.

Structurally, the affairs of the Coalition were conducted through three committees; central, finance and propaganda. The Central Committee was composed of 12 members, four representatives from each of the three groups. Members of the Central Committee were: Maḥmoud Mirfenderesky, ʿAlāʾ-al-Din Mir Moḥammad Ṣādeqi, ʿEzzat-Allāh Ḵalili, Mehdi Bahādorān (the Eṣfahāni mourning group); Ṣādeq Amāni, Moḥammad Ṣādeq Eslāmi, Asad-Allāh Lājevardi, Ḥosayn Raḥmāni (mourning group of the Šayḵ ʿAli Mosque); Mehdi ʿErāqi, Ḥabib-Allāh Asḡarawlādi, Ḥabib-Allāh Šafiq, Abu'l-Fażl Tavakkoli (mourning group of Amindawla's mosque) (Moqaddam, p. 151). This committee was the decision making and steering body of the organization. It was responsible for drafting and preparing plans and projects facilitating the founding of a model Islamic society. The finance and propaganda committee were also composed of the representatives of each group as well as a member of the Central Committee (Moqaddam, p. 157).

Under the six-item rubric of the "Central Committee's Responsibilities," there are three different references (items 1, 2 and 6) to the necessity of establishing close ties with the politically oriented clergy and the religious Sources of Emulation (marājeʿ), seeking their counsel and guidance and obtaining permission and approval from them where and when necessary (Moqaddam, p. 157). The emphasis on seeking official guidance in its decisions from members of the clerical institution became the most distinguishing feature of the Coalition. On paper, it seemed as if the Coalition was voluntarily forfeiting its ultimate decision-making rights to the authority, opinion and leadership of Khomeini.

To formalize their faithful allegiance and subservience to the guiding role of the clergy, the Coalition requested Khomeini to appoint or recommend a group of clerics to supervise their activities. Subsequently the Coalition presented Khomeini with a list of possible clerical advisors. These clerics were to counsel the Organization on matters that required a religious opinion and act as Khomeini's representatives in case he could not be readily reached. From the list, which must have been made up of his students or clerics very close to him, Khomeini confirmed Moṭahhari, Behešti, Moḥi-al-Din Anwāri and ʿAbd-Allāh Mawlāʾi, who subsequently constituted the officially powerful Clerical Council, sitting at the apex of the organization (Bādāmčiān, p. 47). The Clerical Council had two main responsibilities: first, to provide intellectual and ideological guidance to members and second, to pronounce technical/religious opinions, effectively leading the way on religious and political issues. Accepting the politically oriented clergy as the repository of Islamic knowledge and the legitimate custodian of Islamic values, norms and ethics, it was only natural that the Coalition felt obliged to seek the opinion and accord of Islamic jurists in all those realms, where the social or political overlapped or became inter-twined with the religious realm (Moqaddam, p. 153).

Before the Coalition entered its operational stage as a religio-political organization, the recruitment phase was already under way. In his meetings with the leaders of individual mourning groups prior to the merger, Khomeini had informally recommended an organizational network based on 10-men cells. The directive aimed to guarantee the expansion of the organization. According to one report, by January of 1965, the Islamic Coalition of Mourning Groups had 500 operational cells in Iran with some 5,000 members. Some 300 of these cells were operating in Tehran (ʿErāqi, p. 170).

THE 5 JUNE 1963 UPRISING

From the spring of 1963 to the fall of 1964, members of the Coalition played a key role as the propaganda and operational arm of Khomeini in Tehran. On the operational front, the Coalition and its members provided an array of services. They were instrumental in organizing demonstrations, public speeches, religio-political sermons and rallies. In the aftermath of these political activities and agitations, when militants and zealots were imprisoned, the Coalition financially supported them inside the prisons and their families on the outside (Mahallāti, p. 65). During tense moments of confrontation between the regime and Khomeini's partisans in Qom, more experienced members of the Coalition such as Mehdi ʿErāqi acted as Khomeini's bodyguards. The Coalition was instrumental in mobilizing and bringing their zealous sympathizers in the form of religious mourning groups and processions to the streets. The coordination of demonstrations in Tehran with Ayatollah Khomeini's fiery speeches in Qom, to generate a maximum political impact was also the responsibility of the Coalition. In view of the Coalition's very close ties with the bazaar, the closing of the bazaar as a traditional sign of protest against the government was left to Coalition members or sympathizers. Finally, the initial organization and mobilization of the demonstrations that occurred in Tehran after the arrest of Khomeini on 5 June 1963, was the work of the Coalition.

On the propaganda front, the Coalition is credited for printing and effectively distributing the speeches, messages and declarations of Khomeini. It is reported that on one occasion, the Coalition distributed some 200,000 to 250,000 copies of Khomeini's declaration within two hours (10 p.m. and 12 a.m.) in Tehran, Qom, Mashad, Shiraz and Isfahan (ʿErāqi, p. 170). The Coalition played a key role in dispatching fiery preachers to its provincial branches (Aḥmadi, p. 339). It also financed, printed and distributed two clandestine publications, *Beʿṯat* (Prophetic Mission) and *Enteqām* (Revenge). These two journals were written, edited and produced in Qom by a handful of clerics very close to Khomeini (Bādāmčiān, p. 84; Ha-shemi Rafsanjāni, p. 195). *Beʾṯat*, which was the more political and polemical of the two was managed by Rafsanjani, while Moḥammad-Taqi Meṣbāḥ Yazdi, supervised *Enteqām*, the more theoretical and ideological publication (Hashemi Rafsanjani, p. 195). The articles in both *Beʿṯat* and *Enteqām* were used along with more specialized pamphlets as the reading and educational texts discussed in the 10-men cells of the Coalition (Moʾassesa-ye moṭāleʿāt o taḥqiqāt-e siāsi, *Sāzmān-e mojāhedin-e ḵalq* I, Tehran, Political Studies and Research Institute, 2005, pp. 225-26).

The Coalition was an effective and dependable medium for informing Khomeini's supporters in Tehran of the actions, movements and events surrounding and related to the Ayatollah in Qom. It also coordinated the religio-political activities in Tehran with the tempo of Khomeini's activities in Qom. The spectacular show of force of the mourning groups in Tehran on 3 June 1963, the day of *āšurā*, started at 8 in the morning. Soon the religious procession of the mourning groups turned into a political demonstration. The crowd chanted anti-Shah and pro-Khomeini slogans, formulated by Ṣādeq Amāni, one of the Coalition leaders (Moqaddam, pp. 95-96). Around noon, ʿErāqi, another one of the leaders of the Coalition, addressed the large rally in front of Tehran University. Subsequently, the demonstrators/mourning groups moved to the vicinity of Marmar Palace, the Shah's residence, ending their march at the bazaar around three in the afternoon (Moqaddam, p. 96). One hour later, Khomeini went to the Fayżiya Seminary School in Qom and delivered his scathing *āšura* speech against the Shah and Israel, accusing the former of waging war against Islam and the clerical establishment (*ruḥāniyat*) and the latter of scheming to uproot the Qurʾān in Iran (Moqaddam, pp. 97-99). Less than thirty six hours after this speech Khomeini was arrested, triggering off the 15th of Ḵordād (5th of June) uprising.

While the Coalition's responsibility was to disseminate every word and action of the Ayatollah and mobilize the people through demonstrations and rallies, thereby sustaining the religio-political fervor and enthusiasm that Khomeini had generated, the government was intent on insulating Khomeini, his activities and that of his followers. It is reported that early in the morning of 5 June 1963, members of the Coalition were the first to be informed by a young envoy from Qom that Khomeini had been arrested (Bādāmčiān, pp. 66-67). The organization of the initial key demonstrations, which could be argued to have instigated the events of that historical date was planned and orchestrated by the Coalition. The two main protest marches and demonstrations one emanating from the bazaar area and the other which is said to have been led by or had the blessing of Ṭayyeb Ḥāj Reżāʾi from Rey street (meydān-e bārforušān) were organized or directed by the Coalition (ʿErāqi, pp. 183-84; Ruḥāni, p. 484; ʿĀqeli, p. 156; Mirzāʾi, pp. 176, 200-201, 206).

The popular uprising after Khomeini's arrest on 5 June 1963 rapidly spread from Tehran's bazaar area, the focal point of the Coalition's power base across Iran and took the Shah's regime by surprise. Shocked by the magnitude of opposition and the intensity of the protest movement, the regime was temporarily destabilized and was forced to impose Martial Law. The provocative slogans of "Khomeini or death" (*yā marg yā Ḵomeyni*) and "Khomeini, Khomeini may God protect you; may he die, may he die, he who is your bloodthirsty enemy" (*Ḵomeyni Ḵomeyni Ḵodā negahdār-e to, bemirad bemirad došman-e ḵunḵʷār-e to*), chanted by the throng of demonstrators had an unequivocal message and its anti-Shah emphasis was unheard of since the hot August days of 1953 (for the slogans, see Bādāmčiān, p. 67). The 5 June 1963 uprising and the bloody repression that ensued, may be considered as the prelude to the 1979 Revolution in Iran.

The Islamic Coalition of Mourning Groups was in effect the first religio-political organization of its kind, as it was convened and summoned by a prominent religious figure in Iran's predominantly a-political clerical establishment. Neither Ayatollah Kāšāni nor Nawwāb Ṣafawi, who had previously formed their respective political organizations, had Ayatollah Khomeini's scholastic and spiritual stature, record and credentials. This was the first time that an ʿālem (Islamic scholar) and a renowned seminary school teacher in Qom had formed a political arm, members of which were not clerics, yet possessed impeccable religious credentials. Khomeini had meticulously inquired about and examined the religio-political zeal and efficiency of each of the three groups before initiating their merger.

THE COALITION'S ARMED BRANCH

From the inception of the Coalition, a small faction led by Amāni and ʿErāqi leaned towards the formation of an armed branch within the organization (Ṣadri, 2004, p. 96). Both men had been active in Nawwāb Ṣafawi's Devotees of Islam. Ayatollah Akbar Hashemi Rafsanjani (Akbar Hāšemi Rafsanjāni, hereafter Rafsanjani) maintains that ʿErāqi and Amāni's ties to and experience with the activities of Nawwāb Ṣafawi's "Fedāʾiān-e Eslām" was influential in their tendency towards armed struggle and the founding of the Armed Branch (Hashemi Rafsanjani, p. 241). The Armed Branch was to carry out a "positive struggle" in contrast to the propaganda and political struggle, which was dubbed as "negative struggle." The idea of creating an armed branch does not seem to have had the approval of the majority of the Coalition members. Ayatollah Maḥallāti has suggested that the idea of an armed branch caused a theoretical split and division within the Coalition (Maḥallāti, p. 65). According to Ṣādeq Amāni, subsequent to an evaluation of the conditions in the country, the faction within the Coalition which favored armed struggle concluded that the appropriate response to the prevailing problems could only come out of the barrel of the gun (Mojahedin-e Khalq Organization, I, pp. 227-28).

The bloody confrontations of the Fayżiya School and the June uprising created the right conditions for this faction to air its views and present its plans. The Coalition is said to have finally decided to permit the few who wished to establish an armed branch to pursue their project of recruiting suitable members and obtaining weapons (ʿErāqi, p. 205). Soon the Armed Branch became equipped with home-made dynamite, 8 revolvers and ammunition (Moqaddam, p. 273). In the meantime religiously and ideologically devoted and physically fit young men of around 20 were recruited into the Armed Branch and given weapons training (ʿErāqi, p. 206). The Armed Branch was led by Amāni and its members included ʿErāqi, Hāšem Amāni, ʿAbbās Modarresifar and Abu'l-Fażl Ḥāj Ḥaydari of the older generation and Moḥammad Boḵārāʾi, Reżā Ṣaffār Harandi, Mortażā Niknežād, and ʿAli Andarzgu who were the younger recruits of between 19 and 22 years of age (Qāsempur, pp. 36-37; ʿErāqi, pp. 214-15, Amiri, pp. 148,159).

The establishment of the Armed Branch inevitably imposed its own logic, determining the trajectory and fate of the Coalition. Preparation for carrying out armed missions was moving the Coalition from its propaganda and political phase to the execution or armed phase. The security precautions necessary for the survival of a large semi-public organization were very different from that of a small clandestine group committed to armed struggle and political assassinations. The overlap between the two different functions and activities of the Coalition became its Achilles heel. The armed activities of the Armed Branch endangered the existence of the propaganda and political branch just as it had happened with the Muslim Brotherhood in Egypt of 1949. Even though the Coalition tried to shield and insulate itself from the eventual security dangers and threats that assassination missions of the Armed Branch could pose for it, the key positions of the Amāni brothers and ʿErāqi linking the political organization to the military branch compromised and undermined all precautionary provisions (ʿErāqi, p. 205).

As the Coalition considered itself to be the executive arm of Khomeini and felt morally obliged to act according to Khomeini's directives, the decision to found the Armed Branch needed his approval. Three different accounts exist on Khomeini's response. ʿErāqi argues that even though from the beginning the idea of establishing an armed branch was entertained and discussed within the Coalition, Khomeini would not commit himself to approving such a body. A second account, the origin of which is unknown, suggests that Khomeini initially opposed the idea of an armed branch but then conceded to its formation (Bādāmčiān, p. 102). According to a third account, again the source or sources of which are not revealed, after the Fayżiya incident and the June 5 uprising, when certain Coalition members sought Khomeini's position on the creation of an armed branch, he is reported to have said, "It is all right as long as you do not receive weapons from anywhere so that you would become dependent, instead you ought to purchase or manufacture it yourself" (Moqaddam, p. 241). Ayatollah Mahdawi Kani recalls that; "Apparently, the Imam (Khomeini) did not favor armed activities" and that "some knew that he did not approve of armed movements" (K̲ᵛājeh-Sarvi, pp. 122-23).

The establishment of the Armed Branch seems to have been in spite of Khomeini's will and directives and in defiance of the Coalition's Charter. As such, the decision to create the Armed Branch of the Coalition could be considered as disobedience and insubordination. Given the Coalition's public image of the perfectly obedient follower of Khomeini's opinions and convictions, after the 1979 Revolution, the issue of Khomeini's position on the Armed Branch and armed struggle became a highly sensitive one. Through official statements, the Coalition has tried to convince the public that its decision to embark on the path of "armed jihad" was legitimized by a "religious permit" (*ʿAṣr-e āzādagān*, 9 Esfand 1378 Š./28 February 1999).

KHOMEINI'S EXILE AND THE ASSASSINATION OF THE PRIME MINISTER

Khomeini's exile. On 13 October 1964, the Iranian parliament ratified a highly controversial and sensitive extraterritorial agreement by a narrow margin of 74-61. Given the handpicked parliament, the relatively high votes against a government Bill demonstrated the unpopularity of the Bill. The Status of Forces Agreement, known to Iranians as the Capitulations Agreement "provided American military personnel and their dependents stationed in Iran with full diplomatic immunity" (Bill, p. 156). To Iranians the Capitulations Agreement was considered as an affront to Iran's national sovereignty and territorial integrity. The fact that as a result of this Agreement Iranian law would no longer apply to American servicemen infuriated the public.

It is said that the Coalition, through one of its sympathizers in the Iranian parliament, received news of the government's bill concerning the provision of diplomatic immunity to the 1,700 US military advisors in Iran, before it was deliberated in the Majles. Khomeini was informed of the Bill in advance by the Coalition, yet he had insisted on proof before reacting to it (ʿErāqi, p. 207). Once the Majles ratified the Agreement, Khomeini waited for 13 days and then on the birthday of the Shah, which was officially celebrated, he explicitly lashed out against the Capitulations Agreement, the US, Britain, the Soviet Union, Israel, the Majles, the government and the Shah.

In a highly charged and moving speech, Khomeini said, "They have sold out all of us and our independence and still celebrate by illuminating and adorning the streets [reference to the official festivities on the Shah's birthday] the Majles and the government have shamelessly reduced the Iranian people to a status lower than American dogs. This Agreement has made us a colonized country, it has presented the Muslim people of Iran to the world as lower than savages. If the clergy had any influence they would not allow a puppet of the Americans to commit such foulness, they would kick him out. If our country is occupied by the Americans, tell us and deport us from this country. All our problems are because of this USA. All our problems are because of Israel. Israel belongs to the US, these members of the parliament belong to the US, these ministers [in the government] belong to the US and are appointed by them, if they are not why do they not stand up and shout down the Agreement? . . . May God destroy all those who betray this land, this country and betray Islam and the Qurʾān" (Moqaddam, pp. 200-207).

On the night following Khomeini's speech, its text was printed, reproduced and distributed on a very wide scale by members of the Coalition in Tehran and a few provincial centers. ʿErāqi was instrumental in obtaining the text from Khomeini, transporting it to Tehran and printing it on an A-3 format. Given the inflammatory content of the speech and SAVAK's sensitivity to prevent its circulation, the Coalition's ability to efficiently distribute the text without getting arrested, constituted a victory for members of the Coalition (Bādāmčiān, pp. 107-9). Nine days after this fiery speech, Khomeini was arrested and banished. Surprisingly enough, there were no major demonstrations marking his arrest and exile.

Originally, the Armed Branch assessed the possibility of assassinating the Shah, the prime minister Manṣur, two ex-prime ministers and Shah's confidants, Amir Assad-Allāh ʿAlam and Manučehr Eqbāl (q.v.), the police chief, General Neʿmat-Allāh Naṣiri, and General ʿAbd-al-Karim Ayādi, the Shah's special physician who was also known to be a Bahai (ʿErāqi, p. 209; Moqaddam, p. 366). Even though there seems to have been a consensus on the assassination of the Shah, the Armed Branch reached the conclusion that in view of the Coalition's organizational weakness and un-preparedness to take power, such an act may either lead to anarchy or enable other more disciplined and structured organizations to benefit from the situation. Afraid of the consequences of eliminating the Shah, it was therefore decided not to assassinate the Shah and focus on Manṣur (ʿErāqi, pp. 209-10).

The fatwa to assassinate Manṣur. Once the decision had been made to assassinate Ḥassan-ʿAli Manṣur, the Prime Minister, a fatwa had to be obtained in support of this action. Khomeini, the spiritual and temporal father of the Coalition had been approached and asked for his approval, yet he had refused to issue a fatwa or condone the assassination (ʿErāqi, pp. 228-29; Aḥmadi, p. 336; Ḵalḵāli, p. 163; SAVAK sources as reported by Moqaddam, pp. 366, 373).

Within the members of the Armed Branch, two different views competed on the necessity to obtain permission from a religious source of emulation for the act of assassination. One position, which seems to have been advocated by ʿErāqi maintained that the verdict of "corruptor on earth" had already been passed and confirmed in relation to their potential targets and they did not need to seek confirmation for their act.

The other group within the Armed Branch is said to have been represented by Ṣādeq Amāni. In contrast to the first group, this tendency was adamant on obtaining a religious permission from a source of emulation, before it proceed with its assassination project (Moqaddam, p. 245). Having failed to convince Khomeini to issue a religious edict, attempts were made to seek permission from Ayatollah Moḥammad Hādi Milāni in Mashad (Moqaddam, p. 245). Milāni is reported to have said, "If someone can do this, this would be an obligation and should be done with a minimum of collateral damage" (Moqaddam, p. 246). The Armed Branch of the Coalition construed Milāni's verbal statement as a valid permission to assassinate the Shah or Manṣur (Moqaddam, pp. 366, 374). Ḵalḵāli suggests that even though Khomeini had not allowed the assassination, Moḥi-al-Din Anwāri, a member of the Clerical Council had opined that the murder of Manṣur is an obligation and you may act if you want to (Ḵalḵāli, p. 163).

At around ten in the morning of 21 January 1965 Ḥassan-ʿAli Manṣur, the Prime Minister was shot twice at very close range as he got out of his car in front of the Majles by Moḥammad Boḵrāʾi who was immediately arrested; his two other accomplices, Nikneẓād and Ṣaffār Harandi were arrested by the nightfall of January 21. Within ten days of the assassination, members of the Armed Branch, including ʿErāqi and Ṣādeq Amāni as well as all key members of the Coalition including Anwāri, were arrested. Anwāri was a member of the Clerical Council and is said to have had close ties with the Armed Branch (Moqaddam, p. 366; Ḵalḵāli, p.163).

On April 27, 1965, the trial of 13 defendants accused of "attempting to overthrow the regime, murder of Ḥasan-ʿAli Manṣur, possession and sale of illegal arms and hiding the culprits" started in a military tribunal and was over on May 16, 1965. In court, the Armed Branch's weapons were put on display and the military prosecutor, Colonel Mir Ḥosayn ʿĀtefi, presented the pistols used by Boḵrāʾi and Nikneẓād as important exhibits in the trial. In the tradition of "Fedāʾiān-e Eslām," the Colts had a piece of paper glued to their short barrels, which read, "Stop the autocratic rule of the Shah, the people will not accept becoming colonized, the Iranian regime is illegitimate and long live Islam, the world religion" (Moqaddam, pp. 477-78, 541). The prosecutor referred to the slogans on the Colts and concluded that the intentions, goals and objectives of the defendants could be clearly drawn from their content. The operational team of Boḵrāʾi, Nikneẓād and Ṣaffār Harandi, in addition to the Amāni brothers and ʿErāqi were sentenced to death and the remaining seven, including Anwāri were given prison terms. On 15 June ʿErāqi and Hāšem Amāni's death sentences were commuted to life imprisonment, while the other four were executed on 16 June 1965 (Moqaddam, p. 384-85). Those who escaped capture and imprisonment became isolated and marginalized. Some of them became active in newly formed armed organizations that later entered the political stage. The lesson drawn by Muslim zealots from the assassination of Manṣur was that a relatively small operation not only jeopardized but dealt a major blow to the totality of religio-political movements. Rafsanjani argues that the slaying of Manṣur provided the regime with the necessary pretext to apply unrestrained violence against all opposition forces in society (Hashemi Rafsanjani, p. 241). The violent government backlash effectively put an end to the activities of the Coalition. In the years that elapsed between June 1965 and the release of the Coalition's key figures in 1977, the organization went through a period of hibernation and inactivity. In the meantime the baton of political opposition and armed struggle was passed on to other organizations of diverse ideological convictions, most of which had scarcely anything in common with the Coalition.

Bibliography: See ii. below.

ii. JAMʿIYAT-E MOʾTALEFA AND THE ISLAMIC REVOLUTION

After the 1979 Revolution, the "Coalition of Islamic Mourning Groups" changed its expressive and meaningful name to the rather awkward appellation of Jamʿiyat-e moʾtalefa-ye eslāmi (the Society of Islamic Coalition). This change went largely unnoticed in Iranian political circles. Each segment of the society was pre-occupied with defining and propagating its own vision of the future Iranian state and society while adjusting to the revolution and its rapidly evolving leadership. Furthermore, to the recently politicized youth and even to their elders, the "Coalition of Islamic Mourning Groups" was not a common household name. The new name remained loyal to the history of the group, by retaining the term 'Coalition,' yet omitted any reference to the original activities of the groups composing the Coalition. This was a first step towards political modernization. The Coalition was breaking with a past, which projected it as a traditional religious force primarily concerned with the observation and practice of rites and rituals, while emphasizing its political and revolutionary credentials. Replacing the term "mourning groups" simply with "society" was sending a message of continuity and change to those whom it wanted to recruit.

COALITION AND THE MAKING OF THE ISLAMIC REVOLUTION

On the eve of the revolution and in its immediate aftermath, the Coalition did not constitute a major force on the Iranian political scene. The Coalition did not possess a coherent political structure, organization or even an identifiable constituency or base. It did, however, possess influential individual members and sympathizers who had been gradually released from prison and it could depend on a group of affiliates who had been outside prison, essentially engaged in social, charity and educational activities of primarily a religious style rather than a political one. In sum, the "Society of Islamic Coalition" was a loose association of friends and old brothers, sharing a common history, common heroes and martyrs as well as common enemies and friends.

The most important characteristic of the Coalition's sympathizers and members continued to be its long-held firm belief in allying itself with Ayatollah Khomeini and his clerical followers and accepting their religio-political leadership and guidance. This position was the Coalition's winning card in the aftermath of the revolution. The Coalition could hammer at its revolutionary and militant historical credentials among the new generation of Islamic zealots and ride on the wave of Khomeini's popularity. The fact that after some 16 years Ayatollah Khomeini, the Coalition's founder and spiritual leader had become the uncontested leader of the revolution and that their clerical counselors, collaborators and prison cell-mates were occupying key positions of power, provided the Coalition with a golden opportunity to rebuild its organization and carve out a major political position for itself in the post-revolution structure of the state.

The Coalition re-organizes. In the last few months before Khomeini's triumphant return, individual members and affiliates of the Coalition began to re-build their network in cooperation with their clerical allies. Members of the Coalition participated in meetings, discussions and organization of demonstrations and political actions with Khomeini's clerical representatives, preparing and planning for the transfer of power (Rażawi, p. 135). During the mass demonstrations of *tāsuʿā* and *ʿāšurā* (10 and 11 December of 1978) in Tehran, upon the request of Hojjat-al-Eslām Maḥallāti, key Coalition figures were instrumental in channeling and directing the slogans of the demonstrators. During the *ʿāšurā* demonstration, the slogan of "Death to the Shah" orchestrated by Coalition members echoed for the first time in the streets of Tehran (Maḥallāti, p. 104).

As the days of the Shah's regime came to a close, the administration of the transition of power and the running of the state fell upon the revolutionaries. A small group of Khomeini's clerical followers and members of Mehdi Bāzargān's Iran Freedom Movement (Nahżat-e āzādi) to whom Khomeini had confided the lion's share of the responsibilities, needed to rely on people whom they knew and shared a history to relegate more specific tasks and responsibilities. Individual Coalition members were being contacted by Khomeini's clerical representatives, especially Ayatollah Moṭahhari, to participate in various tasks and functions. In the transition of power to the new revolutionary leadership, old acquaintances were gradually re-forged into new networks and organizations.

The Reception Committee. One pressing task was to prepare for Khomeini's safe return to Tehran while the Shah's regime was still in power. The "Committee for the Reception of his Eminence the Imam," (Komita-ye esteqbāl az ḥażrat-e emām) was charged with this task. The Committee was to operate under the supervision of Moṭahhari, who was also in charge of the "Council of the Islamic Revolution," the highest revolutionary authority in Iran in the absence of Khomeini. In January 1979, Khomeini sent a message from France, officially charging this Revolutionary Council, which had been secretly in place since November 1978, with the task of "realizing the Islamic objectives of the people" (Kordedeh, p. 31). Of the six key clerical figures nominated by Khomeini to this Council, three were very closely associated with the Coalition. Moṭahhari and Behešti had been members of the Coalition's "Clerical Council" and Bāhonar along with Behešti had been instrumental in drafting the Coalition's Charter in 1963. Two other members of the Revolutionary Council, Hashemi Rafsanjani and Mahdawi Kani had been in Evin prison with the Coalition leaders and knew of them and their activities since 1963 (for the list of the six clergy, see ibid, pp. 24-25). It is also said that in 1972, Rafsanjani who had founded a company called "Dežsāz," had commercial dealings with certain members and sympathizers of the Coalition such as Rafiqdust, Šafiq, Mirfenderesky, Mir Moḥammad Ṣādeqi and Tawakkoli (Ak̲awān Tawḥidi, pp. 267-69). The Coalition's longstanding, close and untarnished historical connection and relation with Khomeini and the key members of the "Council of the Islamic Revolution," assured them of a fair share in the new Islamic system.

The "Reception Committee" was responsible for facilitating Khomeini's return, assuring his safety, planning his agenda as well as the logistics for what was to be a historical return. The "Reception Committee" enabled Coalition members to systematically re-build their organization and pull together their sympathizers in a coordinated and well-structured manner. Mohsen Rafiqdust, was called upon to join the "Reception Committee" and was placed in charge of finding a suitable residence for Khomeini as well as assisting in his security and safety in Tehran. He suggested the Refāḥ School. A young member of the old Coalition, Rafiqdust was imprisoned and released on the eve of the Revolution (Rafiqdust, pp. 34, 110, 125, 131). Refāḥ was a girl's school that was founded by members of the Coalition (Rowšan-nehād, pp. 88-89, 98-99). The responsibility for maintaining peace and order and assuring Khomeini's security on his arrival in Tehran was entrusted to Ṣādeq Eslāmi, one of the founding members of the Coalition. Eslāmi had divided the task of maintaining order among 12 appointees who were mainly Coalition sympathizers if not members. It is said that Ṣādeq Eslāmi's Orderliness Council (Komita-ye enteẓāmāt) mobilized some 60,000 individuals to assure internal security on the day of Khomeini's return. This impressive number is said to have formed the initial nucleus of what came to be the "Committee of the Islamic Revolution" (Komita-ye Enqelāb-e Eslāmi; see *Šomā*, 12 Tir, 1376 Š./3 July 1997).

Committee of the Islamic Revolution. This committee was a key body not only responsible for state security after the breakdown of the old regime, but for bringing members of the old regime and counter-revolutionaries to justice. Their task included door-to-door searches, setting up check points in cities, confiscations and imprisonments. In effect the "Komita" had replaced the national police. Coalition members were also involved in the Propaganda Branch (Komita-ye tabliḡāt) of the "Reception Committee" which was stationed at Khomeini's residence. At the Propaganda Branch, it seems as though Bādāmčiān, another key Coalition member, played a supervising role in channeling information to the Iranian press (*Šomā*, 17 Bahman 1377 Š./6 February 1998).

In Tehran, Coalition members were actively involved in preparing for the return and rule of Khomeini. ʿErāqi arrived in France shortly after Khomeini and stayed close to the Ayatollah supervising the logistics of his ever-more populated and frequented residence, acting as his body guard and assuring his peace and tranquility. He also acted as the liaison between Khomeini and the "Reception Committee" (Ḡaffāri, pp. 315, 402).

After his arrival at Tehran's Mehrābād airport and a short speech, Khomeini sat in the front seat of a Chevrolet Blazer next to Rafiqdust, who drove through a crowd popularly estimated to be made up of some two million or more well-wishers who had literally "brought Tehran to a standstill to greet the Imam" (it should be noted, however, that this is a very dubious figure if examined carefully; the figure of two million, were it not an exaggerated number, would require a procession of people organized at 20 persons to a row that would need approximately 100 kilometers of space in order to stand).

Once Khomeini reached Tehran, however, it was the Coalition who were at the wheel. Since the foundation of the Islamic Republic, Coalition members have spread out into and occupied key roles in numerous sensitive and decision-making arenas. It would be difficult to provide a precise account of their presence in all aspects and facets of Iran. At best, only a broad overview of the Coalition's spread and scope of power in post-revolution Iran is possible. The Coalition's involvement in the three main domains of financial-economic, political, and judiciary-security-military will be assessed, before presenting the evolution of the Coalition's world outlook.

THE FINANCIAL-ECONOMIC DOMAIN

Less than ten days after the victory of the revolution, Khomeini appointed Askarawlādi to help Maḥallāti supervise the "Cooperative Fund" of Tehran's guilds (Ṣanduq-e taʿāwoni-e aṣnāf; Maḥallāti, p. 134). In the summer of 1980, Askarawlādi was also appointed as director of the Endowments Organization (Sāzmān-e awqāf). In an official edict on 10 March 1979, Khomeini appointed Mehdi Karrubi along with Askarawlādi and Šafiq to establish relief committees across the nation. Accounts were to be opened for this charitable venture and the funds collected were earmarked to alleviate the needs of the poor (*Ṣaḥifa-ye nur* V, p. 188). This committee came to be known as "Imam Khomeini's Relief Committee" (Komita-ye emdād-e Emām Ḵomeyni). After Karrubi's appointment to the Foundation of Martyrs (Bonyād-e šahid), Askarawlādi continued to be Khomeini's representative and subsequently Ayatollah Ali Khamenei's (ʿAli Ḵāmenaʾi) representative at "Imam Khomeini's Relief Committee." This organization, under the control of Askarawlādi to this date (2008) has become an important Coalition stronghold (Nāṭeq Nuri, p. 67). By 1994, this organization provided services to some 2,850,000 people in Iran. These services varied from setting up small-scale production units to providing dowries for newly wedded women and free medical services. In recent years, the Imam Khomeini Relief Organization has expanded its programs beyond Iran's borders and into the Azerbaijan Republic, Afghanistan, Lebanon, Tajikistan, Bosnia and Palestine (see *Salāmirān.org* in bibliography).

Foundation of the Oppressed. Less than a month after taking over power, Khomeini issued a key edict, ordering the establishment of the "Foundation of the Oppressed" (Bonyād-e mostażʿafin), renamed as the "Foundation of the Oppressed and Disabled" (Bonyad-e mostażʿafin wa jānbāzān) after the outbreak of the Iran-Iraq war. This foundation was charged to expropriate all the assets and belongings–movables and immovable of the Pahlavi family as well as those individuals who were affiliated, associated or collaborated with the previous regime. According to Khomeini, the confiscated properties were considered as war booty (*ḡanāʾem*) and as such did not belong to the government, but to the people and were subsequently to be spent in favor of the poor and downtrodden by a non-government organization. Khomeini charged the Foundation to relieve poverty, homelessness and destitution in the entire country (Khomeini [Ḵomeyni], *Ṣaḥifa-ye nur* III, p. 366).

Once the foundation's charter was written in July 1979, ʿAli-Naqi Ḵāmuši was nominated as director of the powerful "Foundation of the Oppressed" and ʿErāqi was appointed as its supervisor (Kāviāni, pp. 44, 65). ʿAli-Naqi Ḵāmuši, an old member of the Coalition, in turn nominated Ḥabib-Allāh Šafiq, who was already appointed to the "Imam Khomeini Relief Organization" and Moṣṭafā Mir Salim, another Coalition member as financial supervisors of the foundation (ibid, p. 65). Six months after Ḵamuši's appointment, in one of his public speeches, Khomeini enquired, "is it true that the Foundation of the Oppressed has become the Foundation of the Rich [and arrogant]?" (ibid, p. 65). Subsequent to the report of a task force appointed by Khomeini to investigate the affairs of the Foundation and fourteen months after Ḵamuši's initial appointment, he was removed from the Foundation.

Ḵamuši returned to the Board of Directors of the Chamber of Commerce, Industries and Mines of Iran (q.v.), joined two Coalition brothers, Askarawlādi and Mir Moḥammad Ṣādeqi and served as the president of the Chamber from 1984 to 2007 (Eʿtemād, *Sāl-nāma* 1385 Š./2006, p. 70). In its role as the strongest lobby of the private sector, the Board of the Chamber is represented on key governmental bodies, including the sensitive councils of Money and Credit, Stock Market, Exports, Coordination of Foreign Affairs and the Arbitration Council of Customs, Taxes and Insurance (*Hammihan*, 31 Ḵordād 1386 Š./21 June 2007).

From September of 1980 until the spring of 1989, the "Foundation of the Oppressed," Iran's financial and economic powerhouse with total administrative autonomy, hardly any mechanism of checks and balances and an annual budget of $10 billion, employing some 150,000 workers, slipped out of the hands of the Coalition (Oxford Analytica, 23 July 1999). However, from 1989 until 1999 when Moḥsen Rafiqdust was nominated by Ayatollah Khamenei as the director of Foundation, this gigantic economic conglomerate came back under the control of a Coalition member.

The decisions concerning investments, production and imports by the industrial, agricultural, construction, service, and commercial units of the Foundation have major consequences for home market prices and profit margins of domestic private firms. The Coalition's control of the para-state foundations as well as its control over an array of market and bazaar organizations such as the Iran Chamber of Commerce, the Guild Affairs Committee, the Islamic Economy Organization, the Union of the Association of Islamic Guilds and Bazaar (Ettehādiya-ye anjomanhā-ye eslāmi-e aṣnāf wa bāzār), provided it with a considerable and asymmetric share of economic and financial power. The scope of the Coalition's activities allowed it to construct and benefit from a widespread network of patron-client structures and relationships. The Guild Affairs Committee and the Islamic Economy Organization were both co-founded by Taqi Ḵamuši, a member of the old Coalition. The "Union of the Association of Islamic Guilds and Bazaar" was founded by Amāni and acted as an important lever in mobilizing the bazaar in support of the Coalition's political demands (Qučāni, p. 7; Ḡolāmi).

The Coalition operated the Iranian economy as a traditional family enterprise, in which brothers would help out one another on the basis of kinship and loyalty rather than efficiency, expertise or merit. In a patrimonial enterprise, it was evident that the family would seek to secure and guarantee the benefits and gains of its members. The exceptional concentration and monopolization of financial power in the hands of the Foundation along with its ironclad political shield from outside investigations and the absence of transparency in its accounts provided it with a highly disproportionate economic and political weight in the country.

THE POLITICAL DOMAIN

The Coalition has vied for political power by actively competing for all elective offices enumerated in the Constitution. It has systematically presented candidates for the President's Office, the Parliament, the Assembly of Experts, Local Councils and all conceivable so-called civil society associations and organizations such as the association of doctors, lawyers and journalists. In tandem with its efforts to seek political power on the elective front, the Coalition has worked behind the scenes employing its brotherhood network to solicit positions on appointed bodies such as the "Guardian Council" (Šurā-ye negahbān) "Expediency Council" (Šurā-ye maṣleḥat-e neẓām) and the para-state organizations.

Islamic Republic Party. On 29 February 1979, the founding of the Islamic Republic Party (IRP) was announced by five influential clerical figures, Behešti, Musawi Ardabili, Rafsanjani, Bāhonar and Khamenei. Behešti, Bāhonar and Rafsanjani were, to different degrees, directly affiliated with the Coalition and had a common history with it. According to an account, from the 21 member Central Council of the IRP, eight were members of the Coalition (*Šomā*, 5 Āḏar 1384 Š./26 November 2005). At least one third of IRP's Central Council was under direct control of the Coalition. The IRP was a broad umbrella organization of various Islamic tendencies, some at ideological odds with one another, united only in their acceptance of Khomeini's religio-political leadership.

Presidential campaigns. From the first presidential elections in 1980 the Coalition played an active role in nominating its members or allies for the office of President. Its nominee for the first election was Jalāl-al-Din Fārsi. The second presidential election occurred during the difficult times of internal instability and the raging Iran-Iraq war in 1981. The Coalition tested its independent strength by fielding two Coalition members, Askarawlādi and ʿAli-Akbar Parvareš. While the Coalition had two of its own members running for presidency, it officially supported Moḥammad-ʿAli Rejāʾi, the IRP candidate, who was eventually elected. This seemingly contradictory behavior demonstrated that the Coalition candidates were not seriously expected to compete for power, but were actors in a show of competitive presidential elections (Ṣāleḥ, p. 672).

Once Khamenei was elected president in October 1981, his first nominee for the powerful post of Prime Minister, ʿAli-Akbar Welāyati, was rejected by the Majles. Subsequently, Khamenei presented a list of five candidates for the Majles to choose from (Ṣāleḥ, pp. 685-86). Among the five, Parvareš, Mir Salim and Ğafurifard were Coalition members, reflecting the influence of the organization at the time. The Majles, however, voted in favor of Mir Ḥosayn Musawi as Prime Minister and the Coalition's political ambitions were curbed.

The Coalition in government. After the departure of President Abu'l-Ḥasan Bani Ṣadr from the political scene, Rejāʾi the second President of the Islamic Republic appointed Bāhonar as his Prime Minister and in Bāhonar's government four Coalition members or affiliates received ministerial posts. The two key ministerial positions of Commerce and Education went to Askarawlādi and Parvareš, (Ẓarifiniā, Appendix). In the provisional government of Ayatollah Mahdawi Kani, following the assassination of Rejāʾi and Bāhonar and subsequently in Mir Hossein Mousavi's (Mir Ḥosayn Musawi) leftist government of November 1981, the four Coalition figures retained their positions.

It was not until the end of August 1983 that Askarawlādi left the cabinet, while the other three Coalition members continued to serve in Musavi's government. In the summer of 1984 Musawi re-shuffled the government and did not include any Coalition members or affiliates. The only exception was Moḥsen Rafiqdust, who had come to occupy the new ministerial position of the Revolutionary Guards. It was not until Rafsanjani's second government in 1993 that the Coalition was once again represented in the government through Āl-e Esḥāq and Mir Salim, occupying the ministries of Commerce and Islamic Guidance. Once again from 1997 to 2005, during Khatami's presidency and since 2005 when Maḥmud Aḥmadinejād served as the president, members of the Coalition were not represented in the cabinet. These cabinets primarily represented the two new ideological configurations in Iran's political scene, which burgeoned in the 1990s: the new reformist and pro-democracy and the new populist, fundamentalist currents with no sympathy for the right wing fundamentalists (see ISLAM IN IRAN xiii).

In the early 1980s, the Coalition's pro-market position was actively supported by the influential Society of Qom Seminary School Teachers (Jāmeʿa-ye modarresin-e ḥawza-ye ʿelmiya-ye Qom). In a joint meeting of Askarawlādi and Nabawi with the members of this Society, the forthright and plainspoken Ayatollah Aḥmad Āḏari Qomi, who later even confronted Khomeini on economic issues, lambasted the economic formulations, policies and positions of the government. Āḏari Qomi, reflecting the common concerns of the Society of Qom Seminary School Teachers as well as that of the Coalition and bazaar, qualified the economic policies of the Mousavi government as leading the country down the path of "Communist societies" and declared these anti-market policies as simply un-Islamic. (Ṣāleḥ, pp. 302-3).

The issue of whether Islamic economics on the basis of traditional legal edicts (*aḥkām-e feqh-e sonnati*) were capable of resolving the economic problems of a revolutionary society with egalitarian aspirations and in the throes of war was not a simple matter. In May of 1982, first the members of the Society of Qom Seminary School Teachers and less than a week later, the members of the Coalition visited Khomeini to complain about the un-Islamic discriminatory policies against the market and owners of capital and wealth. In the meeting between the Society of Qom Seminary School Teachers and Khomeini, the Ayatollah informed the exalted members of the Society that he too was trying to abide by and implement Islamic jurisprudence. Khomeini, however, warned them against giving the people the impression that they were "supporting the capitalists" (Ṣāleḥ, p. 327).

During the Coalition's meeting of June 1981 with Khomeini, the members expressed their anxieties concerning the economic situation in the country and argued that government policies were drifting away from the precepts of Islam based on jurisprudence. Bādāmčiān, representing the interests of the business and commercial classes couched his free-market arguments in strictly Islamic terms. He referred to the Islamic Republic's successful track in dealing with political and military problems and attributed this success to the adoption of policies that relied on that type of Islam which emanated from the clergy. Bādāmčiān concluded that economic problems too should be resolved on the basis of *Islam-e feqāhati* or an Islam based on jurisprudence. Bādāmčiān was astutely arguing that economic policy had to take its lead not from the revolutionary lay in the government, but from the learned jurists of the Society of Qom Seminary School Teachers or the President (Ṣāleḥ, p. 335).

The pro-market position of the Society of Qom Seminary School Teachers, based on their understanding of Islam, brought them ever closer to the Coalition, which also believed in the non-involvement of the government in the economy. The two organizations, one religious and the other political and traditionally linked to the bazaar believed in the simple fact that economic affairs should be left to the bazaar. The extent of Askarawlādi and the Coalition's constant disputes with Mousavi is well documented in Rafsanjani's memoirs. The scope of these differences found its echo in the left-leaning Majles as well (Hashemi Rafsanjani, 2002, pp. 40, 85, 91, 128, 163-64, 170). The standoff between Mousavi's left-leaning government and the alliance of the Society of Qom Seminary School Teachers, the Coalition and the bazaar dragged on. After Khamenei's second Presidential term, the anti-Mousavi bloc including the Coalition campaigned in favor of Mahdawi Kani as the new Prime Minister. The confrontation between the Coalition and Mousavi over economic issues and interests on the one hand and Khomeini's support of Mousavi on the other hand is said to have led the Coalition to abandon its much flaunted loyalty to and blind emulation of Khomeini. Correctly assessing Khomeini's sympathy for Mousavi's egalitarian economic outlook, the Coalition is said to have pragmatically identified and opted for a different Source of Emulation than that of Khomeini on economic issues. An influential Coalition member is said to have opined that: "the Imam [Khomeini] is a mojtahed and Ayatollah

Mahdawi Kani is also a mojtahed and we imitate Mahdawi Kani on this [economic] issue" (Ḡolāmi, part one). Just as the Coalition had sought someone else's opinion, when Khomeini refused to permit them to assassinate Prime Minister Manṣur, once again, the Coalition tried to circumvent Khomeini's position. In spite of President Khamenei's opposition to Mousavi, Khomeini's support for his Prime Minister assured him of a second four year term. During Mousavi's second term (1985-1989) the Coalition lost its power in the government.

LEGISLATIVE CAMPAIGNS

In the first post-revolutionary Iranian parliament, the Coalition was represented. Ever since, with ebbs and flows, the Iranian Majles has had its own Coalition faction. An alliance between the IRP, the Society of Tehran's Militant Clergy and the Society of Qom Seminary School Teachers facilitated the election of Coalition members and sympathizers to the Majles. In the legislative elections for the 2nd Majles (1983), while Tehran could only send 30 members to the Majles, Askarawlādi ranked 32nd in Tehran and was shut-out of the parliament. Other Coalition members such as Zavāreʾi, Amāni and Bādāmčiān, however, succeeded in entering the Majles. In the elections for the 3rd Majles (1987) none of the Coalition's key figures succeeded in obtaining a seat. Yet in the 4th Majles (1991), with the aid of the Guardian Council's newly acquired right to reject the eligibility of certain candidates and the Coalition's usual alliance with the two influential clerical societies, Ḵamuši, Askarawlādi and Bādāmčiān entered an overwhelming right-leaning parliament. The Coalition's election platform was based on improving and rejuvenating the economy through privatization, structural adjustment, attracting foreign investment and the establishment of Free Trade Zones. The Coalition's call for economic welfare after 8 years of war must have fell on receptive ears. Politically, they presented themselves as followers of both Khamenei and Rafsanjani. Their election slogan of "obedience towards the Leader and support for Hashemi" provided them with a secure political position and assured them of certain key ministerial positions in Rafsanjani's government.

The success of the Coalition and its right-leaning clerical allies in the 4th Majles (1992-96) seems to have convinced the Coalition that it could rely on its own support network to push ahead with its agenda. This surge of self-confidence implied that the Coalition had become convinced that it no longer required Rafsanjani's support. The Coalition and Rafsanjani did not have major differences on economic issues such as the role of the private sector in the economy, even though they may have disagreed on sectoral emphases, the modality of economic interaction with the West or the division of the economic pie. Yet in terms of managerial style and the objectives and scope of economic development, disagreements were more than simmering. While Rafsanjani was able to attract and use a well-educated, up to date and relatively efficient group of managers and technocrats, the Coalition continued to look upon these technocratic, sometimes Western-educated newcomers, lacking traditional credentials, with great suspicion. The Coalition was also weary of the cultural and political implications of Rafsanjani's ambitious developmental policies. The Coalition felt that Rafsanjani's policies would erode the kind of Islamic identity that it deemed suitable for Iran. In return, Rafsanjani was weary of allying himself and compromising with the traditional right-leaning Islamic factions, which he regarded as a force restraining him from achieving his objectives of economic welfare and construction.

For the election campaign of the 5th Majles, the Society of Tehran's Militant Clergy and a Coalition dominated constellation of small Islamic organizations such as the Islamic Society of Engineers, the Islamic Society of Workers and the Society of Zeynab—the women's organization of this constellation—announced the formation of an ad hoc umbrella entity with the clumsy name of Society of Tehran's Militant Clergy and their Concordant Organizations (Jāmeʿa-ye ruḥāniyat-e mobārez Tehran wa Tašakkolhā-ye hamsu). At the time, this old political alliance, which had existed in various forms for almost ten years, seemed to be the winning ticket. Certain of their victory in the 5th Majles, the Tehran Militant Clergy and the Concordant Organizations refused Rafsanjani's request for five slots on their common list of 30 candidates for Tehran. It has been suggested that it was not the Society of Tehran's Militant Clerics that vetoed Rafsanjani's request but the Concordant Organizations, namely the Coalition. It has even been insinuated that Askarawlādi, Ḵamuši and Lājevardi were the Coalition members vetoing Rafsanjani's seemingly innocuous demand (*Hafte-nāme-ye Bahār*, 9 Esfand 1374 Š./28 February 1996; Mortaji, p. 12; *Payām-e emruz*, Mordād-Šahrivar, 1376 Š./August-September 1997).

Hashemi Rafsanjani was almost compelled by the Coalition to form his new family, the Functionaries of Construction (Kārgozārān-e sāzandegi). The success of Rafsanjani's technocratic and liberal-minded protégés in the 5th Majles coincided with the political decline of the Tehran Militant Clergy and the Concordant Organizations. The sectarianism of the Coalition sealed the political fate of the Society of Tehran's Militant Clergy as well (*Payām emruz*, Bahman-Esfand,1374 Š./February-March 1996).

The legislative euphoria of the Coalition and their right-leaning allies during the 4th Majles was rather short-lived. In the three subsequent elections, namely the 5th, 6th and 7th Majles, Coalition members proved unsuccessful in entering the Majles. The mixed and recently poor performance of the Coalition in parliamentary elections is a reflection of the degree of their popularity and a measure of their social weight and significance, as a political force. The fact that the eligibility of their candidates has not been questioned by the Guardian Council in elections, while the qualifications of their rivals has been subjected to widespread rejections adds to the significance of the Coalition's relatively unsuccessful record in the electoral process. Yet their limited success in the legislature should not be construed as a setback for their policies and programs especially between 1989 and 1997.

From March 1988 to the death of Khomeini in June 1989, the close clerical ally of the Coalition, namely the Society of Tehran's Militant Clergy, became largely overshadowed by the left-leaning clerical faction of Society of Tehran's Militant Clerics (Majmaʿ-e ruhāniun-e mobārez-e Tehran). This new clerical formation which seceded from the Society of Tehran's Militant Clergy over its conservative Islamic paradigm was favored by Khomeini and his son, Ahmad Khomeini. As long as the Ayatollah was alive, this new clerical group could not be excluded or pushed out of the political scene. After Khomeini's death, the Society of Tehran's Militant Clergy and their allies swiftly regained their influence and power in pivotal institutions such as the Guardian Council, the 2nd Assembly of Experts, and the 4th Majles. The close and symbiotic political relation between the Coalition and the two key conservative clerical "Societies" (Tehran's Militant Clergy and Qom Seminary School Teachers) fused their fates. As the fortunes of the left-leaning Society of Tehran's Militant Clerics started to wane, that of the "Societies" rose. This important change of winds enabled the Coalition to realize its objectives and interests even though it could not muster the constituency allowing it to play a key role in the legislature. Despite appearances, the secure political position of the Coalition has become shakier after the 7th Majles in which a new breed of conservatives gained a majority. The young conservatives that succeeded in the 7th Majles and won the presidency in 2005 were again a different type of conservatives from the Coalition, even though the Coalition wishes to act as their spiritual mentor.

THE JUDICIARY, SECURITY, AND MILITARY DOMAINS

Immediately after the revolution, Lājevardi, ʿErāqi and Kačuʾi took charge of the arrested members of the old regime who were brought to the Refāḥ School. Later, Kačuʾi and Lājevardi went to work at Evin prison (*Šomā*, 12 Tir 1376 Š./3 June 1997; and 30 Dey 1385 Š./20 January 2006). Soon the circle of the enemies of the new Islamic Republic expanded from the relatively old and petrified members of the old regime to the young and militant members of a variety of political opposition groups. In June 1981, concomitant with the Peoples' Mojāhedin's "declaration of war" against the government and the escalation of their armed struggle, Lājevardi, who had a long history of animosity with the Mojāhedin after having collaborated with them for a period, was appointed to the post of the Islamic Revolution's Prosecutor of Tehran (Dādsetān-e enqelāb-e eslāmi-e Irān). This was a sensitive and important judiciary-security position, providing Lājevardi with nearly unlimited powers to uproot the armed opposition. Lājevardi played a key and categorical role in the repression of the Mojāhedin and other political opponents of the Islamic Republic (Hashemi Rafsanjani, 2002, p. 60). He is said to have been in favor of a thorough, uncompromising and violent policy towards political opposition. Lājevardi was not only suspicious of all opposition forces, but viewed the Mojāhedin of the Islamic Revolution, who were committed to Khomeini and were represented in Mousavi's government, with grave mistrust (Bāqi, 2000, pp. 46-49). At this very sensitive juncture of the Islamic Republic's history, the Coalition played an important role in setting a precedent on the manner and intensity in which armed as well as passive confrontation with the state would be dealt with and resolved in the new Islamic Republic (Hashemi Rafsanjani, 1999, p. 440).

The Head of the Judiciary. From 1989 until 1999, Ayatollah Moḥammad Yazdi, who is said to have been close to the Coalition, headed the Judiciary (Oxford Analytica, *Iran: Judicial Battleground*, 23 June 1999). According to the Constitution, the head of the judiciary is appointed by the Supreme Leader. Yazdi was and is not an official member of the Coalition. He traced his sympathy for the Coalition to the first months after the victory of the revolution and applauded them for their "bravery and acceptance of the rule of the jurisconsult (*welāyatpaziri*)." Yazdi recalled that while he was the head of the Judiciary, he was asked by the Coalition to attend their meetings. On a number of occasions he attended their meetings and explained the policies of his office to the Coalition members (Yazdi, p. 349). Upon his appointment to the head of the judiciary, Yazdi appointed Reżā Zavāreʾi, a Coalition member, as his counselor (Dād, p. 69). Zavāreʾi was also a member of the Guardian Council. In 1992, Bādāmčiān, the Coalition's number two figure, was appointed as counselor to the head of the judiciary. Lājevardi's appointment to the directorship of the country's "Prisons and Reformation Organization" was during Yazdi's control over the judiciary. During Yazdi's tenure, Šafiq, an old member of the Coalition was placed in charge of coordinating the affairs of his office in the judiciary (*Šomā*, 30 Dey 1385 Š./20 January 2007). While prior to the appointment of Yazdi, the judiciary was criticized by the Coalition, during his appointment, the Coalition rallied behind him and became one his main supporters (Ḡolāmi).

After Khomeini decreed in 1979 the establishment of the Islamic Revolutionary Guard Corps (IRGC), Moḥsen Rafiqdust, who at the time was active in Tehran's Revolutionary Committee, was summoned to attend the first meeting of the founders (Rafiqdust, 2004, p. 172). Rafiqdust was a member of the five-man team which commanded the IRGC (Sāzgārā, 23/07/06). He participated in drafting the Charter of the Corps and was designated as Director of the Corps' supplies and logistics department. Later, ʿErāqi and Rafiqdust played a key role in merging, consolidating and centralizing various armed groups loyal to the Islamic Republic, under the umbrella of the IRGC. The IRGC started its activities with a minimum of resources and, for the first six months of its operation, its personnel worked on a voluntary basis and the newly created revolutionary corps was directed by a Central Council. The guards of the Corps in certain military barracks such as *Wali-e ʿaṣr* turned against Rafiqdust and accused him of financial wrongdoings and graft (Rafiqdust, 2004, p. 192).

With the outbreak of the Iran-Iraq war, the IRGC experienced a radical transformation. The size of its organization and the resources at its disposal expanded exponentially. While the weakened, disheartened and distrusted Iranian Army found it difficult to confront the Iraqi occupation of Iran on its own, the young and zealous IRGC fighters proved a more potent, promising and trusting force. As the war raged, the IRGC was given greater scope to obtain heavy weapons in order to create a major military force with its own proper army, navy and air force branches. This metamorphosis required the IRGC to engage in the heavy procurement of armaments. Rafiqdust as the Director of logistics played an important role in the arms purchases and financial operations of the IRGC. (Hashemi Rafsanjani, 1999, p. 496; idem, 2001, p. 61).

From the summer of 1982, the idea of creating a Ministry of the IRGC was in the air. The chief function of the Ministry was to act as the supplier of IRGC. This implied greater regulation and supervision over the logistical activities and defense procurements of the IRGC by placing the IRGC's acquisitions and purchases under the purview of the government. This Ministry did not officially come into existence until November 1982. The Maj-les voted in favor of Rafiqdust as the first Minister of IRGC (Hashemi Rafsanjani, 2001, pp. 272, 302). It is reported that in 1987 the IRGC was allocated $700 million in foreign exchange and its overall budget for military procurements was 2.4 times higher than that of the regular army. On 12 September 1988, the Majles refused to reinstate Rafiqdust as Minister of the IRGC and he was ousted after a vote of no-confidence. After six years, Rafiqdust left his place to Ali Šamḵāni and the Coalition lost its leverage on the powerful Ministry of IRGC.

Expediency Council. For the first time since the foundation of the Expediency Council (Majmaʿ-e tašḵiṣ-e maṣleḥat-e neẓām) in February 1988, Coalition members succeeded in entering this highly influential body in March 1997. Two official members of the Coalition, Askarawlādi and Mir Salim, in addition to a close affiliate of the Coalition, Morteżā Nabawi were appointed by Ayatollah Khamenei to the 19-member Council headed by Hashemi Rafsanjani (*Šomā*, 21 Farvardin 1376 Š./10 April 1997).

THE COALITION'S WORLDVIEW

Political platform. The political platform of the Coalition is based on an unshakeable belief in, and devotion to, the religio-political leadership, guardianship and custodianship of the clergy (*ruḥāniyat*). From its inception and long before the establishment of the Islamic Republic, the Coalition believed in "the creation of an ideal Islamic society." It was Ayatollah Khomeini who gave birth to the Coalition and subsequently by ushering the Islamic Revolution provided them with the opportunity to experiment with the "creation of an ideal Islamic society." Therefore, the Coalition identifies and distinguishes itself as a lay political organization totally loyal and devoted to those clergy who consider "Imam Khomeini" as their role-model. The Coalition believes that only such clerics can discern right from wrong and therefore lead the Coalition to make correct and desirable Islamic decisions on social, economic, cultural and political issues.

The promotion of total compliance with and loyalty to the rule of the jurist-guardian, while emphasizing the importance of the peoples' role in the affairs of the state has created a theoretical paradox in the Coalition's discourse. The political opponents of the Coalition have systematically accused it of ignoring the popular vote and promoting a religious oligarchy. At times, certain statements by Coalition leaders have given credence to this criticism. In April 1997, Askarawlādi declared that: "In the absence of the Twelfth Imam, the just jurist as his vice-gerent is responsible for running the affairs of the Muslim community (*omma*). The suggestion of those who argue that the legitimacy of the jurist-guardian's rule (*welāyat*) is based on the peoples' vote is a plot and the wish of the enemies of Islam. The jurist-guardian's rule in an Islamic system is derived from Islamic sources and not from the peoples' vote" (Mortaji, pp. 44-45).

Consistent with its initial objective of "creating an ideal Islamic society" in April 1997, the Coalition suggested that the Expediency Council should explore and assess the process by which the Islamic Republic could be transformed into a 'Government of Islamic Justice' (*Šomā*, 21 Farvardin, 1376 Š./10 April 1997) The Coalition's suggestion implied that the Islamic Republic was a transitional form of government which should eventually be replaced with an Islamic Government. The deletion of the noun Republic could be construed as a call to eliminate the Republican characteristic of the Iranian political system. By purging the political system of its pivotal guarantor of the peoples' partial sovereignty, the Coalition seemed to be promoting a political system where the jurist-guardian would monopolize all power without any checks and balances by the people.

The fact remains that despite its political defeats and deceptions in numerous rounds of political competition, the Coalition's zeal for political participation has not dampened. It seems as if, with the passing of time, the Coalition has become ever more committed to becoming a viable and modern political party, a development not favorably looked upon by many of its clerical allies. With the maturing of the Coalition, it has become difficult to label this political organization as categorically authoritarian, anti-democratic and simply in favor of a hierocracy. At the end of 2005 and some six months after the election of President Ahmadinejad, Ayatollah Meṣbāḥ Yazdi and his students, especially Moḥsen Ḡarawiān, launched and publicized the highly inflammable dual idea that the establishment of an Islamic Government, in contrast to an Islamic Republic, was a religious necessity and that Imam Khomeini neither believed in a Republic nor the legitimizing character of the peoples' vote. These propositions were an echo of the Coalition's suggestions some nine years ago. Meṣbāḥ Yazdi, President Ahmadinejad's chief clerical proponent, even went as far as suggesting that those who would consider the validity of

"Republicanism" as equal to that "Islamism" were infidels (*Šarq*, 20 Dey 1384 Š./10 January 2005).

In view of the Coalition's previous flirtation with the concept of a "Government of Islamic Justice," belittling the people's vote in contrast to the role of the jurist-guardian, its reaction to the wave of anti-Republicanism whipped up by Meṣbāḥ Yazdi and his followers was unexpected if not astonishing. Bādāmčiān and Ḡafurifard rejected the anti-Republican ideas attributed to Khomeini. Bādāmčiān referred to Khomeini's famous dictum of "an Islamic Republic neither a word more nor less" and suggested that the Imam's succinct statement had clearly settled the issue. Ḡafurifard went further and treated the suggestion that Khomeini did not believe in the Republic as a grave accusation against the Imam's ideas. He argued that based on "political rationalism" the Islamic Republic was the best political system as it "obtained its religiosity/legitimacy (*mašruʿiyat*) from Islam and derived its acceptance/desirability (*maqbuliyat*) from the peoples' vote (*Sharq*, 14 Dey 1384 Š./14 January 2005). Amir Moḥebiān, an important and measured theoretical voice always considered very close to the Coalition and a regular contributor to *Resālaat*, argued that "if the Republican aspect of the system is negated it would be important to see what would replace it. The antithesis of Republicanism, a system based on the peoples' participation, is Sultanism in which one or a few people rule. If we reject the Republic, would we want to replace it with Sultanism? Certainly Sultanism was neither the Imam's preferred political system nor was it included in the Constitution, since the Islamic Revolution overthrew this type of government" (*Šarq*, 12 Dey 1384 Š./2 January 2005).

Economic platform. The economic platform of the Coalition constitutes yet another one of its axiomatic principals. Based on the employment record of a good number of its founding fathers and even that of the second generation of its adherents, the Coalition has been viewed as the bazaar faction of Iran's political forces. It has been suggested that the Coalition is probably the only political organization in Iran which possesses an organic relation with its social base of small shopkeepers and merchants (Ẓarifiniā, pp. 94-95).

The Coalition has consistently favored an economic system based on the sanctity of private property and the freedom of profit in commercial and economic activities, without any regulation on the accumulation of wealth as long as the activities engaged in are considered as Islamically permissible. During Mousavi's premiership, the Coalition became the most outspoken critic of the government's interventionist and statist position, condemning it as un-Islamic and socialist. At the time, the Coalition, in alliance with the Society of Qom's Seminary School Teachers, actively campaigned to reduce the purview of the state and cooperative sector to the benefit of the private sector. It also moved to protect the private sector from the state's incursions. The Coalition was intent on freeing the economy of state monopolies, denying the government the power to take over the distribution of certain goods during the war, and shielding the private sector from price controls and the imposition of fines and punishments against businesses accused of speculation and hoarding. The notion that the government may be a good supervisor, but not a good merchant, encapsulated the Coalition's position at the time.

During the war period, the anti-interventionist posture of the Coalition gave it a pro-market and pro-capitalist reputation. Categorizing the Coalition as pro-market and pro-capitalist may erroneously imply that it firmly believes in a perfectly competitive free-market capitalist system. As true as this may have been during the early years of the revolution, the Coalition seems to have outgrown its traditional small shopkeeper and merchant base and has become a major patron and benefactor in all conceivable economic and financial fields. The political and economic resources that it controls and commands have enabled it to widen and deepen its influence by creating a vast and yet largely opaque patron-client network. The increasing significance of political power in securing economic gain has brought about an important change in the Coalition's initial admiration for free markets and disaffection for government intervention in the market.

The Coalition continues to hold private property, entitlement to the proceeds of commercial and economic activities as well as the right to reproduce and increase private property and wealth as an axiomatic principal. However the ever-increasing involvement of the Coalition in various state, para-state and government owned and managed economic units as well as its ability to guarantee profits and gains by influencing economic policy has provided it with a taste for rewards through political networking and favoritism. The shift in the Coalition's economic platform is a function of its increasing reliance on rewards obtained through non-market mechanisms. It can, therefore, no longer be regarded as the bulwark of the free-market that it was during the early days of the revolution.

First in June 2005 and subsequently in July 2006, Ayatollah Khamenei articulated a new reading of the famous Article 44 of the Constitution. He called for an increasing share of activities and resources for the cooperative and the private sector in the national economy. He also evoked the necessity of privatizing state-owned economic units and reducing the state's financial and managerial load. The Coalition supported this important re-orientation in the economy, which had been nominally underway since Rafsanjani's presidency. Moḥammad Nabi Ḥabibi, the Director General of the Coalition party called for the creation of "a centralized and efficient management group dedicated to Article 44, in order to implement and realize the directives of the Leader [i.e., Khamenei]" (*Šomā*, 5 Esfand 1385/24 February 2006). Bādāmčiān, the vice-director of the Coalition Party, shed some light on the composition of this key management group which the Coalition promoted to implement the directives of the Leader. He argued that the reason for the nation's economic failures had been the hegemony of "eclectic thoughts and tendencies" at the governmental level. This distortion, Bādāmčiān argued, had taken root ever since the transitional government of Bāzargān came to power. According to Bādāmčiān, the prevalence of un-Islamic and eclectic thoughts of both the socialist and Western variants during previous governments had produced a situation where 82 percent of the economy was state-owned.

For Bādāmčiān, correction of the ideological-religious deformation which he identified as the prime cause of Iran's economic plight, hinged on "entrusting the economic affairs to individuals possessing healthy Islamic thoughts derived from the ideas of Imam Khomeini." Naturally, these individuals would be expected to be free of any Western or Eastern deviations. Bādāmčiān emphasized that this religiously correct designated group also needed to be experienced managers familiar with he world economy (*Šomā*, 15 Esfand 1385 Š./6 March 2006).

Elaborating on the particulars of this designated group who would take over the economic realm and realize the directives of the Leader, Bādāmčiān's called for "relegating [economic] responsibilities to those individuals who were proponents and upholders of values (*arzešgerāyān*)." The "upholders of values" are defined as those who "during the past three decades" had not been eclectic and who were capable of fostering and managing a 'pro-value revivalism.' Bādāmčiān argued that such a necessary revival needed "authoritative, managerial and thoughtful individuals" (*Šomā*a, 15 Esfand 1385 Š./ 6 March 2006). For Coalition leaders, solving unresolved economic problems was not necessarily related to the dismantling of the state and para-state economic units, privatization, introduction of competition, stamping out corruption and improving transparency, but was contingent upon entrusting and relegating the management of the economy to individuals whose profile resembled the Coalition's first generation. The change in the Coalition's economic platform is well reflected in its emphasis on economic administration, planning and control by "worthy and pro-value" individuals rather than empowering the impersonal market.

The Coalition's control over non-private economic titans, obtained through political networking and brotherhood relations has provided it with a high-yielding power base. Furthermore, the economic gains from these resources are, to a large extent, politically determined. The Coalition has come to realize that it stands to gain much more from the state's politically motivated allocation of oil revenues than from the market's allocation mechanism. It, therefore, finds itself in the favorable dual position of drawing economic advantage in the form of economic rent from control over political levers as well as economic returns from an imperfect market, the rules of which it can influence to its own benefit. Success in an impersonal market system requires transparency, perfect information, minimal state and political interference as well as efficiency. Benefiting from economic rent in a "confraternal capitalist system" requires access to political power; proximity, familiarity and friendship with power brokers; opaqueness and patron-client relationships, requiring loyalty and not necessarily productivity. The Coalition has expanded its power base by relying on and benefiting from an authoritarian "confraternal capitalist system" and will not be able to prosper as much in an impersonal efficiency-seeking market capitalist system.

Cultural platform. The Coalition firmly believes in the truth, validity and legitimacy of its own perception of Islam, which it attributes to a religious jurist. The claim by the Coalition that it obediently follows the lead of a Source of Emulation legitimizes it to treat all its political rivals as effectively un-Islamic. In practice, however, the Coalition has sought and followed the Islamic interpretation that best suits its own interests. The Coalition has consistently claimed that its positions were a pure reflection of Ayatollah Khomeini's. However, following its own interest, the Coalition did not shy away from opposing Khomeini's decision to support Mousavi's economic policies during his Premiership. Yet the Coalition's argument that they represent and uphold true Islamic values because those values have been identified as such by the Islamic jurists, constitutes the main pillar of their claim to legitimacy as a political force. Khatami's alternative Islamic discourse, with its own vocabulary and categorizations, presented a real challenge to the Coalition. During Khatami's presidency, the Coalition was confronted with a young and well-read generation of Islamic intellectuals, which compelled it to define and redefine its ideology in relation to their theories.

According to Bādāmčiān, pluralism has no place in an Islamic government, since it leads to chaos, the emergence of a violent dictatorship or the hegemony of foreigners (*Šomā*, 21 Farvardin, 1378 Š./10 April 1999) The Coalition's dislike for pluralism in all its aspects sets the tone for the cultural platform of this political organization. The notion of "freedom for the opposition" became an important slogan of Khatami's election campaign and gradually gained popularity as a virtue and a value during his presidency. The Coalition's response to the spread and popularity of an invitation to political and cultural tolerance for the "other" was one of anxiety and suspicion. To the Coalition pluralism, tolerance and indulgence befogged the clearly delineated boundaries separating the righteous revolutionary Islamic forces or the Coalition and its concordant forces, who were worthy of running the state, from the undeserving "others." Acceptance of the rights of "others" or pluralism and tolerance weakened categorical distinctions between right and wrong, good and evil, and friends and enemies. The Coalition, however, promoted and needed to homogenize in order to label. It viewed pluralism and the extension of freedom to the opposition as a possible Horse of Troy which could not only pave the way for a parliamentarian overthrow of the Islamic system, but would also undermine Islamic values by promoting moral laxity and gender mixing (*Šomā*, 8 Ḵordād 1378 Š./29 May 1999). To the Coalition, the application of authority and homogenization were undisputed virtues in all domains (*Šomā*, 4 Āḏar 1385).

As the non-clerical custodian of Islamic values, the Coalition is deeply alarmed about the erosion of certain values and principles in the face of what it conceives to be a "cultural assault." Convinced of an ongoing conspiracy against the cultural Islamic values of society, the Coalition adopts an offensive position against all its political rivals who may think differently. In its weekly, *Šomā*, the Coalition officially itemized the cultural strategy of the "enemy." (*Šomā*, 11 Āḏar 1385 Š./2 November 2006). It argued that subsequent to the failure of its military assault against the Islamic Republic, the enemy sought to destabilize the Republic through a "cultural assault." According to the Coalition, the "enemy" conducted its cultural campaign against the Iranian youth on eight different fronts: first, advertisement and propagation of Western lifestyles, worldliness and Westernization; second, propagation of secularism and the division between religion and politics as an ideal political model; third, the propagation of pluralism and the multiplicity of discourses in relation to religion and Islam with the objective of wiping out the original, correct and pure Mohammedan discourse; fourth, presenting a violent and terrorist image of Islam; fifth, mocking Islamic beliefs and sanctities through desecrating otherworldly values; sixth, assaulting and attacking the basis of Islam, the Islamic system and all those institutions guaranteeing the Islamic nature of the system; seven, propagating the notion of duality in the power-structure and the government, while pitting the elected against the appointed in the system; and eight, changing the taste, demand and expectation of people and channeling them to collide with the ideals and objectives of the Islamic Revolution.

The Coalition maintains that the "cultural assault and massacre of the revolution's third generation" has been paved by governments adopting a policy of "tolerance and indulgence." According to the Coalition, this cultural assault was akin to a "silent toppling" of the system, with newspapers, books, films, CDs, DVDs, journals and free tribunes at universities acting as its main foot soldiers. (*Šomā*, 11 Āḏar 1385 Š./2 November 2006). In its reaction to events that could be categorized as "cultural assaults," the Coalition has been accused of supporting a discourse of violence (*Payām-e emruz*, Šahrivar-Mehr 1378 Š./September-October 1999). During the student unrests that followed an attack by the security forces on the main dormitory of Tehran University in July 1999, the notion of "cultural assault" blended with "political assault." Askarawlādi supported Ayatollah Meṣbāḥ Yazdi's position in relation to the use of violence against dissidents, nonconformists and rioters, who were categorized as "corruptors and assailants." Askarawlādi supported Meṣbāḥ as "one of the most outstanding figures of the Qom seminary" and "an astute and deep connoisseur of Islam" (*Šomā*, 28 Mordad, 1378/19 August 1999). Meṣbāḥ Yazdi had justified violence by arguing that: "Islam allows any Muslim to kill a person who insults Islamic sanctities" (*Payām-e emruz*, Shahrivar-Mehr 1378 Š./September-October 1999). In reference to the students, Askarawlādi argued that "undoubtedly those who had participated in Tehran's riots had entered the phase of toppling [the regime] and deserved to be considered as corruptors and assailants since they had taken their orders for such activities from espionage services of the enemy." Having categorized the students involved as "corruptors and assailants," Askarawlādi concurred with Meṣbāḥ that religious punishments (one of which could be death) had to be applied to the culprits and condemned those who criticized Meṣbāḥ as a theoretician of violence (*Šomā*, 28 Mordād, 1378 Š./19 August 1999). According to Bādāmčiān's assessment, the tumult was masterminded by "the Americans, the Zionists and a few dependent foreign governments in collusion with domestic mercenaries" (*Šomā*, 31 Tir, 1378 Š./22 July 1999).

Under the pretext of defending Islamic sanctities, the Coalition is said to have orchestrated waves of opposition against Khatami's government in order to limit constitutionally sanctioned liberties and freedoms. In its effort to curb such liberties, the Coalition is suspected of having compelled the Society of Tehran's Militant Clerics to write an open letter against Khatami in September 1999 (*Payām-e emruz*, Ābān 1378 Š./November 1999).

FROM RELIGIOUS MOURNING GROUPS TO POLITICAL PARTY

The provisional government of Ayatollah Mahdawi Kani in 1981 reflected the delicate balance of power between the very different economic and religious outlooks that had come together under the umbrella of the Islamic Republic Party. In the absence of the widely respected Mahdawi Kani in the subsequent government the differences and rivalries became more pronounced and confrontational. The influential members of the Coalition, especially Askarawlādi, resisted the statist and interventionist economic policies of Mousavi. Economic disagreements over-flowed into religious disputes, with the pro-market Coalition accusing Mousavi's left-leaning interventionist faction of ignoring primary religious edicts. The brawl eventually necessitated the intervention of Khomeini. The topics of dispute and personal disagreements in the government mirrored the tug of war between two main factions in the IRP.

It was not until the differences between the two factions rendered the party effectively inoperative and the disagreements between President Khamenei and Prime Minister Mousavi, each representing a different faction reached new and unmanageable heights that in June 1987, the IRP dissolved itself to prevent the animosities from permeating throughout society. In the same year, the Coalition decided to reorganize itself independently and, having obtained permission from Khomeini, it began the new phase of its political activities and registered its organization under the name of Jamʿiyat-e Moʾtalefa-ye Eslāmi (*Šomā*, Dey 1384 Š./January 2005). The 12 founding members of the new organization were Amāni, Bādāmčiān, Tawakkoli-binā, Moṣtafā Ḥāʾerizādeh, Abu'l-Fażl Ḥāji Ḥaydari, Sayyed Aṣḡar Rokṣefat, Moḥammad Jawād Rafiqdust, Mehdi Saʿid Moḥammadi, Ḥabib-Allāh Šafiq, Ḥabib-Allāh Askarawlādi,

Aḥmad Karimi Eṣfahāni and Jawād Maqṣudi (Qolāmi). Askarawlādi became Director General or the official leader of the organization and remained in that position until 2004, when he stepped down and Ḥabibi, took over from him as the Director General.

The Coalition's first Congress was held in the winter of 1992 (Dey 1370 Š./January 1992), followed by its second Congress two years later. At the 2nd Congress, the Coalition's charter was modified and the number of members on the Central Council was expanded from 15 to 30. The 5th Congress decided to change the name of its plenary meeting to a General Assembly. The most important change in the organization came during the 7th General Assembly, held in 2004. The Coalition members present at the General Assembly voted in favor of changing the Coalition's name to Ḥezb-e moʾtalefa-ye eslāmi or the Party of Islamic Coalition. Until the 3rd Congress in 1995, names of Central Council members as well as the time and place of the plenary meetings were largely kept secret from the public. The 4th Congress broke with this clandestine tradition and the organization became more transparent (Ḡolāmi). The 7th General Assembly was widely publicized by the Coalition. The names of 26 members of the Central Council were published, yet for some reason the names of four other members of the steering 30-person Central Council were concealed. According to the official statistics of the Coalition, there was only one clerical figure and three women among the Central Council members. Thirty percent of the Central Council was reported to be young (*Šomā*, *Viže-nāma*, Dey 1384 Š./January 2006).

In February 1997, the Coalition published its official weekly newspaper. *Šomā*, appeared a few months before the presidential elections during which the Coalition forcefully campaigned for Nāṭeq Nuri. The name of the weekly, *Šomā* was the abbreviation for *šohadā-ye moʾtalefa-ye eslāmi* or the "Martyrs of the Islamic Coalition." During the first nine months of its publication, the expression of "Martyrs of the Islamic Coalition" was systematically printed at the top of the first page. Yet in October 1997, the "Martyrs of the Islamic Coalition" was first replaced by "Society of Islamic Coalition" and later by "Party of Islamic Coalition." During the past ten years, the scant and austere 8-page weekly has grown to a large 18-page tabloid. Before the publication of *Šomā*, the Coalition's positions and opinions were usually reflected in the pages of *Resālat* newspaper, which appeared in January 1986. The editor of *Resālat*, Kāẓem Anbārluʾi, became a member of the Central Council of the Coalition and the director of the Coalition's Political Center.

CONCLUSION

The upward social, economic and political mobility of the Coalition since its inception reflects a phenomenal transformation in the organization and its members. Coalition members have gone from obscurity to fame, from marginality to centrality, from militant contenders of power to influential members of the legislative, judiciary and executive branches. Their mode of organizational interaction was impacted by the milieu from which they came. The Coalition's first generation firmly believed in an all-male community in which relations were based on solidarity, selflessness, brotherhood, loyalty, charity and a sense of chivalry, all for the cause of God. These qualities were virtues to be aspired to in the pre-modern commercial world of Iranian bazaars (see BĀZĀR iii; JAVĀNMARDI). At the time of its inception, the Coalition was a small semi-clandestine, petty-trader, bazaar-based entity with the majority of its all male lower middle-class members in their youth, living very modestly in the popular neighborhoods around Tehran's bazaar. The Coalition's ideal was to be of service to Ayatollah Khomeini, in whom it believed as a religious as well as a political source of emulation, and to help him topple the regime. The Coalition has now developed into an official political party with its own youth, women, regional and international organizations, holding regular open meetings and seminars. Its think-tanks are involved in studies, analysis, planning and policy formulation. The Coalition Party delegates participate in international seminars, pay official visits to countries such as China, Malaysia and Syria and confer with their governmental representatives.

Today, the Coalition has a distinguished place among the political and economic elite of Iran. By 2007, a good number of its members whom in the 1960s were committed to dismantling the Shah's regime would probably appear among the imaginary 1,000 families of power and fortune that is always said to have ruled. The Party and its members have concentrated political and economic power to an unprecedented degree. Even though leading Coalition members still officially meet with the people of the street and the traditional mosque-going folk in Iran, their political and economic success has physically, mentally, inspirationally and ideologically uprooted them from the soil, which nourished their zeal, ideals and aspirations. Caught in the duality of its past and present, the Coalition needs to decide the ideal Islamic behavior which it wishes to promote among its younger members. Would it choose the lifestyle, ethical norms, value systems and aspirations of the likes of Boḵrāʾi, Ṣaffār Harandi, Niknežād, Amāni, and ʿErāqi, who sacrificed their lives for its cause or should it candidly accept the events since the revolution and its own earthly conditions embroiled with economic and political power and all that is associated with it?

The first generation of the Coalition, with its dated ethical norms, has now come to be viewed as "dead wood" and dinosaurs facing extinction by the new generation of Islamic conservatives, emerging primarily from the Revolutionary Guards and Mobilization forces. They have been represented by various short-lived and disposable groupings such as "The Constructors" (*ābādgarān*), "The Sacrificers" (*iṯārgarān*), "The Pleasant Scent of Service" (*rāyeḥa-ye ḵoš-e ḵedmat*), and the recently created rubric of "The United Front of Conservatives" (*Jebha-ye mottaḥed-e oṣulgerāyān*). Yet as upstart political groups, they have no real commitment to playing the game of politics according to the values and norms of the Coalition's first generation.

In the 2nd Local Elections of February 2003 and the 7th Parliamentary Elections of November 2004, under pressure from their young and parvenu political rivals, key Coalition members desisted from running for office, which may result in its gradual elimination from political power. The new conservative rivals of the Coalition, with their new political ethics who attained power in the above Elections, and more specifically in the Presidential Elections of 2005, saw no reason to share the power they had obtained through their own political acumen and tactical astuteness with the Coalition (see further ISLAMIC MOVEMENTS IN 20TH CENTURY IRAN).

Bibliography: Books. Ḥ. Akawān Tawḥidi, *Dar pas parde-ye tazvir*, Paris, 1985. Ḥ. Amiri, *Tāriḵ-e šafāhi-e Hayʾatḥā-ye moʾtalefa-ye eslāmi*, Tehran, 2007. B. ʿĀqeli, *Ruzšemār-e tāriḵ-e Irān*, 2 vols., Tehran, 1991. A. Bādāmčiān, *Āšnāʾi bā Jamʿiyat-e moʾtalefa-ye eslāmi*, n.p., n.d. Idem and Banāʾi, *Hayʾatḥā-ye moʾtalefa-ye eslāmi*, Tehran, 1983. ʿE. Bāqi, *Barāy-e tāriḵ: Goft o gu bā Saʿid Ḥajjāriān*, Tehran, 2000. J. A. Bill, *The Eagle and the Lion*, New Haven, 1988. Sayyed Kāẓem Bojnurdi, *Ḵāṭerāt-e Sayyed Kāẓem-e Bojnurdi*, Tehran, 1999. B. Dād, *Ṣad ruz bā Ḵātami*, Tehran, 1998. J. Fārsi, *Zavāyā-ye tārik*, Tehran, 1994. A. Forāti, *Tāriḵ-e šafāhi-e enqelāb-e eslāmi*, Tehran, 2000. H. Ḡaffāri, *Ḵāṭerāt-e Hādi Ḡaffāri*, Tehran, 1995. N. Ḥamidiān, *Safar bar bālhā-ye ārezu*, Sweden, 2004. A. Hashemi Rafsanjani, *Dowrān-e mobārezeh*, Tehran, 1997. Idem, *ʿObur az boḥrān*, ed. Y. Hāšemi Rafsanjāni, Tehran, 1999. Idem, *Ārāmeš wa čāleš*, ed. M. Hāšemi, Tehran, 2002. Idem, *Pas az boḥrān*, ed. F. Rafsanjāni, Tehran, 2001. Ḥ. Kāviāni, *Bāzḵʾāst az qodrat*, Tehran, 2000. S. Kalkāli, *Ḵāṭerāt-e Ayat-Allāh Ṣādeq Kalkāli*, Tehran, 2000. M. Kāẓemi, *Ḵāṭerāt-e ʿEzzatšāhi*, Tehran, 2006. Ruḥ-Allāh Khomeini (Ḵomeyni), *Ṣaḥifa-ye nur*, 17 vols., Tehran, 1982. F. Mahallāti, *Ḵāṭerāt wa mobārezāt-e šahid Mahallāti*, Tehran, 1997. M.-R. Mahdawi Kani, *Ḵāṭerāt Ayat-Allāh Mahdawi Kani*, ed., G. Kʾājasarvi, Tehran, 2006. L. Mayṯami, *Az Nahżat-e āzādi tā Mojāhedin* I, Tehran, n.d. S. Mirzāʾi, *Ṭayyeb dar gozar-e luṭihā*, Tehran, 2002. Moʾassesa-ye moṭāleʿāt-e siāsi, *Sāzmān-e mojāhedin-e ḵalq*, 2 vols., Tehran, 2005. K. Moqaddam, *Ḵošunat-e qānuni*, Tehran, 2001. Ḥ.-ʿA. Montaẓeri, *Matn-e kāmel-e ḵāṭerāt-e Ayat-Allāh Ḥosayn-ʿAli Montaẓeri*, Europe, 2000. H. Mortaji, *Jenāḥhā-ye siāsi dar Irān-e emruz*, Tehran, 1998. M. Moslem, *Factional Politics in Post-Khomeini Iran*, Syracuse, 2002. M. J. Moẓaffar, "Avvalin raʾis-e jomhur," Tehran, 1999. ʿA.-A. Nāṭeq Nuri, *Ḵāṭerāt-e Ḥojat-al-Eslām Nāṭeq-e Nuri*, ed., M. Mirdār, Tehran, 2005. Oxford Analytica, "Iran: Judicial Battleground," June 23, 1999. Idem, "Iran: Bonyad Reorganization," July 23, 1999. M. Qoučāni, *Pedar-ḵʾāndeh wa čapḥā-ye javān*, Tehran, 2000. Moḥsen Rafiqdust, *Ḵāṭerāt-e Moḥsen Rafiqdust*, ed., D. Qāsempur, Tehran, 2004. M. Rażawi, *Hāšemi wa enqelāb*, Tehran, 1997. N. Rowšan-nahād, *Madāres-e eslāmi dar dawra-ye Pahlavi-e dovvom*, Tehran, 2005. Ḥ. Ruḥāni, *Barrasi wa taḥlili az nahżat Emām Ḵomeyni*, Tehran, 1982. M. Ṣadri, *Zendegi wa amalkard-e Ḥasan-ʿAli Manṣur*, Tehran, 2004. M. Sāʾeli Kordedeh, *Šurā-ye enqelāb-e eslāmi-e Irān*, Tehran, 2005. Sayyed Ḥasan Ṭāheri Ḵorramābādi, *Ḵāṭerāt-e Āyat-Allāh Ṭāheri Ḵorramā-bādi*, ed., M.-R. Aḥmadi, I, Tehran, 1998. Moḥammad Yazdi, *Ḵāṭerāt-e Āyat-Allāh Moḥammad Yazdi*, Tehran, 2001. H. R. Ẓarifiniā, *Kālbodšekāfi-e jenāḥ-hā-ye siāsi-e Irān*, Tehran, 1999.

Electronic sources. Ayatollah Anwāri, *Ḵāṭerāt-e Ayat-Allāh Anwāri*, ed., R. Jaʿfariān <www.baztab.ir/news/64251.pl>. Emrouz, 2/7/2007, http://emrouz.info/print.aspx?ID=5007 Fattāḥ Ḡolāmi, Kalbod Shekafi Motalefeh, I, http://www.baztab.com/index.asp?ID=2525. Idem, Kālbod šekāfi-e moʾtalefeh, II, http://www.baztab.com/index.asp?ID=2649. M. Sāzgārā, "Sepāh wa se enherāf," 23/07/06 http://www.sazgara.net/persian.

(ALI RAHNEMA)

JAMKĀNA. See AHL-E ḤAQQ.

JAMSHEDJI SORAB KUKADARU (b. Surat, 26 May 1831; d. Bombay, 4 October 1900), Parsi Zoroastrian priest. Kukadaru was born in Surat (Gujarat, India) but spent most of his life in Bombay (modern Mumbai). He was known for his simple and ascetic lifestyle and for paying extremely rigorous respect to priestly purity rules. He spent the larger part of his time in prayers and rituals. Although he was a mere ritual priest, as of 1862 he was publicly addressed as Dastur (High-priest; see Patel, II, p. 62).

Kukadaru served as chief instructor at Seth Jijibhai Dadabhai Zand Avesta Madressa in Bombay from its inception in 1863 until it was closed down (Patel, III, p. 804). In 1872 he complained to the Bombay Parsi Panchayat (q.v.) that he had advertised his plan to publish an edition and translation of the *Dēnkard* (q.v.) in five volumes, but that this plan had been subverted by the trustees' decision to entrust this work to Dastur Peshotan Sanjana (1857-1931, see SANJANA, DASTUR DARAB PESHOTAN at *iranica.com*). His request to make him a collaborator of Sanjana was turned down by the trustees (Desai, p. 67).

As a learned priest, Kukadaru lectured on religious and social issues (Patel, II, pp. 95, 692) and contributed religion-related articles to the magazine *Yazdān parast* which was published between 1868 and 1889 (Patel, II, p. 246; III, p. 804). Moreover, he published two booklets—*Kholāsae āfrinagān* (Explanation of the Āfrinagān, 1864) and *Hekāete āfrinagān* (Facts about the xfrx̌ngān, 1866)—taking a stance in the controversy that was raging among the priests about the prayers to be recited within the Āfrinagān and the Jāšān (qq.v.) rituals (Patel, II, p. 62). He was also involved in other controversies and legal cases.

Kukadaru was a reputed astrologer. He was renowned for his spiritual powers, in particular with respect to healing and divination. He is reported to have prophesized several events (including the death of certain persons) and outwitted a Muslim *pir* (spiritual master) who had challenged him.

Dastur Kukadaru was a member of the managing committee of the Anjuman Atash Behram temple in Bombay during the time of its construction (Patel, III, p. 654). He was publicly thanked for his generous donation of Rs. 8,500 towards the building of the temple. In commemoration of his efforts, the main hall on the ground floor of the Anjuman Atash Behram bears Kukadaru's name. In his commitment to this project, he lined up with the Jamasp-Asa family against the Sanjanas, as the latter were in charge of the already existing Atash Behram temple that followed the same (Shenshai) calendar (see CALENDARS iv.).

Possibly as an explanation of how a modest ritual priest could have procured such a large amount of money, the legend started to circulate later that it was the power of his prayers that had materialized gold. Posthumously, Dastur Kukadaru rose to become one of the most famous priests in Parsi history. Rituals on the occasion of his anniversary are performed on popular demand to this day, and a bust of Dastur Kukadaru (showing him bespectacled, wearing a beard and a priestly turban) is one of the most popular iconographical materials within the Parsi community. Prayer in front of his image is said to bring the fulfillment of one's wishes.

Kukadaru's posthumous fame was further reinforced when he began to appear, in the form of a light-aura, to Ervad Nadirshah Aibara (1933-89), another ritual priest. Dastur Kukadaru would transmit prayers to Aibara who would then hand over these ritual prescriptions to his clients. The powerful "vibrations" of these prayers have reportedly "healed" thousands of Zoroastrians. After the death of Aibara, this tradition was continued by his widow (Kreyenbroek and Munshi, pp. 259-66).

From the gifts that devotees wanted to present him, Aibara started the Dastoorji Kookadaru Memorial Fund, which eventually sponsored the consecration (in 1990) of a new fire-temple in Sanjan (Gujarat), the reputed landing-place of the Parsis at the Indian west coast. This is the one and the only Parsi fire temple named in the memory of a priest (Dastoorji Kookadaru Dar-e Mehr). As a priest-saint and posthumous ritual healer, Dastur Kukadaru is a unique figure in the history of modern Zoroastrianism (Stausberg, III, pp. 123-25).

Bibliography: S. F. Desai, *History of the Bombay Parsi Punchayet, 1860-1960*, Bombay, 1977. Ph. G. Kreyenbroek and Sh. N. Munshi, *Living Zoroastrianism. Urban Parsis Speak about their Religion*, Richmond, Va., 2001. B. B. Patel, *Parsee Prakash, Being a Record of Important Events in the Growth of the Parsee Community in Western India, Chronologically Arranged from the Date of Their Immigration into India to the Year 1860 A. D.*, 3 vols., Bombay, 1878-1920. M. Stausberg, *Die Religion Zarathushtras: Geschichte, Gegenwart, Rituale*, 3 vols., Stuttgart, 2002-4.

(MICHAEL STAUSBERG and RAMIYAR P. KARANJIA)

JAMŠID B. MASʿUD ḠIĀṮ-AL-DIN KĀŠI. See ḠIĀṮ-AL-DIN KĀŠI.

JAMŠID (or JAM), mythical king of Iran; Middle Persian J̌am, J̌amšēd, Avestan Yima (Old Indic Yama), with the epithet *xšaēta* (Elamite Persepolis tablets Yamakšedda; Benveniste, 1966, p. 96; Hallock, p. 771; Hinz, p. 273). The common noun, meaning "twin," is attested once in Old Avestan in the dual (*yə̄mā*, see below) and in Old Indic from the *Rigveda* on (singular, dual, plural), and is used to denote one of a pair of twins, twin brothers or sisters, or several individual twins. On the name, see also Mayrhofer, I, no. 406. This entry is divided into two sections.

i. *Myth of Jamšid.*

ii. *Jamšid in Persian Literature.*

i. MYTH OF JAMŠID

In the Avesta (q.v.), several myths are associated with Yima. He ruled the world in a golden age; he saved living beings from a natural catastrophe by preserving specimens in his *var-* (fortress); he possessed the most Fortune (*xᵛarənah-*, Mid. Pers. *xwarrah*) among mortals, but lost it and his kingship as a consequence of lying; and he was "cut" (in half?) by an evil being. The Middle Persian literature has preserved additional myths: Jam and the New Year's Day festival (Nowruz), Jam and his sister, Jam's hybris, Jam and Dahāg (New Pers. Żaḥḥāk), and others; the Zoroastrian and Muslim Persian literature contains the stories about Jamšid and Tahmuraṯ and the discovery of the healing property of bull's urine (*gōmēz*, q.v., where the story is not mentioned), Jamšid as cultural hero, and others. Among the early Muslim historians, the stories about Jam and Jamšid were popular at all times, from Abu Ḥanifa Dinavari (d. betw. 894-903, q.v.), Ṭabari (839-923), Abu ʿAli Amirak Balʿami (d. betw. 992-97, q.v.), etc. to Mirḵᵛānd (1433-98).

The Yima/Jamšid story as known in the West at the time was frequently described by authors who wrote on Iranian religion in the 19th and early 20th centuries (e.g., Stuhr; Windischmann, 1852; idem, 1859; idem, 1863, pp. 19-44; Darmesteter, 1877, pp. 94, 154, 185, etc.; Lindner; Carnoy; Güntert, 1923; Geldner, 1926, pp. 28-31; etc.). Arthur Christensen (q.v., 1918-34, II) collected all sources for Yima and Jamšēd that were known to him, including Vedic, Avestan, Middle Persian, and New Persian Zoroastrian texts, as well as the Muslim historians and miscellaneous others; all the information found in the sources of the Islamic period has been collected by Mahšid Ṣediqiān (on the myths, see also Darmesteter, 1893, II, pp. 19-31, 623-25, with notes; Wesendonk, p. 160 n. 2; on the interpretations of the Yima myths, see Zaehner, 1961, chap. 5; on the sources, Yarshater, pp. 359-66; Boyce, 1975-82, I, pp. 92-96 and n. 54 on literature; Dehḵodā, *Loḡat-nāma.*, ss.v. "Jam" and "Jamšid"; Humbach and Ichaporia, 1998, pp. 103-13 [Av. passages with Pahl. versions]; for early studies on the Indic Yama, see Macdonell, pp. 171-74, for recent thoughts, see Bodewitz, with further references).

It has always been recognized that the Yima story and its later elaborations have parallels in both Indic and

Mesopotamian (incl. Biblical) mythology, although the significance of these facts has been much disputed. This is also true for the question of Indo-European origins.

Yima xšaēta as solar figure. Yima's standing epithet *xšaēta* has received no obviously correct explanation (see Kellens, 1999-2000, p. 727 n. 7). The word is also the epithet of *huuar-* "sun" (*huuar- xšaēta-* and *huuardxšaēta-*, Mid. Pers. *xwaršēd*, New Pers. *k̲ᵛoršid*), the heavenly lights, Tištriia, Apąm Napāt (q.v.), and the Life-giving Immortals (*aməša spəṇtas*, q.v.), and the feminine form *xšōiθnī* (cf. *paiti* "master," fem. *paθnī*) is used with the goddesses Aṣ̌i and Anāhitā (qq.v.), as well as dawn, all of them presumably luminous celestial phenomena. Since Yima is said to be like the sun to look at among men (*huuarə.darəsō maṣ̌iiānąm*; *Yasna* 9.4) and his life is immortal and "sun-filled" (*xᵛanuuaṇt*, *Yasna* 9.1), *xšaēta* would seem to refer to the color of the sun (golden or reddish). It could then be the same term that is used to denote the color of horses, as in the proper name *šēd-asp* (see Benveniste, 1966, pp. 21-22), the name of Jamšid's grandson (son of Ṭur, see below on Dahāg and the "cutting" of Yima) in the *Garšāsb/Garšāsp-nāma* (ed. Huart, pp. 90-91).

The Indian Yama and Iranian Yima are both the sons of a solar figure, Old Ind. Vivasvant, Av. Vīuuaŋᵛhant, "the one who shines far and wide" (Gathic genitive *Vīuuaŋhušō* from *Vīuuaŋᵛhah-*, cf. Old Ind. *vi-vas-*, present stem *vi-uchá-*, Av. *vī.usa-* "light up, shine far and wide"). The Old Indic verb is commonly used of dawn and the Avestan verb in the description of dawn on the third morning after death (*θritiiā̊ xšapō vī.usaiti* "as the third night turns into bright [dawn]"; *Vd*. 19.28).

Yima possessed the divine Fortune in the highest degree (*xᵛarənaŋᵛhastəma*) among those born, like Zarathustra and like Miθra, Ahura Mazdā (q.v.), and his Word, among gods (*Y*. 9.4; *Yt*. 19.35).

The Muslim authors routinely state that *šid* means "shine, radiance, some comparing *k̲ᵛor-šid*. Ebn al-Aṯir (I, p. 64) adds that *jam* means "moon" (cf. Abu'l-Fedā, ed. Fleischer, pp. 66-69, Cairo ed., p. 40: *jam-šid* means "brightness of the moon" [*šoʿāʿ al-qamar*] versus *k̲ᵛor-šid* "brightness of the sun" [*šoʿāʿ al-šams*]).

Friedrich Carl Andreas (q.v.) and Walter B. Henning (q.v.) suggested that the word meant "ruler" (I, p. 15 [187] n. 6: *xwar-šēd* "sun-lord"; presumably from *xšay-* "rule"; see Benveniste, 1966, p. 21: "chief"), but the evidence is slim and complicated by Sogdian *axšēδ* "ruler" (Manichean *smān/βaγān axšēδ* "ruler of the heavens/ the gods"), also mentioned by Muslim authors as a title of the rulers of Sogdiana (see EḴŠĪD; see also the discussion in Benveniste, 1966, pp. 20-22 with refs; Skjærvø, 1995, p. 205, suggested the word is simply a borrowed Mid. Pers. *xšēd*).

In the Kushan empire, Yam-šēd achieved divine status and appears as the god Iamšo on coins (see Grenet, pp. 253-58) and in personal names, such as Iamšo-lado "given by Yamšo" (Sims-Williams, 1997-98, pp. 196-97; idem, 2000, p. 194). François Grenet suggests *-šo* may be a byform of *šao* "king" (or could it be an abbreviation for Yam-šēd?). In the coin representations, Iamšo holds a bird, which has been identified as the Avestan Vārəγna (see below on Yima's sin).

Yima and the heroes of origins. In *Yasna* 9.1-13, the praise-hymn to Haoma (q.v.), Haoma tells Zarathustra that the births of the four most important human beings in history were gifts given as rewards when their fathers pressed the *haoma* for the benefit of the world of the living: Vīuuanᵛhant begot Yima (who made the world immortal); Āθβiia (Mid. Pers. Āspī, New Pers. Ābtin, q.v.) got Θraētaona (Mid. Pers. Frēdōn; see AŽDAHĀ, FERĒDŪN), who overcame and chained Aži Dahāka to Mount Damāvand (q.v.); Θrita of the Sāmas begot Kərəsāspa (New Pers. Garšāsp, see AŽDAHĀ, GARŠĀSP-NĀMA), who will kill Aži Dahāka (New Pers. Żaḥḥāk) at the end of time; and Pourušaspa begot Zarathustra, who will initiate the return to the state of immortality (see Kellens, 2001).

In the Avesta, these heroes are only four in a relatively stable list of hero-sacrificers who sacrifice to various deties in order to be permitted to fulfill specific functions in upholding the cosmic order. The first three in the sequence are Haošiiaŋha (Mid. Pers. Hōšang, New Pers. Hušang), Taxma Urupi (Mid. Pers. Tahmōraf, New Pers. Tahmuraṯ), and Yima, who all three fight evil in their own ways. Yima is followed by Aži Dahāka, the giant dragon who wishes to do evil, but is overcome by Θraētaona. Last in the sequence is a succession of *kauuis*, which concludes with Kauui Vištāspa, who is associated with Zarathustra. Each of the heroes sacrifices in different locations (see Kellens, 1999-2000, pp. 736-39): Haošiiaŋha on the skirts or top of Mount Harā and Yima from High Hukairiia, the high peak of Mount Harā, via which the Heavenly River comes down at Ahura Mazdā's request (*Yt*. 5.3, 85).

In the later tradition, the list has become a chronological sequence of two dynasties. The first is that of the (Mid. Pers.) Pēšdādīs, or Peshdadids, named after Haošiiaŋha's standing epithet *paraδāta* "established before (others)," Mid. Pers. *pēš-dād*, but is expanded to include Gayōmart/d (q.v.) as its first member (Av. Gaiiō Marəta, New Pers. Gayumarṯ, the first to listen to Ahura Mazdā; *Yt*. 13.87). The second is that of the Kāwīs, or Kayanids, named after the title *kauui* (Mid. and New Pers. *kay*), which must originally have referred to poet-sacrificers with special powers (cf. OInd. *kaví*).

The Avesta does not suggest any family relationships between the heroes, but, in the Middle and New Persian epic tradition, they have become members of royal dynasties, and Jamšid has become Tahmōraf/Tahmuraṯ's brother (*Bundahišn* 35.3; brother or brother's brother, e.g., in Banākati, p. 28). There is also no explicit link between Yima and Aži Dahāka in the Avesta.

In the Middle Persian literature, we find several examples that Jam(šēd) was considered to be linked with Zarathustra (the first and last of the four born as a result of their fathers' *haoma* sacrifices). In the *Dēnkard* (q.v.), Zarathustra is said to be of human lineage (*tōhmag*) through Jam and of the lineage of the Life-giving Immortals through Nēryōsang (*Dk*. 7.2.21). Zādspram, remarkably, states that Zarathustra's lineage connects him back to Ohrmazd himself (*Wizīdagīhā* 7: *abāz-paywandišnīh ī Zardušt ō Ohrmazd*, ed. Gignoux and Tafazzoli, pp. 62-63). According to Zādspram, Zarathustra was descended from Nēryōsang through Pōrušasp and from Frēdōn son of Āspīy through Pōrušasp's mother Wēzag and from Jam through the Āspīyān family (cf. *Bundahišn* 35.52, on Frēdōn's descent). Another passage of the *Dēnkard*, however, appears to say that Zarathustra's luminosity made him resemble Jam's lineage (*Dk*. 5.2.2, ed. Amouzgar and Tafazzoli, pp. 24-25). The *Bundahišn* (35.8) also records that Pōrušasp was descended from Manuščihr, a tradition found later as well (Ṭabari, I/2, pp. 681-82, tr., IV, p. 77; see the genealogical tables in Justi, pp. 390-93).

Yima and the golden age. In *Vidēvdād* (chap. 2), Zarathustra asks Ahura Mazdā who he spoke with first among mortals, upon which Ahura Mazdā tells Zarathustra the story of Yima. He originally offered Yima the task of carrying (forth) and memorizing (for practicing and proclaiming) his *daēnā* (i.e., Ahura Mazdā's thoughts, words, and deeds; see DĒN), which Yima declines (Kellens, 1997-98, p. 760 with n. 39, is overly skeptical about the possibility of establishing the meaning of the verbs). Ahura Mazdā then offers him, as an alternative, the role of protector and furtherer of living beings, which Yima accepts, promising that, as long as he is in command, the world will be perfect, there being no excesses of heat and cold and no sickness or death. Ahura Mazdā then gives him two tools, a cattle goad (*aštrā*) and a *suβrā*, either some kind of pick (cf. Pers. *sumb-* "pierce") or a shepherd's flute (cf. *nāḷī* in *RV*. 10.1235.7) or horn (Duchesne-Guillemin, 1980; cf. Kellens, 1994-95, p. 702; see Sims-Williams, 2001, with further references).

Although it is not said explicitly, it may have been Yima's *x*ᵛ*arənah* that enabled him to maintain the world in this state, and one reason that it did not last may have been his refusal to accept the promotion of Ahura Mazdā's *daēnā*. Had he done so, then, according to the Pahlavi *Dēnkard*, by the coming together in him of the royal Fortune (*xwarrah ī xwadāyīh*) and that of the good *dēn*, the Foul Spirit would have been destroyed, as he would have been, had Zarathustra also possessed the royal Fortune (*Dk*. 3.129, tr. Menasce, p. 133). In the *Dēnkard* (7.1.20), however, it is said that it was by the strength of the *paymān* (see below) that he maintained the creation immortal, etc.

As described in the Avesta (*Vd*. 2; *Y*. 9.4, *Yt*. 9.9-10, 15.16, 19.32-33), under Yima's rule the world prospered and the number of people, cattle, and fires increased, while the *daēuuas* (see DAIVA, DĒW) were deprived of their desires and *yearning (*išti* and *saokā*, which are kept in the moon, *Yt*. 7.5), their cattle (*fšaoni*, *vąθβa*), and their fame (*frasasti*, *Yt*. 5.26, 19.32). According to the *Bundahišn* (18.8-10), Jam achieved this with the help of the three major fires, Ādur Farrōbay (Farnbay), Ādur Gušnasp, and Ādur Burzēnmihr (qq.v.), which Ohrmazd had lit as *xwarrahs* for the protection of living beings. According to *Yašt* 9.10, this state lasted 1000 winters, while the total duration described in the *Vidēvdād* is 3 x 300 winters.

Reasons why humanity was immortal are given in the Middle Persian translation of *Yasna* 9.1, where people are said to have become immortal by eating the meat Jam offered them, and in a story in the *Persian Rivāyat*s (see below). Some Middle Persian texts specify that "immortality" did not imply "forever," only a very long time; the *Mēnōy ī xrad* (61.18) has 300 years and the Pahlavi *Vidēvdād* (2.41), 150 years.

According to the Middle Persian texts, Ohrmazd/Ahura Mazdā had made Jam, Frēdōn, and Kay-Us immortal (*MX*. 7.27), but Jam and Kay-Us lost their immortality for their sins (Pahlavi *Vd*. 2.5). Yima's immortality and youth (15 years old), which he inherited from his father (*Y*. 9.5) and passed on to the inhabitants of the golden age, are frequently mentioned in the Avesta. In the *Persian Rivāyats* it is said that nobody could distinguish father from son (tr. Christensen, 1918-34, II, p. 69).

The *Vidēvdād* goes on to tell that, since living beings were eternally young and immortal, after 300 winters the earth became too crowded, and Ahura Mazdā told Yima to use the two tools he had received to expand the earth by one-third its original size. Yima did so three times, after three periods of 300 winters, upon which the earth was presumably twice its original size.

The story in *Vidēvdād* 2 is also in the *Dēnkard*. Here, Jamšēd is also said to have accepted all four "limbs" (*pēšag*) of the *dēn*, the classes of priests, warriors, farmers, and artisans (*āsrōnīh ud artēštārīh ud wāstryōšīh ud hutuxšīh*; see CLASS SYSTEM i. In the Avesta), by which he made the world prosper (*Dk*. 7.1.20-24). Afterward, Frēdōn was assigned a share of Jam's *wāstryōšīh* (*Dk*. 7.1.25-27) and Karišāsp a share of his *artēštārīh* (*Dk*. 7.1.32). The *āsrōnīh*, although not said, may have gone to Zarathustra, and Yima may have reserved the *hutuxšīh* for himself (see below on Yima, culture hero).

Most of the Islamic sources mention his division of society (see below on King Jamšid), but few mention the story of his enlargement of the world. It is reported by Maqdesi, however, according to whom God told Jam to go up on Mount Alborz and, from there, command the earth to expand by 300,000 *farsaḵ*s in circumference (*Bad*ʾ III, pp. 140-42, tr. pp. 145-46, tr. Šafiʿi Kadkani, I, p. 501), and by Abu Rayḥān Biruni (q.v.), who ascribes to God himself the action of enlarging the earth three times (Biruni, ed. Sachau, p. 217, tr. p. 202).

According to the *Fravardin yašt* (q.v.), Yima's *fravaši* (q.v.) is invoked against natural plagues opposite of the perfect conditions during Yima's rule (*Yt*. 13.130: *ainišti* "lack of obtaining one's wishes" *daēuuō.karštā* "dragged forth by the *daēuuas*"; *haēcah auuāstra* "watering without grass," i.e., waterlogged earth[?]; and the *iθiiajah maršaonō* "the *danger of the *maršauuan*"[?], in Mid. Pers. explained as *sēj ī nihān-rawišn* "the *sēj* that moves in secret"). According to Manuščihr's *Dādestān ī dēnīg* (q.v.), it was Jam's *fravaši* that kept *sēj* and terror (*sahm*) away from the creatures (*DD*. 36.67). In book 7 of the *Dēnkard*, a part of Jam's speech to the *dēws* is preserved, which may be from the above story. Here, Jam eplains to the *dēws* that Zarathustra will give them back the non-desire (*a-xwāhišnīh*) they made (cf. *Yt.* 13.130).

King Jamšid and Nowruz. More elaborate stories are told in the Middle and New Persian tradition about Jamšid as king. According to the *Persian Rivāyats* (tr. Christensen, 1918-34, II, pp. 60-67), Jamšid was summoned before God himself and given kingship over the world with its insignia: the signet ring, the throne, and the diadem. Returning to earth, he came down from Mount Alborz, and people who looked in that direction are said to have seen two suns, one of which was Jamšēd (cf. Biruni, ed. Sachau, p. 217, tr. p. 202, ed. Aḏkāʾi, p. 268; see below). Instead of this story, the *Šāh-nāma* explains how he had a throne made for himself, encrusted with jewels (*gowhar*), which the demons (*divs*) then lifted up to the sky at his command, and thus the king sat in the middle of the air, shining like the sun, with the whole world gathered to look at him and scattering jewels on him (ed. Mohl, I, p. 52, ed. Khaleghi, I, p. 44; cf. his house on Hariburz, see below on Yima and the *vara*). According to Abu Manṣur Ṯaʿālebi (p. 13) and Ṭabari (I, p. 180, tr. I, p. 350), Jamšid was thus able to travel from Damāvand to Babylon in one day (cf. Biruni, ed. Sachau, p. 216, tr. p. 111, ed. Aḏkāʾi, p. 266).

A modern version of the story is reported by the Capuchin missionary to Persia and Armenia, Gabriel du Chinon (1668), according to which Gemechid (Jamšid) went into the heaven of the sun every day and brought back the science of the stars, but Chinon ascribed the golden age to Peridon (Ferēdun; Chinon, 1671, pp. 478-79; cf. Darmesteter, 1893, I, p. 13 n. 3). The day on which this took place was the day of Hormoz (the first) of the month of Farvardin, later called the New Day, on which Jamšid gave a party with wine, song, and music. In the Pahlavi *Māh ī frawardīn rōz ī xordad*, it is stated that it was on the day of Xordad (the 6th), after Jam had made ossuaries and ordered people to do likewise that they made the day a new day and called it New (Year's) Day (Jamasp-Asana, ed., p. 103; also *Persian Rivāyats*, tr. Christensen, 1918-34, II, p. 69).

The tradition connecting Nowruz with Jamšid is probably older, as it shows up in a Manichean text, which describes how all the lords of the world would come to Yam on New (Year's) Day (see below, Yima in Manicheism). Moreover, under the Achaemenids, the New Year's Day celebration included a procession of rulers of the various provinces of the empire bringing gifts to the king, as depicted in reliefs at Persepolis. The connection with the legend of Jamšid, whether ancient or more recent, is seen in the name of Taḵt-e Jamšid (the Throne of Jamshid) for the palace ruins. Mirḵᵛānd (1959-72, I, p. 519; ed. Kayānfar, II, p. 597) reports that Jamšid moved his residence from Sejestān (Sistān) to Fārs at the beginning of his reign and that he built the palace now called Čehel Menār (i.e., Persepolis), where the day he ascended the throne in celebration was called Nowruz.

In this connection, the *Persian Rivāyats*, differently from almost all other texts, also describe how Jamšid made humans immortal (tr. Christensen, 1918-34, II, pp. 65-70). Before he proclaimed himself universal monarch on New Year's Day, at the creator's command, he went to the Činwad bridge (q.v.), closed the door to Hell, and locked it so that Ahrimen and the *divs* could not enter, and so no one died during his reign. All this took place on the day of Ḵordād of the month of Farvardin. The myth may well be old, as Jamšid is here acting, like the Achaemenid king, as both supreme secular and supreme religious authority, who bars evil from the world on New Year's Day, thus rejuvenating the world. Among the Muslim historians, only Biruni has the story, but abbreviated (ed. Sachau, p. 217, tr. p. 202; ed. Aḏkāʾi, pp. 267-68): Because Eblis had stopped the benediction on the Great Nowruz (6 Farvardin), God told Jamšid to go to the land of Eblis and his companions. He was there until he had dealt with the problem, then came back and restored order, upon which he appeared as the sun, and people thought they saw two suns in the sky. He also told people to destroy the ancient temples and to build no new ones on that day. Later, Mirḵᵛānd reported that Jamšid had ordered people to destroy the idols (*bothā*) on that day (1959-72, I, p. 516; ed. Kayānfar, II, p. 595).

A story that may be related to this is told in *Māh ī frawardīn rōz ī xordad* (Jamasp-Asana, ed., p. 103). It was on this day that J̌am brought the *paymānag* "right measure" out of Hell, so that it became visible in the world and which, according to the *Dēnkard*, was needed to make the creation immortal, etc. (*Dk.* 7.1.20; see below, J̌am and the *paymān*).

Yima as culture hero. In the Pahlavi and later literature, all the early heroes are credited with certain inventions promoting civilization. The only one mentioned in the Avesta is that Ahura Mazdā, in addition to telling him how to build the *vara* (*Vd.* 2.25-26), taught Yima how to make and use brick from mud (*Vd.* 2.31-32), a task that, in the later Persian tradition, King Jamšid is said to have assigned to the *divs*, who then made all kinds of constructions with brick (*Persian Rivāyats*, tr. Christensen, 1918-34, II, p. 68). The later tradition, however, ascribes to the rule of Jam most aspects of civilization. For instance, Ebn al-Nadim quotes a source according to which the time of Jam was a time of general civilizing of the world that continued until the reign of Ẓaḥḥāk (ed. Tajaddod, p. 299, tr. pp. 572-73). Mirḵᵛānd even places Pythagoras (Fiṯāḡurat) in attendance on Jamšid at this time (1959-72, I, p. 519).

Among religious practices that J̌am(šēd) taught men was the wearing of the kusti. This tradition is reported in the *Dādestān ī dēnīg* (38.21, 25-26, 30), in the *Persian Rivāyats* (tr. Dhabhar, p. 24), and in the prose *Ṣad dar-e naṯr* (pp. 9-10), where the *hamāzōr* (q.v.) is also ascribed to him. In addition, the metrical *Ṣad dar-e naẓm* (tr. Christensen, 1918-34, II, pp. 64-65) attributes to him the institution of the seasonal *gāhānbār* festivals (q.v.; see also *Persian Rivāyats*, tr. Dhabhar, tr., pp. 323-24), to which *Māh ī frawardīn rōz ī xordad* (Jamasp-Asana, ed., p. 103) and the *Persian Rivayats* add the use of ossuaries or *daxmas* (see CORPSE; tr. Christensen, 1918-34, II, p. 69).

Masʿudi (sec. 1372) also refers to a tradition according to which Jam established the fire cult and taught that the fire was the image of the light of the sun and the stars. This may well be an old tradition, since fires feature prominently among the inhabitants of Yima's realm (*Vd.* 2.8, etc.: small and large animals and men, dogs, and birds, and red burning fires), which also brings to mind Vivasvant as the one who sent the sacrificial fire to mankind (*RV.* 6.8.4, cf. 4.7.4, 8.39.3), while Vīuuaŋᵛhan was the first to perform a *haoma* sacrifice, as Haoma tells Zarathustra while he is preparing the sacrificial fire (*Y.* 9.1). Balʿami's report that Jam, taking the advice of Eblis, threw all those who refused to adore him into the fire might, conceivably, be a version of the same story (1962, p. 132; 2000, p. 89).

According to the *Šāh-nāma* (ed. Mohl, I, pp. 48-52; ed. Khaleghi, I, pp. 41-43), the *Persian Rivāyats* (tr. Christensen, 1918-34, II, pp. 66-68), and the *Fārs-nāma* (Ebn Balḵi, pp. 30-32), Jamšid also taught men weaving and how to make fabrics (cotton, silk, wool, linen), and clothes and how to wash them; he made weapons and other necessities of warfare, and taught people sowing; and he divided society into the four classes and defined the various tasks of each. He also invented ships built of wood and used them to fetch pearls for jewelry. He extracted precious stones from the rocks and gold and silver from the earth. He invented the use of furs and selected his favorite perfumes and laid out gardens and parks with trees and flowers. Finally, he taught men medicine. According to Ṭabari, Jamšīd charged the *divs* with producing depilatories, perfumes, and medicines (ed., I, p. 179-81, tr. I, pp. 349-50; see also Faḵr-e Modabber, pp. 7-8, 257-58).

Biruni reports a story told by the *mowbed* Ādurbād of Baghdad, according to which Jamšid also discovered sugar (ed. Sachau, p. 216, tr. p. 200; ed. Aḏkāʾi, p. 266), and Mirḵᵛānd adds the discovery of wine (1959-72, I, p. 518, ed. Kayānfar, II, pp. 596-97; which in the Jewish tradition was ascribed to Noah, contemporary with Jamšid in the Muslim tradition; see also Christensen, 1918-34, II, p. 123 with n. 1). Ebn al-Nadim reports that Jamšid had imposed corvee on Eblis and that he ordered him to teach him how to write (ed. Flügel, I, p. 12, ed. Tajaddod, p. 15, tr. I, p. 23).

Ḥamza Eṣfahāni (ed. p. 31, tr. pp 19-20), *Mojmal al-tawāriḵ* (p. 40), and Ḥamd-Allāh Mostawfi (1915-19, I, p. 44, II, tr., p. 50) also report that Jam founded Ctesiphon and made a bridge across the Tigris that was destroyed by Alexander, but the ruins of which could still be seen (see also Ebn al-Aṯir, I, p. 65). According to Mostawfi, he also finished the construction of Eṣṭaḵr (begun by Kayumarṯ and Hušang) and Hamadān, as well as the bridge over the Tigris (1910-13, p. 87; idem, 1915-19, pp. 71, 120, II, pp. 74, 119). Ebn Balḵi (p. 32) reports that he made Eṣṭaḵr his capital, turned it into a metropolis, and had three fortresses, called Seh Gonbadān, built in the city, and Faḵr-al-Din Banākati says that he built Eṣṭaḵr and a big palace there, which at Banākati's time was called Čehel Menāra (p. 29). The *Šahrestānīhā ī Ērān-šahr* has a note that "Babylon (Bābēl) was made during the reign of J̌am" (ed. Daryaee, pp. 14, 18; on the story of Jamšid's seven wonders destroyed by Alexander, see Christensen, 1918-34, pp. 77, 164-65; *Persian Rivāyats*, pp. 436-37).

Ebn Esfandiār tells from the local history of Ṭabarestān that, in ancient days, the area was inhabitable and in the possession of the *divs* until Jamšid came, who overcame the *divs* and had them level the mountains and fill in the lakes, drain the fens, etc. (pp. 56-57; tr. Browne, pp. 14-15). Faḵr-e Modabber (p. 185) ranks Jamšid's horse, a black one according to him, along with Raḵš (the celebrated steed of Rostam) among the best horses of all-time.

Yima and the vara. After the third enlargement of the earth, any further expansion being apparently impossible, Ahura Mazdā and Yima called a meeting of gods and men, respectively, in which it was decided that the population of the earth must be reduced. This was to be achieved by severe winters, one particularly harsh one, followed by flooding when the snow melted. In order that living beings should not perish completely, Ahura Mazdā described for Yima how to make a kind of fortress (Av. *vara-*, Mid. Pers. *war*, *war ī jamkerd*), in which to keep samples of all creatures of Ahura Mazdā alive during the winter. He specified the architectural features of the building and explained how to use clay. He also explained about the two kinds of lights in the *vara*: those established of themselves (*xᵛaδāta*, probably the eternal lights, cf. *Y.* 1.16), and those established for the duration of the worlds of thought and/or of living beings (*stiδāta*). Yima then brought pairs of all living things into the *vara*, excluding those with bodily defects, and, every forty winters, two children would be born from a human couple.

The Karšipta bird brought the *daēnā* of Ahura Mazdā into the *vara*, and its *ahu* and *ratu* (i.e., the first new beings and models for subsequent beings?) were Zarathustra and his son Uruuataṱ.nara (Mid. Pers. Urwatadnar; cf. *Bdh.* 29.6; specifically, Urwatadnar is said to be the *ratu* of the farmers; *Bdh.* 35.56).

According to the Middle Persian *Mēnōy ī xrad* (61.15), the *war* was underground in Ērān-wēz (q.v.), while, according to the *Bundahišn* (29.14), it was beneath Mount Čamagān (?) in Pārs. It was lit miraculously, unaffected by summer and winter, and contained all things in the world of the living (*Bundahišn* 32.7). J̌am also had a house on Hariburz (high Harā, Alborz, q.v.), made of diamonds (*Bdh.* 32.1, 14: **gōhrēn*, cf. his crystal throne, see above on King Jamšid) and another in Pārs, called J̌amkerd (*Bdh.* 32.7).

The *vara* had a further purpose, which is only explained in the post-Avestan texts. Toward the end of the millennium of Ušēdar, the first of Zarathustra's three eschatological sons, when men and beasts are decimated by the terrible (*sahmgen*) winter or rain of the sorcerer Malkūs (*sēǰ-čihr* "of the lineage of *sēǰ*, *Bdh.* 33.30), the world is repopulated from the *war* (*Bdh.* 33.1, *Dādestān ī dēnīg* 36.80-81; *Dk.* 7.1.24, 7.9.3-4; *Mēnōy ī xrad* 26.24; *Pahlavi Rivāyat* 48.17; *Zand ī Wahman Yasn* 9.14).

The term *vara* (Pahlavi *war*) has been thought to refer to some kind of enclosure (related to English *wall* from Latin *vallum*), or, more precisely, a cavern (Geldner, 1926, p. 30, cited by Hauschild, p. 25 n. 40; Gershevitch, 1974, pp. 66-69; Kellens, 1999-2000, p. 732). It is the same word as Old Indic *valá*, which Indra breaks or splits open to free the imprisoned cows. According to Johannes Hertel, the term refers to the celestial vault; see Keith's critique (pp. 621-23).

In the *Pahlavi Rivāyat*, *war* is explained as "lake" (*Pahlavi Rivāyat* 8e), but Mid. Pers. *war* "lake" is from Avestan *vairi*, a different word. A similar connection, however, appears to have been made in the description of Pahlavi Mount Hugar (= Hukairiia, where Yima sacrificed, see above on Yima and the heroes of origins) in the *Bundahišn*, where the springs and canals of Ardwīsūr are described (*Bdh*. 10.5-6). Here, one canal (*nāwīčag*) is said to go up on high Hugar, where there is a lake (*war*), into which the water pours and is purified. The direct connection is with the Avestan description of Arəduuī Sūrā, who has 1000 *vairi*s (e.g., *Y*. 65.4 = *Yt*. 5.4; see ANĀHĪD), but, in the *Bundahišn*, Hukairiia's epithets "containing all poems, golden" (*vīspō.vahma zaranaēna*; *Yt*. 5.96, 12.24, 15.15) are rendered as "containing all *sūrag*s, golden" (*hamag-sūrag zarrēn*), which appears to be influenced by *Vidēvdād* 2.6 "golden pick" (*suβrąm zaranaēnīm*), Mid. Pers. "containing holes, golden" (*sūrāgōmand ī zarrēn*; in the *Yasna*, *vahma* is usually rendered by *niyāyišn* "song").

Yima and the divine Fortune (x^{v}arənah-). *Yašt* 19, the *Zamyād yašt*, is devoted to a myth of the *x^{v}arənah* that is not at all understood, but involves three kinds of *x^{v}arənah* (cf. *Y*. 1.14): that of the Aryans (*airiianəm x^{v}arənō*), the *unseizable *x^{v}arənah* (*ax^{v}arətəm x^{v}arənō*), and that of the *kauuis* (*kauuaēm x^{v}arənō*). The exact meaning of the word and its precise mythical reference are also not known, except that it appears to possess some luminous quality. It is associated with *išti* "desire," both in the *Gāθās* (*Y*. 51.18 *ištōiš x^{v}arənå* "the *x^{v}arənah*s of [his] *išti*) and later (*Yt*. 18.1 *airiianəm x^{v}arənō pouru.vąθβəm *pouru.ištim*), which occurs frequently in the Yima myth (see above on Yima and the golden age). Middle Persian *Yasna* 9.4, where Yima is said to possess the most *x^{v}arənah* among those born, has the commentary: *xwarrah* is partly one's duty (*xwēškārīh*), partly in a man's body, and that in Jam's body; according to *Yt*. 17.22, it was placed in Zarathustra's body (see also *Bdh*. 14.7-10, 18.16). The *x^{v}arənah* is associated with water (*Yt*. 8.34 *aβždātəm x^{v}arənō* "the *x^{v}arənah* placed in the water"), specifically the heavenly ocean (the Vourukaṣ̌a Sea: the *ax^{v}arətem x^{v}arənō*, *Yt*.19.45-53); it is distributed over the earth by the gods (*yazata*s) when the sun shines (*Niyāyišn* 1.11) and by the Life-giving Immortals when the moon shines (*Niyāyišn* 3.5); and it is associated with the mountains and their births (*Y*. 1.14, *Yt*. 18 and beginning of *Yt*. 19; *Persian Rivāyats* 46.5, see Skjærvø, 1994, p. 218 n. 29a).

Yima's sin and loss of the divine Fortune. As ruler of the world, Yima was endowed with the divine Fortune of the *kauuis*. According to the Avesta, the Fortune left him, however, on account of a particular sin, and, according to the later sources, he had to relinquish his throne and go into exile. Being no longer immortal, he was killed by being cut apart.

In the *Gāθās* (see GATHAS), Yima is mentioned once only (*Y*. 32.8, see below on the Gathic myth): "Yima, in particular, has been renowned (as guilty) of these sins." This statement is followed by a text that has been much discussed, although its exact meaning still escapes us, but, which, in the Pahlavi tradition, is said to mean that Yima taught people to eat meat.

In *Yašt* 19.30-34, the wanderings of the Fortune of the *kauuis* are described and, in particular, how it left Yima in the shape of the Vārəγna bird when he uttered a "deceiving word" (*draogəm vācim*). The passage contains further details about the actual lie, but the text has not yet been satisfactorily eplained (see Kellens, 1999-2000, p. 727). It appears that someone, referred to as "this one" (*aēm*), caused Yima to desire (? *cinmāne*) something that was not real and true (*aŋhaiθiia = a-haiθiia*). The context provides no reference for "this one," but, not mentioned by name, he could be the great seducer, the Evil Spirit (Aŋra Maniiu, New Pers. Ahrimen, q.v.) himself, who wanted Yima's Fortune (*Yt*. 19.46). The word *cinmāne* is derived from *can-* "desire" by Eric V. Pirart (p. 46; Hintze, pp. 189-90, Humbach and Ichaporia, 1998, p. 110); earlier interpretations include "assembly place" (Windischmann, 1863, p. 28: possible connection with the Činwad bridge), infinitive "to think" (Bartholomae, *AirWb*., col. 596), and "in (his) mind" (Lommel, p. 179). With *a-haiθiia*, cf. also Darius's assertion (Bisotun 4.44-45) that his statements about his deeds are "true" (*hašiya* = Av. *haiθiia*), not "said to deceive" (*naiy duruxtam*, cf. *draogəm vācim*), which would imply that, if he knew the Yima story, Darius disavowed the fault of his mythical prototype.

According to the *Zamyād yašt*, the Fortune left Yima three times and was seized by Miθra, who possessed the most Fortune among gods; the son of Āθβiia (i.e., Θraētaona), the most valorous of all (except Zarathustra); and Kərəsāspa, the strongest of all (except Zarathustra). Here, we have again the four sons of *Yasna* 9. According to a later Persian version, when God had taken the light from Jamšid, he gave one-third to Mehr, one-third to Zarathustra, and one-third to Zarathustra's three eschatological sons, Ušēdar, Ušēdarmāh, and Sōšāns (Bartholomae, 1915, p. 88; Christensen, 1918-34, II, p. 76). Friedrich Windischmann (1863, p. 28) had suggested that the three Fortunes represented the three fires of the Sasanian ritual, which, according to the *Bundahišn* had been lit as three *xwarrah*s for the protection of living beings (*Bdh*. 18.8, see, above, Yima ruler of the golden age; also Darmesteter, 1883, II, pp. 615-16).

Yima's lie is mentioned only once in *Yašt* 19, before the description of the three departures of the Fortune, and it is not clear whether it left each time on account of a new lie (as assumed by Christensen, 1918-34, II, pp. 52-54; Kellens, 1997-1998, p. 746, 1999-2000, p. 727), whether it departed three times (thus Christensen, 1931, p. 103; Humbach and Ichaporia, 1998; also Kellens, 1997-1998, p. 746), or whether it departed in three portions (thus Bartholomae, *AirWb.*, col. 964; Pirart, 1992). Almut Hintze proposes that the text simply stresses the finality of the departure of the Fortune (pp. 197-98; see also Kellens, 1997-1998, on the whole myth in *Yašt* 19). The suggestion that the triple departure is related to the triple enlargement of the earth (Panaino, p. 70) has no basis in the texts and explains nothing (see Kellens, 1997-1998, p. 746; less negative: Kellens, 1999-2000, p. 731). What happened after this is also unclear because of difficulties in the Avestan text (*Yt.* 19. 34): Yima "erred" (? *brāsa-*), "devoid of happiness" (*a-śāiti*) and despondent, and, "stunned" (*starəta*), he "lay down" (? *ni-dāra-*) upon the earth.

The length of Jamšid's life and reign varies in the sources. For instance, according to the *Bundahišn*, he lived 616 years and six months before the Fortune left him, then spent a hundred years in exile (*wirēg*; *Bdh.* 36.5); according to the Mid. Pers. *Aogəmadāecā*, he kept the world immortal for 616 years, 6 months, and 13 (or 16) days (*Aog.* 95); and, according to the Pazand *Ayādgār ī Zāmāspīg* (q.v.), he ruled for 717 years, 7 months, and then went away with J̌amī (ed. Messina, pp. 40-42). In Ẓahir-al-Din Marʿaši's *Tāriḵ-e Ṭabarestān* (p. 107), Jamšid's reign is said to have lasted 1000 years, which may reflect the old tradition seen in *Yašt* 9.10 (see above on Yima and the golden age).

According to the *Pahlavi Rivāyat* (31, cf. *Dādestān ī dēnīg* 38.19-21), J̌am's sin was to have refused Ohrmazd's offer of the *dēn* (also *Persian Rivāyats* 47.8) and done the bidding of Ahrimen and the *dēws*, and his lie was to have proclaimed himself creator of the world. For this sin, he was confined to Hell. When Zarathustra questioned him about the worst sinner, Ohrmazd summoned the soul of J̌am and showed it to him. J̌am had done some good things, however, among them the best was to have prevented men from killing good animals in return for getting the elephant from the *dēws* (also *MX.* 26.33a; see Shaked, 1987b, p. 243 n. 15, with refs.). Fighting with the *dēws*, he also made them mortal, so they could be punished. At this, the soul of J̌am repented and told Zarathustra not to listen to the *dēws*, but to accept the *dēn*. For this it was forgiven and was allowed to go to the *hamēstagān* (q.v.; the place of those whose good and evil deeds were of equal weight), where he became the ruler (for later versions of this story, see Christensen, 1918-34, II, p. 76).

The motive of Yima's hybris continues into the post-Sasanian literature, for instance, the *Šāh-nāma* and the *Fārs-nāma*, according to which he assembled the nobles, mowbeds, and the leaders of the army and told them that the world was his and that he had discovered all its properties, concluding with a call for them to hail him as the maker of the world (ed. Mohl, I, pp. 52-54; ed. Khaleghi, I, p. 45; cf. Ebn al-Balḵi, p. 33, "all people and *divs*"). In one *Persian Rivāyat*, Jamšid's hybris is attributed to Ahrimen, who managed to exit from Hell after being confined for seventy years, went to Jamšid, and somehow made him demented, causing him to proclaim himself creator of the world. Having lost his divine Fortune, Jamšid was deposed by Żaḥḥāk and took to the mountains and deserts (tr. Dhabhar, pp. 581-82; tr. Christensen, 1918-34, II, pp. 69-70; cf. Ebn Balḵi, ibid.). According to Balʿami (ed. Bahār, 1962, p. 132, ed. Gonābādi, p. 89), Jamšid was at Damāvand when Bivarasp (Dahāg) came looking for him.

Similarly, according to Balʿami, it was the devil himself who deceived Jamšid into believing that he was the creator of the world. After this, Jamšid required people to adore him as God and arranged to have images of himself adored as those of God; and whoever did not believe in him was thrown into the fire. He also reports that, once Jamšid had organized society into four classes, he asked those of the first class what to do in order not to lose his throne. He was told that he should be just, and so Jamšid began practicing justice (Balʿami, 1962, pp. 130-32). A modernized version is found in Ebn Meskuya/Meskawayh, who attributes Jamšid's fall to pride and tyrannical behavior and his preferring sensual pleasures to governing (ed. Caetani, I, pp. 8-10, ed. Emāmi, p. 7).

The motif of transferring worship from God as creator to another is also found in the story of Mašī and Mašyānī, who first worshiped Ohrmazd as the creator, then Ahriman, thereby committing the sin of uttering a lie (*drō-gōwišnīh*), which sent them to hell (*Bdh.* 14.11-16).

Jam, Tahmuraṯ, and gōmēz. The *Persian Rivāyat*s and a few other Zoroastrian Persian manuscripts contain a story explaining the origin of the beneficent effect of bull's urine (*gōmēz*, q.v., where the story in not mentioned; see also Christensen, 1918-34, I, pp. 184-89, and König, forthcoming, for all details of this story and further references). The story continues an old story alluded to in the Avesta, which included the detail that Taxma Urupi had ridden the Evil Spirit turned into a horse around the world for thirty years (*Yt.* 15.12, 19.29). According to the later story, Ahriman then thought of a ruse to get rid of Tahmuraṯ and swallowed him. Eventually, Jamšid was able to recapture his dead brother from Ahriman's belly by attracting him with a song and an offer to sodomize him (which Soruš told Jamšid were the two things the demon loved the most), and, when Ahriman turned around, Jamšid reached in and pulled Tahmuraṯ out. As a result, however, his hand caught leprosy (*baraṣ*) and driness (*qaḥal*), which made people avoid him because of the foul smell the illness caused. Jamšid therefore took to the mountains, erring like a madman and complaining to God. Exhausted, he fell asleep near a herd of cattle, and a cow/bull happened to urinate on his hand, which was immediately healed. Père Gabriel du Chinon summarizes the story without specifying the names (pp. 457-58).

Yima's sisters and Θraētaona. Θraētaona's regular request to the deities to whom he sacrificed was to overcome Aži Dahāka and to carry off the two most beautiful women in the world, Saŋhauuācī and Arənauuācī "she who speaks solemn announcements" and "she who speaks faults" (*Yt.* 5.34, 9.14, 15.24; see Hoffmann, 1954, for the correct analysis of the text, and Mayrhofer, nos. 24, 275 for the names). In the later tradition, they are Jamshid's sisters (Šahrnāz and Arnvāz), captured by Dahāg and liberated and married by Ferēdun (*Šāh-nāma*, ed. Mohl, I, pp. 98-102; ed. Khaleghi, I, pp. 75-78; *Mojmal al-tawārik*, p. 27).

J̌am and the paymān. Typical of Yima/Jamšid's rule was lack of excess, either too much or too little. This state of "right measure" (*paymān*) is characteristic of Zoroastrian ethics and is discussed at length in the Middle Persian texts, where it is associated in particular with J̌am. In the *Dēnkard*, for instance, it is said that it was by the strength (*ōz*) of the *paymān* that J̌am maintained the creation immortal, etc. (*Dk.* 7.1.20). Once the *paymān* was lost, immortality also became impossible. In two discussions about *paymān* and *frāybūd* and *aibībūd* "too much and too little" in book 3 of the *Dēnkard*, a myth is reported that people in J̌am's perfect world were seduced by the *dēws* and perverted to the extent that they could no longer be immortal. J̌am convoked the *dēws* and asked them who created the world, to which they answered that *they* created it and would now destroy it. J̌am pointed out that it is not possible to be both creator and destroyer, and the lie of the *dēws* was thus revealed and destroyed, ensuring the immortality of humans (*Dk.* 3.227, tr. Menasce, pp. 239-40, 281-83). According to this story, the *āsn(ō)xrad* (the wisdom one is born with) had been stolen (*appurd*) by the *dēws*, but brought back to mankind together with the *paymān* by J̌am, who spent thirteen winters in Hell in the shape of a *dēw*, thereby overcoming the *dēws* and returning to mankind their "desire and profit" (*har dō īšt ud sūd*; *Dk.* 3.286, tr. Zaehner, 1955, pp. 250-51; tr. Menasce, pp. 281-83). In a list of benefits from J̌amšēd in the *Mēnōy ī xrad* (26.33), the third benefit was that "he brought the *paymān* of the world of the living out of the belly of the evil one (*druwand*) who had swallowed it" (on the two stories, see Windischmann, 1863, pp. 202-3; Zaehner, 1955, pp. 250-52; Shaked, 1987; König, forthcoming).

The story appears to be connected with an exegesis of *Yasna* 32.9 *apō mā īštīm [apa]iiaṇtā* "he robs me of my desire," whose Pahlavi rendering is not clear, but *apaiiaṇtā* is rendered by *appurd* "stole," and *īštīm* is explained by *paymān*; *išti*, however, was what Yima had taken from the *daēuuas* (see above Yima and the golden age). Moreover, Mid. Pers. *paymān* is routinely used to render words in *ma-* or *mā-*, including *mā̆iiā* (*Y.* 10.12, 33.9, 43.2, the *paymān* of Wahman), which the exegetes can have linked with *maiiah* "(sexual) pleasure," which was praticed by the *daēuuas* before Zarathustra drove them underground (*Yt.* 19.80; the Mid. Pers. version in *Dk.* 7.4.44 has *māyišn* "sexual pleasure," not *paymān*).

Yima, the dead, and Hell. Yima's connection with the dead is mainly restricted to late narratives, in which he ordered the making of ossuaries and *daxmas* (see above on King Jamšid and Yima as culture hero). There are three references in the narratives above to Yima going to Hell: for his sins, in order to close the door to Hell so that death would be kept out, and in order to bring the *paymān(ag)* out of Hell. In addition, Mary Boyce has suggested that Herodotus' mention (7.114) of a god dwelling underground and ruling over spirits that did not make it to paradise might refer to Yima, since his Indic counterpart Yama was "lord of death" (Boyce, 1975-82, I, pp. 83-84). The description would fit the story of J̌amšēd in the *hamēstagān* better, but it also involves burying people (children) alive to this god (which Boyce does not mention), and so is perhaps more likely to refer to the Evil Spirit. Sacrifice of young people is otherwise associated with Dahāg, who needed them as food for the snakes that grew out of his shoulders (see AŽDAHĀ).

In later Indic, for instance, Buddhist, literature, Yama is the ruler of the underworld, the frightening lord of death. In the Sanskrit translations of the Avesta, he is equated with Astō.vīδātu, Astwihād (q.v.; e.g., *Aogəmadaēca*, p. 107).

The myths of the Indo-Iranian inhabitants of Nuristān (q.v., formerly Kafirestān) and Dardestān contain a figure Im-rō (Imra), known since the 1890s and identified with the Indic King Yama (*yama rāja*), king of the dead (see Parkes, with literature).

The "cutting" of Yima. In *Yašt* 19.46, a story about the contest between the two Spirits (*maniiu*) over the *ax^{v}arəta x^{v}arənа* "the unseizable (?) Fortune," both send emissaries (*ašta*). Those of the Beneficent Spirit were Good Thought (see BAHMAN), Best Order (see ARDWAHIŠT), and the fire (see ĀTAŠ), son of Ahura Mazdā; those of the Evil Spirit were Bad Thought (see AKŌMAN), Wrath with the bloody club (see AĒŠMA), Aži Dahāka, and Spitiiura, the Yima-cutter (*spitiiurəmca yimō.kərəṇtəm*). The *Avesta* contains no other reference to this event, but the Middle Persian texts refer to it in various ways, although the details of it had, apparently, been long forgotten. According to the *Bundahišn* (35.3), J̌am, Tahmōraf, Spitūr, and Narseh were all brothers, and Dahāg and Spitūr collaborated on cutting J̌am apart (*kirrēnīd*; *Bdh.* 35.5; on the use of this verb, see also Lincoln, 1997). Elsewhere, J̌am is said to have been cut apart by the *dēws* at the end of the first millennium of the world of the living (*Bdh.* 33.1) but, when he was cut apart, the Farrōbay fire, which he had enthroned on Mount Xwarrahōmand in Xwārazm, saved him from Dahāg (*Bdh.* 18.9-10).

In the *Pahlavi Rivāyat*, the cutting is presented as the result of J̌am's refusal to promote Ohrmazd's *dēn*. Instead of accepting, J̌am despised (*tar menīd*) Ohrmazd, confident that he could not die (thinking: "Astwihād will not come to me"), and he was then cut apart by *dēws* and men (*PR.* 47.8). In the *Sūdgar nask* commentary on the *Vohuxšaθrā Gāθā* (*Y.* 51) in the *Dēnkard* (*Dk.* 9.21.2-10; Vevaina, 2007, pp. 297-99, 303-4), people complain to Dahāg that the world has become corrupted after the cutting up of J̌am, and all the good things of J̌am's rule have been replaced by bad things. They go on to point out that (different from J̌am), Dahāg is subject to death. In turn, Ohrmazd warns Frēdōn not to cut up Dahāg so that the world does not become full of the harmful animals emerging from his body. In this version of the myth, one of the consequences of the cutting of J̌am was also the "mingling of *dēw*s with people" (*Dk.* 9.21.2), a theme seen in the Avesta in the Zarathustra myth. Before Zarathustra, the *daēuua*s walked on earth in the shapes of men and would abduct human women and have their way with them publicly, but Zarathustra sent them underground, depriving them of their desires (e.g., *Yt.* 19.80, see above on Yima and the golden age). This activity is specifically assigned to the reign of Dahāg in the *Bundahišn* (14B.2), where Dahāg is said to have watched copulation between humans and *dēw*s.

The Persian tradition provides a few further details of this story. In the *Šāh-nāma*, after a hundred years of hiding, Jamšid appeared one day in Čin on the shore of the ocean (cf. Ṯaʿālebi, p. 16, "on some shore,"). Here Żaḥḥāk found him and sawed him apart (ed. Mohl, I, p. 64; ed. Khaleghi, I, p. 52). According to the *Fārs-nāma* and a poem on Jamšid among the *Persian Rivāyat*s, he was killed in China, in a forest, where he had hidden inside a tree according to the *Rivāyat*, by the ocean according to the *Fārs-nāma* (*Persian Rivāyat*s, p. 581; Ebn Balḵi, p. 34; see Christensen, 1918-34, II, pp. 73-75, on this motif, also in Mirḵᵛānd, 1959-72, I, pp. 526-27, ed. Kayānfar, II, pp. 605-6). Satan then told Bivarasp (Żoḥḥāk) where Jamšid was hidden, and he began sawing the tree. When he sawed through Jamšid's body, the sun disappeared, but when they returned the next day, he was again whole. This happened once more before they were able to kill him. There then follows the story of how Jamšid was sent to Hell, but repented, and was sent to *hamēstagān*, where he remained for a thousand years before being admitted into Garōdmān (q.v.).

Additional details include the following: The saw had a thousand edges (*hazār-tēγ*, *Ayādgār ī Zāmāspīg*, p. 42); it was or resembled a fish bone (*Mojmal al-tawāriḵ*, p. 40; Ebn Balḵi, p. 34; Mirḵᵛānd, 1959-72, I, p. 526, ed. Kayānfar, II, p. 604). Spitur was Jamšid's brother (cf. *Bundahišn*, see above), who rebelled and made an attempt on his life, causing him to go into hiding (Ṭabari, ed. I, p. 181, tr. I, p. 350; Ebn al-Balḵi, pp. 33-34). Bivarasp tore out his intestines and swallowed them before sawing him (Ṭabari, ibid.). Dahāg threw him to wild beasts, which tore him apart (Ṯaʿālebi, p. 16). He was burnt at Babylon so that no trace of him remained (*Mojmal al-tawāriḵ*, pp. 40, 462).

Asadi Ṭusi's *Garšāsp-nāma* (qq.v.) contains a long elaboration on the conflict with Dahāg and Jamšid's time in hiding, which is also found in the *Mojmal al-tawāriḵ*. Having escaped from a terrific man-to-man fight with Dahāg, Jamšid came to Zābolestān, where he stayed for twenty years. There, the king's daughter tricked him into marrying her (ed. Huart, pp. 54-71, ed. Yaḡmāʾi, pp. 22-38). The princess bore the son Ṯur (ancestor of Rostam, according to *Mojmal al-tawāriḵ*, p. 25; Tur, in Asadi, p. 42, v. 4). The son, however, looked so much like his father that he generated suspicion that Jamšid himself was there, and the king therefore advised him to leave (Asadi, ed. Huart, pp. 86-87; ed. Yaḡmāʾi, p. 43). He traveled to India (where he ruled a hundred years according to *Mojmal al-tawāriḵ*), and on to China, where he was killed (Asadi, ed. Huart, pp. 88-89, ed. Yaḡmāʾi, p. 43, v. 22; *Šāh-nāma*, ed. Macan, pp. 2125-27; *Mojmal al-tawāriḵ*, pp. 39-40). The *Mojmal al-tawāriḵ* (p. 25) gives the name of the princess as Paričehra, as well as that of another wife as Māhang, daughter of the king of Māčin, with whom he had two sons, Batuʾāl and Homāyun, who was Ābtin's father. According to *Tāriḵ-e Sistān* (p. 2, tr. Gold, p. 1), Sistan (Sejestān) was founded by Garšāsp (also Mirḵᵛānd), descendant of Tur, son of Jamšid, etc., while Mirḵᵛānd has Jamšid as ancestor of both Garšāsp and Rostam (1959-72, I, pp. 526-27, ed. Kayānfar, II, pp. 605-6, tr. p. 118).

A passage in the *Dēnkard* suggests a completely different meaning of the allusion to "cutting." In the *Sūdgar nask* exegesis of the *Vohuxšaθrā Gāθā* (*Dk.* 9.21.5), Dahāg's mother, Ōdag (see Jackson, p. 92; AŽDAHĀ), is alluded to as having harmed J̌amšēd's genitals (*kēr ud gund*), making him a eunuch (*šābestān*) and depriving him of offspring (*bē az ābusīh*) and making him exposed to *sēǰ* (*a-bē-kerd-sēǰ*), for which there was no remedy, so that nothing grew from his body and no lineage (*paywand*) went from him (Vevaina, pp. 298, 304; Skjærvø, 2008, p. 540). If this refers to the "cutting," we have a myth very different from those that ascribed to him and his twin sister offspring (see below).

J̌am and J̌amī (J̌amag). In the *Rigveda*, Yama has a twin sister Yamī, while, in Iran, only Pahlavi J̌am has a twin sister J̌amī (J̌amag). The form J̌am-ī for Av. *Yam-ī is formed like Pah. *ahurān-ī* (spelled with *-ydy*) for Av. *ahurān-ī* (*Y.* 66.1) and J̌am-ag is formed like Rudāb-a, etc.

According to the Pāzand *Ayādgār ī Zāmāspīg*, Wīwanghān had a pair of twins, J̌am and J̌amī, and J̌am took J̌amī with him when he went into exile (see above on Yima's sin; also the *Persian Rivāyat*s, tr. Dhabhar, pp. 580-81). Similarly, according to the *Pahlavi Rivāyat* (8e), after the loss of his kingship, J̌am and his sister J̌amag went into the *war* in order to escape from humans and *dēw*s. When he was nowhere to be found in the world or in Hell, Ahriman suggested he might be in the *war*, and a *dēw* and a *parīg* (a male and female demon) went looking for him. They presented themselves to J̌am and J̌amag as fleeing from the *dēw*s and suggested the four of them be united in marriage, which they were. In the *Bundahišn* (14B1) the background story is omitted and it is only said that, out of fear for the *dēw*s, J̌am took a female *dēw* as his wife and gave J̌amī to a male *dēw*. According to both accounts, it was from these unions that monkeys, bears, and other harmful creatures were born (including the Gandarw, *Pahlavi Rivāyat* (8e9), Żoḥḥāk's evil counselor Kandrow in the *Šāh-nāma*, ed. Khaleghi, I, p. 78). Interestingly, Zādspram has a parallel story about Manuščihr and his othewise unknown sister Manušag, who has the daughter (?) Koxred (Av. *kaxᵛarəiδī*, a kind of sorceress) with Wrath (*hešm*) (Zātspram 9.1, ed. Gignoux and Tafazzoli, pp. 64-65; see also Christensen, 1916-34, I, p. 68).

The *Pahlavi Rivāyat* goes on to tell the story of how, one time Jam and the *dēw* were on a drinking spree, Jamag switched clothes with the *parīg* and took her drunken brother to bed, thus performing *xwēdōdah* (next-of-kin marriage), by the virtue of which the two demons fell back into Hell. The *Bundahišn* also reports that Jam and Jamag had twins, a man named Āspī(g)ān and a woman named *Zrēšom, who married and so continued the lineage (*Bdh.* 35.4). The story is reminiscent of the story of Lot and his daughters, who have intercourse with him when he is drunk, in order to continue the family (*Genesis* 19:31-38).

A later version of this story, perhaps influenced by the story of Yima's sisters, is reported by Ebn Meskawayh, according to whom Jamšid had married his sister to a relative, whom he then made king of Yemen, and she gave birth to Dahāg (ed. Caetani, I, p. 11, ed. Emāmi, p. 8). Biruni, too, mentions that Bivarasp was the son of Jamšid's sister (ed. Sachau, pp. 217-18, ed. Aḏkāʾi, p. 268, tr. p. 202).

Jam's twin sister shows up only in the Pahlavi books and later, but it has been speculated whether this part of the myth is related to the "twins" (*yə̄mā*) of *Yasna* 30.3 "who have ben renowned as the twin 'sleeps'." Since the "twins" in this passage are the two "spirits" (*maniius*), any direct connection with Yima seems to be excluded, although an indirect allusion (typical of the style of the *Gāθās*) can not be ruled out, but discussions have produced nothing convincing (cf. Duchesne-Guillemin, 1962, p. 209). Wolfgang Lentz (1962, pp. 133), for instance, suggested that the passage meant "the twins (Yima and his sister), who have become known by their sleep(ing together)," for which Helmut Humbach (1974, p. 200) suggested "who, because of Yima, have become renowned as the two (kinds of) sleep(ing together)," that is, with the *dēw* and the *parīg*. It is unlikely that the passage in its context has this literal meaning (cf. Skjærvø, 1997, p. 111; idem, 2008), but it is not impossible that the poets expected the listener to make these connections if the myths existed at the time.

The "cutting apart" of Yima, although reminiscent of Plato's myth in the *Symposium* (XIV-XV, 189e-191d), that the primordial androgynes were cut in two to produce men and women, also leads to no futher insight on the matter of the twins. The same is true if the "cutting" was castration, which brings to mind the myth of Uranus and Cronus, where Cronus castrates his father with a sickle with jagged teeth (Hesiod, *Theogony* 178-82; see also Lincoln, 1981b). On the other hand, the story of the incest connects the Iranian myth with the Old Indic myth, in which Yamī tries to seduce here brother.

Yam in Manicheism. The Manichean *Book of Giants* contains two Sogdian fragments of a story about Yam, one in which Yam is presented with five diadems, which he accepts, and one in which he is described as lord of the world, before whom all the lords of the world would assemble on New Year's Day (Sogd. *nawí m[ēθ] = now ruz*; Henning, 1943, p. 74, who read *nwy m[ʾx ?]*; see Skjærvø, 1995, p. 204; the term is found in a Manichean letter with New Year's greetings, Yoshida, 2000, p. 147, line 70), all of which echoes closely Ferdousi's account of the beginning of Jamšid's reign (ed. Mohl, I, p. 48; ed. Khaleghi, I, p. 41). Prods O. Skjærvø (1995) has argued that numerous features of the mythical Yima, Jam(šēd) agree with those of the Manichean Rex Honoris, the second son of the five sons of the Living Spirit, who sits on a throne in the seventh heaven, is the ruler (*smān-xšēδ*) of all ten heavens, and watches over the heavens and the earths, and further with the description of God in *1 Enoch* 14:18, who sits on a throne of crystal with wheels like the shining sun, recalling the description of Jamšid's throne as a glass chariot. The Rex Honoris is also in charge of a wheel that is like a big mirror and allows him to see everything (*Kephalaia* 88.30-33, tr. Gardner, p. 92), which is reminiscent of Jamšid's Cup (see ii, below), which allows him to see everything that goes on in the entire world. According to *1 Enoch* 7-8, the 200 angels, led by Semyaz, taught people medicine, decorations, ornamentation, etc., crafts that, according to the Sogdian fragment, the 200 *δēws* had seen in the heavens among the gods, etc. This may indicate that Mani correlated the Iranian mythical characters with his own in his narrative of the origins of the world in his book *Pragmateia*, deeds of heroes.

Jam in the medieval chronography. The Arab historians, who, following earlier traditions, try to establish synchronisms between the Iranian and Biblical legends, place Jam variously. Ebn Qotayba (q.v.; ed. Wüstenfeld, p. 320; ed. ʿOkāša, p. 652) makes him the Persian Solomon, a tradition also reported by Dinavari (ed. Guirgass, p. 9, ed. ʿĀmer and Šayyāl, p. 6), Maqdesi (text III, pp. 46, 106, tr. pp. 48, 109, tr. Šafiʿi Kadkani, I, pp. 438, 474), Ebn Hawqal (p. 278, tr. p. 273), and Ṯaʿālebi (p. 10). Maqdesi also points out that the Persians assign to Jamšid all the miracles assigned to Solomon (p. 106, tr. p. 109, tr. Šafiʿi Kadkani, I, p. 474); Eṣṭaḵri (pp. 123, 150, tr. pp. 109, 141) and Ebn Ḥawqal (p. 278) refer to Persepolis as the mosque of Solomon (cf. Malʿab Solaymān "Solomon's playground" in Moqaddasi, p. 444) and that Jam was Solaymān; and Ḥamd-Allāh Mostawfi reports that, in the *Ṣowar al-aqālim* (apparently of Abu Zayd Balḵi, [q.v.], lost), the columns in Persepolis were said to be of the Mosque of Solomon and suggests that perhaps Solaymān had turned Jamšid's house into a mosque (Mostawfi, p. 121, tr., p. 120). Ebn al-Nadim simply points out that some say Solaymān was the first to make the demons his subjects, others say it was Jamšid (ed. Flügel, p. 309, ed. Tajaddod, p. 370, tr. p. 727). Several of the Muslim authors criticize the notion that Jamšid was Solomon by referring to the great time span separating them, including Dinavari (ed. Guirgass, p. 9, ed. ʿĀmer and Šayyāl, p. 6: more than 3000 years of difference) and Mirḵᵛānd (1959-72, I, p. 515-16, ed. Kayānfar, II, p. 595, tr. p. 100: more than 2000 years), who produces additional arguments why they cannot have been the same person.

Masʿudi adds that it was also said that the Flood occurred during his reign (ed. Barbier de Meynard and

Courteille II, pp. 112-13, ed. and tr. Pellat, sec. 536), which agrees with Maqdesi, who says that Jamšid lived at the time of Noah (III, pp. 23-24, tr. p. 25, tr. Šafiʿi Kadkani, I, p. 425), while Dinavari has Jam descended from Noah (ed. Guirgass, p. 4, ed. ʿĀmer and Šayyāl, p. 1: son of Vivanjhan son of Arfaḵšad brother of Šāleḵ son of Sām = Šem, son of Noah). Dinavari (ed. ʿĀmer and Šayyāl, pp. 2-3) adds that Jam became king in Babylonia after Sām and that it was during his reign that their language was confused and the sons of Sām settled in various places in the Middle East (*arż Bābel*), including Iranian territories. He also reports that Nimrod was descended from Jam and that all the Arabs are descended from Arfaḵšad (ed. Guirgass, p. 9, ed. ʿĀmer and Šayyāl, p. 6).

Note also Mary Boyce's suggestion that the mention in the *Tansar-nāma* of agriculture in the time of Noah belongs to this tradition (1968, p. 45, n. 2; further on Jamšid's genealogy, see also Christensen, 1918-34, II, pp. 109-11; Wesendonk, 1924, p. 157 with references).

The Iranian Yima and the Indic Yama. The Vedic and Zoroastrian myths agree and differ in crucial details. The one clearly Indo-Iranian element is the shared father, whose functions, however, differ in detail, although they both refer to first sacrifices: Vivasvant sent the sacrificial fire to mankind, while Vīuuaŋᵛhan was the first to perform a *haoma* sacrifice (cf. Keith, pp. 112-13).

Two linguistic formulas in the same Rigvedic hymn make the two myths inseparable, *gātu-* "place to go" + *vinda-* "find" and "assembly of people/mortals": Yama was the first to go along the path into the distance of the great slopes for the sake of the many; he found the way to go (*RV.* 10.14.1, 2: *gātúm viveda*). Yima expanded the earth for the sake of those who did not find a way to go (*Vd.* 2.8 *nōiṯ gātuuō viṇdən*). Yama is the one who assembled people (*RV.* 10.14.1 *saṃgámanaṃ jánānāṃ*), and Yima organized an assembly together with the best men (*Vd.* 2.20: *hanjamanəm frabarata . . . haθra vahištaēibiiō mašiiākaēibiiō*).

Other, less precise, correspondences in the same hymn include the following: Yama presumably acted as a shepherd-king, whose "grazing ground" (*gávyūti* = Av. *gaoiiaoiti*, Miθra's heavenly grazing grounds) can not be taken away (*RV.* 10.14.2). Yima has good flocks (*huuąθβa*), but only the fourth of the first sacrificers, Pōrušāsp, also has a *gaoiiaoiti* (*Dk.* 7.2.29 *gāwyūd ī spitāmān* "the grazing grounds of the Spitāmas"), father of Zarathustra, who will initiate the return of the world to its state of immortality. All mortals will go to this place, where they will no longer see the sun (*RV.* 10.14.12 *dṛśáye sū́ryāya* "give us to see the sun!"; cf. Yima's epithet *huuarə.darəsō*). And Yama guides us among the gods for us to live a long life (*RV.* 10.14.14 *dīrghám ā́yuḥ prá jīváse*, cf. *Y.* 9.19 [request to Haoma] *darəyō.jītīm*).

Yama's mother (daughter of the divine carpenter, Tvaṣṭar), or a substitute (since she disappeared at the wedding), bore the twin Aśvins and left behind a pair (*RV.* 10.17.1-2), perhaps Yama and Manu/Manuṣ, who are both sons of Vivasvant. According to late traditions, Jamšid has a pair of twin sisters (see above) and is, according to the Pahlavi traditions, one of four brothers (see above).

Yama's birth was immortal/among the immortals(?) (*RV.* 1.83.5: *yamásya jātám amṛ́taṃ*), and he became a king "at the barrier of the sky" (*RV.* 9.113.8). His realm of the dead, the abode of the "fathers," was originally in highest heaven (*RV.* 10.14.8: *paramé vyòman*), only later underground. Yima, as king of the golden age, was presumably at first immortal, like his subjects, but it is never suggested he was originally among gods or divine, the *hamēstagān*, of which Jam became king, being located only between earth and the star-level (*Dk.* 5.8.5-6, ed. Amouzgar and Tafazzoli, pp. 40-41). Ṭabari is the only one to state explicitly, that Jamšid was tricked by the Devil (Eblis) to believe himself to be a god and call on people to worship him (I, p. 182, tr. I, 351), on which Balʿami's Devil elaborates: "You are the god of the heavens and earth, but you are not aware of it; you were in heavens, you created this earth, you put the heavens in order and came to the earth to straighten the buisness of the earth, dispense justice, and return to the heavens" (ed. Bahār, p. 131, ed. Gonābādi, p. 89, tr., I, p. 104).

Yama chose death for the sake of(?) the gods (*deva*) or, for the sake of progeny, did not seek immortality (*RV.* 10.13.4, riddle hymn). Yima was killed and went to hell. Yama built a dwelling place (*sā́danā*) for the dead (*RV.* 10.18.13), called "the house of *deva*s" (*RV.* 10.135.7: *yamásya sā́danaṃ deva-mānáṃ*). Yima ruled over men and *daēuua*s and is closely associated with *dēw*s in the later tradition.

In the *Mahābhārata* (book 2 section 8), Yama's assembly house is described in terms similar to the *vara*: It was built by Viśvakarman, bright as gold, covered an area of more than a hundred *yojana*s (a meaure of distance), and possessed the splendor of the sun. It was neither very cool nor very hot, there was no grief or weakness of old age, hunger or thirst. Everything one might desire was to be found there, all kinds of enjoyable things and delicious edibles in abundance, fragrant floral wreaths and fruit trees, and cold and hot waters. All the great heroes of old were there. Also, the house moved wherever Yama wished (Christensen, 1918-34, II, pp. 8-9; *Mahābhārata*, tr. Buitenen, II, pp. 47-48).

The theme of the overpopulation of the earth is also found in India, as well as elsewhere in Indo-European literature. In the *Mahābhārata*, one story is told in the first book (*ādi-parvan*) that, during a golden age populated by immortals, the Asuras were born and multiplied and soon the earth sagged under her burden and, fearful, sought refuge with Brahmā, upon which the gods (*deva*s) descended to earth to destroy their enemies (tr. van Buitenen, I, pp. 136-38). Another story is found in the third book (*vana-parvan*, sec. 141, tr. Chandra Roy, pp. 423-25; cited by Christensen, 1918-34, II, pp. 6-8). Here, during the terrible times of the *kṛta-yuga*, the supreme god (*ādi-deva*) took on "Yama-hood" (*yamatva*) and created a world in which there was immortality, which led to overpopulation. Having sunk 1000 *yojana*s, the earth complained to Nārāyaṇa (= Viṣṇu), who increased his size to enable him to lift the earth back up 1000 *yojanas* on one of his tusks. In the Greek tradition, according to the poem *Cypria* of the Epic Cycle, Zeus devised the Trojan war to rid the earth of the myriad of heroes weighing her down (Hesiod, 1977, pp. 496-97; on further parallels to the story of the overpopulation and expansion of the earth, see Hertel, pp. 23-33, and Keith's critique, pp. 621-23; *Mahābhārata*, tr. Buitenen, II, pp. 203-5; on Flood stories, see Hertel, pp. 26-33).

The Rigvedic dialogue hymn featuring Yama and Yamī has numerous details in common with the Pahlavi stories about Jam and Jamī: Yamī tries to convince Yama to sleep with her, arguing that the immortals wish the one mortal to have offspring (*RV*. 10.10.3); already in the womb, they were made by their engenderer, Tvaṣṭar, to be husband and wife (*RV*. 10.10.5). Yama resists, acknowledging that it may yet happen in coming generations that those closely related (*jāmí*) will perform that which is not proper for them (*ájāmi*; *RV*. 10). They tell one another that they expect the other to be embraced by someone else (*RV*. 13-14).

The Gathic myth of Yima. Numerous attempts have been made to interpret the reference to Yima's sin in *Yasna* 32.8: *yō maṣ̌iiə̄ṇg cixšnušō ahmākə̄ṇg gāuš bagā x^vārəmnō*. Early scholars simply followed the Pahlavi interpretation: *kē-š ō mardōmān čāšīd kū amāgān gōšt pad bazišn xwarēd* "who taught people: eat the meat and distribute(?) it to ours(?)!" In the *Warštmānsr nask* commentary on this strophe in the *Dēnkard*, Av. *cixšnušō* is understood (correctly) as being related to the verb "satisfy (with gifts), make favorable" and the passage as being about how Jam satisfied people by giving them meat to eat (*Dk*. 9.32.12; cf. Pahl. *Y*. 9.1). The Pahlavi rendering is based on several pseudo-etymological interpretations: *gāuš* = *gōšt* "meat," *bagā* = *bazišn* "sharing," and *x^vārəmnō* = *xwarēd* "eat!"

Early scholars usually followed this indigenous tradition; Christian Bartholomae (q.v.), for instance, rendered the line as "he who, in order to satisfy humans, gave our (men) pieces of meat to eat" and maintained it expressed Zarathustra's rejection of Yima and his institutions of the bloody sacrifice and the orgiastic festivals connected with it (*AirWb*., cols. 1866-67 n. 2; 1905, pp. 32-33). Bartholomae, however, assumed that *gāuš* "the bull" (nominative) is for *gaoš* "of bull" (genitive), that is, "of meat" (a meaning *gao-* has nowhere else); *bagā* (instrumental of *baga-* "god") is the same as *bāga-* "share"; and *x^vārəmnō* (unknown meaning) is the causative of of *x^vara-* "eat" (which would be **x^vāraiia-*, but is not attested).

Most translations of the passage in the first half of the 20th century followed this interpretation, for instance, Jacques Duchesne-Guillemin (1962, p. 209), Geo Widengren (pp. 53-54, 66), who also followed Henrik Samuel Nyberg (q.v.; pp. 92-94) in regarding the cult of Yima and the use of *haoma* as typical of the *Männerbund* and therefore proscribed by Zarathustra, a notion that has no basis in the sources (see Boyce, 1987). From the 1950s on, when Bartholomae's (and the Pahlavi translations') arbitrary grammatical analysis of the passage began to be rejected, new attempts to interpret the strophe were made. In 1957, Helmut Humbach returned to the literal interpretation of *gāuš* as "cattle," and, in 1962, Wolfgang Lentz interpreted *bagā* as a form of *baga-* "god," referring to the Zoroastrian tradition that Jam regarded himself as god, while also rejecting the notion that the strophe expressed Zarathustra's disapproval; rather, he used the myths to illustrate his preaching. Then, in a survey of the sources for bloody sacrifices in Zoroastrianism, Mary Boyce questioned the assumption that Zarathustra rejected the bloody sacrifice (or the *haoma*), which was practiced by Zoroastrians till recent times (Boyce, 1966, esp. p. 110; idem, 1975-82, I, pp. 214-18).

Helmut Humbach then suggested *gāuš* could be the verb missing in this phrase and a form of **gau-* "to be deficient, sin," with relatives in Sogdian and Chorasmian meaning "need." He also quoted Karl Hoffmann to the effect that *x^vāra-* could be connected with the Germanic words for *swear* and *oath* (Ger. *Schwur*) and simply mean "swear (an oath)," as in New Pers. *sowgand k̲^vordan*, also comparing the legal Pahlavi term *xwārestān* (Humbach, 1974, p. 199; Bartholomae, 1922, pp. 35, 38: "high court"; Macuch, pp. 108-9: "place of swearing an oath"). In his later translation of the *Gāθās*, Humbach added that *gāuš* could also be from the verb meaning "increase" (1991, I, p. 133, II, p. 82).

Stanley Insler in his *Gāθā* translation (1975) rendered the phrase as "he who wanted to satisfy our men (by) swearing: '*The cow is goddess*'," taking *bagā* as an otherwise unknown feminine of *baga* (Insler, p. 47, with comments, pp. 204, 331; note that there is also no feminine of *yazata* or of *daēuua* in Avestan, *daēuuī-* [*AirWb*., cols. 667-70] probably being a misspelling for *daiuuī-* < *daiβī-* "deceptive"). In 1987, Ilya Gershevitch, building on Humbach and Insler's proposals, suggested that the strophe contained "direct speech uttered by Yima at his trial," and that *bagā* was used by default by "poor pagan Yima" "to address his divine judge" (Gershevitch, 1985-88, pp. 489-90) and proposed various solutions to the problems of *Yašt* 19.30-34, as well. Kellens and Pirart in their edition (1988-91) pointed out the impossibility of finding a convincing interpretation and did not translate.

Yima's time. In the Pahlavi world chronology, the first heroes, Hōšang, Tahmōraf, and Jam, belong to the first millennium after the new-born world of the living was attacked by Ahriman and death was introduced by the killing of Gayōmard and the first Bull (*Bdh*. 1.59 and chap. 4). The story in *Vidēvdād* 2, however, seems to take place before the attack, since, under Yima's reign, there is, as yet, no old age, sickness, or death, nor any of the other evils that were introduced by Ahrimen. When Yima expands the earth, he goes forth "at noon on the road of the sun," which also suggests a time before the attack, when the sun had not yet started to move (*Bdh*. 2.17), that is, in the Pahlavi scheme of things, while the world of the living (*gētīy*) was still in the world of thought (*mēnōy*) or in Ohrmazd's womb (*Bdh*. 1.59).

Moreover, in the Avesta, the first three heroes are typically said to have "had command over men and *daēuuas* on the seven-fold earth" (*Yt.* 19.26-31; cf. Benveniste, 1967; Kellens, 2005) or ask for "command over men and *daēuuas* of all the lands" (*Yt.* 5.21-25), which appears to describe a time not covered by the Pahlavi world chronology, the time when the *daēuuas* walked on earth among men (*Y.* 9.15, *Yt.* 19.80, see above on Yima and the golden age). The coexistence of men and *daēuuas* is clear in the *Gāθās*, as well, and the actual presence of *daēuuas* on earth is suggested by *Yasna* 32.3 ("you, *dāeuuas*, have become renowned on one-seventh of the earth"), and a formerly different status is suggested by *Yasna* 44.20, where the poet asks whether *daēuuas* really once had good rule.

Since Zarathustra was the one who drove the *daēuuas* underground and so put an end to the time of man-*daēuua* mixture and since he is also featured in the *vara*, the Zarathustra myth belongs to this early stage of the world, as well, but he was also the first to sacrifice to Ahura Mazdā and first representative of the three classes in the world of the living (*Yt.* 13.88-90). The myth of the early heroes may therefore reflect a stage of the mythical prehistory before the *daēuuas* were demoted with the sharpening of cosmological dualism (after this, they, like everybody else, had to make a choice, but made the wrong choice, *Y.* 30.6). The Yima/Jam myths even suggest the demotion was connected with Yima. The *Vidēvdād* story may then describe the world after the disappearance of the *daēuuas*. The "chronological" scheme of the *Young Avesta*, although different from that of the later tradition, does not contradict such a possibility, since it is demonstrably the transformation of several older myths (see., e.g., Skjærvø, 1998, on the *kauuis* and the war against Fraŋrasiian). That the chronological indications in the Avesta puzzled the Sasanian priests, however, is clear from the Pahlavi commentary on *Vidēvdād* 2.19, where some commentator found it necessary to spell out the standard teaching of the twelve trimillennia adducing an otherwise lost Avestan passage on the duration of the world of thought and that of living beings (see also Kellens, 1999-2000, pp. 733-34, on the evolution of the old myth under the influence of the millenary scheme).

A different interpretation of *Yasna* 32 may be attempted if we compare the succession of ages in the Iranian mythoepic tradition with the Greek myth of the ages of the world described by Hesiod in his *Works and Days* (lines 110-55). Hesiod's age of gold was, like that of Yima, free from all kinds of worries, including old age. The earth bore abundant and inexhaustible (*áphthonon*) fruits (cf. *Y.* 9.4 = *Yt.* 15.16, 19.32), and people dwelt in peace with abundant flocks (cf. Yima's epithet "having good flocks" *huuąθβa-*). The similarity with Yima's age of gold is obvious, including waters and plants not drying out with inexhaustible (*ajiiamna*) tasty foods (see Skjærvø's review of Humbach and Ichaporia, 1998, pp. 186-87). After this age came to an end, its inhabitants became spirits roaming all over the earth. The men of the silver age were short-lived and characterized by hybris, which led them to sin by refusing to sacrifice and give honor to the gods. As this age, too, came to an end, its inhabitants became spirits (*daimones*) dwelling beneath the earth.

The third age, that of bronze, saw hybris and violence. Men enjoyed war and, killing one another, had to go to Hades, leaving the bright light of the Sun. In *Yasna* 32.6-7, the strophes preceding *Yasna* 32.8, the poet first mentions "the many sins for which he is seeking renown in lack of peace(?)" and then states, "of these sins I declare in *honesty I know none at all, the ones that are renowned as (tales?) of *violence (*jōiiā*), for which (one/he?) is renowned by (his) *shining metal (weapon)." In light of Hesiod's description, the mythoepic references (**srauuahiieitī* "he is seeking renown," *srāuuī* "was renowned") may be to weapon-wielding heroes of great strength, whose violent bent betrayed them into the sin of hybris. The "*shining metal" (*x^vaēnā aiiaŋhā*) is also what the sky is made of (*Yt.*13.2; *Bdh.* 34.5; *MX.* 8.7) and may well refer to (bronze) weapons. There is no evidence that the term refers to the ordeal by fire, as assumed from Bartholomae to Insler and Humbach. Kellens and Pirart, however, suggested the etymology **hu-waina-* "good to look at," which would fit, for intance, mirrors made of shiny bronze.

Hesiod's fourth age, that of iron, was inhabited by a nobler divine race of heroes. This age saw the battles before Thebe and at Troy, which would correspond to the battle of the Kauuis with Fraŋrasiian and the great battle in the *Mahābhārata* (see Skjærvø, 1998). After the wars, the heroes lived in a place free from worries ruled by Cronus, who had become king after castrating his father (*Works and Days* 168-71; cf. Christensen, 1918-34, II, p. 41).

Hesiod's fifth and last age, that of iron, was one of war and good mingled with evil (line 179). Apparently, this was caused by Zeus as a revenge for the theft of the fire by Prometheus (cf. Vivasvant, above on Yima as solar figure), by fashioning Pandora, whose box contained all evils that afterward befell men (the story is told before that of the five ages, *Works and Days* 50-89). This age would correspond to the period of the "mixture" in the Pahlavi scheme.

It is therefore likely, that the Avestan and pre-Avestan myths of the first ages were considerably more archaic than their Pahlavi versions, which explains why it is difficult to reconcile the two. The subsequent fall of Yima, however, is not clarified by these mythical chronologies, but depends on the myth of the Fortune (*x^varənah*), which is not yet understood.

Yima as first man and the cosmogonic sacrifice. Since the 19th century, the *Vidēvdād* Yima myth has been taken to be that of the mythical "first man" as well as "first king." That we are dealing with a first king is clear from the terms *xšaθra* "royal command" and *xšaiia-* "rule, be in command" (on Kellens' objection see below), but the claims that Yima is also the "first man," mainly based on the Indic Yama, are more doubtful and poorly supported by the Iranian sources (cf. Shaked, 1987, p. 238;

Christensen adduces only *Bdh.* 35.4 about the lineage from J̌am and J̌amī through Āspīgān and *Zrēšom, presumably the ancestors of Frēdōn). According to the Avesta, Yima's father, Vīuuaŋᵛhant, was the first mortal to press the *haoma* and thereby obtained a son, Yima, while, in *Vidēvdād* 2, Yima is only the first mortal to be addressed by Ahura Mazdā. As the Iranian Yima had no obvious features of the first man in the Iranian myths, early scholars thought this was an Indo-Iranian part of the myth that had been kept in India but been modified in Iran by Zarathustra, leading to the replacement or displacement of Yima by Gaiia Martān/Gayōmard (cf. Carnoy, 1917, pp. 313-14).

By the turn of the century, it had also been suggested that the Indic Yama and Manu were mythological complementary dublets of the first man (e.g., Macdonell, p. 139; see also, e.g., Lincoln, 1981a, p. 82), an idea that was taken up and applied to the Iranian myth, as well (for a personal interpretation of Yima as originally prophet and Messiah, see Blochet, p. 127.) Christensen also suggested that the Indians had the Flood story from the Babylonians (1916, p. 64; idem, 1918-34, II, pp. 61-62 with n. 1).

The "cutting" of Yima has also been connected with myths about the cutting up of a primordial man or giant to make the world, such as the Rigvedic Puruṣa (*RV.* 10.90) and the Old Norse Ymir. The idea was developed by Hermann Güntert (1923, esp. pp. 333-39), who, to strengthen his case, provided an etymological connection between Yama and Ymir, explaining Ymir as a derivative of **yemo-/yomo-*: Germanic **yum(i)yaz* from Indo-European **yəm(i)yós* (pp. 337-38) with "schwa secundum," a reduced vowel Güntert posited in 1916 in consonant groups that were difficult to pronounce, but on a rather arbitrary basis (Yima/Ymir is not discussed there). He did not, however, explain the function of the suffix, which, at least, ought to mean "belonging to, related to," or, in the case of a proper name, "son of" (another question is whether Indo-European had *-iya-/ -īya-* derivatives with zero grade from this type of nouns). It should be noted that the surface similarity between the two names is deceptive, since the only letter they have in common is *-m-*; the initial *y-* of the Indo-Iranian forms is a consonant (as in *year*), while the initial *y-* of Ymir is a vowel (German *ü-*). There is also no guarantee that the original initial was *y-*, as "**yəm(i)yós*, **wəm(i)yós*, and **Həm(i)yós*" would all become Old Norse *ymir* by Güntert's rule.

Puruṣa, Ymir, and Gayōmard (first man in the Iranian myth) are also not twins, and Yama and Gayōmard are not dismembered to form the parts of the world. Güntert circumvented these problems variously. He interpreted the name of Tacitus' Tuisto, father of Mannus and first ancestor of the Germanic people, as related to German *Zwitter* "hermaphrodite" and *Zwilling* "twin," then compared Ymir, whom he regarded as the factual equivalent of Tuisto (Güntert, 1923, pp. 324-33). The twin nature of Ymir, however, was only preserved in a myth according to which, when Yimir fell asleep, a boy and a girl were born from under his arm, while his two feet engendered a son with six heads (p. 336). From the fact that Gayōmard's offspring were the first two humans (male and female), he concluded that Gayōmard was not yet sexually differentiated (nor was the First Bull), but a hermaphrodite, male-female (pp. 347, 362). The lack of dismembering of Indic Yama was explained by early confusion of Puruṣa "Man," who was really Manuṣ, with Manuṣ's step-brother Yama, which also made Puruṣa a "twin" (pp. 322-24). The (unattested) dismembering of Gayōmard to make the world was replaced by the transformation of his body parts into metals at his death (*Bdh.* 14.3; cf. *MX.* 26.18; Schaeder, p. 228, suggested that this transformation provided a bridge between the legend of the first man and speculations about man as microcosmos).

There are two Pahlavi texts that present the world as consisting of the parts of the human body, but, in neither, the identity of the body is mentioned. The *Pahlavi Rivāyat* contains the cosmogonic part, in which the world is made from a body the creator contains in his own body (*PR.* 46; Güntert, 1923, pp. 330-31), and the *Bundahišn* contains the eschatological part, in which Ohrmazd says he will call back from the world the elements it received in the beginning: the bones from the earth, the blood from the water, the hair from the plants, the soul from the wind (*Bdh.* 34.5).

The myth of Yima in scholarship. Most late-19th- and 20th-century discussions of Old Iranian mythology were based on the axiom of the prophet Zarathustra's reform, in which earlier "pagan" concepts were abandoned in exchange for a modern "ethical" religion. From this point of view, the apparent criticism and rejection of Yima and his sins were part of the prophet's personal doctrine. The appearance of the Yima myth in the Young Avestan and later literature, in spite of the prophet's condemnation, was, like all mythical elements, regarded as a return to pre-Zoroastrian beliefs and a disintegration of the new religion. As there is wide disagreement about the contents of Zarathustra's reform, scholars have used it relatively freely to support their theories.

In the 19th century, a concensus also developed that, based on contents, style, and language, the *Vidēvdād* was a "late" composition, and not to be ascribed to the prophet. For instance, Peter Stuhr (p. 342) found the *Vidēvdād* to be so "pale" and lacking in the "original vivacity of spirit" that it must be a late composition (cited by Wilson, p. 297), echoed over a century later by Ilya Gershevitch (1968, p. 27), to whom "the enjoyment in reading" the *Vidēvdād* was marred by "deadly pedantery" and "dreary repetitions." As for the language, Karl Geldner, for instance, thought that *Vidēvdād* 2 was based on the Iranian epic, but expanded with prose texts by someone with a poor command of the language (Geldner, 1926, p. 28 n. 170); Robert C. Zaehner (1961, p. 162) and Gershevitch (1968, p. 27) both complained about the authors' grammatical confusion and negligence. The notion of the "lateness" of the *Vidēvdād* and its presumed non- or post-Zoroastrian contents, remained throughout the 19th-20th centuries, leading several authors to ascribe the text to the Median Magi (see below). In 1943, Walter Bruno Henning (q.v.) argued that it was post-Alexander, because the units of measure used in it were, he thought, the Greco-Roman ones (Henning, 1943b, pp. 235-36), an argument cited by Boyce (Boyce and Grenet, p. 68). Despite such opinions, which did not take into account the oral and written transmission of the text, the style and language of the *Vidēvdād* do not prove that it is later than the rest of the *Young Avesta* (see Skjærvø, 2006, pp. 112-16), but the common opinion has seriously influenced scholars' study of the Yima myths.

A passage that featured relatively prominently in the early discussions was *Vidēvdād* 2.22 (*auui ahūm astuuaṇtəm aγəm zimō jaŋhəṇti*, twice), first discussed by Bruno Lindner (p. 214) and frequently cited in 19th- and 20th-century scholarship, but rarely questioned (Bartholomae, *AirWb.*, col. 47; Geldner, 1926, p. 28; Christensen, 1918-34, II, p. 59; Boyce, 1975-82, I, p. 94). The adjective *aγəm* "evil," which begins the second octosyllable, agrees in case and number with the preceding "upon the world with bones" rather than with the following "winters," to which it obviously belongs, leading to translations such as "upon the bad corporeal world winters will come" instead of "upon the corporeal world bad winters will come," which is the way the Pahlavi rendering has it. The traditional translation makes it sound as if the winters are a punishment for a humanity gone bad, "sinful humanity" (Lindner, p. 215; Lommel, p. 199), providing an obvious parallel with flood stories such as the one in the Bible. The Avestan adjective is never applied to Ahura Mazdā's creations, however, only those of the Evil Spirit, among them natural disasters (cf. *Y*. 57.14 with *aγå . . . vōiγnå yeiṇti* "evil *floods will come"), and in *Vidēvdād* 7.27, the synonymous adjective *aγauuatō* is applied to "winter" (among the evils characterizing Airiiana Vaējah are the winter and the excess of *vōiγnās*, *Vd*. 1.3). Lommel suggested that the phrase referred to the imperfect humans who were not admitted into the *vara*, but the Avestan adjective is not applied to bodily defects. In view of the poor transmission of the *Vidēvdād*, it is not problematic to assume that *aγəm* has its ending from the previous two words and should be emended to **aγa* to agree with *zimō* (in the manuscript E10, the ending has also been extended to the verb: *zaŋhəṇtəm*). Abraham Anquetil-Duperron, whose translation was based on the Parsi tradition, has "the evil winter," and Martin Haug, realizing the grammatical problem, has the grammatically legitimate translation as "the evil of winter" (Haug, 1862, p. 204 "evils," 1878, p. 233 "evil").

This narrative of a flood released by God to punish a humanity gone bad early on provoked speculations that there might have been at least knowledge of, if not direct borrowings from, Mesopotamian traditions; already in 1871, Alexander Kohut opined that the similarities in the stories about Adam and the flood in the Jewish Talmudic and Midrashic tradition with the Iranian ones were due to interaction between the two peoples when the Jews lived under Iranian government (i.e., in Babylon; Kohut, pp. 59-61, 94). He also suggested that the Yima and the "Meshia" (Mašī) legends were developments of one original legend (p. 68).

Early attempts to interpret the Yima myth include those by the Indologist Rudolph Roth in 1850, who regarded Yama and Yamī as the children of heaven and the thundercloud. Yama was the first man and the first to die and go to the realm of the dead, whose king he became. Yama's paradise was in heaven, that of Yima on earth. Yima's sin was a late development. Yama corresponds to the Indic first man Manu, who gradually replaced him and delegated him to the realm of the dead (see Christensen, 1918-34, II, pp. 32-35 for this and later 19th-century scholarship).

Friedrich Windischmann, building on Roth's study, in his first study (1852) of the Indic Flood story, compared the couple Manuṣ - Yama with Greek Minos and Rhadamanthys, an idea that is occasionally mentioned in subsequent literature (e.g., Lincoln, 1981b, pp. 237-38). In his next study, Windischmann suggested that Gayōmard with his further devolpment into "Meschia" (Mašī) was the first man in the "theosophic form" of the Zoroastrian system, and that Yima was the first man of the old Aryan legend but had to be moved to another place in the system, in spite of the paradisiacal nature of the myth (Windischmann, 1859, p. 76 n. 1). In his later work (1863, p. 27), he suggested that Yima's gift of meat to mankind corresponded to Noah's sacrifice, by which mankind was allowed to eat meat (*Genesis* 8:20, 9:3), and that J̌am's marriage with the *parīg* corresponded to that of Adam with Lilith, (from which union demons, etc. were born) and to the similar union between Eve and a male devil (pp. 31-32).

James Darmesteter, in his early essays on (Indo-)Iranian mythology (1877), interpreted the ancient Indic and Iranian myths in terms of the three battles between the representatives of light and those of darkness, whose weapon is the lightning bolt: in the morning, at new year, and after the storm. In this scenario, the heroes were the agents of the light and came from above, were "men from above." Yima combined the "man from above" and "first man," who, "like all others of his kind," became the king of a legendary kingdom on earth, but was "fatally limited, with a sinister end": he was torn apart by the Serpent with the lightning bolt, an element of the storm myth (Darmesteter, 1877, p. 232). The *vara*, a celestial abode like Yama's *deva-sādana* (correct: *deva-mānam*, see above on the Indic Yama) was originally identical with Garōdmāna, paradise, but the two were separated when Gayōmard became first man and Yima's true title was forgotten (p. 233). The eschatological myth of the destructive winter (not flood!), was the myth of the year, transferred to the life of the universe, but conflicted with the myth of rejuvenation after the storm (p. 234). The replacement of the winter by the rain was one of the rare borrowings from Semitic myth, and "Malkosh" is Hebrew "Malqosh," late-season rain (p. 234 n. 1). Later, in his *Le Zend-Avesta* (1893), Darmesteter relinquished his interpretation of Malkūs, which he had by now connected with Avestan *mahrka* "destruction," and thought the legend was borrowed and the function of Noah transferred to Yima with the necessary adaptations (Darmesteter, 1893, II, pp. 19-20). In the chapter on foreign elements in Zoroastrianism (ibid., III), he devoted a lengthy section to parallels between the Old Testament and Zoroastrian texts; among other things, he suggested that the chronologization of the early history originated in the Bible, which the Avesta used as its model, though the Iranians may have used a Chaldean version of Genesis as model (1893, III, pp. lix-lx). The story of the Flood belonged completely to Noah, whereas it is totally unexpected and incongruous in the story of Yima, so much so that the popular tradition simply dropped it (III, p. lx). The context in which the borrowings could take place was Babylonia and other Jewish diaspora in the Middle East (III, p. lxii).

Bruno Lindner (1893, pp. 215-16) recommended caution in assuming that the Flood story was borrowed in view of the universal existence of Flood stories; rather, one should investigate the Indo-Iranian antecedents of the story. To Zarathustra, the story meant nothing, but he was unable to eradicate it from popular beliefs, and he therefore incorporated the story by putting Yima in charge of furthering the divine creation. The popular development helped out by transposing the Flood story to the eschatological narrative and by recasting it in a framework more suited to Iranian climate and geography. Borrowings or external influence he considered excluded (Lindner, p. 216).

James Hope Moulton, a Wesleyan minister and Methodist missionary in India, focused on the parallels between the Old Testament and the Avestan stories about how sin, death, and misery entered the world (1913, pp. 148-50). Citing *Yasna* 32.8 and the Pahlavi translation of *Yasna* 9.1 (from Bartholomae, *AirWb.*, cols. 1866-67), he concluded that Yima, deceived by the *daēuuas*, who deprive man of good life and immortality, had made his subjects immortal by giving them forbidden food to eat. He pointed out the similarities in the two stories: the spirit of evil was materialized as a serpent and the consequence of the Fall was the loss of the divine Glory; but also the differences: Yima, a man, gave forbidden food (meat) to his subjects, while Eve, a woman, gave a fruit to her husband; Yima was of the fifth, not the first, generation of the world, making him the contemorary of Mahalalel (*Genesis* 5:12); and his brother killed him like Cain killed Abel (Moulton, pp. 307-8). Moreover, the story of the *vara* was similar to that of Noah's ark as well as to the description of the New Jerusalem. Since the Old Testament and its Babylonian parallel stories were older than the Iranian ones, the Iranian ones must have been borrowed, implying that Yima contained elements from Adam, Eve, Abel, Mahalalel, and Noah (p. 308). Moulton also dismissed the *Vidēvdād* as a late work and assigned it to the Magi, whose practices differed from those of the Prophet (pp. 183, 225).

Albert J. Carnoy pointed out that Yima's solar epithets would be incomprehensible if Yima were simply the first man and, instead, suggested that the Yima legend must originally have been that of the setting sun, the perfect image of human life (1917, pp. 313-14).

Johannes Hertel, in his 1924 study, reviewed the Yima myth in *Vidēvdād* 2, comparing Indic Flood myths and myths about the expansion of the earth (pp. 23-33). He concluded that the *vara* (Indic *vala*) must be the vault of heaven (see Keith's critique, 1925, pp. 621-23). To him, the two stories of Yima's golden age and the destructive winter were incompatible. He thought the author could only have been one of the Magi, whom Zarathustra fought, and that the extant story was the result of manipulation of the older myth to make it fit the new religion and make it dogmatically harmless (Hertel, pp. 15-17).

Hermann Güntert, too, who discussed in depth the relationship between Yama/Yima and other Indo-European first men, notably Old Norse Ymir (see above on Yima first man), in a chapter on the Aryan legends of the god-man (1923, Part II, II) was convinced that the name of Gaiia Marətan was the result of artificial speculation (p. 346) and, approving of Windischmann's theory, himself speculated that it was Zarathustra himself who wanted to incorporate Yima into the system, but under the name of Gaiia Marətan, which led to Yima's ouster from the popular traditions (p. 365). He also followed Windischmann in his reconstruction of a Narcissus-like myth, in which Gayōmard fell in love with his "double, *alter ego*" his *fravaši*, by which pederasty and sin entered the world (pp. 361-62).

Karl F. Geldner had studied *Vidēvdād* 2 in detail in 1881, pointing out the Mesopotamian connections (p. 181). In a much later publication (1926), he described the *vara* as preserving a micro-model of Yima's golden age for the continuation of the Aryan race (p. 30, n. 178).

Arthur Christensen began his studies of Iranian "first men" in 1916 with Manu/Manu(š)čihr. The principal conclusion to be drawn from this study, however, is that the evidence for Christensen's conclusion that Manuš.ciθra/Manuščihr replaced *Manuš = the Indic Manuṣ/Manu, first man and first sacrificer (p. 68), is slim at best. His assumption that Manuš.ciθra meant "son of Manuš" is doubtful, in view of the parallel *gaociθra* applied to the moon and meaning "which contains the appearance and/or seed of the bull." Vague connections with Yima include Manu's role in the Indic Flood story and the couple Manuščihr's twin sister Manušag (see above on Yima first man). In the volume devoted to Yima (1934), Christensen relied on *Yašt* 9.10 to assume that Yima's reign originally occupied the entire first millennium of the world of the living, which would include the *Vidēvdād* count of 900 years plus the one century in exile (Christensen, 1918-34, II, pp. 35-36; cf. Darmesteter, 1893, II, p. 18). On this assumption, the Avestan Haošiiaŋha (Hōšang) and Taxma Urupi (Tahmōraf), as well as the Pahlavi Gayōmard, would have been added to the myth from local traditions, which resulted in the new counts of the reign Jam. He proposed explanations of the various myths of the Yima myth complex in the light of comparative mythology, anthropology, and folklore, among them those of first men; the myths of J̌am and J̌amī and Mašī and Mašyānī; Yima's immortality; lands of bliss reserved for heroes (Elysium, Valhalla; 1918-34, II, pp. 36-42); and of the *vara* as land of bliss and Yima, son of the sun and first man, as its first ruler (ibid., pp. 42-45). In Iran, the myth developed in two mutually exclusive directions; on the one hand (original myth), Yima as first man and ruler on earth, and, on the other hand (popular and priestly development), Yima as ruler of the non-terrestrial land of bliss. Subsequently, however, the first took on the characteristics of the second (ibid., pp. 45-46). Christensen cited Windischmann's observation that Yima's gift of meat to mankind corresponds to Noah's sacrifice by which mankind was allowed to eat meat and pointed out that the loss of immortality due to mankind's sins corresponds to Adam's loss of paradise (Christensen, 1918-34, II, pp. 49-50). Following others (e.g., Darmesteter, 1893, p. 20), Christensen also considered the question of a connection between the myth of the *vara* and the winter of Malkūs and that of the Flood, adding the evidence of other Mesopotamian Flood stories, but also pointed out the differences and further compared the Old Norse apocalyptic narratives of a devastating winter (1918-34, II, pp. 58-61). Christensen summed up the development of the myth, beginning with the idea of an Elysium, in which the first man, having become a god, lives with other immortal heroes and gods. This myth was influenced by that of the subterraneous land of the dead and the apocalyptic winter and was moved to the eschatology. Finally, the legend was influenced by the Semitic Flood traditions, widespread in the Near East (ibid., pp. 61-62).

Among more recent discussion of the Yima myth is that by Robert C. Zaehner (1961, chapter 5), who shared Moulton's opinion of the *Vidēvdād* (1961, p. 162). Zaehner gave a detailed description of the Yima myth and its parallels in Indic, but his chief purpose was to explore Yima's relationship with Mithra (cf. Boyce, 1975-82, I, p. 93 n. 54), and his insightful assessments of the myths were evaluated in the light of what he regarded as Zarathustra's teachings. He viewed the Yima legend in the light of Zarathustra's condemnation of Yima as a sinner, who, for his sin, lost immortality for himself and all of humanity. He regarded it as strange that the sin for which Zarathustra denounced him, the animal sacrifice (based on *Y.* 32.8, see above on the Gathic myth of Yima), should not be mentioned in the later tradition and proposed that this reflected the popular tradition, which "developed independently of the Zoroastrian reform" and in which the story of Yima's sin was the more popular. Similarly, the myth of the *vara* "must belong to a very old stratum of Iranian folklore wholly untouched by the teachings of Zoroaster," and Yima was worshipped as a god by those "who had not accepted the Zoroastrian reform" (Zaehner, pp. 134-35).

Marijan Molé, in his discussion of *Y.* 32.8 and its commentary in the *Warštmānsr nask* (*Dk.* 9.32.12), insisted that Yima is presented as first king and that the "sin," which the poet-sacrificer claims not to have committed and for which Yima was renowned, must have been a ritual fault (Molé, 1963, pp. 222-26).

Mary Boyce, too, relieved Zarathustra's teachings of the myths of Yima by assigning them either to pre-Zoroastrian beliefs or to late scholastic speculations. She elaborated on a tradition that Yima dwelt in paradise succeeding that of Yima as the "god beneath earth" (1975-82, I, pp. 94, 116-17, 277-78; see above on Yima, the dead, and Hell), suggesting it developed as the result of Zarathustra's demotion of the subterranean dwelling to Hell; but, since this was no longer a suitable dwelling for King Yima, he was transported into a new, paradisiacal, dwelling, the story of which is told in *Vidēvdād* 2 and, apparently survived in the *Dēnkard* myth of *Nēryōsang* and J̌am bringing Zarathustra's *fravaši* down to earth (ibid., pp. 94, 277). Boyce gives no reference for this last event, which appears to be based on a wrong reading of *Dēnkard* 7.2.21 on the descent of Zarathustra from J̌am and Nēryōsang (see above on Yima and the heroes of the origins; correct tr. by West, see *Dēnkard*, tr. West, p. 23; Molé, 1967, pp. 6-7). Her statement (1975-82, I, p. 95) that, according to the *Vidēvdād*, Yima did not die but withdrew to a hidden place, is unclear, since it is not said explicitly in the Avesta that *Yima* hid in the *vara*, that he dwelt there with his chosen, or, indeed, that he did not die. Boyce followed Moulton and Zaehner (also Henning) in assigning a late date to the *Vidēvdād* and agreed that it is "perfectly possible" that this part of the legend was inspired by the Mesopotamian myth, where it was a punishment wreaked upon the "bad corporeal world," a "wholly unZoroastrian conception," but with the Flood changed into a natural disaster more appropriate for Iranian geography. Boyce regarded the eschatological role of the *war* as due to an apocalyptic tradition that developed later as part of Zoroastrian scholastic learning, but did not become popular, as opposed to Yima's fall (echoing Zaehner). She also regarded Yima's association with first man as "priestly speculation" (Boyce, 1975-82, I, p. 96; cf. Güntert, and Christensen, above).

Bruce Lincoln has written frequently about Yima in the context of "first men," he, too, on the basis of the assumption that the myth was manipulated by Zarathustra (e.g., 1981b, p. 233). Thus, Lincoln believes Zarathustra "stripped" Yima "of his role as lord of paradise" and that the story of the *vara* was "in large measure influenced by the Mesopotamian flood legend" (ibid., p. 234). He aims to reconstruct an Indo-European myth of first sacrificer and first sacrificed man/king, who is dismembered to form the various parts of the world, typified by the Rigvedic Puruṣa "Man" and the Old Norse giant Ymir (Lincoln, 1981a, chap. IV; idem, 1986, p. 174 n. 3). In Indo-Iranian, Lincoln too finds the first sacrificed man/king in Yama, who was replaced by (Pahlavi) Gayōmard in Iran and (Rigvedic) Puruṣa in India (Lincoln, 1981a, pp. 76, 80), and the first sacrificer is Manuš, who is represented as Manušciθra/Manuščihr in Iran (p. 83). Lincoln suggests in conclusion (pp. 83-84) that, because *Manuš as first sacrificer was closely associated with the cattle sacrifice, which had been condemned by Zarathustra, he "was written out of the tradition." He resurfaced, however, in Ahriman ("an original conception of Zarathustra"), first sacrificer [i.e., of Gayōmard, ibid., p. 75]; Spitiiura, as the brother who dismembered Yima [the gods, not Manu, dismembered Puruṣa]; Manuščihr, as the ancestor of the priestly line; and Zarathustra, as "priest par excellence." In Germanic, Ymir was no longer either first man or king by internal developments (ibid., p. 80 n. 142). One of his principal pieces of evidence is the etymological relationship between Yama and Old Norse Ymir proposed by Herrmann Güntert (see above; Lincoln, 1981a, pp. 75-76). He also suggests that the original creative dismemberment of Yima was "transformed along royal lines" into the distribution of the Fortune among representatives of the three classes (Lincoln, 1975, p. 132, cf. 1981a, pp. 78-79). Lincon does not appear to cite the text in the *Pahlavi Rivāyat* about the making of the world from a person (*PR*. 46, cited by Güntert, 1923, pp. 330-31).

Kellens has written on Yima in several articles. In 1984, he developed the theory that the tools given to Yima endowed him with a creative magic that permitted him to perform several tasks received from the gods: make immortality, give the earth its permanent size, and prepare it for the universal cataclysm; thus, he occupied a place between gods and humans. The shared motif of the incest with his sister, however, suggests he was also a first man, ancestor of humanity (Kellens, 1984, pp. 280-81). In 1987 (p. 249, repr. p. 13) and 1988 (pp. 329-34), he suggested that the builder of the Cinuuant Bridge, who "piled" (*ci-*) it up, may have been Yima. In his recent discussions of the myths of Yima (1994-95; 1997-98; 1999-2000, pp. 727-34; 2002-3, pp. 819-26), he questions several of the traditional interpretations of the Avestan evidence. What is more significant, he disputes the interpretation of *xšaθra* as "royal command" and *xšaiia-* as "to rule, be in command" (see 1999-2000, p. 727; wrongly in the present author's opinion), arguing that the two tools given to Yima are those of a magical power, although he points out they are the tools of a shepherd (ibid., p. 729). The notion of the shepherd king is ancient, however, and is found in Iran in the first strophe of the *Gāθās*, the *Yaθā ahū vairiiō* (*Ahunwar*, q.v.). Kellens sums up his comparison between the Indic Yama and Iranian Yima, by asserting that, while Yama was the first man, first to die, and the first to occupy paradise, Yima first construed a paradise (though not really a paradise, since its occupants had not previously died) and was immortal in the first (Pishdadid) period of the world, then mortal and, with his sister, became the "first man" in the sense that, by renewing the *xwēdōdah*, he became the ancestor of the people of the second (Kayanid) period. Thus, Yima provided two elements necessary for the eschatological renewal of immortality: the population that was to repopulate the world in the period of Ušēdar and the *xwēdōdah*, which would lead to the Renovation (*fraškerd*, see FRAŠŌ.KƎRƎTI; Kellens, 1999-2000, pp. 733-34). Yima's was the first of three attempts at immortality, the second being Paradise, to which Zarathustra opened access, and the third the earth itself after the Renovation (cf. Kellens, 1997-98, pp. 759-64).

Shaul Shaked drew the balance of previous studies in an article in 1987. Yima may have been regarded as first mortal and the originator of humanity and civilization. If he was also the first human at some early stage, this was changed in Zoroastrianism when Gaya Marətan became first man and for various other reasons, but, in the extant sources, he is not (Shaked, 1987b, pp. 238. 240). Gaya Marətan/Gayōmard was a new concept introduced by Zoroastrianism, as strongly indicated by the binomial form of his name (like Ahura Mazdā, etc.). His original place in the mythical chronology is not clear (pp. 238-39), as opposed to his function as founder of civilization and first king, which are clear, perhaps also that of first sinner (pp. 240-41). Shaked speculates that "dualism may be inherent in the bright luminosity of the divinity itself," which might explain Yima's ambiguity (p. 244; cf. Carnoy's suggestion that Yima was the setting sun). The pervasive ambiguities in the popular versions of the myths suggest a syncretism by which the different levels influenced one another and the ancient layers filtered up through the more recent ones, while the effects of a cultural syncretism is seen in the attempts at synchronizing Iranian, Biblical, and, later, Islamic characters (Shaked, 1987b, p. 245, cf. ibid., p. 252). In the later tradition, the figures of Yima and Gayōmard are fairly complementary, both being solar figures who received messages from God, but they belong to two different symbolic fields. In the priestly tradition (cf. Güntert, Christensen, Boyce, above), Yima is a semi-divine presence, active and heroic, while Gayōmard represents "humanity as a passive instrument in the cosmic battle." In the popular tradition, they both became mythical first kings (Shaked, 1987b, pp. 251-52).

Bibliography: Abu'l-Fedā ʿEmād-al-Din Esmāʿil, *al-Moḵtaṣar fi aḵbār al-bašar*, ed. Henricus Orthobius Fleischer as *Abulfedae Historia anteislamica; Arabice, e duobus codicibus Bibliothecase regiae Parisiensis*, 101 et 615, Leipzig, 1831; Cairo, n.d., pp. 40-41 (not a critical edition). Raḥim ʿAfifi, *Asāṭir wa farhang-e Irān dar neveštahā-ye Pahlavi*, Tehran, 1995, pp. 486-91. Jaleh Amouzgar and Ahmad Tafazzoli, see *Dēnkard*, book 5. Jāber ʿAnāṣeri, "Dāstān-e Jamšid dar ṭumār-e naqqālān-e ṣāḥeb-qalam," *Čistā* 5, 1988, pp. 688-93. Friedrich C. Andreas and Walter B. Henning, *Mitteliranische Manichäica aus Chinesisch-Turkestan* I, SPAW, Phil.-hist. Kl., 1932, pp. 175-202; repr. in W. B. Henning, 1977, I, pp. 1-48, Behramgore T. Anklesaria, see *Bundahišn*, *Mēnōy ī xrad*. Tehmuras D. Anklesaria, see *Dādestān ī dēnīg*. Abraham Anquetil-Duperron, tr., *Le Zend-Avesta*, 3 vols., Paris, 1771. *Aogəmadaēcā*, see Kaikhusro M. JamaspAsa, ed. and tr., 1982. Asadi Ṭusi, *Garšāsb-nāma*, ed. Ḥabib Yaḡmāʾi, 2nd ed., Tehran, 1975. Avesta, see Anquetil-Duperron; Darmesteter, 1893, 1895; Malandra. *Ayātgār ī Zāmāpig*, ed. and tr. Giuseppe Messina as *Libro apocalittico persiano: Ayātkār i Žāmāspik*, Rome, 1939. Mehrdād Bahār, see *Bundahišn*. Abu ʿAli Moḥammad Amirak Balʿami, *Tāriḵ-e Balʿami*, ed. Moḥammad-Taqi Bahār, Tehran, 1962, pp. 130-32; rev. ed. Moḥammad Parvin Gonābādi, Tehran, 2000; tr. Hermann Zotenberg as *Chronique de . . . Tabari traduite sur la version persane d'Abou-ʿAli Mohammad Balʿami*, 4 vols., Paris, 1867-74. Faḵr-al-Din Dāwud Banākati, *Tāriḵ-e Banākati: Rawżat ule'l-albāb fi maʿrefat al-tawāriḵ wa'l-ansāb*, ed. Jaʿfar Šeʿār, Tehran, 1969. Christian Bartholomae, *Die Zendhandschriften der K. Hof- und Staatsbibliothek in München*, Catalogus codicum manu scriptorum Bibliothecae Regiae Monacensis I/7: Codices Zendicos Complectens, Munich, 1915. Idem, "Zum sassanidischen Recht IV," *Sb. der Heidelberger Akademie der Wissenschaften*, phil.-hist. Kl., 1922, no. 5, Heidelberg, 1922. Parvin Barzin, "Jamšid wa zendagi-e afsānaʾi-e u," *Honar o mardom*, no. 162, 1976, pp. 71-75. Emile Benveniste, *Titres et noms propres en Iran ancien*, Paris, 1966. Idem, "Hommes et dieux dans l'Avesta," in Gernot Wiesner, ed., *Festschrift für Wilhelm Eilers*, Wiesbaden, 1967, pp. 143-47. Abu Rayḥān Biruni, *Ketāb al-āṯār al-bāqia ʿan al-qorun al-ḵālia*, ed. Eduard Sachau as *Chronologie orientalischer Völker von Albêrûnî*, Leipzig, 1878; repr. Leipzig, 1923; ed. with commentary Parviz Aḏkāʾi, Tehran, 2001; tr. Eduard Sachau as *The Chronology of the Ancient Nations*, London, 1879; repr. Frankfurt, 1969.

Edgar Blochet, *Le messianisme dans l'hétérodoxie musulmane*, Paris, 1903. H. W. Bodewitz, "The Dark and Deep Underworld in the Veda," in Joel P. Brereton and Stephanie W. Jamison, eds., *Indic and Iranian Studies in Honor of Stanley Insler on His Sixty-Fifth Birthday*, JAOS 122, 2002, pp. 213-23. Mary Boyce, "*Ātaš-zōhr* and *āb-zōhr*," *JRAS*, 1966, pp. 100-18. Idem, *A History of Zoroastrianism*, 2 vols., Leiden, 1975-82. Mary Boyce and Frantz Grenet, *A History of Zoroastrianism* III: *Zoroastrianism under Macedonian and Roman Rule*, Leiden, 1991. *Bundahišn*, ed. and tr. Behramgore T. Anklesaria as *Zand-ākāsīh: Iranian or Greater Bundahišn*, Bombay, 1956; tr. Mehrdād Bahār as *Bondahešn*, Tehran, 1990. Albert J. Carnoy, "Iranian Mythology," in Louis Herbert Gray, ed., *The Mythology of All Races* VI, Boston, 1917; repr. New York, 1964, pp. 304-19. Arthur Christensen, "Reste von Manu-Legenden in der iranischen Sagenwelt," in *Festschrift Friedrich Carl Andreas zur Vollendung des siebzigsten Lebensjahres am 14. April 1916 dargebracht von Freunden und Schülern*, Leipzig, 1916, pp. 63-69. Idem, *Les types du premier homme et le premier roi dans l'histoire légendaire des Iraniens*, Archives d'études orientales 14.1-2, 2 vols., Stockholm and Leiden, 1918-34. Idem, *Les Kayanides*, Copenhagen, 1931; tr. Ḏabiḥ-Allāh Ṣafā as *Kayāniān*, Tehran, 1957; tr. K. R. Cama Oriental Institute, as *The Kayanians*, Bombay, 1993.

Dādestān ī dēnīg, pt. 1, ed. Tehmuras D. Anklesaria as *The Datistan-i Dinik: Pahlavi Text Containing 92 Questions, Asked by Mitr-Khurshit Atur-Mahan and others, to Manush-Chihar Goshn-Jam, Leader of the Zoroastrians in Persia, about 881 A.D., and Their Answers. Pt. 1. Pursishn I-XL*, Bombay, 1911; ed. and tr. Mahmoud Jaafari-Dehgani as *Dādestān ī dēnīg. Part I. Transcription, Translation and Commentary*, Studia Iranica. Cahier 20, Paris, 1998. *Dēnkard*, book 3, tr. Jean de Menasce as *Le troisième livre du Denkart*, Paris, 1973; book 5, ed. and tr. Jaleh Amouzgar and Ahmad Tafazzoli as *Le cinquième livre du Dēnkard: Transcription, traduction et commentaire*, Studia Iranica. Cahier 23, Paris, 2000; book 7, ed. and tr. Marijan Molé in *La légende de Zoroastre selon les textes pehlevis*, Travaux de l'Institut d'études iraniennes de l'Université de Paris 3, Paris, 1967; book 9, *Sūdgar Nask*, ed. and tr. Yuhan S.-D. Vevaina in idem "Studies in Zoroastrian Exegesis and Hermeneutics with a Critical Edition of the Sūdgar Nask of Dēnkard Book 9," Ph.D. diss., Harvard, 2007. James Darmesteter, *Ohrmazd et Ahriman: leurs origines et leur histoire*, Paris, 1877. Idem, tr., *Le Zend-Avesta: traduction nouvelle avec commentaire historique et philologique*, 3 vols., Paris, 1893; repr. 1960, II, pp. 16-20; idem, tr. as *The Zend-Avesta*, Sacred Books of The East 4, Oxford, 1895. Daryaee, see *Šahrestānīhā ī Ērānšahr*. Bamanji N. Dhabhar, 1909, see *Ṣad dar-e naṯr wa ṣad dar-e Bondaheš*; 1932, see *Persian Rivāyats*. Abu Ḥanifa Dinavari, *Aḵbār al-ṭewāl*, ed. Vladimir Guirgass, Leiden, 1888; ed. ʿAbd-al-Monʿem ʿĀmer and Jamāl-al-Din Šayyāl, Cairo, 1960. Jacques Duchesne-Guillemin, *Zoroastre: Étude critique avec une traduction commentée des Gâthâ*, Paris 1948; tr. Maria Henning as *The Hymns of Zarathustra: Being a Translation of the Gathas Together with Introd. and Commentary*, London, 1961. Idem, *La religion de l'Iran ancien*, Paris, 1962; tr. as *Religion of Ancient Iran*, Bombay, 1973. Idem, "Cor de Yima et trompette d'Isrâfîl: de la cosmologie mazdéenne à l'eschatologie musulmane," *Comptes-rendus de l'Académie des Inscriptions et Belles Lettres 1979*, Paris, 1980, pp. 539-49. Ebn al-Balḵi, *Fārs-nāma*, ed. Guy Le Strange and Reynold A. Nicholson, Cambridge, 1921. Ebn Ḥawqal, *Ketāb ṣurat al-arż*, ed. Johannes Hendrik Kramers, 3rd ed., Leiden, 1967; tr. Johannes Hendrik Kramers and Gaston Wiet as *Configuration de la terre*, 2 vols., Paris and Beirut, 1964. Ebn Esfandiār, *Tāriḵ-e Ṭabarestān*, ed. ʿAbbās Eqbāl, 2 vols., Tehran, 1941; tr. Edward G. Browne as *An Abridged Translation of the History of Ṭabarestán*, Leiden and London, 1905. Ebn Meskawayh, *Tajāreb al-omam*, facs. ed. Leone Caetani, 3 vols., Leiden, 1909-17; ed. Abu'l-Qāsem Emāmi, I, Tehran, 1987, pp. 6-10. Ebn al-Nadim, *Ketāb al-fehrest*, ed. Gustav Flügel, 2 vols., Leipzig, 1871-72; ed. Reżā Tajaddod, Tehran, 1971; tr. Bayard Dodge as *The Fihrist of al-Nadīm: A Tenth-Century Survey of Muslim Culture*, 2 vols., New York and London, 1970. Ebn Qotayba Dinavari, *Ketāb al-maʿāref*, ed. Ferdinand Wüstenfeld as *Ibn Coteiba's Handbuch der Geschichte*, Göttingen, 1850; ed. Ṯarwat ʿOkāša, Cairo, 1960. Eslāmi Šahr-e Bābaki, "Osṭura-ye Jamšid," in Masʿud Rażawi, ed., *Dar pirāmun-e Šāh-nāma*, 1990, pp. 223-44. Abu Esḥāq Ebrāhim Eṣṭaḵri, *Ketāb masālek al-mamālek*, ed., Michaël Jan De Goeje, Leiden, 1967; tr. Moḥammad b. Asʿad Tostari as *Masālek wa mamālek*, ed. Iraj Afšār, Tehran, 1974. Faḵr-e Modabber Moḥammad b. Manṣur Mobārakšāh, *Ādāb al-ḥarb wa'l-šajāʿa*, ed. Aḥmad Sohayli Ḵ*ᵛ*ānsāri, Tehran, 1967. Abu'l-Qāsem Ferdowsi, *Šāh-nāma*, ed. Turner Macan, *The Shah nameh. An Heroic Poem, Containing the History of Persia from Kioomurs to Yesdejird by Abool Kasim Firdousee*, 4 vols., Calcutta, 1829; ed. Djalal Khaleghi-Motlagh, New York, 1987-.

Gabriel du Chinon, posthumous ed. by Louïs Moreri as *Relations nouvelles du Levant ou, Traités de la religion, du gouvernement, & des coûtumes des Perses, des Armeniens, & des Gaures. Avec une description particuliere de l'établissement, & des progrez qui y font les missionnaires, & diverses disputes qu'ils ont eu avec les Orientaux*, Composés par le P. G.-D. C. [Père Gabriel Du Chinon] & donnés au public par le Sieur L. M. P.-D. E. T. [Louïs Moreri, Prêtre, Docteur en Théologie], Lyon, 1671. Iain Gardner, see *Kephalaia*. Gathas, see Helmut Humbach, 1994; Stanley Insler. Karl F. Geldner, "Übersetzungen aus dem Avesta. II: Vendidâd 2, 15, 5," *Zeitschrift für vergleikende Sprachforschung* 25, 1881, pp. 179-212. Idem, *Die Zoroastrische Religion <das Avestā>*, Religionsgeschichtliches Lesebuch, 2nd ed., fasc. 1, Tübingen, 1926. Ilya Gershevitch, "Old Iranian Literature," in *Handbuch der Orientalistik* I: *Der Nahe und der Mittlere Osten* IV: *Iranistik* 2: *Literatur* 1, Leiden, 1968, pp. 1-30. Idem, "An Iranist's View of the Soma Controversy," in Philippe Gignoux and Ahmad Tafazzoli, eds., *Mémorial Jean de Menasce*, Louvain, 1974, pp. 45-75. Idem, "Yima's Beaf-Plea," in Gherardo Gnoli et Lionello Lanciotti, eds., *Orientalia Iosephi Tucci memoriae dicata*, 3 vols., Rome, 1985-88, II, pp. 487-99. Gignoux and Tafazzoli, see Zādspram. Frantz Grenet, "Notes sur le panthéon iranien des Kouchans," *Stud. Ir.* 13, 1984, pp. 253-62. Hermann Güntert, *Indogermanische Ablautprobleme: Untersuchungen über Schwa secundum, einen zweiten indogermanischen Murmelvokal*, Strassburg, 1916. Idem, *Der arische Weltkönig und Heiland. Bedeutungsgeschichtliche Untersuchungen zur indo-iranischen Religionsgeschichte und Altertumskunde*, Halle en der Saale, 1923. Richard T. Hallock, *Persepolis Fortification Tablets*, Chicago, 1969. Abu'l-Ḥasan Ḥamza Eṣfahāni, *Ketāb taʾriḵ seni moluk al-arż wa'l-anbiāʾ*, ed. and Latin tr. J. M. E. Gottwaldt, 2 vols., St. Petersburg and Leipzig, 1844-48, I, p. 31. Martin Haug, *Essays on the Sacred Language, Writings, and Religion of the Parsees*, Bombay, 1862; 2nd ed., ed. E. W. West, Boston, 1878. Richard Hauschild, "Die Tirade von der Wagenwettfahrt des Königs Haosravah und des Junkers Nərəmanah (Yašt 5, 50): Neuer Versuch einer Deutung," *Mitteilungen des Instituts für Orientforschung der Deutschen Akademie der Wissenschaften* 7, 1959, pp. 1-78, esp. p. 25 n. 40. Walter B. Henning, "The Book of the Giants," *BSO(A)S* 11, 1943a, pp. 52-74; repr. in idem, 1977, II, pp. 115-37. Idem, "An Astronomical Chapter of the Bundahishn," *JRAS*, 1943b, pp. 229-48; repr. in idem, 1977, II, pp. 95-114. Idem, *W. B. Henning Selected Paprs*, 2 vols., Acta Iranica 14-15, Tehran and Leiden, 1977. Johannes Hertel, *Die himmelstore im Veda und im Awesta*, Leipzig, 1924. Hesiod, *Theogony* and *Works and Days*, in *Hesiod, the Homeric Hymns and the Homerica*, tr. Martin Litchfield West, Oxford and New York, 1988. Almut Hintze, ed. and tr. *Zamyād-Yašt: Edition, Übersetzung, Kommentar*, Wiesbaden, 1994; reviewed by Antonio Panaino, in *Kratylos* 42, 1997, pp. 63-71. Walther Hinz, *Altiranisches Sprachgut der Nebenüberlieferungen*, Wiesbaden, 1975. Karl Hoffmann, "Jungawestisch *zazāite*," *Münchener Studien zur Sprachwissenschaft* 4, 1952 (repr. 1961), pp. 43-49; repr. in idem, *Aufsätze zur Indoiranistik*, ed. Johanna Narten, 2 vols., Wiesbaden, 1976, II, pp. 373-77. Helmut Humbach, "Zur altiranischen Mythologie," *ZDMG* 107, 1957, pp. 361-71. Idem, *Die Gathas des Zarathustra*, 2 vols., Heidelberg, 1959. Idem, "Methodologische Variationen zur arischen Religionsgeschichte," in Manfred Mayrhofer et al., eds., *Antiquitates Indogermanicae . . . Gedenkschrift f. Hermann Güntert . . .*, Innsbruck, 1974, pp. 193-200. Idem, *The Gāthās of Zarathustra and the Other Old Avestan Texts* I-II, Heidelberg, 1991 (with Josef Elphenbein and Prods Oktor Skjærvø). Helmut Humbach and Pallan Ichaporia, *The Heritage of Zarathushtra: A New Translation of His Gāthās*, Heidelberg, 1994. Idem, ed. and tr., *Zamyād Yasht: Yasht 19 of the Younger Avesta: Text, Translation, Commentary*, Wiesbaden, 1998; reviewed by Prods Oktor Skjærvø in *Bulletin of the Asia Institute* 13, 1999 [publ. 2002], pp. 182-90.

Stanley Insler, *The Gāthās of Zarathustra*, Acta Iranica 8, Tehran and Liège, 1975. Mahmoud Jaafari-Dehgani, see *Dādestān ī dēnīg*. A. W. Jackson, *Zoroastrian Studies: The Iranian Religion and Various Monographs*, New York, 1928. Kaikhusro M. JamaspAsa, ed. and tr., *Aogəmadaēcā: A Zoroastrian Liturgy*, Sb. der Österreichischen Akademie der Wissenschaften, phil-hist. Kl. 397, Vienna, 1982. Jamaspji Dastur Manochehrji Jamasp-Asana, ed., *The Pahlavi Texts*, Bombay, 1897. Judith Josephson, *The Pahlavi Translation Technique as Illustrated by Hōm Yašt*, Uppsala, 1997. Ferdinand Justi, *Iranisches Namenbuch*, Marburg, 1895; repr. Hildesheim, 1963. Arthur B. Keith, *The Religion and Philosophy of the Veda and Upanishads*, 2 vols., Cambridge, 1925. Jean Kellens, "Yima, magicien entre les dieux et les hommes," in *Orientalia J. Duchesne-Guillemin Oblata*, Acta Iranica 23, Leiden, 1984, pp. 267-81. Idem, "Characters of Ancient Mazdaism," *History and Anthropology* 3, 1987, pp. 239-62; repr. in Kellens, 2000, pp. 1-24. Idem, "Yima et la mort," in Mohammad Ali Jazayery and Werner Winter, eds., *Languages and Cultures: Studies in Honor of Edgar C. Polomé*, Berlin, New York and Amsterdam, 1988, pp. 329-34; tr. Prods Oktor Skjærvø, in Kellens, 2000, pp.

95-98. Idem, "Langues et religions indo-iraniennes: L'âme entre le cadavre et le paradis," *Annuaire du Collège de France: résumé des cours et travaux, 1994-1995*, pp. 697-705. Idem, "Langues et religions indo-iraniennes: de la naissance des montagnes à la fin du temps: le Yašt 19," *Annuaire du Collège de France: résumé des cours et travaux, 1997-1998*, pp. 737-65. Idem, "Langues et religions indo-iraniennes: Promenade dans les Yašts à la lumière de travaux nouveaux (suite)," *Annuaire du Collège de France: résumé des cours et travaux, 1999-2000*, pp. 721-51. Idem, *Essays on Zarathustra and Zoroastrianism*, tr. and ed. Prods Oktor Skjærvø, Costa Mesa, Calif., 2000. Idem, "Fils du soleil, fils du sacrifice," in Maria Gabriela Schmidt and Walter Bisang, eds., *Philologica et Linguistica: Historia, Pluralitas, Universitas. Festschrift für Helmut Humbach zum 80. Geburtstag am 4. Dezember 2001*, Trier, 2001, pp. 316-22. Idem, "Langues et religions indo-iraniennes: l'éloge mazdéen de l'ivresse," *Annuaire du Collège de France: résumé des cours et travaux, 2002-2003*, pp. 817-45. Idem, "L'amphipolarité sémantique et la démonisation des daivas," in G. Schweiger, ed., *Indogermanica: Festschrift Gert Klingenschmitt: Indische, iranische und indogermanische Studien dem verehrten Jubilar dargebracht zu seinem fünfundsechzigsten Geburtstag*, Taimering, 2005, pp. 283-88. Jean Kellens and Eric Pirart, ed. and tr., *Les textes vieil-avestiques*, 3 vols., Wiesbaden, 1988-91. *Kephalaia*, see Iain Gardner. *Kephalaia*, tr. Iain Gardner as *The Kephalaia of the Teacher: The Edited Coptic Manichaean Texts in Translation with Commentary*, Leiden etc., 1995. Alexander Kohut, "Die talmudisch-midraschische Adamssage in ihrer Rückbeziehung auf die persische Yima- und Meshiasage," *ZDMG* 25, 1871, pp. 59-94. Götz König, *Die Erzählung von Ṭahmuras und Ǧamšid: Edition des np. Textes in Pahlawi-Schrift MU 29 31.16-47.17 nebst dreier np. Parallelfassungen*, Iranica, Wiesbaden, forthcoming.

Wolfgang Lentz, "Yima and Khwarenah in the Avestan Gathas," in Walter B. Henning and Ehsan Yarshater, eds., *A Locust's Leg: Studies in Honour of S. H. Taqizadeh*, London, 1962, pp. 131-34. Bruce Lincoln, "The Indo-European Myth of Creation," *History of Religions* 15, 1975, pp. 121-45. Idem, *Priests, Warriors, and Cattle: A Study in the Ecology of Religions*, Berkeley etc., 1981a. Idem, "The Lord of the Dead," *History of Religions* 20, 1981b, pp. 224-41. Idem, *Myth, Cosmos, and Society: Indo-European Themes of Creation and Destruction*, Cambridge, Mass., 1986. Idem, "Pahlavi kirrenidan: Traces of Iranian Creation Mythology," *JAOS* 117, 1997, pp. 681-85. Bruno Lindner, "Die iranische Flutsage," in Ernst Kuhn, ed., *Festgruss an Rudolf von Roth zum doktor-jubiläum, 24. August 1893, von seinen freunden und schülern*, Stuttgart, 1893, pp. 213-16. Herman Lommel, tr., *Die Yäšt's des Avesta*, Göttingen, 1927. Arthur A. Macdonell, *Vedic Mythology*, Strassburg, 1897. Maria Macuch, *Rechtskasuistik und Gerichtspraxis zu Beginn des siebenten Jahrhunderts in Iran: Die Rechtssamlung des Farroḫmard i Wahrāmān*, Wiesbaden, 1993. *Mahābhārata*, tr. Protap Chandra Roy as *The Mahabharata of Krishna-Dwaipayana Vyasa* [II], Book 3, Calcutta, 1884; ed. and tr. Johannes A. B. van Buitenen as *The Mahābhārata* I-II, Chicago, 1973-75. William W. Malandra, *An Introduction to Ancient Iranian Religion: Readings from the Avesta and Achaemenid Inscriptions*, Minneapolis, 1983. Manuščihr Gušnǰam/J̌uwānǰam, see *Dādestān ī dēnīg*. Moṭahhar b. Ṭāher Maqdesi, *Ketāb al-badʾ wa'l-taʾriḵ*, ed. and tr. Clément Huart as *Le livre de la création et de l'histoire*, 6 vols., Paris, 1899-1919; tr. Moḥammad-Reżā Šafiʿi Kadkani as *Āfarineš wa tāriḵ*, 2 vols., Tehran, 1995. Ẓahir-al-Din Marʿaši, *Tāriḵ-e Ṭabarestān wa Ruyān wa Māzandarān*, ed. ʿAbbās Šāyān, Tehran, 1954. Abu'l-Ḥasan ʿAli Masʿudi, *Moruj al-ḏahab wa maʿāden al-jawhar*, ed. Barbier de Meynard and Pavet de Courteille, revised new ed. by Charles Pellat, 7 vols., Beirut, 1966-79; tr. Barbier de Meynard and Pavet de Courteille as *Les Prairies d'or*, revised and corrected by Charles Pellat, 3 vols., Paris, 1962-71. Jalāl Matini, "Pāyān-e zendagāni-e Jamšid wa sargoḏašt-e ḵānadān-aš," in *Yaḡmā-ye si-o-dovvom*, Tehran, 1991, pp. 355-64. Manfred Mayrhofer, *Iranisches Personennamenbuch* I, Vienna, 1977. Jean de Menasce see *Dēnkard*, book 3. *Mēnōy ī xrad*, ed. Tahmuras D. Anklesaria as *Dânâk-u mainyô-i khard*, Bombay, 1913; tr. E. W. West as "Dînâ-î maînôgî khirad," in idem, tr., *Pahlevi Texts*, Part 3, Sacred Books of the East 24, 3rd ed., Delhi, 1970, pp. 3-113; tr. Aḥmad Tafażżoli as *Minu-ye ḵerad*, Tehran, 1975; repr. Tehran, 1995. Giuseppe Messina, see *Ayādgār ī Zāmāspīg*. Marijan Molé, *Culte, mythe et cosmologie dans l'Iran ancien: Le problème zoroastrien et la tradition mazdéenne*, Paris, 1963 (also pub. as *Le problème zoroastrien et la tradition mazdéenne*). Idem, 1967, see *Dēnkard*, book 7. Moḥammad Mirḵᵛānd, *Tāriḵ-e rawżat al-ṣafā*, 11 vols., Tehran, 1959-72, I, pp. 516-28; ed. Jamšid Kayānfar as *Tāriḵ-e rawżat al-ṣafā fi sirat al-anbiāʾ wa'l-moluk wa'l-ḵolafāʾ*, 7 vols. in 11, Tehran, 2001. *Mojmal al-tawāriḵ wa'l-qeṣaṣ*, ed. Moḥammad-Taqi Malek-al-Soʿarāʾ Bahār, Tehran, 1939. Abu ʿAbd-Allāh Moḥammad Moqaddasi, *Aḥsan al-taqāsim fi maʿrefat al-aqālim*, ed. Michaël Jan De Goeje, Leiden, 1967. Ḥamd-Allāh Mostawfi, *Tāriḵ-e gozida*, facs. ed. Edward G. Browne, 2 vols., Leiden, 1910-13. Idem, *Nozhat al-qolub*, ed. and tr. Guy Le Strange, 2 vols., Leiden and London, 1915-19. James H. Moulton, *Early Zoroastrianism: Lectures Delivered at Oxford and in London, February to May 1912*, London, 1913.

Nāma-ye Tansar ba Gošnasb, ed. Mojtabā Minovi, Tehran, 1975; tr. Mary Boyce as *The Letter of Tansar*, Rome, 1968. Henrik S. Nyberg, *Irans forntidiga religioner*, Stockholm, 1937; tr. Hans H. Shaeder as *Die Religionen des Alten Iran*, repr. Osnabrück, 1966. *Pahlavi Rivāyat*, ed. and tr. Alan V. Williams, as *The Pahlavi Rivāyat Accompanying the Dādestān ī Dēnīg* I-II, Det Kongelige Danske Videnskabernes Selskab, hist.fil. medd. 60, 1-2, Copenhagen, 1990; tr. Mahšid Mir-Fak̲rāʾi as *Rewāyat-e Pahlavi*, Tehran, 1988. Antonio Panaino, see Hintze. *Persian Rivāyats*, tr. Bamanji Nusserwanji Dhabhar as *The Persian Rivayats of Hormazyar Framarz and Others*, Bombay, 1932. Peter Parkes, "Temple of Imra, Temple of Mahandeu: A Kafir Sanctuary in Kalasha Cosmology," *BSO(A)S* 54, 1991, pp. 75-103. Eric V. Pirart, *Kayân Yasn (Yasht 19.9-96): l'origine avestique des dynasties mythiques d'Iran*, Sabadell-Barcelona, 1992. Ebrāhim Pur(-e) Dāwud, "Jam," in idem, *Yāddāšthā-ye Gāthā*, ed. Bahrām Farahvaši, Tehran, 1957, pp. 425-40. Rudolph Roth, "Die Sage von Dschemschid," *ZDMG* 4, 1850, pp. 417-33. Ḏabiḥ-Allāh Ṣafā, *Ḥamāsa-sarāʾi dar Irān*, Tehran, 1984, pp. 424-51. *Šāh-nāma*, see Ferdowsi. *Šahrestānīhā ī Ērānšahr*, ed. and tr. Touraj Daryaee, as *Šahrestānīhā ī Ērānšahr: A Middle Persian Text on Late Antique Geography, Epic, and History with English and Persian Translations*, Costa Mesa, Calif., 2002. *Ṣad dar-e naṯr wa ṣad dar-e Bondaheš/Saddar Naṣr and Saddar Bundehesh*, ed. Bamanji N. Dhabhar, Bombay, 1909. Mahindok̲t Ṣediqiān, *Farhang-e asāṭiri-ḥamāsi-e Irān ba rewāyat-e manābeʿ-e baʿd az Eslām* I, Tehran, 1976, pp. 76-125. Hans H. Schaeder, "Iranische Lehren," in Richard Reitzenstein and Hans H. Schaeder, *Studien zum antiken Synkretismus aus Iran und Griechenland* II, Leipzig, 1926; repr., 2 vols. in 1, Darmstadt, 1965. Shaul Shaked, "Paymān: An Iranian Idea in Contact with Greek Thought and Islam," in *Transition Periods in Iranian History: Actes du Symposium de Fribourg-en-Brisgau (22-24 mai 1985)*, Studia Iranica. Cahier 5, Leuven, 1987a, pp. 217-40. Idem, "First Man, First King: Notes on Semitic-Iranian Syncretism and Iranian Mythological Transformations," in Shaul Shaked, David Dean Shulman, and Gedaliahu G. Stroumsa, eds., *Gilgul: Essays on Transformation, Revolution, and Permanence in the History of Religions, Dedicated to R. J. Zwi Werblowsky*, Leiden and New York, 1987b, pp. 238-56. Nicholas Sims-Williams, "A Bactrian Deed of Manumission," *Silk Road Art and Archaeology* 5, 1997-98, pp. 191-211. Idem, *Bactrian Documents* I, Studies in the Khalili Collection III, Corpus Inscr. Iran. II/6, Oxford, 2000. Idem, "Avestan *suβrā-*, Turkish *süvre*," *Silk Road Studies* 5 (*De Dunhuang à Istanbul: Hommage à James Russell Hamilton*), 2001, pp. 329-38. Prods Oktor Skjærvø, "Hymnic Composition in the Avesta," *Die Sprache* 36/2, 1994 (publ. 1996), pp. 199-243. Idem, "Iranian Epic and the Manichean *Book of Giants*: Irano-Manichaica III," in *Zsigismond Telegdi Memorial Volume*, AOASH 48/1-2, 1995 (publ. 1997), pp. 187-223. Idem, "The State of Old-Avestan Scholarship," *JAOS* 117, 1997, pp. 103-14. Idem, "Eastern Iranian Epic Traditions II: Rostam and Bhīṣma," *AOASH* 51, 1998, pp. 159-70. Idem, "The *Videvdad*: Its Ritual-Mythical Significance," in Vesta Sarkhosh Curtis and Sarah Stewart, eds., *Birth of the Persian Empire*, London and New York, 2006, pp. 105-41. Idem, "Zoroastrian Dualism," in *Acts of Light against Darkness: Dualism in Ancient Mediterranean Religion and the Contemporary World*, University of North Carolina at Chapel Hill (forthcoming). Peter F. Stuhr, *Die Religions-Systeme der Heidnischen Völker des Orients*, Berlin, 1836.

Abu Manṣur ʿAbd-al-Malek Ṯaʿālebi, *Ḡorar ak̲bār moluk al-fors*, ed. Hermann Zotenberg as *Histoir des rois des Perses*, Paris, 1900. Moḥammad b. Jarir Ṭabari, *Taʾrik̲ al-rosol wa'l-moluk*, ed. Michaël Jan De Goeje, Leiden, 1964, I/1, pp. 179-83; tr. by various scholars as *The History of al-Ṭabari*, 40 vols., Albany, New York, 1985-2007. Aḥmad Tafażżoli, "'Suvrā-ye' Jamšid wa 'suvrā-ya' Żaḥḥāk," *MDAT* 23/4, 1976, pp. 48-50. *Tārik̲-e Sistān*, ed. Moḥammad-Taqi Malek-al-Šoʿarāʾ Bahār, Tehran, ca. 1935; tr. Milton Gold as *The Tārikh-e Sistān*, Rome, 1976. *Vidēvdād* 2, see Malandra. Yuhan S.-D. Vevaina, see *Dēnkard*, book 9, *Sūdgar Nask*. Otto Günther von Wesendonk, *Urmensch und Seele in der iranischen Überlieferung: Ein Beitrag zur Religionsgeschichte des Hellenismus*, Hannover, 1924. Geo Widengren, *Die Religionen Irans*, Stuttgart, 1965. John Wilson, *The Pársí Religion as Contained in the Zand-Avastá, and Propounded and Defended by the Zoroastrians of India and Persia, Unfolded, Refuted, and Contrasted with Christianity*, Bombay, 1843. Friedrich H. H. Windischmann, *Ursagen der arischen Völker*, Munich, 1852. Idem, *Mithra: Ein Beitrag zur Mythengeschichte des Orients*, Abhandlungen für die Kunde des Morgenlandes 1, 1859. Idem, *Zoroastrische Studien: Abhandlungen zur Mythologie und Sagengeschichte des alten Iran*, ed. Fr. Spiegel, Berlin, 1863. *Wizīdagīhā ī Zādspram*, ed. and tr. Philippe Gignoux and Ahmad Tafazzoli as *Anthologie de Zādspram: Edition critique du texte pehlevi*, Studia Iranica. Cahier 13, Paris, 1993. Ehsan Yarshater, "Iranian National History," in *Camb. Hist. Iran* III/1, Cambridge, 1983, pp. 359-477. *Yasna* 9, see Josephson; Malandra. *Yašt* 19, see Humbach and Ichaporia, 1998; Hintze; Pirart. *Yašts*, see Lommel; Malandra. Yutaka Yoshida, and Takao Moriyasu, ベゼクリク出上ソグド語。ウイグル語マニ教徒手紙文 "Manichaen Sogdian and Uighur Letters Recently Unearthed in Bezeklik, Turfan," *Studies on the Inner Asian Languages* (*Nairiku Ajia gengo no kenkyū*) 15, 2000, pp. 135-78. Zādspram, see *Wizīdagīhā ī Zādspram*. Robert Charles Zaehner, *Zurvan: A Zoroastrian Dilemma*, Oxford, 1955. Idem, *The Dawn and Twilight of Zoroastrianism*, London, 1961. *Zāmyād yašt*, see Almut Hintze; Humbach, 1999. *Zand ī Wahman Yasn*, ed. and tr. Carlo G. Cereti as *The Zand ī Wahman Yasn. A Zoroastrian Apocalypse*, Rome, 1995.

(PRODS OKTOR SKJAERVØ)

ii. JAMŠID IN PERSIAN LITERATURE

The name Jamšid often alternates in Persian poetry with the short form Jam in response to metrical requirements. It is also interpreted as such in some Islamic sources (e.g., Meskawayh, 1, p. 6; Balʿami, 1974, I, p. 130; *Mojmal al-tawārik̲*, p. 25; Ebn al-Balk̲i, p. 29; Ebn

Esfandiār, p. 57; Mostawfi, p. 80). Sources all agree that he reigned for several hundred years, but they differ on the exact length of his rule. Ebn Qotayba (p. 652) reports it to be 960 years, while, according to Menhāj-e Serāj (I, pp. 135-36), he ruled for 400 years as a godly king and 400 years more after he was deceived by Satan. The authors of the Persian translation of Ṭabari's Qurʾān commentary assign him 1000 years (II, p. 403), Pseudo-Ḵayyām (pp. 17-18) 800 years, but Ebn al-Balḵi (p. 30), *Mojmal al-tawāriḵ* (p. 39), and Faḵr-e Modabber (p. 8) 716 years. According to Abu ʿAli Moḥammad Balʿami (I, p. 131), Jamšid ruled for either 400 or 700 years; the latter figure is mentioned also in a number of other sources (e.g., *Šāh-nāma* I, p. 41; Ḡazāli, p. 90, Mostawfi p. 80). Abu Rayḥān Biruni (ed. Aḏkāʾi, pp. 122-23) gives Jam's rule as 716 years according to one report and as 616 according to another, and Abu Manṣur Ṯaʿālebi (p. 17) reports 500 years.

Two narrative strands are discernable in Jamšid's biography: the secular epic strand, in which he is the son of king Ṭahmuraṯ (e.g., *Šāh-nāma*, I, p. 41, v. 3; Ebn al-Faqih p. 406; Ṭusi p. 255; Mostawfi, 1362, p. 80), and the priestly or religious strand, according to which he is Ṭahmuraṯ's brother (e.g., Balʿami, I, p. 130; Meskawayh, I, p. 6; *Mojmal al-tawāriḵ*, p. 25; Maqdesi, III, p. 24, tr. Šafiʿi Kadkani, I, p. 425; Pseudo-Ḵayyām, p. 17; Ebn al-Balḵi, pp. 10, 29, who also says that Jam may have been Ṭahmuraṯ's nephew; Menhāj-e Serāj, I, p. 135; *Haft laškar*, p. 6; cf. Dārāb Hormazyār, I, p. 313). A number of other texts do not specify the relationship of Jamšid to Ṭahmuraṯ at all (e.g., ʿAskari, p. 411; Eṣṭaḵri, pp. 123, 150, tr. pp. 109, 141; Ḡazāli, p. 90). The secular tradition, found in the *Šāh-nāma* and related texts, in time overwhelmed the religious story and is also supported by Iranian oral tradition (Enjavi, II, p. 314, III, pp. 17-18).

Jamšid's epic life-story may be divided into the period of his kingship and the period after he was deposed. Jamšid's most coherent epic biography is found in the *Šāh-nāma*, according to which he was Ṭahmuraṯ's son, succeeded his father to the throne, and proclaimed himself to be both king and priest (I, pp. 41, vv. 3-4, 8). He invented a series of important implements and institutions in the following order. He spent fifty years in inventing various weapons and armor (I, pp. 41-42, vv. 10-13), fifty in inventing weaving and tailoring (I, p. 42, vv. 14-17), fifty more in ordering his subjects into separate professions (I, p. 42, vv. 19-26, p. 43, vv. 30-31), and finally fifty more years in instituting social casts according to the functionalities that he had assigned to each group (I, p. 43, vv. 32-34). Although arranging his subjects into different professions is a different task from instituting social casts, these functionalities are often conflated in scholarship on Jamšid. He spends the next fifty years in instructing the demons, whom his father Ṭahmuraṯ had already subdued, to make bricks and buildings such as palaces and bath-houses (I, p. 43, vv. 35-38). It should be noted that, contrary to some readings of these lines, demons did not teach Jamšid how to build anything. It was rather Jamšid who, having taught them brick making (I, p. 43, v. 35), employed them in his building projects. Some demons appear to have been outside his dominion. For instance, the demon Pulādvand claims to have caused much trouble for Jamšid and a number of other kings (III, p. 270, v. 2674). Jamšid goes on to mine precious stones, establish the use of aromatics, and teach the art of medicine. He then builds ships and crosses the waters that separate the seven realms. All of these activities took another fifty years to complete (I, p. 43, vv. 39-46). Following all this, Jamšid builds himself a magnificent bejeweled throne, which he ascends and orders his demons to carry in the air on the first day of the vernal equinox. He thus institutes the festival of the New Year (Nowruz; I, p. 44, vv. 48-55). This period of creative activity lasts 250 years. During the next three hundred years Jamšid rules peacefully and his subjects neither fall sick nor die (I, p. 44, vv. 56-57). At the end of this 550 years, Jamšid grows arrogant, claims divinity, and alienates everyone (I, p. 45, vv. 65-71). He loses his royal gory (*farr*, q.v.), and his realm falls into chaos (I, p. 45, v. 74, p. 51, vv. 166-71). His subjects go over to the land of the Arabs, and ask Żaḥḥāk, a new and powerful Arab ruler, to come to Iran and take over Jamšid's throne. Żaḥḥāk attacks Jamšid's capital at the head of a large army comprised of Arabs and Persians (I, p. 51, vv. 172-78), and Jamšid, unable to resist Żaḥḥāk's forces, escapes and disappears for one hundred years (I, p. 51, vv. 179-82). However, at the end of this period he is captured by Żaḥḥāk, who orders him to be sawed in half (*ba arra-š sarāsar ba do nim kard*; *Šāh-nāma* I, p. 52, vv. 183-86).

The longitudinal sawing of Jam's body is suggestive of a "castration" motif (Omidsalar, 1987, p. 349, see also illustrations). Balʿami (d. 974), who must have had access to Ferdowsi's prose archetype, corroborates Ferdowsi by reporting that the "saw was put on Jamšid's head and he was sawed down to his legs" (Balʿami, I, p. 132). Every illustration in the *Šāh-nāma* Project's data bank of miniatures (http://shahnama.caret.cam.ac.uk/) shows Jamšid being cut longitudinally with the saw blade placed on his head and worked down toward his feet. Therefore, it is not difficult to imagine that the saw is displaced upward to mask the symbolic nature of Jamšid's castration and death. There is evidence that indicates the existence of a story about Jamšid's death, according to which Jamšid does not react to the pain and undergoes his punishment in silence (Ḵāqāni, 1995, p. 860). Another report tells of his execution by being thrown to wild beasts who devour him (e.g., Ṯaʿālebi, p. 17). According to yet another version that must have been available to Faḵr-e Modabber in the early 13th century (ca. 1229 CE or after), he dies peacefully after a long reign (Faḵr-e Modabber, p. 8).

The *Šāh-nāma* has nothing to say about what happened to Jamšid in the century following his defeat. That information is provided in the *Garšāsb-nāma* (comp. in 458/1066) of Asadi Ṭusi, according to which (pp. 21-22), following his ouster, Jamšid is forced to live incognito, because Żaḥḥāk has ordered all the kings under his command to arrest and send him to Iran. In the course of his travels Jamšid meets the beautiful warrior daughter of king Gurang of Zābol. This princess, who is not named in the *Garšāsb-nāma*, but is called Paričehra in the *Mojmal al-tawāriḵ* (p. 25). Many kings and princes ask for her hand in marriage, but she refuses to get married because her father has authorized her to choose her own husband (*Garšāsb-nāma*, p. 23, v. 35) and, besides, her nursemaid has told her that she is destined to marry a great king and give birth to a heroic son (*Garšāsb-nāma*, p. 23). Jamšid comes upon her garden and asks for three cups of wine from one of her attendants and is taken to her. The princess falls in love with him and they begin to feast (pp. 24-27). Soon the feasting leads to a subtle flirtatious discourse centering upon two courting doves on a nearby tree that Jam and the warrior princess kill by arrows (*Garšāsb-nāma*, pp. 29-30). The passage is reminiscent of a similar enigmatic flirtation scene between Cuchulainn and Emer in the Irish epic *Táin Bó Cúailnge* (Kinsella, pp. 26-27). The nurse-maid arrives and reveals Jamšid's identity to the princess, who confronts Jamšid with it. Jamšid denies his identity even when he is shown one of the "wanted posters" (lit. a piece of silk bearing Jamšid's portrait) that Żaḥḥāk had sent far and wide for his arrest, and gives his name as Māhān-e Kuhi (*Garšāsb-nāma*, pp. 31-32, vv. 195-240). Finally, after receiving assurances that he will not be betrayed, Jamšid relents and the two quietly marry (*Garšāsb-nāma*, pp. 33-36). Soon the princess gets pregnant and her father, who has grown suspicious of her behavior, discovers the truth. At first he threatens to arrest Jamšid and send him to Żaḥḥāk, but he changes his mind and agrees to protect his new son-in-law (*Garšāsb-nāma*, pp. 36-40). Jamšid predicts that a great line of heroes will be born of his union with the princess; and that the fifth of them will be an exceptionally powerful paladin (*Garšāsb-nāma*, p. 41, vv. 53-56). This is somewhat contradictory to the story of Jamšid's spiritual fall, because, although according to the *Šāh-nāma*, Jamšid's *farr* (royal glory)—that is, the power that gives legitimate kings their magical abilities including the ability to predict future events—has left him; in the *Garšāsb-nāma*, Jamšid is able to foretell the future as though he still possesses his *farr*. Indeed, the *Garšāsb-nāma* makes no reference to Jamšid's loss of his royal glory at all. In time, Jamšid's wife gives birth to a son whom they name Tur; and although the king tries to keep Jamšid's marriage to his daughter a secret by claiming that the baby is his own son (*Garšāsb-nāma*, p. 42, v. 5), the boy's resemblance to Jamšid's many wanted posters betray his true paternity (*Garšāsb-nāma*, p. 43, vv. 8-9). Rumors about Jamšid grow, and king Gurang advises him to leave lest Żaḥḥāk's spies find out his whereabouts (*Garšāsb-nāma*, p. 43, vv. 13-16). Jamšid leaves Zābolestān and travels first to India, and later to China, but he is captured and surrendered to Żaḥḥāk, who orders him sawed in half. Informed of his death, Jamšid's wife commits suicide after a month of mourning (*Garšāsb-nāma*, pp. 43-44).

Although the *Garšāsb-nāma* gives the impression that Jamšid was killed immediately after his arrest, according to the *Kuš-nāma* (comp. ca. 501/1108) of Irānšāh b. Abi'l-Ḵayr, he lived for fifty years in Żaḥḥāk's prison before his execution (p. 189, v. 740). Jamšid's son, Tur, ascends the throne of Zābolestān following his maternal grandfather's death. His progeny all resemble their ancestor Jamšid in appearance and physical prowess (e.g., *Garšāsb-nāma*, p. 49, v. 81, p. 52, vv. 30-31, p. 244, v. 62). Apparently the reason Jamšid's progeny turn out to be such powerful heroes is that he was quite physically powerful himself and could kill any kind of wild beast by his bare hands (Ebn Balḵi, p. 30).

There are quite a few variations on the *Šāh-nāma* story of Jamšid's life and personality. Aside from the princess of Zābolestān, who is mentioned in the *Garšāsb-nāma*, Jamšid had a number of wives and many children. He had married a Chinese princess because, according to the *Kuš-nāma*, following Żaḥḥāk's attack, Jamšid sends his wife, the daughter of the king of China, along with his two sons, Fārak and Nunak, to a forest in China (Irānšāh, 1998, pp. 187-88). Once assured of his family's safety, he rides against the Indian king Mehrāj at the head of a great army. Unfortunately, the single manuscript of the *Kuš-nāma* has a large lacuna here and the narrative suddenly jumps to the scene of Jamšid's execution (pp. 188-90). Jamšid's adventures in India and his wars with the Indian king are also mentioned in the *Mojmal al-tawāriḵ* (p. 40), which although gives no more details at least corroborates the *Kuš-nāma*'s version. According to the *Šāh-nāma*, a number of paladins aside from the hero Garšāsb/Garšāsp descend from Jamšid (III, p. 289, vv. 21-22). A group of these are called Jamšidiān (*Šāh-nāma*, V, p. 90, v. 143), the most famous of whom are the descendants of king Lohrāsb/Lohrāsp (IV, p. 360, v. 2,947). This accounts for the fact that Jamšid's pavilion, weapons, and other possessions are later found in the possession of Lohrāsb's descendants (e.g., *Šāh-nāma* V, p. 106, v. 309, p. 141, v. 710, p. 366, v. 883, p. 367, v. 890). The epics composed after the *Šāh-nāma* confirm this and tell us that Lohrāsb's great grandson Bahman owned Jamšid's pavilion (*sarā-parda*; Irānšāh, 1991, p. 549, vv. 9,452, 9461, cf. *Haft laškar*, p. 549). In the *Farāmarz-nāma* (q.v.), the hero Farāmarz is mentioned as a Jamšid descendant (*Farāmarz-nāma*, pp. 59-60, vv. 72-91, p. 107: vv. 794-95), and we are also told that Bižan (q.v.), during his adventures, came upon the burial chamber of one of Jamšid's lesser known son, Nušzād (*Farāmarz-nāma*, pp. 87-88, vv. 510-14). Some authorities report that one of Jamšid's descendents was in Noah's arc (Balʿami, 1974, I, p. 146; Menhāj-e Serāj, I, p. 137). Among the later Iranian rulers, Yaʿqub b. Layṯ (r. 861-79) is said to have traced his lineage to him (*Tāriḵ-e Sistān*, pp. 201-2).

Jamšid is described as a man quite handsome, luminous (e.g., *Tarjama-ye Tafsir-e Ṭabari* II, p. 402; Qaṭrān, pp. 367, 525), and huge enough to receive the epithet *piltan* "immense" (lit. "of elephant-like body"; Ḵāqāni, 1995, p. 74), which is ordinarily reserved for his heroic descendants Rostam and Esfandiār in the *Šāh-nāma*. He was physically powerful (e.g., Ebn al-Balḵi, p. 30), and rode a black horse when he was not being carried around by demons (Sanāʾi, p. 72; Fak̲r-e Modabber, p. 185). There may have been a story about his invulnerability to which K̲āqāni alludes (1995, p. 69). Indeed, a folk version of his capture and death confirms his invulnerability (see below). Another story in the *Bustān* of Saʿdi alludes to Jamšid's sorrow for loss of one of his children, but it is not clear if the story is original or was created by Saʿdi in order to make a moral point (Saʿdi, 1363, p. 186 vv. 3,679-82). Unlike the great kings and heroes of old, Jamšid seems to have had a special place in the popular imagination of classical Iran. This may be partly because he was associated with the prophet Solomon, and partly because of his association with the ruins of Persepolis. Ebn al-Balk̲i, the author of the *Fārs-nāma*, who must have seen these ruins considers many of the images that depict various Achaemenid kings to have been representations of Jamšid (Ebn al-Balk̲i, p. 127). Others must have thought the same.

Jamšid's character as an originator of social customs is implied in many literary sources in which certain rites are said to have been practiced according to his "rule." He is viewed as the founder of funerary rites. For instance, the hero Garšāsb orders that his corpse "be dressed according to the prescriptions of Jamšid" (*bapuš-am ba jāma bar āyin-e Jam*) before he is placed in his tomb (*Garšāsb-nāma*, p. 465, v. 51). Since Zoroastrians expose their dead rather than enshroud or bury them, and since Jamšid's practice in this verse implies entombment without a hint of exposure, the verse may be cited as an indication of Jamšid's pre-Zoroastrian character. Jamšid's rules must have included marriage law as well. In the story of Bahrām V Gōr (q.v.), the hero marries the daughters of Borzin "according to the customs of Gayumart and Jamšid" (*Šāh-nāma* VI, p. 483, v. 874).

A number of important discoveries and inventions are ascribed to him in addition to what is mentioned in the *Šāh-nāma*. Some of these are: millstones and water wheel (T̲aʿālebi, pp. 8-9), astronomy and glass-making (Maqdesi, III, p. 140, tr. Šafiʿi Kadkani, I, p. 500), talc paper (*zar-waraq*; Ebn al-Balk̲i, p. 32), roads and paint (Balʿami, 1974, I, p. 130), dyeing (Gardizi, p. 2), sugar (ʿAskari, p. 411; Biruni, p. 266), writing (Ebn al-Nadim p. 15, tr. p. 23), different languages (*Mojmal al-tawārik̲*, p. 145), and locks and keys, as well as domestication of the elephant (Menhāj-e Serāj, I, p. 135). He is said to have built a large number of cities such as Hamadān, Eṣṭak̲r, Ctesiphon (q.v.), and Ṭus (Maqdesi, IV, p. 99, tr. Šafiʿi Kadkani, II, p. 616; Ebn al-Balk̲i pp. 32, 34; *Mojmal al-tawārik̲*, pp. 40, 521; Qomi, pp. 60, 73-77; Mostawfi, p. 81; Gardizi, p. 2), and is also credited with creating important waterworks in the city of Fin in Kāšan and elsewhere (Qomi, p. 77; Maqdesi, IV, p. 60, tr. Šafiʿi Kadkani, II, p. 594). The founding of a number of holy fires are also attributed to Jamšid (e.g., Ṭusi, p. 74; Qomi, p. 88; Gorgāni, p. 358). One of the most important of his innovations is wine, the story of which is associated with a charming narrative that concerns one of his concubines (Ṭusi, pp. 15-16; ʿAwfi, pp. 30-31; Moʿin I, p. 433). It may be deduced from the wording of the *Šāh-nāma* that Jamšid's invention of wine was known to Ferdowsi, because he is the first king in the epic to engage in feasting with wine (*Šāh-nāma* I, p. 44, v. 54). Frequent allusion to his connection with wine throughout Persian literature implies that the story of his invention of wine, though not explicitly stated in the *Šāh-nāma*, must have been quite well-known (e.g., Manučehri, pp. 18, 120; Mok̲tāri, p. 486; K̲āqāni, 1995, p. 661; see also Moʿin, I, pp. 433-35).

Because of his long reign and association with absolute dominion, Jamšid's name is paired with "royal glory" and the concept of the ideal kingship in the *Šāh-nāma* (e.g., II, p. 406, vv. 347-48, V, p. 454, v. 182, VII, p. 16, v. 9, VIII, p. 203, v. 2,664), post-*Šāh-nāma* epics (e.g., *Garšāsb-nāma*, p. 417, v. 13; Zartošt-e Bahrām, p. 7; *Bānugošasb-nāma*, p. 111), as well as Persian court poetry (e.g., Farrok̲i, p. 411; ʿOnṣori, p. 202; Mok̲tāri, p. 618; K̲āqāni, 1995, p. 618; Qaṭrān, p. 473; Ašraf, p. 142; Anwari, I, p. 96) and prose (e.g., Ebn al-Balk̲i, p. 30; Lāhuri, p. 60). Perhaps his reputation as the ideal king is responsible for his further association with wisdom in the *Šāh-nāma*, where frequent reference is made to his dicta (e.g., VI, p. 250, v. 107, VII, p. 34 v. 37), and a number of other Persian and Arabic texts (cf. Fak̲r-al-Din Gorgāni, p. 320, v. 20; Saʿdi, 1363, p. 52, vv. 478-80, p. 186 vv. 3679-82; Moḥammadi, IV, pp. 315-18). He is also associated with the worship of the sun in the *Šāh-nāma* (e.g., V, p. 77, v. 22, p. 83, v. 69). It is not, however, clear whether the pairing of Jamšid and K̲uršid "the sun" in the epic and other poetry (e.g., Farrok̲i, p. 132; Qaṭrān pp. 390, 473 and esp. p. 525; Sanāʾi, p. 500; Moʿezzi p. 170; Mok̲tāri, p. 618; Fak̲r-al-Din Gorgāni, p. 25, v. 12; Suzani, p. 228; K̲āqāni, 2006, p. 86, vv. 10-11, p. 174 v. 7; Ašraf, p. 142; Jamāl-al-Din Moḥammad b. ʿAbd-al-Razzāq p. 373; Mādeḥ, p. 144; K̲ᵛāju, p. 24) is motivated by requirements of meter and rhyme, by the memory of his flying towards the sun in the pre-Islamic religious tradition (see above), or by something else.

Jamšid's grand throne, made for him by the demons, is already mentioned in the *Šāh-nāma* (I, p. 44, vv. 48-51) and other Persian poetry. The famous throne of Ṭāqdis, which was one of the prized possessions of K̲osrow II Parvēz (r. 591-628), is also said to have been originally built by Jamšid (*Mojmal al-tawārik̲*, p. 79). He is also said to have left behind several great treasures, one of which was later discovered by Bahrām Gōr (*Šāh-nāma* VI, pp. 459-60, p. 562, v. 596). A fantastic animal called *Gorg-e guyā*, "the speaking wolf," tells of a great treasure that was hidden by Jamšid in a vast cave built for him by the demons and fairies under his command, and that he had ordered this wolf to guard it. The beast tells of Jamšid's many hidden treasures, and later the hero Bižan finds one of the hordes that contains Jamšid's own crown (*Farāmarz-nāma*, pp. 82-84).

Perhaps Jamšid's most famous magical implements are his wine cup and his ring. Yet, his wine cup is mentioned neither in the *Šāh-nāma* nor in the works of early poets and appears to be a later development, probably from the middle of the 6th/12th century. In all likelihood it was formed under the influence of Kay Ḵosrow's magical cup and the similarity of the word *jām* (cup) with the name Jam which would be tempting to Persian poets. *Jām-e Jam* (Jam's cup) is said to have magical properties that helped the owner to either achieve dominion over the world (e.g., Moʿezzi, p. 491) or enabled him to see the unseen and forecast the future (e.g., Ḵᵛāju, p.55; Moʿin, II, p. 300). Mystics reinterpreted the cup as a metaphor for the heart and the soul (Moʿin II, pp. 302-6). Farid-al-Din ʿAṭṭār uses it as a metaphor for the divine tablet on which all is written (ʿAṭṭār, 1983, p. 122, v. .2, p. 213, v. 5). Ḥāfeẓ employs similar metaphors (e.g., I, p. 112, v. 5 and p. 244 v. 1).

Whereas Jamšid's cup is not mentioned in the *Šāh-nāma*, his ring is explicitly mentioned in a manner that proves that it was part of his legend in the Iranian heroic tradition (II, p. 6, v. 50). The *Šāh-nāma* also alludes to the ring indirectly (I, p. 51, v. 178) and it is further mentioned in the verses of at least two Ghaznavid poets (ʿOnṣori, pp. 202, 229; Sanāʾi, p. 83). Therefore, although it may be tempting to consider Jam's ring as an Iranian manifestation of the famous ring of king Solomon that has been referred to in many religious and legendary texts (e.g., Neysāburi p. 305), and although there must have been some influence from that direction, the objects are common enough and magically potent enough to have grown independently in the Iranian and the Jewish narrative traditions. In other words, because of the similarities between the legends of Solomon and Jamšid in their respective traditions, aspects of these narratives, including that of the magical ring, may have coalesced in the absence of a genetic relationship. Not only are similarities between Solomon and Jamšid noted in classical sources (e.g., Ebn Qotayba, p. 652; Maqdesi, III, pp. 106-7, tr. Šafiʿi Kadkani, I, pp. 474-75; Eṣṭaḵri, p. 123, tr. p. 109), but also often personages or objects of their respective courts are paired in Persian poetry (e.g., Farroḵi, pp. 226, 242; Masʿud-e Saʿd, I, p. 484; Moʿezzi, pp. 43, 478; Ḵāqāni, 1995, pp. 23, 70; Sanāʾi, pp. 375, 500; Qaṭrān, p. 167; Anwari, I, pp. 171, 274). Be that as it may, there may be no doubt that the two legends have merged in the Iranian tradition. For instance, the story of Solomon's encounter with the king of the ants that has been alluded to in the Qurʾān (27:18) and is quite well known from other religious literature (e.g., Neysāburi, pp. 287-88) is attributed to Jamšid in Ḵāqāni's *Divān* (pp. 166, 904) as is the story of Solomon's loss of his ring to the demon Ašmodai (see Krappe; Shaked; and motif K1934.1 "Impostor [magician, demon] takes the place of the king"; see Thompson) in spite of the fact that Jamšid's loss of his throne to Żaḥḥāk, unlike Solomon's loss of his throne to Ašmodai, was quite final (see Ḵāqāni, 1995, pp. 86, 422; Anwari, I, p. 331, II, p. 643; Ḵᵛāju, p. 85). Interestingly enough Ḵāqāni ascribes all the details of Solomon's fall and his employment as a fisherman during the period of his exile to Jamšid (1995, pp. 422, 425; cf. Neysāburi, pp. 303-6). There is reason to believe that what gave Jamšid's ring its potency was the formula that was written on its stone (ʿOnṣori, pp. 202, 229; Moḵtāri, pp. 317, 345, 552; Sanāʾi p. 500; Anwari, I, p. 339) and that the ring's gemstone may have been green (Anwari, I, p. 7; cf. Šahidi, p. 40).

Jamšid has three functionality in Persian folklore. On the one hand, his name, usually in the form of Malek Jamšid, is a common name for the main hero of various folktales. In that general sense, the name has no connection with the Jamšid of the *Šāh-nāma*. Thus, Vladimir Minorski's suggestion that the Jamšid mentioned in the *Vis o Rāmin* (p. 138, v. 50, p. 146, v. 31), which has all the hallmarks of a literary version of a folk story, is necessarily the famous Jamšid of the *Šāh-nāma* may not be taken at face value without corroborating evidence (see Gorgāni, p. 426). Jamšid also appears in a series of folktales that are derived from the *Šāh-nāma* narratives. These tales tend to elaborate upon certain *Šāh-nāma* scenes or persona. For instance, whereas in the *Šāh-nāma* version of Zāl's story an unnamed "man from the land of Indians" appears to Zāl's father in a dream and informs him of the whereabouts of his son (I, p. 168, vv. 93-95), according to the oral versions of this tale, the man in the dream is Jamšid (Enjavi, I, p. 67). Similarly, whereas the *Šāh-nāma* provides no explanation about why Żaḥḥāk kills Jamšid by sawing him in half rather than by a more conventional means of dispatch (I, p. 52, v. 186), the folk version of the story explains that Żaḥḥāk first tried killing his captive by the sword, but, because Jamšid was invulnerable, he could not be killed by the blade. Later, the devil appeared in as an old man and informed the tyrant that Jamšid could be killed only by being cut asunder with a saw (Enjavi, II, pp. 303-4). There are a number of interesting features of Jamšid's legend in the *ṭumārs* (scrolls) of the *naqqāl*s (story-teller). These scrolls, which narrate idiosyncratic versions of Iranian epic literature in prose, are primarily derived from the *Šāh-nāma* and extra *Šāh-nāma* texts; but they also freely mix the literary narratives with elements adopted from Persian folklore (see Omidsalar and Omidsalar). For instance, the story of Jamšid's fall, which in the *Šāh-nāma* merely precedes Żaḥḥāk's appearance, is made into a prerequisite of Żaḥḥāk's legend in one of these scrolls. According to the *Haft laškar*, the very moment when Jamšid begins to entertain the idea of claiming divinity is the moment when "Żaḥḥāk is conceived" (*Haft laškar*, p. 7). Similarly, although the *Garšāb-nāma* tells of how the princess of Zābolestān recognized Jamšid from having seen the "wanted posters" that Żaḥḥāk had sent far and wide, according to the *Haft laškar*, she had already fallen in love with his picture before she ever laid eyes on him (motif T11.2. "Love through sight of picture"; see Thompson).

It is interesting that although Jamšid is held responsible for his sin in the Zoroastrian priestly tradition, which sends him to hell and forgives him only grudgingly (Dārāb Hormozyār, II, pp. 208-9), he has been totally rehabilitated in Persian literature and folklore. Thus, aside from the many positive references to his character that abounds in Persian literature, the *Haft laškar* portrays him as a saint with special knowledge of the activities and mission of the Shiʿite messiah (*Haft laškar*, pp. 133-14).

Bibliography: Awḥad-al-Din Moḥammad Anwari, *Divān-e Anwari*, 2 vols., ed. Moḥammad-Taqi Modarres Rażawi, 3rd ed., Tehran, 1985. Abu Naṣr ʿAli Asadi Ṭusi, *Garšāsb-nāma*, ed. Ḥabib Yaḡmāʾi, Tehran, 1975. Abu Helāl Ḥasan ʿAskari, *al-Awāʾel*, ed. Moḥammad Sayyed Wakil, Ṭanṭa, Egypt, 1987. Sayyed Ḥasan Ašraf Ḡaznavi, *Divān-e Sayyed Ḥasan Ḡaznavi, Molaqqab ba Ašraf*, ed. Moḥammad-Taqi Modarres Rażawi, 2nd rev. ed., Tehran, 1983. Farid-al-Din ʿAṭṭār, *Elāhi-nāma*, ed. Foʾād Ruḥāni, Tehran, 1972. Idem, *Divān*, ed. Taqi Tafażżoli, Tehran, 1983. Idem, *Moṣibat-nāma*, ed. ʿAbd-al-Wahhāb Nurāni Weṣāl, 3rd rev. ed., Tehran, 1985. Sadid-al-Din Moḥammad ʿAwfi, *Jawāmeʿ al-ḥekāyāt*, ed. Jaʿfar Šeʿār, Tehran, 1975. Abu ʿAli Moḥammad Amirak Balʿami, *Tāriḵ-e Balʿami*, ed. Moḥammad-Taqi Malek-al-Šoʿarāʾ Bahār, Tehran, 1962, pp. 130-32; rev. ed. Moḥammad Parvin Gonābādi, Tehran, 1974; tr. Hermann Zotenberg as *Chronique de . . . Tabari traduite sur la version persane d'Abou-ʿAli Mohammad Balʿami*, 4 vols., Paris, 1867-74. Faḵr-al-Din Dāwud Banākati, *Tāriḵ-e Banākati: Rawżat ule'l-albāb fi maʿrefat al-tawāriḵ wa'l-ansāb*, ed. Jaʿfar Šeʿār, Tehran, 1969. *Bānugošasp-nāma*, ed. Ruḥangiz Karachi, Tehran, 2003. Christian Bartholomae, *Altiranisches Wörterbuch*, Berlin, 1961. Abu Rayḥān Biruni, *Ketāb al-āṯār al-bāqia ʿan al-qorun al-ḵālia*, ed. Eduard Sachau as *Chronologie orientalischer Völker von Albêrûnî*, Leipzig, 1878; repr. Leipzig, 1923; ed. with commentary Parviz Aḏkāʾi, Tehran, 2001; tr. Eduard Sachau as *The Chronology of the Ancient Nations*, London, 1879; repr. Frankfurt, 1969. Idem, *Ketāb al-Saydana fi'l-ṭebb*, ed. ʿAbbās Zaryāb Ḵoʾi, Tehran, 1991. Dārāb Hormazyār, *Dārāb Hormazyār's Rivāyat*, ed. Ervad Mnockji Rustamji Unvala, 2 vols, Bombay, 1922. Ebn al-Balḵi, *Fārs-nāma*, ed. Guy Le Strange and Reynold A. Nicholson, Cambridge, 1921; offset printing, Tehran, 1984. Ebn Esfandiār, *Tāriḵ-e Ṭabarestān*, ed. ʿAbbās Eqbāl, 2 vols., Tehran, 1941. Ebn al-Faqih, *Ketāb al-boldān*, ed. Yusof Hādi, Beirut, 1996 (an edition based on the Āstān-e Qods MS no. 5229, which is the complete text of the second half of Ebn al-Faqih's *Ketāb al-Boldān*; the edition published in the series *Bibliotheca Geographrum Arabicorum* is an abridged text and lacks much of what is in the Āstān-e Qods manuscript). Ebn al-Nadim, *Ketāb al-fehrest*, ed. Reżā Tajaddod, Tehran, 1971; tr. Bayard Dodge as *The Fihrist of al-Nadīm: A Tenth-Century Survey of Muslim Culture*, 2 vols., New York and London, 1970. Ebn Qotayba Dinavari, *Ketāb al-maʿāref*, ed. Ṯarwat ʿOkāša, Cairo, 1960. Abu'l-Qāsem Enjavi Širāzi, *Ferdowsi-nāma: mardom wa Ferdowsi*, 3 vols, 2nd ed., Tehran, 1984. Abu Esḥāq Ebrāhim Eṣṭaḵri, *Ketāb masālek al-mamālek*, ed., Michaël Jan De Goeje, Leiden, 1967; tr. Moḥammad b. Asʿad Tostari as *Masālek wa mamālek*, ed. Iraj Afšār, Tehran, 1974.

Faḵr-e Modabber Moḥammad b. Manṣur Mobārakšāh, *Ādāb al-ḥarb wa'l-šajāʿa*, ed. Aḥmad Sohayli Ḵᵛānsāri, Tehran, 1967. *Farāmarz-nāma*, ed. Maḥmud Sarmadi, Tehran, 2004. Farroḵi Sistāni, *Divān-e Ḥakim Farroḵi Sistāni*, ed. Moḥammad Dabirsiāqi, 3rd rev. ed., Tehran, 1984. Abu'l-Qāsem Ferdowsi, *Šāh-nāma*, ed. Djalal Khaleghi-Motlagh, New York, 1987. Abu Saʿid ʿAbd-al-Ḥayy Gardizi *Zayn al-aḵbaār*, ed. ʿAbd-al-Ḥayy Ḥabibi, Tehran, 1968. *Garšāsb-nāma*, see Asadi Ṭusi. Abu Ḥāmed Moḥammad Ḡazāli, *Naṣiḥat al-moluk*, ed. Jalāl Homāʾi, Tehran, 1972. Faḵr-al-Din Asʿad Gorgāni, *Vis o Rāmin*, ed. Moḥammad Rowšan, Tehran, 1998. Šams-al-Din Moḥammad Ḥāfeẓ, *Divān*, ed. Parviz Nātel Ḵānlari, 2 vols., Tehran, 1983. *Haft laškar: ṭumār-e jāmeʿ-e naqqālān az kayumarṯ tā Bahman*, ed. Mehrān Afšāri and Mahdi Madāyeni, Tehran, 1998. Clément Huart and Henri Massé, "Djamshīd," in *EI*[2] II, pp. 438-39. Irānšāh b. Abi'l-Ḵayr, *Bahman-nāma*, ed. Raḥim ʿAfifi, Tehran, 1991. Idem, *Kuš-nāma*, ed. Jalāl Matini, Tehran, 1998. Abu ʿAbd-Allāh Moḥammad b. ʿAbdus Jahšiāri, *Ketāb al-wozarāʾ wa'l-kottāb*, facs. ed. Hans von Mžik as *Das Kitāb al-Wuzarāʾ wa-l-kuttāb des Abū ʿAbdallāh Muḥammad ibn ʿAbdūs al-Ǧahšiyārī, nach dem Handschriftlichen unikum der Nationalbibliothek in Wien, Cod. Mixt. 916*, Leipzig, 1926; ed. Ḥasan Zayn, Beirut, 1988; tr. Abu'l-Fażl Ṭabāṭabāʾi, Tehran, 1969. Jamāl-al-Din Moḥammad b. ʿAbd-al-Razzāq Eṣfahāni, *Divān-e kāmel . . .*, ed. Ḥasan Waḥid Dastgerdi, 2nd ed., Tehran, 1983. Ḵᵛāju Kermāni, *Homāy o Homāyun*, ed. Kamāl ʿAyni, 2nd ed., Tehran, 1991. Abu'l-Fażl Ḵāqāni Šarvāni, *Divān*, ed. Sayyed Ziāʾ-al-Din Sajjādi, 5th ed., Tehran, 1995. Idem, *Ḵatm al-ḡarāyeb (Toḥfat al-ʿErāqayn): nosḵa-bargardān-e nosḵa-ye ḵaṭṭi-e šomāra-ye 845 Ketābḵāna-ye melli-e Oṭriš (Vian), ketābat-e 593/1197*, ed. Iraj Afšār, Tehran, 2006. Pseudo-Ḵayyām, *Nowruz-nāma*, ed., ʿAli Ḥaṣuri, rev. 2nd ed., Tehran, 1978. Thomas Kinsella, tr., *The Táin, Translated from the Irish Epic Táin Bó Cúailnge*, Oxford, 1970. Alexander H. Krappe, "Solomon and Ashmodai," *American Journal of Philology* 54, 1933, pp. 260-68. ʿAbd-al-Sattār b. Qāsem Lāhuri, *Majāles-e Jahāngiri: majleshā-ye šabāna-ye darbār-e Nur-al-Din Jahāngir az 24 Rajab 1017 tā 19 Ramażān 1020 H.Q.*, ed. ʿĀref Nowšāhi and Moʿin Neẓāmi, Tehran, 2006.

Qāsem Mādeḥ, *Jahāngir-nāma*, ed. Sayyed Ziāʾ-al-Din Sajjādi with an introd. by Mahdi Moḥaqqeq, Tehran, 2001. Manučehri Dāmḡāni, *Divān-e Manučehri Dāmḡāni*, ed. Moḥammad Dabirsiāqi, Tehran, 1991. Abu Zayd Moṭahhar b. Ṭāher Maqdesi, *Ketāb al-badʾ wa'l-taʾriḵ*, ed. and tr. Clément Huart as *Le livre de la création et de l'histoire*, 6 vols., Paris, 1899-1919; tr. Moḥammad-Reżā Šafiʿi Kadkani as *Āfarineš wa tāriḵ*, 2 vols., Tehran, 1995. Masʿud-e Saʿd-e Salmān, *Divān-e Ašʿār-e Masʿud-e Saʿd*, ed. Mahdi Nuriān, 2 vols., Isfahan, 1985. Menhāj-e Serāj, *Ṭabaqāt-e nāṣeri*, ed. ʿAbd-al-Ḥayy Ḥabibi, two vols. in one, Tehran, 1984. Abu ʿAli Meskawayh, *Tajāreb al-omam*, ed. Abu'l-Qāsem Emāmi, 5 vols, Tehran, 1987. Abu ʿAbd-Allāh Moḥammad Moʿezzi, *Divān-e Amir-al-Šoʿarāʾ Moḥammad b. ʿAbd-al-Malek Nišāburi*, ed. ʿAbbās Eqbāl, Tehran, 1939. Moḥammad Moḥammadi, *Tāriḵ o far-*

hang-e Irān dar dawrān-e enteqāl az ʿaṣr-e Sāsāni ba ʿaṣr-e eslāmi, 6 vols., Tehran, 2001. Moḥammad Moʿin, *Mazdayasnā wa adab-e pārsi*, 2 vols., ed. Mahindok̲t Moʿin, 2nd ed., Tehran, 2005. ʿOt̲mān Mok̲tāri, *Divān-e Mok̲tāri Ḡaznavi*, ed. Jalāl-al-Din Homāʾi, Tehran, 1962. Ḥamd-Allāh Mostawfi, *Tārik̲-e gozida*, ed. ʿAbd-al-Ḥosayn Navāʾi, 2nd ed., Tehran, 1983. Nāṣer-e K̲osrow, *Divān-e ašʿār*, ed. Ḥasan Taqizāda, 3rd ed., Tehran, 1993. Ebrāhim b. Manṣur Nisāburi, *Qeṣaṣ al-anbiāʾ*, ed. Ḥabib Yaḡmāʾi, 2nd ed., Tehran, 1980. Mahmood Omidsalar, "The Dragon Fight in the National Persian Epic," *International Review of Psycho-Analysis* 14, 1987, pp. 343-56. Mahmood Omidsalar and T. Omidsalar, "Narrating Epics in Iran," in Margaret Read Macdonald, ed., *Traditional Storytelling Today: An International Sourcebook*, Chicago and London, 1999, pp. 326-40. Abu'l-Qāsem Ḥasan ʿOnṣori, *Divān-e ʿOnṣori Balk̲i*, ed. Moḥammad Dabirsiāqi, 2nd ed., Tehran, 1984. Abu Manṣur Qaṭrān Tabrizi, *Divān-e Ḥakim Qaṭrān Tabrizi*, ed. Moḥammad Nak̲javāni, Tehran, 1983. Ḥasan b. Moḥammad Qomi, *Tārik̲-e Qom*, Pers. tr. Ḥasan b. ʿAli Qomi, ed. Sayyed Jalāl-al-Din Ṭehrāni, 2nd ed., Tehran, 1982.

Moṣleḥ-al-Din Saʿdi, *Bustān*, ed. Ḡolām-Ḥosayn Yusofi, 2nd rev. ed., Tehran, 1984. Idem, *Golestān*, ed. Ḡolām-Ḥosayn Yusofi, Tehran, 1989. Ḏabiḥ-Allāh Ṣafā, *Ḥamāsa-sarāʾi dar Irān*, Tehran, 1984, pp. 424-51. *Šāh-nāma*, see Ferdowsi. Jaʿfar Šahidi, *Šarḥ-e loḡāt o moškelāt-e Divān-e Anwari*, 2nd ed., Tehran, 1985. Abu'l-Majd Majdud b. Ādam Sanāʾi, *Divān-e Ḥakim Abu'l-Majd Majdud b. Ādam Sanāʾi Ḡaznavi*, ed. Moḥammad-Taqi Modarres Rażawi, 3rd ed., Tehran, 1983. Mahindok̲t Ṣediqiān, *Farhang-e asāṭiri-ḥamāsi-e Irān ba rewāyat-e manābeʿ-e baʿd az Eslām* I, Tehran, 1976, pp. 76-125. Shaul Shaked, "Iranian Influences on Judaism: First Century B.C.E. to Second Century C.E.," in Willliam D. Davies and Louis Finkelstein, eds., *Cambridge History of Judaism* I, Cambridge, 1984, pp. 308-26. Suzani Samarqandi, *Divān-e Ḥakim Suzani Samarqandi*, ed. Nāṣer Šāh-Ḥosayni, Tehran, 1959.

Abu Manṣur ʿAbd-al-Malek T̲aʿālebi, *Ḡorar ak̲bār moluk al-fors*, ed. Hermann Zotenberg as *Histoir des rois des Perses*, Paris, 1900. *Tārik̲-e Sistān*, ed. Moḥammad-Taqi Malek-al-Šoʿarāʾ Bahār, Tehran, ca. 1935; tr. Milton Gold as *The Tārikh-e Sistān*, Rome, 1976. *Tarjama-ye Tafsir-e Ṭabari*, ed. Ḥabib Yaḡmāʾi, 7 vols., Tehran, 1960. Moḥammad b. Maḥmud Ṭusi, *ʿAjāyeb al-mak̲luqāt wa ḡarāyeb al-mawjudāt*, ed. Manučehr Sotuda, 2nd ed., Tehran, 2003. Zartošt-e Bahrām-e Paždu, *Zartošt-nāma*, ed. F. Rosenberg as *The Book of Zoroaster: Zarātusht Nāma*, rev. ed. by Moḥammad Dabirsiāqi, Tehran, 1959.

(MAHMOOD OMIDSALAR)

JAMŠIDI, one of several semi-nomadic, Persian-speaking, Hanafite Sunni groups of northwestern Afghanistan known as *aymāq* (q.v.; Turk *oymāq*).

The Jamšidi have often been subsumed within the larger category of *čār* (*čahār*) *aymāq* (the four tribes), which not only comprised the Jamšidi, Firuzkuhi, Taymani, and Sunni Hazāra of Qalʿa-ye Now, but, according to some accounts, also included other groups like the Timuri, Zuri, Qepčāq, Čengizi, and Ṭāheri (Janata, p. 141; Mehrabān, p. 34; Schurmann, pp. 50-55). This apparent contradiction can be resolved in the light of the different usages of the Mongol term *aymāq* (q.v.). Originally signifying 'a group of people, a tribe,' it also denoted territorial and administrative subdivisions in the sense of "district" (Doerfer, I, pp. 182, 185). From Mongol times on, the division of territories into four units can be observed in different settings, most notably the partition of Čengiz Khan and Timur's realms among four descendants. The organization of Herat province into four constituent districts (*boluk*) is well established from the 18th century on (Fōfalzay, 1967, pp. 65, 398-400; Lal, p. 10). The troops raised in the environs of Herat during the Sadōzay era were generally known as *čahār oymāq* and also included local Qezelbāš contingents (Fōfalzay, 1958, p. 300). This term thus primarily referred to a type of military and administrative organization rather than a purely ethnic category (Centlivres, p. 33; Janata, p. 149).

There is evidence that the Jamšidi owe their genesis to the formation of a military coalition. This is reflected by the popular etymology tracing their name to *jamʿ šoda* "gathered or collected together." According to Āqā Khan b. Yalangtuš, the leading family was of Kayānid descent and derived its name from the mythical king Jamšid (q.v.). Resettled from Sistān to Bādḡis north of Herat in 1392-93, this group gathered a number of local tribal segments under their command and assisted Timur in the protection of the frontier of Khorasan. As a result, the name Jamšidi was applied collectively to all their followers (Āqā Khan, tr., p. 165). Another version associates the Kayānid migration to Bādḡis with the person of Timur's grandson Oloḡ Beg, during whose reign, according to this tradition, sixty thousand of them moved to Bādḡis, led by two brothers, Ḥaydar-solṭān and Yalangtuš (Adamec, p. 185). From the early Safavid period on, the Jamšidi are mentioned as ancient revenue payers of Herat (Jonābādi, p. 525), and they figure among the groups who entered the service of Shah ʿAbbās I the Great (r. 1588-1629) around 1598 (Eskandar Beg, ed. Afšār, I, p. 573, ed. Reżwāni, p. 921, tr., II, p. 759). Based in Harirud River and Karok̲ east of Herat, they controlled the lands along the first stages along the high-road to Maymana and held service grants in the mountainous region of Ḡarjestān (Eskandar Beg, pp. 1154, 1475; Naṣiri, pp. 158-59, 280-81).

In their own accounts, the members of the Jamšidi *k̲ān k̲ēl* project a continuum of Jamšidi dominance over Bādḡis from the Timurid period to the 18th century (Adamec, p. 185; Āqā Khan, tr., pp. 165-56). In fact, a number of demographic shifts occurred prior and during Nāder Shah Afšār's time. One such event was the arrival of the Abdāli Afghans (later known as Dorrāni Paštuns) around 1592, whose extensive nomadic migrations around Herat also included Bādḡis. In 1717 the Abdāli established control over Herat and conquered all the dependencies of the former Safavid province (Marʿaši, pp. 19, 21). According to the Āqā Khan b. Yalangtuš, Nāder Shah's invasion from 1727 on tipped the scales once more in favor of the Jamšidi. The Jamšidi and other Persian speaking groups were moved to Mashad, Jām, and Langar subsequent to Nāder Shah's second campaign in 1729 (Dorrāni, p. 105), but they were allowed to return to Bādḡis after his conquest of Herat in February 1732. Moreover, their leader was appointed to the command over the four *aymāq* of Herat (Āqā Khan, tr., p. 166). There is evidence, however, that the Jamšidis were not the only group to benefit from the removal of the Abdāli population to various places in Khorasan and their later settlement in Kandahar (Qandahār) (Minorsky, p. 9; Navāʾi, pp. 198-99, 210-11). Nāder Shah's chronicler, Moḥammad-Kāẓem Marvi (I, p. 198), reports that Nāder Shah awarded the government (*salṭanat*) over both the Jamšidi and Sunni Hazāra (*ṭāyefa-ye uymāyqiya-ye Hazāra wa Jamšidi*) to a local Hazāra leader.

In the early 19th century, Khorasan experienced a dramatic increase of political segmentation. With the dissolution of the Sadōzay empire in 1818, the last representatives of the dynasty, Maḥmud Shah (r. 1819-26) and his son, Prince Kāmrān (r. 1826-42), found their sphere of influence reduced to Herat and were situated within the orbit of Qajar territorial claims, which were intermittently enforced by military power. This setting of shifting patterns of authority presented opportunities and hazards for the local tribal leadership. By awarding a service grant in Karok̲, Maḥmud Shah caused one Jamšidi section to separate from the main group based in northern Bādḡis around Košk and along the Morḡāb River at Bālā Morḡāb, Māručāq, and Panjdeh at that time (Adamec, pp. 186, 206; Stirling, pp. 248-60). In the late 1830s the Jamšidi of northern Bādḡis were allied with the militarily and numerically dominant Sunni Hazāras of Qalʿa-ye Now (Forrest, ed., p. 38). Shortly afterwards the efforts of Kāmrān's powerful vizier, Yār-Moḥammad Khan Alekōzay (d. 1851), to build up a more compliant chief as counterpoise to the traditional leadership created another split among the northern section of the Jamšidi. As part of his endeavor to re-populate the valley of Herat after the Persian siege of 1837-38, Yār-Moḥammad forcefully resettled 5,000 Jamšidi families in this region (Adamec, pp. 187-88; Ferrier, pp. 158, 172).

During this time the bulk of the tribe moved to K̲iva, where they joined the service of its amirs, Raḥimqoli Khan (r. 1842-45) and Moḥammad-Amin Khan (r. 1845-55). Estimates of the Jamšidi who settled in K̲iva vary between 5,000, 7,000, 10,000 and 12,000 families (Ferrier, pp. 193-94; Basiner, pp. 202-3; Adamec, p. 188; Vámbéry, p. 355; Āqā Khan, tr., p. 166). While the European sources speak of a forceful removal of the Jamšidi to K̲iva, there is evidence that their leaders entertained a close relationship with the local court. Mir Aḥmad Khan Jamšidi received the title of Khan Āqā from Mohammad-Amin Khan, joined his activities against the Persians in Marv and Sarak̲s in 1854-55, and was killed together with him during the battle of Sarak̲s against the joint Persian and Teke Turkmen forces in Jomādā II 1271/March 1855 (Sepehr, pp. 1202-3, 1248-52; see also CENTRAL ASIA vii). Given the unrest unfolding in K̲iva after the death of the Khan, Mir Aḥmad Khan's brother, Mehdiqoli Khan, and the Jamšidi returned to their erstwhile settlements in Bālā Morḡāb and Māručāq soon afterwards (Adamec, p.189; Khanikoff, p. 376; Stewart, p. 51).

The incorporation of Herat into the Bārakzay/Moḥammadzay (see AFGHANESTAN X; DORRĀNI) kingdom in 1863 also affected the Jamšidi. They gained political leverage during the reign of Amir Šēr ʿAli Khan (r. 1863-66 and 1868-78) but suffered violent inroads into their domain under Amir ʿAbd-al-Raḥmān Khan (r. 1880-1901). Subsequent to the Persian siege of 1856, the Persian appointee, Solṭān-Aḥmad Khan (r. 1857-63), attempted to establish tighter administrative control over the tribes around Herat. The Jamšidi of Karok̲ lost their customary service grants and were forced to pay revenues, and the northern section of the Jamšidi were driven from their stronghold in Bālā Morḡāb (Molloy, p. 10). In order to evade the military pressure exerted by Solṭān-Aḥmad Khan, the Jamšidi of northern Bādḡis supported Amir Dōst Moḥammad Khan Bārakzāy's (r. 1826-63, q.v.) siege of Herat in Ḏu'l-qaʿda-Ḏu'l-ḥejja 1279/May 1863. Mehdiqoli Khan Jamšidi entered a marriage alliance with Dōst Moḥammad Khan's successor, Amir Šēr ʿAli Khan, giving two daughters to Šēr ʿAli Khan's sons, Moḥammad-Yaʿqub and Moḥammad-Ayyub. In 1863 Moḥammad-Yaʿqub Khan was appointed governor of Herat at the age of fourteen. Mehdiqoli Khan Āqā Amin-al-Dawla acted as his guardian and virtually controlled the affairs of the province until Moḥammad-Yaʿqub Khan's recall and imprisonment in 1874. In 1880 he was put to death after an attempt to rebel against Moḥammad-Ayyub, who held Herat during the Second Anglo-Afghan War of 1878-80 (q.v.). In order to evade the ensuing general persecution of the Jamšidi tribe, Mehdiqoli Khan's son, Yalangtuš Khan, fled to Maymana (Adamec, pp. 190-91; Kakar, 1971, pp. 70-71; Lee, pp. 400-402; Āqā Khan, tr., p. 169).

Within the first years of his reign, Amir ʿAbd-al-Raḥmān Khan switched from a policy of patronage to one of relentless persecution. Until 1883 the chiefs of the four *aymāq* received a total subsidy amounting to 60,000 rupees annually (Molloy, p. 9). In recognition of Yalangtuš Khan's services during the conquest of Herat in 1881, the amir awarded him the title of Amin-al-Dawla and confirmed him as leader of the Jamšidi. In 1883 he invited the Jamšidi to re-occupy their erstwhile possessions in Bālā Morḡāb in order to secure the northwestern frontier. In December 1884 Yalangtuš Khan was appointed governor of Panjdeh, and his brother, Amin-Allāh, was placed in charge of Bālā Morḡāb. Yet, subsequent to the Russian occupation of Panjdeh in March 1885, ʿAbd-al-Raḥmān Khan accused Yalangtuš Khan of treachery and had him and Amin-Allāh Khan executed in late 1886. The Jamšidi returned to Košk but were deported to Herat in 1889. Those who were allowed to return to Košk a few years later found that their lands had in the meantime been appropriated by Afghan officials (Adamec, p. 284; Yate, 2003, pp. 163-64). Subsequent to the Panjdeh crisis, Amir ʿAbd-al-Raḥmān entrusted Paštuns rather than local tribesmen with the protection of the northwestern frontier (Adamec, pp. 198-204, 283; Kakar, 1979, pp. 131-32; Tapper, pp. 57-58, 62-64). Yalangtuš Khan's sons and nephews remained in prison until 1903 and eventually fled to Russian territory in 1908. Their flight once again exposed the Jamšidi to persecutions by the Afghan government, causing 3,000 families to flee to the Russian districts of Čaman-e Bēd and Qalʿa-ye Mōr, located on the lower course of the Košk River (Āqā Khan, tr., pp. 170-73). During the unrest accompanying the Bolshevik Revolution of October 1917 and the advent of the Red Army, the Jamšidi were relocated to Kondoz in northeastern Afghanistan but returned to Turkmenistan in 1919 (Rzehak and Pristschepowa, p. 21).

In the course of the 19th century, a number of Jamšidi groups moved to the vicinity of Mashad. These migrations were triggered by vizier Yār-Moḥammad Alekōzay's oppressive policies in 1842, the Persian siege of 1856, and Moḥammad-Ayyub Khan's defeat and flight to Persia in 1881 (Curzon, I, pp. 198-99; Adamec, pp. 207-8; Yate, 1900, pp. 32-33, Napier, p. 246). In 1883 the Jamšidi on Persian soil were estimated at 500 families (Stewart, p. 51).

The Jamšidi population of Herat province hovered around the mark of 10,000 families during the 19th century. In 1839 Henry Pottinger reported a total of 12,000-13,000 families, 8,000 of whom belonged to the northern section (apud Adamec, p. 187). In the 1850s and 1870s the entire tribe was estimated to comprise 10,000-12,000 families and to have a fighting capacity of 4,000-5,000 men. During this period 400 Jamšidi cavalry were in the service of Herat (Daud Khan, p. 8; Napier, p. 243, Taylor, p. 855). The Jamšidi of Košk were thought to number 4,000-5,000 families in the late 1870s and 1880s, while the Jamšidi population of Karok̲ was estimated at 2,000 families (Adamec, pp. 192-93, 204-5; Grodekov, pp. 122, 158; Stewart, p. 50). In the 1950s the Jamšidi centered around Košk and Bālā Morḡāb reportedly amounted to 60,000 souls (Janata, p. 141). The sharpening of ethnic demarcations that evolved along with the anti-Communist resistance and the civil war of the 1980s and the 1990s also affected the Jamšidi, and as Sunni Persian speakers they have increasingly been subsumed within the larger ethnic category of the Tajik.

In the 19th century the Jamšidi were divided into twelve major tax units (*maḥalla-ye pok̲ta*), and 112 subdivisions (*maḥalla-ye k̲ām*), each of which comprised a flock of about 500 sheep and was looked after by a headman (*malek*). The Jamšidi were organized under a hierarchy of leaders, with the *katk̲odā*s representing the major sections and the *arbāb* attending to the affairs of the minor sections (Adamec, p. 196; Elphinstone II, p. 206). The northern section of the Jamšidi followed a semi-nomadic lifestyle. They lived in black goats' hair tents and portable huts, and almost the whole population moved southwards with their flocks into the hills in spring and returned for the summer harvest. The Jamšidi of Karok̲, by contrast, had given up their nomadic habits by the late 19th century (Adamec, pp. 194-95, 207). A portion of the Jamšidi in Persia were likewise settled (Stewart, p. 49). Like other groups in the region, the Jamšidi derived part of their income by participating in the slave trade with K̲iva and Bukhara in the early 19th century (K̲āvari Širāzi, pp. 826, 830). The rich pastures of Bādḡis allowed the upkeep of vast herds of sheep and cattle. The horses of the region, described as small but enduring, formed a major item of export in the 19th century (Moḥammad-Ḥayāt Khan, p. 458). Among the local products are grain, melons, pistachios, pistachio galls for tanning (*bozḡonj*), and Persian manna (*taranjabin, širk̲ešt*). The Jamšidi women were known for the production of fine fabrics from wool and goat's hair, which were sold in Herat and Persia (Mehrabān, p, 36; Vámbéry, p. 261).

Bibliography: Ludwig Adamec, ed., *Historical and Political Gazetteer of Afghanistan* III: *Herat and Northwestern Afghanistan*, Graz, 1975, pp. 184-208. Āqā Khan b. Yalangtuš, *Tārik̲-nāmča-ye Jamšidihā*, tr. A. A. Semenov as "Djemshidi i ikh strana (The Jamšidi and their country)," *Izvestiya turkestanskovo otdela russkovo geograficheskovo obshchestva* (Journal of the Turkistan Branch of the Russian Geographical Society) 16, 1923, pp. 161-74. Theodor Friedrich Julius Basiner, *Naturwissenschaftliche Reise durch die Kirgisensteppe nach Chiwa*, St. Petersburg, 1848, repr., Osnabrück, 1969. Pierre Centlivres, "Groupes ethniques: de l'hétérogénéité d'un concept aux ambiguités de la représentation, l'exemple afghan," in Eckart Ehlers, ed., *Beiträge zur Kulturgeographie des islamischen Orients*, Marburger geographische Schriften 78, Marburg, 1979, pp. 25-37. George N. Curzon, *Persia and the Persian Question*, 2 vols, London, 1892, repr., London, 1966. Daud Khan, *An Account of Daud Khan's Visit to Afghanistan and Khorasan etc.*, Simla, Government Central Branch, India Office Library, L/P & S/5/274 no. 90 of 26 December 1873. Gerhard Doerfer, *Türkische und mongolische Lehnwörter im Neupersischen*, 4 vols., Wiesbaden, 1963-75. Solṭān-Moḥammad b. Musā Dorrāni, *Tārik̲-e solṭāni*, Bombay, 1881. Eskandar Beg Torkamān Monši, *Tārik̲-e ʿālamārā-ye ʿabbāsi*, ed. Iraj Afšār, 2 vols., Tehran, 1955-56; ed. Moḥammad-Esmāʿil Reżwāni, 3 vols., Teheran, 1998; tr. Roger Savory as *History of Shah ʿAbbās the Great*, 3 vol., Boulder, 1979-86. Mountstuart Elphinstone, *An Account of the Kingdom of Caubul, and Its Dependencies in Persia, Tartary, and India, Comprising a View of the Afghaun Nation, and A History of the Dooraunes Monarchy*, 2 vols., New York, 1839, repr., Karachi, 1992. Joseph Pierre Ferrier, *Caravan Journeys and Wanderings in Persia, Afghanistan, Turkistan, and Beloochistan . . .* tr. William Jesse from the original unpub. manuscript, ed. H. D. Seymour, London, 1857. ʿAziz-al-Din Wakili Fōfalzay, *Timur Šāh Dorrāni*, 2 vols., Kabul, 1954, repr., Kabul,

1967. Idem, *Dorrat al-zamān fi taʾrik̲ Šāh Zamān*, Kabul, 1958. George W. Forrest, ed., *Selections from the Travels and Journals Preserved in the Bombay Secretariat*, Bombay, 1906. Nikolai Ivanovich Grodekov, *Colonel Grodekoff's Ride from Samarcand to Herat through Balkh and the Uzbek States of Afghan Turkestan*, tr. Charles Marvin, London, 1880. Edit Gustavorna Gafferberg, "Zhilishche dzhemshidov kushkinskovo raiona" (Jamšidi dwellings in the Kushka District, Turkmenistan), *Sovetskaya Etnografiya* 1/4, 1948, pp. 124-43. Alfred Janata, "Die Bevölkerung von Ghor: Beitrag zur Ethnographie und Ethnogenese der Chahar Aimaq," *Archiv für Völkerkunde* 17-18, 1962-63, pp. 73-156. Mirzā Beg b. Ḥasan Ḥosayni Jonābādi, *Rawżat al-ṣafawiya*, ed. Ḡolām-Reżā Ṭabāṭabāʾi Majd, Tehran, 1999. Hasan K. Kakar, *Afghanistan: A Study in Internal Developments 1880-1896*, Kabul, 1971. Idem, *Government and Society in Afghanistan: The Reign of Amir ʿAbd al-Rahman Khan*, Austin, 1979. Fażl-Allāh K̲āvari Širāzi, *Tārik̲-e d̲uʾl-qarnayn*, ed. Nāṣer Afšār-far, 2 vols., Tehran, 2001. Nicolas de Khanikoff, "Mémoire sur la partie méridionale de l'Asie centrale," *Recueil de voyages et de mémoires publié par la societé de géographie* 7, 1864, pp. 239-451. Mohan Lal, "A Brief Description of Herat," *J(R)ASB* 3, 1834, pp. 9-18. Jonathan L. Lee, *The "Ancient Supremacy," Bukhara, Afghanistan, and the Battle for Balkh, 1731-1901*, Leiden and New York, 1996. ʿAbd-Allāh Mehrabān, "Taḥqiq-e pirāmun-e ḥayāt-e ejtemāʿi wa siāsi-e Jamšidihā," *Melliathā-ye barādar* 3, 1983, pp. 34-37. Vladimir Minorsky, "Esquisse d'une histoire de Nadir-chah," *Publications de la Société des Etudes Iraniennes et de l'Art Persan* 10, 1934, pp. 1-46. Moḥammad-Ḥayāt Khan, *Ḥayāt-e afḡān*, Lahore, 1867; tr. Henry Priestly as *Afghanistan and Its Inhabitants*, Lahore, 1981. Moḥammad-K̲alil b. Dāwud Marʿaši, *Majmaʿ al-tawārik̲ dar tārik̲-e enqerāż-e Ṣafawiyya wa waqāyeʿ-e baʿd tā sāl-e 1207 hejri qamari*, ed. ʿAbbās Eqbāl, Tehran, 1983. Moḥammad-Kāẓem Marvi, *ʿĀlamārā-ye nāderi*, ed. Moḥammad Amin Riāḥi, 3 vols., Tehran, 1985. Moḥammad Taqi Lesān-al-Molk Sepehr, *Nāsek̲ al-tawārik̲*, ed. Jamšid Kayānfar, 3 vols., Tehran, 1998. E. Molloy, *Report on Herat*, National Archives of India, Foreign Dept. A-Pol-E, no. 317 of September 1883. G. C. Napier, *Memorandum on the Condition, Resources, etc. of the Perso-Afghan Border with Some Notes on the Herat Territory*, India Office Library, L/P & S/7/4, part 1, pp. 217-53, 1875. Moḥammad-Ebrāhim b. Zayn al-ʿĀbedin Naṣiri, *Dastur-e šahriārān, sālhā-ye 1105 tā 1110: pādšāhi-e Šāh Solṭān-Ḥosayn Ṣafawi*, ed. Moḥammad-Nāder Nasiri Moqaddam, Tehran, 1994. ʿAbd-al-Ḥosayn Navāʾi, *Nāder Šāh wa bāzmāndagān-aš, hamrāh bā nāmahā-ye salṭanati wa asnād-e siāsi wa edāri*, Tehran, 1989. Eldred Pottinger, *Memoir on the Country between Herat and Kabul, the Paropamisian Mountains and the River Amoo*, India Office Library, L/P & S/5/145 No. 7, Enc. 20, 1839. Lutz Rzehak and Walerija A. Pristschepowa, *Nomadenalltag for den Toren von Merw: Belutschen, Dschamschedi, Hazara*, Dresden, 1994. H. F. Schurmann, *The Mongols of Afghanistan: An Ethnography of the Moghôls and Related Peoples of Afghanistan*, The Hague, 1962. Charles Edwards Stewart, *The Aimak Tribes*, India Office Library, LPS-18-A53 Pt. 1, 1883, pp. 1-79. Edward Hamilton Stirling, *The Journals of Edward Stirling in Persia and Afghanistan*, ed. Jonathan Lee, Naples, 1991. R. L. Taylor, *A Tabular Statement of the Tribes Adjoining the Neighbourhood of Herat*, India Office Library, L/P & S/5/253, pp. 854-55. Nancy Tapper, "The Advent of Pashtun Maldars in North-Western Afghanistan," *BSO(A)S* 36, 1973, pp. 55-79. Armin Vámbéry, *Travels in Central Asia: The account of a Journey from Teheran across the Turkoman Desert . . . to Khiva, Bokhara, and Samarcand, Performed in the Year 1863*, London, 1864. Charles E. Yate, *Khurasan and Sistan*, Edinburgh and London, 1900; tr. Qodrat-Allāh Rowšani and Mehrdād Rahbari as *Safar-nāma-ye K̲orāsān wa Sistān*, Tehran, 1986. Idem, *Northern Afghanistan, or Letters from Afghan Boundary Commission*, Edinburgh and London, 1888, repr., London, 2003.

(CHRISTINE NOELLE-KARIMI)

JĀN MOḤAMMAD KHAN, AMIR ʿALĀʾI,

(b. Tehran, ca 1886; d. Tehran, 1951), brigadier general and commander of Khorasan army during the early Reżā Shah period. His father, Mirzā Aḥmad Khan Alāʾ-al-Dawla (q.v.), was a ranking state officer during the reigns of Nāṣer-al-Din Shah and Moẓaffar-al-Din Shah and held several prominent positions, including the governor of Tehran at the dawn of the Constitutional Revolution (Bāmdād, *Rejāl* I, pp. 89-92). After completing his primary education, Jān Moḥammad entered the Cossack School, where he graduated as an officer and eventually advanced to the rank of a colonel. In the 1921 coup d'etat, he was one of the officers serving under Reżā Khan and arrived in Tehran as a member of his entourage (Makki, I, p. 206). He was promoted to the rank of brigadier general and appointed as the commander of the ʿEšratābād military base, where all the politicians arrested after the coup were jailed. Subsequently, he was appointed as the commander of Erāq Infantry Brigade that was also stationed in ʿEšratābād. He frequently participated in battles aimed at the disarming of the tribes.

In 1924, Reżā Khan Sardār-e Sepah, who was at the same time the prime minister and minister of war, resigned due to certain disagreements that he had with the Majles representatives and left Tehran in protest. The military staged a demonstration in favor of Sardār-e Sepah and against the Majles, and Jān Moḥammad Khan, who was still the commander of the ʿEšratābād brigade, actively threatened the Majles and its deputies by staging a military maneuver in front of the Majles building at the head of his troops in full force (Bahār, II, p. 65). During the same year, he sent his brigade to the south and himself accompanied Sardār-e Sepah in the expedition against Shaikh Ḵazʿal, the Arab shaikh of Moḥammara, the present-day Ḵorram-Šahr (Reżā Shah Pahlavi, p. 7). A year later he became the commander of the Khorasan army (*laškar-e šarq*). As his first mission at this post, he set out to disarm the Turkmans, which he followed with such ruthlessness that many people left their homes and ran to the desert to save their lives (Yakrangiān, p. 374). Among his most cruel acts was the hanging of Sardār Moʿazzaz Bojnurdi along with his brother, his son-in-law, and a number of people working for him. Sardār Moʿazzaz was the governor of Bojnurd, who had adeptly ruled and kept in peace this extensive area on the border with Russia. For a whole century, the entire border in the Northeast had been guarded by his family and, since 1880, the government of Gorgān had been entrusted to them as well (Bahār, II, p. 230; ʿĀqeli, p. 793). Three months after arriving in Mashad, Jān Moḥammad Khan went to Bojnurd. Sardār Moʿazzaz received him warmly and also escorted him on his return trip to Mashad. Once they reached Mashad, Jān Moḥammad ordered the arrest of Sardār Moʿazzaz and his six companions and a few days later had them all hanged. On the same day, ten local leaders of Mashad and sixty-five Turkmen tribal chiefs were executed in Bojnurd and Mashad. Then immediately Jān Moḥammad proceeded to plunder the Sardār's property (Bahār, II, p. 240; ʿĀqeli, pp. 203, 794-95).

Jān Moḥammad continued his cruel bloodshed in Khorasan and the Torkaman Ṣaḥrā with impunity, with every day several people were executed upon his orders (Bahār, II, p. 239). He kept busy accumulating personal wealth at the expense of others and of attending to his official duties. State money was mishandled and the wages of the people working under him were not paid (Yakrangiān, p. 377). As a result, a revolt broke out in Marāva Tappa military base under the command of Captain Lahāk Khan, and the unpaid soldiers overpowered the cities of Darragaz, Qučān, and Širvān and set forth to attack Mashad. They announced the establishment of a republic and in Bojnurd killed the officers that had refused to join them by firing squad (Makki, IV, p. 120). Since it was clear that Jān Moḥammad was unable to stop the rebellion, a force was dispatched from Tehran under the command of Colonel Ruḥ-Allāh Jahānbāni who, reinforced by the air force, succeeded in defeating Lahāk Khan, who fled to Russia. Thereafter, Reżā Shah went to Mashad to investigate the causes of the rebellion personally. Upon arrival in Mashad, he replaced Jān Moḥammad by Brigadier General Amān-Allāh Jahānbāni as the commander of the Khorasan army. Jān Moḥammad was sent back to Tehran in disgrace, where he was incarcerated for some time (Hedāyat, p. 371) and eventually discharged in dishonor from the army. Reżā Shah confiscated all his assets and used them to pay the back wages of the officers in Khorasan. He also arrested and executed twelve people in Bojnurd who had cooperated with Lahāk Khan.

After his dishonorable discharge from the army, Jān Moḥammad started a farming business. He is described as an extremely excitable man with a harsh and cruel mentality, a characteristic reportedly displayed also by his father (Bāmdād, *Rejāl* I, p. 92).

Bibliography: Bāqer ʿĀqeli, *Šarḥ-e ḥāl-e rejāl-e siāsi wa neẓāmi-e moʿāṣer-e Irān*, 3 vols., Tehran, 2001, pp. 201-4, 793-95. Moḥammad-Taqi Bahār, *Tāriḵ-e moḵtaṣar-e aḥzāb-e siāsi-e Irān* II, Tehran, 1984. Mahdiqoli Hedāyat, *Ḵāṭerāt wa ḵaṭarāt*, 2nd ed., Tehran, 1965. Ḥosayn Makki, *Tāriḵ-e bist-sāla-ye Irān*, 4 vols., Tehran, 1979-84. Reżā Shah Pahlavi, *Safar-nāma-ye Ḵuzestān*, Tehran, 1976. M.-Ḥ. Yakrangiān, *Golgun Kafanān*, Tehran, 1947.

(BĀQER ʿĀQELI)

JANĀB (JENĀB) **DAMĀVANDI** (b. village of Aḥmadābād, Damāvand district, 1867; d. Aḥmadābād, 1973), popular name of Moḥammad Fallāḥi, a vocalist of the late Qajar period, who performed in religious assemblies. His father Mollā ʿAli, known as Mirzā-ye Moʿallem, was the personal tutor of Solṭān Morād Mirzā Ḥosām-al-Salṭana, a son of the crown prince ʿAbbās Mirzā.

Mollā ʿAli enrolled Moḥammad at the Ṣadr School in Tehran where, alongside his school work, he received training as a vocalist by Āqā Jaʿfar Lāhiji. There is not much information available about the first thirty years of his life, but what is known is that he gained the title *janāb* (see ALQĀB O ʿANĀWIN) during this period. He lived in era when the traditions and modes (*dastgāh*, q.v.) of Persian music were being transformed by the masters. Damāvandi associated with the Farāhāni brothers, Āqā Ḥosaynqoli and Mirzā ʿAbd-Allāh (qq.v.) and other masters of the time, including Ḥājj ʿAli-Akbar Khan Šahnāzi, Ḡolām-Ḥosayn Darviš Khan, Bāqer Khan, Ṭāherzāda, Eqbāl Āḏar, from each of whom he learned something different ("Yādvāra," p. 67).

Damāvandi's voice is preserved on records dating back to when records of Persian music were first being produced in Tehran, Tbilisi, London, and Paris (1906-15). In these early recordings Damāvandi has sung in the modes of *šur* (accompanied by Mirzā Asad-Allāh Khan on the *tār*), *moḵālef* (accompanied by Ḥosayn Khan on the *kamānča*), *šur-e dašti*, and *bayāt-e Eṣfahān* (accompanied by Āqā Ḥosaynqoli on the *tār*; Sepantā, p. 171). He also made a recording of the call to prayer (*aḏān*) and prayers (*monājāt*; catalogue number G.14.12596-95), which brought him his initial fame. He also made a number of recordings with ʿAli Akbar Šahnāzi on the *tār*, the first of which was when Šahnāzi was only fourteen years old (Sepantā, p. 143, n. 3).

Ḥasan Mašḥun has characterized Damāvandi's style of singing as the Ḵorāsāni style and has compared him to such masters as Sayyed Bāqer Jandaqi, Shaikh Ṭāher

Żiaʾ Reṯāʾi, Ḥāji Tāj Neišāburi, and ʿAli Khan Nāyeb-al-Salṭana (Mašḥun, p. 658). However, in a radio interview on 14 Dey 1350 Š./4 January1971, Damāvandi explained that he learned to sing the call to prayer from Sayyed Jaʿfar Lāhiji in Tehran and singing the repertoire of Persian music (*radif*) from Sayyed Abd-al-Raḥim Eṣfahāni in Isfahan (Mašḥun, p. 417). Despite the difficulty in precisely determining Damāvandi's style of singing from extant records, it can be said that it resembles the Ḵorāsāni style more closely than the Eṣfahāni style.

Damāvandi was buried in his birthplace of Aḥmadābād. He is remembered by his fellow villagers as a generous individual. He built a school in Aḥmadābād, which is still standing and is known as Ḵāna-ye Moʿallem (House of the Teacher). His works have not been reprinted. The Kowṯar House of Culture (Farhang-sarā-ye Kowṯar) in Damāvand commemorated the 30th anniversary of his death with a memorial on 4 Dey 1382 Š./ 24 December 2003 ("Yādvāra," pp. 66-67).

Bibliography: S. A. Mir ʿAlinaqi, "Janāb-e Damāvandi," in *Dāneš-nāma-ye Jahān-e eslām* X, pp. 810-11. Ḥasan Mašḥun, *Tāriḵ-e musiqi-e Irān*, Tehran, 1994. Sāsān Sepantā, *Tāriḵ-e tahawwol-e żabṭ-e musiqi dar Irān*, Isfahan, 1987. "Yādvāra-ye ostād-e āvāz-e Irān: Janāb Damāvandi," *Maqām* 7/11, 2004.

(S. A. MIR ʿALINAQI)

JANĀB. See ALQĀB WA ʿANĀWIN.

JAND, a medieval Islamic town on the right bank of the lower Jaxartes in Central Asia some 350 km from where the river enters the Aral Sea; hence the Aral often appears in geographical works as the "Sea of Jand."

The town is first mentioned by the geographers of the 10th century as an Oghuz (Ḡozz, q.v.) Turkish settlement. Nothing is known of its prior history. Soviet archeologists have suggested that there were "Hunno-Turkish" settlements in the region, perhaps re-fortified in the 10th century but certainly having a lineal descent from early times, especially as one of the three towns of the Oghuz Turks mentioned by Ebn Ḥawqal (q.v., fl. 10th cent.) is called al-Qarya al-ḥadiṯa "the New settlement," later known in Persian as 'Deh-e now' and in Turkish as 'Yengikent' (Ebn Ḥawqal, ed. Kramers, p. 512, tr. Kramers and Wiet, pp. 489-90; *Ḥodud al-ʿālam*, p. 122, commentary p. 371; cf. Tolstov, pp. 263-64). The site of Jand probably lay either near modern Qyzylorda (the Czarist Russian Perovsk) or at an old Kyrgyz cemetery lower down the river at Khorkhut, a station on the Orenburg-Tashkent railway, in either case now in the Kazakhstan Republic.

Jand and other nearby places were significant settlements of the Oghuz. Already in the l0th century, colonies of Muslim traders probably received there the products of the Inner Asian steppes and forestlands. Jand plays a role in the semi-legendary accounts of Seljuq (Saljuq) origins as the place where the eponymous founder Seljuq b. Duqāq became a Muslim. When the Seljuq family and their tribesmen moved south to Transoxania and Khorasan, the town became the seat of a rival branch of the Oghuz under the Yabghus (Barthold, *Turkestan*³, pp. 178, 257). Jand had at this time close links with Khwarazm (Ḵʷārazm; see Chorasmia) and its shahs. Bayhaqi (q.v., d. 1077) mentions a certain Yaʿqub Jandi, who had been a Khwarazsmhah diplomatic envoy to the Samanids at Samarqand (Samarkand) and was involved in the negotiations of the Ma'munid shahs with Maḥmud of Ghazna (r. 998-1030, see GHAZNAVIDS) in 1014 (Bayhaqi, ed. Fayyāż, pp. 911-12). At the time of Maḥmud's son Masʿud I (r. 1031-40), the yabghu of Jand, Abu'l-Fawāres Šāh Malek b. ʿAli, was the sultan's ally against the Saljuqs who were harrying Khorasan, and in 1038 Masʿud appointed him ruler of Khwarazm. But he only enjoyed this power for a few years, since he was expelled from his territories in 1043-44 by the victorious Saljuqs (Barthold, *Turkestan*³, pp. 297-303.)

Jand now entered on its period of greatest florescence, as a frontier outpost of the Saljuqs and then the Khwarazmshahs of Atsïz's line against the pagan Qïpchaqs, although these rulers often had to relinquish control to local chiefs. Thus the Saljuq Alp Arslān (q.v., r. 1063-72) had to lead an expedition to Jand in 1065. The Shah Atsïz used Jand as the base for a punitive expedition into the steppes in ca. 1133, but then lost the town and only recovered it in 1152. The Khwarazmshah's eldest son Il Arslān (q.v., d. 1172) was now appointed governor of Jand, an indication of its importance, and the latter's son, Tekiš (d. 1200) likewise held this office. Various incursions into the Qïpchaq steppe were launched from it, and it was in the course of one of these that Khwarazmian troops first clashed with Čengiz Khan's Mongols (see ČENGIZ KHAN, d. 1227), according to Nasavi (d. 1249-50) in 1215-16.

Jand had to surrender to the Mongols in 1220 but was nevertheless plundered. Čengiz's eldest son, Jochi (d. 1227) used it as the base for his attack on Gorgānj in Khwarazm the following year (Jovayni, tr. Boyle, I, pp. 83, 86-90; Barthold, *Turkestan*³, pp. 415-16). The geographer, Yāqut (d. 1229), visited Jand around this time (*Boldān* (Beirut) II, pp. 168-69; cf. Samʿāni, ed. Yamāni III, p. 350). He noted that its people were Hanafite (q.v.) in *maḏhab* (legal school) and that its famous poet and stylist was Yaʿqub b. Širin Jandi, who had been a pupil of Zamaḵšari (q.v., 1075-1144) in Khwarazm and a Khwarazmshah envoy to Bukhara and Samarqand in 1153.

Jand continued to enjoy modest prosperity under the Mongol Great Khans and the Chaghatayids (see CHAGHATAYID DYNASTY). The town appears on an early 14th-century Chinese map as Jan-di, but towards the end of the century it apparently ceased to exist.

Bibliography (in addition to that given in the text): C. E. Bosworth, "Djand," in *EI*² Suppl., pp. 244-46. S. P. Tolstov, *Auf den Spuren der altchoresmischen Kultur*, tr. O. Mehlitz, Berlin, 1953.

(C. EDMUND BOSWORTH)

JANDAQ, a town and rural district (*dehestān*) in the Ḵor and Biābānak district (*bakš*) of Nāʾin sub-province in the province of Isfahan (q.v.).

The rural district. The rural district of Jandaq is located south of Dašt-e Kavir (q.v.) and in the northern part of the Ḵor and Biābānak district. It is comprised of eleven villages and the town of Jandaq (Markaz-e āmār-e Irān, 1997, p. 6). The mountains of the rural district are part of the lone peaks of central Iran including, among others, Rašid Kuh (highest elevation 2,075 m), Zāluband (highest elevation 1,843 m), and Kalāta (highest elevation 1,726 m; Jaʿfari, I). A number of springs and natural wells are located at the foot of these mountains (Jaʿfari, I, p. 466). The seasonal Čāhgir River also passes through the rural district (*Farhang-e joḡrāfiāʾi*, LI, p. 3), which is also home to numerous stretches of sands (*rigzār*) and temporary farms (Ḥekmat Yaḡmāʾi, 1991, pp. 291, 293). The rural district is also home to a variety of flora, including *gaz* trees, *tāḡ*, *ānḡuza*, *qodduma*, *bālangu*, *esparza*, *āvišan*, *par-e siāvaš*, and *ḵākšir*, and fauna, such as foxes, jackals, mountain goats, *quč*, deer, rabbits, and pheasants (*Farhang-e joḡrāfiāʾi*, LI, pp. 2-10, LXI, pp. 5, 18).

Water for the rural district is obtained from subterranean channels (*qanāt*), deep and semi-deep wells, natural wells, and springs, while farming, gardening, herding, and rug weaving in the style of Nāʾin comprise the major economic activities (*Farhang-e joḡrāfiāʾi*, LI, p. 2). The main agricultural products include wheat, barley, cotton, *senjed*, and sunflower seeds as well as pomegranates, apricots, figs, grapes, almonds, pistachios, apples, berries, dates, alfalfa (*yonja*), and vegetables (*tarabār*; *Farhang-e joḡrāfiāʾi*, LI, pp. 2-3, 7).

According to the 1996 national census, the population of Jandaq's villages comprised of 297 households (or about 1,500-1,600 persons; Markaz-e āmār-e Irān, 1997, p. 6). Its inhabitants are Persian speaking Shiʿite Muslims (*Farhang-e joḡrāfiāʾi*, LI, p. 2).

The town. At an elevation of 980 m, the town of Jandaq is located in the northwestern part of the district, approximately 110 km northwest of Ḵor. With a desert climate, it is located on the southern edge of Dašt-e Kavir, approximately 8 km east of Piškuh and 9 km southwest of Godār-e Jandaq. According to the Synoptic Station of Ḵor and Biābānak, the town's highest temperature has been recorded at 46.6 degrees Celsius in the summer month of Mordād (July-August) and its lowest temperature has been recorded at 6.6 degree Celsius in the winter month of Esfand (February-March; Sāzmān-e hawā-šenāsi-e kešvar, 1996-97). The average annual precipitation is 45.3 mm (Sāzmān-e hawāšenāsi-e kešvar, p. 190). During rainfall, the Vāza dam, located 6 km south of the town, works to increase the level of water in the subterranean channels (*Farhang-e joḡrāfiāʾi*, LI, p. 2; Goli Zavāra, p. 32). Jandaq is also home to lead and copper mines (*Asnād-e maʿāden-e Irān*, pp. 89-90).

In Mehr 1374 Š./October 1995, Jandaq was officially recognized as a town, and, according to the 1996 national census, its population was 4,068 (Markaz-e āmār-e Irān, 1997, p. 74).

The monuments of Jandaq include Jandaq Castle (or Fortress of Ardbil), which seems to date back to the Sasanian period, and which is known as the prison of Anuširvān. (Ḥekmat-Yaḡmāʾi, 1974, pp. 16-19; Idem, 1991, pp. 73-80; Ḥaqiqat, p. 351).

Jandaq was a part of Yazd until the reign of Fatḥ-ʿAli Shah Qājār (r. 1797-1834, q.v.), but during the last decade of his reign it was subsumed under the province of Kumes/Qumes (approximately equivalent to the province of Semnān; ibid.; Honar Yaḡmāʾi, p. 117; Ḥakim-al-Mamālek, p. 48).

Today, despite modern renovations, the town has a traditional look and structure (for a detailed survey of Jandaq, see M. Bādanj).

Bibliography: Asnād-e maʿāden-e Irān 1300-1332 Š., ed. Mahšid Laṭifiniā, Tehran, n.d. Maʿṣuma Bādanj, "Jandaq," in *Dāneš-nāma-ye jahān-e eslām* XI, 2007, pp. 29-33. *Farhang-e joḡrāfiāʾi-e ābādihā-ye kešvar-e jomhuri-e eslāmi-e Irān*, Tehran, n.d. Ḡolām-Reżā Goli Zavāra, *Simā-ye Nāʾin: gowhar-e kavir*, Tehran, 1994. ʿAlinaqi b. Esmāʿil Ḥakim-al-Mamālek, *Ruz-nāma-ye safar-e Ḵorāsān*, Tehran, 1977. ʿAbd-al-Rafiʿ Ḥaqiqat, *Tāriḵ-e Qumes*, Tehran, 1983. Sven Anders Hedin, tr. Parviz Rajabi, *Kavirhā-ye Irān*, Tehran, 1976. ʿAbd-al-Karim Ḥekmat Yaḡmāʾi, *Jandaq: Rustā-i kohan bar karān-e kavir*, Tehran, 1974. Idem, *Bar sāḥel-e kavir-e namak*, Tehran, 1991. Esmāʿil Honar Yaḡmāʾi, *Jandaq wa Qumes dar awāḵer-e dawra-ye Qājār*, Tehran, 1984. ʿAbbās Jaʿfari, *Gitāšenāsi-e Irān*, Tehran, 1989-2000. Markaz-e āmār-e Irān, *Šenās-nāma-ye ābādihā-ye kešvar, ostān-e Eṣfahān, šahrestān-e Nāʾin*, Tehran, 1997. Sāzmān-e Asnād-e Melli-e Irān, n.p., 1997. Sāzmān-e hawā-šenāsi-e kešvar, *Sāl-nāma-ye āmāri-e hawā-šenāsi 1996-1997*, Tehran, 1999. Wezārat-e Kešvar, *Našriya-ye tāriḵ-e taʾsis-e ʿanāṣer-e taqsimāti ba hamrāh-e šomāra-ye moṣawwabāt-e ān*, Tehran, 2003.

(M. BADANJ)

JANGALI MOVEMENT (1915-20), a movement that took shape in the aftermath of the 1905-11 Constitutional Revolution, under the leadership of Mirzā Kuček Khan Jangali (q.v.), in response to the period of political decay brought about by the advent of World War I and the occupation of Iran by Anglo-Russian and Ottoman troops.

POLITICAL BACKGROUND

After the suppression of the Constitutional Revolution by Tsarist forces in 1911, some 17,500 Russian troops were stationed in northern Iran. They formed, together with the Qajar's Cossack Brigade that was officered by Russians, the backbone of the newly established Russian control of the northern provinces and again exerted influence on Persian affairs. The British, however, are alleged to have exerted influence through the Anglophile Abu'l-Qāsem Khan Nāṣer-al-Molk. The Qajar politician had been educated at Oxford (1879-81), and acted between

1910 and 1914 as the regent of Aḥmad Shah. In addition, the gendarmerie (q.v.), known as Žāndāmeri-e dawlati, which had been established in 1910 with the help of Swedish officers to serve as highway patrol and rural police force, was considered to be an instrument of the British. The Anglo-Russian relations were still defined in terms of their secret agreement of 1907 that had divided Persia into British and Russian spheres of influence and defined Tehran as a neutral zone. After the outbreak of World War I, Britain and Russia pressured the Qajar government to declare war on the Central Powers (Germany, Austria-Hungary, Ottoman Empire). Yet Persia declared its neutrality on 1 November 1914 because the outbreak of the war unleashed political forces that tried to secure the constitution.

A number of factors allowed for the re-emergence of the constitutionalists. The first was the withdrawal of a large number of Russian troops in August 1914 for the purpose of reinforcing the Caucasian front (Nikitin, p. 38), while pursuing a less oppressive policy in Iran. A contributory factor was the end of Nāṣer-al-Molk's regency with the coronation of Solṭān Aḥmad Mirzā on 21 July 1914. During the crisis period of 1911 to 1914 the regent had clamped down on the Democratic Party, and by 1914 the Party was on the verge of collapse. Under Aḥmad Shah's reign, the more moderate and liberal-minded statesman, Mostawfi-al-Mamālek, was appointed as prime minister and formed his cabinet in Tehran. On 5 December 1914, the Third Parliament was finally inaugurated and started its work in early January 1915. Now Ottoman and German intrigue and propaganda entered the scene because the parliament soon became an important center of anti-Entente (Britain, France, Russia) activity and pro-German agitation increased (Dailami, 1994, pp. 28-31). It was in the wake of these events, in early 1915, that Russia and Britain drew closer together and came to a full accord with regard to Persia. They signed a new secret agreement in which the neutral zone was added to the British sphere of influence and in return Russia was given a free hand in the northern provinces. Britain no longer opposed Russian efforts to bring those provinces under its control (Miroshnikov, pp. 52-53).

In Tehran, German and Ottoman agitation reached its height in the summer of 1915. German diplomats had established firm contact with leading politicians, many of whom were members of the Democratic Party. A hysterically pro-German atmosphere was created in the capital. In the autumn of 1915, the Germans stepped up their pressure and prepared for the final stage. Some 2,000 gendarmes gathered in Tehran and demanded their unpaid wages. A large number of armed recruits camped outside Tehran, following in the footsteps of the constitutional revolutionaries, as a sign of their readiness to attack the capital. Arms and ammunition were smuggled into Tehran, and plans were made to disarm the Qajar's Cossack Brigade (FO 248/1120: Marling's memo, "Turkish soldiers in Tehran," 22 Oct. 1915; cf. Miroshnikov, p. 53). The Democratic Party increased their pressure on the premier, Mostawfi-al-Mamālek, who began negotiating a Persian-German treaty with the German minister Prinz Heinrich zu Reuss (1879-1942).

Russia, alarmed by a possible Persian declaration of war on the Entente, dispatched a large force under General Nikolai Baratov (1864-1932), and one of its divisions quickly marched to Karaj, thus threatening Tehran. Mostawfi-al-Mamālek decided to move the government and the shah to Isfahan (Bahār, pp. 17-18). This decision triggered the famous migration (*mohājerat*) of the deputies and political activists, the Swedish-officered gendarmerie, which had eventually sided with Germany after the outbreak of the war, and most German, Austrian and Ottoman diplomats, as well as a section of the population. They moved south, leaving Tehran for Qom, yet in the end Mostawfi and the shah remained in Tehran. The emigrants (*mohājerun*) declared war on the Entente, and fought until early 1917 when the Russian army dispersed them in Mesopotamia (Gehrke, tr., I, pp. 228-80).

Subsequent to the suppression of the constitutionalists in 1911, Russian policy had indicated that Russia hoped to secure long-term control of the northern provinces. Russians bought vast tracts of land from the Iranians, and the policy of settling Russian peasants in the Caucasus was extended to include Iran. Russian exports doubled, and their consulate collected taxes for its government (Kazemzadeh, pp. 676-77; Entner, pp. 41, 57). The cornerstone of Russian power was its army and, on the whole, Russian policy in Gilān can be characterized as consisting of little diplomacy and much brute force through which Russia had come to gain almost total control of Gilān's administration during the crisis period from 1911 to 1914 (Kazemzadeh, p. 676). However, the approaching war presented new problems. Russia began to concentrate troops on her Ottoman frontier in the Caucasus, and moved her occupation forces from northern Iran. Moreover, the Russian authorities were instructed to adopt a more relaxed attitude towards the population whose discontent the army could barely control. But Gilān's administration completely collapsed when in August 1914 the Russian forces left for the Caucasus. Chaos ensued, and even the Qajar governors refused to uphold the law and enforce order without the protection of the Russian army. Disobedience began in mild forms. There were collective complaints about landlords and Russian agents, and a few industrial strikes took place. But by the beginning of 1915, Gilān was the scene of widespread unrest. Peasants and city dwellers were firing their weapons at the few hundred Russian soldiers still stationed in the province, while even more forces were called to the Caucasian front (FO 248/1117: Resht news, 4 April 1915).

THE ORIGINS OF THE JANGALI MOVEMENT

Mirzā Kuček Khan became a revolutionary leader because he adapted to this revolutionary situation, exploiting rather than initiating fortuitous circumstances. In his youth he had been a religious student, but in 1908 he abandoned his religious career and joined the constitutionalist social-democrats. Already in 1909, he was a junior commander of the revolutionary force that attacked and captured Tehran, and two years later he was forced into internal exile. Shortly before the court's migration from Tehran to Qom, in late summer of 1915, Kuček Khan returned to Gilān when the activities of the Jangalis began. Their first group took to Gilān's forests (*jangal*) and declared that they intended to free the province of the Russian army (FO 248/1117: Maclaren to Ramsden, 19 Nov. 1915). The Jangalis quickly distinguished themselves from other bandits by trying and executing criminals. They financed themselves by abducting wealthy individual, in particular landowners, to ransom them for large sums of money.

In their dealings with peasants, they were careful to be scrupulously fair and make full payments in any transaction (Dailami, 1994, p. 44; Kazemi, 1991, p. 106). The earliest known Jangali operation took place in October 1915 when the governor of Rašt put a certain landowner, ʿAbd-al-Razzāq Šafti, in charge of the district of Pasiḵān with a view to preventing the Jangalis from approaching Rašt. Subsequently Šafti's men were attacked and defeated by the Jangalis. Those who survived fled in disarray to Rašt. Subsequently, another big landowner, Żarḡām-al-Salṭana's brother, Šojāʿ-al-Divān, was given 200 men and sent to the forests of Fumān where he was defeated on two occasions and his men were disarmed (FO 248/1117: Maclaren to Ramsden, 19 Nov. 1915).

In the meantime, with Tehran on the brink of falling into German hands, Rašt was made the principal base of the Russian army and thousands of troops constantly passed through that city on their way from Baku to Qazvin whence operations against the Migrants were to be directed. Once the Russians were back and established in Rašt, a force of 550 Russian soldiers and 50 men of the Qajar's Cossack Brigade set out to suppress the Jangalis. That expedition failed miserably too and the Jangalis emerged victorious.

Following the defeat of the Russian expedition the Jangalis distributed clandestine broadsheets (*šab-nāmas*) in Rašt, declaring their intention to attack and capture the city. The Russians, who now had more troops at their disposal, effectively declared Martial law and in their attempt to clear Rašt of anti-Russian elements, some 160 houses were burned to the ground (FO 248/1149: Resht news, 8 Jan. 1916).

At about the same time a large number of Russian troops from Rašt, Anzali, Manjil and Zanjān were sent on an expedition against the Jangalis, who were heavily defeated in January 1916, but Baratov's forces stopped just short of completely destroying them. According to Kuček Khan, if the Russian force had remained another few days in the region, the Jangalis would have had to surrender as many had frozen to death and the others were subsisting on a diet of grass and roots (Dailami, 1994, p. 46). Nevertheless, they regrouped within a few weeks, pursuing a defensive policy until 1917 when the February Revolution in Russia allowed them to emerge from the forests. Prior to that their force was composed of numerous petty-bourgeois city dwellers, fishermen from Anzali, itinerant seasonal agricultural workers, petty-landowners who were constantly under pressure by the bigger and more influential landowners, Turkish escapee prisoners of war, perhaps even a good number of Iranian émigrés from the Caucasus, but most important of all, the mass of poor and middle peasantry (Dailami, 1994, p. 51). To the above, we have to add the perennial presence of Bolshevik agitators from the Caucasus in Gilān.

THE JANGALIS AND THE AGRARIAN QUESTION

One of the shortcomings of historiography on the Jangali movement is the ignorance that concerns the activities of the Bolsheviks and the peasantry who both in fact continued to be present in Gilān. Although these have been studied in works on the Constitutional Revolution, their presence in the Jangali movement has been overlooked. Following the occupation of Gilān by the Russian army, Russian commercial activity, especially that of Khostaria, extended from industry into agriculture. Active Russian acquisition of land, the Russian's encouragement of Gilāni landowners to become Russian subjects, and their subsequent efforts to please them by suppressing the peasantry and reinforcing the old 'feudal' regime, provided the backdrop for an alliance of the peasantry, the small working class and the urban petty-bourgeoisie which included the fishermen, the city artisans and small producers whose economic position had been undermined by the great influx of Russian goods into Gilān (Abrahamian, 1979, pp. 391, 394). And it was their joint struggles that were to dominate the scene after the outbreak of the war. The collapse of administration in Gilān brought about economic stagnation, social and political insecurity and demographic instability. At this stage discontent in the countryside was to be directed against Russian interest and 'Russian agents' and once again Tāleš, the hotbed of peasant rebellions, was to be the scene of the most violent unrest. At the end of January 1915, in retaliation for the activities of a Russian agent, "a more than usually disreputable specimen of his class," the factories of Lianozov and Khoshtaria were burned down. (FO 248/1117: Resht news, 31 Jan. 1915). The Russian army's retaliation caused the dislocation of the peasant population (who fled for fear of reprisals) in many parts of Gilān. Russian efforts to maintain order usually resulted in more chaos. Every single expeditionary force, both Russian and Iranian, which had set out to fight the Jangalis, made the pillaging of villages its first priority. The state of chaos in Gilān also allowed the landowners to pillage the countryside. A typical example was that of Żarḡām who pillaged the whole district of Fumān in November 1915 (FO 248/1117: Resht news, 24 Dec. 1915).

Russian efforts pursuing the policy of annexing Gilān, created even more discontent and contributed to the state of chaos. For instance, when a Russian government delegation arrived in Gilān to purchase land, a certain Russian subject took it upon himself to sell them a village that did not belong to him. In this case the peasants who owned the village shot the Russian subject and in retaliation the

Russian consul had seven of the peasants shot and the village burnt down. The remainder of the peasants fled and abandoned the village (FO 248/1149: Maclaren to Marling, 4 Sep. 1916).

The spread of disease among livestock and specially the prevalence of cholera were also contributing factors. The little evidence that exists reveals the great extent of the problem. In December 1915, the number of fatalities in one small village between Rašt and Anzali was recorded to be 36. By April 1916, cholera caused the death of 15 people daily in the Fumān area alone (FO 248/1117: Resht news, 4 Dec. 1915; FO 248/1149: Resht news, 15 April 1916). The stage was thus set for the rapid growth of the Jangali movement, and the Russian factor resulted in an anti-imperialist alliance between the aforementioned classes.

The Gilāni revolutionaries, because of the Russian domination of the cities, inevitably based themselves in the countryside. The great mass of peasants were to form most of the Jangali fighting force, and Kuček Khan, despite the fact that he led an anti-imperialist struggle, also inevitably fostered an agrarian movement. The experience of the Constitutional Revolution shows that he was well aware of the political characteristics of the countryside where the peasantry joined the city artisans and the petty traders in the struggle. The Jangalis immediately set out to hold wealthy individuals to ransom and extracted very large sums of money from them. Apart from a few exceptions, all of those individuals were landowners. Most of them were well known reactionary figures of the constitutional period. As it later became obvious, these actions by the Jangalis were not merely a temporary measure but were part of a long-term revolutionary policy. Those landowner-politicians who actively opposed the Jangalis, were their special targets. The Jangalis also levied tax on the landowners and at the same time tried to force them not to pay tax either to the Russian consul or the governor general of Gilān. After their initial defeat in January 1916, the Jangalis had quickly regrouped and grown into a partisan army. By December 1916, their influence had extended to the gates of Rašt and they levied tax even on lands that were on the outskirts of the provincial capital (FO 248/1149: Resht news, 3 Dec. 1916).

The landowners, who in any case had refrained from paying any proper tax since 1906, eventually declared to the authorities in Gilān that they would not pay their taxes unless the Jangalis were completely suppressed (FO 248/1149: Resht news, 18 Nov. 1916). Ever since the rise of the Jangalis they had financed and raised a number of expeditionary forces against them. All of them had failed. Finally the Russian consul, the governor general and a number of principle landowners of Gilān gathered together to orchestrate their efforts against the Jangalis and they even considered a second attempt at assassinating Kuček Khan, but on the whole they failed to produce a solution (FO 248/1149: Resht news, 10 July 1916).

Apart from holding landowners to ransom, the Jangalis also threatened to carry off the crops of others if the landowners refused to pay (FO 248/1149: Maclaren to Marling, 10 July 1916). Later on the landowners were treated even more harshly. Maclaren once reported, "180,000 tomans have already been collected by the band at Lahijan. They had prepared various instruments of torture and informed their victims that if money was not forthcoming without delay, the instruments would be employed. The threat was sufficient and instruments were not required" (FO 248/1168: Maclaren to Marling, decipher 41, 28 Dec. 1917).

The landowners were not, however, treated in a much better manner by the Iranian and Russian authorities. First of all, the anti-Jangali expeditions had not refrained from looting the properties of some landowners on their way to fight the Jangalis. The leaders of those expeditions also continued, as in the pre-1905 era, to treat even the landowners as absolute subjects. Frequent incidents reminded the men of property that they still had no legal status vis-à-vis the elite of the country who treated them as absolute subjects of a despotic monarchy. The case of a certain Sardār Eqtedār, an aristocratic governor who arrived from Māzandarān in July 1916 to raise another expeditionary force against the Jangalis, is a typical example. Maclaren reported, "It appears that Serdar Iktidar on leaving Shahsavar, had telegraphed to the deputy governor of Lahijan . . . to collect 100 horses for him. The horses were not ready and it so infuriated his excellency that after abusing Ḥāji Emin-ed Diwan, Muftakhar-ul Molk and Salar Muayyed, three of the largest and most distinguished landowners of the district who had come to present themselves to him, he ordered them to be beaten. On representations of some of his friends, however, he commuted the beating to a fine of 1500 tomans which was paid on the spot" (FO 248/1149: Maclaren to Marling, 10 July 1916).

General Baratov too, whose army had been subjected to rapid disintegration in the course of late 1916 and 1917, refrained from taking decisive action against the Jangalis. He also mistreated the landowners. For instance, Żarḡām, who continued to resist the Jangalis, was arrested by the Russian troops and General Baratov did not release him until he extracted a large sum of money from him (FO 248/1168: Maclaren to Marling, deciphers 4 and 22, 6 March and 16 July 1917, resp.). Eventually the landowners, "seeing that they would be totally ruined if they did not come to some arrangement" with the Jangalis, decided to approach Kuček Khan and submit to his authority with the hope of convincing him "to leave them something to live on." They organized a delegation and engaged in fruitless negotiations with the Jangalis (ibid.) who continued to carry out their policy even further and in more radical forms. By the spring of 1917, when the Jangalis were in control of most of Gilān, they confiscated the land of bigger landowners who continued to resist them.

Among those landowners who lost their lands and all their property, were the aristocrats Amin-al-Dawla, and his wife princess Faḵr-al-Dawla. Amin-al-Dawla was arrested after his peasants complained to the revolutionaries. Subsequently he was tried in a revolutionary court, fined 75,000 tomans and was imprisoned. His lands were confiscated and distributed among his peasants. Fak̲r-al-Dawla was treated in a similar manner. She managed to escape arrest by the Jangalis, but a revolutionary court confiscated all her land and property in absentia and distributed them among peasants (FO 248/1168: Maclaren to Marling, decipher 20, 15 June 1917; decipher 32, 20 August 1917; Maclaren to Scott, 29 Oct. 1917; Maclaren to Marling, 30 Oct. 1917). Indeed the Jangali movement had a prominent anti-landlord character. One of the major reasons for its success in its early years was the lack of will and decisiveness displayed by the landowning counter-revolutionary establishment (Tamimi-Ṭāleqāni).

THE 1917 RUSSIAN REVOLUTION

As a result of the Jangali's activities in the countryside, signs of internal conflict appeared. Two reactionary heroes of the Constitutional Revolution, Ḥāji Mirzā Moḥammad-Reżā, the leader of the provincial *anjoman*, and Sālār Fāteḥ, a commander of the insurgent forces in Gilān–abandoned the new revolutionaries.

General Baratov could not maintain the high concentration of Russian troops that he had used to suppress the Jangalis in January 1916. Most of his forces would soon leave Gilān to continue the Russian offensive against the Ottomans. Apart from having to maintain control of the areas taken from the nationalist forces (Hamadan and Kermanshah), Baratov's army had to push further west on the Iranian front to put more pressure on the Ottoman forces that were about to capture Kut al-Amara in Mesopotamia. But soon, in late 1916, Kut al-Amara fell and the groundwork for the return of the nationalist forces to Iran was prepared. In June 1916, once again, the Emigrants appeared at Kermanshah, defeated the Russians and advanced up to and captured Hamadan. The Russian forces retreated to Qazvin where they were to be joined by more troops from Gilān. In the province, the main effect of the second Migrant advance was that both by sending support to the Jangalis and by engaging large numbers of Russian troops, it greatly contributed to their rise to prominence. In the autumn of 1916, just under 1,000 men were engaged in fighting the Jangalis. Most belonged to the Qajar's Cossack Brigade who had arrived from Tehran, and only 150 Russian soldiers participated in those operations (FO 248/1149: Resht news, 9 Sep. 1916; 23 Sep. 1916; 3 Dec. 1916; 23 Dec. 1916).

In December 1916, the last expedition of that period was heavily defeated and as a result the anti-Jangali forces in Gilān disintegrated. The few hundred men of the Cossack Brigade remained, but were confined to their barracks with the consent of the prime minister in Tehran. Rumors that the Jangalis were about to attack and capture the city caused great panic in Rašt (FO 248/1168: decipher 2, 31 Jan. 1917; decipher 3, 13 March 1917).

Up to the beginning of this period the Jangalis on the whole had pursued a defensive policy and had only tried to survive. The new offensive was launched with a view to gaining and consolidating new territories. From January 1917, the Jangalis began to disarm the big and influential landowners and installed their own representatives as government officials wherever their influence was extended. Soon the February Revolution in Russia added to the encouragement that the advance of the nationalist forces into Iran had given to the Jangali movement. The Russians, in the wake of that revolution, established friendly relations with the Jangalis and signed an agreement with them that promised the eventual evacuation of their troops from Gilān. From then on, apart from a few insignificant incidents, even Tsarist diplomatic and military authorities refrained from confronting the revolutionaries. A little later, the return of Ottoman forces to Iranian Azerbaijan and their capture of Tabriz in May 1917 also facilitated their progress.

The Jangalis established themselves in Gilān in a surprisingly short time. Maclaren, the British Acting vice-consul, was probably too late in reporting in August that they had become "to all intents and purposes the masters of Gilān" (FO 248/1168: decipher 32, 20 Aug. 1917).

Throughout 1917, as the influence of the Jangalis increased, all governors and deputy governors, except those who had a history of collaboration with the Jangalis, were replaced. By August, the only exceptions to the rule were the General Governor and the Kārgozār, who as mere official figures, completely submitted to the Jangalis and worked under the supervision of their representatives. After the October Revolution in Russia, they too, as the last remaining officials of the Tehran government, were turned out of Gilān (FO 248/1168: decipher 32, 20 Aug. 1917; decipher 35, 28 Nov. 1917). At the same time the Jangalis began to disarm and bring under control those landlords who were still resisting them. This process continued throughout 1917 and found even more radical dimensions after the October Revolution (FO 248/1168: decipher 20, 15 June 1917; decipher 35, 28 Nov. 1917).

Significant social and political changes were brought about as a result of the rise of the Jangalis. Once again, popular participation in political activity increased. Public meetings were organized by a variety of political forces and *anjoman*s were set up in the towns. There are signs that these were also set up in the countryside. Confiscation and distribution of land in Lašta-nešā had in fact been the result of collective efforts on the part of local peasants of the area who had gone so far as publishing a proclamation in Rašt about the oppression of their landlord, Amin-al-Dawla. A number of newspapers also appeared in the province, the most important and long lasting of them was the organ of the Jangalis, entitled *Jangal*.

In 1917, the Jangalis carried out important reforms. They exempted the peasants (for the time being) from paying tax or dues. They took over and supervised the distribution of water to farms, a perennial source of quarrel between peasants and landlords (FO 248/1168: *Jangal*, No. 2, 17 June 1917; decipher 18, 21 May 1917; decipher 22, 16 July 1917). These measures encouraged productivity and while famine ruled in the rest of Iran, agricultural production in Gilān reached an all time high. The Jangalis in fact sent rice to famine-stricken Tehran, as well as actively feeding the besieged city of Baku in Russian Azerbaijan. The peasants also acquired legal rights and had their complaints attended to by Jangali courts that extended their services to the urban population as well (Dailami, 1994, p. 39).

In the towns more reforms were carried out in the government departments including the police force which was completely taken over. By the end of 1917, out of their revenue of 1,000,000 tomans, extracted from landlords and government departments, the Jangalis were paying 21,000 tomans per month as wages to their employees (FO 248/1168: decipher 35, 28 Nov. 1917). The rest was spent on the revolutionary army.

Throughout 1917, the Jangali movement was hampered by internal dissent. As an anti-imperialist front that included a whole array of political elements, it could not completely fulfill the aspirations of its radical activists. While the right wing of the movement under Ḥāji Aḥmad Kasmāʾi (a disgruntled merchant) did not wholeheartedly oppose the central government, the left wing did, and refused to compromise. Throughout 1917, Kuček Khan stubbornly kept the main Jangali forces in the forests and refused to establish himself in Rašt. Had he done so, it would have meant that he had compromised the objectives of his movement. He was firstly concerned about the presence of Russian troops that the Provisional Government in Petrograd refused to withdraw. Even after establishing good relations with the Russians in Rašt, and signing an agreement with them that promised the evacuation of Russian troops, and despite their efforts to convince him to take up the governorship of Gilān, Kuček Khan categorically refused to leave the forest.

When the Jangalis emerged from the forests in 1917, as a result of the relaxation of Russian hostilities, they adopted the Committee of *Etteḥād-e eslām* (Union of Islam) that appears to have survived the ravages of the constitutional times, as their political arm, when the Tsarist army suppressed the Gilāni *anjoman*s in late 1911. The extent of Kuček Khan's involvement with the Committee is not clear. As it turned out he was no fan of the Turks. The radical Jangali, Esmāʿil Khan, nevertheless wrote that Kuček acquired much support through the adoption of such a populist title for the Jangalis' political organization. He had acquired a "political front" (Jangali, p. 68). The Committee was, however, purged of a number of Muslim clerics before it was set to work. Nevertheless, it was dominated by the right wing (Fak̲rāʾi, p. 96).

The newspaper *Jangal* reflected the ideas of the Committee. The writers of the paper were very much preoccupied with the war situation and the military invasion of Iran by the Entente armies, but there was very little Turkophilia in their writings. The Committee denounced Russia for continuing to occupy northern Iran with the excuse of an Ottoman threat. It also denounced the aristocracy and corrupt officials who opposed reform. It even supported Aḥmad Shah until late 1917, when the Bolshevik Revolution brought about radical change into Iranian politics. Of course, at the time this was the policy of all insurgent Iranians, such as Sayyed Ḥasan Taqizādeh, the leader of the Democratic Party, and Ḥaydar Khan ʿAmu-og̲li, the most radical figure in Iranian politics of the time (Dailami, 2004, p. 96). While the Jangalis demanded elections to reopen the suppressed Majles, they did not cease pushing for government reforms. There is no sign that any faction of the Jangalis hoped to establish an Islamic theocracy in Gilān or in Iran (Dailami, forthcoming). No Muslim cleric was ever to play a role in the leadership of the movement. Nor were the clerics given a privileged position in the Gilāni society or in the movement. Some were even persecuted and imprisoned by the Jangalis (Afšār, 1984, pp. 363-64).

The radicals of the movement went along with the populism of Etteḥād-e eslām Committee. They carried out their agrarian policy with great vigor but played down their underpinning ideological doctrines for the time being. What kept the movement together were the military occupation of the Iranian territory and the common anti-imperialist aspirations of the revolutionaries.

In practice, the Jangalis defied the Shah and the central government but this was not the attitude of the entire movement. For the time being, however, it was the Russians who had to be dealt with. In 1917, the process of the disintegration of the Russian army reached a sensitive point. The signs of this process were visible ever since Baratov's army had entered northern Iran. Mutinies were reported as early as the autumn of 1915 and the Russian authorities were never in sufficient control of their troops. By late 1916, Russian policy in Gilān was practically abandoned and in the wake of the February Revolution, there was an eruption of political activity among Russian soldiers. The governor of Rašt reported to Tehran that "Russian subjects and soldiers" participated in political meetings "with such strange ferocity that even their leaders were unable to restrain them" (*Jangal*, No. 3, 24 June 1917, p. 4).

In 1917, a Russian 'Executive Committee' was formed in Gilān that included Russians, Georgians and Azerbaijanis. In May of that year, the Committee, independently of General Baratov, sent a delegation to Fumān to meet and fraternize with the Jangalis. It was led by the Georgian officer Polkovnik (Major) Dzhardzhadze, and included two Azeris, and was accompanied by the Jangalis' representative in Rašt, ʿEzzat-Allāh Hedāyat. They met Kuček Khan and three other Jangali leaders at one of the schools that had been established for peasant children. They celebrated a new relationship, exchanged presents, and in Rašt the Executive Committee "praised Mirza Kuchik Khan in the most extravagant terms . . . [and declared] that he ought to be made Governor General of Gilān" (FO 248/1203: decipher 18, 21 May 1917). The negotiations were followed up in August when the two sides agreed that Russian evacuation could be delayed to prevent a British takeover of Gilān and allow the Jangalis to strengthen themselves further (Dailami, 1994, pp. 42-43).

RADICALISM AND THE CRISIS OF NATIONALISM

Shortly after the October Revolution in Russia, the Bolsheviks declared the Anglo-Russian agreement of 1907 null and void. They also promised the withdrawal of Russian troops from Iranian territory. They immediately tried to enter into official diplomatic negotiations with the Persian government. They signed the Brest-Litovsk treaty with Germany that allowed for the actual realization of Russian evacuation. All of the above was in line with the aspirations of the Iranian patriots who had campaigned and fought for that since the outbreak of World War I (Dailami, 1999, pp. 63-65). The Iranian socialist leader, Sayyed Ḥasan Taqizādeh, was prompted to send a telegram to the Petrograd Soviet, thanking the Bolsheviks for their actions with regard to Iran.

The Jangalis, too, praised the Bolsheviks for their respect for Iranian sovereignty. In the immediate wake of the October Revolution a number of changes took place in Gilān. First of all, the Jangalis took steps towards monopolizing political power. Some political organizations (such as the terrorist groups) were suppressed while others were absorbed into the movement. It was also at that stage that the Jangalis officially turned against the monarchy. Also at that stage came the formal demand for division of land among peasants. And finally, the Jangalis were to strike a firm alliance with the Bolsheviks in Gilān.

Within the Iranian context the Jangalis relations with the government and the landowners, are most important. While they took over virtually all government departments, their persecution of landowners intensified (FO 248/1168: Maclaren, report 35, 25 Nov. 1917).

In early 1918, the Jangalis sent emissaries to various parts of Iran and southern Russia to rally support and negotiate with potential allies. They recruited volunteers for the partisan army, gathered arms in Tehran and formed numerous secret cells in the capital for the purpose of seizing power.

Indeed the Jangalis intended to move on Tehran. Esmāʿil Khan Jangali, the radical and prominent leader of the movement confirms that the Gilāni partisans had the intention of moving on Tehran. However, he does not explain how they wanted to seize power. The little evidence that is available suggests that they hoped to capture Tehran in the same way that they had during the Constitutional Revolution—that is with the collaboration of other forces such as the Azerbaijanis and the Baḵtiāris (Dailami, 1994, pp. 102-6), but the Azeris had been suppressed by the Ottomans and the Bakhtiaris were under the influence of the British. Soon, in a letter to the Turkish diplomat and alleged master-spy ʿObayd-Allāh Efendi, Kuček Khan wrote that he considered the prerequisite to the seizure of power in Tehran an alliance of Gilān, Iranian Azerbaijan, and Caucasian Bolsheviks (Dailami, 1992, p. 55).

By early 1918, the Jangalis had formed a revolutionary army that has been estimated to have numbered between 3,000 and 8,000 men, but the turn of events did not allow for the pre-conditions of revolution. The consequences of any unilateral seizure of power on the part of the Jangalis cannot easily be assessed. On the other hand, Kuček Khan was a perfectionist and he hesitated to move on Tehran. Hence, despite pressures from some Jangali left-wingers and Turkish agents in Tehran, he did not take that step. It is ironic that while the Turks urged Kuček Khan to seize power in Tehran, they practically prevented him from doing so by their attempt to annex Iranian Azerbaijan and by their siege of Bolshevik Baku. In addition, they suppressed the Democratic Party in Tabriz. Their siege of Baku prevented the formation of any effective alliance between the Jangalis and the Baku Bolsheviks (Dailami, 2006, pp. 152-54).

Moreover, the Jangalis did not have much time. Soon afterwards a British expeditionary force, under General Lionel Charles Dunsterville, arrived in Gilān. Before November 1917, the British had little interest in Gilān; but after that date, their interest was aroused by the evacuation of Gilān. It was now feasible for northern Iran to come under British control and Gilān could become a base for launching expeditionary forces to Transcaucasia. Thus January 1918 saw the formation of the Dunster force in Baghdad, which had fallen into British hands in March 1917. The destination of the Dunster force, as originally planned, was to be Tiflis but this plan was soon changed and Dunsterville was ordered to proceed to Baku to participate in the defense of the city against the Ottomans. The British force had to pass through Gilān to reach the Caucasus. It reached Qazvin on 15 February and there it had to halt to assess the situation. Dunsterville states in his memoirs that at this stage, "Kuchik had vowed not to let the British through and his committee were working at Enzeli in conjunction with the Bolshevik Committee who were equally determined not to allow our passage" (Dunsterville, p. 27).

A detachment of the Dunster force arrived and stayed briefly in Anzali, before returning to Qazvin and later to Hamadān. The Jangali-British antagonism, however, intensified later. In response to the British kidnapping and hostage taking of Solaymān Mirzā Eskandari, the Democrat leader and a "migrant" (*moḥājer*) member of the Iranian Parliament, the Jangalis arrested the British acting vice-consul, Charles Maclaren, and the British agents, Major Noel Oakshot and Captain Edmond Noel, in conjunction with the Bolsheviks in Baku and their representatives in the Anzali Revolutionary Committee. The Jangalis demanded the release of Solaymān Mirzā (FO 248/1212: Cox to Balfour, 13 April 1918).

In the meantime, Dunsterville managed to bring under British pay a counter-revolutionary Russian Colonel, Bicherakhov, with his 1,200 soldiers. The Jangalis had reached an agreement with the Bolsheviks that Bicherakhov could pass through Gilān to go to Baku but as yet the Bolshevik dominated Baku Soviet did not want the British forces in the city and the Dunster force had to be kept back. But as it turned out, not all of the 1,000 strong forces in Anzali were under the control of the Revolutionary Committee. A great number of them were Dašnaks who had secretly reached an agreement with Dunsterville as he reached Qazvin once again. They rescued

Maclaren and Oakshot allowing the combined Dunster force-Bicherakhov force to attack the Jangali positions at Manjil (Dailami, 1994, pp. 113-18). Subsequently, the Dunster force established itself in Rašt.

It should be added that the political situation in Baku had also changed and Dunsterville planned to go to Baku with the greater part of his force as soon as conditions permitted. On 25 July 1918, frightened by the approach of the Ottoman-Azeri "Army of Islam," the non-Bolshevik forces in the Baku Soviet narrowly passed a resolution to ask for British help. The Bolsheviks retaliated by resigning and on 31 July, the Dašnaks, the Russian Social Revolutionaries and the Mensheviks formed the Centro-Caspii Directorate and invited the British to Baku, and this was promptly accepted. The Jangalis lost hope with the political situation in the whole of Iran and the Caucasus. They were also alarmed by the Ottoman advances into Iranian Azerbaijan and their siege of Baku which brought about the collapse of the thus far amicable Jangali-Bolshevik alliance. They thus came to terms with the British and signed an agreement with them on 12 August 1918 (Fakhraii, pp. 153-57).

As a result, the twelve German and Austrian officers who drilled Jangali partisans were expelled from Gilān. Yet, in fact, the Jangalis' relations with the Germans improved after the Anglo-Jangali agreement. Kuček Khan contacted the German Caucasus Mission under General von Kress, who in turn sent large amounts of arms and ammunition (Dailami, 2006, pp. 150-52).

However, the Jangalis' relationship with the Bolsheviks was more important and lasted much longer, although it was temporarily impaired in late 1918. As in the case of the Constitutional Revolution, the Bolsheviks were present in Gilān since 1915 when the movement began. Among their agitators were figures who later became well-known personalities in Soviet politics. Best known were the Georgians Sergo Ordzhonikidze and Budu Mdivani (Dailami, 1990, pp. 44-45).

After the October Revolution and the proclamation of friendly overtures, the Bolsheviks organized themselves in Gilān. In December 1917, a Revolutionary Committee was formed at Anzali that consisted of Bolsheviks and Social Revolutionaries (Miroshnikov, p. 82). Their leader was Anton Cheliabin, and the secretary of the committee was I. O. Kolomiitsev who later became the second Bolshevik diplomatic representative in Tehran. At the time, a number of soldier committees and left-wing political cells were also formed in Gilān. There were, however, in Gilān also White Russians and supporters of the Provisional Government, and this made it difficult to impose complete control over the Russian soldiers (Dailami, 1990, p. 46; 1992, pp. 55-56). The power of the Revolutionary Committee in Gilān depended entirely on the strength of the Bolsheviks in Baku. However, although the Bolsheviks had dominated the political scene and had assumed the leadership of the Baku Soviet, they were yet to capture political power in its entirety. In the Baku Soviet there were a whole array of political parties that represented various interests and the Soviet had, in turn, rivals in the city in the organizations of the Duma and the Executive Committee of Public Organizations (IKOO). At a later stage, new political forces emerged so that the Bolsheviks had to share and contend for power with Armenian and Azerbaijani nationalists. A simplified version of this complexity of political relations was reflected in Gilān, where an "Executive Committee," probably attached to the IKOO, competed with the Revolutionary Committee for power and the control of Russian troops. The Bolshevik Committee was thus in a position of relative weakness in Gilān and was not always capable of controlling the activities of Russian soldiers. This situation continued until early April 1918, when the Bolsheviks seized power and established a Soviet government known as the Baku Commune. Subsequently, the number of Red Guards in Gilān increased to some 1,000. A great number of them were in fact Dašnak fighters who had joined forces with the Bolsheviks in Baku.

For the time being, as the Dunster force approached Gilān, the Jangalis could not come to an agreement with the Executive Committee about the British. They thus allowed 15 days grace for the Dunster force to pass through on its way to Baku (Dailami, 1992, pp. 56-57). At the same time, the Jangalis sent a delegation to Baku where they met the Azeri Bolshevik, Nariman Narimanov, and the Commune's leader, Stepan Shahumian. Baku was in any case unable to help much against the British threat as itself was under siege by the Ottoman army (Dailami, 1992, pp. 59-60).

In any case, as the Dašnaks infiltrated the Bolshevik forces in Gilān and as the British prisoners were rescued at the time of the battle of Manjil, the Jangali-Bolshevik alliance collapsed. In the end the Revolutionary Committee did not last long either. Its life was very much dependent on the life of the Baku Commune. Once the government of the Commune collapsed, the Red Guards who were stationed at Anzali, returned to Baku. In August 1918, according to the intelligence reports of the British War Office, proof was found that the members of the Committee were working for Kuček Khan. Subsequently, the British, who had by then established themselves in Gilān, arrested Cheliabin and his comrades and deported them to Mesopotamia (Dailami, 1990, p. 50).

At about the same time, the frenzy brought about by the Bolshevik Revolution, finally settled in Iran. The British were now in control of most of the Iranian territory and on 7 August 1918, the Anglophile cabinet of Woṯuq-al-Dawla came to power. The end of the Great War was near. The pan-Islamists in the Jangali movement were forced to come to terms with the British and reject Turkish overtures once and for all. At that stage, the Committee of Etteḥād-e Eslām was dissolved in Gilān and the Jangalis bade farewell to pan-Islamism (Chaquèrie, 1984, p. 14; 1995, p. 67; Dailami, forthcoming).

Ideological and organizational development. After the agreement with the British and the dissolution of the Etteḥād-e Eslām Committee, the Jangali movement entered a period of decline and ideological transformation. The above two events represented crises after which the movement had to define its goals anew. Discarding the last remnants of Ottoman influence appears to have been a unanimous decision. While the Left was deeply disillusioned with Turkish actions in Iranian Azerbaijan and the Caucasus, the imminent defeat of the Central Powers in the war was enough for the Right who did not want to continue with the movement anymore. They wished to submit to British domination while the Left considered itself to be in a state of armed truce with the newcomers.

The differences led to new elections for the leadership of the movement and the right-wingers lost. After a few days the leader of the Right, Ḥāji Aḥmad Kasmāʾi, once again expressed discontent and by the end of December 1918, having taken advantage of Kuček's absence, they resolved to come to terms with the Tehran government (FO 248/1203: APO in Resht to political officer Norperforce in Qazvin, 9 Dec. 1918; Oakshot, 28/29 Dec. 1918). Kasmāʾi had already made it clear that he wished to surrender. He was also interested to take as much of the movement with him as possible (FO 248/1203: Oakshot to Percy Cox, 11 Dec. 1918). He secretly obtained a pardon from Tehran and accepted the government's conditions, which included the takeover of 2,000 Jangali partisans and their arms. When Kuček Khan returned from his Ṭāleš expedition and found out about the negotiations, he expressed his anger with the right-wingers and demanded fresh negotiations and the prior opening of the Majles. He also rejected British offers of the governorship of Gilān (FO 248/1243: Warren in Resht, 26 Jan. 1919; Wickham in Resht, decipher R2, 7/8 Feb. 1919). Before the breakdown in negotiations, the British had already decided to attack the Jangalis and afterwards had the central government under Woṯuq-al-Dawla deliver an ultimatum to them. They also began agitating against the Jangalis among the powerful landlords (Dailami, 1994, pp. 148-50).

Action against the revolutionaries started on 29 March 1919, when a detachment of British troops entered Rašt. Landowners and the Mullahs came out in full force to support the British. The Mullahs of Rašt began preaching against the Jangalis in mosques (FO 248/1241: Tehran intelligence summary 22, 31 March 1918; FO 248/1243: Political officer in Qazvin to British minister in Tehran, 6 May 1919). The landowners were quick to organize themselves. Sepahsālār assembled a large force in Tonokābon and the lords of Ṭavāleš headed by Żarḡām-al-Salṭana drove Jangali officials out and attacked the revolutionary forces.

At about the same time the split in the movement deepened. In early February 1919, after Ḥāji Aḥmad made efforts to surrender, the left-wing Jangalis formed a committee that they called the "Bolshevik Committee." This committee, it appears, even presented a radical program to the movement. Better-known members of the Committee included Dr. Hešmat, Eskandar Khan, Mirzā Esmāʿil Jangali, Mirzā Moḥammad, and Ehsān-Allāh Khan Dustdār (FO 248/1243: Extract from Resht situation report 2, 20 Feb. 1919). Kuček Khan did not join the Bolshevik Committee and instead offered to its reconciling members a "Socialist Committee," formed under the influence of the left wing of the Democratic Party, the *Żedd-e taškili*, who had just arrived in Gilān to form their political committees (FO 248/1260: Priority decipher 21, 17 Feb. 1919; Resht situation report 2, 20 Feb. 1919). While Kuček Khan expressed his loyalty to the members of the *Żedd-e taškili*, which had found fresh vigor in early 1919 with leaders such as Sayyed Ḥasan Taqizādeh in Berlin and the notorious revolutionary, Ḥaydar Khan ʿAmu-oḡli in Petrograd, he also showed that he had bade farewell to his "Islam" once and for all. The British Political Officer at Qazvin described the details of a conversation with Kuček Khan in the following manner: "He told me . . . after studying in the local Madresa, he became an Akhund. He seemed to regard this as an enormous jest, his solemn fanatical countenance became wreathed in smiles and his bulky frame heaved with inward mirth as he confessed to his former calling" (FO 248/1243: Political officer in Qazvin, 10 Feb. 1919). Kuček apologized for his own distant religious past but he did not apologize for the Etteḥād-e Eslām. As a staunch populist (he was a popular leader) Kuček Khan had rallied a whole array of political forces and disgruntled classes around himself. An aspect of his populism was his moral correctness in handling the religious and the quasi-national sentiment of the populace with care, and he followed that policy until the end of the soviet republic that he established in June 1920. He was successful in luring the revolution from anti-imperialism to socialist republicanism and he had done so by appealing to numerous discontented forces. The heterogeneous nature of the movement that he led is now reflected in the radical variety of historiography on the subject, reminiscences and books that vary from Islamic fundamentalism to Bolshevism (Dailami, 2006, pp. 138, 207-8).

In the course of internal arguments, the composition of the political organization of the Jangalis appears to have changed a number of times but even that did not consolidate the anti-imperialist front. Kuček Khan came out with the idea of resurrecting the old provincial council (*anjoman-e ayālati*) of the constitutional times. That implied holding elections although his popularity was at an all time low. Tehran promptly instructed the Governor to prevent the elections for the Society from being held (FO 248/1260: Resht situation report 10, 26 March 1919). Negotiations continued for a few more days but after all it was too late. The combined offensive of Qajar and British troops began, and at the end of March 1919, the British delivered their ultimatum to the Jangalis who were demanding their surrender.

The offensive was a military success as those who did not surrender, could not fight either. Before the Jangali Right and Left could get to fighting each other and thus ensuring the end of the movement, the partisan army was dismissed and it melted into the countryside, only to reassemble at a later date.

A number of factors helped the Jangalis to regroup. The populace, after a few years, once again tasted the oppression of the landlords and the Qajar's Cossack Brigade. Hence, partisans and peasants, once again joined the surviving leaders. Furthermore, in August 1919, came the all-Iranian popular discontent with the Anglo-Persian agreement, giving a major boost to the movement (Dailami, 1994, p. 75). But before all that, as early as June, Bolshevik emissaries had begun to infiltrate the province from the Caucasus. The most solid evidence was discovered in July when the Bolsheviks and Iranian communists sent a certain Stepan Afonian to Gilān to seek Jangali assistance in order to 'organize' the Iranian Communist Party in the province. Afonian and others established themselves there and supported the Jangalis while establishing contact between Gilān, Baku, and Tiflis (Dailami, 1990, p. 52).

Soon afterwards, for the second time, the Lankarān communists contacted Kuček Khan, and in August 1919, he set out to meet them there. By the time he reached the area the Caucasian revolutionaries had been driven out by counter-revolutionaries. At the same time, Bolshevik emissaries from Turkistan also arrived in Gilān (Dailami, 1990, p. 53). The involvement of the Baku Bolsheviks and communists in Gilān during 1919 and early 1920 became the central theme in the Jangali story. At the end of the summer of 1919, the Jangali Bolshevik, Mirzā Esmāʿil, was sent to Transcaucasia (FO 248/1260: APO in Enzeli, 21 Sept. 1919; political officer in Resht, 18 Oct. 1919; Enzeli situation report 3, 12 Oct. 1919). After that date, British reports repeatedly spoke of the resurrection of the Jangali movement in collusion with the Bolsheviks. The arrival of the northern radicals had become a foregone conclusion. The British and Tehran decided to try to prop up Kuček Khan against the Bolsheviks. The 11th Red Army, having entered Baku on 28 April 1920, landed in Gilān on 18 May and the Bolsheviks were welcomed by the Jangalis.

The Jangalis Socialist Committee constituted itself into the Socialist Party in the wake of the Bolshevik landing and adopted a program that included demands for internationalism as well as the separation of religion from politics (Gilak, pp. 527-29; Fak̲rāʾi, pp. 56-59). The political demands of the radical leaders of the Jangali movement eventually culminated in the establishment of the Soviet Republic of Gilān on 5 June 1920.

Bibliography: Archive. Foreign Office and Foreign and Commonwealth Office: General correspondence from the British embassy and consulates in Persia (Iran after 1935), 1807-1970, MSS FO 248, National Archives, Kew, UK; in particular: FO 248/1117–1915. To Seistan. From and to Resht. From and to Tabriz. Circulars to consuls. To miscellaneous. FO 248/1120–1915. From Seistan. Nos. 451-703. FO 248/1149–1916. Rafizadeh-Revolt against South Persia Rifles. FO 248/1168–1917. Isfahan consulate–Jungle Band. FO 248/1203–1918. Jarrahi lands–Kashgai. FO 248/1212–1918. Recruits for the British Army–Russian affairs. Nos. 1-50. FO 248/1241–1919. Hamadan grain–Intelligence summaries. FO 248/1243–1919. Italian interests–Jangalis. Nos. 1-150. FO 248/1260–1919. Pushtikuh–Resht.

Studies. R. Abikh, "Natsional'noe i revoliutsionnoe dvizhenie v Persii v 1917-1919 gg. (Vospominania Ekhsan Ully-Khana), *Novyi Vostok* 23-24, 1928, pp. 234-67; nos. 26-27, 1929, pp. 125-61; no. 29, 1930, pp. 88-107. E. Abrahamian, "The Causes of the Constitutional Revolution in Iran," *IJMES* 10, 1979, pp. 381-414. Idem, *Khomeinism: Essays on the Islamic Republic*, Berkeley, 1993. J. Afary, "Peasant Rebellions of the Caspian Region during the Iranian Constitutional Revolution," *IJMES* 23, 1991, pp. 137-61. Idem, "The Contentious Historiography of the Gilan Republic in Iran: A Critical Exploration," *Iranian Studies* 28, 1995, pp. 3-24. I. Afšār, "Asnād-e gereftāri-e Moḥsen Khan Amin-al-Dawla dar Jangal," in Reżā Reżāzāda Langarudi, ed., *Yādgār-nāma: Majmuʿa-ye maqālāt-e taḥqiqi taqdim šoda be ostād Ebrāhim Fak̲rāʾi*, Tehran, 1984, pp. 361-78. I. Afšār, et al. eds., *Barghā-ye jangal: Nāmahā-ye Rašt o asnād-e nahżat-e jangal*, Tehran, 2001. M. Āǰudāni, *Yā marg yā tajaddod: Daftari dar šeʿr o adab-e mašruṭa*, London, 2002. A. H. Arslanian, "Dunsterville's Adventure: A Reappraisal," *IJMES* 12, 1980, pp. 199-216. Moḥammad-Taqi Bahār, *Tārik̲-e mok̲taṣar-e aḥzāb-e siāsi: Enqerāż-e Qājāriya*, Tehran, 1944. C. Chaquèri, *L'Union soviétique et les tentatives de soviets en Iran*, Essais historiques: Antidote 2, Tehran, 1983. Idem, "The Jangali Movement and Soviet Historiography: A Commentary," *Central Asian Survey* 5/1, 1986, pp. 57-64. Idem, *The Soviet Socialist Republic of Iran, 1920-1921: Birth of the Trauma*, Pitt Series in Russian and East European Studies 21, Pittsburgh, 1995.

P. Dailami, "The Bolsheviks and the Jangali Revolutionary Movement, 1915-1920," *Cahiers du monde russe et soviétique* 31, 1990, pp. 43-60. Idem, "The Bolshevik Revolution and the Genesis of Communism in Iran, 1917-1920," *Central Asian Survey* 11/3, 1992, pp. 51-82. Idem, "Nationalism and Communism in Iran: The Case of Gilan, 1915-1921," Ph.D. diss., University of Manchester, 1994. Idem, "Bravin in Tehran and the Origins of Soviet Policy in Iran," *Revolutionary Russia* 12/2, 1999, pp. 63-82. Idem, "The First Congress of the Peoples of the East and the Iranian Soviet Republic of Gilan, 1920-21," in Stephanie Cronin, ed., *Reformers and Revolutionaries in Modern Iran*, New York, 2004, pp. 85-117. Idem, "The Populists of Rasht: Pan-Islamism and the role of the Central Powers in World War I Iran," in Touraj Atabaki, ed., *Iran and the First World War: Battleground of the Great Powers*, London/New York, 2006, pp. 137-62. L. C. Dunsterville, *Adventures of Dunsterforce*, London, 1920; reprint, London, 1932; tr. Ḥosayn Anṣāri as *K̲āṭerāt-e Ženerāl Danstervil-e sarkub-e jangal*, Tehran, 1983. M. L. Entner, *Russo-Persian Commercial Relations, 1828-1914*, Gainesville, 1965. E. Fak̲rāʾi, *Sardār-e jangal*, Tehran, 1965; repeatedly reprinted. U. Gehrke, *Persien in der deutschen Orient-Politik während des Ersten Weltkrieges*, Darstellungen zur auswärtigen Politik 1, 2 vols., Stuttgart, 1960; tr. by Parviz Sadri as *Irān dar siāsat-e šarqi-e Ālmān dar jang-e jahāni-e avval*, 2 vols., Tehran, 1998.

V. L. Genis, "Les bolcheviks au Guilan: La chute du gouvernement de Koutchek Khan (juin-juillet 1920)," *Cahiers du monde russe* 40/3, 1999; available online: http://monderusse.revues.org/document21.html. Idem, *Krasnaia Persiia: Bol'sheviki v Giliane 1920-1921–Dokumental'naia khronika*, Moscow, 2000. Moḥammad-ʿAli Gilak, *Tāriḵ-e enqelāb-e jangal*, Rašt, 1992. A.-H. Hairi, "Kučak Khān Djangali," in *EI*² V, pp. 310-11. Mirzā Esmāʿil Jangali, *Qiām-e jangal*, ed. Esmāʿil Rāʿin, Tehran, 1978. F. Kazemi, "Peasant Uprisings in Twentieth-Century Iran, Iraq, and Turkey," in F. Kazemi and J. Waterbury, eds., *Peasants and Politics in the Modern Middle East*, Miami, 1991, pp. 101-24. F. Kazemi and E. Abrahamian, "The Nonrevolutionary Peasantry of Modern Iran," *Iranian Studies* 11, 1978, pp. 259-304. F. Kazemzadeh, *Russia and Britain in Persia, 1864-1914: A Study in Imperialism*, New Haven, 1968. L. I. Miroshnikov, *Iran in World War I: Lectures Read at Harvard University in November 1962*, Moscow, 1964; tr. A. Dokhaniati as *Irān dar jang-e jahāni-ye avval*, Tehran, 1965. V. P. Nikitin (B. Nikitine), *Irān-i ke man šenāḵta-am*, tr. from French by ʿAli-Moḥammad Farahvaši, Tehran, 1950; reprint, Tehran, 1977. P. Rochard, "Entre réforme et tradition: Le mouvement Jangali de 1915 à novembre 1921," *Luqmān* 11/1, 1994, pp. 67-80. Aḥmad-ʿAli Sepehr, Mowarreḵ-al-Dawla, *Irān dar jang-e bozorg 1914-1918*, Tehran, 1957; reprint, Tehran, 1983. R. G. Suny, *The Baku Commune, 1917-1918: Class and Nationality in the Russian Revolution*, Princeton, 1972; originally, "The Baku Commune, 1917-1918: Political Strategy in a Social Revolution," Ph.D. diss., Columbia University, 1968. Mirzā Moḥammad Tamimi Ṭāleqāni, *Doktor Hešmat ke bude? Jangal-e Gilān če bude?* Tehran, 1945.

(Pezhmann Dailami)

JĀNI BEG/BEYG KHAN BIGDELI ŠĀMLU

(d. 26 Šaʿbān 1055/15 October 1645), *išik-āqāsi-bāši* (master of ceremony) and *qurči-bāši* (head of the tribal guards) under the Safavid Shah Ṣafi I (r. 1629-42) and Shah ʿAbbās II (r. 1642-66). Little is known about Jāni Beg's background. Adam Olearius (p. 671) called him "by origin a peasant's son" who "at the time of Shah ʿAbbās was a humble servant from Šāmlu," which would explain why the Persian sources from the reign of Shah ʿAbbās I are silent on his place in the Šāmlu genealogy and the early years of his public life. The sources call him a *ḡolām-e ḵāṣṣa*, suggesting that, even in the period after Shah ʿAbbās I, not all ḡolāms were of Georgian, Armenian, and Circassian background, and list two brothers of his, Oloḡ Khan and Qara Khan Beg (Eskandar Beg and Moḥammad-Maʿṣum, p. 200; Wāleh Eṣfahāni, p. 117; Waḥid Qazvini, p. 68; Waziri, II, p. 638).

We first encounter Jāni Beg in an official capacity in 1625, when he served in the army of Zaynal Khan Šāmlu and was chosen as envoy to engage in peace talks concerning Baghdad with the Ottoman commander Ḥāfeẓ Aḥmad Pasha (Eskandar Beg, p. 45, tr. Savory, p. 1266). His rise to high officialdom continued with his appointment as *yasāvol-e ṣoḥbat* (aide-de-camp) in 1629, shortly after the accession of Shah Ṣafi I (Moḥammad-Maʿṣum, p. 43). In 1630-31 he left Persia on a diplomatic mission to the Ottoman court in Istanbul, returning in 1631-32 (Moḥammad-Maʿṣum Eṣfahāni, pp. 124, 158; Wāleh Eṣfahāni, p. 160). The following year he was sent to Ardabil to imprison Šarif Beg, the governor of Ardabil and the superintendent (*motawalli*) of its shrine, whose injustice had generated many complaints among the populace (Wāleh Eṣfahāni, pp. 118-19; Eskandar Beg and Wāleh Eṣfahāni, p. 99). When later that same year news broke that the Ottoman general Ḵalil Pasha was threatening Van, Shah ʿAbbās II dispatched Jāni Beg to collect an army in Čoḵur-e Saʿd and to raid and plunder the area around Van (Moḥammad-Maʿṣum, pp. 170-71).

Jāni Beg was made to keep a watchful eye on the northwestern frontier, for in the spring of 1635 the shah put him at the command of an army recruited from Qarabāḡ, Šervān/Šarvān and Čoḵūr-e Saʿd in order to confront the approaching Ottoman army (Moḥammad-Maʿṣum, p. 196; Wāleh Eṣfahāni, p. 213; Eskandar Beg and Wāleh Eṣfahāni, p. 165). During the siege of Erevan he was made išik-āqāsi-bāši (Moḥammad-Maʿṣum, p. 246; Eskandar Beg and Wāleh Eṣfahāni, p. 199; Estrābādi, p. 252).

In the spring of 1637, Jāni Beg succeeded Amir Khan as head of the qurči regiments (qurči-bāši), a function that he would keep until his death in 1645 (Moḥammad-Maʿṣum, 246). With that promotion came an appointment as governor of Kermān in 1646 (Waziri, II, p. 635). He seems to have performed well in the latter function, for Moḥammad-Saʿid Mašizi (pp. 207-9) speaks of the stability and prosperity of Kermān in this period and the good care Jāni Beg took of the peasants. He also founded a village, Jāniābād, near Kermān city (Bigdeli, I, p. 1107; Waziri, II, pp. 636-38). He is not likely to have resided much in Kermān, though, for he let himself be represented by his brother Oloḡ Khan (Waziri, II, pp. 635-37). His other brother, Qara Khan Beg, by then an aide-de camp (*yasāvol-e ṣoḥbat*), benefited from Jāni Beg's promotion as well, for he became *ordubegi* in 1629 (Eskandar Beg and Wāleh Eṣfahāni, p. 240). Shortly after his appointment in Kermān, Jāni Beg was summoned to assemble a contingent of musketeers (*tofangči*) from that town for the defense of Baghdad against a new Ottoman threat (Waziri, II, p. 635).

Already powerful owing to his important function, Jāni Beg moved into primary position at the court with the accession of Shah ʿAbbās II in 1642. In the first year of the adolescent shah's reign, he was one of the three officials who effectively ruled the country (the other two were Mirzā Sāru Taqi and Moḥammad-ʿAli Beg; see, in ARA, VOC 1144, Daghregister Hendrick Walckaert, fol. 561; VOC 1141, 20 Aug. 1642, fol. 547). His landed possessions were vast; pious endowments (*waqf*) in his name were located in places varying from Azerbaijan to Kermān, Isfahan, and Hamadān. His name is also attached to a *madrasa* in Qom (Bigdeli, I, pp. 1100-1101, II, pp. 808-12).

Jāni Beg's ultimate fate is entwined with the death of grand vizier Mirzā Moḥammad Sāru Taqi. In 1643 Jāni Beg became related to Mirzā Sāru Taqi when his daughter was married off to Mirzā Qāsem, a nephew of the grand vizier (Mollā Kamāl, p. 100). This appears to have been meant to solidify a family alliance that also included Shah ʿAbbās II's mother, and that was designed to do away with a mutual rival, Rostam Khan, the *sepahsālār* (ARA, VOC 1144, 14 May 1643, fols. 488-94). This alliance does not seem to have outlived its immediate objective, for Jāni Beg would emerge as the main conspirator in the assassination of Mirzā Sāru Taqi. The reasons for the resentment that led to the conspiracy mostly involved disagreement over fiscal and military policy, with Jāni Beg favoring a strong military and Mirzā Sāru Taqi taking the side of the cash-strapped court. Mirzā Sāru Taqi's curtailing the salaries of the qurčis naturally created resentment among their ranks (ARA, VOC 1158, Daghregister Leonard Winnincx). He also insisted that ʿAli Mardān Khan, the governor of Kandahar (Qandahār), pay his dues to Isfahan or be summoned to court to be replaced. Jāni Beg, concerned about the simultaneous Ottoman threat to Baghdad, counseled the shah against replacing ʿAli Mardān Khan so as not to create turmoil on the eastern border (Falsafi, p. 297; Floor, p. 257).

The author of *ʿAbbās-nāma* (p. 4) claims that Jāni Beg resolved to remove the chief minister after he had been told that the latter was planning to kill him. According to various sources, Jāni Beg made great efforts to poison Shah ʿAbbās II's mind against the grand vizier, pointing to his arrogance and insinuating that the grand vizier was driving the country to ruin and that he was a threat to the shah himself (ARA, VOC 1158, Daghregister Winnincx; Chardin, VII, pp. 308-9). Having received permission from the shah, Jāni Beg, on 22 Šaʿbān 1055/11 October 1645, went to Mirzā Sāru Taqi's house and cut the senior grand vizier down (different interpretations of the circumstances and motives of the murder in Babayan, pp. 123-28, and Floor, pp. 258 ff.).

Following the murder of Mirzā Sāru Taqi, Jāni Beg himself was betrayed by the royal wine-maker (*širači-bāši*) Ṣafiqoli Beg, who feared that the conspiracy would extend to the throne itself and that the objective was to overthrow the shah (especially since Jāni Beg had called up 30,000 troops). But it was the shah's mother, whose protégé Mirzā Sāru Taqi had been, who was instrumental in the terrible revenge that followed. Jāni Beg was assassinated on 15 October 1645, and with him a large number of his co-conspirators and members of his clan perished. Among the victims were Naqdi Khan, ʿArab Khan Šāmlu, and Dāwud Khan Šāmlu, the governor of Gilān, who had been a principal enemy of Mirzā Sāru Taqi, because the latter had indicted him for embezzlement. Dāwud Beg's position was given to Ṣafiqoli Beg (Chardin, VII, pp. 306-7; ARA, VOC 1158, Daghregister . . . Leonard Winnincx). His possessions in Kermān and Hamadān were confiscated, and the post of qurči-bāši devolved on Morteżāqoli Khan, who also took over as governor of Kermān. Jāni Beg's two brothers, Ološ Khan, who had continued to represent Jāni Beg in Kermān, and Qara Khan, who was army commander (*sardār*) in Khorasan, were apprehended and lost their lives as well (Waḥid Qazvini, p. 68; Mašizi Bardsiri, p. 211; Waziri, II, p. 638; ARA, VOC 1152, Daghregister . . . Willem Bastincq, fol. 248). The career of Jāni Beg's son, ʿAbd al-Qāsem Khan, on the other hand, did not suffer in the wake of his father's demise. He would be superintendent of water distribution (*mirāb*) before becoming *divānbegi* (q.v.), mayor of Qazvin, and later khan of Hamadān (Mašizi Bardsiri, pp. 373, 391; Chardin, IX, pp. 361, 571-72; Sanson, in Kroell, p. 40; Sanson, pp. 110-12).

Bibliography: ARA = Algemeen Rijks Archief (Dutch National Archives). Ḡolām-Ḥosayn Bigdeli, ed., *Tāriḵ-e Bigdeli: madārek wa asnād*, 2 vols., Tehran, 1988. Sayyed Ḥosayn b. Mortażā Ḥosayni Estrābādi/Astarābādi, *Tāriḵ-e solṭāni: az Šayḵ Ṣafi tā Šāh Ṣafi*, ed. Eḥsān Ešrāqi, Tehran, 1985. Eskandar Beg Torkamān and Moḥammad-Yusof Wāleh Eṣfahāni, *Ḏayl-e tāriḵ-e ʿālamārā-ye ʿabbāsi*, ed. Aḥmad Sohayli Ḵᵛānsāri, Tehran, 1938. Ann Kroell, ed., *Nouvelles d'Ispahan, 1665-1695*, Société d'Histoire de l'Orient, Paris, 1979. Mir Moḥammad-Saʿid Mašizi Bardsiri, *Taḏkera-ye Ṣafawiya-ye Kermān*, ed. Moḥammad-Ebrāhim Bāstāni Pārizi, Tehran, 1990. Moḥammad-Maʿṣum b. Ḵᵛājagi Eṣfahāni, *Ḵolāṣat al-siar: Tāriḵ-e ruzgār-e Šāh Ṣafi*, Tehran, 1989. Mollā Kamāl, *Tāriḵ-e Mollā Kamāl*, in Ebrāhim Dehgan, ed., *Tāriḵ-e Safawiān*, Arāk, 1955. Adam Olearius, *Vermehrte newe Beschreibung der muscowitischen und persischen Reyse*, Schleswig, 1656, facs repr., Tübingen, 1971; tr. A. Behpūr as *Safar-nāma-ye Ādām Oleʾārius (baḵš-e Irān)*, Tehran, 1984. N. Sanson, *Voyage ou état présent du royaume de Perse*, Paris, 1694; tr. John Savage as *The Present State of Persia: . . . Account of the Manners, Religion, and Government of That People*, London, 1695. VOC (Dutch East India Company) = *Generale Missieven der Vereenigde Oostindische Compagnie*, ed. Willem Philipus Coolhaas, 7 vols., the Hague, 1960-78. Moḥammad-Ṭāher Waḥid Qazvini, *ʿAbbās-nāma yā šarḥ-e zendagāni-e Šāh ʿAbbās ṯāni (1052-1073)*, ed. Ebrāhim Dehgān, Arāk, 1950. Moḥammad-Yusof Wāleh Qazvini Eṣfahāni, *Ḵold-e barin: Irān dar zamān-e Šāh Ṣafi wa Šāh ʿAbbās-e dovvom, 1030-1071 h.q.*, ed. Moḥammad-Reżā Naṣiri, Tehran, 2001. Aḥmad-ʿAli Khan Waziri, *Tāriḵ-e Kermān*, ed. Moḥammad-Ebrāhim Bāstāni Pārizi, 3rd ed., 2 vols, Tehran, 1985.

Studies. Kathryn Babayan, "The Waning of the Qizilbash: The Spiritual and the Temporal in Seventeenth Century Iran," Ph.D. diss., Princeton University, 1993. Naṣr-Allāh Falsafi, "Sargoḏašt-e 'Sāru Taqi' Maḵdum-al-Omarāʾ wa Ḵādem-al-Foqarāʾ," in idem, *Čand maqāla-ye tāriḵi wa adabi*, Tehran, 1963, pp. 287-309. Willem Floor, "The Rise and Fall of Mirza Taqi, the Eunuch Grand Vizier (1043-55/1633-45) Makhdum al-Omara va Khadem al-foqara," *Studia Iranica* 26, 1997, pp. 237-66.

(RUDI MATTHEE)

JANNĀBA. See GONĀBĀD.

JANNĀBI, ABU SAʿID. See, ĀBI, ABU SAʿID JANN

JAPAN AND ITS RELATIONS WITH IRAN. The subject of contact between the two countries will be discussed in the following sub-entries:

i. *Introduction.*
ii. *Diplomatic and commercial relations with Iran.*
iii. *Japanese travelers to Persia.*
iv. *Iranians in Japan.*
v. *Archeological missions to Persia.*
vi. *Iranian studies in Japan, pre-Islamic period.*
vii. *Iranian studies in Japan, Islamic period.*
viii. *Safavid studies in Japan.*
ix. *Centers for Persian studies in Japan.*
x. *Collections of Persian books in Japan.*
xi. *Collections of Persian art in Japan.*
xii. *Translations of Persian works into Japanese.*
xiii. *Translations of Japanese works into Persian.*

i. INTRODUCTION

The seventh-eighth century Japanese annals depict an early ruler (*tennō* "emperor") of Yamato, centered in the area of modern Nara Prefecture, as he hears for the first time about the rich land to the west—meaning Korea; the revelation comes from a god speaking through the king's wife (*Kojiki* 2.92, p. 257; *Nihon Shoki* [*NS*] I, pp. 221-22 [= year 193 C.E. in the archaizing *NS* chronology]). At least by the late 3rd century C.E., the "land of Wa" (the incipient kingdom of Yamato) does appear to be clearly engaged with China and the states of Korea; this is indicated by the early, if brief, account of Japan found in the Chinese history of the kingdom of Wei (tr. Tsunoda). In this same period, across Central Asia, links were being formed to further Sogdian trade (q.v. at *iranica.com*) with China, and these trade connections would facilitate communication and cultural exchange between the Iranian-speaking world and China and its sphere of influence into the Islamic period.

During the fourth-sixth centuries, while the Sasanian empire flourished in western Asia, state formation continued in Japan. Japanese involvement in the politics of the Korean peninsula, the settlement in Japan of Koreans and Chinese bringing their arts and crafts, more general diplomatic contacts, and commerce in luxury goods all created avenues for the Japanese to increase their knowledge of the mainland and, potentially, of what lay farther to the west. The flow of trade and material culture eastward from China to Japan, directly or via Korea, was diverse and continuous enough so that foreign art and technology from the West, in original form as well as in Chinese interpretations, and even foreign artisans, might have been drawn along. The earliest historical immigrants from Korea, whether voluntary or sent as tribute, practice essential trades; they are weavers and seamstresses (*NS* I, pp. 349-50, 362-63 [years 463, 470]; *Kojiki* 127.6, p. 349), tanners (*NS* I, pp. 396, 397 [yr. 493]) and potters (II, p. 117 [587]). Such artisans are presumably meant also by the simple description "immigrants," who continue to arrive in small groups during the following centuries and receive assistance in settling (e.g., I, p. 396; II, pp. 38, 139, 371 [yrs. 493, 540, 608, 685]).

In the sixth century Buddhist proselytizing of Yamato from Korea developed in earnest, and the Japanese weighed the prestige and irresistibility in the west of this religion "from distant India" (*NS* II, p. 66) against the rights of the national gods (II, pp. 66-67 [yr. 552]). Not only clerics were sent to Japan in this effort, but image-makers and architects (p. 96 [yr. 577]), carpenters and metalworkers (II, p. 117 [yr. 588]), and teachers of Chinese language (II, p. 404 [yr. 691]). The products of Buddhism—images, incense-burners, sutras and technical literature (e.g., on geography and astronomy)—as well as the producers, reached Japan [e.g., II, pp. 65, 126 [yrs. 552, 602]). Gifts reported for the year 688 include "all kinds of colored fine silks" (II, p. 387), which, like earlier tribute of curtains and flags [II, p. 86 [yr. 562]), suggest the possible introduction of exotic western motifs (such as the silk shown below; see xi). The pursuit of Chinese dances and Korean music (II, pp. 144, 359 [yrs. 612, 683]) suggests a wide range of influence in court social activities: for example, the Japanese version of backgammon, *suguroku*, perhaps was a fairly recent import from China at the time it was banned (II, p. 395 [yr. 689]). This measure, whether or not it was an attempt to curb frivolity in general, may have a connection with the statement that the previous emperor once made his court gamble with him (II, p. 371 [yr. 685]).

The promotion of Buddhism in the state of Yamato in the seventh century (which was accelerated by Shōtoku Taishi [Prince], d. 622), together with the ongoing emulation of the Chinese imperial administration and Confucian morality, fostered use of the Chinese language and writing system, which gave access to Chinese literature and knowledge of the world. Student priests had begun to travel to China by 608 (*NS* II, p. 139), just four years after the date assigned to the seventeen-article constitution that is attributed to Shōtoku, which proclaimed Confucian ideals for the state and gave Buddhism an official status in it (II, pp. 128-32). Two priests who were sent from Japan to study with Xuan Tsang, who had previously brought relics and copies of the Buddhist scriptures from India (II, p. 254 [yr. 658]), would have heard direct and personal report about the western world.

Also in the mid-seventh century it is reported, as two incidents, that men and women of "Tukhārā" reached Kyushu, blown by a storm (*NS* II, p. 246 [yr. 654]) or having drifted from Amami Island at the northern end of the Ryukyu chain (II, p. 251 [yr. 657]; cf. a made-up story of a ship drifting to the same landfall in Kyushu, II, p. 101 [yr. 583]). The people may be though to be Iranians originally of Ṭoḵārestān in northern Afghanistan (Barthold, *Turkestan*[3], pp. 66-68; *Ḥodūd al-ʿālam*, tr. Minorsky, pp. 108-9). They are not stated to be merchants, nor as pursuing the East China Sea sailing route to Kyushu—from the Yangtze basin, Fukien (modern Fujian Province, China), or southeast Asia—or the northern route to Kyushu from the Yellow Sea and Korea. The fact that both incidents are reported in summer to early fall (4th month and 7th month, respectively), a relatively good sailing time, is inconclusive: in the 4th month of year 570 a Korean envoy is reported to have missed landfall (presumably Kyushu), and his ship was blown well northeastward to the shore of Echigo (Niigata Prefecture; *NS* II, p. 87; cf. Tungus fishermen reaching that area from the north—Hokkaido—or across the Sea of Japan: II, p. 58 [yr. 544]). There are no details to identify the people of Tokhārā as refugees from the recent Arab conquest of Iran or as Sasanian envoys, although Ṭoḵārestān was a last refuge of Sasanian resistance at that time (Pulleyblank, p. 425). At least one of them intended to return to his homeland, apparently by land, after first visiting the T'ang court at the capital, Chang'an (II, p. 266 [yr. 660]), which suggests a possible diplomatic mission. He is referred to by name and appears comfortable in the East Asian milieu; perhaps he belonged to the Sogdian trading network. (See also iv, below.)

Maritime trade between Japan and China and the exchange of Buddhist scholarship continued—more reliably than diplomatic exchanges—through Japan's Heian period (794-1185) and the medieval shogunates. As both Chinese and Arab seafaring expanded and crossed paths in Southeast Asia, opportunities occurred for chance contacts between Persians and Japanese in the course of travel and trade. A relic of such a meeting is described below (see iv). Marco Polo's residence in China took place in the period of consolidation of Mongol control over China, in which there also occurred two failed naval expeditions against Japan (1274, 1281). His information on Japan (*Chipen-gu*, "land of Nippon") probably reflects this recent turbulence as well as the perspective of the Chinese annals (bk. III, chaps. 2-3 and 4; Yule, II, pp. 253-66). He points out the remoteness and independence of the island nation, and the difficulty of access by sea, but he also explains how the seasonal monsoons are utilized for sailing the East China Sea east and west (Yule, II, p. 264). The 7,459 islands mentioned by mariners as found in this "Sea of Chin" (ibid.), and other points in this part of the narrative (bk. III, chap. 4 [Yule]) seem to better indicate the Philippines; and perhaps Marco Polo and his informants viewed all the north-south island chains above Indonesia as one continuous series. Similarly, the Syrian writer Abu'l-Feda (d. 1331), after describing Java, Vietnam (Champa), and Cambodia (Qemār), reports on the many "little islands of China" (p. 369) that lay farther east and aligned north and south, and he does not separately take note of Japan.

The close control of mercantile activity in the Japanese ports during medieval times may help account for the sparseness of foreign merchants there that is mentioned by Marco Polo. Nevertheless, Persian luxury goods reached Japan by trade or diplomacy (see below, xi, for examples). Subsequently, the Tokugawa Shogunate (1603-1857) enforced the isolation of the country more effectively than had the medieval shogunates, and this control is described in detail by the report of the Safavid mission to Siam in 1685 (O'Kane, pp. 193, 194; on this text, see SAFINE-YE SOLAYMĀNI at *iranica.com*). In spite of the limited access to Japan, Westerners had considerable information about it; as they gathered at the Siamese court and vied for the king's favor, they could relate fact as well as hearsay to the Persian merchant community there. The secretary of the mission set down what he heard of the country, people, and king of Japan, craft products and trade practices, precious metals and coinage, besides a Dutch view of the rivalry with the Portuguese there (O'Kane, pp. 188-98). The presence of many Chinese artisans in Japan also is noted (p. 197). (On the Persian presence in Siam, see THAILAND-IRAN RELATIONS at *iranica.com*.)

Direct contact and observation of each other by Persians and Japanese would wait for the establishment of Japan's relations with the world by the modernizing administration of the Meiji period (1868-1912). The remaining sections of this entry discuss the course of Iranian-Japanese official relations and other interaction since that time and the study in Japan of Iranian languages, history, and culture.

For Iranians in East Asia, see also CHINESE-IRANIAN RELATIONS.

Bibliography: Abu'l-Feda, *Taqwim al-boldān*, Paris, 1840. *Kojiki*, tr. Donald L. Philippi, Tokyo, 1968. *Nihon Shoki* [*NS*] W. G. Aston, tr., *Nihongi. Chronicles of Japan from the Earliest Times to A.D. 697*, London, 1924; repr., Rutland, Vt. and Tokyo, 1972. John O'Kane, tr., *The Ship of Sulaiman*, London, 1972. Edwin G. Pulleyblank, "Chinese-Iranian Relations i. In Pre-Islamic Times," in *EIr*. V/4, 1991, pp. 424-31. Ryusaku Tsunoda, tr., "History of the Kingdom of Wei," in *Japan in the Chinese Dynastic Histories: Later Han Through Ming Dynasties*, ed. L. Carrington Goodrich, South Pasadena, 1951, pp. 8-20. Charlotte von Verschuer, "Japan's Foreign Relations 600 to 1200 A.D.: A Translation from Zenrin Kokuhōki," *Monumenta Nipponica* 54/1, 1999, pp. 1-39. Hiromitsu Washizuka, Kim Lena, and Susan K. Smith, *Transmitting the Forms of Divinity. Early Buddhist Art from Korea and Japan*, New York, 2003. Masatoshi M. Yoshino, "Winter and Summer Monsoons and the Navigation in East Asia in Historical Age," *GeoJournal* 3/2, 1979, pp. 161-70. Henry Yule, *The Book of Ser Marco Polo the Venetian, concerning the kingdoms and marvels of the East*, 2 vols., New York, 1903.

(C. J. BRUNNER)

ii. DIPLOMATIC AND COMMERCIAL RELATIONS WITH IRAN

Qajar period, 1796-1925. Although it is not clear when Iran initiated diplomatic contact with Japan, it is believed to have been in 1873, when Nāṣer-al-Din Shah, on his first trip to Europe, met Naonobu Sameshima of Satsuma, who was the then Japanese ambassador to Paris, France. The shah did not include many details about the meeting in his memoir (Nāṣer-al-Din Shah, 1998, p. 215).

Seven years later, Nāṣer-al-Din Shah received a Japanese delegation in Tehran. Masaharu Yoshida, the leader of the delegation, explains in his memoirs that Takeaki Enomoto, the Japanese ambassador to Russia, was offered an opportunity to meet with Nāṣer-al-Din Shah in Saint Petersburg, when the shah was traveling back to Iran after his second trip to Europe. In this meeting, the shah showed an interest in trading with Japan and discussed formulation of a commercial treaty (Yoshida, p. 2; tr., p. 30). This timing is incorrect, however, since in fact the shah did not journey back to Iran through Saint Petersburg. Instead, the meeting must have been held in May 1878, during the shah's passage to Europe. The shah did not mention the meeting in his travelogue, even though he mentions his meeting with a Japanese student at a military school in France and demonstrates his knowledge of Japan (Nāṣer-al-Din Shah, 2000, p. 181).

According to Yoshida, subsequent to the meeting, talks between the two countries continued in Russia; moreover, the Iranian chargé d'affaires in Russia prepared a draft of the commercial treaty and presented it to the Japanese consul. Meanwhile, Enomoto, after returning to Japan, planned a delegation to Iran. The delegation consisted of seven members: Masaharu Yoshida, a diplomat and the chief of the delegation; Nobuyoshi Furukawa, a captain of the Japanese army; two staff members of the Ōkura Trading Company (Ōkura Gumi Shōkai); and three merchants. They reached Bušehr in July 1880 with samples of Japanese products, including some of Japanese tea. In September, they entered Tehran and resided there for over three months. Nāṣer-al-Din Shah granted them an audience at the Šams-al-ʿemāra Palace and inquired about the Japanese political system, army, railways, and other matters, and had an informal meeting with them a few days later (*Ruz-nāma-ye Irān*, no. 432, 29 Šawwāl 1292; Eʿtemād-al-Salṭana, III, p. 2009; Yoshida, pp. 143-55; tr. pp. 181-91). The members of the mission held trading fairs in Bušehr and Tehran in order to exhibit Japanese products; however, they did not draw much interest from the Iranians. The treaty talk never took place, because Japan wished to be treated on a most-favored-nation basis by Iran and obtain the same extraterritorial rights that the European countries enjoyed, which Iran did not agree to. The mission was poorly organized and failed to procure definitive success (Nakaoka, pp. 230-31; Okazaki, pp. 83-84). Nevertheless, the delegation was able to provide the Japanese with first-hand information on Qajar Iran through the detailed travelogues of Yoshida and Furukawa.

After Yoshida and Furukawa, three Japanese travelers—namely, Yasumasa Fukushima, Toyokichi Ienaga, and Masaji Inoue—visited Iran. Fukushima was a lieutenant colonel in the Japanese Army Intelligence and was interested in political and military affairs. He commenced his journey to Bušehr in May 1896 and reached Tehran in July, soon after the assassination of Nāṣer-al-Din Shah. He noted the Persian soldiers' lack of discipline and the frequency with which Persian officers exacted bribes. He was received by Moẓaffar-al-Din Shah at Ṣāḥebqerāniya (Fukushima, pp. 75-78). Ienaga was an officer serving in the Government-General of Taiwan under Japanese rule; he was entrusted with the mission of conducting a survey of opium production in Iran and Turkey. His journey began in July 1899 at Bušehr, and he reached Tehran in September. Moẓaffar-al-Din Shah received him at the summer palace and told him that the shah was hoping for good commercial relations between Iran and Japan. Ienaga also met with Mirzā ʿAli-Aṣḡar Khan Amin-al-Solṭān (q.v.; Ienaga, pp. 101-4). Masaji Inoue was a student of the University of Vienna, and he traveled to Caucasus, Iran, and Central Asia during his summer vacation. He entered Tehran in September 1902. Although he undertook the journey for personal reasons, he met with Mirzā Naṣr-Allāh Nāʾini Mošir-al-Dawla, the minister of foreign affairs, and attended a party at his house as well (Inoue, pp. 274-75, 280-81).

There is no statistical data available regarding the commercial relations between the two countries before the 1920s. Fukushima was delighted when he found Japanese goods at a shop in Tehran. The owner of the shop said that he had visited Japan in 1895 and had imported the goods himself. Fukushima calls him "Ṣarrāf-bāši"; but he must have been Ṣaḥḥāf-bāši, who authored a travelogue about his worldwide travels, as Sugita (p. 180) points out. According to his travelogue, Ebrāhim Ṣaḥḥāf-bāši Tehrāni visited Yokohama in the middle of August 1897 and remained in Japan for approximately fifty days. This was the first account of a visit to Japan by an Iranian; however, his description of Japan is quite short, and little is known about what he really did there (Ṣaḥḥāf-bāši, pp. 85-91). The first Iranian political figure to visit Japan was Mirzā ʿAli-Aṣḡar Khan Amin-al-Solṭān, who began his world tour after he was dismissed from the office of prime minister for the second time. Prior to his pilgrimage to Mecca, he visited Nagasaki via Russia and China in December 1903 and remained in Japan for twenty-eight days. In Tokyo, he was received by Emperor Meiji and also met with the then Prime Minister Taro Katsura as well as the ex-prime minister Hirobumi Itō, who was a powerful statesman. He visited many tourist sites such as Kyoto and Nikkō as well as military facilities and modern schools and was very impressed by Japan's modernization. His fellow traveler, Mahdiqoli Moḵber-al-Salṭana Hedāyat (q.v.), wrote a detailed report on the various aspects of Japan in his travelogue (Hedāyat, pp. 148-226).

In Persian newspapers such as *Aḵtar*, Japan gradually came to be considered as a model of modernization. In particular, Japan's victory in the Russo-Japanese War in 1905 aroused a great deal of interest in Japan among Iranians (Pistor-Hatam; Haag-Higuchi). Ḥosayn-ʿAli Tājer's *Mikādo-nāma*, the *Šāh-nāma* style epic about the war, demonstrates the extent to which Iranians were affected by Japan's victory. Nevertheless, despite this interest, official diplomatic relations between the two countries were not established until 1929, although the diplomats of the two countries held many talks in Europe. Around 1905, an Iranian diplomat offered the Japanese chargé d'affair of the Netherlands, Mitsuhashi, a treaty, but the negotiations did not produce any results. In 1922 in Rome, the Japanese ambassador, Ochiai, officially negotiated with the Iranian chargé d'affair, Esḥāq Khān, and they almost reached an agreement with each other about the draft of the treaty; however, Iran eventually refused to sign it (Nuita, pp. 6-7).

Following several rounds of unsuccessful negotiations, Iran sent its first delegation to Japan in 1922, but the details of this mission have not yet been studied (Nihon Iran Bunkakyōkai, p. 12). On the other hand, Japan sent another delegation to Iran in 1923 in order to observe Iran's political and economic conditions. The chief of the delegation, Eishirō Nuita, who was a diplomat, lived in Tehran for approximately three months and wrote several reports about his journey. He found that Iran was not as modernized as Japan; their visit was as strenuous as Yoshida's visit despite the availability of automobiles. The prevailing circumstances had also changed since Yoshida's time. First, in his memoir, Nuita displays great interest in the oil fields and oil refinery in Ābādān (q.v.), which became a major factor in the relationship between the two countries at a later period. Second, Nuita explains Iran's political situation and pays considerable attention to Reżā Khan Sardār-e Sepah (future Reżā Shah), who had launched major military reforms. Third, he met with many pro-Japanese Iranians in Tehran. He visited the house of an Iranian, the interior walls of which were full of paintings and pictures of the Russo-Japanese War, including portraits of the Japanese emperor and generals (Nuita, pp. 30-34). A part of the pro-Japanese sentiment that Iranians have cultivated in their minds was germinated in this period.

According to Nuita, even at that time, which was when the Soviet Union had abrogated its unequal treaty with Iran, the Japanese government hesitated to conclude a treaty with Iran without consular jurisdictions, because the government was anxious about the treatment of Japanese people under Iranian jurisdiction. This is why the treaty was not concluded before the Pahlavi period.

Nuita includes some data about the two countries' economic relations, which were strengthened by World War I. In 1922-23, Japanese exports to Iran were valued at approximately 800,000 yen, and the volume of Japanese imports was approximately the same. On the other hand, this was only 1 percent of the British trade with Iran. Nuita found some Japanese products in Iran, such as silk handkerchiefs, cotton clothes, matchsticks, and tea; however, with the exception of tea glasses that were frequently used in Iranian daily life, the number of Japanese products was not considerable (Nuita, pp. 49-53).

According to the Yokohama Shōkin Ginkō (Yokohama Specie Bank), in 1924-25, the total value of Iranian imports from Japan was 7,822,088 rials (about GBP 186,240), which was only 1.0 percent of Iran's total imports, thus ranking Japan as the tenth largest among Iran's trading partners (see Table 1). Moreover, the total value of Iranian exports to Japan was 12,396,925 rials (about GBP 295,164), that is, only 1.2 percent of Iran's total exports and merely the ninth highest among the countries. All of the Iranian exports comprised of opium, the amount of 25,003 man (= 74,259 kg) most of which was re-exported to China.

Table 1

DETAILS OF THE IRANIAN IMPORTS FROM JAPAN IN 1924-25

	Amount (man)	Value (rial)	Ranking
Cotton yarns	140,578	4,086,115	Third
Matches	26,201	245,095	Third
Glasses	63,329	750,411	Second
Ceramics	83,906	101,395	Second
Candles	6	50	Seventh

Source: Yokohama Shōkin Ginkō, pp. 78-83.

Pahlavi period, 1926-79. Following the coronation of Reza Shah in April 1926, Iran initiated judicial reforms as well as negotiations with European countries to abrogate their extraterritorial rights. This resulted in the removal of the obstacles that had hindered the official diplomatic relations between Iran and Japan. Moreover, Japan also wished to expand its trade with Iran. In the same year, Japan sent a diplomat to Iran and opened a diplomatic office in Tehran. After negotiations, on 10 Farvardin 1308/30 March 1929, representatives from the two countries signed a provisional commercial treaty, which included the bilateral most-favored-nation clause. In August, Japan established a legation in Tehran, which was located near the Marmar Palace (Kāḵ-e Marmar); Akio Kasama was the first Japanese minister to stay with the legation. In May 1930, Iran established a legation in Tokyo with Avānes Khan Mosāʿed-al-Salṭana as the first envoy extraordinary and minister plenipotentiary (Wezārat-e Omur-e Ḵāreja, p. 7).

Following the establishment of diplomatic relations, commercial relations also developed gradually. In 1939-40, Iranian imports from Japan reached 19,324,000 yen (= 96,620,000 rials), which was more than twelve times that of 1924-25, while Iranian exports to Japan increased to 6,587,000 yen (= 32,935,000 rials), which was more than twice that of 1924-25. Japan became Iran's second largest trading partner, behind Germany, and shared 10.5 percent of the total Iranian trade in 1939. The most important Japanese product was cotton fabrics, which constituted 90 percent of Iran's total imports. Japan was the largest exporting country of cotton fabrics for Iran in 1938-39 and 1939-40, surpassing the United Kingdom and the Soviet Union (Shimizu, p. 243). On the other hand, Iran's most important product was raw cotton,

Table 2
IRANIAN IMPORTS FROM AND EXPORTS TO JAPAN IN 1954

Imports	(in $1,000)	(in %)	Exports	(in $1,000)	(in %)
Cotton fabrics	8,836	37.7	Petroleum	10,761	50.1
Woolen fabrics	1,905	8.1	Raw cottons	9,685	45.0
Staple fiber fabrics	1,249	5.3	Salts	310	1.4
Ceramics	1,197	5.1	Others	743	3.5
Rayon fabrics	1,021	4.4			
Sewing machine	869	3.7			
Woolen yarns	842	3.6			
Others	7,497	32.0			
Total	23,416	100.0	Total	21,499	100.0

Source: Nihon Keizai, p. 194.

Table 3
IRANIAN IMPORTS FROM AND EXPORTS TO JAPAN IN 1968

Imports	(in $1,000)	(in %)	Iranian exports	(in $1,000)	(in %)
Steel manufactures	42,057	30.8	Petroleum	603,890	95.5
Machinery	39,066	28.6	Petroleum products	18,086	2.8
Textile goods	24,292	17.8	Food items	2,808	0.4
Metal goods	10,193	7.5	Others	7,661	1.3
Tire tubes	6,354	4.6			
Others	14,727	10.7			
Total	136,689	100.0	Total	632,445	100.0

Source: Japan External Trade Organization, 1969, pp. 26-27.

which comprised approximately 90 percent of its total exports to Japan (Nihon Iran Bunka Kyōkai, pp. 53-54).

Furthermore, the political situations in Europe had significant effects on Irano-Japanese relations. Reza Shah had close relations with Nazi Germany and shared its anti-communist policy. Japan also concluded an anti-communist pact with Germany in 1936. Thus, it was quite natural that the two governments sought closer ties with each other. In 1938, Iran offered to conclude another treaty with Japan, and after negotiations on 18 October 1939, the Irano-Japanese Treaty of Amity was signed by the respective representatives (Center for Asian Historical Record, AO3022678600). World War II had already begun by then, but the situation changed drastically when Germany invaded the Soviet Union in June 1941. In August, the Soviet and British armies invaded and occupied Iran, and Reza Shah abdicated. Japan, which had concluded the Three-Power Pact with Germany and Italy in September 1940, entered the war with an air attack on the United States base at Pearl Harbor in Hawaii on 7 December 1941.

In January 1942, the Tripartite Treaty was concluded by Iran, the Soviet Union, and the United Kingdom, all of whom intended to support the war against fascism. Iran broke off its diplomatic ties with Japan on 13 April 1942, and the Japanese legation in Tehran was closed. Following the Tehran Conference attended by Joseph Stalin, Winston Churchill, and Franklin Roosevelt, Iran declared war against Japan on 9 Esfand 1323/1 March 1945, although no direct conflict had ever occurred between the two countries.

For the next eight years, there were no diplomatic relations between Iran and Japan, but two years after the end of World War II, Irano-Japanese trading was restarted. The total amount of the trade was worth 12 million rials in 1947, 22 million rials in 1948, and 231 million rials in 1950 (Inoue, p. 215). The most important event for the two countries in this period was related to the Oil Nationalization Movement of Iran (see ANGLO-PERSIAN OIL COMPANY).

After April 1951, the Moṣaddeq government attempted to export "nationalized" oil, but they had little success, because the British government blocked the export of Iranian oil. A small Japanese oil company, Idemitsu, wished to import oil directly from oil-producing countries at attractive prices and began negotiations with the National Iranian Oil Company (Šerkat-e melli-e naft-e Irān; NIOC) in November 1952. They signed an agree-

Table 4
IRANIAN IMPORTS FROM AND EXPORTS TO JAPAN IN 1976

Iranian imports	(in $1,000)	(in %)	Iranian exports	(in $1,000)	(in %)
Machinery	582,642	34.1	Petroleum	4,190,051	94.2
Steel manufactures	553,040	32.4	Petroleum products	114,342	2.6
Textile goods	230,181	13.5	LPG	95,210	2.1
Metal goods	102,379	6.0	Food items	9,184	0.2
Tire tubes	75,944	4.5	Others	39,290	0.9
Others	162,374	9.5			
Total	1,706,560	100.0	Total	4,448,077	100.0

Source: Japan External Trade Organization, 1977, p. 34.

ment in February 1953 in Tehran. Idemitsu secretly sent an oil tanker called Nishshōmaru to Ābādān, where the tanker reached in April. Avoiding British colonial territories, the tanker returned to Japan through the Sunda strait with 18,468 kiloliters of gasoline and 3,325 kiloliters of gas oil (Yomiuri, pp. 259-87; Elwell-Sutton, pp. 298-99). As soon as the tanker reached Yokohama, the Anglo-Iranian Oil Company sued Idemitsu at the district court in Tokyo for stealing its oil, but the court denied its appeal. Between June 1953 and the end of 1954, Idemitsu imported 800,000 kiloliters of oil from Iran. However, the fall of the Moṣaddeq government through the coup d'etat of 1953 (q.v.) and the formation of the oil consortium initiated by the United States prevented Idemitsu from continuing to import oil directly from the NIOC (Yomiuri, pp. 385-86).

Nevertheless, the Nishshōmaru incident provided the two countries with an opportunity to resume their diplomatic relations. Iran signed the Treaty of Peace with Japan in San Francisco in September 1951, and the state of war with Japan legally ended. In Tehran in October 1953, Hirose, the Japanese envoy to Iran, and ʿAbd-Allāh Enteẓām (q.v.), the Iranian minister of foreign affairs, agreed to resume diplomatic relations. Japan reopened its legation in Tehran in November 1953, while the Iranian legation in Tokyo was reopened in December 1954. In the following year, each legation was raised to embassy status. The first Iranian ambassador was Musā Nuri Esfandiāri (Wezārat-e Omur-e Ḵāreja, p. 8). In addition, the Cultural Agreement was concluded between Iran and Japan in April 1957.

The royal houses of the two countries played significant roles in maintaining diplomatic relations. In Ordibehešt 1337/May 1958, the Japanese emperor, Showa (r. 1926-89), officially invited Mohammad Reza Shah Pahlavi to Japan. The latter visited Japan for two weeks, along with Iranian ministers and generals, and was received by the Japanese emperor. He also attended the opening ceremony of both the third Asian Games and the exhibition of Persian Arts in Tokyo, and visited manufacturing facilities in the industrial areas near Tokyo and Osaka. His visit resulted in new agreements between the two countries. In November, the Cultural Agreement came into operation, and in December, the Agreement of Cooperation in Economy and Technology was signed by the representatives of the two countries. In response to an invitation by Mohammad Reza Shah, the Japanese crown prince Akihito (the current reigning emperor) visited Iran in Ābān 1339/November 1960. He stayed in Iran for a week and gave a speech at the Senate.

Japan's trade with Iran developed markedly after the nationalization of oil industry, which resulted in the clash of the Iranian government with the United Kingdom. In 1952-53, Iranian imports from Japan reached 159.4 million rials, while Iranian exports to Japan were valued at 491.7 million rials (see Table 2).

In 1956, Japan was the fourth largest importing country and the eleventh largest exporting country for Iran. On the other hand, Iran was Japan's most important trading partner in the Middle East, although Iran constituted only 1 percent of the total Japanese exports in 1957. In 1959, the International Bank of Iran and Japan was established, and the bank's capital was shared by Iran (65 percent) and Japan (35 percent). The bank played an important role with respect to Japanese investments in Iran in the 1970s (Tōkyō Ginkō, p. 29).

The Iranian government was not satisfied with the trading situation, since, with the exception of petroleum, its trade with Japan was unfavorably balanced for Iran, whose trade deficit reached 8 million US dollars. Iran began to restrict imports from Japan in 1959, which Japan responded to by successfully concluding trade treaties with Iran in 1960 and 1964-65. According to these trade treaties, Japan was obliged to import Iranian products in the amounts that the treaty stipulated. It was difficult for Japan to fulfill this obligation, and as a result, Iran did not continue with the treaties. In 1968, Iran and Japan concluded a more comprehensive trade treaty in which Iran treated Japan on a most-favored-nation basis, while Japan was required to import Iranian products worth 12 million dollars per year, excluding oil. In the wake of this treaty, the volume of Irano-Japanese trade increased considerably; Iranian imports increased by 77 percent and Iranian exports, by 20 percent, between

1967 and 1968 (Japan External Trade Organization, 1969, p. 25).

By 1966-67, Japan had already become the world's largest importer of Iranian products including petroleum, which accounted for 21 percent of Iran's total exports. With regard to exports to Iran, Japan was the fourth largest exporter after West Germany, the United States, and the United Kingdom. For Japan, Iran was its most important trading partner in the Middle East (see Table 3).

The reason for this growth in trading was the swift growth of Japan's economy in the 1960s, leading to Japan's increasing demand for oil, which they imported chiefly from Iran. Moreover, Japan's heavy industries developed considerably in this period, and it began exporting machines, cars, and steel to Iran. This trend did not change significantly in the 1970s, although the volume of trade increased more than tenfold in dollar value. In 1975-76, Japan was the third largest importer of Iranian products, behind the United States and West Germany, and the world's largest importer of Iranian petroleum (see Table 4).

The 1970s witnessed a new trend, namely, an increase in Japanese investments in Iran. After the oil crisis in 1973, Iran came to be considered as one of the safest countries with respect to investments. Iran's close relations with the United States also attracted many Japanese investors. From 1973-74 to 1975-76, Japanese investments reached 6.2 billion rials, which comprised 49.8 percent of total foreign investments in Iran. Japan was the largest investing country in Iran, and more than 100 Japanese companies established offices in Tehran.

From among these companies, the most important project was the Iran-Japan Petrochemical Company (IJPC). It was linked with Japan's acquisition of the mining concession for the oil field in Lorestān in July 1971. Japan needed new oil fields that it could mine by itself because the price of oil was continually increasing at that time, and Japan wished to maintain a secure oil supply. Iran agreed to this oil concession on the condition that Japan would build a petrochemical plant at Bandar-e Šāpur (later Bandar-e Emām). In April 1973, the IJPC was established as a fifty-fifty venture between the National Petrochemical Company of Iran (NPC) and a consortium of Japanese companies headed by Mitsui and Company. In the first stage, the IJPC had funds amounting to 600 million dollars. The construction of the plant commenced in September 1976. The IJPC employed over 3,000 Japanese laborers as well as Iranians and Koreans. In January 1977, the Japanese government established a consulate at Ḵorramšahr to deal with the Japanese businessmen and laborers. In connection with the IJPC project, Japan granted a credit of 28.8 billion yen to Iran in March 1976 in order to deal with the increased costs of the plant's construction (Gaimushō, 1977, I, p. 158).

Other joint ventures included two factories built by Toshiba in Rašt and a tire factory established by Bridgestone in Shiraz. Pars Toshiba Industrial monopolized the market for electric fans in Iran, and Pars Toshiba Lamp enjoyed a market share of 50 percent with respect to electric lamps and fluorescent lighting. Sanyu [San'yū] Consultants Inc. personnel also organized a reclamation project for Hāmun lake in Sistān after 1970.

The economic relations between Iran and Japan were very close; consequently, it was quite natural for the Japanese Prime Minister Takeo Fukuda to visit Iran in September 1978. He was received by the Iranian Prime Minister Jaʿfar Šarif Emāmi and Mohamamd Reza Shah. In a joint statement, the two prime ministers agreed that Japan should continue to import Iranian products regularly and cooperate with Iran in the field of science and technology (Gaimushō, 1979, II, pp. 397-98). At that time, however, the anti-Pahlavi movement had already begun, and Fukuda's visit was rendered insignificant due to the Revolution.

Post-revolutionary period, 1979-2006. In February 1979, the Japanese government officially recognized Iran's new government. The political disorder inconvenienced the Japanese companies in Iran; however, Mehdi Bāzargān, the provisional prime minister, declared that the new government wished to maintain a good relationship with Japan and hoped that the joint projects including the IJPC would be continued. Furthermore, Iran's oil exports to Japan resumed in March. The Japanese government decided to support the IJPC as a national project, but the taking over of the U.S. embassy in Tehran in November 1979 and the ensuing hostage crisis (q.v.) leading to increasing tensions between the United States and Iran obliged Japan to take measures to display its discontent with the situation. Iranian oil exports to Japan were stopped after April 1980, and Japan withdrew its non-visa agreement with Iran in June. The relations between Iran and Japan normalized once the American hostages were released in January 1981.

Nonetheless, the outbreak of the Iran-Iraq War (see IRAQ vii) in September 1980 embarrassed the Japanese government. Japanese companies expected that the situation in Iran would eventually settle down following the Revolution, but it only grew worse due to the war. Since Japan had economic relations with both Iran and Iraq, it maintained a neutral position with respect to the war and, besides, attempted to bring an end to the war as early as possible. In May 1982, Yoshio Sakurauchi, the then Japanese minister of foreign affairs, published Japan's stance on the issue and invited Iran and Iraq to end their conflict and hold talks for reconciliation. In 1985, Japan separately invited Ṭāreq ʿAziz, the foreign minister of Iraq, and ʿAli-Akbar Hāšemi Rafsanjāni, the speaker of the Iranian parliament, to Japan and attempted to persuade them to end the war, but without success. The war inflicted severe damages on the Japanese investments in Iran and the Irano-Japanese joint projects. For example, the IJPC plant was bombarded on as many as twenty occasions and thus remained incomplete. Finally, in October 1989, the Japanese companies retreated entirely from the IJPC project and paid 130 billion yen to the NPC as settlement. Nevertheless, in spite of the Revolution and even during the course of the war, Japan remained a good trading partner for Iran. In 1983-84,

Table 5
IRANIAN IMPORTS FROM AND EXPORTS TO JAPAN IN 1984

Imports	(in $1,000)	(in %)	Exports	(in $1,000)	(in %)
Machinery	990,245	58.5	Petroleum	2,815,986	98.2
Textile goods	239,019	14.1	Petroleum products	32,592	1.1
Steel manufactures	192,778	11.4	Metal materials	11,766	0.4
Chemical products	69,853	4.1	Food items	3,079	0.1
Metal goods	36,744	2.2	Others	5,426	0.2
Others	163,484	9.7			
Total	1,692,123	100.0	Total	2,868,849	100.0

Source: World Economic Information Service, 1986, p. 16.

Table 6
IRANIAN IMPORTS FROM AND EXPORTS TO JAPAN IN 1994

Imports	(in $1,000)	(in %)	Exports	(in $1,000)	(in %)
Machinery	622,200	68.3	Petroleum	2,636,200	95.6
Steel and metal products	117,300	12.9	Textile goods	40,500	1.5
Chemical products	83,300	9.1	Food items	36,700	1.3
Textile goods	3,900	0.4	Metal prod.	19,000	0.7
Others	84,200	9.3	Others	25,900	0.9
Total	910,900	100.0	Total	2,758,300	100.0

Source: World Economic Information Service, 1998, p. 20.

the volume of Japanese exports to Iran was the second largest, behind only West Germany, and the volume of Japan's imports from Iran was the largest among all the countries (see Table 5).

After the end of the Iran-Iraq War in 1988, Japanese exports to Iran recovered to the level of the pre-revolution period for a few years, and Japan remained the second largest exporter behind Germany until 1995. Since then, Japan has maintained its number one ranking in terms of imports from Iran, although they recovered to the level of the pre-revolution period only after 2003 (see Table 6).

The Iranian efforts to export carpets, a major textile item, and food items such as pistachio nuts are evident from this Table. On the other hand, the volume of Japanese textile goods, which had once been a major item of the Iranian imports, is shown to have decreased drastically.

A major problem emerged between Iran and Japan in the early 90s, due to an influx of Iranian illegal laborers into Japan. Taking advantage of the non-visa agreement, the number of Iranian immigrants reached 32,000 in 1990 and 48,000 in 1991, of which the majority were working without work permits; in addition, their stay in Japan exceeded the permissible period as per the non-visa agreement by over three months. The Japanese Immigration Office deported 7,315 arriving Iranians from the New Tokyo International (Narita) Airport, who were considered to have arrived with the intention of working illegally. Finally, in April 1992, Japan and Iran stopped implementing the non-visa agreement, and the Iranian immigration decreased (for details see iv. below).

The political relations between the two countries were comparatively favorable in the 1990s. In 1993, Japan granted a credit of 38 billion yen to Iran for constructing the fourth Kārun Dam, but the D'Amato Act that the United States established in 1996, which imposed sanctions on foreign companies dealing with Iran and Libya, prevented Japan from forging closer ties with Iran. Japan's attitude toward Iran was also affected by tension between Iran and Germany. This was generated by the 1997 verdic of the Berlin High Court in the case of the killing of Kurdish opposition leaders at Mykonos Restaurant in Berlin on 17 September 1992; the court ruled that high-ranking state officials of Iran also were involved in the plot. But the emergence of Moḥammad Ḵātami as the president changed the situation. In 1999, the Japanese government decided to grant an additional credit of 7.5 billion yen to Iran for the fourth Kārun Dam project. In October 2000, Moḥammad Ḵātami paid a visit to Japan. He was received by the Japanese emperor, gave a speech at the House of Representatives, and held talks with the Japanese prime minister Yoshirō Mori. In a joint statement, Iran offered Japan the primary mining rights for the Āzādagān oil field, while Japan promised to pay

Table 7
IRANIAN IMPORTS FROM AND EXPORTS TO JAPAN IN 2004

Imports	(in $1,000)	(in %)	Exports	(in $1,000)	(in %)
Machinery	639,300	57.2	Petroleum	7,964,700	96.4
Steel/metal products	289,900	26.0	LPG	200,600	2.5
Chemical products	49,500	4.4	Textile goods	25,500	0.3
Textile materials	43,900	3.9	Food items	10,500	0.1
Others	94,500	8.5	Others	58,700	0.7
Total	1,117,100	100.0	Total	8,260,000	100.0

Source: World Economic Information Service, p. 36.

Iran 30 billion dollars in advance for three years worth of petroleum imports. In 2004, three Japanese companies and the NIOC concluded a contract to develop jointly the Āzādagān oil field, and the Japanese share was stipulated at 75 percent of the total shares.

The structure of Irano-Japanese trade has changed only marginally since the 1980s; yet, the current total Iranian exports to Japan are more than double of those in the 1990s (see Table 7).

Since the emergence of Maḥmud Aḥmadinežād's presidency in 2005, the political relations between Japan and Iran have become rather strained. The Iranian nuclear program as well as pressure from the United States has made Japan's political position more difficult. In September 2003, Japan had already agreed to be one of the co-sponsors of the proposal drafted by the Board of Governors of the International Atomic Energy Agency against the Iranian nuclear program. This difficult state of affairs is reflected in the reduction of the Japanese share in Āzādagān oil field to 10 percent in 2006.

Bibliography: Japanese archival sources before 1945 are available on the website of the Center for Asian Historical Record, National Archives of Japan at http://www.jacar.go.jp/. Iranian archives also hold many documents, but they have never been studied comprehensively.

Persian Sources. Daftar-e moṭāleʿāt-e siāsi wa bayn-al-melali, *Siāsatgarān wa rejāl-e siāsi dar rawābeṭ-e ḵāreji-e Irān*, Tehran, 1990, pp. 41-42. Moḥammad-Ḥasan Khan Eʿtemād-al-Salṭana, *Tāriḵ-e montaẓam-e nāṣeri*, ed. Moḥammad-Esmāʿil Reżwāni, 3 vols., Tehran, 1984-88. Mahdiqoli Hedāyat (Moḵber-al-Salṭana), *Safar-nāma-ye Makka az rāh-e Sibri, Čin, Žāpon, Amrikā . . . Torkiya*, ed. Moḥammad Dabirsiāqi, Tehran, 1989. ʿAbd-al-Reżā Hušang Mahdawi, *Siāsat-e ḵāreji-e Irān dar dawrān-e Pahlavi*, Tehran, 1974, pp. 423-24, 537-38. Nāṣer-al-Din Shah, *Ruz-nāma-ye ḵāṭerāt-e Nāṣer-al-Din Šāh dar safar-e awwal-e Farangestān*, ed. Fāṭema Qāżihā, Tehran, 1998. Idem, *Ruz-nāma-e ḵāṭerāt-e Nāṣer-al-Din Šāh dar safar-e dovvom-e Farangestān*, ed. Fātema Qāżihā, Tehran, 2000. *Ruz-nāma-ye Irān*, repr. Tehran, 1996. Ebrāhim Ṣaḥḥāf-bāši Tehrāni, *Safar-nāma-ye Ebrāhim Ṣaḥḥāf-bāši Tehrāni*, ed. Moḥammad Moširi, Tehran, 1979. Ḥosayn-ʿAli Tājer-e Sirāzi, *Mikādo-nāma*, ed. ʿAli Amin Anṣāri, Tehran, 2006. Moḥammad Wāredi, ed., *Žāpon*, 3rd ed., Tehran, 2005. Wezārat-e Omur-e Ḵāreja, *Rawābeṭ-e dawlat-e šāhanšāhi-e Irān bā dowal-e ḥawza-ye masʿuliyat-e Edāre-e haftom-e siāsi ṭayy-e panjāh sāl-e šāhanšāhi-e Pahlavi*, Tehran, 1976.

English Sources. L. P. Elwell-Sutton, *Persian Oil: A Study in Power Politics*, London, 1955. Roxane Haag-Higuchi, "A Topos and Its Dissolution: Japan in Some 20th-Century Iranian Texts," *Iranian Studies* 29/1-2, 1996, pp. 71-84. Anja Pistor-Hatam, "Progress and Civilization in Nineteenth-Century Japan: The Far Eastern State as a Model for Modernization," *Iranian Studies* 29, 1996, pp. 111-26. Hashem Rajabzadeh, "Russo-Japanese War as Told by Iranians," *Annals of Japanese Association for Middle East Studies* 3/2, 1988, pp. 144-66. Idem, "Japan as Seen by Qajar Travellers," in Elton L. Daniel, ed., *Society and Culture in Qajar Iran: Studies in Honor of Hafez Farmayan*, Costa Mesa, 2002, pp. 285-309. Hiroshi Shimizu, *Anglo-Japanese Trade Rivalry in the Middle East in the Inter-War Period*, London, 1986.

Japanese Sources. *Asahi Shimbun*, Tokyo, 1945-. Yasumasa Fukushima, *Chūō Ajia kara Arabia e* (From Central Asia to Arabia), ed. A. Ōta, Tokyo, 1943. Nobuyoshi Furukawa, *Perusha kikō* (Journey to Persia), Tokyo, 1891; tr. Hāšem Rajabzāda and Kinji Eura as *Safar-nāma-ye Furukāwā*, Tehran, 2005. Gaimushō (Ministry of Foreign Affairs of Japan), *Gaikō seisho* (Blue book), Tokyo, 1957-. Gaimushō Gaikō Shiryō-kan (Diplomatic Records Office of the Ministry of Foreign Affairs of Japan), *Nihon gaikō jiten* (Dictionary of Japanese diplomacy), Tokyo, 1992. Toyokichi Ienaga, *Nishi-ajia Ryokoki* (Journey to West Asia), Tokyo, 1900. Eiji Inoue, *Waga Kaisō no Iran* (My memory of Iran), Tokyo, 1890; ed. Masayuki Inoue, Tokyo, 1986; tr. Hāšem Rajabzāda as *Irān wa man: ḵāṭerahā wa yāddāšthā-ye Eiji Inuva*, Tehran, 2004. Masaji Inoue, *Chūōajia ryokōki* (Journey to Central Asia), Tokyo, 1903. Shiro Ishiwada, *Orenjiiro no Hono ōtte: Iran sekika-tono jūnen* (Pursuing the orange flame: ten years with the Iran Petroleum Project), Tokyo, 1981. Japan External Trade Organization (JETRO),

Table 8
IRANIAN MINISTERS PLENIPOTENTIARY AND CHARGÉS D'AFFAIRES

Avānes Khan Mosāʿed-al-Salṭana	minister plenipotentiary	Jul. 1930-Aug. 1931
Ḥasan-ʿAli Kamāl Hedāyat	minister plenipotentiary	Sep. 1931-Oct. 1933
Bāqer ʿAẓimi	minister plenipotentiary	Oct. 1933-May 1937
ʿAli-Moḥammad Šaybāni	chargé d'affaires	May 1937-Nov. 1938
Maḥmud Bahādori	chargé d'affaires	Dec. 1938-Mar. 1941
Abu'l-Qāsem Najm	minister plenipotentiary	Mar. 1941-May 1943
Musā Nuri Esfandiāri	minister plenipotentiary	Mar. 1955-April 1955
Ḥasan Ṭāheriān	chargé d'affaires	Nov. 1989-Feb. 1990

Source: Daftar-e moṭālaʿāt-e siāsi wa bayn-al-melali, p. 41.

Table 9
IRANIAN AMBASSADORS

Musā Nuri Esfandiāri	April 1955-August 1956
Ḥosayn Qods Naḵaʿi	November 1956-February 1958
ʿAbbās Ārām	February 1958-August 1959
Jawād Ṣadr	December 1959-December1963
Hormoz Qarib	February 1964-January 1968
Nur-al-Din Kiā	June 1968-July1972
ʿAbd-al-Ḥosayn Ḥamzāwi	July 1972-July 1977
Nāṣer Majd Ardakāni	August 1977-May 1979
Qāsem Ṣāleḥ-ḵu	May 1979-April 1982
ʿAbd-al-Raḥim Govāhi	April 1982-July 1987
Moḥammad-Ḥosayn ʿĀdeli	July 1987-November 1989
Ḥoayn Kāẓem Purardabili	February 1990

Source: Daftar-e moṭālaʿāt-e siāsi wa bayn-al-melali, pp. 41-42.

Table 10
JAPANESE MINISTERS PLENIPOTENTIARY AND CHARGÉS D'AFFAIRES

Akio Kasama	minister plenipotentiary	December 1929-October 1932
Toyokichi Fukuma	chargé d'affaires	October 1932- February 1933
Takezō Okamoto	minister plenipotentiary	February 1933-November 1936
Shunsuke Asada	chargé d'affaires	November 1936- September 1937
Shōichi Nakayama	minister plenipotentiary	September 1937-September 1940
Gorō Asaoka	chargé d'affaires	September 1940- March 1941
Hikotarō Ichikawa	minister plenipotentiary	March 1941- April 1942
Tasuo Hirose	chargé d'affaires	November 1953-May 1954
Suemitsu Kadowaki	minister plenipotentiary	May 1954-February 1955
Uryū Matao	chargéd'affaires	February-April 1955

Source: Gaimushō Gaikō Shiryōkan, appendix, pp. 67-68, 100.

Iran, Osaka. 1969; rev. ed., Tokyo, 1977. Akio Kasama, *Sabaku no kuni* (Land of desert), Tokyo, 1935; tr. Hāšem Rajabzāda as *Safar-nāma-ye Kāzāmā*, Tehran, 2002.

Saneki Nakaoka, "Gaimushō goyōgakari Yoshida Masaharu Perusha to kō ikken (The Japanese government mission of 1880 to Persia and Turkey Headed by Masaharu Yoshida)," *Mikasanomiya-denka Kokikinen Orientogaku Ronshū*, Tokyo, 1985, pp. 221-33. Nihon Iran Bunkakyōkai (Japan-Iran Culture Association), *Shinkōkoku Iran* (An emerging nation, Iran), Tokyo, 1940. Nihon Keizai Shinbunsha (Nihon Keizai Shimbun, Inc.), *Iran to Nippon* (Iran and Japan), Tokyo. 1958. Nihon Kōgyō Kurabu (The industry club of Japan), *Iran Iraku jijō* (Iran and Iraq affairs), Tokyo,

Table 11
JAPANESE AMBASSADORS

Hisanari Yamada	April 1955-March 1958
Kōhei Teraoka	June 1958-January 1960
Hiroshi Chiba	October 1960-July 1963
Yoshimitsu Andō	August 1963-December 1966
Atsushi Uyama	January 1967-May 1969
Kensaku Maeda	August 1969-September 1972
Keisuke Arita	October 1972-April 1974
Katsuichi Igawa	June 1974-November 1978
Chikara Wada	December 1978-May 1981
Shōtarō Takahashi	June 1981-August 1983
Yutaka Nomura	September 1983-March 1987
Yoshio Fujimoto	March 1987-June 1989
Kunihiko Saitō	July 1989

Source: Gaimushō Gaikō Shiryōkan, appendix, p. 100.

1956. Eishirō Nuita, *Persha Mesopotamiya hōmen shisatsudan* (Journey to Persia and Mesopotamia), Tokyo. 1924. Shōkō Okazaki, "Meiji no Nihon to Iran: Yoshida Masaharu shisetsudan (1880) ni tsuite (The first Japanese Mission to Qajar Persia)," *Osaka-gaikokugodaigaku Gakuhō* 70/3, 1985, pp. 71-86; tr. Hāšem Rajabzāda et al. as "Nak̲ostin hay᾽at-e sefārat-e Žapon ba Irān dar dawra-ye Qājāriya," *Āyanda* 15/3-5, 1989, pp. 350-75, 412-14. Hideaki Sugita, *Nihonjin no Chūtō hakken* (The Japanese discovery of the Middle East), Tokyo, 1995. Hitoshi Suzuki, *Iran kakumei to Nihonjin* (The Iranian revolution and the Japanese), Tokyo, 2000. Tōkyō Ginkō (Bank of Tokyo), *Iran no Keiza-to Kinyu-jijo* (The economy and financial affairs of Iran), Tokyo, 1967. World Economic Information Service (WEIS), *ARC Repōto: Iran*, Tokyo, 1986, 1998, 2005. Yokohama Shōkin Ginkō (Yokohama Specie Bank), *Perushia keizai jijō* (The economy of Iran), Tokyo, 1930. The Yomiuri Shimbun, *Nishshomaru jiken: Iran sekiyu o motomete* (The Nishshōmaru affair in quest of Iranian oil), Tokyo, 1981. Masaharu Yoshida, *Kaikyō tanken Perusha no tabi* (Adventures in Muslim Persia), Tokyo, 1894; tr. Hāšem Rajabzādeh as *Safar-nāma-e Yušidā Māsāhāru: nak̲ostin ferestāda-ye Jāpon ba Irān dar dawra-ye Qājār, 1297-98 h.q.*, Mashad, 1994.

(NOBUAKI KONDO)

iii. JAPANESE TRAVELERS TO PERSIA

In Japan the Edo Shogunate (1603-1867) forbade any visits or trade with foreigners other than those from China and the Netherlands. According to the decree of 1635, the Japanese were barred from traveling abroad and, according to the decree of 1639, the Portuguese were forbidden to enter the main islands of Japan. It was only in 1854 that relations with foreign countries were resumed. This process gathered pace with the advent of the Meiji period (1868-1912), when the Japanese were allowed to go on official visits abroad. In 1929 formal diplomatic relations were established between Japan and Persia.

The Japanese mission of 1880-81. In 1879, Nāṣer-al-Din Shah, returning from his second European tour, received the Japanese minister plenipotentiary Enomoto and secretary Tokujirō Nishi while in Saint Petersburg and expressed his interest in establishing relations with Japan (Yoshida, p. 2, tr., p. 30). In response, the Meiji government sent a formal mission to Persia in 1880. It was composed of the following members: Masaharu Yoshida (1852-1921) from the ministry of foreign affairs, who headed the mission; Nobuyoshi Furukawa (1849-1921), who was a captain in the Japanese army; Magoichirō Yokoyama (1848-1911), the vice-president of the Ōkura Gumi trading company; and others, including five merchants (Eʿtemād-al-Salṭana, 1984-88, III. p. 2009; idem, 1984-89, I, p. 331, giving the names as: Yošidā Mosaḥḥaro, Yukuyāma Kuʾijirow, Fukārvā Nuluyoš). On April 8 they left Tokyo's Shinagawa harbor on board the battleship *Hiei*. After transit stops at Hong Kong, Singapore, Ceylon, Bombay, Karachi, and Muscat, the battleship anchored at Bušehr (Bushire) on 9 July 1880. The mission entered Bušehr formally on July 11, and on July 25 began the overland journey to Tehran. For the Japanese party this was their first experience of Persia and the Middle East, and they found much to marvel at and compare and contrast with their own very different culture at home. Their travelogues are a vivid testimonial to their impressions and reactions (e.g., Furukawa, pp. 36, 41, 53; Yoshida, pp. 70-71, 73, 135).

On their way to Tehran, they visited the ruins of Persepolis and Pasargadae on August 13 and 14, and were struck by the extraordinary differences in the appearance and architecture of the monuments of the past in Persia and Japan. At Persepolis they saw the cuneiform inscriptions and noted that the ancient characters were called in Persian *mik̲aki*, derived from the word "nail" (*mik̲*) (Yoshida, pp. 78-81, tr., pp. 115-26). They made their formal entry into the capital on September 10, and were received in audience by Nāṣer-al-Din Shah on September 27 (Furukawa, p. 211, tr., p. 256) or October 2 (Yoshida, p. 145, tr. p. 181). During their stay in Tehran, the party presented and sold their Japanese specialties (lacquer and cloisonné works, swords, etc.) brought from Japan. They left Tehran on December 30, and departed from the port of Anzali on the Caspian Sea for Baku on 12 January 1881 (Yoshida, p. 188, tr. p. 178).

In assessing the nature of this expedition, it must be borne in mind that at the time Japan was actively and successfully engaged in building a modern state, and looked favorably at Persia, a kingdom on the other side of Asia and one of the few countries that had managed to preserve its independence in the colonized Orient. The mission's findings, as reflected in Yoshida's account, were pessimistic. Though he was impressed by the great interest shown by Nāṣer-al-Din Shah in the Japanese modernization effort and its achievements, the embassy found the Persian bureaucracy and army in a parlous state verging on the chaotic. Corruption was rife among those in high positions, and public morale was at a low ebb, with little confidence in the government. Among the dignitaries that Yoshida met, he found much to praise in Mirza Ḥasan Khan Moširal-Dawla (Sepahsālār), the ill-fated minister who was dismissed and exiled a few days after Yoshida's arrival in Tehran. In his travelogue, Yoshida expresses his concern about the fate and fortune of Persia in those turbulent years (Yoshida, pp. 129-31, tr. p. 166).

Yoshida's memoirs also contain some illuminating passages on the life of Zoroastrians and Armenians in Persia and an invaluable account on the background to the trading-house of David Sassoon, the opium merchant in Bušehr (Yoshida, pp 22-23, 89-90; tr. pp. 49-51, 122).

Travelers to Persia in the late Qajar period. Yasumasa Fukushima (1852-1919) worked in the General Staff Office as an army intelligence officer and was known for his bravery. He made a successful crossing of Siberia on horseback during the winter of 1892 to gather intelligence about the construction of the trans-Siberian railroad by imperial Russia. He started from Germany in February and reached Japan in June. Given the strategic and military significance of Russia, Fukushima thought it was vital for Japan to be fully acquainted with conditions in Russia. He performed three overseas explorations to collect military data during his tenure as an intelligence officer, and specifically to verify the disposition of the Russian troops and the state of the progress of the construction of the Central Asia railroad in Turkestan. The secretive aspect of this mission meant that the reports were not released, and many of his activities at the time are still shrouded in mystery. The relevant parts of his *Ajia ryakuhō* (Brief account of Asia) and *Aō nikki* (Diary of Asia and Europe), in which he described his visits to Persia, the Caucasus, and Central Asia, have not yet been made public (Kaneko, p. 122). His travels to Persia were included as one of the itineraries on his third overseas exploration from August 1895 to March 1897.

Fukushima landed at Bušehr by steamer on 22 May 1896 after making a round of calls on Burma (Myanmar), Thailand, and India. He followed the same route as Yoshida, Furukawa, and the others in 1880, and reached Isfahan on June 23 via Kāzerun and Shiraz. At Isfahan he was received in audience by Masʿud Mirzā Ẓell-al-Solṭān, the prince governor. Leaving Isfahan on June 28, Fukushima reached Tehran via Qom on July 3. His aim was to inspect the military system of the Persian army and to prepare for his projected exploration of Russian Turkistan. He was received in audience by the recently enthroned Moẓaffar-al-Din Shah on 19 July 1896.

Leaving Tehran on August 2, via Qazvin and Rašt, Fukushima departed from Anzali harbor on a Russian steamship and reached Baku after two days. He then began a thorough survey of Russian Turkistan from the eastern coast of the Caspian Sea to Ashkabad (ʿEsqābād), Marv, Bukhara, Samarkand, Tashkent, and Kokand. After that, on September 12, he traveled south to Persia again from Ashkabad and arrived at Mashad via Qučān on September 16. He stayed for a week in Mashad, where the British consulate general gave him some assistance. He was back in Tehran on October 2, where he spared no time and effort to observe the military exercises of the Persian soldiers, whom he found in a state of complete disarray and chaos (pp. 143-44). In his travelogue, *Chūō Ajia yori Arabia e* (Traveling from Central Asia to Arabia), he gives an account of his audience with the Persian king under the title "2 or 3 childish questions in a soulless hall" (Fukushima, p. 77). His accounts of his meetings with Ẓell-al-Solṭān, Amin-al-Soltān (the prime minister), the Naẓm-al-Molk (Italian, Conte di Monteforte, former head of the police), and other dignitaries are of special interest. He also gives an informative account on Ṣaḥḥāf-bāši Mirzā Ebrāhim Khan, the first Persian to visit Japan and write his memoirs, and his brother Mirzā Esmāʿil Khan. While in Tehran, Fukushima mainly associated with, and was greatly helped by, Wagner Khan, the Austrian military adviser to the Persian court and a teacher at Dār al-Fonun (q.v.; Fukushima, pp. 41, 65, 70-72, 146-49, 161).

Toyokichi Ienaga (1862-1936) studied politics in the United States and is regarded as one of the Japanese pioneers who acquainted Japan with the politics of the United States. Before embarking on teaching at the University of Chicago, he explored India, Persia, and Turkey from May 1899 to March 1900 upon the request of the governor-general of Formosa Prefecture. Ienaga left Taiwan on 17 May 1899 and arrived in Persia at Bušehr on a steamship from Bombay on July 24 (Ienaga, p. 20). He stayed in Bušehr for three days before he left for Tehran, which he reached on September 10 by traveling via Shiraz, Isfahan, and Qom. On the way, he visited the ancient ruins of Persepolis and Pasargadae on August 20 or 21 (Ienaga, pp. 67-74). He dispatched regular on-the-spot accounts of his travels to *Kokumin shinbun*, a daily Japanese newspaper. These reports were later compiled and printed as a book in 1900. The second to fifth reports relate to Persia. In these, he offered a sketch of contemporary Persian social life, culture, politics, economy, and history, based on his direct and frank personal observations. According to these reports, he suffered greatly from the intense summer heat, something that he had not experienced before, as well as from the woeful accommodations. He also found the landscape monotonous and the royal apparatus pompous but devoid of power, the real authority being exercised by British and Russian legations (Ienaga, pp. 121-22).

Like Fukushima, he frequently used the British telegraph offices as lodging houses while traveling in Persia; he also carried a letter of introduction from the British minister in Japan, which he found useful, given the considerable power and prestige enjoyed by Britain in Persia in those days. On 13 September 1899, he had an audience with the shah, and on September 17 he left Tehran for Rašt via Qazvin, Manjil, and Rostamābād. On September 21 he left Persia from the Anzali harbor on a Russian steamship destined for Baku (Ienaga, pp. 105, 117).

Masaji Inoue (1876-1947) was a typical colonial official of the Meiji Era. He is regarded as one of the earliest Japanese pioneers to visit Central Asia from the Caucasus (Kaneko, p. 127). During his university summer vacations while studying at a European university, Inoue embarked on a journey to Central Asia from Europe (16 August-6 November 1902). On his way back to Europe he traveled through Persia.

On September 10, Inoue arrived at the small Persian port of Mašhadsar (later Bābolsar) on the southeast shore of the Caspian Sea (Inoue, p. 194); this was on the sea route from the Russian harbor Krasnovodsk on the east shore of the Caspian Sea. It was a daring venture to take this obscure route to enter Persia. He crossed the Alborz range and arrived in Tehran on September 15 (Inoue, pp. 229, 333). Inoue stayed in Tehran for five days; he lodged at a hotel under British management, where both Fukushima and Ienaga had also stayed, in 1892 and in 1899 respectively.

Inoue met some eminent Persians in Tehran and also visited the royal palace, but did not have an audience with the shah. After leaving Tehran on September 20, via Qazvin, Zanjān, Solṭāniya, Miāna, and Tabriz, Inoue crossed into Russia at Jolfā on September 30. He observed and wrote frankly in his travelogue about many aspects of his visit, the people he met, modes of transport, industries, and natural scenery. His description of the conditions in Gilān and Māzandarān is informative and rich in detail (Inoue, pp. 216-43).

Naokichi Nakamura (1865-1932) was a merchant whose insatiable curiosity led him to travel first to the United States (1888-98) and subsequently on a world trip (1901-07). Late in May 1902, Nakamura arrived at Bušehr harbor on a British steamship from Karachi. He stayed in Bušehr for five days before he left for Tehran, where he arrived some time around 9 October 1902, traveling via Shiraz, Isfahan, and Kāšān. He traveled with little money and sought the support of various people on the way. He was helped by the manager of the Anglo-Persian Bank at Shiraz, who had also looked after Fukushima when he visited the city. He also stayed at the same lodging house belonging to the British consulate at Isfahan where Fukushima had stayed in 1896. After a week's stay in Tehran, Nakamura left on October 16; passing through Qazvin and Rašt, he reached Anzali to embark for Baku. There are few details in his travel account about the places he visited or even on relevant dates and time, but the book contains vivid recollections of his conversations with people he had met on his travels.

Kakō Ōba (Kageaki, 1872-1921?) traveled to Persia in 1910 and to almost every corner of the world as a reporter for the *Ōsaka mainichi shinbun* newspaper. He left Japan on March 15, on the battleship Ikoma. He reached Persia, arriving in Anzali harbor from Baku, and went to Tehran from Rašt on October 25 via Manjil and Qazvin. Although the length of his stay in Persia was less than two weeks, which included several days in Tehran, his writings contain a very detailed description of the city of Tehran and Māzandarān province, depicting the natural scenery, industry, transportation condition, religion, social custom, issues relevant to women, newspapers, diplomatic relations, etc. He pointed out to the strong influence that Russia and Britain wielded over Persia. Ōba left Persia from Mašhadsar on October 4, returning to Japan on 27 October 1911 by way of Central Asia and such towns as Marv, Bukhara, and Samarkand.

Bibliography: Moḥammad-Ḥasan Khan Eʿtemād-al-Salṭana, *Tāriḵ-e montaẓam-e nāṣiri*, ed. Moḥammad-Esmāʿil Reżwāni, 3 vols., Tehran, 1984-88. Idem, *al-Maʾāṯer wa'l-āṯār*, ed. Iraj Afšār as *Čehel sāl tāriḵ-e Irān dar dawra-ye pādšāhi-e Nāṣer-al-Din Šāh*, commentaries by Ḥosayn Maḥbubi Ardakāni, 3 vols., Tehran, 1984-89. Yasumasa Fukushima, *Chūō Ajia yori Arabia e* (Traveling from Central Asia to Arabia), ed. Azan ota, Tokyo, 1943. Nobuyoshi Furukawa, *Perushya kikō* (Persian journal), Tokyo, 1891; tr. Hashem Rajabzadeh and Kinji Eura as *Safar-nāma-ye Furukawa*, Tehran, 2004. Toyokichi Ienaga, *Nishi Ajia ryokōki* (Record of a west Asian journey), Tokyo, 1900. Masaji Inoue, *Chūō Ajia ryokōki* (Record of a Central Asian journey), Tokyo, 1903. Tamio Kaneko, *Chūō Ajia ni haitta nihonjin* (Japanese who went to Central Asia), Tokyo, 1973. Naokichi Nakamura, *Tekkyaku jūō* (From the East to the West on iron feet), in *Godaishū tankenki* (Records of exploration of the five continents) III, Tokyo, 1910. Kakō Ōba, *Nanboku yonman mailu* (40,000 miles south and north), Tokyo, 1911. Tadahiko Ōtsu, "Meiji 13-nen Perushya hōmondan'in ni tsuite" (On the members of the Persia visit of 1880), *Chashm* 83, 1999, pp. 28-34. Shoko Okazaki, "Naḵostin hayʾat-e sefārat-e Žapon ba Irān dar dawra-ye Qājāriya," tr. Hāšem Rajabzadeh et al., *Āyanda* 15/3-5, 1989, pp. 350-75, 412-14. Kiyoshi Tabohashi, "Sōgyō jidai ni okeru Meiji seifu kōshō" (Foreign relations in the early Meiji era), *Shigaku zasshi* 34, 1923, pp. 806-18. Yuriko Yamanaka, "Meiji Nihonjin no Perusia taiken" (Experiences of Meiji Japanese in Persia), *Hikaku bungaku* 35, 1993, pp. 117-28. Masaharu Yoshida, *Kaikyō tanken Perushia no tabi* (Adventures in Muslim Persia), Tokyo, 1894; tr. H. Rajabzadeh as *Safar-nāma-ye Yušidā Māsāhāru: naḵostin ferestāda-ye Jāpon ba Irān dar dawra-ye Qājār, 1297-98 h.q.*, Tehran, 1994.

(TADAHIKO OHTSU and HASHEM RAJABZADEH)

iv. IRANIANS IN JAPAN

Japanese society is often said to be closed to foreigners, and yet in 2005 the number of foreign residents in Japan reached two million people (1.6 percent of the total population of the country). Among the foreigners in Japan, Iranians total about 5,000 people, constituting a small minority group. In the early 1990s, about 50,000 Iranians were residing in Japan; many of them were illegal workers. Despite the fact that most Iranians were obliged to return to their homeland after the Japanese legislation for immigration underwent changes in the early 1990s, an Iranian community in Japan continues to exist.

Early times. The first mention of Iranians (Persians) coming to Japan can be found in the *Nihon Shoki* (Chronicles of Japan), one of the earliest Japanese historical sources, completed in 720 C.E. It records that in 654 C.E. several people arrived in Japan from Tokhārā (Aston, pp. 246, 251, 259). Though there is some controversy about the location of Tokhārā, some scholars have claimed the name to be a shortened version of Tok̲ārestān, which was part of the territory of Sasanian Persia (Itō, 1980, pp. 5-10). Elsewhere in the *Nihon Shoki*, it is mentioned that in 660, when an Iranian (Persian), whose name was Dārā, returned to his country, he left his wife in Japan and promised the Emperor that he would come back and work for him again (Aston, p. 266; Imoto, 2002, pp. 58-60).

In the 7th to the 9th centuries, foreigners—then known in Japanese as *toraijin*—were coming to Japan mainly from Korea and China, bringing with them technology, culture, religion (Buddhism), and ideas. Eastern Asia, especially the Tang Dynasty of China (618-907), had socio-economic networks with many regions of the world, including southern and western Asia. Chang'an (present-day Xi'an), the capital of the Tang Dynasty, was an international city with people from various countries, including Iranians (Persians), some of whom traveled further to Japan. Iranian names are to be met with in historical documents, and one can find some influence of Persian culture in the architecture, sculptures, and also in the customs and old Japanese rituals at that time. For example, some scholars have claimed that there is some influence of Persian culture in the Omizutori ritual held every February at Tōdaiji temple in Nara (Itō, 1980, pp. 125-33).

The oldest document in Persian, which is preserved in Japan, was procured by the Japanese priest named Kyōsei (1189-1268) from Iranians (Persians) during his trip to southern Asia in 1217. Thinking they were Indians, the priest asked them to write something for him as a keepsake. However, after his return to Japan he found out that they were not Indians, because no one could understand what the writing meant. This document—a single page—was discovered in the late 20th century, when it was established that it is written in Persian and contains a line from Abu'l-Qāsem Ferdowsi's *Šāh-nāma* (qq.v.), a line from Fak̲r-al-Din Gorgāni's *Vis o Rāmin* (qq.v.), and a quatrain of unknown authorship (Okada, 1989).

Early modern times. Due to Japan's policy of isolation in the Edo period (1603-1867), diplomatic and economic relations with foreign countries were much limited. Foreigners were not allowed to reside in Japan except in restricted areas, and there were no foreign communities until the Meiji period (1867-1912). In the 17th century some Iranian merchants arrived from Thailand to Nagasaki, which was the only area that foreign traders were allowed to enter, but this was an exceptional case (Nagashima, 1997). After the Meiji Restoration (1868), Japan wanted to become a modern state like European countries and began to open its doors to foreigners. In 1880, the first Japanese delegation was sent to Persia. The head of the delegation, Masaharu Yoshida (1852-1921), wrote a travelogue and introduced Qajar Persia to the Japanese (Yoshida, 1894).

On the other hand, there is a travelogue about the trip to Japan written by Mehdiqoli Hedāyat Mok̲ber-al-Salṭana (1864-1955, see HEDAYAT [HEDĀYAT], MOK̲BER-AL-SALṬANA, MEHDIQOLI), the Prime Minister of Persia in 1927-33 and a relative of the famous Iranian poet Ṣādeq Hedāyat (1903-51, q.v.; Okazaki, 1992; Rajabzadeh, 2002). He accompanied ʿAli-Aṣg̲ar Khan Amin-al-Solṭān (1858-1907, see ATĀBAK-E AʿẒAM), the prime minister of Persia under the last three Qajar shahs, in his travels to Russia, East Asia, and the U.S.A. in 1903-04. Hedāyat was both his associate and translator during the trip. They entered Japan by ship from Shanghai on 9 December 1903, arriving first at Nagasaki and then sailing on to Kobe. After visiting the ancient capital city of Kyoto, they arrived in Tokyo on 14 December. The Japanese government treated the ex-prime minister of Persia as an official guest. During their 22-day stay in Tokyo until 6 January 1904, they met with the Emperor Meiji (r. 1867-1912), Prime Minister Taro Katsura, the first prime minister of Japan, Hirofumi Itō, Minister of Foreign Affairs Jutarō Komura, and other politicians. They visited several schools (including girls' schools), courts, the naval port of Yokosuka, and other places.

Hedāyat was much impressed by the simple and well-organized life of the Japanese, their intense interest in education, and other aspects of life in Japan. He was especially surprised by the fact that the Japanese attended to their business very seriously and without giving any gratuities. He was also impressed by Japanese patriotism. After the victory over China in the first Sino-Japanese War of 1894-95, Japan was preparing for the Russo-Japanese War that would take place in 1904-05. Hedāyat wrote that, after meeting with politicians and visiting a military school, he felt that war was very near. Japanese victory over Russia impressed Iranian society, which had suffered from Russian domination in the 19th century.

The twentieth century up to 1979. After the Meiji Restoration (1868), foreigners started to settle in Japan. Diplomatic relations between Persia and Japan were officially established in 1929, when the first Japanese legation was opened in Persia. In the next year, the Persian legation in Japan was established. However, there is a record of a consul-general of Persia from before then: a newspaper in Kobe reported on an Iranian consul-general's residence, calling it "Bajaj's House" (*Kōbe shinbun*, 4 January 2003). The house was built in the Taishō period (1912-26) and, upon being sold, became opened to the public and was used as a Persian museum from 1981 to 1994. Unfortunately, the building was completely destroyed in the Great Hansin earthquake that shook Kobe in 1995. Kobe was one of the first Japanese ports opened to foreigners, many of whom settled there soon after the country opened up, so it is likely that there was an unofficial or honorary consul representing the Iranians who lived in the city at that time.

After Japan entered World War II, Iran broke off relations with Japan, and they were restored only in 1953. However, economic ties had already resumed in 1947, and there were small numbers of Iranian traders, especially carpet traders and their families, residing in Japan (Inoue, p. 215). Iranians who stayed in Japan were historically limited to traders, students, skilled workers, and temporary residents who worked for Iranian companies or for the Iranian government. Most of them were highly educated people with relatively high income, and their number was not considerable before the Islamic Revolution of 1979. Records from the Japanese Immigration Office show that there were 76 Iranians in Japan in 1964, 187 in 1974, 543 in 1985, and 1,237 in 1991. Among them were members of well-known and rich Iranian families, but, even though they knew each other, no particular association or community of Iranians existed in Japan.

Japanese cities which had facilities for foreigners, such as international schools, cemeteries, and religious institutions, were few, and therefore foreigners in Japan, especially those from Western, south Asian, and west Asian countries, tended to live mainly in big cities like Tokyo or in the old ports, such as Yokohama and Kobe, which have long been open to foreigners. These cities had communities of different national and religious groups. For example, a Muslim community existed in Kobe from the 1930s, and both a Jewish and a Bahai community from the 1950s. Some Iranian residents in Japan belonged to these communities. In general, the lifestyle of most Iranians in Japan was similar to that of the Westerners. They sent their children to international schools and used shops that sold imported goods. Japanese people usually treated the Iranians living in Japan just in the same way as they did the Westerners.

After the Islamic Revolution of 1979. From 1986 to 1991-92, Japan experienced enormous economic prosperity. However, because the Japanese government prohibited the issue of visas to unskilled workers, a shortage of workers became a serious problem for small businesses and factories in Japan. At first, many of the illegal workers came to Japan from Korea, China, and other countries of the Far East. After that, others followed from South American countries, for example, Brazil and Peru, from southeast Asia, for example, Bangladesh and Pakistan, and from the Middle East, including Iran (Komai, 1996).

After the end of the Iran-Iraq War (see IRAQ vii) in 1988, many young Iranian men who were returning from the battlefields could not find jobs in Iran. Iran and Japan had a bilateral agreement at that time which allowed entry for short-term visits without a visa. The anti-Western Islamic Revolution in Iran caused the West to close the doors to Iranian workers, except for political refugees, but Japan remained a country where Iranians could enter without a visa. Most of the Iranians who came to Japan at that time were single men in their 20s and 30s. They included both ethnic Persian Iranians and ethnic Turkic Iranians, and many of them were from Iran's big cities (Yamagishi and Morita, 2002; Tsukuba Daigaku Shakaigaku Kenkyūshitsu, 1995). As they could not speak any Japanese when they came to Japan, they first had to work as unskilled workers. The Japanese Immigration Office states that, although there were only 764 illegal Iranian residents in 1990, this number increased to 10,915 in 1991 and to 40,001 in 1992. In comparison, the number of legal Iranian residents was 1,237 in 1991, 4,516 in 1993, and 8,645 in 1996.

Many of the Iranian workers had little knowledge of the Japanese language or Japanese culture and social system, and there was no suitable Iranian community to guide them. Therefore, they used public parks in the center of Tokyo, such as Yoyogi Park or Ueno Park, to communicate with each other, to get information about work, housing, and shopping, and to receive news about their home country (Morita, 2003, pp. 161-62). Some Iranians, after losing their jobs, would spend their nights in Ueno Park. Every Sunday these parks became full of Iranian workers. In contrast to the Chinese or Koreans, the Iranians were easily recognized as foreigners, and their presence made foreign workers a visible reality for the Japanese. The majority of the Iranians worked in small businesses and factories in the suburbs of Tokyo. However, a small minority began to commit crimes, such as selling fake cell-phone cards or drugs in the parks. Because the Iranian workers were the latest foreign workers to come to Japan, their working conditions were worse than those of other foreigners. The media treated Iranians especially as the symbol of illegal foreign workers at that time, and controversy among the Japanese about the acceptance of foreign workers heated up (Kura, 2000).

With the sudden increase in illegal Iranian workers, the Japanese government decided to suspend the bilateral agreement in 1992, after which entering Japan became very difficult for Iranians. For many Iranians who had left their wives and children in Iran it also meant they had lost the chance to bring their families to Japan. In 1990 the Japanese government changed the immigration law, and special visas were only granted to people of Japanese descent from Latin America or to those who had been left behind as children when Japan withdrew from China after World War II. This created a kind of hierarchy among the foreign workers in Japan, with Iranian illegal workers in the lowest position. Moreover, the Japanese media often sensationally reported the crimes of Iranians. Following the sudden recession in Japan's economy in 1991-92, the situation of Iranian workers deteriorated drastically. Many Iranians lost their jobs, some of them could not get paid, and if some were injured at work, they could not get any compensation at all. Since they were illegal workers, they received no help. NGOs were established to support the immigrants, and activities to improve this situation began.

After the change in the Japanese immigration legislation, Iranian workers began to return to Iran, and the number of illegal Iranians decreased year by year. From 28,437 illegal Iranians in 1993, 16,252 in 1995, 11,303 in 1997, and 7,304 in 1999, there remained as few as 4,335 in 2001. Generally, there was no way for them to get legal status in Japan, with the exception of those Iranians who had married Japanese women and who could get special legal residential status at the discretion of the minister of justice. But additionally, with the support of some Japanese NGOs, some Iranians and other foreigners applied for legal status in Japanese district courts in September 1999, December 1999, and July 2000. Children born in Japan to Iranian parents with no legal status had in principle to return to Iran. However, the parents and their Japanese supporters from the NGOs insisted that, if the Japanese government deported them, it would violate their human rights. The argument was that, since such children had spent most of their lives in Japan and knew little Persian language or Iranian culture, they would suffer if sent to Iran. In 1994 Japan had ratified the United Nations Convention on the Rights of the Child (of 1989), so the claim was made that the Japanese government must consider the rights of Iranian children born in Japan. As a result, of twelve Iranian families who sued the Japanese government, seven were granted legal status in Japan (Asian People's Friendship Society, 2002, pp. 96-106).

Of 5,227 Iranians residing in Japan in 2005, 1,687 (about 30 percent) were permanent residents, and about five percent (248 people) were students. The number of Iranian students in Japan continues to grow every year. Some Iranian students wish to seek employment in Japan after they graduate from university. The ratio of Iranians who obtained legal residence in Japan by marrying Japanese women has become about 18 percent of all Iranians living in Japan. They have started to set up their own businesses in Japan, such as Iranian restaurants and carpet shops (Sakurai, 2003, pp. 57-61). Sooner or later, a second generation of them will join Japanese society, giving some influence to the Iranian community in Japan.

Bibliography: Asian People's Friendship Society (A.P.F.S.), *Kodomotachi ni amunesuti wo* (Amnesty for children), Tokyo, 2002. W. G. Aston, tr., *Nihongi. Chronicles of Japan from the Earliest Times to A.D. 697*, London, 1924; repr. Rutland, Vt. and Tokyo, 1972. Mehdiqoli Hedāyat Mok̲ber-al-Salṭana, *Safar-nāma-ye tašarrof be Makka-ye moʿaẓẓama az ṭariq-e Čin, Žāpon wa Āmrikā*, Tehran, 1945. E. Imoto, "Asuka no Perushiajin" (Persians in Asuka), *Higashi Ajia no kodai bunka* 113, 2002, pp. 58-68. N. Inaba and N. Higuchi "Iranjin rainichi no haikei to keii" (Background and details of Iranians who came to Japan), *Komyunikēshon gakka ronshū* (Mito) 19, 2006, pp. 157-92. E. Inoue, *Waga kaisō no Iran* (My memory of Iran), Tokyo, 1986. G. Itō, *Perushia bunka toraikō. Shiruku rōdo kara Asuka e* (A thought about the arrival of Persian culture in Japan—from the Silk Road to Asuka), Tokyo, 1980. H. Komai, *Nihon no esunikku shakai* (Ethnic societies in Japan), Tokyo, 1996. S. Kura, "Gaikokujin no imēji" (Images of the alien), *Miyazaki Kōritsu Daigaku Jinbungakubu kiyō* 8/1, 2000, pp. 71-89. T. Morita, "Iranian Immigrant Workers in Japan and Their Networks," in *Global Japan*, ed. R. Goodman, C. Peach, A. Takenaka, and P. White, London and New York, 2003, pp. 159-64.

H. Nagashima, "Persian Muslim Merchants in Thailand and Their Activities in the 17th Century," *Nagasaki Kenritsu Daigaku ronshū* 30/3, 1997, pp. 387-99. E. Okada, "Sok̲an-i digar dar bāzšenāsi-e beyt-i az *Vis o Rāmin* dar kohnatarin nevešta-ye fārsi-e bāzmānda dar Žāpon" (abstract: "Identification of a Line from *Vis and Rāmin* in the Oldest Sample of Persian Writing Found in Japan"), *Irānšenāsi* 1/1, 1989, pp. 70-75 (Persian pagination), pp. 27-28 (English pagination). Idem, *Tonari no Iranjin* (Iranian neighbors), Tokyo, 1998. S. Okazaki, "Iranjin ga mita Meiji no Nihon" (Japan in Meiji period as seen by Iranians)," in *Chūtō sekai* (Middle Eastern World), ed. S. Okazaki, Tokyo, 1992, pp. 160-74. H. Rajabzadeh, "Japan as Seen by Qajar Travelers," in *Society and Culture in Qajar Iran: Studies in Honor of Hafez Farmayan*, ed. E. L. Daniel, Costa Mesa, Calif., 2002, pp. 285-309. K. Sakurai, *Nihon no musurimu shakai* (Muslim society in Japan), Tokyo, 2003. Tsukuba Daigaku Shakaigaku Kenkyūshitsu, "Zainichi Iranjin" (Iranians in Japan), in *Gaikokujin teijū mondai shiryō shūsei* (A collection of materials on the problem of the settlement of foreign immigrants), ed. H. Komai, Tokyo, 1995, pp. 329-587. T. Yamagishi and T. Morita, *The Iranian Experience of Japan Through Narratives*, Tokyo, 2002. M. Yoshida, *Kaikyō tanken Perushia no tabi* (Exploring Islam—a Persian journey), Tokyo, 1894.

(TOYOKO MORITA)

v. ARCHEOLOGICAL MISSIONS TO PERSIA

After World War II Japanese archeologists could not continue their work on sites in Korea and China, and their expertise became available for research in the Middle East and Persia. Japanese excavations, in some contrast to European and North American practices, would all be sponsored by universities, none by museums. In 1955, for the first time, a Japanese team conducted a general survey and an excavation in Persia. By 1979, when the Islamic Revolution and the subsequent Iran-Iraq War (see IRAQ vii) halted all archeological activities, Japanese national universities—those of Kyoto, Tokyo, Tsukuba, Hiroshima, and Hokkaido—had sent nearly 30 missions to Iran.

The archeological missions between 1955 and 1979 had two goals. The first concerned the origin of the farming village in Iran and Mesopotamia. Some archeologists assumed that these regions had an impact on the agricultural civilization of East Asia. For example, the Austrian ethnologist and archeologist Robert Heine-Geldern (1885-1968) suggested the comparative study of painted pottery in order to trace the eastward influence of West Asia. The second goal was the exploration of cultural relations along the Silk Road, whose trade routes crisscrossed Eurasia and ultimately connected Japan with Italy. Parthian and Sasanian artifacts relevant to the study of East-West connections, such as silverware, glasswork, and pottery, were being sold on the art markets in Iran and in the West; most of them lacked provenance and were the result of clandestine digging. The attention of Japanese archeologists was drawn to such objects as Sasanian faceted cut glass bowls (see GLASS, in *EIr*. XI, pp. 10-11, pl. 1), which were allegedly found in tombs in the Deylamān (q.v.) region of Gilān Province. In form, design, and decorative technique, these bowls are quite similar to one in the Shōsōin Repository of the Imperial Treasury in Nara as well as to fragments found in the tumulus of Emperor Ankan (d. 535 C.E.) in Osaka and to fragments unearthed in Kyoto and Kyushu (see below, xi). Other artifacts in the Shōsōin, including glass and silver, also could have been produced in Iran and Central Asia and brought to Japan through China. Thus they may give evidence of the cultural relationship between Iran and East Asia.

Kyoto University. The first of the Japanese scientific missions after 1945 were conducted by Kyoto University and made up of archeologists, architects, art historians, anthropologists, and botanists; its teams worked in Iran, Pakistan, and Afghanistan between 1956 and 1959. The archeologists conducted general surveys in Persia, for example, of the old fort Mināb on the Persian Gulf and of Hormuz (q.v.) island. While they did not excavate any sites, they collected a great number of shards of Chinese porcelain—celadon, white, and blue-and-white wares. (For publications of the work of Kyoto University east of Iran during the 1950s-60s, see Bibliography.)

Tokyo University. Namio Egami (1906-2002), who had specialized in China and Mongolia until 1945, organized the Iraq-Iran Archeological Expedition in 1955. His team conducted excavations and anthropological research until 1966, focusing on the districts of Marv Dašt (Fārs province) and Deylamān (Gilān Province). In addition, Shinji Fukai (b. 1924), led a team of art historians and architects in 1965, 1976, and 1978. They surveyed the rock reliefs of Ṭāq-e Bostān near Kermānšāh (see SASANIAN ROCK RELIEFS at *iranica.com*), with particular interest in the site's location on the Silk Road trade route. Fukai's group employed photogrammetry (stereo camera) to measure the grottoes containing the reliefs.

Marv Dašt district. The goal of this expedition was to investigate the prehistoric farming communities in southern Iran. Archeologists dug the village sites of Tall-e Bākun, Tall-e Gap, Tall-e Jari, Tall-e Muški, and Tepe Saravān (Fahliān district), while the party of architects and art historians investigated the palace of Persepolis (Taḵt-e Jamšid).

Tall-e Bākun. This is a prehistoric site consisting of two mounds (A, B). In 1956, painted pottery, potsherds, and stone sickle blades were found in a dwelling site. The surface of a few potsherds show the impressions of grains and of flat-woven hemp cloth, documenting the cultivation of wheat and the knowledge of spinning and weaving. The pottery from mound A is painted with geometrical patterns and bird and animal motifs that are more elaborate than those on pottery from mound B. The site is dated to 3,500 B.C.E.

Tall-e Gap. The site comprises seven mounds (A-G), and in 1959, the largest mound (A) was selected for excavation. A building on the fourth stratum, with a square platform that contained a large amount of ashes, seems to have been used for animal sacrifice, since fire worship was not practiced on the Iranian plateau in the prehistoric period. The painted pottery, which is dated ca. 3,500-3,200 B.C.E., is characterized by comb-tooth patterns, stylized human and animal motifs, horizontal repetition of triangles and squares, and zigzag lines.

Tall-e Jari. This site (excavated in 1959) is made up of two adjacent mounds (A, B). In mound A, the dwelling of the upper stratum was constructed from plain mud bricks, while the dwelling of the lower stratum had walls painted in red. Coarse pottery and stone blades were found in the upper stratum, and red-polished pottery with geometrical patterns in the lower layer. The finds of mound A included a large number of accessories made from small shells and the bones of wild animals. The coarse pottery from mound B is dated to 5,000 B.C.E.

Tall-e Muški. This site was excavated in 1965. The typical pottery form is keel pottery, decorated only on the shoulder above the keel; it is homogenous throughout the strata, and the majority of it is red-slipped or burnished and buff-slipped. Particularly abundant among the clay objects are earplugs, which have also been interpreted as game pieces or mortars. There are many animal figurines, but neither a mother goddess nor a spindle whorl. Among the stone objects, blades form the most important group of chipped implements. The carbon-14 dating of the Muški objects is 6,690 B.C.E.

Deylamān district. This region comprises the tableland on the northern slope of the Alborz (q.v.) mountains. It lies 1,500 to 2,000 m above sea level, and is strategically situated, easy to defend and difficult to attack. Excavations were conducted in 1960, 1964, 1976, and 1978, and these focused on tombs (and not dwellings) of the late Bronze Age, early Iron Age, and Partho-Sasanian period in the villages of Qalākuti, Ḥasan Maḥalla, Nowruz Maḥalla, Lasulkān, Ḵorramrud, and Ḥalimejān. This mission had two goals: One was to investigate late Bronze and early Iron Age civilization in northern Iran, and the other was to trace the sources of cut-glass vessels which had been found in China and Japan.

The archeological research on the grave sites revealed three main types of construction: dolmen, stone chamber, and shaft or pit. There was also a single instance of an urn burial for a child. Most tombs only housed one body, but the collective burial of two or more persons was also practiced. Such burials are interpreted as indications of the social structure, showing a relationship of master and servant(s) or lord and attendant(s). The largest burial was found in Qalākuti, where one tomb contained the principal deceased and thirteen other corpses; some of these were buried with swords and pikes, others with headgear and vessels.

The grave goods found dated to the late Bronze Age or early Iron Age. They included bronze and iron weapons (swords and spearheads), horse equipage (bits and straps), mirrors, bronze figurines of animals, clay animal figures, accessories of gold and silver with precious stones and agate and glass beads, cylindrical seals, spindle whorls, needles, scissors, and grindstones. Animal bones, including limb bones of an antelope with bronze rings, were found in one pit, and are interpreted as evidence of animal sacrifice. Pottery was polished, in black or brownish red, or coarse. Notable were dishes with high stands or with three legs, large flat-bottomed bowls, and spouted or semi-spouted jars; these document that in Deylamān the manufacture of pottery was technologically well advanced during the Bronze and Iron Ages. The polished black or red pottery was of special interest to the excavators because of the similarities with proto-historic or prehistoric Chinese black or grey pottery.

A second group of finds comprised antiquities of the Parthian and Sasanian periods. They included pottery, iron weapons, blown glassware, accessories of gold, silver, and gems, iron shears, H-shaped bits, and bronze receptacles. These bronze objects are of a peculiar color; their alloy consists of copper, tin, lead, and iron with small quantities of bismuth, arsenic, antimony, zinc, and silver. A similar alloy can be found in Japanese antiquities. In a Parthian-period tomb of a man, the grave goods included swords and harnesses, but also a pair of iron shears 30 cm in length. These could have been used for shearing domestic sheep and goats, suggesting the presence of specialized small-cattle breeding in the local pastoral society. A glass bowl was unearthed at Ḥasan Maḥalla in 1964; it had embossed ornamentation, but was not done in the cut-glass technique.

Tsukuba University. The Prehistoric Archeological Expedition of Tsukuba University (the former Tokyo University of Education) worked in Persia between 1971 and 1977 for four seasons. The team was led by Seiichi Masuda (b. 1922), who had worked on Egami's excavations in Marv Dašt and Deylamān. The goal of this mission was to compare the early stages of development in ancient farming villages of southern and northern Iran. His team focused on two sites: Tepe Jari-A in southwest Iran and the eastern and western mounds at Tepe Sang-e Čaḵamāq (Bastām, Semnān province). They excavated these sites in 1971, 1973, 1975, and the western mound again in 1977.

The excavation at Tepe Jari-A revealed the existence of three strata. At the bottom stratum was a culture with painted white-slip pottery that is comparable to the Jeitun type in Turkmenistan (Sialk I; see CERAMICS i), at the middle stratum a culture without painted pottery, and at the top stratum a culture with painted pottery that is comparable to the Sialk III.

At Sang-e Čaḵamaq, the western mound had five strata. Since potsherds were only found in the third stratum, the invention of pottery is dated to this period. Three types of buildings were excavated. The first contained rooms with a simple beaten earth floor and a hearth at floor level; apparently it was a workshop for everyday use. Another type had a room whose floor was covered with thick plaster painted in red, and this building is believed to have served for religious functions. Here the hearth is on a raised base and so is considered to be some sort of fire altar. The third type of building formed a small room with a raised, plastered floor. This room is interpreted as a sacred place for offerings, because the finds comprise a few clay figurines of mother goddesses and animals as well as bone spatulas, flint blades with microliths, and obsidian blades with flint cores.

The eastern mound (which is larger) had six strata. The pottery ornamentation there consists of geometric patterns in red-brown pigment. Painted pottery of the Jeitun type (Sialk I) was found in all strata, while pottery of the Čašma ʿAli type (Sialk II, 6,500 B.C.E.) also was unearthed in the upper strata. Notable objects were a husking tray, from the third stratum, and a house-shaped model. Other finds included cosmetic implements of clay or stone, round spindle wheels, stone tools, and sickle shafts with animal decoration. A significant find was a small piece of copper tubing, which suggests that metalworking had already begun in this area during the prehistoric period. This mound reveals the early stage of an agricultural settlement of a pre-pottery culture, as well as a more advanced stage with painted pottery.

Hiroshima University. The Hiroshima University Scientific Expedition, led by Hisakazu Matsuzaki (b. 1913) and Hiroshi Shiomi (b. 1930), conducted archeological research in northeastern Iran regarding prehistoric agricultural settlements. In 1971, they conducted a series of general surveys and joined the Tsukuba University group in their excavations of Sang-e Čaḵamaq. The Hiroshima team took charge of the westernmost site of the western mound. They excavated mud-brick dwellings at four of the mound's five strata. As in sites on the eastern mound, a few rooms had a plastered floor, sometimes colored red, which suggests a special function for the room. Finds included stone implements, stone vessels, fragments of clay figurines, and earthen vessels, as well as horn and bone implements, and the site is considered Mesolithic or early Neolithic.

Middle Eastern Culture Center in Japan. Located in Tokyo, the Center was founded in 1979, and its president is the Middle East scholar, H.I.H. Prince Takahito Mikasa (b. 1915). The center conducted its first archeological survey in Persia in 1990. In 2001 a team surveyed the district of Rostamābād in Gilān in cooperation with the Iranian Cultural Heritage Organization, and in 2002 they excavated at Tepe Jalāliya, a site in the Kaluraz valley. The mound's first and second stratum are attributed to the Iron Age, while the third stratum belongs to the Partho-Sasanian period. Although the finds include pottery, terra-cotta spindle whorls, and stone vessels, on the whole they are quite limited in variety and quantity.

Bibliography: All publications are in Japanese with English summaries, unless otherwise indicated.

Publications of Kyoto University. Scientific Expedition to the Karakoram and Hindu Kush (in English):

Kinji Imanishi, ed., *Personality and Health in Hunza Valley*, Kyoto, 1963. Shinobu Iwamura et al., *The Zirni Manuscript; a Persian-Mongolian Glossary and Grammar*, Kyoto, 1961. Shiro Kitamura, *Flora of Afghanistan*, Kyoto, 1960. Idem, ed., *Plants of West Pakistan and Afghanistan*, Kyoto, 1977. Susumu Matsushita and Kazuo Huzita, eds., *Geology of the Karakoram and Hindu Kush*, Kyoto, 1965. Masuzo Uéno, ed., *Insect Fauna of Afghanistan and Hindukush*, Kyoto, 1963. Kosuke Yamashita, ed., *Cultivated Plants and their Relatives*, Kyoto, 1965.

Scientific Mission to the Iranian Plateau and Hindu Kush: Persia. Mitsukuni Yoshida and Koyama Kihei, *Western Asia at Work 1964*, Kyoto, 1966 (in Japanese only). Afghanistan and Pakistan. Seiichi Mizuno, ed., *Haibak and Kashmir-Smast; Buddhist Cave-Temples in Afghanistan and Pakistan Surveyed in 1960*, Kyoto, 1962. Idem, ed., *Hazār-Sum and Fīl-Khāna; Cave-Sites in Afghanistan Surveyed in 1962*, Kyoto, 1967. Idem, ed., *Durman Tepe and Lalma: Buddhist Sites in Afghanistan Surveyed in 1963-1965*, Kyoto, 1968. Idem, ed., *Mekhasanda: Buddhist Monastery in Pakistan Surveyed in 1962-1967*, Kyoto, 1969. Takayasu Higuchi, *Chaqalaq Tepe: Fortified Village in North Afghanistan Excavated in 1964-1967*, Kyoto, 1970. S. Mizuno, ed., *Basāwal and Jelālābād-Kabul: Buddhist Cave-Temples and Topes in South-east Afghanistan, Surveyed Mainly in 1965*, Kyoto, 1970-71. S. Mizuno and T. Higuchi, *Thareli, Buddhist Site in Pakistan Surveyed in 1963-1967*, Kyoto, 1976.

Reports of the Institute for Oriental Culture at Tokyo University in the series: Tokyo University Iraq-Iran Archaeological Expedition. Kikuo Atarashi and Seiji Horiuchi, *Fahlian* I. *The Excavation at Tape Suruvan, 1959*, Tokyo, 1963. Namio Egami and Jirō Ikeda, *Anthropological Studies of West Asia: I–Human Remains from the Tombs in Dailamanistan, Northern Iran*, Tokyo, 1963. N. Egami et al., *Dailaman: I–The Excavations at Ghalekuti and Lasulkan, 1960*, Tokyo, 1965. Idem, *Dailaman: II–The Excavations at Noruzmahale and Khoramrud*, 1960, Tokyo, 1966. N. Egami and Seiichi Masuda, *Marv-Dasht: I–The Excavation at Tall-i Bakun, 1956*, Tokyo, 1962. N. Egami and Toshihiko Sono, *Marv-Dasht: II–The Excavation at Tall-i Gap, 1959*, Tokyo, 1962. Shinji Fukai and Toshino Sono, *Dailaman: III–The Excavation at Hassani Mahale and Ghalekuti, 1964*, Tokyo, 1968. Sh. Fukai and J. Ikeda, *Dailaman: IV– The Excavations at Ghalekuti II & I, 1964*, Tokyo, 1971. Sh. Fukai, Kiyoharu Horiuchi, and Toshio Matsutani, *Marv-Dasht: III–The Excavation at Tall-i Mushki, 1965*, Tokyo, 1973. Sh. Fukai and Kiyoharu Horiuchi, *Taq-i-Bustan: I and II–Plates*, Tokyo, 1969-72. Sh. Fukai, et al., *Taq-i-Bustan: III–Photogrammetric Elevations*, Tokyo, 1983. Idem, *Taq-i-Bustan: IV–Text*, Tokyo, 1984. Sh. Fukai and Toshio Matsutani, *Halimehjan: I–The Excavation at Shahpir, 1976*, Tokyo, 1980. Idem, *Halimehjan: II–The Excavation at Lameh Zamin, 1978*, Tokyo, 1982. J. Ikeda, *Anthropological Studies of West Asia: II–Human Remains from the Tombs in Dailaman, Northern Iran*, Tokyo, 1968.

Publications of Tsukuba University. S. Masuda, "Excavation at Tappe Sang-e Cagmaq," in *Proceedings of the 1st Annual Symposium on Archaeological Research in Iran*, Tehran, 1973a. Idem, "Excavation at Tepe Sang-e Cagmaq," *Japanese Scientific Monthly* 25/12, 1973b, pp. 783-88; in Japanese. Idem, "Excavations at Tappeh Sang-e Caxmaq," in Firouz Bagherzadeh, ed., *Proceedings of the IInd Annual Symposium on Archaeological Research in Iran/Gozārešhā-ye dovvomin majmaʿ-e sālāna-ye kāvešhā wa pažuhešhā-ye bāstān-šenāsi dar Irān*, Tehran, 1974a, pp. 23-33. Idem, "Tepe Sang-e Čaxamaq," *Iran* 12, 1974b, pp. 222-23 and pls. IXb-c. Idem, "Report of the Archaeological Investigations at Šāhrud, 1975," in Firouz Bagherzadeh, ed., *Proceedings of the IVth Annual Symposium on Archaeological Research in Iran/Gozārešhā-ye čahāromin majmaʿ-e sālāna-ye kāvešhā wa pažuhešhā-ye bāstān-šenāsi dar Irān*, Tehran, 1976, pp. 63-70.

Publications of Hiroshima University. Hiroshima University Scientific Expedition, ed., *The Way of the Steppe: Archaeological Research in Iran*, 1971, Tokyo, 1973.

Publications of the Middle Eastern Culture Center in Japan. Tadahiko Ohtsu, Nokandeh Jebrael, and Kazuya Yamauchi, eds., *Preliminary Report of the Iran-Japan Joint Archaeological Expedition to Gilan, First Season, 2001*, Tokyo, 2003. Idem, *Preliminary Report of the Iran-Japan Joint Archaeological Expedition to Gilan, Second Season, 2002*, Tokyo, 2004.

(TOH SUGIMURA)

vi. IRANIAN STUDIES IN JAPAN, PRE-ISLAMIC PERIOD

Scholarly interest in ancient Iran in Japan developed from the early 20th century on, suffered a setback with the advent of World War II, but re-emerged stronger than before from the 1950s on, when archeological research and excavation surpassed philology as the leading field of interest. Although archeological activity was suspended with the advent of the Islamic Revolution of 1978-79, it was resumed in 2001 (see also above, v).

PIONEER DAYS

Ancient Iranian studies in Japan started at the beginning of the 20th century in Tokyo and Kyoto independently. In Tokyo, Shigeru Araki (1884-1932), who had studied ancient Iran under Abraham V. Williams Jackson (q.v.) at Columbia University from 1914 to 1920, began to teach ancient Iranian literature at the Department of Linguistics in Tokyo Imperial University; he served as a part-time lecturer from 1922 to 1931. He continued to collect source materials and scholarly books, with the financial support of the Keimeikai Foundation, until his death in 1932. His main publication is a brief summary of ancient Iranian studies in the West to that date (1922; in Japanese). His collection, currently owned by the Institute of Oriental Culture, Tokyo University, is now the most complete set of such source materials in Japan and the main starting point for students of the literature of ancient Iran (Henri Massé, "Comptes rendus," *JA* 228, Janvier-Mars, 1936, p. 161; see also Aoki and Einoo, eds., forthcoming).

Araki's pupil, Kametarō Yagi (1908-86), was appointed in 1932 as a research assistant at the Department of Linguistics, Tokyo Imperial University, and seemed to be a promising heir of Araki; but Araki's early death and his own induction into the army, which caused him to lose his academic position in 1937, forced him to give up his career as a scholar of ancient Iran. He served in the military in China and Burma during World War II. In 1961, when a Department of Persian Language was established at the Osaka University of Foreign Studies, he was offered a teaching position as professor of Iranian studies, but he declined the offer and spent the rest of his life as a teacher of German. His articles on ancient Iranian studies were collected and published after his death (1988).

Viscount Atsuuji Ashikaga (1901-83), who had studied with Émile Benveniste (q.v.) at École Pratique des Hautes Études in Paris in 1932-35, started in 1942 as an assistant professor at the Department of Indological Studies, Kyoto Imperial University, and became full professor in 1950. His major contributions are an introduction to ancient Iranian religions (1941) and a general survey of ancient Iranian history (1978), both in Japanese.

AFTER WORLD WAR II

Philological studies at Kyoto University. After World War II, it was Kyoto University (renamed from Kyoto Imperial University) which became the academic center for philological studies on ancient Iran. In 1954, Ashikaga, in cooperation with Prince Mikasa, founded the Society for Near Eastern Studies in Japan (Nippon Oriento Gakkai), which started with 64 members, including Ashikaga himself and Gikyo Itō (on whom, see below). This society publishes two academic journals, which have served as the main vehicles for Near Eastern studies conducted by Japanese scholars. They are *Oriento. Bulletin of the Society for the Near Eastern Studies in Japan* (in Japanese, since 1955) and *Orient: Reports of the Society for Near Eastern Studies in Japan* (in English, since 1960). Ashikaga also founded the Society for Western and Southern Asiatic Studies at Kyoto University in 1956, which within a year began publishing its own journal, *Seinan-Ajia Kenkyū. Bulletin of the Society for Western and Southern Asiatic Studies, Kyoto University* (in Japanese). Initially students and graduates of Kyoto University formed the main body of this society's membership, but the high standard maintained by the journal attracted many scholars from other academic centers, and it is now another outlet for ancient Iranian studies in Japan. This society also provided the stimulus for establishing the Department of West Asian History at the same university in 1969.

Gikyo Itō (1909-96), a pupil of Ashikaga, succeeded to his teacher's chair at the Department of Indological Studies, Kyoto University, in 1970. He was chiefly a scholar of Avestan and Pahlavi philology. His major works are his contributions to the syntax of the Gathas (1935), as well as a series of nineteen articles on the Gathas ("Gathica") and another series on Pahlavi ("Pahlavica"); both series, mostly in English, were published in the above-mentioned journal *Orient*. (Some articles, printed but not published, are in the possession of the author.) He also wrote works in which he translated from the Zoroastrian Pahlavi books into Japanese from the viewpoint of his original perspectives on ancient Iranian philology and Zoroastrianism. Most notable among these contributions are "Linguistic Interpretations . . . ," *Ancient Persia*, *Studies on Zoroaster*, and *Selected Papers*. His collection on Iranian philology, containing both source materials and scholarly books, is now owned by the Institute of Oriental Culture of Tokyo University (see Aoki and Einoo, 2004).

Itō's pupil, Ei'ichi Imoto (1930-), concentrates mainly on the cultural connection between ancient Iran and Japan and has published two major contributions on the relationship between these two ancient civilizations. Thanks to his scholarship, the Department of Persian Language at Osaka University of Foreign Studies, where he started as professor in 1964, has become another academic center for ancient Iranian studies in Japan. His chair was eventually held by his pupil Shunsuke Okunishi (1947-), the author of a collation of manuscripts of the Iranian *Bundahišn* (q.v.).

Koji Kamioka (1938-), another student of Itō, had studied ancient Iranian philology under Richard N. Frye at Harvard University; in 1972 he became associate professor at the Research Institute for Languages and Culture of Asia and Africa, Tokyo University of Foreign Studies. Later, however, he turned his concentrated interest away from classroom teaching to fieldwork. He is the co-author of an important report on caravan routes in Sasanian Persia. He also arranged for the purchase of the late Mark J. Dresden's (q.v.) collection on ancient Iranian studies for his Institute's library. Owing to his efforts, the Research Institute became another academic center for ancient Iranian Studies in Japan.

Yutaka Yoshida (1954-) studied Sogdian under Nicholas Sims-Williams at the University of London. He taught at Kobe City University of Foreign Studies before becoming professor at the Department of Linguistics, Kyoto University, in 2006. His proficiency in Sogdian and knowledge of ancient Chinese has led him to conduct notable research concerning pre-Islamic Central Asia. His publications include two contributions to Manichean studies and one on the Sogdian merchants in China and India (see also his PERSONAL NAMES, SOGDIAN, IN CHINESE SOURCES at *iranica.com*).

Yoshida's pupil, Etsuko Kageyama (1972-), succeeded Yoshida at Kobe City University of Foreign Studies. She has published several articles on Sogdian arts, notably one on Sogdians in Kucha.

Toyoko Kawase (1950-) of the Department of Persian Language, Osaka University of Foreign Studies, studied the Elamite Fortification Tablets at the University of

Chicago under Richard T. Hallock (q.v.) and is the author of two notable studies on the subject.

Seiro Haruta (1959-) of the Department of West Asian History, Kyoto University, is the only specialist of Parthian history in Japan. His major contributions are an article on verbal logograms (see HUZWĀREŠ) in Parthian and a new translation of an Avroman (q.v.) parchment.

Archeological studies at Tokyo University. In Tokyo, philological studies on ancient Iranian were discontinued after Araki's death in 1932. After 1956, however, Namio Egami (1906-2002) of the Institute of Oriental Culture, Tokyo University (renamed from Tokyo Imperial University) organized the Tokyo University Iraq-Iran Archaeological Expedition and conducted a good deal of archeological research in Iraq and Iran (see above, v). This included excavations at sites of the earliest farming villages in the Marvdašt area, Fārs, excavations of ancient tombs in the valleys of Deylamān and Ḥalimehjān in Gilān, excavations of the sites of ruins dating back to the Achaemenid period at Fahliān, Fārs (see Atarashi, ed.), and actual measurements of Ṭāq-e Bostān (Fukai and Horiuchi, eds.).

The expedition included Shinji Fukai (1922-85) and his student Katsumi Tanabe (1941-), both art historians specializing in ancient Persia. Fukai, while directing measurement at Ṭāq-e Bostān, became interested in ancient Persian glass; he turned most of his scholarly efforts to this subject and made two notable contributions to the study of Persian glass and ceramics. Tanabe has published a good number of articles, in both English and Japanese, on the study of Sasanian and Kushan arts, including one on the investiture of Ardašir II and the images of Šāpur I and II, several others likewise concerning Ṭāq-e Bostān, and one on the origin of a Buddhist urn. Tanabe was a research staff member at the Ancient Oriental Museum, Tokyo (founded in 1978), which became a center for archeological studies of Iran in Japan. Another member of this expedition, Yoshimasa Chiyonobu (1937-), has devoted his efforts to the repair and measurement of all archeological materials collected by this expedition in Iran. He has classified and published the materials from Deylamān and potsherds from Tepe Sialk in two separate parts of a catalogue.

A separate archeological expedition was carried out by the Japanese Expedition of the Tokyo University of Education for the Prehistoric Sites in Iran, which, led by Sei'ichi Masuda, conducted excavations at Tepe Sang-e Čaḵmāq, Khorasan, between 1973 and 1975.

The political situation in Iran in the late 1970s, culminating in the Revolution of 1978-79 and the establishment of the Islamic Republic, caused the suspension of the Japanese archeological expeditions there until 2001. In that year Tadahiko Ōtsu (1952-) of the Middle Eastern Culture Center in Japan and Kazuya Yamauchi (1961- , who had a master's degree from Tehran University) of the National Research Institute for Cultural Properties, Tokyo, started archeological surveys in Gilān Province in collaboration with the Iranian Cultural Heritage Organization (Sāzmān-e mirāṯ-e farhangi-e Irān).

Archeological studies at Kyoto University. In 1959, Sei'ichi Mizuno (1905-71) of the Institute for Research in Humanities, Kyoto University, organized the Iran, Afghanistan, Pakistan Archaeological Mission of Kyoto University; its main targets were Buddhist cave-temples dug into mountainsides in Afghanistan. The mission, led by Mizuno, conducted research on the Buddhist temples in Haybak (see AYBAK [Afghanistan]) and Kashmir-Smast (Pakistan), on cave sites at Hazār Som near Haybak and Fil-ḵāna near Jalālābād (Afghanistan), and on Buddhist sites at Durman Tepe in the Qonduz plain and Lalma in the Jalālābād basin (Afghanistan); excavation of a monastery constructed atop Mount Mekhasanda near Shahbaz-Garhi (Pakistan); excavation of a Buddhist site on Chaqalaq Tepe in the Qonduz plain (Afghanistan); the survey of the Buddhist stupas in the Jalālābād plain and Kabul; and, led by Takayasu Higuchi, a general survey of Buddhist remains in Bāmiān (q.v.), Afghanistan.

Following Kyoto University's mission, Hiroshima University's Scientific Expedition in Iran in 1974 engaged in mapping archeological sites in Gorgān (see Shiomi).

Philological studies at Tokyo University. In contrast to the active situation of archeological studies, philological Iranian studies at Tokyo University in the second half of the 20th century produced only a few scholars of ancient Iran. Susumu Sato (1930-) of Tokyo University of Education has published many articles (all in Japanese) dealing with the Median and Achaemenid periods. Most notable among them are a contribution on the Achaemenid economy and another on state formation in Media and Persia.

Yumiko Yamamoto (1946-) of the Department of Oriental History, Tokyo University, studied Zoroastrian history under Mary Boyce at the University of London. Her two articles on the cult of fire in the history of Iran are her most notable contributions.

Akinori Okada (1947-), out of his own general interest in mysticism, translated the *Yašts* and *Vidēvdād* of the Avesta into Japanese.

Hiroshi Kumamoto (1948-) studied Middle Iranian languages under Mark J. Dresden at the University of Pennsylvania and specialized in Khotanese. His main contributions are an article on a lyrical poem in Khotanese and another one on some Khotanese texts kept at the Institute of Oriental Studies of the Russian Academy of Sciences in St. Petersburg. He is now preparing an edition of Khotanese Saka documents in the Bibliothèque Nationale collected by Paul Pelliot (to be titled *Saka Document Texts II*). Kumamato became the chairman of the Department of Linguistics at Tokyo University in 1989.

Takeshi Aoki (1972-) of the Department of Islamic Studies, Tokyo University, started his career as a student of Islamic mysticism, but later became interested in Zoroastrian religious thought in the Sasanian and early Islamic periods, which is now the focus of his research and scholarship. His most notable contributions are an article on an annotated translation of *Dēnkard* (Book 3) and another on the philosophical characteristics of Zoroastrianism.

Bibliography: The following is a select list of the contributions by Japanese scholars to pre-Islamic Iranian studies.

Takeshi Aoki, "The Genealogy of Philosophical Zoroastrianism," *Journal of the K. R. Cama Oriental Institute*, no. 64, 2001, pp. 59-78. Idem, "An Annotated Translation of Zoroastrian Book Pahlavi Literature, the *Dēnkard* Book 3.1 from the Posthumous Papers of the Late Prof. Gikyo ITO," *The Memoirs of the Institute of Oriental Culture, Tokyo University* 146, 2004, pp. 41-72 (in Japanese). Takeshi Aoki and S. Einoo, eds., *Catalogue of ITO Gikyo Collection*, Tokyo, 2004. Idem, eds., *Catalogue of Araki Shigeru Collection*, Tokyo, forthcoming. Shigeru Araki, *Considerations on the History of Persian Literature*, Tokyo, 1922 (in Japanese). Viscount Atsuugi Ashikaga, *Persian Religious Thoughts*, Tokyo, 1941 (in Japanese). Idem, *Persian Empires*, Tokyo, 1978 (in Japanese). Kikuo Atarashi and Kiyoharu Horiuchi, *Fahlian*, The Tokyo University Iraq-Iran Archaeological Expedition Report 4, Tokyo, 1965 (the excavation at Tepe Saravān). Yoshimasa Chiyonobu, *Catalogue of Archeological Materials in the Department of Archeology of West Asia* II: *Iran (Metal Remains)*; III: *Iran (Potsherds from Tepe Sialk)*, The University Museum, The University of Tokyo Material Reports 12 and 28, Tokyo, 1986-93 (in Japanese). Namio Egami "Excavations at Two Prehistoric Sites: Tepe Djari A and B in The Marv-Dasht Basin," in *A Survey of Persian Art* XIV, pp. 2936-39. Namio Egami and Jiro Ikeda, *Human Remains from the Tombs in Dailamanistan, Northern Iran*, 2 vols., Tokyo, 1963-68. Namio Egami, Selichi Masuda, and Toshihiko Sono, eds., *Marv-Dasht*, The Tokyo University Iraq-Iran Archaeological Expedition Report 2-3, 2 vols, Tokyo, 1962 (excavations at Tall-e Bākun and Tall-e Gap; in Japanese with Eng. abstract). Idem, eds., *Dailaman*, 3 vols, The Tokyo University Iraq-Iran Archaeological Expedition Report 6-8, Tokyo, 1965-68 (excavations at Qalʿakoti, Nowruz Maḥalla, and K̲orramrud). Shinji Fukai, "A Study of a Glass Bowl at Hassani Mahaleh in Dailaman," *The Memoirs of the Institute of Oriental Culture, Tokyo University* 36, 1965, pp. 1-22. Idem, *Perushia no garasu*, tr. Edna B. Crawford as *Persian Glass*, New York, 1977. Idem, *Perushia no kotōki*, tr. Edna B. Crawford as *Ceramics of Ancient Persia*, New York, 1981. Shinji Fukai, Namio Egami, and Jiro Ikeda, eds., *Dailaman* IV: *The Excavations at Ghalekuti II and I*, Tokyo University Iraq-Iran Archeological Expedition. Report 12, Tokyo, 1964. Shinji Fukai and Kiyoharu Horiuchi, eds., *Taq-i Bustan*, 4 vols, Tokyo, 1969-84. Shinji Fukai, Kiyoharu Horiuchi, and Toshio Matsutani, *Marubu Dashuto/Marv-Dasht* III: *The Excavation at Tall-i Mushki*, The Tokyo University Iraq-Iran Archaeological Expedition 14, Tokyo, 1973 (in Engl. and Japanese). Shinji Fukai and Tashio Matsutani, *Halimehjan* I: *The Excavation at Shahpir, 1976*, Tokyo, 1980; II: *The Excavation at Lameh Zamin, 1978*, The Tokyo University Iraq-Iran Archaeological Expedition 16 and 18, Tokyo, 1982.

Seiro Haruta, "Formation of Verbal Logograms (Aramarograms) in Parthian," *Orient* 28, 1992, pp. 17-36. Idem, "A New Translation of the Avroman Parchment No. 3 (British Library Or. 8115)," *Bulletin of the Society for Near Eastern Studies in Japan* 44/2, 2001, pp. 125-34 (in Japanese). Takayasu Higuchi, ed., *Bāmiān*, 4 vols., Kyoto, 1983-84 (in Japanese). Eiichi Imoto, *Kodai no Nihon to Iran* (Ancient Japan and Iran), Tokyo, 1980. Idem, *Asuka to Perushia* (Asuka and Persia), Tokyo, 1984. Gikyo Ito, *Syntax der Nebensätze der Gathas des Avesta mit steter Rücksicht auf den Rgveda*, Kyoto Imperial University, 1935. Idem, "Lingusitic Interpretations of the Pahlavi Version of the Pahlavico-Chinese Bilingual Epitaph Found at Sian," *Bulletin of the Society for Western and Southern Asiatic Studies, Kyoto University* 13, 1964 (in Japanese). Idem, *Ancient Persia*, Tokyo, 1974 (in Japanese). Idem, *Studies on Zoroaster*, Tokyo, 1979 (in Japanese). Idem, *Selected Papers on Zoroastrianism*, Tokyo, 2001 (in Japanese). Estuko Kageyama, "Sogdians in Kucha: a Study from Archaeological and Iconographical Material," in *Les Sogdians en Chine*, Paris, 2005, pp. 135-62. Koji Kamioka and Hikoichi Yajima, *Iran Zagurosu Sanmyaku goe no ki karaban ruto* (Caravan routes across the Zagros Mountains in Iran), Research Institute for Languages and Culture of Asia and Africa, 1988. Toyoko Kawase, "Female Workers 'pašap' in the Persepolis Royal Economy," *Acta Sumerologica* 6, Dept. of Linguistics, University of Hiroshima, 1984, pp. 19-31. Idem, "Kapnuški in the Persepolis Fortification Texts," in Leon de Meyer, Hermann Gasche, and François Vallat, eds., *Fragmenta Historiae Elamicae: mélange offerts à M. J. Steve*, Paris, 1986, pp. 263-75. Hiroshi Kumamoto, "The Concluding Verses of a Lyrical Poem in Khotanese," in *Haranandalahari: Volume in Honour of Professor Minoru Hara on His Seventieth Birthday*, Reinbek, 2000, pp. 143-54. Idem, "Sino-Hvatanica Petersburgensia," *Manuscripta Orientalia* 7/1, 2001, pp. 3-9.

Selichi Masuda, "Umam Material and the Li-Tripod," in *A Survey of Persian Art* XV, pp. 3213-19, figs. 1217-29. Idem, "Excavations at Tappeh Sang-e Čak̲māq," in *Gozārešhā-ye dovvomin majmaʿ-e sālāna-ye kāvešhā wa pažuhešhā-ye bāstān-šenāsi dar Irān/Proceedings of the Second Annual Symposium on Archaeological Research in Iran*, Tehran, 1974, pp. 23-33. Idem, ed., *Tappeh Sang-i Čak̲māq*, Tokyo, 1977 (in Japanese). Idem, "The Excavation at Tappeh Sang-e Čak̲māq," *Archive für Orientforschung* 31, 1984, pp. 209-12. Seiichi Mizuno, ed., "Haibāk *and Kashmir-Smast*, Kyoto, 1962. Idem, *Hazār-Sum and Fīl-Khāna: Cave Sited in Afghanistan Surveyed in 1962*, Kyoto, 1967. Idem, ed., *Durman Tepe and Lalma: Buddhist Sites in Afghanistan Surveyed in 1963-65*, Kyoto, 1968. Idem, ed., *Mekhasanda: Buddhist Monastery in Pakistan Surveyed in 1962-1967*, Kyoto, 1969. Idem, ed., *Chaqalaq Tepe: Fortified Village in North Afghanistan Excavated in 1964-1967*, Kyoto, 1970. Idem, ed., *Basawal and Jelalabad-Kabul: Buddhist Cave-Temples and Topes in South-East Afghanistan Surveyed Mainly in 1965*,

Kyoto, 1971. Akinori Okada, tr., *Zoroastrianism: Hymns for Gods*, Tokyo, 1982 (in Japanese). Tadahiko Ohtsu, *Archaeological Survey in Northern Iran: Report on the General Survey in Gilan and its Surrounding Areas*, Tokyo, 2003. Shunsuke Okunishi, "The Collation of the Manuscripts of the Bundahishn: Preface and Chapter I, Part I," *Orient* 19, 1983, pp. 63-85. Susumu Sato, "A Study of the Royal Economy of the Achaemenid Empire," *The Bulletin of the Tokyo University of Education, Literature Department*, 91, 1973, pp. 1-26; 106, 1976, pp. 1-17. Idem "Ethnogeny and State-Formation in Media and Persia," *Bulletin of the Society for Near Eastern Studies in Japan*, 38/2, 1995, pp. 16-37. V. H. Shiomi, *Archaeological Map of the Gorgān Plain, Iran*, no. 1, Hiroshima, 1976. Toshihiko Sono, "Recent Excavations at Tepe Gap, Marv Dast," in *A Survey of Persian Art* XIV, pp. 2940-46. Katsumi Tanabe, "Unique Sasanian Silver Plate with Bahram Gur's Ostrich-Hunting Scene and with Gold Inlay," *Bulletin of the Ancient Orient Museum* 2, Tokyo, 1980, pp. 45-68. Idem, "Iconographical and Iconological Study on the Larger Iwan at Taq-i Bustan," *Bulletin of the Okayama Orient Museum* 2, 1982, pp. 61-113 (in Japanese with Eng. abstract). Idem, "Date and Significance of the So-Called Investiture of Ardashir II and the Images of Shahpur II and III at Taq-i Bustan," *Orient* 21, 1985, pp. 102-21. Idem, "The Iranian Origin of the Buddhist Urn," *AMI* 20, 1987, pp. 251-59. "The Kushano-Sasanian Kings Hidden in Roman and Chinese Literary Sources," in Katsumi Tanabe, Joe Cribb, and Helen Wang, eds., *Papers in Honour of Prof. Ikuo Hirayama on His 65th Birthday*, Studies in Silk Road Coins and Culture, Kamakura, 1997, pp. 75-88. Idem, "A Kushano-Sasanian Silver Plate and Central Asian Tigers," *Silk Road Art and Archaeology* 7, 2001, pp. 167-86.

University Library of Tokyo University of Foreign Studies, ed., *The Library of the Late Prof. M. J. Dresden on Indo-Iranian Linguistics and Languages*, Tokyo, 1989. Kametaro Yagi, *Collected Papers of Kametaro Yagi*, 2 vols, Tokyo, 1988 (in Japanese). Yumiko Yamamato, "The Zoroastrian Temple Cult of Fire in Archaeology and Literature," *Orient* 15, 1979, pp. 19-54; 17, 1981, pp. 67-104. Kazuya Yamauchi, *The Vocabulary of Sasanian Seals*, Tokyo, 1993. Idem, "New Discoveries of Iranian Archaeology," *Bulletin of the Ancient Orient Museum* 17, 1996, pp. 123-49; 18, 1995, pp. 233-57. Yutaki Yoshida, "Manichaean Aramaic in the Chinese Hymnscroll," *BSOAS* 46/2, 1983, pp. 326-31. Idem, "Middle Iranian and Old Turkish -Notes on Two Sets of Colophons or Scribbles Found in Manichaean Texts," *Studies on the Inner Asian Languages* 8, 1993, pp. 127-33 (in Japanese). Idem, "Additional Notes on Sims-Williams' Article on the Sogdian Merchants in China and India," in Alfredo Cadonna and Lionello Lanciotti, eds., *Cina e Iran: da Alessandro Magno alla dinastia Tang*, Firenze, 1996, pp. 67-77.

(TAKESHI AOKI)

vii. IRANIAN STUDIES, ISLAMIC PERIOD.

See online at *iranica.com*, forthcoming.

viii. SAFAVID STUDIES IN JAPAN

Among Japanese scholars interested in Iran, the ratio of historians who conduct research on pre-modern Iran is relatively higher than that in Europe and North America. This seems to be due to the fact that, while in Europe and North America researchers interested in Iran are trained either in the departments of Oriental Studies or Middle Eastern Studies, where a variety of related subjects are taught, in Japan they usually come out of the departments of Oriental History. The unique notion of "Oriental history" (*tōyōshi*) is closely related to the Japanese world view at the turn of the 19th-20th centuries. Until quite recently, there have been neither special departments for Persian language and literature or Iranian philosophy, nor a department of Middle Eastern Studies in any large university in Japan. As a result, historical studies has been the only choice for a student who wanted access to Iran.

Japanese scholars began to become interested in Iran and the Middle East in the 1970s, when serious historical research began. The growing interest in the history of a remote country like Iran, which had had no close relations with Japan, seems to reflect the stability and prosperity of Japanese society some thirty years after the end of the Second World War. At the same time, Japanese economic dependence on the Middle East, revealed by the Oil Shock of 1973 and the Iranian Revolution in 1979, raised the general interest in Iran and the Middle East.

Minobu Honda, the founder of Japanese historical studies on Iran and a specialist of the Mongol period, became professor in the department of West Asian History at Kyoto University in 1975. To make Persian primary sources accessible to researchers and students of Iranian studies, he made efforts to furnish the library with published Persian sources as well as microfilms of important Persian manuscripts kept in Western and Iranian libraries. He also invited distinguished Iranian scholars such as Iraj Afšār to Japan to train students in using Persian manuscripts. Under the direction of Honda and Eiji Mano, associate professor in the same department, the Kyoto School of Iranian history became firmly established. The Safavid period was one of its popular topics, because it was regarded as the starting point of modern Iran and the fact that a considerable number of primary sources remain extant and easily accessible, compared with those of the earlier periods. Students such as Tōru Horikawa and Masashi Haneda, the second generation of the Kyoto school, became interested in Iranian and Central Asian history in the 16th and 17th centuries. Haneda, after getting his doctorate in Paris with a thesis on the Safavid military system (pub. as *Le châh et les Qizilbâš*), moved to the University of Tokyo and trained students such as Nobuaki Kondō, Akihiko Yamaguchi, Yukako Gotō, Kazuo Morimoto, Hirotake Maeda, and others, who are all interested in the medieval and modern history of Iran. Teaching of Persian language was done mainly by Koichi Haneda at the Tokyo University of Foreign Studies, who had spent several years in the 1970s in Tehran. Thus, the school of Iranian history was established at the University of Tokyo, in addition to the already existing Kyoto school, from which noted scholars such as the late Shiro Ando, Kazuyuki Kubo, Tomoko Morikawa, and others have emerged. Kondō and Morimoto spent some time in Iran, while Maeda stayed in Georgia for a couple of years. Yamaguchi and Gotō carried out their research in Paris and Bamberg respectively. Only M. Haneda took part in the second Safavid round table held in Cambridge in 1993, but when the fourth Safavid round table was held in Bamberg in 2003, there were five Japanese participants. Japan has now become an important center for the study of Safavid history.

The genesis of Safavid studies in Japan was an outgrowth of the interest in the history of the Mongols and the Turkic people, which is a significant point characterizing Safavid studies there. A second such point is the current strong tendency to place Safavid history within a general framework of Middle Eastern history.

Iranian history has usually been taught as part of Oriental history in most Japanese universities, where the history of the Mongols and Turkic people is a favorite theme and which has had a long tradition of study since the end of the 19th century. Consequently it was quite natural that the first generation of scholars interested in Iranian history, like Honda and Mano, should have started their research through an interest in Mongol and Turkic history. The second generation of scholars, such as Horikawa and Haneda, inherited the outlook of their teachers and, making use of the extensive work already done on Mongol and Turkic history in Japanese, attempted to point out the significance of Turco-Mongol tribal elements in Safavid society. This kind of approach was able to relativize Walther Hinz's (q.v.) theory of the rebuilding the Iranian nation state by the Safavids, which was widely accepted in Japanese academic circles at the time.

In Japan, the tendency to set up a research field called the "Islamic World" is so strong that historians of Iran are usually regarded as being in the same group as historians of Arab countries and the Ottoman Empire. They often exchange research information with one another, and, as a result, find common topics, such as the institution of pious endowments (*waqf*), the "Islamic" slavery system, the comparative military system, the social role of the ulema, and so on. Such communication beyond the borders of ethnicity and political territory is a strongpoint of Japanese studies on Iranian history. On the other hand, Japanese scholars are inclined to establish a framework of the "Islamic world," almost equivalent with the Arabo-Perso-Turkish world of the Middle East, and confine their studies within it.

Bibliography: References are limited to works in Western and Persian languages. Budāq Monši Qazvini, *Jawāher al-aḵbār*, ed. Haneda Koichi and Moḥammad-Reżā Naṣiri, Institute for the Study of Languages and Cultures of Asia and Africa (ILCAA), Tokyo, 1999. Masashi Haneda, *Le châh et les Qizilbâš: Le systeme militaire safavide*, Islamkundliche Untersuchungen 119, Berlin, 1987 (rev. version of the author's diss.). Idem, "La famille Huzani d'Isfahan (15-17e siecles)," *Studia Iranica* 18/1, 1989, pp. 77-92. Idem, "The Character of the Urbanization of Isfahan in the Later Safavid Period," in Charles Melville, ed., *Safavid Persia: The History and Politics of an Islamic Society*, Pembroke Persian Papers 4, London, 1996, pp. 369-87. Idem, "Emigration of Iranian Elites to India during the 16-18th Centuries," in Maria Szuppe, ed., *L'héritage timouride: Iran-Asie Cntral-Inde XVi-XVIII siècles*, Cahiers d'Asie Centrale 3-4, 1997, pp. 129-44. Idem., "Bandar ʿAbbas and Nagasaki: An Analysis of the Reaction of the Safavid Government to Europeans from a Comparative Perspective," *Annals of the Japan Association for Middle Eastern Studies* 20/2, 2005, pp. 119-30. Walther Hinz, *Irans Aufstieg zum Nationalstaat im fünfzehnten Jahrhundert*, Berlin and Leipzig, 1936. Kondo Nobuaki, ed., *Persian Documents: Social History of Iran and Turan in the Fifteenth-Nineteenth Centuries*, London and New York, 2003. Hirotake Maeda, "On the Ethno-Social Background of Four *Gholām* Families from Georgia in Safavid Iran," *Studia Iranica* 32/2, 2003, pp. 243-78.

(MASASHI HANEDA)

ix. CENTERS FOR PERSIAN STUDIES IN JAPAN

University courses. Formal undergraduate and graduate programs of Persian studies in Japan are offered at Osaka University School of Foreign Studies (Ōsaka Daigaku Gaikokugo Gakubū) and Tokyo University of Foreign Studies (Tōkyō Gaikokugo Daigaku).

Osaka University School of Foreign Studies continues the former Osaka School of Foreign Studies, which was founded in 1921 and became a faculty of Osaka University in 2007. It offers, as it has since being reorganized in the 1990s, specialization in 25 foreign languages, as well as minor fields in other languages. The department of Persian studies, the oldest program of its kind in Japan, was founded in 1961, and typically has accepted 15 to 22 new students for undergraduate courses each academic year (which is 1 April to 31 March of the next year, in the Japanese educational system). In the 1990s the separate departments of Persian, Arabic, and Turkish studies were joined to form the new group of Middle Eastern Studies. Around the same time, graduate and doctoral courses were established; as of the spring of 2007 more than a dozen students had obtained their M.A. degree from the department, and one Ph.D. candidate had graduated. In the mid-1990s a School of International Studies was established at the university, and 5 new students of the school were assigned each year to attend Persian classes for two years as their secondary major. This practice increased the number of annual new students to over 20, for a total undergraduate enrollment of 80 students. By the spring of 2007, about 600 students (men and women in almost equal numbers) had completed the courses. Students are required to write and submit a graduation paper on a topic related to Iranian studies.

In April 2007, faculty members of the department consisted of three Japanese, Shigeo Mori (professor, Iranian languages), Yuko Fujimoto (assistant professor, contemporary Persian literature), and Shin Takehara (associate professor, Iranian folklore), as well as an Iranian visiting professor (Dr. Ḥasan Reżāʾi Bāḡbidi, Old and Middle Iranian languages). A number of part-time lecturers also teach in the department's regular class schedule, as well as in summer and winter intensive classes.

Tokyo University of Foreign Studies, one of the oldest centers of higher education in Japan, founded its department of Persian Studies in 1980. The department accepts about 15 new students for its undergraduate course each academic year; and up to 31 March 2007, 381 students had completed this course. Seventeen M.A. degrees and one Ph.D. have been awarded from the department. The general features of teaching methodology, curriculum, and course content are almost the same as in Osaka.

Besides formal courses leading to degrees, the department offers night courses of Persian open to the general public, with focus especially on members of the local community. The program, called "Open Academy," is designed to provide specialized education to business people, housewives, and others residing in the neighborhood as a community service and with the aim of enhancing the image of the university and maintaining good community relations. By the end of March 2007, 61 applicants had attended the "open academy" classes.

As of 1 April 2007, faculty members of the department consisted of 4 Japanese, namely Makoto Hachioshi (professor, modern history of Iran), Morio Fujii (professor, Persian literature with special interest in mysticism), Dr Ayano Sasaki (assistant professor, Persian classical literature with special interest in Hafez), and Yoshie Satoko (associate professor, linguistics and Iranian languages), as well as one Iranian visiting professor, Dr. Zahrā Ṭāheri (Persian literature).

The department has also participated in the program of the university's Research Institute for Languages and Cultures of Asia and Africa (Ajia Afrika Gengo-bunka-kenkyūjo). The latter sponsored intensive five-week Persian courses during the summer school holidays of 1976, 1978, 1988, 1990, and 2000—the first three in Tokyo, the last two in Osaka and with the collaboration of Osaka University of Foreign Studies. The courses were open to students and faculty members of all universities and research institutes in the country, and were completed by 51 students (10, 13, 10, 14, and 4 in the respective years).

Some other major Japanese universities have a long history of Persian studies but lack a Persian department; they include Tokyo, Kyoto, Nagoya, Hokkaido, and Sendai universities; these provide Persian courses to occasional applicants among their students. At Keiō, Waseda, and Tōkai universities, as well as at some other institutions of higher education and high schools affiliated with them, Persian classes are held in most academic years. Ryūkoku University, originally a Buddhist institution going back to the 17th century, is housed in three campuses in Kyoto and Shiga Prefectures, When a Persian course was offered in its graduate school in April 2007 more than 70 students applied, indicating the persisting attraction of Iran and Persian studies in Japan.

Other activities. The Japan-Iran Society (Nippon-Iran Kyōkai) was established in the 1950s by Idemitsu Oil Company (see above, ii) and supported by the Iranian embassy and relevant government departments in Tokyo. One of its activities was to organize elementary Persian courses, mainly for business people. These ended with the Society's closure in the 1990s. Although a new Japan-Iran Friendship Society was established in Tokyo by enthusiasts of Iranian studies, the former courses have not been replaced.

The Japanese Ministry of Foreign Affairs sponsors special intensive Persian courses in its training program for staff, mainly in diplomatic and consular categories, who are scheduled to be assigned to Japanese diplomatic posts in Persian-speaking countries. The courses are given in collaboration with the Persian Department of the Tokyo University of Foreign Studies.

Faculty members of Persian departments have compiled and published a number of textbooks and reference books, especially Persian-Japanese and Japanese-Persian dictionaries, for students of Persian. Notable are those compiled by Y. Fujimoto, Y. Furushima, R. Gamō, T. Kuroyanagi, E. Okada, Sh. Okazaki, H. Rajabzadeh, and F. Satō (see Bibliography). The work of Japanese translators of Persian texts are also used in coursework as supplementary materials.

Bibliography: Yuko Fujimoto and Hashem Rajabzadeh, *Perushiago tegami no kakihō* (How to write letters in Persian), Tokyo, 1993. Yuko Fujimoto, *Ekisupuresu Perushiago* (Express Persian), Tokyo, 1999. Yuriko Furushima, *Perushiago jiten* (Persian[-Japanese] dictionary), Tokyo, 1993. Reiichi Gamō, *Perushiago bunpō nyūmon* (Introduction to Persian grammar), Tokyo, 1983. Takeshi Katsufuji and Hashem Rajabzadeh, *Perushiago kotowaza yōhō jiten* (Dictionary of Persian proverbs and usage), Tokyo, 1993. Tsuneo Kuroyanagi, *Perushiago yon shūkan* (Persian in four weeks), Tokyo, 1982. Idem, *Perushiago-Nihongo daijiten/Farhang-e jāmeʿ-e fārsi be žāponi* (Persian-Japanese collegiate dictionary), Tokyo, 2001. Emiko Okada, *Perushiago kihon tango 2000* (2,000 basic Persian words), Tokyo, 1993. Shoko Okazaki, *Kiso Perushiago* (Basic Persian grammar), Tokyo, 1982. Hashem Rajabzadeh, *Perushiago yōreishū* (Persian words in context), Osaka University of Foreign Studies, 2000.

(HASHEM RAJABZADEH)

x. COLLECTIONS OF PERSIAN BOOKS IN JAPAN

See online at *iranica.com*, forthcoming.

xi. COLLECTIONS OF PERSIAN ART IN JAPAN

Persian works of art in Japanese collections may be classified roughly into two categories: artifacts brought to Japan through China and the Korean peninsula in ancient, medieval, and early modern times, and those purchased in art markets since the 19th century. The first group is historically of great importance, since these objects were brought to Japan mainly by trade with China and western countries and give evidence of a cultural exchange between Persia and Japan that started as early as the 6th century C.E. The most important Persian artifacts of this type are held at two Buddhist temples in Japan—glass vessels and brocade fragment at the Shōsōin of Tōdaiji (Nara) and a silk tabard at Kōdaiji (Kyoto).

The 8th-century imperial treasures of the Shōsōin. The Shōsōin is a log storehouse of Tōdaiji Temple in Nara, the first permanent capital of Japan during the Nara Period (710-84). It was constructed at the command of Emperor Shōmu (r. 724-49), and after his death his belongings and household items were presented to this imperial repository by his widow, the empress Kōmyō. The most interesting of the artifacts stored there since the 8th century include exotic objects brought back from China by Japanese monks, dignitaries, and envoys. Some of these artifacts traveled to China, Korea, and Japan from Persia, Central Asia, and India along the Silk Routes, the system of trade routes linking East Asia with the western world (Hayashi, pp. 85-103).

The most important such pieces among the Shōsōin relics are various types of glass vessels of Sasanian derivation, some with cut decoration or applied coil decoration. Especially noteworthy is a white glass bowl with circular facets (ht. 8.5 cm, diam. 12 cm; PLATE I). A similar bowl (repaired) of 8.1 cm height was excavated from the tumulus of Emperor Ankan (late 6th century) in Osaka. Additionally, a few fragments of glass bowls with similar cut decoration were excavated from the archeological sites in Kyoto (Fukai, 1972, pp. 306-12) and Fukuoka in Kyushu. Some of these bowls, rather than being post-Sasanian imitations of Persian wares, may actually have been produced in Persia during the Sasanian period and brought to Japan via the Silk Roads. A bowl with similar cut decoration found in Gilān Province, now in the Iran Bastan Museum (Muza-ye Irān-e Bāstān), Tehran, tends to substantiate this hypothesis both by the cutting technique and the style of circular decoration (Fukai, 1968, pp. 6-18).

In addition to the cut glass bowl of the Shōsōin, there is a pear-shaped ewer with a handle (ht. 27 cm, diam. 14 cm; PLATE II), the form of which is of Sasanian origin; it can be compared with ewers discovered in Gilān and Qazvin and kept at the Iran Bastan Museum. The chemical composition of these Shōsōin vessels and the bowl fragments is of alkaline-lime, with or without lead, according to Beta-ray backscattering examination.

Among the metalwork in the Shōsōin, the two items most noteworthy morphologically are of elongated, eight-lobed shape (PLATE III); they can be compared to a silver cup of similar shape (said to have been found in Qazvin) in the Iran Bastan Museum (Fukai, 1968, p. 117, fig. 69). Sasanian silver pieces with elliptical and multi-foliated shapes spread extensively throughout Eurasia; and the prototype of these multi-lobed glass and metal vessels

PLATE I

Bowl with cut facets. Alkaline lime glass: ht. 8.5 cm. 8th century. Shōsōin, Nara.

PLATE II

Jug with handle. White glass: ht. 27.2 cm. 8th century. Shōsōin, Nara.

PLATE III

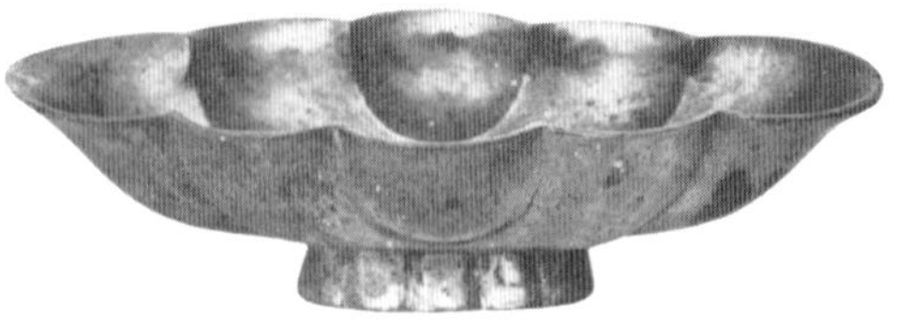

Elliptical foliate cup. Gilt bronze: lth. 19.7 cm, ht. 5.1cm. 8th century, Japan. Shōsōin, Nara.

PLATE IV

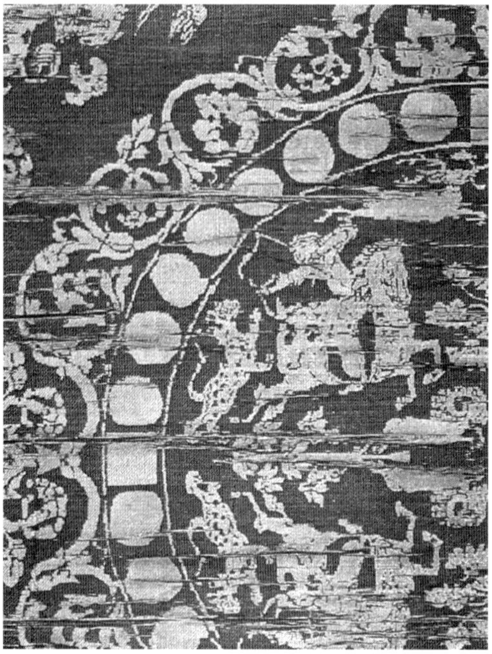

Compound twill-weave silk. Lion hunt roundel design: lth.191.3 cm, w. 70.8 cm. 8th century, Tang China (?). Shōsōin, Nara.

apparently goes back to the Sasanian period, though the provenance of some pieces is either Tang China or Central Asia. The eight-lobed gilt bronze cup in the Shōsōin, based on florescent X-ray analysis, is presumably a local imitation. Nevertheless, it is still an important indication of the intercultural communication between East and West.

An important textile in the Shōsōin is a fragment of silk brocade depicting confronted equestrians shooting lions set within a pearl roundel (PLATE IV). This textile pattern that was originated in the Sasanian empire and diffused westwards to Europe and eastwards to China and Japan (Otavsky, pp. 185-95; Ackerman, pp. 3074-78, figs. 1138 and1139; see also ABRIŠAM).

Kōdaiji Temple. Commerce of the early modern period (before and during the Tokugawa shogunate, 1603-1867) is represented by a 16th-century Persian silk kilim in Kōdaiji Temple, Kyoto, as well as by Persian and Indian carpets preserved in the Tokugawa Museum, Nagoya. These presumably had been presented to the *daimyō*, the feudal lords. Frequent trade with Western countries such as Portugal, Spain, and the Netherlands during the 15th-17th centuries brought to Japan a number of exotic commodities such as glass and woolen products. These objects are assumed to have been either items of tribute or gifts presented to the rulers and high-ranking officials.

The 16th-century kilim at Kōdaiji Temple was later tailored into a tabard (*jinbaori*, a sleeveless coat worn over armor by the samurai) for Toyotomi Hideyoshi (1537?-98), one of the most powerful lords of Japan during the feudal age, in whose memory Kōdaiji was built in 1605. During the age of the Japanese civil wars (1467-1568) many of the daimyōs wore a tabard made of imported woolen fabric in bright colors and showy patterns. In Hideyoshi's case, the tabard was tailored from a Safavid silk kilim partly brocaded with silver and gold threads. The tabard is characterized by the designs of mythological beasts such as dragons, a variety of birds, animal combat scenes, and lion-masks. Interestingly, this tabard is closely related in its patterns, color scheme, and weaving density to the recently acquired silk kilim, formally called the Figdor kilim (Kāšān, 2nd half of the 16th cent.), in the Miho Museum. Their common features lead us to assume that both were woven in the same court workshop in Kāšān during the Safavid dynasty (Pope and Ackerman, XII, pl. 1268; Spuhler, pp. 84-87). The tabard and the Figdor kilim are associated with another piece, the Sanguszko Kermān carpet of the late 16th century, which is one of the masterpieces of Persian carpet weaving (Pope and Ackerman, XII, pl. 1206). These three pieces share the design repertoire of a Chinese dragon, phoenix, and *qilin* (an auspicious horned animal in Chinese mythology) along with the representation of animals in combat. The Sanguszko carpet, once owned by the Polish royal family, is now in the Miho Museum collection (Miho Museum, pp. 307-11).

The Kyoto preservation associations. Persian carpets figure among the decorations of the 32 float-carts (*yamaboko*) which are paraded in the traditional (since 892) July Gion Festival in Kyoto, which is associated with Yasaka Shrine. Each of the 32 neighborhood float-cart preservation associations (*hozonkai*) is responsible for one of the floats and its trappings (assembly, cleaning, disassembly, storage), and their joint activities are coordinated through the Gion Festival Float-cart Federation (Gion Matsuri Yamaboko Rengōkai). Several of the associations, such as the Minami-Kannon-Yama Hozonkai and the Naginata-Boko Hozonkai, own Persian carpets. In the late 16th and 17th centuries the wealthy citizens of Kyoto, mostly textile dealers and artisans, vied with one another in purchasing luxurious imported textiles, some Chinese, some Persian and Indian, in order to

PLATE V

(1)

(2)

Tabard of a feudal lord. Silk with silver and gold threads: ht. 99 cm. 16th century, Kashan. Kōdaiji Temple, Kyoto. (1) Front. (2) Back.

adorn the huge Gion Festival floats. For the past five hundred years these festival trappings have been displayed to the public during the procession through the city (Gonick, pp. 183-209).

Among the float trappings are seven Persian pile carpets, five of which are of the so-called Herat type in exceptionally good condition, while two others are of the so-called Polonaise type made of silk with metallic threads. The piles of the latter two carpets are very worn. They may have been woven under Shah ʿAbbās I (r. 1587-1629) in Kāšān or Isfahan (Walker, pp. 173-74). Their present condition suggests that they may have been sold or given away to the townsfolk after having been used long enough by members of the ruling class. These carpets lack, however, the documentation to prove precisely how and when they were imported into Japan and transferred to their present owners.

Museums and research centers. The majority of the Persian artifacts that came to Japan from the 19th century onward were purchased after World War II. These consist of diverse types of ancient earthenware vessels, modern ceramics, tiles, and glassware. The appeal of earthenware and ceramics to the Japanese is well known; and the considerable quantity of Persian glassware in Japanese public and private collections may be explained by such an attraction, which dates back to the Shōsōin treasures. The following list of major museums and other institutions indicates the main types of their Persian holdings.

(1) National and regional museums. National Museum of Ethnology, Osaka: modern carpets and ceramics, ethnic art, and modern Persian handicrafts. Tokyo National Museum: ancient and Islamic ceramics, glassware, and textiles. Matsudo Museum, Chiba: glassware. Hiroshima Prefectural Art Museum: Islamic metalwork; of particular interest is a Saljuq bronze lantern. Nara International Foundation, commemorating the Silk Road Exposition (N. Egami and J. Gluck Collections): ancient earthenware and Islamic ceramics. Yokohama Museum of Eurasian Cultures (N. Egami collection): ancient and Islamic pottery.

(2) Private museums founded by individuals. Bridgestone Museum of Art, Tokyo: ceramics; glassware. Eisei Bunko Museum of Art, Tokyo: Islamic ceramics; modern carpets. Hakutsuru Fine Art Museum, Kobe: Modern carpets. Matsuoka Museum of Art, Tokyo: ceramics. Miho Museum (Shumei Culture Foundation), Shiga: Achaemenid and Sasanian metalwork; glassware; Saljuq pottery; of particular interest are the Sanguszko carpet, Figdor silk kilim, luster-painted ware, and *mināʾi* wares. Ohara Museum of Art, Okayama: Islamic ceramics and tiles. Hirayama Ikuo Silk Road Museum, Yamanashi: silverware; glassware; tiles; textiles; coins. Tokugawa Art Museum, Nagoya: classical carpets. Toyama Memorial Museum of Art, Saitama: brocades; modern pile carpets. Yamato Bunkakan Museum, Nara: ceramics.

(3) Single-theme collections. Aichi Prefectural Ceramic Museum, Seto: prehistoric, ancient, and Islamic ceramics. Ancient Orient Museum, Tokyo: ancient pottery; clay figurines; Islamic ceramics and coins. Okayama Orient Museum: ancient and Islamic ceramics; tiles; glassware; coins; jewelry; seals; Sasanian metalware; Safavid and Qajar textiles; of particular interest are tiles from Taḵt-e Solaymān. Middle East Culture Center in Japan, Tokyo: prehistoric and ancient earthenware; bronze figurines; ancient and Islamic ceramics; tiles; Sasanian

and Islamic metalwork; glassware; Safavid and Qajar textiles; miniature paintings; coins; of particular interest are a Sasanian silver plate with an equestrian hunting scene and a small prayer niche (*meḥrāb*) tile with the ninety-nine names (*al-asmāʾ al-ḥosnā* "beautiful names") of Allāh.

(4) University collections. Hiroshima University: painted and burnished pottery; archeological materials. Tenri University Sankōkan Museum, Nara: Sasanian or proto-Sasanian silverware and Islamic pottery. Tokyo University Museum: painted pottery, glassware, and archeological materials. University of Tsukuba, Ibaraki: glassware, clay figurines, and archeological materials.

Bibliography: Phyllis Ackerman, "Royal Personages on Sasanian Silks," in Arthur Upham Hope and Phyllis Ackerman, eds., *A Survey of Persian Art from Prehistoric Times to the Present*, 2nd ed., 16 vols., Tehran, 1964, XIV, pp. 3068-79. An Jiayao, *Early Chinese Glassware*, tr. Matthew Henderson, London, 1984. Shinji Fukai, *Perushia kobijutsu kenkyū: garasuki, kinzokuki/Study of Iranian Art and Archaeology: Glassware and Metalwork*, Tokyo, 1968. Idem, "A Fragment of a Sassanian Cut Glass Bowl Recently Found at Kyoto," in M. Y. Kiani and A. Tajvidi, ed., *The Memorial Volume of the Vth International Congress of Iranian Art and Archaeology . . . 11th-18th April 1968/ Yād-nāma-ye panjomin kongera-ye bayn-al-melali-e bāstān-šenāsi wa honar-e Irān . . .*, vol. II, Tehran, 1972, pp. 306-12. Idem, *Perushia no garasu*, tr. Edna B. Crawford as *Persian Glass*, New York and Tokyo, 1977; tr. Ārmān Šišegarān as *Šiša-ye Irāni*, Tehran, 1992. Agnes Geijer, "A Silk from Antinoé and the Sassanian Textile Art," *Oriental Suecana* 12, 1964, pp. 1-36. Roman Ghirshman, *Iran—Parthians and Sassanians*. London, 1962, pp. 203-48. Jay Gluck and Sumi Hiramoto Gluck, eds., *A Survey of Persian Handicraft: a pictorial introduction to the contemporay folk art and crafts of modern Iran*, Tehran, New York, London, and Ashiya, 1977. Gloria G. Gonick, *Matsuri: Japanese Festival Art*, Los Angeles, 2002.

Yoshito Harada, *Shōsōin no garasu/Glass Objects in the Shōsōin*), Tokyo, 1965. Prudence O. Harper, *The Royal Hunter: Art of the Sasanian Empire*, New York, 1978. Ryoichi Hayashi, *Shiruku Rōdo to Shōsōin*, tr. Robert Ricketts as *The Silk Road and the Shoso-in*, New York, 1975. E. J. Laing, "A Report on Western Asian Glassware in the Far East," *Bulletin of the Asia Institute*, N.S. 5, 1991, pp. 109-21. Miho Museum, *Catalogue of the Miho Museum (South Wing)*, Shigaraki, 1997. Nara National Museum, *The Catalogue of the 53rd Annual Exhibition of Shōsō-in Treasures*, Nara, 2001. Karel Otavsky, "Zur Kunsthistorischen Einordnung der Stoffe," in idem, ed., *Entlang der Seidenstrasse: frühmittelalterliche Kunst zwischen Persien und China in der Abegg-Stiftung*, Riggisberg, 1998, pp. 119-214. Arthur Upham Pope and Phyllis Ackerman, eds., *A Survey of Persian Art from Prehistoric Times to the Present*, 4 vols., Oxford, 1938-39; 2nd ed., with corrigenda and addenda, 16 vols., Tehran, 1964. F. Spuhler, *The Thyssen-Bornemisza Collection: Carpets and Textiles*, London, 1998, no. 16. Daniel Walker "Rugs in the Gion Matsuri Preservation Associations," in Nobuko Kajitani and Kōjirō Yoshida, eds., *Gion Matsuri yamaboko kensōhin chōsa hōkokusho: torai senshokuhin no bu* (A survey of the Gion Festival float hangings: imported textiles section), Kyoto, 1992.

(TOH SUGIMURA)

xii. TRANSLATIONS OF PERSIAN WORKS INTO JAPANESE

Japanese scholars in the late 19th century began to embark on Oriental studies outside the traditional fields (out of fashion after the Meiji Restoration of 1868) of Chinese literature and Confucian learning. Some were attracted to Persia, initially by its literary heritage. Thus Japanese readers were introduced to the Persian classics with translations of ʿOmar Ḵayyām's *Robāʿiyāt* and Ferdowisi's *Šāh-nāma*, and these works still serve as the primary representatives in Japan of the field of Iranian literature.

Classical Persian literature. The *Robāʿiyāt* attributed to ʿOmar Ḵayyām was first introduced to Japanese academia by the teacher and scholar Lafcadio Hearn (1850-1904), the celebrated Japanologist and author of many works on Japan and Japanese subjects, in a lecture at Imperial University of Tokyo in September 1896 (cf. the school lecture in Hearn, 1926). Kambara Ariake, who was present at the lecture, was so fascinated and moved by the *Robāʿiyāt* that he translated into Japanese six pieces from Edward FitzGerald's (1809-83, q.v.) version of the quatrains and published them in 1908. Another translation of FitzGerald, by Shun Ōsumi and Shōfu Ōsumi, was published the same year in Tokyo. There followed other translations, mostly based on FitzGerald, by Bunkichi Katano (1914), Shigeru Araki (1920), Sofu Taketomo (1921 and 1947), Hōjin Yano (1935 and 1938), Ryō Mori (1941 and 1948), Ryōho Horii (1947), Ryōsaku Ogawa (1948), Tetsuo Nagiri (1949), Eizō Sawa (1960), Reiichi Gamō (1964, 1973, and 1983), Tsuneo Kuroyanagi (1973), Toshihiko Ōgata (1984), Riō Mori (1986), Katsuyaki Yamaji (1988), and Toshinaga Ida (1989). Katano rendered the *Robāʿiyāt* in Japanese from the English translation of Justin H. McCarthy (*Rubaiyat*, London, 1889). Ogawa was the first to translate the *Robāʿiyāt* from the original Persian, and this version is admired for its eloquence and beautiful expression. Yano in his translations rendered the quatrains with beautiful and poetic expression in the *tanka* form of classical Japanese verse (five lines, 5 + 7 + 5 + 7 + 7 syllables). Ryō Mori used a simpler, more easily understandable language in the second translation. Taketomo's translation became the source of several quotations in the works of the popular novelist Osamu Dazai (1909-48).

Ferdowsi (q.v.) was the next Persian poet to attract the attention of Japanese writers and authors. A number of translations were made of sections of his *Šāh-nāma*

(*Ō-sho* in Japanese), beginning with those that were readily available in 19th-century English, French, German, and Italian versions (on which, see s.v. ŠĀH-NĀMA at *iranica.com*). The first and most frequently treated episode was the tragedy of *Rostam o Sohrāb*. The heroes of the *Šāh-nāma*, with their adventures and tragic fates, hold an appeal for the Japanese, who can find in them a close similarity to the ill-fated heroes of their own mythology and history. The *Šāh-nāma* was introduced to the literary world of Japan in 1916, when Bunmei Tsuchiya (1891-1990), himself a poet, published an abridged translation from English versions. This work, *Perushia shinwa* (Legends of Persia), served as a model for Akijirō Soma's *Perushia no densetsu to rekishi* (Legends and history of Persia, 1922) and Masaharu Higuchi's translation of *Rostam o Sohrāb* (1941). Tsuneo Kuroyanagi was the first to publish abridged tales of the *Šāh-nāma* translated directly from Persian (1969), followed by Emiko Okada's similar work (1999). Abridged translations of stories from the *Šāh-nāma* are also found in Shigeru Araki's literary history of Persia (1922).

Saʿdi, like Ḵayyām and Ferdowsi, has attracted a number of Japanese scholars, who have worked primarily on the *Golestān* (in Japanese, *Bara-en* "Rose garden"). Among them, Gamō and Sawa are notable for the elegance of their translations. Araki (1922) quoted excerpts of Saʿdi's works. Asatori (Chōka) Katō rendered the *Golestān* in beautiful Japanese (1922); Katō is known as one of the first Japanese who converted to Islam and made a pilgrimage to Mecca. Kowashi Takase's translation of *Golestān* was published in 1948. Ryōtan Tokuzawa's *Iran monogatari* (Stories of Iran, 1948) contains an introduction to, and translations of, parts of the *Golestān* (pp. 137-55). Sawa produced an authentic and beautiful, but abridged, translation of it. R. Gamō, having previously published excerpts of his translation of the *Golestān* in several literary journals, was the first scholar to produce a complete translation (1963); it has since been reprinted many times. Gamō's abridged translation of Saʿdi's *Bustān* was published in 1964. Kuroyanagi's translation of *Golestān* was published in 1985.

Gamō was the first scholar to publish (1955) a general survey on the life and time of Hafez (q.v.) and his work, with many references to selected verses of his poems. He was followed by Sawa, who translated selected pieces of the work (1966). Gamō's main source was the Divān of Hafez edited by Ḥosayn Pežmān-e Baḵtiāri (Tehran, 1936). He also refers to a *Ḥayāt-e Ḥāfez* (in Urdu?) by Šebli Noʿmāni as well as E. G. Browne's *A Literary History of Persia*. Gamō makes further reference to Hafez in his work on Persian lyric poetry (1964). Kuroyanagi published a complete translation of the Divān of Hafez in 1976, basing his rendering on a more authentic edition of the work by Moḥammad Qazvini and Qāsem Ḡani (Tehran, 1941). In 1988 he published a more elaborate translation of selected *ḡazal*s of Ḥafez, with annotations.

Of Islamic, mystical, and philosophical works, translations by the scholar of Islam and other Eastern religions, Toshihiko Izutsu (1914-93), stand out for their authenticity and elegance; those of Jalāl-al-Din Moḥammad Rumi's *Fihi mā fihi* and Mollā Ṣadrā's *Ketāb al-mašāʾer* (both in 1978) are notable. R. Gamō was first to publish an introduction to the *Maṯnawi* with examples of its contents (1964). Akiro Matsumoto produced an elaborate translation of ʿAbd-al-Raḥmān Jāmi's *Lawāyeḥ* and Šarif Jorjāni's *Resālat al-wojud* (2002). Kazuo Morimoto of Tokyo University published (2007) a translation of Moḥammad-Ḥosayn Ṭabāṭabāʾi's *Šiʿa dar Eslām*, together with the appendices of Seyyed Hossein Nasr's English translation. Kazuo Morimoto of Tokyo University published his annotated translation of Nāṣer-e Ḵosrow's *Safar-nāma* in four parts in issues of the Scientific Journal (*Shihō*) of Hokkaido University (2005 and 2006). In the area of wisdom literature (*andarz*, q.v.), Neẓāmi Aružiʾs *Čahār maqāla* and ʿOnṣor-al-Maʿāli Keykāvus b. Eskandar's *Qābus-nāma* were translated by Kuroyanagi and published together (1969).

The name of Emiko Okada is associated with translations of lyrical poetry, and she has also produced several elegant examples of the romantic narratives of Neẓāmi Ganjavi's *Ḵosrow o Širin* (1977) and *Layli o Majnun* (1981), and Faḵr-al-Din Asʿad Gorgāni's *Vis o Rāmin* (1990). Translations of Neẓāmi's *Haft peykar* (q.v.) were published by Takeo Nono (1962) and Kuroyanagi (1971).

Many selections from Persian classics have been translated and included in Japanese textbooks for Persian language study, for example, those by Kuroyanagi. Persian proverbs and maxims were introduced, with annotations and examples of their usage, by Takeshi Katsufuji and Hashem Rajabzadeh (1993).

Contemporary Persian literature. Interest in Persian contemporary literature, especially among younger generations, is increasing in Japan, although that interest may often be driven more by current events than by pursuit of literary values. Translation from Persian into Japanese, with its different way of expression, remains difficult. But there is promise in an emerging generation well versed in Persian as well as Japanese, who are open-minded and positive, and who appreciate and enjoy their acquaintance with the works of Iranian writers.

In the category of the novel and short story, Bozorg ʿAlawi's *Ḵāʾen* was among the first to be translated (Ichirō Nono, 1959). Several works of Jalāl Āl-e Aḥmad (q.v.), including *Nefrin-e zamin* and *Jašn-e farḵonda*, have been introduced to Japanese readers. Sādeq Hedāyat's *Buf-e kur* was first translated by Eishō Horii in 1976. In the 1970s and 1980s more than twenty works of Hedāyat were translated by Kiminori Nakamura and published in several literally journals, starting with *Āyena-ye šekasta* (1977 and 1983). Nakamura published his translations of selected works of Hedāyat in one volume in 1984. Moḥammad-ʿAli Jamālzāda (q.v.) is also among Nakamura's favorite writers, from whom he translated *Fārsi šekar ast* and *Rajol-e siāsi* (1980), followed by a collection of his selected works (1987). Other translators of Hedāyat's works include E. Okada (with *Dāwūd-e gužpošt*, 1977) and Sachiko Takayasu (*Ābji Ḵānom*, 1982). A translation of Ṣamad Behrangi's *Pesarak-e labuforūš* by Takashi Iwami was published in 1983. Yuko Fujimoto of Osaka University of Foreign Studies published translations of a number of contemporary literary works, including Ṣamad Behrangi's *Bist o čahār sāʿat dar ḵ^v āb o bidāri* (1983) and *Māhi-e siāh-e kučulu* (1984), Simin Dānešvar's *Šahri čon behešt* (1984), and Goli Taraqqi's *Bozorg-bānu-ye ruḥ-e man* (1991). Her latest published translation is Zoyā Pirzād's "Hastahā-ye ālbālu" (2007).

Modern Persian poetry has been introduced by a few works of some literary figures including Aḥmad Šāmlū and Forūḡ Farroḵzād (Kiminori Nakamura, tr., 1984). Kimie Maeda (Onuma) has introduced several works of Šāmlu and Sohrāb Sepehri.

Other translations. Kametarō Yagi (1908-86)'s translation of the book *Jang*, written in the last years of Reżā Shah (1938) by Aḥmad Naḵjavān, a deputy in the Ministry of War, shows a parallelism between the political cultures of Iran and Japan in the years leading up to World War II. The author tries to justify war as an unavoidable means to provide mankind with qualifications to achieve perfection and a real civilization. He sees the world as a scene of continuous struggle among nation states for hegemony and national goals in which relations are regulated by power and strength and not by fairness and justice (pp. 4-5).

In the field of folklore, translations of Ṣādeq Hedāyat's *Neyrangestān* (tr. Shunsuke Okunishi) and Ḵ^v ansari's (d. 1713) *ʿAqāyed al-nesāʾ* (tr. E. Okada) were published in one volume (1999). Translations of Persian folktales have mainly introduced the work of Abu'l-Qāsem Enjavi Širāzi, including pieces of his *Qeṣṣahā-ye irāni* (tr. Okunishi and Yuko Hamahata, 1983-86). Other such translations include *Jamšid Šāh* by Mehrdād Bahār (1979) and F. Ṭāyerfar's *Mājarā-ye Aḥmad o Sārā* (2006), the fourth of a series translated by Keiko Ikuo. In historical linguistics, Kazuya Yamauchi published a translation (1997) of Aḥmad Tafażżoli and Žāla Āmuzgār's *Pahlavi; adabiyāt wa dastur-e ān.*

Another work dealing with Persian culture is Yoshifusa Seki's beautiful translation into Japanese of *Golestān-e ḵiāl* (Flower garden of imagination, Iranian Cultural Heritage Organization, Tehran, 1988), titled *Yume no hanazono* (Tehran, 1997). The book displays selected works of painting and miniature art, book decoration, calligraphy, wood carving, tiles, glazed vases and vessels, coins, and other art objects preserved in Iranian museums and other public collections.

Bibliography: Classical literature; religion and philosophy. Shigeru Araki, *Perushia bungakushi-kō* (Survey of the literary history of Iran), Tokyo, 1922. Ferdowsi, *Šāh-nāma*, selections tr. Bunmei Tsuchiya as *Perushiya shinwa* (Legends of Persia), Tokyo, 1916; tr. Akijirō Soma as *Perushiya no densetsu to rekishi* (Legends and history of Persia), Tokyo, 1922; tr. Masaharu Higuchi (*Rostam o Sohrāb* as *Rostam to Sohrab*), Tokyo, 1941; tr. Reiichi Gamō, in *Iran no rekishi to bunka* (Iran's history and culture), Tokyo, 1941; abridged tr. Tsuneo Kuroyanagi as *Ō-sho (Shā-nāme)*, Tokyo, 1969; tr. Ts. Kuroyanagi (*Rostam o Sohrāb* as *Rostam to Sohrab*), Tokyo, 1987, and *Perushia no shinwa: Ō-sho (Shā-nāme) yori* (Persian legends from the *Šāh-nāma*), Tokyo, 1989; selections tr. Emiko Okada as *Ō-sho. Kodai Perushiya no shinwa densetsu* (*Šāh-nāma*. Ancient myths and legends of Iran), Tokyo, 1999; selection (Sām va Zāl) tr. Okada in *Perushia no yottsu no monogatari* (Four stories of Iran), Tokyo, 2004. Reiichi Gamō, *Jojō shijin: Shirāzu no Hafez* (The lyric poet; Hafez of Shiraz), Nihon-Iran Kyōkai (Japan-Iran Friendship Society), Tokyo, 1955. Idem, "Jojōshi" (Lyric poetry), in *Arabia-Perushia shū* (Arabic-Persian literature), Sekai bungaku Taikei (Literature of the world, Series) 68, Tokyo, 1964, pp. 374-92. Faḵr al-Din Asʿad Gorgāni, *Vis o Rāmin*, tr. Emiko Okada as *Vīs to Rāmīn. Perushia no koi no monogatari* (Vis and Rāmin: a Persian love story), Tokyo, 1990.

Ḥāfeẓ, *Divān*, tr. Eizō Sawa as "Hafez shishō" (Selected poems of Hāfez), in *Sekai meishishū taisei* (Compilation of famous poetry of the world) 18. *Tōyō* (Orient), Tokyo, 1960, pp. 329-44; tr. Tsuneo Kuroyanagi as *Hāfizu shishū* (Poetic works of Hafez), Tōyō Bunko Series No. 299, Tokyo, 1976; repr. in Perushia Koten Sōsho Series No. 1, Tokyo, 1977; tr. Kuroyanagi as *Hāfizu jojō shishō yakuchū* (Hāfez; annotated translation of selected lyric poems), Tokyo, 1988. Nur-al-Din ʿAbd-al-Raḥmān Jāmi, *Lawāyeḥ*, and Sayyed Šarif Jorjāni, *Resālat al-wojud*, tr. Akirō Matsumoto as *Perushia sonzai issei ronshū* (Collection of Persian ontological works), Tokyo, 2002. Sayyed ʿAli Šarif Jorjāni, see Jāmi. Mollā Ṣadrā Širāzi, *Ketāb al-mašāʾer*, tr. Toshihiko Izutsu as *Sonzai-ninshiki no dō—sonzai to honshitsu ni tsuite* (The path of apprehending existence. On existence and reality), Tokyo, 1978.

ʿOmar Ḵayyām, *Robāʿiyāt*, tr. Shun Ōsumi and Shōfu Ōsumi as *Rubaiyatto*, Tokyo, 1908; tr. Kanbara Ariake, Tokyo, 1908; tr. Bunkichi Katano, Tokyo, 1914; tr. Shigeru Araki, as *Omuma Ḫayamu to yon'gyoushi (Rubaiyatto) zenyaku* (ʿOmar Ḵayyām and the "Quatrains" [*Robāʿiyāt*]—full translation), Tokyo, 1920; tr. Sōfu Taketomo, Tokyo, 1921; tr. Hōjin Yano, Tokyo, 1935 and 1938; tr. Ryō Mori, Tokyo, 1941 and 1948; tr. Ryōho Horii, Tokyo, 1947; tr. Sōfu Taketomo, Tokyo, 1947; tr. Ryōsaku Ogawa, Tokyo, 1948; tr. Tetsuo Nāgiri, Tokyo, 1949; tr. Eizō Sawa, Tokyo, 1960; tr. Tsuneo Kuroyanagi and Reiichi Gamō, Tokyo, 1964; tr. Chōbo Hasegawa, Tokyo, 1967; tr. Kuroyanagi, Tokyo, 1973 and 1983; tr. Toshihiko Ogata, Kyoto, 1984; tr. Riō Mori, Tokyo, 1986; tr. Katsuyuki Yamaji, in *Kagoshima Keizai Daigaku ronshū*, 1988; tr. Toshinaga Ida, Tokyo, 1989.

ʿOnṣor-al-Maʿāli Keykāvus b. Eskandar, *Qābus-nāma*, tr. Tsuneo Kuroyanagi as *Kābūs no sho* (Book of Qābus), in Kuroyanagi, *Perushia itsuwa-shū: Kābūs no sho; Yottsu no kōwa* Tokyo, 1969. Nāṣer-e Ḵosrow, *Safar-nāma*, tr. Kiminori Nakamura as "Tabi no sho," *Harubūza*, No. 111, 1981, pp. 2-18; tr. Kazuo Morimoto, in *Hokkaido Daigaku Shihō*, No. 35, February 2003, pp. 1-29, and No. 38, December 2005, pp. 23-50. Aḥmad Neẓāmi Arużi, *Čahār maqāla*, tr. Tsuneo

Kuroyanagi as *Yottsu no kōwa* (Four discourses), in Kuroyanagi, *Perushia itsuwa-shū: Kābūs no sho; Yottsu no kōwa*, Tokyo, 1969. Neẓāmi Ganjavi, *Haft peykar*, tr. Takeo Nono, Tokyo, 1962; tr. Tsuneo Kuroyanagi as *Shichi ōhi* (Seven queens), Tokyo, 1971. Idem, *K̲osrow o Širin*, tr. Emiko Okada as *Hosurō to Shīrīn*, Tokyo, 1977. Idem, *Layli o Majnun*, tr. Okada as *Raira to Majnūn*, Tokyo, 1981. Selections, tr. Okada in *Perushia no yottsu no monogatari* (Four stories of Iran), Tokyo, 2004. Āgā Jamāl K̲ᵛānsāri, *ʿAqāyed al-nesāʾ*, tr. Emiko Okada, in *Perushia minzoku-shi* (Records of Persian folkways), Tokyo, 1999. Jalāl-al-Din Moḥammad Rumi, *Fihi mā fihi*, tr. Toshihiko Izutsu as *Rūmī goroku* (Rumi's discourses), Tokyo, 1978. Idem, *Maṯnawi-e maʿnawi*, the introductory part, tr. Reiichi Gamō as *Seishinteki Maṯnawi*, in *Sekai bungaku taikei: Arabiya-Perushiya shū*, Tokyo, 1964, pp. 347-73. Saʿdi, *Bustān*, tr. Reiichi Gamō, Tokyo, 1964. Idem, *Golestān*, tr. Chōka Katō as *Bara-en*, Tokyo, 1922; tr. Kowashi Takase as *Bara no sono*, Tokyo, 1948; tr. Eizō Sawa as *Goresutān*, Tokyo, 1951; tr. Reiichi Gamō as *Bara-en*, Tokyo, 1953, and *Bara-en (Gurisutān): Iran chūsei no kyōyō monogatari* (Gulistan: refined tales from Iran's Middle Ages), Tokyo, 1964; tr. Tsuneo Kuroyanagi as *Bara-en*, Tokyo, 1985.

Modern literature and folklore. Jalāl Āl-e Aḥmad, "Jašn-e fark̲onda," tr. Sachiko Takayasu as "Medetai shukujitsu," *Harubūza*, No. 116, 1981, pp. 2-19. Idem, *Nafrin-e zamin*, tr. Minoru Yamada as *Chi no majinai*, Tokyo, 1981. Bozorg ʿAlavi, *K̲āʾen*, tr. Ichirō Nano as "Mikkokusha," *Shin Nihon bungaku* 14/5, 1959, pp. 51-62. Mehrdād Bahār, *Jamšid Šāh*, tr. Sachiko Takayasu as "Jamushido Ō," *Harubūza*, No. 91, 1979, pp. 2-24. Ṣamad Behrangi, *Bist o čahār sāʿat dar k̲ᵛāb o bidāri*, tr. Yuko Fujimoto as "Tehran no nijūyojikan," in *Gendai Ajia seiji ni okeru chiiki to minshū* (Osaka University of Foreign Studies), 1983, pp. 251-70. Idem, *Māhi-e siāh-e kučulu*, tr. Yuko Fujimoto (Kagawa) as *Chisana kuroi sakana*, Tokyo, 1984. Simin Dānešvar, *Šahri čon behešt*, tr. Yuko Fujimoto (Kagawa) as "Tengoku no yōna machi," in *Gendai Ajia ni okeru chiiki seiji no shosō* (Aspects of regional politics in modern Asia), Osaka, 1984, pp. 179-96. Abu'l-Qāsem Enjavi Širāzi, *Qeṣṣahā-ye irāni*: tr. Shunsuke Okunishi as "Iran no mukashi-banashi," *Sekai kōshō bungi kenkyū* [*SKBK*], No. 4, 1983, pp. 409-33; tr. Yuko Hamahata: as "Iran no minwa," in *SKBK*, No. 5, 1984, pp. 573-95; as "Iran no mukashi-banashi," *SKBK*, No. 7, 1986, pp. 339-67, and No. 8, 1986, pp. 157-90. Forūḡ Farrok̲zād, *Tawallod-i digar*, tr. Kiminori Nakamura, Tokyo, 1984.

Ṣādeq Hedāyat, *Buf-e kur*, tr. Eishō Hori as "Mōmoku no fukurō," *Gekkān Shiruku-rōdo*, 2/8, 1976, pp. 85-129, and in *Sekai no bungaku* (Literature of the world), Tokyo, 1983. Idem, *Āyena-ye šekasta*, tr. Kiminori Nakamura as "Kowareta kagami," in *Iran bungaku* 1, 1977. Idem, selected short stories tr. Nakamura as *Mōmoku no fukurō*, Tokyo, 1983; tr. Nakamura as *Sādeku Hedāyato tampenshū* (Short stories of Ṣādeq Hedāyat), Tokyo, 1985; tr. Keiichirō Ishii as *Ikiume. Aru hannin no shuki yori* (Buried alive. From the notes of a criminal), Tokyo, 2000. Idem, *Neyrangestān*, tr. Shunsuke Okunishi, in *Perushia minzoku-shi* (Records of Persian folkways), Tokyo, 1999. Moḥammad ʿAli Jamālzāda, *Fārsi šekar ast*, tr. Kiminori Nakamura as "Perushiago wa sato," *Harubūza*, No. 98, 1980, pp. 2-14. Idem, *Rajol-e siāsi*, tr. Kiminori Nakamura as "Seijika," *Harubūza*, No. 99, 1980, pp. 2-20. Idem, *Jamaruzadei tampenshū* (A selection of Ja-mālzadah's short stories; Persian title: *Bargozida-ye āṯār-e Jamālzāda*), tr. Kiminori Nakamura, Tokyo, 1987. Zoyā Pirzād, "Hastahā-ye ālbālu," tr. Yuko Fujimoto, in *Iran kenkyū* (Osaka University of Foreign Studies) 3, 2007, pp. 168-207. Ryōten Tokuzawa, *Iran monogatari* (Stories from Persia), Tokyo, 1943. Goli Taraqqi, *Bozorg-bānu-ye ruḥ-e man*, tr. Yuko Fujimoto, in *Asian Studies* (Osaka University of Foreign Studies) 1, 1991, pp. 133-47. F. Ṭāyerfar, *Mājarā-ye Aḥmad o Sārā*, tr. Keiko Aikō as *Ahumado no orusuban*, Tokyo, 2006.

Other references. Žāla Āmuzgār and Aḥmad Tafazzoli, *Zabān-e Pahlavi: adabiyāt wa dastur-e ān*, Tehran, 1974; tr. Kazuya Yamauchi as *Pahrabi-go: sono bungaku to bumpō*, Institute of Silk Road Studies, Tokyo, 1997. Lafcadio Hearn, "Edward Fitzgerald and the 'Rubaiyat'," in idem, *Poets and Poems*, comp. Ryuji Tanabé, Tokyo, 1926, pp. 211-32. Iranian Cultural Heritage Organization, *Golestān-e k̲iāl*, Tehran, 1988; tr. Yoshifusa Seki as *Yume no hanazono* (Garden of dreams), Tehran, 1997. Takeshi Katsufuji and Hashem Rajabzadeh, *Perushiago kotowaza yōhō jiten* (Dictionary of Persian proverbs and usage), Tokyo, 1993. Hashem Rajabzadeh (Hāšem Rajabzāda), "Šāh-nāmašenāsi dar Žāpon," *Āyanda* 17/9-19, pp. 675-82. Moḥammad-Ḥosayn Ṭabāṭabāʾi, *Šiʿa dar Eslām*; tr. Seyyed Hossein Nasr as *Shiʿite Islam*, Albany, 1975; tr. Kazuo Morimoto as *Shiʿa-hā no jigazō: rekishi shisō kyōgi* (Self-portrait of Shiʿism: history, thought, doctrine), Tokyo University, 2007. Tōyō Bunko (Oriental Library), *Nihon ni okeru Chūtō-Isuramu kenkyū bunken mokuroku* (Bibliography of Islamic and Middle Eastern studies in Japan [1868-1988]), Tokyo, 1992.

(HASHEM RAJABZADEH)

xiii. TRANSLATIONS OF JAPANESE WORKS INTO PERSIAN

Translation into Persian of works written in French, English, and other European languages began in Nāṣer-al-Din Shah's reign (1848-96). The Government Translation Bureau (Dār-al-tarjama-ye k̲āṣṣa-ye dawlati) under Moḥammad-Ḥasan Khan Eʿtemād-al-Salṭana engaged in translating diverse historical, geographical, and literary works. Perhaps some of these touched on East Asian history and culture, including Japan. But a specific introduction of Japan to Persian readers began when Japanese military victories over China (Sino-Japanese War, 1894-95) and, especially, Russia (Russo-Japanese War, 1904-

05) excited the interest of Iranians and other Western Asian nations. One such notable work was *Mamlakat-e šams-e ṭāleʿ yā dawlat-e Žāpon* compiled and translated by Māṭāvus Khan Melikiān and published in 1904. In 1907 Ḥosayn-ʿAli Tājer Širāzi published an account of the Russo-Japanese War in 2,000 couplets of epic verse. Titled *Mikādo-nāma*, it was based on translated reports and commentaries. For four decades after Iran's Constitutional Revolution (1905-11, q.v.), however, there are no records of any further Persian publications about Japan.

In the early 1940s, after the abdication of Reza Shah in 1941, the changed political atmosphere led to a revival of publishing activities, and several new literary journals appeared. Prominent among them was *Sok̲ān*, founded in 1943 by Parviz Nātel K̲ānlari, who was also its chief editor. *Sok̲an* provided incentives and opportunity for growth to the promising younger generation of writers and translators. Many celebrated literary figures, including K̲ānlari himself and Ṣādeq Hedāyat (q.v.), translated examples of Japanese literature from French or other Western languages, and these were published in *Sok̲an* (see Rajabzadeh, 1997). These include translations of some old Japanese stories and a few stories of Kyōgen (Japanese comic plays) by Hamid ʿEnāyat; "Urāshimā Tārō," a Japanese folk-tale, by Hedāyat; and a representative work of Junichirō Tanizaki (1886-1965) by Zahrā K̲ānlari. Japanese poetry was first introduced to Persian readers by a number of contributors to *Sok̲an*, of whom Ḥamid ʿEnāyat, Sohrāb Sepehri, and Aḥmad Šāmlu are notable. Sepehri rendered a number of *tanka* verses (a classical 31 syllable poetry, comprising five lines of five, seven, five, seven, and seven syllables) into beautiful Persian. Selections of the 14th-century *Tsurezuregusa* (Essays in idleness), a collection of observations and anecdotes by the monk Kenkō Yoshida (d. 1350), were also first introduced in *Sok̲an*—apparently translated by P. N. K̲ānlari.

Translations continued to appear in the 1950s and 1960s in such literary journals as Aḥmad Šāmlu's *Ketāb-e hafta* and Ḡolām-Ḥosayn Ṣāʿedi's *Alefbā*. ʿAbbās Saʿidi (1973) is credited as one of the first authors since Māṭāvus Khan Melikiān to compile an introductory book on Japan, based on sources in European languages. More recent works on modern Japanese history include Aḥmad Birašk's translation (1996) of *The Japan Reader* (ed. Jon Livingston et al.).

Japanese classical poetry is represented in Persian by anthologies of haiku translations (Šāmlu, 1997; Maeda and Pāšāʾi, 2002), as well as *Gol-e ṣadbarg*, a selection from the 8th-century anthology of poems in a number of different verse forms, *Man'yōshū* (Collection of 10,000 leaves), which is the earliest collection of Japanese poetry (selections tr. Rajabzadeh and Fujimoto, 1993). Prose literature is represented by the *Tsurezuregusa* (tr. Rajabzadeh, 1993).

Since the 1950s a considerable number of books containing Persian translations of short stories and novels by Japanese writers has been published, mostly introducing works of Natsume Sōseki (1867-1916), Ryūnosuke Akutagawa (1892-1927), Masuji Ibuse (1898-), Yasunari Kawabata (1899-1972), Kojiro Serisawa (1897-), Yukio Mishima (1925-70), and Kenzaburō Ōe (1935-). Compilations of selected short stories by Japanese writers have also been published, such as the work translated by Ārtuš Budaqiān. In recent years, two literary journals, *Kelk* (no. 65, 1995) and *Pol-e firuza* (1/4, 2002), have published special issues on Japan with Hashem Rajabzadeh as guest editor; these contain a number of articles translated from Japanese.

Japan has also been the subject of original fiction written in Persian. A number of works depict adventures and hardships experienced by unauthorized Iranian workers there in the 1990s. Examples are ʿAbbās Mašhadi's *K̲asta-delān dar Žāpon* (1997) and Ḥamid Mobini's *Man az Žāpon āmada-am* (1977). Mašhadi's is a fascinating work of fiction based on a new image of Japan which took shape among tens of thousands of Iranians, mostly unemployed young men, who in the 1990s adventured to Japan, traveling on tourist visas in search of temporary jobs (see above, iv). The references made in the work to things Japanese, locations, and place names, however, suggest that the writer himself has not lived in Japan, at least for a long time. Mobini's work is a typical and factual diary of an educated young man who has experienced the hardship of living and working in Japan as an illegal worker.

Publications on Japan and Japanese arts translated into Persian include books on Japanese drama and the classical theatrical genres of Nō (Noh), Kabuki, and Kyōgen. Some works related to Japanese films also have been translated, including *Sinemā-ye Yāsujirō Ozu* (Yasujirō Ozu's [1903-63] films) compiled by A. Ṭabāṭabāʾi, which presents the oeuvre of a director noted for his moving depictions of family life, its close bonds and its tensions. In the field of fine arts, *Šiša-ye Irani* is Ārmān Šišegarān's translation (from the English version) of Shinji Fukai's *Persian Glass*.

In the area of philosophy and religion, translated works mostly relate to Zen Buddhism, an example of which is Delārā Qahramān's *Ṣad ḥekāyat-e Zen*, a translation of one hundred selected Zen stories. Hashem Rajabzadeh rendered in Persian the *Bukkyō seiten* (Teaching of Buddha), compiled by the Bukkyō Dendō Kyōkai (Society for the Promotion of Buddhism), as *Čonin goft Budā* (1984).

A number of Japanese travel accounts and memoirs of Japanese who traveled in Iran from 1880 on have been translated by Rajabzadeh, some with the collaboration of Japanese researchers. These include works by Masaharu Yoshida (traveled 1880-81) and his traveling companion Nobuyoshi Furukawa, Atsuuji Ashikaga (1934 to 1964), Iwatarō Uchiyama (1926-27), Akiyo Kasama (1929-32), and Eiji Inoue (1934 to 1984). (See also, above, iii.)

Other non-fiction works include Morio Ono's account of Iranian agriculture, translated by Rajabzadeh as *K̲ayrābād-nāma* (1988). Rajabzadeh has also translated a number of articles by Japanese scholars who are engaged in Iranian studies, including part of Seichō Matsumoto's work on the introduction of Persian art into Japan in ancient times. For the benefit of the Persian-speaking community in Japan, Yoshifusa Seki did the Persian translation in a conversation guide (one of a series) for foreigners with Japanese doctors (Ōnishi and Masumo). A few textbooks used in teaching Japanese to non-Japanese students also have been translated into Persian; the original sources are mainly in English.

Bibliography: Literature. Ryūnosuke Akutagawa, "Rashōmon" and other short stories, tr. Amir-Faridun Gorgāni as *Rāšumun wa dāstānhā-ye digar*, Tehran, 1965. Ārtuš Budāqiān, tr. *Bargozida-ye dāstānhā-ye kutāh az nevisandagān-e moʿāṣer-e Žāpon*, Tehran, 1999. Ḥamid ʿEnāyat, "Nemāyeš-e žāponi" (about Nō [Noh], Kyōgen, and Kabuki theater), *Soḵan* 7/1, 1956, pp. 46-51. Idem, "Šʿer-e žāponi," *Soḵan* 6/10, 1955, pp. 903-5. Idem, "Dāstānhā-ye žāponi" (a survey of Japanese prose), *Soḵan* 6/11, 1956, pp. 1010-13. Sādeq Hedāyat, "Qeṣṣa-ye žāponi-ye Urāshimā," *Soḵan* 2/1, 1944, pp. 43-45. Ḥosayn-ʿAli Tājer Širāzi, *Mikādo-nāma*, Calcutta, 1905-07; ed. ʿAli Amin Anṣāri, Tehran, 2006. Masuji Ibuse, *Kuro ame* (Black rain), Tokyo, 1966; tr. Karim Kešāvarz as *Bārān-e siāh*, Tehran, 1977. Parviz N. Ḵānlari, selections of *Tsurezuregusa*, tr. as *falsafa-ye žaponi*, in *Soḵan* 2/7, 1945, p. 512. Takeshi Katsufuji, Haiku poems on Iran and Afghanistan, tr. H. Rajabzadeh as "Čand hāiku dar bāra-ye Irān wa Afgānestān," *Āyanda* 17/5-8, 1989, pp. 598-99. Yasunari Kawabata, *Yama no oto* (The sound of the mountain), Tokyo, 1954; tr. D. Qahremānpoor as *Āvā-ye kuhestān*, Tehran, 1984.

K. Maeda and ʿA. Pāšāʾi, trs., *Lāk-e pūk-e zanjara: haiku-ye žāponi*, Tehran, 2002. *Man'yōshū*, tr. H. Rajabzadeh and Yuko Fujimoto as *Man'yō hyaku-sen: Gol-e ṣad-barg: gozida-ye māniyushu, šeʾr-e qadim-e Žāpon*, Mashad, 1993. ʿAbbās Mašhadi, *Ḵasta-delān dar Žāpon*, Tehran, 1988. Yukio Mishima, short stories, tr. Aḵtar Eʿtemādi as *Haft pol*, Tehran, 1985. Idem, *Kinkakuji*, tr. M. ʿĀliḵāni as *Maʿbad-e ṭelāʾi*, Tehran, 1993. Ḥamid Mobini, *Man az Žāpon āmada-am*, Tehran, 1997. Kenzaburō Ōe, *Man'en gannen no futtobōru* (Soccer in the year 1860), Tokyo, 1967; tr. J. Bester as *Silent Cry*, Tokyo, 1974; tr. Farzān Sojudi as *Faryād-e ḵāmuš*, Tehran, 1998. Delārā Qahramān, tr., *Ṣad hekāyat-e Zen*, Tehran, 1992. Reżā Saʿid-ḥosayni, "Three classical Japanese poems," in *Soḵan* 9/2, 1958, p. 177. Hashem Rajabzadeh, *Andiša va eḥsās dar šeʿr-e moʿāṣer-e Žāpon*, Tehran, 1979. Idem, "Žāpon dar Soḵan," in Iraj Afšār and Hans Robert Roemer, eds., *Soḵanvāra: panjāh-o-panj goftār-e pažuheši ba yād-e Doktor Parviz Nātel Ḵānlari*, Tehran, 1997, pp. 308-41. Sohrāb Sepehri, "Seven Japanese tanka poems," in *Soḵan* 6/8, 1955, pp. 703-4. Aḥmad Šāmlu, tr., seven Japanese poems, in: *Soḵan* 3/8-9, 1947, pp. 616-20. Ahmad Šāmlu et al., *Haiku: šeʿr-e žāponi az āḡāz tā emruz*, 3rd ed., Tehran, 1997. Kojirō Serisawa, short stories, tr. H. Qadimi and M. Nuri as *Dāstānhā-ye kutāh-e Ḵāvar-e Dur*, Shiraz, 1992. Natsume Sōseki, *Botchan* (Sonny boy), Tokyo, 1906; tr. H. Rajabzadeh as *Botchān*, Tehran, 1980. Junichirō Tanizaki, "Shisei" (Tattooing), tr. Zahrā Ḵānlari as "Ḵālkubi," *Soḵan* 6/8, 1955, pp. 694-702. Kenkō Yoshida, *Tsurezuregusa* (Essays in idleness), various editions and translations, e.g., *The Tsurezuregusa of Kenko*, tr. Donald Keene, New York, 1967; tr. H. Rajabzadeh as *Tsure-zure-gusā: golestān-e žāponi*, Tehran, 1993.

History and travel. Atsuuji Ashikaga, *Iran* (Travels in Iran), in E. Imoto and G. Itō, eds., *Ashikaga Atsuuji chosakushū* (Collected works of Atsuuji Ashikaga), Tōkai University, 1988; comp. and tr. H. Rajabzadeh as *Safar-nāma, ḵāṭerāt, wa yād-nāma-ye Āšikāgā Ātsuuji*, Tehran, 2004. Maḥmud Khan Eḥtešām-al-Salṭana, *Ḵāṭerāt-e Ehtešām-al-Salṭana*, ed. Sayyed Moḥammad-Mahdi Musawi, 3rd ed., Tehran, 1989. Moḥammad-Ḥasan Khan Eʿtemād-al-Salṭana, *Ruz-nāma-ye ḵāṭerāt*, ed. Iraj Afšār, 3rd ed., Tehran, 1987. Nobuyoshi Furukawa, *Perushia kikō* (Travels in Iran), Tokyo, 1890; tr. Kinji Eura and Hashem Rajabzadeh as *Safar-nāma-ye Furukawa*, Tehran, 2005. Eiji Inoue, *Waga kaisō no Iran* (My memories of Iran), ed. Masayuki Inoue, Tokyo, 1986; tr. H. Rajabzadeh as *Irān va man: ḵāṭerahā wa yāddāšthā-ye Eiji Inoue*, Tehran, 2004. Akio Kasama, *Sabaku no kuni: Perushiya, Toruko, Arabiya* (The desert countries: Iran, Turkey, and Arabia), Tokyo, 1935; tr. H. Rajabzadeh as *Safar-nāma-ye Kāsāmā, naḵostin wazir-moḵtār-e Žāpon dar Irān*, Tehran, 2001. Māṭāvus Khan Melikiān, comp. and tr., *Mamlakat-e šams-e ṭāleʿ yā dawlat-e Žāpon*, Tehran, 1904. Iwatarō Uchiyama, "Iran," in *Hankotsu 77 nen: Uchiyama Iwatarō no jinsei* (77 years defiance: the life of Iwatarō Uchiyama), Yokohama, 1968; tr. H. Rajabzadeh as "Safar-nāma wa ḵāṭerāt-e Uchiyāmā Iwātārō, naḵostin ferestāda-ye Žāpon ba Irān dar sada-ye bistom, Mehr 1305-Mehr 1306" in *Kelk*, no. 65, 1995, pp. 305-42. Masaharu Yoshida, *Kaikyō tanken Perushia no tabi* (Adventures in Muslim Persia) (1880-1881), Tokyo, 1894; tr. H. Rajabzadeh as *Safar-nāma-ye Māsāhāru Yoshidā, naḵostin ferestāda-ye Žāpon ba Irān dar dawra-ye Qajar, 1297-98 h.q.–1880-81 milādi*, Mashad, 1994.

Art and culture. Shinji Fukai, *Perushia no garasu*, Kyoto, 1973; tr. Edna Crawford as *Persian Glass*, New York and Tokyo, 1977; tr. Ārmān Šišegarān as *Šiša-ye irāni*, Tehran, 1992. Yukichi Fukuzawa, *Bunmeiron no gairyaku*, Tokyo, 1875; tr. David A. Dilworth and G. Cameron Hurst as *An Outline of a Theory of Civilization*, Tokyo, 1973; tr. Čangiz Pahlavān as *Nāẓariya-ye tamaddon*, Tehran, 1985. Seichō Matsumoto, *Peruseporisu kara Āsukā e* (From Persepolis to Asuka), in part tr. H. Rajabzadeh and Toshimi Itō as "Nemunahā-ye honar-e Iran dar Žāpon," *Pol-e firuza* 1/4, 2002, pp. 118-26. Morio Ono, *Iran nōmin 25 nen no dorama* (A 25-year drama with Iranian farmers), Nippon Hōsō Kyōkai (Japan Broadcasting Corporation), Tokyo, 1990; tr. H. Rajabzadeh as *Ḵayrābād-nāma: 25 sāl bā rūstāʾiān-e Irān*, Tehran, 1998. Hashem Rajabzadeh, *Žāpon: diruz o emruz*, Tehran, 2005. ʿAbbās Saʿidi, comp. and tr., *Žāpon: baḥt-i dar bāra-ye sar-zamin wa mardom-e Žāpon*, Mashad, 1964.

A. A. Ṭabāṭabāʾi, comp. and tr., *Sinemā-ye Yāsujirō Ozu*, Tehran, 1988; based on Tadao Satō, *Yasujirō Ozu no geijutsu* (The art of Yasujirō Ozu), Tokyo, 1978, and other sources. Shūgaku Yamabe et al., *Bukkyō seiten* (Teachings of Buddha), Bukkyō Dendō Kyōkai (Society for the Promotion of Buddhism), Tokyo, 1973; tr. H. Rajabzadeh as *Čonin goft Budā*, Tokyo, 1984.

Other works. Edward Behr, *Hirohito: Behind the Myth*, London, 1990; tr. Arasṭu Āḏari as *Hirohito dar warā-ye osṭura*, Tehran, 1995. Felicien Challaye, *Contes et légendes du Japon*, Paris, 1931; tr. Ardašir Nikpur as *Dāstānhā-ye žāponi*, Tehran, 1961. Herman Kahn, *The Emerging Japanese Super-state*, New York, 1970; tr. Soruš Ḥabibi as *Žāpon*, Tehran, 1979. Jon Livingston et al., eds., *The Japan Reader*, 2 vols., New York, 1973; tr. Aḥmad Birašk as *Šenāḵt-e Žāpon*, Tehran, 1996. Akio Morita, Edwin M Reingold, and Mitsuko Shimomura, *Made in Japan: Akio Morita and Sony*, New York, 1986; tr. M. Shimomura as *Meido-in-Japan: waga teikenteki kokusai senryaku*, Tokyo, 1987; tr. H. Rajabzadeh as *Taraqqi-e Žāpon: talāš-e āgāhāna yā moʿjeza*, Tehran, 1995. Mamoru Ōnishi and Hisashi Masumo, *Gaikokujin to nihonjin ishi no rinshō kaiwa-shū 10. Perushyago-hen* (Clinical diagnostic conversations between foreigners and Japanese doctors, no. 10. Persian language); Persian section (*qesmat-e fārsi*) tr. Yoshifusa Seki with co-title *Majmūʿa-ye mokālamāt-e bālini bayn-e ḵārejiān wa pezeškān-e žāponi*, Tokyo, 1992. Edwin O. Reischauer, *Japan, Past and Present*, New York, 1946, etc.; tr. Maḥmud Moṣāḥab as *Žāpon dar goḏašta wa ḥāl(l)*, Tehran, 2000.

(HASHEM RAJABZADEH)

JĀRČI, a public crier, announcer or herald, derived from the Mongol *jar* (proclamation, announcement) and certainly also related to the Turkish *yar* as in *yarliğ* (Mo. *jarlig*), meaning decree or order (Doerfer, pp. 277-78; see also explicitly in Naṭanzi, pp. 310, 322: *jār farmudan*). The term *jār* is first encountered in the manual by Hendušāh Naḵjavāni, in a context denoting 'summons to service' (e.g., p. 16). In the Persian sources of the 15th century concerning Timur's conquests and the subsequent Timurid period, the compound *jār rasānidan/rasāndan* is found with the meaning 'to order, summon,' chiefly in a military context (see examples in Doerfer, *loc. cit.*, also e.g., Ḥasan b. Šehāb, pp. 32, 116, 119). The term *jārči* is perhaps used in the late 14th century by Zayn-al-Din (p. 122) but little can be learned from the context.

Jārčis are found listed among the members of the private household (*ḵāṣṣa*) at the review of troops carried out by Solṭān Ḵalil in Fārs in 1476, with the imputed role of 'announcers;' in this case, however (as also in Samarqandi, p. 713), the role of shouting orders (*jār*) is assigned to the muster-masters (*tovāčis*) rather than to the *jārčis* (Minorsky, "Review," pp. 154, 160, 161, idem, *Tadhkirat*, 36). However, the *jārčis* certainly had their own established position, at least by the end of the 15th century (Fażl-Allāh b. Ruzbehān Ḵonji Eṣfahāni, p. 242). Both *tovāčis* and *jārčis* had a role in mustering and mobilizing the troops at the beginning and the end of the Safavid period (Ḵoršāh b. Qobād, pp. 7, 101; cf. Naṣiri, pp. 223, 258, 305; Floor, p. 242), although Floor considers that the office of *tovāči-bāši* had given way, by the 1640s, to the *jārči-bāši*.

Criers or heralds naturally have a role in both civilian and military capacities. Evidence of their existence is best documented in the Safavid period, at the end of which *jārčis* are described as attached to several different departments of government, but always with the same essential function of shouting loudly (*be āvāz-e boland*). Thus the *jārčis* of the household guard (*kešik*), who came under the authority of the master of ceremony (*Ešik-āqāsi-bāši*), shouted out the names of the permanent guards of the royal household on duty every night, to be recorded by the royal guard record keepers (*kešik-nevisān*; Mirzā Rafiʿā, pp. 24, 102). Under the same authority, the *jārčis* are described as public announcers of the Divān (Minorsky, *Tadhkirat*, p. 47), thus presumably proclaiming orders and decrees issued by the government (cf. Floor, p. 243, citing Kaempfer, *Am hofe*). *Jārčis* announced the taxes on staple foodstuffs every week and also shouted warnings to the people to remain indoors when the Shah rode out attended by the ladies of his harem (Doerfer, p. 279, citing Chardin and Olearius, respectively). The *jārči-bāši*, at the head of several *jārčis*, was enrolled among the senior cavalrymen in charge of arsenal (*qurčis*) and was in attendance at the Shah's stirrup whether on journeys or in audience. At camp (*ordu*), during the more general roll call of the great *qorčis* than the reviews conducted by the Shah himself or the *qorči-bāši*, his duty was to shout out to each of the soldiers in turn to come for inspection, who was then paid his specified wages on the approval of the *qorči-bāši* (Mirzā Rafiʿā, p. 120).

In a military context, *jārčis* were attached to the musketeers, under the jurisdiction of the commander of the musketeers (*tofangči-bāšis*) (Mirzā Rafiʿā, p. 26, Minorsky, *Tadhkirat*, p. 48; Floor, p. 184), and also to the artillery (*tup-ḵāna*), under the authority of the cannon commander (*tupči-bāšis*) (Mirzā Rafiʿā, p. 32; Minorsky, p. 51; Floor, p. 196), and in each case their payments were endorsed by the viziers of the respective departments (Minorsky, pp. 73-74). In these roles, their duty was presumably to shout orders to the troops, with powerful voices to carry over the din of battle (cf. Floor, p. 266). Evidence of these roles is relatively abundant also for the period of Nāder Shah's campaigns (see e.g., Marvi, pp. 137, 172, 265, 292, 565, 594, 917, etc.).

Bibliography: G. Doerfer, *Die mongolische Elemente im Neupersischen*, Wiesbaden, 1963. Willem Floor, *Safavid Government Institutions*, Costa Mesa, CA, 2001. Ḥasan b. Šehāb Yazdi, *Jāmeʿ al-tawāriḵ-e Ḥasani*, ed. Ḥ. Modarresi Ṭabāṭabāʾi and I. Afšār, Karachi, 1987. Hendušāh Naḵjavāni, *Dastur al-kāteb* II, ed. ʿA. ʿA. ʿAlizādeh, Moscow, 1976. Fażl-Allāh b. Ruzbehān

Ḵonji Eṣfahāni, *Tārik̲-e ʿālamārā-ye Amini*, ed. John E. Woods, London, 1992. Ḵoršāh b. Qobād al-Ḥosayni, *Tārik̲-e ilči-e Neẓāmšāh*, ed. M. R. Naṣiri and K. Haneda, Tehran, 2000. Moḥammad Kāẓem Marvi, *ʿĀlam-ārā-ye Nāderi*, ed. M. A. Riāḥi, 3 vols., Tehran, 1985. Vladimir Minorsky, "A civil and military review in Fars in 881/1476," *BSOS* 10, 1939, pp. 927-60. Idem, *Tadhkirat Al-Muluk. A manual of Safavid Administration*, ed. and tr. V. Minorsky, London, 1943. Moʿin-al-Din Naṭanzi, *Montak̲ab al-tawārik̲-e Moʿini*, ed. J. Aubin, *Extraits du Muntakhab al-tavarikh-i Muʿini (Anonyme d'Iskandar)*, Tehran, 1957. Moḥammad Ebrāhim Naṣiri, *Dastur-e šahriārān*, ed. M. N. Naṣiri Moqaddam, Tehran, 1994. Mirzā Rafiʿā Anṣāri, *Dastur al-moluk*, in I. Afšār, ed. *Daftar-e tārik̲ I. Majmuʿa-ye asnād o manābeʿ-e tāriki*, Tehran, 2001, pp. 477-651. ʿAbd al-Razzāq Samarqandi, *Maṭlaʿ-e saʿdayn* II, ed. ʿA.-Ḥ. Navāʾi, Tehran, 2004. Zayn-al-Din, *Ḏayl-e Tārik̲-e gozida*, ed. I. Afšār, Tehran, 1993.

(CHARLES MELVILLE)

JĀRČI-E MELLAT, a weekly satirical paper published in Tehran with long interruptions between 12 Šawwāl 1328/16 October 1910 and 8 Ḵordād 1307 Š./29 May 1928. It was suspended on numerous occasions, and the two papers, *Jārči-e asrār* (2 Ḏuʾl-ḥejja 1329/23 Nov. 1911) and *Jāsus* (22 Rabiʿ I 1332/18 Feb. 1914; Ṣadr Hāšemi, II, p. 161), that were published as replacements were immediately banned. In the fourth year, and between the ninth and the twelfth year of publication, the paper appeared twice a week before reverting to once a week publication.

The founder, director, and editor-in-chief of *Jārči-e mellat* was Sayyed Ḥosayn Tajriši (Ebrāhimzāda). From the fourteenth issue in the fourth year of publication (29 Ḏuʾl-ḥejja 1332/18 Nov. 1914), the name of ʿAli Ḥosaynzāda (Nedāʾi), started to appear on the paper as the license-holder. Ḥosaynzāda had been formerly in charge of distribution of Tehran newspapers and had published in 1911 a similar satirical paper called *Jangal-e mawlā* (Bayāt and Kuhestāni-nežād, eds., p. 398; Ṣadr Hāšemi, II, pp. 172-74). Its managing director in the fifth year was Ḥasan Monšizāda Tabrizi, who had previously worked in the same position for a while for the newspaper *Ḥayāt-e Irān* (Ṣadr Hāšemi, II, p. 236). In 1917, the paper was incorporated with the establishment of a company (Šerkat-e Ruz-nāma-ye jārči-e mellat) in its name.

Jārči-e mellat was a socio-political newspaper but it also contained serialized fictions and non-fictions. In its early days, it was regarded as being affiliated to the Democrat Party (Ḥezb-e demokrāt), but this was officially denied by the party ("Jārči-e melat," *Irān-e now* 3/1, 24 Rabiʿ I, 1329/25 March 1911). It supported Aḥmad Qawām (Qawām-al-Salṭana) for a while during the his premiership, but it was a steadfast partisan of Reżā Khan Sardar-e Sepah (the future Reżā Shah), who, during his own tenure as prime minister, arranged for secret cash payments to the paper ("Nāma-ye ʿAli Nedāʾi," p. 850). *Jārči-e mellat*, being a satirical paper, contained texts and cartoons vilifying influential people, which led to its numerous suspensions by the government; it, however, faced no such problems during the reign of Reżā Shah (r. 1925-41). From the tenth year of publication, it turned into a paper featuring various kinds of news.

Up to issue 26 in the fourth year of publication, *Jārči-e mellat* was lithographed in the pen of the calligrapher Solṭān-al-Kottāb at Mirzā ʿAli Aṣḡar/Marvi printing house. Afterwards, one half (pp. 1 and 4) continued to be lithographed in the same print shop and the other half was typeset first in the state's printing house (Maṭbaʿa-ye dawlati) and then at those of Bāqerzāda brothers and Kalimiān. Eventually the whole newspaper was produced completely in typeset at Bāqerzāda brothers printing house and, for brief periods, at those of Nahżat-e šarq (1921) and Ṭehrān (1923). According to a report by the German embassy in Tehran, in the years prior to the coup d'etat of 1921 (q.v.), *Jārči-e mellat* had a print run of 1,500 (apud Mehrad, p. 73).

The cartoons and sketches that *Jārči-e mellat* carried were quite popular in those days (ʿAyn-al-Salṭana, p. 3547). They were sometimes in color and in the early years of publication were the work of a certain ʿAli-Reżā. Starting in its tenth year, when it turned into a solely news-reporting paper, *Jārči-e mellat* had no illustrations, except for the last few years when it occasionally carried Reżā Shah's picture.

Jārči-e mellat was printed in four double-column pages of approximately 22 x 35 cm, but the appearance changed a number of times. Some issues, in particular after year fourteen, had only two pages. The annual subscription rate for Tehran was initially six krans and finally fifty krans in the last year. Incomplete sets of *Jārči-e mellat* are kept in major Iranian libraries, and outside Persia at Cambridge University Library, Bibliothèque Nationale in Paris, and the Institute of Manuscripts of Academy of Science in Baku.

Bibliography: Touraj Atabaki and Solmaz Rustamova-Towhidi, *Baku Documents: Union Catalogue of Persian, Azerbaijani, Ottoman Turkish and Arabic Serials and Newspapers in the Libraries of Republic of Azerbaijan*, London and New York, 1995, p. 132. Qahramān Mirzā ʿAyn-al-Salṭana Sālur, *Ruz-nāma-ye k̲āṭerāt-e ʿAyn-al-Salṭana*, ed. Masʿud Sālur and Iraj Afšār, 10 vols., Tehran, 1998-2000. Masʿud Barzin, *Šenās-nāma-ye maṭbuʿāt-e Irān az 1215 tā 1357 Š.*, Tehran, 1992, p. 140. Kāva Bayāt and Masʿud Kuhestāni-nežād, eds., *Asnād-e maṭbuʿāt, 1286-1320 H.Š.*, 2 vols., Tehran, 1993, I, pp. 312, 396-400. Lucien Bouvat "La Presse à Téhéran en 1915," *RMM* 30, pp. 279-80. Edward G. Browne, *The Press and Poetry of Modern Persia*, Cambridge, 1914, pp. 67-68, 70. Šahin Esfandiāri et al., *Maṭbuʿāt-e Irān: fehrest-e taḥlili-e ketāb-k̲āna-ye Majles-e senā*, Tehran, 1979, pp. 76-77. Guʾel Kohan, *Tārik̲-e sānsur dar maṭbuʿāt-e Irān*, 2 vols., Tehran, 1984, II, pp. 691-92. Rudolf Mach and Robert D. McChesney, "A List of Persian Serials in the Princeton

University Library," Unpub. Monograph, Princeton, New Jersey, 1971. Ahmad Mehrad, *Die Deusche Pénétration pacifique des Iranischen pressewesens 1909-1936*, Frankfurt am Main, 1983. "Nāma-ye ʿAli Nedāʾi ba Reżā Ḵān," *Pažuheš-nāma-ye tāriḵ-e maṭbuʿāt-e Irān*, no. 1, 1997. Ali No-Rouze [Ḥasan Moqaddam], "Registre analytyque annoté de la presse persane (deputis la Guerre)," *RMM* 60, 1925, no. 95. Hyacinth Louis Rabino, *Ṣurat-e jarāyed-e Irān wa jarāyed-i ke dar ḵārej az Irān ba zabān-e fārsi čāp šoda ast*, Rašt, 1911, no. 68. Moh.ammad Ṣadr Hāšemi, *Tāriḵ-e jarāʾed o majallāt Irān*, 4 vols., Isfahan, 1948-53, II, pp. 158-60. Bižan Sartipzāda and Kobrā Ḳodāparast, *Fehrest-e ruz-nāmahā-ye mawjud dar Ketāb-ḵāna-ye melli*, Tehran, 1977, no. 165. Ursula Sims-Williams, *Union Catalogue of Persian Serials and Newspapers in British Libraries*, London, 1985, no. 265. Giti Šokri, "Fehrest-e majallahā-ye ketāb-ḵāna-ye Moʾassasa-ye āsiāʾi-e Dānešgāh-e Širāz," *FIZ* 27, 1987, p. 353. Ḥasan Solṭāni, "Čand ruz-nāma-ye fārsi-e qadim," *Rāhnemā-ye ketāb* 17/10-12, 1955, pp. 788-93. Mortażā Solṭāni, *Fehrest-e ruz-nāmahā-ye fārsi dar majmuʿa-ye ketāb-ḵāna-ye markazi wa markaz-e asnād-e Dānešgāh-e Tehrān*, Tehran, 1975, p. 149, nos. 118-19, 121.

(*EIr*.)

JARQUYA, a district located in the eastern region of Isfahan Province.

i. *The district.*
ii. *The dialect.*

i. The District

The toponym is known locally also as Garkuya, with possible components *gar* and *kuh* (cf. Jarquh in Yāqut, II, p. 63), both meaning "mountain"; the first component may alternatively have derived from Av. *gufra-*, *jafra-* (deep), inferring also "lower," in contradistinction to Abarquh (q.v.) "higher/upper mountain," with which the adjoining district Jarquya has been linked throughout history.

Geography and economy. Separated from Isfahan by the Šāhkuh range, Jarquya spreads over 6,500 km^2, stretching in a northwest-southeast direction to the wasteland that separates it from Abarquh. The district is connected to Isfahan and Qomša by roads, but it is separated from Ardakān (q.v.) in Yazd Province by the Gāvḵuni lagoon, into which all Jarquya's streambeds carry floodwater. Jarquya is extremely barren with less than 10 cm annual precipitation. Chronic drought and fuel consumption have resulted in destruction of much of the flora, save for a few stretches of steppes with *gaz* (q.v.) and *ğič* (zygophyllum, bean caper; Šafiʿi, pp. 16-34). The lowland fauna, consisting of the deer, zebra, and leopard, is extant only in the recollections of aged hunters. The Kolāhqāzi heights in the northwest of the district is a protected park. Salt mines are exploited throughout the district, particularly in Siān, Rāmša, and Ḵārā (ʿĀbedi, p. 214).

Jarquya has been subjected to several modern administrative revisions. Traditionally ranked as a rural district (*boluk*) and occasionally grouped with Rudašt and Kuhpāya to its north, Jarquya is naturally and administratively divided into Upper and Lower Jarquya (Jarquya-ye ʿOlyā and Jarquya-ye Soflā, that is, farther and nearer to Isfahan, respectively), each with relatively stable oasis villages (Janāb, pp. 180, 191). Those of Lower Jarquya are Qārna, Ganjābād, Siān/Siun (or Siān-e Namaki, cf. the nearby Siān in Rudašt), Āḏarḵᵛārān (locally Ōḵāron; renamed Ḥabibābād after the Revolution of 1978-79), Ḥosaynābād, Moḥammadābād, Naṣrābād (former Givān), Yangābād (Yanguvā, now Nikābād), Peykān, Saʿādatābād, Mazraʿa-ʿArab, and Ḥaydarābād. Upper Jarquya consists of two clusters of villages: (1) Dastgerd, Kamālābād, Ḥasanābād (center), Ḵārā, Mālvājerd, and Yaḵčāl (renamed Allāhābād after the Revolution), and (2) Fayżābād, Esfandārān, Ḥāreṯābād, Aḥmadābād, Mobāraka, and Rāmša(n). None of these settlements distinguish themselves in terms of population or economy; hence, Jarquya's administrative center has shifted several times in the modern era. The current seat is Nikābād, located 65 km southeast of Isfahan and 1,565 m above the level, with a population 4,800 (1990 estimate; see also ISFAHAN iii). The population of the district decreased from 30,300 in the early 1950s (Razmārā, p. 55) to nearly 27,900 in 1996 (Sāzmān-e barnāma, pp. 2, 6), in contrast to the high national growth. The main cause of depopulation has been migration to Isfahan and Tehran in search of jobs.

The district suffers from chronic water shortages. Its ninety subterranean channels (*qanāt*) have fallen into disrepair since the long period of drought which began in the mid-1960s. More than 200 deep and semi-deep wells have been dug ever since, providing saline water. The declining agriculture has partly been revitalized recently through the project of bringing the water of Zāyandarud River to Lower Jarquya by means of irrigation canals (104 km) via Mobāraka and the Mahyār plain. It is supplemented by 100 km of pipelines carrying drinking water by the rate of 100 liters per second (local interviews).

Rural economy prevails throughout Jarquya. The main produce is beans, beetroots, and fruits such as melons, pomegranates, figs, grapes, mulberry, almond, and pistachio; madder (*ronnās*) and some opium were also produced. The salinity of the water does not allow substantial production of various grains; only small amounts of cereals are sown. The industrial staple is cotton, renowned to be among the best produced in Persia (Eʿtemād-al-Salṭana, IV, p. 2186; Moḥammad-Mahdi, p. 320). The flourishing of textile industries in Isfahan in the early Pahlavi period (see ISFAHAN xiv) had an echo in Jarquya, where a cotton ginning mill was established, only to be relocated to Isfahan in the early 1950s (ʿĀbedi, p. 120). More recently, industrial spinning of the wool has been on the rise. Another thriving business in many villages is mechanized stockbreeding of poultry; a large storehouse in Nikābād supplies the poultry for the entire province (Šafiʿi, p. 415). Many families are engaged in truck transportation. Handicrafts include *giva* (q.v.) and cotton textiles such as *jājim* (a variety of flat-woven carpets), linen (*karbās*), and bed-sheets (*čādor-šab*), as well as carpets, all woven by women. Women would wrap themselves in white or colorful *čādor-šab*s in public while men used to dress richly in dark blue linen tunics (Šafiʿi, pp. 406; Mehryār, p. 48). They dress differently today; women wrap themselves in a loose, sleeveless black cover in compliance with government dress regulations, and men usually dress simply wearing jackets and plain shirts.

The older quarters of Yangābād and other major settlements have attractive desert architecture of vaulted constructions and outstanding wind towers (*bādgir*, q.v.) and domes, all in sun-dried bricks marking the skyline. A few intact Qajar cisterns along the roads are reminiscent of more prosperous times. There are also remnants of mud-brick buildings, mostly fortifications and *čahārṭāq* (q.v.) structures, belonging to the remote past (Šafiʿi, passim; cf. Afšār, p. 64). None of these have received serious archeological attention. The landscape is also dotted with pigeon towers (*borj-e kabutar*), a typically common sight in the rural areas of Isfahan, which was once used for collecting pigeon manure to fertilize melon fields. A notable place in Jarquya is the shrine of Emāmzāda Shah ʿAbd-al-Moẓaffar, located at about 6 km west of Siān, where the festival of Šaṣt-šaši is held from the 66th to 70th days after Nowruz; an associated rite is swimming in a pond watered by Šāh Čašma, the outlet of the Siān's spring. Some local pundits believe that this ritual is a remnant of the Tirgān or Ābpāšān festival. The same festival is held also in other Jarquya settlements, particularly in Mālvājerd and Rāmša (Mehryār, p. 415).

History. There are sporadic citations of individual places of Jarquya in the medieval sources. The castle of Qulanjān is described in the 13th and 14th centuries as a mud fortress at a two-day journey from Isfahan. It received its water from subterranean channels and its products were fruits, cereals, and grapes (Yāqut, II, p. 63; Mostawfi, I, pp. 123-24; Le Strange, p. 283). It is identified with the ruins of Quljān near Esfandārān (Janāb, p. 192; for the picture, see Šafiʿi, p. 73). In two decrees (one dated 971/1564) carved on the stone inscriptions in Isfahan's Friday mosque, Mālvājerd is listed among the villages that were granted tax relief by Shah Ṭahmāsp I (r. 1524-76; Honarfar, pp. 89, 157). It appears that Jarquya had an old tradition of crafting weapons which thrived during the dynastic rivalry following the Afghan invasion (cf. Šafiʿi, p. 338, cf. preface by M.-E. Bāstāni Pārizi).

Droughts and disputes over allocation of water shape the modern history of the region. The drought of 1776-95 set Jarquya against the neighboring Qomša and Izadḵᵛāst (q.v.) for a share of the Izadḵᵛāst streams. As a result of the famine and feuds, Peykān and Yangābād were depopulated in favor of the newly-founded villages of Fayżābād, Mazraʿa-ʿArab, and Ḥaydarābād; the latter was named after the master digger of its subterranean channel (Šafiʿi, pp. 205-23). By Qajar times Yangābād and Peykān had regained their former importance, and Peykān had been designated as the administrative center (*qaṣaba*) of Jarquya (Širvāni, p. 199; Eʿtemād-al-Salṭana, IV, p. 2186).

An insurgency broke out in Jarquya over tax payment during the reign of Moḥammad Shah Qājār (r. 1834-48). The repetition of the rebellion in the summer of 1868 led to an invasion of the district by Isfahan's prince-governor Masʿud Mirzā Ẓell-al-Solṭān, whose troops were defeated by Āqā Moḥammad Yangābādi. Only the severe famine and cholera of 1969-71 could break the local resistance. Later on, Āqā Moḥammad, much praised for his valor (Eʿtemād-al-Salṭana, IV, p. 2186), paid a conciliatory visit to the royal court in Tehran and was eventually appointed the governor of Jarquya and Abarquh (Šafiʿi, pp. 245, 228-57). His son and successor, Mollā ʿAli Khan Mirpanj, tried to evade the hostile people of Yangābād by moving his seat to the newly-founded village of Ganjābād, while his rival Mirzā ʿAbd-al-Ḥosayn Khan Mirpanj built the fortress of Raḥmatābād with a subterranean channel, a watermill, a cistern, and a bathhouse (Šafiʿi, pp. 264, 276).

The open terrain of Jarquya exposed it to nomadic incursions throughout its history. It is reported that Mālvājerd was depopulated following the Afghan invasion of Isfahan. The tribes from Fārs, who were relocated under the Zand dynastic rule, retain a semi-nomadic life near Naṣrābād and Moḥammadābād into this century (Šafiʿi, pp. 150, 415, 446; cf. Perry, pp. 210-11). The nomads belong to the clans of Bāṣeri, Lor, Sanjari, Visikusa, Moʾmeni, Jaʿfari, Dāstāni, and ʿArab, and some still use the Zagros uplands as their summer quarters (local interviews; Razmārā, pp. 55, 198). The occasional raids by the Baḵtiāri and Boir Aḥmadi (qq.v.) tribal men extended into the years following World War II (Šafiʿi, pp. 134, 347).

There seems to have been a sizeable Zoroastrian community in Jarquya as recently as the late Qajar period. An early 20th century report alludes to the Pahlavi idiom (see ii below) as being spoken by the Zoroastrians of the area (Janāb, pp. 128, 247). There are still certain Muslim individuals and families who are referred to as *gabr* (q.v.), the uncomplimentary term referring to Zoroastrians, which is also carried by a quarter in Esfandārān. In the old cemetery of Āḏarḵᵛārān, the Muslim gravestones date no earlier than the 16th century, while the older stones, which bear no inscription, are attributed to Zoroastrians. Remnants of a fire temple still stand in Dastgerd (Šafiʿi, pp. 82-86, 180). In view of the existence of a fire temple and Zoroastrian communities in Jarquya, and the similarity of name Jarquya/Garkuya and Karkōk/Karkōy(a) in Sistān, where a famous fire temple stood (Tāriḵ-e Sistān, pp. 35-37; Markwart, pars. 35-37), drawing a historical connection between the two places appears plausible; nevertheless, from a comparative-historical perspective, it is difficult to relate the two toponyms, for the correspondence between the initial *g* and *k* is rarely found in Iranian languages.

Jarquya appears to have been integrated, against the will of its inhabitants, into Qomša administrative domain under Ẓell-al-Solṭān. It eventually succeeded to secede in 1955 after a decade of intensive, and at times violent, campaign, and to come under Isfahan's jurisdiction (Šafiʿi, pp. 270, 358-65). There is an ongoing political campaign to promote the status of Jarquya from the current *bak̲š* (district) to *šahrestān* (sub-provincial unit).

Bibliography: Ḥasan ʿĀbedi, *Eṣfahān az leḥāẓ,-e ejtemāʿi o eqteṣādi*, Tehran?, 1955. Iraj Afšār, "Ḥalqa-ye Abarquya-Jarquya," *Zamān*, no. 18, 1997, pp. 58-64. Moḥammad-Ḥasan Khan Eʿtemād-al-Salṭana, *Merʾāt al-boldān*, ed. ʿAbd-al-Ḥosayn Navāʾi and Mirhāšem Moḥaddet̲, 4 vols. Tehran, 1989. Loṭf-Allāh Honarfar, *Ganjina-ye āt̲ār-e tārik̲i-e Eṣfahān*, Isfahan, 1965. Mir Sayyed ʿAli Janāb, *Eṣfahān*, ed. ʿAbbās Naṣr, Isfahan, 1992. Guy Le Strange, *The Lands of the Eastern Caliphate*, 2nd ed. Cambridge, 1930. J. Markwart, *A Catalogue of the Provincial Capitals of Eranshahr: Pahlavi Text, Version and Commentary*, ed. G. Messina, Rome, 1931. Moḥammad Mehryār, *Farhang-e nāmhā wa ābādihā-ye kohan-e Eṣfahān*, Isfahan, 2003. Moḥammad-Mahdi b. Moḥammad-Reżā Eṣfahāni, *Neṣf jehān fi taʿrif al-Eṣfahān*, ed. Manučehr Sotuda, Tehran, 1961, 2nd ed., Tehran, 1989. Ḥamd-Allāh Mostawfi Qazvini, *Nozhat al-qolub*, ed. and tr. Guy Le Strange as *The Geographical Part of the Nuzhat-al-qulūb*, 2 vols., Leiden and London, 1915-19. John R. Perry, "Forced Migration in Iran during the Seventeenth and Eighteenth Centuries," *Iranian Studies* 8/4, 1975, pp. 199-215. Ḥosayn-ʿAli Razmārā, ed., *Farhang-e jog̲rāfiāʾi-e Irān (ābādihā)* X, Tehran, 1950, repr. 1976. Sirus Šafaqi, *Jog̲rāfiā-ye Eṣfahān*, Isfahan, 1974. ʿAli Šafiʿi Nikābādi, *Garkuya: sarzamin-i nāšenāk̲ta bar karān-e kavir*, 2nd ed., Isfahan, 1997. Sāzmān-e barnāma wa budja, Markaz-e āmār-e Irān, *Saršomāri-e ʿomumi-e nofus o maskan 1375, Šenās-nāma-ye ābādihā-ye kešvar, Ostān-e Esfahān, Šahrestān-e Esfahān*, pub. no. 6-34, Tehran, 1997. ʿAbd-al-Ḥosayn Sepantā, *Tārik̲ča-ye awqāf-e Eṣfahān*, Isfahan, 1967, p. 44. Zayn-al-ʿĀbedin Širvāni, *Bostān al-siāḥa*, lithograph ed., Tehran, 1898. *Tārik̲-e Sistān*, ed. Moḥammad-Taqi Malek-al-Šoʿarāʾ Bahār, Tehran, ca. 1935. Šehāb-al-Din Abu ʿAbd-Allāh Yāqut Ḥamawi, *Moʿjam al-boldān*, 5 vols., Beirut, 1955-57.

(HABIB BORJIAN)

ii. THE DIALECT

The dialect of Jarquya, together with those of Rudašt and Kuhpāya to its north, belongs to the Isfahani (Provincial) subgroup of the Central Dialects (q.v.; see also ISFAHAN xxi). Only about half of the villages of the district have retained their idioms, namely Ganjābād, Siān, Yangābād, Peykān, Mazraʿa-ʿArab, and Ḥaydarābād in Lower Jarquya (north), and Dastgerd, Kamālābād, Ḥasanābād, K̲ārā, and Yak̲čāl in Upper Jarquya (Šafiʿi, pp. 12-15; see also ISFAHAN xx). Sub-dialectal variation is noticeable, for example, between the dialect of Yangābād in the north and Ḥasanābād in the south: initial /h/ drops in the south, e.g., *hezze* ~ *ezza* "yesterday," *holoki* ~ *oloki* "hole," *hošgi* ~ *ošgi* "cough"; /j/ softens to /ž/ or /y/ in the north: *žan* ~ *jan* "woman," *žaž* ~ *jāj* "a plant used as fuel," *vāyne* ~ *va:jona* "I say"; note also *kāy* ~ *ka(h)a* "game," *yede* ~ *yele* "a bit," *sion* ~ *soni* "such"; and there are lexical variations such as *girye* ~ *barma* "weep(ing)," *sündi* ~ *angona* "watermelon," *süs* ~ *pura* "chaff" (cf. Ebrāhimi, pp. 8-10; Šafiʿi, p. 512). The following sketch of the dialect of Yangābād is based on the author's field notes taken in 2005, with occasional use of the material published by Šafiʿi.

Historical phonology. The affinity of Jarquyi to the Northwest group of Iranian languages can be seen in such characteristic developments as OIr. *ts > s: *mas* "big," *kas* "small"; *dz > z: *zommā* "son-in-law," *hezze* "yesterday," *zon-* "know" (but *bāhü:* "arm"); *tsw > sp: *sibi* "white"; *dzw > zb: *zu(v)on* "tongue"; *dw- > b: *bar* "door," *(i)bi* "other"; *y-, *vy- > y: *i(y)e* [ijɛ, ijjɛ] "barley," *vā-vuz-/voss-* "find," *yā* "place" (but *juš* "boil"); *j- > j/ž: *žan* "woman, wife," *jinji* "wife," *žandegi* "life," *jin-/jind-* "hit," *žang* "rust," *žire* "cumin," *žārt-* (< *jyau-) "chew," *mežon* (< *maig/j-) "mist," and possibly *ješd* "ugly." Later developments: *w- is retained in *vāron* "rain," *varf* "snow," *vid* "willow," *vādom* "almond," *viss* "twenty," *vad* "bad," *vešše* "hungry," *visgi* "so much," *vašd-* "pass." *-č- > ž/j: *žer* "below," *jer-* (in, e.g., *jer-negü:ni* "cellar"), *ruže* "fast(ing)," *ižir* "pretty," *rež-* "pour," *-ji* "also" (cf. Av. *cit̰*), *vāž* "call," and, with further softening of the consonant, in *vā(y)-* "say" (but *peš-* "cook" < *paxša- [*pak-s-]?). *θr, *xr, *fr > *hr > r: *pore* "son," *ār-či* "hand mill," *dār* "sickle" (but *ousan* "pregnant" < *ā-puθra-tanu-); *sür* "red," *čār* "spinning wheel" (but *čarx* "wheel"); *gāre* "down" (< Av. *gufra-*, *jafra-*; but *ferāt-* "sell") and possibly the preverb *hā-* (< *fr-).

The changes *xt, *ft > t are found in just a few lexical items: *dot(i)* "daughter, girl," *sot-* "burn," *ret-* "*pour" (in *der-ham-ret-* "mess up"); *hā-git-* "seize," *dar-kat-* "fall," *vāt-* "say," *ferāt-* "sell" (most potential examples of these developments are lost in favor of regularized past stems in -ā-); otherwise /t/ is normally voiced in the clusters: *āmuxde* "trained," *deraxd* "tree," *taxde* "plywood," *saxdi* "hardship"; *kufd-* "pound," *ā-xofd-* "sleep," *var-ešnofd-* "hear," *čefd* "button"; also note *vaxdi* "when," *ofdöu* "sun," *kufdar* "pigeon." The clusters *št and *st have developed either into /ss/, e.g., *vessā-* "stand," *dar-xoss-* "throw," *vass-* "run," *hessu* "is (there)," or into /šd/, as in *pošd* "back," *müšd* "full," *čāšdone* "breakfast," *dašd* "washbasin," *pāyešd* "weeding," *esbārešd* "order," *sargozašd* "biography," *Rudašd* "Rudašt," *mošderi* "customer," *-šd-* "go," *hā-nišd-* "sit," *dašd-* "sew," *vašd-* "pass," *kāšd-* "sow." *r̥t is retained (in contrast to the Isfahan dialect Sedehi) in past stems: *marte* "dead," *xesart-* "catch a cold," *kart-* "do," *bart-* "carry," *gart-* "turn," *žārt-* "chew," *ošmārt-* "count," and probably *dārt-* "have" (cf. Parthian *dird-*). $*x^w$ > x: *xox* "sister," *xou* "sleep," *xo(č)-* "self," *ā-xus-/xofd-* "sleep," *xer-/xārt-* "eat," *xon-/xond-* "read." $*x^{(w)}$, *h are lost in *üč* "nothing," *ižir* "pretty," *ibize* "melon"; cf. *hü:še* "bunch," *heš* "plowshare," *hürd* "small, chopped," *hošk* "dry," *hošgi* "cough," *hou* "with, to" (< *hada?), *himir* "dough." Mid. WIr. -d- is lost in, e.g., *ke/kie* "house, room," *kāy* "game," *rui* "intestine," *kom(in)* "which," *puo/pou* "father," *mā:* "mother," *jāyü* "witchcraft," *biār* "awake." Loss of other medial consonants include -r- in *ežon* "cheap," *dez-* "sew," *nüfü:n* "curse," *hā-git-* "seize," *katune* (but also *kartone* < *kart-dān-ag) "hen-coop," and -x- in *tāl* "bitter," *tom* "seed." Loss of the final consonant is common: *mü:* "hair," *re:* "road," *či:* "thing," *dü* "smoke," *žü:* "early," *sā* "hundred, *duru* "lie." Note also the *t-* in *tel* "heart," *t-* "hit" ("give," with the preverb *hā-*).

Old labials in medial position are absorbed into adjacent vowels, yielding diphthongs: *ou* "water," *öur* "cloud," *löu* "lip," *souz* "green," *šöu* "night," *noudun* "gutter," *rou-n-* "sweep." *p- is changed sporadically to other labials: *ba'aštā* "five," *fand* "advice," *fātešā* "king," *vesse* "pistachio." Reverse developments include *perdous* "paradise," *pandoq* "hazelnut," and probably *pāxder* (Pers. *fāḵta*) "ringdove"; note also *xape* "strangulation," *qip* "funnel," *lāhāp* "quilt." Vowels: Original back vowels are generally fronted to /ü/, e.g., *dü:r* "late; far," *düm* "on"; face," *müš* "mouse," *ālü* "plum," *āberü* "dignity." *ā is raised before nasals: *jom* "cup," *jon* "soul," *bon* "roof," *kaxdon* "straw-rick," *mon-/mond-* "stay," *yābün* "barren land."

Phonology. The vowel system consists of /a ā e o i u ü/. The distinction between /ü/ and /u/ or /i/ can be seen in *kü* "outside," *ku* "mountain; where is," *dü* "smoke; two," and *du* "buttermilk," *müš* "mouse" ~ *miš* "ewe"; sometimes however, they are used interchangeably: *mü:* ~ *mi* "hair." Diphthongs include /ou ~ öu/ (also heard as *o: ow* ~ *ö: öw əw*; e.g., *kārdoune* "spider," *garöuj* "sieve"), and /ey, ay/ (e.g., *dey* "maternal uncle," *čey* "tea"; *ayn* "mouth," *ayb* "disadvantage"). The consonants correspond to those of Persian, but /v/ is [β] as in other provincial dialects of Isfahan area. As in Isfahani Persian, /k/ and /g/ are markedly palatalized before front vowels: *kü* [kʲy] "outside," *gü(v)e* [gʲyβɛ] "*giva* (q.v.) footwear." Note the retention of the glottal /ḥ/ and /ʿ/ in words of Arabic origin, e.g., *ḥasüd* "jealous," *ḥāl* "fat," *taḥne* (< *ṭaʿna*) "sarcasm," *jemʿa* "Friday." Harmonization of vowels is common, especially among verb morphemes: *bikirind* (< *be-ker-ind) "they do." The suffix *-i* turns optionally to *-y* after vowels: *čuy* (= *ču-í*) "wooden," *yāy* (< *yā-i*) "a place," *boy* (= *bó-i*) "you were," *befarmāy* "treat yourself!" Epentheses or glides include /v/, /h/, and /y/: *mā-v-ā* "mothers," *čā-v-ā-* (secondary past stem) "catch a cold," *qāye-h-ā* "talks," *puo-h-on* "the father," *vesse-h-ā* (past part.) "become," *pušnā-y-e* (past part.) "covered," *vāssā-y-on* "I stood," *beyšo-y-on* "I went," *bešde-y-on* "I have gone." The morphological stress patterns in Jarquyi are similar to those of other Provincial dialects.

Noun phrase. The nouns and pronouns indicate no gender or formal case. The plural ending is a stressed *-ā*: *jinji-ā* "women." The definite article is *-(h)on*, suffixed to singular nouns when they are qualified by *yon* or *okon* (see Demonstratives, below): *okon bāqon* ~ *un bāq* "that garden," *yon asmon sibi u* "this horse is white," *yon asmon-om bidi* "I saw this horse"). The suffix *-(h)on* appears at the end of noun-phrase (*yon pereynon* "this shirt," *yon pereyn iži<u>ron</u>* "this pretty shirt") and is supplanted by the plural marker: *yon axiā/porehā ki bind*? "who are these men/boys?" (cf. *yon axion/porehon ki bu*? "who is this man/boy?"), *yon yo(u)ne čuyyā* "the wooden mortars." As in colloquial Persian, the suffix *-e* (stressed) is a definite marker, e.g., *ibi müše* "the other mouse"; the indefinite markers are *ye* "a, one" and/or an unstressed *-i* (*-y* after vowels), e.g., *ye ru(v)ā-y* "one day." There is no direct object marker in Jarquyi: *yon bebe* "take this away!" *in ri birie* "you know this" (but see Fronting, below).

Modifiers. As in other dialects of the Isfahan area as well as in the Persian variant of Isfahan, the modifiers (possessives and adjectives) follow the noun, with no overt connector, e.g., *dot fātešā* "king"s daughter," *ax mo* "my husband," *angür siā* "black grapes." Occasionally, however, the Persian *eżāfa* (q.v.) marker is heard, more often in affected speech of younger informants: *ādemā-ye duruvāž* "false-saying people," *xox-e kas* "younger sister."

Pronouns. There are two basic sets of personal pronouns: (1) independent *mo, to, un, hamā, šemā, unā*; (2) enclitic *-(o/e)m, -(o)d/t, -(o)š, -(e)mon, -(e)ton, -(e)šon*, which are used also as person endings in the ergative construction (q.v.) of transitive verbs in the past tenses (see below). When functioning as direct object, the enclitics may be inserted within the verb: *un našᵉnāsie* ~ *na-š-šenāsie* "you don't know him," *vā-š-vuz-im* "that we find him," *he-šon-te* "give them!" The reflexive *xo(č)-* takes enclitic pronouns when functioning as a(n): (i) emphatic: *mo xoč-em un-om ru saḥrā bidi* "I myself saw him in the field," *tā zonon xoč-ed üčgi-d ru kie-d meymoni karte*? "have you yourself invited anyone to your house until now?" *kom gamböu-š xo-š besāt*? "which hut did he himself build?" (ii) possessive: *pač yā xo-š berue* "he takes (it) back to its place," (iii) direct object: *qādib xo-m der ša:r beresnon* "I must get (lit. deliver) myself to the town," *ye gorg o ye lubbā xo-šᵒⁿ-šon ru ār xoss* "a wolf and a fox threw themselves in the mill," or (iv) with prepositions: *piš xo-m be-m-vāt* "I said to myself," *čand-od pül hou xo-d bārte*? "how much money have you brought with you."

Demonstratives. These are *yon/in* "this," *okon/un* "that," *yonehā/inehā* "these," *okon(eh)ā/unehā* "those," which act also as personal pronouns: e.g., *sezā-ye yonehā he-šon-te*! "give them their retribution!" A three-way distinction in deixis (near, medium, far) exists in demonstrative adverbs: *yohon* "here," *eče* "there (near the addressee)," *uhun/vā(če)* "there (very distant)." Examples: *ibi müše čel-tā sekke nārue <u>eče</u>* "the mouse doesn't bring the forty coins there any more," *ye-čan-tā ḥayvon boomeynd <u>eče</u> döur-oš ja:m vessāynd* "a few animals came there [and] gathered around him," *naqādib biši <u>vā(če)</u>* "you should not go there," *okon žanon go <u>uhun</u> nišde māxāsu mo u* "the woman who is sitting there is my mother-in-law."

Prepositions. These include *der* "to," *düm* "on, over," *ez* "from," *hou* "with, to," *jer* "under," *löu* "at," *ru* "in(to)," *tel* "at, next to." They normally require no *eżāfa*: *ru xarand* "in the yard," *kenār vāre* "by the dam," *jer nā* "under the throat," *der xiāl-od go ez-od tarsone*? "do you think I am afraid of you?" *ār vāžāre löu rowre u* "the ruined mill is at the alley." The only attested postposition is *rā* "for (someone)": *šā Yaz rā* "for the king of Yazd," *yon bardon xoč-em rā, in tiše ji to rā* "this spade for myself, this chisel for you." The only circumposition is attested in *he-š-rā* "for him." Prepositions are sometimes omitted: *ou mo te* "give me water!"

Verb phrase. Stems. Past stems are either derived from the old participles (e.g., pres./past *endār-/endārt-* "send") or constructed by adding the formant *-ā* to the present stem (e.g., *kol-/kolā-* "cripple"). There are alternate past stems (secondary in *-ā* vs. the old participial form, e.g., *vin-ā-* vs. *di-* "see," *vāšku-ā-* vs. *vāškufd-* "unstitch"), which may distinguish passive vs. active : *ba-^{h}amer-ā* "it broke" ~ *be-š-hamert* "he broke (it)"; *bu-(v)on-ā* "it was cut," *be-š-vond* "he cut." The causative present stem is formed by adding *-n* to the present stem of intransitive verbs: *peš-n-* "cook (trans.)"; the stem may change form in the causative: *čöus-/čafd-* "stick (intr.)" ~ *čöun-/čöunā-* "stick (trans.)," *ā-xus-/xofd-* "sleep" ~ *ā-xoun-/xounā-* "cause to sleep." Note also that the stems in *-r* or *-rt* optionally lose it when not suffixed: *be-š-ke^{rt}* "he did," *be-ker* "do!" Contraction of the stem occurs in some verbs of high frequency: e.g., *vāyne* (< *vā-yon-e) "I say," *vāme* ~ *vāt-om-e* "I said," *voue* (< *vā-u-e) "he says"; *binon* (< *be-vin-on) "that I see," *bine* (< *be-vin-e) "see!"

Preverbs. *(h)ā-*, *dar-*, *vā-*, *var-* often further specify a stem: *t-/tā-* "hit," *hā-~* "give," *vā-~* "take back," *var-~* "lay upon"; *vez-/vass-* "run," *var-~* "jump"; *māl-/mālā-* "rub," *var-~* "flee"; *ker-/kart-* "do," *var-~* "build up," *kār-/kāšd-* "sow," *var-~* "harvest"; *y-/ome-* "come," *var-~* "rise (of the sun/a voice)"; *š-/šo-* "go," *dar-~* "set (of the sun)"; *čin-/čind-* "shear," *dar-~* "arrange," *band-/bass-* "hit," *dar-~* "shut," *(vā-)gart-/gartā-* "(re)turn"; *hā-n-/nā-* "put," *vā-~* "open"; *hā-gir-/git-* "seize; buy," *ver-~* "lift." As in the Jewish dialect (see ISFAHAN xix), *(h)ā-* vanishes optionally in perfective tenses: *(ā)xofdeyon* "I have slept" (for "sit," see Table 1, below).

Modal affixes. (1) The suffixed durative marker *-e* is used in the present and the imperfect: *y-on-e* "I (will) come, I am coming," *omey-n-e* "I used to/would come," *xer-on-e* "I eat," *xārt-om-e* "I would eat." (2) The perfective prefix *b*(V)- is used in the subjunctive (*b-i-on* "that I come," *ba-xer-on* "that I eat"), imperative (*bā-xā^{r}* "eat!"), preterit (*bo-omi(y)-on* "I came," *be-m-xārt* "I ate"), and perfect (*b-onde-yon* "I have come," *be-m-xārte* "I have eaten"), but is suppressed when the verb has a preverb or is in the negative. (3) The negative marker *ná-* comes just before the stem in all present forms and the intransitive past: *na-š-u-e* "he does not go," *na-šo-y* "you did not go," *ā-na-xus-e* "sleep not!" *ā-na-xofde-y* "you have not slept," *ofdöu var-n-onde* (past part.) "(when) the sun (has) not risen," *bar dar-na-band-e*! "don't shut the door!" In the transitive past, the subject marker may come between the negative marker and the stem: *kart-om-e* "I would do," *na-m-kart-e* (neg.).

Verbal nouns. (1) The infinitive marker *-(e)mon/mun* is added to the past stem preceded by the preverb (if any): *endārt-emon* "to send," *jikā-mon* "to dance," *dar-kat-emon* "to fall." (2) The past participle consists of the perfective prefix and/or the preverb (not always), the past stem, and the stressed suffix *-e*: *b-esbārt-e* "handed over, entrusted," *(ā-)xofd-e* "slept"; the glide *-y-* appears in the secondary stems in *-ā*: *pušnā-y-e* "covered," *har hātāye vātāye dāru* "for every giving (lit. given) there is a taking (lit. taken)" . Some secondary past stems have their past participles also in *-ā* when suffixed (*hessā-yon* "I have gotten up") and *-ehā/-āhā* when not: *vessehā/vessāhā bon* "I had gotten up," *be-š beresehā boym* "we would have reached him," *be-šon-dozehā bo* "they had stolen." (3) A curious present participle in *-oni* is also noted: *benā-šon-ke varvezoni bikirind* "they began jumping."

Person endings. These consist of three sets: (1) *-on*, *-i*, *-u*, *-im*, *-i*, *-ind* are used in the present indicative (*xer-i-e* "you eat," *vāss-i-e* "you stand") and subjunctive (*ba-xer-i* "that you eat," *vāss-i* "that you stand"). (2) *-(o)n*, *-i/y*, *-ø*, *-(y)m*, *-i/y*, *-(y)nd* are used in the intransitive preterit (*vāssā-i* "you stood"), imperfect (*vāssā-y-e* "you would stand"), and perfect (*hessā-i/y* "you have been standing"). (3) The enclitic personal pronouns (see above) are used as subject (agent) markers in the transitive verbs: after the stem in the imperfect (*xārt-ot-e* "you would eat"), and before the stem in the preterit (*be-d-xārt* "you ate") and perfect (*be-d-xārte* "you have eaten"); for the movement of this "ending," see Fronting, below. Imperative endings are sing. *-e* (e.g., *be-š-e* "go!") and pl. *-i* (e.g., *ā-xus-i* "sleep!"), with occasional irregular forms such as *bure* "come!" *nöure* "don't come!" *bii* "come ye!"

Notes on conjugation. (1) The subjunctive and the imperative of certain verbs use "be" as auxiliary: *dār bon* "I may have," *dār be* "have!" *dar be* "be in!" *bezom be* (< *be-zon be) "know!" *gu-š bu* "he may wish" (see also Modal verbs and particle, below). (2) The imperfect forms of intransitive verbs have a *-y-* inserted before the person endings (in full view only in the 1st pers. sing. and the 2nd sing./pl.): *ome-y-n-e*, *ome-y-y-e* "I, you would come," *xofde-y-n-e*, *xofde-y-y-e* "I, you would sleep," *vāssā-y-n-e* "I would stand." (3) Old past stems end either in vowels (*ome-* "come," *šo-* "go," *di-* "see," and possibly a few more) or consonants (limited to V*t*, *rt*, *nd*, *fd*, *šd*, and *ss* according to the aforementioned diachronic rules). The latter appear in (a) plain forms used in the infinitive (*git-emon* "to get") and the transitive preterit and imperfect (*hā-mon-git* "we got," *git-mon-e* "we would get"), or (b) fuller forms in *-e*, used in the intransitive preterit and imperfect (except 3rd sing.): *ā-xofde-yon*, *āxofde-i*, *āxofd*, *āxofde-ym*, *āxofde-i*, *āxofde-ynd* "I slept," etc., *xofde-y-n-e*, *xofde-y-y-e*, *xofd-e*, *xofde-ym-e*, *xofde-y-y-e*, *xofde-ynd-e* "I would sleep," etc. Note that *-e* is not epenthetic, since conjugations with the plain stem would be *āxofd-on "I slept," etc. Nor it is likely to be the participial marker *-é*; in the neighboring Rudašti dialects the same element appears mostly as *-ā* (e.g., Kamandāni *āxofto-yon*, *āxoftā-ym-e*), that is, the secondary stem formant. Nevertheless, one should not rule out the possibility that

Table 1
VERB FORMS (3RD PERS. SING.)

	Intransitive		Transitive	
	without preverb	with preverb	without preverb	with preverb
	"go"	*"sit"*	*"eat"*	*"throw"*
present	*š-ú-e*	*ning-ú-e*	*xer-ú-e*	*dar-xus-u-e*
subjunctive	*bé-š-u*	*hā́-ning-u*	*bá-xer-u*	*dár-xus-u*
imperative	*bé-š-e*	*hā́-ning(-e)*	*bā́-xā*^{r}	*dár-xus-e*
preterit	*béy-šo*	*hā́-nišd*	*bé-š-xā(rt)*	*dár-oš-xoss*
imperfect	*šó-y(y)-e*	*níšd-e*	*xā́rt-oš-e*	*xóss-oš-e*
perfect	*be-šdé*	*ø-nišd-é*	*be-š-xārté*	*dar-oš-xosse*
infinitive	*šondemón*	*nišdemón*	*xārtemón*	*dar-xossemón*

the intransitive imperfect is constructed on the past participle, as is the case in Sedehi. (4) Regardless of the origins of the *-e*, it yields preterit forms which are distinguishable from the perfect only by the placement of the stress: *āxofdeynd* "they slept" vs. *āxofdéynd* "they have slept." (5) On the other hand, the intransitive past stems ending in vowels have extra forms, in which an original *d* resurfaces: *béy-šo-yon* "I went," *šó-y-n-e* "I would go," *be-šdé-yon* "I have gone," *šond-emón* "to go"; *bó-ome-ym* "we came," *omé-y-m-e* "we would come," *b-ondé-ym* "we have come," *ond-emón* "to come." (Cf. Isfahani Jewish, where retention of the original *d* is surmised to be applicable to monosyllabic stems ending in a vowel; see ISFAHAN xix; cf. also Jarquyi *jind-emon* "to hit," *der-gind-emon* (< *gir-) "to kindle.") (6) Intransitive compounds with transitive auxiliary verbs receive transitive conjugations: *tou-š-bexā* "it twisted" (cf. trans. *be-š-tounā* "he twisted"), *girye-š-beke* "he cried," *benā-šon-ke* "they began," *pā-m gir-oš-beke* "my foot got stuck."

Fronting. This term was coined by Donald Stilo (see HAMADĀN ix) to signify the mobility of the person endings, set 3 (see above), throughout the sentence. In Jarquyi transitive past tenses as well, there is a strong tendency for the enclitic agents to move off the verb to a preceding word, often to the direct object. Indeed, fronting is preferred because, in the absence of *-rā*, it is the only way to mark direct objects. Examples: *un-om nadi* "I didn't see him" (cf. *na-m-di* "I didn't see"), *nesf-e qezā-m bexārte bo* "I had eaten half of the meal," *ki vāž mo-š betā*? "who called me?" *berā Ahmad-om hou xo-m barte* "I took Aḥmad's brother with me," *to-šon ez kie kü karte* "they have kicked you out of the house," *sou(v)ā-šon ez deraxd bičind* "they picked the apples off the tree." However, it is not uncommon for the agent to move to the indirect object: *čiči-ton hou mo buā*^{t}? ~ *hou mo-ton čiči buāt*? "what did you tell me?" *hou-t-om vāte* "I would tell you," *čand pül-od* (= *čand-od pül*) *hou xo-d bārte*? "how much money have you brought with you?" The agent optionally remains on the verb when no direct object is present (*ez visgi be-š-xārte* "so much he has eaten . . .") or when the object is not in the same clause: *har či pül o telā bo, ver-oš-git o ru tübre-š-oš nā* "he took all the money and gold that was (there) and put (it) into his sack." Fronting to a word that already has an enclitic possessive marker is also possible: *puo-š-om bekošde* "I have killed his father," *ba'anje-m-om ji bu(v)ond* "I cut my fingers as well," *xāšgā rās-*^{o}*š-om hou-š buāte bo* "I wish I had told him the truth." Imperfect transitive person endings are optionally fronted: *āš-<u>oš</u> lesāye vo xārt-<u>oš</u>-e* "he would lap the soup up and eat (it)."

To be. (1) The copula consists of the stems zero (present), *b-* (subjunctive), and *bo-* (past), conjugated regularly with the person-ending sets (1) and (2) listed above; e.g., *yon goloyon čan xāš-u* "how delicious this pear is," *angür feroumun ni-u* "grapes are not plenty," *okon dotion ki b-u*? "who is/might be that girl?" The copula may also express location: *dezār löu öu bo-ø* "the wall was by the water." The past and subjunctive forms are used as auxiliary in periphrastic tenses: the pluperfect *bešde bo-ynd* "they had gone," *be-š-on vāte bo* "they had said"; the perfect subjunctive *bešde b-ind* "they may have seen," *be-š-on vāte bu* "they may have said." (2) The copula combines with the preverb *der-/dar* to form the existential/locative verb for animate nouns: *peysin kie der-on* "I'll be home in the afternoon," *bāxsure kāy der-u*? "where is the father-in-law?" *gusband ru pāgir deru* "the sheep is in the pen," *dar be* "be in!" *mili ru kiri dar bo* "the cat was in the oven." (3) *hess-*, the existential verb for the inanimate nouns, is attested only in the present 3rd sing.: *čerā kāy hessu*? "where is the light?" *sart tel dezār hessu* "the ladder is by the wall."

Become. This is expressed by two verbs: (1) the copula plus the modal affixes *be-* or *-e*; the present tense has the stem *b-*, also derived from "to be": pres. *zü: xasse b-i-e* "you get tired quickly," past: *del-oš rāzi na-bo-ye* "he would not be content"; the pres. 3rd sing. in negative *nabue* (cf. *[be]-b-u-e* "it becomes") functions as an impersonal modal: *tirmā nabue čiā garm vāpuši* "you/one may not wear warm clothes in the summer"; (2) *vess-/vessā-* (also "stand"), with the past part. *vessehā/vessāhā*, e.g., *vesse* "become!" *qāy-šon vessā* (Pers. *harf-ešān šod*) "they began arguing (lit. speaking)," *qāyem vessā-ynd* "they hid from view," *max vessāhā boyon* "I had gotten lost," *temom navessehā bo* "it had not been finished."

The passive is formed analytically with the past participle and "become": *die vessā* "he was seen."

Have. The verb is irregular in that it does not take the modal affixes *be-* or *-e*, and that the transitive endings follow the stem in the past: *(na-)dār-u* "he has (not)," *dārt-oš* "he had," *dār b-e* "have!" Though not common in Jarquyi, progressive forms can be built on "have," on the model of colloquial Persian: *dār-on čiāhā-m vāpušone* "I am putting on my clothes," *dārt-om komze-m vonde* "I was cutting a/the melon."

Modal verbs and particle. (1) *gu-/gā-* "want" is conjugated with the enclitic pronouns as the agent in all tenses: pres. *gu-m(-e), gu-d/t(-e), gu-š(-e)*, subj. *gu-m bu*, etc., past *gā-m(-e)*, etc. Examples: *gum/gām bešon* "I want/wanted to go," *gum bu bešon* "that I want to go," *kue-m-om gu-m-e* "I want my dog as well," *gām(e) bion gāre* " I wanted to come down." The agent maker is optionally fronted (see Fronting, above): *har kār-i go del-od gu-ṣ̌-e beke ~ har kār-i-ṣ̌ go del-od gue beke* "do whatever you wish." (2) *šā-* "can" is conjugated with enclitic pronouns and the 3rd person sing. of "be": pres. and past *be-šā- bo*, subj. *be-šā- bu*. Examples: *tā yā-y go bešā-š bo* "as far as he could," *ibi našā-š bo ez yā-š yeyyu* "he cannot stand up from his place any more," *xāšgā bešā-m bu ye kār-i bekeron* "I wish I could do something." (3) *qādib* "must" is impersonal: *qādib qāy baltarā guš hāti* "you must listen to elder's advice," *hou to-m bu(v)āt go naqādib biši vā(če)* "I told you that you should not go there." See also Become, above.

Bibliography: H. Borjian, "Jogrāfiā-ye guyeshā-ye welāyati-e Eṣfahān," *Irānšenāsi/Irānshenāsi* 17/3, 2005, pp. 466-86. Ḥamida Ebrāhimi Faḵāri, "Tawṣif-e zabānšenāḵti-e guyeš-e manṭaqa-ye Jarquya," M.A. thesis, Univ. of Isfahan, 1997. ʿAli Šafiʿi Nikābādi, *Garkuya: sarzamin-i nāšenāḵta bar karān-e kavir*, 2nd ed., Isfahan, 1997.

(HABIB BORJIAN)

JARRĀḤI RIVER. See KHUZESTAN i. Geography.

JĀRUDIYA. See ZAIDIS.

JĀSK, also written Jāšk ('Jasques' in English East India Company sources), a small Baluchi port on the Makrān coast with palm gardens. Dean William Vincent is credited (Mockler, 1879, p. 141) with having been the first to identify Jāsk with the toponym Badis mentioned in Arrian's account (*Indica* 32.5) of the voyage of Nearchus (Vincent, 1797; cf. Wilson, p. 40; Tarn, p. 481), but this identification is disputed (e.g., d'Anville, pp. 140, identified Jāsk with Claudius Ptolemy's promontory of Carpella; Forbiger, 1844, p. 532, identified Jāsk with Dagasira; Tomaschek, 1890, p. 41; idem, 1970, identifying Badis with Kuh-e Mobārak or Tujek; Berthelot, p. 22, identified Jāsk with Omana of the *Periplus of the Erythraean Sea*, sec. 36, see Vincent, 1800-05). Be that as it may, Jāsk is certainly located in the area inhabited by the *ichthyophagi* (fish-eaters) encountered along the Persian coast by Nearchus (Longo, 1987).

The island of Jāsak mentioned by Yāqut Ḥamawi and Zakariyāʾ Qazvini is thought to have been Lārak (Lockhart, p. 486) and not Jāsk. Aḥmad b. Majid Najdi, better known as Ebn Majid, the 15th-century writer on navigation, gives the alternative name al-Karāri and the plural Jawāšek for Jāšk, noting that the overland journey from Sind to Jāsk took six weeks (Ebn Majid, tr., pp. 212, 448-49).

In December 1616, the English East India Company sent Edward Connock on the British vessel, *James*, to Jāsk with a cargo from Surat, thereby inaugurating English trade with Persia (Curzon, II, p. 427; Sykes, II, p. 189; Wilson, p. 138). In July, 1617, Connock was received by Shah ʿAbbās I (q.v.) himself and successfully negotiated a trade agreement (Steensgaard, p. 308), coming away with a royal edict (*farmān*, q.v.), granting, *inter alia*, the right to construct churches, hold religious services, found a cemetery, imprison and repatriate English outlaws, and exercise criminal jurisdiction in mixed Anglo-Persian cases (Steensgaard, pp. 329-30). A charge for highway policing (*rāhdāri*) was to be paid by the English, although their goods, both imports to and exports from Jāsk, were exempt from any customs charges. In 1618, however, Connock's successor, Thomas Barker, was refused permission to build a fort at Jāsk (Steensgaard, pp. 330, 333). By this time, the Portuguese were taking active steps to pursue and intercept English Company vessels attempting to reach Jāsk from Surat, leading to the Battle of Jāsk in 1620 in which the English captain lost his life, but the Portuguese fleet was defeated (Curzon, II, pp. 427-28; Sykes, II, pp. 190-91; Wilson, p. 142; Steensgaard, pp. 337-41).

In 1809 Jāsk was tributary to the Imam of Muscat (Grant, p. 336). In 1869 it became the site of an Indo-European Telegraph station (Preece, p. 429; Lorimer, p. 917) at which the overland line from Bušehr (q.v.) and Bandar Lenga met the submarine cables coming from Karachi (via Gwādar) and Aden (Holdich, pp. 387-88; Oppenheim, II, p. 322). A post office, barracks for 100 *sepoys* to protect the telegraph line (withdrawn from Qešm in 1879; Curzon, 1892, II, p. 428), and an office of the British India Company were also located at Jāsk, as was a small fort with a Persian governor and about twenty Kurdish soldiers (Oppenheim, II, p. 323).

Bibliography: B. d'Anville, "Recherches géographiques sur le Golfe Persique et sur les bouches de l'Euphrate et du Tigre," *Mémoires de littérature, tirés des registres de l'Académie Royale des Inscriptions et Belles-Lettres* 30, 1764, pp. 132-97. A. Berthelot, "La côte méridionale de l'Iran d'après les géogreaphes grecs," *Mélanges offerts à M. Octave Navarre par ses élèves et ses amis*, Toulouse, 1935, pp. 11-24. George N. Curzon, *Persia and the Persian Question*, 2 vols., London, 1892; repr. Lonon, 1966. Ebn Majid Najdi, *Fawāʾed fi oṣul ʿelm al-baḥr wa'-qawāʾed*, tr. Gerald Randall Tibbetts as *Arab Navigation in the Indian Ocean before the Coming of the Portuguese*, London,

1971. Albert Forbiger, *Handbuch der alten Geographie*, 3 vols., Leipzig, 1842-48. Captain N. P. Grant, "Journal of a Route through the Western Parts of Makran," *JRAS* 5, 1839, pp. 328-42. Colonel T. H. Holdich, "Notes on Ancient and Mediæval Makran," *The Geographical Journal* 7, 1896, pp. 387-405. Lawrence Lockhart, "D̲jāsak," in *EI*^{2} II, p. 486. O. Longo, "A Trip among Fish Eaters," *Newsletter of Baluchistan Studies* 4, 1987, pp. 11-18. John G. Lorimer, *Gazetteer of the Persian Gulf, ʿOman, and Central Arabia*, 2 vols., Calcutta, 1908-15; repr., Westmead, U.K., 2 vols. in 6, IIA, pp. 914-31. Major E. Mockler, "On the Identification of Places on the Makran Coast Mentioned by Arrian, Ptolemy, and Marcian," *JRAS* 11, 1879, pp. 129-54. Max Freiherr von Oppenheim, *Vom Mittelmeer zum Persischen Golf durch den Haurän, die Syrische Wüste und Mesopotamien*, 2 vols., Berlin, 1899-1900. J. R. Preece, "Journey from Shiraz to Jashk, via Darab, Forg, and Minab," *JRGS*, Supplementary Paper 1, 1885, pp. 403-35. Zakariyāʾ b. Moḥammad Qazvini, *ʿAjāʾeb al-mak̲luqāt wa ḡarāʾeb al-mawjudāt*, ed. Ferdinand Wüstenfeld as *Kosmographie*, Wiesbaden, 1967. Ḥosayn-ʿAli Razmārā, ed., *Farhang-e joḡrāfiāʾi-e Irān (ābādihā)* VIII, Tehran, 1953, p. 94. Moḥammad-ʿAli Sadid-al-Salṭana (Kabābi), *Bandar ʿAbbās wa K̲alij-e Fārs*, ed. ʿAli Setāyeš, Tehran, 1984, passim. Paul Schwarz, *Iran im Mittelalter nach den arabischen Geographen*, Leipzig, 1896-35; repr., 9 vols. in 4, Frankfurt on the Main, 1993, II, p. 89. Neils Steensgaard, *Carracks, Caravans and Companies: The Structural Crisis in the European-Asian Trade in the Early 17th Century*, Lund, 1973. Percy M. Sykes, *A History of Persia*, 2 vols., 3rd ed. with suppl. essays, London, 1930; repr., London, 1958. W. W. Tarn, *The Greeks in Bactria and India*, Cambridge, 1951. W. Tomaschek, *Topographische Erläuterung der Küstenfahrt Nearchs vom Indus bis zum Euphrat*, Vienna, 1890. Idem, "Badis," in George Wissowa, Wilhelm Kroll, and Karl Mittlehaus, eds., *Paulys Real-Encyclopädie der classicschen Altertumswissenschaft* II/2, Stuttgart, 1970, col. 2727. W. Vincent, *The Voyage of Nearchus from the Indus to the Euphrates*, London, 1797. Idem, *Periplus of the Erythraean Sea*, 2 vols., London, 1800-05. Arnold T. Wilson, *The Persian Gulf*, Oxford, 1928.

(D. T. POTTS)

JAŠN. See GĀHANBĀR; FESTIVALS ii.

JĀSP. See MAḤALLĀT.

JĀT, a contested and ambiguous label for several non-food-producing peripatetic itinerant communities in Afghanistan (Rao, 1982; idem, 2004; Olesen) and the surrounding region (Akiner; Arnold; Berland; Berland and Rao; Ivanow; Pischel; Sykes). The Jāts are occasionally dubbed gypsy in ethnographic, historic, and travel accounts. In early post-Islamic Arabic historical records the Jāt are called Zoṭṭ and in the Persian and Arab worlds Jāt and Zoṭṭ are referred to as non-food-producing semi-nomadic people with Indian origins (Westphal-Hellbusch, 1984, p. 356), irrespective of their own claims for ethnic or linguistic identity. There are sizeable communities of settled and nomadic Jāts numbering several millions in India and Pakistan, about which we have a limited ethnographic and historical record (Berland; Bingley; Dahiya; Pande; Pradhan; Qanungo). The present article deals with the Jāts of Afghanistan, a heterogeneous ethnic group that consists of several non-food-producing nomadic and semi-nomadic communities, each calling itself by a distinct descent and/or occupational autonym.

The label Qaw(w)āl is occasionally used interchangeably with the exonym Jāt in Afghanistan. The overlapping social categories Jāt and Qawāl in Afghanistan carry pejorative connotations. No one wants to be identified as Jāt or Qawāl. As such, these two labels do not analytically qualify as ethnonyms but are references to ethnic or social categories to which no one wants to belong. In Afghan popular culture, argumentative and quarrelsome behavior, including careless and carefree speech and dress, especially among young women, is characterized as Jāt behavior. All peripatetic communities reject the label Jāt but apply it to other communities in the larger Jāt ethnic universe. For example, a sub-group of the Jāt called Pikrāj will reject being called Jāt but will assign the label to other sub-groups of the larger Jāt category.

Widely known to the people of Afghanistan, the Jāts in that country have received sparse ethnographic attention from scholars. The descriptive accounts of Asta Olesen (especially 1994) and Aparna Rao (especially 1982) are our only sources for academic information about the Jāt peripatetic communities of Afghanistan. Ethnographic research for these studies was conducted during early 1970s.

The major Jāt communities in Afghanistan are identified as Baluch, Ḡorbat, Jalāli, Šādibāz, Pikrāj, Vangāwālā, Jōgi, Šayk̲ Moḥammadi, and Mussali. Most of these communities were segmented into smaller descent units usually identified with the suffix *k̲ēl*. The exception was the Ḡorbat, in which segments were named Faray, Kayāni, and Syawun. Smaller and less known Jāt segments referred to in the literature are Čangar, Jolā, Sadu, Čalu, Kowli, Kutana, Luli, and Mogat. Aparna Rao (2004) lists four general features of the Jāt noted by outsiders to differentiate them from other nomadic and semi-nomadic communities in Afghanistan: (1) They lived in houses in urban areas and in white tents when they lived in rural areas and, in contrast to the black goat's hair tents of the pastoral nomads, in white tents when they lived in rural areas; (2) they were collectively known as outsiders with Indian origins even though a Jāt community itself, as in the case of the Ḡorbat, would claim Iranian roots; (3) they were considered both physically and ritually unclean and associated with undesirable and polluting occupations of feeding on carrion and corpses, bloodletting, prostitution, pimping, and child-abduction; (4) their small and dark physical features validated their Indian, non-Afghan, origins.

Most Jāts in Afghanistan claim to be Sunni Muslims. The Ḡorbat, one of the largest and most dispersed Jāts, are mostly Shiʿite. Jāt communities in Afghanistan were organized around common patrilineal descent. Each community consisted of a minimal lineage, a cluster of a few patrilineally linked nuclear families that consider themselves descendents of a known male ancestor. Some lineages are labeled with a proper name as a prefix to *ḵēl*, for instance, Zaku-ḵēl among the Šayḵ Moḥammadi; others are identified by occupation such as Naddāf-ḵēl (lineage of cotton carders) or by place such as Čahārbāḡi (from Čahārbāḡ), or by objects such as Koluḵi (of lumps of dried mud or mud brick). Most Jāt myths of origin locate them in early Islamic history and link them to putative ancestors with special spiritual powers. The Jāts speak the Persian or Paxtu (Pashtu, Pukhtu) language of the local Afghan communities where they work and engage in trade. Every Jāt community claims to have a secret language (Quzulagi among the Ḡorbat, Adurgari among the Šayḵ Moḥammadi), which outsiders are supposed not to understand (Rao, 1982; idem, 2004; Olson, 1987; idem, 1994).

In general, male members of Jāt communities in Afghanistan engage in barter exchanges mostly in the lower class neighborhoods of urban areas like Kabul and in rural areas of Afghanistan. They make and peddle bird cages (*qafas*) and flat circular drums (*dāyera*, see DAF(F) AND DĀYERA). Cloth, haberdashery, perfumes, and trinkets (*sawdā*) are purchased in urban markets and peddled for a profit. As traders in trinket the Jāts are known as *sawdāgar*, trinket peddler. Some Jāts work as snake charmers, sellers of charms (*taʿwiḏ*) against snake and scorpion bites, monkey handlers (*šādibāz*), jugglers and conjurers (*madari*), chinaware repairer (*patragar*), and cotton carders (*naddāf*). The Šayḵ Moḥammadi and Mussali Jāts of Eastern Afghanistan make and peddle grain sieves (*ḡarbayl* [*ḡalbayl*], *čiḡil* or *maydabiz*) and winnowing trays (*čaj*, *čač*). They work as grain cleaners and threshers, rice millers (*pāykub*), and winnowers of grain in addition to peddling trinkets and other commodities bought in urban markets and sold in rural areas during their summer and fall migrations around Kabul and in Kōhdāman, especially in the area south of Čarikār (q.v.). Jāt women peddle a variety of goods including cloth, haberdashery; bangles (*čoriwāla* or *čoriforuš* in Persian, *bangriwāl* in Paxtu) and other jewelry; thread and needle (*tār o suzan*); comb (*šāna*); hairpins (*siḵak*); make-up for women (*sorḵi o safaydā*, red and white powder); *sorma o sala-yi*, powdered antimony [*kohl*]—used to color eyelashes and the area around the eyes and eyebrows—and a small wooden bodkin for application (in Paxtu these two items are called *ranza aw sala-yi*); tools for personal hygiene (*gel-e saršoi*, a pinkish soft rock that, when soaked in water, produces a paste that was used for cleaning the skull skin; *ḵešt*, a soft rock for removing grime; *sang-e pāy*, a round pumice for cleaning foot soles; *kisa*, a glove made of coarse cloth for removing grime; *lif*, a soft woven glove for lathering soap; *pāki*, blade for removing hair). Some Jāt women engaged in fortune-telling (*fāll-bini*), drawing blood by cupping (*ḵoon-kaši*), and leeching (*jok zadan*). In urban areas Jāt women had a reputation for performing abortions. Drawing blood and abortion are explicitly prohibited in Islam. All these occupations are ranked low in Afghanistan and stereotyped with negative attributes. The Jāts exchanged their services and commodities mainly through barter, receiving used clothes, old shoes, and worn out household goods. General purpose money was rarely involved in these transactions. In the context of these exchanges the Jāts, especially Jāt women, were an important source of information about the outside world for their women customers.

Major communities. During the 1970s the Baluch Jāts in Afghanistan estimated their own numbers at about 2,500 individuals. They were concentrated in northern and northwestern Afghanistan with the largest numbers in the city of Herat. They were locally known as Čalu, Herati, and Jāt-Baluč and were distinguished from the tribal Baluch. The Jāt-Baluč claimed Baluchistan as their ancestral home and were traditionally hosted by the Jamšidi communities, among whom they worked as blacksmiths, coppersmiths, and jewelers. As a result of the 1970s drought in northern Afghanistan, the Baluch Jāts moved out of Jamšidi settlements and adopted music, dance, and female prostitution as their primary economic strategy (Rao, 1986).

The Ḡorbat Jāts were the most widely distributed itinerant peripatitics of about 1,000 nuclear families in Afghanistan. They could be found in all large cities and rural areas of the country. Ḡorbat men peddled cloth and haberdashery and made and peddled sieves and round flat drums. Blood-letting is the most common occupation among the itinerant Ḡorbat. In the 1970s some segments of the Ḡorbat community had become sedentary. The Ḡorbat claim Iranian origin despite outsiders' insistence that they are originally from India. Most Ḡorbat are Shiʿite; only those in Kandahar claim to be Sunni. Their language is generally called Ḡorbati, Magadi in Herat, and Quzulagi in Kabul and Kandahar. It is alleged that the name Ḡorbat and its phonetic variations are used by some itinerant gypsy communities in Central Asia, Western Iran, Europe, North Africa, and even in North America (Rao, 1982).

The Jalāli and Pikrāj (northeast Afghanistan) and Šādibāz and Vangāwālā (eastern Afghanistan) Jāts claim their origin in Dera Esmāʿil Khan and Dera Ḡāzi Khan (west of the Indus River) in what is now Pakistan. Famine and feuds are given as reasons for moving out of the Indus valley into Afghanistan. Among the about 500 Jalāli Jāts, some men are known as professional beggars, musicians, and peddlers of haberdashery. A few Jalāli Jāt men trained monkeys to dance and engage in acrobatics. Jalāli women were known as fruit peddlers. In the 1970s, approximately 2,000 Pikrāj were scattered in small concentrations around the cities of Balkh, Mazār-e Šarif, Maymana, Qondoz, and Ṭālaqān. Pikrāj Jāt men were engaged mostly in buying and selling donkeys and horses and in the repair of cracked or broken china ware. Pikrāj women were known for selling bangles.

The Šādibāz or Šādiwan were estimated at 1,500 strong in the 1970s. They peddled their occupation in and around the cities of Kabul and Jalālābād and throughout the provinces of Lōgar and Parwān. Šādibāz men trained and peddled exhibitions of performing monkeys. The animals were imported from Pakistan. In the 1970s the Šādibāzi trade declined and men of this community started peddling cloth and labor for the production of agricultural harvests. Šādibāz women peddled bangles imported from Pakistan (Rao, 1986).

The Vangāwālā (bangle seller) Jāt numbered about 3,000 individuals (Rao, 1986). Their women peddled bracelets, cloth, and haberdashery in the area south of the Hindu Kush mountains (q.v.) and east of Qalāt and Orozgān plus the Bāmiān Valley and the major cities of northeast Afghanistan. Some Vangāwālā men were jugglers, conjurers, and snake charmers and peddled spells against snake bites and scorpion stings. A few Vangāwālā men had settled in Kabul as shopkeepers selling cloth; others were engaged in peddling used shoes, religious posters, and perfumes on Kabul streets. Some Vangāwālā families were engaged in picking fruit and a few others had become full-time farmers. The Jōgi Jāts claim to have their origin in Bengal and were scattered throughout northern Afghanistan. They were engaged in begging, fortune telling, blood letting and leeching, and selling herbal medicines. Jōgi men were working in the harvesting of cotton and cereals. Some consider them a branch of the Jalāli Jāts (Rao, 1986).

The itinerant Šayk̠ Moḥammadi Jāts lived in and around the village of Maskura in the Ališang valley, Lag̠mān Province. In the 1970s they numbered about 150 related families. They made winnowing trays which their men and women peddled together with thread and needles, hairpins, and trinkets in exchange mainly for wheat. They peddled cloth during market days. A few Šayk̠ Moḥammadi owned shops in Jalālābād and in Mehtarlam, the provincial capital of Lag̠mān. A nearby community of Šayk̠ Moḥammadis outside of Maskura specialized in cotton carding (*naddāfi*) and repairing damaged chinaware (*patragari*). After the spring wheat harvest in Lag̠mān, throughout the summer months and early autumn the Šayk̠ Moḥammadi camped in tents in the area surrounding Kabul and in Kōhdāman around Sarā-ye K̠oja. By exploiting price differences in Lag̠mān, Kabul, and Kōhdāman, they peddle cloth, bangles, hairpins, balloons, and other trinkets in exchange mainly for grapes and raisins. They returned to Lag̠mān after the fruit harvest season (Rao, 1986).

The Mussali Jāts lived in units of 1-3 families per village throughout the densely populated Ališang and Alingar valleys of Lag̠mān Province. Unlike other Jāts, they lived in permanent dwellings and were integrated into the local political economy in a relatively fixed landowner-laborer relationship. They produced labor for threshing, winnowing and cleaning during the late spring harvest season in Lag̠mān. Following the agricultural cycle, during mid to late summer they peddled these services in the heavily populated Kabul and Kōhdāman regions in exchange for grain and other agricultural products.

Although quite limited in scope, the introduction of modern roads and means of transportation and communication, together with industrial agricultural technologies and expansion of urban environments, had a far-reaching transforming impact on Jāt society and culture in Afghanistan. In addition, the collapse of the state structure of Afghanistan and the political and social changes in the surrounding region over the last three decades have produced profound changes in all ethnic communities of Afghanistan. In all likelihood not many Jāts survived these transformations and those that did survive have probably moved to the relative safety and stability of the surrounding countries. No reliable information is available about the Jāt communities currently residing inside Afghanistan.

Bibliography: S. Akiner, "Enduring Strangers: Mughat, Lyuli, and Other Peripatetics in the Social Fabric of Central Asia," in Joseph C. Berland and Aparna Rao, eds, *Customary Strangers: New Perspectives on Peripatetic Peoples in the Middle East, Africa, and Asia*, London, 2004, pp. 299-307. S. Bazmee Ansari, "D̲jāt," in *EI*² II, pp. 488-89. H. Arnold, "Some Observations on Turkish and Persian Gypsies," *The Journal of Gypsy Lore Society (JGLS) 3-4*, 1989-99, pp. 105-22. Joseph C. Berland, *No Five Fingers are Alike: Cognitive Amplifiers in Social Context*, Cambridge, 1982. A. H. Bingley, *History, Caste and Culture of Jāts and Gūjars*, New Delhi, 1978. Clifford E. Bosworth, "Zuṭṭ," in *EI*² XI, pp. 574-75. Bhim Singh Dahiya, *Jāts, The Ancient Rulers: A Clan Study*, New Delhi, 1980. William Crooke, *The Tribes and Castes of the North-Western Provinces and Oudh*, 4 vols., Calcutta, 1986, III, pp. 26-51. W. Ivanow, "On the Language of the Gypsies of Qainat (in Eastern Persia)," *Journal of the Asiatic Society of Bengal (JASB)*, N. S. 10, 1914, pp. 439-55. Idem, "Further Notes on Gypsies in Persia," *JASB*, N. S. 16, 1920, pp. 281-91. Idem, "An Old Gypsy-Darwesh Jargon," *JASB*, N. S. 18, 1922, pp. 375-83. A. Olesen, "The Musallis-the Graincleaners of East Afghanistan," *Afghanistan Journal* 91, 1982, pp. 13-19. Idem, "Peddling in East Afghanistan: Adaptive Strategies of the Peripatetic Sheikh Mohammadi," in Aparna Rao, ed, *The Other Nomads: Peripatetic Minorities in Cross-cultural Perspective*, Koln, 1987, pp. 35-63. Idem, *Afghan Craftsmen: The Culture of Three Itinerant Communities*, London, 1994. Idem, "Adaptive Strategies among Itinerant Craftsmen in Eastern Afghanistan: Mussalis, Shaykh Mohammadis and Ghorbats," in Daniel Balland, ed, *Hommes et Terre d'Islam: mélanges offerts à Xavier de Planhol*, 2 vols., Tehran, 2000, I, pp. 435-48. Ram Pande, *Bharatpur upto 1826: A Social and Political History of the Jāts*, Jaipur, 1970. R. Pischel, "Home of the Gypsies," *JGLS* 2/4, 1909, pp. 292-320. Mahesh Chandra Pradhan, *The Political System of the Jāts of Northern India*, London, 1966. K. R. Qanungo, *History of the Jāts*, Calcutta, 1925. Aparna Rao, "Note préliminaire sur les *Jāt* d'Afghanistan," *Studia Iranica* 8/1, 1979, pp. 141-49.

Idem, "Qui sont les Jāt d'Afghanistan?" *Afghanistan Journal* 8/1, 1981, pp. 55-64. Idem, *Les Gorbat d'Afghanistan: Aspects economiques d'un groupe itinerant "Jāt,"* Paris, 1982. Idem, "Non-food-producing Nomads and the Problem of Their Classification: The Case of the Ghorbat of Afghanistan," *Eastern Anthropologist* 35/2, 1982, pp. 115-34. Idem, "Peripatetic Minorities in Afghanistan," in Erwin Orywal, ed, *Die ethnischen Gruppen Afghanistans: Fallstudien zu Gruppenidentität und Intergruppenbeziehungen*, Wiesbaden, 1986, pp. 254-83. Idem, "Roles, Status and Niches: A Comparison of Peripatetic and Pastoral Women in Afghanistan," *Nomadic Peoples* 21/22, 1986, pp. 153-77. Idem, "Folk Models and Interethnic Relations in Afghanistan: A Case Study of Some Peripatetic Communities," in J-P. Digard, ed, *Le fait ethnique en Iran et en Afghanistan*, Paris, 1988, pp. 109-20. Idem, "Ghorbat," in *Encyclopedia of World Cultures* IX, 1995, pp. 105-7. Idem, "Marginality and Language Use: The Example of Peripatetics in Afghanistan," *JGLS* 5/2, 1995, pp. 69-95. Idem, "Strangers and Liminal Beings: Some Thoughts on Peripatetics, Insiders, and Outsiders in Southwest Asia," in Joseph C. Berland and Aparna Rao, eds., *Customary Strangers: New Perspectives on Peripatetic Peoples in the Middle East, Africa, and Asia*, London, 2004, pp. 270-98. Idem, ed., *The Other Nomads: Peripatetic Minorities in Cross-cultural Perspective*, Koln, 1987. A. Rao and M. J. Casimir, "How Non-food-producing Nomads Obtain Their Food: Peripatetic Strategies in Afghanistan," in I. de Garine and Geoffrey A. Harrison, eds., *Coping with Uncertainty in Food Supply*, Oxford, 1988, pp. 360-78. Percy M. Sykes, "Persian Jāts," *JGLS* 3/4, 1910, p. 320. Sigrid Westphal-Hellbusch, "Jāt," in Richard V. Weeks, ed., *Muslim Peoples: A World Ethnographic Survey*, 2 vols., London, 1984, II, pp. 355-60. Sigrid Westphal-Hellbusch and Heinz Westphal, *The Jāt of Pakistan*, Forschungen zur Ethnologie und Sozialpsychologie, Berlin, 1964.

(M. JAMIL HANIFI)

JĀTAKASTAVA, a Khotanese religious poem in praise (Skt. *stava-*) of the Buddha's former births (Skt. *jātaka-*). It is entirely preserved in a single manuscript that was recovered from the Caves of the Thousand Buddhas (Qianfodong) near Dunhuang (q.v. at *iranica.com*) in northwestern China and is now kept in the British Library. The text, written in formal Late South Turkestan Brāhmī (q.v.) script, occupies fols. 1v-39r and is followed by a colophon in cursive script on fol. 39 (ms. Ch. 00274: Bajley, *KT* I, pp. 198-219; facs. of fol. 1v and 39r in Stein, 1921, pl. cl; complete facs. in Bailey, 1938, pp. 145-83; ed. Dresden, 1955, with tr., grammatical sketch, survey of parallels of the stories and gloss.; corrections and additions in Dresden, *IIJ* 14/1-2 1972, pp. 104-6; cf. Emmerick, 1992, p. 24).

The work, which is written in Late Khotanese and whose title is known from the text itself (stanza 3 and colophon, fol. 39r2), is dedicated to the well-being of the Khotanese King Vīśa' Śūrrä (st. 5) and must thus date from this king's reign (967-78 C.E.). Its aim is to extol the virtues of the Buddha by means of extremely concise summaries (one to five stanzas each) of fifty-two edifying episodes from fifty-one *jātaka* stories (two episodes are taken from the story of Prince Viśvantara, sts. 141-43 and 161-63); for most of the stories, parallels have been traced elsewhere in Buddhist narrative literature. The Khotanese *Jātakastava* is presumably an original composition based on Indian sources and not a real translation, though it is presented as such (cf. Dresden, 1955, pp. 402-3). No precise parallel text has been identified: the Sanskrit *Jātakastava* of Jñānayaśas belongs to the same literary genre but is a different text (Sanskrit and Tibetan texts in Bailey, 1939; rev. Sanskrit and tr. in Shackleton Bailey, 1954).

The praise of the *jātaka*s that forms the main body of the work is preceded by a prologue (sts. 1-10) and followed by an epilogue (sts. 164-69). Most of the summaries close with such short formulas of praise as "Therefore, to you then homage more than a hundred myriad times" (v. 15d), or "Therefore to you, O good being, from me at your feet homage" (v. 29d) and the like, but occasionally the praise extends to half a stanza or to a whole stanza, as in st. 19. Accordingly, the two stanzas that follow the fifty-first story—the future Buddha's gift of his own flesh to ransom a pigeon—are also best regarded as the relevant, otherwise missing, praise (sts. 159-60) and not as an "interlude" as suggested by M. J. Dresden (1955, pp. 401, 444).

The colophon informs us that the text was copied or ordered to be copied by a follower of Vajrayāna (Diamond Vehicle) Buddhism called Cā Kīmä-śanä (i.e., Chinese *Zhang Jinshan*), whose name also occurs in the Khotanese Vajrayanist poems of ms. Ch. i.0021b of the year 971 C.E. (see Skjærvø, 2002, pp. 550-56) and in the Chinese devotional text of ms. Ch. i.0021a of the year 982 C.E. (see Bailey, 1944, p. 11; for the datings see Hamilton, 1979, p. 51). His signature is found in Sogdian script at the end of the colophon (*kymš'n* without the family name) as well as in the last preserved folio of the Khotanese version of the medical text *Siddhasāra* by Ravigupta (*cw kymš'n*, ms. Ch. ii.002, fol. 156v: see Bailey, 1938, p. 67). The Kīma-śanä mentioned without a family name in the burlesque poem of ms. P 2745 (Bailey, *KT* II, pp. 92-93; ed. Kumamoto, 1995, pp. 243-45, with tr. and comm.) could be the same person.

Bibliography: D. R. Shackleton Bailey, "The Jātakastava of Jñānayaśas," in *Asiatica: Festschrift Friedrich Weller zum 65. Geburtstag gewidmet von seinen Freunden, Kollegen und Schülern*, ed. J. Schubert and U. Schneider, Leipzig, 1954, pp. 22-29. H. W. Bailey, *Codices Khotanenses: India Office Library Ch. ii 002, Ch. ii 003, Ch. 00274 Reproduced in Facsimile with an Introduction*, Copenhagen, 1938. Idem, "The Jātakastava of Jñānayaśas," *BSOS* 9/4, 1939, pp. 851-59. Idem, "The Colophon of the *Jātaka-stava*," *Journal of the Greater India Society* 11/1, 1944, pp. 10-12. Idem,

Khotanese Texts [*KT*] I-VII, Cambridge, 1945-85 (several reprs. with corrections). M. J. Dresden, *The Jātakastava or "Praise of the Buddha's Former Births": Indo-Scythian (Khotanese) Text, English Translation, Grammatical Notes and Glossaries*, Philadelphia, 1955. R. E. Emmerick, *A Guide to the Literature of Khotan*, 2nd ed., Tokyo, 1992. J. Hamilton, "Les règnes khotanais entre 851 et 1001," in *Contributions aux études sur Touen-houang*, ed. M. Soymié, Genève, 1979, pp. 49-54. H. Kumamoto, "Miscellaneous Khotanese Documents from the Pelliot Collection," *Tokyo University Linguistics Papers* 14, 1995, pp. 229-58. P. O. Skjærvø, *Khotanese Manuscripts from Chinese Turkestan in The British Library: A Complete Catalogue with Texts and Translations*, with contributions by U. Sims-Williams, Corpus Inscr. Iran. II/V/Texts VI, London, 2002. M. A. Stein, *Serindia: Detailed Report of Explorations in Central Asia and Westernmost China*, Oxford, 1921, 5 vols.

(MAURO MAGGI)

JAUBERT, PIERRE AMÉDÉE ÉMILIEN-PROBE (b. Aix-en-Provence, 3 June 1779; d. Paris, 28 January 1847), French Orientalist who also served as interpreter and diplomat at Napoleon Bonaparte's court. He studied Turkish, Arabic, and Persian languages for two years (1796-98) with Sylvestre de Sacy at the École des Langues Orientales in Paris, and then was appointed interpreter with the title "jeune de langues" at the French legation in Constantinople. Then he took part, as the interpreter, in Napoleon's expedition to Egypt (1798-99) and in 1799 became the senior interpreter in the service of Napoleon (1769-1821). He taught for two years (1800-01) at the École des Langues Orientales, before accompanying French troops in 1802 in their expedition to Alexandria in Egypt. On his return to France in 1803, he was appointed secretary interpreter at the Ministry of Foreign Affairs and professor of Turkish language at the École des Langues Orientales. In 1804, he was charged to announce to the Ottoman Emperor Sultan Selim III (r. 1789-1807) that Napoleon had been crowned emperor. In March of the following year, he was sent to Persia to establish an alliance with Fatḥ-ʿAli Shah Qājār (r. 1797-1834, q.v.) against England and Russia. Jaubert accomplished this mission in spite of many difficulties caused by the Ottomans, such as being imprisoned near the Persian border for eight months (August 1805-March 1806). It was thus only in June 1806 that he was received in audience by the Shah of Persia in Tehran and presented a letter from Napoleon. The negotiations were carried out very well and the court of Persia offered him a large portrait of the shah as well as various Persian manuscripts that Jaubert gave to the Imperial Library after his return to Paris in January 1807 (Robinson, p. 875). Towards the end of April of the same year, he went to the castle of Finkenstein in East Prussia as interpreter for the negotiations between Napoleon and the ambassador of the shah of Persia for a treaty of alliance against Russia and Great Britain. These negotiations were concluded by the Treaty of Finkenstein, which was signed on 4 May 1807 (Hurewitz, I, pp. 184-85), but Napoleon's peace treaty with Russia two months later made the Finkenstein Treaty practically insignificant.

Jaubert received many privileges from Napoleon Bonaparte: the cross of chevalier of the Légion d'honneur, an annual rent of 4,000 franks, the title of Chevalier of the Empire (May 1808), and the position of Master of the requests at the Council of State (1810). During the period known as Hundred Days (20 March 8-July 1815), Jaubert occupied the position of the "Chargé d'affaires" of France in Constantinople. That was why the next French regime did not appreciate his services and he was dismissed. Afterwards, he devoted his time to linguistic research and to teaching. In 1818-19, he embarked on a new trip to the East. In 1921, he published his travel account *Voyage en Arménie et en Perse*, in which he discussed the economic possibilities of Persia (pp. 282-89) using the accounts of other French travelers. He described the Qajar court (pp. 227-34) and various Iranian ceremonies and compared them with those of the Ottomans (pp. 290-319). He devoted a number of pages to an account of the nomads in Iran (pp. 250-63) and also mentioned the situation of the Iranian women vis-à-vis those in the Ottoman Empire (pp. 320-25). In a chapter concerning the population, incomes, and spending, Jaubert compared the situation of that time in Iran with the past and wrote: "The Persians are constantly exposed to the exactions and to the violence of the subaltern agents of the government" (p. 273). Mention should also be made of his translation of Šarif Edrisi's geography.

In 1830, he joined the Académie des inscriptions et belles-lettres while teaching as the professor of the Persian language in the Collège de France. In 1834, he was named president of the Société asiatique. In 1841, he was appointed "Pair de France" in the Chambre des Pairs in Paris. He became Chevalier of the Légion d'honneur (1845) and was president of the Société asiatique until his death on 28 January 1847.

Bibliography: Iradj Amini, *Napoléon et la Perse: les relations franco-persanes sous le Premier Empire, dans le contexte des rivalités entre la France, l'Angleterre et la Russi*, Paris, 1995. Šarif Edrisi, *Nozhat al-moštāq fi ek̲terāq al-āfāq*, tr. Pierre Amédée Jaubert as *Géographie d'Edrisi. tr. . . . d'après deux manuscrits de la Bibliothèque du roi et accompagnée de notes*, 2 vols., Paris, 1836-40. Jacob C. Hurewitz, tr. and ed., *The Middle East and North Africa in World Affaris: A Documentary*, 2 vols., New Haven, 1975-79. Pierre Amédée Jaubert, *Voyage en Arménie et en Perse, fait dans les années 1805 et 1806*, Paris, 1821; tr. ʿAliqoli Eʿtemād

Moqaddam as *Mosāfarat dar Armanestān wa Irān*, Tehran, 1968. Idem, *Éléments de la grammaire turque*, Paris, 1823. B. W. Robinson, "Persian Painting under the Zand and Qājār," in *Cambridge History of Iran* VII: *From Nadir Shah to the Islamic Republic*, Cambridge and New York, 1991, pp. 870-89.

(NADER NASIRI-MOGHADDAM)

JAVĀNMARDI or *FOTOWWA* denote a wide variety of amorphous associations with initiation rituals and codes in the Islamic world, primarily in its eastern regions. They also refers to the ideological or philosophical underpinnings of such associations, namely an ethical system dominated by altruism, magnanimity, liberality, and unquestioning loyalty to fellow members of the association. The personal noun associated with *fotowwa* is *fatā* "young" (pl. *fetyān*).

Fotowwa did not exist as an identifiable institution in the time of the Prophet (Cahen, 1959, pp. 32-34). The term *fatā* nonetheless occurs in the Qurʾān (12:30, 18:60, 21:60, and in the plural forms *fetya* and *fetyān*: 12:36, 12:62, 18:10, 18:13). In the last of these verses, which refers to the People of the Cave (*aṣḥāb al-kahf*), the term may have a laudatory sense: "They were young men who believed in their Lord and We increased them in guidance." It was certainly interpreted in this way by later commentators, such as Rašid-al-Din Meybodi, who pointed out that the Qurʾān refers to a number of prophets including Abraham (Ebrāhim), Joshua (Yušaʿ), and Joseph (Yusof) as *fatā* and used the occasion of elucidating the quoted verse on the *aṣḥāb al-kahf* to sketch the general principles of *javānmardi* (Meybodi, V, pp. 668-69; *Tarjama-ye tafsir-e Ṭabari* III, p. 940, both using the term *javānmard*). Even if such interpretations be questioned as an attribution to the Qurʾān of later semantic developments, it is certain that the term *fotowwa* was sometimes used in pre-Islamic Arabia to designate values such as generosity, hospitality, courage, and solidarity, and it is possible that here, as on other occasions, the Qurʾān infused with partially new content a term already current in the Arabian environment (Farès, pp. 79-80). Worthy of mention in the same connection as well as the later designation of Imam ʿAli b. Abi Ṭāleb (q.v.) as *sayyed al-fetyān* is the well-known account of a divine utterance "*la fatā ellā ʿAli*" (There is no young brave man but ʿAli) during the battle of Oḥod (Ṭabari, III, p. 1402, tr., VII. p. 120; Kohlberg, p. 846). In any event, *fotowwa* was initially an individual quality, lacking in organizational associations.

The use of the term *fotowwa* with social and organizational implications arose outside the Arabian peninsula, in Iraq and Persia, and it may therefore owe its origin to institutions already existing there in pre-Islamic times (Baldick, pp. 352-61). It has thus recently been proposed (Zakeri, 1995b, pp. 303-4) that the earliest attestation of the term *fotowwa* with the connotations attached to it in Islamic culture is to be found in the poetry of Baššār b. Bord (d. 783), an Arabic poet of Persian descent. If this be true, it is possible that Persian *šoʿubi*s such as Baššār were seeking to popularize *fotowwa* in the Islamic milieu as an institution inherited from the Sasanian era. According to this line of thought, *fotowwa* was the social and ethical code practiced by *āzādān*, a class of Persian nobility (see ĀZĀD), which consisted of small landholders and warriors who served as military commanders, administrators, and court bodyguards. Their ethos is said varyingly to have been designated as *āzādagi*, implying bravery and readiness to help actively the defenseless, and as *javānmardi*, with a more abstract meaning of moral and spiritual nobility. On the other hand, in a reference to what may have been the predecessors of *javānmardān*, they are "described in the Pahlavi commentary to *Vidēvdād* 3.41 as those who believed that robbing the rich to give to the poor was a meritorious act." In the Islamic period, *javānmardi* is often used as a synonym for terms such as *ʿayyāri* (see ʿAYYĀR) and *āzādi* that were used in the Persian context (Hanaway, pp. 161-63). The close correspondence in meaning between the Pers. *javānmardi* and the Ar. *fotowwa*, both combining the senses of youth and moral refinement, might be taken to imply a loan translation, in one direction or the other. It is more likely, however, that a confluence took place between similar concepts and traditions.

One argument in favor of a possible Persian origin for the *fotowwa* consists of the initiation ritual surrounding the admission of new members, which always includes the binding on (*šadd*) of a belt, twisted thrice around the waist of a new initiate to represent the three stages of religious knowledge and practice known as *šariʿat*, *ṭariqat*, and *ḥaqiqat* (Taeschner, 1979, p. 495; Massignon, "Shadd"). The *šadd* bears a clear resemblance to the *kustig*, the belt with which a Zoroastrian male is girded on reaching the age of fifteen as a sign of maturity. It, too, is twisted around the waist three times, to signify the three cardinal principles of "Good Speech, Good Thoughts and Good Acts" (Dhabhar, ed., chap. 46). It should, however, be noted that there is a difference between the two practices, the former denoting initiation and the latter being a rite of passage, and that the Zoroastrian *kustīg* is meant to demarcate the noble from the ignoble parts of the body, an element lacking in the *šadd* of the *fotowwa*. It is also noteworthy that Salmān Fārsi (Ar. Fāresi) is generally regarded as having been entrusted with the *šadd* of the Prophet's Companions (Massignon, 1963, tr. Unvala, p. 20), which might further support the thesis of an exclusively Persian origin for *fotowwa*. As pointed out above, however, *fotowwa* had not taken on institutional form in the time of the Prophet, apart from which many roles have been posthumously attributed to Salmān Fārsi in the complete absence of historical evidence.

DIFFERENT FORMS OF THE *FOTOWWA*.

Fetyān as an urban militia or associations in the Omayyad and ʿAbbasid periods. The military units constituted by the *āzādān* under the Sasanians remained mostly intact in the early Islamic period and were affiliated to the Arabs as clients, being employed by them, as by their former masters, to wage war on the frontiers of the empire, to constitute a personal guard or entourage (*ḡelmān/ḡolāmān, šākeriya, mawāli*), or to form a police force (*šorṭa, maʿuna* "auxiliaries," *aḥdāṯ*) in major cities such as Basra and Kufa (Zakeri, 1995b, pp. 112-28). It is in connection with such functions that we find the first mention of *fetyān* as organized groups, in reference to Basra in 683. In that year, Māh Farvardin (var. Māh Afridun), the Persian leader of the auxiliary bands in Basra, addressed his followers as *javānmardān*, a term translated by the Arab narrator as *fetyān* (Moḥammad b. Ḥabib, I, pp. 113-14; Ṭabari, I/1, p. 454; Zakeri, 1995b, p. 200). These urban militias are sometimes also referred to as *aḥdāṯ* "young men" (Moḥammad b. Ḥabib, I, p. 684; Ebn Qotayba, p. 414). Widespread in all Persian cities from the 7th century onwards, where they were known as *abnāʾ al-aḥrār* or *āzādmardiya*, groups of this type formed a significant part of the coalition that helped bring the ʿAbbasids come to power (Zakeri, 1995b, pp. 265-89). Thereafter they are seen in the various quarters of Baghdad securing public order and caring for the weak in their respective localities under the direction of a head known as the *raʾis* or *ṣāḥeb al-rabʿ* (Balāḏori, p. 404). They were also aligned with different and sometimes conflicting religious groups, which accounts not only for their participation in religious festivals as corporate groups but also for their role in factional and sectarian strife, particularly in the events that accompanied the siege of Baghdad in 813 (Hoffmann, pp. 27-44; Cheikh-Moussa, pp. 160-88; for modern scholarship on the part played by these *fetyān* in the life of Baghdad and other urban centers, see Sabari, pp. 77-100; Cahen, 1959).

Al-fetyān al-lāhun were associations of hedonistic youth from whom the ethical principles of *fotowwa* appears to have been conspicuously absent, with the single exception of loyalty to the group. From the early 8th century onwards, chronicles and works of *adab* speak of affluent and often unmarried youths who formed associations dedicated to hedonism and the pursuit of amusement. They called themselves *fetyān al-ṣedq*, vowing to support their comrades at times of need and to keep their proceedings secret from outsiders (Ebrāhim Bayhaqi, pp. 248-53; ʿAbbās b. al-Aḥnaf, p. 256). Their rules of conduct, including prescriptions for eating, drinking, and general public comportment, were enforced by an individual known as the *qāżi al-fetyān* (lit. the *fetyān*'s judge), no doubt by way of parody of the official *qāżi*s named by the Abbasids (Jāḥeẓ, 1958, p. 67; Abu Ḥayyān Tawḥidi, 1965, p. 175; idem, 1966, IV, p. 171). Little concerned with Islamic morality or *šariʿa* ordinances, they were much devoted to gambling, music, and dancing; and for their indulgence they maintained communal houses known by the Persian name of *daskara* "seigniorial estate" (Taeschner, 1979, pp. 86, 206, 208, 610). Affiliated to these circles was the celebrated Persian singer and musician Ebrāhim Mawṣeli (d. 804, q.v.), who was known to his colleagues as *al-fatā al-Mawṣeli* (Abu'l-Faraj Eṣfahāni, V, pp. 154-56, 188). The presence of the Christian singer Ḥonayn Ḥiri (d. ca. 728) among the *fetyān* of Najaf and the welcome he received from the *fetyān* of Ḥemṣ on a visit to their city is an indication that *al-fetyān al-lāhun* were inter-confessional, or at least were open to participation by non-Muslims (Abu'l-Faraj Eṣfahāni, V, II, pp. 341-47). Archery and hunting, especially with trained hounds, also ranked high among the interests of the hedonist *fetyān*; the latter pursuit in particular would often bring them into conflict with the authorities. They had their own mode of dress (*ziyy al-fetyān*), greased and dyed their hair, and were further recognizable by the distinctive batons (*meḵṣara*) they carried (Ebn Qotayba, I, p. 299; Ebn ʿAbd Rabbeh, V, p. 48; Abu'l-Faraj Eṣfahāni, I, p. 408, n. 7). Many of these characteristics of *al-fetyān al-lāhun* were to be found in the poet musician Ebn al-Ṭabib (d. ca. 844). He delighted in hunting with hounds, cultivating lute players and keeping the company of the *šoṭṭār* (Kotobi, I, pp. 163-64). The occurrence here of the term *šoṭṭār* (sing. *šāṭer*) is an indication that it may sometimes have been synonymous with *fetyān*. Abu Ḥayyān Tawḥidi (q.v.), writing around 984, described the *šoṭṭār* not only as muscular youths given to the lifting of heavy stones and talking pugnaciously while twisting their mustaches, but also as claimants to *fotowwa* and *javānmardi* (Abu Ḥayyān Tawḥidi, 1965, p. 293; see also Jāḥeẓ, 1938-47, I, pp. 168-69).

The martial fotowwa of frontier regions. It was centered especially in Khorasan, Transoxania, and Sistān, where it operated as a unifying ideal emphasizing piety, steadfastness, self-sacrifice, courage, and fortitude. It was professed by local associations of armed men fighting initially for the expansion of Islam, and included both volunteers and members of the regular army. They were known varyingly as *ḡāziān, mojāhedun, morābeṭun, motaṭawweʿa*, and *ʿayyārān*, who were referred to by Vasiliĭ V. Barthold (pp. 214-15) as "the guild of warriors for the Faith." The origins of these groups may be sought in the auxiliary forces raised by the Omayyads and the early ʿAbbasids in border areas where their own military resources were limited. In times of peace, these military auxiliaries, for whom fighting had become a way of life and their sole source of income, were easily transformed into brigands and became a threat to the government that had first recruited them. Thus straightforward robbers (*loṣuṣ*) are often called *fetyān* (Ẓahir-a-Din ʿAli Bayhaqi, I, p. 19). These robber bands sometimes acquired a popular dimension of the Robin Hood type. The classical example is Yaʿqub b. Layṯ, founder of the Saffarid dynasty in eastern Persia, who began his career as leader of a band of outlaws claiming to act as volunteers (*motaṭawweʿa*) fighting the Kharijites in Sistān (*Tāriḵ-e Sistān*, pp. 200 ff.; Bosworth, pp. 112-13). Less successful than Yaʿqub but also well known in his own time was a certain Aswad Zobd (d. ca. 974) of Baghdad. He accused the rulers of exploiting and impoverishing the people and sought to justify his own acts of robbery by referring to injustices he had personally suffered. Among the virtues ascribed to him are that he never left his victims entirely destitute, took nothing from people with less than a thousand dirhams, and never molested women (Hamadāni, p. 217; Abu Ḥayyān Tawḥidi, 1939-44, III, pp. 160-61). Such self-restraint may have been inspired in part by the need to gain the support or at least tolerance of the communities, both urban and rural, among whom the bandits led their precarious existence, but it also contributed heavily to the emergence of a rich folkloric literature in Persia extolling the deeds of heroes who robbed the rich while sparing the poor (Gaillard, 1987, *passim*). In general, the line separating the warrior from the rebel, and the militiaman from the outlaw, was extremely diffuse; all were recruited from the same class.

Fotowwa in the context of Sufism. The connections of *fotowwa* with Sufism date from the early 12th century and are first seen in Khorasan, presumably as a result of Sufi participation in the *jehād* (q.v.) and interaction with the frontier warriors (*ḡāzi*) mentioned above. This fusion of the Sufi and the *ḡāzi* is exemplified by a certain Nuḥ, a Sufi and head of the *fetyān* of Nišāpur who also qualified as a warrior *ʿayyār* (Salinger, p. 484). It was buttressed by the Hadith attributed to the Prophet that distinguished two forms of *jehād*: the lesser (*aṣḡar*) waged against the external enemies of the faith, and the greater (*akbar*), waged against the sinful and neglectful tendencies within man's inner being. Viewing the same duality somewhat differently, Henry Corbin speaks of a transition from "chevalerie militaire" to "chevalerie spirituelle," which, according to him, is mirrored in Persian literature in the shift from the heroic epic of Ferdowsi to the mystical epic of Šehāb-al-Din Yaḥyā Sohravardi (Corbin's Introd. to Ṣarrāf, pp. 6-7).

The first author who devoted a full-length treatise to *fotowwa* was the Khorasanian Sufi ʿAbd al-Raḥmān Solami (d. 1021). He prescribed as essential to the concept a universal generosity that extended even to the feeding of stray dogs, a renunciation of one's rights and claims in favor of others, and a view of oneself as inescapably lower than all other creatures. This last feature in particular suggests a connection between *fotowwa* and the Malāmatiya or "People of Blame." It often seems in fact that for Solami *fotowwa* and *malāmat* were entirely analogous concepts (see Solami, ed. ʿAfifi, pp. 86-120). Solami's pupil, Abu'l-Qāsem Qošayri (d. 1073), discussed *fotowwa* at some length (pp. 472-78), and the term entered the general vocabulary of Sufism, although some Sufis sought to define it in idiosyncratic terms.

The absorption by the Sufis of the concept of *fotowwa* led in turn to its assimilation by a group commonly associated with them, the artisan and trade guilds. It is uncertain when the guilds arose and when they established their connections with Sufism; the earliest reliable information about them dates from the 13th century. Louis Massignon's assertion that they came into being in the former Sasanian capital of Ctesiphon (q.v.), where they absorbed the pre-existing principles of *fotowwa* is at best an unproven hypothesis, relying on the oral traditions of some of the guilds (Massignon, 1952, p. 401). In the context of the guilds, the term *fotowwa* acquires a new shade of meaning as the code of rules and conduct for their members, ultimately put down in writing for memorization and recitation, especially during rites of initiation. It thus led to the production of a series of manuals in Arabic, Persian, and Turkish entitled *Ketāb al-fotowwa*, *Fotowwat-nāma* or *Kasb-nāma*, and *Fütüvvet-name* respectively (Gölpınarlı, Ivanow, Mokri, Ṣarrāf). There was some variation among texts of this type, depending on the occupations of the guilds for which they were composed, which were further differentiated by the patrons they invoked (typically a prophet or one of the Companions of the Prophet Moḥammad) and the Sufi lineage to which they were affiliated. Useful information concerning the *fotowwa* of the guilds is to be found in ʿOnṣor-al-Maʿāli Kaykāvus b. Eskandar's *Qābus-nāma* (chap. 44), which significantly groups them together with the *javānmardān* and the Sufis. He distinguishes between the *fotowwa* of guilds or professional associations (those of the merchants, the physicians, the astrologers, and the poets), and that of the *ʿayyārān-e javānmard*. The former includes rules of professional conduct as well as ethical principles, while the latter is a reaffirmation of virtues such as bravery, patience, loyalty, purity, and honesty.

The caliphal fotowwa of al-Nāṣer (r. 1180-1225). The Great Saljuqs were able to reduce the influence of urban *fotowwa* groups by means of strong centralization. Many of their members were absorbed in municipal administration and in policing functions, but, with the decline of the Saljuq dynasty, the *fetyān* reemerged as an unstable and divisive element in the urban centers of Iraq and Persia, forming armed groups that vied for domination. As part of an imaginative attempt to unify his realm under his own spiritual as well as political authority, the caliph al-Nāṣer chose to reform and bring under his control the discordant *fotowwa* groups rather than opposing and combating them. To this end, he first joined one such group two years after becoming caliph and soon thereafter proscribed all other groups. Next he declared himself master of an official Sufi-tinged *fotowwa* organization, inviting all Muslim rulers who nominally recognized his sovereignty to join, thus creating an additional link of obedience to the caliphate. He was assisted in this enterprise by the well-known Sufi shaikh, Šehāb-al-Din ʿOmar Sohravardi (d. 1234), who traveled on his behalf to Konya to enroll Kaykāvus (d. 1220), the Saljuq ruler of Anatolia, in the caliphal *fotowwa* organization. Sohravardi's efforts were successful, and it seems likely that it is to his visit that the origins of *fotowwa* in Turkish Anatolia (from where it spread to the Balkans in the Ottoman era) must be ascribed. Nonetheless, the fact that the adherents of *fotowwa* in Anatolia were designated not as *fati* or as *javānmard* but as *aḵi* may point to the existence of an indigenously Turkish element on to which the traditions of *fotowwa* were grafted. There was for long the tendency to regard *aḵi* simply as the Turkish pronunciation of Ar. *aḵi* (my brother), which would certainly be consonant with the ethos of *fotowwa*, but the possibility of a Turkish etymology is not to be excluded. The word *aqi* is mentioned in Maḥmud Kāšḡari's dictionary of early

Turkish, with the meanings of "generous, courageous, virtuous," and a progression *aqi>aki>ahi* would be entirely consistent with the phonetic development of Anatolian Turkish (Bayram, pp. 3-5). It is also worth noting that the Turkish word *yigit*, like Arabic *fati* and Persian *javānmard*, means both youthful and courageous or virtuous, which may be explained either as the result of loan translation, or of simple coincidence. Apart from Anatolia, al-Nāṣer's initiative also enjoyed some success in Syria and Egypt, where the caliphal *fotowwa* continued to flourish for a while even after the destruction of the caliphate in Baghdad in 1258 (Taeschner, "Fotowwa)

Books composed for al-Nāṣer's aristocratic *fotowwa*, such the *Ketāb al-fotowwa* of the Hanbalite jurist Ebn al-Meʿmār (d. 1244), afford considerable insight into its hierarchical structure, ceremonies of initiation, and rich terminology, much of it derived from the varieties of *fotowwa* detailed above, which the caliph's organization was intended to supersede. According to Ebn al-Meʿmār, the adherents of *fotowwa* are all bound together as "companions" or "comrades" (*refāq* or *rofaqā*ʾ). A familial relationship among them is implied by the use of terms such as "elder" (*kabir*/*pišqadam*) and "younger" (*ṣaḡir*), "father" (*ab*/*pedar*) and "son" (*ebn*/*pesar*), and "grandfather" (*jadd*) for the supreme elder (Pers. equivalents of the Ar. terms as used by Moḥammad Āmoli, *Nafāʾes al-fonun* apud Ṣarrāf, pp. 75-78). Entry into the organization thus signified that it had superseded the family as focus of loyalty. This use of relational terms led naturally to the construction of chains of initiation (*salāsel*) similar to those of the Sufi orders, all of which led back through Salmān Fārsi and Imam ʿAli b. Abi Ṭāleb to the Prophet Moḥammad. Members of the same rank were "brothers" (*ʿadil*, lit. "equal") to each other and insofar as they drank in the name of a particular *kabir* they formed a "party" (*ḥezb*, pl. *aḥzāb*) or "group" (*ṭāʾefa*, pl. *ṭawāʾef*). The combination of several such "parties" or "groups" constituted a "house" (*bayt*, pl. *boyut*/*k̲āndān*), the leader of which was varyingly designated as *zaʿim al-qawm*, *šayk̲*, *moqaddam*, *qāʾed*, *ʿaqid*, *ab*, and *kabir al-bayt*. As in all sodalities and brotherhoods, much emphasis was placed on the initiation ritual, which according to Ebn al-Meʿmār took place in two stages. A young postulant (*ṭāleb*) would seek out a postulator (*maṭlub*) to supervise him for a trial period and recommend him for formal initiation. His actual sponsor for the initiation would be, however, a *kabir* who, after performing the key rite of girding (*šadd*/*miān bastan*) with the waistband (*futa*/*ḥezām*/*kamarband*), received his pledge of loyalty (*ʿaqd*) to *fotowwa* and welcomed him into the group. Although now a "girded" (*mašdud*/*miān-basta*) member, he remained a novice (*morid*) for an indefinite time before becoming a fully-fledged companion (*rafiq*), an advancement signified by the ceremonial donning of the distinctive garment of *fotowwa* (*lebās al-fotowwa*), generally consisting of a pair of trousers (*sarāwil al-fotowwa*). Sometimes weapons were substituted for the trousers. On the same occasion, salted water would be drunk (*šorb*) from the bowl (*kaʾs*, *qadaḥ*) of *fotowwa*. The whole ceremony was known as "completion" (*takmil* or *takfia*). Discipline within a "party" would be administered on behalf of the *kabir* by a *wakil*. The *zaʿim al-qawm* would assign to a chief (*naqib*) the function of supervising all initiation ceremonies for his "house" and delivering the speech (*k̲oṭba*), welcoming the new initiate (Ebn al-Meʿmār, pp. 190-230; Taeschner, 1979, pp. 79-81; Salinger, p. 485).

A tripartite division of the members of *fotowwa* not mentioned by Ebn al-Meʿmār can be gleaned from other sources of the same period (e.g., Najm-al-Din Zarkub, in Ṣarrāf, pp. 187-90). The three classes consisted of those whose adherence was purely verbal (*qawli*), those who drank the salted water (*šorbi*), and those who undertook the obligation of wearing a sword (*sayfi*). These categories may have reflected differing degrees or modalities of commitment to *fotowwa* and have thus been comparable to the lay brothers, the clerics, and the knights in Western knighthood, or the fathers, brothers, and lay people in the European religious orders (Taeschner, 1979, p. 81).

It is resemblances such as these, as well as the nature of the then available sources, that led 19th-century European scholars to conclude that al-Nāṣer's *fotowwa* was a kind of chivalrous or knightly order and to render *fatā* or *javānmard* as "knight," "chevalier," or "Ritter." It should, however, be noted that knighthood was tightly linked to European feudalism, whereas the aristocratic *fotowwa* of al-Nāṣer had no such linkage to a socio-economic system.

Fotowwa in the Mongol and post-Mongol periods. The fall of Baghdad to the Mongols in 1258 brought to an end both the ʿAbbasid caliphate and the particular type of *fotowwa* linked to it. However, the *fotowwa* of the *ʿayyār*s persisted and even flourished in Persia. The resourcefulness they demonstrated in the face of the Mongol invasion of Khorasan combined with their support of the Kart dynasty in Herat (1245-389; see ĀL-e KART) increased their popular appeal considerably. In addition, the Sarbadarids of Khorasan, who rose against the fiscal exactions of the Mongols and managed to dislodge the last of them from Persia, had close ties with the *fotowwa* circles. Describing the early activity of the two brothers who inaugurated the movement in Bayhaq in 1337, Ebn Baṭṭuṭa says that "they were killers (*fottāk*), men of the type known in Iraq as *šoṭṭār*, in Khorasan as *sarbadār*, and in the Maghrib as *soqura* (hawks; Ebn Baṭṭuṭa, p. 383). This characterization points to a revival or persistence of the bandit *fotowwa* well-known from earlier times, but at the same time the egalitarian principles that some modern scholars, especially Ilya P. Petrushevsky (pp. 304-9), have perceived in the Sarbadarid movement has caused them to view it as a type of popular revolution.

The Sufi-tinged *fotowwa* of Sohravardi and his predecessors also enjoyed a prolongation into the Mongol and post-Mongol periods. Persian texts such as the *Fotowwat-nāma* of Najm-al-Din Zarkub (in Ṣarrāf, ed., pp. 167-218) contain a wealth of information concerning the rites of initiation and their significance. Zarkub explains that *fotowwa* is the key to all three stages of religious knowledge: *šariʿat*, *ṭariqat* and *ḥaqiqat*. The initiatic trousers symbolize "chastity" (*ʿeffat*); the belt is a symbol of "bravery" (*šajāʿat*); the water drunk in the initiatic ceremony is a symbol of "wisdom" (*ḵerad*); and the salt mixed into it symbolizes "justice" (*ʿadālat*). Two Kobrawi Sufis, ʿAlāʾ-al-Dawla Semnāni (d. 1336, q.v.) and his pupil Mir Sayyed ʿAli Hamadāni (d. 1384), showed considerable interest in *fotowwa*. Semnāni wrote a brief treatise on the subject, in which he incorporated several chapters of Ebn al-Meʿmār's work as well as the *Toḥfat al-ekwān* of ʿAbd-al-Razzāq Kāšāni (d. ca. 1329). Hamadāni was actively involved in *fotowwa*, having received the *lebās al-fotowwa* from a certain Shaikh Moḥammad Aḏkāni (d. 1376), and also composed a *Resāla-ye fotowwatiya*. For Hamadāni, just as *fotowwa* is an essential part of dervish ethics (*faqr*), the garb of the *fetyān*, consisting of a distinctive cap (*kolāh*) and trousers (*sarāwil*), is mandatory wear for the dervish (Taeschner, 1979, p. 240). The most detailed of all treatises on Sufi-colored *fotowwa*, whether in Arabic or Persian, is the *Fotowwat-nāma-ye solṭāni* of Wāʿeẓ Kāšefi (d. 1505), a Naqšbandi in his Sufi affiliations. This book provides much rare information on the ethics, initiation rites, clothing, and hierarchical relationships prevailing in the associations of the water-sellers, weightlifters, wrestlers, poetry-reciters, storytellers, etc. Above all, it shows that the *fotowwa* was still quite widespread in Persia towards the close of the 15th century.

Later manifestations of *fotowwa* can be found in the popular urban associations known as *dāšhā*, *jāhelān*, *šāterān*, and *yatimān*, all of which were linked to the *zur-ḵāna*, the traditional Persian gymnasium. Most towns had a *zur-ḵāna* in which the wrestlers and athletes performed their exercises before a large portrait depicting Imam ʿAli b. Abi Ṭāleb, their patron. A patron closer in time was Pahlavān Maḥmud Ḵʷārazmi (d. 1322), also known as Puriā-ye Wali, who was considered an epitome of strength and chivalrous character. *Fotowwa* or *javān-mardi* seems to have provided the *zur-ḵāna* with its code of honor, organizational principles, and rites of initiation.

Bibliography: ʿAbbās b. al-Aḥnaf, *Divān*, ed. ʿĀteka Ḵazraji, Cairo, 1954. Moḥammad Aḥmad ʿAbd-al-Mawlā, *al-Ayyārun wa'l-šoṭṭār al-baḡdādiya fi'l-taʾriḵ al-ʿabbāsi*, Alexandria, 1986. ʿAbd-al-Razzāq Kāšāni Samarqandi, *Toḥfat al-ekwān fi ḵaṣāʾes al-fetyān*, in Ṣarrāf, ed., pp. 1-57; ed. Moḥammad Dāmādi, Tehran, 1990 (both the Ar. text and its Pers. tr. rendered by Kāšāni himself). Abu Ḥayyān Tawḥidi, *al-Emtāʿ wa'l-moʾānasa*, ed. Aḥmad Amin and Aḥmad Zayn, 3 vols., Cairo, 1939-44. Idem, *Aḵlāq al-wazirayn*, ed. M. T. Ṭanji, Damascus, 1965. Idem, *al-Baṣāʾer wa'l-ḏaḵāʾer*, ed. E. Kaylāni, 10 vols., Damascus, 1964-66. Abu'l-Faraj Eṣfahāni, *Ketāb al-aḡāni*, 20 vols, 3rd. ed., Cairo, 1345-/1926-. Abu'l-ʿAlā ʿAfifi, *al-Malāmatiya wa'l-Ṣufiyā wa ahl al-fotowwa*, Cairo, 1364/1945. Iraj Afšār, "Fotowwat-nāma-ye āhangarān [comp. after 873/1468]," in *Farḵonda payām: yādgār-nāma-ye ostād Doktor Ḡolām-Ḥosayn Yusofi*, Mashad, 1981, pp. 53-59. Hamid Algar, "Shadd," in EI^2 IX, pp. 166-68. Šams-al-Din Moḥammad b. Maḥmud Āmoli, *Nafāʾes al-fonun fi ʿarāʾes al-ʿoyun*, the chap. on *fotwwa* (mainly based on Ebn al-Meʿmār, pp. 110-28), in Ṣarrāf, ed., pp. 58-88. Reza Arasteh, "The Character, Organization and Social Role of the *lutis* (*Javan-Mardan*) in the Traditional Iranian Society of the Nineteenth Century," *Journal of the Economc and Social history of the Orient* 4, 1961, pp. 47-52. Idem, "The Social Role of the *Zurkhana* (House of Strength) in Iranian Urban Communities during the Nineteenth Century," *Der Islam* 37, 1961, pp. 256-59. G. G. Arnakis, "Futuwwa Traditions in Ottoman Empire: Akhis, Bektashi Dervishes and Craftsmen," *Journal of Near Eastern Studies* 12, 1953, pp. 232-52. Mehrdād Bahār, "Varzeš-e bāstāni-e Irān wa rišahā-ye tāriḵi-e ān," *Čistā* 1, 1981, pp. 140-59; repr in idem, *Jostār-i čand dar farhang-e Irān*, Tehran, 1997, pp. 163-85. Aḥmad b. Yaḥyā Balāḏori, *Ketāb fotuḥ al-boldān*, ed. Michaël Jan de Goeje, Leiden, 1866; repr., Leiden, 1968. Julian Baldick, "The Iranian Origin of the *Futuwwa*," *Istituto Universitario Orientale di Napoli* 50, 1990, pp. 345-61. Vasiliĭ V. Barthold, *Turkestan down to the Mongol Invasion*, 3rd rev. ed., Gibb Memorial Series 5, London, 1968. Alessandro Bausani, "An Islamic Echo of the "Trickster"? The ʿAyyārān of Indo-Persian and Malay Romances," in *Gururajamañjarikā: Studi in onore di Giuseppe Tucci*, Instituto Universitario Orientale, 2 vols., Naples, 1974, pp. 457-67. Ebrāhim b. Moḥammad Bayhaqi, *Ketāb al-maḥāsen wa'l-masāwi*, ed. Friedrich Schwally, Giessen, 1902. Ẓahir-al-Din ʿAli b. Zayd Bayhaqi, *Tatemmat ṣewān al-ḥekma*, ed. M. Šafiʿ, Lahore, 1351. Mikail Bayram, *Ahi evren ve ahi teskilāti'nin kurulusu*, Konya, 1991. Jiri Bečka, "The Folk-novel Samak ʿayyār," *Archiv Orientální* 58, Prague, 1990, pp. 150-55. Clifford E. Bosworth, *Sistan under the Arabs*, Rome, 1968. Nes Çağatay, *Bir Türk kurumu olan ahilik*, Konya, 1981. Claude Cahen, "Aḥdāth," in EI^2, p. 256. Idem, "Mouvements et organisations populaires dans les villes de l'Asie musulmane au moyen âge: milices et associations de Foutouwwa," *Recueils de la Société Jean Bodin* 7, 1955, pp. 273-88. Idem, *Mouvements populaires et autonomisme urbain dans l'Asie Musulmane du Moyen Age*, Leiden, 1959 (originally published in *Arabica* 5, 1958, pp. 225-50; 6, 1959, pp. 25-56, 233-65). Alan Cameron, *Circus Factions: Blues and Greens at Rome and Byzantium*, Oxford, 1976, esp. pp. 341-43 in reply to Vryonis. A. Cheikh-Moussa, "L'historien et la littérature arabe médiévale," *Arabica* 43, 1996, pp. 152-88. Henry Corbin, "Juvenilité et chevalerie (*jawānmardī*) en Islam iranien," *Eranos-Jahrbuch* 40, 1971, pp. 311-56. Idem, "Tradition abrahamique et chevalerie spirituelle (*jawānmardī*)," in idem, *En Islam iranien: aspects spirituels et philosophiques*, 4 vols., Paris, 1971-73, IV, pp. 410-60. Idem, *Traites des compagnons-chevaliers*, tr. Eḥsān Narāqi as *Āyin-e javānmardi*, Tehran, 1984 (the book also contains articles by Iranian scholars).

Moḥammad-Taqi Dānešpažuh, "Do manbaʿ barā-ye tāriḵ-e javānmardi wa fotowwat," *Rāhnemā-ye ketāb* 16/7-9, 1973, pp. 406-13. Darviš ʿAli b. Yusof Karkohri, *Ketāb zobdat al-ṭariq elā Allāh* (comp. 805/1402), chap. 6, in Ṣarrāf, ed., pp. 219-24. Bahmanji N. Dhabhar, ed., *Saddar Naṣr and Saddar Bundahesh*, Bombay, 1909. George Duby, "Les *Jeunes* dans la société aristocratique au xiie siècle," *Annales: économies, société, civilisations* 19, 1964, pp. 835-46. Ebn ʿAbd Rabbeh, *al-ʿEqd al-Farid*, ed. Aḥmad Amin et al., 7 vols., Cairo, 1940-53. Ebn Baṭṭuṭa, *Reḥla*, Beirut, 1960. Ebn Meʿmār Bağdādi, *Ketāb al-fotowwa*, ed. Moṣṭafā Jawād et al., Baghdad, 1958-60, Jawād's Introd., pp. 1-99. Ebn Qotayba Dinavari, *ʿOyun al-Akbār*, 4 vols. in 2, Cairo, 1925-30. I. S. Enderwitz, *Liebe als Beruf: al-ʿAbbās ibn al-Aḥnaf und das Ġazal*, Beirut, 1995, esp. pp. 31-65. Ḡolām-Reżā Enṣāfpur, *Tārik wa farhang-e zur-kāna wa gruhhā-ye ejtemāʿi-e zur-kānarow*, Tehran, 1974. Bichr Farès, "Futuwwa," in *EI*[1], suppl., pp. 79-89. Willem M. Floor, "Aṣnāf," in *EIr* I, pp. 772-78. Idem, "The Guilds of Iran: An Overview from the Earliest Beginnings Till 1972," *ZDMG* 125, 1975, pp. 99-116. Idem, "The Political Role of the lūtīs in Qājār Iran," in *Interdisziplinäre Iran-Forschung*, Wiesbaden, 1979, pp. 179-89. Idem, "Guilds and Futuvvat in Iran," *ZDMG* 134, 1984, pp. 106-14. *Fotowwat-nāma-ye čitsāzān* (comp. after 8th/14th cent.), in Ṣarrāf, ed., pp. 225-39; tr. Henry Corbin, ibid., pp. 87-99.

Marina Gaillard, "La notion de javânmardi à travers les textes anciens d'expression persane," M.A. thesis, University of Paris III, Sorbonne Nouvelle, 1978. Idem, "Samak-e ʿAyyār et Xoršid-Šāh: héroes réel et héroes apparent," *Studia Iranica* 14/2, 1985, pp. 199-221. Idem, *Le livre de Samak-e ʿAyyâr: structure et idéologie du roman persan médiéval*, Paris, 1987. Abdülbaki Gölpınarlı, "İslâm ve Türk illerinde Fütüvvet teşkilatı," in *İstanbul Üniversitesi iktisat fakültesi mecmuası* 11, 1949-50, pp. 1-354. Esmāʿil Ḥākemi, "Āyin-e forowwat wa ʿayyāri," Sokan 17, pp. 271-78, 523-27. Idem, *Āyin-e fotowwat wa Javānmardi*, Tehran, 2003. Mir Sayyed ʿAli Hamadāni, *Resāla-ye fotowwatiya*, ed. Marijan Molé, in *Şarkiyat mecmuası* 4, 1961, pp. 33-72. Moḥammad b. ʿAbd-al-malek Hamadāni, *Takmelat taʾrik al-Ṭabari*, Beirut, 1961. William L. Hanaway, "ʿAyyār ii: ʿAyyār in Persian Sources," in *EIr* III, pp. 161-63. Angelika Hartmann, *an-Nāṣir li-Dīn Allāh (1180-1225): Politik, Religion, Kultur in der späten ʿAbbāsidenzeit*, Berlin, 1975, esp. pp. 30-34, 92-108 (on the sources, purpose, and the impact of al-Nāṣer's reforms). R. Hartmann, "As-Sulamī's *Risālat al-Malāmatīja*," *Der Islam* 8, 1918a, pp. 157-203; note by O. Rescher, *Der Islam* 14, 1925, pp. 387-89. Idem, "Futuwwa und Malāma," *ZDMG* 72, 1918b, pp. 193-98. G. von Hoffman, "al-Amīn, al-Maʾmūn und der "Pöbel" von Baghdad in den Jahren 812/13," *ZDMG* 143, 1993, pp. 27-44. V. I. Ivanow, "Études sur les corporations musulmanes indo-persanes," *Revue des études islamiques* 1, 1927, pp. 249-72. Abu ʿOṯmān ʿAmr b. Baḥr Jāḥeẓ, *Ketāb al-ḥayawān*, ed., ʿAbd-Allāh Moḥammad Hārun, 7 vols., Cairo, 1938-47. Idem, *Ketāb al-bokalāʾ*, ed. Ṭāhā Ḥājeri, Cairo, 1958.

Parviz Nātel Kānlari, "Āʾin-e ʿayyāri," *Sokan* 18, 1968, pp. 1071-77; 19, 1969, pp. 19-26, 113-22, 263-67, 477-80. Maḥmud Kāšḡari, *Divān loğāt al-tork*, ed. K. M. Rifʿat Bilge, Istanbul, 1915-17. E. Khohlberg, "ʿAlī b. Abi Ṭāleb ii," in *EIr*. I, pp. 843-48. H. Koşay, "Small Businessmen's Organizations "Ahilik" (friendship) and Its Traditions," *Études Balkaniques (Sofia)* 15, 1979, pp. 101-9. Abu ʿAbd-Allāh Moḥammad b. Šāker Kotobi, *Fawāt al-wafayāt*, ed. Eḥsān ʿAbbās, 5 vols., Beirut, 1973-78. Moḥammad b. Ḥabib, *Ketāb al-naqāʾeż: Naqāʾeż Jarīr wa al-Farazdaq*, ed. A. A. Bevan as *The Nakāʾiḍ of Jarīr and al-Farazdaq*, 3 vols., Leiden, 1905-12. Moḥammad-Jaʿfar Maḥjub, "Samak-e ʿAyyār: setāyeš-nāma-ye delirihā wa javānmardihā," *Sokan* 11, 1960, pp. 667-77. Idem, "Samak-e ʿAyyār," *Kāveš* 1, 1960, pp. 65-67. Idem, "Āʾin-e ʿayyāri," *Sokan* 19, 1969, pp. 869-83, 1059-73, 1182-95; 20, 1970, pp. 38-51, 173-79, 301-11. Idem, "Oṣul-e fotowwat az naẓar-e Mawlānā Ḥosayn Wāʿeẓ Kāšefi," in Ḡolām-Reżā Sotuda, ed., *Majmuʿa-ye maqālāt-e nakostin kongara-ye taḥqiqāt-e irāni* III, Tehran, 1975, pp. 210-22. Idem, "Ravešhā-ye ʿayyāri wa nofud-e kār o kerdār-e ʿayyārān dar *Šāh-nāma*," *Honar o mardom*, nos. 177-78, 1977, pp. 2-13, no. 180, pp. 20-38. Idem, "Javānmardi dar Irān wa Eslām," *Irān-nāma/Iran-nameh* 11/1, 1993, pp. 7-16. Idem, *Āyin-e javānmardi yā fotowwat*, New York, 2000. Louis Massignon, "Shadd," in *EI*[1] IV, p. 245. Idem, "La 'futuwwa' ou 'pact d'honneur artisanal' entre les travailleurs musulmans au Moyen Age," *La Nouvelle Clio* 4, 1952, pp. 171-98. Idem, "Sur la Futuwwa," in Zeki Velidi Togan, ed., *Proceedings of the Twenty-second International Congress of Orientalists Held in Istanbul Sept. 15th to 22nd 1951* II: *Communications*, Leiden, 1957, pp. 277-79. Idem, "Salmān Pāk et les prémices spirituelles de l'Islam iranien," repr. in idem, *Opera Minora*, ed. Youakim Moubarac, 3 vols, Beirut, 1963; tr. Jamshedji M. Unvala, Bombay, 1955. I. Mélikoff-Sayer, "Abū Muslim, patron des Akhis," in *Proceedings of the XXIV International Congress of Orientalists, München 1957*, Wiesbaden, 1959, pp. 419-21. Idem, *Abū Muslim: le "porte-hache" du Khorassan dans la tradition épique turco-iranienne*, Paris, 1962. Abu'l-Fażl Rašid-al-Din Meybodi, *Kašf al-asrār wa ʿoddat al-abrār*, ed. ʿAli-Aṣḡar Ḥekmat, 10 vols., Tehran, 1952-60. H. G. Migeod, "Die Lūṭīs: Ein Ferment des Städtischen Lebens in Persien," *Journal of the Economic and Social History of the Orient* 2, 1959, pp. 82-91. M. Mokri, "Un traité persan relatif à la corporation prolétaire des porteurs d'eau musulmans," *Revue des études islamiques* 45, 1977, pp. 131-56.

Moḥammad-Rajab Najjār, *Ḥekāyāt al-šoṭṭār wa'l-ʿayyārin fi'l-torāṯ al-ʿarabi*, Kuwait, 1981. Ḥosayn Partow Baydāʾi Kāšāni, *Tārik-e varzeš-e bāstāni-e Īrān (Zur-kāna)*, Tehran, 1958. Najm-al-Din Abu Bakr Moḥammad b. Zarkub Tabrizi, *Fotowwat-nāma*, in Ṣarrāf, ed., pp. 167-218. ʿOnṣor-al-Maʿāli Kaykāvus b. Eskandar, *Qābus-nāma*, ed. Ḡolām-Ḥosayn Yusofi, Tehran, 1973; tr. Reuben Levy as *A Mirror for Princes: The Qābus Nāma*, London, 1951. Ilya P. Petrushevsky, *Islam in Iran*, tr. Hubert Evans, New York, 1985. Angelo M.

Piemontese, "L'organizzazione della 'Zurxâne' e la 'Futuwwa'," *Annali dell'Instituto Orientale di Napoli* 14, 1964, pp. 453-73. Idem, "La leggenda del santo-lottatore Pahlavān Maḥmūd Xvārezmi "Puryā-ye Valī" (m. 722/1322)," *Annali dell'Instituto Orientale di Napoli* 15, 1965, pp. 167-213. Idem, "La moderna terminologia della lotta tradizionale persiana," *Oriente Moderno* 45, 1965, pp. 787-801. Idem, "Il Capitolo sui "Pahlavān" delle "*Badayiʿ al-vaqāyiʿ*" di Vāṣefī," *Annali dell'Instituto Orientale di Napoli* 16, 1966, pp. 207-22. Idem, "Il Trattato Sulla Futuwwa (Fotovvatnāme-ye soltani) di Hosein Vāʿiz Kāšefi," *Atti del trezo Congresso studi arabi e islamici, Ravello, 1-6 Septembre 1966*, Ravello, 1967, pp. 557-63. Abu'l-Qāsem ʿAbd-al-Karim Qošayri, *al-Resāla al-Qošayriya fi ʿelm al-taṣawwof*, ed. ʿAbd-al-Ḥalim Maḥmud, Cairo, 1966; Pers. tr. by Abu ʿAli Aḥmad ʿOṯmāni, ed. Badiʿ-al-Zamān Forūzanfar as *Tarjama-ye Resāla-ye Qošayriya*, Tehran, 1966. A. Raymond, "Shadd 2. In the Trade Guild," in *EI*[2] IX, pp. 168-69. John Renard, *Islam and the Heroic Image: Themes in Literature and Visual Arts*, Columbia, South Carolina, 1993. Moḥammad-Amin Riāḥi, *Zabān o adab-e fārsi dar qalamrow-e ʿOṯmāni*, Tehran, 1980. Moḥammad Riāż Khan, *Aḥwāl o āṯār o ašʿār-e Mir Sayyed ʿAli Hamadāni*, Islamabad, 1364/1945. Idem, "Pirāmun-e fotowwat yā javānmardi," *Helāl* 8, 1970, pp. 8-13. Idem, "Caliph al-Nāṣir li-Dīn Allāh and the System of 'Futuwwat,'" *Journal of Pakistan Historical Society* 18, 1970, pp. 180-90. Idem, "Āḡāz wa erteqā-ye nahżat-e fotowwat-e eslāmi," *Maʿāref-e eslāmi*, N.S., no. 1, 1973, pp. 60-72. Idem, "Moḵtaṣar-i az nahżat-e fotowwat dar Īrān wa jahān-e eslāmi," *Majalla-ye Dāneškada-ye adabiyāt wa ʿolum-e ensāni-e Dānešgāh-e Mašhad* 9, 1973, pp. 507-32, 623-50. Idem, "ʿAyyāri wa šaṭṭāri," *Maʿāref-e eslāmi*, N.S., no. 2, 1974, pp. 68-77. Idem, "Futuwwat," *Maʿāref-e eslāmi*, N.S., no. 3, 1974, pp. 58-68. Idem, "Chivalry in Islamic history," *Journal of the Regional Cultural Institute* 6, 1973, pp. 145-58. E. Rossi, "L'instituzione scolastica militare "al-Futuwwah" nell Iraq," *Oriente Moderno* 20, 1940, pp. 297-302 (in modern Iraq, before World War II, some organizations came into being under the name of al-Fotowwa, which followed the example of Hitler's Jugend and the Italian Balilla, with the purpose of the military training of the youth).

Simha Sabari, *Mouvements populaires a Bagdād à l'époque ʿabbāsside, IX*[e]*- XI*[e] *siècles*, Paris, 1981. G. Salinger, "Was the futūwa an Oriental form of Chivalry?" *Proceedings of the American Philosophical Society* 94, 1950, pp. 481-93. Mortażā Ṣarrāf, ed., *Rasāʾel-e javānmardān moštamel bar haft fotowwat-nāma/Traités des compagnons-chevaliers*, Tehran and Paris, 1973, Introd. by Henry Corbin, pp. 1-109. M. S. Seale, "The Ethics of Malāmatīya Sufism and the Sermon on the Mount," *Muslim World* 58, 1968, pp. 12-23 (contains an abridged tr. of Solami's *Resālat al-Malāmatiya*). Shaikh Šehāb-al-Din ʿOmar Sohravardi "Two *fotowwa-nāma*s," in M. Ṣarrāf, ed., pp. 89-66 (on these see Taeschner, 1979, pp. 242-56). Moḥammad b. Ḥosayn Solami, *Ketāb al-fotowwa*, ed. S. Ateş as *Kitabü'l-fütüvve*, Ankara, 1977; ed. with Introd., ed. Abu'l-ʿAlā ʿAfifi, in his *al-Malāmatiya wa'l-Ṣufiyā wa ahl al-fotowwa*, Cairo, 1945; tr. R. Delarière as *La lucidité implacable: Epître des hommes du blâme*, Paris, 1991; tr. Bayrak Tosun as *The Book of Sufī Chivalry: Lessons to the Son of the Moment, Futuwwah*, London and New York, 1983; tr. Qāsem Anṣāri as *Javānmardi wa Javānmardān: Ketāb al-fotowwa*, Qazvin, 2001. Idem, *Resālat al-Malāmatiya*, ed. Abu'l-ʿAlāʾ ʿAfifi, in his *al-Malāmatiya wa'l-Ṣufiyā* . . . , pp. 71-120; see also R. Hartmann, 1918a, and F. Taeschner. Moḥammad b. Jarir Ṭabari, *Taʾriḵ al-rosol wa'l-moluk*, tr. by various scholars as *The History of al-Ṭabari*, Albany, New York, 1985-. Franz Taeschner, "Futuwwa," in *EI*[2] II, pp. 961-69. Idem, "As-Sulamī's *Kitāb al-futuwwa*," *Studia Orientalia Ioanni Pedersen septuagenario . . . dicata*, Oslo, 1953, pp. 340-51. Idem, "Das Puppentheater nach dem Futuvvatnāme-i Sulṭanī des Ḥusain Vāʿiẓ-i Kāšifī (gest. 910/1504-05)," in Wilhelm Hoenerback, ed., *Der Orient in der Forschung: Festschrift für Otto Spies zum April 1966*, Wiesbaden, 1967, pp. 657-59 (the story of Pahlavān Kačal). Idem, "Ḵalīfa-ye ʿAbbāsī wa āyīn-e fotowwat," tr. M. Baḵtiār, *Waḥid* 5, 1968, pp. 625-36, 788-95. Idem, *Zünfte und Bruderschaften im Islam: Texte zur Geschichte der Futuwwa*, ed. H. Helm, Zurich and Munich, 1979 (Taeschner's *Magnum Opus*, a virtual handbook on *fotowwa*; for the rest of Taeschner's works on *fotowwa*, see his bibliography in *Der Islam* 39, 1964, pp. 261-70. *Tāriḵ-e Sistān*, ed. Moḥammad-Taqi Malek-al-Šoʿarāʾ Bahār, Tehran, n.d. Deborah G., Tor, *Violent Order: Religious Warfare, Chivalry, and the ʿAyyār Phenomenon in the Medieval Islamic World*, Würzburg, 2007.

Süleyman Uludağ and Ahmet Yaşar Ocak, "Fütüvvet," *Türkiye Diyanet Vakfi Islam Ansiklopedisi* XIII, 1996, pp. 259-63. *Tarjama-ye tafsir-e Ṭabari*, ed. Ḥabib Yaḡmāʾi, 7 vols., Tehran, 1962. Jean Claude Vadet, "La *Futuwwa*, morale professionelle ou morale mystique," *Revue des études islamiques* 46, 1978, pp. 57-90 (mainly based on Wāʿeẓ Kāšefi's *Fotowwat-nāma-ye solṭāni*). Speros Vryonis, "Byzantine Circus Factions and Islamic Futuwwa Organizations (neaniai, fityān, ahdāth)," *Byzantinische Zeitschrift* 58, 1965, pp. 46-59 (for counter arguments see A. Cameron, pp. 341-43). Ḥosayn Wāʿeẓ Kāšefi, *Fotowwat-nāma-ye solṭāni*, ed. Moḥammad-Jaʿfar Maḥjub, Tehran, 1971; some parts publ. with Russ. tr. by R. A. Galunov as "Zurkhana, atleticheskaya arena Persii" (Zūr-ḵāna, the Persian athletic arena), *Iran* 1, Leningrad, 1927, pp. 87-110; 2, 1928, pp. 72-88; synopsis of the book by Hellmut Ritter in *Der Islam* 18, 1929, pp. 315 (with some significant details). Ḡolām-Ḥosayn Yusofi, "Dar ārzu-ye javānmardi," *Majalla-ye Dāneškada-ye adabiyāt wa ʿolum-e ensāni-e Dānešgāh-e Mašhad* 10, 1974, pp. 339-68; repr. in idem, *Didār-i bā ahl-e qalam*, Mašhad, 1975, pp. 217-45 (comments on *Samak ʿAyyār*). Mohsen Zakeri, "From Iran to Islam: *ʿAyyārān* and *Futuwwa*," in Bert G. Fragner, et al., eds., *Proceedings of the Second*

European Conference of Iranian Studies, Rome, 1995a, pp. 745-57. Idem, *Sāsānid Soldiers in Early Muslim Society: The Origins of ʿAyyārān and Futuwwa*, Wiesbaden, 1995b. Idem, "Muslim 'Chivalry' at the Time of the Crusaders: The Case of Khurāsān and the Mongol Invasion," In *Proceedings of the 3rd European Conference of Iranian Studies, Cambridge 1995*, forthcoming ʿAbd-al-Ḥosayn Zarrinkub, "Ahl-e malāmat wa rāh-e qalandar: moṭālaʿa-i dar bāb-e vākonešhā-ye daruni dar taṣawwof," *Majalla-ye Dāneškada-ye adabiyāt wa ʿolum-e ensāni-e Dānešgāh-e Tehrān* 22, 1975, pp. 61-100.

(MOHSEN ZAKERI)

JAVĀNRUD, a city and a sub-province (*šahrestān*) in the northwest of Kermānšāhān Province near the border with Iraq at about 110 km southwest of Sanandaj sub-province. Apparently it is so called after the name of the Kurdish tribe Javānrud, a dominant tribe of the area in the past, which is now almost entirely urbanite. The sub-province is divided into the Central and the Kalāši districts and is bounded to the north by Owrāmān Lahun, to the east by Ravānsar district, to the west by Iraq, and to the south by Kermānšāhān. In the past Javānrud was one of the eighteen rural districts (*boluk*) of the loosely defined province of Ardalān, the former designation of the Persian province of Kurdistan. It was a rural district of Sanandaj sub-province until the restructuring the administrative order of the country made it a part of Kermānšāhan Province in the mid 1970s, eventually becoming a sub-province in 1989 (Ḥaydari, pp. 276-77). In 1909, Amān-Allāh Khan Ardalān (r. 1799-1825), then the govornor (*wāli*) of Ardalān (i.e., Kurdistan), built a fortress on a hillock near the center of Javānrud and furnished it with an orchard and elegant buildings for the resisence of tribal leaders. The fortress, known as Qalʿa-ye Javānrud, soon fell into ruin due to the lack of proper maintenance (Marduḵ, II, p. 78). Because of its stategic position near the Ottoman border, until the early 20th century, its rulers were always chosen from among the leaders of the Ardalān tribe, which represented the leading local force.

Javānrud is a mountainous region surrounded on the east and north by the mountains belonging to the Zagros range. The major mountain in the region is Šāhu range that extends for 55 km in the northeast with the highest elevation of 3,390 m (Jaʿfari, III, p. 375; Dehḵodā, p. 140; Ḥaydari, p. 276). Kāvāt Cave, a nature's point of attraction briefly described by Moḥammad Marduḵ, is in this mountain (Marduḵ, p. 79). The cave is now closed to the public, because the running stream inside the cave is now diverted to the town as drinking water (Iraj Afšār, p. 49). The sub-district is comprised of 124 villages, 43 of which are mountainous with a cold climate, while the other 81 are located on the plains and have a moderate climate suitable for farming. The water for the villages is supplied by springs and rivers, mainly the rivers of Sirvān, a tributary of Diāla River, and Leyala. Other noteworthy rivers are Zerešk and Zimakān (Jaʿfari, II, pp. 81, 84, 259-61, 440). Agricultural products include barley, wheat, beans, corn, tobacco, and various fruits, of which pomegranates and figs are known for quality. According to Marduḵ (II, p. 79), the area also produced substantial amounts of tragacanth and *A. adscendens* (*gaz-angobin*; see GAZ) for export. A unique product of the area is a kind of honey, known as Šāh Badram, which tastes differently from the common type. It is cultivated only here and in the Mokri area of Kurdistan (Marduḵ, II, p. 79; Mirzā ʿAli Akbar, p. 69). A part of the district is home to natural forests, and the pastures are used for raising sheep and cattle. As a result, its animal products are plentiful (Edāra-ye koll-e āmār, p. 59).

The population of Javānrud sub-province was reported as 109,518 in the census of 1996, of which 53,464 were urban residents, 55,451 lived in rural areas, and the rest were nomads (Ḥaydari, p. 277). The majority of the inhabitants are Sunni Muslims of the Shafeʿite persuasion and followers of Naqšbandi and Qāderi Sufi orders. They generaly speak Kurdish (Jāfi and Owrāmāni dialects), but Persian is also used in urban areas (Ḥaydari, p. 277). Villagers mostly work as animal herders. They spend winters in villages and move to higher grounds during the summer time. Since local farming products are not enough to meet the need of the growing population, additional foodstuff is imported from other regions (Mirzā Šokr-Allāh, p. 48).

A number of tribes and clans inhabit Javānrud, the most important of which are the Jāf (q.v.) nomads, whose original homeland was here and they referred to it as Jāvānrud or Jāfānrud (Moṣṭafā Jawād, p. 28). Following a battle with the govornor of Ardalān toward the end of the 17th century, in which their leader and his son were taken captive and killed, the larger body of Jāf moved to Solaymāniya district in Ottomon territory, and are referred to as Morādi Jāf. The sections that remained behind became known as Jāf-e Javānrud (Sajjādi, pp. 511-12; see JĀF). Other noteworthy tribes are Emāmi, Rostam Beygi, Bābājāni, Zardōyi, Tāyjōzi and Šabānkāra (*Ilāt wa qabāyel-e Kordestān-e Ardalān*, p. 31; Afšār Sistāni, I, pp. 253-55).

Javānrud was the scene of a number of armed tribal rebellions, at times instigated by the interests of foreign powers, but none of the rebellions spread elsewhere or posed any serious threat to the central government (Afšār Sistāni, pp. 253-54).

Bibliography: Iraj Afšār, *Safar-nāmča: golgašt dar waṭan*, Tehran, 2005. Iraj Afšār Sistāni, *Ilhā, čador-nešinān wa ṭawāyef-e ʿašāyeri-e Irān*, 2 vols., Tehran, 1987, I, pp. 253-55. Mirzā ʿAli-Akbar Waqāyeʿnegār Monši, *Ḥadiqa-ye Nāṣeriya dar joḡrāfiā wa tāriḵ-e Kordestān*, ed. Moḥammad-Raʾuf Tawakkoli, Tehran, 1985. ʿAli Akbar Dehḵodā, *Loḡat-nāma*, Tehran, 1946-79. s.v. Edāra-ye koll-e āmār wa ṯabt-e aḥwāl, *Ketāb-e joḡrāfiā wa asāmi-e dehāt-e kešvar*, 2nd ed., Tehran, 1950. Waḥid Ḥaydari, "Javānrud," in *Dāneš-nāma-ye jahān-e eslām* XI, pp. 276-78. Moḥammad Ḥosaynzāda, *Tāriḵča-ye Javānrud*, Kermānšāh, 1998. *Ilāt wa qabāyel-e Kordestān-e Ardalān*, manuscript. ʿAbbās Jaʿfari, *Gitā-šenāsi-e Irān* II: *Rudhā wa rud-nāma-ye Irān*, Tehran, 1997; III: *Kuhhā wa kuh-nāma-ye Irān*, Tehran, 1989. Moṣṭafā Jawād, "Jāvān: al-qabila al-kordiya al-mansiya wa mašāhir al-jāvānin," *Majalla al-majmaʿ al-ʿelmi al-erāqi* 4, 1956. Shaikh Moḥammad Marduḵ Kordestāni, *Tāriḵ-e Kord wa Kordestān wa tawābeʿ yā tāriḵ-e Marduḵ*, 2 vols, Tehran, 1945; 2nd ed., 2 vols. in 1, Tehran, 1974. ʿAli Mirniā, *Ilhā wa ṭāyefahā-ye ʿašāyeri-e Kord-e Irān*, Tehran, 1990. Basile Nikitine, *Les Kurdes: étude sosiologiquw et historique*, Paris, 1956; tr. Moḥammad Qāżi as *Kord wa Kordestān*, Tehran, 1987. Ḥosayn-ʿAli Razmārā, ed., *Farhang-e joḡrāfiāʾi-e Irān (ābādihā)*, V, Tehran, 1952, pp. 108-9. ʿAlāʾ-al-Din Sajjādi, *Mēju-yi adabi Kordi* (History of Kurdish literature), Baghdad, 2nd ed., 1971. Mirzā Šokr-Allāh Sanandaji, *Toḥfa-ye Nāseriya dar tāriḵ wa joḡrāfiā-ye Kordestān*, ed. Ḥešmat-Allāh Ṭabibi, Tehran, 1987. Moḥammad-ʿAli Solṭāni, *Joḡrāfiā-ye tāriḵi wa tāriḵ-e mofaṣṣal-e Kermānšāhān* II: *Ilhā wa ṭawāyef-e Kermānšāhān*, Tehran, 1991.

(ʿABD-ALLĀH MARDUḴ and *EIr*.)

JAVĀNŠIR QARĀBĀḠI, JAMĀL (b. Ḵājalu village, 1773; d. Ḵājalu village, 13 April 1853), a leader of the Javānšir tribe and an office-holder in Qarābāḡ and Dagestan. He was born in 1773 in Ḵājalu village of Javānšir district near Dizak (present-day Nagorno-Karabakh Republic). He was the son of Moḥammad Khan Beg, the grandson of Salif Beg Minbāši, and the great-grandson of Šarif Beg Javānšir. His grandfather was the chief of the Javānšir tribe. After his death, Jamāl Javānšir's father was named the chief of the Javānšir tribe by Ebrāhim Ḵalil Khan Javānšir (1730-1806, q.v.), the ruler of the Šuši/Šuša fort in Qarābāḡ, and was transferred to the fort as its commander.

Jamāl Javānšir studied Persian and Turkish, and in 1787-88, at the age of fifteen, he became one of the scribes (*dabir*) in Ebrāhim Ḵalil Khan's chancery. After a decade, under threat from Āḡā Moḥammad Khan Qājār (d. 1797, q.v.), he left Šuši together with other members of the Ebrāhim Ḵalil Khan's household and settled in the village of Khoznak. He became the secretary (*mirzā*) to one of the wives of Ebrāhim Ḵalil Khan, Bike Ḵānom, who was the sister of ʿOmma Khan (r. 1774-1801), the ruler of the Avars in Dagestan. He studied Arabic for several years and returned to the Šuši fortress after the death of Āḡā Moḥammad Khan Qajar in 1797. In gratitude for the courage displayed by Moḥammad Khan Beg and his Javānšir tribesmen during Āḡā Moḥammad Khan's attack, Ebrāhim Ḵalil Khan appointed Moḥammad Khan Beg's son, Mirzā Jamāl, to the post of his personal secretary and the vizier of Qarābāḡ. Mirzā Jamāl was thus present during the signing of the agreement of 1805 between Ebrāhim Ḵalil Khan and the Russian Prince Pavel Tsitsianov (1754-1806), which brought Qarābāḡ under Russian tutelage. In the same year, Jamāl Javānšir acted as a secretary to Moḥammad Ḥasan Āqā, the eldest son of Ebrāhim Ḵalil Khan, who led the Qarābāḡ cavalry under the command of General Pyotr Nebol'sin (?-1810) during the First Russo-Persian War (1804-13). In June 1806 Mirzā Jamāl witnessed the battle of Khonashin between the forces of Nebol'sin and ʿAbbās Mirzā (1789-1833, q.v.) and reported on the early stages of the war to Ebrāhim Ḵalil Khan. Soon after, he went to Nakhichevan (Naḵčavān), from where he was put in charge of provisions for the Russian army in the region. After the murder of Ebrāhim Ḵalil Khan in 1806, Mirzā Jamāl remained in the service of Ebrāhim Ḵalil Khan's son, Mehdiqoli Khan, the last Khan of Šuši. When the latter fled to Persia in 1822, Qarābāḡ was officially annexed to Russia, and Mirzā Jamāl retired. During the entire period of the war, he and his extended family of some one hundred people were supported by Russia. After retirement, he received an annual pension of 510 silver rubles, 120 bushels of wheat, and 30 bushels of rice from General Alekseĭ Yermolov (1777-1861), the commander-in-chief of the Russian troops in the Caucasus. When Yermolov ordered an official survey of Qarābāḡ to be made, Mirzā Jamāl was called out of retirement and was appointed by the Russian commandant of Šuši to the post of secretary, in which he served various Russian commanders.

During the second Russo-Persian War (1826-28), Mirzā Jamāl accompanied Prince Valerian Madatov (1782-1829) across the Araxes (Aras) River (q.v.), where, with the help of his nephew Karim Beg, Jamāl managed to move the entire village of Sayyed-Aḥmadlu to Dizak district. In 1840, already in his late sixties, Mirzā Jamāl retired from service again. Subsequently, his pension was terminated, and he was suffering financial difficulties, until the Russian viceroy of the Caucasus Mikhail Vorontsov (1782-1856) granted to him the income from the village of Karga-bāzār in the late 1840s. In addition to his knowledge of the aforementioned languages, Mirzā Jamāl knew the Lezgi and Avar languages, had some knowledge of astronomy, and an excellent knowledge of history and geography. It is reported that he was also familiar with medicine and composed poems in Persian. Jamāl Javānšir Qarābāḡi died on 13 April 1853 in Ḵājalu village.

Mirzā Jamāl is best known for his *Tāriḵ-e Qarābāḡ* (History of Qarābāḡ) written in Persian—which was the literary language of the Muslims in the Caucasus—sometime after 1847, upon the order of the Russian Viceroy of the Caucasus Mikhail Vorontsov. It is clear that Mirzā Jamāl had already possessed a draft of the work and that he simply added the introductory and concluding remarks, as well as a number of short chapters, in order to please the Viceroy and to reinstate his own pension. The book covers the history of Qarābāḡ from the arrival of the Arab armies until its conquest by the Russians. Its primary focus, however, is the history of the Khanate of Qarābāḡ from the time of Nāder Shah (r. 1736-47, q.v.) until the death of Ebrāhim Ḵalil Khan in 1806. The part of his work dealing with the struggle between the Javānšir khans and the Armenian petty princes (meliks) of Qarābāḡ is an especially valuable source, being written by a non-Armenian on the major Armenian presence in the region.

Bibliography: G. Bournoutian, *Two Chronicles on the History of Karabagh: Mirza Jamal Javanshir's Tarikh-e Qarabagh and Mirza Adigözal Beg's Karabagh-name*, Costa Mesa, CA, 2004. Akhmedbek Dzhavanshir, *O politicheskom sushchestvovanii Karabakhskogo khanstva s 1747 po 1805 god* (On the political existence of the Khanate of Qarābāḡ from 1747 until 1805), Baku, 1961. Mirza Jamal Javanšir Garabaghi, *Garabag Tarikhi*, Baku, 1959. Dzhemal Dzhevanshir Karabagi, "Karabag," *Kavkaz* 61-69, 1855. Mirza Cemal Cevansir Karabaghli, *Karabag Tarihi*, Ankara, 1990. Mirzā Dzhamal Dzhevanshir Karabagskiĭ, *Istoriya Karabaga* (History of Qarābāḡ), Baku, 1959. Mirzā Jamāl Javānšir Qarābāḡi, *Tāriḵ-e Qarābāḡ*, MS B-712/11603, Institute of History, Academy of Sciences of Azerbaijan, Baku, Azerbaijan; tr. G. Bournoutian as *A History of Qarabagh: an Annotated Translation of Mirza Jamal Javanshir Qarabaghi's Tarikh-e Qarabagh*, Costa Mesa, Calif., 1994; ed. Ḥosayn Aḥmadi as *Tariḵ-e Qarābāḡ*, Tehran, 2003.

(GEORGE BOURNOUTIAN)

JĀVDĀN-NĀMA (also known as *Jāvdān-nāma-ye kabir* or *Jāvdān-nāma-ye elāhi*), the major work of Fażl-Allāh Astarābādi (d. 1394; q.v.), the founder of the Ḥorufi movement (see HORUFISM). The title, which can be translated from Persian either as the "Eternal Book" or as the "Book of Eternity," has been transcribed here as *Jāvdān* and not *Jāvidān* (although this latter form is more current in Persian and is often used in contemporary literature on the Ḥorufis), because early Ḥorufi authors mostly use the form without the "yā" between the "wāw" and the "dāl."

History and manuscripts. The composition of this voluminous work (the complete copy contains about 500 folios) probably took many years. Interpreting the allusive indications found in the *Korsi-nāma* of ʿAli al-Aʿlā (d. 1419; q.v.; one of the most significant followers of Fażl-Allāh), Hellmut Ritter (1892-1971) suggested that the *Jāvdān-nāma* could have been finished by 1386 (Ritter, pp. 22-23). Moḥammad-ʿAli Tarbiat relates in the *Dānešmandān-e Āḏarbāyjān* (p. 553) that Fażl-Allāh wrote the *Jāvdān-nāma* during his imprisonment in Alinjaq in 1394, but this does not seem very plausible since Fażl-Allāh was executed shortly after his arrest. The *Jāvdān-nāma* does, however, mention Baku, the capital of Shirvan where Fażl-Allāh spent the last few years of his life, and the date 2 Rabiʿ II 796/4 February 1394 (British Library, MS Or. 5957, fol. 85b), that is, just seven months before the most probable date of his execution on 6 Ḏu'l-Qaʿda 796/2 September 1394. It is therefore possible that Fażl-Allāh completed the *Jāvdān-nāma* shortly before his death.

Like most Ḥorufi texts, the *Jāvdān-nāma* is only available in manuscript form, with the exception of the fragments included in the *Vāža-nāma* of Ṣādeq Kiā (pp. 42-45) and those in an unpublished dissertation (Mir-Kasimov, 2007a, pp. 495-733). As for the other Ḥorufi writings, the catalogue descriptions require careful scrutiny, and much work still has to be done in order to identify the manuscripts. Among the dated copies of the work, the one in the Millet Library in Istanbul (MS Ali Emiri Farsi, no. 920, dated 992/1584) is perhaps the oldest of the extant. According to the Gölpınarlı catalogue (pp. 56-59), the Millet Library copy was transcribed in Baku from a manuscript which, in its turn, was copied from the manuscript written by Maḵdumzāda (d. 1441), the daughter of Fażl-Allāh. After the second half of the 15th century, the text of the *Jāvdān-nāma* was essentially preserved and transmitted within the Bektashi order of dervishes, from which some copies of this work found their way to the European libraries in the end of the 19th and the beginning of the 20th centuries (Huart, 1889, pp. 238-70; Browne, 1896, pp. 69-86; Idem, 1907, pp. 533-81). According to manuscript catalogues, there are copies of the *Jāvdān-nāma* in libraries in Istanbul, Cairo, Leiden, Cambridge, and in the British Library in London, as well as in some private collections.

The original *Jāvdān-nāma-ye kabir* (the "great" *Jāvdān-nāma*) was written in an idiosyncratic idiom, which mixes the literary Persian with the archaic dialect of Astarābād; the text starts with the word *ebtedāʾ* (beginning) repeated six times. This version should not be confused with the shorter and simplified version written without the use of the dialect, which is also ascribed to Fażl-Allāh and known as the *Jāvdān-nāma-ye ṣaḡir* (the "little" *Jāvdān-nāma*). Two works in Ottoman Turkish are described as adaptations or translations of the latter version: the *ʿEšq-nāma* (the Book of Love) of ʿEzz-al-Din ʿAbd-al-Majid b. Ferešta Taravi (Firishte-oğlu, d. 1459-60), written in 1430; and the *Dorr-e yatim* (the Unique Pearl), composed by a Bektashi dervish named Mortażā in 1638-39 (Gölpınarlı, pp. 114 and 144-47). The former has been translated into modern Turkish under the title *Ilm-i Cavidan* (see Taravi).

Structure and contents. The account of the text given here is based on the manuscript of the British Library. It is therefore feasible that some of the conclusions made here might need to be modified after the thorough comparison of the extant copies of the work has been made. The *Jāvdān-nāma* is without doubt the main source on the original Ḥorufi doctrine. Notwithstanding its foundational role, the contents of the *Jāvdān-nāma* cannot be easily comprehended. The structural idiosyncrasies and some of the difficulties encountered in this text could be a result of intentional encryption elaborated in the Iranian heterodox milieu of the late medieval period, and there are some indications suggesting this possibility in the *Jāvdān-nāma* itself as well as in some later Ḥorufi works. An attempt to comprehend and analyze the contents of the *Jāvdān-nāma* with the help of the indications found in the *Jāvdān-nāma* itself and in other Ḥorufi works was made in Mir-Kasimov, 2007a.

One of the impediments here is the use of a little known local dialect already mentioned above and of the special signs or abbreviations which replace some of the most recurrent expressions. Fortunately, Ḥorufi manuscripts contain notes that explain the meaning of the abbreviations. Besides, the *Jāvdān-nāma* and other Ḥorufi works provide sufficient contextual information for deciphering these abbreviations without the need to consult any other source. Lists of the special signs used in the Ḥorufi texts have been provided by Clément Huart (1909, pp. 189-90), Ṣādeq Kiā (pp. 39-40), and Abdülbâki Gölpın-arlı (pp. 148-49). Shahzad Bashir has discussed a possible metaphysical dimension of these signs (Bashir, 2005, pp. 77-81). Copies of a brief vocabulary of the Astarābādi dialect are sometimes appended to the manuscripts of the *Jāvdān-nāma*, and a substantially extended version of this vocabulary is now available thanks to the work of Ṣādeq Kiā (pp. 48-209). Another difficulty—the allusive, indirect language of the work, which does not allow any immediate conclusion—is attenuated by the incremental repetition in the text, returning regularly to the same questions with some extra details added on, thus gradually clarifying the intentions of the author. A much more serious obstacle is the fragmented composition of the *Jāvdān-nāma*. Indeed, the work is devoid of any thematic organization: paragraphs follow one another without any logical link, and passages related to the same topic are dispersed throughout different places in the text.

The major thematic divisions of the *Jāvdān-nāma* are suggested in an anonymous note annexed to the manuscript of the British Library. They are six, in accordance with the six words *ebtedāʾ*, with which the text starts. Although they do not cover all the subjects discussed in the *Jāvdān-nāma*, they give a general idea about the contents of the work. These six divisions can be summarized as follows: Time, Cosmogony, Anthropology, Theory of the Creative Imagination (*ʿālam-e meṯāl* or *ʿālam-e ḵayāl*), Prophetology, and Return to the Origin (*taʾwil*). The *Jāvdān-nāma* thus contains a complete theological doctrine, the logical pattern of which seems to be determined by the cycle of the Divine Verb with its 28 and/or 32 aspects (literally "words", *kalema*). This cycle unfolds according to two modalities: the "unconscious" one underlies the laws of evolution of the material Universe with all its components, from the heavenly spheres to the tiniest atoms; while the "conscious" one corresponds to the transmission of the knowledge of the Verb in the line of the Prophets. A close correlation exists, therefore, between the cosmic and prophetic cycles. There are only three points where the "unconscious" and "conscious" currents cross and where the physical Form of the complete Verb, with its 28/32 aspects, meets the complete Knowledge of the Verb. The first is Adam, whose bodily form is the locus of manifestation (*maẓhar*) of the Verb *par excellence*, and to whom God "taught all the names" (Qurʾān 2:31)—which means, according to the *Jāvdān-nāma*, that God taught to Adam all the 28/32 aspects of the Verb. Adam is also the last "crossing point," because he will necessarily appear at the end of the cycle, as the locus of manifestation of the accomplished Verb. Between the two manifestations of Adam comes Jesus, whose body is not produced by the laws of the human heredity, but by the Verb spontaneously taking the form of the human body in the womb of Mary. According to the prophetology of the *Jāvdān-nāma*, Jesus begins a sub-cycle within the major prophetic cycle, and he will come back at its end as Mahdi, the eschatological Savior. This is the sub-cycle of the *Ommiyin*—prophets and saints which have a special connection with the "Mother" (*Omm*), the foundation of the divine Verb. Moḥammad is the second *Ommi* prophet. His mission achieves the period of the "descent" (*tanzil*) of the Verb, and it inaugurates the period of the "return to the origin" (*taʾwil*). The doctrine of the *Jāvdān-nāma* is clearly focused on this last phase of the cycle of the Verb, when the gap separating the 28 aspects of the Verb, revealed by the prophet Moḥammad (figured by the 28 letters of the Arabic alphabet composing the text of the Qurʾān), from the 32 aspects of the complete Verb, revealed by God to Adam, will be filled. This is the mission of the *Ommi* prophets coming after Moḥammad, among whom the author apparently integrates the Shiʿite Imams (only very vaguely outlined in the *Jāvdān-nāma*, without any mention of their affiliations, numbers and names, with the exception of ʿAli b. Abi Ṭāleb and his son, Ḥosayn), and the mysterious Witnesses (*šohadā*). The disclosure of the whole set of the 32 original aspects of the Verb will reveal the ultimate meaning of all sacred books. Simultaneously, the material universe will dissolve as the aspects of the Verb will withdraw from the created world on the way of Return to their source. The "conscious" and the "unconscious" lines of the cycle of the Verb will thus come to the common end in the movement which is the Spiritual Exegesis and the Return to the Origin at the same time, in accordance with the etymological meaning of the Arabic term *taʾwil*.

The doctrinal positions of the *Jāvdān-nāma* are mainly developed through the comments of the scriptural materials: the Qurʾān, the Hadith, and extracts from the Old and the New Testaments. The Qurʾān is the main scriptural source of the *Jāvdān-nāma*. According to some evidence found in the *Jāvdān-nāma* itself as well as in the later Ḥorufi works, the fragmented structure and the allusive language of the *Jāvdān-nāma* could be inspired, to a certain extent, by the specific composition of the Qurʾānic text.

The only title of a Hadith collection mentioned in the *Jāvdān-nāma* is *Maṣābiḥ*, which probably refers to the *Maṣābiḥ al-Sonna* of Abu Moḥammad al-Ḥosayn Baḡawi (d. 1122). However, many Hadith quotations in the *Jāvdān-nāma* are not provided with references, and most of them cannot be found in any of the standard Sunni compilations. It is noteworthy that the author uses the Hadith ranging in a very large spectrum. Some hadiths are quoted in the text under the authority of the prophet Moḥammad's wife, ʿĀyeša, who was particularly unpopular in Shiʿite circles because of her opposition to the caliphate of ʿAli b. Abi Ṭāleb. Yet, her name is accompanied with honorific titles, which is usually not to be expected from an "orthodox" Shiʿite author. At the same time, the *Jāvdān-nāma* frequently quotes theophanic sayings with the extreme-Shiʿite coloration ascribed to ʿAli b. Abi Ṭāleb, which had little credit in the Sunni milieu. Besides, there is no sign in the text of the *Jāvdān-nāma*, which would further corroborate the remarks on its possible Shiʿite or more particularly Twelver or Ismaʿili inspiration made in a number of previous studies (Browne, 1896, pp. 69-70; Huart, 1909, pp. xii-xiii; Corbin, pp. 234 and 255; Amoretti, p. 624; Ivanow, p. 188; Gölpınları, pp. 17-18; Ritter, p. 4). As it stands, the work seems to combine the Sunni and the Shiʿite views without conflict—a circumstance which is not unusual in Iranian mysticism, particularly in the period between the Mongol invasion and the rise of the Safavids (13th-16th centuries; see for instance Molé, pp. 61-142).

Along with the Islamic scriptural materials, the *Jāvdān-nāma* also contains extended comments derived from both the Old and the New Testaments, particularly from the Books of Genesis and Exodus, the Gospel of John, and the Book of Revelation or the Apocalypse of John. The extent of the quotations from the Bible and the importance of the doctrinal positions developed around them may represent another aspect of the eschatological orientation of the *Jāvdān-nāma*: reforming Islam and ensuring its transition towards becoming the universal religion which will reunify humankind at the end of time.

The Jāvdān-nāma and the later Ḥorufi tradition. Although the *Jāvdān-nāma* contains no such claim in itself, the followers of Fażl-Allāh considered it as a divine text (*Jāvdān-nāma-ye elāhi*) containing the secrets of the spiritual exegesis (*taʾwil*) of the Qurʾān and of all the previous Holy Books (it should be noted that Fażl-Allāh was addressed by his disciples as *Ṣāḥeb-e taʾwil*, the Master of the Spiritual Exegesis). This was certainly part of the general tendency to sanctify Fażl-Allāh after his death (cf. Bashir, 2000, pp. 289-308).

Ḥorufi community split into several branches almost immediately after the death of its leader and founder Fażl-Allāh in 1394. Doctrinal controversies between regional Ḥorufi groups are attested already in the early Ḥorufi sources, such as the *Estewā-nāma* of Ḡiāṯ-al-Din Astarābādi (d. 1449; cf. Ritter, pp. 40-50). The comparison of the *Jāvdān-nāma* with the later Ḥorufi works also shows some significant shifts in the interpretation of a number of doctrinal topics as early as in the first generation of Fażl-Allāh's disciples (Mir-Kasimov, 2006, pp. 203-35). It seems reasonable, therefore, to admit that after the death of Faẓl-Allāh there existed not one but several "Horufisms" which evolved along historically and theoretically divergent lines. Being the most comprehensive and the most authentic reference of the original Ḥorufi doctrine, the *Jāvdān-nāma* is the starting point of this evolution and the basis for the study of further developments of Ḥorufi ideas.

Bibliography: B. S. Amoretti, "Religion in the Timurid and Safavid Periods," *Camb. Hist. Iran*, vol. VI, ed. P. Jackson and L. Lockhart, Cambridge, 1986, pp. 610-55. Fażl-Allāh Astarābādi, *Jāvdān-nāma*, British Library, London, MS Or. 5957. Shahzad Bashir, "Enshrining Divinity: the Death and Memorialization of Fazlallah Astarabadi in Hurufi Thought," *The Muslim World* 90, 2000, pp. 289-308. Idem, "Deciphering the Cosmos from Creation to Apocalypse: the Hurufiyya Movement and Medieval Islamic Esotericism," in *Imagining the End: Visions of Apocalypse from the Ancient Middle East to Modern America*, ed. A. Amanat and M. Bernardsson, London and, New York, 2002, pp. 168-84. Idem, *Fazlallah Astarabadi and the Hurufis*, Oxford, 2005. E. G. Browne, *The Catalogue of the Persian Manuscripts in the Library of the University of Cambridge*, Cambridge, 1896. Idem, "Further Notes on the Literature of the Hurufis and Their Connection with the Bektashi Order of Dervishes," *JRAS*, 1907, pp. 533-81. Henry Corbin, *En Islam Iranien: aspects spirituels et philosophiques*, vol. III, Paris, 1972. Abdülbâki Gölpınarlı, *Hurufilik metinleri kataloğu*, Ankara, 1973. Clément Huart, "Notice d'un manuscrit pehlevi-musulman," *JA*, 8th series, 14, 1889, pp. 238-70. Idem, *Textes persans relatifs à la secte des houroûfîs*, Leiden and London, 1909. W. Ivanow, *Ismaili Literature: a Bibliographical Survey*, Tehran, 1963. Orkhan Mir-Kasimov, "Notes sur deux textes hurûfî: le Jâvdân-nâma de Fadlallâh Astarâbâdî et l'un de ses commentaires, le Mahram-nâma de Sayyid Ishâq," *Stud. Ir.* 35/2, 2006, pp. 203-35. Idem, "Étude de textes hurûfî anciens: l'oeuvre fondatrice de Fadlallâh Astarâbâdî," Ph.D. diss., École Pratique des Hautes Études, Paris, 2007a. Idem, "Les dérivés de la racine RḤM: Homme, Femme et Connaissance dans le Jâvdân-nâma de Fadlallâh Astarâbâdî," *JA* 295/1, 2007b, pp. 9-33. Ṣādeq Kiā, *Vāža-nāma-ye Gorgāni*, Tehran, 1951. Marijan Molé, "Les Kubrawiya entre sunnisme et shiisme aux huitième et neuvième siècles de l'hégire," *Revue des Études Islamiques* 29, 1961, pp. 61-142. Hellmut Ritter, "Studien zur Geschichte der islamischen Frömmigkeit. II: Die Anfänge der Hurufisekte," *Oriens* 7/1, 1954, pp. 1-54. ʿEzz-al-Din ʿAbd-al-Majid b. Frešta Taravi (Firishte-oğlu), *ʿEšq-nāma*, tr. R. Tanrıkulu as *Ilm-i Cavidan*, Ankara, 1998. Moḥammad-ʿAli Tarbiat, *Dānešmandān-e Āḏarbāyjān*, ed. Ḡolām-Reżā Ṭabāṭabāʾi, Tehran, 1999.

(ORKHAN MIR-KASIMOV)

JĀVID-NĀMA (Pers. *Jāved-nāma*), title of a Persian *maṯnawi* by Muhammad Iqbal (q.v.); it is often rendered into English as "The Song of Eternity." The work was first published in 1932, only six years before Iqbal's death. Being the longest and most carefully planned of all his poems, it is usually considered to be his greatest work. Early reviewers greeted it with a host of superlatives, proclaiming that it would rank with Rumi's *Maṯnawi* or even the *Divān* of Hafez (q.v.). Iqbal himself was confident of its future success and went so far as to predict that its translator would gain fame in Europe. Such eulogies, of course, contain a high degree of exaggeration, but it is fair to say that even with the declining popularity of Persian in the Subcontinent, the poem has stood the test of time, and no study of Iqbal would be possible without reference to its remarkable style and content. Iqbal dedicated the work to his young son, Javed, but the title surely implies that the poet had no doubts about its everlasting worth and importance.

When Iqbal began to compose the *Jāvid-nāma*, he had already formulated the philosophy and doctrines that are commonly associated with him. The wide canvas he chose for this work gave him, as it were, a final opportunity to repeat and reinforce the ideas that were first put forward in his early Persian *maṯnawi*s, such as *Asrār-e ḵodi* "The Secrets of the Self" (1915), and *Romuz-e biḵodi* "The Mysteries of selflessness" (1918).

The idea of tackling such a work had occurred to him in his early student days, when he somewhat ambitiously stated that he would like to write a book in the style of Milton's *Paradise Lost*. This initial project was, perhaps fortunately, abandoned, and eventually it was Jalāl-al-Din Rumi who became one of his most profound influences. He was also greatly impressed by his reading of Dante. Much later, when writing to a friend about future possibilities, he remarked that he intended to produce "a kind of Divine Comedy in the style of Rumi's *Maṯnawi*" (*Maktūbāt-i Iqbāl*, ed. Sayyid Nazir Niazi, Karachi, 1956, p. 300), and this is exactly what the *Jāvid-nāma* turned out to be. In its form, at least, the lengthy *maṯnawi*, which contains almost 4,000 verses, owes much to these two medieval poets, by whose works Iqbal was greatly inspired. The full text of the work can be found in *Kolliyāt-e Eqbāl, Fārsi* (pp. 589-706).

The *Jāvid-nāma* is the story of the poet's journey through the spheres and the far reaches of the heavens in his unending quest to discover the very secrets of life and salvation. In the Prologue (pp. 601-16), which bears some resemblance to that of Goethe's *Faust*, he describes how Zarvān, the old Iranian god of Time and Space, exhorts him to rid himself of earthly limitations. Only then will he be able to embark upon his celestial journey and hear the song of the stars. This leads him to the place where he meets his mentor, Rumi, who agrees to act as his guide, in the same way that Virgil had accepted Dante's request to lead him through Hell and Purgatory to the confines of Heaven. He is now given the name *Zenda Rud* "Living Stream." In this name Iqbal chose for himself there is perhaps another reminiscence of Goethe. The German poet, in "Mahomets Gesang" (which, incidentally, Iqbal freely translated into Persian in *Payām-e mašreq*; q.v. at *iranica.com*), likens the message of the Prophet to a river. Here one is also reminded of the first stanza of Iqbal's Urdu *Sāqi-nāma*, one of his most popular and most optimistic poems, published in the Urdu collection *Bāl-e Jibrīl* and written about the same time as the *Jāvid-nāma*. In this, a small stream, starting its descent from the summit of a mountain breaks through every rock and barrier in the way of its progress and finally emerges as a gushing torrent.

The first stop is the Moon (pp. 619-44), where Zenda Rud and Rumi discourse with the Hindu sage, Jahān-Dust "Friend of the World" on the respective merits of Western and Eastern culture. In answer to Rumi's comment that the only hope of salvation lies in a synthesis of the two, the ascetic proclaims that for all its shortcomings the East will soon overtake the materialistic West. This optimistic message, which runs through much of Iqbal's later verse, is repeated by the angel Saruš, whose song is one of the most lyrical and enchanting parts of the work. In a valley with the strange name of Yarḡmid, the poet finds the tablets of Buddha, Zoroaster, Christ, and Moḥammad, and this gives Iqbal the opportunity to discuss and comment upon their respective teachings.

On Mercury (pp. 647-71), conversations with Jamāl-al-Din Afḡāni (q.v.) and Saʿd-al-Din Pāšā cover a wide range of near-contemporary political topics from the downfall of the Turks to the merits and deficiencies of Bolshevism. Much of the blame for the ills that beset the present-day Islamic world are, in a manner typical of Iqbal, ascribed to the ravings of the fanatical mullah—*din-e mollā fi sabil Allāh fasād*!

On Venus (pp. 675-86), the two companions encounter, among many others, the arrogant Lord Kitchener, whose clipped Persian well portrays the character of the archetypal British imperialist. On Mars (pp. 689-700), where the inhabitants have completely forsaken materialism, and are thus in every way superior to the inhabitants of the "West," Zenda Rud is confronted by a sorceress, who had been brought there from Earth by Farz Marz, the Martian equivalent of Satan. She shrieks out her doctrine of what in modern terms would be described as "women's liberation," predicting a time when women will be able to conceive by a method of artificial insemination. Naturally, Rumi and Zenda Rud thoroughly disapprove of these modern notions, which were being mooted at the time.

Perhaps one of the most moving episodes of the poems takes place on Saturn (pp. 729-35), where India, portrayed as a beautiful houri, "her eyes intoxicated with divine love," appears before the travelers in the chains of slavery. She is followed by two abject traitors from Mysore and Bengal. Even Hell had rejected them.

Having traversed the outer regions of the heavens, the poet at last hears the Divine Voice, which discloses the secrets he desired to know. These are revealed in a final poem (pp. 787-96) written for his son, Javed, to whom the whole work is dedicated:

Life's only purpose is to soar and fly.
The nest is not the place to rest and lie.

Although it might be argued that the ideas expressed in *Jāvid-nāma* had all been set out in Iqbal's earlier Urdu and Persian works, from which most of them were merely repeated, the sheer scale of the poem and the originality of the work's conception make it one of his best and most enduring.

See also IQBAL, MUHAMMAD.

Bibliography: The full text of *Jāvid-nāma* can be found in *Kolliyāt-e Eqbāl, Fārsi*, Lahore, 1973. Other relevant works are: A. J. Arberry, *Javid-nama*, London, 1966 (a complete English translation with an excellent introduction). A. Schimmel, *Buch der Ewigkeit*, Munich,

1957 (a complete German verse translation). Shaikh Mahmud Ahmad, *The Pilgrimage of Eternity*, Lahore, 1961 (a complete English verse translation with a lengthy introduction).

(DAVID MATTHEWS)

JAWĀD, IMAM ABU JAʿFAR. See forthcoming, online.

JAWĀHER AL-ʿAJĀYEB, a short, rare kind of *taḏkera* in Persian containing biographies of female poets and specimens of their verses (mostly in Persian, some in Chaghatay Turkish). It was compiled by Solṭān-Moḥammad b. Amir(i) Heravi (ca. 1562), known as Faḵri Heravi (q.v.; for variant names, see Rāšedi, p. 13), who had started his literary career in Safavid Herat before emigrating to the court of the Arḡuns in Sind (Storey, pp. 795-97; Rāšedi, pp. 11-74 ; Naqawi, pp. 91-94; Ḵayyāmpur, pp. *y, yḥ*). The *Jawāher al-ʿajāyeb* was most probably written in Šaʿbān 962/June-July 1555 (Rāšedi, p. 66), or rather in 1556 after Jalāl-al-Din Moḥammad Akbar (q.v.) ascended the Mughal throne (Naqawi, p. 98; Ḵayyāmpur, pp. *yb*; Rāšedi, pp. 69-70), and not in 1540-41 (Sprenger, p. 10), at the court of Moḥammad ʿIsā Khan Tarḵān (r. 1554-67), and dedicated to a lady called Māh/Māhom Begom (*Jawāher al-ʿajāyeb*, ed. Rāšedi, pp. 114-15). She could be identified either with the nurse of the Emperor Akbar, Māhom (Naqawi, p. 97; Ḵayyāmpur, p. *yb*), or with Ḥājia Māh Begom, the daughter of Moḥammad Moqim Arḡun, wife first of Šāh-Ḥasan Arḡun and then of Moḥammad ʿIsā Tarḵān (*Jawāher al-ʿajāyeb*, ed. Rāšedi, pp. 114 n. 1, 115).

The *Jawāher al-ʿajāyeb* starts with an introduction containing praises of the ruling kings, Shah Ṭahmāsp Ṣafawi in Iran and Akbar in India, of the author's last patron Moḥammad ʿIsā Khan, and of Māhom Begom, the dedicatee (ed. Rāšedi, pp. 113-15); some copies end with a *qaṣida* dedicated to "Māhom" (ed. Rāšedi, pp. 141-42). Eight known manuscripts are described by Rāšedi (pp. 72-74), which completes the lists of Charles Storey and other catalogues. Number of biographies varies between 20 and 31 according to the copy. They are arranged in a rough chronological order. Some manuscripts start with four entries devoted to legendary or saintly women famous throughout the Muslim world: Delārām, ʿĀyeša, Fāṭema, and Zoleyḵā (see ed. Rāšedi, pp. 117-20). The following four items treat Persian language poetesses who lived prior to the Timurid period (ed. Rāšedi, pp. 120-24), namely Mahsati (at the court of the Seljuq Solṭān Sanjar, 12th cent.); Pādšāh Ḵātun bent Qoṭb-al-Din Moḥammad-Solṭān Qarā Ḵetāy who ruled in Kermān at the end of the 13th cent.; Jahān Ḵātun Širāzi and Bibi Ḥayāt, both wives of a vizier of the Injuid Shah Abu Esḥāq (d. 1357) and contemporaries of ʿObeyd Zakāni (d. 1371).

The majority of the entries are devoted to poetesses who lived mostly in Herat, Khorasan, and Transoxiana, and who were contemporaries or near-contemporaries of the author. They include "Mehri; Moḡul Ḵātun (wife of Moḥammad Khan Šeybāni); Āfāq Bega Jalāyer; Nehāni Kermāni; Bija Monajjema; Bibi ʿEṣmati; Bideli; Nehāni Širāzi; a daughter of the *qāżi* of Samarqand; Faḵr-al-Nesāʾ; Ḵānzāda Torbati; Partovi; Šāhmolk; a daughter of Ḡazali Yazdi; Bibi Ārezu; Żaʿefi; Ḥayāt Heravi; Bibi Ātun (wife of Mawlānā Baqāʾi); Jamāli or Ḥejābi (daughter of Mawlānā Helāli); daughter of ʿEffati Esfarāyeni; Fāṭeme Ḵātun Dusti; Tervi(?) Meymāni, and Nesāʾi.

The *Jawāher al-ʿajāyeb* became itself a source for several later Persian and Mughal authors, who included chapters on female poets (list in Rāšedi, pp. 11-12). The *Jawāher al-ajāyeb* is a valuable complementary source for Timurid and Safavid social and cultural history by a contemporary author, but it is also rather unusual and unique in medieval Persian literature by the fact that it is exclusively devoted to women (see Szuppe). It sheds light on the cultural life of Herat elites close to the court circle and on the part played in it by women, both Persian and Turkic.

Bibliography: Catalogues of manuscripts. Eduard Sachau, Hermann Ethé and Alfred Felix L. Beeston, *Catalogue of the Persian, Turkish, Hindūstāni and Pushtū manuscripts in the Bodleian Library*, Catalogi codicum manuscriptorum bibliothecae Bodleianae 13, 3 vols, Oxford 1889-1954, no. 362 (fol. 190-98). Aloys Sprenger, *Catalogue of the Arabic, Persian and Hindùstàny Manuscripts in the Libraries of the King of Oudh* I, Calcutta 1854, no. 5, pp. 9-11. Maulavi Abdul Muqtadir and Sayyed Athar Sher, *Catalogue of the Arabic and Persian manuscripts in the Oriental Public Library at Bankipore*, Patna, 1908, XI, ms 1098; XXXII. Maulavi Qāsim Hasir Radavi and Maulavi Abd-ul-Muqtadir, *Catalogue raisonné of the Būhār Library* I: *Catalogue of the Persian Manuscripts . . .*, Calcutta, 1905, no. 482(1).

Editions. Faḵri Heravi, *Jawāher al-ʿajāyeb*, lithograph ed., Lucknow, 1873. Idem, *Taḏkera-ye Rawżat al-salāṭin wa Jawāher al-ʿajāyeb* (with Divan Fakhri Harvi), compiled during the reign of Shah Hasan Arghun and Mirza Isa Tarkhan at Tatta, year 1551-56, ed. with annotations Sayyed Ḥosām-al-Din Rāšedi, Hyderabad, 1968, pp. 111-42.

Secondary Sources. Aḥmad Golčin-e Maʿāni, *Tāriḵ-e taḏkerahā-ye fārsi*, 2 vols., Tehran, 1969-71, I, pp. 417-32; II, pp. 839-41. Mir Neẓām-al-Din ʿAli-Šir Navāʾi, *Majāles al-nafāʾes*, two Pers. translations by Solṭān-Moḥammad Faḵri Heravi (as *Laṭāʾef-nāma*) and Ḥakim Šāh-Moḥammad Qazvini, ed. ʿAli-Aṣḡar Ḥekmat, Tehran, 1944, editor's Intro. ʿAbd-al-Rasul Ḵayyāmpur, "Introduction" to Faḵri Heravi, *Taḏkera-ye Rawżat al-salāṭin*, ed. ʿAbd-al-Rasul Ḵayyāmpur, Tabriz, 1966. Sayyed Ḥosām-al-Din Rāšedi, "Introduction" to *Jawāher al-ʿajāyeb* (see above). Ḏabiḥ-Allāh Ṣafā, *Tāriḵ-e adabiyāt dar Irān* VI/3, 1992, pp. 1652-53. Charles A. Storey, *Persian Literature: A Bio-Bibliographical Survey*, 2 vols., London 1927-, I/2, no. 1099, pp. 795-97. Saʿid Nafisi, *Tāriḵ-e naẓm o naṯr dar Irān wa dar zabān-e fārsi*, 2 vols., Tehran, 1965, I, pp. 438-39. Sayyed ʿAli-Reżā Naqawi, *Taḏkera-nevisi-e fārsi dar Hend wa Pākestān*, Tehran, 1968, pp. 91-100. Maria Szuppe, "Female Intellectual Milieu in Timurid and Post-Timurid Herāt: Faxri Haravi's Biography of Poetesses *Javāher al-ʿAjāyeb*," in Michele Bernardini, ed., *La civiltà timuride come fenomeno internazionale*, 2 vols., Rome, 1996, I, pp. 119-37.

(MARIA SZUPPE)

JAWĀHER-E ḴAMSA, title of a Persian work on Sufi meditation practices composed by the well-known and controversial Šaṭṭārī saint, Moḥammad Ḡawṯ Gwāleyārī (1500-63; Ernst, 1999a; Kugle). In the text he gives his full name as Moḥammad b. Ḵaṭir-al-Dīn b. Laṭif b. Muʿin-al-Din Qattāl b. Ḵaṭīr-al-Dīn b. Bāyazīd b. Ḵᵛāja Farid-al-Dīn ʿAṭṭār (MS 1384, Patna, fol. 3a), and he also refers to himself as "Abu'l-Moʾayyad Moḥammad al-Mokāṭab be'l-Ḡawṯ ʿenda Allāh" (fol. 270b). The book, as he explains, is the fruit of the teachings of his master, Shaikh Ẓohur Ḥāji Ḥożur, as well as the result of his experiences in retreat over the course of thirteen, or sixteen, years in the mountainous fortress of Čonār in northern India. At the age of twenty-two, he composed the book and showed it to his master, who confirmed his sainthood and the validity of the book's teachings. Subsequently, when he was exiled in Gujarat during the ascendancy of Šēr Šāh Surī (r. 1540-56), at the urging of his disciples he reworked the book, completing this second edition in 1549, when he was fifty years old; no copies of the earlier version are known to exist.

The *Jawāher-e ḵamsa* is divided into five parts, each called a *jawhar*, addressing the following topics: (I) on the worship of devotees (*ʿebādat-e ʿābedān*) concerning Qurʾānic verses in supererogatory prayer, required Islamic prayers, and devotions for particular times; (II) on the practices of ascetics (*zohd-e zāhedān*), dealing with internal practices that may be attempted after gaining perfection in external devotions; (III) on invocation (*daʿwat*) of the names of God, which requires the instruction of a master; (IV) on the recitations and practices (*aḏkār o ašḡāl*) that are distinctive to the mystics of the Šaṭṭārī path; and (V) the legacy of divine practices belonging to those who have realized the truth.

While the *Jawāher-e ḵamsa* is similar to other well-known manuals of Sufi recitation, it also has distinctive characteristics. Part I is clearly aimed at the ordinary believer. The succeeding parts increasingly aim at more elite audiences. The formulas to be recited are almost invariably in Arabic with a strong Qurʾānic flavor, although Persian quatrains are regularly introduced for emphasis. There is frequent reference to the Prophet Moḥammad and to famous Sufis. What is most characteristic of this treatise, however, is its distinctly practical flavor, with detailed instructions not only for performance, but also in terms of the results (whether spiritual or material) that are to be expected; this practicality is probably the reason for the popularity of this work.

In Part III, the invocations include signs of the zodiac, planets, letters of the Arabic alphabet, and the governing spirits (*mowakkelān*) who control all of the preceding. Certain prayers based on divine names fall into distinct classes according to the number of times they are repeated, which may range well into the thousands; some are even pronounced letter by letter. The influences of some of the divine names are explained in metaphysical terms familiar from the school of Ebn al-ʿArabī (q.v.). Frequent use is made of the numerical properties of the Arabic alphabet according to the *abjad* (q.v.) system. There are remarkably practical applications, including one recitation, inscribed on a silver ring, which will make sultans obedient to one's word. Part IV has a detailed description of *ḏekr* (q.v.) techniques including the number of "beats" (*yak żarbī*, etc.), posture, breath control, visualization of divine names and formulas in different parts of the body, psychic states, and the metaphysical significance of experiences to be encountered, occasionally with multi-circular cosmic diagrams and complicated tables of letters.

The *Jawāher-e ḵamsa* has been an extremely popular work since it was first written, and while the Persian text has not been printed, there are a number of manuscripts (Monzawi, 2003-, III, pp. 1392-94 lists over 20 manuscripts; see also idem, 1969-74, II, p. 1118). It had many sequels among the Persian texts produced by the Šaṭṭāri Sufis of India (Ernst, 1999a). It was especially well known in the Arabic translation *al-Jawāher al ḵams* by Ṣebḡat-Allāh of Broach (d. 1606; his *nesba* Broči is sometimes Arabicized as Barwaji), which became a standard part of Sufi training in the Arabian Peninsula, particularly in the hands of teachers such as the latter's Egyptian-born student Aḥmad Šennawi (d. 1619), who wrote an important commentary on the text entitled *Taḥliat al-baṣāʾer* (*al-Jawāher al-ḵams* I, p. 5). This tradition was continued by a succession of teachers who inherited the Šaṭṭārī teachings, including Ṣafi-al-Din Aḥmad Qošāši (d. 1660-61) and the well-known Ebrāhīm Kurāni (d. 1690), whose works were widely studied as far away as Morocco and Southeast Asia (El-Rouayheb, p. 271; Johns, pp. 432-33; idem, pp. 523-24). This Arabic version was published in Fez in a lithograph edition (1900) in Maḡrebī script (recently reprinted in standard Arabic characters), and also in a modern edition (ed. Aḥmad b.ʿAbbās, Cairo, 1974) based on manuscripts from the Tējāni *zāwia* and from the Dār-al-Kotob library; while the editor of the latter publication was an enthusiastic advocate of its spiritual teachings (I, pp. 3-9), the publisher nevertheless included a disclaimer (I, pp. 211-12), disavowing any misguided teaching that was not firmly based on sound Hadith. There have also been at least six Urdu translations from the Persian, frequently reprinted (Rānjhā, pp. 266-67; see also Gaborieau). Some of the practices of this text, including striking diagrams, were rendered into English in the mid-19th century (Ja'far Sharif, pp. 219-31).

Finally, it should be pointed out that peculiar blinkers of early orientalist scholarship held it axiomatic that all forms of Eastern mysticism were identical, so it has often been alleged that Sufism owes much to yoga. T. P. Hughes actually described the *Jawāher-e ḵamsa* as follows: "This book is largely made up of Hindu customs which, in India, have become part of Muhammadanism" (s.v. "Daʿwah," pp. 72-78). The text in fact contains (*al-Jawahir al-ḵams* II, p. 70) a single *ḏekr* formula in Hindi, attributed, not to any yogi, but to the early Češtī Sufi master Farīd-al-Dīn Ganj-e Šakar (d. 1265, q.v.), which is well known in other Sufi literature. Although Moḥammad Ḡawṯ was certainly knowledgeable about yoga (Ernst, 1996), it would be obsessive to see Indian practices as the basis of this Sufi compilation (Ernst, 2005).

Bibliography: Khaled El-Rouayheb, "Opening the Gate of Verification: The Forgotten Arab-Islamic Florescence of the 17th Century," *IJMES* 38/2, 2006, pp. 263-81. Carl W. Ernst, "Sufism and Yoga According to Muhammad Ghawth," *Sufi* 29, Spring 1996, pp. 9-13. Idem, "Meditations of the Shattari Order," in idem, tr., *Teachings of Sufism*, Boston, 1999a, pp. 53-81. Idem, "Persecution and Circumspection in the Shattari Sufi Order," in Fred De Jong and Berndt Radtke, eds., *Islamic Mysticism Contested: Thirteen Centuries of Controversies and Polemics*, Leiden, 1999b, pp. 416-35. Idem, "Situating Sufism and Yoga." *JRAS*, ser. 3, 15, 2005, pp. 15-43. M. Gaborieau, "L'ésotérisme musulman dans le sous-continent indo-pakistanais: un point de vue ethnologique," *Bulletin d'Études Orientales* 44, 1993, pp. 191-209. Thomas Patrick Hughes, *A Dictionary of Islam*, London, 1885; repr., Delhi, 1973. A. H. Johns, "al-Kūrānī, Ibrāhim," in *EI*[2] V, pp. 432-33. Idem, "al-Ḳūs̲h̲ās̲h̲ī, Ṣafī al-Din Aḥmad," in *EI*[2] V, pp., 523-24. Scott A. Kugle, "Heaven's Witness: The Uses and Abuses of Muhammad Ghawth's Mystical Ascension," *Journal of Islamic Studies* 14, 2003, pp. 1-36. Aḥmad Monzawi, *Fehrest-e nosḵahā-ye ḵaṭṭi-e fārsi*, 6 vols., Tehran, 1974-69. Idem, *Fehrest-e moštarak-e nosḵahā-ye ḵaṭṭi-e fārsi-e Pākestān*, Islamabad, 2003-. Moḥammad Naḏīr Rānjhā, *Barr-e Ṣaḡir Pāk o Hend mēñ taṣawwof ki maṭbuʿāt*, Lahore, 1999. Jaʿfar Sharif, *Islam in India or the Qanun-i-Islam: The Customs of the Musalmāns of India, Comprising . . . Their Various Rites and Ceremonies . . .* , tr. Gerhard Andreas Herklots, ed. William Crooke, Oxford, 1921; reprint, New Delhi, 1972.

(CARL W. ERNST)

JAWĀHER-NĀMA, the title of several Persian works on precious stones, gems, minerals, and metals, as well as on crafts related to them. Persian *gowhar* (or, in its Arabicized form, *jawhar*) originally means a pearl, but also a precious stone, a gem, or a jewel (Dehḵodā, s.v.). Although pearls, coral, amber, bezoars, and the like are not minerals or stones in *stricto senso*, in medieval texts they appear together with real minerals under the non-scientific denomination of "stones." Persian books on stones, jewels, and minerals, usually entitled *Jawāher-nāma*, closely follow their Arabic counterparts. Among the Arabic texts on precious stones, the most reputed is Abu Rayḥān Biruni's (973-1048) *Ketāb al-jamāher fi maʿrefat al-jawāher* (written before 1035, see BIRUNI v.). Biruni mentions in his book a treatise on a similar subject written by Naṣr b. Yaʿqub Dinawari (10th-11th cents.), which was apparently already lost in his days (Biruni, tr. Said, pp. 28-29). He also refers to the treatise of Yaʿqub b. Esḥāq Kendi (d. *ca.* 870), which he considers to be very good (Biruni, tr. Said, pp. 28-29).

The Jawāher-nāma of Moḥammad b. Abi al-Barakāt Jawhari Nišāpuri. The earliest surviving example of a *Jawāher-nāma* written in Persian appears to be the work of Farid-al-Din Moḥammad b. Abi al-Barakāt Jawhari Nišāpuri, dated 1196. The text is dedicated to Neẓām-al-Molk Ṣadr-al-Din Abu'l-Fatḥ Masʿud, the vizier of the Khwarazmshah Tekeš b. Il Arslan (r. 1172-1200). The author, nicknamed Jawhari, was a connoisseur of precious stones and a jewel-maker, and he was also occasionally invited to serve as an expert and mediator for royal jewels (Vesel, Afshar, and Mohebbi, p. 154). Biruni, in his time, was also appointed to a similar position (Biruni, tr. Said, p. 47). Nišāpuri's work is divided into four chapters: 1. minerals; 2. precious stones; 3. metals; 4. various items and techniques, including *minā* (enamel) and *talāwiḥāt* (luster ware, and also porcelain and *ḵatu*, the latter being the term for the horn of a mysterious animal or creature, a kind of unicorn, which was sometimes believed to be rhinoceros). Although some parts of the book are clearly inspired by the text of Biruni (or other, unmentioned, "ancient authors"), the major part of the work comprises anecdotes and observations based on the author's experience. Nišāpuri's information is thus based on "ancient" authors, on his own experience as a connoisseur of precious "stones," and on what he heard from merchants and reliable persons. In such a way, Nišāpuri's text can be regarded as a link between the Arabic tradition and the later Persian texts on this subject.

The text gives many details on prices of gems and pearls, on the techniques of jewelry, stone cutting, and polishing, as well as on the extraction of stones and minerals from the mines, the transformation of ores into metals, the making of swords and weapons, together with numerous indications related to other techniques (such as ceramics- and glass-making, and goldsmithing). Some pieces of Nišāpuri's information give indications to lost works of art; thus, one of the original anecdotes mentions a large green stone (probably an emerald), engraved with the image of an enthroned Sasanian king (see Grenet and Vesel). Very little is known about the biography of Nišāpuri; from his observations on pearls one can guess that he made various travels to Sirāf, Kiš, and Bahrain. These travels allowed him to collect extensive valuable information on various terms for the size, color, and price of pearls. Also very original, and of considerable importance for the knowledge of ceramics, are the formulae for metallic lustre decoration on glass and ceramics, which Nišāpuri calls *talāwiḥāt*. His *Jawāher-nāma* is therefore the earliest known Persian text dealing with technical aspects of ceramics. The most reliable copy of this text (almost complete) is dated from the 14th century and preserved in the Malek Library in Tehran. This copy has an illustration with the picture of an oven (or furnace) used for enamel and *talāwiḥāt*. Such technical illustrations are very rare, and other copies of the text (such as the ones in Tashkent) do not have this illustration. Nišāpuri's text was edited by Iraj Afšār in 2004 on the basis of its four major copies preserved in libraries of Qom, Istanbul, Tehran, and Tashkent.

Later Jawāher-nāmas. As early as 1971 Iraj Afšār pointed out that Nišāpuri's text was probably an inspiration for later texts on precious stones, such as Naṣir-al-Din Ṭusi's (1201-74) *Tansuq-nāma-ye Ilḵāni* (completed ca. 1258) and Abu'l-Qāsem ʿAbd-Allāh Kāšāni's *ʿArāʾes al-jawāher wa nafāʾes al-aṭāʾeb* (written in 1300; see Vesel, Afshar, and Mohebbi). In Ṭusi's text, the whole first chapter on the theory of the minerals in the sublunar world is copied from Nišāpuri's book, while the second chapter on "stones" is Ṭusi's original work. Kāšāni's *ʿArāʾes al-jawāher* is notably famous for its Conclusion (*ḵātema*) on ceramics (*kāšigari* or *ḡażāra*). However, this Conclusion, although also dealing with the metallic luster decoration, is completely different from Chapter Four of Nišāpuri's work in the formulae for making luster decoration. Besides, while Nišāpuri calls lustre *talāwiḥāt*, Kāšāni uses the term *rang-e doātaši* (two-fire color).

Naṣir-al-Din Ṭusi's *Tansuq-nāma-ye Ilḵāni* is divided into four chapters (*maqālat*): 1. on minerals; 2. on precious stones; 3. on metals; and 4. on perfumes. Abu'l-Qāsem Kāšāni's *ʿArāʾes al-jawāher wa nafāʾes al-aṭāʾeb* is probably the best known Persian text on minerals and precious stones. Its structure is similar to that of Ṭusi's work: the first part, divided in three chapters, deals with precious and semi-precious stones, and metals; the second part concerns perfumes and drugs. The conclusion (*ḵātema*), entitled "On the arts of ceramics," is original, and the most well-known text on ceramics in the entire Islamic world. It was first edited and translated into German in 1935 (Ritter et al.) and then translated into English in 1973 (Allan).

At later times, other texts on the subject were produced, such as an anonymous *Jawāher-nāma* (edited by Taqi Bineš) which is dated from the 15th century and related to Timurid patronage, and Moḥammad b. Manṣur Daštaki's *Gowhar-nāma* (or *Jawāher-nāma-ye solṭāni*, edited by Manučehr Sotuda), which is dated 1481 and dedicated to the Āq Qoyunlu ruler Uzun Ḥasan (r. 1457-78). Both texts describe precious stones and minerals and provide references to related techniques, such as metalwork, glass-making, and making of ceramics or enamel (*minā*). These texts are therefore invaluable, not only for the description of precious stones and their relation to the goldsmithing, but also for the knowledge of related techniques and crafts. Later examples of *Jawāher-nāmas*, such as the one by Šāh-Moḥammad b. Mobārakšāh Qazvini (16th century), are listed by Storey (vol. II, pt. 3, pp. 449-55). A copy of the versified *Jawāher-nāma-ye manẓum* by Rašid ʿAbbāsi is recorded in the Malek Library in Tehran (Vesel, Afshar, and Mohebbi).

Bibliography: James Allan, "Abu'l-Qasim's Treatise on Ceramics," *Iran* 11, 1973, pp. 111-20. Taqi Bineš, ed., *Jawāher-nāma*, in *Farhang-e Irānzamin* 12, Tehran, 1964. Abu Rayḥān Biruni, *Al-Jamāher fi maʿrefat al-jawāher*, ed. F. Krenkow, Hyderabad, Deccan, 1936; ed. Yusof al-Hādi as *Al-Jamāher fi al-jawāher*, Tehran, 1995; tr. H. M. Said as *The Book Most Comprehensive in Knowledge on Precious Stones: al-Beruni's Book on Mineralogy (Kitāb al-jamāhir fi maʿrifat al-jawāhir)*, Islamabad, 1989. Moḥammad b. Manṣur Daštaki, *Gowhar-nāma*, ed. M. Sotuda, in *Farhang-e Irānzamin* 4, Tehran, 1956. F. Grenet and Ž. Vesel, "Émeraude royale," in *Yād-nāma, in memoria Alessandro Bausani*, vol. II, ed. B. Scarcia-Amoretti and L. Rostagno, Rome, 1991, pp. 99-116. Abu'l-Qāsem Kāšāni, *ʿArāʾes al-jawāher wa nafāʾes al-aṭāʾeb*, ed. Iraj Afshār, Tehran, 1966. Moḥammad b. Abi al-Barakāt Jawhari Nišāpuri, *Jawāher-nāma-ye Neẓāmi*, ed. Iraj Afšār, Tehran, 2004. Yves Porter, "Textes persans sur la céramique," in *La science dans le monde iranien à l'époque islamique*, ed. Ž. Vesel, H. Beikbaghban, and Th. de Crussol des Epesse, Tehran, 1998, pp. 165-89. Idem, "Le quatrième chapitre du *Javāher-nāme-ye Neẓāmi*," in *Sciences, techniques et instruments dans le monde iranien (Xᵉ-XIXᵉ siècle)*, ed. N. Pourjavady and Ž. Vesel, Tehran, 2004, pp. 341-60. H. Ritter, J. Ruska, F. Sarre, and R. Winderlich, "Orientalische Steinbücher und persische Fayencetechnik," *Istanbuler Mitteilungen des Archäologischen Instituts des deutschen Reiches* 3, 1935, pp. 16-48. C. A. Storey, *Persian Literature: a Bio-bibliographical Survey*, vol. II, pt. 3: *F. Encyclopaedias and Miscellanies; G. Arts and Crafts; H. Science; J. Occult Arts*, Leiden, 1977, pp. 449-55. Naṣir-al-Din Ṭusi, *Tansuq-nāma-ye Ilḵāni*, ed. Modarres Rażavi, Tehran, 1969. Ž. Vesel, I. Afshar, and P. Mohebbi, "«Le Livre des Pierres pour Neẓām [al-Molk] (*Javāher-nāme-ye Neẓāmī*)» (592/1195-6): la source présumée du *Tansūkh-nāme-ye Īlkhānī* de Ṭūsī," in *Naṣīr al-Dīn Ṭūsī, philosophe et savant du XIIIᵉ siècle*, ed. N. Pourjavady and Ž. Vesel, Tehran, 2000, pp. 145-74.

(YVES PORTER)

JAWĀLIQI, HEŠĀM b. Sālem, an Imami jurist and theologian of the 2nd/8th century. He was a close associate of the Imams Jaʿfar al-Ṣādeq and Musā al-Kāẓem (qq.v.). His *nesba* was derived from his vocation, which was the selling of woolen sacks (*jawāliq* < Pers. *govāl*, *jovāl*). He was also called al-ʿAllāf after another trade of his, the selling of fodder (*ʿalaf*), which he turned to later in his life (Kašši, II, p. 566). According to his biographers, Hešām b. Sālem was a captive from Khorasan, hence he became a client (*mawlā*) for the Umayyad prince and governor of Kufa, Bešr b. Marwān. He transmitted 363 Hadiths on the authority of the Imams Jaʿfar al-Ṣādeq and Musā al-Kāẓem. He had heard each Hadith either directly from one of the two Imams or from one of their close associates (Ḵoʾi, XX, p. 330). Therefore, his collection of Hadiths is considered a primary source (*aṣl*) and one of the 400 authoritative collections of Imami Hadith (for a partial list of these collections, see Āḡā Bozorg Ṭehrāni, II, p. 128).

Imami biographers considered Jawāliqi to be among the most trustworthy transmitters of Hadith (Najāši, II. p. 435; Kašši, II, p. 567; Ḥelli, II, p. 290). He compiled three other books (*al-Ḥajj*, *al-Tafsir*, and *al-Meʿrāj*) in addition to his own book (*aṣl*) of Hadith (Najāši, II, p. 435). Jawāliqi narrated Hadith on the authority of prominent companions of Jaʿfar al-Ṣādeq and Musā al-Kāẓem, including Abu Baṣir, Abu Ḥamza Ṭomali, Abān b. Taḡleb, Zorāra b. Aʿyān, Jāber Joʿfi, and ʿAmmār Sābāṭi.

Abu'l-Ḥasan ʿAli Ašʿari refers to Jawāliqi as the head of a Shiʿite sub-sect that was named after him "al-Hešāmiya," alleging that this sect "claimed that their Lord possesses the image of a human (*ṣurat al-ensān*), but they deny His possessing flesh and blood, saying that He is bright light (*nur sāṭeʿ*) and He has five senses like human beings" (Ašʿari, 1950, p. 105; idem, 1980, p. 34). However, no sub-sect with such a belief was reported by Ḥasan Nawbaḵti, whose *Feraq al-Šiʿa* is more authoritative on the subject, and it was written earlier than Ašʿari's book. There is, however, an attribution of this belief to Jawāliqi, reported in a conversation between the Imam ʿAli al-Reżā (q.v.) and an associate named ʿAbd-al-Malek Ḥannāṭ (Kašši, II, pp. 568-69), but Ḵoʾi considers the report as weak and not reliable (Ḵoʾi, XX, p. 329).

We have no record of Jawāliqi's date of death, which must have been before 799, that is, the year in which Imam Musā al-Kāẓem died, since there is no record that he narrated any Hadiths from the following Imam, ʿAli al-Reżā. Besides, he was an accomplished theologian in the time of the Imam Jaʿfar al-Ṣādeq (d. 765), which makes it unlikely that he would outlive the long duration of al-Kāẓem's imamate (765-99). Furthermore, he was influential in settling the dispute over the Imamate after the death of Imam al-Ṣādeq, but his name was not mentioned in the controversy following the death of Imam al-Kāẓem (Nawbaḵti, tr. Maškur, pp. 117 ff., tr. Kadhim, pp. 133 ff.; Kašši, II, pp. 566-68), which indicates that he was not alive at that time.

Bibliography: Abu'l-Ḥasan ʿAli Ašʿari, *Ketāb maqālāt al-eslāmiyin wa eḵtelāf al-moṣellin*, Cairo, 1950; ed. Helmut Ritter, Wiesbaden, 1980. ʿAllāma Ḥasan b. Yusof Ḥelli, *Ḵolāṣat al-aqwāl fi maʿrefat al-rejāl*, Qom, 1996. Moḥammad b. ʿOmar Kašši, *Rejāl al-Kašši*, Qom, 1970. Abu'l-Qāsem Ḵoʾi, *Moʿjam rejāl al-ḥadiṯ wa tafṣil ṭabaqāt al-rowāh*, 24 vols., Beirut, 1992. Abu'l-ʿAbbās Najāši, *Rejāl al-Najāši*, ed. Musā Šobayri Zanjāni as *Fahrasat asmāʾ moṣannefin al-Šiʿa al-moštahar be-Rejāl al-Najāši*, Qom, 1986. Ḥasan b. Musā Nawbaḵti, *Feraq al-Šiʿa*, Najaf, 1931; tr. Moḥammad-Jawād Maškur as *Tarjama-ye Feraq al-Šiʿa-ye Nawbaḵti*, Tehran, 1974; tr. Abbas Kadhim as *Shiʿa Sects*, London, 2007. Āḡā Bozorg Ṭehrāni, *al-Ḏariʿa elā taṣānif al-šiʿa*, Beirut, 1983. Abu Jaʿfar Moḥammad b. Ḥasan Ṭusi, *Fehrest*, Beirut, 1983.

(ABBAS KADHIM)

JAWĀMEʿ AL-***ḤEKĀYĀT WA LAWĀMEʾ*** AL-***REWĀYĀT***, the earliest and the most comprehensive collection of stories in the Persian language, compiled by Sadid-al-Din Moḥammad ʿAwfi (d. after 1232, q.v.), the author of the earliest preserved biographichal dictionary (*taḏkera*) of Persian poets. The title of the book varies somewhat in different manuscripts. For example, it is cited as *Jāmeʿ al-ḥekāyāt wa lāmeʿ al-rewāyāt* in manuscript no. 2229 of the Majles library (Nafisi, p. 186), *Jāmeʿ al-ḥekāyāt wa lawāmeʿ al-rewāyāt* in manuscript no. 1784 of Tashkent Academy of Science (Voronofsk, II, p. 402), and *Jawāmeʿ al-ḥekāyāt* in manuscript no. "Or.6855" of the British Museum (Afšār, p. 672). The author, however, has called the book *Jawāmeʿ al-ḥekāyāt wa lawāmeʿ al-rewāyāt* in the preface of the book, which is borne by the early manuscripts (Qazvini, p. *kb*, n. 3).

ʿAwfi was initially engaged in translating *al-Faraj baʿd al-šedda*, the Arabic collection of stories by Qāżi Abu ʿAli Moḥassen Tanuḵi (Moʿin, p. 34), which eventually led him to compile a larger anthology of his own, the *Jawāmeʿ al-ḥekāyāt*.

After the Mongol invasion of Iran, ʿAwfi immigrated to Sind Province in India, where he resided in Uch (Oččh), at the court of Nāṣer-al-Din Qabāja, the ruler of Sind and Multān (r. 1205-28). He served for a while as judge in Cambay, where he finished his Persian translation of *al-Faraj baʿd al-šedda*, which he called *Jawāmeʿ al-ḥekāyāt*, but, encouraged by Qobāja, he began compiling a more comprehensive collection, the *Jawāmeʿ al-ḥekāyāt wa lawāmeʿ al-rewāyāt* (Qazvini, p. *ka*; Moʿin, pp. 25-26). After the death of Qabāja in 1228, ʿAwfi went to Delhi, where he finished the book. It was dedicated toʿAyn-al-Molk Faḵr-al-Din Ḥasan Asʿari, but afterwards, he dedicated it to Neẓām-al-Molk Jonaydi, the minister of Altotmes/Iltutmiš (Qazvini, pp. *ka-kb*). The latest historical event mentioned in the *Jawāmeʿ al-ḥekāyāt* is the revolt of Eḵtiār-al-Din Dawlatšāh Bolkā Ḵalji, the ruler of Lakahnu in the year 1230, which led Moḥammad Qazvini to conclude that the final date of finishing the book might be about 1232-33 (Qazvini, pp. *ka-kb*; ʿAli-Naqi Monzawi, p. 24).

Jawāmeʿ al-ḥekāyāt is arranged in four chapters (*qesm*), each one charachterized by a special subject matter and divided into twenty-five sections (*bāb*). Each section has a title of its own and contains stories that deal with a special aspect of the general subject matter of the chapter. All in all, the book contains a total of 2,113 stories.

The first chapter is titled "On the recognition of the Almighty, the sanctity and miracles of prophets, the wonderous deeds of saints and history" (*Dar maʿrefat-e āfaridgār-e taʿālā wa taqaddos wa moʿjezāt-e anbiāʾ wa karāmāt-e awliāʾ wa tawāriḵ wa maʾāṯer-e moluk wa ḵolafāʾ*) with sections treating themes such as: "the excellence of fairness" (*fażl-e ʿadl*), "decrees of the kings," "craftiness of those who pass judgments (*arbāb-e raʾy*)" "anecdotes about secretaries," "anecdotes about physicians," etc. The second chapter is on "Praiseworthy dispositions and admirable conduct" (*Aḵlāq-e ḥamida wa siar-e marżia*) with sections illustrating "modesty" (*ḥayāʾ*)," "compassion and pity" (*raḥm wa šafaqat*), "generosity," "silence and speech," "keeping secrets" and "nobility of character" (*makārem-e aḵlāq*). The third chapter is titled "Blameworthy characters" (*Aḵlāq-e madmum*) containing sections on "the differences of human nature," "thieves and anecdotes about them," "anecdotes concerning beggars," "reproach of ignorance," "clever women and their subtle remarks," and "the crafty deeds of women and their tricks." The fourth chapter is called "On the description of people and the wonders of the seas and countries and the nature of animals," illustrated in various section with stories on "wonders of fortune telling and their impacts," "the accounts of successful love affairs," "Rum, Ethiopia and India," "the oddities of strange buildings," "the wonders of the world of talisman," "about the nature of beasts and wilds," and so on (ʿAli-Naqi Monzawi, pp. 28-32).

The oldest manuscript (Ancient fonds 75; see Blochet, IV, p. 28), however, has a unique arrangement different from those of others. According to Moḥammad Moʿin (p. 64), this is the original arrangement of the book, which was later altered as the author revised and expanded his work. It is also possible that the original text was shorter than what we have now, but later on new stories were added either by ʿAwfi himself or others (Aḥmad Monzawi, 1969-74, V, p. 3669).

Stories vary in length according to the subject. For instance, in the Ramażāni's facsimile edition, which contains the last fifteen sections of the first chapter (altogether 518 stories), the shortest story (a command of the caliph "ʿOmar b. ʿAbd-al-ʿAzis) is in four lines, while the longest story (Caesar's daughter questioning her suiters) covers nine pages (ed. Ramażāni, pp. 207, 381-89).

Jawāmeʿ al-ḥekāyāt is the first collection of stories in Persian, but its significance is due not only to its literary merits, but also to the fact that it contains a good deal of information of considerable historical significance. Recording historical events in the framework of storytelling was a common approach of the Persian authors of texts on practical ethics (e.g., Neẓām-al-Molk, passim; Saʿdi, passim). It made the reading more enjoyable and the focal point of a story easier to remember. According to ʿAwfi himself, he used a variety of sources (94 altogether), including Zoroastrian and Manichaean works, Ferdowsi's *Šāh-nāma*, Ṭabari's *Taʾriḵ al-rosol waʾl-moluk*, Abu Rayḥān Biruni's *al-Āṯār al-bāqia* and *Taḥqiq mā leʾl-Hend*, Abu Ḥāmed Ḡazāli's *Naṣiḥat al-moluk* and *Kimiā-ye saʿādat*, etc. (see Nizāmud-Din, pp. 273-76). The book also contains a good number of stories without any indication of any sources; these stories may be based on ʿAwfi's own personal experiences (Moṣaffā, p. 45). His major source, however, has been Tanuḵi's collection, which evidently led him to compile his own *Jawāmeʿ al-ḥekāyāt*. There are sixty-two stories and narratives of Tanuḵi in the fourth section of *Jawāmeʿ al-ḥekāyā*, which indicate the extent of the influence of Tanuḵi's work as a model. Unfortunately, some of the sources mentioned by ʿAwfi are lost, of which only fifteen are known today (see Moṣaffā, 1975, pp. 38-54).

The historical stories narrated in *Jawāmeʿ al-ḥekāyāt*, despite all their literary merits and significance, are not all accurate enough to rely upon, in particular those whose sources are lost. A comparison (e.g., 5th sec. of the 1st chap.) with more reliable books on history reveals errors in names, dates, and even recording of certain historical events concerning the Caliphate period (Ḵalʿatbari, pp. 68-71). Some of these errors may have been made by the copyists, including those of the sources that he used. Moreover, it is not clear whether ʿAwfi just copied what he found in his sources or rewrote them, not to mention the fact that some narratives may have been ʿAwfi's own authorship (Bahār, p. 38).

Jawāmeʿ al-ḥekāyāt is also a worthy source of information concerning social matters. There is hardly any aspect of social interest of the time that is not addressed in this book. It covers philosophy, religions, women, poets, the aged, hazardous adventures, astronomy, ethnology, traditions, ancient monuments, natural history and physical properties of objects, etc., each one treated in a section of its own (Moṣaffā, 1973, pp. 50-51). Thus, it seems that the author intended to provide not only a collection of stories and maxims, but also an encyclopedic source of sciences of the day for his contemporaries in 13th-century India (Fouchecour, pp. 154-55). The real value of ʿAwfi's contribution with this collection to the cultural history of Iran reveals itself when it is compared with the works of his predecessors. None of the latter provides such a comprehensive picture of the various aspects of Persian cultural heritage (Nezāmud-Din, p. 24). What is more, ʿAwfi seems to have tried to portray an example of an ideal human being in this period, a kind, self-controled, honest, generous, brave, patient, grateful, and sagacious man (Fouchecour, p. 157).

ʿAwfi's use of his sources is not only copying; he has also edited them according to his own writing style. Besides, he converted all tales and anecdotes into stories without considering their merits from a historical viewpoint (Fouchecour, p. 155).

ʿAwfi's prose has its ups and downs. At times it is convoluted and too florid, while, in some cases, it resembles in clarity and fluency the works of the 14th-century authors (Bahār, III, p. 38). For instance, ʿAwfi's preface of the book is written in an ornate, heavy style, while the stories adapted from elsewhere still reveal their original styles despite bearing ʿAwfi's editing touches (ʿAli-Naqi Monzawi, p. 26).

ʿAwfi's method on selecting the text and his style of compiling an anthology of stories with different subject matters was an innovation in Persian literature. Its reputation, which was the main cause of establishing ʿAwfi's name as a major author (see Qazvini, p. *kj*) and led to the creation of various collections by later authors, some of whom used ʿAwfi's *Jawāmeʿ al-ḥekāyāt* as the major source of their own work. It was also used by several later historians such as Menhāj-e Serāj, Ḥamd-Allāh Mostawfi, Ḥāfeẓ-e Abru, Hendušāh Naḵjavāni, Reżāqoli Khan Hedāyat, etc. (see Nizāmud-Din, pp. 26-30), as well as a number of Western scholars including William Ouseley, Edward Thomos, Josef Markwart, Vasiliĭ V. Barthold, Edward G, Browne, etc. (Nizāmud-Din, pp. 31-32).

So far, 111 manuscripts of *Jawāmeʿ al-ḥekāyāt*, either complete or imperfect, are known to exist in public or private libraries in Persia (38), Great Britain (19), former Soviet Union (15), India (15), Pakistan (9), Turkey (6), France (5), Germany (2), and Austria (1), and one in an unidentified private collection (see Nizāmud-Din, p. 111; Moʿin, pp. 50-62; Aḥmad Monzawi, 1995-97, I, pp. 308-9). Most of them are dated. The oldest known manuscript, which is kept at Bibliothèque Nationale in Paris (no. Ancien Fonds 75), was copied in Tabriz in 1299-1300 (Moʿin, p. 64), about seventy years after the book had been compiled. A major distinction of this manuscript is the author's own biographical accounts, as well as the 175 extra stories that it contains, neither of which are found in other manuscripts (Moʿin, p. 64).

The fame of *Jawāmeʿ al-ḥekāyāt* led to the production of several selections and translations of the book. Four selections have been identified so far. The oldest selection, compiled by ʿAbd-Allāh Kāteb Eṣfahāni in 1479, is kept at Topkapi Saray Library (ms. H. 1372); the next one, dated to the 16th century, belongs to Salar Jung Library (ms. A.N. 304) in Hyderabad (Ashraf, III, p. 10); the third one in the chronological order, titled *Jawāmeʿ al-kalam*, was compiled in 1690-91 (Pakistan National Museum, ms. N.M. 1969-313; Nušāhi, pp. 674-75). The latest known selection, made in 1721 at Qarṣ (a town in Eastern Turkey) by ʿAli b. Moḥammad Šervāni and called *Ketāb al-ʿajāyeb wa'l-ḡarāyeb*, is kept at the Biritish Museum (ms. Or. 1584; Rieu, II, p. 751).

Hādji Ḵalifa has mentioned three Turkish translations. They were rendered, in chronological order, by Ebn ʿArabšāh (d. 1450) at the order of Sultan Morād II (r. 1446-51), by Mawlānā Najāti Bey (d. 1509) for Prince Solṭān-Maḥmud (d. 1481), and by Jalālzāda Ṣāleh Čelebi (d. 1565; Ḥāji Ḵalifa, p. 540; Yazici, p. 439). There is also a Turkish translation in Vienna Library (ms. N.F. 201), whose translator is not identified in Flügel's list (Flügel, I, p. 413). Ḥāji Ḵalifa also mentions a selection in Turkish translation by Moḥammad b. Asʿad b. ʿAbd-Allāh Tostari (d. after 1330; Ḥāji Ḵalifa, I, p. 540).

There are also two translations in Urdu (Aḥmad Monzawi, 1995-, I, p. 308). Teymur Basim Bayef has translated and published a selection of 250 stories with commentaries in Russian (Rasuli, p. 229).

It is unfortunate that in spite of the significant literary and historical value of the *Jawāmeʿ al-ḥekāyāt* and the comprehensive study of Muḥammad Nizāmud-Din, no critical edition of the entire text has yet been published. The first editing attempt was by Moḥammad-Taqi Malek-al-Šoʿarāʾ Bahār, who published a selection of eighty-two stories in 1945 under the title *Montaḵab-e Jawāmeʿ al-ḥekāyāt*. Bahār's edited selection was followed eleven years later by the facscimile edition of fifteen sections of the first chapter by Moḥammad Ramażāni. The first major critical edition was published in two volumes in 1956 by Moḥammad Moʿin, covering the initial three sections of the first chapter in two volumes. In 1971, Jaʿfar Šeʿār published a selection of stories concerning the history of Iran in the format of a school textbook, and followed it with a small selection published (1973) in the series called "Masterpieces of Persian literature" (Šāhkārhā-ye adabiyāt-e fārsi). The credit for the most comprehensive edition of the *Jawāmeʿ al-ḥekāyāt* belongs to Amir-Bānu Moṣaffā (Karimi), who published the critical edition of the entire third chapter in two volumes (1973-74; the 2nd vol. with the cooperation of Maẓāher Moṣaffā) and followed it six years later with the edition of the first part of the second chapter. The most recent edition of a part of the *Jawāmeʿ al-ḥekāyāt* was done by Jaʿfar Šeʿār, who first published in 1984 a selection of stories concerning the history of Iran and Islam, and three years later another selection of stories relevant only to the history of Islam.

Bibliography: Iraj Afsār, "Nosḵahā-ye ḵaṭṭi," *Nasriya-ye ketāb-ḵāna-ye markazi-e Dānešgāh-e Tehrān* 4, Tehran, 1965. Sayyed ʿAli Āl-e Dāwud, "Bargozida-ye aʿjuba wa maḥjuba: dāstān-e ʿāmmiāna-ye kohan-e fārsi (awāyel-e qarn-e haftom-e hejri)," *Nāma-ye farhangestān* 6, 1999, Supplement. Mohammad Ashraf, *A Concise Descriptive Catalogue of The Persian Manuscripts in The Salar Jung Museum and Library*, Hyderabad, 1966. Sadid-al-Din Moḥammad ʿAwfi, *Pānzdah bāb-e Jawāmeʿ al-ḥekāyāt, az ru-ye noskạ-i ka dar zamān-e moʾallef dar awāyel-e qarn-e haftom-e hejri nevešta šoda*, facs. ed. Moḥammad Ramizāni, Tehran, 1956. Idem, *Jawāmeʿ al-ḥekāyāt wa lawāmeʿ al-rewāyāt* I, ed. Moḥammad Moʿin, 2nd ed., Tehran, 1961; part 3/1 ed. Amir-Bānu Moṣaffā (Karimi), Tehran, 1973; Urdu tr. Aḵtar Širāni, 2 vols., Delhi, 1943. Idem, *Lobāb al-albāb*, ed. Edward G. Browne and Moḥammad Qazvini as *Lubàb 'l-albàb*, 2 vols., Leiden and London, 1903-06. Moḥammad-Taqi Malek-al-Šoʿarāʾ Bahār, *Sabk-šenāsi yā tāriḵ-e taṭawor-e naṯr-e fārsi*, 3 vols., Tehran, 1991. Edgar Blochet, *Catalogue des manuscrits persans de la Bibliothèque nationale*, 4 vols., Paris, 1905-34. Edward G. Browne, *Literary History of Persia*, 4 vols., Cambridge, 1929-30, II, pp. 477-78. Gustav Flügel, *Die arabischen, persischen und türkischen Handschriften Kaiserlich-Königlichen Hofbibliothek zu Wien*, 3 vols., Vienna, 1865-67. Charles-Henri de Fouchécour, *Moralia: Les notions morales dans la littérature persane du 3e/9e au 7e/13e siècle*, Bibliothèque iranienne 32, Paris, 1986. Allāhyār Ḵalʿatbari, "Naẓar-i ba ketāb-e *Jawāmeʿ al-ḥekāyāt wa lawāmeʿ al-rewāyāt*," *Majalla-ye bāstān-šenāsi wa tāriḵ* 2/2, 1988, pp. 68-71. Ḥāji Ḵalifa Kāteb Čalabi, *Kašf al-ẓonun ʿan asāmi al-kotob wa'l-fonun* ed. Moḥammad Šaraf-al-Din Yāltqāyā and K. R. Bilge, 2 vols., Istanbul, 1941-43. Moḥammad Moʿin, "Moqaddema" (Inroduction) to his edition of ʿAwfi, *Jawāmeʿ al-ḥekāyāt*, Tehran, 1961, I, pp. 1-80. Aḥmad Monzawi, *Fehrest-e moštarak-e nosḵahā-ye ḵaṭṭi-e fārsi-e Pākestān* VI: *Dāstānhā*, n.p., n.d., pp. 930-31. Idem, *Fehrest-e nosḵahā-ye ḵaṭṭi-e fārsi*, 5 vols. in 7, Tehran, 1969-74, V, pp. 3669-72. Idem, *Fehrestvāra-ye ketābhā-ye fārsi*, 3 vols., Tehran, 1995-97, I, pp. 308-9. ʿAli-Naqi Monzawi, *Fehrest-e ketāb-ḵāna-ye ehdāʾi-e Āqā Sayyed Moḥammad Meskāt ba ketāb-ḵāna-ye Dānešgāh-e Tehrān*, 2 vols., Tehran, 1951-53. Amir-Bānu Moṣaffā (Karimi), "Moqaddema" (Inroduction) to her edition of ʿAwfi, *Jawāmeʿ al-ḥekāyāt*, Tehran, 1973. Idem, "Manābiʿ-e gomšoda-ye *Jawāmeʿ al-ḥekāyāt*," *Gawhar* 3/1, Farvardin 1354/ March 1975, pp. 38-45. Saʿid Nafisi, *Fehrest-e ketāb-ḵāna-ye Majles-e surā-ye melli* VI, Tehran, 1965. Sayyed ʿĀref Nowsāhi, *Fehrest-e nosḵahā-ye ḵaṭṭi-e fārsi-e muza-ye melli-e Pākestān Karāči*, Islamabad, 1983. Neẓām-al-Molk ʿAli b. Ḥasan *Ṭusi, Siar al-moluk (Siāsat-nāma)*, ed. Hubert Darke, Tehran, 1976; tr. Hubert Darke as *The Book of Government or Rules for Kings*, Richmond, 2002. Muḥammad Nizāmud-Din, *Introduction to the Jawámi'u'l-hikáyát wa lawámi'u'rriwáyát of Sadídu'd-Dín Muḥammad al-'Awfí*, London, 1929. Moḥammad Qazvini, "Moqaddema" (Introduction) and "Tarjama-ye moṣannef" (Author's biography), in ʿAwfi, *Lobāb al-albāb*, ed. Edward G. Browne and Moḥammad Qazvini, Leiden, 1903-06, I, pp. *j-ka*. Ārezu Rasuli, "Tarjama-ye *Jawāmeʿ al-ḥekāyāt* ba zabān-e rusi," *Nāma-ye farhangestān* 7/2, Šahrivar 1384 Š./ September 2005, p. 229. Charles Rieu, *Catalogue of the Persian Manuscripts in the British Museum*, 3 vols. and a Supplement, London, 1876-95. Saʿdi, *Golestān*, ed. Ḵalil Ḵaṭib Rahbar, Tehran, 1992. Ḏabiḥ-Allāh Ṣafā, *Tāriḵ-e adabiyāt dar Irān* II, Tehran, 1960, pp. 1026-30. Charles A. Storey, *Persian Literature: A Bio-Bibliographical Survey* II/2, 1 vols. in 2, London, 1972, pp. 781-84. D. G. Voronofsk, *Sobranie vostochnykh rukopiseĭ Akademii Nauk Uzbekskoĭ SSR* (Collection of Oriental manuscripts of the Academy of sciences of the Uzbek SSR) Tashkent, II, Tashkent, 1954; X, Tashkent, 1975. Tahsin Yazıcı, "*Cevâmiu'l-hikâyât*," in *Türkiye dianet vaqfi Islâm ansiklopedisi* VII, Istanbul, 1977, pp. 439-40.

(DARIUSH KARGAR)

JAWHARI, ABU ʿABD-ALLĀH AḤMAD b. Moḥammad b. ʿObayd-Allāh b. Ḥasan b. ʿAyyāš, 10th century Imami transmitter of Hadith (d. 1010). His *nesba* was derived from his profession, which was the selling of, and working with, gemstones (*jawāher*). It is not clear whether this was his family trade or he was the first to practice it and assume the name, but it is certain that he had enough expertise in the appraisal of jewels and the craft of jewelry to write a book on various kinds of pearls and their craft (*Ketāb al-loʾloʾ wa ṣanʿatohu wa anwāʿohu*), indicating his prominence in this craft (Najāši, I, p. 87; Ebn Šahrāšub, p. 57; Ḵoʾi, III, p. 78).

He was a friend of the Imami biographer, Abu'l-ʿAbbās Najāši and his father, but Najāši did not record the Hadith from him, saying, "I found that our shaikhs consider him weak, therefore I did not report his Hadith" (Najāši, I, p. 87), but Ayatollah Abu'l-Qāsem Ḵoʾi correctly noted that Najāši did indeed rely on Jawhari's Hadith in the biography of Ḥosayn b. Besṭām (Ḵoʾi, III, p. 79). In fact, Najāši had him as a source in more instances than the one time that Ḵoʾi reported; Najāši refered to him as "Abu ʿAbd-Allāh b. ʿAyyāš" or "Ebn ʿAyyāš" (Najāši, I, pp. 40, 52, 167, II, p. 430). Perhaps the reason for considering him weak pertained to the deterioration of his mental condition when he advanced in age (Ḥelli, II, p. 323).

According to his biographers, Jawhari belonged to a very prominent family with close ties to the Qāżi Abu ʿOmar Moḥammad b. Yusof, who was the uncle of Jawhari's mother, Sokayna bent Ḥosayn b. Yusof (Najāši, p. 86).

Among Jawhari's books are: *Ketāb moqtażab al-āṯār fi ʿadad al-aʾemma al-eṯnā ʿašar*, *Ketāb al-aḡsāl*, *Ketāb aḵbār Abu Hāšem Dāwud b. Qāsem Jaʿfari*, *Ketāb šeʿr Abu Hāšem*, *Aḵbār Jāber al-Joʿfi*, *Ketāb al-eštemāl ʿalā maʿrefat al-rejāl wa man rawā ʿan Emām*, *Ketāb mā nazala men al-Qorʾān fi Ṣāḥeb-al-Zamān*, *Ketāb aʿmāl šahr Rajab*, *Ketāb aʿmāl šahr Šaʿbān*, *Ketāb aʿmāl šahr Ramażān*, *Ketāb aḵbār al-Sayyed* [al-Ḥemyari, the poet], *Ketāb aḵbār ʿoqalāʾ al-aʾemma al-arbaʿa*, and *Ketāb ḏekr man rawā al-ḥadiṯ men Bani Nāšera* (Najāši, I, p. 87; Ḵoʾi, III, pp. 78-79). Of all these works only the *Ketāb moqtażab al-āṯār* is known to be extant in manuscripts kept in the Library of Imam Mahdi in Sāmarrāʾ (Iraq) and the Āstān-e Qods Library in Mashad (no. 8130). It was prepared for publication by Beʿṯa Foundation in Qom, 1991. It is divided into three parts: the first two parts contain the statements attributed to the Companions of the Prophet in regards to the twelve Imams, while the third part presents the poetry mentioning the number of the Imams and their names, including poems composed prior to the birth dates of several Imams (*Torāṯonā* 72/2, p. 251; Moḥsen al-Amin, IX, p. 325).

With two books on the biographies of Imami transmitters of Hadith, Jawhari can be considered as one of the earliest scholars of this genre (known as *ʿelm al-rejāl*), which was perfected after him by Najāši and Abu Jaʿfar Moḥammad Ṭusi. Jawhari died in 1010 (Najāši, I, p. 87).

Bibliography: Abu Jaʿfar Moḥammad b. ʿAli Ebn Šahrāšub, *Maʿālem al-ʿolamāʾ fi fehrest kotob al-šiʿa wa-asmāʾ al-moṣannefin menhom, qadiman wa ḥadiṯan*, Tehran, 1934 (supplement of Abu Jaʿfar Ṭusi's *Ketāb al-fehrest*). ʿAllāma Ḥasan b. Yusof Ḥelli, *Ḵolāṣat al-aqwāl fi maʿrefat al-rejāl*, Qom, 1996. Abu'l-Qāsem Ḵoʾi, *Moʿjam rejāl al-ḥadiṯ wa tafṣil ṭabaqāt al-rowāh*, 24 vols., Beirut, 1992. Sayyed Moḥsen al-Amin Ḥosayni ʿĀmeli, *Aʿyān al-šiʿa*, ed. Ḥasan al-Amin, 56 parts, Damascus, 1935-62, IX, pp. 323-25. Abu'l-ʿAbbās Najāši, *Rejāl al-Najāši*, ed. Musā Šobayri Zanjāni as *Fahrasat asmāʾ moṣannefin al-Šiʿa al-moštaher be-Rejāl al-Najāši*, Qom, 1986.

(ABBAS KADHIM)

JAXARTES. See SIR DARYA.

JAZĀʾERI, NEʿMAT-ALLĀH ŠOŠTARI. See forthcoming, online.

ʿABBĀS JAZI (Gazi), DARVIŠ (1847-1905), dialect poet from whom survives a *divān* in the dialect of Gaz (q.v.), an oasis north of Isfahan. All that is known about him is based on the occasional references in his own poetry. His father was from Gaz and his mother, Māndagār, from Murčakort, another village of the Borkʸār rural district (*boluk*) of Isfahan. Darviš ʿAbbās' formal education began at the age of seven, but it was interrupted due to economic hardship. He began composing poems in his mid-teens (*Ğazaliyāt*, pp. xxix-xxx), which had brought him recognition already by the age of thirty-six, when Valentin Alekseevich Zhukovskiĭ collected ten *ğazal*s (q.v.), a *robāʿi*, and a *baḥr-e ṭawil* (q.v.) of him in Isfahan (Zhukovskiĭ, II, pp. 33-41). Darviš ʿAbbās lived a simple life, being supported on occasion by the wealthy, whom he panegyrized (e.g., *Ğazaliyāt*, p. 450). He was connected to the Gonābādi (q.v.) Sufi order, but he probably never joined it, as he held a critical view of all sects (Eilers and Schapka, I, p. 23; cf. *Ğazaliyāt*, p. xxi).

Darviš ʿAbbās left a *divān* of about 10,000 couplets, titled *Eršād al-walad*, which survives in more than one manuscript. It contains chiefly *ğazal*s but also other genres (*qaṣida*, *maṯnawi*, *mosammaṭ*, *tarkib-band*, and *baḥr-e ṭawil*). The principal manuscript, apparently in the poet's own hand and bearing marks of his seals, is in 396 pages, dated 1902 (Eilers and Schapka, I, pp. 22-24). Wilhelm Eilers (q.v.), having had this manuscript hand-copied, appended its facsimile to the first volume of his Gazi collections, which contains also the Roman transcription and German translation of twenty-nine poems (Eilers and Schapka, text nos. 209-37). More recently, the co-villagers of Gaz published, in Perso-Arabic script, 236 *ğazal*s of his based on two manuscripts (*Ğazaliyāt*, pp. xv-xvi), one of which appears to be identical with the one copied by Eilers (Borjiān).

The poems of Darviš ʿAbbās are generally lyrical-mystical and satirical in tone, with a strong sense of humor that has made him popular among not only the people of Gaz but also the speakers of the neighboring dialects and beyond. As did many other composers of the *fahlaviyāt* (q.v.), he felt free in imbuing his work with abstract images of classical Persian literature and a flowing, ornate language suffused with Persian words and idioms. His efforts, however, to cast his dialect verses into the exact meters of classical Persian prosody hardly proved successful (Borjiān). Not the least of its claims to attention is the light that his poetry throws on language development. A number of words and phrases in his poetry are already unintelligible to the speakers of Gazi (e.g., *taklar žantāmun* "to make an effort, to exert oneself," *ewartāmun* "to tear, rip," *šānn-o-wān* "go and say [?]"); thus the meaning of many verses remain obscure. Even more interesting is perhaps the phonological features; for instance, the variations of the third person singular enclitic pronoun from *-š*, to *-ž* and *-y* (see CENTRAL DIALECTS), as in *olokī-š* (*Ğazaliyāt*, no. 48), *ulūkī-ž* (Zhukovskiĭ, II, no. 10, p. 38), and *oloki-y* (current pronunciation) "its hole" (for other developments, see Borjiān).

Bibliography: Darviš ʿAbbās Jazi, *Ğazaliyāt-e Darviš ʿAbbās Jazi, ba guyeš-e gazi bā bargardāni-e kalamāt wa tarkibāt-e maḥalli*, ed. Ḥosayn-ʿAli Moḥammadi, Moḥammad-Reżā Qowwatmand, and Aḥmad Ḵāksār, Isfahan, 1992. Ḥabib Borjiān, "Taṣḥiḥ-e motun-e guyeši: divān-e Darviš ʿAbbās Jazi," *Irān-šenāsi/Iranshenasi* 17/2, 2005, forthcoming. Wilhelm Eilers and Ulrich Schapka, *Westiranische Mundarten aus der Sammlung W. Eilers* II: *Die Mundart von Gäz*, 2 vols., Wiesbaden, 1979. Aḥmad Fāżel, "Barrasi-e vižagihā-ye zabāni o dasturi-e guyeš-e gazi, hamrāh bā šawāhed-i az divān-e Darviš ʿAbbās Jazi," M.A. thesis, University of Isfahan, 1995. Valentin A. Zhukovskiĭ, *Materialy dliya izucheniya persidskikh narechiĭ*, Petrograd, 1888-1922, II; repr. as *Materials for the Study of Iranian Dialects*, 3 vols. in 1, Tehran, 1976.

(HABIB BORJIAN)

JAZIRI, SHAIKH AḤMAD, or Malâ-ye Jizrî, early Kurdish poet. Even today, very little is known about the earliest Kurdish poets. The oldest source of information on Malâ-ye Jizrî is a chapter by the scholar Maḥmud Efendi Bâyazidi, written at the request of Alexandre Jaba, Russian Consul in Erzurum, who published it in his *Recueil de Notices et Récits sur la langue kourmandji* (1860). There we learn that his name was Shaykh Aḥmad and that he came from Jazira Bohtân (or Bukhtân), a prosperous river port which was situated on a former meander of the Tigris. Maḥmud Bâyazidi claimed that Malâ-ye Jizrî lived in the 6th century A.H. Subsequently, scholars proposed various dates until D. N. MacKenzie established (1969, p. 129) that the poet was born ca. 1570 and died ca. 1640.

The oral tradition gives his name as Aḥmad Nishâni. He is said to have begun his studies in Jazira, his native town, and continued in Irak (Baghdad), Syria, Egypt, and finally Persia, where he studied philosophy, astrology, and divination. There he also became familiar with the Persian poets and most particularly, with the great Hafez (q.v.), under whose influence he fell. He then returned to his own country, first establishing himself in Diyarbekir, where he taught, and later in Jazira, where he remained for the rest of his life. He is buried in the Madrasa Sor, which has since been destroyed by the Turkish military. According to Maḥmud Bâyazidi, Malâ fell in love with the sister of Prince ʿEzz-al-Din of Bukhtân, to whom he devoted many ghazals.

Malâ-ye Jizrî, like other learned men of the period, knew Arabic and Persian. However, he chose to express himself in Kurdish Kurmanji, the prince's language. Indeed, the earliest masterpieces of Kurdish literature emerged at the same time as the consolidation of the Ottoman and Safavid empires, when the Kurds, in contrast, failed to establish their own state. Malâ left a *diwān* of nearly 2,000 verses, and, although the published manuscripts reveal many differences in the texts and in the order of the poems, Malâ's poetry gives evidence of a well-established technique. The poet, adopting the basic forms of Arab-Persian poetry, had at his disposal a variety of genres and stylistic means. Knowledge of Arabic enabled Malâ to use the distich (*bayt*), in which the two hemistiches answer each other, as in Persian poetry. He also adopted the meter most frequently used by Hafez in his ghazals: --oo ---o -o -oo (to be read from right to left).

His lyric poetry and ghazals, imbued with a mystical spirit, were inspired by the Sufism of the Naqshbandiya Brotherhood (Order), which dominated the Muslim East at that time. Thus, following the example of his model, Malâ sang of pure love, the wine of ecstasy, metaphysical rapture, and the joys and sufferings of mystical love.

Though Malâ-ye Jizrî's poetry is learned, his many borrowings from Arabic and Persian did nothing to make him popular. His work is still accessible only to men of letters—shaykhs and mullahs, who continue to comment on it in the increasingly rare madrasas of Kurdistan.

Bibliography: Publications of the *Diwan* of Malâ-ê Jizrî (in chronological order). Martin Hartmann, *Der Kurdische Diwan des Schēch Aḥmed von Ğezīret ibn ʿOmar genannt Mäla'i Ğizri*, Leipzig, 1904. *Diwan*, in Kurdish-Latin transliteration, published by pieces in the famous magazine *Hawar* (The Call), nos. 35-57, Damascus, 1941-45; Qedrî Begê Jemîl Pasha is the author of the transcription; Foreword by Herekol Azîzan. *Dīwān al-Shaykh al-Jizrī*, by Ahmad ibn al-Mullā Muḥamad Buhtī al-Zivingī, Muftī of al-Qāmishlī, 1957, 2 vols., p. 843; comm. and critical analysis of the text in Arabic. *Dîwanî Shêx Ahmadî Jizîrî*, by Gîw Mukriyanî, 1st ed., Hewlêr (Irbil) 2576 kurdî/1964, p. 167. *Dîwana Melâ-yê Jizîrî*, by Ṣādiq Bahāʾ-al-dīn Amēdī, printed by the Kurdish Academy Press, Baghdad, 1977, p. 639; transliteration into Arabic-Kurdish script, with comm. and critical analysis of the text in Kurdish-Kurmanji. *Diwanî 'arifî Ribbanî Shêx Ahmedî, mashhūr be Melay Jizîrî*, ʿAbd-al-Rahman Sharafkandî "Hejar," Tehran, 1982; transliteration into Arabic-Kurdish script, with comm. and critical analysis of the text in Kurdish-Sorani. *Melayê Ciziri, Diwan*, transliteration into Kurdish-Latin script by Zenelabidin Kaya and M. Emin Narozi, Stockholm, 1987, pp. 327, 233 (facsimile). *Melayê Cizîrî, dîwan*, foreword by Zeynbidîn Zînar, Firat Yayinlari, without place (Istanbul?) and date (1987?) of publication; transliteration into Kurdish-Latin script with comm. and critical analysis of the text in Kurdish-Kurmanji.

Herekol Azîzan says he has seen a lithographed *diwan*, published in Saint Petersbourg without date, and another *diwan* published in Istanbul in 1919.

Studies. Herekol Azîzan (Jeladet Bedir Khan), "Klasîkên me" (Our classics), *Hawar*, no. 33, 9th year, Damascus, Oct. 1941, pp. 6-14. Thomas Bois, "Coup d'œil sur la littérature kurde," *al-Machriq* 49, 1955, pp. 201-39. ʿIzedîn Mistefa Resûl, *Melay Jizîrî, Shtêk derbarey jiyan ur berhemî* (Malâ-ye Jizrî, some remarks on his life and work), Hewlêr (Irbil), 1990, p. 231. Alexandre Jaba, *Recueil de Notices et Récits en langue kourmanji, servant à la connaissance de la litterature et des tribus du Kurdistan*, collected and translated into French by Alexandre Jaba, Consl of H.M. the Emperor of Russia, at Erzeroum: St. Petersbourg, 1860 (H. 1277), with a foreword by Peter J.A. Lerch; repr., Amsterdam, 1979. Qanatê Kurdo, *Tarixa Edebyeta kurdi* (History of Kurdish literature) I, Stockholm, 1983, pp. 90-102. Roger Lescot, "Littérature kurde," in *Histoire des Littératures* I. *Littératures anciennes, orientales et orales*, Encyclopédie de la Pléiade 1, Paris, 1977, pp. 795-805. D. N. Mackenzie, "Malâ-ê Jizrî and Faqî Tayrân," in *Yād-Nāme-ye Irāni-ye Minorsky*, Tehran, 1969, pp. 125-30.

(JOYCE BLAU)

JAŽN-Ā JAMĀʿIYA (Feast of the Assembly), the great communal festival of the Yazidis. The feast is also called *ʿaydā mazin* (great feast), and is celebrated at the main sanctuary of Yazidis at Lāleš valley, located in a mountain area, 62 km northeast of Mosul in Iraqi Kurdistan. The feast lasts for seven days, from twenty-third of September to the first of October, according to the Eastern calendar, which is thirteen days behind the Gregorian one. It is thus an autumn festival, most rituals of which (e.g., the bull, *semāt*, the "tree stump," *samāʿ*, *bar-ē šebākē*, etc.) are directly connected with Yazidi mythology, especially with the cosmogony. The range of customs and rituals performed at Jažn-ā Jamāʿiya make this one of the richest Yazidi observances. Special rites that are conducted in the course of the festival include:

Samāʿ. *Samāʿ* is a sacred dance that is performed every evening in the courtyard of the sanctuary of Shaikh ʿAdi b. Mosāfer Hakkāri (d. ca 1162), to the accompaniment of the sacred music of tambourine (*daf*) and flute (*šabāb*) and by the singing of religious hymns called *qawl* (q.v.) and *bayt* by members of a hereditary group of hymn reciters (*qawwāl*). Representatives of all three Yazidi castes (Shaikhs, *pirs* "elders," and *morids* "disciples") take part in this observance.

Qapāğ. This is a rite that is carried out on a Wednesday under the supervision of the Yazidi prince (*mir*). During the rite, members of the Qāʿyidi, Māmusi and Terk tribes take a male calf or young bull from the shrine of Shaikh ʿAdi to that of Shaikh Šams (one of the Holy Seven), while many pilgrims are watching along the route. At the shrine of Shaikh Šams the animal is sacrificed in the name of the Lord of the Sun (Ḵodān-ē rojē). Sacred food, known as *semāt*, is prepared from the meat of the sacrificial animal and ground wheat, and is divided among the believers.

Bar-ē šebākē. It is an observance centering around a bier which is said to have been that of Shaikh ʿAdi, and which is also called ʿArš-ē Ēzi (Throne of Ēzi) or Taḵt-ē Šayḵ ʿAdi (Throne of Shaikh ʿAdi). On the Thursday after *Qapāğ*, the bier is carried on the shoulders of prominent Yazidis from the shrine of Shaikh ʿAdi to a spring called Āvā Kālokē (Water of Kālokē) and is immersed in it. After that the bier is restored in its original place inside the shrine.

Pari sewārkeren (Carrying of the Fabric). On Friday, a piece of colored fabric (which may not be blue), called *pari*, is carried on the head of a Yazidi and is "baptized" in the Qāni-ā Sepi (White Spring), then it is brought to the shrine of Shaikh ʿAdi to the accompaniment of a sacred flute (*šabāb*) and is put on the coffin of Shaikh ʿAdi or Shaikh Ḥasan.

Semāt. Semāt is the name of the sacred food prepared during the seven days of the festival by the custodian of Lāleš and those of the other shrines in the valley of Lāleš.

Mor keren (lit. sealing, i.e., approximately "baptism"). During the feast all Yazidis, adults and children, males and females, should undergo the rite of *mor keren* in the water of either the Qāni-ā Sepi or the Zamzam spring (a spring in a subterranean cave under Shaikh ʿAdi's shrine). For those undergoing this rite for the first time it is regarded as their initiation into the religion.

Qorm-ē dārē (Tree Stump). On September 23rd a tree stump is put into the water of the Qāni-ā Sepi. It is taken out again on the first of October, which is the day of the actual feast.

Ziāratibun (Pilgrimage). As this is a festival of gathering (*jamāʿiya*) and mutual contact, Yazidis make pilgrimage to the various holy places and shrines in the Valley of Lāleš.

Throughout the feast of Jamāʿiya, the participants dance and make merry with great enthusiasm, as this is a central part of Yazidi religious life. They believe that, during the festival, a Yazidi's soul feels close to God, Ṭāwus-ē Malak (the foremost among the *Haft sorr* "seven archangels"), and other sacred beings, while on the social side, all Yazidis gather together, interact, and reaffirm their religious identity.

Bibliography: Cecil John Edmonds, *A Pilgrimage to Lalish*, London, 1967. G. Furlani, "Le Feste dei Yezidi," *WZKM* 45, 1937, pp. 65-97. John S. Guest, *The Yezidis: A Study in Survival*, London and New York, 1987. Idem, *Survival among the Kurds: A History of the Yezidis*, London and new York, 1993 (rev. ed. of the former). Philip G. Kreyenbroek, *Yezidism, its Background, Observances and Textual Tradition*, Lewiston, N.Y., 1995. Khalil J. Rashow, *An Approach to the Essence of Yezidis Religion/Naḥwa maʿrefat ḥaqiqat al-diāna al-zaydiya*, Stockholm, 1998.

(KHALIL JINDY RASHOW)

JEBĀL, in Arabic, the plural of *jabal* "mountain," a geographical term used in early Islamic times for the western part of Persia, roughly corresponding to ancient Media (Ar. *māh*, see below).

It received its name from its mountain and upland plateau topography, embracing as it did the central part of the Zāgros mountain chain, including the regions of Kurdistan and Lorestān, between the Safidrud River and the Alborz chain in the north and the lowland region of Ḵuzestān in the south, whilst its western limits were the region where the Zāgros chain meets the Mesopotamian plain and its eastern ones the fringes of the central Great Desert (Dašt-e Kavir; see DESERT). In the administrative geography of the early Islamic period, its borders were somewhat ill-defined and fluctuating, but it was often linked with the city of Ray at its northeastern extremity, marking a point roughly half-way along the great Iraq-Khorasan highway which entered Jebāl at Ḥolvān (q.v.) at its western end. At this time, Jebāl contained six important urban centres, Dinavar; Qarmisin, Qarmāsin (the later Kermānšāh); Hamadān; Qazvin; Isfahan; and Ray (qq.v.).

The Arabs pushed into Jebāl soon after they had overrun Iraq, so that the conquest of the region fell essentially in the latter part of the caliphate of ʿOmar b. al-Ḵaṭṭāb and the early years of ʿOṯmān's caliphate: Dinavar in 642; Qarmisin, after the capture of Ḥolvān in 640; Hamadān in 639 or 641, then definitively in 644-45; Isfahan, in 642 or 644; Qazvin, in 644-45; and Ray, at a date variously given as between 639 and 645 (Balāḏori, pp. 301-2, 309, 312, 319, 321-25; Ṭabari, I, pp. 2637-50, 2653-55, tr. pp. 6-13, 20-21, 24-26).

The towns of Dinavar and Nehāvand, both occupied by the Arabs soon after their victory at Nehāvand in 642, had a particular importance in this expansionary period of the Arab conquest of western Persia. They eventually became known as Māh al-Kufa and Māh al-Baṣra respectively, with the their revenues assigned to the upkeep of the Arab warriors (*moqātela*) for campaigning northwards towards the Caucasus and across the Persian plateau to Khorasan (see Morony, on the complexities of this process; the term 'Māh' probably stems from a toponym Māda, i.e., Media). The conquered towns acquired Arab garrisons, so that Arabs became a permanent population element there, and Arab chiefs acquired rural estates; thus the family of the 9th century Arab poet and paladin, Abu Dolaf Qāsem b. ʿIsā ʿEjli (d. between 840 and 843), possessed large states at Karaj to the east of Nehāvand, so that the place became known as Karaj Abi Dolaf (Le Strange, pp. 197-98).

By the early 11th century, the age of the Ghaznavids and Saljuqs, the older term 'Jebāl' was being replaced by that of ʿErāq-e ʿAjam (q.v.) "Iraq of the Persians" in distinction from ʿErāq-e ʿArab "Iraq of the Arabs," that is, Mesopotamia; the Ghaznavid historian Abu'l-Fażl Bayhaqi (q.v.) always uses ʿErāq [-e ʿAjam] for western Persia (see, e.g., index, p. 1015). Šehāb-al-Din Yāqut Ḥamawi has a brief entry "Jebāl" (II, p. 99), but after the Mongol invasions, Jebāl dropped out of use; thus the geographer Ḥamd Allāh Mostawfi (mid-14th century) nowhere uses it (Le Strange, pp. 185-86). The term ʿErāq-e ʿAjam is now completely obsolete in modern Persia, but the alternative name for the town of Solṭānābād, the present-day Arāk, stems from the medieval ʿErāq (-e ʿAjam) (see ARĀK i; Bosworth, p. 859).

Bibliography: Aḥmad b. Yaḥyā Balāḏori, *Ketāb fotuḥ al-boldān*, ed. Michaël Jan de Goeje, Leiden, 1866; repr., Leiden, 1968. W. Barthold, *An Historical Geography of Iran*, tr. Svat Soucek, Princeton, 1984, pp. 121-32, 169-79, 180-83. Abu'l-Fażl Moḥammad Bayhaqi, *Tāriḵ-e Bayhaqi*, ed. ʿAli-Akbar Fayyāż,

Tehran, 1971. Clifford E. Bosworth, "Solṭānābād i," EI^2 IX, p. 859. Ebn al-Faqih, *Moḵtaṣar Ketāb al-boldān*, ed. Michaël Jan de Goeje, Leiden, 1967, pp. 209 ff. Ebn Ḥawqal, *Ketāb ṣurat al-arż*, ed. Johannes Hendrik Kramers, Leiden, 1938; repr., 1967, pp. 357-73; tr. Johannes Hendrik Kramers and Gaston Wiet as *Configuration de la terre*, 2 vols., Beirut, 1964-65, pp. 348-64. Abu Esḥāq Ebrāhim Eṣṭaḵri, *Ketāb masālek al-mamālek*, ed. Michaël Jan de Goeje, Leiden, 1967, pp. 195-203; tr. Moḥammad b. Asʿad Tostari as *Masālek wa mamālek*, ed. Iraj Afšār, Tehran, 1974, pp. 201-12. Guy Le Strange, *The Lands of the Eastern Caliphate* London 1905, repr., 1966. L. Lockhart, "Djibāl" in EI^2, II, p. 534. Abu ʿAbd-Allāh Moḥammad Moqaddasi, *Aḥsan al-taqāsim fi maʿrefat al-aqālim*, ed. Michaël Jan De Goeje, Leiden, 1906, repr., 1967, pp. 384-402. M. G. Morony, "Māh al-Baṣra" in EI^2, V, pp. 1212-13. Paul Schwarz, *Iran im Mittelalter nach den arabischen Geographen*, Leipzig, 1896-35; repr., 9 vols. in 4, Frankfurt on the Main, 1993, IV, pp. 445 ff. Moḥammad b. Jarir Ṭabari, *Taʾriḵ al-rosol waʾl-moluk*, tr. by various scholars as *The History of al-Ṭabari* XIV: *The Conquest of Iran*, Albany, tr. G. Rex Smith, 1994, pp. 20-21. Šehāb-al-Din Abu ʿAbd-Allāh Yāqut Ḥamawi, *Moʿjam al-boldān*, 5 vols., Beirut, 1955-57.

(C. EDMUND BOSWORTH)

JEBHE-YE MELLI. See NATIONAL FRONT.

JEBRIL B. ʿOBAYD-ALLĀH. See BOḴTIŠUʿ FAMILY.

JEH, name of a female demon in a small number of Zoroastrian Middle Persian texts. The name of Jeh is commonly, but with little justification, translated as "whore." It is the Middle Persian rendering of Avestan *jahī-* (or *jahikā-*). That word is used in a number of different meanings, but it appears to have originally meant "woman" and can still be recognized in this meaning in many Avestan passages. The fact that it originally must have been a neutral term for "woman" can also be substantiated by the Khotanese word *jsicā-*, "girl," which goes back to Old Iranian *jahi-* (Emmerick). In the Avesta it occurs, for example, in the expression *nā jahika*, "man or woman" (*Vd.* 18.54), or in lists of humans and other creatures, where its purported negative meaning is nowhere obvious (*Yt.* 17.54; *Pursišnīhā* 9). Such a neutral meaning can even still be observed in *Dēnkard* 7.3.2, undoubtedly a piece of *Zand*, where "seven women" who were present at Zarathushtra's birth are said to have been frightened by the miracle of his laughter upon being born (*az ōy be tarsīd hēnd haft jeh ī-š pērāmōn nišast hēnd*; Molé's emendation of the clearly legible word *jeh* to $^{+}$*dāyag* "wetnurse" is to be rejected).

In other passages, however, the word *jahī-/jahikā-* is used in a pejorative sense, to denote women who are somehow flawed. In some cases, the word is used to denote women who do not (or no longer) produce children (*Yt.* 17.54, *Yt.* 17.58); in others it refers specifically to adulterous women, who present children to their husbands who were not fathered by them (*Yt.* 17.59, *Vd.* 18.61-65). This theme of adultery, in addition to the theme of sorcery attributed to the *jahikā-* (*Y.* 9.32, *Yt.* 3.9, *Vd.* 21.17) was apparently understood as its basic meaning, when Zoroastrian scholars in the Sasanian period began to study and interpret the whole body of Avestan texts.

Middle Persian *jeh* is not an inherited part of Persian vocabulary, but a learned word taken from Avestan. It did not survive in New Persian, where it is only attested in Zoroastrian texts that are based on Middle Persian traditions (e.g., *Sad Dar Nasr* 59, 67). The word was therefore clearly in need of definition, and several such definitions have been preserved: these stress the fact that *jeh* should be used for adulterous women, who sleep with different men, and—by extension—for women who run the risk of such behavior, for example, by dressing inappropriately or by behaving immodestly. The majority of Pahlavi passages in which the word is used, use it to refer to this kind of immoral women.

A small number of passages, however, speak of a demoness named Jeh, who was made famous as Jeh, the Primal Whore by R. C. Zaehner (esp. pp. 183-92). In the fourth chapter of the *Bundahišn* (q.v.), the story is told of the initial stages of the struggle between Ohrmazd (see AHURA MAZDĀ) and Ahriman (q.v.). When they had sealed the pact that bound them to battle, Ahriman realized that his efforts would be fruitless because of Ohrmazd's creation of the Righteous Man. This brought him into a state of unconsciousness that lasted 3,000 years. One by one, his demons told him of their wicked plans, in order to awaken their lord, but this did not work, until Jeh came and told him of her plan to attack the good creation by perverting the righteous man. This restored Ahriman to consciousness, and he rewarded Jeh by kissing her on her forehead, which caused her to menstruate (the "mark" [*daxšta-*] passed on to mortal women since), and by promising to give her whatever she wanted. At that moment, she was shown (presumably by Ohrmazd) the image of a young man, and she chose as her reward the love of men, which Ahriman grudgingly granted her.

A largely parallel story has been preserved by the Syrian theologian Theodore Bar Koni (Benveniste; see BAR KŌNAY), with one dramatic difference: in his version of the story, it is not a demoness who is rewarded by Ahriman, but it is women themselves, who were created by Ohrmazd, but defected to the Evil Spirit. By combining these two passages, from the *Bundahišn* and from Bar Koni, Zaehner believed he could prove that in Zurvanism (a purported "heretical" variety of Zoroastrianism), women were seen as creatures of Ahriman. He attempted to support this striking idea by collecting various Zoroastrian passages which spoke about women in negative terms and then simply claiming them to be Zurvanite. These suggestions were picked up and elaborated upon by Geo Widengren and others, but they have since been shown to be unsoundly based (De Jong).

A more likely background to the myth of Jeh can be found in two aspects of her personality: the fact that she is Ahriman's wife, daughter, and Queen of Hell and the fact that she threatens the Righteous Man, Ohrmazd's chief aide in the battle against evil. These aspects are the exact inversion of the most important characteristics of the goddess Spandārmad in Middle Persian literature, who is described as Ohrmazd's queen, daughter, and wife. This imagery appears to have developed fairly late in the Zoroastrian tradition and in being thus elevated to the position of "mother of creation," Spandārmad appears to have usurped various aspects of other goddesses (Aši [q.v.] and Anāhitā [see ANĀHĪD]), especially as an image of the desirable behavior of married women. In such a context, where Ohrmazd and Spandārmad embodied and patronized the ideal of good men and women, united in marriage and dedicated to virtue, it is understandable that Ahriman also needed a wife, who would embody those aspects of female behavior that were considered most damaging to the cause of good. Since the word *jeh* was obviously in use for adulterous women who engaged in sorcery, a hypostatized Jeh eminently fitted the profile. But the development was late and remained confined to two texts: the *Bundahišn* and *Zādspram*. It did not develop into a fixed part of Zoroastrian cosmogonical myths and did not eclipse the use of the word *jeh* in its technical, human meaning.

Bibliography: E. Benveniste, 'Le témoignage de Théodore bar Kônay sur le zoroastrisme," *Le Monde Oriental* 26-27, 1932-33, pp. 170-215. J. K. Choksy, *Evil, Good, and Gender. Facets of the Feminine in Zoroastrian Religious History*, New York, 2002. R. E. Emmerick, "'Boys'" and 'Girls' in Khotanese," *BAI*, N.S. 7, 1993, pp. 51-54. A. de Jong, "Jeh the Primal Whore? Observations on Zoroastrian Misogyny," in R. Kloppenborg and W. J. Hanegraaff, eds., *Female Stereotypes in Religious Traditions*, Leiden, 1995, pp. 15-41. G. König, 'Zur Figur des "Wahrhaftigen Menschen" (*mard ī ahlaw*) in der zoroastrischen Literatur," *ZDMG* 155, 2005, pp. 161-88. G. Widengren, 'Primordial Man and Prostitute: A Zervanite Myth in the Sassanid Avesta," in *Studies in Mysticism presented to Gershom G. Scholem*, Jerusalem, 1967, pp. 227-34. R. C. Zaehner, *Zurvan. A Zoroastrian Dilemma*, Oxford, 1955.

(ALBERT DE JONG)

JEJEEBHOY, Sir JAMSETJEE (b. Bombay, 15 July 1783; d. Bombay, 14 April 1859), Parsi businessman and philanthropist. Jamsetjee Jejeebhoy received a knighthood in 1842 and a hereditary baronetcy in 1857; both honors were the first of their kind bestowed upon a British subject in India by Queen Victoria.

There was some uncertainty among Jejeebhoy's biographers regarding the exact place of his birth, with proponents of both Navsari and Bombay. Contemporary documents and general consensus today is that he was born in Bombay on 15 July 1783 (*Bombay Government Gazette Supplement*, 11 and 21 April 1836, cf. Mody, 1959, pp. 159-63). Named Jamshed by his father and mother, Merwanjee Maneckjee Jejeebhoy and Jeevibai Cowassjee, Jejeebhoy grew up in Navsari from the age of five to sixteen. Following the death of both his parents in 1799, Jejeebhoy settled permanently in Bombay and was looked after and apprenticed for three years under his maternal uncle Framjee Nusserwanjee Battliwala, later to be also his father-in-law, when on 1 March 1803 Jejeebhoy married Framjee Nusserwanjee's daughter, Avabai (d. 1870). They had three sons (Cursetjee, Rustomjee and Sorabjee) and a daughter (Pirojbai) together.

Jejeebhoy's first business venture was to collect and sell empty bottles, which earned him the appellation of *Battliwala* or 'dealer in bottles.' Having entered the more religiously and linguistically diverse business world of Bombay, he changed his name from Jamshed to the more common Jamsetjee.

Jejeebhoy was a product of the age of partnership and commercial collaboration begun with the introduction of European imperialism in Asia in the late 18th and early 19th centuries. Jejeebhoy's business dealings was in large-volume trade, and by 1814 he had accumulated enough wealth as a merchant to purchase his first ship, the *Good Success*; he would soon add six more as well as charter other ships (Bulley, 2000, pp. 162-65). Jejeebhoy also formed diverse social contacts with Indians of various communities and Europeans. In 1818 the firm of Jamsetjee Jejeebhoy & Co. was formed with the Jain Motichund Amichund and the Konkani Mahomed Ali Rogay as Jejeebhoy's business associates, later to also be joined by the Catholic Goan Rogeria de Faria. By 1836 Jamsetjee Jejeebhoy & Co. had expanded enough to also require the assistance of Jejeebhoy's sons (Mody, pp. 32-34; Natesan, 1930, pp. 7-8; Ramsay, 1855, p. 8; Siddiqi, 1982, pp. 301-24). Jejeebhoy and associates established a network of trade that supplied resources, particularly cotton and, at its height, opium, for export outside India. Part of Jejeebhoy's initial wealth was made in the cotton trade between India and Great Britain during the Napoleonic Wars. The consignment of Indian opium to East Asia constituted Jejeebhoy's major business enterprise and was responsible for a substantial portion of his wealth (Greenberg, 1951, pp. 150-51; Siddiqi, pp. 301-24). Jejeebhoy emerged as the most prominent Indian merchant dealing with China in the first half of the 19th century, making five trips to China between 1799 (when he was only sixteen) and 1807, and he had contacts with the major Chinese, British, and American traders and commercial houses. Jejeebhoy's most famous business association was with Jardine Matheson & Co. of Canton; Jejeebhoy and William Jardine also established an abiding friendship over the years (Karaka, 1884, I, pp. 79-88).

Jejeebhoy utilized his wealth and contacts to become one of the most influential and well-known Indians in Bombay. In 1823 he became a member of the Parsi Panchayat or internal government of the Parsi community of Bombay. He was also recognized as the chief representative of the Indian community of Bombay by the British imperial authorities. His standing in Bombay was further exemplified when in 1843 he became the only Indian director of the Bombay Bank (E. J. Rapson, 2004).

Philanthropic work. While Jejeebhoy's business acumen is evident as a largely self-made man, it was for his philanthropy that he garnered his reputation. He never forgot the relative poverty from which he had emerged, and when he became one of Bombay and western India's principal philanthropists, he used his wealth not only to help his own community, but in generous donations to help other parts of India through the establishment of schools, hospitals, and relief charities, as well as public works such as the building of causeways and bridges (*Encyclopedia Britannica*, 1911, XV, p. 300). Upon his death, the *Bombay Times* of 16 April 1859 noted that: "To write a history of Sir Jamsetjee's benefactions would be to write a book, and not the obituary notice of a journal."

The first record of Jejeebhoy's public charity dates back to 1822 with his payment of the sum of Rs. 3,040 to clear the debts of the poor in civil jail (Nazir, 1866, p. 31). Among the Parsis, charity was a vital provision for community life. Charity to the larger community also functioned to accommodate the Parsis to their social milieu. Jejeebhoy was notable for his conspicuous charity and desire to promote public charity in cooperation with the British. Jejeebhoy applied the lessons of his successful business activities to the establishment of his charities. The profitable business atmosphere had translated into socio-political collaboration between Indians and the British in Bombay, which Jejeebhoy effectively utilized for the benefit of his charitable projects and his personal elevation in colonial society. Jejeebhoy aimed to involve the British in large charitable schemes or to act as trustee by co-financing large-scale charity alongside the British. Jejeebhoy's largest charitable projects: the Parsi Benevolent Institution (1849) at a cost of Rs. 440,000, the J. J. Hospital (1850) at a cost of Rs. 200,000, and the J. J. School of Art (1857) at a cost of Rs. 100,000 promoted British-Indian cooperation in major charitable enterprises. The Benevolent Institution was the first indigenous educational institution in Western India, educating thousands of students and the foundations of a revised Panchayat. The J. J. Hospital brought public and private interests together for the first time in the cause of public health care in Bombay, while the School of Art made Asia a center of design (Palsetia, 2005, pp. 197-217; Wadia, 1950, pp. 80-85, 165-208).

Jejeebhoy's charitable projects and his loyalty to the British garnered him honors and public acclaim. In 1842 Jejeebhoy was to become the first Indian to receive a knighthood from Queen Victoria. In 1857 the Jejeebhoy family's secret efforts over many years to obtain a hereditary title were also realized when Jamsetjee Jejeebhoy was granted a hereditary baronetcy, becoming first baronet. A sum of 250,000 Pounds Sterling was reserved for the maintenance of the baronetcy (Palsetia, 2003, pp. 55-75), and upon Jejeebhoy's death in 1859, his title passed on to his eldest son, Cursetjee, who took the name of Sir Jamsetjee Jejeebhoy as second baronet. When Cursetjee died in 1877, his eldest son, Maneckjee, became Sir Jamsetjee Jejeebhoy, third baronet. They both continued the first Sir Jamsetjee's philanthropic ways and close relations with the British. Jejeebhoy's wife and three sons were all also dedicated philanthropists, while his daughter, Pirojbai, was noteworthy as one of the first Parsi females to receive a formal education (Wadia, pp. 105-35).

Jejeebhoy's charity, honors, and public accolades made him the most famous Parsi of his time and perhaps the first famous non-European colonial subject. In 1859 the citizens of Bombay honored Jejeebhoy with the erection of a marble statue designed by Baron Marochetti and housed in the Library of the Royal Asiatic Society. Funds were collected from around the empire to the sum of Rs. 46,340, and the statue was the first major public tribute of its kind to an Indian in Bombay. Reporting on the on the fundraising efforts to erect the statue, the British editor of the *Bombay Times* of 6 September 1856 appreciated the historical significance of Jamsetjee Jejeebhoy: "There is something more remarkable in such liberality than its munificence. It is of the most enlightened character, and places this Parsee knight not merely among the foremost men in India, but among the best of the British Empire. His abounding charity proves how truly he appreciates every element of civilization, and how keenly alive he is to the usefulness of schemes which have scarcely as yet been developed among ourselves." Other statues of Jejeebhoy were later created from the marble template, including a bronze statue at Kemp's Corner in Bombay, and another at the Parsi Panchayat Headquarters (J. J. Fort School).

At the time of his death the total value of his charities was noted to be Rs. 2,459,736 (more than 245,000 Pounds Sterling). The will and codicil of Jejeebhoy had in addition valued the property, personal and real, bequeathed to his family and friends at just under Rs. 8,500,000 or in excess of 750,000 Pounds Sterling (Mody, pp. 172-75; Palsetia, 2003, pp. 55-75).

Bibliography: Bombay Government Gazette Supplement 11 and 21 April 1836. *Bombay Times*, 6 September 1856. Ibid., 16 April 1859. Anne Bulley, *The Bombay Country Ships, 1790-1833*, Richmond, U.K., 2000. Michael Greenberg, *British Trade and the Opening of China, 1800-42*, Cambridge, 1951. "Jeejeebhoy, Sir Jamsetjee," in *Encyclopedia Britannica*, Eleventh Edition, Vol. XV, 1911, p. 300. D. F. Karaka, *History of the Parsis*, 2 vols., London, 1884. Jehangir R. P. Mody, *Jamsetjee Jejeebhoy: The First Indian Knight and Baronet (1783-1859)*, Bombay, 1959. G. A. Natesan & Co., ed., *Famous Parsis: Biographical and Critical Sketches*, Madras, 1930. C. S. Nazir, *The First Parsee Baronet*, Bombay, 1866. Jesse S. Palsetia, "'Honourable Machinations': The Jamsetjee Jejeebhoy Baronetcy and the Indian Response to the Honours System in India," *South Asia Research* 23, no. 1 (May 2003), pp. 55-75. Idem, "Merchant Charity and Public Identity Formation in Colonial India: The Case of Jamsetjee Jejeebhoy," *Journal of Asian and African Studies* 40, no. 3 (June 2005), pp. 197-217. E. J. Rapson, 'Jeejeebhoy, Sir Jamsetjee, first baronet (1783-1859)', rev. A.-M. Misra, *Oxford Dictionary of National Biography*, Oxford University Press, 2004; article available at: http://www.oxforddnb.com/view/article/14687, accessed 6 June 2008. Asiya Siddiqi, "The Business World of Jamsetjee Jejeebhoy," *The Indian Economic and Social History Review* 19, nos. 3-4, 1982, pp. 301-24. Jal H. Wadia, *Sir Jamsetjee Jejeebhoy Parsee Benevolent Institution Centenary Volume*, Bombay, 1950. Williamson Ramsay, *Memorandum of the Life and Public Charities of Sir Jamsetjee Jejeebhoy*, London, 1855.

(JESSE S. PALSETIA)

JELD. See ṢAḤḤĀFI

JELWA, ABU'L-ḤASAN b. Moḥammad Ṭabāṭabāʾi (b. Aḥmadābād, Gujarat, July 1823; d. Tehran, April 1897), a leading Shi'ite scholar of the 19th century and master teacher of philosophy and mathematics, as well as a poet. Jelwa, the name by which he is best known, was the pen name he used in his poetry.

His father, Sayyed Moḥammad Ṭabāṭabāʾi "Maẓhar," a physician by profession, left Isfahan at young age for Kandahar and Kabul, eventually reaching Hyderabad in Sind. There he married the daughter of Mirzā Ebrāhimšāh, the vizier of Mir Ḡolām-ʿAli Khan. This marriage raised his social status and brought him close to court circles, particularly Mir Ḡolām-ʿAli Khan, who sent him as his envoy to the court of India in Calcutta. After his return to Hyderabad, he became the target of some unfounded accusations. Noticing that he was losing Ḡolām-ʿAli Khan's favor, he left Hyderabad for Aḥmadābād in Gujarat, leaving behind the house he owned (Jelwa, in *Nāma-ye dānešvarān*, p. 32). There Jelwa was born. Sayyed Moḥammad returned to Isfahan when Jelwa was seven years old. He died about seven years later leaving Jelwa in poverty and a target of ridicule by people around him, which eventually forced him to leave Isfahan for Tehran.

Jelwa received his first formal education at the Kāsagarān School in Isfahan and studied Arabic literature, natural sciences, mathematics, and theology. He seems to have studied rational disciplines (logic, philosophy, mathematics, natural sciences) mostly on his own without a teacher. Jelwa has not named his teachers in his autobiography, but his biographers have mentioned Sayyed Raẓi Lārijāni (d. 1854), Mollā Moḥammad-Jaʿfar Lāhiji (d. before 1877), Mirzā Ḥasan Čini (d, 1848), and Mollā ʿAbd-al-Jawād Tuni Ḵorāsāni (d. 1877) as his teachers. None of his teachers had the fame of Jelwa as an outstanding philosopher and scholar.

Jelwa began teaching rational disciplines first in Isfahan and then at the Dār-al-Šefāʾ school in Tehran. The best known among his students are Mirzā Ḥasan Kermānšāhi (d. 1918), Mirzā Šehāb-al-Din Nirizi Širāzi (d. 1921), Mirzā Moḥammad Tonekāboni (d. 1941), Āḵund Mollā Moḥammad Hidaji (d. 1921), Āqā Sayyed Ḥosayn Bādkubi (d. 1939), Mirzā Yaḥyā Dawlatābādi (d. 1939, q.v.), Āḵund Mollā Moḥammad-Kāẓem Ḵorāsāni (d. 1911, q.v.), and Mirzā Moḥammad-ʿAli Šāhābādi (d. 1950). Jelwa and two of his contemporaries, Āqā Moḥammad-Reżā Qomšaʾi and Āqā ʿAli Modarres, are the outstanding representatives of the philosophical school of Tehran in the 19th century.

Jelwa is best known as a teacher, not as a philosopher with original philosophical concepts of his own. As a philosopher, he subscribed to the Aristotelian (*maššāʾi*) school and criticized the philosophical views of Ṣadr-al-Din Širāzi (Mollā Ṣadrā), although he regarded his philosophy quite highly and used to teach it. He also wrote a detailed commentary on Mollā Ṣadrā's *al-Asfār al-arbaʿa*. He seems to have considered this commentary as his most significant work, since it is the only one among his works that he mentions in his autobiography (p. 34). Jelwa, following Avicenna, was against the theory of the union of the intellect (*ʿāqel*) and the intelligible (*maʿqul*), and criticized Mollā Ṣadrā's views in this regard in a brief treatise called *Fāʾda fi etteḥād al-ʿāqel wa al-maʿqul* and in his commentary on Mollā Ṣadrā. Also, following Avicenna and the illuminationist philosophers (see ILLUMINATIONISM), he disagreed with Mollā Ṣadrā's philosophical idea known as substantial motion (*al-ḥarakat al-jawhariya*) and rejected it in a treatise he wrote on the subject. Sayyed Jalāl Āštiāni, a follower of Mollā Ṣadrā's school of thought, in his edition of Dāwud Qayṣari's *Šarḥ-e Foṣuṣ al-ḥekam*, attributed Jelwa's criticism of Mollā Ṣadrā's ideas to his inability to understand them, because, according to Āštiāni, he had no comprehension of theosophy (*ʿerfān*).

Jelwa was never married. He lost his eyesight towards the end of his life and died in Tehran in 1897 and was buried in the tomb of Ebn Bābuya (Bābawayh) near Tehran.

Works. Jelwa remarked in his autobiography that "[since] composing a new original work is very difficult, rather impossible, I did not write anything original." Concerning poetry, he noted: "Once I could distinguish between good and bad poetry, I noticed that composing good poems, despite being difficult, is of no use, so I gave up the idea" (Jelwa, in *Nāma-ye dānešvarān*, p. 34). He left twenty-five works. They include his commentaries on the works of others, short treatises, and a *divān* of poetry. A memorial ceremony was held for him in Qom and Zavāra in 1994 and a collection of articles were published in a memorial volume. The complete set of his works have been recently published in Tehran. After his death, his entire library was purchased by the Majles Library. He had asked that the proceeds be distributed among the poor.

His major works are: *al-Ḥaraka al-jawhariya*, Arabic, supporting Avicenna's view and criticizing those of Mollā Ṣadrā; *Rabṭ al-ḥādeṯ be'l-qadim*, Arabic, criticizing Mollā Ṣadrā; *Fi etteḥād al-ʿaqel be'l-maʿqul*, Arabic; *Kolli wa aqsām-e ān*, Arabic, lecture notes taken by one of his students; commentary on Avicenna's *al-Šefāʾ*; commentary of *Šarḥ-e Ešārāt* by K̲ᵛāja Naṣir-al-Din Ṭusi and by Fak̲r-al-Din Moḥammad Rāzi; commentary on *Šarḥ-e Foṣuṣ al-ḥekam* by Dāwud Qayṣari; and commentaries on Mollā Ṣadrā's *Mabdaʾ wa maʿād*, *Šarḥ-e al-hedāya al-aṯiriya*, *al-Mašāʾer*, and *al-Asfar al-arbaʿa*.

Bibliography: Āḡā Bozorg Ṭehrāni, *Ṭabaqāt aʿlām al-šiʿa: noqabāʾ al-bašar fi'l-qarn al-rābeʿ ʿašar* I, Najaf, 1954, pp. 42-43. Aḥmad Bānipur, "Ḥakim Jelwa," *Kayhān-e andiša*, no. 10, 1987, pp. 75-79. Anisa Bark̲ᵛāh, "Jelwa," in *Dāneš-nāma-ye jahān-e Eslām* X, Tehran, 1996, pp. 588-92. Ḡolām-Reżā Goli Zavāra, ed., *Golšan-e Jelwa: yād-nāma-ye Ḥakim Jelwa*, Qom, 1994. Mirzā Abu'l-Ḥasan Eṣfahāni Jelwa, "Abu'l-Ḥasan b. Moḥammad Ṭabāṭabāʾi," in *Nāma-ye dānešvarān-e nāṣeri* III, n.p., n.d., pp. 31-35 (autobiography). Idem, *Divān-e Jelwa*, ed. Aḥmad Sohayli K̲ᵛānsāri, Tehran, 1969. Idem, *Majmuʿa-ye āṯār-e Ḥakim Jelwa*, ed. Ḥasan Reżāzāda, Tehran, 2006. Moḥammad-ʿAli Modarres, *Rayḥānat al-adab*, 8 vols., Tabriz, n.d., I, 1967, pp. 419-20. Moḥammad-ʿAli Moʿallem Ḥabibābādi, *Makārem al-āṯār dar aḥwāl-e rejāl-e do qarn-e 13 wa 14 hejri* IV, Isfahan, 1973, pp. 1060-61. Sayyed Moḥsen al-Amin Ḥosayni ʿĀmeli, *Aʿyān al-šiʿa*, ed. Ḥasan al-Amin, 56 parts, Damascus, 1935-62, VI, pp. 214-16. Moṣṭafā Moḥaqqeq Dāmād, "Nok̲bagān-e ʿelm o ʿamal-e Irān: Mirzā Abu'l-Ḥasan Jelwa," *Nāma-ye Farhangestān-e ʿolum* 3/5, 1996. Aḥmad Nikuhemat, "Jelwa," *Waḥid*, no. 224, 1978, pp. 20-23. Dāwud b. Maḥmud Qayṣari, *Šarḥ-e Foṣuṣ al-ḥekam*, ed. Sayyed Jalāl-al-Din Āštiāni, Tehran, 2004 (includes the commentary of Jelwa). Manučehr Ṣadduqi Sohā, *Tārik̲-e ḥokāmā wa ʿorafā-ye moʿāṣer*, Tehran, 2002. Mirzā Ṭāher Tonekāboni, "Mok̲taṣar šarḥ-e aḥwāl-e Mirzā-ye Jelwa," *Āyanda* 2/9, 1927, pp. 654-56.

(MAHDI KHALAJI)

JELWA, KETĀB *AL-* (Kurd. *Kitēba jilwe*, "the Book of splendor"), title of a notional sacred text in Yazidism. Written copies of the text were first discovered in the late 1880s, together with Meṣḥefa reš (*Meṣḥefa reş*, "black book,"), another short text purporting to be a sacred book. The oldest copies of these texts were written in Arabic (rather than in Kormānji Kurdish, the language of the Yazidi community). They usually formed part of collections of short works on Yazidism, where they did not appear to have pride of place. Shortly before this, in a published interview with the French scholar Anastase N. Siouffi (1880), Bābā Shaikh, the religious leader of the Yazidis, had declared that the group possessed two "sacred books," written in Arabic and named *Kitēba jilwe* and *Meṣḥefa reş*. The latter was said to be a commentary upon the former. While the title *Meṣḥefa reš* originally appears to have been no more than a generic name for a sacred book, the other title may be connected with an older work, *Ketāb al-jelwa le-arbāb al k̲alwa*, which the Hanbalite theologian and jurisconsult Ebn Taymiya (d. 1328), ascribed to Ḥasan b. ʿAdi (k. 1246; Ebn Taymiya, I, pp. 262-317). Ḥasan was an early leader of the proto-Yazidi community, whose world-view and beliefs were presumably formed by Sufism. In its present form, the *Ketāb al-jelwa* purports to reveal the words of the Peacock Angel (Ṭāwusi Malek; Guest, 1993, pp. 208-10), which makes it unlikely to have originated from Ḥasan b. ʿAdi's work.

In the early 20th century, at least half a dozen manuscripts containing the Yazidi sacred books had found their way to the West. Their provenance was shrouded in mystery, but it seems clear that Jeremiah Shamir, a former Christian monk who made a living as a dealer in books and manuscripts, played a key role in their sudden appearance (Kreyenbroek, p. 11).

An anonymous publication (known to be by A. N. Andrus) in 1891 contained the first verbatim translations of passages from the *Ketāb al-jelwa* and the *Meṣḥefa reš*. The first full translation, by Edward G. Browne (q.v. [not in bibliography]), appeared in 1895. In 1909, Isya Joseph published the Arabic text of both *Ketāb al-jelwa* and *Meṣḥefa reš*, with an English translation. Two years later, in 1911, the Carmelite Père Anastase-Marie de Saint-Elie announced his discovery of what he believed to be the original Kurdish version of the texts. This was written in an otherwise unknown alphabet that bore no obvious resemblance to any other Middle Eastern script, but strangely had separate characters representing Arabic emphatic consonants which do not normally occur in Kurdish. Father Anastase showed his find to the Austrian orientalist Maximillian Bittner, who published the texts in 1913 with a German translation. Bittner had access to Oskar Mann's work on the Mokri dialect of Kurdish, but was evidently unfamiliar with other forms of the language. On the basis of this limited knowledge, he declared the Kurdish of these texts to be ancient and obviously regarded Father Anastase's texts as authentic.

A few years later this view was challenged by Alphonse M ingana, who gave a number of cogent arguments to suggest that these finds did not represent an ancient manuscript tradition. Mingana claimed that the texts were forgeries made by Jeremiah Shamir. At a later stage, Cecil John Edmonds (p. 88) pointed out that the Kurdish of the "sacred books" was not Kormānji, but the Sōrāni of the Arbil region, that is, the dialect of Kurdish spoken by Shamir. To these arguments one might add the very words of *Ketāb al-jelwa*, where Ṭāwusi Malek asserts: "I teach without a scripture" (cf. Guest, 1993, p. 209).

Bibliography: Père Anastase-Marie de Saint-Elie, "La découverte récente des deux livres sacrées des Yézidis," *Anthropos* 6, 1911, pp. 1-39. Maximillian Bittner, *Die heiligen Bücher der Jeziden oder Teufelsanbeter: Kurdisch und Arabisch*, Denkschriften der kaiserlichen Akademie der Wissenschaften in Wien, Phil.-Hist. Klasse 55, Vienna, 1913. Cecil John Edmonds, *A Pilgrimage to Lalish*, London, 1967. Ebn Taymiya, *Majmuʿat al-rasāʾel al-kobrā*, 2 vols., Cairo 1905, I, pp. 262-317. Rudolf Frank, *Scheich ʿAdî, der grosse Heilige der Jezîdîs*, Berlin, 1911. Anis Frayha, "New Yezīdī Texts from Beled Sinjār, 'Iraq," *Journal of the Americal Oriental Society* 66, 1946, pp. 18-43.

Giuseppe Furlani, *Testi Religiosi dei Yezidi: traduzione, introduzione e note*, Bologna, 1930; tr. Jamshedji Maneckji Unvala as *The Religion of the Yezidis: Religious Texts of the Yezidis*, Bombay, 1940. John S. Guest, *The Yezidis: A Study in Survival*, London and New York, 1987; 2nd revised ed. as *Survival among the Kurds: A History of the Yezidis*, London and New York, 1993. Isya Joseph, "Yezidi Texts," *American Journal of Semitic Languages and Literatures* 25, 1909, pp. 111-56, 218-54. Idem, *Devil Worship: The Sacred Books and Traditions of the Yezidis*, Boston, 1919. Philip G. Kreyenbroek, *Yezidism: Its Background, Observances and Textual Tradition*, Lewiston, New York, 1995. Austen Henry Layard, *Nineveh and Its Remains: with An Account of A Visit to the Chaldaean Christians of Kurdistan, and the Yezidis, or Devil-Worshippers, and An Enquiry into the Manners and Arts of the Ancient Assyrians*, 2 vols, London, 1849. Oskar Mann, *Die Mundart der Mukri-Kurden*, 2 vols, Berlin, 1906-09. Alphonse Mingana, "Devil-Worshippers; Their Beliefs and Their Sacred Books," *Journal of the Royal Asiatic Society*, 1916, pp. 505-26. Idem, "Sacred Books of the Yezidis," *Journal of the Royal Asiatic Society*, 1921, pp. 117-19. Anastase, N. Siouffi, "Notice sur la secte des Yézidis," *Jounal Asiatique*, ser. 7, 18, 1880, pp. 78-83.

(PHILIP KREYENBROEK)

JEM SOLṬĀN (or ŠĀHZĀDA JEM) b. Edirne, 27 Ṣafar 864/23 December 1459; d. Naples, 29 Jomādā I 900/25 February 1495), Ottoman prince and poet. Jem Solṭān was the third and youngest son of the Ottoman Sultan Meḥmet (Moḥammad) II (r. 1444-46 and 1451-81). His mother, Čiček (Çiçek) Ḵātun (d. 1498), was one of the concubines in the harem. He was educated at the palace and, at the age of ten, was appointed governor of the district (*sanjaq*) of Kastamonu in the north of Turkey. When his elder brother Moṣṭafā died in 1474, Jem was sent to replace him as governor of the Qarāmān province in southern Turkey, where he created a cultural and literary environment.

When Meḥmet II died in 1481, Bāyazid (Bāyazid II, r. 1481-1512), Jem's eldest brother, managed to arrive in Istanbul before Jem to ascend the throne. Jem was convinced that the throne should belong to him. Having defeated his brother's army, he declared himself the ruler of Anatolia with the capital at Bursa in 1481. However, it became impossible for him to stay in Bursa because his army was defeated by that of Bāyazid II, and he first returned to Konya and then went to Cairo to seek asylum with the Mamluks. Mamluk Sultan Qāyit Bāy (r. 1468-96) sheltered Jem, who, with the help of Qāsem Beg (d. 1483) of the Qaramanids, went to try his luck in Anatolia once again. He was unable to defeat Bāyazid II, who had already firmly established his power. In 1482 Jem went to seek asylum with the Knights of the Order of St. John on the island of Rhodes with the aim of reaching Rumeli (the European part of the Ottoman Empire).

Within a brief time his freedom became more and more restricted, and he had to live almost like a prisoner. Pierre d'Aubusson (1423-1503), the 40th grandmaster of the Order of St. John, made an arrangement with Bāyazid II to bring Jem first to Villefranche and then to Nice. For more than six years Jem was sent from castle to castle in the south of France. In 1489 he was transferred to the Vatican. For a long time Jem stayed under the control of Pope Innocent VIII (Pope in 1484-92), who planned to use him for a crusade, but European monarchs did not support the idea. The French King Charles VIII (r. 1483-98) forced the Pope to send Jem back to France. Jem died on his way to France on 29 Jomādā I 900/25 February 1495 in Naples. After four years, his corpse was brought to Bursa where he was buried in the graveyard of the Morādiya Mosque in 1499.

Works. Four of Jem's works have come down to us: the Persian *divān* (ed. Ṭoqmāq, 2001); the Turkish *divān* (facsim. ed. Ertaylan, 1951, pp. 67-254; ed. Ersoylu, Ankara, 1981, 2nd ed., 1989); *Jamšid o Ḵoršid* (*Āyāt-e ʿOššāq*; ed. Okur Meriç, 1997; ed. İnce, 2000), a Turkish translation of *Jamšid o Ḵoršid* by Salmān-e Sāvaji (d. 778/1376, q.v.) made by Jem in 1478 at Konya for his father Meḥmed II; and *Fāl-e reyḥān-e Jem Solṭān* (ed. Okur, 1992, pp. 219-22), a small work containing 48 couplets.

Jem's Persian *divān* contains 2,415 couplets and has been recorded in four manuscripts (Bursa, Orhan Haraçcı Library, MS E. 6; Istanbul, Topkapı Sarayı Library, MS Revan 739; Istanbul, Süleymaniye Library, MS Fatih 3794; Istanbul, Millet Library, Ali Emiri Efendi, MS Manzum 328). After the first four parts of the manuscript of Orhan Haraçcı Library had been published in facsimile edition by Ismail Hikmet Ertaylan in 1951, the entire text came out in Tehran in 2001 as a critical edition made by A. Nāji Ṭoqmāq (A. Naci Tokmak). Though not a first-class poet but a specialist in classical Persian literature, Jem wrote powerful visionary poems. He was inspired by Persian poets such as Neẓāmi, Salmān-e Sāvaji, Ḥāfeẓ, and Jāmi (qq.v.), as well as by Turkish poets such as Aḥmed Pāšā, Šayḵi, and Nejāti Beg. Many poems express his loneliness and reveal a very romantic character. The quality of his Persian poems is considered to be better than that of his Turkish poems, and he was highly praised as a poet by compilers of poetic anthologies (*taḏkera*). There are many personal letters of Jem Solṭān written in Persian, which suggests that he had a special interest in this language.

Besides being a poet himself, Jem was also a patron for many other poets and writers, such as Saʿdi (*Jem Saʿdisi*), Sehāʾi, Ḥaydar, Laʾli, and Qandi. Some poets, like ʿAyni-e Termeḏi, Aḥmed Pāšā, Ḥamidi, and Qabuli, wrote poems for him. Shaikh Maḥmud Bayāti, who met Jem during the *ḥājj*, dedicated his work *Jām-e Jem-āyin* (Istanbul, 1912-13) to Jem, and so did Šāhedi, a civil servant under Jem in Konya, with his work *Golšan-e ʿOššāq*.

Bibliography: Works. Halil Ersoylu, ed., *Cem Sultan'ın Türkçe Divanı*, Ankara, 1981, 2nd ed., 1989. Adnan İnce, ed., *Cem Sultan, Cemşîd ü Hurşîd*, Ankara, 2000. İ. Münevver Okur Meriç, ed., *Cem Sultan,*

Cemşîd ü Hurşîd (İnceleme–Metin), Ankara, 1997. ʿAbd-al-Raḥmān Nāji Ṭoqmāq [Abdurrahman Naci Tokmak], *Šarḥ-e ḥāl-e Solṭān Jem wa taḥqiq o taḥlil-e divān-e fārsi-e u*, ed. Wahhāb Wali, Tehran, 2001.

Sources. Kenan Beşirov, "Gurbetnâme-i Sultan Cem. Giriş-inceleme-metin-sözlük," M.A. diss., Istanbul University, Istanbul, 2001, pp. 9-35. Aşıq Çelebi, *Mešāʿir al-šoʿarā or Tezkere of Aşıq Çelebi*, facsim. ed. G. M. Meredith-Owens, London, 1971, fols. 67a-68a. Faridun Beg, *Monšaʾāt al-salāṭin*, 2 vols., Istanbul, 1857-58, vol. I, pp. 290-94. *Fatih devrine âit münşeat mecmuası (Wien, Nationalbibliothek, H.O. 161)*, ed. Necati Lugal-Adnan Erzi, Istanbul, 1956, pp. 6-10, 18-19, 75-81, 87, 100. A. Gallotta and G. Bova, "Venedik Devlet Arşivi'nde Osmanlı Şehzadesi Sultan Cem ile ilgili belgeler," Turk. tr. Mahmut H. Şakiroğlu, *Tarih ve Toplum* 5/30, 1986, pp. 19-27. Mustafa Ali Gelibolulu, *Künhü'l-ahbâr'ın tezkire kısmı*, ed. Mustafa İsen, Ankara, 1994, p. 151. Ḥaydar Beg, *Wāqeʿāt-e Solṭān Jem*, ed. M. Arif, Istanbul, 1911-12, pp. 3-17, 23-32. Ḵ^vāja Saʿd-al-Din Efendi, *Tāj al-tawāriḵ*, 5 vols., ed. İ. Parmaksızoğlu, Ankara, 1999, vol. III, pp. 100-3, 156, 186-89, 192-202, 207-23, 235, 273; vol. IV, pp. 114-15, 119. Latifi, *Latifi tezkiresi*, ed. Mustafa İsen, Ankara, 1990, pp. 73-75. J. Lefort, *Topkapı Sarayı Arşivi'nin Yunanca belgeleri. Cem Sultan'ın tarihine bir katkı*, Turk. tr. H. Gonnet, Ankara, 1981. Moṣṭafā b. Jar-Allāh Bayāni, *Tezkeret al-šoʿarā*, ed. İbrahim Kutluk, Ankara, 1997, pp. 8-9. Qınalızade Ḥasan Çelebi, *Tezkeret al-šoʿarā*, ed. İbrahim Kutluk, 2nd ed., Ankara, 1989, pp. 112-15. Sehi Beg, *Hašt Behešt*, ed. Günay Kut as *Heşt bihişt. Sehi Beg tezkiresi: inceleme, tenkidi metin, dizin (Hesht Bihisht: The Tezkire by Sehi Beg)*, facsim. ed., Cambridge, Mass., 1978, pp. 99-102. Šekāri, *Karaman Oğulları tarihi*, ed. M. Mesud Koman, Konya, 1946, pp. 200-4. İsmail Hakkı Uzunçarşılı, "Cem Sultan'a dâir beş orijinal vesika," *Belleten* 24/95, 1960, pp. 457-83.

Studies. Aḥmad Sayyed al-Darrāj, "Jem Solṭān wa al-deblumāsiya al-dowaliya," *al-Majalla al-taʾriḵiya al-Meṣriya* 8, 1959, pp. 201-42. Sema Çakmak Alpun, "Sultan Cem Divanı'nın psikolojik tahlili," M.A. diss., Fırat University, Elazığ, 2000. Ahmet Refik Altınay, *Sultan Cem*, Istanbul, 2001. Anonym., "Cem Sultan," *Türk Dili ve Edebiyatı Ansiklopedisi* II, Istanbul, 1977, pp. 34-35. F. Babinger, *Sultan Mehmed der Eroberer und seine Zeit*, Munich, 1959, pp. 184, 330-37, 445-46, 466. M. Cavid Baysun, *Cem Sultan. Hayatı ve şiirleri*, Istanbul, 1946, pp. 13-69, 71-97. Idem, "Cem. Cem Sultan," *İslâm Ansiklopedisi* III, 1964, pp. 69-81. W. Björkman, "Der Aufenthalt des Prinzen Cem in Ägypten 1481-1482 und seine politische Bedeutung," in *A. Zeki Velidi Togan'a Armağan*, Istanbul, 1955, pp. 71-76. Bursalı Meḥmed Ṭāhir, *Osmanlı mü'ellifleri*, 3 vols. and index, Istanbul, 1914-28, vol. II, pp. 122-23. G. E. Corretto, "Cem Sultan a Roma," *Erdem* 12/35, 2000, pp. 419-50. İlhan Çeneli, "Sultan Cem ve dört şiiri," *Türk Kültürü* 9/128, 1973, pp. 28-30. *Dāneš-nāma-ye adab-e fārsi*, vol. VI: *Adab-e fārsi dar Ānātuli wa Bālkān*, ed. Ḥasan Anuša, Tehran, 2005, pp. 280-82. İsmail Hikmet Ertaylan, *Cem Sultan*, Istanbul, 1951, pp. 12-91, 111-37. Semavi Eyice, "Sultan Cem'in portreleri hakkında," *Belleten* 28/145, 1973, pp. 1-45. Idem, "Sultan Cem Türbesi," *Diyanet Vakfı İslâm Ansiklopedisi* VIII, 1993, pp. 286-87. Elhāma Meftāḥ and Wahhāb Wali, *Negāh-i be ravand-e nofuḏ wa gostareš-e zabān wa adab-e fārsi dar Torkia*, Tehran, 1995, pp. 211-39. R. S. Hattox, "Qāyitbāy's Diplomatic Dilemma Concerning the Flight of Cem Sultan (1481-82)," *Mamluk Studies Review* 6, 2002, pp. 177-90. Halil İnalcık, "Djem," *EI*² II, 1965, pp. 529-31. Idem, "A Case Study in Renaissance Diplomacy: the Agreement between Innocent VIII and Bayezid II on Djem Sultan," *Journal of Turkish Studies* 3, 1979, pp. 209-30. Ahmet Kartal, "Osmanlı medeniyetini besleyen kültür merkezleri, edebî açıdan (XI. asırdan XVI. asrın sonuna kadar Türk Edebiyatı ile Fars Edebiyatının münasebetleri)," Ph.D. diss., Gazi University, Ankara, 1999, pp. 391-92. Cemal Kurnaz, "Cem Sultan'ın Oğuz Han Mersiyesi bir mersiye mi, üç gazel mi?" *Türk Dili* 530, 1996, pp. 315-20. Günay Kut, "Sultan Cem. II. Edebî Yönü," *Diyanet Vakfı İslâm Ansiklopedisi* VII, 1993, pp. 284-86. Münevver Okur, "Cem Sultan'ın yeni bulunan *Fâl-i Reyhân-i Cem Sultân* isimli eseri," *Tarih ve Toplum* 16/96, 1991, pp. 24-27. Idem, *Cem Sultan. Hayatı ve şiir dünyası*, Ankara, 1992, pp. 54-55, 61, 219-22. Cahit Öztelli, "Cem Sultan'ın yeni bulunan *Cemşîd ü Hurşîd* Mesnevisi," *Türk Dili* 26/248, 1972, pp. 124-28. Moḥammad-Amin Riāḥi, *Zabān wa adab-e fārsi dar qalamrow-e ʿOṯmāni*, Tehran, 1990, pp. 165-67. Mahmut H. Şakiroğlu, "Sultan Cem," *Diyanet Vakfı İslâm Ansiklopedisi* VII, 1993, pp. 283-84. Şerafettin Turan, "Barak Reis'in Şehzade Cem meselesi ile ilgili olarak Savoie'ye gönderilmesi," *Belleten* 26/103, 1962, pp. 539-55. İsmail Hakkı Uzunçarşılı, *Osmanlı tarihi*, 5th ed., vol. II, Ankara, 1988, pp. 108-9, 140-43, 161-79, 455-56. Muammer Yılmaz, *Talihsiz Şehzâde Cem Sultan*, Kayseri, 1981, pp. 9-39. Zaynab Saʿd Abu Sana, "Divān al-Amir Jem: derāsat adabiya," *Majalla kolliyya al-adab Jāmeʿa al-Qāhera* 61/1, 2001, pp. 315-82.

(OSMAN G. ÖZGÜDENLİ)

JEMĀLI, Ottoman poet and writer of the 15th century. In two manuscripts of the supplement (*ḏeyl*), which he wrote for the *Ḵosrow o Širin* of Šayḵi, his name is given as Bāyazid b. Moṣṭafā b. Šayḵ Aḥmad Tarjomāni Āqšahri or as Bāyazid b. Moṣṭafā al-mašhur be Šayḵ-oğlu (Kut, p. 316). In medieval sources he was often confused with Šayḵ-oğlu Moṣṭafā (1340-?; see Akün, pp. 481-85). Very little is known about Jemāli's life. He was apparently born around 1410-12 and originated from Qarāmān in southern Turkey. He was the nephew of Šayḵi, who was an outstanding poet of the 14th-15th century. In the beginning of his career, Jemāli was very close to the Ottoman vizier Çandarlı Ḥalil Pasha (d. 1453). While in Bursa, he came under the protection of Sultan Morād II (r. 1421-44 and 1446-51) and became a highly respected poet at the court. After the Ottoman conquest of Constantinople in 1453 he came to live in Istanbul. Jemāli wrote several poems in praise of Meḥmet (Moḥammad) II (r. 1444-46 and 1451-81) and took part in his campaign to Albania. In comparison with the famous contemporary Ottoman poets such as Šayḵi, Nejāti Beg, and Aḥmed Pasha, he always remained second-class. According to the prevailing opinion, he died in Istanbul during the last years of the reign of Bāyazid II (r. 1481-1512).

Works. Jemāli's Turkish *divān* has come down to us in a unique manuscript which also contains a few Persian couplets (Ankara, Millî Library, MS A. 7978/1; see Erimer, 1974). This *divān* has been dealt with in two different theses, both of them published (Derdiyok, 1988 and 1994; Karaman, 1988 and 2002). Jemāli's *Ḏeyl-e Ḵosrow o Širin*, which is the supplement to the *Ḵosrow o Širin* by Šayḵi, comprises 109 couplets. Most probably it was written in 1430-31. The *Homā vo Homāyun (Golšan-e ʿOššāq)*, for which the *Homāy o Homāyun* by Ḵᵛāju-ye Kermāni (q.v.) had served as a model, was written for Morād II in 1446. It contains 4,593 couplets and has been recorded in two manuscripts (Ilıca, 1961; Alkan, 1966; Horata, 1990). The *Meftāḥ al-faraj*, containing about 5,000 couplets, was completed in 1456 and presented to Meḥmet II (Yıldız, 1992). *Al-Resāla al-ʿajiba fi al-ṣanāʾeʿ wa al-badāʾeʿ* is known by the only manuscript preserved in the Cambridge University Library (MS no. 465, see Kut, p. 317). The *Dar bayān-e mašaqqat-e safar wa żarurat o molāzemat*, a small work of 73 couplets, can be found at the end of Jemāli's *divān*. It deals with the difficulties of Meḥmet II's campaign to Albania (Erimer, 1974).

Bibliography: Works. Kadriye Alkan, "Cemâlî'nin 'Hümâ vü Hümâyûn' (Gülšen-i 'Uššâk) Mesnevisi," B.A. diss., Ankara University, Ankara, 1966. İ. Çetin Derdiyok, *Cemâlî Divanı (İnceleme-Metin)*, M.A. diss., Çukurova University, Adana, 1988. Idem, *Cemâlî, hayatı, eserleri ve divanı*, critical edition and facsimile, Cambridge, Mass., 1994. Osman Horata, *Cemâlî, Hümâ vü Hümâyûn (Gülšen-i 'Uššâk). İnceleme-Tenkidli Metin*, Ankara, 1990. İnciser Ilıca, "Gülšen-i 'Uššâk (Hümâ vü Hümâyûn), Cemâlî," B.A. diss., Istanbul University, Istanbul, 1961. Nihal Nomer Karaman, "Cemâlî divânı," Ph.D. diss., Istanbul University, Istanbul, 1988. Idem, *Cemâlî divânı*, Istanbul, 2002. Osman Yıldız, "Cemâlî-i Karamanî, Miftahu'l-ferec. Dil özellikleri, metin, söz dizini," Ph.D. diss., 4 vols., İnönü University, Malatya, 1992.

Sources. Ašıq Çelebi, *Mešāʿir al-šoʿarā or Tezkere of Âšıq Çelebi*, facsim. ed. G. M. Meredith-Owens, London, 1971, fols. 20a, 354a. Mostafa Ali Gelibolulu, *Künhü'l-ahbâr'ın tezkire kısmı*, ed. Mustafa İsen, Ankara, 1994, p. 123. Latifi, *Latifi tezkiresi*, ed. Mustafa İsen, Ankara, 1990, p. 121. Qınalızāde Ḥasan Çelebi, *Taḏkerat al-šoʿarā*, 2nd ed., ed. İbrahim Kutluk, Ankara, 1989, vol. I, pp. 260-61. Sehi Beg, *Hešt bihišt, the tezkire*, facsim. ed. Günay Kut, Cambridge, Mass., 1978, pp. 55, 107-8, 113. Mehmed Süreya Bey, *Sijill-i ʿOṯmāni*, 4 vols., Istanbul, 1890-97, repr. 1971, vol. II, p. 85.

Studies. Ömer Faruk Akün, "Şeyh-oğlu Mustafa," *İslâm Ansiklopedisi* XI, 1970, pp. 481-85. Hüseyin Ayan, "Cemâlî," *Türk Dili ve Edebiyatı Ansiklopedisi* II, Istanbul, 1977, pp. 38-39. Bursalı Meḥmed Ṭāhir, *Osmanlı mü'ellifleri*, 3 vols., Istanbul, 1914-24, vol. II, p. 122. *Dāneš-nāma-ye adab-e fārsi*, vol. VI: *Adab-e fārsi dar Ānātuli wa Bālkān*, ed. Ḥasan Anuša, Tehran, 2004, p. 280. Faruk Kadri Demirtaş [Timurtaş], "Fâtih devri şâirlerinden Cemâlî ve eserleri," *İstanbul Üniversitesi Türk Dili ve Edebiyatı Dergisi* 4/3, 1951, pp. 189-213. İ. Çetin Derdiyok, "Fâtih devri şâirlerinden Cemâlî'nin divân'ında yer alan iki tarih," *Türk Kültürü* 32/375, 1994, pp. 434-37. Idem, "Miftahü'l-Ferec'in iki yeni nüshası," *Bir* 4, 1995, pp. 61-66. Sadeddin Nuzhet Ergun, *Türk şairleri*, 3 vols., Istanbul, 1936, vol. III, pp. 979-82. Kayahan Erimer, "Gün Işığına Çıkan Değerli Bir Eser," *Türk Dili Araştırmaları Yıllığı, Belleten 1973-1974*, 1974, pp. 265-81. Osman Horata, "Cemâlî'nin hayatı ve eserleri," *Hacettepe Üniversitesi Edebiyat Fakültesi Dergisi* 8, 1991, pp. 51-83. Idem, "Cemâlî'nin *Hümâ vü Hümâyûn* mesnevisi," *Marmara Üniversitesi Türklük Araştırmaları Dergisi, Prof. Dr. Âmil Çelebioğlu Armağanı* 7, 1993, pp. 281-306. Idem, "Hâcû-yı Kirmânî ve Cemâlî'nin *Hümâ vü Hümâyûn* mesnevilerinin karşılaştırılması," *Journal of Turkish Studies* 24/1, *in Memoriam Agâh Sırrı Levend*, ed. Günay Kut, vol. I, Cambridge, Mass., 2000, pp. 121-35. Idem, "Cemâlî," *Türk Dünyası Edebiyatçıları Ansiklopedisi* II, Ankara, 2002, pp. 429-32. Günay Kut, "Cemâlî," *Diyanet Vakfı İslâm Ansiklopedisi* VII, 1993, pp. 316-17. Osman Yıldız, "Cemālī-i Karamanī ve *Miftâhu'l-ferec'i*," *Süleyman Demirel Üniversitesi Fen-Edebiyat Fakültesi Sosyal Bilimler Dergisi* 2, 1996, pp. 271-92.

(OSMAN G. ÖZGÜDENLİ)

JENJĀN, coll. Jenjun, "Jinjun," village in the Dašt-e Rostam-e Yek plain, at the western end of the Fahliān area of the Mamasani region, western Fārs (lat. 30°13.532 N, long. 51°26.792 E, 844 m above sea-level; Razmārā, *Farhang* VII, p. 65). It has given its name to a small (ca. 30 x 5 m, 2 m high, 0.15 ha) archeological site of the Achaemenid period. Jinjun is ca. 125 km northwest of Shiraz and 290 km southeast of Ahwāz (Atarashi and Horiuchi, p. 1). Also known as Tappeh Servan or Qaleh Kali, Jinjun is site MS 46 in the recently completed archeological survey of the Dasht-e Rostam-e Yek and Do plains (Zeidi, McCall, and Khosrowzadeh, p. 166).

Jinjun was first documented by Ernst Herzfeld, who visited the site on 10 April 1924 and was immediately struck by the presence of several Persepolitan-type column bases protruding from the ground, leading him somewhat rashly to suggest that Jinjun held the ruins of an entire Achaemenid city (Herzfeld, 1926, p. 258). In 1935 the site was visited by M. Aurel Stein (Stein, pp. 34-36) but it was not until 1959 that a brief, five-day excavation was undertaken by the Second Tokyo University-Iran Archeological Expedition (Atarashi and Horiuchi, Pl. X). In

PLATE I

The small area of pavement and column bases in situ at the end of the 2007 excavations at Jenjān. (Photograph by the author.)

PLATE II

The small area of pavement and one of the column bases in situ at the end of the 2007 excavations at Jenjān. (Photograph by the author.)

addition to three column bases, the Japanese excavators discovered stepped stone merlons and a small area of flagstone paving (PLATES I-II), suggesting the presence of "a small royal pavilion of the Achaemenian dynasty . . . along the road connecting Susa and Persepolis" (Atarashi and Horiuchi, p. 13). In 2003 a joint expedition from the Iranian Center for Archeological Research and the University of Sydney (Australia) re-visited Jinjun, and in the winter of 2007 (31 January-24 February) initiated new excavations at the site.

The bell-shaped column bases, originally discovered by the Japanese expedition and re-excavated by the Iranian-Australian team, bear decoration in the form of sixteen, seven-petalled palmettes that alternate with fluting (PLATE III). Although generally reminiscent of Persepolitan column bases, those of Jinjun have no exact counterparts at either Persepolis or Susa. Their dimensions, however, are

PLATE III

An upturned Achaemenid column base on the surface of Jenjān. (Photograph by the author.)

nearly as large as those used in the Hall of 100 Columns at Persepolis: A-I was 75.8 cm high, with a base diameter of 1.254 m and an upper surface diameter of 79.4 cm; A-IV was 93 cm high, with a base diameter of 1.24 m and an upper surface diameter of 93 cm, Atarashi and Horiuchi, p. 10. These suggest that the building at Jinjun to which the bases belonged was tall, whatever its surface area may have been.

Other finds from the Iranian-Australian excavations included two large fragments of a limestone door lintel or frame; a great quantity of domestic Achaemenid pottery; half a dozen fragments of élite stone vessels, in a variety of pink, white, and dark green stones (possibly marble, travertine, and serpentine; Potts, Petrie et al., Fig. 12); and a similar quantity of extremely fine, colorless glass cup or bowl rims. The stone vessel fragments from Jinjun are every bit as fine as the so-called royal table ware discovered by Schmidt in the Treasury at Persepolis (Schmidt, p. 94; Simpson, pp. 104-31). Large quantities of coarse, heavy pottery, probably fragments of storage jars, far outnumbered the modest number (under a dozen) of classic Achaemenid 'tulip bowls' found at the site. Finally, a number of extremely fine metal objects were recovered, including a needle and pin of tin bronze, as well as corroded iron nails, studs and hook fragments that may have been door furniture.

The general impression that Jinjun may have been a way station on the road between Persepolis and Susa has not been altered by the Iranian-Australian excavations. However, the placement of the site, on the southern side of the Fahliān river (within sight of the Elamite rock relief at Kurangun, and the multi-period site of Tol-e Spid), just below the mountainside, suggests it was intentionally situated away from the main road, in a protected position. The presence of demonstrably élite architecture and finds (glass, stone vessel fragments, tin bronze) suggests that the site may well have been visited by members of the royal party traveling between the Achaemenid capitals. Many of the "J" texts from the Persepolis fortification archive mention commodities "dispensed before the king" or other members of the royal family, including Darius's wife, Irtašduna (PF 730-732), his son Arsames (PF 733-734, 2035), and his brother-in-law (and father-in-law) Gobryas (PF 688). These disbursements occurred at various places, including Kurdušum, Bessitme, and Liduma, but while Arfa'i (p. 43) has identified Jinjun with Liduma, and Herzfeld suggested it was perhaps Taōke (Herzfeld, 1968, p. 178), it is still too early to say what the ancient name of Jinjun may have been (Potts, in press).

Bibliography: A. Arfa'i, "La grande route Persépolis-Suse: Une lecture des tablettes provenant des Fortifications de Persépolis," *Topoi* 9, 1999, pp. 33-45. K. Atarashi and K. Horiuchi, *Fahlian I. The Excavation at Tape Suruvan, 1959*, Tokyo, 1963. E. Herzfeld, "Reisebericht," *ZDMG*, N.F. 5, 1926, pp. 225-84. Idem, *The Persian Empire*, Wiesbaden, 1968. D. T. Potts, "The Persepolis Fortification Texts (PFTs) and the Royal Road: Another look at the Fahliyan area," in P. Briant and W. Henkelman, eds., *Archives Persépolis*, Paris, forthcoming. D. T. Potts, A. Asgari Chaverdi, C. A. Petrie, A. Dusting, F. Farhadi, I. K. McRae, S. Shikhi, E. H. Wong, A. Lashkari and A. Javanmard Zadeh, "The Mamasani Archaeological Project, Stage Two: Excavations at Qaleh Kali (Tappeh Servan/Jinjun [MS 46])," *Iran* 45, 2007, pp. 287-300. D. T. Potts and K. Roustaei, *The Mamasani Archaeological Project Stage One: A report on the first two seasons of the ICAR - University of Sydney expedition to the Mamasani District, Fars Province, Iran*, Tehran, 2006. E. F. Schmidt, *Persepolis II*, Chicago, 1957. St. J. Simpson, "The Royal Table," in J. Curtis and N. Tallis, eds., *Forgotten Empire: The World of Ancient Persia*, London, 2005, pp. 104-31. M. A. Stein, *Old Routes of Western Iran*, London, 1940. M. Zeidi, B. McCall, and A. Khosrowzadeh, "Survey of Dasht-e Rostam-e Yek and Dasht-e Rostam-e Do," in Potts, and Roustaei, 2006, pp. 147-68.

(DANIEL T. POTTS)

JENKINSON, ANTHONY (b. Market Harborough, 8 October 1529, buried Holy Trinity Church, Teigh, 16 February 1611), merchant and traveler. His writings and his map (Figure 1), which are significant for the study of early Anglo-Russian relations, document England's earliest concerted efforts to establish commercial relations with Safavid Persia. Jenkinson views Persia through the lens of mercantile opportunities, and his descriptions of the political state of affairs and its geography, culture, and religion offer valuable, albeit brief observations.

Life. Little is known about his early life. Jenkinson was trained for a mercantile career and traveled extensively throughout Europe and eastern parts of the Mediterranean between 1546 and 1556. In 1553, he obtained a safe-conduct for trade in the Ottoman Empire from Solaymān II (r. 1520-66), the first documented case of Anglo-Ottoman trade. Against the backdrop of the Ottoman-Safavid conflict, Jenkinson witnessed the procession of Solaymān II into Aleppo, and composed a short, but vivid account of the sultan who then was on his way, "marching toward *Persia* against the Great Sophie" (Hakluyt, II, p. 112).

Jenkinson was appointed captain-general of the Muscovy Company, and on 12 May 1557 he set sail for Russia to obtain a safe-conduct from Tsar Ivan IV (r. 1547-84) to explore the Caspian Sea (q.v.) and beyond. The document was granted, and Jenkinson together with Richard Johnson, Robert Johnson, and an interpreter left Moscow for Bukhara (q.v.), where they arrived on 23 April 1558. Jenkinson noted that the Uzbek city, which belonged to the Šaybānid khanate (1500-99; see ABU'L-ḴAYR KHAN), had been part of Timurid Iran (1370-1507) and that its inhabitants "doe now speake the *Persian* tongue" (Hakluyt, I, p. 331). His chief interest, however, was in the available opportunities for the vending of English goods and the establishment of commercial relations. He decided to pass through Safavid Persia (1501-1722) "to have seen the trade of that Countrey" (I, p. 333) on his way home. But because of the "great warres that did newly begin betwixt the *Sophie*, and the kings of *Tartaria*" (I, p. 333), he could not pursue his plans and retraced his steps back to Moscow from where he returned to London in 1560.

In May 1561, Jenkinson was dispatched again and arrived at Moscow in August 1561. This time he carried a letter from Queen Elizabeth I (r. 1558-1603), addressed to "the Great Sophie of Persia," as the Muscovy Company had given him explicit instructions "to procure letters of privilege or safeconduct of the sayd Sophie or other princes" (Hakluyt, I, p. 342) for trade in these regions. Jenkinson suffered a long delay until he received the tsar's permission to continue his journey into Persia, and he left Moscow on 27 April 1562 in the company of the Safavid ambassador. Jenkinson arrived at Shemakha, in the province of Širvān, on 18 August 1562, and the province's governor-general Obdolowc an (see ʿABDALLĀH KHAN b. ESKANDAR, 1532/33-98) richly entertained him. On 2 November 1562, Jenkinson arrived in Qazvin, the seat of Shah Ṭahmāsp (r. 1524-76). But the shah did not wish to jeopardize his recently concluded peace with the Ottoman Empire, so that Jenkinson was neither well received at court nor did he obtain the desired documents. Jenkinson remained in Qazvin over winter until 20 March 1563. He conferred with Indian merchants about the possibility of trading in spices, and on his return journey he obtained trading privileges from ʿAbdallāh Khān. From Moscow Jenkinson immediately sent three members of the Muscovy Company—among them Thomas Alcock (d. 1564)—to Persia on a second voyage, while he himself continued on to England, where he arrived in 1564.

Jenkinson returned to Russia twice more in 1566 and 1571, but he did not go back to Persia. In 1568 he married Judith Marshe, the daughter of John Marshe (1516-79), an original member of the Muscovy Company in 1555. Jenkinson was granted a coat of arms with a crest featuring

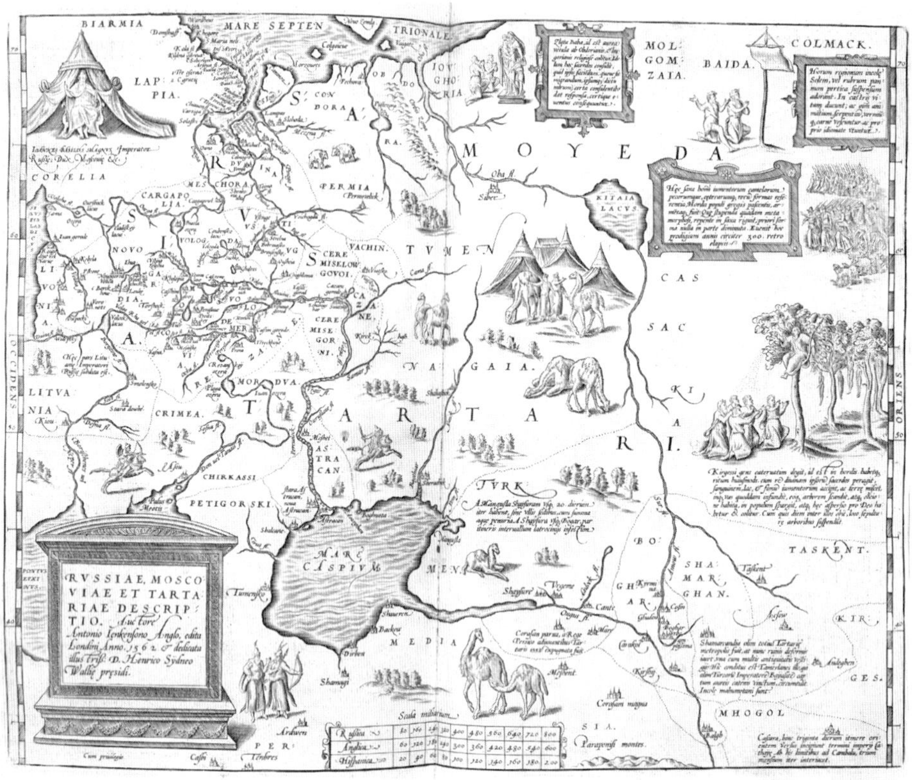

Figure 1. A. Jenkinson, "Russiae, Moscoviae, et Tartariae," in Ortelius, after p. 73 (reduced, orig. size 35 x 43 cm). Courtesy of the Rare Books and Manuscripts Library, Columbia University in the City of New York.

a sea horse on 14 February 1569. His successful missions to Russia as a representative of the Muscovy Company between 1557 and 1571 allowed him to rise to prominence in the Elizabethan diplomatic and mercantile circles, and he was credited with having initiated England's trade with Persia (see GREAT BRITAIN ii. and vii.) during his second journey between 1561 and 1564. Jenkinson remained active in business, and in 1577 he became a member of the Spanish Company. He spent the last years of his life in Ashton where he drew up his will on 13 November 1610.

Safavid Persia. Jenkinson wrote about his travels to Russia and Persia, and produced a map. The travelogues remained unnoticed by his contemporaries until Richard Hakluyt (ca. 1552-1616) incorporated them into his compendious *Principal Navigations*, whose first edition appeared in 1589. But the map was first published in 1562, with a dedication to his patron Henry Sidney (1529-86), Lord President of Wales (Keuning, p. 172). The original version was edited by Clement Adams (ca. 1519-87), engraved by Nicholas Reynolds, and probably printed in Antwerp (Appleby). The map was known in the Netherlands in three different versions, and one was included in the famous *Theatrum orbis terrarum* (Figure 1). Abraham Ortelius (1527-98) compiled this popular atlas, whose first edition appeared 1570 in Antwerp. Although Jenkinson's map is far from accurate according to modern cartographic criteria, the latitudes are nearly correct, and Jenkinson's itinerary is quite clearly represented (Keuning, pp. 174-75). The map's main merit lies in its contribution to the expansion of Elizabethan England's geographical knowledge of these eastern regions.

In his writings, Jenkinson succinctly described, with an eye for commerce and geography, his journeys to regions never before visited by English travelers. In broad strokes he sketched Persia and its borders to other nations. As a merchant he did not fail, of course, to list the commodities that he found at the caravan market in Bukhara (q.v.): "*Craska* [that is, water-colored coarse linen], woollen cloth, linen cloth, pide silkes, Argomacks [that is, horses] and slaves" (Hakluyt, I, p. 332). Jenkinson was shrewd in his interactions with the shah. When the shah asked whom among "the Emperour of Almaine, King Philip, and the great Turke" he considered the most powerful player in the world, Jenkinson avoided any dispraise of the Ottoman sultan because of the "late concluded friendship" (Hakluyt, I, p. 349) between the Ottomans and the Safavids. Jenkinson's personal impression of Shah Ṭahmāsp was that he is "nothing valiant, although his power bee great" (I, p. 351); a quality Jenkinson found confirmed when the Ottoman sultan invaded much of Persia and forced the shah to retreat. Jenkinson considered the Persians in general "comely and of good complexion," though he disapproved of them for being "proude and of good courage, esteeming themselves to bee best of all nations, both for their religion and holiness, which is most erroneous" (I, p. 351).

The Portuguese courier António Tenreiro (fl. 1520s) had already noted the difference between Sunni and Shiʿi Islam (Lockhard, p. 381), but it was Anthony Jenkinson who first familiarized English readers with this distinction. Equally important, Jenkinson's successful acquisition of a safe-conduct from ʿAbdallāh Khan protected English traders from misbehavior, extortion, and misappropriation and thus prepared the way for England's future trade with Safavid Persia.

Bibliography: Sources: R. Hakluyt, *The Principal Navigations, Voyages, Traffiques and Discoveries of the English Nation: Made by Sea or Over-land, to the Remote and Farthest Distant Quarters of the Earth, at Any Time within the Compasse of these 1600 Yeeres . . .*, 2nd ed., 3 vols., London, 1598-1600; esp. I, pp. 324-52 and II, p. 112-13 for Jenkinson's travels; for a modern edition, see E. D. Morgan and C. H. Coote, eds., *Early Voyages and Travels to Russia and Persia by Anthony Jenkinson and other Englishmen: With Some Account of the First Intercourse of the English with Russia and Central Asia by Way of the Caspian Sea*, Works Issued by the Hakluyt Society 72-73, 2 vols., London, 1886. A. Ortelius, *Theatrum orbis terrarum*, Dutch tr., Antwerp, 1598, Jenkinson's map of Russia, including parts of Iran and Central Asia, follows p. 73, orig., Antwerp, 1570. Studies: J. H. Appleby, "Jenkinson, Anthony," in *Oxford Dictionary of National Biography*, ed. H. C. G. Mathew and B. Harrison, Oxford, 2004; available at http://www.oxforddnb.com/view/article/14736 (accessed on 4 January 2008). D. W. Davies, *Elizabethans Errant: The Strange Fortunes of Sir Thomas Sherley and his Three Sons, as well in the Dutch Wars as in Muscovy, Morocco, Persia, Spain, and the Indies*, Ithaca, N.Y., 1967. M. Dimmock, *New Turkes: Dramatizing Islam and the Ottomans in Early Modern England*, Aldershot, Hampshire, 2005. R. W. Ferrier, "The Terms and Conditions under which English Trade was Transacted with Safavid Persia," *BSOAS* 49, 1986, pp. 48-66. J. Keuning, "Jenkinson's Map of Russia," *Imago Mundi* 13, 1956, pp. 172-75, esp. p. 172 and fig. 1 for the version reproduced in Ortelius. L. Lockhart, "European Contacts with Persia, 1350-1736," *Camb. Hist. Iran* VI, 1986, pp. 373-411. M. B. G. Morton, *The Jenkinson Story*, Glasgow, 1962. B. Penrose, *Travel and Discovery in the Renaissance, 1420-1620*, Cambridge, Mass., 1955. T. S. Willan, *The Early History of the Russia Company, 1553-1603*, Manchester, 1956.

(STEPHAN SCHMUCK)

JENN. See GENIE.

JÉQUIER, GUSTAVE,

After G. Jéquier, 1968, no. 44.

Swiss archeologist (b. Neuchâtel, 14 August 1868; died there, 24th March 1946). After completing his secondary education at Neuchâtel and attending its university, and after his military service, he initially pursued his academic studies in 1888 in Berlin, where he attended courses given by the Egyptologist Adolf Erman, and embarked on his thesis in the summer of 1890. Later, after some traveling in Germany, Sweden, Switzerland, and France, he resumed his studies in Paris with another famous Egyptologist, Gaston Maspéro, and received his diploma from the École des Hautes Études under his supervision. At the same time he began his collaboration with Jacques de Morgan (q.v.) in the archeological excavations in Egypt and worked at the following sites: Aswan and Kom-Ombo (1892-93; with Jacques de Morgan); Saqqarah, Sitout, Tell-el-Amarna and Dahchour (1893-94); Licht (1894-95; with J. E.-Gautier); Karnak, Médinet-Habou, and Fayoum (1895-96).

In 1897 he went to Persia as a member of the Délégation scientifique française (see DÉLÉGATION ARCHÉOLOGIQUE FRANÇAISE EN IRAN), directed by Jacques de Morgan, and stayed there until 1902. During these years he excavated hundreds of ancient artifacts at Susa. The most important among these was the third fragment of the Code of Hammurabi, discovered in 1901 during Jéquier's last excavation campaign (assisted by Louis-Charles Watelin). This discovery made it possible to decipher the entire document, on of the most significant objects belonging to the ancient history of Mesopotamia.

During his five year residence in Persia, Jéquier sent home to his family many letters and accounts of his daily life in Persia and these were compiled and published posthumously as a volume entitled *En Perse 1897-1902* (Neuchâtel, 1968) by his son Michel Jéquier. The book provides a vivid description of the archeologist's travels and daily experiences in Persia, and his excavations and discoveries at Susa, and is therefore most informative about the first five years of the archeological expedition by the French delegation in Persia. The many illustrations, including several photographs taken by Jéquier himself, add further historical value to the book. Upon his return to Europe, Gustave Jéquier worked from 1902 to 1904 in Switzerland and in Paris, publishing the reports of the Archeological Delegation.

From 1904 onwards, he resumed his interest in Egypt and visited the country several times In 1913, he was appointed Professor of Egyptology at the University of Neuchâtel where he taught until 1939 and served twice as dean of the Faculty of Letters. In 1914, he chaired the first international congress of ethnography and ethnology at Neuchâtel. During World War I, as well as pursuing his academic research, he worked for the welfare of the prisoners of war and organized teaching programs for internees. In 1924 he was invited by the Egyptian government to carry out excavations at Saqqarah and for the next twelve years he carried out a very productive series of excavations. He returned to Neuchâtel in 1937 and continued for the rest of his life with his research and active participation with the work of the Museum of Ethnography.

Bibliography: Gustave Jéquier, *En Perse 1897-1902, Journal et Lettres de Gustave Jéquier*, ed. Michel Jéquier, Neuchâtel, 1968. It provides a full bibliography of the archeologist's published works (pp. 187-92). J. and E. Gran Aymerich "Gustave Jéquier," *Archéologia*, 218, Nov. 1986, pp. 75-79.

(NADER NASIRI-MOGHADDAM)

JERGA, an assembly or council of local adult men sitting in a circular formation for the resolution of conflicts and discussion of issues and challenges that face the settled and nomadic Pashtun tribal communities of Afghanistan and Pakistan.

The earliest published reference to jerga is provided during the colonial period by Mountstuart Elphinstone (1815), a representative of the British government of India to the court of the ruler of Kabul at his summer capital of Peshawar. English dictionary references to jerga are provided by Henry George Raverty, Henry Walter Bellew, and John Gordon Lorimer, all colonial officers of the British government of India. Other early references to jerga are available in official British colonial records about Pashtuns.

The jerga functions as a sodality, invoked when the need for it appears and disbanded when it is not needed. It is the symbol of the political and legal autonomy of a Pashtun male and his tribe. As such it is an integral part of pashtunwalaey (*paštunwāli*), Pashtun charter for appropriate behavior, including upholding male honor (*nang* or *ʿezzat*) and avoiding shame (*šarm*), both through the proper sexual behavior of his female dependents (*nāmus*, especially wife, daughter, sister, and mother), revenge (*badal*, a form of balanced or negative reciprocity in response to real [bodily] or symbolic [verbal] injury), offering food (*mēlmastia*, hospitality) to those accepted as guests, providing asylum or refuge (*nanawātay*) to those who sue for peace or ask for forgiveness or protection, professing Islam, and abiding by other components of Pashtun custom.

Although the concept of jerga is familiar to non-Pashtuns in the region, it is not their native label for local assemblies or councils for conflict resolution. In Persian, jerga refers to a social network, group, coterie, or clique, but it is not used as the label for tribal or other local mechanisms for conflict resolution. Among the Marri Baluch the term jerga applies to a relatively stable and structured arrangement in which "the hierarchy of tribal leaders, the organs of external administration, and the framework of sections meet and articulate in a manner that is decisive to the function of each" (Pehrson, p. 23). Some contemporary Afghan nationalist writers argue that Pashtun tribes have inherited the concept of jerga from their Aryan ancestors (ʿAṭāʾi, 1978, p. 1; idem, 1979 and 1982 Khadem, p. 52).

Jerga is sometimes interchangeably used with *maraka* (discussion, conversation, or dialogue), but maraka, a form of small-scale jerga, is used among Pashtuns to deliberate and make decisions about specific local policies or problems or to settle minor disputes. Participants in the maraka are male elders of the village or local lineage(s) and are called *marakačiān*. The maraka is convened at the request of an elder or of disputants and is held in the open air courtyard of the local mosque or near a shrine. There are two kinds of marakas. In one the disputants argue in front of the *marakačiān*, who will decide which side has a more persuasive argument. In the other, the maraka examines the evidence and argumentation from each party and acts as an arbitrator and imposes a compromise. In both cases the decision of the maraka is based on consensus and is final (ʿAṭāʾi, 1978).

The jerga, on the other hand, deals with major intra and inter-tribal conflict. In principle the jerga represents the tribe as a whole and acts as a judicial, legislative, and executive agency. In inter-tribal conflict or when a number of tribes wish to participate in a collective response to a challenge or initiative from the state or from another tribe or consortium of tribes, the jerga will include representatives from all tribes involved. Regardless of size or the number of tribes involved, no qualifiers (small, large, etc.) are used with the label jerga. The phrase "great jirga" was once used by the British colonial government of India when it wished to engage the Masʿud tribe as a whole, but the event turned into a "disorderly mob" (Caroe, pp. 401-2). Borrowing from and manipulating European sources, some prominent Afghan authors argue that a *lōya jerga* (great assembly) was convened in two historical settings for the selection of Afghanistan's political leaders: during 1708 for the approval of Mir Ways Hotak's opposition to the Safavid rule in Kandahar (Qandahār), and during 1747 for the selection of Aḥmad Khan Abdāli (q.v.) as the ruler of Afghanistan (Ḡobār, pp. 319, 354). However, neither claim is supported by the historical record.

In its traditional format, the jerga operates on the margins of state structure, in opposition or alternative to the latter. During the colonial and postcolonial period, a jerga from a single tribe or a jerga composed of members from several tribes negotiated with agents of the adjacent state. Such instances are noted in the available ethnographic and historical records. Only landowners may participate in a jerga and, in theory, any adult male member of the tribe can request the convocation of the jerga. Theoretically only a Pashtun tribesman whose father's name appears in tribal genealogical charts can hold land. In practice, however, *mašrān* (elders, sing., *mašr*) or *spingiri* (singular, *spingiray*, white beards, elders) of the constituent lineages (*ḵēl*s or *zai*s) of a tribe initiate and participate in the assembly. The initiative for convening the jerga originates with the tribe(s), not with the state. At least one member of the tribe who knows tribal norms (*narḵ*), including the rules and procedures of the jerga, must participate. This individual is known as a *narḵai* (plural, *narḵiān*). A mullah (a religious leader who leads communal prayers at and keeps up the local mosque) attends the jerga but only to pray for its success and to bless its decision. Some Pashtun tribes allow *sayyeds* (non-Pashtuns who claim descent from Prophet Moḥammad and who usually live among Pashtuns and speak Pashtu) to participate in the jerga. No one officially presides over the jerga and every participant is entitled to speak. The jerga convenes near a local shrine, cemetery, or in the courtyard of a mosque in open space. Open space is explicitly preferred to space under a roof. Every tribe and local community has a designated place for its jerga. Among nomadic Pashtuns, the assembly meets in any open space designated by the elders. The place where the jerga meets is considered sacred and, among some tribes during important jergas, the location is ringed by tribal flags and banners. The Afridi (q.v.) Pashtuns occasionally surround the location of important jergas by black flags. It has been suggested that these flags were supplied to the Afridis by Amir Amān-Allāh (q.v.) of Afghanistan during the 1920s in order to dramatize Afridi opposition to the British government of India (ʿAṭāʾi, 1978, p. 2).

To underscore equality, the jerga participants sit in a circle on bare ground, simple mats, or other floorings of uniform quality. All members of the jerga are considered equal. Non-members may sit near the jerga to listen to its transactions. When the jerga is in session no one shall disrupt or interrupt its transactions. Violators of this rule are subject to punishment. Occasionally a jerga may convene in secrecy in which case no observers are allowed near the jerga. If someone violates its secrecy, he will be severely sanctioned. The punishment ranges from shaving the culprit's mustache and beard to setting his residential property on fire to execution.

A local jerga seldom has more than twenty-five members and rarely more than fifty. Inter-tribal jergas will have larger numbers but seldom more than one hundred. In the past, when jergas were convened in order to deal with the British government of India or the Kabul government, the numbers increased substantially, sometimes running into the hundreds. Both governments regularly distributed allowances or occasional gifts to tribal leaders and other real and potential jerga participants within their spheres of influence. The governments of Afghanistan and Pakistan have, in principle, continued these practices in dealing with tribal Pashtuns within (and occasionally beyond) their borders. It is likely that these policies have directly and indirectly encouraged larger jerga attendance. In general, however, it could be argued that the more remote a tribe was from state influence, the more egalitarian was its format and consequently the larger the number of its jerga participants. The role of the jerga in the resolution of conflict appears to have declined in Pashtun areas that are encapsulated by state structures, as well as in areas where an individual has achieved the status of *malek* (village leader or spokesman), or where the position of khan (village and lineage leader) has evolved into a hereditary rank, or where charismatic Sufi personalities have appeared.

Decisions of the jerga derive from discussion, debate, and mediation and are based on overt consensus or, when there is no explicit disagreement or surrender, to a majority view. Open robust dissent is strongly discouraged and rarely acknowledged. In some local traditions, when during the proceedings of the jerga a minority faction in the assembly disagrees with the prevailing tenor or direction of discussion or debate, its members will express their dissatisfaction by briefly clicking two small stones. When a decision is reached, members of the assembly symbolically express their sincere participation in it by taking a scared oath by collectively placing their hands on a Qurʾān, on which are placed salt (*mālga*) and a sword (*tura*). The attending religious leader presides over this ritual (ʿAṭāʾi, 1978, p. 76).

The decision of the jerga is final and binding on all members of the tribe. The Pashtun jerga generates its own enforcement and executive arrangements. Usually an individual, symbolically called *tsalweḵtai* (one of forty) or *tsalweḵtey* (a set of or group of forty) or *tsalweḵtiān* ([those] of the forty), is assigned to execute the decisions of the jerga. In reality the actual number of the enforcement body varies with the importance and complexity of the task at hand. A person who does not abide by the decision of the jerga risks being expelled from the community and/or having his residential property destroyed. In the forested Pashtun tribal territories, where an active lumber industry exists, the group of men assigned to patrol the forests is also called *tsalweḵtey*. In some Pashtun areas this executive agency is called *arabakey* or *rabakey*. The concepts *tsalweḵtey* and *arabakey*, are symbolic and formulistic and are probably related to the Arabic word *arbaʿun* (forty) and the importance of this number in Muslim rituals and lore.

The popular term in non-Pashtun areas of Afghanistan for a local assembly or a deliberative or advisory body is *šurā-ye maḥalli* (local assembly or council), or *majles-e mašwara* (consultative council attached to the provincial government). During the reigns of Amir Ḥabib-Allāh (1901-19) and Amir Amān-Allāh (1919-29), the Afghan government instituted a *šurā-ye dawlat* (state council) composed of high-ranking members of the central government and the inner circle of the amir, but this practice was discontinued after the fall of Amir Amān-Allāh in 1929 (Hanifi, p. 299). Starting in 1921 and continuing to the present time, governments of Afghanistan have used an ad hoc mechanism in the construction of which the concept of Pashtun tribal jerga has been creatively manipulated. They have used the historical prestige of tribal Pashtuns and the myth of their numerical majority in Afghanistan by convening the so called *lōya jerga* in times of instability and crises, especially during tribal uprisings or widespread discontentment with the central government. On these occasions the government has, at its own expense, summoned "representatives" of the people from Afghan provinces to visit Kabul to participate in an assembly in which it presented and received rubber-stamped approval of its real or potentially controversial policies and programs, including new constitutions and international relations and treaties. About forty percent of the participants in these lōya jergas consisted of the current members of the parliament, members of which had routinely been hand-picked by the government, and the country's high-ranking officials of the military and civil services. Members of these lōya jergas (especially for those from the provinces) received a fully paid visit to and stay for about two weeks in the capital city, with the king and his government acting as the official hosts (Hanifi, pp. 309 ff.). It was this model of the lōya jerga, this time subsidized by the United States and orchestrated by the United Nations, which created the post-Taliban government in Kabul and the current constitution of Afghanistan (Hanifi, pp. 319-21). Since 1921, approximately twelve lōya jergas have been convened by the various governments of Afghanistan.

Over the life span of the state of Afghanistan (1880-present), ideas for the legislative institutions of the central government were inspired by and symbolically associated with the concept of Pashtun tribal jerga. *Majles-e šurā* (consultative assembly) was introduced during the reign of Moḥammad-Nāder (r. 1930-33), and the adjective *melli* (national) was occasionally added (*majles-e šurā -ye melli*) to signify national assembly. In 1933, a *majles-e aʿyān* (assembly of nobles, elders, or grandees) was instituted. During 1964-78, the labels *majles-e šurā* and *majles-e aʿyān* were changed to *wolosi jerga* (people's [i.e., commoners'] assembly) and *da mašrāno jerga* (elders' assembly) respectively (Hanifi, p. 299). The post-2001 constitution of the Islamic Republic of Afghanistan includes specific provisions for the use of these labels for the legislative institutions of the state and for the invocation of the lōya jerga in times of national crises.

See also AFGHANISTAN; PAṢTUNWĀLI.

Bibliography: Akbar S. Ahmed, *Pukhtun Economy and Society: Traditional Structure and Economic Development in a Tribal Society*, London and Boston, 1980. Idem, *Religion and Politics in Muslim Society: Order and Conflict in Pakistan*, London, 1983. Moḥammad-Ebrāhim ʿAṭāʾi (Atayee), *Da Paxtani qabilo eṣṭelāḥi qāmus: ḥoquqi, jazāyi, taʿāmol*, Kabul, 1978; tr. A. Mohammad Shinwary as *A Dictionary of the Terminology of Pashtun's Tribal Customary Law and Usages*, ed. A. Jabar Nader, Kabul, 1979 (condensed translation). Idem, *Da jergo waṭan* (The homeland of jergas), Kabul, 1982. Fredrik Barth, *Political Leadership among Swat Pathans*, London, 1959. Hugh Beattie, *Imperial Frontier: Tribe and State in Waziristan*, London, 2002. Henry Walter Bellew, *A Dictionary of the Pukkhto or Pukshto Language, in Which the Words are Traced to Their Sources*, London, 1867, repr., Karachi, 1980. James Sutherland Broadfoot, *Reports on Parts of the Ghilzi Country and on Some of the Tribes in the Neighbourhood of Ghazni . . .*, ed. William Broadfoot, Royal Geographical Society, Supplementary Papers 1, 1886. Richard Isaak Bruce, *The Forward Policy and Its Results*, London, 1900, 2nd ed., Quetta, 1977. Olaf Kirpatrick Caroe, *The Pathans: 550 B.C.-A.D. 1957*, New York, 1958, pp. 353-56. Cuthbert C. Davis, *The Problem of the North-West Frontier, 1890-1908, with a Survey of Policy Since 1849*, Cambridge, 1932, 2nd rev. ed., London, 1975. Mountsuart Elphinstone, *An Account of the Kingdom of Caubul and Its Dependencies in Persia, Tartary, and India, Comprising a View of the Afghaun Nation, and A History of the Dooraunes Monarchy*, 2 vols., New York, 1839, I, pp. 215-26. Ashraf Ghani, "Afghanistan xi: Administration," in *EIr.* I, pp. 558-64. Moḥammad ʿAlam Fayżzād, *Jergahā-ye bozorg-e melli-e Afḡānestān*, Lahore, 1990. Ḡolām-Moḥammad Ḡobār, *Afḡānestān dar Masir-e Tāriḵ*, Kabul, 1967. John G. Hangin, *A Concise English-Mongolian Dictionary*, Bloomington, 1970. M. Jamil Hanifi, "Editing the Past: Colonial Production of Hegemony through the '*Loya Jerga*,'" *Iranian Studies* 37/2, 2004, pp. 295-322. Evelyn Berkeley Howell, *Mizh, A Monograph on Government's Relations with the Mahsud (Masʿud) Tribe*, Simla, 1931, repr. Karachi, 1979. Erland Jansson, *India, Pakistan or Pakhtunistan?: The Nationalist Movement in the North-West Frontier 1937-47*, Uppsala, 1981. Qiām-al-Din Khadem, *Pahtunwalaey*, Kabul, 1952. L. White King, *Monograph on the Orakzai Country and Clans*, Lahore, 1900, repr. Lahore, 1984. John Gordon Lorimer, *Grammar and Vocabulary of Waziri Pashto*, Calcutta, 1902. Edward E. Oliver, *Across the Border or Pathan and Biloch*, London, 1890, repr., Lahore, 2000. Ram Pande, *Bharatpur Upto 1826: A Social and Political History of the Jats*, Jaipur, 1970. Robert Niel Pehrson, *The Social Organization of the Marri Baluch*, collected and analyzed from his notes by Fredrik Barth, New York, 1966. Theodore Leighton Pennell, *Among the Wild Tribes of the Afghan Frontier*, London, 1914. Henry George Raverty, *A Dictionary of Pukhto or Language of the Afghans*, London, 1860, repr. Lahore, 2001. Idem, *Notes on Afghanistan and Parts of Baluchistan, Geographical, Ethnographical, and Historical*, London, 1888. Willi Steul, *Paschtunwali: Ein Ehrenkodex und Seine rechtliche Relevanz*, Wiesbaden, 1981. R. Tapper, ed, *The Conflict of Tribe and State in Iran and Afghanistan*, New York, 1983. Harold Carmichael Wylly, *From the Black Mountain to Waziristan*, London, 1914. Šaraf-ad-Din ʿAli Yazdi, *Ẓafar-nāma*, ed. Mawlawi Moḥammad Elāhdād, 2 vols., Calcutta, 1885-88; ed Moḥammad ʿAbbāsi, 2 vols., Tehran, 1957; facs. ed, Tashkent, 1972.

(M. JAMIL HANIFI)

JERUSALEM AND IRAN. Twice in its long history Jerusalem came under Persian rule, the first time in the early days of the Achaemenid Empire in the sixth century B.C.E., the second during the westward expansion of the Sasanian state in the early seventh century C.E. Both periods proved formative and entailed far reaching ramifications for the city and its inhabitants.

In the Achaemenid period (539-332 B.C.E). When Cyrus the Great conquered Babylonia in 539 B.C.E., the Jewish community there, which descended from those deported by Nebuchadnezzar in 586 B.C.E., hailed him as God-sent liberator. This is immortalized in (cf. Ezra 1:1-2; see Bickerman):

> In year one of the reign of Cyrus, king of Persia, so that the word of the Lord by the mouth of Jeremiah might be accomplished, the Lord stirred up the spirit of Cyrus, king of Persia, and the king made a proclamation throughout his kingdom, and put it [also] in writing, [saying]: "Thus says Cyrus king of Persia: All the kingdoms of the earth the Lord, the God of heaven, has given to me. And he has charged me to build him a house in Jerusalem, which is in Judah. Whosoever is there among you of all his people, the Lord his God be with him, and let him go up [to Jerusalem]. (2 Chronicles 36:22-23)

Thus ends the canonized Hebrew Bible, a stunning conclusion which invests Jewish hopes of revival and of the rebuilding of Jerusalem's Temple in Persian royal initiative. As "Isaiah" indicates, the rise of the Achaemenids to power, as well as Cyrus's conquest of Babylon and his famed decree of 539 which encouraged the return of exiles from Babylon to Judah (Yehud in the satrapy of Transeuphratis; see EBER NĀRĪ), signaled, in Jewish eyes, the dawn of a new era in the history of Jerusalem.

> [The Lord] says of Cyrus: "He is my shepherd, and he shall fulfill all my purpose"; saying of Jerusalem, "She shall be built," and of the Temple "Your foundation shall be laid." Thus says the Lord to his anointed, to Cyrus, whose right hand I have grasped (Isaiah 44.28-45.1).

Information about Jerusalem in the Persian period is scant (see Grabbe, pp. 13-36; Hope; Talmon), and the Hebrew Bible remains its main source (especially Ezra, Nehemiah, Haggai, Zachariah, Malachi, and "Isaiah"). Ezra 1:2-4 and 6:3-5 provides a Hebrew and Aramaic text of Cyrus's declaration regarding the restoration of the Temple in Jerusalem. The Aramaic original refers to government subsidies for the envisioned "house of God," to its measurements and building materials, and to its endowment, furnished from the gold and silver items which Nebuchadnezzar had removed from the temple in 586 B.C.E. Excavations in various areas of Jerusalem (City of David, Ophel, Tyropean Valley, Mount Zion, Ketef Hinnom, and Mamilla) point to the shrunken size of the city (between 130-40 *dunams* [1 *dunam* = about 1,000 m^2], including 80 *dunams* dedicated to the temple precinct), and to its tiny population of some 1,500 people. (See Carter, pp. 136-48, on excavation sites in Jerusalem pertaining to the so-called First Persian period, 538-450 B.C.E, with map at p. 149 and comprehensive bibliography.)

In spite of an auspicious start, the resettlement and restoration of Jerusalem, especially the rebuilding of the city walls and of the destroyed temple, were slow and intermittent (Ezra 4:24, 6:7; see Schaper; Vanderkam, pp. 194-211). Most of the returning exiles elected to settle in the countryside, only gathering in Jerusalem to celebrate the high holidays (Ezra 3:1-2). Nor did they have sufficient means to engage in major enterprises of construction (Haggai 1:6). Internal divisions between the returning exiles and their own brethren, *Am Haaretz* "people of the land," namely low-born Judahites who had not been exiled, isolated the newly established community, as did its tense relations with the syncretistic environment, which included Samaritans, Ammonites, Ashdodites, and Arabs (Ezra 4:1, 4; Neh. 2:10, 19, 4:1-3, 7:5, 13:23-24). The prophet Haggai (Hag. 1:9) chastises his co-religionists (in 522 B.C.E.) to resume efforts to build the Temple but later complains (in 516 B.C.E.) that the completed structure was vastly inferior to the (memories of the) great Solomonic sanctuary (Hag. 2:3).

Based on an increasingly strict Yahwist monotheism, the centrality of Jerusalem in the theology of the exilic settlers of Yehud (Zachariah 8:3) is reflected in efforts to recreate the city as an exclusive Jewish space ("a holy city," Neh. 11:1) housing an exclusive Jewish sanctuary. In spite of the paucity of finds of material culture from the Persian period in Jerusalem, the small number of idols found in Yehud in general hints at the ultimate success of the drive to establish monotheism throughout the province, including Jerusalem.

Under the guidance of Nehemiah, an enterprising Jewish governor who arrived in Yehud in the middle of the fifth century (the date is debated), Jerusalem's walls were partially restored, although their precise outline remains a matter of controversy among archeologists. Nehemiah refers to a number of gates of Jerusalem: Valley gate, Dung gate, Fountain gate, Sheep gate, Fish gate, Old gate, Horse gate, East gate, and Muster gate. Since Nehemiah claims that it took fifty-two days to complete the rebuilding of the city wall (Neh. 6:15), it seems clear that the rampart embraced a rather small area, perhaps about half of the pre-exilic city. His name, however, remained intimately linked with the great endeavor of the restoration of the city (*Ben Sirah* 49.13).

To resettle the city with exilic Jews, Nehemiah resorted to the imposition of lots (Neh. 11:1), which brought to Jerusalem one out of ten men, each with his family. The concerted efforts to make Jerusalem Jewish again were extended to a campaign against intermarriage, which took place in the course of a popular assembly in Jerusalem summoned by Ezra the scribe (Ezra 9, from mid-fifth cent.?). Although the drive to separate Jewish men from their "non-Jewish" wives appears to have been unsuccessful, it marked an important stage in transforming Jerusalem into a city with a distinct Jewish identity. Nehemiah's re-imposition of Sabbath rules (Neh. 13:8-22), which included the closure of the city gates to commerce and extended to the "cleansing" of the Temple of priests who married "foreign women" (Neh. 13:28-30), likewise contributed to the reshaping of Jerusalem's character according to Torah rules (see Sivan-Zlotnick).

Under the Achaemenids Jerusalem enjoyed an unusual degree of autonomy, which enabled men like Nehemiah and Ezra to recreate Jerusalem and Yehud as a 'Temple-state', namely an entity nominally controlled by Persia but locally managed by Jewish temple priests and scribes according to Jewish law. Documents from Egypt (see Porten and Yardeni) indicate that Jews in Egypt looked for advice and support from Jerusalem (see ELEPHANTINE), and numismatic evidence points to local minting of coins which bore the name of the province (Yehud) in Hebrew script, as well as Jewish symbols, an unusual phenomenon which reflects both the degree of Jerusalem's autonomy and the Jews' own sense of distinct identity.

The Sasanians in Jerusalem, 614-628 C.E. In spite of its brief duration, the Persian conquest and occupation of Jerusalem by the Sasanian army in 614 generated an extraordinary spat of literary works by Jews and Christians alike (Baras, pp. 300-49; Flusin, pp. 151-64; Dauphin, II, pp. 352-60; for archeological evidence, see Magness). For Palestinian Christians the passage into non-Christian hands of a city which Constantine had resolutely turned into an exclusive Christian space some three centuries earlier was a shattering blow, as was the transfer of the true cross to Ctesiphon. Christians also resented the collaboration between Persians and Jews in the early stages of the Sasanian invasion. (On Jewish-Christian polemics as centered on Jerusalem, see Stemberger; Wilken.) Inner divisions among Christians in Jerusalem led to a brief Persian siege in 614 which reportedly culminated in a massive massacre of the city's Christian inhabitants with widespread destruction of Christian sanctuaries. The extent of the damage to human life and to structures is still debated. It seems considerably smaller than the Christian sources suggest. Moreover, barely few months after the conquest, the Persians allowed the Jerusalemite church to gather donations for restoration projects.

For Jews, the coming of the Persians signaled a new era of messianic proportion, after centuries of legal persecution by Byzantine emperors, including a ban on living in Jerusalem. Little known but of special interest are the *piyyutim* (poems composed to accompany service in the synagogue) of the period which touch on the Persian invasion of Palestine, in general, and particularly on Jewish messianic hopes in conjunction with Jerusalem (Yahalom; Sivan). Some *piyyutim* emphasize the continuing affinity between Judaism, Jerusalem, and the temple. Others delineate the resumption of liturgical services in Persian Jerusalem, the emergence of new 'messianic' Jewish leadership, and the execution of this figure by order of the Persian authorities. All in all, little is known of the Sasanian occupation of Jerusalem. What seems clear is that the shift of Persian support from Jews to Christians on the eve of the invasion of Egypt (618/19) entailed the withdrawal of Jewish privileges. The premature death of the 'messiah' (in 618?) signaled the tragic end of hopes of Jewish national revival for centuries. In Jewish memory, the events in Persian Jerusalem between 614 and 618 became beacons of calamity and disappointment. Ḵosrow II was no Cyrus.

Bibliography: Jerusalem in the Achaemenid period. The American Theological Library Association (ATLA) *Religion Database* and *The Cambridge History of Judaism* I. *The Persian Period*, Cambridge, 1984, provide useful points of bibliographic departure. E. J. Bickerman, "The Edict of Cyrus in Ezra I," in *Studies in Jewish and Christian History* I, Leiden, 1976, pp. 72-108. C. E. Carter, *The Emergence of Yehud in the Persian Period. A Social and Demographic Study*, Sheffield, 1999. L. L. Grabbe, *Judaic Religion in the Second Temple Period. Belief and Practice from the Exile to Yavnehpp*, London, 2000, pp. 13-36. L. J. Hoppe, *The Holy City. Jerusalem in the Theology of the Old Testament*, Collegville, Minn., 2000. B. Porten and A. Yardeni, *Textbook of Aramaic Documents from Ancient Egypt* I, [Jerusalem], 1986, A 4.7-9. J. Schaper, "The Jerusalem Temple as an Instrument of the Achaemenid Fiscal Administration," *Vetus Testamentum* 45, 1995, pp. 428-39. H. Sivan-Zlotnick, "The Silent Women of Yehud," *Journal of Jewish Studies* 51, 2000, pp. 3-18. S. Talmon, "The Biblical Concept of Jerusalem," *Journal of Ecumenical Studies* 8, 1971, pp. 300-16. J. C. Vanderkam, *An Introduction to Early Judaism* Grand Rapids, 2001, pp. 194-211.

Jerusalem under the Sasanians. Z. Baras, "The Persian Conquest and the End of Byzantine Rule," in *Eretz Israel from the Destruction of the Second Temple to the Muslim Conquest*, ed. Z. Baras et al., Jerusalem, 1982, pp. 300-49 (in Hebrew). C. Dauphin, *La Palestine byzantine. Peuplement et populations*, 3 vols., Oxford, 1998, II, pp. 352-60. B. Flusin, *Saint Anastase le Perse et l'histoire de la Palestine au début du VIIe siècle* II, Paris, 1992, pp. 151-64. J. Magness, "A Reexamination of the Archaeological Evidence for the Sasanian Persian Destruction of the Tyropoeon Valley," *Bulletin of the American School of Oriental Research* 287, 1992, pp. 67-74. H. Sivan, "From Byzantine to Persian Jerusalem: Jewish Perspectives and Jewish-Christian Polemics," *Greek, Roman and Byzantine Studies* 41, 2000, pp. 277-306. G. Stemberger, "Jerusalem in the Early Seventh Century: Hopes and Aspirations of Christians and Jews," in *Jerusalem. Its Sanctity and Centrality to Judaism, Christianity, and Islam*, ed. L. I. Levine, New York, 1999, pp. 260-72. R. L. Wilken, *The Land Called Holy. Palestine in Christian History and Thought*, New Haven, 1992. J. Yahalom, "The Temple and the City in Liturgical Hebrew Poetry," *The History of Jerusalem. The Early Muslim Period 638-1099*, eds. J. Prawer and H. Ben-Shammai, Jerusalem and New York, 1996, pp. 270-94.

(HAGITH SIVAN)

JESUITS IN SAFAVID PERSIA. The Fathers of the Society of Jesus were the first European missionaries to enter the Persian Gulf in the 16th century. Their pioneer was the Dutchman Gaspar Barzaeus (Berze, 1515-53) who was selected for this task by Franciscus Xavier (1506-52), the founder of the Jesuit mission in Goa, India. Arriving in Hormuz (q.v.) in 1549, Barzaeus wrote extensive reports from the island in the following year (Garcia; Wicki, I, pp. 595-698; Rego, IV, pp. 373-417; Schurhammer, 1963-73, II/2, pp. 291-96). During their stay on the island,

Barzaeus and his men operated in freedom, enjoying the tolerant religious climate of Hormuz. The Portuguese missionaries engaged the resident Jews in religious disputation (Rego, IV, pp. 403-5; Schurhammer, 1933, pp. 279-309). Barzaeus baptized many Muslims, including, according to rumor, Turān Shah, the nominal ruler of the island. He also managed to convert some high-ranking figures, among them the wife and daughter of a Safavid envoy passing through Hormoz *en route* to India. His own intolerant behavior, meanwhile, manifested itself in attempts to ban Jews from Hormuz and to convert mosques to churches, thus risking the wrath of Shah Ṭahmāsp I (r. 1524-76) and the local population (Trigault; Wicki, II, pp. 87-88; Schurhammer, 1963-73, II/3, pp. 409-24; Posch, pp. 78-79, 446-48). The presence of the Jesuits on the island did not lead to further activities on the mainland, however. Faced with an insufferable climate and a populace, whose overall lack of receptivity to their proselytizing did perhaps not suit their purposeful approach, they left Hormuz in 1568.

Only decades later did the Jesuits reenter Persia. From their base in Mughal India, they volunteered to be the first Christian missionaries to go to Isfahan. This followed the news, conveyed by an ex-Jesuit monk by the name of Francisco da Costa who visited Persia on his way back from India in 1599, that Shah ʿAbbās I (r. 1587-1629, q.v.) was ready to convert to the Christian faith and would be willing to allow Christian friars into his territory. Yet the Portuguese viceroy of India chose the Augustinians to organize the next mission on account of their perceived experience in the various missions that they had established in the Persian Gulf, and because the archbishop of Goa offered to pay for the expenses. The Jesuits thus ended up being latecomers to sustained European missionary activity in Persia (Alonso, pp. 250-51).

Unlike the Jesuits and the Augustinians based in Goa, who acted within the jurisdictional framework of the *Padroado* (lit. 'patronage') according to which the Portuguese crown oversaw and funded the overseas dioceses, the activities of the Jesuits operating in Persia took place under other religious and political jurisdictions—most notably those of the Propaganda Fide, established in Rome in 1622, of the French Société des Missions Étrangères, founded in 1658, and of the crowns of France and Poland. Led by French and Polish representatives, their efforts to establish a presence in the country took place in the context of these countries' diplomatic overtures, which themselves trailed those of other European nations. Only in 1642, about forty years after the Augustinians had established themselves in Isfahan, did the Jesuits make preparations to branch out to Persia. The initiative originated in Aleppo, where French Jesuits had arrived in 1625. Its aim was to establish a base on the land route between Near East, India, and China and to be able to work among the Armenians of New Julfa (see JULFA; Richard, 2005-6, p. 7). The original suggestion came from the Bishop of Babylon, Monseigneur Bernard, during a stop in Aleppo while traveling to France. Msgr. Bernard's choice to lead the mission was Aimé Chézaud (1604-64), resident Jesuit in Aleppo who was familiar with that city's many Muslim and Armenian-Persian merchants, but the person who was eventually entrusted with the task was another Frenchman, François Rigordi (1609-79).

Rigordi arrived in Isfahan in early 1646, carrying a recommendation from a Polish ambassador by the name of Jerzy Ilicz who himself was to arrive in Persia shortly. However, Rigordi's initial stay was brief. Arriving as he did in the midst of an episode of anti-Christian measures, taken by the newly acceded grand vizier Ḵalifa Solṭān (1592/93-1654), and faced with resistance and the difficulty of finding housing, Rigordi embarked for India within weeks after arriving. He returned to Isfahan a year later and, with the assistance of the prior of the resident Carmelites, in the fall of 1647 he obtained a decree from Shah ʿAbbās II (r. 1642-66, q.v.) allowing the acquisition of land and the construction of a house in the Safavid capital. It is likely that his promise to seek French assistance and commercial advantage played a role in this success (Rigordi, pp. 32-35; Zimmel, 1969, p. 7).

Rigordi thereupon left Persia, reaching Vienna and Rome via Russia and Poland to report about his achievements and to consult about subsequent initiatives. Eventually he went to France which henceforth became the center of the efforts to establish a Jesuit mission in Isfahan on account of the country's presumed influence in Persia. Alexandre de Rhodes (1591-1660), the famous prior of the Jesuit mission in China and Vietnam until his forcible departure from East Asia, was to be the leading figure in the next phase. It was probably he who first suggested the advantages of Isfahan as a relay station for mail going between Europe and Asia without Portuguese interference, and also as a launching pad for further forays into Central Asia and as far as China (Zimmel, 1969, p. 10; Idem, 1970, p. 884).

Although De Rhodes was commissioned to lead the next mission, it was Father Chézaud who initially went to Persia as his deputy, accompanied by Rigordi. Arriving in 1652, they were at first housed by the resident Carmelites (Raphaël, pp. 210-11; Wilson, pp. 686-87). In the fall of 1653 Rigordi, having traveled to the royal camp in Khorasan, managed to obtain a decree from Shah ʿAbbās II for the establishment of a Jesuit mission in Isfahan and Shiraz. This swift success was, in part, due to the letters of recommendation from the French King, which Rigordi carried, and grandiose promises of French assistance against the Ottomans and other enemies of Persia, which included the prospect of a French assault on Istanbul, of a siege of Surat, and French help with the ouster of the Dutch from Bandar ʿAbbās (Zimmel, 1969, pp. 5-7). As a result, he obtained royal permission for the Jesuits to establish themselves in New Jolfa, Tabriz, and Shiraz (Raphaël, pp. 211-12).

In the short run nothing came out of the venture because of vehement resistance on the part of the Armenians of New Julfa, and more specifically the bishop of the borough's Armenians, who resisted the influx of missionaries into his town for fear that their activities might create divisions in the Armenian community, and who thus sent petitions to the court arguing that the missionaries had come to convert Muslims to Christianity, forcing Chézaud's host, the *kalāntar* ('mayor') of New Julfa, to evict him. These complaints led Moḥammad Beg, the newly appointed grand-vizier, to write to the shah with the request to forbid the Jesuits from establishing themselves in New Julfa until Rigordi's promises and commitments had been met. The result of this pressure was that all missionaries were expelled from Julfa in 1654 (Richard, 1995, II, pp. 215-18). The same circumstances prompted the dispatch of Bernhard Diestel (1623-60)—a young Austrian Jesuit born in Croatia who had joined the mission in Isfahan in 1654—to Poland in order to persuade that country's king to threaten the resident Armenian community with retaliation if the pressure on the Jesuits in Isfahan was not lifted. Before going to Poland, Diestel first went to Rome, where his briefings prompted attempts to reach China via Persia and Central Asia so as to avoid the long maritime journey. In 1656-57 Diestel would lead the first, failed attempt to reach China via this route in early modern times (Zimmel, 1970, pp. 880-88).

The follow-up mission, designed to solidify the creation of a permanent presence in Persia, was again led by De Rhodes. Arriving in Isfahan in late 1656, he and his fellow Jesuits were received in audience by Shah ʿAbbās II, but they did not manage to hand over to the ruler a letter containing a request for a house. The disappointing response De Rhodes brought from France with regard to the promises made by Rigordi created friction and led to frustration as well, and this proved to be a hindrance to a quick implementation of the promise of a convent (Zimmel, 1969, p. 7).

De Rhodes died in 1660 and was succeeded as the superior of the mission by Chézaud. Despite the ill will generated by the broken promises of the French among Persia's officials, Chézaud gained the admiration and even friendship and protection of Moḥammad Beg, the incumbent grand vizier in 1654-61. It was with Moḥammad Beg's assistance and at the latter's recommendation to the shah that Chézaud eventually secured a residence in Isfahan, located near the royal palace (Wilson, pp. 689-705; Zimmel, 1969, pp. 22-24). His erudition, his interest in Persian literature, and his eagerness to engage in religious disputes may have played a role in the good will he created. Having mastered Arabic in Aleppo, Chézaud became proficient in Persian, although not well enough to hold his own in disputations with Shiʿite ulema. He seems to have compiled a Persian dictionary, which now appears to have been lost. Newly discovered manuscripts show that he is also the author of a treatise entitled *Masḥ-e Meṣqal-e ṣafā-ye Āʾina-ye ḥaqqnemā*. Written in the context of the Muslim-Christian controversy provoked in the Islamic world by the missionary presence, this treatise aimed to rebut the *Meṣqal-e Ṣafāʾ dar tajliya-ye Āʾina-ye haqqnemā*, a work of Sayyed Aḥmad b. Zeyn-al-ʿĀbedin ʿAlawi (d. between 1644 and 1650, q.v.), cousin and disciple of Mir Dāmād (d. 1631, see DĀMĀD), in refutation of Christianity, which itself had been written in response to *The Abridgement of the Truth-Revealing Mirror* (*Montaḵab-e Āʾina-ye ḥaqqnemā*), a work written in 1609 by Father Jeronimo Xavier S.J. of India which had been sent to Persia and presented to Shah ʿAbbās I on behalf of the Emperor Jahāngir (r. 1605-27, q.v.; see Richard, 2005-6, pp. 10-18).

Chézaud's other achievement was the founding of a residence in New Julfa. Sometime between 1659 and 1661, upon realizing that his activities in Isfahan proper were futile, Chézaud is said to have sold the house there and moved the mission to New Julfa, where he built a spacious new residence. In 1662 a chapel was consecrated as well; in 1691 it was to be enlarged with the financial assistance of the Catholic-Armenian Shahrimanian family (see SCERIMAN FAMILY at *iranica.com*), so that at the time of Chézaud's death in 1664 the Jesuit mission was in operation. Although we lack specific details, it seems that, at least in the beginning, the endeavor was sponsored by the Polish crown, and in particular by a fund donated by the Polish King John II Casimir (r. 1648-68, d. 1672, himself a Jesuit until he mounted the throne and after he abdicated), and his wife, Queen Marie Louise de Gonzaga-Nevers, who, because of her contributions, was given the honorific title of the founder of the Jesuit missions in Persia (Richard, 1995, II, p. 210). Polish funding may have dried up, for in 1674 it is reported that the Jesuits of Isfahan received a meager allowance of only 90 Spanish reals, which was sent to them from France (Bembo, p. 358).

Chézaud's successor as head of the Jesuit mission in Isfahan was Claude-Ignace Mercier, who arrived in Isfahan in the early summer of 1664, a few months before Chézaud's death. He founded a school for Armenian children as part of the Jesuit compound. Mercier died in 1674 and was succeeded by Jean-Baptiste de la Maze (1624-1709) who had arrived with Mercier and who was to reside in Julfa for the next twenty-five years. He served as the head of the Jesuit mission from 1676 to 1683, when he was succeeded by Father Roux, and held the position again in 1686-1689. De la Maze knew Armenian so well that he lectured in that language to young Armenians (Petis Fils, p. 127; Villotte, pp. 92-96).

The Julfa compound survived the scheming of schismatic Armenians against the missionaries, which in the summer of 1694 led to the expulsion of the Carmelites from New Julfa (Kroell, p. 78). In fact, in subsequent years the Jesuit church in town was the only one allowed to use church bells. By 1700, the Jesuit school taught French, Latin, and Armenian to over one hundred children of local Armenians and resident Europeans. Despite the enthusiasm, industriousness, and perseverance of the fathers, however, they did not make much headway aside from baptizing an unspecified number of young children just before death at the request of their Muslim parents. Even among the Armenian population, their success was limited. In 1658 only six Catholic families were counted among the Armenians of New Julfa.

By the late 17th century the Jesuit field of activity had spread to Shirvan and Armenia as well, where missions were founded in Yerevan, Shemakha (Šemāḵi), and Ganja.

The Yerevan mission came into being as a result of a mission led by Fathers Longeau and Potier, who in 1683 arrived in Isfahan with letters from the French King Louis XIV (r. 1643-1715), requesting permission to establish a mission in Armenia, and who in the following year moved to Yerevan. Located in a suburb of the city, the convent they founded by 1700 consisted of two clerics and one layman, and subsisted on manufacturing wine and on a small annual stipend from the French King (Schillinger, pp. 118-22).

We are better informed about the Shemakha mission, which was chosen because of the Jesuits' perception of the poor state of the Armenians and because Shemakha served as a crossroads of various nationalities and the passageway from Russia and Poland. The Polish contribution was crucial in the founding and administering of this mission and occurred in the double context of trying to find an alternative route to China other than via Siberia, and Polish attempts to lure the Safavids into an anti-Ottoman alliance. The mission resulted from a diplomatic mission by Count Constantin Salomon Siri Zagorski, an Armenian who had been made nobleman in Poland, who in 1686 was sent to Persia as representative of King Jan Sobieski III (r. 1674-96) with the task of probing the shah's interest in joining the European powers in their anti-Ottoman struggle. Having obtained permission from Shah Solaymān I (r. as Ṣafi II in 1666-68, re-enthroned as Solaymān I in 1668 and reigned until 1694) to establish a Jesuit convent in Shemakha, he returned in the company of the French Jesuit Potier, arriving in Shemakha in the middle of 1686. A year later, Potier was killed by the owner of the house he had rented, and De la Maze was sent as his successor (Monier, pp. 44-48). De la Maze would remain in Shemakha until his death in 1709 (De Pradel de Lamase, pp. 251-60). In 1693 or 1694 he wrote an interesting account of conditions in that town as well as in Baku and environs (ARSI, Gall. 97II). He also left a journal of a journey he made from Shemakha to Isfahan in 1698 (De la Maze, pp. 43-90). It is not clear how much he achieved as a missionary, spending much of his time alone in Shemakha. Like all missionaries he was faced with fierce opposition from Schismatic Armenians who actively resisted the catholic missionaries in the northwestern regions of Persia as well. There are also reports about the deterioration of government control in this period, as a result of which the Jesuit Fathers of Shemakha were exposed to popular harassment (De Bruyn, p. 434). After De la Maze's death in 1709, Father Bachoud took over as superior in Shemakha. The city suffered terribly in the last decade of Safavid rule, although the Jesuit convent seems to have been largely spared in the depredations caused by the Lezghi invaders in 1721.

The mission in Ganja came into being as a result of the activities of the Polish Jesuit Ignatius Zapolski, who accompanied Zagorski on the latter's next trip to Persia and who took over from him as Polish ambassador after Zagorski's violent death in 1689. Zapolski's attempts to create new facilities for the Jesuits included a desire to establish a house in Ganja. Shortly before his death in 1703, he obtained a *raqam* ('royal permit') from Shah Solṭān Ḥosayn (r. 1694-1722) authorizing the establishment of a Jesuit convent in Ganja. He died in Sāva, on his way to Ganja, and was succeeded as superior of the new mission by Jan Reuth (AME 354, letter of 18 October 1711, fol. 368; Krzyszkowski, pp. 114, 116).

A total of thirty Polish Jesuits active in Persia in the 17th and 18th centuries have been identified. These include, other than those already mentioned, Michal Więczkzorkowski, Pawel Wrocyński, Andrzej Zielonacki, and Aleksander Kulesza, who worked mainly among Armenians in Shemakha and Ganja. All of them labored under great financial difficulties, tending to plague victims and seeking to end slaving practices and to found envisioned educational projects, but plans for this were cut short owing to rebellion, and they returned to Isfahan where they never managed to establish an independent seminary (Bednarz, pp. 379-82; Pucko, pp. 310-11). The best known of the Polish Jesuits active in Iran was Father Judasz Thaddeus Krusinksi (1675-1756, q.v.), who resided in Persia between 1707 and 1728 and again in the 1740s, and who served the crown as court translator and acted as intermediary between the Papacy and the Safavid court until after 1722.

Little is known about Jesuit activities in Persia following the fall of the Safavids. The Jesuit mission in Isfahan would continue to operate until 1755, and five years later the last Jesuits are said to have left Gilan (Anon., *A Chronicle*, pp. 703-5).

Bibliography: Sources. AME, Archives des Missions Étrangères, Paris. Anonymous, *A Chronicle of the Carmelites in Persia and the Papal Mission of the XVIIth and XVIIIth Centuries*, 2 vols. paginated as one, London, 1939. Anonymous, "Mémoire de la mission d'Erivan," in *Lettres édifiantes et curieuses*, vol. 3, pp. 335-58. Archives des Jésuites de Paris, Perse, no. 30. Archivio di Società de Iesu (ARSI), Rome, Gall. 97II. P. Avril, *Voyage en divers états d'Europe e d'Asie, entreprise pour découvrir une nouveau chemin à la Chine*, Paris, 1692. P. Bachoud, "Lettre de Chamakié, 25 Sept. 1721," in *Lettres édifiantes et curieuses*, vol. 4, pp. 91-100. A. Bembo, *The Travels and Journal of Ambrosio Bembo*, tr. C. Bargellini, ed. and annot. A. Welch, Berkeley, Calif., 2007. C. de Bruyn, *Reizen over Moskovie, door Persie en Indie . . .* , Amsterdam, 1711, 2nd ed., 1714. J. M. Garcia, ed., "Copia de unas cartas del padre maestre Francisco, y del padre M. Gaspar, y outros padres de la compañía de Iesu, que escreuieron de la India a los hermanos del colegio de Iesus, de Coimbra. Trasladadas de Portugués en Castellano. Recibidas el año de M.D.lj. [1551]," facsimile ed. in *Cartas dos Jesuítas do Oriente e do Brasil 1549-1551*, Lisbon, 1993, unpaginated. *Lettres édifiantes et curieuses écrites des missions étrangères*, 8 vols., Toulouse, 1810. J.-B. de la Maze, "Journal du voyage de Père de la Maze de Chamaké à Hispahan par la province du Guilan," in *Lettres édifiantes et curieuses*, vol. 4, pp. 43-90. A. Kroell, ed., *Nouvelles d'Ispahan 1665-1695*, Paris, 1979. J. T. Krusinski, *The History of the Revolutions of Persia*, 2 vols., London, 1728. [P. Monier,] "Mémoire de la province de Sirvan," in *Lettres édifiantes et curieuses*, IV, pp. 11-42. S. Petis, Fils, *Extrait du journal du Sieur Petis, Fils*, in *Relation de Dourry Efendy ambassadeur de la Porte Othomane auprès du Roy de Perse*, ed. L. Langlès, Paris, 1810. *Pis'ma i doneseniya Iezuitov o Rossii kontsa XVII i nachala XVIII veka* (Letters and Reports of Jesuits about Russia in the End of the 17th and in the Beginning of the 18th Century), St. Petersburg, 1904. P. Raphaël, "Mémoire sur les Jésuites circa 1662," in F. Richard, 1995, II, pp. 201-57. A. da Silva Rego, ed., *Documentação para a história das missões do Padorado português do Oriente*, 12 vols., Lisbon, 1947-58. A. de Rhodes, *Relation de la mission des Pères de la Compagnie de Jésus, establie dans le Royaume de Perse*, Paris, 1669. F. Richard, ed., *Raphaël du Mans: missionnaire en Perse au XVIIe s.*, 2 vols., Paris, 1995. F. Rigordi, *Peregrinationes Apostolicae*, Marseilles, 1652. F. C. Schillinger, *Persianische und Ost-Indianische Reis, welche Frantz Caspar Schillinger mit P. Wilhelm Weber und P. Wilhelm Mayr durch das Türckische Gebiet im Jahr 1699 angefangen und 1702 vollendet*, Nuremberg, 1707, repr. 1709, 1716. N. Trigault, *Vita Gasparis Barzaei, Belgae e Societate Iesu B. Xaverii in India socii*, Antwerp, 1610; tr. as *La vie du P. Gaspar Berze Zélandais, de la Compagnie de Jésus et compagnon du B. P. Xavier aux Indes*, Douai, 1612. J. Villotte, *Voyage d'un missionnaire de la Compagnie de Jésus en Turquie, en Perse, en Arménie, en Arabie en en Barbarie*, Paris, 1730. I. Wicki, ed., *Documenta Indica*, 18 vols., Rome, 1948-68. T. Wilson, tr. and ed., "History of the Mission of the Fathers of the Society of Jesus, Established in Persia by the Reverend Father Alexander of Rhodes," *BSOAS* 3, 1925, pp. 675-706.

Studies: C. Alonso, "Una embajada de Clemente VIII a Persia (1600-1609)," *Archivum Historiae Pontificiae* 34, 1996, pp. 7-125. Idem, Nuevas aportaciones para la historia del primer viaje misional de los Carmelitanos Descalzos a Persia (1603-1608), *Missionalia Hispanica* 57, 1962, pp. 249-87. M. Bednarz, "Ignacy Franciszek Zapolski, diplomata i misjonarz w Persji pod koniec wieku" (Ignacius Franciscus Zapolski, Diplomat and Missionary in Persia toward the End the Century), in *Gdy Europa szukata Azji*, ed. F. A. Plattner, Krakow, 1975, pp. 371-86. S. Brzeziński, *Misjonarze i diplomacy polscy w Persji w XVII i XVIII wieku* (Polish Missionaries and Diplomats in Persia in the 17th and 18th Centuries), Potulice, 1935. A. Camps OFM, "Jerome Xavier SJ and the Muslims of the Mughal Empire. Controversial Works and Missionary Activity," *Neue Zeitschrift für Missionswissenschaft*, 1957, pp. 21-22, 175-78. S. Gonçalves SI, *Primeira Parte da História dos Religiosos da Companhia de Jesus e do que fizeram com a divina graça na conversão dos infiéis a nossa sancta fee católica nos reynos e províncias da Índia Oriental*, vol. I, *Vida do Beato Padre Francisco Xavier e começo da História da Companhia no Oriente*, ed. J. Wicki SI, Coimbra, 1957. V. S. Ghougasian, *The Emergence of the Armenian Diocese of New Julfa in the Seventeenth Century*, Atlanta, Ga., 1998. R. Gulbenkian, "The Translation of the Four Gospels into Persian," in Idem, *Estudos Históricos*, vol. 3: *Vária*, Lisbon, 1995, pp. 7-108. R. Jaʿfariān, *Ṣafawiya dar ʿarṣa-ye din, farhang wa siāsat*, 3 vols., Qom, 2000, vol. III, pp. 972-80. J. Krzyszkowski, S.I., "Entre Varsovie et Ispahan. Le P. Ignace-François Zapolski S.I.," *Archivum Historicum Societatis Jesu* 18, 1949, pp. 85-117. S. Kościałkowski, *L'Iran et la Pologne à travers les siècles*, Tehran, 1943, pp. 85-117. M. de Pradel de Lamase, "La religion Chrétienne en Perse et la Mission du P. de la Maze S.J. (1625-1709)," *Revue de l'Histoire des Missions* 4, 1927, pp. 251-60. W. Posch, *Der Fall Alkâs Mîrzâ und der Persienfeldzug von 1548-1549. Ein gescheitertes osmanisches Projekt zur Niederwerfung des safavidischen Persiens*, Marburg, 2000. Z. Pucko, "The Activity of Polish Jesuits in Persia and Neighbouring Countries in the 17th and 18th Centuries," in *Proceedings of the Third European Conference of Iranian Studies*, pt. 2, Mediaeval and Modern Persian Studies, ed. Ch. Melville, Wiesbaden, 1999, pp. 309-15. F. Richard, "Le père Aimé Chézaud controversiste et ses manuscrits persans," *Nāma-ye Bahārestān*, vol. 6-7, No. 1-2, Ser. No. 11-12, 2005-6 (April 2007), pp. 7-18 (Western pagination). G. Schurhammer, "Die Trinitätspredigt Mag. Gaspars in der Synagoge von Ormuz 1549," *Archivum Historicum Societatis Iesu* 1, 1933, pp. 279-309. G. Schurhammer SI, *Franz Xaver, sein Leben und seine Zeit*, 3 vols., Freiburg, Basel, and Vienna, 1963-73. C. Sommervogel, *Bibliothèque de la Compagnie de Jésus*, 9 vols., Brussels, 1890-1916. L. F. F. R. Thomaz, "Descobrimentos e Evangelização. Da Cruzada à missão pacífica," in *Actas de congresso internacional de historia, Missionação Portuguesa e encontro de culturas*, vol. 1, *Cristandade Portuguesa até no século XV*, Braga, 1993, pp. 81-129. C. Wessels, *Early Jesuit Travellers in Central Asia, 1603-1712*, The Hague, 1924. S. Załeski, *Jezuici w Polsce* (Jesuits in Poland), Lvov, 1902. Idem, "Misje w Persji w XVII i XVIII wieku pod protektoratem Polski" (Missions in Persia in the 17th-18th Centuries under the Protectorate of Poland), *Misje Katoloickie* 1, 1882, pp. 3-66. B. Zimmel, "Bernhart Diestel," in *Festschrift für J. Stummvoll*, 2 vols., ed. J. Mayerhöfer and W. Rietzer, Vienna, 1970, vol. II, pp. 880-92. Idem, "Vorgeschichte und Gründung der Jesuitenmission in Isfahan (1642-1657)," *Zeitschrift für Missionswissenschaft und Religionswissenschaft* 53, 1969, pp. 1-26.

(RUDI MATTHEE)

JEVDET, ʿABD-ALLĀH (ABDULLAH CEVDET, b. Arapkir, 9 September 1869; d. Istanbul, 29 November 1932), Ottoman poet, writer, translator, and thinker. He was the son of Ömer Wasfi Bey who belonged to the Ömer-oğulları Kurdish family. Upon finishing primary school in Hozat (Ḳozāt) and Arapkir he studied at the Military Middle School in the city of Maʿmurat al-ʿAziz (today Elazığ) in 1882-85, and then at the Kuleli

Military High School in 1885-88 and at the Gülhane Military Medical School in 1888-94, both in Istanbul. During his military studies he developed an interest in politics and in 1890 became one of the founders and active members of the political group that later became known as the Society for Union and Progress (*İttihad ve Terakki Cemiyeti*). In 1894 he graduated as a medical officer. In 1896 he was exiled to Tripoli for political reasons. In 1897 he went through Tunisia and France to Geneva, where he joined the Young Turks. He wrote various articles for *ʿOṯmānli*, a critical newspaper, and founded the journal *Qahriyāt* which was against the Ottoman political system. In 1899, while continuing his political activities, he accepted the position of medical officer at the Ottoman Embassy in Vienna. After having been expelled from Austria in 1903, he went back to Geneva, where in 1904 he founded the periodical *Ejteḥād*. After some time he was expelled from Switzerland as well and came to Cairo in 1905 and then to Istanbul in 1910, where he renewed the publication of the *Ejteḥād*. Although this periodical was banned many times, he continued publishing it under different names. After World War I, he became director-general of public health for a short time. He wrote an article in which he praised Bahaism (see BAHAI FAITH) as an ideal religion. As a result of this, in 1922 he was summoned to court for having allegedly insulted the Prophet Muhammad, but in 1926 the proceedings were dropped. However, he was never again allowed to take any public post, because he had sided with the British after World War I and also because he had had contacts with *Kürt Teʿâli Cemiyeti* (Society for the Advancement of the Kurds). He died from a heart attack on 29 November 1932 in Istanbul.

ʿAbd-Allāh Jevdet wrote 46 books and translated about 30 books on politics, philosophy, literature, history, psychology, and medicine. He mastered the Persian language and translated two books from Persian into Turkish. The first of them was *Delmasti-e Mowlānā* which contains parts of the *Maṯnawi-e Maʿnawi* and the *Divān-e kabir* by Mowlānā Jalāl-al-Din Rumi (Istanbul, 1921, pp. 3-60). Besides Rumi's poems, it contains two more parts: one of them, entitled *Robāʿiyāt-e Ğazāli* (pp. 61-97), includes Ğazāli's poems, and the other, under the title *ʿUrfi'de şiʿir ve ʿirfân* (pp. 98-128), comprises selected poems from the *divān* by ʿOrfi Širāzi (1555-91). The language of the translation is very clear and impressive; footnotes were added for clarification.

ʿAbd-Allāh Jevdet's second translation from Persian into Turkish is that of ʿOmar Ḵayyām's quatrains (*Robāʿiyāt-e Ḵayyām ve Türkçe'ye tercümeleri*, Istanbul, 1914; 2nd ed. 1926; 3rd ed. 1926; *Rubaîler*, ed. Mehmet Kanar, Istanbul, 2000). Its introduction, entitled *Ḥakim ʿOmar Ḵayyām*, deals with Ḵayyām's biography and poems. The original texts of the *robāʿis* are presented together with the Turkish translation (pp. 42-180), and footnotes have been provided to explain ambiguous places. He also added some Turkish couplets similar to Ḵayyām's *robāʿis*, as well as an index for the *robāʿis* (pp. 182-89). This translation clearly shows the extent to which ʿAbd-Allāh Jevdet had mastered the Persian language as well as Turkish literature. However, this work was later criticized because some of the *robāʿis* were in fact not of ʿOmar Ḵayyām.

Bibliography: "Abdullah Cevdet," *İslâm Ansiklopedisi* I, 1950, p. 46. "Abdullah Cevdet," *Türk Dili ve Edebiyatı Ansiklopedisi* I, Istanbul, 1977, pp. 11-12. Necati Alkan, "'The Eternal Enemy of Islām': Abdullah Cevdet and the Baha'i Religion," *BSOAS* 68/1, 2005, pp. 1-20. *Dāneš-nāma-ye adab-e fārsi*, vol. VI: *Adab-e fārsi dar Ānātuli va Bālkān*, ed. Ḥasan Anuša, Tehran, 2005, pp. 284-86. M. Şükrü Hanioğlu, *Bir siyasal düşünür olarak Abdullah Cevdet ve dönemi*, Istanbul, 1981. Idem, "Abdullah Cevdet," *Diyanet Vakfı İslâm Ansiklopedisi* I, 1988, pp. 90-93. G. L. Lewis, "Djewdet," *EI*[2] II, 1965, p. 533. Şerif Mardin, *Jön Türkler'in siyasî fikirleri, 1895-1908*, Ankara, 1964, pp. 162-80. Karl Süssheim, "ʿAbd Allāh Djewdet," *EI*, Supplement, 1938, pp. 55-60. M. K. Özgül, "Abdullah Cevdet," *Türk Dünyası Edebiyatçıları Ansiklopedisi* I, Ankara, 2002, pp. 46-47. Hilmi Ziya Ülken, *Türkiye'de çağdaş düşünce tarihi*, Istanbul, 1979, pp. 240-54. ʿOmar Ḵayyām, *Robāʿiyāt-e Ḵayyām ve Türkçe'ye tercümeleri*, Istanbul, 1914, 2nd ed. 1926. Idem, *Rubaîler*, Turk. tr. Abdullah Cevdet, Hüseyin Daniş, and Hüseyin Rıfat, ed. Mehmet Kanar, Istanbul, 2000. Jalāl-al-Din Rumi, *Delmasti-e Mowlānā*, Turk. tr. Abdullah Cevdet, Istanbul, 1921.

(OSMAN G. ÖZGÜDENLİ)

JEVDET PASHA (b. Lofça [Lovech, central Bulgaria], 1237/1823; d. Istanbul, 2 Ḏu'l-Ḥejja 1312/26 May 1895), Ottoman writer, historian, jurist, and statesman. His original name was Ahmed (Aḥmad), but he became known under the name Jevdet, which was given to him by his tutor Süleyman Fehim Efendi (d. 1846) in 1843. After finishing primary school in Lofça (modern Lovech), he came to Istanbul in 1839 to continue his studies. He studied theology, mathematics, geology, astronomy, and Arabic literature in several *madrasas*. He studied the Persian language with Mehmed Murad Efendi (d. 1848) and Süleyman Fehim Efendi (d. 1845) and also studied the *divāns* of ʿOrfi (d. 1591) and Šowkat (d. 1695-96). In 1260/1844 he was granted the permission (*ejāzat-nāma*) to teach the *Maṯnawi* of Mowlānā Jalāl-al-Din Rumi. In January 1844 Jevdet was offered a position as a judge (*qāżi*). In 1846 he became the teacher of children of the Prime Minister (Ṣadr-Aʿẓām) Mustafa Rešid Pasha (1800-58), which was a turning point in Jevdet's life and career. Gradually his scientific and scholarly work was taken over by political activities and governmental service. After having held various posts, he became the official state historian (*wāqeʿa-nevis*) in 1855. In 1857 he started his legal career, which he would continue until his death. He successfully accomplished many highly important official tasks. He made a major contribution to the establishment of a new Ottoman legal system and to the publication of the *Majalla*, the Ottoman law-book. Jevdet died in Istanbul on 2 Ḏu'l-Hejja 1312/26 May 1895.

Jevdet Pasha mastered Arabic, Persian, French, and Bulgarian. He wrote more than twenty important books on history, law, grammar, linguistics, logic, and astronomy (for a list of Jevdet Pasha's works see Halaçoğlu and Aydın, 1993, pp. 448-49). Besides, he also completed a Turkish commentary for the Persian *divān* of Ṣāʾeb Tabrizi (d. 1675-76). This commentary, entitled *Tatemma-ye šarḥ-e divān-e Ṣāʾeb*, had been started by Jevdet's tutor, Süleyman Fehim Efendi, who left it unfinished when he died in 1845 (he reached as far as the letter *qāf*). The work was composed according to the classical tradition of writing commentaries for poetic works: the major part of Ṣāʾeb's *divān* and *ḡazal*s (q.v.) are arranged in alphabetical order. The commentary deals not only with the meaning of the couplets, but also with questions of literary art, vocabulary, basic characteristics of inflexion, and grammar, and it is illustrated with samples of poetry. A manuscript of this work can be found at the Bayezid Devlet Library in Istanbul (Veliyüddin Efendi, MS 3302). The commentary by Süleyman Fehim Efendi is on fols. 1b-596b, and the continuation by Jevdet Pasha on fols. 596b-627b. This work has not yet been published.

Bibliography: Works: Ahmed Jevdet Pasha, *Tarih-i Cevdet*, 12 vols., Istanbul, 1891-92. Idem, *Tezâkir*, ed. Cavid Baysun, 4 vols., Ankara, 1953-67, 2nd ed. 1986. Idem, *Ma'rûzât*, ed. Yusuf Halaçoğlu, Istanbul, 1980.

Studies. *Ahmed Cevdet Paşa Semineri*, Istanbul, 1986. Fatima Aliyye, *Ahmed Cevdet Paşa ve zamanı*, Istanbul, 1913-14. M. Cavid Baysun, "Cevdet Paşa, şahsiyetine ve ilim sahasındaki faaliyetlerine dair," *Türkiyat Mecmuası* 11, 1954, pp. 213-30. H. Bowen, "Aḥmad Djewdet Pasha," *EI*² I, 1960, pp. 284-86. Bursalı Meḥmed Ṭāhir, *Osmanlı mü'ellifleri*, 3 vols., Istanbul, 1914-28, vol. II, pp. 129-32. A. Celepoğlu, "Cevdet Paşa," *Türk Dünyası Edebiyatçıları Ansiklopedisi* II, Ankara, 2002, pp. 450-53. Yusuf Halaçoğlu and M. Akif Aydın, "Cevdet Paşa," *Diyanet Vakfı İslâm Ansiklopedisi* VII, 1993, pp. 443-50. E. İhsanoğlu, R. Şeşen, C. İzgi, C. Akpınar, and İ. Fazlıoğlu, *Osmanlı astronomi literatürü tarihi*, ed. E. İhsanoğlu, 2 vols., Istanbul, 1997, vol. II, pp. 665-69. Ahmet Zeki İzgöer, *Ahmet Cevdet Paşa*, Istanbul, 1999. Bekir Kütükoğlu, "Tarihçi Cevdet Paşa," in *Vekâyi'nüvis, Makaleler*, Istanbul, 1994, pp. 367-73. Ebü'l-Ulâ Mardin, *Medenî hukuk cephesinden Ahmed Cevdet Paşa*, Istanbul, 1946. Ümid Meriç, *Cevdet Paşa'nın cemiyet ve devlet görüşü*, Istanbul, 1975. Ch. K. Neumann, *Das indirekte Argument: ein Plädoyer für die Tanzīmāt vermittels der Historie; die geschichtliche Bedeutung von Ahmed Cevdet Paşa's Ta'rih*, Munich, 1992. Idem, "Ahmed Cevdet Paşa'nın tarihçiliğine yansıyan zihniyet dünyası," in *Osmanlı'dan Cumhuriyet'e Problemler, Araştırmalar, Tartışmalar*, Istanbul, 1998, pp. 64-71. Âli Ölmezoğlu, "Cevdet Paşa," *İslâm Ansiklopedisi* III, 1945, pp. 114-23. M. Şakir Ülkütaşır, *Cevdet Paşa, hayatı, şahsiyeti, eserleri (1822-1895)*, Ankara, 1945.

(OSMAN G. ÖZGÜDENLİ)

JEVRI (CEVRI), **AHISKALI** (b. Ahıska, 1805; d. Diyarbakır, 1875), Ottoman poet and translator. His first name was Ahmed (Aḥmad). He was a professional soldier. In 1855 he was transferred to Diyarbakır. In 1867 he became medically unfit for the army. In 1868 he was appointed vice-governor (*mutasarrıf*, Ar.-Pers. *mota-ṣarref*) of Mardin and later became governor of Siverek in 1870 and then of Rıdvan in 1871. He soon left the state service and came back to Diyarbakır, where he died in 1875.

Jevri mastered the Persian language and translated about 5,000 couplets from the *Šāh-nāma* of Ferdowsi into Ottoman Turkish in verse. This translation has never been published. He also wrote some poems in Turkish.

Bibliography: A. B. Alptekin, "Cevrî," *Türk Dünyası Edebiyatçıları Ansiklopedisi* II, Ankara, 2002, p. 456. Sadeddin Nüzhet Ergun, *Türk şairleri*, 3 vols., Istanbul, 1936-45, vol. III, pp. 1049-51. Taḥsin Yāziji (Tahsin Yazıcı), *Pārsinevisān-e Āsiā-ye Ṣaḡir*, Tehran, 1992, p. 30. Idem, "Cevri," *Türk Dili ve Edebiyatı Ansiklopedisi* II, Istanbul, 1977, p. 58.

(OSMAN G. ÖZGÜDENLİ)

JEVRI, EBRĀHIM ČELEBI (CEVRİ İBRAHİM ÇELEBİ, d. 1654), Ottoman poet and calligrapher. Some of his poems seem to suggest that he was born some time between 1595 and 1600 in Edirne. He was brought up in the *Mowlawi-ḵāna* of Ḡalaṭa and in other *Mowlawi-ḵāna*s. He studied with Shaikh Esmāʿil Ankarāvi (d. 1631) who practiced conversational education. Jevri studied calligraphy with Derviš ʿAbdi Mowlawi (d. 1647), who was a very famous calligrapher at that time. For some time Jevri worked as official scribe at the Imperial Council (*divān-e homāyun*), but after a while he left that post and started working as a freelance calligrapher and copier of manuscripts. He transcribed many copies of such voluminous and important works as the *Šāh-nāma*, *Tāriḵ-e Waṣṣāf*, *Maṯnawi-e maʿnawi*, and *Konh al-aḵbār*. Since he was a very famous *nastaʿliq* calligrapher, the manuscripts he copied were of great importance and value for statesmen and intellectuals. It is said that he was a member of the *Mowlawiyya* Sufi order. He died in 1654 in Istanbul.

Works. Jevri produced a voluminous *divān* which contains not only Turkish poems, but also 37 Persian quatrains (*robāʿi*) and two chronograms (*taʾriḵ*). Many manuscripts of his *divān* are found in libraries, among them two autographs dated 1641 and 1645 (Istanbul, Topkapı Sarayı Library, Emanet Hazinesi, MS 1623; Kayseri, Râşid Efendi Library, MS 1286; see Karatay, II, p. 153, no. 2417; Karabulut, 1982, p. 62, no. 57). Jevri's *divān* was published in a critical edition by Hüseyin Ayan (Erzurum, 1981).

In 1627 Jevri reworked the *Selim-nāma*, which was originally composed in 1523 by Šokri-ye Bedlisi (d. after 1530) and which is a biography of Sultan Selim I (r. 1512-20). The only manuscript of Jevri's work (under the same title) is preserved in the Millet Library in Istanbul (Ali Emiri, MS Manzum 1310). Another work of his, a small *maṯnawi* entitled *Ḥelya-ye čahār yār-e gozin*, contains 145 couplets and was published three times (Istanbul, 1876-77, 1891-92, and 1899-1900). In 1635 Jevri rewrote the *Šamsiya*, composed in 1408 by Yazıcı Ṣalāḥ-al-Din, and entitled his work *Malḥama*. Like its original, the *Malḥama* is in verse; it contains 3,617 couplets and was several times published in Istanbul (1855-56, 1877-78, 1888-89, and 1906-7). Another poetic work of Jevri is entitled *Naẓm-e neyāz* and comprises 200 couplets; it deals with the characteristics of the various months of the year. The only available manuscript of it is preserved in the Istanbul University Library (MS TY 714, fols. 98a-100a). Jevri's *Dastur al-ansāb fi al-adab* contains various letters as samples of literary writing (Istanbul, Nurosmaniye Library, MSS 4204 and 4205).

Jevri also made some translations and wrote several commentaries. In his *Ḥall-e taḥqiqāt*, the first 18 couplets as well as 40 further selected couplets from the *Maṯnawi* of Jalāl-al-Din Rumi are commented on in verse form. This work was written in 1647 and contains 415 couplets altogether. It was printed in Istanbul in 1852-53. The *ʿAyn al-foyuż* is Jevri's commentary to the *Jazira-ye Maṯnawi* by Yosuf Sinečāk Dede, who chose 366 couplets in Persian from the *Maṯnawi* of Rumi. Jevri made a verse translation of Dede's work into Ottoman Turkish and provided a commentary. It was written in 1647 and published in Istanbul in 1852-53.

The *Tarjoma-ye aḥwāl-e Kᵛāja Ḥāfeẓ-e Širāzi* was published in Istanbul in 1869-70. It was believed to be Jevri's work, but his name is not mentioned in the manuscripts (Istanbul, Süleymaniye Library, MS Turhan Hatice Sultan 287; Ayan, 1993, p. 461). Some researchers also believe that the *Bayān-e aʿdād-e ṣefathā-ye nafs-e ensāni* and the *Tāriḵ-e Jevri Čelebi*, the latter being published in two volumes in Istanbul in 1874-75, were also written by Jevri. However, there is sufficient doubt about Jevri being their author (Ayan, 1993, p. 461). It is known that Jevri wrote two more books under the titles *Mu'ammâ risâlesi* (*Moʿammā resālesi*) and *Mufredât-i tıbb manzumesi* (*Mofradāt-e ṭebb manẓumesi*), but these works have not been recorded in printed catalogues (Ayan, 1993, p. 461).

Bibliography: Mustafa Aslan, "Cevrî divanında mûsikî," *Türk Kültürü* 36/422, 1998, pp. 361-71. Hüseyin Ayan, "Cevri İbrahim Çelebi," *Türk Dili ve Edebiyatı Ansiklopedisi* II, Istanbul, 1977, pp. 58-59. Idem, *Cevrî: Hayatı, edebî kişiliği, eserleri ve divanının tenkidli metni*, Erzurum, 1981, pp. 4-52. Idem, "Cevri İbrahim Çelebi," *Diyanet Vakfı İslâm Ansiklopedisi* VII, 1993, pp. 460-61. Bursalı Meḥmed Ṭāhir, *Osmanlı mü'ellifleri*, 3 vols., Istanbul, 1914-24, vol. II, pp. 126-28. M. Cunbur, "Cevrî," *Türk Dünyası Edebiyatçıları Ansiklopedisi* II, Ankara, 2002, pp. 455-56. *Dāneš-nāma-ye adab-e fārsi*, vol. VI: *Adab-e fārsi dar Ānātuli wa Bālkān*, ed. Ḥasan Anuša, Tehran, 2005, pp. 290-91. Uğur Derman, "Derviş Abdî-i Mevlevî," *Diyanet Vakfı İslâm Ansiklopedisi* IX, 1994, pp. 190-91. N. Sadeddin Ergun, *Türk şairleri*, 3 vols., Istanbul, 1936-45, vol. I, pp. 104-6. Abdulkadir Erkal, "Türk Edebiyatında hilye ve Cevrî'nin 'Hilye-i Çâr Yâr-ı Güzin'i," *Atatürk Üniversitesi Türkiyat Araştırmaları Enstitüsü Dergisi* 12, 1999, pp. 111-31. ʿAli-Reżā Qarāboluṭ [Ali Rıza Karabulut], *Moʿjam al-maḵṭuṭāt al-mowjuda fi maktabāt Estānbul wa Ānāṭuli*, n.p., n.d., pp. 55-56. Idem, *Kayseri Râşid Efendi Kütüphanesi Türkçe, Farsça, Arapça yazmalar kataloğu*, Kayseri, 1982, p. 62, no. 57. Fehmi Edhem Karatay, *Topkapı Sarayı Müzesi Kütüphanesi Türkçe yazmalar kataloğu*, vol. II, Istanbul, 1961, p. 153, no. 2417. M. Fatih Köksal, "Bir kaside iki şair: Nef'î-Cevrî," *Türklük Bilimi Araştırmaları* 4, 1997, pp. 69-80. Taḥsin Yāziji [Tahsin Yazıcı], *Pārsinevisān-e Āsiā-ye Ṣaḡir*, Tehran, 1992, pp. 29-30.

(OSMAN G. ÖZGÜDENLİ)

JEWS OF IRAN. See JUDEO-PERSIAN COMMUNITIES.

JEYḤUNĀBĀDI, ḤĀJJ NEʿMAT-ALLĀH MOKRI (pen name "Mojrem;" b. Kurdish village of Jeyḥunābād, 1288/1871; d. Jeyḥunābād, 7 Jomādā II 1338/27 February 1920), an influential mystic whose stated mission was to collect and record the previously oral traditions of the Ahl-e Ḥaqq (q.v.) order and to rectify perceived discrepancies and inconsistencies within the established tradition.

Following the migration of Šāh Ḥayās's descendants, Ḥāj Neʿmat's forebears settled in Jeyḥunābād, a village in the Dinavar district of Iran during the reign of Moḥammad Shah Qājār (r. 1834-1848; Calmard). Ḥājj Neʿmat-Allāh lost his father, Mirzā Bayān (Bahrām), in 1880 and his mother, Bibiḵᵛān, the following year, and was thereafter placed under the tutelage of his uncle, Mirzā Ḡolām-ʿAli. After he completed his education, he married Mirzā Ḡolām-ʿAli's daughter, Sakina (1878-1953), with whom he had seven children, of which only three survived: Nur-ʿAli Elāhi (q.v.; also known as Ostād Elāhi, 1895-1974), Malek Jān (also known as Jāni, 1906-93), and Maryam (1909-98). Two years into their marriage, Ḥājj Neʿmat-Allāh began working for the government as the agent (*mobāšer*) of Ḥājj Āqā Ḥasan (or Ḥājj ʿAbd-al-Raḥim) Wakil-al-Dawla (on *wakil al-dawla*s of Kermānšāh see Rāʾin), the secretary (*monši*) of the governor (*ḥākem*) of Kermānšāh, and as deputy-governor (*nāyeb-al-ḥokuma*), respectively, but resigned within a short period and returned to the full-time administration of his family estate (Elāhi, 2007, I, p. 535).

Ḥājj Neʿmat-Allāh describes how he experienced a sudden spiritual awakening (*tajalli*; see Corbin, III, p. 345) in 1900 (Ḥājj Neʿmat-Allāh, *Żiāʾ al-qolub*, fol. 183; Elāhi, *Ḥājj Neʿmat-Allāh*, fol. 2) or 1902 according to his son Nur-ʿAli Elāhi (1981-91, I, p. 554), following a near-fatal illness around the age of twenty-nine. The event drastically changed his attitude toward material preoccupations. He withdrew from all worldly affairs and led a life of ascetic austerity in seclusion in a small retreat (*riāżat-kāna*) in Jeyḥunābād, twelve followers secretly gathered around him in just a year (Elāhi, *Ḥājj Neʿmat-Allāh*, fol. 4; idem, 1981-91, I, pp. 554, 556). During the second year of his retreat (1902), he decided to don the white habit of dervishes and no longer cut his hair and beard. Barefooted and in a state of fasting and asceticism, he undertook a voyage to the shrine of Solṭān Esḥāq (Sohāk, the founder of the Ahl-e Ḥaqq order; see Minorsky, p. 546), a pilgrimage that, in the Ahl-e Ḥaqq tradition, is associated with the status of *ḥāji* "a person who has made the pilgrimage to Mecca" (Minorsky, 1920, p. 239), and he was henceforth called Ḥājj Neʿmat-Allāh. After a cycle of pilgrimages and travels, he stopped meeting with others and engaged in a complete retreat that lasted for two years.

He subsequently emerged from his retreat to live with his family (ca. 1904). The consequence of Ḥājj Neʿmat-Allāh's public revelation was the establishment of his own "mystical path" (*rešta-ye faqr*) within the Ahl-e Ḥaqq order (see Elāhi, 1981-91, II p. 248), complete with its dervish followers and its own center (*ḵānaqāh*). Ḥājj Neʿmat-Allāh did not have a spiritual master during his lifetime, and proclaimed that his source of inspiration was the Lord of the Age (Ṣāḥeb[-e] Zamān). He therefore named his branch Kānadān-e Ṣāḥeb-zamāni, which became the twelfth dynasty (*kānadān*) within the consecrated Ahl-e Ḥaqq dynasties (Elāhi, 1981-91, II, p. 248; on Ahl-e Ḥaqq dynasties see Solṭāni, passim).

The reaction of the hereditary authorities (*sādāt*, i.e., *sayyed*s) of Ahl-e Ḥaqq to the creation of this new branch was mixed, as some feared the loss of their power and responded adversely, while others were receptive or indifferent. It should be noted that among those who became followers of Ḥājj Neʿmat-Allāh were a number of Ahl-e Ḥaqq hereditary authorities, who originated from and belonged to different Ahl-e Ḥaqq dynasties. Ḥājj Neʿmat-Allāh himself enjoyed good personal relations with all of the dynasties, notably with the Ātaš Begi and the descendants of Sayyed Barāka among the Gurān. He also maintained respectful relations with the Shah Ḥayāsi dynasty (Jayḥunābādi, 1984, pp. 328-62; Elāhi, 1981-91, I, p. 553).

Ḥājj Neʿmat-Allāh primarily based his teachings on the principles revealed by Solṭān Esḥāq and sought to preserve the authenticity of the Ahl-e Ḥaqq's core beliefs (Ḥājj Neʿmat-Allāh, *Forqān al-aḵbār*, ms. A, fols. 130-31; Elāhi, 1975, pp. 22-25). He emphasized self-restraint, sincerity, and collective devotion (see Ḥājj Neʿmat-Allāh, *Forqān al-aḵbār*, fols. 34-35, 44-62, 87-88, 130-31, 304-5; see also *naṣāyeḥ* "counsel" in idem, *Šāh-nāma-ye ḥaqiqat*, passim).

Ḥājj Neʿmat-Allāh's dervishes, who were called Darviš-e Ṣāḥeb-zamāni, modeled themselves after him and were known for their piety and ardent faith (Elāhi, *Ḥājj Neʿmat-Allāh*, p. 5; Ḥājj Neʿmat-Allāh, *Forqān al-akbār*, fols. 303-4), roughly 42 percent of his dervishes were women (Elāhi, 1981-91, I, pp. 557, 564, 567). There are also some descriptions of his physical appearance, his habits, and his many gifts (Elāhi, 1981-91, I, pp. 573, 582, 597, II, pp. 17, 87). A good number of extraordinary deeds have been attributed to him (Elāhi, 1981-91, I, p. 28, chap. 23 and passim, II, pp. 27, 114, 268, 390-91; idem, *Ḥājj Neʿmat-Allāh*, fols. 4-5). The most notable feature of his personality is reported to have been his forbearance toward friend and foe alike (Elāhi, 1981-91, II, p. 142).

For the next seven years, from Muḥarram 1325/February-March 1907 to Muḥarram 1332/December 1913 (Elāhi, *Ḥājj Neʿmat-Allāh*, fols. 7-8), Ḥājj Neʿmat-Allāh, his spouse, and their son Nur-ʿAli lived in constant seclusion and asceticism. From early 1914 until his passing, they alternated between six-month periods of contact with others and six-month periods of ascetic retreat.

In 1919, he recorded his will and set out on pilgrimage to Shah Ḥayās, a theophany according to Ahl-e Ḥaqq angelology and an eponym for the Shah Ḥayāsi dynasty, where he acquired the nickname "Ḥāji Wahhāb." Shortly after his return, on 27 Rabiʿ I 1338/20 December 1919, he was bedridden for two months and ten days. He passed away on 7 Jomādā II 1338/27 February 1920 at the age of 49, and was buried in the same small retreat in which he engaged in ascetic practices in Jeyḥunābād, next to the tomb of Yār-ʿAli (d. 1914), his youngest child (Elāhi, *Ḥājj Neʿmat-Allāh*, fol. 9; idem, 1981-91, I, pp. 579-81).

Ḥājj Neʿmat-Allāh authored approximately twenty manuscripts, both in verse and prose, in Kurdish and Persian, which have not yet been fully studied. So far, only two of his works, *Šāh-nāma-ye ḥaqiqat* and *Forqān al-aḵbār*, have been analyzed and edited. He signed his writings with the pen name "Mojrem" (the guilty one) as an acknowledgment of his human fallibility.

As an experienced *kalāmḵᵛān* (scholar-reciter of the *kalām*; on the importance of the exegetic role of the *kalāmḵᵛān*, see Elāhi, 1975, pp. 428-29; van Bruinessen, p. 44 and passim) and the initiator of a new style of *kalām*, Ḥājj Neʿmat-Allāh was sensitive to the divergences that separated the Ahl-e Ḥaqq community.

Ḥājj Neʿmat-Allāh compiled and commented upon the existing material of the Ahl-e Ḥaqq tradition, stating his dismay at how far the Yāresān (i.e., Ahl-e Ḥaqq) had strayed from their core principles, and how those who at one time strove to realize the four pillars of purity, rectitude, self-effacement, and self-abnegation (*pāki*, *rāsti*, *nisti*, *redā*) were now entangled in misguided beliefs and erroneous conduct for the sake of material gains. Throughout almost all of his written works, he thus counseled the Ahl-e Ḥaqq to prefer the eternal (*bāqi*) to the ephemeral (*fāni*) and consistently emphasized devotion to the Truth (see, among others, Jayḥunābādi, 1984, p. 372-75). One of the reasons that Ḥājj Neʿmat attributed to the regression of the Yāresān was their misplaced emphasis on superstitions rather than spiritual truths (see *Forqān al-aḵbār*, ms. A, fol. 76). He also recognized the undue influence exerted by the sayyeds, who had kept the Yāresān in the dark and had even forbidden them from seeking an education solely to preserve their own financial interests (*Forqān al-aḵbār*, ms. A, fols. 79, 82, 299-300; Elāhi 1981-91, I, p. 497). Ḥājj Neʿmat fought for many years against this closed mindset, and despite all the difficulties and obstacles directed toward him by the sayyeds, he did not cease his efforts to rectify these digressions until the end of his life.

Within the context of his tradition, Ḥājj Neʿmat-Allāh's stated mission was to familiarize people with the Ahl-e

Ḥaqq order and record for the Ahl-e Ḥaqq community what no one until then had attempted to do regarding their practices, their goals, and their unity. According to Ḥājj Neʿmat-Allāh, this silence had resulted in confusion and misconceptions, especially with regard to their essential rites and rituals, such as the Marnavi fast (for details see Elāhi, 1975, pp. 141-61; see also the last section of *Forqān al-aḵbār*). From this perspective, his written works were the primary means through which he accomplished his mission of dispelling confusion among the Ahl-e Ḥaqq in order to "end the conflicts that were tearing them apart from within" and "restore the edifice of the religion of Truth" (see *Forqān al-aḵbār*, fols. 67, 83-84).

In his written works, he often used the Persian language, which he considered to be accessible to a wider audience (see, e.g., *Šāh-nāma-ye ḥaqiqat*, p. 324, v. 11291). In an environment where secrecy was of paramount concern, he authored candid and revealing works without fear of the ensuing consequences. His detachment vis-à-vis certain customary habits that were deemed sacred to some Ahl-e Ḥaqq did not fail to scandalize the establishment that claimed guardianship of the "orthodoxy."

Given the interest that Ḥājj Neʿmat-Allāh's written works has garnered both from within the Ahl-e Ḥaqq community in Kurdistan, Iran, and Iraq and from those who have studied them (Minorsky, "Ahl-i Ḥaḳḳ"; Kordestani, 1927; Mokri, Introd. to Ḥājj Neʿmat-Allāh, 1966, pp. 5-21), it can be said that his writings have substantially contributed to the democratization of the *kalām* and the beliefs and practices of the Ahl-e Ḥaqq order (Elāhi, 1981-91, I, p. 569, no. 1804, links this observation to the renewal of the faith that Ḥājj Neʿmat-Allāh is believed to have initiated; see also Mir-Ḥosseini).

Bibliography: Jean Calmard, "Qadjar (les)," in *Encyclopaedia Universalis*, CD-Rom, version 8. Henry Corbin, *En Islam iranien: aspects spirituels et philosophiques. Les fidèles d'amour, shiʿisme et soufisme*, 4 vols., Paris, 1971-72. Jean During, *L'âme des sons: l'art unique d'Ostad Elahi (1895-1974)*, Paris, 2001. Nur-ʿAli Elāhi, *Ḥājj Neʿmat-Allāh Mokri Jeyḥunābādi*, manuscript, Jeyḥunābād, dated 1930. Idem, *Borhān al-ḥaqq*, 3rd ed., Tehran, 1975. Idem, *Āṯār al-ḥaqq*, 2nd ed., 2 vols.,Tehran, 1981-91, 5th ed., Tehran, 2007. Ḥājj Neʿmat-Allāh Jeyḥunābādi, *Forqān al-aḵbār*, manuscript, Jeyḥunābād, dated 1909; ed. Mojan Membrado as "Forqân al-akhbâr," Ph.D. diss., École Pratique des Hautes Etudes, Paris, 2007. Idem, *Żiāʾ al-qolub*, manuscript, Jeyḥunābād, dated 1919. Idem, *Šāh-nāma-ye ḥaqiqat* I, ed. Moḥammad Mokri, Bibliothèque iranienne 14. Tehran and Paris, 1966; full text, Tehran, 1984; ed. with commentary, Nur-ʿAli Elāhi, Tehran, 1995. Saeed Khan Kordestani, "The Sect of Ahl-e Haqq (Ali ilahis)," *The Moslem World* 17, 1927, pp. 31-42. Vladimir Minorsky, "Solṭān Isḥāq," in *EI*[1] IV, p. 546. Idem, "Ahl-i Ḥaḳḳ," in *EI*[2] I, pp. 260-63. Idem, "Notes sur la secte des Ahl-e Haqq," *Revue du Monde Musulman* 40-41, 1920, pp. 19-97. Ziba Mir-Ḥosseini, "Inner Truth and Outer History," *IJMES* 28/2, 1994, pp. 267-85. Esmāʿil Rāʾin, *Ḥoquqbegirān-e Engelis dar Irān*, Tehran, 1983. M. ʿA. Solṭāni, *Tāriḵ-e ḵāndānhā-ye ḥaqiqat wa mašāhir-e motaʾaḵḵer-e Ahl-e Ḥaqq dar Kermānšāh*, 2nd ed., Tehran, 2002. Martin van Bruinessen, "Satan's Psalmists: Some Heterodox Beliefs and Practices among the Ahl-e Ḥaqq of the Gurān District," forthcoming.

(MOJAN MEMBRADO)

JEZYA, the poll or capitation tax levied on members of non-Muslim monotheistic faith communities (Jews, Christians, and, eventually, Zoroastrians), who fell under the protection (*ḏemma*) of Muslim Arab conquerors. It was retained and implemented in most of the Muslim world in a wide variety of ways, was strongly influenced by local economic conditions prevailing before and during the conquest, and varied considerably both over time and geographically. Although early texts tend to use the terms *jezya* and *ḵarāj* interchangeably, or as denoting a general tribute, these terms came to denote two different forms of taxation with the latter levied exclusively on land owners, Muslim and non-Muslim alike.

Muslim Arab conquerors largely retained the taxation systems of the Sasanian and Byzantine empires they had conquered. The word *jezya* itself is most likely a loanword in Arabic and probably derives from the Pahlavi *gazītak*, which denoted a tax levied on the lower classes of society in Sasanian Persia, from which the nobles, clergy, landowners (*dehqāns*), and scribes (or civil servants, *dabirān*) were exempted (Widengren, pp. 123, 149 ff.). The Muslim justification for *jezya* is found in the Qurʾān 9:29, where rejection of Islam is made conditional on the payment of a poll tax—a type of communal taxation to be levied both as a discriminatory tax and as a fee for the protection afforded by the Muslim majority. The Qurʾānic phrase *ḥattā yoʿṭu al-jezyata ʿan yaden wa hom ṣāḡerun* ("till they pay the poll tax out of hand and submissively"; Fakhry, p. 188) was often interpreted literally, with the tax payers subjected to various forms of humiliation, such as bending the back and even being struck. Among Shiʿites, the proper implementation of the *jezya* required the presence of the Imam, but in his prolonged absence, an appropriate jurist, acting as his deputy, could carry out this duty (Tsadik, pp. 62-65).

Much detailed information about the exaction of the *jezya* has survived among the documents of the Cairo Genizah found in Fustat, Egypt. These documents mainly date from 950-1250 C.E. and focus primarily, but not exclusively, on the Mediterranean basin. They also yield data about economic issues affecting Jewish life in the Omayyad and Abbasid caliphates, and thus about specific issues of taxation as well. Information about the far-flung activities of merchants such as the Tustari family, originally from Ḵuzestān, also contributes to our understanding of numerous economic issues, including taxation. In the absence of well-stocked archives or Genizah repositories, it is not possible to arrive at a continuous evaluation of *jezya* and its enforcement in Persia beginning with the Buyid dynasty (10th century, see BUYIDS).

In theory, the *jezya* was supposed to be levied on adult, free, capable males, while children, old people, women, slaves, beggars, and the infirm were supposed to be exempt. The payers of the *jezya* were exempt from military service and the Muslim tax of *zakāt*. Converts to Islam were supposed to have been released from this obligation, but not from land taxes (Gil, pp. 287-91), and this undoubtedly contributed to conversion to Islam in the first two centuries of its advent. But mass conversions that would curtail this revenue caused problems; in the late 7th and early 8th century even the *mawāli* (plur. of *mawlā*, 'client,' 'non-Arab Muslim') were forced to pay *jezya* (Zarrīnkūb, pp. 33-43). Judging by the documents of the Cairo Genizah, the exemptions mentioned above were far from being always implemented.

A uniform rate of taxation or revenue collection never existed throughout the Muslim world. Rates varied on the basis of local economic conditions and taxpayers' wealth, but under the Abbasids they ranged between 1, 2, and 4 *dinārs* (that is, 12, 24, and 48 *dirhams* accordingly; see Cahen, p. 560; Ben Shemesh, II, pp. 42-44; III, pp. 84 ff.), although payment in kind was often accepted as well. This general lack of uniformity led to both commendable flexibility in stressful times and abuse by individual tax collectors and their masters. An instance of the former can be found in Ḥasan b. Moḥammad b. Ḥasan Qomi's (d. 1015) *Tāriḵ-e Qom* (translated into Persian by Ḥasan b. ʿAli b. Ḥasan b. ʿAbd-al-Malek Qomi in the 15th century; see Storey-Bregel, II, no. 869, pp. 1008-9), which shows that a variety of physical conditions was taken into account in Qom in the 9th-10th centuries through the enactment of different tax-paying schedules according to the harvesting of crops (Lambton, 1953, p. 34). According to this source, *ḏemmis* (see PEOPLE OF THE BOOK) paid the *jezya* on the basis of two different schedules, either 24 or 12 *dirhams* (Lambton, 1953, p. 34). Instances of abuse grew with the growth of the *eqṭāʿ* (q.v.) system under the Saljuqs and Il-khanids (qq.v.), when the military castes, awarded various revenues, were far less scrupulous about the welfare of their subjects. Unlike in Egypt, where the *jezya* was collected from individuals and, as the Genizah documents testify, caused great hardships to impoverished Jews (better off individuals were under constant pressure to help their more indigent brethren), the non-Muslim communities throughout Persia and Central Asia were assigned communal tributes of a fixed sum. Since most people, for example in the Saljuq era, were subject also to "uncanonical taxes" (*mokus*; Lambton, 1968, pp. 249-50), the financial burden in medieval Persia must have been considerable. A broad but only periodic reprieve occurred under the early Mongol rulers, when a general poll tax (*saršomāra*, *sarāna*, Mong. *qubchur*) was introduced, only for the *jezya* to be finally reintroduced under Uljāytu (Öljeytü, r. 1304-16). During the reign of the Jalayerid (see JALAYERIDS) ruler Šayḵ Ovays I b. Ḥasan-e Bozorg (r. 1356-74), it is known to have been 8 *dinārs* for the wealthy, 6 for the middle classes, and 4 for the poor (Petrushevsky, p. 533).

For the Safavid period, the scant economic information on this subject is supplemented by the observations of travelers and Judeo-Persian chronicles. Whereas originally Shah ʿAbbās I (r. 1588-1629, q.v.) taxed the Armenians fairly lightly, their *jezya* kept increasing throughout the 17th century in tandem with their wealth. At the same time, the Hindu moneychangers working in Persia were subjected to a special poll tax (Fragner, pp. 548-49). During the reign of Shah ʿAbbās II (r. 1642-66, q.v.), many Jewish communities were forced to convert to Islam for almost seven years from 1656 to 1651-52. During that interim, they apparently did not pay the *jezya*. However, not only was it demanded from them retroactively, when they were allowed to return to their faith, but additional sums were also demanded at that time (Moreen, 1986, pp. 68, 100, 106). Raphaël du Mans (1613-96) notes that in the middle of the 17th century Armenians and Jews had to pay annually one *meṯqāl* of gold (Fragner, p. 548). In 1729-30, in an effort to stave off Ṭahmāsbqoli Khan's (the future Nāder Shah, r. 1736-47) rapacious taxes, the Jewish community of Kāšān converted to Islam and was temporarily exempted from the *jezya*, but only to have it reinstated with a heavy additional fine some six months later (Moreen, 1990, pp. 37-43, 51-56). Evidence of Jews paying the *jezya* in Persia can be found even after 1783; for Zoroastrians, in theory, it was abolished in 1882 (Tsadik, pp. 335-48).

The *jezya*, like other forms of taxation, was supposed to have been used for the common good in the form of salaries and charities, but it was often appropriated by various rulers, local and otherwise. While remission of taxes for Muslims did occur on rare occasions and in order to recover from natural disasters, the *ḏemmis* of Persia and Central Asia were seldom exempted from the payment of the *jezya*.

Bibliography: A. Ben Shemesh, *Taxation in Islam*, 3 vols., Leiden, 1958-69. C. Cahen, "Djizya," *EI*² II, 1965, pp. 559-62. M. R. Cohen, *Poverty and Charity in the Jewish Community of Medieval Egypt*, Princeton, 2005a. Idem, *The Voice of the Poor in the Middle Ages*, Princeton, 2005b. M. Fakhry, *An Interpretation of the Qur'an: English Translation of the Meanings, a Bilingual Edition*, New York, 2004. B. Fragner, "Social and Internal Economic Affairs," *Camb. Hist. Iran* VI, Cambridge, 1986, pp. 491-567. M. Gill, *Jews in Islamic Countries in the Middle Ages*, Leiden, 2004. S. D. Goitein, *A Mediterranean Society*, 5 vols., Berkeley, Calif., 1967-83. A. K. S. Lambton, *Landlord and Peasant in Persia: A Study of Land Tenure and Land Revenue Administration*, London, 1953. Idem, "The Internal Structure of the Saljūq Empire," *Camb. Hist. Iran* V, Cambridge, 1968, pp. 203-82. V. B. Moreen, *Iranian Jewry's Hour of Peril and Heroism: A Study of Bābāī Ibn Lutf's Chronicle (1617-1662)*, New York, 1986. Idem, *Iranian Jewry During the Afghan Invasion: The Kitāb-i Sar Guzasht-i Kāshān of Bābāī Ibn Farhād (1721-1731)*, Stuttgart, 1990. I. P. Petrushevsky, "The Socio-Economic Condition of Iran Under the Īl-Khāns," *Camb. Hist. Iran* V, Cambridge, 1968, pp. 483-537.

Storey-Bregel: *Ch. A. Stori. Persidskaya literatura: bio-bibliograficheskiĭ obzor/C. A. Storey. Persian Literature: a Bio-bibliographical Survey*, tr. into Russian and revised, with additions and corrections, by Yu. E. Bregel, 3 pts., Moscow, 1972. D. Tsadik, "Foreign Intervention, Majority, and Minority: The Status of the Jews during the Latter Part of the Nineteenth Century (1848-1896)," Ph.D. diss., Yale University, 2002. G. Widengren, "The Status of the Jews in the Sassanian Empire," *Iranica antiqua* 1, 1961, pp. 117-62. ʿAbd al-Ḥusain Zarrīnkūb, "The Arab Conquest of Iran and Its Aftermath," *Camb. Hist. Iran* IV, Cambridge, 1975, pp. 1-56.

(VERA B. MOREEN)

JIHAD IN ISLAM. See ISLAM IN IRAN xi.

JIHOṆIKA, a ruler in northwestern India known to us from his coins and an inscription. On the obverse of his bilingual coins, his name is written in corrupt Greek legend as Zeiōnisēs. On the reverse, written in clear Kharoshthi letters he appears as the satrap of Chukhsa and son of the satrap Maṇigula. The inscription engraved on a silver vase found by John Marshall at Sirkap (Taxila, Pakistan) in 1926/7 and published by S. Konow (1929, p. 82) also qualifies him as Jihoṇika the Kshatrapa of Chukhsa, the son of Maṇigula, the brother of the Great King. Though both epigraphic and numismatic evidence points to his paternal ancestry, historians have different views regarding his dynastic affiliation. Though he was considered in the past as a satrap of the Kushans, Indo-Parthians, or Indo-Scythians (qq.v.), he may most probably belong to the clan of Kshaharatas. The Chukhsa satrapy is also known through the Taxila copper scroll of Patika, where Patika's father Liaka Kusuluko is referred as the Kshaharata satrap of Chukhsa. Jihoṇika seems to have succeeded Patika in Chukhsa.

Although, the Taxila silver vase inscription refers to him as the satrap of Chukhsa, scholars are not unanimous when designating the precise location of the area in question. Jihoṇika's coins are not attested in the major discoveries made in the Paropamisadae (Kabul-Begram), and very few are found in the Punjab (Peshawar and Taxila). On the contrary, most of his coins are reported from Kashmir and the eastern part of Hazara. Furthermore, designs of his copper coins are closely linked with those of Azes II depicting bull and lion usually found in the Jammu-Kashmir area. Likewise, there are many reasons today to place Jihoṇika's kingdom in Kashmir, but not in Taxila or Pushkalavati (Peshawar) as believed by many historians in the past.

The precise chronology of Jihoṇika's reign is also controversial. Unfortunately, the epigraphic evidence is not of much use in this respect. The inscription engraved on the neck of the silver vase from Taxila bears a numeral 191. This was interpreted as a date in the so-called Old Saka era, the base year of which was proposed to be 155 B.C.E. Thus the reign of Jihoṇika was placed around 36 C.E. This date would tally with the chronological frame established for Jihoṇika on numismatic evidence (see below). But the problem remains far from being solved. J. Cribb (1999, pp. 196-97), followed by R. C. Senior (2001, pp. 96), categorically refuses to accept this numeral as a date, and they argue that it represents the weight of the vase. Richard Salomon (2005, pp. 374-75) does not exclude this possibility; however, he more cautiously acknowledges that this hypothesis cannot be tested until the weight of the silver vase is determined. Even if the numeral 191 represents a date, it is impossible to relate it to an era that would be accepted by all the scholars.

The numismatic evidence, on the other hand, is of some use in fixing a relative chronology for Jihoṇika. The round copper coins of the bull and lion type of Jihoṇika seem to have been the model for Kujula Kara Kadphises' bull and Bactrian camel coins (MacDowall, 1973, pp. 225-29). Kujula copied not only the denominations and the obverse type of the bull, but the corrupt and misunderstood Greek legend of Jihoṇika. He was certainly a contemporary of the first Indo-Parthian Gondophares (q.v.). The chronology of Gondophares in relation to Jihoṇika is revealed by a series of overstrikes by the latter over the former and the former over the latter. In short, according to the numismatic sequence, the reign of Gondophares should be dated ca. 20-46 C.E. and that of Kujula Kadphises ca. 30-80 C.E. Likewise, once the reign of Kujula Kadphises in relation to Gondophares is well established, the reign of Jihoṇika can be placed between 20 and 40 C.E. (Bopearachchi, pp. 137-39).

Bibliography: O. Bopearachchi, "Recent Coin Hoard Evidence on Pre-Kushana Chronology," in *Coins, Art, and Chronology. Essays on the pre-Islamic History of the Indo-Iranian Borderlands*, ed. M. Alram and D. E. Klimburg-Salter, Vienna, 1999, pp. 99-149. J. Cribb, "The Early Kushan Kings: New Evidence for Chronology. Evidence from the Rabatak Inscription of Kanishka I," in *Coins, Art, and Chronology. Essays on the pre-Islamic History of the Indo-Iranian Borderlands*, ed. M. Alram and D. E. Klimburg-Salter, Vienna, 1999, pp. 177-205. S. Konow, *Corpus Inscriptionum Indicarum, vol. II, Part I, Kharoshthi Inscriptions with the Exception of those of Aśoka*, Calcutta, 1929. D.W. Mac Dowall, "The Azes Hoard from Shaikhan-Dheri: Fresh Evidence for the Context of Jihonika," in *South Asian Archaeology*, ed. N. Hammond, London, 1973, pp. 215-30. R. Salomon, "The Indo-Greek Era of 186/5 B.C. in a Buddhist Reliquary Inscription," in *Afghanistan. Ancien carrefour entre l'Est et l'Ouest*, ed. O. Bopearachchi and M.-F. Boussac, Turnhout, 2005, pp. 359-401. Idem, *Ancient Buddhist Scrolls from Gandhāra. The British Library Kharoṣṭhī Fragments*, Seattle, 1999, pp. 141-45 ("The Jihonika Fragment"). R. C. Senior, *Indo-Scythian Coins and History*, London, 2001.

(O. BOPEARACHCHI)

JIROFT, name of a sub-provincial unit (*šahrestān*), a town, and a dam in Kerman Province.

i. *Geography*.
ii. *Human geography and environment*.
iii. *General survey of excavations*.
iv. *Iconography of chlorite artifacts*.

i. GEOGRAPHY

Jiroft sub-province. Located in the south of Kerman Province, the sub-province of Jiroft is bound by those of Kermān (north), Bam (east), ʿAnbarābād and Kahnuj (south), and Bāft (west). It is comprised of three districts (*bakš*), eleven rural districts, and three towns (Darb-e Behešt, Jebāl-e Bārez, and Jiroft, which is the administrative center of the sub-province).

Jiroft is situated in a relatively wide valley (see JIROFT ii, Figures 1-3; iv, Figures 1-2). The Bārez mountain range, extending for approximately 156 km in a northwest-southeast direction to the east of Jiroft, forms the natural boundary between Jiroft and Bam sub-provinces. The north of the sub-province is marked by Bahr Āsemān range with the highest peak of 3,886 m (Jaʿfari, I, pp. 121-22, 173). Jiroft obtains its water from the Halilrud River (q.v.), which rises in the Hazār Mountain at about 96 km to the northwest of Jiroft town, and its tributaries, one of which contains a waterfall 170 m high (Jaʿfari, II, pp. 86, 236, 300, 432, 480; Ṣafā, pp. 8, 14). The sub-province is also home to one of Iran's tallest waterfalls, Sarandkuh Darin, (177 m high; Ṣafā, p. 154).

Jiroft has three different climate zones: cold, warm, and moderate. Humidity stemming from the Indian Ocean causes torrential rains that result in floods. In the summer a very warm wind, locally called Hušā and Kuhbād, blows from the mountains in the north and north-east towards the plains of Jiroft. This wind, which at times blows for as long as a week, reduces the humidity (Ṣafā, p. 4).

Jiroft is considered the most suitable region in the entire Kerman Province for agriculture. Thanks to its variant climate zones, it produces both warm and cold weather crops and has earned the nickname of "Little India" (Ṣafā, p. 3). The inhabitants of Jiroft are Twelver Shiʿites and speak a local dialect of Persian (Edāra-ye joḡrāfiāʾi, CXIX, p. 56). Several nomadic tribes, such as the Āsiābar, the Jebāl Bārezi, Solaymāni Baluč, and the Mehni do their seasonal migration within the Jiroft sub-province (Markaz-e āmār-e Irān, 1999, pp. 123-25). In 1996 the sub-province of Jiroft had a population of 208,874, among whom 74,790 (36 percent) lived in urban areas while the rest resided in villages (Markaz-e āmār-e Irān, 1997, p. 60).

The main road between Kerman and Bandar ʿAbbās passes through this sub-province. In 1972 the city of Jiroft on the left bank of Halilrud River was connected to the Kahir village on the right bank with the building of a large stone bridge (Ṣafā, p. 13).

In 1937 Jiroft was a sub-provincial unit with three districts in the South Province, and was divided into three districts (*Qawānin wa aḥkām*, p. 75). On Dey 19 of the same year (10 January 1937), with the addition of Sabzevārān, Jiroft became a district of the Bam sub-provincial unit (*Qawānin wa aḥkām*, pp. 89-90) and became a sub-province in 1950 (Wezārat-e kešvar, 1950, II, pp. 368, 440-46). In 1951, Jiroft is mentioned as a sub-provincial unit with four districts (Sabzevārān, Jebāl Bārez, Sārduʾiya, and Kahnuj), with Sabzevārān (i.e., Jiroft) as its administrative center (Razmārā, pp. 95-96, 105-6, 227, 228-29, 343-44). In the administrative divisions of 1976, Jiroft was a sub-provincial unit, consisting of two districts in Kerman Province. In 1990, Jiroft sub-province, with the town of Jiroft as its center, consisted of four districts (Markazi, Jebāl-e Bārez, Sārduʾiya, and ʿAnbarābād) and twenty-two rural sub-districts (*Qawānin wa aḥkām*, 1991, pp. 832-33). In 1998, it included the towns of Jebāl-e Bārez and Darb-e Behešt in addition to 121 rural settlements (*ābādi*). In 2003, the district of ʿAnbarābād became recognized as a sub-provincial unit and separated from Jiroft (Wezārat-e kešvar, 2003, s.v. Ostān-e Kermān).

Jiroft dam (Sadd-e Jiroft). Jiroft or Halilrud Dam is built on Halilrud River (q.v.) at Narāb Gorge (Tang-e Narāb), at its junction with Narāb stream, about 45 km northwest of Jiroft. Jiroft Dam was the 5th concrete dam built in Iran. Construction began in 1975 and was completed in 1993 (Farhangi, p. 96). It is 134 m high and 250 m wide at the crest, with six spillways, a volume of 430 million cubic meters, and the power capacity of 30 megawatts. The lake, with an area of approximately 12 hectares, irrigates nearly 14,200 hectares of Jiroft's and approximately 4,500 hectares of Kohnuj farmlands (Farhangi, p. 96; Ṣafā, pp. 13-14; Niknafs Dehqāni, p. 8).

The town. The town of Jiroft, located approximately 248 km southeast of the city of Kerman at an elevation of 690 m above sea level, is the administrative center of Jiroft sub-province. Jiroft's climate is hot and dry, with the highest temperature of 47 C recorded in Mordād/July-August and the lowest of 2 C in Bahman/January-February. The average annual rainfall has been recorded at approximately 251 mm (Sāzmān-e havā-šenāsi-e kešvar, p. 454). It has an airport serving domestic flights, and is connected by a 282 km highway southwest to Bandar ʿAbbās (q.v.), by a 248 km highway northwest to Kerman city, and by a 95 km highway east to Zāhedān. The city is home to an oil factory and a cotton mill (Edāra-ye joḡrāfiāʾi-e arteš, CXV, p. 28; Niknafs Dehqāni, p. 9). Jiroft was designated as a city in 1951 (Wezārat-e Kešvar, 2003, s.v. Ostān-e Kermān). According to the 1996 national census, it had a population of 59,201 (Markaz-e āmār-e Irān, p. 81).

Jiroft was the center of Kerman Province when the latter was conquered by the invading Arab armies under Sohayl b. ʿAdi in 644, during the caliphate of ʿOmar b. al-Ḵaṭṭāb (Ṭabari, I/V, pp. 2703-705; tr, XXIV, pp, 73-74; Ebn al-Aṯir, pp. 43-44). Jiroft was once more taken during the caliphate of ʿOṯmān b. ʿAffān by the Arab forces under Mojāšeʿ b. Masʿud Solami, who was chasing fleeing Yazdegerd III (Balāḏori, pp. 391-92, tr., p. 147). The inhabitants of Jebāl-e Bārez, which separated the Jiroft area from the rest of Kerman in its northeast, remained Zoroastrian throughout the Omayyad period, converting to Islam towards the end of the 9th century under the Saffarids (Eṣṭaḵri, pp. 164-65, tr. pp. 164-65; Ebn Ḥawqal, p. 221, tr., II, p. 305; Ḥāfeẓ-e Abru, III, p. 20). During the first century of Islam, the region of Kerman, especially Jiroft, was considered a major center of the Kharejites. They were eventually defeated and chased out of the city in 696 by Moḥallab b. Abi Ṣofra Azdi (Ṭabari, II/II, p. 1003, tr., XXII, p. 150).

In the 9th century, Ebn Ḵordādbeh mentioned Jiroft as the largest city Kerman, located 20 leagues (*farsaḵ*) from Bam. In the 10th century, Jiroft was the center of a *kura* (a major administrative unit in a province) of the same name, very prosperous and pleasant, a center commerce with nice markets and clean bathhouses, and larger than Eṣṭaḵar in Fars. It had a fort with four gates (Šāpur, Bam, Sirjān, and Moṣallā). The Friday mosque was made with bricks and gypsum; it was located near the Bam Gate but far from the markets.

Jiroft was referred to as the city of contrasts. It produced fruits of both hot and cold climates, such as dates, walnuts, and citrus fruits. It had a rapid river, and auriferous sands (*ḵāk-e zar*) were found in its canals. Silver was carried to Jiroft from the mines of the area (Eṣṭaḵri, p. 166; Moqaddasi, pp. 461, 466; *Ḥodud al-ʿālem*, p. 126, tr., p. 124).

In the 19th century, Aḥmad-ʿAli Waziri Kermāni (1974, pp. 115, 117-18) described Jiroft as a rural district (*boluk*), with Dosāri as its center and a population of about 8,000 people. According to him, there was no area in the Jiroft district that could be considered a town at that time. The town was already in ruins when the Venetian traveler, Marco Polo (1254-1324) visited the area. He referred it by the name of Camadi, which Vasilĭ Barthold identified with the ruins near the village of Karimābād (Barthold, p. 141 and n. 46; Sykes, 1958, II, p. 105). Sir Percy Sykes mentions a cemetery in Jiroft dating to the 11th century and located the historical city of Jiroft opposite the Kuč plains, 10 km west of the present-day town (Sykes, 1902, pp. 144-45).

Apparently from early 14th century the city was known as Jiroft, center of the Jiroft rural district, which has sometimes been mentioned in sources as Sabzevārān (Kayhān, II, p. 251; Wezārat-e Kešvar, 1950, II, p. 251). Around 1951 Sabzevārān and other districts of Jiroft sub-province were considered the most arable regions of the Eighth Province (i.e., Kermān wa Makrān), where citrus fruits, dates, rice, and cereals were cultivated. Its citrus fruit and rice products were exported. The population of Sabzevārān was lower during the summer, due to the seasonal migration of the nomads, who moved to higher grounds to escape the intense heat (Razmārā, VIII, pp. 105, 228-29). During the middle of this century, particularly in 1962, drought and famine in Jiroft caused the deaths of many of its residents. Droughts still continue to plague the area (Ṣafā, pp. 138-39).

Bibliography: Ludwig Adamec, ed., *Historical Gazetteer of Iran* IV: *Zahedan and SouthEastern Iran*, Graz, 1988, pp. 212-13. Maʿṣuma Bādanj, "Jiroft," in *Dāneš-nāma-ye jahān-e Eslām* XI, Tehran, 2007, pp. 567-71. Abu'l-ʿAbbās Aḥmad b. Yaḥyā Balāḏori, *Ketāb fotuḥ al-boldān*, ed, Michaël de Goeje, Leiden, 1886, repr. Leiden, 1968; partly tr. Āḏartāš Āḏarnuš as *Fotuḥ al-boldān, bakš-e marbuṭ ba Irān*, 2nd ed., Tehran, 1985. Vasilĭ V. Barthold, *An Historical Geography of Iran*, tr. Svat Soucek, Princeton, 1984, pp., 137-38, 140-42. ʿAli Darvišzāda, *Zamin-šenāsi-e Irān*, Tehran, 2001. Ebn al-Aṯir, *al-Kāmel fi'l-taʾriḵ*, ed. C. J. Tornberg, 13 vols., Beirut, 1966. Ebn al-Ḥawqal, *Ketāb ṣurat al-arż*, ed. Johannes Hendrik Kramers, Leiden, 1967; tr. Johannes Hendrik Kramers and Gaston Wiet as *Configuration de la terre*, 2 vols., Beirut, 1964-65, II, pp. 302-7. Ebn Ḵordādbeh, *Ketāb al-masālek wa'l-mamālek*, ed., Michaël Jan De Goeje, Leiden, 1967. Edāra-ye joḡrāfiāʾi-e arteš, *Farhang-e joḡrāfiāʾi-e ābādihā-ye kešvar-e jomhuri-e eslāmi-e Irān* 139 vols., Tehran, 1978-, CXV: *Sabzvārān*. Abu ʿAbd-Allāh Šarif Edrisi, *Ketāb nozhat al-moštāq fi ekterāq al-āfāq*, ed. A. Bombaci et al., Opus Geographicum, Naples, 1970-, fasc. 4, pp. 433-34, 435, 437; tr. with comm. P.-A. Jaubert as *La Géographie d'Edrisi*, 2 vols., Paris, 1836-40; repr. Amsterdam, 1975. Abu Esḥāq Ebrāhim Eṣṭaḵri, *Ketāb masālek al-mamālek*, ed., Michaël Jan De Goeje, Leiden, 1967, pp. 165, 166-67; tr. Moḥammad b. Asʿad Tostari as *Masālek wa mamālek*, ed. Iraj Afšār, Tehran, 1974, pp. 165-71. Bižan Farhangi, *Negareš-i bar sadhā-ye Irān: goḏašta, ḥāl, āyanda*, Tehran, 1993. Firuz Mirzā Farmānfarmā, *Safar-nāma-ye Kermān wa Balučestān*, ed. Manṣura Etteḥādiya (Neẓām Māfi), Tehran, 1981. Ḥāfeẓ-e Abru, *Joḡrāfiā-ye Ḥafeẓ-e Abru*, ed. Ṣādeq Sajjādi, 3 vols., Tehran, 1996-99. ʿAbd-al-Rafiʿ Ḥaqiqat "Rafiʿ," *Farhang-e tāriḵi wa joḡrāfiāʾi-e šahrestānhā-ye Irān*, Tehran, 1997, pp. 186-88. *Ḥodud al-ʿālem*, ed. Manučehr Sotuda, Tehran, 1961; facs. ed. and tr. Vladimir Minorsky as *Ḥodud al-ʿālam: The Regions of the World*, 2nd ed., London, 1970. ʿAbbās Jaʿfari, *Gitāš-enāsi-e Irān*, I: *Kuhhā wa kuh-nāma-ye Irān*, Tehran, 1989; II: *Rudhā wa Rud-nāma-ye Irān*, Tehran, 1997. Masʿud Kayhān, *Joḡrāfiā-ye mofaṣṣal-e Irān*, 3 vols., Tehran, 1932-33, II, pp. 251-52. Guy Le Strange, *The Lands of the Eastern Caliphate* London 1905, repr., 1966, pp. 299, 314-15; tr. Maḥmud ʿErfān as *Sarzaminhā-ye ḵelāfat-e šarqi*, Tehran, 1958, pp. 336-37. Markaz-e āmār-e Irān, *Saršomāri-e ʿomumi-e nofus va maskan 1996: Natāyej-e tafṣili-e koll-e kešvar*, Tehran, 1997. Idem, *Saršomāri-e ejtemāʿi-eqteṣādi-e ʿašāyer-e kučanda 1998: Natāyej-e tafṣili-e koll-e kešvar*, Tehran, 1999. Abu ʿAbd-Allāh Moḥammad Moqaddasi, *Aḥsan al-taqāsim fi maʿrefat al-aqālim*, ed. Michaël Jan De Goeje, Leiden, 1906, repr., Leiden, 1967, pp. 468 ff. Eslām Niknafs Dehqāni, *Barrasi-e guyeš-e Jiroft wa Kohnuj*, Kerman, 1998. Moḥsen Purkermāni, "Padida-i az āṯār-e farʿi-e ātašfašāni dar nawāḥi-e aṭrāf-e Jiroft," *Taḥqiqāt-e joḡrāfiāʾi* 1, 1987, pp. 139-45. *Qawānin wa aḥkām: Majmuʿa-ye qawānin-e sāl-e 1316*, Tehran, n.d. Ḥosayn-ʿAli Razmārā, *Farhang-e jogrāfiāʾi-e Irān* VIII, Tehran, 1953, pp. 105-6. ʿAziz-Allāh Ṣafā, *Tāriḵ-e Jiroft wa Kohnuj*, Kerman, 1994. Sāzmān-e hawā-šenāsi-e kešvar, *Sāl-nāma-ye āmāri-e hawā-šenāsi 1996-97*, Tehran, 1999. Paul Schwarz, *Iran im Mittelalter nach den arabischen Geographen*, Leipzig, 1896-35; repr., 9 vols. in 4, Frankfurt on the Main, 1993, II, pp. 240 ff. Percy M. Sykes, *Ten Thousand Miles in Persia*, London, 1902, pp. 304-5. Idem, *A History of Persia*, 2 vols., London, 1958. Moḥammad b. Jarir Ṭabari, *Taʾriḵ al-rosol wa'l-moluk*, ed. Michaël Jan De Goeje et al., 16 vols., Leiden, 1964; tr. by various scholars as *The History of al-Ṭabari*, 40 vols., Albany, New York, 1985-2007. Aḥmad-ʿAli Waziri Kermāni, *Joḡrāfiā-ye Kermān*, ed. Moḥammad-Ebrāhim Bāstāni Pārizi, Tehran, 1974. Idem, *Tāriḵ-e Kermān*, ed. Moḥammad-Ebrāhim Bāstāni Pārizi, 2 vols., Tehran, 1985. Wezārat-e Kešvar, Edāra-ye koll-e āmār o ṯabt-e aḥwāl, *Ketāb-e joḡrāfiā wa asāmi-e dehāt-e kešvar* II, Tehran, 1950. Wezārat-e Kešvar, Moʿāwenat-e siāsi, Daftar-e taqsimāt-e kešvari, *Našriya-ye tāriḵ-e taʾsis-e ʿanāṣer-e taqsimāti ba hamrāh-e šomāra-ye maṣawwaāt-e ān*, Tehran, 2003.

(M. BADANJ and *EIr*.)

ii. HUMAN GEOGRAPHY AND ENVIRONMENT

Jiroft is the regional capital of the middle section of the Halil Rud (q.v.) valley, south of the Kerman Province in Iran. The Halil Rud valley, oriented northwest to south-east, 400 km long, takes its source in the Zagros mountain range north of Jiroft, and ends in the endorheic Jazmurian basin (Figure 1). Persian and Arab geographers called this river the Demon Stream (*Div Rud*). The works by Guy Le Strange (1854-1933) and Paul Schwarz (1867-1939) provide the main synthetic historical descriptions of the city and its surroundings. In the 10th century C.E., Ebn Ḥawqal (d. after 973?) described Jiroft as a large and important city, covering two miles from one end to the other. The town had a fortified wall, and was closed by the four gates Bāb Šāpur, Bāb Bam, Bāb Sirjan, and Bāb al-Moṣallā. His contemporary Moqaddasi (Miquel) added that at that time Jiroft was larger than the city of Eṣṭaḵr (q.v.) and its houses were mostly built of clay bricks on stone foundations. Waterpower was used to operate 20 to 50 mill wheels. Moḥammad b. Ebrāhim (early 17th century) mentions in his Saljuq chronicle that during the 12th century Qamādin was "a place at the gate of Jiroft where foreign merchants from Rûm (Greece) and Hind had their warehouses and where travellers by sea and land could store their goods" (p. 48; cf. Le Strange, p. 314). Qamādin's shops were filled with "the precious goods from China, Transoxiana, and Khitây, from Hindustân and Khurâsân, from Zanzibâr, Abyssinia, and Egypt, also from Greece, Armenia, Mesopotamia, and Adharbâyjan" (Moḥammad b. Ebrāhim, p. 49). Marco Polo (1254-1324) referred to the Persian Qamādin as Camadi, or even the city of Camadi. According to Moḥammad b. Ebrāhim (p. 83), Qamādi had been a great and noble place, but

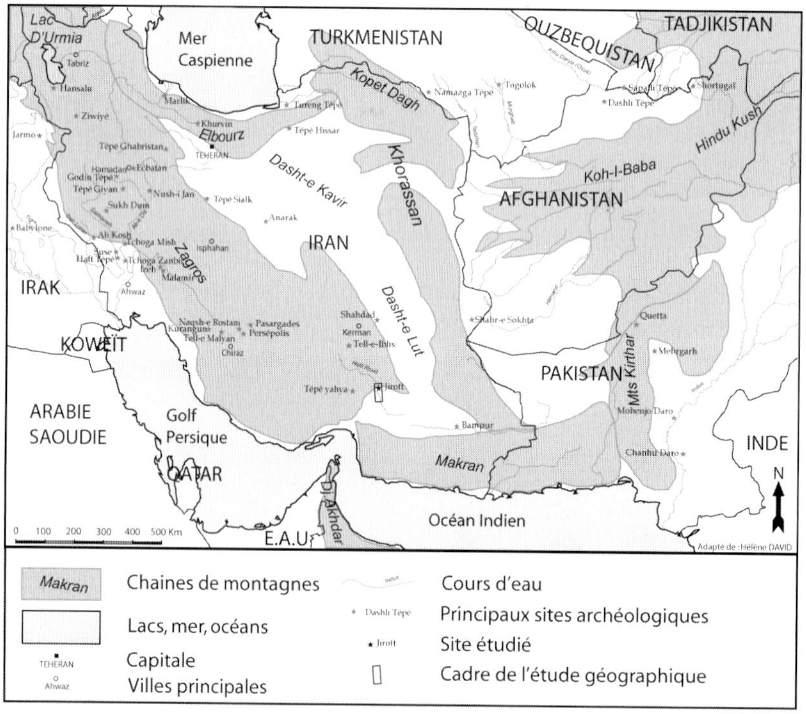

Figure 1. Map of Iran. Courtesy of the author.

already Marco Polo (I, p. 98) saw a city "of little consequence, for the Tartars in their incursions have several times ravaged it." This may explain why both Jiroft and Qamādin disappeared from history after the end of the 13th century C.E., and their names no longer appeared on maps. The vestiges of Jiroft are still visible north of modern Sabzevaran, which has by now recovered its original name of Jiroft.

In 2001, illegal excavation on necropolises, which had been uncovered by a flood of the Halil Rud, south of Jiroft, to the east of the village of Konar Sandal, provided an abundance of vases and chlorite artifacts. The region seems to have been a major centre of their production and distribution during the Bronze Age (q.v.) since the 3rd millennium B.C.E. (Pittman; Madjidzadeh). The Iranian Cultural Heritage and Tourism Organization (ICHO) organized a safeguard program, headed by H. Choubak, and entrusted to Professor Y. Madjidzadeh excavations on the sites of North Konar Sandal and South Konar Sandal. The archaeological project revealed the existence of an important cultural centre, dating back to the Bronze Age in the southeast of Iran that was contemporaneous with the great cities of Mesopotamia (Madjidzadeh; Perrot). Their location in a region reputed to be arid and tough raises the question of environmental constraints and their dynamics during the Holocene. Archeologists wonder to what degree the environmental conditions have been more or less favorable to the blossoming of the Halil Rud civilization, and whether the present archeological map of site distribution conforms to the ancient settlements. All archeological sites inventoried in the valley, including North and South Konar Sandal are located on an alluvial plain, a few meters above the flood plain.

Topography and climate. Between Jiroft and the entry to the Jazmurian basin, the average altitude of the valley bottom is 550 m. High mountains outline this valley: the Jebal Barez massif to the east peaks at almost 4000 m; the Sardouiyeh to the west reaches almost 3000 m, and Mount Hezar to the north has a summit of 4420 m. Downstream of Jiroft, two principal channels drain the alluvial plain, which is 7 km wide: the Halil Rud on the eastern edge and a drain that receives water from several wadis on the western edge and flows together with the Halil Rud in the south of the valley. The valley bottom and the mountain sides are connected through massive flat stretches of alluvial deposits (Pers. *dašt*; q.v.). They are 7 to 12 km wide, slightly inclined (1-1.5 degrees), and imposing torrential alluvial fans dominate their mountain sides. Small mountain chains, easily noticeable in the landscape (Figure 2), line the connection between the alluvial plain and the western *dašt*.

The available climatic data pertain to Kerman, the nearest city which is situated at an altitude of 1649 m and 150 km further north. At this altitude, the annual rainfall ranges from 168 to 203 mm total. Precipitations are concentrated between January and March, while the drought effectively lasts from April to November. The annual temperature averages between 16 and 17.5° C, with a maximum summer temperature of 43° C. The water management service of Jiroft estimates for the Halil Rud valley that the average annual precipitation is 375 mm in the mountains north of Jiroft and 125 mm in the south, in the Jazmurian depression. In other words, the Jiroft basin is situated in a transitional zone between the semi-arid to the north and the arid to the south, and the transitional zone is very sensitive to the consequences of climatic fluctuations. But the impact of the arid fluctuation between 2200 and 1900 B.C.E. is unclear (Roberts and Wright), even though this fluctuation is confirmed for all of the Middle East and Western Asia and seems to coincide with the end of occupancy of the Bronze Age settlements in the Jiroft basin.

Geology and mineral resources. The tectonic collision in the Zagros (Boulin; Alavi) and its subduction under the Makran (Byrn) led to the creation of the Jiroft basin as a combination of a right-slip fault system (Sabzevaran system to the west, Jiroft system to the East), which is positioned north to south with compressive relays from the east and west (Regard). This intermediary position between the systems of Zagros and Makran accounts for the lithological repartition that is visible in the catchment area (i.e., drainage area) of the Halil Rud. To the west, the massif is essentially composed of metamorphic rocks, such as shale, marble, and chlorite. Crystalline (i.e., diorites, granodiorites, granites) and volcanic (i.e., andesite, volcanic ashes) dominate in the east. In the southeast, one finds some limestone massifs. Touching the Jazmurian depression, a large flysch massif rests in discordance with a rhyolitic massif (Figure 2).

This geological context is crucial for understanding the distribution of mineral resources around the Jiroft basin. There is copper (q.v.) in the east, at Jebal Barez, zinc to the west, chlorite (q.v.) and locally gold (q.v.) in the southwest, while the pebbles of the Halil Rud and the *dašt*s offer in abundance a complete sampling of the lithology in the river's catchment area. All of these can be found within a maximum radius of 100 km around the sites of the Konar Sandal.

The natural hazards of seismic activity and flood. During the Holocene the morphogenesis in the Halil Rud valley is active, notably because of neotectonics and especially of the fluvial dynamic. The currently active tectonic dynamics have a strong seismicity as a corollary. The recorded earthquakes (Heydari) over the past 150 years show that the latter are highly concentrated in the Zagros range and characterized by a high frequency and an average magnitude of 4 on the Richter scale. In the Jiroft basin, six earthquakes have been observed, five of which had an epicentre along the Sabzevaran fault system. On the field, many indications indicate the Quaternary activity of these faults. First, the Sabzevaran geological map indicates an average lateral displacement of 3 to 3.5 mm per year and a maximum subsidence of 250 m during the Quaternay, which results in 0.1 mm per year. In his study of the Sabzevaran fault system further to the South, Regard notes the lateral displacement of the fault line at 3 mm per year. Tatar considers it as still active. On the field, the series of small massifs, caused by formations

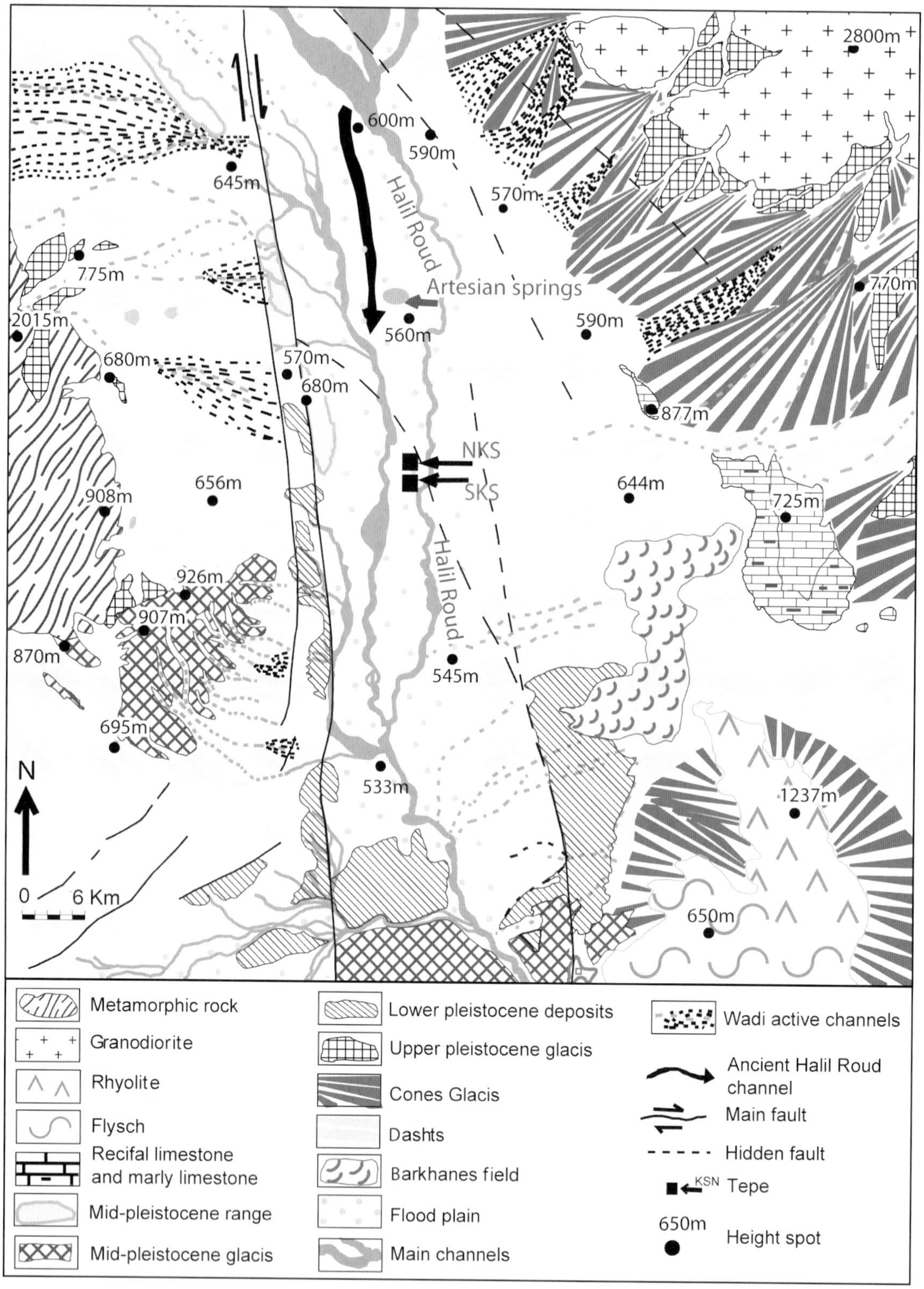

Figure 2. Geomorphological map of the Halil Rud valley. Courtesy of the author.

dating back to the ancient Quaternary that are regularly aligned along the Sabzevaran fault, allow for picturing the displacement.

The Halil Rud valley between Jiroft and the Jazmurian depression corresponds to a pull-apart graben in activity since the Plio-Miocene era. From the Eastern *dašt* two Cretaceous limestone massifs emerge. On the Quaternary scale, the sporadic torrential flash floods that characterize the wadis constitute the most efficient morphological agent. This is particularly true for the flood plains of the Halil Rud during the Holocene (Fouache).

The Halil Rud has the hydrological regime of a wadi: It is characterized by discontinuous and intermittent floods during the winter months, with a very high interannual variability. But the breadth of its catchment area, the presence of snow upstream, and the occurrence of major flash floods caused by precipitations of high intensity, which rarely last more than an hour but can be catastrophic, explain that the fluvial beds can be affected and abundant water resources are available on the plain. The data of the meteorological station at Bam provide estimates, such as the following: an intense rainfall of 64 mm per hour for a duration of 40 minutes is an event that occurs every 100 years; that a rainfall of 56 mm per hour lasting the same time occurs every 50 years; that 36 mm per hours corresponds to one rainfall every 10 years; and that a rainfall of 15 mm per hour occurs every 2 years. The examination of aerial photographs reveals an active, braided stream system that allows for charting with precision the channels and the flood plain of the Halil Rud (Figure 3). Below the terrace on which the archeological sites are located, at a maximum of 1 to 2 m above the flood plain, two levels with traces of stream, the flood plain itself and channels, are visible. The aerial photographs also reveal a paleo-channel, indicating that the Halil Rud overtook the western drain the before the river moved into its present channel at a still undetermined time. The latest large flood event that submerged the whole flood plain occurred in January 1992. The water table is very close to the surface at a depth of less than two meters locally. Naturally put under 8 bars of pressure, the water table even creates artesian wells that sprang naturally in the plain halfway between Jiroft and Konar Sandal until 2001, when they were caught for irrigation and for bottling as mineral water. The main characteristic of this water is an increasing salinity from the upstream towards the downstream, so that it ceases to be potable south of Konar Sandal. The high presence of gypsum in the Neogene formations explains this salinity. The salinitiy, in turn, explains the abundance of tamaris, a halophile species of trees commonly found in marshy areas.

If 4000 to 5000 years ago the seismicity constituted the same risk as today, it did not prevent the imposition of human developments, as witnessed by the recently uncovered archeological vestiges. The floods of the Halil Rud did not constitute a repulsive factor either. Since these societies were careful to settle on the high points of the alluvial terraces, floods may have even constituted a favorable element of human settlement.

A small Mesopotamia. During a major flood event, at the downstream of the Jiroft alluvial fan, the flood plain extends to a maximum width of 7 km, while the water level does not exceed 5 m. If a map of the archaeological sites is superimposed on a map of the Halil Rud flood plain (Figure 3), which indicate zones above water during major floods, they show a perfect correlation. It is equally puzzling to notice that at the time of the last major flood, which occurred in the valley in 1994, the inhabitants of the villages of Konar Sandal sought refuge on the tepe for three days, while at the downstream the water remained high for yet another ten days. Since the floods bring silt that renews the soil, while cleaning the soil saturated with salt, they have a doubly beneficial role. It is important that the date trees, which appear in abundance on the vases of Jiroft and today still form vast plantations, are perfectly adapted to these hydrological and edaphic conditions. The true advantage of this semi-arid region lies in an abundant water table, close to the surface and independent of short drought-cycles.

The presence of this water table explains the abundance of date trees, which were the possible mainstay of an original Neolithic development. Since the Middle Ages, all geographers and travelers mentioned that the valley was fertile and appeared as a small Mesopotamia. Ebn Ḥawkal described Jiroft's environs as a fruitful neighborhood where the crops of both hot and cold regions were grown. At that time the city's main exports were indigo, cardamom, sugar-candy, and *dušāb*, syrup made from grapes or dates, while the surrounding area produced dates, nuts, and oranges. Marco Polo's observations are similar. Today the construction of an irrigation system and green houses on the *dašt*s enrich the agricultural production with important cucumber and tomato harvests. Date trees may well be endemic to the area (Rossignol-Strick). Along the thalwegs, in the higher regions of the *dašt*s, some acacias, well adapted to drought, can be found. Grazing and anthropic pressure caused the forests long ago to disappear. They were already mythic at the time of Ḥamd-Allāh Mostawfi (ca. 1281-ca. 1344; q.v.) who mentioned that lion-haunted forests had originally surrounded the town (p. 140; tr. 139), though in his day there were just immense palm groves. Only shreds of juniper forest subsist at about 3000 m altitude.

It is not yet proven whether the present archeological map correctly reflects human settlement in the Jiroft valley during the Bronze Age because the lower parts of the archeological sites may have been damaged by floods or fossilized by alluvium. The geophysical study conducted at South Konar Sandal (Fouache) shows a major discontinuity between 4 and 10 m depth, which seems to correspond with the level of the first human settlement on this site. Although the age of this site is not yet determined, it is undoubtedly older than Bronze Age, because the Halil Rud river was running west of South Konar Sandal and the necropolis located between the sites of North and South Konar Sandal is today cut in two by the river's channels. But the large urban archeological sites, like those of South and North Konar Sandal, have most

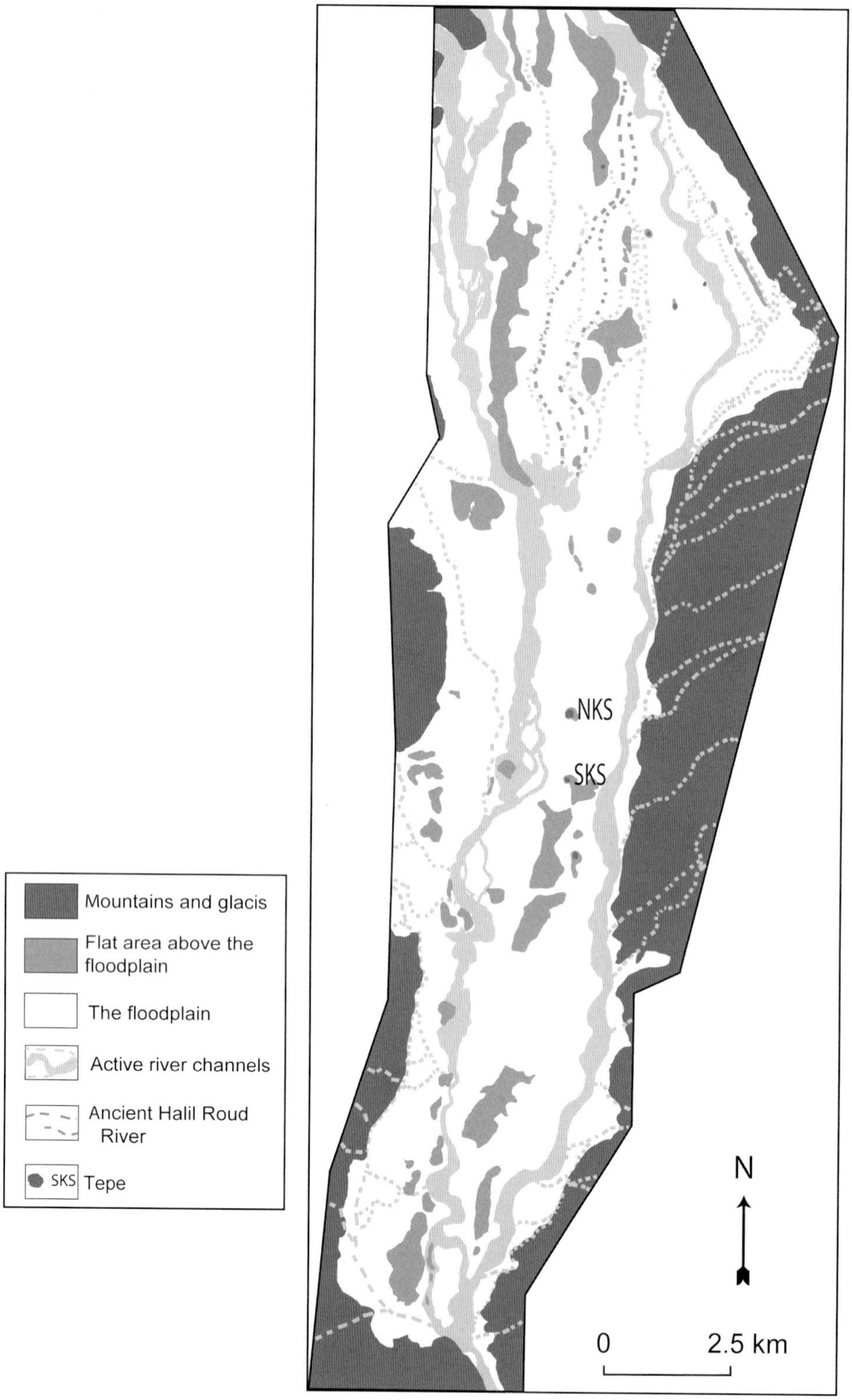

Figure 3. Map of the Halil Rud flood plain. Courtesy of the author.

certainly already subsisted in this landscape, though not in their full extension. The small rural sites, which are located in the flood plain, are buried under several meters of alluvium, probably 2 to 3 m covering.

Bibliography: Travel accounts: Ebn Ḥawqal, *Ketāb ṣurat al-arḍ*, ed. J. H. Kramers, BGA 2, 2nd ed., repr., Leiden, 1967. G. Le Strange, *Lands of the Eastern Caliphate: Mesopotamia, Persia, and Central Asia, from the Moslem Conquest to the Time of Timur*, Cambridge, 1905. Moḥammad b. Ebrāhim, *Histoire des Seljoucides du Kermán*, ed. M. Th. Houtsma, Recueil de texts relatifs à l'histoire des Seljoucides 1, Leiden, 1886. Ḥamd-Allāh Mostawfi, *The Geographical Part of the Nuzhat-al-Qulūb*, ed. G. Le Strange, Leiden, 1915; English tr. by G. Le Strange, Leiden, 1919. Moqaddasi, *Aḥsān al-taqāsim fi maʿrifat al-aqālim*, ed. M. J. de Goeje, BGA 3, repr., Leiden, 1967, pp. 461, 466, 470. M. Polo, *The Book of Ser Marco Polo, the Venetian, Concerning the Kingdoms and Marvels of the East*, tr. by Henry Yule, 3rd ed., 2 vols., London, 1903. P. Schwarz, *Iran im Mittelalter nach den arabischen Geographen*, 9 parts, Leipzig, 1896-Stuttgart, 1936, repr., Hildesheim, 1969; various repr., volume count differs.

Studies. M. Alavi, "Tectonics of the Zagros Orogenic Belt of Iran: New Data and Interpretation," *Tectonophysics* 229, 1994, pp. 211-38. J. Boulin, "Structures in Southwest Asia and Evolution of the eastern Tethys," *Tectonophysics* 196, 1991, pp. 211-68. D. E. Byrn et al. "Great Thrust Earthquakes and Aseismic Slip along the Plate Boundary of the Makran Sabduction Zone," *Journal of Geophysical Research* 97 (B1), 1992, pp. 449-78. E. Fouache et al., "Dynamiques géomorphologique dans la vallée de l'Halil Roud (Iran, région de Jiroft): Perspectives géoarchéologiques," *Paléorient* 31, no. 2, 2005, pp. 107-22. M. Heydari et al., "The Information of Bam Earthquake and its Aftershocks I (2004)," available on the internet: www.iiees.ac.ir/English/bank/Bam/Bam_report_english_aftershock.html (accessed May 23, 2007) A. Miquel, "al-Muḳaddasī," *EI*^{2}, VII, pp. 492-93. Y. Madjdzadeh, ed., "Jiroft: Fabuleuse découverte en Iran," special issue, *Dossiers d'Archéologie*, no. 287, Oct. 2003. J. Perrot, "Jiroft: Un nouveau regard sur les origines de la civilisation orientale," *Dossiers d'Archéologie*, no. 287, Oct. 2003, pp. 2-3. H. Pittman, "La culture de l'*Halil Roud*," *Dossiers d'Archéologie*, no. 287, Oct. 2003, pp. 78-87. N. Roberts and H. E. Wright, "Vegetational, Lake-Level, and Climatic History of the Near East and Southwest Asia," in *Global Climates since the Last Glacial Maximum*, ed. H. E. Wright, Minneapolis, 2003, pp. 194-220. V. Regard, *Variation temporelle et spatiale de la transition subduction-collision: Tectonique de la transition Zagros-Makran (Iran) et modélisation analogique*, Ph.D. diss., Université d'Aix-Marseille III, 2003; available as pdf-file on the internet: http://tel.archives-ouvertes.fr/tel-00003777 (accessed 20 April 2007). M. Rossignol-Strick, "Climat et végétation sur le plateau iranien à l'aube des temps historiques," *Dossier d'archéologie*, no. 287, Oct. 2003, pp. 5-17. M. Tatar et al., "The Present-Day Deformation of the Central Zagros from GPS Measurements," *Geophysical Research Letters* 29, no. 191/927, 2002, doi: 10.1029/2002GL015427.

(ERIC FOUACHE)

iii. GENERAL SURVEY OF EXCAVATIONS

For archeological accuracy the terms "Jiroft" or "Jiroft culture" employed to define a specific ancient Iranian culture and its artifacts should only be cited within quotation marks. All the artifacts known to date that are accorded the Jiroft label have not been excavated; they have in fact been plundered. The plundering seems to have occurred at half a dozen now destroyed cemeteries, none at the modern city of Jiroft in Kerman province in southern Iran, but at loci distanced ca. 28 to ca. 50 km to its south. A number of artifacts have been confiscated from interior thieves and smugglers by local and state authorities at several distant locations within Iran, including Jiroft itself, and others have been confiscated in Europe. In the past year a handful of artifacts have been mentioned as having been excavated by archeologists at tepes within the plundered area (below). Aside from their orphaned, unprovenienced situation, apparently deriving from multiple cemetery sites, all the material remains, baptized by their plunderers and purchasers as "Jiroft antiquities" and accorded the Jiroft cultural appellation both in the popular media and scholarly reports, are known solely from two venues. One is the published popular media reports of the police confiscations in Iran and Europe; the other is their presence in museum, dealer, and collector possessions in many countries, courtesy of the destroyers and smugglers. These facts together with the serious cultural implications involved in knowing and comprehending their apparent proveniences have been ignored (publicly) by archeologists, Iranian and international, and of course the media from the very beginning of modern archeological knowledge of the area.

The background to the recent developments and manifestation of the archeological and cultural term "Jiroft" has been recorded and discussed by Muscarella (2001 [2005]). Beginning in 2001 reports began to emanate from Iran via various Iranian Internet news and other Internet reports that major plundering activity was in progress in Jiroft, or that objects were being "unearthed in the old city of Jiroft . . . ." Soon thereafter countless Western Internet and other printed media outlets began to issue ongoing "reports," some copying Iranian news sources, others making observations directly from the Jiroft region, and all exclusively employing the Jiroft city label to identify artifacts encountered (in reality or from photographs) as well as their alleged locus. This now entrenched de facto archeological use of a city named Jiroft as the sole locus (provenience), as if a single plundered site was under review, was continued thereafter, relentlessly by the media (e.g., Covington, 2004; Lawler, 2004) and regularly by archeologists, for example, "le site de Jiroft" (Madjidzadeh, 2003b, p. 19), "vases [et] . . . 'monde' de

Jiroft," "cimetiéres de Jiroft" (Perrot, 2003, pp. 97, 110; Perrot and Madjidzadeh, 2004; idem, 2005). This contra-archeological solecism generated by scholarly usage continues, notwithstanding that within a couple of years it was determined by archeological surveys that the plundering indeed did not occur at or immediately adjacent to the city of Jiroft, but rather at some distance to its south, at about five or more ancient cemeteries. Perhaps to oppose the single usage "Jiroft" for the loci of the finds, some scholars refer to the area where they have surfaced as "the Jiroft" or "the Jiroft plain" (Lamberg-Karlovsky, 2004; Potts, 2005); the latter general term seems more viable.

Very few objectively determined facts about the "Jiroft culture" are known. One is that plundering did occur at cemeteries south of Jiroft, beginning at some time in 2001 and continuing for most of 2002. Another is that, beginning in 2002, confiscations by local authorities of plundered artifacts, primarily of chlorite, have been accomplished at various locations within Iran—Tehran, Jiroft, Bandar Abbas, etc., that is, in places up to 1,000 km apart; the objects are now deposited in Iranian institutions. But the exact, or approximate, number of confiscated objects remains unknown; undocumented sources (mostly but not solely reported in the media) claim hundreds, "100,000," "tens of thousands," "more than 2,000" or only 500 (Madjidzadeh, 2003b, p. 25; Perrot and Madjidzadeh, 2003, p. 1087). But no authoritative record or reports on the number have yet appeared. Related to these issues is that shortly thereafter scores of similar chlorite objects began to surface in the possession of the plunderers' sponsors, the antiquity dealers, collectors, and museum curators, trustees, and directors.

In as much as it was determined not to conduct excavations or salvage surveys of the plundered cemeteries, the critical issue regarding the number of graves plundered at each cemetery remains unknown to date. Further, specific archeological information no longer possible to determine has been irrevocably destroyed in the hectic plundering: the number and forms of the artifacts recovered from each burial; the nature of the burials, single or multiple; how many actually contained chlorite artifacts, and in what quantities; gender and rank determinations for the burials that contained or did not contain chlorite artifacts; and whether all the plundered cemeteries uniformly contained chlorite artifacts. Internet and media reports have brought forth various figures for the number of objects plundered in "the" cemetery (or cemeteries), from a modest "thousands," to "100,000," to "hundreds of thousands." We will never know (but the upper figures seem too high).

Collectively, many of the published confiscated artifacts share the same cultural and stylistic features (for photographs of a collection of the confiscated objects in Iran, see Madjidzadeh, 2003a; Muscarella, 2001 [2005]; Perrot and Madjidzadeh, 2005). They are thus generally identifiable, if not as "Jiroft" artifacts, as "style de Jiroft" (ibid., p. 135)—at least artifacts from Iran, most probably from the plundered cemeteries in the Kerman area, south of Jiroft. Other confiscated artifacts (both within Iran and surfacing abroad) have features characteristic of another style that is archeologically recorded in other areas of Iran, at Tepe Yahya, ca. 70-80 km northwest of Jiroft (many maps give this site a wrong placement), and from sites in Mesopotamia, Syria, the Gulf, and elsewhere. Archeologists know these as the "Intercultural Style." This dispersed corpus has been excavated in levels at sites attributed to the later phases of the Early Dynastic and to the following early Akkadian periods in Mesopotamian terminology. These cultures flourished in the second half of the third millennium B.C. and, based on disinterested archeological investigation, provide the chronological period in which the culture of the plundered "Jiroft" artifacts is to be realistically situated (Forest, 2003, pp. 131-32; Lamberg-Karlovsky, 2004, pp. 7-8; Amiet, 2002, pp. 95-96; Muscarella, 2001 [2005], pp. 178-79; Potts, 2005).

Not a minor event to be documented in the modern history of "Jiroft" is that, among both the artifacts confiscated within Iran itself and those surfacing and sold abroad, a number are most probably modern forgeries (Muscarella, 2001 [2005], pp. 181-89). In some cases this is recognized by other scholars of ancient Iranian cultures (e.g., Perrot and Madjidzadeh, 2006, pp. 147, 149). Some other objects seem questionable and raise doubts in our minds about their actual birth dates (Muscarella, 2001 [2005], pp. 189-97). Moreover, "Jiroft" forgeries continue to surface among the more recent examples confiscated within Iran itself, and on the Internet, as well as in dealers' possession abroad.

A major component of most "Jiroft" discussions and cultural interpretations, both within the scholarly community and repeatedly echoed by the media and Internet, is the assertion that the "Jiroft" artifact record patently documents a major development in early ancient Near Eastern history, one hitherto archeologically unrevealed. The confiscated artifacts are asserted to reveal not only the existence of a newly recognized, dynamic culture, but, more momentous, the discovery of a hitherto unknown major "civilization." Because of a decreed early chronology for the chlorite artifacts dating them to the late fourth millennium and the first half of the third millennium B.C.E. (Perrot, 2003, pp. 97, 111; Madjidzadeh in Perrot and Madjidzadeh, 2004, p. 1117), the "Jiroft" culture and its polity are proclaimed as historical reality to have preceded the emergence of Sumerian culture. Such a reversal of hitherto perceived interpretations about the nature of the initial diffusion of culture would indicate that the chlorite artifacts (also writing; see below) were exported from southern central Iran to Mesopotamia, and not in the other direction (Perrot and Madjidzadeh, 2006, p. 148). Together with these chronological and cultural assertions, Madjidzadeh has broadened the cultural and geographical issues by claiming that the area of Jiroft is undoubtedly the land of Aratta—a rich cultural center mentioned by the Sumerians and existing to their east, somewhere in Iran—and that Jiroft/Aratta was manifestly the source for the genesis of Sumerian culture.

These non-supportable, non-evidenced assertions are reported continuously, contrary to objective archeological and historical evidence that reference to Aratta occurs in the mid-third millennium B.C.E.

A number of scholars have indeed countered these unanchored pronouncements and firmly challenge them. They argue on the basis of objectively derived data surfacing from excavations that in reality the "Jiroft" artifacts reflect a thriving culture of the 2nd half of the third millennium B.C.E., one that flourished centuries later than the genesis of Sumerian culture. Therefore the "Jiroft" culture was contemporary with a much later phase of Sumerian cultural history (Amiet, 2002; Muscarella, 2001 [2005], Lamberg-Karlovsky, 2004; Covington, 2004, p. 11). To date nothing has changed as regards securing firm, objectively derived information about the plundered cemeteries and the confiscations of objects within Iran, and Internet news and web reports (often repetitious) continue to serve as the main (unverifiable) source for information about "Jiroft."

However, a recent and important opportunity for obtaining objective archeological data of the cultures in the area ca. 28 km south of Jiroft is the excavation of two near-by tepes, named Konar Sandal North and South, or A and B (Covington, 2004, p. 7; Perrot and Madjidzadeh, 2006, p. 125, fig. 2). Although the distance between the tepes is about 2 km (Covington, 2004, p. 7), they are sometimes referred to as if they constitute a single site (a repeat of the "Jiroft" syndrome). Directed by Y. Madjidzadeh, investigations began in 2003, and to date (2007) four campaigns have been completed. But other than a few quite brief, inadequate academic notes (Perrot and Madjidzadeh, 2003, 2004), not one site report providing data on each tepe's architecture and plans, stratigraphical levels, sections, pottery, and so forth, has been published. Nor has the cultural and cultural relationship between the two tepes been discussed and evaluated. Internet reports, Iranian News and others, along with two media reports (Lawler, 2004; Covington, 2004), present short, unconnected sketches or isolated photographs of some of the material recovered, accompanied by the director's cultural conclusions, none of which can be investigated and substantiated by archeologists. In these Internet reports, the term Jiroft is always given as the tepes' cultural attribution, and as the cultural label for all artifacts and writing said to have been recovered there. Sometimes material recovered from the two tepes is conflated, preventing scholars from relating them to a specific tepe locus and to a specific cultural period or phase.

Concerning architecture, for Konar Sandal North scattered references report a terrace upon a broader brick foundation ("haute terrasse . . . 132 m. de côte reposant sur un soubassement en briques 280 m. de côte": Perrot and Madjidzadeh, 2004, p. 1108). This is now identified (Covington, 2004, pp. 4, 7) as a ziggurat 400 x 400 meters, consisting of "four to five million bricks," and on the Internet is dated to 2300 B.C., "one to three centuries older than the most ancient Mesopotamian Ziggurat" (Cultural Heritage News Agency).

For Konar Sandal South, a complex is mentioned ("qui paraît mesurer 300 x 400 meters de côte") set on a platform, also a house (Perrot and Madjidzadeh, 2004, pp. 1114-17, fig. 11) and a fortress wall 10.5 meters thick (Madjidzadeh, 2003c, p. 72). From non-archeologist sources we are informed that a 14-room house was excavated (Lawler, 2004, p. 47) and that there is a two-storied citadel with windows (Covington, 2004, p. 7).

A small number of artifacts from these excavations have been reported, again mostly on the Internet, sometimes with the specific tepe source unmentioned. Fragments of chlorite artifacts are mentioned, all undecorated, as well as a chlorite plaque with an apparent spiral decoration in relief (Madjidzadeh, 2003c, p. 74, photo on p. 72; Perrot and Madjidzadeh, 2005, p. 149; ibid., 2006, p. 103, n. 26); seals and several hundred seal impressions (Covington, 2004, p. 2; Perrot, 2006, p. 108, n. 49); an unbaked mud relief of the lower part of a male, with his arms tied before his chest, from the South tepe ("unearthed in Jiroft"); and two soapstone reliefs depicting men with snake tails (25 x 17 cm); also shark bones and shells from the Gulf (Covington, 2004, p. 10).

One of the most potentially significant finds reported on the Internet from Konar Sandal—but to the Internet from the "excavations in Jiroft," "the Jiroft ancient site"—are a number of alleged inscriptions. It remains unclear how many inscriptions exist, where they were excavated, or if any in fact were recovered from one or both of the tepes. The Internet mentions two inscriptions discovered at Konar Sandal in 2005, but no contexts are mentioned. In the same source, Madjidzadeh is quoted as stating that they should be labeled Proto-Iranian, not Proto-Elamite. Further, two other inscriptions are said to have been recovered in a local farmer's backyard, 300 meters from one of the tepes in 2006, that is, they were not excavated; they measure 18 x 10 cm and 13.5 x 8.5 cm. One Internet-published alleged inscription is on a broken object labeled a brick (20.3 cm) and preserving parts of one and a half lines of indentations. It is proclaimed to be 300 years older than writing from Susa, which signifies to the excavator that the Elamites learned about writing from "Jiroft." Another is a broken but complete tablet alleged to derive from Konar Sandal B (Basello, 2006; no documentation for the source or size is provided); it consists of five lines of incised geometric indentations. Another alleged inscription (still unpublished but circulating among scholars) consists of four lines of geometric incisions (that look as if freshly incised). Not one of the published (not by Madjidzadeh but on the Internet) tablets and their indentations has any relationship with any known system of writing from any ancient culture (see Covington, 2004, p. 11).

Concomitant with the Konar Sandal tepe excavations, Madjidzadeh (2003b, p. 26) briefly mentioned excavations of several burials at two local cemeteries, Riganbar and Konar Sandal, but with no reference to their specific locations relative to the tepes or what was recovered. Only one has been published as a photograph (ibid., p. 25) that shows pottery vessels; it is a Bronze Age burial. An Internet report recorded that the bronze head of a goat "was found in the historical cemetery of Jiroft," a site that eludes us.

Such is the situation about the limited extent of archeological knowledge both of the plunder and the excavations at sites south of Jiroft up to 2007.

Bibliography: Pierre Amiet, review of Madjidzadeh, 2003a, in *Revue d'Assyriologie et d'Archéologie Orientale* 96/1, 2002, pp. 95-96. Gian Pietro Basello, "The Tablet from Konar Sandal B (Jiroft)," at www.elamit.net, accessed on 7 November 2006. Richard Covington, "What was Jiroft?" *Saudi Aramco World*, September/October 2004, pp. 2-11. Cultural Heritage News Agency, "Discovery of the Main Part of Kenar Sandal's Ziggurat," at "Latest Archaeological News from Iran," http://iranarch.blogspot.com/2006/02/discovery-of-main-part-of-kenar.html, accessed on 25 February 2006. Jean Daniel Forest, "La Mésopotamie et les échanges à longue distance aux IV et III millénaires," *Dossiers d'Archeologie*, no. 287, October 2003, pp. 126-34. C. C. Lamberg-Karlovsky, "New Centers of Complexity in the Iranian Bronze Age," *The Review of Archaeology*, Spring 2004, pp. 5-10. Andrew Lawler, "Rocking the Cradle," *Smithsonian*, May 2004, pp. 41-48. Yousef Madjidzadeh, *Jiroft: The Earliest Oriental Civilization*, Tehran, 2003a. Idem, "La découverte de Jiroft," *Dossiers d'Archeologie*, no. 287, October 2003b, pp. 19-26. Idem, "La premiére campagne de fouilles à Jiroft," *Dossiers d'Archeologie*, no. 287, October 2003c, pp. 65-75. Oscar White Muscarella: "Jiroft and 'Jiroft-Aratta'," *Bulletin of the Asia Institute* 15, 2001 (publ. 2005), pp. 173-98. Jean Perrot, "L'iconographie de Jiroft," *Dossiers d'Archeologie*, no. 287, October 2003, pp. 97-113. Jean Perrot and Youssef Madjidzadeh, "Découvertes récentes á Jiroft (sud du plateau Iranien)," *CRAIBL*, 2003, pp. 1087-1102. Idem, "Récentes découvertes à Jiroft (Iran): Résultats de la campagne de fouilles, 2004," *CRAIBL*, 2004, pp. 1105-20. Idem, "L'iconographie des vases et objets en chlorite de Jiroft (Iran)," *Paléorient* 31/2, 2005, pp. 123-52. Idem, "À travers l'ornamentation des vases et objets en chlorite de Jiroft," *Paléorient* 32/1:, 2006, pp. 99-112. Holly Pittman "La culture du Halil Roud," *Dossiers d'Archeologie*, no. 287, October 2003, pp. 78-87. D. T. Potts, "In the Beginning: Marhashi and the Origins of Magan's Ceramic Industry in the Third Millennium BC," *Arabian Archaeology and Epigraphy* 16/1, 2005, pp. 67-78.

(OSCAR WHITE MUSCARELLA)

iv. ICONOGRAPHY OF CHLORITE ARTIFACTS

In the region of Jiroft, a large number of stone (chlorite) vases and objects, carrying human and animal motifs inlaid with semi-precious stones, have recently been discovered. This discovery is of particular importance since little is known about the past of the region on the eve of historical times. However, the material has been collected from illegal excavations and has therefore, unfortunately, lost some of its scientific value.

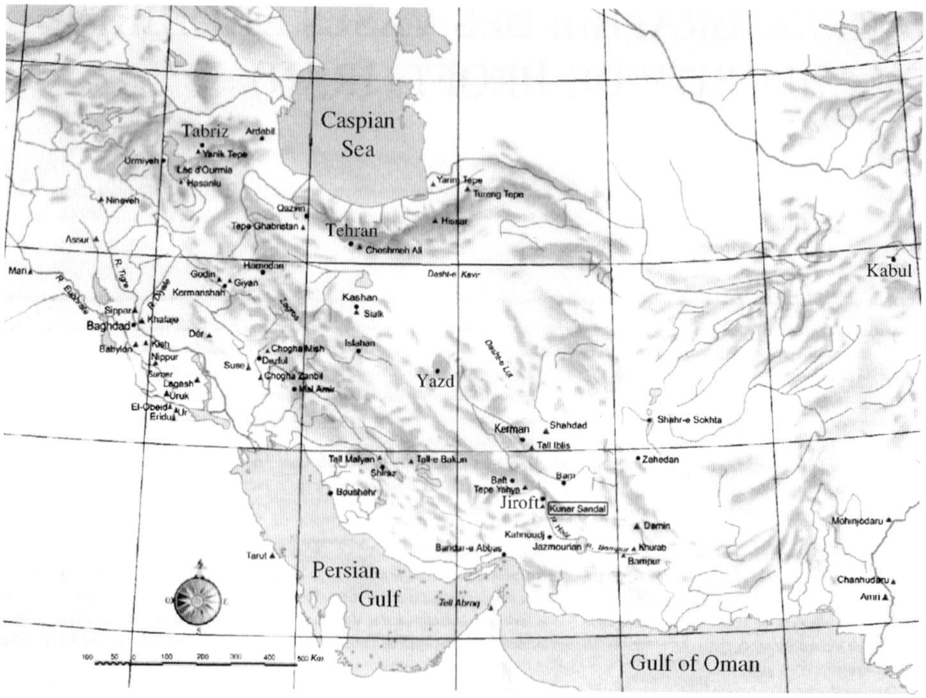

Figure 1. Jiroft, Konār Ṣandal and sites of the 3rd millennium B.C.E. with chlorite vessels.

In the first half of the 3rd millennium B.C.E., the Iranian plateau (fig. 1) was at the crossroads of trade with its neighboring regions. Many settlements are found along the trading routes used for the export of their productions, and this is the case for the Jiroft vases. The Iranian plateau, at that time, looked like a mosaic of cultural areas. To the north were the so-called "grey ware" area with Tureng Tepe in the Gorgān Plain leading to the present-day Turkmenistan, and Tepe Hissar (Ḥeṣār) to the south of the Alborz Range (q.v.); to the east, bordering the Helmand Basin, was Šahr-e Sukta, through which lapis lazuli from the Afghan mountains travels; and to the west lay Malyān (now a large mound ca. 45 km north of Shiraz), then the capital city of the Fars and the zone of contact with Mesopotamia via Susiana and Luristan. In the first half of the 3rd millennium, Fars appears as the development center of the first writing, called "proto-Elamite," which was soon used throughout Iranian plateau. In its southern part of Kerman, tablets have been identified 75 km away to the west of Jiroft at the small site of Tepe Yahya (Yaḥyā), located at about 130 km north of the Strait of Hormuz and the Persian Gulf.

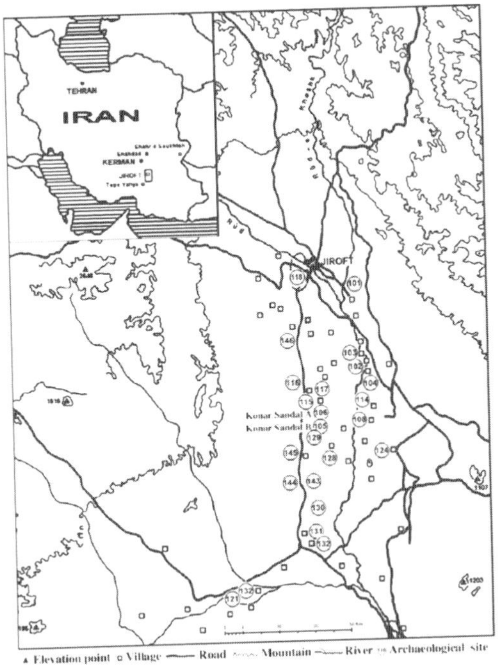

Figure 2. Konār Ṣandal North (105) and South (106), 28 km south of Jiroft.

The region of Jiroft, lying far away from the large centers of civilization, had not until now attracted the attention of researchers. It is located at a distance of 1000 km from the valley of the Euphrates in the west and from the Indus River in the east. Tepe Yahya and Shahdad (Šahdād), 200 km to the north-northeast of Kerman, were occupied at the end of the 3rd millennium and hint at a culture specific to the south of Iran. It is difficult, however, to imagine the population density and the high level of civilization that have been revealed by the current surveys and excavations conducted by Youssef Madjidzadeh on the site of Konār Ṣandal, located 28 km south of Jiroft (fig. 2). The site seems to have been occupied without interruption from the beginning to the end of the 3rd millennium. The settlement spreads over several thousand acres surrounded by a powerful crude brick fortification wall. In the second half of the 3rd millennium, a "citadel" and a high terrace of gigantic proportions were

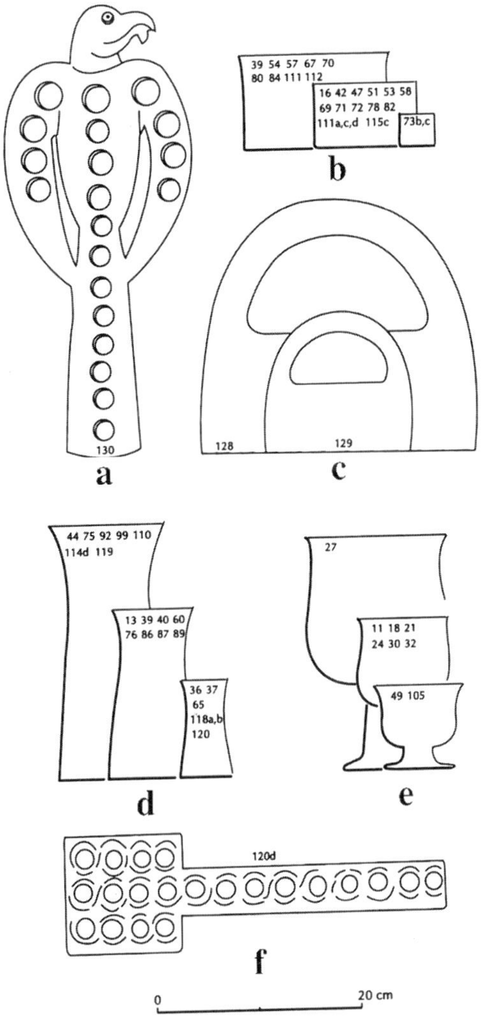

Figure 3. Relative scale of the types of vessels and artifacts; a and f: "gameboards"; b: small cylindrical vessels; c: "handbags"; d: high tronconical vessels; e: cups.

Figure 4. a-b: typical landscape of the Jiroft area and ornamentation of a chlorite vessel; c: candelabrum tree; d: bush; e-f: bushes and ibexes.

Figure 5. a-d: ibexes and bushes.

Figure 6. Zebus: a: details of decoration on a tronconical vessel; b: line of zebus led by a man; c-d lying zebus.

Figure 7. a-b: lions and palm trees; c: young lion and scorpion; d: fighting lionesses over the prey; e: lion and lionesses; f: zebus and lions.

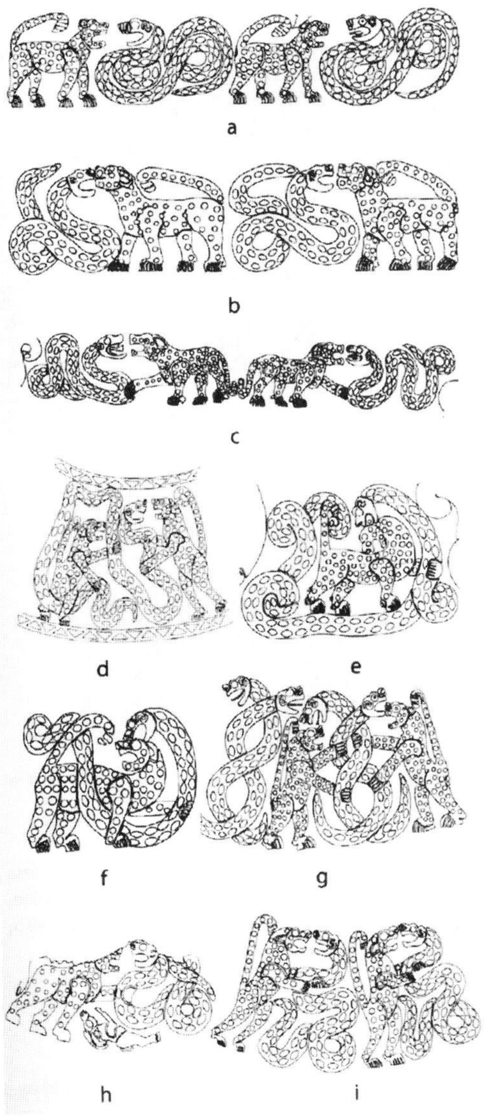

Figure 8. Cheetahs fighting snakes.

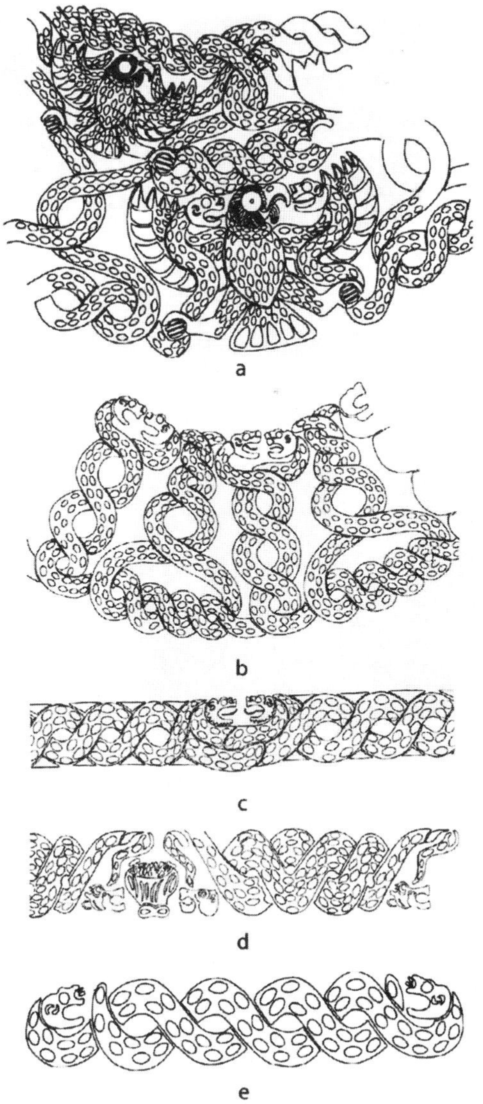

Figure 9. Eagles and snakes: a: two eagles and two snakes, on a tronconical vessel; b-e: intertwined snakes.

towering over it. These monuments rest on remains from the first half of the millennium. They are themselves contemporary of a vast cemetery that seems to have yielded at least a part of the chlorite vases and objects in the present collection.

The exceptional development of the Jiroft culture can be accounted for by the distinctive environment of the site, which is located in a deep depression, very different from the broad basins created on the plateau by the disappearance of large salt lakes (Dašt-e Kavir and Dašt-e Lut; see DESERT). The Jiroft depression is of tectonic origin and results from the subduction of the Arabian plate under the Persian plate. It is 400 km long and, like the folds of the Zagros range, it has a northwest-southeast orientation. The bottom of the depression is at an average height of 600 m, but it seems much deeper because of the steep snow-covered mountains that surround it, reaching their highest point at 4.400 m to the north. These mountains constitute a real water tower feeding the torrential Halilrud River and, in the alluvial plain, artesian wells whose gushing waters irrigate palm groves and gardens. Water collects at the center of the depression in the Jāz Muriān swamps. According to paleo-climatologists, these conditions were the same in the past and have remained

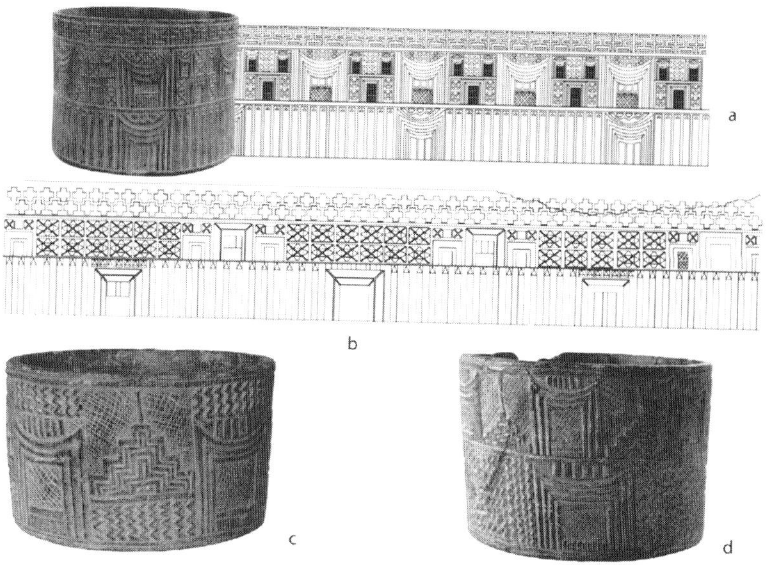

Figure 10. Architectural motives with gates and windows, on cylindrical vessels.

Figure 11. a: mountains landscape and waters; (upper part) a man under an arch with sun and crescent moon symbols; (lower part) man seated on his heels holding zebus; b: man holding a snake; c: two men (drinking) and zebus, on a small cylindrical vassel; d: head of woman protruding from a jar, and snakes; e: man falling from a tree to the trunk of which a zebu is tied; f: man with claws and bull-man playing with cheetahs, and a scorpion in the center (on a cylindrical vessel).

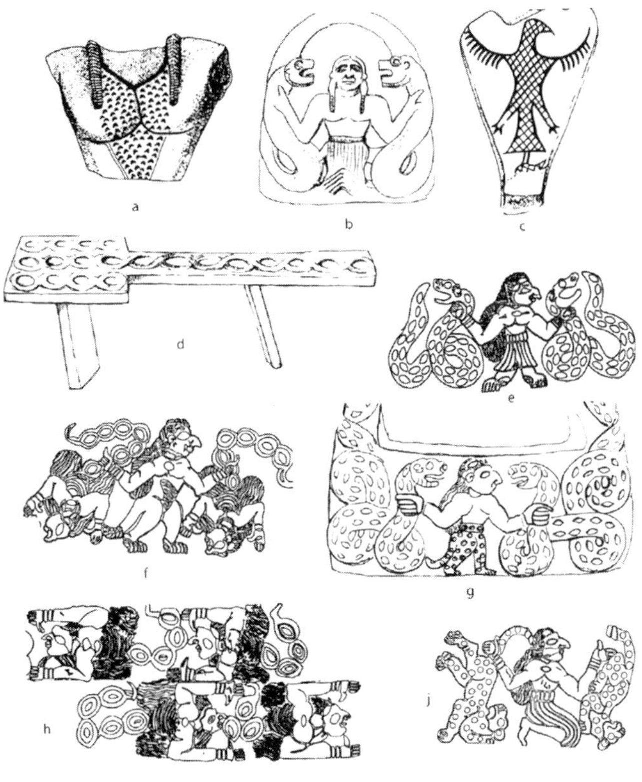

Figure 12. a-c: fragments from Tepe Yahya; d: "gameboard" on supporting tablets; e: man with claws holding two snakes; f: lion-man holding down two scorpion men; h: files of scorpion-man; j: man seated on his heels playing with cheetahs.

almost unchanged in the Northern Hemisphere since the 5th.millennium B.C.E. Another natural asset, also derived from tectonics, is the proximity of diversified mining resources, including copper and chlorite deposits as well as gold bearing lodes.

Chlorite is a soft and easy-to-work rock. It has been in use locally for a long time. Stone vessels are necessary for the long-time conservation of organic products. Given their weight, stone vases rarely exceed 25 cm in height. In smaller dimensions they might have contained aromatic plants and perfumes. They include cylindrical boxes (fig. 3b; PLATE If-h), cups (PLATES Ie, IVm-n), high open-rim vases (fig. 3d; PLATE IIa-e) and a few globular jars (PLATE IVh-k). Along these containers are found large (up to 40 cm), 3 to 4 cm thick indented plate with openwork designs (fig. 3a, c, f; PLATES IIf-k, IIIa-c). Some display a large ring-shaped handle and are reminiscent of the shape of a "handbag" (PLATE IIf-k; a name being more suitable than that of "handle-weight"; they are certainly not weights). Others are "game-boards" (often with twenty small cupules) resting on feet or vertical platelets (PLATE III); they often have the shape of an eagle with folded up wings.

Ornamentation. The figures come out with a slight flat or sculptured relief against a plain background. Technical variations, notably in the inlaying method of colored stones, point to the existence of several workshops. The purpose of inlays was to make the eyes expressive or render spots on the skin and on the coat of animals. Considering style, the aesthetic ratio of the whole is comparatively high; craftsmen endeavored to follow exactly models set by masters whose personality is revealed in some execution details, for instance, the drawing of hands. The ornamentation of certain pieces denotes a truly aesthetic delight. It is possible to speak of a "Jiroft style."

The motifs draw on the natural environment, including landscape, architecture, and vegetation. Plants occupy a relatively large space in the repertoire (Figure 4), and can be explained by the presence of the palm tree, the fruit and wood of which play a predominant role for food and construction. The ornamentation is mainly borrowed from the animal world, not domestic animals (ox, sheep, goat, etc.) but wild animals, among them those having horns, teeth, claws, beaks, talons, or venomous fangs. They include zebus, ibexes, lions, cheetahs, eagles, a small bird of prey, scorpions, and snakes. Man is also included (Figures 6, 11-12). The body is full-frontal, the head in profile, the arms half stretched and raised. He is beardless with long curly hair falling down his back and is either standing or sitting on his heels. He wears a short

PLATE I

Cups: a-b (h 14.5 cm ; diam 11.5 cm); c (h 17.5 cm; diam 12.2 cm); d (h 14.7 cm; diam 10.7 cm); e (h 16 cm; diam 12.3 cm). Cylindrical boxes : f (h 6.5 cm); g (h 10.5 cm; diam 16.5 cm); h (h 7.4 cm; diam 11 cm).

PLATE II

High tronconical vessels: a (h 14.6 cm); b (h 16 cm); c (h 27.8 cm); d (h 17.5 cm); e (h 19.7 cm). "Handbags": f-g (w 24 cm, thks 4.8 cm); h (w 19.5 cm; h 19.4 cm, thks 4 cm); j (w 28 cm ; h 25 cm, thks 3 cm); k (w 18.5, h 18.3 cm, thks 3.2).

PLATE III

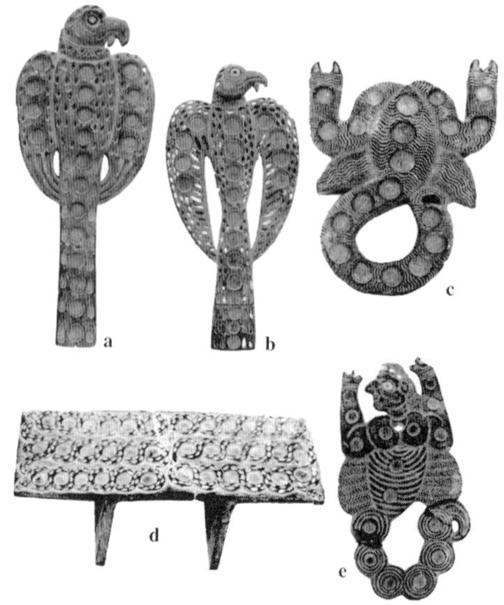

"Gameboards": a : eagle (l 41 cm); b: eagle (l 35 cm); c: scorpion (l 28 cm); d: table on legs (l 35 cm); e: scorpion-man (27 cm).

PLATE IV

Various: miniature vessels a-b: tronconical vessels, single-horned zebu (h 8.2 cm); c : buckles (h 9.3 cm); d: scorpions (h 7 cm); e: bricks and chevrons (h 5.7 cm); f: cylindrical boxes, zebus (h 5.2 cm); g: small gobular jar (h 9.4 cm); h: globular jar with buckles (h 9.4 cm); j: small globular jar with serpents (h 6.9 cm); k: globular jar with rosettes (h 7.5 cm); l: round boxes, buckles (h 6 cm); m: with mat (h 8 cm); n: small cylindrical vessel with scorpion (h 7.5 cm).

kilt tightened by a belt. In the presence of a potentially dangerous animal (e.g., a cheetah or a snake), this man is adorned with bracelets, a necklace supporting a turquoise pendent and wears a headband studded with many colored stones. These presumably magic protective elements may at times be limited to the insertion of one stone only due to shortage of space. They are, however, always shown, at least during the "classical" period of the style; their disappearance corresponds with a stage of technical, stylistic and thematic decline. Ornamentation also includes fantastic images, such as a single horned zebu (PLATE IVa-b), a two-headed eagle and, in particular, hybrid characters. There are human figures whose lower body may be that of a bovid (Figure 11f), a wild "cat" (claws only sometimes, Figure 11f), a scorpion and, in the case of a game-board (unpublished), a snake. Some geometric motifs (hatched triangles, bricks, scales, loops) are present as well. They are inspired by the vegetal world, basketry, architecture (Figure 10). In the latter case, the "gate" motif is often encountered.

Most of these elements are displayed alone or with a different motif, always derived from the same biotope. Animals of the same species are laid out in friezes, possibly designed to create a rhythm, a decorative effect, while snakes intertwine their coils. Miscellaneous elements appear in small narrative scenes like a man falling off a tree to which he has tied a raving zebu (Figure 11e). Animals of the same species are opposing or fighting each other; lionesses stand up against one another (Figure 7); two eagles with deployed wings holding two snakes in their claws (Figure 9a); a cheetah is engaged in an uncertain struggle against the reptile (Figure 8); a zebu gores a lion (the zebu seems to be then on the verge of domestication, Figure 7f). Wearing his protective attire, or as a hybrid figure, man seems to be playing with a cheetah (Figures 11f, 12j), but he maintains a distance from snakes (Figure 12e, g). Over a "hand-bag" (PLATE IIg) two-horned scorpion-men are in confrontation; on a small cylindrical vase, a lion-man brings down a scorpion-man in what could be a mythological battle (Figure 12f).

Significance. The interpretation of images is a risky enterprise. Decorative themes are transmitted, but they sometimes end up expressing an ideology that is different from the one that was initially symbolized. Images have a life of their own, and when they travel in space and time, their meaning may undergo a change. Our interpretations are a function of our culture and of our myths. Moreover, when dealing with the Middle East and its ancient spirituality, we tend to be content with notions found in late Mesopotamian literature, but such notions are anachronistic. Whatever the case, the iconography of the Iranian plateau should not be viewed through the prism of the Mesopotamian civilization.

In the same fashion as there is a certain logic between the containing and the contained in the ornamentation of vases, there may be another between that of an object and its end-use. Since the vases and objects of Jiroft are known to have come from tombs, their ornamentation may relate to funerary rites. This is what the bucolic scenes decorating the high cups suggest, where ibexes of all ages are harmoniously mixing with "blooming bushes" (fig. 5). Such scenes seem intended to alleviate the anguish of the passage leading to the world of the ancestors, especially when, as we may think, the representation of the ibex is loaded with totemic memories and when the plant regularly associated with it is the source of some psychotropic substance possessing the power to facilitate the crossing of the border of the sensorial world. Against a background of this sort, "hand-bags" and "game-boards" also occupy a place of their own. Some motifs of the repertoire, with a specific frequency regarding the motif of the "gate" probably associated with passage rites, are found on both sides of the "bags." The "game-boards" are instruments providing access to destiny, that of the dead as well as that of the living. Whether it relates to a funerary ritual or simply belongs to the deceased, the whole material conveys a way of thinking and an already very sophisticated cosmogony. Where a rite aims at obtaining an advantage, whether visible or invisible, we are nearing magic. When the fantastic, the imaginary are included in the ornamentation, we enter into the domain of the sacred, a blurred concept that will become clear in later historic ages.

The striking thing in the Jiroft iconography and cosmogony is the total absence of a reference to a concept of the divine. Hybrid figures mastering animals exist in the ancient Neolithic tradition, and are still evidenced at the turn of the 5th to the 4th millennium in Susiana, Iran. This heroic image of man stems from a profoundly human urge to dominate and transcend. The "master of animals" has never been worshipped and cannot be considered as a god. Whereas Mesopotamian glyptic art swarms with "deities" and characters engaged in cult-related hunting or war scenes, similar scenes are unknown at Jiroft. Whereas Mesopotamian, Sumerian, or Semitic cosmogony separates reality from a mysterious world inhabited by supernatural transcendent powers whose favor must be gained, Iranian cosmogony is sober and differently oriented. Two opposing principles arise from the Jiroft imagery: one is negative, with the scorpion and the snake, symbols of suffering and death; the other is positive, with the cheetah and the eagle engaged on the side of man against the reptile. It is clearly not be feasible to propose an interpretation of the Jiroft iconography before one can integrate it in the culture it stems from. It, however, seems possible to suggest the idea of a dualistic mode of thinking geared to human pursuits. This particular orientation bears the mark of the strongly contrasted natural environment of the Iranian-Indian plateau. Without falling into geographic determinism, account has to be taken of the extremely particular conditions that prevail in this vast region set against the Zagros Mountain range and turned toward the East and Central Asia. The landscapes may have left their mark on the life of the population, its language, writing, culture, and religion since the dawn of history.

Bibliography: Yusof Madjidzāda (Youssef Madjidzadeh), *Jiroft: kohantarin tamaddon-e Šarq*, Tehran,

2003. Idem, "Jiroft: un nouveau regard sur les origines de la civilisation orientale," *Dossiers d'Archéologie*, no. 287, Oct. 2003, pp. 2-3. Jean Perrot, "L'iconographie de Jiroft," *Dossiers d'archeologie*, no. 287, October 2003, pp. 97-113. Jean Perrot and Youssef Madjidzadeh, "Découvertes récentes á Jiroft (sud du plateau Iranien)," *Comptes-rendus de l'Academie des inscriptiones et belles-lettres*, 2003, pp. 1087-102. Idem, "Récentes découvertes à Jiroft (Iran): résultats de la campagne de fouilles, 2004," *Comptes-rendus de l'Academie des inscriptiones et belles-lettres*, 2004, pp. 1105-120. Idem, "L'iconographie des vases et objets en chlorite de Jiroft (Iran)," *Paléorient* 31/2, 2005, pp. 123-52. Idem, "À travers l'ornamentation des vases et objets en chlorite de Jiroft," *Paléorient* 32/1, 2006, pp. 99-112.

(JEAN PERROT)

JĪVAKAPUSTAKA, a medical text in Sanskrit and Khotanese belonging to the Indian Ayurvedic tradition. It is preserved in a single bilingual manuscript, incomplete and without colophon, that was recovered from the Caves of the Thousand Buddhas (Qianfodong) near Dunhuang (q.v.) in northwest China and is now kept in the British Library.

The manuscript, written in cursive Khotanese Brāhmī (q.v.) script, presumably dates from the 10th century and consists of 71 folios (ms. Ch. ii.003: facing Sanskrit and Khotanese in Bailey, *KT* I, pp. 136-95; facs. of fols. 44 and 64 in Hoernle, 1917, and of fols. 100r and 115r in Stein, 1921, pl. cl; complete facs. in Bailey, 1938, pp. 71-141; ed. of the Khotanese in Konow, 1941, with tr. and gloss.; cf. Emmerick, 1992, pp. 42-43; Meulenbeld, 1999-2002, IIA, p. 126, IIB, pp. 144-45; Skjærvø, 2002, p. 305). A. F. Rudolf Hoernle prepared a study on fols. 44-72r (secs. 1-25 according to Konow's numbering, partly published as Hoernle, 1917: see Emmerick, 1982), which he intended to publish under the title "An ancient medical manuscript from Eastern Turkestan" as the second volume of his *Manuscript Remains of Buddhist Literature Found in Eastern Turkestan* (Oxford, 1916): it is now kept in the India Office and Oriental Collections of the British Library as ms. Eur. D.723 (see Emmerick, 1992, p. 43, and 1997, and Skjærvø, 2002, p. xliv).

The work is an otherwise unknown collection of prescriptions taken from various texts and organized by type of preparation in complementary chapters, which are introduced by the Sanskrit auspicious formula *siddham* 'success', like most of the chapters of the Khotanese *Book of Zambasta* (q.v.). The first chapter is presented (sec. 2) as a teaching of the Buddha to the physician Jīvaka (who is called "the king of physicians" in the Late Khotanese *Mañjuśrīnairātmyāvatārasūtra*, l. 358), hence the conventional title "The book (Skt. *pustaka-*) of Jīvaka" invented by Bailey (*KT* I, p. vii). In the first chapter Sanskrit sentences alternate with Late Khotanese ones, while the other chapters alternate the two languages section by section. Chap. 1 (secs. 1-3; see Hoernle 1917, pp. 420-29, and Emmerick, 1992) contains an antidote (Khotanese *agada-* from Skt. *agada-*); chap. 2 (secs. 4-46; see Emmerick, 1994, for sec. 6 and Hoernle, 1917, pp. 429-32, for sec. 18) deals with drugs mixed with clarified butter (Khot. *gvīha'- rūna-* lit. "cow oil," Skt. *ghṛta-*); chap. 3 (secs. 47-73) with drugs mixed with sesame oil (Khot. *kūṃjsavīnaa- rūna-*, Skt. *taila-*); and chap. 4, which lacks the end (secs. 74-93, sec. 93 being partly extant only in Sanskrit), with powdered medicines (Khot. *cą̄ṇa-* from Skt. *cūrṇa-*). The Khotanese version is based on the corrupt Sanskrit, which the translator could not understand fully, as is indicated by translation mistakes (see Emmerick, 1979, p. 243). For each prescription, the instructions for the preparation are followed by indications on its use. Twenty-nine of the ninety-three prescriptions have been identified in several earlier Indian medical works, including Ravigupta's *Siddhasāra*, which is also extant in Khotanese (see Emmerick, 1979, pp. 235-37).

Bibliography: H. W. Bailey, *Codices Khotanenses: India Office Library Ch. ii 002, Ch. ii 003, Ch. 00274 Reproduced in Facsimile with an Introduction*, Copenhagen, 1938. Idem, *Khotanese Texts* [KT] I-VII, Cambridge, 1945-85 (several reprs. with corrections). R. E. Emmerick, "Contributions to the Study of the *Jīvakapustaka*," *BSOAS* 42, 1979, pp. 235-43. Idem, "Hoernle and the *Jīvaka-Pustaka*," *BSOAS* 45, 1982, p. 343. Idem, *A Guide to the Literature of Khotan*, 2nd ed., Tokyo, 1992. Idem, "The Svastika Antidote," *Journal of the European Āyurvedic Society* 2, 1992, pp. 60-81. Idem, "The Mahāsauvarcalādi Ghee," in *Memoriae munusculum: Gedenkband für Annemarie v. Gabain*, ed. K. Röhrborn and W. Veenker, Wiesbaden, 1994, pp. 29-42. Idem, "The Mahāsauvarcalādi Ghṛta in Hoernle's Unpublished Edition of the '*Jīvakapustaka*'," *Journal of the European Āyurvedic Society* 5, 1997, pp. 76-81. A. F. R. Hoernle, "An Ancient Medical Manuscript from Eastern Turkestan," in *Commemorative Essays Presented to Sir Ramkrishna Gopal Bhandarkar*, Poona, 1917, pp. 415-32. S. Konow, *A Medical Text in Khotanese: Ch. ii 003 of the India Office Library with Translation and Vocabulary*, Oslo, 1941. G. J. Meulenbeld, *A History of Indian Medical Literature*, Groningen, 1999-2002, 3 vols. in 5 pts. P. O. Skjærvø, *Khotanese Manuscripts from Chinese Turkestan in The British Library: A Complete Catalogue with Texts and Translations*, with contributions by U. Sims-Williams, Corpus Inscr. Iran. II/V/Texts VI, London, 2002. M. A. Stein, *Serindia: Detailed Report of Explorations in Central Asia and Westernmost China*, Oxford, 1921, 5 vols.

(MAURO MAGGI)

JIWĀM (Pahl. and Pers. *jīwām*, *jīw*, *jum*, *jām*), "(consecrated) milk," derives from Av. *jīuuiiąm*, *gąm jīuuiiąm*. It is the designation for one of the organic items—now a mixture of milk and consecrated water—used in the Yasna (q.v. at *iranica.com*), Vīsperad, and Vendīdād high or inner liturgical rituals of the Zoroastrians.

According to the Avestan text of the *Nērangestān* and its Pahlavi exegesis, mares, cows, ewes, and goats can be milked during the rite of the taking of *jīwām* (*N.* 2.49.13; Kotwal and Kreyenbroek, pp. 224-25). In Iran, the phrase *nērang jām griftan* or *nīrang jām gereftan*, "rite of taking (consecrated) milk" was used (Jamasp Asa and Nawabi, pp. 68-71). Some magian commentators like Sōshāns even included camels among the ranks of animals whose milk was acceptable for ritual purposes (*N.* 2.49.13), although other commentators such as Abarag (ibid.) ruled that such could be the case only if no other option was available. Both domesticated and wild variants of the animals could be milked, according to Dādweh (ibid.). *Jīwām* could be obtained from more than one animal at a time, with appropriate modification of ritual recitations—although such numerical variation in recitation was not accepted by all priests (see also Meherjirana, pp. 22-23; Anklesaria, pp. 4-5; Kotwal and Boyd, p. 71, n. 39). The animals and their milk should be healthy, free of pollution, and without blemish (*N.* 2.49.16; Kotwal and Kreyenbroek, pp. 226-27; Dhabhar, p. 410; Meherjirana, p. 42; Kotwal and Boyd, p. 70). The animals should be nurtured and tended in an affable manner (Meherjirana, p. 34; Kotwal and Boyd, p. 71, n. 40).

It is a long-cherished Parsi or Indian Zoroastrian tradition to milk only a single goat during the rite of taking *jīwām* (Meherjirana, pp. 22-23; Kotwal and Boyd, pp. 70-71). Milking of cows and other animals for *jīwām* is generally not permitted by Parsi magi, who view the centrality of the goat in this rite as "the custom of the ancients" (Meherjirana, p. 28). It has been recorded that Dastur Jamaspji Edalji Jamaspasa, a learned priest of Pune in India, had taken *jīwām* of a cow for the Yasna ceremony but that the senior priests protested on the grounds that established custom had been violated and declared the ceremony null and void. They also decreed that the retrograde priest and his associates should undergo a Barašnūm (see BARAŠNOM) purification before conducting any further high liturgies (Meherjirana, p. 28; Kotwal and Boyd, p. 71, n. 39). In Parsi praxis, only the goat to be milked can be present; other animals may not be there. Among the Zoroastrians of Iran, however, any number of goats and cows (one, two, or more) can be present—even though only one is milked during the rite—and so the personal pronouns vary, as the case may be, in the recital of the Avestan dedication (Modi, p. 279; Anklesaria, pp. 4-5; Kotwal and Boyd, p. 71, n. 39).

The rite of taking *jīwām* is a separate part of the prefatory service or *Paragṇā* (*N.* 2.49.14; Kotwal and Kreyenbroek, pp. 224-25; Westergaard, p. 333; Anklesaria, pp. 4-5; Modi, pp. 270, 278-79; Jamasp Asa and Nawabi, pp. 68-71; Kotwal and Boyd, pp. 70-72). According to the *Nērangestān* (2.58.1; Kotwal and Kreyenbroek, pp. 264-65; see also Modi p. 319), it originally was the *raēθβiš.kara* (Phl. *rehwiškar*) ritual priest's duty to mix the *jīwām* with the *haoma* (q.v., Pahl. and Pers. *hōm*) juice (now ephedra juice). It is also the duty of the *raēθβiš.kara* to distribute the libation or *zōhr*, prepared by mixing the *haoma* juice and the *jīwām*, among the devotees present at high liturgical rituals. So the rite of taking *jīwām* still is performed by the assistant priest or *rāspī* who, after acquiring ritual power or *ʿamal* through the performance of a Drōn (q.v.) service, goes to a separate ritual area or *pāwī* where the animal has been tethered. The animal is made to stand facing the east. The assistant priest faces south, holds a vase-like metal vessel or *karasyō* called the *jīwāmdān* or *jāmdān*, "place for (consecrated) milk," with consecrated water in his left hand, wipes the goat's udder to cleanse it (make it *sāf*), and then consecrates his right hand and the animal's udder by reciting *xšnaoθra ahurahe mazdå*, "(I do this) for Ahura Mazdā's satisfaction," and the *Aṣ̌əm Vohū* (q.v.) "order is good" prayer while pouring water over the hand and the udder. Next, the *rāspī* stands and recites the antiphonal framing utterance or *bāj* (q.v.) of *jīwām* including a dedicatory formula or *šnūman* (Av. *xšnūmaine*) to Druwāsp (Druuāspā, Drvāsp; see DRVĀSPĀ) who is the female worship-worthy spirit or *yazata* associated with horses, cattle, and goats (and so is also termed Gōš) (for the *šnūman*, see Westergaard, Fragment VI, p. 333). Thereafter, the assistant priest squats and milks the animal while saying the word *aṣ̌əm* "order." The first squirt lands on the ground, the next in the vessel while the *rāspī* recites *aṣ̌a.sara manaŋha* "with orderly thought." That sequence of milking is repeated twice more while reciting the phrases *aṣ̌a.sara vacaŋha* "with orderly speech" and *aṣ̌a.sara šiiaoθna* "with orderly action." The *rāspī* then stands up, pats the animal in thanks, and completes the *bāj* by reciting twice a blessing for all beneficial animals in which he wishes them *hazaŋrəm baēšazanąm baēuurə baēšazanąm*, "thousand-fold good health, ten thousand-fold good health." The assistant priest then returns to the *pāwī* where the high liturgical rituals are conducted and sets the vessel containing *jīwām* in a niche there.

The *jīwām* can then be used in the high liturgical rituals for which its presence is mandatory (Dhabhar, p. 400). During the Yasna ritual, for example, the *jīwām* must be poured into a saucer or *jīwām tašta* by the commencement of the third chapter of the Yasna liturgy both because it will be extolled and praised therein (*Yasna* 3.3), together with other consecrated items on the ritual table, and because the presence of *jīwām* is absolutely necessary from that point onward in the Yasna ritual (Anklesaria, p. 59; Dhabhar, p. 65; Kotwal and Boyd, p. 94; for depictions of *jīwām* on the ritual table, see Kotwal and Boyd, pp. 34-35, fig. 4, no. 13; 43, plate 3; 44, plate 4). The animal that provided the milk comes to be associated—as a symbol of beneficial animals and of those creatures' guardian spirit, the holy immortal or *aməṣ̌a spəṇta* (q.v.) Vohu Manah (Wahman, Bahman, q.v.)—with the ritual in which its product is utilized (on the homology, see Choksy, pp. 119, 126). Therefore, if the animal(s) providing *jīwām* die(s) while the ritual for which the milk was taken is in progress, that ritual is vitiated (Meherjirana, p. 34; Kotwal and Boyd, p. 71, n. 40). The rite of taking *jīwām* is practiced regularly among Parsis in India, but has become rare in Iran due to attenuation in orthopraxy from the 1970s onward. It is not practiced by Zoroastrians in any other countries.

Bibliography: Tahmuras D. Anklesaria, *Yazishne Bā Nirang*, 2nd ed., Bombay, 1926; repr., 1957. Jamsheed

K. Choksy, *Triumph Over Evil: Purity and Pollution in Zoroastrianism*, Austin, 1989. Bamanji N. Dhabhar, *The Persian Rivayats of Hormazyar Framarz and Others*, Bombay, 1932. Kaikhusroo M. Jamasp Asa and Mahyar Nawabi, *The Pahlavi Codices and Iranian Researches*, vol. 36, Shiraz, 1976. Firoze M. Kotwal and James W. Boyd, *A Persian Offering, the Yasna: A Zoroastrian High Liturgy*, Studia Iranica, Cahier 8, Paris, 1991. Firoze M. Kotwal and Philip G. Kreyenbroek, eds. and trans., *The Hērbedestān and Nērangestān, Vol. III: Nērangestān, Fragard 2*, Studia Iranica, Cahier 30, Paris, 2003. Erachji S. Meherjirana, *Pursesh-Pāsokh*, Bombay, 1941; repr., 2005. Jivanji J. Modi, *The Religious Ceremonies and Customs of the Parsees*, 2nd ed., Bombay, 1937; repr., 1986. Niels L. Westergaard, ed., *Zendavesta*, vol. 1, Copenhagen, 1852; repr., Wiesbaden, 1993.

(FIROZE M. KOTWAL and JAMSHEED K. CHOKSY)

JÑĀNOLKADHĀRAṆĪ, lit. "Spell of [the Buddha] Jñānolka," the name of a short Buddhist text of the Mahayanist tradition containing two magic spells (*dhāraṇī*, q.v.) aimed at the protection and deliverance of beings. The only remnants of the Sanskrit original were found in Khotan: a fragment (SHT 4369 = [Hoernle] 142 SC 164) has been identified by Klaus Wille (1996, pp. 390-92, with facs. on p. 405), and three tiny fragments of a single folio from another manuscript of the Sanskrit text with a Khotanese colophon (IOL Khot 195/8-9, 219/4) were published but not recognized by Prods O. Skjærvø (2002, pp. 436, 476). The complete text is known from two Chinese versions (*Taishō Issaikyō: The Tripitaka in Chinese*, ed. J. Takakusu, K. Watanabe and G. Ono, Tokyo, 1924-35, nos. 1397 and 1398), the first of which was translated by the Khotanese monk Devendraprajña (see Forte, 1979), and from a Tibetan translation (Kanjur; see *A Catalogue-Index of the Tibetan Buddhist Canons*, Sendai, 1934, nos. 522, 848, for the Derge ed.).

A virtually complete version of the text in archaizing Late Khotanese is known from thirteen folios and fragments from at least five manuscripts from Khotan. Ernst Leumann (1908, pp. 84-85, 104, and 1920, pp. 157-64) designated the three manuscripts knowm to him as $Jñ^1$, $Jñ^2$ and $Jñ^3$, while two further manuscripts were designated as $Jñ^4$ and $Jñ^5$ by Ronald E. Emmerick (1992, pp. 24-25). The whereabouts of $Jñ^3$ and $Jñ^5$ are unknown. Other fragments in Berlin and London may be referred to as $Jñ^B$ and $Jñ^L$ (see Bibliography). Yet another fragment (H. 144 NS 74: Bailey, 1963, p. 50; Skjærvø, 2002, p. 364, with tr.) contains a *dhāraṇī* which corresponds closely to the second one of the *Jñānolkadhāraṇī*, though the text preceding it differs (cf. Leumann, 1908, p. 85, and Wille, 1996, p. 391). Only the first folio of $Jñ^1$ is missing, but its contents can in part be supplemented by the beginning of $Jñ^4$, which corresponds to $Jñ^1$ [1v-]2v3. The other fragments correspond as follows: $Jñ^2$ = $Jñ^1$ 3r5-5v4; $Jñ^3$ = end of $Jñ^1$ + colophon; $Jñ^5$ = $Jñ^1$ 3r1-5r1; $Jñ^B$ = $Jñ^1$ 2r3-3r4, 5v1-6r2; $Jñ^L$ = $Jñ^1$ 5r-6r3 (side a is the reverse, side b the obverse). The Khotanese text does not agree closely with the Chinese and Tibetan versions according to Leumann (1920, pp. 157, 160-61), and the Khotanese manuscripts seem at times to be at variance among themselves, since $Jñ^4$ v6 and $Jñ^B$ r1 are without parallels in $Jñ^1$ and the wording of the obverse of $Jñ^L$ agrees with the Sanskrit but differs from the overlapping Khotanese manuscripts (e.g. *jaṃb[v]īyā hvąnḍ[ä]* "the men of Jaṃbudvīpa," Skt. *jāṃbudvīpakānāṃ manuṣyāṇ[ā]ṃ*).

Bibliography: Editions. $Jñ^1$ = SI P 3: ed. and tr. Leumann, 1920, pp. 157-63, and Emmerick and Vorob'ëva-Desjatovskaja, 1995, pp. 21-24, with facs. in Emmerick and Vorob'ëva-Desjatovskaja, 1993, pls. 2-6. $Jñ^2$ = H. 142 NS 81-82: Bailey, 1963, p. 105; variants listed by Leumann, 1920, p. 159; ed. and tr. Skjærvø, 2002, p. 349. $Jñ^3$ = a folio once in St. Petersburg: ed. and tr. of the colophon by Leumann, 1920, p. 157. $Jñ^4$ = H. 143 MBL 22: Bailey, 1963, pp. 36-37; ed. and tr. Skjærvø, 2002, p. 355. $Jñ^5$ = Ōtani 1-2: Bailey, 1963, pp. 313-14; facs. in *Seiiki kōku zufu* 2, 1915 (repr. 1972), and *Shin Seiiki-ki*, 1937. $Jñ^B$ = [Hoernle] 143 SC 31 and 185: ed. Skjærvø, 2002, p. 586. $Jñ^L$ = IOL Khot 204/6: ed. and tr. Skjærvø, 2002, p. 451.

Literature. H. W. Bailey, *Khotanese Texts* V, Cambridge, 1963; repr., 1980. R. E. Emmerick, *A Guide to the Literature of Khotan*, 2nd ed., Tokyo, 1992. Idem and M. I. Vorob'ëva-Desjatovskaja, *Saka Documents VII: The St. Petersburg Collections*, Corpus Inscr. Iran. II/V, London, 1993. Idem, *Saka Documents. Text Volume III: The St. Petersburg Collections*, Corpus Inscr. Iran. II/V, with contributions by H. Kumamoto et al., London, 1995. A. Forte, "Le moine khotanais Devendraprajña," *Bulletin de l'École Française d'Extrême-Orient* 66, 1979, pp. 289-97. E. Leumann, "Über die einheimischen Sprachen von Ostturkestan im frühern Mittelalter. Zweiter Teil: Von der arischen Textsprache," *ZDMG* 62, 1908, pp. 83-110. Idem, *Buddhistische Literatur nordarisch und deutsch* I: *Nebenstücke*, Leipzig, 1920; repr., Nendeln, 1966). P. O. Skjærvø, *Khotanese Manuscripts from Chinese Turkestan in The British Library: A Complete Catalogue with Texts and Translations*, with contributions by U. Sims-Williams, Corpus Inscr. Iran. II/V/Texts VI, London, 2002. K. Wille, "Die Hoernle-Fragmente in der Turfan-Sammlung (Berlin)," in *Turfan, Khotan und Dunhuang: Vorträge der Tagung 'Annemarie v. Gabain und die Turfanforschung', veranstaltet von der Berlin-Brandenburgischen Akademie der Wissenschaften in Berlin (9.-12.12.1994)*, ed. R. E. Emmerick et al., Berlin, 1996, pp. 385-408.

(MAURO MAGGI)

JOBBĀʾI, the name of two Muʿtazilite theologians, Abu ʿAli Moḥammad b. ʿAbd-al-Wahhāb (849-915) and his son Abu Hāšem ʿAbd-al-Salām (890-933).

Abu ʿAli was born in 849-50 in Jobbā in Khuzestan (for biographical details, see Gwynne, 1982, pp. 7-31). He came to Baṣra as a youth, presumably before 868, where he studied with Abu Yaʿqub Yusof b. ʿAbd-Allāh Šaḥḥām (ca. 800-71?), who is singled out as his most significant teacher. Šaḥḥām is said to have been "the youngest and most perfect" of the students of Abu'l-Hodayl al-ʿAllāf (ca. 752-841?; q.v.), and, according to later sources, the leadership of the Muʿtazilites fell to him after the death of Abu'l-Hodayl (ʿAbd-al-Jabbār, 1974, pp. 280-81; Ebn al-Mortażā, pp. 71-72). Abu ʿAli left Baṣra for Baghdad some time between 871 and 873. It is reported that Abu'l-Qāsem Balḵi Kaʿbi (q.v.), the leading Muʿtazilite in Khorasan, visited Abu ʿAli's salon (*majles*) for some time before 887, yet the anecdote of a meeting of Abu ʿAli and the heretic Muʿtazilite theologian Ebn al-Rāvandi (q.v.) is without foundation. Some time before 890 or 892, Abu ʿAli left Baghdad and took up residence in ʿAskar Mokram (q.v.) in Khuzestan, where he stayed for the rest of his life. In a mosque in ʿAskar Mokram, Abu ʿAli held public sessions that were open to the general public, and he held classes in which he taught his special students (Ḵošaym, p. 77). It was probably during these years that he met and debated with Abu'l-Qāsem Ḥāreṯ Warrāq in Suq al-Ahvāz (Ebn al-Nadim, pp. 218-19, tr. p. 425). Abu ʿAli died in Šaʿbān 303/Feburary-March 916.

Abu ʿAli had two children, a son, Abu Hāšem ʿAbd-al-Salām, and a daughter who is reported to have been well versed in Muʿtazilite doctrine and to have propagated its teachings among women (ʿAbd-al-Jabbār, 1974, p. 330; Ebn al-Mortażā, p. 109). Abu Hāšem was born 890 (Ḵošaym, p. 306), and, following his father's death in 916, he became the leader of the Baṣran Muʿtazilites. Abu Hāšem apparently spent most of his life in ʿAskar Mokram and in Baṣra (Ḵošaym, p. 310), and in 926-27 or 928-29, he took up residence in Baghdad (Ebn al-Nadim, p. 222, tr., p. 434), where he died in 933.

Works. Abu ʿAli authored numerous works, none of which, with the exception of the first volume of his *Ketāb al-maqālāt* (see Anṣāri), have survived. His oeuvre must have been enormous. Ebn al-Nadim's (d. 995) *Fehrest* is said to have contained a work list comprising seventy titles, yet the relevant portion is not preserved. The Muʿtazilite biographical (*ṭabaqāt*) literature does not provide any information on Abu ʿAli's writings. The most detailed information on his oeuvre is provided by the numerous scattered references in later works, particularly by Muʿtazilites (see Gimaret, 1976; idem, 1984). Apart from numerous independent works devoted to specific issues, responses to questions addressed to him by his students and to refutations, Abu ʿAli wrote a Qurʾān exegesis (Kohlberg, 1992b, p. 342), which was reportedly, together with the commentaries by Abu Bakr Aṣamm (d. 816), Abu'l-Qāsem Balḵi Kaʿbi (d. 931) and Abu Moslem Eṣfahāni (d. 934), among the most significant Muʿtazilite Qurʾān commentaries at that time. It was a massive work of more than 100 parts (*jozʾ*) that was unprecedented in comprehensiveness. Ebn Ṭāwus (d. 1266) offers very precise specifications when he quotes from Abu ʿAli's Qurʾān commentary (*tafsir*). According to Ebn Ṭāwus, it consisted of ten volumes (*mojalladāt*), each volume comprising two parts (*jozʾān*). Each part must have consisted of at least thirteen quires (*korrās*), which at the time comprised, as a rule, either eight or ten folios. Excerpts of Abu ʿAli's commentaries are to be found scattered among numerous later exegeses, most significantly in the *Tahḏib fi tafsir al-Qorʾān* of Ḥākem Jošami (d. 1101), Abu Jaʿfar Moḥammad Ṭusi's (d. 1067) *al-Tebyān fi tafsir al-Qorʾān*, Abu ʿAli Fażl b. Ḥasan Ṭabarsi's (d. ca. 1153) *Majmaʿ al-bayān fi tafsir al-Qorʾān*, and Faḵr-al-Din Moḥammad Rāzi's (d. 1209) *al-Tafsir al-kabir*. Further references to Abu ʿAli's Qurʾān commentary are to be found in ʿAbd-al-Jabbār Hamadāni's (d. 1025) *Motašābeh Qorʾān*, Moḥammad al-Šarif al-Rażi's (d. 1016) *Ḥaqāʾeq al-taʾwil fi motašābeh al-tanzil*, ʿAli b. Ḥosayn al-Šarif al-Mortażā's (d. 1045) *Amāli*, and ʿAli b. Musā b. Ṭāwus' (d. 1266) *Saʿd-al soʿud* (Gwynne, 1982; Kohlberg, 1992b, p. 342; Gimaret, 1994; Nabhā).

Ebn Ṭāwus accused Abu ʿAli of deficiencies in his knowledge of Arabic, and Abu'l-Ḥasan ʿAli Ašʿari (q.v.) states in his own Qurʾān commentary (of which only the introduction is preserved by Ebn ʿAsāker, p. 138) that Arabic was not Abu ʿAli's mother tongue and that he interpreted the Qurʾān in the spoken language of Jobbā. It was the latter's statement that induced some modern scholars (e.g., see Brockelmann, *GAL*, S I, p. 342) to conclude that Abu ʿAli's commentary was in fact a translation of the Qurʾān, either in the dialect spoken at Jobbā or into Turkish. These accusations, however, belong to the realm of polemics (Gimaret, 1994, pp. 32-35). Similarly without foundation is Ebn Ṭāwus' accusation that Abu ʿAli would neither have addressed any historical issues, be it stories of the prophets (*qeṣaṣ al-anbiāʾ*) or the circumstances leading to the revelation of a verse (*asbāb al-nozul*). The same applies to Ašʿari's and Ebn Ṭāwus' accusation that Abu ʿAli completely refrained from taking into account earlier Qurʾān commentaries (Kohlberg, 1992a; idem, 1992b, p. 342). It is from preserved quotations of Abu ʿAli's commentary that some indications as to his school affiliation in legal matters might be gleaned. In most cases, Abu ʿAli opted for Ḥanafi positions, although at times he prefers the view of the Shafiʿites or the Malikites (cf. Gimaret, 1994, pp. 40 ff.).

Abu Hāšem authored numerous works, none of which have survived. The early bio-bibliographical sources give different numbers as to the total number of his writings. Ebn al-Nadim (p. 222, tr. I, p. 434) mentions a list of ten titles, whereas according to Malaṭi (p. 40), Abu Hāšem had authored 160 works in debates (*fi'l-jadal*). The bio-bibliographical notice by Šehāb-al-Din ʿAbd-Allāh Yāqut on Abu Hāšem (s.v. ʿAbd-al-Salām) is presumably among the lost parts of the book. The Muʿtazilite biographical (*ṭabaqāt*) literature does not contain any information on Abu Hāšem's writings. The most detailed information on his writings is provided by the numerous scattered references in later Muʿtazilite works (for references, see the worklist by Gimaret, 1976; idem, 1984). He composed a number of theological summa-type works, the most important among them were apparently *al-Abwāb* (or: *Naqż al-abwāb*), *al-Jāmeʿ* (or *al-Jāmeʿ al-kabir*), and *al-Jāmeʿ al-ṣaḡir*, upon which ʿAbd-al-Jabbār wrote a commentary (ʿAbd-al-Jabbār, 1960-69, IX, p. 69), numerous independent treatises devoted to specific theological issues, responses, and refutations.

Doctrine. Abu ʿAli played a crucial role in the development of Muʿtazilite doctrine formulating a refined theological framework that served as the doctrinal basis for the Basran school of the Muʿtazilites. His theological views apparently underwent some modifications during his life. Since, with the exception of his *Maqālāt*, none of Abu ʿAli's writings are known to be extant, his doctrine can only be learned through the scattered references in later works, particularly those by later Muʿtazilites as well as the *Maqālāt al-eslāmiyin* of his former student Abu'l-Ḥasan Ašʿari. Abu ʿAli saw himself in the tradition of the ideas of Abu'l-Hoḏayl al-ʿAllāf, whose doctrines he set out to revive and to refine, thereby formulating a comprehensive theological system, yet not without disagreeing with Abu'l-Hoḏayl's views regarding a number of issues; he is known to have composed a treatise entitled *Masāʾel al-ḵelāf ʿalā Abi'l-Hoḏayl*.

Abu Hāšem disagreed with his father on a number of doctrinal issues, with regard to which he formulated his own views. The differences of opinion between the two were apparently dealt with by ʿAbd-al-Jabbār in his *al-Ḵelāf bayn al-šayḵayn*, which is lost. He developed the notion of states (*ḥāl*, pl. *aḥwāl*) as an attempt to create a conceptual framework for analysing the ontological quality of God's attributes and their relation to His essence within the established Muʿtazilite view of divine attributes. For this purpose, Abu Hāšem adapted the concept of state employed by the grammarians for a complement in the case of the accusative occurring in a sentence that consists of a subject and a form of *kāna* (to be) as a complete verb. In this case, the accusative cannot simply be taken as a predicate to *kāna* as it would be if *kāna* were incomplete and transitive; it must rather be understood as a *ḥāl*. On this foundation, Abu Hāšem elaborated a system of five different categories of states which he applied to both God and man. These categories are distinguished by the different ontological basis, which brings forth their actuality. According to Abu Hāšem, a state is not an entity or a thing (*ḏāt*, *šayʾ*) and can thus neither be said to be existent (*mawjud*) nor non-existent (*maʿdum*). Not being entities themselves, the states can likewise not be known in isolation. Rather, the essence is known to be qualified through them. Thus, Abu Hāšem speaks of the actuality (*ḥoṣul*) of the states and their initiation (*tajaddod*), while he refrains from asserting for them a coming to be (*ḥoduṯ*) that would imply their coming into existence (Frank, 1978; idem, 1980; Gimaret, 1970; Alami).

The first category is the attribute of essence (*ṣefat ḏātiya*, *ṣefat al-ḏāt*, *ṣefat al-nafs*) through which the essences (*ḏawāt*) differ from each other. The atom (*jawhar*), for instance, is described as an atom not through its essence but through its attribute of essence. The same applies to God, who does not differ from other essences through His mere essence, but rather through His attribute of essence. The second category of states are the essential attributes (*ṣefāt moqtażāt ʿan ṣefat al-ḏāt*), which are by necessity entailed by the attribute of essence as soon as it becomes existent. The attribute of essence of being an atom that is attached to an essence entails the spatiality of the atom whenever it exists. Thus, occupying a space is an essential attribute of an atom. In regard to God, the specific divine quality of His attribute of essence entails His essential attributes. These are His being powerful, knowing, living, and existing. Thus, God must necessarily and eternally be described by these attributes, which cannot cease as long as His eternal attribute of essence lasts. Man's attributes of being powerful, knowing, and living differ in their quality from the corresponding attributes in God. They belong to the third category of states which gain actuality through an entitative determinant (*maʿnā*) or cause (*ʿella*) in the subject. Thus, the qualification of these attributes in man differs from the corresponding attributes in God. Since man's states are caused by entitative determinants, he cannot be described as permanently or necessarily powerful, knowing, etc. Moreover, since these determinants inhere in parts of man's body, he needs his limbs as tools for his actions and his heart in order to know. The determinant itself is therefore not sufficient to actualize man's being powerful and knowing. Further conditions like the health of heart and limbs have to be fulfilled for them to serve as tools in carrying out actions. Thus, the realms of man's power and knowledge are limited by the natural deficiencies of his body. God, in contrast, is unconditionally powerful and knowing since His attributes of being powerful and knowing are essential attributes which do not inhere in any locus and, thus, do not require any limbs. Yet, Abu Hāšem applied this category to God when he reportedly asserted that God is willing or disapproving through a determinant that is His will or His disapproval. Since it is impossible that a determinant may inhere in God, he maintained that God is willing or disapproving through a determinant which does not inhere in a substrate (*lā fi maḥall*).

The fourth category of states are those which are actualized by the action of an agent (*be'l-fāʿel*), in particular the existence of a temporal thing which is founded in its producer's capability. This category is inadmissible in God. While the existence of all created beings is considered as belonging to this category, God's existence is counted as an essential attribute entailed by His attribute of essence. The fifth category are states which gain actuality neither by virtue of the essence nor by an entitative determinant (*lā le'l-ḏāt wa-lā le-maʿnā*). To this category belongs the attribute of "being perceiving" (*kawnohu modrekan*), which is entailed by the perceiver's being living. In regard to God, it gains actuality when the condition (*šarṭ*) of the presence of the perceptible is fulfilled. Man, in order to perceive, must possess healthy senses in addition to the existence of the perceptible. This is not required for God, whose being alive is an essential attribute. Thus, He perceives without senses.

Abu Hāšem reportedly further differed from Abu ʿAli on the issue of how God knows things in their state of non-existence and existence. Abu ʿAli taught that things are not things prior to their being existent since existence (*kawn*) means being found (*wojud*). Yet, a thing may be called a thing and may be known prior to its existence insofar as it is possible to make a statement about it (Ašʿari, pp. 161-62). Owing to his notion of states, Abu Hāšem was not confronted with the issue of whether a thing may be known prior to its existence. The attribute of essence, through which it is what it is, is always attached to it, regardless of whether the thing exists or not (Schmidtke, pp. 197-98, n. 137).

Abu Hāšem is further reported to have differed from his father when arguing that it is good to inflict pain even on the mere supposition that the pain is deserved, as in many cases in which blaming is considered good, the blame is in fact based on supposition rather than knowledge (Heemskerk, pp. 136-37). Abu ʿAli held, by contrast, that supposition cannot take the place of knowledge with respect to deserved pain. He is reported, however, to have made an exception for blame, considering it good to blame someone on the supposition that the person deserved to be blamed. He reportedly explained that this act of blaming is good, not because of the blaming person's supposition (*ẓann*) but because of the benefit that the blamed person derives from the blame; it may prevent him from committing the offence for which he, perhaps undeservingly, has been blamed (Heemskerk, pp. 136-37).

In regard to whether God may inflict illnesses or other calamities upon men because they are deserved, Abu ʿAli held that illnesses inflicted upon infidels and sinners may serve either as a punishment or a trial. This punishment could, in his view, be appropriate in so far as God would render to man there and then some of the punishment he deserves in the hereafter. Abu Hāšem, in contrast, maintained that every illness inflicted by God on men, regardless of whether they are morally obliged or not, can only have the purpose of a trial and never of a deserved punishment. He supported this view by pointing to the principal difference between undeserved pains and deserved punishment: men must be content with their illnesses and bear them patiently, and they are not allowed to be distressed about them just as in regard to favors that God bestows on them. This is, however, not necessary in regard to pains which are a deserved punishment. Owing to these different characteristics, man would therefore be unable to recognize whether a specific illness or calamity is inflicted upon him as a trial or as a deserved punishment. Thus, Abu Hāšem concluded that illnesses can be inflicted by God only for the purpose of trial (ʿAbd-al-Jabbār, 1960-69, XIII, pp. 431 ff.). Abu ʿAli is further reported to have maintained that God may inflict pain upon man for the sake of mere compensation (Mānkdim Šašdiv, p. 493). In arguing against his father's position, Abu Hāšem had reportedly admitted that pain ceases to be unjust when it is compensated. Even with compensation, however, it would by itself still be futile (*ʿabaṯ*) and thus evil is inadmissible for God. Pain inflicted by God thus must result in some kind of benefit (*maṣlaḥa*) in addition to compensation (Mānkdim Šašdiv, p. 493).

On the issue of the nature of passing away and restoration (*fanāʾ wa-eʿāda*), Abu Hāšem had to assert the possibility of passing away without infringing two other vital notions of his teachings. One of these was that all atoms (*jawāher*) and most accidents (*aʿrāż*) endure by themselves. The second notion which he had to take into consideration was that an agent may effect only production (*ijād*) but not annihilation (*eʿdām*). This also applies to God. Thus, He can undo something only through the creation of its opposite. The solution of Abu Hāšem, therefore, was that God causes the passing away of the atoms through the creation of a single accident of passing away (*fanāʾ*). This accident is the opposite of all atoms and, thus, is capable of annihilating any atom. It must itself be existent (*mawjud*), but it cannot inhere in a substrate (*lā fi maḥall*). Furthermore, it does not endure. Most of the points of this concept had been introduced already by Abu ʿAli, but Abu Hāšem disagreed with his father on a number of details. Abu ʿAli is reported to have maintained in his earlier works that there are different types of passing away, each of which causes the annihilation of only the corresponding type of atoms. He is also reported to have revised his position in a later version of his *Naqż al-tāj*, stating that only one passing away is required for all atoms, and that is why the atoms will in fact pass away. Abu Hāšem and his followers disagreed. If it were not for scriptural evidence, there would be no indication that the passing away will actually occur. Abu ʿAli further rejected on principle that anything which does not subsist in a substrate may be defined as an accident. Thus he refrained from classifying passing away as an accident. Abu Hāšem and his school admitted a category of accidents which do not inhere in a substrate (Schmidtke, pp. 211-22).

On the issue of mutual cancellation (*taḥāboṭ*) of man's acts of obedience and disobedience upon which a person's fate in the hereafter is founded, Abu Hāšem disagreed with Abu ʿAli about how this cancellation works. While the latter maintained that the smaller amont of reward or punishment will simply be cancelled by the larger amount, Abu Hāšem adhered to the principle of *mowāzana*, which means that the smaller amount will be deduced from the larger (Mānkdim Šašdiv, pp. 627 ff.).

Abu Hāšem furthermore disagreed with his father whether, and on what grounds, repentance is incumbent upon man for all his sins. Abu ʿAli reportedly held that a sinner is always, by virtue of reason and scriptural evidence, obliged to repent for major and minor sins. Abu Hāšem, on the other hand, considered repentance as obligatory only for the grave sinner (*ṣāḥeb al-kabira*). In respect to minor sins, he denied that repentance is rationally obligatory and held that scriptural authority also does not definitely indicate this obligation. He compared repentance for a minor sin with a supererogatory act (*nāfela*), which is not obligatory in itself. It is, however, good to perform it, since it helps man to perform his duties or, in this case, to repent for his major sins (ʿAbd al-Jabbār, 1960-69, XIV, pp. 393-94). Abu Hāšem is further reported to have held that it is impossible to repent of some sins while still carrying on with others when the penitent is aware of the evil nature of the acts which he is persisting. He reportedly argued that man repents because of the evil nature of the major sin in question. Since the characteristic of evil is shared by all major sins it would be inadmissible that one repents only of some major sins because of their evil, while carrying on with others that are of the same gravity. With this position, Abu Hāšem disagreed with Abu ʿAli who admitted the possibility of repenting of some sins while carrying on with others. The only condition set by Abu ʿAli was that the sin repented and that which was continued must not be of the same kind (*jens*). It would, therefore, be impossible to repent of drinking wine from one pot, while continuing to drink from another, whereas it would be possible to repent of drinking wine, while at the same time carrying on with adultery (Mānkdim Šašdiv, pp. 794-95).

Influence. Apart from his son Abu Hāšem, who was rejected by a number of former followers of his father as his successor, Abu ʿAli had many students. It was apparently Abu ʿAli's student Moḥammad b. ʿOmar Ṣaymari (d. 927) who led the group of the adversaries of Abu Hāšem. This group later became known as the Ek̲šidiya, so called after the name of a student of Ṣaymari, Abu Bakr Aḥmad b. ʿAli b. Maʿjur Ek̲šid (or Ek̲šād; d. 932 or 937). Another famous student of Abu ʿAli was Abu'l-Ḥasan ʿAli Ašʿari (873-935), who, around the year 912-13, repented from Muʿtazilite doctrines; the earliest report about his conversion is given by Ebn al-Nadim, according to whom, Ašʿari's publicly renounced his affilliation with the Muʿtazilites in the congregational mosque of Baṣra on a Friday, but without indicating any reasons or motives on his side. (Ebn al-Nadim, p. 231, tr., pp. 450-51). Later Ašʿari sources relate that Abu ʿAli and his former student Ašʿari engaged in public debates prior to the latter's conversion from Muʿtazilitism around 912, in the course of which Abu ʿAli was defeated which induced Ašʿari to abandon Muʿtazilism; those reports are certainly later inventions designed to inflate the reputation of Ašʿari (cf. Allard, 1965, pp. 37-46; Gwynne, 1985). Other students of Abu ʿAli were ʿAbd-Allāh b. ʿAbbās Rāmahormozi; Abu ʿOmar Saʿid b. Moḥammad Bāheli (d. 912-13); Ebn Abi ʿAllān; Abu'l-Qāsim Ḥāreṯ Warrāq; Abu'l-Qāsem ʿAli Tanuk̲i; Abu ʿAbd-Allāh Wāseṭi; Abu'l-Ḥasan ʿAli b. Farzawayh; Ebn Ḥarb Tostari; Abu Aḥmad ʿAskari ʿAbdaki; Abu'l-Ḥasan Esfarāʾini; Abu ʿAbd-al-Raḥmān Ṣaydalāni; Abu'l-Ḥosayn Ḥosayni; and the three Khorasanis Abu'l-Fażl Kašši, Abu'l-Fażl K̲ojandi, and Abu Saʿid Ošrusani (Heemskerk, pp. 21 ff.).

Among the students of Abu Hāšem mention should be made of Abu ʿAli Moḥammad b. K̲allād (d. 961 ?), Abu ʿAbd-Allāh Baṣri (d. 902 or 905 or 920-79), Abu Esḥāq Ebrāhim b. ʿAyyāš Baṣri, Abu Bakr Bok̲āri, Abu'l-Ḥosayn K̲awāʾefi Bag̲dādi, Abu'l-Ḥasan Farzawi (who formerly had been a student of Abu ʿAli), Abu'l-Qāsem Sirāfi (initially a follower of the Ek̲šidiya), Abu ʿOmrān Sirāfi (who later on became a follower of the Ek̲šidiya), Abu'l-Ḥosayn Azraq, Abu Moḥammad ʿAbdaki, Abu'l-Ḥasan b. Najiḥ (who was also a student of Abu Esḥāq b. ʿAyyāš). It is not clear who succeeded Abu Hāšem as leader of the Bahšamiya following Abu Hāšem's death. ʿAbd-al-Jabbār reports that a group of well-advanced disciples (*motaqaddemun*) transmitted the Muʿtazilite knowledge that they had received from Abu Hāšem, but he mentions by name only Abu ʿAli b. K̲allād and Abu ʿAbd-Allāh Baṣri. By contrast, Ebn al-Mortażā and Abu Moḥammad Esmāʿil Farrazādi mention only one authority to have transmitted knowledge from Abu Hāšem, but they differ on his identification. Ebn al-Mortażā indicates the chain of transmission as: Abu Hāšem and his generation, Abu Esḥāq b. ʿAyyāš, Abu ʿAbd-Allāh Baṣri, and ʿAbd-al-Jabbār Hamadāni (ca. 932-1025). The chain of transmission, according to Farrazādi, was: Abu Hāšem, Ebn K̲allād, Abu ʿAbd-Allāh Baṣri, ʿAbd-al-Jabbār, Abu Rašid Nisāburi (before 970-after 1029), Abu Moḥammad Ḥasan b. Aḥmad b. Mattawayh, Moḥammad b. Mazdak, and Farrazād̲i (Gimaret, 1979, pp. 60 ff.).

It can be surmised that, some years after Abu Hāšem's death, Abu ʿAbd-Allāh became the leader of the Bahšamiya, who in turn was succeeded after his death by ʿAbd-al-Jabbār Hamad̲āni. The latter's successor as leader of the Bahšamiya was Abu Rašid Nisāburi, who in turn was followed by Ebn Mattawayh (Heemskerk, pp. 29 ff.). One of the disciples of ʿAbd-al-Jabbār, Abu'l-Ḥosayn Baṣri (d. 1044), disagreed with his teacher on a number of doctrinal points and later became known as the founder of his own school.

The doctrines of the Bahšamiya were very influential among a number of groups outside Sunni Islam, namely the Zaydiya and the Imamiya, as well as among the Jews, the Karaites, and to a lesser degree, the Rabbanites. Numerous Zaydi scholars were students of representatives of the Bahšamiya, such as the brothers Emām Aḥmad b. Ḥosayn Moʾayyad Be'llāh (d. 1020) and Abu Ṭāleb Nāṭeq (d. ca. 1033), who studied with Abu ʿAbd-Allāh Baṣri and, in the case of Moʾayyad Be'llāh, also with ʿAbd-al-Jabbār, as well as Mānkdim Šašdiw, who was a student of Moʾayyad Be'llāh, and possibly also of ʿAbd-al-Jabbār. During the 11th century, the theological thought of the Caspian Zaydis reached the Zaydis in Yemen, who strove systematically to copy and collect Muʿtazilite, preferably Bahšami, texts. Mention should be made in particular of Imām al-Manṣur Be'llāh ʿAbd-Allāh b. Ḥamza (d. 1217), who founded a library in Ẓafār that was the founding stone of the Motawakiliya, the library of the Great Mosque in Sanʿāʾ. It was from this library that the Egyptian scientific expedition, headed by K̲alil Yaḥyā Nāmi, in 1951 procured microfilms of numerous theological texts of adherents of the Bahšamiya, such as 14 out of 20 volumes of ʿAbd-al-Jabbār's *Mog̲ni*, Mānkdim's critical paraphrase (*taʿliq*) of ʿAbd-al-Jabbār's *Šarḥ al-oṣul al-k̲amsa*, several works by Abu Rašid Nisāburi, Ebn Mattawayh's critical paraphrase (*taʿliq*) of ʿAbd-al-Jabbār's *al-Moḥiṭ fi'l-taklif*, entitled *al-Majmuʿ fi'l-monḥiṭ be'l-taklif*, and his *al-Tad̲kera fi aḥkām al-jawāher wa'l-aʿrāż*. Among the Imamis, mention should be made in particular of al-Sharif al-Mortażā (967-1044), who was a student of ʿAbd-al-Jabbār and who introduced Bahšami doctrine into Twelver Shiʿism (Madelung, 1970, pp. 25 ff.). On the long run, however, the influence of the doctrines of Abu'l-Ḥosayn Baṣri exceeded that of the Bahšamiya by far among the Imamis. The doctrines of the Bahšamis furthermore significantly influenced Jewish thinkers. This holds true for some representatives of the Rabbanites, such as Samuel Ben Ḥofni (d. 1013; see Sklare, 1996), and on a significantly larger scale for the Karaites. The most prominent representative of this current was Yusof Baṣir (d. after 1040; Sklare, 1995; Sklare and Ben-Shammai). Moreover, as was the case with the Zaydis, the Karaites systematically copied Muʿtazilite writings, partly in Hebrew script and partly in Arabic script. One of the very rich, though so far virtually untapped, sources for Bahšami texts in particular, is the Abraham Firkovitch-collection in the Russian National Library of St. Petersburg. It has rich holdings of copies of Bahšami texts produced by the Karaites between the 11th and 13th centuries, part of which was not found in Yemen, such as some further portions of ʿAbd-al-Jabbār's *Moḡni* as well as the latter's *al-Muḥiṭ be'l-taklif* (Borisov; Ben-Shammai; Schmidtke, 2007).

Bibliography: ʿAbd-al-Jabbār b. Aḥmad Hamadāni, "Fażl al-eʿtizāl wa-ṭabaqāt al-Moʿtazila wa-mobāyanatehem le-sāʾer al-mukālefin," in idem, *Fażl al-eʿtezāl wa-ṭabaqāt al-Moʿtazela*, ed. Foʾād Sayyid, Tunis, 1974, pp. 136-350. Idem, *al-Moḡni fi abwāb al-tawḥid wa'l-ʿadl*, ed. Moḥammad Moṣṭafā Ḥelmi et al., 14 vols. in 16, Cairo, 1960-69. Abu Rašid Saʿid b. Moḥammad Nišāburi [attributed to], *Fi'l-tawḥid* [*Diwān al-oṣul* ?], ed. Moḥammad ʿAbd-al-Hādi Abu Rida, Cairo, 1969. Idem, *Ketāb al-masāʾel fi'l-kelāf bayn al-Baṣriyyin wa'l-Baḡdādiyyin: Al-kalām fi'l-jawāher*, ed. Arthur Biram as *Die atomistische Substanzenlehre aus dem Buch der Streitfragen zwischen Basrensern und Bagdadensern*, Berlin, 1902; ed. M. Ziāda and R. Sayyed, Beirut, 1979; tr. Max Horten as *Die Philosophie des Abu Raschid*, Bonn, 1910; repr. as *Studien zur Philosophie des Abu Rashid al-Nisāburi: Nachdruck von Schriften von A. Biram (1902) und M. Horten (1910, 1911)*, ed. Fuat Sezgin, Frankfurt am Main, 1986, pp. 82-170. Ahmed Alami, *L'ontologie modale: étude de la théorie des modes d'Abu Hāšim al-Ǧubbāʾi*, Paris, 2001. M. Allard, *Le problème des attributs divins dans la doctrine d'al-Ašʿari et de ses premiers grands disciples*, Beirut, 1965. Ḥ. Anṣāri, "Abu ʿAli al-Jubbāʾi et son livre *al-Maqālāt*," in Camilla Adang, Sabine Schmidtke, and David Sklare, eds., *A Common Rationality: Muʿtazilism in Islam and Judaism*, Würzburg, 2007, pp. 21-37. Abu'l-Ḥasan ʿAli Ašʿari, *Ketāb maqālāt al-eslāmiyyin wa ektelāf al-moṣallin*, ed. Hellmut Ritter as *Die dogmatischen Lehren der Anhänger des Islam*, 3rd ed., Wiesbaden, 1980. Yusof Ben Abraham Baṣir, *al-Ketāb al-moḥtawi*, ed. and tr. George Vajda as *al-Kitāb al-muḥtawi de Yusuf al-Baṣir: Texte, Traduction et Commentaire*, ed. David R. Blumenthal, Leiden, 1985. Abu'l-Ḥosayn Moḥammad b. ʿAli Baṣri, *Ketāb al-moʿtamad fi oṣul al-feqh*, ed. Moḥammad Ḥamid-Allāh, Damascus, 1965. H. Ben Shammai, "A Note on Some Karaite Copies of Muʿtazilite Writings," *BSOAS* 37, 1974, pp. 295-304. A. Ya. Borisov, "Muʿtazilitskie rukopisi Gosudarstvennoĭ Publichnoĭ Biblioteki v Leningrade (Moʿtazilite manuscripts in the State Public Library of Leningrad)," *Bibliografiya Vostoka* 8-9, 1935, pp. 69-95. Michael Cook, *Commanding Right and Forbidding Wrong in Islamic Thought*, Cambridge, 2000. Ebn ʿAsāker, *Tabyin kaḏeb al-moftari fi mā noseba elā al-Emām Abu'l-Ḥasan al-Ašʿari*, Damascus 1928-29. Ebn Mattawayh, *Ketāb al-majmuʿ fi'l-moḥiṭ be'l-taklif*, ed. Jean Joseph Houben, Daniel Gimaret, and J. R. T. M. Peters, 3 vols., Beirut 1965-99. Idem, *al-Taḏkera fi aḥkām al-jawāher wa'l-aʿrāż*, ed. Sāmi Naṣr Loṭf and Fayṣal Bodayr ʿAwn, Cairo, 1975. Ebn al-Mortażā, *Ṭabaqāt al-Moʿtazela*, ed. Susanna Diwald-Wilzer as *Die Klassen der Muʿtaziliten*, Wiesbaden, 1961. Ebn al-Nadim, *Ketāb al-fehrest*, ed. Reżā Tajaddod, Tehran, 1971; tr. Bayard Dodge as *The Fihrist of al-Nadīm: A Tenth-Century Survey of Muslim Culture*, 2 vols., New York and London, 1970.

Richard M. Frank, "Abu Hāshim's Theory of States: Its Structure and Function," in *Actas do IV Congresso de Estudos Arabes e Islâmicos, Coimbra-Lisboa 1 a 8 septembro de 1968*, Leiden, 1971a, pp. 85-100. Idem, "Several Fundamental Assumptions of the Baṣra School of the Muʿtazila," *Studia Islamica* 33, 1971b, pp. 5-18. Idem, *Beings and Their Attributes: The Teaching of the Basrian School of the Muʿtazila in the Classical Period*, Albany, 1978. Idem, "al-Maʿdum wa'l-mawjud: The Non-Existent, the Existent, and the Possible in the Teaching of Abu Hāshim and his Followers," *Mélanges de l'Institut Dominicain de Études Orientales du Caire* 14, 1980, pp. 185-210. Idem, "Attribute, Attribution, and Being: Three Islamic Views," in Parviz Morewedge, ed., *Philosophies of Existence Ancient and Medieval*, New York, 1982, pp. 258-78. Idem, "Moral Obligation in Classical Muslim Theology," *The Journal of Religious Ethics* 11, 1983, pp. 204-23. Idem, "Can God Do What Is Wrong?" in Tamar Rudavsky, ed., *Divine Omniscience and Omnipotence in Medieval Philosophy: Islamic, Jewish and Christian Perspectives*, Dordrecht, Boston, and Lancaster, 1985, pp. 69-79. Johann Fück, "Neue Materialien zum Fihrist," *ZDMG* 90, 1936, pp. 298-321. Daniel Gimaret, "La théorie des aḥwāl d'Abu Hāšim al-Jubbāʾi d'après des sources ašʿarites," *JA* 258, 1970, pp. 47-86. Idem, "Matériaux pour une bibliographie des Jubbāʾis," *JA* 264, 1976, pp. 277-332. Idem, "Les uṣūl al-ḫamsa du Ġādī ʿAbd al-Ǧabbār et leurs commentaires," *Annales Islamologiques* 15, 1979, pp. 47-96. Idem, *Théories de l'acte humain en théologie musulmane*, Paris 1980, pp. 39 ff. Idem, "Matériaux pour une bibliographie des Jubbāʾi: Note complémentaire," in Michael E. Marmura, ed., *Islamic Theology and Philosophy: Studies in Honor of George F. Hourani*, 1984, pp. 31-38. Idem, "Comment al-Jubbāʾi interprétait les versets 'prédestinationnistes' du Coran," *Annales du Département des Lettres arabes 5*, Université Saint-Joseph (Beyrouth), 1990, pp. 5-22. Idem, *Une Lecture Muʿtazilite du Coran: le Tafsīr d'Abu ʿAlī al-Djubbāʾī (m. 303/915) partiellement reconstitué à partir de ses citateurs*, Louvain and Paris 1994. Rosalind W. Gwynne, "The Tafsir of Abu ʿAli al-Jubbāʾi: First Steps toward a Reconstruction with Texts, Translation, Biographical Introduction and Analytical Essay," Phd diss., University of Washington, 1982. Idem, "Al-Jubbāʾi, al-Ashʿari and the Three Brothers: The Use of Fiction," *Muslim World* 75, 1985, pp. 132-61.

Margaretha T. Heemskerk, *Suffering in the Muʿtazilite Theology: ʿAbd al-Jabbār's Teaching on Pain and Divine Justice*, Leiden, 2000. ʿAli Fahmi Ḵošaym, *al-Jobbāʾiyān: Abu ʿAli wa Abu Hāšem*, Tripoli, 1968. Etan Kohlberg, "ʿAli b. Musā Ibn Ṭāwus and His Polemic against Sunnism," in Bernard Lewis and Friedrich Niewöhner, eds., *Religionsgespräche im Mittelalter*, Wiesbaden, 1992a, pp. 325-50. Idem, *A Medieval Muslim Scholar at Work: Ebn Ṭāwus and His Library*, Leiden, 1992b. Wilferd Madelung, "Imamism and Muʿtazilite Theology," in Toufic Fahd, ed., *Le Shîʿisme imâmite*, Paris, 1970, pp. 13-30. Moḥammad b. Aḥmad Malaṭi, *al-Tanbih wa'l-radd ʿalā ahl al-ahwāʾ wa'l-bedaʿ*, ed. Moḥammad Zāhed Kawṯari, Baghdad and Beirut, 1968. Ḵ. M. Nabhā, *Tafsir Abi ʿAli al-Jobbāʾi*, Beirut, 2007. ʿAbd-al-Karim ʿOṯmān, *Qāżi al-qożāt ʿAbd al-Jabbār b. Aḥmad al-Hamaḏāni*, Beirut, 1968.

Dominik Perler and Ulrich Rudolph, *Occasionalismus: Theorien der Kausalität im arabisch-islamischen und im europäischen Denken*, Göttingen, 2000. J. R. T. M. Peters, *God's Created Speech. A Study in the Speculative Theology of the Muʿtazilite Qāżi al-Qużāt Abu'l-Ḥasan ʿAbd al-Jabbār b. Aḥmad al-Hamaḏāni*, Leiden, 1976. Mānkdim Šašdiw, *Šarḥ al-oṣul al-ḵamsa le-Qāżi'l-Qożāt ʿAbdal-Jabbār . . . al-Hamaḏāni al-Asadābādi*, ed. ʿAbd al-Karim ʿOṯmān [as being by ʿAbd-al-Jabbār], Cairo, 1965. F. Sayyed, "Maḵṭuṭāt al-Yaman," *Majallat maʿhad al-maḵṭuṭāt al-ʿarabiya* 1, 1955, pp. 194-215. Sabline Schmidtke, *The Theology of the ʿAllāma al-Ḥilli (d. 726/1325)*, Berlin, 1991. Idem, "Muʿtazilite Manuscripts in the Abraham Firkovitch Collection," in Camilla Adang, Sabine Schmidtke, and David Sklare eds., *A Common Rationality: Muʿtazilism, Islam and Judaism*, 2007, pp. 377-462. David E. Sklare, "Yusuf al-Baṣir: Theological Aspects of His Halakhic Works," in Daniel Frank, ed., *The Jews of Medieval Islam: Community, Society, and Identity: Proceedings of an International Conference Held by the Institute of Jewish Studies, University College London, 1992*, Leiden, 1995, pp. 249-70. Idem, *Samuel Ben Ḥofni Gaon and His Cultural World: Texts and Studies*, Leiden, 1996. Fuat Sezgin, *Geschichte des arabischen Schrifttums* I: *Qurʾānwissenschaften, Ḥadīṯ Geschicte, Fiqh, Dogmatik, Mystik bis ca. 430 H*, Leiden, 1967, pp. 621-24. David Sklare and H. Ben-Shammai, *Judaeo-Arabic Manuscripts in the Firkovitch Collections: The Works of Yusuf al-Basir, A Sample Catalogue. Texts and Studies*, Jerusalem, 1997. Josef Van Ess, *Theologie und Gesellschaft im 2. und 3. Jahrhundert Hidschra: Eine Geschichte des religiösen Denkens im frühen Islam*, 6 vols., Berlin, 1991-97. ʿAbd al-Salām ʿAbbās Wajih, *Maṣāder al-turāṯ fi'l-maktabāt al-ḵāṣṣa fi'l-Yaman*, 2 vols., Ṣanʿāʾ, 2002. Šehāb-al-Din ʿAbd-Allāh Yāqut Ḥamawi, *Eršād al-arib elā maʿrefat al-adib: al-maʿruf be Moʿjam al-odabāʾ*, ed. David Samuel Margoliouth, 7 vols., Leiden 1907-27. ʿAdnān Moḥammad Zarzur, *al-Ḥākem al-Jašami wa-manhājohu fi tafsir al-Qorʾān*, Beirut, 1972, pp. 133-34.

(SABINE SCHMIDTKE)